MAGAZINES FOR LIBRARIES™

Magazines for Libraries 28th edition
was prepared by ProQuest's Content Department

Editorial
Mark Van Orman, Senior Director, Content
Lisa Heft, Senior Manager, Ingestion & Authorities
Patricia Phillips, Supervisor, Content
Christopher King, Metadata Librarian Lead
Christian Trinidad, Metadata Librarian
J. Angela Wiehagen, Metadata Librarian
Enrique Diaz and Christine Oka, Assistant Editors, Content and Development

MAGAZINES FOR LIBRARIES™

TWENTY-EIGHTH EDITION

Edited by Cheryl LaGuardia

created by

Bill Katz

For the general reader and
school, junior college, college, university
and public libraries

Reviewing the best publications
for all serials collections
since 1969

ProQuest®

Start here.

Published by ProQuest LLC

Printed and bound in the United States of America

International Standard Book Numbers
ISBN 13: 978-1-60030-677-8
International Standard Serial Number 0000-0914
Library of Congress Catalog Card Number 86-640971

ISBN: 978-1-60030-677-8

9 781600 306778

CONTENTS

CONTENTS

PREFACE

Our goal with *Magazines for Libraries (MFL)* is threefold: to help librarians develop your collections, to give library teachers a tool to help researchers assess journals for their research, and, once introduced to the resource by librarians, to enable lifelong learners to consult it for ongoing insight into publications' origins, scope, agendas (if any), and quality. To that end, *MFL* lists and describes the core journals in a host of subjects for which libraries collect journals and magazines. As editor, my definition of core is the essential journals in a subject a library needs to provide their users and researchers to the level that those users are going to need them to carry out their research.

Core journals in one subject may be numerous, while in another area only a few titles are really necessary for researchers' purposes. Given the frequent, ongoing sea changes occurring in journal literature subjects, formats, and costs it can be daunting for librarians to keep up with the progress of the journals in a subject area (or areas, since librarians increasingly select and deselect in multiple subjects). Frankly, that's the main audience we have in mind as we put together each edition of *MFL*: librarians having to make difficult, ongoing decisions in a rapidly developing ocean of information supported by budgets of ever-decreasing size. If we can help librarians with this (seemingly Sisyphean) task we've achieved our main goal.

I give heartfelt thanks to the 160+ *Magazines for Libraries* authors for all the work they do in composing their chapters so expertly. Sincerest thanks, too, to Christian Trinidad (Metadata Librarian) and Patti Phillips (Content Supervisor) at ProQuest, Enrique Diaz (Designer) at Harvard University, and Christine Oka (Library Instruction Specialist) at Northeastern University, for the extraordinary work they contribute to this collaborative resource. And to our readers: please do let me know if there are other subjects you'd like to see covered in *Magazines for Libraries* (cmilkslagu@gmail.com).

May you be well,

Cheryl

STATISTICS FROM THE TWENTY-EIGHTH EDITION

Statistical information on the content of *Magazines for Libraries* continues a feature first introduced in the twelfth edition. The presentation of this information on recommended titles and their publishers is provided as the basis for further analysis-not only of the titles included in or excluded from the current edition of *Magazines for Libraries*, but of trends in the serials publishing industry. All data in the charts and tables should be evaluated by the individual reader within the context of his or her own collection decision-making.

A Closer Look at Publishers and Their Titles

This twenty-eighth edition includes 5,030 titles produced by publishers of all types and sizes - from large commercial publishers, society and association publishers and university presses, to publishing start-ups and newsletter self-publishers. Overall, 1,928 publishers and imprints are represented. While the vast majority of publishers are those with 4 or fewer titles in *MFL*, there are 106 publishers with 5 or more titles selected for this edition.

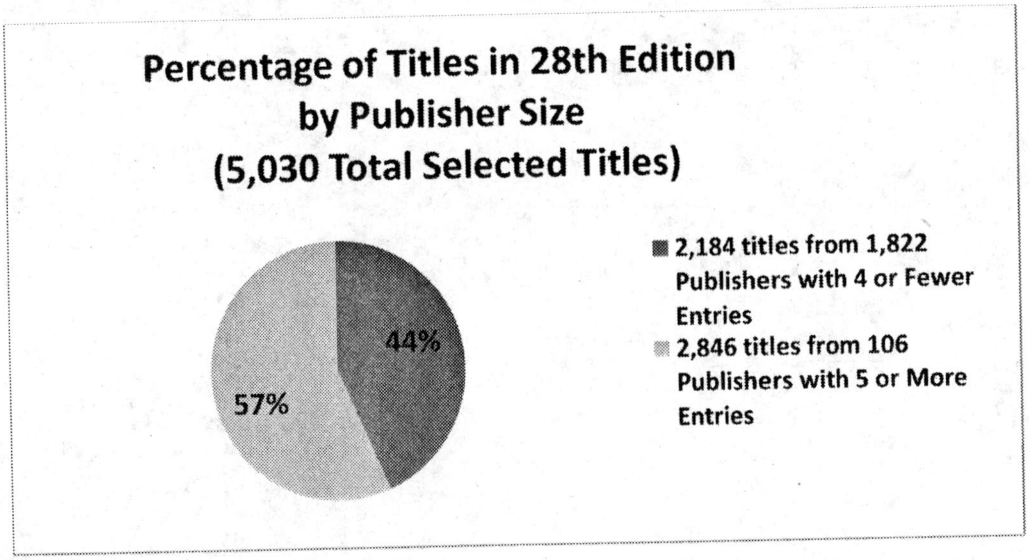

A focused analysis of the 106 publishers with 5 or more entries is provided in **Table 1**, which includes the number of selected titles by feature and format availability. **Table 1** also includes aggregate information on the titles from publishers with 4 or fewer entries.

Table 2 includes a report on the number of publishers in each *MFL* subject chapter. As a benchmark of journal availability and the specific recommendations of the subject section contributors, **Table 3** and **Table 4** contain lists of each of the titles deleted since the last edition of *MFL*, sorted by publisher and by *MFL* subject. The prior edition's record sequence number is provided in both tables to allow the reader to reference the complete listing for a specific title in the older edition.

Commercial Publishers of Scholarly Journals

It is not surprising to see the names and imprints of prominent commercial publishers included in the list of companies with 5 or more entries in *Magazines for Libraries (see* **Table 1**). These names represent publishers in the professional publishing market with large portfolios of titles available for consideration. Their titles include scientific/technical, legal, business, and medical journals utilized by university and college students, professionals in specific research disciplines, and consumers seeking authoritative sources of scholarly information. Many of these companies and their imprints are among the top journal publishers overall.

Table 1 / Publishers with 5 or More Titles in This Edition

Publisher	Number of Titles	Number of Refereed Titles	Percentage Refereed	Number of Online Titles
Routledge	356	345	97%	219
Sage Publications, Inc.	155	153	99%	53
Wiley-Blackwell Publishing, Inc.	124	119	96%	71
Wiley-Blackwell Publishing Ltd.	123	114	93%	87
Elsevier BV	117	113	97%	99
Cambridge University Press	114	109	96%	55
Sage Publications Ltd.	110	109	99%	29
Oxford University Press	109	107	98%	77
Pergamon Press	91	90	99%	89
Springer New York LLC	88	88	100%	66
Springer Netherlands	70	68	97%	52
Taylor & Francis Inc.	57	54	95%	27
Taylor & Francis	53	52	98%	21
Springer	51	50	98%	2
John Wiley & Sons, Inc.	46	42	91%	23
The Johns Hopkins University Press	46	43	93%	0
Elsevier Ltd	45	45	100%	39
Institute of Electrical and Electronics Engineers	44	34	77%	0
University of Chicago Press	43	43	100%	0
John Wiley & Sons Ltd.	42	41	98%	24
Emerald Publishing Limited	39	38	97%	24
Academic Press	36	36	100%	35
Duke University Press	32	30	94%	0
American Psychological Association	31	30	97%	1
Elsevier Inc.	27	27	100%	22
Lippincott Williams & Wilkins	25	25	100%	19
American Chemical Society	23	22	96%	0
Institute of Physics Publishing Ltd.	22	21	95%	0
Indiana University Press	21	18	86%	1
Brill	20	18	90%	0

BioMed Central Ltd.	19	19	100%	0
A I P Publishing LLC	17	16	94%	0
Hearst Magazines	17	0	0%	0
Nature Publishing Group	17	16	94%	11
University of Illinois Press	17	17	100%	0
M I T Press	16	15	94%	0
Scholastic Inc.	16	0	0%	0
University of California Press * Journals Division	16	15	94%	0
Bonnier Corp.	15	0	0%	0
F + W Media Inc.	15	0	0%	0
American Accounting Association	14	11	79%	0
American Library Association	14	6	43%	0
Penton	14	0	0%	0
University of Toronto Press * Journals Division	14	14	100%	0
Conde Nast Publications, Inc.	13	0	0%	0
Time Inc.	13	0	0%	0
Annual Reviews	12	12	100%	0
Pennsylvania State University Press	12	11	92%	1
American Physical Society	11	11	100%	0
Association for Computing Machinery	11	6	55%	0
Wiley - V C H Verlag GmbH & Co. KGaA	11	11	100%	0
American Meteorological Society	10	10	100%	0
B N P Media II, LLC.	10	0	0%	0
Belvoir Media Group, LLC	10	0	0%	0
Cricket Media, Inc.	10	0	0%	0
Mary Ann Liebert, Inc. Publishers	10	9	90%	7
Meredith National Media Group	10	0	0%	0
TEN: The Enthusiast Network	10	0	0%	0
Harvard University	9	6	67%	0
Human Kinetics, Inc.	9	9	100%	0
Intellect Ltd.	9	9	100%	0
American Institute of Aeronautics and Astronautics, Inc.	8	7	88%	0

Table 1 / Publishers with 5 or More Titles in This Edition (cont.)

Publisher	Number of Titles	Number of Refereed Titles	Percentage Refereed	Number of Online Titles
American Society of Civil Engineers	8	8	100%	0
Canadian Science Publishing	8	8	100%	0
Copernicus GmbH	8	7	88%	0
De Gruyter Mouton	8	8	100%	0
Kalmbach Publishing Co.	8	0	0%	0
Optical Society of America	8	8	100%	0
Palgrave Macmillan Ltd.	8	7	88%	1
Royal Society of Chemistry	8	7	88%	0
University of Nebraska Press	8	8	100%	0
Edinburgh University Press Ltd.	7	7	100%	0
Hindawi Publishing Corporation	7	7	100%	0
HistoryNet	7	0	0%	0
Interweave Press, LLC.	7	0	0%	0
University of Hawai'i Press	7	6	86%	0
University of Minnesota Press	7	7	100%	0
University of Texas Press * Journals Division	7	7	100%	0
University of Wisconsin Press * Journals Division	7	7	100%	0
Walter de Gruyter GmbH	7	7	100%	0
Wiley-Blackwell Publishing Asia	7	7	100%	6
American Bar Association	6	2	33%	0
Hanley Wood, LLC	6	0	0%	0
Haymarket Publishing Ltd.	6	0	0%	0
Inderscience Publishers	6	6	100%	0
Institute for Operations Research and the Management Sciences (I N F O R M S)	6	6	100%	0
M D P I AG	6	6	100%	0
Madavor Media, Llc.	6	0	0%	0
PennWell Corporation	6	0	0%	0
Philosophy Documentation Center	6	5	83%	0
Rodale, Inc.	6	0	0%	0

Academy of Management	5	4	80%	0
Active Interest Media	5	0	0%	0
American Real Estate Society	5	5	100%	0
American Society for Microbiology	5	5	100%	0
C C H Inc.	5	0	0%	1
Cell Press	5	5	100%	4
Crain Communications, Inc.	5	0	0%	0
DanceMedia, LLC.	5	0	0%	0
Geological Society of America	5	4	80%	0
Immediate Media Co. Ltd.	5	0	0%	0
Institute of Mathematical Statistics	5	5	100%	0
John Benjamins Publishing Co.	5	5	100%	2
The American Society of Mechanical Engineers	5	4	80%	0
The Taunton Press, Inc.	5	0	0%	0
University of Texas at Austin	5	2	40%	0
Publishers (106) with 5 or more titles	**2846**	**2494**	**88%**	**1168**
Publishers (1822) with 4 or fewer titles	**2184**	**742**	**34%**	**59**
All publishers (1928)	**5030**	**3236**	**64%**	**1227**

Table 2 / No. of Publishers by MFL Subject

Section	No. of Publishers
ACCOUNTING AND TAXATION	38
ADVERTISING, MARKETING, AND PUBLIC RELATIONS	21
AERONAUTICS AND SPACE SCIENCE	37
AFRICA	44
AFRICAN AMERICAN	48
AGRICULTURE	14
ANIMAL RIGHTS/ANIMAL WELFARE	16
ANIME, COMICS, GRAPHIC NOVELS, AND MANGA	12
ANTHROPOLOGY	18
ANTIQUES	15
ARCHAEOLOGY	15
ARCHITECTURE	51
ARCHIVES AND MANUSCRIPTS	13
ART	58
ASIA AND THE PACIFIC	11
ASIAN AMERICAN	9
ASTROLOGY	5
ASTRONOMY	42
ATMOSPHERIC SCIENCES	25
AUTOMOBILES AND MOTORCYCLES	26
BEER, WINE, AND SPIRITS	12
BIBLIOGRAPHY	19
BIOLOGY	32
BIOTECHNOLOGY	18
BIRDS	18
BLIND AND VISUALLY IMPAIRED	13
BOATS AND BOATING	15
BOOKS AND BOOK REVIEWS	17
BOTANY	11
BUILDING AND CONSTRUCTION	11
BUSINESS AND FINANCE	73
CANADA	38
CARTOGRAPHY, GIS, AND IMAGERY	16
CHEMISTRY	13
CHILDREN	33
CIVIL LIBERTIES	18
CLASSICAL STUDIES	12
CLASSROOM MAGAZINES	12
COMMUNICATION	16
COMPUTERS AND INFORMATION TECHNOLOGY	23
COOKING AND COOKERY	11
CRAFTS AND MAKING	19
CRIMINOLOGY AND LAW ENFORCEMENT	22
CULTURAL STUDIES	37
DANCE	12
DEATH AND DYING	15
DIGITAL HUMANITIES	10
DISABILITIES	16
DO-IT-YOURSELF / MAKERS	6

Table 2 / No. of Publishers by MFL Subject (cont.)

Section	No. of Publishers
EARTH SCIENCES AND GEOLOGY	42
ECOLOGY	15
ECONOMICS	21
EDUCATION	45
ELECTRONICS	27
ENERGY	28
ENGINEERING AND TECHNOLOGY	36
ENVIRONMENT AND CONSERVATION	19
EUROPE	25
FAMILY	10
FAMILY PLANNING	7
FASHION AND LIFESTYLE	9
FICTION: GENERAL/MYSTERY AND DETECTIVE	15
FICTION: SCIENCE FICTION, FANTASY, AND HORROR	28
FILMS	28
FIRE PROTECTION	6
FISH, FISHERIES, AND AQUACULTURE	14
FISHING	11
FOLKLORE	16
FOOD AND NUTRITION	7
FOOD INDUSTRY	7
FORENSICS	9
FORESTRY	25
GAMES AND GAMING	14
GARDENING	19
GENDER STUDIES	32
GENEALOGY	15
GENERAL INTEREST	23
GEOGRAPHY	25
GERIATRICS AND GERONTOLOGICAL STUDIES	22
GLOBALIZATION	31
GOVERNMENT PERIODICALS–FEDERAL	13
GOVERNMENT PERIODICALS–STATE AND LOCAL	45
HEALTH AND FITNESS	16
HEALTH CARE ADMINISTRATION	10
HEALTH PROFESSIONS	18
HIKING, CLIMBING, AND OUTDOOR RECREATION	7
HISTORY	18
HOME	10
HOSPITALITY/RESTAURANT	13
HUMAN RESOURCES	8
HUMOR	7
HUNTING AND GUNS	7
INFORMATICS	9
INTERDISCIPLINARY STUDIES	5
INTERIOR DESIGN AND DECORATION	10
INTERNATIONAL MAGAZINES	22
JOURNALISM AND WRITING	16
LABOR AND INDUSTRIAL RELATIONS	23

Table 2 / No. of Publishers by MFL Subject (cont.)

Section	No. of Publishers
LANDSCAPE ARCHITECTURE	12
LATIN AMERICA AND SPAIN	39
LATINO STUDIES	13
LAW	21
LGBT+	7
LIBRARY AND INFORMATION SCIENCE	40
LIFE WRITING/BIOGRAPHY	4
LINGUISTICS	24
LITERARY REVIEWS	30
LITERATURE	39
LITTLE MAGAZINES	22
MANAGEMENT AND ADMINISTRATION	24
MARINE SCIENCE AND TECHNOLOGY	53
MARRIAGE AND DIVORCE	6
MATHEMATICS	21
MEDIA AND AV	17
MEDICINE	17
MENOPAUSE/ANDROPAUSE	4
MIDDLE EAST	12
MILITARY	43
MINDFULNESS	7
MODEL MAKING	7
MULTICULTURAL STUDIES	10
MUSIC	51
MUSIC REVIEWS	4
NATIVE AMERICANS	10
NEWS AND OPINION	20
NUMISMATICS	7
NURSING	7
OCCUPATIONS AND CAREERS	4
PALEONTOLOGY	7
PARANORMAL	7
PARENTING	14
PEACE AND CONFLICT STUDIES	12
PETS	19
PHILATELY	8
PHILOSOPHY	31
PHOTOGRAPHY	10
PHYSICS	18
PHYSIOLOGY	4
POLITICAL SCIENCE	18
POPULATION STUDIES	8
PREGNANCY	7
PRINTING AND GRAPHIC ARTS	28
PSYCHOLOGY	27
PUBLIC HEALTH	10
REAL ESTATE	18
RELIGION	46
ROBOTICS	18

Table 2 / No. of Publishers by MFL Subject (cont.)

Section	No. of Publishers
SAFETY	10
SCIENCE AND TECHNOLOGY	25
SEXUALITY	11
SLAVIC AND EURASIAN STUDIES	21
SOCIAL MEDIA	3
SOCIOLOGY AND SOCIAL WORK	36
SPIRITUALITY AND WELL-BEING	7
SPORTS	52
STATISTICS	20
TEENAGERS	7
TELEVISION, VIDEO, AND RADIO	6
THEATER	16
TRANSPORTATION	61
TRAVEL AND TOURISM	13
URBAN STUDIES	20
VETERINARY SCIENCE	20
WEDDINGS	5
WORLD WIDE WEB	11
ZOOLOGY	15

Table 3 / Titles Deleted Since the Last Edition by Publishers

Publisher	Title	ISSN	27th Edition Sequence No.
African Dream Limited	Bantu	1817-0196	203
American Association of Collegiate Registrars and Admissions Officers	College and University	0010-0889	1923
American Association of School Administrators	School Administrator	0036-6439	1874
American Association of University Professors	Academe	0190-2946	1920
American Federation of Teachers	American Educator	0148-432X	1829
American Geological Institute	Earth	1943-345X	1667
American Marketing Association	Marketing Insights	2327-9117	107
American Radio Relay League, Inc.	Q E X	0886-8093	4900
American Radio Relay League, Inc.	Q S T	0033-4812	4901
American Secondary Education	American Secondary Education	0003-1003	1832
Appalachian State University * National Center for Developmental Education	Journal of Developmental Education	0894-3907	1930
Association for Career and Technical Education	Techniques	1527-1803	1980
Australian National University	Intersections	1440-9151	2584
B M J Group	Occupational and Environmental Medicine	1351-0711	4415
BeerAdvocate	BeerAdvocate		718
BioMed Central Ltd.	B M C Health Services Research	1472-6963	4403
Bloomberg B N A	Government Employee Relations Report	0017-260X	3082
Brewers Association	The New Brewer	0741-0506	725
Brewers Association	Zymurgy	0196-5921	730
C O P Communications	Computer Graphics World	0271-4159	1373
Caddo Gap Press	Journal of Thought	0022-5231	1859
Caddo Gap Press	Teacher Education Quarterly	0737-5328	1972
Cambridge University Press	Disaster Medicine and Public Health Preparedness	1935-7893	4404
Cambridge University Press	Public Health Nutrition	1368-9800	4417
Chautauqua Press	All About Beer	0898-9001	716
cherry bombe, Inc	Cherry Bombe	2326-6945	1403
Chicago Tribune Newspapers, Inc.	Chicago Tribune	1085-6706	3899
Commission on Adult Basic Education	Journal of Research and Practice for Adult Literacy, Secondary, and Basic Education	2169-0480	1940
Cox Newspapers, Inc.	The Atlanta Journal - Constitution	1539-7459	3896
Cricket Media, Inc.	Cicada	1097-4008	4884
Cruz Bay Publishing	Vegetarian Today	2475-0093	1416
Current Publishing Committee	Current (Washington, 1980)	0739-991X	4894
Dalldorf Communications Inc.	Celebrator Beer News	1086-2587	720
Duke University Press	Tikkun	0887-9982	3891
Duke University Press	World Policy Journal	0740-2775	2783
E Q E S, Inc.	Nuclear Plant Journal	0892-2055	4547
Edgewater Park Media, Inc.	Simply Gluten Free Magazine	2326-7925	1413
Elsevier	International Journal of Marine Energy	2214-1669	3556
European Space Agency * Communication Department	E S A Bulletin	0376-4265	138

F D Q Media LLC	F D Q Fashion Doll Quarterly		394
F N O Press	From Now On		1976
Family Reformation, LLC.	Homeschooling Today	1073-2217	1936
Globe and Mail Publishing	The Globe and Mail	0319-0714	3900
Guardian Media Group	The Guardian	0261-3077	3901
Hecate Press	Hecate	0311-4198	2579
Hindwai Publishing Corporation	Advances in Software Engineering	1687-8655	1370
Home Life, Inc.	Practical Homeschooling	1075-4741	1937
I D G Communications Inc.	Computerworld	0010-4841	1393
Institutional Investor, Inc.	Real Estate Finance and Investment	1529-6644	4436
International Civil Aviation Organization (I C A O)	I C A O Journal	1014-8876	143
Interweave Press, LLC	Jewelry Stringing	2165-3631	1429
John Wiley & Sons Ltd.	Statistics in Medicine	0277-6715	4420
Journalism and Discourse Studies	Journalism and Discourse Studies	2056-3191	3054
Journalism Education Association, Inc.	Communication: Journalism Education Today	1536-9129	3070
Justine Magazine	Justine Magazine	1548-8241	4888
Kahrus Institute	KASHRUS Magazine	1074-3502	2458
Kairos	Kairos	1521-2300	1954
KT Press	n.paradoxa	1461-0434	530
Lippincott Williams & Wilkins	Epidemiology (Philadelphia)	1044-3983	4407
Long Story	The Long Story	0741-4242	2287
Los Angeles Times Newspapers, Inc.	Los Angeles Times	0458-3035	3902
Media Concepts Group, Inc.	Native Peoples	0895-7606	3866
Mental Floss LLC	Mental Floss	1543-4702	2645
Meredith Corporation	Martha Stewart Weddings	1534-553X	5096
National Association of Secondary School Principals	NewsLeader		1866
National Association of Secondary School Principals	Principal Leadership	2156-2113	1870
National Catholic Educational Association	Momentum (Washington)	0026-914X	1863
National Council for the Social Studies	Social Education	0037-7724	1967
National Council of Teachers of English	College English	0010-0994	1950
National Council of Teachers of English	English Journal	0013-8274	1952
National Council of Teachers of English	Language Arts	0360-9170	1955
National School Boards Association	American School Board Journal	0003-0953	1831
National Sheriffs' Association	Sheriff Magazine	1070-8170	1497
New Hope Natural Media	Natural Foods Merchandiser	0164-338X	2460
New York Times Company	The Boston Globe	0743-1791	3898
New York Times Company	The New York Times	0362-4331	3904
NewBay Media, LLC	Digital Video	2164-0963	4895
NewBay Media, LLC	Radio	1542-0620	4902
Nordregio	European Journal of Spatial Development	1650-9544	5032
Open University * Knowledge Media Institute	Journal of Interactive Media in Education	1365-893X	1978
Oriental Art Magazine	Oriental Art	0030-5278	532
Oxford University Press	International Journal of Epidemiology	0300-5771	4411
PennWell Corporation	FireRescue Magazine	1094-0529	2368

Table 3 / Titles Deleted Since the Last Edition by Publishers (cont.)

Publisher	Title	ISSN	27th Edition Sequence No.
Pergamon Press	Social Science & Medicine	0277-9536	4419
Project Innovation, Inc.	Education	0013-1172	1837
Public Library of Science	P L o S Neglected Tropical Diseases (Online)	1935-2735	4416
Publishers Development Corp.	Arts and Activities	0004-3931	1943
Quinstreet Inc.	Baseline (New York)	1541-3004	1392
Reporters Committee for Freedom of the Press	News Media and the Law	0149-0737	3057
Romantic Times Publishing Group	R T Book Reviews		2291
Routledge	Action in Teacher Education	0162-6620	1969
Routledge	Art Education	0004-3125	1942
Routledge	Childhood Education	0009-4056	1833
Routledge	Discourse (Abingdon)	0159-6306	1891
Routledge	European Education	1056-4934	1894
Routledge	International Journal of School & Educational Psychology	2168-3603	1908
Routledge	Journal of Broadcasting and Electronic Media	0883-8151	4897
Routledge	Journal of Radio & Audio Media	1937-6529	4898
Routledge	Journal of Student Affairs Research and Practice	1949-6591	1932
Routledge	Kappa Delta Pi Record	0022-8958	1860
Routledge	Learning, Media & Technology (Online)	1743-9892	1956
Routledge	Multicultural Perspectives	1521-0960	1864
Routledge	Royal Musical Association. Journal	0269-0403	3840
Routledge	Studies in Art Education	0039-3541	1946
Routledge	The Educational Forum	0013-1725	1846
Routledge	The Journal of Economic Education	0022-0485	1966
Routledge	The Journal of Educational Research	0022-0671	1858
Routledge	The Social Studies	0037-7996	1968
Sage Publications Ltd.	Diogenes (English Edition)	0392-1921	4035
Sage Publications, Inc.	Health Promotion Practice	1524-8399	4410
Sage Publications, Inc.	Journal of Education	0022-0574	1857
Sage Publications, Inc.	N A S S P Bulletin	0192-6365	1865
Sage Publications, Inc.	Professional School Counseling (Online)	2156-759X	1915
Seattle Times Company	Seattle Times	0745-9696	3905
Seattle University * School of Law	Seattle Journal for Social Justice	1544-1245	1273
Seaways Publishing, Inc.	Seaways' Ships in Scale	1065-8904	3778
Southern Genealogist's Exchange Society, Inc.	Southern Genealogist's Exchange Society Quarterly	1933-1010	2632
Southern Progress Corp.	Cooking Light	0886-4446	1404
Spoonful	Spoonful	2470-1203	1414
Springer Netherlands	Prospects	0033-1538	1900
Springer New York LLC	AIDS and Behavior	1090-7165	4398
Stampington & Company, LLC.	Art Doll Quarterly	1939-5027	390
State University of New York at Cortland	Wagadu	2150-2226	2606
T S L Education Ltd.	Times Higher Education		1903

Taylor & Francis	International Journal of Occupational and Environmental Health	1077-3525	4545
Taylor & Francis Inc.	Literacy Research and Instruction	1938-8071	1957
TechWeb, InformationWeek Business Technology Network	Information Week Online (US Edition)	1938-3371	1395
The Baltimore Sun Company	The Baltimore Sun		3897
The Counselors of Real Estate	Real Estate Issues	0146-0595	4438
The Lancet Publishing Group	The Lancet Infectious Diseases	1473-3099	4414
The McClatchy Company	The Miami Herald	0898-865X	3903
The Weekly Standard	The Weekly Standard	1083-3013	3895
University of Chicago Press	American Journal of Education	0195-6744	1830
University of Illinois * Dalkey Archive Press	The Review of Contemporary Fiction	0276-0045	3417
University of Illinois Press	Feminist Teacher	0882-4843	2567
University of Illinois Press	Visual Arts Research	0736-0770	1947
University of Pittsburgh * University Library System	Radical Teacher (Online)	1941-0832	1871
University of Toronto	Resources for Feminist Research	0707-8412	2599
Univerza v Ljubljani * Filozofska Fakulteta	Azijske Studij	2232-5131	561
Urban Latino Magazine	Urban Latino Magazine	1531-6602	3181
Video Watchdog	Video Watchdog	1070-9991	4907
W S R Publishing	Widescreen Review		4908
Washington Post Co.	The Washington Post	0190-8286	3906
Wiley-Blackwell Publishing, Inc.	Journal of School Health	0022-4391	4413
Wiley-Blackwell Publishing, Inc.	New Horizons in Adult Education & Human Resource Development	1939-4225	1941
Wiley-Blackwell Publishing Ltd.	Review of Education	2049-6613	1901
Women & Environments International Magazine	Women & Environments International Magazine	1499-1993	2608
World Scientific Publishing Co. Pte. Ltd.	International Journal of Humanoid Robotics	0219-8436	4527

Table 4 / Titles Deleted Since the Last Edition by MFL Subject

Section	Title	ISSN	Publisher	27th Ed. Sequence No.
ADVERTISING, MARKETING, AND PUBLIC RELATIONS	Marketing Insights	2327-9117	American Marketing Association	107
AERONAUTICS AND SPACE SCIENCE	E S A Bulletin	0376-4265	European Space Agency * Communication Department	138
AERONAUTICS AND SPACE SCIENCE	I C A O Journal	1014-8876	International Civil Aviation Organization (I C A O)	143
AFRICA	Bantu	1817-0196	African Dream Limited	203
ANTIQUES	Art Doll Quarterly	1939-5027	Stampington & Company, LLC.	390
ANTIQUES	F D Q Fashion Doll Quarterly		F D Q Media LLC	394
ART	n.paradoxa	1461-0434	KT Press	530
ART	Oriental Art	0030-5278	Oriental Art Magazine	532
ASIA AND THE PACIFIC	Azijske Studij	2232-5131	Univerza v Ljubljani * Filozofska Fakulteta	561
BEER, WINE, AND SPIRITS	All About Beer	0898-9001	Chautauqua Press	716
BEER, WINE, AND SPIRITS	BeerAdvocate		BeerAdvocate	718
BEER, WINE, AND SPIRITS	Celebrator Beer News	1086-2587	Dalldorf Communications Inc.	720
BEER, WINE, AND SPIRITS	The New Brewer	0741-0506	Brewers Association	725
BEER, WINE, AND SPIRITS	Zymurgy	0196-5921	Brewers Association	730
CIVIL LIBERTIES	Seattle Journal for Social Justice	1544-1245	Seattle University * School of Law	1273
COMPUTERS AND INFORMATION TECHNOLOGY	Advances in Software Engineering	1687-8655	Hindwai Publishing Corporation	1370
COMPUTERS AND INFORMATION TECHNOLOGY	Baseline (New York)	1541-3004	Quinstreet Inc.	1392
COMPUTERS AND INFORMATION TECHNOLOGY	Computer Graphics World	0271-4159	C O P Communications	1373
COMPUTERS AND INFORMATION TECHNOLOGY	Computerworld	0010-4841	I D G Communications Inc.	1393
COMPUTERS AND INFORMATION TECHNOLOGY	Information Week Online (US Edition)	1938-3371	TechWeb, InformationWeek Business Technology Network	1395
COOKING AND COOKERY	Cherry Bombe	2326-6945	cherry bombe, Inc	1403
COOKING AND COOKERY	Cooking Light	0886-4446	Southern Progress Corp.	1404
COOKING AND COOKERY	Simply Gluten Free Magazine	2326-7925	Edgewater Park Media, Inc.	1413
COOKING AND COOKERY	Spoonful	2470-1203	Spoonful	1414
COOKING AND COOKERY	Vegetarian Today	2475-0093	Cruz Bay Publishing	1416
CRAFTS AND MAKING	Jewelry Stringing	2165-3631	Interweave Press, LLC	1429
CRIMINOLOGY AND LAW ENFORCEMENT	Sheriff Magazine	1070-8170	National Sheriffs' Association	1497
EARTH SCIENCE AND GEOLOGY	Earth	1943-345X	American Geological Institute	1667
EDUCATION	Academe	0190-2946	American Association of University Professors	1920
EDUCATION	Action in Teacher Education	0162-6620	Routledge	1969
EDUCATION	American Educator	0148-432X	American Federation of Teachers	1829
EDUCATION	American Journal of Education	0195-6744	University of Chicago Press	1830
EDUCATION	American School Board Journal	0003-0953	National School Boards Association	1831
EDUCATION	American Secondary Education	0003-1003	American Secondary Education	1832

EDUCATION	Art Education	0004-3125	Routledge	1942
EDUCATION	Arts and Activities	0004-3931	Publishers Development Corp.	1943
EDUCATION	Childhood Education	0009-4056	Routledge	1833
EDUCATION	College and University	0010-0889	American Association of Collegiate Registrars and Admissions Officers	1923
EDUCATION	College English	0010-0994	National Council of Teachers of English	1950
EDUCATION	Discourse (Abingdon)	0159-6306	Routledge	1891
EDUCATION	Education	0013-1172	Project Innovation, Inc.	1837
EDUCATION	English Journal	0013-8274	National Council of Teachers of English	1952
EDUCATION	European Education	1056-4934	Routledge	1894
EDUCATION	From Now On		F N O Press	1976
EDUCATION	Homeschooling Today	1073-2217	Family Reformation, LLC.	1936
EDUCATION	International Journal of School & Educational Psychology	2168-3603	Routledge	1908
EDUCATION	Journal of Developmental Education	0894-3907	Appalachian State University * National Center for Developmental Education	1930
EDUCATION	Journal of Education	0022-0574	Sage Publications, Inc.	1857
EDUCATION	Journal of Interactive Media in Education	1365-893X	Open University * Knowledge Media Institute	1978
EDUCATION	Journal of Research and Practice for Adult Literacy, Secondary, and Basic Education	2169-0480	Commission on Adult Basic Education	1940
EDUCATION	Journal of Student Affairs Research and Practice	1949-6591	Routledge	1932
EDUCATION	Journal of Thought	0022-5231	Caddo Gap Press	1859
EDUCATION	Kairos	1521-2300	Kairos	1954
EDUCATION	Kappa Delta Pi Record	0022-8958	Routledge	1860
EDUCATION	Language Arts	0360-9170	National Council of Teachers of English	1955
EDUCATION	Learning, Media & Technology (Online)	1743-9892	Routledge	1956
EDUCATION	Literacy Research and Instruction	1938-8071	Taylor & Francis Inc.	1957
EDUCATION	Momentum (Washington)	0026-914X	National Catholic Educational Association	1863
EDUCATION	Multicultural Perspectives	1521-0960	Routledge	1864
EDUCATION	N A S S P Bulletin	0192-6365	Sage Publications, Inc.	1865
EDUCATION	New Horizons in Adult Education & Human Resource Development	1939-4225	Wiley-Blackwell Publishing, Inc.	1941
EDUCATION	NewsLeader		National Association of Secondary School Principals	1866
EDUCATION	Practical Homeschooling	1075-4741	Home Life, Inc.	1937
EDUCATION	Principal Leadership	2156-2113	National Association of Secondary School Principals	1870
EDUCATION	Professional School Counseling (Online)	2156-759X	Sage Publications, Inc.	1915
EDUCATION	Prospects	0033-1538	Springer Netherlands	1900
EDUCATION	Radical Teacher (Online)	1941-0832	University of Pittsburgh * University Library System	1871
EDUCATION	Review of Education	2049-6613	Wiley-Blackwell Publishing Ltd.	1901
EDUCATION	School Administrator	0036-6439	American Association of School Administrators	1874
EDUCATION	Social Education	0037-7724	National Council for the Social Studies	1967
EDUCATION	Studies in Art Education	0039-3541	Routledge	1946
EDUCATION	Teacher Education Quarterly	0737-5328	Caddo Gap Press	1972
EDUCATION	Techniques	1527-1803	Association for Career and Technical Education	1980

Table 4 / Titles Deleted Since the Last Edition by MFL Subject (cont.)

Section	Title	ISSN	Publisher	27th Ed. Sequence No.
EDUCATION	The Educational Forum	0013-1725	Routledge	1846
EDUCATION	The Journal of Economic Education	0022-0485	Routledge	1966
EDUCATION	The Journal of Educational Research	0022-0671	Routledge	1858
EDUCATION	The Social Studies	0037-7996	Routledge	1968
EDUCATION	Times Higher Education		T S L Education Ltd.	1903
EDUCATION	Visual Arts Research	0736-0770	University of Illinois Press	1947
FICTION: GENERAL / MYSTERY AND DETECTIVE	R T Book Reviews		Romantic Times Publishing Group	2291
FICTION: GENERAL / MYSTERY AND DETECTIVE	The Long Story	0741-4242	Long Story	2287
FIRE PROTECTION	FireRescue Magazine	1094-0529	PennWell Corporation	2368
FOOD INDUSTRY	KASHRUS Magazine	1074-3502	Kahrus Institute	2458
FOOD INDUSTRY	Natural Foods Merchandiser	0164-338X	New Hope Natural Media	2460
GENDER STUDIES	Feminist Teacher	0882-4843	University of Illinois Press	2567
GENDER STUDIES	Hecate	0311-4198	Hecate Press	2579
GENDER STUDIES	Intersections	1440-9151	Australian National University	2584
GENDER STUDIES	Resources for Feminist Research	0707-8412	University of Toronto	2599
GENDER STUDIES	Wagadu	2150-2226	State University of New York at Cortland	2606
GENDER STUDIES	Women & Environments International Magazine	1499-1993	Women & Environments International Magazine	2608
GENEALOGY	Southern Genealogist's Exchange Society Quarterly	1933-1010	Southern Genealogist's Exchange Society, Inc.	2632
GENERAL INTEREST	Mental Floss	1543-4702	Mental Floss LLC	2645
GLOBALIZATION	World Policy Journal	0740-2775	Duke University Press	2783
JOURNALISM AND WRITING	Communication: Journalism Education Today	1536-9129	Journalism Education Association, Inc.	3070
JOURNALISM AND WRITING	Journalism and Discourse Studies	2056-3191	Journalism and Discourse Studies	3054
JOURNALISM AND WRITING	News Media and the Law	0149-0737	Reporters Committee for Freedom of the Press	3057
LABOR AND INDUSTRIAL RELATIONS	Government Employee Relations Report	0017-260X	Bloomberg B N A	3082
LATINO STUDIES	Urban Latino Magazine	1531-6602	Urban Latino Magazine	3181
LITERATURE	The Review of Contemporary Fiction	0276-0045	University of Illinois * Dalkey Archive Press	3417
MARINE SCIENCE AND TECHNOLOGY	International Journal of Marine Energy	2214-1669	Elsevier	3556
MODEL MAKING	Seaways' Ships in Scale	1065-8904	Seaways Publishing, Inc.	3778
MUSIC	Royal Musical Association. Journal	0269-0403	Routledge	3840
NATIVE AMERICANS	Native Peoples	0895-7606	Media Concepts Group, Inc.	3866
NEWS AND OPINION	The Weekly Standard	1083-3013	The Weekly Standard	3895
NEWS AND OPINION	Tikkun	0887-9982	Duke University Press	3891
NEWSPAPERS	Chicago Tribune	1085-6706	Chicago Tribune Newspapers, Inc.	3899
NEWSPAPERS	Los Angeles Times	0458-3035	Los Angeles Times Newspapers, Inc.	3902
NEWSPAPERS	Seattle Times	0745-9696	Seattle Times Company	3905
NEWSPAPERS	The Atlanta Journal - Constitution	1539-7459	Cox Newspapers, Inc.	3896
NEWSPAPERS	The Baltimore Sun		The Baltimore Sun Company	3897

NEWSPAPERS	The Boston Globe	0743-1791	New York Times Company	3898
NEWSPAPERS	The Globe and Mail	0319-0714	Globe and Mail Publishing	3900
NEWSPAPERS	The Guardian	0261-3077	Guardian Media Group	3901
NEWSPAPERS	The Miami Herald	0898-865X	The McClatchy Company	3903
NEWSPAPERS	The New York Times	0362-4331	New York Times Company	3904
NEWSPAPERS	The Washington Post	0190-8286	Washington Post Co.	3906
PHILOSOPHY	Diogenes (English Edition)	0392-1921	Sage Publications Ltd.	4035
PUBLIC HEALTH	AIDS and Behavior	1090-7165	Springer New York LLC	4398
PUBLIC HEALTH	B M C Health Services Research	1472-6963	BioMed Central Ltd.	4403
PUBLIC HEALTH	Disaster Medicine and Public Health Preparedness	1935-7893	Cambridge University Press	4404
PUBLIC HEALTH	Epidemiology (Philadelphia)	1044-3983	Lippincott Williams & Wilkins	4407
PUBLIC HEALTH	Health Promotion Practice	1524-8399	Sage Publications, Inc.	4410
PUBLIC HEALTH	International Journal of Epidemiology	0300-5771	Oxford University Press	4411
PUBLIC HEALTH	Journal of School Health	0022-4391	Wiley-Blackwell Publishing, Inc.	4413
PUBLIC HEALTH	Occupational and Environmental Medicine	1351-0711	B M J Group	4415
PUBLIC HEALTH	P L o S Neglected Tropical Diseases (Online)	1935-2735	Public Library of Science	4416
PUBLIC HEALTH	Public Health Nutrition	1368-9800	Cambridge University Press	4417
PUBLIC HEALTH	Social Science & Medicine	0277-9536	Pergamon Press	4419
PUBLIC HEALTH	Statistics in Medicine	0277-6715	John Wiley & Sons Ltd.	4420
PUBLIC HEALTH	The Lancet Infectious Diseases	1473-3099	The Lancet Publishing Group	4414
REAL ESTATE	Real Estate Finance and Investment	1529-6644	Institutional Investor, Inc.	4436
REAL ESTATE	Real Estate Issues	0146-0595	The Counselors of Real Estate	4438
ROBOTICS	International Journal of Humanoid Robotics	0219-8436	World Scientific Publishing Co. Pte. Ltd.	4527
SAFETY	International Journal of Occupational and Environmental Health	1077-3525	Taylor & Francis	4545
SAFETY	Nuclear Plant Journal	0892-2055	E Q E S, Inc.	4547
TEENAGERS	Cicada	1097-4008	Cricket Media, Inc.	4884
TEENAGERS	Justine Magazine	1548-8241	Justine Magazine	4888
TELEVISION, VIDEO & RADIO	Digital Video	2164-0963	NewBay Media, LLC	4895
TELEVISION, VIDEO, AND RADIO	Current (Washington, 1980)	0739-991X	Current Publishing Committee	4894
TELEVISION, VIDEO, AND RADIO	Journal of Broadcasting and Electronic Media	0883-8151	Routledge	4897
TELEVISION, VIDEO, AND RADIO	Journal of Radio & Audio Media	1937-6529	Routledge	4898
TELEVISION, VIDEO, AND RADIO	Q E X	0886-8093	American Radio Relay League, Inc.	4900
TELEVISION, VIDEO, AND RADIO	Q S T	0033-4812	American Radio Relay League, Inc.	4901
TELEVISION, VIDEO, AND RADIO	Radio	1542-0620	NewBay Media, LLC	4902
TELEVISION, VIDEO, AND RADIO	Video Watchdog	1070-9991	Video Watchdog	4907
TELEVISION, VIDEO, AND RADIO	Widescreen Review		W S R Publishing	4908
URBAN STUDIES	European Journal of Spatial Development	1650-9544	Nordregio	5032
WEDDINGS	Martha Stewart Weddings	1534-553X	Meredith Corporation	5096

HOW TO USE THIS BOOK

*Title. *ISSN. Date Founded. *Frequency. *Price. Editor. Publisher and Address. *Internet-WWW. Illustrations, Index, Advertising. *Sample. *Refereed. Circulation. *Date Volume Ends. *CD-ROM. Microform. Reprint. *Online. *Indexed. *Book Reviews. *Audience. *Annotation.

The bibliographic data in the entries contain the items shown in the box above. Items preceded by an asterisk are fully explained in the paragraphs that follow. The Abbreviations section lists the general abbreviations found in the bibliographic information in the numbered entries.

The detailed Subject Index enables the user to access the enormous amount of information that may not be readily retrievable from the alphabetically arranged Title Index. All subject classifications used, as well as variations in wording of subject headings, are listed in the Subject Index. The numbers that appear in the indexes refer to the magazine entry numbers, not page numbers.

Title

The periodicals in this book are listed alphabetically, by title, under the subjects given in the Contents. They are numbered sequentially, beginning with 1 on page 1 and ending with 5,030, the last magazine entry in the book, on page 762.

ISSN Numbers

This international standard, which is used all over the world by serial publishers to distinguish similar titles from each other, directly follows the title. *Ulrich's Periodicals Directory* was used to verify this information.

Frequency and Price

The frequency is given immediately after the founding date, and the symbols used are explained in the General Abbreviations section. The price quoted is the annual subscription rate given by the publisher, usually as of 2019. A large number are prices for 2020. Prices are relative and, of course, subject to change-probably upward. Furthermore, the fluctuation of the dollar makes the prices of foreign magazines even more relative.

World Wide Web

The web address (URL) represents the address at the time of the compilation. As anyone knows who uses the Internet, the address may change frequently. In a case where the address does not prove correct, try shortening the address back to the "root" or entering the name of the magazine in the search engine box. Normally this works.

Sample

Publishers were asked whether or not they would send a free copy of the magazine to a library if requested. Those who replied favorably are indicated by the single word "sample". The request should be made by the head of the library, or by the head of the serials department, and written on official stationery. The indication that publishers are willing to send samples to institutions does not mean they are necessarily interested in sending them to individual subscribers. And one additional note: Several publishers would not supply review copies of their publications. So, if there are a few titles not in the list that you might otherwise expect to see here, that is why. *MFL* does depend on publisher cooperation to be able to access and examine titles for possible inclusion.

Refereed

This term is used to indicate that manuscripts published in the journal have been reviewed by experts and specialists in the field before being accepted for publication. Sometimes refereed journals are characterized as "peer-reviewed." This process tends to make scholars trust the reliability of the content of an article more than a non-refereed article.

Date Volume Ends

Librarians find it helpful to know when a publisher ends a volume-obviously for purposes of binding. The information provided is from the publisher.

Online

This includes the basic sources of online access to a particular title. This may be in reference to an index, or it may be in reference to the full-text of articles in the journal.

Indexed

Information on where titles are indexed or abstracted is given-in abbreviated format-following the bibliographic data. Also indicated are major subject indexes in which the periodicals are indexed. Major must be emphasized. The list of the A&Is recommended by *MFL* subject specialist, can be found on page xxix. The term index in the bibliographic description indicates that the publisher has an index to the periodical.

Book Reviews

Information given refers to the approximate number of reviews that appear in a typical issue of the periodical and the average length.

Audience

Ems (elementary and middle school students); Hs (high school students); Ga (General Adult); Ac (Academic audience); Sa (Special Adult). Each magazine has an indication of audience or type of library for which it is suited. The scale is specific, but as most magazines are for more than one audience, several audience levels are usually given for each title. Periodicals for elementary and middle school students (Ems) are not separated because it is often difficult to draw the line between these two age groups. The titles and descriptive annotations leave little doubt as to the level of maturity for which the magazine is intended. Generally, elementary and middle school means the age group from 4 to 14 years and/or those in elementary or middle school. The high school level (Hs) overlaps and may include middle school, but for the most part, these are titles suitable for those from 14 years up to 18 years and/or in high school. Magazines suitable for public libraries and college and university library reading rooms are rated General Adult (Ga). Publications designated Academic audience (Ac) should be considered for junior colleges, colleges, and universities. Magazines rated Special Adult (Sa) are for specialized audiences and will be read by few people other than professionals or students of a particular subject. It is assumed that the audience symbols are only guides, not designations for type of library-which is to say that the symbol Ga does not mean the magazine is only limited to public libraries any more than Ac means a magazine is only for academic libraries. Obviously the choice should be made by the librarian, and this will depend on his or her assessment of the audience to be served. Public libraries will often include many of the same magazines found in all other libraries.

Annotation

The annotations are generally short summaries describing the scope, purpose, and intent of each magazine, bias (if any), and target audience as described above. In making their recommendations chapter authors are assessing the usefulness and readability of articles in each journal for various audiences. The fact that a journal is listed in *Magazines For Libraries* indicates that it is considered to be a core title for the listed audience and recommended to the libraries serving them.

ABBREVIATIONS

■ GENERAL ABBREVIATIONS

a.	Annual
Ac	Academic (Junior Colleges, Colleges, Universities)
adv.	advertising
Aud.	Audience
bi-m.	Every two months
bi-w.	Every two weeks
Bk. rev	Book reviews
Circ.	circulation
CND	Canadian Dollar
d.	Daily
Ed., Eds.	Editor(s)
Ems	Elementary and Middle School
EUR	Euro
fortn.	Fortnightly
Ga	General Adult
GPB	British Pound
Hs	High School
illus.	illustrations
Irreg.	Irregular
ISSN	International Standard Serial Number
m.	Monthly
N.S.	New Series
no., #, nos.	number(s)
q.	Quarterly
rev.	reviews
Sa	Special Adult
s-a.	Twice annually
s-m.	Twice monthly
s-w.	Twice weekly
3/m.	Three times a month
3/w	Three times a week
3/yr.	Three times per year
USD	U.S. Dollars
vol., vols.	volume(s)
w.	Weekly
yr., yrs.	year(s)

Controlled Circ. Controlled circulation (free to certain groups)

ABSTRACTS AND INDEXES

This is a list of the abstracting and indexing tools recommended by *MFL* chapter authors in this edition. For the most current and accurate information on each simply Google the title to locate full product content at the publishers'/providers' web sites.

AATA Online: abstracts of international conservation literature

ABI/INFORM

Abstract Bulletin of Paper Science and Technology

Abstracts in Anthropology

Abstracts in Social Gerontology

Academic OneFile

Academic Search Complete

Academic Search Premier

ACM Computing Reviews

Advanced Technologies & Aerospace Database

African Studies

African Studies Abstracts

AgeLine

AGRICOLA

Air University Library Index to Military Periodicals

Alternative Press Index

America: History and Life

American Bibliography of Slavic and Eastern European Studies (ABSEES)

Annual Bibliography of English Language and Literature (ABELL)

Anthropological Index Online

Anthropological Literature

AnthroSource

Applied Science and Technology Abstracts

Applied Science and Technology Index

Aquatic Sciences and Fisheries Abstracts (ASFA)

Archaeology Data Service (includes British and Irish Archaeological Bibliography)

Art & Architecture Complete

Art Abstracts

Art and Architecture Complete

Art Design & Architecture Collection

Art Full Text

Art Index

ARTbibliographies Modern

Arts and Humanities Citation Index

arXiv.org

ASSIA: Applied Social Sciences Index and Abstracts

Astrophysics Data System

ATLA Catholic Periodical and Literature Index

ATLA Religion Index

Avery Index to Architectural Periodicals

Bibliography of Asian Studies

ABSTRACTS AND INDEXES

BIOBASE

Biography and Genealogy Master Index

Biography in Context

Biography Index Past and Present

Biological & Agricultural Index

Biological Abstracts

Biological Abstracts/RRM

Biological and Agricultural Index

Biology Digest

BioOne Complete

BIOSIS

BIOSIS Previews

Bloomsbury Fashion Central (includes Berg Fashion Library)

Book Review Digest

Book Review Index

Business and Company Resource Center

Business Collection (includes Business and Company ASAP)

Business Periodicals Index

Business Source Complete

Business Source Premier

CAB Abstracts

CAB Direct

Canadian Business & Current Affairs Database

Chemical Abstracts

Chicano Database

Children's Book Review Index

CINAHL

Communication & Mass Media Complete

Communication Abstracts

Communication Abstracts

Compendex (includes Engineering Index)

Computer & Control Abstracts

Computer Database

Computer Society Digital Library (IEEE)

Contemporary Women's Issues

Criminal Justice Abstracts

Criminal Justice Periodical Index

Current Bibliography on African Affairs

Current Contents/Agriculture, Biology & Environmental Sciences

Current Contents/Clinical Medicine

Current Contents/Life Sciences

Current Contents/Physical, Chemical, and Earth Sciences

Current Law Index

Design and Applied Arts Index

Dictionary of Literary Biography Complete Online

Ecology Abstracts

EconLit

Education Abstracts

Education Research Complete

EMBASE

Environment Complete

Environment Index

Environmental Science Collection

Environmental Sciences and Pollution Management

ERIC

Ethnic NewsWatch

Expanded Academic ASAP

Factiva

Family Studies Abstracts

Feminist Periodicals

Film & Television Literature Index

Forest Science Database

Garden, Landscape & Horticulture Index

GenderWatch

GEOBASE

GeoRef

Google Scholar

Health and Safety Science Abstracts

Health Source: Consumer Edition

Health Source: Nursing/Academic

Hein Online

High-Energy Physics Literature Database (INSPIRE)

Hispanic American Periodicals Index (HAPI)

Historical Abstracts

Horticultural Science Abstracts

Hospitality and Tourism Index

Humanities Index

Humanities International Complete

Humanities International Index

International Bibliography of the Social Sciences (IBSS)

IBZ Online

ICONDA

IEEE Xplore

Index Islamicus

Index to Current Urban Documents

Index to Foreign Legal Periodicals

Index to How to Do It Information

Index to Jewish Periodicals

Index to Legal Periodicals and Books

Index Veterinarius

Information Science & Technology Abstracts

INSPEC

International African Bibliography

International Bibliography of Art

International Bibliography of the Social Sciences

International Bibliography of Theatre and Dance

International Index to Black Periodicals Full Text

International Index to Film Periodicals

International Index to Music Periodicals

International Index to the Performing Arts

International Philosophical Bibliography

International Political Science Abstracts

Internet & Personal Computing Abstracts

JSTOR

L'Annee Philologique

LegalTrac

Leisure Tourism Database

Leisure, Recreation and Tourism Abstracts

LexisNexis

LGBT Life

ABSTRACTS AND INDEXES

Library Literature & Information Science Full Text

Linguistics Abstracts Online

Linguistics and Language Behavior Abstracts (LLBA)

LISA: Library and Information Science Abstracts

Literature Online (LION)

MAS Ultra: School Edition

MasterFILE Premier

Maternity and Infant Care

MathSciNet

MEDLINE

Meteorological and Geoastrophysical Abstracts

Middle Search: Main Edition

MLA International Bibliography

Music Index

Music Periodicals Database

National Sea Grant Library Database

New Testament Abstracts

Nursing Resource Center

Nutrition Abstracts and Reviews

Old Testament Abstracts

OmniFile

PAIS International

Peace Research Abstracts

PEDro, the Physiotherapy Evidence Database

Philosopher's Index

PhilPapers: Online Research in Philosophy

Physical Education Index

Physics Abstracts

PIO: Periodicals Index Online

Political Science Complete

Pollution Abstracts

Primary Search

Project Muse

ProQuest Accounting and Tax Database

ProQuest Biological Science Database

ProQuest Central

ProQuest Nursing and Allied Health Database

ProQuest Research Library

PsycArticles

PsycINFO

PubMed

Quarterly Index to Africana Periodical Literature

Race Relations Abstracts

Readers' Guide to Periodical Literature

RILM Abstracts of Music Literature

Risk Abstracts

SafetyLit.org

Science Citation Index

ScienceDirect

Scopus

Social Sciences Citation Index

Social Sciences Index

Social Services Abstracts

Social Work Abstracts

SocINDEX

Sociological Abstracts

SPORTDiscus with Full Text

Studies on Women and Gender Abstracts

TOCS-IN

TRIS Database

Urban Studies Abstracts

Violence & Abuse Abstracts

Web of Science

Women Studies Abstracts

Women's Studies International

World Agricultural Economics and Rural Sociology Abstracts

Worldwide Political Science Abstracts

zbMATH

Zoological Record

CONSULTANTS

Full names and addresses are given for the consultants at the head of each section.

Adams, Christine (Accounting & Taxation)

Albro, Maggie (Energy)

Anderson, Kari (Forestry)

Arguello, Natasha (Travel & Tourism)

Arnold, Nicole (Education)

Ashmun, Julia D. (Boats & Boating)

Bales, Stephen (Religion)

Bauer, Melissa (Library & Information Science)

Beeler, Cynthia J. (Medicine)

Bergfelt, Theodore (Fiction: General/Mystery & Detective)

Bernnard, Deborah F. (Bibliography)

Bickett, Skye (Family Planning)

Bishop, Sasha (World Wide Web)

Bouchard, Karen (Archaeology)

Brooks, Amanda (Folklore)

Brownfield, Lindsay (History; Weddings)

Bruno, Tom (Anime, Comics, Graphic Novels, & Manga)

Burchsted, Fred (Geography)

Burns, Shelly (Health Care Administration)

Bussell, Hilary (Political Science)

Campbell, Nancy F. (Communication)

Carlson, Erica Alice (News & Opinion)

Carter, David S. (Games & Gaming)

Casper, Christianne (Astrology; Paranormal)

Chilcoat, Kristan Majors (Robotics)

Cohen, Laurie (Classical Studies)

Colbert-Lewis, Danielle (Labor & Industrial Relations)

Cole, Rachel (Transportation)

Cook, Kristen (Computers & Information Technology)

Dankert, Holly Stec (Art; Interior Design & Decoration)

Dawson-Andoh, Araba (Africa)

Deards, Kiyomi D. (Physics)

Dearing, Karen (Globalization)

DeMars, Michelle (Nursing)

Dotson, Daniel S. (Statistics)

Duong, Khue (Informatics)

Ehrenhart, David (Fire Protection)

Eichelberger, Michelle A. (Geriatrics & Gerontological Studies)

Esfahani, Bijan (Science & Technology)

Fairall, Jennifer (Model Making)

Ferreira, Nick (Art)

Ferretti, Stephanie (Family Planning)

Flota, Brian (Literature)

Frankosky, Julia (Peace & Conflict Studies)

Garcia, Kenny (Books & Book Reviews)

Gardinier, Lisa (Latino Studies)

Georgas, Helen (Little Magazines)

Gilman Yamada, Susan (Literary Reviews)

Gullen, Amy (Chemistry)

Hall, Lucinda (Cartography, GIS, & Imagery)

Hanlan, Laura Robinson (Science & Technology)

Hannan, Khyle (Business & Finance)

Harter, Odile (Digital Humanities)

Hicks, Elaine R. (Public Health)

Hill, David (Numismatics)

Ijams, Sally (Cooking & Cookery)

Irwin-Smiler, Kate (Occupations & Careers)

Johns-Masten, Kathryn (Birds)

Johnson, Jennifer (Crafts & Making)

Johnson, Nicholas (Music – Popular)

Jones, Julie (Canada)

Keeran, Peggy (Philosophy)

Kendall, Susan K. (Biotechnology)

Kent, Caroline M. (Journalism & Writing; Parenting)

Kepsel, Andrea C. (Animal Rights/Animal Welfare)

Kline, Hilary (LGBT+; Paleontology)

Kohn, Rebecca (Social Media)

Krajewski, Rex J. (Gardening)

Krug, Emily (Fiction: Science Fiction, Fantasy, & Horror)

LaBonte, Kristen (Ecology)

LaGuardia, Cheryl (Abstracts & Indexes; Latin America & Spain; Europe)

Larsen, Alison (Urban Studies; Health& Fitness)

Leigh, Miriam (Civil Liberties; Menopause/Andropause)

Lener, Edward F. (Earth Sciences & Geology)

Leuzinger, Ryne (Books & Book Reviews)

Loa, Berlin (Native Americans; Photography)

Long, Ann Walsh (Marriage & Divorce)

Lowrie, Reed (Literary Reviews)

Lundstrom, Kacy (Classroom Magazines)

Macfarlane, Carrie M. (Do-It-Yourself / Makers)

MacWatters, Kelly S. (Fish, Fisheries, & Aquaculture; Fishing; Forensics; Sociology & Social Work)

Marcus, Elizabeth (Criminology & Law Enforcement)

Mascarenas, Paul (Humor)

McCaffrey, Erin K. (Family)

McClusky, Duncan (Agriculture)

McCutcheon, Camille (Blind & Visually-Impaired; Pets)

McGuire, Nancy (Human Resources)

McKeigue, Elizabeth (International Magazines; Theater)

McMinn, Howard Stephen (Aeronautics & Space Science)

Meier, John J. (Mathematics)

Meszaros, Rosemary L. (Government Periodicals, Federal; Government Periodicals, State & Local)

Moore, Susan (Atmospheric Sciences)

Murray, Tara (Philately)

Nowak, Kristy (Physiology)

O'English, Lorena (News & Opinion)

Oka, Christine K. (Abstracts & Indexes; Asia & the Pacific; Asian American; Hunting & Guns; Safety)

O'Neill, Kimberly (Biology)

Pakhtigian, Alice S. (Death & Dying)

Paranick, Amber (Archives & Manuscripts; Fashion & Lifestyle; General Interest)

CONSULTANTS

Park, Betsy (Sports)

Parker, Joshua (Middle East)

Pascual, Chloe (Gender Studies)

Pfitzinger, Scott G. (Music Reviews)

Phelps, Devin (Fiction: Science Fiction, Fantasy, & Horror)

Plungis, Joan (Management & Administration)

Providenti, Michael J. (Communication)

Raymond, John (Films)

Reed, Andrea (Media & A/V)

Richardson, Diane (Fire Protection)

Roberts, Sarah (Europe; Home)

Robinson, Margaret E. (Food Industry)

Rogers, Kandace (Beer, Wine, & Spirits)

Romito, David (Marine Science & Technology)

Rose, Marie (Psychology)

Ruan, Lian (Fire Protection)

Rudisell, Carol A. (African American)

Ryckman, Brian (Botany)

Sands, Diane T. (Environment & Conservation; Food & Nutrition)

Schwartz, Vanette M. (Cultural Studies)

Scott, Michael (Latin America & Spain)

Seaman, Priscilla (Anthropology)

Sherman, Leah (Dance)

Sittel, Robbie (Genealogy)

Slater, Jillian M. (Linguistics)

Smith, Donna B. (Printing & Graphic Arts)

Sprung, Amy (Teenagers)

St. Martin, Scott (Real Estate)

St. Pierre, Adam (Antiques)

Storm, Paula M. (Electronics)

Stormes, Sheridan (Music - General)

Straw, Joseph E. (Military)

Sugrue, Edward Creighton (Astronomy)

Sullivan, Laura A. (Communication)

Sundheim, Jennifer (Hiking, Climbing, & Outdoor Recreation)

Tarbet, Amanda (Health Professions)

Tchangalova, Nedelina (Disabilities)

Theriault, Pauline (Automobiles & Motorcycles)

Toker, Emily Coolidge (Economics)

Tomlin, Patrick (Landscape Architecture)

Townley, Megan (Population Studies)

Trendler, Amy (Architecture)

Truslow, Hugh (Slavic and Eurasian Studies)

Tsang, Daniel (Sexuality)

Tummon, Nikki (Canada)

Ugaz, Ana (Veterinary Science)

Vogl, Ann (Mindfulness)

Wallace, Lynn (Children)

Walters, Sheryl (Pregnancy)

Watson, Amy (Hospitality/Restaurant)

Wharton, Nicholas (Building & Construction)

Wilde, Michelle (Zoology)

Williams, Austin Martin (Law)

Williams, Barbara (Physics)

Williams, Clay (Advertising, Marketing & Public Relations)

Wilson, Megan (Engineering & Technology)

Wolfe, Mark (Bibliography)

Wood, Wendy (Printing & Graphic Arts)

Worster, Paul M. (Television, Video & Radio)

Writt, Hilary (Beer, Wine, & Spirits)

Young, Courtney L. (Interdisciplinary Studies)

Zieman, Jessica (Multicultural Studies)

MAGAZINES FOR LIBRARIES

■ ACCOUNTING AND TAXATION

Professional/Scholarly/Taxation

See also Business and Finance; Economics; and Law sections.

Christine M. Adams, Government Documents, Business & Economics Librarian, William F. Maag, Jr. Library, Youngstown State University, One University Plaza, Youngstown, OH 44555; cmadams02@ysu.edu

Introduction

The need for authoritative and diverse research literature in the fields of accounting and taxation is continually growing, for a variety of reasons. Rules and regulations are perpetually changing, necessitating the need for accountants to have access to timely details of such changes. Rapid advancements in accounting-related technology require accountants to not only be up to date within their specializations, but also to remain current in new and varying forms of relevant technology. With the multitude of companies conducting business globally, many accountants must become familiar with other cultures as well as with international laws, regulations, and accounting standards. Most areas of accounting require continuing professional education and the attainment of specific certifications, such as Certified Public Accountant, Certified Financial Manager, Certified Internal Auditor, Certified Management Accountant, and so on.

These ongoing governmental, technological, and global changes support the need for authoritative publications, both practical and theoretical, that address accounting in general as well as the different specializations. Professionals and academics are required to stay current regarding new standards and developments, and therefore rely heavily upon the literature of their profession. Titles in this list are presented in three major sections: (1) "Professional" titles that provide practical information to CPAs and accounting professionals; (2) "Scholarly" titles that publish the results of academic research relevant to the profession; and (3) "Taxation" titles that provide information specific to those preparing tax returns and providing tax advice. A balanced blend of information from all three categories is of value to accounting and tax professionals.

Practical information published in professional journals is vital for daily practice, while theoretical academic research is of the utmost importance in order to analyze and improve the profession. This list attempts to strike a balance between the practical and the theoretical, to help libraries build a solid accounting and taxation collection, especially academic libraries that support accounting research and post-graduate programs. With the shift toward International Financial Reporting Standards, journals espousing global perspectives continue to grow in importance. This list attempts to provide sources of information and research not only from the United States but from other cultures and parts of the world as well. Likewise, publications providing information on accounting-related technology and accounting information systems are also represented.

The formats in which titles may be accessed are continuously evolving. Of course, some journals are still available in print format, but all provide for electronic access in some form. Many titles are published by major content providers and are available through database subscriptions, while some are published by associations that provide electronic access through their websites with membership or by subscription. Association websites are especially useful for professionals because of the enhanced features, such as daily updates, blogs, RSS feeds, e-newsletters, searchable archives, professional development opportunities, and more. Most content providers, journals, and associations have social media presences and mobile applications available for various devices.

The resources suggested in this list will assist librarians in building a well-rounded core collection for accounting researchers and practicing professionals, as well as students pursuing careers within these professions. Because accounting and taxation are interrelated with many other subject areas, librarians may also wish to consider sources listed in other sections of this volume, such as "Business and Finance," "Economics," and "Law."

Basic Periodicals

Ac: *Accounting, Organizations & Society, Accounting Review, Accounting Today, Contemporary Accounting Research, The CPA Journal, Journal of Accountancy, Journal of Accounting Research, Journal of Accounting and Economics, Review of Accounting Studies.*

Basic Abstracts and Indexes

ABI/INFORM, ProQuest Accounting and Tax Database, Business & Company ProFile ASAP, Business Periodicals Index, Business Source Complete.

Professional

1. ***Accountancy.*** Formerly (until 1938): *Incorporated Accountants' Journal.* [ISSN: 0001-4664] 1889. m. GBP 99. Croner-i Ltd., 240 Blackfriars Rd, London, SE1 8NW, United Kingdom; info@croner.co.uk; https://www.croneri.co.uk. Illus., index, adv. Vol. ends: Jun/Dec. Microform: PQC. Reprint: PSC. *Indexed:* A22, ATI, B01, BRI. *Aud.:* Sa.

In publication for more than 130 years, *Accountancy* is a monthly professional journal whose focus is on major issues, current news, and technical developments affecting the United Kingdom accounting professions. Published by Croner-i Ltd., each issue provides in-depth insight, topical comment, and authoritative analysis from leading industry professionals, including technical tax specialists, auditors, forensic experts, tax lawyers, and more. The magazine presents technical and authoritative analysis on complex tax, accounting, and audit issues. The U.K. edition concentrates on U.K. developments. The International edition includes both U.K. and international events. The companion website, *Accountancy Daily*, provides electronic access to the publication by subscription.

2. ***The Accountant.*** Incorporates (1989-1996): *Corporate Accounting International.* [ISSN: 0001-4710] 1874. m. Ed(s): Jonathan Minter. V R L Financial News, 40-42 Hatton Garden, London, EC1 N8EB, United Kingdom; info@vrlfinancialnews.com; http://vrl.trimetric.com. Illus., index, adv. Reprint: PSC. *Indexed:* A22, ATI, B03, BRI. *Aud.:* Sa.

Established in 1874, *The Accountant* is one of the oldest and most highly regarded trade publications in the world. This title is published monthly for those involved in the accounting profession, and each issue reports global news, surveys of worldwide accounting bodies, commentary from industry figures, and profiles business and industry leaders. Regular coverage is provided for products and product innovation, country surveys, technological developments, trends and industry developments, opinions of key players, market-sizing and global perspective, and the like. Members of The Association of Chartered Certified Accountants may include reading of *The Accountant* toward Continuing Professional Development qualification if it has helped them to acquire knowledge and skills relevant to their position. Electronic access to recent editions is provided at the magazine's website by subscription.

3. *Accounting & Business.* Former titles (until 1998): *Certified Accountant;* (until 1972): *Certified Accountants' Journal;* (until 1966): *Accountants Journal.* [ISSN: 1460-406X] 19??. 10x/yr. Free to members. Ed(s): Chris Quick, Rosana Mirkovic. Association of Chartered Certified Accountants, 29 Lincoln's Inn Fields, London, WC2A 3EE, United Kingdom; info@accaglobal.com; http://www.accaglobal.com. Illus. *Indexed:* A22, ATI. *Bk. rev.:* 3, 150-400 words, signed. *Aud.:* Sa.

Accounting & Business is a professional magazine for members of the Association of Chartered Certified Accountants, a global body for professional accountants. It is published ten times per year and provides essential information for accountants and business professionals around the world. Each issue features news in pictures, news in graphics, news round-up, and analysis. Business and accounting-related articles are featured in various sections, including "In Focus," "Insights," "Interviews," "Corporate," and "Practice." If an article is relevant to professional development needs, it can count toward verifiable Continuing Professional Development. A full-text archive of the various editions from recent years is freely available at the ACCA website.

4. *Accounting Horizons.* [ISSN: 0888-7993] 1987. q. USD 401. Ed(s): Teri L Yohn. American Accounting Association, 9009 Town Center Pkwy, Lakewood Ranch, FL 34202; info@aaahq.org; http://aaahq.org. Illus., index, adv. Refereed. Vol. ends: Dec. Reprint: PSC. *Indexed:* A22, ATI, B01, IBSS. *Aud.:* Ac, Sa.

Accounting Horizons is a refereed, scholarly journal published quarterly by the American Accounting Association. One of the main objectives of the publication is "to establish a dialogue—a bridge of ideas—between accounting academics and the business community." The content is written for academics and professionals, including researchers, educators, practitioners, regulators, and students of accounting. Articles focus on a wide variety of accounting topics and provide insight into the accounting profession as a whole, from ethics to financial reporting to regulation of the profession. Topics are relevant to current accounting issues and the future of the accounting profession. Also presented are reviews of professional literature, commentaries on practice, and reports of current events.

5. *Accounting Today: the business newspaper for the tax and accounting community.* [ISSN: 1044-5714] 1987. m. Ed(s): Daniel Hood. SourceMedia, Inc., One State St Plz, 27th Fl, New York, NY 10004; custserv@sourcemedia.com; http://www.sourcemedia.com. Illus. *Indexed:* A22, ATI, B01, B03, BRI, C42, CompLI. *Aud.:* Sa.

Accounting Today provides analysis, breaking news, opinion and expert advice, and practical business-building ideas to help practitioners make informed decisions. The monthly publication is geared to public accounting professionals who provide tax preparation, bookkeeping, auditing, financial planning, and business advisory and consulting services to individuals and small businesses. *AT* focuses on the industry's most important concerns, including tax law, accounting standards, technology, audit assurances, and wealth management. The title's annual rankings, especially the Top 100 Firms and the Top 100 Most Influential People in Accounting, are of widespread note in the accounting profession. AccountingToday.com, the companion website, offers breaking news, in-depth features, insightful editorial analysis, and more.

6. *The C P A Journal.* Former titles (until Dec.1975): *The C P A;* (until Jun.1975): *C.P.A. Journal;* (until 1972): *Certified Public Accountant;* (until 1971): *New York Certified Public Accountant: C P A;* (until 1935): *New York State Society of Certified Public Accountants. Bulletin.* [ISSN: 0732-8435] 1930. m. Ed(s): Anthony H Sarmiento. New York State Society of Certified Public Accountants, 3 Park Ave, 18th Fl, New York, NY 10016; http://www.cpaj.com. Illus., adv. Vol. ends: Dec. *Indexed:* A22, ATI, B01, BRI. *Bk. rev.:* 0-1, 250-350 words, signed. *Aud.:* Sa.

The CPA Journal is a monthly, technical-refereed publication of the New York State Society of Certified Public Accountants. It has been one of the leading national accounting publications for almost 90 years. It is "[e]dited by CPAs for CPAs," and its goal is to provide accounting practitioners, educators, regulators, and other financial professionals with analysis, perspective, and debate on developments in the areas of accounting, auditing, taxation, finance, management, technology, and professional ethics. Content includes the latest news and developments for auditing standards, technology, IRS tax issues, legislation and regulation, taxation, e-commerce, budgeting, trends, and more. The focus is on practical information and thoughtful analysis of relevant issues. Article formats include general interest, technical interest, and those that express an opinion, perspective, or viewpoint. The journal's editorial and review process ensures the highest technical quality. The full text of *The CPA Journal* is available online going back to 1989, and digital analysis is offered at cpajournal.com.

7. *C P A Magazine.* Incorporates (1975-2013): *C A Magazine;* Which incorporated (1969-1996): *C I C A Dialogue;* C A Magazine was formerly (until 1974): *Chartered Accountant;* (until 1971): *Canadian Chartered Accountants;* Which incorporated (1949-1953): *Canadian Chartered Accountant Tax Review.* [ISSN: 2292-5627] 1911. 10x/yr. Free to members. Ed(s): Okey Chigbo. Chartered Professional Accountants of Canada, 277 Wellington St, W, Toronto, ON M5V 3H2, Canada; cpamagazineinfo@cpacanada.ca; http://www.cpacanada.ca. *Aud.:* Sa.

CPA Magazine is a professional journal published by CPA Canada, a Canadian association with the goal of unifying the most influential business leaders in Canada. The publication replaces *CA Magazine, CG Magazine*, and *CMA Magazine*, and brings together the award-winning approaches of these legacy publications. Its goal is to echo the thoughts, perspectives, and expertise of the new unified membership. The magazine is published 10 times per year in English and French, with combined issues in January/February and June/July. It has the largest circulation of any Canadian magazine covering financial and management accounting professionals across every business sector. The CPA Canada website provides access to issues of *CPA Magazine*, as well as access to archived issues from the legacy publications.

8. *C P A Practice Advisor: today's technology for tomorrow's firm.* Former titles (until 2011): *The C P A Technology Advisor;* (until 2004): *The C P A Software News;* (until 1991): *N S P A Software News.* [ISSN: 2160-8725] 1991. 6x/yr. USD 3 qualifying associations of 10,000 or more (Non-members, USD 37). Ed(s): Gail Perry. SouthComm Communications, Inc., 1233 Janesville Ave., PO Box 803, Fort Atkinson, WI 53538; info@southcomm.com; https://www.southcomm.com/. Adv. *Indexed:* ATI, B01. *Aud.:* Sa.

The mission of *CPA Practice Advisor* is to serve, inform, educate, and lead tax and accounting professionals in the areas of technology, workflow systems, and best practices so their firms can become more efficient, productive, and profitable. Through in-depth reviews, interactive tools, insightful columns, timely features, and examinations of best practices and strategies, the goal is to help identify the most beneficial combination of technology and processes. *CPA Practice Advisor* is the only profession-focused workflow technology resource that assists public accountants in advising small-business clients regarding business management strategies that can help increase productivity. Content includes technology and software reviews, columns from industry leaders, and user-oriented features. This publication is widely respected for its editorial independence, objectivity, and integrity.

9. *Cost Management.* Formerly (until 1992): *Journal of Cost Management for the Manufacturing Industry.* [ISSN: 1092-8057] 1987. 1 Base Vol(s). Ed(s): Paul Sharman, Jack Nestor. W G & L Financial Reporting & Management Research, 395 Hudson St, New York, NY 10014; ria.customerservices@thomson.com; http://ria.thomson.com. Adv. Reprint: PSC. *Indexed:* A22. *Aud.:* Sa.

Cost Management is a bimonthly trade journal that features research-based papers, experience-based articles, and case studies on topics related to cost management. The goal of the publication is to examine the different systems and methods for controlling and improving companies' activities, processes, products, and services involving all aspects of cost management. Topics addressed include lean accounting/management and Six Sigma; activity-based costing and time-driven ABC; microfinance; balanced scorecard and target costing; non-financial performance measures; budgeting and management reporting; Decision Support Systems; strategic planning; simulation modeling; analytics; and new computing capabilities, among other topics. Articles are written by respected industry professionals for a diverse audience with varying degrees of knowledge and are concise and to the point.

10. *Financial Management.* Former titles (until 2000): *Management Accounting;* (until 1965): *Cost Accountant.* [ISSN: 1471-9185] 1921. 6x/yr. Free to members. Ed(s): Rocky Rosen. Chartered Institute of Management Accountants, 26 Chapter St, London, SW1P 4NP, United Kingdom; cima.contact@cimaglobal.com; http://www.cimaglobal.com. Illus., index, adv. Reprint: SCH. *Indexed:* A22, ATI, B01, BRI. *Aud.:* Sa.

Financial Management is published by the Association of International Certified Professional Accountants, the most influential body of professional accountants, combining the strengths of the American Institute of CPAs and the Chartered Institute of Management Accountants. It is the largest accountancy title and the fifth largest business-to-business publication in the United Kingdom. Each issue covers essential concepts and provides information, technical updates, analysis, and current news. Primary readers include business leaders and key decision makers from leading companies and commercial organizations around the world. It is printed six times a year. Recent digital editions are available at the magazine's website.

11. *Internal Auditing.* [ISSN: 0897-0378] 1986. 1 Base Vol(s). Ed(s): Susan Weisenfeld, Jack Nestor. W G & L Financial Reporting & Management Research, 395 Hudson St, New York, NY 10014; ria.customerservices@thomson.com; http://ria.thomson.com. Adv. *Indexed:* A22, ATI, BRI, C42. *Aud.:* Sa.

Internal Auditing is a bimonthly publication that features practice-oriented content on critical issues facing internal auditors. The goal of the publication is to aid internal auditors in pinpointing and solving audit problems, understanding information technology, conducting effective and efficient audits, managing internal auditing departments, and staying current in audit trends and developments. Articles are written by experts, and are primarily practice-oriented and of interest to those in the internal auditing profession. Issues feature practical advice; study results and summaries of current audit research; analysis of current developments and trends; best practices; case studies; professional standards and issues; and feedback on new initiatives and standards from COSO, the Institute of Internal Auditors, and other organizations. Sample topics include compliance issues, risk assessment, fraud prevention, corporate governance, and IT auditing.

12. *Internal Auditor: global perspectives on risk, control and governance.* Formerly (until 19??): *I I A Research Reports.* [ISSN: 0020-5745] 1944. bi-m. USD 75 combined subscription in North America (print & online eds.); USD 99 combined subscription elsewhere (print & online eds.)). Ed(s): Anne Millage, David Salierno. Institute of Internal Auditors, Inc., 1035 Greenwood Blvd, Ste 401, Lake Mary, FL 32746; customerrelations@theiia.org; http://www.theiia.org. Illus., index. Vol. ends: Dec. Microform: PQC. Reprint: SCH. *Indexed:* A22, ATI, B01, BRI, C42. *Bk. rev.:* 1-2, 500-1,000 words, signed. *Aud.:* Sa.

Internal Auditor is a bimonthly publication of the Institute of Internal Auditors and features global content relevant to the internal auditing profession. The goal of the publication is to provide practitioners with essential information and practices needed for day-to-day operations. Content includes articles that focus on practical application of topics discussed; case studies describing procedures or methodology, including actual or hypothetical examples; and analysis of studies and surveys that draw conclusions from research and analyze the impact on the internal auditing profession. Content of the magazine is divided between in-depth feature articles and departments, which present a more narrow focus or an opinionated tone. Departments include "Reader Feedback," "Fraud Findings," "In My Opinion," "ITAudit," "Back to Basics," "Risk Watch," and "Governance Perspectives." Topics are timely and offer practical insight and expert advice to readers.

13. *Journal of Accountancy.* [ISSN: 0021-8448] 1905. m. Ed(s): Kim Nilsen, Rocky S Rosen. American Institute of Certified Public Accountants, 1211 Ave of the Americas, New York, NY 10036; journal@aicpa.org; http://www.aicpa.org. Illus., index, adv. Sample. Vol. ends: Jun/Dec. *Indexed:* A22, ATI, B01, BRI, CBRI, L14. *Aud.:* Ac, Sa.

In publication for almost 115 years, the *Journal of Accountancy* is the flagship publication of the American Institute of Certified Public Accountants, whose members include finance and accounting professionals from public accounting firms, corporations, government agencies, and nonprofit organizations. Each issue contains feature articles on accounting, financial reporting, auditing, taxation, personal financial planning, technology, business valuation, professional development, ethics, liability issues, consulting, practice management, education, and more. Articles are presented relating to the following categories: "Practical," "Corporate," "Technical," "Professional Issues," and "Future." "Practical" articles discuss business problems and offer actual or hypothetical solutions. "Corporate" articles explore the aspects of corporate finance. "Technical" articles cover new standards or best practices, including regulatory actions. "Professional Issues" articles address issues facing the accounting profession and provide guidance. "Future" articles are based on academic research or fast-moving trends that have an immediate or near-future impact on the accounting profession. Editorial content relates practical guidance and in-depth analysis of relevant issues.

14. *Journal of Corporate Accounting & Finance.* Former titles (until 1989): *Financial Accounting Reporter;* (until 1986): *Corporate Accounting Reporter;* (until 1979): *Financial Regulation Report.* [ISSN: 1044-8136] 1977. q. GBP 745. Ed(s): Paul Munter. John Wiley & Sons, Inc., 111 River St, Hoboken, NJ 07030; cs-journals@wiley.com; http://onlinelibrary.wiley.com. Adv. Refereed. Microform: WSH. Reprint: PSC. *Indexed:* A22, ATI, B01, BRI. *Aud.:* Sa.

Journal of Corporate Accounting & Finance, a quarterly trade journal, offers new insights and approaches to corporate finance and accounting issues. It is directed to CEOs and corporate accounting and financial executives, as well as outside auditors and accountants working with corporations. Articles are informative, analytical, and practical, but not highly technical. Original material is featured that offers new insights into, and new approaches to, corporate accounting and finance issues, including high-quality how-to articles that cover business strategy and operations. Each of the annual four issues is devoted to one or more primary themes: "Information Technology and Data Analytics"; "International Accounting and Finance"; "Treasury and Cash Management"; "Mergers and Acquisitions, and Corporate Restructuring"; "Cost Management, Performance Metrics and Strategic Business Analysis"; and "Auditing: Internal and External." Topics include supply chain management, managerial economics, capital markets and financial value issues, decision-making, governmental impact on business, tools available to accounting and finance personnel, and other emerging topics.

15. *The Journal of Government Financial Management.* Former titles (until 2001): *The Government Accountants Journal;* (until 1976): *The Federal Accountant.* [ISSN: 1533-1385] 1950. q. Free to members; Non-members, USD 95. Ed(s): Maryann Malesardi. Association of Government Accountants, 2208 Mount Vernon Ave, Alexandria, VA 22301; http://www.agacgfm.org. Illus., index. Refereed. Circ: 14260. Vol. ends: Winter. Microform: PQC. *Indexed:* A22, ATI, B01, BRI. *Aud.:* Ac, Sa.

The Journal of Government Financial Management is a refereed, scholarly journal published quarterly by the Association of Government Accountants, a member organization for financial professionals in government. Since 1950, the publication has provided valuable, in-depth information to decision makers at all levels of government. The purpose of the journal is to contribute to the literature of the government financial-management profession. The publication provides in-depth information to government financial managers in federal, state, and local government, as well as the private sector and academia. It is read by accountants, auditors, budget analysts, electronic data processors, finance directors, information-resource managers, chief financial officers, inspectors general, consultants, and systems designers. The journal includes ethics questions each month, which are submitted by readers and answered by a team of ethics experts. CPE credits can be earned by reading the journal and passing an online quiz.

16. *Main Street Practitioner.* Incorporates (1956-2009): *Tax Magazine;* Formerly (until 2004): *The N S A Practitioner.* 19??. 5x/yr. Free to membership. Ed(s): Julene Joy. National Society of Accountants, 1010 N. Fairfax St., Alexandria, VA 22314-1574; http://www.nsacct.org/. *Aud.:* Sa.

Main Street Practitioner is a members-only publication, published five times per year by the National Society of Accountants, an association for "Main Street" tax and accounting professionals. The publication is aimed at all levels of tax professionals, with an emphasis on those who manage or own their own tax-and-accounting businesses. Articles discuss and analyze cutting-edge information, current trends, and best practices. Topics include accounting, amending returns, auditing issues, bankruptcy, building a business, collections, consolidations, mergers and acquisitions, continuing education, corporations, credentials, divorce issues, estate planning, financial planning, government resources, IRS negotiation, leadership, new tax regulations, partnerships, preparer certification concepts, professional development, professional ethics, setting up a new business, Social Security benefits, success stories, succession planning, tax legislation, tax season preparation, and volunteering. Each issue focuses on a particular theme and includes special features, case studies, tax tips, and best-practice advice from experts.

17. ***Public Accounting Report.*** Incorporates (2000-2004): *C P A Financial Services Advisor.* [ISSN: 0161-309X] 1978. m. Ed(s): Julie Lindy. C C H Inc., 2700 Lake Cook Rd, Riverwoods, IL 60015; cust_serv@cch.com; http://www.cchgroup.com/. *Indexed:* ATI, B01. *Aud.:* Sa.

Public Accounting Report is an independent monthly newsletter that provides competitive intelligence for public accounting firms as well as the entire accounting profession. Since 1978, the publication has been "renowned for its straight reporting and analysis of the news, developments, and trends that have defined the profession for...years." The primary audience includes public accounting-firm partners and professionals, opinion leaders, and industry observers. Content features current news, in-depth firm profiles, mergers and acquisitions, office closings, key personnel moves, legal and regulatory issues, competitive intelligence, niche practices, product launches, and more. A subscription includes special reports and extras, including the PAR Top 100, an annual ranking of the 100 largest accounting firms in the United States; the PAR Professors Survey, an annual ranking of the best accounting programs in the United States; and PAR's annual associations directory, largest firms survey, and women's survey.

18. ***Strategic Finance.*** Former titles (until 1999): *Management Accounting;* (until 1968): *N A A Management Accounting;* (until 1965): *N A A Bulletin;* (until 1957): *N A C A Bulletin;* (until 1925): *National Association of Cost Accountants. Official Publications.* [ISSN: 1524-833X] 1919. m. USD 195. Ed(s): Kathy Williams. Institute of Management Accountants, 10 Paragon Dr, Ste 1, Montvale, NJ 07645; ima@imanet.org; http://www.imanet.org. Illus., index, adv. Vol. ends: Jun. Microform: PQC. Reprint: SCH. *Indexed:* A01, A22, ATI, B01, BRI, EconLit. *Aud.:* Sa.

Strategic Finance is the monthly flagship publication of the Institute of Management Accountants, a worldwide professional association for accountants and finance professionals working in business. The goal is to cover all the important topics and trends that impact accountants and financial professionals in business, including sustainability, risk management, strategy, financial planning, the changing roles of the CFO and the finance function, budgeting, capital decisions, technology, careers, leadership, and more. The magazine provides timely and relevant information about practices and trends in finance, accounting, and information management. Articles are written with practitioners in mind and offer advice to help readers perform their jobs more effectively, advance their careers, grow personally and professionally, and make their organizations more profitable. A notable feature is the Annual Career Issue and Salary Survey, where IMA members' salaries are evaluated. Access to select articles is available at the IMA website, and back issues are available for purchase.

Scholarly

19. ***Abacus: a journal of accounting, finance and business studies.*** [ISSN: 0001-3072] 1965. q. GBP 644. Ed(s): Stewart Jones. Wiley-Blackwell Publishing Asia, 155 Cremorne St, Richmond, VIC 3121, Australia; melbourne@wiley.com; http://onlinelibrary.wiley.com. Illus., adv. Sample. Refereed. Reprint: PSC. *Indexed:* A22, ATI, AmHI, B01, C42, E01, IBSS. *Aud.:* Ac.

In publication since 1965, *Abacus* is a refereed, scholarly journal published on behalf of the Accounting Foundation, The University of Sydney. The publication provides a forum for the expression of independent and critical thought on matters of current academic and professional interest in accounting, finance, and business. Articles feature current research, critical evaluation of current developments in theory and practice, analysis of the effects of regulatory framework, and exploration of alternatives to, and explanations of, past and current practices. The content is international in scope, with emphasis on international accounting and accounting history. *Abacus* is published quarterly and is an ISI-listed journal.

20. ***Accounting and Business Research.*** Formerly (until 1970): *Accounting Research.* [ISSN: 0001-4788] 19??. 7x/yr. GBP 613 (print & online eds.)). Ed(s): Vivien Beattie. Routledge, 4 Park Sq, Milton Park, Abingdon, OX14 4RN, United Kingdom; subscriptions@tandf.co.uk; http://www.tandfonline.com. Illus., index, adv. Sample. Refereed. Microform: PQC; WMP. Reprint: PSC. *Indexed:* A22, ATI, B01, BRI, H&TI, IBSS. *Bk. rev.:* 0-4, 750-1,250 words, signed. *Aud.:* Ac.

Accounting and Business Research, a refereed, scholarly journal published seven times per year, publishes papers that present a substantial and original contribution to knowledge in accounting, finance, and business research. The goal of the publication is to contribute to developing and understanding the role of accounting in business. Authors take a theoretical or empirical approach, using either quantitative or qualitative methods. Research articles cover all areas of accounting, including corporate governance, auditing, and taxation. The focus, however, is accounting, rather than corporate finance or general management. While primarily directed to academics, this journal is also of value to practitioners and others who are concerned with the latest developments and new ideas in the field.

21. ***Accounting & Finance.*** Former titles (until 1979): *Accounting Education;* (until 1973): *Australasian Association of University Teachers of Accounting. News Bulletin.* [ISSN: 0810-5391] 1960. q. GBP 612. Ed(s): Tom Smith. Wiley-Blackwell Publishing Asia, 155 Cremorne St, Richmond, VIC 3121, Australia; melbourne@wiley.com; http://onlinelibrary.wiley.com. Adv. Sample. Refereed. Microform: PQC. Reprint: PSC. *Indexed:* A22, ATI, B01, BRI, C42, E01. *Aud.:* Ac.

Accounting and Finance is a refereed, scholarly journal published quarterly on behalf of the Accounting and Finance Association of Australia and New Zealand. The journal publishes theoretical, empirical, and experimental papers that significantly contribute to the disciplines of accounting, finance, business information systems, and related disciplines. The publication applies economic, organizational, and other theories to accounting and finance phenomena and presents periodic special issues with themes such as research methods in management accounting. Authors employ a wide range of research methods, including statistical analysis, analytical work, case studies, field research, and historical analysis, to examine relevant research questions from a wide range of perspectives. Readership includes academics, graduate students, and all those interested in accounting and finance research, including practitioners in accounting, corporate finance, investments, and merchant and investment banking.

22. ***Accounting and the Public Interest.*** [ISSN: 1530-9320] 2001. a. Free to members. Ed(s): Pamela B Roush. American Accounting Association, 9009 Town Center Pkwy, Lakewood Ranch, FL 34202; info@aaahq.org; http://aaahq.org. Adv. *Indexed:* ATI, B01. *Aud.:* Ac.

Accounting and the Public Interest is an academic journal published annually by the Public Interest Section of the American Accounting Association. The goal of the publication is to provide a forum for academic accounting research that addresses the public interest and takes a socially responsive, and responsible, perspective. Alternative theories and methodologies are considered, as well as more traditional ones. Studies and findings are required to be linked to the public interest by situating them within a historical, social, and political context, as well as providing guidance for responsible action. Research articles cover topics in all areas of accounting, such as financial accounting and auditing, accounting in organizations, social and environmental accounting, government and professional regulation, taxation, gender and diversity issues, professional and business ethics, information technology, accounting and business education, governance of accounting organizations, and more.

23. ***Accounting, Auditing and Accountability Journal.*** Formerly (until 1989): *Accounting Auditing and Accountability.* [ISSN: 1368-0668] 1988. 8x/yr. EUR 8682 (print & online eds.) (excluding UK)). Ed(s): Lee Parker, James Guthrie. Emerald Publishing Limited, Howard House,

Wagon Ln, Bingley, BD16 1WA, United Kingdom; emerald@emeraldinsight.com; http://www.emeraldinsight.com. Illus. Sample. Refereed. Vol. ends: No. 5. Reprint: PSC. *Indexed:* A22, ATI, B01, BRI, E01, IBSS, MLA-IB. *Bk. rev.:* 1-2, 500-1,500 words, signed. *Aud.:* Ac.

Accounting, Auditing and Accountability Journal is a refereed, scholarly journal dedicated to the advancement of accounting knowledge and provides a forum for research on the interaction between accounting and auditing and the impact on socioeconomic and political environments. The goal is to present detailed analysis and critical assessment of current practice, discuss implications of new policy alternatives, and explore the impact of accounting on the socioeconomic and political environment. Research and analysis may be international, national, or organization-specific in its approach. Topics include alternative explanations for observed practice; critical and historical perspectives on current issues and problems; limitations in present accounting measurement; political influences on policy making; social and political aspects of accounting standards; and the broadening scope of the reporting constituency, among other topics. Readership includes accounting and management researchers, accountants, administrators, managers, accounting and auditing policy-makers, and accounting students.

24. ***Accounting Education: an international journal.*** [ISSN: 0963-9284] 1992. 6x/yr. GBP 1446 (print & online eds.)). Ed(s): Richard M S Wilson. Routledge, 4 Park Sq, Milton Park, Abingdon, OX14 4RN, United Kingdom; subscriptions@tandf.co.uk; http://www.tandfonline.com. Illus., index, adv. Sample. Refereed. Vol. ends: Dec. Reprint: PSC. *Indexed:* A22, ATI, B01, E01. *Bk. rev.:* 0-2, 500-750 words, signed. *Aud.:* Ac.

Accounting Education is a refereed, scholarly journal dedicated to publishing research-based papers and other information on key aspects of accounting education and training relevant to practitioners, academics, trainers, students, and professional bodies. The primary goal is to enhance the educational base of accounting practice and thereby produce effective accounting practitioners, who in turn improve the quality of accounting practice. The publication is a forum for the exchange of ideas, experiences, opinions, and research results relating to the preparation of students for careers in public accounting, managerial accounting, financial management, corporate accounting, controllership, treasury management, financial analysis, internal auditing, accounting in government, and other non-commercial organizations, as well as continuing professional development for accounting practitioners. Topics are international in scope and coverage includes curriculum issues, computing matters, teaching methods, and research pertinent to accounting education. The journal also includes exemplars and reviews relating to what is taught, how it is taught, and how effective endeavors are in providing an adequate educational and training base for accounting practice.

25. ***Accounting Forum.*** [ISSN: 0155-9982] 1978. q. GBP 464 print & online eds. Taylor & Francis, 5 Howick Pl, London, SW1P 1WG, United Kingdom; https://www.tandfonline.com. Adv. Sample. Refereed. *Indexed:* A22, B01, BRI, E01. *Bk. rev.:* Number and length vary. *Aud.:* Ac.

Accounting Forum is a refereed, scholarly journal, published quarterly, whose goal is to advance the knowledge of theory and practice in all areas of accounting, business, finance, and related subjects. The publication promotes a greater understanding of the role of business in the global environment, and provides a forum for the intellectual exchange of academic research in business fields, particularly within the accounting profession. Coverage includes accounting theory, auditing, financial accounting, finance and accounting education, management accounting, small business, social and environmental accounting, and taxation. The journal is published for the benefit of practitioners, academics, and students. Each issue presents peer-reviewed articles, notes and comments, and a book review section.

26. ***Accounting Historians Journal.*** Formerly (until 1977): *Accounting Historian.* [ISSN: 0148-4184] 1974. s-a. Free to members. Ed(s): Gloria Vollmers. Academy of Accounting Historians, Case Western Reserve University, Weatherhead School of Management, Cleveland, OH 44106; acchistory@case.edu; http://aahhq.org. Illus. Refereed. Vol. ends: Dec. *Indexed:* A22, ATI, B01, BRI, C42. *Bk. rev.:* 4-5, 750-1,500 words, signed. *Aud.:* Ac, Sa.

Accounting Historians Journal is a refereed, scholarly journal published semi-annually in June and December by the Academy of Accounting Historians, a nonprofit organization that encourages research, publication, teaching, and personal interchanges in accounting history and its interrelation with business and economic history. Topics are related to accounting history, including but not limited to research that provides a historical perspective on contemporary accounting issues. Coverage includes history of the accounting profession, biographies, history of accounting changes, entity case studies, development of accounting theory, and critical examinations of new or old research. There is also interesting coverage of accountings from various periods and places, the ancient world, the medieval period, changes in accounting education, case studies of personal accounts, studies of taxation or accounting technologies, changes in corporate disclosure, and the like. Content is international in scope and addresses the evolution of accounting thought and practice. Past issues of the journal are available electronically at the University of Mississippi Libraries' Digital Accounting Collection.

27. ***Accounting History.*** Formerly (until 1989): *Accounting History Newsletter.* [ISSN: 1032-3732] 1980. q. USD 1202 (print & online eds.)). Ed(s): Garry Carnegie, Brian West. Sage Publications Ltd., 1 Oliver's Yard, 55 City Rd, London, EC1Y 1SP, United Kingdom; info@sagepub.com; https://www.sagepub.com/. Illus., adv. Sample. Refereed. Reprint: PSC. *Indexed:* A22, ATI, B01, E01. *Aud.:* Ac.

Accounting History is a refereed, scholarly journal published quarterly in association with the Accounting History Special Interest Group of the Accounting and Finance Association of Australia and New Zealand. The publication encourages critical and interpretative historical research on the nature, roles, uses, and impacts of accounting, and it provides a forum for the publication of high-quality manuscripts on the historical development of accounting. It provides an international perspective and promotes the study of accounting as a social practice as well as a technical practice. The journal seeks to advance an understanding of the interaction of accounting and its socioeconomic and political environments within historical contexts. Research articles address a wide range of topics and periods and a variety of methodological approaches, including biography, prosopography, institutional history, public-sector accounting history, business history through accounting records, comparative international accounting history, and innovative research methods. It is a premier journal in its field and is a valuable resource for academics, practitioners, and students who seek to understand accounting's past, present, and future.

28. ***Accounting History Review.*** Formerly (until 2010): *Accounting, Business and Financial History.* [ISSN: 2155-2851] 1990. 3x/yr. GBP 638 (print & online eds.)). Ed(s): Trevor Boyns, John Richard Edwards. Routledge, 4 Park Sq, Milton Park, Abingdon, OX14 4RN, United Kingdom; subscriptions@tandf.co.uk; http://www.tandfonline.com. Adv. Sample. Refereed. Circ: 600. Reprint: PSC. *Indexed:* A22, ATI, E01, EconLit, IBSS. *Aud.:* Ac.

Accounting History Review, a refereed, scholarly journal published three times per year, is an international forum for research into the history of accounting thought, practice, and institutions. The primary goal is the publication of scholarly articles that investigate accounting and its implication in diverse social, cultural, and multi-faceted institutional contexts. It reflects accounting history that looks outwardly into contexts with which accounting interacts. The scope of the journal includes research that reconsiders accounting's past from differing and competing points of view. *AHR* presents research into the history of accounting and historical accounts that inform and are informed by broader historiographical debates. Cross-disciplinary, interdisciplinary, and multi-disciplinary studies, and submissions from disciplines with which accounting interacts, are encouraged. Special issues and review essays are presented that highlight emerging research and perspective.

29. ***Accounting, Organizations and Society: an international journal devoted to the behavioural, organizational & social aspects of accounting.*** [ISSN: 0361-3682] 1976. 8x/yr. EUR 3329. Elsevier Ltd, The Boulevard, Langford Lane, Oxford, OX5 1GB, United Kingdom; customerserviceau@elsevier.com; http://www.elsevier.com. Illus., adv. Sample. Refereed. Microform: PQC. *Indexed:* A22, ATI, B01, IBSS, MLA-IB. *Aud.:* Ac.

Accounting, Organizations and Society is a refereed, scholarly journal that is international in scope and focuses on aspects of the relationship between accounting and human behavior, organizational structures and processes, and the changing social and political environment of the enterprise. Topics addressed include the social role of accounting; social audit and accounting for scarce resources; the provision of accounting information to employees and trade unions and the development of participative information systems; processes influencing accounting innovations and the social and political aspects of accounting standard setting; behavioral studies of the users of accounting information; information-processing views of organizations; the relationship between accounting and other information systems and organizational structures and processes; organizational strategies for designing accounting and information systems; human resource accounting; the cognitive aspects of accounting and decision-making processes; and the behavioral aspects of budgeting, among other topics. It is published eight times per year and is one of the *Financial Times*' Top 50 Journals Used in Business School Research Rankings.

30. *Accounting Perspectives.* Formerly (until 2006): *Canadian Accounting Perspectives.* [ISSN: 1911-382X] 2001. q. Free to membership. Ed(s): Amin Mawani. Canadian Academic Accounting Association, 245 Fairview Mall Dr, Ste 410, Toronto, ON M2J 4T1, Canada; admin@caaa.ca; http://www.caaa.ca. Refereed. Reprint: PSC. *Indexed:* A22, ATI, B01, E01. *Aud.:* Ac, Sa.

Accounting Perspectives is a refereed, scholarly journal published quarterly on behalf of the Canadian Academic Accounting Association, an organization for those involved in research and education related to accounting. The publication provides a forum for scholarly research, conducted by academics and practitioners, that addresses current issues in the field of accounting. Topics discussed include financial accounting and reporting, auditing and other assurance services, management accounting and performance measurement, corporate governance, information systems and related technologies, tax policy and practice, professional ethics, accounting education, and more. The journal presents applied research, analysis, and commentary of interest to academics, practitioners, financial analysts, financial executives, regulators, accounting policy makers, and accounting students. Content also includes field studies, case histories, essays, discussion forums, instructional cases, and education articles. The journal seeks a global readership, as well as global submissions. All theoretical and methodological perspectives are welcome.

31. *Accounting Research Journal.* [ISSN: 1030-9616] 1988. q. EUR 448 (print & online eds.) (excluding UK)). Ed(s): Reza Monem, Ellie Chapple. Emerald Publishing Limited, Howard House, Wagon Ln, Bingley, BD16 1WA, United Kingdom; emerald@emeraldinsight.com; http://www.emeraldinsight.com. Sample. Refereed. Reprint: PSC. *Indexed:* ATI, B01. *Aud.:* Ac, Sa.

Accounting Research Journal is a refereed, scholarly journal, published four times per year, that provides an international forum for communication between professionals and academics on emerging areas in contemporary accounting research and practice in all areas of accounting, finance, and related disciplines. The focus of the journal is on interdisciplinary studies and research on contemporary accounting issues arising in specific countries and regions and are of relevance to the private sector, public sector, or not-for-profit sector. Topics addressed include reporting for the future, accounting education, taxation policy and outcomes, forensic accounting, identification and detection of fraud, corporate and behavioral governance, reporting on the Internet, alternative reporting formats, integrated reporting, accounting and e-business, non-financial performance measurement and reporting, and more. The audience for this publication includes accounting, finance, and management researchers, educators, practitioners, and policy makers interested in the role of accounting in organizations.

32. *The Accounting Review.* [ISSN: 0001-4826] 1926. bi-m. USD 487 United States. Ed(s): Mark L Defond. American Accounting Association, 9009 Town Center Pkwy, Lakewood Ranch, FL 34202; info@aaahq.org; http://aaahq.org. Illus., index, adv. Refereed. Vol. ends: Oct. Microform: PQC. Reprint: PSC. *Indexed:* A22, ATI, B01, BRI, CBRI, EconLit, IBSS. *Bk. rev.:* 2-3, 350-1,500 words, signed. *Aud.:* Ac.

In publication since 1926, *The Accounting Review* is a refereed, scholarly journal published bimonthly by the American Accounting Association. The AAA promotes worldwide excellence in accounting education, research, and practice, and its policies state that *The Accounting Review* "should be viewed as the premier journal for publishing articles reporting the results of accounting research and explaining and illustrating related research methodology." Areas of coverage include accounting information systems, auditing and assurance services, financial accounting, management accounting, taxation, and all other areas of accounting, broadly defined. The primary audience for this publication is academicians, graduate students, and others interested in accounting research. It is one of the *Financial Times*' Top 50 Journals Used in Business School Research Rankings.

33. *Asia - Pacific Journal of Accounting & Economics.* Formerly (until 2000): *Asia - Pacific Journal of Accounting.* [ISSN: 1608-1625] 1993. 6x/yr. GBP 391 (print & online eds.)). Ed(s): Hong Hwang, Yin-Wong Cheung. Routledge, 4 Park Sq, Milton Park, Abingdon, OX14 4RN, United Kingdom; subscriptions@tandf.co.uk; http://www.tandfonline.com. Refereed. Reprint: PSC. *Indexed:* ATI, EconLit. *Aud.:* Ac.

Asia-Pacific Journal of Accounting & Economics is a refereed, scholarly journal published six times per year on behalf of the City University of Hong Kong and National Taiwan University. The publication provides an international forum for theoretical and empirical research in all areas of economics and accounting in general. Although most articles relate to the Asia-Pacific region, research from scholars that relates to other regions is also included. Coverage is focused on areas including auditing, financial reporting, earnings management, financial analysts, the role of accounting information, international trade and finance, industrial organization, strategic behavior, market structure, financial contracts, corporate governance, capital markets, and financial institutions.

34. *Asian Review of Accounting.* [ISSN: 1321-7348] 1992. q. EUR 524 (print & online eds.) (excluding UK)). Ed(s): Dr. Haiyan Zhou. Emerald Publishing Limited, Howard House, Wagon Ln, Bingley, BD16 1WA, United Kingdom; emerald@emeraldinsight.com; http://www.emeraldinsight.com. Sample. Refereed. Reprint: PSC. *Indexed:* A22, ATI, B01, E01. *Aud.:* Ac.

Asian Review of Accounting is a refereed, scholarly journal published four times per year. The journal publishes accounting-related research papers, commentary notes, review papers, and practitioner-oriented articles that address significant international issues, as well as those that focus on the Asia-Pacific region in particular. Coverage includes financial accounting, managerial accounting, auditing, taxation, accounting information systems, social and environmental accounting, accounting education, and more. The focus is on perspectives or viewpoints that arise from regional, national, or international focus; a private or public-sector information need; or a market perspective or social and environmental perspective. Articles address accounting issues of wide interest among accounting scholars internationally, and especially those in Asia-Pacific countries.

35. *Auditing: a journal of practice and theory.* [ISSN: 0278-0380] 1981. q. USD 131. Ed(s): Jeffery R Cohen. American Accounting Association, 9009 Town Center Pkwy, Lakewood Ranch, FL 34202; info@aaahq.org; http://aaahq.org. Illus., adv. Refereed. Reprint: PSC. *Indexed:* A22, ATI, B01, C42. *Aud.:* Ac, Sa.

Auditing: A Journal of Practice and Theory is a refereed, scholarly journal published quarterly by the Auditing Section of the American Accounting Association. The goal of the publication is to improve the practice and theory of internal and external auditing and to promote communication between research and practice that influences present and future developments in auditing education as well as auditing research and practice. Articles report the results of original research that puts forth improvements in auditing theory or auditing methodology; discussion and analysis of current issues that affect prospects for developments in auditing practice and in auditing research; practices and developments in auditing in different countries; and uses of auditing in new ways and for different purposes.

36. *Behavioral Research in Accounting.* [ISSN: 1050-4753] 1989. s-a. Ed(s): Steve Salterio. American Accounting Association, 9009 Town Center Pkwy, Lakewood Ranch, FL 34202; info@aaahq.org; http://aaahq.org. Adv. Refereed. Reprint: PSC. *Indexed:* A22, ATI, B01, C42, EconLit. *Aud.:* Ac.

Behavioral Research in Accounting is an academic journal published by the Accounting, Behavior and Organizations Section of the American Accounting Association. The mission of the ABO section is to encourage excellence in research and education regarding the interface between behavioral and organizational sciences and accounting. The journal promotes wide dissemination of the results of systematic scholarly inquiries into the broad field of accounting. The focus of the publication is on original research relating to accounting and how it affects and is affected by individuals and organizations. Content includes theoretical papers and papers based on empirical research—mainly field, survey, and experimental. The journal is published semi-annually and is directed primarily to members of the AAA, particularly the ABO section.

37. ***The British Accounting Review.*** [ISSN: 0890-8389] 1969. 6x/yr. EUR 1407. Ed(s): Alan Lowe, Nathan Joseph. Academic Press, 32 Jamestown Rd, Camden, London, NW1 7BY, United Kingdom; corporate.sales@elsevier.com; http://www.elsevier.com/. Adv. Sample. Refereed. Reprint: PSC. *Indexed:* A22, ATI, B01, E01, IBSS. *Aud.:* Ac, Sa.

The British Accounting Review is a refereed, scholarly journal published six times per year on behalf of the British Accounting and Finance Association. The journal features original and scholarly research papers relating to the broad fields of accounting and finance. Papers may be theoretical, supported with analytical applications of the theory, or empirical, demonstrating the use of appropriate data collection methods and motivated by appropriate theory. Research methods may be analytical, archival, experimental, survey, or qualitative, as well as statistical or econometric in nature. Topics include financial reporting and corporate disclosure; management accounting; accounting information systems; public sector accounting; social and environmental accounting; accounting education; accounting history; taxation; financial regulation; auditing and auditing risk; corporate finance; financial markets and institutions; asset pricing; and behavioral finance and risk management, as well as other topics. The audience for this journal includes academics, accountants, auditors, students, finance managers and directors, corporate treasurers, accounting and auditing standards bodies, government departments, and financial regulators.

38. ***Contemporary Accounting Research.*** [ISSN: 0823-9150] 1984. q. Ed(s): Patricia O'Brien. Canadian Academic Accounting Association, 245 Fairview Mall Dr, Ste 410, Toronto, ON M2J 4T1, Canada; admin@caaa.ca; http://www.caaa.ca. Illus., adv. Refereed. Vol. ends: Winter. Microform: PQC. Reprint: PSC. *Indexed:* A22, ATI, B01, E01, EconLit, IBSS. *Aud.:* Ac.

Contemporary Accounting Research is a refereed, scholarly journal published quarterly on behalf of the Canadian Academic Accounting Association. In publication since 1984, it provides a forum for high-quality research that contributes to the understanding of all aspects of accounting's role within organizations, markets, or society. The journal is international in scope, and its goal is to reflect the geographical and intellectual diversity in accounting research. Coverage includes all aspects of accounting, including audit, financial, information systems, managerial, and tax. Research methods may be analytical, archival, case study, empirical, field, or experimental in nature. Topics often cross disciplines to include economics, finance, history, psychology, sociology, or any that help to examine the role of accounting within organizations, markets, or society. Articles may be written in either English or French. *CAR* is one of the *Financial Times*' Top 50 Journals Used in Business School Research Rankings.

39. ***Critical Perspectives on Accounting.*** [ISSN: 1045-2354] 1990. 8x/yr. EUR 1560. Ed(s): C Cooper, M Annisette. Academic Press, 32 Jamestown Rd, Camden, London, NW1 7BY, United Kingdom; corporate.sales@elsevier.com; http://www.elsevier.com/. Illus., adv. Sample. Refereed. Vol. ends: Dec. Reprint: PSC. *Indexed:* A22, ATI, B01, E01, IBSS. *Aud.:* Ac.

Critical Perspectives on Accounting is a refereed, scholarly journal published eight times per year that provides an academic forum for scholars worldwide who are interested in the broader social, economic, and political issues raised by accounting technologies and corporate behavior. Contributors to this publication subscribe to the belief that conventional theory and practice are not suited to the challenges of the modern era, and that accounting practices and corporate behavior are connected with many of today's allocative, distributive, social, and ecological problems. Many of the research articles presented seek to reformulate corporate, social, and political activity, and suggest the theoretical and practical means by which to do so. Research topics include accounting's involvement in gender and class conflicts in the workplace; management accounting's role in organizing the labor process; the relationship between accounting and the state in various social formations; financial accounting's role in the processes of international capital formation and its impact on stock market stability and international banking activities; and antagonisms between the social and private characters of accounting, among other topics.

40. ***Current Issues in Auditing.*** [ISSN: 1936-1270] 2007. s-a. Free. Ed(s): Lisa Milici Gaynor, Dan Sunderland. American Accounting Association, 9009 Town Center Pkwy, Lakewood Ranch, FL 34202; info@aaahq.org; http://aaahq.org. Adv. Refereed. *Indexed:* ATI, B01. *Aud.:* Ac, Sa.

Current Issues in Auditing is an academic journal published semi-annually by the Auditing Section of the American Accounting Association. The goal of the publication is to promote the widespread dissemination of ideas to auditing academics and practitioners, and to advance the dialogue between them on current issues facing the auditing practice community. Coverage includes all aspects of auditing, including practice-related issues in external auditing, internal auditing, government auditing, IT auditing, and assurance services. Topics include new opportunities and challenges, emerging areas, global developments, the effects of new regulations or pronouncements, the effects of technological or market developments on audit processes, and more. The journal presents papers authored by academics, practitioners, and regulators that are comprehensible and contain a substantive, relevant message for those interested in auditing practice. Published in electronic format only, it is freely available at the AAA website.

41. ***European Accounting Review.*** Supersedes (1989-1992): *European Accounting Association. Newsletter.* [ISSN: 0963-8180] 1992. q. GBP 519 (print & online eds.)). Ed(s): Laurence van Lent. Routledge, 4 Park Sq, Milton Park, Abingdon, OX14 4RN, United Kingdom; subscriptions@tandf.co.uk; http://www.tandfonline.com. Adv. Sample. Refereed. Reprint: PSC. *Indexed:* A22, ATI, B01, E01, IBSS. *Bk. rev.:* Number and length vary. *Aud.:* Ac.

European Accounting Review is a refereed, scholarly journal published quarterly on behalf of the European Accounting Association, an organization whose aim is to link together the Europe-wide community of accounting scholars and researchers. As the only accounting journal that provides a European forum for the reporting of accounting research, *EAR* is dedicated to the advancement of accounting knowledge and the publication of high-quality accounting research. The international journal emphasizes openness and flexibility, not only regarding the substantive issues of accounting research, but also with respect to paradigms, methodologies, and styles of conducting that research. With the advent of the single European market and the resulting harmonization of accounting standards and regulations, *EAR* is viewed as an increasingly important forum for the development of accounting theory and practice.

Financial Accountability & Management. See Business and Finance/Scholarly section.

Government Finance Review. See Business and Finance/Scholarly section.

42. ***The International Journal of Accounting.*** Formerly (until 1989): *The International Journal of Accounting Education and Research.* [ISSN: 1094-4060] 1965. q. SGD 1038 (print & online eds.) (includes Asia, except China & India)). Ed(s): A Rashad Abdel-khalik. World Scientific Publishing Co. Pte. Ltd., 5 Toh Tuck Link, Singapore, 596224, Singapore; wspc@wspc.com.sg; http://www.worldscientific.com. Illus., adv. Sample. Refereed. Reprint: PSC. *Indexed:* A22, ATI, B01, IBSS. *Bk. rev.:* 5-6, 1,000-1,500 words, signed. *Aud.:* Ac.

The International Journal of Accounting is a refereed, scholarly journal whose goal is to advance the academic and professional understanding of accounting theory, policies, and practice from an international perspective and viewpoint. Research articles relate the present and potential ability of accounting to aid in analyzing and interpreting international economic transactions and the economic consequences of such reporting, both in profit and nonprofit environments. The journal takes a broad view of the origins and development of accounting with emphasis on its functions in an increasingly interdependent global economy. Another area of focus is research that helps to explain current international accounting practices, with related theoretical justifications, and to identify criticisms of current policies and practice. The journal is published quarterly and each issue contains articles, book reviews, and announcements.

43. ***International Journal of Accounting & Information Management.*** Formerly (until 2004): *The Asia-Pacific Journal of Information Management.* [ISSN: 1834-7649] 1992. q. EUR 448 (print & online eds.) (excluding UK)). Ed(s): Xin Luo, Maggie Liu. Emerald Publishing Limited, Howard House, Wagon Ln, Bingley, BD16 1WA, United Kingdom; emerald@emeraldinsight.com; http://www.emeraldinsight.com. Sample. Refereed. Reprint: PSC. *Indexed:* ATI, B01. *Aud.:* Ac.

International Journal of Accounting & Information Management is a refereed, scholarly journal published quarterly, which is dedicated to the advancement of management accounting. Research is published in accounting, finance, and information management with a special emphasis given to the interaction between these areas of research in an international context and in either the private or public sectors. Research may be theoretical or empirical, in using quantitative or qualitative research methodologies and employing methods such as surveys, experiments, and case studies. Areas of coverage include development of management accounting theory, explanations of management accounting practices, management control and accountability, performance measurement and management, social context of management accounting practices, globalization and localization of management accounting, behavioral effects of management control, environmental management accounting, international perspectives of capital investment decisions, interface between information technology and management accounting, interface between external financial reporting and internal reporting and decision-making, and management accounting practices in SMEs and in emerging and less developed economies, among other topics.

44. ***International Journal of Accounting Information Systems.*** [ISSN: 1467-0895] 2000. q. EUR 885. Ed(s): S Leech, S V Grabski. Pergamon Press, The Blvd, Langford Ln, E Park, Kidlington, OX5 1GB, United Kingdom; JournalsCustomerServiceEMEA@elsevier.com; http://www.elsevier.com. Adv. Sample. Refereed. Reprint: PSC. *Indexed:* ATI, B01, CompLI. *Aud.:* Ac, Sa.

International Journal of Accounting Information Systems is a refereed, academic journal published quarterly, whose goal is to examine the evolving relationship between accounting and information technology and publish research that advances basic theory and provides guidance to practice. Articles written by practitioners and academicians range from empirical to analytical, from practice-based to the development of new techniques, but primarily relate to problems facing the integration of accounting and information technology. Issues addressed include information systems assurance, electronic dissemination of accounting information, control and auditability of information systems, management of information technology, artificial intelligence research in accounting, development issues in accounting and information systems, human-factors issues related to information technology, development of theories related to information technology, methodological issues in information technology research, information systems validation, human-computer interaction research in accounting information systems, and more.

45. ***International Journal of Auditing.*** [ISSN: 1090-6738] 1997. 3x/yr. GBP 830. Ed(s): David Hay. Wiley-Blackwell Publishing Ltd., The Atrium, Southern Gate, Chichester, PO19 8QG, United Kingdom; cs-journals@wiley.com; http://onlinelibrary.wiley.com. Adv. Sample. Refereed. Reprint: PSC. *Indexed:* A22, ATI, B01, E01, IBSS. *Aud.:* Ac, Sa.

International Journal of Auditing is a refereed, scholarly journal, published three times per year, whose goal is to publish the results of original auditing research conducted in research institutions and in practice. The publication also aims to advance knowledge in auditing by publishing critiques, thought-leadership papers, and literature reviews on various aspects of auditing. Articles are presented that have international appeal and address the audit challenges of the present and the future. Research may have an analytical and statistical, behavioral, economic and financial, sociological, critical, or historical basis. Topics include financial statement audits, public sector/governmental auditing, internal auditing, audit education and methods of teaching auditing (including case studies), audit aspects of corporate governance, audit quality, audit fees, audit-related ethical issues, audit regulation, independence issues, legal liability, auditing history, new and emerging audit and assurance issues, and more. Content is accessible and relevant to auditing practitioners and researchers around the world.

46. ***Issues in Accounting Education.*** [ISSN: 0739-3172] 1983. q. USD 405. Ed(s): Lori Holder-Webb. American Accounting Association, 9009 Town Center Pkwy, Lakewood Ranch, FL 34202; info@aaahq.org; http://aaahq.org. Illus., adv. Refereed. Vol. ends: No. 4. Reprint: PSC. *Indexed:* A22, ATI, B01, BRI, C42. *Bk. rev.:* 2-20, 500-1,500 words, signed. *Aud.:* Ac.

Issues in Accounting Education is a refereed, scholarly journal that is published quarterly by the American Accounting Association. The goal of the publication is to present research, commentaries, instructional resources, and book reviews that assist accounting faculty in teaching and that address important issues in accounting education. The journal is divided into two major sections: "Research and Commentary" (mainly empirically derived and statistically analyzed studies) and "Instructional Resources" (cases derived from actual or simulated business activities, including learning objectives, implementation guidance, and teaching notes). Research topics include the learning process, curriculum development, professional certification, assessment, career training, employment, instruction, and more. Content is of interest to an international readership.

47. ***Journal of Accounting and Economics.*** [ISSN: 0165-4101] 1979. 3x/yr. EUR 2555. Ed(s): R W Holthausen, R L Watts. Elsevier BV, Radarweg 29, Amsterdam, 1043 NX, Netherlands; info@elsevier.com; https://www.elsevier.com/. Illus., index, adv. Refereed. Vol. ends: Jun/Dec. Microform: PQC. *Indexed:* A22, ATI, B01, C42, EconLit, IBSS. *Aud.:* Ac.

Journal of Accounting and Economics is a refereed, scholarly journal published three times per year. It encourages economics-based research that advances accounting knowledge and applies economic theory to the explanation of accounting phenomena. The publication provides a forum for the publication of high-quality manuscripts that employ economic analyses of accounting problems. A wide range of research methodologies are accepted. Topics include the role of accounting within the firm, the information content and role of accounting numbers in capital markets, the role of accounting in financial contracts and in monitoring agency relationships, the determination of accounting standards, government regulation of corporate disclosure and/or the accounting profession, the theory of the accounting firm, and more. This journal encourages researchers to address unexplored accounting-related topics and to challenge conventional wisdom using rigorous economic analysis. *JAE* is one of the *Financial Times*' Top 50 Journals Used in Business School Research Rankings.

48. ***Journal of Accounting & Organizational Change.*** [ISSN: 1832-5912] 2005. q. EUR 803 (print & online eds.) (excluding UK)). Ed(s): Zahirul Hoque. Emerald Publishing Limited, Howard House, Wagon Ln, Bingley, BD16 1WA, United Kingdom; emerald@emeraldinsight.com; http://www.emeraldinsight.com. Sample. Refereed. Reprint: PSC. *Indexed:* A22, ATI, B01, E01. *Aud.:* Ac.

Journal of Accounting & Organizational Change is a refereed, scholarly journal, published quarterly, whose goal is to present multidisciplinary research that relates to organizational and accounting systems changes in the global business environment. Emphasis is placed on exploring how organizations change and how the change process affects internal organizations processes. The publication seeks to explain new techniques, processes, and philosophies associated with the rise of strategy-oriented accounting and information systems. Content includes empirical and case-study articles; replications of previously published studies; and review articles on advances in accounting and organizational-change research. Topics include accounting and management control systems in change management, changes in social and environmental accounting reporting, accountability and performance in the public and private sectors, triple-bottom-line reporting and social accountability issues, accounting change in transitional and developing economies, public-sector reform and accounting change, corporate failure and auditing change, multinational organizational change, and more. Content of this journal is useful to accountants and organizational experts from industry, the public sector, consulting, and academia.

49. *Journal of Accounting and Public Policy.* [ISSN: 0278-4254] 1982. 6x/yr. EUR 1401. Ed(s): Lawrence A Gordon, Martin Loeb. Elsevier Inc., 230 Park Ave, Ste 800, New York, NY 10169; journalscustomerservice-usa@elsevier.com; https://www.elsevier.com. Illus., index, adv. Sample. Refereed. Vol. ends: Winter. Microform: PQC. *Indexed:* A22, ATI, B01, BRI, C42, IBSS. *Aud.:* Ac.

Journal of Accounting and Public Policy is a refereed, scholarly journal, published six times per year, whose goal is to publish research papers that focus on the relationship between accounting and public policy. Articles are presented that address, through theoretical or empirical analysis, the effect of accounting on public policy and vice versa. Research articles concentrate on the interrelationship between accounting and various disciplines, including economics, public administration, political science, policy science, social psychology, sociology, and law. A feature of the publication is the "Accounting Letters" section, which publishes short research articles that facilitate the rapid dissemination of important accounting research.

Journal of Accounting Auditing and Finance. See Business and Finance/Scholarly section.

50. *Journal of Accounting Education.* [ISSN: 0748-5751] 1983. q. EUR 1090. Ed(s): Natalie T Churyk. Pergamon Press, The Blvd, Langford Ln, E Park, Kidlington, OX5 1GB, United Kingdom; JournalsCustomerServiceEMEA@elsevier.com; http://www.elsevier.com. Illus., adv. Sample. Refereed. Microform: PQC. *Indexed:* A22, ATI, B01. *Aud.:* Ac.

Journal of Accounting Education is a refereed, scholarly journal, published quarterly, whose goal is to promote and publish research on accounting education issues and contribute to the improvement of the quality of accounting education worldwide. Articles are included that present the results of empirical studies that are useful to accounting educators in the exchange of ideas and relevant instructional resources. The instructional resources featured in *JAEd* meet relevant educational objectives and are available for general use. Topics addressed are relevant to accounting education, including uses of technology, learning styles, assessment, curriculum, and faculty issues. The journal is divided into four separate sections: "Main Articles" (mostly results of empirical studies), "Educational Cases" (case studies), "Teaching and Educational Notes" (instructional resources and short papers on topics of interest), and "Best Practices" (individual and institutional practices related to student recruitment, student advising, student retention, alumni relations, and efforts to integrate accounting practice and accounting education).

51. *Journal of Accounting in Emerging Economies.* Incorporates (1995-2015): *Research in Accounting in Emerging Economies;* Which was formerly (1990-1993): *Research in Third World Accounting.* [ISSN: 2042-1168] 2011. q. EUR 536 (print & online eds.) (excluding UK)). Ed(s): Shahzad Uddin. Emerald Publishing Limited, Howard House, Wagon Ln, Bingley, BD16 1WA, United Kingdom; emerald@emeraldinsight.com; http://www.emeraldinsight.com. Refereed. Reprint: PSC. *Indexed:* ATI. *Aud.:* Ac, Sa.

Journal of Accounting in Emerging Economies is a refereed, scholarly journal, published quarterly, which presents empirical research papers that are based on diverse methodological and theoretical approaches and that highlight the policy and practical implications of the research. Coverage includes education/training and the role of professional accounting bodies, financial reporting and accounting standards, auditing, corporate governance, management accounting issues, the impact of structural adjustment programs and international financial agencies on accounting practices, and accounting/regulation/privatization. Also covered are accounting practices in family businesses, the role of accounting in socioeconomic development and poverty reduction, and theoretical approaches to accounting, among other topics. This is the only journal that focuses primarily on accounting research in emerging economies. The primary audience includes higher education, international financial institutions, government and public sector institutions in emerging economies, managers of private-sector organizations in emerging economies, and NGOs.

52. *Journal of Accounting Literature.* [ISSN: 0737-4607] 1982. s-a. some issues combined. EUR 269. Ed(s): Stephen Kwaka Asare, W R Knechel. Elsevier Inc., 230 Park Ave, Ste 800, New York, NY 10169; https://www.elsevier.com. Illus. Refereed. Reprint: PSC. *Indexed:* A22, ATI, B01. *Bk. rev.:* Number and length vary. *Aud.:* Ac.

Journal of Accounting Literature is a refereed, scholarly journal, published semi-annually, whose goal is to publish synthesis and original research that makes a fundamental and substantial contribution to the understanding of accounting phenomena, specifically papers that synthesize an area of research in a concise and rigorous manner to assist academics and others to gain knowledge and appreciation of diverse research areas or that present high-quality, multi-method, original research on a broad range of topics relevant to accounting, auditing, and taxation. The lead article of each issue is consistently a synthesis article on an important research topic, with the remaining articles comprising a mix of synthesis and original research papers. In addition to traditional research topics and methods, the publication includes meta-analyses, field studies, critiques of papers published in other journals, emerging developments in accounting theory, commentaries on current issues, innovative experimental research, creative archival analyses, book reviews, and more.

53. *Journal of Accounting Research.* [ISSN: 0021-8456] 1963. 5x/yr. GBP 1000. Ed(s): Lisa Johnson. Wiley-Blackwell Publishing, Inc., 111 River St, Hoboken, NJ 07030; http://onlinelibrary.wiley.com. Illus., adv. Sample. Refereed. Microform: MIM; PQC. Reprint: PSC. *Indexed:* A22, ATI, B01, C42, E01, EconLit, IBSS. *Aud.:* Ac.

In publication since 1963, *Journal of Accounting Research* is a refereed, scholarly journal published on behalf of the Accounting Research Center at the University of Chicago's Booth School of Business. It is the oldest private research journal in the field and is ranked as one of the top accounting research journals in the world. *JAR* publishes original research in all areas of accounting using analytical, empirical, archival, experimental, and field-study methods. Economic questions are addressed in accounting, auditing, taxation, and related fields such as corporate finance, investments, capital markets, law, and information economics. Four regular issues are published per year as well as one conference issue, which contains papers and discussions from the annual accounting research conference that takes place at the University of Chicago. *JAR* is published five times per year, is an ISI-listed journal, and is one of the *Financial Times*' Top 50 Journals Used in Business School Research Rankings.

54. *Journal of Applied Accounting Research.* [ISSN: 0967-5426] 1992. q. EUR 653 (print & online eds.) (excluding UK)). Ed(s): Elaine Harris, Dr. Julia Mundy. Emerald Publishing Limited, Howard House, Wagon Ln, Bingley, BD16 1WA, United Kingdom; emerald@emeraldinsight.com; http://www.emeraldinsight.com. Sample. Refereed. Reprint: PSC. *Indexed:* ATI, B01. *Aud.:* Ac, Sa.

Journal of Applied Accounting Research is a refereed, scholarly journal, published quarterly, which provides a forum for the publication of applied research as it concerns issues relevant to the practice of accounting in a wide variety of contexts. The journal seeks to promote a research agenda that allows academics and practitioners to work together to provide sustainable outcomes in a practice setting. *JAAR* presents articles on topics of current interest to the accountancy profession, in particular new solutions to, or new ways of thinking about, established problems or newly identified problems. The journal aims to be of interest to academics interested in the practical application of accounting, as well as all accounting professionals, including specialists in financial, management, or public-sector accounting or in areas of corporate and financial management. Coverage includes corporate reporting, governance structures of accounting, environmental and social aspects of accounting, accounting in developing economies, approaches to management control, management-accounting techniques, public-sector accounting, business and shareholder value, corporate financial management, taxation, and the like.

Journal of Business Finance & Accounting. See Business and Finance/Trade Journals section.

55. *Journal of Emerging Technologies in Accounting.* [ISSN: 1554-1908] 2004. s-a. USD 136 per issue. Ed(s): Miklos Vasarhelyi. American Accounting Association, 9009 Town Center Pkwy, Lakewood Ranch, FL 34202; info@aaahq.org; http://aaahq.org. Adv. Refereed. *Indexed:* ATI, B01. *Aud.:* Ac, Sa.

Journal of Emerging Technologies in Accounting is a refereed, scholarly journal published semi-annually by the Strategic and Emerging Technologies Section of the American Accounting Association. The purpose of this AAA section is to improve and facilitate the research, education, and practice of advanced information systems, cutting-edge technologies, and artificial intelligence in the fields of accounting, information technology, and management advisory systems. The goal of *JETA* is to encourage, support, and disseminate high-quality research focused on emerging technologies and artificial-intelligence issues related to accounting. The journal focuses on studies that include research on strategic and emerging technologies and the impact on accounting and business environments; discovery and exploratory research about technological environments; conceptual research about the technological environment; field research of emerging and new technologies; studies on previously emerging technologies in a historical perspective; integrative plans for emerging technologies in all areas of accounting; and more.

56. *Journal of Financial Reporting.* [ISSN: 2380-2154] 2016. s-a. Ed(s): Rick Lambert. American Accounting Association, 9009 Town Center Pkwy, Lakewood Ranch, FL 34202; info@aaahq.org; http://aaahq.org. Adv. Refereed. *Indexed:* B01. *Aud.:* Ac.

Journal of Financial Reporting is a refereed, scholarly journal published semiannually by the Financial Accounting and Reporting Section of the American Accounting Association. The journal is open to research on a broad spectrum of financial reporting issues related to the production, dissemination, and analysis of information produced by a firm's financial accounting and reporting system. Topics include accounting standard setting; the production and dissemination of accounting information; the relation between financial information and firm policies such as compensation and corporate governance; the role of financial intermediaries; and analysis by decision makers such as equity investors, creditors, and analysts. The target audience of the publication is financial reporting researchers. *JFR* occasionally publishes themed issues dedicated to studies that launch a new question or move the literature forward in an existing area.

57. *Journal of Forensic Accounting Research.* [ISSN: 2380-2138] 2016. a. Ed(s): Charles D Bailey. American Accounting Association, 9009 Town Center Pkwy, Lakewood Ranch, FL 34202; info@aaahq.org; http://aaahq.org. Adv. Refereed. *Indexed:* B01. *Aud.:* Ac.

Journal of Forensic Accounting Research is a refereed, scholarly journal published annually by the Forensic Accounting Section of the American Accounting Association, whose mission is to foster excellence in the teaching, research, practice, continual professional education (CPE) courses, and curriculum development of forensic accounting services. The publication offers a balance among basic research, practice, and education. Accordingly, forensic accounting research is broadly conceived, and not limited to fraud research.

58. *Journal of International Accounting, Auditing and Taxation.* [ISSN: 1061-9518] 1992. s-a. EUR 813. Ed(s): S C Rhoades-Catanach, A H Catanach. Pergamon Press, The Blvd, Langford Ln, E Park, Kidlington, OX5 1GB, United Kingdom; JournalsCustomerServiceEMEA@elsevier.com; http://www.elsevier.com. Illus., adv. Sample. Refereed. Microform: PQC. Reprint: PSC. *Indexed:* A22, ATI, B01, IBSS. *Aud.:* Ac, Sa.

Journal of International Accounting, Auditing and Taxation is a refereed, scholarly journal, published quarterly, which presents research in all areas of international accounting, including auditing, taxation, and management-advisory services. The goal of the publication is to bridge the gap between academic researchers and practitioners by publishing papers that are relevant to the development of the field of accounting. Content includes applied research findings, critiques of current accounting practices, and the measurement of their effects on business decisions. Also presented are general-purpose solutions to problems through models, and essays on world affairs that affect accounting practice.

59. *Journal of International Accounting Research.* [ISSN: 1542-6297] 2002. s-a. USD 131. Ed(s): Ervin L Black. American Accounting Association, 9009 Town Center Pkwy, Lakewood Ranch, FL 34202; info@aaahq.org; http://aaahq.org. Adv. Reprint: PSC. *Indexed:* ATI, B01, BRI. *Bk. rev.:* Number and length vary. *Aud.:* Ac, Sa.

Journal of International Accounting Research is an academic journal published three times per year by the International Accounting Section of the American Accounting Association. The goal of the publication is to increase understanding of the development and use of international accounting and reporting practices and thereby improve those practices. A wide variety of research methods are accepted, including empirical-archival, experimental, field studies, and theoretical. The journal is directed toward a diverse audience and focuses on articles relating to auditing, financial accounting, managerial accounting, tax, and other specialties within the field of accounting. International coverage areas include the reporting of international economic transactions, the study of differences among practices across countries, the study of institutional and cultural factors that shape practices in a single country but have international implications, and the effect of international accounting practices on users, and more.

Journal of International Financial Management and Accounting. See Business and Finance/Scholarly section.

60. *Journal of Islamic Accounting and Business Research.* [ISSN: 1759-0817] 2010. 5x/yr. EUR 607 (print & online eds.) (excluding UK)). Ed(s): Dr. Mohammad Hudaib, Roszaini Haniffa. Emerald Publishing Limited, Howard House, Wagon Ln, Bingley, BD16 1WA, United Kingdom; emerald@emeraldinsight.com; http://www.emeraldinsight.com. Sample. Refereed. Reprint: PSC. *Indexed:* ATI. *Aud.:* Ac, Sa.

Journal of Islamic Accounting and Business Research is a refereed, scholarly journal, published five times per year, whose objectives are to provide a forum for the advancement of accounting and business knowledge based on *Shari'ah* and to publish articles on the interplay between Islamic business ethics, accounting, auditing, and governance in promoting accountability, socioeconomic justice (*adl*), and everlasting success (*al-falah*). The publication presents current theoretical and empirical research and practice in Islamic accounting; auditing and corporate governance; management of Islamic organizations; accounting regulation and policy for Islamic institutions; *Shari'ah* auditing and corporate governance; and financial and non-financial performance measurement and disclosure in Islamic institutions. *JIABR* is the only journal that offers a platform for publishing both theory and practice of Islamic accounting, auditing, and business research beyond Islamic banking, finance, and economics. The audience for this publication includes scholars and researchers, professionals, managers involved in Islamic business organizations, and students pursuing studies related to Islamic business.

61. *Journal of Management Accounting Research.* [ISSN: 1049-2127] 1989. 3x/yr. USD 136 per issue. Ed(s): Karen Sedatole. American Accounting Association, 9009 Town Center Pkwy, Lakewood Ranch, FL 34202; info@aaahq.org; http://aaahq.org. Illus., adv. Refereed. Reprint: PSC. *Indexed:* A22, ATI, B01, C42, EconLit. *Aud.:* Ac, Sa.

Journal of Management Accounting Research is a refereed, scholarly journal published three times per year by the Management Accounting Section of the American Accounting Association. The goal of the journal is to contribute to the expansion of knowledge related to the theory and practice of management accounting by promoting the dissemination of high-quality applied and theoretical research throughout the world. Coverage includes all areas of management accounting, including budgeting, internal reporting, incentives, performance evaluation, and the interface between internal and external reporting, among other topics. Research articles discuss internal reporting and decision making, profit and nonprofit organizations, service and manufacturing organizations, domestic, foreign, and multinational organizations, and more. The publication accepts all types of research methods, including analytical, empirical, archival, case study, conceptual, experimental, and survey. The audience for this journal is the membership of the Management Accounting Section of the AAA and all others interested in management accounting.

62. *Management Accounting Research.* Former titles (until 1990): *Chartered Institute of Management Accountants Abstracts Bulletin;* (until 1987): *Institute of Cost and Management Accountants. Abstracts Bulletin.* [ISSN: 1044-5005] 1983. q. EUR 1017. Ed(s): W A Van der Stede. Academic Press, 32 Jamestown Rd, Camden, London, NW1 7BY, United Kingdom; corporate.sales@elsevier.com; http://www.elsevier.com/. Illus., adv. Sample. Refereed. Vol. ends: Dec. Reprint: PSC. *Indexed:* A22, ATI, B01, E01, IBSS. *Aud.:* Ac.

Management Accounting Research is a refereed, scholarly journal, published quarterly, whose goal is to present original research in the field of management accounting. The publication provides an international forum for the dissemination of research that draws on any relevant source discipline suitable to examine and elicit novel implications for management-accounting practices or systems in use in any type of organization globally. Papers are written by prestigious international authors, discussing and analyzing management accounting in many different parts of the world. Content includes case studies, field work, and other empirical research, analytical modeling, scholarly papers, distinguished review articles, comments, and notes.

63. *Managerial Auditing Journal.* [ISSN: 0268-6902] 1986. 9x/yr. EUR 12802 (print & online eds.) (excluding UK)). Ed(s): Vivek Mande. Emerald Publishing Limited, Howard House, Wagon Ln, Bingley, BD16 1WA, United Kingdom; emerald@emeraldinsight.com; http:// www.emeraldinsight.com. Sample. Refereed. Reprint: PSC. *Indexed:* A22, ATI, B01, E01. *Aud.:* Ac, Sa.

Managerial Auditing Journal is a refereed, scholarly journal, published nine times per year, which provides a global forum for the examination of current research and practice in auditing and assurance. The journal reflects a contemporary approach by taking readers beyond traditional conventions and discussing ways that today's auditors and assurance providers are analyzing governance, risk management, and performance matters. *MAJ* addresses the relationship between theory and practice by exploring trends, paradigms, and perspectives that include the ethical, social, environmental, and economic aspects of contemporary assurance, management performance, and governance issues. Research areas include the regulatory and professional frameworks of corporate and public-sector governance, ethics, risk, and management performance from multidisciplinary perspectives. Studies may have an analytical, theoretical, or methodological focus and may employ a wide range of research methods, including empirical, experimental, explanatory, case-based analysis, surveys, field studies, conceptual, archival, or critical. The audience for this journal includes academics and researchers, internal and external audit and assurance providers, management and directors, regulators and standard setters, risk managers, and audit committees.

64. *Qualitative Research in Accounting & Management.* [ISSN: 1176-6093] 2004. q. EUR 759 (print & online eds.) (excluding UK)). Ed(s): Lukas Goretzki, Deryl Northcott. Emerald Publishing Limited, Howard House, Wagon Ln, Bingley, BD16 1WA, United Kingdom; emerald@emeraldinsight.com; http://www.emeraldinsight.com. Sample. Refereed. Reprint: PSC. *Indexed:* A22, ATI, B01, E01. *Aud.:* Ac, Sa.

Qualitative Research in Accounting & Management is a refereed, scholarly journal, published quarterly, which promotes qualitative research at the interface of accounting and management. The international journal encourages the assessment of practices in the accounting field through a variety of theoretical lenses, and seeks to further knowledge of the accounting-management nexus in its broadest contexts. *QRAM* presents original research papers, conceptual pieces, substantive review articles, and shorter papers such as comments or research notes. Topics include management accounting and control, performance management and accounting metrics, accounting for strategic management, the use and behavioral effects of accounting information in organizational decision-making, public- and third-sector accounting and management, accounting and management controls for sustainability and the environment, historical perspectives on the accounting-management interface, methods and methodologies for research at the interface of accounting and management, accounting and management in developing countries and emerging economies, and technology effects on accounting-management dynamics, among other topics.

65. *Review of Accounting and Finance.* [ISSN: 1475-7702] 2002. q. EUR 1410 (print & online eds.) (excluding UK)). Ed(s): Janis Zaima. Emerald Publishing Limited, Howard House, Wagon Ln, Bingley, BD16 1WA, United Kingdom; emerald@emeraldinsight.com; http:// www.emeraldinsight.com. Sample. Refereed. Reprint: PSC. *Indexed:* A22, ATI, B01, E01. *Aud.:* Ac.

Review of Accounting and Finance is a refereed, scholarly journal that is published quarterly. The scope of the journal is broad. *RAF* publishes innovative empirical, behavioral, theoretical, and historical research that covers a wide range of accounting and finance issues. A global perspective is offered on topics, including the role of accounting internal and external communications on capital market valuation, microstructure, asset pricing, corporate financial decision making, users' and preparers' behavior and public policy, and more. A distinctive feature of this journal is that it recognizes and supports the multi-paradigmatic nature of both accounting and finance. The editors view contributions from all paradigms as essential contribution to the advancement of knowledge in both areas.

66. *Review of Accounting Studies.* [ISSN: 1380-6653] 1996. q. EUR 1107 (print & online eds.)). Ed(s): Paul Fischer. Springer New York LLC, 233 Spring St, New York, NY 10013; customerservice@springer.com; http://www.springer.com. Illus., adv. Sample. Refereed. Vol. ends: No. 4. Reprint: PSC. *Indexed:* A22, ATI, B01, E01, EconLit. *Aud.:* Ac.

Review of Accounting Studies is a refereed, scholarly journal, published quarterly, whose objective is to provide an outlet for significant academic research in accounting, including theoretical, empirical, and experimental work. The international publication is committed to the principle that distinctive scholarship is rigorous, so research must contribute to the discipline of accounting. All research methods are accepted. The audience for this publication includes all who take an active interest in accounting research. *RAS* is one of the *Financial Times*' Top 50 Journals Used in Business School Research Rankings.

Review of Quantitative Finance and Accounting. See Business and Finance/Scholarly section.

Taxation

67. *A T A Journal of Legal Tax Research.* [ISSN: 1543-866X] 2003. s-a. Free to members. Ed(s): Anthony P Curatola, Roby B Sawyers. American Accounting Association, 9009 Town Center Pkwy, Lakewood Ranch, FL 34202; info@aaahq.org; http://aaahq.org. Adv. *Indexed:* ATI, B01. *Aud.:* Ac, Sa.

ATA Journal of Legal Tax Research is an academic journal published semi-annually by the American Taxation Association, the Tax Section of the American Accounting Association. The journal publishes original research studies that employ legal research methodologies. Content addresses important current tax issues including the history, development, and congressional intent of specific provisions. Research articles propose improvements in tax systems and unique solutions to problems. Proposed or recent tax rule changes are critically analyzed from both technical and policy perspectives. The journal is of value to ATA members and all persons with an interest in tax education and research.

68. *American Taxation Association. Journal.* [ISSN: 0198-9073] 1979. s-a. Ed(s): Connie Weaver. American Accounting Association, 9009 Town Center Pkwy, Lakewood Ranch, FL 34202; info@aaahq.org; http:// aaahq.org. Illus., adv. Refereed. Reprint: PSC. *Indexed:* A22, ATI, B01, BRI, C42. *Bk. rev.:* 5-10, 500-1,000 words, signed. *Aud.:* Ac, Sa.

Journal of the American Taxation Association is an academic journal published semiannually by the American Taxation Association, the Tax Section of the American Accounting Association. The ATA promotes the study of, and the acquisition of knowledge about, taxation. The publication is dedicated to disseminating a wide variety of tax knowledge and, to fulfill this responsibility, tax research is accepted that employs quantitative, analytical, experimental, and descriptive methods. Feature articles are followed by discussion submitted by other contributors and a summary of all papers included in the issue. *JATA* also publishes reviews of textbooks and other books of interest to tax scholars. Readership of the journal includes members of the ATA and other persons with an interest in tax education and research.

69. ***Corporate Taxation.*** Formerly (until Jan. 2001): *Journal of Corporate Taxation.* [ISSN: 1534-715X] 1973. 1 Base Vol(s). Ed(s): Sandra K Lewis. R I A, PO Box 6159, Carol Stream, IL 60197; ria.customerservices@thomson.com; http://ria.thomsonreuters.com. Illus., adv. Microform: MIM; PQC. *Indexed:* A22, ATI, B01, BRI, C42, L14. *Aud.:* Sa.

Corporate Taxation is a bimonthly publication. Articles are written by corporate tax professionals for corporate tax professionals. The magazine provides authoritative analysis and guidance from the leading experts in corporate taxation. Each issue delivers timely, in-depth coverage of such topics as corporate organizations and reorganizations, compensation and fringe benefits, international developments, consolidated returns, and so on. Articles are presented that address topics of importance to practitioners and provide guidance on structuring transactions to produce optimal tax consequences and satisfying compliance mandates with maximum efficiency. This publication does not discuss theoretical matters or how the law could or should be changed.

70. ***International Tax Journal.*** [ISSN: 0097-7314] 1974. bi-m. USD 329. Ed(s): Lowell D Yoder. C C H Inc., 2700 Lake Cook Rd, Riverwoods, IL 60015; cust_serv@cch.com; http://www.cchgroup.com/. Illus., adv. *Indexed:* A22, ATI, B01, BRI, L14. *Aud.:* Sa.

International Tax Journal is a bimonthly publication that presents articles on international tax topics for the benefit of tax professionals and multinational businesses. Written by a team of international tax experts, the magazine focuses on U.S. tax on domestic and international business income, as well as the interaction of international tax regimes with U.S. tax law. Also presented are feature articles and columns on specific foreign tax regimes that may be of interest to tax practitioners advising companies on doing business internationally. Topics addressed include anti-deferral and anti-tax avoidance, foreign tax credits, international partnerships, joint ventures and hybrids, international tax controversies, technology and telecommunications, transfer pricing, financing international operations, treaties, subpart F, economic developments, tax rules of foreign countries, pending legislation, international tax opportunities and pitfalls, among others. The readership of this publication is primarily tax attorneys advising international businesses.

71. ***Journal of International Taxation.*** [ISSN: 1049-6378] 1990. 1 Base Vol(s) m. USD 850. Ed(s): Peter M Daub. W G & L Financial Reporting & Management Research, 2395 Midway Rd, Carrollton, TX 75006; ria.customerservices@thomson.com; http://ria.thomson.com. *Indexed:* A22, ATI. *Aud.:* Sa.

Journal of International Taxation is a monthly publication that provides an authoritative, in-depth, and practical analysis of the laws, regulations, treaties, and decisions governing international taxation. The focus is on developing practical strategies to limit tax liability and avoid unnecessary tax penalties. It presents news on the latest major tax developments in the United States and around the world, with a focus on transactions both inbound (foreign businesses in the United States) and outbound (U.S. businesses abroad). Topics include transfer pricing, cross-border M&A, FATCA and information reporting, foreign tax credits, treaties, indirect tax and VAT, customs and trade, and forms and compliance/procedure, among other topics. Along with comprehensive articles, the journal's regular monthly columns include news features from Ernst & Young and a "Customs & Trade" report by a leading trade attorney. Articles are practical and include specific planning advice and strategies.

72. ***Journal of State Taxation.*** [ISSN: 0744-6713] 1982. q. USD 470 combined subscription (print & online eds.)). Ed(s): James T Collins. C C H Inc., 2700 Lake Cook Rd, Riverwoods, IL 60015; cust_serv@cch.com; http://www.cchgroup.com/. Microform: WSH; PQC. *Indexed:* ATI, B01, BRI, L14. *Aud.:* Sa.

Journal of State Taxation is a quarterly publication whose goal is to help practitioners meet, master, and stay ahead of today's complex state tax challenges. Articles provide guidance and insight from leading practitioners in state taxation. The magazine offers many unique features, such as the "Multistate Tax Charts" and "Frequently Asked Multistate Tax Questions." It includes four regular columns by top names in state taxation: "Apportionment News," "Nexus News," "Credits and Incentives," and "Current Developments." Regular alerts are provided to keep practitioners up to date on current topics, such as state tax incentives, sales tax exemptions, refund opportunities, and proposed, pending, or recently enacted legislation. Coverage of important cases is reported, along with assessments of the impact. *JST* publishes easy-to-read and easy-to-understand tips and suggestions on how to reduce state and local tax liabilities.

73. ***Journal of Taxation: a national journal of current developments, analysis, and commentary for tax professionals.*** [ISSN: 0022-4863] 1954. 1 Base Vol(s) m. USD 335; USD 495 combined subscription (print & online eds.)). Ed(s): Joseph I Graf, Sheldon I Banoff. R I A, PO Box 6159, Carol Stream, IL 60197; ria@thomson.com; http://ria.thomsonreuters.com. Illus., index, adv. Circ: 14000. Microform: PQC. *Indexed:* A22, ATI, B01, BRI, C42, L14. *Aud.:* Sa.

Journal of Taxation is published monthly and is dedicated to the needs of tax practitioners. The focus is on practical information and tax-planning ideas that cover individuals and corporations, estates and trusts, partnerships, and so on. In-depth articles from leading practitioners are presented that examine the problems that tax lawyers and CPAs regularly face in practice. The publication also provides current tax news, the latest tax law changes, court decisions, revenue rulings, and administrative actions. It also covers issues arising in tax accounting, real estate transactions, compensation and employee benefits, retirement plans, and cross-border transactions. Topics addressed do not include theoretical matters or policy discussion of how the law should be changed; however, constructive criticism of administrative or judicial interpretations of the law are included.

74. ***Journal of Taxation of Financial Products.*** [ISSN: 1529-9287] 2000. q. Ed(s): Mark H Price. C C H Inc., 2700 Lake Cook Rd, Riverwoods, IL 60015; cust_serv@cch.com; http://www.cchgroup.com/. *Indexed:* ATI, B01. *Aud.:* Sa.

Journal of Taxation of Financial Products is published quarterly and is devoted exclusively to the analysis of tax ramifications of derivatives and other financial products. It emphasizes the tax treatment of hedges, identifying strategies to maximize the tax-inclusive return for investment vehicles and cross-border derivative transactions, and examines the tax uncertainty from new derivative products. The publication includes complete tax coverage, including strategies and insights into regulatory developments, state and local tax, and international tax issues. Comprehensive, in-depth articles are presented, as well as advice and strategies from practicing professionals. Current tax developments on the federal, international, and state and local levels are regularly reported. Perspective columns are featured relating to high-net-worth investors, investments and hedge funds, capital markets, insurance, international taxation, regulatory issues, and state and local developments. The readership for *JTFP* includes tax practitioners, corporate finance managers, and financial services-firm professionals.

75. ***Journal of Taxation of Investments.*** [ISSN: 0747-9115] 1983. q. Ed(s): Erik M Jensen. Civic Research Institute, 4478 US Rte 27, PO Box 585, Kingston, NJ 08528; order@civicresearchinstitute.com; http://www.civicresearchinstitute.com. *Indexed:* A22, ATI, B01, C42, L14. *Aud.:* Sa.

Journal of Taxation of Investments is published quarterly by the Civic Research Institute. The publication focuses on developments and trends that affect the tax aspects of corporate investing. It helps to evaluate financial instruments, to choose the best products and structures for clients, and to limit the tax impact on investment portfolios. Investments surveyed include: equity and debt securities; real estate, REITs, and REMICs; derivatives; domestic and global markets; hedge funds and mutual funds; equity swaps; and more. Topics addressed are of interest to corporate, institutional, or individual investors, to those who offer investments, and to relevant legal and accounting advisors. While the focus of *JTI* is on tax issues, non-tax issues (such as regulatory restrictions on investors and investments) are also covered. Articles are generally practical, but theoretical discussions are sometimes included. Although most of the content covers U.S. tax and regulatory law, issues related to investing in non-U.S. countries are also examined.

76. *National Tax Journal.* Formerly (until 1948): *National Tax Association. Bulletin.* [ISSN: 0028-0283] 1916. q. Individuals, USD 110; Free to members. Ed(s): Dorey A Zodrow, George R Zodrow. National Tax Association, 725 15th St, NW, Ste 600, Washington, DC 20005; natltax@aol.com; http://www.ntanet.org. Illus., index. Refereed. Vol. ends: Dec. Microform: WSH; PQC. *Indexed:* A22, ATI, B01, BRI, EconLit, IBSS, L14. *Aud.:* Ac, Sa.

National Tax Journal is a refereed, scholarly journal that is published quarterly by the National Tax Association, an organization dedicated to advancing the understanding of the theory and practice of public finance. The goal of the publication is to encourage and disseminate high-quality original research on governmental tax and expenditure policies. The focus is on economic, theoretical, and empirical analysis of tax and expenditure issues, with an emphasis on policy implications. Most regular issues include an "NTJ Forum," which features invited papers by leading scholars that examine a current tax or expenditure policy issue. The December issue is devoted to papers presented at the NTA's annual spring symposium. Forum papers and articles in the December issue are not subject to peer review. The readership for *NTJ* is diverse, including academics, private sector and government economists, accountants, and attorneys, as well as business and government tax practitioners. While the full text for articles going back to 1988 is freely available at the NTA website, the most recent two years are only available to NTA members.

77. *Practical Tax Strategies.* Formed by the merger of (1966-1998): *Taxation for Accountants;* (1972-1998): *Taxation for Lawyers.* [ISSN: 1523-6250] 1998. 1 Base Vol(s). Ed(s): Brian M O'Neil. W G & L Financial Reporting & Management Research, 395 Hudson St, New York, NY 10014; ria.customerservices@thomson.com; http://ria.thomson.com. Illus., index, adv. *Indexed:* A22, ATI, C42, L14. *Aud.:* Sa.

Practical Tax Strategies is a monthly publication that provides tax professionals with strategies to reduce client taxes and satisfy statutory and regulatory compliance mandates. It offers practical information and analysis on recent tax developments, as well as planning strategies related to federal income, estate, and gift taxes. Advice is given on how to maximize savings and minimize risk in every major tax area, including corporations, partnerships, S corporations, LLCs, real estate, accounting, estate planning, personal transactions, compensation, and the like. Articles are written by tax practitioners who understand the issues that arise when servicing clients. Insight is provided by columnists who describe new developments in practicing before the IRS, and help readers assess their own knowledge of critical tax concepts. Content focuses on practical information, therefore theoretical matters or how the law could or should be changed are not discussed.

78. *The Tax Adviser: a magazine of tax planning, trends and techniques.* [ISSN: 0039-9957] 1970. m. Free to members. Ed(s): Rocky S Rosen. CPA2Biz, Inc., 100 Broadway 6th Fl, New York, NY 10005; service@cpa2biz.com; https://www.cpa2biz.com. Illus., index, adv. Microform: WSH; PQC. *Indexed:* A22, ATI, B01, BRI, L14. *Aud.:* Sa.

The Tax Adviser is a monthly publication from the American Institute of Certified Public Accountants. In publication since 1970, it is an authoritative source for news, analysis, and guidance on federal and state taxation with a focus on reporting and explaining federal tax issues to tax practitioners. Through articles and regular columns, *TTA* deals primarily with the technical aspects of federal (and some state) taxation, providing practical, administrative, and technical commentary. Readers are kept informed about the latest plans and actions by the IRS, how to take advantage of the latest tax developments, lessons learned from practitioners in the field, updates on laws and regulations, practical advice on the entire breadth of tax topics, and major annual updates, among other topics. Articles are authored by CPAs, lawyers, tax executives, and professors. Special features include "Tax Clinic," "NewsNotes," "Case Study," and "Tax Trends." The publication is of interest to anyone who must stay informed on federal tax matters. Select articles are available full-text at the AICPA website.

79. *The Tax Executive.* [ISSN: 0040-0025] 1944. bi-m. USD 120 in US & Canada; USD 145 elsewhere; USD 22 per issue. Ed(s): Timothy J McCormally. Tax Executives Institute, Inc., 1200 G St N W, Ste 300, Washington, DC 20005; http://www.tei.org/. Illus., adv. Vol. ends: Nov/Dec. Microform: PQC. Reprint: WSH. *Indexed:* A22, ATI, B01, BRI, C42, L14. *Aud.:* Sa.

The Tax Executive is a professional journal published bimonthly by Tax Executives Institute (TEI), a worldwide association for in-house tax professionals. TEI is dedicated to the development of sound tax policy, compliance with and uniform enforcement of tax laws, and minimization of administration and compliance costs to the benefit of both government and taxpayers. The publication covers current issues of tax policy, administration and management, TEI advocacy initiatives, and more. Each issue features original articles by top law and accounting practitioners, as well as the insights and real-world experiences of TEI members. Readership includes accountants, lawyers, and corporate and business employees who are responsible for the tax affairs of their employers in an executive, administrative, or managerial capacity. A subscription to the publication is included as one of the benefits of TEI membership.

80. *Tax Notes: the weekly tax service.* Former titles (until 1996): *Tax Notes Microfiche Data Base;* (until 1981): *Tax Notes.* [ISSN: 0270-5494] 1972. w. Tax Analysts, 400 S Maple Ave, Ste 400, Falls Church, VA 22046; cservice@tax.org; http://www.taxanalysts.com/. Sample. *Indexed:* A22, ATI, B03, BRI, L14. *Aud.:* Sa.

Published by Tax Analysts, *Tax Notes* provides a weekly summary of federal tax news. The publication updates readers with news and commentary that covers all federal tax laws, regulations, and policy developments. Content includes special reports, in-depth analytical articles, investigative reports, and commentary from leading practitioners, scholars, government officials, and Tax Analysts staff. Topics addressed include federal tax law changes and policy shifts; coverage of the latest congressional action and comments from Treasury and IRS officials; and just-released IRS regulations, revenue rulings, revenue procedures, announcements, and chief counsel advice, among other topics. Also covered are White House budget proposals, and tax bills introduced by Congress, along with cost estimates of those proposals. Readership includes tax professionals in law and accounting firms, corporations, and government agencies. A searchable web archive going back to 1972 is available to subscribers at the Tax Analyst website.

81. *Taxes - The Tax Magazine.* Former titles (until 19??): *Taxes;* (until 1939): *Tax Magazine;* (until 1931): *The National Tax Magazine;* (until 1930): *The National Income Tax Magazine.* 1923. m. USD 420; USD 590 combined subscription (print & online eds.)). Ed(s): Kurt Diefenbach, Shannon Fischer. C C H Inc., 2700 Lake Cook Rd, Riverwoods, IL 60015; cust_serv@cch.com; http://www.cchgroup.com/. Illus. Vol. ends: Dec. Microform: PQC. *Indexed:* A22, ATI, C42, L14. *Aud.:* Sa.

Taxes - The Tax Magazine is a monthly publication that provides readers with practice-oriented analysis of federal, state, and international tax issues. Written by tax experts, articles provide guidance for navigating tax rules and regulations and analysis of current tax issues, trends, and legislative developments. Regular columns include: "Corporate Tax Watch," "Employee Benefits Column," "Federal Tax Practice Standards," "The Estate Planner," "Family Tax Planning Forum," "International Tax Watch," "Tax Practice," "Tackling Taxes," "Tax Meetings," and "Tax Trends." Special conference issues, published in March and June, present papers and panel discussions presented at the University of Chicago Law School's Annual Federal Tax Conference and the Tax Council Policy Institute's Annual Symposium.

■ ADVERTISING, MARKETING, AND PUBLIC RELATIONS

See also Business; Communication; and Journalism and Writing sections.

Clay Williams, Deputy Chief Librarian, Hunter College Libraries, Hunter College, New York, NY 10065

Introduction

In choosing the journals for inclusion here, one must recognize the profound influences that the online environment has upon both scholarship and business.

As predicted, the Internet as the medium of the journals themselves has become the medium and the message. The web as a topic of intellectual discussion is not up for discussion, but the online world has become more transparent and a part of everyone's day-to-day life and is now taken for granted by all. The journals directed at practitioners describe uses of the web in the various manifestations of advertising, while the academic journals explore the effects that the Internet is having on advertising, marketing, and public relations, and what effects the authors think it could or should have.

Practitioners continue to discover ways to use the media to succeed, and the Internet is certainly the major game in town. However, comprehending the online world in its many manifestations and sometimes hidden agendas, if you will, makes things difficult to pin down for more than a moment. Many articles appear on these topics in journals that focus ostensibly on business and marketing. No one questions the importance of advertising, and certainly no one can avoid the role that spin doctors or public relations practitioners are playing in the world today in business.

The inherent pitfalls of the Internet become problematic for a work such as *Magazines for Libraries* because some electronic journals (not to mention companies) do not stay around long enough for their importance to even register, particularly in the academic world. Where are these journals archived and for how long, and in what format? Will they be archived somewhere? If not by the vendors, then where? Consider, as well, that the full-text versions of some journals are best reached via such databases as LexisNexis and EBSCO's various databases, which are now ubiquitous in colleges and public libraries and available at home to subscribers. However, occasional lags in the promptness of recent articles in the promised full-text format speak of other forces at work. The inconsistency only frustrates users, as they see excellent articles abstracted and unavailable because of costs.

The variety of formats we see is representative of the transitional period we are in, and the scholarship reflects that as well. Open access does appear more often, and this battle will now take place in plain view. Does the emperor have any clothes? The profound influence the vendors have in bundling the various journals and magazines has a greater impact in the world of academe than in the professional world, where a company would subscribe to an individual title. This is not the case for the college in which a journal is a part of a package, and so are the years subscribed to as well.

Basic Periodicals

Ga: *Advertising Age, Journal of Advertising, Journal of Advertising Research, The Journal of Consumer Marketing, Journal of Consumer Research, Journal of Macromarketing, Journal of Marketing, Journal of Marketing Research, Marketing News, O'Dwyer's P R Newsletter, Public Relations Review.*

Basic Abstracts and Indexes

ABI/INFORM, Business Periodicals Index, Business Source Elite, Expanded Academic ASAP.

82. ***Academy of Marketing Science. Journal.*** [ISSN: 0092-0703] 1973. q. EUR 1187 (print & online eds.)). Ed(s): Robert W Palmatier. Springer New York LLC, 233 Spring St, New York, NY 10013; customerservice@springer.com; http://www.springer.com. Illus., adv. Refereed. Vol. ends: Oct (No. 4). Reprint: PSC. *Indexed:* A22, B01, BRI, E01. *Bk. rev.:* 2-6, 300-1,000 words. *Aud.:* Ac.

This is the official journal of the Academy of Marketing Science. Articles intended for theoreticians disseminate research results related to the international impact of economics, ethics, and social forces. A regular section concerns marketing and the law. Recent issues contain articles that include a study that examines the effects of downsizing on organizational buying behavior, the concept of culture, the definition of organizational memory, and the dimensions of decision-making context. A reasonable price for an important journal that deals largely with theory.

83. ***Advertising Age.*** Incorporates (1935-2013): *B to B;* (2001-2009): *Creativity;* Which was formerly (1993-2001): *Advertising Age's Creativity;* (1979-2004): *American Demographics;* Which incorporated (1994-1998): *Marketing Tools;* (198?-200?): *Focus;* Which was formerly (1982-198?): *Advertising Age's Focus;* (Jan.1974-May 1974): *Promotion;* Which was formerly (until Dec.1973): *Advertising & Sales Promotion;* (until 1961): *Advertising Requirements;* (19??-1958): *Advertising Agency.* [ISSN: 0001-8899] 1930. w. USD 109 combined subscription (print & online eds.)). Ed(s): Roberta Bernstein. Crain Communications, Inc., 685 Third Ave., 10th Fl., New York, NY 10017-4024; info@crain.com; http://www.crain.com. Illus., adv. Microform: CIS; PQC. *Indexed:* A01, A22, B01, B03, BLI, BRI, C37, C42, Chicano, F01, MASUSE. *Aud.:* Ga, Ac, Sa.

For the student and the practitioner, this tabloid contains enormous amounts of fascinating and useful data. The coverage is thorough yet succinct, and touches on all aspects of advertising. Because it is a weekly, the information is current and topical. It covers important campaigns with text and graphics. The "Annual Agency Report" is a statistical issue that covers the top agencies worldwide. The publication has feature articles on people, on issues such as tobacco and alcohol advertising, and on forthcoming campaigns and spots to watch for, such as those during the Super Bowl. Advertising on the web is not ignored. The title is one of the best for the price in this field. Highly recommended for college, public, and special collections.

84. ***Advertising & Society Review.*** [ISSN: 1534-7311] 2000. q. USD 100. Ed(s): Linda Scott. Advertising Educational Foundation, 220 E 42nd St, Ste 3300, New York, NY 10017; sk@aef.com; http://www.aef.com. Adv. Refereed. *Indexed:* A22, E01. *Aud.:* Ac.

This twenty-first-century addition to scholarship attempts to approach advertising as a cultural phenomenon and to look at it as an academic pursuit. The articles are extensive, and the topics covered are far from narrow. Recent articles discuss "Spirituality that Sells: Religious Imagery in Magazine Advertising," while others concern advertising during World War I. These are not just historical treatises or opinion pieces, but are empirical studies as well.

85. ***Campaign (London, 1968).*** Incorporates (1931-2016): *Marketing;* (2010-2016): *MediaWeek.co.uk;* Which was formerly (1985-2010): *Media Week (Print);* (2003-2016): *Event;* Which was formerly (1997-2002): *Marketing Event;* (1992-1997): *Exhibition Management;* Former titles (until 1968): *W P N Advertisers' Review;* (until 1964): *World's Press News and Advertisers' Review.* [ISSN: 0008-2309] 1929. w. GBP 155 (print or online ed.); GBP 230 combined subscription (print & online eds.)). Ed(s): Claire Beale. Haymarket Publishing Ltd., Bridge House, 69 London Rd, Twickenham, TW1 3SP, United Kingdom; info@haymarket.com; http://www.haymarket.com. Illus., adv. *Indexed:* B01, B03, BRI. *Aud.:* Sa.

This title is included because of its prominence in Britain and the European Union. Political articles that affect American companies are available in the online version, *Campaignlive,* which also provides regular international news feeds. Full text is available in mainstream databases as well, which certainly raises the publication's profile. The articles are generally short, 150-500 words.

86. ***Industrial Marketing Management.*** [ISSN: 0019-8501] 1971. 8x/yr. EUR 2347. Ed(s): Peter J LaPlaca. Elsevier Inc., 230 Park Ave, Ste 800, New York, NY 10169; usinfo-f@elsevier.com; https://www.elsevier.com. Illus., adv. Refereed. Microform: PQC. *Indexed:* A22, B01, C42, IBSS. *Aud.:* Ac.

This very important scholarly journal provides eight to ten clear, well-written articles on topics such as product development, production presentation, advertising, sales, and pricing. Articles often focus on statistical analysis techniques, such as a recent one titled "A Conceptual Model for Building and Maintaining Relationships between Manufacturers' Representatives and their Principals." There is diversity, however; for example, other recent topics include modeling of business-to-business partnerships and the impact of antitrust guidelines on competition.

87. ***International Journal of Advertising: the review of marketing communications.*** Formerly: *Journal of Advertising;* Which superseded (1978-1980): *Advertising Magazine;* Which was formerly: *Advertising;* (1964-1978): *Advertising Quarterly.* [ISSN: 0265-0487] 1982. 8x/yr. GBP

967 (print & online eds.)). Ed(s): Charles R Taylor. Routledge, 4 Park Sq, Milton Park, Abingdon, OX14 4RN, United Kingdom; subscriptions@tandf.co.uk; http://www.tandfonline.com. Illus., index, adv. Sample. Refereed. Circ: 800. Reprint: PSC. *Indexed:* A22, B01, BAS, BRI. *Aud.:* Ac.

This refereed scholarly journal is devoted to publishing authoritative studies for practitioners and academics in the fields of marketing, advertising, and public relations. Articles average about ten pages each. Recent articles include such topics as beer brand advertising and market share in the United States between 1977 and 1998, and a study of the response to banner ads on the web. This title is imperative for research libraries that support programs in advertising and marketing.

88. ***International Journal of Design.*** [ISSN: 1991-3761] 2007. 3x/yr. Free. Ed(s): Lin-Lin Chen, Yaliang Chuang. National Taiwan University of Science and Technology, Graduate Institute of Design, 43, Sec. 4, Keelung Rd., Taipei, , Taiwan, Republic of China. Refereed. *Indexed:* ErgAb. *Aud.:* Sa.

This new journal is open access and thus can be difficult to judge for libraries. That being said, open-access journals are marketed by librarians via lists and word of mouth. Recent articles include "Creating Economic Value by Design" and "Cross-Functional Cooperation with Design Teams in New Product Development." Articles such as these will allow the journal to spread far beyond its Asian roots. In fact, the articles are written by Europeans as well as Asian, and English is the lingua franca.

89. ***International Journal of Internet Marketing and Advertising.*** [ISSN: 1477-5212] 2004. q. USD 790 (print or online ed.)). Ed(s): Eldon Li, Dr. HsiuJu Rebecca Yen. Inderscience Publishers, PO Box 735, Olney, MK46 5WB, United Kingdom; info@inderscience.com; https://www.inderscience.com/index.php. Sample. Refereed. *Aud.:* Ac, Sa.

The quarterly focuses on the emerging changes in theories, strategies, and management methods of marketing and advertising, brought about by the Internet and information technology applications, and their implications for the associated processes, products, and services. Emphasis is on the related social, political, and economic issues, as well as emerging issues of interest to professionals and academics. A recent issue included an article entitled "The role of product reviews on mobile devices for in-store purchases: consumers' usage intentions, costs and store preferences."

90. ***International Journal of Research in Marketing.*** [ISSN: 0167-8116] 1984. 4x/yr. EUR 1462. Ed(s): Cecilia Nalagon, Roland Rust. Elsevier BV, Radarweg 29, Amsterdam, 1043 NX, Netherlands; info@elsevier.com; https://www.elsevier.com/. Illus., index, adv. Refereed. Vol. ends: Nov. Microform: PQC. *Indexed:* A22, B01, BRI, C42. *Bk. rev.:* 0-1. *Aud.:* Ac, Sa.

This title is designed to communicate developments in marketing theory and results of empirical research from any country and from a variety of disciplinary approaches. Coverage includes for-profit as well as nonprofit marketing, consumer behavior, products, pricing, marketing communication, marketing channels, strategic marketing planning, industrial marketing, and international marketing. Recent issues include five or six articles on such topics as consumer-choice behavior in online and traditional supermarkets, and the effects of brand name, price, and other search attributes. Another article topic is homeostasis and consumer behavior across cultures. Although expensive for a quarterly, it does cover areas that other journals do not.

91. ***International Marketing Review.*** Incorporates (1986-1988): *Industrial Marketing and Purchasing.* [ISSN: 0265-1335] 1983. bi-m. EUR 13183 (print & online eds.) (excluding UK)). Ed(s): John W Cadogan. Emerald Publishing Limited, Howard House, Wagon Ln, Bingley, BD16 1WA, United Kingdom; emerald@emeraldinsight.com; http://www.emeraldinsight.com. Illus. Sample. Refereed. Vol. ends: No. 5. Reprint: PSC. *Indexed:* A22, B01, BRI, C42, E01. *Bk. rev.:* 2, 1,000 words. *Aud.:* Ac.

International marketing management is a complex and interesting area of marketing research. This expensive journal is part of an expensive group of marketing journals from MCB. Despite its small subscriber base and high cost, it does have an international readership among academicians because of its excellent articles, research reports, literature reviews, and occasional book reviews. Issues are often devoted to a single topic-recently, for example, retailing. Despite its being indexed prominently, the subscription price makes this journal impossible for many libraries. Naturally, this makes document delivery problematic.

92. ***Journal of Advertising.*** [ISSN: 0091-3367] 1972. 5x/yr. GBP 352 (print & online eds.)). Ed(s): Shintaro Okazaki. Routledge, 530 Walnut St, Ste 850, Philadelphia, PA 19106; enquiries@tandfonline.com; http://www.tandfonline.com. Illus., index, adv. Sample. Refereed. Vol. ends: Dec. Microform: PQC. Reprint: PSC. *Indexed:* A22, B01, BLI, BRI, C42, E01, IBSS. *Bk. rev.:* 0-1, 1,000-2,000 words. *Aud.:* Ac.

This journal cleaves closely to the classic academic model: the articles are all well footnoted and abstracted. They are very theoretical, with extensive use of statistics and well-defined methodologies. A recent issue includes an article titled "The Role of Myth in Creative Advertising Design," and another article explores managers' perceptions of the impact of sponsorship on brand equity. The review process is a blind one, but unfortunately, a call for papers does not come through when the journal is reached only through the indexes.

93. ***Journal of Advertising Research.*** [ISSN: 0021-8499] 1960. q. Free to members. Ed(s): John B Ford. World Advertising Research Center, 432 Park Ave S, 6th F, New York, NY 10016; enquiries@warc.com; http://www.warc.com/. Illus., index, adv. *Indexed:* A22, B01, BRI, Chicano, E01. *Aud.:* Ac, Sa.

This trade periodical, published by the Advertising Research Foundation, consists of well-researched and footnoted articles that are easier to read than those found in most academic journals. The charts and illustrations will not intimidate undergraduates with complicated explanations of methodology. A recent issue presents an article titled "Brain-Imaging Detection of Visual Scene Encoding in Long-Term Memory for TV Commercials." The editorial board is a blend of academics and professionals in the field. There is a calendar of foundation events in each issue.

94. ***Journal of Business & Industrial Marketing.*** Incorporates (2006-2019): *The I M P Journal;* (1993-1994): *Journal of International Marketing.* [ISSN: 0885-8624] 1986. 8x/yr. EUR 13368 (print & online eds.) (excluding UK)). Ed(s): Ivan Snehota, Wesley J Johnston. Emerald Publishing Limited, Howard House, Wagon Ln, Bingley, BD16 1WA, United Kingdom; emerald@emeraldinsight.com; http://www.emeraldgrouppublishing.com. Illus., index. Sample. Refereed. Vol. ends: No. 4. Reprint: PSC. *Indexed:* A22, B01, BRI, C42, E01. *Bk. rev.:* 1-4, 750-1,000 words. *Aud.:* Sa.

Academicians provide practical applications and new ideas based on marketing research to demonstrate the relationship of research to practice in each issue. This is another of MCB University Press's (Emerald Group) products. Recent articles explore sales-force automation usage, effectiveness, and cost-benefit in Germany, England, and the United Kingdom; and studying distance learning for Malaysian sales forces. Marketing educators and practitioners are the intended audience.

95. ***Journal of Consumer Marketing.*** Incorporates (1996-1997): *Franchising Research.* [ISSN: 0736-3761] 1983. 7x/yr. EUR 12781 (print & online eds.) (excluding UK)). Ed(s): Patricia Norberg. Emerald Publishing Limited, Howard House, Wagon Ln, Bingley, BD16 1WA, United Kingdom; emerald@emeraldinsight.com; http://www.emeraldgrouppublishing.com. Illus. Sample. Refereed. Vol. ends: Nov. Microform: PQC. Reprint: PSC. *Indexed:* A22, B01, BLI, BRI, E01. *Bk. rev.:* 2, 500-1,000 words. *Aud.:* Ac, Sa.

Articles in this expensive title report on a wide range of research related to all aspects of consumer marketing. Book reviews are extensive and well written. This journal is indexed in mainstream databases, and students will appreciate that the articles are on current topics of interest. For example, a recent article reports on "Baby Boomers and Busters: An Exploratory Investigation of Attitudes toward Marketing, Advertising and Consumerism." A regular feature on franchising adds to the mix.

96. *Journal of Consumer Psychology.* [ISSN: 1057-7408] 1992. 4x/yr. GBP 876. John Wiley & Sons Ltd., EMEA Institutional Sales, 9600 Garsington Rd, Oxford, OX4 2DQ, United Kingdom; cs-journals@wiley.com; http://onlinelibrary.wiley.com. Adv. Sample. Refereed. *Indexed:* A01, A22, ASSIA, B01, E01. *Aud.:* Ac, Sa.

This title is very much directed toward academics in the field. Articles can include collaborations between faculty in management and psychology. There are peer-reviewed articles in the field of consumer psychology that include topics such as the role of advertising, consumer attitudes, decision-making processes, and direct brand experience. Other topics covered include the development and change of consumer attitudes; judgment, choice, and decision processes; and social cognition research. A recent article is titled "Consumers' Responses to Negative Word-of-Mouth Communication: An Attribution Theory Perspective."

97. *Journal of Consumer Research.* [ISSN: 0093-5301] 1974. bi-m. EUR 414. Ed(s): Darren Dahl. Oxford University Press, 2001 Evans Rd, Cary, NC 27513; custserv.us@oup.com; https://academic.oup.com/journals. Illus., index, adv. Sample. Refereed. Vol. ends: Apr. Microform: PQC. Reprint: PSC. *Indexed:* A01, A22, Agr, B01, Chicano, EconLit, ErgAb, H&TI, HRIS. *Aud.:* Ac, Sa.

A dozen associations co-sponsor this journal, which reports on the research results from numerous disciplines in a dozen articles in each issue. Culture swapping, price perception, consumer-choice deferral, and the role of gifts in the reformulation of interpersonal relationships serve to represent the diversity of the contents. This title covers the latest hot topics in consumer research, and it is a good choice for both large public and academic libraries.

98. *Journal of Global Marketing.* Incorporates (1991-2009): *Journal of Euro-Marketing.* [ISSN: 0891-1762] 1987. 5x/yr. GBP 1137 (print & online eds.)). Routledge, 711 3rd Ave, 8th Fl., New York, NY 10017; http://www.routledge.com. Illus., adv. Sample. Refereed. Vol. ends: Winter (No. 4). Microform: PQC. Reprint: PSC. *Indexed:* A01, A22, B01, E01, H&TI. *Bk. rev.:* 3-4, 500-1,000 words. *Aud.:* Ac, Sa.

Under the auspices of the International Business Press, this journal provides relatively inexpensive access to practical, and sometimes comparative, information on specific aspects of marketing in various countries and geographic regions. Topics address transborder information flow, intellectual property issues, counterfeit goods, market penetration strategies, and personal communication. Recent articles include "The Relationship Between Consumer Ethnocentrism and Human Values, On the Marketing of Nations: A Gap Analysis of Managers' Perceptions, Linking Product Evaluations and Purchase Intention for Country-of-Origin Effects" and "Increasing the Effectiveness of Export Assistance Programs: The Case of the California Environmental Technology Industry." This is a highly selective journal, with about half international subscribers. Only information of interest to nonspecialists is considered for inclusion in this title.

Journal of Hospitality Marketing and Management. See Hospitality/ Restaurant section.

99. *Journal of Interactive Advertising.* [ISSN: 1525-2019] 2000. 3x/yr. GBP 127. Routledge, 711 3rd Ave, 8th Fl., New York, NY 10017; http://www.routledge.com. Refereed. *Indexed:* B01. *Aud.:* Ac, Sa.

This publication, as an open-access journal, appears to focus on the leveling aspects of technology. The use of the social web plays a large part in the choice of articles, as does the use of computers by all the family, so to speak. Recent articles have included "Facebook Me: Collective Self-Esteem, Need to Belong, and Internet Self-Efficacy as Predictors of the iGeneration's Attitudes toward Social Networking Sites," which goes far in defining the focus of this journal. Another article is about "The Effectiveness of Product Placement in Video Games." There does, nonetheless, appear to be an effort to present case studies to the users, and these case studies are from both the academic world and the marketplace.

100. *Journal of Macromarketing.* [ISSN: 0276-1467] 1981. q. USD 813 (print & online eds.)). Ed(s): Marc C Patterson. Sage Publications, Inc., 2455 Teller Rd, Thousand Oaks, CA 91320; info@sagepub.com; http://www.sagepub.com. Illus., adv. Sample. Refereed. Vol. ends: Fall (No. 2). Reprint: PSC. *Indexed:* A22, B01, E01. *Bk. rev.:* 2-6, 1,000-3,000 words. *Aud.:* Ac.

The scholarly articles in this journal address a wide range of social issues, international and domestic, and the impact of marketing upon them. The authors approach topics from many perspectives: historical, analytical, theoretical, and general. Articles in recent issues discuss marketing and the natural environment and the role for morality, and there is a study that examines the marketing literature within the publications of the American Economic Association. Each issue has several extensive, signed book reviews. This work is worth the price for a program concerned with business ethics.

101. *Journal of Marketing.* Formed by the merger of (1934-1936): *The American Marketing Journal;* (1935-1936): *The National Marketing Review.* [ISSN: 0022-2429] 1936. bi-m. USD 540 (print & online eds.)). Sage Publications, Inc., 2455 Teller Rd, Thousand Oaks, CA 91320; info@sagepub.com; http://www.sagepub.com. Illus., index, adv. Refereed. Vol. ends: No. 4. Reprint: PSC. *Indexed:* A22, B01, BAS, BRI, C42, CBRI, H&TI. *Bk. rev.:* 3, 1,000-4,000 words. *Aud.:* Ac.

This official publication of the American Marketing Association includes research articles that must provide a practical link to an application. Articles must be theoretically sound, provide new information or a fresh insight into an unsolved problem, and benefit both practitioners and academicians. Articles tend to be thoughtful, well researched, and interesting. This is a core title for any academic library that supports business programs, especially marketing education programs. There are regular, lengthy book reviews. Recent articles discuss the acquisition and utilization of information in new product alliances and two aspects of brand loyalty: purchase loyalty and attitudinal loyalty. Online subscriptions are available directly from the publisher.

102. *Journal of Marketing Education.* [ISSN: 0273-4753] 1979. 3x/yr. USD 943 (print & online eds.)). Ed(s): Donald R Bacon. Sage Publications, Inc., 2455 Teller Rd, Thousand Oaks, CA 91320; info@sagepub.com; http://www.sagepub.com. Illus., index, adv. Sample. Refereed. Vol. ends: Fall (No. 3). Reprint: PSC. *Indexed:* A22, B01, E01, ERIC. *Aud.:* Ac.

This journal is cosponsored by the Western Marketing Educators Association and the publisher. Each issue includes several papers of about ten pages in length on various aspects of marketing education. Recent articles discuss analyzing the perceptions and preferences of master's of business administration (MBA) students regarding face-to-face versus distance-education methods for delivering a course in marketing management; and familiarizing marketing educators with the process of creative problem-solving. A wise investment as the makeup of marketing departments evolves.

103. *Journal of Marketing Research.* [ISSN: 0022-2437] 1964. bi-m. USD 540 (print & online eds.)). Sage Publications, Inc., 2455 Teller Rd, Thousand Oaks, CA 91320; info@sagepub.com; http://www.sagepub.com. Illus., index, adv. Refereed. Vol. ends: Nov. Reprint: PSC. *Indexed:* A22, B01, BRI, C42, EconLit. *Bk. rev.:* Number and length vary. *Aud.:* Ac.

This core journal presents the results of scholarly and empirical research without the restriction (which accompanies the *Journal of Marketing*) of linking it to practical applications. Mathematical marketing research included in this journal requires that readers possess a strong background in quantitative methods. Papers in recent issues examine negative customer feedback and consumer reactions to corporate social responsibility. Each issue includes a section of research notes on topics such as an empirical analysis of the growth stage of the product life cycle, or the design of research studies for maximum impact; and a section of book reviews.

104. *Journal of Public Relations Research.* Former titles (until 1992): *Public Relations Research Annual;* (until 1989): *Public Relations Research & Education.* [ISSN: 1062-726X] 1984. 6x/yr. GBP 900 (print & online eds.)). Routledge, 711 3rd Ave, 8th Fl., New York, NY 10017; http://www.routledge.com. Sample. Refereed. Reprint: PSC. *Indexed:* A22, B01, E01. *Bk. rev.:* Number and length vary. *Aud.:* Ac, Sa.

This academic journal contains long articles aimed at the advanced student or scholar. A recent article is on "Expansion of Ethics as the Tenth Generic Principle of Public Relations Excellence: A Kantian Theory and Model for Managing Ethical Issues," which demonstrates the journal's focus.

105. *Journal of Services Marketing.* [ISSN: 0887-6045] 1987. 7x/yr. EUR 13368 (print & online eds.) (excluding UK)). Ed(s): Rebekah Russell-Bennett, Mark S Rosenbaum. Emerald Publishing Limited, Howard House, Wagon Ln, Bingley, BD16 1WA, United Kingdom; emerald@emeraldinsight.com; http://www.emeraldinsight.com. Illus. Sample. Refereed. Vol. ends: Nov (No. 4). Reprint: PSC. *Indexed:* A22, B01, BRI, C42, E01. *Bk. rev.:* Number and length vary. *Aud.:* Ac, Sa.

This international marketing journal for practitioners provides research reports on a variety of topics related to all aspects of the service economy, including benchmarking, customer perception, customer satisfaction, quality and performance, marketing operations, and marketing management. A recent article concerns perceived managerial sincerity, feedback-seeking orientation, and motivation among front-line employees of a service organization. Each issue contains five to seven articles, 10-15 pages in length; abstracts of current research literature; and book reviews. This important journal is overpriced for many academic programs that could benefit from a subscription.

106. *Marketing.* [ISSN: 0025-3650] 1931. w. Ed(s): Noelle McElhatton. Haymarket Publishing Ltd., Bridge House, 69 London Rd, Twickenham, TW1 3SP, United Kingdom; info@haymarket.com; http://www.haymarket.com. Illus., adv. Circ: 40000. Vol. ends: Dec. *Indexed:* A22, B01, BRI, C37. *Aud.:* Ga, Sa.

This publication is the newspaper of marketing. Functioning much like a trade magazine, it focuses on international marketing news regarding companies, individuals, brands, legal wrangles, technology, and general areas of market research, advertising, use of emerging technologies, image, and market positioning through dozens of short articles. Survey results and awards are reported, such as a recent report on awards for the best direct-marketing campaigns.

107. *Marketing News: reporting on marketing and its association.* Incorporates (1992-2012): *Marketing Management.* [ISSN: 0025-3790] 1967. m. USD 125 Free to members. Ed(s): Elisabeth Sullivan. American Marketing Association, 311 S Wacker Dr, Ste 5800, Chicago, IL 60606; info@ama.org; https://www.ama.org. Illus., adv. Vol. ends: No. 26. *Indexed:* A22, B01, B03, BRI, Chicano. *Aud.:* Ac, Sa.

The American Marketing Association produces this core trade and industry newspaper to provide timely information to practitioners about the most recent innovations and practices of today's leading companies. Content includes a calendar of events, association activities, and a variety of methods and techniques for achieving marketing goals in a company, for a product, or within the industry as a whole, presented in short articles. An annual directory of consultants is published each June. Sample articles include one on digital yellow pages, and another on the actual profile of baby boomers in marketing terms and marketing to them since the dot-com crash.

108. *Marketing Science: the marketing journal of INFORMS.* [ISSN: 0732-2399] 1982. bi-m. USD 696 (print & online eds.)). Ed(s): K Sudhir. Institute for Operations Research and the Management Sciences (I N F O R M S), 5521 Research Park Dr, Ste 200, Catonsville, MD 21228; informs@informs.org; https://pubsonline.informs.org/. Illus., index. Refereed. *Indexed:* A22, B01, EconLit, IBSS. *Aud.:* Ac, Sa.

The Operational Research Society of America and the Institute of Marketing Science produce this journal, in which authors use mathematics and statistics to evaluate marketing science. It presents papers that offer significant new marketing insights and implications for academics and quantitatively oriented practitioners. One example is a paper on "Direct Competitive Pricing Behavior in the Auto Market: A Structural Analysis." The wide variety of methodologies provides researchers with ideas for approaching research, as well as reports on current concerns. Recent topics include "Patterns in Parameters of Buyer Behavior Models: Generalizing from Sparse Replication. A Model for the Analysis of Asymmetric Data in Marketing Research"; "Application, Predictive Test, and Strategy Implications for a Dynamic Model of Consumer Response"; and "Modeling Retail Customer Behavior at Merrill Lynch."

109. *Media Industry Newsletter: for magazine brand leaders.* Incorporates in part (in 2002): *m i n's New Media Report;* Which incorporated (1994-1997): *Interactive Video News;* Which was formed by the merger of (1993-1994): *Video Services News;* (1990-1994): *Video Marketing Newsletter;* Formerly: *Magazine Industry Newsletter.* [ISSN: 0024-9793] 1948. 48x/yr. USD 1049 combined subscription (print & online eds.)). Ed(s): Steven Cohn. Access Intelligence, LLC, 4 Choke Cherry Rd, 2nd Fl, Rockville, MD 20850; clientservices@accessintel.com; http://www.accessintel.com. Illus., index. Vol. ends: Dec. *Indexed:* B01, B03, BRI. *Aud.:* Sa.

This loose-leaf title is devoted to the media industry, especially magazine and newspaper publications. Its eight to ten pages are filled with statistics regarding advertising in the consumer-magazine publishing industry. There is an opinion article in each issue, and many short pieces on the various industries. This title describes itself as "the first source for magazine advertising data (boxscores)," and it does keep its readers up-to-date on what is happening in the field. Despite the importance of the data, it is a bit pricey for what it might bring to an academic library, but fortunately it is indexed in LexisNexis Academic Universe.

110. *O'Dwyer's.* Former titles (until Dec.2009): *O'Dwyer's P R Report;* (until 2006): *O'Dwyer's P R Services Report.* [ISSN: 2153-3148] 1987. m. USD 60 domestic; USD 90 Canada; USD 125 elsewhere. Ed(s): Jack O'Dwyer, Jon Gingerich. J.R. O'Dwyer Co., Inc., 271 Madison Ave, Ste 600, New York, NY 10016; http://www.odwyerpr.com. Adv. Circ: 2000 Paid and controlled. *Indexed:* BRI. *Aud.:* Sa.

This newsletter publishes articles on current topics and trends of interest to PR professionals, including profiles of firms and discussions of legal and financial issues. It includes such columns as "Web Sitings," which reports on recent developments in the field on the web. This work differs from *O'Dwyer's PR Newsletter* in that it contains more news and less opinion. The columns are informational in intent without any particular political slant. Issues include a PR job market section, and are still considered the gold standard by many in the field.

111. *O'Dwyer's P R Newsletter.* Former titles: *Jack O'Dwyer's Newsletter; Jack O'Dwyer's P R Newsletter.* 1968. w. USD 295. Ed(s): Jack O'Dwyer, Kevin McCauley. J.R. O'Dwyer Co., Inc., 271 Madison Ave, Ste 600, New York, NY 10016; john@odwyerpr.com; http://www.odwyerpr.com. Adv. Circ: 20000 Paid. *Aud.:* Sa.

This indispensable weekly provides the latest news and information on public relations firms and professionals. It subdivides the news rather casually in the "PR Opinion/Items" and "Media News" sections. Under each are several stories that the editors have deemed important for professionals to read. The former gives editorial opinions on politics as they affect this field. In the latter, recently, inductees to the CCNY Communications Hall of Fame are found next to the announcement of the winner of the McDonald's account. Recommended for all professionals and large public libraries.

112. *Psychology & Marketing.* [ISSN: 0742-6046] 1984. m. GBP 1806. Ed(s): Dr. Ronald Jay Cohen. John Wiley & Sons, Inc., 111 River St, Hoboken, NJ 07030; cs-journals@wiley.com; http://onlinelibrary.wiley.com. Illus., index, adv. Refereed. Vol. ends: No. 6. Microform: PQC. Reprint: PSC. *Indexed:* A22, B01, BRI. *Aud.:* Ac, Sa.

This title presents research that bridges academic and practical interests in marketing and advertising through the application of psychological principles to marketing strategy. Research reports are based on "fundamental factors that affect buying, social and cultural trends, psychological profiles of potential customers, and changes in customer behavior." Recent papers discuss the dangers of using deceptive practices in the mail-order business; using deception to measure service performance; and "Romancing the Past: Heritage Visiting and the Nostalgic Consumer." The journal is widely indexed, and the in-depth articles are well written. An important, although expensive, addition for academic and special libraries.

113. *Public Relations Review: a global journal of research and comment.* [ISSN: 0363-8111] 1975. 5x/yr. EUR 1183. Ed(s): Ray E Hiebert. Elsevier Ltd, 125 London Wall, London, EC2Y 5AS, United Kingdom; corporate.sales@elsevier.com; http://www.elsevier.com. Illus., adv. Sample. Refereed. Vol. ends: Dec. Microform: PQC. Reprint: PSC. *Indexed:* A01, A22, B01, BRI. *Bk. rev.:* 5-6, 500-1,000 words. *Aud.:* Ga, Ac, Sa.

This journal considers its title an important guide to its content: there are pieces that could be called research, although some might question the format of the methodology section in the articles. There are pieces that comment on how government policy directly affects aspects of a public relations officer's life. The book reviews alone are worth the cover price. They are extensive and could be considered articles in themselves, perhaps thus fulfilling the "review" promise in the title. A fifth issue published midyear is an extensive bibliography that will interest librarians.

114. ***Public Relations Tactics.*** [ISSN: 1080-6792] 1994. m. USD 100 domestic; USD 110 Canada; USD 120 elsewhere. Ed(s): John Elsasser, Amy Jacques. The Public Relations Society of America, Inc., 33 Maiden Ln, 11th Fl, New York, NY 10038; publications@prsa.org; http://www.prsa.org. *Indexed:* B01. *Aud.:* Sa.

This tabloid directs its articles toward professionals, and they are written by their peers. The articles can concern independent practitioners or employees of big firms. Each issue has a listing of upcoming events such as trade shows. Polls are included that are of interest and importance to the audience, but with little analysis. The articles also keep readers abreast of recent court rulings that have an impact upon the field. This publication is an important mouthpiece for the profession.

115. ***Strategies & Tactics.*** Formed by the merger of (1995-2018): *Public Relations Strategist;* (1994-2018): *Public Relations Tactics.* [ISSN: 2576-2028] 2018. m. Free to members; Non-members, USD 125. Ed(s): John Elsasser, Amy Jacques. The Public Relations Society of America, Inc., 120 Wall St, 21st Fl, New York, NY 10005; helpdesk@prsa.org; http://www.prsa.org. Adv. *Indexed:* A22, B01. *Aud.:* Sa.

This journal is included in the price of Public Relations Society membership dues. It contains about ten articles of interest to the trade. The editors wish to emphasize the regular interviews with CEOs of the leading firms in the field. Recent articles include one on the "Ethical Challenge of Global Public Relations."

■ AERONAUTICS AND SPACE SCIENCE

Howard Stephen McMinn, Director of Collections and Scholarly Communication, Brookens Library, Room 234, University of Illinois at Springfield, One University Plaza, Springfield, IL 62703-5407; stephen.mcminn@uis.edu

Introduction

This section reviews the best journals in the areas that encompass aeronautics and space sciences, from general aviation and its various specialty areas (such as powerless flight) to research-level journals that communicate the technical and scientific underpinnings of flight and space research. Trade journals of importance to the practitioners within these areas are also covered. This section concentrates on core journals rather than the legal, medical, or policy aspects in these areas.

The terms *aeronautics, astronautics,* and *space science* do not conjure up the romantic images of early aviators and aviation pioneers, or the excitement of space exploration, but they are the basic elements of these inspiring endeavors. This romantic concept of flying and space exploration is communicated through the popular and historical journals that capture the adventure, excitement, and sport of all types of aviation and aircraft from parasailing to spaceflight.

The journals are split between those focused on the scientific aspects of space science and aeronautical and astronautical engineering that support all types of aviation and fight including spaceflight. These highly technical fields require very specialized information created by experts in their fields.

From a library perspective, the fields of aeronautics, astronautics, and space science have recently seen a marked rise in the number of new technical journals. Although most of these are from highly respected publishers with impressive editorial boards, they are really too new to be considered leading journals in their field. The rise in Unmanned Aerial Vehicles (UAVs) and microgravity research points toward new research areas and there is corresponding growth in journals and articles in this area but at present most journals that cover unmanned systems focus on all types of vehicles and applications, not just aerial vehicles.

There has been little change in terms of the number of general-interest flight and aviation magazines published. The trend toward electronic publishing of both technical journals and the popular aviation and aviation business focused journals continue with the popularly focused and trade journals leading the way in taking advantage of publishing on mobile platforms.

Overall, the journals and magazines reviewed provide information for the development of a core collection that serves aeronautics and space sciences researchers or those interested in the best publications covering space exploration, flying, and general aviation.

Basic Periodicals

Hs: *Air & Space - Smithsonian, Aviation Week & Space Technology, Flying;* Ga: *Air & Space - Smithsonian, A O P A Pilot, Aviation Week & Space Technology, Flying, FlyPast, Plane & Pilot;* Ac (Nontechnical): *Aerospace America, Aviation Week & Space Technology, Flight International, Space Policy, Vertiflite;* Ac (Technical): *Acta Astronautica, The Aeronautical Journal, A I A A Journal, Journal of Aircraft, Journal of Spacecraft and Rockets, Journal of the Astronautical Sciences, Progress in Aerospace Sciences.*

Basic Abstracts and Indexes

Advanced Technologies & Aerospace Database, The Engineering Index Monthly, International Aerospace Abstracts, Scopus, Web of Science.

116. ***A A H S Journal.*** Formerly (until 1980): *American Aviation Historical Society Journal.* [ISSN: 0882-9365] 1956. a. Free to members. Ed(s): Hayden Hamilton. American Aviation Historical Society, PO Box 3023, Huntington Beach, CA 92704; http://www.aahs-online.org. Illus. Vol. ends: No. 4. *Bk. rev.:* Number and length vary (in e-newsletter). *Aud.:* Ac, Sa.

The American Aviation Historical Society (AAHS) produces this journal consisting of well-researched scholarly articles on all areas of aviation history. The primary emphasis is on the history of general aviation and commercial flight technology, not on military or space history and events, as is the case with most other aviation history magazines. All areas of aviation history are included, from famous aviators and engineers to aircraft design and manufacture, to the history of aerospace advancements and technical achievements. The journal contains both color and black-and-white photographs (appropriate for the time periods covered) and illustrations. The articles are written by historians, military personnel, and scholars, and are produced by society members; and most have an American flavor. Ongoing departments include "Forum of Flight" (consisting of interesting or unusual black-and-white photographs of aircraft submitted by members), "News and Comments from our Members" from readers including items of interest, news, and conference activities and a message from the society's president, and the new "Confession Corner," which relays short stories from members highlighting interesting or humorous events. AAHS also publishes an electronic newsletter, *AAHS Flightline*, that provides interesting articles, book reviews, and membership-related information. *AAHS Journal*, scholarly and informative, is appropriate for academic and public libraries with strong history or aviation collections.

117. ***A I A A Journal: devoted to aerospace research and development.*** Formed by the merger of (1958-1963): *Journal of the Aerospace Sciences;* Which was formerly (1934-1958): *Journal of the Aeronautical Sciences;* (1959-1963): *A R S Journal;* Which was formerly (until 1959): *Jet Propulsion;* (until 1954): *American Rocket Society. Journal;* (until 1945): *Astronautics;* (1930-1932): *American Interplanetary Society. Bulletin.* [ISSN: 0001-1452] 1963. m. USD 160. Ed(s): Alexander J Smits. American Institute of Aeronautics and Astronautics, Inc., 12700 Sunrise Valley Dr, Ste 200, Reston, VA 20191-5807; custserv@aiaa.org; http://www.aiaa.org. Illus., index. Sample. Refereed. Vol. ends: No. 12. Microform: PMC; PQC. Reprint: PSC. *Indexed:* A01, A22, BRI. *Bk. rev.:* 1-2, 300-500 words. *Aud.:* Ac.

This is the leading overarching journal covering the wide range of interest to the membership of the American Institute of Aeronautics and Astronautics (AIAA) in contrast to organizations' more specialized journals. All of the AIAA technical or research-level journals are available on their branded platform, ARC (Aerospace Research Central) and now only available electronically. This journal is designed to disseminate original research papers that discuss new theoretical developments or experimental results for the advancement of astronautics and aeronautics. The areas covered include aerodynamics, aeroacoustics, fluid mechanics, reacting flows, hydrodynamics, research instrumentation and facilities, structural mechanics and materials, propulsion, aircraft technology, STOL/VTOL, fluid dynamics, thermophysics and thermochemistry, and interdisciplinary topics. The journal publishes a number of article types including what they refer to as "Express Articles" that differ from the "Technical Note" section to facilitate the rapid communication of new and potentially important in that they are full articles (receiving the same standards as regular articles) with limited word count that are then rapidly reviewed and published. Periodically, special sections or issues devoted to a specific topic are published, such as the recent special section on flow control. Occasionally book reviews, lectures, and survey papers (to provide comprehensive overviews of subjects of interest) are included. Appropriate for all academic, technical, and larger public libraries.

118. ***A O P A Pilot.*** [ISSN: 0001-2084] 1958. m. Free to members. Aircraft Owners and Pilots Association (A O P A), 421 Aviation Way, Frederick, MD 21701; aopahq@aopa.org; http://www.aopa.org. Illus., index, adv. Circ: 284000. Vol. ends: Dec. *Indexed:* HRIS. *Bk. rev.:* 1-2, 300-500 words. *Aud.:* Ga, Sa.

This is the primary journal of the numerous magazines and newsletters published by the Aircraft Owners and Pilots Association, the world's largest aviation organization serving the needs of all pilots. The journal is slanted toward the private pilot and aircraft owner, with an emphasis on ownership-related issues and flight safety. Articles include information on safety; flying tips and techniques; airports, nearby accommodations, and attractions; newly certified aircraft, along with specifications; and, of course, general-interest pieces on aircraft and flying. There are numerous departments that contain general information pertinent to association members and pilots, such as regulatory news, safety-related information, a calendar of events, and information on new aircraft and equipment, along with meeting and organizational notes. The journal provides many photographs, as well as illustrations, for aviation buffs that highlight the text as well as an occasional photography issue. The magazine contains a large commentary section that is usually geared to members, but it also contains information on safety, along with other issues and concerns with piloting aircraft. AOPA also produces *AOPA Flight Training*, which provides in-depth information for pilots and pilots-in-training. It also publishes an expanded version *AOPA Pilot Magazine-Turbine Edition*, which includes all the articles in *AOPA Pilot* plus additional articles of interest to pilots of turbine-powered aircraft. Current electronic newsletters, AOPA ePilot, AOPA ePilot Flight Training, Aviation eBrief, Flight School Business, Club Connector, CFI (Certified Flight Instructor), and Drone Pilot show the scope and value of the organization and its publications. There is also a weekly videocast, AOPA Live this Week. One of the best general-interest aviation publications and an excellent addition to general aviation collections.

119. ***Acta Astronautica.*** Formerly (until 1974): *Astronautica Acta.* [ISSN: 0094-5765] 1955. s-m. EUR 6809. Elsevier Ltd, The Boulevard, Langford Lane, Oxford, OX5 1GB, United Kingdom; customerserviceau@elsevier.com; http://www.elsevier.com. Illus., adv. Sample. Refereed. Microform: PQC. *Indexed:* A01, A22. *Aud.:* Ac.

The International Academy of Astronautics (IAA) produces this research-level publication focused on astronautics and space sciences. Each issue presents peer-reviewed papers in the areas of life sciences, astronautics, space sciences, and space technology, to promote the peaceful scientific exploration of space to aid humanity using both space born and earth bound systems. In addition, it covers the design, development, research, and technological advances necessary to accomplish this goal. Articles cover microgravity, space station technology, spacecraft, interplanetary flight, satellites, power and propulsion, geomagnetism, GPS, and space economics, along with traditional areas of research such as materials science, guidance and control, and so on. The journal frequently publishes special issues or sections devoted to a specific topic or a collection of selected papers from conferences sponsored by the International Academy of Astronautics or the International Astronautical Federation. One such example is the recent issues on tethers in space. The journal strongly encourages the deposit of research data and supplementary content to promote further research. Overall, the journal's broad coverage and depth with an increase to more than 500 articles per year and its international scope make it appropriate for academic and research libraries.

Ad Astra. See Astronomy section.

120. ***Advances in Space Research.*** Formed by the merger of (1978-1981): *Advances in Space Exploration;* (1963-1981): *Life Sciences and Space Research;* (1960-1980): *Space Research.* [ISSN: 0273-1177] 1981. s-m. EUR 5488. Elsevier Ltd, The Boulevard, Langford Lane, Oxford, OX5 1GB, United Kingdom; customerserviceau@elsevier.com; http://www.elsevier.com. Illus., adv. Sample. Refereed. Vol. ends: No. 24. Microform: PQC. *Indexed:* A01, A22. *Aud.:* Ac, Sa.

This journal, primarily of interest to physicists, astronomers, and the general field of space science, publishes information on fundamental research obtained by utilizing aerospace vehicles. As the official journal of the Committee on Space Research (COSPAR), a scientific committee of the International Council for Science (ICSU), *Advances in Space Research* covers all areas of fundamental research that is obtained with the use of all types of space vehicles including balloons, rockets, rocket-propelled vehicles, and other aerospace vehicles, regardless of political considerations. A sampling of the topics covered includes planets and small bodies of the solar system, the ionosphere, solar energy, geomagnetism, cosmic rays, solar radiation, astrophysics, and studies of the upper atmosphere. Much of the information contained in the journal originates from various conferences and symposia sponsored by COSPAR. Therefore, most issues contain papers on similar topics or in a specific area of interest, such as the recent special issues on "Origins of Cosmic Rays" and "Advances in Solar Physics." Articles are often grouped into categories or sections, some of which are astrodynamics and space debris, earth sciences, earth magnetosphere and upper atmosphere, solar system bodies, and so on. The papers submitted from conferences are thoroughly reviewed before inclusion in the journal. Some articles are available to non-subscribers through the journal's open-access program. Most of the items of interest to the organization's membership are provided in *Space Research Today.* Recently the journal no longer publishes articles related to life sciences due to the creation of a journal specializing on this research area entitled *Life Sciences in Space Research.*

121. ***The Aeronautical Journal.*** Incorporates (1949-1983): *Aeronautical Quarterly;* Former titles (until 1968): *Royal Aeronautical Society. Journal;* Which incorporated (1947-1959): *Helicopter Association of Great Britain. Journal;* (until 1923): *Aeronautical Journal;* (until 1987): *Aeronautical Society of Great Britain. Annual Report.* [ISSN: 0001-9240] 1897. m. GBP 639 (print & online eds.)). Ed(s): Holger Babinsky. Cambridge University Press, University Printing House, Shaftesbury Rd, Cambridge, CB2 8BS, United Kingdom; journals@cambridge.org; https://www.cambridge.org. Illus., index, adv. Refereed. Vol. ends: Dec. Reprint: PSC. *Indexed:* A22. *Bk. rev.:* 2-3, 300-500 words. *Aud.:* Ac.

The purpose of this monthly aeronautical engineering research journal, published for more than 120 years by the Royal Aeronautical Society, is to foster the advancement of all aspects of aeronautical, aerospace, and space sciences. The journal publishes six to ten articles per issue related to the research, design, development, construction, and operation of aircraft and space vehicles. Article topics include fluid mechanics and aerodynamics, propulsion, structures and materials, rotorcraft, astronautics, dynamics and control, noise and vibration, guided flight, air transport, and test flying and flight simulation. The journal occasionally publishes review articles, "Survey Papers," which focus on a specific aspect of aeronautics and astronautics, and book reviews. Occasional special issues are published that are focused on a single topic or theme, or composed of selected technical papers presented at major U.K. aeronautical conferences, such as the publication of papers from the International Society of Air Breathing Engines and the Rotorcraft Virtual Engineering Conference. The journal was one of the first to provide metrics and altmetrics (information on tweets and inclusion in Mendeley libraries) to show the impact of its articles.

Membership and related society information are available in the society's companion publication, *Aerospace*. This companion journal is more of a general-interest publication providing both industry news and membership-related information.

122. *AeroSafety World.* Formerly (until 2007): *Aviation Safety World;* Formed by the merger of (1987-2006): *Accident Prevention;* Which was formerly (until 1987): *F S F Accident Prevention Bulletin;* (1987-2006): *Airport Operations;* Which was formerly (until 1987): *F S F Airport Operations Safety Bulletin;* (1954-2006): *Aviation Mechanics Bulletin;* (1987-2006): *Cabin Crew Safety;* Which was formerly (until 1987): *F S F Cabin Crew Safety Bulletin;* (until 1975): *Cabin Crew Safety Exchange;* (1988-2006): *Flight Safety Digest;* Which was formerly (until 1988): *F S F Flight Safety Digest;* (until 1984): *Flight Safety Digest;* (until 1982): *Flight Safety Facts and Reports;* (until 1974): *Flight Safety Facts and Analysis;* (1987-2006): *Helicopter Safety;* Which was formerly (until 1987): *F S F Helicopter Safety Bulletin;* (until 1985): *Helicopter Safety Bulletin;* (1988-2006): *Human Factors & Aviation Medicine;* Which was formerly (until 1988): *F S F Human Factors Bulletin & Aviation Medicine.* [ISSN: 1934-4015] 2006. m. Free to members. Ed(s): Frank Jackman. Flight Safety Foundation, Inc., 601 Madison St, Ste 300, Alexandria, VA 22314; http://www.flightsafety.org. Adv. *Indexed:* HRIS. *Bk. rev.:* Number and length vary. *Aud.:* Ga, Ac, Sa.

This journal, published by the Flight Safety Foundation, provides articles and in-depth analysis of important safety issues that face the industry, along with numerous standard departments. The feature articles deal with all areas of safety within all sectors of the aviation industry such as but not limited to weather, training, regulations, and human factors. The departments contain news items, editorials, letters to the editor, a calendar of events, and information on the foundation and its members. The "DataLink" section provides articles that include data and analysis on topics specific to aviation and safety. There are occasional sections that provides in-depth coverage of selected reports, reviews of books, and websites of interest to those involved with safety. The main sections are the multiple sections covering safety issues such as safety news, a safety calendar, and the "OnRecord" section, which covers important information taken from the final reports in investigations, and provides awareness of problems so that others would avoid them in the future. This journal was created through the merging of seven newsletters produced by the foundation. These newsletters are listed here primarily to provide a glimpse at the subjects covered by this journal: *Accident Prevention, Airport Operations, Aviation Mechanics Bulletin, Cabin Crew Safety, Flight Safety Digest, Helicopter Safety,* and *Human Factors & Aviation Medicine.* There are no special issues just well written thoughtful articles, news, and information focused on the numerous elements comprising flight safety. The journal is an important, timely publication for those working in the industry or interested in aviation safety.

123. *Aerospace America.* Former titles (until 1984): *Astronautics and Aeronautics;* (until 1964): *Astronautics and Aerospace Engineering;* Which was formed by the merger of (1957-1963): *Astronautics;* (1958-1963): *Aerospace Engineering;* Which was formerly (1942-1958): *Aeronautical Engineering Review;* Astronautics and Aeronautics superseded in part (1964-1975): *A I A A Bulletin.* [ISSN: 0740-722X] 1932. m. USD 220. Ed(s): Ben Iannotta. American Institute of Aeronautics and Astronautics, Inc., 12700 Sunrise Valley Dr, Ste 200, Reston, VA 20191-5807; custserv@aiaa.org; http://www.aiaa.org. Illus., index, adv. Sample. Refereed. Vol. ends: No. 12. Microform: PQC. *Indexed:* A01, A22, BRI. *Aud.:* Hs, Ga, Ac.

This is the membership journal of the largest U.S. aerospace engineering professional organization, the American Institute of Aeronautics and Astronautics (AIAA). Each issue contains three to five feature articles covering all aspects of the industry—economic issues, government rules and financing, aircraft, materials, space transportation, spacecraft, and defense. The articles usually provide more of an overview on the topic, and they primarily interpret or review new research, engineering issues, program developments, and future trends in aeronautics or space sciences. The articles are still quite sophisticated and comprehensive, utilizing many color photographs and illustrations. The journal is devoted to keeping AIAA members up to date on major events and issues in their field and serves as the prime vehicle for relaying information on the institute's activities. It contains valuable news of upcoming conferences and events, along with sections such as covering recent industry news, interviews with important people in the industry or those who impact the industry (such as lawmakers), and other standard sections such as opinions, letters to the editor, information on student achievements, engineering problems or topics, aircraft and electronics updates, new systems, software, and materials or products of note. There are also case studies and an engineer's notebook section both of which would be of particular interest to engineers in the field. The "Year in Review" is published every December and is devoted to recalling the highlights, accomplishments, and news of note for the previous year in aerospace. Overall, this journal is a valuable addition for all types of libraries.

124. *Aerospace & Defense Technology: the engineers guide to design & manufacturing advances.* Former titles (until Dec. 2014): *Aerospace Engineering;* (until 2011): *Aerospace Engineering & Manufacturing;* (until 2008): *Aerospace Engineering;* (until 1983): *S A E in Aerospace Engineering; Defense Tech Briefs.* 2014. 7x/yr. Free to qualified personnel. Ed(s): Bruce Bennett, Jean Broge. S A E Inc., 400 Commonwealth Dr, Warrendale, PA 15096; CustomerSales@sae.org; http://www.sae.org. Illus., adv. *Aud.:* Ac, Sa.

This journal, produced by the Society of Automotive Engineers (SAE), provides technical assistance and state-of-the-art technical information of interest to designers, manufacturers, and project managers of aerospace systems and components. Its emphasis is more on applications, testing, and reliability of aerospace components than on theoretical or experimental results. Unlike most trade journals, this title contains very little information on people, events, or the business side of the industry with only two major departments, "Applications Brief" and one on new products. The journal covers all areas of interest to aerospace engineers, including avionics, new materials, system and component design, propulsion systems, system maintainability, structural design, and related engineering topics. It is an important vehicle for new-product information, product literature, computer products, and other technical information. Its focus is on conveying practical timely information to those working in the field. With its expanded coverage of military aviation and defense topics with information from all major branches of the military, plus agencies such as DARPA and NASA, the journal has expanded its scope and coverage. This journal also supports a new website (URL: www.aerodefensetech.com) that offers additional news and information, as well as white papers and webcasts. The journal periodically publishes special supplements on manufacturing and machining or manufacturing and refabrication. The more theoretical and technical research are presented as papers at SAE conferences and symposia and published in the SAE *International Journal of Aerospace.* Appropriate for technical and academic libraries.

125. *Aerospace Manufacturing and Design: dedicated to the design, manufacturing, and mro of aircraft and aerospace components.* 2007. 7x/yr. Ed(s): Robert Schoenberger, Elizabeth Modic. G I E Media Inc., 5811 Canal Rd, Valley View, OH 44125; http://www.giemedia.com/. Adv. *Aud.:* Ac, Sa.

This is one of the most technically oriented trade journals in the field focusing on manufacturing and design of all types of aerospace vehicles and individual systems. The articles are highly technical and focused on all aspects of manufacturing and design in the aerospace industry. Each issue has a cover story, along with three to five other feature articles. Then there are the standard departments that accompany most trade journals, which focus on industry news and opinions, and its outlook. There is little focus on people in the industry, with most of the departments focused on new products, services, or manufacturing techniques. All of the typical aviation subjects are covered, including safety issues, government regulation, and financial outlooks. However, the primary focus is on manufacturing and design, with articles on precision manufacturing, thermal management, composite repair, inspection issues, lean manufacturing, and productivity and leadership, among others. There are periodic special features, such as a yearly forecast issue focused on the state of the industry. Occasionally other special issue are published such as those on the Paris Airshow, a buyer's guide, additive manufacturing guide, inspection targeting, or other special reports. The magazine's website, besides providing access to the magazine's digital issues, also houses specialized information, such as white papers and the searchable Manufacturing Buyers Guide. There is also a "name that plane" contest. This worthwhile trade journal fills an important niche for the aerospace industry.

126. *Aerospace Science and Technology.* Formed by the merger of (1963-1997): *Recherche Aerospaciale;* Which was formerly (1948-1963): *La Recherche Aeronautique;* (1974-1997): *Recherche Aerospatiale (English Edition);* (1977-1997): *Zeitschrift fuer Flugwissenschaften und Weltraumforschung;* Which was formed by the merger of (1953-1977): *Zeitschrift fuer Flugwissenschaften;* (1964-1977): *Raumfahrtforschung;* Which was formerly (1957-1964): *Raketentechnik und Raumfahrtforschung.* [ISSN: 1270-9638] 1997. 12x/yr. EUR 899. Ed(s): J A Ekaterinaris. Elsevier Masson, 62 Rue Camille Desmoulins, Issy les Moulineaux Cedex, 92442, France; http://www.elsevier-masson.fr. Illus., index. Sample. Refereed. Vol. ends: No. 8. *Indexed:* A01, A22. *Aud.:* Ac, Sa.

This international journal presents articles from original research, review articles, and condensed versions of recently completed doctoral theses in all areas of aerospace science and technology. Topics covered include all issues related to aerospace research, from fundamental research to industrial applications for the design and manufacture of aircraft, helicopters, missiles, launch vehicles, and satellites. Other aspects include articles on the environment, aerospace communication systems, test facilities, and aerospace electronic systems. Included are articles on aerodynamics, computational fluid dynamics (CFD), computer simulation, navigation, guidance and control, data fusion, robotics and intelligent systems, signal processing, materials and structures, flight mechanics, automatic systems, propulsion systems, and analysis of experimental data. The journal originated by combining two of the leading aerospace journals from France and Germany, and the addition of research organizations from Italy, Spain, the Netherlands, and Sweden has solidified this journal as one of the leading European journals in the field. Special issues are occasionally published that comprise selected papers from European aerospace conferences or focus on a specific topic, such as the recent issues on diamond wing aerodynamics or instability and control of massively separated flows.

127. *Aerospace Testing International.* [ISSN: 1478-2774] 2002. q. Free. Ed(s): Christopher Hounsfield. U K & International Press, Abinger House, Church St, Dorking, RH4 1DF, United Kingdom; info@ukintpress.com; http://www.ukipme.com. Adv. Circ: 11000. *Aud.:* Ac, Sa.

This trade journal is focused on the testing of aerospace systems and components, providing a wealth of information for those concerned with aerospace testing, evaluation, and inspection. All areas of aviation and aerospace manufacturing are covered, including civil and military aerospace, defense systems, launch vehicles, satellites, and space systems. The journal contains most of the elements of a typical trade publication, that is, news, feature articles, industry interviews, and information on services available for the aerospace testing industry. This journal is focused on testing materials, structures, and ensuring the safety and reliability of equipment and vehicles rather than the human element, that is, pilots and personnel. There is an entire section on products and services with technical profiles of new equipment and services. The journal has regular columns that present news and opinions on safety issues, current information on the people and companies in the industry, announcements, and newsworthy events. The journal's focus is not on breaking news and day-to-day activities as the journal is only published quarterly, but on providing in-depth analysis of issues and trends within this important segment of the aerospace industry. The journal also produces an additional annual showcase issue aimed at experts in the field, which provides greater scientific focus as it describes in detail the latest research, developments, methods, and science behind the technologies. Safety is critical to the aerospace industry and this is an important publication that addresses areas of testing, and evaluation required to ensure performance, reliability, and quality.

The Air & Space Power Journal. See Military section.

128. *Air & Space - Smithsonian.* Formerly (until 1986): *Air & Space.* [ISSN: 0886-2257] 1978. 7x/yr. Free to members; Non-members, USD 22. Ed(s): Linda Musser Shiner. Smithsonian Institution, Air & Space Magazine, MRC 513, PO Box 37012, Washington, DC 20013; airspace@emailcustomerservice.com. Illus., adv. Vol. ends: No. 6. *Indexed:* A01, A22, BRI, CBRI, HRIS, MASUSE. *Bk. rev.:* 4-5, 800-1,000 words. *Aud.:* Ems, Hs, Ga, Ac.

Air & Space - Smithsonian is the best overall journal for general aviation and space enthusiasts, as every aspect of aerospace and aviation is covered in a comprehensive and entertaining fashion, with outstanding photographs and illustrations. It provides up-to-date topical articles on current aviation, space, aeronautics, and astronautical topics; historical information; future trends; and scientific advancements in all areas of aviation and space exploration. The coverage is broad, from military, general, and commercial aviation to articles on space flight and exploration. It profiles people—both aviation pioneers and present-day decision makers and innovators—and highlights technological and scientific advancements. The strength of this publication is that its articles provide in-depth scientific and technical information in a readable, informative, educational, and entertaining manor. This magazine is the closest thing to actually visiting the Air and Space Museum in Washington, D.C., and marveling at the history of aviation and space travel while imagining its future possibilities. Departments are "In the Museum," "Above and Beyond," "Oldies and Oddities," "One More and Higher," and "Sightings." This is one of those rare magazines that should be in every library collection.

129. *Air Power History.* Former titles (until 1989): *Aerospace Historian;* (until 1965): *Airpower History.* [ISSN: 1044-016X] 1954. q. Free to members. Air Force Historical Foundation, PO Box 790, Clinton, MD 20735; execdir@afhistoricalfoundation.org; http://www.afhistory.org/. Illus., adv. Refereed. Vol. ends: Dec. Microform: PQC. *Indexed:* A01, BAS, BRI, C42, CBRI. *Bk. rev.:* 5-10, 500-750 words. *Aud.:* Ac, Sa.

This is the premier scholarly journal for research into the history of aerospace, aviation, and space science, with an emphasis on the United States Air Force and their personnel. Although the majority of articles are concerned with military aviation, as the Air Force Historical Foundation publishes it, the journal chronicles historic events in all fields of aviation including general aviation and space missions. All time periods are covered from the inception of flying to historical events such as the air war in Vietnam. Articles are interesting reading as well as solid history, with extensive bibliographies written by historians, military personnel, museum curators, and others who possess both a strong academic foundation in history along with a background in aviation. Numerous photographs and illustrations bring the text alive, but most are in black and white due to the topics and times covered. The magazine also includes Air Force Historical Foundation Symposium notices, voluminous book reviews, letters, obituaries, reunions, and related society information. This journal is highly recommended for aviation buffs, military history enthusiasts, and a general readership. The History Mystery puzzle is a fun feature that poses a historical question to the readership with the answer geared not only to solving the mystery by answering the question but also educating and informing the readers. It would be appropriate for all types of libraries based on its content, but its limited focus will not appeal to more general libraries. There are numerous popular history magazines covering military air history and aircraft such as *Flypast* or *Air Classics* that would appeal to a more popular aviation or military history collections.

130. *Air Transport World.* [ISSN: 0002-2543] 1964. m. USD 89 domestic (Free to qualified personnel). Penton, 1911 N. Fort Myer Dr, Ste 600, Arlington, VA 22209. Illus., index, adv. Circ: 1611 Paid. Microform: PQC. *Indexed:* A22, B01, B03, BRI, C42, HRIS. *Aud.:* Sa.

This business-oriented journal covers the area of world airline management, embracing all aspects of commercial aviation and the surrounding industries. The primary focus is on the airline industry, commercial air transport, airline manufacturing, airport management, and related issues. The industry aspects of commercial aviation are another area of focus, with several informative segments that include data and statistics on commuter traffic, airport usage, fuel prices, and foreign exchange rates. Broad article categories include technology, airways, airlines, safety, marketing, maintenance, cargo, and passenger service. Articles on the people involved in this side of the aviation spectrum are informative and enlightening with interviews included at the end of most issues. The "Trends" section provides industry snapshots that are presented simply in graphical format and impart important industry data quickly. Another important section is "Analysis," which provides analysis of the industry beyond the simple facts and figures. Periodically, the journal includes directory information on specific topics—such as practical, factual information for industry insiders—such as the annual world aircraft report, maintenance directory, and trends survey. The journal also publishes topically focused issues that provide valuable information to those within the industry, such as an industry forecast issue and market review. The journal is primarily a trade publication for the commercial aviation segment of the industry, but it provides valuable information on all aspects of aviation.

131. *Aircraft Engineering and Aerospace Technology: an international journal.* Formerly (until 1986): *Aircraft Engineering.* [ISSN: 1748-8842] 1929. 10x/yr. EUR 6900 (print & online eds.) (excluding UK)). Ed(s): Askin Isikveren. Emerald Publishing Limited, Howard House, Wagon Ln, Bingley, BD16 1WA, United Kingdom; emerald@emeraldinsight.com; http://www.emeraldinsight.com. Illus. Sample. Refereed. Vol. ends: No. 6. Reprint: PSC. *Indexed:* A01, A22, E01. *Bk. rev.:* 1-3, 100-250 words. *Aud.:* Ac, Sa.

This journal focuses on research related to materials, technologies, and techniques covering the entire aerospace and aircraft industry. The journal is devoted primarily to disseminating innovative scientific methods, along with research and technology ideas. The journal has recently expanded from six issues per year to ten all designed to benefit the design, development, project management, manufacture, or operation of current or future aerospace vehicle systems. The journal's strength is still in getting leading practitioners in the field to contribute articles of interest to both researchers and fellow practitioners. The research articles are categorized as to their content, with most being research papers or technical papers, but there are other categories, including literature reviews, case studies, conceptual papers, and general reviews. The journal has numerous special issues with a couple per year on a single topic, such as the recent issues on current trends in aircraft design (7th EASN AIRTEC Conference). Appropriate for both academic and larger public libraries.

AirForces Monthly. See Military section.

132. *American Helicopter Society. Journal.* [ISSN: 0002-8711] 1956. q. USD 365 (Members, USD 80). Ed(s): Mark Potsdam. A H S International, 217 N Washington St, Alexandria, VA 22314; staff@vtol.org; http://www.vtol.org. Illus. Refereed. Vol. ends: No. 4. *Indexed:* A01, A22. *Aud.:* Ac.

This journal from the American Helicopter Society is composed of original technical papers that deal with all aspects of the design, theory, and practice of vertical flight including drones and related unmanned aerial vehicles. The articles cover three main areas: research and engineering; design and manufacturing; and operations. These articles are intended to foster the exchange of significant new ideas, information, and research about helicopters and V/STOL aircraft. The emphasis is on computational fluid dynamics (CFD), structures, aerodynamics (both basic and applied), handling qualities, and acoustics. Additional areas include vehicle and component design, manufacture, and testing; operational aspects, including support, noise and vibration, control and control failure, safety and reliability, materials, and design criteria; and historical information. The journal primarily publishes full articles but it occasionally publishes a "Technical Notes" section to provide a forum for brief, timely updates on current research topics as well as invited papers and review articles. The invited papers are generally from the Alexander Nikolsky Honorary Lecture, presented at the society's annual forum. This journal focuses on the more technical aspects of vertical flight, with the general interest and membership information included in the organization's companion publication *Vertiflite* (below in this section).

Aviation History. See Military section.

133. *Aviation Week & Space Technology.* Former titles (until 1960): *Aviation Week, Including Space Technology;* (until 1958): *Aviation Week;* Which was formed by the merger of (1943-1947): *Aviation News;* (1922-1947): *Aviation;* Which incorporated (in 1948): *Air Transport.* [ISSN: 0005-2175] 1916. w. USD 129 domestic; USD 139 Canada; USD 175 elsewhere. Ed(s): Joe L Anselmo. Aviation Week Network, 2 Penn Plz, 25th Fl, New York, NY 10121; http://www.aviationweek.com. Illus., adv. Circ: 93190 Paid. Vol. ends: No. 26. Microform: PQC. *Indexed:* A01, A22, B01, B03, BRI, C37, HRIS, MASUSE. *Aud.:* Ga, Ac.

This is the premier weekly newsmagazine covering aviation, aerospace, and aeronautics with news and information. All segments of the aerospace industry are featured and detailed, along with many short but insightful articles. Each issue has 2 to 3 topical focuses or cover stories with occasional special sections or reports. The regular sections provide news items of note, valuable up-to-date information, and other industry happenings into various topical sections such as "Air Transport," which covers commercial and general aviation. The remaining topics include such areas as "Aerospace Business," "Space," "MRO," "Propulsion," and "Defense." Special reports on important topics or issues, such as security, innovation, and privatization, are included when appropriate. In addition, the magazine contains industry outlooks and profiles, features on people within the industry such as the person of the year, a calendar of events, and news and information from government and other regulatory agencies. A special issue, "Aerospace and Defense," is usually published in early January, which provides outlook/specification tables for all areas of the aerospace industry over the previous year. Other major sections include a world military aircraft inventory; prime contractor and major manufacturer profiles; major airline profiles; and commercial satellite operators. Other special issues include art and photography and coverage of the major air shows, Farnborough and Paris. The combination of specific industry coverage and general-interest articles makes this a valuable resource for all types of libraries.

134. *Ballooning.* [ISSN: 0194-6854] 1977. bi-m. Free to members. Ed(s): Glen Moyer. Balloon Federation of America, 1601 N Jefferson, PO Box 400, Indianola, IA 50125; bfaoffice@bfa.net; http://www.bfa.net. Illus., adv. Vol. ends: No. 6. *Indexed:* SD. *Bk. rev.:* 1-4, 300-500 words. *Aud.:* Ga, Sa.

This journal is published by the Balloon Federation of America, and covers the sport both in the United States and from an international perspective. This is the best of the limited number of general-interest magazines for the ballooning enthusiast. Articles cover the full range of topics of interest to ballooning enthusiasts, including but not limited to safety issues, equipment, profiles of members, descriptions of balloon trips, noteworthy events in ballooning, and information on competitions. The magazine includes excellent color and black-and-white photographs, results from rallies, information on new products, reviews of products and literature, and a directory of the federation's officers. The federation also produces an e-newsletter, "Quick Release," to provide membership-related information or topics such as news, events, new members, officer information, awards, competitions, and the like. *Ballooning* provides quality content with a good layout and organization scheme, and is suitable for all ages.

135. *British Interplanetary Society Journal.* Incorporates (1946-1947): *British Interplanetary Society. Bulletin;* Which was formerly (until 1946): *Combined British Astronautical Societies. Official Bulletin.* [ISSN: 0007-084X] 1934. m. Members, GBP 15; Non-members, GBP 40. Ed(s): Kelvin Long. British Interplanetary Society, 27-29 S Lambeth Rd, London, SW8 1SZ, United Kingdom; mail@bis-spaceflight.com; http://www.bis-space.com/. Illus., index. Refereed. Vol. ends: No. 12. Microform: PQC. Reprint: PSC. *Indexed:* A22. *Aud.:* Ac, Sa.

This monthly publication contains articles that cover all aspects of space exploration, with each issue dedicated to one or two specific subjects, topics, or themes. Emphasis is solely on space and space-based applications. Sample topics include the history of rocket development, solar cells, stellar wind, orbital mechanics, solar sails, robotic exploration, space colonization, space debris, space commerce, and related areas of aeronautics, astronautics, and space sciences. Current issue themes or conference topics that are included in the publication are from the Tennessee Valley Interstellar Workshop, the Fermi Paradox Special Issue, and the Reinventing Space Conference. Also covered are science in the cosmos; the 100-Year Starship Study, and the international space station; the economic, legal, educational, and social aspects of developing an interstellar space program; and time-distance solutions. Most issues contain five to ten articles per issue, with some articles taken from IAA's International Astronautical Conference or other conferences. Recently, the journal has stopped producing double issues and is back to publishing 12 issues per year. The journal is focused on both general topics and interstellar topics with interstellar issues in red in contrast to the blue covers of those focused on general topics. The society's companion publication, *Spaceflight,* provides news and membership information, as well as several feature articles on space missions and spaceflight written by those directly involved with particular projects or missions. Also included in this latter title are book reviews and conference information. Appropriate for major research libraries.

Business and Commercial Aviation. See Transportation section.

136. ***C E A S Aeronautical Journal.*** [ISSN: 1869-5582] 2010. 4x/yr. EUR 593 (print & online eds.)). Ed(s): Andreas Dillmann. Springer Wien, Prinz-Eugen-Str 8-10, Wien, 1040, Austria; journals@springer.at; http://www.springer.com. Reprint: PSC. *Aud.:* Ac, Sa.

CEAS Aeronautical Journal is one of the two recently published research journals from the Council of European Aerospace Societies. The journal focuses on disseminating results and findings in all areas of aeronautics-related science and technology as well as reports on new developments in design and manufacturing of aircraft, rotorcraft, and unmanned aerial vehicles. Sample subjects covered include aerodynamics, computational fluid dynamics, aeroelasticity, structural mechanics, aeroacoustics, structures and materials, communication and control systems, navigation and surveillance, aircraft and aircraft design, rotorcraft and propulsion, flight simulators, flight control systems, supersonic aircraft, structural design, flight dynamics, and flow control. Besides support for the journal from CEAS, the German Aerospace Center (DLR) and the European Space Agency (ESA) have collaborated to support this journal. In terms of format, the journal primarily publishes peer-reviewed articles with occasional reviews and short communications. The journal also occasionally publishes special issues such as the recent issue devoted to aircraft noise generation and assessment. The CAES also publishes the research oriented CEAS Space Journal focused on space science and technology and the membership focused publication, Aerospace Europe Bulletin. URL: https://ceas.org/quarterly-bulletin/

137. ***Chinese Journal of Aeronautics.*** [ISSN: 1000-9361] 1988. bi-m. Zhongguo Hangkong Xuehui, 37 Xueyuan Lu, Beijing, 100083, China. Adv. Refereed. *Aud.:* Ac, Sa.

This is an entirely open-access, international journal covering all aspects of aerospace and astronautical engineering. Publishing all types of articles including those based on theory and practice, experimental results, comprehensive reviews, technology briefs, and reports covering all aspects of aeronautical and astronautical engineering. The articles are divided into broad sections such as "Fluid Mechanics and Flight Mechanics," "Solid Mechanics and Vehicle Conceptual Design," "Electronics and Electrical Engineering and Control," and "Material Engineering and Mechanical Manufacturing." All aspects of the field are covered but emphasis recently has been on articles covering aerodynamics, numerical methods, computational fluid dynamics, actuators, and control. The journal is heavily slanted toward Asian-Pacific institutions in terms of its editorial board and authors, but the journal is peer reviewed and provides access to the highest quality scholarship. About ten percent of the articles are review articles. The journal also publishes special columns usually containing seven to ten papers on the topic; for example, there was a recent special column on PHM (Prognosis and Health Management) with Aerospace Applications and More Electric Aircraft Actuation System. The journal has recently expanded to a monthly publication cycle to accommodate the increased number of articles published. Important for engineering library collections.

138. ***F A A Safety Briefing: your source for general aviation news and information.*** Former titles (until 2010): *F A A Aviation News;* (until 1987): *F A A General Aviation News;* (until 1976): *F A A Aviation News;* (until 196?): *United States. Federal Aviation Agency. Aviation News.* 1961. bi-m. USD 21 domestic; USD 29.40 foreign; USD 8 per issue domestic. Ed(s): Tom Hoffmann, Susan Parson. U.S. Federal Aviation Administration, 800 Independence Ave, SW, Washington, DC 20591; http://www.faa.gov. Illus. Microform: MIM; PQC. *Indexed:* HRIS. *Aud.:* Ga.

Produced by the Federal Aviation Administration (FAA), *FAA Safety Briefing* is designed to promote all areas of aviation safety, with information on safety-related regulations, news, and articles. All areas of flight safety are covered with an emphasis on the safety issues faced by pilots and policies. Articles cover new, existing, and proposed regulations, people within the aviation safety arena, FAA facilities, weather, night flying, or any aspect of aircraft, pilots, or equipment as long as it is related to safety. Major departments include "Flight Forum," a feedback section with responses from the FAA; and "Aeromedical Advisory" and "Ask Medical Certification," the latest information on aviation medicine, with more of an emphasis on healthy flying. Other departments include "Checklists," "Nuts, Bolts, and Electrons," and "Angle of Attack," which are written to provide news, maintenance alerts, safety reminders, and other timely information designed to protect pilots and aircraft. The departments "Jumpseat" and "Postflight" include editorials, runway safety issues, and profiles of FAA employees. There is a general news section, "ATIS," and a section for safety issues related to rotorcraft flight entitled "Vertically Speaking." The journal has added a new department specific to drones. The website provides access to Infographics on safety topics, and GA Safety Enhancements (SE) Topic Fact Sheets, which provide concise information on flight safety topics such as pilots and medications or mountain flying. The journal is available electronically in multiple formats (pdf, ePub, and MOBI). Appropriate for research and technical libraries or people interested in flight safety and training. URL: www.faa.gov/news/safety_briefing

139. ***Flight International.*** Formerly (until 1962): *Flight;* Incorporates (1966-1968): *Aeroplane;* Which was formerly (until 1966): *Aeroplane and Commercial Aviation News;* (until 1962): *Aeroplane and Astronautics;* (until 1959): *Aeroplane.* [ISSN: 0015-3710] 1909. w. GBP 159.50 combined subscription (print & online eds.)). Ed(s): Murdo Morrison. Reed Business Information Ltd., Quadrant House, The Quadrant, Sutton, SM2 5AS, United Kingdom; rbi.subscriptions@quadrantsubs.com; http://www.reedbusiness.com/. Illus., index, adv. Vol. ends: Dec. Microform: PQC. *Indexed:* A22, B03, BRI, HRIS. *Aud.:* Ga, Ac.

This weekly international trade publication, which celebrated its 110th anniversary in 2019, is one of the longest standing journals covering the aerospace and aviation industry. It provides a global perspective on the aerospace industry and covers every aspect—airframe systems and components, support equipment, air transport, general aviation, defense, spaceflight, and regulatory agencies and authorities worldwide. The news section is subdivided into sections by area or topic, such as analysis, technology, business aviation, defense, general aviation, and spaceflight. The articles section usually contains two or three feature articles on topics of interest, such as industry forecasts for the upcoming year, market trends, military aircraft, new aircraft, and safety. Other sections contain letters, jobs, classifieds, commentary, aerospace awards, newsmakers, and similar items. The journal periodically publishes directories of world aircraft, maintenance facilities, turbine engine manufacturers, and world airlines, as well as useful ranking information such as the top 100 aerospace companies, airline safety statistics, and space launch calendars. There are also special issues covering the major air shows, or on hot topics or industry trends, plus those interested and search and view the 1st 95 years of the publication (1909-2004) online. The magazine is one of the few that still provides cutaway schematics of new aircraft with two such posters scheduled in 2019. This magazine is similar to *Aviation Week & Space Technology* (above in this section), but with a greater international flavor. Recommended for both academic libraries and larger public libraries.

140. ***Flying.*** Formerly: *Flying Including Industrial Aviation.* [ISSN: 0015-4806] 1927. m. USD 14 domestic; USD 29 Canada; USD 44 elsewhere. Bonnier Corp., 460 N Orlando Ave, Ste 200, Winter Park, FL 32789; http://www.bonniercorp.com. Illus., index, adv. Sample. Circ: 226000. Vol. ends: No. 12. *Indexed:* A22, BRI, C37, CBRI, HRIS. *Aud.:* Hs, Ga, Ac, Sa.

Flying has the broadest scope of the numerous magazines written for the private pilot and flying enthusiast. Every aspect of general aviation is covered; however, the emphasis is on flying, safety or safe flying topics, and contemporary aircraft. The major articles cover the various aspects of flying such as safety issues, historical topics, airports, rules and regulations, aircraft, and aircraft instrumentation. The feature articles are written primarily to excite the reader and instill or convey the love of flying. Other articles are designed to impart practical advice and cover items of interest to the flying public. There are many articles on equipment and pilot gear as well as sections providing news for pilots, letters to the editor, a calendar of flying rallies and events, and other aviation news, along with new product information. Other sections include one on safety information,"T&T (Training and Techniques)," ranging from flight schools to human factors, to accident reports. Many of the sections or standard features informs and aids readers with information imparted in a personal manner through anecdotes and stories, such as "ILAFF (I Learned About Flying From That)," which provides cautionary tales of what not to do. Overall, the magazine is informative and interesting, with excellent photography. It deserves a place in libraries with aviation collections.

141. ***FlyPast: the UK's top selling aviation monthly.*** [ISSN: 0262-6950] 1980. m. GBP 41 includes domestic & USA; GBP 51 elsewhere; GBP 4.10 per issue. Ed(s): Ken Ellis. Key Publishing Ltd., PO Box 300, Stamford, PE9 1NA, United Kingdom; info@keypublishing.com; http://www.keypublishing.com. Illus., index, adv. Vol. ends: No. 12. *Bk. rev.:* Number and length vary. *Aud.:* Ga, Sa.

This publication is advertised as Britain's top-selling aviation monthly and is essentially a general-interest, military history-focused aviation journal. Although the primary emphasis is on military history, there are some general interest historical content. An additional focus is on the restoration and preservation of aircraft. Again, these are primarily focused on restoration of military aircraft. Unlike academic historical aviation magazines, this journal is geared toward a general readership. The magazine is heavily illustrated with numerous photographs (in both color and in black and white), which is expected given the historical focus of the journal. The articles are informative and interesting and cover many of the same topics as the general-interest aviation magazines, including events and news, with additional departments focused on restoration and preservation. There are occasionally special sections that highlight particular topics such as the recent "Spotlight" section, with several articles focused on a different historic WW II aircraft from its origin to its use in combat. The journal also produces special issues such as the helpful air show guide or the recently published "Air War over Vietnam" issue. The product review sections include memorabilia, books, videos, and art prints. Numerous advertisements for memorabilia and related items are found throughout. This magazine appeals to military-history enthusiasts, and to those interested in military aviation and/or aviation history, as well as aircraft restoration and preservation.

142. ***I E E E Aerospace and Electronic Systems Magazine.*** Formerly (until 1986): *I E E E Aerospace and Electronic Systems Society Newsletter.* [ISSN: 0885-8985] 1961. m. USD 675. Ed(s): Peter K Willet. Institute of Electrical and Electronics Engineers, 445 Hoes Ln, Piscataway, NJ 08854; contactcenter@ieee.org; http://www.ieee.org. Illus., index, adv. Vol. ends: No. 12. *Indexed:* A22. *Bk. rev.:* 1, 500-1,500 words. *Aud.:* Ac, Sa.

Produced by the Institute of Electrical and Electronics Engineers (IEEE) and only available electronically, this magazine provides information specifically geared toward its membership. Its focus is on aerospace electrical and electronic systems and related topics such as navigation, avionics, radar systems, UAV, GPS, spacecraft, aerospace power, radar, sonar, telemetry, defense, transportation, automated testing, and command and control. The feature articles are included in each issue in the areas where computer and electrical engineering overlap with the areas of aeronautical and astronautical engineering. The articles deal primarily with the organization, design, development, integration, and operation of complex systems for air, space, and ground environments in the above areas. The journal's objective is to provide timely, useful, and readable systems information for engineers. The articles in this area are published in the society's sister publication, *IEEE Transactions on Aerospace and Electronic Systems*. The journal also includes information of interest to the membership, such as conference reports, columns (editorials), notices of upcoming meetings and conferences, book reviews, and other membership-related information. The journal has an "Industry Insights" section as well as tutorial issues. The journal also publishes special issues devoted to a specific topic, such as the special issues on "quantum radar" and "cybersecurity in aerospace." *IEEE Aerospace and Electronic Systems Magazine* is primarily of importance to academic and technical libraries and members.

143. ***I E E E Transactions on Aerospace and Electronic Systems (Online).*** Formed by the merger of (1963-1965): *I E E E Transactions on Aerospace (Online);* (1963-1965): *I E E E Transactions on Aerospace and Navigational Electronics (Online);* (1963-1965): *I E E E Transactions on Military Electronics (Online);* (1963-1965): *I E E E Transactions on Space Electronics and Telemetry (Online);* Which was formerly (until 1963)· *I R E Transactions on Space Electronics and Telemetry (Online);* (until 1959): *I R E Transactions on Telemetry and Remote Control (Online);* I E E E Transactions on Aerospace and Navigational Electronics was formerly (until 1963): *I R E Transactions on Aerospace and Navigational Electronics (Online);* (until 1961): *I R E Transactions on Aeronautical and Navigational Electronics (Online);* (until 1955): *I R E Professional Group on Aeronautical and Navigational Electronics. Transactions (Online);* (until 1953): *I R E Professional Group on Airborne Electronics. Transactions (Online);* I E E E Transactions on Military Electronics was formerly (until 1963): *I R E Transactions on Military Electronics (Online).* [ISSN: 1557-9603] 1965. bi-m. USD 2905. Ed(s): Michael Rice. Institute of Electrical and Electronics Engineers, 445 Hoes Ln, Piscataway, NJ 08855; customer.service@ieee.org; http://www.ieee.org. Refereed. *Aud.:* Ac, Sa.

This journal, published by the IEEE Aerospace and Electronic Systems Society, is primarily geared toward publishing research articles in support of those individuals working or studying in the areas of aerospace electronic systems, which includes command, control, and communications systems; avionics; systems engineering; aircraft control; aircraft navigation; missile guidance; satellites; multisensor systems; electronic warfare systems; navigation, target tracking, and global positioning systems; energy conversion systems; intelligent systems; radar systems; autonomous systems; space systems; and support systems. The more than 40 research articles per issue range from specific papers on individual systems to those that cover general research, design, and testing of systems and subsystems. The journal prides itself on being one of the top five most-cited scholarly journals in the area of aerospace engineering, which demonstrates the importance that systems, computers, communications, and electronic systems play in the field. Included with the full papers is a correspondence section for brief discussions of new research. Essentially, this is the systems magazine for aerospace engineering. This research publication occasional publishes special sections such as the recent one on spectrum sharing. Membership and related information is provided by the society's sister publication, *IEEE Aerospace and Electronic Systems Magazine* (above in this section). Recommended for all types of academic and technical libraries.

144. ***Institution of Mechanical Engineers. Proceedings. Part G: Journal of Aerospace Engineering.*** Supersedes in part (in 1989): *Institution of Mechanical Engineers. Proceedings. Part D: Transport Engineering;* Which superseded in part (1847-1982): *Institution of Mechanical Engineers. Proceedings.* [ISSN: 0954-4100] 1984. 14x/yr. USD 6574 (print & online eds.)). Ed(s): Rodrigo Martinez-Val. Sage Publications Ltd., 1 Oliver's Yard, 55 City Rd, London, EC1Y 1SP, United Kingdom; info@sagepub.com; https://www.sagepub.com/. Illus. Sample. Refereed. Vol. ends: No. 6. Reprint: PSC. *Indexed:* A22, E01. *Bk. rev.:* 1-2, 500-750 words. *Aud.:* Ac.

Produced by the United Kingdom's mechanical engineering society (IMechE), this journal publishes papers in the field of aeronautical engineering of interest to mechanical engineers and vice versa. The publication's peer-reviewed articles are designed to further the advancement of the field of aeronautical engineering, especially in the areas of civil and military aircraft, space systems, and their components. Topics cover research, design, development, testing, operation, and service and repair of vehicles and their components. Fields covered include aerodynamics, fluid mechanics, propulsion and fuel systems, avionics and flight control systems, structural and mechanical design, materials science, testing and performance, and airports and spaceports. The journal has expanded yet again, now to 16 issues per year with 50 plus articles published per issue focused on aerospace engineering topics aligned with or overlapping mechanical engineering topics. Occasionally, a volume may be devoted to a special topic or theme, such as recent issues on aircraft design from the 7th European Aeronautics Science Network (EASN) International Conference on "Innovation in European Aeronautics Research." The journal provides some open- access content as well as metrics on downloads, tweets, citations, and CrossRef citations. Appropriate for academic and technical libraries.

145. ***The International Journal of Aeroacoustics.*** [ISSN: 1475-472X] 2002. 8x/yr. USD 2062 (print & online eds.)). Sage Publications Ltd., 1 Oliver's Yard, 55 City Rd, London, EC1Y 1SP, United Kingdom; info@sagepub.com; https://www.sagepub.com. Sample. Refereed. Reprint: PSC. *Indexed:* A01. *Aud.:* Ac, Sa.

The subject of aeroacoustics has increased in importance within the aerospace and aeronautical engineering field recently, due to advances in air, space, and high-speed ground transportation and their effects on people and the environment. The issue of noise and its impact on people, structures (both vehicle- and ground-based support structures), vehicle components, and the overall environment comprise much of the focus of this research journal. A sampling of the topics covered includes fluid flow, jet noise, computational fluid mechanics and aerodynamics, the instability of high-speed jets, turbulence, and shock. This title focuses on all areas of aeroacoustics, publishing six to eight research articles per issue on fundamental and applied aeroacoustics topics. The articles associate these topics with all aspects of civil and military aircraft, automobile, and high-speed train aeroacoustics and related phenomena. The journal makes exceptional use of illustrations (in color and black and white) to enhance the technical information. Some issues are composed of selected papers from workshops and conferences related to aeroacoustics, such as a recent special issue on aeroacoustic resonance and aircraft noise generated from rotors. Recommended for academic and research libraries.

146. ***International Journal of Aerospace Engineering.*** [ISSN: 1687-5966] 2007. . USD 595. Hindawi Publishing Corporation, 315 Madison Ave, 3rd Fl, Ste 3070, New York, NY 10017; hindawi@hindawi.com; https://www.hindawi.com. Refereed. *Indexed:* A01. *Aud.:* Ac, Sa.

This international, open-access journal covers all aspects of aerospace engineering, including aerodynamics and fluid mechanics, aeroacoustics, aeroelasticity, avionics and flight control systems dynamics and control, flight mechanics, mechanics of materials, propulsion, structures, and so on. The purpose is to provide an outlet for scholarly research along with practical engineering solutions, and design methodologies for aircraft, space vehicles, and unmanned air vehicles (UAVs). The journal has recently grown considerably up from about 25 articles per year to over a hundred. This open-access journal has been picked up by the major indexing, abstracts in the discipline, and is supported via article process charges paid by the authors, their funding agency, or their supporting institution with all articles licensed as CC-BY. The journal occasionally publishes special issues composed of articles on selected or focused topics within the scope of the journal that have high interest within the community. Some examples are the issues on "Optimal Control Techniques in Aircraft Guidance and Control" and "Theoretical Modelling of Turbulent Flow in Aerodynamic Applications." All articles, including those in special issues, are peer reviewed by an international board of reviewers. Primarily of interest to researchers and practitioners within the aerospace engineering community.

147. ***International Journal of Micro Air Vehicles.*** [ISSN: 1756-8293] 2009. q. USD 594. Sage Publications Ltd., 1 Oliver's Yard, 55 City Rd, London, EC1Y 1SP, United Kingdom; info@sagepub.com; https://www.sagepub.com. Sample. Refereed. Reprint: PSC. *Indexed:* A01. *Aud.:* Ac, Sa.

This completely open-access journal covers the emerging field of unmanned aerial vehicles (UAVs), specifically micro air vehicles (MAVs), which have unique design, manufacturing, and piloting or flying issues. This journal provides a forum for the publication of the multidisciplinary research being conducted in this new and rapidly emerging specialty in the aerospace field. The articles cover many of the same aspects of other aerospace vehicles, including aerodynamics, propulsion systems, control, avionics, structures, and so on. The main differences are the result of the size, mission, and challenges of these unpiloted aircraft, leading to different perspectives on these traditional areas such as nano-structures, micro-propulsion systems, flexible structures, low Reynolds aerodynamics, flapping wing flight, and target search and tracking. The journal's publisher also combines articles from different issues on similar topics and gathered them into subject-based collections such as collections on sustainability of MAV systems, GPS, and MAV navigation. This quarterly journal continues steady growth primarily due to the growing interest in applied research and the fundamental science in this relatively new specialized area and the quality of the publisher. This title is also covering the new and emerging conferences in this area, such as the International Micro Air Vehicle Conference and Competition.

148. ***Jonathan's Space Report.*** 1989. w. Free. Ed(s): Jonathan McDowell. Harvard - Smithsonian Center for Astrophysics, 60 Garden St, Cambridge, MA 02138; http://www.cfa.harvard.edu/. *Aud.:* Ac.

This electronic newsletter is designed to provide information on all space launches, including manned missions and automated satellites. Users interested in this information can also receive the newsletter via e-mail. A recent issue contains information about the international space station as well as all international launches, including suborbital launches. The newsletter is organized into sections by mission or launch vehicle, often with tables such as recent orbital launches and suborbital launches. The newsletter is now available in seven languages, including Italian, German, and Portuguese. "Jonathan's Space Home Page" provides links to image files, historical articles, and other information and sites related to space exploration. Also included are links to a geostationary satellite log, a launch log, and a satellite catalog. The author has recently started to publish an annual study on space activity located on the web page. The newsletter is fully archived and available, back to its original issue in January 1989. The newsletter and site is not very fancy, but if you are looking for space-vehicle launch and satellite information from a reliable source, this is the place. URL: www.planet4589.org/space/jsr/jsr.html

149. ***Journal of Aerospace Engineering.*** [ISSN: 0893-1321] 1988. bi-m. q. until 2016. USD 860. Ed(s): Wieslaw Binienda. American Society of Civil Engineers, 1801 Alexander Bell Dr, Reston, VA 20191; ascelibrary@asce.org; http://www.asce.org. Illus., index, adv. Refereed. Vol. ends: No. 4. *Indexed:* A01, A22, BRI, HRIS. *Aud.:* Ac.

This journal, produced by the American Society of Civil Engineers (ASCE), publishes research on the practical application and development of civil engineering concepts, designs, and methodologies for aeronautics and space applications, along with transferring resulting technologies and applications to other areas of civil engineering. This international publication provides information related to the civil engineering aspects of aerospace engineering, primarily the structural aspects of space engineering and applied mechanics, aeronautics, and astronautics. Sample topics include flight control systems, autopilot, MEMS, smart composite structures, trajectory optimization, aeroacoustic imaging, aerodynamics of structures, aeroelastic stability, aerospace materials, polymers and laminates, remote sensing, and robotics as related to aeronautics and aerospace engineering. All of the papers (approximately 25 per issue) and technical notes are included, with emphasis placed on technical papers that are designed to share information between civil engineers and related engineering disciplines. Special topical issues or special sections are occasionally published, such as the forthcoming special section on "impact dynamics for advanced aerospace materials and structures." A valuable addition to academic and technical libraries.

150. ***Journal of Aerospace Information Systems.*** Formerly (until 2013): *Journal of Aerospace Computing, Information, and Communication.* [ISSN: 2327-3097] 2004. m. USD 585. Ed(s): Ella M Atkins. American Institute of Aeronautics and Astronautics, Inc., 12700 Sunrise Valley Dr, Ste 200, Reston, VA 20191-5807; custserv@aiaa.org; http://www.aiaa.org. Sample. *Aud.:* Ac, Sa.

This electronic-only journal from AIAA is geared primarily toward those individuals who work or study in the areas of aerospace computing, information, and communication systems. The scope of coverage includes such topics as aerospace systems and software engineering, information technology, knowledge management, computational techniques, remotely operated vehicles, UAVs (unmanned aerial vehicles), real-time systems, embedded systems, software engineering and reliability, systems engineering and integration, communication systems, signal processing, high-performance computing systems and software, expert systems, robotics, intelligent and autonomous systems, and human-computer interfaces. Electronics, communication, control, autonomic software systems, and information systems play an increasingly important role in the design and operation of aerospace systems and vehicles and the included articles are designed to highlight current research in three main areas— computing, information, and communications. This research focuses on the design of aerospace components, systems, and vehicles. Along with the full papers, the journal includes survey papers, technical notes, and letters for the brief discussion of new research. The journal periodically publishes special sections or issues devoted to a specific topic or theme, such as the recent issue on intelligent systems for space exploration. This journal is designed to transfer information and technology in these important areas, both from aerospace engineering to other engineering disciplines, and vice versa. Recommended for academic and technical libraries. URL: http://arc.aiaa.org/loi/jais

151. ***Journal of Aircraft (Online): devoted to aeronautical science and technology.*** [ISSN: 1533-3868] 1963. bi-m. USD 1410. Ed(s): Eli Livne. American Institute of Aeronautics and Astronautics, Inc., 12700 Sunrise Valley Dr, Ste 200, Reston, VA 20191-5807; custserv@aiaa.org; http://www.aiaa.org. Illus., index. Sample. Refereed. Vol. ends: No. 6. Microform: PQC. *Indexed:* A01, A22. *Aud.:* Ac.

This completely online AIAA journal is devoted to the advancement of airborne flight with the focus on the promotion of applied science and technology. It publishes articles on significant advances in the operation of aircraft, advances in aircraft themselves, and the application of aircraft technologies to other disciplines. All types of vehicles related to airborne flight are covered, including commercial and military aircraft, STOL and V/STOL aircraft, and subsonic, supersonic, trans-sonic, and hypersonic aircraft. Areas covered include aircraft and aircraft systems design and operation, flight mechanics, flight and ground testing, computational fluid dynamics (CFD), aerodynamics, and structural dynamics. Related areas are covered, such as the application of computer technology to aircraft and aircraft systems, air traffic management, artificial intelligence, production methods, engineering economic analysis, and logistics support. Accompanying the full-length papers (30 to 40 per issue) are "Technical Comment" and "Engineering Note," sections designed to further communication within the field. The journal publishes special issues or sections such as the special section on computational and experimental aerodynamics and stability and control for agile UAVs. The journal also publishes "Design Forum" papers, which range from design case studies to presentations of new methodologies and emerging design trends, survey papers, and lectures. Recommended for academic, technical, and research libraries.

152. ***Journal of Guidance, Control, and Dynamics (Online): devoted to the technology of dynamics and control.*** Formerly (until 1982): *Journal of Guidance and Control.* [ISSN: 1533-3884] 1978. m. USD 1430. Ed(s): Ping Lu. American Institute of Aeronautics and Astronautics, Inc., 12700 Sunrise Valley Dr, Ste 200, Reston, VA 20191-5807; custserv@aiaa.org; http://www.aiaa.org. Illus., index. Sample. Refereed. Vol. ends: No. 6. *Indexed:* A22. *Bk. rev.:* 1, 750-1,000 words. *Aud.:* Ac.

This journal from AIAA is primarily focused on research that promotes the advancement of guidance, control, and dynamics; to this end, it publishes original, peer-reviewed papers that highlight the development, design, and application of new technology in aeronautics, astronautics, celestial mechanics, and related fields. Topics of articles include astrodynamics, control systems design, control theory, dynamics, stability, guidance, control, navigation, systems optimization, avionics, and information processing. There are also articles that highlight advances in the guidance and control of new aircraft, spacecraft, and related systems. In addition to the full-length papers, the journal includes engineering notes, technical comments, and book reviews. It occasionally publishes special issues on a single topic. There have been issues on computational guidance and control, and on aircraft loss of control. The journal has recently formed an advisory board to provide guidance on emerging technologies and research in the field as well as input on the direction of the journal. Given that the numerous topics covered in the areas of guidance, control, and dynamics are important to other engineering fields, this makes the journal a valuable addition to research collections in engineering.

153. ***Journal of Propulsion and Power (Online): devoted to aerospace propulsion and power.*** [ISSN: 1533-3876] 1985. bi-m. USD 1550. Ed(s): Joseph M Powers. American Institute of Aeronautics and Astronautics, Inc., 12700 Sunrise Valley Dr, Ste 200, Reston, VA 20191-5807; custserv@aiaa.org; http://www.aiaa.org. Illus., index. Sample. Refereed. Vol. ends: No. 6. *Indexed:* A22. *Aud.:* Ac.

This AIAA journal focuses specifically on aerospace propulsion and power systems covering combustion, power generation and use, and overall propulsion systems and/or individual propulsion system components as they relate to the fields of aeronautics, astronautics, and space sciences. Topics include air-breathing propulsion systems (from turbine engines to scramjets), electric propulsion systems, solid and liquid rocket systems, hybrid propulsion systems, advanced propulsion systems, and all propulsion system components. Original papers highlight recent advances in the areas of research, development, design, and application in such subjects as fuel and propellants, power generation and transmission in aerospace systems, jet pumps, combustors and combustion chambers, fuel combustion, computational fluid dynamics (CFD), fluid mechanics, and solid mechanics. Accompanying the full-length technical papers (approximately 30 per issue) are sections containing technical notes that are designed for rapid dissemination of research results, technical comments and survey papers. The journal is getting away from publishing special sections or issues. Appropriate for any research-oriented engineering library.

154. ***Journal of Spacecraft and Rockets (Online): devoted to astronautical science and technology.*** [ISSN: 1533-6794] 1964. bi-m. USD 1340. Ed(s): Hanspeter D Schaub. American Institute of Aeronautics and Astronautics, Inc., 12700 Sunrise Valley Dr, Ste 200, Reston, VA 20191-5807; custserv@aiaa.org; http://www.aiaa.org. Illus., index. Sample. Refereed. Vol. ends: No. 6. Microform: PQC. *Indexed:* A01, A22. *Aud.:* Ac.

This journal from AIAA covers recent research, design, and current developments in the broad area of spacecraft and rockets and their accompanying systems, subsystems, and components. The 25 to 30 articles per issue focus on space sciences, including spacecraft, space vehicles, tactical and strategic missile systems and subsystems, applications, missions, and environmental interactions. Information is given on launch and reentry vehicles, transatmospheric vehicles, system and subsystem design, application and testing, mission design and analysis, applied and computational fluid dynamics, and applied aerothermodynamics. In addition, the journal covers such topics as the emerging commercial space industry, astrodynamics, small space vehicles, space processing and manufacturing, operations in space, interactions between space vehicles, ground-support systems design, and the transfer of space technologies to other fields. All areas of aeronautics are covered, including propulsion, guidance and control, aircraft technology (conventional and STOL/VTOL), structural systems of spacecraft and missiles, missile design, and performance of space vehicles. Occasionally, issues include engineering notes, technical comments, and survey papers. Special issues or sections on specific topics are occasionally published, such as the recent section on hypersonic boundary layer transition prediction. Approximately 10 percent of the articles are freely available as open-access publications. Recommended for research libraries or engineering collections.

155. ***Journal of the Astronautical Sciences.*** Supersedes in part (in 1962): *Astronautical Sciences Review;* Which was formerly (until 1958): *Journal of Astronautics;* (until 1955): *Astronautics.* [ISSN: 0021-9142] 1954. q. EUR 179 (print & online eds.)). Ed(s): Kathleen Howell, Henry J Pernicka. Springer, Tiergartenstr 17, Heidelberg, 69121, Germany; subscriptions@springer.com; https://www.springer.com. Illus., index. Refereed. Vol. ends: No. 4. Reprint: PSC. *Indexed:* A22. *Aud.:* Ac.

This journal provides topical information, research, and reviews on state-of-the-art technologies in all areas of astronautics, including astrodynamics, celestial mechanics, flight mechanics, navigation and guidance, and planetary and space sciences. Topics of articles include such areas as altitude dynamics, orbit determination, altitude stability, space debris, solar radiation, orbital mechanics/dynamics, propulsion systems (both conventional and electric), trajectory optimization, space mission analysis, numerical methods, maneuvering of flight vehicles, dynamics and control, and new astronautical systems and their applications. The journal ordinarily consists of original papers, but occasionally it includes technical notes to speed up communication of new technological and scientific advances. Likewise, the journal occasionally publishes papers taken from important conferences or symposia that are sponsored by the American Astronautical Society (AAS). The society also publishes *Space Times,* (URL: www.astronautical.org/spacetimes) which provides excellent general-interest articles on astronautics, space travel, and information for the society's membership, such as news, events, a calendar, new books, and conference reports. This membership-focused journal is freely available online. *JAS* is most appropriate for academic and technical libraries. ULR: https://link.springer.com/journal/40295

156. ***Journal of Thermophysics and Heat Transfer (Online).*** [ISSN: 1533-6808] 1987. q. USD 1130. Ed(s): Greg F Naterer. American Institute of Aeronautics and Astronautics, Inc., 12700 Sunrise Valley Dr, Ste 200, Reston, VA 20191-5807; custserv@aiaa.org; http://www.aiaa.org. Illus., index, adv. Sample. Refereed. Vol. ends: No. 4. *Indexed:* A22. *Aud.:* Ac.

This AIAA publication, like all of the other research journals by the society, transitioned to online only in 2019. It provides a forum for communicating original research in areas utilized by designers of aerospace systems and components, including all methods of heat transfer-radiative, conductive, and convective, and combinations of these methods. In addition, the effects of these heat-transfer methods are also included. Topics of interest in the corresponding area of thermophysics include mechanisms and properties involved in thermal energy transfer and storage in liquids, gases, solids, and systems that compose one or more of the physical states. Articles cover such topics as aerothermodynamics, conduction, phase change, plasmas and applications, radiative heat transfer, thermophysical properties, multiphase heat transfer, numerical heat transfer, nonintrusive diagnostics, vibrational kinetics, thermal control, convective heat transfer, and other areas of thermophysics, thermodynamics, and heat transfer. These issues are of primary importance to many aerospace-related areas of study, from the propulsion and space vehicle design to the impact on computational fluid dynamics due to extreme temperatures and energy transfer. The journal also includes technical comments, technical notes, survey papers, and occasionally special sections on a topic such as "Ab Initio Approaches for Nonequilibrium Flows." The use of color illustrations and photographs greatly aids in enhancing the technical information provided by this publication. Recommended for major research collections, whether academic or technical.

157. ***Kitplanes: your homebuilt aircraft authority.*** Formerly (until 198?): *Guide to Kitplanes.* [ISSN: 0891-1851] 1984. m. USD 29.95 combined subscription domestic (print & online eds.); USD 41.95 combined subscription foreign (print & online eds.)). Ed(s): Paul Dye, Mark Schrimmer. Belvoir Media Group, LLC, PO Box 5656, Norwalk, CT 06856; customer_service@belvoir.com; http://www.belvoir.com. Illus., adv. Vol. ends: No. 12. *Aud.:* Ga, Sa.

This magazine covers the specialized areas of hobbyists and enthusiasts who wish to design, build, and fly their own aircraft. This is the DIY magazine for aircraft enthusiasts, with an emphasis on providing useful how-to tips and other practical advice and information. Articles cover all aspects of traditional pilot-focused aviation magazines, such as flying, training, safety, and maintenance, with an emphasis on home-built aircraft. This journal also covers the theory and other technical issues related to aircraft design, construction, and flying, with most articles focused on the construction and flying of personal aircraft. Along with feature articles dubbed "Flight Reports," the magazine includes articles in such areas as "Builder Spotlight," "Shop Talk," and "Designers Notebook." Other departments include "Exploring" and "Kit Bits," and the remaining sections provide information on new products and tools, a calendar of events, editorial and readers' comments, classifieds, and information on competitions. There are many color and black-and-white photographs and illustrations, plus information on products and services, in-flight reports, and information on new aircraft. The journal devotes issues to specific topics such as the engine buying guide issue or December's annual homebuilt aircraft directory. Geared to the flying public, hobbyists, and enthusiasts and the ultimate "do-it-yourself" crowd.

158. ***Microgravity - Science and Technology: an international journal for microgravity and space exploration.*** Formerly: *Applied Microgravity Technology.* [ISSN: 0938-0108] 1987. bi-m. EUR 802 (print & online eds.)). Ed(s): Dr. Michael Dreyer. Springer Netherlands, Van Godewijckstraat 30, Dordrecht, 3311 GX, Netherlands; http://www.springer.com. Illus., adv. Refereed. Reprint: PSC. *Indexed:* A22, E01. *Aud.:* Ac, Sa.

This journal focuses on the research and scholarship that are carried out under conditions of altered or reduced gravity. Although these conditions can be artificially created on Earth, the development of long-term platforms in space have led to an increase in this research. The journal focuses on both experimental and theoretical research carried out under these conditions. The scope of coverage includes topics such as materials science, heat and mass transfer, fluid mechanics, radiation biology, astrobiology and exobiology, and human physiology. Also covered is research on test methods, and there are articles on instrumentation and theoretical gravity-related topics. The journal has recently increased the number of articles published per year and it appears that this increase will continue. . It also periodically publishes papers devoted to a single topic as well as organizing papers into topical collections such as the collection on multiphase fluid dynamics in microgravity taken from a number of published volumes. Another excellent research journal in this expanding area of space science is *npj Microgravity*, an entirely open-access journal from the Nature Publishing Group. Appropriate for research libraries.

N A S A Tech Briefs. See Science and Technology section.

159. ***Plane and Pilot: mind-controlled airplanes?, anxiety and pilots, unstable approaches.*** Incorporates (in 1987): *Homebuilt Aircraft; Airways.* [ISSN: 0032-0617] 1965. 7x/yr. USD 15.97 domestic; USD 25.97 Canada; USD 30.97 elsewhere. Madavor Media, Llc., 25 Braintree Hill Office Park, Ste 404, Braintree, MA 02184; customerservice@madavor.com; http://www.madavor.com. Illus., adv. Microform: PQC. *Indexed:* A22. *Aud.:* Hs, Ga, Sa.

This journal is devoted primarily to the interests of recreational flyers or private pilots. The previous subtitle, "the excitement of personal aviation & private ownership" highlighted the scope and coverage of the journal. The feature articles cover topics of interest to general aviation enthusiasts, from purchasing aircraft to tips on better piloting and safety, as well as new planes and equipment. It also includes articles on flying, aircraft, new products, pilot aids, safety information and tips, flying events, information on rules and regulations, and other general-interest items for pilots and aviation buffs. Almost every issue provides a review of new aircraft. There are classifieds, editorials, and letters to the editor. Regular columns and departments include sections on aircraft, safety, and training, along with such sections such as "Gear," which highlights and evaluates new aircraft or equipment. "After the Accident" is an important column that covers safety issues. Most other columns provide practical advice and tips for pilots. One of the distinctive features of this journal that makes it more attractive for libraries is the recent buyers' guide and the journal's emphasis on learning to fly, training, and safety.

160. ***Powered Sport Flying: aviation for the rest of us.*** Formerly (until 2010): *UltraFlight Magazine.* 19??. m. USD 36.95 domestic; USD 48 Canada; USD 90 elsewhere. Sport Aviation Press, PO Box 38, Greenville, IL 62246. Adv. Sample. *Aud.:* Ga, Sa.

This magazine focuses on light sport and ultralight aircraft, with emphasis on owning, building, and flying ultralight and light sport aircraft. The topics covered are similar to the other general aviation magazines such as safety, new aircraft, and unique piloting issues with this type of aircraft. Its format is similar to most information presented through feature articles, columns, and departments. The feature articles cover reports from rallies and contests for ultralight and light sport aircraft along with the unique issues related to building and piloting these specialty aircraft. The journal covers these aircraft from all regions of the world with the focus on the type of aircraft as opposed to a region. There are numerous advertisements and photographs. The standard departments, and news and new-products sections, contain reports from events, information on competitions, new-product announcements and reviews, safety-related items, and a calendar of events. The journal provides an abundance of information on products, equipment, and safety. The articles are well written, and the magazine provides excellent practical information for ultralight, powered parachutes, paragliders, and sport aircraft enthusiasts. Although this journal is privately published, it is provided with membership to the following organizations that highlight its scope and coverage: USUA (US Ultralight Association), LAMA (Light Aircraft Manufacturing Association), PRA (Popular Rotorcraft Association), and USPPA (United States Powered Paragliding Association). This journal is appropriate for libraries focused on general aviation.

161. ***Progress in Aerospace Sciences: an international review journal.*** Formerly (until 1970): *Progress in Aeronautical Sciences.* [ISSN: 0376-0421] 1961. 8x/yr. EUR 2810. Ed(s): B E Richards, F Platzer. Pergamon Press, The Blvd, Langford Ln, E Park, Kidlington, OX5 1GB, United Kingdom; JournalsCustomerServiceEMEA@elsevier.com; http://www.elsevier.com. Illus., adv. Sample. Refereed. Microform: PQC. *Indexed:* A01, A22. *Aud.:* Ac.

This review journal is designed to bring together current advances in the field of aerospace sciences for those involved with research and development, and for other researchers seeking highly technical information. The review articles provide a concise and orderly summary of topics with enough detail that academics in all related fields can gain insight into the most recent and advanced research available. All aspects of aeronautical engineering are covered, including aerodynamics and fluid dynamics; aircraft design and performance; avionics; vehicle dynamics; guidance and control; fracture mechanics; combustion and propulsion systems; composite materials; wind-tunnel design and testing; wind shear; and flight safety. Each issue usually contains three to eight in-depth articles that are usually broken down into the typical sections of review articles: extensive background of the subject, a state-of-the-art review, and recommendations for further research. Color illustrations add to the clarity and understanding of the research presented and occasionally supplementary materials are included with the articles. The journal has recently begun to move away from publishing special or theme issue on a topic. Highly recommended for research collections, whether in the research sector or in academe.

162. ***Room: the space journal of Asgardia.*** [ISSN: 2412-4311] 2014. q. USD 34 combined subscription print & online eds. Ed(s): Igor Ashurbeyli. Asgardia Independent Research Center, Stubenring 2/8-9, Vienna, 1010, Austria; director@airc.at ; https://airc.at. *Bk. rev.:* 2-4. *Aud.:* Ems, Hs, Ga, Ac.

This journal is so unique that it is hard to describe, but worth a look by anyone who is interested in the exploration and settlement of space. The most closely related journal would be if *Air and Space: Smithsonian" was strictly devoted to the exploration of space. The journal's stated purpose is the promotion of peaceful exploration of space for the benefit of humankind through the publication of this highly professional, scientific and, at the same time, popular journal, one that will not confound the general reader. The publication will be accessible to everyone with an interest in the aerospace environment. The authors are experts, aerospace industry leaders and scientists from all over the world. The editorial board is extensive with impressive credentials showing the depth of commitment to ensuring that the articles are of the highest quality yet readable and understandable to a wide audience. This combines with the excellent images and illustrations to make this journal both informative and interesting. Given the journal's purpose, the articles are grouped into these key areas: environment, astronautics, and space sciences. Each issues usually has a special reports section or topic such as space law, space security, Apollo 11, space debris, developing Mars, and the like. Besides the standard departments, forward and opinion (editorials and interviews) and reviews, for instance, there is a section entitled "Space Lounge," designed for and to inspire young readers. Recommended to those interested in and inspired by the thought of space exploration.*

Rotor Drone Pro. See Model Making/Model Aircraft section.

163. ***Science at N A S A.*** 19??. d. Free. Ed(s): Kathy Watkins. N A S A Headquarters, Public Communications Office, Ste 5K39, Washington, DC 20546; public-inquiries@hq.nasa.gov; http://www.nasa.gov. *Aud.:* Hs, Ga, Ac.

Science at NASA is a source for informative articles based on the research activities of the National Aeronautics and Space Administration (NASA). The scope, coverage, and offerings have expanded with the addition of content from the Science Mission Directorate at NASA. Its look and feel continues to be updated, keeping it fresh and usable. The site provides a broad range of information on NASA activities and discoveries while also serving as a gathering place for all of NASA's scientific and technical information and news releases. Most of the articles are organized under broad topics such as "Universe," "Earth," "Sun," "Solar System," "Missions," and "Science & Technology." In addition, there is information for specific audiences, i.e., researchers, learners, citizen scientists under "Get Involved.? The current main page provide the most recent feature article, the picture of the day, and the most recent NASA ScienceCasts (videos) all leading to the current offering and previous content. A new update is the science by the numbers section providing interesting factoids about NASA and space exploration. Topics covered include everything that NASA covers such as space weather, planetary science, microgravity, science highlights, and technology transfer. The site provides a wealth of information in all areas of science in a readable, concise format, and highlighted with images and videos becoming a centralized gateway to discovering everything about NASA's activities and discoveries. For an alternative look at NASA's activities, check out the NASA Watch site (www.nasawatch.com). Suitable for almost any age, and recommended for anyone interested in space. URL: http://science.nasa.gov

164. ***Space Policy.*** [ISSN: 0265-9646] 1985. q. EUR 1799. Ed(s): J Stuart. Pergamon Press, The Blvd, Langford Ln, E Park, Kidlington, OX5 1GB, United Kingdom; JournalsCustomerServiceEMEA@elsevier.com; http://www.elsevier.com. Illus., adv. Sample. Refereed. Microform: PQC. *Indexed:* A01, A22, BRI, P61. *Bk. rev.:* 4-5, 500-1,000 words. *Aud.:* Ac, Sa.

This journal, one of the few interdisciplinary titles in the field of aeronautics and space science, is designed to provide a forum for the discussion of how space policies will shape the future of space exploration, utilization, and related issues. The topics discussed include the impact of scientific discoveries obtained through space applications and research, space activities and discoveries that impact industry and society, and the resulting economic, political, social, legal, and moral issues raised. The exchange of ideas and opinions is as much a part of this journal as is the exchange of scientific and technical information on space activities and developments. Many of the articles center on the topics associated with the use of space and the overall implications of this use. Topics range from space law and space commercialization to the history and status of space programs to space exploration and lunar development to satellite systems and global positioning systems. The journal also provides primarily research articles, the occasional review article, along with case studies, opinion pieces, book reviews, and short reports. In addition to this content, the journal also reproduces official documents such as treaties, government reports, and space agency plans. The journal also publishes a number of special issues, such as the recent issues on the popularization of space. This unique approach blending political, philosophical, business, and societal issues with scientific and engineering issues makes this journal appropriate for research and academic libraries.

165. ***Space Science Reviews.*** [ISSN: 0038-6308] 1962. 8x/yr. Ed(s): Hans Bloemen. Springer Netherlands, Van Godewijckstraat 30, Dordrecht, 3311 GX, Netherlands; http://www.springer.com. Illus., adv. Sample. Refereed. Vol. ends: No. 4. Reprint: PSC. *Indexed:* A01, A22, BRI, E01. *Bk. rev.:* 10-12, 100-300 words. *Aud.:* Ac.

This international review journal is composed of papers on the various topics related directly to space sciences, defined as scientific research carried out by means of rockets, rocket-propelled vehicles, stratospheric balloons, and observatories on the Earth and the Moon. The journal is primarily oriented toward the advancement of pure science, leaning more toward astronomy, with limited coverage of the technical aspects of space science. The papers provide a synthesis of the current research and developments in the numerous branches of space science. All areas of space science are covered, including, but not limited to, the Big Bang theory, supernovae, cosmic rays, solar variability and climate, infrared space observation, airborne observatories, solar-wind phenomena, and characteristics of interstellar matter. The number of special issues and topical collections has recently increased, with issues and collections focused on supernova, space weather, cosmic dust, and the InSight mission to Mars. In addition, the journal occasionally provides brief communications, and errata. This research journal provides a large number of open-access articles with up to 35 percent of the articles recently freely available. Appropriate for academic libraries.

Spaceflight. See Astronomy section.

166. ***Sport Aviation.*** Former titles (until 1961): *Sport Aviation and the Experimenter;* (until 1958): *Experimenter.* [ISSN: 0038-7835] 19??. m. Free to members. Experimental Aircraft Association, Inc., 3000 Poberezny Rd, Oshgosh, WI 54902; info@eaa.org; http://www.eaa.org/. Illus., adv. Sample. Vol. ends: Dec. *Aud.:* Ga, Sa.

This is the main publication of the many produced by the EAA (Experimental Aircraft Association). It is a cross between magazines geared for pilots and aviation enthusiasts and those aimed at specific areas of aviation, such as ultralights and ballooning. The magazine promotes general aviation and covers all types of aircraft, from private aircraft to helicopters and rotorcraft, with emphasis on the sport of aviation and sport aircraft. There are numerous feature articles and other information relevant to anyone interested in general aviation and aircraft. The unique aspect of the magazine are the articles focused on the technical aspects of customizing aircraft, building, and restoring aircraft. The magazine contains sections that provide information of interest to the members of the EAA. There are sections providing columns and editorials, news, an events calendar, association news, a memorial section, and member services. Other sections, such as the "Hands-on" section, provide practical information for those building and restoring aircraft, or the sections focused on safety. The magazine contains additional information on experimental aircraft publication after the cessation of *EAA Experimenter*. Also included are periodic special sections that are primarily focused on EAA's educational, preservation, legacy-building activities, and youth initiatives. The society also publishes *Warbirds*, which is focused on restoring and preserving military aircraft and aviation history; *Sport Aerobatics*; and *Vintage Airplane*. *Sport Aviation* is a worthwhile addition to general-interest collections and public libraries.

167. *Vertiflite.* Incorporates (in 19??): *American Helicopter Society. Directory of Members;* Former titles (until 1963): *Verti-flite Newsletter;* (until Apr.1963): *American Helicopter Society. Newsletter.* [ISSN: 0042-4455] 1953. bi-m. Members, USD 40; Non-members, USD 135. Ed(s): Kim Smith. A H S International, 217 N Washington St, Alexandria, VA 22314; staff@vtol.org; http://www.vtol.org. Illus., index, adv. Vol. ends: No. 5. *Indexed:* A01, A22, HRIS. *Bk. rev.:* 1-2, 700-1,000 words. *Aud.:* Ga, Ac.

This is the membership-focused publication of the American Helicopter Society (AHS) similar to AIAA's *Aerospace America*. Its aim is to provide information on the advances being made in the areas of vertical flight and promoting the wider use of helicopters and other vertical-flight aircraft. It consists usually of two to five topical feature articles on rotorcraft technology that can be found in the society's companion publication *Journal of the American Helicopter Society*. *Vertiflite* provides feature articles on helicopters and rotorcraft technology and the broader use of helicopters and other issues relevant or related to the entire industry, such as a recent issue that focuses on noise. The main focus of the publication is to support the society's membership and provide it with relevant information on new aircraft, new technologies, safety issues, and military technology. Along with these feature articles are book reviews, a calendar of events, information on conference activities, industry briefs, a member-update section, and related news items. The topics or types of articles include the military procurement of helicopters; FAA rules; reviews of new helicopters; the world rotorcraft marketplace; market forecasts; and studies on rotoheads in wake fields. Recommended for academic and technical libraries.

■ AFRICA

Araba Dawson-Andoh, Subject Librarian for African Studies and the Social Sciences, Center for International Collections, Alden Library, Ohio University, Athens, OH 45701-2979; 740-593-2547; dawson-a@Ohio.edu

Introduction

The attainment of independence by African nations in the late 1950s and 1960s; the dynamics of the Cold War; and the rise of the civil rights movement in the United States contributed to an interest in a comprehensive understanding of the African continent, its peoples, and its languages. This resulted in the establishment of African Studies programs in universities and colleges in the United States, Europe, and Africa during this period. The study of Africa is interdisciplinary, comprising a diverse area of inquiry including art, culture, society, music, politics, geography, history, literature, environment, economics, religion, health, and philosophy. Publications covered in the Africa section reflect the diverse nature of the field. They were selected for their broad coverage of the subject, and hence this section aims to serve as a guide, for all types of libraries, to the core list of titles. In general usage, North Africa is grouped with the Middle East, so it is not well represented in this section.

This section includes a broad array of periodicals, scholarly journals reporting original research; news magazines that provide timely information and analysis of contemporary African issues; trade and business magazines reporting on important industries such as communications technology, mining and oil; pan-African lifestyle glossy magazines with the latest fashion, culture, and celebrity news, some with empowerment messages specifically aimed at the modern African woman. A few of these periodicals are published in Africa, and they often provide information, analysis, and insight from an African point of view. Many of the periodicals listed will appeal to scholars, researchers, students, policy experts, business, government and non-governmental organizations, and general audiences. Some of the journals are print, but many—especially journals that cover recent scholarship, research, and statistics—are also available in online databases and websites. A select few are freely available as open-access journals. Full-text articles could be downloaded from electronic databases and directly from journal websites.

Other sources of current news on Africa are Africa-related news feeds and blogs; for example: *AllAfrica* http://allafrica.com/; *Google News* https://news.google.com/; *Africa can end poverty* http://blogs.worldbank.org/africacan/; and *Africa is a country* http://africasacountry.com. Other sources of information on Africa are Internet guides such as *Africa South of the Sahara* https://library.stanford.edu/africa-south-sahara, a comprehensive annotated directory of online resources about Africa.

Basic Periodicals

Hs: *Africa Renewal;* Ga: *Africa Research Bulletin. Economic, Financial and Technical Series; Africa Research Bulletin. Political, Social and Cultural Series; African Business; Journal of Modern African Studies; New African; New African Woman, Transition;* Ac: *Africa; Africa Confidential; Africa Today; African Affairs; African Studies Review; History in Africa; Presence Africaine; Research in African Literatures.*

Basic Abstracts and Indexes

African Studies Abstracts, Current Bibliography on African Affairs, International African Bibliography, PAIS International, Quarterly Index to Africana Periodical Literature.

168. *Africa.* [ISSN: 0001-9720] 1928. q. plus a. bibliography. Ed(s): David Pratten, Deborah James. Cambridge University Press, University Printing House, Shaftesbury Rd, Cambridge, CB2 8BS, United Kingdom; online@cambridge.org; https://www.cambridge.org. Illus., index, adv. Sample. Refereed. Circ: 1250. Vol. ends: No. 4. Reprint: PSC. *Indexed:* A01, A22, A47, AmHI, BRI, E01, IBSS, MLA-IB. *Bk. rev.:* 10-15, 750-2,500 words. *Aud.:* Ac, Sa.

Published quarterly in February, May, August, and November by Cambridge University Press, *Africa* is one of the oldest scholarly journals focusing on the continent. In publication for more than 90 years, it is the journal of the International African Institute in London, which has played a seminal role in the development of the field of African Studies. It is interdisciplinary in approach, and its subject coverage includes the social sciences, history, the environment, and life sciences, with strong emphasis on issues of development, links between local and national levels of society, and cultural studies. *Africa* aims to give increased attention to the production of knowledge from Africa by highlighting the work of local African thinkers and writers, and emerging social and cultural trends. Each issue usually contains articles with extensive bibliographies. Articles are accompanied by abstracts in English and French. Book reviews and review essays are substantial. Special issues are published annually, usually the first issue in the volume. *Africa Bibliography* (see below in this section), a comprehensive indexed annual listing of published work in African Studies from the previous year, is included with the full subscription, or it can be purchased separately. Journal information is available at http://www.african-writing.com/eleven/. *Africa* is highly recommended for all academic collections and large general collections.

169. *Africa Bibliography.* [ISSN: 0266-6731] 1985. a. GBP 454 (print & online eds.)). Ed(s): Richard Bartholemew. Cambridge University Press, University Printing House, Shaftesbury Rd, Cambridge, CB2 8BS, United Kingdom; journals@cambridge.org; https://www.cambridge.org/. Illus. Reprint: PSC. *Indexed:* A01, A22. *Aud.:* Ga, Ac, Sa.

Africa Bibliography is an authoritative guide to works in African studies. It has been published since 1985 under the auspices of the London-based International African Institute. Published by Cambridge University Press, this annual compendium (averaging more than 6,000 entries) reports on books, periodical articles, pamphlets, and book chapters on Africa or of interest to students of Africa. Coverage is primarily in the social and environmental sciences, humanities, and arts, and some items from the medical, biological, and natural sciences. It records the previous year's published works in the field, with provision for retrospective inclusion of earlier items. The bibliography includes materials on Africa published in non-specialist scholarly journals, in addition to specialist Africa publications. Coverage is of the entire continent and its associated islands. The vast majority of the material covered is in English, with a good number of items in French and a few in other European languages, such as Portuguese, Spanish, Italian, and German. Aside from Swahili and Afrikaans, no other African-language items are included in the bibliography. Each issue has an introductory article on subjects such as African publishing, libraries and bibliography, bookshops, broadcast media, and new information technologies. *Africa Bibliography* is arranged by region, country, and subject, preceded by a section for the continent as a whole. The sections are divided by subject classes, with author and subject indexes, and include an author index and a detailed thematic index. Since 2011, the online edition is a fully searchable database, including both the current volume and past volumes. The newly introduced search functionality links to the full text of articles or to items in a library catalog. This recommended reference is an easy-to-use resource for locating current, popular, and scholarly African materials. It is useful both for libraries that are developing comprehensive collections and for those who can only afford to select a few items for geographic coverage of current literature. Some libraries may opt to acquire the *Bibliography* with a subscription to *Africa* (above in this section). This title is available for subscription in print and online editions at the publisher website: https://www.cambridge.org/core/journals/africa-bibliography.

170. *Africa Confidential.* Formerly (until 1967): *Africa.* [ISSN: 0044-6483] 1960. fortn. GBP 842 combined subscription (print & online eds.); USD 1389 combined subscription (print & online eds.)). Ed(s): Clare Tauben, Patrick Smith. Asempa Ltd., 73 Farringdon Rd, London, ECIM 3JQ, United Kingdom; info@africa-confidential.com. Illus., adv. Vol. ends: Dec. *Indexed:* A01, A22, E01. *Aud.:* Ga, Ac, Sa.

Africa Confidential, published since 1960, reports on key political, economic, and security developments in Africa. Issues provide a wealth of information on politics, economics, diplomacy, business, and military affairs. The scope of reporting and analysis is unparalleled, providing contexts for readers trying to get a detailed understanding of the continent. Coverage is broad, includes everything from the latest mining deals and rebel uprisings to detailed analysis of elections, written by a network of correspondents throughout Africa. The contributors write on the basis of anonymity, so articles have no bylines. This is a subscription-only news magazine published biweekly (25 issues a year) and available online and in print. Annual subscription includes unlimited access to the web site, including new articles as they are published, and an eighteen-year online archive of more than 4,000 articles. This newsletter remains in heavy demand, and is highly recommended for both general, academic, and special collections. It is pricey; however, reduced subscription rates are available for academic institutions, NGOs, charities, and students. Subscription options available on the journal web site. URL: www.africa-confidential.com

171. *Africa Development.* [ISSN: 0850-3907] 1976. q. USD 32 (Individuals, USD 30). Ed(s): Felicia Oyekanmi. Council for the Development of Social Science Research in Africa, Avenue Cheikh, Anta Diop x Canal IV, BP 3304, Dakar, , Senegal; codesria@sentoo.sn; http://www.codesria.org. Illus., adv. Refereed. Circ: 600. *Indexed:* C45, IBSS, P61. *Bk. rev.:* 2-5, 1,000-1,500 words. *Aud.:* Ac, Sa.

This bilingual quarterly journal (parallel title: *Afrique et Developpement*) is published by the Council for the Development of Social Science Research in Africa (CODESRIA). Published since 1976, *Africa Development* is the oldest regularly published social science journal in Africa. It supports CODESRIA's principal objective of "exchange of ideas among African scholars from a variety of intellectual persuasions and various disciplines." African authors and others working on Africa or comparative analysis of developing world issues contribute articles on cultural, social, political, and economic issues of society in Africa. The focus may be on an issue in a specific country or continent-wide. Abstracts are in English and French, and articles are either French or English; English predominates. This interdisciplinary journal is highly recommended for academic and special libraries. Online issues are open access, and full-text articles are downloadable. Print issues are available on subscription at a low price. Tables of contents, full text of articles, and back issues are available online from the CODESRIA web site: www.codesria.org/Links/Publications/Journals/africa_development.htm. This journal along with other CODESRIA journals, including (see below in this section for the first two) *African Sociological Review, CODESRIA Bulletin,* and *Afrika Zamani* are available from African Journals Online (AJOL): https://www.ajol.info/

172. *Africa Insight.* Formerly (until 1979): *South African Journal of African Affairs.* [ISSN: 0256-2804] 1971. q. ZAR 500 (Individuals, ZAR 250). Ed(s): Elizabeth Le Roux. Africa Institute of South Africa, PO Box 630, Pretoria, 0001, South Africa; ai@ai.org.za. Illus., index, adv. Sample. Refereed. Circ: 5000. Microform: PQC. *Indexed:* A22, C45, IBSS, MLA-IB, P61. *Bk. rev.:* 3-5, 500-700 words. *Aud.:* Ga, Ac, Sa.

Africa Insight is a quarterly, peer-reviewed journal of the African Institute of South Africa, a think tank devoted to production of knowledge on Africa. It is a multidisciplinary journal that primarily addresses African affairs. It provides a forum for discussion of diverse topics, and it focuses on the process of change in Africa. Topics are wide-ranging: "political trends and events, democratization, economic issues, regional cooperation, international relations, conflict resolution, aspects of education and training, health, community development, food security, [and] institutional capacity building." While many articles focus on southern Africa, the scope of the journal is the entire continent. The articles are scholarly, researched, and frequently illustrated. Journal issues include book reviews on current publications of interest to Africanists. This title is of interest to educators, institutions, and decision makers in business and the public sector, but also to general audiences interested in Africa. Recommended for academic and large public libraries, as well as special libraries. It is also available online at AJOL. URL: https://www.ajol.info/index.php/ai

173. *Africa Renewal.* Former titles (until vol.18,no.3, 2004): *Africa Recovery;* (until 1987): *Africa Emergency Report.* [ISSN: 1816-9627] 1985. q. Free to qualified personnel. Ed(s): Masimba Tafirenyika. United Nations, Department of Public Information, United Nations Bldg, L-172, New York, NY 10017; http://www.un.org. *Indexed:* C42. *Aud.:* Hs, Ga, Ac, Sa.

Africa Renewal is a quarterly magazine published by the United Nations. It was formerly published as *Africa Recovery/Afrique Relance.* The colorfully illustrated magazine examines the many issues that confront the people of Africa, its leaders, and its international partners. Coverage includes topics such as economic reform, debt, education, health, women's advancement, conflict and civil strife, climate change, democratization, development, aid, and investment. Reporting tracks policy debates and examines the many different aspects of the UN's involvement in Africa, especially within the framework of the New Partnership for Africa's Development (NEPAD) and the achievement of the Millennium Development Goals. A French edition is also available. Special editions with various Africa-related issues are published every two years. A recent special edition, on youth, explores challenges and opportunities faced by Africa's youth in areas such as technology, skills training, entrepreneurship, among others. The magazine's focus on contemporary issues, vivid illustrations, and easy accessibility make this a suitable choice for all types of audiences interested in Africa. Free print subscriptions to the magazine can be requested from the magazine's website, and online issues are freely available at the magazine website. URL: http://www.un.org/africarenewal//magazine

174. *The Africa Report (Paris).* [ISSN: 1950-4810] 2005. bi-m. EUR 29 domestic; EUR 35 in Europe; EUR 35 in North America. Groupe Jeune Afrique, 57 bis, Rue d'Auteuil, Paris, 75016, France; http://www.groupeja.com. *Aud.:* Ga, Sa.

The Africa Report is Groupe Jeune Afrique's English-language publication. Available in print and digital editions, it "has established itself as the international publication of reference dedicated to African affairs." The journal is aimed at both African and international readers, providing expert analysis on fast-changing political and economic issues in Africa. Each issue contains surveys, sector reports, and country focus. Coverage includes analysis of African business environment with solid analysis of the political situation and assessment of the risks. Like its French-language weekly counterpart *Jeune Afrique* (see below in this section), field writers in all regions of the continent provide in-depth on-the-ground reportage on politics, economy, industry, and governance. Company profiles and CEO interviews, as well as essential maps and data, complete the editorial offerings. Issues contain sections on politics, country focus, business, art, and life, with opinions, debates, and interviews. *The Africa Report* is recommended for academic, public, and special collections. The publishers offer various subscription packages in single or combined print and digital editions at very reasonable prices. Issues are occasionally accompanied by free topical supplements. URL: http://www.theafricareport.com/

175. *Africa Research Bulletin. Economic, Financial and Technical Series.* Former titles (until 1992): *Africa Research Bulletin. Economic Series;* (until 1985): *Africa Research Bulletin. Economic, Financial and Technical Series;* (until Apr.1965): *Africa Research Bulletin. Africa: Economic, Financial and Technical Series;* (until Feb.1965): *Africa Research Bulletin. Africa: Economic, Financial and Technical.* [ISSN: 2053-227X] 1964. m. GBP 1539. Ed(s): Virginia Baily, Veronica Hoskins. Wiley-Blackwell Publishing Ltd., The Atrium, Southern Gate, Chichester, PO19 8QG, United Kingdom; cs-journals@wiley.com; http://onlinelibrary.wiley.com/. Illus., index, adv. Sample. Reprint: PSC. *Indexed:* A22, B01, E01. *Aud.:* Ac, Sa.

Africa Research Bulletin, a monthly economic news digest, provides in-depth coverage and analysis of economic news on Africa. Its aim is to provide readers an in-depth understanding of Africa. It contains impartial summaries and extensive reports on political and economic developments throughout the continent. It draws on text and summaries from media sources, including African newspapers, news agencies, radio broadcasts, and United Nations agency publications. It also draws on information from government gazettes, international organizations, selected European newspapers and journals, the world press, and the World Wide Web. Content includes regional and international conferences, foreign cooperation and trade agreements, trade figures and foreign direct investment, country and regional economic reviews with maps and tables, financial markets, debt tables, budget proposals and highlights, stock markets, and IMF assessments and loans. Each issue is fully indexed and uses cross-references to guide readers to related articles in previous issues of the bulletin. Issues contain a lead article and six sections, with countries and regional entities listed alphabetically. Sections include continental developments; policy and practice; communications and transport; commodities; industries; and economic aid. The publisher issues a companion series, *Africa Research Bulletin: Political, Social and Cultural Series* (see below in this section). The targeted audience is academics and policy specialists. This title is expensive, but (with the *Political* title) it is highly recommended for specialized and large public and academic libraries. With *Political,* it is available for subscription separately or combined in print and online editions. URL: https://onlinelibrary.wiley.com/journal/14676346

176. *Africa Research Bulletin. Political, Social and Cultural Series.* Former titles (until 1992): *Africa Research Bulletin. Political Series;* (until 1985): *Africa Research Bulletin. Political, Social, and Cultural Series;* (until Mar.1965): *Africa Research Bulletin. Africa, Political, Social, and Cultural Series;* (until Feb.1965): *Africa Research Bulletin. Africa, Political, Social, and Cultural.* [ISSN: 0001-9844] 1964. m. GBP 1539. Ed(s): Veronica Hoskins, Virginia Baily. Wiley-Blackwell Publishing Ltd., The Atrium, Southern Gate, Chichester, PO19 8QG, United Kingdom; cs-journals@wiley.com; http://onlinelibrary.wiley.com/. Illus., index, adv. Sample. Reprint: PSC. *Indexed:* A01, A22, E01. *Aud.:* Ga, Ac, Sa.

Africa Research Bulletin: Political, Social and Cultural Series is a companion journal to the *African Research Bulletin. Economic, Financial and Technical Series* (see above in this section). Information is drawn from hundreds of acknowledged sources, including local press, websites, and radio, to provide news and commentary on politics and society. Sources from Africa are complemented by information from government gazettes, international agencies, and the European and American press. Coverage includes major conference reports; government changes and lists of new officials; internal security; the military; international relations; and cultural and social information. This title opens with a lead article, followed by five sections with countries and regional entities listed alphabetically within each. Sections include internal developments; national security; military; overseas relations; and social and cultural. Major political/military events often appear in chronological order; and charts, graphs, and maps illustrate the articles. The online format follows that of the print. In addition to providing a detailed index, the web allows full-text searching. Expensive, but like the *Economic* series, essential for specialists and academics. Recommended for large academic and special libraries.

177. *Africa Spectrum.* [ISSN: 1868-6869] 2009. 3x/yr. Free. Ed(s): Andreas Mehler, Henning Melber. Sage Publications Ltd., 1 Oliver's Yard, 55 City Rd, London, EC1Y 1SP, United Kingdom; info@sagepub.com; https://www.sagepub.com. Adv. Refereed. *Bk. rev.:* 4-5, 700 words. *Aud.:* Ac, Sa.

Africa Spectrum has been published since 1966 by the GIGA Institute of African Affairs (IAA) in Hamburg. It was previously published only in German until 1970, when English and French were added. Originally known as *Afrika Spectrum,* the title was changed in 2009 when it began publishing only in English. It accepts German- and French-language articles but they are translated before publishing. Part of the GIGA journal family, it is the leading German academic journal exclusively devoted to Africa. It is an interdisciplinary, peer-reviewed academic journal that concentrates on the analysis of current issues of development in Africa south of the Sahara. The journal focuses on socially relevant issues related to political, economic, and sociocultural problems and events in Africa, as well as on Africa's role within the international system. In addition to scholarly articles, each issue include in-depth book reviews, debates, and short contributions. Special issues devoted to specific subjects are issued occasionally. Since 2003, the journal has collaborated closely with the African Studies Association in Germany. Recommended for academic libraries with Africana collections. It is currently an open-access journal, and is freely available online in some databases and on the journal website as well as in print. URL: http://journals.sub.uni-hamburg.de/giga/afsp/index

178. *Africa Today.* [ISSN: 0001-9887] 1954. q. USD 219.45 (print & online eds.)). Ed(s): Derek DiMatteo. Indiana University Press, Office of Scholarly Publishing, Herman B Wells Library 350, Bloomington, IN 47405; iuporder@indiana.edu; http://iupjournals.org. Illus., index. Refereed. Vol. ends: Fall. Microform: PQC. Reprint: PSC. *Indexed:* A01, A22, BRI, C45, CBRI, E01, IBSS, MLA-IB, P61. *Bk. rev.:* 5-15, 750 words. *Aud.:* Ga, Ac, Sa.

Africa Today is one of the leading journals for the study of Africa. It "provides access to the best scholarly work from around the world[,] ranging [among] political, economic, and social issues" relating to Africa. Launched in 1954 as the bulletin of the anti-apartheid American Committee on Africa (ACOA), it is now an academic journal published by Indiana University Press. An interdisciplinary publication, it includes occasional articles in the arts and humanities, as well as research in the social sciences. Its multicultural perspective is seen in the range of topics covered in issues. Each issue contains about five or six articles followed by in-depth book reviews. Special issues with introductory essays focusing on thematic topics are issued occasionally. An alphabetical list of books received and brief biographical information on contributors are featured at the end of each issue. *Africa Today* is recommended for both general and academic audiences. It is available for subscription in print and online at very reasonable rates at the journal website. URL: https://purchase.jstor.org/products.php?issn=00019887.

179. *African Affairs.* Former titles (until 1944): *Royal African Society. Journal;* (until 1935): *African Society. Journal.* [ISSN: 0001-9909] 1901. q. EUR 671. Ed(s): Carl Death, Lindsay Whitfield. Oxford University Press, Great Clarendon St, Oxford, OX2 6DP, United Kingdom; onlinequeries.uk@oup.com; http://global.oup.com. Illus., adv. Sample. Refereed. Reprint: PSC. *Indexed:* A01, A22, A47, AmHI, BRI, C45, E01, IBSS, MLA-IB, P61, SSA. *Bk. rev.:* 5-15, 500-1,500 words. *Aud.:* Ac, Sa.

African Affairs was established as the *Journal of the Royal African Society* in 1901; it adopted its current name in 1944. This highly ranked scholarly journal is published on behalf of the Royal African Society (United Kingdom). It has a long tradition of covering Africa from a broad range of social science and cultural perspectives. "It is an inter-disciplinary journal, with a focus on the politics and international relations of sub-Saharan Africa. It also includes sociology, anthropology, [and] economics, and to the extent that articles inform debates on contemporary Africa, history, literature, art, music and more." Each issue includes several scholarly articles that focus on recent political, social, and economic developments in sub-Saharan countries. There are also briefings on contemporary issues, and research notes on ethical and methodological challenges. The journal regularly posts news of meetings of the Royal African Society and includes the society's annual meeting minutes, announcements, and annual report. Very useful to scholars, students, and librarians is the journal's substantial section of book reviews, with occasional review articles. There is also an invaluable list of recently published books by region, and a listing of articles on Africa that have appeared in non-Africanist journals. A valuable resource for a wide audience that includes students, scholars, librarians, and anyone interested in recent and historical literature on sub-Saharan Africa. Freely available online on the journal website are virtual issues that provide informed and critical analysis on a particular topic or country in Africa. These issues comprise significant articles previously published in the journal, as well as new and exclusive content. This title remains a basic choice for all collections. Abstracts and tables of contents for recent and back issues are available at https://academic.oup.com/afraf/issue

180. ***African and Black Diaspora: an international journal.*** [ISSN: 1752-8631] 2008. s-a. GBP 348 (print & online eds.)). Ed(s): Dr. Sandra Jackson, Dr. Fassil Demissie. Routledge, 530 Walnut St, Ste 850, Philadelphia, PA 19106; enquiries@tandfonline.com; http://www.tandfonline.com. Sample. Refereed. Reprint: PSC. *Indexed:* A22, E01, IBSS, MLA-IB. *Bk. rev.:* Number and length vary. *Aud.:* Ga, Ac, Sa.

African and Black Diaspora is a multidisciplinary peer-reviewed "journal that seeks to broaden and deepen our understanding of the lived experiences of people of African descent across the globe." Works published in the journal are theoretical, historical, and empirical. This title focuses on issues such as power, knowledge, gender, race, and other forms of social identity. In addition to research articles, the journal publishes commentaries and book reviews twice a year, with a mix of regular and special-themed issues. The theme of a recent special issue was identity and transnationalism among second generation African immigrants in the United States. This journal is of interest to academics, specialists, and general audiences. It is recommended for libraries that support African Studies, African American, and African diaspora collections. Tables of contents are available online. URL: www.tandf.co.uk/journals/titles/17528631.asp

181. ***African Archaeological Review.*** [ISSN: 0263-0338] 1983. s-a. EUR 770 (print & online eds.)). Ed(s): Adria LaViolette. Springer New York LLC, 233 Spring St, New York, NY 10013; customerservice@springer.com; http://link.springer.com. Illus., adv. Sample. Refereed. Microform: PQC. Reprint: PSC. *Indexed:* A01, A22, A47, AmHI, BRI, E01. *Bk. rev.:* 1-2, 1,000-1,500 words. *Aud.:* Ac, Sa.

This journal features international scholarship on aspects of African archaeology, "highlighting the contributions of the region as they relate to key global issues." Journal issues contain authoritative, and substantial, articles on archaeological research and activities in Africa, providing access to timely continental and subcontinental studies. The journal covers a wide range of topics on the field ranging from evolution of modern humans to advancements of human culture, and to basic African contributions to the field of archaeology. Field data from sites or localities are often reported. The journal usually includes one or two substantive book reviews. It is of importance in the field and is recommended for institutions with an interest in anthropology and archaeology. The journal's first edition was released in 1983, and it has been released continuously every year. Issues are available in print and online editions. Due to Springer's Open Choice option the journal contains both subscription and open-access articles that are freely available on the journal website. The website also features an "Online First" preview of proofed papers scheduled for publication and an archive of past issues. URL: http://link.springer.com/journal/volumesAndIssues/10437

182. ***African Arts.*** [ISSN: 0001-9933] 1967. q. USD 249 (print & online eds.) USD 54 newsstand/cover). M I T Press, One Rogers St, Cambridge, MA 02142-1209; http://mitpress.mit.edu/. Illus., adv. Refereed. *Indexed:* A01, A06, A22, A47, A51, AmHI, BRI, C37, E01, MASUSE, MLA-IB. *Bk. rev.:* 3-4, 200-700 words. *Aud.:* Hs, Ga, Ac, Sa.

African Arts, a quarterly journal (spring, summer, fall, winter), has been published since 1967 by the James S. Coleman African Studies Center at UCLA. This scholarly journal "presents original research and critical discourse on traditional, contemporary, and popular African arts and expressive cultures." The stated aim is to promote investigation of the interdisciplinary connections among the arts, anthropology, history, language, politics, religion, performance, and cultural and global studies. Features include architecture, arts of personal adornment, and contemporary and popular arts as well as music, film, theater, and other forms of expressive culture. Each issue usually includes four to eight articles with beautiful black-and-white and color illustrations and photos. Entire issues are often devoted to topical concerns and discussions; exhibit announcements and previews; features on museum collections; descriptive reviews of major exhibits; and artist portfolios, photo essays, edgy dialogues, and editorials. Book, video, and/or theater reviews appear in each issue. The visually appealing presentation, subject matter, and accessible writing make this a good choice for all types of audiences. Distributed by MIT Press, it is available both in print and online editions, and subscriptions can be requested from the MIT Press website. URL: http://www.mitpressjournals.org/aa

183. ***The African Book Publishing Record.*** [ISSN: 0306-0322] 1975. q. EUR 570. Ed(s): Cecile Lomer. De Gruyter Saur, Rosenheimer Str 143, Muenchen, 81671, Germany; wdg-info@degruyter.com; http://www.degruyter.com/browse?publisher=KGS. Illus., adv. Vol. ends: No. 4. Reprint: PSC. *Indexed:* A22, E01, MLA-IB. *Bk. rev.:* 35-55, 200-400 words. *Aud.:* Ac, Sa.

ABPR provides comprehensive and systematic coverage of bibliographic and acquisitions data on new and forthcoming publications from the African continent. It covers works of all levels in the African languages, as well as English, French, and Portuguese. The titles included in the bibliographical section are arranged according to subject area, country, and author. Features include an extensive book review section, reviews of new journals, and a variety of news, reports, and articles about African book trade activities and developments. The notes and news section, which precedes the bibliography, provides information on new publishers, book fairs, and various book awards and prizes. Indexes of publishers and currencies complete each issue of the journal. It has an annual annotated review of African reference books. Highly recommended for academic, large public, and special libraries interested in acquiring specialized African materials.

184. ***African Business.*** [ISSN: 0141-3929] 1966. 11x/yr. GBP 40 domestic; EUR 80 foreign. Ed(s): Anver Versi. I C Publications Ltd., 7 Coldbath Sq, London, EC1R 4LQ, United Kingdom; icpubs@africasia.com; http://www.africasia.com/. Illus., index, adv. Sample. Microform: PQC. *Indexed:* A22, B01, BRI. *Bk. rev.:* 1-5, 100-500 words. *Aud.:* Hs, Ga, Ac, Sa.

With a pan-African focus, *African Business* provides information on business trends, risks, and opportunities in Africa in a familiar news magazine format. Each issue usually consists of several sections. The "cover story section" has three, or sometimes four or more, substantial articles on current business and economic issues. The "Special Reports" section includes shorter articles that might be on a particular theme. Usually pieces on African telecoms, ports, and mining appear in each issue. The sections about "Aviation," "Shipping," and the "Development" are shorter, with possibly a single article per section. The "Countryfiles" section features several specific-country analyses of economic developments and trends. News of conferences, trade exhibition dates, African currency tables, book reviews, and columnists with opinions and advice are included. *AB* has won awards for business reporting in Africa. It is current and relevant to anyone seeking to understand business in Africa. With content presented in a colorful, lively, and readable manner, it is recommended for general, academic, and special library audiences. *African Business* is among a number of titles published by IC Publications in London, England, including *New African* (below in this section). For in-depth country analysis, see *Country Reports* (below in this section). Available online and in print; subscription information can be found on the website, which also includes sections of current and past issues. http://www.africanbusinessmagazine.com

185. ***African Development Review.*** [ISSN: 1017-6772] 1989. q. GBP 321. Ed(s): John C Anyanwu. Wiley-Blackwell Publishing Ltd., The Atrium, Southern Gate, Chichester, PO19 8QG, United Kingdom;

cs-journals@wiley.com; http://onlinelibrary.wiley.com/. Illus., adv. Sample. Refereed. *Indexed:* A01, A22, ASSIA, B01, BRI, C45, E01, EconLit, IBSS, P61. *Bk. rev.:* Number and length vary. *Aud.:* Ac, Sa.

The *African Development Review,* published quarterly on behalf of the African Development Bank, is a "professional journal devoted to the study and analysis of development policy in Africa." In English or French, it is also *Revue africaine de developpement.* Emphasis is on the relevance of research findings to policy rather than on purely theoretical or quantitative contributions. Topics covered include macroeconomic policies (fiscal, monetary, and exchange rate policy); economic and structural reforms, including issues of financial sector reforms; sectoral issues on agriculture, energy, mining, and industry; issues of building infrastructure and human resource capacity; private sector development; regional and international concerns such as debt, trade, capital flows, regional integration, South-South cooperation and globalization; and socioeconomic issues of income distribution and poverty alleviation. Each issue includes about six scholarly, technical articles on developmental economics, policy, and planning issues. All articles have English and French abstracts. It also features book reviews, conference reports, and comments on reviewed articles. Free online access to institutions in the developing world is provided through United Nations initiatives (AGORA and OARE). This journal is recommended for academic and special libraries. Available in print and online editions for subscribers, back issues and individual articles may be purchased on the publisher's website. URL: http://onlinelibrary.wiley.com/journal/10.1111/(ISSN)1467-8268

186. *African Economic History.* Formerly (until 1976): *African Economic History Review.* [ISSN: 0145-2258] 1974. s-a. a. until 2017. USD 107 print & online eds. Ed(s): Mariana Candido, Toyin Falola. University of Wisconsin Press, Journals Division, 1930 Monroe St, 3rd Fl, Madison, WI 53711; journals@uwpress.wisc.edu; http://www.uwpress.org/. Illus., adv. Sample. Refereed. Reprint: PSC. *Indexed:* EconLit, IBSS. *Bk. rev.:* 8-10, 600-1,000 words. *Aud.:* Ga, Ac, Sa.

African Economic History is published by the African Studies Program, University of Wisconsin, Madison, and the support of University of Notre Dame. It started in 1974 as *African Economic History Review* and its title changed in 1976. It has also been associated with the Harriet Tubman Institute for Research on Africa and its Diasporas, York University, Toronto. "The journal publishes scholarly essays in English and French on economic history of African societies from precolonial times to the present." Articles published feature research in a variety of fields and time periods, including studies on labor; slavery; trade and commercial networks; economic transformations; colonialism; migration; development policies; social and economic inequalities and poverty. The book review section is substantial. This journal is of interest to historians, economists, anthropologists, sociologists, political scientists, policymakers, and a range of other scholars interested in the African present and past. Usually behind in publication, it is recommended for special, academic, and general audiences. It is available for subscription in print from the University of Wisconsin Press. Online access is from Project MUSE and online back issues from JSTOR.

187. *African Geographical Review.* Formerly (until 2001): *East African Geographical Review.* [ISSN: 1937-6812] 1963. q. 3/yr. until 2019, s-a. until 2015. GBP 235 (print & online eds.)). Ed(s): Leo Zulu. Routledge, 2 Park Sq, Milton Park, Abingdon, OX14 4RN, United Kingdom; http://www.routledge.com. Adv. Sample. Refereed. Reprint: PSC. *Indexed:* A01. *Bk. rev.:* Number and length vary. *Aud.:* Ac, Sa.

This is a refereed journal published in association with the African Specialty Group of the Association of American Geographers. Founded in 1963 at Makerere University in Uganda as the *East African Geographical Review,* the journal was renamed and the scope was broadened in 2000 when the African Specialty Group took over. The aim of this publication is to enhance the standing of African regional geography and to promote a better representation of African scholarship. Articles are contributed by scholars throughout the world. Articles may be from any subfield of geography, as well as be theoretical, empirical, or applied in nature. The journal features short commentaries on contemporary issues in Africa, research articles, methodological or field notes, editorials, and a few short book reviews. Some articles are specialized, while many are of broader social-science interest. Recommended for academic and special library audiences. Tables of contents and abstracts available at the journal's website. URL: http://www.tandfonline.com/toc/rafg20/current

188. *African Historical Review.* Formerly (until 2008): *Kleio.* [ISSN: 1753-2523] 1969. s-a. GBP 240 (print & online eds.)). Ed(s): Paul Landau, Russel Viljoen. UniSA Press, PO Box 392, Pretoria, 0003, South Africa; unisa-press@unisa.ac.za; http://www.unisa.ac.za/press. Illus., adv. Refereed. Reprint: PSC. *Indexed:* A22, E01, IBSS. *Bk. rev.:* Number and length vary. *Aud.:* Ac.

The African Historical Review is a peer-reviewed journal co-published by UNISA and Routledge. Published in South Africa for about 35 years as *Kleio: A Journal of Historical Studies from Africa,* it was originally a research and teaching forum for the history department of the University of South Africa, and evolved into an internationally recognized academic journal. Articles cover a wide variety of historical subjects, and aims for a wider audience with contributors from all over Africa. It includes three to five research articles, review articles, and an often-lengthy book review section in each issue. While regional scholarship is still featured, the intent is to include writing and research on an array of historical topics regarding Africa with diverse theoretical frameworks and methodologies. Recommended for collections that support African Studies, and valuable for bringing African scholarship to readers internationally.

189. *African Identities.* [ISSN: 1472-5843] 2003. q. GBP 586 (print & online eds.)). Ed(s): Pal Ahluwalia. Routledge, 4 Park Sq, Milton Park, Abingdon, OX14 4RN, United Kingdom; subscriptions@tandf.co.uk; http://www.tandfonline.com. Adv. Sample. Refereed. Reprint: PSC. *Indexed:* A01, A22, E01, IBSS, MLA-IB. *Bk. rev.:* Number and length vary. *Aud.:* Ga, Ac, Sa.

African Identities "provides a critical forum for the examination of African and diasporic expressions, representations and identities." Each issue features about five to eight articles examining film, drama, literature, popular music, and culture in the context of African identity. Emphasizing "gender, class, nation, marginalization, 'otherness' and difference, the journal explores how African identities, either by force of expediency or contingency, create layered terrains of (ex)change, [and] decentre dominant meanings, paradigms and certainties." This title is available in print and online. The critical and theoretical approach makes this journal appropriate for an academic library audience, especially collections that support cultural studies of Africa and its diaspora. It is available for subscription in print and online. Tables of contents and back issues are available on the journal website. URL: http://www.tandfonline.com/toc/cafi20/current

190. *African Journal of AIDS Research.* [ISSN: 1608-5906] 2002. q. GBP 409 (print & online eds.)). Ed(s): Alan Whiteside. National Inquiry Services Centre, 4 Speke St, PO Box 377, Grahamstown, 6140, South Africa; publishing@nisc.co.za; http://www.nisc.co.za. Illus., adv. Sample. Refereed. Reprint: PSC. *Indexed:* A01, C45, IBSS, P61, SSA. *Aud.:* Ga, Ac, Sa.

African Journal of AIDS Research (*AJAR*) is a peer-reviewed research journal that is co-published by Routledge and the National Inquiry Services Centre (NISC), the latter based in Grahamstown, South Africa. The journal publishes "papers that make an original contribution to the understanding of social dimensions of HIV/AIDS in African contexts." Articles published have a broad disciplinary focus, including sociology, demography, epidemiology, social geography, economics, psychology, anthropology, philosophy, health communication, media, cultural studies, public health, education, nursing science, and social work. Each journal issue contains about nine research articles, and special thematic issues are published occasionally. Recommended for academic and special library audiences, especially those with African Studies and health collections. The journal is on African Journals Online (www.ajol.info/index.php/ajar). Available in print and online editions; tables of contents, abstracts, and back issues are available at the journal website. URL: http://www.tandfonline.com/loi/raar20

191. *African Journal of Ecology.* Former titles (until 1979): *East African Wildlife Journal;* (until 1963): *Wild Life.* [ISSN: 0141-6707] 1959. q. GBP 1288. Ed(s): Jon Lovett. Wiley-Blackwell Publishing Ltd., The Atrium, Southern Gate, Chichester, PO19 8QG, United Kingdom;

cs-journals@wiley.com; http://onlinelibrary.wiley.com/. Illus., index, adv. Sample. Refereed. Vol. ends: Dec. Microform: PQC. Reprint: PSC. *Indexed:* A01, A22, Agr, BRI, C45, E01, S25. *Bk. rev.:* 1-3, 250-800 words. *Aud.:* Ga, Ac, Sa.

African Journal of Ecology is published in association with the East African Wildlife Society (EAWLS). Formerly called *East African Wildlife Journal,* "it is the foremost research journal on the ecology of the continent." The journal "publishes original scientific research into the ecology and conservation of the animals and plants of Africa." It is the official scientific periodical of the EAWLS and is widely circulated both within and outside Africa. Six to eight scholarly scientific articles are included in each issue. Graphs, tables, and high-quality illustrations accompany the articles on wildlife and plant ecology. Articles are in English with brief French summaries. Book reviews are included, and brief communications often round out some of the issues. Comprehensive reviews on topical subjects are sometimes featured. The editors see the readership as wildlife biologists, academics in biological sciences, undergraduates, and schoolteachers. Like many science periodicals, it is expensive, and is recommended for general science, biology, and botany collections; it is also for research and academic libraries with an environment or ecology program. The journal's early view feature allows free online access to articles that have been copy edited and peer reviewed before they are published in the print edition. Access to the journal is available free online for institutions in the developing world through the AGORA Initiative with the Food and Agriculture Organization of the United Nations (FAO) and the OARE Initiative with the United Nations Environment Program (UNEP). Tables of contents and abstracts are available at the journal's website. Available online through Wiley online library. URL: http://onlinelibrary.wiley.com/journal/10.1111/(ISSN)1365-2028

192. ***African Research and Documentation.*** Formed by the merger of (1964-1972): *African Studies Association of the United Kingdom. Bulletin;* (1962-1972): *Library Materials on Africa.* [ISSN: 0305-862X] 1973. s-a. GBP 55 (Individuals, GBP 45; GBP 18 per issue). Ed(s): Terry Barringer. Standing Conference on Library Materials on Africa, Social Science Collections & Research, British Library St Pancras, London, NW1 2DB, United Kingdom; scolma@hotmail.com; http://scolma.org. Illus., index, adv. *Indexed:* A22, BAS, MLA-IB. *Bk. rev.:* 4-6, 250-1,000 words. *Aud.:* Ac, Sa.

This is the journal of SCOLMA, the U.K. Libraries and Archives Group on Africa. *ARD* publishes articles on all aspects of libraries, archives, and bibliographical matters relating to Africa and African Studies. This journal is a good collection-development tool for Africana resources. It provides current information on publishing trends, bibliographic research projects, reference sources, book reviews, major scholarly writings, and announcements relating to African research sources. Articles focus on current topics or research resources. Issues also include information on Africa-related conferences and meetings, especially those taking place in Great Britain. Papers presented at conferences are often included. Periodically, the journal provides an updated listing of African Studies resources on the Internet. The "Notes and News" section provides a summary of activities in various institutions with Africana collections. Book reviews by librarians cover a wide variety of scholarly works, including some very specialized items. Highly recommended as a useful tool for Africana librarians and scholars. Tables of contents for latest and forthcoming issues are available online. URL: http://scolma.org/

193. ***African Review of Business and Technology.*** Former titles (until 1988): *African Technical Review;* (until 1983): *West African Technical Review.* [ISSN: 0954-6782] 1963. m. Ed(s): Andrew Croft. Alain Charles Publishing Ltd., University House, 11-13 Lower Grosvenor Pl, London, SW1W 0EX, United Kingdom; post@alaincharles.com; http://www.alaincharles.com. Adv. *Indexed:* BRI. *Aud.:* Ac, Sa.

African Review of Business and Technology is a Pan African business magazine published in London by Alain Charles Publishing. The organization publishes several other Africa-related trade magazines including *Communications Africa* (see below in this section). This amply illustrated magazine covers industry news, technical features, and exhibition previews. Topics covered include information technology, oil and gas, construction, and power in Africa. Magazine issues contain business-related editorials, news articles on new developments, materials and contracts relevant to the continent. Editorial content covers banking and financial forecasts, management and business, executive travel and international reports. Regular features include information technology and telecommunications, water supply and electricity, vehicles and transport, oil and petrochemicals, mining and quarrying. There are also advertising, annual suppliers and buyer's guides, as well as coverage of regional exhibitions and conferences. Magazine content is very relevant to Africa's key decision makers serving in executive and managerial capacities in government, industry, and commerce operating in Africa. Recommended for academic and special libraries. Like its sister publications, subscription to the print edition is available free of charge to qualified recipients; digital issues are freely available for download together with an archive dating back to September 2014 on the magazine website. URL: /http://www.africanreview.com/

194. ***African Security.*** [ISSN: 1939-2206] 2008. q. GBP 657 (print & online eds.)). Ed(s): James J. Hentz, Gladys Mokhawa. Routledge, 530 Walnut St, Ste 850, Philadelphia, PA 19106; enquiries@tandfonline.com; http://www.tandfonline.com. Reprint: PSC. *Indexed:* IBSS, P61. *Aud.:* Ac, Sa.

African Security is published quarterly by Taylor and Francis. The journal "explores fresh approaches to understanding Africa's conflicts and security concerns. Its investigation of competing analytical approaches to security complements discussions of current security issues in Africa. The journal strives to investigate the myriad issues relating to conflict and security within and between African nations, not only from the more traditional approaches to security studies but also from more novel and innovative perspectives." The theoretical underpinnings of the journal is based in the disciplines of political science, international relations, and international security, and it also welcomes perspectives from anthropology, development studies, environmental studies, and economics. An article in a recent issue discusses the implications of the neglect of other causes of conflict within indigenous groups in Nigeria's Niger delta region to the efforts of state-led peace-building programs to stabilize the region. This journal addresses both academic and policy issues and is recommended for academic and special libraries. It is available by subscription through the publisher's website and several social science databases. Select articles are freely available as open access since it is a hybrid journal that publishes both OA and paid content. Tables of contents and abstracts are available on the journal website. http://www.tandfonline.com/toc/uafs20/current.

195. ***African Sociological Review.*** Incorporates (in 1997): *South African Sociological Review;* Which was formerly (until 1988): *A S S A Proceedings (Association for Sociology in South Africa).* [ISSN: 1027-4332] 1973. s-a. ZAR 80. Ed(s): Jean-Bernard Ouedraogo, Olajide Oloyede. Council for the Development of Social Science Research in Africa, Avenue Cheikh, Anta Diop x Canal IV, BP 3304, Dakar, , Senegal; codesria@ssonatel.senet.net; http://www.codesria.org. Illus., adv. Refereed. *Indexed:* P61, SSA. *Bk. rev.:* 1,200-1,500 words. *Aud.:* Ac, Sa.

African Sociological Review, which has the parallel title in French, *Revue Africaine de Sociologie,* is a semi-annual publication of CODESRIA (Council for the Development of Social Science Research in Africa), which is based in Dakar, Senegal. It serves as a forum for research-based publishing by African scholars to promote sociological and anthropological thought. Each issue generally contains four or five articles, usually in English, but with occasional French-language essays; its abstracts are in English and French. Journal issues are often categorized into the following sections: "General Issues," "Research Papers," and "Book Review." This journal is recommended for academic and special library audiences. The journal is freely available online both from the AJOL website (www.ajol.info) and CODESRIA. URL: www.codesria.org/spip.php. Tables of contents and abstracts are also available on both sites.

196. ***African Studies.*** Formerly (until 1942): *Bantu Studies.* [ISSN: 0002-0184] 1921. 3x/yr. GBP 702 (print & online eds.)). Ed(s): Dr. Dina Ligaga, Dr. Catherine Burns. Routledge, 4 Park Sq, Milton Park, Abingdon, OX14 4RN, United Kingdom; subscriptions@tandf.co.uk; http://www.tandfonline.com. Illus., adv. Sample. Refereed. Reprint: PSC. *Indexed:* A01, A22, A47, AmHI, C45, E01, IBSS, MLA-IB, P61. *Aud.:* Ac, Sa.

This peer-reviewed, international, interdisciplinary journal, editorially based at the University of the Witwatersrand, South Africa, is published three times a year. The journal encourages dialogue between scholars and "aims to publish high quality conceptual and empirical writing relevant to Africa." The disciplines that the journal focuses on "include but are not limited to: anthropology, critical race, gender and sexuality studies, geography, history, literary, cultural and media studies, sociology, and politics." Each issue includes 10 to 12 articles; some issues contain announcements, some have review articles. Special issues devoted to specific themes are frequently published. This journal—available in print and online—is recommended for academic and public library audiences. Tables of contents and full-text articles of current issues are available for download by subscribers and for purchase by non-subscribers at Taylor & Francis Online. URL: http://www.tandfonline.com/toc/cast20/current

197. *African Studies Quarterly: the online journal of African studies.* [ISSN: 2152-2448] 1997. q. Free. Ed(s): R Hunt Davis, Anna Mwaba. University of Florida, Center for African Studies, 427 Grinter Hall, PO Box 115560, Gainesville, FL 32611; http://www.africa.ufl.edu/. Illus., adv. Refereed. *Indexed:* BRI, IBSS. *Bk. rev.:* 5-15, 500-1,000 words. *Aud.:* Ac.

This is an electronic journal published quarterly by the Center for African Studies at the University of Florida, Gainesville. The online open-access journal is "dedicated to publishing the finest scholarship relating to the African continent." This interdisciplinary, refereed academic journal focuses on contemporary Africa. It includes both research and opinion in a full range of topics related to Africa in all areas. The diversity of coverage is evident in a recent issue with articles from a wide range of authors on diverse topics including: "Identity Management: The Creation of Resource Allocative Criteria in Botswana"; "Democratization and Public Accountability at the Grassroots in Tanzania: A Missing Link"; "Ethnicity, Violence and the Narrative of Genocide: The Dangers of a Third Term in Rwanda"; "Rich Undisciplined and Poetic: A New Writing of the Colonial Past." Each issue features approximately six to ten articles, an extensive book review section, and frequent review essays. *ASQ* also publishes special issues that focus on a specific theme with guest editors. This freely available online journal is recommended for an academic library audience and the book review section is a useful tool for collection development. URL: http://web.africa.ufl.edu/asq

198. *African Studies Review.* Incorporates (1975-1980): *A S A Review of Books;* Formerly (until 1970): *African Studies Bulletin;* Which incorporated (1962-1964): *Africana Newsletter.* [ISSN: 0002-0206] 1958. 4x/yr. GBP 393 (print & online eds.)). Ed(s): Shawn Redding, Elliot Fratkin. Cambridge University Press, University Printing House, Shaftesbury Rd, Cambridge, CB2 8BS, United Kingdom; journals@cambridge.org; https://www.cambridge.org/. Illus., adv. Refereed. Vol. ends: Dec (No. 3). *Indexed:* A01, A22, A47, BRI, E01, IBSS, MLA-IB. *Bk. rev.:* Number and length vary. *Aud.:* Ga, Ac.

ASR is a multidisciplinary journal published three times a year (April, September, and December) by Cambridge University Press for the African Studies Association. It is the principal academic and scholarly journal of the ASA. *ASR* states that its mission is "to publish the highest quality articles, as well as book and film reviews in all academic disciplines that are of interest to the interdisciplinary audience of ASA members." The journal aims to encourage scholarly debates across disciplines. Each issue "contains articles based on original research and analysis of Africa," which are written by international scholars. Extensive book reviews are categorized by subject. Film reviews are categorized by feature and documentary films. Both book and film reviews are preceded by review essays. This title also includes commentaries and a list of books received. It is a good resource for library collection development and a must-have for Africana collections, and is recommended for academic libraries. It is available in print and online. Tables of contents, article-abstracts preview, and subscription information are available at the Cambridge University Press website. URL: http://journals.cambridge.org/actiondisplayJournal?jid=ASR

199. *African Vibes: your connection to contemporary Africa.* [ISSN: 1932-1198] 2006. bi-m. USD 3.95 newsstand/cover. African Vibes, PO Box 10203, Canoga Park, CA 91309. Adv. *Aud.:* Ga.

African Vibes is a lifestyle, fashion, and beauty magazine that covers contemporary Africans and Africa. It states its "mission is to connect the world to contemporary Africa and Africans from a positive and uplifting perspective." The content featured is educative, empowering, and motivating. Topics covered include fashion, business, arts and entertainment, food, sports, arts, relationships, and health. Focused on the African diaspora, it claims to be "the pulse of the dynamic African culture, serving up a mix of celebrity, fashion and entertainment news along with in-depth profiles of the most influential and fascinating African personalities." Recommended for public library audiences. Available for subscription in print and online editions. URL: www.africanvibes.com

200. *Afrique Contemporaine: Afrique et developpement.* [ISSN: 0002-0478] 1962. q. EUR 65 domestic; EUR 65 Belgium; EUR 75 elsewhere. Agence Francaise de Developpement, 5 Rue Roland-Barthes, Paris Cedex 12, 75598, France. Illus., index, adv. Circ: 2000. *Indexed:* A22, IBSS, MLA-IB, PdeR. *Bk. rev.:* 95, 50-100 words. *Aud.:* Ac, Sa.

This is a quarterly, peer-reviewed, academic journal published by l'Agence Francaise de Developpement (AFD). This French-language journal focuses on development trends, politics, and economics, and other issues relating to the African continent, as well as international relations in contemporary Africa. It aims to communicate the analysis and opinions of researchers and various French and foreign specialists involved in the development of the African continent as it is aimed toward achieving *sustainable* development. Full-text translations of selected articles in English are available on the journal website. Brief biographies and interviews are included. *Afrique Contemporaine* includes brief book annotations classed by country and topic. Supplements accompany some issues. Recommended for an academic library audience. Available both in print and online editions. Abstracts and tables of contents available at the journal's website. URL: www.cairn.info/revue-afrique-contemporaine.htm

201. *Afrique Magazine.* Former titles (until 1989): *Jeune Afrique Magazine;* (until 1986): *J A Magazine;* (until 1985): *Jeune Afrique Magazine.* [ISSN: 0998-9307] 1981. m. 10/yr. EUR 29. Afrique et Mediterranee International, 31 Rue Poussin, Paris, 75016, France; http://www.afriquemagazine.com/. Adv. Circ: 55000. *Bk. rev.:* Occasional. *Aud.:* Hs, Ga, Ac.

One of several glossy publications from Le Groupe Jeune Afrique. This is a French-language consumer magazine aimed at youthful, upwardly mobile Africans and diasporic Africans. Coverage ranges from lifestyle articles and features on international figures to food, health, sports, fashion, travel, and music. The magazine is mostly informational, but more serious subjects are treated. It is recommended for academic and large public library audiences. This magazine is available for subscription in print only. Summaries of contents of the current issue are available on the magazine's website. URL: www.afriquemagazine.com/

202. *Azania: archaeological research in Africa.* [ISSN: 0067-270X] 1966. q. GBP 264 (print & online eds.)). Ed(s): Peter Mitchell, Peter Robertshaw. Taylor & Francis, 2, 3 & 4 Park Sq, Milton Park, Abingdon, OX14 4RN, United Kingdom; subscriptions@tandf.co.uk; https://www.tandfonline.com. Illus., index, adv. Refereed. Reprint: PSC. *Indexed:* A01, A22, A47, E01, IBSS. *Bk. rev.:* 10-12. *Aud.:* Ac, Sa.

Azania: Archaeological Research in Africa is a journal of the British Institute in Eastern Africa and has been published since 1966. Azania is an ancient name for East Africa. This journal previously published papers only on the archaeology and precolonial history of Eastern Africa, and has expanded its scope and "now covers all aspects of African archaeology, regardless of temporal or spatial boundaries." It is published quarterly, and its peer-reviewed articles or briefer reports address fieldwork, new methodologies, and/or theoretical concerns, or provide a synthesis of key ideas. Articles are technical and accompanied by photos, graphs, and data. Papers may be in English or French, with abstracts in both languages. Available in print and online editions, *Azania* is recommended for an academic library audience, especially those with interest in archaeology and African Studies. Subscription information and tables of contents are available on the journal website. URL: http://www.tandfonline.com/toc/raza20

203. ***C O D E S R I A Bulletin.*** Formerly: *Africana Newsletter.* [ISSN: 0850-8712] 1987. q. Free to qualified personnel. Ed(s): Alexander Bangirana. Council for the Development of Social Science Research in Africa, Avenue Cheikh, Anta Diop x Canal IV, BP 3304, Dakar, , Senegal; codesria@ssonatel.senet.net. *Aud.:* Ac, Sa.

Based in Senegal, CODESRIA is an important pan-African research organization with a primary focus on the social sciences. The organization's *Bulletin* aims to stimulate discussion, encourage cooperation among African researchers, and facilitate an exchange of information on projects, new books, upcoming conferences, and reports on conferences and seminars. Short, accessible articles are grouped as "Debates" on a theme or topical issue, or alternatively as "Perspectives" on current concerns. The organization publishes several other journals, including *Africa Development* (see above in this section), the longest-standing Africa-based social science journal; *Afrika Zamani,* a journal of history; the *African Sociological Review* (see above in this section); and the *African Journal of International Affairs.* Subscription is available, and this title is distributed free to all social science research institutes and faculties in Africa to encourage research cooperation among African scholars. The *Bulletin* is available in English, French, and Arabic. Highly recommended for both academic and special library audiences. Tables of contents, abstracts, and the full text of articles are freely available online at the CODESRIA website. URL: www.codesria.org/spip.php?

204. ***Cahiers d'Etudes Africaines.*** [ISSN: 0008-0055] 1960. q. EUR 83 (Individuals, EUR 50). Ed(s): J L Amselle. College de France, Ecole des Hautes Etudes en Sciences Sociales (E H E S S), 105 bd Raspail, Paris, 75006, France; editions@ehess.fr; http://www.ehess.fr. Illus., adv. Sample. Microform: IDC. *Indexed:* A22, A47, IBSS, MLA-IB, P61, SSA. *Bk. rev.:* 9-14, 100-1,400 words. *Aud.:* Sa.

Cahiers d'Etudes Africaines is "an international and interdisciplinary bilingual journal (French and English) of the social sciences on Africa, West Indies and Black Africa." This title, in publication since 1960, claims its "role is to serve as a forum for social science research on Africa while refusing to remain imprisoned within a specific cultural arena." "Articles published reflect new trends of research, theoretical and from the field and the discussions they generate." In addition to being interdisciplinary, the journal also promotes an anthropological and historical approach to dealing with Africa and the diaspora. Special thematic volumes with essays on a region or a problem are issued frequently. Review essays, critical book reviews, and a list of publications received are included. Recommended for academic and special library audiences. Available for subscription in print and online editions. Articles and abstracts are available at the journal's website. URL: http://etudesafricaines.revues.org/?lang=en; also https://www.cairn.info/revue-cahiers-d-etudes-africaines.htm

205. ***Canadian Journal of African Studies.*** Formerly (until 1967): *Bulletin of African Studies in Canada.* [ISSN: 0008-3968] 1963. 3x/yr. GBP 323 (print & online eds.)). Ed(s): Roger Riendeau, Christopher Youe. Routledge, 4 Park Sq, Milton Park, Abingdon, OX14 4RN, United Kingdom; subscriptions@tandf.co.uk; http://www.tandfonline.com. Illus. Sample. Refereed. Reprint: PSC. *Indexed:* A22, C45, MLA-IB, PdeR. *Bk. rev.:* 30-40, 500-1,000 words. *Aud.:* Ac, Sa.

This scholarly, multi-disciplinary, bilingual journal "publishes articles principally in the areas of anthropology, political economy, history, geography, and development of the continent." The *Canadian Journal of African Studies/ Revue canadienne des etudies africaines* is the official publication of the Canadian Association of African Studies (CAAS). It is committed to facilitating the dissemination of social science research by Africanists worldwide. Most articles appear in English, unless the theme of an issue is a Francophone country. *CJAS* "aims to improve knowledge and awareness of Africa as well as the problems and aspirations of its people, to inform Canadian policy on and in Africa, and to generate public interest in the study and understanding of Africa in Canada." Articles are original research papers in the areas of anthropology/ ethnography, political science, history, sociology, literature, human geography, and development. In addition to original research papers featured sections in each issue include debates and commentaries, book reviews, and a review essay. The extensive reviews and essays serve as a valuable resource for scholars and librarians to stay abreast of research, debates, and publications in the field of African Studies. Some issues include "Research Notes," where contributors present research in progress on African topics. Special thematic issues appear occasionally. Recommended for academic and special library audiences. Available both in print and online; subscription information is on the journal's website. Tables of contents and abstracts are also on the website. URL: http://www.tandfonline.com/toc/rcas20/current

206. ***Communications Africa.*** [ISSN: 0962-3841] 1991. bi-m. Free to qualified personnel. Ed(s): Hiriyti Bairu. Alain Charles Publishing Ltd., University House, 11-13 Lower Grosvenor Pl, London, SW1W 0EX, United Kingdom; post@alaincharles.com; http://www.alaincharles.com. Adv. *Aud.:* Ga, Sa.

Communications Africa/Afrique is a bilingual (English and French) communications technology and broadcast magazine. It is one of a group of Africa-related magazines published by U.K.-based Alain Charles Publishing. It is an essential source of information on telecommunications, broadcasting, and information technology in Africa. Published bimonthly, this magazine is primarily of interest to mobile operators, Internet service providers, local integrators and resellers of hardware and software, broadcasters, and regulators. Featured articles have regional relevance to the public, telecommunication specialists, and the private sector. It is designed to inform them of the latest technologies available to enhance their businesses. Each issue of the magazine includes regional news reports, a country focus, new technological trends, market updates, and exhibition previews and round-ups. The magazine is suitable for general, special, and academic audiences. Subscription to the print edition is free for qualified recipients and a digital edition is downloadable at the magazine website. Also freely available on the website is an archive of past issues dating back to 2012. The website has a weekly news digest reporting on latest news about the industry. URL: http://www.communicationsafrica.com/

207. ***Country Reports.*** 1971. q. Economist Intelligence Unit Ltd., 750 Third Ave, 5th Fl, New York, NY 10017; americas@eiu.com; https://www.eiu.com. *Aud.:* Ga, Ac, Sa.

Published by the Economist Intelligence Unit, this series of analytical reports aims to assist with executive business decisions by providing timely and impartial analysis on worldwide market trends and business strategies for close to 200 countries. The quarterly reports monitor and analyze developments and trends in politics, policy, and economy. Placing recent events in context, the reports provide a two-year outlook for each country. Graphs and charts illustrate the economic trends and data. Subscriptions per country for print or web access include quarterly main reports and a country profile—an annual reference tool that analyzes political, infrastructural, and economic trends over the longer term. From the same group that publishes *The Economist* and *EIU ViewsWire, Country Reports* is a reliable, longstanding source of data and country intelligence. Online access provides timely updates, downloadable Excel tables, HTML or PDF viewing and archives back to 1996. This is an expensive publication; recommended for general, academic, and special collections; specialized collections may want to consider reports on particular countries of interest rather than the entire set.

208. ***Current Writing: text and reception in southern Africa.*** [ISSN: 1013-929X] 1989. s-a. GBP 214 (print & online eds.)). Ed(s): J U Jacobs. Routledge, 4 Park Sq, Milton Park, Abingdon, OX14 4RN, United Kingdom; subscriptions@tandf.co.uk; http://www.tandfonline.com. Illus., index. Refereed. Vol. ends: Oct. Reprint: PSC. *Indexed:* BRI, MLA-IB. *Bk. rev.:* 15-20, 300-1,200 words. *Aud.:* Ac, Sa.

Current Writing is the official journal of the Southern African Association for Commonwealth Literature and Languages (SAACLALS). Originally conceived by four members of the Department of English at the University of Natal (now the University of KwaZulu-Natal) it has been in publication since 1989, first as an annual and biannually since 1993. It includes essays on contemporary and republished texts in southern Africa and on the interpretation of world texts from a southern African perspective. Scholars from southern Africa are the primary contributors. The review section is an important part of the journal, in which new publications are evaluated. The journal issues the "general" issue in April with articles dealing with a range of interests, and the "theme" issue in October, with articles devoted to a particular topic or theme. The journal is of interest to those studying the development in writing and literature in southern Africa. Writing style and content were greatly influenced by political and social changes in the region. This journal is suitable for comprehensive academic and special collections. Subscription information, tables of contents, and abstracts are available on the journal's website. URL: http://www.tandfonline.com/toc/rcwr20/current

209. *Drum: Africa's leading magazine beating to the pulse of the times.* [ISSN: 0419-7674] 1951. w. ZAR 873.60; ZAR 21 newsstand/cover. Ed(s): Charlene Rolls. Media24 Ltd., PO Box 7167, Roggebaai, 8012, South Africa; letters@drum.co.za; http://www.media24.com. Illus., adv. *Indexed:* MLA-IB. *Bk. rev.:* Number and length vary. *Aud.:* Hs, Ga, Ac.

Drum (South Africa) is a popular consumer-oriented magazine published in South Africa since 1951, and it continues to be an integral part of the South African popular media landscape. Mainly aimed at black readers, it is considered part of every black South African's daily life and serves as a unique vehicle for black expression. Content includes market news, entertainment, and feature articles. Sports heroes, models, political figures, and celebrities are featured on the cover of each weekly issue. Sections on children, women, and entertainment appear in most issues, in addition to regular columns that offer advice, horoscopes, puzzles, and so on. This title can be compared to both *People* and *The National Enquirer. Drum* reflects the multicultural, middle-class, youth-oriented "new" country that is South Africa. Highly recommended for all types of library audiences as a colorful and appealing popular source that offers insight on the values and aspirations of South Africans. Available now in digital and print editions; subscription information is available at the magazine's website. URL: http://drum.co.za/

210. *Eastern Africa Social Science Research Review.* [ISSN: 1027-1775] 1985. 2x/yr. USD 23 in Africa; USD 35 elsewhere. Ed(s): Mohamed Salih, Bahru Zewde. Organization for Social Science Research in Eastern Africa, PO Box 31971, Addis Ababa, , Ethiopia; pub.ossrea@telecom.net.et; http://www.ossrea.net. Refereed. Circ: 500. *Indexed:* A22, C45, E01, P61. *Bk. rev.:* Number and length vary. *Aud.:* Ac, Sa.

The Organization for Social Science Research in Eastern Africa (OSSREA), based in Ethiopia, publishes this biannual journal. This interdisciplinary journal's main focus is on the social sciences. *EASSRR* "serves as a regional forum for critical reflection and discourse on the economic, political, and social aspects as well as development concerns of the countries in Eastern and Southern Africa." It contains scholarly articles, book reviews, and shorter communications that are presumed to be of interest to development planners and policymakers, as well as academics. Recent issues have explored the gender differences in the migration of Zimbabwean teachers to South Africa and the situation of street children in selected cities in South Sudan. It is a consistent venue for African scholars and is highly recommended for academic and special library audiences. This journal is available for subscription in print and online editions. Tables of contents, abstracts, and back issues dating back to 2000 are available through African Journals Online. URL: https://www.ajol.info/index.php/eassrr/index

211. *English in Africa.* [ISSN: 0376-8902] 1974. 3x/yr. ZAR 270 (Individuals, ZAR 245; USD 74 foreign). Ed(s): Gareth Cornwell. Rhodes University, Institute for the Study of English in Africa, PO Box 94, Grahamstown, 6140, South Africa; isea@ru.ac.za; http://www.ru.ac.za/isea. Illus., index, adv. Refereed. Vol. ends: May/Oct (No. 2). *Indexed:* A01, A22, AmHI, IBSS, MLA-IB. *Bk. rev.:* Number and length vary. *Aud.:* Ac, Sa.

This title has been published since 1974 by the Institute for the Study of English in Africa at Rhodes University, Grahamstown, South Africa. *English in Africa* is a scholarly journal devoted to the study of African literature in English. Contributors are generally established writers or academics from South Africa, the United Kingdom, and the United States. It "specializes in publishing previously unpublished or out-of-print primary material, including articles and letters by writers of Africa. The journal also publishes scholarly articles on African writing in English with particular emphasis on research in new or under-researched areas in African literature." Most articles are historical or cultural studies rather than theoretical inquiries. Reviews, review articles, or discussions between writers regularly conclude each issue. There are often thematic issues. More literary and broader in scope than *Current Writing* (see above in this section), *English in Africa* is suitable for academic library audiences, especially institutions with a strong emphasis in English, cultural studies, or African Studies. Full-text articles are now available through several subscription databases. Tables of contents, abstracts and archives dating back 2007 are available at African Journals Online. URL: https://www.ajol.info/index.php/eia/index

212. *FabAfriq Magazine.* [ISSN: 2050-2168] 2011. q. GBP 2.95 per issue. Ed(s): Manyi Takor. FabInspired CIC, 67 Christchurch Close, Edgbaston, Birmingham, B15 3NE, United Kingdom. Adv. Circ: 60000. *Aud.:* Ga.

FabAfriq is a quarterly general-interest magazine offering culture and lifestyle information for people of black origin and other individuals interested in African culture. The stated purpose of the magazine is to challenge and dispel the stereotypes and myths about Africa and people of black origin. Published in Birmingham, United Kingdom, this colorful magazine features photographs and informative articles on issues affecting quality of life. Regular features include fashion; lifestyle; sports; tourism; cuisine; health; and culture. Articles cover relationships, health and fitness, fashion and beauty, African society weddings, finance, career tips, parenting, and more. The magazine's covers usually feature up and coming African models, sports icons, and various African celebrities. The magazine is available on subscription in print and online editions at the website. URL: http://www.fabafriq.com/home

213. *Glam Africa.* [ISSN: 2057-7516] 2015. q. Ed(s): Fadakemi Sulaiman. Glam Africa, http://www.glamafrica.com/. *Aud.:* Ga.

Glam Africa is a quarterly glossy magazine that "connects readers to the latest African style and beauty trends." Available in print and online editions, it is one of the many new Pan-African glossy magazines (*New African Woman* and *Move!*) (see below in this section) that portray the modern African woman as strong and proud of her heritage. It uses a team, including African writers, from different parts of the world, to provide a multi-platform approach to deliver dynamic content. This allows its readers to appreciate the talent and contribution of Africans in different parts of the continent and in the diaspora. Articles are current and engaging. Topics include fashion, hair and beauty, lifestyle, food, events, and travel. *Glam Africa* makes for interesting reading; each edition has its own celebrity cover and is packed with colorful images and editorials, in-depth interviews with top celebrities and exciting individuals. The magazine includes simple fashion and beauty ideas, tips and product features that are both relevant and easily accessible. It is recommended for a general audience. The magazine is distributed in the United Kingdom, Nigeria, Ghana, South Africa, and the rest of the world through online sales and subscriptions. URL: http://www.glamafrica.com/

214. *History in Africa: journal of method.* [ISSN: 0361-5413] 1974. a. GBP 181 (print & online eds.)). Ed(s): Michel Doortmont, Dimitri van den Bersselaar. Cambridge University Press, 1 Liberty Plaza, Fl 20, New York, NY 10004; journals@cambridge.org; https://www.cambridge.org. Illus., adv. Refereed. *Indexed:* A22, A47, E01, IBSS, MLA-IB. *Aud.:* Ac, Sa.

History in Africa is published annually by Cambridge University Press for the African Studies Association, United States. This publication "focuses on historiographical and methodological concerns and publishes textual analysis and criticism, historiographical essays, bibliographical essays, archival reports and articles on the role of theory and non-historical data in historical investigation." Articles focus on all aspects of African history and culture, archival research, and reports from within Africa. This title is an important resource for history-teaching programs, and the essays often reflect new trends in African historical research. Like its sister publication *African Studies Review* (see below in this section) abstracts are in English and French. The journal is a valuable resource for historians, researchers, and advanced graduate students. It is an essential journal for institutions that support African history programs, and is highly recommended as a basic journal for academic libraries. Tables of contents, article abstracts, and subscription information is available at the Cambridge University Press website. URL: https://www.cambridge.org/core/journals/history-in-africa

215. *International Journal of African Historical Studies.* Formerly (until 1972): *African Historical Studies.* [ISSN: 0361-7882] 1968. 3x/yr. Ed(s): Michael DiBlasi. Boston University, African Studies Center, 232 Bay State Rd, Boston, MA 02215; ascpub@bu.edu; http://www.bu.edu/africa. Illus., index. Refereed. Vol. ends: No. 3. *Indexed:* A01, A22, A47, AmHI, BRI, IBSS, MLA-IB. *Bk. rev.:* 65-80, 500-800 words. *Aud.:* Ac, Sa.

Published at the African Studies Center at Boston University, this scholarly journal covers all aspects of African history with a "focus on the study of the African past" in Africa and the African diaspora. Norman Bennett, who founded the journal as *African Historical Studies* in 1968, remained the editor for more than 30 years and was the guiding force behind the journal's growth. The journal publishes three issues each year (April, August, and December). Articles, notes, and documents are based on original research and framed in terms of historical analysis. Article topics include archaeology, history, anthropology, historical ecology, political science, political ecology, and economic history. Each issue contains several in-depth articles. Special thematic issues are published. There is an extensive book review section in each issue, and a "books received" section in the first issue of each volume; and the frequent review essays make this journal a significant collection-development tool. Available in print and online editions. It is recommended for academic collections and large public libraries. Subscription information and PDF and back issue purchase information is available at the journal website. URL: www.bu.edu/africa/publications/ijahs/

216. ***Islamic Africa.*** Formerly (until 2010): *Sudanic Africa.* [ISSN: 2333-262X] 1995. s-a. EUR 172. Brill, PO Box 9000, Leiden, 2300 PA, Netherlands; marketing@brill.com; https://brill.com. Index, adv. Refereed. Reprint: PSC. *Bk. rev.:* Number and length vary. *Aud.:* Ac, Sa.

Islamic Africa is a peer-reviewed, multidisciplinary, academic journal published online and in print, in collaboration with the Institute for the Study of Islamic Thought in Africa (ISITA) at the Program of African Studies of Northwestern University. It "publishes original research concerning Islam in Africa from the social sciences and the humanities, as well as primary source material and commentary essays related to Islamic Studies in Africa." Incorporating the journal *Sudanic Africa,* this title promotes the interaction between scholars of Islam and Africa across historical periods. Its "geographic scope includes the entire African continent and adjacent islands." Some issues feature in-depth introductory essays. Each issue contains about three in-depth book reviews. Published twice a year, this title is suitable for academic and special library audiences, especially in institutions with Islamic Studies and African Studies programs. Subscription information is available at: www.brill.com/products/journal/islamic-africa

217. ***Jeune Afrique.*** Former titles (until 2006): *L' Intelligent;* (until 2000): *Jeune Afrique.* [ISSN: 1950-1285] 1960. w. 44/yr. EUR 124 domestic; EUR 154 in Europe; EUR 174 in North Africa. Ed(s): Bechir Ben Yahmed. Groupe Jeune Afrique, 57 bis, Rue d'Auteuil, Paris, 75016, France; redaction@jeuneafrique.com; http://www.groupeja.com. Illus., adv. Circ: 100000. Microform: PQC. *Indexed:* A22, PdeR. *Aud.:* Ga, Ac, Sa.

Jeune Afrique is the flagship French-language weekly newsmagazine of Groupe Jeune Afrique. Published in Paris in print and online editions, it claims to be the most popular French-language news weekly in the world. The group also publishes an English-language monthly, *The Africa Report* (see below in this section). The glossy, colorful, weekly magazine's format is similar to weekly newsmagazines in the United States. For almost 60 years it has provided in-depth coverage of African and international news, leveraging its continent-wide network of journalists with African expertise. It consistently reports on all the countries of the continent providing insights and content related to the vital concerns of Africa as well as discussing Africa's relationship with other parts of the world. Magazine issues include incisive analysis of the fast-changing political and economic landscapes in Africa today. It has very good coverage of North Africa and Francophone sub-Saharan African countries. Each issue has news, opinion columns, and interpretative and editorial commentary on Africa. It includes feature articles on international, political, cultural, and economic developments. Recommended for general, special, and academic collections. To complement the weekly publication, the magazine's website shares daily updates to political, business, and sports news in text and video. Also available on the website is information on subscription packages. URL: www.jeuneafrique.com

218. ***Journal of African Cultural Studies.*** Formerly (until 1998): *African Languages and Cultures.* [ISSN: 1369-6815] 1988. q. GBP 460 (print & online eds.)). Ed(s): Carli Coetzee. Routledge, 4 Park Sq, Milton Park, Abingdon, OX14 4RN, United Kingdom; subscriptions@tandf.co.uk; http://www.tandfonline.com. Illus., index, adv. Sample. Refereed. Vol. ends: Dec. Reprint: PSC. *Indexed:* A01, A22, A47, AmHI, BRI, E01, IBSS, MLA-IB, P61. *Aud.:* Ac, Sa.

This is an international journal that provides "a forum for perceptions of African culture from inside and outside Africa, with a special commitment to African scholarship." It evolved from the journal *African Languages and Cultures,* founded in 1988 in the Department of the Languages and Cultures of Africa at the School of Oriental and African Studies, London. This title's focus is on the dimensions of African culture, including African literature (oral and written), "performance arts, visual arts, music, cinema, the role of the media, the relationship between culture and power, as well as issues within such fields as popular culture in Africa, sociolinguistic topics of cultural interest, and culture and gender." Articles featured are mostly original research. This journal occasionally publishes a "contemporary conversations section," where authors respond to current issues. Special thematic issues are issued frequently. Some articles in this journal are freely available online due to Taylor & Francis Open Select option for authors. Recommended for academic and special libraries with Africana, cultural studies, and literature and linguistics collections. Tables of contents and abstracts are available on the journal's website. URL: www.tandfonline.com/toc/cjac20/current

219. ***Journal of African Economies.*** [ISSN: 0963-8024] 1992. 5x/yr. EUR 855. Ed(s): Francis Teal. Oxford University Press, Great Clarendon St, Oxford, OX2 6DP, United Kingdom; onlinequeries.uk@oup.com; http://global.oup.com. Illus., adv. Sample. Refereed. Reprint: PSC. *Indexed:* A22, B01, C45, E01, EconLit, IBSS. *Bk. rev.:* 1-5, 800-1,200 words. *Aud.:* Ac, Sa.

This scholarly journal offers "rigorous economic analysis, focused entirely on Africa, for Africans and anyone interested in the continent." Tables, graphs, and data often accompany articles that cover theories on African fiscal and monetary policies, trade, agricultural labor, and production. Book reviews and annotated listings of recent working papers in developmental economics are featured in some issues. Supplements featuring the plenary papers of the African Economic Research Consortium (AERC) are issued occasionally. The journal's focus is on audiences within and beyond academia. This title is valuable to consultants, policymakers, traders, financiers, development agents, and aid workers. It is expensive but highly recommended for large academic, special, and public libraries. Online access is available to subscribers, and the site also offers the option to purchase individual articles for a fee. Free or reduced-cost online access is offered to institutions in developing countries. Tables of contents and abstracts are available on the journal's website. URL: https://academic.oup.com/jae

220. ***The Journal of African History.*** [ISSN: 0021-8537] 1960. 3x/yr. GBP 344. Ed(s): Richard Reid, Lynn M. Thomas. Cambridge University Press, University Printing House, Shaftesbury Rd, Cambridge, CB2 8BS, United Kingdom; journals@cambridge.org; https://www.cambridge.org/. Illus., index, adv. Sample. Refereed. Circ: 2000. Microform: PQC. Reprint: PSC. *Indexed:* A01, A22, A47, AmHI, BRI, E01, IBSS, MLA-IB, P61, SSA. *Bk. rev.:* 20-35, 500-1,400 words. *Aud.:* Ac, Sa.

JAH, published by Cambridge University Press, issues "articles and book reviews ranging widely over the African past, from ancient times to the present." The range of topics covered is broad, including social, economic, political, cultural, and intellectual history. Articles have also explored themes that are of growing interest to historians of other regions, such as gender roles, demography, health and hygiene, propaganda, legal ideology, labor histories, nationalism and resistance, environmental history, the construction of ethnicity, slavery and the slave trade, and photographs as historical sources. Research articles in *JAH* issues are grouped in thematic sections. Journal issues occasionally feature the *JAH* "Forum," consisting of two or more essays from invited scholars on a topic of broad interest within African history and beyond. The in-depth reviews of books section are a good resource for library collection development. Online access is available to subscribers. This journal is highly recommended for academic libraries and special libraries with interest in African Studies and history. A searchable digital archive, with all the articles published from 1960 to 1996, is available from the publishers. Tables of contents, abstracts, and subscription information are available on the journal's website. URL: https://www.cambridge.org/core/journals/journal-of-african-history

221. *Journal of African Law.* [ISSN: 0021-8553] 1956. s-a. GBP 243. Ed(s): R. Murray, E. Onyema. Cambridge University Press, University Printing House, Shaftesbury Rd, Cambridge, CB2 8BS, United Kingdom; journals@cambridge.org; https://www.cambridge.org/. Adv. Refereed. Circ: 500. Microform: WSH; PMC. Reprint: PSC; WSH. *Indexed:* A01, A22, BRI, E01, IBSS, L14, MLA-IB. *Bk. rev.:* Number and length vary. *Aud.:* Ga, Ac, Sa.

Journal of African Law is published by Cambridge University Press for the School of Oriental and African Studies, at the University of London. Its coverage encompasses the laws of sub-Saharan African countries. The scope includes criminal law, family law, human rights, and nationality and constitutional law. One of the leading journals in the field, it has evolved from its earlier focus on legal pluralism and customary law to include a focus on issues of international law, post-conflict resolution, constitutionalism, and commercial law. Journal issues contain a separate section on recent legislation, case law, law reform proposals, and recent international developments affecting Africa. This journal is of interest to development workers, policymakers, and academics and professionals. Highly recommended for law libraries, public libraries, and special collections. It is available for subscription in print and online editions. Tables of contents are available on the journal's website. URL: https://www.cambridge.org/core/journals/journal-of-african-law

222. *Journal of Asian and African Studies.* [ISSN: 0021-9096] 1965. 8x/yr. USD 1532 (print & online eds.)). Ed(s): Nigel C Gibson. Sage Publications Ltd., 1 Oliver's Yard, 55 City Rd, London, EC1Y 1SP, United Kingdom; info@sagepub.com; https://www.sagepub.com/. Sample. Refereed. Reprint: PSC. *Indexed:* A01, A22, BAS, BRI, E01, IBSS, MLA-IB, P61. *Bk. rev.:* 2-3. *Aud.:* Ac, Sa.

JAAS is a peer-reviewed journal published since 1965 to further research and study on Asia and Africa. Published articles cover a wide range of topics including development and change, technology and communication, globalization, public administration, politics, economics, education, health, wealth and welfare, poverty and growth, social sciences, humanities, and linguistics. Each journal issue consists of "articles, research communications, and book reviews that focus on the dynamics of global change and development of Asian and African nations, societies, cultures, and the global community." Special issues are often published around certain themes. Available online and in print editions, it is quite expensive, and is suitable for academic collections. It offers "OnlineFirst," where forthcoming articles are published online before they are scheduled to appear in print. Tables of contents and abstracts are available on the journal's website. URL: http://jas.sagepub.com/

223. *Journal of Contemporary African Studies.* [ISSN: 0258-9001] 1981. q. GBP 1153 (print & online eds.)). Ed(s): Fred Hendricks. Routledge, 4 Park Sq, Milton Park, Abingdon, OX14 4RN, United Kingdom; subscriptions@tandf.co.uk; http://www.tandfonline.com. Illus., adv. Sample. Refereed. Vol. ends: No. 2. Reprint: PSC. *Indexed:* A01, A22, ASSIA, C45, E01, IBSS, MLA-IB, P61, SSA. *Bk. rev.:* 5-15, 500-1,000 words. *Aud.:* Ac, Sa.

This is an "interdisciplinary journal seeking to promote an African-centered scholarly understanding of societies on the continent and their location within the global political economy." The scope of the journal covers the social sciences and humanities. Topics covered include (but are not limited to) culture, development, education, gender, government, labor, land, leadership, politics, social movements, society, tourism, and welfare. Journal issues contain original research articles, book reviews, and occasional review essays. Special thematic issues are frequently published. It is expensive, but is an important selection on contemporary Africa, and is recommended for academic and special collections with a strong interest in Africa. It is available in print and online; subscription information, abstracts, and tables of contents are available on the journal's website. URL: www.tandfonline.com/loi/cjca20#.VXHeIkbqX-w

224. *Journal of Eastern African Studies.* [ISSN: 1753-1055] 2007. q. GBP 867 (print & online eds.)). Ed(s): Jason Mosley. Routledge, 4 Park Sq, Milton Park, Abingdon, OX14 4RN, United Kingdom; subscriptions@tandf.co.uk; http://www.tandfonline.com. Adv. Sample. Refereed. Reprint: PSC. *Indexed:* A22, A47, C45, E01, IBSS, P61. *Aud.:* Ac, Sa.

Journal of Eastern African Studies is a publication of the British Institute in Eastern Africa, published four times each year. East African regions covered include Kenya, Tanzania, Uganda, Ethiopia, South Sudan, Sudan, Somalia, Eritrea, Djibouti, Burundi, Rwanda, Democratic Republic of Congo, Mozambique, Malawi, Comoros, Mauritius, Seychelles, Reunion, Madagascar, Zambia, and Zimbabwe. Transnational topics that are meaningfully connected to this region are also covered. It features broad coverage in the humanities and the social sciences, and especially encourages interdisciplinary analysis and comparative perspectives, as well as research with significant theoretical or methodological approaches. The institute also produces the annual journal *Azania* (see above in this section), which is focused more specifically on the archaeology and history of East Africa. Pricey, this title is recommended for large academic libraries. Subscription information, abstracts, and tables of contents are available on the journal's website. URL: http://www.tandfonline.com/toc/rjea20/current

225. *Journal of Modern African Studies.* [ISSN: 0022-278X] 1963. q. GBP 407. Ed(s): Paul Nugent, Leonardo A Villalon. Cambridge University Press, University Printing House, Shaftesbury Rd, Cambridge, CB2 8BS, United Kingdom; journals@cambridge.org; https://www.cambridge.org/. Illus., index, adv. Sample. Refereed. Circ: 1600. Vol. ends: Dec. Microform: PQC. Reprint: PSC. *Indexed:* A01, A22, BAS, BRI, C45, E01, IBSS, MLA-IB, P61, SSA. *Bk. rev.:* 0-25, 500-2,000 words. *Aud.:* Ac, Sa.

The *Journal of Modern African Studies* "offers a quarterly survey of developments in modern African politics and society." This scholarly journal aims to present "a fair examination of controversial issues in order to promote a deeper understanding of what is happening in Africa today." It largely focuses on contemporary Africa, with an emphasis on politics, economics, societies, and international relations. The journal aims to publish original empirical research in order to illuminate broader issues affecting Africa, so research articles derived from fieldwork in Africa is of particular interest. Shorter pieces on literature, culture, and aspects of social history also appear. Articles are not overly technical or of a strict disciplinary approach; the intent is to make it accessible to any informed and interested reader. The journal includes an extensive book review section. This journal is suitable for students, academics, and general readers, and is highly recommended for academic libraries and special collections. It is available in print and online editions. Tables of contents, abstracts, and subscription information are available at the journal's website. URL: https://www.cambridge.org/core/journals/journal-of-modern-african-studies

226. *Journal of Religion in Africa.* Incorporates (1971-1975): *African Religious Research.* [ISSN: 0022-4200] 1967. q. EUR 411. Ed(s): Dianna Bell. Brill, PO Box 9000, Leiden, 2300 PA, Netherlands; marketing@brill.com; https://brill.com. Illus., adv. Refereed. Vol. ends: No. 4. Reprint: PSC. *Indexed:* A01, A22, A47, AmHI, E01, IBSS, MLA-IB, R&TA. *Bk. rev.:* 4-6, 750+ words. *Aud.:* Ac, Sa.

The *Journal of Religion in Africa* is a quarterly academic journal. Established in 1967, it is one of the leading international journals in religious studies. It focuses on religious traditions in all forms and on the history of religion and ritual within the African continent, particularly in sub-Saharan Africa. It is open to every methodology, and contributors are scholars working in history, anthropology, sociology, political science, missiology, literature, and related disciplines. This title occasionally publishes religious texts in their original African language. In addition to research articles, journal issues include book reviews; and longer review articles on works of special interest are regularly issued. Special issues on current topics are regularly published to highlight emerging themes. As one of the few English-language journals with a focus on religion in Africa, it is recommended for academic libraries, and libraries with religious studies, humanities, and social science collections. It is available in print and online editions; subscription information and tables of contents are available at www.brill.com/journal-religion-africa

227. *Journal of Southern African Studies.* [ISSN: 0305-7070] 1974. bi-m. GBP 895 (print & online eds.)). Ed(s): Colin Stoneman. Routledge, 4 Park Sq, Milton Park, Abingdon, OX14 4RN, United Kingdom; subscriptions@tandf.co.uk; http://www.tandfonline.com. Illus., adv. Sample. Refereed. Microform: PQC. Reprint: PSC. *Indexed:* A01, A22, A47, AmHI, C45, E01, IBSS, MLA-IB, P61, SSA. *Bk. rev.:* 4-6, 200-1,000 words. *Aud.:* Ac, Sa.

The *Journal of Southern African Studies* publishes original research articles on issues of interest and concern in the region of Southern Africa. "It aims to generate fresh scholarly inquiry and exposition in the fields of history, economics, sociology, demography, social anthropology, geography, administration, law, political science, international relations, literature and the natural sciences, insofar as they relate to the human condition." Countries of interest include the Republic of South Africa, Namibia, Botswana, Lesotho, and Swaziland; Angola and Mozambique; Zambia, Malawi, and Zimbabwe; and occasionally, Zaire, Tanzania, Madagascar, and Mauritius. Journal issues often include six to ten extensive articles, review essays, and book reviews. Special thematic issues are occasionally published. The journal is a bit pricey, but will be a good addition to the collections of large academic and special libraries. Available in print and online editions. Tables of contents and subscription information are available at www.tandfonline.com/toc/cjss20/current

228. *Journal of Sustainable Development in Africa.* [ISSN: 1520-5509] 1999. q. Free. Ed(s): Valentine Udoh James, Calvin O Masilela. Clarion University, 840 Wood St, Clarion, PA 16214; info@clarion.edu; http://www.clarion.edu. Refereed. *Indexed:* C45. *Bk. rev.:* 2 per issue. *Aud.:* Ac, Sa.

Journal of Sustainable Development in Africa is a refereed online journal published four times a year. It addresses the policy components of Africa's development issues. "The journal focuses on debates of development; development paradigms; social, cultural, economic, and ecological sustainability and the politics of sustainable development with regard to governance." Contributors to the journal are scholars of Africa, with many years of experience working in Africa. Articles cover both broad and local topics. There are four or five articles and a book review in each issue. Slightly behind in publication, this open-access journal is accessible at the journal's website. URL: www.jsd-africa.com/

229. *The Journal of the Middle East and Africa.* [ISSN: 2152-0844] 2010. s-a. GBP 249 (print & online eds.)). Ed(s): J Peter Pham. Taylor & Francis Inc., 711 3rd Ave, 8th Fl, New York, NY 10017; support@tandfonline.com; http://www.tandfonline.com. Adv. Sample. Refereed. Reprint: PSC. *Indexed:* A01. *Bk. rev.:* Number and length vary. *Aud.:* Ga, Ac, Sa.

The Journal of the Middle East and Africa serves as the flagship publication of the Association for the Study of the Middle East and Africa (ASMEA). This journal aims at "exploring the historic social, economic, and political links between these two regions, as well as the modern challenges they face." It is one of the first peer-reviewed academic journals that provide combined inclusion of the two regions. Interdisciplinary in nature, the journal approaches the regions from the perspectives of Middle Eastern and African Studies as well as anthropology, economics, history, international law, political science, religion, security studies, women's studies, and other disciplines of the social sciences and humanities. Each issue of the journal has approximately six to eight articles; also included are commentaries and book reviews. Still relatively new, it is a journal that should not be overlooked. Recommended for African Studies and Middle Eastern collections in academic libraries. Available in print and online, dues-paying members of ASMEA receive journal issues. Tables of contents, abstracts, archives of issues from 2010 and subscription information are available at the journal's website. URL: www.tandfonline.com/toc/ujme20/. Journal information, TOC, and an archive of issues from 2007 is available on the ASMEA website. URL: http://www.asmeascholars.org/publication/journal-of-the-middle-east-and-africa/

230. *The Maghreb Review.* [ISSN: 0309-457X] 1976. q. GBP 295. Ed(s): Mohamed Ben Madani. Maghreb Review, 45 Burton St, London, WC1H 9AL, United Kingdom. Illus. Refereed. *Indexed:* A22, IBSS, MLA-IB. *Bk. rev.:* 4-6, 2,000-4,000 words. *Aud.:* Ac, Sa.

Independent, interdisciplinary, and bilingual, this quarterly journal is one of the oldest English/French publications that are devoted to the study of North Africa and Islamic culture and religion. Its specific focus is the region of the Maghreb: Algeria, Tunisia, Libya, Morocco, and Mauritania. International scholars contribute articles on archaeology, anthropology, politics, history, religion, and literature—the spectrum of the social sciences and humanities—as they relate to the Berber, Arab, and Islamic heritage of this crossroads region and its interaction with sub-Saharan Africa, the Mediterranean, and the Middle East. Six to eight articles appear in each issue, some in both languages and some with translated abstracts. There are frequent special issues on topics of interest to the region. Abstracts of relevant theses or dissertations and conference papers are featured. Suitable for larger academic library audiences and special libraries with an interest in North Africa. Available only in print editions by subscription. URL: http://www.maghrebreview.com/

231. *Matatu: journal for African culture and society.* [ISSN: 0932-9714] 1987. s-a. EUR 294. Ed(s): John Njenga Karugia, Frank Schulze-Engler. Brill - Rodopi, PO Box 9000, Leiden, 2300 PA, Netherlands; marketing@brill.com; http://www.brill.com. Illus., adv. Refereed. Reprint: PSC. *Indexed:* A01, A22, MLA-IB, P61. *Aud.:* Ga, Ac, Sa.

Matatu, named for the crowded mini-buses used as public transport in East Africa, is a semi-annual refereed journal. It is a "journal on African literatures and societies dedicated to interdisciplinary dialogue between literary and cultural studies, historiography, the social sciences and cultural anthropology." The focus is on African (including Afro-Caribbean) culture and literature, providing a forum for critical debates and exploration of African modernities. While older issues of the journal have thematic titles, not all recent issues have specific themes. Articles, introductory essays, interviews, and autobiographical vignettes are just a few of the materials included in this journal. The journal is an excellent addition to the arts, literature, and cultural studies collections in academic libraries. Tables of contents are available at the journal's website. URL: http://booksandjournals.brillonline.com/content/journals/18757421

232. *Move!: a magazine for women.* [ISSN: 1813-5749] 2005. bi-w. Ed(s): Sbu Mpungose. Media24 Ltd., Naspers Centre, 40 Heerengracht St, PO Box 1802, Cape Town, 8000, South Africa; http://www.media24.com. Adv. *Aud.:* Ga.

Move! is an example of a new crop of African glossy magazines that celebrates modern women with messages of empowerment. It is one of South Africa's biggest selling women's weekly magazines aimed at women who want to improve their living standards. The magazine aims "to educate and empower young black women while entertaining them at the same time." This colorful and practical consumer magazine targets ordinary women while competing successfully on South African newsstands with international women's magazines like *Cosmopolitan* and *Homes and Gardens*. The magazine strives to cover issues that its readership identify with and featured stories provide relevant information. It offers readers accessible "tip driven advice and information for a fast paced, on-the-go lifestyle." Magazine issues are full of tips for successful living, including advice on religion, women's health, relationship, fashion and beauty, child rearing, financial and career, affordable shopping, and test recipes with familiar ingredients. Articles are "informative and empowering, knowledgeable and to-the-point, warm and caring but confident and friendly." Also featured are local gossip and celebrity news. This simple and practical magazine is recommended for a general audience. Available for subscription in print and digital editions. Select articles are featured on the magazine website. URL: http://movemag.co.za/

233. *New African.* Former titles (until 1978): *New African Development;* (until 1977): *African Development.* [ISSN: 0142-9345] 1966. 11x/yr. GBP 40 domestic; USD 90 United States; EUR 80 elsewhere. Ed(s): Baffour Ankomah. I C Publications Ltd., 7 Coldbath Sq, London, EC1R 4LQ, United Kingdom; icpublications@alliance-media.co.uk; http://www.icpublications.com/. Illus., adv. Sample. Circ: 55000. Microform: PQC. *Indexed:* A01, A22, BRI, MLA-IB. *Aud.:* Hs, Ga, Ac.

A glossy consumer newsmagazine from the same publisher as that of *African Business* (see above in this section) and *New African Woman* (see below in this section), *New African* covers the entire spectrum of contemporary African life: political reporting, economic and financial analysis, and articles on culture and social affairs. Each issue includes more than one cover story that deals with a major social or political issue or personality. The scope is pan-African and related to the diaspora, although most features focus on sub-Saharan Africa. Each issue has a section called "Around Africa," which reports on news from specific countries and presents longer special reports on a featured country. The letters and comments section contains comments from e-mail, Twitter feed, and Facebook. The same publisher releases the *New African Yearbook,* with facts and figures on each of the 53 countries. As one of the oldest monthly magazines, *New African* is recommended for all types of audiences. Available in print and online editions, subscription information can be found on the magazine website. The website offers summaries of the cover stories and the tables of contents, as well as full text of some special reports. URL: http://newafricanmagazine.com/magazine/

234. ***New African Woman.*** [ISSN: 1758-8383] 2009. bi-m. Ed(s): Regina Jane Jere-Malanda. I C Publications Ltd., 7 Coldbath Sq, London, EC1R 4LQ, United Kingdom. *Indexed:* C42. *Aud.:* Ga, Ac, Sa.

New African Woman is a bi-monthly glossy magazine that claims to be the "only women's publication covering the entire African continent and its Diaspora." *NAW* and its French edition *Femme Africaine* state they "offer intelligent, meaningful and inspirational features and news in areas that embrace and celebrate the African woman's diverse accomplishments and aspirations." Like its competitors *Glam Africa* and *Move!* (see above in this section), this colorful lifestyle magazine provides in-depth coverage on a diverse range of issues that truly speak to and resonate with the modern African woman worldwide. Feature articles range from fashion to politics, entrepreneurship to parenting, beauty to culture, health to women's rights and empowerment. *NAW* celebrates black beauty and culture with a unique indigenous twist. Articles provide insights into the life of the African woman in an intelligent, meaningful, and inspirational manner by mixing high-fashion glamour with features on powerful African women. Features also address serious issues. Like its sister publications *African Business* and *New African* (see above in this section), this magazine is very popular with the African diaspora as well as on the continent. Following its launch in 2009, *New African Woman* has become a popular must-read and is the only pan-African women's magazine distributed across the continent and its Diaspora. It is recommended for general, large academic, and special library audiences. It is available for subscription in print and some online full-text databases.

235. ***Nka: journal of contemporary African art.*** [ISSN: 1075-7163] 1994. s-a. USD 236. Ed(s): Okwui Enwezor, Chika Okeke-Agulu. Duke University Press, 905 W Main St, Durham, NC 27701; orders@dukeupress.edu; https://www.dukeupress.edu. Illus., adv. Refereed. Reprint: PSC. *Indexed:* A47, A51, MLA-IB. *Bk. rev.:* Number and length vary. *Aud.:* Ga, Ac, Sa.

Published by Duke University Press on behalf of Nka Publications. The aim of the journal is "to create an intellectual space for artists, writers, critics, art historians, and curators, in which the work of African artists could be examined with incisiveness, critical acuity, and theoretical reflection in such a way as to bring the subject of contemporary African art and artists to the international mainstream and to show why this work constitutes an important element of an expanded global contemporary art." This beautifully produced semi-annual journal covers contemporary African and African diaspora art from film to poetry to sculpture. *Nka* mainly includes scholarly articles, book and exhibit reviews, interviews, and roundtable discussions. The editors are art critics and curators. Available in print and online editions, it is a good choice for both public and academic libraries. Slightly delayed in publication. Tables of contents are available at http://nka.dukejournals.org/content/current.

236. ***Pambazuka News: Pan-African voices for freedom and justice.*** [ISSN: 1753-6839] 2000. w. Free. Ed(s): Ama Biney. Fahamu - Networks For Social Justice, Fahamu Trust, The Woolpack, 16 Church St, Oxford, OX12 8BL, United Kingdom; http://www.fahamu.org/. Adv. Circ: 26000 Free. *Bk. rev.:* Number and length vary. *Aud.:* Hs, Ga, Ac, Sa.

Pambazuka News is an online weekly newsletter published by Fahamu: Networks for Social Justice. *Fahamu,* means "understanding" or "consciousness" in Kiswahili, and the group named after this is an activist one formed in 1997 to strengthen and nurture the movement for social justice in Africa. *Pambazuka,* which means the "dawn" or "awakening" in Kiswahili, is a platform for analysis and debate for social justice in Africa. Its editorial office is based in Oxford, with offices around Africa; the newsletter is compiled in the South African office. This title has English, French, and Portuguese editions. Contributors to the newsletter are academics, policy makers, social activists, women's organizations, civil society organizations, writers, artists, poets, bloggers, and commentators. The newsletter is described as "providing a cutting edge commentary and in-depth analysis on politics and current affairs, development, human rights, refugees, gender issues and culture in Africa." In addition to articles, issues include podcasts, videocasts, in-depth book reviews, and brief synopses of books published by Pambazuka Press. Readers can submit comments on articles. Special thematic issues on social justice topics in Africa are issued frequently. It is recommended for academic, special, and general audiences who are interested in human rights, refugees, politics, and current affairs in Africa. It is freely available by e-mail subscription or at the newsletter website. URL: www.pambazuka.org/

237. ***Philosophia Africana: analysis of philosophy and issues in Africa and the Black Diaspora.*** Former titles (until 2001): *African Philosophy;* (until 1998): *S A P I N A Newsletter (Society for African Philosophy in North America);* (until 1995): *S A P I N A Bulletin;* (until 1993): *S A P I N A Newsletter.* [ISSN: 1539-8250] 1988. s-a. USD 132 (Individuals, USD 52). Ed(s): Kibujjo M Kalumba. Pennsylvania State University Press, 820 N University Dr, University Support Bldg 1, Ste C, University Park, PA 16802; info@psupress.org; http://www.psupress.org. Adv. Refereed. *Indexed:* A01, A22, AmHI, BRI, E01, MLA-IB. *Bk. rev.:* Number and length vary. *Aud.:* Ac, Sa.

This academic journal publishes "philosophical or philosophically interdisciplinary works that explore pluralistic experiences of Africa and the Black Diaspora from both universal and comparative points of view." Articles also may represent original or critical interpretations of creative and artistic works that are relevant to Africa and its diaspora. Book reviews and occasional conference reports are included. Special issues are occasionally published. This title is recommended for academic library audiences and special libraries that support African Studies and philosophy programs. Slightly behind in publication. Tables of contents and online access are provided by the Philosophy Documentation Center. URL: https://www.pdcnet.org/philafricana

238. ***Politique Africaine.*** [ISSN: 0244-7827] 1981. q. EUR 130 combined subscription domestic (print & online eds.); EUR 130 combined subscription in Europe (print & online eds.); EUR 130 combined subscription in North Africa (print & online eds.)). Ed(s): Richard Banegas. Editions Karthala, 22-24 Bd Arago, Paris, 75013, France; karthala@orange.fr; http://www.karthala.com. Illus., adv. Refereed. Circ: 3500. *Indexed:* A22, IBSS, MLA-IB. *Bk. rev.:* 20-25, 50-200 words. *Aud.:* Ac, Sa.

This French-language quarterly political science journal is published on behalf of the Association des chercheurs de Politique Africaine. It is a multidisciplinary, peer-reviewed journal centered on the analysis of politics in Africa. Its focus is on the developments taking place in Africa and its relations with the rest of the world. It includes articles devoted to a specific theme, or with focus on a particular country. The scope is the entire African continent, especially sub-Saharan Africa. Apart from the thematic articles, the remainder of each issue includes briefer articles, speeches, and recent political developments. It also includes major meeting and conference announcements, book reviews, and lists of books received. Recommended for academic libraries with interest in Francophone Africa. Tables of contents and abstracts in English are available online. A full-text archive (issues 1-72) is freely available on the journal's website. URL: www.politique-africaine.com

239. ***Presence Africaine: revue culturelle du monde noir.*** [ISSN: 0032-7638] 1947. s-a. Societe Africaine de Culture, 25 bis rue des Ecoles, Paris, 75005, France. Illus. Refereed. *Indexed:* A22, IBSS, MLA-IB. *Bk. rev.:* Number and length vary. *Aud.:* Ga, Ac, Sa.

Presence Africaine has a long and illustrious history, and remains the most influential French-language journal on Africa. It was founded in 1947 by Alioune Diop, a Senegalese intellectual and seminal figure in the discourse on Africa. Its early years coincided with the Pan-Africanist movement and struggles against colonialism, as well as the development of the "Negritude" movement. *PA* was the leading journal of anti-colonial intellectuals in France and Africa, and a major publisher of African writers. Issues feature critical and historical articles, book reviews and discussions, and creative writing. This journal remains important for all libraries with serious interest in Africa. Now bilingual (in French and English), *PA* remains a leading cultural journal of the African diaspora, and is indispensable for academic audiences, especially in institutions that support African Studies and literature. It is available for subscription in print edition only; tables of contents are available online. URL: www.cairn.info/revue.php?ID_REVUE=PRESA&NEXT=0

240. ***Research in African Literatures.*** [ISSN: 0034-5210] 1970. q. USD 219.45 (print & online eds.)). Ed(s): Molly Reinhoudt, Kwaku Larbi Korang. Indiana University Press, Office of Scholarly Publishing, Herman B Wells Library 350, Bloomington, IN 47405; iuporder@indiana.edu; http://iupress.indiana.edu/. Illus., index, adv. Refereed. Microform: PQC. Reprint: PSC. *Indexed:* A01, A22, AmHI, BRI, E01, ENW, F01, IBSS, MLA-IB. *Bk. rev.:* 5-21, 1,000-2,000 words. *Aud.:* Ac, Sa.

This quarterly journal is an essential source for scholarly study of the literatures of Africa. *RAL* includes scholarly essays; extensive bibliographies; and long reviews on all aspects of oral and written literatures, music, film, and theater of Africa. Articles are in English; but literatures in English, French, or African languages are included. The scope extends to the literature and arts of the black diaspora as well. Each issue contains up to 20 contributions, including discussions of short and long fiction, poetry, drama, important new writers, music, film, and theater, as well as literary developments. Book reviews, and often review essays, are featured. A forum offers readers the opportunity to respond to issues raised in articles and book reviews. Information is included on African publishing, and there are announcements of importance to Africanists. Each year, one or two special issues or groupings of articles explore themes. This journal is highly recommended for academic and large public libraries, and for anyone interested in African literature and literary criticism.

241. ***Review of African Political Economy.*** [ISSN: 0305-6244] 1974. q. GBP 752 (print & online eds.)). Routledge, 4 Park Sq, Milton Park, Abingdon, OX14 4RN, United Kingdom; subscriptions@tandf.co.uk; http://www.tandfonline.com. Illus., adv. Sample. Refereed. Reprint: PSC. *Indexed:* A22, B01, C45, E01, EconLit, IBSS, MLA-IB, P61, SSA. *Bk. rev.:* 4-7, 900-3,000 words. *Aud.:* Ac, Sa.

ROAPE is published by Routledge and Taylor & Francis Group for the ROAPE international collective. Published since 1974, it "provides radical analyses of trends, issues and social processes in Africa, adopting a broadly materialist interpretation of change." Topics covered include the "political economy of inequality, exploitation and oppression, whether driven by global forces or local ones (such as class, race, community and gender), and to materialist interpretations of change in Africa." Journal issues contain academic articles, debate pieces, briefings and commentary on current events relating to Africa, and a book reviews section. Each themed issue begins with an editorial, and contains five to nine articles. Highly recommended for academic and special library audiences. Free access to downloadable pdfs of all articles that are more than seven years old is available on the ROAPE collective website: www.roape.org/. Subscription information, tables of contents, and abstracts of current and back issues of the journal are available on the journal's website. The website also provides free access to current Briefings & Debates, which are generally short, topical, and informative pieces, including documents, "with a 'stop press' policy for urgent items." The debates take a position on a controversial topic, either engaging with a previous piece or inviting response. URL: http://www.tandfonline.com/toc/crea20/current

242. ***Transition: an international review.*** Former titles (until 1977): *Ch'indaba;* (until no.50, 1975): *Transition.* [ISSN: 0041-1191] 1961. 3x/yr. USD 172.15 (print & online eds.)). Ed(s): Alejandro de la Fuente. Indiana University Press, Office of Scholarly Publishing, Herman B Wells Library 350, Bloomington, IN 47405; iuporder@indiana.edu; http://iupress.indiana.edu/. Illus., adv. Vol. ends: Aug. Reprint: PSC. *Indexed:* A22, BRI, E01, MLA-IB. *Bk. rev.:* 2-3. *Aud.:* Ga, Ac, Sa.

Transition is published by Indiana University Press for the Hutchins Center for African and African American Research at Harvard University. It was founded in Uganda in 1961. It is regarded today as "the premier international forum for the freshest and most compelling ideas about race and ethnicity, giving voice to a new generation of literary legends." Revived as a new series by Henry Louis Gates in 1991, this magazine takes a critical look at culture, cultural icons, literature, visual imagery, and the arts. It features fiction, creative nonfiction, narrative journalism, art and cultural criticism, political commentary, interviews with important figures and thinkers, book and film reviews, and poetry. After some interruptions in recent years, the publication is back on track. The scope of *Transition* is not just Africa but the entire post-colonial world, with a multicultural perspective; it bills itself as "an international review of politics, culture, and ethnicity from Beijing to Bujumbura." It is led by highly respected scholars. Leading intellectuals and literati serve as board members and as contributors. The essays are clearly written, provocative, and engaging. Worthy of notice are the striking illustrations and photographs. A venue for cultural criticism, this journal is very highly recommended for academic and large public libraries. Selected full-text articles from the archive are freely available on the magazine's website. URL: http://hutchinscenter.fas.harvard.edu/transition

243. ***Ufahamu (Online): journal of African studies.*** [ISSN: 2150-5802] 1970. s-a. Free. Ed(s): Madina Thiam, Janice Levi. University of California, eScholarship, California Digital Library, 415 20th St, 4th Fl, Oakland, CA 94612; info@escholarship.org; https://www.escholarship.org. Illus., adv. Sample. Refereed. *Indexed:* A22. *Bk. rev.:* 1-2, 1,000-2,500 words. *Aud.:* Ga, Ac.

Published since 1970 by the African Activist Association, a graduate student organization at the University of California at Los Angeles, *Ufahamu* is "named after the Swahili word for comprehension, understanding, or being." The aim of the journal is to create "a forum and platform for Africans, people of African descent, students, academics, and non-academics to directly engage, create new methodological and thematic spaces, and challenge misconceptions about Africa and the African diaspora." Founded as a journal of opinion on social issues, it continues to provide an interdisciplinary forum for those whose approach is both scholarly and activist. It includes articles and essays on history, politics, economics, sociology, anthropology, law, and planning and development, as well as literature and the arts in the African continent and diaspora. Contributors to the journal are established writers and academics, as well as graduate students and non-academic researchers. Issues include book and exhibition reviews and occasionally short stories. Addressing an audience of both scholars and general readers, it is recommended for academic institutions and larger public libraries. This online journal is freely available. URL: http://escholarship.org/uc/international_asc_ufahamu

■ AFRICAN AMERICAN

See also Africa; Cultural Studies; and Multicultural Studies sections.

Carol A. Rudisell, Librarian and Head, Reference and Instructional Services Department, University of Delaware Library, Newark, DE 19717-5267; rudisell@udel.edu

Introduction

African American periodicals have a long history, dating back to 1827 when Russwurm and Cornish issued *Freedom's Journal,* the first weekly edited by and for African Americans. "We wish to plead our own cause....[T]oo long have others spoken for us," the publishers stated in their first editorial. The desire to set the record straight, to provide an authentic voice, and to define and interpret one's own reality continue as goals of contemporary African American publications.

Titles in this section fall primarily into two categories: popular magazines that target African American audiences, and scholarly journals in the interdisciplinary field of African American Studies. Scholars and laypersons alike use both types of publications. For example, university professors have introduced the scholarly analysis of hip-hop culture into the curriculum, so hip-hop magazines have become valuable primary source material. When selecting periodicals, librarians should consider the interconnectedness of scholarly and popular publications and analyze the informational content that each provides.

POPULAR MAGAZINES

Just as nineteenth-century journals reflected a multiplicity of concerns ranging from literacy to spiritual growth to abolition, contemporary magazines also convey the diverse interests of today's African American "community," which is anything but a monolithic bloc. African American popular magazines cover news and opinion, fashion, lifestyle, personal finance and business management, popular history and culture, religion, and music. There are "aspirational" or lifestyle magazines targeted to middle-class and upper-middle-class readers; there are also hip-hop magazines designed for urban youth, gospel magazines directed at African American Christians, and many more general publications.

Despite the diversity of the publications, readers will find similar storylines appearing in both scholarly and popular titles. One such storyline is that of the past presidency of Barack Obama and its significance to the African American community. The initial pride, joy, and hope brought on by the election of America's first black president has been partially eclipsed by the rise in racist hate speech and aggressive acts toward communities of color following the 2016 election—acts that Dr. Lawrence Bobo, editor of the *Du Bois Review,* astutely describes as "worrisome signs of erosion in the ties needed to keep a diverse democratic society healthy and whole." An especially troubling theme persistently permeating African American magazines concerns police shootings of unarmed black people that has given rise to the #BlackLivesMatter movement. The controversy arising from individual acts of resistance carried out by football player Colin Kaepernick and other celebrities who support this social justice movement has been well documented and debated within the pages of these publications.

Past surveys show that African American and ethnic communities seek out media that cover their cultural and political concerns, and while this continues to be true, declining advertising revenues and other economic pressures have made it difficult for both popular magazines and scholarly journals to stay afloat. To strengthen their brand, publishers have further expanded their web presence and developed apps for mobile devices that have been enthusiastically adopted by African American readers. African American magazines have also embraced social media, especially Facebook, Instagram, Twitter, and YouTube, as a way of strengthening their brand.

In addition to adopting cost-cutting measures such as fewer issues, smaller page counts, less expensive paper, and increased subscription prices, several publications have moved to online access only and have abandoned their serial format. Such is the case with *Jet,* a leading black-owned magazine founded by John H. Johnson in 1951 that had targeted young, working-class adults, and had been a constant source of weekly news and a staple of barber shops and beauty salons throughout African American communities. Other magazines that are now available only as web sites are the music magazines *Vibe* and *Wax Poetics,* as well as the *Journal of Blacks in Higher Education.*

Magazines that are local or regional in scope have not been included in this section unless they have attained a national readership. Librarians seeking to learn of local or regional titles should consult *Ulrich's Periodicals Directory.* Also, local bookstores are a good source of new local publications.

SCHOLARLY JOURNALS

The journals reviewed in this section are primarily interdisciplinary in scope, although some focus on a single discipline such as the *Journal of Black Psychology.* Disciplines represented within the interdisciplinary publications include anthropology, art, art history, communications, creative writing, economics, education, gender studies, history, law, literature, music, political science, psychology, public policy, religion, sociology, and theater and the performing arts.

A growing trend in academia to examine African American issues within a broader international context is reflected in several journals. All scholarly publications reviewed have significant African American content, although some have widened their scope to include "Africana Studies," "Black Studies," "Pan-African Studies," or "the African diaspora." The first three terms are applied interchangeably to the study of people of African descent, regardless of where they live, whereas "the African diaspora" refers to people of African descent living outside of Africa. Other journals have adopted a multicultural or "ethnic" approach, and cover other peoples of color.

The maturation of the critical race theory movement within the legal profession and beyond has resulted in the publication of several law journals that focus on race. While some examine the full range of issues pertaining to race, others focus on narrower topics such as race and poverty, or race and gender. Together these journals provide several avenues for critical race theorists to further explore ideas that have shaped the movement—ideas pertaining to interest convergence, the social construction of race, the critique of color-blindness, differential racialization, and intersectionality, to name but a few.

Basic Periodicals

Ems: *Black History Bulletin, The Crisis;* Hs: *Black Enterprise, Black History Bulletin, Black Scholar, The Crisis, Ebony, Journal of African American History;* Ga: *African American Review, Black Enterprise, Black History Bulletin, Black Scholar, Callaloo, The Crisis, Ebony, Journal of African American History, Journal of Black Studies, Souls;* Ac: *African American Review, Black Enterprise, Black History Bulletin, Black Music Research Journal, Black Scholar, Callaloo, The Crisis, Diverse: Issues in Higher Education, Du Bois Review, Ebony, Journal of African American History, Journal of Black Psychology, Journal of Black Studies, Journal of Negro Education, Race & Class, Souls, Transforming Anthropology.*

Basic Abstracts and Indexes

Academic OneFile, Academic Search Complete, America: History and Life, Ethnic NewsWatch, Humanities International Index, International Index to Black Periodicals Full Text, MasterFILE Premier, MLA International Bibliography, Sociological Abstracts, Web of Science.

African-American Career World: the diversity employment magazine. See Occupations and Careers section.

244. ***African American Review.*** Former titles (until 1992): *Black American Literature Forum;* (until 1976): *Negro American Literature Forum.* [ISSN: 1062-4783] 1967. q. USD 120. Ed(s): Aileen M Keenan, Nathan L Grant. The Johns Hopkins University Press, 2715 N Charles St, Baltimore, MD 21218; http://www.press.jhu.edu. Illus., adv. Sample. Refereed. Reprint: PSC. *Indexed:* A01, A22, AmHI, BRI, CBRI, E01, F01, MASUSE, MLA-IB. *Bk. rev.:* Number and length vary. *Aud.:* Ga, Ac.

Published quarterly, *African American Review* is a peer-reviewed journal that features literary and cultural criticism, interviews, poetry, short fiction, and book reviews. As the official publication of the Modern Language Association's Division of Black American Literature and Culture, this well-established journal provides a venue for scholars and practitioners of the arts and humanities to engage in intellectual discourse. Topics and time periods covered are wide-ranging and include works of lesser-known writers in addition to those of literary giants such as Toni Morrison and James Baldwin. While the primary focus is on the work of African American writers, the journal also includes pieces on African and Caribbean literature. "Forgotten Manuscripts" features fascinating stories of recently uncovered literary works. This is an important publication for libraries that support undergraduate or graduate programs in American literature, creative writing, or dramatic arts. General readers will also appreciate the literary and cultural analysis that the journal provides, so libraries that serve African American communities will also want to have this in their collections.

African and Black Diaspora. See Africa section.

245. ***Africology: the journal of pan african studies.*** Formerly (until 2010): *Journal of Pan African Studies (Online).* [ISSN: 2156-5600] 1987. irreg. Ed(s): Nana Adu-Pipim Boaduo. Journal of Pan African Studies, PO Box 244, Sun Village, CA 93543. Adv. Refereed. *Indexed:* MLA-IB. *Bk. rev.:* Number and length vary. *Aud.:* Ga, Ac.

Formerly known as *The Journal of Pan African Studies, Africology* is an online, open-access, scholarly journal that publishes interdisciplinary, peer-reviewed articles and creative work about black people living in Africa and elsewhere in the world. It aims to include works that "ask questions and seek answers to critical contemporary issues, based on an affirmative African-centered logic and language of liberation." Sporting an attractively designed interface and strong academic content, the journal has an impressive editorial board composed of librarians, university faculty, independent scholars, activists, and publishers. Recommended for academic libraries that support African Studies or Africana programs, and public libraries that serve black communities. URL: http://www.jpanafrican.org

Afro-American Historical and Genealogical Society. Journal. See Genealogy/Specialized Periodicals section.

Afro-Hispanic Review. See Multicultural Studies section.

246. ***Afro-Latin/American Research Association. Publication.*** [ISSN: 1093-5398] 1997. a. USD 25 (Individuals, USD 15; Free to members). Ed(s): William Luis. Dartmouth College, African and African-American Studies, College of Charleston, 66 George St, Charleston, SC 29424; info@alarascholars.org; http://www.alarascholars.org/. *Indexed:* MLA-IB. *Bk. rev.:* Number and length vary. *Aud.:* Ac.

With open access since 2017, *PALARA,* the *Publication of the Afro-Latin/American Research Association,* is an annual journal that publishes research articles, creative writing, and book reviews pertaining to African diaspora studies in the Americas. While pieces written in English, Spanish, French, and Portuguese are welcome, Spanish and English appear to be the predominant languages. The journal is multidisciplinary and solicits works in literature, history, linguistics, and the social sciences; however, the majority of the published work is either literary or historical. Each issue carries approximately five to ten articles and three to five book reviews; poetry and other creative work are also featured. While the journal is international in scope and has an impressive editorial board drawn from nations throughout the world, readers can find in this journal criticism of familiar American authors such as Julia Alvarez and Junot Diaz. Recommended for academic libraries that support Africana Studies, Ethnic Studies, or Latin American Studies. URL: https://journals.tdl.org/palara/index.php/palara/index

Black Camera. See Films section.

247. ***The Black E O E Journal: the employment & entrepreneur magazine.*** 1991. q. USD 16; USD 4.50 per issue. DiversityComm, Inc., 18 Technology Dr., Ste 170, Irvine, CA 92618; aortega@hnmagazine.com; http://diversitycomm.net/. Adv. *Bk. rev.:* Number and length vary. *Aud.:* Ga.

The *Black EOE Journal* is a career magazine that provides information for African Americans who seek employment and business opportunities within corporate America. The glossy, heavily illustrated magazine with an abundance of corporate advertising seeks to "connect, educate and promote equal opportunity thus creating a more diverse environment." The quarterly magazine publishes about four feature articles, many of which profile accomplished professionals, along with regular columns on topics such as workforce diversity, higher education, health, business-to-business, STEM, finance and insurance, government, and utilities and energy. The magazine also publishes book reviews and a calendar of career fairs and events. A companion web site features more up-to-date news and events, and features a searchable job bank. The magazine is available in print and electronic formats. Recommended for public libraries. URL: https://www.blackeoejournal.com

248. ***Black Enterprise.*** [ISSN: 0006-4165] 1970. m. USD 12.95 domestic; USD 3.99 foreign. Ed(s): Derek Dingle, Alisa Gumbs. Earl G. Graves Publishing Co., Inc., 130 Fifth Ave, 10th Fl, New York, NY 10011-4399; hanks@blackenterprise.com. Illus., adv. Sample. Circ: 500000 Paid. Vol. ends: Jul. Microform: PQC. *Indexed:* A01, A22, B01, B03, BLI, BRI, C37, C42, CBRI, ENW, F01, MASUSE. *Bk. rev.:* 2-3, 250-500 words. *Aud.:* Hs, Ga, Ac.

A magazine "whose mission has always centered on closing the black wealth gap and financially empowering African Americans," *Black Enterprise* was established in 1970. A glossy magazine with abundant corporate advertising, it addresses the financial and business concerns of the African American community, especially consumers, employees, professionals, and entrepreneurs. Each issue includes several feature articles that fall into recurring categories, some of which are "Wealth for Life," which presents a biographical profile; "Money [personal finance]"; "Biz"; "BE 100s," which profiles one of the nation's top 100 black-owned companies; and "Power Player" and "Women of Power," which provide interviews. The magazine also offers shorter columns on news, health, technology, popular psychology, and travel and leisure. While *BE* is rich with information on personal finance and corporate success, you won't find much critical analysis of capitalism or discussion of alternative economic systems. The magazine's annual polls, surveys, interviews, and company profiles will interest high school and academic audiences. Highly recommended for public and academic libraries. High school libraries that serve African American students will also want to consider this title.

249. ***Black History Bulletin.*** Formerly (until 2002): *Negro History Bulletin.* [ISSN: 1938-6656] 1937. s-a. USD 135. Ed(s): Alicia L Moore. The Association for the Study of African American Life and History, 2225 Georgia Ave, NW, Ste 331, Washington, DC 20059; info@asalh.net; http://www.asalh.org/. Illus., index. Refereed. Microform: PMC; PQC. *Indexed:* A01, A22, BRI, CBRI, MASUSE, MLA-IB. *Bk. rev.:* 2-3, 250-500 words. *Aud.:* Ems, Hs, Ga, Ac.

Established in 1937 at the urging of Mary McLeod Bethune, *Black History Bulletin* (formerly *Negro History Bulletin*) is published by the Association for the Study of African American Life and History. The *Bulletin* is a semi-annual, peer-reviewed journal that aims to publish "information about African Americans in U.S. history, the African diaspora generally, and the peoples of Africa." Targeting primarily secondary-school educators, the *Bulletin* places emphasis on articles that focus on middle and high school U.S. history, or social studies methods for teachers. The magazine offers lesson plans that address national social studies standards, quizzes, and classroom activities, as well as reproductions of primary documents that may be incorporated into the curriculum. Recent issues have been thematic and have focused on topics such as the Black Arts Movement and black migration. Educators seeking to create Black History Month lessons and activities will find the practical applications within this publication especially helpful. Recommended for school libraries of all levels, but a must for middle and high school libraries that serve African American youth. Also recommended for libraries that support college and university teacher training programs, and public libraries that serve African American communities.

250. ***Black Masks: spotlight on black art.*** [ISSN: 0887-7580] 1984. q. USD 25; USD 4 newsstand/cover. Ed(s): Beth Turner. Black Masks, PO Box 6642, Tallahassee, FL 32314; http://www.blackmasks.com/. Illus., adv. Vol. ends: May/Jun. *Indexed:* ENW, MLA-IB. *Bk. rev.:* Number and length vary. *Aud.:* Ga, Ac.

For more than 30 years, *Black Masks* has celebrated black theater by publishing "articles and papers on performing, literary or visual arts, and artists of African descent." Initially this slender magazine of 16 pages focused primarily on the performing arts in the New York area, but throughout the years its coverage has extended to other states as well. Each issue includes several feature articles and an "Arts Hotline" section that contains notices of new books, televised events, and upcoming performances and exhibitions throughout the United States. The "Arts Hotline" is also available on the magazine's web site and is searchable by geographic location. Recommended for libraries with strong theater and/or African American Studies collections. URL: http://www.blackmasks.com

251. ***Black Music Research Journal.*** [ISSN: 0276-3605] 1980. s-a. USD 125 (print & online eds.)). Ed(s): Melanie Zeck, Gayle Murchison. University of Illinois Press, 1325 S Oak St, MC-566, Champaign, IL 61820; uipress@uillinois.edu; http://www.press.uillinois.edu. Illus., index, adv. Sample. Refereed. *Indexed:* A22, AmHI, E01, ENW, IIMP, MLA-IB, RILM. *Aud.:* Ga, Ac.

This journal began in 1980 at Fisk University's Institute for Research in Black American Music. Since 1983, the journal has formed part of the Center for Black Music Research at Columbia College in Chicago. A scholarly journal published semi-annually, it includes articles about the philosophy, aesthetics, history, and criticism of black music. The journal seeks to promote an understanding of "the common roots of the music, musicians, and composers of the global African diaspora," and supports interdisciplinary scholarship on all genres of black music. In addition to articles on blues, jazz, gospel, rhythm and blues, and hip-hop, there are also pieces on opera and concert music, ring shouts, reggae, meringue, salsa, and other forms of traditional and contemporary Caribbean and African music. Many issues are devoted to a single theme, such as "Music of Black Los Angeles." A required journal for college and research library collections that support music or African American Studies programs. Public libraries that serve black communities will also want to consider this title.

252. ***Black Renaissance.*** [ISSN: 1089-3148] 1996. 3x/yr. USD 60 (Individuals, USD 31.50; USD 15 per issue). Ed(s): Quincy Troupe. New York University, Institute of African American Affairs, New York University, 14A Washington Mews, 4th Fl, New York, NY 10003; http://africanastudies.as.nyu.edu/page/home. Illus. Vol. ends: Spring. *Indexed:* AmHI, BRI, ENW, MLA-IB. *Bk. rev.:* Number and length vary. *Aud.:* Ga, Ac.

Edited by the accomplished writer Quincy Troupe, *Black Renaissance/ Renaissance Noire* "invites Black genius to apply itself to the realities of the twenty-first century with uncompromised thought, generous and readable analysis, and commentary." It publishes essays, poetry, fiction, interviews, letters, book reviews, photography, and art that critically address contemporary issues facing black people throughout the world. Its large format is well suited for the photographs and other pieces of visual art that contribute to the richness of this fine publication. It has published some of the most important black thinkers, writers, and artists, including Chinua Achebe, Amiri Baraka, Maryse Conde, Jean-Michel Basquiat, Edouard Glissant, Ngugi wa Thiong'o, Ishmael Reed, Derek Walcott, and John Edgar Wideman. Highly recommended for academic collections and larger public libraries.

253. ***The Black Scholar: journal of black studies and research.*** [ISSN: 0006-4246] 1969. q. GBP 259 (print & online eds.)). Ed(s): Shannon Hanks. Routledge, 530 Walnut St, Ste 850, Philadelphia, PA 19106; enquiries@tandfonline.com; http://www.tandfonline.com. Illus., adv. Sample. Refereed. Microform: MIM; PQC. Reprint: PSC. *Indexed:* A01, A22, AmHI, BRI, CBRI, MASUSE, MLA-IB. *Bk. rev.:* 2-3, 500-1,000 words. *Aud.:* Hs, Ga, Ac.

Founded in 1969 during the Black Studies movement, *Black Scholar* continues to serve as a place where "college intellectuals, street academicians, and movement leaders come to grips with the basic issues of black America." Each issue is thematic, and although African American concerns feature prominently, *Black Scholar* regularly publishes articles on black culture outside the United States. The breadth of the journal's scope is evident when examining themes of past issues that have included the struggle in Zimbabwe, facets of black masculinity, and rethinking pan-Africanism for the twenty-first century. While it regularly publishes the works of senior scholars and well-known activists, *Black Scholar* also encourages "young, newly developing black writers and black students" to submit their work. Each issue includes several feature articles, book reviews, and current book announcements. Following the retirement of founder and long-time editor Robert Chrisman, the journal was relaunched with new editorship and an expanded board composed of a new generation of scholars and activists. With changes in its editorial staff and focus, *The Black Scholar* seeks to "to chronicle, analyze and debate the conditions of and the emancipatory efforts by black people, against a multitude of oppressions that include and cross class, nationality, gender, generation, sexuality, and ideology." Research articles are peer reviewed, while creative or public pieces are also carefully evaluated. The journal is available in print and electronic format. Recommended for academic and public library collections. High schools with a sizable African American student body will also want to consider this title. URL: http://www.theblackscholar.org/

254. ***C L A Journal.*** [ISSN: 0007-8549] 1957. q. Ed(s): Sandra G Shannon. College Language Association, c/o Yakini B. Kemp, PO Box 38515, Tallahassee, FL 32315; yakini.kemp@famu.edu; http://www.clascholars.org. Illus., index. Refereed. *Indexed:* A01, A22, AmHI, BRI, MLA-IB. *Bk. rev.:* 3-6, 500-1,500 words. *Aud.:* Ac.

The College Language Association (CLA), founded in 1937 by a group of black scholars and educators, is an organization of college teachers of English and foreign languages. Since 1957, the association has published the *CLA Journal*, which features scholarly research and reviews of books in the areas of language, literature, literary criticism, linguistics, and pedagogy. Since only those articles written by CLA members and subscribers are considered for publication, the journal reflects the research interests of the association. While most articles focus on African American literature, West Indian, Afro-Hispanic, and African literatures are also covered. Criticism of black francophone literature is also represented in *CLA Journal*. Although English is the predominant language, articles written in other languages are also published. The journal includes association news and membership lists, publications by members, committee rosters, and conference announcements. Additionally, the journal includes job announcements. Recommended for academic library collections.

255. ***Callaloo.*** [ISSN: 0161-2492] 1976. 5x/yr. USD 230. Ed(s): Kelley A Robbins, Charles Henry Rowell. The Johns Hopkins University Press, 2715 N Charles St, Baltimore, MD 21218; http://www.press.jhu.edu. Illus., adv. Sample. Refereed. Reprint: PSC. *Indexed:* A01, A22, AmHI, BRI, CBRI, E01, MLA-IB. *Bk. rev.:* Number and length vary. *Aud.:* Ga, Ac.

Although it began in 1976 as a venue for Southern African American writers lacking publishing outlets, *Callaloo* now publishes internationally renowned authors and artists and ranks among the premier black literary journals. In keeping with its name - callaloo is a stew served in Louisiana, Brazil, and the Caribbean - it offers an array of cultures and genres. Issues include fiction, poetry, plays, critical essays, cultural studies, interviews, annotated bibliographies, visual art, and photography. The journal regularly features new and emerging writers, including participants of the Callaloo Creative Writing Workshop, a national retreat of fiction writers and poets. Operating on the principle that there is "infinite variety in Black Art," the journal is international in scope and publishes in French and Spanish, in addition to English. Special thematic issues that focus on individual authors, regions, or genres, such as the one on "Jazz Poetics," have garnered awards from major publishing associations, and the journal has been ranked among the top 15 literary magazines in the United States by *Every Writer's Resource*. In 2014, it introduced a companion, annual issue - *Callaloo Art* - that is devoted entirely to visual art and culture. Required for academic libraries and recommended for public libraries.

256. ***Columbia Journal of Race and Law.*** [ISSN: 2155-2401] 2011. s-a. Free. Ed(s): Ashok Chandran, Wyatt Littles. Columbia University, School of Law, 435 W 116th St, New York, NY 10027; Admissions@law.columbia.edu; http://www.law.columbia.edu. *Indexed:* L14. *Bk. rev.:* Number and length vary. *Aud.:* Ac.

The *Columbia Journal of Race and Law* (*CJRL*), a publication of the Columbia Law School, sets out "to establish a dialogue on historic and contemporary notions of socio-political and legal challenges facing racial and ethnic minorities." *CJRL*, which began in 2011, publishes research articles, notes, essays, and book reviews on issues such as affirmative action, immigration, employment law, community development, criminal law, environmental justice, voting rights, and education. The journal is issued twice per year and encourages work from scholars, practitioners, policy makers, and students. Recommended for academic libraries, especially those with legal studies programs, and law school libraries. All volumes are available on the web with open access. URL: https://cjrl.columbia.edu

257. ***The Crisis.*** Former titles (until 2003): *New Crisis;* (until 1997): *The Crisis.* [ISSN: 1559-1573] 1910. q. USD 12; USD 20 combined subscription (print & online eds.)). Ed(s): John M Vella. The Crisis Publishing Company, Inc., 4805 Mt Hope Dr, Baltimore, MD 21215. Illus., adv. Microform: BHP; PQC. *Indexed:* A01, A22, AmHI, BRI, ENW, MASUSE, MLA-IB. *Bk. rev.:* 2-3, 200-500 words. *Aud.:* Ems, Hs, Ga, Ac.

Founded in 1910 by W.E.B. Du Bois, the eminent scholar and founding father of the National Association for the Advancement of Colored People (NAACP), *The Crisis* is one of the oldest continuously published African American periodicals in print. Through the years it has been a "crusading voice for civil rights" and a respected source of thought, opinion, and analysis on issues pertaining to African Americans. Although the magazine is legally a separate entity, it serves as the official publication of the NAACP; news of the organization, both national and local, can be found in the "NAACP Today" section. All other sections of the magazine - including feature stories, current news, music reviews, theater reviews, book reviews, and interviews - reflect the opinion of the individual authors and not the NAACP. Although its issues are slender (each issue is about 50 pages), the magazine's sparse advertising and concentrated focus on the educational, economic, political, and social aspects of race make it a very substantial publication. The magazine states that it is committed to "battle tirelessly for the rights of humanity and the highest ideals of democracy," and it also seeks to "serve as a trustworthy record of the darker races." Back issues are freely available via Google Books, and current subscriptions are available for print and/or digital formats. *The Crisis* is highly recommended for academic, school, and public libraries. URL: https://www.thecrisismagazine.com/

258. *Diverse: Issues in Higher Education.* Formerly (until 2005): *Black Issues in Higher Education.* [ISSN: 1557-5411] 1984. bi-w. USD 26 combined subscription domestic; USD 50 combined subscription Canada; USD 60 combined subscription elsewhere. Ed(s): GE III Branch, Toni Coleman. Cox, Matthews & Associates, Inc., 10520 Warwick Ave, Ste B 8, Fairfax, VA 22030. Illus., adv. Vol. ends: Feb. *Indexed:* A01, A22, BRI, C42, Chicano, ENW, ERIC, MLA-IB. *Aud.:* Ac.

Since its founding in 1984 as *Black Issues in Higher Education, Diverse* has been the premier newsmagazine that covers issues concerning people of color in higher education. As its earlier title suggests, initially its focus was primarily on African Americans, but in recent years it has expanded its scope to include Latino, Asian American, Native American, and other communities such as the LGBTQ, persons with disabilities, the military, and women. Its coverage of African American concerns remains quite strong, however. Its attractive design, liberal use of color photographs, and clear writing make it a very readable publication. Each issue includes feature stories that run the gamut from general educational trends (for example, emergency notification technologies) to issues affecting people of color, such as efforts to create pipelines to college presidencies for Asian American administrators. The magazine also carries news of recent appointments, grant awards, upcoming conferences, and a very substantial section devoted to academic employment opportunities. It publishes many special, thematic editions (for example, technology, or the state of education in a particular state), and its special report on the top 100 institutions that graduate the most students of color is a welcome annual feature. The magazine supports a robust companion web site that provides news, special reports, blogs, opinion, searchable job announcements, and a wide array of multimedia, including slides and videos. Data from the "top 100" annual survey is also presented at the site. This is a required title for academic libraries, and is recommended for public and secondary school libraries that serve diverse communities. URL: http://diverseeducation.com

259. *Du Bois Review: social science research on race.* [ISSN: 1742-058X] 2003. s-a. GBP 225 (print & online eds.)). Ed(s): Lawrence Bobo. Cambridge University Press, University Printing House, Shaftesbury Rd, Cambridge, CB2 8BS, United Kingdom; journals@cambridge.org; https://www.cambridge.org/. Adv. Refereed. Reprint: PSC. *Indexed:* A22, E01, P61. *Bk. rev.:* Number and length vary. *Aud.:* Ga, Ac.

Bearing the name of the gifted scholar W.E.B. Du Bois, this journal seeks to present "the best cutting-edge research on race" from the social sciences. The journal is edited by Lawrence D. Bobo (Harvard University) and is published by Cambridge University Press for the Hutchins Center for African and African American Research at Harvard University. Its editorial board is made up of eminent scholars drawn from many disciplines. *DBR* also provides a forum for discussion of race issues from a range of disciplines, including economics, political science, sociology, anthropology, law, communications, public policy, psychology, and history. Each issue of *DBR* opens with introductory remarks from the editors that set the stage for three subsequent sections: "State of the Discipline," where invited essays and provocative think-pieces appear; "State of the Art," which features articles based on empirical research; and "State of the Discourse," which includes review essays on current scholarly books, controversies, and research threads. Journal subscriptions are available for print or electronic copy. The journal's web site previews articles of upcoming issues in its "FirstView" section, has several interactive features, and supports easy downloading to select e-readers. With exceptionally well-written articles, the *Du Bois Review* is highly recommended for academic and large public libraries. URL: https://www.cambridge.org/core/journals/du-bois-review-social-science-research-on-race

260. *Ebony.* Incorporates (1985-1998): *E M: Ebony Man;* (1970-1976): *Black World;* Which superseded (1950-1970): *Negro Digest.* [ISSN: 0012-9011] 1945. m. Ed(s): Kierna Mayo. Clear View Group, 820 S Michigan Ave, Chicago, IL 60605. Illus. Sample. Vol. ends: Oct. *Indexed:* A01, A22, BRI, C37, MASUSE, MLA-IB. *Bk. rev.:* 9-12, 25-50 words. *Aud.:* Ems, Hs, Ga, Ac.

Founded by John H. Johnson in 1945, *Ebony* continues to be the most widely circulated magazine targeted to African American readers, although in recent years it has suffered financially and eventually changed publishers. Prior to its sale, the editors introduced a fresh logo and look to boost its appeal to younger readers who might be drawn to *Vibe, Upscale,* or one of the other newer entrants to the magazine market. Committed to publishing positive, uplifting images of black people, the magazine includes articles on successful individuals in entertainment, sports, politics, and religion. It also has regular features on culture, fashion, beauty, and lifestyle, which includes relationships, parenting, personal finance, travel, cooking, and medical advice. *Ebony* also has a section on new books. Its relaunched, highly interactive web site is updated daily and features international politics, arts, and culture. Many back issues of *Ebony* are freely available at Google Books and current subscriptions are available for print and digital formats. A popular title that has been credited with "helping promote and record African-American culture and providing important outlets for a community that for too long was neglected by the mainstream media," *Ebony* is highly recommended for all high school, academic, and public libraries. URL: https://www.ebony.com

Essence. See Fashion and Lifestyle section.

Ethnic and Racial Studies. See Multicultural Studies section.

261. *Fire!: the multimedia journal of black studies.* [ISSN: 2156-4078] 2012. s-a. Ed(s): Daryl Michael Scott, Marilyn M Thomas-Houston. The Association for the Study of African American Life and History, 2225 Georgia Ave, NW, Ste 331, Washington, DC 20059; info@asalh.net; http://www.asalh.org/. *Bk. rev.:* Number and length vary. *Aud.:* Ac.

Published semi-annually by the Association for the Study of African American Life and History, this online-only, peer-reviewed journal focuses on research that incorporates "media elements as primary evidence to substantiate or challenge scholarly theories and interpretations of African American life and history." The journal supports many embedded audiovisual formats, and average file size for articles, including media, is 75 MB per article. The journal publishes original articles, essays, and reviews of works containing media elements. Topics have been as disparate as "Using Video in Phenomenographic Research on Senegal's Mental Health Care System: Implications for Black Studies"; "Almighty Fire: The Rise of Urban Contemporary Gospel Music and the Search for Cultural Authority in the 1980s"; and "From Black to eBlack: The Digital Transformation of Black Studies Pedagogy." Highly recommended for academic libraries that support Africana Studies, digital humanities, or multimedia studies programs.

262. *Georgetown Journal of Law & Modern Critical Race Perspectives.* [ISSN: 1946-3154] 2007. s-a. USD 30 (print or online ed.); USD 55 combined subscription (print & online eds.)). Ed(s): Katherine McInnis, Cynthia Frezzo. Georgetown University Law Center, 600 New Jersey Ave, NW, Washington, DC 20001; admis@law.georgetown.edu; http://www.law.georgetown.edu. *Indexed:* BRI, L14. *Bk. rev.:* Number and length vary. *Aud.:* Ac.

Founded in 2007 by law students who were inspired by their experiences with critical race theorists, the *Georgetown Journal of Law & Modern Critical Race Perspectives* (*MCRP*) seeks to "bridge the gap between scholarship and activism by promoting dialogue that extends beyond the normal academic realm." This title, one of a few journals devoted to legal scholarship on race and identity, is grounded in critical race theory and seeks to address and transform "the subordinated relationships that have historically defined race around the world." To further encourage dialogue, *MCRP* often includes reaction papers, along with the four to five research articles that it publishes. The journal also includes notes and book reviews. Published twice per year, *MCRP* features work from faculty, law students, and practitioners from throughout the nation who are dedicated to advancing social justice. Past articles have included "The Crossroads: Being Black, Immigrant and Undocumented in the Era of #BlackLivesMatter" and "Born Native, Raised White: The Divide Between Federal and Tribal Jurisdiction with Extra-Tribal Native American Adoption." Highly recommended for academic libraries that support legal studies programs and law schools. URL: https://www.law.georgetown.edu/mcrp-journal

263. *The Griot.* [ISSN: 0737-0873] 1981. s-a. Free to members. Ed(s): Tashia Bradley. Southern Conference on African-American Studies, Inc., c/o Howard Jones, PO Box 330163, Houston, TX 77233; scaasi6@aol.com; http://www.scaasi.org. Illus., adv. *Indexed:* MLA-IB. *Bk. rev.:* 1-4, 500-1,000 words. *Aud.:* Ac.

The Griot is the official journal of the Southern Conference on African American Studies, an organization that, in 1979, brought together "all interested minds, regardless of color or creed, who were interested in interpreting and preserving African American history and culture, especially that which had originated in and/or affected the south." While the journal primarily publishes articles in the humanities that "further enhance knowledge of the African's (African, African-American, Caribbean) experience," it occasionally includes work written by social scientists. Essays, criticism, poetry, and book reviews are also featured in the journal. Although the publisher does not offer online subscription, the full text of *The Griot* can be found in the Black Studies Center. Recommended for academic libraries that seek to build comprehensive Africana collections.

264. *Harvard Journal of African American Public Policy.* [ISSN: 1081-0463] 1989. a. USD 40 (Individuals, USD 20). Ed(s): Deloris Wilson, Toni Morgan. Harvard University, John F. Kennedy School of Government, 79 John F. Kennedy St, Cambridge, MA 02138; http://www.hks.harvard.edu/. Adv. Refereed. *Indexed:* A01, BRI. *Bk. rev.:* Number and length vary. *Aud.:* Ac, Sa.

Published by graduate students at the John F. Kennedy School of Government at Harvard University, this journal examines the relationship between policy making and the African American experience. Founded in 1989, this scholarly journal aims to "educate and provide leadership that improves the quality of public policies affecting the African American community." The journal, which has published works by leading policy makers, scholars, and political analysts, includes research articles, interviews, essays, and an occasional book review. Published annually, it is available both in print for a modest subscription fee and online as an open-access journal. This excellent title is highly recommended for academic libraries and public policy collections. URL: http://hjaap.hkspublications.org

265. *Hip Hop Weekly: covering the entire hip hop culture.* [ISSN: 1932-5177] 2007. w. USD 69.99. Z & M Media, LLC, 9663 Santa Monica Blvd, Ste 526, Los Angeles, CA 90210. Illus. *Aud.:* Ga.

Published by David Mays and Ray "Benzino" Scott, founders of the pioneering hip-hop magazine *The Source, Hip Hop Weekly* is a glossy celebrity magazine that seeks to be "a more timely and more engaging way to serve today's hip-hop consumer." Despite its title, the publication's frequency varies between biweekly and monthly. Voted Best Magazine at the 2009 Urban Music Awards, *Hip Hop Weekly* records the movements of hip-hop icons through feature articles, interviews, and a liberal use of photography. While most articles focus on the personal lives and musical developments of hip-hop celebrities, artists often weigh in on current news topics unrelated to music. The magazine has regular features on fashion and beauty, and also includes reviews of new albums, mixtapes, DVDs, films, games, and web sites. Columns by "shock-jocktress" Wendy Williams and other media personalities have contributed to the popularity of this publication. Similar in style to *People,* articles are short and easy to read. Strong language used by musicians during interviews has been redacted. Recommended for urban public libraries that serve young adults and older teens. Academic libraries that seek to build comprehensive collections on African American popular culture may also consider this title.

266. *Howard Journal of Communications.* [ISSN: 1064-6175] 1988. 5x/yr. GBP 445 (print & online eds.)). Ed(s): Chuka Onwumechili. Taylor & Francis Inc., 711 3rd Ave, 8th Fl, New York, NY 10017; support@tandfonline.com; http://www.taylorandfrancis.com. Illus., index, adv. Sample. Refereed. Vol. ends: Dec. Reprint: PSC. *Indexed:* A01, A22, B01, BAS, E01, MLA-IB, P61, SSA. *Bk. rev.:* Number and length vary. *Aud.:* Ac.

The *Howard Journal of Communications* is a scholarly journal that examines the influence of ethnicity, gender, and culture on communication issues. The majority of the editorial staff is located at Howard University, a historically black college; the editorial board is highly diverse and located at major research institutions throughout the United States and abroad. While many of the articles focus on African Americans, the scope of this quarterly is highly multicultural. Past articles have included "The Effects of Involvement in Sports on Attitudes toward Native American Sport Mascots," "Hispanic/Latino Identity Labels: An Examination of Cultural Values and Personal Experiences," and "Change and the Illusion of Change: Evolving Portrayals of Crime News and Blacks in a Major Market." In addition to the four to six peer-reviewed articles that appear in each issue, the journal includes an occasional book review. Some issues have a special theme, for example, "Health Communication and Health Disparities." Available in both print and electronic formats, this title is highly recommended for academic libraries that support programs in communications, journalism, social psychology, speech, gender studies, and multicultural studies. URL: https://www.tandfonline.com/loi/uhjc20

International Review of African American Art. See Art/Museum Publications section.

267. *Journal of African American History.* Formerly (until 2002): *Journal of Negro History.* [ISSN: 1548-1867] 1916. q. USD 183. Ed(s): V P Franklin. University of Chicago Press, 1427 E 60th St, Chicago, IL 60637; custserv@press.uchicago.edu; http://www.journals.uchicago.edu. Illus., adv. Refereed. *Indexed:* A01, A22, AmHI, BRI, CBRI, MLA-IB. *Bk. rev.:* Number and length vary. *Aud.:* Hs, Ac, Sa.

Founded in 1916 as the *Journal of Negro History* by Carter G. Woodson, this is the premier journal in the field of African American history. Published by the Association for the Study of African American Life and History, the founders of Black History Month, this peer-reviewed quarterly includes scholarly articles on all aspects of African American history. The journal often releases special thematic issues; past ones include "National and International Perspectives on Movements for Reparations" and "To Be Heard in Black and White: Historical Perspectives on Black Print Culture." Individual issues also include book reviews, memorial tributes, and announcements. Print and digital formats are available. This is an essential title for libraries that support black history programs and is highly recommended for all academic and research libraries. URL: https://www.journals.uchicago.edu/toc/jaah/current

268. *Journal of African American Males in Education.* [ISSN: 2153-9065] 2010. s-a. Free. Ed(s): Kenyatta T Jones. Journal of African American Males in Education, 2689 E Oakleaf Dr, Tempe, AZ 85281; jlukewood@asu.edu. Refereed. *Bk. rev.:* Number and length vary. *Aud.:* Ga, Ac.

The *Journal of African American Males in Education* (*JAAME*) is a peer-reviewed periodical devoted to research on African American boys and men and their engagement with various educational systems. Scholarly articles focus on African American males at all educational levels, from preschool to graduate school, and in multiple roles (for example, students, teachers, faculty, staff, administrators). While *JAAME* authors examine black male underachievement and gaps in educational attainment, they go far beyond this by also looking at factors that have contributed to academic excellence within black male populations. Most articles, about four or five per issue, are based on original research using both quantitative and qualitative methods; some articles are based on literature reviews and conceptual analysis. An occasional book review is included. *JAAME* is published online only and is open access. Recommended for academic libraries, and for public and school libraries that serve African American communities. URL: http://journalofafricanamericanmales.com/

269. *Journal of African American Studies.* Former titles (until 2003): *Journal of African American Men;* (until 1995): *Journal of African American Male Studies.* [ISSN: 1559-1646] 1993. q. EUR 583 (print & online eds.)). Ed(s): Judson L Jeffries. Springer New York LLC, 233 Spring St, New York, NY 10013; customerservice@springer.com; http://www.springer.com. Illus., adv. Refereed. Vol. ends: Aug. Reprint: PSC. *Indexed:* A01, A22, AmHI, BRI, E01, ENW, MLA-IB, SSA. *Bk. rev.:* Number and length vary. *Aud.:* Ac.

Formerly the *Journal of African American Men,* the *Journal of African American Studies* is a peer-reviewed quarterly that publishes theoretical and empirical articles on issues affecting persons, both male and female, of African descent. Although the journal is multidisciplinary in scope, its content is largely sociological, and research dealing with gender or identity is especially strong. Past issues have covered topics such as gendered racial microaggressions among black women college students; negotiating the impact of racism on the career development of African American professional men; and an interdisciplinary analysis of black girls' and women's resistance strategies. The journal also includes scholarly book reviews. Print and digital formats are available. An important title for academic libraries, especially those that support strong sociology and gender studies programs. URL: https://link.springer.com/journal/12111

270. ***Journal of African Diaspora Archaeology and Heritage.*** [ISSN: 2161-9441] 2012. 3x/yr. GBP 424 (print & online eds.)). Ed(s): Christopher C Fennell. Routledge, 530 Walnut St, Ste 850, Philadelphia, PA 19106; enquiries@tandfonline.com; http://www.tandfonline.com. Refereed. Reprint: PSC. *Aud.:* Ac.

Published three times a year and peer-reviewed, the *Journal of African Diaspora Archaeology and Heritage* provides about four research articles or essays per issue, focusing on "interdisciplinary studies in archaeology, history, material culture, and heritage dynamics concerning African descendant populations and cultures across the globe." Articles critically examine the interplay of artifacts - for example, tools and ceramics, natural landscapes, and social systems - to elucidate the historical legacies of African heritage peoples living throughout the world. Having an editorial board composed of scholars at preeminent institutions on four continents, the journal publishes research on communities primarily located in the Caribbean and the Americas, although African societies are also covered. Available in online and print formats. Recommended for academic libraries that support Africana, material culture, or archaeology programs.

271. ***Journal of Africana Religions.*** [ISSN: 2165-5405] 2013. s-a. USD 257 (print & online eds.)). Ed(s): Sylvester A Johnson, Edward E Curtis. Pennsylvania State University Press, 820 N University Dr, University Support Bldg 1, Ste C, University Park, PA 16802; info@psupress.org; http://www.psupress.org. Adv. Refereed. Reprint: PSC. *Aud.:* Ac, Sa.

Co-sponsored by the Association for the Study of the Worldwide African Diaspora, the *Journal of Africana Religions* is a semi-annual, peer-reviewed publication that features articles and review essays that critically examine black religions in global perspective. Interdisciplinary in scope, the journal draws on anthropology, history, and religious studies, as well as interdisciplinary scholarship in ethnic studies, gender studies, and Africana Studies. No particular religion is given preference, so readers will enjoy articles about traditional African religions, Christianity, Islam, and new religious movements such as Rastafarianism. Available in print and online editions. Recommended for academic libraries that support Africana Studies or religious studies.

272. ***The Journal of Black Psychology.*** [ISSN: 0095-7984] 1974. 8x/yr. USD 1153 (print & online eds.)). Ed(s): Kevin Cokley. Sage Publications, Inc., 2455 Teller Rd, Thousand Oaks, CA 91320; info@sagepub.com; http://www.sagepub.com. Illus., adv. Sample. Refereed. Microform: PQC. Reprint: PSC. *Indexed:* A22, ASSIA, BRI, E01, ERIC, IBSS, SSA. *Bk. rev.:* Number and length varies. *Aud.:* Ac, Sa.

Founded in 1974 by the Association of Black Psychologists, the *Journal of Black Psychology* is a peer-reviewed journal that presents empirical, theoretical, and methodological research on the behavior of black populations. It also provides "Black or Afrocentric perspectives" on other populations. While most articles pertain to African Americans, the journal regularly includes articles on African and Caribbean peoples. In addition to original articles, it includes special features such as research briefs, essays, commentary, and media reviews. With an international array of authors, the journal covers areas such as African-centered psychology, counseling and clinical psychology, education, health and social behavior, life span and family issues, organizational psychology, personality, psychology of black children, and therapeutic interventions. Highly recommended for academic and research libraries.

273. ***Journal of Black Sexuality and Relationships.*** [ISSN: 2334-2668] 2014. q. USD 163 domestic; USD 187 foreign. Ed(s): James Wadley. University of Nebraska Press, 1111 Lincoln Mall, Lincoln, NE 68588; journals@unl.edu; https://www.nebraskapress.unl.edu. Refereed. *Bk. rev.:* Occasional. *Aud.:* Ac.

Founded in 2014, this quarterly journal seeks to publish work by educators, researchers, clinicians, and policy analysts on Black sexuality and interpersonal relationships, including familial, friendship, and romantic relationships. Focusing primarily on African American populations, with an occasional article pertaining to Africa, each issue presents four to six articles drawn primarily but not exclusively from the fields of psychology, sociology, education, communications, and health sciences. Research articles, which employ both quantitative and quantitative methods, are refereed. Past issues of the journal have included the following topics: "African American Men on the Dissolution of Marriages and Romantic Relationships," "Their Own Received Them Not: Black LGBT Feelings of Connectedness," and "Black College Women's Reflections on Sexting during High School." The journal also includes clinical studies, as well as opinion pieces designed to stimulate dialogue within the field. Since scholarship on intersectionality is quite robust, the journal should have no shortage of manuscript submissions. During its relatively short tenure, it has given rise to a new professional association, the Association of Black Sexologists and Clinicians. While there are several journals devoted to gender relations within black populations (for example, *Spectrum* and *Palimpsest*), only *JBSR* specifically addresses black sexuality. Focusing its content more sharply on black sexual behavior and sexual identity will allow this journal to further distinguish itself from the others. Recommended for academic libraries, especially those supporting Sexuality Studies.

274. ***Journal of Black Studies.*** [ISSN: 0021-9347] 1970. 8x/yr. USD 1867 (print & online eds.)). Ed(s): Ama Mazama, Molefi Kete Asante. Sage Publications, Inc., 2455 Teller Rd, Thousand Oaks, CA 91320; info@sagepub.com; http://www.sagepub.com. Illus., index, adv. Sample. Refereed. Vol. ends: Jul. Microform: PQC. Reprint: PSC. *Indexed:* A01, A22, ASSIA, AmHI, BRI, CBRI, E01, IBSS, MLA-IB, P61, SSA. *Bk. rev.:* Occasional. *Aud.:* Ga, Ac.

One of the top-tier African American Studies academic journals, the *Journal of Black Studies* began in 1970 during the height of the Black Studies movement. Its current editor, Dr. Molefi Asante, founded the journal, then subsequently headed the nation's first doctoral program in Africana Studies at Temple University. Published eight times per year, the journal explores all aspects of the black experience, focusing not only on African Americans, but also on Africa, the Caribbean region, and the global African diaspora. Issues include five to ten articles, review essays, and an occasional book review. The scholarship presented by*JBS* covers a wide range of subject areas, including contemporary political and social issues, history, economics, literature, art, and more. While the editor is closely affiliated with Afrocentricity, a concept that is well-represented in the journal, articles reflect a variety of philosophical perspectives and research methodologies. Available in print and digital formats. Highly recommended for academic libraries and large public libraries that serve black communities. URL: http://journals.sagepub.com/home/jbs

275. ***Journal of Multicultural Counseling and Development.*** Formerly (until 1985): *Journal of Non-White Concerns in Personnel and Guidance.* [ISSN: 0883-8534] 1972. q. GBP 217. Ed(s): Caroline S Clauss-Ehlers. Wiley-Blackwell Publishing, Inc., 350 Main St, Malden, MA 02148; http://onlinelibrary.wiley.com. Illus., adv. Refereed. Vol. ends: Oct. Microform: PQC. Reprint: PSC. *Indexed:* A01, A22, BRI, C42, Chicano, ENW, ERIC. *Bk. rev.:* Occasional. *Aud.:* Ac.

This journal is published by the Association for Multicultural Counseling and Development, a member association of the American Counseling Association. Each issue includes four or five articles and an occasional book review pertaining to multicultural or ethnic interests in all areas of counseling and human development. While articles are published in English, author abstracts are provided in both English and Spanish. With a special focus on racial and ethnic issues in the United States, the journal accepts articles based on research, theory, or practical application. Native American, Latinx, Asian American, and African American concerns seem to get equal attention. Articles pertaining to immigrant populations and whiteness studies are also featured. Academic libraries that support counseling, human resource management, psychology, social work, or ethnic studies programs will want to consider acquiring this title. Subscriptions are available for print and electronic editions, and the title is also included in several aggregated databases. URL: https://onlinelibrary.wiley.com/journal/21611912

276. *Journal of Negro Education: a Howard University quarterly review of issues incident to the education of black people.* [ISSN: 0022-2984] 1932. q. USD 310 (print & online eds.)). Howard University, School of Education, Howard University,, Washington, DC 20059; http://www.howard.edu/schooleducation/. Illus. Refereed. Microform: MIM; PMC; PQC. Reprint: PSC. *Indexed:* A01, A22, BRI, CBRI, Chicano, ERIC, MLA-IB, SSA. *Bk. rev.:* 4-6, 1,000-2,500 words. *Aud.:* Ac.

For more than 85 consecutive years of publication, the *Journal of Negro Education* has been a major source of scholarship on every aspect of black education. In addition to publishing on professional education, this peer-reviewed journal also encompasses the social sciences, the physical and natural sciences, the arts, and technology. *JNE* has published an interesting array of special issues on topics as diverse as "Looking beyond the Digital Divide: Computers and Technology in Education," "Early Education and One-Room Schoolhouses," and "Hip Hop, Rap, and Oppositional Culture in Education." Although the journal aims to address educational issues that pertain to black people globally, its contents focus primarily on African Americans. Special features include book and media reviews, news, and announcements. Current subscriptions are available for print or digital formats. A core title for academic libraries, especially those that support education programs. URL: https://www.jstor.org/journal/jnegroeducation

277. *The Journal of Race and Policy.* [ISSN: 1540-8450] 2005. s-a. USD 120 (Individuals, USD 70). Ed(s): Donathan L Brown, Michael L. Clemons. Old Dominion University, Department of Political Science and Geography, 5115 Hampton Blvd, Norfolk, VA 23529; http://www.odu.edu/al/research/crrdp/journal. Refereed. *Indexed:* ENW. *Bk. rev.:* Number and length vary. *Aud.:* Ac, Sa.

Founded in 2005 by the Institute for the Study of Race and Ethnicity at Old Dominion University, the *Journal of Race and Policy* is an interdisciplinary journal published annually that includes research on the interplay of race, ethnicity, and public policy. *JRP* also publishes articles on race in the Commonwealth of Virginia, especially the Hampton Roads region. The journal offers a variety of disciplines, approaches, and methodologies, and aims "to achieve both practicality and theoretical relevance among the ranks of national interdisciplinary peer-reviewed journals concerned with race, ethnicity, culture, class and diversity in American society and globally." Book reviews are also included. Subscriptions are available for the print edition only, but the journal is available online in the Black Studies Center and Ethnic NewsWatch. Recommended for academic libraries that support African American studies, ethnic studies, and public policy programs. Collections that document the South will also want to consider this title.

278. *Journal of Race, Ethnicity, and Religion.* [ISSN: 2153-2370] 2010. m. Free. Ed(s): Yung S Kim. Sopher Press, c/o Miguel A De La Torre, Iliff School of Theology, Denver, CO 80210; info@sopherpress.com; http://www.sopherpress.com. *Bk. rev.:* Number and length vary. *Aud.:* Ac.

Founded in 2010 at the Iliff School of Theology as an open-access journal, *JRER* intends to create a space where religion scholars of color "can study the oppression of our communities and ourselves as a network of interdependent histories." The journal seeks to look within communities of color, with their myriad traditions and cultures, for answers to the religious questions that face scholars and society. *JRER,* whose issue numbering is a bit erratic, includes scholarly essays and book reviews. Topics pertaining to African Americans have included the genesis of African American religious scholarship, and African American children's influence on Mennonite religious practice. These articles have been presented alongside those pertaining to Asian American, Arab American, Native American, and Latinx populations. Recommended for academic libraries, especially those that support religious studies or theological schools. URL: http://raceandreligion.com/JRER/JRER.html

279. *Journal of Racial and Ethnic Health Disparities.* [ISSN: 2197-3792] 2014. 6x/yr. Ed(s): Cato Laurencin. Springer, Tiergartenstr 17, Heidelberg, 69121, Germany; subscriptions@springer.com; https://www.springer.com. Refereed. *Aud.:* Ac, Sa.

This is the official journal of the W. Montague Cobb-National Medical Association (NMA) Health Institute, an organization whose mission is to eliminate racial and ethnic health disparities. Thus, this journal seeks to provide scholarship that explores all aspects of health disparities, including underlying causes, interventions, and best practices for their elimination. The journal publishes original research articles, review essays, and "evolutionary" reviews that reflect state-of-the-art thinking on health disparities. Available in print and online editions. Recommended for academic and medical libraries.

Living Blues. See Music/Popular section.

M E L U S. See Literature section.

Meridians. See Gender Studies section.

280. *National Black Nurses Association. Journal.* [ISSN: 0885-6028] 1986. s-a. USD 35. Ed(s): Joyce Newman Giger. National Black Nurses' Association, 8630 Fenton St, Ste 330, Silver Spring, MD 20910; info@nbna.org; http://www.nbna.org. Adv. Refereed. *Indexed:* A22, Agr. *Aud.:* Ac.

The *Journal of the National Black Nurses Association* (*JNBNA*), published twice a year, includes scholarship on issues related to health care in black communities. Written primarily by nursing and health-care faculty from American institutions, articles may also discuss educational, social, economic, or legislative topics. Articles, about ten per issue, are subjected to blind review. Past issues have covered topics such as psychosocial barriers to breast cancer treatment experienced by African American women; employment and breastfeeding outcomes among African American women; and personal characteristics and cognition in older African Americans with hypertension. While providing a venue for black nurses to share their scholarly work regarding clinical practice or research affecting black communities, the journal is open to scholars of other ethnicities as well. Highly recommended for academic libraries with nursing or public health programs.

National Medical Association. Journal. See Medicine section.

281. *National Political Science Review.* [ISSN: 0896-629X] 1989. a. USD 34.95 per issue. Ed(s): Tiffany Willoughby-Herard. Transaction Publishers, 35 Berrue Cir, Piscataway, NJ 08854; trans@transactionpub.com; http://www.transactionpub.com. Refereed. *Bk. rev.:* Number and length vary. *Aud.:* Ac.

The *National Political Science Review* (*NPSR*) is an annual refereed publication of the National Conference of Black Political Scientists (NCOBPS). It seeks to provide lively scholarly discourse on domestic and global politics and policies that "advantage or disadvantage groups by reason of race, ethnicity, gender and/or other such factors." Since the journal serves a broad audience of social scientists, including historians, sociologists, anthropologists, theologians, economists, ethicists, and others, it also considers contributions on any subject that has "significant political and social dimensions." It publishes about four blind-reviewed articles based on theoretical and empirical research, as well as several papers that were presented at the most recent NCOBPS meeting. Collaborative efforts by two or more contributors are encouraged, although works by single authors are also included. *NPSR* has also published a "Works in Progress" section consisting of essays that showcase works of senior political scientists and bring their research agendas to the attention of the political science profession. The personal essays demonstrate how senior scholars craft their research - how they choose their topics and research methodologies - and are intended to help younger scholars design their own research agendas. The journal also publishes about ten critical book reviews per issue. It is available online as part of the Black Studies Center database. Highly recommended for academic libraries.

282. *Negro Educational Review.* [ISSN: 0548-1457] 1950. q. Ed(s): LaDelle Olion, Noran Moffett. Fayetteville State University, 1200 Murchison Rd, Fayetteville, NC 28301; http://www.uncfsu.edu. Illus., index. Sample. Refereed. Vol. ends: Oct. *Indexed:* A01, A22, ERIC, MLA-IB. *Bk. rev.:* 1-2, 500-1,500 words. *Aud.:* Ac.

The *Negro Educational Review* began as a publishing outlet for faculty at historically black colleges and universities; however, current contributors come from all types of educational institutions. This refereed journal aims to publish quarterly issues; however, recent economic conditions have constrained its releases to one or two combined issues per year. *NER* publishes articles on issues related to "Black experiences throughout the African Diaspora." While the journal's title suggests that its focus is solely on education, it actually covers the full spectrum of scholarship and includes articles on the social and behavioral sciences, the biological and physical sciences, and the humanities, as well as on professional education. For example, past issues have included articles on "Middle Passage in the Triangular Slave Trade: The West Indies," "Government Acquisition of Private Property for Public Use: An Analysis of United States Supreme Court Decisions," and "The Socioeconomic Impact of Lymphatic Filariasis in Tropical Countries." The journal also publishes thematic issues such as one that examined underrepresented women in academe. In addition to scholarly articles, the journal also features book reviews, news reports, and announcements. Subscriptions are available for print copies only; however, back issues can be found in the ProQuest Black Studies Center database at http://bsc.chadwyck.com. Recommended for academic libraries and large public libraries that serve black communities.

283. ***The Network Journal: black professionals and small business magazine.*** [ISSN: 1094-1908] 1993. q. USD 15 domestic; USD 21 Canada; USD 40 elsewhere. Network Journal, 39 Broadway, Ste 2120, New York, NY 10006. Illus., adv. Sample. *Indexed:* ENW. *Bk. rev.:* Number and length vary. *Aud.:* Ga, Sa.

Beginning as a black-and-white tabloid newspaper in 1993, *The Network Journal* is now a full-color trade magazine with a wide readership. Targeted to black professionals, business owners, and "upwardly mobile individuals," the quarterly magazine presents feature articles designed to provide readers with innovative business ideas and techniques, inspirational stories, and information regarding legal matters, marketing, office technology, and taxation. While *The Network Journal* occasionally prints items regarding personal finance and consumer news, this type of information is far more abundant in *Black Enterprise* (above in this section). Other features include brief interviews, book reviews, and announcements of upcoming seminars and events. The magazine sponsors the annual "40-Under-Forty Awards," which highlights 40 people for career excellence, and the "25 Influential Black Women in Business Awards." Print and digital subscriptions are available, and the journal is also available in select databases. Articles from back issues of the magazine are available at the journal's companion web site, which also hosts current news, feature articles, an events calendar, photos, and videos. A useful publication for most public libraries and business collections. URL: https://tnj.com

O: The Oprah Magazine. See General Interest section.

284. ***Obsidian: literature and arts in the African diaspora.*** Former titles (until 2006): *Obsidian 3: Literature in the African Diaspora;* (until 1999): *Obsidian 2: Black Literature in Review;* (until 1986): *Obsidian: Black Literature in Review.* [ISSN: 2161-6140] 1975. s-a. Ed(s): Duriel E Harris. Illinois State University, Campus Box 4241, Normal, IL 61790-4241; http://illinoisstate.edu/. Illus. Refereed. *Indexed:* A22, AmHI, BRI, MLA-IB. *Bk. rev.:* Number and length vary. *Aud.:* Ga, Ac.

This literary review publishes contemporary poetry, fiction, drama, nonfiction prose, and visual arts "from within and concerning the African Diaspora." Past issues have also included color reproductions of a featured visual artist. Hosted for many years by the English Department of North Carolina State University, *Obsidian* (previously *Obsidian 3*) is currently being edited by Duriel E. Harris and is hosted by Illinois State University. The journal seeks to support both new and established writers and artists. Scholarly critical studies have been added to the journal and often contribute to an issue's special theme; for example, the centennial celebration of Richard Wright, or the work of Jeffery Renard Allen. Book reviews are also included. *Obsidian* is recommended for academic libraries, especially those that support creative writing and Black Studies programs. Large public libraries will also want to consider acquiring this excellent literary journal.

285. ***Palimpsest: a journal on women, gender, and the black international.*** [ISSN: 2165-1604] 2012. s-a. USD 110 (Individuals, USD 55). Ed(s): Tiffany Ruby Patterson-Myers, T Denean Sharpley-Whiting. State University of New York Press, 353 Broadway, State University Plaza, Albany, NY 12246; info@sunypress.edu; http://www.sunypress.edu. Refereed. *Indexed:* MLA-IB. *Bk. rev.:* Number and length vary. *Aud.:* Ac.

Built through a partnership between Vanderbilt University's African American and Diaspora Studies Program and the State University of New York (SUNY) Press, *Palimpsest* is a peer-reviewed journal that seeks "to engender further explorations of the Black International as a liberation narrative and Black Internationalism as an insurgent consciousness formed over and against retrogressive practices embodied in slavery, colonialism, imperialism, and globalization." The journal is published twice per year and includes interdisciplinary scholarship drawn from fields such as film studies, literature, and women's and gender studies. Creative work and book reviews are also included. Available in print and online editions. Highly recommended for academic and research libraries that support Africana or gender studies programs.

Philosophia Africana. See Africa section.

286. ***Race & Class: a journal on racism, empire and globalisation.*** Formerly (until 1974): *Race.* [ISSN: 0306-3968] 1959. q. USD 740 (print & online eds.)). Ed(s): Hazel Waters, Jenny Bourne. Sage Publications Ltd., 1 Oliver's Yard, 55 City Rd, London, EC1Y 1SP, United Kingdom; market@sagepub.com; https://www.sagepub.com/. Adv. Sample. Refereed. Reprint: PSC. *Indexed:* A01, A22, AmHI, BAS, BRI, E01, IBSS, MLA-IB, P61, SSA. *Bk. rev.:* Number and length vary. *Aud.:* Ac.

Race & Class is a quarterly British journal that is international in scope and examines racism, class bias, and imperialism in contemporary society and historically. Formerly titled *Race,* the journal was established in 1959 by the Institute of Race Relations, a nonprofit organization known for cutting-edge "research and analysis that informs the struggle for racial justice in Britain and internationally." It has an international editorial board that includes African American scholars, and it regularly publishes articles about African American history and life. Its peer-reviewed research articles, commentaries, and book reviews are scholarly, incisive, and usually far left-of-center. Contributors include academics, scientists, artists, novelists, journalists, and politicians. A good example of the journal's interest in American race relations is its special issue entitled "Cedric Robinson and the Philosophy of Black Resistance," which focused on Robinson's studies of black Marxism. The journal is available in print and electronic formats. Highly recommended for academic libraries. URL: http://journals.sagepub.com/home/rac

287. ***Race and Justice: an international journal.*** [ISSN: 2153-3687] 2011. q. USD 731. Ed(s): Jacinta M Gau. Sage Publications, Inc., 2455 Teller Rd, Thousand Oaks, CA 91320; info@sagepub.com; http://www.sagepub.com. Refereed. *Bk. rev.:* Number and length vary. *Aud.:* Ac.

Race and Justice, a peer-reviewed quarterly, is the official journal of the American Society of Criminology, Division on People of Color and Crime. A forum for scholarship on race, ethnicity, and justice, the journal is especially interested in publishing policy-oriented papers that examine how race/ethnicity intersects with justice system outcomes across the globe. Journal articles emanate from varied disciplines and employ methodological approaches that are qualitative and/or quantitative. Past topics have included "Racial Disparity in Iowa Prisons," "Race, Geography, and Juvenile Justice: An Exploration of the Liberation Hypothesis," and "Assessments of Crime Seriousness on an American Indian Reservation." Each issue usually presents four articles. The journal is available in print and electronic formats. Recommended for academic libraries that support criminal justice programs. URL: http://journals.sagepub.com/home/raj

288. ***Race and Social Problems.*** [ISSN: 1867-1748] 2009. q. EUR 443 (print & online eds.)). Ed(s): Gary F Koeske. Springer New York LLC, 233 Spring St, New York, NY 10013; customerservice@springer.com; http://www.springer.com. Sample. Refereed. Reprint: PSC. *Indexed:* A22, E01, SSA. *Aud.:* Ac.

Race and Social Problems, a quarterly journal that is multicultural and multidisciplinary, provides a forum for the publication of articles that address race and its "enduring relationship to psychological, socioeconomic, political, and cultural problems facing present day society." The journal, with an international editorial board, explores topics such as criminal justice, economic conditions, education, elderly, families, health disparities, mental health, race relations, and youth. Nearly all articles pertain to race in the United States, although some offer an international perspective. Black, Asian, and Latino populations are frequently addressed. The journal publishes mostly original empirical articles, about four per issue, which use a variety of methodologies, including quantitative and qualitative. Articles are subjected to a double-blind peer-review process. Occasionally the journal publishes non-empirical articles such as policy proposals, critical analyses, and historical analyses. Journal issues are occasionally edited by a guest editor who focuses on a single social problem; for example, "Race and Mental Health." The journal operates on the premise that "virtually every race-related social problem impacts on every other race-related social problem that we are attempting to understand and ameliorate," and its hope is that each issue will be of relevance to "race-focused scholars." The journal is available in print and electronic editions. Recommended for all academic libraries, especially those that support social work programs. URL: https://link.springer.com/journal/12552

289. ***Savoy: power. substance. style.*** Formerly (until 2000): *Emerge.* [ISSN: 1532-3692] 1989. q. USD 15.95 domestic; USD 25.95 Canada; USD 35.95 elsewhere. L P Green & Partners, Inc., 3379 Peachtree Rd, NE, Ste 230, Atlanta, GA 30326. Adv. *Indexed:* BRI, ENW, MLA-IB. *Aud.:* Ga, Ac.

Savoy is an attractive, glossy magazine that seeks "to celebrate the true African American experience" by highlighting the "achievements, style and culture of the African American and urban community." Named for Harlem's historic ballroom, *Savoy* began publication in 2001, but folded on two separate occasions. Now based in Atlanta under new ownership, *Savoy* targets its publication to affluent African American urban professionals. This stylish lifestyle magazine provides a mix of news and hot topics, entertainment, sports, business, technology, fashion, travel, and health. Especially popular is the "Savoy Top 100 Most Influential Blacks in Corporate America," an annual feature that showcases business leaders who are influential not just within their companies, but also in their surrounding communities. Profiles of the top one hundred are featured on the magazine's companion web site, which also carries a few select news stories on culture, sports, technology, and business. Recommended for public libraries that serve African American populations, especially those located in urban and suburban areas. URL: http://savoynetwork.com

290. ***Slavery and Abolition: a journal of slave and post-slave studies.*** [ISSN: 0144-039X] 1980. q. GBP 751 (print & online eds.)). Ed(s): Gad Heuman. Routledge, 4 Park Sq, Milton Park, Abingdon, OX14 4RN, United Kingdom; subscriptions@tandf.co.uk; http://www.tandfonline.com. Illus., index, adv. Sample. Refereed. Vol. ends: Dec. Microform: PQC. Reprint: PSC. *Indexed:* A01, A22, AmHI, E01, P61. *Bk. rev.:* 9-15+, 500-1,000 words. *Aud.:* Ac.

Slavery and Abolition is a refereed journal devoted to the study of slavery from the ancient period to the present; it also examines issues relating to the dismantling of slavery and to slavery's legacy. The journal provides perspectives on this sensitive and often controversial topic from a variety of disciplines including history, anthropology, sociology, and literature. Although readers will encounter articles on bondage in ancient Greece or in early Asian history, the bulk of the scholarship focuses on the trans-Atlantic slave trade that brought enslaved Africans to Latin America, the Caribbean, and North America. In addition to special thematic issues, the journal provides an important bibliographical supplement on slavery compiled by Thomas Thurston that updates Joseph C. Miller's published bibliography, "Slavery and Slaving in World History." The bibliography is searchable online (through 2009) at www2.vcdh.virginia.edu/bib/about.php. Book reviews and review articles are also included, as is a "Notes and Documents" section. The journal is available in print and online. Highly recommended for academic libraries. URL: https://www.tandfonline.com/loi/fsla20

291. ***Souls: a critical journal of Black politics, culture, and society.*** [ISSN: 1099-9949] 1999. q. GBP 259 (print & online eds.)). Ed(s): Prudence Browne, Barbara Ransby. Taylor & Francis Inc., 711 3rd Ave, 8th Fl, New York, NY 10017; support@tandfonline.com; http://www.taylorandfrancis.com. Sample. Reprint: PSC. *Indexed:* A22, E01, P61. *Bk. rev.:* 1, 1,000-2,000 words. *Aud.:* Ga, Ac.

Souls is an interdisciplinary quarterly journal that is "produced in the spirit of the intellectual activism of W. E. B. Du Bois" and seeks to present "creative and challenging interpretations of the key issues now being confronted by scholars of modern Black America, Africa, and the Caribbean." The journal was established in 1999 with the sponsorship of the Center for Contemporary Black History, the research unit of the Institute for Research in African-American Studies at Columbia University, and was for many years edited by activist scholar Manning Marable. *Souls* brings together intellectual thought from within and without academe to critically examine black history, politics, socioeconomic research, social theory, and culture. It concentrates on the post-1945 period that witnessed anti-colonial movements throughout Africa and the Caribbean, and the civil rights and Black Power movements within the United States. Beginning with a substantive quotation from Du Bois that sets the stage for the following pages, each issue focuses on a central theme that links the six or more feature articles. Also included are book reviews, recommended books, and an occasional poem. Readers will appreciate both the attractive presentation and the hard-hitting analysis provided by this journal. The journal is available in print and online. Highly recommended for academic libraries and for large public libraries, especially those with Black Studies collections. URL: https://www.tandfonline.com/loi/usou20

292. ***The Source (New York, 1988).*** [ISSN: 1063-2085] 1988. m. Northstar Group Publishers, 240 W 35th St, Ste 405, New York, NY 10001. Illus., adv. *Indexed:* IIMP, IIPA. *Aud.:* Ga, Ac.

Founded initially as a newsletter in 1988 by two Harvard University students, *The Source* is now one of the leading hip-hop magazines on the market. Once considered the "hip-hop bible," the magazine covers all aspects of the hip-hop music industry and includes musician interviews, feature stories, and concert and recording reviews. Although music is its heart, this publication also includes some general news and current events, political commentary, and sports items. Its companion web site offers sections on the same categories, but also provides a music channel, videos, and live streaming of music events and artist interviews. *The Source* has embraced mobile technologies and social media, so fans may purchase apps, subscribe to its YouTube channel, or follow it on Twitter. Recommended for urban public libraries that serve 18- to 24-year-old populations. Also recommended for libraries with strong popular music collections. URL: http://thesource.com

Spectrum: a journal on Black men. See Gender Studies section.

293. ***Transforming Anthropology.*** [ISSN: 1051-0559] 1990. s-a. GBP 65 (print & online eds.)). American Anthropological Association, 2300 Clarendon Blvd, Ste 1301, Arlington, VA 22201; https://www.americananthro.org. Adv. Sample. Refereed. Reprint: PSC. *Indexed:* A22, ASSIA, BRI, E01, SSA. *Bk. rev.:* Number and length vary. *Aud.:* Ac.

Transforming Anthropology is the official journal of the Association of Black Anthropologists, and is published by the American Anthropological Association. The journal explores "the contemporary and historical construction of social inequities based on race, ethnicity, class, gender, sexuality, nationality and other invidious distinctions." *Transforming Anthropology* features peer-reviewed research articles, research reports, discussions, briefs on works-in-progress, and interviews. It also publishes book, film, and video reviews. Topics covered are international in scope, although the United States, the Caribbean, and Africa are highly represented. The journal is available in print and electronic formats. Highly recommended for university and research libraries. URL: https://anthrosource.onlinelibrary.wiley.com/journal/15487466

Transition. See Africa section.

294. ***Trotter Review.*** Formerly (until 1992): *Trotter Institute Review.* [ISSN: 1070-695X] 1987. a. Ed(s): George E Curry. William Monroe Trotter Institute, 100 Morrissey Blvd, Boston, MA 02125; trotterinstitute@umb.edu; http://www.trotter.umb.edu/. Adv. *Indexed:* ENW. *Aud.:* Ac, Sa.

An annual open-access publication of the William Monroe Trotter Institute of the University of Massachusetts-Boston, the *Trotter Review* historically published articles addressing race and race relations in the United States and abroad. The journal's strong public-policy content reflected the service orientation of its parent institution, the Trotter Institute, which was founded in 1984 to provide research, technical assistance, and public service to the black community and other communities of color in Boston and Massachusetts. In recent years, the journal modified its focus and now has "one hand in the academic and the other hand in the journalistic," as it "tracks the issues that matter most to blacks (broadly defined and inclusive of the diaspora)." Further, it seeks to encourage scholars, students, members of the public, and elected officials to address key issues, to increase dialogue about social problems, and to contribute to solutions. Published since 1987, the journal covers education, economic development, immigration, religion, politics, and race relations. It takes a thematic approach and has published special issues on "Literacy, Expression and the Language of Resistance," "Reclaiming Humanity in and out of the Cell," and "Homosexuality and the Black Community." *Trotter Review* is available in print and online as an open-access publication. Academic libraries that support urban affairs, public policy, and African American Studies programs will want to consider this title. URL: https://scholarworks.umb.edu/trotter_review

295. ***Upscale.*** [ISSN: 1047-2592] 1989. bi-m. USD 14.95 (print or online ed.)). Upscale Communications, Inc., 2141 Powers Ferry Rd, Ste 300, Marietta, GA 30067; social@upscalemagazine.com. Illus., adv. Sample. *Bk. rev.:* Number and length vary. *Aud.:* Ga, Ac.

Upscale, a glossy, full-color publication, describes itself as "the ultimate lifestyle magazine that addresses the needs of the most stylish and educated African-American." It aims to keep "savvy, trendy and successful African-Americans" informed and entertained as well as enlightened and encouraged. Somewhat similar in scope to *Ebony,* the magazine regularly presents feature articles on up-and-coming people in entertainment and business; current events; fashion, beauty, and style; relationships; health and fitness; interior design and the arts; and travel. *Upscale* also includes brief reviews of books, films, music, and restaurants. The magazine has a strong web and social media presence. Although it reflects a Southern orientation, the magazine clearly has a national reach. Recommended for public libraries that serve African American communities, especially those located in urban and suburban areas. URL: http://upscalemagazine.com

296. ***Uptown (Harlem): luxury, lifestyle & living.*** [ISSN: 2160-4304] 2004. bi-m. Uptown Media Group, 113 E 125th St, 2nd Fl, Harlem, NY 10035; support@uptownmagazine.com. *Bk. rev.:* Number and length vary. *Aud.:* Ga.

Uptown is a beautifully designed magazine with a clean layout, and is lavishly illustrated. It indeed reflects "a new renaissance of luxury, lifestyle and living." Targeting affluent African Americans who reside in urban areas, the magazine initially had a strong focus on New York City and was inspired by the revitalization of Harlem, Black America's cultural Mecca. But while New York cultural events are core to the magazine, readers will also find much to read about other major metropolitan areas. *Uptown* publishes regional editions for Atlanta, Charlotte, Chicago, Detroit, Philadelphia, and Washington, D.C. Feature articles cover a wide array of topics such as politics, business and industry, travel, and biographical profiles of successful African Americans. Briefer articles highlight luxurious goods and services such as real estate, automobiles, wines and spirits, beauty products and spas, restaurants, and electronic gadgetry. Fashion photography, when available, is exceptionally well done, as is all of the magazine's photography. *Uptown* also provides reviews of artists' shows, films, theater, music, and books. Its companion web site features videos, news, product recommendations, and city guides to fine dining, hotels, and hot night spots. Recommended for urban public libraries, especially in those metropolitan areas mentioned above. Suburban public libraries that serve more affluent African American populations will also be interested in this title. URL: http://uptownmagazine.com

297. ***The Western Journal of Black Studies.*** [ISSN: 0197-4327] 1977. q. USD 90 (Individuals, USD 30). Washington State University Press, 314 Cleveland Hall, Pullman, WA 99164; http://wsupress.wsu.edu. Illus., index, adv. Refereed. Vol. ends: Winter. *Indexed:* A01, A22, AmHI, BRI, ENW, MLA-IB, P61, SSA. *Bk. rev.:* Number and length vary. *Aud.:* Ac.

Founded in 1977, *The Western Journal of Black Studies* is an interdisciplinary journal that publishes scholarly articles on "issues related to the African Diaspora and experiences of African/African Americans in the United States." Sponsored by Washington State University, the journal has an editorial board composed of distinguished scholars from throughout the United States who are working primarily in the social sciences and humanities. All articles are subjected to blind peer review. Each issue includes about five feature articles and several scholarly book reviews. The journal has received the C.L.R. James Award for scholarly publication in the field of Black Studies. Subscriptions are available for print only, although the journal is represented in several aggregated databases. A revamped web site allows readers to browse tables of content and select articles from the current issue. The site also lists books available for review. Recommended for academic libraries and large public libraries that serve African American populations. URL: https://education.wsu.edu/wjbs

Women, Gender, and Families of Color. See Gender Studies section.

298. ***XXL: hip-hop on a higher level.*** [ISSN: 1093-0647] 1997. m. Ed(s): Vanessa Satten, Bianca Torres. Harris Publications, Inc., . Illus., adv. *Aud.:* Ga.

XXL, an urban lifestyle magazine, is regarded as one of the best hip-hop insider magazines. Somewhat similar to its rival *The Source* (above in this section), it covers all aspects of hip-hop music and culture, including the business side of the music industry. Published since 1997, the magazine includes feature articles, interviews, commentaries, and reviews. While its primary focus is on musicians, producers, and others affiliated with the industry, the magazine also features actors, filmmakers, comedians, and other entertainment industry personalities, as well as athletes. *XXL* also includes news, current events, and upcoming music releases. An especially popular feature is its annual "Freshman Class" that highlights new, up-and-coming artists. As with the music that it covers, the language of the magazine is "adult" in nature, and although its title suggests otherwise, this is a magazine that's all about music. The magazine is available in print and digital formats; however, an ever-increasing proportion of content is being moved to its companion web site that is highly interactive and frequently updated with news, music reviews, photos, and videos. The magazine is fully engaged with all the major social media outlets. Recommended for urban public libraries that serve older teens and adults. URL: http://www.xxlmag.com

■ AGRICULTURE

Duncan McClusky, Branch Librarian, College of Agricultural and Environmental Sciences, Tifton Campus, University of Georgia, Tifton, GA 31793

Introduction

All people consume products that come from agriculture and some may not understand what goes into providing them with the food. The population is growing and the number of farms are decreasing. The current agricultural producers need to produce more food on the same amount of land or a little less so it is important to keep up with the latest scientific information. Government legislation has an effect on farmer's work and *Agri-Pulse* (https://www.agri-pulse.com) for a price does a good job of keeping individuals or small groups of people informed about what is going on in Washington and state government. The *Farm Journal* magazine has been assisting farmers since 1877 and their webpage (https://www.agweb.com) is a good resource. *Successful Farming* is another easy-to-read magazine with a webpage (https://www.agriculture.com) that can be accessed.

Basic Periodicals

Ac: *Agronomy Journal, American Society of Agricultural and Biological Engineers. Transactions, Crop Science, Journal of Animal Science, Soil Science Society of America Journal.*

Basic Abstracts and Indexes

AGRICOLA, Biological and Agricultural Index, CAB Direct.

299. ***Agricultural History.*** Formerly (until 1927): *Agricultural History Society. Papers.* [ISSN: 0002-1482] 1921. q. USD 300 (print & online eds.)). Ed(s): Albert Way. Agricultural History Society, Department of History, PO Box H, Mississippi State, MS 39762; http://www.aghistorysociety.org. Illus., index. Refereed. Vol. ends: Fall. Microform: PQC. *Indexed:* A01, A22, Agr, AmHI, BAS, BRI, C45, E01, GardL, IBSS, MLA-IB. *Bk. rev.:* 15-30, 150-600 words. *Aud.:* Ac, Sa.

This society journal focuses on international research on agricultural history and is interested in papers that take a new well-researched approach to a subject. There are normally five articles per issue, and more than 20 book reviews separated by wide geographic ranges. The journal website selects an article or two from each issue and makes this available to all to promote comments and discussions. This journal would be of interest to agricultural and historical researchers.

300. ***Agronomy Journal.*** [ISSN: 1435-0645] 1998. bi-m. Free to members. Ed(s): Daniel Sweeney, Susan Ernst. American Society of Agronomy, Inc., 5585 Guilford Rd, Madison, WI 53711; https://www.agronomy.org. Refereed. *Aud.:* Ac, Sa.

This society publication publishes numerous original international scientific research articles under the subject categories of Agronomic Application of Genetic Resources; Crop Ecology and Physiology; Crop Economics, Production and Management; Climatology and Water Management; Biometry, Modeling and Statistics; Soil Fertility and Crop Nutrition; Organic Agriculture and Agroecology; Soil Tillage, Conservation and Management; Agronomy, Soils and Environmental Quality; Review and Interpretations; and Biofuels and Pest Interactions in Agronomic Systems. Articles are posted on the website immediately after acceptance. There is also a section for the most frequently read articles with a count on how many times this article was downloaded. This journal would be valuable to an academic or research facility in agronomy.

301. ***American Society of Agricultural and Biological Engineers. Transactions.*** Formerly (until 2006): *American Society of Agricultural Engineers. Transactions.* [ISSN: 2151-0032] 1907. bi-m. USD 813. Ed(s): Melissa Miller, Glenn Laing. American Society of Agricultural and Biological Engineers, 2950 Niles Rd, St Joseph, MI 49085; hq@asabe.org; http://www.asabe.org. Illus., index. Sample. Refereed. Vol. ends: Nov/Dec. *Indexed:* A01, A22, Agr, C45, S25. *Aud.:* Ac, Sa.

This peer-reviewed publication contains numerous articles per issue divided into sections such as "Education Outreach & Professional Development"; "Energy Systems"; "Information Technology, Sensors & Control Systems"; "Machine Systems"; "Natural Resources & Environmental Systems"; "Plant, Animal & Facility Systems"; and "Processing Systems." A majority of the recent papers are in the "Natural Resources & Environmental Systems" section. This journal should be in any academic library that provides support for agricultural and engineering programs.

302. ***Animal Frontiers.*** [ISSN: 2160-6056] 2011. q. Free to members. Ed(s): James Sartin. Oxford University Press, 2001 Evans Rd, Cary, NC 27513; custserv.us@oup.com; https://academic.oup.com/journals. Adv. Refereed. *Indexed:* C45. *Aud.:* Ac, Sa.

Four professional animal science societies (American Society of Animal Science, Canadian Journal of Animal Science, European Federation of Animal Science, and American Meat Science Association) jointly produce this journal, which contains invited, peer-reviewed articles on the international issues in animal husbandry. The journal is now being published by Oxford University Press and each issue that appears will continue to have a theme. In the department section there are reports from each of the societies and a from the editor's article. This journal is valuable for an international perspective on animal husbandry issues.

303. ***Crop Science.*** [ISSN: 0011-183X] 1961. bi-m. Free to members. Ed(s): C Wayne Smith, Elizabeth Gebhardt. Crop Science Society of America, 5585 Guilford Rd, Madison, WI 53711; membership@crops.org; https://www.crops.org. Illus., adv. Refereed. *Indexed:* A01, A22, Agr, BRI, C45, S25. *Bk. rev.:* Number and length vary. *Aud.:* Ac.

This professional society bimonthly publication has authors from around the world and is a highly ranked journal for the study of crops. Papers are separated into the broad subject areas of crop breeding and genetics; genomics, molecular genetics and biotechnology; crop physiology and metabolism; seed physiology, production and technology; crop ecology, production and management; forage and grazing land ecology and management; germplasm collections and their use; biomedical, health beneficial and nutritionally enhanced plants; and turfgrass science. This journal is useful for anyone researching crops or working with crops.

304. ***Food Outlook: global market analysis.*** [ISSN: 0251-1959] 1975. s-a. Food and Agriculture Organization of the United Nations (F A O), Viale delle Terme di Caracalla, Rome, 00153, Italy; publications-sales@fao.org; http://www.fao.org. Illus. *Indexed:* C45. *Aud.:* Ga, Ac.

This FAO Trade and Markets Division semiannual publication is in English with the market summaries available in Arabic, Chinese, French, Russian, and Spanish. Regular sections include "Market Summaries"; "Market Assessments"; "Major Policy Developments"; "Statistical Tables"; and "Market Indicators." There can be a few articles in a Special Features section. Another quarterly publication from this FAO Division is *Crop Prospects and Food Situation.* This publication would be valuable to those interested in international agricultural economics.

305. ***Frontiers in Plant Science.*** [ISSN: 1664-462X] 2010. . Free. Ed(s): Uwe Sonnewald, Wolf B Frommer. Frontiers Research Foundation, Avenue du Tribunal Federal 34, Lausanne, 1005, Switzerland; info@frontiersin.org; https://www.frontiersin.org. Refereed. *Indexed:* C45. *Aud.:* Ac, Sa.

This international multidisciplinary open-access journal covers plant research in 19 sections. Articles may be original research, a systematic review, methods, protocols, technology reports, a review, a mini review, policy and practice reviews, hypothesis and theory, a perspective, a general commentary, opinion, or book review. The articles are added and there aren't issues or volumes. Papers may also be grouped by research topics. This is a good resource for plant information.

306. ***Journal of Agricultural Education (Online).*** Former titles (until 2010): *Journal of Agricultural Education (Print);* (until 1989): *American Association of Teacher Educators in Agriculture. Journal.* [ISSN: 2162-5212] 1961. q. Free to members. Ed(s): Kate Shoulders. American Association for Agricultural Education, c/o Roger Tormoehlen, Treas., Dept of Youth Development and Agricultural Education, West Lafayette, IN 47907; http://www.aaaeonline.org. Refereed. *Indexed:* A22, Agr, C45, ERIC. *Aud.:* Ac.

This quarterly refereed journal provides people in the field to widely share information and promote the profession. The journal covers extension and teacher education, communications, leadership development, and the agricultural science related areas. Each paper indicates how often it has been accessed. Recent papers have covered the college readiness of Illinois high school agriculture students, professional development of mid-career agriculture teachers, and mentoring experiences. This journal is valuable for agricultural and education programs.

307. ***Journal of Agricultural Safety and Health.*** [ISSN: 1074-7583] 1995. q. USD 276. Ed(s): Fadi Fathallah. American Society of Agricultural and Biological Engineers, 2950 Niles Rd, St Joseph, MI 49085; hq@asabe.org; http://www.asabe.org. Illus., index. Refereed. Vol. ends: Nov. *Indexed:* Agr, C45, ErgAb. *Aud.:* Ga, Ac.

Safety is an important issue in a hazardous occupation with no mandatory retirement age and the average age of farmers is increasing. There are about four or five articles per issue covering engineering, health, and occupational safety. One recent article was about increasing awareness of farm equipment on public roadways. This journal should be available in any rural agricultural area.

308. ***Journal of Agricultural Science.*** [ISSN: 1916-9752] 2009. m. Ed(s): Tunde Akim Omokanye. Canadian Center of Science and Education, 1120 Finch Ave W, Ste 701-309, Toronto, ON M3J 3H7, Canada; info@ccsenet.org; http://www.ccsenet.org. Sample. Refereed. *Indexed:* C45. *Aud.:* Ac, Sa.

This monthly open-access refereed journal from the Canadian Center of Science and Education publishes articles in all aspects of agriculture. The journal has a goal of being a location to share the latest findings. There are usually about 40 articles per issue from around the world. This journal would be useful for studying international agriculture.

309. ***Journal of Animal Science (Online): the premier journal and leading source of new knowledge and perspectives in animal science.*** [ISSN: 1525-3163] 1942. m. GBP 555. Ed(s): James Sartin. American Society of Animal Science, PO Box 7410, Champaign, IL 61826-7410. Refereed. *Bk. rev.:* 1-5, 35-100 words. *Aud.:* Ac, Sa.

This journal, now available through Oxford University Press online, provides coverage of all areas of animal science research with more than 500 entries published each year. Issue supplements can contain meeting or symposium abstracts as well as educational and extension reports. There are numerous subject category headings in each issue and it is possible to also access the most recent, most read, or most cited articles. This journal should be in libraries supporting animal research.

310. ***Journal of Plant Registrations (Online).*** [ISSN: 1940-3496] 2007. 3x/yr. Free to members. Ed(s): C Wayne Smith, Ann Edahl. Crop Science Society of America, 5585 Guilford Rd, Madison, WI 53711; https://www.crops.org. Refereed. *Aud.:* Ga, Ac, Sa.

This online journal provides information on new cultivars, germplasms, and parental lines, mapping populations, and genetic stocks for the Crop Science Society of America. There are three issues per year and articles that have been edited and accepted can be found in the just-published section before being listed in an issue. It is important for farmers to know about new plants that can be more resistant to diseases, drought, insect pests, or produce a better crop.

311. ***Plant Disease: an international journal of applied plant pathology.*** Incorporates (19??-1980): *Phytopathology News;* Former titles (until 1980): *Plant Disease Reporter;* (until 1923): *The Plant Disease Bulletin.* [ISSN: 0191-2917] 1917. m. USD 1010 domestic; USD 1141 foreign. Ed(s): Alison E Robertson. American Phytopathological Society, 3340 Pilot Knob Rd, St. Paul, MN 55121; aps@scisoc.org; http://www.apsnet.org. Illus., adv. Refereed. Microform: MIM; PMC; PQC. *Indexed:* A01, A22, Agr, C45. *Aud.:* Ac, Sa.

Plant diseases can be devastating for an industry and this society journal is the location to find information of new or existing plant diseases. The authors can submit research articles, special reports, feature articles on topics, disease notes for early reports of diseases, and resource announcements. This journal would be valuable in areas where crops are grown.

312. ***Soil Science Society of America. Journal (Online).*** [ISSN: 1435-0661] 1976. bi-m. Free to members. Ed(s): Andrew Sharpley, Rebecca Funck. Soil Science Society of America, 5585 Guilford Rd, Madison, WI 53711; http://www.soils.org/. Refereed. *Aud.:* Ac, Sa.

This bimonthly publication from the Soil Science Society of America covers all aspects of soil science. There are numerous articles in each issue arranged in subject categories and the value of the articles is shown in the average number of times the articles are downloaded. Authors do have an option of making their articles open access and a few do this. This journal would be valuable in a scientific library.

313. ***U.S. Department of Agriculture. National Agricultural Statistics Service. Agricultural Prices.*** Former titles (until 1942): *United States. Bureau of Agricultural Economics. Farm Product Prices;* (until 19??): *Average Prices Received by Farmers for Farm Produce.* [ISSN: 0002-1601] 19??. m. U.S. Department of Agriculture, National Agricultural Statistics Service, 1400 Independence Ave, SW, Stop 9410, Washington, DC 20250; nass@nass.usda.gov; http://www.nass.usda.gov/. *Aud.:* Hs, Ga, Ac.

There are numerous USDA NASS (National Agricultural Statistics Service) publications available through their website and this title can be found by searching by title under publications. The subscription service is maintained by the Cornell University Mann Library. This monthly release publication covers the prices farmers receive. Data from the 1960s is available on the website and archival information from 1910 to 1960 was included in the 1962 issue. The information is presented primarily in tables and graphs. URL: www.nass.usda.gov

314. ***Weekly Weather and Crop Bulletin.*** Incorporates (1899-1932): *Snow and Ice Bulletin;* Which was formerly (until 1899): *Snow and Ice Chart.* [ISSN: 0043-1974] 1872. w. Free. Ed(s): Brad Rippey. The Joint Agricultural Weather Facility, 1400 Independence Ave SW, Washington, DC 20250; http://www.usda.gov/oce/weather/. Illus., index. Vol. ends: Dec. *Indexed:* A22. *Aud.:* Ga, Ac.

This USDA Office of the Chief Economist bulletin is jointly prepared by the U.S. Department of Commerce, the National Oceanic and Atmospheric Administration, and the U.S. Department of Agriculture. Weather information is critical for agriculture and this publication covers international weather, climate and agrometeorological information using text, maps, tables, and graphs.

■ ANIMAL RIGHTS/ANIMAL WELFARE

See also Birds; Horses; Pets; and Veterinary Science sections.

Andrea C. Kepsel, Health Sciences Educational Technology Librarian, Michigan State University Libraries, East Lansing, MI 48824; akepsel@msu.edu

Introduction

Animal welfare refers to a state of an animal and how it is coping with the conditions in which it lives. It concerns the health, nourishment, safety, comfort, and ability to perform innate behaviors, all in the absence of pain, fear, or distress. Animal welfare encompasses both an animal's physical and mental needs, and includes preventing illness or injury, providing appropriate shelter and nutrition, access to veterinary care, and humane handling and management.

Animal welfare is a popular topic because it touches many aspects of everyday life. It concerns animals of all types, from farm animals, poultry and livestock, marine life, and wildlife, to zoo animals, animals in laboratories, and companion animals. It is also reflected in diets and lifestyles such as vegetarianism and veganism.

Related to animal welfare is the concept of animal rights. Animal rights refers to the belief that animals are sentient creatures and should be granted the same considerations for care and well-being as humans. Proponents of animal rights believe that the use of animals by humans should be banned. There are many organizations that support animal rights whose missions include educating the public and fighting for increased legal protections of animals. Many animal rights organizations focus on a particular species or issue, providing many outlets for those who want to get involved in the protection of animals.

Oftentimes animal welfare is a very divisive topic, with passionate responses from individuals on both sides of an argument. It is important for libraries to have publications that represent the many perspectives people may have. This means paying attention to who is producing a publication and what their message is, and trying to strike a balance between opposing viewpoints represented in a collection.

Basic Periodicals

Ems: *KIND News*; Hs: *AWI Quarterly*; Ga: *AWI Quarterly*; Ac: *Animal Welfare, Journal of Animal Ethics, Journal of Applied Animal Welfare Science*; Sa: Animal Law Review, *Journal of Animal and Natural Resource Law.*

Basic Abstracts and Indexes

Academic Search Premier, AGRICOLA, CAB Abstracts, Humans and Other Species, PubMed.

315. *A S P C A Action.* [ISSN: 1554-6624] 2005. 3x/yr. Free to members. American Society for the Prevention of Cruelty to Animals, 424 E 92nd St, New York, NY 10128; information@aspca.org; http://www.aspca.org. Illus. Sample. *Aud.:* Hs, Ga.

The American Society for the Prevention of Cruelty to Animals (ASPCA, www.aspca.org), founded in 1866, was the first humane society to be established in North America and today is one of the largest in the world. *ASPCA Action*, published three times a year, is a full-color newsletter for members of the ASPCA. The focus of *ASPCA Action* is on animal health and welfare, and issues feature news about events and programs, pet care and behavior advice from experts, legislative and animal-advocacy news, information on recent ASPCA grants awarded to animal groups around the nation, and success stories from members. Recommended for public libraries.

316. *The A V Magazine.* Former titles (until 1977): *The A-V;* (until 1939): *Starry Cross;* (until 1919): *Journal of Zoophily.* [ISSN: 0274-7774] 1892. m. Free to members. Ed(s): Jill Howard Church. American Anti-Vivisection Society, 801 Old York Rd, Ste 204, Jenkintown, PA 19046; aavs@aavs.org; http://www.aavs.org/. Illus. Sample. *Aud.:* Hs, Ga.

The AV Magazine is a publication of the American Anti-Vivisection Society (AAVS, www.aavs.org). The mission of the AAVS is to end the use of animals in science through education, advocacy, and the development of alternative methods. Each issue focuses on one important topic related to the use of animals in research, testing, and education. Issues begin with brief news stories on global animal welfare issues, followed by longer feature articles on that issue's theme, and interviews with experts in the field. Articles are accompanied by full-color images and many include citations to relevant literature.

317. *A W I Quarterly.* Former titles (until 1992): *Animal Welfare Institute Quarterly;* (until 1981): *Animal Welfare Institute Information Report.* [ISSN: 1071-1384] 1951. q. Membership, USD 35. Animal Welfare Institute, 900 Pennsylvania Ave, S E, Washington, DC 20003; awi@awionline.org; http://www.awionline.org/. Illus. Sample. Vol. ends: Winter. *Indexed:* A22, Agr. *Bk. rev.:* Number and length vary. *Aud.:* Hs, Ga, Ac.

The Animal Welfare Institute (AWI, www.awionline.org), founded in 1951, is dedicated to reducing animal suffering caused by people. *AWI Quarterly*, published four times a year, reports on current animal welfare issues and includes sections on animals in laboratories, companion animals, farm animals, marine life, wildlife, government affairs, and humane education. Also included is information on other AWI publications and book reviews of titles with an animal welfare focus.

318. *Act'ionLine.* Former titles: *Friends of Animals Reports; Animals (New York); Actionline.* [ISSN: 1072-2068] 1977. q. USD 2 newsstand/cover per issue. Friends of Animals, Inc., 777 Post Rd, Ste 205, Darien, CT 06820-4721; http://www.friendsofanimals.org. Illus., index, adv. Sample. Vol. ends: Winter. *Bk. rev.:* Occasional. *Aud.:* Hs, Ga.

Act'ionLine is the quarterly magazine produced by Friends of Animals (http://friendsofanimals.org), a nonprofit, international animal advocacy organization. Friends of Animals works to cultivate a respectful view of nonhuman animals, free-living and domestic, and their goal is to free animals from cruelty and institutionalized exploitation around the world. Many stories include suggestions for actions that readers can take when concerned about a topic and contact information for related groups.

319. *AllAnimals.* Former titles (until 1999): *H S U S News;* (until 19??): *Humane Society News;* (until 1989): *Humane Society of the United States. News.* [ISSN: 1948-3597] 1954. bi-m. Free. Humane Society of the United States, 1255 23rd St, Suite 450, Washington, DC 20037; http://www.humanesociety.org/. Illus., adv. *Aud.:* Hs, Ga.

The Humane Society of the United States (HSUS, www.humanesociety.org), the nation's largest animal protection organization, publishes the bimonthly magazine *AllAnimals*. *AllAnimals* includes stories about the HSUS and the humane movement, profiles of people on the front lines, tips for pet owners and wildlife watchers, heartwarming tales of rescue and rehab, and actions readers can take. Articles are often accompanied by full-color photographs and each issue is enhanced by web content such as news, videos, and links to additional articles.

320. *Animal Action.* Former titles (until 1994): *Animal World;* (until 1981): *Animal Ways.* [ISSN: 1354-7437] 1975. bi-m. Free to members. Royal Society for the Prevention of Cruelty to Animals (R S P C A), RSPCA Enquiries Service, Wilberforce Way, Southwater, Horsham, RH13 9RS, United Kingdom; http://www.rspca.org.uk. Illus. Sample. Vol. ends: Dec. *Aud.:* Ems.

Published by the Royal Society for the Prevention of Cruelty to Animals (RSPCA, www.rspca.org.uk/home), *Animal Action* is for readers under 12 years of age. Full of animal news, facts, RSPCA rescues, posters, puzzles, and competitions, this magazine aims to educate young readers about animal welfare while also providing entertainment.

321. *Animal Law Review.* [ISSN: 1088-8802] 1994. s-a. USD 35 (Individuals, USD 25). Ed(s): David Rosengard, Carla Edmondson. Lewis & Clark College, Northwestern School of Law, 10015 SW Terwilliger Blvd, Portland, OR 97219; http://law.lclark.edu/. Illus. Reprint: WSH. *Indexed:* BRI, L14. *Bk. rev.:* Number and length vary. *Aud.:* Ac, Sa.

Dating back to 1994 and dedicated to providing a balanced, scholarly forum for discussing animal-related legal issues, *Animal Law Review* is the nation's oldest law journal devoted entirely to this topic. Animal legal issues include topics such as endangered species protection, regulating animals used in agriculture, animal testing, issues facing companion animals, and animal cloning. Issues are published twice a year and content includes articles, essays, notes, comments, book reviews, and other scholarly works that are valuable to attorneys in corporate, governmental, non-profit, or private practice, as well as legislatures, the judiciary, policymakers, students, and the interested public.

322. *Animal Sheltering: rescue, reunite, rehome, rethink.* Formerly (until 1996): *Shelter Sense.* 1978. bi-m. USD 20 domestic; USD 25 foreign. Humane Society of the United States, 1255 23rd St, Suite 450, Washington, DC 20037; http://www.humanesociety.org/. Illus., adv. Vol. ends: Nov/Dec. *Aud.:* Sa.

Available from the Humane Society of the United States, *Animal Sheltering* is "a magazine for anyone who cares about the health and happiness of animals and people in their community." Issues include practical information and advice on animal protection, sheltering, and control. While the magazine is helpful for anybody interested in these topics, it may be of particular use to professionals in the field.

323. *Animal Welfare.* [ISSN: 0962-7286] 1992. q. Institutional members, GBP 240 (print & online eds.); Individual members, GBP 90 (print & online eds.); GBP 135 combined subscription (print & online eds.): individual non-members). Universities Federation for Animal Welfare, The Old School, Brewhouse Hill, Wheathampstead, St Albans, AL4 8AN, United Kingdom; ufaw@ufaw.org.uk; http://www.ufaw.org.uk/. Illus., index. Sample. Refereed. *Indexed:* A22, Agr, C45. *Aud.:* Ac, Sa.

Animal Welfare is an international scientific and technical journal that publishes the results of peer-reviewed scientific research, technical studies, and reviews relating to the welfare of kept animals (e.g., on farms, in laboratories, zoos, and as companions) and of those in the wild whose welfare is compromised by human activities. The journal is peer-reviewed and published four times a year. To be considered for publication articles must have the potential to improve animal welfare by providing new knowledge, new perspectives, or developing new techniques.

324. *Animals.* [ISSN: 2076-2615] 2011. m. Free. Ed(s): Clive J C Phillips. M D P I AG, St. Alban-Anlage 66, Basel, 4052, Switzerland; info@mdpi.com; http://www.mdpi.com. Refereed. *Indexed:* A01, C45. *Aud.:* Ac, Sa.

Animals is an international open-access journal devoted entirely to animals in all fields, including zoology, ethnozoology, animal science, animal ethics, and animal welfare. Peer-reviewed and published monthly, preference is given to articles that incorporate interdisciplinary or transdisciplinary research to provide an integrated understanding of animals and their relationships with humans. Content includes research articles, reviews, communications, and short notes, and is published in one of four subject areas: zoology, ecology and conservation, animal management and welfare science, and animals and society.

325. *The Animals' Advocate.* Formerly (until 1989): *Animal Legal Defense Fund. Newsletter.* 1985. q. Free to members. Ed(s): Elizabeth Putsche. Animal Legal Defense Fund, 525 E Cotati Ave, Cotati, CA 94931; info@aldf.org; http://www.aldf.org. *Aud.:* Hs, Ga.

Founded in 1979, the Animal Legal Defense Fund's (ALDF, www.aldf.org) mission is to protect the lives and advance the interests of animals through the legal system. *The Animals' Advocate* is published quarterly to keep members and supporters posted on ALDF's groundbreaking legal work for animals. This full-color newsletter contains brief articles on current animal law cases and education on related legislation.

Anthrozoos. See Pets section.

Best Friends. See Pets section.

326. *Journal of Animal and Natural Resource Law.* Formerly (until 2012): *Journal of Animal Law.* 2005. a. USD 27 (print or online ed.)). Ed(s): Claire Corsey, Peter Beltz. Michigan State University, College of Law, 648 N. Shaw Lane, Rm 209C, East Lansing, MI 48824; msujanrl@gmail.com; http://www.msujbsl.com/. Refereed. *Bk. rev.:* Number and length vary. *Aud.:* Ac, Sa.

The Journal of Animal and Natural Resource Law (*JANRL*, www.msujanrl.org) is one of only three journals nationally that is devoted to animal law topics and is the premier resource for animal law and natural resource law scholars and practitioners nationwide. Peer-reviewed and published annually, contents include articles, book reviews, notes, and comments. Each article provides an in-depth legal analysis of a topic and references to the associated legislation.

327. *Journal of Animal Ethics.* [ISSN: 2156-5414] 2011. s-a. USD 216 (print & online eds.)). Ed(s): Priscilla N Cohn, Andrew Linzey. University of Illinois Press, 1325 S Oak St, MC-566, Champaign, IL 61820; uipress@uillinois.edu; http://www.press.uillinois.edu. Adv. Refereed. *Indexed:* BRI, C45. *Bk. rev.:* 1,000 words. *Aud.:* Ac, Sa.

The *Journal of Animal Ethics* is the first named journal of animal ethics in the world. It is devoted to the exploration of progressive thought about animals. It is peer-reviewed, multidisciplinary in nature, and international in scope. It covers theoretical and applied aspects of animal ethics of interest to academics from the humanities and the sciences, as well as professionals working in the field of animal protection. Issues include articles, review articles, book reviews, and argument pieces in which authors offer commentary or persuasion for a specific view on a topic. Articles include detailed reference lists that can be used for further research on a topic.

328. *Journal of Applied Animal Welfare Science.* Former titles (until 1998): *Humane Innovations and Alternatives;* (until 1991): *Humane Innovations and Alternatives in Animal Experimentation.* [ISSN: 1088-8705] 1987. q. GBP 674 (print & online eds.)). Routledge, 711 3rd Ave, 8th Fl., New York, NY 10017; http://www.routledge.com. Illus., index, adv. Sample. Refereed. Reprint: PSC. *Indexed:* A01, A22, Agr, C45, E01. *Bk. rev.:* Number and length vary. *Aud.:* Ac, Sa.

The *Journal of Applied Animal Welfare Science* (*JAAWS*) publishes articles, commentaries, and brief research reports on methods of experimentation, husbandry, and care that demonstrably enhance the welfare of all nonhuman animals. Contents are categorized into four areas of welfare issues: laboratory, farm, companion animal, and wildlife/zoo settings. The journal is peer-reviewed and international in scope. *JAAWS* also publishes research reports, commentaries, letters, news, and book reviews.

329. *Kind News.* Formed by the merger of (19??-2017): *K I N D News Sr;* Which was formerly: *Kind News (Senior ed.);* (1983-2017): *K I N D News Jr.* [ISSN: 2575-0550] 2017. 5x/yr. USD 10 domestic; USD 15.50 foreign. RedRover, PO Box 188890, Sacramento, CA 95818; info@RedRover.org; https://redrover.org/. Adv. *Aud.:* Ems.

Kind News is an eight-page publication that helps children understand and respect animals and think about why treating animals and people with kindness matters. The magazine encourages both empathy and critical thinking in children by celebrating the human-animal bond and helps motivate children to take action to improve the lives of animals. *Kind News* is aligned with national teaching standards and can be easily integrated into school curriculum. It is available in two levels: *Kind News Junior* (grades K-2) and *Kind News* (grades 3-6). Home and classroom subscriptions are available, and there are five issues throughout the school year for both subscription types.

330. *P E T A Global: advancing the animal rights revolution.* Former titles (until 2017): *P E T A's Animal Times;* (until 1994): *P E T A News.* [ISSN: 2573-4245] 1981. 3x/yr. Ed(s): Christina Matthies. People for the Ethical Treatment of Animals, Inc., 501 Front St, Norfolk, VA 23510; info@peta.org; http://www.peta.org. Illus. Sample. *Bk. rev.:* Number and length vary. *Aud.:* Hs, Ga.

People for the Ethical Treatment of Animals (PETA, www.peta.org) is the largest animal rights organization in the world, with more than 6.5 million members and supporters. PETA focuses its attention on the four settings in which the largest numbers of animals suffer the most intensely for the longest periods of time: the food industry, the clothing trade, laboratories, and the entertainment industry. *PETA Global*, published three times a year, is a full-color illustrated magazine for members of the organization. Content includes articles on celebrities that support PETA, news on the organization's activities, recipes, and ways for members to get involved.

331. *Society & Animals: journal of human - animal studies.* Incorporates (1997-2001): *Animal Issues;* Former titles (until 1993): *P S Y E T A Bulletin;* (until 1986): *P S Y E T A Newsletter.* [ISSN: 1063-1119] 1983. 7x/yr. EUR 567. Ed(s): Kenneth Shapiro, William S Lynn. Brill, PO Box 9000, Leiden, 2300 PA, Netherlands; marketing@brill.com; https://brill.com. Illus., index, adv. Refereed. Reprint: PSC. *Indexed:* A01, A22, Agr, C45, E01, IBSS, MLA-IB. *Aud.:* Ac, Sa.

Society & Animals publishes studies that describe and analyze our experiences of non-human animals from the perspective of various disciplines within both the social sciences and humanities. The goal of the journal is to stimulate and support the emerging multi-disciplinary field of animal studies. Empirically based studies are emphasized, but the journal also publishes theoretical analyses, literature reviews, methodological contributions, and comments on relevant topics. *Society & Animals* is unique in the breadth of subjects covered, methods of papers published, and diversity of scholarly disciplines represented. It encourages data-based discussion of ethical and policy issues in the current debate over the place of non-human animals in an increasingly human-centered world.

■ ANIME, COMICS, GRAPHIC NOVELS, AND MANGA

Tom Bruno, Associate Director of Resource Sharing and Reserves, Sterling Memorial Library, Yale University, New Haven, CT 06511,tbruno@westportlibrary.org

Introduction

There may have been a time when anime, comics, graphic novels, and manga were unfamiliar subjects to a librarian, but in recent years the market in North America for all of these has exploded dramatically. Bookstores and public libraries now stock entire sections with the latest manga series, while anime films have moved from special screenings at college fan clubs and art house theaters to the suburban multiplex, and comic artists and graphic novelists have been National Book Award finalists and even won the Pulitzer Prize. Having long been relegated to the stuff of juvenile fiction or esoteric enthusiasts, these art forms are beginning to gain mainstream respect among critics and the general public alike.

Over the past few years, manga and anime have experienced a surge in popularity in the United States and Canada, driven by a youth market enamored with Japanese popular culture ("J-pop") and adults who grew up reading comic books and watching early "Japanimation" exports such as *Astro Boy, Star Blazers,* and *Speed Racer* on television. Although this J-pop invasion was accompanied by a host of glossy consumer magazines, such as *Newtype USA, Protoculture Addicts,* and *Wizard,* many of these publications have folded in the past few years in the face of market consolidation and high production costs, though the popular "tankobon" anthologies of popular manga series are still available through publications such as *Weekly Shonen Jump.*

Comics and graphic novels, on the other hand, have finally come into their own with a series of new scholarly publications, as an increasing number of colleges and universities turn to more serious consideration of the medium. With Hollywood scrambling to produce competing film franchises based on superheroes from both the Marvel and D.C. lines of comics—over the next five years, there will be at least 40 movies coming out that feature comic book heroes (such as Marvel's *Avengers*) and villains (such as D.C. Comics' *Suicide Squad*)—areas of study that were once the province of a few erudite pop culture aficionados are now the stuff of mainstream scholarship and academic criticism.

This nascent legitimacy has not come without its backlash, however, as lifelong fans have reacted in various ways to the application of critical theory to their beloved "funny books." At the same time, comics publishers, eager to expand their readership beyond the traditional young white-male demographic, have made significant efforts to bring diversity to their offerings, much to the delight of many readers and the dismay of others.

To say that the world of comics is going through a period of transformation is something of a cliche. What I would argue makes this particular transformation different is the degree to which comics have insinuated themselves into the discourse of contemporary culture—not just our movies and our TV shows, but our metaphors as well. Batman, Superman, and the Incredible Hulk are part of a secular postmodern pantheon that is almost universally recognized and understood, which is probably why any changes or reinterpretations of these characters meet with such white-hot accusations of blasphemy or heresy. But comic books have always been reinventing themselves even before the days of D.C. Comics' Earth One and Earth-2 and the *Crisis On Infinite Earths.* Comics have always been at their best when they have engaged readers with contemporary issues, and this latest series of changes and continuity reboots is an indication that this peculiar genre born and raised in the twentieth century is alive and well in the twenty-first.

Clearly, anime, comics, graphic novels, and manga are art forms that resist easy categorization, and as these modes of expression gain a more secure foothold in popular culture, the more they are blurred into one all-encompassing genre. A fantastic example of this is the work of Bryan Lee O'Malley, a Canadian cartoonist whose award-winning *Scott Pilgrim* series of graphic novels is directly inspired by the manga tradition. At the same time, anime and manga are borrowing increasingly from North American comic books, graphic novels, feature films, and even literature. Consider also director Guillermo del Toro's 2013 giant robot/monster blockbuster film *Pacific Rim*—this is an excellent example of the rich cross-fertilization that occurs back and forth between Japan and Hollywood.

It is perhaps not surprising, then, that such a fluid and dynamic body of multimedia does not yet have many periodicals that cover it exclusively. With the notable exception of *Mechademia,* it is still particularly difficult to find academic or scholarly journals whose sole focus is anime and manga, although critical reception and interpretation of the genre can be found in many periodicals about film animation or contemporary East Asia culture. While it is true that comics and graphic novels have seen the emergence of a body of scholarly literature, the selection of general-interest magazines about anime, manga, comics, and graphic novels has contracted significantly in recent years, as fandom has migrated to blogs and social media for their previews, news, and reviews, or folded entirely into mainstream entertainment publications. This should hardly be considered a surprise, as comics, graphic novels, and manga themselves have migrated to the digital realm as well.

Basic Periodicals

See above.

Basic Abstracts and Indexes

MLA International Bibliography.

332. ***The Best American Comics.*** [ISSN: 1941-6385] 2006. a. USD 20 per issue 2011 edition. Ed(s): Lynda Barry, Matt Madden. Houghton Mifflin Harcourt Publishing Company, 222 Berkeley St, Boston, MA 02116; trade_publicity@hmco.com; http://www.hmhco.com/. *Aud.:* Ga, Ac, Sa.

While some special pleading may be in order to include this publication as a magazine, *The Best American Comics* is the definitive annual sampling of America's emerging talents in the field of comic art. This title was launched by Jessica Abel and Matt Madden, both of them comic book writers and artists themselves (as well as wife and husband). Each annual edition is 352 pages and features a new guest editor chosen every year by the series editor(s). This publication features more than two dozen excerpts that cull "the best stories from graphic novels, pamphlet comics, newspapers, magazines, mini-comics, and the Internet." In a field that is as visual as it is textual, there is no better introduction to the medium of comic art than a selection of cutting-edge authors, and *The Best American Comics* has delivered just that since its launch in 2006. Also noteworthy are the guest editors' forewords and the inclusion of "expanded selection lists" of artists/authors who did not make the cut. This series is an absolutely indispensable resource for any library building a serious comics collection, and will be very helpful to librarians eager to keep up with comics and graphic novels.

333. ***The Comics Grid: journal of comics scholarship.*** [ISSN: 2048-0792] 2011. . Free. Ed(s): Ernesto Priego. Open Library of Humanities, Salisbury House, Station Rd, Cambridge, CB1 2LA, United Kingdom; martin.eve@openlibhums.org; https://www.openlibhums.org. Refereed. *Aud.:* Ac.

The purpose of the open-access journal *The Comics Grid*-launched in 2011-is "to make original, media-specific contributions to the field of comics scholarship and to advance the appreciation of comic art." Rather than focusing solely on the content of comics, the editors of *The Comics Grid* investigate the interconnection of form and format as well, with consideration to such things as page sizes, the arrangement of panels, and the various technologies of comics production. While each "issue" is archived annually, the journal publishes new articles continually and accepts submissions from scholars in the field on a rolling basis. Recent articles have addressed such topics as the relationship between personality and faces in manga characters; a study of representations over time of Marvel Comics' Storm character from *The X-Men*; and, perhaps most intriguingly, a biological/pictorial catalog and analysis of Marvel and D.C. characters that were inspired by arachnids. Research articles are illustrated with black-and-white or color art as appropriate, and are interspersed with reviews, interviews, and original commentary (one recent commentary featured an insightful exploration of comics, copyright, and academic publishing). *The Comics Grid* is an excellent resource for the study of the representation of comic art itself, as well as a refreshing and unorthodox meditation on the state of comics study in the academy.

334. ***The Comics Journal: the magazine of comics news & criticism.*** Formerly (until 1977): *Nostalgia Journal.* [ISSN: 0194-7869] 1974. 3x/yr. USD 75 domestic; USD 90 Canada; USD 120 elsewhere. Ed(s): Timothy Hodler, Dan Nadel. Fantagraphics Books, Inc., 7563 Lake City Way NE, Seattle, WA 98115; http://www.fantagraphics.com. Illus., adv. *Bk. rev.:* 2-4 pages of reviews. *Aud.:* Ga, Ac, Sa.

Fantagraphics' *Comics Journal* is "a magazine that covers the comics medium from an arts-first perspective." Once a semi-monthly publication, *The Comics Journal* has evolved over the years under editor-in-chief Gary Groth into a daily web review, supplemented by an annual print edition. Each print issue contains an eclectic mix of comics news and reviews, as well as interviews with artists and writers from the whole spectrum of the field-from mainstream to indie comics, from newsstand superhero monthlies to more adult-themed graphic novels and underground publications. Recent issues have covered such topics as interviews with Kevin Eastman (creator of *Teenage Mutant Ninja Turtles*), *Mad Magazine* illustrator Will Elder, a tribute to beloved children's illustrator Maurice Sendak, and the response to James Kochalka's infamous 1996 letter/essay "Craft Is The Enemy." Although all of its contributors are clearly fans of comics and graphic novels, *Comics Journal* revels in its contentious relationship with the industry, applying a level of literary criticism and investigative journalism that is unusual for a medium whose major periodicals smack of unqualified mutual appreciation and boosterism. Issues are generously illustrated mostly in black-and-white, with some color prints, and feature artwork from some of the finest comics talent from around the world. *Comics Journal* also maintains a first-rate web presence, with selected excerpts available free to the public, and full online content for print subscribers. This is an essential resource for both general and specialized library collections.

335. *European Comic Art.* [ISSN: 1754-3797] 2008. s-a. USD 199 combined subscription (print & online eds.)). Ed(s): Laurence Grove, Ann Magnussen. Berghahn Books Ltd., 3 Newtec Pl, Magdalen Rd, Oxford, OX4 1RE, United Kingdom; journals@berghahnbooks.com; http://www.berghahnbooks.com. Adv. Sample. Refereed. Reprint: PSC. *Indexed:* A51, BRI, MLA-IB. *Aud.:* Ac, Sa.

A joint publication of American Bande Dessinee Society and the International Bande Dessinee Society from Berghahn Books Ltd., *European Comic Art* is "the first English-language scholarly publication devoted to the study of European-language graphic novels, comic strips, comic books[,] and caricature." Each issue contains four to six articles and several reviews of recent European comics, covering publications in all European languages, with special emphasis on works in French and English, and accompanied by illustrations in black-and-white. Recent topics addressed include the recent terrorist attack on the editorial offices of *Charlie Hebdo,* Vietnamese foodways in the graphic narratives of Clement Baloup, and performing gender in Algerian manga. While this journal is not intended for general audiences, *European Comic Art* is a welcome addition to academic and special library collections and provides an important avenue of access to contemporary European scholarship in the field of comics and graphic novels.

336. *ImageTexT: interdisciplinary comics studies.* [ISSN: 1549-6732] 2004. 3x/yr. Ed(s): Najwa Al-Tabaa, Terry Harpold. University of Florida, Department of English, 4008 Turlington Hall, PO Box 117310, Gainesville, FL 32611; http://www.english.ufl.edu/. Refereed. *Indexed:* MLA-IB. *Bk. rev.:* 1-4, signed. *Aud.:* Ac, Sa.

Given the decidedly postmodern and multimedia nature of the comics/graphic novel genre, it is perhaps surprising that there aren't more open-access online journals covering the field. *ImageTexT,* published by the University of Florida's English Department, makes up for this relative scarcity, however, by offering an academic review of the medium that is as in-depth as it is comprehensive. *ImageTexT* is a free, open-access, peer-reviewed online publication, and each issue features 8–12 articles (including one to four book reviews) written by an international body of contributors including graduate students, professors, and educated laypersons. Articles are formatted specifically for online reading, contain lavish color illustrations, and permit easy browsing and navigation. Recent issues address such topics as "The Epistemology of the Phone Booth: The Superheroic Identity and Queer Theory in Batwoman: Elegy"; gender formulas in *The Walking Dead* and *The Fantastic Four*; sanity and insanity in *The Killing Joke*; and monstrosity and pornography in the underground pamphlets of Jack T. Chick. As of Issue 8.1 (2015), editorial oversight of this journal has passed from founder Donald Ault to Terry Harpold and Anastasia Ulanowicz, who have promised to expand the scope to include animation, video games, film, illustrated fiction, children's picture books, digital-concrete poetics, and visual rhetoric. *ImageTexT* should be on every librarian's short list of comics journals, not just because it's open access and free, but because it's quite simply one of the best periodicals out there representing the intersection of comics and serious scholarship.

337. *International Journal of Comic Art.* [ISSN: 1531-6793] 1999. s-a. USD 100 (Individuals, USD 45). John A. Lent, Ed & Pub, 669 Ferne Blvd, Drexel Hill, PA 19026. Illus. *Indexed:* MLA-IB. *Bk. rev.:* 5-10, signed. *Aud.:* Ac, Sa.

The brainchild of John A. Lent, Professor of Mass Media and Communication at Temple University, the *International Journal of Comic Art* (*IJOCA*) is a scholarly publication of truly international scope that brings together the study of the related genres of anime, comics, graphic novels, and manga all under the same masthead. Each issue ranges between 300 and 800-plus pages and contains a dizzying array of academic articles that cover aspects of comics from over 50 different countries, with equal emphasis on manga and anime and on the comic art forms of the West. The most recent issues addresses topics as diverse as the emergence of Black cartoon animators in South Africa, the place of the wilderness in *Watchmen,* visual representations of comic sound in Edgar Wright's *Scott Pilgrim vs. The World* (2010), and a surprisingly detailed analysis of varying sizes of word balloons in comics. Each issue includes black-and-white illustrations and several book reviews of recent international publications in the field. While such a journal might not appeal to a more general audience, for academic and special libraries the *International Journal of Comic Art* is unparalleled in its global scope and scholarly treatment of the anime and manga genres.

338. *Journal of Graphic Novels & Comics.* [ISSN: 2150-4857] 2010. q. GBP 365 (print & online eds.)). Ed(s): Joan Ormrod, David Huxley. Routledge, 4 Park Sq, Milton Park, Abingdon, OX14 4RN, United Kingdom; subscriptions@tandf.co.uk; http://www.tandfonline.com. Refereed. Reprint: PSC. *Indexed:* A51. *Bk. rev.:* 6-10 per issue, 1-2 pages each, signed. *Aud.:* Ac, Sa.

The *Journal of Graphic Novels and Comics* is a semi-annual publication from editors David Huxley and Joan Ormrod, both members of the Faculty of Art & Design at Manchester Metropolitan University. Although published in the United Kingdom, this journal professes an international scope, with the goal to "establish a dialogue between academics, historians, theoreticians[,] and practitioners of comics." Each issue is between 80 and 110 pages and contains several articles with color illustrations, as well as six to ten reviews of books recently published in the field. The journal covers various aspects of worldwide culture such as comics-collecting culture and the digital marketplace; mirrored discourse in Alison Bechdel's *Fun Home*; and the moral world of Superman and the American war in Vietnam. As comics and graphic novels continue to gain mainstream acceptance both in society and in academia, it is encouraging to see the launch of new scholarly periodicals such as the *Journal of Graphic Novels and Comics,* which is a welcome addition to any research collection that focuses on the field of comic studies.

339. *Mechademia.* [ISSN: 1934-2489] 2006. a. USD 130 (print & online eds.)). Ed(s): Frenchy Lunning. University of Minnesota Press, 111 Third Avenue South, Ste 290, Minneapolis, MN 55401; ump@umn.edu; http://www.upress.umn.edu. Illus., adv. Refereed. *Indexed:* A22, E01, MLA-IB. *Bk. rev.:* 5-10 reviews, signed. *Aud.:* Ga, Ac.

A publication of the University of Minnesota Press, *Mechademia* is the only academic journal dedicated exclusively to the study of anime and manga in the United States. "[W]e see these not as objects but as arts whose production, distribution, and reception generate networks of connections. Thus our subject area extends from manga and anime to game design, fashion, graphics, packaging, and toy industries[,] as well as a broad range of fan practices related to popular culture in Japan, including gaming, cosplay, fan artwork, anime music videos, anime improvisations, etc." In acknowledgment of this broad spectrum of interconnected content, criticism, and cultural reception, the editors of *Mechademia* have cast their net wide, soliciting submissions from not only traditional academics but from filmmakers, writers, artists, and critics at large. The senior advisory board is similarly diverse, with professors of Eastern Asian languages and literature, communications, film studies, and fine arts and design, as well as independent scholars and writers. Each illustrated issue is 184 pages and contains 10-15 scholarly essays and five to ten signed reviews of books, films, and other related media organized around a central theme. Themes have included the works of Tezuka Osamu and the impact of anime and manga on depictions of lines of sight and perspective. The most recent issue has rather provocatively addressed the extent to which "Japan" might be seen as an idea generated by anime, manga, and other texts rather than the other way around. *Mechademia* is ambitious in scope, a delightful exploration of what its editors have dubbed the "Art Mecho" movement that embraces the global J-pop phenomenon from a critical distance. This journal would make a fine addition to both public and academic library collections that treat the subjects of contemporary Japanese culture and its reception abroad.

340. *Otaku U S A.* [ISSN: 1939-3318] 2007. bi-m. USD 19.95; USD 24.95 combined subscription (print & online eds.)). Ed(s): Patrick Macias. Sovereign Media Co., 6731 Whittier Ave, McLean, VA 22101; laura@sovhomestead.com; http://sovmedia.sovhomestead.com. Illus., adv. *Bk. rev.:* 20-25 manga reviews, 5-10 anime reviews. *Aud.:* Hs, Ga.

A relatively new arrival to the field of anime and manga magazines, *Otaku USA* takes its name from the Japanese word *otaku*, which translates roughly as "nerd" or "geek" or, better yet, the more colloquial slang word "fanboy." *Otaku USA* offers a distinctly American fanboy take on the phenomenon of Japanese pop culture, positioning itself as an "independent" alternative to the other glossy, mass-media anime and manga magazines published by the Japanese entertainment industry jointly in North America and Japan. The magazine offers not only the standard fare of anime/manga previews and reviews, along with coverage of the latest video games, toy releases, anime television reviews, Japanese and J-pop-inspired music, and anime and manga conventions. *Otaku USA* also devotes a significant amount of attention to toys-including the emerging subgenres of "gunpla" (based on the Gundam plastic models kits sold worldwide by Bandai) and "cosplay" (dressing in costume as your favorite anime/manga characters-a convention favorite). Recent issues have also featured 3D printing and its growing popularity among anime and manga enthusiasts. Each issue is also accompanied by a manga preview insert, color centerfold posters, and a DVD containing anime short features, trailers of upcoming releases, and playable demos of the latest video games (statistics beyond manga and anime reviews per issue, seen above, include: five to ten video game reviews, three to five music CD reviews). Although it is hard for a newcomer to compete with the established anime and manga magazine titles, *Otaku USA* carves out a niche for itself by emphasizing the American perspective on the genre and the reaction in the United States to the J-pop invasion. Articles may not be as lavishly illustrated as the established competition, but the editors of *Otaku USA* compensate with feature articles that are specifically geared toward the American reader and that are written with a fan's enthusiasm for the genre, tempered with a broader offering of introspection as to the deeper meanings of Japanese pop culture and its two-way creative relationship with the United States and the West. As such a hybrid creation itself, *Otaku USA* is a worthwhile addition to any library collection and a great resource for both young and old would-be American *otaku*. Following the demise of the popular title of *Protoculture Addicts* (which has not folded, but has not released a new issue since 2008), *Otaku USA* is now the only regular publication covering anime news in North America.

341. *Sequart.* 1996. . Ed(s): Mike Phillips. Sequart Organization, sequart@gmail.com; http://sequart.org/. Illus. *Aud.:* Ga, Ac.

Sequart is an online magazine published by the Sequart Organization, and it focuses "on the study of popular culture and the promotion of comic books as a legitimate art form." Thus it is a great example of the transformation of the body of periodicals that cover topics in comic books and popular culture. *Sequart* magazine itself is only the tip of the iceberg of the organization's portfolio of work, which includes books and full-length documentary movies about comic books, writers/artists, and various themes that run through both comics and contemporary American culture. The magazine's mission, in its own words, is "bridging the gap between academia and fandom, [toward] making scholarship accessible to the general reading public, and [toward] putting complex thoughts into the plainest language possible." To this end, *Sequart*'s editors seek as diverse a set of viewpoints as possible, actively soliciting minority and women's voices as being necessary to supporting an authentic criticism of American pop culture and comics. New articles are uploaded to *Sequart* on a daily basis, and address a wide variety of topics-such as racist iconography in depictions of the American South in the *Swamp Thing* comic; an explanation of the scientific accuracy of the science-fiction television thriller *Orphan Black*; and the ongoing gritty legacy of the 1986 graphic novels *Watchmen* and *The Dark Knight Returns* and their influence on the modern superhero entertainment industry (for good or for ill!). As with other titles following this basic format, scholarly articles are interspersed with news, reviews, and other occasional pieces. *Sequart* is a useful guide to the study of comics and pop culture, and this magazine may steer readers or librarians toward other books and documentaries produced by the Sequart Organization that may provide additional depth or breadth to one's collections in this always-changing, always-growing discipline.

342. *Studies in Comics.* [ISSN: 2040-3232] 2010. s-a. GBP 212 (print & online eds.)). Ed(s): Chris Murray, Julia Round. Intellect Ltd., The Mill, Parnall Rd, Fishponds, Bristol, BS16 3JG, United Kingdom; info@intellectbooks.com; http://www.intellectbooks.co.uk/. Adv. Sample. Refereed. Reprint: PSC. *Indexed:* A51, MLA-IB. *Bk. rev.:* 1-10 per issue, 3-6 pages each, signed. *Aud.:* Ac, Sa.

Another recently-launched scholarly periodical from the United Kingdom, *Studies in Comics* is a peer-reviewed journal edited by Julia Round of Bournemouth University and Chris Murray of the University of Dundee. Its aim is "to make available articles of an exceptional academic standard with a strong theoretical focus." Each issue contains between six and 20 articles, interviews with current artists/authors, and several reviews of current monographs in the field of comics studies. Topics covered include violence and romanticism in the Silver Age comics of Steve Ditko; *American Splendor* and the "universe grotesque"; and the semiotic resources of comics in movie adaptation: a case study of Ang Lee's *Hulk* (2003). *Studies in Comics* is an ambitious journal, bringing serious literary criticism to bear on the comic art medium, and it would make an excellent addition to any college or university library collection.

343. *Weekly Shonen Jump.* Former titles (until 2013): *Weekly Shonen Jump Alpha;* (until 2012): *Shonen Jump.* 2003. w. USD 25.99 (print or online ed.); USD 0.99 per issue (print or online ed.)). Viz Media, LLC, PO Box 77010, San Francisco, CA 94107; media@viz.com; http://www.viz.com/. Illus. *Bk. rev.:* 10-15 manga chapter previews. *Aud.:* Hs, Ga.

From the Japanese word *shonen*, meaning boy, *Weekly Shonen Jump* (formerly *Shonen Jump*, then *Weekly Shonen Jump Alpha*) is a monthly American counterpart to Shueisha's Japanese publication of the same name, published in partnership with VIZ Media since 2003. "Made of the characters meaning few and years," reads the editorial statement, "shonen is Japanese for boy but can also mean pure of heart. Manga and anime created for shonen are among the most popular in the world[,] with fans of all ages and genders." As of 2013, *Weekly Shonen Jump* is now solely a digital publication, having transitioned to an all-online format in order to capture some of the revenue lost to "scanlation," i.e., fan-based translation and distribution of popular Japanese manga titles. Each digital issue features manga chapters printed in black-and-white, with several color pages and a few glossy pages at both the beginning and the end of each book. It contains manga news and reviews of anime, video games, toys, and collectible card games. *Weekly Shonen Jump* also contains extensive coverage of video game and collectible card-gaming strategy, as well as interviews with developers and previews of new gaming products (some issues also contain free collectible trading cards from such popular lines as Yu-Gi-Oh). Each serial chapter installment includes a useful introduction for first-time readers, including a summary of plot elements and a description of the major characters. Like its Japanese counterpart, *Weekly Shonen Jump* is printed right-to-left to preserve the aesthetics of the original manga. *Weekly Shonen Jump* is also an excellent overview of the field of available manga publications, and is a good indicator of what is currently popular among younger readers. As such, it is an important part of any library manga collection. URL: http://shonenjump.viz.com/

■ ANTHROPOLOGY

Priscilla Seaman, Subject Librarian, Anthropology/Geography & Planning/Communication University Library, LI-140, University at Albany, SUNY pseaman@albany.edu

Introduction

In the broadest sense, anthropology is the science and study of humankind. More specifically, the discipline studies human beings in their biological, cultural, and social aspects. Four major subdisciplines constitute the field: archaeology; biological/physical anthropology; cultural/social anthropology; and linguistics. Archaeologists, cultural anthropologists, and linguists respectively examine the material, social, and symbolic lives of humans past and present. Physical anthropologists examine humanity as a biological phenomenon, including studying evolutionary history.

Due to the broad scope of anthropological examinations of humankind, and the proliferation of subdisciplines, the number of available journals is extensive. The titles included in this section were chosen for breadth of subject matter and represent the four branches of anthropology. Please note that this volume also includes separate title lists for archaeology and linguistics.

The American Anthropological Association (AAA) is the largest professional society of anthropology in the United States. A library's core collection should contain some of the association's 20-plus serials, including its flagship publication, *The American Anthropologist.* The following selection of anthropological journals provides guidance for building a core periodical collection, in addition to including titles of note that reflect unique perspectives within the field of anthropology.

Basic Periodicals

Ga: *American Anthropologist, Annual Review of Anthropology, Current Anthropology;* Ac: *American Anthropologist, American Ethnologist, American Journal of Physical Anthropology, Current Anthropology, Royal Anthropological Institute. Journal.*

Basic Abstracts and Indexes

Abstracts in Anthropology, Anthropological Index, Anthropological Literature.

344. *American Anthropologist.* Supersedes (in 1988): *Anthropological Society of Washington. Transactions.* [ISSN: 0002-7294] 1888. q. GBP 451 (print & online eds.)). Ed(s): Deborah A Thomas. Wiley-Blackwell Publishing, Inc., 350 Main St, Malden, MA 02148; http://onlinelibrary.wiley.com. Illus., index, adv. Sample. Refereed. Vol. ends: Dec. Microform: PQC. Reprint: PSC. *Indexed:* A01, A22, A47, B01, BAS, BRI, C45, CBRI, Chicano, E01, F01, IBSS, MLA-IB. *Bk. rev.:* 10-20, 250-300 words. *Aud.:* Ga, Ac.

In publication since 1888, this flagship journal of the American Anthropological Association furthers the association's mission by publishing articles, commentaries, and essays on all facets of anthropological knowledge. The journal content is approximately arranged into the following sections: research articles; public anthropology; visual anthropology including film, television, and the occasional YouTube review; distinguished lectures; and an extensive book review section. *American Anthropologist* is a vital resource for anthropologists and most academic libraries.

345. *American Ethnologist.* [ISSN: 0094-0496] 1974. q. GBP 351 (print & online eds.)). Ed(s): Niko Besnier. Wiley-Blackwell Publishing, Inc., 111 River St, Hoboken, NJ 07030; http://onlinelibrary.wiley.com. Illus., index. Refereed. Circ: 3500. Vol. ends: Nov. Microform: PQC. Reprint: PSC. *Indexed:* A01, A22, A47, AmHI, BAS, BRI, C45, CBRI, Chicano, E01, IBSS, MLA-IB. *Bk. rev.:* Number and length vary. *Aud.:* Ac.

In its own description, *American Ethnologist* conveys "the ongoing relevance of the ethnographic imagination to the contemporary world." The journal lives up to its mission by featuring original research on topical cultural events and concerns. International in scope, this journal presents a broad overview of ethnology and ethnographic research. A core title for most academic libraries.

346. *American Journal of Human Biology (Online).* [ISSN: 1520-6300] 1989. bi-m. GBP 1357. Ed(s): Lynette L Sievert. John Wiley & Sons, Inc., 111 River St, Hoboken, NJ 07030; cs-journals@wiley.com; http://www.wiley.com. Refereed. *Bk. rev.:* About 2 per issue. *Aud.:* Ac.

The *American Journal of Human Biology* is the official journal of the Human Biology Association. Its aims and scopes are described as: "a journal that publishes reports of original research, theoretical articles and timely reviews, and brief communications in the interdisciplinary field of human biology...the journal also publishes abstracts of research presented at its annual scientific meeting and book reviews relevant to the field."

347. *American Journal of Physical Anthropology (Online).* [ISSN: 1096-8644] 1996. 4x/yr. GBP 2509. Ed(s): Peter T Ellison. John Wiley & Sons, Inc., 111 River St, Hoboken, NJ 07030; cs-journals@wiley.com; http://onlinelibrary.wiley.com. Refereed. *Bk. rev.:* 5-10, 1,200 words. *Aud.:* Ac.

The *American Journal of Physical Anthropology* is the official journal of the American Association of Physical Anthropologists. As measured by impact factor, it ranks among the top journals listed in the anthropology category of the Social Science Citation Index and Scimago. Articles encompass the evolution of primates, with an emphasis on human variation and evolution. This journal is published monthly and includes two supplements: the *Annual Meeting Issue* and *The Yearbook of Physical Anthropology.*

348. *Annual Review of Anthropology.* Formerly (until 1972): *Biennial Review of Anthropology.* [ISSN: 0084-6570] 1959. a. USD 431 (print & online eds.)). Ed(s): Donald Brenneis, Karen B Strier. Annual Reviews, PO Box 10139, Palo Alto, CA 94303; service@annualreviews.org; http://www.annualreviews.org. Illus. Refereed. Reprint: PSC. *Indexed:* A01, A22, A47, BAS, C45, IBSS, MLA-IB, P61, SSA. *Aud.:* Ga, Ac.

The *Annual Review of Anthropology* keeps readers current with recent trends and research in the discipline. The *Annual Review* series publishes reviews in 40 different scientific fields. "The comprehensive critical review not only summarizes a topic but also roots out errors of fact or concept and provokes discussion that will lead to new research activity." This title covers significant developments in each of the subfields of anthropology, and includes a section for international anthropology and regional studies. Each volume offers several special themes.

Anthropological Linguistics. See Linguistics section.

349. *Anthropological Quarterly.* Formerly (until 1953): *Primitive Man.* [ISSN: 0003-5491] 1928. q. USD 209 (Individuals, USD 132). Ed(s): Roy Richard Grinker, Nicholas Harkness. George Washington University, Institute for Ethnographic Research, 2110 G St, NW, Washington, DC 20052; anth@gwu.edu; http://anthropology.columbian.gwu.edu/. Illus., index, adv. Refereed. Vol. ends: Oct. Microform: MIM; PQC. *Indexed:* A22, A47, B01, BAS, BRI, Chicano, E01, EIP, IBSS, MLA-IB, P61, SSA. *Bk. rev.:* Number and length vary. *Aud.:* Ga, Ac.

A publication of the George Washington University Institute for Ethnographic Research, *Anthropological Quarterly* offers peer-reviewed articles on social and cultural anthropology. In addition to the goal of "the rapid dissemination of articles that blend precision with humanism," this journal contains a section of "Social Thought and Commentary," which is "a forum for scholars within and outside the discipline of anthropology to add their voices to contemporary public debates." The book reviews, including new-book releases, are often in-depth and extensive.

350. *Anthropology & Education Quarterly.* Former titles (until 1976): *Council on Anthropology and Education Quarterly;* (until 1974): *Council on Anthropology and Education Newsletter.* [ISSN: 0161-7761] 1970. q. GBP 116 (print & online eds.)). Ed(s): Laura A Valdiviezo, Sally Campbell Galman. Wiley-Blackwell Publishing, Inc., 111 River St, Hoboken, NJ 07030; info@wiley.com; http://www.wiley.com/. Illus., index, adv. Sample. Refereed. Vol. ends: Dec. Microform: PQC. Reprint: PSC. *Indexed:* A22, A47, BRI, Chicano, E01, ERIC, IBSS, MLA-IB. *Bk. rev.:* Number and length vary. *Aud.:* Ga, Ac.

This journal, the official publication of the Council on Anthropology and Education, publishes anthropological research in education in the United States and internationally, and discusses educational development and the teaching of anthropology. Its peer-reviewed articles use ethnographic research to address problems of practice, in addition to addressing broad theoretical questions. Articles would interest educators, sociologists, and social workers in addition to anthropologists. The titles of books reviewed are listed in each issue, but the full reviews are found only online. URL: www.aanet.org/cae/aeq.html

351. *Anthropology and Humanism.* Formerly (until 1993): *Anthropology and Humanism Quarterly.* [ISSN: 1559-9167] 1974. s-a. GBP 68 (print & online eds.)). Ed(s): David Syring, Jeffrey Ehrenreich. Wiley-Blackwell Publishing, Inc., 350 Main St, Malden, MA 02148; cs-journals@wiley.com; http://onlinelibrary.wiley.com. Illus., adv. Sample. Refereed. Vol. ends: Dec. Reprint: PSC. *Indexed:* A01, A22, A47, AmHI, BRI, E01, IBSS, MLA-IB. *Bk. rev.:* 3-5, 1,200 words. *Aud.:* Ga, Ac.

This scholarly journal accepts contributions from the four subdisciplines of anthropology, and from scholars in the humanities and other social science disciplines. *Anthropology and Humanism* sets itself apart by publishing work in a variety of genres: poetry, fiction, creative nonfiction, photo essays, and drama. *Anthropology and Humanism* focuses its content on the core question of the discipline: What is it to be human? Because of its cross-disciplinary nature and its mission of pushing the boundaries of scholarly inquiry and creativity, this journal makes a unique addition to a core anthropology journal collection.

352. *Anthropology Today.* Formerly (until 1985): *R A I N (Royal Anthropological Institute News).* [ISSN: 0268-540X] 1974. bi-m. GBP 152. Ed(s): Gustaaf Houtman. Wiley-Blackwell Publishing Ltd., The Atrium, Southern Gate, Chichester, PO19 8QG, United Kingdom; cs-journals@wiley.com; http://onlinelibrary.wiley.com/. Illus., adv. Sample. Microform: PQC. Reprint: PSC. *Indexed:* A01, A22, A47, BRI, C37, E01, IBSS, MLA-IB. *Aud.:* Ga, Ac.

A non-refereed publication, *Anthropology Today* publishes articles that apply anthropological analysis to public and current issues. The journal is international in scope and sources, and provides an interface between the discipline of anthropology and applied fields such as medicine and education. Articles are shorter in length than the research articles of many peer-reviewed journals, but the breadth of the discipline is reflected in the array of topics addressed. Journal sections include narratives, comments, news, and conferences, in addition to original articles.

353. *Anthropos: revue internationale d'ethnologie et de linguistique.* [ISSN: 0257-9774] 1906. 2x/yr. CHF 190; EUR 142. Ed(s): Othmar Gaechter. Editions Saint-Paul Fribourg, Perolles 42, Fribourg, 1700, Switzerland; info@paulusedition.ch; http://www.paulusedition.ch. Illus., index. Refereed. *Indexed:* A22, A47, BAS, IBSS, MLA-IB, P61, SSA. *Bk. rev.:* 30, length varies. *Aud.:* Ac.

Anthropos, in publication for more than one hundred years, is a publication of the Anthropos Institute, an organization located in Germany. The journal's original statutes are grounded in theological discourse and "the restless searching of the human spirit in the history of peoples and cultures." Articles are in English, French, and German and delve into matters of anthropology, ethnology, linguistics, and religious studies. Issues are lengthy, containing more than ten articles of 15-20 pages, as well as reports and comments. Approximately one half of each issue is devoted to an extensive book reviews section, sometimes reviewing more than 50 new titles.

354. *Arctic Anthropology.* [ISSN: 0066-6939] 1962. s-a. USD 311 print & online eds. Ed(s): Christyann Darwent. University of Wisconsin Press, Journals Division, 1930 Monroe St, 3rd Fl, Madison, WI 53711; journals@uwpress.wisc.edu; http://www.uwpress.org. Illus., index, adv. Refereed. Microform: PQC. Reprint: PSC. *Indexed:* A01, A22, A47, BAS, E01, IBSS, MLA-IB. *Bk. rev.:* Number and length vary. *Aud.:* Ga, Ac.

Articles in the journal *Arctic Anthropology* concentrate on the study of Old and New World northern cultures and peoples. The subdisciplines of anthropology are represented in the journal content with an emphasis on arctic, subarctic, and contiguous regions. Articles explore topics such as the peopling of the New World, as well as topics of contemporary cultures of northern peoples. A view into the scholarly focus of this journal is provided by recent articles such as "Sami Archaeology and Postcolonial Theory - An Introduction" and "A Bering Strait Indigenous Framework for Resource Management: Respectful Seal and Walrus Hunting."

355. *The Australian Journal of Anthropology.* Formerly (until 1990): *Mankind.* [ISSN: 1035-8811] 1931. 3x/yr. GBP 257. Ed(s): Michael Goddard. Wiley-Blackwell Publishing Asia, 155 Cremorne St, Richmond, VIC 3121, Australia; melbourne@wiley.com; http://onlinelibrary.wiley.com. Illus., index, adv. Refereed. Reprint: PSC. *Indexed:* A01, A22, A47, BAS, BRI, E01, IBSS, MLA-IB, P61, SSA. *Bk. rev.:* Number varies, 800-1,000 words. *Aud.:* Ga, Ac.

Formerly entitled *Mankind,* this refereed journal publishes papers and book reviews in anthropology and related disciplines. A publication of the Australian Anthropological Society, this journal places a special emphasis on anthropological research based in Australia and neighboring countries in the Pacific and Asian regions. One of three annual issues is devoted to a special topic. Articles are 10-20 pages in length, and each issue contains approximately 125 pages.

356. *Cultural Anthropology.* [ISSN: 0886-7356] 1986. q. Ed(s): Marcel LaFlamme. American Anthropological Association, 2300 Clarendon Blvd, Ste 1301, Arlington, VA 22201; https://www.americananthro.org. Illus. Sample. Refereed. Vol. ends: Nov. Reprint: PSC. *Indexed:* A01, A22, A47, AmHI, BAS, BRI, C45, E01, IBSS, MLA-IB. *Bk. rev.:* Number and length vary. *Aud.:* Ac.

Often occurring in the top ten journals in ranking lists, *Cultural Anthropology* promotes scholarship in cultural studies and the theory of culture. The Society of Cultural Anthropology, which publishes this journal, has as its mission to connect anthropology with other disciplines: history, literature, philosophy, and the social sciences. To that end, articles often focus on topics of interest to these disciplines, and include literary criticism and theory. Issues include original articles, special and thematic features, and a smattering of book reviews. In 2014, *Cultural Anthropology* went open-access, which means that all journal content published since 2014 is freely available on the *Cultural Anthropology* web site immediately upon publication. The journal is also in the process of publishing back issues from 2004 to 2013 to its web site. A core title for academic collections.

357. *Current Anthropology.* Formerly (until 1955): *Yearbook of Anthropology.* [ISSN: 0011-3204] 1955. bi-m. USD 461. Ed(s): Laurence Ralph. University of Chicago Press, 1427 E 60th St, Chicago, IL 60637; subscriptions@press.uchicago.edu; http://www.journals.uchicago.edu. Illus., index, adv. Sample. Refereed. Reprint: PSC. *Indexed:* A01, A22, A47, BAS, BRI, IBSS, MASUSE, MLA-IB, P61, SSA. *Bk. rev.:* 3-5, 2,000 words. *Aud.:* Ga, Ac.

Current Anthropology is a transnational journal devoted to research on humankind, including social, cultural, and physical anthropology, as well as ethnology, archaeology, folklore, and linguistics. Issues include articles, discussions, forums, reports, and book and film reviews. The section "Anthropological Currents" summarizes empirical research in other anthropology publications. For professional and general readership.

358. *Dialectical Anthropology: an independent international journal in the critical tradition committed to the transformation of our society and the humane union of theory and practice.* [ISSN: 0304-4092] 1975. q. EUR 888 (print & online eds.)). Ed(s): Winnie Lem, Anthony Marcus. Springer Netherlands, Van Godewijckstraat 30, Dordrecht, 3311 GX, Netherlands; http://www.springer.com. Illus., index, adv. Vol. ends: Dec. Microform: PQC. Reprint: PSC. *Indexed:* A01, A22, A47, AmHI, BAS, BRI, E01, IBSS, MLA-IB, P61, SSA. *Aud.:* Ac.

Dialectical Anthropology provides a "forum for a dialectical approach to social theory and political practice" and "seeks to invigorate discussion among left intellectuals...scholars and activists working in Marxist and broadly political-economic traditions." This journal publishes social critiques of contemporary civilization in the form of peer-reviewed articles, essays, reviews, poetry, memoirs, and more. Occasional issues are thematic. *Dialectical Anthropology* is self-described as "a major contributor to the radical literature of our time."

359. *Ethnography.* [ISSN: 1466-1381] 2000. q. USD 1422 (print & online eds.)). Ed(s): Paul Willis. Sage Publications Ltd., 1 Oliver's Yard, 55 City Rd, London, EC1Y 1SP, United Kingdom; market@sagepub.com; https://www.sagepub.com/. Adv. Sample. Refereed. Reprint: PSC. *Indexed:* A22, A47, E01, IBSS, MLA-IB, SSA. *Aud.:* Ac.

An international and interdisciplinary peer-reviewed journal, *Ethnography* "provides a forum for the study of social and cultural change." Of special note, this journal endeavors to "bridge the chasm between sociology and anthropology." Each issue is composed of four or five articles that average 25-30 pages in length. In addition to the journal's emphasis on sociology and anthropology, authors from other disciplines are represented, such as geography, social work, and economics.

Ethnohistory. See Multicultural Studies section.

360. *Ethnos: journal of anthropology.* [ISSN: 0014-1844] 1936. 5x/yr. GBP 634 (print & online eds.)). Ed(s): Mark Graham, Nils Bubandt. Routledge, 4 Park Sq, Milton Park, Abingdon, OX14 4RN, United Kingdom; subscriptions@tandf.co.uk; http://www.tandfonline.com. Illus., index, adv. Sample. Refereed. Reprint: PSC. *Indexed:* A01, A22, A47, BAS, E01, IBSS, MLA-IB, P61, SSA. *Bk. rev.:* Number varies, 1,000 words. *Aud.:* Ac.

Original papers on theoretical, methodological, and empirical developments in the discipline of sociocultural anthropology are featured in this publication. Each issue averages five articles of about 25 pages, and an occasional issue publishes approximately six book reviews of several pages in length. Articles and contributors are international. As an example of the global scope of *Ethnos,* a recent issue features articles that focus on anthropological topics in Mexico, Morocco, the Republic of Georgia, and South India.

361. ***Ethos (Malden).*** [ISSN: 0091-2131] 1973. q. GBP 95 (print & online eds.)). Ed(s): Edward D Lowe. Wiley-Blackwell Publishing, Inc., 350 Main St, Malden, MA 02148; http://onlinelibrary.wiley.com. Illus., adv. Sample. Refereed. Vol. ends: Dec. Microform: PQC. Reprint: PSC. *Indexed:* A22, A47, ASSIA, BRI, E01, IBSS, MLA-IB. *Bk. rev.:* Number and length vary. *Aud.:* Ac.

Published by the Society of Psychological Anthropology, *Ethos* concentrates its scholarly content on issues of psychology and anthropology. Articles include a variety of psychocultural topics, such as cultural cognition, transcultural psychiatry, ethnopsychiatry, socialization, and psychoanalytic anthropology. Content includes original articles, essays, commentaries, and book and film reviews, as well as many "special topics" issues.

362. ***Evolutionary Anthropology: issues, news, and reviews.*** [ISSN: 1060-1538] 1992. bi-m. GBP 700. Ed(s): John G Fleagle. John Wiley & Sons, Inc., 111 River St, Hoboken, NJ 07030; cs-journals@wiley.com; http://onlinelibrary.wiley.com. Illus., adv. Refereed. Microform: PQC. Reprint: PSC. *Indexed:* A22, BRI, IBSS. *Bk. rev.:* Number and length vary. *Aud.:* Ac.

A top-ranked journal in the ISI Journal Citation Reports, *Evolutionary Anthropology* focuses current interest in biological anthropology, paleoanthropology, archaeology, and osteology, as well as human biology, genetics, and ecology. This journal also publishes general news of relevant developments in the scientific, social, or political arenas. Book reviews, professional news, letters to the editor, and a calendar are included. Most issues feature an editorial column entitled "Crotchets & Quiddities," which addresses evolutionary concepts and questions that are intended to stimulate thought on various evolutionary anthropology topics.

363. ***Field Methods.*** Former titles (until 1999): *Cultural Anthropology Methods Journal;* (until 1995): *C A M: Cultural Anthropology Methods;* (until 1993): *C A M Newsletter.* [ISSN: 1525-822X] 1989. q. Ed(s): H Russell Bernard. Sage Publications, Inc., 2455 Teller Rd, Thousand Oaks, CA 91320; info@sagepub.com; http://www.sagepub.com. Adv. Sample. Refereed. Reprint: PSC. *Indexed:* A01, A22, A47, E01, IBSS, SSA. *Aud.:* Ac.

Formerly entitled *Cultural Anthropology Methods,* this peer-reviewed journal publishes articles about the methods used by field workers in the social and behavioral sciences and the humanities. Articles focus on issues in the methods used and innovations in the collection, management, and analysis data about human thought and behavior. Most issues publish five or six articles in the 10- to 20-page range. This journal, which operates under the motto "methods belong to all of us," aims to reach scholars, students, and professionals who do fieldwork.

Human Ecology. See Environment and Conservation section.

364. ***Human Nature: an interdisciplinary biosocial perspective.*** [ISSN: 1045-6767] 1990. q. EUR 502 (print & online eds.)). Ed(s): Jane Lancaster. Springer New York LLC, 233 Spring St, New York, NY 10013; customerservice@springer.com; http://www.springer.com. Illus., adv. Sample. Refereed. Circ: 250. Reprint: PSC. *Indexed:* A01, A22, E01, IBSS, SSA. *Bk. rev.:* approx. 2, occasional. *Aud.:* Ac.

The primary objective of the journal *Human Nature* is "to advance the interdisciplinary investigation of the biological, social, and environmental factors that underlie human behavior." It focuses on "functional unity and mutually interactive" factors in the fields of evolution, biology, and sociology, and on "the relevance of a biosocial perspective to scientific, social, and policy issues."

365. ***Human Organization.*** Formerly (until 1949): *Applied Anthropology.* [ISSN: 0018-7259] 1941. q. USD 105 (print & online eds.) Free to members). Ed(s): Sarah Lyon. Society for Applied Anthropology, PO Box 2436, Oklahoma City, OK 73101; info@sfaa.net; http://www.sfaa.net. Illus., index, adv. Refereed. Vol. ends: Winter. *Indexed:* A22, A47, B01, BAS, C45, Chicano, IBSS, MLA-IB, P61, SSA. *Aud.:* Ac.

This refereed journal is published by the Society for Applied Anthropology. *Human Organization* features articles on the scientific investigations of how human beings relate to one another and how these principles are applied to practical problems. Included in the journal are sections on government, industry, health care, and international affairs. Research in this journal spans the globe.

366. ***Journal of Anthropological Archaeology.*** [ISSN: 0278-4165] 1982. q. EUR 1175. Ed(s): John M O'Shea. Academic Press, 225 Wyman St, Waltham, MA 02144; JournalCustomerService-usa@elsevier.com; http://store.elsevier.com/Academic-Press/IMP_5/. Illus., adv. Sample. Refereed. Vol. ends: Dec. *Indexed:* A01, A22, A47, AmHI, BAS, E01. *Aud.:* Ac.

This refereed, international journal publishes articles on the theory and methodology of archaeology. Articles center on archaeological topics spanning a time frame from the emergence of human culture to contemporary investigations and observations. In addition to the journal's focus on archaeology, occasional contributions come from ethnographers, sociologists, and geographers. Issues typically contain approximately 15 to 20 scholarly articles that range in length from 15 to 40 pages. An occasional special-topic issue will have shorter contributions.

367. ***Journal of Anthropological Research.*** Former titles (until 1973): *Southwestern Journal of Anthropology;* (until 1945): *New Mexico Anthropologist.* [ISSN: 0091-7710] 1937. q. USD 269 (print & online eds.)). Ed(s): Lawrence Guy Straus. University of Chicago Press, 1427 E 60th St, Chicago, IL 60637; custserv@press.uchicago.edu; http://www.press.uchicago.edu. Illus., index, adv. Refereed. Vol. ends: Winter. Reprint: PSC. *Indexed:* A01, A22, A47, BAS, BRI, IBSS, MLA-IB, SSA. *Bk. rev.:* Number and length vary. *Aud.:* Ga, Ac.

The *Journal of Anthropological Research* publishes peer-reviewed research articles and book reviews in all subfields of anthropology. Formerly the *Southwestern Journal of Anthropology,* this publication gives some weight to articles relating to the American Southwest and northern Mexico. Most issues have four articles, 20 pages in length, and current, critical book reviews averaging one page in length. Book reviews comprise a large portion of the journal's content; they number up to 20 or more per issue.

368. ***Journal of Anthropological Sciences.*** Former titles (until 2004): *Rivista di Antropologia;* (until vol.15, 1910): *Societa Romana di Antropologia. Atti.* [ISSN: 1827-4765] 1893. a. Ed(s): Giovanni Destro-Bisol. Istituto Italiano di Antropologia, c/o Dipartimento di Biologia Animale e dell'Uomo, Universita di Roma "La Sapienza", Rome, 00185, Italy; http://www.scienzemfn.uniroma1.it. *Aud.:* Ac.

The *Journal of Anthropological Sciences* (JASs) is highly ranked on the ISI Journal Citation Reports, and provides free access to articles from 2004 onward. In addition to its commitment to Open Access, authors who publish in JASs are asked to make their research data available. According to the journal's webpage, "The JASs publishes original articles, notes and reviews concerning of evolutionary anthropology (human paleontology, prehistory, biology and genetics of extinct and extant populations), with particular attention towards interdisciplinary approaches."

369. ***Journal of Human Evolution.*** [ISSN: 0047-2484] 1972. m. EUR 3785. Ed(s): Sarah Elton. Academic Press, 32 Jamestown Rd, Camden, London, NW1 7BY, United Kingdom; corporate.sales@elsevier.com; http://www.elsevier.com/. Illus., index, adv. Refereed. Vol. ends: Dec. Reprint: PSC. *Indexed:* A01, A22, A47, E01, IBSS. *Bk. rev.:* Number and length vary. *Aud.:* Ac.

The central focus of this journal is to publish scholarly articles on all aspects of human evolution. Articles cover both paleoanthropological work, including human and primate fossils, and comparative studies of living species. It is a reputed journal in the field of anthropology and highly ranked in its Impact Factor. Its contents include original research, review articles, news, communication of new discoveries, and forthcoming papers.

370. ***The Journal of Latin American and Caribbean Anthropology.*** Former titles (until 2007): *Journal of Latin American Anthropology;* (until 1995): *The Latin American Anthropology Review.* [ISSN: 1935-4932] 1989. 3x/yr. Ed(s): Linda J Seligmann. Wiley-Blackwell Publishing, Inc., 350 Main St, Malden, MA 02148; cs-journals@wiley.com; http://onlinelibrary.wiley.com. Adv. Sample. Refereed. Reprint: PSC. *Indexed:* A22, A47, BRI, E01, IBSS, MLA-IB, P61. *Bk. rev.:* Number and length vary. *Aud.:* Ac.

The official publication of the Latin American Anthropology Section of the American Anthropological Association, this journal is devoted to publishing articles on research in Mexico, Central and South America, and the Caribbean. Articles may be published in Spanish or English. Each issue has five to seven articles, and theme issues are common. Issues often include numerous film and book reviews.

371. ***The Journal of Peasant Studies.*** [ISSN: 0306-6150] 1973. 6x/yr. GBP 869 (print & online eds.)). Ed(s): Saturnino Borras, Jr. Routledge, 4 Park Sq, Milton Park, Abingdon, OX14 4RN, United Kingdom; subscriptions@tandf.co.uk; http://www.tandfonline.com. Illus., index, adv. Sample. Refereed. Microform: PQC. Reprint: PSC. *Indexed:* A22, AmHI, BAS, C45, E01, IBSS, P61, SSA. *Bk. rev.:* 3-7. *Aud.:* Ac.

The publisher's website describes *The Journal of Peasant Studies* as follows: "A leading journal in the field of rural politics and development, *The Journal of Peasant Studies* (JPS) provokes and promotes critical thinking about social structures, institutions, actors and processes of change in and in relation to the rural world. It fosters inquiry into how agrarian power relations between classes and other social groups are created, understood, contested and transformed. JPS pays special attention to questions of 'agency' of marginalized groups in agrarian societies, particularly their autonomy and capacity to interpret and change their conditions."

372. ***Medical Anthropology Quarterly: international journal for the cultural and social analysis of health.*** Former titles (until 1983): *Medical Anthropology Newsletter;* (until 1968): *Medical Anthropology.* [ISSN: 0745-5194] 19??. q. GBP 117 (print & online eds.)). Ed(s): Carole Bernard, Clarence C Gravlee. Wiley-Blackwell Publishing, Inc., 350 Main St, Malden, MA 02148; http://onlinelibrary.wiley.com. Illus., adv. Sample. Refereed. Vol. ends: Dec. Reprint: PSC. *Indexed:* A22, A47, BRI, C45, E01, IBSS, MLA-IB, SSA. *Bk. rev.:* Number and length vary. *Aud.:* Ac.

As the title suggests, this journal publishes research and theory in the field of medical anthropology. It is produced by the Society for Medical Anthropology, and the journal's "broad field views all inquiries into health and disease in individuals from the holistic and cross-cultural perspective distinctive of anthropology." Contents include original articles, book reviews, and an occasional special focus section. A recent specially focused issue centered on the topic of "Comorbidity."

373. ***Oceania.*** [ISSN: 0029-8077] 1930. 3x/yr. GBP 229. Ed(s): Nancy Williams, Jadran Mimica. Wiley-Blackwell Publishing Asia, 155 Cremorne St, Richmond, VIC 3121, Australia; melbourne@wiley.com; http://onlinelibrary.wiley.com. Illus., index. Refereed. Microform: PQC. Reprint: PSC. *Indexed:* A01, A22, A47, ASSIA, AmHI, BAS, BRI, IBSS, MLA-IB. *Bk. rev.:* 7, length varies. *Aud.:* Ac.

Oceania publishes peer-reviewed research and review articles in the field of social and cultural anthropology in Australia, Melanesia, Polynesia, Micronesia, and Southeast Asia. An important source for Australian and Pacific Studies, it covers past and present customs, ceremonies, folklore, and belief systems of the region. Included are guest-edited thematic issues, maps, graphs, and some illustrations. This journal is recommended for academic libraries that serve anthropology programs or Asian, Pacific, or Australian Studies programs.

374. ***Royal Anthropological Institute. Journal.*** Formerly (until 1995): *Man;* Which incorporated (1907-1965): *Royal Anthropological Institute of Great Britain and Ireland. Journal;* Which was formerly (until 1907): *Anthropological Institute of Great Britain and Ireland. Journal;* Which was formed by the merger of (1869-1872): *Ethnological Society of London. Journal;* Which was formerly (until 1869): *Ethnological Society of London. Transactions;* (until 1861): *Ethnological Society of London. Journal;* (1870-1872): *Journal of Anthropology;* Which was formerly (until 1870): *Anthropological Review.* [ISSN: 1359-0987] 1901. q. GBP 536 (print or online ed.)). Ed(s): Matei Candea. Wiley-Blackwell Publishing Ltd., The Atrium, Southern Gate, Chichester, PO19 8QG, United Kingdom; cs-journals@wiley.com; http://www.wiley.com/. Illus., index, adv. Sample. Refereed. Vol. ends: Dec. Microform: BHP; PQC. Reprint: PSC. *Indexed:* A01, A22, A47, BAS, BRI, E01, IBSS, MLA-IB, P61, SSA. *Bk. rev.:* 40, 350 words. *Aud.:* Ac.

Formerly entitled *Man*, the *Journal of the Royal Anthropological Institute* is the principal journal of the long-standing anthropological organization of the same name. Articles are international in scope and cover all branches of anthropology. This journal is known for its extensive book review section; more than 40 reviews are published per issue. In addition to comments, review articles, and original research, most issues contain a lively and readable essay entitled "What I'm Reading."

375. ***Visual Anthropology Review.*** Former titles (until 1991): *Society for Visual Anthropology Review;* (until 1990): *S V A Review;* (until 1990): *S V A Newsletter;* (until 1985): *Society for the Anthropology of Visual Communication. Newsletter;* (until 1973): *P I E F Newsletter.* [ISSN: 1058-7187] 1970. s-a. GBP 46 (print & online eds.)). Ed(s): Jenny Chio, Mark Westmoreland. Wiley-Blackwell Publishing, Inc., 350 Main St, Malden, MA 02148; cs-journals@wiley.com; http://onlinelibrary.wiley.com. Adv. Sample. Refereed. Reprint: PSC. *Indexed:* A01, A22, A47, BRI, E01, IBSS, MLA-IB. *Aud.:* Ac.

The content of this journal focuses on the study of visual aspects of human behavior and the use of visual media in anthropology research and teaching. *Visual Anthropology Review* has been in publication since the 1970s. Its specialized scope may draw a narrower audience; however, the use of and emphasis on visual media in teaching and learning have increased in recent times. Examples of articles, reviews, and commentary featured in this journal include indigenous media, applied visual anthropology, photography, film, video, art, dance, design, and architecture. Given the breadth of visual representation, *Visual Anthropology Review* has cross-disciplinary appeal.

■ ANTIQUES

General/Doll Collecting

Adam St. Pierre, STEM and Reference Librarian, East Baton Rouge Parish Library, 7711 Goodwood Blvd, Baton Rouge, LA 70809; astpierre@ebrpl.com

Introduction

Currently, individual buyers have the ability to search for virtually any product they want on Amazon and eBay. The antiques industry of today is no different, with close ties to online sales and auctions. Sites like Liveauctioneers, ruby lane, and etsy provide antique collectors an avenue to purchase virtually anything at these auction houses from the comfort of their own home. While Liveauctioneers and other antique and collectible digital marketplaces continue to grow, there are several intractable qualities that come from a live antiques show. Humans are still social and a large part of these events involve interaction between buyers and sellers; and the hunt for the perfect item does not always lead to an online marketplace. No, the serious collectors will still head to the antique shows and shops to look for discarded items that were once valueless and discovered to be priceless. It is for these reasons and more that antique and collectible magazines still thrive in shops, stores, and showcasing events that happen around the world.

Antique collecting continues to remain popular among not just the very rich or the very old but cuts across lines of generation and social status. Many young professionals and millennials are entering the antique collecting business and bringing digital expertise to reach more people across social divides than before. This can be seen with creation of a podcast for the magazine *Antiques*, run by two young professionals within the antique collecting business. Those two young professionals founded the New Antiquarians society, based in New York, devoted to millennial networking within the antique world and many more can be found around the globe. Social media giant Instagram has also brought more photos of beautiful antiques to the public than ever before. As evidenced by the numerous photos tagged with things like: #tiffanysilver #sterlingsilver #wristenthuiast #watchcollector.

As the use of social media continues to raise the profile of the antique world and television programs like *Antiques Roadshow* seem to have unending viewership, the public demands more information about their antiques. Libraries have always received many antique-related reference collections and carried a vast amount of materials for their audiences, but seems to grow ever more popular. Events that allow members of the community to have their valuables or collectibles appraised like the various television programs have not seen their popularity wane. The desire to find out the value of something that may have been tucked away in the attic or understand the history of something found in a pawn shop will not go away anytime soon.

The reviews contained in this section are targeted generally toward public libraries, as much of the attention is concentrated toward the general public. However, many of the reviews do look at how academic libraries might incorporate these titles into their collection assuming demand is there. All the selections will depend, of course, on the specific needs of the patron community that is served.

Basic Periodicals

FINE ANTIQUES/OBJETS D'ART. Ga: *Antique Collecting, The Magazine Antiques.*

POPULAR ANTIQUES/COLLECTIBLES. Ga: *Antique Trader, Maine Antique Digest.*

DOLL COLLECTING. Ga: *Dolls: the collector's magazine.*

Basic Abstracts and Indexes

Readers' Guide to Periodical Literature.

General

376. *Antique Bottle and Glass Collector.* [ISSN: 8750-1481] 1984. m. USD 35. American Glass Gallery, c/o John R.Pastor, PO Box 227, New Hudson, MI 48165; jpastor@americanglassgallery.com; https://americanglassgallery.com. Illus., adv. *Aud.:* Ga.

Antique Bottle and Glass Collector is a glossy mostly full-color magazine that will delight glassware and bottle collectors. Readers will enjoy regular columns like "Heard It Through the Grapevine," which educates the reader on a variety of staff-selected glassware topics in history, and "The Medicine Chest," featuring glassware specifically from the pharmacist's shelf to yours. Additionally, readers will enjoy articles that focus on the collecting, buying, and selling of antique bottles and glassware as well as their unique histories. The publication prominently features an extensive calendar of events and auctions for glassware collectors. Advertisements do not overflow throughout the magazine and many are collectors looking to add to their collection seeking help from others coming across bottles on digs or in antique stores. The accompanying website details events published in the magazine, as well as classified ads and a Facebook page full of great photos. Recommended for libraries that serious antique bottle and glass collector groups within their communities. URL: https://americanglassgallery.com/abgc

377. *Antique Collecting: the magazine for collectors and enthusiasts.* Incorporates (1946-2006): *Antique Dealer & Collectors Guide;* Which incorporated (1981-1982): *Art & Antiques;* Which was formerly (until 1981): *Art & Antiques Weekly;* Antique Dealer & Collectors Guide was formerly (until 1946): *Antique Dealers' Weekly and Collectors' Guide.* [ISSN: 0003-584X] 1966. 10x/yr. GBP 32 domestic; GBP 48 in Europe; GBP 64 elsewhere. Antique Collectors Club, Sandy Ln, Old Martlesham, Woodbridge, IP12 4SD, United Kingdom; info@antique-acc.com; http://www.antiquecollectorsclub.com. Illus., adv. Sample. *Bk. rev.:* 2-6, 100-500 words. *Aud.:* Ga, Sa.

Antique Collecting is an elegant publication that succeeds in both depth and breadth of coverage within the antique world. This British magazine has been around since 1968 delivering consistent and quality coverage on topics like furniture, art print collecting, decorative arts, glass, and so much more. Every issue is packed with auction previews, historical collection for antiques, and market analysis for a wide range of antique collecting. Regular editorials include "Marc My Words" by Marc Allum of *Antiques Roadshow* fame, "Why I Collect," a column very personal as well as varied, and "Cool and Collectible," which ties large events and anniversaries to memorabilia like the World Cup or the anniversary of the Woodstock Music Festival. However, every single article, both the regular editorials and special features, demonstrate a dedication to quality that truly elevates the magazine. The glossy photos are well placed throughout and expert columnists weigh in on a breadth of topics. The strong bent toward British and European markets may dissuade American readers from purchasing. All of the advertisements, fairs, and auctions are for establishments within the United Kingdom. The accompanying website and digital strategy is quite well done as well though. Readers will find original content for only the website as well as many of the magazine articles. Additionally, *Antique Collecting* has put together guides for different collecting topics ranging from rare maps and books, art, furniture, ceramics, and even single malt whisky collecting! Recommended for patrons interested in British and U.K. antique markets and antiques. URL: www.antique-collecting.co.uk/

378. *Antique Trader.* Former titles (until 2000): *The Antique Trader Weekly;* (until 19??): *Antique Trader.* 1957. 24x/yr. USD 59.98 United States; USD 129.98 Canada; USD 2.99 per issue. Ed(s): Karen Knapstein. F + W Media Inc., 1140 Broadway, 14th Fl, New York, NY 10001; contact_us@fwmedia.com; http://www.fwcommunity.com/. Illus., adv. Circ: 22230 Paid. *Bk. rev.:* 30, length varies. *Aud.:* Ga.

Antique Trader has led the pack in quality antique and collectibles publishing since its beginnings in 1957. Readers may be aware that *Antique Trader* is responsible for the popular reference annual publication *Antique Trader Antiques and Collectibles Price Guide*, which is America's number 1 best-selling identification guide. The appearance of the magazine is of newsprint quality with approximately the first ten and last ten pages in full color. The color pages contain quite a few advertisements but the last few pages contain multiple articles in full color. *Antique Trader* focuses specifically on the buying of antiques, the selling of antiques, and various auctions. The magazine publishes 24 issues each year on a mostly bi-weekly basis, so readers get up-to-date pricing information and get comprehensive news to stay current within the world of antiques. The articles will appeal to all levels of interest in the antiques and collectibles world from the seasoned veteran to individuals with only a passing interest. Readers will be treated to ask the expert columns where individuals get advice from certified appraisers who offer opinions to the would-be sellers where their profits will be the greatest. Additionally readers will be delighted with an exhaustive calendar of events, and features from various antique collections that cover a huge variety of interests like art, military memorabilia, comics, and so much more. The accompanying website includes many of the same articles from the magazine as well as a consistently updated blog and a very lively Facebook presence. Subscribers of the magazine receive a weekly e-newsletter packed with articles. The magazine may include more advertisements within the print version now, but it is still just as varied and timely. Highly recommended for public libraries of any size due to breadth of coverage and current information. URL: www.antiquetrader.com/

379. *Antiques & Auction News.* Formerly (until 19??): *Joel Sater's Antiques and Auction News.* 1969. w. Fri. USD 28. Ed(s): Karl Pass. Engle Printing & Publishing Co., Inc., 1425 W Main St, PO Box 500, Mt. Joy, PA 17552; http://www.engleonline.com. Adv. *Aud.:* Ga.

This publication primarily focuses on the east coast market of antiques and collectibles. Published since 1969, it boasts the widest distributed weekly marketplace news publication for auctions, shows, forums, and exhibitions. *Antiques & Auction News* is a short, weekly publication that features auction shows, auction news with prices, events along the east coast, and collectors' advice. The strongest features of this magazine are the auction show news with the prices that the items were sold, news of upcoming events, and the frequency of distribution that keep its readers in the know. An auctioneer directory, event and auction calendar, shops directory, and classifieds also appear in the magazine. Each issue is of newsprint type with color photos interspersed throughout. The accompanying website includes many of the articles featured in the magazine, a directory of antique shops, and a classified section for seekers of particular items and those who want to sell items, aptly named "Seekers & Sellers." The website also includes a complete e-edition that prospective readers can view. As the dominant force in auction news in the Northeastern United States, this is a must purchase for all public libraries in the area. URL: www.antiquesandauctionnews.net/

380. ***AntiqueWeek: weekly antique, auction and collectors' newspaper.*** Former titles (until 1986): *Antique Week - Tri-State Trader;* (until 1983): *Tri-State Trader.* [ISSN: 0888-5451] 1968. w. Mon. USD 41 in state; USD 47.25 out of state. Ed(s): Connie Swaim. MidCountry Media USA, 27 N Jefferson St, PO Box 90, Knightstown, IN 46148. Illus., adv. Sample. Circ: 40000. Vol. ends: Mar. *Bk. rev.:* 16, length varies. *Aud.:* Ga.

AntiqueWeek is a partial color newspaper publishing two editions weekly: the Eastern and Central edition. This publication covers antique news, collector interviews, and antique sales throughout the United States. The coverage includes high end antiques, collectibles, and campy collectibles of the Americana variety. Regular features include auction calendars, shows, classifieds, a mall and shop directory, and antiques website listings for the savvy and not so savvy in the "Internet Connections" section. There's a good bit of advertising spread throughout, but not more than any average newspaper. The color photos are much better integrated into the publication than years past. The website provides much of the same coverage and you can even read the entirety of several weeks back for both editions for a free trial. The readability, frequency of publication, and nearly national coverage would make this a worthy addition to any library collection. URL: www.antiqueweek.com/

381. ***Art & Antiques: for collectors of the fine and decorative arts.*** Incorporates (1967-Jan.1994): *Antique Monthly;* Former titles (until 1984): *Art & Antiques;* (until 1980): *American Art and Antiques.* [ISSN: 0195-8208] 1978. 10x/yr. USD 29.50. Ed(s): John Dorfman. CurtCo Robb Media LLC., 29160 Heathercliff Rd, Ste 200, Malibu, CA 90265; support@robbreport.com; http://www.curtco.com. Illus. *Indexed:* A01, A22, A51, AmHI. *Bk. rev.:* 6, length varies. *Aud.:* Ga.

Art & Antiques magazine is a artfully produced publication that evokes the idea of opening an art book in each of its issues. The publication expertly uses negative space and the carefully chosen photographs blend seamlessly into each article, as do the advertisements, which integrate into the magazine without distracting the reader from the editorial content. If the reader desires, there is a helpful advertisement index toward the end of the magazine. However, this magazine is not just a well-designed publication, but there are many regular articles and features each month that demonstrate its dedication to quality reporting. Regular columns include "Objects of Desire," on incredibly rare item finds; "In Perspective," which includes news, market reports, and events; "Collecting," which includes a featured area of antiques collecting; "Record Breaker," which features particular items sold for incredible amounts of money, and the item's history; and in-depth exhibition coverage from the "Exhibitions" column. *Art & Antiques*'s digital presence does need some work though. Although readers will be able to find original content and many of the same articles from the published magazine, it is not as well designed as their physical publication. The advertisements and events place will remind a perspective reader of early web design. However, they do provide a free eNewsletter with content only available online, which includes very high-quality images. Despite the digital presence, this is a beautiful publication with dedication to quality reporting that is recommended for all library collections. URL: www.artandantiquesmag.com/

382. ***Kovels on Antiques and Collectibles: the newsletter for collectors, dealers and investors.*** Former titles (until 1981): *Kovels on Antiques and Collectibles;* (until 1977): *Ralph and Terry Kovel on Antiques.* 1974. m. Antiques, Inc., PO Box 22192, Beachwood, OH 44122; http://www.kovels.com. Illus., adv. Sample. *Bk. rev.:* Number and length vary. *Aud.:* Hs, Ga.

This newsletter is published by one of the most trusted names in the industry, Kovels. The quality and reliability of the information is immediately apparent. As expected, the focus is very much on pricing and consumer interest. It's a short publication full of concise snippets of information, printed in full color, on newsletter paper with plentiful pictures, and is advertisement-free. Regular features include sales reports, which cover a variety of collectibles in each issue, and a brief overview of a recent featured sale. Other regular features include a "Dictionary of Marks," which gives information on specific artist or company markings found on antiques. There is also a "Buyer's Price Guide," which highlights the prices recent sales have fetched, and a "Collector's Gallery." The newsletter has a very specific scope of disseminating pricing information and acting as a visual resource to help readers identify items of value. This is recommended for all libraries and is an excellent supplemental addition to the annual *Kovels' Price Guide.* As expected, with the backing of this publication, the Kovels website is in-depth and includes price guides, an events calendar, and a collector services directory. A good portion of the content is freely accessible, and subscribers to this newsletter get access to an annual index. There is also premium online content that requires an additional subscription. URL: www.kovels.com

383. ***The Magazine Antiques.*** Former titles (until 1971): *Antiques;* (until 1952): *Magazine Antiques;* (until 1928): *Antiques.* [ISSN: 0161-9284] 1922. bi-m. USD 39.95 domestic; USD 79.95 Canada; USD 95 elsewhere. Ed(s): Sammy Dalati, Gregory Cerio. Brant Publications, Inc., 110 Greene St, 2nd Fl, New York, NY 10012; info@artnews.com; http://www.themagazineantiques.com. Illus., index. Vol. ends: Dec. Microform: PQC. *Indexed:* A06, A22, A51, BAS, BRI, CBRI, MLA-IB. *Bk. rev.:* 1-9, length varies. *Aud.:* Ga, Ac, Sa.

The Magazine Antiques considers itself an authority on decorative and fine arts, architecture, preservation, and interior design, which it still succeeds on that dedication to aesthetic. Every issue in the glossy, full-color magazine contains features by experts in the field and well-placed photographs of fine art pieces from furniture, to art prints, ceramics, and so much more. The publication's strength comes from regular featured articles like "Current and Coming," "Critical Thinking/Difficult Issues," and in-depth articles on a wide gamut of fine art topics. "Critical Thinking/Difficult Issues" asks us to re-examine art, literature, and antiques through a critical lens and challenges us to see that work from a different perspective. The publication does a good job explaining the context of many of the pieces in all of the features by various experts in the fine and decorative arts world. This contextual explanation will delight even those with a passing interest in history as well as historians. The publication may see some new restructuring as the editor and publisher have purchased the magazine from their parent company, making it into an employee-owned operation. The accompanying website and social media presence is much better maintained than in the past, and contains a vibrant podcast as well as a well-curated Instagram feed. Past articles from the physical magazine and new content populate the website, but the emphasis is still strongly focused on the magazine, with no digital version available. A newsletter is available but only because the paid newsletter is no longer maintained. This publication is recommended for academic libraries with an active fine arts department and public libraries with a dedicated fine arts community. URL: www.themagazineantiques.com/

384. ***Maine Antique Digest.*** [ISSN: 0147-0639] 1973. m. USD 43 domestic; USD 67 foreign. Ed(s): S Clayton Pennington. Maine Antique Digest, Inc., 911 Main St, PO Box 1429, Waldoboro, ME 04572. Illus., adv. Sample. Vol. ends: Dec. Microform: PQC. *Indexed:* A22. *Bk. rev.:* 2-3, 500-2,000 words. *Aud.:* Ga, Sa.

Maine Antique Digest began publication at the dining table of Sam and Sally Pennington in 1973 and their periodical has delighted its readers ever since. The title of the periodical suggests that only Maine and the northeastern part of the United States are covered, but the scope of it is much larger. The *Maine Antique Digest* includes all the of the United States, Canada, and even features a section called "London Letters." The pages are done in newsprint, blurring the line between magazine and newspaper. Regardless of look and title, this publication aspires to provide must-read information for serious antique collectors, especially those of Americana. The vast majority of images are in full color and well placed within each editorial. Advertisements exist at the very beginning of the publication, although there are some that are placed in-between featured articles. Regular columns include "The Young Collector," "Computer Column," "Antique Jewelry & Gemology," "Books Received," obituaries, and club news. However, the strength of this publication are the detailed columns on the outcomes of specific auctions and shows. These articles tell the story of each show and auction, the most valuable pieces, and the pricing information that antique dealers and serious collectors will delight in reading. While there is much more information available to subscribers, a visit to their website will allow you to read some of their articles, advertisements, and events calendar. Additionally, they are very active on Facebook, Twitter, and Instagram, with links to articles, pictures of auction house finds, and the like. The publisher does put together an annual directory called the *M.A.D. Antiques Trade Directory*, available for download, and includes show promoters, auctioneers, organizations, and dealers. Recommended for libraries that have a specific need for serious antique news coverage and Americana. URL: www.maineantiquedigest.com

385. ***Teddy Bear Times & Friends.*** Formerly (until 2018): *Teddy Bear and Friends;* Incorporates (1986-2012): *Teddy Bear Review.* 1983. bi-m. USD 74.99 combined subscription print & online eds. Ed(s): Joyce Greenholdt. Jones Publishing, Inc., N7528 Aanstad Rd, Iola, WI 54945; http://www.jonespublishing.com. Adv. *Indexed:* BRI. *Aud.:* Ga.

Despite a name change and a publisher change, *Teddy Bear Times & Friends* still delivers a quality content for the teddy bear and soft sculpture animal community. The magazine features plenty of good full-color photographs of teddy bears and toys made from a variety of materials such as alpaca, mohair, and wool. The advertisements are spread throughout each issue, so that they do not detract from the articles and are of much higher quality than years past. Every issue features artist profiles, tips on various design techniques, and stories about how people joined the craft, as well as a calendar of events. Regular features include "Bear Hospital," a column detailing bear restoration, "Bear Market," a showcase of featured bears and artists, and "Collectors Corner," where individuals are interviewed about their collection and passion for soft sculpture animals. The publication also puts on a yearly competition called the "Teddy Bear of the Year" awards, or the "TOBYS," for industry professionals as well as the DIY crowd. The website features an Etsy store directory of various teddy bear creators, and downloadable patterns available for purchase. Recommended for all ages and all public library collections. URL: www.teddybearandfriends.com

386. ***Treasures (Des Moines): vintage to modern collecting.*** Formed by the merger of (1959-2011): *Collectors News;* (1993-2011): *Antiques & Collecting Magazine;* Which was formerly (until Oct.1993): *Antiques and Collecting Hobbies;* (until 1985): *Hobbies: The Magazine for Collectors;* Which was formed by the 1931 merger of: *Sports and Hobbies;* (1901-1931): *Philatelic West; Hobby News; Collector's Work; Eastern Philatelist;* Hobbies: The Magazine for Collectors incorporated: *Shipmodeler.* [ISSN: 2162-3147] 1931. m. USD 24. Heuss Printing Inc, 903 North Second St, Ames, IA 50010. Illus. Vol. ends: Feb. Microform: PQC. *Indexed:* A22, BRI, C37, CBRI, MLA-IB. *Bk. rev.:* 4-6, 30-100 words. *Aud.:* Ga.

Treasures was formed after a merger of *Collectors News* and *Antique & Collecting* magazine, but it has been in existence since 1931 by a variety of different names. The publication's current iteration displays a breadth of coverage that looks at more modern collector's and vintage items. This is a beautifully designed magazine full of vibrant color illustrations. There are advertisements but they are interspersed throughout the publication in a way that feels natural and does not detract from the quality of features written. There's even an advertisers index in the back for readers to reference. As for the editorial content, every issue contains auction news, museum exhibition exposes, book reviews, and collecting trends. *Treasures* digital presence has changed quite a bit, seeming to remove all of the web features and focusing primarily on their Facebook page. Their Facebook page does post quite a bit of the mid-century modern and vintage items they focus on, as well as sharing events readers of the magazine may find of interest. Despite the current digital strategy, *Treasures* is recommended for public libraries with vintage and mid-century modern collector groups, as it is beautifully presented, entertaining, and simplistic. URL: www.treasuresmagazine.com/

387. ***Yesteryear: your monthly guide to antiques and collectibles.*** Former titles (until 1979): *Yester-Year;* (until 1977): *Yester-Year Antique Marketplace.* [ISSN: 0194-9349] 1975. m. USD 19. Ed(s): Michael Jacobi. Yesteryear Publications, Inc., PO Box 2, Princeton, WI 54968; yesteryearantiques@centurytel.net; http://www.antiqueswisconsin.com/. Illus. *Bk. rev.:* 2-10, 200-300 words. *Aud.:* Ga.

This newspaper features antiques and collectibles, with more of a focus on the collectibles side. The strongest aspect, and the backbone of the publication, is the amount of readers' questions answered. There are four "Question & Answer" sections: "Know Your Antiques," with answers from expert Terry Kovel; "Common Sense Antiques" by Fred Taylor, which specifically covers furniture; "Rinker on Collectibles" by Harry Rinker; and "Antique or Junque" by Anne McCollam. In addition to featured articles, the publication offers a detailed calendar of events, sales, and flea markets around Wisconsin and the surrounding North Central states. There is also an antique shop directory and plenty of advertising. The accompanying website contains a sample issue and subscription information, but not much else. There is a newly added social media presence in the form of a Facebook page but it does not have much of a following yet. This is a useful regional publication and would be recommended for public libraries in the geographic area covered. URL: http://yesteryearpublications.com

Doll Collecting

Immediately when someone says the word "dolls," the images of Barbie, G.I. Joe, and American Girl dolls spring to mind. However, there is much more variety and depth to the doll collecting world beyond the giant doll maker franchises that many us grew up around. The Doll collecting world is wonderfully diverse and encompasses a wide array of interests and doll types. Publications that cater to art dolls, vintage dolls, antique dolls, contemporary dolls, miniature accessories, doll homes, and doll fashion abound in the doll collecting world. That is not to say that the Doll collecting world is only a consumer culture but a vibrant community exists where doll crafting is represented as well. There is still very strong support for doll collecting and crafting magazines within the United States and really across the globe. However, this strong support does not completely shield the doll collecting publications from the trend of print magazines ceasing operation as *Doll Collector: for the love of dolls* has ceased publication since the last edition of this book.

Doll collecting and crafting magazines will always have an audience as their publications focus on building communities and engaging other doll artists and makers. Most of the doll making and collecting magazines have embraced digital content and distribution as a means to bring more to their readers. These magazines have listened to the changing types of media and offer more multimedia, social media, and exclusive digital content to supplement their existing product. These additions, and the passion that doll makers and collectors bring to their hobby, keep this community very much alive. The responsive nature of the publishers in this industry and readers who continually share content and ideas with each other bode well for this sector of publishing.

388. ***Antique Doll Collector.*** Formerly (until 1997): *Antique Doll World.* [ISSN: 1096-8474] 1993. m. USD 42.95 domestic; USD 72.95 foreign; USD 6.95 newsstand/cover domestic. Puffin Co., LLC, PO Box 239, Northport, NY 11768. Adv. *Bk. rev.:* Number and length vary. *Aud.:* Ga.

Antique Doll Collector prides itself on being a complete guide to antique, vintage, and collectible dolls. The magazine lives up to that by providing doll history and research, discussions of value and provenance, and entertainment value to its readers. The publication proves itself by having an extremely thorough calendar of events, auction news, featured editorials, and a great many classified ads. While there are many advertisements, they are specifically collectors looking to add to their collection, resellers that span the globe, or doll collecting auction houses the world over. Each issue contains editorials that focus on various doll styles, their history, and years of production that will garner intrigue with those that have only a passing interest in history. They also provide articles on doll care, doll patterns, accessories, and how to identify dolls for their readers. In-depth coverage on collections of varying size and geographic location are included. There is still very little information available on their website other than subscription information for the physical or digital version, back issues, and some events. Despite the digital presence this is a fine magazine for vintage and antique doll collectors or those with any interest in these antiques. Recommended for libraries that have existing antique or vintage doll collecting community. URL: www.antiquedollcollector.com/

389. *Doll Castle News.* [ISSN: 0363-7972] 1961. bi-m. USD 23.95 domestic; USD 30 Canada; USD 60 elsewhere. Castle Press Publications, Inc., PO Box 601, Broadway, NJ 08808; https://www.castlepress.com. Illus., adv. Vol. ends: Jan/Feb. *Bk. rev.:* 3-4, 100-150 words. *Aud.:* Ga, Sa.

Doll Castle News has been around since 1961 when the original editor realized that she loved corresponding with other doll collectors more than operating a doll repair shop. Since then it has maintained a name among quality doll collecting magazines. The magazine itself is in both color and black and white, and features articles from vintage styles to antique and contemporary dolls. The magazine's main strength is the projects and patterns for dolls, and each issue contains a craft project. The instructions are well written enough that this reviewer might be able to tackle at least the first few steps. The entirety of the magazine feels very familiar, and community oriented, but at the same time well researched. Regular features include "From the Antique Doll Cupboard," "Appraising Your Dolls," and "From the Scrapbook." Absolutely recommended for public library patrons who have an interest in the subject. While the website's design could use a facelift, the content is well researched and they offer an e-newsletter during the in-between months of the bi-monthly publication. URL: http://www.dollcastlemagazine.com/

390. *Dolls: the collector's magazine.* Incorporated (1972-2012): *Doll Reader;* (199?-2003): *Doll World.* [ISSN: 0733-2238] 1982. 10x/yr. Jones Publishing, Inc., N 7450 Aanstad Rd, PO Box 5000, Iola, WI 54945; MemberServices@cessnaowner.org; http://www.jonespublishing.com. Illus., adv. Vol. ends: Dec. *Bk. rev.:* 2-4, 100-150 words. *Aud.:* Ga, Sa.

This title merged with *Doll Reader* in 2012 and its scope covers the world of fashion dolls, art dolls, popular manufactured dolls, and cloth-sewn dolls. *Dolls* is a full-color publication with brilliant doll photography and a sleek feel. The magazine contains doll show reviews, events, news, and classifieds. However, it is fairly short and a large amount of the pages are advertisements. Additionally, the articles seem to focus more on popular culture and less on the community-building DIY spirit than many other doll collecting magazines. There is a regular column called "Antique Q&A," where readers can send in photos and ask questions about their antique dolls, usually to get it appraised and learn about its provenance. There is also a longstanding column called "Curious Collector," where readers learn about the history of a particular type of doll and its story. The digital strategy and presence of the publication is quite strong, however. The Facebook page has consistently updated content that is fresh and pulls from its past articles as well as upcoming doll show events. The blog is also consistently updated with content showcasing different doll makers and content tied directly to pop culture. Additionally, there's a doll show calendar and industry directory that points readers to instructors and courses, restoration professionals, doll artists, doll houses and furniture, and much more. The publication seems overly broad in scope, so this is only recommended for libraries just beginning their doll collecting magazine collection or those that need to round it out. URL: www.dollsmagazine.com/

391. *Dolls House World.* Incorporates: *International Dolls House News.* [ISSN: 0961-0928] 1989. m. GBP 59.99; GBP 5.99 newsstand/cover. Ashdown Broadcasting, PO Box 2258, Pulborough, RH20 9BA, United Kingdom; support@ashdown.co.uk; http://www.ashdown.co.uk. Illus., adv. Sample. *Aud.:* Ga, Sa.

Dolls House World bills itself as the United Kingdom's favorite miniaturist magazine. The publication focuses specifically on doll houses and miniature accessories for dolls. This is a sleek full-color magazine filled with fantastic photographs intended to let you see all of the finer details of each miniature created. *Dolls House World* is definitely written by passionate artists and experts in the field of miniature making, which can be seen from its quality reporting. Every issue is filled with artist profiles and stories of how particular miniature houses came to life, detailing every type of material used. However, the real community-building spirit comes from the "Mini Makes" sections that detail how to make particular items that are essential to making miniature houses. Some of these step-by-step instructions will delight prospective readers and may even help some of the less crafty to finish a project or two. The publication also features extensive reports from various shows, show dates, show previews, and advertisements for different miniature makers. In addition to a great print publication, *Dolls House World* has an extensive social media, multimedia, and web presence. They have a digital version of the magazine available in every single app store and, as they are a part of Ashdown Publishing, they have issues available via iMag, a digital provider of magazines. Additionally there is an online education platform called "Dollhouse Classroom" that teaches skills to prospective miniature makers or to help the professionals brush up on topics. Lastly, they have an Etsy directory of miniature artists, so that readers of the magazine can buy other miniatures to alter if they so choose. Since this is a very specific interest, this is only recommended for libraries with an active miniature-making community. URL: www.dollshouseworld.com/

■ ARCHAEOLOGY

Karen Bouchard, Scholarly Resources Librarian, Brown University Library, Providence, RI 02912

Introduction

Archaeology as a discipline interests a broad range of people; the idea of digging up and rediscovering the past holds a romantic appeal that we have seen exploited in popular movies and television shows, though these programs rarely show the many hours of toil and research that are actually required. The general reader might be surprised to learn that archaeology journals tend to be quite technical, written for specialists who understand the techniques, technology, and science that are a part of excavations today. Despite the serious academic nature of most journals, interested readers can also find popular magazines that are geared toward the general public, from high school age upwards. Some archaeological societies divide their publications between more scholarly titles and more accessible popular ones; others simply encourage their writers to avoid jargon and to attempt to write with a more general audience in mind. Almost all now come in electronic as well as print editions and many offer enhanced materials on their websites

Because of the interdisciplinary nature of the field, archaeology journals frequently include articles that also appeal to anthropologists, historians, art historians, classicists, and scholars in other related disciplines. Journals cover the worldwide nature of this scholarship and practice, with some publications accepting articles about any archaeological topic while others concentrate on very narrow geographical locations. In recent decades, the focus has shifted for much of archaeological research to include topics of modern concern such as climate change, social justice, gender, and indigenous studies. As a result, these journals are important to many disciplines outside of the traditional focus areas, and they should therefore be considered essential for academic collections in general.

Basic Periodicals

Hs: *American Archaeology, Archaeology;* Ga: *American Archaeology, Archaeology, Biblical Archaeology Review, Egyptian Archaeology;* Ac: *American Antiquity, American Journal of Archaeology, Antiquity, Archaeology, Journal of Roman Archaeology, Near Eastern Archaeology, North American Archaeologist, Oxford Journal of Archaeology, World Archaeology.*

Basic Abstracts and Indexes

AATA Online: abstracts of international conservation literature, Abstracts in Anthropology, Anthropological Index Online, British and Irish Archaeological Bibliography.

African Archaeological Review. See Africa section.

392. ***American Antiquity.*** [ISSN: 0002-7316] 1935. q. GBP 286 (print & online eds.)). Ed(s): Lynn H Gamble. Cambridge University Press, 1 Liberty Plaza, Fl 20, New York, NY 10004; online@cambridge.org; https://www.cambridge.org/. Illus., adv. Refereed. Circ: 6600. Vol. ends: Oct. Reprint: PSC. *Indexed:* A01, A06, A22, A47, AmHI, BRI, CBRI, MLA-IB. *Bk. rev.:* 6-11 per issue, 1-2 pages, signed. *Aud.:* Ac, Sa.

One of several journals published by the Society for American Archaeology, *American Antiquity* is a quarterly review of New World archaeology, with the focus on the prehistory of the United States and Canada, although historical archaeology is also included. Each issue is published both online and in print, and features three to seven original scholarly papers, field reports from archaeological sites, a varying number of book reviews, and a Forum article on an important topic in archaeology such as faculty jobs or Bayesian chronological modeling. Recent topics have included food security in the seventeenth century North Carolina Piedmont, use of soapstone during the Mission Period in Alta California, and social networks and northern Iroquoian confederacy dynamics. Attention is also paid to scholarship in the field of anthropology. Articles are accompanied by high-quality color and black-and-white illustrations and maps. *American Antiquity* is a free publication for members of the Society for American Archaeology. Its articles will be of interest to archaeologists, anthropologists, historians, and other social scientists and should be considered an essential journal for academic research libraries.

393. ***American Archaeology.*** Formerly (until 1997): *Archaeological Conservancy Newsletter.* [ISSN: 1093-8400] 1980. q. Free to members. Ed(s): Michael Bawaya. Archaeological Conservancy, 1717 Girard Blvd. NE, Albuquerque, NM 87106; tacinfo@nm.net; http://www.americanarchaeology.org. Illus. *Bk. rev.:* 4 per issue, one column, signed. *Aud.:* Ga.

A quarterly publication of The Archaeological Conservancy, located in Albuquerque, New Mexico, *American Archaeology* is "the only popular magazine devoted to presenting the rich diversity of archaeology in the Americas." Each print-only issue contains several articles and is richly illustrated with glossy color photographs. Also included are a listing of events such as museum exhibits, tours, and conferences, and current news stories about archaeology. Recent topics have included the landscape of Thomas Jefferson's Monticello, the Yupik village of Nunalleq, and the archaeology of Native American tattooing. *American Archaeology* also contains information of interest to members of The Archaeological Conservancy and lists the acquisitions of new sites under its aegis, field reports from current conservancy projects, and opportunities for field school and volunteer work. Book reviews are concise but informative. The magazine is highly readable and beautifully illustrated and is an appropriate acquisition for a public library.

394. ***American Journal of Archaeology.*** Formerly (until 1897): *American Journal of Archaeology and of the History of the Fine Arts.* [ISSN: 0002-9114] 1885. q. USD 340 (print & online eds.)). Ed(s): Jane B Carter. Archaeological Institute of America (Boston), 44 Beacon St 2nd Fl, Boston, MA 02108; http://www.archaeological.org. Illus., index, adv. Refereed. Vol. ends: Oct. Microform: PMC; PQC. *Indexed:* A01, A06, A22, AmHI, BAS, BRI, CBRI, Chicano, MLA-IB. *Bk. rev.:* 15-25 per issue, 900-2,000 words, signed, online only. *Aud.:* Ac, Sa.

Published by the Archaeological Institute of America, located at Boston University, the *American Journal of Archaeology* is a quarterly review of current scholarship in "the art and archaeology of ancient Europe and the Mediterranean world, including the Near East and Egypt, from prehistoric to Late Antique times." Each issue includes 4 to 5 scholarly articles of 30 to 40 pages each, with color and black-and-white photographs, line drawings, plans, and maps. Also included are "necrologies" of recently deceased archaeologists of note, field reports, and museum reviews. Book reviews, as well as supplementary content such as image galleries and indexes, and all pre-1923 content are now freely available on the journal's open access website, *AJA Online*. The journal itself is published both in print and online. Recent topics covered include reconstructing the Sacred Way between Miletos and Didyma, clothing from the Royal Tombs at Nimrud, and Greek graffiti of Herculaneum. Academic collections with an interest in Classical Studies will find this journal to be an important addition.

395. ***Ancient Mesoamerica.*** [ISSN: 0956-5361] 1990. 3x/yr. GBP 430. Ed(s): Nancy Gonlin, William R Fowler, Jr. Cambridge University Press, University Printing House, Shaftesbury Rd, Cambridge, CB2 8BS, United Kingdom; journals@cambridge.org; https://www.cambridge.org/. Adv. Refereed. Circ: 800. Reprint: PSC. *Indexed:* A01, A22, A47, E01, IBSS. *Aud.:* Ac, Sa.

An international publication, *Ancient Mesoamerica* is a scholarly journal that covers pre-Columbian Mesoamerican archaeology and its intersection with the allied disciplines of art history, ethnohistory, linguistics, and cultural anthropology. Each issue, published in print and online biannually, contains from 12 to 16 articles written in English or (to a lesser extent) Spanish, accompanied by color and black-and-white maps, line drawings, and other illustrative matter, and ranging in length from 10 to 30 pages. Although scholarly, the journal seeks also to reach the non-specialist reader. The subject matter reflects the interdisciplinary ethos of the journal, with special attention paid to the historical linguistics of indigenous Mesoamerican languages. *Ancient Mesoamerica* also has a strong anthropological focus, reflecting the New World affinity between the fields of archaeology and anthropology. Recent issues have explored such topics as the "Eclipse Glyph" in Maya text and iconography, Altun Ha and the water scroll emblem glyph, and ceramic ethnoarchaeology in Mexico. This is an excellent review of the state of Mesoamerican research, appropriate for scholarly audiences but also accessible to the serious nonprofessional.

396. ***Antiquity: a quarterly review of world archaeology.*** [ISSN: 0003-598X] 1927. bi-m. GBP 357. Ed(s): Robert Witcher. Cambridge University Press, University Printing House, Shaftesbury Rd, Cambridge, CB2 8BS, United Kingdom; journals@cambridge.org; https://www.cambridge.org/. Illus., index, adv. Sample. Refereed. Vol. ends: Dec. Microform: MIM; IDC; PQC. Reprint: PSC. *Indexed:* A01, A06, A22, A47, AmHI, BAS, BRI, IBSS, MLA-IB. *Bk. rev.:* 9-15 per issue, 1-3 pages, signed; 3-4 book review articles, 2-8 pages, signed. *Aud.:* Ac, Sa.

Published six times per year, in print and online, by the Antiquity Trust and edited by the Department of Archaeology at Durham University, *Antiquity* is a peer-reviewed journal of world archaeology that "reports new archaeological research, method and issues of international significance in plain language to a broad academic and professional readership." Each issue features from 12 to 15 articles of 10 to 15 pages each, presenting either original research or newly applied or developed "Debates," a section presenting papers that address contentious issues of interest to the archaeological profession; and "Project Galleries," which showcases new projects, fieldwork discoveries, and innovative applications of technology. These latter articles are short, available online only, and freely accessible. Also included are both book reviews and more substantial thematic book-review articles. Articles are well illustrated with color and black-and-white photographs, charts, maps, and line drawings. Recent topics include the antiquity of bow-and-arrow technology, early art in the Urals, and burnt offerings of jade from the Shang Dynasty. The journal plays an important role in any archaeological research collection.

397. ***Archaeology (Long Island City).*** [ISSN: 0003-8113] 1948. bi-m. USD 14.97 domestic (Free to members). Ed(s): Jarrett A Lobell. Archaeological Institute of America, 36-36 33rd St, Long Island City, NY 11106; aia@aia.bu.edu; http://www.archaeological.org/. Illus., index, adv. Vol. ends: Nov/Dec. *Indexed:* A01, A06, A22, A47, AmHI, BAS, BRI, C37, CBRI, MASUSE, MLA-IB. *Aud.:* Hs, Ga, Ac, Sa.

While the Archaeological Institute of America also publishes the more scholarly *American Journal of Archaeology* for a professional archaeological audience, its bimonthly title *Archaeology* is a general-interest magazine intended for wider circulation, offering "compelling narratives about the human past from every corner of the globe." Its scope covers all ages from prehistoric to the present. Each issue contains five feature articles with glossy color photos, a "World Roundup" of archaeology news, a "From the Trenches" feature offering late-breaking news and notes, a "Letter from..." piece about a current archaeological site, and "Artifact," a one-page essay about a specific object. Recent subjects have included desert agriculture in Israel, a seventeenth-century shipwreck off a Dutch island, and the archaeology of gardens. Like its more academically oriented sister publication, this print magazine boasts a dynamic web presence, including videos, podcasts, and travel information. This well-illustrated, informative, and entertaining magazine is of interest especially to general audiences, but will also be appreciated in college and university libraries.

398. ***Archaeometry.*** [ISSN: 0003-813X] 1958. bi-m. GBP 360. Ed(s): Ina Reiche, Mark Pollard. Wiley-Blackwell Publishing Ltd., The Atrium, Southern Gate, Chichester, PO19 8QG, United Kingdom; cs-journals@wiley.com; http://onlinelibrary.wiley.com/. Illus., adv. Sample. Refereed. Vol. ends: Aug. Reprint: PSC. *Indexed:* A&ATA, A01, A22, BAS, E01. *Aud.:* Ac.

Published bimonthly for the University of Oxford in association with several other societies, *Archaeometry* is "an international journal covering the involvement of the physical and biological sciences with archaeology and art history. The topics covered include dating methods, artifact studies, mathematical methods, remote sensing techniques, conservation science, and the study of man and his environment." Each issue contains 12 to 14 articles of 10 to 25 pages in length and featuring color and black-and-white photographs, plans, maps, and graphs. The geographical and temporal scope of *Archaeometry* is wide-ranging and the language is highly technical. Recent articles discuss stable isotope sourcing of wool from textiles at Pacatnamu, the social and economic complexity of ancient Jerusalem as seen through choices in lighting oils, and the evidence of crucifixion on the Shroud of Turin. This journal is suited to an academic research collection for archaeology.

399. ***Biblical Archaeology Review.*** Incorporates (1998-2006): *Archaeology Odyssey;* (1992-2005): *B R;* Which was formerly (1985-1992): *Bible Review.* [ISSN: 0098-9444] 1975. bi-m. USD 13.97 domestic (Free to members). Ed(s): Hershel Shanks. Biblical Archaeology Society, 4710 41st St, NW, Washington, DC 20016; bas@bib-arch.org; http://www.biblicalarchaeology.org/. Illus., adv. Vol. ends: Nov/Dec. *Indexed:* A01, A22, AmHI, BRI, MLA-IB, R&TA. *Bk. rev.:* 1-2 per issue, 300-1,000 words, signed. *Aud.:* Ga, Ac, Sa.

Biblical Archaeology Review, a bi-monthly publication of the Biblical Archaeology Society, features "articles by top scholars written for the layperson." Each glossy issue offers several feature articles and regular departmental columns that present news, opportunities to go on digs, reviews, editorials, and short takes on varied topics. The magazine is available both in print and online, and also has a web portal with additional features, such as a "Special Collections" section that presents curated articles on a single topic, videos, and links to articles referenced in the print edition. Articles are well illustrated with color and black-and-white photographs and maps. Recent topics have included an Early Roman period landfill in Jerusalem, the Canaanite artistic tradition at Israelite Hazor, and Phoenicia's special relationship with Israel. Articles are highly readable and enjoyable, making this magazine an excellent addition to both public and academic libraries.

400. ***Cambridge Archaeological Journal.*** [ISSN: 0959-7743] 1991. q. GBP 338 (print & online eds.)). Ed(s): John Robb. Cambridge University Press, University Printing House, Shaftesbury Rd, Cambridge, CB2 8BS, United Kingdom; journals@cambridge.org; https://www.cambridge.org/. Illus., index, adv. Refereed. Circ: 1800. Vol. ends: Oct. Reprint: PSC. *Indexed:* A01, A22, A47, AmHI, E01. *Bk. rev.:* 7-10 per issue, 1-4 columns, signed. *Aud.:* Ac, Sa.

Published quarterly and available as an online journal or bundled with print, *Cambridge Archaeological Journal* is "one of the leading international journals for symbolic, social and cognitive archaeology." It covers all periods and areas, focusing on the human intellect of early societies, including art, religion, and symbolism. Each issue features 8 to 10 articles of 15 to 20 pages in length and somewhat sparsely illustrated with color and black-and-white photographs, maps, graphs, and drawings. Also included are book reviews and longer review essays. Recent topics have included ageing and the body in archaeology, an archaeological inquiry into Classic Maya educational practice, and Shona political succession in southern Africa. Articles are suitable for an academic or educated amateur audience and of interest not only to archaeologists but to scholars in such fields as history and the arts.

401. ***Egyptian Archaeology.*** [ISSN: 0962-2837] 1991. s-a. Free to members; Non-members, GBP 5.95. Ed(s): Jan Geisbusch. Egypt Exploration Society, 3 Doughty Mews, London, WC1N 2PG, United Kingdom; http://www.ees.ac.uk. Illus., index, adv. Circ: 2500. *Bk. rev.:* 2-4 per issue, 2-3 columns, signed. *Aud.:* Ga, Ac.

The Egypt Exploration Society, founded in 1882, has published this biannual publication for its members since 1991. Each issue has eight to nine articles of four to six pages in length on a variety of topics in ancient Egyptian archaeology, art, and papyrology, accompanied by glossy photographs, drawings, and computer re-creations. The "Digging Diary" offers a roundup of field reports from ongoing excavations and highlights expeditions headed by the society. Recent issues feature shabtis from tombs in western Thebes, an early temple of Ptah at Karnak, and the Metropolitan Museum's Temple of Dendur. Although this periodical is chiefly targeted toward members of the Egypt Exploration Society, its accessible articles and rich visual content make it a fine resource for anyone with an interest in ancient Egypt.

402. ***Heritage & Society.*** Formerly (until 2011): *Heritage Management.* [ISSN: 2159-032X] 2008. s-a. GBP 382 (print & online eds.)). Ed(s): Elizabeth Brabec. Routledge, 4 Park Sq, Milton Park, Abingdon, OX14 4RN, United Kingdom; subscriptions@tandf.co.uk; http://www.tandfonline.com. Refereed. Reprint: PSC. *Indexed:* A01, C45. *Bk. rev.:* 3-5 per issue, 2-3 pages, signed. *Aud.:* Ga, Ac.

Heritage & Society is "a global, peer-reviewed journal that provides a forum for scholarly, professional, and community reflection on the cultural, political, and economic impacts of heritage on contemporary society." Topics discussed include collective memory, historic preservation, cultural resource management, cultural heritage ethics, and related subjects. The journal is published twice a year in print and online. Each issue contains three to four articles of 20 to 30 pages in length, some of which are illustrated with color photographs and maps. Book reviews are also included. Topics are wide ranging, recently including heritage rights for Tasmanian Aboriginals, Taksim Square in Istanbul as a heritage site, and England's small music venues. The journal is of interest not only to archaeologists, but also to those who work for indigenous communities, governmental agencies, and cultural heritage organizations. Accessible and covering a great variety of topics, *Heritage & Society* is appropriate both for public libraries and for academic collections that focus on archaeology, indigenous studies, and public humanities.

403. ***Hesperia.*** [ISSN: 0018-098X] 1932. q. USD 210 (print & online eds.)). Ed(s): Jennifer Sacher. ASCSA Publications, 6-8 Charlton St, Princeton, NJ 08540-5232. Illus. Refereed. *Indexed:* A06, A22, AmHI, E01, MLA-IB. *Aud.:* Ac, Sa.

A quarterly publication of the American School of Classical Studies at Athens, *Hesperia* "welcomes submissions from all scholars working in the fields of Greek archaeology, art, epigraphy, history, materials science, ethnography, and literature, from earliest prehistoric times onward." Available in print and online, each issue contains four to five articles of 20 to 80 pages in length, illustrated with color and black-and-white photographs, maps, and other illustrative material. Also included with each article are comprehensive scholarly bibliographies. Recent topics have included the decipherment of Linear B as an early form of Greek, the iconography of deceased maidens on Attic grave reliefs, and the acoustics of Byzantine churches in Thessaloniki. A venerable journal, published since 1932, *Hesperia* is an indispensable part of any research collection. Its scholarly articles are useful not only for archaeologists and historians but also for the general reader with an interest in Greek history and culture.

404. ***Historical Archaeology.*** [ISSN: 0440-9213] 1967. q. EUR 551 (print & online eds.)). Ed(s): Christopher N Matthews. Society for Historical Archaeology, 13017 Wisteria Dr #395, Germantown, MD 20874; hq@sha.org; http://www.sha.org. Illus., index, adv. Refereed. Vol. ends: Dec. *Indexed:* A01, A22, AmHI, BRI, IBSS, MLA-IB. *Bk. rev.:* 0-8 per issue, 1-3 pages, signed. *Aud.:* Ac, Sa.

Historical Archaeology is the quarterly journal of the Society for Historical Archaeology and is a benefit of membership. The journal focuses on the sites and material culture of the modern world, with an emphasis on the formation of a global economy following the 15th-century voyages of discovery. Most, though not all, contributors are members of the society. Articles cover an international range of topics in such areas as cultural identity and ethnicity, archaeology of foodways, technological and methodological approaches, major site excavations, and more. Each peer-reviewed print issue contains 6 to 12 feature articles of 12 to 25 pages in length, illustrated with color and black-and-white photographs, maps, and line drawings. Book reviews, interviews, technical briefs, and other archaeological news are included in some issues. Recent topics have included Mashantucket Pequot labor in the later 18th century, the archaeology of maple sugar camps in northern Michigan, and aligning method and theory in the archaeology of plantation slavery. This scholarly journal is appropriate for academic libraries with collections in archaeology, anthropology, history, and related fields.

405. ***Journal of Archaeological Method and Theory.*** Former titles (until 1994): *Archaeological Method and Theory;* (until 1989): *Advances in Archaeological Method and Theory.* [ISSN: 1072-5369] 1978. q. EUR 1149 (print & online eds.)). Ed(s): James M Skibo, Catherine M Cameron. Springer New York LLC, 233 Spring St, New York, NY 10013; customerservice@springer.com; http://www.springer.com. Adv. Refereed. Reprint: PSC. *Indexed:* A01, A22, A47, E01, IBSS. *Aud.:* Ac.

The *Journal of Archaeological Method and Theory* is a quarterly scholarly and international publication, available in print and online versions. Its intent is to present "original articles that address method- or theory-focused issues of current archaeological interest and represent significant explorations on the cutting edge of the discipline." Each issue contains from 12 to 14 articles, somewhat sparsely illustrated with color and black-and-white photographs, maps, charts, and graphs, and ranging in length from 25 to 35 pages. Recent topics have included parental grief and mourning in the Andes, incisions on a Paleolithic cave bear bone, and the structural and functional complexity of hunter-gatherer technology. The journal is geared toward practicing archaeologists and anthropologists and is an important addition to academic collections that serve them.

406. ***Journal of Archaeological Science.*** [ISSN: 0305-4403] 1974. m. EUR 3442. Ed(s): Marcos Martinon-Torres, Robin Torrence. Academic Press, 32 Jamestown Rd, Camden, London, NW1 7BY, United Kingdom; corporate.sales@elsevier.com; http://www.elsevier.com/. Illus., index, adv. Sample. Refereed. Vol. ends: Nov. Reprint: PSC. *Indexed:* A&ATA, A01, A22, A47, E01. *Aud.:* Ac.

Published monthly in print and online versions in association with the Society for Archaeological Sciences, this journal is aimed at "archaeologists and scientists with particular interests in advancing the development and application of scientific techniques and methodologies to all areas of archaeology." The editors aim to publish only "truly innovative studies that have a potential impact on wider research across many times and places, change our perspective on major issues within archaeology, or raise important issues for the future of the discipline." Each month approximately 6 to 20 research articles are presented, illustrated with color photographs, maps, and charts, and ranging from 10 to 25 pages in length. Substantial bibliographies are included. Recent issues have featured articles on ancient tin production in the Iberian Peninsula, early medieval water mill technology, and zooarchaeology in the era of big data. Highly technical in its language, the *Journal of Archaeological Science* is appropriate for academic research collections.

407. ***Journal of Field Archaeology.*** [ISSN: 0093-4690] 1974. 8x/yr. GBP 296 (print & online eds.)). Ed(s): Christina Luke. Routledge, 4 Park Sq, Milton Park, Abingdon, OX14 4RN, United Kingdom; subscriptions@tandf.co.uk; http://www.tandfonline.com. Illus., adv. Sample. Refereed. Vol. ends: Winter. Microform: PQC. Reprint: PSC. *Indexed:* A&ATA, A22, A47, AmHI, BAS, BRI. *Bk. rev.:* Occasional, 2-3 pages, signed. *Aud.:* Ac, Sa.

Boston University publishes the *Journal of Field Archaeology* for "professionals concerned with the interpretation of the archaeological record around the world." With the 2018 volume, this journal now publishes eight issues per year online and prints them twice annually with four issues each. One special open access online issue is additionally planned for each year. Featured are articles containing analyses of archaeological data, technical and methodological studies, and discussions of archaeological heritage and ethics. Issues contain 5 to 6 articles that are 10 to 20 pages in length and illustrated with color and black-and-white photographs, maps, charts and graphs, and line drawings. The journal is international in scope, and some recent topics include a pastoral Neolithic settlement in Tanzania, drawing and digital media in archaeological field recording, and finding mid nineteenth-century Native settlements in California. This publication is appropriate for academic research libraries that serve programs in archaeology.

408. ***Journal of Mediterranean Archaeology.*** [ISSN: 0952-7648] 1988. s-a. USD 488 print & online eds. Ed(s): A Bernard Knapp, Peter van Dommelen. Equinox Publishing Ltd., 415, The Workstation, 15 Paternoster Row, Sheffield, S1 2BX, United Kingdom; info@equinoxpub.com; http://www.equinoxpub.com/. Adv. Refereed. *Indexed:* A01, A22. *Aud.:* Ac.

A biannual publication with a truly regional focus, the *Journal of Mediterranean Archaeology* is "the only journal currently published that deals with the entire multicultural world of Mediterranean archaeology." The journal is available in print and online. Each issue presents 6 to 9 scholarly articles, 20 to 30 pages in length, from an international list of contributors. Special emphasis is put on social interaction and change as well as broader contemporary theoretical approaches to Mediterranean archaeology with respect to "gender, agency, identity, and landscape." The articles are illustrated with color and black-and-white photographs, maps, plans, graphs, and line drawings. Recent topics have included mobility and place making in late Pleistocene and early Holocene Italy, gender performativity in the Knossos frescoes, and the Israelite perception of space. The *Journal of Mediterranean Archaeology* brings an interdisciplinary philosophy and methodology to an area of study that has broad implications for the history of the western world. It will be of interest to academic library collections that serve scholars in history, gender studies, anthropology, and other disciplines in addition to its main focus of archaeology.

409. ***Journal of Roman Archaeology.*** [ISSN: 1047-7594] 1988. a. USD 180; USD 200 combined subscription (print & online eds.)). Ed(s): John H Humphrey. Journal of Roman Archaeology LLC., The Editor, JRA, 95 Peleg Rd, Portsmouth, RI 02871. Illus. Sample. Refereed. *Indexed:* A22. *Bk. rev.:* 80-90 per issue, 3-12 pages, signed. *Aud.:* Ac, Sa.

This international journal, published annually in two fascicules, covers not only the latest developments in Roman archaeology but also topics in ancient Roman art, history, classical philology, and Greco-Roman culture. The first fascicule of each volume contains 8 to 15 scholarly articles of 20 to 30 pages each, followed by 10 to 16 archaeological reports and notes from the field. The second fascicule contains from 80 to 90 "long, synthetic" book reviews. Although submissions are welcomed in English, Spanish, French, Italian, and German, the majority of material is written in English. Subscriptions are available in print and online. Articles are illustrated with color and black-and-white photographs, plans, and drawings. In the most recent volume, articles included the "lost" Nollekens relief from Domitian's Palace; athletes, acclamations and imagery from the end of antiquity; and the water-supply infrastructure of Byzantine Constantinople. Drawing submissions from the most respected academic institutions around the world and including a huge number of in-depth reviews of scholarly publications, the *Journal of Roman Archaeology* is an indispensable resource for scholars in all areas of Greco-Roman civilization.

410. ***Latin American Antiquity.*** Supersedes in part (in 1990): *American Antiquity.* [ISSN: 1045-6635] 1935. q. GBP 207 (print & online eds.)). Ed(s): Maria A Gutierrez, Geoffrey Braswell. Cambridge University Press, 1 Liberty Plaza, Fl 20, New York, NY 10004; online@cambridge.org; https://www.cambridge.org/. Illus., index, adv. Refereed. Vol. ends: Dec. Reprint: PSC. *Indexed:* A01, A22, A47, AmHI, BRI, CBRI. *Bk. rev.:* 8-9 per issue, 2-3 pages, signed. *Aud.:* Ac, Sa.

A sister publication of *American Antiquity* (see above in this section), this quarterly journal of the Society for American Archaeology is "devoted to special reports on archaeology, prehistory, and ethnohistory in Mesoamerica, Central America, and South America, and culturally related areas." Each issue presents 7 to 10 feature articles of 10 to 20 pages in length and written in either English or Spanish (with abstracts in both languages), and available in print and online. The articles include substantial references. Also included are preliminary reports, comments, and book reviews. Illustrative material is relatively sparse and includes color and black-and-white photographs, line drawings, maps, and graphs. Recent topics explored include nineteenth-century roofing traditions in Peru, the early Holocene environment of northwest Guyana, and Maya figurines from Guatemala. *Latin American Antiquity* regularly features some of the most preeminent scholars and archaeologists in the field today, and thus is an essential component of any New World archaeological research collection.

411. *Medieval Archaeology.* [ISSN: 0076-6097] 1957. s-a. GBP 231 (print & online eds.)). Ed(s): Sarah Semple. Routledge, 4 Park Sq, Milton Park, Abingdon, OX14 4RN, United Kingdom; subscriptions@tandf.co.uk; http://www.tandfonline.com. Illus., adv. Refereed. Reprint: PSC. *Indexed:* A&ATA, A01, A22, AmHI, BRI. *Bk. rev.:* 30-50 per issue, 300-1,000 words, signed. *Aud.:* Ac, Sa.

The Society for Medieval Archaeology publishes this biannual scholarly journal of international standing, available in print and online. *Medieval Archaeology* primarily covers the archaeology of Britain and Ireland from the fifth to the sixteenth century, although articles about contemporaneous developments in continental Europe and elsewhere are welcomed by the editors. Each issue contains 6 to 8 feature articles of 10 to 40 pages each and illustrated with color and black-and-white photographs, charts, graphs, maps, and line drawings. Comprehensive bibliographies are included. More general articles focus on theory and methodology or report on fieldwork and other archaeological highlights from the previous year. The journal also publishes a substantial number of book reviews. Recent issues feature articles on monetary practices in early medieval western Scandinavia, early medieval jet-like jewelry in Ireland, and the monumental cemeteries of northern Pictland. This journal is appropriate for academic libraries with collections not just in archaeology, but also in medieval history and the history of the British Isles and Ireland.

412. *Near Eastern Archaeology.* Formerly (until 1998): *Biblical Archaeologist.* [ISSN: 1094-2076] 1938. q. USD 209. Ed(s): Stephanie Budlin. University of Chicago Press, 1427 E 60th St, Chicago, IL 60637; custserv@press.uchicago.edu; http://www.journals.uchicago.edu. Illus., index, adv. Refereed. Vol. ends: Dec. *Indexed:* A&ATA, A01, A06, A22, A47, AmHI, BRI, C26, MLA-IB, R&TA. *Bk. rev.:* 2-4 per issue, 4 columns, signed. *Aud.:* Ga, Ac, Sa.

This glossy, colorful magazine, published four times a year by the American Schools of Oriental Research, "brings to life the ancient world from Mesopotamia to the Mediterranean with vibrant images and authoritative analyses." Each issue usually offers seven to ten articles that are under ten pages in length and well illustrated with color photographs. Special issues on a single topic, such as gender archaeology, can feature as many as 20 articles. Among the recent topics explored are Philistine burial customs, Twelfth Dynasty Egyptian fortresses in Sudan, and the archaeological renaissance in the Kurdistan region of Iraq. The accessible language of the texts and the colorful illustrations make *Near Eastern Archaeology* appropriate both for academic and public libraries.

413. *North American Archaeologist.* [ISSN: 0197-6931] 1979. q. USD 721 (print & online eds.)). Ed(s): Anthony T Boldurian. Sage Publications, Inc., 2455 Teller Rd, Thousand Oaks, CA 91320; info@sagepub.com; http://www.sagepub.com. Illus., adv. Sample. Refereed. Vol. ends: No. 4. Reprint: PSC. *Indexed:* A22, A47, AmHI, MLA-IB. *Bk. rev.:* 1 per issue, 3-4 pages, signed. *Aud.:* Ac, Sa.

This quarterly publication is "the only general journal dedicated solely to North America, offering total coverage of archaeological activity in the United States, Canada, and northern Mexico (excluding Mesoamerica)." Both prehistoric and historic archaeology are included in its purview. The journal is published in print and online, but an "OnlineFirst" feature assures that the latest research is published on the web as quickly as possible, before it appears in either type of publication. Each issue offers 2 to 4 research articles, 25 to 50 pages in length, and sparsely illustrated with color and black-and-white photographs, maps, plans, and graphs. One in-depth book review is generally included in each issue. Recently featured topics include the source of brick clay at Brookgreen Plantation in South Carolina, stock raising and winter sheep camps in Wyoming, and New Deal archaeology in Kansas. *North American Archaeologist* offers readers a scholarly mix of theory and methodology and is appropriate for an academic research library.

414. *Oxford Journal of Archaeology.* [ISSN: 0262-5253] 1982. q. GBP 812. Ed(s): Chris Gosden, Barry Cunliffe. Wiley-Blackwell Publishing Ltd., The Atrium, Southern Gate, Chichester, PO19 8QG, United Kingdom; cs-journals@wiley.com; http://onlinelibrary.wiley.com. Illus., adv. Sample. Refereed. Reprint: PSC. *Indexed:* A&ATA, A01, A22, E01, IBSS. *Aud.:* Ac, Sa.

A quarterly journal published in association with the Institute of Archaeology at the University of Oxford, the *Oxford Journal of Archaeology* provides an unparalleled comprehensive review of the latest scholarship in European and Mediterranean archaeology, covering the Paleolithic era to the medieval. Each issue is published in print and online and consists solely of 5 to 6 articles of 12 to 30 pages each, solicited from some of the most respected scholars in the field. Articles are illustrated with color and black-and-white photographs, maps, charts and graphs, and line drawings. Among the recent topics covered are the central Adriatic wine trade of Italy, Early Bronze Age metalwork deposits in Scotland, and the social meanings of Mycenaean metal cups. Geared to a scholarly audience, this journal is an essential part of any archaeological research collection, valuable to historians of the ancient and medieval world, and required reading for any practitioner of European or Mediterranean archaeology.

415. *Post-Medieval Archaeology.* [ISSN: 0079-4236] 1967. 3x/yr. GBP 326 (print & online eds.)). Ed(s): Katherine Fennelly. Routledge, 4 Park Sq, Milton Park, Abingdon, OX14 4RN, United Kingdom; subscriptions@tandf.co.uk; http://www.tandfonline.com. Adv. Refereed. Reprint: PSC. *Indexed:* A01. *Bk. rev.:* 5-7 in one issue per year, 1-2 pages, signed. *Aud.:* Ac, Sa.

This publication of the Society for Post-Medieval Archaeology is issued three times a year in print and online. The journal is "devoted to the study of the material evidence of European society wherever it is found in the world," documenting the transition from the medieval era to modern industrial society through a multidisciplinary approach that looks at material, textual, iconographic, and scientific evidence. The first and second issues of each volume contain seven to ten feature articles on a variety of topics and varying in length. Articles are illustrated with color and black-and-white photographs, maps, charts, graphs, and line drawings, and include substantial bibliographies. Other features may include obituaries of prominent archaeologists, reports, commentaries, and news. The third issue features fieldwork summaries and five to seven book reviews. Recent topics have included vernacular architecture in Doha, Qatar; the impact of the Great War on the British ceramics industry; and the archaeology of consumption in Ottoman urban centers. The archaeology of this period is of critical importance not just to practitioners of the field but to anyone with an interest in modern history, making *Post-Medieval Archaeology* an important part of any academic research collection.

416. *World Archaeology.* [ISSN: 0043-8243] 1969. 5x/yr. GBP 714 (print & online eds.)). Ed(s): John Schofield. Routledge, 4 Park Sq, Milton Park, Abingdon, OX14 4RN, United Kingdom; subscriptions@tandf.co.uk; http://www.tandfonline.com. Illus., index, adv. Sample. Refereed. Microform: PQC. Reprint: PSC. *Indexed:* A&ATA, A01, A22, A47, AmHI, BAS, E01, IBSS, MLA-IB. *Aud.:* Ac, Sa.

World Archaeology "was established specifically to deal with archaeology on a world-wide multiperiod basis." Published five times a year in print and online, the first four issues contain 6 to 10 articles of 12 to 20 pages in length, organized around a particular theme. The fifth issue, titled "Debates," is a forum for discussion, debate, and comment. Articles are sparsely illustrated with color and black-and-white photographs, maps, charts, graphs, and line drawings, and contain comprehensive bibliographies. Recent issue themes have included the history of archaeology, the archaeology of food surplus, and counter archaeologies. Both the thematic emphasis and the dedicated space for regular discussion make this journal an indispensable resource for any archaeological collection, both for scholars and interested amateurs.

■ ARCHITECTURE

See also Interior Design and Decoration; Landscape Architecture; and Urban Studies sections.

Amy Trendler, Architecture Librarian, Ball State University, Muncie, IN 47306; aetrendler@bsu.edu

Introduction

The readership for architecture magazines and journals is made up of several groups: professional architects, scholars and academics, students, the design savvy, and the general public. The titles in this section all serve at least one of these groups, most titles serve more than one group, and some titles are pertinent to all segments of the architecture audience. Given the wide range of the architecture magazine readership, there is a good chance that a special, academic, or public library will carry one or more of the titles listed in this section, and a sizable architecture library might carry all of the titles in this section.

Within the pages of architecture magazines and journals, readers will find critical reviews of new buildings all over the world, case studies, theoretical musings and essays, opinion pieces, news of the profession, thoroughly researched articles on historical topics, information on cutting-edge materials and trends, and many, many illustrations. It is not unusual for articles in architecture magazines to be accompanied by numerous color photographs, plans, details, architects' sketches, sections, elevations, and more. The visual presentation of architecture is the defining feature of some publications such as *GA Document, Detail*, and *The Plan*, which specialize in documenting new buildings or highlighting details. Other titles focus on research (*Journal of Green Building, Journal of the Society of Architectural Historians*) or writing about architecture (*Architectural Design, Log*), news of the profession (*Architect, Architectural Record, Architects' Journal, Architect's Newspaper, Canadian Architect*), or current trends in the design world (*Metropolis, Azure, Wallpaper*).

Scholarly architecture journals are available online by subscription or open access, and some of these titles are not offered in print at all. The magazines, on the other hand, have largely persisted as print publications. Digital editions of a number of the magazines are available—in some cases only to the individual subscriber and not to the institutional subscriber—but some important architecture magazines exist only in print. The impact for libraries is a continuing need for shelf space to display and store their architecture magazine holdings.

Basic Periodicals

Ga: *Architect, Architectural Record, Azure, Taunton's Fine Homebuilding, Metropolis, Preservation, Wallpaper;* Ac: *A & U, Architectural Design, Architectural Review, El Croquis, Domus, G A Document, Journal of Green Building, R I B A Journal, Society of Architectural Historians. Journal.*

Basic Abstracts and Indexes

Architectural Publications Index, Art & Architecture Complete, Art Full Text, Art Index, Avery Index to Architectural Periodicals.

417. ***A A Files.*** Former titles (until 1981): *A A Quarterly;* (until 1969): *Arena;* (until 19??): *Architectural Association Journal;* (until 195?): *A A Journal.* [ISSN: 0261-6823] 1981. s-a. Free to members; Non-members, GBP 32. Architectural Association Inc., School of Architecture, 36 Bedford Sq, London, WC1B 3ES, United Kingdom; publications@aaschool.ac.uk; http://www.aaschool.ac.uk. Illus. *Indexed:* A06, A22, MLA-IB. *Bk. rev.:* 6-8, 1,500 words. *Aud.:* Ac.

Wide-ranging articles on contemporary architects and their projects, essays on architectural history or theory, and thorough exhibition and book reviews can be found in the richly illustrated, advertisement-free pages of *AA Files*. Published twice a year by the Architectural Association School of Architecture in London, the journal grows out of the research of the school's faculty, the school's impressive lecture and exhibition program, and "a rich and eclectic mix of architectural enquiry from all over the world." Architects, architectural and art historians, academics, and the occasional poet or artist make up the list of contributors. Available as a print subscription, full text from all issues including the current one is also available in JSTOR. Recommended for academic and architecture libraries.

418. ***A & T.*** [ISSN: 1132-6409] 1992. s-a. A + T Editiones, General Alava 15-2 A, Vitoria-Gasteiz, 01005, Spain; aplus@aplus.net; http://www.aplus.net/. Illus. *Aud.:* Ac, Sa.

An issue of this advertisement-free, semi-annual Spanish periodical analyzes several buildings or projects as part of an overall theme such as public space, mixed-use buildings, or domestic architecture. The visual coverage of the selected buildings and projects is exhaustive and includes numerous photographs, plans (for every floor, even for the high-rise projects), sections, and details. In addition, *A & T* is unique in creating graphics that illustrate the analysis. For example, an issue on mixed-use buildings featured graphics detailing the percentage of individual uses (commercial, housing, office space, and so on), comparing floor space and site coverage, and situating the works in context. All text is in both Spanish and English. A preview of some content from the issues is available for free online, but the full text appears only in the printed or digital publication, which can be purchased individually or via subscription. Recommended for architecture libraries.

419. ***A & U.*** [ISSN: 0389-9160] 1971. m. JPY 30; USD 248.18. Shinkenchiku-sha Co. Ltd., Kasumigaseki Bldg. 17F, 3-2-5 Kasumigaseki, Chiyoda-ku, Tokyo, 100-6017, Japan; http://www.japan-architect.co.jp. Illus., index, adv. Circ: 25000. Vol. ends: Dec. *Indexed:* A22. *Bk. rev.:* Number and length vary. *Aud.:* Ac, Sa.

The sister magazine to *JA: the Japan Architect*, *A + U* covers international architecture. Profusely illustrated, it is one of several titles that are largely devoted to building studies (see also, for example, the GA publications such as *GA Document*). Issues focus on an international architect or firm, or architects and architecture in a particular city or region. Essays and interviews appear on the pages of *A + U*, but most pages are filled with the meticulously detailed building studies. Each study is composed of several paragraphs of description and numerous illustrations, details, plans, elevations, and conceptual drawings. Brief biographies of the architects whose work appears in the issues are always included. Text is in both Japanese and English. Tables of contents beginning with issue 353 (2002) are available online; the full text is only available in the printed issues or the digital issues available for purchase by individuals. Recommended for architecture libraries.

420. ***A R Q: Architectural Research Quarterly.*** [ISSN: 1359-1355] 1995. q. q. until 2014. GBP 362. Ed(s): Adam Sharr, Richard Weston. Cambridge University Press, University Printing House, Shaftesbury Rd, Cambridge, CB2 8BS, United Kingdom; journals@cambridge.org; https://www.cambridge.org/. Adv. Refereed. Reprint: PSC. *Indexed:* A22, E01. *Bk. rev.:* Number and length vary. *Aud.:* Ac.

A quarterly published in Great Britain, *ARQ* features "cutting-edge work covering all aspects of architectural endeavour." The lengthy, well-illustrated articles in an issue are grouped into the broad categories of design, theory, history, criticism, practice, perspective, or urbanism. Topics range from the historical to the contemporary. Detailed building studies, book reviews, interviews, or thought pieces complete an issue. Contributors are generally British, but the work of European, Australian, and American authors, educators, and architects also appears in the pages of *ARQ*. Abstracts for issues beginning with volume 1 (1995) are freely accessible online. Available in print only or online only subscriptions to libraries or individuals. Recommended for architecture libraries.

421. ***A V Monografias.*** [ISSN: 0213-487X] 1985. bi-m. 5 / yr. EUR 115 domestic; EUR 140 in Europe; EUR 160 elsewhere. Arquitectura Viva S.L., Calle de Aniceto Marinas 32, Madrid, 28008, Spain. Illus., adv. Circ: 9000. *Aud.:* Ac, Sa.

Each number of *AV Monografias*, a bimonthly journal published in Madrid, Spain, is focused on an international designer or firm such as Alvaro Siza, MVRDV, or Shigeru Ban, all the subjects of recent issues. The occasional historic figure (Le Corbusier, Lina Bo Bardi) or geographic area (Latin America, China, Portugal) may provide the theme of some issues in a given year, and an annual review of Spanish architecture is always the focus of a double issue. All of the journal's issues may contain a few essays, but most pages are devoted to anywhere from 10 to 24 building studies accompanied by a wealth of illustrative matter (photographs, plans, sections, elevations, site plans, sketches, details, and diagrams). Text is in both Spanish and English. Available in print or digital editions; tables of contents and the editor's introduction to each issue may be viewed on the publisher's website. Recommended for architecture libraries.

422. *Abitare: home, town and environmental living.* Formerly (until 1962): *Casa Novita.* [ISSN: 0001-3218] 1961. 11x/yr. R C S Periodici, Via San Marco 21, Milan, 20121, Italy; info@periodici.rcs.it. Illus. *Indexed:* A06. *Aud.:* Ga, Ac, Sa.

First published in 1961, this well-respected international design magazine re-launched in 2014 with a renewed focus and a goal to "promote Italian design culture into the world." Architecture and interiors feature prominently in the lineup of topics, which also includes furniture, product, and many other types of design as well as reports on research and studies related to design. International subjects do appear in the articles, but Italy and Italian designs and designers predominate. This is also true in the news section (called Booster), which features information about products, projects, exhibitions, and events in Milan and other Italian locales. Articles are well-illustrated with large, color photographs, plans, sections, and diagrams. All text is in both Italian and English. Libraries may subscribe in print; the digital edition of the magazine is available for purchase by individuals only. Recommended for architecture and large public libraries.

423. *L'Arca International: la revue internationale d'architecture, design et commmunication visuelle.* [ISSN: 7141-410X] 1996. bi-m. EUR 68.50 France and Italy; EUR 100 in Europe; EUR 125 elsewhere. Arca International, 31 av. Princesse Grace, Monaco, 98000, France. *Bk. rev.:* Number and length vary. *Aud.:* Ac, Sa.

L'Arca International is a bimonthly glossy magazine edited in Monaco and published in Italy that bills itself as the "international magazine of architecture, design and visual communication." A multi-page section at the beginning of an issue compiles short news items and features products, recently completed architectural projects, company profiles, short book reviews, and other brief notes. The rest of the magazine is composed of a couple of topical feature articles or essays and a case study of a new building accompanied by many color photographs, plans, details, models, and sketches. Shorter but similarly well-illustrated articles on an additional 6 to 8 works round out the issue along with the "short" section profiles of one or a handful of new works in one-page spreads that often include a plan or detail alongside a brief description and a couple of color photographs. The exhibition calendar in the "agenda" section, like the rest of the magazine, covers venues worldwide. With the exception of the ads, all the text is printed in French, Italian, and English. Individuals who subscribe to the print edition have access to the online version of the magazine; libraries may subscribe to the print edition. Recommended for architecture libraries.

424. *Architect: the new face of architecture.* Former titles (until 2006): *Architecture;* (until 1983): *A I A Journal;* (until 1957): *American Institute of Architects. Journal;* Architecture Incorporated (1992-1995): *Building Renovation;* (1920-1995): *Progressive Architecture;* Which was formerly (until 1945): *Pencil Points (East Stroudsburg, 1944);* (until 1943): *New Pencil Points;* (until 1942): *Pencil Points (East Stroud, 1920);* Which incorporated: *Monograph Series (New York, 1929);* (1983-1986): *Architectural Technology.* [ISSN: 1935-7001] 2006. m. USD 59 domestic (Free to qualified personnel). Ed(s): Ned Cramer, Greig O'Brien. Hanley Wood, LLC, 1 Thomas Cir, NW, Ste 600, Washington, DC 20005; http://www.hanleywood.com. Adv. Circ: 3213 Paid. *Indexed:* A01, AmHI, B01, MASUSE. *Bk. rev.:* Number and length vary. *Aud.:* Ac, Sa.

This monthly trade publication is also the official magazine of the American Institute of Architects (AIA), and as such it is a great resource of information on architectural practice in the United States. Sent free to AIA members, the magazine includes news items on the organization's events, programs, and awards. These sections and the feature articles and departments focused on the business side of architecture will appeal to the professional; the well-illustrated case studies, news and events, architect interviews, and book, product, and exhibition reviews will also appeal to a wider audience. A ranking of the top 50 U.S. architecture firms is published annually. Some of the content from the magazine is available for free on the *Architect* website as well as additional images of projects that appeared in the print publication, current news, job postings, and blogs. Recommended for architecture libraries and large public libraries.

425. *The Architects' Journal: the home of British architecture.* Former titles (until 1919): *Architects' and Builders' Journal;* (until 1910): *Builders' Journal and Architectural Engineer.* [ISSN: 0003-8466] 1895. bi-w. GBP 165 combined subscription domestic (print & online eds.); GBP 231 combined subscription foreign (print & online eds.)). Ed(s): Christine Murray. E M A P Publishing Ltd., 69 - 77 Paul St, London, EC2A 4NQ, United Kingdom; reception.GLH@topright-group.com; http://www.emap.com. Illus., adv. Sample. Circ: 7415. *Indexed:* A06, A22, AmHI, BRI, HRIS. *Bk. rev.:* Number and length vary. *Aud.:* Ac, Sa.

An issue of this bi-weekly British trade publication contains short news pieces, a couple of longer feature articles on architecture and architectural practice in Great Britain, and three to four detailed building studies. Columns and opinion pieces, information about architectural competitions, and the occasional interview, exhibition, or book review round out an issue. The magazine is well-illustrated and the building studies include many photographs, plans, sections, and thoroughly described and identified details. *The Architects' Journal* is an excellent resource for architects working or contemplating work in Great Britain, and the building studies and feature articles will appeal to anyone interested in contemporary British architecture. The *AJ* website includes content from the magazine but does not re-create the format of the print edition. A digital edition is available online to individual subscribers. Recommended for architecture libraries.

426. *The Architect's Newspaper.* [ISSN: 1552-8081] 2003. 12x/yr. The Architect's Newspaper, Llc., 21 Murray St, 5th Fl, New York, NY 10007. Adv. Circ: 15000 Paid and controlled. *Aud.:* Sa.

As the title implies, this periodical is a glossy, tabloid-format publication filled with news items written for an audience of professional architects. Previously published in several geographic editions (East, West, Midwest), as of 2016 there is just one edition of *Architect's Newspaper* published 12 times a year that covers all of the United States. Three of the 12 issues during the year are *AN Interior*, and the newspaper seeks to serve a readership of interior designers, landscape architects, contractors, and developers in addition to architects. A longer feature article or series of short articles on a theme and 18 to 20 brief articles and short news pieces fill the pages of each issue. Most articles describe newly completed works, projects under development, events, and exhibitions from all over the United States. A critical review or commentary may also make an appearance. Befitting the newspaper format, the articles are illustrated by one or more color photographs, but these do not approach the scale or breadth of the average architecture magazine. Select content and images from an issue are available for free online and occasionally more images accompany the online article, but the full contents of the print issues are not available in a digital edition. A subscription to *The Architect's Newspaper* is free to registered architects. Recommended for architecture libraries.

427. *Architectural Design.* Formerly (until 1947): *Architectural Design & Construction.* [ISSN: 0003-8504] 1930. bi-m. GBP 346. Ed(s): Helen Castle. John Wiley & Sons Ltd., EMEA Institutional Sales, 9600 Garsington Rd, Oxford, OX4 2DQ, United Kingdom; cs-journals@wiley.com; http://onlinelibrary.wiley.com. Illus., index, adv. Sample. Vol. ends: Nov/Dec. *Indexed:* A06, A22, EIP. *Bk. rev.:* 8, 250 words. *Aud.:* Ac, Sa.

Architectural Design is a bimonthly journal well-known for its deep dives into current topics in architecture, landscape architecture, interior design, and urban design. A guest editor or editors curate each issue and introduce the selected topic such as the recent "design for health: sustainable approaches to therapeutic architecture" or "4D hyperlocal: a cultural toolkit for the open-source city." Numerous color illustrations accompany the 15 or more articles, essays, or interviews by architects, architectural historians, theorists, artists, and academics. In addition to print subscriptions, pdf full text of this title is available by subscription from Wiley for 2005 through the present. *AD* can also be purchased as single issues. Recommended for architecture and large academic libraries.

Architectural Digest. See Interior Design and Decoration section.

428. *Architectural Histories.* [ISSN: 2050-5833] 2013. s-a. Free. Ed(s): Petra Brouwer. Ubiquity Press Ltd., 6 Windmill St, London, W1T 2JB, United Kingdom; support@ubiquitypress.com; https://www.ubiquitypress.com/. Refereed. *Bk. rev.:* Number and length vary. *Aud.:* Ac, Sa.

Architectural Histories is the peer-reviewed, open-access journal of the European Architectural History Network. Research articles, position papers, reviews, the occasional interview, and editorials are published online throughout the year forming an annual volume by year's end. Fifteen or more research articles make up each volume and while the focus is largely on European architectural history, North American and Latin American topics also make the occasional appearance. Several "special collections" form subsets across volumes on topics including architecture and travel, how a "culture of crisis" affects the built environment and architectural practice, and "building word image: printing architecture 1800-1950." This title is a useful one for librarians to know about where collections include *Architectural History* and the *Journal of the Society of Architectural Historians*. Recommended for architecture libraries.

429. *Architectural History.* [ISSN: 0066-622X] 1958. a. GBP 174 (print & online eds.)). Ed(s): David Hemsoll. Cambridge University Press, University Printing House, Shaftesbury Rd, Cambridge, CB2 8BS, United Kingdom; journals@cambridge.org; https://www.cambridge.org. Reprint: PSC. *Indexed:* A06, A22. *Bk. rev.:* Number and length vary. *Aud.:* Ac.

Published annually for The Society of Architectural Historians of Great Britain, this peer-reviewed journal is the British counterpart of the *Journal of the Society of Architectural Historians*. The dozen or more lengthy, scholarly articles in each issue are primarily on the architecture of Great Britain and the work of British architects at home and abroad, but the occasional European subject also makes an appearance. Articles in an issue are in chronological order, which is helpful since the time periods covered are extensive and a single issue can range from ancient to gothic to mid-century modern. Beginning with volume 59 in 2016, issues of the journal also includes a number of one- to two-page book reviews. This title is available in print via subscription; full text is available online in JSTOR with a moving wall of three years. Recommended for architecture and academic libraries.

430. *Architectural Record.* Incorporates: *American Architect and Architecture; Western Architect and Engineer.* [ISSN: 0003-858X] 1891. m. USD 49. Ed(s): Robert Ivy, Elisabeth Broome. McGraw-Hill Construction Dodge, 148 Princeton-Hightstown Rd. N1, Hightstown, NJ 08520; http://construction.com. Illus., index, adv. Circ: 115155 Paid. Vol. ends: Dec. *Indexed:* A01, A06, A22, AmHI, B01, BRI, C37, F01, GardL, MASUSE, MLA-IB. *Bk. rev.:* 6, 50-250 words. *Aud.:* Ga, Ac, Sa.

This long-running (the first issue appeared in 1891) glossy trade magazine is a great source of information on contemporary American architecture. The focus is on the United States, but issues often include information on projects and architects from all over the world. Sections devoted to selected building types, product information, architectural technology, interiors, lighting, and current projects are regularly published alongside feature articles, architect interviews, book reviews, exhibition and lecture notices. All of the sections and articles are well illustrated. Much of the content from the print magazine, including images, is available online, but full content is reserved for those who subscribe to the print or digital versions of this title. Recommended for all library types.

431. *The Architectural Review.* Incorporates (in 1909): *Details.* [ISSN: 0003-861X] 1896. 10x/yr. Individuals, GBP 88 (print & online eds.); Free to qualified personnel). Ed(s): Catherine Slessor. Emap Construct Ltd., 69-77 Paul St, London, EC2A 4NW, United Kingdom; http://www.emap.com. Illus., adv. Microform: IDC. *Indexed:* A&ATA, A01, A06, A22, AmHI, BAS, BRI, GardL. *Bk. rev.:* 4-6, 500 words. *Aud.:* Ga, Ac, Sa.

The December 2016/January 2017 issue of *The Architectural Review* celebrated 120 years of the journal with a look back at the archives and a look forward to the future. In looking forward, editor in chief Christine Murray reaffirmed the British journal's commitment to critical reporting and reviews that cover architecture and the built environment the world over. Each of the ten issues published in a year focuses on a different theme such as the recently featured water, Africa, and women in architecture. Most of the feature articles, case studies, opinion pieces, and essays are related to the theme, but some may cover unrelated current topics. All of the pieces in an issue are accompanied by an array of color photographs, plans, sections, and details. Articles on emerging or internationally known architects and firms are always included in an issue, as are investigations of a building typology related to the theme (for example, dams in the issue on water). The full text of some of the content in the print issues is available for free online if individuals register with *The Architectural Review* website; a digital edition is also available to individuals for one-time purchase of issues or by subscription. Recommended for architecture and large public libraries.

432. *Architectural Science Review.* Formerly (until 1958): *Architectural Science.* [ISSN: 0003-8628] 195?. q. GBP 653 (print & online eds.)). Taylor & Francis, 2, 3 & 4 Park Sq, Milton Park, Abingdon, OX14 4RN, United Kingdom. Illus., index, adv. Sample. Refereed. Vol. ends: Dec. Microform: PQC. Reprint: PSC. *Indexed:* A22, BRI, EIP, ErgAb. *Bk. rev.:* Number and length vary. *Aud.:* Ac, Sa.

Founded at the University of Sydney in Australia in 1958, this peer-reviewed quarterly published by Taylor & Francis covers a multitude of topics that fall under the heading of "architectural science." It remains one of the few publications to focus on the subject. The six or more articles and the occasional book reviews in an issue may be on acoustics, structural engineering, environmental systems, sustainability, lighting, digital architecture, or other topics related to the intersections between technology, science, and architecture. Australia is well-represented, but overall the research subjects and case studies are international, as are the scholars and researchers who make up the list of authors. Available to libraries as an online only or print and online subscription. Recommended for architecture or engineering libraries with a strong research focus.

433. *Architecture Asia.* [ISSN: 1675-6886] 2009. q. Free membership. Architects Regional Council of Asia, 1603-55, Seocho 1-dong, Seocho-gu, Seoul, , Korea, Republic of; http://www.arcasia.org/. *Bk. rev.:* Number and length vary. *Aud.:* Ac, Sa.

Architecture Asia is the quarterly journal of the Architects Regional Council Asia (ARCASIA), which is comprised of the national institutes of architects of 18 countries from China to India, the Philippines, Japan, Indonesia, and most everywhere in between. Issues are organized around a theme (neo-futurism and new vernacular architecture are recent examples) and present eight to ten building studies of works spread across the region. Along with descriptions, the building studies include color photographs, plans, and often additional drawings, elevations, or sections. A feature article or two, book reviews, and reports on local design events round out the tables of contents. Interest in this part of the world remains strong, as evidenced by coverage in international design periodicals, and this title is an excellent English-language choice for its focus on both the area and its architects. Beginning with the 2011 issues, an online edition of the journal is available for free to individuals who register on the journal's website. Recommended for architecture libraries.

434. *L'Architecture d'Aujourd'hui.* Formerly: *Architecture Francaise.* [ISSN: 0003-8695] 1930. bi-m. EUR 150. Archipress & Associes, 10 Cite d'Angouleme, Paris, 75011, France; http://www.larchitecturedaujourdhui.fr/en/. Illus., adv. *Indexed:* A06, A22, BAS, PdeR. *Bk. rev.:* Number and length vary. *Aud.:* Ac, Sa.

First published in the 1930s, this well-respected French journal is now overseen by an editorial board that includes a number of internationally known designers (Jean Nouvel, Shigeru Ban, Frank Gehry, Renzo Piano, and others) and goes by the abbreviation *'A'A'*. Six issues are published in a year on themes such as stone, museums, or mixed-use projects, which set the stage for issues or trends that are explored in ten or more projects by international architects, feature articles, essays, interviews, and opinion pieces. Reviews, brief news items, and a products section are also included. In addition to the six bi-monthly thematic issues, *'A'A'* publishes four special issues-AA Projects, AA Projects "Les cahiers de Reinventer Paris," AA Perspectives, and AA Events-comprised of case studies, interviews, and essays exploring projects or the work of a designer or firm. Both the special and the regular issues contain many color photographs, drawings, plans, and details. All text appears in French and English. A digital edition of the journal is available to individual subscribers. Recommended for architecture libraries.

435. *Architecture plus Design.* [ISSN: 0970-2369] 1984. m. Ed(s): Suneet Paul. Media Tranasia (India) Pvt. Ltd., 323, Udyog Vihar Phase 4, Gurgaon, 122 016, India; http://www.mediatransasia.in. Illus., adv. *Aud.:* Ac, Sa.

This monthly publication, "an Indian journal of architecture," covers the architectural scene in India and abroad for its audience of professional architects and interior designers. A theme such as contemporary Indian architecture, "leisure-scapes," or energy efficient design characterizes the five to ten buildings studies in an issue, which are well-documented with photographs, plans, sections, and drawings. The buildings profiled are largely from India, but buildings from all over the world may also be included. Short news items, upcoming events, building material and product manufacturer profiles, and a couple of short articles describing newly completed interiors are sometimes joined by book reviews, an interview, or a travelogue to round out an issue. A useful publication for those interested in contemporary Indian architecture and architectural practice in the country. Recommended for architecture libraries.

436. *Architecture_media_politics_society.* [ISSN: 2050-9006] 2012. 8x/yr. Free. Architecture_Media_Politics_Society, 7 Station Rd., Gateacre, L25 3PY, United Kingdom. Refereed. *Aud.:* Ac, Sa.

This peer-reviewed open-access journal is the publication of a nonprofit research organization, AMPS (Architecture, Media, Politics, Society), which focuses on bringing together the interdisciplinary mix of researchers and scholars who study the intersections between society, culture, architecture, and city planning. The organization hosts conferences, frequently in Great Britain but also in international locales, and posts selected papers online. The journal is published eight times a year and issues consist of a single research article on a contemporary or historical aspect of the built environment. The articles in some volumes focus on a specific theme such as visioning technologies or housing, but most of the 11 volumes published since the journal was founded in 2012 contain articles that focus on diverse research topics related to the built environment. Recommended for architecture libraries.

437. *Azure: design architecture & art.* Former titles (until 1985): *Village Gazette;* (until 1984): *WestClair Gazette.* [ISSN: 0829-982X] 1984. 8x/yr. CAD 39.95 in US & Canada; USD 70 elsewhere; USD 44.95 combined subscription in US & Canada (print & online eds.)). Ed(s): Catherine Osborne. Azure Publishing Inc., 213 Sterling Rd., Ste. 206, Toronto, ON M6R 2B2, Canada; azure@azureonline.com. Illus., adv. Circ: 20000 Paid. *Bk. rev.:* Number and length vary. *Aud.:* Ga, Ac, Sa.

Azure is a Canadian architecture and design magazine that covers both North American and European design in the eight issues that are published during the year. Several issues focus on recurring themes including an annual houses issue, design trends, and the *Azure* awards issue. An issue is composed of feature articles accompanied by shorter pieces on new buildings, news items, a designer or firm profile, products and materials sections, and book reviews. This title will appeal to the same design-conscious audience that reads *Metropolis* or *Wallpaper*. A few of the articles, some of the recurring departments, and select images are available for free online, but the full content of the magazine is reserved for subscribers to the print or digital issue. Recommended for architecture and public libraries.

438. *Blueprint (Chelmsford): architecture, design & contemporary culture.* [ISSN: 0268-4926] 1983. m. GBP 49 domestic; EUR 121 in Europe; USD 179 United States. Progressive Media Group Ltd., John Carpenter House, John Carpenter St, London, EC4Y 0AN, United Kingdom; pmg@progressivemediagroup.com; http://www.progressivemediagroup.com/. Adv. Sample. *Indexed:* A22. *Bk. rev.:* Number and length vary. *Aud.:* Ac, Sa.

Re-launched in 2014 as a "premium bi-monthly," this glossy British magazine continues to offer a critical view of architecture and design in Great Britain and farther afield, now in a larger format (260 pages per issue) and with more detailed articles. Recurring departments feature columns by designers considering a range of current topics, interviews, an architect or firm profile, information on products and materials, and notice of six or more current exhibitions. Recently completed projects, interiors, and exhibitions are considered in several one- to two-page critical reviews. Among the eight to ten longer articles in an issue there may be a well-illustrated building study along with feature articles that consider current practice, ongoing trends, or the occasional historical subject. Individual subscribers can choose a print or digital subscription; libraries can subscribe to the print magazine or access full text of the articles via the ProQuest Engineering Collection. Recommended for architecture libraries.

439. *Buildings & Landscapes: journal of the vernacular architecture forum.* Formerly (until 2007): *Perspectives in Vernacular Architecture.* [ISSN: 1936-0886] 1982. s-a. USD 217 (print & online eds.)). Ed(s): Carl Lounsbury, Anna Vemer Andrzejewski. University of Minnesota Press, 111 Third Avenue South, Ste 290, Minneapolis, MN 55401; http://www.upress.umn.edu. Adv. Refereed. *Indexed:* A22, BRI, E01, MLA-IB. *Bk. rev.:* Number and length vary. *Aud.:* Ac.

Buildings & Landscapes is the biannual journal of the Vernacular Architecture Forum, which is dedicated to studying vernacular architecture in North America. Each issue is composed of five or six articles and five to seven lengthy book reviews that focus on common, everyday spaces in the built environment, including many different types of housing, commercial buildings, churches and meeting houses, public spaces, and regional variations in style, type, and use of all these spaces and more. Articles are based on archival research as well as fieldwork, and although the focus is largely on North America, international subjects may also make an appearance. Black-and-white photographs, illustrations, plans, and diagrams accompany the articles. Available by subscription in print or by full text online. Recommended for academic and architecture libraries.

Built Environment. See Urban Studies section.

440. *Canadian Architect.* [ISSN: 0008-2872] 1956. m. CAD 54.95 domestic; USD 105.95 United States; USD 125.95 elsewhere. Ed(s): Elsa Lam. I Q Business Media Inc., 80 Valleybrook Dr., Toronto, ON M3B 2S9, Canada. Illus., adv. Microform: PQC. *Indexed:* A01, A06, A22, B01, BRI, C37. *Aud.:* Ga, Sa.

The monthly magazine of the Royal Architectural Institute of Canada, *Canadian Architect* consists of building studies, architecture news, product reviews, and reports on exhibitions, conferences, and other events. Most of the content is related to the Canadian built environment or the practice of architecture in Canada. Though this title is slim (at about 50 pages), each issue is well illustrated and contains a full array of plans, sections, and drawings for the building studies. This is a great resource for those interested in Canadian architecture or for architects working in the country. Digital editions of issues beginning with January 2008 are free to view on the magazine's website. Recommended for architecture and public libraries.

441. *Casabella: rivista internazionale di architettura.* Former titles (until 1964): *Casabella Continuita;* (until 1954): *Costruzioni Casabella;* (until 1939): *Casabella;* (until 1932): *La Casa Bella.* [ISSN: 0008-7181] 1928. 11x/yr. EUR 81.90; EUR 12 newsstand/cover. Ed(s): Francesco Dal Co. Arnoldo Mondadori Editore SpA, Via Mondadori 1, Segrate, 20090, Italy; infolibri@mondadori.it; http://www.mondadori.com. Illus., index, adv. Circ: 45000 Paid. *Indexed:* A06, A22. *Bk. rev.:* 8, 150 words. *Aud.:* Ac, Sa.

Casabella is a large format Italian journal that covers international contemporary architecture and the occasional historical subject in issues published 11 times a year. An issue may consist of several building studies and a theoretical essay or article on a historical topic, or a mix of building studies and short articles on a specific theme such as Brazilian architecture or Italian churches. An interview with an influential architect may also be included. The building studies offer numerous plans, details, sections, and color photographs spread across the expansive pages. In the Italian/English edition English translations are printed in the captions for the illustrations and English text for most, but not all, of the articles is printed in the back of the journal. Book and exhibition reviews, shorter articles, and the extensive product review section are in Italian only. Tables of contents for recent issues are free online; a digital edition is available to individuals by subscription. Recommended for architecture libraries.

442. ***Crit.*** Formerly (until 1977): *Telesis;* Incorporates (1986-1995): *A I A S News;* Which was formerly (until 1986): *Newsflash;* (until 1984): *A S C / A I A News;* (until 1978): *American Institute of Architects. Association of Student Chapters. News.* [ISSN: 0277-6863] 1976. s-a. Free to members. Ed(s): George Guarino. American Institute of Architecture Students, 1735 New York Ave, N W, Washington, DC 20006; mailbox@aias.org; http://www.aias.org. Illus., adv. *Aud.:* Ac.

The journal of the American Institute of Architecture Students (AIAS), *Crit* was redesigned in 2015 and refocused to appeal to an audience of new professionals and academics in addition to students in architecture school. The journal is set to be published in print once a year with a second issue to be published online once a year. Student work from the AIAS honor awards or other sources is always included, as are feature articles, essays, and opinion pieces. Most submissions are by undergraduate and graduate student authors and they are illustrated with color photographs, drawings, and plans. An interview with practicing architects may also be featured. Useful as a window onto student interests, projects, and competitions in the United States and Canada. PDF copies of the journal are available on the AIAS website for 2010-present. Recommended for architecture libraries.

443. ***El Croquis: de arquitectura y diseno.*** [ISSN: 0212-5633] 1982. m. EUR 230 domestic; EUR 297 in Europe; EUR 322 in US & Canada. Ed(s): Paloma Poveda. El Croquis Editorial, Av. Reyes Catolicos 9, El Escorial, Madrid, 28280, Spain; elcroquis@elcroquis.es; http://www.elcroquis.es/. Adv. Circ: 30000. *Indexed:* A22. *Aud.:* Ac, Sa.

Although technically a quarterly, an issue of *El Croquis* functions less like a journal and more like a monograph on an international architect, firm, or the occasional theme. Essays, interviews, and short biographies are included, but the exhaustive documentation of built works and projects are the real draw of this publication. Each work is accompanied by page after page of illustrations, plans, details, conceptual drawings, models, sections, and elevations. The illustrative matter far outweighs the textual descriptions, which are printed in both Spanish and English. An excellent source for visual documentation of the work of international architects; also useful for the interviews with architects. Available in print; a library or individual subscription to the *El Croquis* Digital Library offers online access to issues from 2001 to the present. Recommended for architecture libraries.

444. ***Detail (German Edition): Zeitschrift fuer Architektur & Baudetail.*** [ISSN: 0011-9571] 1961. 10x/yr. EUR 192 (Students, EUR 102). DETAIL Business Information GmbH, Messerschmittstr 4, Muenchen, 80992, Germany. Illus., adv. *Indexed:* A22. *Bk. rev.:* Number and length vary. *Aud.:* Ac, Sa.

Like many other architecture journals, *Detail* is devoted to contemporary international architecture and features an impressive array of color photographs of recent works. What sets this journal apart is that the eight to ten profiles of buildings in the "documentation" section are accompanied by large-scale section drawings of details that have been redrawn by *Detail* staff. Photographs, plans, and small-scale sections similar to those found in other journals also appear in the article. Buildings in the documentation section and the articles in the shorter "discussion" and "technology" sections focus on a selected theme such as timber construction, higher-density housing, or refurbishment. Brief news pieces, book and exhibition reviews, and a products section complete each issue. Eight issues of the English edition are published in a year: 6 theme issues and two supplemental issues, titled *Detail Green*, on sustainable architecture. The original German-language publication is published 12 times a year and available in a bilingual German/English edition. Digital editions of these publications are also available to individuals by subscription. Photos and text for some projects are available online, but the details, plans, and other drawings only appear in the full journal. Recommended for architecture libraries. *Detail* readers will also be interested in *The Plan*, the Italian journal that publishes contemporary building details.

445. ***Domus: architettura arredamento arte.*** [ISSN: 0012-5377] 1928. m. 11/yr. EUR 110. Editoriale Domus, Via Gianni Mazzocchi 1/3, Rozzano, 20089, Italy; editorialedomus@edidomus.it; http://www.edidomus.it. Illus. *Indexed:* A06, A22. *Bk. rev.:* 7, 750 words. *Aud.:* Ac, Sa.

An excellent source for information on contemporary architecture and design, *Domus* is a large-format Italian monthly magazine that was first published in 1928. All the text is in both English and Italian, from the extensive exhibition calendar to the feature articles, building studies, interviews, and book and product reviews. Color photographs often fill the pages and extend to double spreads and the building studies contain many plans, sections, and details. The scope is truly international; articles in a single issue often range from Europe to North America, India to China, and everywhere in between. Local editions delve deeper into their geographic areas, which include China, Sri Lanka, India, Germany, and Central America. The table of contents and a short summary of the articles is available for free online; the full content appears only in the printed magazine. Individuals may subscribe to the digital edition or purchase single digital issues. Recommended for architecture and large public libraries.

446. ***Enquiry (Washington D.C.): a journal for architectural research.*** Formerly (until 2011): *A A R C Journal.* [ISSN: 2329-9339] 2003. irreg. Free. Ed(s): Philip D Plowright, Suchi Bhattacharjee. Architectural Research Centers Consortium, http://www.arcc-journal.org/. Refereed. *Aud.:* Ac, Sa.

This peer-reviewed open-access journal is the publication of the Architectural Research Centers Consortium (ARCC), an international organization that seeks to support architectural research in architecture schools, research centers, and elsewhere. Once an outlet for publishing papers from ARCC conferences and themed issues, the journal is now a platform for a wider selection of research-based articles on architecture and the built environment. Primary research, theory, the current state and future directions of the profession, and reflections on architectural education and architectural research are the subjects of the five to six articles included in each annual issue. Recommended for architecture libraries.

447. ***G A Document.*** [ISSN: 0389-0066] q. A.D.A. Edita Tokyo Co. Ltd., 3-12-14 Sendagaya, Shibuya-ku, Tokyo, 151-0051, Japan. *Aud.:* Ac, Sa.

Issues of this large-format journal are focused solely on five or more recently completed buildings designed by a variety of architects and firms from all over the world. In a typical issue, a few paragraphs in both English and Japanese preface a rich collection of photographs, plans, elevations, sections, and details of the chosen works. Special issues may be devoted to the work of a single architect or firm, and an annual yearbook issue highlights international projects from two dozen or more architects. *GA Houses* is a similar title offered by the same Tokyo publisher, A.D.A. Edita. Both are great resources for visual documentation of recent, international architecture. Lists of the works that are included in issues of both publications are available online, but there are only a few small images of pages from the printed issues. Recommended for architecture libraries.

448. ***Grey Room.*** [ISSN: 1526-3819] 2000. q. USD 367 (print & online eds.)). M I T Press, One Rogers St, Cambridge, MA 02142-1209; journals-cs@mit.edu; http://mitpress.mit.edu/. Adv. Refereed. *Indexed:* A01, A22, A51, E01, MLA-IB. *Aud.:* Ac.

A handful of lengthy articles are the main focus of this quarterly, which seeks to "[bring] together scholarly and theoretical articles from the fields of architecture, art, media, and politics to forge a cross-disciplinary discourse uniquely relevant to contemporary concerns." Theory plays a significant role in most articles, which explore a variety of topics in the fields represented. Contributors are largely scholars from North America, but Great Britain, Australia, and Europe are also represented. Institutional subscriptions are available for print only or print and electronic access; articles are available in JSTOR with a moving wall of five years. Recommended for architecture and academic libraries.

449. ***Harvard Design Magazine.*** Former titles (until 1997): *G S D News;* (until 1983): *H G S D News.* [ISSN: 1093-4421] 1977. s-a. USD 27 domestic; USD 30 foreign; USD 20 per issue domestic. Ed(s): Jennifer Sigler. Harvard University, Graduate School of Design, 48 Quincy St, Gund Hall, Cambridge, MA 02138; info@harvarddesignmagazine.org; http://www.gsd.harvard.edu. Illus., adv. Refereed. *Bk. rev.:* Number and length vary. *Aud.:* Ac.

In 2014, the magazine of Harvard University's Graduate School of Design was rededicated to cross-disciplinary dialogue on a wider spectrum of the issues that affect design. Although this title is still organized around a central theme, issues now consider that theme from a wider variety of viewpoints. For example, among the authors of the issue "Wet Matter," which focused on the ocean, article authors included architecture and landscape architecture scholars and practitioners, as well as geographers, anthropologists, a sociologist, a historian, and a chef. Interviews with a physician and activist, an ocean scientist, and a poet were also included. Select articles from the print issues are available for free on the magazine's website; the full text of the magazine is only available in print. Recommended for architecture libraries.

450. ***The International Journal of Architectural Computing.*** [ISSN: 1478-0771] 2003. q. USD 1134 (print & online eds.)). Sage Publications Ltd., 1 Oliver's Yard, 55 City Rd, London, EC1Y 1SP, United Kingdom; info@sagepub.com; https://www.sagepub.com. Sample. Refereed. Reprint: PSC. *Bk. rev.:* Number and length vary. *Aud.:* Ac.

This peer-reviewed quarterly was founded by four international organizations "dedicated to promoting collaborative research and development of computer-aided design." The editorial board continues to be made up of members from the founding organizations-eCAADe, ACADIA, SIGraDi, and CAADRIA-as well as the CAADFutures Foundation. Five to eight research articles prefaced by an editorial make up most issues; occasionally, a book review is also included. This title covers a range of topics, studies, methodologies, and investigations under the umbrella of computer-aided design, and the articles either are papers selected from one of the founding organization's conferences (which have themes such as rethinking comprehensive design or open systems) or speak to a theme the editors have chosen to characterize the issue (for example, design agency). Authors tend to be scholars and researchers from universities the world over. Available as a print, online, or combined subscription. Recommended for architecture libraries.

451. ***International Journal of Islamic Architecture.*** [ISSN: 2045-5895] 2012. s-a. GBP 199 (print & online eds.)). Ed(s): Mohammad Gharipour. Intellect Ltd., The Mill, Parnall Rd, Fishponds, Bristol, BS16 3JG, United Kingdom; info@intellectbooks.com; http://www.intellectbooks.co.uk/. Adv. Sample. Refereed. Reprint: PSC. *Bk. rev.:* Number and length vary. *Aud.:* Ac.

This biannual, peer-reviewed journal publishes scholarly articles on contemporary and historical architecture, landscape architecture, city planning, and urban design in the "historic Islamic world" of the Middle East and portions of Africa and Asia, as well as the contemporary Islamic built environment farther afield. Issues feature five to seven articles, along with book and exhibition reviews. Published in Great Britain, the journal has an editorial board drawn from academics and scholars from all over the world. A useful source of scholarship on the subject. Libraries can subscribe to the journal in print and online, or online only. Recommended for architecture and academic libraries.

452. ***J A.*** Formerly (until 1991): *Japan Architect.* [ISSN: 1342-6478] 1956. q. Ed(s): Yutaka Shikata. Shinkenchiku-sha Co. Ltd., Kasumigaseki Bldg. 17F, 3-2-5 Kasumigaseki, Chiyoda-ku, Tokyo, 100-6017, Japan; http://www.japan-architect.co.jp. Illus., adv. Circ: 18000 Paid. *Indexed:* A06, BAS. *Aud.:* Ac, Sa.

A year's worth of this Japanese quarterly is made up of a yearbook issue and three issues on either a single Japanese architect or firm or a topical theme. This title is virtually advertisement-free, and the large-format pages of every issue are given over to the numerous color photographs, detailed drawings, plans, sections, and elevations that accompany a short description of each building. The emphasis is on works at home and abroad by world-renowned or up-and-coming Japanese architects; works in Japan by international architects are also featured. An essential resource for Japanese architecture. All text is in English and Japanese. Tables of contents and a few page views from an issue are available online, but these represent only a fraction of the content from the printed issue. Recommended for architecture libraries.

Journal of Architectural and Planning Research. See Urban Studies section.

453. ***Journal of Architectural Education.*** Former titles (until 1984): *J A E;* (until 1975): *Journal of Architectural Education.* [ISSN: 1046-4883] 1947. s-a. GBP 386 (print & online eds.)). Ed(s): Marc Neveu. Taylor & Francis Inc., 711 3rd Ave, 8th Fl, New York, NY 10017; support@tandfonline.com; http://www.tandfonline.com. Illus., index. Refereed. Vol. ends: Aug. Microform: PQC. Reprint: PSC. *Indexed:* A01, A06, A22, AmHI, E01, MLA-IB. *Bk. rev.:* 5-6, 1,500 words. *Aud.:* Ac.

This scholarly, refereed journal is published biannually by Taylor and Francis for the Association of Collegiate Schools of Architecture (ACSA). Each issue is composed of a mix of essays and articles-sometimes developed from sessions at the ACSA conference-as well as architectural criticism, and book and exhibition reviews. This title is a good resource for discovering those topics of interest in North American architectural education and current scholarship in the field, which means it will be of interest almost exclusively to an academic audience. Full text of articles published from volume 1 in 1947 to the present are available via subscription; articles from the journal are available in JSTOR with a moving wall of seven years. Recommended for architecture libraries.

454. ***Journal of Architectural Engineering.*** [ISSN: 1076-0431] 1994. q. USD 664. Ed(s): Ece Erdogmus. American Society of Civil Engineers, 1801 Alexander Bell Dr, Reston, VA 20191; ascelibrary@asce.org; http://www.asce.org. Adv. Refereed. *Indexed:* A01, A22, HRIS. *Bk. rev.:* Number and length vary. *Aud.:* Ac.

The *Journal of Architectural Engineering* is a peer-reviewed, quarterly journal published by the American Society of Civil Engineers (ASCE). The topics covered include acoustics, lighting, construction, and sustainability, as well as structural, electrical, and mechanical engineering as they relate to the built environment. Two to five technical papers and two to five case studies make up most issues, along with the occasional book review or "technical note" on a specific detail. The editorial board and the article authors are mainly from North American universities, independent research centers, and companies or firms. Libraries may select a print, online, or combined subscription. Recommended for engineering libraries with civil, architecture, or construction programs and architecture libraries where there is interest.

455. ***The Journal of Architecture.*** [ISSN: 1360-2365] 1996. bi-m. GBP 1603 (print & online eds.)). Ed(s): Charles Rice, Peter Gibbs-Kennet. Routledge, 4 Park Sq, Milton Park, Abingdon, OX14 4RN, United Kingdom; subscriptions@tandf.co.uk; http://www.tandfonline.com. Illus., adv. Sample. Refereed. Reprint: PSC. *Indexed:* A01, A22, B01, E01. *Bk. rev.:* Number and length vary. *Aud.:* Ac.

Jointly published six times a year by Routledge and the Royal Institute of British Architects, this scholarly, peer-reviewed journal has an international scope and an editorial board that includes regional editors from more than 20 countries. Students, academics, and practitioners contribute articles on contemporary and historical topics in architectural theory, methodology, or the intersections between architecture and technology, or architecture and culture. Some issues in a volume may be guest-edited and devoted to special topics; most issues include book, exhibition, or film reviews. Institutions may choose an online-only or combined print-and-online subscription. Recommended for architecture and large academic libraries.

456. ***Journal of Green Building.*** [ISSN: 1552-6100] 2006. q. USD 709 (print & online eds.) Individuals, USD 149 (print & online eds.)). College Publishing, 12309 Lynwood Dr, Glen Allen, VA 23059; collegepub@mindspring.com; http://www.collegepublishing.us. Adv. Sample. Refereed. *Aud.:* Ac, Sa.

Two sections, the "industry corner" and "research articles," make up each issue of this quarterly journal, which is devoted to design and construction topics in green building. The scholarly research articles are peer-reviewed while the industry corner is written for an audience of practitioners by architects, engineers, and other professionals. Taken together, the two sections provide a strong mix of practical information, theory, and research from authors working and teaching all over the world. Small photographs and diagrams accompany the articles, but the focus here is on the research and textual information instead of big, glossy images. Subjects covered include green building materials, techniques, case studies, and education. Libraries have the option of an online only or a print and online subscription; subscriptions include online access to all previous issues. Recommended for architecture libraries.

Landscape Architecture. See Landscape Architecture section.

Landscape Journal. See Landscape Architecture section.

457. ***Log (New York).*** [ISSN: 1547-4690] 2003. 3x/yr. USD 36 domestic; USD 40 in Canada & Mexico; USD 60 elsewhere. Ed(s): Cynthia Davidson. Anyone Corporation, 41 W 25th St, 11th Fl, New York, NY 10010; any@anycorp.com; http://www.anycorp.com. Adv. *Aud.:* Ac.

Published three times a year, *Log* is "an independent journal on architecture and the contemporary city." A dozen or more articles plus shorter "observations" make up an issue, which occasionally focuses on a theme such as "New Ancients," which explored the revival of interest in history in the work of selected architects, curators, theorists, and historians. Deliberately devoid of the glossy images that appear in architecture magazines, the 15 or more articles, essays, conversations, and opinion pieces in an issue are of a literary bent. Authors tend to be scholars in architecture, architectural history, culture, and theory, or practicing architects who also teach. Previews of some articles are available online, but the full content is reserved for the printed journal. Issues are available in JSTOR beginning with 2003 with a two year moving wall. Recommended for architecture libraries.

458. ***Lotus International: rivista trimestrale di architettura - quarterly architectural review.*** Formerly (until 1970): *Lotus.* [ISSN: 1124-9064] 1963. 4x/yr. EUR 86. Editoriale Lotus, Via Santa Maria 19a, Milan, 20123, Italy; abbonamenti@editorialelotus.it. *Indexed:* A06, BAS. *Aud.:* Ac, Sa.

Projects presented in the pages of *Lotus International* are by a roll call of world-renowned international architects. The critical essays, articles, and building studies center on a theme or building type in each issue of this Italian quarterly. Recent subjects included archaeological parks, the current state of architecture in Milan, and displaced populations in the issue on "people in motion." The building studies are accompanied by an array of high-quality photographs, plans, details, and sections, all with detailed captions. Text is in both Italian and English. Tables of contents and small images of some of the printed pages are available for free online; individuals receive access to digital editions as part of their subscription. Recommended for architecture libraries.

459. ***Mark: another architecture.*** [ISSN: 1574-6453] 2005. bi-m. Mark Publishers, Laan der Hesperiden 68, Amsterdam, 1076 DX, Netherlands. Adv. *Aud.:* Ac, Sa.

Issues of this Dutch bimonthly present dozens of projects in Europe, North America, South America, and Asia by world-renowned designers and rising talents, making *Mark* a veritable catalog of what's new in architecture around the world. The "notice board" section posts a color photo and basic facts for 8 to 12 projects on paper, the "cross section" devotes two pages each to a dozen or more newly built works, and the "long section" presents 8 to 12 more buildings in longer articles accompanied by many photographs, plans, and drawings as well as interviews with designers or firms. Several feature articles and a products section complete the issue. Tables of contents are available for free online but the full content is only available in the printed issues, or in digital issues available for purchase or subscription via Zinio. Recommended for architecture libraries.

460. ***Metropolis: architecture and design at all scales.*** [ISSN: 0279-4977] 1981. 11x/yr. USD 19.95 domestic; USD 42.95 Canada; USD 99 elsewhere. Ed(s): Susan S Szenasy, Tamy Cozier. Bellerophon Publications, Inc., 205 Lexington Ave, 17th Fl, New York, NY 10016; MetropolisMagazine@emailcustomerservice.com; http://www.metropolismag.com. Illus., adv. Circ: 61000. Vol. ends: Jun. *Indexed:* A22. *Bk. rev.:* 2. *Aud.:* Ga, Ac, Sa.

This suave design magazine covers the urban international scene in recent architecture, restorations, product and furniture design, and city planning. Alongside news and events, interviews, book reviews, and short essays, the "spectrum" section contain eight to ten short articles on products, materials, exhibitions, and other topics described as "an essential survey of architecture and design today." Three to five or more feature articles may cover similar topics in greater detail or focus on broader themes. Of interest to those working in design fields, *Metropolis* also makes for good reading for the design-conscious and the urban dweller. Subscribers can opt for a print or digital-only subscription. Recommended for architecture, academic, and large public libraries.

461. ***Open House International: the journal of an association of institutes and individuals concerned with housing, design and development in the built environment.*** Formerly (until 1983): *Open House.* [ISSN: 0168-2601] 1976. q. Free to members. Ed(s): Nicholas Wilkinson. Open House International Association, PO Box 74, Gateshead, NE9 5UZ, United Kingdom. Adv. Refereed. *Indexed:* A22. *Aud.:* Ac, Sa.

Most issues of this refereed quarterly are guest-edited and focused on a topical theme related to housing, neighborhoods, or urbanism. Articles are contributed by worldwide educators, scholars, and the occasional designer. Small black-and-white photographs, plans, charts, and maps illustrate the journal, but the main value here is the research and projects detailed by the authors. The journal and archives are available online for subscribers, and the archives may also be purchased on DVD or online. Recommended for architecture libraries.

462. ***Perspecta.*** [ISSN: 0079-0958] 1952. a. USD 29.95 per issue. Yale University, School of Architecture, PO Box 208242, New Haven, CT 06520; http://www.architecture.yale.edu/drupal/. Illus. *Indexed:* A06. *Aud.:* Ac.

The annual *Perspecta* has the distinction of being the oldest student-edited journal of architecture published in the United States (the first issue was published in 1952). It is one of two student-edited publications from the Yale School of Architecture. The other, *Retrospecta,* which is also published annually, features student work and events at the school. Issues of *Perspecta* offer essays and articles by scholars, PhD candidates, and practitioners on topical themes and how they affect architecture. Some issues include interviews with architects, others include reprints of articles from older volumes related to the current theme alongside the contemporary pieces, and some volumes offer extensive illustrations. Issues are sold individually in print. Recommended for architecture libraries.

463. ***The Plan: architecture & technologies in detail.*** [ISSN: 1720-6553] 2002. 3x/yr. Centauro SRL, Via del Pratello 8, Bologna, 40122, Italy; http://www.centauro.it. *Aud.:* Ac, Sa.

The Plan is an Italian journal that compares favorably with both *Detail,* for drawings of contemporary building details, and *GA Document,* for the wealth of visual documentation. Published eight times a year, the issues contain three to five building studies accompanied by a section drawing of a detail and numerous color photographs, plans, site plans, sections, sketches, and diagrams. In addition to the international, contemporary buildings featured in the studies, issues of *The Plan* include a section on "the city plan" that uses maps and other data to tell the story of a world city. Some issues include an "old & new" section documenting an addition or intervention in a historic building illustrated with as many images and detail drawings as the contemporary building studies. The "report" section in the last pages describes and illustrates eight or more new buildings, products, or firms in one or two pages each. Text is in English. Limited content is available for free on *The Plan*'s website; full content is available in the printed issues. Individuals may subscribe to the digital edition. Recommended for architecture libraries.

464. ***Preservation.*** Former titles (until vol.48, no.4, 1996): *Historic Preservation;* (until 1952): *National Council for Historic Sites and Buildings Quarterly Report;* Which incorporated (1990-1995): *Historic Preservation News;* Which was formerly (until 1990): *Preservation News.* [ISSN: 1090-9931] 1949. q. Free to members. Ed(s): James H Schwartz, Arnold Berke. National Trust for Historic Preservation, 1785 Massachusetts Ave, NW, Washington, DC 20036. Illus., adv. Vol. ends: Nov. Microform: PQC. *Indexed:* A&ATA, A06, A22. *Bk. rev.:* 4, 300-500 words. *Aud.:* Ga, Ac, Sa.

A snapshot of preservation activities in the United States, *Preservation* is a glossy quarterly magazine that is sent to National Trust members. Buildings, towns, main streets, and the natural world are all candidates for preservation and subjects for the journal's articles and departments. Issues include book reviews and short pieces on news and events. A recurring travel section highlights historic buildings and sites in the United States and abroad and promotes National Trust tours. The "transitions" section keeps tabs on "places restored, threatened, saved, and lost." Those in the historic preservation field should be aware of this title, but may be more interested in *Forum Journal*, which is also published by the National Trust; members of the general public interested in preservation will consider the magazine essential reading. The text of the printed *Preservation* magazine is available on the National Trust website with selected images; *Forum Journal* articles are available online to members of the National Trust Forum who register with the site and to libraries via Project MUSE. Recommended for all library types.

465. *R I B A Journal.* Incorporates (1986-2003): *R I B A Interiors;* Former titles (until 1993): *Royal Institute of British Architects. Journal;* (until 1987): *Architect;* (until 1986): *R I B A Journal;* (until 1965): *Royal Institute of British Architects. Journal;* Which was formed by the merger of (1879-1893): *Royal Institute of British Architects. Transactions;* Which was formerly (until 1879): *Royal Institute of British Architects. Sessional Papers;* (until 1877): *Sessional Papers Read at the Royal Institute of British Architects;* (until 1854): *Royal Institute of British Architects. Transactions;* (1887-1893): *Royal Institute of British Architects. Journal of Proceedings;* Which was formerly (until 1887): *Royal Institute of British Architects. Journal of Proceedings;* (until 1885): *Royal Institute of British Architects. Proceedings.* [ISSN: 1463-9505] 1893. m. GBP 63 domestic; EUR 120 foreign. Atom Publishing, Clerkenwell House, 45/47 Clerkenwell Green, London, EC1R 0EB, United Kingdom; info@atompublishing.co.uk; http://www.atompublishing.co.uk/. Illus., index, adv. Sample. Circ: 29936. Vol. ends: Dec. Microform: PQC. *Indexed:* A06, A22, AmHI, BAS, EIP. *Bk. rev.:* 3, 200 words. *Aud.:* Ac, Sa.

A rich source of information for architects practicing in Great Britain, the Royal Institute of British Architects' trade journal is also notable for its coverage of British architecture. This title is published monthly, and each issue is made up of one or more well-illustrated building studies, critiques, and firm profiles joined by news, opinion pieces, and reviews. Content is grouped into sections: buildings, culture, products, and the "intelligence" section devoted to short pieces on the issues and concerns of British architectural practice. Classified and display advertisements and recruitment postings complete the issue. Along with *Architect's Journal,* this title is a good resource for those considering work in Great Britain or anyone wanting to stay current on what's new in British architecture. Recommended for architecture libraries.

466. *Society of Architectural Historians. Journal.* Formerly (until 1946): *American Society of Architectural Historians. Journal.* [ISSN: 0037-9808] 1940. q. USD 667 (print & online eds.)). Ed(s): Patricia Morton. University of California Press, Journals Division, 155 Grand Avenue, Ste 400, Oakland, CA 94612-3764; http://www.ucpress.edu/journals.php. Illus., index, adv. Refereed. Circ: 4000. Vol. ends: Dec. Microform: PQC. *Indexed:* A06, A22, BAS, MLA-IB. *Bk. rev.:* 20, 1,500 words. *Aud.:* Ac.

The *Journal of the Society of Architectural Historians (JSAH)* is a scholarly, peer-reviewed quarterly composed of lengthy essays and thoughtful, informative exhibition, book, and media reviews. Beginning with the June 2017 issue (vol. 76, no. 2), the journal also includes one or more shorter (but still peer-reviewed) essays on "new research discoveries and conclusions in architectural history" in the "Findings" section. From ancient to modern, technical to theoretical, all aspects of the built environment, urbanism, and landscape studies fall under the purview of the journal. An indispensable resource for architectural history, the journal is also of interest to those in fields such as urban studies, history, and cultural studies. Sent to JSAH members as part of their membership benefits, the journal is available by subscription in print and online through the University of California Press. Articles are also in JSTOR with a moving wall of three years. Recommended for architecture and academic libraries.

467. *Taunton's Fine Homebuilding.* Formerly (until 1991): *Fine Homebuilding.* [ISSN: 1096-360X] 1981. 8x/yr. USD 37.95 domestic; USD 40.95 Canada; USD 45.95 elsewhere. Ed(s): Chris Ermides. The Taunton Press, Inc., 63 South Main St, PO Box 5506, Newtown, CT 06470; publicrelations@taunton.com; http://www.taunton.com. Illus., adv. Circ: 300000 Paid. *Indexed:* BRI, CBRI. *Bk. rev.:* 3, 500 words. *Aud.:* Ga, Ac, Sa.

A popular magazine for the homebuilder, this journal also makes good reading for homeowners or students in the design and construction fields. Departments and articles cover topics related to construction and home improvement projects, tools and methods, materials and best practices. The focus is on houses that are average or small size and affordable building projects that a skilled do-it-yourselfer could successfully complete. While some articles describe and illustrate tools and techniques step-by-step, *Fine Homebuilding* pays equal attention to the finished products. Many color photographs accompany the feature articles, and the annual houses and kitchen and bath special issues showcase stunning, well-crafted designs. Excerpts and some images from the eight issues published during the year are available online; individual subscribers can choose a digital subscription or print and digital. Recommended for public libraries and architecture libraries where there is interest.

468. *Thresholds (Cambridge).* [ISSN: 1091-711X] 1992. q. USD 77 (print & online eds.)). M I T Press, One Rogers St, Cambridge, MA 02142-1209; journals-cs@mit.edu; http://www.mitpressjournals.org/. Refereed. *Aud.:* Ac.

Begun in 1992 as a monthly zine, this title from the MIT Department of Architecture is now a peer-reviewed journal published annually. The essays and articles are written by scholars, PhD candidates, practitioners, or artists, and they speak to a selected theme in art, architecture, or culture. Recent themes were "workspace," which looks at how current ways of working affect individuals, spaces, and the nature of work, and "scandalous," which "investigate[d] the relevance of scandal in creative practice." Issues can be purchased individually or by subscription; individuals may purchase access to the full text of the journal online. Recommended for architecture libraries.

469. *Volume.* Formed by the merger of (2001-2004): *Archis (English Edition);* (1986-2004): *Archis (Deventer);* Which was formerly (until 1985): *Wonen - T A - B K;* (1960-1972): *Tijdschrift voor Architectuur en Beeldende Kunsten.* [ISSN: 1574-9401] 2005. s-a. Ed(s): Arjen Oosterman, Christian Ernsten. Archis Foundation, PO Box 14702, Amsterdam, 1001 LE, Netherlands; info@archis.org; http://www.archis.org. Illus., adv. Circ: 6000. *Indexed:* A22. *Aud.:* Ac, Sa.

A project of the Archis foundation (an experimental think tank in the Netherlands), AMO (the design and research arm of architectural firm OMA), and C-LAB (Columbia University's Laboratory for Architectural Broadcasting), *Volume* is a biannual magazine that seeks to interrogate the whys of contemporary architecture and the forces and trends that affect it. To this end, the pages of an issue are filled with short essays, opinion pieces, critiques, and artists' projects that dissect, contextualize, or question the theme under consideration. The themes can range from the impact of machines on architecture to how research influences the built environment to considering shelter and all its implications for architecture given current world events. Tables of contents and select articles are available online; the full magazine is available in print only. Recommended for architecture libraries.

470. *Wallpaper.* [ISSN: 1364-4475] 1996. m. GBP 31.99. T I Media, The Blue Fin Bldg, 110 Southwark St, London, SE1 0SU, United Kingdom; ukcontent@timeinc.com; http://www.timeincuk.com. Adv. *Bk. rev.:* Number and length vary. *Aud.:* Ga, Ac, Sa.

Published monthly, *Wallpaper* is a British design and lifestyle magazine composed of both feature articles and sections on architecture, design, art, travel, lifestyle, fashion, and jewelry. In addition to its own section, architecture may appear in the feature articles, the book reviews, and elsewhere throughout the issue. Recently completed international buildings, future projects, materials, and well-known or up-and-coming architects are highlighted. This title is well-suited to architecture audiences and those interested in all forms of world design. The magazine's website is its own entity, offering similar content to the print magazine, but not duplicating issues or articles. The magazine is available to individuals in print or an iPad edition; libraries can subscribe to the print addition. Recommended for architecture, academic, and large public libraries.

471. *Werk - Bauen & Wohnen.* Formed by the merger of (1946-1982): *Bauen und Wohnen;* (1914-1982): *Werk.* [ISSN: 0257-9332] 10x/yr. CHF 200 domestic (Students, CHF 140). Zollikofer AG, Fuerstenlandstr 122, St. Gallen, 9001, Switzerland; leserservice@zollikofer.ch; http://www.zollikofer.ch. Adv. Circ: 9000. *Indexed:* A06, A22, BAS. *Bk. rev.:* Number and length vary. *Aud.:* Ac, Sa.

In issue 6 for the 2013 volume of *Werk bauen und wohnen,* a German-language Swiss publication, there debuted a redesign for this 100-year-old magazine. In addition to a new graphic design, some of the organization of the content has changed, although each issue will continue to be devoted to a theme such as the recently featured "[t]he street as habitat," architecture for children, or brick. Switzerland has long been the primary focus of this title, but international buildings and projects may also appear in the articles, news, or reviews. Feature articles are accompanied by an impressive collection of color photographs, plans, site plans, sections, and details, as well as English and French summaries. Profiles of new buildings and interiors, book and exhibition reviews, news and events, and shorter articles on architectural practice and other topical subjects are in German only. A synopsis of the content of each issue is available online, but the full articles appear only in the printed issue. Recommended for architecture libraries.

■ ARCHIVES AND MANUSCRIPTS

General/National, Regional, and State Newsletters/National, Regional, and State Newsletters—Canada/National, Regional, and State Newsletters—United States/Special-Interest Newsletters

See also Bibliography; History; and Library and Information Science sections.

Amber Paranick, Reference Librarian, Newspaper & Current Periodical Reading Room, Library of Congress, Washington, D.C

Introduction

According to a definition provided by the Society of American Archivists, an archivist is an individual responsible for appraising, acquiring, arranging, describing, preserving, and providing access to records of enduring value, according to the principles of provenance, original order, and collective control to protect the materials' authenticity and context. One could also say that an archivist is an individual with responsibility for management and oversight of an archival repository or of records of enduring value.

The archival mission is to ensure the identification, preservation, and use of the historical record. Those working with archives or manuscripts collections are constantly faced with the decision of which records will be preserved in perpetuity. Exactly what constitutes a record of enduring value is highly debatable, and because of this fact, spirited and lively discussions are often carried out in periodical literature.

The field of archives (not to mention the archival profession itself) has experienced profound changes since its inception, and published literature in this field reflects the changing landscape, while still keeping a firm grasp of past practice. In today's landscape, archivists collaborate with those working in a variety of disciplines, such as information technology, publishing, and knowledge management in order to fulfill their responsibilities.

Journals in this section provide the basic foundation for modern archival practice and theory, and reflect evolving viewpoints about archival theory and practice. Content published within this section reports on hot topics in the field, such as the challenges presented by electronic records (e-records) and born-digital collections; disaster planning; metadata standards like Encoded Archival Description; digitization of records; the archival profession itself; and archival education.

On the whole, published archival literature has largely been written for a scholarly or academic audience. In spite of that, recent efforts in archival advocacy and education have illustrated the need for more personal archiving, drawing a larger audience to the subject. As more and more print journals adapt to the electronic age, publishers are making copies available in electronic format as well. This statement holds true for many of the titles listed here.

Basic Periodicals

Ga: *Prologue; Ac: American Archivist, Archival Issues, Archivaria, Information Management.*

Basic Abstracts and Indexes

America: History and Life, Historical Abstracts, LISA: Library and Information Science Abstracts, Library Literature.

General

472. *The American Archivist.* [ISSN: 0360-9081] 1938. s-a. USD 209 (Free to members). Ed(s): Gregory S Hunter. Society of American Archivists, 17 N State St, Ste 1425, Chicago, IL 60602; info@archivists.org; http://www.archivists.org. Illus., index, adv. Refereed. *Indexed:* A22, BRI, CBRI, ISTA, MLA-IB. *Bk. rev.:* 9-11, 400-1,500 words. *Aud.:* Ac, Sa.

American Archivist is the semi-annual, refereed journal of the Society of American Archivists, a heavily relied-on collection of national archival practice, procedure, and theory. Its content strives to provide contextual analysis of collections, and the relationship of those collections to archivists, students of archival studies, users, and macro and micro communities. Recurring topics include cultural preservation, born-digital archives, and trends in records management. Literature review, case studies, commentaries, and resource lists also appear in every issue. The journal addresses the critical role that technology and copyright play in archives, whether through digital asset-management systems or as a preservation tool. Recent articles include an analysis on archives in the context of the Occupy movement, and using provenance to define third-party privacy. As of this writing, issues beginning in 1938 are available online with a subscription. The journal plays a key role in informing archival theory and policy in the United States, as it is the journal that represents the largest professional archives group in North America. Widely used in archives management programs and continues to offer strong analysis and resources.

473. *Archival Issues: the journal of the midwest archives conference.* Formerly (until 1992): *Midwestern Archivist.* [ISSN: 1067-4993] 1976. s-a. USD 80 (Individuals, USD 35; Free to members). Ed(s): John Fleckner. Midwest Archives Conference, c/o William J Maher, University Archivist, University of Illinois Archives, Urbana, IL 61801; w-maher@illinois.edu; http://www.midwestarchives.org. Illus., index, adv. Refereed. Vol. ends: No. 2. *Bk. rev.:* 6-8, 750-1,500 words. *Aud.:* Ac, Sa.

Archival Issues, a peer-reviewed journal published by the Midwest Archives Conference, purports to address contemporary issues in archives, which it does by publishing many case studies borne out of state and city archives, or local special collections. Recent issues discuss poetry archives in Washington, D.C.; building digital libraries out of small collections; and a discussion of Greene and Meissner's "More Product, Less Process" as applied to the Jim Wright papers at Texas Christian University. Some regional issues related to preservation and climate are also featured, but they would be relevant to any archives. The journal is published twice a year, and features archives professionals and instructors specializing in preservation of film and sound recordings, copyright, and innovative business concepts. Key archival analysis is being discussed, but a collection development department may find acquisition of this title superfluous.

474. *Archival Science: international journal on recorded information.* Incorporates (in 2001): *Archives & Museum Informatics;* Which was formerly (1987-1989): *Archival Informatics Newsletter.* [ISSN: 1389-0166] 2000. q. EUR 600 (print & online eds.)). Ed(s): G Oliver, Elisabeth Yakel. Springer Netherlands, Van Godewijckstraat 30, Dordrecht, 3311 GX, Netherlands; http://www.springer.com. Adv. Refereed. Reprint: PSC. *Indexed:* A22, BRI, E01, ISTA. *Aud.:* Ac, Sa.

Archival Science, published quarterly in the Netherlands, "promotes the development of archival science as an autonomous scientific discipline" and claims to cover "all aspects of archival science theory, methodology, and practice...around the world." These aspects seem to center around archives and cultural heritage as a record of history. This international title is excellent for readers desiring a wider perspective, and issues usually have a general theme. The most recent issue includes articles titled "Personal documentation on a social network site: Facebook, a collection of moments from your life?"; "Diplomatic analysis of technical drawings: developing new theory for practical application"; and "Archival representations of immigration and ethnicity in North American history: from the ethnicization of archives to the archivization of ethnicity." The journal, aimed at archives students and educators, is useful to readers pondering cultural self-determination, and more Derrida-type questions about the legitimacy of records and history. Abstracts of the journal articles are available online.

475. *Archivaria.* Formerly (until 1976): *Canadian Archivist.* [ISSN: 0318-6954] 1963. s-a. CAD 295 (print & online eds.) Free to members). Ed(s): Jennifer Douglas. The Association of Canadian Archivists, 130 Albert St, Ste 1912, Ottawa, ON K1P 5G4, Canada; aca@archivists.ca; https://archivists.ca. Illus., index, adv. Refereed. *Indexed:* A&ATA, A22, BRI, C37, CBRI. *Bk. rev.:* 10-20, 750-2,500 words. *Aud.:* Ac, Sa.

Archivaria functions as the Canadian twin of *American Archivist.* The journal, published twice a year by the Association of Canadian Archivists, centers on the "scholarly investigation" of archives in Canada and wider international circles, and is bilingual for its Quebecois readers. *Archivaria*'s international scope is robust, and its recent contributors, like Terry Cook and Mark Matienzo, are well known in American archives scholarship: Topics include archives as they relate to history, education and instruction around born-digital materials, and archival ethics. Recent book reviews discuss books on digital curation, metadata, and film preservation. The full scope of this journal's content is available electronically, and tables of contents are open to subscribers and non-subscribers. It provides a good complement to *American Archivist* or any other archives education journals. *Archivaria* is available by print or online subscription.

476. *Archives and Manuscripts.* Formerly (until 1955): *Bulletin for Australian Archivists.* [ISSN: 0157-6895] 1954. 3x/yr. GBP 278 (print & online eds.)). Ed(s): Louise Trott, Katrina Dean. Taylor & Francis, 2, 3 & 4 Park Sq, Milton Park, Abingdon, OX14 4RN, United Kingdom; subscriptions@tandf.co.uk; http://www.tandf.co.uk. Illus., adv. Sample. Refereed. Vol. ends: Nov. Reprint: PSC. *Bk. rev.:* 15-20, 500-2,000 words. *Aud.:* Ac, Sa.

The triannually published journal *Archives and Manuscripts,* which is peer-reviewed and published by the Australian Society of Archivists, Inc., aims to inform its national archives community about the "theory and practice of archives and record-keeping." The audience is primarily professionals, educators, researchers, and students. The country's diversity, along with occasional perspective from New Zealand and Fiji, is a basis for critical insight and analysis in articles about adoption records and archives and their use with child-abuse victims; archival education and literacy around indigenous communities; and archival ethics related to such issues. The journal includes an "International Notes" section, which describes regional archival practices, current projects of interest, and literature reviews. Article abstracts are available online. The latest issue was a special issue entitled "Participatory archives in a world of ubiquitous media." Professionals looking to explore nontraditional archives, or collections that pertain to indigenous groups, would find *Archives and Manuscripts* very useful.

477. *Archives and Records.* Former titles (until 2013): *Society of Archivists. Journal;* (until 1955): *Society of Local Archivists. Bulletin.* [ISSN: 2325-7962] 1947. 3x/yr. GBP 479 (print & online eds.)). Ed(s): Jenny Bunn, Charlotte Berry. Routledge, 4 Park Sq, Milton Park, Abingdon, OX14 4RN, United Kingdom; subscriptions@tandf.co.uk; http://www.tandfonline.com. Illus., index, adv. Sample. Refereed. Microform: PQC. Reprint: PSC. *Indexed:* A01, A22, AmHI, E01. *Bk. rev.:* 15-25, 600-1,400 words. *Aud.:* Ac, Sa.

Archives and Records is published twice a year by the Archives and Records Association, and covers archives "challenges and opportunities presented by new media and information technology" in archives in the United Kingdom and Ireland. Yet, libraries elsewhere would find the journal useful in comparing similar concerns around preservation, ethics, provenance, and technology in archives. Issues are generally themed and contain a mix of book reviews, essays, case studies, and relevant cultural analyses. The following articles were published within a recent issue: "Implementation of appraisal regulations including the selection of sample archives[:] A case study on the Swedish country district police"; a book review of *Digital Curation Bibliography: Preservation and Stewardship of Scholarly Works*; and a book review of *Records Management and Knowledge Mobilisation: A Handbook for Regulation, Innovation and Transformation.* This journal is useful to researchers or archivists who work on western European collections or document colonialism and its influence on archives. It is also appealing to those practicing professionals interested in the ever-evolving archival theories. Issues of the title are available in print format, and entire issues are freely accessible online.

478. *Information Management.* Former titles: *The Information Management Journal;* (until 1999): *Records Management Quarterly;* (until Jan.1986): *A R M A Records Management Quarterly;* (until 1976): *Records Management Quarterly;* (until 1967): *Records Review.* 1960. bi-m. A R M A International, 11880 College Blvd, Ste 450, Overland Park, KS 66210; Sales.Dept@armaintl.org; http://www.arma.org. Illus., index. Vol. ends: Dec. *Indexed:* A01, A22, B01, BRI, C42, CompLI. *Bk. rev.:* 1-4, 1,000-2,500 words. *Aud.:* Ac, Sa.

Also referred to as ARMA International, the professional, nonprofit Association of Records Managers and Administrators International produces the peer-reviewed *Information Management* magazine. The target audience for the journal is record and information managers, and its focus is "the application of management principles and appropriate technologies to the production, coordination, acquisition, organization, representation, control, dissemination, use, and ultimate disposition of information, whatever the format...leading to the more effective functioning of organizations of all kinds." The focus of the trade publication's most recent issue was to reinforce the idea of the value of sustained collaboration in every article. These articles included: "Balancing the Risks and Rewards of Cloud-Based Healthcare Information," "Leveraging the Principles in Mergers, Acquisitions, and Divestitures," and "Proposing a Charter of Personal Data Rights." The journal stays current on technology issues, which is critical given the influx of born-digital data that comprises the bulk of recordkeeping in the twenty-first century. The journal publishes six times a year and is available electronically.

479. *Journal of Archival Organization.* [ISSN: 1533-2748] 2002. q. GBP 414 (print & online eds.)). Ed(s): Thomas J Frusciano. Routledge, 530 Walnut St, Ste 850, Philadelphia, PA 19106; enquiries@tandfonline.com; http://www.tandfonline.com. Adv. Refereed. Circ: 42 Paid. Reprint: PSC. *Indexed:* A01, A22, E01, ERIC, ISTA. *Bk. rev.:* Number and length vary. *Aud.:* Ac, Sa.

The quarterly and peer-reviewed *Journal of Archival Organization* "places emphasis on emerging technologies, applications, and standards that range from Encoded Archival Description (EAD) and methods of organizing archival collections for access on the World Wide Web to issues connected with the digitization and display of archival materials." Which is to say that the journal covers all the usual bases in regard to archival scholarship. The publisher, which has frequently published journals and textbooks related to library science, knows its intended audience well, pulling together a series of articles about metadata, book reviews that address digitization texts, and the fate of a historically Black university's college archives. Also featured are a regular web site, book reviews, and interviews with leading archives or history scholars; however, because the journal covers similar ground as some other archives-related journals, libraries may not need to create priority space for the journal on its shelves. It is good work, but ultimately, more compelling scholarship is available. Tables of content and abstracts are available electronically.

480. *Manuscripta: a journal devoted to manuscript studies.* Incorporates in part (in 1956): *Historical Bulletin.* [ISSN: 0025-2603] 1957. 2x/yr. EUR 108 combined subscription (print & online eds.)). Brepols Publishers, Begijnhof 67, Turnhout, 2300, Belgium; periodicals@brepols.net; http://www.brepols.net. Illus., adv. *Indexed:* C26, MLA-IB. *Bk. rev.:* Number and length vary. *Aud.:* Ac, Sa.

Manuscripta, a biannual journal produced by Brepols Publishers, is published for the Knights of Columbus Vatican Film Library at Saint Louis University. This title specifically focuses on Renaissance studies and manuscripts, including the study of paleography, codicology, illumination, and book production/preservation. Such a specialized journal would do well at a university or library with a broad Renaissance or medieval studies program or collection; and more general liberal arts programs may not need something with such a narrow focus. The most recent volume published is volume 57 (2 2013), and its articles include: "The Directory of Institutions in the United States and Canada with Pre-1600 Manuscript Holdings: From its Origins to the Present, and its Role in Tracking the Migration of Manuscripts in North American Repositories"; "Newberry Case MS 153 and the Circulation of Curricular Texts"; and "Jews among Christians: Hebrew Book Illumination from Lake Constance." Issues are available online.

481. *Manuscripts.* Formerly (until 1953): *Autograph Collectors' Journal.* [ISSN: 0025-262X] 1948. q. Free to members. Manuscript Society, 14003 Rampart Ct, Baton Rouge, LA 70810; sands@manuscript.org; http://www.manuscript.org. Illus., adv. Vol. ends: No. 4. Microform: PQC. Reprint: PSC. *Indexed:* A22, MLA-IB. *Bk. rev.:* Number and length vary. *Aud.:* Ga.

The quarterly journal *Manuscripts* was first published in 1948 by the nonprofit Manuscript Society, which was known previously as the National Society of Autograph Collectors. The group's aim is scholarly documentation of historical manuscripts for historians, private collectors, and antiquarians. On the surface, this slim journal centers on the publishing and book trade and is highly specialized. Yet, it is an excellent asset for museum curators, archivists, and special-collections librarians who are looking for analysis on authentication and provenance. Issues include two regular columns: book reviews and auction trends; and the title serves as a resource guide for collectors, containing news items regarding the marketplace. A recent issue featured articles on "Ida S. McKinley: An Autograph Study" and "Harrison as President." The title seeks contributions from both non-members and members, and issues are available in print or by becoming a member of the Manuscript Society.

482. *Prologue (Washington).* Formerly (until 1969): *National Archives Accessions.* [ISSN: 0033-1031] 1940. q. USD 24 domestic; USD 30 per issue foreign; USD 6 per issue. National Archives and Records Administration, 8601 Adelphi Rd, College Park, MD 20740; http://www.archives.gov. Illus., index. Vol. ends: Winter. *Indexed:* A22, AmHI. *Aud.:* Ga.

Prologue magazine is a quarterly title published by the National Archives and Records Administration (NARA), and its articles aim to "bring readers stories based on the rich holdings and programs of the National Archives across the nation-from Washington, DC, to the regional archives and the Presidential Libraries." Issues are available in print, and electronic versions of the title can be downloaded for e-readers from the Scribd and Zinio web sites. *Prologue*'s target audience consists of researchers, educators, historians, genealogists, and other information management professionals; and it serves as a complementary journal to more scholarly resources in the subject. In its most recent issue, content includes a discussion of how the Federal Communications Commission (FCC) colorized television; a feature article entitled "Secret Treaties with California Indians"; and commentary about the " 'Records of Rights' exhibit in the David M. Rubenstein Gallery," by current National Archivist David Ferriero. Selected articles from current and back issues are available online.

483. *Provenance.* Formerly (until 1983): *Georgia Archive.* [ISSN: 0739-4241] 1972. a. USD 40 Free to members. Ed(s): Heather Oswald. Society of Georgia Archivists, PO Box 688, Decatur, GA 30031; president@soga.org; http://www.soga.org. Illus., index. Refereed. Vol. ends: No. 1. *Bk. rev.:* 3-4, 750-1,250 words. *Aud.:* Ac, Sa.

The Society of Georgia Archivists created the journal *Provenance* in 1972, and it was the first journal ever published by a state or regional organization. Since then, the journal has continued to "focus on the archival profession in the theory and practice of archival management" with a much wider audience, as it is currently circulated nationally and internationally. The journal is published annually, and thus it tends to offer more thoughtful perspective on current archives-related events, since enough time has usually passed before any issues are published. Nuanced articles and book reviews from a recent issue include, respectively, "Preservation of the video game" and "Archival Anxiety and the Vocational Calling." Also, because the journal tends to encourage first-time writers, many of the articles bring a fresh voice and insight, as the journal is not weighted down by articles from the more well-known names in the archives field. The journal seems geared toward students in archival studies or library science programs, and is available in print; also, back issues can be ordered from the Society of Georgia Archivists. *Provenance* is an excellent resource to include among archives studies texts, especially for younger professionals and students.

484. *The Public Historian.* [ISSN: 0272-3433] 1978. q. USD 328 (print & online eds.)). Ed(s): James F. Brooks. University of California Press, Journals Division, 155 Grand Avenue, Ste 400, Oakland, CA 94612-3764; http://www.ucpress.edu/journals.php. Illus., index, adv. Refereed. Circ: 1615. Microform: PQC. *Indexed:* A01, A22, AmHI, BRI, CBRI, E01, MLA-IB. *Bk. rev.:* 30-60, 1,000-2,800 words. *Aud.:* Ac, Sa.

The Public Historian, a quarterly journal published by the University of California Press and sponsored by National Council on Public History, refers to itself as the "voice of the public history movement." Individual subscriptions to The Public Historian are included with membership in the National Council on Public History. Issues are generally themed, and a recent issue includes articles entitled "What I've Learned Along the Way: A Public Historian's Intellectual Odyssey"; "Engaging the Contested Memory of the Public Square: Community Collaboration, Archaeology, and Oral History at Corpus Christi's Artesian Park"; and a book review on capturing oral history collections. The title seeks to cover areas such as public policy and policy analysis; federal, state, and local history; historic preservation; oral history; and museum and historical administration. It is a worthwhile addition to a university library or a library with a focus on grassroots movements, ethnic studies, and regional history.

485. *R B M: A Journal of Rare Books, Manuscripts and Cultural Heritage.* Formerly (until 2000): *Rare Books and Manuscripts Librarianship.* [ISSN: 1529-6407] 1986. s-a. USD 49 domestic; USD 55 in Canada & Mexico; USD 65 elsewhere. Ed(s): Jennifer K Sheehan. American Library Association, 50 E Huron St, Chicago, IL 60611; ala@ala.org; http://www.ala.org. Illus., index, adv. Sample. Vol. ends: No. 2. *Indexed:* A22, MLA-IB. *Bk. rev.:* Number and length vary. *Aud.:* Ac, Sa.

RBM: A Journal of Rare Books, Manuscripts, and Cultural Heritage is published biannually by the Association of College and Research Libraries (ACRL). It seeks to publish articles on topics pertaining to special collections libraries and cultural heritage institutions. The journal's main focus is on rare books and preservation, and it is therefore essential reading for anyone interested in preserving cultural heritage, such as special collections librarians, archivists, preservation officers and conservators, artists, museum professionals, collectors, dealers, filmmakers, performance artists, faculty, students, and researchers. *RBM* focuses on the changing environment of rare-book librarianship, and it includes content such as coping with emerging technologies in libraries; new economic models for collecting materials; "the creation of strategic partnerships"; and the ways in which people experience the "authentic." Recent articles include "Build It and S/He Will Come: A Reflection on Five Years in a Purpose-Built Special Collections Space"; "Alchemy and Innovation: Cultivating an Appreciation for Primary Sources in Younger Students"; and "Participant Learning in an Archival Education and Outreach Program to Fraternities and Sororities: An Implementation of Evidence-Based Librarianship and Information Science." Book reviews and annotated rare-book and special collections catalogues are also included in most issues. Issues are available in print and as electronic copies for individual and institutional subscribers.

National, Regional, and State Newsletters

The newsletters of state, provincial, and regional associations provide archivists in the field with current awareness of challenges and opportunities, a sense of community, and a forum for professional development. They track state and provincial legal trends, list professional and public workshops, announce and report on local meetings, describe funding opportunities, publish job announcements, and gather news from member repositories. The larger or most active associations may publish articles on a par with the national journals, but they generally focus on shorter-range issues and resources to support the daily work of their members. Most organizations publish issues in pdf format that are available online, with some restricting recent issues to members only; a few still print newsletters that are a benefit of membership. The following publications of national, regional, state, and provincial archival associations are arranged geographically.

National, Regional, and State Newsletters—Canada

ACA Bulletin. [ISSN: 0709-4604] 6/yr. Larry Dohey. ACA Bulletin, Roman Catholic Archdiocese, P.O. Box 1363, St. John's, NL Canada A1C 5M3 (http://archivists.ca/publications/bulletin.aspx).

ALBERTA

ASA Newsletter. q. Archives Society of Alberta, P.O. Box 4067, South Edmonton Post Office, Edmonton, AB T6E 4S8 (http://www.archivesalberta.org/default.asp?V_ITEM_ID=69).

BRITISH COLUMBIA

AABC Newsletter. [ISSN: 1183-3165] q. Archives Association of British Columbia, 34A - 2755 Lougheed Highway, Suite #249, Port Coquitlam, BC V3B 5Y9 (http://aabc.bc.ca/aabc/newsletter/default.htm).

MANITOBA

ArchiNews/ArchiNouvelles. [ISSN: 1193-9958] q. Association for Manitoba Archives, Box 26005 Maryland P.O., Winnipeg, MB R3G 3R3 (http://www.mbarchives.mb.ca/communique.htm).

NEWFOUNDLAND AND LABRADOR

ANLA Bulletin. [ISSN: 0821-7157] q. Association of Newfoundland and Labrador Archives, P.O. Box 23155, St. John's, NL A1B 4J9 (http://www.anla.nf.ca/).

ONTARIO

Off the Record. q. Archives Association of Ontario, 1444 Queen Street East, Suite #205, Toronto, ON M4L 1E1 (http://aao.fis.utoronto.ca/aa/otr.html).

QUEBEC

La Chronique. 10/yr. L'Association des archivistes du Quebec, C.P. 9768, succ. Sainte-Foy, Quebec G1V 4C3 (http://www.archivistes.qc.ca/publication/chronique.html).

SASKATCHEWAN

SCAA Newsletter. Saskatchewan Council for Archives and Archivists, Kathlyn Szalasznyj, Outreach, 2506 Woodward Avenue, Saskatoon, SK S7J 2E5 (http://scaa.usask.ca/newsletter.html).

YUKON

YCA Newsletter. Yukon Council of Archives, Publications Committee, Box 31089, Whitehorse, Yukon Y1A 5P7 (http://www.yukoncouncilofarchives.ca/sections/newsletter/newsletter.html).

National, Regional, and State Newsletters—United States

Archival Outlook. [ISSN: 1520-3379] 6/yr. Teresa M. Brinati. SAA, 17 North State St., Suite 1425, Chicago, IL 60602-3315 (www.archivists.org/periodicals/ao.asp).

ALABAMA

The Alabama Archivist. s-a. $10. Carol Ellis. Society of Alabama Archivists, P.O. Box 300100, Montgomery, AL 36130-0100 (http://www.alarchivists.org/publications.html).

CALIFORNIA

SCA Newsletter. q. $45. Society of California Archivists, Long Beach Public Library, Collection Services Department, 101 Pacific Ave., Long Beach, CA 90822 (http://www.calarchivists.org/SCANewsletter).

DELAWARE VALLEY

Archival Arranger. 3/yr. $12. Joanne McKinley. Delaware Valley Archivists Group, New Jersey Division of Archives and Records Management, 2300 Stuyvesant Ave., P.O. Box 307, Trenton, NJ 08625 (http://www.dvarchivists.org/).

FLORIDA

The Florida Archivist. q. $20. Michael Zaidman. Society of Florida Archivists, P.O. Box 2746, Lakeland, FL 33806-2746 (http://www.florida-archivists.org/newsletter.htm).

GEORGIA

SGA Newsletter. q. $25. Renna Tuten. Society of Georgia Archivists, P.O. Box 133085, Atlanta, GA 30333 (http://www.soga.org/pubs/nltr/issues.php).

HAWAII

AHA Newsletter. q. $15. Association of Hawai'i Archivists, P.O. Box 1751, Honolulu, HI 96806 (http://www2.hawaii.edu/~wertheim/AHA.html).

INTERMOUNTAIN

CIMA Newsletter. q. $15. Roy Webb. Conference of Inter-Mountain Archivists, J. Willard Marriott Library, 295 South 1500 E., University of Utah, Salt Lake City, UT 84112 (http://www.lib.utah.edu/cima/news.html).

KENTUCKY

The Kentucky Archivist. s-a. $10. Jim Cundy. Kentucky Department for Libraries and Archives, 300 Coffee Tree Road, P.O. Box 537, Frankfort, KY 40602-0537 (http://kyarchivists.org/kyarch.htm).

LOUISIANA

LAMA Newsletter. [ISSN: 1073-1008] s-a. $15. Phyllis Kinnison, Louisiana State University, Special Collections, Hill Memorial Library, Baton Rouge, LA 70803 (http://www.nutrias.org/lama/lama.htm).

LOUISIANA, NEW ORLEANS

Greater New Orleans Archivists Newsletter. 3/yr. $10. Lester Sullivan, Archives & Special Collections, Xavier University Library, 7325 Palmetto St., New Orleans, LA 70125 (http://nutrias.org/gnoa/gnoa.htm).

MICHIGAN

Open Entry. s-a. $20. Bob Garrett, Archives of Michigan: garrettr1@michigan.gov (http://www.maasn.org/).

MID-ATLANTIC

Mid-Atlantic Archivist. [ISSN: 0738-9396] q. $35. Michael P. Martin. Mid-Atlantic Regional Archives Conference, P.O. Box 710215, Oak Hill, VA 20171 (http://www.lib.umd.edu/MARAC/committees/marac-pubs.html).

MIDWEST

MAC Newsletter. [ISSN: 0741-0379] q. $30. Kathy Koch. Midwest Archives Conference, 4440 PGA Boulevard, Suite 600, Palm Beach Gardens, FL 33410 (http://www.midwestarchives.org/macnewsletter.asp).

MINNESOTA, MINNEAPOLIS-ST. PAUL

TCART Newsletter. s-a. Candy Hart. Twin Cities Archives Round Table, Archives MS-C1919, Hamline University, 1536 Hewitt Ave., St. Paul, MN 55104 (http://www.tcartmn.org/).

MISSISSIPPI

The Primary Source. [ISSN: 0741-6563] s-a. Peggy Price. Society of Mississippi Archivists, P.O. Box 1151, Jackson, MS 39215-1151 (http://www.msarchivists.org/theprimarysource/).

MISSOURI, KANSAS CITY

The Dusty Shelf. q. $15. Kathi Whitman. Kansas City Area Archivists, c/o Western Historical Manuscripts Collection, University of Missouri-Kansas City, 320 Newcomb Hall, 5100 Rockhill Road, Kansas City, MO 64110-2499 (http://www.umkc.edu/KCAA/DUSTYSHELF/DUSTY.HTM).

MISSOURI, ST. LOUIS

The Acid Free Press. $7.50. Mike Everman. Association of St. Louis Area Archivists, Saint Louis University Archives Pius Library 307, 3650 Lindell Blvd., St. Louis, MO 63108 (http://www.stlarchivists.org/index.php?pr=Home_Page).

NEW ENGLAND

NEA Newsletter. q. $30. New England Archivists, George C. Gordon Library, Worcester Polytechnic Institute, 100 Institute Road, Worcester, MA 01609 (http://www.newenglandarchivists.org/newsletter/index.html).

NEW YORK, NEW YORK

Metropolitan Archivist. s-a. $25. Rachel Chatalbash. Archivists Round Table of Metropolitan New York, Inc., P.O. Box 151, New York, NY 10274-0154 (http://www.nycarchivists.org/pubMetro.html).

NORTH CAROLINA

North Carolina Archivist. s-a. $25. Cat Saleeby McDowell. Society of North Carolina Archivists, P.O. Box 20448, Raleigh, NC 27619 (http://www.ncarchivists.org/pubs/newslet.html).

NORTHWEST

Easy Access. q. $15. John Bolcer. Northwest Archivists, Inc., Univ. of Washington, UW Libraries, Box 352900, Seattle, WA 98195-2900 (http://www.lib.washington.edu/nwa/EasyAccess.html).

OHIO

The Ohio Archivist. [ISSN: 1047-5400] s-a. $15. Beth Kattelman. Society of Ohio Archivists, Jerome Lawrence and Robert E. Lee Theatre Research Institute, The Ohio State University, 1430 Lincoln Tower, 1800 Cannon Dr., Columbus, OH 43210 (http://www.ohioarchivists.org/newsletter.html).

ROCKY MOUNTAINS

The Rocky Mountain Archivist. [ISSN: 1098-7711] q. $15. Ashley Large. Society of Rocky Mountain Archivists, Colorado State University, 1019 Morgan Library, Fort Collins, CO 80523 (http://www.srmarchivists.org/newsletter/default.htm).

SOUTHWEST

The Southwestern Archivist. [ISSN: 1056-1021] q. $10. Katie Salzmann, Kris Toma. Society of Southwest Archivists, P.O. Box 225, Gaithersburg, MD 20884 (http://southwestarchivists.org/HTML/Publications.htm).

TENNESSEE

Tennessee Archivist. q. $20. Jay Richiuso. Society of Tennessee Archivists, Tennessee State Library and Archives, 403 Seventh Ave. N., Nashville, TN 37243 (http://www.tennesseearchivists.org/newsletter.html).

WASHINGTON, SEATTLE

SAA Newsletter. 3/yr. $15. Seattle Area Archivists, P.O. Box 95321, Seattle, WA 98145-2321 (http://www.historylink.org/saa/Newsletters.htm).

Special-Interest Newsletters

Archivists caring for the same types of records, performing the same functions, working in similar specialized institutions, or collecting in the same areas benefit from sharing knowledge and news in special-interest newsletters. Many relevant newsletters are published by sections and roundtables of the Society of American Archivists. These groups meet at the SAA annual conference, and many post meeting notes as well as periodic news, reviews, and outside resources; some also publish fuller articles. The list below offers all the special-interest publications (and a couple of newsletters/web sites or blogs) that emanate from SAA groups, with selected others, most of which are available online and many of which, published as pdf documents, require Adobe Reader. Newsletters from the allied fields of preservation and conservation are included; individual repositories' publications are not included. Editors of newsletters and web content change frequently, so readers are advised to contact the group directly for current information or SAA where relevant: Society of American Archivists, 17 North State St., Suite 1425, Chicago, IL 60602-3315 (http://archivists.org).

ACQUISITION AND APPRAISAL

Acquisition and Appraisal Section Newsletter, SAA (http://www.archivists.org/saagroups/acq-app/newsletter.asp).

BUSINESS

Business Archives Section web site, SAA (http://www.archivists.org/saagroups/bas/welcome.asp).

COLLEGE AND UNIVERSITY ARCHIVES

The Academic Archivist. College and University Archives Section, SAA (http://www.archivists.org/saagroups/cnu/index.asp).

CONGRESSIONAL PAPERS

Congressional Papers Roundtable Newsletter, SAA (http://www.archivists.org/saagroups/cpr/newsletters.asp).

DESCRIPTION

Descriptive Notes. Description Section, SAA (http://www.archivists.org/saagroups/descr/index.asp).

EAD (ENCODED ARCHIVAL DESCRIPTION)

EAD Roundtable web site, SAA (http://www.archivists.org/saagroups/ead/).

ELECTRONIC RECORDS

Electronic Records Section Newsletter, SAA (http://www.archivists.org/saagroups/ers/news.asp).

Crossroads: developments in electronic records management and information technology. Committee on Electronic Records and Information Systems (CERIS), NAGARA. 4/yr. $75. Membership benefit; two years past and earlier available online to non-members. National Association of Government Archives and Records Administrators, 90 State St., Suite 1009, Albany, NY 12207 (http://www.nagara.org/displaycommon.cfm?an=1&subarticlenbr=79).

FILM

AMIA Newsletter. [ISSN 1075-6477] q. $50. David Lemieux. Association of Moving Image Archivists, 1313 North Vine St., Hollywood, CA 90028 (http://www.amianet.org/resources/newsletter.php).

GOVERNMENT RECORDS

Official Word: The Government Records Section Newsletter. Government Records Section, SAA (http://www.archivists.org/saagroups/gov/newsletters/index.asp).

NAGARA Clearinghouse: news and reports on government records. 4/yr. $75. Membership benefit. National Association of Government Archives and Records Administrators, 90 State St., Suite 1009, Albany, NY 12207 (http://www.nagara.org/displaycommon.cfm?an=1&subarticlenbr=78).

LESBIAN AND GAY

Archival InQueeries. Lesbian and Gay Archives Roundtable, SAA (http://www.archivists.org/saagroups/lagar/newsletters/index.html).

MANAGEMENT

Archives Management Roundtable Newsletter, SAA (http://www.archivists.org/saagroups/archmgmt/newsletters.asp).

MANUSCRIPTS

Manuscript Repositories Section Newsletter, SAA (http://www.archivists.org/saagroups/mss/newsletter.asp).

The Manuscript Society News. 4/yr. $60. The Manuscript Society, 1960 East Fairmont Dr., Tempe, AZ 85282-2844 (http://manuscript.org/publications.html).

RBMS Newsletter. 2/yr. Association of College and Research Libraries, ALA, 50 E. Huron St., Chicago, IL 60611 (http://www.rbms.info/publications/index.shtml#newsletter).

MULTICULTURAL

Archivists and Archives of Color Roundtable Newsletter, SAA (http://www.archivists.org/saagroups/aac/Activities.htm).

Native American Archives Roundtable Newsletter, SAA (http://www.archivists.org/saagroups/nat-amer/index_files/Page435.htm).

MUSEUMS

Museum Archives Section blog, SAA (http://saa-museum.blogspot.com/).

ORAL HISTORY

Oral History Section Newsletter, SAA (http://www.archivists.org/saagroups/oralhist/newsletters.asp).

PERFORMING ARTS

Performance!. Performing Arts Roundtable, SAA (http://www.archivists.org/saagroups/performart/newsletter/index.html).

PRESERVATION AND CONSERVATION

AIC News. [ISSN: 0887-705X] 6/yr. $105. American Institute for Conservation of Historic and Artistic Works, 1156 15th St., NW, Suite 320, Washington, DC 20005-1714 (http://aic.stanford.edu/library/aicnews_archive.html).

Conservation, The GCI Newsletter. [ISSN: 0898-4808] 3/yr. Free. Jeffrey Levin. The Getty Conservation Institute, 1200 Getty Center Dr., Suite 700, Los Angeles, CA 90049-1684 (http://www.getty.edu/conservation/publications/newsletters/).

Guild of Book Workers Newsletter. [ISSN: 0730-3203] 6/yr. $75. Jody Beenk. Guild of Book Workers, 521 Fifth Ave., New York, NY 10175 (http://palimpsest.stanford.edu/byorg/gbw/news.shtml).

Infinity. Preservation Section, SAA (http://www.archivists.org/saagroups/preserv/text/news.htm).

International Preservation News: a newsletter of the IFLA Core Activity for Preservation and Conservation. 3/yr. Library of Congress, 101 Independence Ave., SE, Washington, DC 20540-4500 (http://www.ifla.org/VI/4/ipn.html).

WAAC Newsletter. [ISSN: 1052-0066] 3/yr. $35. Western Association for Art Conservation, 5905 Wilshire Blvd., Los Angeles, CA 90036 (http://palimpsest.stanford.edu/waac/wn/).

RECORDED SOUND

Recorded Sound Roundtable Newsletter, SAA (http://www.archivists.org/saagroups/recsound/newsletters.asp).

RECORDS MANAGEMENT

The Records Manager. Records Management Roundtable, SAA (http://www.archivists.org/saagroups/recmgmt/newsletters.asp).

REFERENCE

RAO News. Reference, Access, and Outreach Section, SAA (http://www.archivists.org/saagroups/rao/index.asp).

RELIGIOUS

The Archival Spirit. Archivists of Religious Collections Section, SAA (http://www.saa-arcs.org/).

NEARI Newsletter. $10. New England Archivists of Religious Institutions, Boston CSJ Archives, 637 Cambridge St., Brighton, MA 02135-2801 (http://www.csjboston.org/neari.htm).

SCIENCE, TECHNOLOGY, AND HEALTH CARE

Archival Elements. Science, Technology, and Health Care Roundtable, SAA (http://www.archivists.org/saagroups/sthc/publications.html).

VISUAL MATERIALS

VIEWS: The Newsletter of the Visual Materials Section. Visual Materials Section, SAA (http://www.lib.lsu.edu/SAA/views.html).

ART

General/Museum Publications

See also Crafts and Making section.

Holly Stec Dankert, Research and Access Services Librarian, The School of the Art Institute of Chicago, John M. Flaxman Library, 37 S. Wabash, Chicago, IL 60603; hdankert@saic.edu

Nick Ferreira, Interim Special Collections Librarian, The School of the Art Institute of Chicago, John M. Flaxman Library, 37 S. Wabash, Chicago, IL 60603; nferre1@saic.edu

Introduction

Although the primary readers of art publications continue to be artists, art dealers, art collectors, museum curators, art historians, and scholars, many of the titles in this section will be of interest to members of the general public, and especially students. The terms *art* and *arts* as used in this section can be defined as two- or three-dimensional visual arts of all media including, but not limited to, paint, pencil, ink, found objects, clay, bronze, other metals, video, film, new media, photography, decorative arts, and performance. However, as museums, scholars, and the artists themselves continue to expand what art is, many of the titles included in this section report on non-object-based arts such as socially engaged art practices, time-based art, or large-scale installations intended to encourage participation with its audience.

The "General" subsection here features core titles for art collections or libraries where there is an interest in artistic work and culture, including general-interest magazines, scholarly and professional journals, and instructional magazines for artists. Also, attempts have been made to include journals that focus on art from various parts of the globe and on specific areas in the art world. Bulletins from major museums highlighting their own collections are divided into a separate category following the "General" subsection.

Most titles exist in some online version and while much of the scholarship in the arts is now conducted using online access to journals, many users still rely on the full-color reproduction of artworks found within magazines. Especially for the casual and general reader of art magazines, print remains relevant. Core titles with additional web content are indicated usually within the description of the apropos titles. Some of these magazines' websites provide only subscription and general information. The present contributors hope that the entries in this section will give librarians a reasonable perspective on the sorts of journals that are available concerning art in all its diverse forms.

Basic Periodicals

GENERAL. Ems: *The Artist's Magazine;* Hs: *American Art, Art in America, The Artist's Magazine;* Ga: *Art in America, Artforum International, The Artist's Magazine;* Ac: *Art Bulletin, Art History, Art in America, Art Journal, Artforum International, Artnews, Journal of Visual Culture, October*.

MUSEUM PUBLICATIONS. The *Metropolitan Museum of Art Bulletin* is the best multipurpose museum publication for all ages. A local museum publication could also be chosen for regional representation.

Basic Abstracts and Indexes

Art Design & Architecture Collection; Art Index; ARTbibliographies Modern; International Bibliography of Art (successor to *BHA: Bibliography of the History of Art*).

General

African Arts. See Africa section.

486. ***Afterall: a journal of art, context and enquiry.*** [ISSN: 1465-4253] 1998. 2x/yr. USD 121. Ed(s): David Morris, Ana Bilbao. University of Chicago Press, 1427 E 60th St, Chicago, IL 60637; custserv@press.uchicago.edu; http://www.journals.uchicago.edu. Adv. Refereed. *Indexed:* A51. *Aud.:* Ga, Ac, Sa.

Afterall is a London-based contemporary arts magazine founded by college of art and design professionals. The editorial staff—now including museum, academic press, and higher education oversight—continues to offer "in-depth analysis of artists' work, along with essays that broaden the context in which to understand it." Each issue provides the reader with lengthy, well-researched articles that include notes and many full-color images about a few selected contemporary artists; and it often includes several different writers discussing the same artists' works from varying perspectives. Adding to the information in the print journal, the website includes exhibition reviews, videos, picture essays, and interviews. Recommended for large public libraries and academic libraries that serve art programs. URL: www.afterall.org

Afterimage. See Photography section.

487. ***American Art.*** Formerly (until 1991): *Smithsonian Studies in American Art.* [ISSN: 1073-9300] 1987. 3x/yr. USD 293. University of Chicago Press, 1427 E 60th St, Chicago, IL 60637; subscriptions@press.uchicago.edu; http://www.journals.uchicago.edu. Illus., adv. Sample. Refereed. Vol. ends: Fall. *Indexed:* A01, A22, A51, AmHI, MASUSE, MLA-IB. *Aud.:* Ga, Ac.

Produced by the Smithsonian American Art Museum, *American Art* encompasses the visual heritage of the United States from its beginning in the colonial era to the present. Interdisciplinary articles range from history to archaeology, anthropology, and cultural studies, all with a focus on visual arts. While the editorial statement indicates that the scope is primarily fine arts, *American Art* includes works of popular culture, public art, film, photography, electronic multimedia, and decorative arts and crafts. Each issue offers a mix of scholarly feature articles and a commentary that focus on an issue or artist of importance to the Smithsonian or to the American art world at large. Articles are written in accessible language, and the mix of color and black-and-white photographs makes this well suited to public libraries and colleges and universities.

488. ***Apollo: the international art magazine.*** [ISSN: 0003-6536] 1925. m. USD 95 combined subscription United States (print & online eds.)). Ed(s): Thomas Marks. Apollo Magazine Ltd., 22 Old Queen St, London, SW1H 9HP, United Kingdom; apollo@cisubs.co.uk. Illus., adv. Vol. ends: Dec. Microform: PQC. Reprint: PSC. *Indexed:* A06, A22, A51, BAS, BRI, CBRI, MLA-IB. *Bk. rev.:* 6-7, 800-1,000 words. *Aud.:* Ga, Ac.

Tastefully illustrated and international in scope, *Apollo*'s issues target ancient through contemporary art, whatever the market is collecting, with six or seven articles aimed at an educated audience and written by curators, professors, and other art experts. The December issue reviews the year, with feature articles on acquisitions, exhibitions, a personality of the year, and more. Each issue includes a diary of museum shows, book reviews, and loads of Paris, London, and New York gallery ads. It is geared toward collectors and curators but is also relevant to academicians. The website of *Apollo* features an agenda of art world happenings, a blog, and a monthly podcast. Appropriate for large public libraries and academic libraries that serve art programs. URL: www.apollo-magazine.com

489. ***Archives of Asian Art.*** Formerly (until 1967): *Chinese Art Society of America. Archives.* [ISSN: 0066-6637] 1946. s-a. USD 246. Ed(s): Mary Gladue. Duke University Press, 905 W Main St, Durham, NC 27701; orders@dukeupress.edu; https://www.dukeupress.edu. Illus., index, adv. Refereed. *Indexed:* A06, A22, BAS, E01, MLA-IB. *Aud.:* Ac, Sa.

Published semi-annually to highlight research and scholarship of South, Southeast, Central, and East Asian art and architecture, *Archives of Asian Art* provides a forum for scholars, with four to six lengthy articles that are generously illustrated. It covers visual arts, archaeology, architecture, and the history of collecting within all time periods. This publication serves as one of the few English-language resources for serious students and scholars. It is highly recommended for research collections in academic libraries.

Art & Antiques. See Antiques/General section.

490. ***Art Asia Pacific.*** [ISSN: 1039-3625] 1993. bi-m. USD 85; USD 15 per issue. Ed(s): John Jervis, Elaine W Ng. Art Asia Pacific Publishing, Llc., 245 Eighth Ave, Ste 247, New York, NY 10011. Illus., adv. *Indexed:* A51, AmHI. *Aud.:* Ac, Sa.

Art Asia Pacific covers leading figures and trends in contemporary art in Asia, the Pacific, and the Middle East. Several feature-length articles cover artists working in every media in this glossy and minimally stylized magazine. Full-color imagery predominates in both features and international gallery ads. Regular departments showcase happenings, art fair and auction reports, profiles of creators, reviews of biennials, and exhibitions internationally and in major U.S. cities. Some essays and other content are available online for current and archived issues. An annual almanac of news, country reports, festivals, and books rounds out the subscription. Written in straightforward language to appeal to a wide audience, *Art Asia Pacific* is recommended for academic and large public libraries. URL: http://artasiapacific.com/

491. ***The Art Bulletin.*** Former titles (until 1919): *College Art Association of America. Bulletin (Print);* (until 1917): *College Art Association. Bulletin (Print).* [ISSN: 0004-3079] 1913. q. Free to members. Ed(s): Kirk Ambrose, Nina Athanassoglou-Kallmyer. College Art Association, 50 Broadway, 21st Fl, New York, NY 10004; nyoffice@collegeart.org; http://www.collegeart.org. Illus., index, adv. Refereed. Vol. ends: No. 4. Microform: IDC; PQC. Reprint: PSC. *Indexed:* A01, A06, A22, A51, AmHI, BAS, BRI, CBRI, MASUSE, MLA-IB. *Bk. rev.:* Numerous, essay length. *Aud.:* Ac.

Published quarterly by the College Art Association (CAA), *The Art Bulletin* serves as a forum for leading scholarship and debate in contemporary art-historical practice. Research articles cover all periods, many in Western art, and are usually accompanied by color and black-and-white images. Abstracts of each article are provided in the table of contents, and articles include bibliographic notes. See CAA's online portal for job listings in the arts and other benefits to members. *The Art Bulletin* is considered essential for all research collections and academic libraries. URL: www.collegeart.org

Art Education. See Education/Specific Subjects and Teaching Methods: The Arts section.

492. ***Art History.*** [ISSN: 0141-6790] 1978. 5x/yr. GBP 850. Ed(s): Genevieve Warwick. Wiley-Blackwell Publishing Ltd., The Atrium, Southern Gate, Chichester, PO19 8QG, United Kingdom; cs-journals@wiley.com; http://onlinelibrary.wiley.com/. Illus., index, adv. Sample. Refereed. Vol. ends: Dec. Microform: PQC. Reprint: PSC. *Indexed:* A01, A22, A51, AmHI, BAS, BRI, E01, MLA-IB. *Bk. rev.:* 9-11, essay length. *Aud.:* Ac.

The Association for Art History publishes *Art History* to provide research in the historical and theoretical aspects of traditional visual arts—primarily two-dimensional works on paper and canvas, with occasional forays into three-dimensional art—from both Western and Eastern hemispheres. Articles that explore the arts in their interdisciplinary context are encouraged. Targeted to art and design professionals and others concerned with the advancement of the history of art, *Art History* seeks to consider related cultural, economic, and social issues as well. Librarians will especially appreciate the extensive scholarly book reviews written by experts in the field. Recommended for all academic libraries.

493. ***Art in America.*** Former titles (until 1939): *Art in America and Elsewhere;* (until 1921): *Art in America.* [ISSN: 0004-3214] 1913. m. USD 45 domestic; USD 85 Canada; USD 100 elsewhere. Ed(s): Lindsay Pollock. Brant Publications, Inc., 575 Broadway, 5th Fl, New York, NY 10012. Illus., adv. Microform: PQC. *Indexed:* A01, A06, A22, A51, AmHI, BRI, CBRI, Chicano, F01, MASUSE, MLA-IB. *Bk. rev.:* 2-3, 1,000 words. *Aud.:* Ga, Ac.

Published since 1913, *Art in America* continues to be a standard in the field of art. Feature articles are focused on both contemporary artists and the current issues in the arts in the United States. The magazine includes brief articles that cover both U.S. and international news, issues, exhibitions, architecture, and regional reports. *Art in America*'s target audience ranges from curators and collectors to the casual art fan. Images are large and in full-color. The magazine's website includes additional features, reviews, interviews, and up-to-the minute news. Highly recommended for public libraries and academic libraries. URL: www.artinamericamagazine.com

494. ***Art India: the art news magazine of India.*** [ISSN: 0972-2947] 1996. q. INR 520 domestic; USD 34 United States; GBP 19 United Kingdom. Art India Publishing Co. Pvt. Ltd., Jindal Mansion, 5-A Dr G Deshmukh Marg, Mumbai, 400 026, India; artindia.info@gmail.com. Adv. *Indexed:* A51. *Bk. rev.:* Number and length vary. *Aud.:* Ac, Sa.

Art India showcases the contemporary Indian art world and promotes a critical platform for exploring new media art, painting, sculpture, photography, and architecture. There is substantial reporting in English that covers cultural and societal issues in the visual arts; profiles and interviews of current visual artists, including reviews of local and international Indian artists; book reviews; and gallery listings. Much current content and access to archives for subscribers are available online. Appropriate for museum, academic, and public libraries that serve visual artists and collectors. URL: www.artindiamag.com

495. ***Art Journal.*** Formerly (until 1960): *College Art Journal;* Which superseded (in 1941): *Parnassus.* [ISSN: 0004-3249] 1941. q. Free to members. Ed(s): Lane Relyea, Gloria Sutton. College Art Association, 50 Broadway, 21st Fl, New York, NY 10004; nyoffice@collegeart.org; http://www.collegeart.org. Illus., adv. Refereed. Microform: PQC. Reprint: PSC. *Indexed:* A&ATA, A01, A06, A22, A51, AmHI, BAS, BRI, CBRI, MASUSE, MLA-IB. *Bk. rev.:* 6, length varies. *Aud.:* Ac.

Art Journal is an academic periodical published by the College Art Association. Peer reviewed, the association's journal focuses on creating a dialogue among educators who teach art, design, criticism and theory, art history, visual culture, and makers of art. Articles are of a scholarly nature and focus on cultural change reflected in the visual arts, with commissioned pieces, artist's projects, exchanges, and interviews covering subjects of the twentieth and twenty-first centuries. Contemporary works and artists are featured, with black-and-white and color illustrations. Highly recommended for all academic libraries, especially those with studio or history of art departments.

496. ***Art Monthly.*** [ISSN: 0142-6702] 1976. 10x/yr. GBP 55 (Individuals, GBP 46; GBP 4.80 per issue domestic). Ed(s): Patricia Bickers. Britannia Art Publications Ltd., 28 Charing Cross Rd, London, WC2H 0DB, United Kingdom. Adv. Sample. *Indexed:* A01, A22, A51, AmHI, BRI. *Bk. rev.:* 1-3, 1,000 words. *Aud.:* Ga, Ac.

This journal is primarily concerned with the contemporary art world as it manifests itself in the United Kingdom. Each issue of *Art Monthly* includes interviews with, and profiles of, leading figures in the art world, as well as emerging artists and critics' explorations of trends in art and the art world. It also contains art news, book reviews, reports from other parts of the globe, and a lengthy section of exhibition listings and reviews from throughout the United Kingdom. Recommended for colleges of art and design, as well as academic libraries that support studio programs.

497. ***Art New England: a resource for the visual arts.*** [ISSN: 0274-7073] 1979. bi-m. USD 28 domestic; USD 33 Canada; USD 40 elsewhere. Art New England, Inc., 560 Harrison Ave, Ste 412, Boston, MA 02118. Illus., adv. Vol. ends: Dec. *Aud.:* Ga, Ac.

This magazine offers regional art and cultural news for the New England area, focusing on artists, exhibitions, performances, and installations from that region. Also useful to local artists are the guides to schools and artists' directories found in each issue, plus advertising for classes, workshops, degrees, and programs in the area, including studio visits. Special themed issues focus on Museums (May/June) and Galleries (September/October). The website offers additional content in blogs and some archived content. Recommended for public and academic libraries that serve studio arts programs in the Northeastern United States. URL: http://artnewengland.com/

498. ***The Art Newspaper (International Edition).*** Incorporated (1988-1989): *Journal of Art.* [ISSN: 0960-6556] 1990. 11x/yr. USD 110 combined subscription in Europe (print & online eds.); USD 115 in US & Canada (print & online eds).). Ed(s): Jane Morris. Umberto Allemandi & C., Via Mancini 8, Turin, 10131, Italy; http://www.allemandi.com. Adv. Sample. *Indexed:* A22, A51. *Aud.:* Ga, Ac, Sa.

The Art Newspaper is a true newspaper in its format and content. Its focus is commentary and news of the international art world. It is divided into two sections. The first section is devoted to what's going on in private, national, and international museums; legislation/regulation in the arts; financial crises and funding issues; the effects of world events on art collections; and scandals from all areas. Columnists and op/ed writers turn a critical eye on governments around the world and the effects that their policies have on the arts; plus, there are other regular commentaries. The second section lists exhibitions around the globe, divided into New York, the rest of the United States, London, the rest of the United Kingdom, France, Germany, and the rest of the world. There is also an auction listing. The website offers some free content and is worth bookmarking. An excellent source for keeping up with world art news and people. Highly recommended for large public libraries and academic libraries that serve art programs. URL: www.theartnewspaper.com

499. ***Art Nexus (English Edition).*** [ISSN: 0122-1744] 1976. q. USD 32. Ed(s): Ivonne Pini, Celia Sredni de Birbragher. ArtNexus Miami, 12500 N E 8th Ave, 2nd Fl, North Miami, FL 33161; customerservice@artnexus.com; http://www.artnexus.com/. Adv. *Indexed:* A51. *Bk. rev.:* 1-3, 1,000 words. *Aud.:* Ga, Ac, Sa.

Art Nexus offers an opportunity to explore many aspects of Central and South American visual arts. Issues include interviews, profiles, discussion, and criticism that focuses on individual artists or groups of artists. These inspections of art at the individual level are augmented by features on international festivals, fairs and conferences, and reviews and discussions of exhibitions by Latin American artists or concentrating on Latin American art held all over the world. There are also book and catalog reviews, as well as an extensive gallery guide. The English-language edition was reviewed. Online, the reader is provided with further information about news, exhibitions, and events throughout the Latin American art world, visual galleries, and a database of contemporary Latin American artists, along with other relevant information. URL: www.artnexus.com

500. ***Art Papers Magazine.*** Formerly (until 1999): *Art Papers;* Which was formed by the merger of (1977-1980): *Contemporary Art - Southeast;* (1980-1981): *Atlanta Art Papers;* Which was formerly (until 1980): *Atlanta Art Workers Coalition Newspaper;* (until 1978): *A A W C Ltd. Newsletter.* [ISSN: 1524-9581] 1981. bi-m. USD 35 domestic; USD 45 in Canada & Mexico; USD 75 elsewhere. Ed(s): Victoria Camblin. Art Papers, Inc., PO Box 5748, Atlanta, GA 31107; creative@artpapers.org. Illus., adv. Vol. ends: Nov/Dec. Microform: PQC. *Indexed:* A22, A51. *Bk. rev.:* 1, 1,000 words. *Aud.:* Ga, Ac, Sa.

Art Papers represents a regional non-profit dedicated to promoting contemporary art practices, bringing an array of programs, critical dialogue, free public lectures and scholarship to Georgia and the surrounding area. Via its magazine and website *Art Papers* lists myriad studio visits, interviews, collecting and art resources, regional artists' gallery shows, and reviews, making this resource valuable for artists and for all those who are interested in contemporary art. Appropriate for public, college, and university libraries. URL: www.artpapers.org

501. ***Art Press: la revue de l'art contemporain.*** [ISSN: 0245-5676] 1972. m. Individuals, EUR 6.50. Ed(s): Catherine Millet. ArtPublications, 8 rue Francois Villon, Paris, 75015, France. *Indexed:* A22, A51. *Bk. rev.:* Number and length vary. *Aud.:* Ac, Sa.

Published bilingually, with French and English integrated side by side, this international monthly explores contemporary visual arts, literature, video, film, performance, electronic arts, music, theater, new media—a broad array of global cultural phenomena. Feature-length articles are sometimes thematic, covering important events, philosophies, and emerging trends in contemporary art and society. Editorials, interviews (with artists, curators, dealers), book and exhibition reviews, and thematic columns (art market, literature) complete each issue. Recommended for research collections in the arts.

502. *Art Review (London).* Former titles (until 1993): *Arts Review;* (until 1961): *Art News & Review.* [ISSN: 1745-9303] 1949. 8x/yr. GBP 39 combined subscription domestic (print & online eds.); GBP 42 in US & Canada (print & online eds.)). Ed(s): Mark Rappolt. Art Review Ltd., 1 Honduras St, London, EC1Y 0TH, United Kingdom; info@art-review.co.uk. Illus., index, adv. *Indexed:* A22, A51. *Bk. rev.:* Number and length vary. *Aud.:* Ga, Ac.

An international contemporary art magazine, *Art Review* is "dedicated to expanding contemporary art's audience and reach." Aimed at both the specialist and a general audience, this magazine brings together reportage, commentary, news, and many (20 to 30 each issue) exhibition reviews from around the globe. Feature-length articles explore current issues in the contemporary art world and are illustrated with full-color images. Many issues also include artist-produced supplements. The magazine's website includes additional features, reviews, blogs, and videos but limits users to five free articles per month and one digital edition in The Magazine Online (the digital archive of *ArtReview* and *ArtReview Asia*, from 2006 to the present day), with the exception of the three most recent issues. Recommended for large public libraries and academic libraries, especially those that serve art programs. URL: www.artreview.com

503. *Art Therapy.* Supersedes in part: *American Journal of Art Therapy.* [ISSN: 0742-1656] 1983. q. GBP 268 (print & online eds.)). Ed(s): Donna Kaiser. Routledge, 530 Walnut St, Ste 850, Philadelphia, PA 19106; enquiries@tandfonline.com; http://www.tandfonline.com. Adv. Refereed. Reprint: PSC. *Indexed:* A22, A51, ERIC. *Bk. rev.:* 3-5, 1,000 words. *Aud.:* Ac, Sa.

This is the official journal of the American Art Therapy Association, and its stated purpose is "advancing research and understanding of how art therapy functions in the treatment, education, development, and life enrichment of people." Each issue contains four to five articles written by art therapy professionals; viewpoints and commentary on issues of concern to the profession; book reviews and news briefs in the field. One of the few scholarly publications devoted exclusively to this profession, *Art Therapy* is appropriate for academic or special libraries that support art programs and a definite for libraries that support art therapy programs.

504. *Artes de Mexico.* [ISSN: 0300-4953] 1953. q. MXN 900 domestic; USD 90 foreign. Ed(s): Ana Maria Perez Rocha. Artes de Mexico y del Mundo S.A., Plaza Rio de Janeiro 52, Col Roma, Mexico City, 06700, Mexico; artesdemexico@artesdemexico.com; http://www.artesdemexico.com/. Illus., adv. Refereed. Circ: 20000 Paid. *Indexed:* A06, A51. *Aud.:* Ac, Sa.

Artes de Mexico is reminiscent of coffee-table art books with its large format and lavishly illustrated blend of vibrantly photographed arts, crafts, and cultural phenomena of Mexico. Each thematic issue offers divergent viewpoints on a single subject. This journal usually contains at least some feature-length articles, and the variety and length of essays, interviews, or poetry make each issue distinctive. All are written in Spanish, with English translations at the back of the issue. Recommended for libraries with strong art and/or multicultural collections.

505. *Artforum International.* Formerly (until 1982): *Artforum.* [ISSN: 1086-7058] 1962. 10x/yr. USD 50 domestic; USD 70 Canada; USD 120 elsewhere. Artforum International Magazine, Inc., 350 Seventh Ave, New York, NY 10001; generalinfo@artforum.com; http://www.artforum.com. Illus., adv. Vol. ends: Sep/Jun. *Indexed:* A01, A06, A22, A51, AmHI, BAS, BRI, C42, F01, MLA-IB. *Bk. rev.:* 1, length varies. *Aud.:* Ga, Ac.

The primary magazine for reporting on international contemporary art, *Artforum International* is accessible to a wide audience. Within this title, the critical articles on all media—sculpture, painting, installation, architecture, video and music art, mixed media, and popular culture—frequently include artist interviews. Glossy ads proliferate, featuring the latest shows at galleries around the world. Regular reviews cover individual artists, gallery exhibits, film, music, books, top-ten lists, and other art world events. Included three times a year are previews of 50 upcoming exhibitions. A calendar of international art events is provided in every issue. The magazine's website offers worthwhile extras: an international museum finder, blogs, festivals/biennials, free art resources, art zines, news briefs, and the like. Essential for all art libraries, collectors, and curators of contemporary art. Highly recommended for all academic and large public libraries. URL: www.artforum.com

506. *The Artist: inspiration, instruction & practical ideas for all artists.* Incorporates (1966-1986): *Art and Artists.* [ISSN: 0004-3877] 1931. m. GBP 32.50 domestic; USD 45 foreign. The Artists' Publishing Company Limited, Caxton House, 63-65 High St, Tenterden, TN30 6BD, United Kingdom. Illus., index, adv. Sample. *Indexed:* A06, A22. *Bk. rev.:* Number and length vary. *Aud.:* Ga, Ac.

The British equivalent to *American Artist, The Artist* provides many instructional articles for professional and amateur artists. A dozen articles offer practical advice on technique, materials, and other helpful technical information, and are illustrated with lots of easy-to-follow color illustrations. The focus is generally representational art, landscapes, and figurative and still-life portrayals. Exhibition reviews, profiles of contemporary artists, interviews, and other current news in the United Kingdom make up the rest of the contents. Recommended for public libraries and schools with fine arts programs. URL: www.painters-online.co.uk/magazines/the-artist.htm

507. *The Artist's Magazine.* [ISSN: 0741-3351] 1984. 10x/yr. USD 22.96 United States; USD 32.96 Canada. Ed(s): Maureen Bloomfield. F + W Media Inc., 1140 Broadway, 14th Fl, New York, NY 10001; info@fwmedia.com; http://www.fwcommunity.com/. Illus., adv. Circ: 72076 Paid. *Indexed:* A22. *Bk. rev.:* 50, 200 words. *Aud.:* Hs, Ga.

The Artist's Magazine is designed for artists of all levels of accomplishment from beginner to professional. Most of the articles instruct and present various working methods, materials, tools, and techniques. Marketing information is provided, plus announcements of study opportunities and art competitions. The magazine is part of a larger resource accessible at the website that offers video tutorials, business tips, technical questions and answers, clinics, and much more. This is an educational and instructive publication that would be most useful for school art programs or public libraries. URL: https://www.artistsnetwork.com/

508. *Artlink.* [ISSN: 0727-1239] 1981. q. AUD 90 (Individuals, AUD 58; AUD 15 per issue). Artlink Australia, PO Box 182, Fullarton, SA 5063, Australia. Illus., adv. *Indexed:* A51. *Aud.:* Ac, Sa.

An Australian contemporary art magazine, *Artlink* has a scope that includes diverse visual-culture expression by the artists of Australia and the Asia-Pacific region. Articles on new media, Internet art, video, electronic arts, performance, photography, mixed media, and outsider and aboriginal art are presented. Each richly illustrated issue offers a wide range of viewpoints, examining broad themes important to the region, including the cultures of Australia and diasporic artists. Also included are a dozen or more short articles, regional news, and exhibition reviews. Recommended for libraries where there is an interest in contemporary art.

509. *ARTnews.* Former titles (until 1923): *American Art News;* (until 1904): *Hyde's Weekly Art News.* [ISSN: 0004-3273] 1902. q. USD 19.95 domestic; USD 29.95 Canada; USD 44.95 elsewhere. Ed(s): Sarah Douglas. ARTnews LLC, 110 Greene St, 2nd Fl, New York, NY 10012; info@artnews.com; http://www.artnews.com. Illus., adv. Circ: 65705. Microform: MIM; PQC. *Indexed:* A&ATA, A01, A06, A22, A51, AmHI, BRI, CBRI, F01, IIPA, MASUSE, MLA-IB. *Bk. rev.:* 3-4, 300-500 words. *Aud.:* Hs, Ga, Ac.

One of the oldest art magazines still in print, *ARTnews* is a primary source for keeping current with American and international contemporary art. In 2016 it went from a monthly to quarterly magazine, still focusing on major issues related to the art world market—"Reshaping the American Museum," "Queer Art," and "Los Angeles" are among the most recent themes. Targeted toward art professionals and serious collectors who wish to follow art trends globally. This standard art magazine is highly recommended for all libraries. The website offers news and information beyond the print issues. URL: www.artnews.com

510. *Beaux Arts Magazine.* [ISSN: 0757-2271] 1983. m. EUR 49. Beaux Arts Magazine, 3, carrefour de Weiden, Issy-les-Moulineaux, Paris, 92130, France; courrier@beauxartsmagazine.com. Illus., index, adv. Sample. Circ: 49000. *Indexed:* A22, A51, PdeR. *Bk. rev.:* Number and length vary. *Aud.:* Ga.

Published in France, *Beaux Arts Magazine* is a beautifully illustrated periodical aimed at the art collector. Articles are written for a general audience, and the scope covers all of Europe. Included are auction news and sales, exhibition announcements, museum events, interviews, a calendar of events, book reviews, and occasional performance and movie reviews. Written in French, but the American edition includes abstracts of the articles in English, which increases the utility of this attractive publication. Recommended for libraries with extensive art holdings. URL: www.beauxartsmagazine.com

511. *The Burlington Magazine.* Formerly (until 1948): *Burlington Magazine for Connoisseurs.* [ISSN: 0007-6287] 1903. m. GBP 870 (print & online eds.) Individuals, GBP 328 (print & online eds.)). Ed(s): Michael Hall. The Burlington Magazine Publications Ltd., 14-16 Dukes Rd, London, WC1H 9SZ, United Kingdom; editorial@burlington.org.uk. Illus., adv. Vol. ends: Dec. Reprint: PSC. *Indexed:* A&ATA, A06, A22, A51, BAS, CBRI, MLA-IB. *Bk. rev.:* 10-15, 1,000 words. *Aud.:* Ac.

Begun in 1903 to lavishly illustrate, attribute, discover, and document Western European art for connoisseurs, *Burlington Magazine* has long maintained a well-respected reputation among art historians and other scholars. Its aim and scope today cover all historical periods from prehistoric art to modern Western art, including works and artists outside of Europe. Its design is elegant, with lots of full-color images. Articles by experts in the field focus on new developments, historical documents, conservation practices, and the history of collecting art. Book reviews, shorter notices, obituaries, exhibition information, and a calendar of events round out this important journal. Limited content is accessible on the website. Recommended for all research collections in academic and special libraries. URL: www.burlington.org.uk/

512. *Canadian Art.* Formed by the merger of (1967-1984): *Arts Canada;* Which was formerly (until 1967): *Canadian Art;* (until 1943): *Maritime Art;* (1974-1984): *Artsmagazine;* Which was formerly (until 1974): *Art;* (until 1969): *Society of Canadian Artists. Journal.* [ISSN: 0825-3854] 1984. q. CAD 24 domestic; CAD 34 United States; CAD 42 elsewhere. Canadian Art Foundation, 215 Spadina Ave, Ste 320, Toronto, ON M5T 2C7, Canada. Illus., adv. Vol. ends: Winter. *Indexed:* A06, A51, BRI, C37. *Bk. rev.:* 1-3, 500 words. *Aud.:* Ga, Ac, Sa.

Published in part by the Canadian government, Canada Council, and the Ontario Arts Council, *Canadian Art* is a quarterly that is devoted to the visual arts of that country. It is beautifully designed, with many full-color images, and the subject matter covers painting, sculpture, illustration, design, architecture, photography, and film. Articles are not limited to any particular time period; however, profiles of individual contemporary artists with reproductions of their works or group shows predominate, making this an invaluable resource for contemporary Canadian art. The magazine's website is also worth bookmarking. This publication is aimed toward a general audience that includes art collectors and regular guests of art galleries. URL: www.canadianart.ca

Critical Inquiry. See Cultural Studies section.

513. *Flash Art.* [ISSN: 0394-1493] 1979. bi-m. Ed(s): Helena Kontova, Giancarlo Politi. Giancarlo Politi Editore, Via Carlo Farini 68, Milan, 20159, Italy; http://www.flashartonline.it. Illus., adv. *Indexed:* A06, A22, A51. *Bk. rev.:* 2-3, 600-900 words. *Aud.:* Ga, Ac.

Flash Art focuses on the international contemporary art world. Each issue contains news, exhibition reviews, interviews, and feature articles on two-dimensional, three-dimensional, performance art, video, and mixed-media works and their creators. Beautifully illustrated with large reproductions/ documentation of artwork, *Flash Art* complements these illustrations with thoughtful and timely writing. *Flash Art*'s website expands on the magazine with news, extra reviews, and commentary from its international contributors. In an effort to give readers and researchers open access to the magazine's history, *Flash Art* has begun to publish its archive online. Access is currently available back to 2006. Recommended as an important basic international source for all libraries with an interest in art and art criticism.

514. *Frieze: contemporary art and culture.* [ISSN: 0962-0672] 1991. 8x/yr. GBP 35 domestic; GBP 41 foreign; GBP 60 combined subscription (print & online eds.)). Ed(s): Rosalind Furness, Jennifer Higgie. Frieze Publishing Ltd., 1 Montclare St, London, E2 7EU, United Kingdom; http://www.frieze.com/. Adv. Sample. Circ: 26520. *Indexed:* A22, A51. *Bk. rev.:* 1, 1,000-1,500 words. *Aud.:* Ac, Sa.

London-based *Frieze* is the self-proclaimed "leading magazine of contemporary art and culture." This claim is supported not only by a half-dozen feature articles on the current European art scene and numerous gallery/ exhibition reviews, but also by extensive coverage of film, performance, books, and music. The editors give exposure to established but also very new artists in reviews, feature articles, and hundreds of full-color gallery ads in each packed issue. *Frieze* organizes multiple art fairs: Frieze London, Frieze New York, and Frieze Masters. The website offers full-text magazine content, art world news, and Frieze Art Fair updates. Recommended for all libraries that wish to provide access to international contemporary art. URL: www.frieze.com

515. *I F A R Journal.* Formerly (until 1998): *I F A R Reports;* Which was formed by the merger of (1981-1985): *Art Research News;* (1980-1985): *Stolen Art Alert;* Which was formerly (until 1980): *Art Theft Archive Newsletter.* [ISSN: 1098-1195] 1984. q. Free to members; Non-members, USD 75. International Foundation for Art Research, Inc., 500 Fifth Ave, New York, NY 10110; http://www.ifar.org. Illus., index, adv. Sample. *Indexed:* A51. *Aud.:* Sa.

IFAR Journal, published by the International Foundation for Art Research (IFAR), informs the art community about recent art theft, authentication, fraud, and art laws through feature articles. From its founding, *IFAR Journal* has been a resource for scholarship in authentication research, authenticating problematic works of art, and providing a clearinghouse for legal issues. Each issue contains four or five well-researched articles, plus brief discussions of art and the law, updates, and news items. Selections of stolen art, recovered and missing art are printed in each issue. As an advocate for the entire art community, *IFAR Journal* provides important research about provenance and attribution not found in other art journals. Appropriate for research and municipal libraries.

Journal of Aesthetic Education. See Cultural Studies section.

The Journal of Aesthetics and Art Criticism. See Cultural Studies section.

516. *The Journal of Canadian Art History.* [ISSN: 0315-4297] 1974. s-a. CAD 70. Ed(s): Martha Langford. Journal of Canadian Art History, Concordia University, 1455 boul. de Maisonneuve ouest, Montreal, QC H3G 1M8, Canada. Illus., index, adv. Refereed. Vol. ends: No. 2. Microform: PQC. *Indexed:* BRI, C37, MLA-IB, PdeR. *Bk. rev.:* 4-5, lengthy. *Aud.:* Ac, Sa.

The national art history journal in Canada, *JCAH* is a scholarly periodical devoted to the research of Canadian art, architecture, decorative arts, and photography. It includes all historical and contemporary periods, with articles that are sparingly illustrated in black-and-white. Both English- and French-language submissions are accepted, and three- or four-page summaries are translated into the other appropriate language. Also included on a regular basis are bibliographies, such as of individual artists and architects; theses and dissertations in Canadian art and architecture; and book reviews and reviews of exhibition catalogues specific to Canadian art. The journal's website provides pdf copies of back issues. Appropriate for research collections in academic libraries. URL: http://jcah-ahac.concordia.ca

517. *Journal of Pre-Raphaelite Studies.* Former titles (until 1992): *Journal of Pre-Raphaelite and Aesthetic Studies;* (until 1987): *Journal of Pre-Raphaelite Studies;* (until 1980): *Pre-Raphaelite Review.* [ISSN: 1060-149X] 1977. s-a. CAD 24; GBP 17. Ed(s): David Latham. Journal of Pre-Raphaelite Studies, c/o David Latham, 208 Stong College, York University, Toronto, ON M3J 1P3, Canada. Illus. Sample. Refereed. *Indexed:* AmHI, BRI, C37, MLA-IB. *Aud.:* Ac.

Founded to create a forum for the study of Pre-Raphaelite, Aesthetic, and Decadent art, culture, and literature of the nineteenth century, *JPRS* publishes research on renowned Pre-Raphaelite artists, as well as the cult of Pre-Raphaelites worldwide and its interaction with Victorian literary figures and Victorian culture and mores. A dozen papers, sparsely illustrated with black-and-white images, are printed in this small-scale, semi-annual journal. Articles include historical examinations and interdisciplinary studies on sexuality, consumerism, and industrial art. Although targeting a fairly narrow topic, *JPRS* is important for academic libraries with studies in nineteenth-century literary and art history programs.

518. ***Journal of the Warburg and Courtauld Institutes.*** Formerly (until 1940): *Warburg Institute. Journal.* [ISSN: 0075-4390] 1937. a. GBP 153.50. Warburg Institute, University of London, Woburn Sq, London, WC1H 0AB, United Kingdom; warburg.books@sas.ac.uk; http://warburg.sas.ac.uk/home/. Illus., index. Refereed. Reprint: PSC. *Indexed:* A06, A22, AmHI, MLA-IB. *Aud.:* Ac.

Published in a single volume, *JWCI* provides an outlet for scholarly research in art history and classical studies, especially as reflected in European art and letters. It is the scholarly journal for the University of London, School of Advanced Study, The Warburg Institute, and the University of London's Courtauld Institute of Art. The half-dozen lengthy scholarly articles in each edition are important not only to art historians but also to scholars in religion, science, literature, sociology, philosophy, and anthropology. Recommended for all academic libraries that support programs of cultural and intellectual history and other special research collections.

519. ***Journal of Visual Culture.*** [ISSN: 1470-4129] 2002. 3x/yr. USD 1043 (print & online eds.)). Ed(s): Marquard Smith. Sage Publications Ltd., 1 Oliver's Yard, 55 City Rd, London, EC1Y 1SP, United Kingdom; info@sagepub.com; https://www.sagepub.com/. Sample. Refereed. Reprint: PSC. *Indexed:* A01, A22, A47, A51, E01, F01, IBSS, MLA-IB. *Bk. rev.:* Number and length vary. *Aud.:* Ac, Sa.

This is an international and interdisciplinary scholarly journal, with editors from the United States and Europe. The *Journal of Visual Culture* "promotes research, scholarship and critical engagement with visual cultures." Authored by professors, scholars, and critics in the humanities and social sciences, six to eight thought-provoking articles that are featured in each issue examine ideas, concepts, metaphors, and philosophies in international visual and cultural practices. Topics covered include copy, reproduction, race, simulation, spectacle, and other critical topics. Issues include authored book reviews relating to the field. Appropriate for academic libraries.

520. ***Juxtapoz: art & culture.*** [ISSN: 1077-8411] 1994. q. USD 29.99 domestic; USD 75 Canada; USD 80 elsewhere. High Speed Productions, Inc., 1303 Underwood Ave, San Francisco, CA 94124; orders@hsproductions.com; http://www.hsproductions.com/. *Indexed:* A51. *Aud.:* Ga.

Juxtapoz is an art and culture magazine that bridges the world of fine art with street art, graffiti, and other alternative forms of art. Regular columns include travel, design, fashion, exhibition reviews and previews, and product reviews. These columns are supported by feature-length articles on early to mid career artists. *Juxtapoz* shines with its focus on large, detailed reproductions of artwork and informative interviews. This magazine is highly recommended for public libraries that are looking for youth culture and arts titles as well as academic libraries that support art programs.

521. ***Koreana: Korean art and culture.*** [ISSN: 1016-0744] 1987. q. KRW 18000 domestic; USD 33 in Japan, Hong Kong, Taiwan & China; USD 37 elsewhere. Korea Foundation, 10th Fl, Diplomatic Center Bldg, 2558 Nambusunhwanno, Seocho-gu, PO Box 227, Seoul, 137-863, Korea, Republic of; http://www.kf.or.kr/. Adv. Circ: 9000. *Indexed:* AmHI, BAS, MLA-IB. *Aud.:* Ga, Ac, Sa.

This beautifully illustrated, quarterly magazine in English is devoted to traditional and contemporary Korean art and culture. Four to six feature articles typically revolve around a theme such as weddings, traditional and contemporary; Korean perceptions of life and death; or national treasures such as the Gyujanggak archives. Regular departments include interviews with architects and artists, cuisine and arts of living, discovering Korea, a featured masterpiece, an art review, and a small section devoted to Korean literature. Much full-text content from current and archived issues can be found for free on the magazine's website. Recommended for academic libraries and large public libraries. URL: www.koreana.or.kr

522. ***Leonardo & Leonardo Music Journal.*** [ISSN: 0024-094X] 1968. 6x/yr. USD 786 (print & online eds.)). Ed(s): Roger F Malina. M I T Press, One Rogers St, Cambridge, MA 02142-1209; journals-cs@mit.edu; http://mitpress.mit.edu/. Illus., adv. Refereed. *Indexed:* A&ATA, A01, A06, A22, A51, E01, EIP, MLA-IB. *Bk. rev.:* 10-15, 2,000+ words. *Aud.:* Ac, Sa.

Leonardo focuses on the arts as they intersect with the scientific disciplines and developing technologies, within an international scope and from an academic perspective. This journal attempts to foster communication between technology-minded artists by providing information on current, emerging, and historical trends in the use of science in the arts. Issues contain artists' statements, interviews, general articles, and special sections all related to the journal's mission. *Leonardo Music Journal* (*LMJ*) began publication in 1991 as a companion to *Leonardo,* documenting the ideas of composers, musicians, sound artists, and instrument builders. *LMJ* is published annually and includes a downloadable audio companion with each issue. The website includes sample articles, cumulative indexing, and general information about the journal, the society, and relevant news and events. Recommended for academic libraries, especially those who serve art, new media, and/or science programs. URL: www.leonardo.info

523. ***Master Drawings.*** [ISSN: 0025-5025] 1963. q. USD 125 domestic; USD 160 foreign; USD 45 per issue. Ed(s): Jane Turner. Master Drawings Association, Inc., 225 Madison Ave, New York, NY 10016-3405; administrator@masterdrawings.org . Illus., index, adv. Refereed. Vol. ends: No. 4. *Indexed:* A06, A22. *Bk. rev.:* Number varies, essay length. *Aud.:* Ac, Sa.

This journal is published by the Master Drawings Association of New York, and its audience is primarily art historians, collectors, and dealers. This academic quarterly provides a venue for the exclusive study of drawings and occasionally other works on paper, for example, engraving and watercolor since the Renaissance. Thematic issues concentrate mainly on the old masters up to 1900, and are written for scholars. Authors tend to be art history fellows, professors, and museum curators, and they focus on new developments and reattributions of specific drawings. Appropriate for academic libraries that support art history programs.

524. ***Modern Painters: art, architecture, design, performance, film.*** [ISSN: 0953-6698] 1988. 8x/yr. USD 59.99 combined subscription domestic (print & online eds.); USD 79.99 combined subscription Canada (print & online eds.); USD 99.99 combined subscription elsewhere (print & online eds.)). BlouinArtinfo Corp, 88 Laight St, New York, NY 10013; http://www.blouinartinfocorp.com/. Adv. *Indexed:* A01, A22, A51. *Bk. rev.:* 5-8, 500 words. *Aud.:* Ac, Sa.

Not devoted exclusively to painting as the title implies, *Modern Painters* brings together leading voices in visual arts criticism and analysis—academics, writers, and artists—to provide stimulating discussions of current practices in international art. Stating a mission to "not only report, but define and shape important events and trends in the art and cultural worlds," *Modern Painters* succeeds admirably. Feature articles are devoted to politics and art, reviews of current practices, introduction of new artists, and examination of important movements and media. Full-page color gallery and exhibition ads predominate in this monthly. Individual artist's studio practices are often featured, and book reviews and extensive not-to-be-missed exhibitions are a regular occurrence. An important international title for all comprehensive art collections in any library.

525. ***Mousse.*** [ISSN: 2035-2565] 2006. q. EUR 40 domestic; EUR 50 foreign. Ed(s): Edoardo Bonaspetti, Chiara Leoni. Mousse Magazine and Publishing, Via De Amicis 53, Milan, 20123, Italy; info@moussemagazine.it; http://moussemagazine.it/. Illus., adv. *Indexed:* A51. *Bk. rev.:* 3-5. *Aud.:* Ac, Sa.

Established in 2006, *Mousse* is a quarterly international contemporary art magazine. The magazine's focus is on interviews, conversations, and essays by artists, scholars, and curators. This large-format magazine was formerly printed on newsprint but newer issues have been printed on glossy stock. It is beautifully illustrated with many large color images. Issues often include micro serial publications that focus on a specific phenomenon within the field of contemporary art or curating. Examples of these past publications include *Ten Fundamental Questions of Curating* and *The Artist as Curator*. Highly recommended for museum and academic libraries that serve art and/or art history programs. URL: www.moussemagazine.it

526. ***New American Paintings.*** [ISSN: 1066-2235] 1993. bi-m. USD 89 domestic; USD 139 Canada; USD 189 elsewhere. Ed(s): Steven T Zevitas. The Open Studios Press, 450 Harrison Ave., 47, Boston, MA 02118. Illus., adv. *Aud.:* Ga, Ac, Sa.

New American Paintings is a unique publication in the art world. Rather than including a number of interviews, critical essays, or artist profiles, each well-constructed, lushly illustrated issue features page after page of paintings (one per page), broken up only by a brief biography, artist statement, and contact information for each of the painters presented. The painters in each issue are usually culled from a specific regional juried exhibition, so a variety of lesser-known artists are brought to light in each issue. Recommended for all libraries that support contemporary art practices.

527. ***New Criterion.*** [ISSN: 0734-0222] 1982. 10x/yr. USD 48 combined subscription domestic (print & online eds.); USD 62 combined subscription Canada (print & online eds.); USD 70 combined subscription elsewhere (print & online eds.)). Ed(s): James Panero, Roger Kimball. Foundation for Cultural Review, 900 Broadway, Ste 602, New York, NY 10003. Illus., adv. Microform: PQC. *Indexed:* A01, A22, A51, AmHI, BRI, MLA-IB. *Bk. rev.:* 3, lengthy. *Aud.:* Ga, Ac.

New Criterion is published by the Foundation for Cultural Review, which gives the magazine a much wider scope than strictly visual arts. Poets, authors, public policy scholars, humanities lecturers, and critics all contribute to create a vehicle for poetry, arts criticism, and commentary on cultural life in America. Departments in theater, art, music, and the media provide substantial reviews, and exhibition listings and book reviews make regular appearances in this periodical. Engaging and interesting to the informed reader, *New Criterion* is recommended for both public and academic libraries.

Nka. See Africa section.

528. ***October.*** [ISSN: 0162-2870] 1976. q. USD 367 (print & online eds.)). M I T Press, One Rogers St, Cambridge, MA 02142-1209; journals-cs@mit.edu; http://mitpress.mit.edu/. Illus., adv. *Indexed:* A01, A22, A51, AmHI, E01, MLA-IB. *Aud.:* Ac.

October is an important voice of art criticism and theory of twentieth and twenty-first century art. Founded in New York by a group of theoreticians, it has focused on themes of Deconstruction, poststructuralist art theory, and other intellectual discourse in America. Frequently monothematic, issues offer approximately a half-dozen lengthy scholarly discourses of the societal, political, or cultural impact of the visual arts. Contributors are scholars, critics, and artists from a variety of academic disciplines, with the arts, film, and literature predominating. Intellectually rigorous, *October* will appeal to many scholars in the humanities. Recommended for academic research collections.

529. ***Oxford Art Journal.*** [ISSN: 0142-6540] 1978. 3x/yr. EUR 440. Ed(s): Jo Applin. Oxford University Press, Great Clarendon St, Oxford, OX2 6DP, United Kingdom; onlinequeries.uk@oup.com; http://global.oup.com. Illus., adv. Sample. Refereed. Vol. ends: No. 2. Reprint: PSC. *Indexed:* A22, A51, E01. *Bk. rev.:* 8, essay length. *Aud.:* Ac.

A venue for critical analysis of the visual arts, primarily Western, the *Oxford Art Journal* has contributed to the reexamination of art history through social context and political interpretations. Seven to ten scholarly, peer-reviewed papers represent research in the visual arts and related historical and philosophical issues, from antiquity to contemporary art practice. This title is well illustrated with color and black-and-white photos. Five or six signed book reviews—and the focus on the historical, social commentary of art—make this title appropriate for college and university libraries.

530. ***Print Quarterly.*** [ISSN: 0265-8305] 1984. q. GBP 85 domestic; GBP 101 in US & Canada; GBP 92 elsewhere. Ed(s): Rhoda Eitel-Porter. Print Quarterly Publications, 10 Chester Row, London, SW1W 9JH, United Kingdom. Illus., adv. Refereed. Vol. ends: Dec. *Indexed:* A22, A51. *Bk. rev.:* Number and length vary. *Aud.:* Ac, Sa.

Print Quarterly is the leading publication in its field. Devoted to the art of the printed image, whether engraving, intaglio, woodprint, lithograph, drypoint, or zincograph, this title covers the history of printmaking from the fifteenth century to the present. Features include three to four peer-reviewed articles and in-depth book reviews. The publication is well illustrated, and the articles are written for academicians, although collectors would also find this a very useful source of information. It includes unique sections devoted to news items in the print and graphic arts world (new attributions, the latest serial publications, brief articles on societies) that go beyond the ordinary current events news. This journal is recommended for academic art libraries, museums, and other special collections.

531. ***Public Art Review.*** [ISSN: 1040-211X] 1989. s-a. USD 60 domestic; USD 84 foreign. Ed(s): Karen Olson. Forecast Public Art, 2324 University Ave W, Ste 104, St. Paul, MN 55114; http://www.forecastpublicart.org. Adv. Refereed. *Indexed:* A22, A51. *Aud.:* Ga, Ac, Sa.

Public Art Review is produced by Forecast Public Art, a St. Paul-based consulting group. The magazine's scope includes not only local public artworks but also regional and national as well. Striving to encourage public art and artists, *PAR* features articles on maintaining and conserving public art; consulting and managing projects—often of city-wide plans; and exploring critically contemporary public art in America, whether smaller-scale individual pieces or large-scale, big-name projects. Occasional pieces cover international public art constructions. Recommended for art, architecture, and urban planning collections in large public and academic libraries.

532. ***R A C A R.*** [ISSN: 0315-9906] 1974. s-a. Free to members. Association d'Art des Universites du Canada, 360 Fairbrooke Court, Arnprior, ON K7S 0E6, Canada. Illus. Refereed. Circ: 900. Vol. ends: No. 2. *Indexed:* A51, BRI, C37. *Bk. rev.:* 6, essay length. *Aud.:* Ac.

RACAR is published by the Universities Art Association of Canada, with the assistance of the Social Sciences and Humanities Research Council of Canada, and it is the leading scholarly Canadian art journal. Peer-reviewed articles feature lengthy treatments of Western art history, written in either French or English and illustrated with black-and-white photos. Recent articles include critical curating in museums, liminal spaces and bodies, and Chris Burden's work as institutional critique, among others. Interviews and exhibition reviews are regularly included. Some articles are available at no charge on their website. Appropriate for academic and research collections. http://www.racar-racar.com/

533. ***Raw Vision.*** [ISSN: 0955-1182] 1989. q. GBP 37 (Individuals, GBP 27). Ed(s): John Maizels. Raw Vision Ltd., PO Box 44, Watford, WD25 8LN, United Kingdom. Adv. *Indexed:* A51. *Bk. rev.:* 5-10, 1,000+ words. *Aud.:* Ga, Ac.

Raw Vision is an international journal dedicated to art and artists working outside of the institutionalized art world. Each issue includes news, exhibition reviews, and feature-length articles on these untrained artists and movements such as art brut, outsider art, and folk art. *Raw Vision*'s intended audience ranges from curators and scholars to the casual fan of art. The journal is heavily illustrated with many large color reproductions. *Raw Vision*'s website includes article excerpts, current news, and obituaries. Recommended for museum and academic libraries that serve art programs and public libraries with an interest in nontraditional art. URL: www.rawvision.com

534. ***Revue de l'Art.*** [ISSN: 0035-1326] 1968. q. EUR 80 domestic; EUR 95 foreign. Ophrys, 25 Rue Ginoux, Paris, 75737, France; editions.ophrys@ophrys.fr; http://www.ophrys.fr. Illus. *Indexed:* A&ATA, A22. *Bk. rev.:* 4-5, essay length. *Aud.:* Ac.

Under the auspices of the French Committee of Art History, this journal provides international scholarship on Western art from the Middle Ages through current times, often focusing on the art of France. Abstracts occasionally summarize the contents of the French-language articles in English and German. Each issue includes book reviews, biographical essays, a calendar of museum exhibitions, and critical bibliographies along with studies in recent art history scholarship. Appropriate for research collections in academic or special libraries in the arts.

535. *Sculpture.* Incorporates (1993-1995): *Maquette;* Which was formerly (until 1993): *Sculpture Maquette;* Former titles (until 1987): *International Sculpture;* (until 1985): *Sculptors International;* (until 1982): *International Sculpture Center. Bulletin;* (until 1977): *National Sculpture Center. Bulletin.* [ISSN: 0889-728X] 196?. 10x/yr. Free to members. Ed(s): Glenn Harper. International Sculpture Center, 19 Fairgrounds Road, Ste B, Hamilton, NJ 08619; http://www.sculpture.org/. Illus., adv. Vol. ends: Dec. *Indexed:* A22, A51. *Bk. rev.:* 10-12, 150 words. *Aud.:* Ga, Ac, Sa.

Published by the International Sculpture Center, this is the only international publication of its kind devoted exclusively to all forms of contemporary sculpture. Richly illustrated with full-color photography, the feature articles concentrate on traditional forms of three-dimensional arts. With gallery ads, news briefs, exhibition announcements, interviews with sculptors, and reviews of installations, this is a useful title to artists, collectors, and scholars. The website offers features, reviews, videos, and other daily content. Recommended for all academic libraries with significant art programs and for larger public libraries.

536. *Tribal Art.* Former titles (until 2006): *Tribal;* (until 2002): *The World of Tribal Arts.* 1994. q. EUR 65 in Europe; USD 85 elsewhere; EUR 20 per issue in Europe. Primedia sprl, B.P. 18, Arquennes, 7181, Belgium. Illus., adv. Sample. *Indexed:* A47, A51, MLA-IB. *Bk. rev.:* 8-12, 1,000+ words. *Aud.:* Ga, Ac, Sa.

Tribal Art is dedicated to fine and antique traditional art from Africa, Oceania, Indonesia, and the Americas. Each extensively illustrated issue features articles and information on art and antiques from specific tribes, geographic areas, and time periods. It also includes features on collectors, collecting, and exhibitions and auctions. *Tribal Art* provides a unique perspective on some of the non-canonical histories of art. Recommended for museum, academic, and public libraries that have an interest in indigenous arts and antiques. URL: www.tribalartmagazine.com/

537. *West 86th: a journal of decorative arts, design history, and material culture.* Formerly (until Mar.2010): *Studies in the Decorative Arts.* [ISSN: 2153-5531] 1993. s-a. USD 212 (print & online eds.)). Ed(s): Paul Stirton. University of Chicago Press, 1427 E 60th St, Chicago, IL 60637; subscriptions@press.uchicago.edu; http://www.journals.uchicago.edu. Illus., adv. Sample. Refereed. Reprint: PSC. *Indexed:* A51, BRI, CBRI. *Bk. rev.:* Number varies, essay length. *Aud.:* Ga, Ac.

West 86th, formerly titled *Studies in the Decorative Arts,* emphasizes analytical and interpretative scholarly research of the decorative arts and design history, regardless of media, culture, era, or geographic location. Recent issues highlight research from all time periods and all regions. Focusing on the designed objects as documents of material culture and placing them within their social and political contexts, the journal provides a forum for new research in the field. Four to six peer-reviewed articles are sparsely illustrated with black-and-white photographs. Each issue includes signed reviews of important new books, often including newly translated tomes, and exhibitions. Recommended for larger public libraries and college and university libraries.

538. *Woman's Art Journal.* [ISSN: 0270-7993] 1980. s-a. USD 111 (print & online eds.) Individuals, USD 44). Ed(s): Joan Marter, Margaret Barlow. Old City Publishing, Inc., 628 N 2nd St, Philadelphia, PA 19123; info@oldcitypublishing.com; http://www.oldcitypublishing.com. Illus., index, adv. Sample. Refereed. Vol. ends: No. 2. Microform: PQC. *Indexed:* A22, A51, BRI, FemPer, MLA-IB. *Bk. rev.:* 5-13, 400-3,500 words, signed. *Aud.:* Hs, Ga, Ac, Sa.

Intended to focus as a platform for re-examining feminist ideas, this publication covers women in the visual arts and related areas from antiquity to the present, although recent issues focus on the modern era through the present decade. Each issue is divided roughly into two sections: "Portraits, Issues and Insights," about individual women artists or genres, and "Reviews," which covers exhibitions and publications by and about women artists. Contributors include artists, critics, art professionals, and academics; all voices are welcome. Issues include high-quality black-and-white and color illustrations. Of interest for art and women's studies collections.

539. *Word & Image: a journal of verbal/visual enquiry.* [ISSN: 0266-6286] 1985. q. GBP 996 (print & online eds.)). Routledge, 4 Park Sq, Milton Park, Abingdon, OX14 4RN, United Kingdom; subscriptions@tandf.co.uk; http://www.tandfonline.com. Illus., adv. Sample. Refereed. Reprint: PSC. *Indexed:* A01, A22, A51, AmHI, B01, E01, MLA-IB. *Bk. rev.:* Number varies, 1 page. *Aud.:* Ac, Sa.

Word & Image is an interdisciplinary journal that focuses on the "study of the encounters, dialogues and mutual collaboration (or hostility) between verbal and visual languages," regardless of media. As such, it is important to literary critics, art historians, linguists, social historians, philosophers, and psychologists alike. Scholarly articles examine the many complicated relationships between words and images. Issues sometimes revolve around a central theme, with guest editors invited to participate, but most cover a variety of subjects from discourse of aesthetics and ontology to Gilded Age political culture. Articles are primarily in English, but French and German occasionally appear. Strictly a scholar's resource, it is recommended for academic libraries. Universities that support programs in linguistics and literature, art history, and communications will find this journal indispensable.

540. *Zeitschrift fuer Kunstgeschichte.* Formed by the merger of (1876-1932): *Repertorium fuer Kunstwissenschaft;* (1866-1932): *Zeitschrift fuer Bildende Kunst;* (1923-1932): *Jahrbuch fuer Kunstwissenschaft;* Which was formerly (1908-1923): *Monatshefte fuer Kunstwissenschaft;* (1905-1908): *Monatshefte der Kunstwissenschaftlichen Literatur.* [ISSN: 0044-2992] 1932. 4x/yr. EUR 98. Deutscher Kunstverlag GmbH, Schlierseestr 5, Muenchen, 81541, Germany; info@deutscherkunstverlag.de; http://www.deutscherkunstverlag.de. Illus., index, adv. Refereed. Vol. ends: No. 4. Reprint: PSC. *Indexed:* A06, A22, A51, MLA-IB. *Bk. rev.:* 3-4, lengthy. *Aud.:* Ac.

The focus is scholarly research, especially issues pertaining to methodology and historiography in all periods of art history, making this leading German publication a standard in the field since the 1930s. Black-and-white and occasionally color photography illustrate the five or six peer-reviewed articles that represent international art history research. Articles appear in German, English, French, or Italian. Lengthy book reviews provide extensive treatment of three or four books in each issue. Appropriate for museum and academic libraries, especially those with art history programs.

Museum Publications

541. *Archives of American Art Journal.* Former titles (until 1964): *Archives of American Art. Quarterly Bulletin;* (until 1962): *Archives of American Art. Bulletin.* [ISSN: 0003-9853] 1960. s-a. USD 88. Ed(s): Emily D Shapiro, Tanya Sheehan. University of Chicago Press, 1427 E 60th St, Chicago, IL 60637; custserv@press.uchicago.edu; http://www.journals.uchicago.edu. Illus. Refereed. *Indexed:* A06, A22, A51, MLA-IB. *Bk. rev.:* Number and length vary. *Aud.:* Ac, Sa.

The Archives of American Art in the Smithsonian Institution provides researchers with access to the largest collection of documents on the history of the visual arts in the United States from the eighteenth century to the recent past. Its journal publishes cultural and social research about the permanent collections of the archives, encouraging new scholarship and writing on primary sources. Three or four articles in each issue feature papers of artists, collectors, art historians, and other art world figures, and records of dealers, museums, and other institutions. Book reviews and regional reports that cover new acquisitions to the archives round out this important resource of historical documentation. Highly recommended for research collections.

542. *International Review of African American Art.* Formerly (until 1984): *Black Art.* [ISSN: 1045-0920] 1976. q. Free to members; Non-members, USD 42. Hampton University Museum, 100 E Queen St, Hampton, VA 23668; museum@hamptonu.edu; http://museum.hamptonu.edu. Illus. Refereed. Vol. ends: No. 4. *Indexed:* A01, A22, A51, AmHI, BRI, MLA-IB. *Bk. rev.:* Number and length vary. *Aud.:* Hs, Ga, Ac, Sa.

The International Review of African American Art (IRAAA), published by the Hampton University Museum, has long provided an important voice for visual and performing artists of African American heritage. This full-color, well-illustrated journal frequently chooses one aspect of African American art for the subject of an issue, most recently focusing on emerging artists, Norman Lewis (1909-1979), and architects of the African Diaspora. It includes a handful of book or exhibition reviews and noteworthy news on contemporary artists or new acquisitions. Cultural history and social themes related to the experience of the African American artist make this of interest to anyone conducting research in African American culture or American Studies. Additional content is available on the website. Recommended for all academic and large public libraries. URL: iraaa.museum.hamptonu.edu/

543. *Metropolitan Museum Journal.* [ISSN: 0077-8958] 1968. a. USD 110. University of Chicago Press, 1427 E 60th St, Chicago, IL 60637; custserv@press.uchicago.edu; http://www.press.uchicago.edu. Illus. Refereed. *Indexed:* A06, A22, BAS, MLA-IB. *Aud.:* Ac, Sa.

This journal publishes new scholarly research that examines works of art in the permanent collection of the Metropolitan Museum of Art and related matters. Articles investigate the cultural context of these art objects and cover archival research and technical analyses. Contributors are usually specialists, researchers, or museum staff. The journal's website provides pdf copies of the entire archive. Because the Metropolitan Museum is one of the premier museums in the United States, this publication is highly recommended for all research collections in academic, museum, and special libraries. URL: www.metmuseum.org/research/metpublications

544. *Metropolitan Museum of Art Bulletin.* Incorporates (1986-1988): *Metropolitan Museum of Art. Recent Acquisitions;* Which was formerly (1979-1985): *Metropolitan Museum of Art. Notable Acquisitions.* [ISSN: 0026-1521] 1905. q. Free to members; Non-members, USD 50. Ed(s): Mark Polizzotti, Sue Potter. Metropolitan Museum of Art, 1000 Fifth Ave, New York, NY 10028; communications@metmuseum.org; http://www.metmuseum.org. Illus. Sample. Vol. ends: No. 4. *Indexed:* A&ATA, A01, A06, AmHI, BAS, MLA-IB. *Aud.:* Ga, Ac, Sa.

One of the two Metropolitan Museum of Art publications, the *Bulletin* focuses on one artist, theme, historical period, or item from the permanent collection, in one lengthy article for each issue. Most contributions are written by museum personnel, but occasionally outside scholars may compose an article. Every two years the fall issue of the Met's quarterly *Bulletin* celebrates notable recent acquisitions and gifts to the collection. Recent acquisitions are noted in the fall issue. The primary audience for this publication is museum members and art historians, but it is highly recommended for all academic libraries.

545. *The Outsider.* 1996. a. Free to members. Ed(s): Janet Franz. Intuit. The Center for Intuitive and Outsider Art, 756 N Milwaukee Ave, Chicago, IL 60622; intuit@art.org; http://www.art.org. *Bk. rev.:* 2-5, 1,000+ words. *Aud.:* Ga, Ac, Sa.

This annual publication from Intuit: the Center for Intuitive and Outsider Art focuses on outsider art, folk art, intuitive art, and art brut, which are all featured at this museum and are within the unique niche of the art world that it serves. *The Outsider* includes features on artists as well as surveys and studies of aspects of outsider art. Recommended for museum and academic libraries with an interest in outsider art.

546. *La Revue des Musees de France.* Former titles (until 2008): *La Revue du Louvre et des Musees de France;* (until 1961): *La Revue des Arts;* (until 1951): *Musees de France;* (until 1948): *Bulletin des Musees de France;* (until 1915): *Les Musees de France;* (until 1911): *Bulletin des Musees de France;* (until 1908): *Musees et Monuments de France.* [ISSN: 1962-4271] 1951. bi-m. EUR 69. Ed(s): Danielle Gaborit Chopin, Jean Pierre Cuzin. Editions de la Reunion des Musees Nationaux, 49 Rue Etienne Marcel, Paris, Cedex 1 75039, France; http://www.rmn.fr. Illus., adv. Refereed. *Indexed:* A&ATA, BAS. *Aud.:* Ac, Sa.

This beautiful publication with lavish illustrations provides coverage of the special collections and works of art in the Louvre and other national museums of France. Information on new acquisitions, temporary exhibitions, and restoration work is regularly featured. Exhibition reviews, subject bibliographies, and calendars of events are also included. The text is in French; abstracts are in English and German. Recommended for all academic and museum libraries.

547. *Studies in Modern Art.* [ISSN: 1058-997X] 1991. irreg. Members, USD 22.50; Non-members, USD 25. Museum of Modern Art, 11 W 53rd St, New York, NY 10019; http://www.moma.org. Illus. *Aud.:* Ga, Ac, Sa.

Although not published with any regularity, these monographs issued serially by the Museum of Modern Art are worth noting. They showcase important collections, individual works of art, and special programs at the museum. The publication maintains high standards of scholarship and makes a significant contribution to the serious study of contemporary art. Issues are frequently monothematic. The most recent issue was published as an ebook exclusively. Issues are appropriate for academic, museum, and large public libraries.

548. *Studies in the History of Art.* Supersedes in part (in 1972): *Report and Studies in the History of Art.* [ISSN: 0091-7338] 1967. irreg. National Gallery of Art, 2000B S Club Dr, Landover, MD 20785; pressinfo@nga.gov; http://www.nga.gov. Illus. *Indexed:* A06, A22. *Aud.:* Ga, Ac, Sa.

Designed to document scholarly symposia, this series-as-a-book is sponsored in part by the National Gallery of Art's Center for Advanced Study of the Visual Arts. Published irregularly, each monothematic volume presents a dozen or so research papers from a single symposium, fostering study of the history, theory, and criticism of art, architecture, and urbanism. Recent topics cover the art and artifacts of the American Civil War, the ancient world of Naples, and modernism and landscape architecture. An important resource for research art collections in all institutions.

549. *Tate Etc.* Formerly (until 2004): *Tate.* [ISSN: 1743-8853] 1993. 3x/yr. GBP 15 domestic; GBP 17 in Europe; EUR 21 in Europe. Ed(s): Simon Grant. Tate Etc., Millbank, London, SW1P 4RG, United Kingdom; subscriptions@tate.org.uk; http://www.tate.org.uk. Adv. *Indexed:* A51. *Aud.:* Ga, Ac, Sa.

The Tate Gallery's contribution to museum literature is refreshing in the presentation of its collections in a contemporary art-magazine format. *Tate Etc* features essays, artist interviews, briefs, artistic collaborations, and updates about the Tate's vast holdings that range from 1500 through contemporary art. A significant portion of the magazine is devoted to modern and contemporary international art in all media. Unlike with most publishers, every past issue is available free online, with many images, but not all. Recommended for large public libraries and academic and special collections. URL: http://www.tate.org.uk/art/tate-etc

550. *Winterthur Portfolio: a journal of American material culture.* Incorporates: *Winterthur Conference Report.* [ISSN: 0084-0416] 1964. 3x/yr. USD 263. Ed(s): Catharine Dann Roeber. University of Chicago Press, 1427 E 60th St, Chicago, IL 60637; subscriptions@press.uchicago.edu; http://www.journals.uchicago.edu. Illus., index, adv. Sample. Refereed. Reprint: PSC. *Indexed:* A01, A06, A22, A51, AmHI, BRI, MLA-IB. *Bk. rev.:* Number and length vary. *Aud.:* Ac.

Winterthur Portfolio is an academic journal published on behalf of the Winterthur Museum. It covers the arts in America with emphasis on the cultural framework in which the objects reside, including American Studies, technology and design, architecture, decorative arts, material culture, as well as fine art. Two to three articles are featured, drawing scholarly expertise from diverse fields of cultural geography, ethnology, anthropology, archaeology, art history, folk studies, and literature, to name a few. Articles are often lavishly illustrated with both color and black-and-white photography. A selection of book reviews of academic note are offered in each issue. Important for special and academic libraries, especially those with American Studies programs.

551. ***Women in the Arts.*** Formerly (until 1991): *National Museum of Women in the Arts News.* [ISSN: 1058-7217] 1983. 3x/yr. Free to members. National Museum of Women in the Arts, 1250 New York Ave, NW, Washington, DC 20005; member@nmwa.org; http://www.nmwa.org. Adv. *Aud.:* Ac, Sa.

Produced by the National Museum of Women in the Arts (NMWA), this glossy magazine recognizes the achievements of women artists, musicians, authors, and other contributors to world culture. The museum exists to promote women in all the visual arts, music, theater, film, and literature throughout the world. This broad mission allows for a wide variety of topics to be featured in each issue while highlighting the museum's collection, contemporary and historical. *Women in the Arts* regularly reports on new acquisitions, regional updates, and other NMWA news, plus it contains a calendar of events and exhibitions. Available with an annual museum membership, *Women in the Arts* is recommended for museum, academic, and large public libraries.

■ ASIA AND THE PACIFIC

Christine K. Oka, Library Instruction Coordinator, 270 Snell Library, Northeastern University, Boston, MA 02115; c.oka@northeastern.edu

Introduction

In this section, you will find a selection of publications that reflect the diversity of area studies, as well as the geographic areas of Asia and the Pacific. The scope of this section is to cover collectively the area of Asia and the Pacific; for this reason, journals about individual countries are not included. Most of the publications are available online, a reflection of the competing space needs of libraries to meet the demand for more collaborative work space, meeting rooms, and makerspaces. Another move to online may be due to the cost of producing and delivering a physical issue; one popular travel magazine about traveling to islands, including those in the Pacific, recently went from glossy print format to online only.

This section aims to help by providing a selection of subscription and open-access titles that could be used in support of research at academic and special libraries, and for public libraries that serve users with an interest in Asia and the Pacific.

Basic Periodicals

Asia Policy, Harvard Journal of Asiatic Studies, Journal of Asian Studies, The Contemporary Pacific.

Basic Abstracts and Indexes

America: History and Life, AnthroSource, Bibliography of Asian Studies (BAS), Historical Abstracts, IBSS, PAIS International, Sociological Abstracts.

Archives of Asian Art. See Art section.

552. ***Asia - Pacific Review.*** [ISSN: 1343-9006] 1994. s-a. GBP 339 (print & online eds.)). Ed(s): Terri Nii. Routledge, 4 Park Sq, Milton Park, Abingdon, OX14 4RN, United Kingdom; http://www.tandfonline.com. Illus., index, adv. Sample. Refereed. Reprint: PSC. *Indexed:* A01, A22, BAS, E01, IBSS, P61. *Aud.:* Hs, Ga, Ac, Sa.

Asia-Pacific Review analyzes global political, economic, security, energy, and environmental issues, with specific emphasis on the Asia-Pacific region. While the publication is a product of the Nakasone Yasuhiro Peace Institute (NPI), "an independent, non-profit research institute founded in Tokyo by former Prime Minister Yasuhiro Nakasone..." the review is published by Taylor & Francis Online. *Asia-Pacific Review* aims to publish peer-reviewed research by "leading scholars, diplomats, politicians and business people who are actively involved in making decisions that affect the Asia-Pacific region in the twenty-first century." Recent articles discuss China's foreign aid—the aid they receive as well as aid they provide to other developing countries; the Trump-Kim Summit; and a comparative study of happiness in Japan and the Netherlands. Articles are clearly written, provide historical background and context for their subjects and are accessible to general readers. The emphasis is to make this information available to all. Highly recommended for academic and special libraries; this also would be a useful resource for high school and public libraries as well.

553. ***Asia Policy.*** [ISSN: 1559-0968] 2006. s-a. USD 150 (Individuals, USD 60). Ed(s): Jessica Keough, Mark W Frazier. National Bureau of Asian Research, 1414 NE 42nd St, Ste 300, Seattle, WA 98105; nbr@nbr.org; http://www.nbr.org. Sample. Refereed. *Indexed:* A22, E01. *Bk. rev.:* Number and length vary. *Aud.:* Ga, Ac, Sa.

This is "a peer-reviewed scholarly journal presenting policy-relevant academic research on the Asia-Pacific that draws clear and concise conclusions useful to today's policymakers." Published twice a year by the National Bureau of Asian Research, *Asia Policy* contains research notes of "new, important, and even exploratory conceptual frameworks or descriptive information" and analyses for policymakers. China's BRI (Belt and Road Initiative), a development and investment initiative to invest in infrastructure to Asia, Europe, and Africa is examined from a number of perspectives—China's cooperation with Pakistan, India's challenge to China, and how the United States responds to changing alliances. Articles are well written and accessible to academics, policy makers, and the general reader interested in these topics. Each issue also includes a "Book Review Roundtable," a collection of reviews and analyses of books, along with author responses. Highly recommended for all libraries.

554. ***Asian Ethnicity.*** [ISSN: 1463-1369] 2000. q. GBP 481 (print & online eds.)). Ed(s): Chih-yu Shih. Routledge, 4 Park Sq, Milton Park, Abingdon, OX14 4RN, United Kingdom; subscriptions@tandf.co.uk; http://www.tandfonline.com. Adv. Sample. Refereed. Reprint: PSC. *Indexed:* A01, A22, E01, IBSS, P61, SSA. *Bk. rev.:* Number and length vary. *Aud.:* Ga, Ac.

Published by Routledge, a member of the Taylor & Francis Group, *Asian Ethnicity* aims to move research on Asian ethnicity and identity away from being treated in a "balkanized" way "with anthropologists, economists, historians, political scientists, sociologists and others publishing their studies in single-discipline journals." This journal provides a cross-disciplinary forum for research "about ethnic groups and ethnic relations in the half of the world where questions of ethnicity now loom largest." While the journal may cover any time period, the emphasis is on the twentieth and twenty-first centuries. The geographical focus "bounded by Lake Baikal to the north, Japan to the east, Java to the south and the Caspian Sea to the west." A recent special issue about Chinese in Africa: "Chineseness" and the Complexities of Identities pushed the time period and geographical scope, as well as challenging the assumption the Chinese in Africa are a homogenous group. According to the article, "The Chinese diaspora in Africa range from descendents of migrants that settled in Africa in the seventeenth century to twenty-first century migrants." In addition to insightful articles, each issue has a section of two- to three-page book reviews; most books reviewed are in English. The Taylor & Francis Online journal website provides enhanced access tools for research with links to "Latest Articles" accessible online, helpful recommendations for related articles under "People also read." *Asian Ethnicity* is one of the Taylor & Francis and Routledge Open Select Journals, which gives authors the option, once their articles have passed peer-review, to publish their research as open access. The accompanying article processing charge (APC) includes the article in a highly regarded scholarly publication that is promoted to researchers, as well as increasing access. This can be measured by the journal platform's metrics for articles: number of article views, citations in CrossRef, Web of Science and Scopus, along with Altmetrics-counting article mentions on the number of times an article is accessed on social media sites, along with breakdowns identifying sources by country. Article mentions are also traced from Wikipedia, blogs, newspapers, policy documents, and many other sources. The interdisciplinary content makes this a good choice for academic libraries.

555. ***Asian Survey: a bimonthly review of contemporary Asian affairs.*** Supersedes (in 1961): *Far Eastern Survey;* Which was formerly (until 1935): *Institute of Pacific Relations. American Council. Memorandum.* [ISSN: 0004-4687] 1932. bi-m. USD 624 (print & online eds.)). Ed(s):

Uk Heo. University of California Press, Journals Division, 155 Grand Avenue, Ste 400, Oakland, CA 94612-3764; http://www.ucpress.edu/journals.php. Illus., index, adv. Sample. Refereed. Vol. ends: Dec. Microform: PQC. *Indexed:* A01, A22, BAS, C45, E01, ENW, IBSS, MLA-IB, P61. *Aud.:* Ac, Sa.

Asian Survey describes itself as "the journal that offers new and original insights on prominent policy issues in the Asian region with a particular focus on qualitative scholarship." With a new editor, there are plans to modify the scope of the journal to include "policy-based quantitative scholarship. . . and open the door to studies of Asian countries and people that use quantitative analysis methods (e.g., cross-national, time-series, game theory)." This is an acknowledgment of changes in academic scholarship by "embracing both qualitative and quantitative analysis." Journal coverage includes, but is not limited to, diplomacy, disarmament, missile defense, military, economic nationalism, and global capitalism. The in-depth analysis and commentary on political, economic, and social developments in Asia are what have made it the "sourcebook for sound analyses of current events, governmental policies, socio-economic development and financial institutions." Articles may be about the politics of inter-caste marriage in India, or the relationship between business and institutions in the China-Vietnam rice trade. At the beginning of the calendar year, there is a thematic issue with an overview of the transitions and potential challenges facing Asia collectively and individually in 25 countries. Accessible online through JSTOR and the University of California Press journals website. Recommended for academic and special libraries.

556. *ASIANetwork Exchange: a journal for Asian studies in the liberal arts.* Formerly (until 1993): *Asian Exchange.* [ISSN: 1943-9938] 1992. s-a. Ed(s): Hong Zhang, Marsha Smith. Open Library of Humanities, Salisbury House, Station Rd, Cambridge, CB1 2LA, United Kingdom; martin.eve@openlibhums.org; https://www.openlibhums.org. Refereed. *Indexed:* A01. *Bk. rev.:* Number and length vary. *Aud.:* Ac, Sa.

The ASIANetwork began in 1992 and grew from a series of conferences to a consortium of approximately 160 North American colleges organized "to strengthen the role of Asian Studies within the framework of liberal arts education." The *ASIANetwork Exchange,* an open-access, peer-reviewed journal published twice a year, "catering primarily to faculty appointed in liberal arts institutions with programs in Asian Studies. . . seeks to publish current research, as well as high-quality pedagogical essays written by specialists and non-specialists alike." The journal is especially interested in submissions of articles and book and media reviews relevant to the needs of the undergraduate classroom. Articles may be observations on how digital is changing research and teaching on Asia to more specific techniques on using manga to help students build visual analysis skills. The publisher, Open Library of Humanities, makes the journal freely available online and also works to ensure permanent access to and preservation of the content by using CLOCKSS and LOCKSS archiving systems. Recommended for academic and special libraries. URL: https://www.asianetworkexchange.org/

The Australian Journal of Anthropology. See Anthropology section.

557. *The Contemporary Pacific: a journal of island affairs.* [ISSN: 1043-898X] 1989. s-a. USD 59 Pacific Islands. Ed(s): Alexander Mawyer. University of Hawai'i Press, 2840 Kolowalu St, Honolulu, HI 96822; uhpjourn@hawaii.edu; http://www.uhpress.hawaii.edu. Illus., index, adv. Sample. Refereed. Vol. ends: Fall. *Indexed:* A01, A22, A47, BAS, BRI, C45, CBRI, E01, IBSS, MLA-IB, P61, SSA. *Aud.:* Ga, Ac, Sa.

Published twice a year by the Center for Pacific Islands Studies, University of Hawai'i at Manoa, *The Contemporary Pacific (TCP)* covers "a wide range of disciplines with the aim of providing comprehensive coverage of contemporary developments in the entire Pacific Islands region, including Melanesia, Micronesia, and Polynesia. It features refereed, readable articles that examine social, economic, political, ecological, and cultural topics, along with political reviews, book and media reviews, resource reviews, and a dialogue section with interviews and short essays." A recent special issue, "Repossessing Paradise" examines the idea of paradise, with articles about contested possession in the case of Hawai'i, the marketing of paradise in reality television, tourism and real estate promotion, and paradise in Polynesian oral tradition as portrayed in film. Article topics range from urbanization, culture change, decolonization, cultural movements, ethnic relations, protecting the environment to social and health problems. In addition to research articles, there are political reviews, with analyses for individual countries in the Pacific area, such as Federated States of Micronesia (FSM), New Caledonia, and Fiji, along with book and media reviews. Each issue features artwork on the cover, and within, of a Pacific artist with a biographical profile. The artwork, whether painting, photography, or collage, complements the articles or theme of the issue. Available by subscription in print or online, or through the Project Muse database of humanities and social science journals. Back issues of *The Contemporary Pacific* are freely accessible through the ScholarSpace, the open-access, digital institutional repository for the University of Hawaii at Manoa. This is an interesting mix of the open-access and subscription-access models. Recommended for academic and special libraries supporting Pacific Studies. Public library users with an interest in Pacific cultures would also find this journal of interest.

558. *Contemporary Southeast Asia: a journal of international and strategic affairs.* [ISSN: 0129-797X] 1979. 3x/yr. SGD 137 in Singapore, Malaysia & Brunei. Ed(s): Ian Storey. Institute of Southeast Asian Studies, 30 Heng Mui Keng Terrace, Pasir Panjang, Singapore, 119614, Singapore; pubsunit@iseas.edu.sg; http://www.iseas.edu.sg/. Illus., index, adv. Refereed. Vol. ends: Dec. Reprint: SCH. *Indexed:* A01, A22, BAS, BRI, E01, IBSS, P61, SSA. *Bk. rev.:* 6-8, 600-1,000 words. *Aud.:* Ac, Sa.

Identified by members of the Bibliography of Asian Studies Advisory Committee as one of the most important journals in Asian Studies, *Contemporary Southeast Asia* is an international, refereed publication. "After more than two decades of existence, *Contemporary Southeast Asia* (CSEA) has entered a new phase of specialization to reflect more directly the changing priorities of the Institute of Southeast Asian Studies (ISEAS) as well as to cater to an increasing demand among our subscribers for a focus on issues related to domestic politics, international affairs, and regional security. . . in keeping with the rapid advances in the field of strategic studies concerning not just Southeast Asia but, indeed, the larger Asia-Pacific environment." Published three times a year, each issue contains "up-to-date analyses of important trends and events as well as authoritative and original contributions from leading scholars and observers on matters of current interest." In addition to research articles and book reviews, there are thematic issues. Articles are well written and provide historic background and context, making them accessible to general readers. In addition to the articles, each issue contains thoughtful book reviews. Access to current issues are available through Project MUSE, EBSCOhost, Gale, and ProQuest platforms. Highly recommended for academic and special libraries, and appropriate for public libraries that serve users with an interest in Asia and international relations.

559. *Cross-Currents: East Asian history and culture review.* [ISSN: 2158-9666] 2011. s-a. USD 150 (Individuals, USD 50). Ed(s): Wen-hsin Yeh, Hyongchan Kim. University of Hawai'i Press, 2840 Kolowalu St, Honolulu, HI 96822; uhpjourn@hawaii.edu; http://www.uhpress.hawaii.edu. *Bk. rev.:* 1,000-2,000 words. *Aud.:* Ga, Ac, Sa.

A product of the Institute of East Asian Studies, UC Berkeley, and the Research Institute of Korean Studies, Korea University, *Cross-Currents: East Asian History and Culture Review* is published by University of Hawaii Press. This peer-reviewed, open-access journal aims to provide "up-to-date research findings, emerging trends, and cutting-edge perspectives concerning East Asian history and culture from scholars in both English-speaking and Asian language-speaking academic communities. . . [and] balance issues traditionally addressed by Western humanities and social science journals with issues of immediate concern to scholars in China, Japan, Korea, and Vietnam." Recent issues include "Articles," usually clustered around a theme, as well as "Individual Submissions," a section of "Review Essays," and "Notes & Bibliographies." Sometimes there is a "Photo Essay" or book review in the section, "Readings from Asia." To give an idea of the disciplinary range covered by *Cross-Currents,* the thematic articles in one issue are about "Buddhist Art of Mongolia: Cross-Cultural Connections, Discoveries, and Interpretations," while another issue looks at "Air-Water-Land-Human: Interdisciplinary Approaches to Health and Environment in East Asia." The "Essays," and "Notes & Bibliographies" contain reviews of books on a similar topic—for example, two books are discussed and compared in "Queer Life, Communities, and

Activism in Contemporary China." The print version of the journal is published semi-annually; the ejournal is published quarterly and packed with interesting topics. Recommended for academic, special, and public libraries.

Europe-Asia Studies. See Slavic and Eurasian Studies section.

560. ***Harvard Journal of Asiatic Studies.*** [ISSN: 0073-0548] 1936. s-a. USD 60 (Individuals, USD 36). Ed(s): Melissa J Brown. Harvard-Yenching Institute, 2 Divinity Ave, Cambridge, MA 02138; http://www.harvard-yenching.org/. Illus., index. Sample. Refereed. Vol. ends: Dec. Microform: MIM; PQC. Reprint: SCH. *Indexed:* A01, A22, AmHI, BAS, BRI, CBRI, E01, IBSS, MLA-IB. *Bk. rev.:* 12-15, 8-12 pages. *Aud.:* Ac, Sa.

This journal is published with support from the Harvard-Yenching Institute, with the stated mission "to disseminate original, outstanding research and book reviews on the humanities in Asia, focusing at present on the areas of China, Japan, Korea, and Inner Asia." Peer-reviewed, "The Editor of *HJAS* is guided by its Editorial Board and acts on the advice of referees worldwide." A semi-annual publication, *Harvard Journal of Asiatic Studies* usually is published in June and December covering the arts, literature, history, and philosophy of Asia. Each issue contains refereed articles, an editorial preface, brief description of the image on the cover of the journal, review essays, and a number of substantial, in-depth book reviews. Article topics in recent issues have ranged from a discussion of the Uyghurs in Central Asia, to Chinese learning in medieval Japan, to Chinese Buddhism from the fifth century to the present. Available online through Project Muse and JSTOR, this journal is of interest to specialists, but provides enough information that students will find it of use as well. The Project Muse platform for *HJAS* supports sharing through social media sites, such as Facebook, Pinterest, Google Bookmark, LinkedIn, and so on. Recommended for special libraries and academic libraries.

561. ***International Journal of Asia - Pacific Studies.*** [ISSN: 1823-6243] 2005. s-a. Free. Penerbit Universiti Sains Malaysia, D34, Penerbit USM, Penang, 11800, Malaysia; http://www.penerbit.usm.my. Refereed. *Bk. rev.:* 1,500-2,000 words. *Aud.:* Ac.

Published under the auspices of the Asian Pacific Research Unit (APRU) at Universiti Sains Malaysia, the *International Journal of Asia-Pacific Studies* is a "multidisciplinary, internationally refereed publication focusing primarily on Asia (West, South, Southeast and East), Australasia and the Pacific Rim regions of the Americas (North, Central and South)." This e-journal carries out the mission of the APRU to disseminate original research in the disciplines encompassing "politics, history, indigenous languages and literature, religion, man and the environment, ethno-history, anthropology, cultural heritage, social issues, economic development, war and conflict resolution, prehistory and archaeology, and the arts" to a global community. The journal is explicit about its open-access policy: "All articles are freely available to read, share and download. In accordance to publication ethics and best practices of scholarly publishing, authors and journals must be properly credited." Published twice a year, articles are double-blind peer-reviewed. Recent articles cover cross-disciplinary topics ranging from student social movements, retirement migration, linguistic landscape analysis, or the function of swear words when American films need subtitles created in Arabic. Along with the research articles, *International Journal of Asia-Pacific Studies* publishes book reviews in every issue. Content is available in pdf and EPUB, an e-book file format that can be downloaded and read on mobile devices, such as tablets, e-readers, or smartphones. Indexed in Google Scholar and the Directory of Open Access Journals (DOAJ), this title is recommended for academic libraries.

Japanese Journal of Religious Studies. See Religion section.

Journal of Asian and African Studies. See Africa section.

562. ***Journal of Asian Studies.*** Former titles (until 1956): *The Far Eastern Quarterly;* (until 1941): *Bulletin of Far Eastern Bibliography.* [ISSN: 0021-9118] 1936. q. GBP 188 (print & online eds.)). Ed(s): Jeffrey N Wasserstrom. Cambridge University Press, University Printing House, Shaftesbury Rd, Cambridge, CB2 8BS, United Kingdom; journals@cambridge.org; https://www.cambridge.org/. Illus., index, adv. Sample. Refereed. Circ: 8300. Vol. ends: Dec. Microform: PQC. Reprint: PSC. *Indexed:* A01, A22, A47, AmHI, BAS, BRI, C45, CBRI, E01, IBSS, MLA-IB, P61. *Bk. rev.:* 40-50. *Aud.:* Ac, Sa.

Essential for any library that supports Asian Studies, the *Journal of Asian Studies (JAS)* is published by Cambridge University Press for the Association for Asian Studies. Since 1936, *JAS* has been committed to publishing "the very best empirical and multidisciplinary work on Asia, spanning the arts, history, literature, the social sciences, and cultural studies." Each issue contains an editorial foreword, research articles, and numerous substantial book reviews with geographical coverage, such as China and Inner Asia, South Asia, Southeast Asia, as well as Transnational and Comparative categories. The journal also publishes clusters of papers to stimulate new observations and discussions on specific themes and issues, ranging from migration, transnationalism, public health, and environmental impacts within countries and regions of Asia and the Pacific. The Cambridge University Press online platform, Cambridge Core, supports the expected "Search," "Browse," and "Latest Issue" links along with metrics for "Most Cited" articles. Social media is prominently displayed, including Facebook, Twitter, and the Cambridge Core Blog. Recommended for academic library collections.

Oceania. See Anthropology section.

563. ***Pacific Dynamics: journal of interdisciplinary research.*** [ISSN: 2463-641X] 2017. s-a. Free. University of Canterbury, Macmillan Brown Centre for Pacific Studies, Te Whare Wananga O Waitaha, Private Bag 4800, Christchurch, 8140, New Zealand; https://www.canterbury.ac.nz/mbc/. Refereed. *Bk. rev.:* 800-1,500 words. *Aud.:* Ga, Ac, Sa.

Pacific Dynamics is an open-access journal published by the Macmillan Brown Centre for Pacific Studies, with the support of the UC Arts Digital Lab, University of Canterbury, New Zealand. Truly interdisciplinary, the journal aims to "promote rigorous debates on theoretical discourses, applied knowledge and policy issues regarding the Pacific Islands, including New Zealand, Australia and the Pacific Rim . . ." and to support a "deeper and critical exploration of diverse paradigms of knowledge in their conceptual and applied forms. This involves reimagining the often fiercely guarded dominant disciplinary boundaries, research discourses and methodologies." Instructions to potential authors describes the two types of articles the journal accepts for peer review and publication: "The first is a standard journal article (6,000-7,000). The second is a short critical and analytical piece (2,000-3,000 words)." Recent article topics range from the evolution of Islam in Fiji, customary land title and indigenous rights in Papua New Guinea, the unusual language dynamics of French Creole as a minority language in New Caledonia, and a study of the music and community resilience of Australian South Sea Islanders of the "Black Pacific." The journal articles are located on the UC Research Repository at the University of Canterbury. The platform provides a search feature for the entire repository or a specific collection, such as *Pacific Dynamics*. The articles have completed a "comprehensive peer review" and are well-written and accessible to general readers as well as academics. Highly recommended for discovery systems at academic and public libraries.

Pacific Philosophical Quarterly. See Philosophy section.

Philosophy East and West. See Philosophy section.

564. ***Positions: Asia critique.*** [ISSN: 1067-9847] 1993. q. USD 460. Ed(s): Tani E. Barlow. Duke University Press, 905 W Main St, Durham, NC 27701; orders@dukeupress.edu; https://www.dukeupress.edu. Adv. Refereed. Reprint: PSC. *Indexed:* A01, A22, BAS, E01, MLA-IB, P61. *Bk. rev.:* Number and length vary. *Aud.:* Ga, Ac, Sa.

The stated purpose of *Positions* is to offer "a fresh approach to East Asia and Asian American studies," and to create a forum for all concerned with the social, intellectual, and political events unfolding in East Asia and within the Asian Diaspora. It accomplishes this with specialties within Asian Studies, but also pushes the boundaries with contributors in anthropology, literature, history, philosophy, economics, film and television studies, and Internet fan forums. The content reflects the diversity of research with "articles, commentaries, poetry, photo spreads, and political and philosophical debates" presenting questions from a wide range of perspectives. A recent thematic special issue—The End of Area: Biopolitics, Geopolitics, History—reflects the multidisciplinary range of *Positions*, drawing from philosophical studies of Lyotard, Derrida, and Marx, as well as examining the relevance of area studies, or the concept of a physical location, in a time of migration and globalization. Articles are scholarly, and of interest to a broad range of researchers. Recommended for academic libraries.

■ ASIAN AMERICAN

Christine K. Oka, Library Instruction Specialist, Northeastern University Libraries, Boston, MA 02115

Introduction

Asian Americans are an incredibly diverse ethnic, religious, and socioeconomic group that defies the single descriptor. This presents a challenge to libraries when it comes to providing Asian American magazines and journals for their users. In a recent Pew Research Center publication, *Key Facts about Asian Americans, a Diverse and Growing Population,* "a record 20 million Asian Americans trace their roots to more than 20 countries in East and Southeast Asia and the Indian subcontinent, each with unique histories, cultures, languages and other characteristics." (Lopez, 2017)

These "official" definitions are only the tip of the iceberg in describing this population. Bibliographically, the situation is further complicated with library resources variously categorizing the group under "ethnic interests" or subsuming Asian American into Asia. The confusion is understandable. As Shawn Wong noted, "Sixty percent of the Asians in America are foreign born, which makes me the exception rather than rule in the country of my birth. People in Asia know I'm foreign and people in America assume that I am foreign born" (Wong, 1998). On the other hand, within the population of 20 million, a number of them are "invisible." There is growing interest in disaggregation of data on Asian Americans, especially in the area of higher education (Teranishi, 2014). Teranishi discovered "the stereotype of Asians as the 'model minority' has obscured any real knowledge about AAPI student populations, with a blanket assumption of success." The stereotype has resulted in making the disadvantaged members of the model minority forgotten and underserved.

Additionally, finding an audience, coupled with the recession, hasn't made it easy for magazines. In recent years, a number of magazines have ceased print publishing as production costs have increased and advertising dollars dwindled. *Koream* and *Audrey Magazine* suspended publication in December 2015 after being acquired by London Trust Media. The publisher, James Ryu, plans future online versions of the magazines, but, he admits "has yet to figure out what that is" (Kim, 2015). In fact, the steady migration to online is evident in this chapter, as almost all of the reviewed publications were accessed online, had volunteer contributors and authors, supported by donations and community support AND put any revenue into the online publication costs.

In the interest of "truth in advertising," with *Magazines for Libraries,* I have identified magazines and online publications for many types of libraries serving a variety of audiences. These titles are likely to be longer-term, continuing publications libraries can reasonably expect to obtain (or link to). They also are of interest to a broad spectrum of library readers throughout the country.

Libraries could meet some of the needs of Asian-born and Asian American users by exploring online news sources and newspapers and open-access journals. One resource for articles would be the Asian American Studies Commons, a Digital Commons network of 79 institutional repositories at http://network.bepress.com/arts-and-humanities/race-ethnicity-and-post-colonial-studies/asian-american-studies/. Also, full text for a variety of Asian American publications is available on the web by subscription; most notably, with *Ethnic NewsWatch,* a database published by ProQuest (www.proquest.com).

REFERENCES

Ampersand: UCLA Ed and IS Online Newsletter. March 11, 2014. Web. Retrieved April 5, 2014. https://ampersand.gseis.ucla.edu/national-study-led-by-robert-teranishi-reveals-underserved-aapi-student-populations/

Harmon, Joanie. "National Study Led by Robert Teranishi Reveals Underserved AAPI Student Populations."

Kim, Victoria. "Archivist of the Korean American Experience Says Goodbye to Print." *Los Angeles Times*, 27 December 2015. Web. Retrieved March 16, 2016. http://www.latimes.com/local/california/la-me-korean-magazine-20151227-story.html

Lopez, Gustavo, et al. "Key Facts about Asian Americans, a Diverse and Growing Population." Pew Research Center. Fact Tank: News in the Numbers. September 8 2017. Web. Retrieved May 16, 2018. http://www.pewresearch.org/fact-tank/2017/09/08/key-facts-abouSt-asian-americans/

Teranishi, Robert; et al. *iCount: A Data Quality Movement for Asian Americans and Pacific Islanders in Higher Education.* Web. Retrieved April 5, 2014. http://aapip.org/publications/icount

Wong, Shawn. "The Chinese Man Has My Ticket." In: Susan Richards Shreve and Porter Shreve, eds. *How We Want to Live: Narrative on Progress.* Boston: Beacon Press, 1998; pp. 142-149.

Basic Periodicals

Hs: *Amerasia Journal, Brown Girl Magazine, Mochi Magazine;* Ga: *Amerasia Journal;* Ac: *Amerasia Journal, Journal of Asian American Studies.*

Basic Abstracts and Indexes

America: History and Life, Ethnic NewsWatch, Race Relations Abstracts, Sociological Abstracts.

565. ***Amerasia Journal.*** [ISSN: 0044-7471] 1971. 3x/yr. GBP 505 print & online eds. University of California, Los Angeles, Asian American Studies Center, 3230 Campbell Hall, 405 Hilgard Ave, Los Angeles, CA 90095; aascpress@aasc.ucla.edu; http://www.aasc.ucla.edu/. Illus., index. Sample. Refereed. Vol. ends: No. 3. Microform: PQC. *Indexed:* A01, A22, AmHI, BAS, BRI, CBRI, MLA-IB. *Bk. rev.:* Number varies, 3-4 pages. *Aud.:* Ga, Ac.

Amerasia Journal is the oldest continuously published academic journal in the interdisciplinary field of Asian American Studies, and is produced three times a year—winter, spring, and fall. In addition to the substantial book and film reviews, each issue, usually thematic, contains articles by writers of all ethnicities and disciplines. Contributors to the most recent issue discuss how Asians, Asian Americans, Asians in the Americas, or Pacific Islanders interpret "home, if not exile or migration." Topics include discussion of Vietnamese identity and displacement, and an interview, "A Unique Voice in the Spanish World" with Chinese-Peruvian author Siu Kam Wen, describing his "experiences living in three countries, among three cultures, and using three languages." His identity as a "triple exile" is confronted "in his daily life and in his fictional writings." A bibliography of his works is included. Additional information is accessible through the journal's social media: a blog (www.amerasiajournal.org/blog/), a Facebook page (https://www.facebook.com/AmerasiaJournal), and a Twitter account (http://twitter.com/uclaaascpress). Thoughtful articles, in-depth interviews, and review articles make this journal essential for all academic libraries that support ethnic and multicultural studies, and this title is highly recommended for large public libraries that serve Asian American and other ethnic communities. Access to the archives of all issues from volume one, 1971, is available with print subscription.

566. ***Asian American Journal of Psychology.*** [ISSN: 1948-1985] 2010. q. USD 723 (Individuals, USD 151; Members, USD 82). Ed(s): Bryan S K Kim. American Psychological Association, 750 First St, NE, Washington, DC 20002; journals@apa.org; http://www.apa.org. Adv. Sample. Refereed. Circ: 300. *Aud.:* Ac, Sa.

The official publication of the Asian American Psychological Association, the *Asian American Journal of Psychology* is "dedicated to research, practice, advocacy, education, and policy within Asian American psychology." The goal of the *AAJP* is to be a resource of "empirical, theoretical, methodological, and practice[-]oriented articles and book reviews covering topics relevant to Asian American individuals and communities, including prevention, intervention, training, and social justice." Recent articles include comparative studies of U.S. raised and non-U.S. raised Asian students, the campus safety experiences of Asian American and Asian international college students, and measuring the intergenerational cultural conflict among Asian Americans. The research articles identify the multiple issues facing Asians and Asian Americans, especially within the educational environment and how institutions may develop interventions and services to support this specific ethnic group. This journal is essential for academic and special libraries that support psychology, counseling, human services, and health-care research within multicultural studies.

567. ***Asian American Literature: discourse and pedagogies.*** [ISSN: 2154-2171] 2010. a. Free. Ed(s): Noelle Brada-Williams. San Jose State University, One Washington Sq, San Jose, CA 95192; http://www.sjsu.edu/. Refereed. *Bk. rev.:* Number and length vary. *Aud.:* Hs, Ga, Ac, Sa.

Asian American Literature: Discourses and Pedagogies is an open-access journal developed for "[t]he production, collection, and distribution of accessible high quality research on Asian American Literature for students, teachers, and the general public." When polling local educators and students about Asian American literature, founding editor Noelle Brada-Williams was surprised to discover how only a few names were mentioned, such as Amy Tan and Pearl S. Buck, and "the tendency for both students and teachers to break apart the term 'Asian American' into separate and seemingly unrelated words...." Published annually at San Jose State University in California (SJSU), the journal is accessible through the institution's repository ScholarWorks at http://scholarworks.sjsu.edu/aaldp/. The repository uses Digital Commons institutional repository software, which not only makes the current volume easy to access, but also provides links to select and browse all volumes, or individual volumes, as well as link to the "Most Popular Papers," or to thematic volumes. With respect to other web sites and spaces, updates and news about this journal are available through Facebook, Twitter, LinkedIn, Google+, and other social media. This peer-reviewed journal does not limit itself to article submissions by academics. The publication will consider original articles from anyone for consideration for publication, "provided he or she owns the copyright to the work being submitted or is authorized by the copyright owner or owners to submit the article." Book reviews are included, with plans to expand into reviewing literature "with the specific focus of how these texts can be used in the classroom." Open access and linking are recommended for academic and public libraries that serve researchers, educators, and general readers interested in Asian American literature and teaching.

568. ***Brown Girl Magazine: smart. hip. beautiful.*** 2008. . Free. Ed(s): Trisha Sakhuja, Kamini Ramdeen. Brown Girl Magazine, LLC, 26811 Monarch Valley Ln, Katy, TX 77494; staff@browngirlmagazine.com; http://www.browngirlmagazine.com/. Illus., adv. *Aud.:* Hs, Ga.

Founded in 2008 as an online publication, *Brown Girl Magazine* "was created by and for South Asian women who believe in the power of storytelling as a vehicle for community building and empowerment." It is open access, and one can subscribe to the magazine and get issues by email, but the website itself is an extensive media platform worth exploring with features on Lifestyle, Entertainment, Health, Relationships and Culture, to name a few. Despite the name, the magazine boasts a 35 percent male readership and celebrates this demographic with "Brown Boy," alongside the other features at the top of the page, as well as adding men to the writing staff. International in scope, the "Community Highlights" feature reaches out to readers in Canada, the United States, South Asia, and the United Kingdom. *Brown Girl* also extends its reach through social media, such as Facebook, Twitter, and Pinterest. The magazine allows people to share their stories online and to build an offline community of like-minded supporters. Recommended for public libraries that serve an Asian American, especially South Asian, community, and for academic libraries that support Asian American and ethnic studies.

569. ***India Currents (Online).*** 1987. m. Free. Ed(s): Nirupama Vaidhyanathan. India Currents, 2670 S White Road, Ste 165, San Jose, CA 95148; info@indiacurrents.com; http://www.indiacurrents.com. Illus., adv. Circ: 200000. *Bk. rev.:* 800-1,000 words. *Aud.:* Hs, Ga, Ac, Sa.

Published since 1987, first as *India Currents Magazine* and later as *India Currents,* this publication became an all-digital magazine in 2017, dedicated to the premise "that all Americans of *all* backgrounds are interested in learning about other world cultures and that they respond to information that is presented to them in an accessible and attractive manner." *India Currents* explores "the heritage and culture of India as it exists in the United States of America." . . . [and] has the largest following among Indian media in the United States." Features include the cover story, articles about business, health, community, youth, and "professional advice" articles regarding the law, taxes, and health and relationship questions. The cover stories highlighted personal experiences, social issues, and historical topics; one article was about a project to create a "historical database on the service and lives of South Asian soldiers" at the United States World War I Centennial Commission in Washington, DC. Under the "Culture" dropdown, articles included reviews of books, films, food, music, and travel. Content is available through ProQuest Ethnic NewsWatch database, but *India Currents* is also available as an open-access resource. Readers may subscribe and receive issues and updates in their email. The updates, photos, and links are accessible through social media, such as Facebook, Twitter, Google+, and LinkedIn.

570. ***Journal of Asian American Studies.*** [ISSN: 1097-2129] 1998. 3x/yr. USD 145. Ed(s): Rick Bonus. The Johns Hopkins University Press, 2715 N Charles St, Baltimore, MD 21218; http://www.press.jhu.edu. Illus., adv. Sample. Refereed. Vol. ends: Oct. Reprint: PSC. *Indexed:* A22, BAS, E01, ENW, MLA-IB. *Bk. rev.:* Number varies, 2-3 pages. *Aud.:* Ga, Ac.

The Association for Asian American Studies was founded in 1979 with the mission of advancing excellence in teaching and research in the field and promoting closer ties and understanding among the various groups within it - Chinese, Japanese, Korean, Filipino, Hawaiian, Southeast Asian, South Asian, and Pacific Islander, among others. The association's official journal, *Journal of Asian American Studies,* publishes original articles that explore the historical, social, and cultural aspects of the Asian American community and the Asian diaspora. The articles document research in these areas, along with new theoretical developments, methodological innovations, public policy concerns, pedagogical issues, and book, media, and exhibition reviews. Recent articles have covered diverse topics, such the political participation of Taiwanese Americans in the early twenty-first century, to examining cross-cultural collaboration in Asian American literature, to the long-reaching significance of *budae jjigae,* or "military base stew" to Koreans and Korean Americans. Each issue also contains four or five thoughtful book reviews. The online version of this journal is available in the Johns Hopkins University Project Muse collection. Essential for academic libraries that support Asian American and other ethnic studies programs.

571. ***Journal of Southeast Asian American Education and Advancement.*** [ISSN: 2153-8999] 2006. a. Free. National Association for the Education and Advancement of Cambodian, Laotian, and Vietnamese Americans, University of Hawai'i, Dept of IPLL, Spalding Hall 255, Honolulu, HI 96822; wayne.wright@utsa.edu; http://jsaaea.coehd.utsa.edu/index.php/JSAAEA/. Index, adv. Refereed. *Bk. rev.:* 3-5 per issue. *Aud.:* Ga, Ac, Sa.

The *Journal of Southeast Asian American Education and Advancement* (*JSAAEA*) is an official publication of the National Association for the Education and Advancement of Cambodian, Laotian, and Vietnamese Americans (NAFEA), with support from the Department of Curriculum and Instruction and the College of Education at Purdue University, along with Purdue Libraries Scholarly Publishing Services and Purdue University Press. This online, open-access, peer-reviewed journal aims to provide "a forum for scholars and writers from diverse fields who share a common interest in Southeast Asian (SEA) Americans and their communities." The journal is published annually and takes an interdisciplinary look at education and advancement, through public policy, social work, health, community development, and political advocacy. Access is provided through institutional repository software, via Digital Commons, at http://docs.lib.purdue.edu/jsaaea/. The latest issue explores a new area of research - the linguistic landscape of Cambodia town in Lowell, Massachusetts, which is only the second recognized Cambodia town in the United States. In addition to the research, there are many in-depth book reviews. Linking to this journal at http://docs.lib.purdue.edu/jsaaea/ is recommended for academic libraries, public libraries, and special libraries for researchers, educators, and professionals who serve Southeast Asian American communities.

572. ***Mochi Magazine: empowering young Asian American women.*** 2008. s-a. Free. Ed(s): Stephanie Wu, Christine Wei. Mochi Magazine, info@mochimag.com; http://www.mochimag.com/. Illus., adv. *Aud.:* Hs, Ga.

The webpage of the publication is direct: "*Mochi Magazine* is an online magazine dedicated to young Asian American women, and is run entirely by an amazing group of volunteers. Any profit, whether via advertising or donations, goes directly into website costs." There are two (sometimes three) issues per year and everything is accessible from the website, https://www.mochimag.com/ or readers can subscribe to get each thematic issue by email. The latest issue, "The Visibility Issue," has article categories such as "Entertainment," "Fashion," "Beauty," "Food & Health," "Relationships," "College & Career," and a link to the blog. This thematic issue contained articles discussing "white-washing" in films, where Asian characters are either changed or played by non-Asian actors. Another type of visibility problem discussed was hate crimes against Asian Americans. "In reality, most Asian American hate crimes are quite frequently underreported, as minorities often feel unsupported by law enforcement and do not come forward with racially-motivated attacks." Additional communication and information are available through social media, such as Facebook, Twitter, Google+, YouTube, and a news feed. The magazine interface helpfully identifies the most popular articles, also groups articles by category, and gathers "Articles You Might Like" from past issues. Recommended for high school and public libraries that support Asian American populations.

573. *Positively Filipino: your window on the Filipino diaspora.* 2013. . Free. Ed(s): Mona Lisa Youchengco. Positively Filipino LLC, 5226 Diamond Heights Blvd, San Francisco, CA 94131; awesomeness@positivelyfilipino.com; http://www.positivelyfilipino.com/. *Aud.:* Hs, Ga, Ac, Sa.

Positively Filpino is upbeat and describes itself as "the premier digital native magazine celebrating the story of Filipinos in the diaspora of nearly 13 million expatriates." The background on this online publication reflects the changing environment and economics of magazine publication. The editor of *Positively Filipino,* Mona Lisa Youchengco, had started the print publication *Filipinas Magazine* in 1992. When advertising revenue for print declined in the new millennium, she moved to the online environment with *Positively Filipino*. The title harkens back to the days when "Filipino immigrants often faced rejection and racism," with signs on hotels saying "Positively No Filipinos Allowed." Here, at *Positively Filipino,* news, editorials, blogs, and videos are accessible as a forum to celebrate Filipino heritage and achievements, while at the same time exploring the "collective challenges both in the homeland and the diaspora." The *Positively Filipino* home page contains sections such as "Community News," "Screening Room," and "Series," with dropdowns to access articles. The "Collections" tab is a reflection of the aim of the magazine to reach all demographics, with sections covering topics such as "Fashion," "Politics," "Achievers & Role Models," "All About Pinoy Food," "Of a Certain Age," and "Health and Wellness." Visit the "Series" tab to, among other things, "Know Your Diaspora," with information about Filipino immigrant communities all over the world, including Australia, Belgium, and Greece, to name a few. *Positively Filipino* is recommended for academic, high school, and college-level libraries, as well as public libraries. URL: www.positivelyfilipino.com/

■ ASTROLOGY

Christianne Casper, Instruction Coordinator, Broward College, South Campus, 7200 Pines Blvd., Pembroke Pines, FL 33024; ccasper@broward.edu

Introduction

Astrology dates back to the Babylonians in the second millennium B.C. Since then, astrology has influenced language, literature, religion, science, philosophy, and psychology. Astrologists study the major planets, stars, and celestial bodies at the time of birth using observations, measurements, and calculations about these celestial bodies to produce a framework of symbolic patterns that affect life events. Analyzing these patterns, astrologists attempt to explain and predict social, political, emotional, and other important aspects of life. People turn to astrology as a way to gain greater insight into their past, present, and future lives.

Some popular astrology journals include *Horoscope Guide, Dell Horoscope,* and *The Mountain Astrologer.* These journals provide information on personal horoscopes and guides to world events. Other journals, such as *Today's Astrologer,* have a more scholarly, research-oriented approach. The following list includes publications for all levels of interest.

Basic Periodicals

Hs: *Horoscope Guide;* Ga: *Dell Horoscope, The Mountain Astrologer;* Ac: *Today's Astrologer*.

Basic Abstracts and Indexes

Academic Search Premier, MasterFILE Premier.

574. *Dell Horoscope: the world's leading astrology magazine.* Formerly (until 199?): *Horoscope.* [ISSN: 1080-1421] 1935. m. USD 34.97 domestic; USD 54.47 foreign. Dell Magazines, 6 Prowitt St, Norwalk, CT 06855; customerservice@pennypublications.com; http://www.pennydellpuzzles.com. Illus., adv. *Indexed:* BRI, CBRI. *Bk. rev.:* 3, signed. *Aud.:* Hs, Ga.

Dell Horoscope is one of the most popular astrology magazines. The articles cover general-interest topics ranging from world and national events to personal forecasts. Also included are yearly, monthly, and daily guides. The regular features include letters to the editor, answers to readers' astrological questions, a monthly planetary data table, and book and product reviews. *Dell Horoscope* is written with both professional astrologers and amateurs in mind. The online version includes daily forecasts, a readers' forum, and links to other astrology web sites. Also of interest is "Cosmic Connections," which lists astrological activities in the United States and Canada.

575. *Horoscope Guide.* [ISSN: 8750-3042] 19??. m. USD 38.30; USD 3.99 per issue. Kappa Publishing Group, Inc., 6198 Butler Pike, Ste 200, Blue Bell, PA 19422; http://www.kappapublishing.com. Illus., adv. *Bk. rev.:* 2-3. *Aud.:* Hs, Ga.

This magazine is designed for the astrology enthusiast. Each monthly issue includes a quick-reference section for daily forecasts regarding each sign for that month. There are three or four feature articles that address such diverse topics as family and personal issues, spiritual wellness, and current events as influenced by astrology. Monthly features include advice columns, a "zodiagram," a planning calendar, and a yearly forecast for the current sign. The online version provides access to an article from the current issue in "Read a Story."

576. *International Astrologer.* Formerly: *Kosmos.* 1968. 3x/yr. Free to members. Ed(s): Vickie Pelz. International Society for Astrological Research, Inc., PO Box 38613, Los Angeles, CA 90038; mmacycles@mail.msn.com; http://www.isarastrology.com. Illus., adv. Refereed. *Aud.:* Ac, Sa.

This journal is designed to advance the field of astrological research, intended for both students and professional astrologers. Feature articles offer diverse discussions of astrological interest, ranging from general community news to political/celebrity analysis, and including how-to columns on research, and financial astrology. The journal also contains conference information for the International Society for Astrological Research, including annual conference reports and evaluations.

577. *The Mountain Astrologer: your gateway to understanding the cosmos.* [ISSN: 1079-1345] 1987. bi-m. USD 38.95 domestic; USD 46 Canada; USD 71 Mexico. Ed(s): Linda Kaye. Mountain Astrologer, PO Box 970, Cedar Ridge, CA 95924. Illus., adv. Sample. Vol. ends: Nov/Dec. *Bk. rev.:* 3-5. *Aud.:* Ga, Ac, Sa.

The Mountain Astrologer provides a wealth of information for professional and amateur astrologers alike. Standard features include a "Forecast Calendar," "Astrology News," "Current Lunations," letters to the editor, a professional directory, and signed book and astrological web site reviews. The web site reviews and the abundance of charts are extremely helpful. The online version lists the table of contents of the current issue and provides an index of articles from 1990 to 2010. Web site recommendations are also available. In addition, there is a "New to Astrology" section, which provides an overview of basic concepts of astrology.

578. *Today's Astrologer.* Former titles (until 199?): *American Federation of Astrologers. Bulletin;* (until 19??): *A F A Bulletin;* (until 1945): *A F S A Bulletin.* [ISSN: 1067-1439] 1938. m. Free to members. American Federation of Astrologers, Inc., 6535 S Rural Rd, Tempe, AZ 85283; http://www.astrologers.com. Illus., index. *Aud.:* Ac, Sa.

Today's Astrologer, the bulletin of the American Federation of Astrologers (AFA), was established as a forum to promote astrology through research and education. There is an average of five articles per issue. Regular departments include "Data Exchange," "The Question Box," and "The Communication Center." This last department is a calendar of activities of member organizations and other astrology affiliates. Finally, a "Lunation/Full Moon" chart is provided. URL: www.astrologers.com

■ ASTRONOMY

See also Aeronautics and Space Science; and Atmospheric Sciences sections.

Edward Creighton Sugrue, Jr., Wolbach Library, Harvard-Smithsonian Center for Astrophysics, 60 Garden St., Cambridge, MA 02138; edsugrue@hotmail.com

Introduction

In 2018, the death of Stephen Hawking recalled the attention of the world from various other concerns to black holes, to cosmology, and to astronomy in general. Many events since, such as LIGO observing the merging of two neutron stars; the great dust storm on Mars threatening the Opportunity rover; and the interstellar object Oumuamua passing through our solar system, almost like something from an Arthur C. Clarke book, have all continued to interest the general public, including, we hope, your own library patrons.

All of these astronomical activities can remind us of the original meaning of the word "awesome." Yet, as truly awesome as they are, none of these pursuits would be possible were it not for a network of timely, topical communication among astronomers, and between the astronomers and the public at large.

Modern astronomers' jobs are made vastly easier by staying well informed about recent developments in their field. One of the best ways to do this is by means of the journals discussed in this section. Similarly, the interested public is well served by being able to follow these astronomers as they work, as their research is published.

The selections put forward here include titles of interest to a diverse range of readers, ranging from Spanish-speaking children, to the average intelligent adult, to hobbyists with a specific astronomical interest, to professional astronomers.

There is a wide range of astronomical periodicals available, many of which are indeed quite democratic in spirit, and aim at a wider audience. However, librarians need to take extra care concerning which periodicals they select in this area of study for their institutions. Although many of the following periodicals are aimed at the general public, other periodicals are so esoteric that even undergraduate astronomy students have trouble wading through them.

Take care, also, not to assume that the periodicals listed under the heading "Basic Periodicals" below are "basic" in the sense of being simple. Many of them are overflowing with high-level equations, and are only basic in that they are invaluable components of any serious academic astronomy library. Also note that "basic" periodicals are distinct from "core" periodicals. Core periodicals are chosen and agreed upon by specialized science libraries. They can be identified by consulting PAMNET, which is described below in this introduction. In general, in determining a periodical's prospective value to your library, pay attention to the audience codes that periodicals have been assigned, and take time to examine their annotations and their web sites.

That said, a lot of these periodicals do provide terrific information to committed amateur astronomers, of whom there are many. Amateur astronomers, after all, make major contributions to the field on a regular basis. The general-audience periodicals serve a role that is at least as valuable as the specialized journals, because many thoughtful people, including children, harbor a great love of astronomy yet simply don't have the time to study it in any great depth. Many periodicals listed here fall somewhere between the abstruse journals and the nontechnical ones. Quite a few of these tend to specialize in a particular area of astronomical research, such as meteors, cosmology, or the planets of our solar system.

Most of these publications, although not all, can be found on the Internet. These days, you might want to tell your library patrons to also look for Facebook groups about particular astronomy topics, or ask if they would care to follow their favorite astronomers on Twitter, and so on. Several excellent periodicals are available free of charge on the web. This section includes a couple of journals that are designed entirely to translate research being done in Russia. For journals with a similar function, seek out *Ulrich's Periodicals Directory*.

A word to the wise: If you are new to this field, do not confuse *Astronomy and Astrophysics Abstracts* with *Astronomy and Astrophysics*. They sound like they should be connected somehow, but they are completely unrelated publications, and the similarity in their titles is merely an annoying coincidence.

Academic librarians who are new to the field also need to be aware of PAMNET. PAMNET is a valuable, professional online forum, useful for discussing astronomy periodicals and other information sources with fellow information professionals and librarians. PAMNET can easily be found online at http://pam.sla.org/manual/pamnet-information/. *Astronomy and Astrophysics Abstracts,* NASA's ADS (http://adswww.harvard.edu), and INSPEC are excellent indexing services.

Basic Periodicals

Ems: *Abrams Planetarium Sky Calendar, SkyWatch;* Hs, Ga: *Astronomy, Griffith Observer, Mercury, Sky & Telescope, SkyWatch;* Ac: *The Astronomical Journal, Astronomy, Astronomy and Astrophysics, Royal Astronomical Society. Monthly Notices.*

Basic Abstracts and Indexes

INSPEC, Astrophysics Data System (ADS).

579. *A A V S O Journal.* [ISSN: 0271-9053] 1972. s-a. USD 65 Free to members; USD 12 per issue. Ed(s): John Percy. American Association of Variable Star Observers, 49 Bay State Rd, Cambridge, MA 02138; aavso@aavso.org; http://www.aavso.org. Illus., index. Refereed. Vol. ends: No. 2. *Bk. rev.:* 1-2, 400-600 words. *Aud.:* Ac, Sa.

The American Association of Variable Star Observers (AAVSO) has members in more than 40 countries and is the largest organization of variable-star observers in the world. Its members include both amateur and professional astronomers, and they first watch and track variable stars (those stars whose luminosity changes over time), then submit their observations to the AAVSO. Amateur astronomers play a very important role in the tracking of variable stars, as there are far too many for only professionals to follow. A typical journal edition may feature one broad editorial, followed by many more tightly focused research articles on photometry of variable stars. In a recent year, one broad editorial sought to provide an overview of the history, current state, and future of the journal itself. The next year, one of these editorials asked readers to think about the value of astronomy itself. The AAVSO web site has such features as: a search engine designed to locate variable stars in the AAVSO charts; a variety of online tools to assist observers in processing their information; and even a "variable star of the month." The electronic, online version of this journal can be found on the web site, as well. This journal publishes refereed, scientific papers on variable-star research; observer observation totals; activities of AAVSO committees; letters to the editor; and the "Annual Report of the Director." It is a valuable, respected source of information within the astronomical community. URL: www.aavso.org/publications/jaavso

580. *Abrams Planetarium Sky Calendar.* [ISSN: 0733-6314] 1969. q. USD 11 domestic; USD 14 foreign. Michigan State University, Talbert & Leota Abrams Planetarium, Michigan State University, 755 Science Rd, East Lansing, MI 48824; http://www.pa.msu.edu/abrams/. Illus. Sample. *Aud.:* Ems, Hs, Ga, Ac.

Sky Calendar is set up in such a way as to call attention to the most interesting goings-on in the heavens, in any given week, or any part of any week. It is an especially useful tool for locating the planets. As the name suggests, this publication is laid out like a calendar, presenting a new page for each month. The reverse side of each page presents a simplified sky map for that month, printed for use at mid-evening, at a latitude selected because it is near the mean latitude of some of the most populous areas in the continental United States (approximately 40 degrees north latitude). In a recent issue, along with the usual conjunctions, eclipses, and so on, the *Sky Calendar* includes assistance for locating the comet 46/P/Wirtanen, which is expected to be visible in mid-December 2018. Diagrams in the boxes for each day invite the reader to track the moon's rapid motion past the planets, and past the brighter stars. Similarly, readers can follow the (apparently) slower pace of the planets, in their conjunctions with bright stars, with other planets, and with the largest asteroids in their orbits. This is a very specialized publication that serves only the purpose described here. You will not find, for example, articles, book reviews, or evaluations of software; you will just find the charts. The highly illustrated format and easy-to-follow guide make the loose-leaf calendar popular. Information presented in the calendar can be used (with permission) as a teaching tool by members of astronomical societies and teachers. URL: www.pa.msu.edu/abrams/SkyCalendar

581. ***Ad Astra.*** [ISSN: 1041-102X] 1989. q. Free to members. National Space Society, P O Box 98106, Washington, DC 20090; nsshq@nss.org; http://www.nss.org. Illus., adv. Vol. ends: No. 6. *Indexed:* A01, A22, BRI. *Bk. rev.:* Number and length vary. *Aud.:* Hs, Ga, Ac, Sa.

Ad Astra contains articles and news stories concerning U.S. and international space programs, federal space policy formation, commercial space endeavors, emerging space technologies, and recent scientific achievements pertinent to astronomy. It is the membership publication of the National Space Society, and its articles can be read both by space and astronomy enthusiasts and by those with extensive education in the field. Recently, this journal published articles discussing the role that Jeff Bezos is positioning himself to play in the future exploration of space. An interview with astronaut Nicole Stott is also included this year, so, that may be of particular interest to your younger female library patrons. Regular departments in the publication include "Launch Pad," "Mission Control," "Countdown," "Space Community," and "Lifting Off." The primary focus is, of course, the space program, but often there are articles dealing with broader astronomical issues such as cosmology, or, on occasion, wholly speculative articles about possible future space-related ventures. The journal sometimes includes reviews for outstanding space-related children's books on its web site. This popular journal has numerous beautiful illustrations and photographs, and has helped spark an early interest in space in many people. A valuable addition to any library, whether it specializes in astronomy or not. URL: www.nss.org/adastra

582. ***Advances in Astronomy.*** [ISSN: 1687-7969] 2008. . USD 495. Hindawi Publishing Corporation, 315 Madison Ave, 3rd Fl, Ste 3070, New York, NY 10017; orders@hindawi.com; https://www.hindawi.com. Refereed. *Indexed:* A01. *Aud.:* Ac, Sa.

Advances in Astronomy is a peer-reviewed, open-access journal publishing original research articles, as well as review articles in all areas of astronomy and astrophysics. Intended for serious astronomers, physicists, and other scientists, it attracts authors from observatories and universities all over the world. Some recent articles touch upon the data provided by the Fermi gamma-ray burst monitor, and the newer Swift BAT (burst alert telescope). Other recent articles discuss Poisson denoising for astronomical images, and the lunar DEM (digital elevation model). URL: www.hindawi.com/journals/aa

583. ***American Astronomical Society. Bulletin (Online).*** [ISSN: 2330-9458] 1969. irreg. Free. American Astronomical Society, 2000 Florida Ave, NW, Ste 300, Washington, DC 20009; aas@aas.org; http://aas.org/. *Aud.:* Ac, Sa.

The *Bulletin* has existed only in an online version since 2016. Its function is to give the American Astronomical Society (AAS) a professional forum in which to present the abstracts of papers from recent conferences and meetings, and to present notices of the society that are likely to be of interest to the professional astronomical community. Annual observatory reports and reports of the society itself are also published here. The observatory reports are particularly useful to people wanting to determine the observational capabilities and major research programs of various observatories. The *Bulletin* sometimes includes such interesting papers as "Temporal Evolution and Spatial Distribution of White-light Flare Kernels in a Solar Flare," "Magnetic Reconnection in the Solar Chromosphere," and "A Database of Flare Ribbon Properties from Solar Dynamics Observatory." The AAS reserves its *Astronomical Journal* and *Astrophysical Journal* (both below in this section) for original research papers. URL: www.aas.org/publications/baas

584. ***Annual Review of Astronomy and Astrophysics.*** [ISSN: 0066-4146] 1963. a. USD 431 (print & online eds.)). Ed(s): Ewine F van Dishoeck, Sandra M Faber. Annual Reviews, PO Box 10139, Palo Alto, CA 94303; service@annualreviews.org; http://www.annualreviews.org. Refereed. Reprint: PSC. *Indexed:* A01, A22. *Aud.:* Ac, Sa.

This is a valuable synthesis of the current state of research in a wide range of topics of astronomical inquiry. It is thoroughly updated once each year. Each volume contains roughly 15 to 20 articles, each dealing with a currently "hot" topic in astronomy. The articles give the reader a detailed overview of what kind of research is being done, and on what specific problems and issues researchers are striving to focus still more resources. Recently, some of the articles deal with "The Origins of Hot Jupiters," the "Interstellar Dust Properties of Nearby Galaxies," and "Debris Disks: Structure, Composition, and Variability." Each article is followed by a selected bibliography of several dozen of the most important published papers in that particular area of inquiry, for the year. These bibliographies are chosen by some of the top people in the world in that particular subfield. Be aware that the articles assume a certain scientific sophistication and awareness on the part of the reader. *ARAA* is a tremendously useful volume for librarians and astronomers, and it is often kept behind the circulation desk in science libraries to keep it safe. URL: http://arjournals.annualreviews.org/loi/astro?cookieSet=1

585. ***Association of Lunar and Planetary Observers. Journal.*** [ISSN: 0039-2502] 1947. q. Free to members. Ed(s): Ken Poshedly. Association of Lunar and Planetary Observers, c/o Matthew L. Will, Secretary, PO Box 13456, Springfield, IL 62791; matt.will@alpo-astronomy.org; http://www.alpo-astronomy.org. Illus. Sample. Refereed. Vol. ends: No. 4. *Bk. rev.:* 1-2, 300-500 words. *Aud.:* Ac, Sa.

Not to be confused with the *Lunar and Planetary Information Bulletin.* Sometimes known by its alternate title, *The Strolling Astronomer,* this journal is a publication of the Association of Lunar and Planetary Observers (ALPO). It specializes in publishing astronomical studies and articles relating to the study of our own solar system. Some recent articles discuss the research of ALPOSS Coordinator and Scientific Advisor Richard Hill, on solar Carrington Rotations. Cosmology, or the study of other star systems, is not covered here. The journal is regularly mailed to members of ALPO, an international organization of amateur and professional astronomers. Not an easy magazine to leaf through, it can be a learning experience for the novice astronomer who is not afraid of a challenge. Contents often include calls for papers, book reviews, and updates and surveys of specific organized observing programs. ALPO has many subdivisions, each with its own publication, and subscriptions to these other publications need to be handled directly with each division. The ALPO web site can help settle questions concerning which publications might be best for you. *The Strolling Astronomer* is considered to be the means of coordinating all the various areas of ALPO research under a single cover. Reports and observations from readers and staff are always welcome for all publications, provided they have not been published elsewhere. Useful for serious science libraries. URL: www.alpo-astronomy.org

586. ***The Astronomical Almanac.*** Supersedes (1960-1981): *Astronomical Ephemeris;* (1852-1980): *American Ephemeris and Nautical Almanac;* (1766-1852): *Nautical Almanac and Astronomical Ephemeris.* [ISSN: 0737-6421] 1766. a. USD 49 domestic; USD 68 foreign. U.S. Naval Observatory, 3450 Massachusetts Ave, Washington, DC 20392; http://www.usno.navy.mil/. *Aud.:* Hs, Ga, Ac, Sa.

The Astronomical Almanac is one of the fruits of a long-standing collaboration between American and British nautical almanac services. It features invaluable, authoritative tables and charts, as opposed to discursive articles. It contains precise ephemerides of the Sun, moon, planets, and satellites, data for eclipses, and information on other astronomical phenomena for a given year. Most data are tabulated at one-day intervals. This journal includes geocentric positions of the Sun, moon, planets, dwarf planets and small solar system bodies, and bright stars; heliocentric positions of the planets and their orbital elements; universal and sidereal times; daily polynomials for the moon's position; physical ephemerides of the Sun, moon, and planets; elongation times and differential coordinates of selected satellites of the planets; rise, set, and transit times of the Sun and moon; eclipse data and maps; tables of reference data for various celestial objects; useful formulae; and other information. Don't miss the "Explanatory Supplement" to this publication. The supplement is an authoritative source on astronomical phenomena and calendars, and offers detailed directions for performing practical astronomy. All in all, this is a very valuable, time-honored, esteemed resource - generally given pride of place in any serious astronomy collection. URL: www.usno.navy.mil/USNO/astronomical-applications/publications/astro-almanac

587. ***The Astronomical Journal (Online).*** [ISSN: 1538-3881] 1849. m. USD 635. Institute of Physics Publishing, Inc., 190 North Independence Mall West, Ste 601, Philadelphia, PA 19106; info@ioppubusa.com; http://iopscience.iop.org. Illus., index. Refereed. Vol. ends: No. 6. Reprint: PSC. *Indexed:* A22. *Aud.:* Ac, Sa.

Considered to be one of the five or six "core" journals in any serious astronomy collection, *AJ* is essential for any academic institution with an astronomy program, and is indispensable to serious astronomers. A preferred vehicle for publishing original observations and research with a fairly short publication time, this journal publishes many seminal papers. Emphasis is placed on scientific results derived from observations, as opposed to concepts extrapolated from theory. Recent articles discuss the size distribution of small Hilda asteroids, stellar companions of exoplanet host stars in K2, and the Grism Lens-amplified Survey from Space (GLASS). Coverage in this journal includes the traditional areas of astronomy, and expanded topics, including all currently "hot" subjects, such as detection of new planets; large-scale structure of the universe; asteroids that are likely to strike the Earth; and every imaginable other topic pertaining to astronomy. This journal and *Astrophysical Journal* (below in this section) comprise the main U.S. publications of new research in the fields of astronomy and astrophysics, similar to the European *Astronomy and Astrophysics* (below in this section). URL: www.iop.org/EJ/journal/-page=scope/1538-3881

588. ***Astronomical Society of the Pacific. Publications.*** [ISSN: 0004-6280] 1889. m. USD 599 (print & online eds.)). Ed(s): Jeff Mangum. Institute of Physics Publishing, Inc., 190 North Independence Mall West, Ste 601, Philadelphia, PA 19106; info@ioppubusa.com; http://iopscience.iop.org. Illus., index, adv. Sample. Refereed. *Indexed:* A01, A22. *Aud.:* Ac, Sa.

The Astronomical Society of the Pacific (ASP) publishes several titles, among them *Universe in the Classroom* and *Mercury* (both below in this section), *Publications of the ASP*, and *Selectory*, a catalog of equipment for astronomy. The ASP's mission is "to advance the science of astronomy and disseminate astronomical information," and it uses some of its publications to this end. Be aware that *Publications* is an actual title - it does not simply refer to a group of publications, but rather constitutes an actual periodical in and of itself. *Publications* is the ASP's technical journal, which includes refereed reports on current research, Ph.D. thesis abstracts, and review articles on astronomy and astrophysics. It prides itself on giving equal coverage to "all wavelengths and distance scales" of astronometric data. Recent articles delve into Wolf-Rayet stars formed by chemically homogenous evolution, a discussion of how peer review in astronomy really works, and how it could be improved, and a search for dust emission from (24) Themis, using the Gemini-North Observatory. URL: www.journals.uchicago.edu/page/pasp/brief.html

589. ***Astronomy.*** [ISSN: 0091-6358] 1973. m. USD 42.95 domestic; USD 54.95 Canada; USD 58.95 elsewhere. Ed(s): Kathi Kube, David J Eicher. Kalmbach Publishing Co., 21027 Crossroads Circle, PO Box 1612, Waukesha, WI 53187; customerservice@kalmbach.com; http://www.kalmbach.com. Illus., adv. Vol. ends: Dec. *Indexed:* A01, A22, BRI, C37, CBRI, MASUSE. *Bk. rev.:* 5-6, 50-500 words. *Aud.:* Hs, Ga, Ac.

This is one of the most popular astronomy publications among casual sky watchers. Insightful, well-written articles, aimed at a popular audience, are brought together here with some truly spectacular full-color photographs of some of the most "stellar" sights in the heavens. *Astronomy* provides readers with space news reports, monthly observing tips, reviews of telescope-related products, hobby information, and the latest news on space exploration. The web site includes extremely user-friendly podcasts, blogs, and an online Q&A readers forum. A very helpful sky chart, as well as observing tips for locating specific objects in the sky, are to be found in the periodical, in a visually appealing format that is both pleasant and stimulating to read. Recent articles discuss the identification of the mysterious object Oumuamua as a comet, not an asteroid; a huge dust storm on Mars affecting the robotic rover Opportunity, in June, 2018; and the status of the troubled Webb space telescope, currently expected to be launched in 2021. This magazine would be a welcome addition to virtually any library. URL: www.astronomy.com

590. ***Astronomy and Astrophysics (Online).*** Incorporates (1996-2000): *Astronomy and Astrophysics. Supplement Series (Online).* [ISSN: 1432-0746] 2001. 24x/yr. EUR 3215. E D P Sciences, 17 Ave du Hoggar, Parc d'Activites de Courtaboeuf, Les Ulis, 91944, France; contact@edpsciences.org; https://www.edpsciences.org. Refereed. *Aud.:* Ac, Sa.

Sponsored by the European Southern Observatory, this publication represents scientific organizations in 17 European countries. The journal is a cooperative effort that grew out of the merger of the publications of several of the represented organizations. It once had a supplement, published separately, but today the main journal and the supplement are published under a single cover. Or, the journal can be accessed through its web site. Papers relate to all aspects of astronomy and astrophysics (theoretical, observational, and instrumental), regardless of the techniques used to obtain the results. Some items that will *not* be found in this journal include observatory reports, review papers, and conference proceedings. Especially since the merging of this title with its supplement, coverage includes all areas of astronomy and astrophysics, including connected fields. Some recent articles touch upon analyses and observations of the plane of the Milky Way, as surveyed by the multi-national High Energy Stereoscopic System (HESS) Collaboration. Also, there has been some discussion of the history and significance of the journal itself, as this year marks the fiftieth anniversary of its founding. This journal intends to review all important fields relevant to the study of astronomy and astrophysics from time to time, while frequency of review is dictated by the amount of activity in an area. This research publication is comparable to *The Astronomical Journal* and *The Astrophysical Journal*. Recently added features include the ability for registered readers to view the most recent issue on the web site. These readers can also sign up for e-mail alerts concerning their favorite astronomical topics. URL: www.aanda.org

591. ***Astronomy and Computing.*** [ISSN: 2213-1337] 2013. 4x/yr. EUR 463. Ed(s): A Accomazzi, T Murphy. Elsevier BV, Radarweg 29, Amsterdam, 1043 NX, Netherlands; info@elsevier.com; https://www.elsevier.com/. Refereed. *Aud.:* Hs, Ga, Ac, Sa.

The importance of computers in astronomy is already enormous, and will continue to grow. This journal is aimed at computer science specialists, but if you have a young library patron who is serious about astronomy, you would be doing her a big favor by exposing her to this journal, and advising her to just make an effort to understand as much as possible. *Astronomy and Computing* focuses on the broad area between astronomy, computer science, and information technology. The journal aims to publish the work of scientists and (software) engineers in all aspects of astronomical computing, including the collection, analysis, reduction, visualization, preservation, and dissemination of data, and the development of astronomical software and simulations. Recent articles deal with topics such as unsupervised learning of structure in spectroscopic cubes; the DES science portal: creating science-ready catalogs; and a web service framework for astronomical remote observation in Antarctica by using satellite link. This journal covers applications for academic computer science techniques to astronomy, as well as novel applications of information technologies within astronomy.

592. ***Astronomy & Geophysics.*** Formerly (until 1997): *Royal Astronomical Society. Quarterly Journal.* [ISSN: 1366-8781] 1960. bi-m. GBP 345. Ed(s): Sue Bowler. Oxford University Press, Great Clarendon St, Oxford, OX2 6DP, United Kingdom; jnls.cust.serv@oup.com; https://academic.oup.com/journals/. Illus., index, adv. Sample. Refereed. Circ: 3700. Vol. ends: No. 6. Microform: PQC. Reprint: PSC. *Indexed:* A01, A22, E01. *Bk. rev.:* Number and length vary. *Aud.:* Ac, Sa.

After a redesign in 1996, *Astronomy & Geophysics* replaced the *Quarterly Journal of the Royal Astronomical Society* as its topical publication. One objective of the journal is to promote communication among general astronomers and planetary scientists. Therefore, it often has exceptionally strong coverage of planetary sciences, yet it also has excellent coverage of cosmology, black holes, astrophotography, and the like. Articles are written in accessible language, without many equations or formulae, and include related topics such as interdisciplinary research, information about upcoming international conferences, science policy, the history of the fields of study of astronomy- or geophysics-related topics, social issues within the astronomical community, astronomy-related news, and topical book and software reviews. Many traditions from the *Quarterly Journal* remain, such as the journal's being a forum for discussion of fundamental and controversial scientific issues. In 2018, the late, great Stephen Hawking's final scientific paper on the concept of the multiverse has provoked discussion of that topic, often calling upon an article by George Ellis published in this journal in 2008, entitled "Opposing the Multiverse." Other recent articles celebrate female Fellows of the Royal Astronomical Society, clouds of hydrogen sulphide at Uranus, and the role of gravitational waves in revealing neutron stars. Among other new features, available for consideration on the web site, is the ability for readers to alert their librarian to any given article, in case the librarian is engaged in creating new subject guides, and so on. URL: www.blackwellpublishing.com/journal.asp?ref=1366-8781&site=1

593. *Astronomy Reports.* Former titles (until 1993): *Soviet Astronomy;* (until 1974): *Soviet Astronomy A.J.* [ISSN: 1063-7729] 1924. m. EUR 6609 (print & online eds.)). Ed(s): Aleksandr A Boyarchuk. M A I K Nauka - Interperiodica, Profsoyuznaya ul 90, Moscow, 117997, Russian Federation; compmg@maik.ru; http://www.maik.ru. Illus., index. Sample. Refereed. Vol. ends: No. 6. Reprint: PSC. *Indexed:* A01, A22, E01. *Bk. rev.:* Number and length vary. *Aud.:* Ac, Sa.

This journal is displayed prominently at any serious astronomy library. *Astronomy Reports* is a cover-to-cover translation of the principal Russian astronomy journal *Astronomicheskii Zhurnal*, and is available simultaneously with the Russian edition from Maik Nauka/Interperiodica Publishing. Russia has a long and proud tradition of producing great astrophysicists, and a lot of cutting-edge science is first reported in the Russian journals. Issues consist of about 10 to 20 articles in many areas of astronomy, including radio astronomy, theoretical and observational astrophysics, physics of the Sun, planetary science, stellar astronomy, celestial mechanics, astronomical methods and instrumentation, and issues having to do with cosmological large-scale structure. Recent articles in 2018 have discussed perspectives for distributed observations of near-Earth space using a Russian-Cuban observatory, and segregation of calcium isotopes in the atmospheres of chemically peculiar (CP) stars. Proceedings of international conferences and book reviews are also included. URL: www.springer.com/astronomy/journal/11444

594. *The Astrophysical Journal (Online): an international review of astronomy and astronomical physics.* Formerly (until 1895): *Astronomy and Astro-Physics.* [ISSN: 0004-637X] 18??. 18x/yr. USD 2280. Ed(s): Ethan T Vishniac. Institute of Physics Publishing, Inc., 190 North Independence Mall West, Ste 601, Philadelphia, PA 19106; info@ioppubusa.com; http://iopscience.iop.org. Illus., index. Refereed. *Indexed:* A01, A22. *Aud.:* Ac, Sa.

This is widely deemed to be the most important research journal in the world related to astronomy and astrophysics. Many astronomical and astrophysical discoveries of the twentieth and twenty-first centuries were first reported in this peer-reviewed official publication of the American Astronomical Society. Any major astronomy library considers this to be part of its "core" collection. Be aware that the astrophysics presented here is extremely esoteric, with many elaborate equations and graphs in every single article. Recent topics covered include the Mouse Pulsar Wind Nebula; how galaxies form stars, the connection between local and global star formation in galaxy simulations; and photometric variability of quasars in the Sloan Digital Sky Survey. A supplement series accompanies this journal, its main purpose being to present substantial and extensive support for material found in the main journal. Access to a full-text electronic version is free with a paid print subscription. URL: http://iopscience.iop.org/0004-637X/

595. *Astrophysics.* [ISSN: 0571-7256] 1965. q. EUR 5209 (print & online eds.)). Ed(s): David M Sedrakian. Springer New York LLC, 233 Spring St, New York, NY 10013; customerservice@springer.com; http://www.springer.com. Illus., index, adv. Sample. Refereed. Vol. ends: No. 4. Microform: PQC. Reprint: PSC. *Indexed:* A01, A22, E01. *Aud.:* Ac, Sa.

The Consultants Bureau, a subsidiary of Plenum Publishing, is responsible for publishing dozens of English translations of Russian journals, including *Astrophysics*, a cover-to-cover translation of the Russian *Astrofizika*. This journal presents data obtained at Sternberg Astronomical Institute and all principal observatories in Russia, along with recent theoretical and experimental advances in astrophysics. Like *Astronomy Reports*, this is full of cutting-edge Russian science and is geared toward a higher-level audience. Articles deal with the entire range of astronomical and astrophysical phenomena. Topics of papers include planetary atmospheres, interstellar matter, solar physics, and space astrophysics, along with a broad range of related topics. Recently, attention has been given to high energy gamma-ray emission from PKS 0625-35, among other topics. URL: www.springer.com/astronomy/practical+astronomy/journal/10511

596. *Astrophysics and Space Science: an international journal of astronomy, astrophysics and space science.* Incorporates (1970-1972): *Cosmic Electrodynamics;* (1975-1981): *Space Science Instrumentation.* [ISSN: 0004-640X] 1968. m. Ed(s): J Mould, E Brinks. Springer Netherlands, Van Godewijckstraat 30, Dordrecht, 3311 GX, Netherlands; http://www.springer.com. Illus., index, adv. Sample. Refereed. Vol. ends: No. 2. Microform: PQC. Reprint: PSC. *Indexed:* A01, A22, E01, MSN. *Aud.:* Ac, Sa.

This respected journal publishes original contributions, invited reviews, and conference proceedings over the entire range of astronomy and astrophysics. It includes observational and theoretical papers, as well as those concerned with the techniques of instrumentation. Observational papers can include data from ground-based, space, and atmospheric facilities. *Astrophysics and Space Science* has published, and continues to publish, landmark papers in its field. It is widely considered an indispensable source of information for professional astronomers, astrophysicists, and space scientists. Recent coverage has been given of cosmic strings in a five dimensional spherically symmetric background, and the global modulation of galactic and jovian electrons in the heliosphere. The supplemental publication *Experimental Astronomy* (below in this section) is included with the subscription at no extra cost. URL: www.springer.com/astronomy/journal/10509

597. *Astrum.* [ISSN: 0210-4105] 1960. bi-m. Membership, EUR 115. Agrupacio Astronomica de Sabadell, Apdo de Correos 50, Sabadell, Barcelona, 08200, Spain; secretaria@astrosabadell.org; http://www.astrosabadell.org. Illus., adv. Circ: 2000. *Aud.:* Hs, Ga.

Astrum is a colorful astronomy magazine in Spanish, aimed at a popular audience. ProQuest has chosen to survey some astronomy periodicals in Spanish, so that librarians serving constituencies with a growing Spanish-speaking population can accommodate the needs of those patrons. *Astrum* serves this role quite well. It is not a commercial magazine - it is mailed free to members of the Agrupacio Astronomica de Sabadell and to astronomical centers and libraries. However, if your library seeks to foster an interest in science in Hispanic children, you might consider e-mailing the publishing part of the Agrupacio. *Astrum* includes articles, sky charts, ephemerides, and even surveys of Spanish-language Internet resources having to do with astronomy. Furthermore, this title is full of very colorful, high-resolution photographs of many of the more beautiful areas in the sky. URL: www.astrosabadell.org/html/ca/publicacions.htm

598. *British Astronomical Association. Journal.* [ISSN: 0007-0297] 1890. bi-m. Free to members. Ed(s): Hazel McGee. British Astronomical Association, Burlington House, Picadilly, London, W1J 0DU, United Kingdom; office@britastro.org; http://britastro.org/. Illus., index. Refereed. Vol. ends: No. 6. *Indexed:* A01, A22, BRI. *Bk. rev.:* 6-20, 500-1,000 words. *Aud.:* Ac, Sa.

Since its founding in 1890, this journal has published the observations and work of British Astronomical Association (BAA) members, and members receive the journal free. However, nonmembers are eligible to receive the journal if they contact the publisher. Many articles and items of interest to all amateur astronomers are published, along with the observations and work of BAA members. The letters to the editor are often lively and opinionated, with discussions on any subject having to do with astronomy, especially at the amateur level. Subscribers are offered special deals on astronomy-related products from time to time, such as CD-ROMs or software. A recent sampling of articles would include a discussion of how to define the size of an asteroid using amateur observations; analysis of the patterns of cyclones at Jupiter's poles as revealed by the Juno spacecraft; and observing the dark nebulae, AKA "holes in the heavens," visible in the summer months. Although this publication is geared to amateur astronomers and professionals who focus on observational techniques, it does not include the star charts and viewing guides that are published by equivalent American publications, such as *Astronomy* and *Sky & Telescope*. URL: www.britastro.org/jbaa

599. ***Celestial Mechanics and Dynamical Astronomy: an international journal of space dynamics.*** Formerly (until 1989): *Celestial Mechanics.* [ISSN: 0923-2958] 1969. m. Ed(s): Sylvio Ferraz-Mello. Springer Netherlands, Van Godewijckstraat 30, Dordrecht, 3311 GX, Netherlands; http://www.springer.com. Illus., index, adv. Sample. Refereed. Vol. ends: No. 4. Microform: PQC. Reprint: PSC. *Indexed:* A01, A22, BRI, E01, MSN. *Aud.:* Ac, Sa.

This international publication is concerned with the entire scope of dynamical astronomy and its applications, as well as with peripheral fields. It is heavily math- and physics-oriented, which can make reading difficult for those not well-versed in these fields. Articles cover all aspects of celestial mechanics: mathematical, physics-related, and computational, including computer languages for analytical developments. The majority of the articles are in English. Recent articles have delved into the Sitnikov Problem for several primary bodies configurations, and the energy integral for post-Newtonian approximation. This noteworthy publication is considered in the astronomical community to be the journal of record in its area, and it belongs in any complete astronomical library. URL: www.springer.com/astronomy/astrophysics+and+astroparticles/journal/10569

600. ***Communicating Astronomy with the Public Journal.*** [ISSN: 1996-5621] 2007. q. Free to qualified personnel. Ed(s): Georgia Bladon, Anne Rhodes. International Astronomical Union, IAU-UAI Secretariat, 98bis Blvd Arago, Paris, 75014, France; iau@iap.fr; http://www.iau.org. Refereed. *Indexed:* A01. *Bk. rev.:* Number and length vary. *Aud.:* Ac, Sa.

CAP is designed to provide a forum for professionals in the area of astronomy education, at planetariums, and in astronomy-related public outreach, to share insights, methods, and viewpoints. It hopes to make it easier for people in these fields to share both the excitement of science and the actual new information about the universe that today's astronomers are coming to comprehend. Many people in the world today do not realize the awesome magnitude of the leaps forward that our knowledge of the universe is taking, due to advances in technology, in our lifetime. *CAP* seeks to help remedy this situation. Recent articles have been devoted to the public discussion of science in the age of Facebook and Twitter (get used to it); a view ahead to events and activities planned for 2019, which will be the one hundredth anniversary of the founding of the International Astronomical Union; and a discussion of the Hands-On Universe project, developed by Roberto Trotta, which seeks to spread an appreciation of astronomy using various workshops and activities employing all five senses. URL: www.capjournal.org/index.php

601. ***Earth, Moon, and Planets: an international journal of solar system science.*** Former titles (until 1984): *Moon and the Planets;* (until 1978): *Moon.* [ISSN: 0167-9295] 1969. 6x/yr. EUR 953 (print & online eds.)). Ed(s): Murthy S Gudipati. Springer Netherlands, Van Godewijckstraat 30, Dordrecht, 3311 GX, Netherlands; http://www.springer.com. Illus., index, adv. Sample. Refereed. Vol. ends: Dec. Microform: PQC. Reprint: PSC. *Indexed:* A01, A22, BRI, E01. *Bk. rev.:* Number and length vary. *Aud.:* Ac, Sa.

This international journal publishes original contributions on subjects ranging from star and planet formation and the origin and evolution of the solar and extra-solar planetary systems to asteroids, comets, meteoroids, and near-Earth objects. The research done in this journal on near-Earth objects (NEOs) includes studies on asteroids that are considered likely candidates to one day strike Earth. A point to bear in mind is that the planets covered in this journal include exoplanets, which means native to star systems beyond our own. This is very quickly becoming a much more significant area of study than it was just a few years ago. This journal also publishes relevant special issues and topical conference proceedings, review articles on problems of current interest, and book reviews. For example, recently published articles discuss the central symmetry analysis of wrinkle ridges in lunar Mare Serenitatis; scatter radar studies of daytime plasma lines; and the formation of patterns in a self-gravitating isentropic gas. The editor welcomes proposals from guest editors for special thematic issues. URL: www.springer.com/astronomy/journal/11038

602. ***Experimental Astronomy: astrophysical instrumentation and methods.*** [ISSN: 0922-6435] 1989. bi-m. EUR 1434 (print & online eds.)). Ed(s): Peter von Ballmoos. Springer Netherlands, Van Godewijckstraat 30, Dordrecht, 3311 GX, Netherlands; http://www.springer.com. Illus. Sample. Refereed. Vol. ends: No. 4. Microform: PQC. Reprint: PSC. *Indexed:* A01, A22, E01. *Aud.:* Ac, Sa.

Experimental Astronomy acts as a medium for the publication of papers on the instrumentation and data handling necessary for the conduct of astronomy at all wavelength fields, including radio, X-rays, and the like. *Experimental Astronomy* publishes full-length articles, research letters, and reviews on developments in detection techniques, instruments, data analysis, and image-processing techniques. These technical specializations are evolving so quickly that the coverage provided in this journal is of great importance to anyone with a professional interest in having truly current technical information. Occasionally, special issues are published to provide in-depth coverage on the instrumentation or analysis connected with a particular project, such as satellite experiments. Recent articles touch upon the characterization of the chemical composition of exoplanet atmospheres using next-generation space telescopes/observatories such as ARIEL and the Webb space telescope; and the use of logistic regression for stellar classification. Subscribers to *Astrophysics and Space Science* (above in this section) receive this publication as a supplement, but it can also be purchased alone. URL: www.springer.com/astronomy/journal/10686

603. ***Griffith Observer.*** [ISSN: 0195-3982] 1937. m. USD 23 domestic; USD 35 foreign; USD 2.50 per issue. Griffith Observatory, 2800 E Observatory Rd, Los Angeles, CA 90027; http://www.griffithobs.org. Illus. *Indexed:* MLA-IB. *Aud.:* Hs, Ga.

Published monthly by the observatory, this journal provides information about the activities at the Griffith Observatory and popular articles about astronomy. It is comparable in aims and scope to the Spanish-language journal *Astrum.* Sky charts, illustrations, guides to useful Internet links, and photographs enhance this publication, which strives to create a lifelong interest in science in its readers. Recent articles include discussion of artist Lia Halloran's artistic representations of the contributions of female astronomers to the world heritage of astronomy, and the "Super Blue Blood Moon" eclipse of January 2018. For its efforts at popularizing astronomy, the *Griffith Observer* has been characterized as "the Carl Sagan of astronomy periodicals." URL: www.griffithobs.org/Observer.html

604. ***Icarus.*** [ISSN: 0019-1035] 1962. 18x/yr. EUR 9710. Ed(s): P D Nicholson. Academic Press, 225 Wyman St, Waltham, MA 02144; JournalCustomerService-usa@elsevier.com; http://store.elsevier.com/Academic-Press/IMP_5/. Illus., index, adv. Sample. Refereed. Vol. ends: No. 2. *Indexed:* A01, A22, BRI, E01. *Bk. rev.:* 2-3, 150-2,000 words. *Aud.:* Ac, Sa.

Devoted to publishing original contributions in planetary science and the study of solar systems (be they our own solar system, or other, recently discovered planetary systems orbiting more distant stars), this is another very prominent journal for academic libraries. Librarians should note that these fields are focused primarily on relatively local astronomy. Articles are generally about planets, moons, the Sun, or asteroids within our solar system. Coverage of cosmology, black holes, quasars, or theoretical physics is very rarely included. Articles concerning extrasolar planets, or "exoplanets" (planets revolving around stars other than the Sun), are included on the grounds that stars with exoplanets constitute solar systems in their own right. This field is quite new, but it is increasingly important. All aspects of planetary-system research are included, such as results of new research and observations. Recent articles deal with the temperature on Jupiter as observed from the FORCAST camera on

SOFIA; the origin of internal layers in comet nuclei; and the mixing of lunar regolith (soil, or surface dust). Special sections or issues are also a feature. All articles appear in English, but occasional abstracts are in German, French, or Russian. URL: www.elsevier.com/wps/find/journaldescription.cws_home/622843/bibliographic

605. ***International Astronomical Union. Minor Planet Center. Minor Planet Circulars - Minor Planets and Comets (Print).*** Former titles (until 1979): *M P C;* (until 1978): *Minor Planet Circulars.* [ISSN: 0736-6884] 1947. m. International Astronomical Union, Minor Planet Center, Harvard-Smithsonian Center for Astrophysics, 60 Garden St, MS-18, Cambridge, MA 02138; http://www.minorplanetcenter.net/. Illus. *Aud.:* Ac, Sa.

Generally published on the date of the full moon (hence, the approximately monthly frequency), *Minor Planet Circulars* are available both in print and electronically as the *Minor Planets Electronic Circulars.* Astrometric observations on comets and on particularly unusual minor planets are included, although some information is summarized in observatory code. For those who may not be aware of this, "minor planets" is another accepted term for "asteroids." These circulars are published by the agency in charge of keeping an eye out for asteroids that may one day strike Earth. The circulars were once sent out as telegrams, and even today they retain the pithiness of the telegram. No space is wasted, and there is seldom anything resembling actual articles. New numberings and namings of asteroids/minor planets are also announced in the *Circulars.* URL: www.minorplanetcenter.net/iau/services/MPCServices.html

606. ***International Journal of Astrobiology.*** [ISSN: 1473-5504] 2002. bi-m. Ed(s): Rocco Mancinelli. Cambridge University Press, University Printing House, Shaftesbury Rd, Cambridge, CB2 8BS, United Kingdom; journals@cambridge.org; https://www.cambridge.org/. Adv. Refereed. Circ: 450. Reprint: PSC. *Indexed:* A22, E01. *Bk. rev.:* Number and length vary. *Aud.:* Ga, Ac, Sa.

This fascinating journal provides an introduction to the burgeoning world of "astrobiology." This topic includes not only the search for intelligent extraterrestrial life, but also the study of interstellar chemical conditions that are conducive to the appearance of primitive life-forms. The possibility of life on Mars is discussed, as are the (relatively) high chances of discovering life on Saturn's moons Titan and Enceladus, or in the water of Jupiter's moons Europa, Ganymede, and Callisto. Recent articles deal with the possibility of Dyson Spheres (artificially constructed spheres encircling entire stars), which may be observable in some of the less obvious radiation wavelengths; the emerging discipline of robotic astrobiology; and the so-called Silurian Hypothesis, which posits the query whether we could recognize the ruins of extremely ancient industrial civilizations, possibly left by temporary visitors from alien space-faring civilizations, in deep sedimentary layers on Earth. Related inquiries are made into such issues as adaptations made by terrestrial life-forms to extreme environments on Earth. The journal includes peer-reviewed research papers, book reviews, and overviews of this fast-evolving discipline. There has been much excitement about the possibility of life on Enceladus, another moon of Saturn. This journal is intended primarily as a forum for biochemists, astronomers, and other professionals in allied fields, but the inherently fascinating nature of the topic could make some readers choose to put in the extra effort required to wade through an issue. URL: http://journals.cambridge.org/action/displayJournal?jid=IJA

607. ***Journal for the History of Astronomy.*** Incorporates (1979-2002): *Archaeoastronomy.* [ISSN: 0021-8286] 1970. q. USD 723 (print & online eds.)). Ed(s): Michael Hoskin. Sage Publications Ltd., 1 Oliver's Yard, 55 City Rd, London, EC1Y 1SP, United Kingdom; info@sagepub.com; https://www.sagepub.com. Illus. Refereed. Vol. ends: No. 4. Reprint: PSC. *Indexed:* A01, A22, A47, BRI, MLA-IB. *Bk. rev.:* 6-16, 300-1,000 words. *Aud.:* Ac, Sa.

The only journal of its type, *Journal for the History of Astronomy* covers the history of astronomy from its earliest times. The research presented is a pleasant, fascinating change of pace from the heavily math- and science-oriented publications so common (and so important) in astronomy. Few journals capture more successfully the spirit of astronomy, in the sense of the important role it has played throughout the historical struggle between reason and superstition. This journal's subject matter is not rigidly restricted to the history of astronomy per se. For example, sometimes intellectual forays are made into relevant topics in the study of the history of mathematics, or of physics. Recent articles discuss the possible astronomical significance of the mysterious Antikythera mechanism; the solar dial in the Olsztyn castle in Poland, and how it pertains to Copernicus and his discoveries; and a discussion of the assumptions behind Ptolemy's so-called proof of Earth's centrality in the universe. A supplemental publication, *Archaeoastronomy,* is included with a subscription. This supplement is dedicated to investigating astronomical practice and celestial lore in ancient societies from all over the world. Sample articles might include, for example, discussion of ancient Mayan, Inca, Greek, or Egyptian astronomical traditions and edifices, by experts who are learned in these fields. URL: www.shpltd.co.uk/jha.html

608. ***Journal of Cosmology and Astroparticle Physics.*** [ISSN: 1475-7516] 2003. m. USD 2605. Institute of Physics Publishing Ltd., Temple Circus, Temple Way, Bristol, BS1 6HG, United Kingdom; custserv@iop.org; http://iopscience.iop.org. Sample. Refereed. *Indexed:* MSN. *Aud.:* Ac, Sa.

A fairly new journal, *JCAP* is an ambitious, selective online periodical that focuses on the interrelationships between the smallest of subatomic particles and the nature of the universe at its grandest scales, "in the large." Common topics include string theory, gravitational waves, "p-brane democracy," M-theory, brane cosmology, black holes, implications of subatomic particles upon the large-scale structure of the universe, and other cosmological issues. Recent articles hold forth upon luminosity and cooling of highly magnetized white dwarfs; cosmogenic neutrino flux predictions; and the search for dark matter gamma-ray emission from the Andromeda Galaxy. Criteria for article acceptance are "scientific quality, originality and relevance." This journal is probably too advanced for most amateur hobbyists, but it has been placed on many "core" reading lists for academic science libraries, even in these financially strapped times. URL: www.iop.org/EJ/journal/JCAP

609. ***Living Reviews in Solar Physics.*** [ISSN: 1614-4961] 2004. irreg. Free. Ed(s): Sami Solanki. SpringerOpen, Tiergartenstr 17, Heidelberg, 69121, Germany; info@springeropen.com; http://www.springeropen.com. Refereed. *Indexed:* A01. *Aud.:* Ac, Sa.

This is a peer-reviewed, online forum for cutting-edge research and discussion of solar and heliospheric physics. The word "living" is built into this journal's title because authors keep their articles "alive" by means of frequent online updates. *Living Reviews* also wishes to be known for its up-to-date, critical reviews of the particular subfield of solar research covered by a given article. Some recent topics of articles include semiclassical approximations of the Wheeler-DeWitt equation, and relativistic dynamics and extreme mass ratio inspirals. Bibliographic subject guides to assist in further research are always appended. These guides are updated often by the authors, and include links to helpful web sites. This journal aims to become an online starting point for graduate students; and for professionals in the field, it aims to open the most significant doors of online research as they emerge. URL: http://solarphysics.livingreviews.org

610. ***Lunar and Planetary Information Bulletin (Online).*** Former titles (until 2003): *Lunar & Planetary Information Bulletin (Print);* (until 1978): *Lunar Science Information Bulletin.* [ISSN: 1534-6587] 1974. q. Free. Ed(s): Paul Schenk. Lunar and Planetary Institute, 3600 Bay Area Blvd, Houston, TX 77058; order@lpi.usra.edu; http://www.lpi.usra.edu. Illus. *Bk. rev.:* Number and length vary. *Aud.:* Ga, Ac.

Not to be confused with the *Association of Lunar and Planetary Observers Journal.* This is a real treat for the layperson who has the background and command of vocabulary. The Lunar and Planetary Institute provides support services to NASA, and to planetary scientists. Their publication covers astronomical topics that are likely to be of interest to the average involved reader, such as potential fossils on Mars, or the adaptation of hydroponic plant cultures to possible long-term space missions for life-support purposes. A regular section titled "Spotlight on Education" focuses on events and programs that provide planetary scientists and astronomers with an opportunity to do outreach work to the community. There is a "New in Print" section that takes the reader on a tour of recently published books in the field. Often, one of these titles is singled out for an in-depth review, which sometimes includes an interview with the author. Also, the "News from Space" section is excellent, containing six or seven short articles about exciting goings-on in astronomy.

Recent articles discuss the twenty-fifth anniversary of the Shoemaker/Levy 9 comet, and its impact into Jupiter; and an interesting article on planetary nomenclature, or how planets are named. Intelligent, well-written discussions can be found dealing with such questions as the origin of the solar system or of the asteroid belt. An objective and scientific approach, written in a delightfully accessible style. URL: www.lpi.usra.edu/publications/newsletters/lpib

611. *Mercury (Online).* Former titles (until 2008): *Mercury (Print);* (until 1972): *Astronomical Society of the Pacific. Leaflet.* [ISSN: 2373-2857] 1925. q. USD 72 Free to members. Ed(s): Paul Deans. Astronomical Society of the Pacific, 390 Ashton Ave, San Francisco, CA 94112; astro@astrosociety.org; http://www.astrosociety.org. Illus., index, adv. Circ: 3500. Vol. ends: No. 6. *Indexed:* A01, A22, BRI, MASUSE. *Bk. rev.:* 2-6, 50-200 words. *Aud.:* Hs, Ga, Sa.

Mercury is now entirely online, and its purpose is to provide the necessary perspective for understanding astronomy. This nonspecialist magazine is geared toward a broad public audience, and features articles on topics ranging from astronomy research and education, to archaeoastronomy, history, and public policy. It is the most widely read online publication of the Astronomical Society of the Pacific (ASP), a nonprofit organization whose goal is to promote public interest and awareness of astronomy through education and outreach programs. As the online membership magazine of the ASP, this title has made a name for itself as *the* resource by which teachers may follow innovations in astronomy education. Frequently, there are articles dealing with the role of education in science, and the role of science in society. The magazine includes sky calendars and sky maps for use in the Northern Hemisphere. Recent articles discuss the pluses and minuses of high altitude balloons for bearing instruments aloft for space research; NASA's Transiting Exoplanet Survey Satellite, and our hopes that it could discover 20,000 alien worlds; and how NASA's InSight lander will be able to study the interior and geological history of Mars. Book reviews are included, as are regular sections on current observing prospects, "armchair astrophysics," and news highlights from the world of astronomy. URL: www.astrosociety.org/pubs/mercury/mercury.html

612. *The Messenger.* [ISSN: 0722-6691] 1974. q. Free. Ed(s): Jeremy R Walsh. European Southern Observatory, Karl Schwarzschild Str 2, Garching, 85748, Germany; ips@eso.org; http://www.eso.org. Illus., index. Sample. *Aud.:* Ac, Sa.

Published by the European Southern Observatory (ESO) in La Silla, Chile, this magazine presents the activities of the ESO to the public. Subscription is free of charge. The periodical is roughly comparable to the *Griffith Observer*, in that it acts as a window into the activities of a major observatory, but it adds an international flavor. The primary significance of this journal is that it emphasizes the astronomy of the Southern Hemisphere, which is often given short shrift in many astronomy journals. As the audience codes indicate, many of the articles are quite high-level, full of equations, graphs, and so on. However, the photographs of the ESO staff happily toiling away at their astro-projects make the reader feel like a guest in the home of an interesting extended family. Recent articles discuss newly enhanced data discovery services for the ESO science archive; the imaging of stellar surfaces; and the stellar initial mass function of dusty starburst galaxies. The ESO observatory is supported by eight countries: Belgium, Denmark, France, Germany, Italy, Sweden, Switzerland, and the Netherlands, and it receives eight hundred proposals a year for research that would require use of the facility. URL: www.eso.org/sci/publications/messenger

613. *Meteoritics and Planetary Science.* Formerly (until 1996): *Meteoritics;* Which superseded (in 1953): *Contributions of the Meteoritical Society;* Which was formerly (until 1947): *Contributions of the Society for Research on Meteorites;* Meteoritics superseded in part (in 1953): *Popular Astronomy.* [ISSN: 1086-9379] 1935. m. GBP 1594 (print & online eds.)). Ed(s): Agnieszka P Baier, A J Timothy Jull. John Wiley & Sons, Inc., 111 River St, Hoboken, NJ 07030; cs-journals@wiley.com; http://onlinelibrary.wiley.com. Illus., adv. Refereed. Microform: PQC. Reprint: PSC. *Indexed:* A01, A22, BRI, E01. *Aud.:* Ac, Sa.

This scholarly journal is published by the Meteoritical Society, an international organization that studies the smallest bodies in the solar system. It is free to society members. Articles are peer reviewed and are always original, and articles published here cannot be found elsewhere. *MaPS* provides a forum for discussing the study of extraterrestrial matter and history, including asteroids, comets, tektites, impact craters, and interplanetary dust - uniting professionals from a variety of backgrounds including geology, physics, astronomy, and chemistry. Planetary science is also given coverage. This means that articles can sometimes be found here that deal with the planets and moons of our solar system, including our own moon. Of the several journals that deal largely with meteors and asteroids, this is the one that deals most directly with what we can *learn* from meteors, especially what we can learn about the origins of our solar system. This journal is different from, for example, the *Minor Planet Circulars*, in that it includes articles as well as raw data. Recent articles deal with the interior evolution of the asteroid Ceres, as elucidated by the science from the Dawn probe, and the significance of iddingsite in nakhlite meteorites. URL: http://meteoritics.org

614. *Nature Astronomy.* [ISSN: 2397-3366] 2017. m. USD 99. Nature Publishing Group, The MacMillan Bldg, 4 Crinan St, London, N1 9XW, United Kingdom; nature@nature.com; https://www.nature.com. Refereed. *Bk. rev.:* Number and length vary. *Aud.:* Ga, Ac, Sa.

Nature Astronomy is a new journal from the Nature group of publications. It deals with all aspects of astronomy, including observational astronomy, theoretical astrophysics, computational techniques, exoplanets, galactic astronomy, and cosmology. It features comments, book reviews, news and views, and correspondence. Some recent articles discuss the increasing popularity of moons of the outer planets of our solar system, as possible cradles of life; how to incorporate input from non-astronomers such as biologists and chemists, in the search for extraterrestrial life, as we become better able to understand conditions on exoplanets; and studies that seek to correlate the shape of galaxies with their age. URL: https://www.nature.com/natastron/about

615. *New Astronomy.* [ISSN: 1384-1076] 1996. 8x/yr. EUR 846. Ed(s): P S Conti, G Brunetti. Elsevier BV, Radarweg 29, Amsterdam, 1043 NX, Netherlands; info@elsevier.com; https://www.elsevier.com/. Illus. Sample. Refereed. Vol. ends: No. 8. *Indexed:* A01, A22. *Aud.:* Ac, Sa.

This journal includes full-length research articles and letter articles. In recent years, it has shifted its focus to emphasize computational astronomy, i.e., computer modeling, and mathematical methodology and applications, and *NA* hopes to become the leading journal in this area. It aims to have a very short publication time, which keeps it very close to the cutting edge of astronomy. It prides itself on sending personal e-mails to astronomers about upcoming articles in their specialties. It covers solar, planetary, stellar, galactic, and extragalactic astronomy and astrophysics, and reports on original research in all wavelength bands, ranging from radio to gamma-ray. Topics include all fields of astronomy and astrophysics: theoretical, observational, and instrumental. Recent articles discuss such topics as estimates of supermassive black hole spins for the standard accretion disk model, and V1719 Aql, a solar-type twin binary. An institutional subscription provides web access for everyone at a subscribing institute, an archival paper edition, and an electronic copy for LAN distribution. Slightly lower prices for smaller institutions and for individuals are available on request, and a two-month free trial is available for individuals. URL: www.elsevier.com/locate/newast

616. *New Astronomy Reviews.* Formerly (until 1998): *Vistas in Astronomy;* Incorporates (1977-1991): *Astronomy Quarterly.* [ISSN: 1387-6473] 1958. 6x/yr. EUR 1070. Ed(s): J Audouze, P A Charles. Elsevier BV, North-Holland, Postbus 211, Amsterdam, 1000 AE, Netherlands; JournalsCustomerServiceEMEA@elsevier.com; http://www.elsevier.com. Illus., index, adv. Sample. Refereed. Vol. ends: No. 45. Microform: PQC. *Indexed:* A01, A22, BAS. *Aud.:* Ac, Sa.

Although the name of this journal has changed, there has been no significant content change from years past. The journal still includes historical perspectives and in-depth reports, review articles, and surveys of findings on major activities in astronomical research. Contributions include reprints in specific areas and in-depth review articles that survey major areas of astronomy. The journal covers solar, planetary, stellar, galactic, and extragalactic astronomy and astrophysics. It reports on original research in all wavelength bands, ranging from radio to gamma-ray. Some articles in 2018 have delved into the terrestrial (Earth) record of Late Heavy Bombardment by asteroids and other bolides, around 2.5 to 3.5 billion years ago, and star clusters in evolving galaxies. This journal might be seen as taking the broad-based coverage of *Mercury* to a higher level, for reading by professional scientists. Written for astronomers, astrophysicists, and space scientists. URL: www.journals.elsevier.com/new-astronomy-reviews/#description

617. *The Observatory: a review of astronomy.* [ISSN: 0029-7704] 1877. bi-m. GBP 70 (Individuals, GBP 15). Ed(s): D J Stickland. Observatory, 16 Swan Close, Grove, OX12 0QE, United Kingdom. Illus., index, adv. Refereed. Vol. ends: No. 6. *Indexed:* A22. *Bk. rev.:* Number and length vary. *Aud.:* Ga.

This journal is sent free to members of the Royal Astronomical Society (RAS), and it is owned and managed by the editors. Meetings of the RAS are reported, but information does not generally overlap with what appears in the official RAS publications *Monthly Notices* and *Astronomy and Geophysics*. Those two are considered the most important publications of this society, while *The Observatory* is more of a supplement. Papers and correspondence tend to be short but scholarly, with few illustrations. *The Observatory* prides itself on publishing "the most comprehensive set of book reviews in astronomy." URL: www.ulo.ucl.ac.uk/obsmag

618. *Planetarian.* [ISSN: 0090-3213] 1972. q. Free to members. International Planetarium Society, Griffith Observatory, 2800 E Observatory Rd, Los Angeles, CA 90027; http://www.griffithobservatory.org. Illus., adv. Refereed. Vol. ends: No. 4. *Indexed:* A01, A22. *Aud.:* Hs, Ac, Sa.

Planetarian is free with membership in the International Planetarium Society, but there is also the option for libraries to purchase the journal separately. The majority of the publication is devoted to astronomy education, with special emphasis on the role planetariums can play. For example, an article may discuss the value of planetariums as teaching aids to help students develop a three-dimensional vision of the structure of our galaxy. Another topic is planetariums acting as aids in helping students visualize actual or potential space voyages. Recent articles discuss planetarium-related issues in Turkey, Mexico, and Sweden; and how to build and train an effective planetarium staff. This is a fairly specialized journal, but certainly a very interesting and very readable one. It includes much information of interest to astronomers, academic libraries, school libraries, and science teachers. URL: www.ips-planetarium.org/?plntrn

619. *Planetary and Space Science.* [ISSN: 0032-0633] 1959. 15x/yr. EUR 5627. Ed(s): R Schulz. Pergamon Press, The Blvd, Langford Ln, E Park, Kidlington, OX5 1GB, United Kingdom; JournalsCustomerServiceEMEA@elsevier.com; http://www.elsevier.com. Illus., adv. Sample. Refereed. Microform: PQC. *Indexed:* A01, A22. *Aud.:* Ac, Sa.

This is the official journal of the European Geophysical Society, Planetary and Solar Systems Sciences Section. It includes both articles and "short communications" (letters). While this journal still focuses primarily on coverage of planetary and solar system research, as in times past, its scope has now broadened to include extra-solar systems and astrobiology, comprehensive review articles, and meetings papers. Articles still tend to be focused on planetary systems - but with recent advances in astronomy, some of the planets studied lie outside of our solar system. Articles dealing with such topics as cosmology, black holes, active galactic nuclei, or quasars will not be found, as they do not relate to planetary systems. Ground-based and space-borne instrumentation and laboratory simulation of solar system processes are included. This journal has a fairly similar mission and audience to *Icarus*, and libraries may want to compare these two excellent journals to consider which best meets their needs. The intended audience includes professional astronomers, astrophysicists, atmospheric physicists, geologists, and planetologists. Some articles in 2018 discussed determining Mars rotation using data from a moving rover, and the performance of the BepiColombo Laser Altimeter. URL: www.elsevier.com/wps/find/journaldescription.cws_home/200/description#description

620. *Popular Astronomy.* Formerly (until 1981): *Hermes;* Incorporates (in 1981): *S P A News Circular.* [ISSN: 0261-0892] 1953. q. Free to members. Society for Popular Astronomy, c/o Guy Fennimore, 36 Fairway, Nottingham, NG12 5DU, United Kingdom; secretary@popastro.com; http://www.popastro.com/. Illus. *Indexed:* MLA-IB. *Aud.:* Hs, Ga, Ac.

This highly readable British publication covers all aspects of astronomy. Each issue is packed with articles and photographs, many in color. Regular features include a review of developments in astronomy and space science; methods, advice, and ideas for the practical amateur astronomer; and a sky diary of what's upcoming in the next week. There is an unusual section called "Amateur Scene," which provides interviews and surveys dealing with the very active amateur astronomy scene - astronomy clubs, "open sky nights" at college observatories, and the like. Recent articles discuss the evolution of planetaria, looking at Earth through alien eyes, and a guide to imaging the Perseid meteors. The clear, readable style will appeal to beginners and more experienced amateurs alike. This journal is roughly comparable in scope and approach to *Astronomy* and *Sky & Telescope*. URL: www.popastro.com/spapop/home.htm

621. *Royal Astronomical Society. Monthly Notices.* Formerly (until 1833): *Astronomical Society of London. Monthly Notices.* [ISSN: 0035-8711] 1827. 36x/yr. GBP 5490. Ed(s): D R Flower. Oxford University Press, Great Clarendon St, Oxford, OX2 6DP, United Kingdom; jnls.cust.serv@oup.com; https://academic.oup.com/journals/. Illus., adv. Sample. Refereed. Microform: PQC. Reprint: PSC. *Indexed:* A01, A22, E01. *Aud.:* Ac, Sa.

This journal is considered to be a "core" publication for any high-level astronomy library. Since 1827, it has published timely articles, from contributors all over the world (not just from the United Kingdom), on all areas of astronomy, including positional and dynamical astronomy, astrophysics, radio astronomy, cosmology, space research, instrument design, and more. Replete with equations, this periodical is indispensable for the serious astronomer, but rather slow going for anyone but the most committed amateur. Recent articles discuss such topics as neutron star bulk viscosity, spin-flip, and newly born magnetars. This journal includes some new keyword search features, so if you have perused this journal in the past, be ready for some pleasant surprises. Note that *The Observatory: A Review of Astronomy* (above in this section) is an optional companion to this journal. URL: www.blackwellpublishing.com/journal.asp?ref=0035-8711

622. *Royal Astronomical Society of Canada. Observer's Handbook.* Formerly (until 1911): *Canadian Astronomical Handbook.* [ISSN: 0080-4193] 1907. a. CAD 27.95 per issue domestic; CAD 38.20 per issue United States; CAD 44.20 per issue elsewhere. Ed(s): David M F Chapman. Royal Astronomical Society of Canada, 203-4920 Dundas St W, Toronto, ON M9A 1B7, Canada; mempub@rasc.ca; http://www.rasc.ca. Illus., index. Circ: 8500. Microform: PQC. *Aud.:* Ems, Hs, Ga, Ac, Sa.

The *Observer's Handbook* is a guide published annually since 1907 by The Royal Astronomical Society of Canada. Please note: there is now an American version of this publication, set up to be even more user-friendly to American astronomy enthusiasts. Through its long tradition and the highly respected expertise of its contributors, it has come to be regarded as the standard North American reference for data concerning the sky. The material in it is of interest to professional and amateur astronomers, scientists, teachers at all levels, students, science writers, campers, scout and guide leaders, and others. The guide is an integral part of many astronomy courses at the secondary and university levels, and it is on the reference shelf of many libraries of various kinds. URL: www.rasc.ca/handbook

Science. See Science and Technology/General section.

623. *The Science Teacher.* Formerly (until 1937): *Illinois Chemistry Teacher.* [ISSN: 0036-8555] 1934. 9x/yr. Free to members. Ed(s): Caroline Barnes, Scott Stuckey. National Science Teachers Association, 1840 Wilson Blvd, Arlington, VA 22201; nstapress@nsta.org; http://www.nsta.org/. Illus., index, adv. Sample. Refereed. Circ: 22800. Vol. ends: May. Microform: PQC. *Indexed:* A01, A22, BRI, ERIC. *Aud.:* Ems, Hs.

The Science Teacher is not exclusively an astronomy periodical, but it frequently devotes a lot of coverage to astronomy. This is one of the publications of the National Science Teachers Association (NSTA), and is aimed at secondary school teachers. *Science and Children* is a parallel journal published by the same association, directed at teachers of a younger age bracket. Both of these are highly respected journals that take a hands-on approach to education.

They are each constantly brimming over with specific ideas for age-appropriate activities, as opposed to the jargon of educational theory. Recent articles are devoted to making science interesting and accessible to all students, including LGBT students, and the slowing of light in glass, which of course is a helpful way of making telescopes more interesting. If your library includes teachers among its patrons, you should be aware of these journals for their utility in the communication of the wonder of astronomy to young minds. NSTA journals are a member benefit and are not available by subscription. URL: www.nsta.org/highschool

624. ***Sky & Telescope: the essential guide to astronomy.*** Formed by the merger of (1933-1941): *The Telescope;* (1936-1941): *The Sky;* Which superseded (in 1936): *Drama of the Skies;* Which was formerly (until 19??): *American Museum of Natural History. Hayden Planetarium. Bulletin.* [ISSN: 0037-6604] 1941. m. USD 42.95 United States; USD 49.95 Canada; USD 5.99 per issue. Ed(s): Peter Tyson. F + W Media Inc., 1140 Broadway, 14th Fl, New York, NY 10001; contact_us@fwmedia.com; http://www.fwcommunity.com/. Illus., index, adv. Sample. Circ: 64432 Paid. Vol. ends: Jun/Dec. Microform: PQC. *Indexed:* A01, A22, BRI, CBRI, MLA-IB. *Bk. rev.:* 4-5, 350-1,000 words. *Aud.:* Hs, Ga, Ac.

Since it began publication in 1941, *Sky & Telescope* has been a leader in providing accurate and up-to-date information on astronomy and space science. The magazine chose its subtitle of "the essential guide to astronomy" itself, but it is able to get away with it. It is written so that it appeals to all astronomy enthusiasts, from the youngest novice to the most seasoned professional. Its articles are painstakingly edited to be easily understood by both technically savvy readers and those who benefit from clear descriptive language and graphics. Regular features include book reviews, a sky calendar, news notes, and tips on imaging the sky. Recent articles touch upon NASA's MAVEN spacecraft, and what it told us about how Mars lost its original atmosphere; how to clean up space junk; and how nineteenth-century economic history on Earth affected how we thought about Mars and its so-called canals. Annually, this journal prints a directory of organizations, institutions, and businesses related to astronomy. URL: www.skyandtelescope.com

Sky Calendar. See *Abrams Planetarium Sky Calendar.*

625. ***SkyNews: the Canadian magazine of astronomy and stargazing.*** [ISSN: 0840-8939] 1988. bi-m. CAD 26 domestic; USD 36 United States; CAD 41 elsewhere. Ed(s): Terence Dickinson. SkyNews Inc, PO Box 10, Yarker, ON K0K 3N0, Canada; gseronik@skynews.ca. Illus., adv. *Indexed:* BRI, C37. *Aud.:* Hs, Ga, Ac.

A useful, very popular publication for novice stargazers. Each colorful issue contains news, columns, features, an excellent sky chart, and equipment reviews. Articles are directed primarily, but not exclusively, to a Canadian audience. What this may mean to an American library is simply that some of the tables presented will have been calibrated with more northerly latitudes in mind. This may have a certain impact on the utility of *some* of the information provided, but the articles and equipment reviews, of course, will still be quite useful, enjoyable, and engrossing. Recent articles discuss observing the Ring Nebula in Lyra; how to get the ideal pair of binoculars for your own stargazing habits; and ideas and methods for how to get data-noise-free astro-images. URL: www.skynewsmagazine.com

626. ***SkyWatch.*** [ISSN: 1089-4888] 1996. a. USD 8.99 (print or online ed.)). Sky Publishing Corp., 90 Sherman St, Cambridge, MA 02140; http://www.skyandtelescope.com. Adv. Microform: PQC. *Aud.:* Ems, Hs, Ga.

Published by the people who bring us *Sky & Telescope,* this annual listing of sky events is meant for beginners or serious amateurs. A portable, uncomplicated guide to the night sky, *SkyWatch* is a useful observing tool. Included are star charts from September of one year through December of the following year; a map of the lunar surface; a gallery of state-of-the-art astrophotography; and articles on choosing telescopes, binoculars, and other astronomy gear. Recent articles discuss the size of the universe, the best astronomy apps for your phone, and the times for observing the various planets and meteor showers over the course of the year. Also helpful is the featured how-to article on finding 16 of the most popular objects for viewing in the night sky. This publication can be compared to the *Observer's Handbook* (see *Royal Astronomical Society of Canada. Observer's Handbook,* above in this section). URL: www.shopatsky.com/skywatch-2016; or Google "Skywatch 2016" in quote marks.

627. ***Solar Physics: a journal for solar and solar-stellar research and the study of solar terrestrial physics.*** [ISSN: 0038-0938] 1967. m. Ed(s): Lidia van Driel-Gesztelyi, John Leibacher. Springer Netherlands, Van Godewijckstraat 30, Dordrecht, 3311 GX, Netherlands; http://www.springer.com. Illus., index, adv. Sample. Refereed. Vol. ends: No. 14. Reprint: PSC. *Indexed:* A01, A22, BRI, E01. *Aud.:* Ac, Sa.

Solar Physics was founded in 1967 and is the principal journal for the publication of the results of fundamental research on the Sun. It is meant to be read by serious scientists. The journal treats all aspects of solar physics, ranging from the internal structure of the Sun and its evolution, to the outer corona and solar wind in interplanetary space. Papers on solar-terrestrial physics and on stellar research are also published when their results have a direct bearing on our understanding of the Sun. Recent articles touch upon morphological predictors of flaring activity on the sun, and flux rope formation due to shearing and zipper reconnection. URL: www.springer.com/astronomy/astrophysics/journal/11207

628. ***Solar System Research.*** [ISSN: 0038-0946] 1967. bi-m. EUR 7497 (print & online eds.)). Ed(s): Mikhail Ya Marov. M A I K Nauka - Interperiodica, Profsoyuznaya ul 90, Moscow, 117997, Russian Federation; compmg@maik.ru; http://www.maik.ru. Illus. Sample. Refereed. Vol. ends: No. 6. Reprint: PSC. *Indexed:* A01, A22, BRI, E01. *Aud.:* Ac, Sa.

This journal is translated into English by MAIK Nauka/Interperiodica Publishing and is published simultaneously with the Russian edition. Review papers appear regularly, along with notes on observational results and communications on scientific meetings and colloquiums. *Solar System Research* is the only journal from Russia that deals with the topics of planetary exploration, including the results of original study obtained through ground-based and/or space-borne observations and theoretical/computer modeling. In recent years, the journal has significantly expanded the scope of its interest through the involvement of new research fields such as planetary geology and cosmophysics, planetary plasma physics and heliosphere, atmospheric sciences, and general problems in comparative planetology. Yet, as in the past, the journal's focus remains on our own solar system, as opposed to exoplanets. One recent article discusses calibrating the albedo of asteroids, and another deals with Saturn's moon Iapetus, and how the equatorial ridge on its surface was formed. URL: www.springer.com/astronomy/journal/11208

629. ***Spaceflight.*** [ISSN: 0038-6340] 1956. m. Free to members; Non-members, GBP 4.50. British Interplanetary Society, 27-29 S Lambeth Rd, London, SW8 1SZ, United Kingdom; mail@bis-spaceflight.com; http://www.bis-space.com/. Illus., index, adv. Vol. ends: No. 12. Microform: PQC. *Indexed:* A22, B03. *Aud.:* Hs, Ga, Ac, Sa.

Published since 1956, this is considered to be a core journal by most astronomy libraries. Regarded as an authoritative periodical, *Spaceflight* focuses primarily upon national, international, and commercial efforts to explore space. Articles cover such topics as ongoing space shuttle missions, details of space station life, and educational efforts aimed at popularizing these initiatives. In general, articles are aimed at a presumably intelligent audience that may or may not be professionally involved in space exploration. Recent articles discuss the European Space Agency's upcoming Ariane 6, a new generation of heavy load launcher; an interesting chapter in the history of astronomy, the East German populace's ways of finding out about advances in astronomy when they were behind the Iron Curtain; and the significance of Jeff Bezos in the exploration of the solar system. URL: www.bis-space.com/products-page/magazines-and-journals/spaceflight-magazine/

630. ***SpringerBriefs in Astronomy.*** [ISSN: 2191-9100] 2012. irreg. Springer, Tiergartenstr 17, Heidelberg, 69121, Germany; subscriptions@springer.com; https://www.springer.com. *Aud.:* Hs, Ga, Ac, Sa.

If your institution values and appreciates the content of the *Annual Review of Astronomy and Astrophysics* (above in this section), then you may wish to take a look at this series. *SpringerBriefs in Astronomy* covers the full range of topics under the rubric of astronomy, but they strive to go into greater depth, and give a fuller account of the subjects they cover, than might be possible in some other publications. Thus, *SpringerBriefs* serves as a set of timely, concise tools for students, researchers, and professionals. Typical texts for publication might include: a snapshot review of the current state of a hot or emerging field; a concise introduction to core concepts that students must understand in order to make independent contributions; an extended research report that gives more details and discussion than is possible in a conventional journal article; a manual describing underlying principles and best practices for an experimental technique; an essay exploring new ideas within astronomy and related areas; or broader topics such as science and society. Recent articles touch upon extrasolar planets and their host stars, research on teaching astronomy in the planetarium, and three-body dynamics and its application to exoplanets.

631. ***StarDate.*** Formerly (until 1986): *McDonald Observatory News.* [ISSN: 0889-3098] 1972. bi-m. USD 26 domestic; USD 32 in Canada & Mexico; USD 45 elsewhere. Ed(s): Rebecca Johnson. University of Texas, Austin, McDonald Observatory, 1 University Station A2100, Austin, TX 78712; http://mcdonaldobservatory.org. Illus. Sample. *Aud.:* Ems, Hs, Ga.

StarDate is known to many as a radio show, but you can find the same information and more in the online edition or by purchasing a paper copy. The magazine is perfect for amateur astronomers and anyone interested in celestial events and space exploration. It is updated daily, and includes such helpful features as an astronomical "Tip of the Day," which concerns interesting things to observe in the sky; a section called "Today on StarDate," which presents articles on all kinds of topics from astronomy and the history of astronomy, including archaeo-astronomy; and daily astronomical questions to ponder. There are also Internet links about astronomy and an astronomical search engine for online research. Recent articles discuss the idea of seeds of life spread by comets and asteroids, perhaps to worlds other than Earth, and other articles go into cosmic superlatives, such as what are the fastest, largest, and oldest things in the universe. For Spanish-speaking children, *StarDate* is available in Spanish. Look for "Universo Online," on the right-hand side of the web site. URL: http://stardate.org

The Strolling Astronomer. See *Association of Lunar and Planetary Observers. Journal.*

632. ***The Universe in the Classroom.*** [ISSN: 0890-6866] 1984. q. Free. Ed(s): Jeff Mangum. Astronomical Society of the Pacific, 390 Ashton Ave, San Francisco, CA 94112; service@astrosociety.org; http://www.astrosociety.org. Illus. *Aud.:* Ems, Hs.

This is an electronic educational newsletter for teachers. Published by our old friend, the Astronomical Society of the Pacific, *The Universe in the Classroom* assumes no background in astronomy on the part of the teacher. It is designed to suggest activities and lesson plans that the teacher can employ for her or his students, to enhance their natural wonder at the night sky. Efforts are made to keep the content of each issue relevant, in some way, to astronomical topics that may currently be in the news. The web site strives to include updated links to resources and to assist the educator in developing her or his own understanding of various topics. One recent issue seeks to help educators show students how to construct telescopes from a simple pinhole viewer to more complex instruments. URL: www.astrosociety.org/education/publications/tnl/about.html

■ ATMOSPHERIC SCIENCES

See also Marine Science and Technology section.

Susan Moore, Catalog Librarian and Unit Coordinator, Cataloging Metadata Unit, Rod Library, University of Northern Iowa, Cedar Falls, IA 50613; susan.moore@uni.edu

Introduction

"Atmospheric sciences" include a number of specific disciplines, such as atmospheric chemistry, climatology, meteorology, atmospheric physics, and weather forecasting. Other disciplines concerned with weather and the study of the atmosphere are also included. While the United States withdrew from an international agreement, interest continues in the fluctuations that many regions are experiencing with their weather and how these changes are related to climate change.

The publications listed in this section focus on research journals and general-interest periodicals devoted to the study of atmospheric sciences and weather. Listed here are titles for libraries in North America that primarily publish articles concerning meteorology, climatology, atmospheric chemistry, atmospheric physics, weather forecasting, and related areas.

The list contains only journals published in English; however, as researchers are interested in weather phenomena wherever they happen, some journals from regions outside North America published in English are included.

Many federal publications once issued in print are now only available on the web. Changing to an online publication allows for faster updating and increased interactivity. These sites include:

National Weather Service. http://weather.gov/. This very useful web site of weather and forecasting data from the National Weather Service includes links to areas covered by watches and warnings, as well as links to *Active Alerts, Forecast Maps, Radar, Air Quality, Satellite,* and *Past Weather.*

National Centers for Environmental Information. www.ncdc.noaa.gov/oa/about/about.html. The National Centers for Environmental Information maintains the archive of climate data (according to the web site, the largest archive of its kind in the world). The Centers develop national and global datasets and serve as the country's leading authority for environmental information.

Weather and Climate. www.usda.gov/oce/weather/index.htm. A joint project of the World Agricultural Outlook Board of the U.S. Department of Agriculture and the National Oceanic and Atmospheric Administration, the site includes links to publications that provide important meteorological information to those engaged in agriculture and related fields. Titles included are *Daily U.S. Agricultural Weather Highlights, Weekly Weather and Crop Bulletin, Major World Crop Areas and Climatic Profiles,* and *Monthly World Agricultural Weather Highlights.* Many of these publications include specific information for commodity buyers and farmers, such as current agricultural weather highlights and crop production reviews.

Basic Periodicals

Hs: *Weatherwise;* Ga: *American Meteorological Society. Bulletin; Weather; Weatherwise; WMO Bulletin;* Ac: *American Meteorological Society. Bulletin; Atmospheric Chemistry and Physics; Atmospheric Science Letters; Climate Dynamics; Journal of Applied Meteorology and Climatology; Journal of Climate; Journal of Geophysical Research: Atmospheres; Journal of the Atmospheric Sciences; Monthly Weather Review; Royal Meteorological Society. Quarterly Journal; Weather; Weather and Forecasting; Weather, Climate, and Society; Weatherwise; WMO Bulletin.*

Basic Abstracts and Indexes

Chemical Abstracts, GEOBASE, INSPEC, Meteorological and Geoastrophysical Abstracts, Science Citation Index.

633. ***Advances in Atmospheric Sciences.*** [ISSN: 0256-1530] 1984. bi-m. EUR 1247 (print & online eds.)). Ed(s): Daren Lu, Huijun Wang. Chinese Academy of Sciences, Institute of Atmospheric Physics, PO Box 9804, Beijing, 100029, China; http://www.iap.ac.cn/. Refereed. Circ: 1000. Microform: PQC. Reprint: PSC. *Indexed:* A01, A22, C45, E01, S25. *Aud.:* Ac.

Publishes original scholarly articles on the "dynamics, physics, and chemistry of the atmosphere and ocean." The sponsoring bodies are the Chinese Committee for International Association of Meteorology and Atmospheric Sciences and the Institute of Atmospheric Physics, Chinese Academy of Science. A majority of articles have a geographic focus on Asia and the Pacific. Meant for researchers in meteorology and atmospheric sciences, the articles are fairly technical. Papers covering weather systems, numerical weather prediction, climate dynamics and variability, satellite meteorology, air chemistry and the boundary layer, and clouds and weather modification are welcome.

634. *American Meteorological Society. Bulletin.* [ISSN: 0003-0007] 1920. m. Free to members; Non-members, USD 175. Ed(s): Jeffrey Rosenfeld. American Meteorological Society, 45 Beacon St, Boston, MA 02108; amsinfo@ametsoc.org; http://www.ametsoc.org. Illus., index, adv. Sample. Refereed. Circ: 13000. Vol. ends: Dec. Microform: PMC. *Indexed:* A01, A22, BRI, C45, E01, S25. *Bk. rev.:* Occasional, 200-500 words. *Aud.:* Ga, Ac.

This title serves as the official forum of the American Meteorological Society. It normally contains "editorials, topical reports to members, articles, professional and membership news, conference announcements, programs and summaries, book reviews, and coverage of society activities." Each issue includes a calendar of professional meetings. There is also a section called "Nowcast" that contains short articles on developments in atmospheric and related sciences that are often not peer-reviewed. Regular supplements include a list of the society's current publications and the annual report of the society. This title is recommended for any library in the United States that supports teaching and research in atmospheric science, meteorology, climatology, and related fields. It is also available to members through the society's web site.

635. *Asia-Pacific Journal of Atmospheric Sciences.* Formerly (until 2008): *Hangug Gisang Haghoeji.* [ISSN: 1976-7633] 1965. 4x/yr. EUR 772 (print & online eds.)). Ed(s): Soon-Il An. Korean Meteorological Society, Youngdungpo-gu, Shingil-dong 508, Ciwon Bldg 704, Seoul, 150-050, Korea, Republic of; komes@komes.or.kr; http://www.komes.or.kr. Refereed. Reprint: PSC. *Aud.:* Ac.

A publication of the Korean Meteorological Society, this is a refereed international journal that publishes original scientific research in all areas of atmospheric science. It does have a strong emphasis on the Asia-Pacific region. Review articles, research notes, and communications of preliminary results are also published. Special issues and supplements are occasionally published as well.

636. *Atmosfera.* [ISSN: 0187-6236] 1988. q. USD 80 (Individuals, USD 60; MXN 300 domestic). Ed(s): Carlos Gay. Universidad Nacional Autonoma de Mexico, Centro de Ciencias de la Atmosfera, Circuito Exterior, Ciudad Universitaria, Mexico City, 04510, Mexico. Illus., index. Refereed. Vol. ends: Dec. *Indexed:* A22. *Aud.:* Ac.

This journal publishes theoretical, basic, empirical, and applied research on topics related to the atmospheric sciences. Contributions relating to the characterization and understanding of air-sea interactions as they relate to meteorological phenomena and interactions of the atmosphere and the biosphere, and how these relate to climate, are particularly welcomed. Short contributions and correspondence are also occasionally published. Articles are in English, with abstracts in English and Spanish. The journal is particularly strong in its coverage of Latin America and the neighboring oceans. Recent topics include economic growth in Latin America and the Caribbean and carbon dioxide emissions, a cost-benefit analysis of flood protection in Tabaso, Mexico, and the impact of climate of farm inputs in developing countries' agriculture.

637. *Atmosphere.* [ISSN: 2073-4433] 2010. q. Free. Ed(s): Dr. Robert Talbot. M D P I AG, St. Alban-Anlage 66, Basel, 4052, Switzerland; http://www.mdpi.com. Refereed. *Indexed:* A01, C45. *Bk. rev.:* Number and length vary. *Aud.:* Ac.

This open-access international scholarly journal publishes scientific studies that concern the atmosphere, and it is particularly interested in cross-disciplinary articles in the areas of atmospheric chemistry, atmospheric physics, air quality (including climate interactions), and meteorology. The stated aim is "to encourage scientists to publish their experimental and theoretical research in as much detail as possible." There is, therefore, no length restriction on papers. Book reviews, communications, and short notes are also published. Occasionally, special issues covering a specific topic are published.

638. *Atmosphere - Ocean.* Formerly (until 1978): *Atmosphere.* [ISSN: 0705-5900] 1963. 5x/yr. GBP 183 (print & online eds.)). Ed(s): Guoqi Han, Douw Steyn. Routledge, 4 Park Sq, Milton Park, Abingdon, OX14 4RN, United Kingdom; subscriptions@tandf.co.uk; http://www.routledge.com. Illus., index. Sample. Refereed. Reprint: PSC. *Indexed:* A22, C45, S25. *Bk. rev.:* Occasional, 750-1,000 words. *Aud.:* Ac, Sa.

As the principal scientific journal of the Canadian Meteorological and Oceanographic Society, this title is very good at publishing studies, both original research and review articles, that have a Canadian focus. Many of the researchers are Canadian, but foreign contributions covering other regions are also published. Geographic areas of particular interest are Arctic, coastal, and mid- to high-latitude regions. The journal publishes occasional special issues on topics of interest in meteorology and related fields. Articles may be in English or French, although most are in English. Abstracts are in both languages.

639. *Atmospheric Chemistry and Physics.* [ISSN: 1680-7316] 2001. 24x/yr. Copernicus GmbH, Bahnhofsallee 1e, Goettingen, 37081, Germany; info@copernicus.org; http://www.copernicus.org. Refereed. *Indexed:* S25. *Aud.:* Ac.

This open-access, interactive journal is an international journal that publishes studies that investigate the atmosphere of the Earth and the chemical and physical processes that occur there. Layers of the atmosphere that are covered range from the surface of the land and ocean up to the turbopause. The main subject areas included are "atmospheric modelling, field measurements, remote sensing, and laboratory studies of gases, aerosols, clouds and precipitation, isotopes, radiation, dynamics, biosphere interactions, and hydrosphere interactions," with a focus on studies that have general implications for atmospheric science. Recent articles cover topics such as dust modeling in summertime West Africa, the potential impact of emission policies on tropospheric ozone, and the surface impacts of the Quasi Biennial Oscillation. Meant for researchers in meteorology and atmospheric sciences, the articles are fairly technical.

640. *Atmospheric Environment.* Formed by the merger of (1990-1994): *Atmospheric Environment. Part A, General Topics;* (1990-1994): *Atmospheric Environment. Part B, Urban Atmosphere;* Both of which superseded in part (in 1990): *Atmospheric Environment;* Which superseded in part (in 1967): *Air and Water Pollution;* Which was formerly (until 1963): *International Journal of Air and Water Pollution;* (until 1961): *International Journal of Air Pollution.* [ISSN: 1352-2310] 1967. 24x/yr. EUR 12270. Elsevier Ltd, The Boulevard, Langford Lane, Oxford, OX5 1GB, United Kingdom; customerserviceau@elsevier.com; http://www.elsevier.com. Illus., adv. Sample. Refereed. Microform: MIM; PQC. *Indexed:* A01, A22, C45, S25. *Aud.:* Ac.

Atmospheric Environment puts an emphasis on original research that covers "atmospheric composition and its impacts," including such topics as "atmospheric relevance of emissions and depositions of gaseous and particulate compounds, chemical processes and physical effects in the atmosphere, as well as impacts of the changing atmospheric composition on human health, air quality, climate change, and ecosystems." Of particular interest are papers concerning the impacts of natural and human-induced changes to the atmosphere of the Earth that have a degree of novelty to them. Some review articles are published. Some issues publish papers presented at specific conferences. There are also thematic issues. Articles are written for researchers and scientists.

641. *Atmospheric Research.* Formerly (until 1986): *Journal de Recherches Atmospheriques.* [ISSN: 0169-8095] 1963. 16x/yr. EUR 4008. Ed(s): J L Sanchez. Elsevier BV, Radarweg 29, Amsterdam, 1043 NX, Netherlands; info@elsevier.com; https://www.elsevier.com. Illus., index. Refereed. *Indexed:* A01, A22, C45, S25. *Aud.:* Ac.

This journal publishes research papers, review articles, letters, and notes concerning "the part of the atmosphere where meteorological events occur." While all processes from the ground to the tropopause are covered, continuing to be the major topics of focus are: the physics of clouds, mesoscale meteorology, and air pollution, i.e., atmospheric aerosols; microphysical processes; cloud dynamics and thermodynamics; and numerical simulation, climatology, climate change, and weather modification. Special issues are published occasionally. Articles are primarily in English. Recent topics covered include diurnal variation of atmospheric stability and turbulence during different seasons at two tropical stations in the Indian Peninsula; seasonal cycles of precipitation over major river basins in South and Southeast Asia; and the impact of aerosol and freezing level on orographic clouds.

642. *Atmospheric Science Letters.* [ISSN: 1530-261X] 2000. q. Free. Ed(s): Rev. Ian N James. John Wiley & Sons Ltd., EMEA Institutional Sales, 9600 Garsington Rd, Oxford, OX4 2DQ, United Kingdom; cs-journals@wiley.com; http://onlinelibrary.wiley.com. Adv. Refereed. *Indexed:* A01, A22, E01. *Bk. rev.:* Number and length vary. *Aud.:* Ac, Sa.

This online open-access journal of the Royal Meteorological Society serves as a peer-reviewed route to publication for shorter contributions to the atmospheric and closely related sciences. Topics of particular interest include dynamical meteorology, ocean-atmosphere systems, climate change, variability and impacts, new or improved observations from instrumentation, hydrometeorology, numerical weather prediction, data assimilation, physical processes of the atmosphere, and land surface-atmosphere systems. Recent topics include intraseasonal variation of the East Asian monsoon associated with the Madden-Julian Oscillation; time trends and persistence of maximum and minimum temperatures in the United States; and changes in air quality in the United Kingdom monitored from space.

643. *Boundary-Layer Meteorology: an international journal of physical, chemical and biological processes in the atmospheric boundary layer.* [ISSN: 0006-8314] 1970. m. EUR 4725 (print & online eds.)). Ed(s): John R Garratt, E Fedorovich. Springer Netherlands, Van Godewijckstraat 30, Dordrecht, 3311 GX, Netherlands; http://www.springer.com. Illus., index, adv. Refereed. Vol. ends: Dec. Microform: PQC. Reprint: PSC. *Indexed:* A01, A22, Agr, C45, E01, S25. *Bk. rev.:* Occasional, 350-500 words. *Aud.:* Ac.

This journal covers "the physical, chemical and biological processes occurring in the lowest few kilometres of the Earth's atmosphere." It publishes "theoretical, numerical and experimental studies of the atmospheric boundary layer over both land and sea surfaces." Articles are intended for professionals in atmospheric science. Occasionally, special issues that focus on a particular topic are published. The subject areas included are air-sea interactions, micrometeorology, air-quality control, agriculture and forestry, surface processes, and the planetary boundary layer. Recent topics include wind tunnel simulations of weakly and moderately stable atmospheric boundary layers; a simulation of the effect of building heights on turbulent flows over an actual urban area; and the impact of three-dimensional effects on the simulation of turbulence in an Alpine valley.

644. *Climate Dynamics: observational, theoretical and computational research on the climate system.* [ISSN: 0930-7575] 1986. 16x/yr. EUR 10862 (print & online eds.)). Ed(s): Dr. Jean-Claude Duplessy, Edwin K Schneider. Springer, Tiergartenstr 17, Heidelberg, 69121, Germany. Adv. Refereed. Reprint: PSC. *Indexed:* A01, A22, Agr, C45, E01, S25. *Aud.:* Ac.

This journal covers all aspects of the dynamics of the global climate system. The articles and the editorial board are international in scope. The journal especially welcomes papers that cover "original paleoclimatic, diagnostic, analytical or numerical modeling research on the structure and behavior of the atmosphere, oceans, cryosphere, biomass and land surface as interacting components of the dynamics of global climate," particularly as these topics relate to climate dynamics on particular scales of space or time. Recent topics include analysis of return periods and return levels of yearly July-September extreme droughts in the West African Sahel; global diurnal temperature range changes since 1901; and the role of the Indian summer monsoon variability on Arabian Peninsula summer climate.

645. *Climatic Change: an interdisciplinary, international journal devoted to the description, causes and implications of climatic change.* [ISSN: 0165-0009] 1977. 25x/yr. EUR 4910 (print & online eds.)). Ed(s): Gary Yohe, Michael Oppenheimer. Springer Netherlands, Van Godewijckstraat 30, Dordrecht, 3311 GX, Netherlands; http://www.springer.com. Illus., index, adv. Refereed. Microform: PQC. Reprint: PSC. *Indexed:* A01, A22, Agr, BRI, C45, E01, S25. *Bk. rev.:* Number and length vary. *Aud.:* Ac.

This interdisciplinary journal focuses on "the totality of the problem of climatic variability and change." Articles come from a variety of disciplines in the sciences, social sciences, and other fields interested in climatic variation. There are occasional special issues on topics of particular interest. Given the wide range of disciplines covered and the growth of interest in interdisciplinary research, this journal should be of interest to academic libraries in general. Topics recently covered include the impact of risk communication on cooperation in climate change mitigation; indicators of climate change in agricultural systems; and distribution of the global carbon budget using climate justice criteria.

646. *Dynamics of Atmospheres and Oceans.* [ISSN: 0377-0265] 1977. 4x/yr. EUR 1277. Ed(s): L Shay. Elsevier BV, Radarweg 29, Amsterdam, 1043 NX, Netherlands; info@elsevier.com; https://www.elsevier.com. Illus., index, adv. Sample. Refereed. Vol. ends: Jan. Microform: PQC. *Indexed:* A01, A22, S25. *Aud.:* Ac, Sa.

This international journal includes research "related to the dynamical and physical processes governing atmospheres, oceans, and climate." Papers can be theoretical, computational, experimental, or observational investigations. Of particular interest are "papers that explore air-sea interactions and the coupling between atmospheres, oceans, and other components of the climate system." Most articles are technical in nature and assume reader familiarity with mathematical modeling. In addition to scholarly articles, short contributions as well as scholarly reviews are published. Fields represented by the authors include meteorology, atmospheric science, environmental engineering, Earth sciences, and other fields. There are occasional special issues that focus on a particular topic.

647. *Earth Interactions.* [ISSN: 1087-3562] 1997. irreg. Free. Ed(s): Rezaul Mahmood, Joseph A Santanello. American Geophysical Union, 2000 Florida Ave, NW, Washington, DC 20009; service@agu.org; http://sites.agu.org/. Illus. Refereed. *Indexed:* A01, A22, E01, S25. *Aud.:* Ac.

Earth Interactions is a joint publication of the American Geophysical Union, the American Meteorological Society, and the Association of American Geographers and is fully open access. The focus of this journal is articles concerning "the interactions among the atmosphere, hydrosphere, biosphere, cryosphere, and lithosphere, including, but not limited to, research on human impacts, such as land cover change, irrigation, dams/reservoirs, urbanization, pollution, and landslides." The types of articles published include reports on original research, review articles, and brief reports concerning data or models. Since the journal is completely electronic, authors are encouraged (but not required) to use animations or other components. URL: http://earthinteractions.org

648. *International Journal of Biometeorology: the description, causes, and implications of climatic change.* Formerly (until 1960): *International Journal of Bioclimatology and Biometeorology.* [ISSN: 0020-7128] 1957. bi-m. EUR 1626 (print & online eds.)). Ed(s): Scott C Sheridan. Springer, Tiergartenstr 17, Heidelberg, 69121, Germany. Illus., index, adv. Refereed. Vol. ends: Mar. Reprint: PSC. *Indexed:* A01, A22, Agr, C45, E01, S25. *Aud.:* Ac.

This title publishes original research papers, review articles, and short communications on "the interactions between living organisms and factors of the natural and artificial atmospheric environment." Articles cover the impact that the environment has on the full range of living organisms from single-cell organisms to humans. Recent topics include pollen distribution in the northeastern Indian Ocean and its significance; the changes in urban plant phenology in the Pacific Northwest from 1959 to 2016; and managing the risk of extreme climate events in Australian major wheat production systems. This title may be of interest to biologists and medical professionals, as well as Earth and atmospheric scientists.

649. *International Journal of Climatology.* Formerly (until 1989): *Journal of Climatology.* [ISSN: 0899-8418] 1981. 15x/yr. GBP 2779. Ed(s): Dr. Radan Huth. John Wiley & Sons Ltd., EMEA Institutional Sales, 9600 Garsington Rd, Oxford, OX4 2DQ, United Kingdom; cs-journals@wiley.com; http://onlinelibrary.wiley.com. Illus., index, adv. Sample. Refereed. Vol. ends: Dec. Microform: PQC. Reprint: PSC. *Indexed:* A22, C45, S25. *Bk. rev.:* 300-500 words. *Aud.:* Ac, Sa.

The title "aims to span the well established but rapidly growing field of climatology." Thus, it covers climate system science, from local to global-scale climate observations and modeling; seasonal to interannual climate prediction; and climatic variability and climate change. Approaches covered include synoptic, dynamic, and urban climatology; hydroclimatology; human bioclimatology; ecoclimatology; dendroclimatology; palaeoclimatology; marine climatology; atmosphere-ocean interaction; the application of climatological knowledge to environmental assessment and management and economic production; and climate and society interactions. Though this is a publication of the Royal Meteorological Society, the journal expects articles to contribute significantly to the international literature. Research papers, reviews of progress, and reports are published here, as well as book reviews.

650. ***The International Journal of Meteorology.*** Formerly (until Sep.2005): *Journal of Meteorology.* [ISSN: 1748-2992] 1975. 10x/yr. GBP 120 (Individuals, GBP 41.50). Ed(s): Samantha J A Hall. Artetech Publishing Co., 20 Massey Ave, Lymm, WA13 0PJ, United Kingdom. Illus., index, adv. Sample. Refereed. Vol. ends: Dec. *Indexed:* A22. *Bk. rev.:* 750-1,000 words. *Aud.:* Ga, Ac.

Published by the Tornado and Storm Research Organisation (TORRO), this title specializes in severe weather and meteorology, especially events that occur in the United Kingdom and Ireland. This well-illustrated journal is of interest to meteorologists and weather enthusiasts. There are occasional special issues that usually cover notable weather events. There is also an annual special issue that covers all of TORRO's research results of the previous year, including an annual summary of significant weather events.

651. ***Journal of Applied Meteorology and Climatology.*** Formerly (until 2006): *Journal of Applied Meteorology;* Which superseded in part (in 1987): *Journal of Climate and Applied Meteorology;* Which was formerly (1962-1983): *Journal of Applied Meteorology.* [ISSN: 1558-8424] 1962. m. Members, USD 160 (print & online eds.); Non-members, USD 1775 (print & online eds.)). Ed(s): David A Kristovich. American Meteorological Society, 45 Beacon St, Boston, MA 02108; amspubs@ametsoc.org; http://www.ametsoc.org. Illus., index. Refereed. Vol. ends: Dec. *Indexed:* A01, A22, E01, S25. *Aud.:* Ac, Sa.

This journal is a publication of the American Meteorological Society and publishes applied research related to "weather modification, satellite meteorology, radar meteorology, boundary layer processes, physical meteorology, air pollution meteorology, agricultural and forest meteorology, mountain meteorology, and applied meteorological numerical models." Articles concerning applied climatological topics are also considered. Examples of recent topics published include a formula for calculating the saturation vapor pressure of water and ice; the use of urban heat islands as a shield from extreme cold events; and the evaluation and postprocessing of fire weather predictions in the northeastern United States.

652. ***Journal of Atmospheric and Oceanic Technology.*** [ISSN: 0739-0572] 1984. m. Members, USD 155 (print & online eds.); Non-members, USD 1465 (print & online eds.)). Ed(s): William J Emery, Luca Baldini. American Meteorological Society, 45 Beacon St, Boston, MA 02108; amsinfo@ametsoc.org; http://www.ametsoc.org. Illus., index. Refereed. Vol. ends: Dec. *Indexed:* A01, A22, C45, E01, S25. *Aud.:* Ac.

A publication of the American Meteorological Society, this journal focuses on research on "describing instrumentation and methods used in atmospheric and oceanic research, including remote sensing instruments; measurements, validation, and data analysis techniques from satellites, aircraft, balloons, and surface-based platforms; in situ instruments, measurements, and methods for data acquisition, analysis, and interpretation and assimilation in numerical models; and information systems and algorithms." The articles are written for researchers in the subject and not practicing meteorologists. Brief articles on works in progress are occasionally included in a notes-and-correspondence section. Articles are marked to indicate their focus on atmospheric or oceanic topics. Recent topics include evaluating humidity and sea salt disturbances on carbon dioxide flux measurements; the application of the EMD method to river tides; and proposing a correction for the thermal mass-induced errors of CTD tags mounted on marine mammals. This title is primarily of interest to researchers in the atmospheric sciences.

653. ***Journal of Atmospheric Chemistry.*** [ISSN: 0167-7764] 1983. 4x/yr. EUR 1609 (print & online eds.)). Ed(s): Elliot L Atlas. Springer Netherlands, Van Godewijckstraat 30, Dordrecht, 3311 GX, Netherlands; http://www.springer.com. Illus., adv. Refereed. Microform: PQC. Reprint: PSC. *Indexed:* A01, A22, Agr, BRI, C45, E01, S25. *Aud.:* Ac.

This publication concerns research on the chemistry of the Earth's atmosphere, especially the region below 100 kilometers. The journal focuses on topics such as studies of the composition of air and precipitation and the physiochemical processes in the Earth's atmosphere (excluding air pollution problems that are primarily of local importance only); the role of the atmosphere in biogeochemical cycles; the chemical interaction of the oceans, land surface, and biosphere with the atmosphere; laboratory studies of the mechanics in homogeneous and heterogeneous transformation processes in the atmosphere; and descriptions of major advances in instrumentation. Recent topics covered include the impact of freezing and compaction on iron solubility in natural snow; water-soluble inorganic ions of size-differentiated atmospheric particles from a suburban site of Mexico City; and role of precursor emissions on ground level ozone concentration during summer season in Poland. Articles are written for scientists and researchers.

654. ***Journal of Climate.*** Supersedes in part (in 1988): *Journal of Climate and Applied Meteorology;* Which was formerly (1962-1983): *Journal of Applied Meteorology.* [ISSN: 0894-8755] 1962. s-m. Members, USD 195 (print & online eds.); Non-members, USD 2730 (print & online eds.)). Ed(s): Anthony J Broccoli, John C Chiang. American Meteorological Society, 45 Beacon St, Boston, MA 02108; amsinfo@ametsoc.org; http://www.ametsoc.org. Illus., index. Refereed. Vol. ends: Dec. *Indexed:* A01, A22, Agr, C45, E01, S25. *Aud.:* Ac, Sa.

Published by the American Meteorological Society, this journal concentrates on articles concerned with research on topics such as large-scale variability of the atmosphere, oceans, land surface, and cryosphere; past, present, and projected future changes in the climate system (including those caused by human activities); and climate simulation and prediction. Brief reports and comments are also published. Review articles must be approved by the chief editor prior to submission. Recent articles explore assessing the impact of volcanic eruptions on climate extremes; climate forecasting of the tropical Indo-Pacific Ocean using model-analogs; and probabilities of causation of climate changes.

655. ***Journal of Geophysical Research: Atmospheres.*** Supersedes in part (in 2013): *Journal of Geophysical Research;* Which was formerly (until 1949): *Magnetism and Atmospheric Electricity;* (until 1899): *Terrestrial Magnetism.* [ISSN: 2169-897X] 1896. s-m. Ed(s): Minghua Zhang. Wiley-Blackwell Publishing, Inc., 111 River St, Hoboken, NJ 07030; info@wiley.com; http://onlinelibrary.wiley.com. Illus. Refereed. Reprint: PSC. *Indexed:* C45, S25. *Aud.:* Ac, Sa.

A publication of the American Geophysical Union, this journal publishes articles "that advance and improve understanding of atmospheric properties and processes, including the interaction of the atmosphere with other components of the Earth system." Recent topics include agricultural fire impacts on ozone photochemistry over the Yangtze River delta region, East China; numerical evaluation of the modern and future origins of atmospheric river moisture over the West Coast of the United States; and the role of wave-induced diffusion and energy flux in the vertical transport of atmospheric constituents in the mesopause region. Articles are written for professionals and graduate students.

656. ***Journal of Hydrometeorology.*** [ISSN: 1525-755X] 2000. bi-m. Members, USD 145 (print & online eds.); Non-members, USD 825 (print & online eds.)). Ed(s): Christa D Peters-Lidard. American Meteorological Society, 45 Beacon St, Boston, MA 02108; amspubs@ametsoc.org; http://www.ametsoc.org. Refereed. *Indexed:* A01, A22, C45, E01, S25. *Aud.:* Ac, Sa.

This journal publishes articles on "research on modeling, observing, and forecasting processes related to fluxes and storage of water and energy, including interactions with the boundary layer and lower atmosphere, and including processes related to precipitation, radiation, and other meteorological inputs." As with most American Meteorological Society publications, this title also publishes brief reports and comments. Recent topics include the characterization of rain microphysics; vapor condensation in rice fields and its contribution to crop evapotranspiration in the subtropical monsoon climate of China; and estimating the landscape soil water losses from satellite observations of soil moisture.

657. ***Journal of Meteorological Research.*** Formerly (until 2013): *Acta Meteorologica Sinica.* [ISSN: 2095-6037] 1987. bi-m. EUR 1232 (print & online eds.)). Ed(s): Guoxiong Wu, Dalin Zhang. Chinese Meteorological Society, 46 Zhongguancun Nan Dajie, Haidian District, Beijing, 100081, China. Illus., index, adv. Refereed. Circ: 300 Paid. Reprint: PSC. *Aud.:* Ac, Sa.

This title is the English version of the official Chinese Meteorological Society journal. Areas of emphasis include pure and applied meteorology, climatology, and climate change; atmospheric physics and chemistry; cloud physics and weather modification; numerical weather prediction; atmospheric sounding and remote sensing; marine meteorology; and air pollution meteorology. Many of the articles cover Asia. Review articles are accepted. Articles recently published cover topics such as an investigation into the formation, structure, and evolution of an EF4 tornado in East China; atmospheric circulation patterns over East Asia and their connection with summer precipitation and surface air temperature in Eastern China during 1961-2013; and diurnal and seasonal variations of thermal stratification and vertical mixing in a shallow fresh water lake. Recommended for research collections.

658. ***Journal of Operational Meteorology.*** Formed by the merger of (2001-2012): *Electronic Journal of Operational Meteorology;* (1976-2012): *N W A Digest.* [ISSN: 2325-6184] 2013. . USD 60. Ed(s): Adam Clark. National Weather Association, 3100 Monitor Ave, Ste 123, Norman, OK 73072. Refereed. *Aud.:* Ac, Sa.

This publication of the National Weather Association focuses on operational meteorology. Areas covered by the publication include "new or improved forecasting and warning techniques, verification studies, applications of observations and models to improve forecasts and warnings, and case studies of major weather events." Related topics will be considered if they relate to operational meteorology. This publication primarily targets meteorologists and meteorology students in the United States.

659. ***Journal of Southern Hemisphere Earth Systems Science (Online).*** Formerly (until 2016): *Australian Meteorological and Oceanographic Journal (Online).* 2009. irreg. Free. Ed(s): David Karoly, Dr. Sophie Lewis. Australia. Bureau of Meteorology, GPO Box 1289, Melbourne, VIC 3001, Australia; http://www.bom.gov.au. Refereed. *Aud.:* Ga.

This journal was formed from the merger of the *Australian Meteorological and Oceanographic Journal* and the *Australian Meteorological Magazine.* Focusing on the southern hemisphere, it publishes articles on meteorology, climate, oceanography, hydrology, coastal zone processes, and space weather. Not surprisingly, given the focus and the publisher, a number of articles cover Australia and the rest of the Southern Hemisphere.

660. ***Journal of the Atmospheric Sciences.*** Formerly (until 1962): *Journal of Meteorology.* [ISSN: 0022-4928] 1944. m. Members, USD 170 (print & online eds.); Non-members, USD 2480 (print & online eds.)). Ed(s): Walter A Robinson, William H Brune. American Meteorological Society, 45 Beacon St, Boston, MA 02108; amsinfo@ametsoc.org; http://www.ametsoc.org. Illus., index. Refereed. *Indexed:* A01, A22, E01, S25. *Aud.:* Ac, Sa.

This journal from the American Meteorological Society publishes "basic research related to the physics, dynamics, and chemistry of the atmosphere of Earth and other planets, with emphasis on the quantitative and deductive aspects of the subject." Most of the articles are quantitative, although there are occasional brief articles and notes. Recent topics include the local view of atmospheric available potential energy; how environmental conditions influence vertical buoyancy structure and shallow-to-deep convection transition across different climate regimes; and linear and nonlinear dynamics of North Atlantic oscillations.

661. ***Meteorological Applications.*** [ISSN: 1350-4827] 1994. q. GBP 436. Ed(s): P J Burt. John Wiley & Sons Ltd., EMEA Institutional Sales, 9600 Garsington Rd, Oxford, OX4 2DQ, United Kingdom; cs-journals@wiley.com; http://onlinelibrary.wiley.com. Adv. Sample. Refereed. Reprint: PSC. *Indexed:* A01, A22, BRI, C45, E01, S25. *Aud.:* Ac.

Written for applied meteorologists, forecasters, and other users of meteorological services, this journal of the Royal Meteorological Society covers a range of topics, including applications of meteorological and climatological data and their benefits; forecasting; warning-service delivery techniques and methods; analysis and prediction of weather hazards; performance and verification of numerical models and forecasting services and their value; training techniques; and practical applications of ocean and climate models. There are occasional special issues that deal with topics of current interest. Recent topics include a new approach to statistical-dynamical downscaling for long-term wind resource predictions; drying trends under changing climate conditions using four meteorological drought indexes; and the impact of the hottest day on record on the rail system in the United Kingdom.

662. ***Meteorological Society of Japan. Journal.*** [ISSN: 0026-1165] 1882. bi-m. Ed(s): Tetsuya Takemi, Masaki Satoh. Nihon Kisho Gakkai, c/o Japan Meteorological Agency, 1-3-4, Ote-machi, Chiyoda-ku, Tokyo, 100-0004, Japan; metsoc-j@aurora.ocn.ne.jp; http://www.metsoc.or.jp/index.html. Illus. Refereed. Vol. ends: Dec. *Indexed:* A01, A22, C45. *Aud.:* Ac.

The journal publishes research in areas of meteorology including "meteorological observations, modeling, assimilations, analyses, global and regional climate research, satellite remote sensing, chemistry and transport, and dynamic meteorology including geophysical fluid dynamics." All articles are in English. Since this is the research journal of the Meteorological Society of Japan, the geographic areas of East Asia and the western Pacific Ocean are well covered. The journal welcomes articles on Asian monsoons, climate and mesoscale models, and numerical weather forecasts. Special issues that focus on a particular topic are occasionally published. Recent topics include the outer-core wind structure of tropical cyclones; climate variability in monsoon and arid regions attributable to dynamic vegetation in a global climate model; and structure and environment of tornado-spawning extratropical cyclones around Japan.

663. ***Meteorology and Atmospheric Physics.*** Formerly (until 1986): *Archives for Meteorology, Geophysics, and Bioclimatology. Series A: Meteorology and Geophysics - Archiv fuer Meteorologie, Geophysik und Bioklimatologie. Series A.* [ISSN: 0177-7971] 1948. m. EUR 4179 (print & online eds.)). Ed(s): C Simmer. Springer Wien, Prinz-Eugen-Str 8-10, Wien, 1040, Austria; journals@springer.at; http://www.springer.com. Illus., adv. Sample. Refereed. Vol. ends: Dec. Reprint: PSC. *Indexed:* A22, Agr, BRI, E01. *Bk. rev.:* 200-500 words. *Aud.:* Ac, Sa.

This title publishes articles of original research in the areas of physical and chemical processes in both clear and cloudy atmospheres. Atmospheric dynamics, general circulation in the atmosphere, synoptic meteorology, analysis of weather systems in specific regions, and atmospheric energetics are a few of the topics covered. The journal is international in scope, and authors and research are from around the world. Recent articles cover such topics as the effects of ice microphysics on the inner core thermal structure of the hurricane boundary layer; an investigation on the Bay of Bengal branch of summer monsoon during normal and delayed onset over Gangetic West Bengal; and the synoptic thermodynamic and dynamic patterns associated with Quitandinha River flooding events in Petropolis, Rio de Janeiro (Brazil).

664. ***Monthly Weather Review.*** [ISSN: 0027-0644] 1872. m. Members, USD 185 (print & online eds.); Non-members, USD 2645 (print & online eds.)). Ed(s): David M Schultz. American Meteorological Society, 45 Beacon St, Boston, MA 02108; amsinfo@ametsoc.org; http://www.ametsoc.org. Illus., index, adv. Refereed. Vol. ends: Dec. *Indexed:* A01, A22, C45, E01, S25. *Aud.:* Ac, Sa.

This American Meteorological Society journal publishes research related to the analysis and prediction of observed atmospheric physics and circulations, especially on those phenomena that have seasonal or subseasonal time scales. Review articles and articles on high-impact weather events, such as hurricanes, are published on occasion. A recurring column is the "Picture of the Month," which features a photograph of interesting weather phenomena. Recent topics covered include ensemble sensitivity analysis for targeted observations of supercell thunderstorms; the microphysics and radiation effect of dust on the Saharan air layer; and the influence of the monsoon trough and Arabian heat low on summer rainfall over the United Arab Emirates.

665. *The Open Atmospheric Science Journal.* [ISSN: 1874-2823] 2007. . Free. Ed(s): Yoav Yair. Bentham Open, Executive Suite Y-2, PO Box 7917, Sharjah, , United Arab Emirates; subscriptions@benthamscience.org; http://www.benthamscience.com. Refereed. *Aud.:* Ac.

This online, open-access journal publishes "reviews, research articles, letters, and guest[-]edited single topic issues in all areas of climate research and atmospheric science." The editorial board is international in scope. Topics that have been published recently include the assimilation of GPS radio occultation data for tropical cyclogenesis in the eastern Atlantic; a case study of municipal solid waste landfills impact on air pollution in south areas of Italy; and a study on the contamination by coal dust in the neighborhood of the Tarragona Harbor of Spain.

666. *Royal Meteorological Society. Quarterly Journal: a journal of the atmospheric sciences, applied meteorology, and physical oceanography.* Incorporates (1922-1950): *Bibliography of Meteorological Literature.* [ISSN: 0035-9009] 1871. 8x/yr. GBP 823. Ed(s): Douglas J Parker, Lesley P Gray. John Wiley & Sons Ltd., EMEA Institutional Sales, 9600 Garsington Rd, Oxford, OX4 2DQ, United Kingdom; cs-journals@wiley.com; http://onlinelibrary.wiley.com. Illus., index, adv. Sample. Refereed. Vol. ends: Oct. *Indexed:* A01, A22, C45. *Bk. rev.:* Number and length vary. *Aud.:* Ac, Sa.

One of the major research journals in meteorology, this title focuses on original research in atmospheric sciences and associated fields. The papers are scholarly and technical and are written by scholars from around the world. Review articles, short articles, and comments on previously published articles are considered. Book reviews appear in some issues. Also, special issues publish the papers from a particular scientific meeting or on specific topics. Recommended for libraries that support atmospheric and Earth sciences programs.

667. *Russian Academy of Sciences. Izvestiya. Atmospheric and Oceanic Physics.* Formerly: *Academy of Sciences of the U S S R. Izvestiya. Atmospheric and Oceanic Physics;* Which superseded in part (in 1965): *Academy of Sciences of the U S S R. Bulletin. Geophysics Series.* [ISSN: 0001-4338] 1957. bi-m. EUR 3679 (print & online eds.)). Ed(s): Georgii S Golitsyn. M A I K Nauka - Interperiodica, Profsoyuznaya ul 90, Moscow, 117997, Russian Federation; compmg@maik.ru; http://www.maik.ru. Refereed. Reprint: PSC. *Indexed:* A01, A22, C45, E01. *Aud.:* Ac, Sa.

This is the English translation of *Izvestiya Rossiiskoi Akademii Nauk-Fizika Atmosfery i Okeana,* and it "publishes original scientific research and review articles on vital issues in the physics of the Earth's atmosphere and hydrosphere and climate theory." Papers on research techniques and brief communications are published occasionally. Articles are technical in nature and written primarily by scientists from Russia. Recent articles include a history of boundary-layer studies at the Institute of Atmospheric Physics; an estimate of the boundary of the Rossby Regime Zone in the atmosphere; and wave activity and its changes in the troposphere and stratosphere of the Northern Hemisphere in the winters of 1979-2016.

668. *Tellus. Series A: Dynamic Meteorology and Oceanography (Online).* Supercedes in part: *Tellus (Online).* [ISSN: 1600-0870] 1990. 5x/yr. Free. Ed(s): Peter Lundberg. Co-Action Publishing, Ripvaegen 7, Jaerfaella, 17564, Sweden; info@co-action.net; http://www.co-action.net. Refereed. *Indexed:* C45. *Aud.:* Ac, Sa.

This peer-reviewed open-access journal of the International Meteorological Institute in Stockholm focuses on "dynamic meteorology, physical oceanography, data assimilation techniques, numerical weather prediction, climate dynamics and climate modelling." The journal publishes original research. Review articles, brief research notes, and letters to the editor are also published, along with occasional special issues on topics of current interest, and conference proceedings. Recent topics include the role of convective available potential energy in tropical cyclone intensification; the changing relationship between the convection over the western Tibetan Plateau and the sea surface temperature in the northern Bay of Bengal; and an analysis of ensemble prediction of the uncertainty in the location of winter storm precipitation. Recommended for libraries that serve atmospheric scientists and oceanographers.

669. *Tellus. Series B: Chemical and Physical Meteorology (Online).* Supercedes in part: *Tellus (Online).* [ISSN: 1600-0889] 1990. 5x/yr. Free. Ed(s): Hans-Christen Hansson. Co-Action Publishing, Ripvaegen 7, Jaerfaella, 17564, Sweden; info@co-action.net; http://www.co-action.net. Refereed. *Indexed:* C45. *Aud.:* Ac, Sa.

This open-access peer-reviewed journal of the International Meteorological Institute in Stockholm focuses on "all aspects of atmospheric chemical cycling related to Earth science processes; long-range and global transport and dispersion; aerosol science; chemical reactions; cloud physics and chemistry related to cloud radiative effects, physical/chemical transformation and wet removal; biogeochemical cycles of carbon and other atmospheric constituents important to climate, air quality and the environment." The journal publishes original research. Review articles, brief research notes, and letters to the editor are also published. Special issues that cover conference proceedings or topics of current interest are published as warranted. Recommended for libraries that serve those studying hydrology, geography, atmospheric sciences, and oceanography.

670. *Theoretical and Applied Climatology.* Formerly (until 1985): *Archives for Meteorology, Geophysics, and Bioclimatology. Series B: Climatology, Environmental Meteorology, Radiation Research - Archiv fuer Meteorologie, Geophysik und Bioklimatologie. Series B.* [ISSN: 0177-798X] 1948. m. EUR 8347 (print & online eds.)). Ed(s): H Grassl. Springer Wien, Prinz-Eugen-Str 8-10, Wien, 1040, Austria; journals@springer.at; http://www.springer.com. Adv. Sample. Refereed. Reprint: PSC. *Indexed:* A01, A22, BRI, C45, E01, S25. *Aud.:* Ac, Sa.

This journal covers research in the areas of "climate modeling, climatic changes and climate forecasting; micro- to mesoclimate; applied meteorology as in agro- and forest meteorology; biometeorology; building meteorology and atmospheric radiation problems as they relate to the biosphere; effects of anthropogenic and natural aerosols or gaseous trace constituents; [and] hardware and software elements of meteorological measurements, including techniques of remote sensing." Articles are technical and scholarly in nature and are not limited to one geographic area. Recent articles cover such topics as determining optimum tilt angles of solar surfaces in Sakarya, Turkey; precipitation and temperature trends and dryness/wetness pattern during 1971-2015 in Zhejiang Province, southeastern China; and characteristics of drought in Southern China under climatic warming, the risk, and countermeasures for prevention and control.

671. *W M O Bulletin.* [ISSN: 0042-9767] 1952. s-a. CHF 30. Ed(s): L Lengoasa. World Meteorological Organization, 7 bis Avenue de la Paix, Case postale 2300, Geneva, 1211, Switzerland; pubsales@gateway.wmo.ch; http://www.wmo.int. Illus., index, adv. Circ: 6500. Vol. ends: Oct. *Indexed:* A22, C45, S25. *Bk. rev.:* 2-5, 300-500 words. *Aud.:* Ga, Ac.

This is the official journal of the World Meteorological Organization (WMO), a specialized agency of the United Nations. Each issue has a theme with a target readership of the WMO scientific community, with extended outreach to the broader informed public. Recent themes have been water, sustainable development goals, and communicating the linkages between extreme events and climate change. It publishes scholarly articles on meteorology, climatology, hydrology and the environment, and related fields. The stated aim of the *Bulletin* is "to inspire readers to improve their operations and reach out to their user communities, by providing interviews, features, case studies and best practices in the areas of weather, climate and water." Recommended.

672. *Weather.* Incorporates (1965-2003): *Weather Log.* [ISSN: 0043-1656] 1946. m. GBP 97. Ed(s): Jim Galvin. John Wiley & Sons Ltd., EMEA Institutional Sales, 9600 Garsington Rd, Oxford, OX4 2DQ, United Kingdom; cs-journals@wiley.com; http://onlinelibrary.wiley.com. Illus., index, adv. Sample. Refereed. Vol. ends: Dec. Reprint: PSC. *Indexed:* A01, A22, BRI, C45, S25. *Aud.:* Hs, Ga, Ac.

This journal is meant for the meteorological professional and those having a general interest in weather. Technical terminology and mathematical equations are kept to a minimum. Topics covered include case studies of interesting and important weather events, climatic change, weather observation (including the use and interpretation of satellite and radar imagery), weather and climate as environmental hazards, developments in weather forecasting, meteorology, climatology, and oceanography, and the history of meteorology and climatology. There are also regular series of articles that include such topics as historic and notable weather stations; interpretation of weather maps and weather information on the web; and pen portraits of historic figures in meteorology. Because it is a publication of the Royal Meteorological Society, there is a slight emphasis on the United Kingdom. This title is the house journal of the Royal Meteorological Society and includes news of the society, such as reports of meetings and conferences. There is a letters section, with most letters coming from the United Kingdom. Recommended for both academic and public libraries.

673. *Weather and Forecasting.* [ISSN: 0882-8156] 1986. bi-m. Members, USD 145 (print & online eds.); Non-members, USD 880 (print & online eds.)). Ed(s): Paul M Markowski. American Meteorological Society, 45 Beacon St, Boston, MA 02108; amsinfo@ametsoc.org; http://www.ametsoc.org. Illus., index. Refereed. *Indexed:* A01, A22, E01. *Aud.:* Ac.

With the target audience of weather forecasters and researchers, the articles are technical in nature. Research covered includes "papers on significant weather events, forecasting techniques, forecast verification, model parameterizations, data assimilation, model ensembles, statistical postprocessing techniques, the transfer of research results to the forecasting community, and the societal use and value of forecasts." Authors are from around the world, and the articles submitted cover numerous parts of the world as well. As with most publications of the American Meteorological Society, sections for brief reports and comments are included in many issues.

674. *Weather, Climate, and Society.* [ISSN: 1948-8327] 2009. q. Members, USD 120 (print & online eds.); Non-members, USD 590 (print & online eds.)). Ed(s): Amanda Helen Lynch. American Meteorological Society, 45 Beacon St, Boston, MA 02108; amsinfo@ametsoc.org; http://www.ametsoc.org. Refereed. *Indexed:* A22, E01. *Bk. rev.:* Number and length vary. *Aud.:* Ga, Ac.

This quarterly journal of the American Meteorological Society covers "economics, policy analysis, political science, history, and institutional, social, and behavioral research that relates to weather and climate, including climate change." Since the focus is interdisciplinary, articles that involve both natural/physical scientists and social scientists are welcomed. Recent articles cover topics such as the effect of risk and protective decision aids on flood preparation in vulnerable communities; social connections and their effect on evacuation decisions during Hurricane Irma; and the attributes of weathercasters who engage in climate change education.

675. *Weatherwise.* [ISSN: 0043-1672] 1948. bi-m. GBP 156. Ed(s): Margaret Benner. Taylor & Francis Inc., 711 3rd Ave, 8th Fl, New York, NY 10017; support@tandfonline.com; http://www.tandfonline.com. Illus., index, adv. Sample. Circ: 6000. Microform: PQC. Reprint: PSC. *Indexed:* A01, A22, BRI, C37, E01, MASUSE. *Bk. rev.:* Number and length vary. *Aud.:* Ga, Ac, Sa.

This popular magazine has as its target audience the intelligent layperson interested in weather. It publishes general-interest articles on weather that showcase "the power, beauty, and excitement of weather." The articles present the latest discoveries and issues in meteorology and climatology. Expert responses to reader questions and a review of weather over North America during the preceding two months are regular columns. Photographs are in color, and there is an annual photography contest. The March/April issue includes a summary of weather events from the previous year. Recommended for all libraries that serve users with an interest in weather.

Weekly Weather and Crop Bulletin. See Agriculture section.

■ AUTOMOBILES AND MOTORCYCLES

Pauline Theriault, Reference Librarian, Multnomah County Library, 801 SW 10th Ave., Portland, OR 97205; paulinet@multcolib.org

Introduction

From the first self-propelled vehicle, created by Frenchman Nicholas Joseph Cugnot in 1769, to the ongoing race to create the first fully autonomous self-driving car, and from the first electric hansom cabs that operated in New York City in 1897 to the rise of ride-sharing companies Uber and Lyft, the automotive industry has always been at the forefront of revolution.

Nowhere is this more apparent than in the automobile's role in the fourth industrial revolution, where a focus on affordable electric power, connectivity, cybersecurity, and self-driving cars has dominated the industry in the last few years. Even more changes may be on the horizon in the near future: changes in fuel efficiency regulations and the threat of tariffs on auto imports roil lawmakers and the public alike. And while ride-sharing and car-sharing has increased, North American car, and particularly truck sales, continue to climb and Americans still continue to log more driving miles than in previous years. The collector car market continues to increase and has expanded to include older pickup trucks and muscle cars. Auto sports, collector cars, motorcycles, and car shows appeal to a large portion of the population, and there are plenty of magazines published to prove it.

Whether the vehicle of choice is an aging wood-paneled station wagon, a Honda motorcycle, a shared vehicle, a Vespa, or a Ferrari, everyone has their favorite mode of getting around. Partial to BMWs? Drag racing? Green transportation? Mini-trucks? Whatever the interest, there is undoubtedly a magazine geared to the specific audience. Whether your patrons are classic car enthusiasts, armchair race enthusiasts, automotive industry professionals, proprietors of a small auto repair shop, or just average Americans wanting to dream about the latest new cars, there is a title for everyone.

The selected list of titles below reflects only a small portion of the magazines published for car and motorcycle enthusiasts. If a particular autosport or auto lifestyle is popular locally, librarians may wish to seek out specialized titles to support that interest.

Basic Periodicals

Automobile Magazine, Car and Driver, Cycle World, Motor Trend, Motorcyclist.

Basic Abstracts and Indexes

Academic Search Premier, MasterFILE Premier, Readers' Guide to Periodical Literature.

676. *American Bagger: the original American v-twin performance touring and customizing authority.* [ISSN: 2159-2810] 2006. m. USD 24.95 domestic; USD 54.95 foreign. Maverick Publications, 3105 W Fairgrounds Loop, Ste 200, Spearfish, SD 57783; info@maverickpub.com; http://www.maverickpub.com. Adv. *Aud.:* Ga.

American Bagger is a fine example of just one of the highly specialized titles available in the world of motorcycles. This magazine is aimed at the enthusiast who loves custom touring cycles with saddlebags - a.k.a. "Baggers" - and is packed with stunning color photos and information on one-of-a-kind, customized v-twin touring bikes. For larger public libraries.

677. *American Iron Magazine: for people who love Harley-Davidsons.* Formerly (until 1989): *American Iron.* [ISSN: 1059-7891] 19??. m. T A M Communications Inc., 5610 Scotts Valley Dr, Ste B552, Scotts Valley, CA 95066; http://www.tamcom.com. Adv. *Aud.:* Ga.

American Iron covers American-made motorcycles including Indian and Victory, with a heavy emphasis on Harley-Davidson. For the serious motorcycle enthusiast, this no-nudity title's features include bike reviews, safety skills, technical articles, classic and custom bikes, accessory reviews, and route recommendations.

678. *American Motorcyclist.* Former titles (until 1977): *A M A News;* (until 19??): *American Motorcycling.* [ISSN: 0277-9358] 1947. m. Free to members. Ed(s): James Holter. American Motorcyclist Association, 13515 Yarmouth Dr, Pickerington, OH 43147; http://www.americanmotorcyclist.com. Illus., adv. Sample. Vol. ends: Dec. *Bk. rev.:* 1-5, 500-2,000 words. *Aud.:* Ga, Sa.

American Motorcyclist is distributed monthly to the more than 280,000 members of the American Motorcyclist Association (AMA). The AMA acts as a political lobby for motorcyclists, and this title often includes reports on legislative issues that affect your right to ride, along with feature stories and rider profiles. Activities, both state-by-state and national, are also included. Readers should expect to find photos of dirt bikes, road races, new bikes, and families on the glossy, full-color pages. Recommended for large public libraries.

679. ***Antique Automobile.*** Formerly (until 19??): *Antique Automobile Club of America. Bulletin.* [ISSN: 0003-5831] 1937. bi-m. Free to members. Ed(s): West Peterson. Antique Automobile Club of America, Inc., 501 W Governor Rd, PO Box 417, Hershey, PA 17033; general@aaca.org; http://www.aaca.org. Illus., adv. Sample. *Indexed:* A22. *Aud.:* Ga.

Published by the Antique Automobile Club of America (AACA), *Antique Automobile* is the first historical automotive society publication. The goal of the club is to perpetuate "the pioneer days of automobiling by furthering the interest in and preserving of antique automobiles," and this title will be of interest to all serious antique automobile enthusiasts. The AACA uses the term *automobile* to include all "self-propelled vehicles intended for passenger use," including cars, race vehicles, trucks, fire vehicles, and motorcycles. Approximately half of the magazine is in full color. Columns, news, a calendar of events, and a comprehensive list of all AACA regions and chapters are included in each issue.

680. ***Automobile Magazine.*** Former titles (until 1989): *Automobile;* (until 1987): *Automobile Magazine.* 1986. m. USD 10 domestic; USD 22 Canada; USD 34 elsewhere. Ed(s): Michael Floyd, Rusty Kurtz. TEN: The Enthusiast Network, 1 Discovery Place, Silver Spring, MD 20910; http://www.enthusiastnetwork.com. Illus., adv. Sample. *Indexed:* A22, BRI. *Aud.:* Hs, Ga, Ac.

Automobile is geared to the general car enthusiast, covering new vehicles, preview vehicles, and collector cars. The full-color photos of auto interiors and exteriors are excellent; the car reviews are primarily subjective, and lack the technical data included in other general-interest automobile magazines such as *Car and Driver* and *Road & Track.* This title's columns are well written, entertaining, and occasionally irreverent; *Automobile* is a fun read. Although somewhat slender, this magazine will be popular in any public library and its reasonable price makes it a must-have purchase.

681. ***Automotive Engineering (Warrendale).*** Former titles (until 2014): *Automotive Engineering International (Print);* Which incorporates (1989-1998): *Truck Engineering (Print);* (until 1998): *Automotive Engineering (Print);* (until 1972): *S A E Journal of Automotive Engineering (Print);* Which superseded in part (in 1970): *S A E Journal (Print);* Which was formerly (until 1928): *Society of Automotive Engineers. Journal (Print);* (until 1917): *S A E Bulletin (Print).* [ISSN: 2331-7639] 1917. m. Free to members. S A E Inc., 400 Commonwealth Dr, Warrendale, PA 15096; CustomerSales@sae.org; http://www.sae.org/automag. Illus. Vol. ends: Dec. Microform: PMC. *Indexed:* A22, C42, HRIS. *Aud.:* Ac, Sa.

This publication of the Society of Automotive Engineers is the premier source for technology and product information for vehicle design, development, and manufacture. Aimed at the automotive professional, articles are technical and in depth, covering everything from aerodynamics to instrument panels. Features include editorials, sections on global vehicles, technology reports, insiders and insights, and regulations and standards. Highly recommended for academic libraries and specialized collections.

682. ***Automotive Industries.*** Former titles (until 1994): *Chilton's Automotive Industries;* (until 1976): *Automotive Industries;* (until 1972): *Chilton's Automotive Industries;* (until 1970): *Automotive Industries;* (until 1947): *Automotive and Aviation Industries;* (until 1942): *Automotive Industries;* (until 1917): *Automobile and Automotive Industries;* Incorporated (1923-1934): *Automotive Abstracts;* and incorporated in part (in 1917): *The Horseless Age.* [ISSN: 1099-4130] 1895. m. Ed(s): Edward Richardson. Diesel & Gas Turbine Publications, 20855 Watertown Rd, Ste 220, Waukesha, WI 53186; http://www.dieselpub.com. Illus., adv. Microform: CIS; PMC; PQC. *Indexed:* A22, B01, B03, BRI, C42, HRIS. *Aud.:* Ga, Ac, Sa.

Automotive Industries is "devoted to providing global coverage on all aspects of the automobile marketplace, with an emphasis on the people, products and processes that shape the industry." With in-depth news, information, insight, and analysis on the global events that affect the auto industry, this title is geared to automotive manufacturers and suppliers. Recent articles, for example, cover autonomous driving, vehicle-generated data, and driver monitoring systems. Highly recommended for all libraries that support the automotive industry, as well as academic libraries with automotive design programs.

683. ***Automotive News.*** Incorporates (1939-1942): *Automotive Service;* Formerly (until 1938): *Automotive Daily News.* [ISSN: 0005-1551] 1925. w. Mon. USD 159 domestic (print or online ed.)). Ed(s): Jason Stein. Crain Communications, Inc., 1155 Gratiot Ave, Detroit, MI 48207; info@crain.com; http://www.crain.com. Illus., adv. Microform: CIS; PMC; PQC. *Indexed:* A22, B01, B03, BRI, C37, HRIS. *Aud.:* Ac, Sa.

Automotive News is the leading source of news information for the automotive industry, providing in-depth coverage of the industry from North America to Europe to Asia. All aspects of the industry are covered, from engineering, design, and production to marketing, sales, and service. Opinion articles, a calendar, sales figures, and classifieds are included in every issue. Required reading for the automotive professional and recommended for larger library collections.

684. ***AutoWeek.*** Formerly (until 19??): *Autoweek and Competition Press.* [ISSN: 0192-9674] 1958. bi-w. USD 29.95; USD 1.25 per issue. Crain Communications, Inc., 1155 Gratiot Ave, Detroit, MI 48207; info@crain.com; http://www.crain.com. Illus., adv. *Indexed:* A22, B01, B03, BRI, C37, MASUSE. *Aud.:* Ga.

AutoWeek is a weekly publication for auto enthusiasts and, thanks to its frequency, it is often the first to publish photographs of pre-production car models. Content includes car reviews, news, motorsports coverage (including rally, Le Mans, NASCAR, and Formula One), and automotive trends. Readers of *Automotive News* also tend to enjoy this title, which is highly recommended for all collections.

685. ***Car.*** Formerly (until 1965): *Small Car;* Incorporates (1983-2010): *Performance Car;* Which was formerly (until 1983): *Hot Car.* [ISSN: 0008-5987] 1962. m. GBP 48.60 domestic; GBP 69.99 foreign. H. Bauer Publishing Ltd., Media House, Lynchwood, Peterborough, PE2 6EA, United Kingdom; http://www.bauermedia.co.uk. Illus., adv. Sample. *Aud.:* Ga.

This U.K. publication focuses on high-performance models primarily for the European car enthusiast. Entertaining and attractive, its features include news, reviews, first drives, and road tests, and the popular section "The Good the Bad and the Ugly," which details new cars on sale in the United Kingdom. The "Spy Shot" section gives scoops, illustrations, and shots of cars still under development. Due to price, this title is recommended for specialized collections.

686. ***Car and Driver.*** Formerly (until 1961): *Sports Cars Illustrated.* [ISSN: 0008-6002] 1956. m. USD 15; USD 4.99 per issue (print or online ed.)). Ed(s): Eddie Alterman. Hearst Magazines, 1585 Eisenhower Pl, Ann Arbor, MI 48108; HearstMagazines@hearst.com; http://www.hearst.com. Illus., adv. *Indexed:* A01, A22, BRI, C37, HRIS, MASUSE. *Aud.:* Hs, Ga.

Car and Driver is one of the most recognized and respected general-interest automobile magazines, and for good reason. Filled with well-written reviews, high-quality photography, car comparisons, road tests, and car previews, this title both educates and entertains car enthusiasts with authoritative information and a large dose of humor. The annual "10 Best Cars" issue is not to be missed. Highly recommended for all public libraries.

687. ***Car Craft: Loud Fast Real.*** Formerly: *Honk.* [ISSN: 0008-6010] 1953. m. USD 12 domestic; USD 24 Canada; USD 36 elsewhere. TEN: The Enthusiast Network, 1 Discovery Place, Silver Spring, MD 20910; http://www.sourceinterlink.com. Illus., adv. *Indexed:* A22, BRI. *Aud.:* Hs, Ga.

Car Craft is aimed at the hands-on, do-it-yourself car enthusiast who is interested in rebuilding, maintaining, and customizing high-performance, American-made street cars built after 1955, primarily muscle cars. Articles include technical topics (such as floorpan installation), how-to pieces (painting laser-straight body lines), and project cars. Columns are humorous and well written. For public libraries.

688. *Collectible Automobile.* Formerly (until 19??): *Consumer Guide Elite Cars.* [ISSN: 0742-812X] 1984. bi-m. USD 39.95 domestic; USD 68.95 Canada; USD 79.95 elsewhere. Ed(s): John Biel. Publications International Ltd., PO Box 8508, Big Sandy, TX 75755; http://www.pilbooks.com. Illus., adv. *Bk. rev.:* 1-5. *Aud.:* Ga, Sa.

Collectible Automobile is a vintage car-lover's dream. Each issue details the design and technical history of three or four automobiles, along with photo features, segments on collectible commercial vehicles, and personality profiles. Featured cars range from early models to models produced only 20 years ago. This title is full of high-quality, full-color photographs on glossy paper, many of which feature close-ups of unique car details. With little advertising and excellent writing, this magazine is the top choice for collectible-car fanatics and the casual enthusiast looking for eye candy. Highly recommended for all public libraries and libraries with automotive collections.

689. *Cycle World.* Incorporates (1950-1991): *Cycle.* [ISSN: 0011-4286] 1962. m. USD 12 combined subscription domestic (print & ipad eds.); USD 22 combined subscription Canada (print & ipad eds.); USD 31.93 combined subscription elsewhere (print & ipad eds.)). Bonnier Corp., 15215 Alton Pky, Ste 100, Irvine, CA 92618; intake@cycleworld.com; http://www.bonniercorp.com. Illus., adv. *Indexed:* A22, BRI, C37, MASUSE. *Bk. rev.:* Number and length vary. *Aud.:* Hs, Ga.

This high-quality magazine covers the entire spectrum of motorcycling, including sport bikes, dirt bikes, standards, and cruisers. Each issue contains plenty of color photographs, technical articles, road tests with detailed technical and performance data, race coverage, interviews, and special features, along with well-written columns. This well-liked, well-known publication is recommended for public libraries.

690. *Dirt Rider.* [ISSN: 0735-4355] 1982. m. USD 12 combined subscription domestic (print & ipad eds.); USD 22 combined subscription Canada (print & ipad eds.); USD 32 combined subscription elsewhere (print & ipad eds.)). Bonnier Corp., 15215 Alton Pky, Ste 100, Irvine, CA 92618; http://www.bonniercorp.com. Illus., adv. *Aud.:* Ga.

Dirt Rider focuses on off-road motorcycling for enthusiasts of all ages and abilities. Features include stories about how and where to ride, new equipment, motorcycles, and prominent individuals in the sport. Regular articles include dirt bike tests and comparisons, technical how-to tips, race reports and upcoming races, and product information, such as a recent comparison of chest protectors. Recommended for public libraries.

691. *F 1 Racing.* [ISSN: 1361-4487] 1996. m. USD 69 domestic; USD 75 combined subscription domestic (print & online eds.)). Ed(s): Anthony Rowlinson. Haymarket Publishing Ltd., Bridge House, 69 London Rd, Twickenham, TW1 3SP, United Kingdom; info@haymarket.com; http://www.haymarket.com. Adv. *Aud.:* Ga.

Formula 1, the world's most expensive sport, has been popular everywhere around the globe, with the exception of the United States, since 1950. The 2012 opening of the Circuit of the Americas F1 track in Austin, Texas, marked the return of the U.S. Grand Prix and recent years have shown an increase in the popularity of F1 racing in the United States. Aimed at F1 enthusiasts, this magazine features high-quality photographs, comprehensive coverage of drivers, races, race tracks, and technical information on the cars and the teams, as well as F1 developments. The global popularity of F1 racing, coupled with the return of the U.S. Grand Prix, make this a title for serious consideration for public libraries.

692. *Four Wheeler Magazine: world's leading four wheel drive magazine.* [ISSN: 0015-9123] 1962. m. USD 10 domestic; USD 22 Canada; USD 34 elsewhere. TEN: The Enthusiast Network, 831 South Douglas St, El Segundo, CA 90245; http://www.sourceinterlink.com. Illus., adv. Vol. ends: Dec. *Aud.:* Ga.

Four Wheeler covers 4x4 trucks, SUVs, and off-road vehicles. It presents a wide range of articles including domestic trail rides, event coverage, new-vehicle testing and evaluation, and technical articles designed for four-wheelers of all abilities. It also includes how-to installation articles, equipment guides, and comprehensive product testing. Feature issues include "Four Wheeler of the Year" and "Pickup Truck of the Year." Recommended for public libraries.

693. *Green Car Journal.* [ISSN: 1059-6143] 1992. q. Ed(s): Ron Cogan. RJ Cogan Specialty Publications Group, Inc., 1241 Johnson Ave, San Luis Obispo, CA 93401; www.greencargroup.com. Adv. *Aud.:* Ga, Ac, Sa.

Green Car Journal "emphasizes the joy of driving while recognizing the need to harmonize the automobile's impact on energy and our environment." This title contains information on electric, alternative-fuel, and low-emission vehicles, and features articles on issues such as green fleets, top fuel-economy favorites, auto trends, and top picks for green cars and trucks. In addition, the magazine awards an annual "Green Car of the Year." Highly recommended for all collections.

694. *Hemmings Classic Car.* [ISSN: 1550-8730] 2004. m. USD 18.95 domestic; USD 29.48 Canada; USD 32.95 elsewhere. Hemmings Publishing, 222 Main St, PO Box 256, Bennington, VT 05201; hmnmail@hemmings.com; http://www.hemmings.com. *Aud.:* Ga, Sa.

Self-described as "the definitive all-American collector-car magazine," *Hemmings Classic Car* focuses on American-built collector cars, targeting enthusiasts, owners, collectors, dealers, restorers, and parts manufacturers. This title features all eras of autos with a primary focus on postwar vehicles. Of special interest is the buyers' guide in each issue, which focuses on a particular make and model for particular years, detailing technical aspects of the vehicle, parts prices, and what you can expect to pay. Recommended for large public libraries and automotive collections.

695. *Hemmings Motor News.* 1954. m. USD 31.95 domestic; USD 56.14 Canada; USD 98.95 Mexico. Ed(s): Richard Lentinello, Nancy Bianco. Hemmings Publishing, 222 Main St, PO Box 256, Bennington, VT 05201; hmnmail@hemmings.com; http://www.hemmings.com. Adv. *Aud.:* Ga.

Hemmings Motor News describes itself as the "world's largest collector car marketplace," and indeed it is. Each issue is more than 500 pages long; approximately 80 pages are dedicated to features and articles, while the remaining pages are classifieds and other advertising. As with *Hemmings Classic Car,* each issue provides a buyers' guide as well as interesting features that profile vehicles, car design, auto show coverage, and upcoming events. Recommended for public libraries and automotive collections.

696. *Hot Rod.* Formerly (until 1953): *Hot Rod Magazine.* [ISSN: 0018-6031] 1948. m. USD 14 domestic; USD 26 Canada; USD 38 elsewhere. Ed(s): David Freiburger. TEN: The Enthusiast Network, 1 Discovery Place, Silver Spring, MD 20910; http://www.sourceinterlink.com. Illus., adv. Vol. ends: Dec. Microform: PQC. *Indexed:* A22, BRI, C37, MASUSE. *Bk. rev.:* 1-3, 200-500 words. *Aud.:* Hs, Ga.

Hot rodding, the art of modifying automobiles for performance and appearance, is hugely popular and this magazine is filled with wonderful photos of heavily modified cars, such as a recent tricked out first-generation Ford Bronco. Articles cover how-to information, people, races, and technical know-how. Each issue of *Hot Rod* is in full color with lots of advertising. Recommended for all public libraries.

697. *Motocross Action.* [ISSN: 0146-3292] 1973. m. USD 15.99 domestic; USD 31.99 Canada; USD 45.99 elsewhere. Hi - Torque Publications, Inc., 25233 Amza Dr, Valencia, CA 91355; http://www.hi-torque.com. Adv. *Indexed:* SD. *Aud.:* Ga.

Aimed at the motocross racing enthusiast, this action-packed magazine features riding tips, race reports, bike tests, technical tips, interviews, and equipment reviews. This title will be of interest to both motocross racers and spectators. Recommended for public libraries.

698. ***MOTOR: covering the world of automotive service.*** [ISSN: 0027-1748] 1903. m. USD 48 domestic (Free to qualified personnel). Ed(s): John Lypen. Hearst Business Media, 1301 W. Long Lake Rd, Ste 300, Troy, MI 48098; http://www.hearst.com. Illus., index, adv. Sample. Microform: PQC. *Indexed:* A22. *Aud.:* Sa.

MOTOR is a specialized magazine aimed at owners, managers, and technicians of retail automotive service and repair shops and car dealerships. Articles cover technical aspects, such as which model of car has windows that won't open, and business management aspects, such as how to turn your good shop into a great shop. Diagnostic techniques and service procedures, new-product information, and industry news are also included. Recommended for vocational and technical schools, automotive collections, and collections that serve the small-business community.

699. ***Motor Age: for the professional automotive import & domestic service industry.*** Incorporates (1921-2002): *Motor Service;* Former titles (until 1997): *Chilton's Motor Age;* (until 1970): *Motor Age;* (until 1961): *Chilton's Motor Age;* (until 1950): *Motor Age;* (until 1943): *Motor Age for Automotive Servicemen;* (until 1940): *Motor Age.* [ISSN: 1520-9385] 1899. m. USD 70 domestic (Free to qualified personnel). Ed(s): Tschanen Brandyberry. U B M Advanstar Communications, Inc., 6200 Canoga Ave, 2nd Fl, Woodland Hills, CA 91367; info@advanstar.com; http://ubmadvanstar.com//. Illus., adv. Circ: 139000 Controlled. Microform: PQC. *Indexed:* A22, B01, BRI, C42, MASUSE. *Aud.:* Sa.

Motor Age strives to "advance the automotive service professional," and it has been doing so since 1899. This title covers all aspects of running an independent auto service shop, focusing on operations, trends, and products. Issues include shop profiles, technical tips and techniques, and articles on best practices in management. Recommended for vocational and technical schools, automotive collections, and collections that serve the small-business community.

700. ***Motor Trend.*** Incorporates (in 19??): *Car Life;* (in 1971): *Sports Car Graphic;* (in 1971): *Wheels Afield.* [ISSN: 0027-2094] 1949. m. USD 10 domestic; USD 22 Canada; USD 34 elsewhere. TEN: The Enthusiast Network, 831 South Douglas St, El Segundo, CA 90245; info@enthusiastnetwork.com; http://www.enthusiastnetwork.com. Illus., index, adv. Vol. ends: Dec. *Indexed:* A01, A22, BRI, C37, MASUSE. *Aud.:* Hs, Ga, Ac.

Motor Trend is one of the most well-known consumer automotive magazines, thanks in part to its highly coveted "Motor Trend Car of the Year Award." Chock-full of automobile reviews, interviews, and consumer information, the magazine covers a wide spectrum of vehicles. Reviews include first tests, long-term tests, and side-by-side car comparisons, and contain specs, test data, and consumer information. Inexpensive, informative, and entertaining at the same time, this magazine is highly recommended for all collections.

701. ***Motorcycle Classics: ride 'em, don't hide 'em.*** [ISSN: 1556-0880] 2005. bi-m. USD 24.95 domestic; USD 39.95 foreign; USD 29.95 combined subscription domestic (print & online eds.)). Ed(s): Richard Backus. Ogden Publications, Inc., 1503 SW 42nd St, Topeka, KS 66609; http://www.ogdenpubs.com. Adv. *Aud.:* Ga.

Many motorcycle magazines focus on a particular type of motorcycle. *Motorcycle Classics* is dedicated to the classic and vintage motorcycles of yesteryear, whether made in the United States or overseas; whether cruisers, touring, or standard bikes; or whether BMW, Honda, or Harley. Each issue features articles on motorcycle and equipment reviews, restoration projects, and future collectibles. Recommended for large public libraries.

702. ***Motorcycle Consumer News.*** Former titles (until Nov.1993): *Road Rider's Motorcycle Consumer News;* (until 1993): *Road Rider;* (until 1970): *Road Rider News.* [ISSN: 1073-9408] 1969. m. USD 20 combined subscription (print & online eds.); USD 7 newsstand/cover). Ed(s): David Hilgendorf. Lumina Media, LLC, 2030 Main St, Ste 1400, Irvine, CA 92614; info@luminamedia.com; http://luminamedia.com. Illus., adv. Sample. *Aud.:* Ga.

Motorcycle Consumer News is often described as the *Consumer Reports* of the motorcycle world. Unlike the vast majority of motorcycle magazines, it accepts no advertising, is printed on glare-free paper, and is not sold at newsstands. Each issue features recalls, first impressions of bikes, extensive model evaluations, product comparisons, an events calendar, and feature articles. This unbiased magazine deserves a place in every public library.

703. ***Motorcyclist.*** Incorporates (1970-1988): *Motorcycle Buyer's Guide.* [ISSN: 0027-2205] 1912. m. USD 10 combined subscription domestic (print & ipad eds.); USD 22 combined subscription Canada (print & ipad eds.); USD 34 combined subscription elsewhere (print & ipad eds.)). Bonnier Corp., 2 Park Ave, 9th Fl, New York, NY 10016; http://www.bonniercorp.com. Illus., adv. *Indexed:* A22, BRI. *Aud.:* Hs, Ga.

Motorcyclist is the premier title for all-around, general motorcycle enthusiasts, covering racing, street motorcycling (including cruising, touring, and commuting), and the occasional historical race. International motorcycle shows are often covered, and each issue contains well-written, lengthy evaluations of new bikes that include superb color photographs and technical details. Regular sections include "First Rides," "Road Tests," "Flashback," "Gearbox," and "Motorcycle Escapes." Highly recommended for all public libraries.

704. ***National Dragster.*** Incorporates: *N H R A Souvenir Program;* Which was formerly: *N H R A Souvenir Yearbook.* [ISSN: 0466-2199] 1960. 25x/yr. Membership, USD 39. Ed(s): Juan Torres. National Hot Rod Association, 2035 Financial Way, Glendora, CA 91741; http://www.nhra.com. Illus., adv. *Aud.:* Ga.

National Dragster covers all facets of the drag racing world, from motorcycle drag racing to "Top Fuel," "Top Alcohol," "Pro Stock," and "Funny Car." Features include news, tech columns, and competition coverage. Stunning full-color photos make this an especially entertaining view of life at the track. Recommended for all public libraries.

705. ***Petersen's 4 Wheel & Off-Road.*** Formerly (until 19??): *Hot Rod Magazine's 4 Wheel and Off-Road.* [ISSN: 0162-3214] 1977. m. USD 12 domestic; USD 24 Canada; USD 36 elsewhere. Ed(s): Rick Pewe. TEN: The Enthusiast Network, 831 South Douglas St, El Segundo, CA 90245; http://www.enthusiastnetwork.com. Illus., adv. Sample. *Indexed:* BRI. *Aud.:* Hs, Sa.

Like the title says, *Petersen's 4 Wheel and Off-Road* is aimed at the enthusiast interested in four-wheel drive trucks and in driving them off-road. Each issue includes vehicle reviews and road tests, how-to and technical information, project vehicles, off-road and vehicle news, and plenty of color photos. Recommended for large public libraries.

706. ***Racer.*** [ISSN: 1066-6060] 1992. 8x/yr. USD 39 combined subscription domestic (print & online eds.); USD 59 combined subscription Canada (print & online eds.); USD 79 combined subscription elsewhere (print & online eds.)). Ed(s): Laurence Foster. Racer Media & Marketing, Inc., 17030 Red Hill Ave, Irvine, CA 92614. *Aud.:* Ga.

Racer is the largest general-interest motorsports magazine in the United States. It covers all flavors of auto racing events: Formula 1, Indycar, NASCAR, NHRA, sports and GT cars, and World Rally. With in-depth features, interviews, and stunning full-color photography, *Racer* gives readers a behind-the-scenes look at the world of racing. Each issue includes a day-by-day listing of all live and taped television motorsports events for the month. Recommended for all public libraries.

707. ***Rider: motorcycling at its best.*** [ISSN: 1522-9726] 1974. m. USD 14.97 domestic; USD 24 Canada; USD 36 elsewhere. Ed(s): Mark Tuttle, Jenny Smith. EPG Media, LLC, 1227 Flynn Rd, Ste 304, Camarillo, CA 93012; info@epgmediallc.com; http://epgmediallc.com/. Illus., index, adv. Sample. *Indexed:* BRI. *Aud.:* Ga.

Rider is a general-interest motorcycling magazine aimed at the road and street motorcycle enthusiast. It focuses on touring, cruising, and sport bikes. Regular features include equipment reviews, ride reports, maintenance tips, and how-to articles on riding skills and gear. This title focuses more on the rides themselves, rather than the equipment, with a nod to those who use their bikes to commute. Recommended for public libraries.

708. *Road & Track.* [ISSN: 0035-7189] 1947. m. USD 15; USD 5.99 newsstand/cover. Ed(s): Kim Wolfkill, Michael Fazioli. Hearst Magazines, 1499 Monrovia Ave, Newport Beach, CA 92663; HearstMagazines@hearst.com; http://www.hearst.com. Illus., adv. Circ: 608337. Vol. ends: Dec. *Indexed:* A01, A22, BRI, C37, MASUSE. *Bk. rev.:* 1-2, 2,000 words. *Aud.:* Hs, Ga.

Road & Track is one of the oldest automobile enthusiast magazines in the United States, founded in 1947. Its full-color, glossy pages feature everything from the latest concept cars from auto shows worldwide, to production and sports cars. Regular features include road tests - both first looks and long-term - as well as technical and styling analysis, and trends. Each issue also includes coverage of at least one automobile race. Recommended for all public libraries.

709. *RoadRUNNER: motorcycle touring & travel.* Formerly (until 2007): *Road Runner Motorcycle Cruising & Touring.* [ISSN: 1939-7976] 2001. bi-m. USD 29.95. Ed(s): Christian Neuhauser, Florian Neuhauser. RoadRUNNER Publishing, 206 N Spruce St, Ste 2B, Winston-Salem, NC 27101. Adv. *Aud.:* Ga.

RoadRUNNER magazine is "dedicated to serving active motorcycle enthusiasts by providing them with a comprehensive resource of national and international tours, exciting and picturesque new places to ride, and valuable information on new motorcycles and products that enhance their riding experience." Each issue lives up to this mission, with the inclusion of six to seven touring articles from the United States and abroad; motorcycle and product reviews; and fantastic color photographs. This title is for both motorcycle enthusiasts who enjoy touring and those who just prefer to armchair travel. Recommended for public libraries.

710. *Truckin': world's leading truck publication.* [ISSN: 0277-5743] 1975. 13x/yr. USD 24.95 domestic; USD 37.95 Canada; USD 50.95 elsewhere. Ed(s): Courtney McKinnon, Jeremy Cook. TEN: The Enthusiast Network, 831 South Douglas St, El Segundo, CA 90245; http://www.enthusiastnetwork.com. Illus., adv. *Aud.:* Hs, Ga.

This title is dedicated to the truck enthusiast and covers trucks, SUVs, 4x4 lifted off-road vehicles, mini-trucks, and custom trucks. Customization, new model reviews, and technical tips are all regular features. The majority of the trucks in this magazine are recent vehicles, and readers are likely to encounter lots of color photos of trucks with painted flames. Recommended for large public libraries.

711. *Vintage Motorsport: the journal of motor racing history.* [ISSN: 1052-8067] 1982. bi-m. USD 45 domestic; USD 60 Canada; USD 75 elsewhere. Vintage Motorsport Inc., 8712 E. Via De Commercio, Ste. 9, Scottsdale, AZ 85258. Adv. *Bk. rev.:* Number and length vary. *Aud.:* Hs, Ga, Ac.

This title provides a fascinating look into the history of auto racing. Filled with stunning old and new photos of vintage race cars, *Vintage Motorsport* also contains racer profiles and articles covering auto races, both current and historic. The magazine covers current vintage racing news, event schedules, and commentary. Recommended for comprehensive collections.

712. *Ward's AutoWorld (Online).* Former titles: *Ward's AutoWorld (Print); Ward's Quarterly.* 1964. m. Free. Ed(s): David E Zoia. Ward's Automotive Group, 3000 Town Ctr, Ste 2750, Southfield, MI 48075; wards@wardsauto.com; http://www.wardsauto.com. Illus., index, adv. Circ: 68200 Controlled. *Indexed:* A22, B01, BRI, HRIS. *Aud.:* Ac, Sa.

Ward's Automotive Group has covered the auto industry for more than 80 years. This publication covers a wide spectrum of the industry, with articles on vehicle technology, global industry trends, labor and management issues, the latest in manufacturing and materials, and economic, political, and legal issues. Special issues include Ward's ten best engines, an annual suppliers' issue, and a state-of-the-industry issue. Recommended for specialized academic collections and large public libraries.

■ BEER, WINE, AND SPIRITS

Kandace Rogers, krogers@sullivan.edu

Hilary Writt, hwritt@sullivan.edu; Sullivan University Library, Lexington Campus

Introduction

A strong economy continues to have a positive effect on the beer, wine, and spirits industry, resulting in significant growth in all sectors, particularly premium and specialty spirits. The spirits market boom, which started in the whisky and bourbon sectors, has expanded with tequila, gin, and rye all featured prominently. Breweries remain popular and have begun to expand their offerings by adding teas, ciders, and other artisanal beverages to respond to consumer demand for variety as well as use of local and fresh ingredients.

The publications of the beverage industry reflect the current movements of American culture and economy, with articles about the #MeToo movement; women in leadership; diversity; cannabis and CBD; locally sourced, sustainable, biodynamic, and organic products; and climate change. The merger and acquisition trend carries into the beverage periodical market too.

One of the major mergers involves *Wines & Vines* and *Wine Business Monthly.* As of 2019, *Wines & Vines* is no longer publishing and has been incorporated into *Wine Business Monthly.* The merged trade publication, which is producer-focused, has both depth and breadth. Articles containing research on women in leadership roles in the industry come alongside ones about irrigation techniques, digital advertising, and sales figures and analysis. In addition, a new whiskey publication, *American Whiskey,* enters the fray publishing four issues a year and covering whiskey with the consumer in mind.

Reader expectations for electronically available text has prompted a change in publication models for many titles. Moving from traditional print, publications are shifting to all online, mostly online with supplementary print, or ceasing publication altogether—a consequence for titles *All About Beer, Beer Advocate, Celebrator Beer News,* and *Draft Magazine.*

All publications offer supplemental website content with a variety of features that are only available online, via e-mail newsletter, or in a companion app. Basic annual subscriptions are now tiered and may include access to online material free with print subscription, additional fee with print, or electronic-only access.

Basic Periodicals

Chilled, Whisky Advocate, Wine Spectator.

Basic Abstracts and Indexes

Academic Search Premier; Hospitality and Tourism Index; MasterFILE Premier.

713. *American Whiskey.* [ISSN: 2516-855X] 2018. q. USD 24.95 United States; USD 34.95 Canada; USD 49 elsewhere. Paragraph Publishing Inc., 12812 Cardinal Lane, Urbandale, IA 50323; office@paragraphpublishing.com; http://www.paragraphpublishing.com. Adv. *Aud.:* Ga, Sa.

With its launch in 2018, *American Whiskey* entered the publishing world releasing four issues a year. Covering whiskey with the consumer in mind, articles include distiller and distillery profiles, industry standards and regulations, whiskey and cigar pairings, and tasting recommendations. Reflecting the current U.S. cultural climate, issues also touch on whiskey clubs for women and minorities and environmental concerns related to whiskey production. Advertisements for various whiskeys accompany the articles.

714. *The Beer Connoisseur.* [ISSN: 2151-4356] 2009. q. USD 15. Ed(s): Lynn Davis. On Tap Publishing, PO Box 420903, Atlanta, GA 30342. Adv. *Bk. rev.:* Number and length vary (on web site). *Aud.:* Ga, Sa.

With a writing focus on beer appreciation similar to the more lofty wine titles, *The Beer Connoisseur* combines reviews and articles that highlight all aspects of beer brewing and consumption. Articles promote beer as a cultured accompaniment to fine cuisine and dining with a global scope. Each issue offers scored beer reviews from blind taste tests conducted by industry experts, with extensive commentary and distribution information. Discontinued as a bi-monthly print magazine in 2015, *The Beer Connoisseur* splits publishing between five online-only issues and one hard-copy printing each year. The "mega print edition," *The Beer in Review,* is a 200-page issue ranking the top 100 beers of the year and publishing in early to mid-January. Supplemental website content includes free weekly e-newsletters, best-of lists, and an extensive directory.

715. *Brew Your Own: the how-to homebrew beer magazine.* [ISSN: 1081-826X] 1995. 8x/yr. USD 28. Ed(s): Betsy Parks. Brew Your Own, 5515 Main St, Manchester Center, VT 05255; byo@byo.com. Illus., adv. Sample. *Bk. rev.:* Number and length vary. *Aud.:* Ga, Sa.

Publishing since 1995, *Brew Your Own* magazine is dedicated to providing a wide range of content for the homebrewer. All aspects of homebrewing are explored, with articles and advertising designed to keep the homebrewer informed, at every expertise level. Issues include brewing recipes; recommendations for both ingredient and hardware selection and purchase; and a supplier directory arranged by state/country, and book reviews. The extensive website contains both free and subscriber content, with issues available both in print and digital. Emphasis on brewing on a small scale make subscription necessary only for libraries with beverage programs or public demand.

716. *Chilled: raise your spirits.* [ISSN: 2373-8243] 2008. bi-m. Free to qualified personnel. Ed(s): Gina Farrell. Chilled Media LLC, 350 Motor Pkwy, Ste 200, Hauppauge, NY 11788; info@chilledmagazine.com. Illus., adv. *Aud.:* Ga, Sa.

With an emphasis on "new products within the drinking and nightlife community," content in *Chilled* magazine combines coverage of celebrity drinking with craft cocktail recipes and mixology. Focusing primarily on liquor and spirits, *Chilled* offers short articles of 1-2 pages each, with recipes designed to highlight a specific ingredient or spirit. Advertisements focus on new products and releases, to build reader interest and product recognition. In early 2017 the magazine shifted from paid to free subscription for print, with digital issues also available on the magazine website back to volume 5 (2013).

717. *Craft Beer & Brewing.* [ISSN: 2334-119X] 2014. q. USD 29.99 domestic; USD 49.99 foreign. Ed(s): Jamie Bogner. Unfiltered Media Group, LLC, 311 S College Ave, Fort Collins, CO 80524; customerservice@beerandbrewing.com; http://unflt.com/. Adv. *Indexed:* B01. *Aud.:* Ga, Sa.

As they celebrate their fifth year publishing, *Craft Beer & Brewing* magazine continues to provide a stylish and informative publication for a broad audience of beer enthusiasts. Following the same template from the initial issues, current content focuses on beer appreciation for both the consumer and brewer. Recent article topics include advice on brewing styles and process from professional brewmasters; and examination of trends in brewing, such as use of unusual ingredients or ways brewers are incorporating processes from other spirits into their beer creation. Since its beginning in 2014, content evolution has become more focused on brewing and beer consumption and less emphasis on food/beer pairings and cooking with beer. A companion website offers both free content, with reviews and brewing recipes, as well as subscription content with instructional videos, weekly e-mail newsletter, and access to back issues. As the craft beer industry continues to grow and expand, this title demonstrates continued quality and solid coverage of a popular topic.

718. *Imbibe.* [ISSN: 1557-7082] 2006. bi-m. USD 21.95 domestic; USD 31.95 Canada; USD 41.95 elsewhere. Imbibe Media Inc, 1001 SE Water Ave, Ste 285, Portland, OR 97214. Illus., adv. *Aud.:* Ga, Sa.

Publishing since 2006, *Imbibe* offers a well-rounded exploration of the world of drinks and beverage appreciation. Self-described as the "ultimate guide to liquid culture," attention is paid to not only beer, wine, and cocktails but also to homemade sodas, tea, and coffee. Articles explore beverage destinations such as a bourbon distillery in Kentucky or tea in Taipei. The companion website has access to portions of the magazine archive as well as unique articles and a large recipe collection for drinks, food, and more. Specific issues highlight topics such as the fall beer guide, a holiday issue, and the annual Imbibe 75, a list of who and what will be trending in the upcoming year. A multiple award winner, each issue offers an extensive coverage of all aspects of drink consumption. Print only, digital only, and print plus digital subscriptions are available.

719. *Market Watch (New York).* [ISSN: 0277-9277] 1981. 10x/yr. USD 60 domestic; USD 85 elsewhere. Ed(s): Marvin R Shanken. Marvin R. Shanken Communications, Inc., 825 Eighth Ave, 33rd Fl, New York, NY 10019; mmorgenstern@mshanken.com; http://www.mshanken.com/. Adv. *Indexed:* H&TI. *Aud.:* Ga, Sa.

With a design similar to its fellow publications *Wine Spectator* and *Whisky Advocate, Market Watch* examines the spirits consumption from a business perspective. Articles promoting new products contain data and suggest marketing strategies. Content varies from features on wine from different countries, cocktail machines, and industry trends to merchandising news and profiles of on- and off-premise operations. The companion website supplements the print version with news coverage, including restaurant openings and interviews with mixologists and sommeliers of renown. Designed for the beverage manager or retailer, content could be informative for hospitality and event management studies as well as spirits classes to analyze sales and track trends. Non-industry subscribers receive both the print and digital versions of the magazine.

720. *Robert M. Parker Jr.'s the Wine Advocate.* [ISSN: 0887-8463] 1978. bi-m. Ed(s): Lisa Perrotti-Brown. Wine Advocate, Inc., 855 Bordeaux Way, Suite 200, Napa, CA 94558; support@robertparker.com ; https://www.robertparker.com/. *Aud.:* Ga, Sa.

Publishing since 1978, *The Wine Advocate* is the creation of Robert M. Parker Jr., an internationally renowned oenophile. An independent reviewing source, *Robert Parker's Wine Advocate* presents reviews without bias or editorial influence and with no photographs or advertisements. Wine ratings use the *Parker Points* 50-100 scale and are intended as an impartial, uncensored review for consumer use. Reviews are grouped by region, and essays from the editors accompany individual reviews, elaborating on conditions, such as weather, that existed during the wine-making process and could have affected the final product. Website content is a separate subscription and supplements the print subscription with tasting notes, articles and editorials, restaurant reviews, and additional material.

721. *The Tasting Panel.* Former titles (until 2009): *Patterson's The Tasting Panel;* (until 2007): *Patterson's Beverage Journal;* (until 1987): *Patterson's California Beverage Journal.* [ISSN: 2153-0122] 1941. 8x/yr. USD 36. Ed(s): Ruth Tobias. Patterson's The Tasting Panel Magazine, 6345 Balboa Blvd. Suite 111, Encino, CA 91316; subscriptions@tastingpanelmag.com; https://www.tastingpanelmag.com. Adv. *Indexed:* A01. *Aud.:* Ga, Sa.

The *Tasting Panel* produces articles about the adult beverage industry. Within eight issues a year, *The Tasting Panel* covers industry trends; chefs, sommeliers, and mixologists of note; wine and spirits producers; travel destinations; and wine and spirit reviews. Advertisements for wine, spirits, and food and beverage events abound with the publication, and accessibly written articles do not overwhelm those new to the industry. Subscribers get two issues in one, as each issue flips over to reveal additional content and reviews. Both the editor-in-chief and the publisher contribute to the wine and spirits reviews, and their reviews reflect their distinctive styles. Visitors to the publication's website find web exclusive stories, recipes, and access to archived issues back to 2016. Similar to *Market Watch* (above in this section) in the depth of coverage it provides, *The Tasting Panel* is an additional voice, at a lower price point, for those interested in the wine and spirits industry. Only U.S. residents can subscribe.

722. *Whisky Advocate.* Former titles (until 2011): *Malt Advocate;* (until 1994): *On Tap.* 19??. q. USD 22 domestic; USD 24 Canada; USD 40 elsewhere. Marvin R. Shanken Communications, Inc., 825 Eighth Ave, 33rd Fl, New York, NY 10019; http://www.mshanken.com/. Illus. *Aud.:* Ga, Sa.

Renamed in the fall of 2011, *Whisky Advocate* (formerly *Malt Advocate*) has been the leading publication on all things whisky since the early 1990s. Covering all types of malt beverages, issues have topics such as craft bourbons, ryes from Canada, how to build a personal collection, and advice for shopping at bottle auctions. Issues also feature travel suggestions (great hotel whisky bars and Tucson, AZ), interviews with master distillers, and drink recipes. Each issue has a buying guide that rates whiskies from around the world, by region of production. Entries from the buying guide are available on the website, searchable and dating back 20+ years. The magazine is also the presenter of the annual Whisky Fest, a sampling and educational event hosted in major U.S. cities.

723. ***Wine & Spirits.*** Formerly (until 198?): *Wine & Spirits Buying Guide.* [ISSN: 0890-0299] 1982. 8x/yr. USD 29.95 combined subscription (print & online eds.)). Ed(s): Joshua Greene. Wine & Spirits Magazine, Inc., 2 W 32nd St, Ste 601, New York, NY 10001; subscription@wineandspiritsmagazine.com. Illus., adv. *Indexed:* H&TI. *Aud.:* Ga, Sa.

Launched in 1982, *Wine & Spirits* is a mainstream alternative to the formal wine magazines. Utilizing polls and lists for many of its reviews and rankings, *W&S* makes the information accessible and easy to understand for a broad audience of readers. Issues often have a theme such as Top 50 wines, Canary Islands wines, and Farm-to-Table travel. Articles focus not only on wine quality and tasting, but also examine wine makers, their vineyards, and how they create their bottles. The *Wine & Spirits* web page features supplemental content like reviews for everything from wine books to cocktail bars, along with videos from various Wine & Spirits events. Its lower annual subscription rate makes it worth consideration to reach a wide readership.

724. ***Wine Enthusiasts.*** Formerly (until 1993): *Wine Enthusiast Magazine.* [ISSN: 1078-3318] 1988. 13x/yr. USD 29.95 domestic; USD 49.95 Canada; USD 85.95 elsewhere. Ed(s): Lauren Buzzeo, Adam Strum. Wine Enthusiast, 200 Summit Lake Dr 4th Fl, Valhalla, NY 10595; custserv@wineenthusiast.net; http://www.wineenthusiast.com. Illus., adv. *Aud.:* Ga, Sa.

Founded in 1988 by Adam and Sybil Strum, *Wine Enthusiast* grew out of their Wine Enthusiast Company, which began in 1979. With a large trim size and full-color pages, the magazine has an attractive presentation that is useful to both consumers and producers. Issues typically have a theme like Top Best Buys, 40 under 40 Producers and Tastemakers, and New World Wines; while special editions, like an issue dedicated to the Pacific Northwest, are also published. Articles about the hottest wine regions and varietals mingle with reviews, travel guides, profiles, and recipes and pairings. The focus is not exclusively on wine either, as issues include articles about spirits, beer, and winemakers transitioning to spirits distillers. Print subscriptions are available for domestic and international subscribers, and the publication has a significant online presence with access to online editions.

725. ***Wine Spectator.*** [ISSN: 0193-497X] 1976. 13x/yr. USD 59.95. Ed(s): Kim Marcus. Marvin R. Shanken Communications, Inc., 825 Eighth Ave, 33rd Fl, New York, NY 10019. Illus., adv. *Indexed:* B01, BRI, H&TI. *Aud.:* Ga, Sa.

Publishing since 1976, *Wine Spectator* has a glossy format and open design that make it the most recognized wine magazine in the industry. Issues cover current oenophile news; personalities in the industry; food and cooking with wine; travel; and selected upscale spirits. Ratings offer guidance and recommendations with scores and reviews of new wine releases worldwide. Subscription options include print, print and digital, or digital only. The print plus digital includes access to more than 300,000 ratings and an e-newsletter with advance wine ratings. Online content also includes access to other Shanken publications, discussion forums, daily news updates, and a classified section for jobs, shopping, and much more.

726. ***WineMaker: creating your own great wines.*** 2003. bi-m. USD 26.99 domestic; USD 29.99 Canada; USD 46.99 elsewhere. Ed(s): Betsy Parks. Battenkill Communications LLP, 5515 Main St., Manchester Center, VT 05255. Adv. Circ: 108500 Paid and controlled. *Aud.:* Ga, Sa.

Younger sister magazine of the publishing group behind the beer title *Brew Your Own, WineMaker* is written for the amateur winemaker. Vintners from beginner to expert will find articles written for a variety of knowledge levels and expertise. Issues examine a range of topics from growing your own grapes to simple brewing with wine kits and pairing food with wine. *WineMaker*'s subscription model offers a print edition, a digital membership, or a combination. The digital membership provides additional content including access to current and back issues;, a searchable database of wine making questions and answers; articles with techniques for different grape varietals; and an extensive resource guide for the hobby viticulturalist. *WineMaker* also sponsors the world's largest wine competition devoted to hobby wines, the WineMaker International Amateur Wine Competition, and hosts the annual WineMaker Magazine Conference.

■ BIBLIOGRAPHY

See also Books and Book Reviews; Library and Information Science; and Printing and Graphic Arts sections.

Deborah F. Bernnard, Director of Public Services, University at Albany, Albany, NY 12222; dbernnard@albany.edu

Mark Wolfe, Curator of Digital Collections, M. E. Grenander Department of Special Collections and Archives, Science Library, University at Albany, Albany, NY 12222; mwolfe@albany.edu

Introduction

Bibliography is the study of books as physical objects. While the term is often limited to the practice of *enumerative* bibliography, as in (for example) the process of making lists of books by author, the domain of knowledge is much broader and deeper. Bibliography, as it pertains to the magazines listed in this section, is predominantly concerned with the broader category of *analytical* bibliography.

In *Book Collecting: A Modern Guide* (Bowker, 1977), Terry Belanger divides *analytical* bibliography into several types: *historical* ("the history of books broadly speaking, and the persons, institutions, and machines producing them"); *textual* ("the relationship between the printed text as we have it before us and that text as conceived by its author"); and *descriptive* ("the close physical description of books"). The subject of bibliography is of interest to rare-book librarians, curators, bibliophiles, and scholars who are interested in medieval studies and the history of the book.

Journals that cover bibliography are often produced by bibliographical societies. These societies are not necessarily affiliated with an educational institution, and their membership consists of anyone who has an interest in bibliography. The Bibliographic Society of America is one example of a national society. Included here are publications by American, British, Australian, New Zealander, and Canadian societies. Other important journals for the field are published by research universities whose collections are often the subject of the articles found in these journals. Also important for bibliography collections are journals that specialize in specific aspects of bibliography, such as *Gutenberg-Jahrbuch*, which is devoted to Johannes Gutenberg. Other journals may be specific to book history and book collecting.

Basic Periodicals

Ac, Sa: *Bibliographical Society of America. Papers; The Library; Studies in Bibliography.*

Basic Abstracts and Indexes

America: History and Life, Historical Abstracts, Library Literature & Information Science, MLA International Bibliography.

727. ***La Bibliofilia: rivista di storia del libro e di bibliografia.*** [ISSN: 0006-0941] 1899. 3x/yr. EUR 190 print & online eds. Ed(s): Edoardo Barbieri. Casa Editrice Leo S. Olschki, Viuzzo del Pozzetto 8, Florence, 50126, Italy; celso@olschki.it; http://www.olschki.it. Illus., adv. Vol. ends: Sep/Dec. *Indexed:* A22, MLA-IB. *Bk. rev.:* 6-10, 300-3,000 words. *Aud.:* Ac, Sa.

First published in 1899, *La Bibliofilia* is a venerable Italian publication that covers publishing, printing, and the book trade in Italy. Articles are written in German, English, French, and Italian, with English or Italian abstracts included at the end of each article. Research articles, book reviews, and a notes section are found in each issue. Most of the reviews are of books published in Italian, although some issues include an Americana section in which books published in the United States are reviewed in English. Each volume is beautifully produced on high-quality stock. Recommended for special collections and academic libraries that support substantial Italian Studies programs.

728. *Bibliographical Society of America. Papers.* Incorporates (1907-1912): *Bibliographical Society of America. Bulletin;* Formerly (until 1909): *Bibliographical Society of America. Proceedings and Papers.* [ISSN: 0006-128X] 1905. q. USD 348 (print & online eds.)). Ed(s): David L Gants. University of Chicago Press, 1427 E 60th St, Chicago, IL 60637; custserv@press.uchicago.edu; http://www.press.uchicago.edu. Illus., index, adv. Refereed. Vol. ends: Dec. Reprint: PSC. *Indexed:* A01, A22, AmHI, BRI, CBRI, MLA-IB. *Bk. rev.:* 7-10 of 500-2,500 words; plus 4-6 more of 200-500 words. *Aud.:* Ac, Sa.

Published since 1905, the *Papers of the Bibliographical Society of America* contains articles on book and manuscript printing, distribution, and collecting in all disciplines. Each issue contains several peer-reviewed articles; many include black-and-white reproduced illustrations. The *Papers* presents a nice mix of articles that explore both historical publications and newer formats, such as Zines. Book reviews, bibliographical notes, and review essays may also be included in select issues. Each issue contains a section titled "Society Information," in which Bibliographical Society information, news, and notes are published. The *Papers of the Bibliographical Society of America* is published quarterly and an index to the whole volume is available in issue four. Recommended for special collections and large academic libraries.

729. *Bibliographical Society of Canada. Papers.* Former titles (until 1963): *Bibliographical Society of Canada. Newsletter;* (until 1955): *Bibliographical Society of Canada. Bulletin.* [ISSN: 0067-6896] 1949. s-a. Ed(s): Ruth-Ellen St. Onge. Bibliographical Society of Canada, 360 Bloor St W, PO Box 19035 WALMER, Toronto, ON M5S 3C9, Canada; secretary@bsc-sbc.ca; http://www.bsc-sbc.ca/en/. Refereed. *Indexed:* BRI, C37, MLA-IB. *Bk. rev.:* Number and length vary. *Aud.:* Ac, Sa.

The *Papers of the Bibliographical Society of Canada* is the official publication of the society, which is the premiere journal in Canada on the study of bibliography. The journal features three regular sections, research articles, "Books in Review," and "Notes." The journal averages one to three articles per issue with roughly one quarter of them published in French, some of which are accompanied by illustrations. Articles range in topics on printing and publishing history as well as textual studies, many of which draw on Canadian history and its connections to bibliography. Recent issues include titles such as "Tried, Tested, but not Proved: The Home Cook Book and the Development of a Canadian Culinary Identity" and "The Geopolitics of Nineteenth-Century Canadian Copyright, as seen by some British Authors." Each issue includes numerous book reviews of scholarship printed in English and French. This is a high quality publication and would be at home in any academic library, especially those wanting a Canadian perspective on the subject.

730. *Bodleian Library Record.* Formerly (until 1938): *Bodleian Quarterly Record.* [ISSN: 0067-9488] 1914. s-a. GBP 50 (Individuals, GBP 40). Bodleian Library, Broad St, Oxford, OX1 3BG, United Kingdom; fob@bodley.ox.ac.uk; http://www.ouls.ox.ac.uk. Illus., index. Refereed. Circ: 1500 Paid. Vol. ends: Oct. Microform: PQC. *Indexed:* A22, AmHI, MLA-IB. *Bk. rev.:* 2-4, approx. 2,000 words each. *Aud.:* Ac, Sa.

The *Bodleian Library Record,* published semiannually, contains articles made possible by engaging in research with the library's collections. The Bodleian is Oxford University's main library and dates back to 1602. With such a long history there is no end to possible research topics. Each issue contains a "Notes and News" section, in which information is imparted about past and present library staff and events; reviews of monographs published by The Bodleian Library; notable accessions; and a "Notes and Documents" section, in which scholars describe selected manuscripts in the collection. There are also several feature articles in each issue that delve deeply into Bodleian collections. Recommended for special collections and larger academic libraries.

731. *The Book Collector.* Supersedes (in 1952): *Book Handbook.* 1952. q. GBP 80 (Individuals, GBP 60). Collector Ltd., PO Box 1163, St Albans, AL19WS, United Kingdom; editor@thebookcollector.co.uk. Illus., adv. Sample. Vol. ends: Winter. Microform: PQC. Reprint: PSC. *Indexed:* A22, AmHI, BRI, CBRI, MLA-IB. *Bk. rev.:* 4-8, 500-3,000 words. *Aud.:* Ac, Sa.

Created in 1952 by Ian Fleming of James Bond fame, *The Book Collector* contains scholarly essays, lists, catalogs, and news from the rare-book and antiquarian trade worlds in the United Kingdom, with some coverage of the United States. Long-time editor Nicolas Barker retired in 2016. Ian Fleming's nephew, James Ferguson, is carrying on his uncle's legacy as the current editor. Each issue includes eight to ten research articles or essays, which often include high-quality images. Recent issues include a profile of rare books collector Mark Samuels Laster and a "History of the Festival Publications Poetry Pamphlets." All issues contain a "News and Comments" section, which reports on all things related to the printed book. The journal is published quarterly. Reviews of relevant publications are included at the end of each issue. Recommended for special collections and larger academic and public libraries.

732. *Book History.* [ISSN: 1098-7371] 1998. a. USD 80. The Johns Hopkins University Press, 2715 N Charles St, Baltimore, MD 21218; http://www.press.jhu.edu. Illus., adv. Sample. Refereed. Reprint: PSC. *Indexed:* A01, A22, AmHI, E01, MLA-IB. *Aud.:* Ac, Sa.

There is an immense variety and depth of scholarship to be gleaned from the history of the book. *Book History,* the official journal of the Society for the History of Authorship, Reading and Publishing, serves as the publication venue for this scholarship. This annual, hardcover publication contains about a dozen well-researched articles on topics ranging from authorship to university presses. Illustration, censorship, and ebooks are also among the many topics covered. A short biography of each contributor is listed at the end of each issue. The journal publishes only scholarly essays and articles. It does not include reviews or commentary. However, each issue contains a valuable literature review article on a specific print, publishing, or book history topic. Recommended for special collections and larger academic and public libraries.

733. *Cambridge Bibliographical Society. Transactions.* [ISSN: 0068-6611] 1949. a. Cambridge Bibliographical Society, c/o Cambridge University Library, W Rd, Cambridge, CB3 9DR, United Kingdom; cbs@lib.cam.ac.uk; http://www.lib.cam.ac.uk/cambibsoc. Illus. Refereed. *Indexed:* A22, MLA-IB. *Aud.:* Ac, Sa.

Published annually, the *Transactions of the Cambridge Bibliographical Society* focuses on University of Cambridge-related research. This may include articles on works found in Cambridge libraries, works written by Cambridge authors, or works published by Cambridge University establishments. The most recent volume contains research articles as well as a "summary of the Society's activities." High-quality reproductions of illustrations, book and parchment pages, and photographs accompany many of the articles. Each volume also includes a short summary of the society's activities during the year. Recommended for larger academic and special collections libraries.

734. *Gutenberg-Jahrbuch.* [ISSN: 0072-9094] 1926. a. EUR 85 per issue. Ed(s): Stephan Fuessel. Harrassowitz Verlag, Kreuzberger Ring 7b-d, Wiesbaden, 65205, Germany; service@harrassowitz.de; https://www.harrassowitz.de. Illus. *Indexed:* MLA-IB. *Aud.:* Ac, Sa.

Gutenberg-Jahrbuch is an annual devoted to scholarship on the life of Johannes Gutenberg and the history of the book. Although it is published in Germany, articles are written in German, English, Italian, Spanish, and French. Articles written in languages other than English are prefaced with an English-language abstract. Each volume is beautifully produced with both color and black-and-white reproductions. Selected recent titles of English-language articles are "The Variant Typesetting of the Editio Princeps of Augustinus, De civitate dei 1467" and "Forming a Collection of Fifteenth Century Books in the Twenty-first Century." Recommended for academic libraries and special collections.

735. *Harvard Library Bulletin.* Former titles (until 1947): *Harvard University Library. Notes;* (until 1941): *Harvard Library Notes.* [ISSN: 0017-8136] 1920. q. USD 35 in North America; USD 41 elsewhere; USD 15 per issue. Ed(s): William P Stoneman. Harvard University Library, Wadsworth House, 1341 Massachusetts Ave, Cambridge, MA 02138; http://hul.harvard.edu. Illus. Refereed. Vol. ends: Winter. *Indexed:* A22, BAS, MLA-IB. *Aud.:* Ac, Sa.

The *Harvard Library Bulletin* is broad in scope; articles may be about an exhibition at the library, a collection, a notable work, or a person with a Harvard connection such as Ralph Waldo Emerson (who attended Harvard at age 14). Most issues contain two or three disparate-topic articles. However, themed issues are occasionally published. Recommended for large academic libraries.

Please note that the publishers have announced a hiatus for the "Bulletin" after the release of volumes 27.3 and 28.103 in 2019.

736. ***Huntington Library Quarterly: studies in English and American history and literature.*** Formerly (until 1937): *The Huntington Library. Bulletin.* [ISSN: 0018-7895] 1931. q. USD 260 combined subscription (print & online eds.)). Ed(s): Jean Patterson. University of Pennsylvania Press, 3905 Spruce St, Philadelphia, PA 19104; journals@pobox.upenn.edu; http://www.pennpress.org. Illus., index, adv. Sample. Refereed. Circ: 429. Microform: PQC. *Indexed:* A01, A22, AmHI, BRI, E01, MLA-IB. *Bk. rev.:* 1-4, 2,000-7,500 words. *Aud.:* Ac, Sa.

The Huntington Library, a private library founded in 1919 by American philanthropist Henry E. Huntington, houses a large and rich collection of rare books and manuscripts in British and American history and literature. However, articles in the *Huntington Library Quarterly* cover more than just materials in the collection. The publishers invite submissions on "the literature, history, and art of Brtain and America from the sixteenth century through the long eighteenth century." Often, themed issues are interspersed throughout a volume. Issues that are not themed may contain substantial review sections as well as a "Notes and Documents" feature, in which scholars provide bibliographical notes on selected rare items in the collection. "Intramuralia," a listing of Huntington Library acquisitions for a year, is published approximately two years after the actual acquisition. Black-and-white reproductions of manuscript pages, paintings, drawings, or photographs are included as appropriate. Recommended for academic libraries and special collections.

737. ***John Rylands Library. Bulletin.*** Former titles (until 2014): *John Rylands University Library of Manchester. Bulletin;* (until 1972): *John Rylands Library. Bulletin.* [ISSN: 2054-9318] 1903. s-a. GBP 186 (print & online eds.)). Ed(s): Cordelia Warr, Stephen Mossman. Manchester University Press, Fl. J, Renold Bldg., Altrincham St., Manchester, M1 7JA, United Kingdom; mup@manchester.ac.uk; http://www.manchesteruniversitypress.co.uk/. Illus., index, adv. Sample. Refereed. Reprint: PSC. *Indexed:* A22, AmHI, BAS, MLA-IB, R&TA. *Aud.:* Ac, Sa.

The *Bulletin of the John Rylands Library* is a forum for scholarship on a wide range of subjects pertaining to the collections of the library, which houses "one of the world's finest collections of rare books and manuscripts." The John Rylands University Library of Manchester is part of the University of Manchester, located in Manchester, England. The library's collections are vast and boast a large collection of early Methodist papers. Its holdings include "12,500 books printed between 1475 and 1640, and 45,000 printed between 1641 and 1700." Publication is now reliably up to date due to a recent change in publishers. Recommended for large academic and special collections.

738. ***The Library: the transactions of the Bibliographical Society.*** Incorporates (1893-1919): *Bibliographical Society. Transactions;* Formerly (until 1889): *Library Chronicle.* [ISSN: 0024-2160] 18??. q. EUR 398. Ed(s): James Willoughby, William Poole. Oxford University Press, Great Clarendon St, Oxford, OX2 6DP, United Kingdom; onlinequeries.uk@oup.com; http://global.oup.com. Illus., index, adv. Sample. Refereed. Vol. ends: Dec. Microform: PQC. Reprint: PSC. *Indexed:* A22, BRI, CBRI, E01, MLA-IB. *Bk. rev.:* 10-13, 1,000-2,000 words. *Aud.:* Ac, Sa.

The Library is a publication of the Bibliographical Society, and is the premier scholarly journal on the study of bibliography and book history in the United Kingdom. "All aspects of descriptive, analytical, textual and historical bibliography come within" the scope of *The Library*. The journal typically devotes each issue to two or three full-length scholarly articles, as well as extensive book reviews. Each issue devotes space to three regular sections: "Books Received" contains a listing of new monographs, such as *Street Literature of the Long Nineteenth Century: Producers, Sellers, Consumers*. "Recent Books" features an annotated listing relevant to the field of bibliography; and "Recent Periodicals" features published articles germane to bibliography that are categorized by language or place of publication. Recent issues include article titles such as "From Restorer to Editor: The Evolution of Lewis Theobald's Textual Critical Practice" and "The Writing Tables of James Roberts." The journal is indexed yearly. This excellent journal should be subscribed to by research universities and those libraries that support programs in the history of the book and rare-book librarianship.

739. ***Matrix (Herefordshire).*** [ISSN: 0261-3093] 1981. a. Whittington Press, Lower Marston Farm, Leominster, HR6 0NJ, United Kingdom; rose@whittingtonpress.plus.com; http://www.whittingtonpress.com. Illus. *Indexed:* A51. *Bk. rev.:* 12-25, 100-2,500 words. *Aud.:* Ac, Sa.

Matrix is a book-length, large-format journal that is published yearly and printed using a letterpress on handmade paper. *Matrix* is an exquisite publication that is a collectible object itself. It features numerous tipped-in illustrations, pull-out posters printed with woodblock type, glossy color plates, and other expressive features typical of the book arts. The journal will inspire scholars of the book arts, typography, and book historians. *Matrix* is truly unique and stands out among nearly all of the bibliography journals for the amount of care and quality of materials spent on each issue. The articles are well written and engaging, and the journal proves that rigorous scholarship need not look drab or unpleasing to the eye. Recent issues include articles such as "Doing the Odd Linocut," "Allamanda Press: Now We Are Six," and "In the Shadow of Dunbar Bay." This journal is appropriate for any size academic institution, and those that support programs in book arts, rare-book librarianship, and the history of the book, as well as bibliophiles.

740. ***Princeton University Library Chronicle.*** Incorporates (in 19??): *Princeton University Library. Biblia.* [ISSN: 0032-8456] 1939. 3x/yr. Friends of Princeton University Library, 1 Washington Rd, Princeton, NJ 08544; principi@princeton.edu; http://www.fpul.org. Illus., index. Refereed. Vol. ends: Spring. *Indexed:* A22, AmHI, BAS, MLA-IB. *Aud.:* Ac, Sa.

The *Princeton University Library Chronicle* is a publication of the Friends of the Princeton University Library. The journal covers many aspects of bibliography; aiming to "publish articles of scholarly importance and general interest based on research in the rare book and manuscripts collection of the Princeton University Library." Each issue typically features three or four well-documented research articles that are generously illustrated, sometimes in color. Articles such as "Rare Books in Princeton's Korean Collection" and "The First Jewish Americans: Freedom and Culture in the New World" are featured. Recent acquisitions of books, coins, manuscripts, and art that are new and notable to the library collections are described by curators and librarians of the collections. The *Chronicle* features meeting notes under the section "Friends of the Library." Also, there is a short "Cover Note" that describes the cover illustration. There can be thematic issues, such as one themed around Irish writers and literature that include original submissions or extracts from works in progress. A comprehensive index of each volume is published yearly with the journal. This journal would be appropriate in any academic library that supports programs in the humanities or information studies programs.

Printing Historical Society. Journal. See Printing and Graphic Arts section.

Printing History. See Printing and Graphic Arts section.

741. ***The Private Library.*** Formerly (until 1958): *P L A Quarterly.* [ISSN: 0032-8898] 1957. q. Private Libraries Association, c/o Jim Maslen, 29 Eden Dr, Hull, HU8 8JQ, United Kingdom; http://www.plabooks.org/. Illus., index. Refereed. *Indexed:* MLA-IB. *Bk. rev.:* 1-3, 500-3,000 words. *Aud.:* Sa.

The Private Library is published quarterly by the Private Libraries Association. Each issue is slim but inviting and refreshing nonetheless. The journal features academic articles that will appeal to the scholar of bibliography as well as to book collectors. Each issue typically features two or three articles that include checklists of the books mentioned, typically illustrated, and sometimes in color. The journal focuses "on books that can be collected today" and features "printed essays by members' libraries, specialised collections, the work of the private press, illustrators and, indeed, any aspect of the mania likely to appeal to collectors," many of which focus on book collection in the United Kingdom. *The Private Library* presents one of the most enjoyable publications in the field of bibliography for the specialist and non-specialist, while maintaining academic rigor and excellence. Recent issues feature articles like "A Collector's Journey to the Stanbrook Abbey Press" and "John William North: A Radical Illustrator." The journal is appropriate for bibliophiles, academic libraries, and some larger public libraries.

Quaerendo: a journal devoted to manuscripts and printed books. See Printing and Graphic Arts section.

R B M: A Journal of Rare Books, Manuscripts and Cultural Heritage. See Archives and Manuscripts/General section.

742. ***Script & Print.*** Formerly (until 2004): *Bibliographical Society of Australia and New Zealand. Bulletin.* [ISSN: 1834-9013] 1970. q. Free to members. Ed(s): Shef Rogers. Bibliographical Society of Australia & New Zealand, c/o Bryan Coleborne, PO Box 390, Yass, NSW 2582, Australia; http://www.bsanz.org. Illus., adv. Sample. Refereed. *Indexed:* MLA-IB. *Bk. rev.:* 2-3, 800-1,400 words. *Aud.:* Ac, Sa.

Script & Print is a quarterly journal that has been in publication since 1970, and is the premier journal of its kind in Australia and New Zealand. *Script & Print* publishes on all aspects of bibliography, including "physical bibliography: the history of printing, publishing, bookselling, type founding, paper making, bookbinding; paleography and codicology; [and] writing, editing and textural bibliography." Each issue features four or five scholarly articles that are well referenced and occasionally illustrated, and there are typically three or four full-length book reviews. Recent issues feature articles entitled "Ships' Newspapers and the Graphic Universe Afloat in the Nineteenth Century," "The Materials of Which I Am Made: Evelyn Waugh and Book Production," and a book review of "The Noblest Roman: A History of the Centaur Type of Bruce Rogers." *Script & Print* will appeal to an international audience, and is appropriate for any large academic library that seeks to support programs in rare-book librarianship and the history of the book.

743. ***Scriptorium: international review of manuscript studies and bulletin codicologique (book reviews).*** [ISSN: 0036-9772] 1947. s-a. Ed(s): O Legendre, P Cockshaw. Centre d'Etude des Manuscrits, Bd de l'Empereur 4, Brussels, 1000, Belgium. Illus., adv. Refereed. Circ: 900. Vol. ends: No. 2. *Indexed:* A22, MLA-IB. *Bk. rev.:* 300-350, 50-1,500 words. *Aud.:* Ac, Sa.

Scriptorium is a bi-yearly, multi-language international publication, founded in 1947, on the study of medieval manuscript research. The book-length journal covers the subject of codicology, which is the "...material description of any aspect of manuscripts: supporting material, page-setting, binding, paleography, miniatures..."; and the journal "inform[s] on cultural environment and offer[s] a bibliography regarding mediaeval manuscripts through Western, Eastern and Central Europe." In addition, the *Scriptorium* devotes nearly half of each issue to the *Bulletin codicologique,* which features more than 100 pages or as many as 300 book review entries per issue. It includes brief reviews of books and recent papers published by French, English, Spanish, German, and Italian scholars. Color plates are featured (on glossy paper at the back of the journal) that correspond to the research articles. The journal's editors write that the *Bulletin codicologique* "presents in fact a state of affairs regarding manuscript-related studies and serves as a thread for the scholar who risks losing his way amidst documentation that has become labyrinthine." An essential resource for any serious teaching and research programs in medieval studies.

744. ***Studies in Bibliography.*** Formerly (until 1950): *University of Virginia. Papers of the Bibliographical Society.* [ISSN: 0081-7600] 1948. a. USD 70 per issue. Ed(s): David L Vander Meulen. University of Virginia Press, PO Box 400318, Charlottesville, VA 22904; upressva@virginia.edu; http://www.upress.virginia.edu. Illus. Refereed. *Indexed:* A22, E01, MLA-IB. *Aud.:* Ac, Sa.

Studies in Bibliography is a publication of the Bibliographical Society of the University of Virginia. The journal purports to being "one of the pre-eminent journals in the fields of analytical bibliography, textual criticism, manuscript study, and the history of printing and publishing." *Studies in Bibliography* was founded in 1948 by Fredson Bowers, who was one of the most important bibliography scholars of the twentieth century; the journal has continued its commitment to excellence under the editorship of David L. Vander Meulen. Many articles published in the journal have become part of the core curriculum in courses on bibliography. Recent issues feature articles such as "Errors in the Malory Archetype: The Case of Vinaver's Wight and Balan's Curious Remark"; "Joyce's Library *Ulysses*"; and "Lines Per Page, Engravings, and Catchwords in Milton's 1720 *Poetical Works.*" The notable American scholar Thomas Tanselle is a regular contributor to the journal. *Studies in Bibliography* is published annually as one volume. Recent volumes feature seven to nine full-length articles, but these generally lack illustration. This is a must for academic libraries that support or serve library science, rare-book librarianship, the history of the book, and private book collectors.

745. ***Textual Cultures (Online).*** [ISSN: 1933-7418] 2006. s-a. Free. Ed(s): Dan O'Sullivan. Indiana University Press, Office of Scholarly Publishing, Herman B Wells Library 350, Bloomington, IN 47405; journals@indiana.edu; http://www.iupress.indiana.edu/. Refereed. *Bk. rev.:* 4-12, 800-2,400 words. *Aud.:* Ac, Sa.

Textural Cultures is a publication of the Society for Textual Scholarship. The journal is published twice a year in English, French, German, Spanish, and Italian, and each issue includes English abstracts for every article, although the majority of submissions are published in English. The journal features many topics that range from historical studies to theoretical issues that confront the field of bibliography. The journal has transitioned to publishing online only as of 2013. The journal's self-described focus deals with "textual editing, redefinitions of textuality, the history of the book, material culture, and the fusion of codicology with literary, musicological, and art historical interpretation and iconography." Recent issues have featured articles that cover broad topics, such as "Rethinking Scholarly Commentary in the Age of Google" and "Deep Mapping in Edward Hitchcock's Geology and Emily Dickinson's Poetry." Each issue contains five or six research articles under "Essays," and two or three substantial book reviews. This is a rigorous academic journal that would be appropriate for any academic library that supports programs in literature, history of the book, and rare-book librarianship.

■ BIOLOGY

General/Biochemistry and Biophysics/Cell and Molecular Biology/ Developmental Biology/Genetics/Microbiology

See also Agriculture; Biotechnology; Birds; Botany; Environment and Conservation; Marine Science and Technology; and Science and Technology sections.

Kimberly O'Neill, Associate Professor, Research and Instruction Librarian, Regis University, Dayton Memorial Library, Denver, CO 80221

Introduction

The biological sciences permeate all aspects of our existence and interactions on this planet. The desire to attain knowledge in this broad scientific discipline starts at an early age when we become interested in our environment, the bugs on the ground, the flowers in our gardens, and the functions of our bodies. We seek to find answers to the fascinating questions that come up in our daily lives. The information available in biological sciences is vast, covering so many subgroups that it can be overwhelming.

This section of *Magazines for Libraries* breaks down some of the main areas of publishing in the biological sciences into subsections that include "General Biology," "Biochemistry and Biophysics," "Cell and Molecular Biology," "Developmental Biology," "Genetics," and "Microbiology." The fields of Botany, Ecology, Forestry, Marine Science, Medicine, Zoology, and others have large numbers of publications by themselves, so these publications are left to their own sections.

The titles included here are targeted to the academic and special library to suit the subject-specific researcher, student, educator, and general biologist. Almost all titles have an online as well as a print element. Some of these titles offer free online content. Many of the general titles are widely indexed in the popular subject indexes.

Open Access (OA) publishing has increased in recent years, with many journals offering an OA option. In offering this option, these journals usually require a fee from the author. This allows publications to be freely available to non-subscribers. The National Institutes of Health (NIH) Public Access Policy began requiring that any researcher funded by the NIH must submit an electronic version of the final, peer-reviewed manuscript on acceptance for publication. These articles must be made publicly available no later than 12 months after the official date of publication to the National Library of Medicine's PubMed Central (PMC). PMC is the NIH digital archive of full-text, peer-reviewed journal articles.

There is also a growing amount of content published under the Creative Commons Attribution License. Under this agreement, authors will retain copyright, but anyone is allowed to download, use, reuse, distribute, or even modify the content as long as the original author and source are cited. This license eliminates the need to contact the publisher or author directly. Scientific publishing sets the standard by offering more opportunities for access and flexibility in publishing models.

Basic Periodicals

Ga: *BMC Biology; Nature; PLoS Biology;* Ac: *Biochemistry; Cell; Genetics; Microbiology and Molecular Biology Reviews; National Academy of Sciences. Proceedings; The Quarterly Review of Biology.*

Basic Abstracts and Indexes

Biological Abstracts, Biological and Agricultural Index, Biology Digest, BIOSIS Previews, Current Contents/Agriculture, Current Contents/Life Sciences, MEDLINE, Proquest Biological Science Database, PubMed, Web of Science.

General

746. *B M C Biology.* [ISSN: 1741-7007] 2004. irreg. Free. Ed(s): Miranda Robertson. BioMed Central Ltd., Fl 6, 236 Gray's Inn Rd, London, WC1X 8HB, United Kingdom; info@biomedcentral.com; https://www.biomedcentral.com. Adv. Refereed. *Indexed:* A01, C45. *Aud.:* Ga, Ac, Sa.

B M C Biology is the flagship, open-access biology journal of the B M C series published by BioMed Central. The journal publishes research and methodology articles of special importance and broad interest in any area of biology and biomedical sciences. Types of articles include reviews, opinion pieces, and research articles. There are also methodology articles that present a new experimental or computational method, test, or procedure and software articles in which authors of software applications, tools, or algorithm implementations publish descriptions of their code using the software article type. *B M C Biology* is a full-text online journal. All articles are published online on the journal's web site without barriers to access immediately upon acceptance. Full text is also available free through PubMed Central. Research articles are published after full peer review. Highly recommended for academic and special libraries that support a biology program. Also recommended for public libraries that support a science collection. URL: http://bmcbiol.biomedcentral.com

747. *Biochimica et Biophysica Acta. General Subjects.* Supersedes in part (in 1964): *Biochimica et Biophysica Acta.* [ISSN: 0304-4165] 1947. 12x/yr. EUR 5803. Elsevier BV, Radarweg 29, Amsterdam, 1043 NX, Netherlands; info@elsevier.com; https://www.elsevier.com/. Refereed. Microform: PQC. *Indexed:* A01, A22, C45. *Aud.:* Ga, Ac.

Articles published in *BBA General Subjects* cover a wide variety of general biology topics. Examples include: medically important biochemistry/biophysics research, nanobiology, systems biology, chemical biology, structural biology, novel complexes, cellular signaling, glycobiology, redox biology, stem cells, imaging methodologies, and mechanistic characterization. This journal is one of the nine topical journals from *Biochimica et Biophysica Acta* (*BBA*). It contains "original, hypothesis-driven studies or reviews covering subjects in biochemistry and biophysics that are considered to have general interest for a wide audience." The journal supports innovations such as 3D models and crystallographic data, audioslides, a database linking tool, and a protein viewer. Online open access and paid-subscription access are available from 1964 to the present via ScienceDirect. Appropriate for academic and general libraries. URL: www.journals.elsevier.com/bba-general-subjects/

748. *Biological Reviews (Online).* [ISSN: 1469-185X] 1935. bi-m. GBP 432. Wiley-Blackwell Publishing Ltd., The Atrium, Southern Gate, Chichester, PO19 8QG, United Kingdom; cs-journals@wiley.com; http://www.wiley.com/. Refereed. *Indexed:* C45. *Aud.:* Ac, Sa.

Covering the entire range of the biological sciences, *Biological Reviews* presents review articles aimed at general biologists as well as specialists in the field. Each issue contains several review articles. Articles are up to 20,000 words long, and each contains an abstract, a thorough introduction, and statement of conclusions. Reviews of books are not published. Online, full-text content is provided through Wiley Online Library from 1923 to the present. This journal is appropriate for experts, researchers, and scholars, however authors may consider writing for a broader audience. An excellent resource for general academic as well as research collections that support biology programs. URL: http://onlinelibrary.wiley.com/journal/10.1111/(ISSN)1469-185X

749. *Biology Open.* [ISSN: 2046-6390] 2011. m. Free. Ed(s): Jordan Raff. The Company of Biologists Ltd., 140 Cowley Rd, Cambridge, CB4 0DL, United Kingdom; sales@biologists.com; http://www.biologists.com. Refereed. *Indexed:* C45. *Aud.:* Ga, Ac, Sa.

Biology Open (*BiO*) is an open-access online journal published by The Company of Biologists. This peer-reviewed journal covers all aspects of biological science, including cell science, developmental biology, and experimental biology. The journal was launched to alleviate the delays in the acceptance process and create an avenue for publishing research that lacked a perceived impact. Included in the journal are research articles, reviews, and correspondence. Since 2012, articles have appeared immediately in PubMed Central. This journal would be of interest to public, academic, and special libraries. URL: http://bio.biologists.org/

750. *BioScience: a forum for integrating the life sciences.* Formerly (until 1964): *A I B S Bulletin.* [ISSN: 0006-3568] 1951. m. EUR 622. Ed(s): Dr. Timothy M Beardsley. Oxford University Press, 2001 Evans Rd, Cary, NC 27513; https://academic.oup.com/journals. Illus., index, adv. Refereed. Vol. ends: Dec. Microform: PQC. Reprint: PSC. *Indexed:* A01, A22, Agr, BRI, C45, CBRI, E01, ERIC, GardL, MASUSE, MLA-IB, S25. *Bk. rev.:* 2-7, 600-2,000 words. *Aud.:* Ga, Ac, Sa.

BioScience is a peer-reviewed, heavily cited, monthly journal with content written and edited for accessibility to researchers, educators, and students. It is published by the American Institute of Biological Sciences (AIBS). Its content includes authoritative overviews of current research in biology, accompanied by essays and discussion sections on education, public policy, history, and basic concepts of the biological sciences. Also included are articles about research findings and techniques, advances in biology education, feature articles about the latest frontiers in biology, discussions of professional issues, book reviews, news about AIBS, a policy column ("Washington Watch"), and an education column ("Eye on Education"). Selected sections are available for free access online each month. Full text is available with a subscription. All AIBS members receive free subscriptions to print and online issues. Recommended for special, academic, and large public libraries. URL: http://bioscience.oxfordjournals.org/

751. *Current Biology.* [ISSN: 0960-9822] 1991. 24x/yr. EUR 2860. Ed(s): Geoffrey North. Cell Press, 600 Technology Sq, Ste 5, Cambridge, MA 02139; http://www.cell.com. Illus., adv. Sample. Refereed. Vol. ends: Dec. *Indexed:* A01, A22, C45, E01. *Aud.:* Ga, Ac, Sa.

Current Biology's primary goal is to foster communication across fields of biology by publishing important findings of general interest from diverse fields and by providing highly accessible editorial articles that aim to inform non-specialists. The journal includes articles that present findings of broad biological interest, as well as news. Non-subscribers have free online access to the featured article of the current issue, as well as free sponsored articles. Additionally, *Current Biology* publishes papers online ahead of the print issue each week. This title is appropriate for special and academic libraries, especially those that support biology programs, and large public libraries. All articles older than one year are free online through the Cell Press web site archive. URL: www.cell.com/current-biology/home

752. *Evolution (Online).* [ISSN: 1558-5646] m. GBP 746. Ed(s): Mohamed Noor. John Wiley & Sons Ltd., EMEA Institutional Sales, 9600 Garsington Rd, Oxford, OX4 2DQ, United Kingdom; cs-journals@wiley.com; http://onlinelibrary.wiley.com. Refereed. *Bk. rev.:* 0-2, 1,000-3,000 words. *Aud.:* Ac, Sa.

The main objectives of *Evolution* are the promotion of the study of organic evolution and the integration of the various fields of science concerned with evolution. The journal is published for the Society for the Study of Evolution. As of 2017, the journal has been published exclusively online. Contents include regular papers, perspectives, brief communications and comments, as well as book reviews. The Evolution App is available for the iPad through the Apple App Store. Authors may use *Evolution*'s open-access option, called OnlineOpen, which allows free immediate access to their article for subscribers and non-subscribers. Non-subscribers also have limited access to sample full-text issues online. Highly recommended for all academic libraries and some special libraries. *Evolution*'s full-text content is online for subscribers via Wiley Online Library. URL: http://onlinelibrary.wiley.com/journal/10.1111/(ISSN)1558-5646

753. *The F A S E B Journal.* Supersedes (in 1987): *Federation of American Societies for Experimental Biology. Federation Proceedings.* [ISSN: 0892-6638] 1987. m. Ed(s): Gerald Weissmann. Federation of American Societies for Experimental Biology, 9650 Rockville Pike, Bethesda, MD 20814; staff@faseb.org; http://www.faseb.org. Illus., index, adv. Refereed. *Indexed:* A01, A22, Agr, C45. *Bk. rev.:* Number and length vary. *Aud.:* Ac, Sa.

The FASEB Journal (Federation of American Societies for Experimental Biology) publishes papers that have integrated one or more of the member disciplines. This title is one of the world's most highly cited biology journals. It consistently ranks among the top biology publications. *The FASEB Journal* is a preferred venue for the latest research reports and reviews of epigenetics, iRNA mechanics, histone acetylation, nitric oxide signaling, eicosanoid biochemistry, angiogenesis, tumor suppressor genes, apoptosis, cytoskeletal function, and human stem-cell research. The journal publishes peer-reviewed, multidisciplinary, original research articles, as well as editorials, reviews, and news of the life sciences. Online, full-text access is provided from July 1987 to the present. Recommended for most biology collections in special and academic libraries. URL: www.fasebj.org

754. *National Academy of Sciences. Proceedings.* [ISSN: 0027-8424] 1914. w. Ed(s): Inder M Verma. National Academy of Sciences, 500 Fifth St NW, NAS 340, Washington, DC 20001; http://www.pnas.org. Illus., index, adv. Sample. Refereed. Vol. ends: Dec. Microform: PQC. *Indexed:* A01, A22, Agr, BRI, C45. *Aud.:* Ac, Sa.

PNAS is a multidisciplinary scientific journal that covers the physical, biological, and social sciences. This journal includes papers in the categories of research reports, commentaries, reviews, colloquium papers, perspectives, and reports on the National Academy of Sciences. *PNAS* is the world's most-cited multidisciplinary scientific journal. The biological sciences are covered across many disciplines from cell biology to evolution, genetics, immunology, and more. It is published weekly in print and daily online. Full text is available online with a subscription. There is free access to tables of contents, abstracts, early edition highlights, content older than six months, and more. Individual and institutional subscriptions are available. Appropriate for academic and special libraries, and essential for most science collections. URL: www.pnas.org

Natural History. See Science and Technology/General section.

755. *Nature: international weekly journal of science.* Incorporates (1971-1973): *Nature. Physical Science;* (1971-1973): *Nature. New Biology;* Both of which superseded in part (in 1971): *Nature.* [ISSN: 0028-0836] 1869. 51x/yr. EUR 5448. Ed(s): Dr. Philip Campbell. Nature Publishing Group, The MacMillan Bldg, 4 Crinan St, London, N1 9XW, United Kingdom; feedback@nature.com; https://www.nature.com. Illus., index, adv. Sample. Refereed. Vol. ends: Dec. *Indexed:* A&ATA, A01, A22, Agr, B03, BAS, BRI, C37, C45, CBRI, MASUSE, MLA-IB, S25. *Aud.:* Ga, Ac, Sa.

Nature is the most-cited weekly international science journal. The mission of *Nature* is "to serve scientists through prompt publication of significant advances in any branch of science, and to provide a forum for the reporting and discussion of news and issues concerning science." *Nature* provides rapid, authoritative, insightful, and arresting news and interpretation of topical and coming trends that affect science, scientists, and the wider public. Online content is available with a subscription. Free sample issues and trials are available. Online features include podcasts, webcasts, blogs, career listings, and select content in full text. SpringerNature publications cover a wide variety of scientific literature especially in the life sciences. Highly recommended for any library that supports the sciences. URL: www.nature.com/nature/index.html

756. *Open Biology.* [ISSN: 2046-2441] 2011. . Free. Ed(s): Jonathan Pines. The Royal Society Publishing, 6-9 Carlton House Terr, London, SW1Y 5AG, United Kingdom; publishing@royalsociety.org; http://royalsociety.org/journals. Refereed. *Indexed:* C45. *Aud.:* Ac, Sa.

Open Biology is the Royal Society's peer-reviewed online journal that focuses on research in cell and developmental biology, molecular and structural biology, biochemistry, neuroscience, immunology, microbiology, and genetics. The journal publishes research articles, reviews, invited perspectives, invited commentaries, comments, and invited replies. All papers are immediately available in PubMed Central. The journal offers open peer review for all manuscripts to make the review process as transparent as possible. Reviewer reports, decision letter and associated author responses are accessible alongside published articles. Recommended for academic and special libraries. URL: http://rsob.royalsocietypublishing.org/

757. *P L o S Biology (Online).* [ISSN: 1545-7885] 2003. m. Free. Ed(s): Chris Ferguson, Emma Ganley. Public Library of Science, 1160 Battery St, Koshland Bldg E, Ste 100, San Francisco, CA 94111; plos@plos.org; http://www.plos.org. Adv. Refereed. *Aud.:* Ga, Ac, Sa.

PLoS Biology is a peer-reviewed, open-access journal that presents significant and original works in all areas of biological science. It also encompasses works that intersect other disciplines, such as chemistry, medicine, and mathematics. The journal's audience is international in scope including the scientific community as well as educators, policy makers, patient advocacy groups, and interested members of the public. *PLoS Biology* is highly selective in accepting primary research articles, short reports, methods and resource articles and meta-research articles that examine how research is (or should be) designed, carried out, communicated, and evaluated. *PLoS Biology* is part of a suite of journals from PLoS. It is indexed in major databases, such as PubMed, CAS, and Web of Science. Suited for libraries supporting a Biological Sciences program. URL: http://journals.plos.org/plosbiology/

758. *Perspectives in Biology and Medicine.* [ISSN: 0031-5982] 1957. q. USD 190. Ed(s): Solveig C Robinson, Martha Montello. The Johns Hopkins University Press, 2715 N Charles St, Baltimore, MD 21218; http://www.press.jhu.edu. Illus., index, adv. Sample. Refereed. Vol. ends: Summer. Reprint: PSC. *Indexed:* A01, A22, BRI, C45, E01, MLA-IB. *Bk. rev.:* Number and length vary. *Aud.:* Ac, Sa.

Perspectives in Biology and Medicine is "an interdisciplinary scholarly journal whose readers include biologists, physicians, students, and scholars, interested in the intersections of biology and medicine." Authorship takes an informal style to "preserve the humanity, excitement, and color of the biological and medical sciences." Also included are book reviews, essay reviews, and letters to the editors. Most essays range from 4,000 to 7,000 words, in addition to an abstract. Although many essays are invited, voluntary contributions are welcomed. Print and online subscriptions are available for individuals and institutions. Full text is provided online by The Johns Hopkins University Press Project Muse, from 1958 to the present. A free sample is available online. Appropriate for academic, special, and medical libraries. URL: http://muse.jhu.edu/journals/perspectives_in_biology_and_medicine/

759. *Quantitative Biology.* [ISSN: 2095-4689] 2013. q. Ed(s): M Zhang, C Tang. Springer, Tiergartenstr 17, Heidelberg, 69121, Germany; https://www.springer.com. Refereed. Reprint: PSC. *Aud.:* Ac, Sa.

Quantitative Biology is an interdisciplinary journal that concentrates on original research that uses quantitative approaches and technologies to analyze and integrate biological systems, construct and model engineered life systems, and gain a deeper understanding of the life sciences. Content is focused in two main areas: bioinformatics and computational biology, and systems and synthetic biology. Research articles, reviews, and perspectives articles are accepted. Issues from 2013 to the present are available through Springer. Suitable for academic libraries that support a biology program or specialized libraries with a life sciences focus. URL: www.springer.com/life+sciences/systems+biology+and+bioinformatics/journal/40484

760. *The Quarterly Review of Biology.* [ISSN: 0033-5770] 1926. q. USD 504. Ed(s): Daniel E Dykhuizen. University of Chicago Press, 1427 E 60th St, Chicago, IL 60637; subscriptions@press.uchicago.edu; http://www.journals.uchicago.edu. Illus., index, adv. Sample. Refereed. Vol. ends: Dec. Reprint: PSC. *Indexed:* A01, A22, BRI, C45, CBRI, MLA-IB, S25. *Bk. rev.:* 250-3,000 words. *Aud.:* Ga, Ac, Sa.

The Quarterly Review of Biology (QRB) is the foremost review journal in biology. Articles are published in all areas of biology, but with a traditional emphasis on evolution, ecology, and organismal biology. *QRB*'s papers offer important new ideas, concepts, and syntheses. Content includes concise, authoritative articles, theoretical papers, comprehensive book reviews arranged by subject, and timely assessments of the life sciences. Scholars in associated areas of study will also find policy studies and the history and philosophy of science that are useful to their research. Online full text is available from 1926 to the present, through the University of Chicago Press. Individual and institutional subscriptions are available. Appropriate for general biology collections and special, academic, and large public libraries. URL: www.journals.uchicago.edu/loi/qrb

Science. See Science and Technology/General section.

761. *Systematic Biology.* Formerly (until 1992): *Systematic Zoology.* [ISSN: 1063-5157] 1952. bi-m. EUR 399. Ed(s): Thomas J Near. Oxford University Press, Great Clarendon St, Oxford, OX2 6DP, United Kingdom; onlinequeries.uk@oup.com; http://global.oup.com. Illus., index, adv. Sample. Refereed. Vol. ends: Dec. Microform: PQC. Reprint: PSC. *Indexed:* A01, A22, Agr, C45, E01. *Bk. rev.:* 800-2,000 words. *Aud.:* Ac, Sa.

Systematic Biology is a bimonthly publication of the Society of Systematic Biologists. The contents include original theoretical or empirical research papers on methods of systematics as well as phylogeny, evolution, morphology, biogeography, paleontology, genetics, and the classification of all living things. There is a "Points of View" section that offers discussion; book reviews; and news. Full text from 1952 to the present is available online with a subscription. There are select open-access articles within some issues. "Advance Access" articles are available online before the print edition. Recommended for special and academic libraries. There is a mobile version of the web site. URL: http://sysbio.oxfordjournals.org/

Biochemistry and Biophysics

762. *Analytical Biochemistry: methods in the biological sciences.* [ISSN: 0003-2697] 1960. 24x/yr. EUR 11308. Ed(s): William Jakoby. Elsevier Inc., 1600 John F Kennedy Blvd, Philadelphia, PA 19103; journalscustomerservice-usa@elsevier.com; https://www.elsevier.com. Illus., index, adv. Sample. Refereed. *Indexed:* A01, A22, C45, E01. *Bk. rev.:* 0-2, 240-500 words. *Aud.:* Ac, Sa.

Analytical Biochemistry places an emphasis on methods in the biological and biochemical sciences. More specifically, it publishes methods in analytical techniques, membranes and membrane proteins, molecular genetics, protein purification, immunological techniques applicable to biochemistry, immunoassays that introduce a unique approach, cell biology, general cell and organ culture, and pharmacological and toxicological research techniques. Contents include original research articles, review articles on methods for biological and biochemical sciences, and notes and tips, which include methods summarized in a short format. Full-text articles are available online for the entire run of the publication through ScienceDirect. There is an open-access publishing option for authors. This journal is geared specifically to biochemists and would be a useful resource for academic and research libraries. URL: www.journals.elsevier.com/analytical-biochemistry-methods-in-the-biological-sciences/

763. *Biochemical and Biophysical Research Communications.* [ISSN: 0006-291X] 1959. 52x/yr. EUR 18652. Ed(s): W Baumeister. Elsevier Inc., 1600 John F Kennedy Blvd, Philadelphia, PA 19103; journalscustomerservice-usa@elsevier.com; https://www.elsevier.com. Illus., index, adv. Sample. Refereed. *Indexed:* A01, A22, Agr, C45, E01. *Aud.:* Ac, Sa.

Biochemical and Biophysical Research Communications is known as the "premier international journal devoted to the very rapid dissemination of timely and significant experimental results in diverse fields of biological research." Contents include the "Breakthroughs and Views" section, which contains mini-reviews and collections of special-interest manuscripts. The broad range of research areas includes biochemistry, biophysics, bioinformatics, cancer research, cell biology, developmental biology, immunology, molecular biology, neurology, plant biology, and proteomics. Print and online subscriptions are available to individuals and institutions. This is a open-access journal. Full text is available online via the ScienceDirect web site. Useful for biochemists and biophysicists, as well as academic and research libraries. URL: www.journals.elsevier.com/biochemical-and-biophysical-research-communications/

764. *Biochemical Journal.* Formed by the merger of (1973-1984): *Biochemical Journal. Cellular Aspects;* (1973-1984): *Biochemical Journal. Molecular Aspects;* Both of which superseded in part (in 1973): *Biochemical Journal.* [ISSN: 0264-6021] 1984. s-m. EUR 5200 (print & online eds.)). Portland Press Ltd., 3rd Fl, Charles Darwin House, 12 Roger St, London, WC1N 2JU, United Kingdom; editorial@portlandpress.com; http://www.portlandpress.com/. Illus., index, adv. Refereed. Microform: PMC; PQC. *Indexed:* A01, A22, Agr, C45. *Aud.:* Ac, Sa.

Biochemical Journal publishes high-impact research on all aspects of biochemistry, cellular bioscience, and molecular biology. Theoretical contributions will be considered equally with papers that deal with experimental work. Contents include research papers that make a significant contribution to biochemical knowledge, including new results obtained experimentally, descriptions of new experimental methods or new interpretations of existing results, research communications, and reviews. Published by Biochemical Society's Portland Press, free trials and some open-access content are offered through the journal's web site. Archived journal content is available from 1906-2007 via PubMed Central. Recommended for special and academic libraries. URL: www.biochemj.org

765. *Biochemistry: including biophysical chemistry & molecular biology.* [ISSN: 0006-2960] 1962. w. USD 6605. Ed(s): Alanna Shepartz. American Chemical Society, 1155 16th St NW, Washington, DC 20036; help@acs.org; http://www.acs.org. Illus., index, adv. Sample. Refereed. Vol. ends: Dec. *Indexed:* A01, A22, Agr, BRI, C45. *Aud.:* Ac, Sa.

Published weekly by the American Chemical Society (ACS), *Biochemistry* "publishes research from the arena where biochemistry, biophysical chemistry and molecular biology meet." Articles cover structure, functions, and regulation of biologically active molecules; gene structure and expression; biochemical mechanisms; protein biosynthesis; protein folding, and global protein analysis and function; membrane structure/function relationships; biochemical methods; bioenergetics; and bioinformatics and immunochemistry. *Biochemistry* publishes manuscripts under Research articles, New Concepts, Current Topics, Viewpoints Communications, Perspectives, and From the Bench articles, which report new or improved methods of interest to the biological chemistry community. "Articles ASAP" offers recently approved online content on an expedited schedule. Dynamic ACS ActiveView pdfs are provided for most full-text articles. Open-access options for authors are available through the ACS

AuthorChoice program. Institutional subscriptions through ACS Web Editions, covering content from 1962 to the present, may be purchased. Appropriate for special and academic libraries. URL: http://pubs.acs.org/journal/bichaw

766. ***Biochemistry and Cell Biology.*** Former titles (until 1986): *Canadian Journal of Biochemistry and Cell Biology/Revue Canadien de Biochimie et Biologie Cellulaire;* (until 1983): *Canadian Journal of Biochemistry;* Which supersedes in part (in 1963): *Canadian Journal of Biochemistry and Physiology;* Which was formerly (until 1954): *Canadian Journal of Medical Sciences;* (until 1950): *Canadian Journal of Research. Section E: Medical Sciences.* [ISSN: 0829-8211] 1929. bi-m. CAD 1181 (print & online eds.)). Ed(s): Dr. James R Davie. Canadian Science Publishing, 65 Auriga Dr, Ste 203, Ottawa, ON K2E 7W6, Canada; pubs@cdnsciencepub.com; http://www.nrcresearchpress.com. Illus., index, adv. Sample. Refereed. *Indexed:* A01, A22, Agr, C37, C45, E01. *Aud.:* Ac, Sa.

Biochemistry and Cell Biology "explores every aspect of general biochemistry, and includes up-to-date coverage of experimental research into cellular and molecular biology." Contents include review topics of current interest and notes contributed by international experts. Special issues are dedicated each year to expanding new areas of research in biochemistry and cell biology. First published in 1929, this Canadian journal presents papers in both French and English, although the majority are in English. Full-text online content is available from 1964 through the present by subscription only. There is a sample issue to review via the publisher's web site. Recommended for special and academic libraries. URL: www.nrcresearchpress.com/journal/bcb

767. ***Biochimica et Biophysica Acta. Proteins and Proteomics.*** Former titles (until 2002): *B B A - Protein Structure and Molecular Enzymology;* (until 1982): *B B A - Protein Structure.* [ISSN: 1570-9639] 1967. 12x/yr. EUR 5991. Ed(s): Helmut Meyer, Irene Lee. Elsevier BV, Radarweg 29, Amsterdam, 1043 NX, Netherlands; info@elsevier.com; https://www.elsevier.com/. Refereed. Microform: PQC. *Indexed:* A01, A22, C45. *Aud.:* Ac, Sa.

Articles published in *BBA Proteins and Proteomics* cover "protein structure conformation and dynamics; protein folding; protein-ligand interactions; enzyme mechanisms, models and kinetics; protein physical properties and spectroscopy; and proteomics and bioinformatics analyses of protein structure, protein function, or protein regulation." This journal is one of the nine topical journals from *Biochimica et Biophysica Acta.* It contains regular papers, reviews, and mini-reviews on recent developments. The journal supports innovations such as 3D models and crystallographic data, audioslides, a database linking tool, an interactive network viewer, a PubChem chemical compound viewer, and a protein viewer. Print and online subscriptions are available. Online access is available from 2002 to the present via ScienceDirect. There is online open-access content. Appropriate for academic and special libraries. URL: www.journals.elsevier.com/bba-proteins-and-proteomics/

768. ***Biochimica et Biophysica Acta. Reviews on Cancer.*** Supersedes in part (in 1974): *Biochimica et Biophysica Acta: N. Nucleic Acids and Protein Synthesis;* Which was formerly (until 1965): *Biochimical et Biophysica Acta. Specialized Section on Nucleic Acids and Related Subjects.* [ISSN: 0304-419X] 1963. 4x/yr. EUR 2407. Elsevier BV, Radarweg 29, Amsterdam, 1043 NX, Netherlands; info@elsevier.com; https://www.elsevier.com/. Refereed. Microform: PQC. *Indexed:* A01, A22. *Aud.:* Ac, Sa.

Reviews published in *BBA Reviews on Cancer* focus on "the whole field of the biology and biochemistry of cancer, emphasizing oncogenes and tumor suppressor genes, growth-related cell cycle control signaling, carcinogenesis mechanisms, cell transformation, immunologic control mechanisms, genetics of human (mammalian) cancer, control of cell proliferation, genetic and molecular control of organismic development, and rational anti-tumor drug design. In short, the journal presents critical invited reviews on new developments in cancer investigation at the molecular level." This journal is one of the nine topical journals from *Biochimica et Biophysica Acta.* It contains reviews and mini-reviews. The journal supports innovations such as 3D models and crystallographic data, audioslides, and a protein viewer. Print and online subscriptions are available. Online access is available from 1974 to the present via ScienceDirect. Appropriate for academic and special libraries. URL: www.journals.elsevier.com/bba-reviews-on-cancer

769. ***Biophysical Journal.*** Incorporates (1970-1973): *Biophysical Society. Program and Abstracts;* Which was formerly (until 1970): *Biophysical Society. Meeting. Abstracts;* (until 1959): *Biophysical Society. Meeting. Program and Abstracts.* [ISSN: 0006-3495] 1958. s-m. EUR 1494. Ed(s): Jane Dyson. Cell Press, 11830 Westline Industrial Dr, St. Louis, MO 63146; feedback@cell.com; http://www.cell.com/cellpress. Illus., index, adv. Refereed. Microform: PQC. *Indexed:* A22, Agr, C45. *Aud.:* Ac, Sa.

Research published in *Biophysical Journal* will be of interest to the quantitative biologist in a variety of specialties. There are original research articles, letters, comments to the editor, reviews of current interest in biophysics, and new and notable commentaries that highlight papers found in the same issue. The journal is edited by the Biophysical Society, and all programs and abstracts for annual meetings are included with a subscription. Full-text online content is available from 1960 to the present through PubMed Central. The journal has a 12-month embargo policy, after which the journal submits the final published article on behalf of the author to PubMed Central automatically. There is an open-access option for authors who would like their work freely available immediately. URL: www.cell.com/biophysj/

770. ***The F E B S Journal.*** Former titles (until 2005): *European Journal of Biochemistry;* (until 1967): *Biochemische Zeitschrift;* Which incorporated (1901-1908): *Beitrage zur Chemischen Physiologie und Pathologie.* [ISSN: 1742-464X] 1906. fortn. Free. Ed(s): Seamus Martin. Wiley-Blackwell Publishing Ltd., The Atrium, Southern Gate, Chichester, PO19 8QG, United Kingdom; cs-journals@wiley.com; http://onlinelibrary.wiley.com. Illus., index, adv. Sample. Refereed. Microform: PQC. Reprint: PSC. *Indexed:* A01, A22, Agr, C45, E01. *Aud.:* Ac, Sa.

The FEBS Journal (Federation of European Biochemical Societies) is an international title "devoted to the rapid publication of full-length papers describing original research in all areas of the molecular life sciences." Publishing preference is given to research that advances new concepts or develops new experimental techniques. Contents include research papers, reviews, virtual reviews, and meeting reports. Article topics are broad and inclusive. The journal also publishes commissioned works under Reviews, Minireviews, Viewpoints, and Snapshots on a wide range of topics. Special issues on a specific scientific topic are also offered. Areas of interest include, but are not limited to, immunology, molecular genetics, nucleic acids, protein synthesis, developmental biology, bioenergetics, systems biology, pathogens and infection, and proteomics. The journals can be accessed through Wiley at http://febs.onlinelibrary.wiley.com/hub/journal/10.1111/(ISSN)1742-4658

771. ***F E B S Letters.*** [ISSN: 0014-5793] 1968. 24x/yr. Ed(s): Felix Wieland. John Wiley & Sons Ltd., EMEA Institutional Sales, 9600 Garsington Rd, Oxford, OX4 2DQ, United Kingdom; cs-journals@wiley.com; http://onlinelibrary.wiley.com. Illus., index, adv. Refereed. *Indexed:* A01, A22, C45. *Aud.:* Ac, Sa.

FEBS Letters, published by the Federation of European Biochemical Societies, is an "international journal established for the rapid publication of essentially final short reports in the fields of molecular biosciences." Contents include biochemistry, structural biology, biophysics, computational biology, molecular genetics, molecular biology, and molecular cell biology. Studies may be on microbes, plants, or animals. Found within each issue are mini-reviews, hypotheses, and research letters, all on an international level. *FEBS Letters* Reviews, Hypotheses, Special Issues and select Research Letters are immediately made freely available, at no extra cost for the authors. Online, full-text access is available through Elsevier's ScienceDirect through 2015, after which it moved to Wiley Publishing. After a 12-month embargo, articles are made available to non-subscribers for free. Appropriate for special and academic libraries. URL: http://febs.onlinelibrary.wiley.com/hub/journal/10.1002/%28ISSN%291873-3468/

772. ***Journal of Biochemistry.*** [ISSN: 0021-924X] 1922. m. EUR 658. Ed(s): Kenji Kadomatsu. Oxford University Press, Great Clarendon St, Oxford, OX2 6DP, United Kingdom; onlinequeries.uk@oup.com; http://global.oup.com. Illus., index, adv. Sample. Refereed. Microform: PMC. Reprint: PSC. *Indexed:* A01, A22, Agr, C45, E01. *Aud.:* Ac, Sa.

The *Journal of Biochemistry* publishes articles on biochemistry, biotechnology, molecular biology, and cell biology. Contents include regular research articles and rapid communications written in English. It is published by Oxford University Press on behalf of the Japanese Biochemical Society, and full text is available online with a subscription. Additional online features include e-mail alerts. There is an open-access publishing option for authors. Articles are freely available 12 months after publication through PubMed Central. Recommended for special and academic libraries that support scientists, biologists, physicians, and physiologists. URL: http://jb.oxfordjournals.org/

773. *Journal of Biological Chemistry (Online).* [ISSN: 1083-351X] 1905. w. USD 1245. Ed(s): Herbert Tabor. American Society for Biochemistry and Molecular Biology, Inc., 11200 Rockville Pike, Ste 302, Rockville, MD 20852; asbmb@asbmb.org; http://www.asbmb.org. Adv. Refereed. *Aud.:* Ac, Sa.

This weekly online journal focuses on original research reports in biochemistry and molecular biology, and includes such topics as developmental biology, computational biology, metabolism, protein chemistry, and nucleic acids. Contents include original research papers that make novel and important contributions to the understanding of any area of biochemistry or molecular biology. Accelerated publication that presents new information of high importance and interest to the broad readership is by invitation only. Online features include "Papers in Press," which are author versions of accepted research papers and mini-reviews that are posted and freely available within 24 hours of acceptance. There is some online, full-text access available from 1905 to the present. Content from 2005 to the present is available in full text through PubMed Central. Highly recommended for special libraries and academic libraries that support biology programs. URL: www.jbc.org

774. *Molecular Genetics and Metabolism.* Former titles (until 1998): *Biochemical and Molecular Medicine;* (until 1995): *Biochemical Medicine and Metabolic Biology;* (until 1986): *Biochemical Medicine.* [ISSN: 1096-7192] 1967. m. EUR 3602. Ed(s): Dr. Edward R B McCabe. Academic Press, 225 Wyman St, Waltham, MA 02144; JournalCustomerService-usa@elsevier.com; http://store.elsevier.com/Academic-Press/IMP_5/. Adv. Sample. Refereed. *Indexed:* A01, A22, Agr, C45, E01. *Aud.:* Ac, Sa.

Molecular Genetics and Metabolism is the official journal of the Society for Inherited Metabolic Disorders. The journal is a contribution to the understanding of the metabolic basis of disease. The journal publishes articles that describe investigations that use the tools of biochemistry and molecular biology for studies of normal and diseased states. Research areas include inherited metabolic diseases, systems biology, intercellular and intracellular metabolic relationships, cellular catalysts, and disease pathogenesis and treatment. Full-text access is available online from ScienceDirect. An open-access publishing option is available to authors to provide access to their articles on Elsevier's electronic publishing platforms. Recommended for special and academic libraries with a strong biological program. URL: www.journals.elsevier.com/molecular-genetics-and-metabolism/

Cell and Molecular Biology

775. *Annual Review of Cell and Developmental Biology.* Formerly (until 1995): *Annual Review of Cell Biology.* [ISSN: 1081-0706] 1985. a. USD 431 (print & online eds.)). Ed(s): Ruth Lehmann. Annual Reviews, PO Box 10139, Palo Alto, CA 94303; service@annualreviews.org; http://www.annualreviews.org. Illus. Refereed. Reprint: PSC. *Indexed:* A01, A22, C45. *Aud.:* Ac, Sa.

The *Annual Review of Cell and Developmental Biology* presents the most important "developments in the field of cell and developmental biology, including structure, function, and organization of the cell, development and evolution of the cell as it relates to single and multi-cellular organisms, and models and tools of molecular biology." This journal, published since 1985, is part of the Annual Reviews series of journals, which continues to grow and cover topics in many scientific and social science disciplines. Both print and online subscriptions are available at various levels for single journals or collections. Great for academic or specialized libraries. URL: https://www.annualreviews.org/journal/cellbio

776. *B M C Molecular and Cell Biology.* Formerly (until 2019): *B M C Cell Biology.* [ISSN: 2661-8850] 2000. . Free. Ed(s): Alison Cuff. BioMed Central Ltd., Fl 6, 236 Gray's Inn Rd, London, WC1X 8HB, United Kingdom; info@biomedcentral.com; https://www.biomedcentral.com. Adv. Refereed. *Indexed:* A01, C45. *Aud.:* Ac, Sa.

B M C Cell Biology is an open-access journal that publishes original peer-reviewed research articles in all aspects of cell biology, including cellular compartments, traffic, signaling, motility, adhesion, and division. Types of articles include research articles; database articles that describe either a new biomedical database or a database that has been substantially changed and improved since it was last described in a journal; and methodology articles that present a new experimental or computational method, test, or procedure. *B M C Cell Biology* is a full-text online journal. All research articles are published after full peer review. All articles are published, without barriers to access, immediately upon acceptance. Full text is available free at PubMed Central from 2000 to the present, or via the publisher's site. Recommended for academic and special libraries that support a biology program. URL: http://bmccellbiol.biomedcentral.com/

777. *Biochimica and Biophysica Acta. Molecular and Cell Biology of Lipids.* Former titles (until 1999): *B B A - Lipids and Lipid Metabolism;* (until 1965): *Biochimica et Biophysica Acta. Lipids and Related Subjects.* [ISSN: 1388-1981] 1963. 12x/yr. EUR 5771. Ed(s): Rudolf Zechner, Judith Storch. Elsevier BV, Radarweg 29, Amsterdam, 1043 NX, Netherlands; info@elsevier.com; https://www.elsevier.com/. Refereed. Microform: PQC. *Indexed:* A01, A22, C45. *Aud.:* Ac, Sa.

Articles published in *BBA Molecular and Cell Biology of Lipids* focus on "original research dealing with novel aspects of molecular genetics related to the lipidome, the biosynthesis of lipids, the role of lipids in cells and whole organisms, the regulation of lipid metabolism and function, and lipidomics in all organisms." This journal is one of the nine topical journals from *Biochimica et Biophysica Acta (BBA).* It contains original research papers and papers that detail novel methodology with insight in the area of lipids. Print and online subscriptions are available. Online access is available from 1999 to the present via ScienceDirect. The journal supports innovations such as 3D models and crystallographic data, audioslides, a database linking tool, lipid structures, and a protein viewer. An open-access publishing option is available to authors. Appropriate for academic and special libraries. URL: https://www.journals.elsevier.com/bba-molecular-and-cell-biology-of-lipids/

778. *Biochimica et Biophysica Acta. Bioenergetics.* Formed by the merger of (1965-1966): *Biochimica et Biophysica Acta. Biophysics including Photosynthesis;* Which was formerly (1963-1964): *Biochimica et Biophysica Acta. Specialized Section on Biophysical Subjects;* (1965-1966): *Biochimica et Biophysica Acta. Enzymology and Biological Oxidations;* Which was formerly (1963-1964): *Biochimica et Biophysica Acta. Specialized Section on Enzymological Subjects.* [ISSN: 0005-2728] 1963. 12x/yr. EUR 5096. Ed(s): Fabrice Rappaport, Susanne Arnold. Elsevier BV, Radarweg 29, Amsterdam, 1043 NX, Netherlands; info@elsevier.com; https://www.elsevier.com/. Refereed. Microform: PQC. *Indexed:* A01, A22, C45. *Aud.:* Ac, Sa.

Articles published in *BBA Bioenergetics* "focus on biological membranes involved in energy transfer and conversion. In particular, the focus is on the structures obtained by X-ray crystallography and other approaches, and molecular mechanisms of the components of photosynthesis, mitochondrial and bacterial respiration, oxidative phosphorylation, motility, and transport. It spans applications of structural biology, molecular modeling, spectroscopy and biophysics in these systems, through bioenergetic aspects of mitochondrial biology and including biomedicine aspects of energy metabolism in mitochondrial disorders, neurodegenerative diseases like Parkinson's and Alzheimer's, aging, diabetes, and even cancer." This journal is one of the nine topical journals from *Biochimica et Biophysica Acta (BBA).* It contains full-length research articles and review papers. Print and online subscriptions are available. Online access is available from 1967 to the present via ScienceDirect. The journal supports innovations such as 3D models and crystallographic data, audioslides, a database linking tool, and a protein viewer. An open-access publishing option is available to authors. Appropriate for academic and special libraries. URL: www.journals.elsevier.com/bba-bioenergetics

779. ***Biochimica et Biophysica Acta. Biomembranes.*** Incorporates (1972-2002): *B B A - Reviews on Biomembranes.* [ISSN: 0005-2736] 1947. 12x/yr. EUR 7231. Ed(s): Hans Vogel, Yechiel Shai. Elsevier BV, Radarweg 29, Amsterdam, 1043 NX, Netherlands; info@elsevier.com; https://www.elsevier.com/. Refereed. Microform: PQC. *Indexed:* A01, A22, C45. *Aud.:* Ac, Sa.

Articles published in *BBA Biomembranes* "focus on membrane structure, function and biomolecular organization, membrane proteins, receptors, channels and anchors, fluidity and composition, model membranes and liposomes, membrane surface studies and ligand interactions, transport studies, and membrane dynamics." This journal is one of the nine topical journals from *Biochimica et Biophysica Acta (BBA)*. It contains regular papers, reviews, and mini-reviews. Print and online subscriptions are available. Online access is available from 1967 to the present via ScienceDirect. The journal supports innovations such as 3D models and crystallographic data, audioslides, a database linking tool, lipid structures, and a protein viewer. An open-access publishing option is available to authors. Appropriate for academic and special libraries. URL: www.journals.elsevier.com/bba-biomembranes

780. ***Biochimica et Biophysica Acta. Molecular Cell Research.*** [ISSN: 0167-4889] 1982. 12x/yr. EUR 5400. Ed(s): Athar Chishti, Nikolaus Pfanner. Elsevier BV, Radarweg 29, Amsterdam, 1043 NX, Netherlands; info@elsevier.com; https://www.elsevier.com/. Refereed. Microform: PQC. *Indexed:* A01, A22, C45. *Aud.:* Ac, Sa.

Articles published in *BBA Molecular Cell Research* focus on "understanding the mechanisms of cellular processes at the molecular level. These include aspects of cellular signaling, signal transduction, cell cycle, apoptosis, intracellular trafficking, secretory and endocytic pathways, biogenesis of cell organelles, cytoskeletal structures, cellular interactions, cell/tissue differentiation, and cellular enzymology." This journal is one of the nine topical journals from *Biochimica et Biophysica Acta*. It contains studies at the interface between cell biology and biophysics, and reviews and mini-reviews on timely topics. The journal supports innovations such as 3D models and crystallographic data, antibody data, audioslides, a database linking tool, and a protein viewer. Online access is available from 1982 to the present via ScienceDirect. An open-access publishing option is available to authors. Appropriate for academic and special libraries. URL: www.journals.elsevier.com/bba-molecular-cell-research/

781. ***BioEssays (Online).*** [ISSN: 1521-1878] 1984. m. GBP 1412. Ed(s): Andrew Moore. John Wiley & Sons Ltd., EMEA Institutional Sales, 9600 Garsington Rd, Oxford, OX4 2DQ, United Kingdom; cs-journals@wiley.com; http://onlinelibrary.wiley.com. Refereed. *Bk. rev.:* Number and length vary. *Aud.:* Ac, Sa.

As one of the leading review journals in biology, *BioEssays* "is a review-and-discussion journal publishing novel insights, forward-looking reviews, and commentaries in contemporary biology with a molecular, genetic, cellular, or physiological dimension. A further aim is to emphasise transdisciplinarity and integrative biology in the context of organismal studies, systems approaches, through to ecosystems where appropriate." Contents are divided into three main sections, "Insights & Perspectives" (for ideas, hypotheses, and commentaries), "Prospects & Overviews" (for review-style articles), and "Thoughts & Opinion" (for meeting reports, book reviews, and letters to the editor). The "Prospects & Overviews" section contains mini-reviews that highlight very recent research articles, and longer papers that present a field, its developments, and prospects for a broad readership. In addition, this journal has "Virtual Issues" that are online compilations of previously published articles that highlight a topical area of interest. Those collections are updated regularly, and the articles are freely available for a limited period of time. This title is affiliated with EpiGenesys, the European Network of Excellence for epigenetics research. Wiley Publishing offers authors an open-access model through OnlineOpen. A good source for all biology collections as well as special and academic libraries. URL: http://onlinelibrary.wiley.com/journal/10.1002/(ISSN)1521-1878

782. ***Cell.*** [ISSN: 0092-8674] 1974. bi-w. EUR 3120. Ed(s): Emilie Marcus. Cell Press, 600 Technology Sq, Ste 5, Cambridge, MA 02139; http://www.cell.com/cellpress. Illus., index, adv. Sample. Refereed. *Indexed:* A01, A22, BRI, C45. *Aud.:* Ac, Sa.

Launched in 1974, *Cell* publishes findings of unusual significance in any area of experimental biology, including but not limited to, cell biology, molecular biology, neuroscience, immunology, virology and microbiology, cancer, human genetics, systems biology, signaling, and disease. The basic criterion for considering papers is whether the results provide significant conceptual advances into, or raise provocative questions and hypotheses regarding, an interesting biological question. In addition to primary research articles in four formats, *Cell* features review and opinion articles on recent research advances and issues of interest to its broad readership in the "Leading Edge" section. Online access to full text is available via ScienceDirect. The web site features articles from the current issue of *Cell Online*; supplemental data (web-based material not available in the printed journal); and tables of contents for all archived issues of *Cell Online*. Recommended for academic and special libraries. URL: www.cell.com

783. ***Cell Discovery.*** [ISSN: 2056-5968] 2015. . Free. Ed(s): Gang Pei. Nature Publishing Group, The MacMillan Bldg, 4 Crinan St, London, N1 9XW, United Kingdom; nature@nature.com; http://www.nature.com/reviews. Refereed. *Aud.:* Ac, Sa.

Cell Discovery is an open-access journal, making its content freely available to researchers. The journal, which is published by Nature Publishing in partnership with Shanghai Institutes for Biological Sciences, of the Chinese Academy of Sciences, was established as a sister journal to *Cell Research*. Topics include cell growth and differentiation, signal transduction, apoptosis, stem cells, immunology, neurosciences, plant cell biology, chromatin modulation, epigenetics, and transcription. *Cell Discovery* is a high-quality, peer-reviewed journal indexed in the Directory of Open Access Journals. Its contents would serve academic and specialized science libraries. URL: https://www.nature.com/celldisc/

784. ***The E M B O Journal.*** [ISSN: 0261-4189] 1982. s-m. Wiley-Blackwell Publishing Ltd., The Atrium, Southern Gate, Chichester, PO19 8QG, United Kingdom; cs-journals@wiley.com; http://onlinelibrary.wiley.com. Illus., index, adv. Sample. Refereed. Vol. ends: Dec. Reprint: PSC. *Indexed:* A01, A22, Agr, C45, E01. *Aud.:* Ac, Sa.

The EMBO Journal (European Molecular Biology Organization) "publishes papers describing original research of broad general interest in molecular and cell biology - [and] a particular emphasis is placed on molecular mechanism and physiological relevance." Articles report novel findings of wide biological significance in such areas as ageing, cancer, structural biology, immunology, plant biology, RNA, proteins, cellular metabolism, and molecular biology of disease. Full text is available online with a subscription. Non-subscribers have a limited access to sample issues online. Open access is available through PubMed Central from 1982. This journal offers an open-access option to authors. Established as one of the most influential molecular biology journals, it is recommended for academic and research libraries. URL: http://emboj.embopress.org/

785. ***E M B O Molecular Medicine (Online).*** [ISSN: 1757-4684] 2008. m. Free. Ed(s): Stefanie Dimmeler, Celine Carret. Wiley - V C H Verlag GmbH & Co. KGaA, Postfach 101161, Weinheim, 69451, Germany; cs-germany@wiley.com; http://www.wiley-vch.de. Refereed. *Aud.:* Ac, Sa.

EMBO Molecular Medicine is a peer-reviewed open-access online journal "dedicated to a new research discipline at the interface between clinical research and basic biology." Topics covered include: aging, angiogenesis, cancer biology, channelopathies, differentiation and development, endocrinology/metabolic disease, genetics/epigenetics, genomics, transcriptomics, proteomics, metabolomics of disease, systems medicine, gene therapy, immunology and inflammation, infectious diseases, neurodegeneration, neurological diseases and myopathies, sensory defects, stem cells and regenerative medicine, and vascular and cardiovascular biology. It contains research articles as full-length research papers and short reports. In addition, the journal publishes editorials and review articles in innovative formats that target a broad and non-specialized audience. Online access is available from 2009 to the present. Appropriate for academic and special libraries. URL: http://embomolmed.embopress.org/

786. *Experimental Cell Research.* [ISSN: 0014-4827] 1950. 20x/yr. EUR 9526. Ed(s): U Lendahl. Academic Press, 225 Wyman St, Waltham, MA 02144; JournalCustomerService-usa@elsevier.com; http://store.elsevier.com/Academic-Press/IMP_5/. Illus., index, adv. Sample. Refereed. *Indexed:* A01, A22, Agr, C45, E01. *Aud.:* Ac, Sa.

Experimental Cell Research "promotes the understanding of cell biology by publishing experimental studies on the general organization and activity of cells." Research is published on all aspects of cell biology, from the molecular level to cell interaction and differentiation. Contents include papers that provide novel and significant insights into important problems within these areas. Specific topics include cancer research, developmental biology, meiosis and mitosis, RNA processing, and stem cell biology. Online full-text access is provided by ScienceDirect. Some content innovations include antibody data, audioslides, a database linking tool, a genome viewer, and a virtual microscope. An open-access publishing option is available for authors. This journal is recommended for molecular and cell biologists, and cancer researchers, and for academic and research libraries that support research in those areas. URL: www.journals.elsevier.com/experimental-cell-research/

787. *Journal of Cell Biology.* Formerly (until 1962): *Journal of Biophysical and Biochemical Cytology (Print).* [ISSN: 0021-9525] 1955. bi-w. USD 5810 (print & online eds.)). Ed(s): Jodi Nunnari. Rockefeller University Press, 950 Third Ave., 2nd Fl, New York, NY 10022; subs@rockefeller.edu; http://jgp.rupress.org. Illus., index, adv. Sample. Refereed. *Indexed:* A01, A22, Agr, BRI, C45. *Aud.:* Ac, Sa.

The *Journal of Cell Biology* publishes papers on all aspects of cellular structure and function. Articles must provide novel and significant mechanistic insight into a cellular function that will be of interest to a general readership. Published materials are limited in size but may include concise articles and reports that have the potential to open new avenues of research. The biweekly journal is published by the Rockefeller University Press with the assistance of Stanford University Libraries, a nonprofit organization. Editors are scientists who review articles only within their chosen field. All articles are available in full text online through PubMed Central from 1962 through the present, after six months in print. This journal provides news and short reviews that are useful to students, researchers, and professionals. Appropriate for academic and special libraries. URL: http://jcb.rupress.org/

788. *Journal of Cell Science.* Formerly (until 1966): *Quarterly Journal of Microscopical Science.* [ISSN: 0021-9533] 1852. s-m. USD 3180 (print & online eds.)). Ed(s): Michael Way. The Company of Biologists Ltd., 140 Cowley Rd, Cambridge, CB4 0DL, United Kingdom; sales@biologists.com; http://www.biologists.org. Illus., index. Sample. Refereed. Vol. ends: Dec. Microform: BHP. *Indexed:* A01, A22, Agr, C45. *Aud.:* Ac, Sa.

Covering the complete range of topics in cell biology, *Journal of Cell Science* is also of key interest to developmental biologists, molecular biologists, and geneticists. Contents include research articles, review articles, brief syntheses of important areas, commentaries, "Cell Science at a Glance," and "Sticky Wickets," which provides controversial views of life-science research. The journal is published twice a month by the Company of Biologists, a nonprofit organization determined to promote research and knowledge in the study of biology. Full-text online content of all subsections and some open-access research articles are provided for free in each issue. Some content is also available through PubMed Central. Recommended for special and academic libraries. URL: http://jcs.biologists.org

789. *Journal of Molecular Biology.* [ISSN: 0022-2836] 1959. 24x/yr. EUR 5853. Ed(s): Peter Wright. Academic Press, 32 Jamestown Rd, Camden, London, NW1 7BY, United Kingdom; corporate.sales@elsevier.com; http://www.elsevier.com/. Illus., index, adv. Sample. Refereed. *Indexed:* A01, A22, Agr, C45, E01. *Aud.:* Ac, Sa.

The *Journal of Molecular Biology* contains "high quality, comprehensive and broad coverage in all areas of molecular biology." Specific research areas include biomolecular interactions, cell cycle, cell death, autophagy, cell signaling and regulation, chemical biology, computational biology, DNA replication, stem cells, epigenetics, and gene expression. Online, full-text access is provided by ScienceDirect from 1964 to the present, and includes one free sample issue. An open-access publishing option is available for authors. Appropriate for any academic library or research institution that supports biologists. URL: www.journals.elsevier.com/journal-of-molecular-biology/

790. *Molecular and Cellular Biology (Online).* [ISSN: 1098-5549] 1981. s-m. USD 1713. Ed(s): Roger J Davis. American Society for Microbiology, 1752 N St, NW, Washington, DC 20036; journals@asmusa.org; http://journals.asm.org. Index, adv. Refereed. *Aud.:* Ac, Sa.

Molecular and Cellular Biology publishes high-quality papers that are "devoted to the advancement and dissemination of fundamental knowledge concerning the molecular biology of all eukaryotic cells." The journal went totally online in 2016. Full text is available through PubMed Central from 1981. This title has been rated in the top 100 most influential research journals by the Special Libraries Association in the biochemistry and molecular biology fields. Recommended for undergraduates and researchers in special and academic libraries. URL: http://mcb.asm.org/

791. *Molecular Biology and Evolution.* [ISSN: 0737-4038] 1983. m. EUR 1190. Ed(s): Sudhir Kumar. Oxford University Press, 2001 Evans Rd, Cary, NC 27513; https://academic.oup.com/journals. Illus., index, adv. Sample. Refereed. Vol. ends: Nov. Microform: PMC; PQC. Reprint: PSC. *Indexed:* A22, C45, E01. *Aud.:* Ac, Sa.

Molecular Biology and Evolution is published by the Society for Molecular Biology and Evolution. This journal presents "research at the interface of molecular (including genomics) and evolutionary biology." It reports fundamental discoveries of broader scope and impact, new and improved methods, resources, technologies, and theories that will significantly advance evolutionary research. Full text is available online from 1983 to the present, with a number of open-access articles available in the archive. Articles are available at PubMed Central from 2008 to the present. Appropriate for academic and research libraries. URL: http://mbe.oxfordjournals.org/

792. *Molecular Biology of the Cell (Online).* Formerly (until 1992): *Cell Regulation (Online).* [ISSN: 1939-4586] 1990. 2x/m. Free to members. Ed(s): David G Drubin. American Society for Cell Biology, 8120 Woodmont Ave, Ste 750, Bethesda, MD 20814; ascbinfo@ascb.org; http://www.ascb.org. Adv. Sample. Refereed. *Aud.:* Ac, Sa.

Molecular Biology of the Cell (*MBoC*) is published twice monthly online by the American Society for Cell Biology. The journal publishes original research articles and essays that present conceptual advances of broad interest and significance within all areas of cell biology, genetics, and developmental biology. Articles include supplementary datasets, video data, and previously unpublished data and methods that support the conclusions drawn. Accepted articles are published rapidly after acceptance and ahead of a print version. *MBoC* is an online journal with full-text content available from 1989 to the present with subscription. Non-subscribers have access to tables of contents, abstracts, and a full sample issue at no cost and without having to register. Unredacted accepted manuscripts are accessible immediately through *MBoC In Press.* Final published versions are accessible two months after publication. *MBoC* is also available online through PubMed Central. Access earlier than two months is available through subscription or membership in the ASCB. Recommended for academic and special libraries that support a biology program. URL: www.molbiolcell.org

793. *Molecular Cell.* [ISSN: 1097-2765] 1997. s-m. EUR 2849. Ed(s): Lauren Shipp, John Pham. Cell Press, 600 Technology Sq, Ste 5, Cambridge, MA 02139; http://www.cell.com. Adv. Refereed. *Indexed:* A01, A22. *Aud.:* Ac, Sa.

The goal of *Molecular Cell* is to publish reports of the best research in the field. Topics focus on molecular biology including replication, recombination, repair, gene expression, RNA processing, translation, and protein folding, modification, and degradation. Papers considered for publication must provide interesting mechanistic insights or answer longstanding questions and hypotheses. The majority of each issue consists of research articles, and shorter papers that make up a small section. Free online full text is available 12 months after publication on the journal's website. Additionally, "Online Now" is a feature in which the journal publishes articles online prior to print publication. Appropriate for special and academic libraries. URL: www.cell.com/molecular-cell/home

794. ***Nucleic Acids Research.*** [ISSN: 0305-1048] 1974. 22x/yr. EUR 5253. Ed(s): Barry Stoddard, Keith Fox. Oxford University Press, Great Clarendon St, Oxford, OX2 6DP, United Kingdom; jnls.cust.serv@oup.com; https://academic.oup.com/journals/. Illus., index, adv. Sample. Refereed. Vol. ends: Dec. Reprint: PSC. *Indexed:* A22, Agr, C45, E01. *Aud.:* Ac, Sa.

Nucleic Acids Research is an open-access journal that provides for rapid publication of cutting-edge research into nucleic acids within chemistry, computational biology, genomics, molecular biology, nucleic acid enzymes, RNA, and structural biology. Print contents include standard papers, surveys, and summaries that present brief, formal reviews relevant to nucleic acid chemistry and biology. Online contents include all articles and methods papers that describe novel techniques or advances in existing techniques that are highly significant, and supplemental materials. The January issue is devoted to biological databases, and a July issue presents papers describing web-based software resources of value to the biological community. This journal is published by Oxford University Press, and all issues, from 1974 to the present, are freely available online under an open-access model. Content is also available through PubMed Central. Recommended for academic and research libraries with biology, medical, and chemistry collections. URL: http://nar.oxfordjournals.org/

Developmental Biology

795. ***B M C Developmental Biology.*** [ISSN: 1471-213X] 2000. irreg. Free. Ed(s): Philippa Harris. BioMed Central Ltd., Fl 6, 236 Gray's Inn Rd, London, WC1X 8HB, United Kingdom; info@biomedcentral.com; https://www.biomedcentral.com. Adv. Refereed. *Indexed:* A01, C45. *Aud.:* Ac, Sa.

B M C Developmental Biology is an open-access journal that publishes original peer-reviewed research articles on all aspects of cellular, tissue-level, and organismic aspects of development. Emphasis is on publishing work that makes a significant contribution to the field rather than having wide appeal. *B M C Developmental Biology* is a full-text online journal. All research articles are published after full peer review. Articles are published, without barriers to access, immediately upon acceptance. Full text is available free online through PubMed Central from 2001 to the present, or via the publisher's web site. Recommended for academic and special libraries. URL: http://bmcdevbiol.biomedcentral.com

796. ***Development (Cambridge): for advances in developmental biology and stem cells.*** Formerly (until 1987): *Journal of Embryology and Experimental Morphology.* [ISSN: 0950-1991] 1953. s-m. USD 3728 (print & online eds.)). Ed(s): Olivier Pourquie. The Company of Biologists Ltd., 140 Cowley Rd, Cambridge, CB4 0DL, United Kingdom; sales@biologists.com; http://www.biologists.org. Illus., index. Sample. Refereed. Vol. ends: Dec. *Indexed:* A01, A22, C45. *Aud.:* Ac, Sa.

Known as a primary research journal, *Development* provides "cutting edge research articles across the spectrum of plant and animal development." It acts as a forum for all research that offers genuine insight into developmental mechanisms. Experimental papers are given top priority. Studies can address any aspect of the developmental process, including evolutionary studies, stem cells and nuclear reprogramming, regional specification, morphogenesis, and organogenesis. Published by The Company of Biologists, this journal includes research articles and meeting reviews. Full text is available online, from 1953 to the present. Additionally, *Development* publishes articles online ahead of their being published in print. Recommended for academic and special libraries. URL: http://dev.biologists.org/

797. ***Developmental Biology.*** [ISSN: 0012-1606] 1959. 24x/yr. EUR 12077. Ed(s): Marianne Bronner. Academic Press, 3251 Riverport Ln, Maryland Heights, MO 63043; JournalCustomerService-usa@elsevier.com; http://www.elsevier.com/. Illus., index, adv. Sample. Refereed. *Indexed:* A01, A22, Agr, C45, E01. *Aud.:* Ac, Sa.

Developmental Biology is the official journal of the Society for Developmental Biology. Original research, letters, reviews, and technical reports are published concerning "research on the mechanisms of development, differentiation, and growth in animals and plants at the molecular, cellular, and genetic levels." Research areas of particular interest include molecular genetics of development, control of gene expression, cell and cell-matrix interactions, mechanisms of differentiation, growth factors and oncogenes, regulation of stem cell populations, gametogenesis and fertilization, developmental endocrinology, plant development, and the evolution of developmental control. Contents include original research papers that contribute new information to the understanding of developmental mechanisms, and review articles intended to reach a broad readership. There are two special sections, "Genomes and Developmental Control" and "Evolution of Developmental Control Mechanism." Online, full-text access is provided through ScienceDirect. There is an open-access publishing option for authors. All articles published after 12 months have unrestricted access and will remain permanently free to read and download. This journal is considered the best in its field. Recommended for academic and special libraries. URL: www.journals.elsevier.com/developmental-biology/

798. ***Genes & Development.*** [ISSN: 0890-9369] 1987. s-m. Individuals, USD 145. Ed(s): T Grodzicker. Cold Spring Harbor Laboratory Press, 500 Sunnyside Blvd, Woodbury, NY 11797; cshpress@cshl.edu; http://www.cshlpress.com. Illus., adv. Sample. Refereed. Reprint: PSC. *Indexed:* A01, A22, C45. *Aud.:* Ac, Sa.

Genes & Development publishes "high quality research papers of broad general interest and biological significance in the areas of molecular biology, molecular genetics and related fields." This title has been named one of the top five research journals in the field of molecular biology and genetics, and is published in association with the Genetics Society. Contents include research papers, research communications, and resource/methodology papers, as well as commissioned review articles and perspectives. Online and print subscriptions are available separately. Some articles are published online in advance of print. Free sample issues are found online, as well as access to tables of contents and abstracts. Open access is available for some archived editions. Recommended for special and academic libraries. URL: http://genesdev.cshlp.org/

Genetics

799. ***American Journal of Human Genetics.*** [ISSN: 0002-9297] 1948. m. EUR 1459. Ed(s): Emilie Marcus, David L Nelson. Cell Press, 600 Technology Sq, Ste 5, Cambridge, MA 02139; celleditor@cell.com; http://www.cell.com. Illus., index, adv. Refereed. Vol. ends: Dec. Microform: MIM; PQC. Reprint: PSC. *Indexed:* A01, A22, BAS, BRI, C45, Chicano. *Bk. rev.:* 0-3, 200-1,200 words. *Aud.:* Ac, Sa.

Published for The American Society of Human Genetics, the primary professional organization for human geneticists in the Americas, this journal is a "record of research and review relating to heredity in humans and to the application of genetic principles in medicine and public policy, as well as in related areas of molecular and cell biology." Papers appear on such topics as behavioral genetics, biochemical genetics, clinical genetics, cytogenetics, dysmorphology, gene therapy, genetic counseling, genetic epidemiology, genomics, immunogenetics, molecular genetics, neurogenetics, and population genetics. Also included are review articles, reports, conference announcements, employment notices, and letters to the editors. Online access is provided through multiple full-text sources. New articles are published ahead of final publication on the journal's web site. All *AJHG* articles, from 1949 to the present, are freely available at PubMed Central starting six months after publication. A good source for special and academic libraries. URL: www.cell.com/AJHG/

800. ***B M C Genetics.*** [ISSN: 1471-2156] 2000. irreg. Free. Ed(s): Simon Harold. BioMed Central Ltd., Fl 6, 236 Gray's Inn Rd, London, WC1X 8HB, United Kingdom; info@biomedcentral.com; https://www.biomedcentral.com. Adv. Refereed. *Indexed:* A01, C45. *Aud.:* Ac, Sa.

B M C Genetics is an open-access online journal that publishes original peer-reviewed research articles on all aspects of inheritance and variation in individuals and among populations. Attention is given to articles that significantly contribute to scientific knowledge in the field rather than broad interests. Coverage includes animal population genetics, complex traits and quantitative genetics, epigenetics and chromosome biology, functional genetics, human population genetics, plant population genetics, and statistical and computational genetics. All research articles are published after full peer review. All articles are published, without barriers to access, immediately upon acceptance. Full text is available online through PubMed Central from 2000 to the present, or via the publisher's web site. Recommended for academic and special libraries that support a biology program. URL: http://bmcgenet.biomedcentral.com

801. ***Biochimica et Biophysica Acta. Gene Regulatory Mechanisms.*** Formerly (until 2008): *B B A - Gene Structure and Expression;* Which superseded in part (in 1982): *Biochimica et Biophysica Acta: N. Nucleic Acids and Protein Synthesis;* Which was formerly (until 1965): *Biochimica et Biophysica Acta. Specialized Section on Nucleic Acids and Related Subjects.* [ISSN: 1874-9399] 1962. 12x/yr. EUR 4623. Ed(s): Joseph Reese. Elsevier BV, Radarweg 29, Amsterdam, 1043 NX, Netherlands; info@elsevier.com; https://www.elsevier.com/. Refereed. Microform: PQC. *Indexed:* A01, A22, C45. *Aud.:* Ac, Sa.

BBA Gene Regulatory Mechanisms includes "reports that describe novel insights into mechanisms of transcriptional, post-transcriptional, and translational gene regulation. Special emphasis is placed on papers that identify epigenetic mechanisms of gene regulation, including chromatin, modification, and remodeling. This section also encompasses mechanistic studies of regulatory proteins and protein complexes; regulatory or mechanistic aspects of RNA processing; regulation of expression by small RNA; genomic analysis of gene expression patterns; and modeling of gene regulatory pathways." This journal is one of the nine topical journals from *Biochimica et Biophysica Acta*. It contains descriptive reports and research papers. The journal supports innovations such as 3D models and crystallographic data, audioslides, a database linking tool, a genome viewer, and a protein viewer. An open-access publishing option is available to authors. Print and online subscriptions are available. Online access is available from 2008 to the present via ScienceDirect. Appropriate for academic and special libraries. URL: www.journals.elsevier.com/bba-gene-regulatory-mechanisms

802. ***Biochimica et Biophysica Acta. Molecular Basis of Disease.*** [ISSN: 0925-4439] 1990. 12x/yr. EUR 3384. Ed(s): Ronald Oude Elferink, Jeffrey Keller. Elsevier BV, Radarweg 29, Amsterdam, 1043 NX, Netherlands; info@elsevier.com; https://www.elsevier.com/. Refereed. Microform: PQC. *Indexed:* A01, A22. *Aud.:* Ac, Sa.

BBA Molecular Basis of Disease covers "the biochemistry and molecular genetics of disease processes and models of human disease." Specifically "aspects of aging, cancer, and metabolic-, neurological-, and immunological-based disease." This journal is one of the nine topical journals from *Biochimica et Biophysica Acta*. Articles emphasize the underlying mechanisms of disease pathways and provide novel contributions to the understanding and/or treatment of these disorders. The journal supports innovations such as 3D models and crystallographic data, audioslides, a database linking tool, and a protein viewer. Print and online subscriptions are available. An open-access publishing option is available for authors. Online access is available from 1990 to the present via ScienceDirect. Appropriate for academic and special libraries. URL: www.journals.elsevier.com/bba-molecular-basis-of-disease

803. ***Genetics (Online).*** [ISSN: 1943-2631] 1916. m. Free. Ed(s): Mark Johnston. Genetics Society of America, 9650 Rockville Pike, Bethesda, MD 20814; staff@dues.faseb.org; http://www.genetics-gsa.org/. Adv. Refereed. *Aud.:* Ac, Sa.

Genetics, published by the Genetics Society of America, is an international peer-reviewed, peer-edited journal. *Genetics* publishes high-quality, original research that reports novel findings in the fields of genetics and genomics. Included in each issue are Reviews, Commentary, Perspectives, Educational Primers, Toolbox Reviews, plus the series YeastBook, FlyBook, and WormBook. Time-sensitive material needing quick dissemination of a noteworthy finding or observation may be published in the "Communications" column. Subscriptions include archived content back to 1916 and the open-access journal G3: Genes | Gnomes | Gnetics. There is also some non-subscription open- access content and a blog "Genes to Genomes." Pubmed Central indexes this journal back to 1916 with a 12-month embargo on current content. *Genetics*' rising impact factor make it a good addition to an academic science collection. URL: http://www.genetics.org/

804. ***Genome Research.*** Formerly (until 1995): *P C R Methods and Applications.* [ISSN: 1088-9051] 1991. m. Cold Spring Harbor Laboratory Press, 1 Bungtown Rd, Cold Spring Harbor, NY 11724; cshpress@cshl.edu; http://www.cshlpress.com. Illus. Sample. Refereed. Circ: 50000. Reprint: PSC. *Indexed:* A01, A22, C45. *Aud.:* Ac, Sa.

Genome Research is an international, continuously published, peer-reviewed journal that features outstanding original research that provides novel insights into the genome biology of all organisms, including significant advances in genomic medicine. The journal also provides high-quality reviews and perspectives written by respected leaders in the field, and reports cutting-edge computational biology and high-throughput methodologies. Submitted articles selected by the editor are peer reviewed, and all accepted papers must present original research; researchers should be prepared to make available all materials needed to duplicate their work. There is an open-access publishing option for authors. *Genome Research* follows the guidelines for fair use of community resource data. Complete datasets are made available on the journal's web site. Print and online subscriptions are available. Online access is available from 1991 to present via the publisher's web site, six months after print publication. Appropriate for academic and special libraries. URL: http://genome.cshlp.org/

805. ***Heredity.*** [ISSN: 0018-067X] 1947. m. EUR 1493. Ed(s): Manfred J Muller. Nature Publishing Group, The MacMillan Bldg, 4 Crinan St, London, N1 9XW, United Kingdom; nature@nature.com; https://www.nature.com. Illus., index, adv. Sample. Refereed. Microform: PQC. *Indexed:* A01, A22, Agr, BRI, C45, E01. *Bk. rev.:* 4-5, 400-2,000 words. *Aud.:* Ac, Sa.

Heredity is published for The Genetics Society, as part of the Nature Publishing Group. The journal presents "high-quality articles that describe original research and theoretical insights in all areas of genetics." Contents include original research articles, short reviews, book reviews, news, and commentaries that keep researchers and students updated on advances in the field. Topics explored include population genetics (including human), genomics, functional genomics and proteomics, evo-devo, biometrical and statistical genetics, ecological and evolutionary genetics, animal and plant breeding, and cytogenetics. Free online features include the monthly "Heredity Podcast" and a number of feature articles. Archived content is freely available after 12 months. Appropriate for special and academic libraries. URL: www.nature.com/hdy/index.html

806. ***Human Biology (Detroit).*** [ISSN: 0018-7143] 1929. q. USD 510 (print & online eds.)). Ed(s): Brian M Kemp, Ripan S Malhi. Wayne State University Press, The Leonard N Simons Bldg, 4809 Woodward Ave, Detroit, MI 48201; tara.reeser@wayne.edu; http://wsupress.wayne.edu/. Illus., index, adv. Refereed. Vol. ends: Dec. Microform: PQC. *Indexed:* A01, A22, A47, BAS, BRI, C45, Chicano, E01, IBSS. *Bk. rev.:* 1-3, 500-1,400 words. *Aud.:* Ac, Sa.

Human Biology is the official journal of the American Association of Anthropological Genetics. This international, peer-reviewed journal publishes ideas, methods, and techniques in the human biology field. Topics include evolutionary and genetic demography, behavioral genetics, population genetics, quantitative genetics, anthropological genetics, genetic epidemiology, molecular genetics, ancient-DNA studies and paleogenomics, and growth physiology focusing on genetic/environmental interactions. *Human Biology* is available in print and electronic format through the publisher's web site. Subscriptions are available to individuals and institutions, and student/senior discounts are offered. Appropriate for academic and special libraries with collections in anthropology, biology, and medicine. URL: http://wsupress.wayne.edu/journals/humanbio

807. ***Journal of Heredity.*** Formerly (until 1914): *American Breeders' Magazine.* [ISSN: 0022-1503] 1903. 7x/yr. EUR 656. Ed(s): C Scott Baker, Anjanette Baker. Oxford University Press, Great Clarendon St, Oxford, OX2 6DP, United Kingdom; onlinequeries.uk@oup.com;

http://global.oup.com. Illus., index, adv. Refereed. Circ: 900. Vol. ends: Nov/Dec. Microform: IDC; PMC; PQC. Reprint: PSC. *Indexed:* A01, A22, Agr, BRI, C45, E01, MLA-IB. *Bk. rev.:* 0-5, 300-900 words. *Aud.:* Ac, Sa.

Journal of Heredity is published on behalf of the American Genetic Association. To be included in this journal, articles must significantly contribute to the topics of genomics and gene mapping, gene action, regulation and transmission, bioinformatics and computational genetics, molecular adaptation and selection, reproductive strategies and kinship analysis, quantitative genetics and Mendelian inheritance, molecular systematics and phylogenetics, population structure and phylogeography, conservation genetics, or biodiversity. Contents include research papers, brief communications, announcements, and review articles. Also included are papers on rapidly advancing fields such as genome organization, comparative gene mapping, animal models of human disease, and molecular genetics of resistance to infectious disease in plants and animals. Full text is available online from 1905 to the present with a subscription, or open access via PubMed from 2008 through the present with a 12-month embargo. Recommended for a wide range of biologists, as well as special and academic libraries. URL: http://jhered.oxfordjournals.org/

808. ***Molecular Genetics and Genomics.*** Former titles (until 2001): *Molecular and General Genetics;* (until 1966): *Zeitschrift fuer Vererbungslehre;* (until 1957): *Zeitschrift fuer Induktive Abstammungs- und Vererbungslehre.* [ISSN: 1617-4615] 1908. m. EUR 8627 (print & online eds.)). Springer, Tiergartenstr 17, Heidelberg, 69121, Germany; subscriptions@springer.com; https://www.springer.com. Illus., index, adv. Sample. Refereed. Reprint: PSC. *Indexed:* A01, A22, Agr, C45, E01. *Aud.:* Ac, Sa.

Molecular Genetics and Genomics publishes peer-reviewed research in all areas of genetics and genomics. Contents cover all areas of genetics and genomics that encompass experimental and theoretical approaches to all organisms. Full text is available online from 1908 to the present by subscription. Very early content is in German. An open-access option is offered through Springer Open Choice. Intended for biologists and recommended for special and academic libraries. URL: http://link.springer.com/journal/438

809. ***Nature Genetics.*** [ISSN: 1061-4036] 1992. m. EUR 6648. Ed(s): Myles Axton. Nature Publishing Group, 75 Varick St, 9th Fl, New York, NY 10013; nature@natureny.com; http://www.nature.com. Illus., index, adv. Sample. Refereed. *Indexed:* A01, A22, Agr, BRI, C45. *Aud.:* Ac, Sa.

Nature Genetics publishes genetic and functional genomic studies on human traits and other organisms, including the mouse, fly, nematode, and yeast. It focuses on the genetic basis for common and complex diseases as well as the mechanism, architecture, and evolution of gene networks. Contents include editorials, research articles, letters, news and views, and meeting reports. Online features include the "Free Association" blog, which contains links and editorial comments on research and news in genetics, as well as reader feedback. Articles are published online in advance of the print publication. Online full text is available from 1992 to the present, with a subscription. Sample issues are available. Appropriate for special and academic libraries that support biology programs. URL: www.nature.com/ng/index.html

810. ***R N A.*** [ISSN: 1355-8382] 1995. m. Individuals, USD 320. Ed(s): Dr. Timothy W Nilsen. Cold Spring Harbor Laboratory Press, 1 Bungtown Rd, Cold Spring Harbor, NY 11724; cshpress@cshl.edu; http://www.cshlpress.com. Adv. Sample. Refereed. *Indexed:* A22, C45, E01. *Aud.:* Ac, Sa.

RNA is a publication of the RNA Society that serves as an international forum for publishing a broad array of RNA research. It is a monthly publication that "provides rapid publication of significant original research in all areas of RNA structure and function in eukaryotic, prokaryotic, and viral systems." Topics covered include structural analysis; rRNA, mRNA, and tRNA structure, function, and biogenesis; alternative processing; ribosome structure and function; translational control; RNA catalysis; RNA editing; RNA transport and localization; regulatory RNAs; large and small RNP structure, function, and biogenesis; viral RNA metabolism; RNA stability and turnover; in vitro evolution; and RNA chemistry. Papers are considered in six areas: "Reports," "Articles," "Bioinformatics," "Hypotheses," "Methods," and "Letters to the Editor." It also publishes "Reviews," "Perspectives," "Commentaries," and "Mini-reviews." Subscriptions to the print journal include full online access; online-only subscriptions are available to institutions. Full text from 1995 to the present (with a 12-month embargo) is provided by PubMed Central or via the publisher's web site. Appropriate for special and academic libraries. URL: http://rnajournal.cshlp.org/

Microbiology

811. ***Canadian Journal of Microbiology.*** [ISSN: 0008-4166] 1954. m. CAD 1400 (print & online eds.)). Canadian Science Publishing, 65 Auriga Dr, Ste 203, Ottawa, ON K2E 7W6, Canada; pubs@cdnsciencepub.com; http://www.nrcresearchpress.com. Illus., index, adv. Sample. Refereed. Vol. ends: Dec. *Indexed:* A01, A22, Agr, C37, C45, E01, S25. *Aud.:* Ac, Sa.

Published since 1954, *Canadian Journal of Microbiology* presents new research in microbiology. Topics include "applied microbiology and biotechnology; microbial structure and function; fungi and other eucaryotic protists; infection and immunity; microbial ecology; physiology, metabolism, and enzymology; and virology, genetics, and molecular biology." Contents include articles, notes, mini-reviews, reviews, and letters. Although papers in French are accepted, the majority of the journal is in English. e-First articles are published before they appear in the print edition. Just-IN manuscripts are pdf versions of authors' accepted manuscripts prior to copy editing and page composition. There is an open-access option for authors as well. Online content is available in full text from 1954 to the present, with subscriptions. A recommended source for academic and special libraries. URL: www.nrcresearchpress.com/journal/cjm

812. ***Current Microbiology.*** [ISSN: 0343-8651] 1978. m. EUR 2266 (print & online eds.)). Ed(s): Erko Stackebrandt. Springer New York LLC, 233 Spring St, New York, NY 10013; customerservice@springer.com; http://www.springer.com. Illus., adv. Refereed. Microform: PQC. Reprint: PSC. *Indexed:* A01, A22, Agr, BRI, C45, E01. *Aud.:* Ac, Sa.

Current Microbiology offers "rapid publication of new research on all aspects of microbial cells, including prokaryotes and eukaryotes and, where appropriate, viruses." Content covers general, medical, and applied microbiology and virology, drawing on physiology, biochemistry, genetics, biotechnology, morphology, taxonomy, diagnostic methods, and immunology as applied to microorganisms. The journal has an open-access publishing option for authors. Some articles are published online first before the print publication. The journal has an online version with content from 1978 to the present. Recommended for biology collections in special and academic libraries. URL: http://link.springer.com/journal/284

813. ***International Journal of Systematic and Evolutionary Microbiology.*** Former titles (until 2000): *International Journal of Systematic Bacteriology;* (until 1966): *International Bulletin of Bacteriological Nomenclature and Taxonomy.* [ISSN: 1466-5026] 1951. m. Ed(s): Martha Trujillo. The Microbiology Society, Charles Darwin House, 12 Roger St, London, WC1N 2JU, United Kingdom; journals@microbiologysociety.org; http://www.microbiologysociety.org/. Illus., index, adv. Sample. Refereed. Vol. ends: Oct/Dec. *Indexed:* A22, Agr, C45. *Bk. rev.:* 1,000-1,200 words. *Aud.:* Ac, Sa.

IJSEM is published by the Society for General Microbiology. It includes papers dealing with "all phases of the systematics of bacteria, including taxonomy, nomenclature, identification, characterization, and culture preservation," featuring descriptions of the majority of all new prokaryotic and yeast species. It is the official journal of record for bacterial names of the International Committee on Systematics of Prokaryotes and of the International Union of Microbiological Societies. Online access is provided by the Microbiology Society to print subscribers. Issues are also available through PubMed Central from 2007 with a 12-month embargo. OpenMicrobiology is the journal's open-access publishing option. Appropriate for special and academic libraries. URL: http://ijs.sgmjournals.org/

814. ***Journal of Bacteriology (Online).*** [ISSN: 1098-5530] 1916. s-m. USD 1580. Ed(s): Thomas J Silhavy. American Society for Microbiology, 1752 N St, NW, Washington, DC 20036; journals@asmusa.org; http://journals.asm.org. Index, adv. Refereed. *Aud.:* Ac, Sa.

This journal "publishes research articles that probe fundamental processes in bacteria, archaea and their viruses, and the molecular mechanisms by which they interact with each other and with their hosts and their environments." Contents include guest commentaries, mini-reviews, meeting reviews, presentations, and research articles on genetics and molecular biology. There is online access to articles from 1916 to the present. Access is free six months or less after an issue is published through PubMed Central. Highly recommended for biology collections in special and academic libraries. URL: http://jb.asm.org/

815. ***The Journal of Eukaryotic Microbiology (Online).*** [ISSN: 1550-7408] 1950. bi-m. GBP 365. Ed(s): Roberto Docampo. Wiley-Blackwell Publishing, Inc., 111 River St, Hoboken, NJ 07030; info@wiley.com; http://onlinelibrary.wiley.com. Illus. Refereed. *Aud.:* Ac, Sa.

The Journal of Eukaryotic Microbiology is an online journal that is published on behalf of International Society of Protistologists. Content includes "original research on protists, including lower algae and fungi." Topics cover all aspects of these organisms, including behavior, biochemistry, cell biology, chemotherapy, development, ecology, parasitology, and systematics. Journal contents include research articles, communications, and reviews by invitation only. Occasionally, special reports make up supplements. Online access from 1954 to the present is available with a subscription. Free access is available from 1997 to the present via Wiley Online Library. Additional online features include free e-mail alerts and free sample issues. Effective with the 2014 volume, this journal moved to an online-only format. URL: http://onlinelibrary.wiley.com/journal/10.1111/

816. ***Journal of Virology (Online).*** [ISSN: 1098-5514] 1967. s-m. USD 1976. Ed(s): Rozanne M Sandri-Goldin. American Society for Microbiology, 1752 N St, NW, Washington, DC 20036; journals@asmusa.org; http://journals.asm.org. Adv. Refereed. *Aud.:* Ac, Sa.

Known as a premier source concerning viruses, the *Journal of Virology* is the most cited journal in virology. Topics include virion structure and assembly, viral genome replication and regulation of gene expression, genetic diversity and evolution, virus-cell interactions, cellular responses to infection, transformation and oncogenesis, gene delivery, viral pathogenesis and immunity, and vaccines and antiviral agents. Much content is focused on viruses that impact humans, through guest commentaries, mini-reviews, and spotlight features. Online access to full text is provided for through PubMed Central six months after articles have been published in print. This highly regarded title is recommended for academic and special libraries. URL: http://jvi.asm.org

817. ***Microbiology.*** Formerly (until 1994): *Journal of General Microbiology.* [ISSN: 1350-0872] 1947. m. Ed(s): Dr. Tanya Parish. The Microbiology Society, Charles Darwin House, 12 Roger St, London, WC1N 2JU, United Kingdom; journals@microbiologysociety.org; http://www.microbiologysociety.org/. Illus., index, adv. Sample. Refereed. Vol. ends: Dec. *Indexed:* A01, A22, Agr, C45. *Aud.:* Ac, Sa.

Microbiology, one of the world's leading microbiological journals, is published by the Microbiology Society. Contents include research papers, reviews, mini-reviews, a microbiology comment section for readers' responses, and the occasional special issue. Sections include "biochemistry and molecular biology, biodiversity and evolution, cell and developmental biology, environmental microbiology, genes and genomes, pathogens and pathogenicity, physiology, plant-microbe interactions, and theoretical microbiology." Full text is available online from 1947 to the present with subscription. There is some open-access content. A free sample issue can be found online. Some content is also available through PubMed Central after a 12-month waiting period. Appropriate for academic and special libraries. URL: http://mic.sgmjournals.org

818. ***Microbiology and Molecular Biology Reviews (Online).*** Formerly (until 1997): *Microbiological Reviews (Online).* [ISSN: 1098-5557] 1997. q. USD 921. Ed(s): Michael J Buchmeier. American Society for Microbiology, 1752 N St, NW, Washington, DC 20036; journals@asmusa.org; http://journals.asm.org. Index, adv. Refereed. *Aud.:* Ac, Sa.

This journal is recognized as the "definitive broad-based review journal in the disciplines of microbiology, immunology, and molecular and cellular biology." It is published by the American Society for Microbiology. Articles provide the latest findings on bacteria, viruses, parasites, fungi, and other eukaryotes. Contents include mostly review articles on the following topics: cellular biology, ecology, genetics, host-parasite relationships leading to disease, molecular biology, physiology and enzymology, and virology. Subscriptions are available as print and online with full text from 1937 to the present. Non-subscribers have free full-text access up to one year after an issue's publication through PubMed Central. A good source for special libraries and academic biology collections. URL: http://mmbr.asm.org/

819. ***MicrobiologyOpen.*** [ISSN: 2045-8827] 2012. . Free. Ed(s): Pierre Cornelis. John Wiley & Sons Ltd., EMEA Institutional Sales, 9600 Garsington Rd, Oxford, OX4 2DQ, United Kingdom; cs-journals@wiley.com; http://onlinelibrary.wiley.com. Refereed. *Indexed:* C45. *Aud.:* Ac, Sa.

MicrobiologyOpen is a peer-reviewed open-access journal that delivers rapid decisions and fast publication of microbial science on topics such as eukaryotic microorganisms, prokaryotes (bacteria and archaea), and viruses infecting or interacting with microorganisms, including genetic, biochemical, biophysical, bioinformatic, and structural analyses. It contains journal features, original research articles, reviews, and editorials. All articles published by *MicrobiologyOpen* are fully open access via Wiley Open Access Journals. Articles are immediately and freely available to read, download, and share. Online access is available from 2012 to the present. Appropriate for academic and special libraries. URL: http://onlinelibrary.wiley.com/journal/10.1002/%28ISSN%292045-8827

820. ***Nature Microbiology.*** [ISSN: 2058-5276] 2016. m. Free. Ed(s): Andrew Jermy. Nature Publishing Group, The MacMillan Bldg, 4 Crinan St, London, N1 9XW, United Kingdom; nature@nature.com; https://www.nature.com. Refereed. *Indexed:* C45. *Aud.:* Ac, Sa.

Nature Microbiology is an editorially independent publication of Nature Publishing and is exclusively online. Topics cover all aspects of microorganisms, including evolution, physiology, cell biology, interactions, and societal significance. The journal publishes research articles as soon as they are ready. Other features include "News & Views," "Reviews," and "Comment and Opinion." Articles may be purchased individually online or through an annual online subscription. This journal would suit an academic or special science-library audience. URL: https://www.nature.com/nmicrobiol/

821. ***Virology.*** [ISSN: 0042-6822] 1955. 13x/yr. EUR 11245. Ed(s): M Emerman. Academic Press, 225 Wyman St, Waltham, MA 02144; JournalCustomerService-usa@elsevier.com; http://store.elsevier.com/Academic-Press/IMP_5/. Illus., index, adv. Refereed. *Indexed:* A01, A22, Agr, C45, E01. *Aud.:* Ac, Sa.

Virology publishes results of basic research in all areas of virology, including the viruses of vertebrates and invertebrates such as plants, bacteria, yeasts, and fungi. Contents include regular articles that present results of basic research that break new ground; rapid communications, which are brief, definitive reports of high significance; and mini-reviews, which discuss cutting-edge developments and themes in virology. Topics include virus replication, virus structure and function, virus-cell biology, gene therapy, viral pathogenesis and immunity, and emerging viruses. ScienceDirect provides online access to full text. This journal is recognized as a leading resource for current information in this field. There is free access to articles after 12 months, and free access to reviews and special issues, and an open-access publishing option for authors. Recommended for academic and special libraries, and appropriate for undergraduates as well as researchers. URL: www.journals.elsevier.com/virology/

■ BIOTECHNOLOGY

See also Biology section.

Susan K. Kendall, Ph.D., Health Sciences Coordinator and Biology Librarian, Michigan State University Libraries, East Lansing, MI 48824

Introduction

Biotechnology is a dynamic and growing field with exciting potential. It is an applied science, meaning knowledge from the basic biological sciences, particularly from biochemistry, genetics, molecular biology, or cell biology, is applied to practical purposes in medicine, agriculture, food science, or environmental studies, and developed into commercial products. In some cases, biological sciences are combined with other areas of study like engineering, material science, computer science, or chemistry, in interdisciplinary ways.

There are always new areas of biotechnology receiving attention. Gene editing using the CRISPR-CAS system was *Science Magazine*'s "Breakthrough of the Year" in 2015, and all the potential applications have yet to be discovered. Other areas of importance are stem cells research, regenerative medicine, nanotechnology for drug delivery, nanomedicine, implantable sensors, and synthetic biology to manufacture organisms. Environmentalists, bioethicists, and the public have viewed some of the advances of biotechnology with concern. Nevertheless, most people seem to believe that being able to translate biological findings into useful products to improve our lives is the main reason to support biological research.

Scientists doing biotechnology work publish their research in many different kinds of journals ranging from basic biology to medical, chemical, or engineering journals, depending on their focus. There are a number of journals devoted specifically to biotechnology and all its subfields. Some of the most highly regarded are listed in this section. However, none of the journals focusing solely on biotechnology quite reaches the importance of the most prestigious journals in biology or medicine. The librarian collecting in this area should be aware that, depending on the topic, the very best biotechnology-related papers may be published in interdisciplinary journals such as *Nature, Science, Nature Genetics, Cell,* and *The New England Journal of Medicine.*

Like journals in the other sciences, biotechnology journals are all available in electronic format, and often only in electronic format. The older issues of most journals have been digitized back to the first volume. For current issues, the electronic version is usually now considered the version of record, and many print journals, if they exist at all, are stripped down to only a subset of the total number of published articles, without much of the image or, of course, any of the video or data content. It is actually astonishing that print versions of some of these journals still remain since they seem more and more irrelevant. It is very common for articles to be published online after they are reviewed and accepted in journal issues that are "in progress." Reading journals online is increasingly comfortable and easy for users on mobile devices. Most journal web sites have responsive design to the size of the device being used, and there are app versions of some journals available for download. Only a couple of scientific publishers have created journal apps that allow readers to pair their device with their institutional subscription to gain access to the full journal. Others have apps created only for individual subscribers. What works better for institutional subscribers are third party apps like BrowZine that allow for browsing and reading journals in a tablet-friendly version but work directly with libraries to enable access to subscribed material.

Publishers have tried to push their electronic journals into the social side of science with varying results. Almost all of them include capabilities for social bookmarking and sharing of articles by email, Facebook, CiteULike, Del.icio.us, Digg, Reddit, LinkedIn, Google+, Mendeley, Twitter, and others, and some of them make a point of highlighting articles that have been top rated by Altmetrics.com for having many mentions on social media. A few publishers have tried to create online communities around a single journal or set of journals in a subject area to take advantage of the Internet beyond displaying journal volumes, issues, and articles in a more traditional way that mimics print. Some years ago, these online communities were started as busy web portals with news feeds, blogs, discussion forums, and events calendars. A few of these still remain, but most online communities around journals have moved to Facebook. The more successful of these online communities on Facebook are by society publishers who more naturally draw member scientists who support and are interested in the work of the society, its conferences, and its publications. Commercial publishers tend to have Facebook pages and Twitter updates that highlight articles from their publications or from the scientific news in general, but they cannot generate a sense of community like a society can. It turns out that scientists are not really looking to publishers to stimulate social interaction. They may be communicating with others on Twitter about articles they are reading or bypassing the publishers altogether to interact on social networking sites for scientists such as the highly criticized ResearchGate, where they can maintain profiles and upload their own articles, sometimes illegally. The use of online forums for open peer review of articles (as an alternative to traditional peer review) is an idea that may never be realized. Publishers unsuccessfully tried to generate interest in this in the past, and now ResearchGate has tried to generate interest in its open review system. The fact still remains that scientists have little time to pursue activities that do not directly lead to career rewards. Peer review done right is time consuming and requires a high level of in-depth scrutiny. Scientists will do peer review for the papers assigned to them and receive credit for that kind of activity, but they cannot spend the same kind of time with other papers on the web.

Predictions of the demise of the scholarly journal as a medium for communication have not been borne out. In fact there are more journals than ever. Electronic publishing has driven a trend toward the steady breakdown of the importance of traditional volumes or issues of journals, however. The individual article is the important unit. This has always been somewhat true when users find articles by searching an index like Medline, but it seems even more to be the case now. Scientists still value the journal name and reputation to give them an idea of the trustworthiness of the content. Volumes and issues still exist for many online journals, it seems, primarily to allow for efficient citation. The rapid publication of individual articles online as they are peer reviewed and accepted, but perhaps not yet copy edited, is very common and expected by scientists in a rapidly changing field like biotechnology. Where scientists used to subscribe to table of contents services and browse new issues of their favorite journals when they were published, perhaps monthly, they now must daily monitor what is new on the journal's web site, perhaps by using automatic RSS feeds or by following a journal or publisher on Twitter. Publishers' web gateways or portals further break up journal issues by listing highlighted articles, most downloaded articles, or groups of articles with a similar theme, pulling content from different issues or from different journals (by the same publisher, of course) to create a virtual issue. Scientists clicking on these hyperlinks to individual articles and creating their own lists of favorites are like most users of any kind of information on the Internet. They have become used to following information and ideas from one place to the next without regard for hierarchy, and they enjoy customizing websites to suit their own particular needs and interests.

Open-access publishing with the author-pays model is widespread in the biological sciences, and biotechnology is no exception. The open access philosophy says that information should be immediately freely available electronically to everyone, and the publishing costs of editing, peer-review, or putting the papers online should be covered by something other than a personal or library subscription. The funding source could be a granting agency or the authors themselves. While the majority of important journals in biotechnology are still primarily subscription-based, several on this list have always been open access or have gone totally open access in recent years. Most of the major publishers also have a hybrid model for their journals, allowing authors who wish to pay an extra fee to make their articles open access to choose that option. Access to the results of publicly funded biomedical research has now been a reality for more than ten years in several countries with policies from the United States National Institutes of Health (NIH), the Canadian Institutes of Health Research, and Research Councils UK requiring no more than six months embargo on research publications until they are available for free in a repository. Expanded public access policies have also been passed in the United States to include non-biomedical research funded by other government agencies, and success depends on whether these agencies can develop plans for centralized repositories like the NIH has in PubMed Central. All of these public access policies are compromises for open-access proponents who insist that immediate free access to research is the goal. European Union leaders have recently announced a goal for publicly funded research to become fully open access by 2020, and other countries and publishers will be watching to see how that progresses. The publishers of all of the journals listed in this section advertise that they will work with authors to make sure they are in compliance with the current requirements of their funding agencies.

Some of the discussion has moved on from open-access publishing to open data and data archiving issues. Government funding agencies in many countries are beginning to think about how to preserve valuable data so that it is not lost to future generations of scientists. Policies are just starting to require scientists to include data management plans in their grants, and many librarians are learning about the issue of preservation and access to digital information. This is certainly an issue for biotechnologists, many of whom generate particularly large datasets in their work. But repositories need to be developed, and these would likely be more complex than repositories for archiving articles. For example, the NIH supports more than 50 data sharing repositories, particularly for genomic, protein, or chemical structure data of different types, and there is also a clinical trials results database. Other independent repositories exist for neuroscience, phylogenetic, and environmental data, to name just a few. But for some kinds of data, there is no clear repository. Some journals listed in this section require adherence to data citation principles laid out by the Data Citation Synthesis Group in their *Joint Declaration of Data Citation Principles*. Many of the journals also provide some kind of storage and access for machine-readable supplementary datasets associated with published articles, but long-term preservation plans remain unclear.

The number of serials in the biotechnology area is already quite large and continues to grow along with the field. The journals or magazines listed here were chosen from that large number based on several criteria, but the librarian should be aware that for any given subfield of biotechnology, many other quality journals should be considered. In particular, there is overlap in subject matter with several other sections of this book, so the reader should look to sections such as Energy, Engineering and Technology/Biomedical Engineering, or Biology/Genetics for titles specific to those areas. For example, most journals about biofuels research are not listed here but are in the Energy section. Titles chosen for this section tended to be journals that are interdisciplinary, covering biotechnology from agriculture to medicine, with a few specialized journals that would be unlikely to appear in other sections of this book. In choosing journals for the list that follows, impact factor as published in the database Journal Citation Reports from Clarivate Analytics was taken into account. A journal's impact factor is based primarily on citation data, with the assumption that journals containing highly cited articles, particularly in biomedical areas, tend to be of higher quality. The impact factor of 160 journals classified in the biotechnology subject area are tracked by the Journal Citation Reports. Other criteria were also taken into consideration when generating the list below. Journals of different types and from different publishers were chosen to diversify the list. Both journals publishing primarily original research and journals publishing primarily reviews were included, and journals commenting on the ethical, legal, or regulatory issues surrounding biotechnology are noted. Both open-access and traditional journals made the list. The newness and emerging quality of the field can be noted from some of the information about the journals listed. Many are not very old. Still others have undergone name changes or expansions into sister journals to reflect trends. All of the journals listed are indexed in at least one major bibliographic database such as Medline, Web of Science, or Biological Abstracts. A good academic or corporate research and development library that serves scientists in biotechnology will have a mix of both the general and relevant subject-specific journals to include the range of primary research, review, and news or regulatory articles. A library serving non-scientists interested in biotechnology from a business or other angle will likely have only the journals that contain a news section or articles with a business, legal, or regulatory slant. These are the ones noted as also appropriate for a general audience. Only a couple of the most general journals or magazines listed would be appropriate for a public library.

Basic Periodicals

Ac, Sa: *Nature Biotechnology, Trends in Biotechnology.*

Basic Abstracts and Indexes

Biological Abstracts, MEDLINE, Scopus, Web of Science.

822. ***Applied and Environmental Microbiology (Online).*** Formerly (until 1976): *Applied Microbiology (Online).* [ISSN: 1098-5336] 1953. s-m. USD 1383. Ed(s): Harold L Drake. American Society for Microbiology, 1752 N St, NW, Washington, DC 20036; journals@asmusa.org; http://journals.asm.org. Index, adv. Refereed. *Aud.:* Ac, Sa.

Published by the American Society for Microbiology, this journal, while not solely focused on biotechnology, contains a significant number of articles devoted to research in biotechnology; industrial, environmental, and food microbiology; and applied areas where new products or practical benefits are the results of microbial research. Each issue is divided into anywhere from 12 to 15 subject sections, so researchers can easily skip to the sections that interest them the most: for instance, food microbiology or biodegradation, or physiology. Almost all of the articles are peer-reviewed research articles, but occasional issues will contain a mini-review, guest commentary, or meeting review article at the beginning. Research scientists in many different applied microbiology fields would be interested in this journal.

823. ***Applied Microbiology and Biotechnology.*** Former titles (until 1984): *European Journal of Applied Microbiology and Biotechnology; European Journal of Applied Microbiology.* [ISSN: 0175-7598] 1975. 18x/yr. EUR 13262 (print & online eds.)). Ed(s): Alexander Steinbuechel. Springer, Tiergartenstr 17, Heidelberg, 69121, Germany. Refereed. Reprint: PSC. *Indexed:* A01, A22, Agr, BRI, C45, E01, S25. *Aud.:* Ac, Sa.

This journal covers a wide range of topics that qualify as applied microbiology and biotechnology, including molecular biotechnology, genomics, proteomics, applied microbial physiology, bioprocess engineering, and environmental biotechnology. Most of the papers are original, peer-reviewed research articles; however, each issue usually has several short five- to six-page mini-reviews that summarize and provide perspective on a research area or trend. The focus is mostly on the science, although very occasional mini-reviews cover policy issues. The journal would primarily be of interest to scientists in the field.

824. ***Bioinformatics.*** Incorporates (1993-2000): *International Conference on Intelligent Systems for Molecular Biology. Proceedings;* Formerly (until 1998): *Computer Applications in the Biosciences.* [ISSN: 1367-4803] 1985. fortn. EUR 3708. Ed(s): Alfonso Valencia, J Kelso. Oxford University Press, Great Clarendon St, Oxford, OX2 6DP, United Kingdom; onlinequeries.uk@oup.com; http://global.oup.com. Illus., adv. Sample. Refereed. Reprint: PSC. *Indexed:* A01, A22, Agr, C45, CompLI, E01. *Aud.:* Ac, Sa.

This is the leading and one of the oldest journals in the field of bioinformatics and an official publication of the International Society for Computational Biology. Bioinformatics is the collection, processing, and analysis of biological information using computers and computer algorithms. The subject matter can include genetic or genomic analysis, systems biology data, text mining, databases, and even bioimage informatics. Much of the information and data generated today in biotechnology is on a large scale, making manipulation by computers essential. While bioinformatics started out as a combination of biology and computer science, it has evolved into a scientific discipline in its own right. The journal publishes both original research and review articles about new developments in the field. Two sections within the journal, "Discovery Notes" and "Application Notes," publish shorter papers - respectively, the first describes "biologically interesting discoveries using computational techniques," and the second are "short descriptions of novel software, databases, or applications." Instructions to authors require that all supporting data upon which article conclusions rest must be made available in a public repository. Directly relevant supplementary data cited in the paper will be archived on the journal site.

825. ***Biosensors and Bioelectronics.*** Formerly (until 1989): *Biosensors.* [ISSN: 0956-5663] 1985. 12x/yr. EUR 5049. Ed(s): Anthony P F Turner. Elsevier BV, Radarweg 29, Amsterdam, 1043 NX, Netherlands; info@elsevier.com; https://www.elsevier.com. Illus., adv. Refereed. *Indexed:* A01, A22, Agr, C45. *Bk. rev.:* Occasional. *Aud.:* Ac, Sa.

According to the journal web site, "the field of bioelectronics seeks to exploit biology in conjunction with electronics in a wider context." Analytical devices that incorporate biological or biomimetic material with a transducer to transmit a digital electronic signal to indicate the presence of a specific substance are called biosensors. Biosensors and bioelectronics have been applied to problems in medicine, pharmaceuticals, the environment, food processing, or security. This journal publishes primarily original, peer-reviewed research articles as full papers or short communications. Often there are a couple of review article per issue. Some issues have contained special topic sections or groups of papers from a conference. This journal would be of interest to research scientists.

826. ***Biotechnology Advances: research reviews.*** [ISSN: 0734-9750] 1983. 8x/yr. EUR 3712. Ed(s): E A Bayer. Elsevier Inc., 230 Park Ave, Ste 800, New York, NY 10169; usinfo-f@elsevier.com; https://www.elsevier.com. Adv. Sample. Refereed. Microform: PQC. *Indexed:* A01, A22, Agr, C45. *Bk. rev.:* Occasional. *Aud.:* Ac, Sa.

This is a journal devoted to publishing reviews of important advances in all areas of biotechnology, and would be of interest to students or researchers in industry, government, and academia. Each issue contains research review papers on such topics as tissue engineering, chemical engineering, food and agricultural technologies, bioremediation, environmental technologies, drug discovery, and genetic technologies. Special issues publish papers from conferences, or on one theme such as "trends in *in vitro* diagnostics and mobile healthcare."

827. *Biotechnology and Bioengineering.* Formerly (until 1962): *Journal of Biochemical and Microbiological Technology and Engineering.* [ISSN: 0006-3592] 1959. m. GBP 7779. Ed(s): Douglas S Clark. John Wiley & Sons, Inc., 111 River St, Hoboken, NJ 07030; cs-journals@wiley.com; http://onlinelibrary.wiley.com. Illus., adv. Refereed. Microform: PQC. Reprint: PSC. *Indexed:* A22, Agr, C45, S25. *Aud.:* Ac, Sa.

This journal covers every area of biotechnology: environmental, food, plant, pharmaceutical, medical, and industrial. Articles on topics such as tissue engineering, stem cells, biofuels, protein engineering, biosensors, bioinformatics, and bioremediation, all also covered by more narrowly focused journals mentioned in this book, are accepted. Some issues contain review articles. "Communications to the Editor" are shorter research papers found at the end of each issue. The journal covers only the scientific advancements in biotechnology and not the business, legal, or other sides of the field, and so is of interest primarily to scientists or engineers.

828. *Biotechnology for Biofuels.* [ISSN: 1754-6834] 2007. irreg. Free. Ed(s): Michael Himmel, Charles Wyman. BioMed Central Ltd., Fl 6, 236 Gray's Inn Rd, London, WC1X 8HB, United Kingdom; info@biomedcentral.com; https://www.biomedcentral.com. Adv. Refereed. *Indexed:* A01, C45. *Aud.:* Ac, Sa.

This is an open-access, peer-reviewed journal from BioMed Central (BMC), the open-access division of the publisher Springer Nature that relies on the author-payment model for support. The company publishes several journals of interest in biotechnology, and this fairly new journal seems to have risen in importance. The journal covers articles that describe advances in the technology of biofuels and bioproducts, and applications of biotechnology to the production of these products from plants, biomass, and carbon dioxide. Articles are published immediately upon acceptance, and there are no discrete issues. Volumes of the journal correspond to the year of publication. The journal publishes peer-reviewed research articles, methodology articles, and review articles. Other BMC journals of interest to biotechnologists include *BMC Bioinformatics* and *BMC Biotechnology.* Of interest to researchers in the field.

829. *Biotechnology Journal (Online).* [ISSN: 1860-7314] 2006. m. GBP 2270. Ed(s): Alois Jungbauer, Sang Yup Lee. Wiley - V C H Verlag GmbH & Co. KGaA, Postfach 101161, Weinheim, 69451, Germany; service@wiley-vch.de; http://www.wiley-vch.de. Refereed. *Aud.:* Ac, Sa.

Published in liaison with the Asian Federation of Biotechnology, the European Biosafety Association, and the European Society of Biochemical Engineering Sciences, this online-only (as of 2014) journal publishes mostly "special" or "focus" issues around a particular topic or conference, with a few regular issues. The focus issues each have different expert editors who write an editorial on the topic. The journal is comprehensive in scope, covering subjects such as systems biotechnology, nanobiotechnology, plant/agricultural/environmental/industrial biotechnology, medical biotechnology, gene therapy, regenerative medicine, ethics and biosafety. Published papers can include research articles, rapid communications, technical reports, reviews, biotech methods, perspectives, commentary, and editorials. The journal web site links to relevant conferences and other Wiley journals. Of interest primarily to researchers and other professionals in the field.

830. *Briefings in Bioinformatics.* [ISSN: 1477-4054] 2000. bi-m. EUR 748. Ed(s): Martin Bishop. Oxford University Press, Great Clarendon St, Oxford, OX2 6DP, United Kingdom; onlinequeries.uk@oup.com; http://global.oup.com. Adv. Sample. Refereed. Reprint: PSC. *Indexed:* A01, A22, B01, C45, E01. *Bk. rev.:* Number and length vary. *Aud.:* Ac, Sa.

This online-only journal (as of January 2018) publishes reviews and articles in the field of bioinformatics, in which biological information is processed and analyzed using computer algorithms. Most bioinformatics journals only contain original research articles of use to researchers in the bioinformatics field who are developing new tools and programs. This journal claims to be unique in providing practical help and advice for the non-bioinformatics specialist who may be using or teaching the tools or databases but does not develop them. As a result, the papers can vary in scope and depth. Articles can even be on such topics as bioinformatics education. There are occasional special issues on one topic or inspired by a conference. Issues can also contain some book or software/database reviews. A sister journal, *Briefings in Functional Genomics,* is likely to also be of interest to researchers in this area.

831. *Critical Reviews in Biotechnology.* [ISSN: 0738-8551] 1983. q. GBP 2454 (print & online eds.)). Ed(s): Inge Russell, Graham Stewart. Taylor & Francis Inc., 530 Walnut St, Ste 850, Philadelphia, PA 19106; support@tandfonline.com; http://www.tandfonline.com. Adv. Sample. Refereed. Reprint: PSC. *Indexed:* A01, A22, Agr, C45, E01. *Aud.:* Ac, Sa.

This journal is a forum for critical evaluation of recent publication in all areas of biotechnology from agricultural and industrial to genomics and medical biotechnology. It publishes only review articles to help scientists keep up on the latest methodologies, findings, and ideas. This journal would be of interest to research scientists in academic and industrial settings.

832. *Current Opinion in Biotechnology.* [ISSN: 0958-1669] 1990. bi-m. EUR 4520. Ed(s): Jan van der Meer, Greg Stephanopoulos. Elsevier Ltd., Current Opinion Journals, The Blvd, Langford Ln, Kidlington, OX5 1GB, United Kingdom; JournalsCustomerServiceEMEA@elsevier.com; http://www.current-opinion.com. Illus., adv. Sample. Refereed. Vol. ends: No. 12. *Indexed:* A01, A22, C45, E01, S25. *Aud.:* Ac, Sa.

The Current Opinion series of journals is geared toward helping researchers keep up to date with the large amount of information published in their fields by providing authoritative, expert opinion on recent advances and annotations of select recently published original papers. *Current Opinion in Biotechnology* covers all areas of biotechnology by dividing the subject into ten topics, each of which is reviewed once a year. Each of the six issues per year reviews one or two of these topics, and an expert section editor is assigned to each: analytical biotechnology; plant biotechnology; food biotechnology; energy biotechnology; environmental biotechnology; nanobiotechnology; systems biology; tissue, cell, and pathway engineering; chemical biotechnology; and pharmaceutical biotechnology. The journal is geared toward scientists and focuses on scientific advances rather than business or regulatory issues. Articles would be excellent for classroom use to introduce advanced students to important topics.

833. *Drug Discovery Today.* Incorporates (in Dec.2004): *Drug Discovery Today. Targets;* Which was formerly (2002-Feb.2004): *Targets;* Incorporates (in Nov.2004): *Drug Discovery Today. Biosilico;* Which was formerly (2003-Mar.2004): *Biosilico.* [ISSN: 1359-6446] 1996. m. EUR 6036. Ed(s): Steve L Carney. Elsevier Ltd., Trends Journals, 32 Jamestown Rd, London, NW1 7BY, United Kingdom; JournalsCustomerServiceEMEA@elsevier.com; http://www.elsevier.com. Sample. Refereed. *Indexed:* A01, A22. *Aud.:* Ac, Sa.

Similar to Elsevier's Trends series, this journal publishes reviews for scientists to help them maintain currency in their research and technological areas and also to address commercial and regulatory issues that play a part in planning research and development. The short front section contains editorials on current topics and perspectives pieces. The majority of the journal is the "Reviews" section, with keynote, foundation, and short reviews. Keynotes cover broad topics, foundation reviews are written for beginners and are an introduction to fundamental principles, and short reviews cover fast moving research topics in three categories: "Gene to Screen," "Informatics," and "Postscreen." The related *Drug Discovery Today* online-only journal collection contains two themed review journals published quarterly: *Drug Discovery Today: Disease Models* and *Drug Discovery Today: Technologies.* Besides the scholarly journals, *Drug Discovery Today* is also available as a digital magazine at the drugdiscoverytoday.com web site. The site functions as a portal and, besides the journal, it also features news about the biotechnology industry in the United Kingdom and upcoming biotechnology conferences. The site doesn't seem to be a priority for Elsevier, however, since other kinds of content linked from the portal, such as podcasts, webinars, and features, have not been updated from 2009-2012. Some of the journal articles are available as free downloads from the site, but much of the review content from *Drug Discovery Today* is not, and readers are pointed back to Elsevier's Science Direct platform. Geared toward both a research and industry audience, particularly in the United Kingdom. URL: http://drugdiscoverytoday.com

834. ***Genome Biology (Online).*** Formerly (until 2001): *GenomeBiology.com (Online).* [ISSN: 1474-760X] 2000. . Free. Ed(s): Barbara Cheifet. BioMed Central Ltd., Floor 6, 236 Gray's Inn Rd, London, WC1X 8HB, United Kingdom; info@biomedcentral.com; https://www.biomedcentral.com. Sample. Refereed. *Indexed:* C45. *Aud.:* Ac, Sa.

BioMed Central (BMC), which is part of Springer Nature, publishes this online-only journal, which is open access. It is a forum for all areas of biology and biomedicine informed by genomic and post-genomic research: molecular, cellular, organismal, and population biology, as well as clinical applications. It is a highly ranked and more selective journal that publishes "outstanding" research in these areas. Articles that are rejected may be recommended for publication in lesser ranked BMC journals such as *BMC Genomics*. Article types include original research, methods, software, opinions, reviews, and commentaries on the field. Because the journal is online-only, articles in *Genome Biology* are published as soon as they are available. There are no issues of the journal, and a volume is simply all of the articles from a particular year of publication, however special issues are created out of groups of articles on a similar topic. BMC discontinued its web subject portals but does publish tweets and a blog covering highlights from the whole BMC series of journals, and these are highlighted on the web site of this journal.

Genome Research. See Biology/Genetics section.

835. ***Human Gene Therapy.*** [ISSN: 1043-0342] 1990. 22x/yr. USD 11027. Ed(s): Terence R Flotte. Mary Ann Liebert, Inc. Publishers, 140 Huguenot St, 3rd Fl, New Rochelle, NY 10801; info@liebertpub.com; http://www.liebertpub.com. Adv. Sample. Refereed. Vol. ends: Dec. Reprint: PSC. *Indexed:* A01, A22, E01. *Aud.:* Ac, Sa.

Like another journal listed in this section, *Molecular Therapy*, this journal publishes peer-reviewed scientific papers on all aspects of gene therapy, which involves the correction of diseases by replacing abnormal genes with normal ones. All stages of gene therapy research are covered, from preclinical laboratory investigations to clinical trials. It is the official journal of several European countries' gene therapy societies. Besides the research articles, there are sometimes reviews, editorials, and commentaries, particularly in special focus issues. One recent special issue was on Chinese gene and cell therapy research. The journal has instant online publishing of all manuscripts in unedited format within 72 hours of peer review and acceptance. Later, copy editing and proofreading will yield a final archived version of the paper. Two sister journals, the bimonthly *Human Gene Therapy Methods* and quarterly *Human Gene Therapy Clinical Development* focus on technological advances and clinical trials data relevant to regulatory review respectively. Of interest to scientific researchers or clinicians in this area.

836. ***Journal of Biotechnology.*** [ISSN: 0168-1656] 1984. 24x/yr. EUR 8059. Ed(s): A Puehler. Elsevier BV, Radarweg 29, Amsterdam, 1043 NX, Netherlands; info@elsevier.com; https://www.elsevier.com. Adv. Refereed. Microform: PQC. *Indexed:* A01, A22, Agr, C45. *Aud.:* Ac, Sa.

This multidisciplinary journal is divided into sections that cover all aspects of biotechnology: biochemistry and physiology; food and agricultural biotechnology; genomics; molecular biology and bioinformatics; medical biotechnology; industrial processes; and bioprocess engineering. This title provides for rapid publication of peer-reviewed research articles, both long and short. It particularly seeks to publish interdisciplinary articles that are not suitable for publication in a journal for a more specific discipline. There are also quite frequent "whole genome announcement" papers that report the complete sequencing of the genome of a bacterium used in biotechnology. The focus is on primary research articles, rather than reviews or other types of articles. Of interest to researchers in many areas of biotechnology.

837. ***Metabolic Engineering.*** [ISSN: 1096-7176] 1999. bi-m. EUR 1393. Ed(s): Greg N Stephanopoulos. Academic Press, 225 Wyman St, Waltham, MA 02144; JournalCustomerService-usa@elsevier.com; http://store.elsevier.com/Academic-Press/IMP_5/. Adv. Refereed. *Indexed:* A01, A22, E01. *Aud.:* Ac, Sa.

Metabolic engineering involves the alteration or manipulation of the metabolic pathways of organisms (often by genetic engineering) for commercial objectives, to produce chemicals or fuels for environmental, agricultural, or medical purposes. The research in this area is interdisciplinary, drawing on ideas and techniques from molecular biology, physiology, and biochemistry, as well as modeling and data analysis from the fields of engineering, bioinformatics, and computational biology. This journal publishes original peer-reviewed research and reviews, and would be useful for research scientists.

838. ***Molecular Therapy.*** [ISSN: 1525-0016] 2000. m. USD 2801. Cell Press, 50 Hampshire St, 5th Flr, Cambridge, MA 02139; feedback@cell.com; http://www.cell.com. Adv. Sample. Refereed. *Indexed:* A01, A22, E01. *Aud.:* Ac, Sa.

The official publication of the American Society for Gene and Cell Therapy, this journal publishes papers on all aspects of gene, peptide, protein, oligonucleotide, and cell-based therapeutics research for human disease. Primary research articles can report basic or preclinical studies, translational research, or the results of clinical research. Besides these papers, each issue may also contain review articles, commentaries, or a meeting report. There are three sister journals with a more targeted audience: *Molecular Therapy: Nucleic Acids*; *Molecular Therapy: Methods & Clinical Development*; and *Molecular Therapy: Oncolytics*. All of these journals would be of interest to scientists or clinicians working in this field.

839. ***Nanomedicine.*** [ISSN: 1743-5889] 2006. 24x/yr. GBP 2785 (print & online eds.)). Ed(s): Bethany Small, Jon Wilkinson. Future Medicine Ltd., Unitec House, 2 Albert Pl, London, N3 1QB, United Kingdom; info@futuremedicine.com; http://www.futuremedicine.com/. Adv. Sample. Refereed. Circ: 14100. *Indexed:* BRI. *Aud.:* Ac, Sa.

This emerging field grew out of nanotechnology, and this journal "addresses the important challenges and advances in medical nanoscale-structured material and devices, biotechnology devices and molecular machine systems and nanorobotics." Nanomedicine offers new opportunities for novel approaches to the prevention and cure of diseases. It is still in its infancy, and this journal aims to be a tool to shape this exciting field. The journal covers principles of nanomedicine plus basic research, nanotechnological advances, preclinical testing and applications for nanomedical tools, ethical, regulatory, and legal issues and commercialization. Each issue might contain editorials, short communications, reviews, or research articles, with occasional special focus issues. Of interest to academic, industrial, and clinical researchers as well as regulatory authorities.

840. ***Nature Biotechnology.*** Formerly (until 1996): *Bio-Technology.* [ISSN: 1087-0156] 1983. m. EUR 6648. Ed(s): Andrew Marshall. Nature Publishing Group, 75 Varick St, 9th Fl, New York, NY 10013; nature@natureny.com; http://www.nature.com. Illus., adv. Sample. Refereed. Microform: PQC. *Indexed:* A01, A22, Agr, BRI, C45. *Aud.:* Ga, Ac, Sa.

If a librarian wants to subscribe to only one journal in the field of biotechnology, this should be it, because it has something for everyone. This journal has one of the highest impact factors among biotechnology journals ranked by Clarivate Analytics, and it covers both the scientific and business aspects of the field. The scope of the journal includes all of biotechnology from the agricultural and environmental to the biomedical. The beginning section of the journal is devoted to international news from business and research communities, and essays, editorials, and articles covering the current political, ethical, legal, and societal issues surrounding biotechnology and new products. Regular columns include the "Bioentrepreneur" (with advice on building a business), a "Patents" section with advice and lists of recent patent applications, a "Data Page" covering drug approvals and stock prices, and "News and Views." There is also a section on careers and a "People" section at the end that announces new appointments or retirements of CEOs and other leaders at biotechnology companies. The rest of the journal contains scientific articles, both longer and shorter communications. The web site has been streamlined from its past busy portal look and is now designed simply to highlight recent scientific and news articles from the latest issue. There are feeds from Nature Jobs and Nature Events and also a podcast series, but some past resources like a blog or multimedia content have been discontinued. While the research articles and some other sections of the journal will be of most use to scientific academic and special libraries, the news and business content will be valuable for both business and public libraries.

841. ***Nature Reviews. Drug Discovery.*** [ISSN: 1474-1776] 2002. m. EUR 6648. Ed(s): Peter Kirkpatrick. Nature Publishing Group, The MacMillan Bldg, 4 Crinan St, London, N1 9XW, United Kingdom; NatureReviews@nature.com; https://www.nature.com. Adv. Sample. Refereed. *Indexed:* A01, A22. *Aud.:* Ga, Ac, Sa.

This journal is part of the Nature Reviews series of journals that are geared toward keeping researchers informed and up to date. The scope of the journal is the entire field of drug discovery and development including industry trends, patent law, and drug approvals. There are four main sections. There is usually one article published in each issue for the "Comment" section, which covers broader issues: opinions, implications of science on society, new developments, future directions, and business outlooks. This is followed by a "News and Analysis" section, which contains current stories on the scientific or business aspects of drug discovery, and information on patents and the latest drugs. Interviews with key people might also be included. A "Research Highlights" section provides short updates on recently published research papers. Finally, a "Reviews" section contains commissioned review articles by leading researchers in their field. The journal is geared toward scientists in the field but also non-scientists and business people working in the pharmaceutical industry.

842. ***New Biotechnology.*** Former titles (until 2008): *Biomolecular Engineering;* (until 1999): *Genetic Analysis: Biomolecular Engineering - Techniques and Applications;* (until 1990): *Genetic Analysis Techniques.* [ISSN: 1871-6784] 1983. 6x/yr. EUR 1331. Ed(s): Mike L Taussig. Elsevier BV, Radarweg 29, Amsterdam, 1043 NX, Netherlands; info@elsevier.com; https://www.elsevier.com/. Refereed. Microform: PQC. *Indexed:* A01, A22, Agr, C45. *Aud.:* Ac, Sa.

This is the official journal of the European Federation of Biotechnology, and it publishes papers on the entire spectrum of biotechnology subject areas from health to food and agriculture to genomics to bioremediation to biofuels. Naturally, it has a European focus, but it is international. A recent special issue on bioeconomy covered all parts of the world including Asia, Latin America, and Canada. It claims to cover the science and the political, business, and financial issues involved in the industry, including safety, regulations, and ethics. Many recent issues are solely made up of original scientific research articles, however, so there is not regular coverage of industry or societal issues. Primarily of interest to researchers in the field.

843. ***Plant Biotechnology Journal (Online).*** [ISSN: 1467-7652] 2003. 9x/yr. Free. Ed(s): Henry Daniell. Wiley-Blackwell Publishing Ltd., The Atrium, Southern Gate, Chichester, PO19 8QG, United Kingdom; cs-journals@wiley.com; http://onlinelibrary.wiley.com. Adv. Refereed. *Aud.:* Ac, Sa.

This online-only, open-access journal is published in association with two societies, the Society for Experimental Biology and the Association of Applied Biologists. It publishes molecular plant sciences with a strong focus on application rather than model plants used mostly in laboratories. Practical applications of plant studies can be found in such wide-ranging fields as agriculture, biodiversity, biomaterials, bioremediation, conservation, food sciences, forestry, pharmaceuticals, and medicine. A large number of the articles are devoted to genomics, functional genomics, and transgenic technologies. There are primary, peer-reviewed research articles, reviews, commentary, and special issues devoted to a single topic such as molecular farming. Of interest to researchers in the field.

Scientific American. See Science and Technology/General section.

844. ***Stem Cells and Development.*** Former titles (until 2004): *Journal of Hematotherapy & Stem Cell Research;* (until 1999): *Journal of Hematotherapy.* [ISSN: 1547-3287] 1992. s-m. USD 4251. Ed(s): Graham C Parker. Mary Ann Liebert, Inc. Publishers, 140 Huguenot St, 3rd Fl, New Rochelle, NY 10801; info@liebertpub.com; http://www.liebertpub.com. Adv. Sample. Refereed. Reprint: PSC. *Indexed:* A01, A22, C45, E01. *Aud.:* Ac, Sa.

This journal is the official publication of the British Society for Gene and Cell Therapy. It is a forum for the publication of original, peer-reviewed research articles on human or animal stem cell research and its potential therapeutic applications, and it claims to provide "critical and even controversial" coverage of emerging findings. Basic, clinical, and translational research are included. Original research articles seem to take up most issues, but the journal also publishes comprehensive reviews, cutting-edge communications, and technology reports. Like other Mary Ann Liebert journals, instant online access is provided to peer-reviewed articles 72 hours after their acceptance for publication and before final copy editing. This journal would be of interest to research scientists in the field.

845. ***Stem Cells (Durham): the international journal of cell differentiation and proliferation.*** Formerly (until 1993): *International Journal of Cell Cloning.* [ISSN: 1066-5099] 1983. m. GBP 679. Ed(s): Jan A Nolta, Ann Murphy. AlphaMed Press, Inc., 318 Blackwell St, Ste 260, Durham, NC 27701; http://www.alphamedpress.org/. Adv. Sample. Refereed. Circ: 3000. Reprint: PSC. *Indexed:* A22. *Aud.:* Ac, Sa.

Stem Cells (not to be confused with Hindawi's *Stem Cells International*) is one of the leading and oldest journals in this specialty subject area and one of only three journals published by AlphaMed Press. It is co-published by Wiley-Blackwell and available on the Wiley platform. The journal covers all aspects of stem cell research from basic laboratory investigations to the translation of findings to clinical care. Embryonic stem cells, adult tissue-specific stem cells, cancer stem cells, regenerative medicine, the stem cell niche, technology development, proteomics, and genomics of stem cells and translational and clinical research are the separate subsections of many issues. Most of the articles are original research reports, but there are occasional concise reviews of topics in any of these sections. A sister journal on the AlphaMed Press platform, *Stem Cells Translational Medicine*, publishes original research and reviews focused more on the clinical aspects of stem cells including clinical trial and regulatory information. A separate Stem Cells Portal web site claims to be a hub for the two journals, however it does not directly link into either journal's issues. It does link to some highlighted articles from both of these journals and includes a round-up of news articles, press releases, headlines, links to clinical trial information, and reviews of relevant articles published in other journals. There is a journal club on the site where reviews of recent articles are published with proposed discussion points, and users must register and login to make comments. It is still unclear how much of a community is generated at this portal, however, since there are almost no comments. There are more comments on the journal's Facebook page, which is where most journals are now creating community.

846. ***Tissue Engineering. Parts A, B and C.*** Supersedes in part (in 2008): *Tissue Engineering.* [ISSN: 2152-4947] 1995. 42x/yr. USD 9320. Ed(s): Antonios G Mikos, John A Jansen. Mary Ann Liebert, Inc. Publishers, 140 Huguenot St, 3rd Fl, New Rochelle, NY 10801; info@liebertpub.com; http://www.liebertpub.com. Adv. Sample. Refereed. Reprint: PSC. *Aud.:* Ac, Sa.

This is the official journal of the Tissue Engineering and Regenerative Medicine International Society. The goal of this emerging field is eventually to be able to regenerate tissues or create new tissues and artificial organs using biological cells and biomaterials along with biotechnology techniques. Such current topics of research as nanobiotechnology, gene therapy, and stem cells are included. Much of this is still in the experimental rather than the clinical stage, but the field is growing by leaps and bounds. The journal is in three parts. Part A is the flagship journal, publishing peer-reviewed, hypothesis-driven research articles. Part B comes out six times a year and publishes reviews that give a broader and summarized view of the tissue engineering field, new developments, and new areas of research. Part C is monthly and presents methods and protocols that will be adapted by the tissue engineering community. As mentioned for other journals from this publisher, instant access is provided to articles from all three parts of the journal within 72 hours of their acceptance for publication and before final copy editing. Research scientists in the field would be interested in all three parts of the journal.

847. *Trends in Biotechnology.* [ISSN: 0167-7799] 1983. m. EUR 2942. Ed(s): Matthew Pavlovich. Elsevier Ltd., Trends Journals, The Blvd, Langford Ln, Kidlington, Oxford, OX5 1GB, United Kingdom; JournalsCustomerServiceEMEA@elsevier.com; http://www.elsevier.com. Illus., adv. Sample. Refereed. Vol. ends: No. 19. *Indexed:* A01, A22, Agr, C45. *Aud.:* Ac, Sa.

Part of the Trends journal series from Elsevier's Cell Press, this journal aims to highlight new developments in biotechnology by publishing many different types of articles to update readers on scientific findings and their agricultural, environmental, or biomedical impact on the world. The core of the journal is review articles that summarize and discuss recent research in all areas of biotechnology. "Opinions" articles present a personal viewpoint on a research topic rather than a balanced review. There are also short articles written for a broader audience, including the "Science and Society" articles, written in a journalistic style on biotechnological issues relevant to policy and society, and the "Forum" articles, which raise awareness about a new development in the field. "Spotlights" articles update readers about one or two recent important articles, and "Scientific Life" articles discuss issues relevant to the scientific community such as career paths, publishing, and ethics. This journal could have a varied readership, from scientific researchers to students newer to the field who could benefit from the more journalistic articles. Articles from the journal would be very useful for classroom teaching. Like other Cell Press journals, this journal is published on two separate platforms. The version on Elsevier's ScienceDirect points users directly to volumes and issues and is likely the one to which libraries will link. The version on the Cell Press platform is slightly more portal-like and, besides the journal issues, points to articles from other Trends journals, a Cell Press blog, podcast, and career network.

■ BIRDS

See also Environment and Conservation; and Pets sections.

Kathryn Johns-Masten, Associate Librarian, Penfield Library, SUNY Oswego, Oswego, NY 13126; kathryn.johnsmasten@oswego.edu

Introduction

"Birds have wings; they're free; they can fly where they want when they want, they have the kind of mobility people envy."

—Roger Tory Peterson

The titles in this section will appeal to amateur birders, students of ornithology, researchers, and professional ornithologists. They encompass a wide range of geographic areas. Some focus on a specific area; others focus on specific types of birds—for example, waterbirds or predators. The titles appropriate for a general audience, or for those new to birding, provide color photographs and articles from ornithologists as well as fellow amateur birders. The professional academic journals contain in-depth articles that include scientific studies and field research.

Web sites provide birders with the ability to interact with each other, submit bird counts, listen to bird songs, and communicate with researchers and professional ornithologists. The majority of the journals are available online and provide additional features such as supplemental information, sightings, photographs, and video and sound files.

These print and online publications were selected based on their appeal to a range of readers, from amateur to professional.

Basic Periodicals

Hs: *Bird Watcher's Digest, BirdWatching, Living Bird;* Ga: *Bird Watcher's Digest, Birding, BirdWatching, Living Bird;* Ac: *British Birds, Emu, Journal of Avian Biology, North American Birds, Wilson Journal of Ornithology.*

Basic Abstracts and Indexes

Biological Abstracts.

848. *The Auk: ornithological advances.* Supersedes (in 1884): *Nuttall Ornithological Club. Bulletin;* Which was formerly (until 1976): *Nuttall Ornithological Club. Quarterly Bulletin.* [ISSN: 0004-8038] 1884. q. Ed(s): Mark E. Hauber. Central Ornithology Publication Office, 151 Petaluma Blvd. S., Ste. 301, Petaluma, CA 94952-5183; aoucospubs@gmail.com; http://www.aoucospubs.org/. Illus., index, adv. Refereed. Vol. ends: Oct (No. 4). Microform: IDC; PQC. *Indexed:* A01, A22, BRI, C45, E01, MLA-IB. *Bk. rev.:* 10, 500 words. *Aud.:* Ac, Sa.

The Auk is an international, peer-reviewed journal that publishes original research and scholarship that advances the fundamental scientific knowledge of bird species, both living and extinct; and broad biological concepts through studies of bird species. Articles often introduce or employ innovative empirical and theoretical approaches and analyses. By impact factor, this title continues to be ranked among the top peer-reviewed journals in the field of ornithology. The online format provides a weekly posting of articles, while the print format is published quarterly. Recommended for academic and special libraries that support ornithology and ecology programs.

849. *Bird Conservation International.* [ISSN: 0959-2709] 1991. q. GBP 441. Ed(s): Phil Atkinson. Cambridge University Press, University Printing House, Shaftesbury Rd, Cambridge, CB2 8BS, United Kingdom; journals@cambridge.org; https://www.cambridge.org/. Illus., adv. Sample. Refereed. Reprint: PSC. *Indexed:* A22, C45, E01. *Aud.:* Ac, Sa.

This journal publishes original peer-reviewed papers and reviews, including targeted articles and recommendations of leading experts. It seeks to promote worldwide research and conservation action to ensure the protection of bird life and fragile habitats they depend upon. It provides international up-to-date coverage of all aspects of the conservation of birds and their ecosystems. In addition, it uses birds to illustrate wider issues of biodiversity, conservation, and sustainable resource use. Recommended for academic and special libraries that support ornithology studies.

850. *Bird Study: the science of pure and applied ornithology.* Incorporates (in 1963): *Bird Migration;* Which was formerly (1934-1954): *British Trust for Ornithology. Bulletin.* [ISSN: 0006-3657] 1954. 4x/yr. USD 424 (print & online eds.)). Ed(s): I R Hartley. Taylor & Francis, 2, 3 & 4 Park Sq, Milton Park, Abingdon, OX14 4RN, United Kingdom; subscriptions@tandf.co.uk; https://www.tandfonline.com. Illus., index, adv. Refereed. Vol. ends: No. 3. Microform: PQC. Reprint: PSC. *Indexed:* A22, C45, E01. *Bk. rev.:* 1, 50 words. *Aud.:* Ac, Sa.

This journal from the British Trust for Ornithology publishes high-quality, original research papers on field ornithology, especially related to evidence-based bird conservation. It especially covers patterns of distribution and abundance, movements, and habitat preferences; developing field census methods; and ringing and other techniques for marking and tracking. The journal focuses on birds in the Western Palearctic, which includes Europe, North Africa, and the Middle East, although research on their biology outside of the Western Palearctic is accepted. In addition, the journal includes scientific reviews, articles covering general ornithological issues, and short articles that make scientific criticisms of papers published recently in the journal. Recommended for the professional and for serious students of bird life.

851. *Bird Watcher's Digest.* [ISSN: 0164-3037] 1978. bi-m. USD 19.99 combined subscription (print & online eds.); USD 4.99 newsstand/cover). Pardson, Inc., 149 Acme St, PO Box 110, Marietta, OH 45750. Illus., adv. Vol. ends: Jul/Aug. Microform: PQC. *Bk. rev.:* 8, 50 words. *Aud.:* Hs, Ga.

Bird Watcher's Digest is a popular magazine that offers articles for the amateur birder written by ornithologists. Regular columns cover attracting birds, bird behavior, backyard birdwatching, and helpful hints for new birders. Other regular features include letters from readers, gardening tips, and wonderful color photographs. This magazine covers North American species and birding hotspots in North America and beyond. The field-guide size of this publication makes it convenient to carry outdoors, and this title is available in print and online formats. Recommended for general audiences.

852. *Birding.* [ISSN: 0161-1836] 1969. bi-m. Free to members. Ed(s): Ted Floyd. American Birding Association, Inc., 1618 W Colorado Ave, Colorado Springs, CO 80904; members@aba.org; http://www.aba.org. Illus., index, adv. Vol. ends: Dec (No. 6). *Bk. rev.:* 3, 200 words. *Aud.:* Ga, Ac.

This is the magazine of the American Birding Association, with a mission to educate the general public in the appreciation of birds and their relationship to the environment. It focuses on North American and foreign birdfinding, bird conservation, behavior, field identification techniques, and birder education. In addition, it includes reviews of books, media, and equipment. Additional online content is available, including sightings, supplemental information for articles, bird songs, and links to books reviewed in issues. Recommended for public and academic libraries.

853. ***BirdWatching.*** Formerly (until 2011): *Birder's World.* [ISSN: 2158-3838] 1987. bi-m. USD 26.95 domestic; USD 32.95 Canada; USD 34.95 elsewhere. Ed(s): Matt Mendenhall, Chuck Hagner. Madavor Media, Llc., 85 Quincy Ave, Ste 2, Quincy, MA 02169; customerservice@madavor.com; http://www.madavor.com. Illus., adv. *Indexed:* A01, BRI. *Bk. rev.:* Number and length vary. *Aud.:* Hs, Ga.

For nearly 30 years, *BirdWatching* has been one of North America's top magazines about wild birds and birding. The magazine is for enthusiasts who are new to birding as well as to experienced birders, and offers readers superb color photography. It contains feeding and attracting tips, reviews of books and new products, conservation news, useful info about the best birding locations in North America, and articles by the well-known ornithologists. In addition, feature articles and regular columns cover identification tips, photography pointers, worldwide bird movement, and travel tips for birders. The web site contains a blog, photo galleries, a birding basics section, and a "hotspots near you" section. Highly recommended for all birders.

854. ***British Birds.*** [ISSN: 0007-0335] 1907. m. GBP 99 (Individuals, GBP 53). Ed(s): Dr. Roger Riddington. B B 2000 Ltd., 4 Harlequin Gardens, St Leonards on Sea, TN37 7PF, United Kingdom; subscriptions@britishbirds.co.uk. Illus., index, adv. Sample. Refereed. Vol. ends: Dec. *Indexed:* A22, MLA-IB. *Bk. rev.:* 2, 200 words. *Aud.:* Ac.

British Birds is considered by many to be "*the* journal of record in Britain," and publishes original research from the Western Palearctic, which includes Europe, North Africa, and the Middle East. The journal publishes articles on a wide variety of topics, including behavior, conservation, distribution, identification, status, and taxonomy. Regular features include book reviews, news and comments, recent reports of rarities, and information on equipment and travel for birders. In addition, it publishes annual reports of the Rarities Committee and the Rare Breeding Birds Panel. The web site provides search for articles from 1907 to 2011. Contributors include professionals and knowledgeable amateurs, and articles are written for all levels of birdwatcher.

855. ***The Condor: ornithological applications.*** Formerly (until 1900): *Cooper Ornithological Club. Bulletin.* [ISSN: 0010-5422] 1899. q. Ed(s): Philip C Stouffer. Central Ornithology Publication Office, 151 Petaluma Blvd. S., Ste. 301, Petaluma, CA 94952-5183; aoucospubs@gmail.com; http://www.aoucospubs.org/. Illus., index, adv. Refereed. Circ: 1712. Vol. ends: Nov. Microform: PQC. *Indexed:* A01, A22, BRI, C45, E01. *Bk. rev.:* 1, 2,000 words. *Aud.:* Ac, Sa.

The Condor is an international, peer-reviewed scientific journal that publishes original research, syntheses, and assessments that address ornithological applications. It focuses on the application of scientific theory and methods to the conservation, management, and ecology of birds; and it advocates for the application of ornithological knowledge to conservation and management policy and other issues of importance to society. It is considered the premier journal in avian conservation and applied work on birds. The online format provides a weekly posting of articles, while the print format is published quarterly. Recommended for libraries that serve research ornithologists and practitioners.

856. ***Emu: austral ornithology.*** [ISSN: 0158-4197] 1901. q. GBP 479 (print & online eds.)). Ed(s): Kate Buchanan. Taylor & Francis Australasia, Level 2, 11 Queens Rd, Melbourne, VIC 3004, Australia; enquiries@tandf.com.au; http://www.tandfonline.com/. Illus., index, adv. Sample. Refereed. Vol. ends: Dec. Reprint: PSC. *Indexed:* A01, A22, Agr, C45, E01. *Bk. rev.:* 2, 1,000 words. *Aud.:* Ac, Sa.

Emu publishes original high-quality papers and reviews in all areas of ornithology, and is considered the premier journal for ornithological research in the Southern Hemisphere and the adjacent tropics. While scholarly articles are the main feature, book reviews are also included. Topics range from the effects of climate change on birds to DNA analysis. Students and researchers interested in the biology and management of birds will find this title useful. The variety of species covered by this geographic area makes it a recommended title for research libraries that serve ornithologists.

857. ***Ibis: the international journal of avian science.*** [ISSN: 0019-1019] 1859. q. GBP 639. Ed(s): Paul F Donald. Wiley-Blackwell Publishing Ltd., The Atrium, Southern Gate, Chichester, PO19 8QG, United Kingdom; cs-journals@wiley.com; http://onlinelibrary.wiley.com/. Illus., index, adv. Sample. Refereed. Vol. ends: Oct. Reprint: PSC. *Indexed:* A22, Agr, BRI, C45, E01, MLA-IB. *Bk. rev.:* 25, 300 words. *Aud.:* Ac, Sa.

Ibis is a peer-reviewed journal that publishes original papers, reviews, and short communications. The journal is at the forefront of research activity in ornithology, with an emphasis on conservation, ecology, ethology, taxonomy, and the systematics of birds. Union conference proceedings are occasionally published as supplements to *Ibis*. Online subscribers are able to view a wide range of supplementary material hosted online for many *Ibis* papers, including data and supporting research, and video and sound files. Recommended for research and academic libraries that support ornithological research.

858. ***Journal of Avian Biology (Online).*** [ISSN: 1600-048X] 1970. bi-m. GBP 412. Ed(s): Thomas Allerstam, Jan-Ake Nilsson. Wiley-Blackwell Publishing Ltd., The Atrium, Southern Gate, Chichester, PO19 8QG, United Kingdom; cs-journals@wiley.com; http://onlinelibrary.wiley.com. Refereed. *Aud.:* Ac, Sa.

The *Journal of Avian Biology* publishes empirical and theoretical research in all areas of ornithology, with an emphasis on behavioral ecology, evolution, and conservation. In addition to peer-reviewed research articles, the journal publishes reviews, letters, communications, and short point-of-view papers. Topics include habitat, conservation, distribution, migration, ecology, and behavior of birds. Recommended for academic and research libraries that support ornithological research.

859. ***Journal of Field Ornithology.*** Former titles (until 1980): *Bird-Banding;* (until 1930): *Northeastern Bird-Banding Association. Bulletin.* [ISSN: 0273-8570] 1930. q. GBP 362. Ed(s): Gary Ritchison. Wiley-Blackwell Publishing, Inc., 350 Main St, Malden, MA 02148; http://onlinelibrary.wiley.com. Illus., index, adv. Sample. Refereed. Vol. ends: No. 4. Microform: PQC. Reprint: PSC. *Indexed:* A22, Agr, BRI, C45, E01. *Bk. rev.:* 4, 200 words. *Aud.:* Ac, Sa.

The journal of the Association of Field Ornithologists publishes original articles with a focus on the descriptive or experimental study of birds in their natural habitats. A specific focus is placed on field studies conducted in the Neotropics and those involving participation by nonprofessional ornithologists. Bird banding, conservation, habitat, and fieldwork are emphasized. Technology used to perform or aid in the study of birds is discussed in detail, such as solar-powered transmitters and audio-video systems. Studies that involve participation by amateur ornithologists in research are encouraged. Recommended for academic and research collections.

860. ***Journal of Ornithology.*** Formerly (until 2004): *Journal fuer Ornithologie;* Which incorporated (1851-1858): *Naumannia.* [ISSN: 2193-7192] 1853. q. EUR 1003 (print & online eds.)). Ed(s): Franz Bairlein. Springer, Tiergartenstr 17, Heidelberg, 69121, Germany; orders-hd-individuals@springer.com; https://www.springer.com. Illus., adv. Refereed. Reprint: PSC. *Indexed:* A01, A22, BRI, C45, E01, MLA-IB. *Aud.:* Ac, Sa.

The *Journal of Ornithology* has been published for over 150 years. It contains original papers, reviews, technical notes, and commentaries that cover all aspects of ornithology. The editorial board is international, consisting of subject editors from around the world. Topics include behavior, ecology, environment, and conservation of birds. Recommended for institutions that support advanced ornithological research.

861. *The Journal of Raptor Research.* Former titles (until 1987): *Raptor Research;* (until 1972): *Raptor Research News.* [ISSN: 0892-1016] 1967. q. Free to members. Raptor Research Foundation, Inc., c/o Cheryl Dykstra Editor-in-Chief, Raptor Environmental, West Chester, OH 45069; http://www.raptorresearchfoundation.org/. Illus., index, adv. Sample. Refereed. Vol. ends: No. 4. *Indexed:* A01, A22, C45. *Bk. rev.:* 3, 800 words. *Aud.:* Ac, Sa.

The Journal of Raptor Research is an international scientific journal that publishes original peer-reviewed research reports and review articles focused on all aspects of predatory birds throughout the world. Features include book reviews, letters, short communications, and articles with extensive references. Research includes raptor ecology, behavior, life history, conservation, and techniques. Membership in the Raptor Research Foundation includes receiving the newsletter *Wingspan.* Recommended for academic and research libraries.

862. *Living Bird.* Former titles (until 1991): *Living Bird Quarterly;* (until 1982): *The Living Bird.* [ISSN: 1059-521X] 1962. q. USD 39 (print or online ed.)). Ed(s): Tim Gallagher. Cornell University, Laboratory of Ornithology, 159 Sapsucker Woods Rd, Ithaca, NY 14850; cornellbirds@cornell.edu; http://www.allaboutbirds.org. Illus., adv. *Indexed:* A22. *Bk. rev.:* Number and length vary. *Aud.:* Hs, Ga, Ac.

Living Bird is published by the Cornell Laboratory of Ornithology and contains articles on all aspects of bird life, including bird watching, behavior, and environmental concerns. It reviews current research and activities related to ornithology, and includes birders' guides to various countries and travel adventures. The magazine contains high-quality color photos, articles from experts in birding and ornithology, and reviews of the latest books, binoculars, and equipment. Recommended for amateur birders.

863. *The Loon.* Formerly (until 1964): *The Flicker.* [ISSN: 0024-645X] 1929. q. Free to members. Minnesota Ornithologists' Union, J F Bell Museum of Natural History, University of Minnesota, Minneapolis, MN 55455; mou@moumn.org; http://moumn.org. Illus., index. *Bk. rev.:* 1, 200 words. *Aud.:* Ga, Ac.

The Loon, the publication of the Minnesota Ornithologists' Union (MOU), is a peer-reviewed journal on the birds of Minnesota. It includes field studies, observation of birds, a seasonal report on bird migration, and book reviews. Although the journal concentrates on birds in the Minnesota area, it is one of the best regional bird journals available. Recommended for professional ornithologists in the field, and for research libraries with ornithology programs, especially those in the Minnesota region.

864. *North American Bird Bander.* Incorporates (1979-1981): *Inland Bird Banding;* Formed by the merger of (1938-1976): *E B B A News;* (1924-1976): *Western Bird Bander.* [ISSN: 0363-8979] 1976. q. Free to members. Western Bird Banding Association, c/o C John Ralph, Redwood Sciences Lab, USFS, Arcata, CA 95521; jdw@klamathbird.org; http://www.westernbirdbanding.org. Illus., index, adv. Sample. Vol. ends: Oct/Dec. Microform: PQC. *Bk. rev.:* 1, 250 words. *Aud.:* Ac, Sa.

This peer-reviewed journal is for the serious bird bander. It includes research from the Eastern, Inland, and Western Bird Banding Associations. Some of the topics covered are bird banding equipment and basics of banding, netting, and trapping. This journal also contains reports from banding stations and on original research by banders. Recent literature and books on banding, annual reports of the associations, regional news, and notes and comments are included. Recommended for professional ornithologists in the field.

865. *North American Birds.* Former titles (until 1999): *National Audubon Society Field Notes;* (until 1994): *American Birds;* (until 1971): *Audubon Field Notes.* [ISSN: 1525-3708] 1947. q. USD 60 (Members, USD 30; Non-members, USD 32). Ed(s): Ned Brinkley. American Birding Association, Inc., 1618 W Colorado Ave, Colorado Springs, CO 80904; members@aba.org; http://www.aba.org. Illus., index, adv. Circ: 4000 Paid. Vol. ends: Winter. Microform: PQC. *Indexed:* A22. *Aud.:* Ga, Ac, Sa.

North American Birds, called the "journal of record" for birders, provides a complete overview of the changing panorama of North America's bird life. It publishes reports that cover all of the continent's bird life, including range extensions and contractions, migration patterns or seasonal occurrences of birds, and population dynamics. Regional reports contained in each issue provide articles that cover migration sightings and the effects of climate and weather patterns on bird movement specific to that region. Articles on outstanding bird records augment the regional reports. Also includes color photographs of the most interesting birds of the season. Recommended for academic libraries and special libraries that serve ornithologists.

Owl. See Children section.

866. *Pacific Seabirds.* Formerly (until 1994): *Pacific Seabird Group. Bulletin.* [ISSN: 1089-6317] 1974. s-a. Free to members. Ed(s): Vivian M Mendenhall. Pacific Seabird Group, c/o Lindsay Young, Treasurer, PO Box 61493, Honolulu, HI 96839-1493; info@pacificseabirdgroup.org; http://www.pacificseabirdgroup.org. Illus. Sample. Vol. ends: Fall (No. 2). *Bk. rev.:* 2,500 words. *Aud.:* Ac, Sa.

Pacific Seabirds is published by the Pacific Seabird Group to improve communication among Pacific seabird researchers. Topics relating to the conservation of seabirds in the Pacific Ocean and regional seabird research keep members and the general public informed. The journal covers the entire Pacific region (including Russia, Alaska, Canada, Southeast Asia, the west coast of the United States, and all Pacific Islands). It contains technical articles, reports, book reviews, artwork, and abstracts of papers presented at meetings. Recommended for researchers and academic libraries.

867. *Waterbirds: the international journal of waterbird biology.* Former titles (until 1999): *Colonial Waterbirds;* (until 1981): *Colonial Waterbird Group. Proceedings.* [ISSN: 1524-4695] 1977. 3x/yr. Free to members. Ed(s): Stephanie L Jones. Waterbird Society, 5400 Bosque Blvd, Ste 680, Waco, TX 76710; membership@osnabirds.org; http://www.waterbirds.org. Illus. Refereed. *Indexed:* A22, C45. *Bk. rev.:* Number and length vary. *Aud.:* Ac, Sa.

Waterbirds is an international scientific journal that publishes original research on all types of waterbird species living in marine, estuarine, and freshwater habitats internationally. It has been published by the Waterbird Society for over two decades, to promote and encourage communication about the world's waterbird population. Topics cover conservation, management, biology, and techniques used to study the world's waterbirds. Waterbirds include seabirds, wading birds, shorebirds, and waterfowl. Recommended for researchers and academic libraries.

868. *Western Birds: quarterly journal of Western Field Ornithologists.* Formerly (until 1973): *California Birds.* [ISSN: 0160-1121] 1973. q. Free to members. Western Field Ornithologists, c/o Philip Unitt, San Diego Natural History Museum, PO Box 121390, San Diego, CA 92112; http://www.westernfieldornithologists.org. Illus., index, adv. Refereed. *Indexed:* A22. *Bk. rev.:* 1, 1,000 words. *Aud.:* Ga, Ac.

This quarterly journal provides articles for both amateur and professional field ornithologists, while maintaining a high level of quality. This journal includes lengthy articles, reports, and book reviews. It covers topics on identification, conservation, behavior, population dynamics, migration status, geographic variation, and effects of pollution. Also contains techniques for censusing, sounds recording, and photographing birds in the field. Reports and studies focus on birds from the Rocky Mountain and Pacific states and provinces, including Hawaii and Alaska, western Texas, northwestern Mexico, and the northeastern Pacific Ocean. Recommended for academic libraries and researchers interested in this geographic area.

869. *The Wilson Journal of Ornithology.* Former titles (until 2006): *The Wilson Bulletin;* (until 1894): *Wilson Ornithological Chapter of the Agassiz Association. Journal;* (until 1893): *Agassiz Association. Wilson Ornithological Chapter. Wilson Quarterly;* (until 1892): *Agassiz Association. Department of the Wilson Chapter. The Semi-annual;* (until 1981): *The Ornithologists' and Oologists' Semi-annual.* [ISSN: 1559-4491] 1889. q. Free to members. Ed(s): Mary Bomberger Brown.

Wilson Ornithological Society, c/o Dale Kennedy, Biology Department, Albion College, Albion, MI 49224; DKennedy@albion.edu; http://www.wilsonsociety.org/. Illus., index. Refereed. Vol. ends: Dec. Microform: PQC. *Indexed:* A01, A22, BRI, C45, E01, MLA-IB. *Bk. rev.:* 3, lengthy. *Aud.:* Ac, Sa.

Since 1889, *The Wilson Journal of Ornithology* has provided scholarly research from around the world on all aspects of ornithology. It is a major journal in the field, containing articles based on original studies of birds and short communications that describe observations of particular interest. It includes reviews of new books on birds and related subjects, as well as ornithological news. Articles are accessible to both professional and amateur ornithologists. Most articles focus on the western hemisphere (including research on Neotropical birds), though the geographic coverage of the journal is global. Recommended for research libraries that serve ornithologists.

■ BLIND AND VISUALLY IMPAIRED

See also Disabilities section.

Camille McCutcheon, Assistant Dean of the Library, Coordinator of Collection Management, University of South Carolina Upstate, 800 University Way, Spartanburg, SC 29303; CMcCutcheon@uscupstate.edu

Introduction

There are many print and electronic periodicals available to address the needs of blind and visually impaired individuals and their support networks. The intended audiences of these publications include individuals with low vision, parents of blind children, teachers and professionals who work with deaf-blind individuals, and blinded veterans of the U.S. Armed Forces. The subject matter of these periodicals varies widely: poetry or prose submitted by the blind and visually impaired; improvements in assistive technology; ways to adjust to vision loss late in life; and tips on day-to-day living with blindness or a visual impairment. Other titles contain reprints and compilations of articles from mainstream newspapers and magazines.

Publishers of the resources featured in this section all have web sites and can be contacted via e-mail. In addition to the electronic journals, there are several other magazine titles that have current and back issues available online. Most of the publications included here are in the large print format, which is 14-point type or higher. Other available formats for some of these titles include braille, e-mail, digital cartridge, digital text, digital braille, hard-copy braille, CD, USB flash drive, and podcast.

Four titles in this section, *Braille Book Review* (*BBR*), *Magazines in Special Media*, *Musical Mainstream*, and *Talking Book Topics* (*TBT*), are published by the National Library Service for the Blind and Physically Handicapped (NLS), Library of Congress. NLS administers the braille and talking-book program, a free library service available to U.S. residents and American citizens living abroad whose low vision, blindness, or disability makes reading regular printed material difficult. Through its national network of libraries, NLS mails books and magazines in talking book and braille formats and playback equipment directly to enrollees at no cost. Music instructional materials are also available in large print, ebraille, braille, and recorded formats. *BBR*, *Magazines in Special Media*, *Musical Mainstream*, and *TBT* are not available to libraries outside of the NLS network. Information can be found at loc.gov/ThatAllMayRead.

Basic Periodicals

FOR THE BLIND AND VISUALLY IMPAIRED. *The ACB Braille Forum, Braille Book Review, Braille Monitor, Dialogue, Guideposts, The New York Times Large Print Weekly, Reader's Digest Large Print, Seeing It Our Way, Syndicated Columnists Weekly, Talking Book Topics.*

BASIC REFERENCE MATERIALS. *National Library Service for the Blind and Physically Handicapped, Library of Congress.*

ORGANIZATIONS.

American Council of the Blind, 1703 N. Beauregard St., Suite 420, Arlington, VA 22311, www.acb.org, info@acb.org.

American Association of the Deaf-Blind, 3825 LaVista Road, W-2, Tucker, GA 30084, www.aadb.org, aadb-info@aadb.org.

American Foundation for the Blind, 1401 South Clark Street, Suite 730, Arlington, VA 22202, www.afb.org.

American Printing House for the Blind, 1839 Frankfort Avenue, Louisville, KY 40206, www.aph.org, info@aph.org.

Blinded Veterans Association, 125 N. West Street, 3rd Floor, Alexandria, VA 22314, www.bva.org, bva@bva.org.

Clovernook Center for the Blind and Visually Impaired, 7000 Hamilton Avenue, Cincinnati, OH 45231, www.clovernook.org.

Helen Keller National Center for Deaf-Blind Youths and Adults, 141 Middle Neck Road, Sands Point, NY 11050, www.helenkeller.org/hknc, hkncinfo@hknc.org.

Lighthouse Guild, 250 West 64th Street, New York, NY 10023, www.lighthouseguild.org.

National Braille Press, 88 St. Stephen Street, Boston, MA 02115, www.nbp.org, contact@nbp.org.

National Federation of the Blind, 200 East Wells Street at Jernigan Place, Baltimore, MD 21230, nfb.org.

National Library Service for the Blind and Physically Handicapped, Library of Congress, Washington, DC 20542, www.loc.gov/nls, nls@loc.gov.

Basic Abstracts and Indexes

Academic Search Complete.

870. ***The A C B Braille Forum.*** [ISSN: 0006-8772] 1962. m. Ed(s): Sharon Lovering. American Council of the Blind, 1703 N. Beauregard St., Suite 420, Arlington, VA 22311; info@acb.org; http://www.acb.org. Adv. Sample. Vol. ends: Jun. *Aud.:* Sa.

The official publication of the American Council of the Blind, *The ACB Braille Forum* is a resource for blind and visually impaired individuals. It contains news, human interest stories, information about legislation, and announcements of new products and services. Information and updates about the American Council of the Blind (ACB) are also featured. The current issue, along with issues dating back to 2010, is accessible via the ACB web site. Issues published during odd-numbered months are available in print as *The ACB Braille Forum*, while issues published during even-numbered months are available as *The ACB E-Forum. The ACB Braille Forum* is also available in the following formats: braille, 20-point type, digital cartridge, podcast, and e-mail. URL: http://acb.org

871. ***A F B Directory of Services Database.*** 1926. . Free. American Foundation for the Blind, 2 Penn Plz, Ste 1102, New York, NY 10121; http://www.afb.org. *Aud.:* Ga, Sa.

Provides information on organizations and agencies in the United States and Canada that offer services for people who are blind or visually impaired. Each organizational profile in this free online resource provides full contact information, including web site address and key personnel, as well as useful descriptions of services offered that help in identifying the appropriate agency. An excellent reference source. URL: www.afb.org

872. ***AccessWorld (Online): technology news for people who are blind or visually impaired.*** [ISSN: 1526-9574] 2000. m. Free. Ed(s): Lee Huffman. American Foundation for the Blind, 2 Penn Plz, Ste 1102, New York, NY 10121; afbinfo@afb.net; http://www.afb.org. Illus. *Aud.:* Ga, Sa.

AccessWorld has news and articles concerning technology for the blind and visually impaired. It also includes product reviews and information on access issues. The *AccessWorld* archives contain issues that date back to 2000 and are accessible via the American Foundation for the Blind web site. URL: www.afb.org

873. ***The B V A Bulletin.*** [ISSN: 0005-3430] 1946. bi-m. Free to members. Blinded Veterans Association, National Board of Directors, 125 N W St, 3rd Fl, Alexandria, VA 22314; bva@bva.org; http://www.bva.org. Illus. Sample. *Aud.:* Sa.

Information in *The BVA Bulletin* is written by blinded veterans *for* blinded veterans. This publication contains news, legislation, feature articles, information from the president of the Blinded Veterans Association, recent and upcoming association activities, letters to the editor, and an "In Remembrance" section for blinded veterans who have recently died. The current issue, along with issues dating back to 2006, is accessible via the BVA web site. *The BVA Bulletin* is also available in the following formats: 14-point type, CD, an MP3 downloadable audiofile, and e-mail. URL: www.bva.org

874. *Braille Book Review.* [ISSN: 0006-873X] 1932. bi-m. Free to blind and physically handicapped. U.S. Library of Congress, National Library Service for the Blind and Physically Handicapped, 1291 Taylor St, Washington, DC 20542; nls@loc.gov; http://www.loc.gov/nls. Illus., index. Sample. *Bk. rev.:* Number and length vary. *Aud.:* Ems, Hs, Ga, Sa.

Braille Book Review contains announcements of braille books recently added to the Library of Congress collection, along with news and developments in library services for blind individuals. The braille edition includes one-line annotations from *Talking Book Topics* (below in this section) and a braille order form. The current issue of *BBR*, along with issues dating back to 2014, is accessible via the NLS web site. This publication is also available in the following formats: 14-point type, ebraille, and hard-copy braille. URL: www.loc.gov/nls

875. *Braille Monitor.* [ISSN: 0006-8829] 1956. 11x/yr. Free to visually impaired. Ed(s): Gary Wunder. National Federation of the Blind, 200 E Wells St, at Jernigan Pl, Baltimore, MD 21230; nfb@nfb.org; http://www.writers.nfb.org/. Illus., index, adv. Sample. Vol. ends: Dec. *Aud.:* Sa.

The leading publication of the National Federation of the Blind (NFB), the *Braille Monitor* is read by the blind, their families, and the professionals who serve them. The *Braille Monitor* contains recipes, human interest stories, profiles of blind individuals, and highlights of NFB activities and programs. It also addresses concerns of the blind, such as civil rights, social issues, legislation, employment, and education, and provides information on technology and aids/appliances used by the blind. The current issue, along with issues dating back to 1957, is accessible via the NFB web site. Other available formats of the *Braille Monitor* include 14-point type, braille, USB flash drive, and e-mail. URL: http://nfb.org

876. *Connect! (Sands Point).* 2010. 3x/yr. Free. Ed(s): Beth Jordan, Allison Burrows. Helen Keller National Center for Deaf - Blind Youths and Adults, 141 Middle Neck Rd, Sands Point, NY 11050; hkncinfo@hknc.org; http://www.hknc.org. *Aud.:* Ga, Sa.

CONNECT! is the electronic newsletter for the Helen Keller National Center for Deaf-Blind Youths and Adults (HKNC). Featured in the newsletter are activities at the HKNC and across the United States that would be of interest to deaf-blind individuals. The current issue of *CONNECT!*, along with selected back issues, is accessible via the HKNC web site. URL: www.helenkeller.org/hknc

877. *Dialogue (Salem): a world of ideas for visually impaired people of all ages.* Incorporates (1983-1995): *Lifeprints.* [ISSN: 1069-6857] 1961. q. USD 42. Blindskills, Inc., PO Box 5181, Salem, OR 97304; info@blindskills.com; http://www.blindskills.com. Sample. Vol. ends: Winter. *Bk. rev.:* Number and length vary. *Aud.:* Ga, Sa.

Dialogue contains informative articles written by people who are blind or visually impaired. Living with low vision, technology, sports and recreation, careers, education, and cooking are some of the topics covered. News and information on ways to obtain new products and services are also included. This publication is available in the following formats: 18-point type, braille, and e-mail. URL: www.blindskills.com

878. *Future Reflections.* [ISSN: 0883-3419] 1981. q. Free. Ed(s): Deborah Kent Stein. National Federation of the Blind, 200 E Wells St, at Jernigan Pl, Baltimore, MD 21230; nfb@nfb.org; http://www.writers.nfb.org/. Sample. *Indexed:* P01. *Aud.:* Sa.

Future Reflections is a resource for parents and educators of blind children. It contains profiles of blind children and their parents and educators, as well as information on the National Federation of the Blind (NFB). Also included are articles on issues concerning blind children, educational programs for blind students, and resources for parents and teachers. The current issue, along with issues dating back to 1981, is accessible via the NFB web site. *Future Reflections* is available in standard print (12-point type) and through e-mail. URL: http://nfb.org

879. *Guideposts: true stories of hope and inspiration.* [ISSN: 0017-5331] 1945. m. 11/yr. USD 22.97. Ed(s): Edward Grinnan. Guideposts, 39 Old Ridgebury Rd, Ste 2AB, Danbury, CT 06810; http://www.guideposts.org. Illus., index, adv. Sample. Vol. ends: Mar. *Aud.:* Ga, Sa.

Guideposts, an inspirational, interfaith publication, presents first-person narratives that encourage readers to achieve their "maximum personal and spiritual potential." This publication is available in 15-point type. URL: www.guideposts.org

880. *Magazines in Special Media.* Incorporates (1993-1995): *Magazines.* [ISSN: 0889-6518] 1968. irreg. U.S. Library of Congress, National Library Service for the Blind and Physically Handicapped, 1291 Taylor St, Washington, DC 20542; nls@loc.gov; http://www.loc.gov/nls. *Aud.:* Sa.

Divided into two parts, *Magazines in Special Media* provides information on periodicals and newsletters that are produced in a variety of formats, including large print, digital text, and ebraille. The first part is an alphabetical listing of magazines that are available through the National Library Service for the Blind and Physically Handicapped (NLS) and its network of cooperating libraries. The second is an alphabetical listing of magazines that are not a part of the NLS program and cannot be requested from network libraries. *Magazines in Special Media* is accessible via the NLS web site. This publication is also available in 14-point type and in hard-copy braille. An excellent reference source. URL: www.loc.gov/nls

881. *Musical Mainstream.* Former titles (until Dec.1976): *New Braille Musician; Braille Musician.* [ISSN: 0364-7501] 1942. q. Free to blind and physically handicapped. U.S. Library of Congress, National Library Service for the Blind and Physically Handicapped, 1291 Taylor St, Washington, DC 20542; nls@loc.gov; http://www.loc.gov/nls. Sample. *Bk. rev.:* Number and length vary. *Aud.:* Ga, Sa.

Musical Mainstream contains selected articles from national magazines about classical music, music criticism, and music teaching and lists new National Library Service music acquisitions. This publication is available in 14-point type, digital cartridge, ebraille, and hard-copy braille. URL: www.loc.gov/nls

882. *The New York Times Large Print Weekly.* Formerly (until 2007): *New York Times Large Type Weekly.* 1967. w. USD 209.60. Ed(s): Tom Brady. New York Times Company, 620 8th Ave, New York, NY 10018. Illus., adv. Sample. Vol. ends: Feb. *Aud.:* Ga, Sa.

This publication contains selected articles that have appeared throughout the past week in *The New York Times.* Graphics and color photographs enhance stories on national and international news, science and health, business, the arts, and sports. An editorial and a crossword puzzle are also included. *The New York Times Large Print Weekly* is available in 16-point type. URL: www.nytimes.com

883. *Our Special: a braille magazine edited for and by blind women.* [ISSN: 0030-6959] 1927. bi-m. USD 15. Ed(s): Kesel Wilson. National Braille Press, 88 St Stephen St, Boston, MA 02115; orders@nbp.org; http://www.nbp.org. *Aud.:* Sa.

Our Special is a resource especially for blind women. It contains both original articles and ones reprinted from newspapers and women's magazines. Topics featured in *Our Special* include career issues, crafts, health, dating, cooking, travel, poetry, shopping, and fashion. *OS* is available as an electronic text file and in paper braille and electronic braille. URL: www.nbp.org

884. *Reader's Digest (Large Print for Easier Reading).* Former titles (until 2001): *Reader's Digest (Large Print); Reader's Digest Large Type Edition.* 1964. m. USD 35.96. Ed(s): Bruce Kelley. Reader's Digest Association, Inc, Reader's Digest Rd, Pleasantville, NY 10570; http://www.rd.com. Adv. *Aud.:* Ga, Sa.

Reader's Digest Large Print contains in-depth feature articles and departments such as "Word Power," "Life in These United States," "Laughter, the Best Medicine," and "Humor in Uniform." In addition to being available in large print, this periodical is available from the American Printing House for the Blind (APH) in the following formats: braille, four-track cassette, digital flash cartridge, and as a Digital Talking Book download. The advertising has been removed from the editions produced by the APH. URL: www.rd.com

885. ***Seeing It Our Way: recipes, crafts, and much more!*** 1997. m. USD 30 (print or braille ed.)). Ed(s): Bunny Kerner. Horizons for the Blind, 125 Erick St, A103, Crystal Lake, IL 60014; mail@horizons-blind.org; http://www.horizons-blind.org. *Aud.:* Ga, Sa.

Seeing It Our Way is a magazine published by Horizons for the Blind, an organization "dedicated to improving the quality of life for people who are blind or visually impaired by increasing accessibility to consumer products and services, education, recreation, and the cultural arts." Recipes, gardening, crafts, sports, technology, and poetry are some of the topics covered in *Seeing It Our Way*. This publication is available in 22-point type and in braille. URL: http://horizons-blind.org

886. ***Slate & Style.*** [ISSN: 1536-4321] 1982. q. USD 10. Ed(s): Eve Sanchez. National Federation of the Blind, 200 E Wells St, at Jernigan Pl, Baltimore, MD 21230; nfb@nfb.org; http://www.writers.nfb.org/. *Bk. rev.:* Number and length vary. *Aud.:* Ga, Sa.

Slate & Style is a magazine published by the National Federation of the Blind Writers' Division. Although this publication features literary writing, it also contains information about other writing styles. Selected issues dating back to 2010 are accessible via the National Federation of the Blind Writers' Division web site. *Slate & Style* is also available through e-mail. URL: writers.nfb.org

887. ***Syndicated Columnists Weekly.*** 1984. w. USD 24. National Braille Press, 88 St Stephen St, Boston, MA 02115; http://www.nbp.org. *Aud.:* Sa.

Syndicated Columnists Weekly contains the best editorials written by syndicated columnists that have appeared that week in major U.S. newspapers such as *The Wall Street Journal, The New York Times, The Washington Post,* and *The Boston Globe. SCW* is available in paper braille and in electronic braille. URL: www.nbp.org

888. ***T X SenseAbilities: a bi-annual publication about visual impairments and deafblindness for families and professionals.*** 2010. s-a. USD 10. Ed(s): Holly Cooper. Texas School for the Blind and Visually Impaired, 1100 W 45th St, Austin, TX 78756; htpp://www.tsbvi.edu. *Aud.:* Sa.

TX SenseAbilities is published by the Texas School for the Blind and Visually Impaired and by the Department of Assistive and Rehabilitative Services, Division for Blind Services. This newsletter contains articles, news, and announcements about visual impairments and deaf-blindness for families and professionals. The current issue, along with issues dating back to 2007, is accessible via the *TX SenseAbilities* web site. URL: www.tsbvi.edu/tx-senseabilities

889. ***Talking Book Topics.*** [ISSN: 0039-9183] 1935. bi-m. Free to blind and physically handicapped. U.S. Library of Congress, National Library Service for the Blind and Physically Handicapped, 1291 Taylor St, Washington, DC 20542; nls@loc.gov; http://www.loc.gov/nls. Index. Sample. *Aud.:* Ems, Hs, Ga, Sa.

Talking Book Topics contains announcements of recorded books recently added to the Library of Congress collection, along with news and developments in library services for blind and physically handicapped individuals. One-line annotations from *TBT* are included in *Braille Book Review* (above in this section). The current issue of *TBT,* along with issues dating back to 2014, is accessible via the NLS web site. This publication is also available in the following formats: digital cartridge, 14-point type, and digital text. URL: www.loc.gov/nls

■ BOATS AND BOATING

See also Fishing; Hunting and Guns; and Sports sections.

Julia D. Ashmun, Managing Partner, Dirty Dog Software, P.O. Box 1623, Plaistow, NH 03865; julia@dirtydogsoftware.com

Introduction

Magazines in this section will appeal to current and future boaters who own, rent, charter, crew, or dream of having a boat. Titles here cover a variety of boats ranging from paddleboats to yachts. Most titles are focused on particular types of boats (for example, canoes/kayaks, personal watercraft, motor boats, pontoons, sailboats, trawlers, or yachts) and/or particular aspects of boating (such as cruising, crewing, building and maintenance, boat and equipment reviews, or showboats). Magazine topics typically include boat and equipment reviews, favorite destinations, boating skills, maintenance, navigation, and boating safety.

Over the last seven years, the boating industry has continued to show a steady single-digit growth in sales (6 percent growth in 2017 new motor boat sales). Leading the growth is still small versatile boats (under 26 ft.) aimed at meeting a range of family activities (e.g., skiing, wake boarding, tubing, and fishing) but even large yacht sales are rebounding. Participation in kayaking has had steady annual growth from 6.1 million in 2006 to 15.69 million in 2016. Plus 90 percent of new powerboats sold in the United States over the past 15 years are still in use today. So many magazines continue to cover smaller boats and include a maintenance section.

Basic Periodicals

Hs: *Boating World, Canoe & Kayak, Cruising World, Practical Sailor, The Woodenboat;* Ga: *Boating World, Canoe & Kayak, Cruising Outpost, Cruising World, PassageMaker, Practical Sailor, The Woodenboat;* Ac: *Canoe & Kayak, Practical Sailor, The Woodenboat.*

Basic Abstracts and Indexes

Readers' Guide to Periodical Literature.

890. ***Blue Water Sailing.*** [ISSN: 1091-1979] 1996. m. USD 29.95 domestic; USD 44.95 Canada; USD 64.95 elsewhere. Ed(s): George Day. Blue Water Sailing, 747 Aquidneck Ave, Ste 201, Middletown, RI 02842; http://www.bwsailing.com. Adv. *Aud.:* Ga, Sa.

Focused at providing solutions for extended offshore sailing, this magazine is geared toward current and future blue-water sailors. *Blue Water Sailing* includes practical tips for offshore seamanship, detailed boat reviews with many photographs, gear review, chartering, cruising news; personal stories; and amazing destinations ranging from Bahamas and Cuba, to Thailand and Polynesia. Special articles include offshore navigation, navigation electronics, Automatic Identification System (AIS), radar, weather, safety, solar, and more. Recommended for public libraries that serve offshore and blue water boaters. URL: www.bwsailing.com

891. ***Boat International.*** Former titles (until 2016): *ShowBoats International;* (until 1983): *Showboats.* [ISSN: 2572-505X] 1988. m. EUR 54 domestic; USD 98 United States; EUR 66 combined subscription domestic print & online eds. Boat International Media, First Fl, 41-47 Hartfield Rd, London, SW19 3RQ, United Kingdom; info@boatinternational.co.uk; https://www.boatinternational.com/. Illus., index, adv. *Aud.:* Ga, Sa.

Originally launched as *ShowBoats International* in 1983, this publication has changed the title to *Boats International* and is the definitive magazine covering multi-billion dollar luxury yachts and associated fabulous destinations, lifestyles, events, and market intelligence. Yacht reviews include vessel specifications, design layouts, designer information, and plenty of gorgeous interior and exterior photos. These yachts are the highest of the high-end, high-concept vessels typically costing in the millions of dollars. Your readership will probably not be buying these boats, but boating enthusiasts and aspiring millionaires can always dream. URL: www.boatinternational.com

892. *Boating.* Incorporates (in 1980): *Motorboat;* Which incorporated (in 1975): *Family Houseboating;* Formerly (until 1966): *Popular Boating.* [ISSN: 0006-5374] 1956. 10x/yr. USD 12 combined subscription domestic (print & ipad eds.); USD 22 combined subscription Canada (print & ipad eds.); USD 32 combined subscription elsewhere (print & ipad eds.)). Bonnier Corp., 460 N Orlando Ave, Ste 200, Winter Park, FL 32789; http://www.bonniercorp.com. Illus., adv. *Indexed:* A22, BRI, C37. *Aud.:* Ga, Sa.

One of the magazines with the highest circulation in the genre, *Boating* offers a wide range of information for power boaters with a focus on review and evaluation of boat, marine accessories, and watersport equipment. Other topics include "how to" features on installing equipment, boat maintenance, fishing, troubleshooting, trailering, and DIY projects plus articles on safety and industry news. This is a highly polished, visually satisfying journal with extensive use of color and graphics. Although there is a substantial amount of advertising, it is generally integrated well with the text. The emphasis is on runabouts, cruising and fishing boats, performance boats, pontoon boats, personal power crafts, and watersports boats. URL: www.boatingmag.com

893. *Boating World.* Former titles (until 1991): *Boat Journal;* (until 1990): *Small Boat Journal.* [ISSN: 1059-5155] 1979. 9x/yr. USD 10 combined subscription for 2 yrs. print & online eds. Ed(s): Mike Werling. Duncan McIntosh Co. Inc., 18475 Bandilier, Fountain Valley, CA 92708. Illus., adv. *Indexed:* BRI. *Aud.:* Hs, Ga, Sa.

This magazine's focus is on power boats under 35 feet, a popular size for family boating trips, water-sports activities, and fishing. There's a very wide range of articles covering gear, DYI, engines, water sports, trailering, new, legal issues, and a fun section called "Bonehead Blunders." Articles offer practical advice for hands-on upkeep and maintenance, as well as consumer tips (such as buying a used boat, insuring boats, asking a maritime attorney about boat liens). A colorful production, with good graphics and broad coverage. Because it focuses on boats of such a popular size, this publication merits strong consideration as part of a library's core collection. URL: www.boatingworld.com

894. *Canoe & Kayak.* Formerly (until 1993): *Canoe;* Which was incorporated (in 1941): *American Canoeist.* [ISSN: 1077-3258] 1973. q. Ed(s): Dave Shively. TEN: Action Outdoor Group, 2052 Corte Del Nogal, Ste 100, Carlsbad, CA 92011. Illus., adv. Vol. ends: Dec. *Indexed:* A22, S25, SD. *Aud.:* Ems, Ga, Ac, Sa.

An excellent offering of information for canoe and kayak enthusiasts of all levels and expanded to include kayak fishing. Primary emphasis is on descriptions of paddling trips, ranging from casual day outings to rigorous whitewater excursions along with coverage of the newest boats and accessories. There is considerable coverage of paddling techniques, skills, safety, travel, travelers, and health. The feature stories on places and people, along with the stunning photos, are capturing. This is topped off by material on boat design and construction, and "Rides" (photos of personal kayak and canoes). Tastefully done, the magazine is both informative and very enjoyable to read. *Canoe & Kayak* will be appreciated by a wide audience of paddlers. URL: www.canoekayak.com

895. *Cruising Outpost Magazine: the boating & cruising lifestyle.* [ISSN: 2372-3335] 2013. q. USD 45 combined subscription (print & online eds.); USD 25 (print or online ed.)). Ed(s): Sue Morgan, Bob Bitchin. Cruising Outpost, Box 100, Berry Creek, CA 95916; bob@cruisingoutpost.com; http://cruisingoutpost.com. Illus., adv. *Aud.:* Ga, Sa.

Cruising Outpost Magazine, on the boating and cruising lifestyle, is a relatively new magazine that became extremely popular in its first year. This is not surprising, since it was started by the editors and writers of *Latitudes & Attitudes.* This sailing magazine is not only captivating and informative but also fun. Primary topics are destinations, cruising stories, boat and equipment reviews, news, and humor. Other topics include galley tips, rigging, babies onboard, pets onboard, health, and weather. Cruisers and boaters who read *Latitudes & Attitudes* will surely enjoy *Cruising Outpost Magazine.* URL: www.cruisingoutpost.com

896. *Cruising World.* [ISSN: 0098-3519] 1974. m. USD 28 combined subscription domestic (print & ipad eds.); USD 44 combined subscription Canada (print & ipad eds.); USD 60 combined subscription elsewhere (print & ipad eds.)). Ed(s): Mark Pillsbury. Bonnier Corp., 460 N Orlando Ave, Ste 200, Winter Park, FL 32789; http://www.bonniercorp.com. Illus., adv. Sample. Microform: PQC. *Indexed:* A22, BRI, C37, SD. *Bk. rev.:* 3, 50 words. *Aud.:* Hs, Ga.

This is a popular magazine dedicated to open-water sailing and beautiful destinations. *Cruising World*'s content centers on descriptive narratives of cruising destinations, boat reviews and book reviews, how-to articles, chartering and practical solutions, and techniques for long-term cruising. Trip narratives convey a good sense of the open-water experience, and provide interesting glimpses of the character, history, and culture of international areas visited. Practical material covers such topics as navigational techniques, seamanship, safety, live-aboards, systems, and boat maintenance including refits and upgrades. The writing is sound, the photos are pleasing, and the overall quality of the magazine is excellent. This title is useful and informative for current and future blue water sailors. URL: www.cruisingworld.com

897. *Dockwalk.* Incorporates (2001-2005): *Captain's Log.* 1998. m. USD 75 domestic; USD 150 foreign. Ed(s): Lauren Beck, Steve Davis. Boat International Media, First Fl, 41-47 Hartfield Rd, London, SW19 3RQ, United Kingdom; info@boatinternational.co.uk; https://www.boatinternational.com/. Adv. *Aud.:* Hs, Ga, Sa.

Dockwalk Magazine enables captains and crew of super yachts to keep up to date on their industry, especially when their jobs may take them around the world. This title includes articles on training, maintenance, team dynamics, health, insurance, finance, new gear, new electronics, recipes, social events, destinations, and activities for the captain and crew (such as deckhands, mates, engineers, stews, and chefs). This is a great magazine for current crew or those considering this occupation. URL: www.dockwalk.com

898. *Good Old Boat: the sailing magazine for the rest of us!* [ISSN: 1099-6354] 1998. bi-m. USD 39.95 (print or online eds.); USD 8 per issue in US & Canada). Ed(s): Michael Robertson. Partnership for Excellence, Inc., 1300 Evergreen Dr N W, Jamestown, MD 58401; http://www.goodoldboat.com. Adv. *Bk. rev.:* Number and length vary. *Aud.:* Ga, Sa.

Good Old Boat magazine is aimed at average, do-it-yourself sailors who are not sailing the latest and greatest new yachts but are instead "celebrating older-model sailboats." This magazine focuses on furthering a sailor's knowledge of boat design, maintenance, upgrades, seamanship, and do-it-yourself (DIY) improvement projects. To this end, their in-depth boat review includes not only the description and attractive photos of the boat but also the history, design layout, designer's biography, and feedback from the owners of that model. Other topics include design lessons, book and equipment reviews, and features about fellow sailors relating their experiences ranging from DIY projects to favorite cruising spots. URL: www.goodoldboat.com

899. *Houseboat Magazine.* 1971. bi-m. USD 13.95 combined subscription domestic (print & online eds.); USD 20 combined subscription foreign (print & online eds.)). Ed(s): Jess Carpenter. Harris Publishing, Inc. (Idaho Falls), 360 B St, Idaho Falls, ID 83402; customerservice@harrispublishing.com; http://www.harrispublishing.com. Illus., adv. *Aud.:* Ga, Sa.

This title covers all facets of houseboat ownership, rental, interior design, maintenance, lifestyles, activities, recipes, news, and fun destinations. One of the defining features of this magazine is its focus on different destinations, including some of the history, scenic qualities, and services found there. The usage of houseboats has expanded beyond vacation rental boats on large lakes and rivers in the Western and Midwestern regions to include live-aboards, rentals, and vacations anywhere in the world. URL: www.houseboatmagazine.com

900. *Ocean Navigator: marine navigation and ocean voyaging.* Formerly (until Dec. 1986): *Navigator.* [ISSN: 0886-0149] 1985. 7x/yr. USD 27.95. Ed(s): Tim Queeney. Navigator Publishing LLC., 58 Fore St, Portland, ME 04101; http://www.oceannavigator.com. Illus., adv. Sample. *Bk. rev.:* 2-4, 75-200 words. *Aud.:* Ga.

Ocean Navigator is dedicated to marine navigation and ocean voyaging. Ocean and coastal passages requires considerable knowledge of navigation, weather, electronics, and seamanship covered in this magazine. Articles also include other aspects of ocean voyaging, such as boat maintenance, gear reviews, and cruise destination information. Some articles give accounts of voyages in which navigational skills or equipment have been a significant or crucial factor in the trip's outcome. Most articles offer detailed, in-depth coverage and are interesting and informative. Also covered are events, news, and ocean racing. Although most of the material applies to sailing craft, the navigational features can be valuable for all boaters and they have added "Voyaging under power" (e.g., trawlers). URL: www.oceannavigator.com

901. ***PassageMaker: the power cruising authority.*** [ISSN: 1095-7286] 1996. 8x/yr. USD 34.95 domestic; USD 45.95 Canada; USD 53.95 elsewhere. PassageMaker Magazine, Inc., 105 Eastern Ave, Ste 203, Annapolis, MD 21403; http://www.passagemaker.com. Adv. Circ: 32500. *Aud.:* Ga, Sa.

PassageMaker is the leader in covering trawlers and the cruising-under-power lifestyle. Each issue has boat and equipment reviews, destination reviews ranging from local rivers to the "Great Loop" and international destinations, and an in-depth technical section on all aspects of boating maintenance and upgrades (for example, electronics, engine maintenance, fuel systems, painting, running gear, seamanship, and weather). It also includes human interest stories about cruisers, their boats and pets, and upcoming events of interest. This will be both a practical help and a cozy read for a growing segment of aging Baby Boomers who don't relish the rigors of other kinds of boating and who are fast becoming trawler enthusiasts. URL: www.passagemaker.com

902. ***Pontoon & Deck Boat.*** 1971. m. USD 19.95 combined subscription domestic (print & online eds.); USD 40 combined subscription foreign (print & online eds.)). Harris Publishing, Inc. (Idaho Falls), 360 B St, Idaho Fall, ID 83402; customerservice@harrispublishing.com; http://www.harrispublishing.com. Illus., adv. *Aud.:* Ga, Sa.

This publication focuses exclusively on all aspects of pontoon and deck boats. The main topics are boat reviews, equipment testing, gear and product reviews, fishing tips, industry news, interviews, destinations, and do-it-yourself information. This is a thin but attractively packaged publication that fills a need for a unique and growing group of boaters. URL: www.pdbmagazine.com

903. ***Power and Motoryacht.*** Formerly (until 19??): *Guide to Marine Electronics.* [ISSN: 0886-4411] 1985. m. USD 12 domestic; USD 27 Canada; USD 42 elsewhere. Ed(s): Dan Harding, Simon Murray. Active Interest Media, 5720 Flatiron Pkwy, Boulder, CO 80301. Illus., adv. Circ: 100000. Vol. ends: Dec. *Indexed:* A22. *Aud.:* Ga, Sa.

Power and Motoryacht covers large powerboats in detail, with feature stories about new boats, electronics, sports fishing, mega yachts, destinations, interesting boaters, communication, navigation, and maintenance tips. Also includes a list of upcoming boat shows and fishing tournaments. This glossy magazine is aimed at readers seeking information about large powerboats and is heartily recommended to libraries that serve them. URL: www.powerandmotoryacht.com

904. ***Practical Sailor: guide to sailing gear.*** [ISSN: 0161-8059] 1974. m. USD 84 combined subscription in US & Canada (print & online eds.); USD 120 combined subscription elsewhere (print & online eds.)). Ed(s): Darrell Nicholson. Belvoir Media Group, LLC, PO Box 5656, Norwalk, CT 06856; customer_service@belvoir.com; http://www.belvoir.com. Sample. *Indexed:* SD. *Aud.:* Hs, Ga, Sa.

Practical Sailor is the *Consumer Reports* of sailing and does not accept any advertising. The focus of this magazine is on product testing, boat reviews, boat maintenance, and boat safety. The title's content is an invaluable resource to current or future boat owners. The detailed equipment reviews describe the types of testing, how each product tested, a conclusion, and often include result matrices. The sailboats reviews are also in-depth and contain quotes from boat owners about items they like or don't like; value/price graphs over the years, starting with original cost; interior, exterior, hull, and manufacturing quality information; and how the boat handles under sail. This publication is a "must have" resource for boaters and would complement any boating collection. URL: www.practical-sailor.com

905. ***Sail.*** [ISSN: 0036-2700] 1970. m. USD 15. Ed(s): Peter Nielsen. Active Interest Media, 5720 Flatiron Pkwy, Boulder, CO 80301. Illus., adv. Circ: 75000. Vol. ends: Dec. *Indexed:* A22, BRI. *Bk. rev.:* 1-2, 200 words. *Aud.:* Ga, Sa.

A popular magazine that provides a balanced selection of material, with an emphasis on boating knowledge and skills as applied to equipment, maintenance, navigation, seamanship, cruising, charting, and racing activities. Articles address these issues in very practical terms. There are also narratives that describe interesting cruise destinations or situations that demonstrate sailing skills and experiences. The magazine's content applies to both small and large sailboat boats along with multihulls with a consistent focus on the enhancement of sailing skills for both novice and expert sailors. This magazine should be a core holding for most boating collections. URL: www.sailmagazine.com

906. ***Sailing.*** [ISSN: 0036-2719] 1966. 10x/yr. USD 28 domestic; USD 39 Canada; USD 70 elsewhere. Port Publications, Inc., 125 E Main St, PO Box 249, Port Washington, WI 53074. Illus., adv. Sample. Vol. ends: Aug. Microform: PQC. *Indexed:* A22, BRI. *Bk. rev.:* 2-4, 200-400 words. *Aud.:* Ga.

Set apart from its competition by its oversize pages, this magazine combines lengthy feature articles with pictorial beauty. Its primary content is balanced between cruising locales and reviews of boats and equipment. Additional material covers maintenance skills, sailing techniques, and sailing news. What separates this magazine from others is its large format, which allows full-page photos to convey the panorama of certain places or the sensation of skimming through the water. URL: www.sailingmagazine.net

907. ***Sailing World.*** Former titles (until 1986): *Yacht Racing and Cruising;* (until 1983): *Yacht Racing;* (until 1972): *One-Design and Offshore Yachtsman;* (until 1965): *One-Design Yachtsman.* [ISSN: 0889-4094] 1962. 8x/yr. USD 19.97 combined subscription domestic (print & ipad eds.); USD 31.97 combined subscription Canada (print & ipad eds.); USD 43.97 combined subscription elsewhere (print & ipad eds.)). Bonnier Corp., 55 Hammarlund Way, Middletown, RI 02842; http://www.bonniercorp.com. Illus., adv. Microform: PQC. *Indexed:* BRI, C37. *Aud.:* Ga.

The definitive periodical for performance- and competition-oriented sailors. *Sailing World* coverage includes narratives about competitive events and articles that focus on sailing techniques, boat technology, and racing tactics. The material is primarily oriented toward larger boats, but it is also applicable to smaller ones. Most articles are thorough and informative, with the intent of enhancing sailing skills and performance. The magazine also includes boat reviews and evaluations of high-performance equipment and gear. Racing news and results are included for many levels of competition. This is a visually appealing publication, with attractive photography, graphics, and layout design. Intended for serious sailors involved in competitions, this is an excellent choice for libraries near sailing centers. URL: www.sailingworld.com

908. ***The Watercraft Journal: America's most popular pwc magazine.*** 2013. . Free. Ed(s): Kevin Shaw. Shaw Group Media, kevin.shaw@shawgroupmedia.com; http://www.watercraftjournal.com. *Aud.:* Hs, Ga, Sa.

Devoted to personal watercraft (PWCs), this magazine offers product, gear, and watercraft reviews and features "How to articles," "Editorials," "Interviews," and "Shop tours." There are sections for a large variety of PWC usages: endurance, fishing, meets, offshore, racing, surfing, touring, and freerides (like freestyle). Unlike most PWC sites that "evoke a sensation of speed, glamour, and performance, with graphics, action photographs, and splashy color," this journal, aside from manufacturers' product photos, is straightforward coverage of the topics with lengthy, in-depth descriptions. The "How to articles" have enough technical information, photos, and videos for riders who do their own maintenance and repair. PWCs represent about a quarter of new boat sales and would probably be well placed in many collections.

909. ***The Woodenboat: the magazine for wooden boat owners, builders and designers.*** [ISSN: 0095-067X] 1974. bi-m. USD 34; USD 44 combined subscription (print & online eds.); USD 7.95 per issue (print or online ed.)). Ed(s): Matthew P Murphy. WoodenBoat Publications, Inc., 41 WoodenBoat Ln, PO Box 78, Brooklin, ME 04616; http://www.woodenboat.com. Illus., adv. Sample. Vol. ends: Nov/Dec. *Indexed:* A22. *Bk. rev.:* 2, 500-1,000 words. *Aud.:* Hs, Ga, Ac, Sa.

Although most modern boats are made of synthetic materials there are still boaters, boat schools, and boat builders devoted to wooden boats. This magazine is dedicated to preserving that tradition. The wooden boat logo (a Viking boat) on clothing items is recognized at any waterfront. The publication covers the history, design, building, and preservation of wooden boats of all styles and sizes. Featured articles include highly detailed descriptions and plans for building or restoring a boat as well as historical pieces on a style of boat. Other articles have substantive biographical profiles of individuals prominent in the wooden-boat industry. And there is information on upcoming courses and events. The color photography, illustrations, and design all lend a sense of artistry not found in many other boating periodicals. This elegant publication is a pleasure to read and is highly recommended for the core collection. URL: www.woodenboat.com

910. ***Yachting.*** [ISSN: 0043-9940] 1907. m. USD 16 combined subscription domestic (print & ipad eds.); USD 39 combined subscription Canada (print & ipad eds.); USD 62 combined subscription elsewhere (print & ipad eds.)). Bonnier Corp., 460 N Orlando Ave, Ste 200, Winter Park, FL 32789; http://www.bonniercorp.com. Illus., adv. Microform: PQC. *Indexed:* A22, BRI, C37, CBRI, MASUSE, SD. *Aud.:* Ga.

This periodical emphasizes large, upscale yachts, brokers, gear, activities, and destinations associated with yachts and yacht charting. It is intended for experienced yachtsmen and prospective owners of both powerboats and sailboats. It contains well-written articles on a variety of boating topics. Evaluations of new boats are numerous, as are cruise narratives describing interesting, exotic, or out-of-the-way places to visit. The magazine has high production values and a very good sense of style. URL: www.yachtingmagazine.com

■ BOOKS AND BOOK REVIEWS

See also Archives and Manuscripts; Bibliography; Library and Information Science; and Printing and Graphic Arts sections. Book reviews in subject areas are located within their specific subject areas (e.g., *Science Books and Films* in the Science and Technology section).

Kenny Garcia, Research and Instruction Librarian, California State University, Monterey Bay, 100 Campus Center, Seaside, CA 93955; kengarcia@csumb.edu.

Ryne Leuzinger, Research and Instruction Librarian, California State University, Monterey Bay, 100 Campus Center, Seaside, CA 93955; rleuzinger@csumb.edu

Introduction

The number of books published each year is now at an all-time high. This marked growth shows no sign of slowing down as self-publishing, e-books, and tablet apps continue to alter the publishing world. This abundance of new books makes informative book review publications more important than ever. Luckily there is no dearth of useful, well-written resources available for us to utilize in discovering the best new releases. It is to our great benefit that these resources continue to add to their assortment of features that provide information on newly published books, with offerings such as videos, blogs, podcasts, and easily searchable archives.

While the Internet, and in particular social media, has provided us with more opportunities than ever for discovering new books, mainstays like *The New York Review of Books* and *Publishers Weekly* continue to hold significant influence. Technology has brought great change to the ways in which books are discovered by readers, yet much remains the same. Many of the resources listed below have been used by generations of librarians and readers who seek reliable, critical information on book publishing and selection.

Basic Periodicals

Ems: *Book Links, Center for Children's Books. Bulletin, The Horn Book Magazine;* Hs: *Booklist, Kirkus Reviews;* Ga: *Booklist, Kirkus Reviews, New York Review of Books, New York Times Book Review, Publishers Weekly;* Ac: *Choice, New York Review of Books, New York Times Book Review, Publishers Weekly, T L S.*

Basic Abstracts and Indexes

Book Review Digest, Book Review Index, Children's Book Review Index, Library Literature and Information Science Index.

911. ***American Book Review.*** [ISSN: 0149-9408] 1977. bi-m. USD 30 (Individuals, USD 24; USD 35 foreign). Ed(s): Jeffrey R Di Leo. University of Houston at Victoria, School of Arts & Sciences, 3007 N Ben Wilson, Victoria, TX 77901. Illus., adv. Sample. Circ: 5000. Vol. ends: Sep/Oct. *Indexed:* A01, A22, AmHI, BRI, CBRI, Chicano, E01, MLA-IB. *Bk. rev.:* 25-30, 500-2,500 words. *Aud.:* Ac, Sa.

American Book Review has been in publication for more than 40 years and features reviews of overlooked fiction and poetry written by and for writers. *ABR* also publishes reviews of nonfiction, including works of criticism, biographies, and cultural studies. Items chosen for review favor the avant-garde and are most often small-press releases. *ABR* is published six times a year and every issue includes a "focus" section with several articles selected by a guest editor. Recent topics have included biofiction and geocriticism. John Ashbery, William H. Gass, Joyce Carol Oates, and a number of other highly influential American authors have served as contributing editors. Article excerpts from each edition of *ABR* are freely available on its web site, and digital subscriptions are available via Project Muse. Academic libraries with strong collections in modern American literature will appreciate this resource. URL: http://americanbookreview.org/

912. ***Book Links: a quarterly supplement to Booklist.*** [ISSN: 1055-4742] 1991. q. Ed(s): Bill Ott. American Library Association, 50 E Huron St, Chicago, IL 60611; ala@ala.org; http://www.ala.org. Illus., index, adv. Vol. ends: Aug. *Indexed:* A01, A22, AmHI, BRI, C37, MASUSE. *Bk. rev.:* 50-75, 50-150 words. *Aud.:* Ems, Ga.

Published by the American Library Association, *Book Links* is a quarterly supplement to *Booklist* and is designed for teachers, youth librarians, school library media specialists, reading specialists, curriculum coordinators, and others interested in providing children with literature-based resources. *Book Links* includes book reviews, interviews with authors/illustrators, and articles on how to incorporate reviewed books into classroom activities. The book reviews include an appropriate grade-level range. The web site provides a searchable article index and a link to browse through archived articles. Current *Book Links* articles can be accessed through the *Booklist Online* database. The *Booklist Online* web site also provides Common Core State Standards resources originally published in the *Book Links* magazine. *Book Links* is available digitally through web and/or mobile device apps. *Book Links* is recommended for school libraries, public libraries, and academic libraries that have a teacher education and/or children's literature collection. URL: www.booklistonline.com/booklinks

913. ***Book Page.*** 1988. m. Individuals, USD 30. Ed(s): Lynn Green. ProMotion, Inc., 2143 Belcourt Ave, Nashville, TN 37212; contact@bookpage.com. Illus., adv. Sample. Circ: 400000. *Indexed:* CBRI. *Aud.:* Ga.

Book Page is a monthly publication that is distributed freely to readers at subscribing bookstores and libraries. *Book Page*'s goal is to "recommend the best books for readers of all types." Most of the books featured are from large publishers, and reviews are limited to books published within the last month. *Book Page* includes short review sections that focus on highlights in specific categories, such as mysteries, cooking, romance, audio books, and book club picks. Longer review sections cover fiction, nonfiction, and children's books. In addition to book reviews, *Book Page* features interviews with authors and columns on a variety of book-related topics. *Book Page*'s web site contains a free pdf version of current and past issues. A useful, easily readable resource for public libraries. URL: http://bookpage.com/

914. *Booklist.* Formerly (until 1969): *The Booklist and Subscription Books Bulletin;* Which was formed by the merger of (1930-1956): *Subscription Books Bulletin;* (1917-1956): *The Booklist;* Which was formerly (1905-1917): *A L A Booklist.* [ISSN: 0006-7385] 1969. s-m. 22/yr. USD 169.50 domestic; USD 188.50 elsewhere. Ed(s): Bill Ott. American Library Association, 50 E Huron St, Chicago, IL 60611; customerservice@ala.org; http://www.ala.org. Illus., index, adv. Circ: 13200 Paid. Vol. ends: Sep. Microform: PQC. *Indexed:* A01, A22, AmHI, BRI, C37, CBRI, Chicano, MASUSE, MLA-IB. *Bk. rev.:* 200-250, 75-150 words. *Aud.:* Ems, Hs, Ga, Ac.

Booklist has been published by the American Library Association for more than a century and has a yearly run of 22 issues. Its reviews are primarily written by librarians and academics, and it describes its audience as "librarians, book groups, and book lovers." Quality and anticipated demand are factors in deciding which books to review, and special consideration is given to the interests of small and medium-sized libraries. Columns, interviews, special features, bibliographies, and full coverage of ALA awards as well as "best of" lists accompany *Booklist*'s concise and engaging reviews. "Spotlight" issues focus on popular genres, topics, and themes, such as graphic novels, biography, and romance. Each issue has a separate section for reference book reviews. Subscriptions include a quarterly supplement, *Book Links,* which is targeted to teachers and youth librarians. *Booklist*'s web site includes an archive, blogs, and other resources that support librarians in collection development and readers' advisory. The *Booklist Online* database, which has a multi-user subscription option, features searchable full text of more than 160,000 reviews. A highly recommended resource for school and public librarians. URL: www.booklistonline.com/booklinks

915. *Boston Review.* Formerly (until 1982): *New Boston Review.* [ISSN: 0734-2306] 1975. bi-m. USD 25 domestic; USD 35 in Canada & Mexico; USD 43 elsewhere. Ed(s): Deborah Chasman, Joshua Cohen. Boston Critic, Inc., PO Box 425786, Cambridge, MA 02142. Illus., adv. Vol. ends: Dec/Jan. Microform: LIB; PQC. *Indexed:* A22, AmHI, BRI, CBRI, MLA-IB. *Bk. rev.:* 20-25, 250-2,000 words. *Aud.:* Ga, Ac, Sa.

The *Boston Review* is an independent and nonprofit magazine co-published with MIT Press that covers a variety of topics such as class and inequality, gender and sexuality, global justice, law and justice, literature and culture, philosophy and religion, politics, race, science and nature, and war and security, and it publishes book reviews, essays, fiction, and poetry. The *Boston Review* web site provides free access to most of the content of the current issue and all of the content of archived issues. *Boston Review* is also available digitally through web and/or mobile device apps. *Boston Review* is recommended for public and academic libraries. URL: http://bostonreview.net/

C M Magazine. See Canada section.

916. *Center for Children's Books. Bulletin.* Former titles (until 1958): *Children's Book Center. Bulletin;* (until 1950): *University of Chicago. Center for Instructional Materials. Service Bulletin;* (until 1947): *Children's Books Received by the Center for Instructional Materials.* [ISSN: 0008-9036] 1945. 11x/yr. USD 120. Ed(s): Deborah Stevenson. The Johns Hopkins University Press, 2715 N Charles St, Baltimore, MD 21218; http://www.press.jhu.edu. Illus., adv. Sample. Vol. ends: Jul/Aug. Reprint: PSC. *Indexed:* A22, BRI, CBRI, E01. *Bk. rev.:* 70, 50-100 words. *Aud.:* Ems, Hs, Ga, Ac.

Founded in 1945, the *Bulletin of the Center for Children's Books* reviews current books for children. The *Bulletin* is published monthly by the Graduate School of Library and Information Science at the University of Illinois at Urbana-Champaign. Each review evaluates the book's content, reading level, strengths, weaknesses, and quality of format. It also provides concise summaries and suggestions for curricular use. Each review is rated using one of six categories: "Recommended" (R), "Additional Book of Acceptable Quality" (Ad), "Marginal Book" (M), "Not Recommended" (NR), "Specialized Collections" (SpC), and "Special Reader" (SpR). The regular features of the *Bulletin* are: "Bulletin Blue Ribbons" (annual selection of most distinguished books); "The Big Picture" (monthly editorial on new titles and trends); "Professional Connections" (bibliographies, reviews of professional books, and research article abstracts); and "Subject and Use Index" (searchable index by subject, curricular use, or genre). The *Bulletin*'s web site includes links to the current "Big Picture" article, "Blue Ribbon List," "Bulletin Stars List," and an annotated guide book to gift books. The *Bulletin* is recommended for school libraries, public libraries, and academic libraries that have a teacher education and/or children's literature collection. URL: http://bccb.ischool.illinois.edu/

917. *Choice: current reviews for academic libraries.* [ISSN: 0009-4978] 1963. m. USD 489 domestic; USD 525 in Canada & Mexico; USD 629 elsewhere. Ed(s): Mark Cummings. Association of College and Research Libraries, 575 Main St, Ste 300, Middletown, CT 06457; acrl@ala.org. Illus., index, adv. Vol. ends: Jul/Aug. *Indexed:* BAS, BRI, CBRI, Chicano, MLA-IB. *Bk. rev.:* 600, 100-250 words. *Aud.:* Ga, Ac.

Published monthly by the Association of College and Research Libraries, *Choice* publishes 500+ new book reviews, a bibliographic essay, and a forthcoming title list each month. The reference materials and web sites are mostly reviewed by academic librarians. The primary goal of *Choice* is to support academic libraries at the undergraduate level. Reviewed titles are given one of five possible recommendations: "essential," "highly recommended," "recommended," "optional," and "not recommended." Reviews are organized by subject areas. The recommendation and the appropriate audience/academic level are listed in the "Summing Up" section. *Choice* is also available digitally through web and/or mobile device apps. *Choice* is recommended for academic libraries, especially those that serve undergraduates. URL: http://www.choice360.org/products/reviews

918. *Horn Book Guide to Children's and Young Adult Books.* [ISSN: 1044-405X] 1989. s-a. USD 60 domestic; USD 77 Canada; USD 81 elsewhere. Ed(s): Roger Sutton. Horn Book, Inc., 56 Roland St, Ste 200, Boston, MA 02129; info@hbook.com; http://www.hbook.com. Illus., index, adv. Sample. Vol. ends: Jan/Jun. *Indexed:* BRI, CBRI. *Bk. rev.:* 2,000, 40-50 words. *Aud.:* Ems, Hs, Ga, Ac.

Published twice a year, the *Horn Book Guide* reviews more than 2,000 books every six months. The reviews in *Horn Book Guide* provide a short description, a rating between one (outstanding) and six (unacceptable), appropriate grade levels, and illustration information. The *Guide* also presents a unique and colorful cover for each issue. The *Horn Book* web site provides free access to a semi-annual title index list of the reviewed books. Available as a separate subscription, the *Horn Book Online* is a fully searchable database of more than 100,000 reviews published between 1989 to the present. *Horn Book Online* is searchable by author, illustrator, title, subject, bibliographic data, and rating. *Horn Book Guide* is recommended for school libraries, public libraries, and academic libraries that have a teacher education and/or children's literature collection. URL: www.hbook.com/horn-book-guide/

919. *The Horn Book Magazine: about books for children and young adults.* [ISSN: 0018-5078] 1924. bi-m. USD 72. Ed(s): Roger Sutton. Horn Book, Inc., 56 Roland St, Ste 200, Boston, MA 02129; info@hbook.com; http://www.hbook.com. Illus., index, adv. Sample. Vol. ends: Nov/Dec. Microform: NBI; PQC. *Indexed:* A01, A22, BRI, C37, CBRI, Chicano, MLA-IB. *Bk. rev.:* 70-120, 100-300 words. *Aud.:* Ems, Hs, Ga, Ac.

Published bimonthly, *The Horn Book Magazine* provides books reviews, editorials, and interviews with authors of fiction, nonfiction, poetry, and picture books for children and young adults. The book reviews include a short description of the book, appropriate grade level, and, if deemed outstanding, a starred indicator. *Horn Book* editors choose the best children's and young adult books of the year for the "Fanfare" list, which is published annually in the January/February issue. The *Horn Book* web site features links to some of the book reviews, "Notes from the Horn Book" (a monthly newsletter), and "Talks with Roger" (a monthly interview with an author, which supplements "Notes from the Horn Book"), blog links, and weekly app reviews. *The Horn Book*

Magazine is recommended for school libraries, public libraries, and academic libraries that have a teacher education and/or children's literature collection. URL: www.hbook.com/horn-book-magazine-2/

920. *Journal of Scholarly Publishing.* Formerly (until 1994): *Scholarly Publishing.* [ISSN: 1198-9742] 1969. q. USD 158. Ed(s): Robert Brown, Alex Holzman. University of Toronto Press, Journals Division, 5201 Dufferin St, Toronto, ON M3H 5T8, Canada; journals@utpress.utoronto.ca; http://www.utpjournals.com. Illus., index, adv. Sample. Refereed. Vol. ends: Jul. Microform: PQC. *Indexed:* A01, A22, BAS, E01, ISTA, MLA-IB. *Bk. rev.:* 1-4, 400-500 words. *Aud.:* Ac, Sa.

For nearly 50 years, the *Journal of Scholarly Publishing* has been an authoritative voice on academic publishing. It describes itself as "a resource for academics and publishers that addresses the new challenges resulting from changes in technology, funding and innovations in publishing." *JSP* features articles on topics like the future of scholarly publishing, scholarship on the web, digitization, copyright, editorial policies, computer applications, marketing, and pricing models. It is published by the University of Toronto Press, and digital access is available via UTP's web site, as well as through Project Muse, both of which offer full searching of articles. Online articles sometimes include enhanced features not available in the print version - photos, videos, and audio - encouraging further exploration and research. Published quarterly, *JSP* will appeal to authors, editors, marketers, and publishers of scholarly books and journals, and is recommended for academic and research libraries. URL: www.utpjournals.com/Journal-of-Scholarly-Publishing.html

921. *Kirkus Reviews.* Former titles (until 1991): *Jim Kobak's Kirkus Reviews;* (until 1985): *Kirkus Reviews;* (until 1969): *Kirkus Service;* (until 1967): *Virginia Kirkus' Service;* (until 1964): *Virginia Kirkus' Service. Bulletin;* (until 1955): *Virginia Kirkus' Bookshop Service. Bulletin.* [ISSN: 1948-7428] 1933. bi-w. USD 199 combined subscription domestic (print & online eds.); USD 229 combined subscription foreign (print & online eds.)). Ed(s): Claiborne Smith. Kirkus Media LLC, 6411 Burleson Rd, Austin, TX 78744; customers@kirkusreviews.com; http://www.kirkusreviews.com. Illus., index, adv. *Indexed:* A01, BRI, CBRI, MASUSE. *Bk. rev.:* Number and length vary. *Aud.:* Ems, Hs, Ga, Ac.

Founded in 1933, *Kirkus Reviews* publishes book reviews, book apps, and self-published books twice a month. The magazine is available digitally or in print. *Kirkus* reviews fiction, nonfiction, children's, teen, and indie books. Books of exceptional merit are awarded a "Kirkus Star" and are automatically entered into the Kirkus Prize contest, which awards the Kirkus Prize for Fiction, the Kirkus Prize for Nonfiction, and the Kirkus Prize for Young Readers' Literature. The web site provides links to independent, young adult, children's, and adult print indexes, book reviews, author interviews, video interviews with authors, blogs, a ProConnect service (which connects publishers, agents, and film executives with self-published books), and services for authors. *Kirkus Reviews* is recommended for school libraries, public libraries, and academic libraries. URL: https://www.kirkusreviews.com/

922. *Lambda Literary Review.* Former titles (until 2010): *Lambda Book Report;* (until 1991): *Lambda Rising Book Report.* 1987. q. Ed(s): William Johnson. Lambda Literary Foundation, 5482 Wilshire Boulevard #1595, Los Angeles, CA 90036; http://www.lambdalit.org. Illus., adv. *Indexed:* A01, A22, AmHI, BRI, C37, C42, CBRI, GW, MASUSE, MLA-IB. *Aud.:* Hs, Ga, Ac.

Prior to the publication of the web magazine, the *Lambda Literary Review,* the Lambda Literary Foundation published the *Lambda Book Report.* The *Lambda Literary Review* covers anthologies, drama, erotica, general fiction, illustrated, memoirs, mystery, nonfiction, poetry, romance, speculative fiction, and young adult books. The *Lambda Literary Review* also publishes interviews, editorials, essays, poetry, an online book club, and LGBT-themed arts news articles. The Lambda Literary Awards, an annual literary awards ceremony presented by the Lambda Literary Foundation, celebrates the best lesbian, gay, bisexual, and transgender books of the year. The Lambda Literary Foundation web site provides links to the Lambda Literary Awards, Writers' Retreat for Emerging LGBT Voices, Lambda LitFest Los Angeles, LGBT Writers in Schools Program, and literary resources such as book clubs, literary magazines, organizations, publishers, bookstores, and book groups. The *Lambda Literary Review* is recommended for school, public, and academic libraries. URL: www.lambdaliterary.org/

923. *London Review of Books.* [ISSN: 0260-9592] 1979. fortn. GBP 29.95 domestic; GBP 37.20 elsewhere including Europe; USD 35 United States. Ed(s): Mary-Kay Wilmers. L R B Ltd., 28 Little Russell St, London, WC1A 2HN, United Kingdom. Illus., index, adv. Vol. ends: Dec. Microform: PQC. *Indexed:* A01, A22, AmHI, BRI, C37, CBRI, MLA-IB. *Bk. rev.:* 15-20, 1,500-2,500 words. *Aud.:* Ga, Ac.

Founded in the late 1970s, *The London Review of Books* has the largest circulation of any literary magazine in Europe. It is published 24 times a year, and each issue contains up to 15 lengthy reviews and essays on social and political issues written by academics, writers, and journalists. There are also shorter art and film reviews, as well as poems. The *LRB* web site features an easily browsable archive, a podcast in which authors read their essays, and a blog that focuses on current affairs. The web site has some freely available articles from both current and past issues; the electronic version of the current issue and the complete online archive are available to subscribers. Recommended for academic and larger public libraries. URL: www.lrb.co.uk/

924. *New York Review of Books.* [ISSN: 0028-7504] 1963. s-m. USD 79.95 domestic; USD 95 Canada; USD 115 elsewhere. Ed(s): Ian Buruma. N Y R E V, Inc., 435 Hudson St Ste 300, New York, NY 10014. Illus., adv. Circ: 132976. Vol. ends: Jan. Microform: PQC. *Indexed:* A&ATA, A01, A22, AmHI, BRI, CBRI, MASUSE, MLA-IB. *Bk. rev.:* 15-20, 2,000-3,500 words. *Aud.:* Ga, Ac, Sa.

Founded in 1963, *The New York Review of Books* is often thought of as one of the English language's premier literary magazines. The *NYRB* is published twice a month and features thoughtful, in-depth articles on politics, books, and culture. Most of its articles are written by writers who are themselves a major force in world literature. A recent issue contained contributions by Christian Wiman, Claire Messud, James Wolcott, and Darryl Pinckney. In addition to reviews, interviews, and articles, the *Review* features original poetry and extensive advertising from academic publishers promoting newly published books. Its web site features robust content, including a blog and a podcast. Many of the *NYRB*'s articles are freely available on its web site, and subscribers have access to a complete archive dating back to 1963. An essential resource for academic and public libraries. URL: www.nybooks.com/

925. *New York Times Book Review.* Former titles (until 1923): *New York Times Book Review and Magazine;* (until 1920): *New York Times Review of Books;* (until 1911): *New York Times Saturday Review of Books and Art;* (until 1896): *New York Times Saturday Book Review Supplement.* [ISSN: 0028-7806] 1896. w. New York Times Company, 620 8th Ave, New York, NY 10018; public@nytimes.com; http://www.nytimes.com. Illus., index. Vol. ends: Dec. Microform: PQC. *Indexed:* A01, A22, AmHI, BRI, CBRI, Chicano, MLA-IB. *Bk. rev.:* 45-50, 250-2,500 words. *Aud.:* Ga, Ac, Sa.

The *New York Times Book Review* is a weekly publication that is available as both part of the Sunday edition of *The New York Times* and via its own subscription. The *NYTBR* is regarded as one of the most influential and widely read book review publications. It features reviews written by journalists, academics, and writers of both fiction and nonfiction books that have been published by primarily large publishers. *NYTBR* is known for its in-depth, full-page reviews and its influential weekly bestsellers list, as well as its end-of-the-year best-of lists. Its web site features a book review podcast as well as an archive dating back to 1981, which is freely accessible to subscribers and allows non-subscribers to view ten free articles per month. An essential source for all libraries. URL: www.nytimes.com/pages/books/review/

926. *Publishers Weekly: the international news magazine of book publishing.* Formerly (until 1873): *Publishers' and Stationers' Weekly Trade Circular;* Incorporates (in 1872): *American Literary Gazette and Publishers' Circular;* Which was formerly (until 1863): *American Publishers' Circular and Literary Gazette;* (until 1855): *Norton's Literary Gazette and Publishers' Circular.* [ISSN: 0000-0019] 1872. w. Free to qualified personnel; USD 249 combined subscription domestic (print &

online eds.)). PWxyz, LLC, 71 West 23 St. #1608, New York, NY 10010. Illus., index, adv. Sample. Vol. ends: Dec. *Indexed:* A01, A22, B01, B03, BAS, BRI, C37, C42, CBRI, Chicano, F01, MASUSE, MLA-IB. *Bk. rev.:* 70, 50-150 words. *Aud.:* Ems, Hs, Ga, Ac, Sa.

Publishers Weekly is a weekly newsmagazine that features articles, news stories, bestsellers lists, industry statistics, and book reviews. It publishes more than 175 book reviews in each issue, with notable books assigned a red star. Its targeted audience include publishers, booksellers, librarians, literary agents, authors, and the media. The *Publishers Weekly* website provides links to news stories; book reviews; bestsellers lists; children's and young adult book reviews and industry news; author interviews and profiles; announcements; e-book and digital publishing news; international book publishing news and trade shows; and opinion pieces. *Publishers Weekly* now also covers self-published books through "BookLife," *Publishers Weekly*'s website dedicated to independent authors. Subscribers can choose to subscribe to the print and digital edition or just the digital edition, which includes access to the *Publishers Weekly* book reviews database of more than 200,000 book reviews, 95,000 articles, and 9,000 author interviews. *Publishers Weekly* is recommended for school and public libraries. URL: www.publishersweekly.com/

927. ***Rain Taxi: review of books.*** [ISSN: 1535-9352] 1996. q. USD 16 domestic; USD 25 in Canada & Mexico; USD 45 elsewhere. Ed(s): Eric Lorberer. Rain Taxi, Inc., PO Box 3840, Minneapolis, MN 55403; orders@raintaxi.com. Illus., adv. Circ: 16000. *Aud.:* Ems, Hs, Ga, Ac.

Published quarterly, *Rain Taxi* publishes reviews of fiction, poetry, nonfiction, graphic novels, art, drama, and children's and young adult books; it also includes essays and interviews, in print and digital form. The online edition includes material not found in the print edition, including short book reviews. *Rain Taxi* also publishes a chapbook series and hosts literary events. The *Rain Taxi* web site provides links to videos of author interviews, pedagogical resources, bookstores, literary magazines, and "Rain Taxi Rewind," which is a curated look at archived reviews published by *Rain Taxi* in the last 20 years. *Rain Taxi* is recommended for public and academic libraries. URL: www.raintaxi.com/

928. ***T L S: the Times literary supplement.*** Formerly (until 1969): *Times Literary Supplement.* [ISSN: 0307-661X] 1902. w. Ed(s): James MacManus, Peter Stothard. Times Newspapers Ltd., 3 Thomas More Sq, London, E98 1XY, United Kingdom; custserv@timesonline.co.uk; http://www.timesonline.co.uk. Illus., index, adv. Vol. ends: Dec. Microform: RPI. *Indexed:* A01, A22, AmHI, BRI, CBRI, F01, MLA-IB. *Bk. rev.:* Number and length vary. *Aud.:* Ga, Ac.

Founded more than a century ago, the *Times Literary Supplement* is a weekly publication based in London that describes itself as offering "comprehensive coverage of the latest and most important publications, in every subject, and in several languages." Reviews in *TLS* are divided by subject: cultural history, classics, biography, fiction, history, language, and others. Contributors to *TLS* have included literary icons such as Orhan Pamuk, Italo Calvino, and Gore Vidal. *TLS* is available as part of the *Sunday Times* or via its own subscription. Its web site contains a comprehensive text archive, with articles from 1994 to the present, which is available to subscribers. There is a separate historical archive available via Cengage Learning, which contains content published between 1902 and 2007 and features full-text searching. Highly recommended for both public and academic libraries that seek a resource that covers literature through an international lens. URL: www.the-tls.co.uk/tls/

929. ***The Women's Review of Books.*** [ISSN: 0738-1433] 1983. bi-m. USD 133 (Individuals, USD 46; USD 6 per issue). Ed(s): Amy Hoffman. Old City Publishing, Inc., 628 N 2nd St, Philadelphia, PA 19123; info@oldcitypublishing.com; http://www.oldcitypublishing.com. Illus., index, adv. Sample. Vol. ends: Sep. Microform: PQC. *Indexed:* A01, A22, AmHI, BRI, C37, C42, CBRI, FemPer, MASUSE, MLA-IB, WSA. *Bk. rev.:* 15-20, 1,000-1,500 words. *Aud.:* Ga, Ac, Sa.

The Women's Review of Books, a collaborative project between the Wellesley Centers for Women and Old City Publishing, began publishing essays, book reviews, and poetry by and about women in 1983. As a bimonthly publication, *The Women's Review of Books* covers fiction, poetry, art, memoirs/biographies, theory, history, and other nonfiction topics. It also publishes original artwork, illustrations, photography, and poetry by women. Selected articles from as far back as 2006 are made available through the Wellesley Centers for Women web site. *WRB* is recommended for public and academic libraries. URL: www.wcwonline.org/Women-s-Review-of-Books/womens-review-of-books

■ BOTANY

See also Biology; and Ecology sections.

Brian Ryckman, STEM Librarian, Southern New Hampshire University, 2500 N. River Rd., Manchester, NH 03106

Introduction

Botany traces its origins back millennia when peoples sought to improve agricultural output recognizing plant hardiness, diversity, and sustainability as factors directly related to survival. The field has expanded considerably and touches many disciplines but it's interesting to consider how these early concerns still resonate in modern study. The treatment of these issues has broadened from an individual level to that of global significance as we look to plants as harbingers of environmental change while holding potential solutions to food scarcity and security, medicinal applications, biofuels, environmental management, and other challenges. Botany is generally divided into the following sub-disciplines: morphology, physiology, ecology, and systematics, further dividing into smaller subcategories. In this section the study of plants is treated from a scientific perspective but we should also consider the social, medicinal, and humanistic fields in which the history of the study of plants has played a significant role.

While this section focuses on botany as its core, other sections within *MFL,* such as "Biology" or "Ecology," may also be of interest to libraries looking to collect in this subject area to provide associated information for patrons. Researchers and laypersons may consider titles that address specific issues within the field such as Gardening, Biotechnology, Agriculture, Horticulture, and Forestry as examples. Many professional societies and organizations exist within the field of botany and several serve as publisher of their own journal. Because of this, many of the publications have a research or scholarly focus in both general and more specialized areas, but several would fit well in public libraries with special collections or a strong user interest in the subject matter. Several of the journals also offer online open access either at the article level or regarding the publication as a whole.

Basic Periodicals

Ac: *American Journal of Botany, Annals of Botany, International Journal of Plant Sciences.*

Basic Abstracts and Indexes

AGRICOLA, BIOBASE, Biological Abstracts, Biological & Agricultural Index, CAB Abstracts, Chemical Abstracts, Horticultural Science Abstracts, Science Citation Index.

930. ***A O B Plants.*** [ISSN: 2041-2851] 2009. m. Free. Ed(s): J Hall Cushman. Oxford University Press, Great Clarendon St, Oxford, OX2 6DP, United Kingdom; onlinequeries.uk@oup.com; https://academic.oup.com/journals/. Refereed. *Indexed:* C45. *Aud.:* Ac, Sa.

Managed by the Annals of Botany Company with the support of Oxford University Press, this open-access, not-for-profit journal was established in 2009 in response to overwhelming numbers of submissions to its sister journal, *Annals of Botany. AOB Plants* maintains open-access position with relatively low author fees adhering to the philosophy that scientific research should be made available to the public. This journal features timely and transparent high-quality research on all aspects organismal, environmental, ecological, and evolutionary plant biology with an eye toward current interest. The types of articles published include research and technical articles, reviews, commentaries, and short communications. Because of the general scope and wide intended audience, this publication will be of interest for public, academic, and special botany collections.

931. ***American Journal of Botany.*** Incorporates (19??-1982): *Botanical Society of America. Meeting. Abstracts;* Which was formerly (until 198?): *Botanical Society of America. Abstracts of Papers to be Presented at the Meetings;* (until 1977): *American Journal of Botany.* [ISSN: 0002-9122] 1914. m. Ed(s): Pamela Diggle, Amy McPherson. John Wiley & Sons Ltd., EMEA Institutional Sales, 9600 Garsington Rd, Oxford, OX4 2DQ, United Kingdom; cs-journals@wiley.com; http://onlinelibrary.wiley.com. Illus., adv. Sample. Refereed. Microform: IDC; PMC. *Indexed:* A01, A22, Agr, BRI, C45, S25. *Bk. rev.:* Number and length vary. *Aud.:* Ac, Sa.

This journal is published by the Botanical Society of America, featuring peer-reviewed research articles, news and views, and reviews. According to the author submission guidelines, the journal publishes in all areas of plant biology (including ecology, evolution, physiology, biodiversity, systematics, development, genetics, paleobotany, structure, and function), all levels of organization (ecosystem to molecular), and all organisms studied by botanical researchers (including land plants, algae, fungi, lichen, cyanobacteria). With its general focus on all plant groups and allied organisms, this journal is of interest to plant scientists in all areas of plant biology. Recommended for academic and special botany collections.

932. ***Annals of Botany.*** [ISSN: 0305-7364] 1887. 14x/yr. EUR 1803. Ed(s): J S Heslop-Harrison, David Frost. Oxford University Press, Great Clarendon St, Oxford, OX2 6DP, United Kingdom; onlinequeries.uk@oup.com; http://global.oup.com. Illus., adv. Sample. Refereed. Microform: IDC; PMC. Reprint: PSC. *Indexed:* A01, A22, Agr, C45, E01, S25. *Bk. rev.:* Number and length vary. *Aud.:* Ac, Sa.

First published in 1887, the *Annals of Botany* is the oldest continuously published plant science journal. The journal is managed by the Annals of Botany Company, a not-for-profit educational charity, and is recognized for its rigorous review process. Topics range from applying molecular, analytical, mathematical, and statistical techniques to examine topical questions at any level of biological organization ranging from cell to community, from tissue culture to crop production, and from microclimate to ecosystem. Published monthly, this journal also produces at least two extra issues per year on a particular theme of interest in plant biology. Articles include research papers, review articles (both invited and submitted), and book reviews. This journal is of interest to plant biology researchers across specialties and is recommended for academic and special botany collections.

933. ***Annual Review of Plant Biology.*** Former titles (until 2002): *Annual Review of Plant Physiology and Plant Molecular Biology;* (until 1988): *Annual Review of Plant Physiology.* [ISSN: 1543-5008] 1950. a. USD 431 (print & online eds.)). Ed(s): Sabeeha Merchant. Annual Reviews, PO Box 10139, Palo Alto, CA 94303; service@annualreviews.org; http://www.annualreviews.org. Refereed. Reprint: PSC. *Indexed:* A01, A22, Agr, C45, GardL. *Aud.:* Ac, Sa.

Since 1950, researchers have turned to *Annual Review of Plant Biology* for review articles that cover a wide range of plant biology subdisciplines including biochemistry and biosynthesis, genetics, genomics and molecular biology, cell differentiation, tissue, organ and whole plant events, acclimation and adaptation, and methods and model organisms. Plant biology is covered from the cellular to the community level, with a focus on significant contributions to advancement in the previous year. This journal will be of great use to keep plant biology researchers aware of important annual advances across the field. It should be a core component of an academic or special library collection that supports such researchers.

934. ***B M C Plant Biology.*** [ISSN: 1471-2229] 2001. irreg. Free. Ed(s): Julia Simundza. BioMed Central Ltd., Floor 6, 236 Gray's Inn Rd, London, WC1X 8HB, United Kingdom; info@biomedcentral.com; https://www.biomedcentral.com. Adv. Refereed. *Indexed:* A01, Agr, C45. *Aud.:* Ac, Sa.

BMC Plant Biology is an open access, peer-reviewed journal that considers articles on all aspects of plant biology, including molecular, cellular, tissue, organ, and whole organism research. Especially useful features of this online-only journal include large datasets, large numbers of illustrations and moving pictures, and data displayed in a form that can be manipulated by readers. This journal is freely available online, and offers comprehensive articles on topics of interest to general plant scientists and specialized botanists. It is recommended for all academic, special botany collections, and could prove a useful, free addition to a public library collection as well.

935. ***The Botanical Review.*** [ISSN: 0006-8101] 1935. q. EUR 223 (print & online eds.)). Ed(s): Dennis W M Steven, Brian Boom. Springer New York LLC, 233 Spring St, New York, NY 10013; customerservice@springer.com; http://www.springer.com. Illus., adv. Sample. Refereed. Vol. ends: Oct/Dec. Microform: IDC; PMC; PQC. Reprint: PSC. *Indexed:* A01, A22, Agr, BRI, C45, E01. *Aud.:* Ac, Sa.

The Botanical Review has been a leading international journal noted for its in-depth articles on a broad spectrum of botanical fields. Its detailed review articles cover a wide range of topics within the field of botany, including systematics, phytogeography, cladistics, evolution, physiology, ecology, morphology, paleobotany, and anatomy. The goal of the journal is to synthesize the current research done by various scientists on a particular topic within the field of plant biology in order to identify current gaps and research needs within that particular area. Articles are mainly by invitation. This journal will be of interest to any researcher wishing to keep current in the field of plant biology, and is recommended for academic and special botany collections.

936. ***Botany.*** Former titles (until Jan.2008): *Canadian Journal of Botany;* (until 1950): *Canadian Journal of Research. Section C: Botanical Sciences;* Which superseded in part (in 1935): *Canadian Journal of Research.* [ISSN: 1916-2790] 1929. m. USD 1973 (print & online eds.)). Ed(s): Christian R Lacroix. Canadian Science Publishing, 65 Auriga Dr, Ste 203, Ottawa, ON K2E 7W6, Canada; pubs@cdnsciencepub.com; http://www.nrcresearchpress.com. Illus., index, adv. Refereed. Vol. ends: Dec. *Indexed:* A01, A22, Agr, C37, C45, E01, S25. *Aud.:* Ac, Sa.

This well-respected international journal has been a source of original research articles, review articles, and commentary in all areas of plant science since 1929. The National Research Council of Canada, the journal's publisher, ensures a rigorous peer-review process for each article. Topics covered include cell and molecular biology, ecology, mycology and plant-microbe interactions, phycology, physiology and biochemistry, structure and development, genetics, systematics, and phytogeography. The journal is of interest to general and specialized plant science researchers, and is recommended for public, academic, or special botany collections.

937. ***Current Opinion in Plant Biology.*** [ISSN: 1369-5266] 1998. bi-m. EUR 3561. Ed(s): Ottoline Leyser, James Carrington. Elsevier Ltd., Current Opinion Journals, The Blvd, Langford Ln, Kidlington, OX5 1GB, United Kingdom; JournalsCustomerServiceEMEA@elsevier.com; http://www.current-opinion.com. Adv. Sample. Refereed. *Indexed:* A01, A22, Agr, C45, GardL. *Aud.:* Ac, Sa.

Current Opinion in Plant Biology is focused on presenting the most significant developments in plant biology each year. It grows increasingly more difficult to keep up with the many diverse research developments that impact the field of botany. In response to this trend, this journal utilizes experts within the field of study to identify and analyze the most significant advances in botany over the previous year. This journal is primarily written for botany researchers, and is divided into themed sections including growth and development, genome studies and molecular genetics, physiology and metabolism, biotic interactions, cell signaling and gene regulation, and cell biology. The journal commissions section editors (authorities in their field) for each of these topics, who then decide which subtopics will be covered in their section. These editors then invite individual authors to compose short review articles in which they present recent developments they feel were most significant in the previous year for each subtopic. Additionally, these authors select original research articles they found most interesting and annotate those articles for inclusion. This publication will be of primary interest to academic and special botany collections; however, it could play a useful role in a comprehensive public library collection where researchers need to keep abreast of current botany research.

938. ***International Journal of Plant Sciences.*** Former titles (until 1992): *Botanical Gazette;* (until 1876): *Botanical Bulletin.* [ISSN: 1058-5893] 1875. 9x/yr. USD 1734 (print & online eds.)). Ed(s): Christina Caruso. University of Chicago Press, 1427 E 60th St, Chicago, IL 60637; subscriptions@press.uchicago.edu; http://www.journals.uchicago.edu. Illus., index, adv. Sample. Refereed. Vol. ends: Nov. Reprint: PSC. *Indexed:* A01, A22, Agr, BRI, C45, GardL, S25. *Bk. rev.:* Number and length vary. *Aud.:* Ac, Sa.

This journal, internationally recognized as a major forum for botany research, presents original, peer-reviewed research in all areas of the plant sciences. Focused on presenting new contributions in plant biology from around the world, the journal covers a wide variety of topics including biochemistry, cell and developmental biology, ecology, evolution, genetics, genomics, physiology, morphology and anatomy, systematics, plant-microbe interactions, and paleobotany. In addition, the journal publishes special issues on topics of current interest, including research presented at major botanical conferences. This journal is written for general and specialized plant biologists who are interested in current research in the field, and is recommended for any academic or special botany collection.

939. ***New Phytologist (Online).*** [ISSN: 1469-8137] 1998. 16x/yr. GBP 2757. Ed(s): Alistair Hetherington. Wiley-Blackwell Publishing Ltd., The Atrium, Southern Gate, Chichester, PO19 8QG, United Kingdom; cs-journals@wiley.com; http://onlinelibrary.wiley.com. Refereed. *Bk. rev.:* Number and length vary. *Aud.:* Ac, Sa.

New Phytologist, published on behalf of the nonprofit New Phytologist Trust, is dedicated to the promotion of original and current plant-science research. The journal presents peer-reviewed, original research on topics of current interest in plant science that fall into four major areas: physiology and development, environment, interaction, and evolution. These topics are covered at levels ranging from cellular to the global environment. Other features of the journal include a forum section that hosts letters, commentary, meeting reports, and opinion pieces; short research reviews on topics of current interest; rapid reports; modeling/theory papers; and methods papers. Special issues of the journal are published to highlight key areas of current research. There are open-access options available to authors, so some of this journal's articles are freely available online. This journal is recommended for general plant scientists who need to keep up-to-date with current research developments and scholarly discussion. It would be key for any academic or special botany collection.

940. ***The Plant Cell.*** [ISSN: 1040-4651] 1989. m. Ed(s): Sabeeha Merchant. American Society of Plant Biologists, 15501 Monona Dr, Rockville, MD 20855; info@aspb.org; http://www.aspb.org. Illus., index, adv. Sample. Refereed. *Indexed:* A01, A22, Agr, C45. *Aud.:* Ga, Ac, Sa.

The Plant Cell is a highly regarded source of cutting-edge original research that is of broad interest to all plant biologists, not just specialists. The journal places special emphasis on cellular biology, molecular biology, biochemistry, genetics, development, and evolution. Published monthly by the American Society of Plant Biologists, this journal prides itself on a rigorous but very expedient peer-review process that provides rapid turnaround on research articles. As part of the journal's mission to increase interactive discussion in the plant biology research community, the front section of the journal is devoted to commentaries, editorials, meeting reports, review articles, and summaries of featured research papers. There are some open-access articles available for this journal via the journal's website. Since *The Plant Cell* is written for a general audience of plant biology researchers, it is recommended for any public, academic, or special botany collection.

941. ***Plant, Cell & Environment.*** [ISSN: 0140-7791] 1978. m. GBP 4771. Ed(s): Anna Amtmann. Wiley-Blackwell Publishing Ltd., The Atrium, Southern Gate, Chichester, PO19 8QG, United Kingdom; cs-journals@wiley.com; http://www.wiley.com/. Illus., adv. Sample. Refereed. Microform: PQC. Reprint: PSC. *Indexed:* A01, A22, Agr, C45, E01, S25. *Aud.:* Ac, Sa.

This high-impact journal focuses on the ways plants respond to their environment. The journal publishes original research articles, technical reports, reviews, and commentaries that provide readers with new awareness about these interactions. Because this is such an interdisciplinary focus, the topics covered include plant biochemistry, molecular biology, biophysics, cell and whole plant physiology, crop physiology, physiological ecology, genetics, and pathology. These topics are examined at many different levels, from molecular to the whole community. This is an excellent journal for botany researchers who want a wide breadth of knowledge about divergent plant/environment interactions, and it would be particularly useful in an academic or special library setting.

942. ***The Plant Journal (Online).*** [ISSN: 1365-313X] 1991. s-m. GBP 4133. Wiley-Blackwell Publishing Ltd., The Atrium, Southern Gate, Chichester, PO19 8QG, United Kingdom; cs-journals@wiley.com; http://www.wiley.com/. Refereed. *Indexed:* C45. *Aud.:* Ac, Sa.

This journal, published in association with the Society for Experimental Biology, is one of the most highly cited by the general plant science community. *The Plant Journal* presents highly significant advances in international botany research. Topics covered range across all areas of plant biology, including molecular and cell biology, biochemistry, genetics, and protein function in plants. Original research articles, technical advance articles, and resource articles are all included in the journal; special issues are published periodically on topics of current interest. There are open-access options available for some of the journal articles via the publisher's website. As a high-quality, rigorous research publication intended to keep any botany researcher up-to-date, this journal is suitable for academic or special botany collections.

943. ***Plant Physiology (Online).*** [ISSN: 1532-2548] 1926. m. Free. Ed(s): Michael R Blatt, Patti Lockhart. American Society of Plant Biologists, 15501 Monona Dr, Rockville, MD 20855; info@aspb.org; http://www.aspb.org. Adv. *Aud.:* Ac, Sa.

Plant Physiology is a highly regarded, international journal that presents basic research on how plants live, function, and interact with their biotic and abiotic environments. The topics covered include physiology, cellular and molecular biology, biochemistry, genetics, biophysics, and the environmental biology of plants. Some articles are available for free via the journal's website, and they are labeled accordingly. This journal is written for scientists interested in the physiology of plants, but presents a wide range of topics within that discipline. It is a necessary journal for any academic or special botany collection that supports plant physiology researchers.

944. ***Taxon: international journal of plant taxonomy, phylogeny and evolution.*** [ISSN: 0040-0262] 1951. bi-m. EUR 698. Ed(s): Dirk C. Albach. Wiley - V C H Verlag GmbH & Co. KGaA, Postfach 101161, Weinheim, 69451, Germany; service@wiley-vch.de; http://www.wiley-vch.de. Illus., adv. Refereed. *Indexed:* A22, Agr, C45. *Bk. rev.:* Number and length vary. *Aud.:* Ac, Sa.

As the official journal of the International Association for Plant Taxonomy, this is an important source for current information regarding plant and fungal systematic and evolutionary botany. Topics covered include, but are not limited to, systematics, molecular phylogenetics, morphology, taxonomy and plant classification, methods and techniques, paleobotany, and nomenclature. In addition to original, peer-reviewed research articles and review articles, the journal also includes features such as proposals to conserve or reject names, proposals to amend the code, current reports on plant systematics from around the world, and book reviews. As it is written for an international research audience with a particular interest in taxonomy, phylogeny, systematics, and nomenclature, this journal will be of interest to any academic and special libraries that support such specialized interests.

945. ***Trends in Plant Science.*** [ISSN: 1360-1385] 1996. m. EUR 3657. Ed(s): Susanne C Brink. Elsevier Ltd., Trends Journals, The Blvd, Langford Ln, Kidlington, Oxford, OX5 1GB, United Kingdom; JournalsCustomerServiceEMEA@elsevier.com; http://www.elsevier.com. Illus., adv. Sample. Refereed. Vol. ends: No. 6. *Indexed:* A01, A22, Agr, C45, GardL. *Aud.:* Ac, Sa.

This highly cited journal presents review articles on a broad range of topics of current interest to both plant science researchers and technicians. Topics presented include (but are not limited to) growth and development, genetics and evolution, cell biology, physiology, nutrition, pathology, and plant interactions with both abiotic and biotic environments. These topics are covered at levels ranging from molecular to ecosystem. Invited and refereed review articles, as well as opinion articles, focus on basic research topics or controversies that illuminate important developments on a particular specialty topic. The journal is designed as a tool for academic and applied plant scientists across specialties to stay current with the latest botany research developments. It is appropriate for academic and special library collections that serve either researchers or field technicians.

■ BUILDING AND CONSTRUCTION

See also Architecture; Home; and Interior Design and Decoration sections.

Nicholas Wharton, Head, Reference and Public Services, Mortensen Library, University of Hartford, 200 Bloomfield Ave., West Hartford, CT 06117; wharton@hartford.edu

Introduction

Construction information can be passed along from skilled practitioner to apprentice or trade student through example, trial and error, and even drawing up or writing one's own how to's. Having the best information and locating the correct tools to be able to take on and complete minor or major construction projects, becomes as important to the skilled contractor as the correct procedures and tools for a physician performing surgery. Architects design the specifications for a project. Installers then must interpret those plans to build anything from a renovated bathroom to the tallest skyscraper. All of the pieces have to fit to create a final project safely built with quality materials and up to code. As long as there have been projects, which is about as long as humanity has been using tools to aid in the domestication and building of cities, towns, and roads, there have been trade secrets or blueprints that can be taught by hand or written out with steps and drawings or pictures and passed down. For hundreds of years, construction organizations have highlighted those steps by producing books, magazines, and newsletters to help guide humanity to continue to build and rebuild our societies.

This section of *Magazines for Libraries* highlights some of the best journals and magazines that a patron may be looking for to gain new ideas, learn how to design or build, learn about new products and comparisons, or just get to see what other projects have been successful over the years. This section caters to the men and women in the construction business who do this masterful work day in and day out. Engineers, architects, project managers, carpenters, masons, heavy equipment drivers, glaziers, and laborers need guidance that may require more than what a supervisor or colleague may impart from prior knowledge over the years. Ways to complete tasks may become obsolete or dangerous, and building processes may become more streamlined, more or less expensive, and safer. Materials may fall out of fashion as green technologies and different materials will improve building performance or longevity with less maintenance.

This chapter highlights all of these factors, the practical, the theoretical, and the informational can be found in these magazines that focus on a multitude of types of construction. The magazines represent industries in concrete, new construction, light construction, remodeling, HVAC, steam fitting, machinery, and electrical maintenance. Each magazine has an online presence and some have shifted to exclusively online. On each website there is helpful information that is freely available to help with the specific areas that are highlighted on each page or section. Product information, best practices, newsletters, access to archives, and article searches represent the common online options for each journal.

Many types of libraries will require access to many or all of these journals. Patrons in public libraries across the globe, special libraries that serve engineering, construction and architectural patrons, school libraries with trade programs and classes, and academic libraries that support construction, design, and engineering programs all may have needs served by one or more of the journals in the Building and Construction chapter. Whatever the library and whoever the patron is, these magazines will help to mold the construction worker or engineer into a more rounded, knowledgeable, and safer member in their field.

Basic Periodicals

Sa: *Builder* (Washington), *Building Design & Construction, Constructor, Professional Builder.*

Basic Abstracts and Indexes

Applied Science and Technology Index, Engineering Index, TRIS Database.

946. ***A C I Materials Journal.*** Supersedes in part (until 1987): *American Concrete Institute. Journal.* [ISSN: 0889-325X] 1905. bi-m. Individuals, USD 172; Free to members. American Concrete Institute, 38800 Country Club Dr, Farmington Hills, MI 48331; BKStore@concrete.org; http://www.concrete.org. Illus., index, adv. Sample. Refereed. *Indexed:* A22, HRIS. *Aud.:* Ac, Sa.

The peer-reviewed *ACI Materials Journal* offers insights into the technical aspects of concrete construction through mixing techniques, maintaining, refurbishing, and strengthening facilities, forms, and walls. The journal touches on factors that range from the technical like electrical resistivity, to maintenance like concrete cracking mitigation, and to current topics like climate change effects on concrete. Abstracts of articles are easily accessible at the American Concrete Institute website (ACI). The ACI suite of journals and reports are available for free to members and all abstracts can be accessed through the International Concrete Abstracts Portal dating back to the first issue of each title. Most articles can be purchased for $14.50 each. Memberships to the American Concrete Institute includes a subscription to the *ACI Materials Journal.* Nonmembers may purchase access for $249/year, $124/year if under 28, free e-membership for students, and organizational memberships at $1,100/year. URL: https://www.concrete.org/publications/acimaterialsjournal.aspx

947. ***A C I Structural Journal.*** Supersedes in part (until 1987): *American Concrete Institute. Journal.* [ISSN: 0889-3241] 1905. bi-m. USD 172 domestic (Free to members). American Concrete Institute, 38800 Country Club Dr, Farmington Hills, MI 48331; BKStore@concrete.org; http://www.concrete.org. Illus., index, adv. Refereed. Microform: PQC. *Indexed:* A22, HRIS. *Aud.:* Ac, Sa.

Dealing with the structural aspects of concrete construction, the peer-reviewed *ACI Structural Journal* focuses on analysis and design of concrete structures and reinforcing technologies and techniques. Topics may include concrete beams use and construction, steel and fiber reinforcements, seismic performance, anti-cracking control, and corrosion protection. Abstracts of articles are easily accessible at the American Concrete Institute website (ACI). The website also offers access to codes and standards, other handbooks and manuals, symposia reports, and other guides. The ACI suite of journals and reports are available for free to members and all abstracts can be accessed through the International Concrete Abstracts Portal dating back to the first issue of each title. Most articles can be purchased for $14.50 each. Memberships to the American Concrete Institute includes a subscription to the *ACI Structural Journal.* Non-members may purchase access for $249 per year, $124 per year if under 28, free e-membership for students, and organizational memberships at $1,100 per year. URL: https://www.concrete.org/publications/acistructuraljournal.aspx

948. ***Builder (Washington).*** Incorporates (1978-1982): *Housing;* Which was formerly (until 1978): *House & Home;* (until 1952): *The Magazine of Building (House & Home Edition);* (until 19??): *Architectural Forum;* Supersedes in part (in 1981): *N A H B Builder;* Which was formerly (until 1980): *Builder;* Which superseded (in 1978): *N A H B Journal-Scope;* Which was formed by the merger of: *N A H B Journal; N A H B Washington Scope.* [ISSN: 0744-1193] 1942. m. Free to qualified personnel. Ed(s): Denise Dersin. Hanley Wood, LLC, 1 Thomas Cir, NW, Ste 600, Washington, DC 20005; fanton@hanleywood.com; http://www.hanleywood.com. Illus., adv. Microform: PQC. *Indexed:* A22, BRI. *Aud.:* Ac, Sa.

Builder takes on all aspects of new building construction highlighting modern trends such as prefabrication and tiny homes, going green with passive solar and smart homes, economic trends in the housing industry and building tricks. *Builder* is one of several Hanley Wood publications to support the home builder, carpenter, general contractor, and designer. The *Builder* website has links to online news articles, links to *Builder* articles, and helpful sections with videos, products, design, and resources to help the general contractors, designer, and carpenters create homes for all interested buyers and developers to enjoy. The online magazine has a browse archive to 2006, with searchable articles back to 2001. Email subscriptions are free as is an opt in daily newsletter. Print subscriptions are free to those who qualify or $8 per issue for those not qualified. Qualification criteria is not fully explained on site.

949. ***Building Design & Construction: the magazine for the building team.*** Formerly (until 1958): *Building Construction.* [ISSN: 0007-3407] 1950. m. Free to qualified personnel. S G C Horizon LLC, 3030 W Salt Creek Ln, Ste 201, Arlington Heights, IL 60005-5025; tmancini@sgcmail.com; http://www.sgchorizon.com/. Illus., index, adv. Sample. Circ: 76006 Controlled. *Indexed:* A22, B03, BRI. *Aud.:* Ac, Sa.

Architects, designers, engineers and contractors will find helpful articles from *Building Design & Construction* magazine. The magazine offers full-color images to go with well written and edited articles to aide in building construction and design whether highlighting products, offering solutions, or highlighting award-winning projects. The online experience offers more than just the magazine with podcasts, videos, blogs, product analysis, and other resources available. The current magazine is highlighted on the home page and can be accessed in magazine format as well. Online access is free and subscriptions are free for email notifications and free for print within the United States. One may also subscribe to several helpful newsletters and online alerts for free. Rates for non-U.S. subscribers is not available. Online archives can be browsed or searched back to September 2010.

950. ***Buildings: smarter facility management.*** Formerly (until 1947): *Buildings and Building Management;* Incorporates (1910-1958): *National Real Estate and Building Journal;* (199?-2002): *Building Interiors.* [ISSN: 0007-3725] 1906. m. Free to qualified personnel. Stamats Business Media, Inc., P O Box 1888, Cedar Rapids, IA 52406; http://www.stamats.com/. Illus., index, adv. Vol. ends: Dec. Microform: PQC. *Indexed:* A22, B01, BRI. *Aud.:* Ac, Sa.

Geared toward facility managers and building owners who oversee building operations, *Buildings* offers insights into care and maintenance of facilities of residential, commercial, and government buildings. Topics include energy-saving options, how to repair or refurbish without disrupting tenants, recycling, and green projects. The online version offers a navigable Table of Contents and page-turning capabilities. You also can download the magazine if you so desire. Online access is free at their website. There is a free online archive dating back to 2015 with a special section for "Vintage Issues," which currently showcases the years 1913 and 1963. Qualified subscribers may receive *Buildings* in print or as "enhanced digital" for free. There is no listed criteria or cost for those deemed not qualified. Interested users may also sign up for various *Buildings* newsletters. URL: https://www.buildings.com/

951. ***Concrete Construction.*** Former titles (until 1999): *Aberdeen's Concrete Construction;* (until 1990): *Concrete Construction.* [ISSN: 1533-7316] 1956. m. USD 30 domestic; USD 39 in Canada & Mexico; USD 93 elsewhere. Ed(s): Stephanie Johnston. Hanley Wood, LLC, 8725 W Higgins Rd, Ste 600, Chicago, IL 60631; fanton@hanleywood.com; http://www.hanleywood.com. Illus., index, adv. Microform: PQC. *Indexed:* A22, BRI, HRIS. *Aud.:* Ac, Sa.

Concrete Construction is part of the Hanley-Wood suite of construction journals. Contractors will find in the *Concrete Construction* magazine well written and informative articles on construction methods and materials, including mixing techniques and best practices. Codes and standards, innovative techniques for controlling mixtures and set times, robotics and machinery are highlighted on the website and in each issue of the magazine. The online experience offers access to web-based areas that includes a "Resource Center," a "How To" section, a product and projects guide, and business resources. Print subscriptions are free, and access is free online to the current issue and the archives. Locating the current online edition requires a scroll to the footer at the bottom of the page; and to find the archives you must scroll to the bottom of the main page and choose "magazine" in the footer. Archives of the journal are available digitally from July 1956 to the present. One may also subscribe to the magazine by filling out an online form linked from the footer of the page. URL: https://www.concreteconstruction.net/

952. ***Concrete International.*** [ISSN: 0162-4075] 1979. m. USD 181 (Members, USD 54). American Concrete Institute, 38800 Country Club Dr, Farmington Hills, MI 48331; BKStore@concrete.org; http://www.concrete.org. Refereed. *Indexed:* A22, HRIS. *Aud.:* Ac, Sa.

Concrete International (*CI*) offers professional contractors, architects, engineers, and technicians insights into guidance, innovations, ACI codes and standards for the development, engineering, and building of concrete structures. For further concrete research, the online journal offers access to abstracts of the current issue and a link to the American Concrete Institute (ACI) abstracts database for all of its publications including *ACI Structural Journal* and *ACI Materials Journal* dating back to its inception. The ACI suite of journals and reports are available for free to members, and all abstracts can also be freely accessed through the International Concrete Abstracts Portal dating back to the first issue of each title. URL: https://www.concrete.org/publications/concreteinternational.aspx

953. ***Construction Equipment: ideas and insight for the equipment pro.*** Former titles: *Construction Equipment Magazine; Construction Equipment and Materials Magazine.* [ISSN: 0192-3978] 1949. 13x/yr. Free to qualified personnel. S G C Horizon LLC, 3030 W Salt Creek Ln, Ste 201, Arlington Heights, IL 60005-5025; tmancini@sgcmail.com; http://www.sgchorizon.com/. Illus., index, adv. Sample. Circ: 80000 Controlled. *Indexed:* A22, B03, BRI. *Aud.:* Sa.

Construction Equipment offers feature articles on the heavy equipment used on construction sites including pavers, cement mixers, loaders, cranes, trucks, and all of the machinery that moves, digs, and builds structures, infrastructure, and landscaping. From Bobcats to skyscraper cranes, the construction engineer, general contractor, and project planner can learn about available equipment to purchase, lease, or rent to complete construction projects. The online experience allows access to the published articles plus access to videos in each issue regarding evaluations, news, and views of machines getting the work done. However, the site is rife with pop-up advertising with each new page accessed. Subscriptions are free for print and email. Just fill out an online form. The online journal is freely available with archives dating back to August 2012. There are also newsletters and product ratings on the website. URL: https://www.constructionequipment.com/

954. ***The Construction Specifier.*** [ISSN: 0010-6925] 1950. m. USD 59 domestic; USD 69 Canada; USD 199 elsewhere. Construction Specifications Institute, 110 S Union St, Ste 100, Alexandria, VA 22314; csi@csinet.org; http://www.csinet.org. Illus., index. *Indexed:* A22. *Aud.:* Sa.

The peer-reviewed articles in the *Construction Specifier* offer insights for those responsible for estimating and buying materials and labor for construction jobs. Coding specifications, materials management, and product pricing will aid all architects, designers, and estimators in determining the best ways to present and land the next construction project; and will also help to maintain the documents and methodology needed to complete the specification process. Subscriptions are free and online. Archives date back to January 2008 and its accompanying newsletter dates back to July 2014. These articles are accessible with a subscription. One may purchase high-quality magazine reprints for $350 per article. URL: https://www.constructionspecifier.com/

955. ***Constructor.*** Supersedes in part (in 1922): *General Contractors Association. Bulletin;* Which was formerly (until 1921): *Associated General Contractors. Bulletin;* (until 1919): *General Contractors Association. Bulletin.* [ISSN: 0162-6191] 1919. bi-m. Ed(s): Jeanne J Clapp. A G C, 2300 Wilson Blvd, Ste 400, Arlington, VA 22201; info@agc.org; http://www.agc.org. Illus., index, adv. *Indexed:* A22, HRIS. *Aud.:* Sa.

Published by the Associated General Contractors of America (AGC), *Constructor* brings articles regarding construction management to the forefront. Articles highlight ways to help the AGC bring projects from design to completion, including articles on safety issues, drone technology, opportunities for women, and ways to save time, effort, and expense. Subscriptions and access to the web content and archives are free. Email and print subscriptions have a quick form. The back issues to May/June 2012 are keyword searchable or may be accessed from a list. There is also an archive to two newsletters and its sponsored content from construction advertisers. URL: https://www.constructormagazine.com/

956. ***Contractor: the newsmagazine of mechanical contracting.*** [ISSN: 0897-7135] 1954. m. USD 99 (Free to members). Ed(s): Robert P Mader. Penton, 1100 Superior Ave., Cleveland, OH 44114; information@penton.com; http://www.penton.com. Illus., adv. Circ: 50377 Controlled. *Indexed:* A22, B01, B03, BRI. *Aud.:* Sa.

Contractor serves the plumbing community, which includes, contractors and engineers who work with piping, heating, fire sprinklers, and general plumbing to better aid those professionals in maintenance, repair, design, and installation of plumbing materials. Online nets the subscriber access to two other online journals, *Contracting Business* and *HPAC Engineering*. The online archive of the digital editions is searchable or browsable to January 2012, but articles are only accessible with a subscription. Subscriptions for online are free, and the print versions of *Contractor* are currently set at $99 per year or $149 for 2 years. A weekly newsletter is available for subscribers, as well. URL: https://contractormag.com

957. *Custom Home.* Incorporates (1987-1999): *Custom Builder;* Which was formerly (until 1987): *Progressive Builder;* (until 1986): *Solar Age;* Which incorporated (in 1985): *Progressive Builder;* (until 1976): *Solar News and Views.* [ISSN: 1055-3479] 1991. bi-m. USD 36 in US & Canada (Free to qualified personnel). Ed(s): Katie Gerfen. Hanley Wood, LLC, 1 Thomas Cir, NW, Ste 600, Washington, DC 20005; fanton@hanleywood.com; http://www.hanleywood.com. Illus., adv. *Indexed:* A22, BRI. *Aud.:* Sa.

Custom Home delivers information to the home remodeler or builder, designer, and architect. Articles offer insights into different types of home construction and materials. Articles may have interactive videos and graphics depicting projects completed or ongoing. Some of the articles highlight the economic outlook of the market and areas where home building is growing or declining. Online you can access information about products, green resources, content about houses or specific rooms, and information written for builders or architects. There is also access to various newsletters and its archives after signing up. Archived articles may be searched or browsed back to 2004. Access to the online content is free with sign up. Registering nets you an online version to your email every other month with options to access *Resident Architect* and *Design Studio*, free as well. Online you can access information about products, green resources, content about houses or specific rooms, and information written for builders or architects. There is also access to various newsletters and its archives after signing up. URL: https://www.customhomeonline.com/

958. *E C & M.* Incorporates (in 2002): *Power Quality Assurance;* Formerly (until 199?): *Electrical Construction & Maintenance.* [ISSN: 1082-295X] 1901. m. USD 55 domestic (Free to qualified personnel). Ed(s): Michael Eby, Ellen Parson. Penton, 330 N Wabash Ave, Ste 2300, Chicago, IL 60611; information@penton.com; http://penton.com. Illus., adv. Circ: 104000 Controlled. *Indexed:* A22, B01, BRI, C42. *Aud.:* Ac, Sa.

Electrical engineers will find up-to-date news and industry trends for all aspects of electrical design and maintenance. The *EC&M* offers practical options for the professional electrician, written by experts in the field. Articles touch on topics such as safety issues, compliance rules, green technologies, and troubleshooting ideas. The website offers a Discover menu with links to online magazines *Electrical Wholesaling* and *Electrical Marketing*. The Menu tab allows you access to various extra tools including white papers, webinars, newsletters, subscriptions, and access to the digital archives. The Digital Archive is searchable and dates back to most issues. The format of the archive lists each article by date of publication and you must continue scrolling to browse. The search box will search by relevance with no other options. You must be a registered user to access the archives and older articles, but registration is free and easy. Print subscriptions are also free with access to eight e-newletters. URL: https://www.ecmweb.com/

The Family Handyman. See Do-It-Yourself/Makers section.

959. *H P A C Engineering.* Formerly (until 1999): *Heating, Piping and Air Conditioning;* Which incorporated (1915-1929): *American Society of Heating and Ventilating Engineers. Journal.* [ISSN: 1527-4055] 1929. m. Free to members. Ed(s): Scott Arnold. Penton, 1100 Superior Ave., Cleveland, OH 44114; information@penton.com; http://www.penton.com. Illus., adv. Microform: PQC. *Indexed:* A01, A22, B03, BRI, C42. *Aud.:* Ac, Sa.

Plumbers, pipefitters, steamfitters, and HVAC engineers will find well-written articles offering information on trends, safety, efficiencies, and automation regarding all aspects of mechanical systems engineering. Intended to aid in the day-to-day work of the HVAC practitioner, *HPAC Engineering* highlights reliable installation solutions and economic outlooks for all to the HVAC technologies. The online experience offers links to other magazines from the publisher and a pinpointed menu that allows one to move quickly to specific sections. Other helpful tools—such as webinars, subscriptions, white papers, and newsletters—are offered as well. The Digital Archive is searchable and dates back to most issues. The format of the archive lists each article by date of publication and you must continue scrolling to browse. The search box will search by relevance with no other options. You must be a registered user to access the archives and older articles, but registration is free and easy. Print subscriptions are also free. URL: https://www.hpac.com/

960. *Journal of Light Construction (New England Edition).* Supersedes in part (in 1989): *The Journal of Light Construction;* Which was formerly (until 1988): *New England Builder.* [ISSN: 1050-2610] 1982. m. USD 39.95 domestic; USD 54.95 foreign. Hanley Wood, LLC, 186 Allen Brook Ln, Williston, VT 05495; fanton@hanleywood.com; http://www.hanleywood.com. Illus., index, adv. Sample. *Aud.:* Sa.

Light construction refers to work that is part of its whole, which would include roofing, siding, fireplaces, renovations, and drywall finishing. These tasks may be completed by subcontractors or handymen. The tasks at hand require differing skill levels and expertise in joining the job at hand to the whole of the building or structure needing work. The *Journal of Light Construction* has been serving this community with easy-to-read and ready-to-use articles and ideas. Subscriptions to the print journal and the *JLC Field Guide* is available for $39.95 per year for U.S. residents and $54.95 internationally, which includes access to the digital version and its archives. Online access is free, yet by registering it allows access to pdf downloads of articles and access to a free weekly newsletter. Archives date back to 1986, but very difficult to locate as the user must scroll to the bottom of the site and click the "Magazine" link at the very bottom. The site and online journal are provided by construction publisher Hanley-Wood. Pop-up ads when you first enter the site detract from the online experience. URL: https://www.jlconline.com/subscribe/default

Old-House Journal. See Do-It-Yourself/Makers section.

961. *P M Engineer.* [ISSN: 1080-353X] 1995. m. Free to qualified personnel (print or online eds.)). Ed(s): John McNally. B N P Media II, LLC., 2401 W Big Beaver Rd, Ste 700, Troy, MI 48084; portfolio@bnpmedia.com; http://www.bnpmedia.com. Adv. Sample. *Indexed:* B01, BRI, C42. *Aud.:* Ac, Sa.

For the plumbing or mechanical engineer, the *PM Engineer* offers in-depth coverage of topics that discuss codes and safety issues, fire protection, medical gas lines, pipe fitting, and HVAC issues. News and business ideas as well as in-depth coverage of products and highlights of successful projects fill up each issue. Access to the online edition and archive are free to anyone, but you must register to gain access. Subscriptions to the print version are free to U.S. residents who can receive up to four other relevant eNewsletters, as well. The magazine has a digital archive back to April 1998. The website offers "Web Exclusives," various multimedia articles and tutorials, market areas, and product highlights. Each online article has an interactive user-edited comment feed. You may also select the text to be translated in several different languages. URL: https://www.pmengineer.com/

962. *Plumbing Engineer.* [ISSN: 0192-1711] 1973. m. Ed(s): John Mesenbrink, James Schaible. T M B Publishing, 1838 Techny Ct, Northbrook, IL 60062; info@tmbpublishing.com; http://plumbingengineer.com/. Illus., adv. Circ: 25920 Controlled. *Indexed:* A22. *Aud.:* Ac, Sa.

Covering the piping industry from fire protection to HVAC, and pipefitting to ASHRAE codes, *Plumbing Engineer* offers highly detailed and helpful articles for plumbers, steamfitters, pipefitters, engineers, and contractors. Articles are laid out in easily accessible format and take an in-depth look at the trends and potential problems faced by the plumbing industry and its engineers. Online there are specific portals for "Engineers & Specifiers," "Contractors & Intallers," and "Wholesalers & Distributers." There is a buyer's guide, a section on standards and codes, how to's, business outlook, and product highlights. Subscriptions are free to any of the PHCP Pros journals, but the publisher reserves the right to disqualify subscription applications. Online archival issues dating back to 2014 are accessible from a pull-down menu. Searching for articles on a topic offers access to articles dating back to 2009. URL: https://www.phcppros.com/publications/1-plumbing-engineer

963. ***Professional Builder.*** Former titles (until 1993): *Professional Builder and Remodeler;* (until 1990): *Professional Builder;* (until 1985): *Professional Builder and Apartment Business;* (until 1973): *Professional Builder;* (until 1968): *Practical Builder.* [ISSN: 1072-0561] 1936. m. Free to qualified personnel. Ed(s): Amy Albert. S G C Horizon LLC, 3030 W Salt Creek Ln, Ste 201, Arlington Heights, IL 60005-5025; tmancini@sgcmail.com; http://www.sgchorizon.com/. Illus., adv. Sample. Circ: 120833. Microform: CIS. *Indexed:* A22, BRI. *Aud.:* Sa.

Since 1936, *Professional Builder* has been informing builders, designers, and project managers on all aspects of building and construction. The magazine provides information on issues in the housing and building industry including coding, innovations, product analysis, business content, economic industry trends, and how-to guides. Online you may access the current feature articles and locate information on design and construction, business or sales, new products in the field, and upcoming events. Print and online subscriptions are free after filling out a short form. Access to the full-text online archive goes back to July 1999. You may also subscribe to a suite of other magazines including newsletters and blogs offered by the publisher. URL: https://www.probuilder.com/

964. ***Qualified Remodeler: best practices, products & design ideas.*** Incorporates (1985-1991): *Kitchen and Bath Concepts.* [ISSN: 0098-9207] 1975. m. USD 81 domestic (Free to qualified personnel). S O L A Group Inc., 1880 Oak Ave., Ste. 350, Evanston, IL 60201; http://www.solabrands.com. Illus., adv. Circ: 82510. *Indexed:* BRI. *Aud.:* Sa.

The *Qualified Remodeler* offers timely articles regarding the home remodeling industry with design solutions for homes and rooms that require updating or expansion. Geared to contractors, designers, and builders, the articles offer product highlights, recent renovations, industry trends, and business tips. Each issue is freely available online and you can browse the site or access through the online "Flipbook" feature. Anyone can apply for free to subscribe to the print or online version of the magazine by filling out a form and answering a short questionnaire. If you do not qualify, you may still access the magazine from the website. The digital archive dates back to July 2018. URL: https://www.qualifiedremodeler.com/

965. ***Remodeling.*** Formerly (until 1985): *Remodeling World;* Incorporates (1983-1987): *Remodeling Contractor;* Which was formerly (until 1983): *Home Improvement Contractor;* (until 1976): *Home Improvements;* (until 1969): *Building Specialties and Home Improvements.* [ISSN: 0885-8039] 1982. m. USD 19.95 domestic (Free to qualified personnel). Hanley Wood, LLC, 1 Thomas Cir, NW, Ste 600, Washington, DC 20005; fanton@hanleywood.com; http://www.hanleywood.com. Illus., adv. Microform: PQC. *Indexed:* BRI. *Aud.:* Sa.

Geared toward general contractors and restoration professionals, *Remodeling* magazine offers cover and feature stories plus regular features that include editorials, "You Build It," "Your Business," and product highlights. The magazine guides and informs on reconstruction and renovation projects with product reviews, industry trends, standards and best practices. The print magazine formats in traditional magazine style and the online experience duplicates page-by-page turning if you prefer, as well as a web style. Online content offers news and insights in the field of restoring and replacing aspects in existing homes and buildings and the complete remodel with access to the Hanley-Wood publisher's suite of trade magazines. Online subscriptions are free after a brief sign up for all online content. The print *Remodeling Magazine* subscriptions are free to professionals who qualify, and access to the "Remodeling Daily Update" email newsletter is free. Archives are complete back to October 2009 and selected back to January 2002. URL: www.remodeling.hw.net

This Old House. See Do-It-Yourself/Makers section.

966. ***Welding Journal.*** Former titles (until 1937): *American Welding Society Journal;* (until 1934): *American Welding Society. Journal;* (until 1922): *American Welding Society. Proceedings.* [ISSN: 0043-2296] 1922. m. Free to members. Ed(s): Andy Cullison. American Welding Society, 550 N W LeJeune Rd, Miami, FL 33126; info@aws.org; http://www.aws.org. Illus., adv. Refereed. Microform: PMC; PQC. *Indexed:* A22. *Aud.:* Sa.

Welding Journal, published by the American Welding Society, features articles on trends, technology, and latest products for the professional welder. The peer-reviewed articles offer tips on cost savings, techniques, design, and safety, and are nicely illustrated in full color. Industry news, product spotlights, member profiles, and editorial letters are featured each month. There is also a Spanish version of the magazine, *Welding Journal en Espanol,* which is published quarterly and is free. Also free is the quarterly *Welding Marketplace,* which features welding products and services. Subscriptions to the *Welding Journal* comes with membership in the American Welding Society. Choose one- to three-year memberships with savings for multiple years. One year is $88 for a regular member plus a $12 fee, or $15 for students with no fee. Corporate memberships are also offered. The online archives date back to 2000; however, using the search tool for articles returns articles back to 1930. Searching is freely available to all. Articles may be purchased for $10 or Interlibrary Loan may serve without a subscription. Also available to nonmembers are many of the article research papers dating back to 1970, and these are freely available for PDF download with Acrobat reader. URL: https://www.aws.org/publications/weldingjournal

BUSINESS AND FINANCE

General/Computer Systems and Forecasting/Ethics/International/Small Business/State and Regional/Trade and Industry/Banking/Insurance/Investment/Scholarly/Trade Journals

See also Accounting and Taxation; Advertising and Public Relations; Economics; Management and Administration, Human Resources; and Real Estate sections.

Lisa Junghahn, Research Librarian, University of California, Irvine, 401 E. Peltason, Irvine, CA 92697; ljunghahn@law.uci.edu

Introduction

The Business and Finance section of *Magazines for Libraries* has one additional title since the last edition.

This section contains a diverse selection of business journals. These journals will be of value for public and academic librarians as well as faculty members and business professionals.

Business and finance are complex subjects that require comprehensive and detailed publications. This list is a helpful guide to a broad selection of core business journals.

Basic Periodicals

GENERAL. Ga: *Barron's, Fast Company, Forbes, Harvard Business Review, Industry Week;* Ac: *Business History Review, Business Horizons, Journal of Business Research, Journal of Education for Business, Journal of Retailing.*

COMPUTER SYSTEMS AND FORECASTING. Ga: *CIO;* Ac: *International Journal of Forecasting.*

ETHICS. Ac: *Business and Society Review, Journal of Business Ethics.*

INTERNATIONAL. Ga: *The Journal of Commerce;* Ac: *Journal of International Business Studies, Journal of World Business.*

SMALL BUSINESS. Ga: *Entrepreneur, Franchising World;* Ac: *Entrepreneurship: Theory and Practice, Journal of Small Business Management.*

STATE AND REGIONAL. Will vary.

TRADE AND INDUSTRY. Will vary.

Basic Abstracts and Indexes

ABI/INFORM, Business Abstracts, Business and Company Resource Center, Business Source Complete.

General

967. *Barron's.* Former titles (until 1994): *Barron's National Business and Financial Weekly;* (until 1942): *Barron's.* [ISSN: 1077-8039] 1921. w. Ed(s): Greg Bartalos, Phil Roosevelt. Dow Jones & Company, 1211 Ave of the Americas, 4th Fl, New York, NY 10036; support@barrons.com; https://www.dowjones.com/. Illus., adv. Vol. ends: Dec. *Indexed:* A22, ATI, BRI, CBRI. *Bk. rev.:* Number and length vary. *Aud.:* Ga.

This weekly newspaper format provides general business information that serves the needs of investors. Articles on current business, economic, and political trends are accompanied by reports on industries, individual companies, and people in the news. The "Market Week" center section covers securities analysis and performance statistics, including stock tables, economic indicators, commodities, money markets, and major indexes. This is a core business and investment title for public and academic libraries. URL: www.barrons.com/

968. *Bloomberg Markets.* Formerly (until 2000): *Bloomberg.* [ISSN: 1531-5061] 1992. 13x/yr. USD 29.95 domestic; USD 38.95 Canada; USD 54.95 elsewhere. Bloomberg Finance L.P., 499 Park Ave, New York, NY 10022; magazine@bloomberg.com; http://www.bloomberg.com. Adv. *Aud.:* Sa.

The subjects here are money, money-making, and how to build wealth. Regular features include financial predictions, international news, company profiles, Wall Street news, and op-ed pieces. Articles are global in scope, covering everything from the infrastructure of developed countries to the educational attainment and potential of populations in emerging markets. Pieces cover both macro-factors, like security in shipping lanes, and micro-factors, like management performance at specific companies. This serial is ideal for public libraries with a broad collection, and academic institutions with finance degree programs. URL: www.bloomberg.com/markets-magazine/

969. *Business and Professional Communication Quarterly.* Former titles (until 2014): *Business Communication Quarterly;* (until 1995): *Association for Business Communication. Bulletin;* (until 1985): *A B C A Bulletin (American Business Communication Association);* (until 1969): *A B W A Bulletin (American Business Writing Association).* [ISSN: 2329-4906] 1935. q. USD 617 (print & online eds.) Free to members). Ed(s): James M Dubinsky, Melinda Knight. Sage Publications, Inc., 2455 Teller Rd, Thousand Oaks, CA 91320; info@sagepub.com; http://www.sagepub.com. Illus., index, adv. Sample. Refereed. Microform: PQC. Reprint: PSC. *Indexed:* A22, B01, BRI, E01, ERIC. *Bk. rev.:* 2-3, 750-1,000 words. *Aud.:* Ac.

This interdisciplinary journal is aimed primarily at an international readership involved directly in the teaching of business communication. As with its sister publication, *Journal of Business Communication,* submissions are invited from educators in a wide variety of fields, including management, rhetoric, organizational behavior, composition, speech, mass communication, psychology, linguistics, advertising, sociology, information technology, education, and history. Topics cover teaching methods in a variety of settings: technical institutes, community colleges, four-year colleges, universities, and corporate-training programs. Article formats include case studies of specific classroom techniques, reports on program development strategies, research on classroom teaching and assessment, and book reviews of textbooks and other titles of interest to faculty. URL: http://bcq.sagepub.com/

970. *Business and Society Review.* Formerly (until 1974): *Business and Society Review/Innovation;* Which was formed by the merger of (1962-1973): *Innovation; Business and Society Review.* [ISSN: 0045-3609] 1972. q. GBP 405. Ed(s): Robert E Frederick. Wiley-Blackwell Publishing, Inc., 111 River St, Hoboken, NJ 07030; http://onlinelibrary.wiley.com. Illus. Microform: PQC. Reprint: PSC. *Indexed:* A22, B01, BRI, C42, E01, L14. *Aud.:* Ac.

This scholarly publication includes a dozen articles of 10 to 20 pages in length, which cover a wide range of ethical issues, corporate citizenship, and social responsibility. Some issues are thematic. Articles are of interest to businesspeople, academics, and others involved in the contemporary debate about the proper role of business in society. Expect to find this title in academic collections that support business programs and in larger public libraries. URL: http://onlinelibrary.wiley.com/journal/10.1111/(ISSN)1467-8594

Business Economics. See Economics section.

971. *Business History Review.* Formerly (until 1954): *Business Historical Society. Bulletin.* [ISSN: 0007-6805] 1926. q. GBP 229 (print & online eds.)). Ed(s): Geoffrey G Jones, Walter A Friedman. Cambridge University Press, 1 Liberty Plaza, Fl 20, New York, NY 10004; journals@cambridge.org; https://www.cambridge.org/. Illus., index, adv. Refereed. Circ: 2000. Vol. ends: No. 4. Microform: PQC. *Indexed:* A22, B01, BAS, BRI, CBRI, EconLit, IBSS, MLA-IB. *Bk. rev.:* 25-30, 750-1,000 words. *Aud.:* Ac.

Each issue is composed of three feature articles, of 40 to 50 pages in length, along with numerous book reviews. Subjects cover biographical profiles, corporate culture, and studies of specific industries, with emphasis on North American history. Photographs and illustrations appear on the cover and accompany some articles. The online archives offer article abstracts back to 1954, and pdf images of book reviews back to 2002. Of interest to all social scientists, historians, and fans of Americana. URL: http://journals.cambridge.org/action/displayJournal?jid=BHR

972. *Business Horizons.* Supersedes in part (in 1958): *Indiana Business Review.* [ISSN: 0007-6813] 1957. 6x/yr. EUR 673. Ed(s): L F Miller, M J Dollinger. Elsevier Inc., 230 Park Ave, Ste 800, New York, NY 10169; usinfo-f@elsevier.com; https://www.elsevier.com. Illus., index, adv. Sample. Refereed. Vol. ends: No. 6. Reprint: PSC. *Indexed:* A22, B01, BAS, BRI, CBRI. *Bk. rev.:* 0-3, 1,500 words. *Aud.:* Ga, Ac.

This bimonthly title is edited by the Kelley School of Business, Indiana University. Approximately ten scholarly articles, seven to ten pages in length, address a wide range of business disciplines, business ethics, and the impact of business on society. Editors strive to strike a balance between the practical and the academic; contributors are encouraged to avoid nontechnical language. Each issue contains a cumulative index for the current volume year. Of interest to all academic libraries. URL: www.sciencedirect.com/science/journal/00076813

973. *Business India: the magazine of the corporate world.* [ISSN: 0254-5268] 1978. bi-w. INR 750. Business India Group, Nirmal, 14th Fl, Nariman Pt, Mumbai, 400 021, India; biedit.mumbai@businessindiagroup.com; http://www.businessindiagroup.com. Illus., adv. Vol. ends: Dec. *Indexed:* B01, C37. *Aud.:* Sa.

This biweekly magazine is aimed at Indian business and corporate executives. In addition to business news, it includes editorials on the political and economic climate, interviews with prominent business figures, and articles on technology, energy, advertising, manufacturing, and banking. There are brief news reports on companies and occasional articles on social issues. A good source of coverage of Indian business news. URL: www.businessindiagroup.com/bi-about.aspx

974. *Business Today (Princeton).* Formerly (until 1968): *Princeton Business Today.* [ISSN: 0007-7100] 1968. s-a. Free to qualified personnel. Ed(s): B J Sullivan. Foundation for Student Communication, Inc., 48 University Pl, Princeton, NJ 08544. Illus., adv. Circ: 200000. Microform: MIM; PQC. *Indexed:* A22. *Aud.:* Ga, Ac, Sa.

This student-run magazine serves as a forum for diverse topics and is designed to give undergraduates a broader understanding of business leadership, industry innovation, government policies, international perspectives, and career track advice. The content will appeal to a wider college audience, not just business majors. Ideal for browsing collections in academic libraries. URL: www.businesstoday.org/

Consumer Reports. See General Interest section.

975. ***Fast Company.*** [ISSN: 1085-9241] 1995. 10x/yr. USD 5 domestic; USD 25 Canada; USD 35 elsewhere. Ed(s): Jonathan Brenden Clark, Robert Safian. Fast Company, Inc., 7 World Trade Ctr, New York, NY 10007. Illus., adv. Circ: 782043 Paid. *Indexed:* A22, B01, BRI, C37. *Aud.:* Ga.

Articles of varying lengths profile executives, managers, and business owners who drive innovation. Emphasis is placed on covering the new, novel, and trendy in the business world. The writing style is irreverent. Bold graphics and content that are pushed to the very edges of the page speak to a reader who is most likely comfortable with multitasking. Conclusions are frequently enumerated or distilled to bullet points; lists of companies or products are ranked, all for the purpose of providing information - fast. Online access to the current issue and archives is available at the web site, complemented by video and other web exclusives. URL: www.fastcompany.com/

976. ***Forbes.*** [ISSN: 0015-6914] 1917. bi-w. USD 20. Forbes, Inc., 499 Washington Blvd, Jersey City, NJ 07310; readers@forbes.com; http://www.forbes.com. Illus., index, adv. Vol. ends: Dec. Microform: PQC. *Indexed:* A22, ATI, AgeL, Agr, B01, B03, BLI, BRI, C37, Chicano, F01. *Aud.:* Ga.

The focus of this title is on news and analysis that impact executives, managers, and investors. In addition to the cover story, a typical issue contains numerous short articles, each analyzing economic trends or profiling industries, corporations, and key individuals. Recurring sections include "Marketing," "Entrepreneurs," "Technology," "Money and Investing," and "Health." A subscription is complemented by occasional supplements: *Forbes Asia* and *Forbes Life,* which contain lifestyle features. Current issue and archives content are available at the web site. A core title for both public and academic libraries. URL: www.forbes.com/forbes

Fortune. See General Interest section.

977. ***Harvard Business Review.*** [ISSN: 0017-8012] 1922. bi-m. Harvard Business School Publishing, 60 Harvard Way, Boston, MA 02163; corpcustserv@hbsp.harvard.edu; http://harvardbusiness.org/. Illus., index, adv. Vol. ends: Dec. Microform: PQC. *Indexed:* A22, B01, BAS, BLI, BRI, C42, CBRI. *Bk. rev.:* Number and length vary. *Aud.:* Ga.

Each issue contains about a dozen articles, ten pages in length, along with a short case study. *HBR* provides readers with the current thinking of scholars and industry leaders on the topics of human resources management, manufacturing, strategic planning, globalization of markets, competitiveness, and related general business interests. Articles - although rarely containing footnotes - are highly regarded if not considered scholarly. This is a core business title for academic libraries and larger public libraries. URL: https://hbr.org/

978. ***IndustryWeek: the management resource.*** Incorporates (1985-1995): *Electronics;* Which was formerly (1984-1985): *Electronics Week;* (1930-1984): *Electronics.* [ISSN: 0039-0895] 1882. 22x/yr. USD 69 domestic (Free to qualified personnel). Ed(s): Patricia Panchak. Penton, 1100 Superior Ave., Cleveland, OH 44114; information@penton.com; http://www.penton.com. Illus., index, adv. Circ: 236248 Controlled. Vol. ends: Dec. Microform: PQC. *Indexed:* A01, A22, B01, B03, BRI, C42, MASUSE. *Aud.:* Ga.

This trade magazine profiles individuals and companies active in manufacturing industries. Approximately five feature articles in each issue cover a wide range of topics of interest to executives and managers, including innovation, competition, infrastructure, globalization, supply chains, distribution, labor relations, regulatory pressures, and best practices in management and marketing. Recurring departments address emerging technologies, leadership, e-business, continuous improvement, and economic policies. Features and departments from the current and previous issues are freely available online at the web site. Web-only content is highlighted alongside the magazine's table of contents. Of interest to all business collections. URL: www.industryweek.com

979. ***Journal of Business and Economic Statistics.*** [ISSN: 0735-0015] 1983. q. GBP 190 (print & online eds.)). Ed(s): Shakeeb Khan, Rong Chen. Taylor & Francis Inc., 711 3rd Ave, 8th Fl, New York, NY 10017; support@tandfonline.com; http://www.tandfonline.com. Illus. Refereed. Vol. ends: Oct. Reprint: PSC. *Indexed:* A22, B01, EconLit, MSN. *Aud.:* Ac.

One of the official journals from the American Statistical Association, this scholarly title focuses on a broad range of topics in applied economics and business statistical problems. Using empirical methods, authors of these highly technical articles presume a reader's knowledge of mathematical theory. Topics covered include demand and cost analysis, forecasting, economic modeling, stochastic theory control, and impact of societal issues on wages and productivity. Recommended for academic libraries.

980. ***Journal of Business Research.*** Formerly (until 1973): *Southern Journal of Business.* [ISSN: 0148-2963] 1966. 12x/yr. EUR 4409. Ed(s): Arch G Woodside. Elsevier Inc., 230 Park Ave, Ste 800, New York, NY 10169; usinfo-f@elsevier.com; https://www.elsevier.com. Illus., index. Sample. Refereed. Vol. ends: Nov. Microform: PQC. *Indexed:* A22, B01, BRI, C45, IBSS. *Aud.:* Sa.

Each issue presents a dozen articles (of 8-20 pages in length) that cover theoretical and empirical advances in buyer behavior, finance, organizational theory and behavior, marketing, risk and insurance, and international business. Issues are frequently devoted to a theme, e.g., cross-cultural consumer studies, electronic marketing theory, Asian business research, etc. Emphasis is placed on linking theory with practical solutions. Intended for executives, researchers, and scholars alike. URL: www.sciencedirect.com/science/journal/01482963

Journal of Business Strategy. See Management and Administration section.

Journal of Consumer Research. See Advertising, Marketing, and Public Relations section.

981. ***Journal of Education for Business.*** Former titles (until 1985): *The Journal of Business Education;* (until 1929): *The Business School Journal.* [ISSN: 0883-2323] 1928. 8x/yr. GBP 220 (print & online eds.)). Ed(s): James L Morrison. Routledge, 530 Walnut St, Ste 850, Philadelphia, PA 19106; enquiries@tandfonline.com; http://www.tandfonline.com. Illus., adv. Refereed. Reprint: PSC. *Indexed:* A01, A22, B01, BRI, C42, CBRI, ERIC. *Bk. rev.:* Irregular; 500-750 words. *Aud.:* Ac.

This is a forum for authors reporting on innovative teaching methods and curricula or proposing new theories and analyses of controversial topics in accounting, communications, economics, finance, information systems, management, marketing, and other business disciplines, trends, and professional information. Each issue contains eight to ten features that aid educators in preparing business graduates who will need new competencies and leadership skills to thrive. This would be most interesting to higher-education administrators and faculty members. URL: www.tandfonline.com/loi/vjeb20#.V5gLCOgrKUk

982. ***Journal of Retailing.*** [ISSN: 0022-4359] 1925. q. EUR 694. Ed(s): M Mantrala, S Brown. Pergamon Press, The Blvd, Langford Ln, E Park, Kidlington, OX5 1GB, United Kingdom; JournalsCustomerServiceEMEA@elsevier.com; http://www.elsevier.com. Illus., adv. Sample. Refereed. Microform: PQC. Reprint: PSC. *Indexed:* A22, B01, BRI, C45. *Aud.:* Ac.

Each issue offers five or six articles, 20-25 pages in length. Retailing is defined as the act of selling products and/or services to consumers for their personal or family use. Thus, the scope of this journal is explicitly limited to consumer behavior, retail strategy, marketing channels, location analysis, the marketing mix, merchandise management, store and operations management, store atmospheric issues, and retail services. Other topics may be addressed so long as retailing is the focus of the submission. Examples include benchmarking retail productivity, supply chain management, marketing impact assessment, and public policy issues. There is liberal use of mathematical models for the benefit of other academicians; a general readership will appreciate the nontechnical executive summaries. URL: www.journals.elsevier.com/journal-of-retailing

Computer Systems and Forecasting

983. *C I O: the magazine for information executives.* Incorporates (1995-1997): *WebMaster.* [ISSN: 0894-9301] 1987. 23x/yr. USD 95 in US & Canada (Free to qualified personnel). Ed(s): Brian Carlson, Elana Varon. C X O Media Inc., 492 Old Connecticut Path, PO Box 9208, Framingham, MA 01701; http://www.cxo.com/. Illus., adv. Circ: 140000. *Indexed:* A22, B01, B03, BRI, CompLI. *Aud.:* Ga.

This major trade title provides semi-monthly industry updates, news and events, tips, trends, and opinions by and for managing executives in the information technology and computer systems departments of medium-to-large organizations. Feature articles cover management skills, outsourcing, recruiting and other human resource management topics, emerging technologies, e-commerce, and IT strategies. Although aimed at the working professional, *CIO* is well suited for public libraries that serve the business community, and academic libraries that support advanced business degrees and computer science programs. Current and previous issues' content is available at the website. URL: www.cio.com/magazine

Decision Sciences. See Management and Administration section.

984. *Decision Support Systems.* [ISSN: 0167-9236] 1985. 12x/yr. EUR 2612. Ed(s): James R Marsden. Elsevier BV, Radarweg 29, Amsterdam, 1043 NX, Netherlands; info@elsevier.com; https://www.elsevier.com/. Illus., index, adv. Refereed. *Indexed:* A22, B01, CompLI, ErgAb. *Aud.:* Ac.

This is a highly technical and scholarly journal that covers the concept of using computers for supporting the managerial decision process. Articles discuss artificial intelligence, cognitive science, computer-supported cooperative work, database management, decision theory, economics, linguistics, management science, mathematical modeling, operations management psychology, and user-interface management systems. The relatively high subscription price and theoretical focus limit holdings to academic libraries that offer programs in advanced business administration, MIS, or computer science. URL: www.elsevier.com/locate/issn/01679236

eWEEK. See Computers and Information Technology/Popular Titles section.

985. *Information & Management.* Incorporates (1981-1985): *Systems, Objectives, Solutions;* Former titles (until 1977): *Management Datamatics;* (until 1975): *Management Informatics;* (until 1972): *I A G Journal.* [ISSN: 0378-7206] 1968. 8x/yr. EUR 1905. Ed(s): P Y K Chau. Elsevier BV, Radarweg 29, Amsterdam, 1043 NX, Netherlands; info@elsevier.com; https://www.elsevier.com/. Illus., index, adv. Refereed. Microform: PQC. *Indexed:* A22, B01, C42, CompLI. *Bk. rev.:* Number and length vary. *Aud.:* Sa.

Aimed at managers, database administrators, and senior executives, this scholarly journal covers a wide range of developments in applied information systems, such as knowledge management, data mining, and CRM. Articles focus on trends in evaluation methodology and models; managerial policies, strategies, and activities of business, public administration, and international organizations; and guidelines on how to mount successful information technology initiatives through case studies. The technical nature of the writing will appeal primarily to researchers and practitioners active in the MIS field. URL: www.sciencedirect.com/science/journal/03787206

986. *International Journal of Forecasting.* [ISSN: 0169-2070] 1985. 4x/yr. EUR 1041. Ed(s): Rob J Hyndman. Elsevier BV, Radarweg 29, Amsterdam, 1043 NX, Netherlands; info@elsevier.com; https://www.elsevier.com/. Adv. Refereed. Microform: PQC. *Indexed:* A22, B01, BAS, BRI, C42, EconLit, P61. *Bk. rev.:* Number and length vary. *Aud.:* Ac, Sa.

This official publication of the International Institute of Forecasters is the leading journal of forecasting for all aspects of business. It strives to bridge the gap between theory and practice for those policy and decision makers who utilize forecasting methods. Articles by international scholars are featured each quarter, along with notes, book and software reviews, and reviews of current research in forecasting. Although not published as often as the *Journal of Forecasting,* at half the cost, this title is an economical alternative. Recommended for academic libraries. URL: www.sciencedirect.com/science/journal/01692070

987. *International Journal of Technology Management.* [ISSN: 0267-5730] 1986. m. USD 2200 (print or online ed.)). Ed(s): MA Dorgham, Dr. M A Dorgham. Inderscience Publishers, PO Box 735, Olney, MK46 5WB, United Kingdom; info@inderscience.com; https://www.inderscience.com/index.php. Illus., index. Sample. Refereed. *Indexed:* A01, A22, Agr, B01, BRI, CompLI, IBSS, ISTA. *Bk. rev.:* Number and length vary. *Aud.:* Ac, Sa.

This refereed journal disseminates advances in the science and practice of technology management, with the goal of fostering communication between government officials, technology executives, and academic experts worldwide. Each issue contains research reports and case studies on technology transfers, supply chain management, sourcing, R&D systems, and information technology. Geared to academics, researchers, professionals, and policy makers, *IJTM* is best suited to academic libraries with advanced degree programs in the management and engineering sciences.

988. *The Journal of Business Forecasting.* Formerly (until 2005): *Journal of Business Forecasting Methods and Systems.* [ISSN: 1930-126X] 1981. q. Free to members; Non-members, USD 95. Ed(s): Chaman L Jain. Graceway Publishing Co., PO Box 670159, Flushing, NY 11367. Illus., index, adv. Sample. Vol. ends: No. 4. Microform: PQC. *Indexed:* A01, A22, ATI, B01, BRI, C42. *Bk. rev.:* 1, 750 words. *Aud.:* Ac, Sa.

Executives and managers comprise the primary audience of this highly specialized publication. Clearly written and jargon-free articles provide practical information for decision makers on inventory control, supply chain management, production scheduling, budgeting, marketing strategies, and financial planning. Also featured are international and domestic economic outlooks and corporate earnings analysis by industry. Of most interest to academic business collections and corporate libraries.

989. *Journal of Forecasting.* [ISSN: 0277-6693] 1982. 8x/yr. GBP 1540. Ed(s): Derek W Bunn. John Wiley & Sons Ltd., EMEA Institutional Sales, 9600 Garsington Rd, Oxford, OX4 2DQ, United Kingdom; cs-journals@wiley.com; http://onlinelibrary.wiley.com. Illus., adv. Sample. Refereed. Vol. ends: Nov. Reprint: PSC. *Indexed:* A22, B01, BRI, C42, EconLit, IBSS, MSN. *Aud.:* Sa.

Edited by an international board of scholars, this title is multidisciplinary, welcoming submissions dealing with any aspect of forecasting: theoretical, practical, computational, and methodological. A broad interpretation of the topic is taken with approaches from various subject areas, such as statistics, economics, psychology, systems engineering, and social sciences, which are all encouraged. This journal presupposes a knowledge of mathematical theory; it is appropriate for academic and corporate libraries. URL: http://onlinelibrary.wiley.com/doi/10.1002/for.v35.4/issuetoc

Long Range Planning. See Management and Administration section.

Ethics

990. *Business Ethics: a European review.* [ISSN: 0962-8770] 1992. q. GBP 1421. Ed(s): Dima Jamali. Wiley-Blackwell Publishing Ltd., The Atrium, Southern Gate, Chichester, PO19 8QG, United Kingdom; cs-journals@wiley.com; http://onlinelibrary.wiley.com/. Illus., adv. Sample. Refereed. Reprint: PSC. *Indexed:* A22, B01, BRI, E01, IBSS. *Bk. rev.:* Brief; number varies. *Aud.:* Ac.

This primarily European-focused journal provides a forum for dialogue through original theoretical research and refereed scholarly papers. The range of contributions reflects the variety and scope of ethical issues faced by businesses and organizations worldwide. Articles address ethical challenges and solutions, analyze business policies and practices, and explore the concept of good ethical thinking. Submissions that are responsive to changing concerns and emerging issues are encouraged. Interviews, brief book reviews, comments, and responses to previously published articles round out the content. Appropriate for academic institutions with a tradition of comparative studies. URL: http://onlinelibrary.wiley.com/journal/10.1111/(ISSN)1467-8608

991. ***Business Ethics Quarterly.*** [ISSN: 1052-150X] 1991. q. GBP 274. Ed(s): Denis G Arnold. Cambridge University Press, 1 Liberty Plaza, Fl 20, New York, NY 10004; journals@cambridge.org; https://www.cambridge.org/. Adv. Sample. Refereed. Microform: PQC. Reprint: PSC. *Indexed:* A22, B01, BRI, IBSS. *Bk. rev.:* 2-3, 1,000-2,000 words. *Aud.:* Ac.

This official journal of the Society for Business Ethics publishes peer-reviewed articles on a broad range of topics, including the internal ethics of business organizations; the role of business organizations in larger social, political, and cultural frameworks; and the ethical quality of market-based societies and market-based relationships. There are approximately four to six feature articles in each issue, accompanied by one or more review articles. Recognizing that contributions to the better understanding of business ethics can come from any quarter, the journal encourages submissions from the humanities, social sciences, and professional fields. Of most interest to academic business collections. URL: http://journals.cambridge.org/action/displayJournal?jid=BEQ

992. ***Journal of Business Ethics.*** Incorporates (1997-2004): *Teaching Business Ethics;* (1988-2004): *International Journal of Value-Based Management.* [ISSN: 0167-4544] 1982. 28x/yr. EUR 5397 (print & online eds.)). Ed(s): Alex C Michalos, Deborah C Poff. Springer Netherlands, Van Godewijckstraat 30, Dordrecht, 3311 GX, Netherlands; http://www.springer.com. Illus., adv. Refereed. Vol. ends: Dec. Microform: PQC. Reprint: PSC. *Indexed:* A22, B01, BRI, E01, IBSS. *Aud.:* Ac.

This journal has aimed to improve the human condition by providing a public forum for discussion and debate about ethical issues related to business. The number of submissions and general interest in ethics have greatly expanded in recent years; two sister publications have been absorbed, and new section editors have been named to handle business law, codes of ethics, corporate governance, gender issues, philosophic foundations, small business, teaching business ethics, and value-based management. An important title for collections that support academic programs in business. URL: www.springer.com/social+sciences/applied+ethics/journal/10551

International

African Business. See Africa section.

993. ***China Business Review.*** Formerly (until 1977): *U S China Business Review.* [ISSN: 0163-7169] 1974. bi-m. USD 89 combined subscription domestic (print & online eds.); USD 99 combined subscription foreign (print & online eds.)). United States - China Business Council, 1818 N St, N W, Ste 200, Washington, DC 20036-2406; info@uschina.org; http://www.chinabusinessreview.com/. Illus., index, adv. Sample. Circ: 3500 Paid. Vol. ends: Nov/Dec (No. 6). Microform: PQC. *Indexed:* A22, B01, B03, BAS, C42. *Aud.:* Ga, Sa.

This official magazine of the U.S.-China Business Council provides an in-depth picture of the China market, and unique insight into the business and investment environment in China, legal developments, impending legislation, and industrial-sector issues. Each issue contains a few articles that examine one particular topic. Topics include all sectors of the Chinese economy and all business issues, from human resources and management to operational issues and broader policy issues. Intellectual property-rights issues, looking after China's elderly, and the growing Chinese health-care industry are examples in recent issues. URL: www.chinabusinessreview.com/

The Economist. See Economics section.

994. ***Japan Spotlight: Economy, Culture & History.*** Formerly (until 2003): *Journal of Japanese Trade and Industry.* [ISSN: 1348-9216] 1982. bi-m. JPY 6000; JPY 1200 newsstand/cover. Japan Economic Foundation, 11th Fl, Jiji Press Bldg., 5-15-8 Ginza Chuo-Ku, Tokyo, 104-0061, Japan; info@jef.or.jp; http://www.jef.or.jp/. Illus., adv. Circ: 35000. *Indexed:* A22, B01, B03, BAS, BRI, C42. *Aud.:* Sa.

This journal covers not only economy, industry, and trade, but also international politics, history, culture, and other topics that fit the primary goal of the Japan Economic Foundation, i.e., to create a deeper understanding of Japan and the world. Writers include business executives, government officials, university professors, specialist researchers, and leading journalists. Current issue contents and searchable archives are available at the web site only to print subscribers. Recommended for academic collections that support programs in international business or Japanese Studies; a must for corporations doing business with Japan. URL: www.jef.or.jp/journal

995. ***The Journal of Commerce.*** Incorporates (1923-2009): *Shipping Digest;* (1913-2009): *The Traffic World;* Formerly (until 2002): *J o C Week;* Which superseded in part (in 2000): *Journal of Commerce;* Which was formerly (until 1996): *Journal of Commerce and Commercial;* (until 1927): *Journal of Commerce.* [ISSN: 1542-3867] 1827. w. Free to members. Ed(s): Chris Brooks. Journal of Commerce, Inc., 2 Penn Plz E, Newark, NJ 07105; http://www.joc.com. Microform: PQC. *Indexed:* B01, BRI. *Aud.:* Ga.

This weekly provides authoritative editorial content for international business executives to help them plan their global supply chain and better manage their day-to-day international logistics and shipping needs. This information is delivered through news, analysis of the political landscape that surrounds the latest regulatory issues, case studies, and perspective pieces. Recommended for all international business and transportation collections. Page thumbnails from the digital edition can be viewed at the web site, but only selected full-screen content can be displayed to nonsubscribers. URL: www.joc.com

996. ***Journal of International Business Studies.*** [ISSN: 0047-2506] 1970. 9x/yr. GBP 484. Ed(s): Anne Hoekman. Palgrave Macmillan Ltd., Macmillan Building, 4 Crinan St, London, N1 9XW, United Kingdom; onlinesales@palgrave.com; http://www.palgrave-journals.com. Adv. Sample. Refereed. Reprint: PSC. *Indexed:* A22, B01, BAS, BRI, C37, E01, EconLit, IBSS. *Bk. rev.:* Infrequent. *Aud.:* Ac.

Each issue contains a short editorial and eight empirical and hypothetical research articles, 15-20 pages in length, and research presented is cutting-edge and breaks new ground, rather than merely making an incremental contribution to international business research. Submissions should address real-world phenomena, problems, or puzzles and build on relevant prior research to highlight what is interesting and different. Contents can include occasional articles identified as "perspectives" that are deliberately controversial or challenging to mainstream views. Recommended for all academic business collections.

997. ***Journal of Multinational Financial Management.*** [ISSN: 1042-444X] 1990. 5x/yr. EUR 691. Ed(s): P G Szilagyi. Elsevier BV, Radarweg 29, Amsterdam, 1043 NX, Netherlands; info@elsevier.com; https://www.elsevier.com/. Refereed. Microform: PQC. *Indexed:* A22, B01, EconLit, IBSS. *Aud.:* Ac, Sa.

Corporate executives buying and selling goods and services, and making financing and investment decisions across national boundaries, have developed policies and procedures for managing cash flows denominated in foreign currencies. These policies and procedures, and the related managerial actions of executives, change as new relevant information becomes available. This title offers original articles that deal with the management of the multinational enterprise. Some of the topics covered include: foreign exchange risk management; cost of capital; political risk assessment; international tax management; and international liability management. URL: www.journals.elsevier.com/journal-of-multinational-financial-management

998. ***Journal of World Business.*** Formerly (until 1997): *Columbia Journal of World Business.* [ISSN: 1090-9516] 1965. bi-m. q. until 2016. EUR 1015. Ed(s): Jonathan Doh. Pergamon Press, The Blvd, Langford Ln, E Park, Kidlington, OX5 1GB, United Kingdom;

JournalsCustomerServiceEMEA@elsevier.com; http://www.elsevier.com. Illus., index, adv. Sample. Refereed. Vol. ends: No. 4. Microform: PQC. *Indexed:* A22, B01, BRI, Chicano, EconLit, IBSS. *Aud.:* Ac.

Each issue includes half-a-dozen articles written by leading academic researchers, top government officials, and prominent business leaders on issues related to financial markets, free trade, transition economies, emerging markets, privatization, joint ventures, mergers and acquisitions, human resource management, and marketing. Separate editorial review boards are designated for contributors in the United States, Europe, Latin America, and the Pacific Rim. Recommended for all academic collections that support international business studies. URL: www.journals.elsevier.com/journal-of-world-business

999. ***Latin Trade: your business source for Latin America.*** Formerly (until 1996): *U S - Latin Trade.* [ISSN: 1087-0857] 1993. bi-m. USD 149. Miami Media, 75 Valencia Ave, Ste 1000, Coral Gables, FL 33134; info@latintrade.com. Illus. *Indexed:* A01, A22, B01, B03, BRI, C42. *Bk. rev.:* Number and length vary. *Aud.:* Ac, Sa.

This pan-regional newsmagazine covers all aspects of corporate business in Central and South America. Feature articles tend to be few and short in length. Four departments fill out the remainder of each issue, providing timely information, statistics, and opinion pieces on people, companies, regulations, technology, import/export, travel destinations, and various trade and industry topics of the region. Special issues include the annual Bravo Awards, which recognize outstanding leadership in Latin America, and the annual ranking of Latin America's 100 largest publicly traded companies. The web site provides current economic indicators, along with a shallow archive of recently published articles. URL: www.latintrade.com

1000. ***Thunderbird International Business Review.*** Formerly (until 1998): *International Executive;* Incorporates (1988-2001): *Global Focus;* Which was formerly (until 1999): *Global Outlook;* (until 1998): *Business and the Contemporary World.* [ISSN: 1096-4762] 1959. bi-m. GBP 716. Ed(s): Suzy Howell, Mary B Teagarden. John Wiley & Sons, Inc., 111 River St, Hoboken, NJ 07030; cs-journals@wiley.com; http://onlinelibrary.wiley.com. Adv. Refereed. Microform: PQC. Reprint: PSC. *Indexed:* A22, B01, BRI. *Bk. rev.:* 0-8, 450-2,000 words. *Aud.:* Ac.

With the goal of exchanging ideas and research between scholars and practitioners worldwide, this refereed journal addresses the unique challenges of global human management, analysis of multinational corporations, small business development, marketing ethics, market entry, doing business in specific countries, and international trade policies. Of primary interest to libraries that support graduate degree programs in business or international relations. URL: http://onlinelibrary.wiley.com/journal/10.1002/(ISSN)1520-6874

Small Business

Black Enterprise. See African American section.

1001. ***Entrepreneur (Irvine).*** Former titles (until 1978): *International Entrepreneurs;* (until 1977): *Insider's Report.* [ISSN: 0163-3341] 1973. m. USD 9.99 (print or online ed.); USD 10.99 combined subscription (print & online eds.)). Ed(s): Jason Feifer, Linda Lacina. Entrepreneur Media, Inc., 18061 Fitch, Irvine, CA 92614; subscribe@enterpreneurmag.com; http://www.entrepreneur.com. Illus., adv. Sample. *Indexed:* A22, B01, BRI. *Aud.:* Ga.

A leading magazine that covers trends, issues, and problems associated with starting and running a business. Short features written in an engaging style include individual and company profiles; success stories; strategies for improvement; and rankings of top companies and individuals. News coverage includes national, global, women-oriented, industry-specific, and hot topics. Each issue contains tips on technology, money, management, and marketing; classified ads; and a products-and-services directory. The web site contains full-text features and columns from the current issue and archives, along with online exclusives. A core title for business collections in most public and academic libraries. URL: www.entrepreneur.com/magazine

1002. ***Entrepreneurship & Regional Development.*** [ISSN: 0898-5626] 1989. 10x/yr. GBP 1052 (print & online eds.)). Ed(s): Alistair R Anderson. Routledge, 4 Park Sq, Milton Park, Abingdon, OX14 4RN, United Kingdom; subscriptions@tandf.co.uk; http://www.tandfonline.com. Adv. Sample. Refereed. Reprint: PSC. *Indexed:* A22, B01, E01, EconLit, IBSS. *Bk. rev.:* Infrequent. *Aud.:* Ac.

This title focuses on the diverse and complex characteristics of local and regional economies (primarily European) that lead to entrepreneurial vitality. It provides a multidisciplinary forum for researchers, students, and practitioners in the fields of entrepreneurship and small- to medium-sized enterprise (SME) development within the larger context of economic growth and development. Each issue contains four or five articles, each 15–25 pages in length. Of interest to academic collections that cater to small-business studies or economics.

1003. ***Entrepreneurship: Theory and Practice.*** Formerly (until 1988): *American Journal of Small Business.* [ISSN: 1042-2587] 1976. bi-m. USD 967 (print & online eds.)). Sage Publications, Inc., 2455 Teller Rd, Thousand Oaks, CA 91320; info@sagepub.com; https://us.sagepub.com. Illus., index, adv. Refereed. Vol. ends: No. 4. Reprint: PSC. *Indexed:* A22, ATI, B01, C42, E01, IBSS. *Aud.:* Ac.

Blending theoretical and applied methods, this official journal of the U.S. Association for Small Business and Entrepreneurship features refereed articles on a wide range of topics in the field of entrepreneurship studies, including creation of enterprises, management of small firms, and issues in family owned businesses. Case studies, research notes, announcements, and guest editors' commentary occur sporadically throughout the year. Most appropriate for academic libraries.

1004. ***Family Business Review.*** [ISSN: 0894-4865] 1988. q. USD 632 (print & online eds.)). Ed(s): Pramodita Sharma. Sage Publications, Inc., 2455 Teller Rd, Thousand Oaks, CA 91320; info@sagepub.com; http://www.sagepub.com. Illus., index, adv. Sample. Refereed. Vol. ends: No. 4. Reprint: PSC. *Indexed:* A22, B01, BRI, E01. *Bk. rev.:* Number and length vary. *Aud.:* Ac.

An international editorial board oversees this scholarly publication, which is dedicated to furthering knowledge and increasing interdisciplinary skills of educators, consultants, and researchers of family owned businesses. Four features, comprised of method papers and case studies, are presented in each issue, along with invited commentaries, interviews, and book reviews. Occasional special issues are devoted to family owned business practices in a particular region of the world. Recommended for academic libraries that support entrepreneurship programs. URL: http://fbr.sagepub.com/

1005. ***Franchising World.*** Former titles (until Dec.1990): *Franchising Opportunities;* (until Feb.1990): *Franchising Opportunities World;* (until 1989): *Franchising World; International Franchise Association. Quarterly Legal Bulletin; International Franchise Association. Legal Bulletin.* [ISSN: 1524-4814] 1960. m. Free to members; Non-members, USD 50. Ed(s): Terry Hill. International Franchise Association, 1501 K St, NW, Ste 350, Washington, DC 20005; ifa@franchise.org; http://www.franchise.org. Adv. Circ: 25600. Microform: PQC. *Indexed:* A22, B01, BRI. *Aud.:* Ga.

The official publication of the International Franchise Association. Each issue contains eight articles that offer practical advice for both franchisors and franchisees. Anybody interested in franchising as a small-business opportunity will want to consult this publication. Regular columns address management and operations, industry trends, case studies, legal and regulatory issues, minority ownership opportunities, international development, and association events and activities. Digital issues of the magazine from the past two years can be viewed at the web site by selecting "News" from the navigation bar. URL: www.franchise.org/franchising-world-digital-version

1006. ***Home Business Magazine.*** Formerly: *National Home Business.* [ISSN: 1092-4779] 1994. q. USD 15 domestic; USD 31 Canada; USD 47 elsewhere. Ed(s): Stacy Ann Henderson, Sherilyn Colleen. United Marketing & Research Company, Inc., 20664 Jutland Pl, Lakeville, MN 55044; http://www.homebusinessmag.com. Illus., adv. *Indexed:* B01. *Aud.:* Ga.

Featuring five or six articles on strategy, along with an individual success story, this magazine exudes practical advice. There is a strong online presence at the web site, a useful bookmark in libraries that do not subscribe to this bimonthly in print. Information is organized by channels: "Start Up," "Marketing/Sales," "Money Corner," "Management," "Home Office," "Telecommuting," and "Community." High-resolution digital images of recent issues permit online viewing, page by page. Of most interest to public libraries. URL: www.homebusinessmag.com

1007. ***Journal of Business Venturing: entrepreneurship, entrepreneurial finance, innovation and regional development.*** [ISSN: 0883-9026] 1985. 6x/yr. EUR 2008. Ed(s): Dean A Shepherd. Elsevier Inc., 230 Park Ave, Ste 800, New York, NY 10169; usinfo-f@elsevier.com; https://www.elsevier.com. Illus., index, adv. Sample. Refereed. Microform: PQC. *Indexed:* A22, B01. *Aud.:* Sa.

Leading scholars and practitioners contribute developed theoretical and empirical studies to fulfill the editor's stated aims of knowledge advancement in four key areas: entrepreneurship, new business development, industry evolution, and technology management. Approximately five refereed articles of 20-30 pages in length make up each issue. Occasionally included are invited papers by selected authors, with a topic of special concern. The last issue of each volume includes a cumulative index for the volume year. An important journal for academic libraries that support programs for advanced degrees in business.

1008. ***Journal of Small Business Management.*** [ISSN: 0047-2778] 1963. q. GBP 393. Ed(s): George T Solomon. Wiley-Blackwell Publishing, Inc., 111 River St, Hoboken, NJ 07030; http://onlinelibrary.wiley.com. Illus., index, adv. Sample. Refereed. Vol. ends: Nov. Reprint: PSC. *Indexed:* A22, B01, BLI, BRI, C42, E01, IBSS. *Aud.:* Ac.

This official journal of the International Council for Small Business publishes research in entrepreneurship studies and fosters the exchange of ideas dealing with marketing, financing, accounting, management, education, technology, law, and cross-cultural ramifications. Each issue contains five or six rigorously researched articles aimed at the international academic community. Appropriate for academic institutions that offer advanced degrees in business administration.

1009. ***Minority Business Entrepreneur.*** [ISSN: 1048-0919] 1984. bi-m. USD 18. Ed(s): Emily Richwine. Minority Business Entrepreneur, 3528 Torrance Blvd, Ste 101, Torrance, CA 90503. Illus., index, adv. Vol. ends: No. 6. *Indexed:* ENW. *Bk. rev.:* Number and length vary. *Aud.:* Ga.

This title serves to inform, educate, and inspire business owners who are women or in an ethnic minority. Articles profile individual entrepreneurs, report on success stories, analyze failures, and provide best-practice examples designed to enhance small-business management. Typical articles describe corporate and government programs and the positive benefits of supplier diversity. Ideal for public libraries that serve small businesses; of interest to academic collections that support entrepreneurship programs. URL: www.mbemag.com/

1010. ***Small Business Economics: an entrepreneurship journal.*** [ISSN: 0921-898X] 1989. 8x/yr. EUR 2526 (print & online eds.)). Ed(s): David B Audretsch, Zoltan J Acs. Springer New York LLC, 233 Spring St, New York, NY 10013; customerservice@springer.com; http://www.springer.com. Illus., index, adv. Sample. Refereed. Microform: PQC. Reprint: PSC. *Indexed:* A22, B01, BRI, E01, EconLit, IBSS. *Bk. rev.:* 0-1, 750-1,000 words. *Aud.:* Ac.

This title provides a forum for theoretical, empirical, and conceptual papers in entrepreneurship. The scope is interdisciplinary and cross-national research from a broad spectrum of disciplines and related fields, including economics, finance, management, psychology, regional studies, sociology, and strategy. Each issue features six to eight articles of research and analysis that address personal characteristics of entrepreneurs, new ventures and innovation, firms' life cycles, and the role played by institutions and public policies. Of most interest to academic libraries. URL: http://link.springer.com/journal/11187

1011. ***Technovation: the international journal of technological innovation, entrepreneurship and technology management.*** [ISSN: 0166-4972] 1981. m. EUR 2358. Ed(s): Jonathan Linton. Pergamon Press, The Blvd, Langford Ln, E Park, Kidlington, OX5 1GB, United Kingdom; JournalsCustomerServiceEMEA@elsevier.com; http://www.elsevier.com. Illus., adv. Sample. Refereed. *Indexed:* A22, B01, BRI, IBSS. *Bk. rev.:* 1-3, 500-1,000 words. *Aud.:* Ac.

All facets of the process of technological innovation, from conceptualization through commercial utilization, are covered. Topics include technological trends and breakthroughs, availability of capital for new product development and introduction, displacement of existing products, management of entrepreneurial ventures, management of innovation in small and medium enterprises (SMEs), investment strategies related to new science- or technology-based innovations, the innovator as an individual and as a personality type, and technology transfer to developing nations. Case studies that illustrate how innovation occurs from business and technical standpoints are also included, together with reviews and analyses of governmental and industrial policy that inhibit or stimulate technological innovation. Recommended for academic collections that support small business studies. URL: www.sciencedirect.com/science/journal/01664972

State and Regional

Several states and major cities produce some form of business newsmagazine. The Alliance of Area Business Publications provides a directory of members' titles at its web site, www.bizpubs.org.

1012. ***Los Angeles Business Journal.*** [ISSN: 0194-2603] 1979. w. Mon. USD 99.95 combined subscription domestic (print & online eds.); USD 199 combined subscription foreign (print & online eds.)). Ed(s): Laurence Darmiento, Charles Crumpley. California Business Journals, 5700 Wilshire Blvd, Los Angeles, CA 90036; https://www.pubservice.com/CJ.htm. Adv. Microform: PQC. *Indexed:* BRI. *Aud.:* Ga.

This weekly newspaper covers local business activity in the second-largest metropolitan area in the United States. Regular columns feature articles on media and technology, small business, finance, investment, and real estate. Each issue has a special report that contains several brief articles on a specific industry or subject. Topical rankings of companies known as "The Lists," along with selected articles from the current newsstand issue, are now available online after free registration through the web site. Links are provided to regional editions that cover Orange County, San Diego, and the San Fernando Valley. URL: www.labusinessjournal.com

Trade and Industry

Beverage Industry. See Food Industry section.

1013. ***Beverage World: intelligence for the global drinks business.*** Incorporates (in 2002): *Beverage World International;* Former titles (until 1975): *Soft Drinks;* (until 1966): *National Bottler's Gazette.* [ISSN: 0098-2318] 1882. m. Free to qualified personnel. Ed(s): Jeff Cioletti, Andrew Kaplan. Ideal Media LLC, PO Box 2054, Skokie, IL 60076; http://www.idealmediallc.com. Illus., index, adv. Circ: 34000. Vol. ends: Dec. Microform: PQC. *Indexed:* A22, B01, H&TI. *Aud.:* Sa.

This journal tracks all aspects of the global beverage industry: manufacturers, bottlers, distributors, and retailers of soft drinks, fruit juices, iced teas, coffees, wines, spirits, and bottled waters. Articles and interviews cover diverse topics, including industry statistics, market share, packaging, vending, quality control, consumer preferences, marketing efforts, and fleet management. Only the current digital edition is viewable at the website; however, this website does offer complementary special reports, new product profiles, and "Lists & Rankings." An ideal candidate for a large public library with a patron group involved in the beverage industry, and academic institutions with patrons looking for market and industry data. URL: www.beverageworld.com

Billboard. See Music/Popular section.

Boxoffice Pro. See Films section.

Broadcasting & Cable. See Television, Video, and Radio section.

Builder. See Building and Construction section.

1014. ***Chain Store Age: the news magazine for retail executives.*** Former titles (until 1995): *Chain Store Age Executive with Shopping Center Age;* (until 1975): *Chain Store Age Executives Edition Including Shopping Center Age;* Which was formed by the merger of (1959-1964): *Chain Store Age (Executives Edition);* Which was formerly (until 1959): *Chain Store Age (Administration Edition);* (until 1928): *Chain Store Age;* (1962-1964): *Shopping Center Age.* [ISSN: 1087-0601] 1964. 8x/yr. Free to qualified personnel. Ed(s): Marianne Wilson. Lebhar-Friedman, Inc., 425 Park Ave, New York, NY 10022; info@lf.com; http://www.lf.com. Illus., adv. Sample. Circ: 26674. Vol. ends: Dec. Microform: CIS. *Indexed:* A22, B01, B03, BRI, C42. *Aud.:* Sa.

This title, from the same publisher as *Retailing Today* (below in this section), serves the decision makers who manage chain stores and shopping centers. Nearly two dozen short articles in each issue discuss current news, events, and issues related to real estate, store planning, operations, electronic retailing, payment systems, related products, and technologies. Appropriate for larger public libraries and for academic libraries that support business programs. Free registration is required to access published article content and detailed industry data. URL: www.chainstoreage.com

1015. ***Chemical Week.*** Incorporates (in 2003): *Soap & Cosmetics. Blue book;* Former titles: *Chemical Industries Week;* (until 1951): *Chemical Industries;* (until 1933): *Chemical Markets.* [ISSN: 0009-272X] 1914. w. USD 149.97 domestic; USD 169.97 Canada; USD 449 elsewhere. Ed(s): Roberte Westervelt, Kate Phillips. Access Intelligence, LLC, 4 Choke Cherry Rd, 2nd Fl, Rockville, MD 20850; info@accessintel.com; http://www.accessintel.com. Illus., index, adv. Sample. Circ: 9533 Paid. Microform: PQC. *Indexed:* A&ATA, A01, A22, Agr, B01, B03, BRI, C42. *Aud.:* Sa.

Weekly news source for chemical manufacturers and related industries, including pharmaceuticals and plastics. A cover story, running two or three pages, accompanies brief business and finance news articles organized by region: United States/Americas, Europe/Mideast, and Asia/Pacific. Other sections cover construction projects, mergers and acquisitions, information technology, specialty chemical production, environmental issues, laws and regulations, company and market profiles, management trends, and newsmakers in the industry. Online content of the magazine is restricted to current subscribers only at the website. URL: www.chemweek.com

Constructor. See Building and Construction section.

ENR. See Engineering and Technology/Civil and Environmental Engineering section.

Fleet Owner. See Transportation section.

1016. ***Footwear News.*** [ISSN: 0162-914X] 1945. w. USD 72 domestic; USD 149 in Canada & Mexico; USD 295 elsewhere. Ed(s): Neil Weilheimer. Fairchild Publications, Inc., 750 3rd Ave, 3rd Fl, New York, NY 10017; customerservice@fairchildpub.com; http://www.fairchildpub.com. Illus., adv. Circ: 17189. *Indexed:* B01, B03, BRI, C42. *Aud.:* Sa.

The readership of this weekly includes designers, retailers, manufacturers, importers, wholesalers, suppliers, tanners, finishers, and members of related fields. It offers extensive coverage of trends in women's, men's, and children's footwear across the dress, casual, and athletic categories. A typical issue is more visual than textual in content; articles tend to be brief profiles of designer lines and manufacturers. The web site offers only a few features and current news items; it lacks the graphic punch of its print counterpart. Of most interest to libraries that collect in fashion design. URL: www.footwearnews.com

1017. ***Global Cosmetic Industry.*** Former titles (until 1999): *D C I;* (until 1997): *Drug and Cosmetic Industry;* (until 1932): *Drug Markets;* (until 1926): *Drug and Chemical Markets;* Drug and Cosmetic Industry incorporated (1957-1988): *Drug and Cosmetic Catalog;* Which was formerly (until 1957): *Drug and Cosmetic Review;* (until 1939): *Drug and Cosmetic Catalog.* [ISSN: 1523-9470] 1914. m. Free. Ed(s): Jeff Falk. Allured Publishing Corp., 336 Gundersen Dr, Ste A, Carol Stream, IL 60188; customerservice@allured.com; http://www.allured.com. Illus., index, adv. Circ: 15089. Vol. ends: Dec. Microform: PMC; PQC. *Indexed:* A22, B01, B03, BRI, C42. *Aud.:* Sa.

GCI, primarily intended for cosmetics and personal-care product professionals, is a showcase of research and development, market trends, and marketing efforts. Features are short and mix the practical (product application) with the technical (formulas and ingredient analysis). Of interest to academic collections that support marketing programs and to special libraries that support personal-care product manufacturers, marketers, and retailers. Also somewhat of interest to public libraries because of the practical information imparted to consumers, e.g., new product previews and general fashion forecasts. Current issue contents and archives are available at the web site. URL: www.gcimagazine.com

1018. ***H F N.*** Former titles (until 1995): *H F D - Home Furnishing Daily;* (until 19??): *H F D - Retailing Home Furnishings;* (until 1976): *Home Furnishings Daily;* (until 1929): *Women's Wear Daily. Saturday.* [ISSN: 1082-0310] 19??. w. Free to qualified personnel. Ed(s): Duke Ratliff, Warren Shoulberg. Macfadden Communications Group, LLC, 333 Seventh Ave, 11th Fl, New York, NY 10001; http://www.macfad.com. Illus., index, adv. Sample. Circ: 18111. *Indexed:* B03, BRI, C42. *Aud.:* Sa.

This is a key news source for suppliers, manufacturers, wholesalers, and retailers in and associated with the interior design industry. It covers the broad spectrum of what constitutes home furnishings. In addition to the obvious furniture, there are major appliances, housewares, tableware, bedding, floor coverings, lighting and decorative accessories, do-it-yourself decorating products, and giftware. Articles address new materials, products, and processes; news and newsmakers; market conditions; and industry trends. Online content at the web site is limited to article summaries from the current issue only. However, today's news briefs, job postings, and a trade-show calendar will nicely complement a paid print subscription. Of interest to larger business collections. URL: www.hfndigital.com/

Logistics Management. See Transportation section.

1019. ***Packaging Digest.*** Incorporates (in 1985): *Packaging;* Which was formerly (until 1985): *Package Engineering Including Modern Packaging;* Which was formed by the merger of (1927-1979): *Modern Packaging;* (1956-1979): *Package Engineering;* Which incorporated (in 1974): *Package Engineering New Products;* Which was formerly (until 1973): *Package Engineering New Products News.* [ISSN: 0030-9117] 1963. m. Free to qualified personnel (print or online ed.)). Canon Communications LLC, 1200 Jorie Blvd., Ste.230, Oak Brook, IL 60523; info@cancom.com; http://www.cancom.com. Illus., adv. Sample. Circ: 91681. Vol. ends: Dec. Microform: PQC. *Indexed:* A22, B01, B03, BRI, C42. *Aud.:* Sa.

Aimed at managers, marketers, and manufacturers in the packaging industry, this monthly tabloid presents the fusion of art, design, and functionality. Ten to 12 short articles feature company and product information; new materials, technologies, and manufacturing methods; environmental concerns; and retail display. Recurring departments report on industry news, pending legislation, regulatory pressures, and new product spotlights. Illustrations abound. Current and past issue articles, daily news updates, industry links, and a few web-based exclusives are available online at the web site. An important source for marketing and branding trends. URL: www.packagingdigest.com

1020. ***Progressive Grocer (New York, 2002).*** Formed by the merger of (1922-2002): *Progressive Grocer (New York, 1922);* (1979-2002): *Supermarket Business;* Which was formerly (1969-1979): *Supermarketing;* (1946-1969): *Food Topics.* 2002. m. USD 135 domestic (Free to qualified personnel). Ed(s): Meg Major. Stagnito Media, 570 lake Cook Rd, Ste 106, Deerfield, IL 60015; http://www.stagnitomedia.com. Illus., adv. Circ: 40082 Paid and controlled. *Indexed:* A22, B01, B03, BRI. *Aud.:* Ga, Sa.

Intended for the supermarket manager, this title covers such topics as personnel and labor issues, security, customer service, new products, store design, and market conditions in general. Retailers, both foreign and domestic, who utilize unique approaches to management are spotlighted in a "Store of the Month" feature. Articles are categorized as grocery, fresh food, or nonfoods business. Regular departments address consumer preferences, in-store promotions, technology, equipment, distribution, and issues unique to independent stores. This title is of interest to academic libraries that support marketing and management programs, and to public libraries because of the general appeal of food. Current issue contents, web exclusives, and daily news updates are available online at the web site. URL: www.progressivegrocer.com

1021. *Recycling Today.* Formed by the merger of (1990-1992): *Recycling Today (Scrap Market Edition);* (1990-1992): *Recycling Today (Municipal (Post-Consumer) Market Edition);* Both of which superseded in part (in May 1990): *Recycling Today;* Which was formerly (until 1963): *Secondary Raw Materials.* [ISSN: 1096-6323] 1992. m. Free to qualified personnel. Ed(s): Brian Taylor, DeAnne Toto. G I E Media Inc., 5811 Canal Rd, Valley View, OH 44125; http://www.giemedia.com/. Illus., adv. Circ: 30000. *Indexed:* A22, B03, BRI, C42. *Aud.:* Sa.

This title addresses social, political, and environmental issues that impact, and are impacted by, recycling efforts from both a local and global perspective. Articles monitor trends in waste management technologies and processes, environmental regulations, and the volatility of recycled commodity prices. Each issue provides updates on the status of the nonmetallic, ferrous, nonferrous, paper, electronics, scrap, and construction/demolition debris sectors. Current issue contents and archives are available to subscribers at the web site; nonsubscribers may register there for free online access. URL: www.recyclingtoday.com/magazine

1022. *Retail Merchandiser: strategies for growth.* Formerly (until May 2000): *Discount Merchandiser.* [ISSN: 1530-8154] 1961. bi-m. Free to qualified personnel. Ed(s): Amanda Gaines. RedCoat Publishing, 900 Cummings Center, Ste 222-T, Beverly, MA 01915; http://www.redcoatpublishing.com/. Illus., adv. Circ: 20000. Vol. ends: Dec. *Indexed:* A22, B01, BRI. *Aud.:* Ac, Sa.

All aspects of merchandising are covered in this publication, including manufacturing, distribution, marketing, advertising, and sales. Articles discuss product lines, famous brands, private labels, store security, technology enhancements, staffing, and related issues. Industry news, newsmakers, and competition are spotlighted. The special convention issue contains 20 pages of editorial commentary on the current and future state of mass retailing. This is a useful publication for libraries that support professionals and some academics with a focus on retail and marketing. URL: www.retail-merchandiser.com/

1023. *Retail Traffic.* Formerly (until May 2003): *Shopping Center World;* Incorporates (1975-1991): *Shopping Center World Product and Service Directory.* [ISSN: 1544-4236] 1972. m. USD 109 domestic (Free to qualified personnel). Ed(s): David Bodamer. Penton, 249 W 17th St, New York, NY 10011; information@penton.com; http://www.penton.com. Illus. Circ: 36553 Controlled. Microform: PQC. *Indexed:* A22, B01, B03, BRI, C42. *Aud.:* Sa.

This trade title caters to commercial real estate executives, shopping center developers, owners and managers, retail chain store executives, construction personnel, marketing professionals, leasing agents, brokers, architects, and designers. Articles report on successful shopping center properties, projects proposed and underway, specific design elements and materials, financing, and retail store profiles. Regular departments include "Shows and Events," "Retail Design Trends," "Lease Language," "International News," and "Sales Figures of Major Retailers." Content is available online after free registration. URL: http://nreionline.com/

1024. *Rock Products.* Former titles (until 1994): *Rock Products Mining & Processing;* (until 1963): *Rock Products;* (until 1917): *Rock Products and Building Materials;* Rock Products incorporated (1896-1924): *Cement and Engineering News;* (1918-193?): *Concrete Products.* [ISSN: 0747-3605] 1897. m. USD 62 in US & Canada (Free to qualified personnel). Ed(s): Mark S Kuhar. Mining Media International, 8751 E Hampden Ave, Ste B-1, Denver, CO 80231; info@mining-media.com; http://www.mining-media.com. Illus., adv. Vol. ends: Dec. Microform: PQC. *Indexed:* A22, C42. *Aud.:* Ga, Ac, Sa.

Topics covered are associated with the quarried stone, sand, gypsum, lightweight aggregate, and earthmoving industries. Regular features include a handful of articles on manufacturing technologies, business practices, community relations, labor, regulatory, and safety issues. Additional trade-specific departments include industry news, environmental issues, a Washington letter, new products, and a calendar of events, in addition to an annual buyers' guide and dealer directory. Current and previous issues are available online at the web site. Apart from special libraries, this title is of interest to academic libraries that support civil engineering programs and public libraries in communities with quarry operations. URL: www.rockproducts.com

1025. *Rubber World.* Former titles (until 1954): *India Rubber World;* (until 1899): *India Rubber World and Electrical Trades Review.* [ISSN: 0035-9572] 1889. 16x/yr. USD 34 domestic; USD 39 Canada; USD 149 elsewhere. Ed(s): Jill Rohrer, Don R Smith. Lippincott & Peto, Inc., 1867 W Market St, Akron, OH 44313. Illus., adv. Vol. ends: Dec. Microform: PMC; PQC. *Indexed:* A22, B01, BRI. *Aud.:* Sa.

Feature articles provide up-to-date technical service information for rubber chemists and formulators, give R&D personnel current technical know-how, and inform plant engineering personnel about the latest equipment and production technology. Regular departments include "Business Briefs," "Patent News," "Market Focus," "Tech Service," "Process Machinery," "Supplies Showcase," "Meetings," and "Calendar of Events." The subscription includes additional quarterly issues devoted to special topics. Digital edition of the current issue is offered after free registration at the web site; articles from previous issues must be purchased. Libraries that support industrial marketing, chemistry, or engineering research and development should find this title useful in their collections. URL: www.rubberworld.com

Sea Technology. See Marine Science and Technology section.

Snack Food & Wholesale Bakery. See Food Industry section.

1026. *Special Events Magazine.* Formerly: *Special Events.* [ISSN: 1079-1264] 1982. bi-m. USD 19.95 domestic (Free to qualified personnel). Ed(s): Lisa Hurley. Penton, 11500 W Olympic Bl. #574, Los Angeles, CA 90064; information@penton.com; http://www.penton.com. Circ: 5763 Paid and controlled. *Indexed:* B01, BRI, C42. *Aud.:* Ga, Sa.

A resource for event professionals who design and produce social, corporate, and public events in hotels, resorts, banquet facilities, and other venues. Coverage of galas is extensive; photos are a feast for the eyes. Departments provide practical advice on event management and tout new products and innovative ideas. The publication has a cooperative alliance with the International Special Events Society. In each issue, five pages are reserved for news and promotion of the society's web site. Contents of the current and back issues are available online. URL: www.specialevents.com

1027. *Stores.* Former titles (until 1947): *National Retail Dry Goods Association. Bulletin;* (until 1925): *National Retail Dry Goods Association. Confidential Bulletin.* [ISSN: 0039-1867] 1912. m. USD 120 (print or online ed.) (Free to qualified personnel). Ed(s): Susan Reda. N R F Enterprises, Inc., 325 7th St, NW, Ste 1100, Washington, DC 20004. Illus., adv. Vol. ends: Dec. *Indexed:* A22, B01, B03, BRI. *Aud.:* Sa.

This title features corporate and industry news for all kinds of retail chain stores and wholesale clubs, restaurants, drug stores, direct mail, and marketing firms engaged in specialty and general merchandising. The focus is on technology, management, and operations. Special issues include ranked lists of department stores in July and specialty chains in August, both including sales and earnings figures. Appropriate for larger public libraries and for academic libraries that support business programs. URL: https://nrf.com/connect-us/stores-magazine

1028. *Textile World.* Formerly (until 1921): *Textile World Journal;* Which was formed by the merger of (1903-1915): *Textile World Record;* (1894-1915): *Textile Manufacturers Journal;* Incorporates (1907-1923): *Posselt's Textile Journal;* (1894-19??): *Textile Advance News;* (1916-19??): *Textiles;* Which was formerly (until 1916): *Knit Goods;* Incorporates (2001-2001): *Textile Industries;* Which was formerly (until 2001): *America's Textile Industries;* (until 2000): *America's Textiles*

International; (until 1986): *America's Textile;* Which was formed by the merger of (19??-1983): *America's Textiles. Knitter - Apparel Edition;* Which incorporated (1962-1982): *Knitting Industry;* (1971-1983): *America's Textiles. Reporter - Bulletin;* Which was formed by the merger of (1908-1971): *America's Textile Reporter;* Which was formerly (until 1908): *The American Wool and Cotton Reporter;* (1933-1971): *Textile Bulletin;* Which was formerly (1911-1933): *Southern Textile Bulletin.* [ISSN: 0040-5213] 1915. m. Free to qualified personnel. Billian Publishing, Inc., 2100 RiverEdge Pky, Ste 1200, Atlanta, GA 30328; info@billian.com; http://www.billian.com. Illus., adv. Vol. ends: Dec. Microform: PMC; PQC. *Indexed:* A22, B01, C42. *Aud.:* Sa.

Included in this title are reports on technologies such as yarn manufacturing; fabric forming; chemical treatment and finishing; industrial and specialty textiles; carpet manufacturing and marketing; manufacturing systems; and management issues on an international basis. Articles and advertisements introduce suppliers, new products, innovative techniques, and industry trends. Recurring departments provide industry news, statistics, legal developments, legislation, profiles of companies, interviews with executives, and occasional special reports. The current issue and archives are freely available online. URL: www.textileworld.com

1029. ***W W D: the retailer's daily newspaper.*** Incorporates (199?-2004): *Fairchild's Executive Technology;* (2000-2002): *W W D, The Magazine;* (2001-200?): *W W D Beautybiz;* Which was formerly (in 2001): *Beautybiz;* Former titles (until 1976): *Women's Wear Daily;* Which incorporated (1931-1940): *Retail Executive;* (until 1927): *Women's Wear.* [ISSN: 0149-5380] 1892. w. daily until Apr., 2015. USD 99 domestic (print or online ed.); USD 312.70 Canada; USD 595 elsewhere). Ed(s): Edward Nardoza. Fairchild Publications, Inc., 750 3rd Ave, 3rd Fl, New York, NY 10017; customerservice@fairchildpub.com; http://www.fairchildpub.com. Illus., adv. Circ: 46728. Microform: PQC. *Indexed:* B01, B03, BRI, C42. *Aud.:* Ga.

This newspaper-format publication provides extensive coverage of the women's apparel and couture fashion industries. Each weekday issue of this "fashion bible" focuses on a rotating theme of accessories, ready-to-wear, sportswear, or beauty, along with commentary on the season's colors, styles, and fabrics. Designers are profiled and their runway shows are lavishly photographed. There is extensive reporting on the social scene that is intrinsic to the concept of "image." Manufacturing problems, marketing, distribution channels, and retail issues are discussed in brief. To view content from today's paper and previous issues at the web site requires a separate subscription. Of interest to libraries with a flair for fashion. URL: www.wwd.com

1030. ***Woodworking Network.*** Former titles (until 2014): *Wood Products;* (until 2013): *Wood & Wood Products;* (until 1952): *Wood Combined with Wood Products;* Which was formed by the merger of (1946-1951): *Wood;* (190?-1951): *Wood Products;* Wood & Wood Products incorporated (in 1960): *The Wood-Worker;* (in 1960): *Veneers and Plywood;* Which was formerly (until 1934): *Veneers.* [ISSN: 2375-2106] 1951. m. C C I Media LLC, 2240 Country Club Pkwy, SE, Cedar Rapids, IA 52403; http://ccimedia.net/. Illus., adv. Microform: PQC. *Indexed:* A22, B01, C42. *Aud.:* Sa.

This publication is intended for management and operating personnel in the woodworking industry. Articles address machining trends and developments; management and marketing techniques; and automation, hardware, and design for the markets for residential furniture, business and institutional furniture, cabinet, millwork, and paneling. Archives, industry news, and other web exclusives are available at the web site. URL: www.woodworkingnetwork.com/

Banking

1031. ***American Banker: on focus and in depth.*** Formerly (until 1887): *Thompson's Bank Note and Commercial Reporter;* Incorporates (in 2002): *Financial Services Marketing.* [ISSN: 0002-7561] 1836. d. USD 995 combined subscription (print & online eds.)). Ed(s): Neil Weinberg. SourceMedia, Inc., One State St Plz, 27th Fl, New York, NY 10004; custserv@sourcemedia.com; http://www.sourcemedia.com. Illus., index, adv. *Indexed:* ATI, B01, B03, BLI, BRI, C42. *Bk. rev.:* Number and length vary. *Aud.:* Ac, Sa.

This highly regarded daily financial paper reports on trade and industry news and newsmakers. It covers trends in community banking, mortgages, investment products, debt and credit, technology, ATMs, and finance. Bank ratings, marketing, court cases, regulations, and news about movers and shakers in the banking industry are also included. Because of the in-depth coverage of banking and the concise reports of related general business and industry news, this is a must for bankers and for academic as well as larger public libraries. URL: www.americanbanker.com/

1032. ***The Banker.*** [ISSN: 0005-5395] 1926. m. GBP 645 combined subscription (print & online eds.)). Ed(s): Brian Caplen. The Financial Times Ltd., 1 Southwark Bridge, London, SE1 9HL, United Kingdom; help@ft.com; http://www.ft.com/. Illus., index, adv. Sample. Circ: 28974. Vol. ends: Dec. Microform: PQC. Reprint: SCH. *Indexed:* A22, B01, B03, BLI, BRI. *Bk. rev.:* Number and length vary. *Aud.:* Ac, Sa.

This international banking newsmagazine provides insights into the international retail and investment-banking climates. Each issue includes summary reports of economic and industry conditions in a dozen or more countries, along with brief reports that cover banking, capital markets, foreign exchange, derivatives, trade finance, risk analysis, technology, and interviews. Recent contents include discussions of covered bonds, the credit derivatives market, the strengthening of firms' compliance departments, and a host of other issues for each geographic region. Ranked lists of top banks and directories of foreign banks are often provided. This is a great choice for any academic or large public library whose patrons are interested in international finance, development, and banking news. URL: www.thebanker.com/

1033. ***Credit Union Magazine: for credit union elected officials, managers and employees.*** Formerly: *Credit Union Bridge.* [ISSN: 0011-1066] 1924. m. USD 64. Ed(s): Kathryn Kuehn. Credit Union National Association, Inc., PO Box 431, Madison, WI 53701; http://www.cuna.org. Illus., index, adv. Circ: 30900. Microform: PQC. *Indexed:* A22, B01, BLI. *Aud.:* Ac, Sa.

This important trade magazine, produced by the Credit Union National Association, reports on news and newsmakers, new products and technologies, target markets, new services, and information related to credit unions in general. Recent topics include discussions of student loans, vehicle repossession, and measuring customer loyalty. This title is worthwhile for large public libraries and academic libraries that support finance programs or a campus credit union. The website provides free articles from the current issue and archives. URL: http://news.cuna.org/

1034. ***Mortgage Banking: the magazine of real estate finance.*** Formerly (until 1981): *Mortgage Banker;* Which superseded (in 1939): *M B A News Review.* [ISSN: 0730-0212] 1936. m. Members, USD 80; Non-members, USD 95. Ed(s): Janet Reilley Hewitt. Mortgage Bankers Association, 1919 M Street NW, 5th Fl, Washington, DC 20036; info@mortgagebankers.org; http://www.mortgagebankers.org. Illus., index, adv. Sample. Vol. ends: Sep. Microform: CIS; PQC. *Indexed:* A22, B01, B03, BLI, BRI. *Aud.:* Ac, Sa.

This journal provides practical and timely articles about all aspects of real estate finance. Departments cover trends, technology, software, key people, the secondary mortgage market, statistics, sources of demographics and research, mortgage revenue bonds, and servicing. The companion web site highlights the current issue and provides a searchable archive. Libraries that support business programs that focus on real estate should consider this title. URL: www.newslibrary.com/sites/mbkb/

Insurance

1035. ***Best's Review.*** Formed by the merger of (1969-2000): *Best's Review. Life - Health Insurance Edition;* Which was formed by the merger of (1920-1969): *Best's Insurance News. Life - Health Edition;* Which was formerly (19??-1920): *Best's Life Insurance News;* (1964-1969): *Flitcraft Courant;* Which was formerly (until 1964): *Life Insurance Courant;* (until 19??): *Insurance Courant;* (1977-2000): *Best's Review. Property - Casualty Insurance Edition;* Which was formerly (until 1977): *Best's*

Review. Property - Liability Edition; (until 1969): *Best's Insurance News. Fire and Casualty.* [ISSN: 1527-5914] 2000. m. USD 57; USD 15.50 per issue. A.M. Best Co., Inc., Ambest Rd, Oldwick, NJ 08858; http://www.ambest.com. Illus., index, adv. Vol. ends: Apr. *Indexed:* A22, AgeL, B01, B03, BRI. *Aud.:* Ac, Sa.

This trade magazine provides wide coverage of the insurance industry under a single title. This integrated edition includes company and industry news, political and regulatory information, new-product announcements, newsmakers in the industry, and reports of court cases in each issue. This publication "best" represents the insurance industry as a whole, and therefore is a core title for large public and academic libraries. URL: www.ambest.com/review/

1036. ***Insurance: Mathematics and Economics.*** [ISSN: 0167-6687] 1982. 6x/yr. EUR 2675. Ed(s): Rob Kaas. Elsevier BV, Radarweg 29, Amsterdam, 1043 NX, Netherlands; info@elsevier.com; https://www.elsevier.com/. Illus., index, adv. Sample. Refereed. Vol. ends: No. 4. Microform: PQC. *Indexed:* A22, B01, EconLit, IBSS, MSN. *Aud.:* Ac, Sa.

Each issue contains five to eight papers of international interest, 10-15 pages in length, concerned with the theory of insurance mathematics or the inventive application of it, including empirical or experimental results. Articles evaluate mathematical and economic applications related to actuarial science and a variety of insurance-related concerns. Libraries that support programs in actuarial science, mathematics, and economics should evaluate this journal despite its hefty price. URL: www.sciencedirect.com/science/journal/01676687

1037. ***Journal of Risk and Insurance.*** Formerly (until 1964): *Journal of Insurance;* Which was formed by the merger of (1954-1957): *Review of Insurance Studies;* (1933-1957): *American Association of University Teachers of Insurance. Journal;* Which was formerly (until 1937): *American Association of University Teachers of Insurance. Proceedings of the Annual Meeting.* [ISSN: 0022-4367] 1957. q. USD 814 print & online eds. Ed(s): Joan T Schmit. Wiley-Blackwell Publishing, Inc., 111 River St, Hoboken, NJ 07030; info@wiley.com; http://onlinelibrary.wiley.com. Illus., index. Sample. Refereed. Vol. ends: Dec. Microform: PQC. Reprint: PSC. *Indexed:* A22, B01, BRI, E01, EconLit. *Bk. rev.:* 1-3, 1,000+ words. *Aud.:* Ac.

This is the flagship journal of the American Risk and Insurance Association. Each issue contains roughly ten articles that present original theoretical and empirical research in insurance economics and risk management. The focus is on the organization of markets, managing pure risk, insurance finance, the economics of employee benefits, utility theory, insurance regulation, actuarial and statistical methodology, and economics of insurance institutions. Large public libraries and academic libraries that support business programs should consider this title. URL: http://onlinelibrary.wiley.com/journal/10.1111/(ISSN)1539-6975

1038. ***National Underwriter. Life & Health.*** Former titles (until 2004): *National Underwriter. Life and Health Financial Services;* (until 1986): *National Underwriter. Life and Health Insurance Edition;* (until 1970): *National Underwriter. Life Insurance Edition.* [ISSN: 1940-1345] 197?. bi-w. USD 249 (Free to qualified personnel). The National Underwriter Company, 5081 Olympic Blvd, Erlanger, KY 41018; customerservice@nuco.com; http://www.nationalunderwriter.com. Illus., adv. Vol. ends: Dec. Microform: PQC. *Indexed:* A22, B01, B03, BRI, C42. *Aud.:* Sa.

This is a core newspaper for the life, health, and financial-services segments of the insurance industry. A variety of topics are covered, including new product information; changes in the tax law; new federal and state legislation; company, agent, and brokerage activities; and trade association meetings. Special in-depth issues are offered throughout the year that focus on particularly hot topics or issues of importance. Public libraries with a balanced business collection and all academic libraries that support insurance programs should have this title. The companion web site offers current news and past issues. URL: www.nationalunderwriter.com/magazines

1039. ***National Underwriter Property & Casualty.*** Former titles (until Sep.2013): *Property Casualty 360;* (until Jan.2013): *National Underwriter. P & C;* (until 2004): *National Underwriter. Property & Casualty - Risk & Benefits Management Edition;* (until 1989): *National Underwriter. Property and Casualty - Employee Benefits Edition;* (until 1986): *National Underwriter. Property and Casualty Insurance Edition;* (until 1970): *The National Underwriter;* (until 1917): *The Western Underwriter;* (until 1899): *Ohio Underwriter.* [ISSN: 2331-5326] 1897. m. USD 249 domestic; USD 289 Canada; USD 369 elsewhere. Ed(s): Shawn Moynihan. The National Underwriter Company, 5081 Olympic Blvd, Erlanger, KY 41018; customerservice@nuco.com; http://www.nationalunderwriter.com. Illus., adv. Microform: PQC. *Indexed:* A22, B01, B03, BRI, C42. *Aud.:* Ac, Sa.

This is a core newspaper for the international property, casualty, and risk-management insurance industry. Regularly featured sections include industry trends, agent and broker activities, corporate risk management, employee benefits, product and marketing information, stock activity, international events, and reinsurance. In addition, special, in-depth issues throughout the year focus on hot topics or issues of importance. Public libraries with a balanced business collection and all academic libraries that support insurance programs should have this title. The companion web site offers current news and past issues.

Investment

1040. ***Better Investing.*** [ISSN: 0006-016X] 1951. m. Free to members. Betterinvesting, PO Box 220, Royal Oaks, MI 48068; corporate@betterinvesting.org; http://www.betterinvesting.org. Illus., index, adv. Sample. Microform: PQC. *Indexed:* A22. *Bk. rev.:* Number and length vary. *Aud.:* Ga, Ac, Sa.

A popular choice for personal-investing collections in public libraries, this title presents news and information related to money management, investment clubs, and National Association of Investors Corporation (NAIC) events. Each issue includes an editorial, letters to the editor, "Ask Mr. NAIC," a growth-fund report, a technology report, and regional notices. The stocks and funds section includes an undervalued stock, a stock to study, a contrary opinion, a "five years ago stock to study," an undervalued stock, and an 18-month undervalued review. Public and academic libraries that serve individual investors or support investment courses should certainly consider this title. URL: www.betterinvesting.org/Public/StartLearning/BI+Mag/default.htm

1041. ***C F A Digest.*** [ISSN: 0046-9777] 1971. q. USD 50 combined subscription (print & online eds.)). Ed(s): Nicole R Lee. C F A Institute, 915 E High St, Charlottesville, VA 22902; info@cfainstitute.org; http://www.cfainstitute.org. Illus. Sample. *Indexed:* B01. *Aud.:* Ac, Sa.

The Association for Investment Management and Research, composed of the Institute of Chartered Financial Consultants and the Financial Analysts Federation, produces this digest. Each issue provides 600-word abstracts of 30 articles, drawn from a pool of more than 100 investment-related journals. Included are scholarly articles on alternative investments, corporate finance, corporate governance, debt investments, derivatives, equity investments, financial markets, investment theory, portfolio management, quantitative tools, and risk measurement and management. Publishers' names, addresses, and article order forms are included. In each issue, the editor summarizes the general content and the uses of the research articles. This is a core title for academic libraries that support programs in investment and finance. URL: www.cfapubs.org/toc/dig/current

1042. ***Euromoney.*** Incorporates (1989-2005): *Corporate Finance;* Which was formerly (1984-1989): *Euromoney Corporate Finance;* Incorporates (1991-2001): *Central European.* [ISSN: 0014-2433] 1969. m. GBP 499 combined subscription (print & online eds.); EUR 656 combined subscription (print & online eds.); USD 877 combined subscription (print & online eds.)). Ed(s): Clive Horwood. Euromoney Institutional Investor Plc., 8 Bouverie St, London, EC4Y 8AX, United Kingdom; customerservices@euromoneyplc.com; http://www.euromoneyplc.com/. Illus., index, adv. Sample. Vol. ends: Dec. *Indexed:* A22, B01, B03, BLI, BRI. *Bk. rev.:* Number and length vary. *Aud.:* Ac, Sa.

This title monitors the global financial marketplace, including financial institutions, securities, and commodities in established and emerging economies. It provides profiles of companies, industries, and the family trees and business interests of the people who control the wealth. Related aspects of international finance are covered. Each issue provides information from a dozen or more countries and regions. This is a core industry publication for anyone interested in international finance, and is appropriate for academic, special, and larger public libraries that support finance programs or professionals, especially with patrons seeking a comparative perspective. URL: www.euromoney.com/

1043. ***Institutional Investor (America's Edition).*** Incorporates (1972-1973): *Pensions;* (1970-1973): *Corporate Financing;* Which was formerly (until 1970): *Investment Banking and Corporate Financing.* [ISSN: 0020-3580] 1967. 10x/yr. GBP 385 combined subscription United Kingdom (print & online eds.); EUR 519 combined subscription in Europe (print & online eds.); USD 599 combined subscription elsewhere (print & online eds.)). Institutional Investor, Inc., 225 Park Ave S, New York, NY 10003; http://www.institutionalinvestorsalpha.com/. Illus., index, adv. Vol. ends: Dec. *Indexed:* A22, ATI, B01, B03, BLI, BRI, C42. *Bk. rev.:* 1-2, 1,000-1,500 words. *Aud.:* Ac, Sa.

This practitioner's magazine is known for its benchmark rankings and ratings of analysts, asset managers, banks, and country credit globally. These rankings are designed to assist financial professionals in making sound investment decisions. The journal provides detailed coverage of commercial and investment banking and many other areas of finance and investing. It also addresses policies, strategies, and the political activities in the social arenas that influence investment decisions. This publication is a must for academic and research libraries that support programs in business and finance.

1044. ***Investor's Business Daily.*** Formerly (until 1991): *Investor's Daily.* [ISSN: 1061-2890] 1984. d. (Mon.-Fri.). USD 319. Ed(s): Wesley Mann. Investor's Business Daily, Inc., 12655 Beatrice St, Los Angeles, CA 90066. Illus., adv. Circ: 264699. *Indexed:* B01, BLI, BRI. *Aud.:* Ga, Sa.

This daily newspaper provides timely information for individual and institutional investors. It reports on the economic, social, and political trends that drive markets and the individuals, companies, industries, and funds that make up the competitive landscape. Regular features include a weekly list of the 100 top-rated stocks, a list of stocks traded heavily by institutional investors, unbiased market analysis, profiles of innovative companies, and "Investor's Corner," lessons for successful investing. This newspaper is an excellent source for evaluating the global investment climate, and is a necessity for academic libraries that support business programs and for large public libraries. URL: www.investors.com/

1045. ***Investors Chronicle.*** Former titles (until 1983): *Investors Chronicle & Financial World;* (until 1979): *Investors Chronicle;* (until 1971): *Investors Chronicle and Stock Exchange Gazette;* Which was formed by the merger of (1901-1967): *Stock Exchange Gazette;* (1914-1967): *The Money Market Review & Investors' Chronicle;* Which was formerly (until 1914): *The Money Market Review.* [ISSN: 2052-725X] 1967. w. GBP 145 domestic includes Northern Ireland; GBP 191 in Europe; GBP 225 elsewhere. Ed(s): John Hughman. The Financial Times Ltd., 1 Southwark Bridge, London, SE1 9HL, United Kingdom; help@ft.com; http://www.ft.com/. Illus., adv. Sample. Circ: 26938. Vol. ends: Dec. Microform: RPI; PQC. *Indexed:* BLI, BRI. *Bk. rev.:* Number and length vary. *Aud.:* Ac, Sa.

This weekly British financial newsmagazine has been providing private investors with market information since 1860. Articles are grouped by category under general business news, features, tips, markets, sectors, and companies. Stock tips, statistics, and a survey article appear in each issue. Special supplements are issued with a subscription that report on insurance, investing for children, and other topics of interest to investors. This title provides a more international perspective than most U.S.-produced magazines of its kind.

1046. ***The Journal of Portfolio Management.*** [ISSN: 0095-4918] 1974. bi-m. USD 1590. Ed(s): Frank J Fabozzi. Portfolio Management Research, 41 Madison Ave, 20th Fl, New York, NY 10010; pm-research@pageantmedia.com; https://www.pm-research.com. Illus., adv. Refereed. *Indexed:* A22, ATI, B01, BLI, BRI, C42, EconLit. *Bk. rev.:* Number and length vary. *Aud.:* Ac, Sa.

This journal for investment professionals is focused on all aspects of institutional investing. Substantive articles are written in a layperson's terms by both practitioners and academics. Articles are not longer than 20 pages each, and recent ones cover topics such as innovation and portfolio management, embedded tax liabilities and portfolio choice, and investing under inflation risk. Recommended for academic and large public libraries. URL: www.iijournals.com/toc/jpm/current

1047. ***Kiplinger's Personal Finance: we rank the top mutual funds.*** Former titles (until 2000): *Kiplinger's Personal Finance Magazine;* (until 1991): *Changing Times;* (until 1949): *Kiplinger Magazine.* [ISSN: 1528-9729] 1947. m. USD 12 combined subscription domestic (print & online eds.) ; USD 29 combined subscription foreign (print & online eds.) ; USD 7 newsstand/cover). Ed(s): Knight A Kiplinger, Barbara Hoch Marcus. Kiplinger Washington Editors, Inc., 1100 13th St NW Ste 750, Washington, DC 20005; http://www.kiplinger.com. Illus. *Indexed:* A01, A22, ATI, AgeL, B01, BRI, C37, CBRI, MASUSE. *Bk. rev.:* Number and length vary. *Aud.:* Ga, Sa.

Aimed at anyone who wants to take an active role in his or her own personal-finance decisions, this title offers practical strategies for investing, managing, and spending your money. Articles cover topics that range from paying for college to planning your retirement, and everything in between. Regular departments monitor and report on mutual funds, money market funds, blue chips, and taxes. Personal-interest columns discuss travel, health, personal finances, and family finances. A handful of articles in each issue discuss general concerns related to investing. Special issues evaluate and chart mutual fund performance. The web site provides online access to selected content. URL: www.kiplinger.com/

1048. ***Morningstar FundInvestor.*** Former titles (until 1999): *Morningstar Investor;* (until 1995): *Five Star Investor.* [ISSN: 1099-0402] 1992. m. USD 125 combined subscription (print & online eds.)). Ed(s): Russel Kinnel. Morningstar, Inc., 22 W Washington St, Chicago, IL 60602; productinfo@morningstar.com; http://www.morningstar.com. *Indexed:* B01. *Aud.:* Ga, Ac, Sa.

The firm Morningstar produces both stock and mutual-fund investment newsletters and a user-friendly web site with helpful free content that includes fund data, calculators, and market news. The mutual fund title evaluated here comprises monthly issues that contain detailed coverage of the mutual fund industry, including 500 selected funds. This publication offers ratings, statistics, and interviews with top financial planners and fund industry leaders, as well as news, updates, and emerging trends in the industry. All public and academic libraries that provide investment information should have this title. URL: http://mfi.morningstar.com/

1049. ***Pensions & Investments.*** Former titles (until 1990): *Pensions and Investment Age;* (until 1981): *Pensions and Investments.* [ISSN: 1050-4974] 1973. bi-w. USD 325; USD 1650 combined subscription (print & online eds.)). Ed(s): Nancy Webman. Crain Communications, Inc., 711 Third Ave, New York, NY 10017; info@crain.com; http://www.crain.com. Illus., adv. Microform: CIS; PQC. *Indexed:* A22, ATI, B01, B03, BLI, BRI. *Aud.:* Ga, Sa.

This weekly newsmagazine for money managers provides information, explanation, analysis, and updates on all aspects of pensions and institutional investments. Regular departments cover news, interviews, opinions, a "pensions and investments" index, and updates on newsmakers. The "Annual Databook" issue includes a ranking of top managers and funds, statistics on pension plans, mutual funds, savings plans, life insurance, and more. Recent feature articles address the state of municipal pension plans, the impact of same-sex marriage laws on pension planning, and overall retirement confidence. URL: www.pionline.com/

1050. ***Worth.*** Former titles (until 2006): *Robb Report Worth;* (until 2003): *Worth;* (until 1992): *Investment Vision;* Which incorporated (1985-1991): *Personal Investor.* [ISSN: 1931-9908] 1987. q. USD 75 domestic; USD 100 foreign; USD 18.95 per issue. Ed(s): Richard Bradley. Worth Group LLC, 101 Park Ave, 4th Fl, New York, NY 10178; PRESS@WORTH.COM. Illus. *Bk. rev.:* Number and length vary. *Aud.:* Ga, Sa.

This personal investing magazine is aimed at high-net-worth individuals and their advisors. The magazine's features cover topics ranging from top wealth advisors, philanthropy, and tax havens, to profiles of CEOs and prominent business people. Even if you do not own a second home or a yacht, this publication provides savvy investment advice that could benefit all types of investors. Recommended for browsing collections in public libraries and larger academic libraries. URL: www.worth.com/

Scholarly

This section provides recommended purchases. To get more detailed evaluation and rankings of academic journals in the subject area, visit Harzing.com at www.harzing.com/jql.htm.

1051. ***Applied Mathematical Finance.*** [ISSN: 1350-486X] 1994. bi-m. GBP 1857 (print & online eds.)). Ed(s): Christoph Reisinger, Dr. Ben Hambly. Routledge, 4 Park Sq, Milton Park, Abingdon, OX14 4RN, United Kingdom; subscriptions@tandf.co.uk; http://www.tandfonline.com. Adv. Sample. Refereed. Reprint: PSC. *Indexed:* A22, B01, BLI, E01, EconLit, MSN. *Aud.:* Ac, Sa.

Aimed at financial practitioners, academics, and applied mathematicians, this title includes 15- to 20-page articles by worldwide academics that are designed to encourage the "confident use" of applied mathematics and mathematical models for finance. Papers cover such topics as economic primitives (interest rates, asset prices, and the like), market behavior, market strategy (such as hedging), financial instruments, reviews of new developments in financial engineering, general mathematical finance, models and algorithms, new products, and reviews of practical tools. Recent articles explore modeling electricity prices with forward-looking capacity constraints, and trader behavior and its effect on asset price dynamics. URL: www.tandfonline.com/toc/RAMF20/current

1052. ***Financial Accountability & Management.*** [ISSN: 0267-4424] 1985. q. GBP 738. Ed(s): Irvine Lapsley. Wiley-Blackwell Publishing Ltd., The Atrium, Southern Gate, Chichester, PO19 8QG, United Kingdom; cs-journals@wiley.com; http://onlinelibrary.wiley.com/. Adv. Sample. Refereed. Reprint: PSC. *Indexed:* A22, ATI, B01, BLI, C42, E01. *Aud.:* Ac, Sa.

This interdisciplinary journal draws from the fields of economics, social and public administration, political science, management sciences, accounting, and finance. The focus is on financial accountability, accounting, and financial and resource management for governmental and nonprofit organizations. Articles discuss everything from optimal tax and audit structures to strategies for private-public financing, to public-sector adoption of corporate practices. URL: http://onlinelibrary.wiley.com/journal/10.1111/(ISSN)1468-0408

1053. ***Financial Management.*** [ISSN: 0046-3892] 1972. q. GBP 412 (print & online eds.)). Ed(s): Raghavendra Rau, Marc Lipson. Wiley-Blackwell Publishing, Inc., 111 River St, Hoboken, NJ 07030; http://onlinelibrary.wiley.com. Illus., index. Refereed. Vol. ends: Winter. Microform: PQC. Reprint: PSC. *Indexed:* A22, ATI, B01, BRI, C42, E01, EconLit, IBSS. *Aud.:* Ac, Sa.

This is a core publication for financial management because of its high-quality, often groundbreaking research. Editors include the most widely published scholars in the field, and each volume addresses a variety of topics related to the practical applications and economic aspects of operating large public companies. Articles report on a range of topics, such as company ownership structures, takeover strategies and risks, and corporate finance solutions. Sources of data are provided, and some articles are presented as tutorials intended for classroom use. Strictly for academic and research libraries. URL: http://onlinelibrary.wiley.com/journal/10.1111/(ISSN)1755-053X

1054. ***Financial Markets, Institutions and Instruments.*** Former titles (until 1992): *Monograph Series in Finance and Economics;* (until 1977): *New York University, Center for the Study of Financial Institutions. Buletin.* [ISSN: 0963-8008] 1928. 5x/yr. GBP 724. Ed(s): Mary Jaffier, Anthony Saunders. Wiley-Blackwell Publishing, Inc., 111 River St, Hoboken, NJ 07030; http://onlinelibrary.wiley.com. Illus., adv. Sample. Refereed. Reprint: PSC. *Indexed:* A22, B01, BLI, E01, EconLit, IBSS. *Aud.:* Ac, Sa.

This journal attempts to bridge the gap between the academic and professional finance communities by covering topics that are relevant to both groups. Contributors include both financial practitioners and academics. Each issue has in-depth articles on a single topic, while the year-end issue features the year's most significant developments in corporate finance, money and banking, derivative securities, and fixed-income securities. A recent issue, for example, focuses on CEO bonus compensation and bank default risk. Recommended for academic and corporate libraries. URL: http://onlinelibrary.wiley.com/journal/10.1111/(ISSN)1468-0416

1055. ***Government Finance Review.*** Formed by the merger of (197?-1985): *Government Financial Management Resources in Review;* (1926-1985): *Governmental Finance;* Which was formerly (until 1971): *Municipal Finance.* [ISSN: 0883-7856] 1985. bi-m. USD 35. Ed(s): Anne Spray Kinney, Marcy Boggs. Government Finance Officers Association, 203 N LaSalle St, Ste 2700, Chicago, IL 60601; publications@gfoa.org; http://www.gfoa.org. Illus., index, adv. Circ: 16000 Paid. Microform: PQC. *Indexed:* A01, A22, ATI, B01, BLI, BRI. *Bk. rev.:* Number and length vary. *Aud.:* Ac, Sa.

The membership magazine of the Government Finance Officers Association of the United States and Canada reflects a broad spectrum of theory and practice in finance and financial management for state and local governments. Recent article topics include a 25-year retrospective of the GASB; the importance of cash-flow analysis in times of fiscal stress; and misunderstandings about accounting for capital assets. A core title for public-finance collections. URL: www.gfoa.org/GFR

1056. ***International Journal of Finance & Economics.*** [ISSN: 1076-9307] 1996. q. GBP 783. Ed(s): Michael P Dooley, Keith Cuthbertson. John Wiley & Sons Ltd., EMEA Institutional Sales, 9600 Garsington Rd, Oxford, OX4 2DQ, United Kingdom; cs-journals@wiley.com; http://onlinelibrary.wiley.com. Illus., adv. Sample. Refereed. Vol. ends: Dec. Reprint: PSC. *Indexed:* B01, BLI, EconLit. *Bk. rev.:* 1, signed, 5,000 words. *Aud.:* Ac, Sa.

Each issue includes a small number of lengthy articles on topics related to some aspect of international finance. Each article has a 500-word nontechnical abstract. Occasionally, an article will be published that is academically rigorous but less technical. The content of this journal appears to be more empirical than theoretical; it is positioned as a step between practitioner and theoretical titles that focus on similar content. Recent article topics include the Euro as a reserve currency; announcement effects on exchange rates; and nonlinear interest rate dynamics and forecasting. Although pricey, this title is appropriate for international finance collections in larger libraries. URL: http://onlinelibrary.wiley.com/journal/10.1002/(ISSN)1099-1158

1057. ***International Review of Economics & Finance.*** [ISSN: 1059-0560] 1991. 6x/yr. EUR 933. Ed(s): C R Chen, H Beladi. Elsevier BV, Radarweg 29, Amsterdam, 1043 NX, Netherlands; info@elsevier.com; https://www.elsevier.com/. Illus., index. Refereed. Microform: PQC. Reprint: PSC. *Indexed:* A22, B01, BAS, BLI, EconLit. *Bk. rev.:* Number and length vary. *Aud.:* Ac, Sa.

This journal presents a global perspective in empirical and theoretical papers on financial and market economics. Articles in recent issues explore country size and tax policy; privatizing by merger; and manager compensation related to cash flow. The half-dozen lengthy articles in each issue require a working knowledge of statistics to be fully appreciated. Libraries that support finance students and professionals will want to consider this title.

1058. ***Journal of Accounting Auditing and Finance.*** [ISSN: 0148-558X] 1977. q. USD 598 (print & online eds.)). Ed(s): Bharat Sarath. Sage Publications, Inc., 2455 Teller Rd, Thousand Oaks, CA 91320; info@sagepub.com; http://www.sagepub.com. Illus., adv. Refereed. Reprint: PSC. *Indexed:* A22, ATI, B01, BLI, EconLit. *Aud.:* Ac.

This journal aims to publish high-quality original research in accounting and accounting issues that relate to finance, economics, and operations. Empirical, analytical, and experimental research is included. Recent topics include carbon business accounting, the role of auditor specialization, and a study of fiscal year-ends. Academic libraries that support accounting and finance programs should consider this title. URL: http://jaf.sagepub.com/

1059. ***Journal of Banking & Finance.*** Incorporates (1985-1989): *Studies in Banking and Finance.* [ISSN: 0378-4266] 1977. 12x/yr. EUR 5482. Ed(s): Geert Bekaert, Carol Alexander. Elsevier BV, Radarweg 29, Amsterdam, 1043 NX, Netherlands; info@elsevier.com; https://www.elsevier.com/. Illus., index, adv. Sample. Refereed. Vol. ends: Dec. Microform: PQC. *Indexed:* A22, ATI, B01, BAS, BLI, BRI, EconLit, IBSS. *Bk. rev.:* Number and length vary. *Aud.:* Ac, Sa.

This journal aims to provide a platform for scholarly research that concerns financial institutions and the capital markets in which they function. Many of this journal's issues contain a special section of five or six themed articles, and an additional seven to ten regular papers on topics related to financial institutions, money, and capital markets. The editorial board includes top U.S. and international finance faculty, as well as some practitioners, mainly from the U.S. Federal Reserve system. Recent articles have discussed bank capital and financial constraints on private firms; ETF arbitrage; and corporate social responsibility in banking.

1060. ***The Journal of Derivatives.*** Incorporates (1992-1999): *The Journal of Financial Engineering.* [ISSN: 1074-1240] 1992. q. USD 929. Ed(s): Joseph Pimbley. Portfolio Management Research, 41 Madison Ave, 20th Fl, New York, NY 10010; pm-research@pageantmedia.com; https://www.pm-research.com. Illus., index, adv. Refereed. *Indexed:* A22, B01, BLI, BRI, C42, EconLit. *Aud.:* Ac, Sa.

Aimed at bridging the gap between academic theory and practice, this title is a leading analytical journal on derivatives. Readers need to be well versed in mathematics. Articles range from 10 to 20 pages in length, include charts and graphs, and offer analysis and evaluative commentary on all aspects of the use of derivatives: hedging, management of foreign exchange risk, maximization of transaction costs, measuring swap exposures on a balance sheet, comparison of price models, evaluation of new products, embedded options, arbitrage between cash and futures markets, and similar themes. An interesting recent article discusses how to apply academic derivatives theory and research to real-world problems. Suitable for libraries that support graduate finance programs or finance professionals. URL: www.iijournals.com/toc/jod/current

1061. ***Journal of Emerging Market Finance.*** [ISSN: 0972-6527] 2002. 3x/yr. USD 450 (print & online eds.)). Ed(s): S Maheshwaran. Sage Publications India Pvt. Ltd., B-1/I-1 Mohan Cooperative, Industrial Estate, Post Bag 7, New Delhi, 110 044, India; info@sagepub.in; http://www.sagepub.in. Sample. Refereed. Reprint: PSC. *Indexed:* A22, E01, EconLit, IBSS. *Aud.:* Ac.

This journal aims to highlight the theory and practice of finance in emerging markets. Emphasis is on articles that are of practical significance, but the journal covers theoretical and conceptual topics as well. Recent articles examine such diverse topics as foreign institutional investor behavior in Turkey and fixed-income managed funds in Eastern Europe. Academic libraries that support global finance programs should consider this title. URL: http://emf.sagepub.com/

1062. ***The Journal of Finance.*** [ISSN: 0022-1082] 1946. bi-m. GBP 439 (print & online eds.)). Ed(s): Campbell R Harvey. Wiley-Blackwell Publishing, Inc., 111 River St, Hoboken, NJ 07030; info@wiley.com; http://onlinelibrary.wiley.com. Illus., index. Sample. Refereed. Vol. ends: Dec. Microform: MIM; PQC. Reprint: PSC. *Indexed:* A22, ATI, B01, BLI, BRI, C42, CBRI, E01, EconLit, IBSS. *Bk. rev.:* 3-4, 1,500-2,000 words. *Aud.:* Ac, Sa.

This is the official publication of the American Finance Association and is a core publication for business collections. It is one of the most widely cited academic journals in finance and economics. A single issue generally includes six to ten feature articles of 20-50 pages in length, plus six to ten shorter papers that report on original scholarly research, in addition to announcements, commentaries, and lectures. This journal highlights research from all major fields of financial research, and would be a welcome addition in large public and academic libraries. URL: http://onlinelibrary.wiley.com/journal/10.1111/(ISSN)1540-6261

1063. ***Journal of Financial and Quantitative Analysis.*** [ISSN: 0022-1090] 1966. bi-m. GBP 455. Ed(s): Jarrad Harford, Stephen Brown. Cambridge University Press, University Printing House, Shaftesbury Rd, Cambridge, CB2 8BS, United Kingdom; online@cambridge.org; https://www.cambridge.org/. Illus., index, adv. Sample. Refereed. Vol. ends: Dec. Microform: PQC. Reprint: PSC. *Indexed:* A22, ATI, B01, C42, EconLit, IBSS. *Aud.:* Ac, Sa.

In this academic journal, theoretical and empirical research on corporate finance, investments, financial markets, and related concepts are approached from a quantitative perspective. As articles tend to be data-heavy, knowledge of finance and statistics is needed to fully appreciate this journal. Academic libraries with extensive programs in finance or economics should consider this title. URL: http://journals.cambridge.org/action/displayJournal?jid=JFQ

1064. ***Journal of Financial Economics.*** [ISSN: 0304-405X] 1974. 12x/yr. EUR 5376. Ed(s): G William Schwert. Elsevier BV, Radarweg 29, Amsterdam, 1043 NX, Netherlands; info@elsevier.com; https://www.elsevier.com/. Illus., index, adv. Sample. Refereed. Vol. ends: No. 2. Microform: PQC. *Indexed:* A22, ATI, B01, EconLit, IBSS. *Bk. rev.:* Number and length vary. *Aud.:* Ac, Sa.

The focus of this journal is on reports of analytical, empirical, or clinical research in capital markets, corporate finance, corporate governance, and economics of organizations and financial institutions. Feature articles are usually 15-50 pages long. Recent articles discuss corruption in bank lending, collateral pricing, and the effects of social norms on markets. Large academic libraries with graduate programs in finance and economics may be the only ones that will want to invest in this costly journal. URL: www.sciencedirect.com/science/journal/0304405X

1065. ***Journal of Financial Intermediation.*** [ISSN: 1042-9573] 1990. q. EUR 1370. Ed(s): M Campello, C Calomiris. Academic Press, 3251 Riverport Ln, Maryland Heights, MO 63043; JournalCustomerService-usa@elsevier.com; http://www.elsevier.com/. Illus. Sample. Refereed. *Indexed:* A22, B01, BLI, E01, EconLit. *Aud.:* Ac, Sa.

The focus of this title is on the design of financial contracts and institutions. Research topics have included the theory of financial intermediation; informational bases for the design of financial contracts; the role of insurance firms in influencing allocations and the efficiency of market equilibrium; the economics of financial engineering; and interactions between real and financial decisions. Articles are 20-30 pages in length, and recent issues include articles on broad topics such as bank runs, pension funding, and credit derivatives. This journal would be appropriate for large public libraries that serve educated investors, and for many academic libraries. URL: www.sciencedirect.com/science/journal/10429573

1066. ***The Journal of Financial Research.*** [ISSN: 0270-2592] 1978. q. GBP 536. Ed(s): Drew B Winters, Scott E Hein. Wiley-Blackwell Publishing, Inc., 111 River St, Hoboken, NJ 07030; http://onlinelibrary.wiley.com. Illus., index, adv. Sample. Refereed. Microform: PQC. Reprint: PSC. *Indexed:* A22, ATI, B01, BRI, E01, EconLit. *Bk. rev.:* Number and length vary. *Aud.:* Ac, Sa.

This journal presents original research in investment and portfolio management, capital markets and institutions, and corporate finance, corporate governance, and capital investment. Each issue contains eight to ten articles that are 15-20 pages long. Recent articles examine the linkage between financial risk tolerance and risk aversion, mutual fund governance, and debt financing. Large academic libraries that support finance programs and public libraries that serve educated investors should consider this title. URL: http://onlinelibrary.wiley.com/journal/10.1111/(ISSN)1475-6803

1067. *The Journal of Fixed Income.* [ISSN: 1059-8596] 1991. q. USD 910. Ed(s): Stanley J Kon. Portfolio Management Research, 41 Madison Ave, 20th Fl, New York, NY 10010; pm-research@pageantmedia.com; https://www.pm-research.com. Illus., adv. *Indexed:* A22, ATI, B01, BLI, C42. *Aud.:* Ac, Sa.

The associate editors are mostly academics from top universities and professionals from investment firms. Each issue contains six to ten articles, each about 20 pages long, that report original applied research on all aspects of fixed-income investing. Articles discuss market conditions and methods of analysis of a variety of fixed-income investments. Recent articles discuss return chasing in bond funds and inflation risk premiums. Libraries that support graduate finance programs or investment professionals should consider this title. URL: www.iijournals.com/toc/jfi/current

1068. *The Journal of Futures Markets.* [ISSN: 0270-7314] 1981. m. GBP 2372. Ed(s): Robert I Webb. John Wiley & Sons, Inc., 111 River St, Hoboken, NJ 07030; cs-journals@wiley.com; http://onlinelibrary.wiley.com. Illus., index, adv. Sample. Refereed. Vol. ends: Dec. Reprint: PSC. *Indexed:* A22, B01, B03, BRI, C42, EconLit, IBSS. *Aud.:* Ac, Sa.

Each issue of this journal focuses on futures, options, and other derivatives. The articles range from the highly theoretical to the very practical. Recent topics discuss the effects of after-hours trading, employee stock options, and credit default swaps. Articles include charts and tables. Recommended for academic and research libraries that support finance programs.

1069. *Journal of International Financial Management and Accounting.* [ISSN: 0954-1314] 1989. 3x/yr. GBP 774. Ed(s): Richard Levich, Sidney Gray. Wiley-Blackwell Publishing Ltd., The Atrium, Southern Gate, Chichester, PO19 8QG, United Kingdom; cs-journals@wiley.com; http://onlinelibrary.wiley.com. Illus., adv. Sample. Refereed. Reprint: PSC. *Indexed:* A22, ATI, B01, E01, IBSS. *Bk. rev.:* 1-2, 1,500 words. *Aud.:* Ac, Sa.

Each issue contains three to five original research articles, each 20-30 pages long, on topics related to international aspects of financial management and reporting, banking and financial services, auditing, and taxation. Issues include an "Executive Perspective" (written by a practitioner), a case, comments concerning earlier papers, or a book review. Recent articles discuss choosing between IAS and U.S. GAAP accounting practices; the impact of the Euro on the European economy; and capital budgeting and political risk. Libraries that support finance programs and professionals may want to consider this specialized title.

1070. *Journal of International Money and Finance: theoretical and empirical research in international economics and finance.* [ISSN: 0261-5606] 1982. 10x/yr. EUR 2452. Ed(s): K G Koedijk. Pergamon Press, The Blvd, Langford Ln, E Park, Kidlington, OX5 1GB, United Kingdom; JournalsCustomerServiceEMEA@elsevier.com; http://www.elsevier.com. Illus., adv. Sample. Refereed. Microform: PQC. *Indexed:* A22, B01, BLI, C42, EconLit, IBSS. *Bk. rev.:* Number and length vary. *Aud.:* Ac, Sa.

This publication presents research in all areas of international finance, monetary economics, and the increasing overlap between the two. Topics include foreign exchange, balance of payments, international markets, fiscal policy, foreign aid, and international economic institutions. Articles in recent issues discuss currency predictability; exchange-rate pass-through; and central bank swap line effectiveness. Each article is roughly 15-30 pages long. The scope of this journal makes it an appropriate choice for academic and research libraries.

1071. *Public Finance Review.* Formerly (until 1997): *Public Finance Quarterly.* [ISSN: 1091-1421] 1973. bi-m. USD 1707 (print & online eds.)). Ed(s): James Alm. Sage Publications, Inc., 2455 Teller Rd, Thousand Oaks, CA 91320; info@sagepub.com; http://www.sagepub.com. Illus., adv. Refereed. Circ: 800 Paid. Microform: PQC. Reprint: PSC. *Indexed:* A22, ATI, B01, BRI, E01, EconLit, IBSS, P61. *Bk. rev.:* Number and length vary. *Aud.:* Ac, Sa.

This scholarly journal explores the theory, policy, and institutions related to the allocation, distribution, and stabilization functions within the public sector of the economy. Each issue includes five lengthy articles in which authors present theoretical and empirical studies of the positive or normative aspects of (primarily) U.S. federal, state, and local government policies. Recent article topics include a history of tax collection, social security benefits, and public education. Academic libraries that support programs in public administration and finance should consider this title. URL: http://pfr.sagepub.com/

1072. *Quantitative Finance.* [ISSN: 1469-7688] 2001. m. GBP 2999 (print & online eds.)). Ed(s): Michael Dempster, Jim Gatheral. Routledge, 4 Park Sq, Milton Park, Abingdon, OX14 4RN, United Kingdom; subscriptions@tandf.co.uk; http://www.tandfonline.com. Adv. Sample. Refereed. Reprint: PSC. *Indexed:* A22, B01, BLI, BRI, E01, EconLit, MSN. *Bk. rev.:* Number and length vary. *Aud.:* Ac, Sa.

This interdisciplinary journal presents original research that reflects the increasing use of quantitative methods in the field of finance. Just a few of the applications covered in this journal are experimental finance, price formation, trading systems, corporate valuation, risk management, and econometrics. This journal has a well-respected editorial board from universities and research institutions around the world, and this fact makes the journal a good pick to add depth to quantitative areas in finance collections of research libraries. URL: www.tandfonline.com/loi/rquf20#.V5lcwugrKUk

1073. *The R M A Journal.* Former titles (until Sep. 2000): *The Journal of Lending & Credit Risk Management;* (until 1996): *Journal of Commercial Lending;* (until 1992): *Journal of Commercial Bank Lending;* (until 1967): *Robert Morris Associates Bulletin.* [ISSN: 1531-0558] 1918. 10x/yr. Members, USD 70; Non-members, USD 110. Ed(s): Frank M Devlin. Risk Management Association, 1801 Market St, Ste 300, Philadelphia, PA 19103; customers@rmahq.org; http://www.rmahq.org/. Illus., index, adv. Refereed. Circ: 3000 Paid. *Indexed:* A22, ATI, B01, BLI, BRI. *Bk. rev.:* Number and length vary. *Aud.:* Ac, Sa.

The official journal of the Risk Management Association (RMA), this is a key source of information for commercial loan officers. It covers risk management issues in addition to commercial lending. Each issue contains 10-12 feature articles as well as regular departments on management strategies, commercial lending and risk management issues, accounting actions, and a cautionary case study. The RMA web site serves as a portal to all RMA products and services, including a searchable archive of journal articles. An essential title for libraries that support finance programs and banking professionals. URL: www.rmahq.org/tools-publications/the-rma-journal

1074. *The Review of Financial Studies.* [ISSN: 0893-9454] 1988. bi-m. EUR 682 in Europe (except the UK). Ed(s): Andrew Karolyi. Oxford University Press, Great Clarendon St, Oxford, OX2 6DP, United Kingdom; onlinequeries.uk@oup.com; https://academic.oup.com/journals/ . Illus., adv. Sample. Refereed. Reprint: PSC. *Indexed:* A22, B01, BLI, E01, EconLit, IBSS. *Bk. rev.:* 1, signed, 1,000-2,500 words. *Aud.:* Ac, Sa.

This scholarly journal interprets the scope of finance as to broadly allow for much interplay between finance and economics. Each issue presents a balance of new theoretical and empirical research in the form of 10-12 lengthy articles. Recent papers examine such topics as corporate leverage, corporate bond returns, and entangled financial systems. Academic libraries should consider this a core finance title. URL: https://rfs.oxfordjournals.org/

1075. *Review of Quantitative Finance and Accounting.* [ISSN: 0924-865X] 1991. 8x/yr. EUR 2658 (print & online eds.)). Ed(s): Cheng-Few Lee. Springer New York LLC, 233 Spring St, New York, NY 10013; customerservice@springer.com; http://www.springer.com. Illus., adv. Sample. Refereed. Vol. ends: No. 4. Microform: PQC. Reprint: PSC. *Indexed:* A22, ATI, B01, BLI, E01, EconLit, IBSS. *Aud.:* Ac, Sa.

The articles in this journal are original research that involves the interaction of finance with accounting and economic and quantitative methods. This interdisciplinary journal is international in scope and includes five or six lengthy articles per issue. A strong background in mathematics and economic statistics is required to understand these articles, so only specialists and research libraries should consider this journal for purchase. URL: http://link.springer.com/journal/11156

Trade Journals

1076. ***Financial Analysts Journal.*** Formerly (until 1960): *The Analysts Journal.* [ISSN: 0015-198X] 1945. q. GBP 330 (print & online eds.)). Ed(s): Barbar S Petitt, Steven Thorley. Routledge, 530 Walnut St, Ste 850, Philadelphia, PA 19106; enquiries@tandfonline.com; http://www.tandfonline.com. Illus., index, adv. Sample. Refereed. Vol. ends: Nov/Dec. Microform: PQC. *Indexed:* A22, ATI, B01, BRI, C42, EconLit, IBSS. *Bk. rev.:* 1-2, 500 words. *Aud.:* Ac, Sa.

Each issue of this title, which is aimed at academics and practitioners, contains nearly a dozen articles of varying length on financial and investment analysis. Primary emphasis is on valuation, portfolio management, market structure, market behavior, and professional conduct and ethics. Articles also involve accounting, economics, and securities law and regulations. Recent issues include articles on a simple theory of the financial crisis using Fischer Black, and measurement biases in hedge fund performance data. Association content, such as speeches, commentary, and association policy statements, is also included. The editorial board has representatives from highly respected universities and capital management firms. Suited for academic or public libraries that support finance programs or financial analysts. URL: www.cfapubs.org/toc/faj/current

1077. ***Journal of Business Finance & Accounting.*** [ISSN: 0306-686X] 1974. 10x/yr. GBP 1675. Ed(s): Peter F Pope, Martin Walker. Wiley-Blackwell Publishing Ltd., The Atrium, Southern Gate, Chichester, PO19 8QG, United Kingdom; cs-journals@wiley.com; http://onlinelibrary.wiley.com. Illus., index, adv. Sample. Refereed. Vol. ends: Dec. Reprint: PSC. *Indexed:* A22, ATI, B01, C42, E01, EconLit, IBSS. *Aud.:* Ac, Sa.

This journal covers both theoretical and empirical analysis of accounting and finance relating to financial reporting, asset pricing, financial markets and institutions, market microstructure, corporate finance, corporate governance, and the economics of internal organization and management control. Each issue delivers eight to ten research articles that are 15-20 pages in length. Even though this is a more expensive journal, the large number of articles and the variety of topics make it an impressive title. URL: http://onlinelibrary.wiley.com/journal/10.1111/(ISSN)1468-5957

1078. ***Journal of Financial Planning.*** Formerly (until 1988): *Institute of Certified Financial Planners. Journal.* [ISSN: 1040-3981] 1979. m. Free to members. Financial Planning Association, Ste 600, 7535 E Hampden Ave, Denver, CO 80231; info@onefpa.org; http://www.plannersearch.org. Illus., index, adv. Sample. Refereed. Vol. ends: No. 4. *Indexed:* A22, ATI, AgeL, B01. *Aud.:* Ac, Sa.

This practitioner-focused title serves as a forum for the exchange of ideas and information related to the financial planning profession. Roughly a dozen short articles focus on professional issues, retirement, portfolio management, investment research, technology, noteworthy people, and strategies. Departments report on legal and legislative news, institutional resources, continuing education, letters to the editor, and contacts. The web site includes full-text articles from current and past issues, and features additional content that does not appear in the print edition. Academic and large public libraries that support programs, and professionals in insurance and finance, should consider this title. URL: https://www.onefpa.org/journal/Pages/default.aspx

1079. ***Mergers & Acquisitions (New York, 1965): the dealmakers' journal.*** Incorporates (1967-1967): *Mergers and Acquisitions Monthly.* [ISSN: 0026-0010] 1965. m. USD 1595. Ed(s): Ken MacFadyen. SourceMedia, Inc., One State St Plz, 27th Fl, New York, NY 10004; custserv@sourcemedia.com; http://www.sourcemedia.com. Illus., index, adv. Sample. Circ: 3000 Paid. *Indexed:* A22, B01, B03, C42, L14. *Aud.:* Ga, Sa.

Corporate mergers and acquisitions (M&A) are the specialized focus of this core trade magazine. Joint ventures are reported on, but are not regularly charted. Data are gathered from a number of sources, including Thomson's Merger and Corporate Transaction Database, and they are used to develop league tables that rank the leading financial advisers in the M&A industries, as well as sales volumes of target companies, industries most attractive to foreign investment, countries with the largest role in M&A in the United States, and the top transactions. Quarterly rosters give data on U.S. acquisitions by SIC code, foreign acquisitions in the United States, and U.S. acquisitions overseas. In addition, this title includes a feature cover story, guest articles from M&A professionals, current industry news, and the "industry's most comprehensive calendar of events."

1080. ***Site Selection.*** Former titles (until 1994): *Site Selection and Industrial Development;* (until 1984): *Site Selection Handbook;* (until 1977): *Industrial Development's Site Selection Handbook;* (until 1976): *Site Selection Handbook;* (until 1970): *Industrial Development's Site Selection Handbook;* Incorporated (in 1984): *Industrial Development;* Which was formerly (until 1967): *Industrial Development and Manufacturers Record;* Which was formed by the 1958 merger of: *Manufacturers Record;* (1954-1958): *Industrial Development.* [ISSN: 1080-7799] 1956. bi-m. USD 95 domestic (Free to qualified personnel). Ed(s): Mark Arend, Adam Bruns. Conway Data, Inc., 6625 The Corners Pky, Ste 200, Norcross, GA 30092; circulation@siteselection.com; http://www.conway.com. Illus., adv. Circ: 44000. Microform: PQC. *Indexed:* A22, B01, BRI, C42. *Aud.:* Ac, Sa.

This title offers original research and analysis, interviews, and case studies for expansion-planning decision-makers: CEOs, corporate real estate executives, facility planners, human resource managers, and consultants. Industry overviews provide forecasts and address key topics such as new plant construction, utilities and other infrastructure concerns, political and business climates, and labor demographics. Detailed economic development reports on specific cities, states, regions, and foreign countries fill out each issue. Current and back issue content, along with exclusive web content, is offered at the web site. URL: www.siteselection.com

1081. ***Venture Capital Journal.*** Former titles (until 1980): *Venture Capital; S B I C-Venture Capital; S B I C-Venture Capital Service.* [ISSN: 0883-2773] 1961. m. Ed(s): Alastair Goldfisher. Thomson Reuters, 3 Times Sq, New York, NY 10036; general.info@thomson.com; http://thomsonreuters.com/en.html. Adv. *Indexed:* A22, B01, BRI. *Aud.:* Ac, Sa.

This is a core journal for libraries that cater to venture capitalists, entrepreneurs, or entrepreneurship programs. It offers news, analysis, and insight into the venture capital and private equity markets, with stories on recent deals, new sources of capital, and fund formations. There are profiles of leading venture capital firms and their portfolios, interviews with institutional investors, an event calendar, and up-to-date reports on the latest venture-backed IPOs. Recent issues have focused on angel investors, consumer goods, and health-care innovations.

1082. ***Wall Street & Technology: for senior-level executives in technology and information management in securities and investment firms.*** Formerly (until 1992): *Wall Street Computer Review;* Which Incorporated (in 1991): *Wall Street Computer Review. Buyer's Guide.* [ISSN: 1060-989X] 1983. m. USD 85 domestic (Free to qualified personnel). Ed(s): Gregory MacSweeney. TechWeb, Financial Technology Network, 11 W. 19th St., New York, NY 10011; http://www.techweb.com/. Illus., index, adv. Sample. Circ: 25000 Controlled. Vol. ends: Dec. *Indexed:* A22, B01, BLI, BRI, C42. *Aud.:* Ac, Sa.

This trade publication is one of an important group of niche titles that provide information on the technology of financial services (others include *Insurance & Technology* and *Bank Systems & Technology*). The technology and communications aspects of the financial-services industry are discussed in articles and departments that report on trading, regulation, and money management. Regular coverage includes risk management, trading and exchange, investment technology, inside operations, and a calendar. Recent articles discuss timely topics such as the credit crisis, data security, global markets, new software platforms, and IT outsourcing. The web site has current and past articles arranged by topic and type of article, plus a buyers' guide. URL: www.wallstreetandtech.com/

■ CANADA

Julie Jones, Simon Fraser University Library, 8888 University Drive, Burnaby, BC, Canada; julie_jones@sfu.ca.

Nikki Tummon, McGill University Library, 3459 McTavish St., Montreal, PQ, Canada H3A 0C9; nikki.tummon@mcgill.ca

Introduction

The magazines and journals in this section have been selected for their focus on Canada, and the glimpse into various aspects of life in this vast and diverse country that they provide. All titles are published in Canada, with split-run publications (foreign-published but with some Canadian content) excluded. Some academic journals devoted to research about Canada are represented here, as well as magazines for general audiences that cover all aspects of Canadian life, including politics, economics, arts and culture, geography, fashion and lifestyle, travel, and history. This section aims to provide representation at the national and provincial/territorial level.

Most publications are in English. However, a healthy number of them contain articles in either English or French, and some are completely bilingual. (Canada's two official languages are English and French.) For the most part, subject-specific titles are not included. This means that while many magazines and journals are published in and about Canada on a range of narrowly defined topics (e.g., cooking, gender studies, engineering, nursing, etc.), especially at the provincial level, this carefully curated list contains titles that have a broader focus. For more magazines not included in this listing (or to learn more about the magazine industry in Canada), see *Magazines Canada* (www.magazinescanada.ca) or *Masthead Online* (www.mastheadonline.ca).

Two new entries made it into the Canada section this year: *Chatelaine* and *Spacing*. First published in 1928 and currently enjoying a renaissance, it seemed right to include Canada's current number one women's magazine, *Chatelaine*. Focusing on topics affecting all Canadian women, *Chatelaine* has a rich history and contemporary relevance. Canadians are also increasingly interested in and engaged with urban issues and how their cities function and are planned. *Spacing* is an award-winning magazine with a focus on urban issues and city planning in Canada. These new entries reflect a modern-day Canada and are responding to Canadians' demand for excellent journalism concerned with the issues that affect them in the day-to-day, in an accessible format.

The Canadian magazine industry continues to evolve and adjust to the digital reality of the twenty-first century. Trends such as a decrease in the number of pages of print editions and increased digital content and branding continue. Content is increasingly geared toward online and mobile users, with supplementary material frequently available online and via apps.

Canadian academic journals are also prioritizing digital content, and in many cases this is a boon for both the publisher and reader. For example, online publication allows for rolling publication, which removes the need to compile a complete issue, allowing for more timely publication of individual articles and, thus, speedier dissemination of knowledge. Open access continues to gain strength and be a goal within Canadian academic publishing. This is being helped along by the fact that the federal research funding agencies in Canada (the Tri-Agency of CIHR, NSERC, and SSHRC) have recently enacted the Tri-Agency Open Access Policy on Publications, which mandates that all peer-reviewed journal publications resulting from Tri-Agency funding must be freely available online within 12 months of publication.

Magazines and academic journals continue to play an important role in the Canadian publishing industry, providing a forum for research by, for, and about Canadians, as well as ongoing snapshots of Canadian lifestyles and interests. There is incredible value in providing access to the titles listed here and continuing to maintain a healthy collection of Canadian periodicals, whether in a public library or academic setting.

Basic Periodicals

Hs, Ga, Ac: *Canadian Geographic, Maclean's, The Walrus.*

Basic Abstracts and Indexes

Canadian Business & Current Affairs Database (CBCA).

1083. *Above & Beyond: Canada's arctic journal.* [ISSN: 0843-7815] 1988. q. CAD 30 domestic; CAD 45 foreign; CAD 5.95 newsstand/cover. Ed(s): Tom Koelbel. Above & Beyond, PO Box 683, Mahone Bay, NS B0J 2E0, Canada; info@arcticjournal.ca. Adv. Circ: 16000. *Indexed:* A47, BRI. *Bk. rev.:* 1, 1 page, signed. *Aud.:* Hs, Ga.

Above & Beyond: Canada's arctic journal is dedicated to detailing life in Canada's arctic. Articles are diverse, covering topics related to science, travel and tourism, arts, culture, education, business, government, Indigenous issues, and history particular to the North. Increasingly, articles cover topics related to climate change and the impact it is having on the North. In its print form, this publication serves as the official in-flight magazine for First Air, a commercial airline that services Nunavut and the Northwest Territories. Digital subscriptions are also available, and the most recent issue may be viewed for free on the web site via the Issuu digital publishing interface. Select articles from issues past and present are available on the web site in html. *Above & Beyond* provides excellent content for a general or public library audience and provides an important glimpse into life in Canada's North. URL: www.arcticjournal.ca/

1084. *Acadiensis: journal of the history of the Atlantic region.* [ISSN: 0044-5851] 1971. s-a. CAD 35 (Individuals, CAD 25). Ed(s): Stephen Dutcher, Bill Parenteau. University of New Brunswick, Department of History, Campus House, PO Box 4400, Fredericton, NB E3B 5A3, Canada; http://www.unbf.ca/arts/History. Illus., index, adv. Sample. Refereed. Vol. ends: Spring (No. 2). Microform: PQC. *Indexed:* A22, BRI, C37, IBSS, MLA-IB. *Bk. rev.:* 2-4, 12-24 pages. *Aud.:* Ga, Ac.

Acadiensis is a scholarly journal established in 1971 that is focused on the regional history of Atlantic Canada. Articles are accepted and published in either English or French. The scope is broadly defined: it includes not only the territory of Canada's four Atlantic Provinces but also northern New England, the Gulf of St. Lawrence, and the North Atlantic as they relate to the history of the region. Historians are the most highly represented group among authors, but the journal also contains research articles, book reviews, and essays by specialists in historical geography, economic history, folklore, literature, political science, anthropology, sociology, law, and other fields. The journal is published twice a year and is now open access, with online access to all articles. Acadiensis Press publishes books on the history and culture of Atlantic Canada and journal subscribers receive a 20 percent discount. This journal is well suited for public libraries and academic libraries, especially those with Canadian or Atlantic Studies programs in their region. URL: http://journals.hil.unb.ca/index.php/Acadiensis/index

1085. *L'Actualite.* Incorporates (1971-1976): *Maclean;* Which was formerly (1961-1971): *Magazine Maclean;* Formerly (until 1960): *Ma Paroisse.* [ISSN: 0383-8714] 1976. 20x/yr. CAD 35. Ed(s): Carole Beaulieu. Rogers Publishing Ltd., 1200 McGill College Ave, Off 1700, Bureau 800, Montreal, QC H3B 4G7, Canada; http://www.rogerspublishing.ca. Illus., adv. Microform: PQC. *Indexed:* A22, BRI, C37, MLA-IB, PdeR. *Bk. rev.:* 1, 1-2 pages, signed. *Aud.:* Hs, Ga, Ac.

L'Actualite, the most popular French-language newsmagazine in Canada, is published 18 times a year and includes provincial, national, and global news; politics; business; and Quebec entertainment, as well as regular features on health, sports, travel, and food and wine. Some content is available for free online, and online subscriptions are available for the full journal. The web site also contains additional information including contests, blogs, and readers' comments on articles. *L'Actualite* is suited for libraries who wish to offer publications that are in French and about French-Canadian and Quebecois news and culture. URL: www.lactualite.com

1086. *Alberta History.* Formerly (until 1975): *Alberta Historical Review.* [ISSN: 0316-1552] 1953. q. Free to members. Historical Society of Alberta, Sta C, PO BOX 4035, Calgary, AB T2T 5M9, Canada; info@albertahistory.org; http://www.albertahistory.org/. Illus., index. Refereed. Microform: PQC. *Indexed:* A22, BRI, C37. *Bk. rev.:* 15-20, 1-2 pages. *Aud.:* Ga, Ac.

Alberta History is the journal of the Historical Society of Alberta (HSA). The journal contains research articles, primary source material, and book reviews dealing with Alberta history. Photos and illustrations are typically included with articles. The journal is published quarterly and, at the time of writing, issues published between 1953 and 2005 are available online via the University of Alberta's Peel's Prairie Provinces (http://peel.library.ualberta.ca). This is a good addition to the collections of large public libraries and an important title for academic libraries that support research in the areas of Albertan, Western Canadian, or Canadian history.

1087. *Arctic.* [ISSN: 0004-0843] 1948. q. Free to members; Non-members, USD 25. Ed(s): Karen McCullough. University of Calgary, Arctic Institute of North America, 2500 University Dr NW, Calgary, AB T2N 1N4, Canada; arctic@ucalgary.ca; http://www.arctic.ucalgary.ca. Illus., index. Sample. Refereed. Vol. ends: Dec (No. 4). Microform: PQC. *Indexed:* A01, A22, BRI, C37, C45, MLA-IB, S25. *Bk. rev.:* 7-10, 1-3 pages. *Aud.:* Ac.

Arctic is the journal of the Arctic Institute of North America, an arctic and circumpolar research center based at Alberta's University of Calgary. With a goal of supporting cross-disciplinary understanding of the North, *Arctic* publishes contributions dealing with polar and subpolar regions from any area of scholarship. Content is mainly composed of peer-reviewed original research articles, but the journal also publishes book reviews and commentaries, as well as profiles of significant people, places, and northern events. Institute news is reported via a special section entitled *InfoNorth*. Research articles represent rigorous scholarship from many disciplines, including anthropology, astronomy, biology, ecology, education, engineering, fine arts, geography, medicine, and paleontology. Articles are increasingly concerned with climate change research. This quarterly has been published continuously since 1948, and its archives are freely available online on the Open Journal Systems platform (http://arctic.journalhosting.ucalgary.ca/arctic/index.php/arctic/index). Access to the research articles in recent issues requires a subscription. Highly recommended for any libraries focused on the North, environmental studies, or climate change.

1088. *B C Studies: the British Columbian quarterly.* [ISSN: 0005-2949] 1969. q. CAD 125 (Individuals, CAD 70). Ed(s): Leanne Coughlin, Graeme Wynn. University of British Columbia, 6303 NW Marine Dr, Rm 2, Vancouver, BC V6T 1Z1, Canada; http://www.ubc.ca. Illus., index, adv. Sample. Refereed. Microform: PQC. Reprint: PSC. *Indexed:* A01, BRI, C37, IBSS. *Bk. rev.:* 4-20, 2-6 pages, signed. *Aud.:* Ga, Ac.

BC Studies is a peer-reviewed scholarly journal devoted to the study of social, cultural, historical, political, and economic aspects of life in British Columbia. Content is drawn from a number of fields, including anthropology, archaeology, archives, art, art history, demography, economics, education, gender studies, geography, history, linguistics, literature, museology, music, First Nations studies, photography, political science, and sociology. Established in 1969, the journal notes on its web site that it is an important publishing venue of original research from a diverse group of scholars, and a training ground for students. Content is composed of articles, book reviews by authorities in the field, and bibliographies of often obscure books, articles, theses, and government publications on British Columbia. "Review Essays," "Photo Essays," "Case Comments" (commentaries on particular court cases), and "Forums" are published from time to time, as are themed issues. Examples of themed issues are: Vancouver's social history (no. 69/70); labor, work, and welfare (nos. 103 and 118); park history (no. 170); and 11 special issues devoted to aspects of the First Nations of British Columbia (nos. 19, 57, 89, 95, 101, 115/116, 120, 125/126, 153, 138/139, and 152). *BC Studies* is based at the University of British Columbia, but it is also supported by Simon Fraser University and the University of Victoria. Archives dating back to the first issue are freely available online on the Open Journal Systems platform (http://ojs.library.ubc.ca/index.php/bcstudies/index), but access to the research articles in recent issues requires a subscription. Recommended for large public libraries and for academic libraries that support Canadian or British Columbia Studies programs. URL: http://bcstudies.com/

1089. *Border Crossings.* Formerly (until 1985): *Arts Manitoba.* [ISSN: 0831-2559] 1977. q. CAD 40 (Individuals, CAD 32; CAD 9.95 per issue). Ed(s): Meeka Walsh. Arts Manitoba Publications Inc., 500-70 Arthur St, Winnipeg, MB R3B 1G7, Canada. Illus., index, adv. Vol. ends: No. 4. Microform: PQC. *Indexed:* A51, AmHI, BRI, C37. *Bk. rev.:* 1-3, 2 pages, signed. *Aud.:* Ga, Ac.

Border Crossings is a quarterly arts and culture magazine that is edited and published in Winnipeg. Content is "more curated than edited," according to the web site, and themes and ideas are investigated through articles, reviews and criticism, interviews, and portfolios of photographs and drawings. Each issue includes a section called "Artist's Pages," which is a three- to five-page section where a selected artist constructs visual content. Coverage of the magazine includes visual art, photography, dance, writing, film, theater and performance, music, architecture, and popular culture, and it aims to be interdisciplinary (that is, to "cross borders"). A searchable index goes back to 1977's volume 1, issue 1. Some current and archival content is available for free on the web site. A good addition to public and academic library collections alike. URL: http://bordercrossingsmag.com/

1090. *British Columbia Magazine.* Formerly (until 2002): *Beautiful British Columbia.* [ISSN: 1709-4623] 1959. q. CAD 25.95 domestic; CAD 29.95 United States; CAD 31.95 elsewhere. Ed(s): Jane Zatylny. Destination British Columbia, 12th Fl, 510 Burrard St, Vancouver, BC V6C 3A8, Canada; cs@bcmag.ca; http://www.destinationbc.ca. Illus., adv. *Indexed:* BRI, C37. *Aud.:* Hs, Ga.

British Columbia Magazine is a quarterly devoted to the scenic geography of British Columbia, with a focus on travel and tourism. The well-researched stories are highly visual: photographs are a major emphasis of this publication. Examples of topics covered include parks, wilderness, and wildlife, travel destinations, outdoor recreation, geography, ecology, conservation, science and natural phenomena, remarkable people, First Nations culture, heritage places, and history. The magazine was launched in 1959 and, as of writing, boasted a readership of over one million from around the world. Digital and print subscriptions are offered. Some content from the magazine is available on the web site. Print back-issues are available for purchase, and many are considered collector's issues. An excellent addition to high school and public libraries. URL: http://bcmag.ca/

1091. *C M Magazine: Canadian review of materials.* Former titles (until 1995): *C M: Canadian Materials for Schools and Libraries;* (until 1980): *Canadian Materials.* [ISSN: 1201-9364] 1971. w. Free. Ed(s): John Tooth, Dave Jenkinson. Manitoba Library Association, 167 Houde Dr, Winnipeg, MB R3V 1C6, Canada; http://www.umanitoba.ca/. Illus. *Indexed:* BRI, C37, CBRI. *Bk. rev.:* 30, 1 page, signed. *Aud.:* Ems, Ga, Ac.

CM Magazine is a free online journal concerned with reviewing Canadiana of interest to children and young adults, including publications produced in Canada, or published elsewhere but of interest or significance to Canada. Books and DVDs are reviewed. Teachers, school librarians, public librarians, and university professors who have expertise in materials for juveniles write the reviews. Reviews include recommended age ranges and grades for the materials. In a nod to the school librarians who are especially likely to use it, the journal is published from September to June. Other users that the publication is aimed at are children, parents, teachers, and other types of librarians, and professionals working with young people. This publication was previously published by the Canadian Library Association, but now is published by the Manitoba Library Association. URL: www.umanitoba.ca/cm/

1092. *Canada's History.* Formerly (until 2010): *The Beaver.* [ISSN: 1920-9894] 1920. bi-m. CAD 31.38; CAD 38.05 combined subscription (print & online eds.)). Canada's National History Society, Bryce Hall, Main Fl, 515 Portage Ave, Winnipeg, MB R3B 2E9, Canada; memberservices@canadashistory.ca; http://www.canadashistory.ca. Illus., index, adv. Circ: 37000 Paid. Vol. ends: Dec/Jan (No. 6). *Indexed:* A01, A22, BRI, C37, CBRI, MASUSE. *Bk. rev.:* 3-6, 1-3 pages. *Aud.:* Hs, Ga, Ac.

Canada's History (formerly *The Beaver*) is a bimonthly popular magazine that aims to educate and entertain via stories that bring past events and people to life. Initially published by the Hudson's Bay Company, this is the oldest history magazine in Canada. Canada's National History Society, a charitable organization, took over publishing responsibilities in 1994, and the magazine is its main tool in its efforts to promote interest in Canadian history. Under the former name, online access for the publication became complicated due to modern sexual connotations of the word, and the name change occurred in March 2010. Content is aimed at a diverse audience that is made up of professional historians as well as general readers of all age groups, in Canada and beyond. Articles and photographs detail Canadian history topics such as social history, politics, exploration, discovery and settlement, aboriginal peoples, war, culture, and business and trade. Subscriptions are available for print copies, but there is some content available on the web site and some that is only available online. URL: www.canadashistory.ca/Magazine

Canadian Art. See Art/General section.

1093. *Canadian Dimension: for people who want to change the world.* [ISSN: 0008-3402] 1963. bi-m. CAD 39.99 (Individuals, CAD 29.99). Dimension Publishing Inc., 2E-91 Albert St, Winnipeg, MB R3B 1G5, Canada; info@canadiandimension.com. Illus., index, adv. Sample. Circ: 3500. Vol. ends: Nov/Dec (No. 6). Microform: PQC. *Indexed:* A01, A22, BAS, BRI, C37. *Aud.:* Hs, Ga, Ac.

Canadian Dimension is a left-leaning magazine published six times per year, including two double issues. Founded in 1963, the magazine bills itself on its web site as "an independent forum for Left-wing political thought and discussion-including just about the entire range of what passes for the Left in Canada." Articles are written in plain language and aimed at an audience composed of activists, community organizers, trade unionists, students, academics, and anyone else interested in challenging mainstream ideas and debating for social change. Content includes feature articles; regular columns; cartoons, illustrations, and photographs; and in-depth reviews of film, web sites, and books. Topics covered include but are not limited to politics and foreign policy, education, labor, food and agriculture, family, and globalization. Issues typically have a theme-some examples of recent themes for issues: "Economies in Transition" (volume 48, issue 2), "What's to Eat?" (volume 48, issue 1), "The Battle for Canada's North" (volume 47, issue 3), and "Labour and Austerity" (volume 63, issue 3). This magazine is available in print or digital format and is appropriate for high school, public, and academic libraries. Some content, including blog posts and podcasts, is freely available online. URL: http://canadiandimension.com/

1094. *Canadian Ethnic Studies.* [ISSN: 0008-3496] 1969. 3x/yr. CAD 160. Canadian Ethnic Studies Association, c/o Department of History, University of Calgary, 2500 University Dr, NW, Calgary, AB T2N 1N4, Canada. Illus., index, adv. Sample. Refereed. Vol. ends: No. 3. Microform: PQC. Reprint: PSC. *Indexed:* A01, A22, A47, AmHI, BRI, C37, E01, ENW, IBSS, MASUSE, MLA-IB, P61, SSA. *Bk. rev.:* 15-20, 1-4 pages, signed. *Aud.:* Ga, Ac.

Canadian Ethnic Studies/Etudes ethniques au Canada is a refereed scholarly journal that focuses on the study of ethnicity, immigration, inter-group relations, and the history and cultural life of ethnic groups in Canada. The journal is interdisciplinary and was founded in 1969. Published three times per year, it is the official publication of the Canadian Ethnic Studies Association. Content is composed of journal articles, primary sources (often translated), opinion pieces, immigrant memoirs, an "Ethnic Voices" section, book and film reviews, and an annual index. Articles are accepted and published in either English or French. Access to content is dependent on having a print or online subscription. Recommended for academic and large public libraries.

1095. *Canadian Geographic.* Formerly (until 1978): *Canadian Geographical Journal.* [ISSN: 0706-2168] 1930. bi-m. CAD 28.52 domestic; CAD 37.95 United States; CAD 59.95 elsewhere. Ed(s): Rick Boychuk. Canadian Geographical Enterprises, Ste 200, 1155 Lola St, Ottawa, ON K1K 4C1, Canada; editorial@canadiangeographic.ca. Illus., index, adv. Sample. Vol. ends: Nov/Dec (No. 6). *Indexed:* A01, A22, BAS, BRI, C37, CBRI, MASUSE, P01. *Bk. rev.:* 1-5, 1 page, signed. *Aud.:* Hs, Ga, Ac.

Canadian Geographic is published six times per year by the Royal Canadian Geographical Society. Through the disciplinary lens of geography, the magazine reports on science, environment, travel, natural resource, and human and cultural stories from across Canada. As well as feature articles, the publication features regular columns, maps, and book reviews. Production values are high: the photographs and art direction are both notable. The supplement *Canadian Geographic Travel* is published four times a year. The web site provides some material supplementary to current content. Some back-issue material, including the magazine covers dating back to 1975, is also available on the web site. URL: www.canadiangeographic.ca

1096. *Canadian Historical Review.* Formerly (until 1920): *Review of Historical Publications Relating to Canada.* [ISSN: 0008-3755] 1896. q. USD 180. Ed(s): Dimitry L Anastakis, Mary-Ellen Kelm. University of Toronto Press, Journals Division, 5201 Dufferin St, Toronto, ON M3H 5T8, Canada; journals@utpress.utoronto.ca; http://www.utpjournals.com. Illus., index, adv. Sample. Refereed. Circ: 883. Vol. ends: Dec (No. 4). Microform: PMC; PQC. *Indexed:* A01, A22, AmHI, BRI, C37, CBRI, E01, IBSS, MLA-IB, P61, SSA. *Bk. rev.:* 20-30, 1-3 pages, signed. *Aud.:* Ga, Ac.

Canadian Historical Review (*CHR*) has been published for over 115 years and is the primary, and most prestigious, Canadian history scholarly journal. From 1897 to 1920, the journal was published as *Review of Historical Publications Relating to Canada.* As of 1920, the University of Toronto Press has been publishing the journal under its current name. Authoritative scholarship that examines and analyzes ideas, people, and events that have impacted Canada's history is presented via the peer-reviewed articles published in the journal. Book reviews written by experts in the field are also included, as are bibliographies of recent books, media, and dissertations that will be of interest to Canadian historians at all levels. This journal is published four times per year. Abstracts are provided in both English and French, and articles are accepted and published in either language. Some full-text content is open access, but much of it is dependent on a subscription. The *Canadian Historical Review* is recommended for academic libraries and large public libraries. URL: www.utpjournals.com/Canadian-Historical-Review.html

1097. *Canadian House & Home: the magazine of home & style.* Former titles (until 1984): *House and Home;* (until 1982): *House & Home Magazine;* (until 19??): *Moving House & Home.* [ISSN: 0826-7642] 1979. m. CAD 26.95; CAD 6.50 newsstand/cover. House & Home Media, 511 King St W, Ste 120, Toronto, ON M5V 2Z4, Canada; subscriptions@hhmedia.com. Adv. Sample. *Indexed:* BRI, C37. *Bk. rev.:* 5-10, 100 words. *Aud.:* Ga.

Canadian House & Home is devoted to home design and decorating. Content includes profiles of remarkable homes across the country, home decor and renovation trends, how-to information on the organization and updating of interiors, gardening ideas and techniques, and recipes and entertainment ideas. Each issue also includes a source (buying) guide. Photographs and art direction figure prominently, given the focus of the magazine. Additional content-including supplementary photo galleries, video content, "H & H Online TV" episodes, and blogs-is available on the web site. Both print and digital subscriptions are offered. Recommended for public libraries. URL: http://houseandhome.com/

1098. *Canadian Issues.* Incorporates (1994-1999): *A C S Bulletin;* Which was formerly (until 1994): *A C S Newsletter;* (until 1982): *Association for Canadian Studies. Association Newsletter.* [ISSN: 0318-8442] 1975. q. CAD 50 domestic; CAD 90 United States; CAD 124 elsewhere. Ed(s): Victor Armony, Randy Boswell. Association for Canadian Studies, 1822-A Sherbrooke Ouest W, Montreal, QC H3H 1E4, Canada; general@acs-aec.ca; http://www.acs-aec.ca. Microform: PQC. *Indexed:* BRI, C37, PdeR. *Bk. rev.:* 1-2, 1 page, signed. *Aud.:* Hs, Ga, Ac.

Canadian Issues/Themes Canadiens is the flagship publication of the Association for Canadian Studies (ACS). The ACS is dedicated to supporting the development of the field of Canadian Studies via a number of initiatives, including "encouraging interdisciplinary exchanges that complement and connect the efforts of scholars in diverse fields as well as leaders in the public and private sectors" (www.acs-aec.ca/en/the-acs/mandate/). Thus, *Canadian Issues* is a bilingual (French/English), multidisciplinary magazine that publishes articles and opinion pieces on Canadian society, government, history, and economics. The publication is aimed at a broad audience composed of history educators, librarians, archivists, academics, researchers, and policymakers. Issues are typically themed-some recent examples of themes include "Towards a New Blueprint for Canada's Recorded Memory" (Spring 2014), "50 Years of the Royal Commission on Bilingualism and Biculturalism" (Fall 2013), "The War of 1812: History and the Canadian Identity" (Fall 2012), and "The Academic Achievement of Immigrant Origin Students" (Winter 2011). This publication is suited to high school, academic, and public libraries. URL: www.acs-aec.ca/en/publications/canadian-issues/

1099. ***Canadian Living: smart solutions for everyday living.*** [ISSN: 0382-4624] 1975. m. CAD 23.98 domestic; CAD 61.98 United States. T C Media, 25 Sheppard Ave, Ste 100, Toronto, ON M2N 6S7, Canada; info@transcontinental.ca; http://www.transcontinental-gtc.com/. Adv. Circ: 555118 Paid. *Indexed:* BRI, C37, GardL. *Aud.:* Hs, Ga.

Canadian Living is a popular Canadian family/lifestyle magazine aimed at women. It is especially known for recipes that are well tested and reliable; but content also focuses on health, fashion, relationships, beauty, home and gardening projects, parenting, and work-life balance. It frequently features regional stories about people and places around the country. In addition to supplementary content, much of the content from the magazine can be viewed on the web site. Print and digital subscriptions are available. URL: www.canadianliving.com/

1100. ***Canadian Public Policy.*** [ISSN: 0317-0861] 1975. q. USD 220. Ed(s): Michael Veall. University of Toronto Press, Journals Division, 5201 Dufferin St, Toronto, ON M3H 5T8, Canada; journals@utpress.utoronto.ca; http://www.utpjournals.com. Illus., index, adv. Sample. Refereed. Circ: 747. Vol. ends: Dec (No. 4). Microform: PQC. *Indexed:* A01, A22, B01, BRI, C37, E01, EconLit, P61, SSA. *Bk. rev.:* 15-25, 1-2 pages, signed. *Aud.:* Ga, Ac.

Canadian Public Policy is an academic journal concerned with economic and social policy. The journal aims to stimulate research and discussion of policy issues in Canada. This title is published quarterly by the University of Toronto Press, and articles are accepted and published in either French or English. Given the interdisciplinary nature of public policy issues, articles are from a variety of disciplinary perspectives. The readership to which the journal is directed includes decision makers and advisers in business organizations and governments, and policy researchers in private institutions and universities. Articles are refereed, and themed supplements are published from time to time. Examples of recent supplements include "Environmental Policy in Canada" (August 2013), "Life Course as a Policy Lens: Challenges and Opportunities" (February 2011), and "The Automobile and its Industry in Canada" (April 2010). Editorial content and reviews are included alongside refereed articles. Some content is open access. Published quarterly, this journal is recommended for academic libraries and large public libraries. URL: https://www.utpjournals.com/Canadian-Public-Policy.html

1101. ***Canadian Wildlife.*** Supersedes in part (in 2002): *International Wildlife.* [ISSN: 1201-673X] 1995. bi-m. CAD 29 domestic; CAD 47 United States; CAD 55 elsewhere. Ed(s): Martin Silverstone. Canadian Wildlife Federation, 350 Michael Cowpland Dr, Kanata, ON K2M 2W1, Canada; http://www.cwf-fcf.org. Adv. Sample. *Indexed:* A01, BRI, C37, MASUSE. *Aud.:* Hs, Ga.

Canadian Wildlife is a popular nature magazine published bimonthly by the nonprofit Canadian Wildlife Federation (CWF). Articles are published on topics such as climate change, wildlife and habitats, conservation, and politics related to nature. This publication is available in French as *Biosphere.* Though some content is available on the web site, access to articles is primarily subscription-based. Digital and print subscriptions are available. This magazine is suited for school and public libraries. URL: http://cwf-fcf.org/en/discover-wildlife/resources/magazines/canadian-wildlife/

Canadian Woman Studies. See Gender Studies section.

1102. ***Chatelaine (English Edition).*** Incorporates (in 1958): *Can. Home J;* Which was formerly (1906-1910): *The Home Journal.* [ISSN: 0009-1995] 1928. bi-m. m. until 2017. CAD 14.95 domestic; CAD 73 United States; CAD 85 elsewhere. Ed(s): Jane Francisco. Rogers Publishing Ltd., One Mount Pleasant Rd, Toronto, ON M4Y 2Y5, Canada; http://www.rogerspublishing.ca. Illus., adv. Sample. Circ: 571545. Microform: MIM; PQC. *Indexed:* A22, BRI, C37, MASUSE, PdeR. *Aud.:* Ga.

Chatelaine is an exciting magazine for today's Canadian woman. More than simply a lifestyle magazine, *Chatelaine* is the modern woman's guide to fashion, health and wellness, food and drink, homemaking, home decor, parenting, and personal financial management. In the last few years, *Chatelaine* has undergone a bit of a makeover, and the result is a more contemporary publication, featuring regular columns that reflect the realities of Canada's diverse population. It goes out of its way to promote Canadian brands, companies, artists, and entrepreneurs. There is also a French edition [ISSN: 0317-2635]. *Chatelaine* is published monthly. The web site (www.chatelaine.com, English; fr.chatelaine.com, French) offers online content in an attractive format that does not necessarily correspond to the print content. This magazine is suitable for public libraries.

Etudes Inuit Studies. See Native Americans section.

1103. ***Insights on Canadian Society.*** Formerly: *Canada. Statistics Canada. Canadian Social Trends.* 1986. s-a. Ed(s): Sebastien LaRochelle-Cote. Statistics Canada, 170 Tunney's Pasture Driveway, 7th floor, Jean Talon Building, Ottawa, ON K1A 0T6, Canada; infostats@statcan.ca; http://www.statcan.gc.ca. Illus., index, adv. Vol. ends: No. 4. Microform: PQC. *Indexed:* A01, C37, PdeR. *Aud.:* Hs, Ga, Ac, Sa.

Covering a broad range of topics through short, accessible articles, this replacement publication for the former *Canadian Social Trends* "aims to provide policy makers, media[,] and the general public with a better understanding of socioeconomic issues faced by Canadians through innovative, policy-relevant, and timely analysis." Contributors are expert researchers from various divisions of *Statistics Canada* (www.statcan.gc.ca/start-debut-eng.html). Topics covered include labor, income, education, and social and demographic issues. Charts, statistics, overviews, and links to related material are included with articles. This publication is available online, with articles provided in html and pdf versions; it is an important publication for all types of libraries. URL: www.statcan.gc.ca/pub/75-006-x/75-006-x2012001-eng.htm

1104. ***International Journal of Canadian Studies.*** [ISSN: 1180-3991] 1990. s-a. CAD 80 domestic; USD 100 domestic; CAD 110 combined subscription domestic (print & online eds.)). Ed(s): Oriana Palusci, Melissa Haussman. University of Toronto Press, Journals Division, 5201 Dufferin St, Toronto, ON M3H 5T8, Canada; journals@utpress.utoronto.ca; http://www.utpjournals.com. Adv. Refereed. *Indexed:* BRI, C37, MLA-IB, P61, PdeR. *Aud.:* Ga, Ac.

The *International Journal of Canadian Studies* is a multidisciplinary bilingual (English/French) scholarly journal. It is published twice a year by the International Council of Canadian Studies (www.iccs-ciec.ca) and is intended for an academic audience of teachers and researchers from various disciplines interested in the field of Canadian studies. It would also be of interest to a general audience. The International Council of Canadian Studies at University of Alberta makes past issues available online (1990-2006) in pdf. This journal would be of interest to academic, special, and large public libraries. URL: www3.csj.ualberta.ca/iec-csi/

1105. ***Journal of Canadian Studies.*** [ISSN: 0021-9495] 1966. 3x/yr. CAD 155. Ed(s): Marian Bredin. University of Toronto Press, Journals Division, 5201 Dufferin St, Toronto, ON M3H 5T8, Canada; journals@utpress.utoronto.ca; http://www.utpjournals.com. Illus., index, adv. Refereed. Circ: 380. Vol. ends: No. 4. Microform: PQC. *Indexed:* A01, A22, AmHI, BRI, C37, E01, IBSS, MLA-IB. *Bk. rev.:* 1-2, 8-15 pages, signed. *Aud.:* Ga, Ac.

The *Journal of Canadian Studies* is a multidisciplinary scholarly journal published three times a year by University of Toronto Press. It is intended for audiences both in Canada and abroad, and strives to publish the best original research about Canadian history, culture, sociology, and political science.

Articles are primarily in English but can be in French. Some but not all issues include a book review section and/or a listing of new books published in the field of Canadian Studies. Available in print and online for a fee. This journal would be of interest for academic and large public libraries.

1106. ***Labour: journal of Canadian labour studies - revue d'etudes ouvrieres Canadiennes.*** [ISSN: 0700-3862] 1976. s-a. CAD 35. Ed(s): Charles W. Smith, Joan Sangster. Canadian Committee on Labour History, a/s Athabasca University Press, Peace Hills Trust Tower, Edmonton, AB T5J 3S8, Canada; cclh@athabascau.ca; http://www.cclh.ca. Illus., index, adv. Sample. Refereed. Vol. ends: No. 2. *Indexed:* A01, B01, BRI, C37, C42, IBSS. *Bk. rev.:* Number and length vary. *Aud.:* Ga, Ac.

Labour/Le Travail is a bilingual, interdisciplinary journal published semi-annually by the Canadian Committee on Labour History. With a particular focus on the history of Canadian workers, articles cover the fields of Canadian working-class history, industrial sociology, labor economics, and labor relations. Aside from articles, the journal also features conference reports, review essays, book and film reviews, and presentations. It also contains minutes from the Annual Meeting of the Canadian Committee on Labour History. This journal would be of interest to large public libraries, resource centers with a historical focus, and academic libraries with Canadian Studies collections. An archive of the journal is available for free online through the web site, except for the most recent year. URL: www.lltjournal.ca/index.php/llt/issue/archive

1107. ***Literary Review of Canada: a review of Canadian books on culture, politics and society.*** [ISSN: 1188-7494] 1991. 10x/yr. CAD 72 (Individuals, CAD 59). Ed(s): Bronwyn Drainie. Literary Review of Canada Inc., 170 Bloor St W, Ste 710, Toronto, ON M5S 1T9, Canada; info@reviewcanada.ca; http://reviewcanada.ca. Adv. *Indexed:* BRI, C37, MLA-IB. *Bk. rev.:* 12, 1-2 pages, signed. *Aud.:* Ga, Ac.

The *Literary Review of Canada* publishes high-quality reviews written by reputable critics, of primarily Canadian books, both fiction and nonfiction. It also features essays on politics, culture and society, Canadian poetry, and original artwork. The web site offers a table of contents for all issues from 2006, up to and including the current issue, with select full-text access. This journal would be appropriate for any public or academic library collection. URL: www.reviewcanada.ca/magazine/back-issues/

1108. ***Maclean's.*** Former titles (until 1911): *Busy Man's Magazine;* (until 1905): *Business Magazine.* [ISSN: 0024-9262] 1905. m. w. until 2017. CAD 49.95 domestic. Ed(s): Kenneth Whyte, Mark Stevenson. Rogers Publishing Ltd., One Mount Pleasant Rd, Toronto, ON M4Y 2Y5, Canada; RMS@rci.rogers.com; http://www.rogerspublishing.ca. Illus., index, adv. Sample. Circ: 355054. Microform: NBI; PQC. *Indexed:* A01, A22, B01, BRI, C37, CBRI, F01, MASUSE. *Bk. rev.:* 1-2, 2-4 pages. *Aud.:* Hs, Ga, Ac.

Maclean's is a weekly general-interest magazine. It features opinion and editorial columns as well as investigative journalism, covering Canadian and international news and current events. The magazine looks at a broad range of topics, including politics, economy, education, culture, society, and work. Color photos accompany just about every column and article. The web site offers online content in an attractive format, which does not necessarily correspond to the print content. Suitable for public and academic libraries. URL: www.macleans.ca

1109. ***Maisonneuve: a quarterly of arts, opinion & ideas.*** [ISSN: 1703-0056] 2002. q. CAD 20 domestic; CAD 29 in the Americas; CAD 42 elsewhere. Ed(s): Derek Webster. Maisonneuve, 1051 boul Decarie, PO Box 53527, Saint Laurent, QC H4L 5J9, Canada; submissions@maisonneuve.org; http://www.maisonneuve.org. Adv. *Aud.:* Hs, Ga, Ac, Sa.

Maisonneuve is an award-winning quarterly magazine published in Montreal with a focus on arts, culture, news, and ideas. Commentary on Canada and, notably, Quebec figure prominently. The magazine features essays, opinion, fiction, and visual art, and has been called "a new *New Yorker* for a younger generation." Educated, urban readers are drawn to *Maisonneuve* for its eclectic content and balanced perspective on the day's news and events. Select articles are available for free online through the web site. This magazine would be of interest to public and academic libraries. URL: www.maisonneuve.org

1110. ***Manitoba History.*** Formerly (until 1980): *Manitoba Pageant.* [ISSN: 0226-5044] 1956. 3x/yr. Free to members. Ed(s): Robert Coutts. Manitoba Historical Society, 61 Carlton St, Winnipeg, MB R3C 1N7, Canada; info@mhs.mb.ca; http://www.mhs.mb.ca/. Illus., adv. Refereed. *Indexed:* BRI, C37. *Bk. rev.:* 4-8, 1-3 pages. *Aud.:* Hs, Ga, Ac.

Manitoba History is a semi-annual scholarly journal published by the Manitoba Historical Society. It contains feature-length academic articles that cover Manitoba's political, social, economic, and cultural history. It also includes brief articles, book reviews, photo essays, events and announcements, and other popular information for a general Manitoba audience. Many articles are available for free online (www.mhs.mb.ca/docs/mb_history/). Archived issues go back to 1983. This journal would be of interest to large public libraries, resource centers with a historical focus, and academic libraries with Canadian Studies and Canadian history collections.

1111. ***Newfoundland and Labrador Studies.*** Formerly (until 2005): *Newfoundland Studies.* [ISSN: 1719-1726] 1985. s-a. CAD 30 (Individuals, CAD 20). Ed(s): Alison Carr, James Feehan. Memorial University of Newfoundland, Department of English, Arts and Administration 3026, Elizabeth Ave, St. John's, NL A1C 5S7, Canada; harlow@mun.ca; http://www.mun.ca. Illus., index. Refereed. *Indexed:* BRI, C37, MLA-IB. *Bk. rev.:* 6-7, 2-5 pages, signed. *Aud.:* Ga, Ac.

Newfoundland and Labrador Studies is a scholarly journal published biannually by Memorial University's Faculty of Arts. It provides a venue for refereed academic articles on the history and culture of Newfoundland and Labrador, written in either English or French. The interdisciplinary nature of the scholarship makes this journal appealing to a broad audience from across Newfoundland and Labrador and elsewhere. Most issues include book reviews, and some include a historical document (edited and annotated), and review articles. The full archive, including the current issue, is available for free online (https://journals.lib.unb.ca/index.php/NFLDS/issue/archive). This journal would be of interest to large public libraries and academic institutions with Canadian Studies collections.

1112. ***Ontario History.*** Formerly (until 1947): *Ontario Historical Society. Papers and Records;* Incorporates (1944-1948); *Ontario Historical Society. Newsletter.* [ISSN: 0030-2953] 1899. s-a. CAD 42 (Individuals, CAD 31.50; Free to members). Ed(s): Dr. Thorold Tronrud. The Ontario Historical Society, 34 Parkview Ave, Willowdale, ON M2N 3Y2, Canada; http://www.ontariohistoricalsociety.ca/. Illus., index. Refereed. Reprint: PSC. *Indexed:* BRI, C37, MLA-IB. *Bk. rev.:* 5-12, 500-1,000 words. *Aud.:* Ga, Ac.

Ontario History is a biannual, peer-reviewed journal published in the spring and fall. Articles are devoted to the history of Ontario and all aspects of its diverse heritage. Each issue includes book reviews and sometimes feature-length essays, and reports and/or case studies. Published by the Ontario Historical Society, it is considered Ontario's premier history journal. Only available in print. This journal is suitable for large public libraries and academic libraries with a Canadian history collection.

1113. ***Outdoor Canada: the total outdoor experience.*** [ISSN: 0315-0542] 1972. 8x/yr. CAD 19.95 domestic; CAD 34.95 United States; CAD 126 elsewhere. Cottage Life Media, 54 St Patrick St, Toronto, ON M5T 1V1, Canada; clmag@cottagelife.com; http://cottagelife.com. Illus., adv. Sample. *Indexed:* BRI, C37. *Aud.:* Ga.

Outdoor Canada is an award-winning national fishing and hunting magazine published six times a year. Entertaining and informative, it boasts a nice mix of knowledge and skill-building articles, as well as travelogues, photography, buyers' guides, cooking and recipe columns, and detailed and extensive reporting on Canada's heritage outdoor sports. Available in print and online for a fee. This leisure magazine is best suited for public libraries in communities with an interest in the great outdoors, in particular hunting and fishing.

1114. *Policy Options.* [ISSN: 0226-5893] 1979. 10x/yr. CAD 45.93 in state; CAD 41.95 out of state; CAD 59.95 United States. Institute for Research on Public Policy, 1470 Peel St, Ste 200, Montreal, QC H3A 1T1, Canada; irrp@irrp.org; http://www.irpp.org. Illus., adv. Circ: 3000. *Indexed:* BRI, C37. *Bk. rev.:* 0-1, 500 words. *Aud.:* Ga, Ac.

Policy Options is considered Canada's premier public-policy magazine, and comes out ten times a year from the Institute for Research on Public Policy. This useful and informative magazine publishes short independent research on a broad range of public policy issues, in either English or French. The journal's web site offers some full-text content for free, otherwise a complete online version of the magazine is available for a subscription fee. It is intended for readers with an interest in policy debate and Canadian politics, and would be suitable for academic and larger public libraries. URL: www.policyoptions.irpp.org/issues/public-square/

1115. *Prairie Forum.* [ISSN: 0317-6282] 1976. s-a. Ed(s): JoAnn Jaffe, Curtis Shuba. Canadian Plains Research Center, University of Regina, 3737 Wascana Parkway, Regina, SK S4S 0A2, Canada; canadian.plains@uregina.ca; http://www.cprc.ca. Illus., index. Refereed. Vol. ends: Fall (No. 2). Microform: PQC. *Indexed:* BRI, C37, MLA-IB. *Bk. rev.:* 2-10, 2-4 pages. *Aud.:* Ga, Ac, Sa.

Prairie Forum is a multidisciplinary journal devoted to publishing research related to the Canadian Plains region, and it comes out twice a year, in spring and fall. The focus is not on just one province but rather the entire region (Alberta, Saskatchewan, and Manitoba). As well, it aims to bridge an interdisciplinary gap by encouraging contributions from a wide variety of disciplines in writing on Canadian prairies' nature, environment, history, politics, and culture. oURspace, hosted at the University of Regina, makes the entire archive available for free online (http://ourspace.uregina.ca/). This journal would be of interest to large public libraries and academic libraries with a Canadian Studies collection.

1116. *Queen's Quarterly: a Canadian review.* [ISSN: 0033-6041] 1893. q. Queen's Quarterly, Queen's Quarterly, 144 Barrie St, Kingston, ON K7L 3N6, Canada; http://info.queensu.ca/quarterly. Illus. Refereed. Microform: PQC. *Indexed:* A22, BAS, BRI, C37, C42, CBRI, MLA-IB. *Bk. rev.:* Number and length vary. *Aud.:* Ga, Ac.

Queen's Quarterly is an academic journal that aims to both educate and entertain. It is published by Queen's University and is intended for both an academic and a general audience. It offers feature-length articles, critical essays, book and movie reviews, photography, short fiction and poetry, travel writing, and more in the humanities and social sciences disciplines. *Queen's Quarterly* is a cross between an intellectual general-interest magazine and an academic journal, making it suitable for both public and academic libraries. Full text is available online for a subscription fee.

1117. *Quill and Quire: Canada's magazine of book news and reviews.* Incorporates (in 1989): *Books for Young People.* [ISSN: 0033-6491] 1935. 10x/yr. CAD 79.50 domestic; CAD 125 foreign. Ed(s): Stuart Woods. St. Joseph Media, 111 Queen St E, Ste 320, Toronto, ON M5C 1S2, Canada; communications@stjoseph.com; http://www.quillandquire.com/. Illus., adv. Circ: 5400 Paid. Microform: MMP. *Indexed:* BRI, C37, CBRI, MLA-IB. *Bk. rev.:* Number and length vary. *Aud.:* Hs, Ga, Ac.

Quill and Quire is the go-to magazine for the Canadian book trade. Published ten times a year, it offers industry commentary and news, author profiles, and reviews of new adult and children's titles, of around 400 new titles a year. This makes it constitute the most comprehensive coverage of books by Canadian authors. On the web site, expect to find events and job announcements, as well. Digital subscription available. Recommended for public and academic libraries. URL: www.quillandquire.com

1118. *Report on Business Magazine.* Former titles (until 1985): *Report on Business;* (until Feb.1985): *Report on Business 1000.* [ISSN: 0827-7680] 1984. 11x/yr. Ed(s): Gary Salewicz. Globe and Mail Publishing, 351 King St. E., Ste. 1600, Toronto, ON M5A 0N1, Canada; globeandmail@publicitas.com; http://globelink.ca. Illus., adv. Circ: 264640. *Indexed:* BRI, C37. *Bk. rev.:* 1-3, 500 words, signed. *Aud.:* Hs, Ga, Ac.

Report on Business is published by *The Globe and Mail,* one of Canada's largest national newspapers. The magazine was launched over 30 years ago and continues to cover industry developments, market activity, and current and upcoming business opportunities. Aside from feature articles and news, it also contains trend tracking, critical commentary, and some lighter lifestyle fare. It is essential reading for business executives, entrepreneurs, owners, investors, up-and-coming professionals, and a general audience with an interest in the Canadian business environment. Available in print and online. Suitable for public and academic libraries. URL: www.theglobeandmail.com/report-on-business/rob-magazine/

1119. *Revue d'Histoire de l'Amerique Francaise.* [ISSN: 0035-2357] 1947. q. Institut d'Histoire de l'Amerique Francaise, Universite de Montreal, Dept. d'Histoire, Montreal, QC H3C 3J7, Canada; ihaf@ihaf.qc.ca; http://www.ihaf.qc.ca. Adv. Refereed. Microform: PQC. *Indexed:* BRI, C37, MLA-IB, PdeR. *Aud.:* Ac.

Revue d'Histoire de l'Amerique Francaise is a scholarly French-language journal that is published four times a year by Institut d'histoire de l'Amerique francaise (www.ihaf.qc.ca/IHAF/). It is devoted to the history of Quebec, French Canada, and French North America. It publishes articles, historiographic assessments, research notes, criticism, and summaries on all aspects of the French settlement in America, and is widely lauded for its impeccable research and writing from leading scholars from around the world. Although this journal appears to be active, the latest issue was published in the fall of 2012. This journal would complement a collection of other journals with a focus on Canadian and North American history. Available in print and online for a fee. It is suitable for large public libraries and academic libraries with a Canadian history collection.

1120. *Saltscapes: Canada's east coast magazine.* [ISSN: 1492-3351] 2000. bi-m. CAD 26.95. Ed(s): Heather White. Saltscapes Publishing Limited, 30 Damascus Rd, Ste 209, Bedford, NS B4A 0C1, Canada; subscriptions@saltscapes.com. Adv. *Aud.:* Hs, Ga.

Saltscapes is a lively lifestyle magazine that features the best that Atlantic Canada has to offer. This magazine is intended for a general audience with an interest in Atlantic Canada, those who plan on visiting there, and those who live in the region. Sections include "Food & Drink"; "Home & Cottage"; "People & Culture"; and "Healthy Living." The focus is more on rural lifestyles than urban ones. Available in print and online for a fee. This magazine is recommended for public libraries across Canada and especially those on the east coast.

1121. *Saskatchewan History.* [ISSN: 0036-4908] 1948. s-a. CAD 15 domestic; CAD 17.50 foreign. Saskatchewan Archives Board, Murray Bldg, Rm 91, Saskatoon, SK S7N 5A4, Canada; info.saskatoon@archives.gov.sk.ca; http://www.saskarchives.com/. Illus., index, adv. *Indexed:* BRI, C37, MLA-IB. *Bk. rev.:* 7-8, 1-2 pages. *Aud.:* Ga, Ac.

Saskatchewan History is published by the Saskatchewan Archives and comes out twice a year, in the spring and in the fall. This magazine is intended for general and academic audiences and has something for everyone, including scholarly articles, heritage reports, archive news, and book reviews. Photographs and colorful illustrations complement the text and document Saskatchewan's history and its citizens. This magazine would be of interest to public libraries and academic libraries with Canadian history collections.

1122. *This Magazine.* Former titles (until 1998): *This Magazine - Education, Culture, Politics;* (until 1973): *This Magazine is about Schools.* [ISSN: 1491-2678] 1966. bi-m. CAD 27.99. Ed(s): Lauren McKeon. Red Maple Foundation, 417-401 Richmond St W, Toronto, ON M5V 3A8, Canada; publisher@thismagazine.ca. Illus., index, adv. Circ: 5000. Microform: PQC. *Indexed:* A22, BRI, C37. *Bk. rev.:* 1-2 pages. *Aud.:* Hs, Ga, Ac.

This Magazine is published six times a year and aims to provide an alternative perspective on Canadian politics, art, and pop culture. It classifies itself as edgy and subversive and focuses on social issues and activism in Canada. It combines investigative reporting with commentary and in-depth arts coverage and prides itself on showcasing young and up-and-coming writers and artists. Select content is available on the web site. This publication would be relevant to public libraries and academic libraries with an interest in Canadian social issues. URL: www.this.org

1123. *Toronto Life.* Incorporates (1969-1982): *Toronto Calendar Magazine;* (1962-1966): *Ontario Homes and Living.* [ISSN: 0049-4194] 1966. m. CAD 24.86 domestic. Ed(s): Angie Gardos, Sarah Fulford. Toronto Life Publishing Co. Ltd., 111 Queen St East, Ste 320, Toronto, ON M5C 1S2, Canada; guides@torontolife.com; http://www.torontolife.com. Illus., index, adv. Sample. *Indexed:* BRI, C37. *Aud.:* Ga.

Toronto Life is a monthly general-interest magazine for Torontonians interested in food and wine, fashion, real estate, entertainment, culture, municipal politics, and Toronto society. It also caters to those seeking the city as a travel destination. Highlights include a listing of restaurants organized by neighborhood and cuisine type and arts and entertainment listings. With articles, advice columns, opinion pieces, and "best of" lists, all presented with a colorful layout of photographs and illustrations, *Toronto Life* appeals to a general audience living in Toronto and wanting to stay abreast of the best the city has to offer. Select content from the print version as well as supplementary content is available on the web site. This magazine is suitable for public libraries, especially those in the Greater Toronto Area (GTA). URL: www.torontolife.com/

University of Toronto Quarterly. See Literature section.

1124. *The Walrus.* [ISSN: 1708-4032] 2003. 10x/yr. CAD 29.75. Walrus, 411 Richmond St. East, Ste. B15, Toronto, ON M5A 3S5, Canada. Adv. *Bk. rev.:* Number and length vary. *Aud.:* Hs, Ga, Ac, Sa.

The Walrus, often unofficially referred to as the Canadian *Harper's,* is a monthly general-interest magazine about Canada for educated and curious readers. Articles focus on current affairs, social and political issues, and arts and culture. It also contains commentary, opinion, and analysis. Some of the best writers and artists from Canada and beyond contribute to *The Walrus.* Special issues include an annual summer reading issue, featuring some of the best short fiction by Canadian authors, as well as a special winter double issue. Select content is available on the web site. This magazine would be relevant to all public and academic libraries. URL: www.thewalrus.ca

1125. *Zoomer Canada.* Former titles (until 2010): *Zoomer;* (until Oct. 2008): *C A R P;* (until 2008): *C A R P Fifty Plus;* (until 2001): *C A R P News Fifty Plus;* (until 1999): *C A R P News;* (until 1994): *C A R P;* (until 1992): *C A R P News;* (until 1986): *C A R P Newsletter.* [ISSN: 1928-0920] 1985. 9x/yr. CAD 19.95 domestic; CAD 79.95 foreign. Canadian Association of Retired Persons, 30 Jefferson Ave, Toronto, ON M6K 1Y4, Canada; support@carp.ca; http://www.carp.ca. Adv. *Indexed:* BRI, C37. *Aud.:* Ga, Ac, Sa.

Zoomer is a magazine for the Baby Boomer generation: men and women ages 45 and up. The articles and columns focus on all aspects of life after 45: health, beauty, finances, travel and leisure, arts, and lifestyle. This magazine aims to help this demographic stay energetic and passionate and make the most out of life. Select content is available on the web site. Recommended for public libraries. URL: www.everythingzoomer.com

■ CARTOGRAPHY, GIS, AND IMAGERY

See also Environment and Conservation; Earth Sciences and Geology; and Geography sections.

Lucinda M. Hall, Map Librarian, Evans Map Room, Dartmouth College Library, 25 N Main St, Hanover, NH 03755; lucinda.m.hall@dartmouth.edu

Introduction

Cartography, geographic information systems (GIS), and imagery are separate but related fields. Cartography is the science and practice of creating analog or digital maps. GIS is a framework for capturing, managing, analyzing, and visualizing spatial data. Imagery includes aerial photography, satellite imagery, and remote sensing images used in many disciplines. Cartography, GIS, and imagery are part of everyday life, employed by the tools we use daily to navigate, make decisions, and learn about the world.

Literature in the field focuses heavily on the collection, analysis, and applications of spatial data (including maps) and imagery across disciplines. The use and study of cartography, GIS, and imagery is found in what would be considered the more traditional fields. Examples include geology, environmental sciences, and architecture, but has also seen growth in humanities and social sciences, including history, English, and sociology. One would be hard-pressed to find a field where cartography, GIS, and imagery is not being utilized.

The titles in this section range from industry magazines, to society publications, to academic journals. The majority of the titles are applicable to upper-level undergraduates, graduates, and professional-level researchers with some titles intended for practitioners and general readers. They offer a mix of theoretical articles, empirical research reports, book reviews, conference proceedings, and special issues focused on a particular topic or theme.

Basic Periodicals

Cartography and Geographic Information Science, Computers & Geosciences, GeoInformatica, IEEE Transactions on Geoscience and Remote Sensing, Imago Mundi, International Journal of Geographical Information Science, International Journal of Remote Sensing, Journal of Geographical Systems, Photogrammetric Engineering and Remote Sensing, Surveying and Land Information Science.

Basic Abstracts and Indexes

GEOBASE, GeoRef, Scopus.

1126. *A C S M Bulletin: promoting advancement in surveying and mapping.* Formerly (until 1981): *American Congress on Surveying and Mapping. Bulletin.* [ISSN: 0747-9417] 1950. bi-m. USD 100 domestic; USD 115 foreign; USD 126 combined subscription domestic (print & online eds.)). Ed(s): Ilse Alipui. American Congress on Surveying and Mapping, 5119 Pegasus Court, Ste Q, Frederick, MD 21704; curtis.sumner@nsps.us.com; http://www.acsm.net. Illus., adv. Circ: 8000. *Indexed:* A22. *Bk. rev.:* Number and length vary. *Aud.:* Ac, Sa.

This trade magazine covers current events in geospatial technologies and the related fields of geodesy, GIS, GPS, and others. It reflects the interest of members of four American Congress on Surveying and Mapping (ACSM) professional organizations: the American Association for Geodetic Surveying (AAGS), the Cartography and Geographic Information Society (CaGIS), the Geographic and Land Information Society (GLIS), and the National Society of Professional Surveyors (NSPS). This magazine also includes conference reports, articles, book reviews, and association news. An online "Webmazine" is free. For academics and practitioners.

1127. *Annals of G I S (Online).* [ISSN: 1947-5691] q. Free. Taylor & Francis Inc., 530 Walnut St, Ste 850, Philadelphia, PA 19106; enquiries@taylorandfrancis.com; http://www.tandfonline.com. Refereed. *Aud.:* Ac, Sa.

This international peer-reviewed journal is published in cooperation with the International Association of Chinese Professionals in Geographic Information Sciences. The journal encourages the interdisciplinary exchange of original ideas on theory, methods, development, and applications in the fields of geo-information science. Papers cover developments in remote sensing and data acquisition, geographic information systems, geo-visualization and virtual geographic environments, spatial analysis, and uncertainty modeling.

1128. *Arc News.* [ISSN: 1064-6108] 1987. q. Free to qualified personnel. Ed(s): Citabria Stevens. Environmental Systems Research Institute, Inc., 380 New York St, Redlands, CA 92373; requests@esri.com. Adv. *Aud.:* Ac, Sa.

Arc News is a industry magazine geared toward a range of GIS professionals, IT/GIS support, researchers, and educators. It covers the latest developments in GIS technology, applications of GIS in industry and government, conferences, and trends in GIS teaching and learning. Its target audience is the Environmental Systems Research Institute (ESRI) user community, but others will find material of interest here. The electronic version offers articles that appear exclusively online, as well as web-only content and supplemental podcasts. URL: http://www.esri.com/esri-news/arcnews

1129. ***ArcUser.*** [ISSN: 1534-5467] 1998. q. Ed(s): Monica Pratt. Environmental Systems Research Institute, Inc., 380 New York St, Redlands, CA 92373. Adv. *Aud.:* Ac, Sa.

ArcUser is an industry magazine that publishes articles on the developments in GIS technology and the use of GIS software. It features technical information including tutorials, tips, and best practices. The target audience is the Esri user community, but the information published in the magazine will be of use to GIS professionals, managers, or developers. The print version of the magazine is available within the United States for free, and online access is freely available globally.

1130. ***The Cartographic Journal: the world of mapping.*** [ISSN: 0008-7041] 1964. q. GBP 585 (print & online eds.)). Ed(s): Adam King. Taylor & Francis, 2, 3 & 4 Park Sq, Milton Park, Abingdon, OX14 4RN, United Kingdom; subscriptions@tandf.co.uk; https://www.tandfonline.com. Illus., index, adv. Sample. Refereed. Vol. ends: Dec. Reprint: PSC. *Indexed:* A01, A22, MLA-IB. *Bk. rev.:* Number and length vary. *Aud.:* Ac, Sa.

This long-standing peer-reviewed title is the official journal of the British Cartographic Society. The journal is international in scope and includes scholarly articles and professional papers on all aspects of cartography and mapping, remote sensing, geographical information systems (GIS), the Internet, and global positioning systems. The journal also publishes articles on social, political, and historical aspects of cartography and book and software reviews. Geared toward scholarly readers.

1131. ***Cartographic Perspectives.*** Former titles (until 1989): *Cartographic Information;* (until 1987): *Map Gap.* [ISSN: 1048-9053] 1981. 3x/yr. Ed(s): Amy L Griffin, Patrick Kennelly. North American Cartographic Information Society, 2311 E Hartford Ave, Milwaukee, WI 53211; business@nacis.org; http://nacis.org/. Refereed. *Indexed:* A01, MLA-IB. *Bk. rev.:* Number and length vary. *Aud.:* Ga, Ac, Sa.

Cartographic Perspectives is the journal of the North American Cartographic Information Society (NACIS), with members representing academia, cartographic publishers, and the GIS and digital mapping communities, as well as educators, map curators, and librarians. The open-access journal contains research and descriptive papers on all aspects of cartography, maps, and related topics in eight sections: "Practical Cartographer's Corner," "Cartographic Collections," "Reviews," "Views on Cartographic Education," "Opinions," "Peer-Reviewed Articles," "Marginalia," and "Visual Fields." Appropriate for academic libraries that support a map collection or geography department, and for special libraries that support cartographic work.

1132. ***Cartographica: the international journal for geographic information and geovisualization.*** Incorporates (1964-1980): *Canadian Cartographer;* Which was formerly (until 1968): *Cartographer.* [ISSN: 0317-7173] 1964. q. USD 270. Ed(s): Monica Wachowicz, Emmanuel Stefanakis. University of Toronto Press, Journals Division, 5201 Dufferin St, Toronto, ON M3H 5T8, Canada; journals@utpress.utoronto.ca; http://www.utpjournals.com. Illus., index. Sample. Refereed. Circ: 433. Vol. ends: No. 4. Microform: PQC. *Indexed:* A01, A22, BRI, C37. *Bk. rev.:* Number varies; 750 words. *Aud.:* Ac, Sa.

Cartographica is the official publication of the Canadian Cartographic Association. This international and interdisciplinary peer-reviewed journal publishes articles on cartographic thought, the history of cartography, cartography and society, as well as material on geo-visualization research. Abstracts are in both English and French. A "Technical Notes and Ephemera" section includes research notes, technical information, opinions, news items, and occasional humor and trivia. For a scholarly audience.

1133. ***Cartography and Geographic Information Science.*** Former titles (until Jan.1999): *Cartography and Geographic Information Systems;* (until 1990): *American Cartographer.* [ISSN: 1523-0406] 1974. 5x/yr. GBP 228 (print & online eds.)). Ed(s): Scott M Freundschuh, Nicholas Chrisman. Taylor & Francis, 2, 3 & 4 Park Sq, Milton Park, Abingdon, OX14 4RN, United Kingdom; subscriptions@tandf.co.uk; https://www.tandfonline.com. Illus., adv. Refereed. Vol. ends: Oct. Reprint: PSC. *Indexed:* A01, A22, BRI. *Aud.:* Ac, Sa.

This is the official publication of the Cartography and Geographic Information Society (CaGIS), which is a member organization of the American Congress on Surveying and Mapping (ACSM). The society "supports research, education, and practices that improve the understanding, creation, analysis, and use of maps and geographic information." *CaGIS* became one of the three official journals of the International Cartographic Association (ICA) in 2004, and has since expanded coverage globally, inviting international submissions to the journal, as well as international participation in the editorial and review processes. This journal "houses" the U.S. National Report to the ICA. Articles include research on cartographic representations, GIS, spatial analysis, web-based mapping, and other topics.

1134. ***Computers & Geosciences: an international journal.*** Incorporates (1985-1989): *C O G S Computer Contributions.* [ISSN: 0098-3004] 1975. 12x/yr. EUR 4605. Elsevier Ltd, The Boulevard, Langford Lane, Oxford, OX5 1GB, United Kingdom; customerserviceau@elsevier.com; http://www.elsevier.com. Illus., index, adv. Sample. Refereed. Vol. ends: Dec (No. 27). *Indexed:* A01, A22, C45, CompLI, S25. *Bk. rev.:* Number and length vary. *Aud.:* Ac.

Computers & Geosciences publishes scholarly research and application articles that describe new computation methods for the geosciences. It covers computational and informatics elements including computational methods, data models, remote sensing data analysis, and programming languages. It also contains articles on the scientific and social use of geoscience information. Recent special issues were on "Big data and natural disasters" and "Statistical learning in geoscience modelling." For a scholarly audience.

1135. ***The G I S Professional.*** Former titles (until 2010): *U R I S A News;* (until 1982): *U R I S A;* (until 19??): *U R I S A News.* 196?. bi-m. Free to members. Ed(s): Wendy Nelson. Urban and Regional Information Systems Association, 701 Lee St, Ste 680, Des Plaines, IL 60016; info@urisa.org; http://www.urisa.org/. *Aud.:* Ac, Ga, Sa.

The GIS Professional is an official publication of the Urban and Regional Information Systems Association (URISA). It contains news of the association and the GIS world in general. URISA members can submit articles of all types about GIS-related subjects for possible publication.

1136. ***Geocarto International.*** [ISSN: 1010-6049] 1986. 14x/yr. GBP 1086 (print & online eds.)). Ed(s): M D Nellis, Kamlesh C Lulla. Taylor & Francis, 2, 3 & 4 Park Sq, Milton Park, Abingdon, OX14 4RN, United Kingdom; subscriptions@tandf.co.uk; https://www.tandfonline.com. Illus., adv. Sample. Refereed. Reprint: PSC. *Indexed:* A01, A22, E01, S25. *Bk. rev.:* Number and length vary. *Aud.:* Ac.

Geocarto International is a professional academic journal serving the international scientific and user community in the fields of remote sensing, GIS, geoscience, and environmental sciences. Among its goals is to promote multidisciplinary research and to enhance the international exchange of information in the fields of remote sensing, GIS, and related professions. It includes reviews, news, evaluation of equipment and software, and conference reports. Appropriate for academic libraries with collections that include remote sensing as well as GIS and environmental sciences.

1137. ***Geodesy and Cartography (Online).*** Formerly (until 2011): *Geodezija ir kartografija (Online).* [ISSN: 2029-7009] 1997. q. Free. Ed(s): Eimuntas Parseliunas. Vilniaus Gedimino Technikos Universitetas, Leidykla Technika, Sauletekio aleja 11, Vilnius, 10223, Lithuania; knygos@vgtu.lt; http://leidykla.vgtu.lt. Refereed. *Aud.:* Ac, Sa.

This journal is co-published with the Vilnius Gediminas Technical University. *Geodesy and Cartography* features original research articles on geodesy, cartography, remote sensing, geoinformation systems, geoscience, land management, and environmental sciences in the following languages: Lithuanian, English, German, French, and Russian.

1138. ***Geoinformatica: an international journal on advances of computer science for geographic information systems.*** [ISSN: 1384-6175] 1997. q. EUR 1329 (print & online eds.)). Ed(s): Shashi Shekhar, E Bertino. Springer New York LLC, 233 Spring St, New York, NY 10013; customerservice@springer.com; http://www.springer.com. Adv. Sample. Refereed. Reprint: PSC. *Indexed:* A01, A22, CompLI, E01, S25. *Aud.:* Ac.

The aim of the journal is to "promote the most innovative results coming from the research in the field of computer science applied to geographic information systems." Among the topics addressed are spatial modeling, spatial databases, human-computer interfaces for GIS, digital cartography, space imagery in GIS, spatio-temporal reasoning, parallelism, distribution, and communication through GIS. Recent special issues were on "Spatial Computing in Emergency Management" and "Advances in Spatio-Temporal Data Analysis and Management."

1139. ***GIScience and Remote Sensing.*** Former titles (until 2004): *Mapping Sciences and Remote Sensing;* (until 1984): *Geodesy, Mapping and Photogrammetry;* (until 1973): *Geodesy and Aerophotography.* [ISSN: 1548-1603] 1962. 8x/yr. GBP 888 (print & online eds.)). Ed(s): Jungho R Im. Taylor & Francis, 2, 3 & 4 Park Sq, Milton Park, Abingdon, OX14 4RN, United Kingdom; subscriptions@tandf.co.uk; https://www.tandfonline.com. Illus. Refereed. Reprint: PSC. *Indexed:* A22, C45. *Aud.:* Ac, Sa.

This journal publishes original, peer-reviewed articles associated with geographic information systems, remote sensing of the environment, digital image processing, geocomputation, spatial data mining, and geographic environmental modeling. The specialized content includes both basic and applied topics. Articles are written for scholarly audiences.

1140. ***I E E E Geoscience and Remote Sensing Letters.*** [ISSN: 1545-598X] 2004. m. USD 575. Ed(s): Avik Bhattacharya. Institute of Electrical and Electronics Engineers, 445 Hoes Ln, Piscataway, NJ 08855; contactcenter@ieee.org; http://www.ieee.org. Adv. Refereed. *Indexed:* S25. *Aud.:* Ac.

This journal, from the IEEE Geoscience and Remote Sensing Society, publishes short papers with a maximum length of five pages, focusing on new ideas and concepts in the area of remote sensing. As soon as they are accepted, articles are published online and follow that exposure with publication in the printed quarterly version, grouped by topic. The journal accommodates extended objects such as image animations and multimedia.

1141. ***I E E E Journal of Selected Topics in Applied Earth Observations and Remote Sensing.*** [ISSN: 1939-1404] 2008. m. USD 1635. Ed(s): Qian Jenny Du. Institute of Electrical and Electronics Engineers, 445 Hoes Ln, Piscataway, NJ 08854; contactcenter@ieee.org; http://www.ieee.org. Adv. Refereed. *Indexed:* S25. *Aud.:* Ac.

I E E E Journal of Selected Topics in Applied Earth Observations and Remote Sensing (*J-STARS*) publishes articles focused on remote sensing and Earth observations and their use in understanding the Earth. This peer-reviewed journal is sponsored by the IEEE Geoscience and Remote Sensing Society (GRSS) and the IEEE Committee on Earth Observations. The journal strives to serve as a communication venue for the application themes that arise from the annual IEEE conferences and the collaboration of the two founding groups. *J-STARS* publishes the special issue topics formerly found in *Transactions.* Recent special issue topics include "Hyperspectral Remote Sensing and Imaging Spectroscopy" and "Quality Improvements of Remote Sensing Data."

1142. ***I E E E Transactions on Geoscience and Remote Sensing.*** Formerly (until 1980): *I E E E Transactions on Geoscience Electronics.* [ISSN: 0196-2892] 1963. m. USD 1985. Ed(s): Simon H Yueh, Antonio J Plaza. Institute of Electrical and Electronics Engineers, 445 Hoes Ln, Piscataway, NJ 08854; contactcenter@ieee.org; http://www.ieee.org. Illus., adv. Refereed. *Indexed:* A01, A22, B01, C45, S25. *Aud.:* Ac, Sa.

IEEE Transactions on Geoscience and Remote Sensing (*TGARS*) focuses on the techniques, theory, and concepts of remote sensing of the Earth, oceans, atmosphere, and space. It also contains discussion of the processing, interpretation, and dissemination of the sensing data. *TGARS* has peer-reviewed technical and research papers, reviews, and correspondence articles. It is widely indexed. Popular articles include "Accurate Object Localization in Remote Sensing Images Based on Convolutional Neural Networks" and "Self-Taught Feature Learning for Hyperspectral Image Classification." Essential for libraries with remote sensing collections and geosciences collections.

1143. ***I S P R S Journal of Photogrammetry and Remote Sensing.*** Formerly (until 1989): *Photogrammetria.* [ISSN: 0924-2716] 1938. 12x/yr. EUR 1116. Ed(s): Q Weng, D Lichti. Elsevier BV, Radarweg 29, Amsterdam, 1043 NX, Netherlands; info@elsevier.com; https://www.elsevier.com/. Illus., adv. Refereed. Microform: PQC. *Indexed:* A01, A22, C45, S25. *Bk. rev.:* Number and length vary. *Aud.:* Ac.

Referred to as *P&RS,* this is the official journal of the International Society for Photogrammetry and Remote Sensing (ISPRS). With a long publishing history and extensively indexed, this is among the highest-rated journals in the field. *P&RS* publishes high quality, peer-reviewed articles on photogrammetry, remote sensing, spatial information systems, and computer vision. Occasionally theme issues are released; recent theme issues include "State-of-the-art in photogrammetry, remote sensing and spatial information science" and "Visualization and exploration of geospatial data."

1144. ***Imago Mundi: the international journal for the history of cartography.*** [ISSN: 0308-5694] 1935. s-a. GBP 288 (print & online eds.)). Ed(s): Dr. Catherine Delano-Smith. Routledge, 4 Park Sq, Milton Park, Abingdon, OX14 4RN, United Kingdom; subscriptions@tandf.co.uk; http://www.tandfonline.com. Illus., index, adv. Sample. Refereed. Reprint: PSC. *Indexed:* A01, A22, AmHI, BRI, E01, MLA-IB. *Bk. rev.:* Number and length vary. *Aud.:* Ac, Sa.

Imago Mundi is the leading scholarly journal on early maps worldwide. Founded in 1935, it is interdisciplinary and has an international readership. It covers research and occasional review articles about antique maps and historic cartography. Each issue includes book reviews, an indexed bibliography of current literature, and an extensive news-and-notices section on conferences, exhibits, map acquisitions, and so on. The editorship is largely American and British, with an international editorial board. The full-text back issues through 2002 are available through JSTOR free of charge for current individual subscribers of the journal. *Imago Mundi* is important for academic libraries that support a geography department or map collection.

1145. ***International Journal of Applied Earth Observation and Geoinformation.*** Formerly (until 1999): *I T C Journal.* [ISSN: 1569-8432] 1973. 10x/yr. EUR 880. Ed(s): F van der Meer. Elsevier BV, Radarweg 29, Amsterdam, 1043 NX, Netherlands; info@elsevier.com; https://www.elsevier.com/. Illus., adv. Refereed. *Indexed:* A01, A22, C45, S25. *Bk. rev.:* Number and length vary. *Aud.:* Ac.

This journal publishes papers that apply earth observation data to the management of natural resources and environmental issues, such as industrial pollution, biodiversity, or natural hazards. The journal encourages both discussion and review articles, especially those that emphasize economic and social issues related to developing countries. Recent special issues are "Advances in the validation and application of remotely sensed soil moisture" and "Earth observation for habitat mapping and biodiversity monitoring."

1146. ***International Journal of Digital Earth: a new journal for a new vision.*** [ISSN: 1753-8947] 2008. m. GBP 829 (print & online eds.)). Ed(s): Guo Huadong. Taylor & Francis, 2, 3 & 4 Park Sq, Milton Park, Abingdon, OX14 4RN, United Kingdom; subscriptions@tandf.co.uk; https://www.tandfonline.com. Adv. Sample. Refereed. Reprint: PSC. *Indexed:* A01, A22, C45, E01, S25. *Bk. rev.:* Number and length vary. *Aud.:* Ac.

This peer-reviewed journal was founded by the International Society for Digital Earth in 2008, and has quickly gained a solid reputation. Its goal is to integrate and share information regarding digital Earth's science and technology. Specifically, it includes papers on digital Earth theory and framework, geoinformatics, visualization and simulation, data mining, and integration of remote-sensing GIS-GPS. Additionally, it includes topics on digital Earth in societal issues. Full research papers, shorter papers, reports, and book reviews are included. A number of papers are freely available as an "Editor's Choice" selection. Appropriate for libraries with geographic or information technology collections.

1147. *International Journal of Geographical Information Science.* Formerly (until 1997): *International Journal of Geographical Information Systems.* [ISSN: 1365-8816] 1987. m. GBP 3233 (print & online eds.)). Ed(s): Brian Lees. Taylor & Francis, 2, 3 & 4 Park Sq, Milton Park, Abingdon, OX14 4RN, United Kingdom; subscriptions@tandf.co.uk; https://www.tandfonline.com. Illus., index, adv. Sample. Refereed. Vol. ends: Dec. Reprint: PSC. *Indexed:* A01, A22, C45, CompLI, E01, ErgAb. *Aud.:* Ac.

International Journal of Geographical Information Science (IJGIS) focuses on geographical information science (GIScience) and geocomputation and is international in scope. It is of interest to those who research, design, analyze, and plan using GIS in natural resources and environmental studies, as well as those involved in the information and database management aspect of GIS. Recent special issues were on "Human Dynamics in the Mobile and Big Data Era" and "Cyberinfrastructure, GIS and Spatial Optimization." Appropriate for libraries with geography, GIS, or information science research collections.

1148. *International Journal of Remote Sensing.* Incorporates (1983-2001): *Remote Sensing Reviews.* [ISSN: 0143-1161] 1980. m. USD 15256 (print & online eds.)). Ed(s): Warner A Timothy. Taylor & Francis, 2, 3 & 4 Park Sq, Milton Park, Abingdon, OX14 4RN, United Kingdom; https://www.tandfonline.com. Illus., index, adv. Sample. Refereed. Vol. ends: Dec. Reprint: PSC. *Indexed:* A01, A22, C45, E01, S25. *Aud.:* Ac.

This is the official journal of the Remote Sensing and Photogrammetry Society. It is a research journal focused on the science and technology of remote sensing and its applications. Topics include data collection, analysis, and interpretation; surveying from space, air, water, and ground platforms; and use of remote sensing data. In 2010, the section "Remote Sensing Letters" split off to form its own journal of the same name [ISSN 2150-704X]. *International Journal of Remote Sensing* also publishes an online-only "Open Access Section." Editorship and authorship are international. Appropriate for remote-sensing professionals and academic libraries with collections that support environmental studies, geography, and related programs that study remote sensing.

1149. *Journal of Geodesy.* Formed by the merger of (1924-1995): *Bulletin Geodesique;* (1978-1995): *Manuscripta Geodaetica.* [ISSN: 0949-7714] 1995. m. EUR 2938 (print & online eds.)). Ed(s): Roland A Klees. Springer, Tiergartenstr 17, Heidelberg, 69121, Germany. Adv. Refereed. Reprint: PSC. *Indexed:* A01, A22, E01. *Aud.:* Ac, Sa.

The *Journal of Geodesy* is a peer-reviewed, international journal that covers scientific problems of geodesy and related sciences, such as positioning, reference frame, geodetic networks, and remote sensing. It is highly rated, has a long publishing history, and is widely indexed. It is a publication of the International Association of Geodesy. In addition to original research papers, the journal publishes commissioned review papers on topical subjects and special issues arising from chosen scientific symposia or workshops. "Reference Systems" is the journal's most recent special issue published in 2018.

1150. *Journal of Geographical Systems: geographical information, analysis, theory and decision.* Formerly (until 1998): *Geographical Systems.* [ISSN: 1435-5930] 1999. q. EUR 593 (print & online eds.)). Ed(s): Antonio Paez, Manfred M Fischer. Springer, Tiergartenstr 17, Heidelberg, 69121, Germany. Adv. Sample. Refereed. Reprint: PSC. *Indexed:* A01, A22, B01, E01, EconLit. *Aud.:* Ac.

Journal of Geographical Systems is a peer-reviewed publication with an international editorial board. It covers geographical information and its analysis, theory and decision systems, and gives special attention to regional issues, urban and regional economics, spatial economics, geography, GIScience, and environmental sciences. The journal is widely indexed and ranks high on impact factors.

1151. *Journal of Map & Geography Libraries: advances in geospatial information, collections, and archives.* [ISSN: 1542-0353] 2004. 3x/yr. GBP 636 (print & online eds.)). Ed(s): Paige G Andrew, Katherine H Weimer. Routledge, 530 Walnut St, Ste 850, Philadelphia, PA 19106; enquiries@tandfonline.com; http://www.tandfonline.com. Sample. Refereed. Reprint: PSC. *Indexed:* A01, A22, C45, E01. *Aud.:* Ac.

Journal of Map & Geography Libraries covers a wide variety of map, cartography, and geospatial research and applications. It ranges from historic cartography and modern map publishing to emerging GIS and geospatial data topics. It is aimed primarily at the library and archives community, and its international board covers a wide span of cartographic and geospatial data-related specializations. Recent themed issues cover "Education for Organization, Access, and Use of Geographic Information" and "Geospatial Data Management, Curation, and Preservation." Appropriate for libraries, archives, and universities with map or GIS collections and areas of specialization.

1152. *Photogrammetric Engineering and Remote Sensing.* Former titles (until 1975): *Photogrammetric Engineering;* (until 1936): *News Notes of the American Society of Photogrammetry.* [ISSN: 0099-1112] 1934. m. USD 959 domestic; USD 1013 Canada; USD 974 elsewhere. Ed(s): Dr. Russell G Congalton. American Society for Photogrammetry and Remote Sensing, 5410 Grosvenor Ln, Ste 210, Bethesda, MD 20814-2160; asprs@asprs.org; http://www.asprs.org. Illus., index, adv. Refereed. Vol. ends: Dec. *Indexed:* A22, Agr, C45, HRIS, S25. *Bk. rev.:* Number and length vary. *Aud.:* Ac, Sa.

Photogrammetric Engineering and Remote Sensing (*PE&RS*) is the official journal of the American Society for Photogrammetry & Remote Sensing, and society members have complete online access to the journal. Non-member access on the society's web page is limited to a "public version flip book" that does not contain the full peer-reviewed articles. The journal covers new technologies and applications relating to photogrammetry, remote sensing, and spatial sciences. The journal also includes book reviews and the columns "Grids and Datums" and "Signatures."

1153. *The Photogrammetric Record: an international journal of photogrammetry.* [ISSN: 0031-868X] 1953. q. Ed(s): Stuart I Granshaw. Wiley-Blackwell Publishing Ltd., The Atrium, Southern Gate, Chichester, PO19 8QG, United Kingdom; cs-journals@wiley.com; http://onlinelibrary.wiley.com. Illus., adv. Sample. Refereed. Reprint: PSC. *Indexed:* A01, A22, BRI, E01, HRIS. *Aud.:* Ac, Sa.

This international journal publishes articles that reflect modern advancements in photogrammetry, 3D imaging, computer vision, and other related non-contact fields. It is published on behalf of the Remote Sensing and Photogrammetry Society (RSPSoc) and includes an international board, with Europe heavily represented. The scope includes various applications of photogrammetry, including topographic mapping, spatial data acquisition, digital cartography, virtual reality, agriculture and forestry, and other subject-focused works.

1154. *Remote Sensing Letters.* [ISSN: 2150-704X] 2010. m. GBP 432 (print & online eds.)). Ed(s): Giles Foody, Arthur P Cracknell. Taylor & Francis, 2, 3 & 4 Park Sq, Milton Park, Abingdon, OX14 4RN, United Kingdom; subscriptions@tandf.co.uk; https://www.tandfonline.com. Illus. Refereed. Reprint: PSC. *Indexed:* A01, C45. *Aud.:* Ac, Sa.

This journal is peer-reviewed with an international editorial board committed to the rapid publication of articles advancing the science and technology of remote sensing as well as its applications. It previously was printed as a section contained in the *International Journal of Remote Sensing* from 1983 to 2009, and expanded to 12 issues per year in 2013. Articles cover remote sensing of the atmosphere, biosphere, cryosphere, and the terrestrial earth, as well as human modifications to the earth system.

Remote Sensing of Environment. See Environment and Conservation section.

1155. ***Surveying and Land Information Science.*** Former titles (until 2002): *Surveying and Land Information Systems;* (until 1990): *Surveying and Mapping;* (until 1944): *American Congress on Surveying and Mapping. Bulletin;* (until 1942): *National Congress on Surveying and Mapping. Bulletin;* (until 1941): *National Congress on Surveying and Mapping. Report on the ... Meeting.* [ISSN: 1538-1242] 1941. q. USD 180 (print & online eds.) Individuals, USD 130 (print & online eds.); USD 115 domestic). Ed(s): Charles Ghilani. American Congress on Surveying and Mapping, 5119 Pegasus Court, Ste Q, Frederick, MD 21704; curtis.sumner@nsps.us.com; http://www.acsm.net. Illus., index, adv. Sample. Refereed. Vol. ends: Dec. Microform: PQC. *Indexed:* A22, HRIS. *Bk. rev.:* Number and length vary. *Aud.:* Ac, Sa.

This journal is the official publication of the American Association of Geodetic Surveying (AAGS) and the Geographic and Land Information Society (GLIS). The journal publishes research on geodetic surveying, land surveying, and geographic information systems. Articles cover theoretical, technical, administrative, and policy developments in surveying, mapping, and land information systems through research articles, technical papers, surveying notes, surveying education, surveying history, book reviews, and current literature reviews. Every four years, the journal publishes the *U.S. Report to the International Federation of Surveyors* (FIG). The *Proceedings of the Surveying Teachers Conference* is published biannually. *SaLIS* is important for any library—academic, public, or special—that supports research or teaching in any of the numerous applications of GIS and related technologies.

1156. ***Transactions in G I S (Online).*** [ISSN: 1467-9671] 1996. bi-m. GBP 1622. Ed(s): Dr. John P Wilson. Wiley-Blackwell Publishing Ltd., The Atrium, Southern Gate, Chichester, PO19 8QG, United Kingdom; cs-journals@wiley.com; http://onlinelibrary.wiley.com. Refereed. *Bk. rev.:* Number and length vary. *Aud.:* Ac.

Transactions in GIS is an international scholarly journal that contains original research articles, reviews, and brief notes on both applied and theoretical aspects of spatial science. The journal focuses on topics including GIS, GPS, remote sensing, and related geospatial technologies; geospatial data acquisition and sensing; and GIS education and certification. Free access to the journal is provided to institutions in the developing world through the Online Access to Research in the Environment (OARE) initiative. The journal is highly rated, extensively indexed, and geared toward academic and professional audiences.

1157. ***xyHt.*** Formerly (until 2014): *Professional Surveyor (Print).* [ISSN: 2373-7018] 1981. m. Free. Ed(s): Shelly Cox. Flatdog Media Inc., 20 West 3rd St., Frederick, MD 21701; http://www.xyht.com/surveying/flatdog-media/. Adv. *Bk. rev.:* GeoRef. *Aud.:* Ga, Ac.

This trade magazine is a source for news about surveying, global positioning systems, GIS, unmanned drones, hydrography, and 3D imaging.

■ CHEMISTRY

General/Analytical/Inorganic/Organic/Physical

Amy Gullen, Life and Health Sciences Librarian, University of Dayton, 300 College Park Dr., Dayton, IL 45469; gullen@udayton.edu

Introduction

The United Nations Educational, Scientific and Cultural Organization (UNESCO) and the International Union of Pure and Applied Chemistry (IUPAC) partnered to declare 2011 the International Year of Chemistry, "a worldwide celebration of the achievements of chemistry and its contributions to the well-being of humankind," with a theme of "Chemistry - our life, our future." The objectives were to raise awareness and appreciation of chemistry's role in meeting world needs, and to interest youth in chemistry. Coinciding with the one hundredth anniversary of Madame Curie's Nobel Prize, the initiative also provides an opportunity to highlight the contributions of women to the discipline. Many journals have dedicated pages this year to related content.

In October 2004, the Chemical Sciences Roundtable of the Board on Chemical Sciences and Technology of the National Academy of Sciences sponsored a workshop, "Are Chemistry Journals Too Expensive and Inaccessible?" The published summary (Heindel et al., 2005, National Academies Press) describes the many challenges peculiar to chemistry, as well as those facing scholarly publishing in general. It is recommended reading as a primer on past, current, and proposed models of scholarly communication.

Among the challenges highlighted by Heindel et al. (2005) are the complex graphical information and the unique "language" of chemistry that requires both special authoring and special search and retrieval tools. Providing sufficient data to allow others to use published research is also challenging in traditional print formats. Such concerns were part of the rationale behind the now-defunct *Internet Journal of Chemistry. IJC*'s editor noted that the journal had intended to demonstrate the benefits of electronic over print publication - for example, with respect to graphical content not easily rendered in print. This SPARC leading-edge title ended its run in 2005, but innovation in online publishing in chemistry continues (SPARC is the Scholarly Publishing and Academic Resource Coalition).

Journal proliferation may also influence cost of and access to chemistry research. *Ulrich's Periodicals Directory* lists 81 active, English-language, refereed print journals with "chemistry" as part of the subject that began publication in 2000 or later, which is about 14 percent of the total of such journals in *Ulrich's* that began publication within the last decade. Only 20 English-language, refereed print journals with "chemistry" as part of the subject are reported in *Ulrich's* as having ceased. Similarly, between 2005 and 2010, *Journal Citation Reports* added 74 titles to chemistry categories (analytical applied, inorganic/nuclear, medicinal, multidisciplinary, organic, physical, crystallography, and electrochemistry), which represent 13 percent growth in the number of chemistry titles tracked, with 37 percent growth in the total citable articles. The amount of information available for scientists to read and libraries to acquire is clearly growing.

Subdiscipline growth-trends are also interesting. Medicinal chemistry had the greatest percentage increase in titles (58 percent) and articles (68 percent) tracked since 2005. However, physical chemistry is the largest *JCR* category, both in number of titles and in articles tracked, and it also had the largest number of titles added (16) between 2005 and 2010. *JCR* also indicates physical chemistry had the greatest increase in impact, with 49 percent increase in aggregate impact factor, and 37 percent increase in median impact factor between 2005 and 2010. The *JCR* categories of electrochemistry and multidisciplinary chemistry also had remarkable increases (~45 percent) in aggregate impact factor between 2005 and 2010.

The chemistry journal literature has become more complex, as chemistry research thrives at interfaces with other disciplines. Identification of "chemistry" titles is a challenge. Active, refereed, English-language journals in *Ulrich's* with chemistry subject headings may also have subject headings involving engineering (61 of 550 titles, or 11 percent), physics (122 titles, or 22 percent), biology (42 titles, or 8 percent), or some form of medicine or pharmacy (37 titles, or 7 percent). Similarly, many titles reviewed in this section are found in *JCR* chemistry categories and other categories, including engineering, physics, biology, medicinal, nanoscience, and nanotechnology.

High-cost titles have faced targeted competition, and there are a growing number of open-access titles available, as well as open-access content within traditionally published titles. The American Chemical Society partnered with SPARC to develop *Organic Letters* (1999) and *Crystal Growth and Design* (2001) as alternatives to Elsevier's *Tetrahedron Letters* and *Journal of Crystal Growth,* respectively. *Organic Letters* now ranks well above *Tetrahedron Letters* by *JCR* impact factor. *Crystal Growth and Design* ranks second among crystallography titles by 2010 impact factor. Whether competition has kept prices down is difficult to assess, but the targets have continued publication. The outcome for libraries has been the need to purchase two titles, but the overall benefit to the discipline has been the publication of more research.

During review for the sixteenth edition of *MFL,* I reported that print issues for review were less readily available in libraries, as libraries trimmed costs by eliminating print subscriptions in favor of online packages. Some publishers are now finding the cost of producing print prohibitive. The American Chemical Society now prints most of their titles in a reduced two-pages-per-sheet format, a change implemented since the last edition of *MFL.* Subscribers were also offered incentives to replace print with online access. James Milne, editorial director of the Royal Society of Chemistry, indicated that RSC has "no plans to follow suit" (www.rsc.org/chemistryworld/News/2009/June/22060901.asp, retrieved July 2, 2009).

Much chemistry research is freely available online. Examples include *Aldrichimica Acta, Acta Crystallographica Section E: Structure Reports*

Online, the Beilstein Institute titles, and *Chemistry Central Journal.* Bentham publishes a number of open-access chemistry titles, which are excluded from this section in the wake of a 2009 incident involving another Bentham Open title accepting a "fake" paper, as reported on *The Scientist* news blog at www.the-scientist.com/blog/display/55756 (retrieved June 15, 2009).

Many publishers offer authors the option to pay to open-access articles. In August 2006, ACS introduced "AuthorChoice" to allow authors the option of paying to make their work openly available online. The Royal Society of Chemistry has Open Science; Wiley offers OnlineOpen. The result is access for researchers to at least a subset of chemistry content, whether or not their institutions subscribe. One result of the impact of the open-access movement and ongoing dialogue on scholarly publishing has been more options for authors, and more evident mechanisms for requesting permissions for authors and for readers. Some publishers (e.g., Elsevier, NRC) have partnered with the Copyright Clearance Center and have come to provide contextual "Rightslink" forms on their websites.

Acquisition of packages can be more economical than title-by-title selection in many cases, in some ways rendering reviews of individual titles an anachronistic practice. Licensed online access for institutions is ubiquitous, and is offered in various combinations with and without print. Back files continue to fill in and are typically sold separately. Participation by many major publishers in digital archiving initiatives such as Portico, consortial print-archiving agreements, and the cost of maintaining subscriptions in two formats have, to some degree, quieted objections to canceling print subscriptions.

Online value-added features make electronic journals attractive. Most titles reviewed here offer supplementary information online, including chemical image files, video content, and data sets. The widespread assignment of Digital Object Identifiers (DOIs) to research articles facilitates reference-linking both cited and citing articles. Forward linking may be through proprietary platforms; for example, Elsevier uses *Scopus* to link to citing articles. Nearly all journals reviewed here offer e-mail and RSS alerts of new content and other alerting functionality. Additional "Web 2.0" features, which allow readers to share articles via Facebook, Twitter, and other social networking venues, can now be found on American Chemical Society and Wiley journal sites, but not on those of the Royal Society of Chemistry or Elsevier. The American Chemical Society now offers functionality for mobile devices via ACS Mobile, which is available for various smartphone and tablet platforms.

Other recent developments of interest in chemical information include the 2008 launch of the *SciFinder Web,* and the 2009 acquisition of ChemSpider from its originator Antony Williams by the Royal Society of Chemistry. *SciFinder* is the premier abstracting and indexing service for chemistry, and has long been offered only as a desktop client. The web version has added new functionality and customizable features for users, including an alerting service. From RSC's May 11, 2009, press release, "ChemSpider is a free online service providing a structure[-]centric community for chemists" and is "the richest single source of structure[-]based chemistry information." It was originally developed by Williams and a team of volunteers. The ChemSpider website was relaunched under the RSC brand on its own web domain. This free federated search tool retrieves chemical formulas and structures, reference data and suppliers, patents, article citations, and content from Wikipedia. Web APIs, free to academic users, allow web developers to include ChemSpider searches in their own web services.

Reviewed in this section are 48 titles from 13 publishers, representing general chemistry and four subdisciplines. In annotations, if no mention of DOIs is made, the reviewer found no evidence of DOIs assigned. For more information on DOIs, see www.doi.org. *Journal Citation Reports* for 2007 (Thomson-ISI) was used to gather supporting evidence for inclusion and recommendation of journals; where impact factors and other *JCR* measures are mentioned outside of publisher quotes, they are from this source. OpenURL linking levels are reported from the targets-list compiled and posted by Ex Libris on its website as found in April-June 2009; reporting these data does not constitute endorsement of Ex Libris or its link resolver. Most titles in this section are offered on platforms that are to some degree COUNTER-compliant for some usage reports, based on the list of vendors evaluated against Release 3 of the Code of Practice for Journals and Databases at www.projectcounter.org/compliantvendors.html, accessed May-July 2011. Compliant publishers/vendors in this section include ACS, RSC, Elsevier, Wiley, AIP, Thieme, Nature Publishing Group, and BioMed Central. For detailed information on usage statistics reporting, see www.projectcounter.org/compliantvendors.html.

Basic Periodicals

Ac: *Accounts of Chemical Research, Analytical Chemistry, Chemical Reviews, Inorganic Chemistry, Journal of Chemical Education, The Journal of Organic Chemistry, American Chemical Society. Journal.*

Basic Abstracts and Indexes

Chemical Abstracts; Current Contents/Physical, Chemical, and Earth Sciences; Science Citation Index.

General

1158. *Accounts of Chemical Research.* [ISSN: 0001-4842] 1968. m. USD 1013. Ed(s): Cynthia Burrows. American Chemical Society, 1155 16th St NW, Washington, DC 20036; help@acs.org; http://pubs.acs.org. Illus., index, adv. Sample. Refereed. *Indexed:* A01, A22. *Aud.:* Ac, Sa.

Offers short, readable accounts of "basic research and applications in all areas of chemistry and biochemistry" that "describe current developments, clarify controversies, and link the latest advances with past and future research." One or more thematic special issues come out per year. In 2008, article abstracts were replaced with a conspectus that the publisher claims provides greater detail and improves discovery in online searches; such items are longer than abstracts, and typically include an image. This journal has a 2017 Impact Factor of 20.955. Recommended for academic libraries that support chemistry programs and special libraries.

1159. *American Chemical Society. Journal.* Incorporates (1879-1913): *American Chemical Journal;* (1891-1893): *Journal of Analytical and Applied Chemistry;* Which was formerly (until 1891): *Journal of Analytical Chemistry.* [ISSN: 0002-7863] 1879. w. USD 6101. Ed(s): Peter J Stang, Sonja Krane. American Chemical Society, 1155 16th St NW, Washington, DC 20036; help@acs.org; http://pubs.acs.org. Illus., index, adv. Sample. Refereed. *Indexed:* A01, A22, BRI, S25. *Bk. rev.:* Number and length vary. *Aud.:* Ac, Sa.

The flagship journal of the American Chemical Society is "devoted to the publication of research papers in all fields of chemistry" and publishes articles, communications, and book and software reviews. Most articles are accompanied by online supporting information, which includes text, image, and/or video files. In the 2017 Journal Citation Reports from Clarivate Analytics, the American Chemical Society / Journal recorded its highest-ever Impact Factor at 14.357. Strongly recommended for academic and research libraries that support chemistry programs.

1160. *Angewandte Chemie (International Edition).* Formerly (until 1998): *Angewandte Chemie: International Edition in English.* [ISSN: 1433-7851] 1961. 52x/yr. GBP 10181. Ed(s): Peter Goelitz. Wiley - V C H Verlag GmbH & Co. KGaA, Postfach 101161, Weinheim, 69451, Germany; cs-germany@wiley.com; http://www.vchgroup.de. Illus., index, adv. Sample. Refereed. Vol. ends: Dec. Reprint: PSC. *Indexed:* A01, A22, Agr, BRI, C45. *Bk. rev.:* Typically 1 per issue, signed, 1-2 pages in length. *Aud.:* Ac, Sa.

The *International Edition* is the English translation of the German-language publication of the *Gesellschaft Deutscher Chemiker.* It offers review articles, highlights, communications, news, graphical abstracts, author profiles, and Nobel lectures in chemistry and related fields. Critically selected communications on current research results comprise the majority of content. Graphical abstracts, highlights, reviews, and mini-reviews are also published. This title had a 2017 impact factor of 12.102. Recommended for academic and special libraries that support research in chemistry.

1161. *B M C Chemistry.* Formerly (until 2019): *Chemistry Central Journal;* Which incorporated (2011-2015): *Organic and Medicinal Chemistry Letters.* [ISSN: 2661-801X] 2007. . Free. BioMed Central Ltd., Fl 6, 236 Gray's Inn Rd, London, WC1X 8HB, United Kingdom; info@biomedcentral.com; https://www.biomedcentral.com. Adv. Refereed. *Indexed:* A01, A22, C45, E01. *Aud.:* Ac, Sa.

This title is published independently on the BioMed Central platform, and it covers "research in all areas of chemistry." There are sections for organic, inorganic, physical, biological, analytical, environmental, materials and polymer, and food science chemistry. It offers authors rapid publication in an open-access medium. Authors pay processing charges for publication that are waived if author's institution is a BioMed Central member, or at the discretion of the publisher. It publishes full research articles, preliminary communications, methodology papers, commentary, and software reviews. Occasional supplements with meeting abstracts are published. Recommended for academic and special libraries that support research in chemistry.

ChemComm. See *Chemical Communications.*

1162. *Chemical & Engineering News.* Former titles (until 1942): *American Chemical Society. News Edition;* (until 1940): *Industrial and Engineering Chemistry. News Edition.* [ISSN: 0009-2347] 1923. w. USD 685. Ed(s): Bibiana Campos, Amanda T Yarnell. American Chemical Society, 1155 16th St NW, Washington, DC 20036; help@acs.org; http://pubs.acs.org. Illus., index, adv. *Indexed:* A&ATA, A01, A22, Agr, B01, B03, BRI, C42. *Bk. rev.:* up to 1 per issue, 1-2 pages each, signed. *Aud.:* Ga, Ac, Sa.

A magazine of the American Chemical Society (ACS) that provides international coverage of "science and technology, business and industry, government and policy, education, and employment," with relevance to chemistry in concise, accessible articles. Content includes summarized research reports from chemistry and related disciplines and current events. "News of the Week" highlights news headlines with a chemistry focus, including references to published research. Regular sections address business, education, and government policy. Also included are award announcements and ACS news. Online version includes links to companies, agencies, individuals discussed, and cited research. Recommended for academic libraries that support science curricula, research libraries that support chemists, and larger public libraries.

1163. *Chemical Communications (Print).* Former titles (until 1996): *Chemical Society. Chemical Communications. Journal;* (until 1972): *Chemical Communications;* Which superseded in part (in 1965): *Chemical Society. Proceedings;* Which superseded in part (in 1957): *Chemical Society. Journal;* Which was formerly (until 1924): *Chemical Society. Transactions. Journal;* Which superseded in part (in 1878): *Chemical Society. Journal;* Which was formerly (until 1862): *Chemical Society of London. Quarterly Journal;* (until 1849): *Chemical Society of London. Memoirs and Proceedings;* Which was formed by the merger of (1841-1843): *Chemical Society of London. Memoirs;* (1841-1843): *Chemical Society of London. Proceedings;* Chemical Society. Journal incorporated (1891-1914): *Chemical Society. Proceedings;* Which was formerly (1885-1891): *Chemical Society. Abstracts of the Proceedings.* [ISSN: 1359-7345] 1843. 100x/yr. GBP 3207 combined subscription (print & online eds.); USD 5647 combined subscription (print & online eds.)). Royal Society of Chemistry, Thomas Graham House (290), Science Park, Milton Rd, Cambridge, CB4 0WF, United Kingdom; sales@rsc.org; http://www.rsc.org. Illus., adv. Refereed. *Indexed:* A01, A22, E01. *Aud.:* Ac, Sa.

"The largest publisher of high[-]quality communications within the general chemistry arena." The audience is "academic and industrial chemists in all areas of the chemical sciences." Feature review articles are also published. "Web themed issues on cutting[-]edge areas of chemical research" continue to be published throughout the year, as well as an annual "Emerging Investigator" issue. Now publishes 100 issues per year, which is much more frequent than other journals in this section. Recommended for libraries that support academic and industry chemists and related programs.

1164. *Chemical Reviews.* [ISSN: 0009-2665] 1924. s-m. USD 1880. Ed(s): Sharon Hammes-Schiffer. American Chemical Society, 1155 16th St NW, Washington, DC 20036; help@acs.org; http://pubs.acs.org. Illus., index, adv. Sample. Refereed. *Indexed:* A01, A22. *Aud.:* Ac, Sa.

Provides "comprehensive, authoritative, critical, and readable reviews of important recent research in organic, inorganic, physical, analytical, theoretical, and biological chemistry." Several thematic issues are published annually. This is a core title, ranked first among multidisciplinary chemistry titles by 2017 impact factor. Supporting information (primarily text) for some papers is available online at no charge. Recommended for academic libraries that serve chemistry departments and special libraries.

1165. *Chemical Society Reviews (Print).* Formed by the merger of (1947-1972): *Chemical Society. Quarterly Reviews;* (1968-1972): *Royal Institute of Chemistry. Reviews;* Which was formerly (until 1968): *Royal Institute of Chemistry. Lecture Series;* (until 1961): *Royal Institute of Chemistry. Lectures, Monographs, and Reports.* [ISSN: 0306-0012] 1972. s-m. GBP 1201 combined subscription (print & online eds.); USD 1906 combined subscription (print & online eds.)). Royal Society of Chemistry, Thomas Graham House (290), Science Park, Milton Rd, Cambridge, CB4 0WF, United Kingdom; sales@rsc.org; http://www.rsc.org. Illus., adv. Refereed. *Indexed:* A01, A22, E01. *Aud.:* Ac, Sa.

"Publishes accessible, succinct and reader-friendly articles on topics of current interest in the chemical sciences." This title includes both critical and tutorial reviews, the latter appropriate for advanced undergraduates or researchers new to the field, as well as experts. It publishes articles of social interest, broadening the potential reader base beyond research chemists. It also includes RSC Awards reviews. Guest-edited themed issues are published. It ranks third among multidisciplinary chemistry journals by 2017 impact factor. Recommended for academic and research libraries with chemistry collections.

1166. *Chemistry & Industry.* Incorporates (2001-2006): *In the Loop;* Which was formerly (until 2004): *S C I News;* Formerly (until 1932): *London. Society of Chemical Industry. Review Section. Journal;* Which superseded in part (in 1917): *London. Society of Chemical Industry. Journal;* Which was formerly (until 1882): *London. Society of Chemical Industry. Proceedings.* [ISSN: 0009-3068] 1881. m. Fortnightly until 2012. GBP 806. Ed(s): Neil Eisberg. Wiley-Blackwell Publishing Ltd., The Atrium, Southern Gate, Chichester, PO19 8QG, United Kingdom; cs-journals@wiley.com; http://onlinelibrary.wiley.com/. Illus., adv. Sample. Circ: 5500. Vol. ends: No. 24. Reprint: PSC. *Indexed:* A22, B01, BRI. *Bk. rev.:* 1-5 per issue. Signed. *Aud.:* Ac, Sa.

"A news[-]breaking, topical and international chemistry-based magazine-bridging the gap between scientific innovation and industrial and consumer products." This is a useful current-awareness source for industrial chemists, tailored to industry needs and interests but accessible to a lay audience. Issues feature a number of regular sections including news, business, and commentary. "Highlights" summarize recent published research. Recommended for libraries that support academic and industry chemists.

1167. *Chemistry World.* Formerly (until 2004): *Chemistry in Britain;* Which was formed by the merger of (1957-1965): *Chemical Society. Proceedings;* Which superseded in part (in 1957): *Chemical Society. Journal;* (1950-1965): *Royal Institute of Chemistry. Journal;* Which was formerly (until 1950): *Royal Institute of Chemistry. Journal and Proceedings;* (until 1949): *Royal Institute of Chemistry of Great Britain and Ireland. Journal and Proceedings;* (until 1944): *Institute of Chemistry of Great Britain and Ireland. Journal and Proceedings;* (until 1920): *Institute of Chemistry of Great Britain and Ireland. Proceedings.* [ISSN: 1473-7604] 1965. m. GBP 1006 combined subscription (print & online eds.); USD 1811 combined subscription (print & online eds.)). Royal Society of Chemistry, Thomas Graham House (290), Science Park, Milton Rd, Cambridge, CB4 0WF, United Kingdom; sales@rsc.org; http://www.rsc.org/. Illus., adv. *Indexed:* A&ATA, A22. *Bk. rev.:* 6 or more per month, signed. *Aud.:* Ga, Ac, Sa.

Covers research advances, international business news, and government policy as it affects the chemical science community and product applications. Includes job advertisements. Each issue contains several feature articles on timely or timeless topics related to chemistry, plus news items from current research and an opinion section. This title is an excellent source for current awareness in chemistry and the myriad related disciplines, and it is especially well suited for a broad academic audience that includes undergraduates and seasoned researchers. In January 2011, the Royal Society of Chemistry supplements *Highlights in Chemical Science, Highlights in Chemical Biology,* and *Highlights in Chemical Technology* moved to the *Chemistry World* news page, and are no longer published as separate supplements. Free supplementary content on the web site includes the *Chemistry World* blog. Recommended for academic libraries and research libraries that support chemists, as well as large public libraries.

1168. ***Green Chemistry (Print).*** [ISSN: 1463-9262] 1999. s-m. GBP 2307 combined subscription (print & online eds.); USD 4065 combined subscription (print & online eds.)). Royal Society of Chemistry, Thomas Graham House (290), Science Park, Milton Rd, Cambridge, CB4 0WF, United Kingdom; sales@rsc.org; http://www.rsc.org/. Adv. Refereed. *Indexed:* A01, A22, C45, E01. *Aud.:* Ac, Sa.

Publishes original research "that attempts to reduce the environmental impact of the chemical enterprise by developing a technology base that is inherently non-toxic to living things and the environment." Content is intended to be broadly accessible to chemists and technologists, including upper-level undergraduate students. Original research papers, communications, perspectives, and review articles are published; editorials and news (usually conference news) are also included. Institutional online access is available. Electronic supplementary information for articles is available free of charge and includes text and graphics. Recommended for academic libraries that support chemistry or environmental science curricula and research libraries that support chemists.

1169. ***Journal of Chemical Education.*** Incorporates (1896-1942): *New England Association of Chemistry Teachers. Report.* [ISSN: 0021-9584] 1924. m. USD 255. Ed(s): Norbert J Pienta. American Chemical Society, 1155 16th St NW, Washington, DC 20036; help@acs.org; http://pubs.acs.org. Illus., index, adv. Sample. Refereed. *Indexed:* A&ATA, A01, A22, BRI, CBRI, ERIC, MLA-IB. *Bk. rev.:* One or more book/media reviews per issue. *Aud.:* Hs, Ac, Sa.

"The world's premier chemistry education academic journal." Monthly issues contain "a wide range of interesting articles and activities useful in both the classroom and laboratory." Topical coverage runs the gamut from classroom activities to scholarship of teaching and learning chemistry. True to its mission of supporting education, *JCE* has liberal use policies for print and online content. Highly recommended for academic libraries that support chemistry, chemistry education, or general science education curricula, as well as for high school and middle-school chemistry educators.

1170. ***Journal of Physical and Chemical Reference Data.*** [ISSN: 0047-2689] 1972. q. Ed(s): Donald R Burgess, Allan H Harvey. A I P Publishing LLC, 1305 Walt Whitman Rd, Melville, NY 11747; aipinfo@aip.org; http://www.aip.org. Illus., index, adv. Sample. Refereed. *Indexed:* A22. *Aud.:* Ac, Sa.

Published by the American Institute of Physics (AIP) for the National Institute of Standards and Technology (NIST), this journal has the aim "to provide critically evaluated physical and chemical property data, fully documented as to the original sources and the criteria used for evaluation, preferably with uncertainty analysis." It defines reference data as "the best available values for the relevant properties." Critical reviews of measurement techniques that evaluate available data accuracy may be included. This journal includes contributions that originate from the National Standard Reference Data System (NSRDS) as administered by NIST under the Standard Reference Data Act (Public Law 90-396). Recommended for academic and research libraries that support research in chemistry and related disciplines.

1171. ***Macromolecules.*** [ISSN: 0024-9297] 1968. s-m. USD 5024. Ed(s): Marc Hillmyer. American Chemical Society, 1155 16th St NW, Washington, DC 20036; help@acs.org; http://pubs.acs.org. Illus., index, adv. Sample. Refereed. *Indexed:* A01, A22. *Aud.:* Ac, Sa.

Publishes research on "fundamental aspects of macromolecular science including synthesis, polymerization mechanisms and kinetics, chemical modification, solution/melt/solid-state characteristics, and surface properties of organic, inorganic, and naturally occurring polymers." Comprehensive reports, brief communications, technical notes, and topical reviews (perspectives) are published. Supplementary information is available online at no charge, and includes text, data sets, and image files. Recommended for academic and research libraries that support polymer research.

1172. ***Nano Today: an international rapid reviews journal.*** [ISSN: 1748-0132] 2006. 6x/yr. EUR 1273. Ed(s): J Y Ying. Elsevier Ltd, 125 London Wall, London, EC2Y 5AS, United Kingdom; corporate.sales@elsevier.com; http://www.elsevier.com. Adv. Sample. Refereed. *Aud.:* Ac, Sa.

"Publishes original articles on all aspects of nanoscience and nanotechnology" in the form of review articles, rapid communications, and news and opinions. It has a 2017 Impact Factor of 17.753. Recommended for academic and research libraries that support nanotechnology.

1173. ***Nature Chemistry.*** [ISSN: 1755-4330] 2009. m. EUR 6648. Ed(s): Stuart Cantrill. Nature Publishing Group, The MacMillan Bldg, 4 Crinan St, London, N1 9XW, United Kingdom; nature@nature.com; https://www.nature.com. Illus., adv. Sample. Refereed. *Indexed:* A01. *Bk. rev.:* Approx. 1 per issue. *Aud.:* Ga, Ac, Sa.

A multidisciplinary chemistry journal that publishes primary research, reviews, news and research highlights from other journals, commentary, and "analysis of the broader chemical picture beyond the laboratory, including issues such as education, funding, policy, intellectual property, and the impact chemistry has on society." The publisher claims rapid production and independence from "academic societies and others with vested interests" as advantages for prospective authors. *Journal Citation Reports* data for 2012 ranks it third by impact among multidisciplinary chemistry titles. The publisher's web site hosts supplementary chemical information. Recommended for academic, research, and large public libraries.

1174. ***Pure and Applied Chemistry.*** Formerly: *International Congress of Pure and Applied Chemistry. Lectures.* [ISSN: 0033-4545] 1960. m. EUR 1790. Ed(s): Hugh D Burrows. Walter de Gruyter GmbH, Genthiner Str 13, Berlin, 10785, Germany; service@degruyter.com; https://www.degruyter.de. Illus., index. Sample. Refereed. Vol. ends: Dec. *Indexed:* A&ATA, A01, A22, C45, E01. *Aud.:* Ac, Sa.

The official monthly journal of the International Union of Pure and Applied Chemistry (IUPAC) has "responsibility for publishing works arising from those international scientific events and projects that are sponsored and undertaken by the Union," and is the "designated medium for publication of recommendations, technical reports on standardization, recommended procedures, data compilations, and collaborative studies of IUPAC bodies." It also publishes proceedings of IUPAC-sponsored symposia and other events. Occasional special topic features with submission by invitation are published. All but the "current and most recently completed volumes" are freely available on the IUPAC web site. Authors may immediately "deposit copies of their own articles online" in the "IUPAC published pdf form." Technical reports and recommendations are open access upon publication. Recommended for academic and research libraries that support chemistry programs.

Analytical

1175. ***American Society for Mass Spectrometry. Journal.*** [ISSN: 1044-0305] 1990. 12x/yr. EUR 704 (print & online eds.)). Ed(s): Michael L Gross. Springer New York LLC, 233 Spring St, New York, NY 10013; journals-ny@springer.com; http://link.springer.com. Illus., index, adv. Sample. Refereed. Circ: 5110 Paid. Vol. ends: Dec. Reprint: PSC. *Indexed:* A01, A22, BRI. *Bk. rev.:* Occasionally 1 per issue, length varies, signed. *Aud.:* Ac, Sa.

Covers research on "fundamentals and applications" of mass spectrometry, in the disciplines of "chemistry, physics, geology, and environmental science as well as the biological, health, and life sciences." This title publishes research papers, communications, application notes, signed book reviews, accounts, and perspectives, the latter two typically invited by the editor. Annual society conference proceedings and a society directory are published in supplements. The society transferred the publisher to Springer in 2011. Content is free online after a 12-month embargo; some articles are published open access. Recommended for academic and research libraries that support chemistry programs.

1176. *Analyst (Print).* Incorporates (in 1996): *Analytical Communications;* Which was formerly (until 1996): *Analytical Proceedings;* (until 1980): *Chemical Society. Analytical Division. Proceedings;* (until 1975): *Society for Analytical Chemistry, Analytical Division, Chemical Society. Proceedings;* (until 1972): *Society for Analytical Chemistry. Proceedings.* [ISSN: 0003-2654] 1876. s-m. GBP 2053 combined subscription (print & online eds.); USD 3593 combined subscription (print & online eds.)). Ed(s): Duncan Graham. Royal Society of Chemistry, Thomas Graham House (290), Science Park, Milton Rd, Cambridge, CB4 0WF, United Kingdom; sales@rsc.org; http://www.rsc.org/. Illus., adv. Sample. Refereed. *Indexed:* A&ATA, A01, A22, C45, E01, S25. *Aud.:* Ac, Sa.

Offers "the latest developments in theory and application of analytical and bioanalytical techniques." Publishes urgent communications, full papers, and review articles on "interdisciplinary detection science." The emphasis is on rapid publication-typically 50 days from submission to publication for rapid communications, and 90 days from submission to publication for full articles. Communications may be subsequently featured in *Chemical Science* or *Chemical Technology*. Recommended for academic and research libraries that support chemistry programs.

1177. *Analytica Chimica Acta.* Incorporates: *Analytica Chimica Acta - Computer Technique and Optimization.* [ISSN: 0003-2670] 1947. 48x/yr. EUR 14394. Ed(s): R P Baldwin, L Buydens. Elsevier BV, Radarweg 29, Amsterdam, 1043 NX, Netherlands; info@elsevier.com; https://www.elsevier.com/. Illus., index, adv. Sample. Refereed. Microform: PQC. *Indexed:* A01, A22, C45, S25. *Aud.:* Ac, Sa.

"Provides a forum for the rapid publication of original research, and critical reviews dealing with all aspects of fundamental and applied modern analytical science." The emphasis is on innovative methodologies, rather than application of existing methods to new systems. Reviews and invited articles are published. Special issues may feature proceedings from conferences or workshops. Recommended for libraries that support analytical chemistry research programs.

1178. *Analytical Chemistry.* Formerly (until 1948): *Industrial and Engineering Chemistry. Analytical Edition;* Which superseded in part (in 1929): *Industrial & Engineering Chemistry;* Which was formerly (until 1923): *The Journal of Industrial and Engineering Chemistry.* [ISSN: 0003-2700] 1909. s-m. USD 2651. Ed(s): Jonathan Sweedler. American Chemical Society, 1155 16th St NW, Washington, DC 20036; help@acs.org; http://pubs.acs.org. Illus., index, adv. Sample. Refereed. *Indexed:* A01, A22, BRI, C45, S25. *Aud.:* Ac, Sa.

"Concerned with measuring important chemical things," this title publishes research on analytical theory or "any phase of analytical measurements and concepts thereof." Included in this journal are features, letters, news articles, and product reviews of interest to analytical chemists, in addition to accelerated and regular research articles and technical notes. Supporting information for some papers is available online. Recommended for academic libraries that support chemistry and related curricula.

***Biosensors and Bioelectronics*. See Biotechnology section.**

1179. *Journal of Applied Crystallography (Online).* [ISSN: 1600-5767] 1968. bi-m. GBP 851. Ed(s): S S Hasnain. Wiley-Blackwell Publishing Ltd., The Atrium, Southern Gate, Chichester, PO19 8QG, United Kingdom; cs-journals@wiley.com; http://onlinelibrary.wiley.com. Refereed. *Aud.:* Ac, Sa.

Publishes research in crystallographic methods and their "use in identifying structural and diffusion-controlled phase transformations, structure-property relationships, structural changes of defects, interfaces[,] and surfaces," as well as instrumentation and crystallographic apparatus development, theory and interpretation, and numerical analysis. Supplementary content accompanies articles, including three-dimensional images. Recommended for academic and research libraries that support chemistry programs.

1180. *Journal of Chromatography A.* Incorporates (1959-1971): *Chromatographic Reviews;* Supersedes (in 1958): *Chromatographic Methods.* [ISSN: 0021-9673] 1956. 52x/yr. EUR 17563. Ed(s): J G Dorsey, C F Poole. Elsevier BV, Radarweg 29, Amsterdam, 1043 NX, Netherlands; info@elsevier.com; https://www.elsevier.com/. Illus., index, adv. Refereed. Microform: PQC. *Indexed:* A01, A22, Agr, C45. *Aud.:* Ac, Sa.

Publishes "original research and critical reviews on all aspects of fundamental and applied separation science." Published here are primarily full-length research papers, but some short communications, discussions, technical notes, and invited review articles are also included. Articles are arranged by technique. Occasional symposium volumes are published. Its audience comprises analytical chemists, biochemists, clinical chemists, and others who are "concerned with the separation and identification of mixtures or compounds in mixtures."

Inorganic

1181. *Coordination Chemistry Reviews.* [ISSN: 0010-8545] 1966. 24x/yr. EUR 10632. Ed(s): Dr. A B P Lever. Elsevier BV, Radarweg 29, Amsterdam, 1043 NX, Netherlands; info@elsevier.com; https://www.elsevier.com/. Illus., adv. Refereed. Vol. ends: No. 206 - No. 223. Microform: PQC. *Indexed:* A01, A22. *Aud.:* Ac, Sa.

This journal "[o]ffers rapid publication of review articles on topics of current interest and importance in coordination chemistry," which is interpreted broadly to include organometallic, theoretical, and bioinorganic chemistry. Themed special issues are published. Issues may also be dedicated to conference proceedings. This title had a 2017 Impact Factor of 14.499. Issues are combined in pairs, so that only 12 pieces are published each year. The audience comprises inorganic and organometallic chemists. Recommended for academic and research libraries that support research in coordination chemistry.

1182. *Inorganic Chemistry: including bioinorganic chemistry.* [ISSN: 0020-1669] 1962. s-m. USD 5019. Ed(s): William B Tolman, Tamara Hanna. American Chemical Society, 1155 16th St NW, Washington, DC 20036; help@acs.org; http://pubs.acs.org. Illus., index, adv. Sample. Refereed. *Indexed:* A01, A22, BRI. *Aud.:* Ac, Sa.

Publishes "experimental and theoretical reports on quantitative studies of structure and thermodynamics, kinetics, mechanisms of inorganic reactions, bioinorganic chemistry, and relevant aspects of organometallic chemistry, solid-state phenomena, and chemical bonding theory. Emphasis is placed on the synthesis, structure, thermodynamics, reactivity, spectroscopy, and bonding properties of significant new and known compounds." Brief communications, full articles, and invited award addresses are published. Each year, up to three thematic forum issues are published on a "multidisciplinary topic of growing interest." Supplementary information for some papers, including text and images, is available online at no charge. A core title for academic and research libraries that support chemistry programs.

1183. *Inorganica Chimica Acta: the international inorganic chemistry journal.* Incorporates: *Chimica Acta Reviews.* [ISSN: 0020-1693] 1967. 15x/yr. EUR 6729. Ed(s): J M Smith, U Belluco. Elsevier BV, Radarweg 29, Amsterdam, 1043 NX, Netherlands; info@elsevier.com; https://www.elsevier.com/. Illus., index, adv. Sample. Refereed. Microform: PQC. *Indexed:* A01, A22. *Aud.:* Ac, Sa.

Publishes "research in all aspects of inorganic chemistry" in the form of full research articles, short research reports (notes), and regular reviews. Frequent "Protagonists in Chemistry" special issues provide profiles of researchers and collections of appropriately themed articles to honor them. Recommended for libraries that support research programs in inorganic chemistry.

1184. *Organometallics.* [ISSN: 0276-7333] 1982. s-m. USD 4730. Ed(s): Paul J Chirik. American Chemical Society, 1155 16th St NW, Washington, DC 20036; help@acs.org; http://pubs.acs.org. Illus., index, adv. Sample. Refereed. *Indexed:* A01, A22. *Aud.:* Ac, Sa.

This journal records advances in organometallic, inorganic, organic, and materials chemistry. It covers "synthesis, structure, bonding, chemical reactivity and reaction mechanisms, and applications of organometallic and organometalloidal compounds." *Organometallics* publishes communications, mini-reviews, notes, and correspondence. Supporting information for some papers is available online at no charge, and includes text and images. Recommended for libraries that support research programs in organometallic, inorganic, organic, and materials chemistry.

Organic

1185. *Aldrichimica Acta.* Supersedes: *Kardinex Sheets.* [ISSN: 0002-5100] 1967. q. Free. Ed(s): Sharbil J Firsan. Aldrich, Sigma-Aldrich Corporation, 6000 N Teutonia Ave, Milwaukee, WI 53209; aldrich@sial.com; http://www.sigma-aldrich.com. Illus., adv. Sample. *Indexed:* A22. *Aud.:* Ac, Sa.

Publishes review articles on chemistry research written by chemists. Issues are typically thematic, "usually...involving organic, organometallic, bio-organic, or inorganic chemistry." The title began as a marketing tool for Aldrich, and it boasts the highest impact factor of organic chemistry titles for nine of the past ten years. Issues are available online at no charge. That and the fact that articles are all extensive reviews may account for the high impact of the title relative to other titles in its subcategory. Note that articles are not parsed on the online platform; each issue is offered as a single file. Recommended for academic and special libraries that support work in pure and applied chemistry.

1186. *Bioconjugate Chemistry.* [ISSN: 1043-1802] 1990. m. USD 1612. Ed(s): Vincent M Rotello, Ranjini Prithviraj. American Chemical Society, 1155 16th St NW, Washington, DC 20036; help@acs.org; http://pubs.acs.org. Adv. Sample. Refereed. *Indexed:* A22. *Aud.:* Ac, Sa.

Publishes articles, reviews, communications, technical notes, and comments on all aspects of the joining of different molecular functions by chemical or biological means. Recommended for libraries that support research or related programs in biochemistry and organic chemistry.

1187. *Biomacromolecules.* [ISSN: 1525-7797] 2000. m. USD 2426. Ed(s): Ann-Christine Albertsson. American Chemical Society, 1155 16th St NW, Washington, DC 20036; help@acs.org; http://pubs.acs.org. Adv. Sample. Refereed. *Indexed:* A01, A22. *Aud.:* Ac, Sa.

Publishes "interdisciplinary investigations exploring the interactions of macromolecules with biological systems and their environments[,] as well as biological approaches to the design of polymeric materials." Research articles comprise most of the content, but critical reviews, brief communications, and notes are also published. This journal had an SJR of 1.950 in 2017. Recommended for libraries that support polymer research or related programs in organic chemistry.

1188. *The Journal of Organic Chemistry.* [ISSN: 0022-3263] 1936. s-m. USD 4127. Ed(s): Scott Miller. American Chemical Society, 1155 16th St NW, Washington, DC 20036; help@acs.org; http://pubs.acs.org. Illus., index, adv. Sample. Refereed. Vol. ends: Dec. *Indexed:* A01, A22, BRI. *Aud.:* Ac, Sa.

Publishes "novel, important findings of fundamental research in all branches of the theory and practice of organic and bioorganic chemistry," in full articles, notes, and perspectives. This title publishes "Brief Communications" of preliminary results that have warranted "immediate disclosure," and short reviews of current topics called "*JOC*Synopses," in addition to "Articles," "Notes," and "Perspectives." Supplementary information, including text and image files, is offered online. A core title for the subdiscipline, it is recommended for academic libraries that support graduate chemistry programs.

1189. *Natural Product Reports (Print).* Formed by the merger of (1971-1984): *Biosynthesis;* (1970-1984): *The Alkalois;* (1969-1984): *Terpenoids and Steroids;* (1977-1984): *Aliphatic and Related Natural Product Chemistry;* Which superseded in part (in 1977): *Aliphatic Chemistry;* (in 1974): *Aliphatic, Alicyclic, and Saturated Heterocylic Chemistry. Part I. Aliphatic Chemistry.* [ISSN: 0265-0568] 1984. m. GBP 1125 combined subscription (print & online eds.); USD 1979 combined subscription (print & online eds.)). Royal Society of Chemistry, Thomas Graham House (290), Science Park, Milton Rd, Cambridge, CB4 0WF, United Kingdom; sales@rsc.org; http://www.rsc.org/. Adv. Refereed. *Indexed:* A01, A22, Agr, E01. *Aud.:* Ac, Sa.

Primarily publishes reviews on "natural products research including isolation, structural and sterochemical determination, biosynthesis, biological activity and synthesis." This title includes review articles, shorter highlight articles, viewpoint articles, and hot-off-the-press articles. It has a 2017 impact factor of 11.406. Recommended for academic and research libraries that support organic chemistry research.

1190. *Organic Letters.* [ISSN: 1523-7060] 1999. s-m. USD 6484. Ed(s): Erick Carreira. American Chemical Society, 1155 16th St NW, Washington, DC 20036; help@acs.org; http://pubs.acs.org. Adv. Sample. Refereed. *Indexed:* A01, A22. *Aud.:* Ac, Sa.

Publishes brief reports of research on organic chemistry, organometallic and materials chemistry, physical and theoretical organic chemistry, natural products isolation and synthesis, new synthetic methodology, and bio-organic and medicinal chemistry. The emphasis is on rapid communication of research. Established in 1999 as a Scholarly Publishing and Academic Resource Coalition (SPARC) alternative to Elsevier's *Tetrahedron Letters.* It should be noted that *Tetrahedron Letters* costs thousands of dollars more than *Organic Letters.* However, major research institutions now likely subscribe to both titles. Supporting information, including text and image files, is available online at no charge. Recommended for academic and research libraries that support organic chemistry research.

1191. *Tetrahedron: the international journal for the rapid publication of full original research papers and critical reviews in organic chemistry.* [ISSN: 0040-4020] 1957. 52x/yr. EUR 12618. Pergamon Press, The Blvd, Langford Ln, E Park, Kidlington, OX5 1GB, United Kingdom; JournalsCustomerServiceEMEA@elsevier.com; http://www.elsevier.com. Illus., adv. Sample. Refereed. Microform: MIM; PQC. *Indexed:* A01, A22, C45. *Aud.:* Ac, Sa.

Publishes experimental and theoretical research in "organic chemistry and its application to related disciplines, especially bio-organic chemistry." Its specific topical coverage includes organic synthesis, organic reactions, natural products chemistry, reaction mechanism, and spectroscopy. It publishes full research papers, commissioned critical reviews ("Tetrahedron Reports"), and "Tetrahedron Symposia-in-print." Other features include *Tetrahedron* Young Investigator Award papers. It is widely accepted as a core title and is recommended for libraries that support substantial research programs in organic or bio-organic chemistry.

Physical

1192. *A C S Nano.* [ISSN: 1936-0851] 2007. m. USD 2126 domestic; USD 2330 foreign. Ed(s): Paul S Weiss, Heather Tierney. American Chemical Society, 1155 16th St NW, Washington, DC 20036; help@acs.org; http://pubs.acs.org. Adv. Sample. Refereed. *Aud.:* Ac, Sa.

This title "[p]ublishes comprehensive articles on synthesis, assembly, characterization, theory, and simulation of nanostructures (nanomaterials and assemblies, nanodevices, and self-assembled structures), nanobiotechnology, nanofabrication, methods and tools for nanoscience and nanotechnology, and self- and directed-assembly." Research articles, reviews, perspectives, and "conversations" with leading researchers in this emerging discipline are included. Most articles are accompanied by online supporting information, which includes text, image, and/or video files. Recommended for academic and research libraries.

Advanced Materials. See Engineering and Technology/Materials Engineering section.

1193. *Chemistry of Materials.* [ISSN: 0897-4756] 1989. s-m. USD 2688. Ed(s): Jillian M Buriak, Carlos Toro. American Chemical Society, 1155 16th St NW, Washington, DC 20036; help@acs.org; http://pubs.acs.org. Illus., index, adv. Sample. Refereed. *Indexed:* A01, A22. *Aud.:* Ac, Sa.

Publishes "fundamental research at the interface of chemistry, chemical engineering, and materials science," including "theoretical and experimental studies which focus on the preparation or understanding of materials with unusual or useful properties." Solid-state inorganic and organic chemistry, polymer materials, biomaterials, nanomaterials, coatings, thin films, and more are covered. Typical issues offer full articles and short communications. Occasional thematic issues are published. Supporting information for some papers is available online at no charge. Recommended for academic and research libraries that support materials-related research across a range of disciplines.

Journal of Catalysis. See Engineering and Technology/Chemical Engineering section.

Journal of the American Society for Mass Spectrometry. See *American Society for Mass Spectrometry. Journal* under Chemistry/Analytical section.

1194. *Langmuir: the A C S journal of surfaces and colloids.* [ISSN: 0743-7463] 1985. w. USD 6736. Ed(s): Francoise Winnik. American Chemical Society, 1155 16th St NW, Washington, DC 20036; help@acs.org; http://pubs.acs.org. Illus., index, adv. Sample. Refereed. *Indexed:* A01, A22. *Aud.:* Ac, Sa.

Publishes research on surfactants and self-assembly, dispersions, emulsions, foams, adsorption, reactions, films, forces, biocolloids, biomolecular and biomimetic materials, nano- and meso-structured materials, polymers, gels, liquid crystals, interfacial charge transfer, charge transport, electrocatalysis, electrokinetic phenomena, bioelectrochemistry, sensors, fluidics, patterning, catalysis, and photonic crystals. This journal's issues offer brief letters and full articles, the latter arranged into topical categories: materials, colloids, electrochemistry, interfaces, biological interfaces, and devices and applications. Recommended for academic and research libraries that support research in physical chemistry.

1195. *Nano Letters.* [ISSN: 1530-6984] 2001. m. USD 2415. Ed(s): Charles M Lieber, A Paul Alivisatos. American Chemical Society, 1155 16th St NW, Washington, DC 20036; help@acs.org; http://pubs.acs.org. Adv. Sample. Refereed. *Indexed:* A01, A22. *Aud.:* Ac, Sa.

"Reports on fundamental research in all branches of the theory and practice of nanoscience and nanotechnology." This title has ranked in the top eight titles in six different *JCR* subject categories based on impact factor, including multidisciplinary chemistry (eighth) and physical chemistry (fifth). Recommended for academic and research libraries that support research in physical chemistry.

Nature Materials. See Engineering and Technology/Materials Engineering section.

1196. *Physical Chemistry Chemical Physics.* Formed by the merger of (1991-1999): *Berichte der Bunsen-Gesellschaft;* Which was formerly (until 1991): *Berichte der Bunsengesellschaft fur Physikalische Chemie;* (until 1963): *Zeitschrift fuer Elektrochemie;* (1904-1952): *Zeitschrift fuer Elektrochemie und Angewandte Physikalische Chemie;* (1990-1999): *Chemical Society. Faraday Transactions. Journal;* Which was formed by the merger of (1972-1990): *Chemical Society. Faraday Transactions I. Journal;* (1972-1990): *Chemical Society. Faraday Transactions II. Journal;* Which incorporated (1972-1984): *Chemical Society. Faraday Symposia;* Which was formerly (until 1972): *Faraday Society. Symposia;* Both Faraday Transactions I. Journal and Faraday Transactions II. Journal superseded in part (in 1972): *Faraday Society. Transactions.* [ISSN: 1463-9076] 1999. 48x/yr. GBP 4837 combined subscription (print & online eds.); USD 8522 combined subscription (print & online eds.)). Ed(s): Seong Keun Kim. Royal Society of Chemistry, Thomas Graham House (290), Science Park, Milton Rd, Cambridge, CB4 0WF, United Kingdom; sales@rsc.org; http://www.rsc.org. Illus., adv. Refereed. *Indexed:* A22, E01. *Aud.:* Ac, Sa.

Publishes rapid communications, invited articles, and research papers on topics at the interface of physics and chemistry, including biophysical chemistry. This title's coverage includes "spectroscopy, dynamics, kinetics, statistical mechanics, thermodynamics, electrochemistry, catalysis, surface science, quantum mechanics, and theoretical developments." Frequent themed issues are published. The publisher claims this is "the fastest physical chemistry journal," with submission-to-publication time of less than 80 days. It is run by an ownership board with equal representation from 16 societies, mostly European and none North American. Recommended for academic and research libraries that support physical chemistry research.

■ CHILDREN

See also Classroom Magazines; Parenting; and Teenagers sections.

Lynn Wallace, MLIS, Library Director, OSU-Tulsa Library, 700 N. Greenwood, Tulsa, OK 74146; lynn.wallace@okstate.edu

Introduction

Children's magazines provide as many choices as adult magazines, from lifestyle entertainment to serious historical and scientific subject magazines, and each reach out and engage young audiences from birth to age 14.

Magazines for children with strong content and engaging layout help to bridge the practical with the developmental: understanding the world around them; connecting with and enjoying stories and experiences of other people; learning about animals; building self-concept, social understanding, and sometimes just simply being entertained on an appropriate emotional and social level; as well as enhancing and enriching today's STEAM curriculum.

Magazines for children purposefully provide specific recurring departments that help beginning and advanced readers have a sense of familiarity with each issue and include appropriate skill development activities. The best children's magazines support the development of children into creative, critical thinkers who embrace and become "thinkers, changers and makers" within the world.

Several general-interest publishers are now providing three content-tiered magazine titles for the infant and toddler, the early beginning elementary reader, and the independent upper-elementary reader. Equally important is the inclusion of both fiction and nonfiction titles for the lower- and upper-elementary reader to enhance literacy quality and experience. Printing, writing, illustration, and photograph quality varies, but excellence in the overall product guides decision for inclusion.

Fully digitized diverse magazine subscription packages or title-by-title selection options are becoming more common in libraries with available budgetary funds. Digital versions now have an advantage by allowing multiple children access via a printer to those pencil-activity-heavy activities, puzzles, and games.

The breadth of serials available for children is endless, so there are some specific exclusions that are not being included title by title: heavy pop-culture, television, product, and movie-character-based magazines. Exclusion of these is not to say they have no redeeming quality, since they do have literacy building, entertaining, and educational contents, but each title is specific to the fans of that product or character and some, like "Daniel Tiger Neighborhood," are award winners. Redan Publishing (American), DC Thomson & Co. Ltd., Kennedy Publishers, and Egmont Publishers (British) have the most titles in this category and strive to provide a great interactive product, especially for those children obsessed by a certain character; these magazines can be considered a gateway to other publications. English titles are exclusively included, but for the library that does serve a multi-lingual clientele, there are children's publications that are of high quality, like the Spanish titled *Chicos, Caracola,* and *Muy Interesante Junior.* Many more international products like *Tinkle* are available in multiple languages, but are not included here for brevity.

Also not included are highly consumable serials like activity and puzzle books; magazines that show extreme bias; titles that have no basis in fact; web sites that claim to be serialized; individual sport or game titles; and those magazines that serve specific groups or population needs like *Hearing Our Way,* which serves the young deaf community.

In addition, magazines that have an unclear status or that were unable to be vetted, and those regionally focused publications, could not be included due to space constraints. There are a number of good-quality faith-based magazines for different religions that are not being included as well. Examples being *Shine Brightly, Sparkle,* and *Kol Hat'nua.*

There has been a stabilization in the titles available since the last edition. A wealth of returning publications that at their core provide pleasant, informative, entertaining, and challenging content are described based on their most current issues. There are a number of British titles included in this edition because of the high quality and uniqueness of content, and while there is additional cost to American libraries for shipping, these titles are worth considering for inclusion in collections.

As society evolves one can see patterns of new or shifting titles and content enhancing the market by focusing on specific lifestyles such as *Military Kids' Life*; building happiness like *Anorak*; DIY content that focuses on STEM projects from *Beanz*; titles focusing on nutrition and combating obesity in *ChopChop*, *Ingredient*, and *Butternut*. A handful of girl empowerment magazines focus on re-establishing empowerment of girls: *Girls' World* and *Kazoo*, which do not contain sexualized images or content. The trend toward a large market of quality girl magazines however, has created an unbalanced and untapped need for boy-centric titles that address the same types of self-concept content. Representational images in magazines including diversity in photographs, illustrations, and stories are starting to evolve as well.

Only publications serving readers ages 0-14 are covered in this section; for readers after age 14, please refer to the "Teenagers" section of this volume. Several of the inclusions in this section are wonderful publications to incorporate in libraries, classrooms, or homeschooling curricula covering literature, math, geography, social studies, biographies, STEM concepts, consumer information, health, art, music, and creative writing.

Magazines included seek to entertain, teach, explore the world, provide practice of skill sets, allow for intellectual inquiry, and hopefully nurture a generation to be kind, creative, informed, and engaged. With shrinking library budgets and so many titles from which to choose, it is our hope that these annotations have enough accurate and relevant information to provide a starting point for the selection process.

Basic Periodicals

Ask, Babybug, Boys' Life, Chickadee, Chirp, Click, Cobblestone, Cricket, Dig into History, Faces, Fun for Kidz, Highlights for Children, Highlights High Five, Ladybug, Muse, National Geographic Kids, National Geographic Little Kids, Owl, Ranger Rick, Spider, Sports Illustrated for Kids.

Basic Abstracts and Indexes

MAS Ultra: School Edition, Middle Search, Primary Search, Readers' Guide to Periodical Literature.

1197. ***Adventure Box.*** [ISSN: 1366-9001] 1995. 10x/yr. GBP 50 domestic; GBP 73 in the European Union; GBP 79 elsewhere. Ed(s): Simona Sideri. Bayard Presse, 18 Rue Barbes, Montrouge, 82128, France; redactions@bayard-presse.com; http://www.bayard-jeunesse.com. Illus., adv. Sample. *Aud.:* 6-9 yrs.

Small (5 1/2 x 7 1/2 inches) but substantial in content and intent, *Adventure Box* is an attractive and inviting publication for boys and girls alike. With sturdy front and back covers, full-color illustrated pages, and a glued spine, this publication mimics actual beginning chapter books. The main focus of the magazine is the multi-chapter story (approximately 40-45 pages) that varies in writing style and genre (realistic, fantasy, and adventure) with each issue. A recurring department of "Naturebox," which explores the world of nature (animals, insects, plants, and so on), provides full-color photographs and information. Educational games, puzzles, a comic strip, a write-in contest, and, lastly, a back-cover reading comprehension mini-quiz round out the issue. For American readers, please note that there is a tiny sprinkling of British spelling of words such as *colour* and *mum*, but overall, this is a solid magazine for newly independent readers. A subscription is available two ways: the magazine alone or, for an extra price, the magazine with an accompanying CD for read alongs. For educators, the web site provides value-added classroom guides. This is a Parents' Choice Recommended Title. Recommended for public libraries and school libraries.

1198. ***Animal Tales (Englewood Cliffs).*** [ISSN: 2373-8278] 2014. bi-m. USD 29 domestic; USD 35 Canada; USD 41 elsewhere. Ed(s): Brittany Galla. Bauer Publishing, Inc., 270 Sylvan Ave, Englewood Cliffs, NJ 07632; http://www.bauerpublishing.com/. Illus., adv. *Aud.:* Ems, Ga.

An animal "lifestyle" magazine highlighting domestic and wild animals of all sort, this unique title provides stylistically bright, cheerful, glossy-page, rich-looking content that girls will probably find more appealing than boys. Content includes plenty of pull-out animal posters, news and facts, adorable and silly photography, a fiction story, quizzes, pet care, hero pet stories, reader drawings, and contests in each issue. Pull-out posters include unique animal poses and adorable photography, but since animals are not identified the reader may not recognize the animal in the poster. Not like other more serious educational wildlife titles, *Animal Tales* presents animals from more of a "lifestyle" viewpoint, by giving some animal information to the young pet owner, and overviews of wild animals. *Animal Tales* does have advertisements and some doubles as actual content. This title keeps a web site for contest entries and polls. Appropriate for individual subscribers and very large public libraries.

1199. ***Aquila: big ideas for inquisitive kids.*** [ISSN: 0965-4003] 1994. m. GBP 55 domestic; GBP 60 in Europe; GBP 70 elsewhere. Ed(s): Anji Anstey-Holroyd, Freya Hardy. New Leaf Publishing Ltd, Studio 2, 67A Willowfield Rd, Eastbourne, BN22 8AP, United Kingdom; office@aquila.co.uk. Illus., adv. Sample. *Aud.:* 8-13 yrs.

This oversized, thematically based monthly publication is intended to "expand well beyond the school curriculum." Math, science, art, and history are incorporated into the wide range of themes each month. They provide a creative table of contents that will entice new readers and unique illustrations make the pages leap out for interaction. Each theme is handled differently with very few regular column areas, which adds for a unique experience. Most entries open in the two-page spread and are colorfully illustrated. Included are art projects, fiction writing, jokes, experiments, quizzes, and games to enhance the theme. This magazine will appeal to those gifted students who are highly engaged in extracurricular learning. The wording is dense throughout the magazine, but it is frequently broken up by call-out boxes, different fonts and styles of writing, illustrations, and text boxes. There is an "Over to You" page for reader's write-ins. Their online presence includes Facebook and Twitter. Recommended for public libraries and school libraries.

1200. ***Ask: arts & sciences for kids.*** Incorporates (1998-2015): *Appleseeds*. [ISSN: 1535-4105] 2002. 9x/yr. USD 33.95 domestic; CAD 48.95 Canada; USD 39.95 combined subscription domestic (print & online eds.)). Cricket Media, Inc., 7926 Jones Branch Dr, Ste 870, McLean, VA 22102; support@cricketmedia.com; www.cricketmedia.com. Illus., adv. Sample. *Indexed:* P01. *Aud.:* 6-9 yrs.

Ask: arts & sciences for kids is an engaging nonfiction magazine that seeks to cover thematic topics and explore a wide range of topics including technology, science, nature, the human body, and cultures. *Ask* is for the younger elementary reader with nonfiction articles, engaging photographs, helpful illustrations, and maps that enhance demonstrated facts and interesting news about the subject. Integral to the content layout is Marvin, the cartoon raccoon who along with his regular cartoon friends provide comic relief, pose additional questions, and help simplify complex information. Regular departments include the comic "Nestor's Dock" and "Nosy News," a short news section. *Ask* has no advertisements, general arts and crafts, fiction stories, and puzzles and games. Use of photographs and quirky cartoon illustrations are inviting and youthful. Digital subscriptions are available across multiple platforms and teacher's guides are available online. This is a Parent's Choice Gold Award winner for multiple years running. Highly recommended for personal subscriptions, school libraries, classroom subscriptions, and public libraries.

1201. ***Babybug.*** [ISSN: 1077-1131] 1994. 9x/yr. USD 33.95. Cricket Media, Inc., 70 E. Lake St Ste. 800, Chicago, IL 60601; support@cricketmedia.com; www.cricketmedia.com. Illus., adv. Sample. Vol. ends: Nov/Dec. *Aud.:* 0-3 yrs.

This beginner's magazine is the perfect start to engage in pre-emergent literacy activities with children birth to preschool by reading aloud, acting out, and following activity guides available. This small, sturdy, water-resistant magazine provides rounded corners, non-toxic ink and no staples, for a safe reading experience time and again. Predictable sections in each issue include the illustrated story of "Kim and Carrots"; exploring the world around us in "Let's Explore"; and "First Concepts," which introduces age-appropriate subjects like shapes, colors, and counting. Original, adapted and classic poems, action and nursery rhymes, songs, and seek-and-finds round out this little booklet-like magazine. The inside-back cover provides a "Guide to Caregivers" with tips, activities, and child-development information. Digital subscriptions and individual issues are available across multiple platforms. This is a Parent's Choice Gold Award winner for multiple years. Recommended for early childhood resource libraries and public libraries.

1202. ***Bazoof!*** Formerly (until 2016): *Zamoof.* [ISSN: 2369-6389] 2007. bi-m. CAD 29.95 in US & Canada; KHR 39 elsewhere. Dream Wave Publishing, Inc., 1879 2nd Ave West, Vancouver, BC V6J 1J1, Canada; mail@zamoofmag.com; http://zamoofmag.com/. Adv. *Aud.:* Ems; 7-12 yrs.

This Canadian publication, *Bazoof!*, focuses on articles, activities, and stories that promote a whole person exploring personal care, nutrition, fitness, character development, and more. The magazine is loosely set in the "metropolis on the Planet GLAK," and some pages are set in the main town on the planet. The entire magazine has a very inviting comic-book feel in layout and coloring, and boasts pencil-friendly paper. The departments have smartly edited background pages, short-paragraph story bits, and a large number of overlaid side panels. While this is a general magazine, its styling gives it a more boy-oriented feel, but girls will enjoy the magazine as well. Recently launched is a companion magazine, *AbaJub*, that is completely online and interactive with clickable images taking you to different content areas. Digital subscriptions are available across all platforms. There is a social media, blog, and web presence for *Bazoof!*. For public libraries that want to include a kid-friendly, healthy-lifestyle title.

1203. ***Beanz.*** Formerly (until 2017): *Kids, Code and Computer Science.* [ISSN: 2573-3958] 2013. bi-m. USD 29.99 combined subscription domestic print & online eds.; USD 35 combined subscription elsewhere print & online eds. Ed(s): Tim Slavin. Owl Hill Media, LLC, 378 Eastwood Rd., Woodmere, NY 11598; hello@kidscodecs.com. Sample. *Bk. rev.:* Number and length vary. *Aud.:* Ems, Ga.

Undergoing a name change in 2017, "Beanz" was chosen as the title because of its use in coding language to mean "reusable bits of code" that are applied to create new applications. This magazine fills a gap in the STEM market, focusing on varied aspects and skills needed in computer science: math skills, computer language, coding, and computer engineering. The magazine up front may be intimidating for novices; however, readers can begin to understand subject matter once they dig into the links and tutorials offered online. Articles discuss the history of computers and computer components, fun projects, binary number projects, computer language, and coding tutorials for the beginning and experienced computer student. Also included are specific tutorial instructions utilizing the latest hardware and software available. The news section and reviews of board games, robots, books, and apps are timely and relevant. This is a Parent's Choice Silver Award winner. Digital subscription is available on multiple platforms. Recommended for personal subscriptions, school libraries, computer science classrooms, and public libraries.

1204. ***Boys' Life: the magazine for all boys.*** [ISSN: 0006-8608] 1911. m. USD 24 combined subscription domestic (print & online eds.); USD 45 combined subscription foreign (print & online eds.)). Ed(s): Michael Goldman. Boy Scouts of America, 1325 W. Walnut Hill Ln, PO Box 152079, Irving, TX 75015; http://www.bsa.scouting.org. Illus. Microform: NBI; PQC. *Indexed:* A22, BRI, C37, MASUSE, P01. *Bk. rev.:* Number and length vary. *Aud.:* 8-18 yrs.

Published by the Boy Scouts of America since 1911, this is the quintessential outdoor boy's magazine, which publishes two split publications for two different age ranges. Both magazines have the same design elements. For ages 6-10, the language is simpler, with comic strips, feature articles that interest younger scouts, and several pages of youthful games, brain teasers, and puzzles. For ages 11-18, the content is aimed at older Boy Scouts, such as westward-bound adventures, holding down a job, taking trips, and a fiction story. These monthly issues are packed with comics, faith-based stories, fitness tips, social issues, real-life Boy Scout stories, popular games, sports, reviews of books and movies. There are areas in each magazine that are more Boy Scout-centric, such as "Merit Badge Minute," which helps boys complete tasks needed to earn certain merit badges, and "Scouting Around," which highlights a variety of atypical scouting adventures. Each issue has a workshop section with instructions and equipment lists for building projects, but the degree of difference in difficulty between the two publications is noticeable. Several, but not all, of the articles will interest non-scouting boys, but the real appeal is for the boy who is interested in the scouting, outdoor, or adventure lifestyle. Some commercial and Boy Scout-specific advertisements are found throughout the magazine. The highly engaging, interactive web site has its own features, games, and photos. The publications also keep an active social media presence across multiple platforms. Digital subscriptions are available across most devices. Recommended for personal subscriptions, public libraries, and Boy Scouts.

1205. ***Brainspace: where great young minds go to grow.*** [ISSN: 2291-8930] 2013. q. CAD 24 domestic; CAD 33 United States; CAD 60 elsewhere. Brainspace Publishing Inc., 394 Ontario St, Newmarket, ON L3Y 2K4, Canada; brainspacemagazine@bell.net; http://www.brainspacemagazine.com/. *Aud.:* Ga.

Incorporating "Blippar" app technology to make the pages come alive on a mobile device, *Brainscape* is an augmented reality publication for children, merging the print with digital content for added value. The magazine, published in Canada, can be enjoyed even without the app technology; however, while the digital natives will thrive using the additional content via a smart device, those without access to proper technology will not have equal access, especially with the new feature that requires the application to access the content, although there are only four back pages in some issues that have a few pages. *Brainspace* has a broad appeal to those bright or gifted children who thrive on learning at more of an in-depth level. Subjects span science, math, language, botany, money management, space, history (not human social history), geology, French, and random facts, with the additional content on the app. Science experiments suggested can typically be done with items around the house, and the magazine has additional video content for help. Working through the magazine front to back, readers may have the sense they are going from one class in school to another with each subject, so it lends itself well for the homeschooling community. Print subscriptions are best due to the incorporation of the "Blippar" app. Additional downloadable content is available on the title's web page for all of children, parents, and educators. Recommended for personal subscriptions, school libraries, and public libraries with appropriate technology support.

1206. ***Chickadee.*** [ISSN: 0707-4611] 1979. 10x/yr. Ed(s): Mandy Ng. Bayard Canada, Owlkids, 10 Lower Spadina Ave, Ste 400, Toronto, ON M5V 2Z2, Canada; bayard@owl.on.ca; http://www.owlkids.com/. Illus., index, adv. Sample. Vol. ends: Dec. *Indexed:* BRI, C37, P01. *Bk. rev.:* Number and length vary. *Aud.:* 6-9 yrs.

This is a magazine for the younger elementary student, which is jammed with a variety of news articles, comic stories, nonfiction and fiction pieces to delight those in grades 1-3. Each issue starts with a one-page "Chick and DEE" comic, in which the two namesake comic characters join their friends in some comic relief, and ends with "Mish and Mash," which is full of jokes and tongue twisters. An animal of the month is featured, with vibrant pictures, facts, and an accompanying puzzle or activity page. While some standard maze and hide-and-seek puzzles are included, several of the games and puzzles are original in design and can't be found in other publications for this age range. Factual information blurbs, a book or movie review, and articles round out *ChickaDEE.* This title is a Parent's Choice Gold Award winner. Recommended for personal subscriptions, school libraries, and public libraries.

1207. ***ChildArt.*** [ISSN: 1096-9020] 1998. q. USD 30 domestic; USD 40 foreign. Ed(s): Ashfaq Ishaq. International Child Art Foundation, PO Box 58133, Washington, DC 20037; http://www.icaf.org/. Adv. Sample. *Indexed:* BRI, P01. *Aud.:* 8-12 yrs.

The International Child Art Foundation, a nonprofit organization, works at engaging children in the arts with its programming, research, hosting a world festival, and by publishing a unique academic type magazine. *ChildArt,* published quarterly, is geared toward the seriously innovative and creative pre-teen child seeking depth of the creations of art and its role and use in society. Guest editors are masters of their individual craft providing overview of subjects like architecture, color, and design. Articles highlight one subsection of the theme, including in-depth interviews, dissections of the topic, and examples of projects to try. Each issue is published on quality paper with normal layout with stunning photography and art pieces. Sample issues are available for download at the magazine's web page. Print and electronic subscriptions are available, and the foundation has a large social media presence across platforms. An appropriate title for arts education facilities, schools, and public libraries.

1208. ***Chirp.*** Formerly: *Tree House.* [ISSN: 1206-4580] 1992. 10x/yr. CAD 34.95 in US & Canada; CAD 64.95 foreign. Ed(s): Jackie Farquhar. Bayard Canada, Owlkids, 10 Lower Spadina Ave, Ste 400, Toronto, ON M5V 2Z2, Canada; bayard@owl.on.ca; http://www.owlkids.com/. Illus. Sample. *Bk. rev.:* Number and length vary. *Aud.:* 3-6 yrs.

Touted as "The See and Do, Laugh and Learn Magazine," this little pre-school title provides young beginning readers tools to start to read independently. Chirp, the little mascot, is featured in a very short, easy-to-follow comic. Content throughout is multi-leveled to appeal to the varying skill levels. Included is a three- to four-page fiction story or poem for a great read aloud. Other simple, short-sentence, and rebus stories for those pre-reader children provide a reading bridge. Printed on consumable newsprint paper, the games, arts and crafts, cutouts, and physical-activity suggestions provide high interaction with content. The "Playhouse" section has monthly contests, with prizes for reader-contributed items. Skills for practice include counting, sequencing, fine motor skills, language development, gross motor skills, and sight-word recognition. Libraries should expect a large amount of pencil marks throughout this very inviting publication. A parent's advisory board and child experts help establish the content guidelines. A large web site presence for both parent and child is available, with a "Family Literacy Blog" and a "Chirp Blog." This is a frequent Parent's Choice Gold Award winner. Highly recommended for personal subscriptions, school libraries, and public libraries.

1209. ***ChopChop: the fun cooking magazine for families.*** [ISSN: 2169-0987] 2010. q. USD 16.95. Ed(s): Catherine Newman. ChopChopKids, 32 Calvin Rd, Watertown, MA 02472; http://www.chopchopmag.org. *Aud.:* Ems, Ga.

A children's cooking magazine that promotes learning to cook with an adult. Each issue provides several recipes focusing on healthy, real ingredients as a way to combat childhood obesity. The recipes are typically seasonal and come with clear instructions. Design of the magazine includes crisp scrumptious photos that will make readers hungry if not curious about new foods just paging through each issue. Other non-recipe food topics include interviews with chefs and those leading healthy lifestyles, food safety, cooking vocabulary, and food science. Parents will want to help their children with completing some of the recipes included for safety and proper technique. Some of the recipes may not appeal to the general child eater, but rather to a "foodie." A frequent Parent's Choice Gold Award winner, the magazine is endorsed by the American Academy of Pediatrics and is guided by a nutrition advisory board. Highly recommended for school and public libraries.

Cicada. See Teenagers section.

1210. ***Click: opening windows for young minds.*** [ISSN: 1094-4273] 1998. 9x/yr. USD 33.95 domestic; USD 48.95 foreign. Ed(s): Amy Tao. Cricket Media, Inc., 70 E. Lake St Ste. 800, Chicago, IL 60601; support@cricketmedia.com; www.cricketmedia.com. Illus., adv. Sample. Vol. ends: Dec. *Indexed:* P01. *Aud.:* 3-6 yrs.

A visually appealing, informational pre-school magazine, *Click* provides readers a way to become inquisitive and knowledgeable with each unique monthly topic. Topics are covered with a variety of fiction stories, articles, a tear-out activity, and comics. "Click" and "Jane," comic characters at the beginning of each issue, learn about the month's theme. Illustrations are whimsical, and vocabulary and sentence structure are age-appropriate. "Click" and her friends are then sprinkled throughout the magazine and sometimes help clarify information. Most nonfiction pieces provide various aspects of the subject and are simple enough to understand, and include effective photographs. A tear-out game section on the back cover provides the child with a thematic game or activity to play, and provides skill practice with scissors instead of the typical pencil-to-paper activity pages and without damage to the rest of the issue. This is a Parent's Choice Gold Award winner for multiple years. Highly recommended as a standard title in early childhood center libraries and school libraries, for personal subscriptions, and for public libraries.

1211. ***Cobblestone: discover American history.*** [ISSN: 0199-5197] 1980. 9x/yr. USD 33.95 domestic; USD 48.95 foreign. Ed(s): Meg Chorlian. Cricket Media, Inc., 70 E. Lake St Ste. 800, Chicago, IL 60601; support@cricketmedia.com; www.cricketmedia.com. Illus., index. Sample. Vol. ends: Dec. *Indexed:* A22, BRI, MASUSE, P01. *Bk. rev.:* 10, length varies. *Aud.:* 9-14 yrs.

This American history-focused children's magazine delves deep into myriad very specific thematic issues, topics, and periods in our rich history. A consulting expert editor is chosen to help steer each issue exploring a single, highly focused topic. Themes can include a social cause, a type of industry, a single historical event, natural resources, a specific decade, politics and government, a specific region and any other relevant issue in America's past, present, or future. Content includes biographies of key historical figures, pivotal moments, facts and figures, and multiple photographs. A department of note includes "Going Global," which compares cultures. *Cobblestone* doesn't shy away from difficult topics and issues and provides factual non-biased coverage. This magazine contains no advertisements, and a digital subscription is available across multiple platforms. This is a Parent's Choice Gold Award winner. Highly recommended to public and school libraries for inclusion.

1212. ***Cousteau Kids.*** Formerly (until 2004): *Dolphin Log.* [ISSN: 1946-7133] 19??. q. Individuals, USD 30. Cousteau Society, Inc., Greeley Sq. Station, 4 E 27th St, PO Box 20321, New York, NY 10001; communication@cousteau.org; http://www.cousteau.org. Illus. *Indexed:* A22. *Aud.:* Ems, Ga.

The Cousteau Society publishes a slim quarterly magazine to promote love of all things aquatic. The nonprofit organization provides educational information in this 20-page, over-sized, glossy-paper publication. Each thematically driven issue provides readers an inside look at fascinating underwater creatures, their behavior, and their habitat. The design layout is fresh, with ample space between photography and informational vignettes. Cute design elements are incorporated throughout, like the starfish-outlined page numbers. Regular content departments include "Creature Feature," focusing on a specific underwater animal, and "Sea Queries," which provides answers to burning questions. The Cousteau Society focuses on ecological conservation and content reflects this mission. A crossword or word-search puzzle with relevant vocabulary is included. Appropriate for personal subscriptions, school libraries, public libraries, or classroom subscriptions.

1213. ***Cricket: the realm of imagination.*** [ISSN: 0090-6034] 1973. 9x/yr. Ed(s): Lonnie Plecha. Cricket Media, Inc., 70 E. Lake St Ste. 800, Chicago, IL 60601; support@cricketmedia.com; www.cricketmedia.com. Illus., adv. Sample. Vol. ends: Jul/Aug. *Indexed:* A22, P01. *Aud.:* 9-14 yrs.

A substantive literary experience for the oldest child reader, 9-14 years old. *Cricket* has been the best in the field for decades. This highly glossy-page magazine touts a very well respected editorial board of academics, authors, illustrators, and children's literature specialists. Each issue is filled with a good mix of multi-cultural poetry, science fiction, folk tales, fantasy, historical and contemporary fiction, and highly researched nonfiction pieces. Some fiction pieces are multiple pages, and run serially spanning several issues. Regular features include "The Letterbox," which prints two full pages of reader letters; "Cricket Country," a graphical story; and the closing, "Old Cricket Says," which imparts wisdom on a topic. "Cricket League" presents recurring contests for fiction story, photo, and poetry. The ever-present cartoon cricket characters chatter in the margins, explaining concepts and vocabulary to the reader. *Cricket* has been a Parent's Choice Gold Award winner for several years. Highly recommended as a standard inclusion for school and public libraries.

1214. ***Curious Jane Magazine.*** [ISSN: 2572-3863] 2014. q. USD 38. Ed(s): Samantha Razook. Curious Jane, 400 3rd Ave, Brooklyn, NY 11215; info@curiousjanecamp.com; https://www.curiousjanecamp.com. *Aud.:* Ems.

A new project-based magazine, "Curious Jane Magazine" delivers DIY inventive content specifically marketed toward the creative and active girl. Creator and editor Samantha Razook developed the quarterly publication as an outgrowth of the Curious Jane Summer Camps held in New York each summer. Each issue is filled with just DIY projects that promote invention, engineering, science, design, and group projects and there are no advertisements. Each project comes with a "maker checklist," step by step instructions with pictures and illustrations, as well as a "Fun Fact." Issues are thematic and include different types of projects including paper to pencil activities, creating games, crafts, and science experiments. Materials needed to complete each project vary from household items like baking soda and food ingredients to potentially budget restrictive and difficult to source consumables like copper wire and convex glass lenses. Appropriate for large public libraries with DIY programming and large girls groups like Girl Scouts.

1215. ***Dig into History.*** Former titles (until 2015): *Dig;* (until 2001): *Archaeology's Dig.* 1999. 9x/yr. USD 33.95 domestic; USD 48.95 foreign. Ed(s): Rosalie Baker. Cricket Media, Inc., 70 E. Lake St Ste. 800, Chicago, IL 60601; support@cricketmedia.com; www.cricketmedia.com. Illus. Sample. Vol. ends: Nov/Dec. *Indexed:* BRI, P01. *Bk. rev.:* 3-5, 20-40 words. *Aud.:* 9-14 yrs.

This serial incorporates world history, archaeology, and anthropology. Contributing scholars and consulting editors provide thoroughly researched articles and labeled artifact photographs. Controversial or sensitive topics like Islam in history and Syria today after civil war provide factual, non-biased information. "Ask Away," answers children's questions about archaeology and history. The section "Let's Go Dig-ging" highlights current and historical archaeology research and discovery. This publication is advertisement- and pop-culture free, and should appeal to both boys and girls with its enjoyable layout. This is a Parent's Choice Gold Award winner for multiple years. Highly recommended for school libraries, public libraries, and personal subscriptions.

1216. ***Discovery Box.*** [ISSN: 1366-9028] 1995. 10x/yr. EUR 72 in Europe; EUR 79 elsewhere; GBP 50 United Kingdom. Ed(s): Simona Sideri. Bayard Presse, 18 Rue Barbes, Montrouge, 82128, France; redactions@bayard-presse.com; http://www.bayard-jeunesse.com. Illus., adv. Sample. *Aud.:* 9-12 yrs.

This British publication provides an over-sized magazine focused on science, nature, history, and human interests. Each thematic issue includes double-page illustrations, with word call-outs to identify parts of the illustration, photographs, comic stories, diverse writing styles, well-researched articles, and wide-ranging content. The layout and design of this publication is innovative, with great visual appeal, but standard contents can be disjointed and unrelated to the chosen theme. Experiments, games, jokes, pet care, and a comprehension quiz round out this sister publication to *Storybox* and *Adventure Box.* Several different topics are covered issue to issue, with no advertisements to distract. Appropriate for personal subscriptions, school libraries, and public libraries.

1217. ***Discovery Girls: a magazine created by girls, for girls.*** [ISSN: 1535-3230] 2000. bi-m. USD 22.95 domestic. Ed(s): Sarah Verney. Discovery Girls, 445 S San Antonio Rd, Ste 205, Los Altos, CA 94022. Illus., adv. Vol. ends: Oct. *Bk. rev.:* Number and length vary. *Aud.:* 8-13 yrs.

This bimonthly magazine is specifically geared toward pre-teen ("tween") girls. The readers of *Discovery Girls* are featured in photo shoots, fashion spreads, hair design, and biographical sketches, all age-appropriate. An advice column called "Ask Ali" gives relevant advice on fashion, boys, parents, school, diet, exercise, and many other typical concerns for this age range. Articles, polls, information on relationships, health, beauty, fashion, trends, decorating, school, and many other issues important to today's young busy girl are in each issue. The magazine digs a little deeper than a typical lifestyle magazine, but it is American in focus. The content addresses important issues of girl's changing bodies, embarrassing moments, and difficulties with relationships. There are a few advertisements in this magazine, including self-promotion of girl guides that the publisher produces. Available across multiple platforms. Appropriate for public libraries and personal subscriptions.

1218. ***Dot: think and play.*** [ISSN: 2057-5025] 2015. q. GBP 20 domestic; GBP 26 in US & Canada; GBP 28 elsewhere. Studio Anorak, Unit L/M, Reliance Wharf, 2-10 Hertford Rd, London, N1 5EW, United Kingdom; press@anorakmagazine.com; http://www.anorakmagazine.com. *Aud.:* 1-5 yrs.

Dot is a general-interest variety magazine that is unique in its focus on being the "happy mag for preschoolers." Published quarterly, each issue has a theme such as "Jobs," "Food," and "Woodlands," and the contents throughout each issue focuses its activities and stories to the theme. Drawing activities, traditional rhymes, comic pages, relevant activity pages, some fiction stories, a craft with instructions, and a variety of coloring and drawing prompts is standard. The most notable feature that sets *Dot* apart from its companion older magazine, *Anorak,* is the engaging art and graphic design under the guidance of the art director and featuring a number of different artists. The art is perfect for preschoolers with simplistic illustrations and vibrant colors. Pages vary between sparse drawings to very busy pages with plenty of content to absorb. Stiff paper and a slightly smaller than normal size makes the magazine feel more substantial. This title is filled with original developed content that celebrates the innocence of puddle jumping and the intelligence of resourceful young children. Recommended for large public libraries.

1219. ***Eco Kids Planet.*** [ISSN: 2056-5437] 2014. m. Individuals, GBP 36. Eco Kids Planet, 41 Claremont Rd, Barnet, EN4 0HR, United Kingdom; hello@ecokidsplanet.co.uk; http://www.ecokidsplanet.co.uk/. *Aud.:* Ems, Ga.

This monthly magazine has been quickly gaining large respect in the children's magazine publishing world. *Eco Kids Planet* stands out by focusing on special ecological topics around the globe. This over-sized, thick, recycled and biodegradable, glossy-paged magazine boasts 34 pages focused on the animals, terrain, conservation efforts, and cultural studies related to a different eco-system each month. The magazine's layout and design, illustrations, and photography engage each reader with vocabulary, fun facts, and scientific information. The cartoon figure "Eco Planet Kids" guides the reader through diaries, interviews, and projects; and the title includes several pages of puzzles, games, and activities. A detailed, illustrated pull-out paper map of the region is included. Since the magazine is published in the United Kingdom, occasional British spellings of words or unfamiliar phrases can be found. This title has international appeal, even with the extra postage cost. Sets of back issues are available for bulk purchase. Highly recommended for school libraries, homeschoolers, and science and geography classrooms, as well as public libraries.

1220. ***Faces: people, places, and cultures.*** Formerly: *Faces Rocks.* [ISSN: 0749-1387] 1984. 9x/yr. USD 33.95 domestic; USD 48.95 foreign. Ed(s): Elizabeth Crooker. Cricket Media, Inc., 70 E. Lake St Ste. 800, Chicago, IL 60601; support@cricketmedia.com; www.cricketmedia.com. Illus., index. *Indexed:* A22, BRI, MASUSE, P01. *Bk. rev.:* 1. *Aud.:* 9-14 yrs.

Specifically published for readers 9-14 years old, *Faces: people, places, and cultures,* strives toward the best of anthropology and culture studies with geography and social issues, literature and history, combined into one issue. Topics include culture, customs, food, architecture, politics, history, fiction stories or plays, art, music, foreign language, science, local habitat, animals, and a glimpse into youth of the area. *Faces* includes informational articles, fiction, photography, folklore, activities, and illustrations. Commonalities that exist around the world are highlighted effectively. Articles vary in length, and excellent eye-catching photography helps spur readers to understand better. The regular department "High Five" at the beginning of each issue provides five simple facts to know about the topic. The layout of the magazine is very crisp and refreshing. The magazine boasts a large academic and subject-specialist advisory board. Teacher resources are available on the title's web page. This has been a Parent's Choice Gold Award winner for multiple years. Highly recommended for school libraries, geography classrooms, and public libraries.

1221. ***Fun for Kidz.*** Incorporates (1989-201?): *Hopscotch;* (1995-201?): *Boys' Quest.* [ISSN: 1536-898X] 2002. bi-m. USD 32.95 domestic; USD 50.59 Canada; USD 70.45 elsewhere. Ed(s): Marilyn Edwards. Bluffton News Publishing & Printing Co., 103 N Main St, Bluffton, OH 45817-0164. *Indexed:* BRI, C37, P01. *Aud.:* Ems, 5-12 yrs.

Fun for Kidz, a bimonthly gender-neutral magazine, is filled with stories, games, puzzles, crafts, and projects. The title, 30 pages in length, includes full-color and numerous illustrations, and some photographic content. Each issue features a stand-alone topic, with articles enhancing the issue's theme, including a multi-page comic strip, poetry, a variety puzzle page, factual reporting, and fiction stories. Sections such as "Science" are consistent issue to issue. Some nice features are the thorough table of contents, puzzle solutions, and age-appropriate fiction. The "Riding with Max & Grace" page, about two golden retrievers who travel around America, is simple, but endearing. The intent of the magazine is to "encourage literacy and reading comprehension." Back issues are available for purchase from the publisher, as are the out-of-print *Hopscotch for Girls* and *Boy's Quest*. Recommended for public libraries, homeschoolers, and personal subscriptions.

1222. *Fun to Learn - Friends (American Edition).* Formerly (until 2010): *Fun to Learn - Playroom;* (until 2001): *Preschool Playroom.* [ISSN: 2155-5818] 2001. 6x/yr. USD 27.50. Redan Publishing, Inc., 1115 Inman Ave. Ste 123, Edison, NJ 08820; customerservice@redan.com; http://www.redan.com. Illus., adv. *Aud.:* Ems.

Preschool children's most recognizable and favorite television and book characters come together to create a familiar and fun, highly consumable pre-school magazine. "Curious George," "Max and Ruby," "PJMasks," "Peppa Pig," and more, create the main content pages including a rebus story, a sequentially numbered story, and plenty of pencil seat work to help the pre-literate with counting, coloring, matching, and letters. Famous children's stories such as "The Ugly Duckling" or "Elmer the Elephant" are featured at the end of the magazine. Redan publishes a large number of pencil-friendly pulp-paper magazines including these character-specific titles: "Marvel Super Heroes," "Paw Patrol," "Barbie," "Disney Jr.," "Thomas & Friends," "Scooby-Doo!," "Disney Frozen," "Peppa Pig," "Disney Junior," "Sparkle World," "Disney Princess," and "Ultimate Spider-Man." Best for personal subscriptions due to how consumable the pages are, but also appropriate for public libraries and early childhood centers.

Girls' Life. See Teenagers section.

1223. *Girls' World.* [ISSN: 2332-4511] 2013. 7x/yr. USD 31.50 domestic; USD 37.50 Canada; USD 43.50 elsewhere. Ed(s): Brittany Galla. Bauer Publishing, Inc., 270 Sylvan Ave, Englewood Cliffs, NJ 07632; http://www.bauerpublishing.com/. Illus., adv. *Aud.:* Ems, Ga.

An introductory "lifestyle" magazine for young elementary and middle-school readers, *Girls' World* combines young celebrities and American homogeneous lifestyle content. This glossy, bright, over-sized-format magazine is full of advice, quizzes, animals, fiction, and nonfiction writing and games. The "Express Yourself" section provides reader-submitted artwork. Crafts, quizzes, pencil activities, and lifestyle tips are featured prominently in between longer article content. All of the photographs provide a mostly age-appropriate image of multicultural girls, as well as their favorite young stars of today. Several full-page, pull-out posters are splattered throughout. Simple advertisements are placed throughout the magazine and mimic real content. This title's web page provides small interactive content for "Freebies, Polls, and Artwork." Appropriate for personal subscriptions and large public libraries.

1224. *Highlights for Children.* Incorporates (1953-1960): *Children's Activities;* Which was formerly (until 1953): *Children's Activities for Home and School.* [ISSN: 0018-165X] 1946. m. Ed(s): Christine French Cully. Highlights for Children, Inc., 1800 Watermark Dr, Columbus, OH 43216; http://www.highlights.com. Illus., index. Vol. ends: Dec. Microform: PQC. *Indexed:* A22, BRI, P01. *Aud.:* 6-12 yrs.

Highlights has been the standard in children's magazines for more than 70 years, and continues to be a strong publication today. With the beloved "Goofus and Gallant" and "Puzzles," this magazine continues producing high-quality stories, nonfiction articles, crafts, and pencil activities, all on pencil-friendly paper. Science, animals, history, and culture are covered in both fiction and nonfiction articles. "Your Own Pages" feature reader-submitted poems, jokes, and art. "Dear Highlights," at the back of each issue, provides real-life advice on homework, friendship, and a variety of other life issues. The magazine's 42 pages is packed with visuals and text, and standard departments. Illustrations and stories do include a much more multicultural, yet wholesome, view of the world. Interactive material is in the kids section of the title's web page, while there are also very robust sections for parents and teachers. For those who love the hidden picture-puzzles, *Highlights for Children* produces a monthly "club" magazine that is extremely consumable as well. Due to its high quality and popularity, this publication should be a requirement for public libraries, and is highly recommended for school libraries.

1225. *Highlights Hello.* [ISSN: 2166-0514] 2013. m. USD 39.96 domestic; USD 57.08 Canada; USD 49.44 elsewhere. Highlights for Children, Inc., 1800 Watermark Dr, PO Box 269, Columbus, OH 43216; eds@highlights.com; http://www.highlights.com. *Indexed:* P01. *Aud.:* 0-2 yrs.

An infant and toddler magazine, *Highlights Hello* is specifically published for the youngest of audiences, 0-2 years. This title has an updated design with large pictures, rounded corners, durable pages, and a safely stitched seam. Content begins with an engaging "Hello" and ends with a real child photo and the endearing "bye-bye." Sections are labeled with colorful corner indicators breaking pages into reliable sections including "story, song, poem, puzzle and silly." Each issue helps the caregiver share the joy of reading, and gives toddlers realistic glimpses of the world around them and supports language-acquisition skills. Adult interactive suggestions are included right on the page in a smaller font. An interactive web page has child-development articles for the parent. Highly recommended for early childhood center libraries, personal subscriptions, and public libraries where appropriate.

1226. *Highlights High Five: celebrating early childhood.* [ISSN: 1943-1465] 2007. m. USD 48 combined subscription domestic (print & online eds.); USD 57.08 combined subscription Canada (print & online eds.); USD 65.16 combined subscription elsewhere (print & online eds.)). Ed(s): Christine French Cully. Highlights for Children, Inc., 1800 Watermark Dr, Columbus, OH 43216; eds@highlights.com; http://www.highlights.com. Illus. Sample. *Indexed:* P01. *Aud.:* 2-6 yrs.

This sister publication of *Highlights* provides pre-emergent skills to the preschool audience, and is one of the top preschool magazines published. Its "fun with purpose" mission is to provide pre-reading, math, and other skills necessary in preparation of entering school. "Spot" the dog is always in the first set of pages, in a very simple comic. Three content areas dispersed throughout each issue are: "Reading," providing brief fiction and nonfiction stories and poems with recognizable, repeated characters; "Puzzles," providing the famous hidden pictures, matching games, and silly pages; and "Activities," which consists of crafts, physical activities, and simple food recipes for healthy eating. Regularly, there is a read-aloud story in English and Spanish, which includes some Spanish vocabulary. On the back page, there is one more matching game and a look-and-find game to get the student back into the issue. The *Highlights* family of magazines has introduced a companion magazine titled *High Five Bilingue,* which provides the same great content but one half of the magazine is completely in Spanish and then the content repeats in English. The web page provides downloadable age-appropriate apps, a podcast, a parent's guide, and an educator's guide. Highly recommended as a standard for personal subscriptions, the homeschooler, early-childhood education libraries, school libraries, and public libraries.

1227. *Humpty Dumpty Magazine.* Formerly (until 1979): *Humpty Dumpty's Magazine for Little Children.* [ISSN: 0273-7590] 1952. bi-m. USD 29.94 domestic; USD 39.94 elsewhere. Ed(s): Steven Slon. Children's Better Health Institute, 1100 Waterway Blvd, Indianapolis, IN 46202; editor@saturdayeveningpost.com; http://www.uskidsmags.com. Illus., index, adv. Vol. ends: Dec. Microform: PQC. *Indexed:* A22, BRI, P01. *Aud.:* 2-6 yrs.

Humpty Dumpty provides content for a large-ranged demographic (ages 2-6). This magazine is non-sequentially broken into three separate areas - labeled as "Read," "See," and "Do." Familiar friends "Ted, Ed and Caroll" appear in a new story in each issue. Crafts, pencil puzzles, and games are included, and some require scissors, as in their cut, draw, play features, but it will disturb the content on the reverse side of the page. A reader-submitted art and picture area provides for reader-submitted interaction. Advice from the title's health editor comes in "4-ever Fit," which teaches children about physical activity. The "Let's Draw" section provides step-by-step instructions to allow children the chance to practice drawing skills. The magazine does provide for the entire demographic in contents, which might not fit the entire targeted age range really well, both in reading level and in interest level, but adult interaction with the magazine may help bridge the gap for younger children. Appropriate for personal subscriptions and public libraries.

1228. ***Jack and Jill.*** [ISSN: 0021-3829] 1938. bi-m. USD 29.94 domestic; USD 39.94 elsewhere. Ed(s): Steven Slon. Children's Better Health Institute, 1100 Waterway Blvd, Indianapolis, IN 46202; editor@saturdayeveningpost.com; http://www.uskidsmags.com. Illus., adv. Microform: PQC. *Indexed:* A22, BRI, MASUSE, P01. *Bk. rev.:* Number and length vary. *Aud.:* 6-12 yrs.

This magazine "promotes the healthy physical, educational, creative, social and emotional growth" of elementary school boys and girls. *Jack and Jill* magazine is printed on pulp paper for easy pencil to paper activities, and has revamped some of its content for its 80-year anniversary. "Forever Fit" section provides advice on exercise, nutrition, and family health tips. "Let's Grow" provides gardening information for the beginner. The "Safety" section provides reporting on children's current concerns like bullying and football safety. Also included are several page fiction and non-fiction stories, interactive quizzes, recipes, crafts, reader-submitted drawings, poems, and pet pictures. Content is very similar to the publisher's younger offering, *Humpty Dumpty,* making fans of the younger magazine look forward to graduating to this title. Prepare to have these magazines marked up by enthusiastic children. Appropriate for personal subscriptions and public libraries.

1229. ***Kayak: Canada's history for kids.*** [ISSN: 1712-3984] 2004. q. CAD 14.95 domestic; CAD 19.95 United States; CAD 24.95 elsewhere. Canada's National History Society, Bryce Hall, Main Fl, 515 Portage Ave, Winnipeg, MB R3B 2E9, Canada; memberservices@canadashistory.ca; http://www.historysociety.ca. Illus. Sample. *Indexed:* C37, P01. *Aud.:* 7-11 yrs.

Kayak: Canada's History for Kids introduces children to Canada's rich history, natural resources, and notable citizens. The magazine reports on a variety of time periods, geographic locations, historical retrospectives, and cultural heritage. Notable Canadian citizens and their achievements are featured, and celebrates Canadian culture and diversity, which gives children an appreciation of their own country's values and history. A multi-page comic written by Alex Diochon overtly tackles racism and racial history and provides didactic glimpses of this part of Canada's history without sugar coating events. Each issue includes word games, puzzles, jokes, fun facts, and contests. A tiny bit of advertising is included. Recommended for Canadian public libraries and bordering states in North America.

1230. ***Kazoo.*** 2016. q. USD 50 domestic; USD 65 Canada; USD 78 elsewhere. Ed(s): Erin Bried. Kazoo Media LLC, PO Box 150274, Brooklyn, NY 11215. *Aud.:* 5-10 yrs.

Kazoo is for "girls who aren't afraid to make some noise" and joins the other girl-centric magazine offerings that help to empower the next generation of women to develop skills and talents without barriers of gender. Specifically geared toward 5-10 year-old girls, content of this variety magazine includes thematic representations of concepts. "Small but Mighty" focuses on how one little change whether ecological, social, or personal in the world can make a big difference in impacting the world in a positive way. Content is delivered through comic stories, one-page vignettes, question-and-answer pages, the content of the pencil seat work activities, along with fiction and non-fiction pieces written by famous authors. Editors intentionally include information and seek expert submissions from strong women in science, literature, leadership, artistry, and more. Currently this magazine is only available via a print subscription. Recommended to large public library systems.

1231. ***Ladybug: the magazine for young children.*** [ISSN: 1051-4961] 1990. 9x/yr. USD 33.95 combined subscription domestic (print & online eds.); USD 48.95 combined subscription foreign (print & online eds.)). Ed(s): James M O'Connor. Cricket Media, Inc., 70 E. Lake St Ste. 800, Chicago, IL 60601; support@cricketmedia.com; www.cricketmedia.com. Illus., adv. Sample. Vol. ends: Aug. *Indexed:* P01. *Aud.:* 3-6 yrs.

This glossy, full-sized, 35-page magazine for very young children provides an introduction to stories, songs, and poetry. Well-known children's writers and artists provide quality stories and illustrations. Included in every issue is a song with the musical score; "I Spy" and other pencil puzzles; crafts and activities. The magazine provides the emergent reader a simply written and illustrated short adventure story, while other longer stories are written and meant for story time by caregivers. High-quality poetry and traditional rhymes break up the stories in the magazine. Stories can include fiction, nonfiction, fantasy, and cartoons, and a recurring "Ladybug, Muddle & Thud" round out the magazine toward the back of each issue. Special activity tear-out pages at the back involve an interactive learning activity. Ladybug and friends, who are cartoon characters, are placed throughout each issue to provide predictability. This has been a Parent's Choice Gold Award winner for multiple years. Highly recommended as a standard for early-childhood school libraries, school libraries, personal subscriptions, and public libraries.

1232. ***Magic Dragon: presenting young writers and artists.*** 2005. q. USD 22 domestic; USD 29 Canada. Ed(s): Patricia Roesch. Association for Encouragement of Children's Creativity, PO Box 687, Webster, NY 14580; http://www.magicdragonmagazine.com/. Illus., adv. Vol. ends: Fall. *Aud.:* Ems, Ga.

Art and writing comprise a great creative expression for children. This publication "presents writing and art created by children 12 years old and younger," with the purpose of "encouraging creative thinking and expression in young children." *Magic Dragon* prints a large amount of full-color and three-dimensional art pieces intermixed with the writing submissions, on a heavy matte paper stock. There are "How To's" and "Write It" instructions in both art and writing pieces, to encourage the reader to continue to explore the craft and create. Art is visually stimulating and not always perfect, which is a great representation of the fact that art is not ever perfect. Most featured art pieces are gathered from the Northeast part of the United States. Contributors' names, ages, and locations are printed next to the published pieces, and contributors are all ages from 6 to 12. There is a Facebook page that also publishes works. Subscriptions can be for one or two years, or single issues can be purchased. Discounted classroom subscriptions are available. Recommended for public libraries and schools committed to art programs.

1233. ***Military Kids' Life.*** [ISSN: 2378-5470] 2015. q. USD 18.95. Chameleon Kids, LLC, 8 Sloop Hill Rd, New Windsor, NY 12553; info@chameleonkids.com; http://www.chameleonkids.com/. *Aud.:* Ems.

A special population of children, who sometimes get overlooked, now has an entire magazine devoted to its different life experiences. *Military Kids' Life* strives to encourage military children to look at the fun/bright side of their sometimes unpredictable lives by providing tips, information, ideas, activities, puzzles, and stories to which they will relate. This publication is independent from any branch of the U.S. government and does not discuss war, violence, politics, or the dangerous side of military life. Instead, it focuses on travel, moving, making friends, going to a new school, trying new foods, and becoming the best person you can strive to become. Biographical sketches of successful adults who were traveling military kids, or of current kids living in a foreign country, or of pets around the globe, help personalize the common experience. Several articles are written by military children. Graphic design layout for this magazine is eye-catching, inviting, and engaging, and there are few advertisements, mostly related to military life. This title's web site includes a small blog, and a parent's and teacher's guide. The magazine does keep a presence on other social media platforms, and can be purchased digitally. This is a Parent's Choice Silver Award winner. Recommended for public, school, or base libraries that serve a large child military population.

1234. ***Muse (Chicago).*** [ISSN: 1090-0381] 1996. 9x/yr. USD 33.95 domestic; USD 48.95 foreign. Ed(s): Johanna Arnone. Cricket Media, Inc., 70 E. Lake St Ste. 800, Chicago, IL 60601; support@cricketmedia.com; www.cricketmedia.com. Illus., adv. Sample. Vol. ends: Dec. *Indexed:* P01. *Aud.:* 9-14 yrs.

Muse provides a glossy paper eclectic magazine filled with informational nonfiction articles, facts, biographical sketches and STEM information. This title is a solid nonfiction choice for curious readers looking for in-depth information developed on one theme and goes beyond just history and science. All articles are written with extreme detail and provide factually based research from the magazine's highly reputable advisory board. A recent issue on "helping" gives examples of a science hero in history, how chimpanzees help each other, and how to help the environment and reduce trash. *Muse* is advertisement-free and atypically devoid of most of the most common puzzles and games; but instead it includes challenging experiments and problems to continue exploration. This has been a Parent's Choice Gold Award winner for multiple years. Highly recommended for school libraries, classroom subscriptions, and public libraries.

1235. ***National Geographic Kids.*** Formerly (until Oct.2002): *National Geographic World;* Which superseded (in 1975): *National Geographic School Bulletin;* Which was formerly (until 1961): *Geographic School Bulletins;* (until 1941): *Geographic News Bulletins.* [ISSN: 1542-3042] 1975. 10x/yr. USD 25 domestic; USD 29.95 Canada; USD 34.95 elsewhere. Ed(s): Rachel Buchholz. National Geographic Partners, LLC, 1145 17th St N W, Washington, DC 20036-4688. Illus., index, adv. Microform: PQC. *Indexed:* A22, BRI, C37, MASUSE, P01. *Aud.:* 6-12 yrs.

From the publishers of the world-renowned *National Geographic* is a kids' magazine for ages 6 to 12. This frenetic but organized title will delight readers and keep their attention. A large number of topics are included in this slim serial: animals, wacky facts, places, people, technology, entertainment, and photographs. There is between one and three main articles in each issue, each varying between two and four pages and small vignette facts throughout the rest of the pages. A few advertisements for food, toothpaste, and other *National Geographic* products are included in the magazine. A section denoted by the yellow band on the page border, headed "Fun Stuff," includes matching, hidden picture, and other puzzles. The web page provides robust free content to non-subscribers, but offers special downloads to subscribers. Recommended for personal subscription and public libraries.

1236. ***National Geographic Little Kids: the magazine for young explorers.*** [ISSN: 1934-8363] 2007. 6x/yr. USD 18 domestic; USD 24.95 Canada; USD 28 elsewhere. Ed(s): Rachel Buchholz. National Geographic Society, 1145 17th St, NW, Washington, DC 20036; askngs@nationalgeographic.com; http://www.nationalgeographic.com/. *Indexed:* P01. *Aud.:* 3-6 yrs.

Young animal lovers will enjoy exploring geography, animals, nature, and the world around them in this small-sized, glossy, bimonthly magazine with the distinctive yellow borders. Vibrant photographs, excellent editing and artwork, age-appropriate activities, and short facts with pictures about animals are in each issue. Pull-out collector cards in the stapled middle section have a picture and name of an animal on the front of the card, and fun facts on the back. Frequent educational pages provide interactivity with counting, sorting, naming, matching, and logic. An interactive web page with additional activities is not restricted to subscribers, but parents must sign up children for an account. This is a Parent's Choice Silver Award winner for 2018. Highly recommended for personal subscriptions, early-childhood resource libraries, public libraries, and school libraries.

1237. ***New Moon Girls.*** Formerly (until 2008): *New Moon.* [ISSN: 1943-488X] 1993. bi-m. USD 40.95 domestic; USD 49.95 elsewhere. Ed(s): Helen Cordes. New Moon Publishing, PO Box 161287, Duluth, MN 55816. Illus., index, adv. Vol. ends: Jul/Aug. *Indexed:* BRI, GW, MASUSE. *Bk. rev.:* Number and length vary. *Aud.:* 8-14 yrs.

Now celebrating 25 years, this magazine and its accompanying online social network provides a feminist viewpoint and global content. Written by girls for girls, mentors advise contributors and moderate both the print issue as well as the online community. Their web site states the magazine is for girls aged 8-14, but some information slants to an older "teen" market. Feature articles cover topics such as "Body and Mind," which discusses physical body changes," and "Your Way," which provides comparisons of cultures, styles, and beliefs. "How Aggravating," where girls can voice concerns about the status of the female gender in society, is one example of the feminine empowerment viewpoint. Included in each issue is a two- to four-page girl-written item of fiction loosely tied to that month's theme. Opportunities abound for reader participation, including the submission of opinions, ideas, advice, book reviews, poetry, and fiction, as well as artwork and letters. A monthly calendar, with interesting facts and important dates to remember, provides the reader ideas for an entire month. "The Last Word" features interviews with inspirational female role models. Subscriptions can be either in print or online, but both come with a very active safe social media platform access, which girls must sign up for, and which is closely edited and monitored. Recommended for personal subscriptions for just that right delicate age, as well as for school and public libraries.

1238. ***Owl: the discovery magazine for kids.*** [ISSN: 0382-6627] 1976. 10x/yr. CAD 34.95 in US & Canada; CAD 64.95 elsewhere. Ed(s): Kim Cooper. Bayard Canada, Owlkids, 10 Lower Spadina Ave, Ste 400, Toronto, ON M5V 2Z2, Canada; bayard@owl.on.ca; http://www.owlkids.com/. Illus., index. Sample. *Indexed:* BRI, C37, P01. *Bk. rev.:* Number and length vary. *Aud.:* 9-13 yrs.

This well-designed magazine for upper-elementary and middle-school independent readers provides a wide range of subjects. Contents include social studies, science, current events, and science information. The "Weird Zone" section highlights true-but-weird science stories and facts; "Insider," provides the cover story in a few pages designed with side panels, photos, and call-out boxes, and the "Maker Space" section provides craft, building, and science experiments. A small amount of advertising is included, but overall, this is a very satisfying discovery magazine for boys and girls, with bold colors, excellent comic strips, and advice columns. Design elements include inviting side panels, running heads, and call-out boxes. The web site provides the "OWL Blog" videos, polls, activity sheets, and more news information. This title has received a Parent's Choice Gold Award. Highly recommended for personal subscriptions and public libraries.

Plays. See Theater section.

1239. ***Ranger Rick.*** Formerly (until 1983): *Ranger Rick's Nature Magazine.* [ISSN: 0738-6656] 1967. m. 10/yr. USD 24.95 domestic; USD 36.95 foreign. Ed(s): Mary Dalheim. National Wildlife Federation, 11100 Wildlife Ctr Dr, Reston, VA 20190; pubs@nwf.org; https://www.nwf.org. Illus., index, adv. Vol. ends: Dec. Microform: NBI; PQC. *Indexed:* A22, BRI, C37, MASUSE, P01. *Aud.:* 7-14 yrs.

Ranger Rick is the quintessential children's magazine for in-depth animal and nature coverage, published by the National Wildlife Federation. Stunning wildlife photography is intermixed with a spacious layout and interesting fact vignettes. A multi-page comic titled "Ranger Rick Adventures," starring the raccoon and his friends exploring nature, start each issue. Fun facts are listed in side panels, and bubble balloons appear next to a variety of animal and insect photography. The few standard departments besides the comic and a games page come and go, given the issue's main focus. The games section is at least three pages of ciphering, word searches, and matching activities. The web site is robust with extra activities and is free to non-subscribers. Downloadable apps and subscriptions on multiple platforms are available. This title has been a Parents' Choice Gold Award winner for several years. Highly recommended for personal subscriptions and school libraries, and as a standard title in public libraries.

1240. ***Ranger Rick Cub: a first look at animals.*** [ISSN: 2473-7291] 2017. bi-m. USD 19.96 domestic; USD 31.96 foreign. Ed(s): Lori Collins. National Wildlife Federation, 11100 Wildlife Ctr Dr, Reston, VA 20190; pubs@nwf.org; https://www.nwf.org. *Aud.:* 0-4.

Launched in 2017, National Wildlife Federation now provides a third tiered magazine to their holdings for the youngest of animal lovers. *Ranger Rick Cub* is the perfect start to a wildlife magazine with simple full-colored photography of the most common and recognizable animals in simple and clean poses or action shots. Illustrated stories, matching, letter discovery, and rhyming text help with pre-emergent literacy skill development. Design and layout of the magazine is clean and simple with a "Grown-ups" call-out box on most pages with additional activity or discussion suggestion for further developmental activities. A small Ranger Rick cub is sprinkled throughout the issue and the back page of the magazine provides a hide-and-seek game to have the child revisit the magazine to practice discovery and counting skills. A Parents' Choice Award winner, this new title will grow in popularity coming from such a longstanding publisher in the wildlife field. Highly recommended for public libraries and early childhood centers.

1241. ***Ranger Rick Jr.*** Former titles (until 2012): *Big Backyard;* (until 2011): *Your Big Backyard.* [ISSN: 2169-2750] 1980. 10x/yr. USD 24.95 domestic; USD 36.95 foreign. Ed(s): Lori Collins. National Wildlife Federation, 11100 Wildlife Ctr Dr, Reston, VA 20190; pubs@nwf.org; https://www.nwf.org. Illus. *Indexed:* P01. *Aud.:* 3-6 yrs.

The National Wildlife Federation's *Ranger Rick Jr.* magazine provides nature and animal lovers a great resource with the cartoon character Ricky the Raccoon, guiding the young beginning reader. Each issue features a specific animal or concept with at least two feature pieces, and with accompanying full-color photographs and artwork. There is a fun hide-and-seek game with Sammy the Skunk, for counting skills practice, on the table of contents page. Each issue has very consistent departments like "Ricky's Playhouse," which features games; "Ricky and Pals," a multi-paged fiction story; and "Ricky's Mail," where readers submit photos or artwork. The text is simple, large, and sparse on each page, and enhances the pictures and drawings. One rebus story for emergent readers and a hands-on craft help the child engage more. The title's web site includes videos, activities, printouts, and games, as well as downloadable apps even for the non-subscriber. This has been a Parent's Choice Gold Award winner for numerous years. Highly recommended for personal subscriptions and for public and school libraries.

1242. ***Skipping Stones: a multicultural literary magazine.*** [ISSN: 0899-529X] 1988. q. USD 35. Ed(s): Arun Narayan Toke. Skipping Stones, Inc., 166 W 12th Ave, PO Box 3939, Eugene, OR 97403; info@skippingstones.org. Illus. Sample. *Indexed:* BRI, P01. *Bk. rev.:* 16, 30-50 words. *Aud.:* 8-15 yrs.

Skipping Stones is a nonprofit publication that stresses "cooperation, creativity and celebration of cultural and linguistic diversity" in each quarterly issue. The inside contents are text heavy with black-and-white drawings and photos that are printed on recycled, oversized white paper. The exterior of the magazine has full-color, reader-submitted artwork with matte/glossy paper. Reader-submitted work by both youth and adults from around the world fosters "communication among children from different lands." Nonfiction, fiction, biographies, essays, book reviews, and poetry make up the majority of content. The content can be very deep and thoughtful, with world views of global warming, nature and beauty, injustice, racism, immigration, and everyday life in other regions of the world. Yearly, the magazine recognizes young writers with its youth honor award, as well as book awards for diverse books published for children. Appropriate for public libraries, especially those with diverse clientele.

1243. ***Spider: the magazine for children.*** [ISSN: 1070-2911] 1994. 9x/yr. USD 33.95 domestic; USD 48.95 foreign. Ed(s): Alice Letvin. Cricket Media, Inc., 70 E. Lake St Ste. 800, Chicago, IL 60601; support@cricketmedia.com; www.cricketmedia.com. Illus. Sample. Vol. ends: Dec. *Indexed:* P01. *Bk. rev.:* Number and length vary. *Aud.:* 6-9 yrs.

This literary magazine combines high-quality historical, realistic, and fantasy fiction, nonfiction, folktales, poetry, and a few activities to give the newly independent reader an overall delightful reading experience. Geared toward graduates of *Ladybug* magazine, this literary chronicle's contents are similar to those of its sister publication, featuring a thematic traveling through, but not a complete inundation by, the topic. "Doodlebug and Dandelion" characters start each issue with a story that introduces the theme, like animals or fairies. A number of the stories and folktales are several pages long and are intermixed with the poetry, comic pages, and nonfiction articles. Some of the best writers and illustrators contribute their talent to *Spider.* The character of Spider and his cartoon friends add spice to the magazine by commenting, sometimes adding definitions, clarifying ideas, and joking throughout the margins. The layout of departments and stories is fairly consistent across issues, and is very appealing with interesting fonts, full-color illustrations, and regularly placed letter and craft departments. A tear-out page at the back of each issue provides the reader an extra game or activity, but few actual interactive pages of puzzles are included in this glossy-paged title. This has been a Parent's Choice Gold Award winner for multiple years. Highly recommended as a standard for school libraries, public libraries, and personal subscriptions.

1244. ***Sports Illustrated for Kids.*** [ISSN: 1042-394X] 1989. m. 10/yr. USD 31.95 domestic. Time Inc., Time & Life Bldg, Rockefeller Center, 29th Fl, New York, NY 10020-1393; information@timeinc.com; http://www.timeinc.com. Illus., adv. *Indexed:* A22, BRI, C37, MASUSE, P01. *Aud.:* 8-14 yrs.

This sports-focused magazine is a kid's version of the extremely popular adult magazine, but written in easier language that includes athletic achievements, puzzles, and games. Issues vary but can include pull-out collectible cards and posters of famous athletes. Multiple sports that appeal to girls and boys are covered seasonally, with player sketches, equipment highlights, play strategy, and human-interest stories revolving around the sport played. Stunning action shots, freeze-frame shots, and other full-color photography provide stimulating coverage. Also included is the recurring "What's the Call" segment that asks readers to judge sports rules interpretation. A back-page comic titled "Buzz Beamer" puts the character Buzz in different sports situations. Advertisements are sparse and are focused on sports gear, related publications, and some food. The *SIKIDS* web page is updated frequently and includes online games, photos, blogs, polls, and videos. Sign-up is free and not limited to subscribers. Highly recommended as a standard for public libraries and school libraries, and for personal subscriptions.

1245. ***Stone Soup: the magazine by young writers and artists.*** [ISSN: 0094-579X] 1973. bi-m. USD 47 combined subscription domestic (print & online eds.); USD 53 combined subscription in Canada & Mexico (print & online eds.); USD 59 combined subscription elsewhere (print & online eds.)). Ed(s): William Rubel, Gerry Mandel. Children's Art Foundation, 245 Eighth Ave, Ste 256, New York, NY 10011; info@childrenartfoundation.org; http://www.childrenartfoundation.org. Illus., adv. Vol. ends: Summer. *Indexed:* BRI, P01. *Bk. rev.:* Number and length vary. *Aud.:* 8-13 yrs.

Young writers and artists from around the globe submit creative writing and hand-drawn illustrations to help create a subdued but authentic magazine run by the non-profit Children's Art Foundation. This title has no advertisements or flashy editing, and the subtlety of presentation of the magazine provides a peaceful break from overly designed and flashy layouts of today's popular magazines. Each issue includes real-life experiences, adventure, and imaginative poems and stories that are relevant to readers today. Published six times per year, the magazine selects the highest quality of writing and illustration by both boys and girls, with appropriate author acknowledgement; they even acknowledge non-published authors that submitted quality work in their honor roll. Book reviews are several paragraphs long and focus on recently published English-language children's books. Bonus materials and free archives are available on the web site without a subscription. The publication also keeps an active social media presence across multiple platforms. In addition to print subscriptions, subscriptions are available in a print/digital combination; and digital-only is available. Recommended as the gold standard of magazines for creative writing done by children. For all types of libraries, classrooms, creative writing centers, and for personal subscriptions to those young writers and artists.

1246. ***Story Box.*** [ISSN: 1366-901X] 1995. 10x/yr. EUR 88 in Europe; EUR 94 elsewhere. Ed(s): Simona Sideri. Bayard Presse, 18 Rue Barbes, Montrouge, 82128, France; redactions@bayard-presse.com; http://www.bayard-jeunesse.com. Adv. Sample. *Aud.:* 3-6 yrs.

This is the best of a full-length picture-book and a richly engaging magazine combined into one "quality magazine to share and enjoy with children." Each issue centers on a fully illustrated, picture book-length, read-aloud story for read-aloud time. The stories range from realistic fiction to folktales and imaginary adventures, and are written by reputable authors and illustrators. After the stories come several other magazine features, including information about animals; a rhyming story; and fascinating facts about science and nature. SamSam, a well-loved comic character, goes on fast-paced futuristic adventures that don't always turn out quite right. There are also plenty of age-appropriate mazes, word searches, dot-to-dot puzzles, coloring pages, phonetic practice, and word games. Another wonderfully produced, wordless comic strip, "Polo," will delight pre-readers with a story they can follow all on their own. American readers should note that this is a British publication, with British spellings like "mum," but the overall content has international appeal. There are two subscription options available, print and print with accompanying CDs for an enhanced audio experience. The publisher's web site has a few interactive coloring pages and other activities, and now provides a few downloadable story apps for purchase on Apple products. Recommended for early education center libraries and public libraries.

1247. ***Storytime.*** [ISSN: 2055-639X] 2014. m. USD 69.99. Luma Works, 90 London Rd, Studio 2B18, London, SE1 6LN, United Kingdom; hello@lumaworks.com; http://lumaworks.com. Illus., adv. *Aud.:* Ems.

Traditional literature and well-developed stories continues to have large value in children's development, and the *Storytime* magazine's entire focus is on storytelling. The seven included stories selected are multi-page stories, myths, legends, shortened books, world tales, and poems. Interactive call-out boxes ask readers to participate in a look-and-see, acting the scene out, drawing, or craft within each story. Most illustrations provide nostalgic styles reminiscent of 1940s-to-1960s picture books. The magazine itself is the size and paper quality of a picture book, and the intent is as a read-aloud between caregivers and children. At the back of each issue is the "Storytime Playbox," with dot-to-dots, word search, crafts, counting, coloring, and simple arithmetic. This is a British publication, so the expense may prohibit purchasing for American readers who have options of obtaining the same stories from other sources. Appropriate for public and school libraries.

Time for Kids Around the World. See Classroom Magazines/Social Studies and Current Events section.

1248. ***Wild: Canada's wildlife magazine for kids.*** Formerly (until 1995): *Ranger Rick (Ottawa);* Which superseded in part (in 1984): *Ranger Rick;* Which was formerly (until 1982): *Ranger Rick's Nature Magazine.* [ISSN: 1492-014X] 1967. 6x/yr. CAD 22 domestic; CAD 49 United States; CAD 59 elsewhere. Canadian Wildlife Federation, 350 Michael Cowpland Dr, Kanata, ON K2M 2W1, Canada; info@cwf-fcf.org; http://www.cwf-fcf.org. Adv. *Indexed:* BRI, C37, MASUSE. *Aud.:* 5-13 yrs.

Canada's wildlife magazine *Wild* is a nature and wildlife publication for ages 5-13. Content includes stories, games, activities, and a recurring comic that features the characters Moose and Weasel, teaching elementary-aged children about wildlife around the world, and Canada specifically. In some of the issues, important explorers are interviewed and discuss their explorations in detail. Articles are written on different academic levels to try and appeal to a wide age range. A beautiful pull-out poster and amazing photography are included. Appropriate for personal subscriptions and public libraries.

■ CIVIL LIBERTIES

General/Bioethics: Reproductive Rights, Right-to-Life, and Right-to-Die/ Freedom of Expression and Information/Freedom of Thought and Belief/ Groups and Minorities/Political-Economic Rights

See also News and Opinion; and Political Science sections.

Miriam Leigh, Business Analyst, Harvard University Information Technology; miriam.leigh@gmail.com

Introduction

The journals reviewed in this section document the crucial role of civil liberties in democracy. Civil liberties—the rights to freedom of thought, expression, and action without interference from government—have been at the forefront of debate in the United States since the Founding Fathers wrote the Bill of Rights with the specific intent to safeguard individual liberties against the power of a strong central government.

Civil liberties have traditionally been concerned with freedom of expression and due process, but the specific focus has changed as public attitudes have shifted from one generation to the next. Civil liberties have expanded and, during times of national crisis such as war, have contracted. Judicial activism has had significant impact on civil liberties. The Warren Court (1953-1969) carved out the constitutional right of privacy that later became the basis of *Roe v. Wade*. The Burger Court shifted rightward and weakened civil liberties, notably in the area of criminal procedure protections.

Toward the end of the twentieth century, technology became the First Amendment battleground. Free speech on the Internet and the right to privacy relating to individuals' genetic profiles entered the debate. The terrorist attacks of September 11, 2001, and the USA PATRIOT Act, giving government unprecedented investigative powers, heightened civil liberties concerns. Government actions to prevent future terrorist attacks have made the defense of civil liberties more complex than at any time in our history.

In 1822, James Madison wrote, "A people who mean to be their own governors must arm themselves with the power which knowledge gives." Articles in journals in this section give historical review of civil liberties issues and also chronicle contemporary discussion by intellectuals and policymakers. Medical crowdfunding, worker rights, preservation of indigenous culture, civil disobedience, health care reform, taxation and regulation, and the Establishment Clause are issues that citizens, students, and scholars will want to fully explore in order to be more fully able to participate in American discourse and democracy. Journals in this section inform Americans about issues that touch on their daily lives and on the future of their country, as well as issues faced by people all over the world.

Librarians should review titles in other sections of *Magazines for Libraries*, most notably the ones dedicated to individual groups ("African American," "Asian American," "Disabilities," "Latino Studies," "Native Americans," and "Gender Studies") to augment titles in this section.

Basic Periodicals

Hs: *Journal of Intellectual Freedom and Privacy, Liberty* (Hagerstown), *Reason;* Ga: *Cultural Survival Quarterly, Free Inquiry, Journal of Intellectual Freedom and Privacy, Liberty* (Hagerstown), *Northwestern Journal of International Human Rights, Reason, The International Journal of Human Rights;* Ac: *American Journal of Bioethics, Bioethics, Columbia Human Rights Law Review, Cultural Survival Quarterly, George Mason University Civil Rights Law Journal, Harvard Civil Rights—Civil Liberties Law Review Human Rights Law Review, Human Rights Quarterly, The International Journal of Human Rights, Journal of Human Rights Practice, Journal of Intellectual Freedom and Privacy, Journal of Law, Medicine, & Ethics, Kennedy Institute of Ethics Journal, Law & Inequality, Northwestern Journal of International Human Rights, Reason, Stanford Journal of Civil Rights & Civil Liberties, Texas Journal on Civil Liberties & Civil Rights;* Sa: *American Journal of Bioethics, American Journal of Law & Medicine, Bioethics, Columbia Human Rights Law Review, Free Inquiry, Harvard Civil Rights–Civil Liberties Law Review, Human Rights Law Review, Human Rights Quarterly, The International Journal of Human Rights, Journal of Human Rights Practice, Journal of Law, Journal of Law and Religion, Kennedy Institute of Ethics Journal, Medicine & Ethics, Law & Inequality, Northwestern Journal of International Human Rights, Stanford Journal of Civil Rights & Civil Liberties, Texas Journal on Civil Liberties & Civil Rights.*

Basic Abstracts and Indexes

Alternative Press Index.

General

1249. ***Columbia Human Rights Law Review.*** Formerly (until 1972): *Columbia Survey of Human Rights Law.* [ISSN: 0090-7944] 1967. 3x/yr. Ed(s): Brian Yin, Daniel Ravitz. Columbia University, School of Law, 435 W 116th St, New York, NY 10027; Admissions@law.columbia.edu; http://www.law.columbia.edu. Microform: WSH; PMC. Reprint: WSH. *Indexed:* A22, BRI, L14, MLA-IB. *Aud.:* Ac, Sa.

The student-run *Columbia Human Rights Law Review* is "one of the oldest and the most recognized human rights journals in the world." Published three times a year, it aims to analyze and discuss civil liberties in both a domestic and international context. Recent topics have included the rights of workers under various regulatory regimes; the use of firearm prohibitions in preventing intimate violence; and burnout faced by human rights advocates. Articles are dense and technical in nature, making them most appropriate in law libraries and libraries affiliated with law schools.

Criminal Justice Ethics. See Criminology and Law Enforcement section.

1250. ***George Mason University. Civil Rights Law Journal.*** [ISSN: 1049-4766] 1990. 3x/yr. USD 60 in US & Canada; USD 70 elsewhere. Ed(s): Theresa Dalmut, Christine Fries. George Mason University, Antonin Scalia Law School, 3301 Fairfax Dr, Arlington, VA 22201; gmlr@gmu.edu; http://www.gmu.edu. Reprint: WSH. *Indexed:* A01, BRI, L14. *Aud.:* Ac, Sa.

The *George Mason University Civil Rights Law Journal* was founded in 1990, and "serves as a forum for thought-provoking scholarly articles written by leading academics." Recent articles have addressed such issues as open records requests and their effects on academic freedom; current iterations of civil disobedience; and firearm manufacturer liability. Articles are of a complex legal nature, and thus would be most appropriate in a legal library or in the library at a law school. This title is available both as a paid print subscription and for free at the website. URL: https://sls.gmu.edu/crlj/

1251. ***Harvard Civil Rights - Civil Liberties Law Review.*** [ISSN: 0017-8039] 1966. s-a. USD 42 domestic; USD 52 foreign. Ed(s): Katherine Cielinski, Joseph Breen. Harvard University, Law School, 1563 Massachusetts Ave, Cambridge, MA 02138; http://www.law.harvard.edu/. Illus. Reprint: WSH. *Indexed:* A01, A22, B01, BRI, L14, P61. *Aud.:* Ac, Sa.

This publication, the leading progressive law journal in the United States, focuses on civil rights and the American people's loss thereof. Written from a perspective of social justice, the *Harvard Civil Rights-Civil Liberties Law Review* offers dialogues on a variety of controversial topics. It was founded with the goal "to catalyze progressive thought and dialogue through publishing innovative legal scholarship and from various perspectives and in diverse fields of study." Recent issues explore sexual harassment claims and mandatory arbitration; indigenous environmental rights; and the role of non-traditional labor organizations in improving migrant worker conditions. In addition to its availability as a paid print subscription, the *CRCL* is available for free online. URL: http://harvardcrcl.org/

1252. ***Human Rights Law Review.*** Formerly (until 1994): *Student Human Rights Law Centre. Newsletter.* [ISSN: 1461-7781] 19??. q. EUR 463. Ed(s): David Harris. Oxford University Press, Great Clarendon St, Oxford, OX2 6DP, United Kingdom; onlinequeries.uk@oup.com; http://global.oup.com. Adv. Sample. Reprint: PSC; WSH. *Indexed:* A22, BRI, CJPI, E01, L14, P61. *Bk. rev.:* 2-4, 1,500-2,200 words. *Aud.:* Ac, Sa.

Human Rights Law Review is published quarterly with the intent to "promote knowledge, awareness and debate of human rights law and policy." It offers a range of articles, updates on recent cases, and book reviews on human rights issues around the world. This journal is written with an academic focus, but is also intended for a wider audience of anyone involved in human rights work. Recent issues have published articles on the constitutionality of same-sex relations bans in India; the prohibition of detaining immigrant children; and the legal right of equal recognition for people with cognitive disabilities. Because of its broad appeal, this journal would be appropriate in any academic library.

1253. ***Human Rights Quarterly: a comparative and international journal of the social sciences, humanities, and law.*** Formerly (until 1981): *Universal Human Rights.* [ISSN: 0275-0392] 1979. q. USD 250. Ed(s): Bert B Lockwood, Jr., Verjine Adanalian. The Johns Hopkins University Press, 2715 N Charles St, Baltimore, MD 21218; http://www.press.jhu.edu. Illus., adv. Sample. Refereed. Vol. ends: Nov. Reprint: PSC; WSH. *Indexed:* A01, A22, BAS, BRI, CJPI, E01, IBSS, L14, MLA-IB, P61, SSA. *Bk. rev.:* 1-9, 1,100-3,000 words. *Aud.:* Ac, Sa.

Human Rights Quarterly, published by the Johns Hopkins University Press, offers award-winning articles in the field of human rights. It uses as its focus the Universal Declaration of Human Rights, publishing articles from experts in a variety of disciplines that include the law and the humanities. This title includes book reviews, essays, and analytical articles, intending to "provide decision makers with insight into complex human rights issues." Recent articles are on such topics including the use of a human rights framework to protect children's health in tobacco control enforcement; an assessment of reparations programs; and the prosecution of sexual violence at war crimes tribunals. Although *Human Rights Quarterly* is intended primarily for policymakers, it is also edited to be of use to the "intelligent reader," making it extremely appropriate for any academic library.

1254. ***Law & Inequality: a journal of theory and practice.*** [ISSN: 0737-089X] 1981. s-a. USD 18 (Free to qualified personnel). Ed(s): Andrew Glasnovich. University of Minnesota, Law School, 229 19th Ave S, Minneapolis, MN 55455; law@umn.edu; http://www.law.umn.edu. Illus., adv. Refereed. Vol. ends: Jun. Microform: WSH. Reprint: WSH. *Indexed:* A22, BRI, CJPI, L14. *Bk. rev.:* 1, 2,000 words. *Aud.:* Ac, Sa.

Law & Inequality, published twice a year under the umbrella of the University of Minnesota Law School, provides articles, essays, and letters "addressing issues of inequality in law and society." Recent topics include Confederate monuments and compelled speech issues; legalization of polygamy in the West; and race and charter schools. Although most articles are written in the traditional legal format, they are also intended to appeal to a wider audience, both within and outside the legal community. Thus, this title would be appropriate in both legal and academic libraries.

New Perspectives Quarterly. See News and Opinion section.

1255. ***Northwestern Journal of International Human Rights.*** [ISSN: 1549-828X] 2003. s-a. Free. Ed(s): Stephanie Le, Daniel Hooks. Northwestern University, School of Law, 375 E Chicago Ave, Chicago, IL 60611; reprint-permissions@law.northwestern.edu; http://www.law.northwestern.edu. Reprint: WSH. *Indexed:* A01, L14. *Aud.:* Ga, Ac, Sa.

The *Northwestern Journal of International Human Rights* is published twice a year, and is "dedicated to providing a dynamic forum for the discussion of human rights issues and international human rights law." The journal offers traditional legal articles as well as presentations from the Annual Transatlantic Dialogue conference between the Center for International Human Rights at Northwestern University School of Law and the Catholic University in Leuven, Belgium. Recent articles cover such topics as school desegregation; a comparison of North Korean defectors and refugee-seekers in America; and the concept of extending a statute of limitations in filing workers compensation claims to maintain worker dignity. Available only in full text online, for free. URL: www.law.northwestern.edu/journals/jihr

Social Philosophy and Policy. See Philosophy section.

Social Theory and Practice. See Cultural Studies section.

1256. ***Stanford Journal of Civil Rights & Civil Liberties.*** [ISSN: 1553-7226] 2005. s-a. USD 42 domestic; USD 47 foreign; USD 24 per issue. Ed(s): Sabrina Forte, Margo Watson. Stanford University, Stanford Law School, Crown Quadrangle, 559 Nathan Abbott Way, Stanford, CA 94305-8610; communications@law.stanford.edu; https://law.stanford.edu. *Indexed:* CJPI, L14. *Aud.:* Ac, Sa.

The *Stanford Journal of Civil Rights & Civil Liberties,* published twice a year by the students of Stanford Law, has as its mission "to explore the changing landscape of the civil rights and civil liberties dialogue, the real world implications of these changes on society, and the larger structural and systemic implications of these issues." The most recent issues explore mandatory individual arbitration agreements and workers rights; proposed rules to curtail certain juvenile incarceration practices; and the Fourth Amendment in light of recent technological advances. Although this title's intended audience is the legal community, the articles are clear and the topics are highly relevant in today's world. This journal would be a good fit for both legal and academic libraries.

1257. ***Texas Journal on Civil Liberties & Civil Rights.*** Formerly (until 2003): *Texas Forum on Civil Liberties and Civil Rights.* [ISSN: 1930-2045] 1992. s-a. USD 40 domestic; USD 50 foreign; USD 20 per issue. University of Texas at Austin, School of Law Publications, 727 E Dean Keeton St, Ste 4.134B, Austin, TX 78705; webmaster@law.utexas.edu; https://law.utexas.edu/publications/. Adv. Reprint: WSH. *Indexed:* A01, CJPI, L14. *Aud.:* Ac, Sa.

The *Texas Journal on Civil Liberties & Civil Rights* explores "the state of civil rights in America by publishing cutting edge articles at the intersection of law, politics, and society written by judges, lawyers, professors and fellow students." It publishes in-depth explorations of legal issues, as well as letters to the editor. This journal covers such timely topics as Native American representation on juries, improving educational outcomes on formerly incarcerated youths, and religious freedom and same-sex marriage in Texas. The articles are well written and scholarly, and would be well-suited to an academic library.

Bioethics: Reproductive Rights, Right-to-Life, and Right-to-Die

1258. ***The American Journal of Bioethics.*** [ISSN: 1526-5161] 2001. m. USD 1950 (print & online eds.) Individuals, USD 230 (print & online eds.)). Ed(s): David Magnus. Routledge, 530 Walnut St, Ste 850, Philadelphia, PA 19106; enquiries@tandfonline.com; http://www.tandfonline.com. Illus. Refereed. Reprint: PSC. *Indexed:* A01, A22, BRI, E01. *Bk. rev.:* Number and length vary. *Aud.:* Ac, Sa.

The *American Journal of Bioethics*, launched in 2001, has rapidly become one of the most widely read publications in the field. It offers two primary, or "target," articles and then several peer commentaries on each article, allowing for a varied and in-depth exploration of each topic. In addition, *AJOB* publishes book reviews and correspondence from readers. In 2007, this journal moved from being published six times per year to 12. Recent issues touch on such topics as the use of social media in supporting clinical research, informed consent in medical research, and the ethics of withholding or withdrawing medical supports. Readers will also enjoy the companion website for thought-provoking news, editorials, and even a blog. The institutional subscription price includes *AJOB Neuroscience* and *AJOB Primary Research* in a bundle. URL: www.bioethics.net

1259. ***Bioethics.*** [ISSN: 0269-9702] 1987. 9x/yr. GBP 1006 (print or online ed.)). Ed(s): Udo Schueklenk, Ruth Chadwick. Wiley-Blackwell Publishing Ltd., The Atrium, Southern Gate, Chichester, PO19 8QG, United Kingdom; cs-journals@wiley.com; http://www.wiley.com/. Illus., adv. Sample. Refereed. Reprint: PSC. *Indexed:* A01, A22, ASSIA, BRI, E01, IBSS, P61, SSA. *Aud.:* Ac, Sa.

This journal, published under the aegis of the International Association of Bioethics, explores contemporary ethical concerns raised in the course of biomedical research. These debates reflect those in today's popular discourse. Recent topics include human genome editing, anti-fat bias, medical crowdfunding, and the ethical implications of humanitarian medical aid in Syria. Issues occasionally focus on a single theme, allowing authors to explore topics on a more in-depth level, such as the July 2019 issue on "The Ethics of Embryo Donation." The articles are a mix of scientific studies and more accessible popular-style articles.

1260. ***The Journal of Law, Medicine & Ethics.*** Formerly (until 1993): *Law, Medicine and Health Care;* Which was formed by the merger of (1973-1981): *Medicolegal News;* (1980-1981): *Nursing Law and Ethics.* [ISSN: 1073-1105] 1981. q. USD 1071 (print & online eds.)). Ed(s): Kevin Cutterson. Sage Publications, Inc., 2455 Teller Rd, Thousand Oaks, CA 91320; info@sagepub.com; http://www.sagepub.com. Illus., adv. Sample. Refereed. Vol. ends: Winter. Microform: WSH; PQC. Reprint: PSC. *Indexed:* A01, A22, BRI, CJPI, E01, L14. *Bk. rev.:* Number and length vary. *Aud.:* Ac, Sa.

Published quarterly by the American Society of Law, Medicine & Ethics, *The Journal of Law, Medicine & Ethics* aims to be "a leading peer-reviewed journal for research at the intersection of law, health policy, ethics, and medicine." Issues contain topical sections, and this title publishes articles based on a single symposium. This allows the journal to explore a given subject in depth and from a variety of perspectives. Recent issues have discussed bio-medical data sharing; best practices for breastfeeding and HIV; and health care reform. In addition to these symposium articles, each issue also contains standalone articles, regular columns, a calendar of professional events, and the occasional book review. Articles are scholarly, and would be most appropriate in academic, legal, and medical libraries.

1261. ***Kennedy Institute of Ethics Journal.*** [ISSN: 1054-6863] 1991. q. USD 225. Ed(s): Rebecca Kukla, Hailey Huget. The Johns Hopkins University Press, 2715 N Charles St, Baltimore, MD 21218; http://www.press.jhu.edu. Illus., adv. Sample. Refereed. Vol. ends: Dec. Reprint: PSC. *Indexed:* A01, A22, E01. *Bk. rev.:* Number and length vary. *Aud.:* Ac, Sa.

This interdisciplinary journal provides a wide view of bioethics, social issues, practical and philosophical ethics, and currently has a particular focus on "ethical and social issues in science practice, as well as philosophical approaches to health, environmental, and science policy, especially those that situate philosophical and ethical issues in a global context." The articles are thoughtful and readable. Recently published topics include rehabilitation criteria for older hospitalized patients, the possible irrelevance of using binary sex to describe patients, and drug tests for welfare recipients.

Freedom of Expression and Information

Journal of Information Ethics. See Library and Information Science section.

1262. ***Journal of Intellectual Freedom and Privacy.*** Formerly (until 2016): *Newsletter on Intellectual Freedom (Online).* q. bi-m. until 2016. USD 100 (Individuals, USD 50). American Library Association, 50 E Huron St, Chicago, IL 60611; ala@ala.org; http://www.ala.org. *Bk. rev.:* 1-4, 500-700 words. *Aud.:* Hs, Ga, Ac.

Renamed in May 2016 as the *Journal of Intellectual Freedom and Privacy,* this title is published by the American Library Association's Office of Intellectual Freedom. It is the only journal that reports on challenges to materials from schools and libraries nationwide. It provides articles on thought-provoking topics such as obscenity and censorship during the Comstock period; library patron confidentiality; and free speech on university campuses. It also offers several smaller news pieces of interest. This periodical is available both in print format and in full text online. URL: https://journals.ala.org/jifp

Freedom of Thought and Belief

1263. ***Free Inquiry.*** [ISSN: 0272-0701] 1981. bi-m. USD 24.95 domestic; USD 36.95 foreign. Council for Secular Humanism, PO Box 664, Amherst, NY 14226; info@secularhumanism.org; http://www.secularhumanism.org. Illus., adv. Microform: PQC. *Indexed:* A01, A22, BRI, MLA-IB. *Bk. rev.:* 3-5, 500-1,500 words. *Aud.:* Hs, Ga, Sa.

Free Inquiry is published as the mouthpiece of the Council for Secular Humanism. It takes as its focus the exploration of complex contemporary ethical issues through the lens of secular humanism. Its "Statement of Purpose" specifies that the journal's aim is "to promote and nurture the good life—life guided by reason and science, freed from the dogmas of god and state, inspired by compassion for fellow humans, and driven by the ideals of human freedom, happiness, and understanding." Recent articles cover such topics as voters with no religious affiliation in a contentious election cycle; clergy sex abuse scandals; and current bans on religious facial coverings. Sections in the magazine include letters to the editor, op-eds, feature articles, book reviews, poetry, and more. These timely articles reflect issues being discussed in the American popular press.

The Humanist. See Religion section.

Journal of Church and State. See Religion section.

1264. ***Journal of Law and Religion.*** [ISSN: 0748-0814] 1983. 3x/yr. GBP 140 (print & online eds.)). Ed(s): Silas W Allard. Cambridge University Press, 1 Liberty Plaza, Fl 20, New York, NY 10004; online@cambridge.org; https://www.cambridge.org. Illus., index, adv. Refereed. Microform: WSH; PMC. Reprint: PSC; WSH. *Indexed:* A01, A22, BRI, CJPI, L14, P61, R&TA. *Bk. rev.:* 10-20, 2,000 words. *Aud.:* Ac, Sa.

Dedicated to exploring the intersection of law and religion, this journal offers an international perspective on relevant topics. In the "Statement of Perspective," the editor identifies the six major focuses of the journal: historical, theoretical, ethical, global, professional, and spiritual. Issues often focus on recent news, with topical articles, editorials, and legal papers from writers from a variety of religious and legal backgrounds. Recent topics include approaches in accommodating religious law within a civil legal system; the impact a judge's religious worldview may have on their work; and early Tibetan Buddhist law. Although this journal is largely intended for a legal audience, many of the articles can be enjoyed by the general public.

1265. *Liberty (Hagerstown): a magazine of religious freedom.* [ISSN: 0024-2055] 1906. bi-m. USD 7.95. Ed(s): Lincoln Steed. Review and Herald Publishing Association, 55 W Oak Ridge Dr, Hagerstown, MD 21740; info@rhpa.org; http://www.reviewandherald.com/. Illus., adv. Circ: 200000. Vol. ends: Nov/Dec. Microform: PQC. *Indexed:* A22. *Aud.:* Hs, Ga.

Published six times per year by the Seventh Day Adventist Church, *Liberty* offers a variety of thought-provoking articles, essays, and editorials. Its "Declaration of Principles" states the journal's position that "[r]eligious liberty entails freedom of conscience: to worship or not to worship; to profess, practice, and promulgate religious beliefs, or to change them." This focus on the separation of church and state yields strong viewpoints on pressing contemporary topics. Recent issues of *Liberty* include multiple interpretations of the establishment clause; the Huguenot roots in American religious freedom; and a religious perspective on school shootings. This magazine is highly readable, and is available both by print subscription and for free online. URL: www.libertymagazine.org

Groups and Minorities

The Advocate. See LGBT+ section.

Children's Legal Rights Journal. See Sociology and Social Work/ General section.

1266. *Cultural Survival Quarterly.* Formerly (until 1981): *Cultural Survival Newsletter.* [ISSN: 0740-3291] 1976. q. USD 4.99 newsstand/cover domestic; USD 6.99 newsstand/cover Canada. Cultural Survival, Inc., 2067 Massachusetts Ave, Cambridge, MA 02140. Illus. Reprint: PSC. *Indexed:* A22, A47, ENW. *Bk. rev.:* 1-3, 300-700 words. *Aud.:* Ga, Ac.

Cultural Survival Quarterly was founded as a society newsletter. Over the last 40-plus years, it has become an authoritative resource on important issues that affect indigenous and ethnic minority communities around the world. Recent topics covered include the preservation of the Yuchi language; indigenous-led philanthropic funding; and indigenous-led land conservation initiatives. This magazine publishes thought-provoking essays, book reviews, and photographs with the intent of expanding public understanding about indigenous rights and cultures, with writers from indigenous communities or working closely with indigenous groups. In addition to a paid print subscription, this journal is also available for free at their website. URL: www.culturalsurvival.org/publications/ cultural-survival-quarterly.

Political-Economic Rights

Employee Relations Law Journal. See Labor and Industrial Relations section.

1267. *The International Journal of Human Rights.* [ISSN: 1364-2987] 1997. 8x/yr. GBP 1169 (print & online eds.)). Ed(s): Damien Short. Routledge, 4 Park Sq, Milton Park, Abingdon, OX14 4RN, United Kingdom; subscriptions@tandf.co.uk; http://www.tandfonline.com. Adv. Sample. Refereed. Circ: 9000. Reprint: PSC. *Indexed:* A01, A22, E01, IBSS, P61. *Bk. rev.:* Number and length vary. *Aud.:* Ga, Ac, Sa.

Published eight times per year, the *International Journal of Human Rights* has an ambitiously broad scope. It covers a wide spectrum of topics, including "human rights and the law, race, religion, gender, children, class, refugees and immigration." Articles are academic but readable, designed to appeal to a range of readers such as academics, lawyers, politicians, NGO workers, activists, and the interested general public. The journal primarily publishes original research, but also offers essays, comments, literature surveys, and more, with occasional special issues devoted to a single topic. A recent special issue covers human rights monitoring and implementation. Other recent issues cover such topics as indigenous rights in Morocco; Isis and the sexual slavery of Yazidi women and girls; and human rights for people with intellectual disabilities.

1268. *Journal of Human Rights Practice.* [ISSN: 1757-9619] 2009. 3x/yr. Ed(s): Paul Gready, Richard Carver. Oxford University Press, Great Clarendon St, Oxford, OX2 6DP, United Kingdom; onlinequeries.uk@oup.com; https://academic.oup.com/journals/. Refereed. Circ: 2848 Paid. Reprint: PSC. *Bk. rev.:* Number and length vary. *Aud.:* Ac, Sa.

Written primarily for human rights practitioners (NGO workers, anthropologists, etc.) and academics, the *Journal of Human Rights Practice* intends to "capture learning and communicate the lessons of practice across professional and geographical boundaries," in order to encourage and stimulate new approaches and ideas in the field. The journal publishes interviews, research articles, review articles, book reviews, and more, allowing for a wide perspective. Recent topics include the issue of statelessness from a human rights perspective; the use of public libraries as sanctuary spaces; and the use of international jurisprudence to decriminalize homosexuality in Belize. The journal is academic but clearly written, and would be an appropriate fit in academic and legal libraries.

The Progressive. See News and Opinion section.

1269. *Reason: free minds and free markets.* [ISSN: 0048-6906] 1968. 11x/yr. USD 14.97 (print or online ed.); USD 19.97 combined subscription (print & online eds.)). Ed(s): Katherine Mangu-Ward, Stephanie Slade. Reason Foundation, 5737 Mesmer Ave, Los Angeles, CA 90230; chris.mitchell@reason.org; http://reason.org/. Illus., index, adv. Vol. ends: Apr. Microform: PQC. *Indexed:* A01, A22, BRI, CBRI. *Bk. rev.:* 3-4, 1,500-2,500 words. *Aud.:* Hs, Ga, Ac.

Founded in 1968 as a student publication based at Boston University, *Reason* has since become an independent publication dedicated to "making a principled case for liberty and individual choice in all areas of human activity." It is published 11 times a year by the Reason Foundation, a nonprofit research organization dedicated to advancing libertarian principles, although the journal remains editorially independent. *Reason* is written for a general audience, with recent articles on such timely topics as Kim Kardashian, Donald Trump, and criminal justice reform; the high cost of housing; and taxes and regulation in California. The journal is available in full text online, although the most recent issue is available only at newsstands and by subscription.

■ CLASSICAL STUDIES

See also Archaeology; Art; History; Linguistics; and Literature sections.

Laurie Cohen, Liaison Librarian for Classics, Education, Jewish Studies, and Religious Studies, Hillman Library, University of Pittsburgh, Pittsburgh, PA 15260

Introduction

Despite the longevity of the field of Classical Studies in academia, the current campus climate has been adversarial to many of the humanities and social sciences fields. Oddly enough, this change occurs at the same time that Greek and Roman civilization is enjoying a resurgence in popular culture. Fewer Classics journals are still being published, and they mainly fall into two categories: the established, rigorously reviewed publications that are used by faculty, graduate students, and researchers; and the less restrictive journals used by laypeople with a more casual interest in Classics. Within the latter category are journals published for use by high school Greek and Latin teachers, which include curriculum guides, listings of new materials, and forums for pedagogical discussion. There are also publications that address topics from Ancient Greek and Roman culture, such as narrative fiction, poetry, drama, or dance, which are of interest to modern artists, contemporary scholars, and other performers who have been inspired by Classical artists and their themes. The ongoing crisis in scholarly publishing has not been kind to many academic disciplines, and Classical Studies has proven to be no exception in this regard. A number of publications have attempted to move to an open-access format with varying levels of success. While the necessity of publication in peer-reviewed journals for the purposes of receiving tenure will ensure that the most respected of scholarly publications in Classical Studies will survive, the current movement to question the validity and necessity of academic tenure could also have an effect on journal publication.

Basic Periodicals

American Journal of Philology, Ancient Narrative, Arethusa, Arion, Bryn Mawr Classical Review, Classical Antiquity, The Classical Journal, Classical Outlook, Classical Philology, The Classical Quarterly, The Classical Review, Classical World, Didaskalia, Greece & Rome, Mnemosyne, Phoenix (Toronto), T A P A.

Basic Abstracts and Indexes

L'Annee Philologique, Humanities International Index, MLA International Bibliography, TOCS-IN, Web of Science.

1270. *American Journal of Philology.* [ISSN: 0002-9475] 1880. q. USD 215. Ed(s): David H J Larmour. The Johns Hopkins University Press, 2715 N Charles St, Baltimore, MD 21218; http://www.press.jhu.edu. Illus., adv. Sample. Refereed. Vol. ends: Winter. Reprint: PSC. *Indexed:* A01, A22, AmHI, BRI, CBRI, E01, MLA-IB. *Bk. rev.:* 5-7, 2-5 pages. *Aud.:* Ac.

Founded in 1880 by American classical scholar Basil Lanneau Gildersleeve, the *American Journal of Philology* is a quarterly publication of the Johns Hopkins University Press. Each issue offers several scholarly articles that highlight the latest research in Greek and Roman literature, classical linguistics, and related topics in Greek and Roman history, society, religion, philosophy, and cultural and materials studies. There are five to seven book reviews as well. Recent articles have covered such topics as performance and fiction in Synaesius' *De Regno*; Cato at Utica; geometry and genre in Columella; and Ovid's books and their fate in the exile poetry. There are also occasional special issues, such as one on Roman dining. Few journals are as prestigious and influential to the field of Classical Studies as the *AJP*, making it an indispensable part of any academic library collection with a strong focus on Latin and Greek or the humanities.

1271. *Ancient Narrative.* [ISSN: 1568-3532] 2001. 3x/yr. Ed(s): Dr. Maaike Zimmerman, Gareth Schmeling. Barkhuis Publishing, Kooiweg 38, Eelde, 9761 GL, Netherlands; info@barkhuis.nl; http://www.barkhuis.nl. Refereed. *Bk. rev.:* 1-4, 3,000-5,500 words. *Aud.:* Ac.

A continuation of the *Petronian Society Newsletter* and the *Groningen Colloquia on the Novel*, *Ancient Narrative* is "an interdisciplinary peer-reviewed electronic journal publishing articles on Greek, Roman, and Jewish novels and narrative from the ancient and Byzantine periods." Although its focus primarily consists of Classical and religious scholarship, *Ancient Narrative* welcomes contributions from any scholars interested in the birth and development of narrative fiction. Authors are encouraged to revise their articles based on reader feedback; at the end of each year, the revised articles are made available in both electronic and print form. Recent issues have featured articles on topics such as depictions of violence in Greek novels; a Petronian brothel in the *Great Gatsby*; Heliodorus and late antique historiography; and the defence of Isis and the horse goddess in Apuleius' *Metamorphoses*. Each issue also contains several reviews of recent monographs published in the field. *Ancient Narrative* has recently transitioned from a subscription-based publishing model to an open-access format, which is consistent with the editors' vision of facilitating scholarship as a fruitful dialogue between authors and readers.

1272. *Arethusa.* [ISSN: 0004-0975] 1968. 3x/yr. USD 130. Ed(s): Madeleine S Kaufman, Martha Malamud. The Johns Hopkins University Press, 2715 N Charles St, Baltimore, MD 21218; http://www.press.jhu.edu. Illus., adv. Sample. Refereed. Vol. ends: Fall. Reprint: PSC. *Indexed:* A22, AmHI, E01, MLA-IB. *Aud.:* Ac.

Published three times a year by the Johns Hopkins University Press, *Arethusa* is an interdisciplinary journal that highlights literary and cultural studies of the ancient Graeco-Roman world. Each issue offers four to eight scholarly articles, with a focus on literary criticism. Recent issues have covered such topics as the rhetoric of desire in *Philostratus' Letters*; the gendered economics of Greek bronze mirrors; Tacitus's critique of corruption; Arion and Roman elegy; narrative circles in Plato's *Timaeus*; and tracking scents in Aeschylus's *Oresteia*. *Arethusa* prides itself on embracing a mix of contemporary literary theory and more traditional modes of Classical scholarship; thus, making it a more accessible publication about Ancient Greek and Latin literature than those whose emphasis in on philology and linguistics.

1273. *Arion: a journal of humanities and the classics at Boston University.* [ISSN: 0095-5809] 1962. 3x/yr. USD 60 (print & online eds.)). Ed(s): Herbert Golder, Nicholas Poburko. Boston University, 1 Silber Way, Boston, MA 02215. Illus., adv. Vol. ends: Fall. Microform: PQC. Reprint: PSC. *Indexed:* A22, AmHI, MLA-IB. *Bk. rev.:* 2-5, 5-20 pages. *Aud.:* Ac, Ga.

Launched in 1990 by Boston University, *Arion* continues to push the envelope of Classical Studies, offering its erudite and eclectic mix of scholarly essays, reviews, and translations, as well as original fiction and poetry inspired by ancient authors and Classical themes. In its "Advice to Prospective Contributors," the editor states "the literary essay, rather than the usual academic article, is best suited to Arion's purpose of integrating learning and imagination. We value most the contributor who speaks across the disciplines; the author who can write on Sophocles, say, in a way that engages the student of Shakespeare." Recent issues have offered a breadth of topics, such as Catallus, hip-hop, and masculinity; Robert Frost in Roman mode; historical Greece and European myths; and reading Virgil on a salary. Few academic publications in any discipline would make for scintillating reading to laypersons, but *Arion* is a notable exception to this rule, and would be an excellent addition to any large academic or public library's collection.

1274. *Bryn Mawr Classical Review (Online).* [ISSN: 1063-2948] 1990. irreg. Ed(s): Camilla MacKay, James O'Donnell. Bryn Mawr College, 101 N Merion Ave, Bryn Mawr, PA 19010; info@brynmawr.edu; http://www.brynmawr.edu. Illus. Refereed. *Indexed:* AmHI. *Bk. rev.:* 1,500-2,000 words. *Aud.:* Ac.

Not a magazine or journal per se, the *Bryn Mawr Classical Review* is an open-access online collection of reviews of current scholarly work in the field of Classical Studies, including ancient Greek and Roman archaeology. New book reviews are added irregularly and are written by experts in the respective field that each monograph addresses. The *BMCR* blog permits readers to comment on individual reviews, permitting some degree of interactivity between readers, reviewers, and occasionally the original authors of the books being reviewed as well. The *Bryn Mawr Classical Review* is one of the best resources available for keeping abreast of new books being published in the field, and thus could serve as a valuable tool for collection development as well.

1275. *Classical Antiquity (Online).* [ISSN: 1067-8344] 1982. s-a. USD 261. Ed(s): Mark Griffith. University of California Press, Journals Division, 155 Grand Avenue, Ste 400, Oakland, CA 94612-3764; http://www.ucpress.edu/journals.php. *Aud.:* Ac.

A biannual publication of the University of California Press, *Classical Antiquity* is "a journal that combines the pleasures, politics, intellectualism, cultural production, sciences, and linguistics of European traditions, centuries past." Each issue features five or six articles about Classical Studies, with an emphasis on comparative literature and interdisciplinary studies. "The object of *Classical Antiquity* is to publish significant research on topics from the entire spectrum of ancient Greek and Roman cultures in the context of the ancient Mediterranean." Recent topics have included sightseeing at Colonus; slave religiosity in the Roman middle republic; unified cityscapes and elite collaboration in Roman Asia Minor; the diffusion of the codex; and Greek-Anatolian language contact and the settlement of Pamphylia. In a field of publications that can often sag under the weight of their own scholarship, *Classical Antiquity* manages to strike a balance between respectable research and broader cultural relevance, making it a lively addition to most academic library collections.

1276. *The Classical Journal.* [ISSN: 0009-8353] 1905. q. USD 139 (print & online eds.)). Ed(s): Antony Augoustakis. Classical Association of the Middle West and South, Department of Classics, Monmouth College, Monmouth, IL 61462; camws@camws.org; https://www.camws.org. Illus., index, adv. Refereed. Microform: PMC; PQC. *Indexed:* A22, AmHI, BRI, CBRI, IIMP, MLA-IB. *Bk. rev.:* 3-5, 1-5 pages. *Aud.:* Hs, Ac.

The Classical Association of the Middle West and South, the largest regional Classics association in the United States and Canada, has been publishing *The Classical Journal* for more than one hundred years. Each issue of this quarterly publication contains several articles that cover topics in ancient Graeco-Roman literature, history, or culture (including book reviews), as well as articles that discuss teaching Greek and Latin in high schools and colleges. Each issue also contains a "forum" in which a specific topic or event is examined in detail. Recent issues have included articles about "Tragedy and Succession in Nicander's *Theriaca*; "Latin and the American Civil War"; and "Melampus in Callimachus and Hesiod." While there are many Classical Studies publications that offer a healthy range of solid scholarship, *The Classical Journal*'s strong pedagogical focus makes it of special interest to library collections that support the education of future Greek and Latin teachers.

1277. *Classical Outlook.* Formerly (until 1936): *Latin Notes.* [ISSN: 0009-8361] 1923. q. Free to members; USD 15 per issue. Ed(s): Ronnie Ancona. American Classical League, 860 NW Washington Blvd, Ste A, Hamilton, OH 45013; info@aclclassics.org; http://www.aclclassics.org. Illus., adv. *Indexed:* A22, BRI, CBRI, MLA-IB. *Bk. rev.:* 6-8, 300-1,000 words. *Aud.:* Hs, Ac, Ga.

Classical Outlook, "the most widely circulated Classics journal in North America," is a quarterly publication of the American Classical League, which since 1919 has fostered the study of classical languages in the United States and Canada. This is primarily a journal for teachers, and each issue of *Classical Outlook* includes short essays, scholarly articles, committee or research reports, classroom materials, original artwork and poetry, and reviews of books or other media. One unique feature is the "Teaching Materials and Resource Center." Items are selected for publication by the editors for the dual purpose of offering information that can be used by active teachers of Latin and Greek, and keeping ACL members up to date on recent scholarship in the field of Classical Studies. Thus, this journal is not only an essential tool for educators, but it can also provide an excellent overview to lay readers or other amateur enthusiasts for the Classics.

1278. *Classical Philology: a journal devoted to research in classical antiquity.* [ISSN: 0009-837X] 1906. q. USD 376. Ed(s): Sarah Nooter. University of Chicago Press, 1427 E 60th St, Chicago, IL 60637; subscriptions@press.uchicago.edu; http://www.journals.uchicago.edu. Illus., index, adv. Sample. Refereed. Vol. ends: Oct. Reprint: PSC. *Indexed:* A01, A22, AmHI, BRI, MLA-IB. *Bk. rev.:* 4-6, 3-5 pages. *Aud.:* Ac.

A quarterly publication of the University of Chicago Press, *Classical Philology* is one of the most respected journals in the field of Classical Studies. From its statement of editorial policy, *CP* "is devoted to publishing the best scholarly thought on all aspects of Graeco-Roman antiquity, including literature, languages, anthropology, history, social life, philosophy, religion, art, material culture, and the history of classical studies." Each issue features four to six scholarly articles, a section on "Notes and Discussions," and several book reviews. Recent articles include "Sophoclean Moments in Greek Comedy"; "Helen and the Divine Defense"; and "Conversation Analysis and Particles in Greek Tragic Dialogue." There are also special issues with a specific focus. *Classical Philology* is a first-rate academic journal with international repute, and is therefore a "must-have" for any library collection that supports the Classics.

1279. *The Classical Quarterly.* [ISSN: 0009-8388] 1906. s-a. GBP 229 (print & online eds.)). Ed(s): Andrew Morrison, Bruce Gibson. Cambridge University Press, University Printing House, Shaftesbury Rd, Cambridge, CB2 8BS, United Kingdom; journals@cambridge.org; https://www.cambridge.org/. Illus., index, adv. Sample. Refereed. Microform: PQC. Reprint: PSC. *Indexed:* A01, A22, AmHI, E01, MLA-IB. *Aud.:* Ac.

One of the premier academic journals dedicated to classical scholarship, *The Classical Quarterly* is a biannual publication of the Classical Association of Great Britain. Each issue features from 20 to 30 articles, with a strong focus on philology. While there are no book reviews in *The Classical Quarterly*, they do appear in *The Classical Review*, which is also published by the Classical Association. Recent issues have covered such topics as "Greek Local Historiography and Its Audiences"; "Protagoras' Great Speech"; "Memmius the Epicurean"; and "Anaximander's Spartan Sundial." Although *Classical Quarterly* may not appeal to laypersons or amateur enthusiasts of the Classics, it is an indispensable resource for serious scholars and professional classicists.

1280. *The Classical Review.* [ISSN: 0009-840X] 1886. s-a. GBP 229 (print & online eds.)). Ed(s): Roger Rees, Mike Edwards. Cambridge University Press, University Printing House, Shaftesbury Rd, Cambridge, CB2 8BS, United Kingdom; journals@cambridge.org; https://www.cambridge.org/. Illus., index, adv. Sample. Refereed. Microform: PMC; PQC. Reprint: PSC. *Indexed:* A01, A22, AmHI, BRI, CBRI, E01, MLA-IB. *Bk. rev.:* 150, 100-2,000 words. *Aud.:* Ac.

The Classical Review, also published by the Classical Association of Great Britain, is a semi-annual collection of book reviews "covering the literatures and civilizations of ancient Greece and Rome." Each issue features about 150 reviews and 50 brief notes, providing an impressive swath of current scholarship in the Classics. Recent issues have included "The Homeric Epics and Other Texts"; versions of history in ancient Greece; "Plutarch's Versatility"; and a re-consideration of Cassius Dio. Like the *Bryn Mawr Classical Review*, *Classical Review* is an important tool for any librarian seeking to build a strong collection in Classical Studies.

1281. *Classical World: a quarterly journal on antiquity.* Formerly (until 1957): *The Classical Weekly;* Which superseded (in 1907): *The New York Latin Leaflet.* [ISSN: 0009-8418] 1907. q. USD 85. Ed(s): Lee T Pearcy, Robin Mitchell-Boyask. The Johns Hopkins University Press, 2715 N Charles St, Baltimore, MD 21218; http://www.press.jhu.edu. Illus., adv. Sample. Refereed. Vol. ends: Jun/Aug. Reprint: PSC. *Indexed:* A22, AmHI, BRI, CBRI, E01, MLA-IB. *Bk. rev.:* 15-20, 300-500 words. *Aud.:* Hs, Ac.

A quarterly publication of the Classical Association of the Atlantic States, *Classical World* covers the literature, history, and society of ancient Greece and Rome, especially from a pedagogical perspective. "The ideal reader of *Classical World* is a scholarly teacher or a teaching scholar, and the ideal contributor has something to say to this reader." Every issue features original articles, research bibliographies, and reviews of scholarly monographs, textbooks, and other teaching materials. Each issue also includes information about scholarships, fellowships, conferences, and other programming of interest both to teachers and students of the Classics. Recent issues have focused on themes such as slavery, the Harvard School, and writing imperial politics in Greek. *Classical World* is a first-rate journal that would appeal to both high school and collegiate readers.

1282. *Didaskalia.* [ISSN: 1321-4853] 1994. irreg. Free. Ed(s): Amy R Cohen. Randolph College, 2500 Rivermont Ave, Lynchburg, VA 24503; helpdesk@randolphcollege.edu; http://www.randolphcollege.edu/. Illus. Refereed. *Indexed:* IIPA. *Bk. rev.:* 2-3, 1,000-2,000 words. *Aud.:* Ga, Ac.

Started in 1994 as a "notice board" for discussing productions of ancient drama, *Didaskalia* is an open-access online journal that features the study of all Greek and Roman performance, both ancient and modern. Each issue offers scholarly articles on the performance of Classical drama, dance, and music, as well as reviews of contemporary productions, previews of upcoming productions, and interviews with artists and scholars. A recent issue "takes a snapshot of a tiny fraction of the computer-aided projects and initiatives that are rapidly changing how we study ancient performance." *Didaskalia* also publishes opinions or essays reflecting personal views on aspects of ancient performance. Given the cultural importance of performance in the Classical world and the diachronic interplay between ancient Greek and Roman authors and modern artists, a publication such as *Didaskalia* is a wonderful resource for both scholars of ancient performance and contemporary performers.

1283. *Greece & Rome.* [ISSN: 0017-3835] 1931. s-a. GBP 146 (print & online eds.)). Ed(s): Robert Shorrock, Vedia Izzet. Cambridge University Press, University Printing House, Shaftesbury Rd, Cambridge, CB2 8BS, United Kingdom; online@cambridge.org; https://www.cambridge.org/. Illus., adv. Sample. Refereed. Microform: PQC. Reprint: PSC. *Indexed:* A01, A22, AmHI, BRI, E01, MLA-IB. *Bk. rev.:* 2-3, 500-1,000 words. *Aud.:* Hs, Ga, Ac.

Greece & Rome, another publication by the Classical Association of Great Britain, aims to deliver classical scholarship "to a wider audience." Each issue features several articles of general interest on various aspects of Greek and Roman literature, history, and culture. Reviews of recently published books are also included, as well as subject reviews that provide concise updates for different disciplines within the field of Classical Studies. Recent issues have covered a wide range of topics: "Understanding Delphi Through Tibet"; "Diplomacy and Language between Greece and Rome"; "The Beginnings of Roman Naval Power"; and "Greek Culture in Afghanistan and India: Old Evidence and New Discoveries." It is rare to find a journal that makes academic scholarship more accessible to the layperson without oversimplifying the subject matter, but *Greece & Rome* manages to challenge readers of all levels of expertise while at the same time engaging them.

1284. *Mnemosyne: a journal of classical studies.* [ISSN: 0026-7074] 1852. bi-m. EUR 981. Brill, PO Box 9000, Leiden, 2300 PA, Netherlands; marketing@brill.com; https://brill.com. Illus., adv. Refereed. Vol. ends: Nov. Microform: SWZ. Reprint: PSC. *Indexed:* A01, A22, AmHI, BRI, E01, MLA-IB. *Bk. rev.:* 10-12, 500-1,500 words. *Aud.:* Ac.

Published four times a year, *Mnemosyne* is one of the oldest journals in the field of Classical Studies. Each issue features between 12 and 20 articles that focus primarily on ancient Greek and Latin philology and textual criticism, with extensive short notes and occasional book reviews. The subject matter is highly technical and requires subject expertise in Classical languages. Recent articles have included "Women and the Language of Food in the Plays of Aristophanes"; "The Art and Rhetoric of Lucian's Hippias"; "Proclus on the Forms of Attributes"; and "Odysseus as Storyteller." Although this journal will appeal only to a limited audience, *Mnemosyne* is the ne plus ultra of Classical philology, and thus is a required title for any college or university that offers advanced study in Greek or Latin.

1285. *Phoenix (Toronto, 1946).* [ISSN: 0031-8299] 1947. s-a. USD 151 (print & online eds.)). Ed(s): Judith K Schutz, B Akrigg. Classical Association of Canada, Trinity College, 6 Hoskin Ave, Toronto, ON M5S 1H8, Canada; http://www.cac-scec.ca. Illus., index. Refereed. *Indexed:* A22, MLA-IB. *Bk. rev.:* 15-20, 500-1,000 words. *Aud.:* Ac.

Published by the University of Toronto Press for the Classical Association of Canada, *Phoenix* features "the literature, language, history, philosophy, religion, mythology, science, archaeology, art, architecture, and culture of the Greek and Roman worlds from earliest times to about AD 600." Each issue contains several articles and 15 to 20 book reviews written in English and French. Recent issues have included "Gendered Speech in Sophocles' Electra"; "The Size of the Tragic Chorus"; and "Debt, Land, and Labor in the Early Republican Economy." With no recent publications from *Mouseion*, the Classical Association of Canada's other professional journal, *Phoenix* is now an essential resource for keeping abreast of scholarly research in the Classics in Canada, and as such it is an excellent addition to any academic library collection.

1286. *T A P A.* Formerly (until 201?): *American Philological Association. Transactions;* Which superseded (in 1974): *American Philological Association. Transactions and Proceedings;* Which was formerly (until 1897): *American Philological Association. Transactions.* [ISSN: 2575-7180] 1870. s-a. USD 150. The Johns Hopkins University Press, 2715 N Charles St, Baltimore, MD 21218; http://www.press.jhu.edu. Illus., adv. Sample. Refereed. *Indexed:* A01, A22, AmHI, E01, MLA-IB. *Aud.:* Ac.

The official research publication of the American Philological Association, *TAPA* (formerly *Transactions of the American Philological Association*) is the main clearinghouse of scholarship in the field of Classical Studies. This journal is now published two times a year, and each issue contains between six and ten articles on various topics in Greek and Latin literature, Classical philology, and ancient history. Each Autumn issue includes an address from the current APA president, as well. Recent articles have featured such topics as citizenship and empire before and after Augustus; "Authorial Pagination in the Eclogues and Georgics"; and "Plato's Defense of Athens." Although it goes without saying that *TAPA* is an essential title for any library collection that supports studies of Ancient Greek and Latin, it is also an excellent snapshot of the current state of Classical Studies, and as such would be a welcome addition to any academic research library.

■ CLASSROOM MAGAZINES

Art/Foreign Language/Language Arts/Life Skills/Mathematics/Science/ Social Studies and Current Events/Teacher and Professional

See also Children; Education; and Teenagers sections.

Kacy Lundstrom, Instruction Coordinator, Utah State University, Logan, UT 84322-3000; kacy.lundstrom@usu.edu

Introduction

These magazines provide creative, hands-on ways for students in the K–12 classroom to enjoy learning. They also provide ways for teachers to support this learning, including providing teachers with tips and ideas for how they can facilitate learning by using these resources. These magazines give students introductory practice with discipline-specific vocabulary and research. They can also garner student interest in unique and visual ways, and can also help save teachers' time by providing ideas or specific instructions for lessons that are relevant and creative.

The magazines listed in this section target students and specify target ages relating to reading level. Some magazines are primarily or solely found in online formats, while nearly all have moved toward having a strong online presence. For easy identification of how these magazines would correspond with classroom content or student interests, sources are listed by subject.

Since the latest edition of *MFL*, one major change is the merger of the Weekly Reader company and Scholastic. Due to market pressures and decreasing school budgets, titles such as *Current Events, Current Science,* and *Weekly Reader* have been folded into related Scholastic publications. According to Scholastic's web site, this merger allows them to offer "a line of classroom magazines that combine the classic curriculum support of Weekly Reader with the educational expertise of Scholastic."

A number of these titles cater specifically to teachers, identifiable mainly by the integration of direct tips, lesson plans, and activities for how to use magazine content in the classroom. The titles can be found within the "Teacher and Professional" subsection. Suggestions for integration include ideas for (1) how to use unique art or current-event stories to stimulate critical thinking; (2) how to create collaborative learning opportunities for students; and (3) classroom discussion. Material is designed to help students meet learning objectives and to enrich classroom curriculum. To assist in giving specific instructions and guides for how to integrate magazine content into the classroom, many of these resources are accompanied by supplementary web sites, CDs, learning goals, and assessment ideas. Magazines such as *Scope* have new online interactive features, as well as classroom resources designed for use on a whiteboard or projector.

Most of the magazines in this section are published in the U.S., although similar magazines are also produced in other countries (e.g., Canada or Australia). One major foreign language publisher, Authentik Language Learning Resources Ltd., a campus company of Trinity College, Dublin, was also forced into liquidation due to market challenges.

The education pedagogy reflected in these magazines through its content and instruction ideas tends to mirror the goals of current pedagogy in today's educational research. Magazines that specifically focus on theory are listed in the "Education" section of this volume or in the corresponding subject discipline section, such as "Art," or "Marine Science and Technology."

The titles listed here are likely to be classroom subscriptions, while the titles that are more likely to be personal subscriptions are listed in the "Children" and "Teenagers" sections, although a number of those titles could also be applicable in a classroom setting. Subscriptions are available as classroom sets or at a discounted per-issue price.

Basic Periodicals

Select by subject and audience level.

Basic Abstracts and Indexes

Academic Search Premier, Education Research Complete, ERIC, MAS Ultra: School Edition, Primary Search, OmniFile (Wilson).

Art

Dramatics. See Theater section.

1287. ***Scholastic Art: grades 7-12.*** Formerly (until 1992): *Art and Man;* Incorporates: *Artist Junior.* [ISSN: 1060-832X] 1970. 6x/yr. Students, USD 8.99. Scholastic Inc., 557 Broadway, New York, NY 10012; news@scholastic.com; http://www.scholastic.com. Illus., index. Sample. Vol. ends: Apr/May. *Indexed:* A22. *Aud.:* Ems, Hs.

This beautifully illustrated magazine introduces students to classical and contemporary art and artists from around the world. The "Artist of the Month" column features an interview with a student artist from among the winners of the Scholastic Art and Writing Award. Each issue features a "Masterpiece of the Month," with a poster of the featured artist's work in the teacher's edition and mini-posters in each student issue. "Art Spotlight" and "Critics Corner" are regular skills features. The new "Career Corner" page features an interview with an art professional, as well as a career profile with salary and education information and advice on what a student can do to prepare for a career in that particular field. The teacher's edition for grades 7-12 (free with orders of ten or more student subscriptions) includes discussion questions, an answer key for the skills sections, a lesson plan for the "Art Workshop," a reproducible question sheet for the featured theme, and a list of the National Content Standards for the Visual Arts to which each article correlates. An additional teacher's edition for working with students in grades 4-6 is also included. The web site includes an editorial calendar, with topics and artists for the year's upcoming issues, that teachers can use to plan future lessons. URL: http://teacher.scholastic.com

Stone Soup. See Children section.

Foreign Language

1288. ***Ciao Italia: il mensile per il tuo italiano.*** [ISSN: 0997-0290] 6x/yr. European Language Institute (E L I), Casella Postale 6, Recanati, 62019, Italy; editorial@elionline.com; http://www.elimagazines.com. Illus. *Aud.:* Ems, Hs.

One of many foreign-language magazines from this publisher, *Ciao Italia* is intended for students in their second year of Italian ("lower intermediate" level). Other magazines target various levels of language proficiency from elementary school through college. All include comic strips, puzzles, and games to teach vocabulary. Topical articles provide reading practice and enhance comprehension. Elementary-level magazines include colorful pictures, games, and classroom activities. Intermediate levels place greater emphasis on civilization and culture and contain articles about music, sports, movies, and the Internet. More advanced levels provide excerpts from contemporary literature, enhanced glossaries, and a wider variety of articles. Teachers' guides include reproducible activities as well as a list of the lessons, goals, and grammar to be covered in each of the year's issues. Audio CDs accompany classroom orders for most of the magazines. Other magazines from this publisher include: Italian: *Azzurro,* for students of various ages beginning to learn Italian; *Ragazzi* (intermediate); *Tutti Insieme* (upper intermediate); and *Oggitalia,* for advanced students. German: *Fertig...los,* for students beginning to study German; *Kinder* (lower intermediate); *Freunde* (intermediate); and *Zusammen* (upper intermediate). Spanish: *Vamos!,* for students beginning to study Spanish; *Chicos* (lower intermediate); *Muchachos* (intermediate); and *Todos Amigos* (upper intermediate). French: *Voila,* for beginning French in elementary school; *C'est Facile,* for the next level of beginning study; *Mome* (lower intermediate); *Jeunes* (intermediate); *Ensemble* (upper intermediate); and *Presse-Papiers,* for advanced students. Latin: *Adulescens,* for students with a beginning knowledge of Latin; and *Iuvenis* (lower intermediate). Russian: *Davai,* for students studying Russian at an intermediate level. For students of English as a Second Language, ELI publishes *Ready for English,* for primary school; *Let's Start,* for secondary beginners; *A Tot for English* (lower intermediate to one year of English); *Kid* (intermediate to two years of English); *Teen* (upper intermediate to three years of English); and *Sure!,* for advanced students. The web site also includes teacher resources, such as reading texts, song lyrics, activities, and professional development materials. The "Play & Learn" section has games, comics, picture dictionaries, tests in the various languages, and e-mail postcards. URL: www.elimagazines.com

1289. ***Que Tal - Grades 6-12.*** Formerly: *Oye.* [ISSN: 0033-5940] 1966. bi-m. Students, USD 7.99 6 issues. Mary Glasgow Magazines, Westfield Rd, Southam, CV47 0RA, United Kingdom; orders@maryglasgowplus.com; http://maryglasgowplus.com. Illus. Sample. *Aud.:* Hs.

Distributed through Scholastic, this colorful Mary Glasgow (London) magazine is aimed at first-year students of Spanish. Teen-interest content-such as interviews, activities, puzzles, and games-helps build language proficiency and cultural awareness. "Teacher's Notes" (in English), free with class subscriptions, provides additional teaching ideas, background information to complement articles, reproducible worksheets, activities, and quizzes. For each title, two audio CDs (with tracks corresponding to each issue) include an engaging radio show format, games, contests, original songs for singing along, and an illustrated booklet with full audio transcripts. The price per student is $6.95 for six issues. Other Mary Glasgow magazines include: Spanish: *Ahora,* for advanced beginners; and *El Sol,* for intermediate and advanced learners. French: *Allons-y!,* for beginners and near-beginners; *Bonjour,* for advanced beginners; *Ca Va?,* for intermediate; and *Chez Nous,* for advanced. German: *Das Rad,* for beginners and near-beginners; and *Schuss,* for intermediate. In addition, several Mary Glasgow titles are distributed only in Canada. *La Petite Press* is a French-language magazine for ages 7-11 with teacher's notes available in English or French. A series for English language learners includes *Click* (beginner level), *Crown* (pre-intermediate), *Team* and *Club* (intermediate), and *Current* (advanced).

Language Arts

Cricket. See Children section.

1290. ***Scholastic Action.*** [ISSN: 0163-3570] 1977. 12x/yr. Students, USD 85. Ed(s): Janice Behrans. Scholastic Inc., 557 Broadway, New York, NY 10012; news@scholastic.com; http://www.scholastic.com. Illus. Sample. *Indexed:* MASUSE, P01. *Aud.:* Hs.

Action is a reading and language arts magazine that covers teen topics for middle and high school students reading at a third- to fifth-grade level. Celebrity profiles, debate topics, and real-life skill activities provide engaging reading material for teens. A series of read-aloud plays based upon current movies, TV shows, and classic books is designed to be integrated into the curriculum and help students with decoding, fluency, and class participation. Every story is followed by a reading comprehension quiz. The "True Teen" nonfiction articles highlight teens who have overcome personal and social challenges. A teen advice column appears in every issue. Graphic organizers and other tools accompanying the articles help students to improve their reading comprehension and suggest strategies for reading, writing, and vocabulary building. The teacher's edition includes "Issue at a Glance," which ties articles to skills, activities, and related standards. It contains lesson plans and reproducible worksheets as well as a planning calendar. This magazine could also be useful for ESL students.

1291. ***Scholastic Let's Find Out: my weekly reader.*** Incorporates (in 201?): *Let's Find Out;* Formerly (until 1995): *My First Magazine.* [ISSN: 0024-1261] 19??. 32x/yr. Students, USD 5.25. Scholastic Inc., 557 Broadway, New York, NY 10012; news@scholastic.com; http://www.scholastic.com. Illus. Sample. Vol. ends: May/Jun. *Aud.:* Ems.

Each month, *LFO* provides teaching ideas for the five critical areas of early reading: phonemic awareness, phonics, fluency, vocabulary, and comprehension in four themed issues. Pictures, stories, and activities help pre-K and kindergarten children discover the world around them. Regular sections include "Kids Can Do It," "Science," "People and Places," and "Early Reader." "My Rebus Reader" is a new mini-book format featured in each issue, which began in March 2009. There is also a section, "Look What I'm Learning at School" (which includes "Let's Find Out Goes Home"), that comprises activities to be done with parents or family, with instructions in both English and Spanish. Free classroom posters in full color are included in each issue. The teacher's guide, included with each subscription, contains cross-curricular activities, tips for teaching with the posters, NAEYC guidelines and connections to state and national standards, and links to additional resources.

1292. ***Scholastic Scope: the language arts magazine.*** Incorporates: *Read Magazine.* [ISSN: 0036-6412] 1964. bi-w. during school year. Scholastic Inc., 557 Broadway, New York, NY 10012; custserv@scholastic.com; http://www.scholastic.com. Illus., adv. Sample. *Indexed:* A01, A22, P01. *Bk. rev.:* Number and length vary. *Aud.:* Ems.

Scholastic Scope, which absorbed Weekly Reader's *READ* when the two companies merged, provides literature and writing activities for sixth- to tenth-grade students, including read-aloud plays, writing workshops, vocabulary builders, and reading strategies. Each issue provides writing prompts, puzzles, a "Readers Theater" play, and regular features such as "You Be the Editor," which works on particular grammar elements such as pronouns or quotations, and the "Scope 100," challenging words taken from SAT/ACT lists. The "Having Your Say" writing program invites readers to submit their poetry, book reviews, music reviews, essays, and stories for publication in the magazine. Skill-building features and test-preparation lessons are tied to state and national standards. *Scholastic Scope* works on skills such as sequencing, listening, graph reading, and comprehension. The teacher's edition includes lesson plans with pre-reading activities and post-reading discussion questions, as well as reproducible pages. Now includes digital lessons on the web site. URL: www.scholastic.com/scopemagazine/index.html

1293. ***Storyworks - Grades 3-6: language arts.*** [ISSN: 1068-0292] 1993. 6x/yr. Students, USD 6.99. Scholastic Inc., 557 Broadway, New York, NY 10012; custserv@scholastic.com; http://www.scholastic.com. Illus. Sample. Vol. ends: Apr/May. *Indexed:* BRI, P01. *Bk. rev.:* 4-5, 125 words. *Aud.:* Ems.

A literature magazine for grades 3-6, *Storyworks* features fiction, nonfiction, poetry, plays, and illustrations by award-winning children's authors and artists. Activities that develop grammar, writing, vocabulary, and test-taking skills complement the readings. "Reviews by You" publishes students' reviews of books they've read. "Sentence Chef" and "Writing Rescue" provide writing skills exercises. "Word Nerd" introduces vocabulary, and "Grammar Cop" and "WordWorks" supply practice with grammatical concepts and parts of speech. "Micro Mystery" builds comprehension with reading for detail. Writing activities in the "Yesterday and Today" feature present side-by-side articles for students to compare and contrast an event or person from the past with the contemporary equivalent. Contests and author interviews offer students the opportunity to experience literature in more active and personal ways. In the teacher's guide, the feature "At a Glance" lists articles with corresponding themes and standards. The web site has additional lessons, quizzes, activities, and contests.

Life Skills

1294. ***Choices with Current Health - Grades 7-12.*** Incorporates (in 1999): *Health Choices;* Supersedes (in 1985): *Co-Ed;* Incorporates (in 1991): *Forecast for the Home Economist;* Which superseded (in 1986): *Forecast for Home Economics;* (1963-1966): *Practical Forecast for Home Economics.* [ISSN: 0883-475X] 1956. 8x/yr. USD 9.49. Scholastic Inc., 557 Broadway, New York, NY 10012; custserv@scholastic.com; http://www.scholastic.com. Illus., index, adv. Sample. Vol. ends: May. *Indexed:* A01, A22, BRI, C37, C42, MASUSE, P01. *Aud.:* Ems, Hs.

This life skills magazine for grades 7-12 features articles about health and nutrition, family life, decision making, careers, and personal development, using examples of interest to this age group. Weight and healthy lifestyles, sportsmanship and competition, teen pregnancy, and personal responsibility are some of the topics covered. Each article includes an activity that encourages students to apply what they've learned. Features include "Sticky Situation," in which students help other students as positive peer role models with issues such as substance abuse and personal relationships, and "Recipe 101," featuring recipes from an 18-year-old chef. The teacher's edition summarizes the articles, ties them to applicable standards, and provides discussion questions and additional activities for the featured stories. The tone is upbeat and not condescending; difficult issues are presented honestly. Because of the high interest of the subject matter, this magazine could be used as discussion material in a variety of subjects or settings-for example, language arts, health, or social studies.

1295. ***Imagine (Baltimore): big ideas for bright minds.*** [ISSN: 1071-605X] 1993. 5x/yr. USD 50. Ed(s): Melissa Hartman. The Johns Hopkins University Press, 2715 N Charles St, Baltimore, MD 21218; http://www.press.jhu.edu. Sample. *Indexed:* A22, E01. *Bk. rev.:* Number and length vary. *Aud.:* Hs.

Written for gifted students in grades 7-12, this exciting periodical is a five-time winner of the Parents Choice Gold Award. Each issue focuses on a general subject area, such as public health, politics and government, writing, philosophy, or "the art and science of games." Emphasis is given to activities that students can do *now* to pursue that interest, as well as career opportunities in that field. Each issue includes articles about summer programs and extracurricular activities across the country (written by student participants), student reviews of selective colleges, advice on planning for college, career profiles of accomplished professionals, puzzles, web resources, and book reviews written by students.

Mathematics

1296. ***Scholastic Dynamath.*** Formerly (until 1982): *Scholastic Math Power.* [ISSN: 0732-7773] 1992. 8x/yr. Students, USD 6.99. Ed(s): Jack Silbert. Scholastic Inc., 557 Broadway, New York, NY 10012; news@scholastic.com; http://www.scholastic.com. Illus. Sample. Vol. ends: May. *Indexed:* P01. *Aud.:* Ems.

A workbook/magazine for grades 3-6, *Dynamath* reinforces basic math skills with colorful pictures, problems, and puzzles. Telling time, measurements, map reading, and problem solving are among the skills taught. Features include "Math on the Job," "Numbers in the News," and "Money Math" to help students with problem solving. The teacher's edition includes an answer key; lesson plans and extension activities; a "Problem of the Day" planning calendar to introduce math lessons with a warm-up exercise; and a table that correlates math features with national math standards (National Council for Teachers of Mathematics; NCTM).

1297. ***Scholastic Math - Grades 6-9.*** [ISSN: 0198-8379] 1980. 5x/yr. Scholastic Inc., 557 Broadway, New York, NY 10012; custserv@scholastic.com; http://www.scholastic.com. Illus., adv. Sample. *Indexed:* MASUSE, P01. *Aud.:* Ems, Hs.

Scholastic Math for grades 6-9 is designed to prepare junior high students for pre-algebra. Math problems are illustrated in articles on current, real-world, age-appropriate topics. Features include "Fast Math" brainteasers, "Sports by the Numbers," "Math at Work," "Math in Literature," and "Math for Your Daily Life." Skills exercises, quizzes, and practice tests help prepare students for standardized tests. Movies, celebrities, sports, consumer math, and math-related news make complex concepts accessible and entertaining. The teacher's edition contains teaching tips, extension activities, and a skills guide that correlates the articles to National Council for Teachers of Mathematics (NCTM) standards that are covered in each issue.

Science

1298. ***National Geographic Explorer.*** Formerly (until 2003): *National Geographic for Kids.* [ISSN: 1541-3357] 2001. 7x/yr. USD 4.75 combined subscription (print & online eds.)). National Geographic Society, 1145 17th St, NW, Washington, DC 20036; http://www.nationalgeographic.com/. Illus., adv. Sample. *Indexed:* BRI, MASUSE. *Aud.:* Ems.

The National Geographic Society offers two editions of this colorful magazine, which helps students to develop nonfiction reading skills using science, social studies, and geography content. The *Pioneer Edition* is written at a second- to third-grade reading level and the *Pathfinder Edition* is written for fourth- to sixth-graders. Both editions look alike and feature the same topics, maps, graphs, and illustrations, but vary the text and concepts in terms of length and complexity. The editions can be used separately for a specific grade level or combined for differentiated instruction so that teachers can mix and match to address students' individual reading levels. The standards-based articles help teachers to meet NCLB goals. The "Teacher's Guide," included with each issue, contains suggested teaching strategies, "fast facts" about the featured subject matter, reproducible worksheets for checking comprehension, and extension activities for writing practice and making connections between disciplines. Supplementary content, such as games, e-cards, puzzles, and additional links can be found on the web site, as well as one article from each issue translated into Spanish (URL: www.nationalgeographic.com/ngexplorer). *National Geographic Young Explorer* [ISSN 1930-8116] is geared to a kindergarten-grade 1 reading level. This magazine develops literacy skills and introduces word patterns and rhymes through poetry while teaching standards-based science and social studies content. Designed for reluctant readers in grades 6-12, *National Geographic Extreme Explorer* [ISSN 1938-8004] uses engaging science and social studies-based stories and photographs to reinforce literacy skills. Specific reading strategies are highlighted at the beginning of each story.

1299. *Scholastic Science World - Grades 6-10.* Incorporates (in 19??): *Current Science;* Former titles (until 19??): *Science World;* (until 1987): *Scholastic Science World;* (until 1974): *Science World (1965);* Which incorporated (1965-1968): *Senior Science (1965);* Which was formerly (1960-1965): *Science World. Edition 2;* Science World (1965) was formerly (until 1965): *Science World. Edition 1;* Both of which superseded in part (in 1960): *Senior Science.* 1957. m. during school year. Scholastic Inc., 557 Broadway, New York, NY 10012; news@scholastic.com; http://www.scholastic.com. Illus., index, adv. Sample. Circ: 390298. Vol. ends: May. *Indexed:* A22, BRI, C37, MASUSE, P01. *Aud.:* Ems, Hs.

Newly titled *Science World Current Science* due to its merger with Weekly Reader, this magazine shares articles and hands-on experiments for grades 6-10. Each issue features interesting articles on topics in the fields of physical, earth/space, life/health, and environmental sciences, as well as technology. Hands-on experiments with photos, diagrams, maps, graphs, and charts are regular features, as are puzzles, quizzes, and brain-teasers that help students understand scientific processes. Regular features include "I Want That Job," an interview with a career professional in the sciences, and "Gross Out," which looks at aspects of nature or scientific phenomena that may be outside our comfort zone or experience. The teacher's edition provides lesson plans and a table that connects content to appropriate National Science Education Standards. It also contains an answer key, reproducible skills pages, and additional quizzes to test vocabulary, reading comprehension, and understanding of graphs and maps.

1300. *Scholastic SuperScience - Grades 3-6.* Formed by the merger of (1989-1997): *SuperScience Blue;* (1989-1997): *SuperScience Red.* 1997. 8x/yr. Students, USD 6.99. Ed(s): Britt Norlander. Scholastic Inc., 557 Broadway, New York, NY 10012; custserv@scholastic.com; http://www.scholastic.com. Illus., index. Sample. Vol. ends: Apr/May. *Indexed:* BRI, C37, MASUSE, P01. *Aud.:* Ems.

A cross-curricular science newsmagazine for grades 3-6, *SuperScience* is theme-based and includes many color photos that teach earth, life, and physical science concepts. Hands-on activities, experiments, and quizzes on the news stories actively engage students in the content. The teacher's guide provides background information, teaching strategies, discussion prompts, additional activities, reproducible worksheets, and answer keys. Regular features include "Science Mystery," where students read a fictional text, then use scientific method and data to solve the case; and the "You Asked" column, which answers a student-generated question in each issue. "Cool Science Jobs" features an interview with a scientist and gives information about preparation, skills, and salary for that career. Feature articles are tied to curriculum areas through process skills addressed in each activity (e.g., observe, compare, use numbers, hypothesize, etc.). *SuperScience* features help teachers meet local, state, and National Science Education standards.

1301. *Science News: magazine of the society for science and the public.* Former titles (until 1966): *Science News Letter; Science News Bulletin.* [ISSN: 0036-8423] 1922. 26x/yr. Ed(s): Tom Siegfried. Science Service, 1719 N St, NW, Washington, DC 20036; subnews@sciserv.org; http://www.sciencenews.org/. Illus., index, adv. Circ: 133000 Paid. Vol. ends: Dec. Microform: PQC. *Indexed:* A01, A22, Agr, BRI, C37, MASUSE. *Bk. rev.:* 6-8, 125 words. *Aud.:* Hs, Ga.

Science News is packed with information about what's happening in the science community. Brief news articles that cover a broad spectrum of science can provide material for class discussion or student writing assignments. Sections include "Atom and Cosmos," "Body and Brain," "Matter and Energy," "Earth," "Numbers," "Humans," and "Science and Society." *Science News Online* provides an archive of past issues with free access to cover stories and additional access for subscribers. Also available on the web site are special features, such as blogs and book listings. RSS feeds are available for topic, department, blogs, and columns. The "Science News for Kids" section of the web site links to articles on topics of particular interest to younger readers. Although the magazine is not specifically aimed at K-12 students, it is very popular in middle and high schools, and is highly recommended. URL: www.sciencenews.org

Social Studies and Current Events

Cobblestone. See Children section.

1302. *Junior Scholastic: the current events magazine.* [ISSN: 0022-6688] 1937. bi-w. Scholastic Inc., 557 Broadway, New York, NY 10012; custserv@scholastic.com; http://www.scholastic.com. Illus., index, adv. Sample. *Indexed:* C37, P01. *Aud.:* Ems.

Junior Scholastic merged with Weekly Reader's *Current Events.* It remains a colorful current events magazine for grades 6-8. *Junior Scholastic: Current Events* features U.S. and world news, American and world history, biographical profiles, and maps. Articles focus on people and topics in the news, and the many photos and illustrations help students understand complex issues. The U.S. news section covers a wide variety of topics from anthropology and the environment to sports and entertainment. The "Debate" feature presents a controversial question with pro and con viewpoints to initiate classroom discussion. "MapSearch" and "GeoSkills" provide examples of different types of maps and guidance in how to read them. Additional features include key vocabulary at the end of each article, and questions to encourage further analysis of the topics. The teacher's edition contains supplementary material for the stories in the issue with references to additional resources, skills masters, activities, quizzes, and answer keys. The *Junior Scholastic* page on the *Scholastic News* web site contains additional supporting material, such as test-prep and skills reproducibles and links to online resources. URL: www.scholastic.com/juniorscholastic

1303. *The New York Times Upfront (Student Edition): the news magazine for teens.* Formerly (until 1999): *Scholastic Update;* Which was formed by the merger of (1972-1983): *Scholastic Search;* (1920-1983): *Senior Scholastic;* Which incorporated (in 19??): *American Observer;* Which was formerly (until 19??): *World Week.* [ISSN: 1525-1292] 1983. 14x/yr. Scholastic Inc., 557 Broadway, New York, NY 10012; custserv@scholastic.com; http://www.scholastic.com. Illus., index, adv. Sample. Vol. ends: May. *Indexed:* A01, A22, BRI, C42, MASUSE, P01. *Aud.:* Hs.

Upfront is a newsmagazine for teens that features in-depth coverage of current events, entertainment, and trends. Informative articles about national and international events, special reports, and interviews encourage high school students to consider various points of view. Recent articles examine the presidential election, the impact of the economy on the U.S. auto industry, education of girls in Afghanistan, and twenty-first-century piracy. The teacher's edition includes lesson plans for the national, international, economy, and "times past" sections with teaching objectives, classroom strategies, writing prompts, and quizzes. "Cartoon Analysis" and "Photo Analysis" activities in the teacher's edition promote media literacy with thought-provoking questions. Each student issue includes political cartoons from around the country and a debate question with pro and con viewpoints. A subscription also includes two special series: "Coming of Age," which focuses on the challenges teens face in the world today, and "Immigration in America," about the current debate over who gets to be an American. The web site supplements the print newsletter and links to additional teacher resources. URL: http://teacher.scholastic.com/upfront

1304. ***Scholastic News. Grade 5-6 Edition.*** Formed by the merger of (1952-1998): *Scholastic News (Edition 6);* Which was formerly (until 1993): *Scholastic Newstime;* (until 1989): *Scholastic News (Newstime Edition);* (until 1982): *Scholastic Newstime;* (1941-1998): *Scholastic News (Citizen Edition);* Which was formerly (until 1982): *Scholastic News Citizen;* (until 1973): *Young Citizen.* [ISSN: 1554-2440] 1998. 24x/yr. Students, USD 4.75. Ed(s): Lucille Renwick. Scholastic Inc., 557 Broadway, New York, NY 10012; news@scholastic.com; http://www.scholastic.com. Illus., index. *Indexed:* P01. *Aud.:* Ems.

This colorful current-events weekly, published in several editions, targets various reading levels and interests. This magazine absorbed Weekly Reader when the company merged with Scholastic. *Scholastic News,* in first-grade and second-grade editions (32 issues per year), helps students learn phonics, vocabulary, fluency, and comprehension skills by introducing them to real-world events, seasons, and holidays. Grade 1 and 2 editions also include posters, take-home activity pages, graphic organizers for teachers, and three big issues on "pencil-friendly paper" each month for guided reading. Editions 3 and 4 (24 issues each per year) build on those skills and introduce science, history, and geography topics. Both include a "Test Prep Program" with online quizzes, reproducibles, and diagnostic tests to help focus on improving standardized testing skills. Grade 3 includes "Place in the News," a current events and geography feature, and "Find It," which comprises mini-lessons that provide an activity for each story. Grade 4 and the senior edition (for fifth- and sixth-grade students) focus on current events, civic awareness, and geography with features such as "News Zone" and "News Map." "Graph of the Week" incorporates charts and graphs that illustrate data on topics of interest to readers, such as popular sports activities or favorite format for books they read. Editions sometimes include two-sided posters, and all have teacher's guides with lesson plans, reproducible pages, and additional resources. All content can be extended with material from the *Scholastic News Online* web site (www.scholasticnews.com). Meanwhile, *Scholastic News English/Espanol* (Levels 1 and 2) has a flip format that lets students read in their native language and then flip the magazine over to read the same content in English. Every issue has "Exploring Your World" sidebars that connect topics to Latino cultures. The teacher's edition contains "Let's Learn English with Maya and Miguel," which comprises reproducible pages that are meant to reinforce spelling and vocabulary.

1305. ***Time for Kids Around the World.*** Formerly (until 2010): *Time for Kids World Report;* Which superseded in part (in 1997): *Time for Kids.* 1995. 6x/yr. Time Inc., 1271 Ave of the Americas, New York, NY 10020; information@timeinc.com; http://www.timeinc.com. Illus. Vol. ends: May. *Bk. rev.:* Number and length vary. *Aud.:* Ems.

Time for Kids is a weekly newsmagazine that is published in three editions: *Big Picture* for grades K-1 (ages 4-7), *News Scoop* for grades 2-3 (ages 7-10), and *World Report* for grades 4-6 (ages 10-12). Each colorful issue is theme-based and contains articles, puzzles, and contests relating to the featured topic. Recent themes include "Green Schools," "Amazing Inventions," and "Animal Habitats." Issues also include spotlights on people with notable accomplishments, short book reports, and opinion columns. The web site contains highlights from the issues (including the cover story in both English and Spanish), quizzes, mini-lessons, a teacher's guide, and worksheets. *Time for Kids Around the World,* an eight-page magazine with a companion web site, integrates geography, reading, math, and science while introducing students to the people, languages, and culture of countries around the world. It is available to subscribers to the *World Report* and *News Scoop* editions for one dollar per student. URL: www.timeforkids.com

Teacher and Professional

Arts and Activities. See Education/Specific Subjects and Teaching Methods: The Arts section.

1306. ***Entrsekt.*** Former titles (until 2014): *Learning & Leading with Technology;* (until 1995): *The Computing Teacher; Oregon Computing Teacher.* [ISSN: 2334-2587] 19??. m. International Society for Technology in Education, 1710 Rhode Island Ave NW, Ste 900, Washington, DC 20036; iste@iste.org; http://www.iste.org. Illus., index. Sample. Vol. ends: May. Microform: PQC. *Indexed:* A22, BRI, ERIC. *Aud.:* Sa.

This membership publication that the International Society for Technology in Education (ISTE) calls its "flagship periodical" is for K-12 teachers and teacher educators with a broad range of experience in integrating technology into the classroom. Articles emphasize practical applications of technology. "Learning Connections" focuses on uses of technology for specific subjects (language arts, social studies, math, science, and physical education) and service learning. "Leading Connections" offers teacher-to-teacher advice on technology issues, professional development topics, and projects for the connected classroom. Each issue reviews new products and emerging technologies for teaching and learning. "Point/Counterpoint" provides opposing viewpoints on current education questions, and "Bloggers Beat" provides coverage of hot topics from bloggers and those who comment on their posts. The web site (www.iste.org) provides members with access to the full text of articles.

1307. ***Internet at Schools: an educator's guide to technology and the web.*** Former titles (until 2011): *MultiMedia & Internet at Schools;* (until 2003): *MultiMedia Schools.* [ISSN: 2156-843X] 1994. 5x/yr. USD 49.95 domestic; USD 64 in Canada & Mexico; USD 73 elsewhere. Ed(s): Kathie Felix, David Hoffman. Information Today, Inc., 143 Old Marlton Pike, Medford, NJ 08055; custserv@infotoday.com; http://www.infotoday.com. Illus., adv. Sample. *Indexed:* A01, A22, BRI, C37. *Bk. rev.:* 4. *Aud.:* Ac, Sa.

A practical how-to magazine for librarians, teachers, and media specialists, *MultiMedia & Internet@Schools* reports on, reviews, and discusses a wide array of electronic media, including Internet resources and online services, library systems, curriculum software, and administrative systems and tools to improve learning. Articles and columns address issues associated with using electronic information resources in K-12 schools. Regular features include "Cyberbee," informing on web resources for classroom use; "The Pipeline," which focuses on new technologies and new uses of current technologies; and various "Watch" columns, which highlight product and industry news. All are contributed by practicing educators who use new technologies in the classroom or media center. *MultiMedia & Internet@Schools* is addressed primarily to K-12 librarians and media specialists, but it also will be of interest to technology coordinators, principals, and other administrators. Register for a free account on the web site for links to current and archived content from the magazine, with free full text for some articles (the rest available on a pay-per-view basis) and all product reviews. Special discounts are available for first-time subscribers. You can also sign up to receive the *MMIS Xtra* newsletter via e-mail. URL: www.mmischools.com

1308. ***The Mailbox: the idea magazine for teachers.*** [ISSN: 0199-6045] 1972. bi-m. USD 29.95 domestic; USD 40.95 foreign. The Education Center, Inc., PO Box 9753, Greensboro, NC 27429; customerservice@themailbox.com; http://www.theeducationcenter.com. Illus., index, adv. Sample. Vol. ends: Dec/Jan. *Aud.:* Sa.

A colorful and engaging resource for teachers, *The Mailbox* is published in five editions: "Preschool," "Kindergarten," "Grade 1," "Grades 2-3," and "Intermediate." The "Preschool" edition includes arts and crafts, story time, circle time, songs, and science, among other activities that promote counting and pre-reading skills. A fold-out centerfold activity is included in each issue. "Kindergarten and Grade 1," formerly a combined edition, is now two separate editions. The "Kindergarten" edition contains many reproducibles as well as a centerfold pullout, and focuses on basic skills in math, literacy and literature, science, and social studies. "Grade 1" builds on those skills, introducing two-digit addition, fractions, and themed writing ideas. The "Grade 2-3" edition takes the math, reading, science, and cross-curricular activities to the next level, with the introduction of more grammar and additional emphasis on comprehension. The "Intermediate" edition features activities in the broad subject areas as well as a "Seasonal" category, with writing prompts and skills practice relating to the holidays and events of the season. The "Teachers Resource" section in all of the editions includes resources for classroom displays, management tips and timesavers, and activities sent in by subscribers in "Our Readers Write." *Mailbox Companion Online* is a free online service for subscribers that complements the print issue and contains a homepage specifically for the subscriber's edition of the magazine, additional reproducibles, and other magazine extenders to complement the units in every issue. "The Mailbox Blog" is searchable by topic and keyword and provides information about news, publications, and areas of interest to teachers.

Additionally, there is *Teacher's Helper: classroom skill builders* [ISSN 1078-6570]. 6/yr. USD 24.95. The Education Center, P.O. Box 9753, Greensboro, NC 27429-0753; www.themailbox.com. Illus. Vol. ends: Dec./Jan. *Aud:* Sa. Provides skill-based reproducible activity worksheets in four editions: "Kindergarten," "Grade 1," "Grades 2-3," and "Intermediate."

Mathematics Teacher. See Mathematics/General section.

1309. *Onestopenglish.* 200?. d. GBP 42; USD 68; EUR 53. Macmillan Education, Macmillan Oxford, Between Towns Rd, Oxford, OX4 3PP, United Kingdom; permissions@macmillan.com; http://www.macmillaneducation.com. Adv. *Aud.:* Sa.

Onestopenglish, a teacher's resource site published by Macmillan English Campus, part of the Macmillan Education Group, publishes materials developed for teachers of English as a first or second language. Currently there are over 420,000 users in over 100 countries. Materials are available in British and American English. There are three ways to access *Onestopenglish* resources: (1) You can browse the categories for free; all material is available for downloading for classroom use. (2) You can sign up as a registered user (also free) for access to expanded content, an interactive forum in which to share ideas with teachers around the world, and a monthly newsletter with up-to-date information about what's new on the site. Finally, (3) you can subscribe to the "Staff Room" for access to a database of over 6,500 resources searchable by age, level, and language focus. Resources include lesson plans, games, worksheets, and tips and suggestions for teachers of preschoolers through teenagers. Weekly news lessons from the *Guardian Weekly,* audio and podcasts, songs, games, music videos, and flashcards are also available, along with the series "Onestop Phonics." An individual subscription costs $62, and institutional subscriptions are based upon the number of teachers, starting at $288 for up to five teachers. A full-featured site for both English and ESL instruction, this is a very useful resource for teachers and students. URL: www.onestopenglish.com

1310. *Scholastic Early Childhood Today (Online).* [ISSN: 2168-2283] 1986. 8x/yr. Free. Scholastic Inc., 557 Broadway, New York, NY 10012; custserv@scholastic.com; http://www.scholastic.com. Adv. *Aud.:* Ac, Sa.

Early Childhood Today has transitioned from a print magazine to a solely online presence. The web site offers free access to a wealth of material from an archive that spans 22 years of serving early childhood professionals. *Early Childhood Today* features teaching tips and resources, online interactive learning activities, and management strategies. Articles focus on leadership issues as well as behavior and development. The "School-Home Connection" section includes articles about parent/teacher communication, as well as recommended send-home activities. The "Connect" section provides a discussion forum for teachers and tools for students to communicate as well. Professional resources include articles by experts in behavior and development in children from birth to age six, and reports from the field.

1311. *Scholastic.com.* Formerly (until 19??): *Scholastic Network.* 1920. w. Scholastic Inc., 557 Broadway, New York, NY 10012; custserv@scholastic.com; http://www.scholastic.com. *Aud.:* Ems, Sa.

An excellent source of information and classroom resources with separate areas for each of its target audiences (kids, parents, teachers, administrators, and librarians), the *Scholastic.com* web site emphasizes participation and interaction. The teacher's section includes lesson plans, printables and mini-books, teaching tips, and activities for pre-K through 12th grade. Dropout prevention strategies, assessment in the differentiated classroom, and content area writing are some of topics covered under the "Teaching Strategies" section. The "Tools" section provides teaching templates for creating rubrics, flash cards, and graphic organizers. The site also includes a "Classroom Homepage Builder" and "TeacherShare," a free, worldwide learning network for K-8 classroom teachers to create, edit, collaborate on, and share classroom content. URL: www.scholastic.com/home/

School Arts. See Education/Specific Subjects and Teaching Methods: The Arts section.

1312. *Science and Children.* Formerly (until 1963): *Elementary School Science Bulletin.* [ISSN: 0036-8148] 1952. 9x/yr. Free to members. National Science Teachers Association, 1840 Wilson Blvd, Arlington, VA 22201; nstapress@nsta.org; http://www.nsta.org/. Illus., index, adv. Sample. Refereed. Circ: 21000. Vol. ends: May. *Indexed:* A22, BRI, ERIC, WSA. *Bk. rev.:* 6, 300 words. *Aud.:* Sa.

Science and Children is a peer-reviewed journal from the National Science Teachers Association (NSTA) for elementary science teachers, science teacher administrators, and teacher educators. It features articles that discuss pedagogy and educational issues relevant to science teaching. The table of contents indicates whether articles apply to particular grade ranges (K-2, 3-6, K-6, etc.). "In the News" highlights discoveries and current research of interest to the science community. Regular features include "Finds & Sites," a list of free or inexpensive materials, publications, and events; "Teaching Through Trade Books," activities inspired by children's literature; and "Every Day Science Calendar," a monthly calendar with "facts and challenges for the science explorer." "Science 101" experts answer teachers' questions about everyday science. "NSTA Recommends" reviews both student texts and professional literature for science teachers. These reviews and others are also available online. URL: www.nsta.org/recommends

1313. *Science Scope.* Formerly (until 19??): *Middle Jr. High Science Bulletin.* [ISSN: 0887-2376] 1978. 9x/yr. Free to members. Ed(s): Ken Roberts. National Science Teachers Association, 1840 Wilson Blvd, Arlington, VA 22201; nstapress@nsta.org; http://www.nsta.org/. Illus., index, adv. Sample. Refereed. Vol. ends: May. *Indexed:* A22, BRI, ERIC. *Bk. rev.:* 3-4, 300 words. *Aud.:* Sa.

Produced by the National Science Teachers Association (NSTA), this is a professional journal for middle-level and junior high school science teachers. Peer-reviewed articles provide ready-to-use activities and teaching strategies for life science, physical science, and earth science. Regular features include "Science Sampler," descriptions and templates for classroom activities and field trips; "Tried and True," classic demonstrations and experiments; "Tech Trek," incorporating the latest technology in the classroom; "Scope on Safety," safety information for the classroom; and "Scope's Scoops," summaries of recent scientific news. "NSTA Recommends" highlights trade books. These reviews and others are available online. URL: www.nsta.org/recommends

The Science Teacher. See Astronomy section.

■ COMMUNICATION

See also Education; Journalism and Writing; Media and AV; and Television, Video, and Radio sections.

Laura A. Sullivan, Research and Information Services Librarian, Northern Kentucky University, Steely Library, Highland Heights, KY 41099; FAX: 859-572-6181; sullivanl@nku.edu.

Nancy F. Campbell, Assistant to the Dean for Library Services, Northern Kentucky University, Steely Library, Highland Heights, KY 41099; FAX: 859-572-6181; campbelln@nku.edu.

Michael J. Providenti, Web Development Librarian, Steely Library, Highland Heights, KY 41099; FAX: 859-572-6181; providenti@nku.edu

Introduction

This section features representative, critical publications in the discipline of communication. Titles chosen reflect scholarship and analysis in all fields of communication: mass, speech, interpersonal, organizational, rhetorical, and applied, among others. A large number of articles reflect the political times, with a particular current spotlight on "fake news," as well as social media's political influence. All titles of the National Communication Association are featured (it is the oldest and largest national organization to advance communication scholarship and education), including its online publications. In general, the list includes many well-known core periodicals within the discipline.

Recent titles added include *communication+1*; *Discourse & Communication*; *International Journal of Listening*; and *Journal of Intercultural Communication Research*. While it is recognized that there are numerous communication periodicals that focus on a specific type of communication - such as political, business, visual, health, and so on - for purposes of consistency, the current list concentrates on key, broad publications, although these titles publish articles on specialized communication areas. The trend of open-access publications is reflected in our selections. Emphasis is on academic titles; however, the necessary titles for larger public libraries are represented, as well.

Basic Periodicals

Ac: *Argumentation & Advocacy, Communication Education, Communication Monographs, Communication Quarterly, Communication Reports, Communication Research, Communication Research Reports, Critical Studies in Media Communication, Human Communication Research, Journal of Applied Communication Research, Journal of Communication, Quarterly Journal of Speech, Southern Communication Journal, Western Journal of Communication.*

Basic Abstracts and Indexes

Communication & Mass Media Complete, Communication Abstracts, ERIC, Humanities Index, PsycINFO, Sociological Abstracts.

1314. *Advances in the History of Rhetoric.* [ISSN: 1536-2426] 1997. s-a. GBP 214 print & online eds. Ed(s): Ekaterina Haskins. Routledge, 530 Walnut St, Ste 850, Philadelphia, PA 19106; enquiries@tandfonline.com; http://www.tandfonline.com. Refereed. Circ: 160 Paid and controlled. Reprint: PSC. *Indexed:* AmHI, MLA-IB. *Bk. rev.:* Number and length vary. *Aud.:* Ac.

As the annual research publication of the American Society for the History of Rhetoric, this title "welcomes contributions from scholars who take a historical approach to the study of rhetoric," including theory, discourse, criticism - across disciplines and across all historical periods. Recent article subjects include William Jennings Bryan and rhetoric and rhetoric in ancient Greece. Recommended for academic libraries.

1315. *American Communication Journal.* [ISSN: 1532-5865] 1997. q. Free. Ed(s): Wei Zha. American Communication Association, c/o Anita K. McDaniel, Editor, Department of Communication Studies, Wilmington, NC 28403; mcdaniela@uncw.edu; http://www.americancomm.org/. Refereed. *Bk. rev.:* Irregular. *Aud.:* Ac, Sa.

This title's goal is to be a primary online source for "interdisciplinary scholarship on communication," enabling authors to incorporate multimedia into their submissions. The featured "Practitioners' Corner" seeks reports and research from authors who apply classroom theories and principles to the real world. A check of the journal's web site finds the following topics addressed in recent issues: social media news characteristics; uses of live blogs; and millennials and message style. A recent special issue is devoted to "The Role of Trust in the 2016 Presidential Campaign." Occasional book reviews are focused on emerging trends within communication and other disciplines.

1316. *Argumentation and Advocacy.* Formerly (until 1988): *American Forensic Association. Journal.* [ISSN: 1051-1431] 1964. q. GBP 247 (print & online eds.)). Ed(s): Catherine Langford. Routledge, 530 Walnut St, Ste 850, Philadelphia, PA 19106; enquiries@tandfonline.com; http://www.tandfonline.com. Illus. Refereed. Reprint: PSC. *Indexed:* A01, A22, AmHI, BRI, MLA-IB. *Bk. rev.:* 2-5, lengthy. *Aud.:* Ac.

This "flagship" journal of the American Forensic Association advances the study of argumentation. Any research methodology is encouraged in the areas of argumentation theory (contemporary or historical), public and political argument, culture and argument, legal argument, interpersonal arguing, and forensics and pedagogy. A particular focus is on argumentative and performance aspects of public speaking. Special issues occur on an occasional basis - e.g., volume 54 (1 and 2), 2018, is devoted to political campaign debates in the 2016 election. Book reviews are included. Article topics from recent issues include gender and performance and campaign debate scholarship. A title for academic collections.

1317. *Atlantic Journal of Communication.* Formerly (until 2004): *New Jersey Journal of Communication.* [ISSN: 1545-6870] 1993. 5x/yr. GBP 292 (print & online eds.)). Ed(s): Gary P Radford. Routledge, 530 Walnut St, Ste 850, Philadelphia, PA 19106; enquiries@tandfonline.com; http://www.tandfonline.com. Illus., adv. Sample. Refereed. Reprint: PSC. *Indexed:* A01, A22, AmHI, E01. *Bk. rev.:* Number and length vary. *Aud.:* Ac, Sa.

The focus of this academic journal is on problems and issues in the field of communication studies, with particular concentration on theory, practice, and policy. Submissions are subject to a blind editorial review. Representative article topics from recent issues include gender bias in sports journalism, Michelle Obama's Twitter rhetoric, and presidential candidates and campaign materials.

Broadcasting & Cable. See Television, Video, and Radio section.

Columbia Journalism Review. See Journalism and Writing/Journalism section.

1318. *Communication +1.* [ISSN: 2380-6109] 2012. a. Free. University of Massachusetts Amherst, Arnold House, 715 N Pleasant, Amherst, MA 01003; umassmag@admin.umass.edu; http://www.umass.edu/. Refereed. *Aud.:* Ac, Sa.

Beginning in 2012, this online-only, peer-reviewed title provides a "forum for exploring and sharing ideas about communication across modes of inquiry and perspectives." The most recent volume concentrates on media and cultural studies, featuring articles on topics such as rhetoric and food politics and the role of culture in city planning communication. The focus in the next call for articles is on "intersectionalities and media archaeologies," scheduled for availability in Fall 2018.

1319. *Communication and Critical/Cultural Studies.* [ISSN: 1479-1420] 2004. q. GBP 332 (print & online eds.)). Ed(s): D Robert DeChain. Routledge, 530 Walnut St, Ste 850, Philadelphia, PA 19106; enquiries@tandfonline.com; http://www.tandfonline.com. Sample. Reprint: PSC. *Indexed:* A22, E01. *Bk. rev.:* 1 or more, lengthy. *Aud.:* Ac.

A journal of the National Communication Association, *CCCS* "publishes original scholarship that situates culture as a site of struggle and communication as an enactment and discipline of power." Within that framework, topics may include class, race, ethnicity, gender, sexuality, the public sphere, the nation, globalization, and environment. The journal features "critical inquiry that cuts across academic and theoretical boundaries and welcomes a variety of methods including textual, discourse, and rhetorical analyses alongside auto/ethnographic, narrative, and poetic inquiry." Topics discussed in recent issues include communication support among incarcerated women, the vernacular of graffiti, and affect theory in the age of Trump. *CCCS* publishes occasional reviews of major new books, as well. A relevant publication for today's world, this journal belongs in comprehensive communication collections.

1320. *Communication Currents: knowledge for communicating well.* 2006. bi-m. Free. Ed(s): Katherine Hawkins. National Communication Association, 1765 N St, N W, Washington, DC 20036; inbox@natcom.org; http://www.natcom.org. *Aud.:* Ac.

This online web magazine of the National Communication Association looks at current communication research that is published in scholarly journals of the NCA, and translates them into a "form understandable and usable for broad audiences, including communication experts working with lay audiences, instructors and students, the press, and other interested members of the public." In addition to the essays, there are two sections included: first is "Cross Current," which provides short pieces (no more than 1,200 words) that are invited and solicited from NCA members, and that assert a position on a contemporary communication issue. Second is "Comments for Opening the Lines of Communication," which are short and an opportunity for communication scholars to address "how communication issues are presented or positioned in the popular press and other media outlets." Submissions may be in response to a recent event, film, or book, for example, on a communication issue, or may deal in general with a topical communication matter. Recent topics include the role of listening in civil discourse, Billy Graham as media celebrity, and humor in the classroom. A recommended title for its comprehensible presentation of timely communication research.

1321. ***Communication Education.*** Formerly (until 1976): *The Speech Teacher.* [ISSN: 0363-4523] 1952. q. GBP 293 (print & online eds.) Individuals, USD 121). Ed(s): Jon Hess. Routledge, 530 Walnut St, Ste 850, Philadelphia, PA 19106; enquiries@tandfonline.com; http://www.tandfonline.com. Illus., index, adv. Sample. Refereed. Vol. ends: Oct. Microform: PQC. Reprint: PSC. *Indexed:* A01, A22, BRI, CBRI, E01, ERIC, MLA-IB. *Aud.:* Ac, Sa.

Covering original instructional communication scholarship in all methodologies, this title's areas of focus include technology in mediated instruction, classroom discourse, life-span development of communication competence, and diverse backgrounds of learners and teachers in instructional settings. Research beyond the classroom, such as community service learning and instructional intervention activities, is also examined. Issues will offer occasional special sections, such as one on mental health stigma; for example, accommodations in public speaking courses. Recent topics published include defining diversity, public speaking and student fears, and hate speech and freedom of speech. This journal, a critical publication for communication faculty, and researchers, is valuable for its focus, and a necessary resource for academic libraries.

1322. ***Communication Methods and Measures.*** [ISSN: 1931-2458] 2007. q. GBP 440 (print & online eds.)). Ed(s): Andrew F Hayes. Routledge, 530 Walnut St, Ste 850, Philadelphia, PA 19106; enquiries@tandfonline.com; http://www.tandfonline.com. Adv. Sample. Refereed. Reprint: PSC. *Indexed:* A22, E01. *Aud.:* Ac.

This title aims to bring attention to new developments in methodological tools and approaches, with recent emphasis on digital and social media research, and to introduce new methods of measurement useful to the discipline. Editors encourage articles focused on "methods for improving research design and theory testing using quantitative and/or qualitative approaches." Subjects of recent publications include computational communication science; content analysis; and measuring personal news media value. Recommended for upper-division studies in academic libraries.

1323. ***Communication Monographs.*** Formerly (until 1976): *Speech Monographs.* [ISSN: 0363-7751] 1934. q. GBP 320 (print & online eds.)). Ed(s): Kory Floyd. Routledge, 530 Walnut St, Ste 850, Philadelphia, PA 19106; enquiries@tandfonline.com; http://www.tandfonline.com. Illus., index. Sample. Refereed. Vol. ends: Dec. Microform: PQC. Reprint: PSC. *Indexed:* A01, A22, BAS, E01, MLA-IB, SSA. *Aud.:* Ac.

Communication Monographs publishes original research, theoretical papers, and original reviews on human communication processes. The journal seeks research that "bridge[s] boundaries that have traditionally separated scholars within the communication discipline," within rigorous review and high intellectual standards. It especially features content that offers answers to current communication questions that are of "theoretical, conceptual, methodological, and/or social importance." This title now offers open-access options for its authors. A recent article topic includes family communication patterns and hope communication. A recent special issue on advances in methods and statistics introduces articles on Big Data and AI and crowdsourcing research. Recommended for academic libraries.

1324. ***Communication Quarterly.*** Formerly (until 1976): *Today's Speech.* [ISSN: 0146-3373] 1953. 5x/yr. Individuals, USD 100. Ed(s): Benjamin R Bates. Routledge, 530 Walnut St, Ste 850, Philadelphia, PA 19106; enquiries@tandfonline.com; http://www.tandfonline.com. Illus., index, adv. Sample. Refereed. Vol. ends: Fall. Microform: PQC. Reprint: PSC. *Indexed:* A01, A22, AmHI, BRI, E01, F01, MLA-IB. *Aud.:* Ac.

This journal publishes all types of refereed manuscripts (topical interest papers, research reports, state-of-the-art reviews, supported opinion, and critical studies) that advance the understanding of human communication. A diverse, "eclectic" mix of topics is covered; recent articles focus on beauty ideals and reality television and verbal aggression in romantic relationships. Six to eight articles are published in each issue. A 2018 special issue on rhetoric in the 2016 presidential election features articles on demographic rhetoric and the 2016 election through the eyes of *Saturday Night Live. Communication Quarterly* is a regional communication association publication, and a core title for academic libraries.

1325. ***Communication Reports.*** [ISSN: 0893-4215] 1988. s-a. Ed(s): Dr. William F Sharkey. Routledge, 4 Park Sq, Milton Park, Abingdon, OX14 4RN, United Kingdom; subscriptions@tandf.co.uk; http://www.tandfonline.com. Illus., adv. Sample. Vol. ends: Summer. Reprint: PSC. *Indexed:* A01, A22, B01, E01. *Aud.:* Ac.

This journal seeks short, original, data-based articles on broadly defined human communication topics. Theoretical or speculative reports are not accepted; rather, emphasis should be on research data analysis, and submissions should reflect this. Themed issues occur frequently. Topics from recent issues include family communication patterns; risky adult behavior; role study of working college students; and communication in supervisor/employee relationships. Recommended for academic collections.

1326. ***Communication Research.*** [ISSN: 0093-6502] 1974. 8x/yr. USD 1890 (print & online eds.)). Ed(s): Silvia Knobloch-Westerwick, Jennifer Gibbs. Sage Publications, Inc., 2455 Teller Rd, Thousand Oaks, CA 91320; info@sagepub.com; http://www.sagepub.com. Illus., index, adv. Sample. Refereed. Vol. ends: Dec. Reprint: PSC. *Indexed:* A01, A22, AmHI, B01, BRI, E01, F01, MLA-IB, P61, SSA. *Aud.:* Ac.

The editorial goal of *Communication Research* is to publish articles that explore communication across societal systems, such as mass media, new technology, and intercultural, from a multidisciplinary perspective. Similar to other journals in the field, this title now offers "Online First" (forthcoming articles published ahead of print). Several themed issues for 2018 focus on entertainment, romantic relationships and politically related discussion; a sampling of article topics includes globalization of popular music and supernatural affects. Although a costly title, it should be required for academic collections.

1327. ***Communication Research Reports.*** [ISSN: 0882-4096] 1984. q. GBP 65 combined subscription (print & online eds.)). Ed(s): Theodore A Avtgis. Routledge, 530 Walnut St, Ste 850, Philadelphia, PA 19106; enquiries@tandfonline.com; http://www.tandfonline.com. Illus., index, adv. Sample. Refereed. Microform: PQC. Reprint: PSC. *Indexed:* A22, E01. *Aud.:* Ac.

A publication of the Eastern Communication Association, *Communication Research Reports* publishes brief, empirical articles on human communication in a wide variety of areas, including intercultural, interpersonal, aging/life span, health, organizational, persuasive, mass, political, nonverbal, instructional, relational, or mediated. Articles emphasize reporting and interpretation of the results rather than theory. Editor-solicited articles are also featured in the Spotlight on Method or Analysis. Recent article topics include news-sharing behavior, body image and media, and instructor-student email analysis. For academic collections.

1328. ***The Communication Review.*** Formerly: *Communication (Langhorne).* [ISSN: 1071-4421] 1975. q. GBP 396 (print & online eds.)). Ed(s): Bruce A Williams, Andrea L Press. Routledge, 530 Walnut St, Ste 850, Philadelphia, PA 19106; enquiries@tandfonline.com; http://www.tandfonline.com. Adv. Sample. Refereed. Reprint: PSC. *Indexed:* A01, A22, B01, E01, IBSS, MLA-IB. *Bk. rev.:* Number and length vary. *Aud.:* Ac.

This title "seeks a synthesis of concerns [that are] traditional to the fields of communication and media studies." Scholarship is sought in three divisions: communication and culture; communication as a social force; and communication and mind. The editors are particularly interested in "historical work, feminist work, and visual work," and seek non-traditional examination and review of controversial topics within the discipline. Book reviews and lengthy essays are also encouraged. Upon recent examination, submissions have included articles on news coverage of U.S. immigration issues; child limits on technology use and future impact on academic achievement; and character analysis in *Modern Family* (television program). Recommended for academic libraries.

1329. *Communication Studies.* Formerly (until 1989): *Central States Speech Journal.* [ISSN: 1051-0974] 1949. 5x/yr. GBP 328 (print & online eds.)). Ed(s): Robert Littlefield. Routledge, 4 Park Sq, Milton Park, Abingdon, OX14 4RN, United Kingdom; subscriptions@tandf.co.uk; http://www.tandfonline.com. Illus., index, adv. Sample. Refereed. Vol. ends: Winter. Reprint: PSC. *Indexed:* A01, A22, E01, MLA-IB. *Aud.:* Ac.

A publication of the Central States Communication Association, *Communication Studies* publishes high-quality original research on communication theory and research processes, with the expectation that the essays and studies advance human communication scholarship. There are no restrictions as to methodology or philosophy. Article topics vary - for example, Facebook and civility, birth order as it relates to communication patterns. A special issue on replications in 2018 revisited topics such as Facebook as a predictor of students' social capital. An important title for academic libraries.

1330. *Communication Teacher (Online).* Formerly (until 1999): *Speech Communication Teacher (Online).* [ISSN: 1740-4630] 1986. q. GBP 98. Ed(s): Marian Houser. Routledge, 4 Park Sq, Milton Park, Abingdon, OX14 4RN, United Kingdom; subscriptions@tandf.co.uk; http://www.routledge.com. Adv. Sample. Refereed. *Aud.:* Ac.

Published by the National Communication Association, *Communication Teacher* is a quarterly publication dedicated to the identification, assessment, and promotion of quality teaching practices in the K-12, community college, and university communication classrooms. The journal focuses on original teaching activities and communication education assessment. Examples of recent articles include "Integrating critical and trans-affirming pedagogies in argumentation and debate: A heuristic narrative," "Illuminating everyday performances of privilege and oppression," and "Encouraging participation in face-to-face lectures: The index card technique." Each issue is available electronically to current subscribers in January, April, July, and October. Subscribers then receive a printed volume at the end of the year.

1331. *Communication Theory.* [ISSN: 1050-3293] 1991. q. GBP 1239 (print & online eds.)). Ed(s): Karin Gwinn Wilkins. Wiley-Blackwell Publishing, Inc., 350 Main St, Malden, MA 02148; cs-journals@wiley.com; http://onlinelibrary.wiley.com. Illus., adv. Sample. Refereed. Vol. ends: Nov. Reprint: PSC. *Indexed:* A22, BRI, E01, IBSS, MLA-IB, P61. *Aud.:* Ac, Sa.

This journal publishes "high quality, original research into the theoretical development of communication." Many disciplines are represented, including communication studies, psychology, cultural/gender studies, sociology, political science, philosophy, linguistics, and literature. Articles that examine technology, ethnicity and race, global and intercultural communication, gaming, and intergroup studies are among those works welcomed. Recent articles include "Using Semantic Networks to Define the Quality of Arguments," "On Social Networking and Psychosis," and "In Search of a Latin American Approach to Organizational Communication: A Critical Review of Scholarship (2010-2014)." Recommended for larger research libraries.

1332. *Communication World.* Former titles (until 1982): *Journal of Communication Management;* (until 1981): *Journal of Organizational Communication;* (until 1974): *I A B C Journal.* [ISSN: 0744-7612] 1973. m. Free to members. Ed(s): Natasha Nicholson, Sue Khodarahmi. International Association of Business Communicators, 601 Montgomery St, Ste 1900, San Francisco, CA 94111; http://www.iabc.com. Illus., adv. *Indexed:* A01, A22, B01, BRI, C42, F01. *Aud.:* Ga, Ac, Sa.

The official publication of the International Association of Business Communicators combines practical articles with global communication issues in the area of communication management. *CW* is published bimonthly, and its online version, *CW Online,* is updated regularly. Articles serve an international audience and include interviews with communication innovators and case studies on current topics. A wide variety of subjects is covered, including marketing communication, strategic planning, crisis communication, employee communication, public relations, career advice, and speechwriting/presentations. The publication's goals are to "stay at the forefront of developments in the communication profession, engaging and informing readers in an interactive and dynamic way." Current article topics have included building trust, CEO activism, and technology trends. For large public libraries and academic business and communication collections.

1333. *Critical Studies in Media Communication.* Formerly (until 2000): *Critical Studies in Mass Communication.* [ISSN: 1529-5036] 1984. 5x/yr. GBP 358 (print & online eds.)). Ed(s): Katherine Sender, Peter Dechernev. Routledge, 530 Walnut St, Ste 850, Philadelphia, PA 19106; enquiries@tandfonline.com; http://www.tandfonline.com. Illus., index, adv. Sample. Refereed. Vol. ends: Dec. Reprint: PSC. *Indexed:* A01, A22, AmHI, BRI, E01, F01, IBSS, MLA-IB, P61, SSA. *Aud.:* Ac.

Critical Studies in Media Communication publishes original research and analytical and interpretive articles that reflect a concentration on mediated communication. Interest is in "original scholarship in mediated and mass communication from a cultural studies and/or critical perspective." Recent articles include "An impulse to exploit: the behavioral turn in data-driven marketing" and "(Not) getting paid to do what you love: Gender, social media, and aspirational work." A publication of the National Communication Association, this is a valuable source for academic libraries due to its expansive approach to mediated communication theory and research.

1334. *Discourse & Communication.* [ISSN: 1750-4813] 2007. q. Ed(s): Teun A van Dijk. Sage Publications Ltd., 1 Oliver's Yard, 55 City Rd, London, EC1Y 1SP, United Kingdom; info@sagepub.com; https://www.sagepub.com/. Adv. Sample. Refereed. Reprint: PSC. *Indexed:* A22, E01, IBSS. *Bk. rev.:* 3, lengthy. *Aud.:* Ac.

Scholars who are interested in qualitative, discourse analytical approaches to issues of communication and/or linguistics, pragmatics, discourse studies, semiotics, and related disciplines will turn to this international, interdisciplinary journal. In addition to texts/conversation, this discipline "has extended its field to the study of the cognitive, interactional, social, cultural, political and historical 'contexts' of discourse." Book reviews and discussion notes are included in addition to the research articles. Sample articles are "Resolving a Gender and Language Problem in Women's Leadership: Consultancy Research in Workplace Discourse," and "Exploring Australian Journalism Discursive Practices in Reporting Rape: The Pitiful Predator and the Silent Victim." Recommended for academic research libraries.

1335. *Discourse & Society: an international journal for the study of discourse and communication in their social, political and cultural contexts.* [ISSN: 0957-9265] 1990. bi-m. USD 2577. Ed(s): Teun A van Dijk. Sage Publications Ltd., 1 Oliver's Yard, 55 City Rd, London, EC1Y 1SP, United Kingdom; market@sagepub.com; https://www.sagepub.com/. Adv. Sample. Refereed. Reprint: PSC. *Indexed:* A01, A22, BRI, E01, IBSS, MLA-IB, P61, SSA. *Bk. rev.:* Number and length vary. *Aud.:* Ac.

Discourse & Society is an international, multidisciplinary journal of discourse analysis. The journal studies "society through discourse and discourse through an analysis of its sociopolitical and cultural functions or implications." Social, political, or cultural problems of the day that require a multidisciplinary approach are featured. The journal requires accessibility as one criterion; that is, articles should be accessible to readers of various levels of expertise and specialization, and to readers from varied disciplines and countries. Articles from a recent issue include "Opposition as victimhood in newspaper debates about same-sex marriage" and "In the theater of political style: Touches of populism, pluralism and elitism in speeches of politicians." Lengthy book reviews are included, and issues are occasionally devoted to special topics. An expensive title, but appropriate for research libraries.

1336. *Electronic Journal of Communication.* [ISSN: 1183-5656] 1990. q. Free to members. Ed(s): Teresa Harrison. Communication Institute for Online Scholarship, PO Box 57, Rotterdam Junction, NY 12150. Illus. Refereed. *Bk. rev.:* Occasional. *Aud.:* Ac, Sa.

Presented in English with French abstracts, this academic journal addresses all areas of communication studies, including theory, research, practice, and policy. Each issue is devoted to a specific theme such as "Impact of Technology on Interpersonal Relationships" and "Risk, Crisis, Emergency, and Disaster: On Discourse, Materiality, and Consequentiality of Communication." Nonsubscribers may access the editor's introduction to the issue and view abstracts for each article. A subscription is required to access the articles and the search engine that indexes every word in the issue. Occasionally, an issue will include special features with book reviews.

1337. ***First Amendment Studies.*** Former titles (until 2013): *Free Speech Yearbook;* (until 1970): *Speech Association of America. Committee on Freedom of Speech. Yearbook; Freedom of Speech Yearbook.* [ISSN: 2168-9725] 1960. s-a. GBP 123 (print & online eds.)). Ed(s): David Dewberry. Routledge, 530 Walnut St, Ste 850, Philadelphia, PA 19106; enquiries@tandfonline.com; http://www.tandfonline.com. Refereed. Circ: 700. Reprint: PSC. *Indexed:* BRI, L14, MLA-IB. *Bk. rev.:* Number and length vary. *Aud.:* Ac, Sa.

This journal publishes original essays that make a significant contribution to theory and/or policy, on all aspects of free speech. Essays may be historical or contemporary, on topics such as free speech law and legislation analysis, and the role of free speech in various contexts such as popular culture and organizations. All methodologies are accepted. Book reviews are included, and an issue may be devoted to a special topic, such as "trigger warnings." A National Communication Association journal that would fit well in law libraries and research libraries.

Howard Journal of Communications. See African American section.

1338. ***Human Communication Research.*** [ISSN: 0360-3989] 1974. q. GBP 1239 (print & online eds.)). Ed(s): Eun-Ju Lee. Wiley-Blackwell Publishing, Inc., 350 Main St, Malden, MA 02148; http://onlinelibrary.wiley.com. Illus., adv. Sample. Refereed. Vol. ends: Jun. Microform: PQC. Reprint: PSC. *Indexed:* A01, A22, B01, E01, ERIC, MLA-IB, SSA. *Aud.:* Ac, Sa.

This official journal of the International Communication Association offers a broad social science focus to the study of human communication. It is touted as one of the top ten journals in human communication, and articles emphasize human symbolic processes in the areas of interpersonal, nonverbal, organizational, intercultural, and mass communication; language and social interaction; new technologies; and health communication. Emphasis is on theory-driven research, human communication methodologies, and critical synthesis. The journal will appeal not only to communication studies scholars but also to those in psychology, sociology, linguistics, and anthropology. In fact, the editors welcome submissions from those within and outside the communication field. For large public and academic libraries.

1339. ***International Journal of Communication.*** [ISSN: 1932-8036] 2007. irreg. Ed(s): Arlene Luck, Larry Gross. University of Southern California, Annenberg Center for Communication, 3502 Watt Way, Los Angeles, CA 90089-0281. Refereed. *Bk. rev.:* Number and length vary. *Aud.:* Ac.

This international, online, academic, multimedia, peer-reviewed journal is broadly targeted at the many interdisciplinary aspects of communication, rather than being narrowly focused on any particular subset of the discipline. Articles are presented in pdf format and are available without subscription. Users are encouraged to register with the site (so that the journal can collect usage statistics, and users can be notified via e-mail of new issues), although there is no subscription fee. Along with the articles, book reviews are also published. Recommended for academic libraries.

1340. ***International Journal of Listening.*** Formerly (until 1995): *International Listening Association. Journal.* [ISSN: 1090-4018] 1987. 3x/yr. GBP 373 (print & online eds.)). Ed(s): Margarete Imhof. Routledge, 530 Walnut St, Ste 850, Philadelphia, PA 19106; enquiries@tandfonline.com; http://www.tandfonline.com. Adv. Sample. Refereed. Reprint: PSC. *Indexed:* A01, A22, E01, ERIC. *Bk. rev.:* Number and length vary. *Aud.:* Ac.

The *International Journal of Listening,* an International Listening Association journal, publishes scholarship on listening in a wide range of contexts, including professional, interpersonal, public/political, media or mass communication, educational, intercultural, and international. Methodologies accepted are empirical, pedagogical, philosophical, and historical. The journal scope does not include listening as it pertains to speech and language pathology, hearing/auditory neurology, and strict cognitive psychology. Articles address listening as it relates to many disciplines (mass communication, intercultural communication, business communication, rhetorical studies, and so forth). Issues may have an organizing topic (for example, "listening in mediated contexts") and may include book reviews. Recommended for academic libraries.

1341. ***Journal of Applied Communication Research.*** [ISSN: 0090-9882] 1973. q. GBP 504 (print & online eds.)). Routledge, 711 3rd Ave, 8th Fl., New York, NY 10017; http://www.routledge.com. Illus., adv. Sample. Refereed. Vol. ends: Nov. Microform: PQC. Reprint: PSC. *Indexed:* A01, A22, BRI, E01, ERIC, MLA-IB, SSA. *Aud.:* Ac, Sa.

This journal publishes articles that bring communication theory and practice together. Articles report on actual communication situations or show results that can be applied to the solution of communication problems. Articles can be any of the following: original research applied to practical situations/problems; application articles that offer ways of improving or expanding upon a particular communication setting through specific research or theory; or commentaries on applied communication issues. Any methodological or theoretical approach is considered, although rigorous application is expected. Examples of articles include "Efficacy and authority of the message sender during emergency evacuations: a mixed methods study" and "Yes means yes and no means no, but both these mantras need to go: communication myths in consent education and anti-rape activism." Valuable for its pertinent topics, and recommended for academic libraries.

1342. ***Journal of Communication.*** [ISSN: 0021-9916] 1951. q. USD 2029 (print & online eds.)). Oxford University Press, Great Clarendon St, Oxford, OX2 6DP, United Kingdom; jnls.cust.serv@oup.com; https://academic.oup.com/journals/. Illus., index, adv. Sample. Refereed. Microform: PQC. Reprint: PSC. *Indexed:* A01, A22, AmHI, B01, BAS, BRI, C45, CBRI, E01, F01, IBSS, MLA-IB, P61, SSA. *Bk. rev.:* 4 or more, length varies. *Aud.:* Ac.

Considered a flagship journal in the communication studies field, this publication is interdisciplinary and concentrates broadly on communication theory, research, practice, and policy. The journal is "especially interested in research whose significance crosses disciplinary and sub-field boundaries." Articles are written by scholars, professors from a variety of disciplines, and graduate and doctoral students. Recent articles include "Deception in Mobile Dating Conversations," "Media, Communication, and the Environment in Precarious Times," and "The Pipeline of Online Participation Inequalities: The Case of Wikipedia Editing." There is an extensive book review section, with review essays and shorter book reviews. A necessary publication for large public libraries and academic libraries.

1343. ***Journal of Communication Inquiry.*** [ISSN: 0196-8599] 1974. q. USD 661 (print & online eds.)). Ed(s): Andrea Weare. Sage Publications, Inc., 2455 Teller Rd, Thousand Oaks, CA 91320; info@sagepub.com; http://www.sagepub.com. Illus., adv. Sample. Refereed. Vol. ends: Oct. Reprint: PSC. *Indexed:* A01, A22, AmHI, B01, BRI, E01, MLA-IB, P61, SSA. *Bk. rev.:* 1-3, lengthy. *Aud.:* Ac.

This journal approaches the study of communication and mass communication from cultural and historical perspectives. The interdisciplinary aspects of communication are emphasized, as articles reflect a variety of approaches, from philosophical to empirical to legal. International contributors regularly represent such diverse areas as mass communication, cultural studies, journalism, sociology, philosophy, and political science. Recent articles include "Access, Deconstructed: Metajournalistic Discourse and Photojournalism's Shift Away From Geophysical Access" and "The Grotesque Protest in Social Media as Embodied, Political Rhetoric." Valuable for its commitment to providing a place for alternative viewpoints on communication and media studies. Includes critical essays and book reviews. For large research collections.

1344. ***Journal of Computer-Mediated Communication.*** [ISSN: 1083-6101] 1995. q. Free. Ed(s): S Shyam Sundar. Wiley-Blackwell Publishing, Inc., 111 River St, Hoboken, NJ 07030; http://onlinelibrary.wiley.com. Illus., index, adv. Sample. Refereed. *Indexed:* A22, E01. *Aud.:* Ac, Sa.

This journal provides a broad interdisciplinary forum for research and essays based on any of the social sciences on the topic of computerized communication. Articles address research on media technologies in communication, business, education, political science, sociology, psychology, media studies, and information science. Examples of articles include "Structure of Ego-Alter Relationships of Politicians in Twitter" and "Object Touch by a Humanoid Robot Avatar Induces Haptic Sensation in the Real Hand." A recommended open-access journal.

1345. ***Journal of Intercultural Communication.*** [ISSN: 1404-1634] 1999. q. Free. Ed(s): Jens Allwood, Miguel Benito. Immigrant Institutet, c/o Moetesplats Goeteborg Soedra Allegatan 1B, Goeteborg, 413 01, Sweden; info@immi.se; http://www.immi.se. Refereed. *Indexed:* IBSS. *Aud.:* Ac.

With a focus on the similarities and differences of global cultures and linguistic patterns, this journal promotes research that may have a positive impact on intercultural communication. Issues are published gradually to the web as articles are accepted for publication through a peer-review process. Examples of articles include "Intercultural Sensitivity - A Study of Pre-service English Language Teachers" and "Developing Intercultural Competence via Social Media Engagement in a Language Learning Framework." For those interested in submitting articles to the journal, statistics are presented to demonstrate the number of accepted and rejected articles broken down by nation of origin.

1346. ***Journal of Intercultural Communication Research.*** Former titles (until 2002): *World Communication;* (until 1985): *Communication.* [ISSN: 1747-5759] 1972. 4x/yr. GBP 545 (print & online eds.)). Ed(s): Stephen M Croucher. Routledge, 4 Park Sq, Milton Park, Abingdon, OX14 4RN, United Kingdom; subscriptions@tandf.co.uk; http://www.tandfonline.com. Adv. Sample. Refereed. Reprint: PSC. *Indexed:* A22, E01. *Aud.:* Ac.

Published by the World Communication Association, the *Journal of Intercultural Communication Research* focuses on "cross-cultural comparative research or results from other types of research concerning the ways culture affects human symbolic activities." The journal is published 6 times per year. Recent articles include "Negotiating Structural Absences: Voices of Indigenous Subalterns of Eastern India" and "Perpetuation of Whiteness Ideologies in U.S. College Student Discourse." Recommended for large academic libraries.

1347. ***Journal of International and Intercultural Communication.*** [ISSN: 1751-3057] 2008. q. GBP 237 (print & online eds.)). Ed(s): Rona Tamiko Halualani. Routledge, 530 Walnut St, Ste 850, Philadelphia, PA 19106; enquiries@tandfonline.com; http://www.tandfonline.com. Sample. Reprint: PSC. *Indexed:* A22, E01. *Aud.:* Ac.

A National Communication Association title, *JIIC* publishes scholarship on international and intercultural communication. All types of communication are considered (interpersonal, mass) within the framework of a global perspective. Theoretical and empirical submissions are invited in the following viewpoints and methods: qualitative, quantitative, critical, and textual. Issues are asked to be significant in the realm of the environment, gender and sexuality, democracy, postcolonialism, identity, health, organizing, the workplace, pedagogy, and more. Recommended for academic research libraries.

1348. ***Journal of Nonverbal Behavior.*** Formerly (until 1979): *Environmental Psychology and Nonverbal Behavior.* [ISSN: 0191-5886] 1976. q. EUR 1341 (print & online eds.)). Ed(s): Jessica Dennis, Howard S Friedman. Springer New York LLC, 233 Spring St, New York, NY 10013; customerservice@springer.com; http://www.springer.com. Illus., adv. Sample. Refereed. Vol. ends: Winter. Microform: PQC. Reprint: PSC. *Indexed:* A01, A22, E01, MLA-IB. *Aud.:* Ac, Sa.

This specialized journal publishes original theoretical and empirical research on the varying components of nonverbal communication, such as proxemics, distance, eye contact, facial expressiveness, nonverbal emotional expression, gestures, and related behaviors. The journal recognizes the interdisciplinary nature of nonverbal communication, and manuscripts are welcomed from a variety of research fields. Special issues are also published. A worthwhile title for comprehensive research collections.

1349. ***Journal of Social and Personal Relationships.*** [ISSN: 0265-4075] 1984. 8x/yr. USD 3121 (print & online eds.)). Ed(s): Mario Mikulincer, Geoff MacDonald. Sage Publications Ltd., 1 Oliver's Yard, 55 City Rd, London, EC1Y 1SP, United Kingdom; market@sagepub.com; https://www.sagepub.com/. Adv. Sample. Refereed. Reprint: PSC. *Indexed:* A01, A22, B01, E01, IBSS, SSA. *Bk. rev.:* 0-3, length varies. *Aud.:* Ac.

This international journal publishes important scholarship on social and personal relationships. The nature of the field results in articles that are multidisciplinary in scope, drawing from social, clinical, and developmental psychology, sociology, and communication. Recent article titles include "A grounded theory of online coping by parents of military service members" and "Exploring the role of the romantic relationship context in weight loss." There is a book review section, and issues are occasionally devoted to special topics. The journal is a member of the Committee on Publication Ethics (COPE) and has a podcast series, "Relationship Matters." A necessary addition to fully round out a basic academic communication collection.

Journalism & Mass Communication Educator. See Journalism and Writing/Pedagogy section.

1350. ***Mass Communication and Society.*** Formerly (until 1998): *Mass Communications Review.* [ISSN: 1520-5436] 1973. bi-m. GBP 748 (print & online eds.)). Ed(s): Ran Wei. Routledge, 530 Walnut St, Ste 850, Philadelphia, PA 19106; enquiries@tandfonline.com; http://www.tandfonline.com. Illus., adv. Sample. Refereed. Vol. ends: Summer/Fall. Reprint: PSC. *Indexed:* A01, A22, AmHI, BRI, E01, P61, SSA. *Bk. rev.:* 1-2, lengthy. *Aud.:* Ac.

This is the official journal of the Mass Communication and Society Division of the Association for Education in Journalism and Mass Communication. Research and scholarship are published on mass communication theory from various perspectives, although the macrosocial and societal perspectives are encouraged. Methodologies include quantitative, qualitative, surveys, ethnography, laboratory experiments, legal analysis, and historical. This is a cross-disciplinary publication that draws from sociology, law, philosophy, history, psychology, and anthropology. Recent titles include "The Psychology of Marathon Television Viewing: Antecedents and Viewer Involvement" and "Changing Policy With Words: How Persuasive Words in Election Pledges Influence Voters' Beliefs About Policies." Book reviews on mass communication processes, media effects, and social impacts are also included as is the Special Issue, such as "Refugees, Media, and Public Opinion." Worthwhile for academic collections.

Philosophy and Rhetoric. See Philosophy section.

1351. ***Popular Communication: the international journal of media and culture.*** [ISSN: 1540-5702] 2003. q. GBP 476 (print & online eds.)). Ed(s): Miyase Christensen, Patrick Burkart. Routledge, 530 Walnut St, Ste 850, Philadelphia, PA 19106; enquiries@tandfonline.com; http://www.tandfonline.com. Adv. Sample. Refereed. Reprint: PSC. *Indexed:* A01, A22, E01. *Bk. rev.:* 1-4, lengthy. *Aud.:* Ac, Sa.

This international journal is a "forum for scholarly investigation, analysis and dialogue about communication symbols, forms, materiality, systems and networks within the context of transnational and globalized popular culture and communication." All aspects of popular culture communication are covered, such as legacy and new media, the Internet, consumer culture, games, print, radio, music, dance, sports, film and television, fandom, and social media. The publication is relevant to many fields - mass communication, media studies, sociology, gender studies, and so on. Diverse theoretical and methodological scholarly perspectives are encouraged. A reader will find some issues devoted to a particular topic, such as "Podcasting, the Popular, and the Public Sphere." Book reviews of both academic and nonacademic titles on popular communication/culture are included, as is an occasional review essay. This is a title to round out academic communication collections, due to the continuing influence of popular culture in today's world.

1352. ***Qualitative Research Reports in Communication.*** [ISSN: 1745-9435] 2000. a. USD 52 per issue. Ed(s): Janie Harden Fritz. Routledge, 4 Park Sq, Milton Park, Abingdon, OX14 4RN, United Kingdom; subscriptions@tandf.co.uk; http://www.tandfonline.com. Adv. Sample. Refereed. Reprint: PSC. *Indexed:* A01, A22, E01. *Aud.:* Ac.

An Eastern Communication Association journal, *QRRC* publishes numerous qualitative and critical research essays that cover the spectrum of human communication topics (legal, interpersonal, rhetorical, intercultural, mediated, political, and organizational) from "all geographical regions of the globe." The brief essays are 2,500 words or less. Recent articles include "Television Spoilers Recast as Narrative Teasers" and "Social Media and Active Shooter Events: A School Crisis Communication Challenge." A solid title for academic collections.

1353. ***Quarterly Journal of Speech.*** Former titles (until 1928): *Quarterly Journal of Speech Education;* (until 1918): *Quarterly Journal of Public Speaking.* [ISSN: 0033-5630] 1915. q. USD 437 (print & online eds.) Individuals, USD 96). Ed(s): Raymie E McKerrow. Routledge, 530 Walnut St, Ste 850, Philadelphia, PA 19106; enquiries@tandfonline.com; http://www.tandfonline.com. Illus., index, adv. Sample. Refereed. Vol. ends: Nov. Microform: PMC; PQC. Reprint: PSC. *Indexed:* A01, A22, AmHI, BRI, CBRI, E01, ERIC, MLA-IB, P61, SSA. *Bk. rev.:* 4 or more, lengthy. *Aud.:* Ac.

A respected and established journal in the field, *QJS* publishes scholarship "under rhetoric's broad purview." The understanding of rhetoric goes beyond the traditional approach, and the journal embraces the fact that "many different intellectual, archival, disciplinary, and political vectors, traditions, and methods" are represented. Both established views of rhetoric and contemporary are evident in recent titles such as "Black hands push back: Reconsidering the rhetoric of Booker T. Washington" and "Containing Sotomayor: Rhetorics of personal restraint, judicial prudence, and diabetes management." Book reviews are included. A necessary title for academic libraries.

1354. ***The Review of Communication.*** [ISSN: 1535-8593] 2001. q. GBP 266. Ed(s): Pat J Gehrke. Routledge, 530 Walnut St, Ste 850, Philadelphia, PA 19106; enquiries@tandfonline.com; http://www.tandfonline.com. Sample. Refereed. *Indexed:* A22, E01. *Bk. rev.:* Number and length vary. *Aud.:* Ac, Sa.

This peer-reviewed National Communication Association title welcomes "substantive" essays on both communication controversies and advances in the field. Studies may be historical, theoretical, philosophical, qualitative, quantitative, rhetorical, or syncretic and can "build theory, advance our understanding of a method, extend or challenge a current paradigm, bridge a divide, clarify a term or concept, or demonstrate a pragmatic function." A well-respected title with original communication scholarship to solidify a communication collection.

1355. ***Rhetoric Society Quarterly.*** Formerly (until 1976): *Rhetoric Society Newsletter.* [ISSN: 0277-3945] 1969. 5x/yr. GBP 290 (print & online eds.)). Ed(s): Susan C Jarratt. Taylor & Francis Inc., 711 3rd Ave, 8th Fl, New York, NY 10017; support@tandfonline.com; http://www.taylorandfrancis.com. Illus., index, adv. Sample. Refereed. Vol. ends: Oct. Reprint: PSC. *Indexed:* A22, BRI, E01, MLA-IB. *Bk. rev.:* 3 or more, length varies. *Aud.:* Ac.

A publication of the Rhetoric Society of America, *RSQ* features cross-disciplinary scholarship on all aspects of rhetorical studies to engage an "interdisciplinary audience of scholars and students of rhetorics who work in communication studies, English studies, philosophy, politics and other allied fields." Approaches include historical, theoretical, pedagogical, and practical criticism. Editorial expectations are that the scholarship submitted will advance and/or contribute to a multidisciplinary field. To serve its mission as a publication for the society, *RSQ* also publishes book reviews, announcements, and general information. A solid journal in its field, and recommended for academic collections.

1356. ***Southern Communication Journal.*** Former titles (until 1988): *Southern Speech Communication Journal;* (until 1971): *The Southern Speech Journal;* (until 1942): *Southern Speech Bulletin.* [ISSN: 1041-794X] 1935. 5x/yr. GBP 281 (print & online eds.)). Ed(s): Leroy G Dorsey. Taylor & Francis Inc., 711 3rd Ave, 8th Fl, New York, NY 10017; support@tandfonline.com; http://www.taylorandfrancis.com. Illus., index, adv. Sample. Refereed. Vol. ends: Summer. Microform: PQC. Reprint: PSC. *Indexed:* A01, A22, BRI, E01, MLA-IB. *Bk. rev.:* Number and length vary. *Aud.:* Ac.

A well-established, long standing publication of a regional communication association, *SCJ* publishes original scholarly research on human communication. The journal is not limited to any topic, simply those topics of interest to scholars, researchers, teachers, students, and practitioners in the communication field. Known for "advancing both communication theories and practical applications in tandem," any methodological and theoretical orientation is welcome, as long as the topic is established as important, the methodology is sound, and the theoretical viewpoint is appropriate. Recent articles illustrate the varied content: "Spiritual Support Experienced at a Cancer Wellness Center" and "Sharing Emergency Alerts on a College Campus: How Gender and Technology Matter." Book reviews are also included. A recommended title for academic libraries.

1357. ***Text and Performance Quarterly.*** Formerly (until 1989): *Literature and Performance.* [ISSN: 1046-2937] 1980. q. GBP 366 (print & online eds.)). Ed(s): Mindy E Fenske. Routledge, 4 Park Sq, Milton Park, Abingdon, OX14 4RN, United Kingdom; subscriptions@tandf.co.uk; http://www.tandfonline.com. Illus., adv. Sample. Refereed. Vol. ends: Oct. Reprint: PSC. *Indexed:* A22, AmHI, E01, MLA-IB. *Aud.:* Ac, Sa.

This peer-reviewed journal publishes readable scholarship that examines and advances the study of performance as a "social, critical, communicative practice; as a theoretical lens; as a critical method; as a technology of representation and expression; and as a hermeneutic." Material is often presented in diverse styles, such as narratives, interviews, performance texts/scripts, and photographic essays. A variety of perspectives and methodologies of performance are considered. In addition to essays, "The Performance Space" section analyzes performances from all types of venues as they relate to performance studies theory and praxis. For comprehensive communication collections.

1358. ***Toastmaster.*** Formerly: *The Toastmasters International.* [ISSN: 0040-8263] 1933. m. Free to members. Ed(s): Suzanne Frey. Toastmasters International, PO Box 9052, Mission Viejo, CA 92690; letters@toastmasters.org; http://www.toastmasters.org/. Illus., index. Vol. ends: Dec. *Aud.:* Ga, Sa.

This is a monthly magazine for members of Toastmasters International, a nonprofit educational organization, although libraries may purchase a subscription. The publication provides helpful information and practical tips to those interested in acquiring and improving their communication and leadership skills. Articles have a how-to focus as they cover topics such as humor, public speaking, leadership, famous speakers, speech writing, presentation technology, language, team building, and mentoring. Regular features include a Member Success Story or Portrait of a Toastmaster and a Members Forum. Since the majority of readers are experienced and knowledgeable public speakers, submissions are reviewed for "originality, depth of research, timeliness and excellence of expression." Notices and articles about the activities of the organization are also included. Of benefit to business professionals and other people with these special interests, this is a title for public libraries.

1359. ***Vital Speeches of the Day.*** [ISSN: 0042-742X] 1934. m. McMurry, Inc., 1010 E Missouri Ave, Phoenix, AZ 85014; info@mcmurry.com; http://www.mcmurry.com. Adv. Sample. *Indexed:* A22, AgeL, BAS, C37. *Aud.:* Hs, Ga, Ac.

Vital Speeches of the Day, according to the web site, is a "monthly collection of the best speeches in the world." Critical speeches are presented by leaders in the fields of business, politics, education, government, and more. "From Franklin Roosevelt to Ronald Reagan, from Mahatma Gandhi to Lady Gaga, we've published every thoughtful, useful, inspiring or provocative speech we've gotten our hands on for more than three quarters of a century." The speeches serve dual purposes - as models of excellent current oratory and as informative discussions on key issues. Speeches are printed in full (unless otherwise stated), and editorial policy is committed to covering both sides of public questions. Speeches primarily focus on subjects of North American concern. (There is an international sister publication, *Vital Speeches International,* with speeches from all over the world.) Examples of *VS*, speeches are "Global Peace Effort," an address by Lyndon Baines Johnson, 1968, and "Media Reform," an address by journalist Bill Moyers, 2007. Not only is this title important for the general public, it is also an excellent resource for the student of public speaking. Recommended for school, public, and academic libraries.

1360. ***Western Journal of Communication.*** Former titles (until 1992): *Western Journal of Speech Communication;* (until 1977): *Western Speech Communication;* (until 1975): *Western Speech.* [ISSN: 1057-0314] 1937. 5x/yr. GBP 267 (print & online eds.)). Routledge, 4 Park Sq, Milton Park, Abingdon, OX14 4RN, United Kingdom; subscriptions@tandf.co.uk; http://www.tandfonline.com. Illus., index, adv. Sample. Refereed. Microform: PQC. Reprint: PSC. *Indexed:* A01, A22, BAS, E01, ERIC, MLA-IB. *Aud.:* Ac.

One of two scholarly journals of the Western States Communication Association, *WJC* publishes original scholarly articles in all areas of human communication, including rhetoric, communication theory, health, family, interpersonal, and small-group communication, language behavior, critical and cultural studies, oral interpretation, performance studies, freedom of speech, and health and family communication. All methodological and theoretical perspectives are encouraged. Editorial policy encourages research that is accessible to both a scholarly audience and a learned public. A consistently strong title for academic libraries.

1361. ***Women's Studies in Communication.*** Formerly (until 1982): *O R W A C Bulletin.* [ISSN: 0749-1409] 1977. 4x/yr. GBP 156 (print & online eds.)). Ed(s): Joan Faber McAlister. Routledge, 530 Walnut St, Ste 850, Philadelphia, PA 19106; enquiries@tandfonline.com; http://www.tandfonline.com. Illus., adv. Refereed. Vol. ends: Fall. Reprint: PSC. *Indexed:* A01, A22, AmHI, BRI, C42, F01, FemPer, GW, MLA-IB, WSA. *Bk. rev.:* Number and length vary. *Aud.:* Ac, Sa.

The editorial policy of *WSIC* states that it provides a "feminist forum for diverse research, reviews, and commentary addressing the relationships between communication and gender." This journal seeks research where gender, power, class, race, ethnicity, and nationality "intersect." The publication is open to any methodology, perspective, scope, and context in various areas of communication including performance, rhetoric, media, interpersonal, organizational, and cultural studies. Also, "feminist studies concerning queer and transgender politics, masculinity, dis/ability, labor, transnationalism, postcolonialism, and critical race theory are especially encouraged at this time." The journal has a Conversation and Commentary section on a chosen topic (for example, "The Gendered/Racial Politics of Citizenship: Violence, Inclusion, and Exclusion"), includes essays as well as articles, and has book and media reviews. As the official journal of the Organization for Research on Women and Communication, this is a necessary title for academic libraries.

■ COMPUTERS AND INFORMATION TECHNOLOGY

Professional Journals/Popular Titles/Trade Journals

See also Business; Electronics; Engineering and Technology; and Library and Information Science sections.

Kristen Cook, Research Librarian, McLennan Community College Library, Waco, TX; kcook@mclennan.edu

Introduction

Computers and information technology is a broad subject area encompassing computer science theory, software design, human factors, practical applications, consumer technology, problem solving, and product and process selection. Some areas within the scope of this list are multidisciplinary. The audience is varied in this subject area including scholars, industry experts, decision-makers, designers, practitioners, researchers, librarians, hobbyists, and consumers.

Technology publications are impacted by rapidly evolving technology and the online publishing industry. Fortunately, longstanding and flagship titles continue their importance. The range of topics for some publications has increased with technological development while other titles are publishing less often and increasingly with special topic issues. Popular titles offer additional content via blogs and web publishing, open-access is growing even in traditional journals, and publishers have phased out print subscriptions.

Publications across all types continue to address security. Focus in the theoretical and practical journals is on cloud-based computing, blockchain, Internet of Things, data management, real-world applications, and the future of user-centered design. Topics such as social media, photography, gaming, ethics, the digital life, and emerging mobile technology frequent the popular computing periodicals.

Most of the popular titles are recommended for public libraries, while scholarly journals are most suited to academic libraries. There is a new category for trade journals to differentiate those publications that are not peer-reviewed journals, but are more theoretical and methodological than a popular title.

Basic Periodicals

Ga: *Macworld, PC Magazine, PC World;* Ac: *Association for Computing Machinery. Journal, The Computer Journal, Educause Review, Journal of Computer Science and Technology.*

Basic Abstracts and Indexes

Computer and Control Abstracts, Computing Reviews, INSPEC, Internet & Personal Computing Abstracts, Information Science & Technology Abstracts, Scopus, Web of Science.

Professional Journals

1362. ***A C M Queue (Online).*** [ISSN: 1542-7749] 2003. 6x/yr. Free. Association for Computing Machinery, 2 Penn Plaza, Ste 701, New York, NY 10121; acmhelp@acm.org; https://www.acm.org. *Aud.:* Ac.

ACM Queue is a bimonthly magazine published by the Association for Computing Machinery that is aimed at practicing software engineers and is oriented toward addressing topics, technologies, practices, and issues that are on the horizon or have just begun to impact the computing field, economy, and society. Contributors are by invitation only and include many significant researchers and practitioners from within the field. Topics cover a wide spectrum, including system administration, computing performance, development, visualization, power management and "the soft side of software." *ACM Queue* is available online and is also translated into Portuguese. This title is highly recommended for academic libraries, as the topics covered are of general and current interest within the field of computer science and the magazine's audience includes both students and researchers.

1363. ***A C M Transactions.*** q. Free. Association for Computing Machinery, 2 Penn Plaza, Ste 701, New York, NY 10121; acmhelp@acm.org; https://www.acm.org. *Aud.:* Ac.

ACM Transactions is the umbrella under which a collection of more than 40 peer-reviewed, discipline-specific journals are published by the Association for Computing Machinery. Each specific journal maintains a direct relationship to one of the ACM's many special-interest groups. For instance, the *ACM Transactions on Database Systems* is steered by the ACM Special Interest Group on Management and Organization of Data. Each of these journals is released on their own schedule and focuses on original, previously unpublished research within the given discipline. Articles address new areas of research or new experiences with applications of existing research, and all articles are peer reviewed. Recommended for academic libraries. A list of *Transactions* titles can be found at: https://www.acm.org/publications/journals

1364. ***A I Magazine.*** [ISSN: 0738-4602] 1980. q. Free to members. Ed(s): David B Leake. A A A I Press, 2275 East Bayshore Rd, Ste 160, Palo Alto, CA 94303; info@aaai.org; http://www.aaai.org. Illus., index, adv. Refereed. Vol. ends: Dec. *Indexed:* A22, BRI, CompLI. *Bk. rev.:* Number and length vary. *Aud.:* Ac.

This professional journal is the official publication of the Association for the Advancement of Artificial Intelligence. The organization itself has been active since 1979, and began publishing this journal in 1980. *AI Magazine* has maintained its quarterly release schedule ever since. This peer-reviewed journal, though its title includes "Magazine," features articles, conference reports, editorials, and association news. The issues previously had centered on themes, but as of Spring 2018, the topics vary in their relationship to AI. Recent articles cover such topics as AI ethics, autonomous vehicles, teaming intelligence, reinforced learning, and military applications. Recommended for academic libraries.

1365. *Advances in Multimedia.* [ISSN: 1687-5680] 2007. . USD 395. Hindawi Publishing Corporation, 315 Madison Ave, 3rd Fl, Ste 3070, New York, NY 10017; info@hindawi.com; https://www.hindawi.com. Refereed. *Aud.:* Ac, Sa.

Advances in Multimedia is an open-access, peer-reviewed journal that publishes both original research and review articles in the subject area of multimedia systems. The journal's aim and scope is to present experimental and theoretical studies and to provide its readership with current multimedia technology and applications, awareness of emerging trends, and discussion of the future of digital information processing, storage, transmission, and representation. The journal initiated publication in 2007, and produces the occasional special issue dedicated to a specific topic of interest (examples include visual analyses and machine learning) as part of its regular publication schedule. All articles are available freely online, and print subscriptions are available as well. Recommended for academic libraries.

1366. *Association for Computing Machinery. Journal.* [ISSN: 0004-5411] 1954. bi-m. USD 1035. Ed(s): Eva Tardos. Association for Computing Machinery, PO Box 30777, New York, NY 10087; acmhelp@acm.org; https://www.acm.org. Illus., index. Refereed. Microform: PQC. *Indexed:* A22, B01, CompLI, MSN. *Aud.:* Ac.

The *Journal of the Association for Computing Machinery* is a bimonthly publication of the Association for Computing Machinery that has been in continuous publication since 1954. The journal is a "best of" publication with the stated goal of including only "original research papers of lasting value in computer science." All articles are peer reviewed, and each article must meet the rigorous criteria of being "truly outstanding in its field and to be of interest to a wide audience." The timely and relevant articles cover the entire spectrum of research in the field of computer science, broadly construed and changing over the course of time as computing technology evolves. Recommended for academic libraries.

1367. *Communications of the A C M.* Formerly (until 1959): *Association for Computing Machinery. Communications.* [ISSN: 0001-0782] 1958. m. USD 1149. Ed(s): Moshe Y Vardi. Association for Computing Machinery, PO Box 30777, New York, NY 10087; acmhelp@acm.org; https://www.acm.org. Illus., index, adv. Sample. Vol. ends: No. 12. *Indexed:* A01, A22, B01, BRI, CompLI, ErgAb, MLA-IB. *Aud.:* Ac.

Considered the flagship publication of the ACM, this monthly magazine has remained an essential title for academics and computing professionals for more than 60 years. The publication, available in print, online, and with a new digital edition, reflects the diversity of the ACM membership in the scope and content of the contributed and invited articles, news, and reviews. In 2008, the magazine's format and editorial process was significantly changed in order to appeal to a wider field of industry professionals and academics, as well as to bring in international topics and authors. Some content may be in the web format of *Communications* that is not included in the print publication, due to page limits. Topics include news, opinion, research, practical applications, and coverage of leading and emerging trends in information technology. The more heavily research-oriented sections of the magazine ("Review Articles" and "Contributed Articles") are peer reviewed. The "Practice" articles are submitted by invitation from the editorial board. Due to its wide range of content, the magazine is of relevant interest to both technology practitioners and researchers, and is recommended for both academic and public libraries.

1368. *The Computer Journal.* [ISSN: 0010-4620] 1958. m. EUR 1988. Ed(s): Fionn Murtagh. Oxford University Press, Great Clarendon St, Oxford, OX2 6DP, United Kingdom; onlinequeries.uk@oup.com; https://academic.oup.com/journals/. Illus., index, adv. Sample. Refereed. Vol. ends: No. 8. Microform: PQC. Reprint: PSC. *Indexed:* A01, A22, BRI, CompLI, E01, ErgAb, MLA-IB. *Aud.:* Ac.

The Computer Journal is published by Oxford University Press on behalf of England's BCS - The Chartered Institute for IT. The journal is academically oriented. All articles are refereed, and the journal's objective is to serve all branches of the computer science community by publishing high-quality papers concerning original research and new developments in the field of computer science. The journal publishes articles in four broad areas, with editors dedicated to that section: (1) computer science, methods, and tools; (2) computer and communication networks and systems; (3) computational intelligence; and (4) security in computer systems and networks. Recent topics include cloud computing, data encryption, computer security, algorithms, and mathematical optimization. This journal is highly regarded within the field, and is recommended for academic libraries.

1369. *Computer (New York).* Formerly (until 1970): *I E E E Computer Group News.* [ISSN: 0018-9162] 1966. m. USD 2825. Ed(s): David Alan Grier. Institute of Electrical and Electronics Engineers, 445 Hoes Ln, Piscataway, NJ 08855; contactcenter@ieee.org; http://www.ieee.org. Illus. Refereed. *Indexed:* A01, A22, BRI, CompLI, ErgAb. *Aud.:* Ac.

Computer magazine is considered the flagship publication of the IEEE Computer Society. This monthly, peer-reviewed journal aims to provide more practicality than a traditional peer-reviewed journal and more technical information than most trade magazines. The overall focus of the magazine is all aspects of computer science, including "research, trends, best practices, and changes in the profession." Recent issues have included articles discussing trojan detection, quantum computing, cyberbullying, security, and the Internet of Things. Recommended for academic libraries.

1370. *Computers in Libraries: complete coverage of library information technology.* Formerly (until 1989): *Small Computers in Libraries;* Which incorporated (1986-1988): *Systems Librarian and Automation Review;* (1985-1987): *Bulletin Board Systems;* (1986-1987): *Public Computing.* [ISSN: 1041-7915] 1981. m. USD 109.95 (Individuals, USD 69.95). Ed(s): Richard T Kaser. Information Today, Inc., 143 Old Marlton Pike, Medford, NJ 08055; custserv@infotoday.com; http://www.infotoday.com. Illus., index, adv. Vol. ends: Dec. *Indexed:* A01, A22, B01, B03, BRI, C42, ERIC, ISTA. *Bk. rev.:* Number and length vary. *Aud.:* Ac.

Computers in Libraries is arguably the preeminent magazine dedicated to covering the intersection of technology and libraries. The magazine is published on a monthly basis by Information Today, which also hosts the annual Computers in Libraries conference in Arlington, Virginia. The magazine's central focus is on the practical application of technologies for all types of libraries, including academic, public, school, and special libraries. Each issue offers case studies, educational technology case studies, stories, and opinions. Topical themes for the 2019 publishing year include cloud computing, emerging technology, open access, all things social, privacy and security, and the digital experience. This journal is recommended for academic libraries, and is a highly recommended professional resource for library staff in all types of libraries.

1371. *Human - Computer Interaction (Mahwah): a journal of theoretical, empirical, and methodological issues of user psychology and of system design.* [ISSN: 0737-0024] 1985. bi-m. GBP 838 (print & online eds.)). Ed(s): Steve Whittaker. Taylor & Francis Inc., 711 3rd Ave, 8th Fl, New York, NY 10017; support@tandfonline.com; http://www.taylorandfrancis.com. Adv. Sample. Refereed. Reprint: PSC. *Indexed:* A01, A22, B01, CompLI, E01, ErgAb. *Aud.:* Ac.

This interdisciplinary, scholarly journal explores topics of usable design and how users react to and use technology. The journal offers original research, commentaries, editorials, and special topic issues. Recent issues address manufacturing and the maker movement, digital life experiences, the future of usability theory, and 3D printing. Some open-access articles are published and available online. This journal is highly recommended for the study of interaction and system design. Recommended for academic libraries.

1372. *Human Technology.* [ISSN: 1795-6889] 2005. 3x/yr. Free. Ed(s): Jukka Jouhki. Jyvaskylan Yliopisto, Open Science Center, University of Jyvaskyla, PO Box 35, Jyvaskyla, 40014, Finland. Refereed. *Aud.:* Ac.

Human Technology is an open-access journal that offers research on the human element in a society integrated with information and communication technologies. This peer-reviewed publication aims to bring original research from all subject disciplines related to technology's effect on and integration with human existence. Nontraditional ideas and controversial topics are welcomed, provided the research is of high scientific quality. Recent topics covered in relationship to ICT were immigration, dating relationships, demographics and educational gaming. Recommended for academic libraries.

1373. ***I E E E Pervasive Computing: mobile systems, ubiquitous computing, internet of things.*** [ISSN: 1536-1268] 2002. q. USD 960. Ed(s): Marc Langheinrich. Institute of Electrical and Electronics Engineers, 445 Hoes Ln, Piscataway, NJ 08854; contactcenter@ieee.org; http://www.ieee.org. Adv. Refereed. *Indexed:* A22, CompLI, ErgAb. *Aud.:* Ac.

This IEEE magazine examines theory and practices related to the integration of ubiquitous computing across mediums and activities, and throughout daily life. *IEEE Pervasive Computing* publishes peer-reviewed papers, interviews, case studies, product reviews, conference reports, and more. In addition to computing topics such as Internet of Things, wearable technology, mobile technology, 3D printing, and augmented reality, also covered are topics such as attention management and monitoring, awareness and technology, and other psychological areas in relation to its scope. Each issue is published on a special topic, with additional regular columns on hot topics. Recommended for academic libraries.

1374. ***I E E E Software.*** [ISSN: 0740-7459] 1984. bi-m. USD 1465. Ed(s): Ipek Ozkaya. Institute of Electrical and Electronics Engineers, 445 Hoes Ln, Piscataway, NJ 08854; contactcenter@ieee.org; http://www.ieee.org. Illus., adv. Refereed. Vol. ends: No. 6. *Indexed:* A01, A22, B01, BRI, CompLI. *Aud.:* Ac.

Targeted at software professionals, *IEEE Software* is "the authority on translating software theory into practice." This is mainly achieved through a focus on all aspects of the software industry in peer-reviewed articles by experts working in the real world. In addition to the peer-reviewed content, *IEEE Software* offers editorials, letters to the editor, debates, and other contributions to challenge readers. Although articles are written for professionals, the language used and subjects discussed are substantially less formal than those seen in the various IEEE journals. Recent topics include hybrid software development, project management, and automated testing of software. Recommended for academic libraries.

1375. ***I E E E Transactions.*** m. I E E E Computer Society, 2001 L St NW, Ste 700, Washington, DC 20036; customer.service@ieee.org; http://www.computer.org. Refereed. *Aud.:* Ac.

Similar to *ACM Transactions, IEEE Transactions* is the umbrella under which the IEEE Computer Society publishes many individual journals that cover separate aspects of the field of computer science. Each journal is oriented toward a specific aspect of computer science, including computer architecture, parallel and distributed computing, software engineering, computer graphics, learning technologies, mobile computing, multimedia, bioinformatics, and networking. Each of the titles publishes peer-reviewed original research. The current list of journals, including *Transactions* titles is available on their website. This collection of titles is recommended for academic libraries. URL: https://www.ieee.org/publications/index.html#ieee-publications

1376. ***Information Systems: databases: their creation, management and utilization.*** [ISSN: 0306-4379] 1975. 8x/yr. EUR 3053. Ed(s): Dennis Shasha, Gottfried Vossen. Elsevier Ltd, The Boulevard, Langford Lane, Oxford, OX5 1GB, United Kingdom; customerserviceau@elsevier.com; http://www.elsevier.com. Illus., adv. Sample. Refereed. Vol. ends: No. 8. Microform: PQC. *Indexed:* A01, A22, CompLI. *Aud.:* Ac.

Information Systems is a peer-reviewed journal exploring topics in data creation, management, and utilization. Accepted topics are of relevance to the major international conferences (ACM SIGMOD/PODS, for example). It is published eight times a year and includes a range of article types, including original research, reviews, and implementation papers. Articles cover the design and implementation of languages, data models, process models, algorithms, software and hardware for information systems, data mining, information retrieval, and cloud management of data. Of particular interest is the journal's strong focus on practice-based article topics. The journal's online presence includes "virtual special issues" that compile previously published papers on a common theme. Recommended for academic libraries.

1377. ***Interacting with Computers.*** [ISSN: 0953-5438] 1989. 6x/yr. Ed(s): Russell Beale. Oxford University Press, Great Clarendon St, Oxford, OX2 6DP, United Kingdom; onlinequeries.uk@oup.com; https://academic.oup.com/journals/. Illus., adv. Refereed. Microform: PQC. Reprint: PSC. *Indexed:* A01, A22, CompLI, ErgAb. *Bk. rev.:* Number and length vary. *Aud.:* Ac.

Interacting with Computers is the official peer-reviewed publication of the BCS (Chartered Institute for IT/British Computer Society) and Interaction Specialist Group. The founding and current editorial boards include interaction experts from around the world. Jakob Nielsen is listed among the founding editors and advisory board. The intent of the publication and the editorial policy is to enable scholarly communication between academics and practitioners on such topics as HCI, user interface design, usability, accessibility, and user assessment technologies and strategies. The readership community includes designers, ergonomists, human factors practitioners, educational technology experts, and researchers in social, computers, and information sciences. Articles are timely, globally diverse, and relate to consumer technology as well as applications in accessibility, medicine, psychology, and education. Recommended for academic libraries, particularly students and scholars in design, information technology, and information science.

1378. ***Interactions (New York).*** [ISSN: 1072-5520] 1994. bi-m. USD 805. Ed(s): Simone Barbosa, Gilbert Cockton. Association for Computing Machinery, PO Box 30777, New York, NY 10087; acmhelp@acm.org; https://www.acm.org. Adv. *Indexed:* A22, ErgAb. *Aud.:* Ac.

Interactions is a bimonthly magazine published by the Association for Computing Machinery. The publication works to make "engaging human-computer interaction research accessible to practitioners" and "practitioners' voices heard by researchers." The magazine is less formal than the ACM's scholarly research-oriented journals. Instead of focusing on the publishing of original or cutting-edge research, *Interactions* aims to publish articles, stories, and other less traditional content that illustrates the interconnections between technology and human experience. Recent topics include the need for empathy, automation of the power grid, robotics, sustainable cities, and self-care technologies. Recommended for academic libraries.

1379. ***Journal of Computer Science and Technology.*** [ISSN: 1000-9000] 1986. bi-m. EUR 1583 (print & online eds.)). Ed(s): Guo-Jie Li. Springer New York LLC, 233 Spring St, New York, NY 10013; customerservice@springer.com; http://www.springer.com. Illus., adv. Sample. Refereed. Reprint: PSC. *Indexed:* A22, BRI, CompLI, E01, MSN. *Aud.:* Ac.

The *Journal of Computer Science and Technology* is international in focus and provides a forum for computer science and technology scientists and engineers. The journal is sponsored by the Institute of Computing Technology, Chinese Academy of Sciences, and China Computer Federation. Papers are of original research, accompanied by occasional special issues devoted to conference proceedings, and cover a range of topics, including formal methods, algorithms and complexity, computer architecture, high-performance computing, software engineering, distributed computing systems, artificial intelligence, bioinformatics, data mining, database systems, information security, and computer graphics and visualization. Recommended for academic libraries.

1380. ***Journal of Database Management.*** Formerly (until 1992): *Journal of Database Administration.* [ISSN: 1063-8016] 1990. q. USD 800. Ed(s): Keng Siau. I G I Global, 701 E Chocolate Ave, Ste 200, Hershey, PA 17033; eresources@igi-global.com; http://www.igi-global.com. Refereed. *Indexed:* A22, B01, BRI, CompLI, E01. *Aud.:* Ac.

The *Journal of Database Management* is a professional journal publishing peer-reviewed articles of three types: research articles, research notes, and research reviews. Articles that are accepted for publication should cover novel topics or contribute to the field in promoting the understanding of existing theory. Topics cover a broad range of areas in database management and administration, including artificial intelligence, augmented and virtual reality, geographic information systems, Internet of Things, the semantic web, machine learning, and data quality. The intended audience for this journal, which is published in print and online and indexed in many reputable A&I sources, includes academics and IT professionals. Recommended for academic libraries.

Journal of Digital Information. See Library and Information Science section.

1381. ***Journal of Usability Studies.*** [ISSN: 1931-3357] 2005. q. Free. Ed(s): James Lewis, William Albert. User Experience Professionals' Association, 140 N Bloomingdale Rd, Bloomingdale, IL 60108; office@uxpa.org; https://uxpa.org. Refereed. *Indexed:* A01, ErgAb. *Aud.:* Ac.

The *Journal of Usability Studies* is an online only, scholarly publication from the User Experience Professionals' Association (UXPA). The UXPA, founded in 1991, supports practitioners in the field of user-oriented study and design. The journal is peer-reviewed and provides a forum for original research, case studies, best practices, and opinion in this field and related fields. Recent topics included a tribute issue to Nigel Bevan, older adults and user experience, long-term user experience, perceived usability and aesthetics, and the future of user-oriented design. Recommended for academic libraries.

1382. ***S I A M Journal on Computing.*** [ISSN: 0097-5397] 1972. bi-m. USD 1063 (print & online eds.)). Ed(s): Robert Krauthammer. Society for Industrial and Applied Mathematics, 3600 Market St, 6th Fl, Philadelphia, PA 19104; siam@siam.org; http://www.siam.org. Illus., adv. Sample. Refereed. Vol. ends: Dec. *Indexed:* A01, A22, B01, CompLI, MSN. *Aud.:* Ac.

This journal, published in print and digitally, by the Society for Industrial and Applied Mathematics, provides articles that make a technical and significant contribution to mathematical and formal computer science. The bimonthly journal was founded in 1972, and publishes articles that cover a very broad range of topics, including designing algorithms, data structures, computational complexity, computational algebra, robotics, artificial intelligence, mathematical aspects of programming languages, databases and information retrieval, cryptography, distributed computing, and parallel algorithms. Full tables of contents are available on the journal's website, and access to full-text articles is available to subscribing institutions and individuals. Recommended for academic libraries.

1383. ***Software: Practice and Experience.*** [ISSN: 0038-0644] 1971. m. GBP 4042. Ed(s): Kendra N Cooper, Rajkumar J Buyya. John Wiley & Sons Ltd., EMEA Institutional Sales, 9600 Garsington Rd, Oxford, OX4 2DQ, United Kingdom; cs-journals@wiley.com; http://www.wiley.com. Illus., index, adv. Sample. Refereed. Vol. ends: No. 15. Reprint: PSC. *Indexed:* A22, CompLI. *Aud.:* Ac, Sa.

Software: Practice and Experience is a thoroughly refereed journal offering original research by software practitioners for practitioners and academics. Accepted articles must contribute meaningful and novel content in the areas of software design, implementation, and problem solving. The aim is not to cover all aspects of software engineering, but to concentrate on how-tos for others, programming techniques, new techniques and tools, survey papers, and case studies. Recent topics include technological and data-driven dairy farming, design patterns and structural problems, modeling and simulation in applied situations, and blockchain in business process management. This journal is published in print and online. Recommended for academic libraries.

Popular Titles

1384. ***eWEEK (Online).*** 1983. . Quinstreet Inc., 950 Tower Ln, 6th Fl, Foster City, CA 94404; http://quinstreet.com/. Adv. *Aud.:* Ga.

This trade-oriented web-only magazine is part of the Ziff-Davis/Quinn Street Enterprise collection of publications. All aspects of the computer industry are covered, with a general orientation toward a readership composed of decision makers and technology leaders in business environments. Topics covered include IT security, CIO roles, Android and Apple news, networking, enterprise applications, networking, and other related subjects. The publication is available for free. Recommended for high school and public libraries.

1385. ***iPhone Life.*** [ISSN: 1949-2014] 2008. q. USD 15.97. Ed(s): Donna Cleveland. Mango Life Media, 402 N B St, Ste 108, Fairfield, IA 52556. Illus., adv. *Aud.:* Ga.

This magazine covers the rapidly changing world of iOS-related technology, specifically looking at the iPhone and iPad and the technology landscape they have created. It is published in both print and digital format. Each issue features a number of articles, including reviews of applications, games, and peripherals, tips and tricks, and case studies of iOS-device power-users. The magazine's companion website does not repeat any of this content, and instead focuses on adding value by publishing timely news and reviews and aggregating iOS-related information from other sources. Recommended for public libraries.

1386. ***MacWorld (Online).*** Incorporates (1985-1997): *MacUser.* 1984. m. IDG Consumer & SMB, 501 Second St, 5th Fl, San Francisco, CA 94107; http://www.macworld.com. Illus., adv. Vol. ends: Dec. *Indexed:* A01, A22, B01, B03, BRI, C37, MASUSE. *Aud.:* Hs, Ga.

Published monthly since 1984, *MacWorld* is the leading magazine devoted to coverage of the Apple market. The magazine is a vital source for end users and practitioners. It publishes a range of article types, including in-depth analyses, hardware and software reviews, usage tips, surveys, and editorials and opinion pieces. The focus is on Apple hardware and related peripherals, software for Apple computers and mobile devices, and the computer industry as related to Apple and its products. An accompanying website offers a wealth of information to supplement the digital magazine. Recommended for public libraries.

1387. ***Online Searcher: information discovery, technology, strategies.*** Formed by the merger of (1977-2013): *Online;* (1993-2013): *Searcher.* [ISSN: 2324-9684] 2013. bi-m. USD 159.95 domestic; USD 175 in Canada & Mexico; USD 202 elsewhere. Ed(s): Marydee Ojala. Information Today, Inc., 143 Old Marlton Pike, Medford, NJ 08055; custserv@infotoday.com; http://www.infotoday.com. Illus., adv. Sample. Vol. ends: Dec. *Indexed:* A01, A22, B01, B03, BRI, C42, ISTA. *Aud.:* Ac, Sa, Ga.

Online Searcher is a bimonthly magazine oriented toward information professionals working in a range of industries and disciplines. Each issue offers regular columns, original articles and case studies, news, and reviews. Regular columnists include Mary Ellen Bates, William Badke, Nancy Herther, Barbie Keiser, Carly Lamphere, and Greg Notess. Common topics within this trade magazine include search engine news and tips, commercial search engines, accessibility, web design, Internet research on special topics, Internet of Things, information and digital literacy, and social media. The website includes tables of contents, full text of selected articles, and additional content that supplements the magazine. Recommended for academic and public libraries.

1388. ***P C Magazine (Online).*** [ISSN: 2373-2830] m. USD 19.99; USD 1.25 per issue. Ziff Davis Media Inc., 28 E 28th St, New York, NY 10016; info@ziffdavis.com; http://www.ziffdavis.com. *Indexed:* A01, B01, MASUSE. *Aud.:* Ga.

PC Magazine is part of the family of digital-only Ziff Davis magazines. The digital edition retains the same look and feel of the previous print edition for both mobile and desktop devices. The magazine covers all areas of technology, with emphasis on consumer technologies ranging from smart phones to network area storage devices. As with most consumer technology magazines, it includes a number of article types, such as independent reviews, tips and how-tos, editorials by prominent technology writers, and business-oriented case studies. The website provides additional free content, but is supported by numerous ads. This is an essential publication for end users and IT experts. Recommended for public libraries.

1389. ***P C World (Online).*** [ISSN: 1944-9143] 19??. m. USD 19.97. I D G Consumer & S M B, 501 2nd St, San Francisco, CA 94107; http://www.idgcsmb.com/. Adv. *Aud.:* Ga.

PC World is part of the same family of publications that includes *Macworld.* This digital-only magazine is oriented toward both hardware and software professionals and consumers, with a focus on offering industry news, product reviews, and technological solutions. Articles cover a broad range of topics and are not platform-specific, focusing on issues of relevance to users throughout the technology spectrum, with a particular emphasis on analysis and reviews of new technologies and products. Recent topics include a review of a foldable tablet, Windows XP patches, mobile device cameras, and gaming on PCs. An accompanying ad-run website offers timely information to supplement the digital edition. Recommended for public libraries.

Trade Journals

C I O. See Business and Finance section.

1390. ***Educause Review: why it matters to higher education.*** Former titles (until 2000): *Educom Review;* (until 1989): *Educom Bulletin;* (until 1984): *Educom;* Incorporates (2000-2011): *The EDUCAUSE Quarterly;* Which was formerly (197?-2000): *Cause/Effect.* [ISSN: 1527-6619] 1966. q. Free to members; Non-members, USD 54. Ed(s): Teddy Diggs. Educause, 1150 18th St, NW, Ste 1010, Washington, DC 20036; info@educause.com; http://www.educause.edu. Illus., adv. Circ: 22000. Vol. ends: Dec. *Indexed:* A01, A22, CompLI, ERIC. *Aud.:* Ac.

Educause Review is published by Educause, a nonprofit organization that brings together IT leaders and professionals in academia. The magazine is published in both print and online formats. All articles in the print edition are freely available online including a PDF download, but the web version includes additional articles, blog content, and columns not covered in the print subscription. The magazine's goal is to take a broad look at current developments in the information technology industry and how they affect higher education, and it is aimed at a readership that includes administrators and managers in the technology field, as well as non-IT staff such as academic administrators and leaders, librarians, and faculty. Recent articles cover such topics as digital lecture capture, MOOCs, cybersecurity, and open access. Recommended for academic libraries.

1391. ***Linux Journal.*** [ISSN: 1938-3827] 1994. m. USD 34.50. Ed(s): Doc Searls. Linux Journal, LLC., 9597 Jones Rd, #331, Houston, TX 7706. Adv. *Aud.:* Ga.

Linux Journal is a magazine devoted to the coverage of the Linux operating system with a focus on Apple computers running macOS. The magazine is available as an online subscription and a companion website offers additional reviews and technical articles. Articles in this publication range from consumer use, server administration, and software development, and would appeal to macOS send-users and practitioners. Article types include reviews, news, opinion, technical information, best practices, and future trends. Recommended for public libraries.

1392. ***Operating Systems Review.*** Formerly (until 1970): *S I G O P S Bulletin.* [ISSN: 0163-5980] 1967. 3x/yr. Members, USD 20; Non-members, USD 30. Ed(s): Kishore Pusukuri, Christopher Rossback. Association for Computing Machinery, 2 Penn Plaza, Ste 701, New York, NY 10121; acmhelp@acm.org; https://www.acm.org. Illus., index, adv. *Indexed:* A22. *Aud.:* Ac.

Operating Systems Review is a publication of the Association for Computing Machinery's Special Interest Group on Operating Systems. Each issue is oriented around a specific theme with articles solicited by guest editors. Several types of articles are published, including polemics, works in progress, results of repeated research, historical accounts, novel approaches to operating system education, and tutorials. The journal's scope covers a range of subjects, including computer operating systems and architecture for multiprogramming, multiprocessing, and time sharing; resource management; evaluation and simulation; reliability, integrity, and security of data; communications among computing processors; and computer system modeling and analysis. Recent articles include such topics as heterogeneous computing, memory management, ARM servers, and system performance in virtualized systems. Recommended for academic libraries.

1393. ***T H E Journal.*** [ISSN: 0192-592X] 1974. bi-m. Free to qualified personnel. 1105 Media Inc., 9201 Oakdale Ave, Ste 101, Chatsworth, CA 91311; info@1105media.com; http://www.1105media.com. Illus., adv. *Indexed:* A01, A22, B01, BRI, ERIC, MLA-IB. *Bk. rev.:* Number and length vary. *Aud.:* Hs, Ga, Ac.

T.H.E. Journal is a bimonthly magazine for technology leaders, practitioners, and decision makers within education. The content covers topics relevant to all levels of education, but is focused on K-12. This magazine was the first publication in the area of educational technology. The magazine is available in print and online. The website offers additional content including trends, information and industry reviews. A free digital format is offered by email subscription. Topics that have been addressed in recent issues include esports, teaching technology to parents, wifi on school buses, blockchain deployment, and teaching robotics. This publication is recommended for high school, public, and academic libraries.

■ COOKING AND COOKERY

Sally Ijams, Knowledge and Learning Services Librarian, Darien Library, 1441 Post Road, Darien, CT 06820; sijams@darienlibrary.org

Introduction

Culinary trends over the past several years find us eating at home more, seeking out locally grown foods, leaning toward a more plant-based diet, and expanding our palates with international foods and flavors. The rapid growth of online grocery shopping can now deliver once rare ingredients with relative ease, putting even the more exotic recipes within reach for the home cook. Cooking magazines today offer a plethora of recipes that emphasize quick preparation, high flavor, and fewer ingredients— perfect for the busy home cook. All of the titles included in this 28th edition are geared toward general library audiences, are relevant to current culinary trends, and are recommended for inclusion in library collections.

Basic Periodicals

Bon Appetit, Cook's Illustrated, EatingWell.

Basic Abstracts and Indexes

Reader's Guide to Periodical Literature.

1394. ***Bon Appetit.*** [ISSN: 0006-6990] 1956. 10x/yr. USD 15 domestic; USD 28 Canada; USD 38 elsewhere. Ed(s): Adam Rapoport. Conde Nast Publications, Inc., 1 World Trade Center, New York, NY 10007; communications@condenast.com; http://www.condenast.com. Illus., adv. *Indexed:* A22, BRI, C37. *Aud.:* Ga, Ac, Sa.

Bon Appetit continues to be the gold standard of American cooking magazines. Each issue offers recipes, entertaining ideas, travel stories, and wine reviews and recommendations. While aimed at the adult palate, Deb Perelman of Smitten Kitchen blog fame writes the Picky Eaters' Club, a monthly recipe that is decidedly kid-friendly. In addition, *Bon Appetit* explores the hottest options in cooking gear and tableware. Regular features offer tips, products, and techniques that complement the recipes. Strongly recommended for public libraries. URL: www.bonappetite.com

1395. ***Christopher Kimball's Milk Street Magazine.*** 2016. bi-m. USD 29.95 combined subscription print & online eds. Christopher Kimball's Milk Street, 177 Milk St, Boston, MA 02109; info@177milkstreet.com; https://www.177milkstreet.com. Adv. *Aud.:* Ga.

The Milk Street philosophy focuses on high-flavor recipes from around the world with ingredients that are readily available to the average home cook. Each issue contains a selection of easy weeknight meals, book reviews, and lessons and discoveries from the Milk Street staff. Recommended for anyone looking to expand their repertoire or who enjoys food writing.

1396. ***Cook's Illustrated.*** Former titles (until 1992): *Cook's;* (until 1985): *The Cook's Magazine.* [ISSN: 1068-2821] 1980. bi-m. USD 24.95 domestic; USD 30.95 Canada; USD 36.95 elsewhere. America's Test Kitchen, 17 Station St, Brookline, MA 02445; customerservice@americastestkitchen.com; http://www.americastestkitchen.com. Illus., index. Sample. *Indexed:* H&TI. *Aud.:* Ga, Ac, Sa.

Cook's Illustrated is dedicated to presenting the science behind the essential recipes, setting it apart from the crowd. A cooking manual once known for its distinctive covers and pen-and-ink drawings, it now offers photographs of techniques and finished dishes. Through exhaustive testing of not only recipes but also of kitchen equipment and ingredients, the magazine is also thorough without being overly scholarly. Strongly recommended for public libraries. URL: www.cooksillustrated.com

1397. ***Cuisine at Home.*** Former titles (until 2001): *Cuisine;* (until 2000): *August Home's Cuisine.* [ISSN: 1537-8225] 1996. bi-m. USD 29 for 2 yrs. domestic; USD 49 Canada. Ed(s): Joy Taylor. August Home Publishing Co., PO Box 842, Des Moines, IA 50304; orders@augusthome.com; http://www.augusthome.com. Illus., adv. Sample. Vol. ends: Nov. *Aud.:* Ga.

The best in basic home cooking with an emphasis on a rich array of comfort foods. Recipes are presented in activity/ingredient order, and accompanying instructional photos beautifully illustrate helpful techniques. Nutritional facts for each recipe included. Nice addition for collections that need basic cookery skill instructionals.

1398. ***EatingWell: where good taste meets good health.*** [ISSN: 1046-1639] 1990. bi-m. USD 10. Ed(s): Jessie Price. EatingWell, Media Group, 20 Graham Way, Ste 100, Shelburne, VT 05482. Illus., index, adv. Vol. ends: Nov/Dec. *Aud.:* Ga, Sa.

With the subtitle "Where Good Taste Meets Good Health," this magazine not only offers healthy recipes, but also has great articles and stories on current food and lifestyle trends. There are recipes for all levels of cooks, with a special nod to those who are looking for fast and flavorful main courses. Inspiring articles for those who want to maintain a healthy lifestyle. Recommended for all public libraries. URL: www.eatingwell.com

1399. ***Fine Cooking: for people who love to cook.*** [ISSN: 1072-5121] 1994. bi-m. USD 29.95 in US & Canada; USD 36 elsewhere. Ed(s): Jennifer Armentrout. The Taunton Press, Inc., 63 South Main St, PO Box 5506, Newtown, CT 06470; publicrelations@taunton.com; http://www.taunton.com. Illus., index, adv. Circ: 240000 Paid. *Indexed:* H&TI. *Bk. rev.:* Number and length vary. *Aud.:* Ga, Ac, Sa.

Fine Cooking definitely places the emphasis on food for the home cook who wants to eat well. The "Great Finds" feature is a showcase for seasonal foods and how to best prepare them. "Books That Cook" is an excellent collection development tool for librarians and cookbook lovers alike. Menus help the cook mix and match recipes in the issue. Many recipes include beer and wine pairings. Recommended for public libraries. URL: www.finecooking.com

1400. ***Food & Wine.*** Former titles (until 1983): *Monthly Magazine of Food and Wine;* (until 1981): *International Review of Food and Wine.* [ISSN: 0741-9015] 1978. m. USD 15 combined subscription domestic (print & online eds.)). Ed(s): Dana Cowin. Time Inc., Time & Life Bldg, Rockefeller Center, 29th Fl, New York, NY 10020-1393; information@timeinc.com; http://www.timeinc.com. Illus., index, adv. Sample. Vol. ends: Dec. *Indexed:* A22, H&TI. *Aud.:* Ga, Sa.

Food & Wine is the final word on what's going on in the culinary industry. From coverage of new and notable restaurants to the chefs who staff their stoves, it is the perfect resource for the home cook pondering what to make for dinner. The recipe index at the front of each issue includes notes, recipes that are fast, vegetarian, staff favorites, and of course, most are accompanied by a wine pairing. Strongly recommended for public libraries. URL: www.foodandwine.com

1401. ***Rachael Ray Every Day.*** Formerly (until 2015): *Every Day with Rachael Ray.* [ISSN: 2381-3830] 2005. 10x/yr. USD 9.98. Meredith National Media Group, 805 Third Avenue, New York, NY 10022; http://www.meredith.com. Adv. *Aud.:* Ga.

Like her eponymous television show, this upbeat, colorful magazine offers a mix of fast, affordable, and flavorful recipes, while a nice array of instructional articles are balanced with recipes that assume some experience in the kitchen. In addition, there are lifestyle articles, equipment advice, and kitchen how-to's. Recommended for public libraries. URL: www.rachaelraymag.com

1402. ***Saveur.*** [ISSN: 1075-7864] 1994. 9x/yr. USD 29.95 domestic. Ed(s): Adam Sachs. Bonnier Corp., 460 N Orlando Ave, Ste 200, Winter Park, FL 32789; http://www.bonniercorp.com. Illus., index, adv. *Indexed:* BRI, H&TI. *Aud.:* Ga, Ac, Sa.

Equal parts travelogue, culinary history, and recipes from all over the globe, *Saveur* packs a lot of information in its nine issues a year. Each issue tells a story about a place and its food, or takes an ingredient and focuses on how the world uses it. The recipe index is minimal, divided by recipe type with no key provided. "Notes from the Saveur Test Kitchen," located at the back of every issue, explores knowledge gleaned during the making of the issue. Recommended for public libraries with a high interest in travel and culinary history. URL: www.saveur.com

1403. ***Sift.*** [ISSN: 2380-7075] 2015. 3x/yr. King Arthur Flour Company, 58 Billings Farm Rd, White River Junction, VT 05001; customercare@kingarthurclour.com; http://www.kingarthurflour.com/. Illus., adv. *Aud.:* Ga.

Decades of knowledge from the King Arthur Flour test kitchens go into each issue. With recipes for novice bakers as well as experienced bread mavens, the beautifully illustrated instructions ensure baking success nearly every time. This magazine caters to all dietary needs, including gluten free. *Sift* is not yet available for subscription but can be purchased per issue. It is an exceptionally worthy addition to library collections where baking is of interest. Highly recommended.

1404. ***Taste of Home: cooking,caring & sharing.*** [ISSN: 1071-5878] 1993. bi-m. USD 19.98 domestic; CAD 36.98 Canada (for 12 issues); USD 25.98 elsewhere). R D A Enthusiast Brands, LLC, 1610 N 2nd St, Ste 102, Milwaukee, WI 53212; customercare@rd.com; http://www.rda.com/. Illus., index, adv. Sample. Circ: 3100000 Paid. Vol. ends: Nov/Dec. *Aud.:* Ga.

This magazine is devoted to the home cook who needs to get dinner on the table. All the recipes are sourced from readers and with an emphasis on simple, fresh ingredients and include nutritional information. Easy, instructional tips and tricks make it a great choice for the new cook. Recommended for public libraries. URL: www.tasteofhome.com

■ CRAFTS AND MAKING

General/Clay/Fiber/Jewelry - Metal/Knitting and Crochet/Needlework/Quilting/Wood/Papercrafts/Sewing

Jennifer Koenig Johnson, Reference Librarian, Springdale Public Library, Springdale, AR 72764

Introduction

The traditionally overlapping nature of crafts, hobbies, art, mixed media, do-it-yourself (DIY), home repair, and anything else made by hand, have become even more entangled with the emergence of the maker movement, STEAM (or the alternate STEM and STREAM), increased popularity of DIY, Pinterest, and other websites and apps focused on crafts, hobbies, and creating art. It is important to understand the differences between crafts and hobbies and professional products such as art, photography, and other sellable outcomes.

According to the Merriam-Webster dictionary, crafts are "skill[s] in planning, making, or executing," while hobbies are "a pursuit outside one's regular occupation engaged in especially for relaxation." DIY takes it a step further to add in the handicraft aspect. For crafts and making, it is safe to limit it to subjects that are performed for non-occupational or professional outcomes and that are created by hand with the purpose of enjoyment. While this chapter will have periodical titles that are academic in nature, most of these titles are for the crafters, hobbyist, and novices.

There are a wide variety of mediums that crafts can be made from—plastics, paper, fibers and textiles, wood, glass, metal, and so on. This chapter will include general craft periodicals and periodicals focused on clay and glass, fiber, jewelry—metal, knitting and crochet, needlework, papercraft, quilting, and wood. Due to the historically blurry lines between hobbyist/crafter and practitioner, it is important to utilize cross-referencing and review periodical titles held elsewhere in those related subjects.

Like many resources, online access has become increasingly popular and many traditionally print resources have added an online format, maintained only a print format, or ceased publication. This results in content that was available can now be easier or harder to find and, in some cases, the content is not available at all. Most of the periodicals included in the Crafts and Making chapter have an online version or additional resources online. That online content, for some of the titles and topics, enhances the usage and value of the periodical. In some cases, the website simply exists as a way for subscribers to access, renew, update, or end the print subscription. Not all listed periodicals are equal—some titles have bonus content that is packaged with the issue while others have additional content online for subscribers. Some titles are available for print and digital subscription, while others are in only print or digital format.

There are a lot of periodicals available in print and online that cover the ever-growing subject area of crafts and making. These are just a selection of titles that have been evaluated as excellent titles for libraries to consider adding to their collections. For this edition of *Magazines for Libraries*, eight new periodical titles were added to the Crafts and Making chapter along with a new periodical category, papercraft.

Basic Periodicals

GENERAL. *American Craft*

CLAY AND GLASS. *Ceramic Review*

FIBER. *Piecework*

JEWELRY - METAL. *Bead & Button*

NEEDLEWORK. *World of Cross Stitching*

PAPERCRAFT. *Papercraft Inspirations*

QUILTING. *Quilting Arts*

WOOD. *Woodsmith*

Basic Abstracts and Indexes

Readers' Guide to Periodical Literature.

General

1405. ***American Craft.*** Former titles (until 1979): *Craft Horizons with Craft World;* (until 1978): *Craft Horizons;* Incorporates: *Craft World.* [ISSN: 0194-8008] 1941. bi-m. Free to members. Ed(s): Monica Moses. American Craft Council, 1224 Marshall St NE, Ste 200, Minneapolis, MN 55413; council@craftcouncil.org; http://www.craftcouncil.org. Illus., adv. Microform: PQC. *Indexed:* A06, A22, A51, BAS, BRI, CBRI, MLA-IB. *Bk. rev.:* Number and length vary. *Aud.:* Ga, Ac, Sa.

With more than 75 years' experience, it would be almost impossible to find a better resource that has the same quality, scope, and expertise. *American Craft* covers crafts from the Ancient World to the Modern Era, from the Americas throughout the world. Despite the periodical's title, it has a wholistic world view and shows the audience that all craft is art. Like most magazines, it has the traditional periodical features such as notes from the editor, profiles, news and trends, featured articles, and advertisements. What makes this title so unique is the coverage, scope (as previously mentioned) and the highlight of artists, continuing education and career advancement opportunities, emerging mediums such as modernism meets craft, and almost a dozen articles. This beautifully designed periodical is well thought through, which makes it ideal for libraries with an active artist community.

1406. ***Cloth Paper Scissors.*** [ISSN: 1551-8175] 2004. bi-m. USD 34.95 United States; USD 43.95 Canada. Interweave Press, LLC., 133 W 19th St, New York, NY 10011; customerservice@interweave.com; http://www.interweave.com/. Adv. Circ: 40229 Paid. *Aud.:* Ga, Ac, Sa.

Utilizing the popular mixed-media trend, this periodical pulls a wide variety of arts and crafts together into one expertly laid out and beautifully designed magazine. *Cloth Paper Scissors* pulls all types of fiber and collage art as well as altered books, a/v materials, stamping, and embroidery. Each issue features approximately six-plus feature articles, which range in topic, theme, and style. It includes collage work, studio profiles, news and trends, testing out new products and techniques, artist profiles, call for art submissions, reader challenges and results, and more. It is a fun and creative periodical that can assist in supporting library programming for adults and young adults as well as support an active craft and art community. It is ideal for libraries with a maker movement collection.

1407. ***Die-cutting Essentials.*** [ISSN: 2631-4398] 2014. m. Practical Publishing International Ltd., Ste G2, St Christopher House, 217 Wellington Rd S, Stockport, SK2 6NG, United Kingdom; info@practicalpublishing.co.uk; http://www.practicalpublishing.co.uk. *Aud.:* Ga.

In recent years, die-cutting has become a trendy craft that allows crafters to extend their creativity and make new crafts with paper, vinyl, and a variety of other materials utilizing a die-cutting machine. *Die-cutting Essentials* is one of many U.K.-based publications that is content heavy and is user oriented. Each issue has more than 50 projects and ideas for readers and includes news, hints and tips, shopping recommendations, and giveaway. *Die-cutting Essentials* is a lovely blend of tradition, papercrafts, and modern ideas. Recommended for libraries with an active maker community.

1408. ***Make (Sebastopol).*** [ISSN: 1556-2336] 2005. bi-m. USD 34.99; USD 6.99 per issue. O'Reilly Media, Inc., http://www.oreilly.com. Illus. *Aud.:* Ga.

With a print and online format, this is a technology-based DIY periodical that can appeal to a wide audience of different ages and educational backgrounds. It combines the DIY mindset with the technology in everyday life. *Make* highlights projects, readers, and their stories. Each issue has approximately two columns, three-plus featured articles, and various sections with ideas, eight-plus projects, and continual education and skill improvement. It also showcases tools (with a section devoted to tool reviews), products, and reader-created projects. It is user focused and highlights the flexibility of the maker movement. This is an interesting and forward-moving periodical that could benefit libraries with a technology and maker movement focus.

Clay

1409. ***Ceramic Review.*** Formerly (until 1970): *C P A Newsheet.* [ISSN: 0144-1825] 19??. bi-m. Members, GBP 32; Non-members, GBP 36; GBP 7.50 per issue domestic. Ed(s): Bonnie Kemske. Ceramic Review Publishing Ltd., 63 Great Russell St, London, WC1B 3BF, United Kingdom. Illus., index, adv. *Indexed:* A06, A22. *Aud.:* Ac, Sa.

Ceramic Review captures the technical and practical aspects of ceramics while also incorporating an international scope and feel. With rotating themes throughout the year, it succeeds in providing a holistic view of ceramics both in style, age, and origin while ensuring that articles focus on challenging, in-depth topics. It also provides information on methods, techniques, and the craft. Highlighting potters, artists, and studios, it showcases both the knowledge of ceramics and those actively working in the field of study. With stories, reviews, and advice, it is sure to appeal to those working with or who study ceramics.

1410. ***Ceramics Monthly.*** [ISSN: 0009-0328] 1953. 10x/yr. USD 3.49 per month. Ed(s): Sherman Hall. American Ceramic Society Inc., 600 N Cleveland Ave, Ste 210, Westerville, OH 43082; customerservice@ceramics.org; http://www.ceramics.org. Illus., index, adv. Microform: NBI; PQC. *Indexed:* A&ATA, A01, A06, A22, A51, BAS, BRI, CBRI. *Aud.:* Sa.

Ceramics Monthly, which has celebrated more than 65 years of publication, is geared to those working in the ceramics industry and less to those studying or teaching ceramics. It features articles on established potters or new artists and highlights a different type of pottery in each issue. It contains sections on clay culture, exposure, studio showcase, techno file, tips and tools, and working potter recipes, which are geared toward those working in a ceramics studio. It also includes a call for submissions section. While an important title, it should only be considered by libraries with a strong ceramic community or patronage.

Fiber

1411. ***Piecework.*** [ISSN: 1067-2249] 1993. bi-m. USD 24 domestic; USD 29 Canada; USD 34 per issue foreign. Interweave Press, LLC., 133 W 19th St, New York, NY 10011; customerservice@interweave.com; http://www.interweave.com/. Illus., adv. Circ: 27182 Paid. *Bk. rev.:* Number and length vary. *Aud.:* Ga, Sa.

Piecework is a fun and cultured periodical that uniquely discusses the history and diversity in fabric handicrafts. Readers can access projects, tips, recommendations, and articles on knitting, crochet, and embroidery. Difficulty levels vary from pattern to pattern but all skill levels can benefit from this periodical (although novice users may feel intimidated by the patterns in some issues). Each issue contains a calendar of upcoming events, products needed by fiber users, abbreviations, and techniques. There are approximately 13 feature articles in each issue and the issues rotate through themes, fiber styles, historical styles, and pattern types. *Piecework* is a beautiful and high-quality periodical that provides an excellent blend of past and present in the fiber arts. It also provides a then and now piece that shows, for example, what a sewing machine looked like then versus now. It a good periodical for libraries with a strong fiber arts collection.

1412. ***Rug Hooking.*** [ISSN: 1045-4373] 1989. 5x/yr. USD 34.95. Ampry Publishing, LLC, 3400 Dundee Rd, Ste 220, Northbrook, IL 60062; https://www.amprycp.com/. Illus., index, adv. *Bk. rev.:* Number and length vary. *Aud.:* Ga, Sa.

Rug Hooking, which focuses on traditional patterns and historical methods, is one of the few titles still available that focuses specifically on making handmade rugs. Though rug hooking, like many fiber crafts, waxes and wanes in popularity, it is a topic that should be available in some format or another in libraries. Each issue of *Rug Hooking* consists of featured articles, projects, expert profiles, advice, and techniques. Though *Rug Hooking* only comes out five times per year, each issue is themed and focused so that it is concise, detailed, and informative. Through the website, readers can access giveaways, instructions, current and back issues, subscription services, book club, videos, and events. While adding the periodical may not be high on anyone's list of magazines to order, libraries should consider offering materials on rug hooking.

1413. ***Spin-Off: it's about making yarn by hand.*** [ISSN: 0198-8239] 1977. q. USD 30 domestic; USD 34 Canada. Interweave Press, LLC., 133 W 19th St, New York, NY 10011; customerservice@interweave.com; http://www.interweave.com/. Illus., adv. Circ: 23424 Paid. *Bk. rev.:* Number and length vary. *Aud.:* Ga, Ac, Sa.

Spin-Off is an excellent periodical source for those interested in all aspects related to hand-spinning. It covers fiber art aspects well and provides in-depth articles on varied materials, techniques, and trends in the world of yarn spinning. Each issue includes a highlight on a fiber, which can expose the reader to a new material or assist them in better understanding that fiber. There are approximately ten featured articles and three projects included in each issue. Readers can access reviews of books, products, trends, and techniques as well as artist interviews and profiles. It is a solid periodical and does well in covering fiber arts. As an Interweave publication, the periodical is available in print and digital formats. Recommended for libraries with a strong fiber arts community.

Jewelry - Metal

1414. ***Bead & Button.*** [ISSN: 1072-4931] 1994. bi-m. USD 28.95 domestic; USD 36.95 Canada; USD 42.95 elsewhere. Ed(s): Julia Gerlach. Kalmbach Publishing Co., 21027 Crossroads Circle, PO Box 1612, Waukesha, WI 53187; customerservice@kalmbach.com; http://www.kalmbach.com. Illus., adv. *Aud.:* Ga.

Bead & Button, a solid beading periodical, provides in-depth articles and projects for those of various skill levels. Each issue has approximately three columns and ten-plus patterned projects, which seamlessly blend into the theme for each issue. Readers can access new techniques, tips, and ideas, as well as learn more about gemstones and beads. It also has a section to showcase readers' projects and current trends. With an international feel and a lot of varied beadwork and jewelry, readers will be delighted by this creative periodical and inspired to start making jewelry (as the reviewer was inspired to do so!). There is also an advertisement index, website director, and directories for classes, shops, and societies in each issue. Additional content is found online. Highly recommended for libraries looking for a beading periodical that currently do not have one.

1415. ***Beadwork.*** Incorporates (2003-2010): *Step by Step Beads;* Former titles (until Dec.2011): *Super Beadwork;* (until 1998): *Interweave Beadwork.* [ISSN: 1528-5634] 1996. bi-m. USD 29.95 domestic; USD 34.95 Canada. Interweave Press, LLC., 133 W 19th St, New York, NY 10011; customerservice@interweave.com; http://www.interweave.com/. Illus., adv. Circ: 48098 Paid. *Bk. rev.:* Number and length vary. *Aud.:* Ga.

Beadwork, like *Bead & Button*, is geared for the more artistic and professional scale jewelry enthusiast. While the periodical does include information about all types of beadwork, it focuses primarily on beadwork as jewelry. Each issue has a "designer of the year" project, which consists of approximately three projects. Besides those designer projects, there are approximately 10-plus projects per issue as well as stitch tips, artist profiles, tips and techniques, stitch index, project skill level ratings, and bead information. This periodical appears to be geared toward the serious jewelry enthusiast and those with a higher skill level than novice. It also includes international designs. Still, a good title for consideration for libraries with a strong beading or jewelry-making collection.

Knitting and Crochet

1416. ***Crochet!*** Formed by the merger of (199?-2002): *Annie's Crochet to Go;* Which was formerly (199?-199?): *Annie's Quick & Easy Crochet to Go;* (199?-199?): *Annie's Quick & Easy Pattern Club;* (1980-199?): *Annie's Pattern Club Newsletter;* (1999-2002): *Crochet Home & Holiday;* Which was formerly (1989-1999): *Crochet Home;* (1987-1989): *Crochet Fun.* [ISSN: 1539-011X] 2002. q. USD 21.97 combined subscription (print & online eds.); USD 7.99 per issue). Ed(s): Ellen Gormley, Carol Alexander. Annie's Publishing, 306 E Parr Rd, Berne, IN 46711; http://www.annies-publishing.com/. Adv. Circ: 60000. *Aud.:* Ga.

Crochet! is a good periodical to be considered for libraries looking for a general audience crochet magazine. Most issues contain 15+ projects, along with featured articles and tips and techniques. Many issues will have patterns geared for various skill levels and provides tutorials and instructions for learning crochet. Patterns range from clothing, accessories, home decor, and gifts. Through the publisher website, readers can access some free content. It's a solid periodical to consider adding to your crochet collection.

1417. ***Inside Crochet.*** [ISSN: 2040-1051] 2009. m. GBP 48 domestic; GBP 66 in Europe; GBP 75 elsewhere. Ed(s): Claire Montgomerie. Tailor Made Publishing Ltd., PO Box 6337, Bournemouth, BH1 9EH, United Kingdom; contact@tailormadepublishing.co.uk; http://www.tailormadepublishing.co.uk/. Illus., adv. *Bk. rev.:* Number and length vary. *Aud.:* Ga, Sa.

Inside Crochet, a periodical published in the United Kingdom, succeeds at providing excellent quality in both their print and online formats. Through the magazine website, users can access information about the print magazine and subscription, patterns and tutorials, competitions, the marketplace, and FAQs. Similar content is available through the print format. Most issues are easy to navigate and include a variety of approximately 15+ patterns. With featured articles and news, readers can access information on techniques, how-to guides, and information specific for beginners. While subscriptions in North America are more expensive, it is a great resource to consider.

1418. ***Interweave Crochet.*** [ISSN: 1937-0008] 2004. q. USD 26.95 United States; USD 30.95 Canada. Interweave Press, LLC., 133 W 19th St, New York, NY 10011; customerservice@interweave.com; http://www.interweave.com/. Adv. Circ: 39573 Paid. *Bk. rev.:* Number and length vary. *Aud.:* Ga.

Interweave Crochet is a creative, inspiring, and sophisticated publication that leaves the reader wanting to make all the projects and knowing there is never enough time to do so. Each issue has a good selection of patterns, which are well designed and tied into the theme of the issue. The featured articles are well written and on point with current trends, topics, and news. Most issues have a thread and hook review, new products review, and a glossary and project index. All skill levels will find a pattern in most issues and, if not, users can access the online content for more patterns, tutorials, and instructions. This well-crafted periodical will benefit any crafter who uses it. Print and digital editions are available through Interweave Press. Recommended for public libraries with a crochet collection.

1419. ***Interweave Knits.*** [ISSN: 1088-3622] 1996. q. USD 26.95 United States; USD 30.95 Canada. Interweave Press, LLC., 133 W 19th St, New York, NY 10011; customerservice@interweave.com; http://www.interweave.com/. Illus., adv. Circ: 85292 Paid. *Aud.:* Ga.

Interweave Knits is a staple periodical of any knitting collection. With a variety of projects and featured articles per issue, along with tips and techniques, how-to instructions, and recommendations for tools and supplies, it is a smart, sophisticated, and well-written periodical that should be a core title in any public library. Each issue leaves the knitter wishing they could make each project and knowing there will never be enough time. An inspiring periodical for all knitters and those who wish to learn.

1420. ***Vogue Knitting International.*** Formerly (until 198?): *Vogue Knitting.* [ISSN: 0890-9237] 1982. 5x/yr. USD 27.97 domestic; USD 32.97 Canada; USD 7.99 per issue. Soho Publishing Company, 104 West 27 St, 3rd Fl, New York, NY 10001; http://www.sohopub.com/. Illus., adv. *Aud.:* Ga.

After more than 35 years of publication, *Vogue Knitting International* is still a core title for knitting periodicals. While patterns and design are not always trendy or popular, the designs are classic, timeless, and sophisticated. Most issues contain three-plus featured articles, five-plus fashion articles (which include patterns), and guides for how to knit, fiber recommendations, news and trends, yarn shop profiles, events, tips and techniques, and abbreviations and patterns. For libraries wanting to add a second knitting periodical, this is a good title to consider.

Needlework

1421. ***Cross Stitch Gold.*** [ISSN: 1471-3667] 2000. 9x/yr. GBP 44.99; GBP 5.99 newsstand/cover. Ed(s): Sarah Trevor. Immediate Media Co. Ltd., Vineyard House, 44 Brook Green, London, W6 7BT, United Kingdom; enquiries@immediatemedia.co.uk; http://www.immediate.co.uk. Adv. Sample. *Aud.:* Ga.

Another personal favorite, *Cross Stitch Gold* is a title boasted as one of the best and it is high on the ranking list. Each issue is full of helpful, insightful information, tips, and techniques along with patterns, articles, interviews, and more. Each issue contains a theme and themed projects (approximately eight per issue) along with letters from readers, subscription information, freebies and contests, preview of next issue, stitching guides and reviews, and puzzles. It's not as thick as other cross stitch periodicals, but is a good title to consider. An added bonus: through the website, users can access tutorials, patterns, and more! URL: http://www.cross-stitching.com/

1422. ***Just Cross Stitch.*** [ISSN: 0883-0797] 1983. 7x/yr. USD 21.97 combined subscription (print & online eds.); USD 6.99 per issue). Ed(s): Lillian Anderson, Christy Schmitz. Annie's Publishing, 306 E Parr Rd, Berne, IN 46711; http://www.annies-publishing.com/. Illus., adv. Circ: 75000. *Aud.:* Ga.

While most cross stitch magazines are published in the United Kingdom, *Just Cross Stitch* is based in North America. It is relatively low in cost and is a solid periodical that provides a good mixture of articles, information, and patterns. Each issue consists of featured articles (approximately four with patterns) and approximately 16 projects showcased. Readers can access news, stitch illustrations, marketplace, instructions, and a project gallery in each issue. Besides the print content, there is additional information found online through the periodical website. *Just Cross Stitch* is another personal favorite and should be a serious contender when selecting a cross stitch periodical.

1423. ***Stitch.*** Formerly: *Stitch With the Embroiderers Guild.* [ISSN: 1467-6648] 1999. bi-m. GBP 25.50 domestic; GBP 30.60 in Europe; GBP 37.50 in the Americas. Ed(s): Kathy Troup. E G Enterprises Ltd., 1 Kings Rd, Walton on Thames, KT12 2RA, United Kingdom; administrator@embroiderersguild.com; http://www.embroiderersguild.com. Adv. *Aud.:* Ga.

Stitch, an embroidery magazine and publication of the Embroiderers Guild of the United Kingdom, is a well-rounded periodical that covers a variety of stitches, their history and background, and contemporary patterns and projects. In the reviewed issues, there were seven projects and three articles. Both issues contained news, craft events in the United Kingdom, Q & A section, subscription information, stitching supplies, a preview of the next issue, distance learning opportunities, and a reader gallery. *Stitch* provides a stitch guide, patterns, and templates in all issues. *Stitch* is not limited to embroidery, though that is a large part of its coverage, and the included patterns are easy to follow and are geared for various difficulty levels. Through the Embroiderers Guild of the United Kingdom website, users can access additional online content such as special magazine discounts, guild projects, membership, shop, *Embroidery Magazine,* retailer discounts, and upcoming events. *Stitch* is a contemporary and inspiring periodical that should be considered for strong needlework collections or maker space programs.

1424. ***The World of Cross Stitching.*** [ISSN: 1460-1974] 1997. m. GBP 48.50. Ed(s): Ruth Southorn. Immediate Media Company Origin Ltd., Tower House, Fairfax St, Bristol, BS1 3BN, United Kingdom; info@immediatemedia.co.uk; http://www.immediatemediaorigin.com. Adv. Sample. *Aud.:* Ga.

There are a handful of United Kingdom-based periodicals that boast the "best in Britain" label, but *The World of Cross Stitching* is truly an excellent, content heavy periodical. Each issue is well thought through, laid out appropriately, and contains beautiful patterns, interesting and creative ideas, and tips and techniques that are inspiring. Included patterns are easy to read and follow with charts in color and the needed materials clearly labeled. Each issue has a monthly panel that provides tips, advice, and Q & A. The issues have seasonal, monthly themes and the associated patterns, articles, and other content mesh well in that monthly theme. Each issue also contains a puzzle, competitions, news, events, supplies for products shown in the issue, access to back issues, a preview of the next month, and tutorial information. Of the many cross stitch magazines available, this is one to consider.

Quilting

1425. ***American Patchwork & Quilting.*** [ISSN: 1066-758X] 1993. bi-m. Meredith National Media Group, 1716 Locust St, Des Moines, IA 50309; http://www.meredith.com. *Bk. rev.:* Number and length vary. *Aud.:* Ga, Sa.

American Patchwork & Quilting is a good, basic periodical with easy-to-follow instructions for various skill level quilters. Each issue comes with approximately eight projects, plus additional patterns that can be viewed online (subscription required to access the online patterns), and new techniques, tips, and ideas. Through allpeoplequilt.com, readers can access more quilt patterns, other fabric-based projects, instructions on how to quilt, and back issues of the periodical. Book recommendations are also included. It is an informative and quality periodical that should be included in quilting collections. Recommended for public or special libraries.

1426. *American Quilter.* [ISSN: 8756-6591] 1985. bi-m. Free to members. American Quilter's Society, PO Box 3290, Paducah, KY 42002; http://www.americanquilter.com/. Adv. *Bk. rev.:* Number and length vary. *Aud.:* Ga.

In recent years, a shift from guild-based periodicals to project-based periodicals has occurred, with the latter being more common. *American Quilter* is one of many project-based titles. It consists of eight patterned projects per issue as well as approximately six non-project articles. Each issue contains information on the online content, creative ideas, new products and techniques, and designer profiles. It also includes an advertisement index, which may be useful for hardcore quilting patrons. The American Quilting Society also has online resources available through iQuilt.com. Each issue also contains upcoming events and exhibitions. A worthy title to consider for any collection. Recommended for public libraries.

1427. *Quilting Arts.* [ISSN: 1538-4950] 2001. bi-m. USD 34.95 United States; USD 43.95 Canada. Ed(s): Vivika DeNegre. F + W Media Inc., 1140 Broadway, 14th Fl, New York, NY 10001; contact_us@fwmedia.com; http://www.fwcommunity.com/. Adv. Circ: 44256 Paid. *Aud.:* Ga, Sa.

Quilting Arts, a publication by the Quilting Company, is an excellent contemporary quilting publication that provides new techniques, tips, and modern methods. It attempts to showcase how to be creative with fiber and thread. Each issue consists of approximately seven-plus patterns, gallery and studio profiles, and reader challenges. For those wanting quilting supplies, new products, and shop information, *Quilting Arts* also provides an advertisement index, Q & A, and marketplace. The Quilting Company website also provides additional resources and quilting information as a supplement to *Quilting Arts*. The main difference between *Quilting Arts* and other quilting periodicals is that *Quilting Arts* has a focus on the art of quilting, which can be a refreshing perspective. Recommended for libraries interested in adding a contemporary, inspiring quilting periodical to their collection.

1428. *Quiltmaker: step-by-step patterns, tips & techniques.* [ISSN: 1047-1634] 1982. bi-m. USD 29.97 United States; USD 35.97 Canada. Ed(s): Carolyn Beam. F + W Media Inc., 1140 Broadway, 14th Fl, New York, NY 10001; contact_us@fwmedia.com; http://www.fwcommunity.com/. Illus., index. Sample. Circ: 125975. Vol. ends: Nov/Dec. *Indexed:* BRI. *Aud.:* Ga.

Like other titles, *Quiltmaker* is full of projects and patterns. With varying difficulty levels, this periodical can appeal to quilters of all experience levels. Unlike other quilting titles, it attempts to provide a wide view to quilting styles, layouts, fabrics, and colors so that it has something that will appeal to a wide readership. Each issues contains approximately six-plus patterns, three feature quilts and columns, and guides for learning to quilt, utilizing scraps, and a spotlight feature. Through the parent company, the Quilting Company, readers can access the print and online formats with a subscription or by purchasing individual issues. Through the original website, readers can access back issues, patterns, and more. *Quiltmaker* is a good recommendation for libraries looking to add a quilting periodical to their collection.

Wood

1429. *Fine Woodworking.* Incorporates (in 1998): *Home Furniture;* Which superseded (in 1997): *Taunton's Home Furniture;* (in 1996): *Fine Woodworking's Home Furniture;* Formerly (until 1993): *Fine Woodworking.* [ISSN: 0361-3453] 1975. bi-m. USD 34.95 domestic; USD 36.95 Canada; USD 41.95 elsewhere. The Taunton Press, Inc., 63 South Main St, PO Box 5506, Newtown, CT 06470; publicrelations@taunton.com; http://www.taunton.com. Illus., index, adv. Sample. Circ: 292000 Paid. *Indexed:* A06, A22. *Aud.:* Ga, Sa.

Meant for the professional woodworkers, *Fine Woodworking* is an excellent trade publication for those seeking a high-quality periodical that is laid out well and contains a lot of useful information. Each issue contains approximately five-plus featured articles as well as information on the online resources. With tips and suggestions, information about tools and materials, handwork, designing projects, woodworking fundamentals, and new products, readers will find more than enough information to keep them inspired while also providing new and innovative information. There is also an index for advertisements and a woodworker's market. Recommended for libraries with an interest in woodworking, craft professions, and structure.

1430. *Popular Woodworking Magazine.* Former titles (until 1985): *Popular Woodworker;* (until 1984): *Pacific Woodworker.* [ISSN: 0884-8823] 1981. 7x/yr. USD 24.95 United States; USD 32.95 Canada. Ed(s): Megan Fitzpatrick. F + W Media Inc., 1140 Broadway, 14th Fl, New York, NY 10001; contact_us@fwmedia.com; http://www.fwcommunity.com/. Illus., adv. Circ: 152121 Paid. *Indexed:* MASUSE. *Bk. rev.:* Number and length vary. *Aud.:* Ga.

Popular Woodworking Magazine is meant for the intermediate level woodworker, someone who has previously completed a wood project. Chock full of helpful information, issues of *Popular Woodworking Magazine* contain approximately four projects and four articles, written by experts in the field, as well as references to additional online content, letters from readers, staff tips and tricks, tool testing, and articles on the various stages of the woodworking process. Between the print format and the online content, this is an ideal resource for libraries with a high circulating woodworking collection.

The Woodenboat. See Boats and Boating section.

1431. *Woodsmith.* [ISSN: 0164-4114] 1979. bi-m. USD 29 for 2 yrs. domestic; CAD 60 Canada; USD 43 elsewhere. August Home Publishing Co., 2200 Grand Ave, Des Moines, IA 50312; orders@augusthome.com; http://www.augusthome.com. Illus. Sample. Vol. ends: Dec. *Aud.:* Ga.

Woodsmith is an easy-to-use, high-quality periodical that provides projects, tips and suggestions, and plans for woodworkers. Projects are listed by categories and each issue contains woodworking recommendations, techniques, highlights on tools, products, and materials, and instructions. Most issues have approximately five projects and six articles. It is a user-focused periodical full of excellent advice, recommendations, and projects. Recommended for novice and advanced woodworkers.

Papercrafts

1432. *Papercraft Inspirations.* [ISSN: 1744-4381] 2004. m. GBP 53.49. Ed(s): Angela Poole. Immediate Media Co. Ltd., Vineyard House, 44 Brook Green, London, W6 7BT, United Kingdom; enquiries@immediatemedia.co.uk; http://www.immediate.co.uk. Adv. *Aud.:* Ga, Sa.

While scrapbooking has traditionally been the main type of papercraft, over the past decade papercrafting has expanded to cover a wide variety of things. *Papercraft Inspirations*, advertised as "Britain's best-selling paper craft magazine," is one of many periodicals devoted to crafts that involve paper. This periodical has a wide scope that allows it to cover a variety of topics and styles while also meeting the varying needs of their readers. Each issue contains letters from readers, best buys, news and trends, preview of the next issue, supplier list for products shown in the issue, and templates and paper to use for included projects. Most issues will contain approximately 100+ projects that will appeal to a wide audience. *Papercraft Inspirations* provides projects, tips, and information for all skill levels. The projects that are covered come from various categories such as gifts, occasions, home, and so on. This is a fun and creative publication that is best suited for libraries with patrons who enjoy doing papercrafts.

Sewing

1433. ***Sew News: the trusted sewing source.*** [ISSN: 0273-8120] 1980. bi-m. USD 23.98 United States; USD 29.98 Canada. Interweave Press, LLC., 133 W 19th St, New York, NY 10011; customerservice@interweave.com; http://www.interweave.com/. Illus., adv. Circ: 58133 Paid. *Indexed:* BRI. *Bk. rev.:* Number and length vary. *Aud.:* Ga.

One of many sewing magazines available, *Sew News* is a good staple periodical to have in any strong sewing collection. Available in both print and online formats, *Sew News* specializes in giving creative ideas, techniques, and options for all skill levels. It is a fun and inspiring periodical that covers a wide variety of sewing areas: clothing, accessories, home, office, gifts, occasions, and more! Most craft magazines are plagued by a lot of advertisement and this periodical is no exception. Each issue contains articles and patterns, profiles of designers, techniques, and themes. It also provides staff picks, book recommendations, and ten-plus feature articles and approximately eight columns. Sewing popularity has increased over the years, so this is a good periodical to consider adding to any maker collection. Ideal for academic and public libraries.

1434. ***Threads: for people who love to sew.*** [ISSN: 0882-7370] 1985. bi-m. USD 32.95 domestic; USD 34.95 Canada; USD 38.95 elsewhere. The Taunton Press, Inc., 63 South Main St, PO Box 5506, Newtown, CT 06470; publicrelations@taunton.com; http://www.taunton.com. Illus., index, adv. Circ: 130000 Paid. Vol. ends: Dec. *Indexed:* BRI. *Aud.:* Ga, Sa.

With more 30 years in print, *Threads* is a foundation periodical for sewing. Each issue contains informative and in-depth articles per issue as well as tips, techniques, fabric information, embellishments, a creative thread article, and pattern reviews, hacks, and Q & A. Besides the print content, there is also additional content online. Through the periodical website, users can access additional information such as a magazine index and tutorials. Good title for consideration for libraries looking to add additional sewing periodicals.

■ CRIMINOLOGY AND LAW ENFORCEMENT

See also Law; and Sociology and Social Work sections.

Elizabeth Marcus, Undergraduate Experience Librarian, Western Carolina University, Cullowhee, NC 28723; emarcus@email.wcu.edu

Introduction

In the field of criminology, there are two basic types of magazines: scholarly journals and trade and professional publications. Both types are reviewed in this section. Scholarly journals are sometimes published by commercial publishers in association with an academic society, and these relationships are noted in the reviews. These partnerships have flourished in the last decade or so, no doubt due to the presence of online versions of the journals and the technology needed to support that format. Sage Publications and Routledge are both examples of publishers that have successfully embraced this model.

Scholarly journals frequently favor empirical research over theoretical works and commentary, but there are several titles that provide both, and this is noted in the annotations. The intended audience for these journals comprises researchers and policy makers, and they are good choices for academic and special libraries. As one would expect, the trade magazine articles are the more practical, and would be of the most help to those who work in the field.

Most of the titles reviewed in this section are published in the United States, but international publications are included, and many of the U.S.-based journals publish content that is both international and interdisciplinary. Those two adjectives frequently appear in journal subtitles.

The present reviewer relied on three resources to determine which journals appear in this section, all of which proved very helpful and informative: (1) the previous edition of *Magazines for Libraries*; (2) *Ulrich's Periodicals Directory*; and (3) *Cabell's Directories of Publishing Opportunities*. For this edition, one new title, *Criminology, Criminal Justice, Law & Society*, was added, reflecting a trending focus on criminal theory and increasing availability of quality open-access journals.

In addition, the U.S. government's National Criminal Justice Reference Service is an excellent resource, and publishes numerous reports and statistical bulletins that are not reviewed here, primarily due to the vast number of them. Readers are referred to the service's website at www.ncjrs.gov. Several of the most popular and important U.S. government publications are, however, reviewed, such as *Federal Probation*.

Basic Periodicals

Ga: *American Jails, Corrections Today, Law and Order Magazine, Police Chief;* Ac: *The British Journal of Criminology, Crime & Delinquency, Criminal Justice and Behavior, Criminal Justice Ethics, Criminology, The Howard Journal of Criminal Justice, Journal of Offender Rehabilitation, Journal of Research in Crime and Delinquency, Justice Quarterly, Policing and Society, The Prison Journal.*

Basic Abstracts and Indexes

Criminal Justice Abstracts, Criminal Justice Periodicals Index, SocINDEX.

1435. ***Aggression and Violent Behavior.*** [ISSN: 1359-1789] 1996. bi-m. EUR 1464. Elsevier Ltd, The Boulevard, Langford Lane, Oxford, OX5 1GB, United Kingdom; customerserviceau@elsevier.com; http://www.elsevier.com. Adv. Sample. Refereed. *Indexed:* A01, A22, ASSIA, CJPI, IBSS, N13. *Aud.:* Ac, Sa.

Aggression and Violent Behavior is a bimonthly, peer-reviewed publication that has become one of the premier journals of the criminology field since its inception in 1996. The journal is a compilation of "substantive and integrative review articles, as well as summary reports of innovative ongoing clinical research programs on a wide range of topics relevant to the field of aggression and violent behavior." Reoccurring topics explored in this journal include homicide, family and workplace violence, sexual assault, and genetic and physiological associations with aggression. As a multidisciplinary periodical, *Aggression and Violent Behavior* holds significance for a variety of researchers and professionals, including those in criminal justice, psychology, sociology, social work, law, forensic studies, and many other fields. This publication is available in print, as well as online in its entirety via ScienceDirect.

1436. ***American Jails.*** [ISSN: 1056-0319] 1987. bi-m. Free to members. American Jail Association, 1135 Professional Ct, Hagerstown, MD 21740; http://www.aja.org. Illus., index, adv. Sample. Vol. ends: Nov/Dec. *Indexed:* A01, BRI, CJPI. *Aud.:* Ga, Ac, Sa.

American Jails is the official trade publication of the American Jail Association and a six-time APEX Award-winner for Publication Excellence. It is published bimonthly, with the first issue printed in 1987. The magazine's audience comprises association members and government personnel at local, state, and federal levels, also including private sector teams. *American Jails'* content is typical of professional association publications. Included are industry and association news stories; a column that summarizes recent pertinent federal court cases; and policy advocacy and training opportunities. The majority of articles address American matters, but foreign coverage is occasionally provided. Each issue of the magazine has an editorial spotlight. Recent spotlights include "Suicide Prevention: Everybody's Business"; "The Need for Pay Parity"; and "Mental Health: A Little Advice." There is also a column by the association's chaplain that discusses the spiritual care of inmates and corrections staff. Most issues contain in-depth articles that offer operational best-practice advice—for example, the May/June 2019 issue features an article on responding to jail deaths. Research review articles and essays, sometimes authored by academics, appear in many issues, and they are written in clear language and fully referenced. This publication is a good choice for large public libraries, colleges, and universities with criminal justice programs, and special libraries that serve the corrections industry.

1437. *American Journal of Criminal Justice.* Formerly (until 1984): *Southern Journal of Criminal Justice.* [ISSN: 1066-2316] 1975. q. EUR 434 (print & online eds.)). Ed(s): Wesley G Jennings, Caitlyn Meade. Springer New York LLC, 233 Spring St, New York, NY 10013; customerservice@springer.com; http://www.springer.com. Adv. Refereed. Reprint: PSC. *Indexed:* A22, CJPI, E01, N13, P61, SSA. *Aud.:* Ac, Sa.

American Journal of Criminal Justice is the official, peer-reviewed journal of the Southern Criminal Justice Association (SCJA). Formerly titled *Southern Journal of Criminal Justice,* this quarterly title was first published in 1975. Topic coverage includes a wide variety of "items pertaining to the criminal justice process, the formal and informal interplay between system components, problems and solutions experienced by various segments, innovative practices, policy development and implementation, evaluative research, the players engaged in these enterprises, and a wide assortment of other related interests." Recent article topics include the cost of cyberstalking; the role of self-control in texting while driving; and the social origins of radicalization. Special issues are published occasionally, with the latest issue introducing a variety of research on school safety. *American Journal of Criminal Justice* is a valuable resource for academics and professionals in the fields of criminal justice, social work, sociology, psychology, and law. This publication is available in print and online through EBSCOhost, ProQuest, and SpringerLINK.

1438. *Asian Journal of Criminology: an interdisciplinary journal on crime, law and deviance in Asia.* [ISSN: 1871-0131] 2006. q. EUR 562 (print & online eds.)). Ed(s): Jianhong Liu. Springer Netherlands, Van Godewijckstraat 30, Dordrecht, 3311 GX, Netherlands; http://www.springer-sbm.de. Refereed. Reprint: PSC. *Indexed:* A22, BRI, CJPI, E01. *Bk. rev.:* 1-2, signed. *Aud.:* Ac, Sa.

Asian Journal of Criminology is a quarterly, peer-reviewed publication that is relatively new, being first published in 2006. The journal seeks to "advance the study of criminology and criminal justice in Asia, to promote evidence-based public policy in crime prevention, and to promote comparative studies about crime and criminal justice." Articles are multidisciplinary, relating to a variety of fields including sociology, psychology, forensic science, social work, urban studies, history, and geography. Special issues are released annually, with the latest issue focusing on public and criminal justice systems. Each issue includes four articles and occasional book reviews. Although this journal is geographically focused, it maintains a global appeal through comparative studies with other countries and research methodologies that translate to different settings. *Asian Journal of Criminology* would be most appropriate for academic institutions with criminology, criminal justice, or Asian Studies programs.

1439. *Australian and New Zealand Journal of Criminology.* [ISSN: 0004-8658] 1968. 4x/yr. USD 1375 (print & online eds.)). Ed(s): Mark Halsey, Andrew Goldsmith. Sage Publications Ltd., 1 Oliver's Yard, 55 City Rd, London, EC1Y 1SP, United Kingdom; info@sagepub.com; https://www.sagepub.com/. Illus., index, adv. Sample. Refereed. Vol. ends: No. 3. Reprint: PSC. *Indexed:* A01, A22, BRI, CBRI, CJPI, HRIS, IBSS, L14, P61, SSA. *Bk. rev.:* 3-5, 1,000 words; signed. *Aud.:* Ac, Sa.

Australian and New Zealand Journal of Criminology is the official journal of the Australian and New Zealand Society of Criminology (ANZSOC). As a quarterly publication, this journal is "dedicated to advancing research and debate on a range of criminological problems and embraces diverse, methodological approaches, being home to a wide range of criminological and interdisciplinary work in the field of crime and criminal justice." As one would expect, most of the articles are authored by Australian or New Zealand researchers, and address issues pertaining to those countries, but articles by American, Canadian, and other international criminologists are also included. Each issue contains six to eight peer-reviewed research articles, and frequently opens with an editorial introduction. Book reviews are often included. Full-text access is available through Sage.

1440. *The British Journal of Criminology: an international review of crime and society.* Formerly (until 1960): *British Journal of Delinquency.* [ISSN: 0007-0955] 1950. bi-m. EUR 1055. Ed(s): Sandra Walklate. Oxford University Press, Great Clarendon St, Oxford, OX2 6DP, United Kingdom; onlinequeries.uk@oup.com; http://global.oup.com. Illus., adv. Sample. Refereed. Reprint: PSC; WSH. *Indexed:* A01, A22, BRI, CJPI, E01, IBSS, L14, N13, P61, SSA. *Bk. rev.:* 8-10; signed. *Aud.:* Ac, Sa.

The British Journal of Criminology: An International Review of Crime and Society (*BJC*) is published by Oxford University Press under the auspices of the Centre for Crime and Justice Studies, an independent charity located in London. The journal was launched in 1950 as *The British Journal of Delinquency* and changed its title in 1960. It has evolved into one of the top academic criminology journals (for the rationale for this assessment, see the introduction to this section for information on selection/ranking criteria). The content has both an international and an interdisciplinary focus, and its advisory board is composed of academics from around the globe. The editorial policies do not prescribe that submissions be only original research, or empirically based, as is the case with many other peer-reviewed journals in this section, but that they "contribute new knowledge to an understanding of crime and society." Each issue contains from 5 to 12 articles, and a number of scholarly book reviews. *BJC* is a valuable resource for academics and researchers in crime, whether they are from the fields of criminology, sociology, anthropology, psychology, law, economics, politics, or social work. It is also appropriate for professionals and policy makers.

1441. *Canadian Journal of Criminology and Criminal Justice.* Former titles (until 2003, vol.45): *Canadian Journal of Criminology;* (until 1978): *Canadian Journal of Criminology and Corrections;* (until 1971): *Canadian Journal of Corrections.* [ISSN: 1707-7753] 1958. q. USD 220. Ed(s): Simon J Verdun-Jones. University of Toronto Press, Journals Division, 5201 Dufferin St, Toronto, ON M3H 5T8, Canada; journals@utpress.utoronto.ca; http://www.utpjournals.com. Illus., index. Sample. Refereed. Circ: 690. Vol. ends: Oct. Microform: PQC. *Indexed:* A01, A22, ASSIA, BRI, C37, CJPI, E01, IBSS, L14, N13, PdeR, SSA. *Bk. rev.:* 5-8, 500-1,000 words; signed. *Aud.:* Ac, Sa.

The *Canadian Journal of Criminology and Criminal Justice* is published quarterly by the University of Toronto Press for the Canadian Criminal Justice Association (CCJA). The articles are peer-reviewed and bilingual, available in French or English, with the abstract available in both languages. The journal's scope is broad—it seeks to be a "forum for original contributions and discussions in the fields of criminology and criminal justice," and the coverage is theoretical as well as empirical. Most of the articles relate directly to Canadian criminal justice concerns, but the research would be of interest to U.S. practitioners and criminal justice scholars and students. This journal is available full-text from several vendors: Project Muse, EBSCOhost, and ProQuest.

1442. *Corrections Today.* Former titles (until 1979): *American Journal of Correction;* (until 1954): *Prison World;* (until 1941): *Jail Association Journal.* [ISSN: 0190-2563] 1939. bi-m. Free to members. American Correctional Association, 206 N Washington St, Ste 200, Alexandria, VA 22314; jeffw@aca.org; http://www.aca.org. Illus., index, adv. Sample. Vol. ends: Dec. Microform: MIM; PQC. Reprint: PSC. *Indexed:* A01, A22, BRI, CJPI, N13. *Bk. rev.:* 1-2, 300-500 words; signed. *Aud.:* Ga, Ac, Sa.

Corrections Today is a bimonthly trade magazine published by the American Correctional Association (ACA). Recent article topics address challenges in monitoring inmate communication, improving staff morale, and implementing mentoring programs for youth in confinement. These articles are written by professionals in the corrections industry and public agencies. Guest editorials, ACA news items, research notes, book reviews, and other columns are also provided. *Corrections Today* is a recommended resource for special libraries that serve the industry and academic libraries in institutions with a criminal justice department. It is available in print and online from the association. EBSCOhost and ProQuest's Criminal Justice Periodicals Index provides full-text access from 1994 to the present.

1443. *Crime & Delinquency.* Incorporates (1960-1972): *N C C D News;* Which was formerly (1955-1960): *N P P A News;* Former titles (until 1960): *National Probation and Parole Association Journal;* (until 1955): *National Probation and Parole Association. Yearbook;* (until 1947): *National Probation Association. Year Book;* (until 1929): *National Probation Association. Proceedings;* (until 1928): *National Probation Association. Annual Conference. Annual Report and Proceedings.* [ISSN: 0011-1287] 1955. bi-m. USD 3336 (print & online eds.)). Ed(s): Paul E

Tracy. Sage Publications, Inc., 2455 Teller Rd, Thousand Oaks, CA 91320; info@sagepub.com; http://www.sagepub.com. Illus., index, adv. Sample. Refereed. Vol. ends: Oct. Reprint: PSC. *Indexed:* A01, A22, BRI, CJPI, E01, ERIC, IBSS, L14, N13, SSA. *Aud.:* Ac, Sa.

Crime & Delinquency is one of the most highly respected journals in the study of criminology. The journal dates back to 1955, when it was published by the National Probation and Parole Association (NPPA). Sage began publishing the journal for the organization in 1984, and now works directly with the editor, who is not associated with the former NPPA (presently named the National Council on Crime and Delinquency). *Crime & Delinquency*'s articles are policy-oriented, and span the breadth of all criminal justice issues, including juvenile and adult offenders, victims, police and other law enforcement agencies, and crime prevention. They consist of qualitative or quantitative research, reviews of recent literature, debates of current issues, or discussions of future directions in the field. Contributors are primarily American academics from the disciplines of sociology, criminology, family therapy, social work, and other related subjects. However, some articles are written by international scholars, practitioners from public-policy think tanks, or governmental agencies. The journal has an editorial policy requiring authors to present their conclusions, particularly statistical information, in a manner that is accessible to non-academic practitioners. Its audience is policy makers, academics, and criminal justice researchers in any setting. The quality of the articles and the clarity of the writing also make this an excellent resource for college students studying criminal justice, sociology, social work, counseling, or public administration. The journal is available in print and online from Sage. The online archive includes issues from 1955 to the present.

1444. *Crime, Law and Social Change: an interdisciplinary journal.* Formerly (until 1991): *Contemporary Crises;* Incorporates (1986-1992): *Corruption and Reform.* [ISSN: 0925-4994] 1977. 10x/yr. EUR 1738 (print & online eds.)). Ed(s): Nikos Passas. Springer Netherlands, Van Godewijckstraat 30, Dordrecht, 3311 GX, Netherlands; http://www.springer.com. Illus., adv. Sample. Refereed. Microform: PQC. Reprint: PSC. *Indexed:* A22, BAS, BRI, CJPI, E01, IBSS, P61, SSA. *Bk. rev.:* Number and length vary. *Aud.:* Ac, Sa.

Crime, Law and Social Change is a well-regarded peer-reviewed journal. Its articles focus on the "political economy of organized crime" around the world, including international, national, regional, or local emphasis. These articles are interdisciplinary essays and reviews, and they cover a broader range of topics than might first be expected. According to the publisher, primary topics include financial crime, political corruption, environmental crime, and the expropriation of resources from developing nations. The journal thoroughly covers the topic of human rights through reports on compensation and justice for survivors of mass murder and state-sponsored terrorism, essays on gender, racial, and ethnic equality, and a number of other related articles. Contributors are academics and practitioners from throughout the world. The number of articles per issue varies, from 4 to 12, and book reviews are included often. Many issues have themes and are introduced by guest editors. For example, the April 2019 issue focuses on the politics of hate. Additional recent special issues cover "The Collective Action against Corruption" and "The Role of Law in Curbing Corruption." *Crime, Law and Social Change* is available in print and online from Springer. EBSCOhost and ProQuest offer full-text access, with a one-year embargo. Each volume has five numbered issues, although some issues are combined into one. This journal is recommended for academic libraries, due to the quality of its articles and its appeal to many other social science disciplines.

1445. *Criminal Justice and Behavior: an international journal.* Supersedes (in 1974): *Correctional Psychologist.* [ISSN: 0093-8548] 1973. m. USD 1502 (print & online eds.)). Ed(s): Emily J Salisbury. Sage Publications, Inc., 2455 Teller Rd, Thousand Oaks, CA 91320; info@sagepub.com; http://www.sagepub.com. Illus., index, adv. Sample. Refereed. Vol. ends: Dec. Microform: WSH; PMC; PQC. Reprint: PSC. *Indexed:* A22, ASSIA, BRI, CBRI, CJPI, E01, L14, N13, SSA. *Bk. rev.:* Number and length vary. *Aud.:* Ac, Sa.

Criminal Justice and Behavior: An International Journal is published monthly by Sage for the International Association for Correctional and Forensic Psychology. The journal "promotes scholarly evaluations of assessment, classification, prevention, intervention, and treatment programs to help the correctional professional develop successful programs based on sound and informative theoretical and research foundations." The journal began publishing monthly in 2007, and changed its editorial policy to include literature reviews, commentary, and other submissions, in addition to the empirical research that had been and remains its primary focus. It occasionally contains book reviews. Academics author the majority of articles for this journal, but behavioral scientists from medical institutions and public organizations contribute as well. Ranked as a first-tier journal (for rationale for this assessment, see section introduction for information on selection/ranking criteria), *CJB* is a good choice for academic libraries and special libraries that serve criminal justice professionals. Available in print and online. The online archive goes back to volume one in 1974.

1446. *Criminal Justice Ethics.* [ISSN: 0731-129X] 1982. 3x/yr. GBP 211 (print & online eds.)). Ed(s): Margaret Leland Smith, Jonathan Jacobs. Routledge, 530 Walnut St, Ste 850, Philadelphia, PA 19106; enquiries@tandfonline.com; http://www.tandfonline.com. Illus. Sample. Refereed. Vol. ends: Summer/Fall. Microform: PQC. Reprint: PSC. *Indexed:* A01, A22, BRI, CJPI, L14. *Bk. rev.:* 1-2, review essays. *Aud.:* Ac, Sa.

Criminal Justice Ethics is published by Taylor & Francis in association with the Institute for Criminal Justice Ethics at John Jay College of Criminal Justice, the City University of New York. The articles are largely philosophical; in fact, many are authored by professors of philosophy or law. They stand in contrast to quantitative and empirical articles that populate many of the other scholarly journals in this section. The journal "addresses ethical issues arising in all of the contexts of criminal justice, exploring their conceptual, normative, and empirical aspects and the relations between them." In 2010, the publication frequency changed from twice to three times a year. Recent issues cover topics such as algorithmic sentencing, responsibilities of using lethal force, and preventive detention for terrorists. This journal's coverage of ethical matters is excellent, and it is essential for law schools and highly recommended for other academic libraries. However, the content is more appropriate for faculty, graduate, and upper undergraduates than for freshmen.

1447. *Criminal Justice Policy Review.* [ISSN: 0887-4034] 1986. 9x/yr. USD 2312 (print & online eds.)). Ed(s): David L Myers. Sage Publications, Inc., 2455 Teller Rd, Thousand Oaks, CA 91320; info@sagepub.com; http://www.sagepub.com. Adv. Refereed. Reprint: PSC. *Indexed:* A01, A22, CJPI, E01, N13, P61, SSA. *Bk. rev.:* Number and length vary. *Aud.:* Ac, Sa.

Criminal Justice Policy Review (*CJPR*) was first published in 1986 by the Indiana University of Pennsylvania's criminology department. It is now published nine times per year by Sage, but the current editor remains associated with that university. The editorial introduction to the first issue stated: "Because criminal justice policy is studied by scholars, debated by politicians, enacted into law by legislators, executed by scores of functionaries, and is the focus of diverse commentary from a broad range of interests[,] the CJPR wishes to be the medium through which all of these perspectives can be presented." The articles reflect this broad mission, and include essays, research (quantitative and qualitative), commentary, and interviews. Contributors are primarily academics; however, professionals are also encouraged to submit. There are frequent special issues with guest editorials; recent ones cover the topics of hate crimes and police accountability. This journal is highly recommended for academic and special libraries. It is available in print and online.

1448. *Criminal Justice Review.* [ISSN: 0734-0168] 1976. q. USD 582 (print & online eds.)). Ed(s): William Alex Pridemore. Sage Publications, Inc., 2455 Teller Rd, Thousand Oaks, CA 91320; info@sagepub.com; http://www.sagepub.com. Adv. Sample. Refereed. Microform: PQC. Reprint: PSC; WSH. *Indexed:* A22, BRI, CJPI, E01, N13, P61, SSA. *Bk. rev.:* 1-2 review essays, 15-20, 700-1,000 word, signed reviews. *Aud.:* Ac, Sa.

Criminal Justice Review is published by Sage in association with Georgia State University. It is a quarterly, peer-reviewed publication that is "dedicated to presenting a broad perspective on criminal justice issues within the domestic United States." The journal publishes quantitative and qualitative research, research notes, and commentary, and encourages contributors to take an interdisciplinary approach. Each issue contains five to seven articles and a large book review section, frequently containing ten or more reviews. There are occasional special issues—the most recent presents research on "Crime and Control in the Digital Era." This journal would be a good choice for academic libraries with criminal justice departments, and may also be of interest to faculty and students in political science. It is available in print and online. The online archive goes back to the first issue in 1976.

1449. *Criminal Justice Studies: a critical journal of crime, law and society.* Formerly (until 2003): *The Justice Professional.* [ISSN: 1478-601X] 1986. q. GBP 411 (print & online eds.)). Ed(s): Richard Tewksbury. Routledge, 530 Walnut St, Ste 850, Philadelphia, PA 19106; enquiries@tandfonline.com; http://www.tandfonline.com. Sample. Refereed. Reprint: PSC. *Indexed:* A22, B01, CJPI, E01, IBSS, P61, SSA. *Aud.:* Ac, Sa.

Criminal Justice Studies: A Critical Journal of Crime, Law and Society is a quarterly, multi-disciplinary journal that publishes articles that address issues in criminal justice, public policy, administration, and public affairs. The articles may be quantitative or qualitative studies, research notes, literature reviews, or summary reports. Recent examples include "Police Use of Force: an Examination of the Minority Threat Perspective" and "Social Psychological Risk Factors, Delinquency and Age of Onset." Special issues are published periodically, addressing topics like cybercrime and desistance from sexual offending. The journal is available online from Taylor & Francis, starting with volume 7, issue 2, when it was published under its original title *The Justice Professional.* This journal would be useful to faculty and students in criminal justice and political science programs.

1450. *Criminology: an interdisciplinary journal.* Formerly (until 1970): *Criminologica.* [ISSN: 0011-1384] 1963. q. USD 405 (print & online eds.)). Ed(s): Bianca Bersani, Denise Gottfredson. Wiley-Blackwell Publishing, Inc., 111 River St, Hoboken, NJ 07030; info@wiley.com; http://onlinelibrary.wiley.com. Illus., index, adv. Sample. Refereed. Circ: 3569 Paid. Vol. ends: Nov. Microform: PQC. Reprint: PSC; WSH. *Indexed:* A01, A22, BRI, CJPI, E01, IBSS, N13, SSA. *Aud.:* Ac, Sa.

Criminology is a quarterly publication of the American Society of Criminology (ASC). It is consistently ranked as a first-tier criminology journal (see section introduction for information on selection/ranking criteria). The content is interdisciplinary, with articles from sociology, psychology, and other social sciences that is "devoted to crime and deviant behavior." Most of the articles are empirical studies, but theoretical discussions and literature reviews are also included. Most articles are authored by American academics and relate to U.S. crime and policies; however, this isn't always the case, as the society has international members and welcomes articles that cover international issues. An example is a recent article titled "Roads Diverged: An Examination of Violent and Nonviolent Pathways in the Aftermath of the Bosnian War." Other topics discussed in recent publications include homicide and suicide connections, criminal group dynamics, and prison sentence increases. This journal is essential for academic libraries, and is useful for criminal justice, sociology, social work, and psychology programs. It is available online and in print from Wiley (formerly Blackwell). The online archive goes back to the first issue in 1963. The ASC also publishes *Criminology and Public Policy,* which is reviewed in this section.

1451. *Criminology & Criminal Justice: an international journal.* Formerly (until 2006): *Criminal Justice.* [ISSN: 1748-8958] 2001. 5x/yr. USD 1315 (print & online eds.)). Ed(s): Adam Crawford. Sage Publications Ltd., 1 Oliver's Yard, 55 City Rd, London, EC1Y 1SP, United Kingdom; info@sagepub.com; https://www.sagepub.com/. Adv. Sample. Refereed. Reprint: PSC. *Indexed:* A01, A22, ASSIA, CJPI, E01, IBSS, P61, SSA. *Bk. rev.:* 2-4, signed. *Aud.:* Ac.

Criminology & Criminal Justice (*CCJ*) is the official journal of the British Society of Criminology. Launched in 2001 under the title *Criminal Justice, CCJ* is peer reviewed and produced five times per year. Although it is published under the auspices of a British society and the majority of authors are from U.K. universities, the journal also encourages submission of articles written by authors from other countries. Recent issues included contributions from the United States, Norway, Czech Republic, and Japan. The articles can be theoretical or empirical, and discuss policy and practice from all areas of the study of criminal justice, including policing, prisons, drug use, crime prevention, and more. Most issues contain several book reviews. Special issues are published occasionally, with the most recent addressing coercive control in domestic abuse. The journal is published by Sage, and is available online and in print. The online archives begin with volume one. This journal is recommended for academic libraries with a criminal justice department.

1452. *Criminology and Public Policy.* [ISSN: 1538-6473] 2001. q. Ed(s): L Sergio Garduno, William D Bales. Wiley-Blackwell Publishing, Inc., 111 River St, Hoboken, NJ 07030; http://onlinelibrary.wiley.com. Adv. Sample. Refereed. Reprint: PSC; WSH. *Indexed:* A01, A22, CJPI, E01, N13. *Aud.:* Ac, Sa.

Criminology and Public Policy was first published in 2001 by the American Society of Criminology (ASC) as a forum to present policy-related research findings in a meaningful way to policy makers. The society also publishes *Criminology* (see above in this section), which contains empirical research articles aimed at criminal justice researchers rather than at policy makers. Each issue of *Criminology and Public Policy* addresses several current policy issues, such as sentencing reform, juvenile delinquency, electronic monitoring, and terrorism. An editorial introduces each topic, followed by a research article, which is written in a slightly different format than is the case in most academic peer-reviewed journals, due to its intended audience. Two or three related policy essays follow. Like its sister publication, this journal is a good choice for academic libraries and special libraries that serve those who study criminal justice policy issues. This journal would also be an excellent choice for undergraduates. The articles are scholarly but more accessible than those of other scholarly research journals. Available online and in print from Wiley (formerly Blackwell).

1453. *Criminology, Criminal Justice, Law & Society.* Formerly (until 2014): *Western Criminology Review.* [ISSN: 2332-886X] 1998. 3x/yr. Free. Ed(s): Stuart Henry, Christine Curtis. Western Society of Criminology, 1305 Corona Pointe Court, Corona, CA 92879; Secretary-Treasurer@WesternCriminology.org; http://westerncriminology.org//. Refereed. *Indexed:* CJPI. *Aud.:* Ac; Sa.

Criminology, Criminal Justice, Law & Society is a peer-reviewed publication that promotes "understanding of the causes of crime; the methods used to prevent and control crime; the institutions, principles, and actors involved in the apprehension, prosecution, punishment, and reintegration of offenders; and the legal and political framework under which the justice system and its primary actors operate." Recent issues explore topics such as the evolution of occupational stressors for law enforcement officers, the impact of social intervention on improved self-control as a criminogenic need, and exploration of presidential rhetoric and use of crime control theater. This publication is open access and would be appropriate for academic institutions with criminology, criminal justice, or criminal law programs.

1454. *Critical Criminology: international journal.* Formerly (until 1996): *Journal of Human Justice.* [ISSN: 1205-8629] 1989. 4x/yr. EUR 799 (print & online eds.)). Ed(s): David Kauzlarich. Springer Netherlands, Van Godewijckstraat 30, Dordrecht, 3311 GX, Netherlands; http://www.springer.com. Adv. Refereed. Reprint: PSC. *Indexed:* A22, BRI, C37, CJPI, E01. *Bk. rev.:* 1-2, 1,500-2,500 words, signed. *Aud.:* Ac, Sa.

Critical Criminology is the official journal of two related professional bodies: the Division of Critical Criminology of the American Society of Criminology, and the Academy of Criminal Justice Sciences Section on Critical Criminology. The journal publishes articles that focus on "issues of social harm and social justice" that are written from alternative criminological perspectives, such as feminist, Marxist, and postmodernist. *Critical Criminology* is published quarterly, and each issue contains five to ten articles and scholarly, in-depth book and film reviews. There are occasional special issues with introductions by guest editors. The March 2019 issue was entitled "Crucial Critical Criminologies—Revisited and Extended." This journal provides interesting and provocative articles that would be of interest to faculty and students studying criminology, political science, and sociology, especially if they were interested in exploring alternative methodologies. It is favorably rated by the journal-ranking sources consulted for this review (see section introduction for information on selection/ranking criteria). This publication is available in print and electronically from Springer.

1455. *European Journal of Criminology.* [ISSN: 1477-3708] 2004. bi-m. USD 1614 (print & online eds.)). Ed(s): Lisa Burns, Paul Knepper. Sage Publications Ltd., 1 Oliver's Yard, 55 City Rd, London, EC1Y 1SP, United Kingdom; info@sagepub.com; https://www.sagepub.com/. Adv. Sample. Refereed. Reprint: PSC. *Indexed:* A22, ASSIA, CJPI, E01, IBSS. *Aud.:* Ac, Sa.

European Journal of Criminology is offered by Sage in association with the European Society of Criminology. The society was formed in 2000 and the journal's first issue appeared in 2004 to address issues that were particularly relevant to that continent and its various member countries. The articles present scholarly research, including theoretical, quantitative, qualitative, or comparative studies. They contain evaluations of various criminological interventions, institutions, or political processes. Each issue has four to eight articles, and is sometimes thematic. The latest special-themed issue addresses European jihadists. The journal frequently includes a country survey that summarizes the featured country's criminal justice system, trends in crime and punishment, and major publications. This journal is recommended for academic libraries with programs concerned with European criminology, including political science, sociology, European Studies, and criminal justice. Available in print and online.

1456. *Federal Probation (Online): a journal of correctional philosophy and practice.* [ISSN: 1555-0303] 2004. 3x/yr. Free. Administrative Office of the United States Courts, Federal Corrections and Supervision Division, 1 Columbus Cir, NE, Washington, DC 20544; http://www.uscourts.gov. *Indexed:* N13. *Bk. rev.:* June and Dec. issues. *Aud.:* Ga, Ac, Sa.

Federal Probation is published three times a year by the Administrative Office of the United States Courts. It first appeared in 1937, and continued to be published in print until 2004. This publication is also freely available online, as are many U.S. federal documents. The contributors are scholars, practitioners, lawyers, and policy researchers. The articles are essays, policy analyses, and research studies. They are written using scholarly language, but are not laden with legal jargon beyond the comprehension of students. When appropriate, references are provided. Each September issue focuses on a special topic; the latest issue discusses topics related to "Pretrial Services: Front-End Justice" in the federal probation system. June and December issues contain a column that focuses on juvenile justice; and there is an annual index in December. This journal is an excellent resource for students, scholars, and practitioners, especially those who work with the courts.

1457. *Feminist Criminology.* [ISSN: 1557-0851] 2006. q. USD 926 (print & online eds.)). Ed(s): Rosemary Barberet. Sage Publications, Inc., 2455 Teller Rd, Thousand Oaks, CA 91320; info@sagepub.com; http://www.sagepub.com. Adv. Sample. Refereed. Reprint: PSC. *Indexed:* A22, ASSIA, CJPI, E01, FemPer. *Aud.:* Ac, Sa.

Feminist Criminology is a relatively new journal that presents criminological research from a feminist perspective. It is the official journal of the Division on Women and Crime of the American Society of Criminology, and was launched in 2006. The following excerpt from the introductory editorial of that inaugural issue explains the journal's scope and editorial intent: "The main aim of this journal is to focus on research related to women, girls, and crime. The scope includes research on women working in the criminal justice profession, women as offenders and how they are dealt with in the criminal justice system, women as victims, and theories and tests of theories related to women and crime. This journal will highlight research that takes a perspective designed to demonstrate the gendered nature of crime and responses to crime. The main focus of the journal will be empirical research and theory, although the editor welcomes practice-oriented manuscript." It is available in print and online from Sage at http://fcx.sagepub.com. Readers interested in this title should also consider *Women & Criminal Justice,* also reviewed in this section.

1458. *Homicide Studies: an interdisciplinary & international journal.* [ISSN: 1088-7679] 1997. q. USD 1229 (print & online eds.)). Ed(s): Lynn A Addington. Sage Publications, Inc., 2455 Teller Rd, Thousand Oaks, CA 91320; info@sagepub.com; http://www.sagepub.com. Illus., adv. Sample. Refereed. Reprint: PSC. *Indexed:* A01, A22, CJPI, E01, N13. *Bk. rev.:* Occasional, 800-1,000 words, signed. *Aud.:* Ac, Sa.

Homicide Studies: An Interdisciplinary & International Journal is a quarterly publication of the Homicide Research Working Group, which was organized in 1991 at the American Society of Criminology meeting. The group saw its mission as interdisciplinary and international—much broader than just American criminology. Its goal, and the focus of the journal, is to present "the latest thinking and discussion in homicide studies aiding more effective public policies to help reduce and possibly prevent future homicides." The first issue of *Homicide Studies* appeared in 1997. Each issue contains four to seven articles; some include commentaries, responses to research articles, and book reviews. Examples of topics covered in recent articles are police homicide rates, the rise of homicides from 2014 to 2016, and factors that influence solved cases. Authors are academics, professionals, and policy experts from the fields of criminology, sociology, public health, anthropology, social work, and more. A good choice for academic and special libraries concerned with homicide crimes and policy. Available in print and online. URL: http://hsx.sagepub.com

1459. *The Howard Journal of Criminal Justice.* Former titles (until Feb.1984): *Howard Journal of Penology and Crime Prevention;* (until 1965): *Howard Journal.* [ISSN: 2059-1098] 1921. 5x/yr. GBP 767. Ed(s): Anita Dockley, Penny Green. Wiley-Blackwell Publishing Ltd., The Atrium, Southern Gate, Chichester, PO19 8QG, United Kingdom; cs-journals@wiley.com; http://onlinelibrary.wiley.com. Illus., adv. Sample. Refereed. Vol. ends: Nov. Microform: PQC. Reprint: PSC. *Indexed:* A01, A22, CJPI, E01, N13. *Bk. rev.:* 2-3, 700-1,200 words. *Aud.:* Ac, Sa.

The Howard Journal of Crime and Justice is an international, peer-reviewed journal published by Wiley for the Howard League for Penal Reform, a U.K.-based charity founded in 1866. The journal is published four times a year, and each issue contains five to seven articles relating to both theory and practice. These articles address "all aspects of the relationship between crime and justice across the globe." As with other journals reviewed in this section, the editors seek to inform practitioners as well as academics, so the writing is clear and accessible. Contributors are primarily U.K. academics, but the journal welcomes submissions written by practitioners, and occasionally scholars in the United States, Canada, or other countries are represented. The most articles are research based, but commentary, essays, and book reviews are also included in each volume. Special issues are published periodically, with the latest title being "Interpreting Penal Policymaking." *The Howard Journal of Crime and Justice* is available in print and online from Wiley. The online archive goes back to 1921. Although this journal is U.K.-based, the policies and issues discussed are applicable to U.S. criminal justice practitioners, faculty, and students.

1460. *International Criminal Justice Review.* [ISSN: 1057-5677] 1991. q. USD 494 (print & online eds.)). Ed(s): William Alex Pridemore. Sage Publications, Inc., 2455 Teller Rd, Thousand Oaks, CA 91320; info@sagepub.com; http://www.sagepub.com. Adv. Sample. Refereed. Reprint: PSC; WSH. *Indexed:* A22, CJPI, E01, IBSS, N13, SSA. *Bk. rev.:* 7-10, 800-1,300 words, signed. *Aud.:* Ac, Sa.

The *International Criminal Justice Review* (*ICJR*) is a publication of Georgia State University's Department of Criminal Justice, which also publishes *Criminal Justice Review* (reviewed in this section). Sage is the publisher of both journals since 2005. The journal's articles focus on one particular country, or compare two or more countries. They may use quantitative or qualitative methodologies, and commentary is also welcome. The main criteria are that they present "strong interest in cross-national criminology." Each quarterly issue contains three to eight articles and numerous book reviews. Recent articles address corruption among prospective elites in Ghana and lethal violence, childhood, and gender in Mexico City. The authors are academics from throughout the world; however, most are affiliated with U.S. universities. *ICJR* is available in print and online from Sage, back to the inaugural issue in 1991. URL: http://http://journals.sagepub.com/home/icj

1461. *International Journal of Offender Therapy and Comparative Criminology.* Former titles (until 1972): *International Journal of Offender Therapy;* (until 1966): *Journal of Offender Therapy;* (until 1961): *Association for Psychiatric Treatment of Offenders. Journal.* [ISSN: 0306-624X] 1957. 14x/yr. USD 1996 (print & online eds.)). Ed(s): Mark T Palermo. Sage Publications, Inc., 2455 Teller Rd,

Thousand Oaks, CA 91320; info@sagepub.com; http://www.sagepub.com. Illus., index, adv. Sample. Refereed. Vol. ends: Winter. Microform: PQC. Reprint: PSC. *Indexed:* A01, A22, ASSIA, BRI, CJPI, E01, L14, N13, P61, SSA. *Bk. rev.:* Occasional, 300-1,000 words, signed. *Aud.:* Ac, Sa.

International Journal of Offender Therapy and Comparative Criminology publishes articles that focus on research and theory as they inform treatment practices for criminal offenders. The journal addresses three primary aspects of offender therapy: psychological, due to the preponderance of offenders with serious psychological disorders; genetic/biological, to help inform those treating offenders to recognize and deal with these factors; and environmental, which looks at the influences of offenders' life histories on their behavior. Examples of recent article topics include adolescent delinquency and its connection to general strain theory of crime; effects of culture on death penalty views in Mexico and the United States; and risk taking in China's commercial sex industry. Contributors to this journal come from a variety of disciplines, and include psychologists, social workers, counselors, health scientists, legal studies scholars, sociologists, and medical professionals, as well as corrections and criminal justice researchers and policy makers. In keeping with the editorial intent to present articles from international scholars, research from other countries is included. Sage publishes this journal, which is available in print and online. The online archive is complete, beginning with volume one in 1966. URL: http://journals.sagepub.com/home/ijo

1462. *Journal of Contemporary Criminal Justice.* [ISSN: 1043-9862] 1978. q. USD 1000 (print & online eds.)). Ed(s): Chris Eskridge. Sage Publications, Inc., 2455 Teller Rd, Thousand Oaks, CA 91320; info@sagepub.com; http://www.sagepub.com. Illus., adv. Sample. Refereed. Vol. ends: Nov. Reprint: PSC. *Indexed:* A01, A22, B01, CJPI, E01, IBSS, N13. *Aud.:* Ac, Sa.

Journal of Contemporary Criminal Justice is a quarterly journal that examines current criminal justice issues in depth to inform academics, professionals, and policy makers. It is interdisciplinary, with contributors from most social science fields, including anthropology, criminology, economics, history, legal studies, political science, psychology, public administration and policy, sociology, and social work. Each issue addresses a single topic, and most have a guest editor who is an expert on that topic. For example, the May 2019 issue is subtitled "Health and Crime at Crime Hot Spots." Guest editors for each issue write a detailed introductory essay that presents an overview of the topic at hand and the research that follows. The journal's unique theme-based coverage makes this title a good choice for academic and special libraries. URL: http://ccj.sagepub.com

1463. *Journal of Correctional Education.* Former titles (until 1974): *Correctional Education;* (until 1973): *Journal of Correctional Education.* [ISSN: 0740-2708] 1949. q. Free to members. Ed(s): John J Dowdell, Russell L Craig. Ashland University, 401 College Ave, Ashland, OH 44805; http://www.ashland.edu/. Illus., index, adv. Sample. Refereed. Vol. ends: Dec. Microform: PQC. *Indexed:* A01, A22, CJPI, ERIC, N13. *Aud.:* Ac, Sa.

The *Journal of Correctional Education* is published by Ashland University for the Correctional Education Association, whose members serve as educators for juveniles and adults in criminal justice settings. The journal contains research articles, discussions, and guidelines on best practices, and reports that cover current issues and legislative updates. Examples of current article topics are self-monitoring interventions in juvenile justice facilities and self-care strategies for staff stress and burnout. The articles are well written, and even the research articles are composed in language that is accessible to the layperson. Full-text articles are available through ProQuest's Criminal Justice Periodicals database and EBSCOhost. This journal is appropriate for correctional educators and other practitioners such as social workers, as well as those in academia studying criminal justice or related social science disciplines. URL: https://www.ashland.edu/founders/programs/correctional-education/journal-correctional-education

1464. *Journal of Criminal Justice.* [ISSN: 0047-2352] 1973. 6x/yr. EUR 2271. Ed(s): Matthew DeLisi. Pergamon Press, The Blvd, Langford Ln, E Park, Kidlington, OX5 1GB, United Kingdom; JournalsCustomerServiceEMEA@elsevier.com; http://www.elsevier.com. Illus., adv. Sample. Refereed. Microform: PQC. *Indexed:* A01, A22, ASSIA, BRI, CJPI, Chicano, L14, N13, SSA. *Aud.:* Ac, Sa.

Journal of Criminal Justice: An International Journal is published six times a year by Elsevier. Its scope is broad in that it covers all aspects and elements of criminology, but its editorial intent is to publish creative and innovative thought and research in the discipline. Two special issues are released each year, with the most recent issues discussing mental health and crime and a study of race and ethnicity in criminology. Examples of topics addressed in recent articles include sex buying behavior of U.S. adult males; vaping and adolescent delinquency; and accuracy in self-reported arrests. The majority of articles represent U.S.-based research, but many issues contain at least one article that analyzes international criminal justice concerns. The quality of the research and writing in this journal is excellent, and it belongs in academic libraries with criminal justice programs, and in special libraries interested in criminological research. More information is available at the website. URL: https://www.journals.elsevier.com/journal-of-criminal-justice

1465. *Journal of Criminal Justice Education.* [ISSN: 1051-1253] 1990. q. GBP 594 (print & online eds.)). Ed(s): George Higgins. Routledge, 4 Park Sq, Milton Park, Abingdon, OX14 4RN, United Kingdom; subscriptions@tandf.co.uk; http://www.tandfonline.com. Illus., index, adv. Sample. Refereed. Vol. ends: Fall. Reprint: PSC; WSH. *Indexed:* A01, A22, CJPI, E01, N13. *Bk. rev.:* Number and length vary. *Aud.:* Ac, Sa.

The *Journal of Criminal Justice Education* (*JCJE*) is published by Routledge for the Academy of Criminal Justice Sciences (ACJS) to serve as a "forum for the examination, discussion and debate of a broad range of issues concerning post-secondary education in criminal justice, criminology, and related areas." Articles include reviews of various pedagogical approaches, such as concept mapping to teach criminological theory; or using classical literature to encourage students' independent thinking skills. There was also an analysis of different active-learning exercises, such as film analysis and jail tours. In addition to pedagogy, some articles address criminal justice departments' administrative concerns, such as a review of the characteristic of criminal justice scholars who are successful at obtaining research grants, and bibliometric and citation analysis of criminal justice journals. Special issues are produced occasionally; the most recent special-issue theme was "How to Find Success as a Criminal Justice Faculty Member." *JCJE* also contains book reviews and book review essays. In 2010, the journal became a quarterly publication; it had been published three times a year. More information is available at the web site. URL: http://www.tandfonline.com/toc/rcje20/current

1466. *Journal of Experimental Criminology.* [ISSN: 1573-3750] 2005. q. EUR 779 (print & online eds.)). Ed(s): Lorraine Mazerolle, Adele Somerville. Springer New York LLC, 233 Spring St, New York, NY 10013; journals@springer-ny.com; http://link.springer.com. Refereed. Reprint: PSC. *Indexed:* A22, CJPI, E01, N13. *Aud.:* Ac.

Journal of Experimental Criminology was launched in 2005 to publish experimental and quasi-experimental research, systematic reviews, and other evidence-based methodologies in the disciplines of criminology and criminal justice. The journal is international in scope, with an editorial board from institutions that span the globe. However, the majority of article authors are individuals based in the United States. They include academics, practitioners from public-policy institutes, and individuals from think tanks. The articles include presentations of empirical research, articles that discuss research methodologies as they pertain to the discipline, and discussions of criminal justice problems and concerns. There are occasional special issues; for example, June 2018 was devoted to experimental tests of interventions to reduce violence, injury, and harm. This journal is best suited for academic institutions with criminal justice programs.

1467. *The Journal of Forensic Psychiatry & Psychology.* Formerly (until 2003): *Journal of Forensic Psychiatry (Print).* [ISSN: 1478-9949] 1990. bi-m. GBP 1032 (print & online eds.)). Ed(s): Jenny Shaw. Routledge, 4 Park Sq, Milton Park, Abingdon, OX14 4RN, United Kingdom; subscriptions@tandf.co.uk; http://www.tandfonline.com. Adv. Sample. Refereed. Reprint: PSC. *Indexed:* A01, A22, ASSIA, CJPI, E01, IBSS. *Aud.:* Ac, Sa.

The Journal of Forensic Psychiatry & Psychology was first published in 1990 as the *Journal of Forensic Psychiatry.* As the journal became multidisciplinary, its aim has been to publish "papers relating to aspects of psychiatry and psychological knowledge (research, theory and practice) as applied to offenders and to legal issues arising within civil, criminal, correctional or legislative contexts." A variety of topics are explored in recent issues of this peer-reviewed publication, including weekend and holiday homicides, mental health of mothers in prison, and self-harm among patients. With an international scope, this publication is valuable to a number of legal, health, and academic institutions. This publication is available in print and online via Taylor & Francis Online, EBSCOhost, and other full-text databases.

1468. *Journal of International Criminal Justice.* [ISSN: 1478-1387] 2003. 5x/yr. EUR 899. Ed(s): Salvatore Zappala. Oxford University Press, Great Clarendon St, Oxford, OX2 6DP, United Kingdom; onlinequeries.uk@oup.com; http://global.oup.com. Adv. Sample. Refereed. Reprint: PSC. *Indexed:* A22, BRI, CJPI, E01, L14. *Aud.:* Ac, Sa.

The *Journal of International Criminal Justice* was first published in 2003 by the Oxford University Press. The journal's mission is to address "the major problems of justice from the angle of law, jurisprudence, criminology, penal philosophy, and the history of international judicial institutions." New issues are published five times per year, and the journal provides a valuable forum for discussion of international law issues and trends. Special issues are published periodically. *Journal of International Criminal Justice* is available in print and online via EBSCOhost, LexisNexis, Oxford University Press, and other full-text sources.

1469. *Journal of Interpersonal Violence: concerned with the study and treatment of victims and perpetrators of physical and sexual violence.* [ISSN: 0886-2605] 1986. 24x/yr. USD 3079 (print & online eds.)). Ed(s): Jon R Conte. Sage Publications, Inc., 2455 Teller Rd, Thousand Oaks, CA 91320; info@sagepub.com; http://www.sagepub.com. Illus., index, adv. Sample. Refereed. Vol. ends: Dec. Reprint: PSC. *Indexed:* A01, A22, BRI, CJPI, E01, ERIC, N13, SSA. *Bk. rev.:* 1, 700-1,000 words, signed. *Aud.:* Ac, Sa.

Journal of Interpersonal Violence's subtitle states the journal is "concerned with the study and treatment of victims and perpetrators of physical and sexual violence," and this succinctly explains the unique editorial focus of this journal, on both the victims and offenders in interpersonal violence. Contributors are academics and practitioners from a variety of disciplines, including sociology, social work, public health and health administration, pediatrics, clinical psychology, and criminal justice. They are primarily associated with U.S. universities and policy centers; however, submissions from international researchers are frequently included. The articles "address the causes, effects, treatments, and prevention of all types of violence." Recent examples of research in this journal include studies of contempt and anger in intimate partner violence as well as narcissism's role in cyberbullying. In addition to research articles, the journal publishes regular features that include commentary, practice notes, discussions of methodology, and book reviews. The *Journal of Interpersonal Violence* is published by Sage and available in print and online. The online archive goes back to the first issue in 1986. This journal is useful for faculty, students, and practitioners, and is recommended for most academic libraries. URL: http://intl-jiv.sagepub.com

1470. *Journal of Offender Rehabilitation: a multidisciplinary journal of innovation in research, services, and programs in corrections and criminal justice.* Former titles (until 1990): *Journal of Offender Counseling, Services and Rehabilitation;* (until 1980): *Offender Rehabilitation.* [ISSN: 1050-9674] 1976. 8x/yr. GBP 1620 (print & online eds.)). Ed(s): Creasie Finney Hairston. Routledge, 530 Walnut St, Ste 850, Philadelphia, PA 19106; enquiries@tandfonline.com; http://www.tandfonline.com. Illus., adv. Sample. Refereed. Circ: 328 Paid. Vol. ends: Spring/Summer. Microform: PQC. Reprint: PSC. *Indexed:* A01, A22, CJPI, E01, ERIC, N13, SSA. *Aud.:* Ac, Sa.

Journal of Offender Rehabilitation is an interdisciplinary journal that publishes qualitative, quantitative, and theoretical articles covering research, services, and programs related to the treatment of offenders. Recent article topics include "female employment struggles postincarceration; rescue dog programs in maximum-security prisons; literacy and education evaluation of incarcerated individuals; examination of veterans treatment courts (VTCs); risk assessment of criminal offenders," and more. Contributors come from the fields of criminal justice, psychology, psychosocial and community health, social work, and related fields, and include academics and practitioners. This journal is recommended for practitioners, faculty, and students in the fields of social work, counseling, and therapy. It is published eight times a year by Routledge. Readers interested in this journal should also review the *International Journal of Offender Therapy* (reviewed in this section) and *Comparative Criminology.* URL: www.tandf.co.uk/journals/WJOR

1471. *Journal of Quantitative Criminology.* [ISSN: 0748-4518] 1985. q. EUR 1420 (print & online eds.)). Ed(s): David Weisburd, Badi Hasisi. Springer New York LLC, 233 Spring St, New York, NY 10013; customerservice@springer.com; http://www.springer.com. Illus., index, adv. Refereed. Vol. ends: Dec. Microform: PQC. Reprint: PSC. *Indexed:* A01, A22, ASSIA, CJPI, E01, N13, SSA. *Aud.:* Ac, Sa.

The *Journal of Quantitative Criminology* (*JQC*) is a quarterly journal that presents studies using quantitative research methodologies to investigate criminological concerns. Most articles are original research, but the journal also accepts critiques of quantitative methodologies and discussions of advances in the field of criminological research. The coverage is interdisciplinary, arising from the fields of sociology, statistics, political science, geography, economics, and engineering. Contributors are primarily U.S. academic criminologists; however, some are professors in related disciplines, or practitioners and researchers at public policy institutions. The first issue of *JQC* appeared in 1985, before the rise in popularity of quantitative research. Many of the scholarly journals reviewed in this section publish quantitative research, but this journal was the first to focus on it. It is ranked as first-tier journal (see section introduction for information on selection/ranking criteria), which speaks to quality of the articles. *JQC* is highly recommended to faculty, graduate students, and professionals interested in criminological research. The articles are a bit heavy for most undergraduates unless the students are statistically inclined. Available in print and online from Springer.

1472. *Journal of Research in Crime and Delinquency.* [ISSN: 0022-4278] 1964. q. USD 1380 (print & online eds.)). Ed(s): Michael Maxfield. Sage Publications, Inc., 2455 Teller Rd, Thousand Oaks, CA 91320; info@sagepub.com; http://www.sagepub.com. Illus., index, adv. Sample. Refereed. Vol. ends: Nov. Microform: WSH; PMC. Reprint: PSC. *Indexed:* A01, A22, BRI, CJPI, E01, ERIC, IBSS, N13, SSA. *Aud.:* Ac, Sa.

Journal of Research in Crime and Delinquency is published by Sage in cooperation with the Rutgers School of Criminal Justice. From its inaugural issue in 1964 until volume 45 in 2008, the journal was sponsored by the National Council on Crime and Delinquency (NCCD). This U.S. nonprofit was founded in 1907 to promote research to support humane solutions to family, community, and justice problems. Rutgers faculty members have been involved in the editorial process since the 1990s, and state that the scope and mission remain as they were under the NCCD watch. The journal publishes original research, research notes, and essays. It is ranked among the top criminal justice journals (see section introduction for information on selection/ranking criteria). Each issue contains three to five articles, and presents the results of original quantitative or qualitative research into delinquency. In February 2011, the journal resumed publishing special issues after a several-year hiatus. The theme for the latest issue was "Crime Caught on Camera." Examples of topics covered in other recent issues include family support during prison reentry; evaluation of juvenile drug treatment courts; crime comparison across neighborhoods; virtual reality in criminal decision-making research and vacant housing's role in criminal activity. This journal would be helpful to anyone interested in current research on delinquency, including criminologists, social workers, and psychologists. Available online and in print from Sage. URL: http://journals.sagepub.com/home/jrc

1473. *Justice Quarterly.* [ISSN: 0741-8825] 1984. bi-m. GBP 863 (print & online eds.)). Ed(s): Lisa M Dario, Cassia C Spohn. Routledge, 4 Park Sq, Milton Park, Abingdon, OX14 4RN, United Kingdom; subscriptions@tandf.co.uk; http://www.tandfonline.com. Illus., adv. Sample. Refereed. Reprint: PSC; WSH. *Indexed:* A01, A22, CJPI, E01, N13, SSA. *Bk. rev.:* 2, 1,000-2,000 words, signed. *Aud.:* Ac, Sa.

Justice Quarterly is the official publication of the Academy of Criminal Justice Sciences, which also publishes the *Journal of Criminal Justice Education* (reviewed above in this section). *Justice Quarterly* is highly regarded by criminal justice scholars and is ranked among the top criminal justice journals in surveys (see section introduction for information on selection/ranking criteria). The articles are multidisciplinary and employ a variety of quantitative, qualitative, and other empirical research methodologies. For example, in recent issues, scholars examine the effects of race on homeless youths' interaction with police. This journal is appropriate for academic libraries, being useful for social science students and faculty researchers. It is published by Routledge and available electronically and in print.

1474. ***Law and Order Magazine: the magazine for police management.*** [ISSN: 0023-9194] 1953. m. Free to qualified personnel. Ed(s): Yesenia Salcedo, Jennifer Gavigan. Hendon Media Group, 130 N Waukegan Rd, Ste 202, Deerfield, IL 60015; info@hendonpub.com; http://www.hendonpub.com. Illus., index, adv. Sample. Circ: 37000. Vol. ends: Dec. Microform: PQC. *Indexed:* A22, CJPI, N13. *Bk. rev.:* 0-5, 75-150 words. *Aud.:* Ga, Ac, Sa.

Law and Order Magazine is a monthly trade magazine for law enforcement professionals. The coverage is comprehensive and touches on all aspects of the profession, including equipment and products, training, techniques, office management, and best practices. Each issue has a thematic focus, and several articles touch on the same topic. For example, a recent focus was drones in law enforcement. The magazine also contains a calendar of upcoming events, an editorial introduction, feature articles, product reviews, news, and other columns. Many issues are available full-text through ProQuest's Criminal Justice Periodicals database. Some content is free online from the journal's website. The publisher, Hendon, offers a searchable online archive of *Law and Order* and three other related magazines that it publishes. This magazine is useful for law enforcement professionals, especially those in management positions, and academic libraries that support programs that offer law enforcement courses and degrees. URL: www.hendonpub.com/publications/lawandorder/

1475. ***Legal and Criminological Psychology.*** [ISSN: 1355-3259] 1996. s-a. GBP 326 (print & online eds.)). Ed(s): Paul Taylor. John Wiley & Sons Ltd., EMEA Institutional Sales, 9600 Garsington Rd, Oxford, OX4 2DQ, United Kingdom; cs-journals@wiley.com; http://onlinelibrary.wiley.com. Adv. Sample. Refereed. Reprint: PSC. *Indexed:* A01, A22, ASSIA, CJPI, E01, N13, SSA. *Aud.:* Ac, Sa.

Legal and Criminological Psychology is one of 11 journals published by the British Psychological Society (BPS). The journal was first released in 1996, with two issues printed each year. According to the BPS, this publication's goal is to "advance professional and scientific knowledge in the conjunction of legal psychology and criminological psychology." Most of the articles featured in each journal issue contain original research, but book reviews, hot-topic debates, and article commentary (with author response) are also included periodically. The range of topics discussed in this journal includes mental health and the law, management of offenders, witness and jury roles, crime detection and prevention, and aspects of deception. *Legal and Criminological Psychology* is available in print and online through EBSCOhost, Wiley, and other full-text providers.

1476. ***National Institute of Justice Journal.*** Superseded in part (in 1992): *National Institute of Justice Reports;* Which was formerly (until 1991): *N I J Reports;* (until 1983): *S N I: Selective Notification of Information.* [ISSN: 1067-7453] 1972. s-a. Ed(s): Jolene Hernon. U.S. Department of Justice. National Institute of Justice, 810 Seventh St, NW, Washington, DC 20531; http://www.ojp.usdoj.gov/nij/. Illus. Circ: 80000. *Aud.:* Ga, Ac, Sa.

The National Institute of Justice is the research, development, and evaluation agency of the U.S. Department of Justice. It is charged with providing independent, evidence-based research and tools for crime control and on justice issues, especially on the state and local levels. The *National Institute of Justice Journal* is published several times a year by the institute. Its intended audience is criminal justice professionals and policy makers, but college and advanced high school students researching current topics in criminal justice would find the journal useful as well. The articles are well written and clear. They present the results of recent research in language that the layperson can understand. The authors are U.S. government personnel, policy researchers, university professors, and other experts. Footnotes and citations are often included. Recent articles present research about the impact of incarceration on dependent children, the prevalence of sexual assault on college campuses in the United States, the impact of foreclosures on neighborhood crime rates, and more. The online archive dates back to 1994. The journal is available in print and online. URL: www.nij.gov/journals/Pages/welcome.aspx

1477. ***The Police Chief: professional voice of law enforcement.*** Former titles (until 1953): *Police Chiefs News;* (until 1947): *Police Chiefs' Newsletter.* [ISSN: 0032-2571] 1934. m. Free to members; Non-members, USD 30. Ed(s): Kerry Sullivan, Danielle Gudakunst. International Association of Chiefs of Police, Inc., 515 N Washington St, Alexandria, VA 22301; http://www.theiacp.org/. Illus., index. Circ: 23382. Vol. ends: Dec. Microform: PQC. *Indexed:* A22, BRI, CJPI, HRIS, N13. *Aud.:* Ga, Ac, Sa.

The Police Chief is the official publication of the International Association of Chiefs of Police, the world's oldest and largest police chief organization. The association has more than 20,000 members in almost 100 countries. Contributors to the magazine are most often law enforcement professionals from local, state, and federal agencies, but some pieces are written by academics or professionals from related fields. The content is typical of trade and association magazines—association news; legislative updates and other legal news; new equipment, products, and technology reviews; training and professional development advice and best-practice examples; and employment opportunities. *The Police Chief* is published monthly, and is available in print and online. The online access is free and available back to September 2003 through the journal website. This journal is recommended for all law enforcement special libraries and academic libraries that serve institutions offering a criminal justice degree. URL: http://policechiefmagazine.org

1478. ***Police Quarterly.*** [ISSN: 1098-6111] 1998. q. USD 1043 (print & online eds.)). Ed(s): Dr. John L Worrall. Sage Publications, Inc., 2455 Teller Rd, Thousand Oaks, CA 91320; info@sagepub.com; http://www.sagepub.com. Refereed. Reprint: PSC. *Indexed:* A01, A22, CJPI, E01, N13. *Bk. rev.:* 1-2, 2-6 pages, signed. *Aud.:* Ac, Sa.

Police Quarterly is published by Sage in association with the Police Executive Research Forum and the Police Section of the Academy of Criminal Justice Sciences. The former is a national membership organization of metropolitan, county, and state police executives. It was formed in 1977 to improve the profession through research and public policy debate. The latter is a section of a prominent international association of scholars and professionals, and is the publisher of two other journals reviewed in this section, *Justice Quarterly* and the *Journal of Criminal Justice Education.* The journal reviewed here, *Police Quarterly,* publishes research that is policy oriented to inform both those in academia and practitioners. The articles are in the form of "theoretical contributions, empirical studies, essays, comparative analyses, critiques, innovative program descriptions, debates, and book reviews." Examples of topics addressed recently include marijuana legalization and law enforcement in Colorado's neighbor states; use of mine-resistant ambush-protected vehicles in law enforcement response; and body-worn cameras and police officer burnout. Although this journal is perhaps too specialized for some academic libraries, it should be included in the collections of those who serve criminal justice students and faculty. It also should be considered by large public libraries and special libraries. URL: http://intl-pqx.sagepub.com

1479. ***Policing and Society: an international journal of research and policy.*** [ISSN: 1043-9463] 1990. 9x/yr. GBP 1961 (print & online eds.)). Ed(s): Jenny Fleminge. Routledge, 4 Park Sq, Milton Park, Abingdon, OX14 4RN, United Kingdom; subscriptions@tandf.co.uk; http://www.tandfonline.com. Illus., adv. Sample. Refereed. Reprint: PSC. *Indexed:* A01, A22, ASSIA, CJPI, E01, IBSS, P61, SSA. *Aud.:* Ac, Sa.

Policing and Society: An International Journal of Research and Policy is published nine times a year and specializes in the study of policing institutions throughout the world. Coverage includes "social scientific investigations of police policy and activity; legal and political analyses of police powers and governance; and management oriented research on aspects of police organization." There are occasional special issues; a recent one covered comparison between public and private policing. Each issue is truly international—for example, a recent one contained articles covering Belgium, Canada, South Korea, and Trinidad and Tobago. URL: www.tandfonline.com/toc/gpas20/current

1480. ***Policing (Bingley): an international journal of police strategies and management.*** Formed by the merger of (1978-1996): *Police Studies;* (1981-1996): *American Journal of Police.* [ISSN: 1363-951X] 1978. bi-m. EUR 4170 (print & online eds.) (excluding UK)). Ed(s): Wesley G Jennings, Lorie A Fridell. Emerald Publishing Limited, Howard House, Wagon Ln, Bingley, BD16 1WA, United Kingdom; emerald@emeraldinsight.com; http://www.emeraldinsight.com. Illus. Sample. Refereed. Microform: PQC. Reprint: PSC; WSH. *Indexed:* A01, A22, ASSIA, CJPI, E01, P61, SSA. *Bk. rev.:* 1, 900-1,500 words, signed. *Aud.:* Ac, Sa.

Policing: An International Journal of Police Strategies and Management looks at policing through an international lens. Each issue contains 7 to 15 research articles that are interdisciplinary and cover all aspects of law enforcement, including training, policies, practice, technology, and more. Recent issues contain research on management of deaf suspects in the United States; methods for detecting spatial-temporal clusters of violence in South Korea; and the effects of body-worn cameras on complaints against police in Latin America. Although this is not a top-tier research journal, articles are thorough and scholarly. *Policing* is a good choice for academic libraries that offer a criminal justice degree. The journal is available online from Emerald beginning with volume 20, 1997.

1481. ***Policing (Oxford): a journal of policy and practice.*** [ISSN: 1752-4512] 2007. 4x/yr. Ed(s): Peter Neyroud, P Waddington. Oxford University Press, Great Clarendon St, Oxford, OX2 6DP, United Kingdom; onlinequeries.uk@oup.com; https://academic.oup.com/journals. Adv. Refereed. Reprint: PSC. *Indexed:* CJPI. *Bk. rev.:* 6, signed. *Aud.:* Ac, Sa.

Policing: A Journal of Policy and Practice is a quarterly, peer-reviewed publication launched in 2007 by Oxford University Press. According to the journal's home page, its audience is "law enforcement leaders, police researchers, analysts and policy makers." The primary editorial board is composed of U.K.-based academics, professionals, and policy analysts, although there is also an international editorial board with members from other European countries, and the United States, Australia, Canada, and South Korea. The journal's first issue was a special issue devoted to policing terrorism. Each subsequent issue has contained original research articles, usually around ten, and several scholarly book reviews. Many issues also have editorials and other opinion pieces, and some have case studies. Although this title is relatively new, this journal's prestigious publisher and the quality of its content should guarantee its success. Even with its U.K.-centered content, it is highly recommended for all academic libraries and special libraries that serve clientele interested in policing policy and theory.

1482. ***The Prison Journal: an international forum on incarceration and alternative sanctions.*** Supersedes (in 1921): *Journal of Prison Discipline and Philanthropy.* [ISSN: 0032-8855] 1845. q. Ed(s): Rosemary L Gido. Sage Publications, Inc., 2455 Teller Rd, Thousand Oaks, CA 91320; info@sagepub.com; http://www.sagepub.com. Illus., index, adv. Sample. Refereed. Vol. ends: Dec. Microform: PQC. Reprint: PSC. *Indexed:* A01, A22, BRI, CJPI, E01, N13, SSA. *Aud.:* Ac, Sa.

The Prison Journal: An International Forum on Incarceration and Alternative Sanctions was first published in 1921 by the Pennsylvania Prison Society, a social justice and prison reform organization founded in 1787. It remains the official publication of the society, and is now published by Sage. The journal's mission is to be a "central forum for studies, ideas, and discussions of adult and juvenile confinement, treatment interventions, and alternative sanctions." The journal is published at least four times per year, and each issue contains three to seven articles. Examples of recent papers include an analysis of Ethiopian prison society; a comparison of parents in prisons across the United States; and development of training for health care providers of transgender patients. There are topical special issues—a recent topic was prison higher education. The contributors are academics and practitioners from the United States and other countries, specializing in the fields of public administration and ethics, criminal justice studies, psychiatric nursing, and related disciplines. The articles are scholarly and written in clear language, making this journal a good choice for social science undergraduates. It is also appropriate for faculty and professionals who are interested in social justice issues as they apply to prisons. URL: http://intl-tpj.sagepub.com

1483. ***Probation Journal: the journal of community and criminal justice.*** Formerly (until 1974): *Probation.* [ISSN: 0264-5505] 1929. q. USD 1059 (print & online eds.)). Ed(s): Lol Burke. Sage Publications Ltd., 1 Oliver's Yard, 55 City Rd, London, EC1Y 1SP, United Kingdom; info@sagepub.com; https://www.sagepub.com/. Adv. Sample. Refereed. Reprint: PSC. *Indexed:* A22, CJPI, E01. *Bk. rev.:* 5-6, 300-600 words, signed. *Aud.:* Ga, Ac, Sa.

Probation Journal: The Journal of Community and Criminal Justice is a peer-reviewed journal published by Sage in association with Napo, a U.K.-based trade union and professional association for family court and probation staff. It was first published in 1929 (by an earlier incarnation of Napo) as a trade magazine but has evolved into a quarterly scholarly journal that addresses U.K. and international probation and related issues. Napo, although still involved in the publication of the journal, exercises no editorial control. Since *Probation Journal* is a U.K. publication, most of the articles discuss issues directly related to that country, but the research and theory are applicable to an international audience; according to the journal's website, subscribers span 25 countries. The journal features articles that present the results of quantitative and qualitative research, discuss best practices, and present recent theoretical debates. Each issue also contains book reviews and a column, "In Court," that "reviews recent appeal judgements and other judicial developments that inform sentencing and early release." URL: http://journals.sagepub.com/home/prb

1484. ***Psychology, Crime & Law.*** [ISSN: 1068-316X] 1994. 10x/yr. GBP 1057 (print & online eds.)). Ed(s): Dr. Theresa Gannon, Brian H Bornstein. Routledge, 4 Park Sq, Milton Park, Abingdon, OX14 4RN, United Kingdom; subscriptions@tandf.co.uk; http://www.tandfonline.com. Adv. Sample. Refereed. Reprint: PSC. *Indexed:* A01, A22, CJPI, E01, IBSS. *Aud.:* Ac, Sa.

Psychology, Crime & Law is the official journal of the European Association of Psychology and Law (EAPL). Since its release in 1994, the journal's purpose has been "to promote the study and application of psychological approaches to crime, criminal and civil law, and the influence of law on behavior." Articles within this publication explore procedures and individuals of the law process from a psychological standpoint. For example, a recent issue includes a study of dementia in prisoners with sexual convictions. *Psychology, Crime & Law* is uniquely valuable to special libraries, such as law libraries, but is broad enough in scope that it is beneficial for academic institutions with criminal justice, law, or related programs of study. This publication is available in print as well as online through Taylor & Francis Online, EBSCOhost, and other full-text providers.

1485. ***Punishment & Society: the international journal of penology.*** [ISSN: 1462-4745] 1999. 5x/yr. USD 1620 (print & online eds.)). Ed(s): Dario Melossi. Sage Publications Ltd., 1 Oliver's Yard, 55 City Rd, London, EC1Y 1SP, United Kingdom; info@sagepub.com; https://www.sagepub.com/. Adv. Sample. Refereed. Reprint: PSC. *Indexed:* A01, A22, CJPI, E01, IBSS, N13, P61, SSA. *Bk. rev.:* 4-5, lengthy, signed. *Aud.:* Ac, Sa.

Punishment & Society: The International Journal of Penology is a highly regarded international and interdisciplinary journal that presents research on punishment, penal institutions, and penal control. A typical issue contains five or six articles and a number of scholarly book reviews and review symposiums. Recent articles include an examination of fathers and masculinity in prison; a study in public views about publicizing arrest records; and an exploration of femininity in prison drug treatment programs. Special issues are published annually, with the latest issue covering the journal's twentieth anniversary, reflecting on scholarly accomplishments and recognizing opportunities for research expansion. This journal is recommended for all academic libraries that serve institutions with criminal justice departments, and related special libraries. It is available in print and online, going back to the first issue in 1999. URL: http://journals.sagepub.com/home/pun

Sexual Abuse. See Psychology section.

1486. *Theoretical Criminology: an international journal.* [ISSN: 1362-4806] 1997. q. USD 1592 (print & online eds.)). Ed(s): Simon A Cole, Mary Bosworth. Sage Publications Ltd., 1 Oliver's Yard, 55 City Rd, London, EC1Y 1SP, United Kingdom; info@sagepub.com; https://www.sagepub.com/. Illus. Sample. Refereed. Vol. ends: Nov. Reprint: PSC. *Indexed:* A01, A22, CJPI, E01, IBSS, SSA. *Bk. rev.:* 7-8, 1,400 words, signed. *Aud.:* Ac, Sa.

Theoretical Criminology, as the title suggests, looks at the theoretical aspects of criminology. Within that constraint, however, the coverage is interdisciplinary, international, and broad. Most issues contain three to seven articles and several book reviews. There are special thematic issues; the latest was titled "The State of the State," an examination of how various criminal justice systems help produce particular political entities and how specific political entities affect correctional institutions. This journal is highly regarded by criminal justice scholars (see section introduction for information on selection/ranking criteria). It is recommended for academic libraries and practitioners interested in the subject. It is available in print and online, back to issue 1 in 1997 from Sage. URL: http://journals.sagepub.com/home/tcr

1487. *Trauma, Violence & Abuse (Online): a review journal.* [ISSN: 1552-8324] 2000. q. USD 960. Ed(s): Jon R Conte. Sage Publications, Inc., 2455 Teller Rd, Thousand Oaks, CA 91320; info@sagepub.com; http://www.sagepub.com. Adv. Sample. Refereed. *Indexed:* N13. *Aud.:* Ac, Sa.

Trauma, Violence & Abuse (*TVA*) is a peer-reviewed journal that is "devoted to organizing, synthesizing, and expanding knowledge on all forms of trauma, abuse, and violence." This journal is particularly useful for practitioners, as it is composed of review articles that summarize current practices and subjects of interest in the field. A number of topics are explored in this journal, including sexual abuse, domestic violence, child abuse, and post-traumatic stress disorder. The journal's interdisciplinary scope makes it useful to most academic institutions as well as to professionals in many fields, including criminology, psychiatry, psychology, social work, and law. Unfortunately, *Trauma, Violence & Abuse* ceased to be published in print in 2009, but the journal is still available online through Sage Publications.

1488. *Trends and Issues in Crime and Criminal Justice.* [ISSN: 1836-2206] 1986. 20x/yr. Free. Australian Institute of Criminology, GPO Box 1936, Canberra, ACT 2601, Australia; aicpress@aic.gov.au; http://www.aic.gov.au. *Aud.:* Ac, Sa.

Trends and Issues in Crime and Criminal Justice is a serial publication of the Australian Institute of Criminology, which is part of the Australian government. The institute publishes and makes freely available several serial publications and other reports, and its offered content and services are similar to that of the United States National Criminal Justice Research Service. The *Trends and Issues* homepage describes the publication as "concise, peer-reviewed papers on criminological topics for policy makers and practitioners." This journal first appeared in 1986, and the papers in the series are numbered, rather than dated. For the last few years, 18 to 40 studies have been published annually. They are data rich, referenced, and scholarly, but as they are written for a non-academic audience, the language is straightforward and clear. Some recent titles are "Predicting Online Fraud Victimisation in Australia" and "Benevolent Harm: Orphanages, Voluntourism, and Child Sexual Exploitation in South-East Asia." These reports primarily concern crime issues in Australia, but include broader regional and international topics periodically. URL: www.aic.gov.au/publications/current%20series/tandi.aspx

1489. *Trends in Organized Crime.* [ISSN: 1084-4791] 1995. q. EUR 542 (print & online eds.)). Ed(s): Klaus Von Lampe. Springer New York LLC, 233 Spring St, New York, NY 10013; customerservice@springer.com; http://www.springer.com. Sample. Refereed. Reprint: PSC. *Indexed:* A01, A22, BRI, CJPI, E01. *Bk. rev.:* 3, signed. *Aud.:* Ac, Sa.

Trends in Organized Crime is published by Springer in association with the International Association for the Study of Organized Crime (IASOC). The journal, which has been published since 1995, contains original research, essays, and commentary, and analyses of current and historical organized-crime issues, along with pertinent reports from national governmental agencies. A recent special issue was devoted to organized crime in Latin America. Examples of other topics covered include outlaw bikers in Europe; human trafficking in Portugal; and gang violence intervention. Book reviews and listings of related publications are included in each issue. In addition to the association's members, the journal is a good resource for interested criminologists, policy makers, and academics.

1490. *Victims & Offenders.* [ISSN: 1556-4886] 2005. q. GBP 868 (print & online eds.)). Ed(s): James M Byrne. Taylor & Francis Inc., 711 3rd Ave, 8th Fl, New York, NY 10017; support@tandfonline.com; http://www.tandfonline.com. Adv. Sample. Refereed. Reprint: PSC. *Indexed:* A22, ASSIA, CJPI, E01, SSA. *Aud.:* Ac.

Victims & Offenders is a peer-reviewed publication that provides "an interdisciplinary and international forum for the dissemination of new research, policies, and practices related to both victimization and offending throughout the life course." Journal articles cover a variety of topics, including recent studies about general strain theory and sexual assault, female-perpetrated domestic violence, and mental health of older prisoners. The journal is published at least four times annually and each issue contains five to seven original articles. Special issues are released periodically, addressing topics like problem-solving courts, police response to individuals with behavioral health challenges, and school victimization. *Victims & Offenders* is ideal for academic institutions with criminology and criminal justice programs, but would also be of interest to scholars in the fields of psychology, sociology, and social work.

Violence Against Women. See Gender Studies section.

1491. *Women & Criminal Justice.* [ISSN: 0897-4454] 1989. 6x/yr. GBP 852 (print & online eds.)). Ed(s): Frances P Bernat. Routledge, 530 Walnut St, Ste 850, Philadelphia, PA 19106; enquiries@tandfonline.com; http://www.tandfonline.com. Illus., adv. Sample. Refereed. Circ: 397 Paid. Vol. ends: No. 2. Microform: PQC. Reprint: PSC. *Indexed:* A22, BRI, C42, CJPI, E01, FemPer, GW, N13, SSA, WSA. *Bk. rev.:* 5-10, 500-1,500 words. *Aud.:* Ac, Sa.

Women & Criminal Justice is an international and interdisciplinary journal that covers all aspects of the intersection of women and criminal justice, including women victims, professionals, or offenders. The articles present the results of qualitative and quantitative research, or are theoretical studies. Contributors are academics and professionals from the disciplines of women's studies, sociology, social work, criminal justice, law, and human rights. This title is published six times a year by Routledge. It is available from the publisher in print and online, and the full text is offered through LexisNexis, Taylor & Francis, and EBSCOhost with a one-year embargo. This journal would be of interest to criminologists, sociologists, and those in gender studies. Readers should also consider *Feminist Criminology* (reviewed in this section).

■ CULTURAL STUDIES

See also History; Literature; and Political Science sections.

Vanette M. Schwartz, Social Sciences Librarian, 8900 Milner Library, Illinois State University, Normal, IL 61790-8900; vmschwa@ilstu.edu

Introduction

Cultural studies journals offer scholars and general audiences an ever expanding and diverse combination of theoretical, philosophical, historical, social, and critical writing. The geographical emphasis of publications ranges from East and South Asia to Europe, Canada, and the American Midwest and South, while individual articles detail research from every continent and region. Many cultural studies journals blend history, area studies, politics, and communication with literature, the arts, and philosophy. Other publications span eras from the Renaissance to the early modern period to the future. International and transnational aspects of cultural studies have gained prominence along with global/local emphasis. Cultural studies research shows increased attention to science, technology, and social media, especially as related to popular culture. Interdisciplinary writings remain a foundation of cultural studies as are race, class, and gender. Other cultural studies journals offer varied formats, with expanded use of online videos, photos, musical excerpts, and graphics. Open-access publications have broadened the spectrum of cultural studies by offering added venues for scholars and students to distribute their writing. The field of cultural studies continues to offer an engaging and compelling range of research and writing in the interrelated areas of the social sciences and humanities.

Basic Periodicals

Ga: *Humanities, Journal of Popular Culture;* Ac: *American Quarterly, Critical Inquiry, Humanities, Journal of Popular Culture, Social Science Quarterly.*

Basic Abstracts and Indexes

Academic Search Complete, America: History and Life, Humanities International Complete, MLA International Bibliography, SOCIndex, Sociological Abstracts.

1492. ***American Journal of Cultural Sociology.*** [ISSN: 2049-7113] 2013. 3x/yr. GBP 1454. Ed(s): Jeffrey C Alexander, Philip Smith. Palgrave Macmillan Ltd., Macmillan Building, 4 Crinan St, London, N1 9XW, United Kingdom; onlinesales@palgrave.com; http://www.palgrave.com. Adv. Sample. Refereed. Reprint: PSC. *Aud.:* Ac.

Within the growing study of culture and sociology, this publication explores how patterns of meaning affect inequality, race, gender, crime, and social movements, and aims to "conceptualize these complex cultural processes." Each issue contains several original research articles on topics such as the mobility of working class youth, faith based community organizing, veganism, folk music, and national solidarity. Although many articles cover contemporary topics, others focus on historical subjects including Boston school desegregation and contentious politics in Lowell, Massachusetts, from 1825-1845. Many authors are from U.S. and Canadian universities, with scholars from Europe, Scandinavia, Australia, and Africa also represented. Some issues include responses and rejoinders that provide contrasting views on previously published articles. This journal builds on earlier work in cultural sociology and extends scholarship in this developing field.

1493. ***American Quarterly.*** [ISSN: 0003-0678] 1949. q. USD 210. Ed(s): Jeanette Hall, Mari Yoshihara. The Johns Hopkins University Press, 2715 N Charles St, Baltimore, MD 21218; http://www.press.jhu.edu. Illus., adv. Sample. Refereed. Vol. ends: Dec (No. 4). Reprint: PSC. *Indexed:* A01, A22, AmHI, BAS, BRI, CBRI, Chicano, E01, F01, MLA-IB, P61. *Bk. rev.:* 5-8, essay length. *Aud.:* Ac.

As the premier publication in American Studies, this journal has been published for seven decades. Still the journal continues to keep pace with the continuous advancements in the field of American culture. *American Quarterly* publishes lengthy research articles and review essays on American culture. Recent articles cover such topics as the history of air playing, kawaii-style racist caricature, privatization of prisons as related to migrant detention centers, and settler colonialism in Latin America. In addition to book reviews, event reviews cover art exhibitions and film festivals. Digital project reviews have also been added in selected issues. Special issues are published each September, focusing on themes such as the role of digital humanities or American Studies as related to Pacific and East Asian studies. This journal covers the activities of the American Studies Association, and serves as the major avenue of scholarship in the discipline.

1494. ***American Studies: with American Studies International.*** Former titles (until 1971): *Midcontinent American Studies Journal;* (until 1962): *Central Mississippi Valley American Studies Association. Journal;* (until 1960): *Central Mississippi Valley American Studies Association. Bulletin;* Incorporates (1975-2004): *American Studies International;* Which was formerly (until 1975): *American Studies;* (until 1970): *American Studies News;* Which incorporated (1983-1996): *American Studies International Newsletter.* [ISSN: 0026-3079] 1957. q. USD 50 (Individuals, USD 35; USD 14 per issue). Ed(s): Randal Maurice Jelks, Sherrie J Tucker. University of Kansas, American Studies Department, 1440 Jayhawk Blvd, Rm 213, Lawrence, KS 66045; amerst@ku.edu; http://americanstudies.ku.edu. Illus., index, adv. Refereed. Circ: 1200 Paid. Vol. ends: No. 3. Microform: PQC. *Indexed:* A01, A22, AmHI, BRI, E01, MLA-IB. *Bk. rev.:* Occasional, 10-45, 400-500 words. *Aud.:* Ga, Ac.

The wide spectrum of research on United States cultures and histories is the focus of *American Studies*. Research articles on U.S. literature and the arts, politics, social issues, and popular culture are the foundation of this journal, along with American Studies pedagogy. Recent articles explore such topics as Washington, D.C.'s African American community during the Great Depression, 1920s radical sentiment among immigrant mine workers in Illinois, the silk trade in antebellum northern commerce and youth, and race and crime. Some issues are devoted to a single theme, such as food culture or Latinx civil rights. Review essays and book reviews appear in most issues. The Mid-America American Studies Association, the University of Kansas College of Liberal Arts and Sciences, and the Department of American Studies and the Kansas University Libraries jointly sponsor *American Studies*. The aim of this journal is to be interdisciplinary/transdisciplinary and to widen the field of American Studies discourse, including comparative, international, and transnational coverage. Both specialists and nonspecialists will find engaging articles here.

1495. ***Atlantic Studies: global currents.*** [ISSN: 1478-8810] 2004. q. GBP 666 (print & online eds.)). Ed(s): Manuel Barcia, David Lambert. Routledge, 4 Park Sq, Milton Park, Abingdon, OX14 4RN, United Kingdom; subscriptions@tandf.co.uk; http://www.tandfonline.com. Adv. Sample. Refereed. Reprint: PSC. *Indexed:* A22, AmHI, E01, IBSS, MLA-IB. *Aud.:* Ac.

This international journal brings together scholarship on the cultures and societies of the overall Atlantic world, with emphasis on the "transnational, transhistorical, and transdisciplinary." It deals primarily with the areas of history and literature, along with cultural and critical theory. Articles in recent issues cover topics such as return migration to Haiti in the early nineteenth century, Portuguese immigrants in Brazil, the cross-Atlantic knowledge divide and connections between Atlantic and (Trans)Pacific studies. The diasporic, historical, and literary studies of the region as well as their global effects are the focus of the writing in this journal. *Atlantic Studies* is the official journal of the Society for Multi-Ethnic Studies: Europe and the Americas. Recommended for academic libraries with an emphasis on this region.

1496. ***Body & Society.*** [ISSN: 1357-034X] 1995. q. USD 1471 (print & online eds.)). Ed(s): Mike Featherstone, Lisa Blackman. Sage Publications Ltd., 1 Oliver's Yard, 55 City Rd, London, EC1Y 1SP, United Kingdom; info@sagepub.com; https://www.sagepub.com/. Adv. Sample. Refereed. Reprint: PSC. *Indexed:* A01, A22, E01, IBSS, SSA. *Bk. rev.:* Occasional, 1-4 reviews, 500-1,000 words. *Aud.:* Ac.

Body studies continues to be an ever increasing field of research with new developments appearing constantly. This journal covers disciplines from cultural history and the environment to health studies, film studies, sociology, philosophy, and sport studies. Focusing on the social and cultural analysis of human and non-human bodies, articles in this journal center on issues of communication and media practices, feminism, technology, ecology, medicine, ethics, and performance art. Recent articles in *Body & Society* cover such topics as robot bodies, the biopolitics of synthetic blood, facial feminization surgery and transgender women, the sense of touch and affective studies, and the Ironman triathlon. Special issues are also published on topics such as skin studies and indeterminate bodies. The Theory, Culture and Society Centre at Nottingham Trent University sponsors this journal, along with its joint publication *Theory, Culture and Society.* For scholars interested in a wide-ranging combination of theory, society, culture, and science.

1497. ***Cabinet.*** [ISSN: 1531-1430] 2000. q. USD 38 (Individuals, USD 32; USD 10 per issue). Ed(s): Sina Najafi, Christopher Turner. Immaterial Incorporated, 300 Nevins St, Brooklyn, NY 11217. Sample. *Indexed:* MLA-IB. *Aud.:* Ga, Ac.

The focus of *Cabinet* is "culture," in the most expansive sense of the word. An incredibly wide-ranging magazine, this publication covers primarily art and culture, but combines many other aspects in the mix. This title is both international and interdisciplinary, and each issue contains regular columns and essays along with interviews, photography, works of art, and postcards. Issues begin with regular columns on "Ingestion," "Colors," "Inventory," "Sentences," and "Leftovers." The main section includes both articles and art projects ranging from picture frames to book burning and from eye charts to birch bark drawings. A thematic section is featured in each issue on subjects such as knowledge, milk, the desert, and the nose. Contributors range from academics to freelance writers, artists, filmmakers, sound designers, and musicians. The magazine's website contains a table of contents and information on contributors, along with additional readings, artwork, soundtracks, and musical works. This award-winning publication provides fascinating reading, along with engaging art and photography.

1498. *Canadian Review of American Studies.* Formerly (until 1970): *C A A S Bulletin.* [ISSN: 0007-7720] 1965. 3x/yr. USD 185. Ed(s): Priscilla L Walton. University of Toronto Press, Journals Division, 5201 Dufferin St, Toronto, ON M3H 5T8, Canada; journals@utpress.utoronto.ca; http://www.utpjournals.com. Illus., index, adv. Sample. Refereed. Circ: 289. Vol. ends: No. 3. *Indexed:* A01, A22, AmHI, E01, MLA-IB, P61. *Bk. rev.:* 2-3, 1,000-1,500 words. *Aud.:* Ac.

American culture from the perspective of our northern neighbors is the focus of this publication by the Canadian Association for American Studies, supported by Carleton University in Ottawa. This journal emphasizes cross-disciplinary studies of U.S. culture from both historical and contemporary perspectives. It also includes articles on the relationship between U.S. and Canadian cultures. Each issue includes research articles and review essays written primarily by Canadian academics, with some content by U.S. and international scholars. Many articles focus on literary works or films, while others explore social and cultural issues. Recent articles cover such topics as Cuba and U.S. sovereignty, public mourning at the 9/11 memorial museum, and women's writing in urban captivity narratives. Special issues or sections are published occasionally on topics such as *Game of Thrones*, the Vietnam War, legacies of lynching, and U.S. and Canadian relations in the Trump era. Libraries with an emphasis on American Studies scholarship from varying viewpoints will want to include this journal in their collection.

1499. *City, Culture and Society.* [ISSN: 1877-9166] 2010. q. EUR 746. Ed(s): Francesco Bandarin. Elsevier Ltd, The Boulevard, Langford Lane, Oxford, OX5 1GB, United Kingdom; journalscustomerserviceemea@elsevier.com; http://www.elsevier.com. Refereed. *Indexed:* P61. *Aud.:* Ac.

With more than half the world's population currently living in cities, the study of urban areas has become increasingly significant. The publication *City, Culture and Society* focuses on "urban governance in the 21st century," especially as related to "cultural creativity and social inclusion." The journal covers topics such as urban economics, sustainability, cultural technology, and social inclusion. International in scope, the journal has editorial board members from Europe, the Far East, Australia, the United Kingdom, and the United States. Each issue includes several original articles, with some issues covering a specific theme such as city food governance, innovation and identity in smart cities, or cultural mapping. Other individual articles examine topics such as live music cities, urban street culture, sustainability and community planning, urban art districts, and the placement of city parks. Specific articles focus on an individual city from Naples or Toronto, to Detroit, Sydney, or Bogota. This journal will primarily interest academic libraries, but may also appeal to large public libraries.

1500. *Communication, Culture & Critique.* [ISSN: 1753-9129] 2008. q. GBP 1239 (print & online eds.)). Ed(s): Laurie Ouellette, Sarah Banet-Weiser. Wiley-Blackwell Publishing Ltd., The Atrium, Southern Gate, Chichester, PO19 8QG, United Kingdom; cs-journals@wiley.com; http://onlinelibrary.wiley.com. Reprint: PSC. *Indexed:* A22, BRI, C45, E01, MLA-IB. *Bk. rev.:* 1-2 in some issues; 2-3 pages in length. *Aud.:* Ac.

The International Communication Association publishes this title along with five additional journals. The editors aim to "provide an international forum for critical research in communication, media and cultural studies" with the focus on "questions of power, inequality and justice." Original research articles comprise the bulk of each issue, with reviews and commentary included occasionally. Article content ranges from Beirut's media waste to female domestic workers in Beijing and from cultural fusion theory to populist discourse in social media. Special issues or sections have featured themes from media and the extreme right to sexual harassment in academe. This publication offers a wide range of international subjects, such as Israeli television commercials, advice media in China, and film regulation in contemporary India. With increased emphasis on worldwide media availability and global networking, this journal explores transnational issues from a larger theoretical framework within the social sciences and humanities. This journal will be of interest to researchers not only in communication studies, but also in global politics, economics, and social inquiry.

1501. *Comparative American Studies: an international journal.* [ISSN: 1477-5700] 2003. q. GBP 744 (print & online eds.)). Routledge, 4 Park Sq, Milton Park, Abingdon, OX14 4RN, United Kingdom; subscriptions@tandf.co.uk; http://www.tandfonline.com. Adv. Refereed. Reprint: PSC. *Indexed:* A22, AmHI, E01, IBSS, MLA-IB. *Bk. rev.:* 2-6 reviews, essay length. *Aud.:* Ac.

Scholarship on American Studies from outside the United States is the focus of *Comparative American Studies.* The journal aims to place the discourse on American culture in an international framework. With the contemporary focus on globalization and on the relationship between the United States and other nations, *Comparative American Studies* seeks to draw out the conflicts and common themes, especially in the areas of literature, film, popular culture, photography, and visual arts. Each issue contains six to eight articles on topics such as the political radicalism and the arts, comparative border studies, and cross-cultural influence in American literature. Some articles cover comparative themes in the works of American, Canadian, and Latin American writers and artists. Since its beginning in 2003, this journal has filled a major gap in the literature of American Studies by providing a much-needed international viewpoint.

1502. *Critical Discourse Studies: an interdisciplinary journal for the social sciences.* [ISSN: 1740-5904] 2004. q. GBP 663 (print & online eds.)). Ed(s): John E Richardson. Routledge, 4 Park Sq, Milton Park, Abingdon, OX14 4RN, United Kingdom; subscriptions@tandf.co.uk; http://www.tandfonline.com. Adv. Sample. Refereed. Reprint: PSC. *Indexed:* A22, AmHI, E01, IBSS, MLA-IB, P61. *Bk. rev.:* 2-3, 500-1,000 words. *Aud.:* Ac.

Reaching far beyond language and linguistic studies, this publication has something for every discipline in the social sciences, as well as literary and media studies and racial, ethnic, and gender studies. This journal aims to "publish critical research that advances our understanding of how discourse figures into social processes, social structures, and social change." Connecting academic research with discussion of practical and activist approaches is an additional goal of *Critical Discourse Studies.* Each issue is primarily composed of original articles, with a few book reviews in many issues. Recent articles cover such topics as discourses of political resistance, immigration terminology, media framing of the abortion controversy, as well as racist language on Facebook pages and the rhetoric of identity creation. Some special issues focus on one topic such as socio-economic inequality and media treatment, Marx and discourse, or ethics in critical discourse studies. This journal enhances the range of scholarship on critical discourse, a vital and expanding area of interdisciplinary study.

1503. *Critical Historical Studies.* [ISSN: 2326-4462] 2014. s-a. USD 220 (print & online eds.)). Ed(s): William H Sewell, Jr., Andrew Sartori. University of Chicago Press, 1427 E 60th St, Chicago, IL 60637; custserv@press.uchicago.edu; http://www.journals.uchicago.edu. Adv. Refereed. *Indexed:* A01, AmHI. *Aud.:* Ac.

"Historical reflections on politics, culture, economy, and social life" from all time periods and areas of the world is the focus of this interdisciplinary journal, published under the auspices of the Chicago Center for Contemporary Theory. Editors and authors are primarily from U.S. universities, with additional writers from Europe, the United Kingdom, South Africa, China, and Japan. Each issue includes original lengthy articles followed by review essays, forums, or reflections. Articles provide a well-documented, in-depth analysis of such subjects as the Chinese cultural revolution, Caribbean slave plantations, peasant resistance in nineteenth-century Ireland, as well as corporations and income inequality or the rise and fall of pensions. Scholars in history, political science, and sociology are the primary audience for this publication, but academics in related areas of the social sciences and humanities will also find the content appealing.

1504. ***Critical Inquiry.*** [ISSN: 0093-1896] 1974. q. USD 358. Ed(s): W J T Mitchell. University of Chicago Press, 1427 E 60th St, Chicago, IL 60637; subscriptions@press.uchicago.edu; http://www.journals.uchicago.edu. Illus., index, adv. Sample. Refereed. Vol. ends: Summer. Reprint: PSC. *Indexed:* A01, A22, A51, AmHI, BRI, MLA-IB, P61. *Aud.:* Ac.

For 45 years, *Critical Inquiry* has set the standard for publishing interdisciplinary criticism in the arts and humanities. Each issue includes several articles on topics from the arts, philosophy, literature, film, history, politics, and social issues. Recent issues include articles on such subjects as early colonial Native American literature, collateral damage in war, white military veterans in an era of diversity, and memory and mourning of the battle of Gettysburg. Some volumes include a special section or issue on a single topic such as the occupied and occupier in Israel and Palestine. Most issues contain several original articles, along with critical responses to previous articles. This journal provides a forum for both traditional and currently developing areas of criticism. In *Critical Inquiry,* authors engage in theoretical debate and spar in critical responses. A significant journal for most academic libraries.

1505. ***Critical Review (Philadelphia): a journal of politics and society.*** [ISSN: 0891-3811] 1987. q. GBP 411 (print & online eds.)). Ed(s): Jeffrey Friedman. Routledge, 711 3rd Ave, 8th Fl., New York, NY 10017; http://www.routledge.com. Illus., index. Sample. Refereed. Vol. ends: Fall. Microform: PQC. Reprint: PSC. *Indexed:* A22, BRI, E01, EconLit, IBSS, P61, SSA. *Bk. rev.:* 1-3 review essays. *Aud.:* Ac.

This journal will interest academics in all areas of the social sciences, especially political scientists and economists. *Critical Review* focuses on political theory, while also including articles on political psychology, political economy, and public opinion. Contributors are primarily from U.S. academic circles, with a few authors from other countries. Articles are theoretical or historical but do not advocate or criticize proposed policies. Each issue contains several research articles or essays that are well written and extensively documented. Articles explore topics ranging from religion as a cause of violence to human behavior within politics and from political competence to improving democratic accountability. Some issues concentrate on a particular theme or devote a section to a specific topic including democracy for realists and capitalism, socialism, and democracy. One or more review essays are included in most issues. This journal presents lively writing and debate on major political, economic, and social ideas.

1506. ***Cross-Cultural Research: the journal of comparative social science.*** Former titles (until 1993): *Behavior Science Research;* (until 1974): *Behavior Science Notes.* [ISSN: 1069-3971] 1966. 5x/yr. USD 1198 (print & online eds.)). Ed(s): Carol R Ember. Sage Publications, Inc., 2455 Teller Rd, Thousand Oaks, CA 91320; info@sagepub.com; http://www.sagepub.com. Illus., index, adv. Sample. Refereed. Vol. ends: Nov. Microform: PQC. Reprint: PSC. *Indexed:* A01, A22, A47, BAS, E01, IBSS, MLA-IB, P61, SSA. *Aud.:* Ac.

Cross-Cultural Research aims to publish comparative studies in many areas of the social and behavioral sciences from anthropology, psychology, and sociology to political science, economics, human ecology, and evolutionary biology. The journal articles cover systematic comparisons of cross-cultural issues, including statistical measures linking dependent and independent variables. Recent articles have covered subjects such as cultural consensus theory, altruism, and community collectivism, cross-national variation in attitudes toward premarital sex, cultural differences in privacy during interviews, and slavery from cross-cultural perspectives. Occasional special issues are published on such themes as cross-cultural variations of gratitude, parental power and prestige, or evolutionary approaches to cross-cultural anthropology. The journal is sponsored by Human Relations Area Files, Inc., and is the official journal of the Society for Cross-Cultural Research. Scholars in many areas of the social sciences will find this publication valuable for its analysis and range of coverage.

1507. ***Cultural & Social History.*** [ISSN: 1478-0038] 2004. q. GBP 395 (print & online eds.)). Ed(s): Barry Doyle, Sarah Pearsall. Routledge, 4 Park Sq, Milton Park, Abingdon, OX14 4RN, United Kingdom; subscriptions@tandf.co.uk; http://www.tandfonline.com. Illus., adv. Sample. Refereed. Reprint: PSC. *Indexed:* A22, BRI, E01, P61. *Bk. rev.:* 10-12, essay length. *Aud.:* Ac.

This journal is sponsored by the Social History Society and based in the United Kingdom. The purpose of this publication is to blend the historical study of culture and society beyond the traditional borders of these two areas of history. Although many articles focus on aspects of British or Irish history, the journal also has additional international coverage. Most contributors are from Britain, the United States, or Western Europe. Each issue includes research articles, review essays, and several individual book reviews. Articles cover such topics as glass in late medieval and early modern domestic architecture, the peasant arts movement and country life in England, investigative methods of crime reporters in Leeds, England, during World War II, and settler press efforts to continue publication in German colonies. Occasional special issues have been published on subjects from rethinking gender and justice in South Asia to social mobility in modern Britain. By interweaving the cultural and social aspects of historical research, this journal is keeping pace with disciplinary trends. *Cultural & Social History* will be of interest to scholars and students in history and related areas such as literature, art, and cultural studies.

1508. ***Cultural Critique (Minneapolis, 1985).*** [ISSN: 0882-4371] 1985. 3x/yr. USD 203 (print & online eds.)). Ed(s): John Mowitt, Simona Sawhney. University of Minnesota Press, 111 Third Avenue South, Ste 290, Minneapolis, MN 55401; http://www.upress.umn.edu. Illus., index, adv. Refereed. Vol. ends: Oct. *Indexed:* A22, AmHI, BRI, E01, IBSS, MLA-IB. *Aud.:* Ac.

This journal focuses on analysis, interpretation, and debate of culture in the broadest sense. An international and interdisciplinary publication, *Cultural Critique* deals with aspects of culture from the political and economic to the ethical and artistic. Most contributors are scholars from U.S. institutions, although some international writers and researchers are included. Most issues are devoted to a single topic or a few main subjects. Some articles involve literary criticism, while others focus on sociological, anthropological, and philosophical issues. Both historical topics and contemporary social and aesthetic studies are included. Recent articles cover such subjects as the recording of oral Jewish tradition, reconfiguring the Turkish cultural public sphere, artistic versus ideological sublimation, and intellectual property and emerging religions. *Cultural Critique* will appeal to scholars in literature, film, politics, media, art, and sociology.

1509. ***Cultural History: journal of the international society for cultural history.*** [ISSN: 2045-290X] 2012. s-a. GBP 79 (print & online eds.)). Ed(s): Christopher E Forth. Edinburgh University Press Ltd., The Tun, Holyrood Rd, 12 (2f) Jackson's Entry, Edinburgh, EH8 8PJ, United Kingdom; journals@eup.ed.ac.uk; http://www.euppublishing.com. Adv. Sample. Refereed. *Bk. rev.:* Number and length vary. *Aud.:* Ac.

The International Society for Cultural History publishes this journal, which aims to be a forum for discussion and debate about the theory, methods, issues, and trends in the expanding nexus of culture and history. The journal is international in scope, although most authors and editorial board members are from Europe, Scandinavia, and the United States. Each issue includes several research articles on topics such as defining cultural history in nineteenth-century Finland, private letters in Iberian immigration history, reproduction in Spain's medical literature during the 1950s/1960s and transnational music and immigrant life in Buenos Aires. Occasionally special issues are published on a single theme such as suffering, visuality, emotion or emotions in history, and the arts. Each issue also includes several reviews; review essays discuss a group of books on a specific topic, while individual books are reviewed in both lengthy essays as well as in brief commentaries. *Cultural History* provides a new venue of international writing for historians as well as for scholars in museums, galleries, and archives.

1510. ***Cultural Politics.*** [ISSN: 1743-2197] 2005. 3x/yr. USD 436. Duke University Press, 905 W Main St, Durham, NC 27701; orders@dukeupress.edu; https://www.dukeupress.edu. Adv. Refereed. Reprint: PSC. *Indexed:* ASSIA, BRI, IBSS, MLA-IB, P61. *Bk. rev.:* 2 in some issues; 4-5 pages in length. *Aud.:* Ac.

In a contemporary world that links politics with virtually every aspect of society, this journal explores "what is cultural about politics and what is political about culture." Each issue consists of several articles on topics such as mainstreaming the alt-right, European border politics and necropower, the environmentalization of thinking, power, and capital, "cubanness" in state-sponsored art, and the U.S. resurgence of race versus the myth of the postracial era. Occasional special issues or sections focus on themes such as questioning the super-rich, the cultural politics of luxury and the work of Zygmunt Bauman. The writing links philosophical and political discussions with literary works, performance media, and current online communication. The articles are engaging and provide a unique approach to the integration of culture with contemporary local, national, and transnational political issues. This journal will interest academics and students, especially in political science, but also in related areas of the social sciences, humanities, and fine arts.

1511. ***Cultural Sociology.*** [ISSN: 1749-9755] 2007. q. USD 1000 (print & online eds.)). Ed(s): David Inglis, Matthias Zick Varul. Sage Publications Ltd., 1 Oliver's Yard, 55 City Rd, London, EC1Y 1SP, United Kingdom; info@sagepub.com; https://www.sagepub.com/. Adv. Sample. Refereed. Reprint: PSC. *Indexed:* A22, E01, IBSS, MLA-IB. *Bk. rev.:* 4-5, essay length. *Aud.:* Ac.

This journal merges the fields of sociology and cultural studies into a specialized publication. An official publication of the British Sociological Association, *Cultural Sociology* aims to "consolidate, develop, and promote the arena of sociological understandings of culture." The editors and contributors are primarily from universities in the United Kingdom, with some from the United States and Europe; however, the journal deals with sociology and culture internationally. Articles cover such topics as popular music consumption practices, marketing of food products, cultural interaction in feminist bookstores, human trafficking and media narratives, and aging and barriers to cultural participation. Special issues appear from time to time focusing on subjects such as youth, music, and do-it-yourself careers or producing and consuming inequality. Although scholarship in culture and sociology has been published in many other types of journals, this publication provides a gathering place for research and discourse in this expanding area. Scholars in sociology, cultural studies, gender studies, post-colonial studies, art history, history, and literary and film studies will find this journal of great interest.

1512. ***Cultural Studies.*** Formerly (until 1987): *Australian Journal of Cultural Studies.* [ISSN: 0950-2386] 1983. bi-m. GBP 898 (print & online eds.)). Ed(s): Bryan Behrenshausen, Lawrence Grossberg. Routledge, 4 Park Sq, Milton Park, Abingdon, OX14 4RN, United Kingdom; book.orders@tandf.co.uk; http://www.tandfonline.com. Illus., adv. Sample. Refereed. Vol. ends: Oct. Reprint: PSC. *Indexed:* A01, A22, AmHI, BRI, C45, Chicano, E01, IBSS, MLA-IB, P61, SSA. *Bk. rev.:* 2-6, essay length. *Aud.:* Ac.

In defining the term culture inclusively, *Cultural Studies* seeks to promote and challenge the non-traditional within this interdisciplinary area. Its aim is to "explore the relation between cultural practices, everyday life, material, economic, political, geographical and historical contexts." This journal emphasizes race, class, and gender, while addressing major questions of community, identity, agency, and change. Contributors are mainly from the United States, the United Kingdom, and Australia, with occasional articles by authors from other countries. Each issue contains several original articles, with book reviews included in some issues. Frequently, special issues concentrate on single themes including Chinese cultural studies, racism after recognition, cultural production in Putin's Russia, and mediating affect. Other individual articles have explored such topics as genetically modified foods (GMOs), surveillance art, participatory art as spectacle, the history of the telephone and digital payment technologies, and racial accountabilities and police actions against African Americans. *Cultural Studies* will be of interest to scholars and students seeking dynamic, international coverage of cultural issues.

1513. ***Cultural Studies - Critical Methodologies.*** [ISSN: 1532-7086] 2001. bi-m. USD 308. Ed(s): Norman K Denzon. Sage Publications, Inc., 2455 Teller Rd, Thousand Oaks, CA 91320; info@sagepub.com; http://www.sagepub.com. Adv. Sample. Refereed. Reprint: PSC. *Indexed:* A01, A22, AmHI, E01, IBSS, MLA-IB, P61. *Aud.:* Ac.

While other titles concentrate on the wider range of cultural studies or the specific area of cultural critique, this journal combines both, with an emphasis on "moving methods talk to the forefront." Articles that combine "critical moral discourse, experimental, interpretative methodology, and cultural criticism" are the aim of contributions to this journal. Many issues are composed of several original articles on themes such as Latina adolescence and modes of resistance, refugee stories, the politics of silence, and media culture and the politics of fear. Special issues have also been published on hybrid bodies, transdisciplinary travels of ethnography, and the concept of outsideness especially among girls of color. Analysis of popular culture, media, and new communication technologies is also integral to the writing in this publication. *Cultural Studies - Critical Methodologies* blends methodology with the full expanse of cultural studies and cultural critique to make a vital and engaging addition to the literature in this interdisciplinary field.

1514. ***Culture Unbound: journal of current cultural research.*** [ISSN: 2000-1525] 2009. a. Free. Linkoeping University Electronic Press, Linkoeping Universitet, Linkoeping, 58183, Sweden; ep@ep.liu.se; http://www.ep.liu.se. Refereed. *Bk. rev.:* Occasional. *Aud.:* Ac.

Based in Sweden, this journal combines scholarship from the academic units of the Advanced Cultural Studies Institute of Sweden and the Department of Culture Studies at Linkoeping University. The aim of this publication is to offer "border-crossing cultural research, including cultural studies as well as other interdisciplinary and transnational currents." Each issue is composed of a thematic section with some issues including an open section or independent article on varying topics. Thematic sections range from the unbound brain to critical future studies and from media modernity in India to new methods of knowledge production. Other articles focus on topics such as emotions and career insecurity, the adaptation of books into films and video games, and reading/writing gestures. Contributors are primarily Swedish, European, and U.S. scholars. This open-access journal provides an international forum for cultural research and scholarship.

1515. ***East Asian Journal of Popular Culture.*** [ISSN: 2051-7084] 2015. 2x/yr. GBP 184. Ed(s): Kate Taylor-Jones, John Berra. Intellect Ltd., The Mill, Parnall Rd, Fishponds, Bristol, BS16 3JG, United Kingdom; info@intellectbooks.com; http://www.intellectbooks.co.uk/. Refereed. *Indexed:* BRI, MLA-IB. *Bk. rev.:* 1-2, essay length. *Aud.:* Ac.

From cartoons and toys to fashion and sports, popular culture continues to be on the rise in East Asian countries. This multidisciplinary journal features articles on both local and global trends in the popular culture of Japan, China, Korea, and other area countries. Editors and authors are from universities in the region as well as from the United Kingdom, United States, and Europe. Recent articles explore contemporary topics such as Taiwanese popular culture, Japanese subcultural street styles, German and Chinese Internet censorship, and adult anime/manga fans in Australia. Some articles cover historical topics such as comparative texts on the Long March, images of the Demilitarized Zone (DMZ) and translation in museum exhibitions. Others focus on digital and performance art, folk music, cinema, and technology. While appealing to scholars of popular culture as an academic discipline, this journal also will draw readers interested in current and emerging aspects of cultural interaction with East Asia.

1516. ***European Journal of Cultural and Political Sociology.*** [ISSN: 2325-4823] 2014. 4x/yr. GBP 490 (print & online eds.)). Ed(s): Ricca Edmondson, Charles Turner. Routledge, 4 Park Sq, Milton Park, Abingdon, OX14 4RN, United Kingdom; subscriptions@tandf.co.uk; http://www.tandfonline.com. Refereed. Reprint: PSC. *Bk. rev.:* 2-4, essay length. *Aud.:* Ac.

Published under the auspices of the European Sociological Association, this journal complements the association's long-running publication *European Societies.* This venue aims to publish writings that "explore the relationship between culture and politics through a sociological lens." Editors and authors range from western and eastern Europe and the United Kingdom to Australia, Japan, Israel, and South America. Each issue includes original articles on topics ranging from global corporations and local variations to vital employees and entitlement, and from Italian collective identity to the governance technique of non-enforcement. Occasionally, a special issue is published on a theme such as patterns of power and the sociological imagination, or world culture and global/

local entanglements. Reviews of a few recent books are also included in each issue. This journal will be of interest especially to researchers in sociology, and also to a range of academic readers in the social sciences.

1517. ***Futures: the journal of policy, planning and futures studies.*** [ISSN: 0016-3287] 1968. 10x/yr. EUR 1644. Elsevier Ltd, The Boulevard, Langford Lane, Oxford, OX5 1GB, United Kingdom; customerserviceau@elsevier.com; http://www.elsevier.com. Illus., adv. Sample. Refereed. Microform: PQC. *Indexed:* A22, BRI, C45, ISTA, MLA-IB, P61, SSA. *Bk. rev.:* 2-4, 500-1,500 words. *Aud.:* Ac, Sa.

This journal covers future studies from a cultural, social, scientific, economic, political, and environmental perspective. *Futures* has an international advisory board, but authors are mainly from the United States and the United Kingdom, with some from other countries. The papers that begin each issue cover such subjects as master planning, scenarios for sustainable futures, artificial intelligence evolution, and environmental factors informing decision making. Many volumes include special issues on such themes as the social and ethical dimensions of human colonization and socio-technical futures and the governance of innovation process. Shorter review articles, essays, and reports are included, along with book reviews. *Futures* aims "to examine possible and alternative futures of all human endeavors." This journal will appeal to scholars in the sciences and social sciences, and to members of the business and government communities.

Gender & Society. See Gender Studies section.

1518. ***History of Humanities.*** [ISSN: 2379-3163] 2016. s-a. USD 275 (print & online eds.)). Ed(s): Rens Bod, Thijs Weststeijn. University of Chicago Press, 1427 E 60th St, Chicago, IL 60637; custserv@press.uchicago.edu; http://www.press.uchicago.edu. Adv. Refereed. *Bk. rev.:* 7-10, essay length. *Aud.:* Ac.

Within the range of journals that comprise the humanities, this one is unique. As the official journal of the Society for the History of the Humanities, this publication "explores humanities across time and civilizations and takes a critical look at the concept of humanities itself." Researching the range of humanities fields from inception through transformation into formal university disciplines, and on to present day academia, is the aim of this journal. Several authors are from the University of Amsterdam, with others from European universities as well as the United States, Israel, South Africa, China, and Peru. Articles cover topics such as literary criticism in the modern humanities, the science of grammar, the bibliometric perspective on humanities history and the marginalization of the humanities. Thematic sections have been published on dehumanizing human beings, and the long-range perspective of the division between the humanities and sciences. The journal also includes essays "comparing scholarly practices across disciplines and comparing intellectual traditions in different cultures and civilizations." Researchers interested in broader historical concepts within humanities disciplines will find this journal engaging.

1519. ***History of the Human Sciences.*** [ISSN: 0952-6951] 1988. 5x/yr. USD 2290 (print & online eds.)). Ed(s): Felicity Callard, Angus Nicholls. Sage Publications Ltd., 1 Oliver's Yard, 55 City Rd, London, EC1Y 1SP, United Kingdom; info@sagepub.com; https://www.sagepub.com/. Illus., index, adv. Sample. Refereed. Reprint: PSC. *Indexed:* A01, A22, AmHI, BRI, E01, IBSS, MLA-IB, P61, SSA. *Bk. rev.:* 1-2, essay length. *Aud.:* Ac.

Based on a broad definition of the human sciences, this publication offers a range of scholarly articles that link research from traditional social science disciplines—including sociology, psychology, anthropology, and political science—with the areas of philosophy, literary criticism, art history, linguistics, psychoanalysis, aesthetics, and law. Some issues focus on one theme such as the future of the human sciences, psychotherapy in Europe, or subjectivity and universality in data analysis. Other issues cover a variety of topics from the resurgence of sociobiology to the artificially constructed society. Reviews of individual books as well as review essays appear regularly. Most contributors are academics from British, European, and U.S. institutions. This journal will appeal to scholars and advanced students who are interested in the complex relationships between social science and humanities research.

1520. ***Human Arenas: an interdisciplinary journal of psychology, culture, and meaning.*** [ISSN: 2522-5790] 2018. q. EUR 242 (print & online eds.)). Ed(s): Luca Tateo, Giuseppina Marsico. Springer International Publishing AG, Gewerbestr 11, Cham, 6330, Switzerland; http://www.springer.com. Refereed. *Bk. rev.:* Occasional. *Aud.:* Ac.

Focusing on the general theory of human psyche, this journal is organized around themes of human activity including movement, creation, and regulation. It provides an interdisciplinary publication to foster debate on what psychology can learn from other disciplines, and what other social and behavioral sciences can learn from psychology. Each issue contains several research articles on topics such as human relations, green living, artificial intelligence, the asymmetric in relationships, reintegration of veterans, and non-western worldviews. Articles are organized by arenas from origins to auto-ethnography, and from the body to movement. Occasional interviews or dialogues are included as are book reviews in some issues. This is a very scholarly journal that will appeal most to academics in psychology and philosophy.

1521. ***Humanities: the magazine of the national endowment for the humanities.*** [ISSN: 0018-7526] 1980. bi-m. USD 24 domestic; USD 33.60 foreign. Ed(s): Anna Maria Gillis, David Skinner. U.S. National Endowment for the Humanities, 400 7th St SW, Washington, DC 20506; info@neh.gov; http://www.neh.gov. Illus., index. Sample. Vol. ends: Nov/Dec. Microform: PQC. *Indexed:* A01, A22, AmHI, C45, MASUSE. *Aud.:* Hs, Ga, Ac.

This publication reports on the activities and projects sponsored by the U.S. government's National Endowment for the Humanities (NEH). *Humanities* includes articles on history, literature, music, art, film, theater, and photography. Contributors are academics, freelance writers, and NEH staffers and administrators. Articles cover such topics as Unicode and ancient Mayan hieroglyphs, recalling the nineteenth amendment for women's suffrage, the Atlantic world and early America, and the memoirs of Ulysses S. Grant. Specialized sections appear in many issues. "Statements" describes exhibits and programs sponsored by state humanities councils, and "Executive Function" profiles state humanities council leaders. "One Off" offers brief descriptions of NEH-funded publications and projects, while "Around the Nation" describes activities sponsored by state humanities councils. This publication includes engaging, well-illustrated articles that will appeal to general readers, and it offers information for scholars interested in obtaining NEH funding.

International Journal of Cultural Studies. See Globalization section.

1522. ***International Journal of Politics, Culture, and Society.*** Formerly (until 1987): *State, Culture, and Society.* [ISSN: 0891-4486] 1984. q. EUR 1457 (print & online eds.)). Ed(s): Patrick Baert. Springer New York LLC, 233 Spring St, New York, NY 10013; customerservice@springer.com; http://www.springer.com. Illus., index, adv. Sample. Refereed. Vol. ends: Summer. Microform: PQC. Reprint: PSC. *Indexed:* A01, A22, BRI, E01, IBSS, P61, SSA. *Bk. rev.:* Occasional, essay length. *Aud.:* Ac.

Scholarship derived from the "intersection of nations, states, civil societies, and global institutions and processes" forms the basis for this journal. Each issue includes essays and research articles on global political and economic issues, social classes and ethnic and religious groups, mass culture and communication and social transformation and cultural changes as they impact societies in general. Recent articles cover issues such as political icons, partisanship and its effects on public services, concepts used in digital war games, and NGOs use of social media in developing countries. Some issues focus on particular themes including faith and social activism in Europe, global sociology or space and mobility. Articles frequently cover political and social issues in the context of a particular nation or region. Essay-length book reviews, or a review and commentary section, are included in some issues. The journal's editorial board is centered at the New School for Social Research, but contributors are drawn from many countries. This publication will appeal to social scientists and scholars interested in societal change, especially as it relates to international political and cultural issues.

1523. ***International Review of Social History.*** Formerly (until 1956): *International Institute for Social History. Bulletin.* [ISSN: 0020-8590] 1937. 3x/yr. GBP 243. Ed(s): Aad Blok. Cambridge University Press, University Printing House, Shaftesbury Rd, Cambridge, CB2 8BS, United

Kingdom; journals@cambridge.org; https://www.cambridge.org/. Adv. Refereed. Circ: 1200. Microform: PQC. Reprint: PSC. *Indexed:* A22, BRI, E01, IBSS, MLA-IB, P61, SSA. *Bk. rev.:* 8-12, 1,000 words, some essay length. *Aud.:* Ac.

Sponsored by the International Institute for Social History, this journal publishes much of the leading scholarship in social history. Contributors are mainly from American and British institutions, with some from European countries. The research articles that begin each issue cover a range of countries, often European states, but also China, Japan, India, and South Africa. Many articles explore issues of workers' groups and labor history, but other topics from indigenous workers' dissent to equal pay for men and women, and from human rights campaigns to charismatic leadership are also included. Articles are in English, with occasional reviews in French or German. The extensive annotated bibliography of books on many aspects of social history is a vital section of this journal. The bibliography begins with a general section and is then subdivided by continent and country. The annual supplement is another strength of the journal; this special issue draws together articles on a major theme such as Brazilian labor history, free and unfree labor in Atlantic and Indian Ocean Port Cities from 1700-1850, or convicts and penal colonies in the nineteenth and twentieth centuries. This journal will appeal to historians and social scientists, especially scholars with an interest in labor history.

1524. *Internet Histories: digital technology, culture and society.* [ISSN: 2470-1475] 2017. 4x/yr. GBP 266 (print & online eds.)). Ed(s): Niels Bruegger, Naglaa Abdallah. Taylor & Francis Inc., 530 Walnut St, Ste 850, Philadelphia, PA 19106; enquiries@taylorandfrancis.com; http://www.tandfonline.com. Refereed. *Indexed:* A01. *Bk. rev.:* 3-4 in most issues. *Aud.:* Ac.

Although research on the evolution and development of the digital world has been published in a variety of journals, this journal aims to bring together the range of "cultural, social, political and technological histories of the internet and associated digital cultures." The editors are drawn from Europe, Canada, and Australia, while the editorial board includes scholars from the United States, United Kingdom, South Korea, and South Africa. Each issue contains several articles on topics such as search engines, network neutrality, cybercrime, online communities, photo sharing on Instagram, online archives of primary sources for historians, web archives, Arpanet history, evolution of Facebook, development of streaming, and digital cultural history in various countries and regions of the world. In addition to the research articles, this journal also contains interviews along with book and film reviews. For scholars, students, and tech enthusiasts, this journal will provide a lens to the past and a rich source from which to explore the future of the digital world.

1525. *Jeunesse: Young People, Texts, Cultures.* Formerly (until 2009): *Canadian Children's Literature.* [ISSN: 1920-2601] 1975. s-a. Ed(s): Larissa Wodtke. University of Winnipeg, Centre for Research in Young People's Texts and Culture, 515 Portage Ave, Winnipeg, MB R3B 2E9, Canada; crytc@uwinnipeg.ca; http://crytc.uwinnipeg.ca/home.php. Refereed. *Indexed:* A22, BRI, C37, CBRI, E01, MLA-IB. *Bk. rev.:* Review essays, 3-10 per issue. *Aud.:* Ac.

The aim of this journal is to provide scholarly articles on "cultural productions for, by, and about young people." Both interdisciplinary and international, *Jeunesse* publishes articles in English and French. This publication covers children's and young adult literature, art, and film, including material and digital culture focusing on the roles of "the child." Each issue has several articles on subjects ranging from storytelling memories of street youth to young people and digital piracy to bisexual representation in young adult literature. Some issues include a special section on topics such as the cultures of children and youth or Canadian youth culture in transnational perspective. A forum with divergent views on a common topic appears in various issues. Each issue also includes lengthy review essays on one or more works covering topics such as strength and disability, adolescent sexuality, or children in pop music. *Jeunesse* offers a fresh perspective on international children's and young-adult literature and culture. This journal will appeal most to scholars of children's literature, although some articles will also be of interest to librarians and elementary school teachers.

1526. *Journal for Early Modern Cultural Studies.* [ISSN: 1531-0485] 2001. s-a. USD 80 (Individuals, USD 35). Ed(s): Mark Kelly. University of Pennsylvania Press, 3905 Spruce St, Philadelphia, PA 19104; journals@pobox.upenn.edu; http://www.upenn.edu/pennpress. Adv. Sample. Refereed. *Indexed:* A22, AmHI, BRI, E01, MLA-IB. *Bk. rev.:* 2, 1,000-1,500 words. *Aud.:* Ac.

Although other publications in cultural studies also focus on history, this journal specializes in the era from the late fifteenth to the late nineteenth centuries. As the official publication of the Group for Early Modern Cultural Studies, this publication combines scholarship from many areas of the humanities, social sciences, and area studies with research on gender, colonialism and post-colonialism, race and empire, transnationalism, and globalization. Editors and contributors are largely from U.S. and Canadian universities. Recent articles focus on topics from poor relief in England and France in the twelfth to eighteenth centuries, to British writing on the mechanization of the cotton industry in the eighteenth century to narratives of sleep and biopolitics. Occasional issues focus on an overall theme such as political theology, China in early modern cultural studies, or alternative histories of the East Asia Company. This journal will be of interest to scholars in many disciplines whose research centers on the early modern time period.

1527. *Journal of Aesthetic Education.* [ISSN: 0021-8510] 1966. q. USD 166 (print & online eds.)). Ed(s): Pradeep Dhillon. University of Illinois Press, 1325 S Oak St, MC-566, Champaign, IL 61820; uipress@uillinois.edu; http://www.press.uillinois.edu. Illus., index, adv. Refereed. Vol. ends: Winter. Microform: MIM; PQC. *Indexed:* A22, A51, AmHI, BAS, BRI, CBRI, E01, ERIC, MLA-IB. *Bk. rev.:* 3-5, 500-1,500 words. *Aud.:* Ac.

Journal of Aesthetic Education draws together the threads of philosophy, theory, and pedagogy as applied to the full range of the arts. The journal provides a forum to explore issues in aesthetic education, both in instructional settings and in society at large. Contributors cover issues of arts and humanities instruction, aesthetics and new communications media, environmental aesthetics, and philosophy in aesthetics. Individual issues include articles on theory and philosophy, and analysis of specific works in literature, art, or music. Recent issues feature articles on such topics as music education and social change, core aspects of dance, the art of body movement, and the avant-garde in arts education. Special issues have covered themes from children's literature to pragmatism in aesthetics and arts education curriculum projects. Some issues contain commentary sections with brief essays or responses to earlier articles. This journal will appeal to scholars and artists, as well as to teachers and administrators in arts education.

1528. *The Journal of Aesthetics and Art Criticism.* [ISSN: 0021-8529] 1941. q. GBP 258. Ed(s): Robert Stecker, Theodore Gracyk. Wiley-Blackwell Publishing, Inc., 111 River St, Hoboken, NJ 07030; http://onlinelibrary.wiley.com. Illus., index, adv, Sample. Refereed. Vol. ends: Fall. Microform: MIM; PQC. Reprint: PSC. *Indexed:* A01, A06, A22, A51, AmHI, BAS, BRI, CBRI, E01, F01, IIMP, IIPA, MLA-IB. *Bk. rev.:* 7-15, 1,000-2,000 words. *Aud.:* Ac.

The philosophy of art from a wide-ranging perspective combined with aesthetics within and beyond the arts is the focus of *The Journal of Aesthetics and Art Criticism.* The journal covers both fine and decorative arts, as well as film, photography, performance, and popular culture. Most issues include several research articles, occasional discussion segments, and book reviews. Articles cover theoretical and philosophical research on aesthetics, as well as critical analyses of specific works and artists, historical treatment of the arts, and social and political questions related to aesthetics. Some issues focus on one theme, such as environmentalism and aesthetics or race and aesthetics. Individual articles cover such topics as realism in social media, culinary authenticity, video games as interactive fiction, and socially engaged art. As the journal of the American Society for Aesthetics, this publication will appeal to scholars in the philosophy of the arts, to critics of art, and more broadly to students of aesthetics.

Journal of American Ethnic History. See Multicultural Studies section.

1529. ***Journal of American Studies.*** Formerly (until 1967): *British Association for American Studies. Bulletin.* [ISSN: 0021-8758] 1956. q. GBP 525. Ed(s): Bevan Sewell, Celeste-Marie Bernier. Cambridge University Press, University Printing House, Shaftesbury Rd, Cambridge, CB2 8BS, United Kingdom; journals@cambridge.org; https://www.cambridge.org/. Illus., index, adv. Refereed. Circ: 2000. Vol. ends: Dec. Microform: PQC. Reprint: PSC. *Indexed:* A01, A22, AmHI, BRI, CBRI, E01, IBSS, MLA-IB, P61. *Bk. rev.:* 30-40, 250-750 words. *Aud.:* Ac.

American Studies from an international perspective is the focus of this publication. United States literary works, politics, history, and economics are covered, along with art, music, film, and popular culture. Most contributors are from British universities, although some articles are by U.S. and European authors. Many articles explore American literary classics or historical topics, but cross-disciplinary and comparative cultural studies are also included. Recent articles cover such subjects as interwar Germany through the lens of African American reporters, domestic debate over the Vietnam War, the air war in Korean war films and discerning states of emergency. Some issues feature special forums focusing on topics including the global history of American evangelicalism or the U.S. South and the Black Atlantic. Each issue includes many book reviews, and review essays appear in some issues. The journal is sponsored by the British Association for American Studies. This journal will be of interest to scholars of American Studies in the United States and the United Kingdom as well as internationally.

1530. ***Journal of British Studies.*** Incorporates (1969-2005): *Albion.* [ISSN: 0021-9371] 1961. q. GBP 229. Ed(s): Holger Hoock. Cambridge University Press, 1 Liberty Plaza, Fl 20, New York, NY 10004; journals@cambridge.org; https://www.cambridge.org. Illus., index, adv. Sample. Refereed. Vol. ends: Oct. Microform: PQC. Reprint: PSC. *Indexed:* A01, A22, AmHI, BRI, IBSS, MLA-IB. *Bk. rev.:* 3-5, essay length. *Aud.:* Ac.

Covering British culture from the Middle Ages to the present, this publication includes a range of research articles, review essays, and book reviews. Contributors to the journal include authors from the United States, Britain, Canada, and Australia, as well as a number of other countries. Articles most often cover British history in combination with politics, economics, religion, and social issues. In addition, the journal includes articles on comparative history, gender and cultural studies, the arts, and health and disease. Geographically, most writing in this journal deals with England; however, some articles focus on Ireland and areas of the former British Empire. Recent articles cover such topics as democracy and the British monarchy, 19th century British public schools, the Northern Irish "Troubles," French and Spanish slave law, and dueling and Victorian masculinity. A new column titled, "One British Thing" includes short pieces on items of material culture including clay pipes and fifth century ceramic beakers. Sponsored by the North American Conference on British Studies, this journal will be of significant interest internationally to students and scholars of the culture, society, and history of the United Kingdom.

1531. ***Journal of Cultural Economy.*** [ISSN: 1753-0350] 2008. 6x/yr. GBP 776 (print & online eds.)). Ed(s): Melinda Cooper, Michael Pryke. Routledge, 4 Park Sq, Milton Park, Abingdon, OX14 4RN, United Kingdom; subscriptions@tandf.co.uk; http://www.tandfonline.com. Adv. Sample. Refereed. Reprint: PSC. *Indexed:* A22, E01, MLA-IB. *Bk. rev.:* Occasional essays. *Aud.:* Ac.

The Economic and Social Research Council's Centre for Research on Socio-Cultural Change is the sponsoring organization for this journal, which aims to be the "premiere forum for debating the relations between culture, economy and the social in all their manifestations." Based at the Open University in the United Kingdom, other members of the editorial board are from universities in the United Kingdom, Australia, the United States, and Canada, as well as Europe and South America. Most issues include several scholarly articles, along with review essays, book reviews and commentaries. Special sections are published occasionally on topics such as intersections of cultural studies and finance or mundane market matters. Individual articles cover topics ranging from money and power in the capitalist economy to children's market researchers, and from personalizing prices to workfulness versus digital distractions. This publication will be of interest to scholars and students of economics and social sciences, as well as cultural aspects of these disciplines.

1532. ***Journal of European Popular Culture.*** [ISSN: 2040-6134] 2010. 2x/yr. GBP 186 (print & online eds.)). Ed(s): Owen Evans, Cristina Johnston. Intellect Ltd., The Mill, Parnall Rd, Fishponds, Bristol, BS16 3JG, United Kingdom; info@intellectbooks.com; http://www.intellectbooks.co.uk/. Adv. Sample. Refereed. Reprint: PSC. *Indexed:* AmHI. *Aud.:* Ac.

The increase in popular culture worldwide has brought about a growing interest in publications like the *Journal of European Popular Culture.* This journal "investigates the creative cultures of Europe, present and past," from literature, music, and art to film, media, and drama. Each issue contains scholarly articles on topics such as food culture as related to the Slow Food movement, Italian media coverage of immigrants, the rise of Bollywood films and Glamrock musicians influencing European youth culture. Special issues have appeared on the overall theme of Thatcherism relating the politics of Margaret Thatcher to popular music and culture. There are also articles on specific films and writers. Contributors are faculty members from British, Canadian, and European universities. As a complement to the long-running U.S. *Journal of Popular Culture,* this publication will appeal to academic audiences, as well as to readers interested in popular culture from the European perspective.

1533. ***Journal of Popular Culture.*** [ISSN: 0022-3840] 1967. bi-m. GBP 369. Ed(s): Ann E Larabee. Wiley-Blackwell Publishing, Inc., 111 River St, Hoboken, NJ 07030; http://onlinelibrary.wiley.com. Illus., index, adv. Sample. Refereed. Vol. ends: Spring. Microform: PQC. Reprint: PSC. *Indexed:* A01, A22, AmHI, BAS, BRI, C45, CBRI, Chicano, E01, F01, IBSS, IIMP, IIPA, MLA-IB, SD. *Bk. rev.:* 15-20, 100-500 words. *Aud.:* Ga, Ac.

The articles in this journal explore popular culture and its effects on people and society as a whole. The journal brings to the forefront the aspects of "low culture" that fascinate and consume so much of contemporary U.S. and global society. Each issue contains several articles on a wide variety of topics ranging from animation to professional wrestling to working class heroes, from Facebook and neoliberalism to the American Girl phenomenon, and from indigenous graphic narratives to mental illness in young adult literature. Occasionally special issues are published on themes such as global fashions and revisiting adventure. In addition to its interdisciplinary coverage of U.S. culture, the *Journal of Popular Culture* also includes international coverage. Recent articles focus on Chinese cinema, romance novels in India, and Australian film and television in World War I. This journal is the official publication of the Popular Culture Association. Scholars studying popular literature, film, and television will be interested in this publication, as will students and general readers who are fans of pop culture.

1534. ***Journal of Posthuman Studies: philosophy, technology, media.*** [ISSN: 2472-4513] 2017. s-a. USD 176 (print & online eds.)). Ed(s): Stefan L Sorgner. Pennsylvania State University Press, 820 N University Dr, University Support Bldg 1, Ste C, University Park, PA 16802; info@psupress.org; http://www.psupress.org. Adv. Refereed. *Aud.:* Ac.

This journal aims to analyze "what it is to be human in an age of rapid technological, scientific, cultural and social evolution." Theories of posthumanism along with transhumanism are examined through the lens of a host of disciplines from anthropology, medicine, philosophy and media to environment, sociology and literary/visual arts. Research articles explore such topics as humans syncing with artificial intelligence, human enhancement and species limitations, transhumanist political parties and niche party theory, procedural dimensions in moral decision making, implant technology, evolutionary anthropology, and gene analysis privacy issues. The Ewha Institute for the Humanities at Ewha Womans University in Seoul, Korea, sponsors this publication. This journal will appeal to researchers in bio and medical ethics, as well as philosophy and the entire range of literary, cultural, gender, disability, and queer studies.

1535. ***Journal of Science & Popular Culture.*** [ISSN: 2059-9072] 2018. s-a. GBP 186; USD 279. Ed(s): William Lott, Steven Gil. Intellect Ltd., The Mill, Parnall Rd, Fishponds, Bristol, BS16 3JG, United Kingdom; info@intellectbooks.com; http://www.intellectbooks.co.uk/. Refereed. *Aud.:* Ac.

The interaction of traditionally separate areas of science and culture is brought together in this new journal. Launched by an editorial board of primarily Australian, U.K., and U.S. scholars, this journal aims to establish a forum for the analysis and interpretation of scientific information as it relates to popular culture. At the same time, the journal also publishes emerging scholarship in which popular culture influences the sciences. Recent articles address such topics as science fiction, how television and the film industry portrays scientists and their work, gender in science books for children, art and science collaboration, wildlife documentary films, and how Hollywood presents physics. Each issue includes several research articles along with additional features such as essays, reviews, interviews, and creative works. This journal will appeal to both academics as well as general audiences with an interest in science and its contemporary forms of popular expression.

1536. *Journal of the History of Ideas.* [ISSN: 0022-5037] 1940. q. USD 129 (print & online eds.) Individuals, USD 47 (print & online eds.)). Ed(s): Hilary Plum. University of Pennsylvania Press, 3905 Spruce St, Philadelphia, PA 19104; journals@pobox.upenn.edu; http://www.upenn.edu/pennpress. Illus., index, adv. Sample. Refereed. Vol. ends: Oct/Dec. Microform: PMC; PQC. *Indexed:* A01, A22, AmHI, BAS, BRI, CBRI, E01, IBSS, MLA-IB. *Aud.:* Ga, Ac, Sa.

Intellectual history, very broadly defined, is the focus of this publication. The journal aims to cover a wide range of geographical areas, time periods, and methods, encompassing philosophy, literature, the social sciences, religion, and the arts. Most articles deal with philosophical writings, historiography, theology, scientific theories, or literary works. Each issue contains several scholarly articles that cover such topics as Victorian conflict between science and religion, Darwin's theory of moral sentiments, Jewish influence on medieval Christian thought, and the language of political science in early modern Europe. Special sections or forums appear occasionally on themes including Christianity and human rights and Latin American revolutions of independence. Contributors to the journal are academics, mostly historians, with some authors from the fields of philosophy, classics, and literature. This journal, sponsored by the Society for the History of Ideas, contains superior research and writing that will appeal to scholars in several areas of the humanities.

1537. *Journal of Transnational American Studies.* [ISSN: 1940-0764] 2009. s-a. Free. Ed(s): Erika Doss, Nina Morgan. University of California, eScholarship, California Digital Library, 415 20th St, 4th Fl, Oakland, CA 94612; info@escholarship.org; https://www.escholarship.org. Refereed. *Indexed:* MLA-IB. *Aud.:* Ac.

Sponsored by the University of California at Santa Barbara's American Cultures and Global Contexts Center and Stanford University's Program in American Studies, the *Journal of Transnational American Studies* provides a forum for scholars in American Studies to "bring together innovative transnational work from diverse but often disconnected sites in the US and abroad." Each issue includes several original articles, a "Forward" section and a "Reprise" section. The scholarly articles in each issue span a wide range of topics from archaeological representations of Maya statues to African American black nationalists in Haiti, and from FBI surveillance of the Cuban Venceremos Brigade to the development of the Zionist movement. Special forums appear on occasion covering themes such as globalization and American literature, and Florida, France and the Francophone world. The "Forward" section offers excerpts from new or upcoming publications that point to new developments in the field. The "Reprise" section provides reprinted online access to important works in the field. This journal expands both the scope of American Studies and open access to new scholarship on transnationalism.

1538. *Journal of Urban Cultural Studies.* [ISSN: 2050-9790] 2014. 3x/yr. GBP 209 (print & online eds.)). Ed(s): Benjamin Fraser. Intellect Ltd., The Mill, Parnall Rd, Fishponds, Bristol, BS16 3JG, United Kingdom; info@intellectbooks.com; http://www.intellectbooks.co.uk/. Adv. Refereed. Reprint: PSC. *Indexed:* MLA-IB. *Aud.:* Ac.

Within the field of urban studies, this journal's aim is to combine the aspects of the humanities and social sciences in order to better understand the culture(s) of cities. Articles in this journal draw together the arts, from literature and music to film and digital art, and social aspects of cities, from landscape and architecture to city planning and transportation. Editors and authors are primarily from U.S., Canadian, and British universities, but the journal is international in scope, with coverage of cities from New York and Pittsburgh to Barcelona and Tokyo. Topics covered range from populist art to digital personal space and from skyscrapers to images of the global earth in visual culture. This journal will appeal primarily to scholars in the humanities and urban studies, but also will attract readers with interests in cities and their cultural representation.

1539. *Journal of War and Culture Studies.* [ISSN: 1752-6272] 2008. q. GBP 428 (print & online eds.)). Routledge, 4 Park Sq, Milton Park, Abingdon, OX14 4RN, United Kingdom; subscriptions@tandf.co.uk; http://www.tandfonline.com. Adv. Sample. Reprint: PSC. *Indexed:* AmHI, MLA-IB. *Aud.:* Ac.

The international and multidisciplinary study of war and its cultural impact is the focus of this publication. The Group for War and Cultural Studies, based at the University of Westminster, publishes the journal. Each issue includes several scholarly articles on a wide range of topics related to armed conflict and the many people it involves. Many issues focus on a specific theme, such as war-related tourism, nursing in World War I, remote warfare, and memory and guilt in twentieth-century Europe. Some articles deal with literary works including drone fiction, civil defense magazines, and poetry from World War II. Other writings focus on specific groups such as Polish children as refugees and draftees versus volunteers. Other studies focus on war films, war correspondents, members of the resistance, and bonding among fighting men. Collections with an emphasis on military science and history will find this journal of interest.

1540. *Memory Studies.* [ISSN: 1750-6980] 2008. q. Ed(s): Andrew Hoskins. Sage Publications Ltd., 1 Oliver's Yard, 55 City Rd, London, EC1Y 1SP, United Kingdom; info@sagepub.com; https://www.sagepub.com/. Adv. Sample. Refereed. Reprint: PSC. *Indexed:* A22, E01. *Bk. rev.:* 4-6 (in most issues), 800-1,000 words. *Aud.:* Ac.

How individuals, groups, societies, and nations remember events and aspects of history is a growing area of scholarly research. The journal *Memory Studies* brings together social, cultural, and political scholarship on remembering and forgetting. It is international in coverage, and its editors and editorial board are largely from the United Kingdom, the United States, and Australia, although scholars from other countries are also included. Each issue offers several scholarly articles on one or more topics or problems. Thematic issues appear often on subjects such as memories of joy, the early modern in memory and the transnational effect on cultural memory studies. Articles have been published on subjects varying from the 9/11 museum, to earthquake disaster memories and from resilience in memories of the Spanish civil war to memory as revealed in obituaries of U.S. veterans. Book reviews appear in each issue, along with occasional conference reviews and roundtable discussions. Although primarily for an academic audience, this journal will also appeal to non-specialists with an interest in how and why things are remembered.

1541. *Middle West Review.* [ISSN: 2372-5664] 2014. s-a. USD 103 domestic; USD 115 foreign. Ed(s): Jon Lauck. University of Nebraska Press, 1111 Lincoln Mall, Lincoln, NE 68588; journals@unl.edu; https://www.nebraskapress.unl.edu. Refereed. *Bk. rev.:* 20-25, essay length. *Aud.:* Ac, Ga.

Reinvigorating the study of the American Midwest is a major aim of this journal along with "providing a forum for scholars and non-scholars alike to explore the contested meanings of Midwestern identity, history, geography, society, culture, and politics." Editors and authors are mainly from universities in the region with some freelance writers included. Although not an official publication of any professional organization, the Midwestern History Association supports the objectives and priorities of the review. Topics range from essays on regionalism and the heartland to research articles on politics and Union soldiers after the Civil War, the growth of women suffrage in the late nineteenth and early twentieth centuries, and punk rock in the 1980s. Special issues have been published on regional studies across the United States along with an extensive symposium on Midwestern history. This journal will appeal to both an academic and a general audience with interest in the Midwest region and its influence on the country overall.

1542. ***The Midwest Quarterly: a journal of contemporary thought.*** Supersedes (in 1959): *The Educational Leader.* [ISSN: 0026-3451] 1959. q. Ed(s): James B M Schick. Pittsburg State University, English Department, 406b Grubbs Hall, 1701 S Broadway, Pittsburg, KS 66762; http://www.pittstate.edu/department/english/. Index. Refereed. Vol. ends: Summer. Microform: PQC. *Indexed:* A01, A22, AmHI, BAS, BRI, MLA-IB. *Bk. rev.:* 2-5, 500-750 words. *Aud.:* Ac.

For 60 years, *The Midwest Quarterly* has published both writings of literary analysis and many original poems. Despite its title, the content of this journal has no geographical limitations. It focuses on "analytical and speculative treatment of its topics, rather than heavily documented research studies." Most articles analyze specific literary themes and works, although some cover philosophical, social, and historical topics. Articles exploring the writings of major authors from Geoffrey Chaucer and Alexander Pope to Toni Morrison and Cormac McCarthy are included, as are articles on specific works of art, and articles on specific films or film genres. Other articles cover such subjects as teaching history through a local/regional lens, the Civil War in Washington, D.C., and conspiracy theories in literature. Poetry is a major emphasis of this journal, with each issue including several poems by well-known writers. This journal will appeal to poets as well as scholars in literature and the humanities in general.

1543. ***Modern Intellectual History.*** [ISSN: 1479-2443] 2004. 3x/yr. GBP 346. Ed(s): Samuel Moyn, Duncan Kelly. Cambridge University Press, University Printing House, Shaftesbury Rd, Cambridge, CB2 8BS, United Kingdom; journals@cambridge.org; https://www.cambridge.org/. Adv. Refereed. Reprint: PSC. *Indexed:* A22, E01. *Bk. rev.:* 3-5, essay length, c. 5,000 words. *Aud.:* Ac.

The historical meanings and origins of texts from 1650 to the present are the focus of this journal. European and American history are the major areas covered, but articles on transnational history of other regions are also included. The journal draws upon writings from a wide range of disciplines, including not only the social sciences and literature but also philosophy, religion, natural sciences, visual arts, communications, economic thought, and music. Each issue contains several scholarly articles, along with review essays and an occasional forum containing articles and commentary on a specific theme. Recent articles cover topics including the origins of neoliberal economic geography, nature of property in Napoleonic France, universal language and the question of global English, and the origins of digital humanities. This journal will be of interest to scholars in many disciplines, especially history, philosophy, and political science.

1544. ***Modernism/Modernity.*** [ISSN: 1071-6068] 1994. q. USD 195. Ed(s): John T Crawford, Caitlyn Doyle. The Johns Hopkins University Press, 2715 N Charles St, Baltimore, MD 21218; http://www.press.jhu.edu. Illus., index, adv. Sample. Refereed. Vol. ends: Sep. Reprint: PSC. *Indexed:* A01, A22, A51, AmHI, BRI, E01, MLA-IB, P61. *Bk. rev.:* 10-20, 500-1,500 words. *Aud.:* Ac.

This journal is an interdisciplinary forum for scholars of modernist studies to explore the theories, methods, philosophy, and history of the late-nineteenth through the twentieth centuries. The coverage of *Modernism/Modernity* is international and cross-disciplinary, encompassing primarily the arts and history, along with other areas of the humanities. Many articles are devoted to literary works of modernist writers such as Gertrude Stein, James Joyce, Ayn Rand, Henry James, and D. H. Lawrence. Other articles cover art, music, theater, philosophy, and politics. Recent articles focus on topics such as the Dada movement in Paris, modernism and money, London's avant-garde drama societies, the lack of health care for African Americans in the Jim Crow era, and traces of the Warsaw ghetto boundaries. This publication is the journal of the Modernist Studies Association. It will appeal to academics and literary scholars studying this time period in general and its prominent writers and trends.

1545. ***New Formations: a journal of culture/theory/politics.*** [ISSN: 0950-2378] 1987. 3x/yr. GBP 225 (Individuals, GBP 40). Ed(s): Jeremy Gilbert. Lawrence & Wishart Ltd, 99a Wallis Road, London, E9 5LN, United Kingdom; info@lwbooks.co.uk; http://www.lwbooks.co.uk. Illus., adv. Refereed. Vol. ends: Winter. *Indexed:* A01, A22, BRI, IBSS, MLA-IB. *Bk. rev.:* 2-3, 1,000-3,000 words. *Aud.:* Ac.

As the subtitle suggests, this journal uses the basis of cultural studies and examines it through the critical lens of theory and politics. The purpose of this publication is to explore and critically investigate contemporary culture, its ideology, its politics, and its impact. Each issue includes several articles and essays, many of which focus on one specific theme such as spaces and stories, memory, territory, and moods, posthumanist temporalities and righting feminism. Themes are explored from many points of view—from political and social to literary and philosophical. Articles range from modern applications of classical philosophy to popular culture essays. *New Formations* provides a fresh perspective on historical and contemporary international culture and politics. This journal will be of interest to cultural studies scholars and students, especially in the areas of politics and philosophy.

1546. ***Philosophy & Technology (Dordrecht, 1988).*** Former titles (until 2011): *Knowledge, Technology and Policy;* (until 1998): *Knowledge and Policy;* (until 1991): *Knowledge in Society.* [ISSN: 2210-5433] 1988. q. EUR 458 (print & online eds.)). Ed(s): Luciano Floridi. Springer Netherlands, Van Godewijckstraat 30, Dordrecht, 3311 GX, Netherlands; http://www.springer.com. Illus., index, adv. Refereed. Vol. ends: Winter. Reprint: PSC. *Indexed:* A01, A22, BRI, CompLI, E01, P61. *Bk. rev.:* 2-6, 500-1,000 words. *Aud.:* Ac, Sa.

The impact of technology on individuals and the larger global society continues to draw researchers and theorists. This journal focuses on "the conceptual nature and practical consequences of technologies," and the intersection of philosophy and technology. Each issue includes several scholarly articles, with sections of an issue often centered on a specific theme such as the ethics of biomedical big data analytics, governance of algorithms, cyber deterrence, financial technologies and rethinking art in the age of creative machines. Other research articles cover topics including the qualitative assessment of energy practices, individual versus group privacy, predictive data modeling and promoting biodiversity. Authors are primarily from universities in the United States, United Kingdom, and European countries, with a few from China, Japan, and India. This journal will be of interest to those teaching and researching ethical and philosophical issues of current and developing technologies.

1547. ***Public Culture.*** [ISSN: 0899-2363] 1988. 3x/yr. USD 404. Ed(s): Stephen Twilleym, Shamus Khan. Duke University Press, 905 W Main St, Durham, NC 27701; orders@dukeupress.edu; https://www.dukeupress.edu. Illus., index, adv. Refereed. Vol. ends: Spring. Reprint: PSC. *Indexed:* A01, A22, A47, AmHI, E01, IBSS, MLA-IB, P61, SSA. *Aud.:* Ac.

This journal focuses on cultural studies from a global perspective. *Public Culture* includes research articles and essays on cultural, social, and political issues, including contemporary media, urban issues, consumerism, and advertising. Individual articles and thematic sections cover such topics as human rights, secularism, security practices, street art, refugees and displaced peoples and rural transformation. Photos, drawings, and paintings often accompany articles, and photo-essays are included in most issues. Sponsored by New York University's Institute for Public Knowledge, *Public Culture* has won awards from the Council of Editors of Learned Journals four times. This publication's engaging articles will appeal to readers with an interest in globalization and the internationalization of cultural studies.

1548. ***R S F: The Russell Sage Foundation Journal of the Social Sciences.*** [ISSN: 2377-8253] 2015. q. Russell Sage Foundation, 112 E 64th St, New York, NY 10065; pubs@rsage.org; http://www.russellsage.org. Refereed. *Aud.:* Ga, Ac.

For more than a century the Russell Sage Foundation has been both a social sciences research center and a source of funding for scholars. In addition to the many books published by the foundation, the *RSF Journal of the Social Sciences* also provides an avenue for disseminating original empirical research studies. The journal is "designed to promote cross-disciplinary collaborations on timely issues of interest to academics, policymakers, and the public at large." A central theme is the focus of each issue. Topics range from the immigrant labor market to anti-poverty policies in the United States and from administrative data used for science and policy and regulating the underground gun market. Some issues focus on the long-term consequences of a specific law or report such as Kerner

Commission report on the 1967 race riots or the Coleman Report on educational inequality. The wide-ranging issues covered in this open-access journal will be of interest to the general public as well as researchers in public policy and socioeconomic change.

1549. ***Renaissance Quarterly.*** Incorporates (1954-1974): *Studies in the Renaissance;* Formerly (until 1967): *Renaissance News.* [ISSN: 0034-4338] 1954. q. USD 256 (print & online eds.)). Ed(s): W David Myers, Jessica Lynn Wolfe. Cambridge University Press, 1 Liberty Plaza, Fl 20, New York, NY 10004; journals@cambridge.org; https://www.cambridge.org. Illus., index, adv. Sample. Refereed. Vol. ends: Winter. Reprint: PSC. *Indexed:* A01, A06, A22, AmHI, BRI, CBRI, E01, MLA-IB. *Bk. rev.:* 40-50, 400-500 words. *Aud.:* Ac.

As the leading journal in Renaissance studies, this publication offers research studies, review essays, and a large section of book reviews. Literary works and themes are the focus of many articles, in addition to specialized studies in the arts, religion, or social aspects of the Renaissance. Recent articles cover such topics as ethnography in the Ottoman Greek world, the plague and violence in early modern Italy, Islam in seventeenth-century Europe, and exorcism and religious politics. Review essays and reviews of individual works make up nearly half of each issue. English-language works predominate, but some titles in French and Italian are included. As this is the official publication of the Renaissance Society of America, it includes reports of society meetings. This journal will interest scholars and students of the Renaissance, both for its scholarly articles and for its extensive reviews of current books.

1550. ***Representations.*** [ISSN: 0734-6018] 1983. q. USD 435 (print & online eds.)). Ed(s): Alan Tansman, Kent Puckett. University of California Press, Journals Division, 155 Grand Avenue, Ste 400, Oakland, CA 94612-3764; http://www.ucpress.edu/journals.php. Illus., index, adv. Refereed. Circ: 965. Microform: PQC. *Indexed:* A01, A22, A51, AmHI, E01, MLA-IB, P61. *Aud.:* Ac.

For more than 35 years, *Representations* has provided a multidisciplinary forum for scholars of literature, culture, and history. Most issues include several articles on a variety of topics, with occasional issues focusing on one particular theme. Many articles analyze aspects of a particular literary or philosophical writing, while other essays examine historical, political, or social issues. Recent articles explore topics ranging from Arabic literature to photographic landscape imagery, and from Victorian comparative religious writings to fact and fiction in historical films. The essays are written in a very engaging style and present original perspectives on literary, historical, or social subjects. Occasional special issues focus on such themes as visual history, the social life of pain, and exhibitions in contemporary history. Most contributors are scholars in English or other areas of the humanities. This journal will appeal to a wide range of academics, especially in literature and the humanities.

1551. ***The Sixties: a journal of history, politics and culture.*** [ISSN: 1754-1328] 2008. s-a. GBP 255 (print & online eds.)). Ed(s): Jeremy Varon, John McMillian. Routledge, 530 Walnut St, Ste 850, Philadelphia, PA 19106; enquiries@tandfonline.com; http://www.tandfonline.com. Sample. Refereed. Reprint: PSC. *Bk. rev.:* 8-10, 2-3 pages. *Aud.:* Ga, Ac.

The decade of the 1960s, along with the years just before and after, has come to symbolize a period of major social, political, and cultural change. This journal looks at the history and politics, arts, and media of the time, but also at the ways the 1960s continue to be construed in contemporary popular culture. Each issue begins with original research articles on topics including the birth of punk rock, the Americans for Democratic Action, Chicago's Latino politics, and Vietnam and the United States in the International War Crimes Tribunal, 1966-67. Although many articles focus on the United States, the journal has also included articles on British counterculture cinema, the Iranian student movement, and China's Red Guards. Special issues or forums are occasionally offered on topics such as transpacific alliances by activists and 50 years after 1968. Reviews of books, movies, and art exhibitions are also included. Some issues conclude with a section titled "Our Back Pages," which offers brief accounts of specific events or major people from this era. The journal will appeal to a wide range of scholars and students interested in the 1960s, especially in the disciplines of history, sociology, media, and politics.

Social Epistemology. See Philosophy section.

1552. ***Social Identities: journal for the study of race, nation and culture.*** [ISSN: 1350-4630] 1995. bi-m. GBP 1098 (print & online eds.)). Ed(s): Toby Miller, Pal Ahluwalia. Routledge, 4 Park Sq, Milton Park, Abingdon, OX14 4RN, United Kingdom; subscriptions@tandf.co.uk; http://www.tandfonline.com. Illus., index, adv. Sample. Refereed. Vol. ends: Dec. Reprint: PSC. *Indexed:* A01, A22, E01, IBSS, MLA-IB, P61, SSA. *Bk. rev.:* 1-3, essay length. *Aud.:* Ac.

Current international conflicts and hostilities underscore the critical role of race and ethnicity in contemporary societies. *Social Identities* provides a forum to address global racial, ethnic, and national issues in the context of social and cultural studies. Postmodernism and postcolonialism underscore much of the writing in this journal, as do the theories of how racial, national, and cultural identities are developed, changed, and affected by political and economic power. Each issue begins with several research articles on topics that range from the politics of birthright citizenship to globalization and diaspora communities, and from gentrification and multiculturalism to preserving the Palestinian Arab heritage in Israel. Special thematic issues are published occasionally on subjects such as war and visual technologies, race in urban life, Roma migrants in the European Union and multinational corporations and their effect on business and society. Contributors are mainly from U.S. and U.K. universities, with some writers from Latin America, the Middle East, and Africa. This journal will be of interest to scholars and students in many disciplines, especially politics, history, and sociology, but also humanities and the arts.

1553. ***Social Justice Research.*** [ISSN: 0885-7466] 1986. q. EUR 1257 (print & online eds.)). Ed(s): Kjell Tornblom, Ali D Kazemi. Springer New York LLC, 233 Spring St, New York, NY 10013; customerservice@springer.com; http://www.springer.com. Illus., index, adv. Refereed. Vol. ends: Dec. Microform: PQC. Reprint: PSC. *Indexed:* A01, A22, BAS, BRI, CJPI, E01, IBSS, P61, SSA. *Bk. rev.:* 2-3, essay length. *Aud.:* Ac.

The theory and practice of social justice has become an expanding area of contemporary social science research and scholarship. This journal aims to explore "the origins, structures and consequences of justice in human affairs." This publication takes a cross-disciplinary view of justice, covering social science and policy studies nationally and internationally. Each issue includes articles on the application of justice to such areas as environmental policies, age discrimination, human rights, income inequality, conflict of interest, and immigration policies. Recent articles cover topics such as the influence of skin color on local police practices, victimization across cultures, attacks on children in public schools and churches, and justice in management control systems. From time to time special issues are published on topics such as justice and neuroscience. The articles are well written and thoroughly documented. Contributors are mainly from U.S., Canadian, and European universities. As the official journal of the International Society for Justice Research, this publication will be of interest to scholars in the social sciences, particularly in political science, criminal justice, sociology, and law.

1554. ***Social Science History.*** [ISSN: 0145-5532] 1976. q. GBP 250. Ed(s): Jeffrey K. Beemer, Anne McCants. Cambridge University Press, 1 Liberty Plaza, Fl 20, New York, NY 10004; https://www.cambridge.org. Illus., index, adv. Sample. Refereed. Vol. ends: Winter. *Indexed:* A01, A22, BAS, E01, IBSS, P61, SSA. *Aud.:* Ac.

Social aspects of history have become a major focus of contemporary scholarship within the discipline. This publication focuses on interdisciplinary studies that combine history with the fields of sociology, economics, political science, anthropology, and geography. Articles "combine empirical research with theoretical work," and include comparative and methodological studies. Research covers the family, demography, economic issues, social classes, the labor force, religion, crime, and poverty. Each issue includes articles on such subjects as prohibition and local vs. state control of alcohol policies, U.S. racial inequality trends in the late twentieth century, lynching and racialized terrorism in the American South, African American mobility after emancipation, and cross-cultural migrations in Eurasia since 1500. Some issues publish special sections or symposia on such topics as Ottoman legacies of the state and the politics of diversity. Many articles focus on the United States and Europe with some articles covering history in other areas of the world. As the official journal of the Social Science History Association, this title will have broad appeal not only to historians, but also to scholars in related social science fields.

1555. *Social Science Information.* Formerly (until 1962): *International Social Science Council. Information.* [ISSN: 0539-0184] 1954. q. USD 1442 (print & online eds.)). Ed(s): Anna Rocha Perazzo. Sage Publications Ltd., 1 Oliver's Yard, 55 City Rd, London, EC1Y 1SP, United Kingdom; info@sagepub.com; https://www.sagepub.com/. Illus., index, adv. Sample. Refereed. Vol. ends: Dec. Reprint: PSC. *Indexed:* A22, A47, ASSIA, BAS, C45, E01, IBSS, MLA-IB, P61, SSA. *Aud.:* Ac.

With an international focus, this journal publishes research on theory and method in the social sciences, often emphasizing comparative and cross-cultural research. Articles on such subjects as the emotional roots of right-wing political populism, Facebook surveillance, consumer studies in critical social theory, social determinants of identity in communities, and data on historical climatology indicate the range of issues covered by *Social Science Information.* Occasionally, special issues or symposia are published on such topics as the historical sociology of scientific research instrumentation or the AnthropOcean. The text of articles may be in English or French. This journal is affiliated with the Maison des Sciences de l'Homme in Paris, and will appeal to researchers across a broad spectrum of the social sciences.

1556. *The Social Science Journal.* Formerly (until 1976): *The Rocky Mountain Social Science Journal.* [ISSN: 0362-3319] 1963. q. EUR 754. Pergamon Press, The Blvd, Langford Ln, E Park, Kidlington, OX5 1GB, United Kingdom; JournalsCustomerServiceEMEA@elsevier.com; http://www.elsevier.com. Illus., adv. Sample. Refereed. Reprint: PSC. *Indexed:* A01, A22, B01, BRI, Chicano, IBSS, P61, SSA. *Aud.:* Ac.

Although this publication began as a regional journal, over the past 50 years of its history *The Social Science Journal* has expanded into a national and international forum. This journal publishes research articles, statistical analyses, and case studies. Articles on society, history, economics, politics, and gender are included, along with coverage of social theories, research methods, and curricular issues. Representative articles have covered such subjects as social network effects on academic achievement, state trends in environmental public opinion, part-time employment and worker health, as well as cyberbullying, genetically modified foods, and graffiti and street art. Occasional special issues have covered economics, methods, and policy and social science contributions from South East Asia. As the official publication of the Western Social Science Association, this journal will be of interest to scholars and students in all geographical areas, and in many fields of the social sciences and beyond.

1557. *Social Science Quarterly (Online).* [ISSN: 1540-6237] 1920. 5x/yr. GBP 473. Ed(s): Kim Gaddie, Keith Gaddie. Wiley-Blackwell Publishing, Inc., 111 River St, Hoboken, NJ 07030; info@wiley.com; http://onlinelibrary.wiley.com. Illus. Refereed. *Bk. rev.:* 10-15, 500 words. *Aud.:* Ga, Ac.

For nearly a century, *Social Science Quarterly* has published top-quality research in a wide range of the social sciences from history, political science, and economics, to geography, sociology, and women's studies. The journal is international in scope and covers social and public policy issues, including both theoretical approaches and quantitative research. General-interest articles explore such topics as racial disparities in access to health care, Internet use and the digital divide, the impact of protest on elections in the United States, income levels and life expectancy, gender and the politics of marijuana and how arrests affect the fear of crime. In some issues, articles are grouped around a category such as politics, economics, race and ethnicity, education, media, comparative studies, environment and health, and social research. Special issues appear at least annually on topics such as immigration and changing politics, the selling of outer space, and comparative political communication. This journal offers superior coverage of contemporary social questions from a research standpoint. *Social Science Quarterly* is the official publication of the Southwestern Social Science Association. This journal will interest scholars and students, as well as policy researchers.

1558. *Social Science Research.* [ISSN: 0049-089X] 1972. bi-m. EUR 2035. Ed(s): Stephanie Moller. Academic Press, 3251 Riverport Ln, Maryland Heights, MO 63043; JournalCustomerService-usa@elsevier.com; http://www.elsevier.com/. Illus., index, adv. Sample. Refereed. Vol. ends: Dec. *Indexed:* A01, A22, BAS, Chicano, E01, IBSS, P61, SSA. *Aud.:* Ac.

Although qualitative studies have expanded in the social sciences, much of the current research in these fields remains quantitatively based. This journal covers quantitative research studies as well as methodologies in all areas of the social sciences. Empirical research is the focus of this publication, especially research that emphasizes cross-disciplinary issues or methods. Each issue offers lengthy articles in fields such as cross-national studies, environmental sociology, social inequalities, migration and immigration, gender studies, and political sociology. Recent articles cover such topics as economic growth and human rights, political activists, the effect of unemployment on psychological well-being, physical beauty and social mobility, and social network resources in later life. Contributors are drawn from U.S. colleges and universities, as well as from universities abroad and from private research groups. *Social Science Research* will appeal to scholars and upper-level students in the disciplines of sociology, economics, politics, criminal justice, and demography.

1559. *Social Text.* [ISSN: 0164-2472] 1979. q. USD 408. Ed(s): Marie Buck, Tavia Nyong'o. Duke University Press, 905 W Main St, Durham, NC 27701; orders@dukeupress.edu; https://www.dukeupress.edu. Illus., adv. Refereed. Vol. ends: Winter. Reprint: PSC. *Indexed:* A01, A22, AmHI, E01, MLA-IB, P61, SSA. *Aud.:* Ac.

Addressing cultural theory with an emphasis on "questions of gender, sexuality, race and the environment," *Social Text* offers a lively forum for discussions involving post-colonialism, postmodernism, and popular culture. Contributors are largely U.S. scholars, critics, artists, and writers, although works of international writers are also included. Articles deal with a range of topics from refugee concept and experience to archives of slavery and from human rights poetry to sounds of dissent. Special segments or issues on a single theme have covered such subjects as economies of dispossession, race, religion, and war, and political culture. *Social Text* places current social issues in the larger context of national and international cultural transformation. This journal will appeal to scholars and students interested in the latest cultural theory applied to the critical areas of race, gender, and class.

1560. *Social Theory and Practice: an international and interdisciplinary journal of social philosophy.* [ISSN: 0037-802X] 1970. q. USD 75. Ed(s): Mark LeBar. Florida State University, Department of Philosophy, 151 Dodd Hall, Tallahassee, FL 32306; philosophy@admin.fsu.edu; http://philosophy.fsu.edu/. Illus., adv. Refereed. Microform: PQC. Reprint: PSC. *Indexed:* A01, A22, BRI, IBSS, MLA-IB, P61, SSA. *Aud.:* Ac.

Social Theory and Practice addresses "theoretical and applied questions in social, political, legal, economic, educational and moral philosophy." The Department of Philosophy at Florida State University along with the Philosophy Documentation Center publishes the journal. The articles examine theories of historical figures in philosophy including Kant, Mill, Locke, Marx, and Engels, as well as more contemporary theorists such as Rawls, Habermas, and Foucault. Other writings address questions on racism and hate speech, animal rights, terrorism, nonviolent resistance, abortion, gun control, parental responsibilities, and social identity. Occasional special issues have appeared on topics such as dominating speech, self-deception, and preference, choice, and paternalism. Most contributors are from American and Canadian universities. The writing is scholarly and encompasses a broad range of the humanities and social sciences, as well as public policy issues. This journal will be of interest to scholars and students of philosophy, but also to academics in many other disciplines.

1561. *South Asian History and Culture.* [ISSN: 1947-2498] 2010. q. GBP 476 (print & online eds.)). Ed(s): Boria Majumdar. Routledge, 4 Park Sq, Milton Park, Abingdon, OX14 4RN, United Kingdom; subscriptions@tandf.co.uk; http://www.tandfonline.com. Adv. Sample. Refereed. Reprint: PSC. *Indexed:* AmHI, BAS. *Bk. rev.:* 1-3 review essays, 8-10 book reviews. *Aud.:* Ac.

This multidisciplinary journal focuses on the countries of India, Pakistan, Bangladesh, Sri Lanka, Nepal, and other parts of South Asia. It blends the traditional disciplines of history, economics, and politics with more contemporary areas of gender studies, minority rights, and sexuality studies. The publication also includes research on film, media, photography, sports, medicine, and the environment as related to this region of the world. Authors and editors are primarily from India, Australia, the United Kingdom, and the United States. Each issue contains research articles and book reviews, with some issues featuring commentary, interviews, and photo essays. Special issues or sections are published frequently on subjects ranging from religion and law in modern India to the politics of writing in South Asia, to ideology and representations in women's movements. Other articles focus on topics such as mobility and migration, the politics of exclusion, military organization in early modern South Asia, and family biographies in transnational identities. This publication is aimed at historians and scholars in social sciences and humanities disciplines.

1562. ***Southern Quarterly: a journal of the arts in the south.*** [ISSN: 0038-4496] 1962. q. USD 65 (Individuals, USD 35; USD 91 combined subscription (print & online eds.)). Ed(s): Diane DeCesare Ross, Philip C Kolin. University of Southern Mississippi, 118 College Dr, Box 5078, Hattiesburg, MS 39406; gcadmissions@usm.edu; http://www.usm.edu. Illus., index. Refereed. Vol. ends: Summer. Microform: PQC. *Indexed:* A01, A22, AmHI, BRI, F01, MLA-IB. *Bk. rev.:* 4-10, 400-1,000 words. *Aud.:* Ga, Ac.

The arts and culture of the southern United States are the focus of this journal, including the areas of the fine arts, film, photography, and popular culture, as well as folklore, history, anthropology, and material culture. Each issue presents articles on southern writers and artists, including interviews, critical analyses of particular works, or themes from southern literature, music, visual arts, or cultural studies. Frequently, special issues or features on one theme or author are published. Recent special issues have focused on the Caribbean South, re-playing *Gone with the Wind* and children in the South. *Southern Quarterly* also contains review essays and bibliographies, along with photographic essays, book reviews, and occasional film and exhibition reviews. *Southern Quarterly* is a fascinating and thoroughly enjoyable publication for readers in the South and across the country.

1563. ***Systems Research and Behavioral Science.*** Formed by the merger of (1984-1997): *Systems Research;* (1956-1997): *Behavioral Science.* [ISSN: 1092-7026] 1997. bi-m. GBP 716. Ed(s): M C Jackson. John Wiley & Sons Ltd., EMEA Institutional Sales, 9600 Garsington Rd, Oxford, OX4 2DQ, United Kingdom; cs-journals@wiley.com; http://onlinelibrary.wiley.com. Illus., adv. Sample. Refereed. Vol. ends: No. 4. Microform: PQC. Reprint: PSC. *Indexed:* A22, B01, BAS, BRI, IBSS. *Bk. rev.:* 5-6, 700-1,000 words. *Aud.:* Ac.

As the official publication of the International Federation for Systems Research, this journal aims to publish theoretical and empirical articles on "systems theories, methodologies, and applications—on all strands of the systems movement." The journal has a very broad, interdisciplinary scope, covering systems in society, organizations, and business and management, as well as systems related to social cognition, modeling, values, and the quality of life. Each issue includes research articles on such topics as integrating methodologies in management, industry chains and networks, food and nutrition security, and systems for innovation in large organizations. Special issues appear occasionally on such subjects as modeling sustainability pathways, systemic innovation for a thrivable future, and natural resource management. Some issues include shorter news items or research notes, along with book reviews. The well-written and documented articles range from highly technical studies to theoretical approaches. This journal will be of interest to scholars as well as researchers in business, government, and technology.

1564. ***Thesis Eleven: critical theory and historical sociology.*** [ISSN: 0725-5136] 1980. bi-m. USD 1659 (print & online eds.)). Sage Publications Ltd., 1 Oliver's Yard, 55 City Rd, London, EC1Y 1SP, United Kingdom; info@sagepub.com; https://www.sagepub.com/. Illus., index, adv. Sample. Refereed. Vol. ends: Nov. Microform: PQC. Reprint: PSC. *Indexed:* A01, A22, E01, IBSS, P61, SSA. *Bk. rev.:* 4-6, 1,000-3,000 words. *Aud.:* Ac.

For more than 35 years, *Thesis Eleven* has published some of the leading work in the field of social theory. The journal is international and interdisciplinary, with a focus on "cultivating diverse critical theories of modernity." Incorporating both social sciences and liberal arts disciplines, from sociology and politics to philosophy, cultural studies, and literature, this publication includes European social theory as well as theory from other areas of the world. The editors are from Australian universities, while contributors to the journal are primarily from Europe, Canada, Australia, and the United States. Several research articles make up each issue, along with review essays and book reviews. Shorter essays or commentaries on earlier articles are also included. Recent articles have focused on topics such as public opinion in modern politics, indigenous identities, movements and pathways, populism in the twenty-first century, sustainable water management, and the political in art. This journal will appeal to academics, especially in the fields of sociology, politics, and philosophy.

■ DANCE

Leah Sherman, Visual & Performing Arts Librarian, Robert Manning Strozier Library, Florida State University, Tallahassee, FL

Introduction

Given that the field of Dance remains diverse in its history, study, and practice, so, too, are current dance periodicals notable for their wide range of topical interests, level of inquiries, and proposed readerships. Journals in dance speak to students, educators, researchers, and professionals of all levels, reporting back on a multitude of trends and topics of concern in every issue. The journals available to dance researchers, professionals, and appreciators alike run the gamut across popular and scholarly topics and approaches. Further, because Dance is interdisciplinary in its study and practice, regularly overlapping in conversation with fields such as Theater, Psychology, and History, the breadth of subjects covered across titles touches on a tremendously wide network of ideas and methodologies.

Three major trends on the rise in Dance periodicals have emerged in recent years, namely the growing inclusion of world dance and non-western dance traditions, an increased interest and awareness in Dance history, and new attention to the burgeoning field of Dance Sciences. As for the first of these points, there is also parallel growth in the importance and need for international scholarly voices, in order to facilitate some of these conversations and also to both broaden and strengthen the very pool of dance scholarship. As for new scholarship on the history of Dance, this trend is evidenced in periodicals ranging from scholarly journals to popular magazines; consideration is given not just to famous companies or choreographers, but also notable, individual dancers. Dance periodicals continue to include more and more historical and documentary images in their publications, as well, and these additions add a new level of richness to articles and features, ultimately lending a fuller understanding of dance history beyond textual record. This is especially true of details such as costuming and technical production designs, which may not have been as well-documented in much earlier iterations of dance history literature. Finally, new contributions have also emerged in the field of Dance Sciences, which derives from the sports science of Dance and focuses on the physical performance of dancers as athletes.

As we move into the twenty-first century, publishing practice continues to grow electronically, with expanding indexing online, full-text availability, but also with more informal sites such a magazine websites and blogs. These tides can all be felt in the Dance periodicals, as a number of titles now include supplementary material online, besides offering simultaneous digital versions of print articles. These electronic additions to traditional print media are exceptionally rich in illustrations such as photographic content, but they also allow for streaming media and more interactive elements. This latter inclusion complements the performative nature uniquely found within fields such a Dance, Theater, Music, and even Film, by bridging a communicative gap left by print media alone.

Basic Periodicals

Ems: *Dance Magazine;* Hs: *Dance Magazine, Dance Spirit, Pointe;* Ga: *Dance Magazine, Dance Spirit, Dance Teacher, Dance Today!, Pointe;* Ac: *Ballet Review, Choreologica: Papers on Dance History, Dance Chronicle, Dance Research Journal, Dancing Times, Journal of Dance Medicine and Science, Pointe, Research in Dance Education;* Sa: *American Journal of Dance Therapy, Dance Research Journal, Dance Teacher.*

Basic Abstracts and Indexes

Arts and Humanities Citation Index, Humanities Index, International Index to the Performing Arts, Music Index, SPORTDiscus with Full Text.

1565. *American Journal of Dance Therapy.* Supersedes (in 1977): *American Dance Therapy Association. Monograph.* [ISSN: 0146-3721] 1968. s-a. EUR 834 (print & online eds.)). Ed(s): David A Harris, Christina Devereux. Springer New York LLC, 233 Spring St, New York, NY 10013; customerservice@springer.com; http://www.springer.com. Illus., index, adv. Sample. Refereed. Reprint: PSC. *Indexed:* A22, BRI, E01, IIPA. *Bk. rev.:* 4-5, 500 words. *Aud.:* Ac.

The *American Journal of Dance Therapy* focuses on links between behavior, movement, physical condition, and mental health in its attention to the significance of dance in therapeutic practice. The articles included in this journal are scholarly, covering a variety of aspects of the psychology of movement and dance. Recent issues largely consist of original research, interviews with prominent scholars in the field, and conference abstracts. Journal contributors are varied in their demographics, as they are established scholars, clinicians, educators, and advanced student researchers. This is an excellent resource for a variety of practitioners interested in a wide range of arts disciplines, including but not limited to administrators, educators, psychologists, and arts therapists.

1566. *Ballet Review.* [ISSN: 0522-0653] 1965. q. USD 48 (Individuals, USD 27; USD 12 per issue). Ed(s): Marvin Hoshino. Dance Research Foundation, Inc., 37 W 12th St 7J, New York, NY 10011; http://www.balletreview.com. Illus., adv. *Indexed:* A22, AmHI, BRI, IIPA, MLA-IB. *Bk. rev.:* Number and length vary. *Aud.:* Ac, Ga, Sa.

Ballet Review remains an essential title in the field of dance studies for academic and specialized research collections alike. This journal hosts well-written and well-researched texts as well as important reviews of dance companies specializing in ballet, modern, and contemporary dance styles. Issues generally offer multiple illustrations including historical and documentary photographs; and established scholars of dance history contribute articles to each issue. Other content included spans features on dancer biographies, criticism, and elements of production such as dance music and costuming.

1567. *Choreographic Practices.* [ISSN: 2040-5669] 2010. s-a. GBP 199 (print & online eds.)). Ed(s): Jane M Bacon, Vida L Midgelow. Intellect Ltd., The Mill, Parnall Rd, Fishponds, Bristol, BS16 3JG, United Kingdom; info@intellectbooks.com; http://www.intellectbooks.co.uk/. Adv. Sample. Refereed. Reprint: PSC. *Aud.:* Ga, Ac.

This journal is devoted to the interdisciplinary study of performance, covering a variety of methodologies and scholarly perspectives. Theory, process, and practice are the driving interests of the articles offered by this peer-reviewed publication, and the audience in mind would include researchers of dance studies and history as well as performance studies. *Choreographic Practices* began in 2010 and is published two to three times each year. Recent issues contain multiple scholarly articles and interviews, and many of these entries are generally accompanied by either color or black and white illustrations. This title would be appropriate in any academic or specialized library collection working the dance or greater performance community.

1568. *Choreologica.* [ISSN: 1746-5737] 2005. a. Free to members. Ed(s): Giannandrea Poesio. The European Association for Dance History, 41 Talma Gardens, Twickenham, TW2 7RB, United Kingdom; eadhcommittee@gmail.com; http://www.eadh.com/. Refereed. *Bk. rev.:* 1-4. *Aud.:* Ac.

A fairly new publication, *Choreologica* provides a venue for "historical and theoretical explorations of dance histories and practices." This journal focuses on scholarly discourse within the European context of dance history, and is a product of the European Association for Dance History in effort to raise public interests in the historical legacy of dance culture and practice. Notably, *Choreologica* is a peer-reviewed publication that welcomes contributions from the entire landscape of dance studies, not only scholarly audiences. Besides offering informative articles, each issue also includes several book reviews as well as announcements for professional activities such as upcoming conferences.

1569. *Contact Quarterly: dance & improvisation journal.* Formerly (until 1976): *Contact Newsletter.* [ISSN: 0198-9634] 1975. s-a. USD 45. Ed(s): Melinda Buckwalter, Nancy Stark Smith. Contact Collaborations, Inc., PO Box 603, Northampton, MA 01061; info@contactquarterly.com; http://www.contactquarterly.com. Illus., index. Sample. *Indexed:* IIPA. *Bk. rev.:* Number and length vary. *Aud.:* Ac, Sa.

Contact Quarterly was initially founded in 1975 to cover dance improvisation, and, indeed, the journal continues to publish semi-annual issues devoted to this topic. Described as the "longest living, independent, artist-made, not-for-profit, reader-supported magazine devoted to the dancer's voice," *Contact Quarterly* is a staple of any academic collection. Issues of this magazine generally include a mix of articles, interviews, notices of worldwide dance events, as well as information on dance programs. This title is equally appropriate for dancers, researchers, and educators interested in the philosophy, practice, and social culture of improvisation in dance today.

1570. *Dance Chronicle: studies in dance & the related arts.* Formerly (until 1977): *Dance Perspectives.* [ISSN: 0147-2526] 1959. 3x/yr. GBP 1107 (print & online eds.)). Ed(s): Joellen A Meglin, Lynn Matluck Brooks. Taylor & Francis Inc., 711 3rd Ave, 8th Fl, New York, NY 10017; support@tandfonline.com; http://www.tandfonline.com. Illus., index, adv. Sample. Refereed. Circ: 450. Vol. ends: Winter. Microform: RPI. Reprint: PSC. *Indexed:* A01, A22, AmHI, BRI, E01, IIPA, MLA-IB, RILM. *Bk. rev.:* 3-5 signed, 500-1,000 words. *Aud.:* Ac, Sa.

The content of *Dance Chronicle* remains diverse, since the publication's inception as the first journal created solely for the scholarship of dance. As the oldest title of its kind, *Dance Chronicle* is a necessary entry in any academic or specialized library collection working with dance researchers and practitioners. This peer-reviewed journal covers all aspects of dance history, choreographic studies, performance practice and theory, and dance criticism. The articles published here are well-researched and well-written, and the bibliographic information provided is excellent. Each issue also includes multiple book reviews; these are authored by dance historians and scholars alike.

1571. *Dance Europe: the international dance magazine published in London.* [ISSN: 1359-9798] 1995. 11x/yr. GBP 75. Dance Europe, PO Box 12661, London, E5 9TZ, United Kingdom. Adv. *Bk. rev.:* 1 signed, 500-1,000 words. *Aud.:* Hs, Ga, Ac, Sa.

Dance Europe is an international dance magazine published 11 times each year in both English and in Spanish. The publication offers editorials from current and former professional dancers whose careers sample a range of styles such as ballet and modern dance. Issues contain reports and reviews from Asia beyond its essential emphasis on current European dance practices. *Dance Europe* includes information about upcoming auditions in addition to recurring interviews with both established and up-and-coming dancers. This title is important for collections, given its continued dedication to a far-reaching coverage of the contemporary, global dance community.

1572. *Dance Magazine.* Former titles (until 1948): *Dance;* (until 1945): *Dance Magazine;* (until 1943): *Dance;* (until 1942): *The American Dancer;* Incorporates (in 2006): *Dance Annual Directory;* Which was formerly (until 2004): *Stern's Directory;* (until 2000): *Stern's Performing Arts Directory;* (until 1989): *Performing Arts Directory;* (until 1986): *Dance Magazine Annual;* (until 1974): *Dance Magazine;* (until 1970): *Dance Magazine Annual.* [ISSN: 0011-6009] 1927. m. USD 14.95 domestic; USD 46.95 Canada; USD 66.95 elsewhere. Ed(s): Jennifer Stahl, Madeline Schrock. DanceMedia, LLC., 333 7th Ave, New York, NY 10001; http://dancemedia.com. Illus., index, adv. Sample. Vol. ends: Dec. Microform: PQC. *Indexed:* A01, A22, AmHI, BRI, C37, CBRI, F01, IIPA, MASUSE. *Bk. rev.:* 250-2,500 words. *Aud.:* Ems, Hs, Ga, Ac.

This monthly publication remains a pillar of any library's core collection in dance, as it provides comprehensive treatment of both dance performance and dance education in the United States. *Dance Magazine* is, perhaps, the longest running dance periodical in the country, and it can be confidently referenced for dance news, event listings, advice, and profiles geared toward the entire dance community nationwide. The publication also includes regular features covering a breadth of practitioners across ballet, modern, and theatrical dance. The information found here would be of equal value to dance educators, practitioners, and students desiring to learn and stay connected to contemporary trends in American dance.

1573. ***Dance Research Journal.*** Formerly (until 1975): *C O R D News.* [ISSN: 0149-7677] 1969. 3x/yr. GBP 161. Ed(s): Helen Thomas. Cambridge University Press, 1 Liberty Plaza, Fl 20, New York, NY 10004; journals@cambridge.org; https://www.cambridge.org. Illus., adv. Sample. Refereed. Reprint: PSC. *Indexed:* A01, A22, AmHI, BRI, CBRI, E01, IIPA, MLA-IB, RILM, SD. *Bk. rev.:* Numerous, lengthy, signed. *Aud.:* Ac, Sa.

Dance Research Journal is a strongly academic, peer-reviewed publication published by the Congress on Research in Dance. The information included within this title consists of readable, well-researched articles by renowned scholars of dance studies and dance history. The scholarship published in *Dance Research Journal* covers aspects of international dance studies; the research in this journal is of an extremely high caliber. Each issue contains lengthy book reviews that are well written and thoughtful in their inquiry. This publication is an excellent resource for new and established researchers of dance and its related disciplines.

1574. ***Dance Spirit.*** [ISSN: 1094-0588] 1997. 10x/yr. USD 8.95 domestic; USD 35 Canada; USD 45 elsewhere. Ed(s): Margaret Fuhrer, Courtney Bowers. DanceMedia, LLC., 333 7th Ave, New York, NY 10001; http://dancemedia.com. Adv. Sample. *Indexed:* A01, IIPA, MASUSE. *Aud.:* Ems, Hs, Ga.

This publication is geared toward dance instructors, professionals, and dance students who hope to become professionals. The magazine, written for younger audiences, has bright and colorful photography paired with more abbreviated articles devoted to a variety of dance styles. Tap, swing, ballet, ballroom, and hip hop are all featured here, and the topics of concern vary as well as cover everything from education, to training, to dance competitions. Notably, *Dance Spirit* comes from the same publisher as *Dance Magazine, Dance Teacher,* and *Pointe.*

1575. ***Dance Teacher.*** Formerly (until 1999): *Dance Teacher Now.* [ISSN: 1524-4474] 1979. m. USD 14.95 domestic; USD 28 Canada; USD 38 elsewhere. Ed(s): Karen Hildebrand, Joe Sullivan. DanceMedia, LLC., 333 7th Ave, New York, NY 10001; http://dancemedia.com. Illus., index, adv. *Indexed:* IIPA. *Bk. rev.:* 3, 250 words. *Aud.:* Ga, Ac.

The value of *Dance Teacher* is its unique attention toward instructors across all aspects of dance instruction, ranging from elementary-aged students to adult learners. The only periodical of its kind, *Dance Teacher* includes material on tap, ballroom, Irish dance, ballet, and hip hop, among other genres of dance. Each issue has a variety of features on dance history, institutional profiles, dance music, as well as marketing for dance courses. The corresponding website also offers rich, additional content in the form of videos, guides to collegiate dance programs, "how-to" advice, and also an area devoted to trending topics within the larger dance community.

1576. ***Dance Today!*** Formerly (until 2001): *Ballroom Dancing Times.* [ISSN: 1475-2336] 1956. m. Ed(s): Nicola Rayner. Dancing Times Ltd., 36 Battersea Square, London, SW11 3RA, United Kingdom; subscriptions@dancing-times.co.uk; http://www.dancing-times.co.uk. Illus., adv. Vol. ends: Sep. *Indexed:* IIPA. *Aud.:* Ga, Sa.

Dance Today! is for the dancer but also for the dance lover, too. This title, a sister publication of *Dancing Times,* is specifically for "people who love to dance and watch dancing." Ballroom dance of all varieties is the main school covered in *Dance Today!,* including features on styles such as flamenco and musical theater. Issues contain notes on recent dance competitions, tips and tricks for the budding dancer, and regular notes on new dance books. This publication is rich with color illustrations, and with its clear, readable text, affords a fun and interesting read for a general audience.

1577. ***Dancing Times.*** Incorporates (2001-2015): *Dance Today;* Which was formerly (1956-2001): *Ballroom Dancing Times;* Incorporates (1930-1934): *The Amateur Dancer;* (19??-19??): *Dancing & the Ballroom;* (1964-19??): *The Ballet Annual and Year Book;* Which was formerly (1947-1964): *The Ballet Annual.* [ISSN: 0011-605X] 1910. m. GBP 38.50 domestic; GBP 44.75 foreign. Ed(s): Jonathan Gray. Dancing Times Ltd., 36 Battersea Square, London, SW11 3RA, United Kingdom; subscriptions@dancing-times.co.uk. Illus., adv. *Indexed:* A22, IIPA, MLA-IB. *Bk. rev.:* 4-5. *Aud.:* Hs, Ga, Ac.

This British magazine is the single oldest, continuous publication devoted solely to dance. *Dancing Times,* from the same publisher as *Dance Today!,* appeals to readers interested in contemporary dance, especially as it pertains to the British dance scene. *Dancing Times* covers a wide variety of featured topics, including reports on dance festivals, theatrical productions, dance companies, dance programs, choreography, and dance news. This magazine is also available online. Readers of the electronic version are treated to rich supplementary content including interviews and blog posts. Both the print and online editions of *Dancing Times* contain colorful illustrations to accompany the readable text. Like *Dancing Today!,* this magazine is most appropriate for a general readership. URL: www.dancing-times.co.uk

1578. ***Journal of Dance & Somatic Practices.*** [ISSN: 1757-1871] 2009. s-a. GBP 212 (print & online eds.)). Ed(s): Sarah Whatley. Intellect Ltd., The Mill, Parnall Rd, Fishponds, Bristol, BS16 3JG, United Kingdom; info@intellectbooks.com; http://www.intellectbooks.co.uk/. Adv. Sample. Refereed. Reprint: PSC. *Indexed:* IIPA. *Bk. rev.:* Number varies. *Aud.:* Ac.

The *Journal of Dance & Somatic Practices* is a semi-annual publication focused on the somatic practice in dance, and the way this body of practice impacts performing arts more broadly. This peer-reviewed journal includes multiple scholarly articles in each issue, concerned with topics such as dance therapy, psychology, self-expression, motion, and perception. The entries published in the *Journal of Dance & Somatic Practices* are thorough in their research, and their bibliographic quality is exceptional. This title is meant for scholars of dance, especially dance therapy, and is a must have for both academic and specialized library collections.

1579. ***Journal of Dance Education.*** [ISSN: 1529-0824] 2001. q. GBP 248 (print & online eds.)). Ed(s): Wendy Oliver. Routledge, 530 Walnut St, Ste 850, Philadelphia, PA 19106; enquiries@tandfonline.com; http://www.tandfonline.com. Refereed. Reprint: PSC. *Indexed:* ERIC, SD. *Bk. rev.:* 4-5. *Aud.:* Ac.

This official publication of the National Dance Education Organization (NDEO) hosts original, scholarly articles focusing on the issues and trends of professional dance education. The audience for the *Journal of Dance Education* is broad, targeting a readership comprising teachers, researchers, administrators, choreographers, and students of dance. Many of the features in this journal would also appeal to professional dancers and professional dance trainers, as well as members of community-based dance programs. Contributions to the *Journal of Dance Education* are peer-reviewed, and are welcomed from international scholars and professionals. Issues typically contain a balance of featured scholarly articles, practical offerings, book and media reviews, and a report from the NDEO.

1580. ***Journal of Dance Medicine & Science.*** [ISSN: 1089-313X] 1997. q. USD 218 (Individuals, USD 145). Ed(s): John Solomon, Ruth Solomon. J Michael Ryan Publishing, Inc., 24 Crescent Dr N, Andover, NJ 07821; info@jmichaelryan.com; http://www.jmichaelryan.com/. Adv. Refereed. *Indexed:* BRI, IIPA, SD. *Bk. rev.:* Number and length vary. *Aud.:* Ac.

Journal of Dance Medicine & Science constitutes a quarterly report on current clinical and experimental research from the field of Dance sciences. This publication offers the most up-to-date facts and figures on core topics such as anatomy, sports medicine, physical therapy, kinesiology, and nutrition—all in the context of Dance. The content in this journal would be equally appropriate for a student of medicine as one of dance education, and would be at home in any academic research library. Each issue includes scientific articles, case studies, book reviews, recent news from the field, as well as letters to the editor.

Journal of Physical Education, Recreation and Dance. See Sports/ Physical Education, Coaching, and Sports Sciences section.

1581. *Performance Research: a journal of the performing arts.* [ISSN: 1352-8165] 1996. bi-m. GBP 780 (print & online eds.)). Ed(s): Richard Gough, Ric Allsopp. Routledge, 4 Park Sq, Milton Park, Abingdon, OX14 4RN, United Kingdom; subscriptions@tandf.co.uk; http://www.tandfonline.com. Illus., adv. Sample. Refereed. Reprint: PSC. *Indexed:* A22, A51, E01, IIPA, MLA-IB. *Bk. rev.:* Number and length vary. *Aud.:* Ac, Sa.

Founded in 1996, *Performance Research* describes itself as the "standard for thematic and cross-disciplinary ways of bringing together the varied materials of artistic and theoretical research in the expanded field of performance." The journal emphasizes contemporary performance, hosting contributions from designers, artists, researchers, and practitioners. Recent issues include articles on performance history, politics and theory, pedagogy, and also book reviews. This title would be a good addition to any academic dance collection, but it would also have interest to a population where an established theater program exists, too.

1582. *Pointe: ballet at its best.* Formerly (until 2000): *Points.* [ISSN: 1529-6741] 2000. bi-m. USD 16.95 domestic; USD 25 Canada; USD 35 elsewhere. Ed(s): Hanna Rubin. DanceMedia, LLC., 333 7th Ave, New York, NY 10001; http://dancemedia.com. Illus., adv. *Indexed:* IIPA, MASUSE. *Aud.:* Hs, Ga, Ac, Sa.

Pointe has been a dynamic title in ballet studies since its first issue. Published six times a year, the issues of this magazine include professional and business-orientated content for current and aspiring ballet dancers. Notably, *Pointe* includes more features dedicated to individual dancers rather than entire ballet companies. The articles in each issue consider a wide range of topics such as physical health and injury prevention, professional development, dancing technique, and performance reviews. The best audience for this publication remains professional dancers as well as dance students, and this title should be considered for any organization servicing such practitioners.

1583. *Research in Dance Education.* [ISSN: 1464-7893] 2000. 3x/yr. GBP 457 (print & online eds.)). Ed(s): Angela Pickard. Routledge, 4 Park Sq, Milton Park, Abingdon, OX14 4RN, United Kingdom; subscriptions@tandf.co.uk; http://www.tandfonline.com. Adv. Sample. Refereed. Reprint: PSC. *Indexed:* A01, A22, E01, ERIC, IIPA. *Bk. rev.:* Number and length vary. *Aud.:* Ac.

This journal invites international contributors to discuss the most current trends in research and practice in dance education. Each issue focuses on dance education in many aspects, including but not limited to all ages of study, the theory and practice of teaching and learning in dance, integration of new technologies, dance therapy, community dance, research methods, and aesthetic and artistic education. *Research in Dance Education* offers relevant content to those researchers and instructors alike working on "issues related to pedagogy, philosophy, sociology, and methodology in relation to creating, performing, and viewing dance." Three times a year readers may expect a collection of articles on a wide variety of such topics, as well as an editorial introduction to the issue.

■ DEATH AND DYING

See also Medicine section.

Alice Pakhtigian, Collection Development/Reference Librarian (Temp), Francis Harvey Green Library, West Chester University of Pennsylvania, West Chester, PA 19383; apakhtigia@wcupa.edu

Introduction

Death and dying touch everyone at some point in their lives. There are magazines and periodicals that benefit everyone in all walks of life. Most of the journals listed here are for professionals, academicians, and students. One periodical, *Compassion and Choices*, is a great fit for not just professionals, academicians, and students, but those who are facing death themselves. The topic of death and dying touches the psychological, anthropological, sociological, educational, and religious aspects of life.

The journals listed here research those aspects in depth. The journals will fit universities and colleges that have those particular programs. Certain ones such as *Journal of Hospice & Palliative Nursing, Journal of Palliative Medicine*, and *Progress in Palliative Care* are chiefly aimed at practitioners and students in the health professions. These are essential for libraries that support medical schools and nursing programs as well as hospital libraries.

The journals in general are international in scope and studies. They are also interdisciplinary and diverse within their contents. The journals are published in the United States, Canada, Great Britain, Australia, and New Zealand. Academic, specialized, and medical libraries would benefit from the use of any of the journals listed.

Basic Periodicals

Ac, Sa: *American Journal of Hospice and Palliative Medicine; Death Studies; European Journal of Palliative Care; Journal of Hospice and Palliative Nursing; Journal of Palliative Care; Journal of Palliative Medicine; Mortality; Omega: Journal of Death and Dying; Palliative & Supportive Care; Palliative Medicine; Suicide and Life-Threatening Behavior.*

Basic Abstracts and Indexes

AgeLine, CINAHL, MEDLINE, PsycINFO, Scopus, Social Work Abstracts.

1584. *The American Journal of Hospice and Palliative Medicine.* Formerly (until 1990): *The American Journal of Hospice Care;* Incorporates (2002-2003): *Journal of Terminal Oncology.* [ISSN: 1049-9091] 1984. 8x/yr. USD 2423 (print & online eds.)). Ed(s): Robert E Enck. Sage Publications, Inc., 2455 Teller Rd, Thousand Oaks, CA 91320; info@sagepub.com; http://www.sagepub.com/. Illus., index, adv. Sample. Refereed. Reprint: PSC. *Indexed:* A22, AgeL, E01. *Bk. rev.:* Number and length vary. *Aud.:* Ga, Ac, Sa.

This peer-reviewed journal, published by Sage, is available both in print and online. It offers editorials, commentaries, opinions, original research articles, ongoing topical series, and review articles. A regular topic of research is hospice in an international context. The target audience comprises students in the health care field, practitioners, and counselors. Recent articles include "Novel Therapeutic Strategies for Delirium in Patients With Cancer: A Preliminary Study," "Viewing Hospice Decision Making as a Process," and "The Experiences of Stress of Palliative Care Providers in Malaysia: A Thematic Analysis." Tables of contents are available for all issues online. One can see a sample issue and read sample articles online at: http://ajh.sagepub.com/

1585. *B M C Palliative Care.* [ISSN: 1472-684X] 2002. irreg. Free. Ed(s): Hayley Henderson. BioMed Central Ltd., Fl 6, 236 Gray's Inn Rd, London, WC1X 8HB, United Kingdom; info@biomedcentral.com; https://www.biomedcentral.com. Illus., adv. Refereed. *Indexed:* A01, Agr. *Aud.:* Ac, Sa.

This is one of the many online, open-access, peer-reviewed journals published by BioMed. The names of the reviewers and their reviews are made available. Blogs and tweets share the same page as the table of contents. The publication is aimed toward students and practitioners in the field. Full-text pdf articles are available on the web site. Altmetric scores are listed. Some examples of articles include: "Favored subjects and psychosocial needs in music therapy in terminally ill cancer patients: a content analysis," "Sedation at the end of life - a nation-wide study in palliative care units in Austria," and "Cultural perspectives of older nursing home residents regarding signing their own DNR directives in Eastern Taiwan: a qualitative pilot study." Articles are accessible online. URL: http://bmcpalliatcare.biomedcentral.com/

1586. *Bereavement Care: an international journal for those who help bereaved people.* [ISSN: 0268-2621] 1982. 3x/yr. GBP 217 (print & online eds.)). Ed(s): Kate Mitchell. Routledge, 4 Park Sq, Milton Park, Abingdon, OX14 4RN, United Kingdom; subscriptions@tandf.co.uk; http://www.tandfonline.com. Illus. Sample. Refereed. Reprint: PSC. *Indexed:* A01, A22, E01. *Bk. rev.:* Number and length vary. *Aud.:* Ac, Sa.

This journal is available both online and in print through Taylor and Francis publishers. The journal's goal is to increase the understanding of grief and to increase the care and quality of support to those grieving the loss of a loved one. The publication is aimed toward practitioners, academics, researchers, and non-academics. A sample issue and the table of contents and abstracts beginning with volume 1 (1982) can be found on the journal's web site. This title is published three times a year, and has original studies editorials, book reviews, and first-person stories. *Bereavement Care* is published in association with the United Kingdom's largest bereavement support charity, a national voluntary organization called Cruse Bereavement Care. URL: www.tandfonline.com/toc/rber20/current

1587. *Compassion and Choices Magazine.* Former titles (until 2005): *End-of-Life Choices;* (until 2002): *Timelines;* (until 1994): *Hemlock Quarterly.* [ISSN: 1949-8829] 1980. q. Free to members. Ed(s): Marcia Angell. Compassion & Choices, PO Box 101810, Denver, CO 80250; info@compassionandchoices.org; http://www.compassionandchoices.org. Illus., adv. *Bk. rev.:* Number and length vary. *Aud.:* Ga.

This magazine is available both online and in print through a nonprofit organization called Compassion and Choices, which is committed to improving care and expanding choice at the end of life. This magazine is aimed toward people facing death. It also is aimed for a general audience, lawmakers, and health-care workers, and is published quarterly. This is a good magazine for public libraries. One can freely read the current issue online. The print issue comes with membership in the organization. URL: https://www.compassionandchoices.org/magazine/

1588. *Death Studies: counseling - research - education - care - ethics.* Formerly (until 1985): *Death Education.* [ISSN: 0748-1187] 1977. m. GBP 997 (print & online eds.)). Ed(s): Robert A Neimeyer. Routledge, 530 Walnut St, Ste 850, Philadelphia, PA 19106; enquiries@tandfonline.com; http://www.tandfonline.com. Illus., index. Sample. Refereed. Vol. ends: Dec. Microform: PQC. Reprint: PSC. *Indexed:* A01, A22, BRI, E01, ERIC, MLA-IB, SSA. *Bk. rev.:* Number and length vary. *Aud.:* Ac, Sa.

Published twice a year in print, with five issues in each publication, this peer-reviewed journal is also available online via Taylor and Francis publishers' web site and the different databases. The journal's focus is on research, scholarship, and practical approaches to death; bereavement and loss; grief therapy; attitudes toward death; suicide; and death education. Some article titles include "Development and Validation of the Perceived Life Significance Scale," "On Social Death: Ostracism and the Accessibility of Death Thoughts," and "Dyadic Coping of Parents After the Death of a Child." This journal serves students in the health-care field, counselors, practitioners, and academics. A sample copy is available online, as well as the table of contents and abstracts from volume 1 (1977) onward. The journal contains original research, news from the field, best practices, and in-depth book reviews. URL: www.tandfonline.com/loi/udst20#.V0SG_U0UVaR

1589. *European Journal of Palliative Care.* [ISSN: 1352-2779] 1994. bi-m. Ed(s): Julia Riley. Hayward Medical Communications Ltd., 8-10 Dryden St, Covent Garden, London, WC2E 9NA, United Kingdom; edit@hayward.co.uk; http://www.hayward.co.uk. Illus., adv. *Bk. rev.:* Number and length vary. *Aud.:* Ac, Sa.

The *European Journal of Palliative Care* is the official journal of the European Association for Palliative Care (EAPC). Published bimonthly, this journal is published online and in print. It publishes mostly review articles, but does accept relevant original studies. It covers both social and clinical aspects of palliative care, and is recommended for students, practitioners, and counselors. A special feature of this journal is titled "case study masterclass." A detailed case history, and a question-and-answer format, gives professionals a chance to test their skills in patient management. The answers to the case questions are then provided in the following month's issue. URL: www.haywardpublishing.co.uk/ejpc.aspx

1590. *Grief Matters: the Australian journal of grief and bereavement.* [ISSN: 1440-6888] 1998. 3x/yr. Free to members. Ed(s): Penny Brabin. Australian Centre for Grief and Bereavement, 253 Wellington Rd, Mulgrave, VIC 3170, Australia; info@grief.org.au; http://www.grief.org.au. Illus., adv. Refereed. Vol. ends: Summer. *Indexed:* A01. *Bk. rev.:* Number and length vary. *Aud.:* Ac, Sa.

Published three times a year, *Grief Matters: The Australian Journal of Grief and Bereavement* is the official publication for the Australian Centre for Grief and Bereavement. Published both online and in print, the journal can be found in a range of academic databases. This peer-reviewed title benefits practitioners, students, and faculty in the mental health, pastoral, and social work fields. There are no sample articles online. One needs to contact the Australian Centre for Grief and Bereavement for sample back issues. *Grief Matters* contains research articles, book reviews, and abstracts of relevant articles in other journals. Sample titles from a recent issue include: "Treating the narrative fixations of traumatic grief" and "Attachment, empathy and compassion in the care of the bereaved." Information on the journal and the organization can be located at the web site. URL: www.grief.org.au/ACGB/Publications/Grief_Matters/ACGB/ACGB_Publications/GM/Grief_Matters.aspx

1591. *Illness, Crisis, and Loss.* [ISSN: 1054-1373] 1991. q. USD 1266 (print & online eds.)). Ed(s): Jason Powell. Sage Publications, Inc., 2455 Teller Rd, Thousand Oaks, CA 91320; info@sagepub.com; http://www.sagepub.com. Illus., index, adv. Sample. Refereed. Reprint: PSC. *Indexed:* A01, A22, ASSIA, E01, SSA. *Bk. rev.:* Number and length vary. *Aud.:* Ac, Sa.

This journal is associated with the Center for Death Education and Bioethics, and is a member of the Committee on Publication Ethics. It is peer-reviewed and published quarterly both in print and online. Started in 1991, it publishes original articles, editorials, book reviews, commentaries, "Final Voices," and personal reflections on experiences in dealing with illnesses and bereavement. It covers issues in the social sciences and medical sciences. This title is good for both practitioners and students in the field. A sample issue is available online. Tables of contents are available, from the first issue onward, from the journal's web site. Abstracts are available from 1998 onward. Some examples of titles from a recent issue include: "Parental Responsibility and Respondent Anger, Sympathy, and Willingness to Help Following Child Death" and "Death After Life, Life After Death." URL: https://us.sagepub.com/en-us/nam/illness-crisis-loss/journal200976

1592. *International Journal of Palliative Nursing.* [ISSN: 1357-6321] 1995. m. Individuals, GBP 183. Ed(s): Craig Nicholson. Mark Allen Group, St Jude's Church, Dulwich Rd, London, SE24 0PB, United Kingdom; subscriptions@markallengroup.com; http://www.markallengroup.com. Adv. Refereed. *Indexed:* A01, A22. *Bk. rev.:* Number and length vary. *Aud.:* Ac, Sa.

Available in print and online, this peer-reviewed journal is published monthly by the Mark Allen Group. It features original research in the care of the dying, case studies, and book reviews. Each issue has two regular columns, "Research Roundup" and "Politics and Palliative Care." The former reports on research on palliative care in recent publications; the latter examines the issues that affect palliative care in a particular country. In addition to that focus on individual countries, articles in the journal cover research on end-of-life nursing worldwide. Recent research articles have included "The Role of Subcutaneous Infusion in Integrated, Patient-Centred Palliative Care," "Patients' Experiences of Ongoing Palliative Chemotherapy for Metastatic Colorectal Cancer: A Qualitative Study," and "Impact of a Legislative Framework on Quality of End-of-Life Care and Dying in an Acute Hospital in Spain." Tables of contents and abstracts from volume 4 (1998) to the present are available on the journal's web site. URL: www.magonlinelibrary.com/toc/ijpn/current

1593. *The Internet Journal of Pain, Symptom Control and Palliative Care.* [ISSN: 1528-8277] 2000. 2x/yr. Free. Internet Scientific Publications, Llc., 23 Rippling Creek Dr, Sugar Land, TX 77479; support@ispub.com; http://ispub.com/. Refereed. *Aud.:* Ac, Sa.

This is an open-access, online-only, peer-reviewed journal, published twice a year; it includes original articles, reviews, and case reports. The focus is on pain management and palliative care. Practitioners and students in the medical and social fields would find this journal extremely helpful. Recent titles include: "Influence of Social Modeling and Learning on Somatic, Emotional and Functional Disability in Children with Headache" and "Palliative Care Experience In Breast And Uterine Cervical Cancer Patients In Ibadan, Nigeria." URL: http://ispub.com/IJPSP

1594. ***Journal of Hospice and Palliative Nursing.*** [ISSN: 1522-2179] 1999. 6x/yr. USD 379. Ed(s): Dr. Betty Rolling Ferrell. Lippincott Williams & Wilkins, Two Commerce Sq, 2001 Market St, Philadelphia, PA 19103; customerservice@lww.com; http://www.lww.com. Adv. Refereed. *Aud.:* Ac, Sa.

This is the official journal of the Hospice and Palliative Nurses Association (HPNA). It's available both online and in print, is peer-reviewed, and publishes six times a year. This title started in 1999, and focuses on palliative care, nursing practice, hospice, education, research, and administration. Some articles in a recent issue include "Discovering the Strength of Parents Whose Children Are at End of Life" and "Nursing and End-of-Life Care in the Intensive Care Unit: A Qualitative Systematic Review." The journal also gives continuing education opportunities with the attached articles. Nurses completing and sending the tests offered in the journals receive CE hours after passing the tests. There is a new section called the "Ethics" series-a series of shorter, published articles that focus on the ethical aspects of palliative care. Tables of contents are available for each issue on the journal's web site. URL: http://journals.lww.com/jhpn/pages/default.aspx

1595. ***Journal of Loss & Trauma: international perspectives on stress and coping.*** Incorporates (1994-2006): *Stress, Trauma and Crisis;* Which was formerly (until 2004): *Crisis Intervention and Time-Limited Treatment;* Formerly (until 2001): *Journal of Personal & Interpersonal Loss.* [ISSN: 1532-5024] 1996. 6x/yr. GBP 771 (print & online eds.)). Ed(s): John H Harvey. Routledge, 530 Walnut St, Ste 850, Philadelphia, PA 19106; enquiries@tandfonline.com; http://www.tandfonline.com. Adv. Sample. Refereed. Reprint: PSC. *Indexed:* A01, A22, ASSIA, E01, ERIC. *Bk. rev.:* Number and length vary. *Aud.:* Ac, Sa.

This title is available in both online and print, and is peer reviewed. The *Journal of Loss & Trauma* publishes in print two times a year in June and December, from the Taylor and Francis Group. It is published online six times a year. Formerly known as the *Journal of Personal and Interpersonal Loss* (1996-2000), this journal also incorporates *Stress, Trauma, and Crisis: An International Journal* (2004-2006). This title focuses on issues relating to the social sciences, and is good for practitioners, faculty, and students in the mental health, social work, and counseling fields. Some examples of articles include: "Posttraumatic Stress and Well-Being Following Relationship Dissolution: Coping, Posttraumatic Stress Disorder Symptoms from Past Trauma, and Traumatic Growth" and "Suicide and Older Adults: Risk Factors and Recommendations." Tables of contents and abstracts are available for all issues, starting from volume 1 (1996), on the journal's web site. URL: www.tandfonline.com/loi/upil20#.V2RTnDWGN6l

1596. ***Journal of Pain & Palliative Care Pharmacotherapy.*** Formerly (until 2002): *Journal of Pharmaceutical Care in Pain & Symptom Control;* Incorporates (1985-2002): *The Hospice Journal.* [ISSN: 1536-0288] 1993. q. GBP 893 (print & online eds.)). Taylor & Francis, 2, 3 & 4 Park Sq, Milton Park, Abingdon, OX14 4RN, United Kingdom; subscriptions@tandf.co.uk; https://www.tandfonline.com. Illus., adv. Sample. Refereed. Reprint: PSC. *Indexed:* A01, A22, E01. *Bk. rev.:* Number and length vary. *Aud.:* Ac, Sa.

Formerly known as the *Hospice Journal* (1985-2001), this title incorporates the *Journal of Pharmaceutical Care in Pain & Symptom Control* (1993-2001). It publishes four times a year in print and online, and is peer reviewed, covering advances in acute, chronic, and end-of-life symptom management. The web site offers tables of contents and abstracts. The journal includes original articles, editorials, book reviews, and case reports. This title is good for practitioners, faculty, and students in the fields of bioethics, medicine, nursing, pharmaceutical sciences, psychology, social work, and health-care policy. URL: www.tandfonline.com/toc/ippc20/current

1597. ***Journal of Palliative Care.*** [ISSN: 0825-8597] 1984. q. USD 189 (print & online eds.)). Ed(s): Dr. Keith M. Swetz. Sage Publications, Inc., 2455 Teller Rd, Thousand Oaks, CA 91320; info@sagepub.com; http://www.sagepub.com/. Illus. Sample. Refereed. Vol. ends: Winter. Microform: PQC. *Indexed:* A22, C37. *Bk. rev.:* Number and length vary. *Aud.:* Ac, Sa.

This international, peer-reviewed journal from Canada publishes quarterly, both online and in print. The publisher is the Centre de recherche, Institut universitaire de geriatrie de Montreal. This title was first published in 1985, and it publishes original research, opinion papers, current reviews, case reports, book reviews, and reports on international activities. Article examples include "Healthcare Needs of Patients with Amyotrophic Lateral Sclerosis (ALS) in Singapore: a patient-centred qualitative study from multiple perspectives" and "Hope in Palliative Care: Cultural implications." Tables of contents are available online from 2009 (volume 25) to the present on the journal's web site. URL: http://criugm.qc.ca/journalofpalliativecare/

1598. ***Journal of Palliative Care & Medicine.*** [ISSN: 2165-7386] 2012. m. Free. Ed(s): Michael Silbernan, Karen Jubanyik. Omics Publishing Group, 5716 Corsa Ave, Ste 110, Los Angeles, CA 91362; info@omicsonline.org; http://www.omicsonline.org. Refereed. *Aud.:* Ac, Sa.

This open-access, peer-reviewed, online journal began publishing relatively recently, its first issue appearing in December 2011. There is a simultaneously published edition in French. The journal publishes original research, review articles, and personal reflection/opinion pieces on end-of-life care; it would interest health-care professionals and students. Recent articles have included "The Prevalence and Impact of Invasive Procedures in Women with Gynecologic Malignancies Referred to Hospice Care," "Role of Palliative Radiotherapy for Bone Metastasis," and "Early Contact with Palliative Care Services: A Randomized Trial in Patients with Newly Detected Incurable Metastatic Cancer." At least one special issue is published each year; a recent issue focused on palliative surgery. Articles are available in html and pdf formats. URL: http://omicsgroup.org/journals/palliative-care-medicine.php

1599. ***Journal of Palliative Medicine.*** [ISSN: 1096-6218] 1998. m. USD 2155. Ed(s): Charles F von Gunten, Lisa Pelzek-Braun. Mary Ann Liebert, Inc. Publishers, 140 Huguenot St, 3rd Fl, New Rochelle, NY 10801; info@liebertpub.com; http://www.liebertpub.com. Illus., adv. Sample. Refereed. Vol. ends: Dec. Reprint: PSC. *Indexed:* A01, A22, E01. *Bk. rev.:* Number and length vary. *Aud.:* Ac, Sa.

This is the official journal of the Hospice & Palliative Nurses Association, the Japanese Society for Palliative Medicine, the Australian & New Zealand Society of Palliative Medicine, and the Center to Advance Palliative Care. Published both online and in print, it's peer-reviewed and published monthly. This title started in 1998, and it covers medical, psychological, and legal issues regarding end-of-life care and the relief of suffering for patients with incurable/relentless pain. The journal is aimed toward practitioners, academicians, and students. It includes original articles such as "The Effect of Community-Based Specialist Palliative Care Teams on Place of Care"; reports such as "The Growth of Palliative Care in U.S. hospitals: A Status Report"; fast facts and concepts; case discussions; and reviews and personal reflections. Tables of contents and abstracts, from the first volume onward, are available online at the journal's web site. URL: www.liebertpub.com/jpm

1600. ***Journal of Social Work in End-of-Life & Palliative Care.*** Formerly (until 2005): *Loss, Grief & Care.* [ISSN: 1552-4256] 1986. q. GBP 555 (print & online eds.)). Routledge, 711 3rd Ave, 8th Fl., New York, NY 10017; http://www.routledge.com. Illus., adv. Sample. Refereed. Vol. ends: Winter. Microform: PQC. Reprint: PSC. *Indexed:* A01, A22, ASSIA, E01, SSA. *Bk. rev.:* Number and length vary. *Aud.:* Ac, Sa.

Associated with the Social Work in Hospice and Palliative Care Network, this journal is peer-reviewed and publishes both online and in print quarterly. Previously known as *Loss, Grief & Care* (1987-2004), it has original articles and reflections from social workers in the field. This journal, published by Routledge, goes back to 1987, and it has the table of contents and abstracts, or a first-page review, listed online. Some examples of article titles include "Missed Opportunity: Hospice Care and the Family" and "Adult Hospice Social Work Intervention Outcomes in the United States." URL: www.tandfonline.com/loi/wswe20#.VuqXEuJ97cs

1601. ***Mortality: promoting the interdisciplinary study of death and dying.*** [ISSN: 1357-6275] 1996. q. GBP 773 (print & online eds.)). Ed(s): Kate Woodthorpe, Arnar Arnason. Routledge, 4 Park Sq, Milton Park, Abingdon, OX14 4RN, United Kingdom; subscriptions@tandf.co.uk; http://www.tandfonline.com. Illus., adv. Sample. Refereed. Reprint: PSC. *Indexed:* A01, A22, AmHI, E01, SSA. *Bk. rev.:* Number and length vary. *Aud.:* Ac, Sa.

Mortality is published with the support of the Association for the Study of Death and Society (ASDS). It is an internationally peer-reviewed journal and is published quarterly. Started in 1996, it's of particular interest to practitioners, students, and faculty in counseling, social work, the health professions, psychology, sociology, anthropology, religion, and literature. An annual thematic issue comes out every year and treats the topic in depth. This year's thematic issue was titled "Death, memory and the human in the Internet Era." Some articles listed from other issues include: "A 'good death' for all?: examining issues for palliative care in correctional settings" and "Funerals against death." A sample issue and tables of contents, and abstracts beginning with volume 1 (1996), are available on the journal's web site. URL: www.tandfonline.com/toc/cmrt20/current#.VNExtPldVPM

1602. ***Omega: Journal of Death and Dying.*** [ISSN: 0030-2228] 1970. 8x/yr. USD 1008 (print & online eds.)). Ed(s): Kenneth J Doka. Sage Publications, Inc., 2455 Teller Rd, Thousand Oaks, CA 91320; info@sagepub.com; http://www.sagepub.com. Illus., index, adv. Sample. Refereed. Vol. ends: No. 4. Reprint: PSC. *Indexed:* A01, A22, ASSIA, AgeL, BRI, MLA-IB, SSA. *Bk. rev.:* Number and length vary. *Aud.:* Ac, Sa.

Published online and in print, eight times a year, and peer reviewed, this journal has been around for many years (since 1970). This is the official journal of the Association for Death Education and Counseling. This title's focus is toward practitioners in counseling, social work, and the health fields. It's also helpful for students studying in the field. Some examples of the areas of crisis management the readers will learn about in this journal include terminal illness, fatal accidents, catastrophe, suicide, and bereavement. Sample issues are available online. Recent articles include "Because I'm Also Part of the Family. Children's Participation in Rituals After the Loss of a Parent or Sibling: A Qualitative Study From the Children's Perspective" and "Examining the Importance of Mental Pain and Physical Dissociation and the Fluid Nature of Suicidality in Young Suicide Attempters." Tables of contents and abstracts are available on the journal's web site. URL: https://us.sagepub.com/en-us/nam/omega-journal-of-death-and-dying/journal202394

1603. ***Palliative & Supportive Care.*** [ISSN: 1478-9515] 2003. 6x/yr. Ed(s): William Breitbart. Cambridge University Press, University Printing House, Shaftesbury Rd, Cambridge, CB2 8BS, United Kingdom; journals@cambridge.org; https://www.cambridge.org/. Adv. Sample. Refereed. Reprint: PSC. *Indexed:* A22, E01. *Aud.:* Ac, Sa.

Available in print and online, six times a year, this peer-reviewed journal is published by Cambridge University Press. It started in 2003, and has the abstracts and table of contents online from 2010. This title offers original articles, review articles, case reports, personal reflections, and poetry/fiction. It is directed toward practitioners, faculty, and students in the field of counseling, social work, education, pastoral counseling, and health. Some examples of the more recent articles offered include "Two worlds: Adolescents' strategies for managing life with a parent in hospice," "Assessment of discomfort in patients with cognitive failure in palliative care," and "The positioning of palliative care in acute care: A multiperspective qualitative study in the context of metastatic melanoma." URL: http://journals.cambridge.org/action/displayJournal?jid=PAX

1604. ***Palliative Care and Social Practice.*** Formerly (until 2019): *Palliative Care: Research and Treatment.* [ISSN: 2632-3524] 2008. . Free. Ed(s): Paraq Bharadwaj. Sage Publications Ltd., 1 Oliver's Yard, 55 City Rd, London, EC1Y 1SP, United Kingdom; info@sagepub.com; https://www.sagepub.com. Refereed. *Indexed:* A01. *Bk. rev.:* Number and length vary. *Aud.:* Ac, Sa.

This is an open-access, online-only, peer-reviewed journal from New Zealand, and its frequency is irregular. Active since 2008, this journal covers clinical, scientific, and policy issues in palliative care. It is available through the Directory of Open Access as well as through major databases. Articles can be downloaded in a pdf format. One is given an opportunity to comment on and discuss an article within the title's web site. Article metrics are available. The layout of the journal is not that many articles appear at once in one volume, but rather that articles are placed on the web site as they are published, and all are put together as one volume per year. Some of the article titles include "Death in Long-term Care: A Brief Report Examining Factors Associated with Death within 31 Days of Assessment" and "Clinical Prediction Rule for Patient Outcome after In-Hospital CPR: A New Model, Using Characteristics Present at Hospital Admission, to Identify Patients Unlikely to Benefit from CPR after In-Hospital Cardiac Arrest." The articles can be found on the journal's web site. URL: www.la-press.com/journal-palliative-care-research-and-treatment-j86

1605. ***Palliative Medicine: a multiprofessional journal.*** [ISSN: 0269-2163] 1987. 10x/yr. USD 4931 (print & online eds.)). Ed(s): Catherine Walshe. Sage Publications Ltd., 1 Oliver's Yard, 55 City Rd, London, EC1Y 1SP, United Kingdom; info@sagepub.com; https://www.sagepub.com/. Illus., index, adv. Sample. Refereed. Vol. ends: Dec. Reprint: PSC. *Indexed:* A01, A22, ASSIA, E01. *Bk. rev.:* Number and length vary. *Aud.:* Ac, Sa.

Published both online and in print, this peer-reviewed journal from United Kingdom has been around since 1987. As of 2013, it started publishing ten issues a year. This journal is a member of the Committee on Publication Ethics (COPE). The aim of the journal to improve the knowledge and clinical practice in the care of patients with advanced diseases. Articles are published online before they get to print. As with other Sage publications, abstracts and table of contents are available online. This title covers reviews, case reports, and original research. Some examples of original research article titles include "Perceptions of health professionals on subcutaneous hydration in palliative care: A qualitative study" and "Measuring healthcare integration: Operationalization of a framework for a systems evaluation of palliative care structures, processes, and outcomes." URL: http://pmj.sagepub.com

1606. ***Progress in Palliative Care: science and the art of caring.*** [ISSN: 0969-9260] 1993. bi-m. GBP 646 (print & online eds.)). Ed(s): Mellar Davis. Taylor & Francis, 2, 3 & 4 Park Sq, Milton Park, Abingdon, OX14 4RN, United Kingdom; subscriptions@tandf.co.uk; https://www.tandfonline.com. Adv. Refereed. Reprint: PSC. *Aud.:* Ac, Sa.

This is an international, peer-reviewed journal available both online and print. It has been around since 1993, but online access to the abstracts or the first page and table of contents is from 2003 onward. The journal covers all aspects of palliative care, with the emphasis on current trends and controversies. The journal also publishes an occasional special themed issue. The journal is aimed at palliative care professionals, faculty, and students in the field. Some current articles in the special issue on "Public Health" include "Future directions for community engagement as a public health approach to palliative care in Australia" and "Research in public health and end-of-life care-Building on the past and developing the new." Open-access and other articles are available on the journal's web site. URL: www.tandfonline.com/loi/yppc20#.V2hXajWGN6k

1607. ***Suicide and Life-Threatening Behavior.*** Former titles (until 1976): *Suicide;* (until 1975): *Life Threatening Behavior.* [ISSN: 0363-0234] 1970. bi-m. GBP 756. John Wiley & Sons, Inc., 111 River St, Hoboken, NJ 07030; cs-journals@wiley.com; http://www.wiley.com/. Illus., index, adv. Sample. Microform: PQC. Reprint: PSC. *Indexed:* A01, A22, BRI, CJPI, Chicano, E01, ERIC, SSA. *Bk. rev.:* Number and length vary. *Aud.:* Ac, Sa.

The official journal of the American Association of Suicidology, and published by John Wiley & Sons, this publication has been around since 1970, under other titles. It's international, interdisciplinary, and peer reviewed. One can get a sample issue online. Access to abstracts and table of contents is available on the web site. This title keeps professionals apprised of the latest research, theories, and intervention approaches regarding suicidal behavior and life-threatening behavior. The approaches cover biological, psychological, and sociological angles. Some examples of articles include: "Physical Activity, Suicide Risk Factors, and Suicidal Ideation in a Veteran Sample" and "Effect of Problem-Solving Therapy on Depressed Low-Income Homebound Older Adults' Death/Suicidal Ideation and Hopelessness." This journal is good for practitioners, faculty, and students in the medical, counseling, pastoral, mental health, and social work fields. URL: http://onlinelibrary.wiley.com/journal/10.1111/(ISSN)1943-278X

■ DIGITAL HUMANITIES

Odile Harter, Research Librarian, Harvard College Library, Cambridge, MA 02138; oharter@fas.harvard.edu

Introduction

Digital humanities (DH) is a relatively new academic field whose definition continues to be the subject of vigorous, sometimes acrimonious, debate. In general, "digital humanities" refers to a set of interdisciplinary practices that combine computational tools with humanistic modes of inquiry. The range of scholarly activity that might be referred to as digital humanities falls into three broad categories: (1) the use of computational methods to analyze texts and other objects traditionally within the purview of the humanities, as in mapping, text mining, or network analysis; (2) the rendering of artistic production into digital formats via the creation of digital libraries, web portals, and so on, which often entails the encoding of literature, art, or music so that it can be navigated in a digital environment; and finally, (3) the application of humanistic interpretive analysis to the objects of computation, such as software code, algorithmic culture, or large datasets.

Scholarly work in the field is scattered across a number of different venues: the best digital scholarship often appears in the major journal of a traditional humanities discipline (sometimes as part of a special issue on "data" or "the digital"). There are also important contributions from journals in technical fields and from journals devoted to media studies, information science, libraries, and publishing (*The Journal of Electronic Publishing, Digital Journalism*). A significant portion of the field's scholarly debate and sharing of new work takes place in dedicated web communities and professional association websites, such as Digital Medievalist or the Association for Computers in the Humanities. Rich discussion also takes place on individual project websites, in blog posts, and on Twitter or other social media platforms. There are also a number of sites dedicated to aggregating and curating DH content, such as the excellent *Digital Humanities Now* from the Roy Rosenzweig Center for History and New Media at George Mason University. Books, often with innovative digital components, play an equally important role. See, for example, the *Debates in the Digital Humanities* series of edited collections from the University of Minnesota Press.

DH journals nonetheless offer a forum for the ongoing debate about how to define and shape the field, reports on new projects, and the discussion and refinement of new technical methods. They also offer an opportunity for experimenting with new formats for the academic journal. Many journals are online only and take advantage of the ability to incorporate data and code, publish on a rolling basis, embed media, and use tagging systems to group individual articles in multiple ways. Even high-quality journals can be quite short-lived, reflecting the relative youth of the field as well as its interest in new, sometimes unstable technologies as well as collaborative, crowd-sourced projects.

Basic Periodicals

Digital Humanities Quarterly; Journal of the Text Encoding Initiative.

Basic Abstracts and Indexes

Arts and Humanities Citation Index, Historical Abstracts, Linguistics and Language Behavior Abstracts, MLA International Bibliography.

1608. *Big Data & Society.* [ISSN: 2053-9517] 2014. . Free. Ed(s): Evelyn Ruppert. Sage Publications, Inc., 2455 Teller Rd, Thousand Oaks, CA 91320; info@sagepub.com; http://www.sagepub.com. Adv. Refereed. *Aud.:* Ac.

Big Data & Society focuses on the use of big data to "access and assess" the social sciences. The scope is interdisciplinary, and the journal does welcome (and occasionally publishes) work by humanists, but most corresponding authors hail from the social sciences. Recent topics have included a special issue on "Veillance and Transparency," algorithms in culture, artworks such as the Crowd-Sourced Intelligence Agency and Tracing You, and big data in law and policy. Articles are published on a rolling basis: each issue is accumulated over the course of a six-month period, for two issues a year. The journal is online only and open access; authors are charged a publication fee. Recommended for academic libraries.

1609. *Computational Culture: a journal of software studies.* [ISSN: 2047-2390] 2011. s-a. Free. Ed(s): Matthew Fuller. Computational Culture, http://computationalculture.net/. Refereed. *Bk. rev.:* Number and length vary. *Aud.:* Ac.

While it lacks some of the rigor and polish of more established academic journals, *Computational Culture* stakes out important territory in the emerging field of software studies. This field engages with the "fundamental reconstitution that computing has brought to contemporary life" by applying humanistic interpretive analysis to the "computational objects, processes, and mentalities" that shape forms of governance, thought, "modes of being and sensing," and culture. Recent articles have discussed computational representations of the human body, posited a "computational episteme" that theorizes language for analysis rather than meaning, and considered the subtle ways that PowerPoint shapes public speech. A recommended supplement for academic collections.

1610. *Digital Humanities Quarterly.* [ISSN: 1938-4122] 2007. q. Free. Ed(s): Julia Flanders. The Alliance of Digital Humanities Organizations, Snell Library 213, Northeastern University, Boston, MA 02115; editors@digitalhumanities.org; http://digitalhumanities.org. Refereed. *Indexed:* MLA-IB. *Bk. rev.:* Number and length vary. *Aud.:* Ac.

Started in 2007, this is one of the field's core journals. A major focus is reflection on the identity, definition, and impact of the still-emerging field of digital humanities, but the broad range of topics covered also include specific tools and methodologies, metadata creation and digital curation practices, and pedagogy. Article formats range from the traditional argumentative essay and conference proceedings to project write-ups to more experimental formats such as timelines or creative compositions. Special issues have focused on classical studies, feminisms, transdisciplinarity, multilingual DH, and undergraduate education. *DHQ* is designed for a web-based environment: there are no article pdfs, and each paragraph has its own html anchor. An essential title for academic collections.

1611. *Digital Philology (Online): a journal of medieval cultures.* [ISSN: 2162-9552] 2012. s-a. USD 90. Ed(s): Albert Lloret. The Johns Hopkins University Press, 2715 N Charles St, Baltimore, MD 21218; http://www.press.jhu.edu. Adv. Sample. *Bk. rev.:* Number and length vary. *Aud.:* Ac.

The beautiful manuscripts that form the evidence base for Medieval Studies are a high priority for library digitization projects, with the result that digital Medieval Studies is an active area of inquiry with several journals devoted to the topic. Issues of *Digital Philology* tend to be themed around a particular text or author. Most articles address the application of digital methods to medieval texts, either via the use of computational analysis to gain insight, or via the influence of digital library platforms on the modern reader's experience, though some address the digital more directly than others. Recent articles argue about the nature of medieval narrative; analyze how size and layout influence the ordering of polyphonic musical works in the Machaut manuscripts; and use digital tools to reassess scribal hands in the *Parker Chronicle*. A supplement for academic collections.

1612. *Digital Scholarship in the Humanities.* Formerly (until 2015): *Literary and Linguistic Computing;* Which was formed by the merger of (1980-1986): *A L L C Journal;* (1981-1986): *A L L C Bulletin;* Which was formerly (until 1981): *Association for Literary and Linguistic Computing. Bulletin.* [ISSN: 2055-7671] 1986. q. EUR 567. Ed(s): Edward Vanhoutte. Oxford University Press, Great Clarendon St, Oxford, OX2 6DP, United Kingdom; onlinequeries.uk@oup.com; http://global.oup.com. Illus., adv. Sample. Refereed. Vol. ends: Nov. Reprint: PSC. *Indexed:* A01, A22, AmHI, BAS, CompLI, E01, MLA-IB. *Bk. rev.:* Number and length vary. *Aud.:* Ac.

This title was begun in 1986 as *Literary and Linguistic Computing* and retitled *Digital Scholarship in the Humanities* in 2015. The editors invite contributions "on all aspects of digital scholarship in the Humanities," though the contents are still heavily weighted toward topics in computational linguistics. Recent articles discuss spatial analysis of California journalists' word choices; a study of the rate of decline in the introduction of unique words in different genres of novels; a reconstruction of the chronological sequence of Shakespeare's plays based on patterns of vocabulary and punctuation; and a stylometric model for detecting oaths in Koranic texts. The emphasis on methodology and technical questions in corpus linguistics makes *DSH* an important journal for digital humanists who work in text mining.

1613. *Digital Studies / Le champ numerique.* [ISSN: 1918-3666] 1992. . Free. Ed(s): Daniel Paul O'Donnell. Open Library of Humanities, Salisbury House, Station Rd, Cambridge, CB1 2LA, United Kingdom; martin.eve@openlibhums.org; https://www.openlibhums.org. Refereed. *Indexed:* MLA-IB. *Bk. rev.:* Number and length vary. *Aud.:* Ac.

This title is published on a rolling basis by the Canadian Society for Digital Humanities, a member of the Alliance of Digital Humanities Organizations. There is wide variation in the shape and size of individual issues, as volumes are accumulated over the course of a year, and articles are often grouped into special issues and "clusters." "Volume 0," which runs from 1998 to 2008, consists of working papers from the Congress of the Humanities and Social Sciences; the journal broadened its scope with the launch of volume 1 in 2009, inviting any "well-researched article" in the field, but with particular interest in interdisciplinary work and work that is international in scope. Abstracts are in English and French; most articles are in English, though occasionally in French or other languages. Topics of frequent interest include digital publishing, new digital tools, and gaming. Recent articles have discussed critical copyright studies, the textual traditions of digital editing, the organization of academic programs in computational humanities, and the complex issues involved in archiving web material that is involved in a legal dispute. A supplement for academic collections.

1614. *International Journal of Humanities and Arts Computing.* Formerly (until 2007): *History and Computing.* [ISSN: 1753-8548] 1989. s-a. GBP 91 (print & online eds.)). Ed(s): Dr. David Bodenhamer, Dr. Paul Ell. Edinburgh University Press Ltd., The Tun, Holyrood Rd, 12 (2f) Jackson's Entry, Edinburgh, EH8 8PJ, United Kingdom; journals@eup.ed.ac.uk; http://www.euppublishing.com. Adv. Sample. Refereed. *Indexed:* A01, A22, AmHI, CompLI. *Aud.:* Ac.

This title was begun in 1989 as *History and Computing* and retitled in 2007 to reflect a broadened scope. In 2008, the editors announced a series of special double issues devoted to "key fields of humanities and arts computing." In 2012, the journal shifted its focus eastward by partnering with TELDAP (Taiwan e-Learning and Digital Archives Program), and essays from TELDAP's international conference now appear as occasional supplements. Special-issue topics have included geocultural space, complex datasets, and European research infrastructure. Recent articles have discussed space visualization in film studies; a proof-of-concept for using linked open data to organize and interrelate thirteenth-century French motets; and lessons learned from mapping Samuel Beckett's life in the Digital Literary Atlas of Ireland. Many articles have two or more authors, reflecting the collaborative nature of DH projects. This journal will be of interest to DH practitioners with at least some technical background. A recommended supplement for academic collections.

1615. *Journal of Cultural Analytics.* [ISSN: 2371-4549] 2016. irreg. approx. monthly. Free. Ed(s): Andrew Piper. McGill University, 853 Sherbrooke St W, Montreal, QC H3A OG4, Canada; servicepoint@mcgill.ca; https://www.mcgill.ca/. Refereed. *Aud.:* Ac.

An open-access journal "dedicated to the computational study of culture." Launched in 2016 by Andrew Piper, who retains a strong influence as editor and occasional contributor, as well as via the contributions of scholars from his NovelTM project. The journal has been publishing steadily at the rate of about one article a month. It is closely linked with its sister journal *Post45* (dedicated to post-1945 American literature and culture), with which it shares many design elements, such as rolling publication and using the category name "peer-reviewed" for articles. "Clusters" offer themed groupings, and they're the format used to create special issues. While young, the journal offers high-quality digital scholarship that interweaves computational methods with more traditional ones, and consistently uses computational analysis to inform and critique current scholarly inquiry in a number of humanities disciplines, with a heavy emphasis on literature. Recent articles have used comparative computational analysis of audio recordings to assess the literature on poets' reading styles, taken a deep dive into Ball State's data set of 19th-century library circulation records to illuminate the role of gender in adolescent reading habits, and a comparison of how physical appearance and geo-spatial concepts are used in verbal constructions of race across a large corpus of English texts contemporary with Shakespeare's *Othello*. A recommended supplement for academic libraries.

1616. *Journal of Interactive Technology and Pedagogy.* [ISSN: 2166-6245] 2012. s-a. Ed(s): Laura Wildemann Kane. City University of New York, Graduate Center, 365 Fifth Ave, New York, NY 10016; mwasem@gc.cuny.edu; http://www.gc.cuny.edu. *Aud.:* Ac.

A journal devoted to "critical and creative uses of technology in teaching, learning, and research," with a clear emphasis on classroom practice. The bulk of the articles concern topics in the humanities, and many are squarely within the digital humanities proper. Each issue has a different pair of guest editors, and many tackle a specific theme. The journal is based at the City University of New York (CUNY), but now draws authors and editors from increasingly farther afield. The May 2017 issue celebrated the journal's first ten issues and took stock of the digital humanities in general. Recent themed issues have taken on Art History, ePortfolios, and Disability Studies, while individual articles have addressed such topics as a critical examination of how digital platforms and course content impact students' interpretations of the material, as well as their expectations of privacy in learning; a case study of an information literacy course; and reporting on a decade-long collaborative project between electrical engineers and art conservators, curators, and historians that produced a new method for analyzing paintings. A recommended supplement for faculty who are bringing digital humanities into the classroom.

1617. *Journal of the Text Encoding Initiative.* [ISSN: 2162-5603] 2011. q. Free. Ed(s): John Walsh. Text Encoding Initiative, 30 Addison St., Arlington, MA 02476; info@tei-c.org; http://www.tei-c.org. Refereed. *Indexed:* MLA-IB. *Aud.:* Ac.

The Text Encoding Initiative (TEI), which began discussing the digital encoding of humanities data in 1987, pioneered many of the practices and resources now known as "digital humanities," and the TEI Consortium continues to pursue its mission "to develop and maintain guidelines for the digital encoding of literary and linguistic texts." Begun in 2011, the *Journal of the Text Encoding Initiative* publishes selected papers from the TEI conference, papers focused on a special theme (for example, linguistics or infrastructures), and, starting in 2014, solicits articles via open calls for papers. Frequency varies, with a minimum of one issue per year. Some issues are published on a rolling basis. Text encoding is fundamentally technical: most articles offer detailed technical discussions of programming and markup practices, often with a view to improving interoperability. But the encoding of humanities data inevitably raises more interpretive questions, and the journal offers a forum for general discussions of "the role of technological standards in the digital humanities." Recent articles have discussed the evaluation of digital humanities work for promotion and tenure; how to represent and connect Greek and Latin text fragments; and the importance of encoding dictionaries in ways that optimize compatibility with word-frequency corpora. An essential source for technically advanced scholars who wish to learn about digital projects and stay abreast of developments in best practices and methodologies for text encoding.

Kairos: A Journal of Rhetoric, Technology, and Pedagogy. See Education/Specific Subjects and Teaching Methods: Communication Arts section.

■ DISABILITIES

See also Education; and Medicine and Health sections.

Nedelina Tchangalova, Public Health Librarian/STEM Library, University of Maryland, College Park, MD 20874; nedelina@umd.edu

Introduction

Since the passage of the Americans with Disabilities Act in 1990, there is a constant growth in the alertness and recognition of people with disabilities through the distinction and prestige of many journals and magazines included in this chapter. The style and language of the publications are all-inclusive and empowering. The focus is on the abilities of people who are physically or mentally challenged rather than on their disabilities. All people who have a connection to a person with a (dis)Ability or are themselves a person with a (dis)Ability will find helpful information and life inspiration in several magazines in this section. For the scholarly community, academic journals provide clinical practice based on evidence and showcase recent research developments related to people with a broad spectrum of abilities. These publications show consciousness for disabilities when examining certain applied issues in an upfront style.

The periodicals described in this chapter are representative samples of publications covering various aspects of disabilities, including news in technology development and research; career opportunities; policy, practice, and perspectives; sports; and education. Periodicals related to disabilities are included in other sections of this volume, such as Blind and Visually Impaired; Education; Family; and Occupations and Careers. With the globalization of scientific research, an attempt was made to add publications offering international experiences of individuals with disabilities, practitioners, and researchers. The listing of periodicals here offers many well-known periodicals for the general audience, as well as scholarly publications that connect researchers and practitioners around the globe.

Basic Periodicals

Adapted Physical Activity Quarterly, American Annals of the Deaf, American Journal on Intellectual and Developmental Disabilities, Education and Training in Autism and Developmental Disabilities, Hearing Health, New Mobility, Review of Disability Studies, Sports 'n Spokes, Technology and Disability, Topics in Language Disorders.

Basic Abstracts and Indexes

Academic Search Premier, CINAHL, Education Abstracts, ERIC, Linguistics and Language Behavior Abstracts, PsycINFO, SocIndex, SPORTDiscus with Full Text.

1618. *Ability.* Formerly (until 200?): *Ability Magazine.* [ISSN: 1062-5321] 1992. bi-m. USD 29.70 domestic; USD 9.95 per issue. C.R. Cooper Publishing, 8941 Atlanta Ave, Huntington Beach, CA 92646. Illus., adv. *Aud.:* Hs, Ga, Ac, Sa.

Ability magazine "strives to change public perception of what it means to have a disability by focusing on ability, shattering myths and stereotypes that surround disabilities." The bi-monthly issues include articles ranging from celebrity interviews to CEO profiles in the areas of health, environmental protection, assistive technology, employment, sports, the arts, travel, universal design, mental wellness, and much more. Writers come from a wide range of backgrounds including researchers, best-selling authors, U.S. senators, and advocates. Colorful layouts that incorporate photographs and graphic design elements add flair, with cover stories that feature prominent celebrities, politicians, business leaders, athletes, or similar role models with stories to tell about facing and surmounting challenges related to disabling health conditions. Regular editorial features include interviews, humor, and a crossword puzzle. The journal is searchable on the publisher's website. It has embedded VOICEYE, a high-density matrix barcode system, which allows greater access to its content and enables its readers to hear print through smartphones and tablets in 58 languages. This is a good choice for libraries that collect popular magazines.

1619. *Able Magazine: your favourite disability lifestyle magazine.* Formerly (until 2004): *Disability View.* [ISSN: 1472-4839] 1994. bi-m. GBP 15. Craven Publishing Ltd, 15-39 Durham St, Kinning Park, Glasgow, G41 1BS, United Kingdom; enquiries@cravenpublishing.co.uk; http://www.cravenpublishing.com/. Adv. *Aud.:* Ga.

The magazine's editorial is all about "what disabled people can do, not what they can not." The general lifestyle magazine is intended for people with mobility, sensory, and learning impairments; their families and caregivers; and health and social care professionals. The magazine covers the entire disability spectrum: news, travel, leisure, research, and the latest products as well as sports, activities, and competitions, offering advice and inspiration to readers. A digital edition preview is available on the magazine's website. It features a user-friendly website design. The digital edition provides options for content searching and for expanding the layout of the magazine's print version of the article. An embedded listening tool on the magazine's website provides another way of access to the articles.

AccessWorld (Online). See Blind and Visually Impaired section.

1620. *Adapted Physical Activity Quarterly.* [ISSN: 0736-5829] 1984. q. USD 731. Ed(s): Jeffrey Martin. Human Kinetics, Inc., PO Box 361, Birmingham, AL 35201-0361; humankineticsjournals@subscriptionoffice.com; http://journals.humankinetics.com. Illus., index, adv. Refereed. Vol. ends: Oct. Reprint: PSC. *Indexed:* A01, A22, C45, ERIC, SD. *Bk. rev.:* Number and length vary. *Aud.:* Ac, Sa.

This research journal offers readers the latest "scholarly inquiry relating to physical activity that is adapted in order to enable and enhance performance and participation in people with disability." This is the official journal of the International Federation of Adapted Physical Activity. Each issue is divided into seven sections featuring primary research articles, case studies, techniques for adapting equipment, facilities, methodology, and clinical settings; an editor's column; abstracts of research articles; and books and media reviews. The journal publishes with person-first, nonsexist language. It is multidisciplinary in scope, inviting research from the fields of corrective therapy, gerontology, health care, occupational therapy, pediatrics, physical education, dance, sports medicine, physical therapy, recreation, and rehabilitation. The journal is searchable on the publisher's website. The website also provides access to tables of contents and abstracts. The journal is widely indexed. Recommended for academic libraries.

1621. *ADDitude: strategies and support for adhd & ld.* [ISSN: 1529-1014] 1998. 4x/yr. USD 19.99 combined subscription domestic print & online eds.; USD 27 combined subscription Canada print & online eds. Ed(s): Wayne Kalyn. New Hope Media, LLC, 108 West 39th St., New York, NY 10018; http://www.newhopemedia.com. Illus., adv. *Bk. rev.:* 2-3 per issue. *Aud.:* Hs, Ga, Sa.

This readable quarterly magazine is of interest to families and adults living with Attention Deficit Disorder (ADD) and the professionals who work with them. *ADDitude*'s multi-platform resource network serves its readers each month through print and digital, video, webinars, social media, and more. Subscriptions include a print issue, a digital edition for a tablet, computer, or smartphone, plus subscriber-only digital archive access. Subscribers get the free "ADHD Medication & Treatment" e-book when they order. Colorful layouts deliver three or four cover stories; more than a dozen regular columns, such as self-help, legal issues, and relationship advice; and many additional articles presented in sections—symptom tests and info; medications and treatments; for parents and for adults; blogs and forums; downloads, webinars, and tools for professionals. Many articles are written in the first person by people with ADD, family members, and authors of current books. Each issue features letters from readers and a reader poll. There is an annual guide to schools and camps. The website offers free access to web-exclusive content. The magazine is not indexed in any known databases. Recommended for public libraries.

1622. *American Annals of the Deaf.* Formerly (until 1886): *American Annals of the Deaf and Dumb.* [ISSN: 0002-726X] 1847. q. USD 95 (Individuals, USD 55). Ed(s): Peter V Paul. Gallaudet University Press, College Hall, 4th Floor, 800 Florida Avenue, NE, Washington, DC 20002; gupress@gallaudet.edu; http://gupress.gallaudet.edu. Illus., index, adv. Refereed. Vol. ends: Dec. Microform: PQC. *Indexed:* A01, A22, BRI, E01, ERIC, MLA-IB. *Aud.:* Ac, Sa.

This is a professional journal that targets teachers, administrators, and researchers in the field of deaf education. It is the official publication of the Council of American Instructors of the Deaf (CAID) and the Conference of Educational Administrators of Schools and Programs for the Deaf (CEASD) and is directed and administered by a Joint Annals Administrative Committee made up of members of the executive committees of both of these organizations. The scope of the journal extends beyond education of deaf students to include such topics as communication methods and strategies; language development; mainstreaming and residential schools; parent-child relationships; and teacher training and teaching skills. Each regular issue opens with an editorial. In addition to *Annals*' four issues each year (spring, summer, fall, and winter), subscriptions include an annual reference issue with a directory of deaf education schools; information on programs in the United States and Canada; and demographic data about the schools and students who are deaf or hard-of-hearing. The publisher's website includes indexes by subject, author, and individual volume/issue, and an annual print index is published in the winter issue. This is an essential resource for libraries that serve populations who are deaf or that support professional preparation for those entering the deaf education field.

1623. *American Journal on Intellectual and Developmental Disabilities.* Former titles (until 2008): *American Journal on Mental Retardation (Print);* (until 1987): *American Journal of Mental Deficiency;* (until 1939): *American Association on Mental Deficiency. Proceedings and Addresses of the Annual Session.* [ISSN: 1944-7515] 1876. bi-m. USD 383 (print & online eds.)). Ed(s): Deborah Fidler. American Association on Intellectual and Developmental Disabilities, 501 3rd St, NW, Ste 200, Washington, DC 20001; aaidd@allenpress.com; http://www.allenpress.com. Illus., adv. Sample. Refereed. Vol. ends: Nov. Microform: PQC. *Indexed:* A22, BRI, CBRI, Chicano, ERIC, MLA-IB. *Aud.:* Ac, Sa.

This peer-reviewed journal is dedicated to multidisciplinary scholarly research into the causes, treatments, and prevention of intellectual disabilities. Articles include empirical research on characteristics of people with intellectual and developmental disabilities, systematic reviews of relevant research literature, and evaluative research on new treatments. It is published bimonthly by the American Association on Intellectual and Developmental Disabilities. The journal is widely indexed, including ERIC, PsycINFO, PubMed, Scopus, Web of Science, and many more. Recommended for libraries that serve researchers, clinicians, students, policymakers, and other professionals interested in the fields of disabilities, life science, biology, neuroscience, and behavioral and health sciences as they pertain to intellectual and related disabilities.

Behavior Modification. See Psychology section.

Careers and the Disabled. See Occupations and Careers section.

1624. *Education and Training in Autism and Developmental Disabilities.* Former titles (until 2010): *Education and Training in Developmental Disabilities;* (until 2003): *Education and Training in Mental Retardation and Developmental Disabilities;* (until 1994): *Education and Training in Mental Retardation;* (until 1987): *Education and Training of the Mentally Retarded.* [ISSN: 2154-1647] 1966. q. USD 249 (Individuals, USD 100; Free to members). Ed(s): Stanley H Zucker. Council for Exceptional Children, Division on Autism and Developmental Disabilities, 2900 Crystal Dr, Ste 1000, Arlington, VA 22202; http://www.cec.sped.org/. Illus., index. Refereed. Circ: 6000 Paid. Vol. ends: Dec. Microform: PQC. *Indexed:* A22, ERIC. *Aud.:* Ac, Sa.

This quarterly journal is published by the Council for Exceptional Children, Division on Autism and Developmental Disabilities. Each issue features scholarly research articles related to identification, assessment, educational programming, characteristics, training of instructional personnel, rehabilitation, prevention, community understanding, and legislation. Content includes qualitative and quantitative empirical research and critical reviews of the literature. The publisher provides RSS feeds for most viewed articles, and a section to most commented articles. Users can search the archives online using keywords and limiting searches to content types, publication date, issues, and authors' names. The December issue includes an annual author and title index. Formerly published as *Education and Training in Developmental Disabilities,* the new title demonstrates increased focus on Autism Spectrum Disorder. This title is widely indexed in library databases including ERIC, PsychInfo, PubMed, and Web of Science, which makes it an excellent choice for academic libraries.

Exceptional Parent (Online). See Family section.

1625. *Hearing Health.* Formerly (until 1992): *Voice.* 1984. q. Free to qualified personnel. Ed(s): Yishane Lee. Hearing Health Foundation, 363 7th Ave, 10th Fl., New York, NY 10001; info@hhf.org; http://hearinghealthfoundation.org/. Illus., adv. *Aud.:* Sa.

Hearing Health is a quarterly consumer magazine with articles that focus primarily on news about the latest trends on technology, personal stories from those with hearing loss, and the most current research developments in hearing and balance science. Each issue includes articles organized in several regular columns, such as "Living with Hearing Loss," "Advocacy," "Research," "Meet the Researcher," and more. Topics include managing hearing loss, assistive technology, personal interest and success stories, and disability rights and education. A special online feature is the "Summer Camp Guide," which lists summer camps by regions in the United States. Helpful links include resources in the areas of advocacy, career resources, and student and college resources. The website provides access to the full content of each issue. Subscriptions are free with registration and include both print and online access. It is an optional acquisition for public libraries that serve a significant population of individuals with hearing problems.

1626. *Intellectual and Developmental Disabilities: journal of policy, practice, and perspectives.* Formerly (until 2007): *Mental Retardation.* [ISSN: 1934-9491] 1963. bi-m. Ed(s): James R Thompson. American Association on Intellectual and Developmental Disabilities, 501 3rd St, NW, Ste 200, Washington, DC 20001; anam@aaidd.org; http://www.aamr.org. Illus., index, adv. Sample. Refereed. Vol. ends: Dec. *Indexed:* A01, A22, MLA-IB. *Aud.:* Ac, Sa.

This peer-reviewed publication is a multidisciplinary journal of policy, practices, and perspectives in intellectual and related developmental disabilities. The journal is dedicated to serve researchers, clinicians, students, policymakers, and other professionals interested in disabilities relevant to emerging policies, innovative practices, and transformative concepts. Each bimonthly issue has articles in the categories of policy, practice or research, and perspectives. It also includes abstracts of the articles in French and Spanish. It is widely indexed, including in Academic Search Complete, CINAHL Plus, EMBASE, PsycINFO, Scopus, and Web of Science. Recommended for academic libraries.

Journal of Developmental Education. See Education/Higher Education section.

1627. *Journal of Disability Policy Studies.* [ISSN: 1044-2073] 1990. q. USD 265 (print & online eds.)). Ed(s): Antonis Katsiyannis, Mitchell Yell. Sage Publications, Inc., 2455 Teller Rd, Thousand Oaks, CA 91320; info@sagepub.com; http://www.sagepub.com. Illus., adv. Sample. Refereed. Microform: PQC. Reprint: PSC. *Indexed:* A01, A22, C42, E01, P61, SSA. *Aud.:* Ac, Sa.

According to the publisher's website, this quarterly journal "addresses compelling variable issues in ethics, policy, and law related to individuals with disabilities." Discussions on issues related to a particular disability area are featured in the "From My Perspective" section of the journal. In addition, ethical issues affecting individuals with disability are discussed in the "Point/Counterpoint" column. Articles encompass a broad number of disciplines and range from disability and aging, policy concerning families of children with disabilities, oppression and disability, school violence policies and interventions, to systems change in supporting individuals with disabilities. This is a truly scholarly journal that is indexed in at least a dozen or so commercial indexes and online databases. Academic and research collections should consider this title, especially in view of the extensive indexing.

1628. *Journal of Intellectual Disabilities.* Former titles (until 2005): *Journal of Learning Disabilities;* (until 2000): *Journal of Learning Disabilities for Nursing, Health and Social Care.* [ISSN: 1744-6295] 1997. q. USD 1696 (print & online eds.)). Ed(s): Ruth Northway. Sage Publications Ltd., 1 Oliver's Yard, 55 City Rd, London, EC1Y 1SP, United Kingdom; info@sagepub.com; https://www.sagepub.com/. Sample. Refereed. Reprint: PSC. *Indexed:* A01, A22, ASSIA, E01, MLA-IB. *Aud.:* Ac, Sa.

The journal publishes international studies that "combines practice development innovation with robust research methodology." It provides a forum for both practitioners and researchers to make significant contributions to enhancing the quality of life for people with intellectual disabilities and their supporters. The journal is widely indexed in many databases from various publishers. Academic and research collections should consider this title, especially in view of the extensive indexing.

Journal of Learning Disabilities. See Education/Educational Psychology and Measurement, Special Education, Counseling section.

Learning Disability Quarterly. See Education/Educational Psychology and Measurement, Special Education, Counseling section.

1629. *New Mobility: the magazine for active wheelchair users.* Former titles (until 1994): *Spinal Network's New Mobility;* (until 1992): *Spinal Network EXTRA.* [ISSN: 1086-4741] 1989. m. No Limits Communications Inc., PO Box 220, Horsham, PA 19044. Illus., adv. Sample. *Aud.:* Hs, Ga.

This glossy, upbeat magazine helps fill the need for popular, general-interest publications for people with disabilities, especially for those with mobility impairments. *New Mobility*, acquired by the United Spinal Association in 2010, covers medical news and current research; jobs; benefits; civil rights; sports, recreation, and travel; and fertility, pregnancy, and child care. Feature articles from current issues can be read on the magazine's website. The site also features a search engine for finding written materials grouped in several categories including "Accessibility," "Advocacy," "Health," "Humor," "Lifestyle," "Technology & Products," and many more. Both the magazine and the website represent an upbeat and positive lifestyle. *New Mobility* is a good choice for public libraries.

1630. *P N.* Formerly (until 1992): *Paraplegia News;* Which Incorporated: *Journal of Paraplegia.* 1946. m. USD 26 domestic; USD 38 foreign; USD 5 per issue. Ed(s): Tom Fjerstad. P V A Publications, 2111 E Highland Ave, Ste 180, Phoenix, AZ 85016; info@pnnews.com; http://www.pvamagazines.com. Illus., index, adv. Vol. ends: Dec. *Indexed:* BRI, SD. *Aud.:* Ga, Ac, Sa.

Each monthly issue features news, research, and information about new products, disability legislation, veteran's affairs, accessible travel, assistive technology, housing, employment, and health care for individuals with spinal-cord injuries. Published by the Paralyzed Veterans of America, the magazine is international in scope and is dedicated "to bringing the very best of real-time, up to the moment news and information, for wheelchair users, family members, and medical professionals on the go." The website features tables of contents and article abstracts for each issue, and is searchable. The content is varied, interesting, and of great potential use to wheelchair users and their caregivers. Recommended for public libraries.

1631. *Palaestra: adapted sport, physical education, and recreational therapy.* [ISSN: 8756-5811] 1984. q. USD 326 print & online eds. Ed(s): Martin Block. Sagamore Publishing, 1807 N Federal Dr, Urbana, IL 61801; books@sagamorepub.com; http://www.sagamorepub.com. Illus., index, adv. *Indexed:* A01, A22, BRI, C42, SD. *Bk. rev.:* 5-7, 150-200 words. *Aud.:* Ga, Sa.

The magazine's title is a Greek word for "sport school" or "gymnasium." It is published four times a year in cooperation with Professional Association of Therapeutic Horsemanship International (PATH Intl.); American Association for Physical Activity and Recreation (AAPAR); and United States Paralympics. Articles are focused on people, not disabilities, and is of interest to individuals with disabilities, their caregivers, and professionals in the field. Each issue includes articles on teaching adapted physical education, legislative updates, travel, editorials, sports nutrition, and book and video reviews. The table of contents and article abstracts from the most current issue are available on the publisher's website. Archives are available for limited past issues. The website is searchable. Recommended for libraries that cater to in-service or pre-service physical education teachers, and for public libraries.

Remedial and Special Education. See Education/Educational Psychology and Measurement, Special Education, Counseling section.

1632. *Review of Disability Studies.* [ISSN: 1553-3697] 2003. q. Ed(s): Megan A Conway. University of Hawaii at Manoa, Center on Disability Studies, 1776 University Ave, UA 4-6, Honolulu, HI 96822; rdsj@hawaii.edu; http://www.rds.hawaii.edu. Refereed. *Bk. rev.:* Number and length vary. *Aud.:* Ac, Sa.

This open-access, peer-reviewed, quarterly academic journal is international and interdisciplinary in scope. The culture of disability is the main focus of research articles, essays, and bibliographies included in the journal. Part of the journal's content is forums on disability topics and disability studies, dissertation abstracts, as well as poetry, short stories, creative essays, photographs, and artwork related to disability. Some most recent articles can be read as open-access articles. The full text of the journal from the archives are freely available as downloadable pdf and .doc files. The embedded search box on the site is a tool for locating individual articles on an topic of interest. The website conforms with the standards established by the World Wide Web Consortium for content accessibility (WCAG 2.0), and includes keyboard accessibility, clear and consistent navigation systems, and a consistent structural markup. Indexing is limited to PubMed, SocIndex, Current Abstracts, and TOC Premier. Recommended for academic libraries.

1633. *Sports 'n Spokes: the magazine for wheelchair sports and recreation.* [ISSN: 0161-6706] 1975. bi-m. USD 21 domestic; USD 27 foreign. Ed(s): Tom Fjerstad. P V A Publications, 2111 E Highland Ave, Ste 180, Phoenix, AZ 85016; info@pnnews.com; http://www.pvamagazines.com. Illus., adv. *Indexed:* SD. *Aud.:* Hs, Ga, Sa.

Sports 'n Spokes is a source for wheelchair sports and recreation published by the Paralyzed Veterans of America. This magazine is packed with stories of disability-defying athletic feats. Each bimonthly issue includes a wide range of sports from the traditional basketball, golf, and tennis to the less-well-known fencing, fishing, and rugby. Colorful photographs add to the action. Coverage is inclusive of women, men, and youth, and extends to international events. Four or five feature articles anchor the magazine, with regular departments such as letters to the editor and a calendar of events. Personality profiles and assistive technology are also included. Expanded content and limited full text are freely available on the publisher's website, along with an article search feature. Indexing is limited to SPORTDiscus with Full Text, TOC Premier, and Physical Education Index (Online). Recommended for public libraries, and as a supplemental purchase for recreational reading in academic and special libraries, depending on their missions.

1634. *Technology and Disability.* [ISSN: 1055-4181] 1991. q. EUR 545; USD 670; EUR 654 combined subscription (print & online eds.)). Ed(s): Luc de Witte. I O S Press, Nieuwe Hemweg 6B, Amsterdam, 1013 BG, Netherlands; info@iospress.nl; http://www.iospress.nl. Illus. Refereed. *Indexed:* A01, A22, E01, ErgAb. *Aud.:* Ac, Sa.

This peer-reviewed, quarterly academic journal focuses on the field of assistive technology devices and services for individuals with disabilities and their family members. Although the topics are technical in nature, the journal's content is written with the broader general and academic audience in mind, regardless of training or education. Articles range from research and development efforts, education and training programs, and service and policy activities, to consumer experiences. Indexed in Academic Search Complete, CINAHL, Educational Research Abstracts, Embase, Ergonomics Abstracts, Exceptional Child Education Resources (ECER), Science & Technology Collection, and Scopus. Recommended for academic libraries.

1635. ***Topics in Language Disorders.*** [ISSN: 0271-8294] 1980. q. USD 521. Ed(s): Nickola Wolf Nelson. Lippincott Williams & Wilkins, Two Commerce Sq, 2001 Market St, Philadelphia, PA 19103; customerservice@lww.com; http://www.lww.com. Illus., adv. Sample. Refereed. Vol. ends: Aug. *Indexed:* A01, A22, BRI, ERIC, MLA-IB. *Aud.:* Ac, Sa.

This double-blind, peer-reviewed, scholarly journal targets researchers and clinicians in the field of language development and disorders. The journal strives to provide relevant information to support theoretically sound, culturally sensitive, research-based clinical practices by respected experts. The publisher's website offers access to a keyword search of journal content. In collaboration with the Continuing Education Board of the American Speech-Language-Hearing Association (ASHA), the publisher offers continuing education credits to subscribers and non-subscribers on passing a short test based on the topical issue and the payment of a small fee. It is widely indexed. Recommended for academic libraries that support advanced studies in language development.

■ DO-IT-YOURSELF / MAKERS

See also Building and Construction; Craft; Home; and Interior Design and Decoration sections.

Carrie M. Macfarlane, Director of Research & Instruction, Middlebury College, Middlebury, VT 05753; cmacfarl@middlebury.edu

Introduction

The do-it-yourself genre has evolved. No longer does it simply provide utilitarian advice for thrifty homeowners. Now, it includes mini manuals for hobbyists, and code samples for tech-savvy makers who eschew the disposables of consumer culture.

Even the couch potatoes among us will be inspired by the magazines in this chapter. Can you build a Z80 computer? Refinish a peeling deck? Tune up the lawn mower as the summer months approach? Yes! Anything seems possible when you have a good set of instructions.

The magazines in this chapter will add eye-catching color to your periodicals section with photos and advice from professionals on how to select paints for a living room makeover, how to refresh a mid-century home, or how to create a rainbow lightbox. All of these titles have one goal in common: helping people who want to learn how to get a job done for themselves, rather than asking someone else to do it for them.

You'll notice that some publications are geared toward a specific audience. Is your library in an urban setting? Are you in the vicinity of a historic district? Have you received requests for a makerspace? Consider these factors when you choose your subscriptions, and do-it-yourselfers will thank you as they prepare for their latest projects. Magazines are putting lots of content on their web sites, Facebook, and Instagram pages these days, so it should be easy to select a title without waiting for a sample issue. Make sure your regulars are aware of magazine-themed smartphone apps, too!

For professionals and dedicated hobbyists, consult other sections in this volume, such as Building and Construction, and Crafts and Making. For patrons interested in homemaking, entertaining in the home, and interior design, useful titles can be found in sections such as Home, and Interior Design and Decoration.

Basic Periodicals

Ga: *Better Homes and Gardens Do-It-Yourself, This Old House.*

Basic Abstracts and Indexes

Index to How to Do It Information, Readers' Guide to Periodical Literature.

1636. ***Better Homes and Gardens Do-It-Yourself.*** 1968. q. USD 9.99. Meredith National Media Group, 1716 Locust St, Des Moines, IA 50309; http://www.meredith.com. Adv. *Aud.:* Ga.

This glossy quarterly features advice of interest to home-decorating, remodeling, and gardening hobbyists. Projects are both approachable and affordable, with detailed instructions and plenty of photos. One recent issue showed readers how to decorate with plants, while another showed how to update a hollow-core door using stencils and other embellishments. Now with a regular column called, "Handy Girl," this magazine is more accessible than ever. It is recommended for public libraries that have a large *Better Homes and Gardens* readership. The do-it-yourself section of the web site has a blog with feeds from relevant publications, projects, and design ideas.

1637. ***Extreme How-To: the enthusiast's guide to home improvement.*** [ISSN: 1540-5346] 2002. 9x/yr. USD 18.97; USD 24.95 combined subscription (print & online eds.); USD 3 per issue). Ed(s): Matt Weber. Latitude3 Media Group, Llc., 2300 Resource Dr, Ste B, Birmingham, AL 35242; http://latitude3.com. Adv. *Aud.:* Ga.

Homeowners with some carpentry and repair skills will find this magazine full of useful information regarding home, lawn, and auto maintenance. Recent issues have included tips on springtime yard cleanup, reviews of the best routers for woodwork projects, and advice on how to design and install a sturdy privacy fence. All instructions assume prior fix-it experience. Every year, look for a product guide and directory for home improvement projects. If your library is frequented by builders, carpenters, and serious do-it-yourselfers, this magazine might be a good fit. The web site has how-to videos and guides, Q&A, and product reviews.

1638. ***The Family Handyman.*** Incorporates (1972-1973): *Home Garden's Natural Gardening Magazine;* Which was formerly (1967-1972): *Home Garden & Flower Grower;* (1918-1967): *The Flower Grower.* [ISSN: 0014-7230] 1951. 10x/yr. USD 10; USD 3.99 newsstand/cover. Home Service Publications, Inc., 2915 Commers Dr, Ste 700, Eagan, MN 55121-2398; editors@thefamilyhandyman.com; http://www.familyhandyman.com. Illus., index, adv. Vol. ends: Dec. *Indexed:* A22, BRI. *Aud.:* Ga.

Dedicated do-it-yourselfers can advance from novice to intermediate to expert, all in this one publication. Issues are packed with illustrated step-by-step instructions for projects and repairs for the home and garden, helpful tips, and reviews of new products. Instructions include a complexity ranking (simple to advanced), estimated cost, and time required. Highly recommended for all public libraries. The magazine's web site offers a significant amount of content including a categorized collection of full-text how-to articles, DIY quizzes, a newsletter signup, and info about the online "Family Handyman DIY University."

1639. ***HackSpace: technology in your hands.*** [ISSN: 2515-5148] 2017. m. GBP 55 domestic; GBP 90 United States; GBP 95 elsewhere. Raspberry Pi Foundation, info@raspberrypi.org; http://www.raspberrypi.org. *Aud.:* Ga.

Makerspaces are now popping up even in the most rural and agrarian of communities, as many librarian/makers know. What some of us might not know is that there's a new publication on the magazine stand that will inspire and delight even more of our current and future users. *HackSpace* is an ambitious, full-color monthly aimed at "fixers and tinkerers of all abilities." Its diverse maker profiles and project photos ensure its robust content will feel inviting to all genders and backgrounds, too. So go ahead, follow *HackSpace*'s instructions on how to build an automated herb box, or use its Python code samples to tap into the Internet of Things. You'll not only build something cool, but you'll also feel good about your investment in opening up the maker world to even more library users. The *HackSpace* website has projects, inspiring stories, and back issues.

Make. See Crafts and Making section.

1640. ***Old-House Journal.*** Incorporates (1995-2013): *Old-House Interiors.* [ISSN: 0094-0178] 1973. 8x/yr. USD 24.95 domestic; USD 36.95 Canada; USD 42.95 elsewhere. Ed(s): Demetra Aposporos. Home Buyer Publications, Inc., 4125 Lafayette Ctr Dr, Ste 100, Chantilly, VA 20151; http://www.homebuyerpubs.com. Illus., adv. *Indexed:* A&ATA, A22, BRI, GardL. *Aud.:* Ga.

Designers, homeowners and wannabes all will enjoy paging through the content-rich issues of *Old House Journal*. Divided into 3 sections ("Design," "Restore," and "Inspire"), the magazine is easy to browse and easy to use. An "Inspire" article about a nineteenth century mansard-roofed townhouse in Hoboken, New Jersey, is a perfect illustration of the beauty of this well-rounded magazine: it labels and explains style elements typical of the period. It even provides a glossary of terms! Step-by-step instructions, product reviews, and advice make it easy to highly recommend this title for libraries in communities with old and historic homes. The web site offers an enormous amount of content, including the full text of selected feature articles, a product directory, virtual house tours, and a community forum.

1641. ***This Old House.*** Incorporates (in 2001): *Today's Homeowner Solutions;* Which was formerly (until 2001): *Today's Homeowner;* (until 1996): *Home Mechanix;* (until 1985): *Mechanix Illustrated;* Which was formerly (until 1938): *Modern Mechanix;* Mechanix Illustrated incorporated (in 19??): *Electronics Illustrated.* [ISSN: 1086-2633] 1995. 8x/yr. USD 16 domestic; CAD 26 Canada; USD 5.99 newsstand/cover. Ed(s): Donna Sapolin. Time Inc., 225 Liberty St, New York, NY 10281; http://www.timeinc.com. Illus., adv. *Indexed:* C37, MASUSE. *Aud.:* Ga.

This Old House offers a full complement of advice for owners of old homes. With full-scale carpentry projects, practical decorating tips and Q&A-style tricks of the trade, the magazine lives up to the reputation of the long-running television show from which it originated. Recent issues feature the restoration of an 1830s schoolhouse, garden art, and a buyer's guide to fiberglass windows. Most projects are appropriate for weekend do-it-yourselfers but instructions are careful to advise calling in a professional when a job becomes too big. If your patrons are interested in house and yard maintenance and interior design then this publication should be in your collection. The web site offers categorized projects with videos and step-by-step instructions.

■ EARTH SCIENCES AND GEOLOGY

See also Agriculture; Engineering and Technology; Geography; and Paleontology sections.

Edward F. Lener, Associate Director for Collection Management and College Librarian for the Sciences, University Libraries, Virginia Tech, 560 Drillfield Dr., Blacksburg, VA 24061; lener@vt.edu

Introduction

Due to dramatic coverage of natural disasters such as floods, earthquakes, and landslides in the news media, geologic hazards such as these are often the first thing that comes to mind when one mentions the earth sciences. In fact, the earth sciences touch on many aspects of daily life, from the water we drink to the energy and mineral resources that power our industries and transportation. Research can range from field reconnaissance, using such traditional tools as rock hammer, geological compass, and hand lens, to data-intensive modeling techniques and sophisticated laboratory equipment designed to simulate conditions deep within the earth. The earth sciences are also highly interdisciplinary, drawing on work in biology, chemistry, geography, mathematics, and physics.

As a general rule, publications in the earth sciences tend to have a long lifespan of usefulness. The importance of older literature is reflected by the fact that indexing coverage in the American Geosciences Institute's GeoRef database extends well over 300 years for North America. Of course, while much of the older research and descriptive material is still valid, new theories and more refined analytical techniques often allow for a better understanding of the processes involved. Also, the use of color illustrations and data visualizations in today's earth science journals can help readers to grasp complex information more easily.

The number of publications for general audiences continues to be limited, a problem exacerbated by the demise of *EARTH* magazine in 2019, but there are many excellent academic and specialist journals in the field. When selecting materials in the earth sciences, it is also necessary to consider the issues of geographic coverage and time frame. Work done at sites from around the world and examining different periods of geologic history are essential to developing a well-rounded collection. Obtaining a good mix of both theoretical and applied research is also important.

Nearly all major earth science journals are now published online, often with excellent retrospective coverage available. The GeoScienceWorld journal collection, launched in 2005, features a growing title list, including those of many professional societies in the field. Journal back-file coverage on the platform continues to improve, and ebook collections were added in 2014. The full journal title list may be viewed at the GeoScienceWorld website (pubs.geoscienceworld.org).

The American Geosciences Institute maintains a list of "priority journals." These are serial titles recommended by the GeoRef Users Group Steering Committee to receive the highest priority for database indexing as new issues come out. These journals are indicated in the annotations where applicable. While this is a good indication of the importance of these titles, one should always be cautious about relying too heavily on any single metric. For the full list of priority journals, go to the American Geosciences Institute's website at www.americangeosciences.org/georef/priority-journals.

Basic Periodicals

Hs, Ga: *Geology Today, Rocks and Minerals;* Ac, Sa: *Geological Society. Journal, Geological Society of America. Bulletin, Geology, Geophysics, The Journal of Geology.*

Basic Abstracts and Indexes

GeoRef.

1642. ***A A P G Bulletin.*** Former titles (until 1974): *The American Association of Petroleum Geologists Bulletin;* (until 1967): *American Association of Petroleum Geologists. Bulletin;* (until 1918): *Southwestern Association of Petroleum Geologists. Bulletin.* [ISSN: 0149-1423] 1917. m. Free to members. Ed(s): Michael L Sweet. American Association of Petroleum Geologists, PO Box 979, Tulsa, OK 74101; info@aapg.org; http://www.aapg.org. Illus., index. Refereed. Microform: PMC; PQC. *Indexed:* A22. *Bk. rev.:* 0-4, 300-700 words, signed. *Aud.:* Ac, Sa.

This technical journal recently celebrated its centennial. It serves as the official journal of the American Association of Petroleum Geologists (AAPG) and is targeted toward the association's members, as well as other professionals in the energy industry. The high-quality research and technical articles address such topics as reservoir characterization, well logging, depositional environments, and basin modeling. The AAPG Datapages Archive offers full-text content from 1917 forward for subscribers or by pay-per-view. More recent content includes the option to download whole issues as well as individual articles. Citations and abstracts are available on GeoScienceWorld from 1921 forward, with full text for 2000 to the present. Some open-access articles are available. Readers may register for free RSS feeds or e-mail alerts. Suitable for academic and specialized collections. A GeoRef priority journal.

1643. ***American Journal of Science: an international earth science journal.*** Former titles (until 1880): *American Journal of Science and Arts;* (until 1820): *American Journal of Science.* [ISSN: 0002-9599] 1818. 10x/yr. USD 225 (print & online eds.) Individuals, USD 75 (print & online eds.)). Ed(s): Danny M Rye, Page C Chamberlain. American Journal of Science, 217 Kline Geology Laboratory, Yale University, PO Box 208109, New Haven, CT 06520. Illus., index. Sample. Refereed. Vol. ends: Dec (No. 10). Microform: PMC; PQC. *Indexed:* A01, A22, BRI. *Aud.:* Ac, Sa.

The oldest continuously published journal in the United States devoted to geology and related sciences. Coverage is international in scope. Articles provide in-depth scientific analysis, typically with two to four articles per issue. There are occasional special issues. Designated special volumes and special issues are made available free of charge in digital form. The journal's website provides free tables of contents and abstracts, along with full text for subscribers, from 1860 to the present. Readers may register for free e-mail alerts. Appropriate for academic and research collections. A GeoRef priority journal.

1644. *The American Mineralogist (Print): an international journal of earth and planetary materials.* Former titles (until 1916): *The Mineral Collector;* (until 1894): *Minerals;* (until 1893): *Mineralogists' Monthly;* (until 1890): *Exchanger's Monthly.* [ISSN: 0003-004X] 188?. 6x/yr. EUR 862. Ed(s): Keith D Putirka, Ian Swainson. Walter de Gruyter GmbH, Genthiner Str 13, Berlin, 10785, Germany; service@degruyter.com; https://www.degruyter.de. Illus., index, adv. Sample. Refereed. Vol. ends: Nov/Dec (No. 11 - No. 12). Reprint: PSC. *Indexed:* A01, A22, BRI. *Bk. rev.:* 0-3, 500-1,200 words, signed. *Aud.:* Ac, Sa.

For more than 100 years this journal has been a key title in the field of mineralogy and it serves as an official publication of the Mineralogical Society of America. Research articles cover many topics, including crystal structure, crystal chemistry, and mineral occurrences and deposits. Work in closely related areas such as crystallography, petrology, and geochemistry is also included. In addition, many issues include a section that features newly named minerals, with a brief description and citation to the literature for each of them. Tables of contents for journal issues published from 1916 to the present are available on the Mineralogical Society of America website. Full text of all articles published from 1916 to 1999 is freely accessible online. More recent years are accessible only to subscribers and society members, with some open-access articles available. The GeoScienceWorld website also provides full text to subscribers from 1916 forward, and readers may register for free RSS feeds or e-mail alerts. A GeoRef priority journal.

1645. *Annales Geophysicae: atmospheres, hydrospheres and space sciences.* Formed by the merger of (1983-1988): *Annales de Geophysicae. Serie A: Upper Atmosphere and Space Sciences;* (1983-1988): *Annales Geophysicae. Serie B: Terrestrial and Planetary Physics;* Both of which superseded in part (in 1985): *Annales Geophysicae;* Which was formed by the merger of (1944-1983): *Annales de Geophysique;* (1948-1983): *Annali di Geofisica.* [ISSN: 0992-7689] 1983. m. EUR 386.67. Ed(s): Wlodek Kofman. Copernicus GmbH, Bahnhofsallee 1e, Goettingen, 37081, Germany; info@copernicus.org; http://www.copernicus.org. Illus., index, adv. Sample. Refereed. Vol. ends: Dec (No. 12). *Indexed:* A01, A22, S25. *Aud.:* Ac, Sa.

This open-access journal of the European Geosciences Union (EGU) presents research articles and short communications on a broad range of topics in geophysics. Areas of major emphasis include atmospheric processes and dynamics, the Earth's magnetosphere and ionosphere, and solar and heliospheric physics. Special issues may feature conference papers or an in-depth report on selected geophysical studies. Free online access is available for all articles published from late 1996 forward. Readers may sign up for RSS feeds and topical e-mail alerts.

1646. *Applied Geochemistry.* [ISSN: 0883-2927] 1986. m. EUR 2566. Elsevier Ltd, The Boulevard, Langford Lane, Oxford, OX5 1GB, United Kingdom; customerserviceau@elsevier.com; http://www.elsevier.com. Illus., adv. Sample. Refereed. Microform: PQC. *Indexed:* A01, A22, C45, S25. *Bk. rev.:* 0-2, 400-2,000 words. *Aud.:* Ac, Sa.

This journal emphasizes research in geochemistry that has practical application to such areas as environmental monitoring, resource exploration, and water chemistry. Features full-length reports of original research, shorter rapid communications, and occasional review articles. This title is the official publication of the International Association of GeoChemistry (IAGC), and some issues include reports of association activities. The website provides free access to tables of contents and abstracts for issues published from 1986 to the present, with full-text articles available to subscribers. Some open-access articles are available. Readers may register to receive alerts for specific searches or when new issues become available. Appropriate for academic or corporate research collections. A GeoRef priority journal.

1647. *Basin Research.* [ISSN: 0950-091X] 1988. bi-m. Ed(s): Cynthia Ebinger. Wiley-Blackwell Publishing Ltd., The Atrium, Southern Gate, Chichester, PO19 8QG, United Kingdom; cs-journals@wiley.com; http://onlinelibrary.wiley.com/. Illus., index, adv. Sample. Refereed. Vol. ends: No. 4. Reprint: PSC. *Indexed:* A01, A22, C45, E01, S25. *Bk. rev.:* 0-4, 500-1,500 words, signed. *Aud.:* Ac, Sa.

This journal is a joint publication of the European Association of Geoscientists and Engineers and the International Association of Sedimentologists. It features interdisciplinary work on sedimentary basins with articles that address such issues as sediment transport, fluid migration, and stratigraphic modeling. Special thematic issues are also published from time to time. Free tables of contents and abstracts can be found on the website beginning with 1988, with the full text of articles available for subscribers. Some open-access articles are available. Recommended for comprehensive collections, but libraries on a tight budget may first want to consider its more general counterpart, *Sedimentology,* also published by the International Association of Sedimentologists. Readers may register for a free account to receive RSS feeds or e-mail alerts about new journal content.

1648. *Biogeosciences.* [ISSN: 1726-4170] 2003. fortn. EUR 3058.67; EUR 140.19 newsstand/cover. Copernicus GmbH, Bahnhofsallee 1e, Goettingen, 37081, Germany; info@copernicus.org; http://www.copernicus.org. Refereed. *Indexed:* C45, S25. *Aud.:* Ac, Sa.

This open-access journal of the European Geosciences Union (EGU) examines the interaction of biological and geological processes as living systems, natural processes, and inorganic materials and how they all affect one another in myriad ways. This interdisciplinary title includes research articles, short communications, and reviews. The website also allows for interactive discussion of recent article postings, and readers may register for a free account to receive RSS feeds or e-mail alerts about new journal content.

1649. *Boreas: an international journal of quaternary research.* [ISSN: 0300-9483] 1972. q. GBP 331. Ed(s): Jan A Piotrowski. Wiley-Blackwell Publishing, Inc., 111 River St, Hoboken, NJ 07030; http://onlinelibrary.wiley.com. Illus., index, adv. Sample. Refereed. Vol. ends: Dec (No. 4). Microform: PQC. Reprint: PSC. *Indexed:* A01, A22, BRI, C45, E01. *Bk. rev.:* 0-3, 500-1,200 words, signed. *Aud.:* Ac, Sa.

Sponsored by a partnership of geologists in several Nordic countries, this journal deals exclusively with research on the Quaternary period. This extends from approximately 2.6 million years ago to the present, and many of the topics covered, such as climatic variations and sea-level changes, are of particular relevance today. Other papers examine the stratigraphy, glacial dynamics and landforms, and the flora and fauna of the period. Tables of contents and abstracts are freely available on the website beginning with 1972, with full text for subscribers. Some open-access articles are available. Readers may register to receive free alerts via e-mail or RSS feeds. A GeoRef priority journal.

1650. *Bulletin of Volcanology.* Formerly (until 1984): *Bulletin Volcanologique.* [ISSN: 0258-8900] 1924. 12x/yr. Ed(s): A Harris. Springer, Tiergartenstr 17, Heidelberg, 69121, Germany. Illus., index, adv. Sample. Refereed. Vol. ends: Jul (No. 8). Reprint: PSC. *Indexed:* A01, A22, BRI, E01. *Aud.:* Ac, Sa.

The official journal of the International Association of Volcanology and Chemistry of the Earth's Interior (IAVCEI). As suggested by its title, the emphasis is on volcanoes, including their characteristics, behavior, and associated hazards. Coverage is international in scope and contains related material on magmatic systems and igneous petrology. The website offers free tables of contents and abstracts as well as full-text access from volume 1 forward for subscribers. Some open-access articles are available. Readers may register to receive table of content alerts via e-mail, or sign up for an RSS feed. A GeoRef priority journal.

1651. *Canadian Journal of Earth Sciences.* [ISSN: 0008-4077] 1963. m. CAD 1983 (print & online eds.)). Ed(s): Dr. Ali Polat. Canadian Science Publishing, 65 Auriga Dr, Ste 203, Ottawa, ON K2E 7W6, Canada; pubs@cdnsciencepub.com; http://www.nrcresearchpress.com. Illus., index, adv. Refereed. Vol. ends: Dec (No. 12). *Indexed:* A01, A22, C37, E01, HRIS, S25. *Aud.:* Ac, Sa.

This journal is published by the National Research Council of Canada in affiliation with the Geological Society of Canada. The majority of its articles are in English, and those in French include English abstracts. Articles are more technical than those found in *Geoscience Canada.* As one might expect, for site-specific topics the focus is heavily on Canadian geology, but many of the underlying principles are transferable to other regions. The website offers free tables of contents and abstracts from 1964 on, with full-text access for subscribers. Readers may sign up for RSS feeds or e-mail alerts to learn when new content is published. A GeoRef priority journal.

1652. *Canadian Mineralogist.* Formerly (until 1957): *Contributions to Canadian Mineralogy.* [ISSN: 0008-4476] 1921. bi-m. CAD 525 (print & online eds.) Free to members). Ed(s): Vicki Loschiavo. Mineralogical Association of Canada, 490 Rue de la Couronne, Quebec, QC G1K 9A9, Canada; office@mineralogicalassociation.ca; http://www.mineralogicalassociation.ca. Illus. Sample. Refereed. Vol. ends: Dec. *Indexed:* A22. *Bk. rev.:* 0-2, 300-1,000 words. *Aud.:* Ac, Sa.

This academic journal publishes research papers on crystallography, geochemistry, mineralogy, mineral deposits, and petrology at sites around the world. This title generally has one or more thematic issues each year, often in tribute to an individual or reporting on symposia sponsored by the Mineralogical Association of Canada. Articles are primarily in English, while some include French summaries. Abstracts for papers from 1957 to present are available on the association's website, with full text for subscribers. GeoScienceWorld offers the same years of coverage. Readers may register for free RSS feeds or e-mail alerts. A GeoRef priority journal.

1653. *Canadian Petroleum Geology. Bulletin.* Former titles (until 1963): *Alberta Society of Petroleum Geologists. Journal;* (until 1955): *A S P G News Bulletin.* [ISSN: 0007-4802] 1953. q. Free to members; Non-members, CAD 150. Ed(s): Denis Lavoie, Denise Then. Canadian Society of Petroleum Geologists, 600, 640 8th Ave S W, Calgary, AB T2P 1G7, Canada; http://www.cspg.org. Illus., index, adv. Refereed. Vol. ends: Dec (No. 4). *Indexed:* A22. *Bk. rev.:* 0-4, 500-1,200 words, signed. *Aud.:* Ac, Sa.

This is the official publication of the Canadian Society of Petroleum Geologists, and many of its issues include society business, such as awards and a report of activities. More importantly, the journal also features high-quality research articles on various aspects of petroleum geology in a wide range of geologic environments. Regional coverage emphasizes Canada and Alaska, but the title is still a valuable addition to larger academic or special libraries. Abstracts and tables of contents are available for free from 1965 to the present, and online access is available through GeoScienceWorld from 2000 to the present. Readers may register for free e-mail alerts when new journal content is published. The AAPG Datapages Archive offers full-text coverage from 1953 forward for subscribers or by pay-per-view. A GeoRef priority journal.

1654. *Chemical Geology.* Incorporates (in 1993): *Chemical Geology. Isotope Geoscience Section;* Which was formerly (1983-1985): *Isotope Geoscience.* [ISSN: 0009-2541] 1966. 28x/yr. EUR 8212. Ed(s): Catherine Chauvel, Don Dingwell. Elsevier BV, Radarweg 29, Amsterdam, 1043 NX, Netherlands; info@elsevier.com; https://www.elsevier.com/. Illus., index, adv. Sample. Refereed. Vol. ends: No. 4. Microform: PQC. *Indexed:* A01, A22, S25. *Aud.:* Ac, Sa.

This title serves as an official publication of the European Association of Geochemistry. It has an international scope and provides broad coverage of the field of organic and inorganic geochemistry, including reports about Earth and other planets. Papers address topics such as low-temperature geochemistry, aqueous solutions, analytical techniques, isotope studies, environmental geochemistry, geochronology, and experimental petrology. The website provides free access to tables of contents and abstracts from the journal's inception in 1966, with full-text access available for subscribers. Some open-access articles are available. Readers may register to receive table of contents alerts via e-mail, or sign up for an RSS feed. A GeoRef priority journal.

1655. *Clay Minerals.* Formerly (until 1965): *Clay Minerals Bulletin.* [ISSN: 0009-8558] 1947. q. Ed(s): George Christidis. Cambridge University Press, University Printing House, Shaftesbury Rd, Cambridge, CB2 8BS, United Kingdom; journals@cambridge.org; https://www.cambridge.org/. Illus., index, adv. Refereed. Vol. ends: Dec (No. 4). *Indexed:* A01, A22, E01. *Bk. rev.:* 0-2, 600-1,000 words, signed. *Aud.:* Ac, Sa.

Published on behalf the Mineralogical Society of Great Britain and Ireland, this journal represents the combined efforts of several clay research groups across Europe. Papers are predominantly in English. Many articles focus on research concerning hydrothermal interactions related to clay weathering and diagenesis. Analytical techniques and their use in the determination of structure and physical properties of clay minerals are also emphasized. All issues are available on the publisher's website for subscribers. Some open-access articles are available. Abstracts from mid-1975 onward, and full text from 1996 forward, are available online to subscribers of GeoScienceWorld. Readers may register to receive free e-mail alerts or RSS feeds about new journal content. A GeoRef priority journal.

1656. *Clays and Clay Minerals.* Former titles (until 1965): *Clays and Clay Minerals;* (until 1953): *National Conference on Clays and Clay Technology. Proceedings.* [ISSN: 0009-8604] 1952. bi-m. Ed(s): Joseph W Stucki. Springer Nature Switzerland AG, .
Illus., index. Refereed. Vol. ends: Dec (No. 6). Reprint: PSC. *Indexed:* A22, C45, S25. *Aud.:* Ac, Sa.

This journal serves as the official publication of the Clay Minerals Society and focuses on all aspects of clay science. The publisher's website provides full text from 1952 forward for subscribers. Some open-access articles are available. GeoScienceWorld offers free tables of contents and abstracts beginning with 1975, and subscribers may view full text from 2000 to 2018. As a result of a change in publisher in 2019, new content will no longer continue to be added to GeoScienceWorld. Coverage is similar to that of *Clay Minerals,* but with a greater emphasis on interdisciplinary applications. Together, the two journals provide very thorough coverage of the field. A GeoRef priority journal.

1657. *The Compass (Norman).* Former titles (until 1984): *The Compass of Sigma Gamma Epsilon;* (until 1921): *Sigma Gamma Epsilon Compass.* [ISSN: 0894-802X] 1920. q. Free to members. Ed(s): Aaron W. Johnson, Larry E Davis. Society of Sigma Gamma Epsilon, c/o James C Walters, Sigma Gamma Epsilon, Department of Earth Science, Cedar Falls, IA 50614; walters@uni.edu; http://www.uni.edu/earth/SGE/info.html. Illus., index. Sample. Refereed. *Aud.:* Ac.

Sigma Gamma Epsilon is an honorary scientific society devoted to the earth sciences. Published since 1920, this compact quarterly presents society- and chapter-related news and historical information. It also features research articles on a wide range of topics, with many of them written by students presenting their findings. Research papers are peer reviewed and indexed in the major sources. Long offered only in print form, this title became available online for free beginning in 2012 and articles are included in the Earth Sciences Commons. Readers may register to receive e-mail alerts or RSS feeds about new journal content.

Computers & Geosciences. See Cartography, GIS, and Imagery section.

1658. *Contributions to Mineralogy and Petrology.* Former titles (until 1965): *Beitraege zur Mineralogie und Petrographie;* (until 1957): *Heidelberger Beitraege zur Mineralogie und Petrographie.* [ISSN: 0010-7999] 1947. m. EUR 4884 (print & online eds.)). Ed(s): T L Grove. Springer, Tiergartenstr 17, Heidelberg, 69121, Germany. Illus., index, adv. Refereed. Reprint: PSC. *Indexed:* A01, A22, E01. *Aud.:* Ac, Sa.

This journal provides in-depth technical coverage on the petrology and genesis of igneous and metamorphic rocks. Heavy emphasis is placed on geochemistry, and many of the articles consist of theoretical and experimental work such as determining mineral phase relations and chemical equilibria. Related areas such as isotope geology and element partitioning are also featured. The publisher's website offers free tables of contents and abstracts from 1947 on, with full-text access for subscribers. Some open-access articles are available. Readers may register for free table of contents alerts via e-mail or RSS feed. A GeoRef priority journal.

1659. *Cretaceous Research.* [ISSN: 0195-6671] 1980. bi-m. EUR 2658. Ed(s): E A M Koutsoukos. Academic Press, 32 Jamestown Rd, Camden, London, NW1 7BY, United Kingdom; corporate.sales@elsevier.com; http://www.elsevier.com/. Illus., index, adv. Sample. Refereed. Vol. ends: Dec (No. 6). Reprint: PSC. *Indexed:* A22, E01. *Bk. rev.:* 0-2, 700-1,000 words, signed. *Aud.:* Ac, Sa.

Like *Quaternary Research,* this journal is interdisciplinary and focuses on a single major geological time period. The Cretaceous Period ended about 66 million years ago, a time best known for the extinction of the dinosaurs, but this is by no means the only subject covered. Stratigraphy and paleontology, in particular, receive considerable attention. Special topical issues on significant sites or geologic events from the Cretaceous Period are also featured. The website provides free access to tables of contents and abstracts beginning with 1980 with full-text for subscribers. Some open-access articles are available. Recent articles often include a graphical abstract. Readers may register to receive free e-mail alerts or RSS feeds when new issues are published.

1660. *The Depositional Record.* [ISSN: 2055-4877] 2015. s-a. Free. John Wiley & Sons Ltd., EMEA Institutional Sales, 9600 Garsington Rd, Oxford, OX4 2DQ, United Kingdom; cs-journals@wiley.com; http://www.wiley.com. Refereed. *Aud.:* Ac, Sa.

This open-access journal is an official publication of the International Association of Sedimentologists and complements their flagship journal *Sedimentology.* All articles are published with a Creative Commons license. Content spans the field of sedimentology and includes original research, reviews, and methods papers. Occasional special issues focus more closely on specific sedimentological topics.

1661. *E O S.* Formerly (until 1969): *American Geophysical Union. Transactions.* [ISSN: 0096-3941] 1919. fortn. American Geophysical Union, 2000 Florida Ave, NW, Washington, DC 20009; service@agu.org; http://sites.agu.org/. Illus., index, adv. Sample. Vol. ends: No. 52. Reprint: PSC. *Indexed:* A&ATA, A22, HRIS. *Bk. rev.:* 0-2, 100-400 words. *Aud.:* Ac, Sa.

This science newsmagazine publishes on items of current interest in geophysics research. Along with the feature articles and short news items, there are announcements from the American Geophysical Union, meeting reports, and information on employment opportunities. The journal's website provides free access to recent news and other items in a web-friendly format, along with complete issues for download. Earlier issues are hosted on the Wiley Online platform, from 1920 forward with full text for subscribers and society members. Content for the years 1997 to 2014 is freely available to all. Readers may register for free table of contents alerts via e-mail or RSS feed. A GeoRef priority journal. URL: https://eos.org/

1662. *Earth and Planetary Science Letters.* [ISSN: 0012-821X] 1966. 24x/yr. EUR 8554. Elsevier BV, Radarweg 29, Amsterdam, 1043 NX, Netherlands; info@elsevier.com; https://www.elsevier.com/. Illus., index. Sample. Refereed. Vol. ends: No. 4. Microform: PQC. *Indexed:* A01, A22, S25. *Aud.:* Ac, Sa.

Publishes research on physical and chemical properties of the Earth's crust and mantle as well as its atmosphere and hydrosphere. Other topics include lunar and planetary studies, plate tectonics, ocean floor spreading, and continental drift. The journal focuses on shorter communications with rapid turnaround. The website offers free access to tables of contents and article abstracts for all years of publication. Recent articles often include a graphical abstract. Data sets and other supplementary content are provided online. Full-text articles from 1966 forward are available to subscribers. Some open-access articles are available. Readers may register for free e-mail alerts or an RSS feed when new journal content is available. A GeoRef priority journal.

1663. *Earth Surface Dynamics.* [ISSN: 2196-6311] 2013. irreg. Ed(s): Tom Coulthard. Copernicus GmbH, Bahnhofsallee 1e, Goettingen, 37081, Germany; info@copernicus.org; http://www.copernicus.org. Refereed. *Indexed:* A01. *Aud.:* Ac, Sa.

This international open-access journal focuses on the many different processes that shape the Earth's surface and their interactions. Occasional special issues cover topics such as modeling, monitoring, remote sensing, and software as they relate to geomorphology and landforms. Articles include original research, review articles, and short communications. The website also allows for interactive discussion of recent article postings, and readers may register for a free account to receive RSS feeds or e-mail alerts about new journal content.

1664. *Earth Surface Processes and Landforms.* Formerly (until 1981): *Earth Surface Processes.* [ISSN: 0197-9337] 1976. 15x/yr. GBP 3585. Ed(s): S N Lane. John Wiley & Sons Ltd., EMEA Institutional Sales, 9600 Garsington Rd, Oxford, OX4 2DQ, United Kingdom; cs-journals@wiley.com; http://onlinelibrary.wiley.com. Illus., index, adv. Sample. Refereed. Vol. ends: No. 13. Microform: PQC. Reprint: PSC. *Indexed:* A22, C45, S25. *Bk. rev.:* 0-2, 200-600 words, signed. *Aud.:* Ac, Sa.

This wide-ranging journal from the British Society for Geomorphology publishes on all aspects of Earth surface science and geomorphology. This encompasses the complex process of landform evolution by the processes of weathering, erosion, transport, and deposition. Landslides and other natural hazards are also considered. Much of the work is highly interdisciplinary in nature and shows in what way different chemical, mechanical, and hydrologic factors all interact to shape the landscape. Free tables of contents and abstracts from 1976 forward are provided at the website, with full-text access for subscribers. Some open-access articles are available. Readers may register for free e-mail alerts or RSS feeds. A GeoRef priority journal.

1665. *Economic Geology and the Bulletin of the Society of Economic Geologists.* Formerly (until 1930): *Economic Geology;* Which superseded in part (in 1906): *American Geologist.* [ISSN: 0361-0128] 1905. 8x/yr. Free to members. Ed(s): Mabel J Peterson, Lawrence D Meinert. Society of Economic Geologists, Inc., 7811 Shaffer Pky, Littleton, CO 80127; seg@segweb.org; http://www.segweb.org. Illus., index. Sample. Refereed. Vol. ends: Dec (No. 8). Microform: PMC; PQC. *Indexed:* A22. *Bk. rev.:* 0-4, 600-1,000 words. *Aud.:* Ac, Sa.

Articles feature research on theoretical and experimental aspects of economic geology; these are balanced with papers on field research. Each issue also contains tables of contents information for recent papers of interest from selected other earth science journals. GeoScienceWorld provides free tables of contents and abstracts from 1905 forward, and with full-text articles for all years available for subscribers or society members. Some open-access articles are available. Readers may register for free e-mail alerts or RSS feeds when new journal content is published. A GeoRef priority journal.

1666. *Elements (Quebec): an international magazine of mineralogy, geochemistry, and petrology.* Formed by the merger of (1985-2005): *The Lattice;* (1961-2005): *M A C Newsletter; C M S News.* [ISSN: 1811-5209] 2005. bi-m. USD 150 Free to members. Ed(s): Pierrette Tremblay. Mineralogical Association of Canada, 490 Rue de la Couronne, Quebec, QC G1K 9A9, Canada; office@mineralogicalassociation.ca; http://www.mineralogicalassociation.ca. Adv. Sample. Refereed. *Indexed:* A22. *Aud.:* Ac, Sa.

Elements is a joint effort among 18 participating professional societies in the mineralogical sciences. Issues are each thematic in nature—for example, comets, radioactive waste disposal, urban geochemistry, and specific rock or mineral types. This title also includes news of society events, short courses, awards, and conference reports. Available free to members and offered to subscribers through the website. Full text from 2005 forward is also available online through the GeoScienceWorld platform. Readers may register for free e-mail alerts or RSS feeds. A GeoRef priority journal. URL: http://elementsmagazine.org/

1667. *Engineering Geology.* Incorporates (1983-1991): *Mining Science and Technology.* [ISSN: 0013-7952] 1965. 16x/yr. EUR 4077. Ed(s): C H Juang, C Carranza-Torres. Elsevier BV, Radarweg 29, Amsterdam, 1043 NX, Netherlands; info@elsevier.com; https://www.elsevier.com/. Illus., index, adv. Sample. Refereed. Vol. ends: No. 4. Microform: PQC. *Indexed:* A01, A22, C45, HRIS, S25. *Bk. rev.:* 0-2, 500-1,000 words. *Aud.:* Ac, Sa.

This international journal publishes studies relevant to engineering geology and geotechnical engineering including related topics such as environmental concerns and geological hazards. Article types include research papers, case histories, and reviews. The website provides free access to tables of contents and abstracts from 1965 forward with full-text access for subscribers. Some open-access articles are available. Readers may register for free e-mail alerts or RSS feeds. A GeoRef priority journal.

1668. *Environmental and Engineering Geoscience.* Former titles (until 1995): *Association of Engineering Geologists. Bulletin;* (until 1968): *Engineering Geology.* [ISSN: 1078-7275] 1963. q. USD 295. Ed(s): Ira D Sasowsky, Abdul Shakoor. Geological Society of America, PO Box 9140, Boulder, CO 80301; gsaservice@geosociety.org; http://www.geosociety.org. Illus., index, adv. Sample. Refereed. Vol. ends: Dec (No. 4). *Indexed:* A22, HRIS, S25. *Bk. rev.:* 0-9, 800-3,000 words. *Aud.:* Ac, Sa.

This quarterly title is co-published by the Association of Environmental and Engineering Geologists and the Geological Society of America. It features research articles, case histories, review papers, and technical notes in areas of interest to hydrologists, environmental scientists, and engineering geologists. Topics include site selection, feasibility studies, design and construction of civil engineering projects, waste management, and groundwater. Appropriate for corporate and academic collections. Free tables of contents and abstracts are available on the GeoScienceWorld website from 1976 to the present, with full-text coverage for subscribers. Readers may sign up for free e-mail alerts or RSS feeds when new issues are published. A GeoRef priority journal.

1669. *Environmental Earth Sciences.* Former titles (until 2010): *Environmental Geology;* (until 1993): *Environmental Geology and Water Sciences;* (until 1984): *Environmental Geology.* [ISSN: 1866-6280] 1975. 24x/yr. EUR 6474 (print & online eds.)). Ed(s): Gunter Doerhoefer, James W LaMoreaux. Springer, Tiergartenstr 17, Heidelberg, 69121, Germany. Illus., index, adv. Sample. Refereed. Reprint: PSC. *Indexed:* A22, Agr, BRI, C45, E01, HRIS, S25. *Bk. rev.:* 2-7, 300-1,800 words, signed. *Aud.:* Ac, Sa.

The application of geological principles and data to environmental issues has become increasingly important. This international journal includes both research articles and applied technical reports on specific cases and solutions. Much of the work is multidisciplinary in nature and covers such areas as soil and water contamination, radioactive waste disposal, remediation techniques, and the effects of mining and industrial activities. Special thematic issues often focus in greater detail on some aspect of these subject areas. The website offers tables of contents and abstracts from 1975 to the present, with full-text access for subscribers. Some open-access articles are available. E-mail alerts and RSS feeds are available to track new additions. A GeoRef priority journal, listed under its earlier title of *Environmental Geology.*

1670. *Environmental Geosciences.* Former titles (until 1995): *A A P G Division. Environmental Geosciences Journal.* [ISSN: 1075-9565] 1994. q. Members, USD 8; Non-members, USD 15. Ed(s): Kristin M Carter. American Association of Petroleum Geologists, PO Box 979, Tulsa, OK 74101; info@aapg.org; http://www.aapg.org. Adv. Refereed. *Indexed:* A01, A22, E01. *Aud.:* Ac, Sa.

This quarterly journal is published by AAPG's Division of Environmental Geosciences. Research articles focus on a range of environmental issues such as carbon capture, groundwater monitoring, pollution remediation, and remote sensing. Full-text coverage is available on the "AAPG Datapages" website from mid-1994 forward, with online access to division members and subscribers. GeoScienceWorld offers full text from 1997 onward, along with e-mail alerts and RSS feeds for new content. A GeoRef priority journal.

1671. *Episodes: journal of international geoscience.* Formerly (until 1978): *International Union of Geological Sciences. Geological Newsletter.* [ISSN: 0705-3797] 1963. q. INR 1500 domestic; USD 30 foreign. Ed(s): B R Krishna, Fareeduddin . Geological Society of India, Kavitha Apartments, No 63, 12th Cross, Basappa Layout, PO Box 1922, Bangalore, 560 019, India; gsocind@gmail.com ; http://www.geosocindia.org. Illus. Sample. Refereed. *Indexed:* A22, C45. *Bk. rev.:* 0-4, 500-1,500 words. *Aud.:* Ac, Sa.

Truly international in its scope, this open-access journal covers developments in earth science research, organizations, techniques, and policy. The International Union of Geological Sciences (IUGS) is a large nongovernmental scientific organization that facilitates international cooperation and promotes study in the earth sciences. In addition to research articles, many issues include information about IUGS news and activities or brief reports from international conferences and meetings. There are occasional special issues on specific regions or topics. The full text of articles is freely accessible from 1978 forward via the journal website. URL: www.episodes.org/

1672. *European Journal of Mineralogy: an international journal of mineralogy, geochemistry and related sciences.* Formed by the merger of (1950-1988): *Fortschritte der Mineralogie;* (1968-1988): *Rendiconti della Societa Italiana di Mineralogia e Petrologia;* (1878-1988): *Bulletin de Mineralogia;* Which was formerly (until 1978): *Societe Francaise de Mineralogie et de Cristallographie. Bulletin;* (until 1949): *Societe Francaise de Mineralogie. Bulletin;* (until 1886): *Societe Mineralogique de France. Bulletin.* [ISSN: 0935-1221] 1988. 6x/yr. EUR 430 combined subscription (print & online eds.)). Ed(s): Christian Chopin. E. Schweizerbart'sche Verlagsbuchhandlung, Johannesstr 3A, Stuttgart, 70176, Germany; order@schweizerbart.de; http://www.schweizerbart.de. Illus., index, adv. Sample. Refereed. Vol. ends: Nov/Dec (No. 6). *Indexed:* A22. *Aud.:* Ac, Sa.

This journal is the result of a cooperative effort among several European mineralogical societies, and it replaced several of their individual titles when it began publication in 1989. Papers are international in scope, with an emphasis on European localities. Most articles are in English and they cover a wide range of topics in mineralogy, petrology, and crystallography. Free tables of contents from 1989 forward are offered, along with full text for subscribers on GeoScienceWorld. Some open-access articles are available. Readers may register for free e-mail alerts or RSS feeds. Full text is also available through Ingenta to subscribers or on a per-article basis. A GeoRef priority journal.

1673. *G3: Geochemistry, Geophysics, Geosystems: an electronic journal of the earth sciences.* [ISSN: 1525-2027] 1999. m. GBP 507. Ed(s): Claudio Faccenna. Wiley-Blackwell Publishing, Inc., 111 River St, Hoboken, NJ 07030; http://onlinelibrary.wiley.com. Refereed. *Indexed:* C45, S25. *Aud.:* Ac, Sa.

Published by the American Geophysical Union, this electronic-only journal publishes original research, reviews, and technical briefs in geophysics and geochemistry. The focus is on interdisciplinary processes that pertain to understanding the Earth as a system, and contributions span a wide range of topics. Many submissions include material such as data sets, sound clips, movies, and visualizations that could not readily be included in a print journal. Full-text articles from 2000 to the present are available to subscribers, with the older content free to all. Some open-access articles are available. Readers may register for free e-mail alerts or RSS feeds. A GeoRef priority journal.

1674. *Geo-Marine Letters: an international journal of marine geology.* [ISSN: 0276-0460] 1980. bi-m. EUR 1414 (print & online eds.)). Ed(s): Burg W Flemming. Springer, Tiergartenstr 17, Heidelberg, 69121, Germany. Illus., index, adv. Sample. Refereed. Vol. ends: No. 4. Reprint: PSC. *Indexed:* A01, A22, BRI, E01, S25. *Bk. rev.:* 0-3, 700-1,200 words, signed. *Aud.:* Ac, Sa.

Newer exploratory techniques and advanced equipment have opened up vast areas of Earth's oceans to intensive study. *Geo-Marine Letters* publishes original research and reviews that address geology, geophysics, and geochemistry in a marine environment. Some topics of coverage include depositional environments, sedimentary processes, stratigraphy, and post-depositional movement. The website offers free tables of contents and abstracts from 1981 to the present, with full-text access available for subscribers. Some open-access articles are available. Readers may register to receive free e-mail alerts or RSS feeds when new issues are published.

1675. *Geobiology (Online).* [ISSN: 1472-4669] 2003. 6x/yr. GBP 685. Ed(s): Kurt Konhauser. Wiley-Blackwell Publishing Ltd., The Atrium, Southern Gate, Chichester, PO19 8QG, United Kingdom; cs-journals@wiley.com; http://onlinelibrary.wiley.com/. Adv. Sample. Refereed. *Aud.:* Ac, Sa.

This interdisciplinary journal focuses on the complex interaction of life and the geology and chemistry of the Earth's environment over time. Topics include the origin of life, evolutionary ecology, and the sedimentary rock record. There are occasional special issues. The website offers free tables of contents and abstracts from 2003 forward, with full-text access for subscribers. Some open-access articles are available. A GeoRef priority journal.

1676. *Geochemical Perspectives.* [ISSN: 2223-7755] 2012. s-a. EUR 50. Ed(s): Marie-Aude Hulshoff. European Association of Geochemistry, IPGP-Gopel-Bureau 566, 1, rue Jussieu, Paris, 75238, France. Refereed. *Aud.:* Ac, Sa.

This open-access journal is published by the European Association of Geochemistry. Each article features a single, in-depth article about a specific area of geochemical research from the personal perspective of a long-time researcher in that field. Examples include hydrothermal processes, trace element partitioning, mineral resources, and microanalysis. This unusual approach helps present complex scientific research in a more holistic way. Full-text content is available from the society's website as well as from GeoScienceWorld. URL: http://www.geochemicalperspectives.org/

1677. *Geochemical Transactions.* [ISSN: 1467-4866] 2000. irreg. Free. Ed(s): Yoko Furukawa, Greg Druschel. BioMed Central Ltd., Fl 6, 236 Gray's Inn Rd, London, WC1X 8HB, United Kingdom; info@biomedcentral.com; https://www.biomedcentral.com. Adv. Refereed. *Indexed:* A01, A22, C45, E01, S25. *Aud.:* Ac, Sa.

This open-access electronic publication is freely available online and compares favorably with other titles in the field. *Geochemical Transactions* publishes peer-reviewed articles related to such areas as organic and inorganic geochemistry, marine and aquatic chemistry, chemical oceanography, biogeochemistry, applied geochemistry, astrobiology, and environmental geochemistry. Topical collections of articles are offered on the publisher's website. Free RSS feeds and e-mail alerts are available. An important electronic journal for academic libraries that support earth science research and teaching.

1678. *Geochemistry: Exploration, Environment, Analysis.* [ISSN: 1467-7873] 2001. q. GBP 411 combined subscription domestic (print & online eds.); GBP 465 combined subscription in Europe (print & online eds.); USD 929 combined subscription elsewhere (print & online eds.)). Ed(s): Scott Wood. Geological Society Publishing House, Unit 7, Brassmill Enterprise Ctr, Brassmill Ln, Bath, BA1 3JN, United Kingdom. Illus. Refereed. *Indexed:* C45, S25. *Aud.:* Ac, Sa.

This quarterly is produced by the Geological Society of London and the Association of Applied Geochemists. It covers the application of geochemistry to the exploration and study of mineral resources. Some topics include geochemical exploration, sampling and analytical techniques, and the environmental impacts of mining. Frequent special issues, known as thematic sets, cover selected conferences or hot topics in the field. Full text for subscribers is available on GeoScienceWorld, along with free abstracts from 2001 forward. Readers may register to receive free alerts via e-mail when new content is published. The journal is also available online as part of the Lyell Collection from the Geological Society of London. Recommended for academic and special libraries. A GeoRef priority journal.

1679. *Geochemistry International.* Formerly (until 1963): *Geochemistry.* [ISSN: 0016-7029] 1956. m. EUR 7709 (print & online eds.)). M A I K Nauka - Interperiodica, Profsoyuznaya ul 90, Moscow, 117997, Russian Federation; compmg@maik.ru; http://www.maik.ru. Illus., index, adv. Refereed. Circ: 675. Vol. ends: Dec (No. 12). Microform: PQC. Reprint: PSC. *Indexed:* A01, A22, E01, S25. *Aud.:* Ac, Sa.

Articles are translated from the Russian journal *Geokhimiya.* Research papers address theoretical and applied topics in geochemistry, with a focus on Eurasia. Occasional reports appear from symposia and international meetings. Full text is available to subscribers, beginning with volume 44 published in 2006. Readers may register for free e-mail alerts or RSS feeds. Appropriate for comprehensive collections.

1680. *Geochimica et Cosmochimica Acta.* [ISSN: 0016-7037] 1950. s-m. EUR 5691. Ed(s): M Norman. Pergamon Press, The Blvd, Langford Ln, E Park, Kidlington, OX5 1GB, United Kingdom; JournalsCustomerServiceEMEA@elsevier.com; http://www.elsevier.com. Illus., adv. Sample. Refereed. Microform: PQC. *Indexed:* A01, A22, C45, S25. *Aud.:* Ac, Sa.

Publishes original research papers that cover geochemistry in both terrestrial and planetary settings. Topics include chemical processes and environmental interactions, petrology, isotope analysis, meteoritics, and lunar studies. The website provides free access to tables of contents and abstracts beginning with 1950, with full-text articles available to subscribers. Some open-access articles are available. Readers may register for free alerts via e-mail or RSS feeds. Appropriate for academic and corporate research collections. A GeoRef priority journal.

1681. *Geological Journal.* Formerly (until 1964): *Liverpool and Manchester Geological Journal;* Which was formed by the merger of (1926-1950): *Manchester Geological Association. Journal;* (1874-1950): *Liverpool Geological Society. Proceedings;* Which was formerly (until 1874): *Liverpool Geological Society. Abstract. Proceedings.* [ISSN: 0072-1050] 1951. bi-m. GBP 1543. Ed(s): I D Somerville. John Wiley & Sons Ltd., EMEA Institutional Sales, 9600 Garsington Rd, Oxford, OX4 2DQ, United Kingdom; cs-journals@wiley.com; http://www.wiley.com. Illus., index, adv. Sample. Refereed. Reprint: PSC. *Indexed:* A01, A22, BRI, S25. *Bk. rev.:* 0-7, 500-2,000 words. *Aud.:* Ac, Sa.

This journal provides broad coverage of geology with an emphasis on interdisciplinary work and regional case studies from around the world are included. Frequent special issues cover a broad range of topics. This title is a good complement to others of a general nature, such as *Geology* or *Geological Magazine,* and is appropriate for comprehensive collections. Free tables of contents and abstracts from 1951 to the present are provided on the website, along with full-text access for subscribers. Book reviews are also available free to all. Readers may register for free e-mail alerts or RSS feeds announcing new journal content.

1682. *Geological Magazine.* Formerly (until 1864): *Geologist.* [ISSN: 0016-7568] 1842. 12x/yr. GBP 1039. Ed(s): M B Allen. Cambridge University Press, University Printing House, Shaftesbury Rd, Cambridge, CB2 8BS, United Kingdom; journals@cambridge.org; https://www.cambridge.org/. Illus., index, adv. Sample. Refereed. Circ: 1700. Vol. ends: Nov (No. 6). Microform: BHP. Reprint: PSC. *Indexed:* A01, A22, BRI, C45, E01, MASUSE. *Bk. rev.:* 3-12, 100-500 words. *Aud.:* Ac, Sa.

A strong and well-established general journal in the field, this title publishes research and review articles in all areas of earth sciences. It includes interdisciplinary papers on regional geology, with an emphasis on descriptive work, mineralogy, and paleontology. GeoScienceWorld offers free tables of contents and abstracts from 1940 forward, and subscribers may view full text of articles from 2000 to present. Some open-access articles are available. Readers may sign up for free e-mail alerts or RSS feeds announcing new journal content. Cambridge University Press offers a digitized archive extending back to 1864. A GeoRef priority journal.

1683. *Geological Society. Journal.* Incorporates (1952-1971): *Geological Society of London. Proceedings;* Which superseded in part (in 1971): *Geological Society of London. Quarterly Journal;* Which was formerly (until 1845): *Geological Society of London. Proceedings.* [ISSN: 0016-7649] 1826. bi-m. GBP 1608 combined subscription domestic (print & online eds.); GBP 1785 combined subscription in Europe (print & online eds.); USD 3570 combined subscription elsewhere (print & online eds.)). Ed(s): Graham Shields. Geological Society Publishing House, Unit 7, Brassmill Enterprise Ctr, Brassmill Ln, Bath, BA1 3JN, United Kingdom. Illus., adv. Refereed. Vol. ends: Nov (No. 6). *Indexed:* A01, A22. *Aud.:* Ac, Sa.

This is the flagship journal of the Geological Society of London, one of the oldest geological societies in the world. It is international in scope, with papers covering the full range of the earth sciences. These include both full-length research articles and shorter, rapid-publication "specials." The editors also often publish thematic sets of papers as all or part of an issue. Free tables of contents and abstracts are available on GeoScienceWorld, along with full text for subscribers from 1971 forward. Readers may sign up for free e-mail alerts or RSS feeds. Archival coverage back to 1845 is available as part of the Lyell collection. Highly recommended for academic and special library collections. A GeoRef priority journal.

1684. ***Geological Society of America Bulletin.*** Formerly (until 1961): *Geological Society of America. Bulletin.* [ISSN: 0016-7606] 1890. bi-m. USD 1325 combined subscription print & online eds. Geological Society of America, PO Box 9140, Boulder, CO 80301; gsaservice@geosociety.org; http://www.geosociety.org. Illus., adv. Sample. Refereed. Vol. ends: Dec (No. 12). *Indexed:* A01, A22, C45, HRIS, S25. *Aud.:* Ac, Sa.

This is the lead research journal published by the Geological Society of America (GSA) and contains longer articles than does *Geology.* Although coverage of international topics is included, work in North America is emphasized. All issues from 1890 forward are available on GeoScienceWorld, with full text for subscribers. Some open-access articles are available. Readers may sign up for free e-mail alerts or RSS feeds about new articles. Strongly recommended for academic and corporate collections. A GeoRef priority journal.

1685. ***Geology (Boulder).*** [ISSN: 0091-7613] 1973. m. USD 1325 combined subscription print & online eds. Ed(s): Lyne Yohe. Geological Society of America, PO Box 9140, Boulder, CO 80301; gsaservice@geosociety.org; http://www.geosociety.org. Illus., adv. Sample. Refereed. Vol. ends: Dec (No. 12). *Indexed:* A01, A22, BRI, S25. *Aud.:* Ac, Sa.

This title, published by the Geological Society of America, provides short, thought-provoking articles on a wide range of geological topics of interest to a broad audience. *Geology* is oriented more toward new investigations and recent discoveries in the field than is *Geological Society of America Bulletin.* A "Research Focus" feature highlights additional information on research issues that are related to selected articles. Free abstracts are offered on GeoScienceWorld from 1973 to present, with full-text access for subscribers or society members. Some open-access articles are available. Readers may sign up for e-mail alerts or RSS feeds to stay up to date with new articles. Strongly recommended for academic and corporate collections. A GeoRef priority journal.

1686. ***Geology Today.*** [ISSN: 0266-6979] 1985. bi-m. GBP 864. Ed(s): Peter Doyle. Wiley-Blackwell Publishing Ltd., The Atrium, Southern Gate, Chichester, PO19 8QG, United Kingdom; cs-journals@wiley.com; http://onlinelibrary.wiley.com/. Illus., index, adv. Sample. Refereed. Microform: PQC. Reprint: PSC. *Indexed:* A01, A22, BRI, C37, E01, S25. *Bk. rev.:* 0-10, 200-500 words. *Aud.:* Ga, Ac.

Published on behalf of the Geologists' Association and the Geological Society of London, this journal provides news and current awareness briefings, along with short feature articles. The latter often gravitate toward popular topics, but are well written and illustrated. Free tables of contents with abstracts can be found on the website beginning with 1985, with full-text access for subscribers. Recent years include graphical abstracts. Readers may sign up for free e-mail alerts or RSS feeds to keep up with new content.

1687. ***Geomorphology.*** [ISSN: 0169-555X] 1987. 24x/yr. EUR 4854. Ed(s): T Oguchi. Elsevier BV, Radarweg 29, Amsterdam, 1043 NX, Netherlands; info@elsevier.com; https://www.elsevier.com/. Illus., adv. Sample. Refereed. *Indexed:* A01, A22, C45, S25. *Bk. rev.:* 0-3, 500-1,000 words. *Aud.:* Ac, Sa.

Publishes research papers and review papers on geomorphic studies of all types and scales. Frequent special issues present papers on such topics as karst, fluvial processes, seismic hazards, and planetary geomorphology, or publish conference papers in the field. The website provides free access to tables of contents and abstracts from 1987 onward, with full-text access for subscribers. Some open- access articles are available. Readers may register to receive free e-mail alerts or RSS feeds to track new articles. Appropriate for academic library collections. A GeoRef priority journal.

1688. ***Geophysical Journal International.*** Formerly (until 1989): *Geophysical Journal;* Which was formed by the merger of (1986-1987): *Annales Geophysicae. Series B: Terrestrial and Planetary Physics;* (1958-1987): *Royal Astronomical Society Geophysical Journal;* Which was formerly (until 1958): *Royal Astronomical Society. Monthly Notices. Geophysical Supplement;* (1986-1987): *Annales Geophysicae. Series A: Upper Atmosphere and Space Sciences.* [ISSN: 0956-540X] 1958. m. GBP 1798. Ed(s): J Renner. Oxford University Press, Great Clarendon St, Oxford, OX2 6DP, United Kingdom; jnls.cust.serv@oup.com; https://academic.oup.com/journals/. Illus., adv. Sample. Refereed. Microform: PQC. Reprint: PSC. *Indexed:* A01, A22, E01. *Bk. rev.:* 0-2, 700-1,500 words, signed. *Aud.:* Ac, Sa.

Formed by a merger of three journals, this title continues the numbering of the *Geophysical Journal of the Royal Astronomical Society.* Subject areas covered include seismology, crustal structure, gravity, geomagnetism, and rock rheology. Tables of contents and abstracts can be found on the website from 1958 forward, with full-text access available for subscribers. Some open-access articles are available. Readers may register for free e-mail alerts or RSS feeds about new journal content. A GeoRef priority journal.

1689. ***Geophysical Prospecting.*** [ISSN: 0016-8025] 1953. bi-m. GBP 1364. Ed(s): Tijmen Jan Moser. Wiley-Blackwell Publishing Ltd., The Atrium, Southern Gate, Chichester, PO19 8QG, United Kingdom; cs-journals@wiley.com; http://onlinelibrary.wiley.com/. Illus., adv. Sample. Refereed. Microform: PQC. Reprint: PSC. *Indexed:* A01, A22, C45, E01. *Aud.:* Ac, Sa.

Published on behalf of the European Association for Geoscientists and Engineers, *Geophysical Prospecting* covers research on geophysics as applied to resource exploration and assessment. Many articles report on work in the mineral and energy industries and have a practical emphasis. However, the journal is also appropriate for academic researchers in geophysics. Free tables of contents and abstracts from 1953 to the present are available at the website, along with full-text access for subscribers. Some open-access articles are available. Readers may sign up for free e-mail alerts or RSS feeds to track new journal content.

1690. ***Geophysical Research Letters.*** [ISSN: 0094-8276] 1974. s-m. USD 4794. Ed(s): Noah Diffenbaugh. Wiley-Blackwell Publishing, Inc., 111 River St, Hoboken, NJ 07030; http://onlinelibrary.wiley.com. Illus., index. Sample. Refereed. Vol. ends: Dec. Reprint: PSC. *Indexed:* A22, C45, S25. *Aud.:* Ac, Sa.

This journal is aimed at scientists in diverse disciplines related to geophysics, and issues contain topics such as atmospheric science, oceans, and climate; solid Earth and planets; and hydrology and climate. Manuscripts are of limited length in order to expedite review and publication. The website offers free access to tables of contents and abstracts back to 1974 with full-text access for subscribers. Recent years include graphical abstracts. Some open-access articles are available. Content older than 24 months is freely accessible to all. Readers may register for e-mail alerts and RSS feeds for new journal content. A GeoRef priority journal.

1691. ***Geophysics.*** Formerly (until 1936): *Society of Petroleum Geophysicists. Journal.* [ISSN: 0016-8033] 1931. bi-m. USD 810 (print & online eds.) Corporations, USD 4310 (print & online eds.)). Ed(s): Evert Slob. Society of Exploration Geophysicists, PO Box 702740, Tulsa, OK 74170; meetings@seg.org; http://www.seg.org. Illus., index, adv. Refereed. Vol. ends: Nov/Dec (No. 6). Microform: PQC. *Indexed:* A22, S25. *Aud.:* Ac, Sa.

Published by the Society of Exploration Geophysicists, this is one of the leading journals in the field. Many of the articles focus on seismic data acquisition, processing, and interpretation. Other areas such as mechanical properties of rock, borehole analysis, and remote sensing are also covered. Free tables of contents and article abstracts from 1936 to the present are available on the SEG Digital Library, with full-text articles for subscribers. GeoScienceWorld also offers full-text coverage from 1936 forward for subscribers. Some open-access articles are available. Readers may sign up for free e-mail alerts or RSS feeds. Highly recommended. A GeoRef priority journal.

1692. ***Geoscience Canada.*** Formerly (until 1974): *Geological Association of Canada. Proceedings.* [ISSN: 0315-0941] 1948. q. Individuals, CAD 50; Members, CAD 40; Non-members, CAD 185. Ed(s): Reginald A Wilson. Geological Association of Canada, c/o Dept. of Earth Sciences, Memorial Univ. of Newfoundland, St. John's, NL A1B 3X5, Canada; gac@mun.ca; http://www.gac.ca. Illus., adv. Sample. Refereed. Vol. ends: Dec (No. 4). Microform: PQC. *Indexed:* A01, A22, BRI, C37. *Bk. rev.:* 1-7, 400-1,200 words, signed. *Aud.:* Ac, Sa.

This engaging quarterly is the main journal of the Geological Association of Canada (GAC) and is geared toward the non-specialist. Many of the papers deal with historical and policy issues related to the geology of Canada. Others address topics of broader geologic interest, such as sedimentation processes, glacial geology, geothermal energy, and plate tectonics. For many years, this journal has published an excellent series on mineral deposit models; other series feature such topics as environmental marine geoscience, igneous rock associations, and even geology and wine. Full text of articles is available to GAC members and subscribers from 1974 to the present. Articles from issues older than three years are freely available to all.

1693. ***Geosphere.*** [ISSN: 1553-040X] 2005. bi-m. Free. Ed(s): Bridgette Moore. Geological Society of America, PO Box 9140, Boulder, CO 80301; gsaservice@geosociety.org; http://www.geosociety.org. *Indexed:* A01, S25. *Aud.:* Ac, Sa.

Casting a broad net, *Geosphere* is an online-only, open-access journal that publishes research articles in all fields of the geosciences. Many papers include extras such as animations and links to supplementary data. Themes in some recent special issues include continental rifts, geothermal energy, subduction zones, and grand challenges in the earth and space sciences. All content from 2005 forward is freely available on GeoScienceWorld. Readers may set up an e-mail alert or RSS feed to receive notification when new issues are published. A GeoRef priority journal.

Geothermics. See Energy section.

1694. ***Groundwater.*** [ISSN: 0017-467X] 1963. bi-m. GBP 575. Ed(s): Hendrik M Haitjema. Wiley-Blackwell Publishing, Inc., 111 River St, Hoboken, NJ 07030; http://onlinelibrary.wiley.com. Illus., index. Sample. Refereed. Vol. ends: Nov/Dec (No. 6). Microform: PQC. Reprint: PSC. *Indexed:* A01, A22, Agr, BRI, C45, E01, S25. *Bk. rev.:* 0-5, 300-800 words, signed. *Aud.:* Ac, Sa.

An official journal of the National Ground Water Association (NGWA), this title emphasizes ground water hydrology in aquifers and other geologic environments. Physical and chemical interactions as well as solution transport are also given considerable attention. Monitoring and cleanup techniques, however, are more fully addressed by its sister publication, *Groundwater Monitoring and Remediation.* Tables of contents and abstracts from volumes from 1963 forward are available free online, with full-text access for subscribers and members of the NGWA Scientists and Engineers Division. Some open-access articles are available. Readers may sign up to receive free alerts via RSS feed when new articles are published. A GeoRef priority journal.

1695. ***Hydrogeology Journal.*** Formerly (until 1994): *Applied Hydrogeology.* [ISSN: 1431-2174] 1992. bi-m. EUR 1603 (print & online eds.)). Ed(s): Clifford Voss. Springer, Tiergartenstr 17, Heidelberg, 69121, Germany. Illus., index, adv. Sample. Refereed. Vol. ends: No. 6. Reprint: PSC. *Indexed:* A01, A22, Agr, BRI, C45, E01, S25. *Bk. rev.:* 0-2, 300-800 words, signed. *Aud.:* Ac, Sa.

Hydrogeology Journal is the official journal of the International Association of Hydrogeologists and publishes theoretical and research-oriented papers, as well as applied reports. Occasional special issues are published on topics such as groundwater characterization, land subsidence, and the economics of groundwater. The website offers full-text access from 1992 forward for subscribers. Free tables of contents and abstracts are available along with selected open-access articles. Readers may set up free alerts to learn when new articles are published.

1696. ***Hydrological Processes (Online).*** [ISSN: 1099-1085] 1986. s-m. GBP 4300. Ed(s): Doerthe Tetzlaff. John Wiley & Sons Ltd., EMEA Institutional Sales, 9600 Garsington Rd, Oxford, OX4 2DQ, United Kingdom; cs-journals@wiley.com; http://onlinelibrary.wiley.com. Adv. Sample. Refereed. *Bk. rev.:* 0-1, 500-1,000 words. *Aud.:* Ac, Sa.

This international journal publishes original scientific and technical papers in hydrology. Articles present research on physical, biogeochemical, mathematical, and methodological aspects of hydrologic processes, as well as reports on instrumentation and techniques. Occasional special issues focus on a theme or feature a conference topic. Free tables of contents and abstracts are available on the website from 1986 forward, with full-text access for subscribers. Some open-access articles are available. Readers may sign up to receive alerts when new articles are published. A GeoRef priority journal.

1697. ***Hydrological Sciences Journal.*** Former titles (until 1982): *Hydrological Sciences Bulletin;* (until 1972): *International Association of Scientific Hydrology. Bulletin;* (until 1958): *Bulletin de l'Association Internationale d'hydrologie Scientifique;* (until 1957): *Bulletin d'information de l'Association Internationale d'hydrologie Scientifique.* [ISSN: 0262-6667] 1956. 16x/yr. GBP 1011 (print & online eds.)). Ed(s): Zbigniew W Kundzewicz, Demetris Koutsoyiannis. Taylor & Francis, 2, 3 & 4 Park Sq, Milton Park, Abingdon, OX14 4RN, United Kingdom; subscriptions@tandf.co.uk; https://www.tandfonline.com. Illus., index, adv. Sample. Refereed. Vol. ends: Dec (No. 6). Reprint: PSC. *Indexed:* A01, A22, C45, E01, S25. *Aud.:* Ac, Sa.

This official journal of the International Association of Hydrological Sciences publishes research articles, scientific notes, and discussions. The range of topics covered is quite broad and includes modeling of hydrologic systems, use of water resources, runoff and erosion, and groundwater pollution and chemistry. Current material is all in English but some older articles are in French. The website offers free tables of contents and abstracts from 1956 forward with full-text access for subscribers. Some open-access articles are available.

1698. ***Hydrology and Earth System Sciences.*** [ISSN: 1027-5606] 1997. m. EUR 1929.33; EUR 176.86 newsstand/cover. Ed(s): Hubert H G Savenijeh. Copernicus GmbH, Bahnhofsallee 1e, Goettingen, 37081, Germany; info@copernicus.org; http://www.copernicus.org. Refereed. *Indexed:* C45, S25. *Aud.:* Ac, Sa.

This interdisciplinary, open-access journal publishes research in all areas of hydrology, with an emphasis on interactions with physical, chemical, and biological processes. Topics covered include the hydrological cycle, transport of dissolved and particulate matter, water budgets and fluxes, climate and atmospheric interactions, and the effects of human activity. Special issues address such themes as urban hydrology, hydrologic modeling, and forecasting of droughts and floods. This is a "two-stage open access journal," with papers first posted for comment and discussion in *Hydrology and Earth System Sciences Discussions* (*HESSD*). Upon final acceptance, the revised papers appear in *HESS.* A GeoRef priority journal.

Icarus. See Astronomy section.

1699. ***International Geology Review.*** [ISSN: 0020-6814] 1958. 18x/yr. GBP 2096 (print & online eds.)). Ed(s): Robert Stern. Taylor & Francis Inc., 711 3rd Ave, 8th Fl, New York, NY 10017; support@tandfonline.com; http://www.tandfonline.com. Illus., index, adv. Refereed. Vol. ends: No. 12. Reprint: PSC. *Indexed:* A01, A22, E01. *Bk. rev.:* 0-2, 300-800 words, signed. *Aud.:* Ac, Sa.

This scholarly publication features in-depth review articles and original research. Specific areas of emphasis include petrology, tectonics, and mineral and energy resources. Coverage is truly global in scope, with particular attention to such parts of the world as Africa, Asia, and South America, making this a useful resource for those geographic areas. Tables of contents and article abstracts are freely available online for all volumes from 1959 to present with full-text access for subscribers. Some open-access articles are available. Readers may set up alerts via e-mail or RSS feed to learn when new content is published. A GeoRef priority journal.

1700. ***International Journal of Coal Geology.*** [ISSN: 0166-5162] 1981. 16x/yr. EUR 4267. Ed(s): C O Karacan, S Dai. Elsevier BV, Radarweg 29, Amsterdam, 1043 NX, Netherlands; info@elsevier.com; https://www.elsevier.com/. Illus., adv. Sample. Refereed. Vol. ends: No. 4. Microform: PQC. *Indexed:* A01, A22. *Bk. rev.:* 0-2, 500-1,000 words. *Aud.:* Ac, Sa.

This journal publishes both basic and applied research articles on the geology and petrology of coal from around the world. Some areas of special focus are the geology of coal measures, coal genesis and modern coal-forming environments, and coal-bearing strata. Proceedings of symposia appear in some issues. The website provides free access to tables of contents and abstracts from

1980 forward, with full-text access for subscribers. Some open-access articles are available. Readers may set up alerts via e-mail or RSS feed to learn when new articles are published. Appropriate for comprehensive research collections. A GeoRef priority journal.

1701. ***International Journal of Earth Sciences.*** Formerly (until 1998): *Geologische Rundschau.* [ISSN: 1437-3254] 1910. 8x/yr. Ed(s): Wolf-Christian Dullo. Springer, Tiergartenstr 17, Heidelberg, 69121, Germany; subscriptions@springer.com; https://www.springer.com. Illus., index, adv. Sample. Refereed. Vol. ends: Dec (No. 4). Reprint: IRC; PSC. *Indexed:* A01, A22, Agr, C45, E01, S25. *Aud.:* Ac, Sa.

This journal publishes original research papers and review articles on a wide range of geologic processes. Some areas of focus include tectonics, volcanology, sedimentology, mineral deposits, and surface processes. Coverage is international in scope but with emphasis on Europe. Occasional special issues often address the geology of a specific region. The website offers free tables of contents and abstracts for all volumes from 1910 forward with full-text access for subscribers. Some open-access articles are available. Readers may set up free alerts to receive tables of contents when new issues are published. Listed as a GeoRef priority journal under its earlier title, *Geologische Rundschau.*

1702. ***Interpretation (Tulsa).*** [ISSN: 2324-8858] 2013. q. USD 530 (print & online eds.)). Ed(s): Yonghe Sun. Society of Exploration Geophysicists, PO Box 702740, Tulsa, OK 74170; books@seg.org; http://www.seg.org. Refereed. *Aud.:* Ac, Sa.

This quarterly from the Society of Exploration Geophysicists and the American Association of Petroleum Geologists focuses on interpreting seismic and well-logging data about the Earth's subsurface to draw useful conclusions. It has a more applied emphasis than some other geophysics journals, and many papers address techniques and other methodological considerations. It is available from the SEG Digital Library with free tables of contents and abstracts. Full text from 2013 forward is available to subscribers. It is also offered on GeoScienceWorld with full text of all issues for subscribers. Some open-access articles are available. Readers may sign up for free e-mail alerts or RSS feeds. Recommended primarily for comprehensive academic and corporate collections.

1703. ***Journal of Advances in Modeling Earth Systems.*** [ISSN: 1942-2466] 2009. q. Free. Ed(s): Robert Pincus. Wiley-Blackwell Publishing, Inc., 111 River St, Hoboken, NJ 07030; http://onlinelibrary.wiley.com. Adv. Refereed. *Indexed:* A01, S25. *Aud.:* Ac, Sa.

This gold open-access journal from the American Geophysical Union (AGU) focuses on the development and application of Earth system models, often at regional or global scales. Highly interdisciplinary in nature, the articles focus on a wide range of areas such as atmospheric and oceanic dynamics, climate, and land surface changes. Readers may register for alerts to learn about new articles.

1704. ***Journal of Applied Geophysics.*** Formerly (until 1992): *Geoexploration.* [ISSN: 0926-9851] 1963. 12x/yr. EUR 2510. Ed(s): J Behura, J Xia. Elsevier BV, Radarweg 29, Amsterdam, 1043 NX, Netherlands; info@elsevier.com; https://www.elsevier.com/. Illus., adv. Refereed. Microform: PQC. *Indexed:* A01, A22, S25. *Aud.:* Ac, Sa.

This journal emphasizes methodology and applied aspects of geophysical techniques as used in geological and environmental sciences and engineering. Special issues focus on current topics and conference reports. The website provides free access to tables of contents and abstracts for volumes from 1963 to present with full-text access for subscribers. Some open-access articles are available. Readers may set up free alerts to learn of new articles published in subscription editions or for open-access articles.

1705. ***Journal of Geochemical Exploration.*** [ISSN: 0375-6742] 1972. 12x/yr. EUR 3015. Ed(s): B De Vivo, R A Ayuso. Elsevier BV, Radarweg 29, Amsterdam, 1043 NX, Netherlands; info@elsevier.com; https://www.elsevier.com/. Illus., index. Sample. Refereed. Vol. ends: No. 3. Microform: PQC. *Indexed:* A01, A22. *Bk. rev.:* 0-2, 800-2,000 words. *Aud.:* Ac, Sa.

This monthly journal emphasizes the application of geochemistry in the exploration and study of mineral deposits. Papers present international research on geochemical exploration, sampling and analytical techniques, and uses of geoinformatics data. Some special issues feature a theme on such topics as polluted soils, fluid inclusions, or mapping of geochemical distributions. Free access to tables of contents and article abstracts for all volumes from 1972 forward is available on the website, with full-text access for subscribers. Readers may set up alerts via RSS feed to learn when new articles are published. Appropriate for comprehensive and research collections. A GeoRef priority journal.

1706. ***Journal of Geodynamics.*** [ISSN: 0264-3707] 1984. 10x/yr. EUR 2974. Ed(s): I M Artemieva. Pergamon Press, The Blvd, Langford Ln, E Park, Kidlington, OX5 1GB, United Kingdom; JournalsCustomerServiceEMEA@elsevier.com; http://www.elsevier.com. Adv. Sample. Refereed. Microform: PQC. *Indexed:* A01, A22. *Aud.:* Ac, Sa.

This journal provides an international forum for research in the solid earth sciences with an emphasis on large-scale processes. Papers address a wide range of topics, such as physical properties of rocks and changes with pressure and temperature, mantle convection and heat flow, plate tectonics and kinematics, and magma generation, transport, and emplacement. Occasional issues report on symposia or feature a special topic. Some examples of topics are crustal fluids, geodynamic modeling and subduction zones, and mountain building. Tables of contents and abstracts are available free from 1984 forward with full-text access for subscribers. Some open-access articles are available. Readers may set up free alerts via RSS feed to learn when new articles are published.

1707. ***The Journal of Geology.*** [ISSN: 0022-1376] 1893. bi-m. USD 343. Ed(s): David Rowley. University of Chicago Press, 1427 E 60th St, Chicago, IL 60637; subscriptions@press.uchicago.edu; http://www.journals.uchicago.edu. Illus., index, adv. Sample. Refereed. Vol. ends: Nov. Reprint: PSC. *Indexed:* A01, A22, BRI, S25. *Bk. rev.:* 0-4, 300-750 words. *Aud.:* Ac, Sa.

This prestigious geoscience journal is a key title for academic and special libraries. Articles address a broad range of topics in the discipline of geology and are chosen for their wide applicability or use of innovative approaches and methods. Both the full-length articles and the shorter geological notes reflect high editorial standards, adding to the archival value of this core publication. Tables of contents and abstracts from 1893 forward are available free on the web, with full-text access for subscribers. Back years are also accessible to subscribers via the JSTOR platform. Readers may sign up to receive alerts via e-mail or RSS feed when new issues are published. A GeoRef priority journal.

1708. ***Journal of Geophysical Research.*** Former titles (until 1949): *Terrestrial Magnetism and Atmospheric Electricity;* (until 1899): *Terrestrial Magnetism.* [ISSN: 0148-0227] 1896. m. Wiley-Blackwell Publishing, Inc., 111 River St, Hoboken, NJ 07030; info@wiley.com; http://onlinelibrary.wiley.com. Refereed. Reprint: PSC. *Indexed:* A22. *Aud.:* Ac, Sa.

This comprehensive, interdisciplinary journal presents research on the physics and chemistry of the Earth, its environment, and the solar system. *JGR* is published in seven parts that may be purchased as a package or separately (these parts include atmospheres, biogeosciences, Earth surface, oceans, planets, solid Earth, and space physics). Individual issues often contain special sections with multiple papers devoted to one topic. Tables of contents and abstracts are freely available, while subscribers may view full-text articles. Some open-access articles are available. Content older than 24 months is accessible to all. Readers may sign up to receive free publication alerts via e-mail or RSS feed. Some parts, including *Solid Earth, Oceans,* and *Planets,* are GeoRef priority journals.

1709. ***Journal of Geophysics and Engineering.*** [ISSN: 1742-2132] 2004. bi-m. Ed(s): Shouli Qu, Yanghua Wang. Oxford University Press, Great Clarendon St, Oxford, OX2 6DP, United Kingdom; jnls.cust.serv@oup.com; https://academic.oup.com/journals. Sample. Refereed. *Indexed:* C45, S25. *Aud.:* Ac, Sa.

This bimonthly is issued in partnership with the Sinopec Geophysical Research Institute in China. It publishes research articles in all areas of geophysics, with an emphasis on applied science and engineering. It covers topics like geodynamics, mineral exploration, petroleum engineering, and reservoir geophysics. Free tables of contents and abstracts from 2004 forward with many articles available open access. Readers may get alerts about newly published articles via e-mail or RSS feed.

1710. *Journal of Geoscience Education.* Formerly (until 1996): *Journal of Geological Education.* [ISSN: 1089-9995] 1951. q. GBP 191 print & online eds. Ed(s): Kristen St. John. Taylor & Francis, . Illus., index, adv. Refereed. Vol. ends: Nov (No. 5). Microform: PQC. *Indexed:* A01, A22. *Bk. rev.:* 5-10, 200-800 words. *Aud.:* Ac, Sa.

Earth science teachers are the target audience for this quarterly journal, which reports on techniques, resources, and innovations useful for pedagogy and assessment. Materials span the K-12 level as well as college and university instruction. Occasional special issues cover themes such as sustainability, climate literacy, and the future of geoscience education research. The website of the National Association of Geoscience Teachers (NAGT) offers full-text access to NAGT members. Institutional subscribers may access full text from 1951 forward on the Taylor and Francis website. Readers can sign up for free e-mail alerts or RSS feeds to learn about newly published articles. A GeoRef priority journal.

1711. *Journal of Glaciology.* Formerly (until 1947): *Association for the Study of Snow and Ice. Papers and Discussions.* [ISSN: 0022-1430] 19??. bi-m. International Glaciological Society, Scott Polar Research Institute, Lensfield Rd, Cambridge, CB2 1ER, United Kingdom; igsoc@igsoc.org; http://www.igsoc.org/. Illus., index. Refereed. Reprint: PSC. *Indexed:* A01, A22, S25. *Bk. rev.:* 0-1, 600-1,200 words. *Aud.:* Ac, Sa.

This journal of the International Glaciological Society publishes findings and theories on all aspects of snow and ice, with particular emphasis on studies of glaciers and their formation, movement, and changes over time. Many issues also feature one or more articles that cover new techniques and equipment for glacial investigation. Formerly a subscription journal, since 2016 this title has been published under a gold open-access model.

1712. *Journal of Hydrology.* [ISSN: 0022-1694] 1963. 12x/yr. EUR 11908. Ed(s): A Bardossy, K P Georgakakos. Elsevier BV, Radarweg 29, Amsterdam, 1043 NX, Netherlands; info@elsevier.com; https://www.elsevier.com/. Illus., index, adv. Sample. Refereed. Vol. ends: No. 4. Microform: PQC. *Indexed:* A01, A22, Agr, C45, S25. *Aud.:* Ac, Sa.

Publishes research papers and reviews related to all areas of the hydrological sciences, including physical, chemical, biogeochemical, and systems aspects of surface and groundwater hydrology. Special issues focus on such water-related topics as subsurface systems, flood risk management, and flow and transport in aquifers. Tables of contents and abstracts are available on the website for all volumes from 1963 to present, with full-text access for subscribers. Some open-access articles are available. Readers may set up free alerts via RSS feed. Appropriate for comprehensive academic and research collections. A GeoRef priority journal.

1713. *Journal of Metamorphic Geology.* [ISSN: 0263-4929] 1983. 9x/yr. GBP 2413. Wiley-Blackwell Publishing Ltd., The Atrium, Southern Gate, Chichester, PO19 8QG, United Kingdom; cs-journals@wiley.com; http://onlinelibrary.wiley.com. Illus., adv. Sample. Refereed. Vol. ends: Nov (No. 6). Reprint: PSC. *Indexed:* A01, A22, E01. *Aud.:* Ac, Sa.

This title publishes papers on a full range of metamorphic topics. Research is presented on mineral properties, theoretical and experimental studies of metamorphic reactions, structural deformation and geochemical changes associated with metamorphism, and regional analysis of metamorphic terrains. Occasional special issues focus on particular geologic environments or dynamics. The website provides free tables of contents and abstracts for all volumes from 1983 forward, with full-text access for subscribers. Some open-access articles are available. Free alerts are available via RSS feed or through an account on the publisher's site. A GeoRef priority journal.

Journal of Paleontology. See Paleontology section.

1714. *Journal of Petroleum Geology.* [ISSN: 0141-6421] 1978. q. GBP 700 (print & online eds.)). Ed(s): Christopher Tiratsoo. Wiley-Blackwell Publishing Ltd., The Atrium, Southern Gate, Chichester, PO19 8QG, United Kingdom; cs-journals@wiley.com; http://onlinelibrary.wiley.com. Illus., index, adv. Sample. Refereed. Vol. ends: Oct (No. 4). Reprint: PSC. *Indexed:* A01, A22, E01. *Bk. rev.:* 0-3, 500-1,200 words, signed. *Aud.:* Ac, Sa.

This quarterly presents research on the geology of oil and natural gas, with an emphasis on regions outside of North America. Topics include petroleum exploration and development, basin evolution and modeling, and reservoir evaluation. Free tables of contents and abstracts are available on the website from 1978 forward, with full-text access for subscribers. Some open-access articles are available. Readers may sign up to receive RSS feeds for new issues. Older years are also available on the AAPG Datapages Archive. A GeoRef priority journal.

1715. *Journal of Petrology.* [ISSN: 0022-3530] 1960. m. EUR 2264. Ed(s): Marjorie Wilson. Oxford University Press, Great Clarendon St, Oxford, OX2 6DP, United Kingdom; onlinequeries.uk@oup.com; http://global.oup.com. Illus., index, adv. Sample. Refereed. Circ: 380. Vol. ends: Dec (No. 12). Microform: PQC. Reprint: PSC. *Indexed:* A01, A22, BAS, E01. *Bk. rev.:* 0-2, 600-1,000 words, signed. *Aud.:* Ac, Sa.

This journal features research in igneous and metamorphic petrology. Some subjects covered include magmatic processes, petrogenesis, trace element and isotope geochemistry, and experimental studies and theoretical modeling. Occasional issues feature special themes or papers from selected conferences. Tables of contents with abstracts are available for all volumes on the website from 1960 forward, with full-text access for subscribers. Some open-access articles are available. Readers may sign up to receive free alerts via e-mail. Recommended for academic and special libraries. A GeoRef priority journal.

1716. *Journal of Quaternary Science.* [ISSN: 0267-8179] 1986. 8x/yr. GBP 1787. Ed(s): A J Long. John Wiley & Sons Ltd., EMEA Institutional Sales, 9600 Garsington Rd, Oxford, OX4 2DQ, United Kingdom; cs-journals@wiley.com; http://onlinelibrary.wiley.com. Illus., index, adv. Sample. Refereed. Vol. ends: No. 8. Microform: PQC. Reprint: PSC. *Indexed:* A22, C45, S25. *Bk. rev.:* 2-10, 300-1,000 words, signed. *Aud.:* Ac, Sa.

Published for the Quaternary Research Association, this journal focuses on the Earth's history during the last 2.6 million years. This time period is the same as that covered by the journal *Boreas,* and there are many similarities between the two journals. Papers span a wide range of topics, and many are interdisciplinary in nature. In particular, there is an emphasis on the stratigraphy, glaciation, and paleoclimatology of the period. Occasional special issues often focus on a particular region or environment. Full-length research papers, short contributions intended for rapid communication, and invited reviews are all included. Free tables of contents and abstracts for volumes from 1986 to the present are provided on the website, with full-text access for subscribers. Some open-access articles are available. Readers may sign up to receive alerts when new articles are published. A GeoRef priority journal.

1717. *Journal of Sedimentary Research.* Formed by the merger of (1994-1996): *Journal of Sedimentary Research. Section A: Sedimentary Petrology and Processes (Print);* (1994-1996): *Journal of Sedimentary Research. Section B: Stratigraphy and Global Studies (Print);* Both of which superseded in part (in 1994): *Journal of Sedimentary Petrology.* [ISSN: 1527-1404] 1996. bi-m. Free to members. Ed(s): Melissa B Lester, Gene Rankey. Society for Sedimentary Geology (S E P M), 4111 S Darlington, Ste 100, Tulsa, OK 74135; foundation@sepm.org; http://www.sepm.org. Illus., adv. Refereed. *Indexed:* A22, C45, S25. *Bk. rev.:* 0-3, 200-600 words. *Aud.:* Ac, Sa.

This monthly journal of the Society for Sedimentary Geology publishes papers on topics from all branches of sedimentary geology, including the processes of transport and deposition, inherent characteristics of sediments, and their impacts on other aspects of the geologic record. These range from detailed papers that concentrate on very specific, often small-scale topics to research reports on much larger spatial and temporal scales. The AAPG Datapages archive offers full-text content for subscribers from 1931 forward. Tables of contents and abstracts are also available free on GeoScienceWorld for all volumes, with full-text access for subscribers. A GeoRef priority journal.

1718. ***Journal of Seismology.*** [ISSN: 1383-4649] 1997. q. EUR 854 (print & online eds.)). Ed(s): Mariano Garcia Fernandez. Springer Netherlands, Van Godewijckstraat 30, Dordrecht, 3311 GX, Netherlands; http://www.springer.com. Adv. Refereed. Microform: PQC. Reprint: PSC. *Indexed:* A01, A22, BRI, E01, S25. *Aud.:* Ac, Sa.

This journal specializes in the study of earthquakes and their occurrence around the world. Areas of particular focus include seismicity, fault systems, earthquake prediction and modeling, seismic hazards, and earthquake engineering. Many papers are regional or historical studies. However, broader theoretical work is also included, along with short communications on new analytical techniques and instrumentation. The website provides free tables of contents and abstracts for all volumes from 1997 forward and subscribers may view full text of articles. Some open-access articles are available. Readers may sign up for free alerts via RSS feed.

1719. ***Journal of Structural Geology.*** [ISSN: 0191-8141] 1979. m. EUR 3564. Ed(s): C W Passchier. Pergamon Press, The Blvd, Langford Ln, E Park, Kidlington, OX5 1GB, United Kingdom; JournalsCustomerServiceEMEA@elsevier.com; http://www.elsevier.com. Illus., adv. Sample. Refereed. Microform: PQC. *Indexed:* A01, A22, S25. *Bk. rev.:* 0-2, 500-1,000 words. *Aud.:* Ac, Sa.

This international journal publishes research and review articles on structural geology, tectonics, and the associated rock deformation processes. Topics include faults, folds, fractures, strain analysis, rock mechanics, rheology, and theoretical and experimental modeling. Occasional special issues address specific themes or regions. Tables of contents and article abstracts are accessible free on the website for all volumes from 1979 forward, with full-text access for subscribers. Some open-access articles are available. Readers may set up alerts via RSS feed to learn when new articles are published. Recommended for academic and special libraries. A GeoRef priority journal.

1720. ***Journal of Volcanology and Geothermal Research.*** [ISSN: 0377-0273] 1976. 20x/yr. EUR 6018. Ed(s): M T Mangan, J W Neuberg. Elsevier BV, Radarweg 29, Amsterdam, 1043 NX, Netherlands; info@elsevier.com; https://www.elsevier.com/. Illus., index, adv. Sample. Refereed. Vol. ends: No. 4. Microform: PQC. *Indexed:* A01, A22, S25. *Aud.:* Ac, Sa.

This journal publishes research on geochemical, petrological, geophysical, tectonic, and environmental aspects of volcanic and geothermal activity around the world. Occasional special issues address particular processes, locales, or topics such as volcanic gases, magma genesis, and risk assessment. Tables of contents and abstracts are available free on the website for volumes from 1976 forward, with full-text access for subscribers. Some open-access articles are available. Readers may set up alerts via RSS feed to learn when new articles are published. A GeoRef priority journal.

Lethaia. See Paleontology section.

1721. ***Lithos.*** [ISSN: 0024-4937] 1968. 28x/yr. EUR 3275. Ed(s): Sun-Lin Chung, Andrew Kerr. Elsevier BV, Radarweg 29, Amsterdam, 1043 NX, Netherlands; info@elsevier.com; https://www.elsevier.com/. Illus., index, adv. Sample. Refereed. Vol. ends: No. 4. Microform: PQC. *Indexed:* A01, A22. *Bk. rev.:* 0-3, 800-1,000 words. *Aud.:* Ac, Sa.

This international journal publishes research papers, invited reviews, discussions, and letters in the fields of mineralogy, geochemistry, and petrology. Occasional special issues feature proceedings of meetings such as the Hutton Symposium on Granites and Related Rocks or focus on particular regions. Free access to tables of contents and article abstracts for all volumes is available on the website from 1968 forward, with full-text access for subscribers. Some open-access articles are available. Readers may set up free alerts via RSS feed to learn when new articles are published. A GeoRef priority journal.

1722. ***Lithosphere (Online).*** [ISSN: 1947-4253] 2009. bi-m. Free. Ed(s): Matt Hudson, Jon D Pelletier. Geological Society of America, 3300 Penrose Pl, PO Box 9140, Boulder, CO 80301; pubs@geosociety.org; http://www.geosociety.org. Refereed. *Aud.:* Ac, Sa.

This open-access journal in the solid earth sciences focuses on tectonic processes in the crust and upper mantle, and publishes papers about relationships among geomorphic, lithospheric, and upper-mantle processes. It includes a mix of short articles, longer research papers, and invited reviews. All issues are freely available online. This journal is offered by the Geological Society of America as part of the GeoScienceWorld collection. Alerts to new content are available via e-mail or RSS feed. A GeoRef priority journal.

1723. ***Marine and Petroleum Geology.*** Former titles (until 1984): *Underwater Information Bulletin;* (until 1974): *Underwater Journal Information Bulletin.* [ISSN: 0264-8172] 1971. 10x/yr. EUR 4460. Ed(s): O Catuneanu. Elsevier Ltd, 125 London Wall, London, EC2Y 5AS, United Kingdom; corporate.sales@elsevier.com; http://www.elsevier.com. Illus., index, adv. Sample. Refereed. Microform: PQC. *Indexed:* A01, A22. *Aud.:* Ac, Sa.

Providing a forum for all aspects of marine and petroleum geology, this journal presents papers that focus on research in topics such as basin analysis, estimation of reserves, continental margins, and techniques for analysis and interpretation. Seismic sections and full-color illustrations enhance journal text. Thematic issues are occasionally published on selected basins or depositional environments. Tables of contents and abstracts for all volumes from 1984 forward are available free at the website, with full-text articles accessible to subscribers. Some open-access articles are available. Publication alerts are available via RSS feed.

Marine Geology. See Marine Science and Technology section.

1724. ***Mathematical Geosciences.*** Former titles (until 2008): *Mathematical Geology;* (until 1986): *International Association for Mathematical Geology. Journal.* [ISSN: 1874-8961] 1969. 8x/yr. EUR 2156 (print & online eds.)). Ed(s): Roussos Dimitrakopoulos. Springer, Tiergartenstr 17, Heidelberg, 69121, Germany; subscriptions@springer.com; https://www.springer.com. Illus., adv. Refereed. Vol. ends: Nov (No. 8). Reprint: PSC. *Indexed:* A01, A22, BRI, E01, MSN, S25. *Bk. rev.:* 0-5, 400-700 words, signed. *Aud.:* Ac, Sa.

As in many disciplines, techniques and methods to analyze large amounts of numerical data efficiently are crucial to research in the earth sciences. As suggested by the title, papers in *Mathematical Geosciences,* the official journal of the International Association for Mathematical Geosciences, are primarily concerned with the application of quantitative methods in the earth sciences. Some specific areas of concentration include modeling and simulation, filtering techniques, stochastic processes, and spatial analysis. Occasional special issues focus on particular geologic environments. Tables of contents and article abstracts are freely available for all volumes from 1969 forward on the website, with full-text access for subscribers. Some open-access articles are available. Readers may sign up for free alerts via RSS feed or e-mail. A GeoRef priority journal.

Meteoritics and Planetary Science. See Astronomy section.

1725. ***Mineralium Deposita: international journal of geology, mineralogy, and geochemistry of mineral deposits.*** [ISSN: 0026-4598] 1966. 8x/yr. EUR 2641 (print & online eds.)). Ed(s): Georges Beaudoin, Bernd Lehmann. Springer, Tiergartenstr 17, Heidelberg, 69121, Germany. Illus., index, adv. Sample. Refereed. Vol. ends: No. 8. Reprint: PSC. *Indexed:* A01, A22, BRI, E01. *Bk. rev.:* 0-5, 400-700 words, signed. *Aud.:* Ac, Sa.

This is the official journal of the Society for Geology Applied to Mineral Deposits. It focuses on economic geology, including field studies, mineralogy, experimental and applied geochemistry, and ore deposit exploration. Many of the illustrations are in color, especially those of mineral thin sections. Coverage is international in scope and includes such often under-represented areas as Africa, Asia, Australia, and South America. Occasional thematic issues cover selected ore deposits or mineral types. The website offers free tables of contents and abstracts for all volumes from 1966 forward, with full-text access for subscribers. Some articles are available open access. Readers may sign up for free alerts via RSS feed or e-mail alerts. A GeoRef priority journal.

1726. *Mineralogical Magazine (Print).* Formerly (until 1969): *Mineralogical Magazine and Journal of the Mineralogical Society.* [ISSN: 0026-461X] 1876. bi-m. Ed(s): Pete Williams, Roger Mitchell. Mineralogical Society, 12 Baylis Mews, Amyand Park Rd, Twickenham, TW1 3HQ, United Kingdom; http://www.minersoc.org. Illus., index, adv. Sample. Refereed. Vol. ends: Dec (No. 6). *Indexed:* A01, A22, E01. *Bk. rev.:* 3-8, 500-900 words. *Aud.:* Ac, Sa.

Published by the Mineralogical Society, this well-respected journal has been in print for more than 140 years. Topics covered span not only the field of mineralogy but also related areas such as geochemistry and petrology. Both full-length original research papers and shorter letters for rapid communication are included. Along with *American Mineralogist,* this title is highly recommended for larger academic library collections. Cambridge University Press offers free tables of contents and abstracts from 1876 forward with full-text access for subscribers. GeoScienceWorld also offers full-text access for subscribers beginning with 1997. Some open-access articles are available. Publication alerts are available via RSS feed. A GeoRef priority journal.

1727. *The Mineralogical Record.* [ISSN: 0026-4628] 1970. bi-m. USD 190 (Individuals, USD 62). Ed(s): Wendell E Wilson. Mineralogical Record, Inc., 7413 N Mowry Pl, Tucson, AZ 85741. Illus., index, adv. Sample. Vol. ends: Nov/Dec (No. 6). Microform: PQC. *Indexed:* A01, A22, BRI. *Bk. rev.:* 0-4, 100-800 words. *Aud.:* Ga, Ac, Sa.

Publishes both nontechnical and technical articles for mineral collectors, curators, and researchers. Each issue has numerous high-quality, often rather dramatic, color photographs of minerals. Reports from mineral shows around the world appear in a column called "What's New in the Minerals," and articles include topics such as minerals of a particular region, equipment used by mineralogists, and historically significant mines. The International Mineralogical Association publishes abstracts of new mineral descriptions in *The Mineralogical Record.* The website provides searchable tables of contents back to the first issue, published in 1970. Recommended for larger public and academic libraries. URL: http://www.mineralogicalrecord.com/

1728. *Natural Hazards and Earth System Sciences.* [ISSN: 1561-8633] m. EUR 1362.67; EUR 124.91 newsstand/cover. Ed(s): Fausto Guzzetti. Copernicus GmbH, Bahnhofsallee 1e, Goettingen, 37081, Germany; info@copernicus.org; http://www.copernicus.org. Refereed. *Indexed:* C45, S25. *Aud.:* Ac, Sa.

This well-established, open-access journal from the European Geosciences Union publishes interdisciplinary research concerning the detection, monitoring, risk assessment, and impact of natural hazards. Topics include flooding, landslides, tsunamis, earthquakes, avalanches, and volcanic eruptions. Many of the articles focus on Europe and the Mediterranean region but coverage is international in scope. Full text articles are available to all on the website for this open-access, peer-reviewed journal.

1729. *Nature Geoscience.* [ISSN: 1752-0894] 2008. m. EUR 6648. Ed(s): Heike Langenberg. Nature Publishing Group, The MacMillan Bldg, 4 Crinan St, London, N1 9XW, United Kingdom; nature@nature.com; https://www.nature.com. Adv. Sample. Refereed. *Indexed:* A01, C45, S25. *Bk. rev.:* 0-3, 600-900 words, signed. *Aud.:* Ac, Sa.

This research journal, launched in 2008, carries on the tradition of quality of its namesake. Coverage spans all major areas of the earth sciences, with an emphasis on interdisciplinary work. Articles include primary research, reviews, research highlights, news, and commentary. Tables of contents and abstracts are freely accessible on the website for all issues and full-text articles are available to subscribers. Publication alerts are available by registering for a free account with *Nature*. Some open-access articles are available. A GeoRef priority journal.

1730. *Netherlands Journal of Geosciences.* Former titles: *Geologie en Mijnbouw;* (until 1931): *Mijnwezen;* (until 1928): *Mijnwezen en Metallurgie;* (until 1925): *Mijnwezen;* Incorporates (1946-1999): *Nederlands Instituut voor Toegepaste Geowetenschappen T N O. Mededelingen;* Which was formerly (until 1997): *Rijks Geologische Dienst. Mededelingen;* (until 1977): *Rijks Geologische Dienst. Mededelingen. Nieuwe Serie;* (until 1968): *Geologische Stichting. Mededelingen. Nieuwe Serie.* 1921. q. GBP 360 (print & online eds.)). Ed(s): Johan Ten Veen. Cambridge University Press, University Printing House, Shaftesbury Rd, Cambridge, CB2 8BS, United Kingdom; journals@cambridge.org; https://www.cambridge.org/. Illus., index, adv. Refereed. Vol. ends: No. 4. Microform: SWZ; PQC. Reprint: PSC. *Indexed:* A22, E01. *Aud.:* Ac, Sa.

This is the official journal of the Royal Geological and Mining Society of the Netherlands, also known as KNGMG. It began publication in 2010 and represents a merger of two titles, *Geologie en Mijnbouw* and *Mededelingen Nederlands Instituut voor Geowetenschappen-TNO.* Articles feature research on geology and mining, with an emphasis on the Netherlands, the North Sea, and neighboring areas. A special strength is in geological aspects of coastal and deltaic lowlands, both ancient and modern. Free tables of contents and abstracts are available, with full-text access for subscribers or individual purchase.

1731. *Organic Geochemistry.* [ISSN: 0146-6380] 1977. m. EUR 5813. Ed(s): J K Volkman, E Idiz. Pergamon Press, The Blvd, Langford Ln, E Park, Kidlington, OX5 1GB, United Kingdom; JournalsCustomerServiceEMEA@elsevier.com; http://www.elsevier.com. Illus., adv. Sample. Refereed. Microform: PQC. *Indexed:* A01, A22, C45, S25. *Bk. rev.:* 0-2, 300-1,000 words. *Aud.:* Ac, Sa.

The official journal of the European Association of Organic Geochemists, this monthly publishes papers on all aspects of organic geochemistry, including biogeochemistry, environmental geochemistry, and geochemical cycling. Types of articles include original research papers, comprehensive reviews, technical notes, and meeting announcements. The website provides free tables of contents and article abstracts for all volumes from 1977 forward, with full-text access for subscribers. Some open-access articles are available. Free publication alerts are available via RSS feed. A GeoRef priority journal.

Palaeontology. See Paleontology section.

1732. *Petroleum Geoscience.* [ISSN: 1354-0793] 1994. q. GBP 681 combined subscription in Europe (print & online eds.); USD 1362 combined subscription elsewhere (print & online eds.)). Ed(s): Philip Ringrose. Geological Society Publishing House, Unit 7, Brassmill Enterprise Ctr, Brassmill Ln, Bath, BA1 3JN, United Kingdom. Illus., adv. Refereed. Vol. ends: Nov (No. 4). *Indexed:* A22. *Bk. rev.:* 0-6, 250-600 words, signed. *Aud.:* Ac, Sa.

This quarterly is published by the Geological Society of London and the Petroleum Division of the European Association of Geoscientists and Engineers. Coverage is international in scope and includes both theoretical and applied articles related to petroleum and hydrocarbon resources. Tables of contents and abstracts are freely available online from 1995 to the present. Full-text access is provided to subscribers from multiple sources including the Lyell Collection and GeoScienceWorld. Some open-access articles are available. Free publication alerts are available via e-mail or RSS feed. A GeoRef priority journal.

1733. *Physics and Chemistry of Minerals.* [ISSN: 0342-1791] 1977. 10x/yr. EUR 3917 (print & online eds.)). Ed(s): C McCammon, M Rieder. Springer, Tiergartenstr 17, Heidelberg, 69121, Germany. Illus., index, adv. Sample. Refereed. Vol. ends: No. 10. Reprint: PSC. *Indexed:* A01, A22, E01. *Aud.:* Ac, Sa.

This technical journal focuses on the chemistry and physics of minerals and related solids. Some areas of coverage include atomic structure, mineral surfaces, spectroscopy, chemical reactions and bonding, and analysis of physical properties. The website offers free access to tables of contents and article abstracts for all volumes from 1977 forward, with full-text access for subscribers. Some open-access articles are available. Readers may sign up for free publication alerts via RSS feed or e-mail. Recommended for larger academic or special libraries. A GeoRef priority journal.

1734. *Physics of the Earth and Planetary Interiors.* [ISSN: 0031-9201] 1967. 12x/yr. EUR 3244. Ed(s): K Hirose, G Helffrich. Elsevier BV, Radarweg 29, Amsterdam, 1043 NX, Netherlands; info@elsevier.com; https://www.elsevier.com/. Illus., index. Sample. Refereed. Vol. ends: No. 124 - No. 129. Microform: PQC. *Indexed:* A01, A22. *Bk. rev.:* 0-1, 300-800 words. *Aud.:* Ac, Sa.

This journal is devoted to the study of planetary physical and chemical processes. Papers present observational and experimental studies, along with theoretical interpretation. Occasional special issues present papers from symposia or thematic reports on special topics. The website offers free access to tables of contents and abstracts for all volumes from 1967 forward, with full-text access for subscribers. Some open-access articles are available. Readers may register for free publication alerts. A GeoRef priority journal.

1735. *Precambrian Research.* [ISSN: 0301-9268] 1974. 16x/yr. EUR 5653. Ed(s): R R Parrish, G C Zhao. Elsevier BV, Radarweg 29, Amsterdam, 1043 NX, Netherlands; info@elsevier.com; https://www.elsevier.com/. Illus., index, adv. Sample. Refereed. Vol. ends: No. 4. Microform: PQC. *Indexed:* A01, A22. *Bk. rev.:* 0-2, 200-600 words. *Aud.:* Ac, Sa.

The Precambrian era lasted for some four billion years, representing the bulk of Earth's history on the geologic time scale. This journal emphasizes interdisciplinary studies and publishes research on all aspects of the early history and development of Earth and its planetary neighbors. Topics include the origin of life, the evolution of the oceans and atmosphere, the early fossil record, paleobiology, geochronology, and Precambrian mineral deposits. Free tables of contents and abstracts are available on the website for all volumes from 1974 to present, with full-text for subscribers. Some open-access articles are available. Readers may register for free publication alerts via RSS feed. A GeoRef priority journal.

1736. *Pure and Applied Geophysics.* Formerly: *Geofisica.* [ISSN: 0033-4553] 1939. m. EUR 4579 (print & online eds.)). Ed(s): B Mitchell, R Dmowska. Birkhaeuser Science, Picassoplatz 4, Basel, 4052, Switzerland; info@birkhauser-science.com; http://www.springer.com/birkhauser/. Illus. Refereed. Vol. ends: No. 4. Reprint: PSC. *Indexed:* A01, A22, BAS, BRI, E01, S25. *Bk. rev.:* 0-12, 400-1,200 words, signed. *Aud.:* Ac, Sa.

Often referred to as *PAGEOPH,* this journal features full-length papers on all aspects of geophysics, including solid earth, atmospheric, and ocean sciences. Special issues include themes like tsunami science, mesoscale processes, earthquake physics, properties of fractured rock, and induced seismicity. The website offers free tables of contents and abstracts from 1939 forward, with access to full-text articles for subscribers. Some open-access articles are available. Readers may sign up for alerts via RSS feed or e-mail. Strongly recommended for academic and special libraries. A GeoRef priority journal.

1737. *Quarterly Journal of Engineering Geology and Hydrogeology.* Formerly (until 2000): *Quarterly Journal of Engineering Geology.* [ISSN: 1470-9236] 1967. q. GBP 746 combined subscription domestic (print & online eds.); GBP 833 combined subscription in Europe (print & online eds.); USD 1667 combined subscription elsewhere (print & online eds.)). Ed(s): Jane Dottridge. Geological Society Publishing House, Unit 7, Brassmill Enterprise Ctr, Brassmill Ln, Bath, BA1 3JN, United Kingdom. Illus., adv. Refereed. Vol. ends: Nov (No. 4). *Indexed:* A22, HRIS, S25. *Bk. rev.:* 0-7, 300-800 words, signed. *Aud.:* Ac, Sa.

Upholding the high standards of the Geological Society of London, this publication focuses specifically on geology as applied to civil engineering, mining, and water resources. This makes it of value to both engineers and earth scientists. Coverage is international in scope. In addition to original research, it includes review articles, technical notes, and lectures. Tables of contents and abstracts are freely available on the website from 1967 forward, with full-text offered to subscribers by multiple vendors including the Lyell Collection and GeoScienceWorld. Some open-access articles are available. A GeoRef priority journal.

1738. *Quaternary International.* [ISSN: 1040-6182] 1989. 36x/yr. EUR 2248. Ed(s): M-T Chen. Pergamon Press, The Blvd, Langford Ln, E Park, Kidlington, OX5 1GB, United Kingdom; JournalsCustomerServiceEMEA@elsevier.com; http://www.elsevier.com. Illus., adv. Sample. Refereed. Microform: PQC. *Indexed:* A01, A22. *Aud.:* Ac, Sa.

The official journal of the International Union for Quaternary Research (INQUA), this title publishes interdisciplinary research on the Quaternary period, which includes approximately the last 2.6 million years of the Earth's history. This title reports on studies of environmental changes and interactions, with connections as appropriate to both present-day processes and future climatological implications. Most issues are thematic, often presenting collected papers from symposia and workshops sponsored by INQUA. Free access to tables of contents and abstracts is available on the website for all volumes from 1989 forward, with full-text access for subscribers. Some open-access articles are available. Readers may register for free publication alerts via RSS feed.

1739. *Quaternary Research.* [ISSN: 0033-5894] 1970. bi-m. GBP 1074. Ed(s): Dr. Derek B Booth, Dr. Lewis A Owen. Cambridge University Press, 1 Liberty Plaza, Fl 20, New York, NY 10004; online@cambridge.org; https://www.cambridge.org/. Illus., index, adv. Sample. Refereed. Vol. ends: Nov (No. 3). *Indexed:* A01, A22, Agr, C45, E01, S25. *Bk. rev.:* 0-2, 500-1,000 words. *Aud.:* Ac, Sa.

Papers in this journal, published on behalf of the Quaternary Research Center, present interdisciplinary studies in the earth and biological sciences that span the Quaternary period. Articles explore a diverse range of topics related to the recent past, including botany, climatology, ecology, geochemistry and geophysics, geochronology, geomorphology, and glaciology. Free tables of contents and abstracts for articles for all volumes are available on the website from 1970 forward, with full-text access for subscribers. Some open-access articles are available. Readers may register for free publication alerts via RSS feed. A GeoRef priority journal.

1740. *Rocks and Minerals: mineralogy, geology, lapidary.* [ISSN: 0035-7529] 1926. bi-m. GBP 175. Ed(s): Marie E Huizing. Taylor & Francis Inc., 711 3rd Ave, 8th Fl, New York, NY 10017; support@tandfonline.com; http://www.tandfonline.com. Illus., index, adv. Refereed. Vol. ends: No. 6. Reprint: PSC. *Indexed:* A01, A22, BRI, CBRI, E01, MASUSE. *Bk. rev.:* 0-7, 100-800 words, signed. *Aud.:* Hs, Ga, Ac, Sa.

Affiliated with several mineralogical societies, this journal features spectacular full-color photographs and accessible articles, making it a candidate for libraries of all types. The emphasis is on minerals more than on rocks, and the specimens featured are generally of "museum quality." There is also a considerable amount of other material to interest collectors, such as mineral localities, sample preparation, and historical background. In addition, museum notes, announcements, and a calendar of upcoming events are included. Available online from multiple vendors, with varying years of coverage.

1741. *Sedimentary Geology: an international journal of pure and applied sedimentology.* [ISSN: 0037-0738] 1967. 16x/yr. EUR 5666. Ed(s): J Knight, B Jones. Elsevier BV, Radarweg 29, Amsterdam, 1043 NX, Netherlands; info@elsevier.com; https://www.elsevier.com/. Illus., index, adv. Sample. Refereed. Vol. ends: No. 4. Microform: PQC. *Indexed:* A01, A22, S25. *Bk. rev.:* 0-4, 300-3,000 words. *Aud.:* Ac, Sa.

This research journal publishes papers on all aspects of sediments and sedimentary rocks. Examples of topics addressed include analytical techniques such as numerical modeling; regional studies of sedimentary systems and basin; and sediment transport and deposition. There are occasional special issues on topics such as determining provenance, sediment dynamics, and tsunami deposits, among other subjects. Tables of contents and abstracts are available at the website for all volumes from 1967 forward, with full-text access for subscribers. Free publication alerts are available via RSS feed. A GeoRef priority journal.

1742. *Sedimentology.* [ISSN: 0037-0746] 1962. 7x/yr. GBP 1712. Ed(s): Dr. T D Frank, Dr. N P Mountney. Wiley-Blackwell Publishing Ltd., The Atrium, Southern Gate, Chichester, PO19 8QG, United Kingdom; cs-journals@wiley.com; http://onlinelibrary.wiley.com. Illus., index, adv. Sample. Refereed. Vol. ends: Dec (No. 6). Microform: PQC. Reprint: PSC. *Indexed:* A01, A22, Agr, C45, E01, S25. *Aud.:* Ac, Sa.

This publication is the official journal of the International Association of Sedimentologists. Full-length papers deal with every aspect of sediments and sedimentary rocks. These are well illustrated and of consistently high quality. Free tables of contents and abstracts from 1962 forward are accessible on the website, with full-text access for subscribers. Some open-access articles are available. Readers may sign up to receive free alerts when new articles are published. Recommended for academic and special library collections. A GeoRef priority journal.

1743. *Seismological Research Letters.* Formerly (until vol.57, 1986): *Earthquake Notes;* Which superseded in part: *Seismological Society of America, Eastern Section. Bibliography.* [ISSN: 0895-0695] 1929. bi-m. USD 190 combined subscription domestic (print & online eds.); USD 256 combined subscription India (print & online eds.); USD 213 combined subscription elsewhere (print & online eds.)). Ed(s): Luciana Astiz. Seismological Society of America, 201 Plaza Professional Bldg, El Cerrito, CA 94530-4003; info@seismosoc.org; http://www.seismosoc.org. Illus. Refereed. Circ: 2200 Paid. Microform: PQC. *Indexed:* A22. *Aud.:* Ac, Sa.

This journal complements the *Bulletin of the Seismological Society of America* and provides a mechanism for rapid publication and less formal communications as suggested by the original title *Earthquake Notes*. Many articles report on recent earthquakes or new analytical or interpretive techniques. The website provides free tables of contents and abstracts, while full text is available to subscribers and society members via GeoScienceWorld. A GeoRef priority journal.

1744. *Seismological Society of America. Bulletin.* [ISSN: 0037-1106] 1911. bi-m. USD 664 combined subscription in North America (print & online eds.); USD 809 combined subscription India (print & online eds.); USD 751 combined subscription elsewhere (print & online eds.)). Ed(s): Carol Mark, Andrew Michael. Seismological Society of America, 201 Plaza Professional Bldg, El Cerrito, CA 94530-4003; info@seismosoc.org; http://www.seismosoc.org. Illus., index. Sample. Refereed. Circ: 2500 Paid. Vol. ends: Dec (No. 6). *Indexed:* A22, E01. *Aud.:* Ac, Sa.

This journal publishes research papers, reviews, short notes, comments, and replies in the areas of seismology, earthquake geology, and earthquake engineering. Specific topics include investigation of earthquakes, studies of seismic waves, hazard and risk estimation, and seismotectonics. The website provides free tables of contents from 1911 to the present along with abstracts for newer material, while full text is available via GeoScienceWorld. A GeoRef priority journal.

1745. *Solid Earth (Online).* Formerly (until 2010): *eEarth (Online).* [ISSN: 1869-9529] 2006. s-a. Free. Copernicus GmbH, Bahnhofsallee 1e, Goettingen, 37081, Germany; info@copernicus.org; http://www.copernicus.org. *Aud.:* Ac, Sa.

This open-access journal of the European Geosciences Union (EGU) includes research articles, short communications, and reviews related to the Earth's geology and interactions. Coverage areas are broad, including geodynamics, geophysics, petrology, seismology, soils, and structural geology, among others. Occasional special issues focus on particular topics such as rheology, deformation, and subduction zones. Online access to all articles published is available from 2010 forward. Readers may sign up for free RSS feeds and e-mail alerts.

1746. *Stratigraphy.* [ISSN: 1547-139X] 2004. q. USD 370 USD 17.50 per issue. Ed(s): John A Van Couvering, Lucy E. Edwards. Micropaleontology Press, 256 Fifth Ave, New York, NY 10001; http://micropress.org/. Refereed. *Indexed:* A01. *Aud.:* Ac, Sa.

This quarterly is the journal of record for the North American Commission on Stratigraphic Nomenclature. It publishes research articles on all aspects of stratigraphy, including biostratigraphy, chronostratigraphy, cyclostratigraphy, sequence stratigraphy, tectonostratigraphy, and others. Supplements report on conferences and associated field trips. Tables of contents and abstracts are freely accessible on the website from 2004 forward, while subscribers may view full text. Some open access articles are available.

1747. *Tectonics.* [ISSN: 0278-7407] 1982. m. Ed(s): Claudio Faccenna, John Geissman. Wiley-Blackwell Publishing, Inc., 111 River St, Hoboken, NJ 07030; http://onlinelibrary.wiley.com. Illus., index. Sample. Refereed. Vol. ends: Dec (No. 6). Reprint: PSC. *Indexed:* A22. *Aud.:* Ac, Sa.

Cosponsored by the American Geophysical Union (AGU) and the European Geosciences Union, this journal publishes reports of original analytical, synthetic, and integrative studies on the structure and evolution of the terrestrial lithosphere. Emphasis is on continental tectonics, including such topics as thrusting and faulting, mountain-building, volcanism, and rifting. Tables of contents and graphical abstracts are freely available from 1982 forward, with full-text access for subscribers. Some open-access articles are available. Content older than 24 months is accessible to all. Readers may sign up to receive publication alerts via e-mail or RSS feed. A GeoRef priority journal.

1748. *Tectonophysics.* [ISSN: 0040-1951] 1964. 28x/yr. EUR 9763. Ed(s): R Govers, R Carbonell. Elsevier BV, Radarweg 29, Amsterdam, 1043 NX, Netherlands; info@elsevier.com; https://www.elsevier.com/. Illus., adv. Sample. Refereed. Vol. ends: No. 327 - No. 343. Microform: PQC. *Indexed:* A01, A22, S25. *Bk. rev.:* 0-3, 400-1,500 words. *Aud.:* Ac, Sa.

This title publishes research papers on the geology and physics of the Earth's crust and interior, addressing topics such as regional and plate tectonics, seismology, crustal movements, rock mechanics, and structural features. Articles often include large-scale geological maps, seismic sections, and other diagrams. Numerous special issues cover specific geologic events or environments. The website provides free access to tables of contents and abstracts from 1964 forward, with full-text access for subscribers. Some articles are available open access. Readers may set up free alerts via RSS feed. A GeoRef priority journal.

1749. *Terra Nova: the European journal of geosciences.* Supersedes in part (in 1989): *Terra Cognita.* [ISSN: 0954-4879] 1981. bi-m. GBP 1173. Wiley-Blackwell Publishing Ltd., The Atrium, Southern Gate, Chichester, PO19 8QG, United Kingdom; cs-journals@wiley.com; http://onlinelibrary.wiley.com. Illus., index, adv. Sample. Refereed. Vol. ends: No. 6. Microform: PQC. Reprint: PSC. *Indexed:* A01, A22, E01. *Aud.:* Ac, Sa.

Terra Nova is the result of a collaboration among numerous national geoscience societies throughout Europe. It primarily features short, original research papers that cover the solid earth and planetary sciences, including interfaces with the hydrosphere and atmosphere. Occasional debate articles are a unique feature, and each presents a different side of an issue. Free tables of contents and abstracts are available on the website from 1964 forward, with full-text articles accessible to subscribers. Some open-access articles are available. Readers may sign up to receive alerts when new articles are published.

1750. *Water Resources Research.* [ISSN: 0043-1397] 1965. m. Ed(s): Alberto Montanari. Wiley-Blackwell Publishing, Inc., 111 River St, Hoboken, NJ 07030; http://onlinelibrary.wiley.com. Illus., index. Sample. Refereed. Vol. ends: No. 12. Reprint: PSC. *Indexed:* A22, Agr, C45, EconLit, S25. *Aud.:* Ac, Sa.

Articles present interdisciplinary research on water-related studies that encompass aspects of both the social and natural sciences. Areas of focus include the physical, chemical, and biological sciences in hydrology, as well as economics, policy analysis, and water law. Issues include original research articles along with technical notes, commentaries, and replies. Tables of contents and abstracts are freely accessible for all volumes from 1965 to present, with full-text access for subscribers. Some open-access articles are available. Content older than 24 months is accessible to all. Readers may sign up for alerts to new publications via e-mail or RSS feed. A GeoRef priority journal.

■ ECOLOGY

See also Biology; Botany; Physiology; and Zoology sections.

Kristen LaBonte, Life and Environmental Sciences Librarian, UCSB Library, University of California-Santa Barbara, Santa Barbara, CA 93106-9010

Introduction

Ecology is an interdisciplinary science that studies species, systems, and/or ecosystems and the relationships between them and other systems, such as the physical environment. Studies vary from the micro to the macro, and can range from examining an aspect of a gene to the functioning of a biome. Ecologists often conduct field and laboratory research on behavior, evolution, physiology, and genetics. The impact of this research can be far-reaching and is applied in the fields of natural resource management, wildlife biology, wetland management, resource economics, public health, agriculture, city planning, and conservation policy.

Journals can be broad and comprehensive in scope but can be narrowly focused on an application or field of study, such as *Restoration Ecology* or *Molecular Ecology.* Most have rigorous standards for peer review, with strict deadlines to ensure timely dissemination of research that may be featured as a pre-print on the publication's web site prior to being formally published. Some articles within paid, subscription-based journals are open access, and many journal web sites offer RSS feeds.

Basic Periodicals

Ac: *Ecology, Ecology Letters, Journal of Animal Ecology, Journal of Ecology, Trends in Ecology & Evolution.*

Basic Abstracts and Indexes

Academic Search Premier, AGRICOLA, Aquatic Sciences and Fisheries Abstracts (ASFA), Biological Abstracts, BIOSIS, Current Contents/Life Sciences, Expanded Academic ASAP, Science Citation Index, Web of Science, Zoological Record.

1751. *Acta Oecologica.* Formed by the merger of (1980-1990): *Oecologia Applicata;* (1980-1990): *Oecologia Generalis;* (1966-1990): *Acta Oecologica. Oecologia Plantarum;* Which was formerly (until 1980): *Oecologia Plantarum.* [ISSN: 1146-609X] 1981. 8x/yr. EUR 1069. Ed(s): R Arditi. Elsevier Masson, 62 Rue Camille Desmoulins, Issy les Moulineaux Cedex, 92442, France; http://www.elsevier-masson.fr. Refereed. Microform: MIM; PQC. *Indexed:* A01, A22, C45, S25. *Aud.:* Ac, Sa.

Acta Oecologica publishes studies in all fields of ecology, including evolutionary, conservation, ecosystem, population, and community. Empirical or theoretical papers are sought for publication, but combinations are desired. Review papers and short communications are also published. There is a forum section for short papers on current issues in ecology, feedback on previously published papers, and comments on new books (although book reviews are not published). URL: www.journals.elsevier.com/acta-oecologica/

African Journal of Ecology. See Africa section.

1752. *American Midland Naturalist.* Formerly (until Apr.1909): *The Midland Naturalist.* [ISSN: 0003-0031] 1909. q. USD 95 (Individuals, USD 55). University of Notre Dame, Department of Biological Sciences, Rm 285 GLSC, PO Box 369, Notre Dame, IN 46556; biology.biosadm.1@nd.edu; http://www.nd.edu. Illus., index. Refereed. Microform: IDC; PQC. *Indexed:* A01, A22, Agr, BRI, C45, E01, GardL, S25. *Aud.:* Ac, Sa.

American Midland Naturalist publishes original field and experimental biology articles as well as "review articles of a critical nature on topics of current interest in biology." It covers all areas of natural history and publishes many articles on biodiversity. The scope covers ecology, evolution, and the natural environment. Published since 1909 for the University of Notre Dame, this academic journal no longer is limited in geographic scope to the middle of America. Rather, it covers the North American continent and has occasional articles from other regions. Two volumes, containing two issues each, are published per year. The issues are composed of many full-length articles and a few short "Notes and Discussion" articles. All subject areas related to plant and animal ecology are covered in this diverse journal. URL: www.bioone.org/loi/amid

1753. *The American Naturalist.* [ISSN: 0003-0147] 1867. m. USD 863. Ed(s): Daniel Bolnick. University of Chicago Press, 1427 E 60th St, Chicago, IL 60637; subscriptions@press.uchicago.edu; http://www.journals.uchicago.edu. Illus., index, adv. Sample. Refereed. Reprint: PSC. *Indexed:* A01, A22, Agr, BRI, C45, GardL, MLA-IB. *Aud.:* Ac, Sa.

Advancing the knowledge of organic evolution and examining broad biological principles comprise the focus of *The American Naturalist.* Peer-reviewed articles relating to "ecology, evolution, and behavior research" are published. The journal emphasizes articles "that are a broad interest to the readership, pose new and significant problems, introduce novel subjects, develop conceptual unification, and change the way people think." The electronic edition offers a citation manager, RSS, pdfs, direct Medline and CrossRef linking, table and figure galleries, free text to some recent electronic articles, and ASCII versions of tables. Published for the American Society of Naturalists, this journal is appropriate for academic libraries and professionals. URL: www.journals.uchicago.edu/loi/an

1754. *Animal Conservation: the rapid publication journal for quantitative studies in conservation.* [ISSN: 1367-9430] 1998. bi-m. GBP 560. Ed(s): Darren Evans, Res Altwegg. Wiley-Blackwell Publishing Ltd., The Atrium, Southern Gate, Chichester, PO19 8QG, United Kingdom; cs-journals@wiley.com; http://onlinelibrary.wiley.com. Adv. Sample. Refereed. Reprint: PSC. *Indexed:* A01, A22, Agr, C45, E01. *Aud.:* Ac, Sa.

Conservation of animal species and their habitats is the focus of this peer-reviewed journal, published for the Zoological Society of London. Quantitative studies on species, populations, and communities that are either theoretical or empirical are published, with less emphasis on specific species and more on "new ideas of broad interest and with findings that advance the scientific basis of conservation." The journal covers topics on animal conservation, population biology, conservation biology, physiology, epidemiology, evolutionary ecology, population genetics, biodiversity, biogeography, paleobiology, conservation economics, conservation, ecology, biology, animal science, animal biology, freshwater biology, and marine biology. Editorials, feature papers, commentaries, responses, and original articles are available. URL: onlinelibrary.wiley.com/journal/14691795

1755. *Annual Review of Ecology, Evolution and Systematics.* Formerly (until 2003): *Annual Review of Ecology and Systematics.* [ISSN: 1543-592X] 1970. a. USD 431 (print & online eds.)). Ed(s): Douglas J Futuyma. Annual Reviews, PO Box 10139, Palo Alto, CA 94303; service@annualreviews.org; http://www.annualreviews.org. Refereed. Reprint: PSC. *Indexed:* A01, A22, Agr, C45, S25. *Aud.:* Ac, Sa.

Annual Review of Ecology, Evolution, and Systematics is a core academic journal that provides review articles in one volume each year. The reviews summarize the primary literature, noting significant developments and highlighting conflicts of previous research. It "covers significant developments in the fields of ecology, evolutionary biology, and systematics, as they apply to all life on Earth." This title is a critical starting point for ecologists in conducting research, and is also a great resource for undergraduate assignments. The reviews are written by distinguished authors and editors in the field and are highly cited. URL: www.annualreviews.org/journal/ecolsys

1756. *Applied Soil Ecology.* [ISSN: 0929-1393] 1994. 12x/yr. EUR 2830. Ed(s): C A M van Gestel, H Insam. Elsevier BV, Radarweg 29, Amsterdam, 1043 NX, Netherlands; info@elsevier.com; https://www.elsevier.com/. Index. Refereed. Microform: PQC. *Indexed:* A01, A22, Agr, C45, S25. *Aud.:* Ac, Sa.

Applied Soil Ecology features articles on the function of soil organisms and their association with soil processes, soil structure, soil fertility, nutrient cycling, and agricultural productivity, along with the "impact of human activities and xenobiotics on soil ecosystems and bio(techno)logical control of soil-inhabiting pests, diseases, and weeds." Original research and review articles are published in the journal, and the web site offers announcements, conferences, most downloaded articles, most cited articles, special issues, and recent open-access articles. This peer-reviewed journal is recommended for academic and special libraries. URL: www.elsevier.com/locate/apsoil

1757. ***Aquatic Toxicology.*** [ISSN: 0166-445X] 1981. 12x/yr. EUR 5005. Ed(s): R S Tjeerdema, M J Nikinmaa. Elsevier BV, Radarweg 29, Amsterdam, 1043 NX, Netherlands; info@elsevier.com; https://www.elsevier.com/. Illus., adv. Refereed. *Indexed:* A01, A22, Agr, C45, S25. *Aud.:* Ac, Sa.

Increasing the knowledge and understanding of the impact of toxicants on aquatic organisms and ecosystems is the aim of *Aquatic Toxicology.* This journal publishes field and laboratory studies that relate to the "mechanisms of toxicity and the responses to toxic agents in aquatic environments at the community, species, tissue, cellular, subcellular, and molecular levels, including aspects of uptake, metabolism and excretion of toxicants." The journal has special issues pertaining to specific topics or proceedings related to symposia; and each regular issue is made up exclusively of research articles. It is recommended for academic and special libraries. The online version offers sections on recent open-access articles, conferences, articles with the most social media attention, most downloaded articles, most cited articles, special issues, recent articles, and editors' choice. URL: www.journals.elsevier.com/aquatic-toxicology/

1758. ***Basic and Applied Ecology.*** [ISSN: 1439-1791] 2000. 8x/yr. EUR 934. Ed(s): Teja Tscharntke. Elsevier GmbH, Hackerbruecke 6, Muenchen, 80335, Germany; info@elsevier.com; https://www.elsevier.com. Adv. Refereed. *Indexed:* A22, Agr, C45, E01, S25. *Aud.:* Ac, Sa.

This is the official journal of the Ecological Society of Germany, Austria, and Switzerland, but ecologists from around the world are invited to publish articles on basic and applied ecology from all geographical areas. Original contributions, perspectives, and reviews are included in the journal, which "provides a forum in which significant advances and ideas can be rapidly communicated to a wide audience." The web site features recent articles, most cited articles, recent open-access articles, and most downloaded articles. This journal is recommended for special and academic libraries. URL: www.elsevier.com/locate/baae

Behavioral Ecology. See Zoology/General section.

Behavioral Ecology and Sociobiology. See Zoology/General section.

1759. ***Biological Conservation.*** [ISSN: 0006-3207] 1969. 12x/yr. EUR 6212. Ed(s): Richard B Primack. Elsevier BV, Radarweg 29, Amsterdam, 1043 NX, Netherlands; info@elsevier.com; https://www.elsevier.com. Illus., adv. Sample. Refereed. Microform: PQC. *Indexed:* A01, A22, Agr, C45. *Bk. rev.:* Number and length vary. *Aud.:* Ac, Sa.

Shifting conservation science into conservation practice is a goal of the journal *Biological Conservation,* which is interdisciplinary and international in scope. Articles published span "a diverse range of fields that contribute to the biological, sociological, and economic dimensions of conservation and natural resource management." Areas of focus are broad and encompass various aspects of biological conservation to aid in policy creation and natural resource management. For example, topics covered may include ecological restoration, resource economics, impacts on biodiversity from global change, invasive organism spread, or ecological reserve design. Journal issues have sections for letters to the editor, reviews, regular papers, short communications, and book reviews, or may have a special section on a given topic. The journal is appropriate for institutions with natural resource managers, environmental policy makers, environmental scientists, and ecologists. URL: www.elsevier.com/locate/biocon

1760. ***Biotropica (Online).*** [ISSN: 1744-7429] 1969. bi-m. GBP 436. Ed(s): Emilio Bruna. Wiley-Blackwell Publishing, Inc., 350 Main St, Malden, MA 02148; cs-journals@wiley.com; http://onlinelibrary.wiley.com. Adv. Sample. Refereed. *Bk. rev.:* Number and length vary. *Aud.:* Ac, Sa.

Biotropica, the official journal of the Association for Tropical Biology and Conservation, publishes original research on the behavior, population biology, and evolution of tropical organisms and the conservation, ecology, and management of tropical ecosystems. Academic papers are divided into sections for tropical biology and tropical conservation, alongside reviews of current topics, commentaries that initiate debate and discussions, book reviews, and short communication insights. The journal is available online and is suggested for academic and public libraries that serve researchers interested in tropical biology and conservation. The most cited articles from the previous three years are featured online. URL: onlinelibrary.wiley.com/journal/17447429

1761. ***Conservation Biology.*** [ISSN: 0888-8892] 1986. bi-m. GBP 1203. Ed(s): Mark A Burgman. Wiley-Blackwell Publishing, Inc., 350 Main St, Malden, MA 02148; cs-journals@wiley.com; http://onlinelibrary.wiley.com. Illus., index, adv. Sample. Refereed. Reprint: PSC. *Indexed:* A01, A22, Agr, BRI, C45, E01, GardL, S25. *Bk. rev.:* Number and length vary. *Aud.:* Ac, Sa.

Published for the Society for Conservation Biology *Conservation Biology* is focused on the "science and practice of conserving Earth's biological diversity." Articles define key issues of conservation relating to ecosystems or species in any geographic region, with emphasis given to those that have a scope beyond that particular ecosystem or species. The journal publishes papers in nine sections: contributed papers, research notes, reviews, essays, conservation practice and policy, comments, diversity, letters, and invited book reviews. *Conservation Biology* is a core title for institutions that serve professional physical geographers, environmental scientists, and ecologists. URL: onlinelibrary.wiley.com/journal/15231739

Diversity and Distributions: a journal of conservation biogeography. See Geography section.

1762. ***Ecography (Online): pattern and diversity in ecology.*** [ISSN: 1600-0587] 1978. m. GBP 661. Ed(s): Miguel Araujo. Wiley-Blackwell Publishing, Inc., 350 Main St, Malden, MA 02148; cs-journals@wiley.com; http://onlinelibrary.wiley.com. Adv. Sample. Refereed. *Aud.:* Ac, Sa.

Contemporary ecological spatial and temporal patterns are the primary focus of this academic journal. Issued by the Nordic Ecological Society OIKOS, *Ecography* publishes "studies of population and community ecology, macroecology, biogeography, and ecological conservation." Types of articles included are original research papers, forum, review and synthesis, commentaries, brevia, and software notes. The journal is recommended for academic and special libraries. URL: onlinelibrary.wiley.com/journal/16000587

1763. ***Ecological Applications.*** [ISSN: 1051-0761] 1991. 8x/yr. Ed(s): David Schimel. John Wiley & Sons, Inc., 111 River St, Hoboken, NJ 07030; cs-journals@wiley.com; http://www.wiley.com. Illus., adv. Refereed. Reprint: PSC. *Indexed:* A22, Agr, C45, GardL, S25. *Aud.:* Ac, Sa.

Ecological Applications, a journal of the Ecological Society of America, "publishes papers that develop scientific principles to support environmental decision-making, as well as papers that discuss the application of ecological concepts to environmental issues, policy and management." The journal contains articles that describe original and significant research and communications of short length for urgent application and scientific debate. There are also invited features, forums, and letters to the editor. The journal is a core title for university and special libraries with scholars and practitioners in the ecological and environmental science fields. URL: hesajournals.onlinelibrary.wiley.com/journal/19395582

1764. ***Ecological Complexity.*** [ISSN: 1476-945X] 2004. 4x/yr. EUR 1091. Ed(s): Sergei Petrovskii. Elsevier BV, Radarweg 29, Amsterdam, 1043 NX, Netherlands; info@elsevier.com; https://www.elsevier.com. Refereed. *Indexed:* C45. *Aud.:* Ac, Sa.

Ecological Complexity is an interdisciplinary, peer-reviewed journal that focuses on "all aspects of biocomplexity in the environment, theoretical ecology, and special issues on topics of current interest." Quantitative research that integrates social and natural processes that are applied at broad spatial-temporal scales are published. Ecologists with interest in integrated and quantitative research will find this journal of particular interest, along with those whose research intersects natural and socioeconomic systems. URL: www.elsevier.com/locate/issn/1476945X

1765. ***Ecological Indicators.*** [ISSN: 1470-160X] 2001. m. bi-m. until 2015. EUR 1276. Ed(s): F M Mueller. Elsevier BV, Radarweg 29, Amsterdam, 1043 NX, Netherlands; info@elsevier.com; https://www.elsevier.com. Refereed. *Indexed:* A01, C45. *Bk. rev.:* Number and length vary. *Aud.:* Ac, Sa.

Sound management practices can be informed by the assessment and monitoring of environmental and ecological indicators and indices. *Ecological Indicators* "provides a forum for the discussion of the applied scientific development and review of traditional indicator approaches as well as for theoretical, modelling and quantitative applications such as index development." The journal publishes original research papers, review articles, short notes and case studies, viewpoint articles, letters to the editor, and book reviews; and it features special themed issues. The web site offers journal metrics, articles in press, articles that have had the most social media attention, most downloaded articles, recent open-access articles, and news. It is recommended for academic and special libraries. URL: www.journals.elsevier.com/ecological-indicators/

1766. ***Ecological Modelling.*** [ISSN: 0304-3800] 1975. 24x/yr. EUR 7168. Ed(s): B D Fath. Elsevier BV, Radarweg 29, Amsterdam, 1043 NX, Netherlands; info@elsevier.com; https://www.elsevier.com/. Illus., index, adv. Refereed. Microform: PQC. *Indexed:* A01, A22, C45, S25. *Bk. rev.:* Number and length vary. *Aud.:* Ac, Sa.

Ecological processes and sustainable resource management are described through the use of systems analysis and mathematical models in *Ecological Modelling.* The journal publishes works with a strong emphasis on "process-based models embedded in theory with explicit causative agents," rather than on models that only have correlative or statistical descriptions. Basic ecosystem functions are described using "mathematical and conceptual modelling, systems analysis, thermodynamics, computer simulations, and ecological theory." Original research articles, review articles, short communications, letters to the editor, and book reviews are published. The activities of the International Society of Ecological Modelling are supported by the journal, which has occasional special issues. The is recommended for special libraries and academic institutions that have research bridging ecology and mathematical modeling. URL: www.elsevier.com/locate/ecolmodel

1767. ***Ecological Monographs.*** [ISSN: 0012-9615] 1931. q. Ed(s): Aimee Classen. John Wiley & Sons, Inc., 111 River St, Hoboken, NJ 07030; cs-journals@wiley.com; http://www.wiley.com. Illus., adv. Refereed. *Indexed:* A01, A22, Agr, C45, S25. *Aud.:* Ac, Sa.

Published for the Ecological Society of America, *Ecological Monographs* features articles that "are integrative, synthetic papers that elaborate new directions for the field of ecology." The article length is generally more than 16 printed pages, and the content typically includes many factors that describe complicated ecological processes and phenomena. The journal's mission states that papers published "will provide integrative and complete documentation of major empirical and theoretical advances in the field and will establish benchmarks from which future research will build." It is recommended for academic and special libraries. URL: esajournals.onlinelibrary.wiley.com/journal/15577015/

1768. ***Ecology.*** Formerly (until 1920): *Plant World;* Which incorporated (1893-1900): *The Asa Gray Bulletin.* [ISSN: 0012-9658] 1897. m. Ed(s): Donald R Strong. John Wiley & Sons, Inc., 111 River St, Hoboken, NJ 07030; cs-journals@wiley.com; http://www.wiley.com. Illus., adv. Refereed. Reprint: PSC. *Indexed:* A01, A22, Agr, BRI, C45, CBRI, S25. *Bk. rev.:* Number and length vary. *Aud.:* Ac, Sa.

Ecology focuses on the publishing of concise articles that contain "research and synthesis papers on all aspects of ecology, with particular emphasis on papers that develop new concepts in ecology, that test ecological theory, or that lead to an increased appreciation for the diversity of ecological phenomena." *Ecology* "publishes a broad array of research that includes a rapidly expanding envelope of subject matter, techniques, approaches, and concepts: paleoecology through present-day phenomena; evolutionary, population, physiological, community, and ecosystem ecology, as well as biogeochemistry; inclusive of descriptive, comparative, experimental, mathematical, statistical, and interdisciplinary approaches." The publication provides reports, concept and synthesis articles, full-length articles, notes, statistical reports, comments, data papers, book reviews, and "books and monographs received" along with "The Scientific Naturalist" and "Spotlight" sections. The journal is a core title for academic and special libraries that support ecologists. URL: esajournals.onlinelibrary.wiley.com/journal/19399170

Ecology and Society. See Environment and Conservation section.

1769. ***Ecology Letters (Online).*** [ISSN: 1461-0248] 1998. m. GBP 2159. Ed(s): Tim Coulson. Wiley-Blackwell Publishing Ltd., The Atrium, Southern Gate, Chichester, PO19 8QG, United Kingdom; cs-journals@wiley.com; http://onlinelibrary.wiley.com. Refereed. *Aud.:* Ac, Sa.

Current worldwide ecological research is rapidly published in *Ecology Letters.* The concise, primary literature published in this scholarly journal relates to new developments in ecology or is general-interest in scope. There are sections on "Letters," "Ideas and Perspectives," "Reviews and Syntheses," and "Technical Comments." The web site offers recommended reading, virtual special issues, news, and announcements. This is an important journal for academic libraries that serve ecologists. URL: onlinelibrary.wiley.com/journal/14610248

Ecology of Freshwater Fish. See Fish, Fisheries, and Aquaculture section.

1770. ***Ecosystems.*** [ISSN: 1432-9840] 1998. 8x/yr. EUR 1274 (print & online eds.)). Ed(s): Stephen R Carpenter, Monica G Turner. Springer New York LLC, 233 Spring St, New York, NY 10013; customerservice@springer.com; http://www.springer.com. Illus., adv. Sample. Refereed. Reprint: PSC. *Indexed:* A01, A22, Agr, C45, E01, S25. *Aud.:* Ac, Sa.

Ecosystem science, which incorporates "fundamental ecology, environmental ecology and environmental problem solving," is published in this academic journal focused on management. Spatial and temporal scales of all sizes are examined in large experiments, theoretical research, modeling, comparative research, and long-term investigations. Research published integrates natural and social processes that can be terrestrial or aquatic. The journal features research articles, but also publishes editorials, special features on complex topics, and invited mini-reviews of emerging topics. URL: www.springer.com/life+sciences/ecology/journal/10021

Evolution: international journal of organic evolution. See Biology/General section.

1771. ***Evolutionary Ecology.*** [ISSN: 0269-7653] 1987. bi-m. EUR 902 (print & online eds.)). Ed(s): John A Endler. Springer Netherlands, Van Godewijckstraat 30, Dordrecht, 3311 GX, Netherlands; http://www.springer.com. Adv. Refereed. Reprint: PSC. *Indexed:* A22, Agr, C45, E01. *Aud.:* Ac, Sa.

The focus of *Evolutionary Ecology* is on the ecological influences on evolutionary processes, as well as the evolutionary influences on ecological processes. Behavioral and population ecology are explored with respect to evolutionary aspects, and the journal publishes empirical and theoretical articles on all systems and organisms. Research articles, ideas and perspectives, review articles, and comments on recent articles are published in this academic journal, which is recommended for academic and special libraries. URL: link.springer.com/journal/10682

Forest Ecology and Management. See Forestry section.

1772. ***Freshwater Biology (Online).*** [ISSN: 1365-2427] 1998. m. GBP 5227. Ed(s): Dr. David Dudgeon. Wiley-Blackwell Publishing Ltd., The Atrium, Southern Gate, Chichester, PO19 8QG, United Kingdom; cs-journals@wiley.com; http://onlinelibrary.wiley.com/. Adv. Sample. Refereed. *Bk. rev.:* 0-3, 500-2,000 words. *Aud.:* Ac, Sa.

Freshwater Biology publishes research papers related to all ecological aspects of surficial inland waters. Studies can be focused at any level in the ecological hierarchy that relate to "micro-organisms, algae, macrophytes, invertebrates, fish and other vertebrates, as well as those concerning whole ecosystems and related physical and chemical aspects of the environment." Applied science papers related to the management and conservation of inland waters are published. The journal also has review articles and editorial discussion papers and special issues dedicated to a topic or theme are occasionally published. This journal is appropriate for academic and special libraries that support ecologists, limnologists, biologists, and environmental scientists. URL: onlinelibrary.wiley.com/journal/13652427

1773. *Frontiers in Ecology and the Environment.* [ISSN: 1540-9295] 2003. 10x/yr. GBP 329 (print & online eds.)). Ed(s): Sue Silver. John Wiley & Sons, Inc., 111 River St, Hoboken, NJ 07030; cs-journals@wiley.com; http://onlinelibrary.wiley.com. Adv. Refereed. Reprint: PSC. *Indexed:* C45, GardL. *Aud.:* Ac, Sa.

Frontiers in Ecology and the Environment is published for the Ecological Society of America and is included with membership or via subscription. It is a broad, interdisciplinary journal that focuses on environmental threats and current issues in ecology. The journal "consists of peer-reviewed, synthetic review articles on all aspects of ecology, the environment, and related disciplines, as well as short, high impact research communications of broad interdisciplinary appeal." The journal also features a letters section, editorials, special columns, job ads, and domestic and international breaking news. This title is recommended for academic, college, and special libraries. URL: www.frontiersinecology.org/fron/

1774. *Functional Ecology (Online).* [ISSN: 1365-2435] 1987. bi-m. GBP 1309. Ed(s): Ken Thompson, Charles W Fox. Wiley-Blackwell Publishing Ltd., The Atrium, Southern Gate, Chichester, PO19 8QG, United Kingdom; cs-journals@wiley.com; http://onlinelibrary.wiley.com. Adv. Refereed. *Aud.:* Ac, Sa.

This diverse journal has articles focused on the relationship between the development of organisms and their function in the environment. Standard papers, forum articles, and reviews with perspectives ranging from genetics, life history, behavioral, and physiological characteristics in relationship to an ecosystem are published. Current issues are divided into sections that *Functional Ecology* may spotlight or offer perspectives on: plant morphology, behavioral ecology, evolutionary biology, plant physiological ecology, animal physiological ecology, evolutionary ecology, ecosystems ecology, animal morphology and coloration, plant growth and development, plant-animal interactions, and community ecology. This peer-reviewed journal is recommended for academic and special libraries. URL: www.functionalecology.org/

1775. *Global Change Biology.* [ISSN: 1354-1013] 1995. m. GBP 4384. Ed(s): Steve Long. Wiley-Blackwell Publishing Ltd., The Atrium, Southern Gate, Chichester, PO19 8QG, United Kingdom; cs-journals@wiley.com; http://www.wiley.com/. Adv. Sample. Refereed. Reprint: PSC. *Indexed:* A01, A22, Agr, C45, E01, S25. *Aud.:* Ac, Sa.

Global Change Biology seeks to "promote understanding of the interface between biological systems and all aspects of environmental change that affects a substantial part of the globe." The scope is from the micro to the macro, and it covers topics that include atmospheric pollution, ocean warming, land-use change, climate change, carbon sequestration, and global food security. Primary research articles are the main feature, but the journal also publishes technical advances, research reviews, letters, and commentaries. URL: onlinelibrary.wiley.com/journal/13652486

1776. *Global Ecology and Biogeography: a journal of macroecology.* Formerly (until 1999): *Global Ecology and Biogeography Letters.* [ISSN: 1466-822X] 1991. m. GBP 4791 (print or online ed.)). Wiley-Blackwell Publishing Ltd., The Atrium, Southern Gate, Chichester, PO19 8QG, United Kingdom; cs-journals@wiley.com; http://onlinelibrary.wiley.com. Illus., adv. Sample. Refereed. Reprint: PSC. *Indexed:* A01, A22, Agr, C45, E01, S25. *Aud.:* Ac, Sa.

Global Ecology and Biogeography: a journal of macroecology is an academic journal that contributes "to the growth and societal relevance of the discipline of biogeography." Articles published within this journal are wide in scope and focus on global or regional issues that pertain to biodiversity, ecology, and biogeography. The journal consists of primary research articles and some meta-analyses, methods, and research reviews. Occasional special issues are published. It is a peer-reviewed publication that is appropriate for institutions with faculty that study global change, biodiversity, geography, ecology, biogeography, and environmental science. URL: onlinelibrary.wiley.com/journal/14668238

Human Ecology. See Environment and Conservation section.

1777. *Hydrobiologia: the international journal of aquatic sciences.* Incorporates (in 2003): *Journal of Aquatic Ecosystem Stress and Recovery;* Which was formerly (1991-1997): *Journal of Aquatic Ecosystem Health;* Incorporated (1992-2000): *International Journal of Salt Lake Research.* [ISSN: 0018-8158] 1948. 21x/yr. EUR 18212 (print & online eds.)). Ed(s): Koen Martens. Springer Netherlands, Van Godewijckstraat 30, Dordrecht, 3311 GX, Netherlands; http://www.springer.com. Adv. Refereed. Microform: PQC. Reprint: PSC. *Indexed:* A01, A22, Agr, C45, E01, S25. *Bk. rev.:* Number and length vary. *Aud.:* Ac, Sa.

Limnology and oceanography topics are covered at the levels of molecular, organism, community, and ecosystem. In addition to hypothesis-driven and theoretical research, reviews and opinions are published in this peer-reviewed journal, which is aimed at a "broad hydrobiological audience." The journal has special issues and guest editors and publishes more than 20 volumes each year. Regular volumes are mainly composed of primary research papers. This journal is recommended for academic and special libraries. URL: www.springer.com/life+sciences/ecology/journal/10750

1778. *The I S M E Journal: multidisciplinary journal of microbial ecology.* [ISSN: 1751-7362] 2007. m. EUR 1491. Ed(s): George Kowalchuk, Mark J Bailey. Nature Publishing Group, The MacMillan Bldg, 4 Crinan St, London, N1 9XW, United Kingdom; nature@nature.com; https://www.nature.com. Adv. Sample. Refereed. *Indexed:* A01, C45.

The ISME Journal is a Nature publication that "seeks to promote diverse and integrated areas of microbial ecology spanning the breadth of microbial life, including bacteria, archaea, microbial eukaryotes, and viruses." The scope of the journal is broad and includes microbial population and community ecology, microbe-microbe and microbe-host interactions, evolutionary genetics, integrated genomics and post-genomics approaches in microbial ecology, microbial engineering, geomicrobiology, microbial ecology functional diversity of natural habitats, and microbial ecosystem impacts. The journal has full-length articles, brief communications, perspectives, and some review articles. URL: www.nature.com/ismej/

1779. *Ideas in Ecology and Evolution.* [ISSN: 1918-3178] 2008. a. Free. Ed(s): Lonnie Aarssen. Queen's University, c/o Lonnie Aarssen, Editor, Department of Biology, Kingston, ON K7L 3N6, Canada. Refereed. *Indexed:* A01. *Aud.:* Ac, Sa.

Ideas in Ecology and Evolution is an open-access, peer-reviewed electronic journal published by Queens University in Canada. It serves as a repository of opinion pieces that researchers and students can peruse for ideas for research. There is a section on the "Future of Publishing" that is focused on scholarly communication, and the scope of the journal is broad and focused on any aspect of ecology or evolution. The journal is published annually, with occasional special issues with topics like "Data Sharing in Ecology and Evolution." It is recommended for libraries that serve academics and students in higher education. URL: http://ojs.library.queensu.ca/index.php/IEE

1780. *Journal of Chemical Ecology.* [ISSN: 0098-0331] 1975. m. EUR 2961 (print & online eds.)). Ed(s): John T Romero. Springer New York LLC, 233 Spring St, New York, NY 10013; customerservice@springer.com; http://www.springer.com. Adv. Sample. Refereed. Microform: PQC. Reprint: PSC. *Indexed:* A01, A22, Agr, C45, E01, S25. *Aud.:* Ac, Sa.

The interdisciplinary *Journal of Chemical Ecology* publishes articles that "contain both chemical and ecological/behavioral elements." It is "devoted to promoting an ecological understanding of the origin, function, and significance of natural chemicals that mediate interactions within and between organisms."

Original research articles, review articles, letters to the editor, and rapid communications are included in the publication for the International Society of Chemical Ecology. URL: link.springer.com/journal/10886

1781. ***Journal of Ecology.*** [ISSN: 0022-0477] 1913. bi-m. GBP 1285. Ed(s): Amy Austin, Mark Rees. Wiley-Blackwell Publishing Ltd., The Atrium, Southern Gate, Chichester, PO19 8QG, United Kingdom; cs-journals@wiley.com; http://onlinelibrary.wiley.com. Illus., index. Sample. Refereed. Vol. ends: Dec. Microform: PQC. Reprint: PSC. *Indexed:* A01, A22, Agr, BRI, C45, E01, GardL, S25. *Aud.:* Ac, Sa.

The British Ecological Society offers original research related to the ecology of plants in the *Journal of Ecology.* Experimental papers using any kind of ecological approach are published, along with those focusing on theoretical approaches or papers with historical or descriptive accounts. The journal has a broad scope and an international audience. Each article has a numbered, point-by-point abstract, which makes browsing more efficient. Papers from all geographical regions are published, along with essay reviews and forum (opinion) articles. The journal is appropriate for academic programs related to plant ecology and for professionals. URL: www.journalofecology.org

1782. ***Landscape Ecology.*** [ISSN: 0921-2973] 1987. 10x/yr. EUR 2375 (print & online eds.)). Ed(s): Jianguo Wu. Springer Netherlands, Van Godewijckstraat 30, Dordrecht, 3311 GX, Netherlands; http://www.springer.com. Adv. Refereed. Reprint: PSC. *Indexed:* A22, Agr, BRI, C45, E01, GardL. *Aud.:* Ga, Ac, Sa.

The development and maintenance of sustainable landscapes, informed by the understanding of the relationships between ecological processes and spatial patterns is the primary focus of *Landscape Ecology.* Transdisciplinary and interdisciplinary studies are published that bring "together expertise from both biophysical and socioeconomic sciences to explore basic and applied research questions concerning the ecology, conservation, management, design/planning, and sustainability of landscapes as coupled human-environment systems." The peer-reviewed journal informs researchers and practitioners in the fields of landscape design and planning, biodiversity conservation, broad-scale ecology, and ecosystem management. URL: www.springer.com/life+sciences/ecology/journal/10980

Marine Ecology - Progress Series. See Marine Science and Technology/Marine Biology section.

1783. ***Methods in Ecology and Evolution.*** [ISSN: 2041-210X] 2010. m. GBP 1275. Ed(s): Rob Freckleton, Bob O'Hara. Wiley-Blackwell Publishing Ltd., The Atrium, Southern Gate, Chichester, PO19 8QG, United Kingdom; cs-journals@wiley.com; http://onlinelibrary.wiley.com. Refereed. Reprint: PSC. *Indexed:* A22, E01. *Aud.:* Ac, Sa.

Published for the British Ecological Society, *Methods in Ecology and Evolution* "promotes the development of new methods in ecology and evolution, and facilitates their dissemination and uptake by the research community." Methodological papers are published in all areas of ecology and evolution. The journal's first issue was in 2010, and this title has subsequently become a clearinghouse for the development of new methods. New technology has increased the amount of tools available to ecologists and evolutionary biologists, and the published articles span from being specific to a species, problem, or system to broad applicability at the ecosystem scale. The journal also publishes videos and podcasts with method and tool demonstrations. This title is recommended for academic institutions and special libraries that serve practicing ecologists and evolutionary biologists. URL: www.methodsinecologyandevolution.org

1784. ***Molecular Ecology.*** [ISSN: 0962-1083] 1992. s-m. GBP 7306 (print or online ed.)). Ed(s): Loren Rieseberg. Wiley-Blackwell Publishing Ltd., The Atrium, Southern Gate, Chichester, PO19 8QG, United Kingdom; cs-journals@wiley.com; http://www.wiley.com/. Illus., adv. Sample. Refereed. Microform: PQC. Reprint: PSC. *Indexed:* A01, A22, Agr, C45, E01. *Aud.:* Ac, Sa.

Questions in ecology, behavior, evolution, and conservation are addressed in *Molecular Ecology.* Papers published must employ molecular genetic techniques to address the research issue. Each journal issue has a concentration on primary research articles, but also may have invited reviews, opinion articles (perspectives), and commentaries. Institutions that serve molecular ecologists should include this journal in their collection. Available online and in print. URL: onlinelibrary.wiley.com/journal/1365294x

1785. ***Oecologia.*** Formerly: *Zeitschrift fuer Morphologie und Oekologie der Tiere.* [ISSN: 0029-8549] 1924. 16x/yr. EUR 8490 (print & online eds.)). Ed(s): Roland Brandl, Hannu Ylonen. Springer, Tiergartenstr 17, Heidelberg, 69121, Germany. Illus., adv. Sample. Refereed. Reprint: PSC. *Indexed:* A01, A22, Agr, C45, E01, S25. *Aud.:* Ac, Sa.

Oecologia publishes "innovative ecological research of general interest" related to plant and animal ecology, and is aimed at an international audience. Most published manuscripts are original research based on physiological ecology, behavioral ecology, population ecology, plant and animal interactions, community ecology, ecosystem ecology, global change ecology, or conservation ecology. The journal has a new initiative to "highlight exceptional, original research publications that are part of graduate or undergraduate student theses and carry the name of the student as lead author." It is appropriate for scholars and professionals, and is available online and in print. URL: link.springer.com/journal/442

1786. ***Oikos (Malden, Online): a journal of ecology.*** [ISSN: 1600-0706] 1948. m. GBP 1474. Ed(s): Dries Bonte, Asa Langefors. Wiley-Blackwell Publishing Ltd., The Atrium, Southern Gate, Chichester, PO19 8QG, United Kingdom; cs-journals@wiley.com; http://onlinelibrary.wiley.com. Refereed. *Aud.:* Ac, Sa.

Published for the Nordic Society, *Oikos* features theoretical and empirical work related to all aspects of ecology from all regions of the world. *Oikos* publishes articles that emphasize "theoretical and empirical work aimed at generalization and synthesis across taxa, systems and ecological disciplines." Articles are available online ahead of print in the "EarlyView" feature. The forum section features articles "that aim to stimulate discussion by promoting ideas and synthesis of high novelty." *Oikos* is appropriate for academic institutions with an ecology program or for professionals. URL: http://www.oikosjournal.org/

1787. ***Restoration Ecology (Online).*** [ISSN: 1526-100X] 1993. bi-m. GBP 811. Ed(s): Stephen Murphy. Wiley-Blackwell Publishing, Inc., 111 River St, Hoboken, NJ 07030; info@wiley.com; http://onlinelibrary.wiley.com. Refereed. *Aud.:* Ac, Sa.

Restoration Ecology. is published for the Society for Ecological Restoration. Topics in interdisciplinary science are covered in the journal, which "addresses global concerns" yet also highlights specific issues within ecological communities. Original research articles based on marine, freshwater, and terrestrial ecology are integrated with social science "in the fight to not only halt ecological damage, but also to ultimately reverse it." "Contributions span the natural sciences, including ecological and biological aspects, as well as the restoration of soil, air and water when set in an ecological context; and the social sciences, including cultural, philosophical, political, educational, economic and historical aspects." Restoration practitioners and academic researchers will find valuable information that can be applied on a variety of spatial and temporal scales. URL: https://onlinelibrary.wiley.com/journal/1526100x

1788. ***Trends in Ecology & Evolution.*** [ISSN: 0169-5347] 1986. m. EUR 3903. Ed(s): Paul Craze. Elsevier Ltd., Trends Journals, The Blvd, Langford Ln, Kidlington, Oxford, OX5 1GB, United Kingdom; JournalsCustomerServiceEMEA@elsevier.com; http://www.elsevier.com. Illus., index, adv. Sample. Refereed. Vol. ends: No. 16. *Indexed:* A01, A22, C45. *Bk. rev.:* Number and length vary. *Aud.:* Ac, Sa.

Trends in Ecology & Evolution is a highly regarded journal that focuses on current developments in ecology and evolutionary science. Its topics range from microbiology to global ecology, and it features pure and applied science articles. The journal "is the major forum for coverage of all the important issues concerning organisms and their environments." This is a core journal for university and college libraries that have ecology, evolution, microbiology, biology, and environmental studies departments. It can be found in print and online. URL: www.cell.com/trends/ecology-evolution/home

1789. ***The Wildlife Professional.*** [ISSN: 1933-2866] 2007. q. Free to members. Ed(s): Lisa Moore. Alliance Communications Group, 810 E 10th St, PO Box 368, Lawrence, KS 66044; info@allenpress.com; http://allenpress.com/. Adv. Circ: 8300 Paid. *Aud.:* Ga, Ac, Sa.

Published as a free membership benefit to the Wildlife Society, this magazine is aimed to keep the professional wildlife manager informed of "critical advances in wildlife science, conservation, management, and policy." Each issue has a theme highlighted by a cover story, along with an in-focus topic area, rotating features, and departments with items like policy watch, field notes, and photos from readers. This magazine is recommended for college and academic libraries with wildlife programs and for special libraries, such as career centers. URL: drupal.wildlife.org/publications/twp

■ ECONOMICS

Emily Coolidge Toker, Learning Technology Specialist, Lamont Library, Harvard University; emily_coolidgetoker@harvard.edu

Introduction

The majority of titles listed here are targeted at the skilled researcher. However, as the general public continues to take a strong interest in empirical research, selectors must continue to provide core, generalist staples such as *Challenge: The Magazine of Economic Affairs, The Economist, The American Economic Review,* and *The World Bank Research Observer.* Several prestigious journals have embraced new publishing models, regularly featuring open-access articles and providing additional online-only content. As this shift continues, selectors should prioritize titles with the most value for their readers, generalist laypeople, and experts alike. When expanding a core collection, determine which specialized subfields are gaining the interest of your readers and go from there.

Basic Periodicals

Ga: *Challenge, The Economist, The Journal of Economic History, Journal of Economic Literature, O E C D Observer, World Bank Research Observer;* Ac: *Brookings Papers on Economic Activity, Economic History Review, The Economic Journal, Economica, Journal of Economic Literature, Journal of Economic Theory, Journal of Political Economy, O E C D Observer, Quarterly Journal of Economics, RAND Journal of Economics, The World Bank Economic Review.*

Basic Abstracts and Indexes

ABI/INFORM, Business Source Complete, EconLit, International Bibliography of the Social Sciences, PAIS International, Social Sciences Citation Index, World Agricultural Economics and Rural Sociology Abstracts.

1790. ***The American Economic Review.*** Formed by the 1911 merger of: *American Economic Association Quarterly; Economic Bulletin.* [ISSN: 0002-8282] 1911. m. USD 470. Ed(s): Esther Duflo. American Economic Association, 2014 Broadway, Ste 305, Nashville, TN 37203; aeainfo@vanderbilt.edu; http://www.vanderbilt.edu/AEA/. Illus., index, adv. Refereed. Vol. ends: Dec. Microform: MIM; PMC; PQC. *Indexed:* A22, Agr, B01, BAS, BRI, CBRI, Chicano, EconLit, F01, IBSS. *Aud.:* Ac, Sa.

As the premier journal of the American Economic Association, *The American Economic Review* is a must for any academic or special library. Since 2011, the articles are single blind-reviewed. Quality has not suffered. The field of economics is becoming increasingly interdisciplinary, and the breadth of *AER* content provides sufficient coverage accessible both to laypeople and experts. "Papers and Proceedings of the American Economic Association" are included in each May issue.

American Statistical Association. Journal. See Statistics section.

1791. ***Brookings Papers on Economic Activity.*** [ISSN: 0007-2303] 1970. s-a. USD 110 (Individuals, USD 70). Ed(s): James Stock, Janice C Eberly. Brookings Institution Press, 1775 Massachusetts Ave, NW, Washington, DC 20036; communications@brookings.edu; http://www.brookings.edu. Illus., index. Refereed. Microform: PQC. *Indexed:* A22, B01, BRI, C42, E01, EconLit. *Aud.:* Ga, Ac, Sa.

Brookings Papers on Economic Activity, the flagship publication of The Brookings Institution, publishes content that "emphasize innovative analysis that has an empirical orientation, take real-world institutions seriously, and is relevant to economic policy." Articles are rigorous but accessible to generalists and laypeople. Past issues are freely available online. Academic libraries should seriously consider this publication for their collections.

1792. ***Business Economics: designed to serve the needs of people who use economics in their work.*** [ISSN: 0007-666X] 1965. q. GBP 238. Ed(s): Charles Steindel. Palgrave Macmillan Ltd., Macmillan Building, 4 Crinan St, London, N1 9XW, United Kingdom; onlinesales@palgrave.com; http://www.palgrave.com. Illus., adv. Sample. Refereed. Vol. ends: Oct. Microform: PQC. Reprint: PSC. *Indexed:* A22, Agr, B01, BRI, E01, EconLit. *Bk. rev.:* 1-4, 1,000-1,500 words. *Aud.:* Ga, Ac.

Published by the National Association for Business Economists, this refereed journal provides articles, analyses, summaries, and best practices in business matters. The journal serves as "a leading forum for debating solutions to critical business problems or the analysis of key business issues." Each issue has features on statistics, industries and markets, economics at work, and book reviews. Attributed book reviews are included. All of it is very accessible to the non-economist. Academic and large public libraries should consider this journal for their collections.

1793. ***Challenge (Armonk).*** Former titles (until 1954): *Challenge Magazine;* (until 1952): *Popular Economics.* [ISSN: 0577-5132] 1950. bi-m. GBP 387 (print & online eds.)). Ed(s): Jeff Madrick. Routledge, 530 Walnut St, Ste 850, Philadelphia, PA 19106; orders@taylorandfrancis.com; http://www.tandfonline.com. Illus., index, adv. Sample. Vol. ends: Nov/Dec. Reprint: PSC. *Indexed:* A22, B01, BAS, BRI, E01, EconLit, IBSS. *Bk. rev.:* 1, 2-4 pages. *Aud.:* Hs, Ga, Ac.

Challenge serves "as an approachable and timely source of ideas, information, and public policy proposals," established as a "progressive" outlet for "new Keynesian ideas." Articles are written in a clear, nontechnical manner by well-respected economists and scholars. Each issue has a rough theme, and recent articles include "The Fracturing of Globalization," and "Giving Workers What They Need." In-depth book reviews are also included. Highly recommended for high school, public, academic, and government libraries.

1794. ***Economic Development and Cultural Change.*** [ISSN: 0013-0079] 1952. q. USD 507. Ed(s): Marcel Fafchamps. University of Chicago Press, 1427 E 60th St, Chicago, IL 60637; custserv@press.uchicago.edu; http://www.journals.uchicago.edu. Illus., index, adv. Sample. Refereed. Vol. ends: Jul. Reprint: PSC. *Indexed:* A22, ASSIA, Agr, B01, BRI, C45, EconLit, HRIS, IBSS, P61, SSA. *Bk. rev.:* 8-9, lengthy. *Aud.:* Ga, Ac, Sa.

Published by the University of Chicago Press, this journal is composed of "studies that use modern theoretical and empirical approaches to examine both the determinants and the effects of various dimensions of economic development and cultural change." The journal features "empirical papers with analytic underpinnings" and covers a variety of topics related to economic development. Cited by scholars and researchers in economics, sociology, political science, and geography, this journal is recommended for academic libraries.

Economic Geography. See Geography section.

1795. ***The Economic History Review: a journal of economic and social history.*** [ISSN: 0013-0117] 1927. q. GBP 366. Wiley-Blackwell Publishing Ltd., The Atrium, Southern Gate, Chichester, PO19 8QG, United Kingdom; cs-journals@wiley.com; http://onlinelibrary.wiley.com. Illus., index, adv. Sample. Refereed. Vol. ends: Nov. Microform: IDC; PQC. Reprint: PSC. *Indexed:* A22, AmHI, B01, BRI, E01, EconLit, IBSS. *Bk. rev.:* 28-40, 600-1,200 words, some signed. *Aud.:* Ga, Ac, Sa.

This quarterly journal provides a "broad coverage of themes of economic and social change, including the intellectual, political and cultural implications of these changes." Articles are well-written and accessible to laypeople and experts alike. Recommended for academic and public libraries that serve historians, students, and researchers.

1796. *The Economic Journal.* [ISSN: 0013-0133] 1891. 8x/yr. GBP 531. Oxford University Press, Great Clarendon St, Oxford, OX2 6DP, United Kingdom; jnls.cust.serv@oup.com; https://academic.oup.com/journals. Illus., index, adv. Sample. Refereed. Vol. ends: Nov. Reprint: PSC. *Indexed:* A22, Agr, B01, BAS, BRI, C45, CBRI, E01, EconLit, HRIS, IBSS. *Bk. rev.:* 25, lengthy. *Aud.:* Ac, Sa.

Published on behalf of the Royal Economic Society (U.K.), this classic and frequently cited periodical continues to be a preeminent source on economic issues, both theoretical and empirical. Each issue typically contains 9-11 papers. A discussion forum, data sets, and book notes can be found on its website. The best papers from the annual conference of the Royal Economic Society are published in each May issue. Recent articles include "Can Internal Migration Foster the Convergence in Regional Fertility Rates? Evidence from 19th Century France," "Distributional Implications of Joint Tax Evasion." Highly recommended for academic, government, business, and financial libraries.

1797. *The Economic Record.* [ISSN: 0013-0249] 1925. 5x/yr. USD 689. Ed(s): Garry Barrett. Wiley-Blackwell Publishing Asia, 155 Cremorne St, Richmond, VIC 3121, Australia; melbourne@wiley.com; http://onlinelibrary.wiley.com. Illus., index, adv. Sample. Refereed. Vol. ends: Dec. Reprint: PSC. *Indexed:* A22, B01, BAS, BRI, E01, EconLit, IBSS. *Bk. rev.:* 3-7, lengthy, signed. *Aud.:* Ac, Sa.

A generalist publication produced by the Economic Society of Australia, *The Economic Record* provides a forum for theoretical, applied, and policy research on the economies Australia and New Zealand. Recent articles include "The Role of Tax and Subsidy Policy in Driving Australian House Prices" and "Financial Stress and Indigenous Australians." Recommended for economists and university libraries with international interests.

1798. *Economica.* [ISSN: 0013-0427] 1921. q. GBP 425. Ed(s): Frank Cowell, Lena Edlund. Wiley-Blackwell Publishing Ltd., The Atrium, Southern Gate, Chichester, PO19 8QG, United Kingdom; cs-journals@wiley.com; http://www.wiley.com/. Illus., index, adv. Sample. Refereed. Vol. ends: Nov. Reprint: PSC. *Indexed:* A22, B01, BAS, BRI, E01, EIP, EconLit, IBSS. *Bk. rev.:* 5-11, 275-1,800 words. *Aud.:* Ac, Sa.

A top journal for general economics, published on behalf of the London School of Economics and Political Science, *Economica* is international in scope. Some recent articles include "Some Misconceptions About Public Investment Efficiency and Growth" and "The Consequences of Job Loss in a Flexible Labour Market." The journal contains numerous book reviews and an annual author/title index. Recommended for academic libraries, professional economists, and researchers.

1799. *The Economist.* [ISSN: 0013-0613] 1843. w. 51/yr. USD 160 combined subscription (print & online eds.)). Ed(s): Zanny Minton Beddoes. The Economist Newspaper Ltd., 25 St James's St, London, SW1A 1HG, United Kingdom; intelligentlife@economist.com; http://www.economist.com. Illus., index, adv. Sample. Vol. ends: Dec. *Indexed:* A01, A22, AmHI, B01, B03, BAS, BRI, C37, CBRI, Chicano, F01, MASUSE. *Bk. rev.:* 3-4, 450-500 words. *Aud.:* Ems, Hs, Ga, Ac, Sa.

This popular magazine was founded more than 175 years ago to support free trade and is read in more than 180 countries. It is well respected and considered authoritative on "world politics, global business, finance and economics, science and technology, and the arts." Its timely coverage includes summaries on politics and business, short articles on world leaders, science, technology, finance and economics, surveys of countries and regions, obituaries, and more. Well known in the back of each issue are economic, financial, and market statistics, especially the World GDP. The magazine's website offers additional features such as an online archive, apps, and audio recordings of all content. A must-have for all libraries.

1800. *The Economists' Voice.* [ISSN: 1553-3832] 2004. a. EUR 285. Walter de Gruyter GmbH, Genthiner Str 13, Berlin, 10785, Germany; service@degruyter.com; https://www.degruyter.de. Sample. Refereed. *Indexed:* A22, B01, E01, EconLit. *Aud.:* Ga, Ac, Sa.

The Economists' Voice was founded in 2004 to provide a nonpartisan, peer-reviewed forum for leading economists to share their views on important issues with a general audience. It "seeks to fill the gap between op-ed pages of newspapers and scholarly journal articles." Recent special issues have included "The Future of the European Monetary Union" and "Nutrition and Poverty." Economists, policy makers and analysts, and students of economics will be interested in this online journal. It is strongly recommended for academic and public libraries.

Energy Economics. See Energy section.

The Energy Journal. See Energy section.

Gender and Development. See Gender Studies section.

Harvard Business Review. See Business and Finance/General section.

1801. *History of Political Economy.* [ISSN: 0018-2702] 1969. bi-m. USD 974. Ed(s): Claude Misukiewicz, Kevin D Hoover. Duke University Press, 905 W Main St, Durham, NC 27701; orders@dukeupress.edu; https://www.dukeupress.edu. Illus., index, adv. Refereed. Vol. ends: Winter. Reprint: PSC. *Indexed:* A22, B01, BAS, BRI, E01, EconLit, IBSS, P61. *Bk. rev.:* 3-7, 1-3 pages. *Aud.:* Ga, Ac, Sa.

This is the leading journal in its field, and its scholarly articles focus on topics such as the development of economic thought, the historical context of major figures in the field, and the interpretation of economic theories. Recent articles include "The Power of a Single Number: A Political History of GDP by Philipp Lepenies" and "Virtue, Production and the Politics of Commerce." Early political economists such as Marshall, Adam Smith, Keynes, Malthus, Ricardo, and Marx are heavily featured. Each issue has six or seven articles and attributed book reviews. There is a browsable online archive. Recommended for large public libraries and academic libraries.

1802. *I M F Economic Review.* Former titles (until 2010): *I M F Staff Papers;* (until 1999): *International Monetary Fund. Staff Papers.* [ISSN: 2041-4161] 1950. q. GBP 210. Ed(s): Linda Tesar. Palgrave Macmillan Ltd., Macmillan Building, 4 Crinan St, London, N1 9XW, United Kingdom; onlinesales@palgrave.com; http://www.palgrave.com. Illus., adv. Sample. Refereed. Reprint: PSC. *Indexed:* A01, A22, B01, BAS, BLI, BRI, C42, E01, EIP, EconLit. *Aud.:* Ga, Ac, Sa.

This official research journal for the International Monetary Fund is written for a "general audience including policymakers and academics." The authors are IMF staff, primarily professional economists, and invited guests, and articles cover topics such as "Macroeconomic implications of financial crises; Economic and financial spillovers; Policy responses to crises; Fiscal policy and stabilization; Policy responses to commodity price movements; and Monetary and macroprudential policies." Recent articles include "Capital Controls and the Cost of Debt" and "Financial Development and Technology Diffusion." This journal, published quarterly, is highly recommended for large public, special, and academic libraries

Journal of Banking & Finance. See Business and Finance/Scholarly section.

Journal of Business and Economic Statistics. See Business and Finance/General section.

Journal of Business Ethics. See Business and Finance/Ethics section.

1803. ***Journal of Comparative Economics.*** [ISSN: 0147-5967] 1977. q. EUR 1478. Ed(s): Alessandro Pavan. Academic Press, 225 Wyman St, Waltham, MA 02144; JournalCustomerService-usa@elsevier.com; http://store.elsevier.com/Academic-Press/IMP_5/. Illus., index, adv. Sample. Refereed. Vol. ends: Dec. *Indexed:* A22, B01, BAS, BRI, E01, EconLit. *Bk. rev.:* 2-23, 500-2,000 words, some signed. *Aud.:* Ac, Sa.

A publication of the Association for Comparative Economic Studies, this journal addresses such questions as "what institutions are critical for successful growth; how should institutions be measured; why are certain institutions, such as courts and regulatory culture, slow-moving while others, such as constitutions and electoral procedures, relatively fast-moving; why is there so much cross-sectional variance in the quality of institutions, and what kinds of initial conditions or historic natural experiments can be employed to estimate the causal impact of institutions on economic performance?" Recent articles include "National levels of corruption and foreign direct investment" and "Ex-ante labor market effects of compulsory military service." The journal is particularly strong in coverage of the economies of China, Central Europe, and the former Soviet Union. This journal is the most general of those specializing in economic theory, and as such is recommended for large academic libraries and other institutions with international programs.

Journal of Consumer Research. See Advertising, Marketing, and Public Relations section.

1804. ***Journal of Economic Growth.*** [ISSN: 1381-4338] 1996. q. EUR 1124 (print & online eds.)). Ed(s): Frank Cowell. Springer New York LLC, 233 Spring St, New York, NY 10013; customerservice@springer.com; http://www.springer.com. Adv. Refereed. Reprint: PSC. *Indexed:* A22, Agr, B01, BAS, E01, EconLit, IBSS. *Aud.:* Ac, Sa.

This well-regarded journal publishes research that "explores the role of income distribution, the demographic transition, human capital formation, technological change, and structural transformation in the growth process, as well as the role [of] deeply-rooted geographical, cultural, institutional and human characteristics in the comparative economic development." Highly recommended for academic and special libraries.

1805. ***The Journal of Economic History.*** Incorporates (1941-1950): *Tasks of Economic History.* [ISSN: 0022-0507] 1941. q. GBP 271. Ed(s): Paul W Rhode, Ann Carlos. Cambridge University Press, University Printing House, Shaftesbury Rd, Cambridge, CB2 8BS, United Kingdom; journals@cambridge.org; https://www.cambridge.org/. Illus., index. Refereed. Circ: 3300. Vol. ends: Dec. Microform: MIM; PQC. Reprint: PSC. *Indexed:* A01, A22, Agr, B01, BAS, BRI, CBRI, Chicano, E01, EconLit, IBSS, MLA-IB. *Bk. rev.:* 39-63, 600-1,800 words. *Aud.:* Ac, Sa.

Of interest to economists and economic, social, and demographic historians, the journal has a broad coverage in terms of methodology and geography, *The Journal of Economic History* covers topics such as "money and banking, trade manufacturing, technology, transportation, industrial organization, labor, agriculture, servitude, demography, education, economic growth, and the role of government and regulation." This excellent and approachable journal will appeal to the student and the general public. Recommended for colleges, universities, and public libraries.

1806. ***Journal of Economic Literature.*** Formerly (until 1968): *Journal of Economic Abstracts (Print).* [ISSN: 0022-0515] 1963. q. USD 550. Ed(s): Steven Durlauf. American Economic Association, 2014 Broadway, Ste 305, Nashville, TN 37203; aeainfo@vanderbilt.edu; http://www.aeaweb.org. Illus., index, adv. Refereed. Vol. ends: Dec. *Indexed:* B01, BRI, C45, EconLit, IBSS. *Bk. rev.:* 40, lengthy. *Aud.:* Ac, Sa.

The *Journal of Economic Literature* is the official publication of the American Economic Association (AEA), and is one of the highest ranked journals in the field. It contains four to six research articles written by outstanding economists, numerous book reviews, and new-book listings by *JEL* classification. *e-JEL,* the electronic edition, has the current issue hyperlinks. Each December issue lists dissertations and recipients of doctoral degrees in economics conferred in U.S. and Canadian universities during the previous academic year. Highly recommended for colleges, universities, and larger public and special libraries.

1807. ***Journal of Economic Theory.*** [ISSN: 0022-0531] 1969. bi-m. EUR 5997. Ed(s): Alessandro Pavan. Academic Press, 3251 Riverport Ln, Maryland Heights, MO 63043; JournalCustomerService-usa@elsevier.com; http://www.elsevier.com/. Adv. Sample. Refereed. *Indexed:* A22, B01, E01, EconLit, IBSS, MSN. *Aud.:* Ac, Sa.

This well-established, heavily cited, core scholarly journal publishes "research on economic theory and emphasizes the theoretical analysis of economic models, including the related mathematical techniques." Themes include "mechanism design, information, finance, matching, decision theory, game theory, political economy, market design, macroeconomics and monetary economics." Full text is available on ScienceDirect. An excellent journal for libraries that support theoretical economics.

1808. ***Journal of Economics.*** Formerly (until 1986): *Zeitschrift fuer Nationaloekonomie.* [ISSN: 0931-8658] 1930. 9x/yr. EUR 1744 (print & online eds.)). Ed(s): Giacomo Corneo. Springer Wien, Prinz-Eugen-Str 8-10, Wien, 1040, Austria; journals@springer.at; http://www.springer.com. Illus., index, adv. Sample. Refereed. Reprint: PSC. *Indexed:* A22, Agr, B01, BRI, E01, EconLit, IBSS. *Bk. rev.:* 6-8, lengthy. *Aud.:* Ac.

Focusing on mathematical economic theory, this excellent journal has technical articles that cover mainly microeconomics and some macroeconomics. While not terribly accessible to the layperson, the typical issue has four to five extensive articles and one to two lengthy book reviews. Supplemental issues are devoted to current issues. Authors are academic and international. Recommended for large academic libraries.

1809. ***Journal of Environmental Economics and Management.*** [ISSN: 0095-0696] 1975. 6x/yr. EUR 2975. Academic Press, 3251 Riverport Ln, Maryland Heights, MO 63043; JournalCustomerService-usa@elsevier.com; http://www.elsevier.com/. Illus., adv. Refereed. *Indexed:* A01, A22, Agr, B01, C42, C45, E01, EconLit, IBSS, S25. *Aud.:* Ac, Sa.

This is the official journal of the Association of Environmental and Resource Economists. Devoted to the worldwide coverage of theoretical and empirical research, it "concentrates on the management and/or social control of the economy in its relationship with the management and use of natural resources and the natural environment." The majority of authors are academic economists, and it includes interdisciplinary papers from fields of interest. Recently published articles include "Effects of stricter environmental regulations on resource development," and "The Kyoto protocol: Empirical evidence of a hidden success." Recommended for university and large public libraries.

The Journal of Finance. See Business and Finance/Scholarly section.

Journal of Financial and Quantitative Analysis. See Business and Finance/Scholarly section.

Journal of Financial Economics. See Business and Finance/Scholarly section.

1810. ***Journal of Human Development and Capabilities: a multi-disciplinary journal for people-centered development.*** Formerly (until 2009): *Journal of Human Development.* [ISSN: 1945-2829] 2000. q. GBP 557 (print & online eds.)). Ed(s): Siddiq Osmani. Routledge, 4 Park Sq, Milton Park, Abingdon, OX14 4RN, United Kingdom; subscriptions@tandf.co.uk; http://www.tandfonline.com. Adv. Sample. Refereed. Reprint: PSC. *Indexed:* A01, A22, C45, E01, EconLit, IBSS, P61. *Aud.:* Ac, Sa.

The official publication of the Human Development and Capability Association, founded by Amartya Sen in 2000, this peer-reviewed journal reflects human development as a new school of thought in economics, and thus it is a must-purchase for academic libraries. Its aim is to "promote new perspectives on challenges of human development, capability expansion, poverty eradication, social justice and human rights." Highly recommended for academic and larger public libraries.

1811. *Journal of Institutional and Theoretical Economics.* Formerly (until 1986): *Zeitschrift fuer die Gesamte Staatswissenschaft.* [ISSN: 0932-4569] 1844. q. EUR 489 (Individuals, EUR 199). Ed(s): Gerd Muehlheusser. Mohr Siebeck GmbH & Co. KG, Wilhelmstr 18, Tuebingen, 72074, Germany; info@mohr.de; https://www.mohrsiebeck.com. Illus., index, adv. Refereed. Reprint: SCH. *Indexed:* A22, BAS, BRI, EconLit, IBSS. *Bk. rev.:* 10-14, 600-2,200 words. *Aud.:* Ga, Ac, Sa.

This interdisciplinary journal publishes research on "the problems of economics, social policy, and their legal framework." Since 2013, all accepted articles have been published in an Online First version, although this is removed after the issue is physically available. Recent articles include "Microfinance and Prosocial Behaviors: Experimental Evidence of Public-Good Contributions in Uganda" and "Social Norm and Giving with Indivisibility of Money: An Experiment on Selfishness, Equity, and Generosity." Articles and book reviews may be in English or German, but most are in English; papers have a summary in both languages. Notable are the papers from the Symposium on New Institutional Economics, presented in a single issue annually. Recommended for large public and university libraries.

Journal of Labor Economics. See Labor and Industrial Relations section.

The Journal of Law and Economics. See Law section.

1812. *Journal of Money, Credit & Banking.* [ISSN: 0022-2879] 1969. 8x/yr. GBP 546 (print & online eds.)). Wiley-Blackwell Publishing, Inc., 111 River St, Hoboken, NJ 07030; info@wiley.com; http://onlinelibrary.wiley.com. Illus., index, adv. Sample. Refereed. Vol. ends: Feb/Nov. Microform: PQC. Reprint: PSC. *Indexed:* A22, ATI, B01, BLI, BRI, E01, EconLit, IBSS. *Bk. rev.:* 1-5, 2-4 pages. *Aud.:* Ac, Sa.

A classic in the field of macroeconomics, this widely read and cited journal presents "major findings in the study of monetary and fiscal policy, credit markets, money and banking, portfolio management, and related subjects." Recent articles include titles such as "The Interaction of Monetary and Macroprudential Policies" and "The Role of Durables Replacement and Second-Hand Markets in a Business-Cycle Model." A section called "Shorter Papers, Discussions, and Letters" is for quickly publishing concise new results, models, and methods. The journal provides an online data archive for papers' empirical findings. Both JSTOR and Project Muse have archives. Recommended for libraries catering to policy makers, professional and academic economists, and bankers.

1813. *Journal of Political Economy.* [ISSN: 0022-3808] 1892. m. USD 787. Ed(s): Harald Uhlig. University of Chicago Press, 1427 E 60th St, Chicago, IL 60637; custserv@press.uchicago.edu; http://www.journals.uchicago.edu. Illus., index, adv. Sample. Refereed. Vol. ends: Dec. Reprint: PSC. *Indexed:* A22, B01, BAS, BRI, C45, CBRI, ERIC, EconLit, IBSS, MLA-IB, P61. *Bk. rev.:* 1-2, 2-4 pages. *Aud.:* Ac, Sa.

One of the most prestigious economic journals, the *Journal of Political Economy* publishes "analytical, interpretive, and empirical studies" in such traditional areas as monetary theory, fiscal policy, labor economics, planning and development, micro- and macroeconomics theory, international trade and finance, industrial organization, the history of economic thought, and social economics. Authors are from international academic institutions and government agencies, including the Federal Reserve Board. Each issue is composed of five or six articles, occasionally followed by review articles, comments, and book reviews. In January 2020, the journal will be moving to a monthly publication schedule. It would be wise for academic and larger public libraries to subscribe to this publication.

Journal of Risk and Insurance. See Business and Finance/Insurance section.

Journal of Transport Economics and Policy. See Transportation section.

1814. *Kyklos: international review for social sciences.* [ISSN: 0023-5962] 1947. q. GBP 688. Ed(s): Bruno Frey, Rene L Frey. Wiley-Blackwell Publishing Ltd., The Atrium, Southern Gate, Chichester, PO19 8QG, United Kingdom; cs-journals@wiley.com; http://www.wiley.com/. Illus., index, adv. Sample. Refereed. Vol. ends: Nov. Microform: PQC. Reprint: PSC. *Indexed:* A01, A22, B01, BAS, BRI, E01, EconLit, IBSS. *Bk. rev.:* 15-20, 550-1,600 words. *Aud.:* Ga, Ac, Sa.

This interdisciplinary journal is widely recognized around the world, and published by an international nonprofit organization whose main purpose is "to analyze socio-economic problems of our time and to bridge the gap between scholarship and economic policy makers by means of public conferences and publications." Recent issues include such disparate inquiries as "Join to Prosper? An Empirical Analysis of EU Membership and Economic Growth" and "Why Female Decision-Makers Shy Away from Promoting Competition." Recommended for public and academic libraries catering to researchers, economists, sociologists, policy makers, and students.

1815. *Land Economics.* Formerly (until 1948): *The Journal of Land and Public Utility Economics.* [ISSN: 0023-7639] 1925. q. USD 484 print & online eds. Ed(s): Daniel J. Phaneuf. University of Wisconsin Press, Journals Division, 1930 Monroe St, 3rd Fl, Madison, WI 53711; journals@uwpress.wisc.edu; http://www.uwpress.org. Illus., index, adv. Refereed. Vol. ends: Nov. Microform: PQC. Reprint: PSC. *Indexed:* A22, Agr, B01, BAS, BRI, C45, EconLit, IBSS, S25. *Bk. rev.:* 1-2, 1-6 pages. *Aud.:* Ac, Sa.

Launched in 1925 by Richard Ely, the founder of the American Economic Association, the journal covers topics such as "environmental quality, natural resources, housing, urban and rural land use, transportation, and other areas in both developed and developing country contexts." Recent articles include "Fire, Tractors, and Health in the Amazon: A Cost-Benefit Analysis of Fire Policy" and "Timberland Investment under Both Financial and Biophysical Risk." Highly recommended for scholars and economists in government, business, and finance, as well as academic and special libraries.

Meridians. See Gender Studies section.

1816. *National Institute Economic Review.* [ISSN: 0027-9501] 1959. q. Ed(s): Jagjit Chadha. Cambridge University Press, University Printing House, Shaftesbury Rd, Cambridge, CB2 8BS, United Kingdom; online@cambridge.org; https://www.cambridge.org. Illus., index, adv. Sample. Refereed. Reprint: PSC. *Indexed:* A22, B01, BRI, C42, E01, EconLit, IBSS. *Aud.:* Ga, Ac, Sa.

This periodical was established in 1959 and is from one of Britain's oldest established independent economic research institutes. It covers quantitative research that illustrates a "deeper understanding of the interaction of economic and social forces that affect peoples' lives so that they may be improved." The institute receives no funding from private or public sources. There are five basic sections: "Forecast Summaries," "Commentary," "The World Economy," "The UK Economy," and "Research Articles." Strongly recommended for libraries with large economics collections or those that support international studies.

National Tax Journal. See Accounting and Taxation/Taxation section.

1817. *O E C D Observer.* [ISSN: 0029-7054] 1962. 4x/yr. EUR 100 (print & online eds.)). Organisation for Economic Cooperation and Development (O E C D), 2 Rue Andre Pascal, Paris, 75775 Cedex 16, France; sales@oecd.org; http://www.oecd.org. Illus., index, adv. Vol. ends: Dec/Jan. *Indexed:* A22, B01, BRI, EIP, HRIS, PdeR. *Bk. rev.:* 1-2. *Aud.:* Ga, Ac.

The Organisation for Economic Co-operation and Development (OECD), an international organization composed of 30 member-countries, "is a unique forum permitting governments of the industralised democracies to study and formulate the best policies possible in all economic and social spheres." In contributing to this goal, it "collects and analyses a unique body of data that allows comparison of statistics across countries and provides macro-micro economic research and policy advice in fields that mirror policy-making ministries in governments." Other excellent OECD publications include *OECD Foreign Trade Statistics, OECD Main Economic Indicators, OECD Economic*

Studies, and *OECD Economic Outlook*. The *OECD Observer* is written for a popular audience. It has a wealth of information on the member countries, and also covers transitional economies, dynamic nonmember economies, and the developing world. The journal has a wide scope, encompassing "economic growth, labour markets, education, social policy, demography, industry, services, energy, finance trade, fiscal policy, public-sector management, environment, science and technology, investment and multinational enterprises, transport, agriculture and fisheries, taxation, competition and consumer policy, research and development, urban affairs, telecommunications, tourism, and rural development." Every issue has an editorial, articles on a theme, and additional titles. A very useful feature is the two to six pages of current statistics on the GDP, the consumer price index, and the leading indicators. Highly recommended for academic and public libraries.

Post-Communist Economies. See Slavic and Eurasian Studies section.

Post-Soviet Affairs. See Slavic and Eurasian Studies section.

1818. *The Quarterly Journal of Economics.* [ISSN: 0033-5533] 1886. q. EUR 623. Oxford University Press, 2001 Evans Rd, Cary, NC 27513; orders.us@oup.com; https://academic.oup.com/journals. Illus., index, adv. Refereed. Vol. ends: Nov. Microform: PQC. Reprint: PSC. *Indexed:* A22, B01, BAS, C45, E01, EconLit, IBSS. *Aud.:* Ac, Sa.

The Quarterly Journal of Economics is the second most highly cited of 344 economic journals in the social science edition of the database Journal Citation Reports. It is edited at Harvard University's Department of Economics, and one of its editors, Robert Barro, is considered one of the founders of new classical macroeconomics. A typical issue has ten lengthy articles, which are sometimes controversial and always interesting. The authors are leading American economists, often affiliated with Harvard. This prestigious journal is essential for libraries that serve professionals, academic economists, and students of economics.

1819. *The RAND Journal of Economics.* Former titles (until 1984): *Bell Journal of Economics;* (until 1975): *Bell Journal of Economics and Management Science.* [ISSN: 0741-6261] 1970. q. GBP 355 (print & online eds.)). Ed(s): James R Hosek. Wiley-Blackwell Publishing, Inc., 111 River St, Hoboken, NJ 07030; info@wiley.com; http://www.wiley.com/. Illus., index, adv. Sample. Refereed. Vol. ends: Winter. Microform: PQC. Reprint: PSC. *Indexed:* A22, B01, BRI, C45, E01, EconLit, HRIS, IBSS. *Aud.:* Ac, Sa.

Published by the RAND Corporation, this journal supports and encourages research on "the behavior of regulated industries, the economic analysis of organizations, and applied microeconomics." Empirical and theoretical papers in law and economics are accepted, and authors are usually connected to American universities. Recent articles of note include "The price effects of cross-market mergers: theory and evidence from the hospital industry" and "Dynamic financial contracting with persistent private information." Each issue typically contains about 13 articles arranged around a broad theme; there may be symposium papers as well. Highly recommended for large academic, government, business, and public libraries.

The Review of Financial Studies. See Business and Finance/Scholarly section.

1820. *Review of World Economics.* Formerly (until 2003): *Weltwirtschaftliches Archiv.* [ISSN: 1610-2878] 1914. q. EUR 370 (print & online eds.)). Springer, Tiergartenstr 17, Heidelberg, 69121, Germany. Illus., index, adv. Refereed. Vol. ends: No. 4. Reprint: PSC. *Indexed:* A22, B01, BAS, BRI, C42, E01, EconLit, IBSS. *Bk. rev.:* 10-16, 700-2,100 words. *Aud.:* Ac, Sa.

Internationally renowned and affiliated with the esteemed Kiel Institute for the World Economy, *Review of World Economics* focuses on international economics. Topics include "research in trade and trade policies, foreign direct investment, global supply chains, migration, international finance, currency systems and exchange rates, [and] monetary and fiscal policies in open economies." Contributing authors tend to be well-known scholars; recent articles include "Accumulation of reserves in emerging and developing countries: mercantilism versus insurance" and "Does corruption matter for sources of foreign direct investment?" Each issue has six or seven articles, shorter papers, comments, reports, book reviews, and announcements of new books. An excellent choice for international economists and graduate students.

Theory and Decision. See Philosophy section.

Transitions Online. See Slavic and Eurasian Studies section.

1821. *The World Bank Economic Review.* [ISSN: 0258-6770] 1986. 3x/yr. EUR 361. Oxford University Press, 2001 Evans Rd, Cary, NC 27513; https://academic.oup.com/journals. Illus. Sample. Refereed. Microform: PQC. Reprint: PSC. *Indexed:* A22, B01, BAS, C45, E01, EconLit, IBSS, P61. *Aud.:* Ac, Sa.

The World Bank Economic Review "encourage[s] and support[s] research in the field of development economics," and in particular is a good source for World Bank-sponsored research on development economics. Its international readers are "economists and social scientists in government, business, international universities, and development research institutions," and policy is emphasized over theoretical or methodological issues. Recent articles include "The Effect of Compulsory Schooling Expansion on Mothers? Attitudes Toward Domestic Violence in Turkey" and "Saving Water with a Nudge (or Two): Evidence from Costa Rica on the Effectiveness and Limits of Low-Cost Behavioral Interventions on Water Use." Recommended for academic libraries and larger public libraries.

1822. *The World Bank Research Observer.* [ISSN: 0257-3032] 1986. s-a. EUR 267. Ed(s): Peter Lanjouw. Oxford University Press, Great Clarendon St, Oxford, OX2 6DP, United Kingdom; onlinequeries.uk@oup.com; http://global.oup.com. Illus., adv. Sample. Microform: CIS; PQC. Reprint: PSC. *Indexed:* A22, B01, E01, EconLit, IBSS. *Aud.:* Ga, Ac, Sa.

The World Bank Research Observer is written for nonspecialist readers, and covers "research being undertaken within the Bank and outside the Bank in areas of economics relevant for development policy." Articles are not refereed, but are assessed and vetted by the editorial board. Highly recommended for public and academic libraries.

■ EDUCATION

General, K-12/Comparative Education and International/Educational Psychology and Measurement, Special Education, Counseling/Higher Education/Specific Subjects and Teaching Methods

See also Classroom Magazines; and Parenting sections.

Nicole Arnold, Education Librarian, University of California Irvine, Irvine, CA 92623; nsarnold@uci.edu

Amanda Melilli, Head, Teacher Development and Resources Library, University Libraries, University of Nevada Las Vegas, Las Vegas, NV 89154; amanda.melilli@unlv.edu

Samantha Godbey, Education Librarian, University Libraries, University of Nevada Las Vegas, Las Vegas, NV 89154; samantha.godbey@unlv.edu

Introduction

Resources abound for those who are looking to affect policy, study pedagogy, and gain new skills and knowledge to freshen up their own classroom practices. However, with the budget constraints that many libraries continue to face, the goal of this section was to highlight only the pre-eminent and essential publications.

With the field finding itself more interdisciplinary and diverse than ever before, this section has something for everyone whether they be scholars in pursuit of highly theoretical papers or school teachers looking for tips on classroom management. The selections have a broad disciplinary and age range, with each major or subject, such as math, art, history, and English, represented in at least one of these highly regarded and well-circulated publications. Journals and magazines that focus on student ability and disability topics too, have been carefully selected. In addition to subject-based and ability-focused publications, a number of comparative and international journals and magazines have been included in order to better demonstrate and monitor how the field is changing across the globe. Other journals focus on educational psychology and measurement, counseling, policies, and administration at K-12 and higher education institutions. Schools outside of the public sphere are also covered, whether they be private Catholic, urban, independent, or home schools. The scholarly journals, many of which are peer reviewed, contain evidence-based studies, literature reviews, analyses, and theoretical papers. From time to time, book and media reviews can also be located within these scholarly journals. The popular journals are written and designed in an aesthetically pleasing and thoughtful manner and include articles focusing on tip and resource sharing, lesson planning, policy discussions, and current events in education.

Nearly all of the journals listed here have online editions plus hard copies available, with some of them also being open access.

Basic Periodicals

Ems (teachers): *The Elementary School Journal, Middle School Journal, The Reading Teacher, School Arts;* Hs (teachers): *The American Biology Teacher, History Teacher*; Ga: *Change, The Education Digest, Phi Delta Kappan*; Ac: *The Chronicle of Higher Education, Harvard Educational Review, Teachers College Record.*

Basic Abstracts and Indexes

ERIC.

General, K-12

1823. *American Educational Research Journal.* [ISSN: 0002-8312] 1964. bi-m. USD 1284 (print & online eds.)). Sage Publications, Inc., 2455 Teller Rd, Thousand Oaks, CA 91320; info@sagepub.com; http://www.sagepub.com. Illus., adv. Sample. Refereed. Vol. ends: Winter. Reprint: PSC. *Indexed:* A22, Chicano, E01, ERIC. *Bk. rev.:* Number and length vary. *Aud.:* Ac.

Within each issue, articles are published in two sections under separate editorships and editorial boards: "Social and Institutional Analysis" and "Teaching, Learning, and Human Development." This journal addresses an audience of researchers, practitioners, and policymakers from many disciplines, and its articles are lengthy and substantive, generally about 30 pages long, representing the publication's stated focus on original empirical and theoretical studies and analyses in education. In the first section, the research centers on major political, cultural, social, economic, and organizational issues in education. This section is followed by articles that examine various aspects of teaching, learning, and human development in different types of educational settings. Approximately six articles per issue provide in-depth research findings and analyses with extensive notes, tables, figures, and references. An essential resource for advanced undergraduates, graduate students, and academics. URL: www.aera.net/Publications/Journals/iAmericanEducationalResearchJournali/tabid/12607/Default.aspx

1824. *The Clearing House: a journal of educational strategies, issues, and ideas.* Former titles (until 1936): *Junior-Senior High School Clearing House;* (until 1929): *The Junior High Clearing House;* (until 1928): *The Junior High School Clearing House;* (until 1923): *The Junior High Clearing House.* [ISSN: 0009-8655] 1920. bi-m. GBP 175 (print & online eds.)). Ed(s): Thomas R McDaniel, Pamela B Childers. Routledge, 530 Walnut St, Ste 850, Philadelphia, PA 19106; enquiries@tandfonline.com; http://www.tandfonline.com. Illus., index, adv. Refereed. Reprint: PSC. *Indexed:* A01, A22, BRI, E01, ENW, ERIC, MLA-IB. *Aud.:* Ac.

This peer-reviewed journal is geared toward middle and high school teachers and administrators, with articles authored by academicians, administrators, and consultants in the field. Articles focus on reporting successful school practices as well as occasional theoretical pieces. Emphasis is placed on instructional techniques, leadership, administrative procedures, school programs, and teacher education, with recent topics including teacher attitudes, youth culture in the classroom, teacher self-efficacy and retention, practical strategies for teaching in inclusive environments, mentoring novice teachers, and online instruction. Recommended for academic and school libraries with resources for educators. URL: www.tandfonline.com/loi/vtch20

1825. *Curriculum Review.* Former titles (until 1976): *C A S Review;* (until 1975): *C S Review.* [ISSN: 0147-2453] 1960. m. USD 169. Ed(s): Jessica Polledri. PaperClip Communications, 125 Paterson Ave, Little Falls, NJ 07424; info@paper-clip.com; http://www.paper-clip.com. Illus., adv. Sample. Vol. ends: Sep/May. Microform: PQC. *Indexed:* A01, A22, BRI, CBRI, ERIC, MLA-IB. *Bk. rev.:* Varies by issue. *Aud.:* Ga, Ac.

This is a practical report issued monthly during the school year. It provides teachers and administrators with examples of successful school programs and initiatives. Recent topics have included the implementation of recycling programs, bus drivers and their relationships with students, top three ways for kids to show friendship at school, 3D printers, and school lunches. Columns include highlights of schools successfully using technology to solve problems, positive stories involving teachers and students, and examples of successful school programs. A section on resources for the classroom provides an abstract of useful books for students. Recommended for public, academic, and school libraries with resources for educators. URL: www.curriculumreview.com/

1826. *Early Childhood Education Journal.* Formerly (until 1995): *Day Care and Early Education.* [ISSN: 1082-3301] 1973. 6x/yr. EUR 1589 (print & online eds.)). Ed(s): Mary Renck Jalongo. Springer Netherlands, Van Godewijckstraat 30, Dordrecht, 3311 GX, Netherlands; http://www.springer.com. Illus., adv. Sample. Refereed. Vol. ends: Summer. Microform: PQC. Reprint: PSC. *Indexed:* A01, A22, BRI, CBRI, Chicano, E01, ERIC. *Bk. rev.:* 1-5, 50-500 words; signed. *Aud.:* Ac, Sa.

Intended for early childhood practitioners such as classroom teachers and child-care providers, this peer-reviewed publication focuses on the education and care of young children from birth through age eight. The journal publishes articles that address the issues, trends, policies, and practices of the field. Contributors have covered topics of curriculum, child care programs, administration, staff development, family and school relationships, equity issues, multicultural units, health nutrition, facilities, special needs, employer sponsored care, infant toddler programs, child development, advocacy, and more. Highly recommended for academic libraries that serve education programs and for libraries that serve early childhood professional institutions or organizations. URL: http://link.springer.com/journal/10643

1827. *Education and Urban Society: an independent quarterly journal of social research.* [ISSN: 0013-1245] 1968. 9x/yr. USD 1809 (print & online eds.)). Sage Publications, Inc., 2455 Teller Rd, Thousand Oaks, CA 91320; info@sagepub.com; http://www.sagepub.com. Illus., index, adv. Sample. Refereed. Vol. ends: Aug. Reprint: PSC. *Indexed:* A01, A22, ASSIA, Chicano, E01, ERIC, IBSS, SSA. *Aud.:* Ac, Sa.

This peer-reviewed journal provides a multidisciplinary forum for research articles focused on the role of education in society. The intended audience includes school board members, sociologists, educational administrators, urban anthropologists, political scientists, and other professionals in fields aligned with education. The emphasis is on current issues in the field and new ideas regarding educational practices. The relationship between society and the educator is emphasized. Topics addressed have included: religion and the politics of education, privatization in public education, America's changing demographics and the educational policy implications, as well as educating homeless students in urban settings. Highly recommended for academic libraries with resources for educators. URL: http://eus.sagepub.com

1828. *The Education Digest: essential readings condensed for quick review.* [ISSN: 0013-127X] 1935. 9x/yr. USD 58 domestic; USD 78 foreign. Prakken Publications, Inc., 832 Phoenix Dr, Ann Arbor, MI 48107. Illus., index, adv. Sample. Microform: PQC. *Indexed:* A01, A22, BRI, C37, ERIC. *Bk. rev.:* 2-3, length varies. *Aud.:* Ga, Ac.

This publication provides a condensation of current articles found in a wide variety of publications, allowing educators, students, and other interested readers an opportunity to review current issues in education in one place. Topics include teacher and school diversity, at-risk students, school culture, social justice, instructional technology, and education reform. It also covers the latest reports on state and federal education policy. In addition, there are regularly published book/media reviews. Recommended for public, academic, and school libraries with resources for educators. URL: www.eddigest.com

1829. *Education Finance and Policy.* [ISSN: 1557-3060] 2005. q. USD 432 (print & online eds.)). M I T Press, One Rogers St, Cambridge, MA 02142-1209; journals-cs@mit.edu; http://mitpress.mit.edu/. Adv. Refereed. *Indexed:* A22, E01, ERIC, EconLit. *Aud.:* Ac.

This publication, the official journal of the Association for Education Finance and Policy, includes scholarly articles to inform research and policy in the area of education finance. Articles present theoretical, statistical, and qualitative research from many different viewpoints. Most articles focus on the K-12 system, but some explore issues in early childhood or higher education. Recent topics have included school accountability, school choice, education standards, equity and adequacy in school finance within and across school and district resource allocation, teacher compensation, training and labor markets, instructional policy, higher education productivity and finance, and special education. Policy briefs have focused on current education issues such as student debt, the fiscal impacts of charter schools, early childhood education, and educational resource equity. Recommended for academic and research institutions. URL: www.mitpressjournals.org/efp

1830. *Education Policy Analysis Archives.* [ISSN: 1068-2341] 1993. a. Free. Ed(s): Gustavo E Fischman. Arizona State University, Mary Lou Fulton Teachers College, PO Box 37100, Phoenix, AZ 85069; education@asu.edu; http://education.asu.edu. Refereed. *Indexed:* ERIC. *Aud.:* Ga, Sa.

A peer-reviewed, open-access journal that publishes articles on educational policy at all educational levels worldwide. Articles are in Spanish, Portuguese, or English. Single-article issues are published at roughly weekly intervals, in addition to longer special issues on specific issues in educational policy. Special issues cover topics such as school accountability, special education, Teach for America, and school curriculum. The journal will be of interest to researchers, practitioners, policymakers, and development analysts. Highly recommended for academic libraries. URL: http://epaa.asu.edu/ojs/

1831. *Education Week: American education's newspaper of record.* [ISSN: 0277-4232] 1981. 37x/yr. USD 89.94 domestic; USD 135.94 combined subscription Canada (print & online eds.); USD 208.84 combined subscription elsewhere (print & online eds.)). Ed(s): Anthony Rebora, Ms. Virginia B Edwards. Editorial Projects in Education Inc., 6935 Arlington Rd, Ste 100, Bethesda, MD 20814-5233; http://www.edweek.org. Illus., index, adv. Sample. Vol. ends: Aug. *Indexed:* A01, A22, BRI, ERIC. *Aud.:* Ga, Ac.

This weekly provides full coverage of state and national education news in a newspaper format. There are articles on current topics and issues in the field, information about recent education reports, profiles and interviews, and weekly commentaries. It contains letters to the editor; events listings; advertisements, including for books and curriculum products and services; and job postings. From time to time, there is an in-depth report that appears as a series. *EW* also provides several special issues, such as the yearly review of education in the 50 states, *Quality Counts*. This is essential weekly reading for graduate education students, educators, and administrators in the field. Highly recommended for school, public, and academic libraries. URL: www.edweek.org

1832. *Educational Administration Quarterly: the journal of leadership for effective & equitable organizations.* [ISSN: 0013-161X] 1964. 5x/yr. USD 1255 (print & online eds.)). Sage Publications, Inc., 2455 Teller Rd, Thousand Oaks, CA 91320; info@sagepub.com; http://www.sagepub.com. Illus., index, adv. Sample. Refereed. Vol. ends: Nov. Microform: PQC. Reprint: PSC. *Indexed:* A01, A22, E01, ERIC. *Bk. rev.:* 0-3, essay length. *Aud.:* Ac, Sa.

This peer-reviewed, scholarly journal consists of empirical investigations, conceptual and theoretical perspectives, policy and legal analyses, reviews of research and practice, and analyses of methodology related to broad concepts of leadership and policy issues of educational organizations. The editors are especially interested in papers on educational leadership; governance and reform in colleges of education; teaching of educational administration; and the professional preparation of educational administrators. Faculty, principals, and teachers, national and international, have contributed research articles on topics such as instructional coaching, responsible leadership, and school segregation. Articles are lengthy, generally 30 to 40 pages, with extensive references, tables, and figures. Some issues have a book review or review essay. Each year, *EAQ* grants the William J. Davis Award to the author of the most outstanding scholarly article published in the journal in the previous year. This social justice in principal preparation programs title is published in cooperation with the University Council for Educational Administration. Highly recommended for academic and school libraries. URL: http://eaq.sagepub.com

1833. *Educational Assessment, Evaluation and Accountability.* Formerly (until 2008): *Journal of Personnel Evaluation in Education.* [ISSN: 1874-8597] 1987. q. EUR 734 (print & online eds.)). Ed(s): Karen Edge. Springer Netherlands, Van Godewijckstraat 30, Dordrecht, 3311 GX, Netherlands; http://www.springer.com. Illus., index, adv. Sample. Refereed. Vol. ends: Dec. Reprint: PSC. *Indexed:* A22, E01, ERIC. *Aud.:* Ac, Sa.

This peer-reviewed, scholarly journal offers discussion and analyses of current issues, programs, and research on evaluation, assessment, and accountability in education settings, both national and international. This journal encourages studies that focus on the theory, research, values, and practice of evaluation and assessment pertaining to K-12 teachers, students, administrators, support personnel, and faculty in colleges and universities. Recommended for academic libraries. URL: www.springer.com/education+&+language/journal/11092

1834. *Educational Evaluation & Policy Analysis.* [ISSN: 0162-3737] 1979. q. USD 548 (print & online eds.)). Sage Publications, Inc., 2455 Teller Rd, Thousand Oaks, CA 91320; info@sagepub.com; http://www.sagepub.com. Illus., adv. Sample. Refereed. Vol. ends: Winter. Microform: PQC. Reprint: PSC. *Indexed:* A22, E01, ERIC. *Bk. rev.:* Varies, 0-2, 500-1,200 words. *Aud.:* Ac.

This peer-reviewed journal of the American Educational Research Association publishes theoretical and practical articles for the interest and benefit of researchers involved in educational evaluation, decision making, or policy analysis. In brief, the editorial instructions for submission indicate that contributions should include economic, demographic, financial, and political analyses of education policies; syntheses of policy studies, evaluation theories, and methodologies; results of important evaluation efforts; and overviews of evaluation studies. Book reviews are also included. Articles are generally approximately 20 pages long, with extensive references. An important resource for academic libraries. URL: http://epa.sagepub.com

1835. *Educational Leadership.* Formed by the merger of (1928-1943): *Educational Method;* Which was formerly (1921-1928): *Journal of Educational Method;* (1935-1943): *Curriculum Journal;* Which was formerly (1930-1935): *News Bulletin.* [ISSN: 0013-1784] 1943. 8x/yr. Free to members; USD 47 combined subscription (print & online eds.)). Ed(s): Marge Scherer. Association for Supervision and Curriculum Development, 1703 N Beauregard St, Alexandria, VA 22311; member@ascd.org; http://www.ascd.org. Illus., adv. Circ: 160000. Vol. ends: May. Microform: PQC. *Indexed:* A01, A22, BRI, C37, CBRI, Chicano, ERIC, MASUSE, MLA-IB. *Bk. rev.:* 5, 300 words. *Aud.:* Ga, Ac, Sa.

This magazine's focus is on educators with leadership roles in elementary, middle, secondary, and higher education and all those with an interest in curriculum, instruction, supervision, leadership, and new trends and practices. Authored by teachers, administrators, higher education faculty, and other professionals in the field, articles and essays (generally three to six pages) are organized under such themes as the principalship; faces of poverty; technology-rich learning; the Common Core; and teacher evaluation. Departments include a section on perspectives written by the editor, a research feature that provides an article/commentary, book reviews, letters to the editor, a principal's column, and descriptions of useful websites. Each issue contains a wide selection of illustrated and referenced articles, and advertisements of interest to teachers and administrators. An important resource for academic, public, and school libraries. URL: www.ascd.org/publications/educational-leadership.aspx

1836. *Educational Researcher.* [ISSN: 0013-189X] 1972. 9x/yr. USD 686 (print & online eds.)). Ed(s): Vivian L Gadsden, Carolyn D Herrington. Sage Publications, Inc., 2455 Teller Rd, Thousand Oaks, CA 91320; info@sagepub.com; http://www.sagepub.com. Illus., index, adv. Sample. Refereed. Vol. ends: Dec. Microform: PQC. Reprint: PSC. *Indexed:* A22, E01, ERIC, MLA-IB. *Aud.:* Ac.

This journal of the American Educational Research Association (AERA) publishes scholarly articles of "general significance to the education research community." The journal consists of featured research articles, research reviews or essays, and briefs. The features section contains articles that may report, analyze, or synthesize research inquiries or explore developments of importance to the field of research in education. Responses to articles within an issue may appear in the form of "commentaries," offering a dialogue that highlights divergent approaches and interpretations. Book reviews are included in most issues, as well as some reviews of multimedia, websites, and so on. This title provides AERA news, with annual meeting highlights, council minutes, and meeting events. Contains advertisements for job openings. Occasional special issues cover topics such as value-added measures. An important journal for graduate education students, faculty, and researchers in the field. URL: http://edr.sagepub.com

1837. *Educational Studies.* [ISSN: 0013-1946] 1970. bi-m. GBP 520 (print & online eds.)). Ed(s): Stephanie L Daza, Roland Sintos Coloma. Routledge, 530 Walnut St, Ste 850, Philadelphia, PA 19106; enquiries@tandfonline.com; http://www.tandfonline.com. Illus., index. Sample. Refereed. Microform: PQC. Reprint: PSC. *Indexed:* A01, A22, BRI, CBRI, E01, ERIC, MLA-IB. *Bk. rev.:* Varies by issue. *Aud.:* Ac.

The official journal of the American Educational Studies Association (AESA), *Educational Studies* brings a critical, multidisciplinary approach to the disciplines of social and educational foundations, with research articles, media reviews, essays on pedagogical issues, and other creative works relevant to these disciplines. Articles may focus on teaching within this field, analyze research methodologies, or report on significant findings. Articles have discussed qualitative research in education; images of people in textbooks; community building in social justice work; and the socialist revolution. The time-exposure section provides a glimpse of a historically interesting image, illustration, or publication. Two special-theme issues per year address topics such as postcolonial education and eco-democratic reforms in education. A valuable journal for undergraduate and graduate education students and faculty. URL: www.educationalstudies.org/publications.html

1838. *Educational Theory: a medium of expression.* [ISSN: 0013-2004] 1951. bi-m. GBP 310. Ed(s): Joyce Atkinson, Chris C Higgins. Wiley-Blackwell Publishing, Inc., 111 River St, Hoboken, NJ 07030; http://onlinelibrary.wiley.com. Illus., index, adv. Refereed. Circ: 1455 Paid. Vol. ends: Fall. Microform: PQC. Reprint: PSC. *Indexed:* A01, A22, BRI, CBRI, E01, ERIC, MLA-IB. *Bk. rev.:* 1-3, essay length. *Aud.:* Ac.

Founded by the John Dewey Society and the Philosophy of Education Society, this journal fosters ongoing development of educational theory and discussion of theoretical problems in the education profession. *ET* publishes scholarly articles on the educational foundations of education and related disciplines that contribute to the advancement of educational theory, as well as book reviews. Issues may present articles on a single theme, or there may be a collection of articles on a variety of topics. Symposium issues have guest editors who focus on the special topic—for example, Cheating Education. The "Afterwords" section provides authors' essay-length responses to previously published book reviews. Recommended for academic libraries. URL: http://onlinelibrary.wiley.com/journal/10.1111/(ISSN)1741-5446

1839. *The Elementary School Journal.* Former titles (until 1914): *The Elementary School Teacher;* (until 1902): *The Elementary School Teacher and Course of Study;* (until 1901): *The Course of Study.* [ISSN: 0013-5984] 1900. q. USD 281. Ed(s): Jeanne Wanzek, Michael Coyne. University of Chicago Press, 1427 E 60th St, Chicago, IL 60637; subscriptions@press.uchicago.edu; http://www.journals.uchicago.edu. Illus., index, adv. Sample. Refereed. Reprint: PSC. *Indexed:* A01, A22, Chicano, ERIC, MLA-IB. *Aud.:* Ac.

This peer-reviewed journal publishes articles that focus on educational theory/research and their implications for teaching elementary and middle school. Articles that relate research in child development, cognitive psychology, and sociology to school learning and teaching are also included. This publication is directed toward an audience of researchers, teacher educators, and practitioners. Recently published topics have included function-based interventions in K-8 general education settings, the effects of symbolic and nonsymbolic equal-sign intervention, and the quality of mathematics instruction in Kindergarten. A major title for academic and school libraries with resources for educators. URL: www.press.uchicago.edu/ucp/journals/journal/esj.html

Gender and Education. See Gender Studies section.

1840. *Harvard Educational Review.* Formerly (until 1937): *The Harvard Teachers Record.* [ISSN: 0017-8055] 1931. q. USD 410 (print & online eds.) Individuals, USD 59 (print & online eds.)). Harvard University, Graduate School of Education, 8 Story St, 1st Fl, Cambridge, MA 02138; HEPG@harvard.edu; http://www.gse.harvard.edu. Illus., index. Refereed. Vol. ends: Nov. Microform: PQC. *Indexed:* A01, A22, BAS, BRI, CBRI, Chicano, ERIC, MLA-IB. *Bk. rev.:* Number and length vary. *Aud.:* Ac.

The *Harvard Educational Review* (*HER*) is a journal of opinion pieces and research articles, focusing on teaching and practice in the United States and in international educational settings. Articles and other contributions are authored by teachers, practitioners, policymakers, scholars, and researchers in education and related fields. Authors have focused on such topics as the ethics of community-based research; the maker movement in education; urban schools; and educating diverse students. It contains book reviews of recent publications. The journal is published by an editorial board of doctoral students at the Harvard Graduate School of Education. Highly recommended for academic libraries. URL: http://hepg.org/her-home/home

1841. *The High School Journal.* Formerly (until 1918): *The North Carolina High School. Bulletin.* [ISSN: 0018-1498] 1910. bi-m. USD 80 (Individuals, USD 45). Ed(s): Summer Pennell. University of North Carolina Press, 116 S Boundary St, Chapel Hill, NC 27514; uncpress@unc.edu; http://www.uncpress.unc.edu. Illus., index. Sample. Refereed. Circ: 250. Vol. ends: Apr/May. Microform: PQC. Reprint: PSC. *Indexed:* A01, A22, BRI, E01, ERIC. *Bk. rev.:* 1, 500 words. *Aud.:* Ac.

Managed by the students and faculty at the School of Education at the University of North Carolina at Chapel Hill, this journal publishes research, scholarship, essays, and reviews that examine the field of secondary education. Issues contain a collection of topics of interest for teacher educators and other professionals/individuals who are interested in student success in secondary schools. Recently published topics have included teaching students about Islamophobia; college access and inequity; and tracking college for all reform. Recommended for academic and school libraries with resources for educators. URL: http://soe.unc.edu/hsj/

1842. *History of Education Quarterly.* Formerly (until 1961): *History of Education Journal.* [ISSN: 0018-2680] 1949. q. GBP 176. Cambridge University Press, University Printing House, Shaftesbury Rd, Cambridge, CB2 8BS, United Kingdom; journals@cambridge.org; https://www.cambridge.org/. Illus., index, adv. Sample. Refereed. Vol. ends: Winter. Reprint: PSC. *Indexed:* A01, A22, BAS, BRI, E01, ERIC, MLA-IB. *Bk. rev.:* 5-10, 500 words. *Aud.:* Ac.

This publication of the international and scholarly History of Education Society covers topics that span the history of "formal, non-formal and informal" education, including the history of childhood, youth, and the family. The articles are universal in scope and vary greatly in content and time period. There are two or three lengthy articles per issue, in addition to a historiographical essay. Recently published articles focus on the rise and fall of experimental colleges;

school vaccinations; history education; and the practice of school naming. This title offers an average of ten book reviews per issue. A major journal for education historians, and recommended for academic libraries. URL: http://ojs.ed.uiuc.edu/index.php/heq

1843. ***Independent School.*** Former titles (until 1976): *Independent School Bulletin;* (until 1941): *Secondary Education Board. Bulletin.* [ISSN: 0145-9635] 1935. q. Members, USD 32; Non-members, USD 54. Ed(s): Michael Brosnan. National Association of Independent Schools, 1620 L St, NW, Ste 1100, Washington, DC 20036; info@nais.org; http://www.nais.org. Adv. Microform: PQC. *Indexed:* A01, A22, ERIC, MLA-IB. *Bk. rev.:* 2. *Aud.:* Ac, Sa.

Independent School is published to provide an open forum for the exchange of general information about elementary and secondary education in independent schools. Each issue has a theme, including most recently student health and well-being, foundations for student success, and helping students navigate digital lives. This title contains interviews, profiles, opinion pieces, and a book review section. Recommended for public, academic, and school libraries with resources for educators. URL: https://www.nais.org/magazine/independent-school/about-the-magazine/

1844. ***Journal of Classroom Interaction.*** Formerly (until 1976): *Classroom Interaction Newsletter.* [ISSN: 0749-4025] 1965. s-a. USD 49.50 (Individuals, USD 40). Ed(s): Dr. H Jerome Freiberg. Journal of Classroom Interaction, University of Houston College of Education, 442 Farish Halll, Houston, TX 77204; http://www.jciuh.org/. Illus., index. Sample. Refereed. Vol. ends: Winter. *Indexed:* A22, ERIC. *Aud.:* Ac.

This semi-annual journal publishes articles on empirical research and theory that deal with observation techniques, student and teacher behavior, and other issues connected with classroom interaction. Geared for an audience of faculty, practitioners, and education students, this journal has presented a range of investigations and studies authored by national and international researchers and teacher educators. Topics have included time management in classrooms; the impact of teachers' beliefs and behaviors; facilitation of peer discourse; and encouraging student elaboration in discussing texts. Recommended for academic and school libraries with resource for educators. URL: www.jciuh.org/

1845. ***Middle School Journal.*** [ISSN: 0094-0771] 1970. 5x/yr. GBP 87 (print & online eds.)). Ed(s): Dan Bauer, Joanne L Previts. Taylor & Francis Inc., 711 3rd Ave, 8th Fl, New York, NY 10017; support@tandfonline.com; http://www.taylorandfrancis.com. Illus. Sample. Refereed. *Indexed:* A22, ERIC. *Bk. rev.:* No. *Aud.:* Ac., Ga.

The articles in this official journal of the Association for Middle Level Education are focused on middle-level education and the educational and developmental needs of students aged 10 to 15. Written by teacher educators, professionals in the field, and directed at an audience of middle school practitioners, articles report on successful programs or discuss effective practices and research applications. Sometimes, the journal has calls for student submissions. Issues may be thematic or of general interest to the readership. Coverage of topics has included fostering middle school students' autonomy, building sustainable school-wide adolescent literacy, and reading attitudes. This title includes an editorial section. Recommended for school libraries and academic libraries that serve education programs. URL: www.amle.org/ServicesEvents/MiddleSchoolJournal

1846. ***Mind, Brain, and Education.*** [ISSN: 1751-2271] 2007. q. GBP 318 (print & online eds.)). Ed(s): Jay Giedd, David B Daniel. Wiley-Blackwell Publishing, Inc., 111 River St, Hoboken, NJ 07030; http://onlinelibrary.wiley.com. Adv. Sample. Refereed. Reprint: PSC. *Indexed:* A22, E01, ERIC. *Aud.:* Ac.

The International Mind, Brain, and Education Society created this interdisciplinary, peer-reviewed journal that combines education, biology, and cognitive science to introduce the new field of "mind, brain, and education." Articles include basic and applied research on learning and development. This journal targets an audience comprising educators, school personnel, teacher educators, educational policy professionals, and researchers in general, who wish to explore careful, high-quality research and practice-based evaluation relevant to education. Highly recommended for academic and research institutions. URL: http://onlinelibrary.wiley.com/journal/10.1111/(ISSN)1751-228X

1847. ***Peabody Journal of Education.*** Formerly (until 1970?): *Peabody Journal of Education.* [ISSN: 0161-956X] 1923. 5x/yr. GBP 653 (print & online eds.)). Ed(s): Robert Crowson. Routledge, 530 Walnut St, Ste 850, Philadelphia, PA 19106; enquiries@tandfonline.com; http://www.tandfonline.com. Illus., adv. Sample. Refereed. Vol. ends: Summer. Reprint: PSC. *Indexed:* A01, A22, BAS, Chicano, E01, ERIC, MLA-IB, SSA. *Aud.:* Ac.

Peabody Journal of Education seeks to enhance the understanding and practice among institutions and individuals concerned with human learning and development, from early childhood to tertiary education levels and those at vocational schools. Articles are focused primarily on educational research, practice, and policy, with contributions from practitioners, academicians, policy makers, and researchers. Recent topics have included college readiness for English-language learners, Latinx parents' literacy practices, and the politics of local control funding. An important journal for academic libraries. URL: http://peabody.vanderbilt.edu/faculty/pje/

1848. ***Phi Delta Kappan.*** Formerly (until 1916): *National News Letter of Phi Delta Kappa;* Which Superseded (in 1915): *Phi Delta Kappa Inter-Chapter News Letter.* [ISSN: 0031-7217] 1915. 8x/yr. USD 300 (print & online eds.)). Ed(s): Joan Richardson. Sage Publications, Inc., 2455 Teller Rd, Thousand Oaks, CA 91320; info@sagepub.com; http://www.sagepub.com. Illus., index, adv. Sample. Vol. ends: Sep/Jun. Microform: CIS; PQC. *Indexed:* A01, A22, BRI, C37, CBRI, Chicano, ERIC, MLA-IB. *Aud.:* Ga, Ac.

Phi Delta Kappan publishes accessible articles on education research and leadership, with an emphasis on classroom practice, policy, research, professional issues, and innovations in education. Authored by faculty, practitioners, independent researchers, and consultants in the field, articles report on research or provide commentary on topics of concern and interest for educators at all levels. Recent topics have focused on public school financing, handling aggressive parents, and addressing the teacher quality gap across the nation. A section titled "Backtalk" provides an opportunity for readers to submit comments on previously published articles. This publication also publishes a section of cartoons that offer commentary on current topics. Regular columnists contribute to the magazine in columns such as "Washington View" and "ED Law." News from Phi Delta Kappa is also included. An important resource for educators at all levels. URL: www.kappanmagazine.org/

1849. ***Principal (Alexandria).*** Formerly (until Sep.1980): *National Elementary Principal.* [ISSN: 0271-6062] 1921. 5x/yr. Members, USD 35. Ed(s): Vanessa St Gerard. National Association of Elementary School Principals, 1615 Duke St, Alexandria, VA 22314; publications@naesp.org; http://www.naesp.org. Illus., index, adv. Circ: 28000. Vol. ends: May. Microform: PQC. *Indexed:* A22, Chicano, ERIC. *Bk. rev.:* Number and length vary. *Aud.:* Ac.

This journal is published to serve elementary and middle school principals and educators, particularly those who work with children in the K-8 range. Articles are written by teachers, principals, administrators, and other professionals to address current issues and to present ideas and information for practical applications in the schools. Regular columns include feature articles and commentaries for practitioners, parents and schools, the reflective principal, and school law issues. Recent articles have discussed grief support for students, supportive mental health programs, teacher professional development and motivation, engaging parents, safe schools, and digital literacy. Books of interest to principals are also reviewed. Recommended for academic and school libraries with resources for educators. URL: www.naesp.org/publications-0

1850. ***Review of Educational Research.*** [ISSN: 0034-6543] 1931. bi-m. USD 702 (print & online eds.)). Ed(s): Frank C Worrell. Sage Publications, Inc., 2455 Teller Rd, Thousand Oaks, CA 91320; info@sagepub.com; http://www.sagepub.com. Illus., index, adv. Refereed. Vol. ends: Winter. Microform: PMC; PQC. Reprint: PSC. *Indexed:* A01, A22, Chicano, E01, ERIC, MLA-IB. *Aud.:* Ac.

RER, a peer-reviewed journal of the American Educational Research Association, publishes critical reviews of educational research literature on substantive and methodological issues. Reviews of research relevant to education may be from any discipline. Authored by faculty, doctoral students, and professionals in the field, recent articles have reviewed employees' involvement in work-related learning; reading interventions for students with reading disabilities; assessment feedback in higher education; and the effects of school racial composition on K-12 mathematics outcomes. This journal does not publish original empirical research under most circumstances. Highly recommended for academic libraries. URL: http://rer.sagepub.com/

1851. ***Roeper Review: a journal on gifted education.*** [ISSN: 0278-3193] 1978. q. GBP 139 (print & online eds.)). Ed(s): Dr. Don Ambrose. Routledge, 530 Walnut St, Ste 850, Philadelphia, PA 19106; enquiries@tandfonline.com; http://www.tandfonline.com. Illus., index, adv. Sample. Refereed. Vol. ends: Jun. Reprint: PSC. *Indexed:* A01, A22, BRI, Chicano, E01, ERIC. *Bk. rev.:* 2-3 per issue, 200-800 words. *Aud.:* Ac, Sa.

This journal publishes articles that reflect on research, observation, experience, theory, and practice with regard to the growth, emotions, and education of gifted and talented learners. The internationally focused articles seek to put more attention on giftedness, talent development, and creativity. Faculty authors and professionals have written articles that address issues such as theories and philosophical analyses pertinent to giftedness, talent, and creativity; gender issues; curriculum studies; instructional strategies; educational psychology; elementary/early childhood/secondary education of the gifted; emotional, motivation, and affective dimensions of gifted individuals; differentiating instruction; teacher education; tests, measurement, and evaluation; and program development. Some themed issues are published. An interview with a noted person in the field is also included, along with book reviews and a column on timely topics. This is an informative and important journal in gifted education. Recommended for academic libraries that serve education programs. URL: www.roeper.org/Roeper-Review

1852. ***Teachers College Record: the voice of scholarship in education.*** Former titles (until 1970): *Columbia University. Teachers College. The Record;* (until 1967): *Teachers College Record;* Which incorporated (1910-1914): *The Household Arts Review;* Which was formerly (1908-1910): *The Domestic Art Review.* [ISSN: 0161-4681] 1900. m. Free to members; Non-members, USD 145. Ed(s): Lyn Corno. EBSCO Publishing, 10 Estes St, PO Box 682, Ipswich, MA 01938; information@ebsco.com; http://www.ebscohost.com. Illus., index, adv. Sample. Refereed. Microform: MIM; PQC. *Indexed:* A01, A22, BRI, CBRI, Chicano, E01, ERIC, MLA-IB. *Bk. rev.:* 6-8, 750 words. *Aud.:* Ac.

Teachers College Record is a peer-reviewed scholarly journal of research, analysis, and commentary on a broad range of issues and topics in the field of education. Articles have focused on data and education, student perceptions of school justice, curricular development, and educational policy. The journal also publishes themed issues, such as one in a recent issue focused on high-stakes teacher evaluation. One issue is entirely devoted to book reviews, organized topically under administration, assessment and evaluation, curriculum, diversity, early childhood education, higher education, learning, research methods, social context, teacher education, teaching, and technology. Highly recommended for academic libraries. URL: www.tcrecord.org/

1853. ***Theory into Practice.*** Supersedes (in 1962): *Educational Research Bulletin.* [ISSN: 0040-5841] 1922. q. GBP 206 (print & online eds.)). Ed(s): Eric M Anderson. Routledge, 530 Walnut St, Ste 850, Philadelphia, PA 19106; enquiries@tandfonline.com; http://www.tandfonline.com. Illus., index, adv. Sample. Refereed. Microform: PQC. Reprint: PSC. *Indexed:* A01, A22, B01, BRI, E01, ERIC, MLA-IB. *Aud.:* Ac.

Theory into Practice focuses on the important issues in education. Each issue is theme-based and offers a comprehensive overview of the particular education topic, with articles covering all levels and areas of education, including learning and teaching; assessment; educational psychology; teacher education and professional development; classroom management; counseling; administration and supervision; curriculum; policy; and technology. A guest editor with that specific subject expertise develops the theme. Articles authored by faculty and other professionals in the field are directed at an audience of teachers, education researchers, students, professors, and administrators. Recommended for academic libraries that serve education programs. URL: www.tandfonline.com/loi/htip20

1854. ***Today's Catholic Teacher.*** [ISSN: 0040-8441] 1967. bi-m. USD 15.95 domestic (Free to qualified personnel). Ed(s): Mary Noschang, Betsy Shepard. Peter Li Education Group, 2621 Dryden Rd, Ste 300, Dayton, OH 45439; service@peterli.com; http://www.peterli.com. Illus., adv. Sample. Vol. ends: Apr. *Indexed:* A22, C26. *Aud.:* Ga, Sa.

This journal is written for educators in K-12 Catholic schools, with the goal of helping teachers succeed in the classroom. Content is written from a Catholic viewpoint, and each issue contains practical articles that are related to classroom activities and includes news, ideas for class projects, educator resources, and other teaching aids. A column on technology in the classroom and a parent partnership handbook are also included. Topics have included alternatives to science field trips; helping students evaluate information; digital textbooks; bullying; Common Core assessment; and subject-specific lesson plans. This title contains extensive advertising information on products and services for classroom use. Recommended for Catholic school libraries with resources for educators. URL: www.catholicteacher.com/

1855. ***Urban Education.*** [ISSN: 0042-0859] 1966. bi-m. USD 1907 (print & online eds.)). Sage Publications, Inc., 2455 Teller Rd, Thousand Oaks, CA 91320; info@sagepub.com; http://www.sagepub.com. Illus., adv. Sample. Refereed. Vol. ends: Jan. Microform: PQC. Reprint: PSC. *Indexed:* A01, A22, BRI, Chicano, E01, ERIC, SSA. *Bk. rev.:* Number and length vary. *Aud.:* Ac.

This journal provides research and conceptual reviews that examine issues of concern for inner-city schools. Issues are presented from a gender-balanced and racially diverse perspective and contribute to new and expanded knowledge regarding theory, research, and practice in the field. The journal is organized around multiple interdisciplinary areas, including curriculum and instruction, counseling and social services, policy, equity in urban education, leadership and teacher education, psychology and human development, and special education. This title includes book reviews and an editorial. Recommended for academic libraries. URL: http://uex.sagepub.com

1856. ***Voices from the Middle.*** [ISSN: 1074-4762] 1994. q. Members, USD 25; Non-members, USD 75. Ed(s): Shelbie Witte, Sara Kajder. National Council of Teachers of English, 1111 W Kenyon Rd, Urbana, IL 61801-1096; customerservice@ncte.org; http://www.ncte.org. Sample. Refereed. *Indexed:* BRI, ERIC. *Bk. rev.:* Number and length vary. *Aud.:* Ac.

Recognizing that middle school teachers are challenged with "a unique set of circumstances and issues," this journal is dedicated to supporting the middle school language arts teacher. Each issue provides a forum for the sharing of ideas, practices, reflections, solutions, and theories from classroom teachers and others involved with reading, writing, speaking, and listening in the visual and language arts at the middle school level. Each issue has a featured theoretical article, with additional articles focused on classroom practices for sixth through eighth grades. Specifically, this is for middle schools with a professional library, as well as education libraries. URL: www.ncte.org/journals/vm

1857. ***Y C - Young Children.*** Former titles (until 2002): *Young Children;* (until 1964): *Journal of Nursery Education;* (until 1956): *National Association for Nursery Education. Bulletin.* [ISSN: 1538-6619] 1945. 5x/yr. USD 110 (Individuals, USD 70; Free to members). Ed(s): Derry Koralek, Deanna Ramey. National Association for the Education of Young Children, PO Box 97156, Washington, DC 20090; naeyc@naeyc.org; http://www.naeyc.org. Illus., index, adv. Refereed. Vol. ends: Sep. Microform: PQC. *Indexed:* A22, Agr, ERIC, MLA-IB. *Bk. rev.:* 1-8, 400-800 words. *Aud.:* Ga, Ac.

This peer-reviewed journal of the National Association for the Education of Young Children (NAEYC) addresses an audience of teachers and directors of programs involved with children from birth through age eight within child care, preschool, Head Start, and primary-grade settings. It is also directed at teacher educators, local and state decision-makers, and researchers in child development. Practical articles provide ideas for teaching children and administering programs, and scholarly articles refer to current research and theory as a basis for practical recommendations. Articles also describe program changes that have occurred as an outcome of experts' experience and research about how young children learn. Essays discuss important issues and ideas concerning the education, care, and development of young children. Issues include NAEYC organization information, and brief book reviews of professional publications, as well as of children's books. Articles are primarily written in English, with a few being written in Spanish. Recommended for school, public, and academic libraries. URL: www.naeyc.org/yc/

Comparative Education and International

1858. *Australian Journal of Education.* [ISSN: 0004-9441] 1957. 3x/yr. USD 1312 (print & online eds.)). Ed(s): Petra Lietz. Sage Publications Ltd., 1 Oliver's Yard, 55 City Rd, London, EC1Y 1SP, United Kingdom; info@sagepub.com; https://www.sagepub.com/. Illus., index, adv. Sample. Refereed. Vol. ends: Nov. Reprint: PSC. *Indexed:* A01, A22, BRI, ERIC, MLA-IB. *Bk. rev.:* Number and length vary. *Aud.:* Ac.

This journal publishes papers on the theory and practice of education, especially as related to Australia and its neighboring countries. Embracing all fields of education and training, it aims to inform educational researchers as well as educators, administrators, and policymakers about issues of contemporary concern in education. Articles include original research, research reviews, policy analyses, commentary on previously published articles, and occasional book reviews. The authors represent an international corps of scholars from a broad range of disciplines, such as philosophy, psychology, political science, economics, history, anthropology, medicine, and sociology. Recent articles have discussed transitions for students with disabilities in New South Wales, program evaluation, the use of tablets in the classroom and beyond, and the handwriting experiences of left-handed primary school students in Australia. Publication preferences are given to those who utilize quantitative methodologies. Recommended for academic libraries. URL: http://aed.sagepub.com/

1859. *British Educational Research Journal.* Supersedes in part (in 1978): *Research Intelligence.* [ISSN: 0141-1926] 1978. bi-m. GBP 2019 (print & online eds.)). Ed(s): Mark Connolly, Chris Taylor. Wiley-Blackwell Publishing Ltd., The Atrium, Southern Gate, Chichester, PO19 8QG, United Kingdom; cs-journals@wiley.com; http://onlinelibrary.wiley.com. Illus., index, adv. Sample. Refereed. Reprint: PSC. *Indexed:* A01, A22, E01, ERIC, IBSS, MLA-IB. *Bk. rev.:* Number and length vary. *Aud.:* Ac, Sa.

This peer-reviewed publication of the British Educational Research Association (BERJ) is interdisciplinary in its approach and includes reports of case studies, experiments and surveys, discussions of conceptual and methodological issues and of underlying assumptions in educational research, accounts of research in progress, and book reviews. Although scholarly articles primarily focus on British educational research, the journal's scope is international. Articles have examined family and school interactions, the relationship between school expenditures and school performance, improving reasoning skills through working memory training, and student teachers' perceptions of themselves as civic educators. Recommended for academic libraries. URL: www.bera.ac.uk/researchers-resources/publications/british-education-research-journal

1860. *British Journal of Educational Studies.* [ISSN: 0007-1005] 1952. bi-m. GBP 918 (print & online eds.)). Ed(s): Gary McCulloch. Routledge, 4 Park Sq, Milton Park, Abingdon, OX14 4RN, United Kingdom; subscriptions@tandf.co.uk; http://www.tandfonline.com. Illus., index, adv. Sample. Refereed. Circ: 1300. Vol. ends: Nov. Microform: PQC. Reprint: PSC. *Indexed:* A01, A22, BAS, E01, ERIC, IBSS, MLA-IB. *Bk. rev.:* Numerous, around 16 per issue, 500-1,000 words. *Aud.:* Ac.

This peer-reviewed journal publishes scholarly, research-based articles on education, drawing upon historical, philosophical, and sociological analysis and sources. This international education journal from the United Kingdom addresses the wide range of perspectives in the areas of educational philosophy, history, psychology, sociology, management, administration, and comparative studies. Articles are written for an audience of nonspecialists in the field, in keeping with the journal's interest in clearly expressed and nontechnical contributions to scholarship. Articles have discussed participation in higher education, technology-mediated collaborative learning environments for culturally and linguistically diverse children, privatizing of school-based education in England, and educational effects on individual life chances. Annual special issues address topics such as new directions in teacher education; learning and life chances in knowledge economies and societies; education, security, and intelligence studies. Extensive book review section. Recommended for academic libraries. URL: www.soc-for-ed-studies.org.uk/journal/

1861. *British Journal of Sociology of Education.* [ISSN: 0142-5692] 1980. 8x/yr. GBP 2417 (print & online eds.)). Ed(s): David James. Routledge, 4 Park Sq, Milton Park, Abingdon, OX14 4RN, United Kingdom; subscriptions@tandf.co.uk; http://www.tandfonline.com. Illus., index, adv. Sample. Refereed. Reprint: PSC. *Indexed:* A01, A22, ASSIA, E01, ERIC, IBSS, P61, SSA. *Bk. rev.:* Number and length vary. *Aud.:* Ac, Sa.

This peer-reviewed journal publishes high-quality original, theoretically informed analyses of the relationship between education and society. The journal addresses the major global debates on the social impact of educational policy and practice from an international perspective. International academic authors have contributed articles on school choice, widening participation in higher education, and homework for young children. Annual special issues address topics such as the sociologies of elite schooling, educational inclusion, and education and social mobility. Notices of recently completed doctoral theses in the sociology of education are also included. Different types of reviews are included: review articles, book reviews, and review essays. Recommended for academic libraries. URL: www.tandfonline.com/loi/cbse20

1862. *Canadian Journal of Education.* Formerly (until 1976): *Canadian Society for the Study of Education. Bulletin.* [ISSN: 0380-2361] 1974. q. Ed(s): Katy Ellsworth, Rollande Deslandes. Canadian Society for the Study of Education, 260 Dalhousie St, Ste 204, Ottawa, ON K1N 7E4, Canada; csse-scee@csse.ca; http://www.csse-scee.ca. Illus., index. Refereed. Vol. ends: Fall. Microform: PQC. *Indexed:* A22, BRI, C37, C42, ERIC. *Bk. rev.:* 3-7, 600-1,500 words. *Aud.:* Ac.

The Canadian Journal of Education (the CJE) is the peer-reviewed journal of the Canadian Society for the Study of Education. It publishes bilingual articles that are broadly but not exclusively related to Canadian education. Short research notes, discussions on topics, and book reviews are also included. Articles are published either in English or French, with the abstracts in both languages. The journal publishes issues on early, lifelong, and Francophone education, and from rural, aboriginal, cultural, pre-service, and inclusive perspectives. Topics have included teacher perspectives on inclusive classrooms in rural Canada, collaborative teacher inquiry, student persistence in STEM programs, service learning and student engagement, and academic entitlements in the context of learning styles. Authors are required to demonstrate that their writing and article is relevant to Canada's education community. This is an important and well-indexed Canadian education journal. Recommended for academic libraries. URL: http://journals.sfu.ca/cje/index.php/cje-rce

1863. *Chinese Education and Society.* Formerly (until Jan.1993): *Chinese Education.* [ISSN: 1061-1932] 1968. bi-m. GBP 1416 (print & online eds.)). Routledge, 711 3rd Ave, 8th Fl., New York, NY 10017; enquiries@tandfonline.com; http://www.routledge.com. Illus., index, adv. Sample. Refereed. Vol. ends: Nov/Dec. Microform: PQC. Reprint: PSC. *Indexed:* A01, A22, BAS, E01, ERIC. *Aud.:* Ac, Sa.

This journal provides unabridged English translations of important articles on education from Chinese sources, including scholarly journals and collections of articles in book form, as well as refereed research on specific themes. The journal provides insight on educational policy and practice, reform and development, pedagogical theory and methods, higher education, and schools and families. Articles have covered such topics as rethinking the national education reform blueprint, the growth and changes of higher education in Taiwan, basic education curriculum reform and teachers' challenges in China, and a study on entrance exam reform in Shanghai. Each issue is edited by a guest editor with expertise on a particular topic. Recommended for academic libraries. URL: www.tandfonline.com/loi/mced20

1864. ***Comparative Education: an international journal of comparative studies.*** [ISSN: 0305-0068] 1964. q. GBP 1607 (print & online eds.)). Ed(s): David Phillips. Routledge, 4 Park Sq, Milton Park, Abingdon, OX14 4RN, United Kingdom; subscriptions@tandf.co.uk; http://www.tandfonline.com. Illus., index, adv. Sample. Refereed. Vol. ends: Oct. Reprint: PSC. *Indexed:* A01, A22, BAS, E01, ERIC, IBSS, SSA. *Bk. rev.:* Number and length vary. *Aud.:* Ac, Sa.

This international, peer-reviewed research journal provides current information and analyses of significant world problems and trends in the field of education, with particular emphasis on comparative analysis of educational issues in national, international, and global contexts. It also has an interest in the associated disciplines of government, management, sociology, technology, and communications, with a view to the impact of these areas on educational policy decisions. Special issues have examined the opportunities and challenges of religious schools in Europe, knowledge in numbers, and the significance of space, place, and scale in the study of education. Each issue includes an editorial, as well as book reviews. Recommended for academic libraries. URL: www.tandfonline.com/toc/cced20/current

1865. ***Comparative Education Review.*** [ISSN: 0010-4086] 1957. q. USD 392. Ed(s): Bjorn H. Nordtveit. University of Chicago Press, 1427 E 60th St, Chicago, IL 60637; subscriptions@press.uchicago.edu; http://www.journals.uchicago.edu. Illus., index, adv. Sample. Refereed. Vol. ends: Nov. Reprint: PSC. *Indexed:* A01, A22, BAS, BRI, C45, ERIC, SSA. *Bk. rev.:* Multiple, length varies. *Aud.:* Ac.

The official journal of the Comparative and International Education Society (CIES), this peer-reviewed publication seeks to advance knowledge of education policies and practices throughout the world and the teaching of comparative education studies. Articles authored by international faculty and researchers discuss the social, economic, and political forces that shape education throughout the world. In addition to scholarly articles, issues contain book reviews and media reviews. Special issues have addressed topics such as fair access to higher education, and the local and the global in reforming teaching and teacher education. The journal also produces an annual supplemental bibliography of refereed journal articles on topics relevant to comparative and international education. Highly recommended for academic libraries. URL: www.press.uchicago.edu/ucp/journals/journal/cer.html

1866. ***Current Issues in Comparative Education.*** [ISSN: 1523-1615] 1998. s-a. Free. Ed(s): Sandra Sirota. Columbia University, Teachers College, 525 W 120th St, New York, NY 10027; http://www.tc.columbia.edu/. *Indexed:* ERIC. *Bk. rev.:* Varies by issue. *Aud.:* Ac.

An international open-access journal from Teachers College, Columbia University, dedicated to publishing scholarly debate and discussion on educational policies and comparative studies. With academic and practical experience-based contributions, the journal has a wide and diverse audience. Each issue is themed, and generally includes three to five articles and occasional book reviews. Issue topics have included social movements, activism, and education; comparative and international education as a field; education for social change and transformation; and education in small states. Articles are written by professors, researchers, students, advocates, policymakers, and practitioners from around the world. Recommended for academic libraries. URL: www.tc.columbia.edu/cice/

1867. ***Curriculum Inquiry.*** Formerly (until 1976): *Curriculum Theory Network.* [ISSN: 0362-6784] 1971. 5x/yr. GBP 676 (print & online eds.)). Ed(s): Ruben Gaztambide-Fernandez. Routledge, 530 Walnut St, Ste 850, Philadelphia, PA 19106; enquiries@tandfonline.com; http://www.tandfonline.com. Illus., index, adv. Sample. Refereed. Circ: 760 Paid. Vol. ends: Winter. Reprint: PSC. *Indexed:* A01, A22, E01, ERIC. *Bk. rev.:* Varies by issue. *Aud.:* Ac.

This journal, sponsored by the University of Toronto's Ontario Institute for Studies in Education, focuses on curriculum and pedagogy. Within each issue, international authors from a variety of disciplines offer articles on a wide range of issues and topics related to curriculum development, teaching and learning, teacher education, cultural practice, and educational policy. Each issue includes an intentionally provocative editorial essay. Articles have addressed such topics as class mobility in Newbery Award titles; critical literacy among preservice teachers; and peacebuilding in education. Highly recommended for academic libraries that support colleges of education. URL: www.tandfonline.com/loi/rcui20

1868. ***Economics of Education Review.*** [ISSN: 0272-7757] 1981. bi-m. EUR 1895. Elsevier Ltd, The Boulevard, Langford Lane, Oxford, OX5 1GB, United Kingdom; customerserviceau@elsevier.com; http://www.elsevier.com. Illus., adv. Sample. Refereed. Microform: PQC. *Indexed:* A01, A22, B01, BAS, ERIC, EconLit. *Aud.:* Ac.

This peer-reviewed journal provides a forum in which to share ideas and research findings in the economics of education and to create an interaction between economists and scholars interested in decisions surrounding the economics of education. It also seeks to encourage theoretical, empirical, and policy research that points out the role of economic analysis for an improved understanding of educational problems and issues. The articles cover a wide range of topics, are authored by international faculty, and are documented with references, tables, and other data. Recent articles have focused on the economic impact of universities, improving college access and the related barriers and policy responses, and the impact of computer usage on academic performance. Recommended for academic libraries. URL: www.journals.elsevier.com/economics-of-education-review/

1869. ***Educational Research.*** [ISSN: 0013-1881] 1958. q. GBP 572 (print & online eds.)). Ed(s): Felicity Fletcher-Campbell, Frances Brill. Routledge, 4 Park Sq, Milton Park, Abingdon, OX14 4RN, United Kingdom; subscriptions@tandf.co.uk; http://www.tandfonline.com. Illus., index, adv. Sample. Refereed. Vol. ends: Nov. Microform: SWZ. Reprint: PSC. *Indexed:* A01, A22, E01, ERIC, IBSS, MLA-IB. *Aud.:* Ac.

This peer-reviewed journal is published by the National Foundation for Education Research (NFER), a major British research institution. It presents articles on contemporary issues in education, conveying research findings in language understandable to both scholars and non-expert readers. With its objective of comprehensively describing for readers the problems and research outcomes of a wide range of concerns in all areas of education, this forum for NFER is meant to assist professionals in making practical decisions and to aid those who mediate research findings to policymakers and practitioners. Faculty authors and researchers have written articles on student holistic development, bullying, the framework of habitual trust. Yearly special issues are organized around themes. This publication also includes reviews of research, discussion pieces, short research reports, and book reviews. Recommended for academic libraries. URL: www.tandf.co.uk/journals/titles/00131881.asp

1870. ***European Journal of Education: research, development and policy.*** Formerly (until 1979): *Paedagogica Europaea.* [ISSN: 0141-8211] 1965. q. GBP 1893. Ed(s): Richard Desjardins, Janet Looney. Wiley-Blackwell Publishing Ltd., The Atrium, Southern Gate, Chichester, PO19 8QG, United Kingdom; cs-journals@wiley.com; http://onlinelibrary.wiley.com/. Illus., index, adv. Sample. Refereed. Reprint: PSC. *Indexed:* A01, A22, ASSIA, E01, ERIC, MLA-IB. *Aud.:* Ac.

This international, peer-reviewed journal is produced by the European Institute for Education and Social Policy, a nonprofit organization with expertise in the analysis of education and training policies in Europe and the partner countries of the European Union. The journal offers a European perspective on policymaking, focusing on European research projects and policy analysis of interest to policymakers and international organizations. The journal seeks to contribute to the policy debate at the national and European levels by providing comparative, up-to-date data; examine, compare, and assess education policies, trends, and reforms across Europe; and disseminate policy debates and research results to a wide audience of scholars and practitioners. Each issue is themed, with three to five articles that address the selected theme, and a guest editor with expertise on the topic. A second section of each issue includes articles on other themes. Recent journal themes have included the question of what learning is for, the changing role of teachers, teacher education and professional development, and university rankings. Recommended for academic libraries. URL: http://onlinelibrary.wiley.com/journal/10.1111/(ISSN)1465-3435

1871. *Higher Education: the international journal of higher education research.* [ISSN: 0018-1560] 1971. 12x/yr. EUR 2145 (print & online eds.)). Ed(s): Jussi Valimaa, Simon Marginson. Springer Netherlands, Van Godewijckstraat 30, Dordrecht, 3311 GX, Netherlands; http://www.springer.com. Illus., index, adv. Sample. Refereed. Vol. ends: No. 4. Microform: PQC. Reprint: PSC. *Indexed:* A01, A22, BRI, C42, E01, ERIC, IBSS, MLA-IB. *Bk. rev.:* 0-1, length varies. *Aud.:* Ac.

This publication provides a forum for the exchange of information, experiences, and research results in the field of higher education studies. Developments in higher education institutions at all levels, both public and private, and across the world are reported. International authors reflect on higher education problems and issues, offer comparative reviews and analyses of country policies and education systems, and consider how these contributions may impact future planning. They address problems of teachers, students, administrators, and policymakers. Recent articles have discussed the link between high-impact practices and student learning, faculty mobility, predictors of the acquisition and portability of transferable skills, and the effects of economic status and educational expectations on university pursuit. Recommended for academic libraries. URL: http://link.springer.com/journal/10734

1872. *International Journal of Leadership in Education: theory & practice.* [ISSN: 1360-3124] 1998. q. GBP 905 (print & online eds.)). Ed(s): Duncan Waite. Routledge, 4 Park Sq, Milton Park, Abingdon, OX14 4RN, United Kingdom; subscriptions@tandf.co.uk; http://www.tandfonline.com. Adv. Sample. Refereed. Reprint: PSC. *Indexed:* A01, A22, B01, E01, ERIC. *Aud.:* Ac.

This international journal provides a forum for theoretical and practical discussions of educational leadership. The journal explores conceptual, methodological, and practical issues in a variety of settings. Its stated goal is to publish cutting-edge research on instructional supervision, curriculum and teaching development, and educational administration; it presents alternative theoretical perspectives, methodologies, and leadership experiences. The journal's broad definition of leadership includes teachers as leaders, shared governance, site-based decision making, and community-school collaborations. Issues are divided into three main sections for peer-reviewed, theoretically based research papers; practical shorter articles from academicians and practitioner-researchers; and commentary. Special theme-based issues are published infrequently. Recommended for academic libraries. URL: www.tandfonline.com/toc/tedl20/current

1873. *International Review of Education: journal of lifelong learning.* [ISSN: 0020-8566] 1955. bi-m. EUR 729 (print & online eds.)). Ed(s): Stephen Roche. Springer Netherlands, Van Godewijckstraat 30, Dordrecht, 3311 GX, Netherlands; http://www.springer.com. Illus., index, adv. Sample. Refereed. Vol. ends: Dec (No. 6). Microform: PQC. Reprint: PSC. *Indexed:* A01, A22, BAS, BRI, E01, ERIC, IBSS. *Bk. rev.:* 2-4, length varies. *Aud.:* Ac.

Edited by the UNESCO Institute for Lifelong Learning, this publication is directed at institutes of education, teacher-training institutions and ministries, nongovernment organizations, and individuals throughout the world. It provides an international forum for scholarly articles on the comparative theory and practice of formal and informal education as it relates to lifelong learning and education. As many as three thematic issues might be published in a given year. Recent thematic issues have explored topics such as literacy and lifelong learning in rural Africa, sustainable developmental goals, and indigenous knowledge's role in sustainability. Some articles are non-English, but with an English abstract. Recommended for academic libraries. URL: http://link.springer.com/journal/11159

1874. *Journal of Philosophy of Education.* Former titles (until 1978): *Philosophy of Education Society of Great Britain. Proceedings;* (until 1971): *Philosophy of Education Society of Great Britain. Annual Conference. Proceedings.* [ISSN: 0309-8249] 1966. q. GBP 981. Ed(s): Bob Davis. Wiley-Blackwell Publishing Ltd., The Atrium, Southern Gate, Chichester, PO19 8QG, United Kingdom; cs-journals@wiley.com; http://onlinelibrary.wiley.com. Illus., index, adv. Sample. Refereed. Vol. ends: No. 2. Reprint: PSC. *Indexed:* A01, A22, BRI, E01, ERIC. *Bk. rev.:* Yes, varies. *Aud.:* Ac.

This journal, published on behalf of the Philosophy of Education Society of Great Britain, explores the philosophical dimensions of educational theory. Authors discuss basic philosophical issues related to education, or they may provide critical examinations of current educational practices or policies from a philosophical perspective. This title promotes rigorous thinking on education, and the philosophical and ideological forces that shape the field. The authors are international, as is the editorial board. Articles have focused on such topics as historical reconstruction and the modern university, teacher exclusion and Levina's philosophy for education. One themed special issue is published each year, devoted to topics such as relationships in education, education and the growth of knowledge, and policy. Some issues include special sections with articles on a common theme. This title generally includes a book review or review article. Recommended for academic libraries. URL: http://onlinelibrary.wiley.com/journal/10.1111/(ISSN)1467-9752

1875. *Times Educational Supplement.* [ISSN: 0040-7887] 1910. w. GBP 49 domestic; GBP 210 in Europe; GBP 255 elsewhere. T S L Education Ltd., 26 Red Lion Sq, London, WC1R 4HQ, United Kingdom; info@tsleducation.com; http://www.tsleducation.co.uk. Illus., index, adv. Microform: RPI. *Indexed:* A01, BRI, CBRI. *Aud.:* Ac, Sa.

Times Educational Supplement is the British counterpart to the American publication *Education Week*. It is the United Kingdom's major weekly publication for news concerning "primary, secondary, and further education." It includes background analyses of a wide range of current issues in education, local and national news, and a section on job openings for predominantly K-12 and also higher-education positions. While the emphasis is on Britain, *TES* includes international coverage of Europe, North America, and the Commonwealth nations. This title provides frequent special supplements to the news edition, such as separate job advertising supplements that include international openings. Highly recommended for academic libraries. URL: https://www.tes.com/magazine

Educational Psychology and Measurement, Special Education, Counseling

1876. *Applied Measurement in Education.* [ISSN: 0895-7347] 1988. q. GBP 676 (print & online eds.)). Ed(s): Gus F Geisinger. Routledge, 530 Walnut St, Ste 850, Philadelphia, PA 19106; enquiries@tandfonline.com; http://www.tandfonline.com. Illus., adv. Sample. Refereed. Vol. ends: No. 4. Reprint: PSC. *Indexed:* A01, A22, E01, ERIC. *Aud.:* Ac.

This research journal's prime mission is to improve communication between theory and practice. Articles address original research studies, innovative strategies for solving educational measurement problems, and integrative reviews of current approaches to contemporary measurement issues. The intended audience of researchers and practitioners will find articles on applied research, educational measurement problems and considered solutions, and research reviews of current issues in testing. Research studies with accompanying tables, figures, graphs, and other supporting material address topics such as validating automated essay scoring, estimating variance components in large-scale educational assessments, and the quantification of language acquisition among English-language learners. Occasional special issues cover themes such as "Levels of Analysis in the Assessment of Linguistic Minority Students" and "Teachers' and Administrators' Use of Evidence of Student Learning to Take Action." Contributors are from academic and testing institutions such as the American Council of Testing and the Education Testing System. This journal also features some articles that are open access. Strongly recommended for academic libraries that serve teachers and related education professionals. URL: www.tandfonline.com/loi/hame20

1877. *Counselor Education and Supervision.* [ISSN: 0011-0035] 1961. q. GBP 216. Ed(s): Danica G Hays. Wiley-Blackwell Publishing, Inc., 111 River St, Hoboken, NJ 07030; http://onlinelibrary.wiley.com. Illus., index, adv. Refereed. Circ: 3200. Vol. ends: Jun. Microform: PQC. Reprint: PSC. *Indexed:* A01, A22, BRI, C42, ERIC. *Bk. rev.:* Varies by issue. *Aud.:* Ac, Sa.

This official publication of the Association for Counselor Education and Supervision (ACES) is designed for professionals engaged in the teaching and supervising of counselors. The journal's scope encompasses a broad range of workplaces, from schools to agencies and private institutions. Each issue contains about six articles written by authors, predominantly from academe, which are organized into sections such as "Current Issues," "Counselor Preparation," "Pedagogy," and "Supervision." Articles range from pedagogical methods to practical teaching methods. The inclusion of ACES executive council minutes supports the professional orientation of the journal. A focused journal for a specific audience. URL: www.acesonline.net/

1878. ***Educational Measurement: Issues and Practice.*** Supersedes: *National Council on Measurement in Education. Measurement News;* Formerly: *N C M E Newsletter.* [ISSN: 0731-1745] 1982. q. USD 559 (print or online ed.)). Ed(s): Adam Martin, Derek C Briggs. Wiley-Blackwell Publishing, Inc., 111 River St, Hoboken, NJ 07030; info@wiley.com; http://onlinelibrary.wiley.com. Illus. Refereed. Vol. ends: Winter. Reprint: PSC. *Indexed:* A01, A22, E01, ERIC. *Bk. rev.:* Varies, 0-1, 5,000 words. *Aud.:* Ac.

A journal of the National Council on Measurement in Education (NCME) that is designed to both highlight and inform its professional audience on issues and practices in the field of educational measurement. Each issue contains three articles that range in length from five to ten pages. Journal articles cover such topics as educational assessment knowledge and skills for teachers; the impact of an argument-based approach to validity; testing rubrics for elementary school students' writing; standard-setting methods as measurement processes; models of cognition used in educational measurement; the security of web-based assessments; and large-scale testing in other countries. As a membership publication, the journal also reports on NCME member activities, the annual conference, and organizational news. URL: http://ncme.org/publications/emip/

1879. ***Educational Psychology Review.*** [ISSN: 1040-726X] 1989. q. EUR 1342 (print & online eds.)). Ed(s): Daniel H Robinson. Springer New York LLC, 233 Spring St, New York, NY 10013; customerservice@springer.com; http://www.springer.com. Illus., adv. Sample. Refereed. Vol. ends: Dec. Microform: PQC. Reprint: PSC. *Indexed:* A01, A22, BRI, E01, ERIC. *Aud.:* Ac, Sa.

An international, peer-reviewed publication that supports the field of general educational psychology. Averaging four to six substantial articles per issue, this journal covers the history, profession, and issues of the educational psychology field. Essays on previous research or new research directions, research into practice articles, review articles, and interviews are included. Special thematic issues are common, covering themes like Cognitive Load Theory and relational reasoning in STEM domains. Recommended for academic libraries that serve education and psychology faculty and graduate students. URL: http://link.springer.com/journal/10648

1880. ***J E M.*** Former titles (until 1978): *Journal of Educational Measurement;* (until 1964): *National Council on Measurement in Education. Yearbook.* [ISSN: 0274-838X] 19??. q. USD 527 (print or online ed.)). Ed(s): Jimmy de la Torre. Wiley-Blackwell Publishing, Inc., 111 River St, Hoboken, NJ 07030; info@wiley.com; http://www.wiley.com/. Illus., index, adv. Sample. Refereed. Vol. ends: Winter. Microform: PQC. Reprint: PSC. *Indexed:* A01, A22, ASSIA, BRI, Chicano, E01, ERIC. *Bk. rev.:* Various number and length. *Aud.:* Ac.

Published by the National Council on Measurement in Education, *JEM* (*The Journal of Educational Measurement*) intends to "promote greater understanding and improved use of measurement techniques." The journal's content consists of research studies and reports on educational measurement such as test-score reliability, item clusters and computerized adaptive testing, scaling performance assessments, assessing the dimensionality of NAEP reading data, trace lines for testlets, and the impact of interruptions during online testing. There is a review section for books, software, and published tests and measurements. In addition, the journal solicits and publishes comments on previously published articles and reviews. The authors come from a broad range of testing and measurement backgrounds, such as the National Board of Medical Examiners, Microsoft Corporation, Research Triangle Institute, and CTB/McGraw-Hill. A scholarly research journal for those in the field of educational testing and measurement. URL: http://ncme.org/publications/jem/

1881. ***Journal of Educational and Behavioral Statistics.*** Formerly (until 1994): *Journal of Educational Statistics.* [ISSN: 1076-9986] 1976. bi-m. USD 771 (print & online eds.)). Ed(s): Daniel McCaffrey, Li Cai. Sage Publications, Inc., 2455 Teller Rd, Thousand Oaks, CA 91320; info@sagepub.com; http://www.sagepub.com. Illus., index, adv. Sample. Refereed. Microform: PQC. Reprint: PSC. *Indexed:* A22, E01, ERIC. *Bk. rev.:* Various number and length. *Aud.:* Ac.

Co-sponsored by the American Educational Research Association and the American Statistical Association, this journal is intended for people applying a statistical approach to the field of educational or behavioral research. The journal publishes papers on methods of analysis, as well as reviews of current methods and practices. *JEBS*'s articles inform readers about the use of statistical methods: the "why, when, and how" of statistical methodology. Four to five articles are included per issue, along with the occasional column "Teachers Corner," which presents brief essays on the teaching of educational and behavioral statistics. Articles have addressed issues such as estimating entropy rates of finite Markov chains in regards to behavior studies and the detection and treatment of careless responses to improve item parameter estimation. A focused journal important to those interested in educational and behavioral statistics. Recommended for academic libraries. URL: http://jeb.sagepub.com/

1882. ***Journal of Educational Psychology.*** [ISSN: 0022-0663] 1910. 8x/yr. USD 1051 (Individuals, USD 271; Members, USD 131). Ed(s): Steve Graham. American Psychological Association, 750 First St, NE, Washington, DC 20002; journals@apa.org; http://www.apa.org. Illus., adv. Sample. Refereed. Circ: 900. Vol. ends: Feb. Microform: PMC; PQC. Reprint: PSC. *Indexed:* A01, A22, Chicano, ERIC, MLA-IB. *Aud.:* Ac.

This peer-reviewed scholarly journal's stated purpose is to publish current research in the field of educational psychology, with a secondary purpose of the publication of "exceptionally important" theoretical and review articles of interest to the field. Well-referenced research articles are supported by tables, figures, and appendixes. Article coverage includes learning, cognition, instruction, motivation, social issues, emotion, and special populations at all education levels. This title is published by the American Psychological Association, and is highly recommended for researchers, students, and practitioners in the field of educational psychology. URL: www.apa.org/pubs/journals/edu/

1883. ***The Journal of Experimental Education.*** [ISSN: 0022-0973] 1932. q. GBP 267 (print & online eds.)). Ed(s): Avi Kaplan. Routledge, 530 Walnut St, Ste 850, Philadelphia, PA 19106; enquiries@tandfonline.com; http://www.tandfonline.com. Illus., index, adv. Refereed. Microform: PMC. Reprint: PSC. *Indexed:* A01, A22, Chicano, E01, ERIC, MASUSE, MLA-IB. *Aud.:* Ac.

This peer-reviewed journal publishes basic and applied-research studies that use quantitative or qualitative methodologies in the behavioral, cognitive, and social sciences. Intended for researchers and practitioners, the journal is dedicated to promoting educational research in areas such as teaching, learning, and schooling in the United States and abroad. Contributed articles are divided into three sections: learning, instruction, and cognition; motivation and social processes; and measurement, statistics, and research design. Articles have covered such topics as the usefulness of common SES measures, student mobility in multilevel growth modeling, enjoyment, boredom, and anxiety in elementary schools and their relations with achievement. A journal intended for and useful to the professional researcher in the field of education, and related social sciences. URL: www.tandfonline.com/loi/vjxe20

1884. ***Journal of Learning Disabilities.*** [ISSN: 0022-2194] 1967. bi-m. USD 397 (print & online eds.)). Ed(s): H Lee Swanson. Sage Publications, Inc., 2455 Teller Rd, Thousand Oaks, CA 91320; info@sagepub.com; http://www.sagepub.com. Illus., adv. Sample. Refereed. Vol. ends: Dec. Microform: PQC. Reprint: PSC. *Indexed:* A01, A22, ASSIA, BRI, Chicano, E01, ERIC, MLA-IB. *Aud.:* Ac, Sa.

This journal publishes articles on practice, research, and theory related to learning disabilities. Contributions include feature articles, research articles, and intervention articles, as well as special series that provide in-depth coverage of topics in the field. In covering the multidisciplinary field of learning disabilities, articles have presented topics such as stability of risk status during preschool, reading intervention for English Language Learners, and attitudes and knowledge about learning disabilities in Arabic- and Hebrew-speaking students. Special issues are also published. This title includes a classified advertising section with professional position postings. A professional calendar lists seminars and conferences on learning disabilities. Highly recommended for academic libraries. URL: http://ldx.sagepub.com/

1885. ***Learning Disability Quarterly.*** [ISSN: 0731-9487] 1978. q. USD 263 (print & online eds.)). Ed(s): Diane Pedrotty Bryant, Brian R Bryant. Sage Publications, Inc., 2455 Teller Rd, Thousand Oaks, CA 91320; info@sagepub.com; http://www.sagepub.com. Illus. Refereed. Vol. ends: Fall. Reprint: PSC. *Indexed:* A01, A22, Chicano, ERIC, MLA-IB. *Aud.:* Ac, Sa.

Published by the Hammill Institute on Disabilities and Sage in association with the Council for Learning Disabilities, this journal focuses on educational practices and theories regarding children, youth, and adults with learning disabilities. Articles represent a broad range of formats, including assessment or remediation reports, literature reviews, theory and issue papers, original or applied research, and professional education program models. With usually six articles an issue, this title's contents cover professional development, current issues in the field, the development of effective teaching methods, teaching in inclusive classrooms, and increasing student achievement. Special series have covered topics such as reading and universal design for learning. An important journal of value to both the academician and practitioner. URL: http://ldq.sagepub.com/

1886. ***Psychology in the Schools.*** [ISSN: 0033-3085] 1964. 10x/yr. GBP 672. Ed(s): David E McIntosh. John Wiley & Sons, Inc., 111 River St, Hoboken, NJ 07030; cs-journals@wiley.com; http://onlinelibrary.wiley.com. Illus., index, adv. Sample. Refereed. Vol. ends: Oct. Microform: PQC. Reprint: PSC. *Indexed:* A01, A22, ASSIA, Chicano, ERIC. *Bk. rev.:* 1-5, 600-2,000 words. *Aud.:* Ac, Sa.

This peer-reviewed journal is intended for the school practitioner and others working in educational institutions, including psychologists, counselors, and administrators. Recent articles cover the barriers concerning students' college transition plans, classroom management's relationship to math achievement, and parent-implemented reading interventions. One or two special issues are published annually on current topics such as the school and life experiences of highly mobile pupils and working with gifted students. Occasional test and book reviews. An important journal for school and academic libraries. URL: http://onlinelibrary.wiley.com/journal/10.1002/%28ISSN%291520-6807

1887. ***Remedial and Special Education.*** Formed by the merger of (1981-1984): *Topics in Learning and Learning Disabilities;* (1980-1984): *Exceptional Education Quarterly;* (1978-1983): *Journal for Special Educators;* Which was formed by the 1978 merger of: *Special Children; Journal for Special Educators of the Mentally Retarded;* Which was formerly: *Digest of the Mentally Retarded;* Incorporates: *Retarded Adult.* [ISSN: 0741-9325] 1984. bi-m. USD 364 (print & online eds.)). Ed(s): Kathleen Lane, Karrie A Shogren. Sage Publications, Inc., 2455 Teller Rd, Thousand Oaks, CA 91320; info@sagepub.com; http://www.sagepub.com. Illus., index. Sample. Refereed. Microform: PQC. Reprint: PSC. *Indexed:* A01, A22, ASSIA, BRI, E01, ERIC. *Bk. rev.:* Number and length vary. *Aud.:* Ac, Sa.

A journal dedicated to the issues and practices of remedial and special education. Each issue averages five or six articles, which may be literature reviews, position papers, or research reports. Topics cover a broad range of issues concerning the population of underachieving and exceptional individuals. Recent article topics include teaching math to students with moderate and severe developmental disabilities, self advocacy instruction, and interventions for struggling readers. Special issues are also published. Contributing authors are predominantly academics, including graduate students. Book reviews and a professional calendar are regular features. A journal of importance for the special education teacher and regular classroom teacher, as well as those teaching in the field. URL: http://rse.sagepub.com/

1888. ***Studies in Educational Evaluation.*** [ISSN: 0191-491X] 1975. q. EUR 1415. Ed(s): P Van Petegem. Pergamon Press, The Blvd, Langford Ln, E Park, Kidlington, OX5 1GB, United Kingdom; JournalsCustomerServiceEMEA@elsevier.com; http://www.elsevier.com. Illus., adv. Sample. Refereed. Microform: PQC. *Indexed:* A01, A22, ASSIA, ERIC. *Bk. rev.:* Number and length vary. *Aud.:* Ac.

This is an internationally authored journal that publishes original reports on evaluation studies for practitioners, students, and researchers. Focused on presenting both empirical and theoretical studies, this title seeks articles that report on educational systems, evaluation practices, and current evaluation issues of educational programs, institutions, and educational personnel and student assessment. Article topics have included evaluating the impact of differentiated instruction on literacy and reading in mixed-ability classrooms; pre-service teachers' attitudes toward racial minority students; equivalence among test results for performance-based critical thinking tests for undergraduate students; and the effect of peer assessment on problem-solving skills. Special issues are also published. Special sections occasionally delve into topics such as quality assurance in assessment or data use in schools. Book reviews and brief abstracts of evaluation studies are included in each issue. A high-quality, focused journal with international coverage that is recommended for libraries that serve patrons with an interest in testing and evaluation. URL: www.journals.elsevier.com/studies-in-educational-evaluation/

Higher Education

1889. ***A A U W Outlook.*** Former titles (until 1989): *Graduate Woman;* (until 1978): *A A U W Journal;* (until 1962): *American Association of University Women. Journal;* (until 1921): *Association of Collegiate Alumnae. Journal;* (until 1911): *Association of Collegiate Alumnae. Publications.* [ISSN: 1044-5706] 1884. 3x/yr. Free to members. American Association of University Women, 1111 16th St, NW, Washington, DC 20036; connect@aauw.org; http://www.aauw.org. Illus., adv. Microform: PQC. *Bk. rev.:* 1-2, 200-500 words. *Aud.:* Ga, Ac.

Published by the American Association of University Women for its members, this magazine informs and promotes the organization's mission of "advancing equity for women and girls through advocacy, education, philanthropy, and research." Regular features include an equity watch and "Leaders' Message." Illustrated throughout with photos, the magazine contains classified ads that include job opportunities. Brief feature articles on a common theme have considered aspects of issues such as pay equity, the birth control backlash, paid parental leave, and coming out at work. Member surveys, organizational news, the "Leaders' Message," and an issue devoted to the AAUW's annual conference exemplify the outreach focus of the magazine to its members. An important magazine for academic libraries and for public or private libraries that serve women's organizations. URL: www.aauw.org/resource/aauw-outlook/

1890. ***Change: the magazine of higher learning.*** Formerly (until 1970): *Change in Higher Education.* [ISSN: 0009-1383] 1969. bi-m. GBP 212. Ed(s): Margaret A Miller. Routledge, 530 Walnut St, Ste 850, Philadelphia, PA 19106; enquiries@tandfonline.com; http://www.tandfonline.com. Illus., index, adv. Circ: 12868 Paid. Reprint: PSC. *Indexed:* A01, A22, BRI, C42, CBRI, Chicano, E01, ERIC, MLA-IB. *Bk. rev.:* Varies by issue. *Aud.:* Ac.

A magazine for the practitioner, *Change* presents views and opinions on current higher education issues and trends. This journal, using a magazine format, is intended for all practitioners in higher education institutions, organizations, and government offices, and its focus is on discussion and analysis of educational programs and practices. Articles cover all aspects of higher education, including technology, teaching and learning, curriculum, students, educational philosophy, economics and finance, higher education management and administration, public policy, and the social role of higher education. Each issue contains about six articles, ranging from a brief point of view to a featured article. Article topics have included sexual consent policies, strategies to boost completion rates, college ratings, the history and future of the credit hour, and the evaluation of undergraduate teaching. Regular departments feature an editorial and a column of items of current interest to those in the field. A title important to all those in the field of higher education from administrators and department heads to faculty. URL: www.changemag.org

1891. ***The Chronicle of Higher Education.*** [ISSN: 0009-5982] 1966. w. 43/yr. USD 91 combined subscription domestic (print & online eds.); USD 187 combined subscription Canada (print & online eds.); USD 318 combined subscription elsewhere (print & online eds.)). Chronicle of

Higher Education, Inc., 1255 23rd St, NW, 7th Fl, Washington, DC 20037; help@chronicle.com. Illus., index, adv. Sample. Vol. ends: Aug. Microform: CIS; PQC. *Indexed:* A&ATA, A01, A22, Agr, BRI, C37, C42, CBRI, Chicano, ERIC, F01, MLA-IB. *Aud.:* Ga, Ac.

Published weekly, *The Chronicle of Higher Education* is academia's premier resource for news and information. Although the journal is intended for higher education faculty and administrators, the contents are relevant for others interested in the field of higher education, such as researchers, students, federal and state legislators, government policymakers, and taxpayers. This weekly is organized into sections: current developments and issues in higher education; regular features on faculty, research, money and management, government and politics, international, students, and athletics; the chronicle review, with letters to the editor and opinion articles; listings of coming events; and a section on career networking, with hundreds of job listings. Additionally, twice a year "Events in Academe" indexes meetings, events, and deadlines for fellowships, grants, papers, and prizes. An annual almanac issue covers facts and statistics about U.S. higher education at both the national and state level. Supplementary materials are available online with additional sections like blogs, career-building tools, and a searchable archive with content back to the 1970s. The online version is updated every weekday. A required standard for all academic libraries, as well as higher education institutions and organizations. URL: http://chronicle.com

1892. *College Teaching.* Formerly (until 1985): *Improving College and University Teaching.* [ISSN: 8756-7555] 1953. q. GBP 195 (print & online eds.)). Ed(s): Scott P Simkins, Barbara J Millis. Routledge, 530 Walnut St, Ste 850, Philadelphia, PA 19106; enquiries@tandfonline.com; http://www.tandfonline.com. Illus., adv. Refereed. Reprint: PSC. *Indexed:* A01, A22, BRI, E01, ERIC, MLA-IB. *Aud.:* Ac.

Improving student learning is the core focus of this peer-reviewed journal, with an emphasis on providing new and practical strategies to faculty and instructors in all disciplines. Interdisciplinary full-length articles report research on instructional methods and practices, assessment, evaluation, educational technology, course design, and classroom management. One to two short, 500-word "Quick Fix" articles in each issue provide solutions to common instructional problems. The occasional commentary gives authors a chance to reflect on teaching. Recent articles have addressed topics such as using reflection to enhance faculty and curriculum development, cell phone policies in the college classroom, experiential learning, engagement and online learners, and charismatic teaching. With a broad range of topics, this journal effectively covers the higher education classroom. An important and informative tool for higher education instructors. URL: www.tandfonline.com/toc/vcol20/current

1893. *Community College Journal.* Former titles (until 1992): *Community, Technical, and Junior College Journal;* (until 1985): *Community and Junior College Journal;* (until 1972): *Junior College Journal.* [ISSN: 1067-1803] 1930. bi-m. Free to members; Non-members, USD 36. American Association of Community Colleges, One Dupont Cir, NW, Ste 410, Washington, DC 20036; http://www.aacc.nche.edu. Illus., index, adv. Sample. Circ: 10000. Vol. ends: Jun/Jul. Microform: PQC. *Indexed:* A22, ERIC, MLA-IB. *Bk. rev.:* 4-7, 100-300 words. *Aud.:* Ac.

This journal of the American Association of Community Colleges supports the advancement of community colleges as institutions of higher learning. The journal contents include feature articles, opinion pieces, news items, and coverage of issues in the field of higher education. Each issue is dedicated to a theme, with five or six brief articles. Recent themes include the future of community college reform, community college completion, and workforce development. The intended audience of presidents, board members, administrators, faculty, and staff at two-year institutions is presented with practical content. Articles focus on trends and issues in the field, such as training future faculty, leadership, campus security, community colleges and changing technology needs, and the public image of community colleges. For all community college libraries and graduate education program libraries that support those working in or preparing to work in the field. URL: www.aacc.nche.edu/Publications/CCJ/Pages/default.aspx

1894. *Community College Review.* [ISSN: 0091-5521] 1973. q. USD 751 (print & online eds.)). Ed(s): Jaime Lester. Sage Publications, Inc., 2455 Teller Rd, Thousand Oaks, CA 91320; info@sagepub.com; http://www.sagepub.com. Illus., adv. Sample. Refereed. Vol. ends: Spring. Microform: PQC. Reprint: PSC. *Indexed:* A01, A22, BRI, E01, ERIC, MLA-IB. *Bk. rev.:* Number and length vary. *Aud.:* Ac.

This peer-reviewed journal publishes scholarly research and commentary on community colleges, in the United States and other equivalent schools internationally. With an emphasis on issues of administration, education, and policy, the journal includes blind peer-reviewed qualitative and quantitative research studies, essays, literature reviews, and book reviews. Integrating theory and practice, articles are meant to further the study and understanding of community college students, administrators, and faculty, and the educational environment of community college. Recent articles have focused on who is succeeding in the online STEM classroom, academic momentum and educational outcomes, trajectories of change in community college mission statements, developmental education programs, and success among Latino/a community-college students. An important title for libraries that serve the higher education community, the journal supports the work of administrators, faculty, graduate students, researchers, and policymakers with an interest in community colleges. URL: http://crw.sagepub.com

1895. *Innovative Higher Education.* Formerly (until 1983): *Alternative Higher Education.* [ISSN: 0742-5627] 1976. 5x/yr. EUR 1541 (print & online eds.)). Ed(s): Libby V Morris. Springer Netherlands, Van Godewijckstraat 30, Dordrecht, 3311 GX, Netherlands; http://www.springer.com. Illus., index, adv. Sample. Refereed. Vol. ends: Summer. Microform: PQC. Reprint: PSC. *Indexed:* A01, A22, E01, ERIC, MLA-IB. *Aud.:* Ac, Ga.

This is a refereed academic journal dedicated to emerging and current trends in higher education. Its focus is on providing practitioners and scholars with current strategies, programs, and innovations to enhance the field of higher education. The publication focuses on articles that consider current innovative trends and practices with application beyond the context of higher education; discuss the effect of innovations on teaching and students; present diverse scholarship and research methods; and cover practice and theory appropriate for both faculty and administrators. Recent issues feature topics relevant to the field such as labor market outcomes for those with STEM Master's degrees, the evolving understanding of academic dishonesty and cheating, and the academic coaching of at-risk college students. Highly recommended for libraries at higher education institutions or organizations. URL: www.springer.com/education+%26+language/higher+education/journal/10755

1896. *Journal of College Student Development.* Formerly (until 1988): *Journal of College Student Personnel;* Which superseded (in 1959): *Personnel-o-Gram.* [ISSN: 0897-5264] 19??. 6x/yr. USD 195. Ed(s): Deborah L Liddell. The Johns Hopkins University Press, 2715 N Charles St, Baltimore, MD 21218; http://www.press.jhu.edu. Illus., adv. Sample. Refereed. Vol. ends: Nov. Reprint: PSC. *Indexed:* A22, Chicano, E01, ERIC, MLA-IB. *Bk. rev.:* 0-4, 700-1,000 words. *Aud.:* Ac, Sa.

The official journal of the American College Personnel Association, this title focuses on research about college students and the field of student affairs. Student development, professional development, administrative issues, and innovative programs to enhance student services at institutions in the United States and internationally are discussed. Authors contribute quantitative or qualitative research articles, research reviews, and essays on theoretical, organizational, and professional topics. Shorter research studies present tools and methods that administrators may find useful in providing services. Examples of recent articles are the role of discomfort in collegiate learning and development, characteristics of friend networks and the risk of alcohol, marijuana, and behavioral problems in college, and bereavement leave policies for college students. This title includes book reviews and international research. A professional journal recommended for academic libraries. URL: http://muse.jhu.edu/journals/journal_of_college_student_development/

1897. *Journal of Computers in Mathematics and Science Teaching.* [ISSN: 0731-9258] 1981. q. USD 210. Ed(s): Gary Marks. Association for the Advancement of Computing in Education, PO Box 719, Waynesville, NC 28786; info@aace.org; http://www.aace.org. Illus. Refereed. *Indexed:* A22, CompLI, ERIC. *Aud.:* Ac, Sa.

An academic journal that provides a venue for the exchange of information on using information technology in teaching mathematics and science. This title is published by the Association for the Advancement of Computing in Education, and its aim is to promote the teaching and learning of computing technologies. With an international authorship, the journal is directed to faculty, researchers, classroom teachers, and administrators. Article formats include research papers, case studies, courseware experiences, review papers, evaluations, and opinions. Issues have four to six research articles on such topics as perceptions of pre-service elementary mathematics teachers on their TPACK regarding geometry, how viewers orient toward student dialogue in online math videos, and piloting innovative learning experiences as they relate to digital fabrication. A subject-specific journal of value to both practitioner and researcher at all education levels. URL: www.aace.org/pubs/jcmst/default.htm

1898. ***The Journal of Higher Education.*** [ISSN: 0022-1546] 1930. 6x/yr. GBP 348 (print & online eds.)). Ed(s): Mitchell J Chang. Routledge, 530 Walnut St, Ste 850, Philadelphia, PA 19106; enquiries@tandfonline.com; http://www.tandfonline.com. Illus., adv. Refereed. Reprint: PSC. *Indexed:* A01, A22, BRI, CBRI, Chicano, E01, ERIC, MLA-IB. *Bk. rev.:* Various number and length. *Aud.:* Ac.

The leading scholarly journal in the field of higher education, *The Journal of Higher Education,* publishes research or technical papers, professional practice papers, literature reviews, and policy papers of interest to faculty, administrators, and program managers. Article content focuses on topics of interest and importance to the higher education community. A small number of substantial articles cover the current trends and issues in the field such as university rankings, state higher education governance structures, higher education spending, and access and equity in higher education. Occasional special issues examine topics in depth, such as research and methodology, the faculty in the new millennium, or higher education's social role in the community at large. Highly recommended for all libraries that serve higher education institutions and organizations. URL: www.ohiostatepress.org/Journals/JHE/jhemain.htm

1899. ***Liberal Education.*** Former titles (until 1958): *Association of American Colleges. Bulletin;* Which incorporated (19??-1951): *College and Church;* (until 1940): *Association of American Colleges. Bulletin;* (until 1931): *Association of American Colleges. Bulletin.* [ISSN: 0024-1822] 1915. q. Individuals, USD 50; Members, USD 10; Non-members, USD 14. Association of American Colleges and Universities, 1818 R St NW, Washington, DC 20009; pub_desk@aacu.org; http://www.aacu.org. Illus., index. Vol. ends: Nov/Dec. Microform: PQC. *Indexed:* A01, A22, BRI, C42, ERIC, MLA-IB. *Aud.:* Ac.

This is a journal of the Association of American Colleges and Universities dedicated to improving liberal learning and undergraduate education. This title is the voice of the association and a resource for the higher education community, and its contents highlight liberal education theory and its practical application. Articles seek to enrich undergraduate education by focusing on institutional change, leadership, teaching and learning, and faculty innovation. Three sections include a featured topic with three or four supporting articles; a perspectives section with practical how-to pieces; and an opinion article. For all libraries that serve the undergraduate education community and graduate schools of education. URL: www.aacu.org/liberaleducation/index.cfm

1900. ***Research in Higher Education.*** [ISSN: 0361-0365] 1973. 8x/yr. EUR 2134 (print & online eds.)). Ed(s): Robert K Toutkoushian. Springer Netherlands, Van Godewijckstraat 30, Dordrecht, 3311 GX, Netherlands; http://www.springer.com. Illus., adv. Refereed. Vol. ends: No. 4. Microform: PQC. Reprint: PSC. *Indexed:* A01, A22, E01, ERIC. *Aud.:* Ac.

This journal of the Association for Institutional Research is dedicated to improving the functioning of higher education institutions. Articles are written for an audience of higher education personnel, including institutional planners and researchers, administrators, and student personnel specialists who wish to have a better understanding of higher education institutions for the purpose of improved decision-making, effectiveness, and efficiency. Professional papers focus on quantitative studies of higher education procedures. Areas of focus include administration and faculty, curriculum and instruction, student characteristics, alumni, and recruitment and admissions. Each issue contains about five lengthy, well-referenced articles that address subjects such as student loans and student persistence; international mobility among researchers; sociodemographic diversity and distance education; and student involvement in ethnic student organizations. A standard journal for all academic libraries and higher education institutions and organizations. URL: http://link.springer.com/journal/11162

1901. ***The Review of Higher Education.*** Formerly (until 1978): *Higher Education Review.* [ISSN: 0162-5748] 1977. q. USD 205. Ed(s): Kirsten Robbins, Gary Pike. The Johns Hopkins University Press, 2715 N Charles St, Baltimore, MD 21218; http://www.press.jhu.edu. Illus., adv. Sample. Refereed. Reprint: PSC. *Indexed:* A01, A22, E01, ERIC, MLA-IB. *Bk. rev.:* 12-18 per issue, essay length. *Aud.:* Ac.

The official journal of the Association for the Study of Higher Education (ASHE), this scholarly title reports on the issues and trends affecting the field of higher education. The journal contains peer-reviewed articles, essays, reviews, and research findings. Issues are analyzed, examined, investigated, and described in articles that focus on topics with practical implications for higher education. Recent issues have included articles on high impact college experiences, the manipulation of metrics in higher education; and grounded theory of education for sustainability in the postsecondary classroom. Numerous book reviews are included. An important journal to inform all those working or interested in the field of higher education. URL: www.press.jhu.edu/journals/review_of_higher_education

Specific Subjects and Teaching Methods

ADULT EDUCATION

1902. ***Adult Education Quarterly: a journal of research and theory.*** Formerly (until 1983): *Adult Education;* Which was formed by the merger of (1942-1950): *Adult Education Journal;* (1936-1950): *Adult Education Bulletin;* Both of which superseded in part (in 1941): *Journal of Adult Education;* Which was formerly (until 1929): *American Association for Adult Education. Journal.* [ISSN: 0741-7136] 1950. q. USD 584 (print & online eds.)). Ed(s): Philip Shaw. Sage Publications, Inc., 2455 Teller Rd, Thousand Oaks, CA 91320; info@sagepub.com; http://www.sagepub.com. Illus., index, adv. Sample. Refereed. Vol. ends: Summer. Microform: PQC. Reprint: PSC. *Indexed:* A01, A22, BRI, CBRI, E01, ERIC, MLA-IB. *Bk. rev.:* 3, 1,000 words. *Aud.:* Ac, Sa.

A quarterly, refereed journal dedicated to promoting the practice and understanding of adult and continuing education. Geared to practitioners at all levels of adult and continuing education, policymakers, scholars, and students, this journal aims to be inclusive regarding adult and continuing education topics and issues. Interdisciplinary and internationally focused articles, as well as critical problem-oriented research reports of value to practitioners, are of particular interest. In addition to qualitative and quantitative research reports, the journal publishes theoretical and philosophical analyses, critical literature reviews, position statement essays, book reviews, and editorials. Recent research includes studies on vocational education, older men as learners, practice-based learning among immigrants, and math anxiety in adult learners. Book reviews consider publications that are indirectly related, such as cultural studies, work and the economy, distance learning, and international development. A standard title for academic libraries, as well as adult education organizations. Broadly indexed in a variety of databases URL: http://aeq.sagepub.com

Educational Media International. See Media and AV section.

1903. ***Journal of Adolescent & Adult Literacy.*** Former titles (until 1995): *Journal of Reading;* (until 1964): *Journal of Developmental Reading.* [ISSN: 1081-3004] 1957. 8x/yr. GBP 157 (print & online eds.)). Ed(s): Emily Neil Skinner, Margaret Carmody Hagood. John Wiley & Sons,

Inc., 111 River St, Hoboken, NJ 07030; cs-journals@wiley.com; http://onlinelibrary.wiley.com. Illus., index, adv. Refereed. Circ: 14425. Vol. ends: May. Microform: PQC. Reprint: PSC. *Indexed:* A01, A22, BRI, CBRI, Chicano, ERIC, MLA-IB. *Bk. rev.:* Various number and length. *Aud.:* Ac.

A journal dedicated to providing a forum for educators working in the field of literacy and language arts for learners over the age of 12. This title is published by the International Reading Association. Feature articles have recently focused on participatory literacy, linked text to promote advocacy and agency, and increasing authenticity in writing. Each issue includes practical instructional ideas; student and teacher resource reviews; information on how to apply technology and media in the classroom; and reflections on current reading research, issues, and trends. Each issue contains lengthy reviews of books for adolescents, professional materials, and classroom materials. Recommended for academic libraries. URL: www.reading.org/general/Publications/Journals/JAAL.aspx

THE ARTS

1904. ***Arts Education Policy Review.*** Former titles (until 1992): *Design for Arts in Education;* (until 1977): *Design;* (until 1930): *Design-Keramic Studio;* (until 1924): *Keramic Studio.* [ISSN: 1063-2913] 1899. q. GBP 267 (print & online eds.)). Ed(s): Colleen Conway. Routledge, 530 Walnut St, Ste 850, Philadelphia, PA 19106; enquiries@tandfonline.com; http://www.tandfonline.com. Illus., index, adv. Refereed. Microform: PQC. Reprint: PSC. *Indexed:* A01, A06, A22, BRI, ERIC, IIMP, IIPA, MLA-IB. *Bk. rev.:* 1-3, essay length. *Aud.:* Ac.

This journal provides a forum for the discussion of arts education policy issues in grades pre-K-12, nationally and internationally. With a focus on presenting current and controversial ideas and issues, articles focus on the application of policy analysis to arts education topics. Articles have covered topics such as out-of-school arts education, dance education teacher preparation, music teacher evaluation, professional learning communities to improve teacher efficacy, poetry in the curriculum, and arts education for students with diverse needs. Readership includes teachers, university faculty, education students, graduate students, policymakers, legislators, stakeholders, and others interested in arts in education. Recommended for school libraries and academic libraries with art education programs. URL: www.tandfonline.com/toc/vaep20/current

1905. ***School Arts: the art education magazine for teachers.*** Formerly (until 1935): *School Arts Magazine.* [ISSN: 0036-6463] 1901. 10x/yr. USD 24.95 domestic; USD 39.95 in Canada & Mexico. Ed(s): Nancy Walkup. Davis Publications, Inc. (Worcester), 50 Portland St, Printers Bldg, Worcester, MA 01608; contactus@davis-art.com; http://www.davisart.com/. Illus., index, adv. Sample. Vol. ends: May/Jun. Microform: NBI; PQC. *Indexed:* A01, A06, A22, BRI, CBRI, ERIC, MLA-IB. *Aud.:* Ga, Ac.

This is a magazine dedicated to inspiring art and classroom teachers at the elementary and secondary levels. Issues, often with a theme, address topics such as elementary and high school studio lessons; environment and nature; interdisciplinary connections; and managing the art classroom. Short, focused articles present curriculum ideas and plans; art technique applications; exemplary art programs; instruction and assessment methods; teaching art to special populations; and professional development. Each issue includes different showcases related to materials and resources, including showcases on clay, websites, and technology. Highly recommended for school libraries and academic libraries with art education programs. URL: www.davisart.com/Promotions/SchoolArts/Default.aspx

COMMUNICATION ARTS

1906. ***College Composition and Communication.*** [ISSN: 0010-096X] 1950. q. Members, USD 25; Non-members, USD 75. Ed(s): Jonathan Alexander. National Council of Teachers of English, 1111 W Kenyon Rd, Urbana, IL 61801-1096; customerservice@ncte.org; http://www.ncte.org. Illus., index, adv. Sample. Refereed. Vol. ends: Dec. *Indexed:* A22, AmHI, BRI, CBRI, ERIC, MLA-IB. *Bk. rev.:* Varies. *Aud.:* Ac.

This academic journal, published by the Conference on College Composition and Communication, addresses the issues and concerns of college composition instructors. Articles provide a forum for critical work on the study and teaching of college-level composition and reading. Article content covers all aspects of the profession, including teaching practices, the historical or institutional background of an educational practice, and current issues and trends in related disciplines. Although focused on those responsible for the teaching of composition at the college level, this journal will be of interest to administrators of composition programs, community college instructors, researchers, technical writers, graduate assistants, and others involved with college writing instruction. Each issue contains feature articles, review essays, book reviews, and contributor responses to published research theory or practice. Contributors have considered writing assessment, design thinking and writing, feminist historiography and digital humanities, and adult students and process knowledge transfer. Occasional special issues explore topics such as political economies of composition studies, locations of writing, and indigenous and ethnic rhetoric. Some content has free online access. A highly recommended title for academic libraries. URL: www.ncte.org/cccc/ccc

1907. ***English Education.*** Formerly (until 1969): *Conference on English Education. Selected Addresses Delivered.* [ISSN: 0007-8204] 1963. q. Members, USD 25; Non-members, USD 75. Ed(s): Tara S Johnson. National Council of Teachers of English, 1111 W Kenyon Rd, Urbana, IL 61801-1096; customerservice@ncte.org; http://www.ncte.org. Illus., index, adv. Sample. Refereed. Vol. ends: Dec. *Indexed:* A22, ERIC, MLA-IB. *Aud.:* Ac.

Dedicated to the education of teachers of English, reading, and language arts, the Conference on English Education focuses its journal on pre-service training and in-service development. Issues relevant to the profession are considered, such as pre-service and in-service education, professional development, student teacher evaluation, English curriculum, and trends in teacher education programs nationwide. Each issue has three to five articles that cover such topics as censorship, digital literacy pedagogy, and LGBTQ teacher ally work. Readership is aimed at a broad range of teacher education personnel, including college and university instructors of teachers; in-service educators; teacher consultants; curriculum coordinators; and classroom teachers supervising student teachers. A highly recommended journal for academic libraries that serve education programs. URL: www.ncte.org/journals/ee

1908. ***Journal of Spanish Language Teaching.*** [ISSN: 2324-7797] 2014. s-a. GBP 275 (print & online eds.)). Ed(s): Javier Munoz-Basols. Routledge, 4 Park Sq, Milton Park, Abingdon, OX14 4RN, United Kingdom; subscriptions@tandf.co.uk; http://www.tandfonline.com. Refereed. Reprint: PSC. *Indexed:* MLA-IB. *Bk. rev.:* Various number and length. *Aud.:* Ac.

This peer-reviewed, international journal focuses on the research, methods, materials, and theories of teaching and learning Spanish as a foreign language, with the goal of creating an environment for dialogue between researchers and practitioners worldwide. The majority of the articles are research papers, but the occasional critical survey in a related field of research is also included. This title is aimed at practitioners of all educational levels, and relevant areas of interest include language acquisition, language-teaching methodologies, professional development, curriculum development, and new technologies. Recommended for academic libraries with Spanish language programs and resources for educators. URL: www.tandfonline.com/loi/rslt

1909. ***Reading Improvement: a journal for the improvement of reading teaching.*** Formerly (until 164): *Reading in High School.* [ISSN: 0034-0510] 1963. q. USD 200 (print & online eds.)). Ed(s): Phillip Feldman. Project Innovation, Inc., Spring Hill Sta, PO Box 8508, Mobile, AL 36689; http://www.projectinnovation.biz. Illus., index, adv. Sample. Refereed. Vol. ends: Winter. Microform: PQC. *Indexed:* A01, A22, Chicano, ERIC, MLA-IB. *Bk. rev.:* 0-3, 200-300 words. *Aud.:* Ac.

A journal dedicated to improving the pedagogy and practice of the teaching of reading. Covering all levels of instruction, this title publishes investigative reports and theoretical papers. Each issue contains five to seven articles that cover a broad range of topics, such as encoding and decoding, special education, handwriting, art, and literature in relation to K-12. Recommended for school and academic libraries. URL: www.projectinnovation.com/Reading_Improvement.html

1910. *Reading Research Quarterly.* [ISSN: 0034-0553] 1965. q. GBP 162 (print & online eds.)). Ed(s): Susan B Neuman, Linda Gambrell. John Wiley & Sons, Inc., 111 River St, Hoboken, NJ 07030; cs-journals@wiley.com; http://onlinelibrary.wiley.com. Illus., index, adv. Refereed. Circ: 12280. Vol. ends: Fall. Microform: PQC. Reprint: PSC. *Indexed:* A01, A22, BRI, ERIC, MLA-IB. *Bk. rev.:* 1, length varies. *Aud.:* Ac.

Published by the International Reading Association, *RRQ* is a peer-reviewed, scholarly journal dedicated to presenting and examining the issues of literacy for all learners. Each issue includes reports on important studies, multidisciplinary research, various modes of investigation, and diverse viewpoints on literacy practices, teaching, and learning. Articles include qualitative and quantitative research, integrative reviews, and conceptual pieces that promote and contribute to the understanding of literacy and literacy research. Recent topics have included the influence of peer feedback and author response, children's literacy experiences in low-income families, and teaching bilingual learners. Letters to the editor and commentaries contribute to the journal's dialogue on literacy research. Highly recommended for academic and school libraries. URL: http://onlinelibrary.wiley.com/journal/10.1002/(ISSN)1936-2722

1911. *The Reading Teacher.* Formerly (until 1951): *International Council for the Improvement of Reading Instruction. Bulletin.* [ISSN: 0034-0561] 1948. 8x/yr. GBP 157 (print & online eds.)). Ed(s): Maria Mallette, Diane Barone. International Literacy Association, 800 Barksdale Rd, PO Box 8139, Newark, DE 19714; customerservice@reading.org; http://www.reading.org. Illus., index, adv. Refereed. Circ: 46000. Vol. ends: May. Microform: PQC. Reprint: PSC. *Indexed:* A01, A22, AmHI, BRI, C37, CBRI, Chicano, ERIC, MLA-IB. *Bk. rev.:* Number and length vary. *Aud.:* Ga, Ac.

A peer-reviewed journal by the International Reading Association, *The Reading Teacher* considers practices, research, and trends in literacy education and related disciplines. This journal is published for educators and other professionals involved with literacy education for children to the age of 12. The journal's goal to promote and affect literacy education is realized with article topics such as using word painting to enhance vocabulary, using guided inquiry with multimodal text sets, and re-conceptualizing sight words. An important journal for academic and school libraries with resources for educators. URL: https://ila.onlinelibrary.wiley.com/journal/19362714/

1912. *Research in the Teaching of English.* [ISSN: 0034-527X] 1967. q. Members, USD 25; Non-members, USD 75. Ed(s): Gerald Campano, Ebony Elizabeth Thomas. National Council of Teachers of English, 1111 W Kenyon Rd, Urbana, IL 61801-1096; customerservice@ncte.org; http://www.ncte.org. Illus., adv. Sample. Refereed. Vol. ends: Dec. *Indexed:* A22, ERIC, MLA-IB. *Aud.:* Ac.

RTE's definition of research in the teaching of English is broad and inclusive. The journal is dedicated to publishing multiple approaches to conducting research such as teacher-based research, historical articles, narratives, and current methodology. Additionally, the journal seeks articles that consider literacy issues regardless of language, within schools or other settings, and in other disciplines, and explore the relationship between learning and language teaching. General themes are supported with scholarly, well-referenced articles. Recent topics include professional development learning and its connection to teaching; becoming a social commentary composer; and the ethics of literacy research. A semi-annual selected bibliography of recent research in the teaching of English further supports *RTE*'s mission. Recommended for academic libraries. URL: www.ncte.org/journals/rte

1913. *T E S L - E J.* [ISSN: 1072-4303] 1994. q. Ed(s): Seyed Abdollah Shahrokni, Maggie Sokolik. T E S L - E J, University of California, Berkeley, Technical Communication Program, College of Engineering, Berkeley, CA 94720; http://www.tesl-ej.org/. Illus., index. Refereed. *Indexed:* BRI, CBRI, ERIC, MLA-IB. *Bk. rev.:* Number and length vary. *Aud.:* Hs, Ac.

This is a refereed academic journal focused on the research and practice of English as a second or foreign language. *TESL-EJ* covers a broad range of issues, from research to classroom practices for all education levels. Wide-ranging topics that are covered include language assessment, second-language acquisition, applied socio- and psycholinguistics, and EFL and ESL pedagogy. Issues present original articles and book or media reviews. Recommended for academic libraries with resources for educators. URL: http://tesl-ej.org/

BIOLOGY

1914. *The American Biology Teacher.* [ISSN: 0002-7685] 1938. 9x/yr. USD 303. Ed(s): William F. McComas. University of California Press, Journals Division, 155 Grand Avenue, Ste 400, Oakland, CA 94612-3764; http://www.ucpress.edu/journals.php. Illus., index, adv. Refereed. Vol. ends: Nov/Dec. Microform: PQC. *Indexed:* A01, A22, Agr, BRI, E01, ERIC, GardL. *Bk. rev.:* 4-8, 300-800 words. *Aud.:* Ac, Sa.

This is the award-winning official journal of the National Association of Biology Teachers, and it is aimed at teachers of K-16 and undergraduate biology and life science students. The journal publishes two or three feature articles per issue, which may include reviews of biology research or topics of current interest, discussion of social and ethical issues in biology education, results of studies on teaching techniques, or approaches for use in the classroom. The "Inquiry & Investigations" section includes articles that focus on specific projects for the laboratory or field. Curricular and laboratory-based activities are presented in the "Tips, Tricks & Techniques" section. Most issues have reviews of audiovisual materials or computer resources in "Classroom Media Reviews." Announcements and society news are also featured. Recommended for academic and school libraries with resources for educators. URL: www.nabt.org/websites/institution/index.php?p=26

ENVIRONMENTAL EDUCATION

1915. *The Journal of Environmental Education.* Formerly (until 1971): *Environmental Education.* [ISSN: 0095-8964] 1969. 6x/yr. GBP 328 (print & online eds.)). Ed(s): John Shultis, Paul Hart. Routledge, 530 Walnut St, Ste 850, Philadelphia, PA 19106; enquiries@tandfonline.com; http://www.tandfonline.com. Illus., index. Refereed. Reprint: PSC. *Indexed:* A01, A22, BRI, E01, ERIC, S25. *Bk. rev.:* Varies by issue. *Aud.:* Ac, Sa.

With a focus on environmental education, this journal publishes original articles that promote and inform on instruction, theory, methods, and practice from primary grades through college. Peer-reviewed research articles include project reports, programs, review articles, critical essays, analyses, and qualitative or quantitative studies. The emphasis is on how to instruct on environmental issues and how to evaluate existing programs. There are four to six articles per issue. Topics have included community engagement, sustainable community development, integrating multiple perspectives on the human-nature relationship, and the role of environment clubs in promoting ecocentrism in secondary schools. Readership consists of teachers and others involved with environmental education programs for schools, parks, camps, recreation centers, and businesses. A recommended title for academic libraries with resources for environmental educators. URL: www.tandfonline.com/toc/vjee20/current

MORAL EDUCATION

1916. *Journal of Moral Education.* Formerly (until 1971): *Moral Education.* [ISSN: 0305-7240] 1969. q. GBP 348 (print & online eds.)). Ed(s): Darcia Narvaez. Routledge, 4 Park Sq, Milton Park, Abingdon, OX14 4RN, United Kingdom; subscriptions@tandf.co.uk; http://www.tandfonline.com. Illus., index, adv. Sample. Refereed. Vol. ends: Dec. Reprint: PSC. *Indexed:* A01, A22, ASSIA, E01, ERIC, IBSS, R&TA. *Bk. rev.:* Various number and length. *Aud.:* Ac.

Journal of Moral Education focuses on all aspects of moral education and development. A multidisciplinary approach and inclusive age range contribute to the journal's broad content scope. Authors provide philosophical analyses, empirical research reports, evaluations of educational practice, and overviews of international moral education theories and practices. Five or six articles per issue cover moral education research, such as interpersonal communication competence and digital citizenship, exemplarist moral theory, and educating for inquisitiveness. Curriculum materials and book reviews, as well as special thematic issues, further the academic value of the journal. A standard journal for all academic libraries. URL: www.tandfonline.com/toc/cjme20/current

SOCIAL STUDIES (INCLUDING HISTORY AND ECONOMICS)

1917. *The History Teacher.* [ISSN: 0018-2745] 1967. q. USD 65 (Individuals, USD 38; Free to members). Ed(s): Richard H Wilde, Jane A Dabel. Society for History Education, California State University, 1250 Bellflower Blvd, PO Box 1578, Long Beach, CA 90840; lazarowi@csulb.edu. Illus., index, adv. Sample. Refereed. Vol. ends: Aug. *Indexed:* A01, A22, BAS, Chicano, ERIC, MLA-IB. *Bk. rev.:* Number and length vary. *Aud.:* Ac.

A membership journal of the Society for History Education, this title is dedicated to the teaching of history in the primary, secondary, and higher education classroom. Each issue includes featured articles on the craft of teaching, and additional articles related to history education. Some recent featured articles have dealt with using digitized primary sources, integrating foreign language learning into history classes, and teaching the History of Science in Latin America in English-speaking classrooms. Recommended for academic libraries. URL: www.thehistoryteacher.org/

TEACHER EDUCATION

1918. *Journal of Education for Teaching: international research and pedagogy.* Formerly (until 1981): *British Journal of Teacher Education.* [ISSN: 0260-7476] 1975. 5x/yr. GBP 1447 (print & online eds.)). Ed(s): Peter Gilroy. Routledge, 4 Park Sq, Milton Park, Abingdon, OX14 4RN, United Kingdom; subscriptions@tandf.co.uk; http://www.tandfonline.com. Adv. Sample. Refereed. Reprint: PSC. *Indexed:* A01, A22, E01, ERIC, MLA-IB. *Bk. rev.:* Number and length vary. *Aud.:* Ac.

Journal of Education for Teaching publishes original articles on the subject of teacher education. The journal's definition of teacher education is inclusive of initial training, in-service education, and professional staff development. Primarily British, but with an international orientation, this title seeks to promote academic discussion of issues, trends, research, opinion, and practice on teacher education. Contributors have assessed such issues as student teachers's engagement in Facebook-assisted peer assessment, enhancing preservice teacher's professional competence through experiential learning, and the changes that have occurred to university level EFL teachers' teaching practices. Annually, one issue is devoted to a special topic. Recommended for academic libraries with resources for educators. URL: www.tandfonline.com/loi/cjet20

1919. *Journal of Teacher Education: the journal of policy, practice, and research in teacher education.* [ISSN: 0022-4871] 1950. 5x/yr. USD 827 (print & online eds.)). Sage Publications, Inc., 2455 Teller Rd, Thousand Oaks, CA 91320; info@sagepub.com; http://www.sagepub.com. Illus., adv. Sample. Refereed. Vol. ends: Nov/Dec. Microform: PQC. Reprint: PSC. *Indexed:* A01, A22, BRI, CBRI, Chicano, E01, ERIC, MLA-IB. *Bk. rev.:* 0-1, essay length. *Aud.:* Ac.

A professional journal of the American Association of Colleges for Teacher Education, *Journal of Teacher Education* considers teacher education as a field of study, with a focus on policy, practice, and research. The goal of this peer-reviewed journal is to provide educators with information that will help future teachers deal with the issues, challenges, and demands of the instructional environment. Recent articles have addressed such topics as reexamining coherence in teacher education, multicultural education reform, and the implementation of the co-teaching model in student teaching. Occasionally, essay-length book reviews are included. Highly recommended for academic libraries that serve teacher education programs. URL: http://jte.sagepub.com/

1920. *Teaching and Teacher Education: an international journal of research and studies.* [ISSN: 0742-051X] 1985. 8x/yr. EUR 2727. Ed(s): Terence Lovat, Jennifer Gore. Pergamon Press, The Blvd, Langford Ln, E Park, Kidlington, OX5 1GB, United Kingdom; JournalsCustomerServiceEMEA@elsevier.com; http://www.elsevier.com. Illus., adv. Sample. Refereed. Microform: PQC. *Indexed:* A01, A22, ASSIA, ERIC. *Aud.:* Ac.

This international journal covers all aspects and levels of teaching, teachers, and teacher education. A multidisciplinary title, it is of value to all concerned with teaching, including researchers in teacher education, educational and cognitive psychologists, and policymakers and planners. It is committed to promoting teaching and teacher education through the publication of theory, research, and practice. Special issues, virtual and print, have considered the topics of scholarly work beyond written texts; equity and social justice; teacher education for inclusive education; and teaching learning and development in the United Kingdom. Recommended for all libraries that serve teacher education programs. URL: www.journals.elsevier.com/teaching-and-teacher-education

1921. *Teaching Education.* [ISSN: 1047-6210] 1987. q. GBP 559 (print & online eds.)). Ed(s): Diane Mayer, Julianne Moss. Routledge, 4 Park Sq, Milton Park, Abingdon, OX14 4RN, United Kingdom; subscriptions@tandf.co.uk; http://www.tandfonline.com. Illus., index, adv. Sample. Refereed. Reprint: PSC. *Indexed:* A22, E01, ERIC. *Bk. rev.:* 2, 800 words to essay length. *Aud.:* Ac.

Dedicated to providing a forum for innovative practice and research, this journal focuses on challenge and change in teacher education. Contributors address social, cultural, practical, and theoretical aspects of teacher education, from K-12 to university settings. The journal's contents include critical and theory-based research; scholarly reflections on current teacher education issues; innovative approaches to undergraduate and graduate teaching; new practices in the K-12 classroom; and reviews of scholarly works. Special issues are also published. Recommended for all academic libraries with resources for educators. URL: www.tandf.co.uk/journals/cTED

TECHNOLOGY

1922. *Educational Technology Research & Development.* Formed by the merger of (1978-1989): *Journal of Instructional Development;* (1978-1989): *Educational Communications and Technology Journal;* Which was formerly (unil 1978): *A V Communication Review;* (until 1964): *Audio Visual Communication Review.* [ISSN: 1042-1629] 1989. bi-m. EUR 634 (print & online eds.)). Ed(s): J Michael Spector, T E Johnson. Springer New York LLC, 233 Spring St, New York, NY 10013; customerservice@springer.com; http://www.springer.com. Illus., index, adv. Refereed. Vol. ends: No. 4. Microform: PQC. Reprint: PSC. *Indexed:* A01, A22, BRI, E01, ERIC. *Bk. rev.:* Varies, 0-2, essay length. *Aud.:* Ac.

A publication of the Association for Educational Communications and Technology, this journal serves to promote educational technology and its application to the learning process and focuses entirely on research and development in educational technology. Each issue has five or six articles that cover research, both practical aspects and applied theory, and development topics, including planning, implementation, evaluation, and management. Recent topics have included cognitive domains and computer programming knowledge in young children, TPACK design scaffolding, and digital game based learning for struggling readers. This is the only scholarly journal that focuses entirely on research and development in educational technology. Each issue also includes book reviews, international reviews, and research abstracts. Recommended for academic libraries with resources for educators. URL: http://aect.site-ym.com/?page=ed_technology_r_d

1923. *Journal of Educational Computing Research.* [ISSN: 0735-6331] 1985. 8x/yr. USD 1059 (print & online eds.)). Ed(s): Robert H Seidman. Sage Publications, Inc., 2455 Teller Rd, Thousand Oaks, CA 91320; info@sagepub.com; http://www.sagepub.com. Illus., index. Sample. Refereed. Reprint: PSC. *Indexed:* A22, CompLI, ERIC, MLA-IB. *Aud.:* Ac.

This refereed journal publishes original articles on various aspects of educational computing like the outcome effects of educational computing applications, development and design of new hardware and software, interpretation and implications of research, and theory and history. Interdisciplinary articles are intended for a readership of practitioners, researchers, scientists, and educators from classroom teachers to faculty, and the goal of each issue is to advance knowledge and practice in the field of educational computing through empirical research, analyses, design and development studies, and critical reviews. Authors have presented recent research on adaptive e-learning environments, using speech translation and shadowing in familiar authentic contexts, and electronic books for promoting emergent math. This journal is recommended for academic libraries with education programs. URL: www.baywood.com/journals/previewjournals.asp?id=0735-6331

1924. ***Tech Directions: linking education to careers.*** Former titles (until 1992): *School Shop - Tech Directions;* (until 1990): *New School Shop - Tech Directions;* (until 1989): *School Shop;* (until 1948): *School Shop for Industrial Arts and Vocational Education Teachers.* [ISSN: 1062-9351] 1941. 10x/yr. USD 30 domestic (Free to qualified personnel). Ed(s): Susanne Peckham. Prakken Publications, Inc., 832 Phoenix Dr, Ann Arbor, MI 48107; vanessa@techdirections.com. Illus., index, adv. Sample. Vol. ends: May. Microform: PQC. *Indexed:* A01, A22, B01, ERIC. *Bk. rev.:* 6, 150 words. *Aud.:* Ga, Ac.

This publication focuses on the fields of technology, industrial, and vocational education. Contributors cover teaching techniques, classroom projects, laboratory/classroom administrative procedures, and issues facing the applied educational technology field. The magazine is intended for technology, vocational-technical, and applied science educators at all educational levels, and its articles and columns are curriculum-oriented. Readers will also find cartoons, funny anecdotes, puzzles, and brain teasers that educators can use. Recommended for academic and school libraries with vocational education programs. URL: www.techdirections.com

1925. ***Technology and Engineering Teacher.*** Former titles (until 2010): *The Technology Teacher;* (until 1983): *Man, Society, Technology;* (until 1970): *Journal of Industrial Arts Education;* (until 1964): *The Industrial Arts Teacher.* [ISSN: 2158-0502] 1939. 8x/yr. Free to members. Ed(s): Kathleen B de la Paz. International Technology and Engineering Educators Association, 1914 Association Dr, Ste 201, Reston, VA 20191; iteea@iteea.org; http://www.iteea.org/. Illus., index, adv. Sample. Refereed. Vol. ends: May/Jun. Microform: PQC. *Indexed:* A01, A22, BRI, ERIC. *Bk. rev.:* 1, 100 words. *Aud.:* Ac.

This is the journal of the International Technology Education Association. Its goal is to be a resource tool for technology education practitioners. The audience ranges from elementary school to high school classroom teachers, as well as teacher educators. Article content is focused on the sharing of current trends, classroom ideas, and applications. A section on classroom challenges showcases interesting projects such as radio-controlled cars; creating an electric vehicle; creating a greenhouse; and developing a watershed. As a membership journal, this title also includes association events and news. Recommended for all school and academic libraries with resources for educators. URL: www.iteea.org/Publications/ttt.htm

■ ELECTRONICS

Paula M. Storm, Assistant Professor, Science Technology Librarian, Bruce T. Halle Library, Eastern Michigan University, Ypsilanti, MI 48197; pstorm@emich.edu

Introduction

Trade magazines and journals in the field of electronics range in perspective from technical and scientific to business and consumer. Readers from a variety of backgrounds and educational levels use these publications as a way to keep current in this rapidly changing environment. Those in business need to know how to incorporate electronic equipment into their workflow, how to monitor the electronics industry, and how to improve, assemble, or package their electronic products.

Readers with technical and scientific backgrounds will want to keep current on trends and research, and also to use these journals to communicate their own research findings. Consumers will find the trade magazines invaluable in obtaining information on construction and repair, as well as for explanations, reviews, and ratings of new products. Public librarians who collect in the area of electronics will want to include the trade magazines, and those in an academic environment will supplement those titles with scholarly journals, especially those published by IEEE.

Basic Periodicals

IEEE Transactions on Consumer Electronics; IEEE Transactions on Electron Devices; IEEE Transactions on Industrial Electronics; IEEE Transactions on Power Electronics; IEEE Proceedings; International Journal of Electronics; Solid-State Electronics.

Basic Abstracts and Indexes

ABI/INFORM, Applied Science and Technology Abstracts, Business and Company ASAP, Business Source Premier, Compendex, Computer Database, Electronics and Communications Abstracts, Computer Society Digital Library (IEEE), INSPEC, Physics Abstracts, ScienceDirect, Scopus, Web of Science.

1926. ***Audioxpress: advancing the evolution of audio technology.*** Formed by the merger of (1989-2001): *Glass Audio;* (1980-2001): *Speaker Builder;* (1996-2001): *Audio Electronics;* Which was formerly (1970-1996): *Audio Amateur.* [ISSN: 1548-6028] 2001. m. USD 50 domestic (print or online ed.); USD 65 Canada; USD 75 elsewhere). Ed(s): Joao Martins. Circuit Cellar, Inc., 111 Founders Plz, Ste 300, East Hartford, CT 06108; custservice@circuitcellar.com; http://www.circuitcellar.com/. Illus., adv. *Bk. rev.:* Number and length vary. *Aud.:* Hs, Ga.

For the do-it-yourself audiophile, *AudioXpress* covers subjects that range from amplifiers to vacuum tube technology. Articles feature new projects as well as tips to help upgrade current equipment. Includes reviews of equipment and columns with advice from experts in audio technology.

1927. ***Digital Signal Processing.*** [ISSN: 1051-2004] 1991. m. bi-m. until 2015. EUR 1460. Ed(s): Ercan E Kuruoglu. Academic Press, 225 Wyman St, Waltham, MA 02144; JournalCustomerService-usa@elsevier.com; http://store.elsevier.com/Academic-Press/IMP_5/. Illus., adv. Sample. Refereed. *Indexed:* A01, A22, CompLI, E01, MSN. *Bk. rev.:* Number and length vary. *Aud.:* Ac, Sa.

Digital Signal Processing consists of peer-reviewed research articles and reviews that cover new technologies in the field. This journal is for electronic engineers, scientists, and business managers engaged in digital signal processing. The diverse subjects covered include digital signal processing applications in biomedicine, astronomy, telecommunications, geology, and biology. This journal is available online via Swets, EBSCOhost, Elsevier, and other vendors.

1928. ***E E Times: the industry newspaper for engineers and technical management.*** [ISSN: 0192-1541] 1972. w. United Business Media Llc, TechInsights, Inc., 600 Harrison St, 6th Fl, San Francisco, CA 94107; pmiller@techinsights.com; http://www.techinsights.com. Adv. *Indexed:* A01, A22, B01, B03, BRI, C42. *Bk. rev.:* Number and length vary. *Aud.:* Ga, Ac, Sa.

This trade publication is focused on the key trends and news in the electronics industry. Written for engineers and technical managers, it is a weekly tabloid that contains statistics, charts, and tables on the electronics industry sector. A free online subscription is available. Also available via Gale, LexisNexis, ProQuest, and other vendors. URL: www.eetimes.com

1929. ***Electronic Design.*** Incorporates (1941-2007): *E E Product News.* [ISSN: 0013-4872] 1952. bi-w. USD 120 domestic (Free to qualified personnel). Ed(s): Nancy Friedrich. Penton, 1100 Superior Ave., Cleveland, OH 44114; information@penton.com; http://www.penton.com. Illus., index, adv. Sample. Circ: 145000 Controlled. Vol. ends: No. 28. Microform: PQC. *Indexed:* A01, A22, B01, B03, BRI. *Bk. rev.:* Number and length vary. *Aud.:* Ac, Sa.

Electronic Design features short, practical articles on various subjects of interest to design engineers such as electronic design automation, test and measurement, and communications. Two longer features include "Design Solutions," written by contributors who provide more in-depth advice and problem solutions, and "Technology Report," which addresses current topics in the world of electronic design. Full text is available online via Gale, ProQuest, and other vendors. It is free to qualified subscribers. URL: www.electronicdesign.com

Electronic House. See Home section.

1930. ***Electronics.*** [ISSN: 2079-9292] 2012. q. Free. Ed(s): Dr. Mostafa Bassiouni. M D P I AG, St. Alban-Anlage 66, Basel, 4052, Switzerland; http://www.mdpi.com. Refereed. *Bk. rev.:* Number and length vary. *Aud.:* Ac.

This open-access, peer-reviewed, English-language journal is published in Switzerland by Molecular Diversity Preservation International (MDPI). It covers all aspects of electronics. It is available online from MDPI.

1931. ***Electronics and Communications in Japan.*** Formed by the merger of (1985-2008): *Electronic and Communications in Japan. Part 1: Communications;* (1985-2008): *Electronic and Communications in Japan. Part 2: Electronics;* (1989-2008): *Electronic and Communications in Japan. Part 3: Fundamental Electronic Science;* All of which superseded in part (1963-1985): *Electronic and Communications in Japan.* [ISSN: 1942-9533] 2008. m. GBP 16329. Ed(s): Takatoshi Shindo. Wiley-Blackwell Publishing, Inc., 350 Main St, Malden, MA 02148; cs-journals@wiley.com; http://onlinelibrary.wiley.com. Adv. Sample. Reprint: PSC. *Indexed:* A01, B01. *Aud.:* Ac, Sa.

This scholarly journal publishes original research in the area of electronics. The articles are translated from the Japanese, from papers originally published in the *Transactions of the Institute of Electronics, Information and Communication Engineers of Japan.* Available online via EBSCOhost, Wiley-Blackwell, and Swets.

1932. ***Electronics Letters.*** [ISSN: 0013-5194] 1965. bi-w. GBP 2562 (print & online eds.)). Ed(s): Ian H White, Christofer Toumazou. The Institution of Engineering and Technology, Michael Faraday House, Six Hills Way, Stevenage, SG1 2AY, United Kingdom; postmaster@theiet.org; http://www.theiet.org/. Illus., index, adv. Sample. Refereed. Vol. ends: No. 25. *Indexed:* A01, A22, B01. *Aud.:* Ac, Sa.

Electronics Letters contains short research papers that address the most current international developments in electronics. This journal is published by the Institution of Engineering and Technology, an association formed by the joining together of the IEE (Institution of Electrical Engineers) and the IIE (Institution of Incorporated Engineers). Each issue contains about 30 refereed papers that cover both the science and technology of electronics. Full text is available online from a variety of vendors.

1933. ***Elektor.*** Former titles (until 2007): *Elektor Electronics;* (until 1984): *Elektor.* [ISSN: 1757-0875] 1974. 11x/yr. Free to members. Elektor Electronics (Publishing), Regus Brentford, 1000 Great West Rd, Brentford, TW8 9HH, United Kingdom; sales@elektor-electronics.co.uk; http://www.elektor.com. Illus., adv. Circ: 17500. *Indexed:* A22. *Bk. rev.:* Number and length vary. *Aud.:* Ga, Ac, Sa.

Elektor is a magazine for both consumers and professional engineers. The articles focus on current projects in the electronics industry and newsworthy new products in electronics technology.

1934. ***Embedded Systems Design: creative solutions for senior systems designers and their teams.*** Formerly (until 2005): *Embedded Systems Programming.* [ISSN: 1558-2493] 1988. m. USD 55 domestic (Free to qualified personnel). Ed(s): Rich Nass. United Business Media Llc, TechInsights, Inc., 600 Harrison St, 6th Fl, San Francisco, CA 94107; pmiller@techinsights.com; http://www.techinsights.com. Adv. Circ: 45000. *Indexed:* A01, A22, B01, BRI, C42, CompLI. *Bk. rev.:* Number and length vary. *Aud.:* Ac, Sa.

Embedded Systems Design is a magazine for electronic systems designers who are responsible for selecting, integrating, and building hardware and software components and systems for their companies. Each issue contains short articles that highlight featured products, and longer feature articles that address specific problems encountered by system designers. Available full-text online via ProQuest, Dow Jones Factiva, and Gale.

1935. ***Engineering & Technology.*** Incorporates (2007-2008): *I E T Manufacturing;* Which was formerly (until 2007): *Manufacturing Engineer;* (1921-1989): *Production Engineer;* (2004-2008): *Information Professional;* (2003-2008): *Power Engineer;* Which was formerly (1987-2002): *Power Engineering Journal;* (2007-2008): *I E T Electronics;* Which was formerly (Jun.2003-Jul.2007): *Electronics Systems & Software;* (200?-2008): *Engineering Management;* Which was formerly (1991-200?): *Engineering Management Journal;* (2007-2008): *Control & Automation;* Which was formerly (1990-2007): *Computing & Control Engineering;* Which incorporated (1983-1992): *Computer-Aided Engineering Journal;* (2003-2008): *Communications Engineer;* Which was formerly (until 2003): *Electronics & Communication Engineer;* (until 1998): *Institution of Electronic and Radio Engineers. Journal;* (until 1985): *Radio and Electronic Engineer;* (1939-1963): *British Institute of Radio Engineers. Journal;* Which incorporated: *Institution of Electronic and Radio Engineers. Proceedings;* Engineering & Technology was formed by the merger of (1988-2006): *I E E Review;* Which incorporated (in 2003): *I E E News;* Which incorporated: *Interlink;* I E E Review was formerly (until 1987): *Electronics and Power;* (1949-1954): *Institution of Electrical Engineers. Journal;* Which incorporated (1949-1954): *Institution of Electrical Engineers. Proceedings. Part 1: General;* (1941-1948): *Institution of Electrical Engineers. Journal. Part 1: General;* (1941-1948): *Institution of Electrical Engineers. Journal. Part 2: Power Engineering;* (1941-1948): *Institution of Electrical Engineers. Journal. Part 3: Radio and Communication Engineering;* Part 1, 2 & 3 superseded in part (in 1940): *Institution of Electrical Engineers. Journal;* Which was formerly (until 1888): *Society of Telegraph Engineers and Electricians. Journal;* (until 1972): *Students Quarterly;* (1998-2006): *Engineering Technology;* Which was formed by the merger of (1973-1998): *Electrotechnology;* Which was formerly (1966-1972): *Electrical & Electronics Technician Engineers;* (1988-1998): *Mechanical Incorporated Engineer;* Which was formed by the merger of (1981-1988): *Mechanical Engineering Technology;* (1973-1988): *General Engineer;* Which was formerly (until 1972): *Institution of General Technician Engineers. Journal;* (until 1971): *Junior Institution of Engineers. Journal and Record of Transactions;* (1990-1998): *Electronic and Electrical Engineering;* Which was formerly (until 1990): *Electrical and Electronics Incorporated Engineer;* (until 1983): *Incorporated Engineer;* (until 19??): *I E E I E Bulletin;* (until 1962): *I E E T E Bulletin.* [ISSN: 1750-9637] 2006. 10x/yr. GBP 962 (print or online ed.)). Ed(s): Dickon Ross, Jonathan Wilson. The Institution of Engineering and Technology, Michael Faraday House, Six Hills Way, Stevenage, SG1 2AY, United Kingdom; postmaster@theiet.org; http://www.theiet.org/. Adv. *Indexed:* A22. *Bk. rev.:* Number and length vary. *Aud.:* Ga, Ac, Sa.

Published by the Institution of Engineering and Technology, this monthly publication targets professional engineers. In addition to regular features such as news, research and development, events, and editorials, articles by high-profile contributors are included on a variety of subjects, ranging from technology to management. This title is available in print and via IEEE, the IET Digital Library, EBSCOhost, and other vendors.

1936. ***Everyday Practical Electronics.*** Incorporates (1971-1998): *E T I - Electronics Today International;* Which was formerly (until 1989): *Electronics Today International;* (until 1972): *Electronics Today;* Formerly (until 1995); *Everyday with Practical Electronics;* Which incorporates: *Electronics Monthly;* Which was formed by the merger of (1971-1992): *Everyday Electronics;* (1964-1992): *Practical Electronics.* [ISSN: 1367-398X] 1992. m. GBP 43 domestic; GBP 70 foreign. Ed(s): Michael Kenward. Wimborne Publishing Ltd., Sequoia House, 398a Ringwood Rd, Ferndown, BH22 9AU, United Kingdom; enquiries@wimborne.co.uk. Illus., adv. *Bk. rev.:* Number and length vary. *Aud.:* Ga.

Everyday Practical Electronics [*EPE*] *Online* is a magazine from the United Kingdom for electronics and computer enthusiasts. Each issue contains numerous building projects in electronics, for every level of expertise.

1937. ***I E E E Electron Device Letters.*** Formerly (until Feb.1980): *Electron Device Letters.* [ISSN: 0741-3106] 1980. m. USD 2140. Ed(s): Jesus del Alamo. Institute of Electrical and Electronics Engineers, 445 Hoes Ln, Piscataway, NJ 08855; contactcenter@ieee.org; http://www.ieee.org. Illus. Sample. Refereed. *Indexed:* A22. *Bk. rev.:* Number and length vary. *Aud.:* Ac, Sa.

This journal is published by the IEEE Electron Device Society. It publishes original research and significant contributions relating to the theory, design, and performance of electron and ion devices, solid-state devices, integrated electronic devices, and optoelectronic devices and energy sources. Available online from IEEE.

1938. ***I E E E Journal of Quantum Electronics.*** [ISSN: 0018-9197] 1965. bi-m. USD 2830. Ed(s): Hon Ki Tsang. Institute of Electrical and Electronics Engineers, 3 Park Ave, 17th Fl, New York, NY 10016; contactcenter@ieee.org; http://www.ieee.org. Illus. Refereed. *Indexed:* A01, A22, B01, BRI. *Bk. rev.:* Number and length vary. *Aud.:* Ac, Sa.

Each issue highlights specific subjects, and the articles are grouped accordingly. Published by the IEEE Lasers and Electro-Optics Society, this journal covers technology in which quantum electronic devices are used. Available online via IEEE.

1939. ***I E E E Journal on Emerging and Selected Topics in Circuits and Systems.*** [ISSN: 2156-3357] 2011. q. USD 1100. Ed(s): Eduard Alarcon. Institute of Electrical and Electronics Engineers, 445 Hoes Ln, Piscataway, NJ 08855; corporate-communications@ieee.org; http://www.ieee.org. Adv. Refereed. *Aud.:* Ac.

This journal is published by IEEE and has an emphasis on developing new areas in circuits and system technology. There are special issues on specific topics, including the theory, analysis, design, tools, and implementation of circuits and systems.

1940. ***I E E E Journal on Selected Topics in Signal Processing.*** [ISSN: 1932-4553] 2007. s-a. Ed(s): Lina Karam. Institute of Electrical and Electronics Engineers, 3 Park Ave, 17th Fl, New York, NY 10016; contactcenter@ieee.org; http://www.ieee.org. Refereed. *Bk. rev.:* Number and length vary. *Aud.:* Ac, Sa.

This publication from the IEEE contains solicited papers on special topics on all aspects of signal processing. Useful for academics and practitioners in electronics and electrical engineering.

1941. ***I E E E. Proceedings.*** Former titles (until 1963): *Institute of Radio Engineers. Proceedings;* (until 1939): *Institute of Radio Engineers. Proceedings;* (until 1913): *Wireless Institute. Proceedings of the Meeting Held.* [ISSN: 0018-9219] 1909. m. USD 1380. Ed(s): Gianluca Setti. Institute of Electrical and Electronics Engineers, 3 Park Ave, 17th Fl, New York, NY 10016; contactcenter@ieee.org; http://www.ieee.org. Illus. Refereed. *Indexed:* A22, ErgAb, MLA-IB. *Aud.:* Ga, Ac, Sa.

Published since 1913 and renowned as the most highly cited general-interest journal in electrical engineering and computer science, the *Proceedings of the IEEE* contains in-depth tutorial and review articles in the areas of electrical engineering and technology. Its alternate title is *Proceedings of the I E E E.* Included are survey articles that review an existing technology. Each issue focuses on a special topic, preceded by an editorial that reviews the included papers. Articles are written for the IEEE member or the general reader who has some background in electrical engineering. Available online via IEEE and from EBSCOhost.

1942. ***I E E E Transactions on Circuits and Systems. Part 1: Regular Papers.*** Formed by the merger of (1992-2004): *I E E E Transactions on Circuits and Systems Part 1: Fundamental Theory and Applications;* (1992-2004): *I E E E Transactions on Circuits and Systems Part 2: Analog and Digital Signal Processing;* Both of which superseded in part (in 1992): *I E E E Transactions on Circuits and Systems;* Which was formerly (until 1974): *I E E E Transactions on Circuit Theory;* (until 1963): *I R E Transactions on Circuit Theory;* (until 1955): *I R E Professional Group on Circuit Theory. Transactions.* [ISSN: 1549-8328] 2004. m. USD 1690. Ed(s): Andreas Demosthenous. Institute of Electrical and Electronics Engineers, 445 Hoes Ln, Piscataway, NJ 08855; contactcenter@ieee.org; http://www.ieee.org. Illus. Refereed. Vol. ends: No. 12. *Indexed:* A01, A22, B01, CompLI, MSN. *Bk. rev.:* Number and length vary. *Aud.:* Ac, Sa.

Published by the IEEE Circuits and Systems Society, *IEEE Transactions on Circuits and Systems* contains peer-reviewed papers on the theory and applications of circuits and systems, both analog and digital. Articles contain numerous charts and tables, as well as short biographies of the authors. Available online via IEEE.

1943. ***I E E E Transactions on Circuits and Systems. Part 2: Express Briefs.*** Formerly (until 2004): *I E E E Transactions on Circuits and Systems Part 2: Analog and Digital Signal Processing;* Which superseded in part (in 1992): *I E E E Transactions on Circuits and Systems;* Which was formerly (until 1974): *I E E E Transactions on Circuit Theory;* (until 1963): *I R E Transactions on Circuit Theory;* (until 1955): *I R E Professional Group on Circuit Theory. Transactions.* [ISSN: 1549-7747] 1952. m. USD 1410. Ed(s): C.K Michael Tse. Institute of Electrical and Electronics Engineers, 445 Hoes Ln, Piscataway, NJ 08855; contactcenter@ieee.org; http://www.ieee.org. Illus. Refereed. *Indexed:* A22, CompLI. *Aud.:* Ac, Sa.

The intent of *IEEE Transactions on Circuits and Systems. Part 2: Express Briefs* is rapid dissemination of original innovations and ideas on the subject of digital and analog circuits and systems. If an article is accepted, it is scheduled to be published four months from the date of receipt. Authors may send more in-depth articles to the sister publication *IEEE Transactions on Circuits and Systems. Part 1: Regular Papers,* (above in this section). Available online via IEEE.

1944. ***I E E E Transactions on Computer - Aided Design of Integrated Circuits and Systems.*** [ISSN: 0278-0070] 1982. m. USD 1460. Ed(s): Rajesh Gupta. Institute of Electrical and Electronics Engineers, 3 Park Ave, 17th Fl, New York, NY 10016; subscription-service@ieee.org; http://www.ieee.org. Refereed. *Indexed:* A01, A22, B01, CompLI. *Aud.:* Ac, Sa.

Published by the IEEE Circuits and Systems Society, this journal contains articles on analog, digital, optical, or microwave integrated circuits that emphasize the practical applications and the resulting products of original research. All such research papers are published in this journal, whereas briefer papers that report recent important results are published in the *IEEE Transactions on Circuits and Systems. Part 2: Express Briefs.*

1945. ***I E E E Transactions on Consumer Electronics.*** Former titles (until 1975): *I E E E Transactions on Broadcast and Television Receivers;* (until 1963): *I R E Transactions on Broadcast and Television Receivers;* (until 1955): *I R E Professional Group on Broadcast and Television Receivers. Transactions.* [ISSN: 0098-3063] 1952. q. Ed(s): Fernando Pescador. Institute of Electrical and Electronics Engineers, 445 Hoes Ln, Piscataway, NJ 08855; contactcenter@ieee.org; http://www.ieee.org. Illus. Refereed. *Indexed:* A01, A22, B01, CompLI. *Bk. rev.:* Number and length vary. *Aud.:* Ac, Sa.

This IEEE publication emphasizes new technology in consumer electronics. Consumer electronics includes products and components used for leisure, education, or entertainment. Many of the papers in this journal have been presented at the International Conference on Consumer Electronics. It is available online via IEEE.

1946. ***I E E E Transactions on Electromagnetic Compatibility.*** Former titles (until 1964): *I E E E Transactions on Radio Frequency Interference;* (until 1963): *I R E Transactions on Radio Frequency*

Interference. [ISSN: 0018-9375] 1959. 8x/yr. USD 615. Ed(s): Tzong-Lin Wu. Institute of Electrical and Electronics Engineers, 445 Hoes Ln, Piscataway, NJ 08855; contactcenter@ieee.org; http://www.ieee.org. Illus. Refereed. *Indexed:* A01, A22, B01. *Bk. rev.:* Number and length vary. *Aud.:* Ac, Sa.

Topics covered in this journal include measurement techniques and standards, spectrum conservation and utilization, and equipment and systems related to electromagnetic compatibility. This IEEE publication includes correspondence, brief articles, and longer papers. Available in full text online via IEEE and EBSCOhost.

1947. *I E E E Transactions on Electron Devices.* Former titles (until 1963): *I R E Transactions on Electron Devices;* (until 1955): *I R E Professional Group on Electron Devices. Transactions.* [ISSN: 0018-9383] 1952. m. USD 3350. Ed(s): Giovanni Ghione. Institute of Electrical and Electronics Engineers, 445 Hoes Ln, Piscataway, NJ 08855; contactcenter@ieee.org; http://www.ieee.org. Illus. Refereed. *Indexed:* A01, A22, B01, CompLI. *Bk. rev.:* Number and length vary. *Aud.:* Ac, Sa.

The IEEE Electron Device Society publishes this monthly journal, which covers the theory, design, performance, and reliability of electron devices. Two types of papers are selected for inclusion: peer-reviewed, in-depth regular papers; and briefs covering preliminary results or reporting of recently completed projects. There is also a section for letters to the editor. Full text is available online through the IEEE and from EBSCOhost.

1948. *I E E E Transactions on Industrial Electronics.* Former titles (until 1982): *I E E E Transactions on Industrial Electronics and Control Instrumentation;* (until 1964): *I E E E Transactions on Industrial Electronics;* (until 1963): *I R E Transactions on Industrial Electronics;* (until 1955): *I R E Professional Group on Industrial Electronics. Transactions.* [ISSN: 0278-0046] 1953. m. USD 2140. Ed(s): Emil Levi. Institute of Electrical and Electronics Engineers, 445 Hoes Ln, Piscataway, NJ 08855; contactcenter@ieee.org; http://www.ieee.org. Illus. Refereed. *Indexed:* A01, A22, B01. *Bk. rev.:* Number and length vary. *Aud.:* Ac, Sa.

Each issue of *IEEE Transactions on Industrial Electronics* features a special section of reviewed papers covering a specific topic on the application of electronics to industrial and manufacturing systems and processes. Each section is preceded by a guest editorial that explains the special topic that is to be covered. Following the special section papers are papers on various topics, letters, and comments. As in all *IEEE Transactions* journals, short biographies and photos of authors are included. Online availability is via IEEE and from EBSCOhost.

1949. *I E E E Transactions on Power Electronics.* [ISSN: 0885-8993] 1986. m. USD 2025. Ed(s): Brad Lehman. Institute of Electrical and Electronics Engineers, 3 Park Ave, 17th Fl, New York, NY 10016; contactcenter@ieee.org; http://www.ieee.org. Illus., adv. *Indexed:* A01, A22, B01. *Bk. rev.:* Number and length vary. *Aud.:* Ac, Sa.

Published by the Power Electronics Society of the IEEE, *IEEE Transactions on Power Electronics* has the highest impact factor of any journal in power electronics, according to its editor-in-chief, Frede Blaabjerg. This publication contains both long research papers and shorter letters that introduce new developments and ideas. Online availability is via IEEE and from EBSCOhost.

1950. *I E T Power Electronics.* [ISSN: 1755-4535] 2008. 16x/yr. GBP 977 (print & online eds.)). Ed(s): Volker Pickert, Miguel Castilla. The Institution of Engineering and Technology, Michael Faraday House, Six Hills Way, Stevenage, SG1 2AY, United Kingdom; postmaster@theiet.org; http://www.theiet.org/. Adv. Refereed. *Aud.:* Ac, Sa.

This journal contains articles on the current research and development in power electronics, circuits, devices, techniques, and the performance management of power systems. Five-year Impact Factor is 1.65.

1951. *International Journal of Computer Technology and Electronics Engineering.* [ISSN: 2249-6343] 2011. bi-m. Free. Ed(s): Ajay Somkuwar, Himanshu Mehta. National Institute of Science Communication and Information Resources, Dr K S Krishnan Marg, Pusa Campus, New Delhi, 110 012, India; sales@niscair.res.in; http://www.niscair.res.in. Refereed. *Aud.:* Ac.

This open-access, peer-reviewed, independent academic journal published in India contains original research papers on electronics and related topics.

1952. *International Journal of Electrical and Electronics Engineering Research.* [ISSN: 2250-155X] 2011. bi-m. USD 525. Ed(s): Taheri Abkenar. Transstellar Journal Publications and Research Consultancy Private Ltd., Transstellar Enclave, 12, Periya Kannara St, Mayiladuthurai, 609 001, India; editor@tjprc.org; http://www.tjprc.org. Illus., adv. Refereed. *Bk. rev.:* Number and length vary. *Aud.:* Ac.

This is an English-language open-access journal published in India that covers research in electronics and electrical engineering. *JCR* impact factor is 5.96.

1953. *International Journal of Electronics.* Supersedes in part (in 1965): *Journal of Electronics and Control;* Which was formerly (until 1957): *Journal of Electronics.* [ISSN: 0020-7217] 1955. m. USD 6902 (print & online eds.)). Ed(s): Ian Hunter, Dr. Alaa Abunjaileh. Taylor & Francis, 2, 3 & 4 Park Sq, Milton Park, Abingdon, OX14 4RN, United Kingdom; https://www.tandfonline.com. Illus., index, adv. Sample. Refereed. Reprint: PSC. *Indexed:* A01, A22, B01, E01. *Bk. rev.:* Number and length vary. *Aud.:* Ac, Sa.

International Journal of Electronics originates in the United Kingdom and publishes articles in these topic areas of electronics: solid state, power, analogue, RF and microwave, and digital. Each issue contains fewer than ten full-length papers that report a theoretical or experimental perspective on one of the above topics. Full text is available online via various vendors, including EBSCOhost and Swets.

1954. *International Journal of Industrial Electronics and Drives.* [ISSN: 1757-3874] 2009. s-a. USD 485 (print or online ed.)). Ed(s): Ehab H E Bayoumi. Inderscience Publishers, PO Box 735, Olney, MK46 5WB, United Kingdom; info@inderscience.com; https://www.inderscience.com/index.php. Sample. Refereed. *Aud.:* Ac, Sa.

This journal contains research work in the area of industrial electronics, power converters, and drives, especially those that have commercial potential. It is available online via EBSCOhost and Academic OneFile.

1955. *Journal of Active and Passive Electronic Devices.* [ISSN: 1555-0281] 2005. q. USD 969 (print & online eds.) Individuals, USD 201). Ed(s): Robert Castellano, Guy Campet. Old City Publishing, Inc., 628 N 2nd St, Philadelphia, PA 19123; info@oldcitypublishing.com; http://www.oldcitypublishing.com. Adv. Sample. Refereed. *Bk. rev.:* Number and length vary. *Aud.:* Ac, Sa.

International in scope, this academic journal fills the subject gap of active and passive electronic devices. This peer-reviewed journal includes review articles, short communications, long articles, and book reviews on the subject of electronic components. Full text is available online via EBSCOhost and Old City Publishing Co.

1956. *Journal of Electrical and Electronics Engineering.* [ISSN: 2250-2424] 2011. q. Transstellar Journal Publications and Research Consultancy Private Ltd., 153D, 2nd Main Rd, First Fl, Bhuvaneswari Nagar, Chennai, 600 042, India; editor@tjprc.org; http://www.tjprc.org. Illus. Refereed. *Bk. rev.:* Number and length vary. *Aud.:* Ac.

This English-language journal is published in India and contains research and review articles on all aspects of electrical engineering.

1957. *Journal of Electrical and Electronics Engineering.* Formed by the merger of (2005-2007): *Universitatea din Oradea. Analele. Fascicula Electrotehnica. Sectiunea Inginerie Electrica;* (1999-2007): *Universitatea din Oradea. Analele. Fascicula Electrotehnica, Sectiunea Electronica;* Both of which superseded in part (1993-1999): *Analele Universitatii din Oradea. Fascicula Electrotehnica;* Which superseded in part

(1991-1992): *Analele Universitatii din Oradea. Fascicula Electrotehnica si Energetica;* Which superseded in part (1976-1990): *Lucrari Stiintifice - Institutul de Invatamant Superior Oradea. Seria A, Stiinte Tehnice, Matematica, Fizica, Chimie, Geografie;* Which was formed by the merger of (1971-1973): *Lucrari Stiintifice - Institutul Pedagogic Oradea. Geografie;* (1971-1973): *Lucrari Stiintifice - Institutul Pedagogic Oradea. Matematica, Fizica, Chimie;* Both of which superseded in part (1969-1970): *Lucrari Stiintifice - Institutul Pedagogic Oradea. Seria A;* Which superseded in part (1967-1968): *Lucrari Stiintifice - Institutul Pedagogic Oradea.* [ISSN: 1844-6035] 1967. s-a. Free to qualified personnel. Editura Universitatii din Oradea, Universitatii st, 1, Geotermal Bldg, 2nd Fl, Oradea, 410087, Romania; editura@uoradea.ro; http://webhost.uoradea.ro/editura/. Illus., index. Sample. Refereed. *Indexed:* A01, C45. *Aud.:* Ac, Sa.

This peer-reviewed journal contains original papers in the fields of electronics and electrical engineering. Published in Romania, it has an international scope. This is an open-access journal.

1958. ***Journal of Electronic and Electrical Engineering.*** [ISSN: 0976-8106] 2010. q. Individuals, USD 425. Ed(s): Dr. Yevgen Baganov, Ching-shun Chen. Bioinfo Publications, B2-401, Crimson Crest, SNO-168, Tupe Nagar, DP Rd, Pune, 411 028, India; editor.bioinfo@gmail.com; http://www.bioinfopublication.org. Refereed. *Aud.:* Ac.

Published in India, this English-language journal contains both research and review articles on all aspects of electronics. It is available through EBSCO.

1959. ***Journal of Electronic Materials.*** [ISSN: 0361-5235] 1972. m. EUR 1698 (print & online eds.)). Ed(s): Shadi F Shahedipour-Sandvik. Springer New York LLC, 233 Spring St, New York, NY 10013; customerservice@springer.com; http://www.springer.com. Illus., index, adv. Sample. Refereed. Vol. ends: No. 12. Microform: PQC. Reprint: PSC. *Indexed:* A22, E01. *Bk. rev.:* Number and length vary. *Aud.:* Ac, Sa.

This journal is published by The Minerals, Metals and Materials Society (TMS) and the Institute of Electrical and Electronics Engineers (IEEE). Written for practicing materials engineers and scientists, the *Journal of Electronic Materials* contains peer-reviewed technical papers about new developments in the science and technology of the materials used in electronics, as well as review papers, letters, and selected papers from conferences and meetings of TMS. Several special issues are published during the year containing articles that focus on the same aspect of electronic materials. Available in full text from ProQuest, EBSCOhost, and other vendors.

1960. ***Journal of Electronics Cooling and Thermal Control.*** [ISSN: 2162-6162] 2011. q. USD 398. Ed(s): Dayong Gao. Scientific Research Publishing, Inc., PO Box 54821, Irvine, CA 92619; service@scirp.org; http://www.scirp.org. Refereed. *Aud.:* Ac.

This journal contains original research, technical notes, and reviews about electronic cooling and thermal system-control technology in the computer and electronics industries.

1961. ***Journal of Low Power Electronics.*** [ISSN: 1546-1998] 2005. bi-m. USD 2040. Ed(s): Patrick Girard. American Scientific Publishers, 26650 The Old Rd, Ste 208, Valencia, CA 91381; order@aspbs.com; http://www.aspbs.com. Adv. Refereed. *Bk. rev.:* Number and length vary. *Aud.:* Ac, Sa.

Journal of Low Power Electronics is a peer-reviewed journal with a focus on recent research in the area of low-power electronics, including optoelectronic and electromagnetic devices, wireless communications, VLSI systems, computer systems, signal processing, and more. Full text is available from Ingenta and EBSCOhost.

1962. ***Journal of Low Power Electronics and Applications.*** [ISSN: 2079-9268] 2010. q. Free. Ed(s): Alexander Fish. M D P I AG, St. Alban-Anlage 66, Basel, 4052, Switzerland; info@mdpi.com; http://www.mdpi.com. Refereed. *Aud.:* Ac.

This open-access, English-language journal contains papers related to low-power electronics. Published in Switzerland, it is available from Molecular Diversity Preservation International, and through the Directory of Open Access Journals.

1963. ***Journal of Nanoelectronics and Optoelectronics.*** [ISSN: 1555-130X] 2006. bi-m. USD 2160. Ed(s): Ahmad Umar. American Scientific Publishers, 26650 The Old Rd, Ste 208, Valencia, CA 91381; order@aspbs.com; http://www.aspbs.com. Adv. Refereed. *Bk. rev.:* Number and length vary. *Aud.:* Ac, Sa.

This peer-reviewed journal contains research and review articles on nanoscale and optoelectronic devices and materials. Published by American Scientific Publishers, it is international and interdisciplinary in scope. Special issues highlighting a single subject are published regularly. Indexed in Web of Science, Compendex, and SCOPUS. Full text is available online via EBSCO.

1964. ***Journal of Quantum Electronics and Spintronics.*** [ISSN: 1949-4882] 2010. q. USD 295. Ed(s): M I Miah. Nova Science Publishers, Inc., 415 Oser Ave, Ste N, Hauppauge, NY 11788; nova.main@novapublishers.com; https://www.novapublishers.com. Refereed. *Aud.:* Ac.

This peer-reviewed, international journal publishes original theoretical and experimental research, as well as reviews related to quantum electronic and spin properties. Subject matter also includes quantum electronic and spintronic devices and applications.

1965. ***Microelectronics Journal.*** Formerly (until 1978): *Microelectronics;* Incorporates (1983-1991): *Journal of Semi-Custom I Cs;* (1983-1991): *Semi-Custom I C Yearbook.* [ISSN: 0959-8324] 1967. 12x/yr. EUR 3632. Ed(s): Eby G. Friedman. Elsevier Ltd, 125 London Wall, London, EC2Y 5AS, United Kingdom; corporate.sales@elsevier.com; http://www.elsevier.com. Illus., index, adv. Sample. Refereed. *Indexed:* A01, A22. *Bk. rev.:* Number and length vary. *Aud.:* Ac, Sa.

International in scope, *Microelectronics Journal* covers research on and applications of microelectronics circuits, systems, physics, and devices. Review articles are included, as are papers that present an unusual or new system design or device. Papers are peer reviewed and contain an abstract and keywords.

1966. ***Microelectronics Reliability.*** Formerly (until 1964): *Electronics Reliability & Microminiaturization.* [ISSN: 0026-2714] 1962. m. EUR 6390. Ed(s): N D Stojadnovic. Pergamon Press, The Blvd, Langford Ln, E Park, Kidlington, OX5 1GB, United Kingdom; JournalsCustomerServiceEMEA@elsevier.com; http://www.elsevier.com. Illus., adv. Sample. Refereed. Microform: PQC. *Indexed:* A01, A22. *Bk. rev.:* Number and length vary. *Aud.:* Ac, Sa.

Microelectronics Reliability is composed of research articles that discuss the most current research results and related information on microelectronic device reliability. Topics covered include physics and analysis; evaluation and prediction; design, packaging, and testing; modeling and simulation; and methodologies and assurance. The majority of the remaining articles are primarily case studies. Special issues are sporadically published that report on significant conferences or timely topics in the area of microelectronics. Book reviews are also included in many of the issues. Electronic availability is provided from a number of vendors.

1967. ***Nuts & Volts: evcrything for electronics.*** Formerly (until 1999): *Nuts & Volts Magazine.* [ISSN: 1528-9885] 1980. m. USD 26.95 domestic; USD 33.95 Canada; USD 44.95 foreign. T & L Publications, Inc., 430 Princeland Ct, Corona, CA 92879; display@NutsVolts.com. Illus., adv. *Bk. rev.:* Number and length vary. *Aud.:* Hs, Ga.

Written for the electronics hobbyist, design engineer, and electronics technician, *Nuts & Volts* contains information on equipment and do-it-yourself projects in robotics, lasers, circuit design, computer control, automation, and data acquisition. There are also columns that feature new technology, products, and electronics news. Available in print and online. URL: www.nutsvolts.com

1968. ***Progress in Quantum Electronics: an international review journal.*** [ISSN: 0079-6727] 1969. bi-m. EUR 1000. Ed(s): C Jagdish. Pergamon Press, The Blvd, Langford Ln, E Park, Kidlington, OX5 1GB, United Kingdom; JournalsCustomerServiceEMEA@elsevier.com; http://www.elsevier.com. Adv. Sample. Refereed. Microform: PQC. *Indexed:* A01, A22. *Bk. rev.:* Number and length vary. *Aud.:* Ac, Sa.

Progress in Quantum Electronics is an international journal that contains review articles on current topics in quantum electronics and its applications. The papers are either theoretical or experimental in focus and emphasize various aspects of physics, technology, and engineering related to quantum electronics. Potential readers would include materials scientists, solid state scientists, optical scientists, and electrical and electronic engineers. It is available online from numerous vendors.

1969. ***Radioelectronics and Communications Systems.*** Formerly (until 1967): *Soviet Radio Engineering.* [ISSN: 0735-2727] 1965. m. EUR 4831 (print & online eds.)). Pleiades Publishing, Inc., Pleiades House, 7 W 54th St, New York, NY 10019; info@pleiadesonline.com; http://pleiades.online. Illus. Sample. Refereed. *Indexed:* A22, E01. *Bk. rev.:* Number and length vary. *Aud.:* Ac, Sa.

Radioengineering and electronics are the focus of this scholarly journal, published by Allerton Press. Articles include those that report new research in microwave technology, solid-state electronics, radioengineering systems, integral circuit technology, quantum electronics, radiolocation and radionavigation systems, and biomedical electronics. Importantly, many of the articles report research on subjects that not too long ago would have been classified information.

1970. ***Semiconductor Science and Technology.*** [ISSN: 0268-1242] 1986. m. USD 5175 (print & online eds.)). Ed(s): K Nielsch. Institute of Physics Publishing Ltd., Temple Circus, Temple Way, Bristol, BS1 6HG, United Kingdom; custserv@iop.org; http://iopscience.iop.org. Illus. Sample. Refereed. Vol. ends: No. 12. *Indexed:* A01, A22, CompLI. *Bk. rev.:* Number and length vary. *Aud.:* Ac, Sa.

Published by the Institute of Physics, *Semiconductor Science and Technology* is an international journal that covers semiconductor research and its applications. Research papers, review articles, and rapid communications are all peer reviewed and are written for the scientist or engineer. Occasionally, an issue will cover a specific topic; two such special issues were "Carbon Nanotubes" and "Optical Orientation." Full text is available online from a number of vendors.

1971. ***Solid-State Electronics: an international journal.*** [ISSN: 0038-1101] 1960. m. EUR 2538. Ed(s): Enrique Calleja, Young Kuk. Pergamon Press, The Blvd, Langford Ln, E Park, Kidlington, OX5 1GB, United Kingdom; JournalsCustomerServiceEMEA@elsevier.com; http://www.elsevier.com. Illus., adv. Sample. Refereed. Microform: MIM; PQC. *Indexed:* A01, A22. *Bk. rev.:* Number and length vary. *Aud.:* Ac, Sa.

This international journal consists of collections of original research papers that cover the theory, design, physics, modeling, measurement, preparation, evaluation, and applications of solid-state electronics, crystal growth, semiconductors, and circuit engineering. The letters, review papers, and research papers emphasize the new and innovative and the connection of theory and practice. Full text is available online from Elsevier, EBSCO, and other vendors.

1972. ***Solid State Technology.*** Incorporates (2001-2011): *Small Times;* (1992-2008): *Advanced Packaging;* Which was formerly (1984-1992): *Hybrid Circuit Technology;* Former titles (until 1968): *Semiconductor Products and Solid State Technology;* (until 1962): *Semiconductor Products.* [ISSN: 0038-111X] 1958. 9x/yr. USD 258 domestic (Free to qualified personnel). Ed(s): Peter Singer. PennWell Corporation, 1421 S Sheridan Rd, Tulsa, OK 74112; Headquarters@PennWell.com; http://www.pennwell.com. Illus., index, adv. Sample. Circ: 41136. Vol. ends: No. 12. *Indexed:* A01, A22, B01, B03, C42. *Bk. rev.:* Number and length vary. *Aud.:* Ac, Sa.

Solid State Technology is a trade magazine for managers and engineers in the semiconductor manufacturing industry. Each issue covers the news and technology of such topics as nanotechnology, MEMS, flat panel displays, atomic layer deposition, wafers, and waste handling, as well as the materials, software, products, and processes used in the manufacturing of semiconductors. Occasional special issues cover the state of the industry in specific geographic regions, or report on important conferences and trade shows. Available online from a variety of vendors.

■ ENERGY

Maggie Albro, STEM Librarian, Shippensburg University, Ezra Lehman Memorial Library, 1871 Old Main, Shippensburg, PA 17257; mhalbro@ship.edu

Introduction

From trying to harness power for use in homes to the search for an efficient and ongoing source of energy, the topic of energy has been of interest to everyone from homeowners to utility suppliers to researchers for centuries. The addition of more than 90 new titles added to Ulrichsweb in the past year goes to show the ongoing relevance of the many broad and multidisciplinary titles in today's world.

This section contains reviews for research journals (and a few journals from a non-research perspective) that represent the major publications in new, alternative, and traditional energy fields. A good number of these publications offer open-access options, which is noted within the review, and almost all of the journals are available electronically, which is to be expected of a journal in the field of technology.

As library budgets dwindle, selection of individual journal titles is becoming an increasingly less common practice. For libraries looking to add several energy titles to their collections, publishers may offer an "energy package" with multiple titles at a reduced price. While this takes away the flexibility of single-title subscriptions, benefits, such as the reduced price per title and access to archives and additional titles, may make this option worth the trade-off.

Basic Periodicals

Ga: *Home Power, Power Engineering, World Oil;* Ac: *Energy, Energy & Environmental Science, Energy & Fuels, The Energy Journal, Journal of Energy Engineering.*

Basic Abstracts and Indexes

Applied Science and Technology Index, Engineering Index, Web of Science.

1973. ***Advanced Energy Materials (Online).*** [ISSN: 1614-6840] 2011. bi-m. GBP 8552. Wiley - V C H Verlag GmbH & Co. KGaA, Postfach 101161, Weinheim, 69451, Germany; cs-germany@wiley.com; http://onlinelibrary.wiley.com. Refereed. *Aud.:* Ac.

Begun as a section of *Advanced Materials, Advanced Energy Materials* became a journal in its own right in 2011. The focus of the journal is "materials used in all forms of energy harvesting, conversion, and storage," but the applications are largely for renewable energy sources or, more generally, non-carbon based energy sources. The point is to find the correct materials to use for specific types of energy generation, such as which organics work best in organophotovoltaic systems, or what materials can handle the problems of generating and storing hydrogen (embrittlement, pressurization, temperature). Beyond the choosing of materials is the implementation, such as how the layering of catalytic material affects electrode performance. Issues are comprised of reviews, communications, and full articles. The reviews are lengthy, the communications are relatively short (4 to 6 pages on average), and the articles range from 5 to 15 pages. Some articles include "supplementary material" that ranges from graphics to complex datasets. The title fills a niche in the energy field, and will be useful in cross-disciplinary collections as well.

1974. ***Applied Energy.*** [ISSN: 0306-2619] 1975. 24x/yr. EUR 6535. Elsevier Ltd, The Boulevard, Langford Lane, Oxford, OX5 1GB, United Kingdom; customerserviceau@elsevier.com; http://www.elsevier.com. Illus., adv. Sample. Refereed. Microform: PQC. *Indexed:* A01, A22, C45. *Aud.:* Ac.

Applied Energy discusses energy conversion, conservation, and management from the engineering point of view. Research here is not to develop new energy sources, but to better utilize the ones presently in use. Issues average 35-45 articles, with occasional reviews and short communications. Open-access articles are also available. Authors are almost exclusively academics or from government-sponsored research institutions. It is one of the top ten journals in price, and it should be considered only for an extensive academic library collection.

1975. ***Applied Thermal Engineering: processes, technologies, systems production, storage, utilization.*** Former titles (until 1996): *Heat Recovery Systems and C H P;* (until 1987): *Journal of Heat Recovery Systems.* [ISSN: 1359-4311] 1981. 18x/yr. EUR 5259. Elsevier Ltd, The Boulevard, Langford Lane, Oxford, OX5 1GB, United Kingdom; customerserviceau@elsevier.com; http://www.elsevier.com. Adv. Sample. Refereed. Microform: PQC. *Indexed:* A22, B01. *Aud.:* Ac, Sa.

This journal covers thermal energy applications in depth, from the theoretical to the extremely practical. In general, work involves energy production and large-scale use (such as manufacturing or building heating plants). Although the journal is academic in thrust, often co-authors will work for commercial concerns; the editor himself maintains a private practice as well as an academic appointment. Articles average less than ten pages but can be lengthy. The lag time between submission and electronic publication is often within two to four months of receipt, but print readers can expect to wait another three or four months. However, corrected proofs of articles in press for the upcoming two volumes are fully searchable. Open-access articles are also available. Occasionally, an issue is devoted to the proceedings of a conference, but the bulk of the papers are current, independent research. Those libraries with strong interests in energy and mechanical engineering would find this a welcome title, but compare it to *Applied Energy* (above in this section).

1976. ***Biofuels, Bioproducts and Biorefining.*** [ISSN: 1932-104X] 2007. bi-m. GBP 935. Ed(s): Bruce E Dale. John Wiley & Sons Ltd., EMEA Institutional Sales, 9600 Garsington Rd, Oxford, OX4 2DQ, United Kingdom; cs-journals@wiley.com; http://onlinelibrary.wiley.com. Adv. Sample. Refereed. Reprint: PSC. *Indexed:* A01, C45. *Aud.:* Ac, Sa.

Since its initial publication in 2007, this journal has rapidly become an important title in energy. It is a mix of engineering and business, which may be the important factor in its appeal. With many colorful illustrations and a magazine layout, *Biofpr*, as it calls itself, is in the style of many professional society magazines, rather than a scholarly journal. The scope is larger than biomass as fuel, and includes using biomass for carbon reduction and integrating biomass fuel into power systems. Most of each issue is composed of articles, but there are several regular sections: business highlights, technology news, patents, modeling and analysis (formerly "market trends"), interviews, and the occasional commentary. The articles are categorized as features, perspectives, and reviews. The economic/political articles slightly outnumber the technical material, but both topic areas have complex titles. The modeling and analysis section often highlights a particular fuel type; the patent section will not only list and discuss new patents of interest, but also illustrate trends in number of patents in various countries. Libraries that subscribe to *Biomass & Bioenergy* (below in this section) will find this title a useful addition. Libraries that have little in the bioenergy area might find that this fills the gap.

1977. ***Biomass & Bioenergy.*** [ISSN: 0961-9534] 1991. m. EUR 3880. Elsevier Ltd, The Boulevard, Langford Lane, Oxford, OX5 1GB, United Kingdom; customerserviceau@elsevier.com; http://www.elsevier.com. Adv. Sample. Refereed. Microform: PQC. *Indexed:* A01, A22, Agr, C45. *Aud.:* Ac.

As the title indicates, the coverage of this journal is very mixed, as its scope "extends to the environmental, management and economic aspects of biomass and bioenergy." Some articles will appeal mostly to agribusiness endeavors, discussing harvesting methods, agricultural waste, pesticide runoff, and the like. Others will appeal to the energy engineer, with BTU figures and combustion problems associated with biofuels. Still others will appeal to economists and managers, with long-range forecasting of biofuel production and usage. Authors are from academia and government-sponsored research laboratories, with a wide range of backgrounds: engineering, agriculture, economics, and more. Some open-access articles are available. Institutions with strong agriculture as well as energy collections will find this a core title. Some geographic areas will have a strong interest in this type of energy source, while others will find this a niche topic. Libraries looking for broader coverage should consider *Biofuels, Bioproducts and Biorefining* (above in this section).

1978. ***Energies.*** [ISSN: 1996-1073] 2008. m. Free. Ed(s): Dr. Enrico Sciubba. M D P I AG, St. Alban-Anlage 66, Basel, 4052, Switzerland; info@mdpi.com; http://www.mdpi.com. Refereed. *Indexed:* A01, C45. *Aud.:* Ac.

Energies has a broad a scope, as its title suggests. Largely a technical research journal, it also covers policy and management. As well as the primary energy sources, articles discuss the theory of energy, exploration, delivery, and conversion systems. Environmental issues are raised, but usually in the contexts of policy or management. One troublesome issue is the very short delay between article submission and publication, which is often less than two months. Authors, of course, find this a plus, but it is difficult to see how peer review by more than one reviewer can be accomplished in such a short time. The online interface has several good features, such as article-download statistics, versioning, and links to more works by the same authors, but it lacks links to cited references. As an open-access title, the "subscription price" fits all budgets, but libraries should judge it on how it fits their collection goals.

1979. ***Energy.*** [ISSN: 0360-5442] 1976. 24x/yr. EUR 5713. Ed(s): Henrik Lund. Elsevier Ltd, 125 London Wall, London, EC2Y 5AS, United Kingdom; corporate.sales@elsevier.com; http://www.elsevier.com. Illus., index, adv. Sample. Refereed. Vol. ends: Dec. Microform: PQC. *Indexed:* A01, A22, BAS, C45. *Aud.:* Ac.

One of the first scholarly journals in the energy field, this title covers the full spectrum: all types of energy sources, all aspects of energy production, and economic/political/social factors. *Energy* emphasizes development, assessment, and management of energy programs. Most papers involving technical matter average fewer than eight pages; those concerned with economic issues tend to be twice as long. Technical issues often have an economic or societal aspect; economic issues often have a technical flavor. Periodically, an issue will be devoted to a theme (such as "Energy & Environment: Bringing Together Economics and Engineering") or a symposium (such as "Sustainable Development of Energy, Water and Environment"). Open- access articles are available. Bibliographies, maps, and statistics abound; graphs and tables are often in color. On average, articles are published within six months of receipt, although some take much longer. RSS feeds, open-URL linking, social bookmarking, citations, related articles, and downloading to citation managers are added features. A primary journal, but expensive for all except large academic or industry libraries.

1980. ***Energy and Buildings.*** [ISSN: 0378-7788] 1978. 24x/yr. EUR 4153. Ed(s): Mattheos Santamouris, Janlei Niu. Elsevier BV, Radarweg 29, Amsterdam, 1043 NX, Netherlands; info@elsevier.com; https://www.elsevier.com. Illus., index, adv. Sample. Refereed. Vol. ends: No. 6. Microform: PQC. *Indexed:* A01, A22, ErgAb. *Aud.:* Ac, Sa.

The emphasis here is on the "buildings," with the "energy" portion largely devoted to energy conservation, architectural design for passive energy use/savings, use of solar energy, manipulation of lighting, insulation materials, and cost/benefit analyses for energy consumption. "Sustainability" has been added to the mix, and the journal is also a likely source for distributed energy material, so often used in multi-occupant facilities. The buildings can be anything from high-rise complexes to grass huts, and from classrooms in the tropics to crawlspaces in Finland. Although scholarly in treatment, this journal is practical in outlook; articles have discussed energy consumption in old school buildings, low-cost insulation, pressure air-flow models for ventilation, and heat transfer in insulated concrete walls. Occasionally a theme issue is published. Authorship is international. Articles tend to be short (six to ten pages). Some open-access articles are available. Not for all collections, this title is best for libraries with interest in civil engineering or architecture, as well as energy.

1981. ***Energy & Environment.*** [ISSN: 0958-305X] 1990. 8x/yr. USD 2246 (print & online eds.)). Sage Publications Ltd., 1 Oliver's Yard, 55 City Rd, London, EC1Y 1SP, United Kingdom; info@sagepub.com; https://www.sagepub.com. Illus. Sample. Refereed. Reprint: PSC. *Indexed:* A22. *Aud.:* Ac.

Energy & Environment is described by its editor as an interdisciplinary journal aimed at scientists, engineers, and social scientists, discussing energy's impact on the environment. More to the point, the editor sees it as a forum for all parties to discuss the issues, and actively encourages and publishes their debates. To that end, "Fuel for Thought" is a regular issue feature. Most of the articles are sociopolitical or socioeconomic; the technology issues are raised but, perforce, this is done at a relatively superficial level. The articles themselves are scholarly treatments, and extensively documented, but the authors vary in level of expertise. Very few institutions subscribe to this title, but it deserves a wider audience; regardless of the merits of the debates published here, the fact that the debates occur should help drive out bad science, bad politics, bad economics, and bad blood. Recommended with reservations to libraries with strong programs in economics and politics, as well as energy.

1982. ***Energy & Environmental Science (Online).*** [ISSN: 1754-5706] 2008. m. GBP 1374; USD 2486. Royal Society of Chemistry, Thomas Graham House (290), Science Park, Milton Rd, Cambridge, CB4 0WF, United Kingdom; sales@rsc.org; http://www.rsc.org. Refereed. *Aud.:* Ac.

The title of this journal should actually be Energy, Environmental Science, and Chemistry because the coverage is all from the chemist's perspective. Articles range from full papers to reviews, with an equally broad range of prior knowledge necessary to understand the topics presented. The online version is excellent, with a tabbed display for articles, table of contents, special issues, and "most read" options, making navigation simple and providing more content on a single screen. The entire journal can be searched by field or full text; chemical structure searching is also available through the ChemSpider system. Social bookmarking, RSS feeds, export to bibliographic managers, and finding cites to particular articles are supported. The title is included in some Royal Society of Chemistry packages, but the regular price limits this to collections with strong chemistry and energy programs.

1983. ***Energy & Fuels.*** [ISSN: 0887-0624] 1987. m. USD 2116. Ed(s): Michael T Klein. American Chemical Society, 1155 16th St NW, Washington, DC 20036; help@acs.org; http://pubs.acs.org. Illus., index, adv. Sample. Refereed. *Indexed:* A22. *Bk. rev.:* 1, 1,000 words. *Aud.:* Ac, Sa.

One of the many American Chemical Society (ACS) journals, this is a scholarly publication concerned with both the discovery of non-nuclear fuels and their development as power sources. Each issue's content is arranged by category. Individual issues often contain selected papers from symposia, reviews, and "communications" (brief notes on techniques). Authorship is from academia and includes chemists and geologists as well as engineers. Publication is often within two months of manuscript submission, but can be longer. The site has tabbed views, RSS feeds, social bookmarking, DOI links, html and three types of pdf views, citation alerts, related articles, other articles by the same authors, and the option to download references to the major bibliographic managers. This is a core, quality title.

1984. ***Energy Conversion and Management.*** Former titles (until 1980): *Energy Conversion;* (until 1968): *Advanced Energy Conversion.* [ISSN: 0196-8904] 1961. 24x/yr. EUR 8449. Ed(s): Moh'd Ahmad Al-Nimr. Elsevier Ltd, 125 London Wall, London, EC2Y 5AS, United Kingdom; corporate.sales@elsevier.com; http://www.elsevier.com. Illus., index, adv. Sample. Refereed. Vol. ends: No. 18. Microform: PQC. *Indexed:* A01, A22, C45. *Aud.:* Ac, Sa.

Another of the many energy-related scholarly publications in the Elsevier stable, this journal is concerned with technical development of all types of fuels and energy resources, ranging from hydrocarbons through biomass, solar, wind, and other renewable sources. The topics are defined broadly, so that titles representing published papers include both "Enhancing the performance of energy recovery ventilators" and "Potential of reactivity controlled compression ignition (RCCI) combustion coupled with variable valve timing (VVT) strategy for meeting Euro 6 emission regulations and high fuel efficiency in a heavy-duty diesel engine." While its sister publication, *Energy: the international journal,* discusses large-scale management issues, *Energy Conversion* presents detailed technical papers on the ultimate production of many of the same resources. Authorship is international. Article length averages under ten pages. Although one of the most expensive titles in the field, this publication has a relatively high subscription base, probably because of the emphasis on application and its wide coverage of energy sources.

1985. ***Energy Economics.*** Incorporates (1996-2001): *Journal of Energy Finance and Development.* [ISSN: 0140-9883] 1979. 8x/yr. EUR 2371. Ed(s): U Soytas, B W Ang. Elsevier BV, Radarweg 29, Amsterdam, 1043 NX, Netherlands; info@elsevier.com; https://www.elsevier.com/. Illus., index, adv. Sample. Refereed. Vol. ends: No. 6. Microform: PQC. *Indexed:* A22, B01, EconLit, HRIS, IBSS. *Aud.:* Ac.

True to its name, this scholarly journal discusses the economic and tax issues of energy, generally on the macro scale. Recent issues feature "Does voluntary disclosure create a green lemon problem? Energy-efficiency ratings and house prices," "Manure management coupled with bioenergy production: An environmental and economic assessment of large dairies in New Mexico," and "A higher rebound effect under bounded rationality: Interactions between car mobility and electricity generation." This title is definitely international in scope, and its lengthy articles have covered Indian coal, oil-price sticker shock in Europe, price rigidity in the New Zealand petroleum industry, and the Colombian electricity market. Although other types of fuel sources appear in this title occasionally, most issues deal with oil, coal, and the electricity markets. This is a journal for larger collections with an active local interest in economics; other libraries should consider *The Energy Journal* (below in this section).

1986. ***Energy Engineering.*** Former titles (until 1980): *Building Systems Design;* (until 1969): *Air Conditioning, Heating and Ventilating;* (until 1955): *Heating and Ventilating;* (until 1929): *The Heating and Ventilating Magazine.* [ISSN: 0199-8595] 1904. bi-m. GBP 367 (print & online eds.)). Taylor & Francis Inc., 711 3rd Ave, 8th Fl, New York, NY 10017; support@tandfonline.com; http://www.tandfonline.com. Illus., index. Sample. Refereed. Microform: PMC; PQC. Reprint: PSC. *Indexed:* A22, E01. *Aud.:* Ac, Sa.

This is the energy magazine for the plant engineer, high-rise building supervisor, and town engineer. Articles range from tips on energy auditing to financing renewable energy projects. Most articles are written by practitioners or consultants, but some are by academics. Some have lengthy reference lists and others are obviously "expert-advice" columns. Coverage includes alternative fuels, fuel cells, co-generation, energy control systems, and "green systems." Two other journals from the same publisher (which are not reviewed in this section) are *Strategic Planning for Energy and the Environment* and *Cogeneration and Competitive Power Journal,* the former is addressed to managers, and the latter discusses the technical aspects of "co-generation" (using the byproduct of one power source to produce yet another form of energy). Subscribers can download a pdf of full issues, as well as individual full-text articles. This is a good choice for a large public library and/or undergraduates in an engineering curriculum.

1987. ***The Energy Journal.*** [ISSN: 0195-6574] 1980. q. Free to members; Non-members, USD 475. International Association for Energy Economics, 28790 Chagrin Blvd, Ste 350, Cleveland, OH 44122; iaee@iaee.org; http://www.iaee.org. Illus., index, adv. Sample. Refereed. Vol. ends: No. 4. Microform: PQC. *Indexed:* A01, A22, B01, BRI, CBRI, EconLit. *Bk. rev.:* 4, 1,000 words. *Aud.:* Ac.

This is a scholarly publication that covers the economic and social/political aspects of energy. Generally, this means electric power, oil, and natural gas, but there is some attention to renewable sources. Currently, there is much attention paid to climate and carbon emission issues, electricity demand/distribution economics, and energy consumption patterns. Articles are lengthy, often more than 20 pages, with extensive bibliographies, and they use charts and graphs as illustrations. Authors are from the international academic and government-policy community. Announcements of association conferences and book reviews complete the issues. There are occasional special issues. The web site includes tables of contents and subject category indexes for the entire run of the journal, plus the option for subscribers to download issues rather than receive them by mail. This title is available in full text from several sources; a good choice for libraries with strong energy and economics programs.

1988. ***Energy Law Journal.*** [ISSN: 0270-9163] 1980. s-a. USD 35 domestic (Corporations, USD 41; Free to members). Ed(s): Robert S Fleishman. University of Tulsa, College of Law, 3120 E 4th Pl, Tulsa, OK 74104; news@utulsa.edu; http://www.utulsa.edu/law. Adv. Microform: WSH. Reprint: WSH. *Indexed:* A22, B01, BRI, L14. *Bk. rev.:* 2, 1,000 words. *Aud.:* Ac, Sa.

As much about economics and environment as about law, the *Energy Law Journal* is a scholarly work devoted to lengthy analyses of energy issues and how they affect the law or how the law affects them. Issues are not only reviewed but debated as well. Papers are written by attorneys, judges, and experts from government agencies. Most of the discussions involve U.S. law, but there are occasional works specific to other countries or international in scope. Emphasis is on electricity supply with some attention to oil, natural gas, the environment, and alternative energy forms, such as hydrogen. Book reviews, committee reports on energy and administrative law, and what passes for short notes in the legal world round out the issues. The complete run of issues may be browsed or searched via keyword on the Energy Bar Association web site. A special feature is a list of "cited cases," instances where articles from the journal are cited in opinions, cases, and other legal documents. Pdfs are freely available for all issues. Widely owned by law libraries and with a very modest price, it deserves consideration by libraries with strong energy collections and public-policy collections.

1989. ***Energy Policy: the international journal of the political, economic, planning, environmental and social aspects of energy.*** [ISSN: 0301-4215] 1973. 12x/yr. EUR 5054. Ed(s): Stephen P A Brown, Michael Jefferson. Elsevier Ltd, 125 London Wall, London, EC2Y 5AS, United Kingdom; corporate.sales@elsevier.com; http://www.elsevier.com. Illus., index, adv. Sample. Refereed. Vol. ends: No. 15. Microform: PQC. *Indexed:* A22, B01, BRI, C45, EconLit, HRIS, IBSS. *Aud.:* Ac.

This journal should be compared with *Energy Economics*, also from Elsevier. First, the emphasis is on renewable energy forms (such as wind, solar, and biomass), as opposed to the primarily oil and electric power interests of its sister title. Second, the theme is policy decisions by government and by industry as opposed to financial considerations. Renewable energy, carbon emissions, and energy efficiency are current topics. Both publications have international authorship and interest, but *Energy Policy* often discusses specific countries and regions while *Energy Economics* is often global in focus. The publication lag is very short, often only two to three months. While most of the articles are research reports, many issues also contain a "Viewpoints" section with one or two persuasive analyses. Recommended for libraries with international relations and public policy collections in conjunction with energy research.

1990. ***Energy Sources. Part A. Recovery, Utilization, and Environmental Effects.*** Supersedes in part (in 2006): *Energy Sources;* Which incorporated (1974-1991): *Energy Systems and Policy.* [ISSN: 1556-7036] 1973. s-m. GBP 4981 (print & online eds.)). Ed(s): James G Speight. Taylor & Francis Inc., 711 3rd Ave, 8th Fl, New York, NY 10017; support@tandfonline.com; http://www.tandfonline.com. Illus., index, adv. Sample. Refereed. Reprint: PSC. *Indexed:* A01, A22, BAS, C45, E01. *Aud.:* Ac.

Energy Sources split into two sections in January 2006. Part A, still the major section with 20 issues per year, retained the technical papers; Part B (also reviewed in this section) covers economics, policy, and planning. It is possible to subscribe to each part separately, so that libraries that emphasize the technical aspects of energy are not required to accept the policy addition (and vice versa). There is also a combined subscription option. This journal's theme is fuel sources: carbon-based (petroleum, natural gas, oil tars and shales, organic waste), nuclear, wind, solar, and geothermal. The focus is on extraction and conversion to energy, and what is reported is "completed" research as opposed to theory or in-process updates. Issue topics tend to clump, with a string of issues devoted to carbon-based fuels, then a single issue that covers mostly other forms. Dates are now provided for the publishing process from submission to online publication; the delay is more than two years and often three, despite the publisher's stated aim for rapid publication. This title should only be considered for the comprehensive collection.

1991. ***Energy Sources. Part B. Economics, Planning, and Policy.*** Supersedes in part (in 2006): *Energy Sources;* Which incorporated (1974-1991): *Energy Systems and Policy.* [ISSN: 1556-7249] 1973. q. GBP 708 (print & online eds.)). Ed(s): James G Speight. Taylor & Francis Inc., 711 3rd Ave, 8th Fl, New York, NY 10017; support@tandfonline.com; http://www.tandfonline.com. Sample. Refereed. Reprint: PSC. *Indexed:* A01, A22, C45, E01. *Aud.:* Ac.

Energy Sources split in 2006 into Parts A and B. Part A is the "parent" title and is also reviewed above in this section. As isn't the case with many title splits, it is possible here to subscribe to each title separately or to get both at a reduced price. Part A contains the highly technical papers; Part B contains the analysis papers. This does not mean that they are light reading; recent titles include "Parametric CAPEX, OPEX, and LCOE expressions for offshore wind farms based on global deployment parameters" and "Oil production cost, financial development, and economic growth in Russia." Many of the articles published are reviews in nature.

1992. ***Energy Systems: optimization, modeling, simulation, and economic aspects.*** [ISSN: 1868-3967] 2010. 4x/yr. EUR 679 (print & online eds.)). Ed(s): Panos Pardalos. Springer, Tiergartenstr 17, Heidelberg, 69121, Germany; subscriptions@springer.com; https://www.springer.com. Refereed. Reprint: PSC. *Aud.:* Ac.

Although articles may mention specific energy sources or production process, this is primarily a mathematical modeling journal devoted to the systems of distributing and using energy. Many articles include "grid" or "wind" in their titles, implying the chief energy form is electricity. The treatment is highly mathematical and the authors are just as likely to be economists as engineers. Combinations of academic researchers and production supervisors are also common. Lag time between submission and publication averages six months, but it can be as much as one year. Issues are skimpy, with only four to six articles, but they are relatively lengthy at about 20 pages each. This title will be a good fit in both industry and academic libraries with interests in electric power production.

1993. ***Fuel: the science and technology of fuel and energy.*** Formerly (until 1948): *Fuel in Science and Practice.* [ISSN: 0016-2361] 1922. 24x/yr. EUR 6863. Ed(s): John W Patrick. Elsevier Ltd, The Boulevard, Langford Lane, Oxford, OX5 1GB, United Kingdom; journalscustomerserviceemea@elsevier.com; http://www.elsevier.com. Illus., index, adv. Sample. Refereed. Vol. ends: No. 15. Microform: PQC. *Indexed:* A01, A22. *Bk. rev.:* Number and length vary. *Aud.:* Ac.

One of the oldest professional journals devoted to energy sources, *Fuel* publishes highly technical articles on coal (and coal tar), petroleum (oil, oil shale, oil sands, and derivatives), natural gas, and biomass. Most of the articles concern the production of electrical energy, but there is some attention to transportation (gasoline, diesel fuel, and the like). Authorship is international and largely academic, with some coauthors from commercial enterprises. The articles are under ten pages, well referenced, and illustrated with charts, tables, and line drawings, some in color to enhance readability. Most of each issue is devoted to "full papers," but the occasional review article, brief communication, or book review pops up. Open-access articles are available. The extra issues in this "monthly" are proceedings of conferences. This is a relatively expensive title but is useful in a number of engineering disciplines and has a proven track record. Libraries that subscribe to this title should also consider its sister publication, *Fuel Processing Technology,* below in this section.

1994. ***Fuel Cells (Online).*** [ISSN: 1615-6854] bi-m. GBP 1106. Ed(s): Ulrich Stimming. Wiley - V C H Verlag GmbH & Co. KGaA, Postfach 101161, Weinheim, 69451, Germany; cs-germany@wiley.com; http://www.wiley-vch.de. Refereed. *Aud.:* Ac.

Fuel Cells is a highly technical journal in a highly technical field. The average issue is composed of original research, but special issues on a theme, such as new ceramic materials, often include one or two review articles and editorial comment on the topic. Original articles are short, averaging five or six pages; review articles are much lengthier at 10-15 pages. The journal's scope covers everything about fuel cells from "their molecular level to their applications," but most articles appear to address very specific issues on the laboratory scale. Beginning in 2011, the journal dropped its print version and became online only. Relatively inexpensive for a scholarly journal in a specialized field, this one still requires a strong local interest.

1995. ***Fuel Processing Technology.*** [ISSN: 0378-3820] 1978. 12x/yr. EUR 4971. Ed(s): C Z Li. Elsevier BV, Radarweg 29, Amsterdam, 1043 NX, Netherlands; info@elsevier.com; https://www.elsevier.com/. Illus., index. Sample. Refereed. Microform: PQC. *Indexed:* A01, A22, C45. *Aud.:* Ac.

Fuel Processing Technology should be compared to its sister publication, *Fuel* (above in this section). The two titles cover the same types of fuels: hydrocarbons (coal, oil, shale) and biomass. The first title emphasizes "processing" (the conversion of the raw materials to higher forms of fuels) and the second title also includes papers similar in scope. However, *Fuel Processing Technology* uses a less theoretical approach. The articles make for dense reading, with such titles as "A new catalyst of Co/La2O3-doped La4Ga2O9 for direct ethanol synthesis from syngas." However, there are occasional review articles and special issues. Open-access articles are available. Article authorship, length, illustration, and referencing are also similar. Consider the pair of this title and *Fuel* for those libraries with strong programs in petroleum technology, as well as energy.

1996. ***Geothermics: international journal of geothermal research and its applications.*** [ISSN: 0375-6505] 1972. bi-m. q. until 2015. EUR 2414. Ed(s): E Schill, C Bromley. Pergamon Press, The Blvd, Langford Ln, E Park, Kidlington, OX5 1GB, United Kingdom; JournalsCustomerServiceEMEA@elsevier.com; http://www.elsevier.com. Illus., adv. Sample. Refereed. Microform: PQC. *Indexed:* A01, A22, C45, S25. *Aud.:* Ac.

Geothermal energy sources are more widespread than is commonly thought. Of specialized research interest, this topic also intrigues consumers because of the novelty and the idea of "free energy." In recent years, private homes have begun using ground loop heat exchangers instead of heat pumps; this is basically the same idea but with a more stable environment and fewer moving parts. Most of the articles in *Geothermics* are practical in nature: applied research. Topics include using ground-coupled condensers in air conditioning systems, problems associated with boreholes, surveys of geothermal sites, and similar items. Articles average about ten pages, with color illustrations where appropriate. Open-access articles are available. This is a good title for a strong mechanical engineering collection, as well as for energy.

1997. ***Home Energy.*** Formerly (until 1988): *Energy Auditor and Retrofitter.* [ISSN: 0896-9442] 1984. bi-m. USD 170 (print or online ed.)). Energy Auditor and Retrofitter, Inc., 2124 Kittredge St, #95, Berkeley, CA 94704. Illus., adv. Sample. Vol. ends: Nov/Dec. *Indexed:* BRI. *Aud.:* Ga, Sa.

Home Energy is published by a nonprofit organization, which states that its mission is "to provide objective and practical information for residential energy conservation." Originally intended for the professional home remodeler, since 1997 it has addressed the homeowner as well, partly with consumer guide information and partly with self-help tips. The thrust is efficient use of energy, not necessarily the source of energy, so that home insulation, lighting, water usage, and the like are considered. Each issue has a few articles that are factual in nature, cite publications or refer to web links, and include many photographs and line illustrations. The rest of the issue is "Trends," covering product information, an events calendar, industry news, and briefs. The web site is not just a reproduction of the printed product, but includes a do-it-yourself tips section, a blog, and a training directory. Only subscribers have access to the current content, although the 1993-1999 archive (searchable) has many free articles. There is an extensive list of short, colorfully illustrated information articles for both the consumer and the contractor, plus links to sites of interest. With its wide geographic range, even in states where the winter sun can be hard to find, this is good title for any public library.

1998. ***Home Power.*** [ISSN: 1050-2416] 1987. bi-m. USD 34.95 combined subscription domestic (print & online eds.)). Ed(s): Claire Anderson. Home Power, Inc., PO Box 520, Ashland, OR 97520. Illus., adv. *Aud.:* Ga, Sa.

Home Power has revamped itself several times over its history. The current version is better organized and more "professional" than the early years (although the early years had many offbeat and fun articles). The magazine promulgates "homemade" electric power using renewable energy resources. Two new sections cover energy-efficient vehicles and "home efficiency." Many articles are success stories from the readership. *Home Power* solicits articles but does not offer payment, and the author keeps some publication rights. The web site includes the full digital versions of all issues (free with a three-year subscription), some useful files/data from earlier issues, links to related sites, and job and "experts" lists. The archives are searchable by keyword, and many of the articles are available for free. An excellent choice for public libraries and two-year colleges with technical programs.

1999. ***I E E E Power & Energy Magazine.*** Formed by the merger of (1988-2003): *I E E E Computer Applications in Power;* (1981-2003): *I E E E Power Engineering Review.* [ISSN: 1540-7977] 2003. bi-m. USD 505. Ed(s): Michael Henderson. Institute of Electrical and Electronics Engineers, 445 Hoes Ln, Piscataway, NJ 08854; contactcenter@ieee.org; http://www.ieee.org. *Indexed:* A22. *Bk. rev.:* 1, 1,000 words. *Aud.:* Ac, Sa.

This title is another of the highly relevant, highly useful IEEE Magazines series (as distinct from the often dense IEEE Transactions). It is designed for the "electric power professional." Each issue is based on a theme chosen by the editor, then illustrated with three or four articles. This journal is executed in the usual colorful, glossy style of the IEEE Magazines, and its articles are eight to ten pages in length but with minimal references (often simply URLs). The treatment is suitable for undergraduates and professionals outside the electric power field. The remainder of the issues includes letters, columns, society and industry news, book reviews, new products, and an events calendar. The IEEEXplore site identifies the content type of each title on the contents page, an exceedingly welcome addition when the titles themselves are ambiguous. When searching by journal title, the front matter is included along with links to the latest published articles and popular articles. Well worth considering for many libraries, especially for those where the equivalent IEEE Transactions are either too expensive or too weighty.

2000. ***I E E E Transactions on Energy Conversion.*** Supersedes in part (in 1986): *I E E E Transactions on Power Apparatus and Systems;* Which was formed by the merger of (1952-1963): *Power Apparatus and Systems;* (1952-1963): *American Institute of Electrical Engineers. Transactions. Part 3. Power Apparatus and Systems;* Which superseded in part (in 1952): *American Institute of Electrical Engineers. Transactions.* [ISSN: 0885-8969] 1986. q. USD 1230. Ed(s): Juri Jatskevich. Institute of Electrical and Electronics Engineers, 445 Hoes Ln, Piscataway, NJ 08854; contactcenter@ieee.org; http://www.ieee.org. Adv. Refereed. *Indexed:* A01, A22, B01. *Aud.:* Ac.

The thrust of this journal is efficient conversion of energy-producing mechanisms (usually motors in small or large scale) to electrical energy. Therefore, it contains a significant number of articles that cover wind, solar, and renewable energy production problems. As usual with IEEE Transactions publications, the papers are written for and by academics, but there are highly practical problems under discussion. Large engineering collections will be pleasantly surprised to discover they have a good, economical source of material on niche energy topics. Commercial entities in solar or wind power will find this an inexpensive source of research material. It is also a good title for those electric-car enthusiasts found in engineering schools. This title should be considered in conjunction with *IEEE Transactions on Smart Grid* (below in this section) and the *IEEE Transactions on Power Delivery* (not reviewed in this section), as all three deal with generation and delivery of electricity.

2001. ***I E E E Transactions on Smart Grid.*** [ISSN: 1949-3053] 2010. bi-m. USD 655. Ed(s): Jianhui Wang. Institute of Electrical and Electronics Engineers, 445 Hoes Ln, Piscataway, NJ 08854; contactcenter@ieee.org; http://www.ieee.org. Adv. *Aud.:* Ac, Sa.

Smart Grid may sound like a journal for a small set of specialists within the field of electrical engineering. In fact, though, the aim of the journal is to be cross-disciplinary, and it is cited by *Applied Energy, Energy Policy, Renewable Energy*, and even *Neural Computing Applications.* The reason for these cites is that *Smart Grid* models the power loads and distributions across the entire system, and those models can be used in other applications such as siting plug-ins for hybrid vehicles. As does *Energy Systems* (above in this section), this journal seeks the best ways to use the energy we now produce. In contrast with

Energy Systems, economists are unlikely to submit articles to this highly technical publication, though they could. Libraries with strong energy and electrical/power engineering will be best served by this title; others may prefer *Energy Systems* for its wider scope.

2002. *I E E Transactions on Sustainable Energy.* [ISSN: 1949-3029] 2010. q. USD 845. Ed(s): Badrul Chowdhury. Institute of Electrical and Electronics Engineers, 445 Hoes Ln, Piscataway, NJ 08854; contactcenter@ieee.org; http://www.ieee.org. Adv. Refereed. *Aud.:* Ac.

Sustainable Energy concentrates on articles that demonstrate how to implement wind, photovoltaic, wave, and renewable energy forms and add them to the energy grid. The current emphasis is on wind, with many articles covering the integration of wind power with the more conventional systems. The treatment may be modeling or practical. The articles themselves are highly mathematical, often supplemented with black-and-white illustrations. This will be a useful title for engineering collections, but libraries that seek broader coverage of renewable energy sources will prefer *Renewable Energy* or *Renewable & Sustainable Energy Reviews* (below in this section).

2003. *I E T Renewable Power Generation.* [ISSN: 1752-1416] 2007. 16x/yr. GBP 606 (print & online eds.)). Ed(s): David Infield. The Institution of Engineering and Technology, Michael Faraday House, Six Hills Way, Stevenage, SG1 2AY, United Kingdom; postmaster@theiet.org; http://www.theiet.org/. Adv. Refereed. *Aud.:* Ac.

IET Renewable Power Generation is a research journal that discusses the practical generation of power from several renewable energy sources, from both the technical and the managerial sides of the system. The scope of the journal also includes solar, marine current, geothermal, biomass, wind, wave, photovoltaic, and fuel-cell power sources. Unlike many new titles that have overview articles with broad outlines, *IET Renewable Power Generation* got down to business from the start. This monthly journal has a reasonable price (but compare it to the IEEE publications), and its coverage of the energy outliers will be of value to institutions with active research in these fields.

2004. *Institution of Mechanical Engineers. Proceedings. Part A: Journal of Power and Energy.* Formerly (until 1990): *Institution of Mechanical Engineers. Proceedings. Part A: Journal of Power Engineering;* Which superseded in part (in 1988): *Institution of Mechanical Engineers. Proceedings. Part A: Power and Process Engineering;* Which superseded in part (in 1983): *Institution of Mechanical Engineers. Proceedings;* Which incorporated (1948-1970): *Institution of Mechanical Engineers. Automobile Division. Proceedings;* Which was formerly (until 1948): *Institution of Automobile Engineers, London. Proceedings;* (until 1906): *Incorporated Institution of Automobile Engineers. Proceedings.* [ISSN: 0957-6509] 1983. 8x/yr. USD 4501 (print & online eds.)). Ed(s): C R Stone. Sage Publications Ltd., 1 Oliver's Yard, 55 City Rd, London, EC1Y 1SP, United Kingdom; info@sagepub.com; https://www.sagepub.com/. Illus., index. Sample. Refereed. Vol. ends: No. 6. Microform: PMC; PQC. Reprint: PSC. *Indexed:* A22, E01. *Bk. rev.:* 3, 500 words. *Aud.:* Ac, Sa.

Normally, the journal of a professional society outside the United States would not be included in this section, especially when there are relevant titles available from U.S. equivalents (*IEEE Transactions on Energy Conversion* and *Journal of Solar Energy Engineering,* both reviewed in this section). However, this publication is well worth consideration for a broadly based energy collection. First, it covers a lot of territory: electric power, wind power, ocean wave energy, power production from coal, nuclear energy, gas, fuel cells, and solar energy. Its focus is the conversion of energy forms into electricity; much of the content concerns the design and upkeep of mechanical systems that do the actual conversion. Second, although the publisher is a British society, the journal has an international authorship made up of a combination of academic and industry researchers. Third, it has a relatively rapid turnaround time (often less than three months) from submission to publication. Fourth, the articles are readable (it is indexed in *Applied Science and Technology Abstracts*), well referenced, and well illustrated. Its major shortcoming is that it is relatively expensive for a college library. Most university collections will already have it, as part of the complete IME Proceedings, and therefore at a cheaper rate. Now published by Sage for the Institution of Mechanical Engineers, it enjoys all of the features of the Sage web site.

2005. *International Journal of Energy Research.* [ISSN: 0363-907X] 1977. 15x/yr. GBP 5313. Ed(s): I Dincer. John Wiley & Sons Ltd., EMEA Institutional Sales, 9600 Garsington Rd, Oxford, OX4 2DQ, United Kingdom; cs-journals@wiley.com; http://onlinelibrary.wiley.com. Adv. Sample. Refereed. Microform: PQC. Reprint: PSC. *Indexed:* A01, A22, BRI. *Aud.:* Ac.

The "aims and scope" for this journal are to discuss energy issues with all types of researchers: engineers, scientists, developers, planners, and policy makers. However, the content is quite technical; an engineering degree will be quite helpful. Articles range from short to 20 or more pages. Not only are the authors international, but it is not unusual to find an article co-authored by a team from three or more institutions. Issues are composed of research articles, technical notes, and the occasional review. As it is, the price makes this a hard title to justify; once again, it has the dubious distinction of being the most expensive journal reviewed in this section, if not in the entire energy field. For the comprehensive academic collection.

2006. *International Journal of Green Energy.* [ISSN: 1543-5075] 2004. m. GBP 2453 (print & online eds.)). Ed(s): Xianguo Li. Taylor & Francis Inc., 711 3rd Ave, 8th Fl, New York, NY 10017; support@tandfonline.com; http://www.tandfonline.com. Adv. Sample. Refereed. Reprint: PSC. *Indexed:* A22, C45, E01. *Aud.:* Ac.

This journal - an official journal of the Association of Energy Engineers - publishes research on "the forms and utilizations of energy that have no, minimal, or reduced impact on environment and society." To that end, a large percentage of the articles deal with wind, solar, biomass, and other alternative/renewable sources. Financial considerations play a part, as illustrated by the wonderful merger of economics and technology in individual articles. Niche subjects, rather than mainstream research thrusts, are common within issues. Libraries with interests in sustainable development as well as energy should consider this one.

2007. *International Journal of Hydrogen Energy.* [ISSN: 0360-3199] 1976. 48x/yr. EUR 5043. Ed(s): E A Veziroglu. Elsevier Ltd, 125 London Wall, London, EC2Y 5AS, United Kingdom; corporate.sales@elsevier.com; http://www.elsevier.com. Illus., adv. Sample. Refereed. Microform: PMC; PQC. *Indexed:* A01, A22. *Aud.:* Ac.

This may be the only journal (there are a few magazines) devoted to hydrogen as an energy source, and, as such, it covers both the technical aspects and the social aspects (economics, environment, and international impact). Each issue generally contains about 25 papers, categorized as dealing with economy, electrolysis, solar, chemical/thermochemical, biology, storage, several types of fuel cells, and many others. There is also a goodly number of articles on hydrogen-powered vehicles. Recent articles include "An alkaline water electrolyzer with nickel electrodes enables efficient high current density operation" and "Deep deoxidization from liquid iron by hydrogen plasma arc melting." Several issues each year include an average of 60 conference papers organized around a theme such as "Alternative Energies for Sustainability." Open-access articles are available. This is a niche area in energy research, but a very active one. A good title for a strong energy collection.

2008. *International Journal of Photoenergy.* [ISSN: 1110-662X] 1999. a. USD 895. Hindawi Publishing Corporation, 315 Madison Ave, 3rd Fl, Ste 3070, New York, NY 10017; hindawi@hindawi.com; https://www.hindawi.com. Refereed. *Indexed:* A01, C45. *Aud.:* Ac.

This is a journal with an extremely narrow focus, but one that has caught the attention of many in the photovoltaic and/or solar energy field in its relatively short publishing life. Aimed at the chemistry/chemical engineering researcher, articles cover fine details in photoreactivity, degradation, and, conversely, energizing of materials due to "photoenergy." This is precisely why some researchers in solar energy, fuel cells, and the like read and cite this journal. Resolving materials problems in these fields is critical to success, and much of this is uncharted territory. The web site has some nice features, such as RSS feeds, links to references through the publisher and through Google Scholar, and even a "how to cite" format. There are no volumes or issues; articles are published online as soon as they pass review, which is generally within two months. It is possible to search all articles (and determine which were published in a given year) when a specific reference is needed. This is an open-access publication (a print version is available via subscription), but the treatment is so specialized that only libraries with strong solar/photovoltaic collections will find it useful.

2009. ***Journal of Energy Engineering.*** Former titles (until 1983): *American Society of Civil Engineers. Energy Division. Journal;* (until 1979): *American Society of Civil Engineers. Power Division. Journal;* Which superseded in part (in 1956): *American Society of Civil Engineers. Proceedings.* [ISSN: 0733-9402] 1873. bi-m. q until 2016. USD 759. Ed(s): Chung-Li Tseng. American Society of Civil Engineers, 1801 Alexander Bell Dr, Reston, VA 20191; ascelibrary@asce.org; http://www.asce.org. Illus., adv. Refereed. *Indexed:* A01, A22, BRI, HRIS. *Aud.:* Ac, Sa.

This journal is part of the American Society of Civil Engineers collection of engineering journals and has been focused on energy since 1983. The primary interest is "planning, development, management, and finances of energy-related programs"; this translates to construction of power plants, energy efficiency of buildings, selecting/implementing the optimal power source for a project, and regulatory/environmental issues. This journal is served from the ASCE Library, whose underlying software was designed by Atypon (which also works with many other sci/tech publishers). One of the features of the design is tabs; there is a tab for "most cited" and another for "most viewed," and none of the titles on the one list is on the other. This is probably true for many journals, but it's a good reminder that citation counts are just one of many decision criteria. Compare this title with *Energy and Buildings* (above in this section) for coverage and relevancy to local collections.

2010. ***Journal of Power Sources: the international journal on the science and technology of electrochemical energy systems.*** [ISSN: 0378-7753] 1976. 36x/yr. EUR 10482. Ed(s): Stefano Passerini. Elsevier BV, Radarweg 29, Amsterdam, 1043 NX, Netherlands; info@elsevier.com; https://www.elsevier.com/. Refereed. *Indexed:* A01, A22. *Aud.:* Ac.

Think photovoltaics: the power sources here are fuel cells and batteries for portable power supplies, electric vehicles, satellites, and the like. This journal discusses the conversion of energy from solar, wind, and other sources into storage devices such as fuel cells. Much of the work involves materials properties, electrochemical reactions, and the application of photovoltaics to practical devices. Issues are lengthy, often running to 500 pages, and the publication lag is quite short, sometimes under two months between submission and online publication. The contents are arranged in subject sections, then divided by topic (fuel cells, batteries, review, and so on). This is convenient for the reader, but the pagination is then out of order - with, say, the article on pages 1-4 in the section on fuel cells, after the article on pages 63-73 in the reviews section. Open-access articles are available. This is quite expensive (although not on a cost-per-page basis); libraries with strong engineering collections as well as renewable-energy interests should consider it. However, it should be compared with *Progress in Photovoltaics* (below in this section).

2011. ***Journal of Renewable and Sustainable Energy.*** [ISSN: 1941-7012] 2009. bi-m. Ed(s): P Craig Taylor, John A Turner. A I P Publishing LLC, 1305 Walt Whitman Rd, Melville, NY 11747; aipinfo@aip.org; http://www.aip.org. Adv. Sample. Refereed. *Indexed:* A01, S25. *Aud.:* Ac, Sa.

A number of new energy-related journals and magazines have appeared recently that feature "sustainable" in their titles. *The Journal of Renewable and Sustainable Energy* appears to be the best of the lot in terms of quality and variety of content, range of topics, and its own sustainability. As part of the American Institute of Physics (AIP) journals collection, it is likely to continue long after "sustainable" ceases to be the fashion. Other titles of interest, though, include the *IEEE Transactions on Sustainable Energy* and *Renewable and Sustainable Energy Review* (both reviewed in this section). The new AIP journal contains peer-reviewed articles, which average 15-20 pages, on topics such as solar space heating in a passive house; blended biodiesel fuel; economical inverters for grid-tied generators; and treatment of wastewater by solar power to alleviate water scarcity. Authors are largely from academia; the lag from submission to publication is usually less than six months. The online version of the journal includes a blog, podcasts, a newsletter, interviews, and energy-related news clips, thus separating the research material from the topical. This will be a welcome addition to academic libraries with interests in renewable energy forms, sustainable development, and systems engineering.

2012. ***Journal of Solar Energy Engineering.*** [ISSN: 0199-6231] 1980. bi-m. q. until 2016. USD 914; USD 1099 combined subscription (print & online eds.)). Ed(s): Robert Boehm. The American Society of Mechanical Engineers, Two Park Ave, New York, NY 10016; CustomerCare@asme.org; http://www.asme.org. Illus., index. Sample. Refereed. Vol. ends: Nov. *Indexed:* A01, A22, BRI. *Aud.:* Ac, Sa.

This is an engineering research journal, with short articles (around six pages) on applied research into solar energy production, materials used in solar energy, and applications of solar energy to other engineering problems. Most readers are familiar with the use of solar power to dry fruits and heat water, but many will be surprised to learn that it can also be used in aluminum smelting and fullerene synthesis. The journal should really be titled "Solar and Wind Energy"; every issue has an article or two on wind power. Recent articles range from "Solar Thermal Application for Decentralized Food Baking Using Scheffler Reflector Technology" to "Efficiency Improvement of a Photovoltaic Module Using Front Surface Cooling Method in Summer and Winter Conditions." This is a good value for the research dollar, and it will be useful at industrial as well as academic sites.

2013. ***Nuclear Engineering International.*** Formerly (until 1968): *Nuclear Engineering;* Which incorporated (1956-1968): *Nuclear Power.* [ISSN: 0029-5507] 1956. m. GBP 380.49 domestic; EUR 585.99 in Europe; USD 774.99 in North America. Ed(s): Caroline Peachey. Wilmington Media & Entertainment, Progressive House, 2 Maidstone Rd, Foots Cray, Sidcup, DA14 5HZ, United Kingdom; investorinfo@wilmington.co.uk; http://www.wilmington.co.uk/. Illus., index, adv. Microform: PQC. *Indexed:* A22, B03, BRI, C42. *Aud.:* Ac, Sa.

There are many research journals devoted to nuclear energy, but few devoted to the nuclear industry. A number of "power plant" titles include nuclear (as well as coal, oil, and so on) as fuel sources. *Nuclear Engineering International* is perhaps the earliest magazine in the field; certainly it is among the longest running. Although produced by a British trade press, it is, perforce, international in coverage and orientation. The web site includes the standard features: news, buyers guide, upcoming events, trade shows, and links. It also features videos, including freely available videos of the Fukushima Daiichi plant post-tsunami. For years, the magazine has published "wallcharts" of nuclear plants; many of these, covering all types of reactors, are available for sale as pdfs or prints, providing useful illustrations for nuclear engineering courses. Thanks go, however, to the University of New Mexico's Digital Collections for making low-resolution, color versions available for free (see http://econtent.unm.edu/cdm/search/collection/nuceng). Feature articles are short (two or three pages) with a mix of technical updates, economic trends, and safety issues: in short, anything that affects a nuclear power plant. The subscription price is about three times that of the average specialty trade magazine, precluding most public and academic library purchases, but the web site has many free features and it is indexed in the standard abstract services.

2014. ***Nuclear Technology.*** Former titles (until 1971): *Nuclear Applications and Technology;* (until 1969): *Nuclear Applications.* [ISSN: 0029-5450] 1965. m. GBP 2379 (print & online eds.)). Ed(s): Andrew Klein. Taylor & Francis Inc., 530 Walnut St, Ste 850, Philadelphia, PA 19106. Illus., index. Refereed. Vol. ends: No. 3. Reprint: PSC. *Indexed:* A&ATA, A22. *Bk. rev.:* Occasional. *Aud.:* Ac, Sa.

One of several publications from the American Nuclear Society (ANS), *Nuclear Technology* publishes papers on applications of research to the nuclear field, as opposed to theoretical work; the scope includes medical use as well as a power source. Each issue is subdivided into sections, such as nuclear reactor safety, fission reactors, radioactive waste management, and others as appropriate. The layout is crisp and has such features as keyword descriptors at the head of each paper, which help the reader target relevant papers. The authorship is international, often from industry. Papers average 10-15 pages; there are per-page charges to defray the society's expenses. Occasionally, technical notes (one- or two-page items) and papers from conferences are included. Book reviews are encouraged but rarely appear. Libraries with active physics researchers will probably have all of the ANS publications; others may prefer the specialized titles.

2015. *Oil & Gas Journal.* Formerly (until 1910): *Oil Investors' Journal.* [ISSN: 0030-1388] 1902. m. USD 199 domestic; USD 209 Canada; USD 249 elsewhere. Ed(s): Bob Tippee. PennWell Corporation, 1455 W Loop S, Houston, TX 77027; http://www.pennwell.com. Illus., index, adv. Vol. ends: No. 52. *Indexed:* A22, B03, BRI, HRIS. *Aud.:* Ga, Ac, Sa.

Decade after decade, this has been a reliable source for topical industry news, special features, and lots of data. Articles comprise a large portion of the contents, either short reviews (one to three pages) by staff writers or somewhat longer, referenced papers by industry specialists. Each issue follows the section format of focus articles, general interest news, exploration and development, drilling and production, and processing and transportation, with columns on equipment and statistics. There are a number of annually repeating issues, such as forecast and review or worldwide refining. The best section for librarians is the multi-page statistics analysis at the end of each paper issue. American Petroleum Institute data and prices (crude and refined, U.S. and world regions) are reported weekly, but other analyses pop up from time to time, such as country-by-country current/previous-year production comparison figures. For many years it was included in the *Web of Science* (formerly *Science Citation Index*) because its content was primary for the industry. The print version is found in aggregator databases, but the online version is superior, with daily updates.

2016. *Power Engineering.* Former titles (until 1950): *Power Generation;* (until 1948): *Power Plant Engineering;* Which was formed by the merger of (1896-1917): *Practical Engineer;* (19??-1917): *Power Plant.* [ISSN: 0032-5961] 1917. m. USD 111 domestic; USD 124 in Canada & Mexico; USD 300 elsewhere. Ed(s): Russell Ray. PennWell Corporation, 1421 S Sheridan Rd, Tulsa, OK 74112; http://www.pennwell.com. Illus., index, adv. Vol. ends: Dec. *Indexed:* A01, A22, B01, BRI. *Aud.:* Ga, Ac, Sa.

One of those trade magazines that have been around forever, partly because it knows how to change with the times, *Power Engineering* is concerned with the electric power-producing industry with a concentration on solid fuels, and with a section featuring "renewables." Although it does not ignore the "big picture," its focus is on running the power plant. In addition to short articles, it is chock-full of ads, industry briefs, and regular columns on the environment, business, and field notes (which plant is doing what about which). The articles are often by staff writers, but can also be tips from experts in the industry. Although they usually do not include references, the articles are well illustrated with color photographs, charts, tables, and line drawings. The buyers' guide is continuously updated and freely available on the web. Other features include the "Project of the Year," the big industry conference, Power-Gen, webcasts, podcasts, and white papers. Access to the archives search and articles is free, but features such as the white papers require a subscription. The web site is actually a combination of three PennWell titles: *Power Engineering, Power Engineering International,* and *Cogeneration & On-Site Power Production,* which sometimes makes it difficult to determine the actual source of the information. Aside from the scope, the major difference between this magazine and *Power* (below in this section) is the latter's special reports.

2017. *Power (Houston).* Incorporates (1977-2007): *International Power Generation;* (1976-2007): *Middle East Electricity;* (1981-2007): *European Power News;* Which was formerly (1976-1981): *Power Generation Industrial.* [ISSN: 0032-5929] 1882. m. Free to qualified personnel. Ed(s): Gail Reitenbach. The TradeFair Group, Inc., 11000 Richmond, Ste 500, Houston, TX 77042; info@tradefairgroup.com; http://www.tradefairgroup.com/. Illus., index, adv. Vol. ends: No. 9. Microform: PQC. *Indexed:* A01, A22, B01, B03, BRI, C42. *Aud.:* Ga, Ac, Sa.

After more than a century of publication, McGraw-Hill sold *Power* to the TradeFair Group (Houston, Texas) in 2006. In some areas, there have been some big changes, but much of the familiar format remains. There are still dated issues that have the feature articles and various departments (global monitor, operations and management, new products, and more). Every other issue seems to have a "special report" on something, and there are annual features, such as the "Plant of the Year Award" and the "Top Plants" survey. The concentration is on "traditional" power plants, which run on fossil fuels or nuclear power, but renewable energy sources are also included. Although technical, the articles are written with management in mind, which makes them approachable for the undergraduate or lay reader. They are also often illustrated with statistics that are difficult to find elsewhere. Few articles have references; the author's credentials and e-mail contact are the "cited sources." There are columns on fuels, labor, the environment, and the latest technologies and management practices. Obviously a rival to *Power Engineering* (above in this section), *Power* seems to have the edge on in-depth special issues, but these are not available at the web site except to registered subscribers.

2018. *Progress in Energy and Combustion Science: an international review journal.* [ISSN: 0360-1285] 1975. bi-m. EUR 2803. Ed(s): H Wang, C Schulz. Pergamon Press, The Blvd, Langford Ln, E Park, Kidlington, OX5 1GB, United Kingdom; JournalsCustomerServiceEMEA@elsevier.com; http://www.elsevier.com. Illus., index, adv. Sample. Refereed. Microform: PQC. *Indexed:* A01, A22, C45. *Aud.:* Ac.

This is a review journal that publishes papers on efficient combustion of fuels (fossil and biomass), with the aim of conserving resources and protecting the environment. Although much of the "conserving" is for power-plant energy production, a fair percentage of coverage is devoted to jets and internal combustion engines. Articles are not for the fainthearted; the editors solicit papers from experts in the field, and they do a thorough job. Many articles are lengthy, and it is not unusual for an issue to have only three or four papers, each of 40 pages or more. This journal is heavily illustrated with tables and charts. Very few open-access articles are available. This title is consumed by the academic market, but some papers are deliberately designed for the practicing engineer or manager. This is an expensive publication, but well worth considering for the complete research collection.

2019. *Progress in Photovoltaics: research and applications.* [ISSN: 1062-7995] 1993. 12x/yr. GBP 1906. Ed(s): Martin A Green, Tim M Bruton. John Wiley & Sons Ltd., EMEA Institutional Sales, 9600 Garsington Rd, Oxford, OX4 2DQ, United Kingdom; cs-journals@wiley.com; http://onlinelibrary.wiley.com. Adv. Sample. Refereed. Microform: PQC. Reprint: PSC. *Aud.:* Ac.

For *photovoltaics* in the title, the reader should substitute the term *solar cells.* Issues are arranged by articles being alternately categorized via "accelerated," "research," "applications," or "broader perspective." "Accelerated" is reserved for papers that show significant improvements in technique or reliability, innovations, and/or new theories. There is a deliberate mix of academics, practitioners, and policy makers on the review board to provide the same mix in the journal. Although the editors state that part of the intended readership is policy makers, generally the articles are highly technical and narrowly focused. About once a year there will be a themed issue. The photovoltaics literature survey section, culled from other research journals in the field, is very current and appears in each issue. This is a good title for universities with strong interests in energy and electrical engineering.

2020. *Public Utilities Fortnightly: energy, money, power.* Incorporates (2000-2003): *Fortnightly's Energy Customer Management;* Former titles (until 1994): *Public Utilities Reports. Fortnightly;* (until 1993): *Public Utilities Fortnightly;* (until 1929): *Public Utilities Reports Fortnightly.* [ISSN: 1078-5892] 1928. m. USD 172 for 2 yrs. domestic; USD 232 for 2 yrs. foreign. Public Utilities Reports, Inc., 11410 Isaac Newton Sq, Ste 220, Reston, VA 20190; pur_info@pur.com; http://www.pur.com. Circ: 6500 Paid. Microform: PQC. *Indexed:* A22, B03, BRI, C42, L14. *Aud.:* Ga, Sa.

This classic title hasn't been "fortnightly" since 2003; it is now a monthly, at least for the print version. Gone are the flimsy newsprint pages, replaced by glossy paper, full-color layouts, and eye-catching advertisements. Issues have three or four articles and several columns. The articles average four pages, often with nicely formatted data, and, unless they are opinion pieces, they include numerous references. This is a magazine for the investor, addressing new plant technology, regulatory issues, international economics, and supply/distribution problems for electricity, natural gas, nuclear power, and other large-scale energy suppliers. The brevity of the articles, coupled with the overview approach, makes this a useful source for undergraduates as well. The web site has tables of contents for issues back to 1995; the entire set is searchable, but full text is restricted to subscribers.

2021. ***Renewable & Sustainable Energy Reviews.*** [ISSN: 1364-0321] 1997. 14x/yr. EUR 3374. Ed(s): Dr. Lawrence L Kazmerski. Pergamon Press, The Blvd, Langford Ln, E Park, Kidlington, OX5 1GB, United Kingdom; JournalsCustomerServiceEMEA@elsevier.com; http://www.elsevier.com. Adv. Sample. Refereed. *Indexed:* A01, C45. *Aud.:* Ac.

This publication is a mix of engineering, economics, and policy journal, which, as the title suggests, features review articles. However, the length of the reviews varies considerably: some are more than 30 pages, and others are as short as seven. Authors are either faculty at universities or researchers for government-supported organizations. The energy sources covered are biomass, geothermics, hydrogen, hydroelectric, ocean/tide, solar, and wind. Illustrations are often tables and graphs, which serve as an excellent data source. Open-access articles are included. Libraries should compare this title with its sister publication *Renewable Energy* as well as with *Renewable Energy World* and the *Journal of Renewable and Sustainable Energy* (all reviewed in this section) to determine which title(s) may be most useful for their collections.

2022. ***Renewable Energy: an international journal.*** Formerly (until 1991): *Solar and Wind Technology.* [ISSN: 0960-1481] 1984. 15x/yr. EUR 5165. Ed(s): S A Kalogirou. Pergamon Press, The Blvd, Langford Ln, E Park, Kidlington, OX5 1GB, United Kingdom; JournalsCustomerServiceEMEA@elsevier.com; http://www.elsevier.com. Illus., adv. Sample. Refereed. Microform: PQC. *Indexed:* A01, A22, C45, S25. *Bk. rev.:* 1, 1,000 words. *Aud.:* Ac.

At the other end of the spectrum from such magazines as *Home Power* and *Windpower Monthly* (also reviewed in this section), in both type of content and price, *Renewable Energy* is a scholarly publication. Originally emphasizing solar and wind energy (and still heavily cited in the major solar energy titles), it now includes ocean wave and geothermal material. The intended audience includes manufacturers as well as academics and policy groups. A small percentage of the articles is nontechnical, covering social, political, and economic aspects of renewable energy development; but most articles are technical in nature, and the focus is on implementation rather than theory. Open-access articles are available. The authorship is international, with a high rate of Third World contributors, reflecting the sites that emphasize development and use of low-cost (economically and environmentally) power sources.

2023. ***Renewable Energy World (Online).*** Formerly (until 2013): *Renewable Energy World (Print);* Which incorporated (1996-1998): *Sustainable Energy Industry Journal.* [ISSN: 2373-5023] 1996. bi-m. USD 61 (Free to qualified personnel). Ed(s): Jennifer Runyon. PennWell Corporation, 98 Spit Brook Rd, Nashua, NH 03062; http://www.pennwell.com. Illus., adv. Sample. Circ: 52000. *Aud.:* Ac, Sa.

A colorful trade publication with a well-designed web presence, this magazine covers all of the "renewable" energy sources, but emphasizes solar and wind. The coverage is international, both in terms of articles and of suppliers: it's easy to find wind power companies in, say, Colombia. This journal is designed for the practitioner rather than the scholar, and issues are crammed with current news, include ten or so articles, and contain the usual conference/trade show announcements, letters, editorials, and the like. The web site includes links to suppliers, related material, archives of selected articles from back numbers, and a few videos. The articles themselves often have the kinds of tables, charts, and engineering data that are hard to acquire elsewhere. For public libraries and those serving practitioners.

2024. ***Resource and Energy Economics: a journal of resource, energy and environmental economics.*** Formerly (until 1993): *Resources and Energy.* [ISSN: 0928-7655] 1978. 4x/yr. EUR 1437. Ed(s): G L Poe, S Ambec. Elsevier BV, Radarweg 29, Amsterdam, 1043 NX, Netherlands; info@elsevier.com; https://www.elsevier.com/. Illus., index, adv. Sample. Refereed. Microform: PQC. *Indexed:* A22, B01, C45, EconLit. *Aud.:* Ac.

This journal should be compared with its sister publication *Energy Economics* (above in this section). *Resources and Energy Economics* emphasizes use of resources, of which energy is just one. The papers are scholarly and lengthy (often more than 20 pages). A limited number of open-access articles are available. Recent titles include: "Local labor market shocks and residential mortgage payments: Evidence from shale oil and gas booms" and "Profitable pollution abatement? A worker productivity perspective." The publication delay averages more than one year. Libraries whose interest is primarily in energy will prefer *Energy Economics*, while those with strong economics and/or business collections should consider both journals.

2025. ***Solar Energy.*** Formerly (until Jan.1958): *The Journal of Solar Energy, Science and Engineering.* [ISSN: 0038-092X] 1957. 18x/yr. EUR 4178. Ed(s): Y Goswami. Elsevier Ltd, The Boulevard, Langford Lane, Oxford, OX5 1GB, United Kingdom; http://www.elsevier.com. Illus., index, adv. Sample. Refereed. Vol. ends: No. 6. *Indexed:* A01, A22, Agr, BRI. *Bk. rev.:* 1, 500 words. *Aud.:* Ac.

Solar Energy was once the premier journal in solar research, encompassing biomass and wind energy, as well as the engineering and physical aspects of solar energy. In early 2009, the editors revised the journal's scope to limit the publication of articles on solar radiation and solar resource assessment to novel and universally applicable techniques, resulting in articles' reflecting advances in modeling techniques that render inadequate the "data analysis" approach of earlier years. This title is strictly a scholarly publication, and most of its authors are academics from all of the engineering disciplines, with a few applied physicists included for good measure. Illustrations are limited to charts, tables, and line drawings, although an occasional candid photograph of field work appears. Every few months, there is a topical issue and the occasional "brief note," a brief methodology description. Open-access articles are included. The publication lag time can be more than a year, but most of the lag seems to be in the review process; once accepted, an article is promptly published. Institutions with an emphasis on materials and electronics might prefer its sister publication, *Solar Energy Materials & Solar Cells* (below in this section).

2026. ***Solar Energy Materials & Solar Cells.*** Formerly (until 1992): *Solar Energy Materials;* Incorporates (1979-1991): *Solar Cells.* [ISSN: 0927-0248] 1979. 15x/yr. EUR 5651. Ed(s): C M Lampert. Elsevier BV, North-Holland, Postbus 211, Amsterdam, 1000 AE, Netherlands; JournalsCustomerServiceEMEA@elsevier.com; http://www.elsevier.com. Illus., index. Sample. Refereed. Vol. ends: No. 4. Microform: PQC. *Indexed:* A01, A22. *Bk. rev.:* 1, 500 words, signed. *Aud.:* Ac.

Aptly named, this journal publishes highly technical papers on the materials used in solar energy production and products. Aside from solar cells, it includes light control, optical and photochemical properties of materials, and photothermal devices (used in energy storage). Unlike *Progress in Photovoltaics* (above in this section), this is an applications-centered publication. Open-access articles are available. Publication can be swift (within two months of submission) or as long as a year's lag. This is one of the top ten most-cited journals in energy, but it is best for scholarly collections that encompass materials chemistry as well as energy.

2027. ***Solar Today: leading the renewable energy revolution.*** Formerly: *A S E S News.* [ISSN: 1042-0630] 1987. q. Free to members. American Solar Energy Society, Inc., 2525 Arapahoe Ave, Ste E4-253, Ste 106, Boulder, CO 80302; ases@ases.org; http://www.ases.org. Illus., index, adv. Circ: 18424 Paid. Vol. ends: Nov/Dec. *Indexed:* A22. *Aud.:* Ga, Sa.

This is the members' magazine for the American Solar Energy Society, the "local" correlate of the international solar community; the latter group is served by *Solar Energy*. The latter title is for researchers; *Solar Today* is for everybody. As is true of many magazines in the solar field, wind power is included as an also-ran. Many of the articles describe success stories on a small scale. Others take the larger view, covering potential world markets for wind energy or green power. Although the topics may be technical, the treatment usually is not. The letters section is extensive, there are lots of ads (for both includes links to conferences and events, educational and informational sites, government agencies, utilities, businesses (by specialty), and society business and information on the annual National Solar Tour (formerly, the National Tour of Solar Buildings). There is also a "digital version" of the print the contractor and the homeowner); and society news and conference programs complete the issue.

The web site magazine with the same content but with a glossy display. To top it off, video interviews are now featured. This is an inexpensive title suitable for public libraries, but academic institutions will be better served by *Solar Energy* or *Solar Energy Materials & Solar Cells*.

2028. *Wind Energy.* [ISSN: 1095-4244] 1998. 12x/yr. GBP 923. Ed(s): Scott Schreck, Rebecca Barthelmie. John Wiley & Sons Ltd., EMEA Institutional Sales, 9600 Garsington Rd, Oxford, OX4 2DQ, United Kingdom; cs-journals@wiley.com; http://www.wiley.com. Adv. Sample. Refereed. Reprint: PSC. *Aud.:* Ac.

For many years, there were only two scholarly journals covering wind sources of energy, the *Journal of Wind Engineering & Industrial Aerodynamics* and *Wind Engineering* (the latter reviewed in this section). *Wind Energy* was launched in 1998, evidently in direct competition with *Wind Engineering.* They both cover the technical aspects of generating power from wind sources; they both have an international scope, including papers authored largely by academic institutions and government-funded agencies; they also have lengthy articles and references, and include the occasional historical or economic review. The chief differences between the two journals are price (*Wind Energy* costs twice as much as *Wind Engineering*) and inclusion in ISI's Web of Science (*Wind Energy* is, while *Wind Engineering* is not). However, *Wind Energy* cites *Wind Engineering* and vice versa. Libraries with large collections may want both, but the less expensive title seems the best bet.

2029. *Wind Engineering.* [ISSN: 0309-524X] 1977. bi-m. USD 1700 (print & online eds.)). Sage Publications Ltd., 1 Oliver's Yard, 55 City Rd, London, EC1Y 1SP, United Kingdom; info@sagepub.com; https://www.sagepub.com. Sample. Refereed. *Indexed:* A22. *Aud.:* Ac.

Wind Engineering claims to be the oldest English-language journal devoted entirely to the technical issues of wind power, which is largely true, although the *Journal of Wind Engineering & Industrial Aerodynamics* has been in existence longer, beginning as the *Journal of Industrial Aerodynamics.* Topics covered are wind turbines, turbine blade design, and economic and historical aspects of wind energy, and there is a good deal of emphasis on wind farms and offshore wind energy production. It is very similar in coverage and quality to *Wind Energy* (above in this section), and libraries with restricted budgets or tangential interest in wind power will want to carefully compare the two, especially as *Wind Engineering* offers a discount for libraries whose faculty members publish in the journal.

2030. *Windpower Monthly.* [ISSN: 0109-7318] 1985. m. Ed(s): Jacki Burst. Haymarket Publishing Ltd., Bridge House, 69 London Rd, Twickenham, TW1 3SP, United Kingdom; info@haymarket.com; http://www.haymarket.com. Illus., adv. Sample. Circ: 5000. Vol. ends: No. 12. *Indexed:* C42. *Aud.:* Ac, Sa.

Begun in Denmark, distributed from the United States, and with a web site originating in the United Kingdom, *Windpower Monthly* is truly an international publication. The audience is wind energy businesses, investors, and power plant component manufacturers. Although each issue will have a small number of articles (one of which is the "Focus Article"), the bulk of the magazine is devoted to wind energy news reports, arranged by regions/countries of the world. Some of the news is technical, but most of it is economic or policy news. The "Windicator," a quarterly supplement, is a chart of wind power capacity worldwide, identifying industrial, political, technical, and economic trends. A new feature is "Windpower TV," which comprises video reports and interviews. The magazine also publishes the *Windstats* newsletter, available at an extra cost. One of the few magazines for the wind energy "trade," it is useful only for large collections. Others might rely on aggregators for access to material from 5/1/2013 and newer.

2031. *World Oil.* Former titles (until 1947): *The Oil Weekly;* (until 1918): *Gulf Coast Oil News.* [ISSN: 0043-8790] 1916. m. USD 299. Ed(s): Pramod Kulkarni. Gulf Publishing Co., PO Box 2608, Houston, TX 77252; publications@gulfpub.com; http://www.gulfpub.com. Illus., adv. Circ: 35393. Microform: PQC. *Indexed:* A22, B01, B03, BRI, C42. *Aud.:* Ac, Sa.

One of the many petroleum-related trade magazines (see also the *Oil & Gas Journal* above this section), this one covers oil around the world. Each issue follows the pattern of focus articles, feature articles, columns, news, and departments. Focus and feature articles are short (two or three pages), but they are well illustrated in color. The web site includes supplements and case studies, plus extensive statistics (both production and price), reference tables, forecasts, and analyses, most requiring registration and some requiring a paid subscription. The data alone are worth the price of subscription. An excellent, inexpensive addition to a good energy collection.

■ ENGINEERING AND TECHNOLOGY

General/Biomedical Engineering/Chemical Engineering/Civil and Environmental Engineering/Computer, Control, and Systems Engineering/Electrical Engineering/Industrial and Manufacturing Engineering/Materials Engineering/Mechanical Engineering/Nuclear Engineering

See also Aeronautics and Space Science; Atmospheric Sciences; Biology; Chemistry; Computers and Information Technology; Earth Sciences; Mathematics; Physics; Robotics; and Science and Technology sections.

Megan Wilson, Science & Agriculture Librarian, Murray State University, Murray, KY 42071; mwilson70@murraystate.edu

Introduction

In this *Magazine for Libraries* edition, the selection of journals in the Engineering and Technology section provides a sampling of the engineering and technology research literature for each area. This list includes scholarly and peer-reviewed research journals as well as trade magazines addressing the advances, challenges, and applications of engineering and technology within a variety of industries.

The titles in this edition include some of the most highly ranked and specialized journals in their fields. Many of the journals included here provide options for content alerts and recommended article lists, as well as easy access to the most read and most cited articles. Social media sharing options are often available, providing a seamless way to share research with peers in the research community. Altmetrics continue to see growth and are included on many articles from commercial publishers. These non-traditional metrics provide readers a snapshot of the impact a research paper is having outside the immediate research community including mentions by news organizations, on blogs, and in social media feed.

Open-access publishing continues to gain acceptance by the engineering and technology research community, with many of the publishers offering a hybrid open-access model. Allowing authors the option to pay a processing fee to the publisher or alternatively uploading a copy of the accepted manuscript to an online repository (Green Open Access model). Embargos and format restrictions may apply. As publishers seek to comply with Plan S requirements, several of the journals on this list are now experimenting with "mirror" and "partner" journals as a alternative to the hybrid open-access model. Expect to see some changes in this area in the coming years.

Basic Periodicals

CHEMICAL ENGINEERING. Ga, Ac, Sa: *A I Ch E Journal*.

CIVIL ENGINEERING. Ac, Sa: *E N R*.

COMPUTER, CONTROL, AND SYSTEMS ENGINEERING. Ac, Sa: *Association for Computing Machinery. Journal*.

ELECTRICAL ENGINEERING. Ac, Sa: *IEEE Journals, Proceedings, and Transactions*.

MANUFACTURING ENGINEERING. Ac, Sa: *Journal of Manufacturing Systems*.

MATERIALS ENGINEERING. Ac, Sa: *Journal of Materials Research;*

MECHANICAL ENGINEERING. Ac, Sa: *Mechanical Engineering*.

Basic Abstracts and Indexes

Applied Science and Technology Index, Computer & Control Abstracts, Engineering Index, Compendex, INSPEC, Metals Abstracts.

General

2032. *A S E E Prism.* Formed by the merger of (1974-1991): *Engineering Education News;* (1924-1991): *Engineering Education;* Which was formerly (until 1969): *Journal of Engineering Education.* [ISSN: 1056-8077] 1991. 8x/yr. Free to members. Ed(s): Mark Matthews. American Society for Engineering Education, 1818 N St, NW, Ste 600, Washington, DC 20036; pubsinfo@asee.org; http://www.asee.org/. Illus., index, adv. Microform: CIS; PQC. *Indexed:* A22. *Bk. rev.:* Number and length vary. *Aud.:* Ga, Ac, Sa.

ASEE Prism, published by the American Society for Engineering Education (ASEE), is an engaging and visually attractive trade magazine covering all areas of engineering. Through its variety of special features and regular columns and other content, *Prism* provides readers with information on research and trends in technology, issues in engineering education (K-12 and college level), statistics related to engineering graduates, salaries in academia and industry, programs, and more. Recent issues included articles on urban sanitation, stabilizing ice caps, diversity in engineering, among others. Available in print and online, this popular magazine will appeal to anyone with an interest in engineering and engineering education including students, K-12 teachers, engineering faculty, and practitioners. URL: http://www.asee.org/papers-and-publications/publications/prism

2033. *The Bridge (Washington).* [ISSN: 0737-6278] 1969. q. Free. Ed(s): Cameron H Fletcher. National Academy of Engineering, 500 5th St NW, Washington, DC 20001; http://www.nae.edu. *Indexed:* S25. *Aud.:* Ga, Ac, Sa.

The Bridge, an informative publication, publishes timely thematic issues discussing and analyzing trends, developments, and policies related to the present and future of engineering. Published quarterly by the National Academy of Engineering, *The Bridge* will appeal to engineers as well as policymakers, educators, NAE members, and others. Available in print and online (open access), readers can access current and back issues on *The Bridge* website. PDF versions of entire issues (since 1999) and articles can be downloaded from the website. Because of its broad appeal, both academic and large public libraries may consider making *The Bridge* available to their users. URL: https://www.nae.edu/19582/Bridge.aspx

2034. *Computers & Structures: solids, structures, fluids, multiphysics.* [ISSN: 0045-7949] 1971. 16x/yr. EUR 9161. Elsevier Ltd, The Boulevard, Langford Lane, Oxford, OX5 1GB, United Kingdom; customerserviceau@elsevier.com; http://www.elsevier.com. Illus., adv. Sample. Refereed. Microform: PQC. *Indexed:* A01, A22, CompLI, HRIS. *Aud.:* Ac, Sa.

The peer-reviewed *Computers & Structures* disseminates research advancing the state-of-the-art of computing and modeling methods used to solve problems in all areas of mechanics (e.g., biomechanical, civil, aeronautical, mechanical engineering, and more). It publishes original research and review articles examining the use of novel and general computational techniques to solve problems in engineering or explore new insights into existing methods. Published 16 times per year, the journal publishes special thematic issues and supports open-access publishing. The online version features links to most downloaded, most cited, recent, and open-access articles. Individual articles provide access to recommended and cited articles and may display research highlights in the results list. This journal is highly technical, but will be of interest to researchers in academia, government, or industrial research laboratories. URL: https://www.journals.elsevier.com/computers-and-structures

Engineering & Technology. See Electronics section.

2035. *Engineering Inc.* Former titles (until 2002): *A C E;* (until 2001): *American Consulting Engineer.* [ISSN: 1539-2694] 1990. bi-m. USD 65 (Members, USD 24; Non-members, USD 45). Ed(s): Corey Murray. American Council of Engineering Companies, 1015 15th St, 8th Fl, NW, Washington, DC 20005; acec@acec.org; http://www.acec.org. Adv. *Aud.:* Ga, Ac.

Engineering Inc., a trade magazine published bi-monthly by the American Council of Engineering Companies (ACEC), is a good source of engineering business and economic news, legislative/regulatory proposals for practicing engineers, faculty, and students. Available in print, each issue includes regular features and columns (business news, legislative actions, market watch) as well as full-length articles on topics of current interest. Recent issues include thoughtful discussions of sustainable infrastructure, enhancing disaster preparedness, waterfront restoration, Lean manufacturing, and more. *Engineering Inc.* will be at home in both corporate and academic libraries, as well as public libraries with a strong business orientation. URL: http://www.acec.org/publications/engineering-inc/

2036. *I E E E Transactions on Engineering Management.* Former titles (until 1963): *I R E Transactions on Engineering Management;* (until 1955): *I R E Professional Group on Engineering Management. Transactions.* [ISSN: 0018-9391] 1954. q. USD 665. Ed(s): Tugrul Daim. Institute of Electrical and Electronics Engineers, 445 Hoes Ln, Piscataway, NJ 08854; contactcenter@ieee.org; http://www.ieee.org. Illus., adv. Refereed. *Indexed:* A01, A22, B01, BRI, C42. *Aud.:* Ac, Sa.

Published quarterly, *IEEE Transactions on Engineering Management*, sponsored by the IEEE Technology & Engineering Management Society, publishes literature reviews and peer-reviewed research related to the management of technical functions as it relates to research, design, and engineering. The online version provides easy access to the journal archive, early-access papers, and popular papers. This journal supports open- access publishing. Researchers, practitioners, and faculty who are interested in using technology to manage the engineering process will find relevant research published here. URL: http://ieeexplore.ieee.org/xpl/RecentIssue.jsp?punumber=17

2037. *International Journal for Numerical Methods in Engineering.* Formerly (until 1969): *Numerical Methods in Engineering.* [ISSN: 0029-5981] 19??. 52x/yr. GBP 10668. Ed(s): Charbel Farhat, Rene de Borst. John Wiley & Sons Ltd., EMEA Institutional Sales, 9600 Garsington Rd, Oxford, OX4 2DQ, United Kingdom; cs-journals@wiley.com; http://onlinelibrary.wiley.com. Illus., index, adv. Sample. Refereed. Microform: PQC. Reprint: PSC. *Indexed:* A22, CompLI, MSN. *Bk. rev.:* Number and length vary. *Aud.:* Ac, Sa.

The *International Journal for Numerical Methods in Engineering* publishes research discussing novel applications of numerical methods to engineering problems. This journal accepts original, peer-reviewed research papers in many areas of computational engineering including model reduction, optimization, verification and validation, and more. Recent issues include papers on topology optimization of plane structures, wave filtering in multiscale couplings, finite element methods, scale bridging in multi-scale simulations, and more. Special, thematic issues are published. Available in print and online, the journal supports open-access publishing. The online version provides access to the entire journal archive, early view and accepted articles, as well as links to most accessed and most cited papers. Engineering researchers in academia and industry are the main audience for this journal. URL: http://onlinelibrary.wiley.com/journal/10.1002/(ISSN)1097-0207

Issues in Science and Technology See Science and Technology/History and Philosophy of Science section.

2038. *Journal of Engineering Education.* [ISSN: 1069-4730] 1993. q. GBP 430. Ed(s): Michael C Loui. Wiley-Blackwell Publishing, Inc., 111 River St, Hoboken, NJ 07030; http://onlinelibrary.wiley.com. Adv. Refereed. Reprint: PSC. *Indexed:* A01, A22. *Aud.:* Ac, Sa.

The *Journal of Engineering Education* (*JEE*) (in print and online) is a journal focused on Education as well as Engineering. Published by Wiley for the American Society for Engineering Education, *JEE* is published quarterly and provides readers access to peer-reviewed, current research covering engineering epistemologies, learning mechanisms and systems, diversity, and assessment. Previously published articles discuss motivators of graduate teaching assistants, an analysis of student versus practitioner writing in civil engineering, empathy as a core engineering skill, developing inter-disciplinary competence in engineers and more. *JEE*'s online version provides easy access to the most accessed and cited articles as well as the journal archive. This journal is recommended for all educators, even non-engineering faculty, who work with engineering students. URL: http://onlinelibrary.wiley.com/journal/10.1002/(ISSN)2168-9830

2039. *Journal of Pre-College Engineering Education Research.* [ISSN: 2157-9288] 2011. s-a. Free. Ed(s): Senay Purzer. Purdue University Press, Stewart Ctr 190, 504 W State St, West Lafayette, IN 47907; pupress@purdue.edu; http://www.thepress.purdue.edu. Adv. Refereed. *Aud.:* Ga, Ac.

The *Journal of Pre-College Engineering Education Research* (*J-PEER*), published by Purdue University Press, is an online-only open-access journal that publishes research articles and practitioner reports related to pre-college engineering education. Published twice a year, each issue contains three peer-reviewed research articles and a practitioner report. Issues of *J-PEER* are available online. Pre-college STEM educators will find the research and other reports in *J-PEER* very useful when planning the integration of engineering design into their courses. URL: http://docs.lib.purdue.edu/jpeer/

2040. *Journal of Testing and Evaluation.* Formerly (until 1973): *Journal of Materials;* Which incorporated (in 1966): *Gillett Memorial Lecture;* Superseded in part (in 1961): *American Society for Testing and Materials. Proceedings;* Which was formerly (until 196?): *American Society for Testing Materials. Proceedings;* (until 1945): *American Society for Testing Materials. Proceedings of the Annual Meeting;* (until 1902): *International Association for Testing Materials. American Section. Bulletin.* [ISSN: 0090-3973] 1899. bi-m. USD 422 (Individuals, USD 273). Ed(s): Dr. M R Mitchell. A S T M International, 100 Barr Harbor Dr, PO Box C700, West Conshohocken, PA 19428-2959; service@astm.org; https://www.astm.org. Illus., index. Refereed. Vol. ends: Nov. Microform: PMC; PQC. *Indexed:* A22, E01. *Aud.:* Ac, Sa.

The *Journal of Testing and Evaluation* (*JOTE*) is all about testing and evaluating the materials used in many disciplines of science and engineering. Published six times a year by ASTM International, *JOTE* seeks original, peer-reviewed research papers and briefs, review articles and technical notes, related to material testing and evaluation done in the field and laboratory in the major areas of materials fatigue and fracture, and mechanical and fire testing. This flagship journal supports open-access publishing and publishes thematic issues. The online version provides access to the most current issues, the complete journal archive, and to First Look Papers (online when accepted). *JOTE* is a must read for engineering researchers and practitioners who are developing models and simulations or need information about materials testing and methodologies for their work. Available in print and online. URL: https://compass.astm.org/journals/jote/

Measurement Science and Technology. See Physics section.

National Academy of Sciences. Proceedings. See Biology/General section.

2041. *Quality Engineering.* [ISSN: 0898-2112] 1988. q. GBP 1191 (print & online eds.)). Ed(s): Peter Parker. Taylor & Francis Inc., 711 3rd Ave, 8th Fl, New York, NY 10017; support@tandfonline.com; http://www.tandfonline.com. Adv. Sample. Refereed. Microform: RPI. Reprint: PSC. *Indexed:* A22, B01, E01. *Aud.:* Ac, Sa.

Quality Engineering (in print, online, and microform) publishes peer-reviewed papers on quality engineering solutions. The research topics covered include six sigma methods, quality control, process optimization, reliability engineering, and more. The journal seeks papers describing new methods for use in industry, or giving examples of existing techniques being used in new applications. Published quarterly, *Quality Engineering* supports open-access publishing. The online version from Taylor & Francis provides access to the entire journal archive, the latest articles posted online, and information about calls for papers. Individual articles include easy access to figures and data, references, citations, and more on the abstract page. This journal is recommended for engineering faculty, academic and corporate researchers, and graduate students working on quality engineering problems. URL: http://www.tandfonline.com/loi/lqen20

R & D Magazine. See Science and Technology/General section.

Science and Engineering Ethics. See Science and Technology/History and Philosophy of Science section.

Biomedical Engineering

American Chemical Society. Journal. See Chemistry/General section.

2042. *Annals of Biomedical Engineering.* Incorporates (1976-1978): *Journal of Bioengineering.* [ISSN: 0090-6964] 1972. m. Ed(s): Stefan Duma. Springer New York LLC, 233 Spring St, New York, NY 10013; journals@springer-ny.com; http://www.springer.com. Illus., index, adv. Refereed. Reprint: PSC. *Indexed:* A22, Agr, BRI, E01. *Bk. rev.:* Number and length vary. *Aud.:* Ac, Sa.

The peer-reviewed *Annals of Biomedical Engineering,* official journal of the Biomedical Engineering Society, publishes original research and review articles related to bioengineering, biomedicine, biophysics, biomedical engineering, and more. The journal supports open-access publishing and publishes special, thematic issues and sections. Past themes include additive manufacturing of biomaterials, biomedical design, cardiovascular biomechanics, frontiers in bioengineering, and more. Available in print and online, the publisher aims for quick publication of submitted papers usually posting accepted papers online within two weeks of acceptance. The online version provides easy access to "Online First," "Open Access," and "Latest" articles. Readers can set up RSS feeds or register for journal updates via email. This journal is recommended for academic and other libraries in institutions where significant biomedical research activities take place. URL: http://www.springer.com/biomed/journal/10439

Biochemistry. See Biology/Biochemistry and Biophysics section.

2043. *Biofabrication.* [ISSN: 1758-5082] 2009. q. Ed(s): W Sun. Institute of Physics Publishing Ltd., Temple Circus, Temple Way, Bristol, BS1 6HG, United Kingdom; custserv@iop.org; http://iopscience.iop.org. Sample. Refereed. *Aud.:* Ac, Sa.

Biofabrication covers the use of biologic materials (e.g., cells and proteins) and biomaterials to fabricate biological systems and therapeutic products. The official journal of the International Society for Biofabrication, this journal is peer-reviewed and publishes original research papers, notes, topical reviews, and comments. Major topics of interest include cell, tissue, and organ printing, 3D tissue scaffold fabrication, modeling of biofabrication processes, and more. *Biofabrication* is published quarterly and the online version provides easy access to current and archived issues and accepted manuscripts, as well as most cited, latest, review and feature articles. Open-access articles are clearly marked. This journal is very specialized and will appeal to biomedical researchers, practitioners, and designers in academia and industry who are working in the emerging area of biofabrication. URL: http://iopscience.iop.org/journal/1758-5090

2044. *Biomaterials.* Incorporates (1986-1995): *Clinical Materials;* Which incorporated (in 1991): *Critical Reviews in Biocompatibility.* [ISSN: 0142-9612] 1980. 38x/yr. EUR 11174. Ed(s): K W Leong. Elsevier BV, Radarweg 29, Amsterdam, 1043 NX, Netherlands; info@elsevier.com; https://www.elsevier.com/. Illus., adv. Refereed. Microform: PQC. *Indexed:* A01, A22, C45. *Bk. rev.:* Number and length vary. *Aud.:* Ac, Sa.

Biomaterials is a peer-reviewed, international journal covering many aspects of the physical, biological, and chemical sciences related to the design and use of biomaterials. It publishes original research papers, reviews, and opinion papers discussing the foundational sciences behind biomaterials as well as the clinical application of biomaterials to cancer diagnosis, delivery of drugs and vaccines, implantable devices, regenerative medicine, and more. Available in print, online, and in microform, *Biomaterials* supports open-access publishing and is published 38 times per year. The online version provides easy access to current and archived issues, "Articles in Press," and "In Progress Issues." This journal will appeal to biomaterials and biomedical engineers and researchers in academic, hospital, and corporate settings. URL: https://www.journals.elsevier.com/biomaterials

2045. *Biomedical Microdevices.* [ISSN: 1387-2176] 1998. bi-m. EUR 1120 (print & online eds.)). Ed(s): Mauro Ferrari. Springer New York LLC, 233 Spring St, New York, NY 10013; customerservice@springer.com; http://www.springer.com. Adv. Sample. Refereed. Reprint: PSC. *Indexed:* A22, Agr, E01. *Aud.:* Ac, Sa.

Research and applications of MEMS, microfabrication and nanotechnology for diagnostic or therapeutic applications, are the main focus of *Biomedical Microdevices*. Published bi-monthly, this peer-reviewed research publication focuses on the design, testing, and clinical validation of microdevice systems. The journal supports open-access publishing and the online version is available from Springer. It provides researchers with easy access to "Open Access" and "Latest articles" as well as the journal archive. The website provides social media sharing options and readers can stay up to date by subscribing to RSS feeds or email updates. This journal will appeal to researchers in biomedical and biomaterials engineering and medicine, especially those working on very small-scale devices. URL: https://link.springer.com/journal/10544

Biophysical Journal. See Biology/Biochemistry and Biophysics section.

Biotechnology and Bioengineering. See Biotechnology section.

2046. *I E E E Transactions on Biomedical Engineering (Online).* Formerly (until 1964): *I E E E Transactions on Bio-Medical Electronics (Online);* (until 1963): *I R E Transactions on Bio-Medical Electronics (Online);* (until 1961): *I R E Transactions on Medical Electronics (Online);* (until 1955): *I R E Professional Group on Medical Electronics. Transactions (Online).* [ISSN: 1558-2531] 1953. m. USD 2485. Ed(s): Xiaochuan Pan. Institute of Electrical and Electronics Engineers, 445 Hoes Ln, Piscataway, NJ 08855; subscription-service@ieee.org; http://www.ieee.org. Refereed. *Indexed:* ErgAb. *Aud.:* Ac, Sa.

IEEE Transactions on Biomedical Engineering is a peer-reviewed research journal published monthly by the IEEE Engineering in Medicine and Biology Society. This journal accepts original papers highlighting the use of physics and engineering in all aspects of biomedical engineering. Available in print and online, this journal provides open-access publishing options to authors. The online version has many value-added features including links to current and past issues as well as links to popular, early-access, and related articles as well as automatic content alert notifications. Biomedical research scientists and engineers as well as medical professionals are the target audience of this journal. URL: http://ieeexplore.ieee.org/xpl/RecentIssue.jsp?punumber=10

International Journal of Medical Robotics and Computer Assisted Surgery. See Robotics section.

The International Journal of Robotics Research. See Robotics section.

JAMA: The Journal of the American Medical Association. See Medicine section.

2047. *Journal of Biomaterials Applications.* [ISSN: 0885-3282] 1986. 10x/yr. USD 3604 (print & online eds.)). Ed(s): Jonathan Knowles. Sage Publications Ltd., 1 Oliver's Yard, 55 City Rd, London, EC1Y 1SP, United Kingdom; info@sagepub.com; https://www.sagepub.com/. Sample. Refereed. Reprint: PSC. *Indexed:* A01, A22, E01. *Aud.:* Ac, Sa.

The *Journal of Biomaterials Applications* publishes original research and review papers related to biomaterials. The content is multidisciplinary and discusses all aspects of biomaterials development (especially new developments) and manufacture as well as the clinical applications of biomaterials and biocompatibility issues. The journal is especially interested in research on new and emerging biomaterials technologies. Recent papers in this international, peer-reviewed journal cover topics in hard tissues and materials, soft tissues and materials, biomaterials for organs, functional biomaterials surfaces, and biomaterials processing. Available in print and online. The online version of the journal provides readers with most read, most cited, and OnlineFirst paper lists as well as access to the current issue and the journal archive. Sharing options and permissions information are prominent on each paper, and supplemental materials and altmetrics information are provided when available. Researchers in materials science, biomedical device engineering, and medicine will all find information they can use in this journal. URL: http://journals.sagepub.com/home/jba

2048. *Journal of Biomechanics.* [ISSN: 0021-9290] 1968. 16x/yr. EUR 8029. Ed(s): Dr. Farshid Guilak. Pergamon Press, The Blvd, Langford Ln, E Park, Kidlington, OX5 1GB, United Kingdom; JournalsCustomerServiceEMEA@elsevier.com; http://www.elsevier.com. Illus., adv. Sample. Refereed. Microform: PQC. *Indexed:* A01, A22, C45, ErgAb, SD. *Bk. rev.:* Number and length vary. *Aud.:* Ac, Sa.

The *Journal of Biomechanics* is an international, peer-reviewed journal that publishes original research examining the use of mechanics principles to find solutions to biological problems. The journal publishes original research papers discussing novel approaches and whose findings are significant, as well as relevant, to the journal's scope. Other items published include surveys and perspectives (both by editor invitation), book reviews, and letters to the editor. Research topics of particular interest include cardiovascular and respiratory biomechanics, dental biomechanics, orthopedic, injury, and sports biomechanics, functional tissue engineering, and more. A joint publication of several biomechanics associations, the *Journal of Biomechanics* publishes special, thematic issues, supports open-access publishing, and is available in print, online, and in microform. The online version provides access to recent, most downloaded, most cited, and open-access articles. Individual papers may include full-color figures and photographs as well as supplemental materials (e.g., data files). This journal is recommended for academic and other research libraries serving biomedical engineers, medical researchers, and clinicians. URL: https://www.journals.elsevier.com/journal-of-biomechanics

The Journal of Cell Biology. See Biology/Cell and Molecular Biology section.

2049. *Journal of Tissue Engineering and Regenerative Medicine.* [ISSN: 1932-6254] 2007. m. GBP 1227. Ed(s): Rui L Reis. John Wiley & Sons, Inc., 111 River St, Hoboken, NJ 07030; cs-journals@wiley.com; http://onlinelibrary.wiley.com. Refereed. Reprint: PSC. *Aud.:* Ac, Sa.

The *Journal of Tissue Engineering and Regenerative Medicine* is a multidisciplinary journal specializing in rapid review and publication of research on the combination of stem cells, biomaterials and scaffolds, bioreactive agents, and their constructs in the development of therapeutic approaches. This monthly journal publishes research papers, perspectives and reviews (both by invitation), and clinical case reports. Research topics of interest include cell encapsulation, novel drug discovery/testing methods and models, stem cell use in drug discovery, cell transplantation technologies, and more. This journal supports open-access publishing and is available in print and online. Special issues and supplements are occasionally published. Individual papers in the online version include color graphics and photographs, supporting information (e.g., data files) when available, and more. Sharing options are available and altmetrics are provided for papers when available. This journal will appeal to a many researchers including cell and molecular biologists, biomedical engineers, chemists, medical researchers, clinicians, and surgeons. URL: http://onlinelibrary.wiley.com/journal/10.1002/(ISSN)1932-7005

2050. *Medical Image Analysis.* [ISSN: 1361-8415] 1996. 8x/yr. EUR 1874. Ed(s): Dr. Nicholas Ayache, Dr. James Duncan. Elsevier BV, Radarweg 29, Amsterdam, 1043 NX, Netherlands; info@elsevier.com; https://www.elsevier.com/. Refereed. *Indexed:* A01, A22, E01.

Medical Image Analysis (in print and online) is a well-regarded journal that covers the basic science of processing and analyzing medical imaging data on all scales from cellular to tissue or organ scale. This multidisciplinary journal is peer reviewed and publishes original research papers (eight times per year) covering new developments and implementation of algorithms to improve the representation of pictorial data, visualization, feature extraction, image guide surgery (robots), digital anatomical atlases, and more. A variety of technologies are discussed including magnetic resonance, ultrasound, CT scans, nuclear medicine, X-rays, among others. *Medical Image Analysis* supports open-access publishing and publishes special issues occasionally. Articles in the online version may include 3D radiological data and audio files or videos. This journal is recommended for academic and research libraries where medical imaging research is conducted. URL: https://www.journals.elsevier.com/medical-image-analysis/

Tissue Engineering. Part A. See Biotechnology section.

Chemical Engineering

2051. *A C S Sustainable Chemistry & Engineering.* [ISSN: 2168-0485] 2013. m. Free to members. Ed(s): David T Allen. American Chemical Society, 1155 16th St NW, Washington, DC 20036; service@acs.org; http://www.acs.org. Adv. Refereed. *Indexed:* C45. *Aud.:* Ac, Sa.

The *ACS Sustainable Chemistry & Engineering* journal is an online-only publication focusing on green chemistry and manufacturing, alternative energies and energy resources, and more. This peer-reviewed journal publishes research articles, letters (preliminary works requiring rapid publication), perspectives (topical literature reviews), features, and more. The journal publishes special, thematic issues, supports open-access publishing (hybrid model), and features easy access on its website to recent articles (Articles ASAP), just accepted manuscripts, most read articles, and more. The information in this journal will be of interest to any researcher interested in green chemistry and sustainability including chemical researchers and engineers in academia and industry, as well as environmental scientists. URL: http://pubs.acs.org/toc/ascecg/current

2052. *A I Ch E Journal.* [ISSN: 0001-1541] 1955. m. GBP 2131. Ed(s): Michael P Harold. John Wiley & Sons, Inc., 111 River St, Hoboken, NJ 07030; cs-journals@wiley.com; http://onlinelibrary.wiley.com. Illus., index, adv. Refereed. Circ: 3000 Paid. Vol. ends: Dec. Reprint: PSC. *Indexed:* A22, Agr, BRI, S25. *Bk. rev.:* Number and length vary. *Aud.:* Ac, Sa.

The multi-disciplinary *A I Ch E Journal* is well known among academic researchers and practicing engineers in chemical, biochemical, electrochemical, and environmental engineering, and more. This peer-reviewed, monthly publication includes research papers reporting on significant new theoretical or experimental findings, reviews of important research areas in chemical engineering, A I Ch E letters (on any topic) and perspectives. Manuscripts are solicited on topics including bio- and biomolecular engineering, particle technology and fluidization, process system engineering, reaction engineering, thermodynamics, and more. The online version provides access to early view, most cited, most accessed and accepted articles. URL: http://onlinelibrary.wiley.com/journal/10.1002/(ISSN)1547-5905

2053. *Biochemical Engineering Journal.* [ISSN: 1369-703X] 1998. 12x/yr. EUR 3183. Ed(s): Colin Webb, Masahito Taya. Elsevier BV, Radarweg 29, Amsterdam, 1043 NX, Netherlands; info@elsevier.com; https://www.elsevier.com/. Refereed. *Indexed:* A01, A22, C45. *Aud.:* Ac, Sa.

Published monthly, the peer-reviewed *Biochemical Engineering Journal* accepts original research papers, short communications, and review papers related to the chemical engineering aspects of biological process development. Topics of interest include biocatalysis and biotransformations, biosensors and devices, bioreactor systems, environmental bioengineering, industrial biotechnology, and more. The journal supports open access and provides easy access to open access, most downloaded, recent, and most-cited articles on its home page. Individual articles may include research highlights, graphical abstracts, and supplementary content (when available). Research scientists and practicing engineers in academic, industry, and government, especially those developing new industrial bioprocesses, are the expected audience for this journal. URL: https://www.journals.elsevier.com/biochemical-engineering-journal

Chemical & Engineering News. See Chemistry/General section.

2054. *Chemical Engineering & Technology (Online).* [ISSN: 1521-4125] m. GBP 4006. Wiley - V C H Verlag GmbH & Co. KGaA, Postfach 101161, Weinheim, 69451, Germany; service@wiley-vch.de; http://onlinelibrary.wiley.com. Refereed. *Aud.:* Ac, Sa.

Chemical Engineering & Technology is a peer-reviewed monthly sponsored by three German technical societies: VDI, GDCh, and DECHEMA. It accepts review articles, original research articles, and communications and essays discussing cutting-edge research and new chemical engineering developments. Topical issues are published frequently and recent topics covered include bioenergy, chemical engineering in China, environmental biotechnology, and more. This well-regarded journal (39/135 in Journal Citation Reports Chemical Engineering journals list) supports open-access publishing. The online version provides links to early view, accepted, most accessed, most cited, and editor's choice articles. Article altmetrics data, options for social media sharing, and content alerts are also available. Industrial chemists, chemical and process engineers, biotechnology researchers and designers in academic and industry, especially process and biotechnology industries, will benefit most from the research published herein. URL: http://onlinelibrary.wiley.com/journal/10.1002/(ISSN)1521-4125

2055. *Chemical Engineering Journal.* Former titles (until 1996): *Chemical Engineering Journal and Biochemical Engineering Journal;* (until 1983): *Chemical Engineering Journal.* [ISSN: 1385-8947] 1970. 24x/yr. EUR 6680. Ed(s): J Santamaria, S J Allen. Elsevier BV, Radarweg 29, Amsterdam, 1043 NX, Netherlands; info@elsevier.com; https://www.elsevier.com/. Illus., adv. Refereed. Microform: PQC. *Indexed:* A01, A22, C45. *Aud.:* Ac, Sa.

The *Chemical Engineering Journal* is an international, peer-reviewed journal that disseminates research in three main topic areas: environmental chemical engineering, chemical reaction engineering, and materials synthesis and processing. Published twice a month, this journal accepts original research papers, review articles, short communications and letters to the editor. Available in print and online, this publication supports open-access publishing; special, topical issues are also published. Individual articles in the online version may include research highlights, graphical abstracts, and supplementary content (when available). Researchers in chemical engineering, environmental engineering, materials scientists and engineers will all be interested in the research in this journal. URL: https://www.journals.elsevier.com/chemical-engineering-journal

2056. *Chemical Engineering Science.* [ISSN: 0009-2509] 1951. 18x/yr. EUR 11452. Elsevier Ltd, The Boulevard, Langford Lane, Oxford, OX5 1GB, United Kingdom; customerserviceau@elsevier.com; http:// www.elsevier.com. Illus., adv. Sample. Refereed. Microform: PQC. *Indexed:* A01, A22. *Bk. rev.:* Number and length vary. *Aud.:* Ac, Sa.

The peer-reviewed *Chemical Engineering Science* journal publishes research papers and critical reviews of fundamental topics in chemical engineering and cutting-edge research (experimental or theoretical) 18 times per year. The research published spans all physical scales from the molecular level to production plant scale and is applicable in many fields. Research areas of interest include biochemical engineering, process systems engineering, materials synthesis and processing, reaction engineering, and more. This journal publishes special, topical issues and supports open-access publishing through its mirror journal *Chemical Engineering Science: X.* The online version features easy access to most downloaded, most cited, and recent articles lists. Social media sharing and article feeds are also available. Individual articles include research highlights, graphical abstracts, and supplementary content. Chemical engineers in all areas of the field will find the research in this journal helpful. URL: https://www.journals.elsevier.com/chemical-engineering-science/

Chemical Week. See Business and Finance/Trade and Industry section.

2057. *Computers & Chemical Engineering: an international journal of computer applications in chemical engineering.* [ISSN: 0098-1354] 1977. 12x/yr. EUR 5894. Ed(s): E N Pistikopoulos. Elsevier Ireland Ltd., Elsevier House, Brookvale Plz, E Park, Shannon, , Ireland; nlinfo@elsevier.nl; http://www.elsevier.nl. Illus., adv. Sample. Refereed. Vol. ends: No. 25. Microform: PQC. *Indexed:* A01, A22, CompLI. *Aud.:* Ac, Sa.

The focus of *Computers & Chemical Engineering* is the use of computers in solving chemical engineering problems. This well-regarded journal seeks papers on process systems engineering and newly developed applications or new applications of existing methods of computing and technology to chemical engineering. Topics of interest include modeling and simulation, process and product synthesis/design, plant operations, process safety, domain specific applications, and more. This peer-reviewed monthly journal publishes full-length articles, perspective papers, journal reviews, short notes, and letters to the editor. Special issues are published periodically. The journal supports open-access publishing and the online version provides easy access to articles in press as well as recent, most downloaded, and most cited, and open-access articles. Individual articles include research highlights, recommended articles, and supplementary content. Professional chemical engineers and researchers in any of the process industries will likely find the research published here relevant to their work. URL: https://www.journals.elsevier.com/computers-and-chemical-engineering

Fuel. See Energy section.

2058. *Industrial & Engineering Chemistry Research.* Formed by the merger of (1962-1987): *Industrial and Engineering Chemistry Process Design and Development;* (1962-1987): *Industrial and Engineering Chemistry Fundamentals;* (1978-1987): *Industrial and Engineering Chemistry Product Research and Development;* Which was formerly (until 1978): *Product R & D;* (until 1969): *I & E C Product Research and Development.* [ISSN: 0888-5885] 1987. w. USD 3922. Ed(s): Phillip E Savage. American Chemical Society, 1155 16th St NW, Washington, DC 20036; help@acs.org; http://pubs.acs.org. Illus., adv. Sample. Refereed. *Indexed:* A01, A22, S25. *Aud.:* Ac, Sa.

Published weekly by the American Chemical Society, *Industrial & Engineering Chemistry Research* (available in print and online) publishes peer-reviewed, original research by industrial or academic researchers that is related to chemical engineering. Topics of interest include fundamental research on thermodynamics, reaction kinetics, and engineering catalysis, chemical engineering facets of product research and development, and process design and development including synthesis, process control, modeling, scale-up, and more. Papers on emerging areas of science and technology related to the journal's scope are also sought. The journal supports open-access publishing and the online version provides access to accepted manuscripts, "Articles ASAP," most read, current, and open-access articles. Engineers and scientists working on industrial applications of chemical engineering are the target audience of this journal. URL: http://pubs.acs.org/journal/iecred

2059. *Journal of Catalysis.* [ISSN: 0021-9517] 1962. m. 16/yr. until 2012. EUR 12424. Ed(s): J A Lercher. Academic Press, 3251 Riverport Ln, Maryland Heights, MO 63043; JournalCustomerService-usa@elsevier.com; http://www.elsevier.com/. Illus., adv. Sample. Refereed. *Indexed:* A01, A22, E01. *Bk. rev.:* Number and length vary. *Aud.:* Ac, Sa.

The *Journal of Catalysis* (available in print and online) is an important journal in chemical engineering. This peer-reviewed journal publishes original research related to hetero- and homogeneous catalysis, catalytic properties and their relationships to chemical processes, the development of new inorganic materials catalytic properties, and more. Research articles, priority communications, research notes, and letters to the editor are all accepted; the journal supports open-access publishing. The online version provides easy access to "Articles in Press" and open-access articles, most downloaded, most cited, and recent articles. Individual articles have research highlights, graphical abstracts, supplementary content, and recommended articles. Altmetrics are provided for top-rated articles. Industrial chemists and chemical engineers working on processes requiring catalysts will want to keep abreast of the research in this top journal. URL: https://www.journals.elsevier.com/journal-of-catalysis

The Journal of Chemical Physics. See Physics section.

2060. *Journal of Industrial and Engineering Chemistry.* [ISSN: 1226-086X] 1995. m. bi-m. until 2015. EUR 585. Ed(s): Bok Ryul Yoo. Elsevier BV, Radarweg 29, Amsterdam, 1043 NX, Netherlands; info@elsevier.com; https://www.elsevier.com/. *Aud.:* Ac, Sa.

Published monthly by Elsevier for the Korean Society of Industrial and Engineering Chemistry, the *Journal of Industrial and Engineering Chemistry* (available in print and online) is a multi-disciplinary journal that strives to disseminate information covering all facets of the research and development processes related to industrial and engineering chemistry. This peer-reviewed journal accepts original research papers, reviews, short communications, and notes. The online version provides access to recent and most cited articles and recent open-access articles. At the article level, readers can access "Articles in Press" and set up content alerts. Individual articles may provide graphical abstracts, research highlights, and supplementary content when available. Research chemical engineers as well as research chemists working in the process industries and academia will be interested in this journal. URL: https:// www.journals.elsevier.com/journal-of-industrial-and-engineering-chemistry

Journal of Physical and Chemical Reference Data. See Chemistry/ General section.

Langmuir. See Chemistry/Physical section.

Macromolecules. See Chemistry/General section.

Physical Review Letters. See Physics section.

Physics of Fluids. See Physics section.

Civil and Environmental Engineering

The ASCE Library provides electronic access to all 33 journals that are published by the American Society of Civil Engineers. This core group of journals represents the backbone for any academic library that supports a civil engineering department. From the *Journal of Engineering Mechanics* (which was first published in 1875) to the *Journal of Nanomechanics and Micromechanics* (which was introduced in 2011), the ASCE Library will often prove to be the first stopping place for both the practicing engineer and the academic researcher.

2061. *Building and Environment: the international journal of building science and its applications.* Formerly (until 1976): *Building Science.* [ISSN: 0360-1323] 1965. 16x/yr. EUR 4499. Ed(s): Qingyan Chen. Elsevier BV, Radarweg 29, Amsterdam, 1043 NX, Netherlands; https://www.elsevier.com/. Illus., adv. Sample. Refereed. *Indexed:* A22. *Aud.:* Ac, Sa.

Building and Environment disseminates new knowledge related to the environmental performance of buildings. It publishes peer-reviewed, original research and review articles (16 times per year) and is particularly interested in research related to technologies and systems for high-performing buildings and cities, the impact on humans of the thermal and acoustic visual and air quality factors of buildings, tools for building and city designers and decision makers and solutions for mitigating the environmental impacts of buildings. *Building and Environment* supports open-access publishing and the online version provides easy access to open-access papers as well as RSS feeds. Altmetrics for top-rated articles are also provided. Other features include audio slide options for authors, links to most downloaded, cited, and recent articles. Full-color figures, research highlights, graphical abstracts, and supplementary content are also provided. This multidisciplinary journal will appeal to engineers, designers, community or industry decision makers and policy makers who are interested in the built environment. URL: https://www.journals.elsevier.com/building-and-environment/

2062. *Computer-Aided Civil and Infrastructure Engineering.* Formerly (until 1998): *Microcomputers in Civil Engineering.* [ISSN: 1093-9687] 1986. m. GBP 1537. Ed(s): Hojjat Adeli. Wiley-Blackwell Publishing, Inc., 111 River St, Hoboken, NJ 07030; info@wiley.com; http://onlinelibrary.wiley.com. Illus., adv. Sample. Refereed. Reprint: PSC. *Indexed:* A01, A22, E01, HRIS. *Aud.:* Ac, Sa.

This highly ranked journal seeks to tie advances in IT and computation to advances in civil and infrastructure engineering (CIE). It publishes peer-reviewed research focusing on novel computational methods and models as well as innovative applications of computing in CIE in the major practice areas of CIE (e.g., construction, environmental, highway engineering, and more). Technologies of interest include artificial intelligence and virtual reality, cognitive modeling, genetic algorithms, neural network computing, robotics, and more. This monthly publication accepts original research contributions, state-of-the-art review articles, and articles on novel industrial applications and the use of computers in education. Available in print and online, it supports open-access publishing and publishes special thematic issues. Individual articles contain quick links to full text, figures references, and citing literature. This journal is a must read for any research or practicing engineer in CIE who uses computational techniques on projects. URL: http://onlinelibrary.wiley.com/journal/10.1111/(ISSN)1467-8667

2063. *E N R: the construction weekly.* Formerly (until 1987): *Engineering News-Record;* Which incorporated (1898-1918): *Contractor;* (in 1928): *Sanitary Engineer;* Engineering News-Record was formed by the merger of (1902-1917): *Engineering News;* Which was formerly (until 1902): *Engineering News and American Railway Journal;* (until 1888): *Engineering News and American Contract Journal;* (until 1882): *Engineering News;* (until 1875): *Engineer, Architect and Surveyor;* (until 1874): *Engineer and Surveyor;* (1910-1917): *Engineering Record;* Which was formerly (until 1910): *Engineering Record, Building Record and Sanitary Engineer;* (until 1897): *Engineering Record, Building Record & the Sanitary Engineer;* (until 1890): *Engineering & Building Record and the Sanitary Engineer;* (until 1887): *Sanitary Engineer and Construction Record;* (until 1886): *Sanitary Engineer;* (until 1880): *Plumber & Sanitary Engineer.* [ISSN: 0891-9526] 1917. 46x/yr. USD 82 combined subscription domestic (print & online eds.); USD 89 combined subscription Canada (print & online eds.); USD 195 combined subscription elsewhere (print & online eds.)). Ed(s): Janice L Tuchman, John J Kosowatz. McGraw-Hill Construction Dodge, 2 Penn Plaza, 25th Fl, New York, NY 10121; http://www.fwdodge.com. Illus., adv. Circ: 71255 Paid. Microform: PQC. *Indexed:* A01, A22, B01, BRI, HRIS. *Bk. rev.:* Number and length vary. *Aud.:* Ga, Ac, Sa.

ENR (*Engineering News-Record*) is an important construction trade magazine. Published 46 times per year, *ENR* is known as one of the major sources of industry news about construction firms, project announcements and progress reports, legislation and regulations, product information, technology, business management, and more. Viewpoint articles and editorials are also featured. Two valuable features of *ENR* are the construction economics data they have collected and published since 1913 as well as their annual rankings of the top projects, contractors, design, environmental, and construction management firms, and more. The print edition is visually appealing, containing many full-color photographs and figures. The online version has some open-access content, but a subscription is required to access all its features. It also features some items that are not available in print. This magazine is recommended for academic libraries serving civil engineering programs, and it will also be at home in corporate libraries in contractor or consulting firms working in the construction industry and larger public libraries. URL: www.enr.com

2064. *Earthquake Engineering & Structural Dynamics.* [ISSN: 0098-8847] 1972. 15x/yr. GBP 4887. Ed(s): Anil K Chopra, Masayoshi Nakashima. John Wiley & Sons Ltd., EMEA Institutional Sales, 9600 Garsington Rd, Oxford, OX4 2DQ, United Kingdom; cs-journals@wiley.com; http://onlinelibrary.wiley.com. Illus., index, adv. Sample. Refereed. Microform: PQC. Reprint: PSC. *Indexed:* A22, S25. *Bk. rev.:* Number and length vary. *Aud.:* Ac, Sa.

This highly ranked journal seeks to tie advances in IT and computation to advances in civil and infrastructure engineering (CIE). It publishes peer-reviewed research focusing on novel computational methods and models as well as innovative applications of computing in CIE in the major practice areas of CIE (e.g., construction, environmental, highway engineering, and more). Technologies of interest include artificial intelligence and virtual reality, cognitive modeling, genetic algorithms, neural network computing, robotics, and more. This monthly publication accepts original research contributions, state-of-the-art review articles and articles on novel industrial applications and the use of computers in education. Available in print and online, it supports open-access publishing and publishes special thematic issues. Individual articles contain quick links to full-text, figures references, and citing literature. This journal is a must read for any research or practicing engineer in CIE who uses computational techniques on projects. URL: http://onlinelibrary.wiley.com/journal/10.1111/(ISSN)1467-8667

Engineering Geology. See Earth Sciences and Geology section.

2065. *Environmental Science & Technology.* Incorporates (1991-1993): *Environmental Buyers' Guide.* [ISSN: 0013-936X] 1967. s-m. USD 2909. Ed(s): David L Sedlak, Ariel Grostern. American Chemical Society, 1155 16th St NW, Washington, DC 20036; help@acs.org; http://pubs.acs.org. Illus., index, adv. Sample. Refereed. *Indexed:* A01, A22, Agr, B01, BRI, C45, S25. *Bk. rev.:* Number and length vary. *Aud.:* Ac, Sa.

Environmental Science & Technology is a hybrid publication that is part research journal and part trade magazine. Published by the American Chemical Society, this well-ranked journal is an important source of new research, news, and general information for environmental science researchers and engineers. The journal publishes news, features and papers containing original research, policy analyses, or critical reviews; guest commentary and viewpoints may also appear. Published semi-monthly, *Environmental Science & Technology* supports open-access publishing. The online version includes access to Articles ASAP (early online). Individual articles have full-color figures and graphs, and offer access to supporting information and social media sharing options. URL: http://pubs.acs.org/loi/esthag

I E E E Transactions on Intelligent Transportation Systems. See Transportation section.

2066. *Journal of Construction Engineering and Management.* Formerly (until 1983): *American Society of Civil Engineers. Construction Division. Journal;* Which superseded in part (in 1957): *American Society of Civil Engineers. Proceedings.* [ISSN: 0733-9364] 1873. m. USD 1894. Ed(s): Jesus M de la Garza. American Society of Civil Engineers, 1801 Alexander Bell Dr, Reston, VA 20191; ascelibrary@asce.org; http://www.asce.org. Illus., adv. Refereed. *Indexed:* A01, A22, B01, ErgAb, HRIS. *Aud.:* Ac, Sa.

Published by the American Society of Civil Engineers (ASCE), the *Journal of Construction Engineering and Management* (in print and online) is a peer-reviewed journal that publishes technical papers, notes, and case studies, and more that advances the field of construction engineering while harmonizing practices with design theories. Topics of interest include construction material handling, scheduling, cost estimating, productivity, contract administration, construction management, and more. The online version supports open-access publishing and provides access to related content, most read, and most cited articles. Users can create individual accounts to save searches or implement RSS feeds or content alerts. The content herein will interest engineering researchers, civil and construction engineers, and others working in the field. URL: http://ascelibrary.org/journal/jcemd4

2067. *Journal of Hydraulic Engineering (Reston).* Formerly (until 1983): *American Society of Civil Engineers. Hydraulics Division. Journal;* Which superseded in part (in 1956): *American Society of Civil Engineers. Proceedings.* [ISSN: 0733-9429] 1873. m. USD 2492. Ed(s): Thanos Papanicolaou. American Society of Civil Engineers, 1801 Alexander Bell Dr, Reston, VA 20191; ascelibrary@asce.org; http://www.asce.org. Illus., adv. Refereed. *Indexed:* A01, A22, BRI, C45, HRIS, S25. *Bk. rev.:* Number and length vary. *Aud.:* Ac, Sa.

Published monthly by the American Society of Civil Engineers (ASCE), the *Journal of Hydraulic Engineering* seeks contributions providing analysis of and solutions to problems in hydraulic engineering. Topics of interest include flows in many different situations from free-surface to confined flows, environmental fluid dynamics, multiphase flows, and heat and gas transfer. The journal accepts technical papers and notes, case studies, discussions and closures, and more. This peer-reviewed journal is available in print and online, and the online version features most recent, most read, and most cited articles on its website. Individual articles include links to related articles and social media sharing options. Hydraulic and civil engineers in academia and industry will find the content in this journal relevant to their work. URL: http://ascelibrary.org.mutex.gmu.edu/journal/jhend8

Journal of Hydrology. See Earth Sciences and Geology section.

2068. *Journal of Soils and Sediments: protection, risk assessment and remediation.* [ISSN: 1439-0108] 2001. bi-m. EUR 1046 (print & online eds.)). Ed(s): Philip N Owens, Zhihong Xu. Springer, Tiergartenstr 17, Heidelberg, 69121, Germany; orders-hd-individuals@springer.com; https://www.springer.com. Adv. Refereed. Reprint: PSC. *Indexed:* A22, Agr, BRI, C45, E01, S25. *Aud.:* Ac, Sa.

The peer-reviewed *Journal of Soils and Sediments* (in print and online) publishes research related to contaminated, disturbed, or intact soils and sediments or examines the differences and similarities between them. Several of the major research areas covered include the effects caused by disturbances and contamination, technologies and strategies for treatment, remediation and reuse of soils, international regulations and legislation. Published monthly, the journal accepts original research articles, review articles, short commentary papers, and more. The journal supports open-access publishing. The online version provides quick access to special issues, "Online First Articles," options for content alerts, and social media sharing. This inter-disciplinary journal will appeal to researchers and practitioners in both academia and industry, especially environmental scientists, managers or engineers, biologists, chemists, hydrologists, geologists, lawyers, and more. URL: http://www.springer.com/environment/soil+science/journal/11368

2069. *Water Research.* Supersedes in part (in 1967): *Air and Water Pollution;* Which was formerly (until 1963): *International Journal of Air and Water Pollution;* (until 1961): *International Journal of Air Pollution.* [ISSN: 0043-1354] 1958. 20x/yr. EUR 10161. Elsevier Ltd, The Boulevard, Langford Lane, Oxford, OX5 1GB, United Kingdom; customerserviceau@elsevier.com. Illus., index, adv. Sample. Refereed. Vol. ends: Dec (No. 35). Microform: MIM; PQC. *Indexed:* A01, A22, Agr, C45, S25. *Bk. rev.:* Number and length vary. *Aud.:* Ac, Sa.

Water Research, a highly ranked environmental engineering journal, is a periodical of the International Water Association. It publishes peer-reviewed original research papers and reviews that examine the science and technology of water quality and management. Specific topics of interest include treatment processes for water and wastewater; water-quality assessment and monitoring; groundwater remediation; computational techniques for use in water research; public health and risk assessment; and more. This title is available in print and online. The journal's website offers access to recent articles and most downloaded and most cited articles, as well as conference news and Altmetrics information. ScienceDirect readers can access "In Progress," "In Press," and open-access articles. Article highlights are available, as are linked lists of references and citing articles, recommended articles, and supplementary data. "AudioSlides," an interactive map viewer, and links to datasets are also available. Researchers interested in the management and protection of surface and groundwater resources will find this journal useful, especially those in environmental, chemical, or civil engineering, the life sciences, and limnology. URL: www.journals.elsevier.com/water-research/

2070. *Water Resources Management: an international journal.* [ISSN: 0920-4741] 1987. 15x/yr. EUR 1995 (print & online eds.)). Ed(s): George Tsakiris. Springer Netherlands, Van Godewijckstraat 30, Dordrecht, 3311 GX, Netherlands; http://www.springer.com. Refereed. Microform: PQC. Reprint: PSC. *Indexed:* A22, Agr, BRI, C45, E01, S25. *Aud.:* Ac, Sa.

Water Resources Management (in print and online) is a peer-reviewed, multidisciplinary journal published by Springer for the European Water Resources Association (EWRA). This journal promotes the exchange of water resources management research and experience among researchers, engineers, planners, and policy makers working in water resources management. To accomplish this, the journal publishes original, peer-reviewed papers and brief communications. The topics of interest include water resources assessment, conservation and control (especially policies), planning and design of water resources systems, as well as systems administration, operations, and maintenance. Special thematic issues are also available. Open-access publishing is supported and the online version features links on "Online First" and open-access articles, as well as access to the complete journal archive. URL: https://www.springer.com/earth+sciences+and+geography/hydrogeology/journal/11269

Computer, Control, and Systems Engineering

2071. *A C M Transactions on Algorithms.* [ISSN: 1549-6325] 2004. q. USD 1174 (print & online eds.)). Ed(s): Aravind Srinivasan. Association for Computing Machinery, PO Box 30777, New York, NY 10087; acmhelp@acm.org; https://www.acm.org. Refereed. *Indexed:* MSN. *Aud.:* Ac, Sa.

ACM Transactions on Algorithms is a peer-reviewed, quarterly publication focusing on research on the mathematics of discrete algorithms. The journal is especially interested in papers discussing new algorithms, data structures, new analyses, and more. Specific topics include algorithms (for graphs, number theory, geometry, and more), discrete algorithms for specific applications, as well as counting, coding, data compression, cryptography, and more. The journal publishes special issues and the online version provides access to citing articles and social media sharing options for individual papers. Algorithms are used in many areas of the STEM fields and this journal will interest researchers in mathematics, sciences, and engineering who are developing algorithms for use in their work. URL: http://talg.acm.org/

2072. *A C M Transactions on Computer - Human Interaction.* [ISSN: 1073-0516] 1994. bi-m. USD 831 (print & online eds.)). Ed(s): Ken Hinckley. Association for Computing Machinery, PO Box 30777, New York, NY 10087; acmhelp@acm.org; https://www.acm.org. Refereed. *Indexed:* A22, CompLI, ErgAb. *Aud.:* Ac, Sa.

ACM Transactions on Computer-Human Interaction (*TOCHI*) is a peer-reviewed, multidisciplinary publication focusing on all aspects of human-computer interaction (HCI). Published bi-monthly, *TOCHI* publishes original research papers and research essays on HCI in a wide variety of fields; for example, computer science, IT, education, and medicine. The journal is especially interested in papers on HCI that are systems-focused or long term in perspective. Special thematic issues are published periodically. Through the online version, readers can access the journal archive, including issues in progress. Social media sharing and content alert options are also provided. HCI is a very broad field and *TOCHI*'s contents reflect that in the breadth of the research. Consequently, this journal will appeal to any one doing HCI research and developing applications in any field especially computer science, IT, psychology, education, and medicine. URL: http://tochi.acm.org/

Association for Computing Machinery. Journal. See Computers and Information Technology/Professional Journals section.

2073. *Control Engineering Practice.* [ISSN: 0967-0661] 1993. m. EUR 3415. Elsevier Ltd, The Boulevard, Langford Lane, Oxford, OX5 1GB, United Kingdom; customerserviceau@elsevier.com; http://www.elsevier.com. Adv. Sample. Refereed. Microform: PQC. *Indexed:* A01. *Aud.:* Ac, Sa.

Control Engineering Practice is a peer-reviewed, monthly journal published by Elsevier for the International Federation of Automatic Control (IFAC). The journal publishes application-oriented original research papers on topics including the direct application of control theory in all areas of automation. This includes the automotive, aerospace, chemical, and mining industries as well as applications in traffic control, power systems, and many more. The journal publishes special issues periodically and supports open-access publishing, but only a very small number of open articles are currently available. The online version provides access to most downloaded, most cited, recent, and open-access articles as well as articles-in-press. Individual articles may include research highlights, recommended articles, graphical abstracts, and supplementary content. Process automation and control engineering are found in many industries and the audience for this journal includes industrial control engineers in manufacturing, process and other industries, as well as researchers in academia. URL: https://www.journals.elsevier.com/control-engineering-practice

2074. *Engineering Applications of Artificial Intelligence: the international journal of intelligent real-time automation.* [ISSN: 0952-1976] 1988. 10x/yr. EUR 2723. Elsevier Ltd, The Boulevard, Langford Lane, Oxford, OX5 1GB, United Kingdom; customerserviceau@elsevier.com; http://www.elsevier.com. Adv. Sample. Refereed. Microform: PQC. *Indexed:* A01, A22, CompLI. *Aud.:* Ac, Sa.

Sponsored by the International Federation of Automatic Control (IFAC), *Engineering Applications of Artificial Intelligence* publishes peer-reviewed papers on artificial intelligence (AI) theory as well as papers on its industrial applications. The journal seeks research papers on decision support systems, distributed AI systems, application of chaos theory and fractals, big data analytics, neural networks, and more. Published ten times per year, special issues, including virtual ones, are published and recent ones feature robotics and mining the humanities. The journal supports open-access publishing but only a very small number of articles are currently available. The online version features most downloaded, most cited, recent, and open-access articles as well as articles-in-press. Individual articles may include video or audio slides (or both), research highlights, and graphical abstracts. Since the focus of the journal is AI applications, engineers in any engineering field or industry who are integrating AI into their work will find this journal helpful. Academic researchers in AI may also use this journal. URL: https://www.journals.elsevier.com/engineering-applications-of-artificial-intelligence

2075. *I E E E Systems Journal (Online).* [ISSN: 1937-9234] 2007. q. USD 555. Ed(s): Vincenzo Piuri. Institute of Electrical and Electronics Engineers, 445 Hoes Ln, Piscataway, NJ 08855; contactcenter@ieee.org; http://www.ieee.org. *Aud.:* Ac, Sa.

The *IEEE Systems Journal* is a quarterly, scholarly journal for systems engineering. Published by the IEEE Systems Council, this journal seeks application papers with a system level focus that concentrate on complex systems as well as important national and global system-of-systems. The journal also publishes topical special issues. This journal supports open-access publishing. The online version of the journal provides easy access to popular and early-access articles, latest published and related articles, citing literature, and media. This journal will appeal to researchers and practitioners in systems engineering, computer science, and information systems. URL: http://ieeexplore.ieee.org/servlet/opac?punumber=4267003

2076. *I E E E Transactions on Evolutionary Computation.* [ISSN: 1089-778X] 1997. bi-m. USD 1700. Ed(s): Kay Chen Tan. Institute of Electrical and Electronics Engineers, 445 Hoes Ln, Piscataway, NJ 08854; contactcenter@ieee.org; http://www.ieee.org. Adv. *Indexed:* A22, CompLI. *Aud.:* Ac, Sa.

A top journal in artificial intelligence, *IEEE Transactions on Evolutionary Computation* is a scholarly publication of the IEEE Computational Intelligence Society. Published bi-monthly, the journal—in print, online, CD-ROM, and microform—seeks research papers and letters discussing the theoretical underpinnings of evolutionary computation or application papers providing insights on the areas covered by the journal. Research areas of interest include population-based methods, nature-inspired algorithms, optimizations, and hybrid systems. The journal supports open-access publishing. The online version provides easy access to popular and early-access articles. Individual articles also may provide access to related articles and citing literature as well as supplemental content, for example, media. Computer scientists, systems engineers, and researchers in other science and engineering fields using AI will be interested in the theoretical and applied research published herein. URL: http://ieeexplore.ieee.org/servlet/opac?punumber=4235

2077. *I E E E Transactions on Fuzzy Systems.* [ISSN: 1063-6706] 1993. m. USD 3700. Ed(s): Jonathan Garibaldi. Institute of Electrical and Electronics Engineers, 445 Hoes Ln, Piscataway, NJ 08854; contactcenter@ieee.org; http://www.ieee.org. Adv. Refereed. *Indexed:* A22, CompLI. *Aud.:* Ac, Sa.

Sponsored by the IEEE Computational Intelligence Society, *IEEE Transactions on Fuzzy Systems* (*TFS*), is a top artificial intelligence journal. This peer-reviewed technical journal seeks to publish papers that examine the theory, design, and application of fuzzy systems in a broad spectrum of fields, including aerospace, computing and processing, power generation, robotics and control, signal processing, and more. In addition to technical papers, *TFS* publishes letters, article commentary, and author replies. This title is published monthly in print and online and the online version provides easy access to latest-published, popular, and early-access articles. Individual articles feature linked references and citing articles, article metrics, and social-media sharing. Systems engineers, control engineers, and computer scientists who are interested in the development and application of fuzzy systems will all find this journal relevant. URL: http://ieeexplore.ieee.org/servlet/opac?punumber=91

2078. *I S A Transactions.* [ISSN: 0019-0578] 1961. bi-m. q. until 2012. EUR 836. Ed(s): A B Rad. Elsevier Inc., 230 Park Ave, Ste 800, New York, NY 10169; usinfo-f@elsevier.com; https://www.elsevier.com. Illus., index, adv. Sample. Refereed. Microform: PQC. *Indexed:* A22. *Aud.:* Ac, Sa.

The peer-reviewed *ISA Transactions*, a journal of the International Society of Automation (ISA), focuses on the state-of-the-art and advances in theory and practice in the areas of measurement and automation. In both these areas, it publishes research and practice papers, reviews, technical notes, and more; special issues are also published. Measurement papers published cover sensors, perception systems, fault detection, and more, as well as measurement support techniques—for instance, fuzzy logic. In automation, several areas of interest are system reliability, quality, loss prevention, modeling and simulation, and more. Papers that discuss equipment and techniques that support measurement and automation are also published. This title is published bimonthly in print and online and the online version features access to special issues and most-cited and recent articles. Individual articles feature research highlights, and provide access to citing, related articles, and reference works. This journal will appeal to researchers and practitioners across academia and industry who research or design automated measurement systems. URL: http://www.journals.elsevier.com/isa-transactions/

2079. *The Journal of Artificial Intelligence Research.* [ISSN: 1076-9757] 1993. 2x/yr. USD 90. Ed(s): Francesca Rossi. A A A I Press, 2275 East Bayshore Rd, Ste 160, Palo Alto, CA 94303; info@aaai.org; http://www.aaai.org. Illus. Refereed. *Indexed:* MSN. *Aud.:* Ac, Sa.

The Journal of Artificial Intelligence Research (*JAIR*), a periodical of the Association for the Advancement of Artificial Intelligence (AAAI), publishes research and survey articles, as well as technical notes and topical article collections ("Special Tracks") in artificial intelligence research. One of the first electronic science journals, *JAIR* is an open-access, refereed journal that publishes articles as soon as the final copy is received. Published twice yearly, *JAIR* invites authors to include supplementary materials (for example, data appendices), for posting with their final papers. Recent articles discuss coactive learning, diagnosing multi-agent plans, agent-based artifact systems, choosing trust models, and more. Researchers in all areas of artificial intelligence will find this relevant information in this journal. URL: www.jair.org/

2080. ***Neural Networks.*** [ISSN: 0893-6080] 1988. m. 10/yr. until 2012. EUR 3498. Ed(s): Deliang Wang, Kenji Doya. Pergamon Press, The Blvd, Langford Ln, E Park, Kidlington, OX5 1GB, United Kingdom. Illus. Sample. Refereed. Microform: PQC. *Indexed:* A01, A22, CompLI. *Bk. rev.:* Number and length vary. *Aud.:* Ac, Sa.

Neural Networks (in print, online, and microform) is a top artificial intelligence journal. This peer-reviewed monthly, the journal of the International Neural Network Society, European Neural Network Society, and Japanese Neural Network Society, accepts submissions addressing advances in all areas of neural network research. The major topic areas of interest are cognitive science, neuroscience, learning systems, mathematical and computational analysis, engineering, and applications. The journal publishes research articles, letters and topical reviews, editorials, software surveys, patent information, and more. Special thematic issues are published. The journal supports open-access publishing. Researchers and professionals in computer science, engineering, neurobiology, psychology, and physics who are using or interested in neural networks and their applications may find this journal relevant. URL: https://www.journals.elsevier.com/neural-networks

Robotics and Autonomous Systems. See Robotics section.

Electrical Engineering

The Institute of Electrical and Electronics Engineers (IEEE) publications are core to any engineering collection, and are among the most highly cited journals in engineering. This society produces technical periodicals, conference papers, standards, reports, tutorials, and other specialized publications. The flagship journal, *Proceedings of the IEEE* [0018-9219], is a monthly that presents papers that have broad significance and long-range interest in all areas of electrical, electronics, and computer engineering. The *Index to IEEE Publications* is an annual publication that indexes, by author and subject, all the publications of the society. All of the content mentioned here can be found in the full-text, subscription-based electronic product called IEEE Xplore. Check for current products at http://shop.ieee.org/store.

2081. ***I E E E Network: the magazine of global internetworking.*** [ISSN: 0890-8044] 1987. bi-m. USD 795. Ed(s): Nei Kato. Institute of Electrical and Electronics Engineers, 445 Hoes Ln, Piscataway, NJ 08854; contactcenter@ieee.org; http://www.ieee.org. Illus., adv. Vol. ends: No. 6. *Indexed:* A01, A22, B01, BRI, CompLI. *Bk. rev.:* Number and length vary. *Aud.:* Ga, Ac, Sa.

IEEE Network is a bi-monthly scholarly magazine published by the IEEE Communications Society. This publication focuses on all things network: network architecture, protocols (including design and validation, network control and management, integrated voice/data networks, and more. Recent articles discuss security threats to Hadoop, multi-casting over 5G networks, software defined network forensics, and more. The journal supports open access publishing. The online version (http://ieeexplore.ieee.org/xpl/RecentIssue.jsp?punumber=65) provides access to early access, latest published, and popular articles. Individual articles also provide links to citing articles and supplemental media files. The digital magazine version of the print (http://digital.comsoc.org/publication/ieee-network) is an engaging publication with color photos. This magazine will appeal to network engineers, designers, and researchers in electrical and electronics engineering, transportation, telecommunications, and many other areas.

I E E E Proceedings. See Electronics section.

2082. ***I E E E Transactions on Antennas and Propagation.*** Former titles (until 1963): *I R E Transactions on Antennas and Propagation;* (until 1955): *I R E Professional Group on Antennas. Transactions.* [ISSN: 0018-926X] 1952. m. USD 2595. Ed(s): Danilo Erricolo. Institute of Electrical and Electronics Engineers, 445 Hoes Ln, Piscataway, NJ 08854; contactcenter@ieee.org; http://www.ieee.org. Illus., adv. Refereed. *Indexed:* A01, A22, B01, BRI, CompLI, MSN. *Aud.:* Ac, Sa.

Published monthly, *IEEE Transactions on Antennas and Propagation* is a peer-reviewed research journal published by the IEEE Antennas and Propagation Society. The journal disseminates both theoretical research and experimental advances related to antennas, electromagnetics, and wave propagation. The scope of the topics covered is broad and includes antenna design, development and testing, wireless, arrays and periodic structures, and numerical techniques, as well as related areas such as applied optics, radiation aspects of communication, radio astronomy, and more. The journal supports open-access publishing. The online version provides access to latest, early access, and popular articles. Individual articles have links to related articles, citing literature and media. This journal will be of interest to practicing engineers and academic researchers working in electrical engineering, antennas design, electromagnetics, and telecommunications (especially wireless communications). URL: http://ieeexplore.ieee.org/xpl/RecentIssue.jsp?punumber=8

2083. ***I E E E Transactions on Pattern Analysis and Machine Intelligence.*** [ISSN: 0162-8828] 1979. m. USD 3665. Ed(s): Sven Dickinson. Institute of Electrical and Electronics Engineers, 445 Hoes Ln, Piscataway, NJ 08854; contactcenter@ieee.org; http://www.ieee.org. Adv. *Indexed:* A01, A22, B01, CompLI. *Aud.:* Ac, Sa.

IEEE Transactions on Pattern Analysis and Machine Intelligence (available in print, online, CD-ROM, and microform) is an academic journal published monthly by the IEEE Computer Society. This journal focuses on computer vision, pattern analysis, and machine intelligence. Specific topic areas include visual search, document and handwriting analysis, medical image analysis, video and image sequence analysis, content-based retrieval of image and video, face and gesture recognition, and more. The journal supports open-access publishing. The online version provides easy access to latest, popular, early access, related, and citing articles as well as supplemental media. Academic and industry researchers in electrical engineering, computer science, information science, and biomedical engineering are the primary audience for this journal. URL: http://ieeexplore.ieee.org/xpl/RecentIssue.jsp?punumber=34

2084. ***I E E E Transactions on Power Systems.*** Supersedes in part (in 1986): *I E E E Transactions on Power Apparatus and Systems;* Which was formed by the merger of (1952-1963): *American Institute of Electrical Engineers. Transactions on Power Apparatus and Systems. Part 3;* Which superseded in part (1952): *American Institute of Electrical Engineers. Transactions;* (1952-1963): *Power Apparatus and Systems.* [ISSN: 0885-8950] 1986. bi-m. USD 1565. Ed(s): Nikos Hatziargyriou. Institute of Electrical and Electronics Engineers, 445 Hoes Ln, Piscataway, NJ 08854; contactcenter@ieee.org; http://www.ieee.org. Adv. *Indexed:* A01, A22, B01. *Aud.:* Ac, Sa.

The research in *IEEE Transactions on Power Systems* (available in print, online, CD-ROM, and microform) provides a system-level view of power systems, covering the requirements, planning, analysis, reliability, operation, and economics of electric generating, transmission, as well as distribution systems for general industrial, commercial, public, and domestic consumption. Published bi-monthly by the IEEE Power & Energy Society, this academic journal supports open-access publishing. The online version of the journal provides access to latest published, popular, early access, related, and citing articles as well as supplemental media. This journal will appeal to electrical engineers, power system design engineers, economists, and other professionals working in all areas of the power industry. URL: http://ieeexplore.ieee.org/servlet/opac?punumber=59

2085. ***I E E E Wireless Communications Magazine.*** Formerly (until 2002): *I E E E Personal Communications.* [ISSN: 1536-1284] 1994. bi-m. USD 895. Ed(s): Yi Qian. Institute of Electrical and Electronics Engineers, 445 Hoes Ln, Piscataway, NJ 08854; contactcenter@ieee.org; http://www.ieee.org. Adv. *Indexed:* A22. *Bk. rev.:* Number and length vary. *Aud.:* Ga, Ac, Sa.

IEEE Wireless Communications (available in print, online, CD-ROM, and microform) is a scholarly magazine reporting on current topics and issues in wireless communications. Published bi-monthly by the IEEE Communications Society, this publication disseminates information on the latest innovations in wired and wireless communications and related topics, including networking, protocols, policies and regulations, computing devices, and others. The magazine, which supports open-access publishing, includes guest editorials, book reviews, and synopses of research articles from journals in the field. This magazine will appeal to a broad base of readers, especially professional engineers, researchers, and designers working on communications and networking in industry and academia, as well as policy makers. It may also appeal to general readers who are interested in advances in wireless communications and networking. URL: http://ieeexplore.ieee.org/xpl/aboutJournal.jsp?punumber=7742

2086. ***International Journal of Wireless Information Networks.*** Formerly (until 1994): *International Journal of Wireless Communication.* [ISSN: 1068-9605] 1994. q. EUR 925 (print & online eds.)). Ed(s): Kaveh Pahlavan. Springer New York LLC, 233 Spring St, New York, NY 10013; customerservice@springer.com; http://www.springer.com. Adv. Sample. Refereed. Reprint: PSC. *Indexed:* A01, A22, CompLI, E01. *Aud.:* Ac, Sa.

The *International Journal of Wireless Information Networks* (in print and online) was the first wireless networking journal when it began publication in 1994. The quarterly, peer-reviewed journal seeks manuscripts that focus on wireless applications, performance-prediction methodologies, antennas, modulation and coding, security and privacy, network signaling, and more. The journal publishes original technical papers, invited topical reviews, overviews of standards and field trials, and the like. The journal supports open-access publishing and special issues are published periodically. This magazine will be at home in academic and corporate libraries catering to researchers and practitioners in IT, electrical, telecommunications, aerospace, and biomedical engineering who are designing or working with wireless networks. URL: http://www.springer.com/engineering/electronics/journal/10776

Progress in Quantum Electronics. See Electronics section.

2087. ***S I A M Journal on Imaging Sciences.*** [ISSN: 1936-4954] 2008. . USD 491. Ed(s): Michael Elad. Society for Industrial and Applied Mathematics, 3600 Market St, 6th Fl, Philadelphia, PA 19104; siam@siam.org; http://www.siam.org. Adv. Sample. Refereed. *Indexed:* MSN. *Aud.:* Ac, Sa.

The *SIAM Journal on Imaging Sciences* is an online-only journal published by the Society of Industrial and Applied Mathematics (SIAM). This peer-reviewed journal is published continuously, is grounded in mathematics and computation, and features new ideas and methods in the imaging sciences. It seeks innovative papers related to new applications as well as imaging fundamentals. The research areas covered by the journal include processing and analysis, computer graphics, computer vision, visualization, image understanding, pattern analysis, machine intelligence, remote sensing, signal processing, geoscience, medical and biomedical imaging, seismic imaging, and others. The journal publishes both research and survey articles and supports open-access publishing (Green Model). Supplementary materials are peer-reviewed and may include datasets, figures, code, animations, and more. Because of the importance of imaging in many industries, this journal will appeal to engineers and researchers in many different areas including electrical engineering, computer science, biomedical and health sciences, physical sciences, and more. URL: https://www.siam.org/journals/siims.php

Semiconductor Science and Technology. See Electronics section.

2088. ***Signal Processing.*** [ISSN: 0165-1684] 1979. 12x/yr. EUR 6213. Ed(s): B Ottersten. Elsevier BV, Radarweg 29, Amsterdam, 1043 NX, Netherlands; info@elsevier.com; https://www.elsevier.com/. Illus., adv. Refereed. Microform: PQC. *Indexed:* A01, A22, CompLI. *Aud.:* Ac, Sa.

The monthly, peer-reviewed journal *Signal Processing* (in print, online, and microform) is the journal of the European Association for Signal Processing. Rapid dissemination of signal processing research to engineers and scientists in the field is the goal of this journal, which covers all aspects of signal processing theory and its applications. It publishes original research, tutorial and review articles, and accepts manuscripts on a very wide variety of topics. Select topics of interest include signal theory, signal processing technologies and systems, optical, digital and communication signal processing, radar and sonar signal processing, signal processing in specific fields—for instance, biomedical, geophysical, astrophysical, and Earth resources signal processing, industrial applications, and many more. The journal publishes special issues. Open-access publishing is supported. Engineers working in signal processing, acoustics, control systems, and automation, as well as other industrial settings, will find the content in *Signal Processing* relevant to their work. URL: https://www.journals.elsevier.com/signal-processing/

2089. ***Vehicular Communications.*** [ISSN: 2214-2096] 2014. 4x/yr. EUR 145. Ed(s): M Atiquzzaman. Elsevier BV, Radarweg 29, Amsterdam, 1043 NX, Netherlands; info@elsevier.com; https://www.elsevier.com/. *Aud.:* Ac, Sa.

The *Vehicular Communications* journal (in print and online) is a timely publication on an emerging technology topic. Published quarterly, the journal publishes original research and review papers related to real-time vehicular communications (vehicle-to-vehicle and vehicle-to-infrastructure). The journal publishes print and virtual special issues. The journal supports open-access publishing. Electrical, computer, and telecommunications engineers and researchers working on wireless vehicular communications for any type of vehicle will want to read this journal. URL: https://www.journals.elsevier.com/vehicular-communications

Industrial and Manufacturing Engineering

2090. ***3D Printing and Additive Manufacturing.*** [ISSN: 2329-7662] 2014. bi-m. 4/yr. until 2019. USD 2826. Ed(s): Skylar Tibbits. Mary Ann Liebert, Inc. Publishers, 140 Huguenot St, 3rd Fl, New Rochelle, NY 10801; info@liebertpub.com; http://www.liebertpub.com. Adv. Sample. Reprint: PSC. *Aud.:* Ga, Ac, Sa.

3D Printing and Additive Manufacturing is a bimonthly, peer-reviewed journal publishing research on 3D printing and related fields. The journal seeks quality research on topics related to additive manufacturing (industrial and consumer scales), including the opportunities and issues presented by the processes and materials used, simulation and design tools, applications, policy and law, intellectual property concerns, data standards and others. The journal provides full color pdfs, easy access to article collections (e.g., most cited), social media sharing options, and supports open-access publishing. The potential audience for this journal includes engineers, software developers, lawyers, academic administrators, and researchers in industry, academia, medicine, and government research centers. URL: http://www.liebertpub.com/3dp

2091. ***Computers & Industrial Engineering.*** [ISSN: 0360-8352] 1977. m. EUR 5637. Elsevier Ltd, The Boulevard, Langford Lane, Oxford, OX5 1GB, United Kingdom; customerserviceau@elsevier.com; http://www.elsevier.com. Illus., adv. Sample. Refereed. Microform: PQC. *Indexed:* A22, B01, B03, C42, CompLI, ErgAb. *Bk. rev.:* Number and length vary. *Aud.:* Ac, Sa.

Computers & Industrial Engineering (*CAIE*) is a peer-reviewed, monthly publication that provides an international forum for the exchange of ideas and research related to the use of computers in industrial engineering. To do this, *CAIE* publishes original research papers detailing new methodologies and their application to problems in industrial engineering and related areas. The journal seeks papers that evaluate state-of-the-art computer applications, report on the application of computer methods in industrial engineering to solve problems, or examine the use of computers in the education of industrial engineers. The journal publishes special, topical issues and supports open-access publishing and it will appeal to a broad readership, including academic and industrial researchers, educators, and working professionals in industrial engineering and associated fields. URL: https://www.journals.elsevier.com/computers-and-industrial-engineering

IndustryWeek. See Business and Finance/General section.

2092. *Journal of Manufacturing Processes.* [ISSN: 1526-6125] 1999. q. EUR 673. Ed(s): S G Kapoor. Elsevier Ltd, 125 London Wall, London, EC2Y 5AS, United Kingdom; corporate.sales@elsevier.com; http://www.elsevier.com. Adv. Refereed. *Aud.:* Ac, Sa.

Published by the SME (Society of Manufacturing Engineers), the *Journal of Manufacturing Processes* (available in print, online, and microform) is a peer-reviewed, quarterly publication that disseminates research information on current and emerging manufacturing processes that will improve process efficiency as well as product quality. The journal is interested in manufacturing research, development, and applications in many areas including fabrication (multiple scales), welding, joining and assembly, rapid prototyping, tribology, and more. In the interest of rapid dissemination of ideas, the journal also publishes research from related areas. Recent articles discuss laser surface modification, manufacturing of bio-composite sandwich structures, welding processes, surface roughness modeling, material issues in additive manufacturing, and more. Engineers (mechanical, industrial, chemical, and others) and scientists in industry and academia working to improve existing manufacturing processes and develop new ones to meet the needs of a changing world will find the research in this journal relevant to their work. URL: https://www.journals.elsevier.com/journal-of-manufacturing-processes

2093. *Journal of Manufacturing Science and Engineering.* Formerly (until 1996): *Journal of Engineering for Industry;* Which superseded in part (in 1959): *American Society of Mechanical Engineers. Transactions.* [ISSN: 1087-1357] 19??. m. q. until 2007, b-m. until 2016. USD 1160; USD 1393 combined subscription (print & online eds.)). Ed(s): Y Lawrence Yao. The American Society of Mechanical Engineers, Two Park Ave, New York, NY 10016; CustomerCare@asme.org; http://www.asme.org. Sample. Refereed. *Indexed:* A01, A22, BRI. *Aud.:* Ga, Ac.

Published monthly by the American Society of Mechanical Engineers (ASME), the peer-reviewed *Journal of Manufacturing Science and Engineering* (available in print, online, and microform) is a top journal for manufacturing engineering. The journal publishes original articles discussing theoretical or applied research in all areas of manufacturing. Specific topics of interest include emerging manufacturing technologies, data-science enhanced manufacturing, fabrication, machining and nontraditional manufacturing processes, process engineering, and more. In addition to research articles, the journal accepts technical briefs, design papers, topical reviews, book reviews, and more. The journal supports open-access publishing. The intended audience for this journal is researchers and engineering (mechanical, industrial, among others), and professionals working in manufacturing. URL: http://manufacturingscience.asmedigitalcollection.asme.org/journal.aspx

2094. *Journal of Manufacturing Systems.* [ISSN: 0278-6125] 1982. q. EUR 1115. Ed(s): N Duffie. Elsevier Ltd, 125 London Wall, London, EC2Y 5AS, United Kingdom; corporate.sales@elsevier.com; http://www.elsevier.com. Illus., index, adv. Sample. Refereed. *Indexed:* A22, B01. *Aud.:* Ac, Sa.

The peer-reviewed *Journal of Manufacturing Systems* (available in print and online) is published quarterly by the SME (Society of Manufacturing Engineers). The journal's goal is to publish original research advancing the state of the art of manufacturing systems or encouraging innovation in the development of new systems. To accomplish this, it accepts original research articles and review papers addressing all areas of manufacturing on a variety of scales. In addition, the papers published often address manufacturing challenges and issues in specific industries including aerospace, automotive, medical device manufacturing, and more. Papers examining new and emerging topics in manufacturing systems are also accepted. Topics of interest include complexity management, product and systems life cycles, flexible manufacturing systems, production networks, data sharing, distributed system control, additive manufacturing, and others. The journal publishes special issues on new or emerging topics and an upcoming one will focus on smart manufacturing. This journal will be at home in an academic or corporate library where manufacturing systems researchers, engineering professionals, and managers can easily access it. URL: https://www.journals.elsevier.com/journal-of-manufacturing-systems

2095. *Journal of Quality Technology: a quarterly journal of methods, applications and related topics.* Supersedes in part (in 1969): *Industrial Quality Control.* [ISSN: 0022-4065] 1944. q. GBP 1006 print & online eds. Ed(s): Bradley Jones. Taylor & Francis, . Illus., index, adv. Refereed. Reprint: PSC. *Indexed:* A22, B01, BRI. *Bk. rev.:* Number and length vary. *Aud.:* Ga, Ac, Sa.

Published by the American Society for Quality (ASQ), the *Journal of Quality Technology* (available in print and online) is a peer-reviewed, quarterly publication focusing on the use of new statistical methods in designing experiments, monitoring processes, determining reliability, and the like. The journal publishes technical research papers on new methods, review papers, case studies, book reviews, and more. The journal supports open-access publishing, but users must register for a free account and log in to read open-access content. Readers of this very technical publication will include quality managers in manufacturing or service industries, professional engineers (manufacturing, industrial), and researchers in industry and academia who are working to solve quality issues and problems in their industry. URL: http://docs.lib.purdue.edu/jpeer/

2096. *Manufacturing Engineering.* Former titles (until 1975): *Manufacturing Engineering and Management;* (until 1970): *Tool and Manufacturing Engineer;* (until 1960): *Tool Engineer;* (until 1935): *American Society of Tool Engineers. Journal.* [ISSN: 0361-0853] 1932. m. Free to members; Non-members, USD 12. Ed(s): James D Destefani, Brian J Hogan. Society of Manufacturing Engineers, One SME Dr, PO Box 930, Dearborn, MI 48121; service@sme.org; http://www.sme.org. Illus., adv. Circ: 102500 Controlled. Microform: PQC. *Indexed:* A22, B01. *Bk. rev.:* Number and length vary. *Aud.:* Ga, Ac, Sa.

Manufacturing Engineering (*M.E.*) magazine, (in print, online, and microform), is a trade publication affiliated with the SME (Society of Manufacturing Engineers). This practical monthly magazine contains feature articles, industry news, product reviews, guest editorials, and more. Topics covered by *M.E.* include alternative machining methods, controls and software, fabrication, lean manufacturing R&D, work force development, and more. Special topical issues are published periodically. The digital magazine version of *M.E.* is open access (including the archives). Advertising is accepted. The variety of topics covered by this magazine will help any reader stay up to date on news and technology changes in manufacturing in different industries. It will be of interest to engineers, managers, and other personnel in any type of manufacturing, but may also interest academic and corporate researchers in this area as well. URL: http://advancedmanufacturing.org/series/manufacturing-engineering-magazine/

2097. *Packaging Technology and Science.* [ISSN: 0894-3214] 1988. 12x/yr. GBP 2230. Ed(s): David Shires, Diana Twede. John Wiley & Sons Ltd., EMEA Institutional Sales, 9600 Garsington Rd, Oxford, OX4 2DQ, United Kingdom; cs-journals@wiley.com; http://onlinelibrary.wiley.com. Adv. Sample. Refereed. Microform: PQC. Reprint: PSC. *Indexed:* A22, B01, C45. *Aud.:* Ac, Sa.

Packaging Technology and Science (in print, online, and microform) is an international peer-reviewed journal affiliated with the International Association of Packaging Research Institutes. Published 12 times per year, it covers all aspects of packaging science including aseptic, sterile and barrier packaging, design methods, materials, environmental factors, ergonomics, and more. Research on novel developments, packaging for food, medical and pharmaceutical items, chemicals, hazardous materials, and high volume consumer goods is of interest to the editors. In addition to research articles, the journal also accepts review and applications articles and notes. The journal supports open-access publishing and publishes special issues. Because packaging information is needed in many different industries, the readership of this journal is very broad. Researchers and professionals in packaging engineering, toxicology, and regulatory oversight, as well as environmental, materials, food, polymer scientists, and analytical chemists will all find relevant information herein. URL: http://onlinelibrary.wiley.com/journal/10.1002/(ISSN)1099-1522

2098. *Plant Engineering: the problem-solving resource for plant engineers.* [ISSN: 0032-082X] 1947. m. Free to qualified personnel. C F E Media, 1111 W. 22nd St., Ste 250, Oak Brook, IL 60523; http://www.cfemedia.com/. Illus., adv. Sample. Circ: 90063. *Indexed:* A22, B01, BRI. *Bk. rev.:* Number and length vary. *Aud.:* Ga, Ac, Sa.

The monthly trade magazine *Plant Engineering* (in print, online, and microform) is an engaging and colorful publication whose goal is to provide reliable information to readers to help them ensure the safe and efficient operations of their manufacturing plants. After a redesign of the magazine's format, issues are now divided into three sections called "Insights," "Innovations," and "Solutions." The main website has additional content available, including current and archived webinars on plant engineering topics, editorial research studies, and topical sections on plant automation, safety, energy management, new products, electrical, industry news, and more. Digital versions of the print magazine are open access. Advertising is accepted. This practical publication is highly recommended for plant engineers, plant managers, and other plant personnel to learn about new technologies and emerging trends in plant operations and engineering. URL: http://www.plantengineering.com/

2099. ***Quality Progress.*** Supersedes in part (in 1968): *Industrial Quality Control.* [ISSN: 0033-524X] 1944. m. Members, USD 55; Non-members, USD 80. American Society for Quality, P O Box 3005, Milwaukee, WI 53203; help@asq.org; http://www.asq.org. Illus., index, adv. Circ: 80374. Reprint: PSC. *Indexed:* A22, BRI. *Bk. rev.:* Number and length vary. *Aud.:* Ga, Ac, Sa.

Quality Progress (in print and online) is a monthly trade magazine published by the American Society for Quality (ASQ). The journal publishes articles and case studies examining quality control techniques and ideas in multiple manufacturing and service industries. Topics of interest include auditing and standards, quality management, customer loyalty, measurement, statistics, and more. The journal supports open-access publishing and regular features include news, columns (five are open access), most popular articles, and upcoming industry events. To read open-access content, readers must register for a free account; some regular features, however, require a subscription to read them online. The online version of articles includes a link to related articles, keywords, ability to comment, and social bookmarking options. This magazine will appeal to engineers, scientists, and other researchers working on quality control and quality assurance projects and research in the areas of healthcare, government, military, manufacturing, service industries, and education. URL: http://asq.org/qualityprogress/index.html

Materials Engineering

2100. ***Advanced Materials.*** [ISSN: 0935-9648] 1989. s-m. GBP 10263. Ed(s): Peter Gregory. Wiley - V C H Verlag GmbH & Co. KGaA, Postfach 101161, Weinheim, 69451, Germany; cs-germany@wiley.com; http://www.wiley-vch.de. Adv. Sample. Refereed. Reprint: PSC. *Indexed:* A22. *Aud.:* Ac, Sa.

Advanced Materials is a highly ranked materials science journal. This peer-reviewed, interdisciplinary journal seeks submissions focusing on new materials and methods for their preparation, modification, and investigation. The journal publishes original research and review papers, communications, and research news. Selected topics of interest include materials science, nanotechnology, ceramics, biomaterials, photonics, drug delivery, batteries, semiconductor, polymers, carbon, and more. Special issues focusing on specific themes or topics are available and the journal supports open-access publishing. The intended audience for this important materials science publication is anyone in academia or industry who conducts materials research including materials scientists, chemists, physicists, ceramicists, engineers (biomedical, civil, electrical, mechanical) and metallurgists. URL: http://onlinelibrary.wiley.com.mutex.gmu.edu/journal/10.1002/(ISSN)1521-4095

Applied Physics Letters. See Physics section.

Chemistry of Materials. See Chemistry/Physical section.

2101. ***Corrosion Science: the journal on environmental degradation of materials and its control.*** [ISSN: 0010-938X] 1961. m. EUR 6926. Elsevier Ltd, The Boulevard, Langford Lane, Oxford, OX5 1GB, United Kingdom; customerserviceau@elsevier.com; http://www.elsevier.com. Illus., adv. Sample. Refereed. Microform: PQC. *Indexed:* A&ATA, A01, A22, S25. *Aud.:* Ac, Sa.

Corrosion Science is a peer-reviewed, monthly journal that focuses on original research and reviews of corrosion-related topics. This journal is interested in submissions covering a very wide range of corrosion-related topics, disciplines, and industries. It publishes original research papers ranging from theoretical discussions to extremely practical treatments of the topic. Specific research areas of interest include high temperature oxidation, biochemical corrosion, stress corrosion cracking, corrosion control, and more. Topical review papers are also published and the journal supports open-access publishing. This publication will appeal to a wide audience due to the applicability of the content in different research areas and industries. This journal is highly recommended for materials scientists, chemists, metallurgists, engineers, and designers in aerospace, automotive, civil, mechanical, nuclear, petroleum, and transportation industries. URL: https://www-journals-elsevier-com.mutex.gmu.edu/corrosion-science

2102. ***Engineering Failure Analysis.*** [ISSN: 1350-6307] 1994. 12x/yr. EUR 1845. Elsevier Ltd, The Boulevard, Langford Lane, Oxford, OX5 1GB, United Kingdom; customerserviceau@elsevier.com; http://www.elsevier.com. Adv. Sample. Refereed. Microform: PQC. *Indexed:* A01, A22. *Aud.:* Ac, Sa.

Affiliated with the European Structural Integrity Society (ESIS), the international journal *Engineering Failure Analysis* is a well-ranked, peer-reviewed journal. It publishes original research (case studies are especially encouraged), reviews, and short communications that discuss the analysis of engineering failures. The journal is particularly interested in papers where a detailed application of materials parameters is made to structural problems in engineering as well as discussions of research to reduce the number of failures while expanding the uses of engineering materials. Discussion of the mechanical properties of materials and how they are influenced by structure, process, and environment is important. Some of the materials covered by the journal include metals, polymers, ceramic, and natural materials. The journal is published monthly and supports open-access publishing. The audience of *Engineering Failure Analysis* will comprise academic and industrial researchers and engineers including materials scientists and engineers, as well as chemical, civil, mechanical, manufacturing, chemical, and other types of engineers. URL: https://www.journals.elsevier.com/engineering-failure-analysis

Journal of Applied Physics. See Physics section.

2103. ***Journal of Composite Materials.*** [ISSN: 0021-9983] 1967. 30x/yr. USD 12537 (print & online eds.)). Ed(s): H Thomas Hahn. Sage Publications Ltd., 1 Oliver's Yard, 55 City Rd, London, EC1Y 1SP, United Kingdom; info@sagepub.com; https://www.sagepub.com/. Illus., index. Sample. Refereed. Microform: PQC. Reprint: PSC. *Indexed:* A01, A22, E01. *Aud.:* Ac, Sa.

The *Journal of Composite Materials* (available in print, online, email, and microform) is a leading, peer-reviewed journal that disseminates research on advanced composite materials. Published in association with the American Society for Composites, this international journal publishes original research papers discussing theoretical and experimental research related to the properties of multiphase materials. Major research areas covered include analysis, ceramic-, metal-, and polymer- matrix composites, coatings, damage mechanics, environmental effects, processing and manufacturing, structural reliability, and more. The journal supports open-access publishing and is published 30 times per year. The popularity and use of composites in many different technical and consumer applications means that this journal will appeal to a wide audience of materials scientists, researchers, and engineers from academia, industry, and government, especially military and protective services. URL: http://journals.sagepub.com/home/jcm/

Journal of Electronic Materials. See Electronics section.

2104. ***Journal of Materials Research.*** [ISSN: 0884-2914] 1986. 24x/yr. GBP 1584 (print & online eds.)). Ed(s): Gary L Messing. Cambridge University Press, 1 Liberty Plaza, Fl 20, New York, NY 10004; journals@cambridge.org; https://www.cambridge.org. Illus., index, adv. Refereed. Vol. ends: Dec. *Indexed:* A22. *Aud.:* Ac, Sa.

Sponsored by the Materials Research Society (MRS), the *Journal of Materials Research* (available in print and online) is a peer-reviewed publication that seeks submissions on important advances in materials science. Specific research topics of interest include fundamental materials science, advanced materials (ceramics, metals, polymers, among others), energy-, electrical-, and optical-related material combinations, advanced methods and techniques for analysis, and more. The journal publishes topical "Focus Issues" several times per year, supports open-access publishing, and is published 24 times per year. The journal's website provides access to additional content including the journal's blog and Twitter feed, calls for papers for future issues, and a link to technical talks and other videos on the journal's YouTube channel. The wide coverage of materials science topics in this journal ensures that it will appeal to materials science researchers and engineers in many different disciplines and industries. URL: https://www.cambridge.org/core/journals/journal-of-materials-research

2105. ***Journal of Materials Science.*** Incorporates (1993-2004): *Interface Science;* (1982-2003): *Journal of Materials Science Letters.* [ISSN: 0022-2461] 1966. s-m. EUR 41247 (print & online eds.)). Ed(s): C Barry Carter. Springer New York LLC, 233 Spring St, New York, NY 10013; customerservice@springer.com; http://www.springer.com. Illus., index, adv. Refereed. Vol. ends: Dec. Reprint: PSC. *Indexed:* A&ATA, A01, A22, BRI, E01. *Aud.:* Ac, Sa.

The *Journal of Materials Science* (available in print, online, and CD-ROM) is a peer-reviewed, international publication focused on the structures and properties of engineering materials. Published 24 times per year, the journal publishes papers and reviews of original research or investigation methods for determining the relationships among structure, properties, and material applications. It also publishes viewpoint articles (since 2016) and special issues. Specific areas of interest are biomaterials, ceramics, composites, metals, nanocomposites, polymers, and more. The journal supports open-access publishing. This journal is most relevant for members of the global materials science research community and is recommended for academic and research libraries including corporate libraries. URL: https://www.springer.com/materials/journal/10853

2106. ***M R S Bulletin.*** Incorporates: *J M R Abstracts.* [ISSN: 0883-7694] 1976. m. GBP 493 (print & online eds.)). Ed(s): Lori Wilson, Gopal R Rao. Cambridge University Press, 1 Liberty Plaza, Fl 20, New York, NY 10004; journals@cambridge.org; https://www.cambridge.org. Illus., adv. Refereed. *Indexed:* A22. *Aud.:* Ac, Sa.

Published by Cambridge University Press for the Materials Research Society, the *MRS Bulletin* (in print and online) focuses on disseminating materials science research, technical information, news, and so on, to its readers. Each monthly issue features a thematic section containing peer-reviewed research papers discussing the state-of-the-art. The *MRS Bulletin* also has departments for "News & Analysis," "Opinion," "Features," and "Society News." A special section on energy is published quarterly for researchers working toward sustainable energy solutions. Other content on the journal website includes policy news, an image gallery, book reviews, and "Beyond the Lab," whose goal is to take basic research into the real world, and includes educational and career information. Multimedia content is also available. The *MRS Bulletin* supports open-access publishing and a digital magazine edition of the print is available on the website. Free to members of the Materials Research Society, this publication is valuable to researchers and engineers in materials science and related fields and will help them stay up to date on materials science research and its applications as well as materials science news and policies. Recommended for academic and other research libraries that support material science researchers. URL: https://www.cambridge.org/core/journals/mrs-bulletin

2107. ***Materials Today.*** [ISSN: 1369-7021] 1998. 12x/yr. EUR 852. Elsevier Ltd, The Boulevard, Langford Lane, Oxford, OX5 1GB, United Kingdom; journalscustomerserviceemea@elsevier.com; http://www.elsevier.com. Adv. Refereed. *Indexed:* A01. *Bk. rev.:* Number and length vary. *Aud.:* Ac, Sa.

Materials Today (in print and online) is an academic journal that is the flagship publication in a family of more than 100 specialty materials science publications. This journal's goal is the rapid publication of papers and short communications discussing ground-breaking discoveries and technical advances in materials science. Review articles on emerging topics and developing fields are also published. The journal is published 12 times per year and supports open-access publishing. Currently, its entire archive except for the current year, is completely open access to readers. The *Materials Today* website features additional content including news, webinars, features, podcasts, product announcements, jobs, and more. Social media sharing options are also available. This journal will appeal to a very multidisciplinary audience comprising anyone conducting fundamental materials research or developing new applications for both known and new materials. URL: https://www.journals.elsevier.com/materials-today

2108. ***Nature Materials.*** [ISSN: 1476-1122] 2001. m. EUR 6648. Ed(s): Vincent Dusastre. Nature Publishing Group, The MacMillan Bldg, 4 Crinan St, London, N1 9XW, United Kingdom; nature@nature.com; https://www.nature.com. Adv. Sample. Refereed. *Indexed:* A01, A22. *Aud.:* Ac, Sa.

Nature Materials (in print and online) is the premier multidisciplinary materials science journal. This is a peer-reviewed journal that publishes original research papers, review papers, research highlights (reports on research in other journals), and news. The journal encourages the sharing of research across disciplines and it seeks papers discussing cutting-edge research in all fundamental and applied areas related to materials synthesis and processing, structure, composition, and properties, among others. Select topics of interest include engineering, structural, organic and superconducting materials, as well as materials for electronics and energy, biomedical and biomolecular materials, and design, synthesis, processing, and characterization techniques. Published monthly, this journal supports limited open access by allowing authors to post a copy of their submitted manuscript on non-commercial pre-print servers (e.g., arXiv or biorxiv). *Nature Materials* is a must read for materials researchers and engineers in academia, government, and industry. This journal is a good addition to research library collections anywhere materials research is conducted. URL: http://www.nature.com/nmat/index.html

2109. ***Progress in Materials Science.*** Formerly (until 1961): *Progress in Metal Physics.* [ISSN: 0079-6425] 1949. 8x/yr. EUR 3733. Ed(s): Eduard Arzt. Pergamon Press, The Blvd, Langford Ln, E Park, Kidlington, OX5 1GB, United Kingdom; JournalsCustomerServiceEMEA@elsevier.com; http://www.elsevier.com. Sample. Refereed. Microform: PQC. *Indexed:* A01, A22. *Aud.:* Ac, Sa.

Progress in Materials Science (in print, online, and microform) is an important peer-reviewed journal in materials science. This journal publishes critical reviews of advances in materials science and their applications. The journal focuses on the fundamentals of many areas including microstructure and nanostructure and their relationship to properties. Other subjects of interest include thermodynamics, modeling of processes, engineering, healthcare, and other applications and experimental research explaining the microscopic mechanisms affecting macroscopic properties. Review articles published here are generally very detailed and lengths vary from fewer than 30 pages to more than 100. The journal supports open-access publishing. *Progress in Materials Science* is highly recommended for academic and other research libraries (including corporate). The reviews published herein are very useful to researchers who need to refresh their knowledge of an area and learn about recent advances, or even new areas. URL: https://www.journals.elsevier.com/progress-in-materials-science

Solid-State Electronics. See Electronics section.

Mechanical Engineering

2110. ***Experimental Mechanics: an international journal.*** [ISSN: 0014-4851] 1961. bi-m. EUR 1363 (print & online eds.)). Ed(s): Hareesh V Tippur. Springer New York LLC, 233 Spring St, New York, NY 10013; customerservice@springer.com; http://www.springer.com. Illus., adv. Refereed. Circ: 3000 Paid and controlled. Microform: PQC. Reprint: PSC. *Indexed:* A01, A22, E01. *Aud.:* Ac, Sa.

The official journal of the Society for Experimental Mechanics (SEM), *Experimental Mechanics* is a peer-reviewed journal that publishes research in solid and fluid mechanics and experimental mechanics at all scales, including theoretical and computational analysis. In addition, the journal publishes original research contributions that discuss the design and implementation of experiments to characterize materials, structures, and systems. Specific topics of interest include structural and system-health monitoring, smart materials, metrology, biotechnology, nanotechnology, MEMs, NEMs, and more. In addition to research papers, the journal publishes brief review papers, technical notes, and articles on applications. The journal supports open-access publishing and publishes topical issues periodically. This title is available in print and online and the journal's website provides access to online first, open-access, and sample articles. Individual articles feature linked references and supplementary material. This journal will appeal to researchers in academia, industry, and government, including mechanical and other engineers as well as research scientists in physics, chemistry, and biology who are studying problems using experimental mechanics techniques. URL: www.springer.com/engineering/mechanics/journal/11340

2111. ***I E E E - A S M E Transactions on Mechatronics.*** [ISSN: 1083-4435] 1996. bi-m. USD 1200. Ed(s): George Chiu. Institute of Electrical and Electronics Engineers, 445 Hoes Ln, Piscataway, NJ 08854; contactcenter@ieee.org; http://www.ieee.org. Illus., index, adv. Refereed. Vol. ends: No. 4. *Indexed:* A22. *Aud.:* Ac, Sa.

IEEE-ASME Transactions on Mechatronics is a scholarly journal focusing on the integration of mechanical engineering with electronics and computer science for the development of industrial products and processes. Sponsored by the ASME Dynamic Systems and Control Division and the IEEE Industrial Robotics and Robotics and Automation Societies, the focus of the journal is the theory and methods of mechatronics and their practical applications. Subjects and applications of interest include design, modeling, manufacturing, as well as motion, vibration and noise control, micro-devices, robotics, automotive systems, and the like. Published bi-monthly, the journal features topical focus sections. The journal also offers open-access publishing options. Mechatronics, by definition, is multidisciplinary, so this journal will have a very broad audience. It is recommended reading for researchers and professionals from mechanical, electrical, and electronic and systems engineering, control systems, and computer science who are working on the development of new systems and processes. URL: http://ieeexplore.ieee.org/xpl/RecentIssue.jsp?punumber=3516

2112. ***International Journal of Heat and Mass Transfer.*** [ISSN: 0017-9310] 1960. m. EUR 12127. Ed(s): W Minkowycz. Pergamon Press, The Blvd, Langford Ln, E Park, Kidlington, OX5 1GB, United Kingdom; JournalsCustomerServiceEMEA@elsevier.com; http://www.elsevier.com. Illus., adv. Sample. Refereed. Microform: MIM; PQC. *Indexed:* A01, A22. *Bk. rev.:* Number and length vary. *Aud.:* Ac, Sa.

Published monthly, the *International Journal of Heat and Mass Transfer* (available in print, online, and microform) is a peer-reviewed publication focused on analytical and experimental research on the fundamentals of heat and mass transfer. The journal seeks original research papers, reviews, short communications, letters, and so on, that further the understanding of basic transfer processes and their applications. Specific topics of interest include energy engineering, environmental applications of heat or mass transfer, and new methodologies for measuring transport-property data. The journal supports open-access publishing. This well- regarded journal is recommended for academic, government, and other research libraries that serve users working on heat and mass transfer research. URL: https://www.journals.elsevier.com/international-journal-of-heat-and-mass-transfer

2113. ***International Journal of Plasticity.*** [ISSN: 0749-6419] 1985. 12x/yr. EUR 5015. Ed(s): Akhtar S Khan. Pergamon Press, The Blvd, Langford Ln, E Park, Kidlington, OX5 1GB, United Kingdom; http://www.elsevier.com. Illus., adv. Sample. Refereed. Microform: PQC. *Indexed:* A01, A22. *Aud.:* Ac, Sa.

The *International Journal of Plasticity* (available in print, online, and microform) is a highly ranked journal focusing on plastic deformation of solids. This peer-reviewed journal disseminates original theoretical, experimental, or numerical research discussing plastic deformation, damage, and fracturing of isotropic and anisotropic solids. Research is sought detailing the plastic behavior of crystals, metals, ceramics; shape memory alloys, ceramics, polymers, fracture and fracture mechanics, applications of new plasticity models, and many more. Published 12 times per year, the journal supports open-access publishing and releases topical special issues periodically. This journal is a must read for researchers and engineers (mechanical, structural) who are conducting research in this area. URL: https://www.journals.elsevier.com/international-journal-of-plasticity

2114. ***Journal of Fluid Mechanics.*** [ISSN: 0022-1120] 1956. s-m. Ed(s): M G Worster. Cambridge University Press, University Printing House, Shaftesbury Rd, Cambridge, CB2 8BS, United Kingdom; journals@cambridge.org; https://www.cambridge.org/. Illus., index, adv. Refereed. Circ: 2100. Microform: PMC; PQC. Reprint: PSC. *Indexed:* A22, E01, MSN, S25. *Bk. rev.:* 3, length varies. *Aud.:* Ga, Ac, Sa.

The *Journal of Fluid Mechanics* (available in print, online, and microform) is an important international publication that is a leader in the dissemination of fluid mechanics research. Published semi-monthly, this refereed publication provides readers access to research detailing theoretical, experimental, and computational studies of all areas of fluid mechanics. The journal publishes papers discussing the application of fluid mechanics research in other areas including aeronautics, biology, engineering (chemical, biomedical, mechanical), hydraulics, geology, oceanography, and more. The journal accepts original research papers and papers called "JFM Rapids," which are high-impact papers designated for rapid publication. The journal supports open-access publishing. The journal's website has additional content that may interest readers including the JFM Focus articles (one is featured in each issue) and the JFM Perspectives, which are invited, comprehensive reviews of a specific topic in fluid mechanics. Research scientists (biology, earth and oceanographic sciences, physics) and engineers (aerospace, mechanical, biomedical, hydraulic, chemical) whose research involves fluid mechanics will find the research in this journal relevant to their work. URL: https://www.cambridge.org/core/journals/journal-of-fluid-mechanics

2115. ***Journal of Mechanical Design.*** Formerly (until 1990): *Journal of Mechanisms, Transmissions and Automation in Design;* Which superseded in part (in 1983): *Journal of Mechanical Design.* [ISSN: 1050-0472] 1978. m. q. until 2004, b-m. until 2007. USD 1160; USD 1393 combined subscription (print & online eds.)). Ed(s): Wei Chen. The American Society of Mechanical Engineers, Two Park Ave, New York, NY 10016; CustomerCare@asme.org; http://www.asme.org. Sample. Refereed. *Indexed:* A01, A22, BRI. *Bk. rev.:* Number and length vary. *Aud.:* Ac, Sa.

Sponsored by the American Society of Mechanical Engineers (ASME), the *Journal of Mechanical Design* (in print and online) seeks papers on all areas of design, but especially those discussing design synthesis. This monthly journal publishes peer-reviewed original research papers, topical review papers, technical briefs, books reviews, and more. Design areas featured in the journal include design automation, education, innovation, design theory and methodology, design of mechanisms and robotic systems, direct contact systems, and more. The journal supports open-access publishing, features design innovation papers frequently, and publishes special issues. In addition to the current and past issues, the journal website provides easy access to "Accepted Manuscripts" and "Published ahead of Print" papers. This journal will appeal to educators and researchers working in engineering design education, but especially those in mechanical engineering and associated fields (e.g., energy and power, manufacturing, among others). URL: http://mechanicaldesign.asmedigitalcollection.asme.org/journal.aspx

2116. ***Journal of Microelectromechanical Systems.*** [ISSN: 1057-7157] 1992. bi-m. USD 1210. Ed(s): Christofer Hierold. Institute of Electrical and Electronics Engineers, 445 Hoes Ln, Piscataway, NJ 08854; contactcenter@ieee.org; http://www.ieee.org. Adv. Refereed. *Indexed:* A01, A22, CompLI. *Aud.:* Ac, Sa.

The *Journal of Microelectromechanical Systems* (in print, online, CD-ROM, and microform) is a bi-monthly, peer-reviewed publication focusing on micromechanics and microdynamical systems. Sponsored by the American Society for Mechanical Engineers (ASME) and three IEEE sub-societies (Electronic Devices, Industrial Electronics, and Robotics and Automation), the journal publishes original research papers and letters on topics including micro- and nanofabrication techniques, MEMS functional interfaces to biosystems and the environment, materials properties and functional materials for MEMS, interface issues affecting MEMS, wear, reliability, MEMS standards, examples of MEMS applications, and more. The journal supports open-access publishing. The research presented herein is applicable to many different disciplines and will appeal to researchers and professionals in engineering (biomedical, chemical, electrical, mechanical) as well as medical researchers, biologists, computer scientists and others. URL: http://ieeexplore.ieee.org/xpl/RecentIssue.jsp?punumber=84

Journal of Power Sources. See Energy section.

2117. *Mechanical Engineering.* Incorporates (1982-1988): *Computers in Mechanical Engineering;* Former titles (until 1919): *American Society of Mechanical Engineers. Journal;* (until 1908): *American Society of Mechanical Engineers. Proceedings.* [ISSN: 0025-6501] 1880. m. Free to members. Ed(s): John G Falcioni. The American Society of Mechanical Engineers, Two Park Ave, New York, NY 10016; CustomerCare@asme.org; http://www.asme.org. Illus., index, adv. Microform: PMC; PQC. *Indexed:* A01, A22, B01, BRI, HRIS, S25. *Bk. rev.:* Number and length vary. *Aud.:* Ga, Ac, Sa.

Mechanical Engineering (in print and online) is an informative and engaging magazine on trends and advances in mechanical engineering. Published by the American Society of Mechanical Engineers (ASME), this magazine is a membership of benefit to ASME members and may be available to others through vendors, including ProQuest and EBSCO, in academic and public libraries. The *Mechanical Engineering* website makes some open-access content available to nonmembers, including an archive of cover stories with links to related content and resources and an energy forum webinar archive. This attractive magazine is recommended for mechanical engineering educators, researchers, and students. URL: https://www.asme.org/network/media/mechanical-engineering-magazine

2118. *Mechanical Systems and Signal Processing.* [ISSN: 0888-3270] 1987. 16x/yr. EUR 3424. Ed(s): J E Mottershead. Academic Press, 32 Jamestown Rd, Camden, London, NW1 7BY, United Kingdom; corporate.sales@elsevier.com; http://www.elsevier.com/. Adv. Sample. Refereed. Reprint: PSC. *Indexed:* A01, A22, E01. *Aud.:* Ac, Sa.

The goal of *Mechanical Systems and Signal Processing* (in print and online) is to disseminate high-quality original research and review papers related to signal processing, sensing, instrumentation, modeling, and control of dynamic systems. Contributions are peer reviewed and the journal's focus is interdisciplinary in nature, covering mechanical engineering as well as aerospace and civil engineering. Major research areas of interest include actuation, sensing and control, measurement and signal processing, nonlinearity, rotating machines and machinery diagnostics, and vibrations. The journal is especially interested in papers including both theoretical and experimental aspects as well as theoretical papers that are very relevant to practical applications. The journal publishes 16 issues per year, special topical issues, and supports open-access publishing. This journal will appeal to engineering researchers and professionals in mechanical, aerospace, and civil engineering, and it is recommended for academic, research, and corporate libraries serving users in these areas. URL: https://www.journals.elsevier.com/mechanical-systems-and-signal-processing

Progress in Energy and Combustion Science. See Energy section.

2119. *Wear: an international journal on the science and technology of friction, lubrication and wear.* [ISSN: 0043-1648] 1958. 24x/yr. EUR 12270. Ed(s): P H Shipway, P J Blau. Elsevier BV, Radarweg 29, Amsterdam, 1043 NX, Netherlands; info@elsevier.com; https://www.elsevier.com/. Illus., adv. Refereed. Vol. ends: No. 249 - No. 251. Microform: PQC. *Indexed:* A01, A22, HRIS. *Aud.:* Ac, Sa.

Wear (in print, online, and microform) is an international journal focusing on the mechanisms and nature of wear in materials. This refereed journal publishes original research papers, review papers, and short communications that help advance the basic and applied knowledge in this field. Topics of interest include modeling and physical validation of models, the development and applications of new testing methods and diagnostic tools, wear-related engineering standards, application of wear knowledge in the development of wear-resistant materials and coatings, the relationship between a material's composition, structure, and properties and its wear behavior, and the role of lubricants in the wear process. Published 24 times per year, the journal supports open-access publishing and publishes special issues. Since research on wear and related topics is important to many fields, this journal will be relevant to engineering professionals (mechanical, civil, industrial, manufacturing, biomedical, aerospace, automotive) and researchers in academia, government, and corporate settings. URL: https://www.journals.elseviercom/wear

Nuclear Engineering

Arms Control Today. See Peace and Conflict Studies section.

2120. *Fusion Engineering and Design: an international journal for fusion energy and technology devoted to experiments, theory, methods and design.* Formerly (until 1986): *Nuclear Engineering and Design. Fusion.* [ISSN: 0920-3796] 1984. 12x/yr. EUR 7642. Ed(s): M A Abdou. Elsevier BV, Radarweg 29, Amsterdam, 1043 NX, Netherlands; info@elsevier.com; https://www.elsevier.com/. Refereed. *Indexed:* A01, A22. *Aud.:* Ac, Sa.

Fusion Engineering and Design publishes original research papers and technical engineering notes related to all aspects of nuclear technology. The peer-reviewed experimental papers published in this journal are highly technical in nature and cover all aspects of nuclear fusion technology, models, methods, and design. Selected topics of interest are technologies and materials for fusion, reactor designs, operations and maintenance and plasmas, fuel cycle analysis, safety, waste management, decommissioning, and more. *Fusion Engineering and Design* publishes 12 issues per year and supports open-access publishing. Altmetrics for top-rated papers are provided. Nuclear and mechanical engineers and scientists in both academic and corporate settings who are working on the research and design of fusion reactors and systems need to read this journal to keep informed about advances in this area. URL: https://www-journals-elsevier-com.mutex.gmu.edu/fusion-engineering-and-design

2121. *I E E E Transactions on Nuclear Science.* Former titles (until 1963): *I R E Transactions on Nuclear Science;* (until 1955): *I R E Professional Group on Nuclear Science. Transactions.* [ISSN: 0018-9499] 1954. m. USD 2730. Ed(s): Zane Bell. Institute of Electrical and Electronics Engineers, 445 Hoes Ln, Piscataway, NJ 08854; contactcenter@ieee.org; http://www.ieee.org. Illus., adv. Refereed. *Indexed:* A01, A22, B01, BRI. *Aud.:* Ac, Sa.

The monthly *IEEE Transactions on Nuclear Science* (available in print, online, CD-ROM, and microform) is a peer-reviewed journal published by the IEEE Nuclear and Plasma Sciences Society. The journal publishes articles on theoretical research and applications of nuclear science and engineering. The main topics of interest include tools for the detection and measurement of ionizing radiation, particle accelerators, nuclear medicine and its applications, reactor instrumentation and controls, radiation in space and radiation's effect on materials, components, and systems. In addition to research and application articles, the journal also accepts tutorial and historical articles as well as shorter articles (correspondence) reporting on significant research in the above areas. The journal supports open-access publishing. Nuclear scientists and engineers, physicists and astronomers, biomedical engineers and medical researchers, will benefit from the research published in this journal. URL: http://ieeexplore.ieee.org/xpl/aboutJournal.jsp?punumber=23

2122. *International Journal of Pressure Vessels and Piping: design, manufacture and operation of pressurized components; structural integrity; plant life management.* Incorporates (1980-1991): *Res Mechanica.* [ISSN: 0308-0161] 1973. m. 8/yr. until 2016. EUR 6201. Ed(s): M Smith, P Dong. Elsevier Ltd, 125 London Wall, London, EC2Y 5AS, United Kingdom; corporate.sales@elsevier.com; http://www.elsevier.com. Illus., index, adv. Sample. Refereed. Microform: PQC. *Indexed:* A01, A22. *Aud.:* Sa.

The *International Journal of Pressure Vessels and Piping* (available in print, online, and microform) is a peer-reviewed, monthly publication providing readers with current research on pressure vessels and piping. The journal publishes original research articles and critical topical reviews and is also interested in articles about practical applications. Specific topics of interest include pressure vessel engineering, structural integrity assessment, codes and standards, fabrication, materials requirements, maintenance, quality management, and more. Special thematic issues are published. The journal supports open-access publishing. Since pressure vessels are used in a number of different industries, this publication will be relevant for engineering professionals in industries including energy, petrochemicals and other process industries, transport, and academic and corporate researchers in these areas. URL: https://www.journals.elsevier.com/international-journal-of-pressure-vessels-and-piping

2123. *Journal of Nuclear Materials.* [ISSN: 0022-3115] 1959. 15x/yr. EUR 9681. Ed(s): G S Was. Elsevier BV, North-Holland, Postbus 211, Amsterdam, 1000 AE, Netherlands; JournalsCustomerServiceEMEA@elsevier.com; http://www.elsevier.com. Illus., adv. Refereed. Microform: PQC. *Indexed:* A01, A22. *Aud.:* Ac, Sa.

The *Journal of Nuclear Materials* publishes articles focusing on materials science and engineering for nuclear applications. Published 15 times per year, this peer-reviewed journal (in print, online, and microform) seeks original research submissions as well as critical review papers that cover the fundamentals and applications of nuclear materials from a theoretical, experimental, or computational perspective. Subjects of interest include fission and fusion reactor materials, material aspects of the entire fuel cycle, performance of nuclear waste materials and their immobilization, radiation effects in materials, and more. Special issues are published periodically. The journal supports open-access publishing. It is highly recommended reading for materials scientists and engineers (nuclear, mechanical) working in the nuclear energy and related fields as well as biomedical engineers and researchers in nuclear medicine. URL: https://www.journals.elsevier.com/journal-of-nuclear-materials

2124. *Journal of Radiological Protection.* Formerly (until 1988): *Society for Radiological Protection. Journal.* [ISSN: 0952-4746] 1981. q. USD 980 (print & online eds.)). Ed(s): R Wakeford. Institute of Physics Publishing Ltd., Temple Circus, Temple Way, Bristol, BS1 6HG, United Kingdom; custserv@iop.org; http://iopscience.iop.org. Sample. Refereed. *Indexed:* A01, A22. *Aud.:* Ac, Sa.

The *Journal of Radiological Protection* (available in print, online, and microform) is published quarterly by the Society for Radiological Protection. This peer-reviewed journal publishes original research papers, review papers, practical matter articles describing a radiological protection problem and its resolution, and more. Topics covered by the journal include biological effects, risk and environmental impacts of radiation, instrument development, radiation measuring techniques, epidemiology, among others. This journal supports open-access publishing. It is highly recommended to scientists, engineers, public health officials, and epidemiologists, policy makers, and medical personnel researching radiation's effects on living and non-living systems, designing protection systems, writing safety protocols and standards, or working in nuclear medicine or with radiological imaging tools. URL: http://iopscience.iop.org/journal/0952-474

2125. *Nuclear Engineering and Design: an international journal devoted to all aspects of nuclear fission energy.* Formerly (until 1966): *Nuclear Structural Engineering.* [ISSN: 0029-5493] 1965. 15x/yr. EUR 10454. Ed(s): Y A Hassan. Elsevier BV, Radarweg 29, Amsterdam, 1043 NX, Netherlands; info@elsevier.com; https://www.elsevier.com/. Adv. Refereed. Vol. ends: No. 203 - No. 210. Microform: PQC. *Indexed:* A01, A22. *Aud.:* Sa.

The peer-reviewed journal *Nuclear Engineering and Design* (available in print, online, and microform) covers all areas of nuclear fission energy. Published 15 times per year, this journal presents original research papers, technical notes, summary reports of new regulatory codes or guidelines, overviews of major programs or case histories, and more. The papers published in this journal are technical in nature on topics including reactor engineering, components and protection, properties of materials, fuel engineering, waste management, safety and risk analysis, economics of nuclear plants, licensing issues, and others. The journal supports open-access publishing and provides altmetrics for top-rated papers on its website. Since this journal focuses on all aspects of fission energy, its readers will include nuclear physicists and engineers, as well as economists, plant designers and managers, safety engineers, and more. URL: https://www.journals.elsevier.com/nuclear-engineering-and-design/

Nuclear Engineering International. See Energy section.

2126. *Nuclear Instruments & Methods in Physics Research. Section A: Accelerators, Spectrometers, Detectors, and Associated Equipment.* Supersedes in part (in 1984): *Nuclear Instruments and Methods in Physics Research;* Which was formerly (until 1981): *Nuclear Instruments and Methods;* (until 1958): *Nuclear Instruments.* [ISSN: 0168-9002] 1957. 36x/yr. EUR 10030. Ed(s): William Barletta. Elsevier BV, Radarweg 29, Amsterdam, 1043 NX, Netherlands; info@elsevier.com; https://www.elsevier.com/. Illus., index, adv. Refereed. Vol. ends: No. 456 - No. 474. Microform: PQC. *Indexed:* A&ATA, A01, A22. *Aud.:* Ac, Sa.

This peer-reviewed journal (in print, online, and microform) publishes papers on the design, manufacture, and performance of scientific instruments. Published 36 times per year, the journal accepts both experimental and theoretical submissions on topics including instruments (e.g., particle accelerators, ion sources, radiation detection instruments, spectrometers) as well as control systems and computerization of measurements. The journal supports open-access publishing and publishes special thematic issues. The research in this journal will be relevant to the work of engineers (nuclear, electrical, electronic, biomedical) and scientists (physicists and astronomers) who are working to design, develop, and validate instrumentation and sensors for use in a number of applications in nuclear energy, medicine, astronomy, and more. URL: https://www.journals.elsevier.com/nuclear-instruments-and-methods-in-physics-research-section-a-accelerators-spectrometers-detectors-and-associated-equipment/

2127. *Nuclear Instruments & Methods in Physics Research. Section B: Beam Interactions with Materials and Atoms.* Supersedes in part (in 1984): *Nuclear Instruments and Methods in Physics Research;* Which was formerly (until 1981): *Nuclear Instruments and Methods;* (until 1958): *Nuclear Instruments.* [ISSN: 0168-583X] 1957. 24x/yr. EUR 6774. Ed(s): M B H Breese, C Trautmann. Elsevier BV, Radarweg 29, Amsterdam, 1043 NX, Netherlands; info@elsevier.com; https://www.elsevier.com/. Illus., index, adv. Refereed. Vol. ends: No. 173 - No. 185. Microform: PQC. *Indexed:* A01, A22. *Bk. rev.:* Number and length vary. *Aud.:* Ac, Sa.

The *Journal of Nuclear Instruments & Methods in Physics Research Section B* (online and microform) is a peer-reviewed journal that focuses on energetic beams and their interaction with matter. Selected topics of interest include the modification of materials by energetic beams (neutrons, positrons and muons, plasmas, electron beams, and others), the effects of ion, laser and electron beams on different materials, and the application of beam analysis in other research areas (archaeology, biology, geology, planetary science). The journal occasionally publishes special topical issues. This journal supports open-access publishing. The intended audience for this journal is scientific researchers (physical, life sciences, materials science) conducting fundamental or applied research on the effects of energetic beams on physical materials at different scales. (https://www.journals.elsevier.com/nuclear-instruments-and-methods-in-physics-research-section-b-beam-interactions-with-materials-and-atoms/)

2128. *Nuclear News.* Incorporates (198?-1995): *American Nuclear Society News.* [ISSN: 0029-5574] 1959. m. Free to members; Non-members, USD 575. Ed(s): Betsy Tompkins. American Nuclear Society, Inc., 555 N Kensington Ave, La Grange Park, IL 60526; members@ans.org; http://www.ans.org. Illus., adv. *Indexed:* A22. *Bk. rev.:* Number and length vary. *Aud.:* Ga, Ac, Sa.

Published by the American Nuclear Society (ANS), *Nuclear News* (in print and online) is a go-to publication for news and other information related to the nuclear power industry. Content in this monthly trade magazine (an annual buyers' guide is issued as a supplement) is divided by major topics including Power, Security, Policy and Legislation, Fuel, Waste Management, Industry, and others. Special sections are included in regular issues several times a year. The journal includes an industry calendar and accepts advertising. The content in *Nuclear News* is a must read for anyone working in the nuclear power industry, associated industries (e.g., construction, equipment), government, and regulatory agencies. In addition, it will appeal to non-industry readers who are interested in learning more about the nuclear power industry worldwide. URL: http://www.ans.org/pubs/magazines/nn/

Nuclear Technology. See Energy section.

2129. ***Science and Technology of Nuclear Installations.*** [ISSN: 1687-6075] 2007. . USD 495. Ed(s): Francesco D'Auria. Hindawi Publishing Corporation, 315 Madison Ave, 3rd Fl, Ste 3070, New York, NY 10017; hindawi@hindawi.com; https://www.hindawi.com. Refereed. *Indexed:* A01. *Aud.:* Ac, Ga.

Science and Technology of Nuclear Installations (in print and online) is an Open-Access Gold journal that provides free access to the technical research it publishes to all online readers. This peer-reviewed journal is published continuously online and accepts submissions on industrial applications of nuclear technology, especially the design, operation, and decommissioning of power plants, industrial use of radioisotopes, research reactors, quality assurance, safeguards, management, and more. Specific areas of interest include fuel cycle management, design and construction of nuclear power plants, safety and licensing issues, waste management, and others. Special issues are published and a recent one features papers related to safety features of high temperature gas-cooled reactors. The intended audience of this publication is professionals working to design and build nuclear reactors, utility companies, regulatory bodies, as well as researchers in government and academia. URL: https://www.hindawi.com/journals/stni/

■ ENVIRONMENT AND CONSERVATION

See also Biology; Fishing; Hiking, Climbing, and Outdoor Recreation; Hunting and Guns; and Sports sections.

Diane T. Sands, Librarian, Ratcliff, Emeryville, CA 94608

Introduction

The environment is the backbone of our planet. In the same way, scholarly research journals are the backbone of this section. Ecosystem change has broad implications for health and sustainability at local, regional, and global levels.

Environment-and-conservation-focused periodicals exist to help readers make sense of the increasingly abundant information available. Environmental news journals have value-added, online components that supplement traditional subscriptions. This is an interdisciplinary topic that cannot be covered under a single heading. Readers should look to the other sections of "Zoology," "Science and Technology," "Travel and Tourism," and "Urban Studies," among others, for further information.

Basic Periodicals

Ecology and Society, Environmental Hazards, Environment: Science and Policy for Sustainable Development.

Basic Abstracts and Indexes

Academic Search Premier, AGRICOLA, BIOSIS, Ecology Abstracts, Environment Index, Environmental Sciences and Pollution Management, GEOBASE, Pollution Abstracts, Web of Science.

2130. ***Ambio: a journal of the human environment.*** Incorporates (1972-1979): *Ambio Special Report.* [ISSN: 0044-7447] 1972. 8x/yr. EUR 579 (print & online eds.)). Ed(s): Bo Soderstrom. Springer Netherlands, Van Godewijckstraat 30, Dordrecht, 3311 GX, Netherlands; http://www.springer.com. Illus., index, adv. Refereed. Vol. ends: Dec. Reprint: PSC. *Indexed:* A01, A22, BRI, C45, CBRI, CJPI, E01, S25. *Aud.:* Ac, Sa.

Sponsored by the Royal Swedish Academy of Sciences, this internationally focused publication contains topics that range from ecology, environmental economics, and geological sciences to hydrology, water resources, and earth sciences. "Significant developments in environmental research, policy and related activities" are the core areas for this peer-reviewed journal. References are well documented, even in the personal "Perspective" segment.

American Forests. See Forestry section.

2131. ***American Water Resources Association. Journal (Online).*** [ISSN: 1752-1688] 1965. bi-m. GBP 466. Ed(s): Venki Uddameri. Wiley-Blackwell Publishing, Inc., 111 River St, Hoboken, NJ 07030; http://onlinelibrary.wiley.com. Adv. *Bk. rev.:* Number and length vary. *Aud.:* Ac, Sa.

The *Journal of the American Water Resources Association* (*JAWRA*) says that "[a]s the preeminent multidisciplinary water resources journal, [it] must play an increasing role in communicating emerging scholarly information that will improve our understanding of water systems and how they are best managed. To do this, it is essential [that it] publish innovative, high[-]quality journal articles dealing with both the biophysical and the human dimensions of water resources and aquatic ecosystems." Each issue of this highly respected scholarly journal highlights a "Feature Collection" of articles that are related to a designated topic. Additional articles relate to water chemistry, economic and policy issues, hydrology, or pollution and conservation. Authors can now choose to publish their articles as Open Access.

2132. ***Biodiversity and Conservation.*** [ISSN: 0960-3115] 1991. 14x/yr. EUR 4434 (print & online eds.)). Ed(s): David L Hawksworth. Springer Netherlands, Van Godewijckstraat 30, Dordrecht, 3311 GX, Netherlands; http://www.springer.com. Illus., adv. Refereed. Reprint: PSC. *Indexed:* A22, Agr, BRI, C45, E01, GardL, S25. *Aud.:* Ac, Sa.

This peer-reviewed, academic journal is international in scope and explores "all aspects of biological diversity; description, analysis and conservation, and [the environment's] controlled rational use by humankind." Technical articles use extensive analysis of data and statistics to examine human impact on biodiversity. The journal's issues incorporate political, economic, and social perspectives, as well as editorials and research notes. Subscriptions offered through Springer allow the authors to choose an Open Access option when publishing.

Climatic Change. See Atmospheric Sciences section.

Conservation Biology. See Ecology section.

2133. ***E & E Publishing Online.*** d. Environment and Energy Publishing, LLC, 122 C St, NW, 7th Fl, Washington, DC 20001; pubs@eenews.net; http://www.eenews.net. *Aud.:* Ga, Ac.

This is an online publisher of *Climatewire, Environment & Energy Daily,* and *Greenwire*, as well as a compendium of topical news videos and the service's own online news program. *E&E Publishing* is the leading source for comprehensive, daily coverage of environmental and energy policy and markets. A good source for academic and public libraries that serve political constituents. URL: www.eenews.net/

2134. ***E (Online): the environmental magazine.*** 1990. bi-m. Free. Ed(s): Brita Belli. Earth Action Network, 28 Knight St, Norwalk, CT 06851. Adv. *Aud.:* Hs, Ga, Ac, Sa.

E: the environmental magazine is a general-interest magazine with an international scope that is now published exclusively online. Excellent for public libraries or online research guides. URL: www.emagazine.com/

2135. ***EcoHealth: conservation medicine: human health: ecosystem sustainability.*** Formed by the merger of (2000-2004): *Global Change and Human Health;* (1995-2004): *Ecosystem Health.* [ISSN: 1612-9202] 2004. q. EUR 940 (print & online eds.)). Ed(s): Peter Daszak. Springer New York LLC, 233 Spring St, New York, NY 10013; customerservice@springer.com; http://www.springer.com. Refereed. Reprint: PSC. *Indexed:* A22, BRI, C45, E01. *Bk. rev.:* Number and length vary. *Aud.:* Ac, Sa.

This journal is a central platform for fulfilling the mission of the International Association for Ecology & Health to strive for sustainable health of people, domestic animals, wildlife, and ecosystems by promoting discovery, understanding, and transdisciplinarity. *EcoHealth* hopes to reach researchers, policy makers, and educators through articles on integrated ecology and health challenges arising in public health, human and veterinary medicine, conservation and ecosystem management, rural and urban development and planning, and other fields that address the social-ecological context of health.

Ecology. See Ecology section.

2136. *Ecology and Society: a journal of integrative science for resilience and sustainability.* Formerly: *Conservation Ecology.* [ISSN: 1708-3087] 1997. s-a. Free. Ed(s): Lance Gunderson, Carl Folke. Resilience Alliance Publications, PO Box 40037, Waterloo, ON N2J 4V1, Canada; questions@consecol.org; http://www.consecol.org. Illus. Refereed. *Indexed:* A01, C45, S25. *Bk. rev.:* Number and length vary. *Aud.:* Ac, Sa.

Articles in this open-access, electronic, peer-reviewed journal include occasional special features and groups of articles on the same theme. Articles are published as accepted in an "Issue in Progress" capacity. They are also written for a wide audience that includes "an array of disciplines from the natural sciences, social sciences, and the humanities [that are] concerned with the relationship between society and the life-supporting ecosystems."

Ecosystems. See Ecology section.

2137. *Electronic Green Journal: professional journal on international environmental information.* Formerly (until 1994): *Green Library Journal.* [ISSN: 1076-7975] 1992. a. Free. Ed(s): Maria Anna Jankowska. University of California, eScholarship, California Digital Library, 415 20th St, 4th Fl, Oakland, CA 94612; info@escholarship.org; https://www.escholarship.org. Illus. Sample. Refereed. *Indexed:* A01, BRI, C45, CBRI. *Bk. rev.:* Number and length vary. *Aud.:* Ga, Ac, Sa.

A publication of the UCLA Library, this open-access publication has provided scholarly, international environmental information since 1994. It is a "professional peer-reviewed publication devoted to disseminating information concerning environmental protection, conservation, management of natural resources, and ecologically-balanced regional development."

2138. *Environment: science and policy for sustainable development.* Former titles (until 1969): *Scientist and Citizen;* (until 1964): *Nuclear Information.* [ISSN: 0013-9157] 1958. bi-m. GBP 192. Ed(s): Margaret Benner. Taylor & Francis Inc., 711 3rd Ave, 8th Fl, New York, NY 10017; support@tandfonline.com; http://www.tandfonline.com. Illus., adv. Refereed. Reprint: PSC. *Indexed:* A01, A22, Agr, BRI, C37, C45, CBRI, E01, IBSS, MASUSE. *Bk. rev.:* Number and length vary. *Aud.:* Hs, Ga, Ac, Sa.

Environment analyzes the problems, places, and people where environment and development come together, illuminating concerns from the local to the global. Scientific research is presented, accompanied by photographs, illustrations, and understandable explanations that are accessible to those who want to stay current on questions of environmental policy. This is a general-interest publication that provides peer-reviewed articles, editorials, essays, and suggestions for interesting web sites, books, and articles.

2139. *Environment and Development Economics.* [ISSN: 1355-770X] 1996. bi-m. GBP 410. Ed(s): Eswaran Somanathan. Cambridge University Press, University Printing House, Shaftesbury Rd, Cambridge, CB2 8BS, United Kingdom; journals@cambridge.org; https://www.cambridge.org/. Illus., adv. Refereed. Circ: 1950 Controlled. Reprint: PSC. *Indexed:* A22, B01, BAS, C45, E01, EconLit. *Aud.:* Ac, Sa.

Each issue of *Environment and Development Economics* provides a mix of scientific and policy papers, with a heavy emphasis on economic theory and modeling. This academic journal focuses on "the environmental problems associated with economic development," particularly of developing countries. Occasionally, articles may be available under the Open Access tab to all readers.

2140. *Environment, Development and Sustainability: a multidisciplinary approach to the theory and practice of sustainable development.* [ISSN: 1387-585X] 1999. bi-m. EUR 1016 (print & online eds.)). Ed(s): Luc Hens. Springer Netherlands, Van Godewijckstraat 30, Dordrecht, 3311 GX, Netherlands; http://www.springer.com. Refereed. Reprint: PSC. *Indexed:* A22, Agr, B01, BRI, C45, E01, IBSS, S25. *Aud.:* Ac, Sa.

Environment, Development and Sustainability is an international, multidisciplinary journal that covers environmental impacts of socioeconomic development. This title is concerned with the complex interactions between development and environment, and its purpose is to seek ways and means for achieving sustainability in all human activities aimed at such development. Articles cover different angles of the environmental impacts related to socioeconomic development, particularly in developing and developed areas.

2141. *Environmental Conservation: an international journal of environmental science.* [ISSN: 0376-8929] 1974. q. GBP 707. Ed(s): Nicholas V C Polunin. Cambridge University Press, University Printing House, Shaftesbury Rd, Cambridge, CB2 8BS, United Kingdom; journals@cambridge.org; https://www.cambridge.org/. Illus., adv. Sample. Refereed. Circ: 1800. Vol. ends: Winter. Microform: PQC. Reprint: PSC. *Indexed:* A22, BAS, C45, E01, S25. *Bk. rev.:* Number and length vary. *Aud.:* Ac, Sa.

One of the longest-standing, most highly cited of the interdisciplinary, peer-reviewed, academic environmental science journals. It includes research papers, reports, comments, subject reviews, and book reviews that address environmental policy, practice, and natural and social science of environmental concern at the global level, informed by rigorous local level case studies. The journal's scope is very broad, including issues in human institutions, ecosystem change, resource use, terrestrial biomes, aquatic systems, and coastal and land use management.

2142. *Environmental Ethics: an interdisciplinary journal dedicated to the philosophical aspects of environmental problems.* [ISSN: 0163-4275] 1979. q. USD 80. Ed(s): Eugene C Hargrove. Environmental Philosophy, Inc., 1155 Union Cir, 310980, Denton, TX 76203; cep@unt.edu; http://www.cep.unt.edu. Illus., index. Refereed. Microform: PQC. *Indexed:* A01, A22, Agr, AmHI, BRI, MLA-IB, R&TA, S25. *Bk. rev.:* Number and length vary. *Aud.:* Ac.

Environmental Ethics publishes articles, reviews, and discussions exploring the philosophical aspects of environmental problems. This title provides a peer-reviewed forum for diverse interests and attitudes, bringing together the nonprofessional environmental philosophy tradition with the professional interest in the subject. It is published by the Center for Environmental Philosophy at the University of North Texas.

2143. *Environmental Hazards: human and policy dimensions.* Formerly (until 2006): *Global Environmental Change Part B: Environmental Hazards;* Which superseded in part (in 1999): *Global Environmental Change.* [ISSN: 1747-7891] 1990. 5x/yr. GBP 559 (print & online eds.)). Ed(s): Edmund Penning-Rowsell. Earthscan Ltd., 4 Park Sq, Milton Pk, Abingdon, Oxford, OX14 4RN, United Kingdom; earthinfo@earthscan.co.uk; http://www.tandfonline.com/. Adv. Sample. Refereed. Reprint: PSC. *Indexed:* A01, C45, IBSS, S25. *Aud.:* Ac, Sa.

Written for academics and those with an interest in regulations and governance, *Environmental Hazards* addresses the full range of hazardous events from extreme geological, hydrological, atmospheric and biological events, such as earthquakes, floods, storms, and epidemics, to technological failures and malfunctions, such as industrial explosions, fires, and toxic material releases. This international, peer-reviewed publication, "with a genuinely international perspective, highlights issues of human exposure, vulnerability, awareness, response and risk. The role of hazards in affecting development, and issues of efficiency, social justice and sustainability are also explored in the journal."

2144. *Environmental Justice.* [ISSN: 1939-4071] 2008. bi-m. USD 1088. Ed(s): Sylvia Hood Washington. Mary Ann Liebert, Inc. Publishers, 140 Huguenot St, 3rd Fl, New Rochelle, NY 10801; info@liebertpub.com; http://www.liebertpub.com. Adv. Sample. Refereed. Reprint: PSC. *Indexed:* C45. *Aud.:* Hs, Ac, Sa.

This journal is appropriate for community planners and organizers, academic libraries, and public health professionals. *Environmental Justice* "covers the adverse and disparate health impact and environmental burden that affect marginalized populations all over the world. The Journal facilitates open dialogue among the many stakeholders involved in environmental justice struggles." It is international in scope, and its topics include siting for nuclear power plants, cleanup of toxic environments in low-income areas, disparities in grocery stores between racially dissimilar communities, and community health issues and their underlying environmental causes.

2145. ***Environmental Science & Policy.*** [ISSN: 1462-9011] 1998. m. 10/yr. until 2015. EUR 1794. Ed(s): Dr. M. C Beniston. Elsevier Inc., 230 Park Ave, Ste 800, New York, NY 10169; usinfo-f@elsevier.com; https://www.elsevier.com. Illus., adv. Sample. Refereed. *Indexed:* C45, IBSS. *Bk. rev.:* Number and length vary. *Aud.:* Ac, Sa.

Environmental Science & Policy is written for those "who are instrumental in the solution of environmental problems," including non-governmental and governmental organizations, and business and academic research labs. It also considers the interplay between environmental, social, and economic issues. The journal emphasizes the linkages between these environmental issues and social and economic issues such as production, transport, consumption, growth, demographic changes, well-being, and health.

Ethics, Policy & Environment. See Geography section.

Global Biogeochemical Cycles. See Marine Science and Technology/Ocean Science section.

Global Change Biology. See Ecology section.

Global Ecology and Biogeography: a journal of macroecology. See Ecology section.

Green Places. See Landscape Architecture section.

2146. ***Green Teacher: education for planet earth.*** [ISSN: 1192-1285] 1991. q. Green Teacher, 95 Robert St, Toronto, ON M5S 2K5, Canada. Illus., adv. Sample. *Indexed:* BRI, C37. *Bk. rev.:* Number and length vary. *Aud.:* Hs, Ga, Ac.

Recommended for school and public libraries, *Green Teacher* is a magazine about global and local environmental issues, making it easy to merge lessons into existing school subjects or during students' time outside of school, including at camps or day care, or at home. Activities are designed to empower and engage students to become part of the solution.

2147. ***High Country News: for people who care about the West.*** [ISSN: 0191-5657] 1970. bi-w. USD 29.95 combined subscription (print & online eds.)). Ed(s): Jonathan Thompson. High Country Foundation, 119 Grand Ave, PO Box 1090, Paonia, CO 81428. Illus., index, adv. Circ: 22637 Paid. Vol. ends: Dec. *Indexed:* S25. *Bk. rev.:* Number and length vary. *Aud.:* Hs, Ga, Ac, Sa.

High Country News is an award-winning, "nonprofit media organization that covers the important issues and stories that define the American West. Its mission is to inform and inspire people - through in-depth journalism - to act on behalf of the West's diverse natural and human communities." A good choice for public libraries, particularly in the western United States. Published online as well as in hard-copy form.

2148. ***Human Ecology (New York): an interdisciplinary journal.*** [ISSN: 0300-7839] 1972. bi-m. EUR 2025 (print & online eds.)). Ed(s): Daniel G Bates. Springer New York LLC, 233 Spring St, New York, NY 10013; customerservice@springer.com; http://www.springer.com. Illus., index, adv. Refereed. Reprint: PSC. *Indexed:* A01, A22, Agr, BAS, BRI, C45, E01, P61, SSA. *Bk. rev.:* Number and length vary. *Aud.:* Ac, Sa.

This peer-reviewed journal focuses on the "interaction between people and their environment." Articles examine the problems of adaptation in urban environments, and scrutinize the effects of population density on environmental quality, social organization, and health. International in focus, this journal is recommended for academic libraries.

Journal of Environmental Economics and Management. See Economics section.

The Journal of Environmental Education. See Education/Specific Subjects and Teaching Methods: Environmental Education section.

2149. ***Journal of Environmental Health.*** Former titles (until 1963): *Sanitarian's Journal of Environmental Health;* (until 1962): *Sanitarian.* [ISSN: 0022-0892] 1938. 10x/yr. USD 135 domestic; USD 160 foreign. Ed(s): Kristen Ruby. National Environmental Health Association, 720 S Colorado Blvd, Ste 1000-N, Denver, CO 80246; staff@neha.org; http://www.neha.org. Illus., adv. Refereed. Microform: PQC. *Indexed:* A01, A22, BRI, C45, S25. *Aud.:* Ac, Sa.

From the National Environmental Health Association (NEHA) comes this peer-reviewed journal, with articles concerning the public health field. Published ten times per year, this title "keeps readers up-to-date on current issues," and offers research in such fields as air quality, food safety and protection, occupational safety and health, and water quality. Recommended for both academic and public libraries.

2150. ***Local Environment: the international journal of justice and sustainability.*** [ISSN: 1354-9839] 1996. 12x/yr. GBP 1512 (print & online eds.)). Ed(s): Julian Agyeman. Routledge, 4 Park Sq, Milton Park, Abingdon, OX14 4RN, United Kingdom; subscriptions@tandf.co.uk; http://www.tandfonline.com. Adv. Sample. Refereed. Reprint: PSC. *Indexed:* A01, A22, C45, E01, IBSS. *Aud.:* Ac, Sa.

Local Environment: the international journal of justice and sustainability is a refereed journal that serves as "a forum for the examination, evaluation and discussion of the environmental, social and economic policies and strategies which will be needed in the move towards 'Just Sustainability' at local, national and global levels." Recommended for academic libraries with an urban planning focus, and for libraries that support local policymakers and community advocates.

2151. ***Natural Hazards Review.*** [ISSN: 1527-6988] 2000. q. USD 657. Ed(s): Nasim Uddin. American Society of Civil Engineers, 1801 Alexander Bell Dr, Reston, VA 20191; ascelibrary@asce.org; http://www.asce.org. Adv. Refereed. *Indexed:* A22, C45, HRIS. *Bk. rev.:* Number and length vary. *Aud.:* Ac, Sa.

Published by the American Society of Civil Engineers and the Hazards Center at the University of Colorado at Boulder, *Natural Hazards Review* is "dedicated to bringing together the physical, social, and behavioral sciences; engineering; and the regulatory and policy environments to provide a forum for cutting edge, holistic, and cross-disciplinary approaches to natural hazards loss and cost reduction." International in scope, this journal is recommended for academic libraries.

2152. ***The Natural Resources Journal.*** [ISSN: 0028-0739] 1961. q. USD 20 per issue. Ed(s): Lance Hough, Natalie Zerwekh. University of New Mexico, School of Law, MSC11 6070, 1 University of New Mexico, Albuquerque, NM 87131; journals@law.unm.edu; htttp://lawschool.unm.edu. Illus., index, adv. Refereed. Vol. ends: Fall. Microform: WSH; PMC. Reprint: WSH. *Indexed:* A01, A22, Agr, BAS, BRI, CBRI, EconLit, IBSS, L14, P61, S25. *Bk. rev.:* Number and length vary. *Aud.:* Ac, Sa.

Published by the University of New Mexico School of Law, *The Natural Resources Journal* "is an international, interdisciplinary forum devoted to the study of natural and environmental resources." Policy-oriented, this peer-reviewed academic journal provides analysis of both policy issues and legal cases. Recommended for law libraries or those that support urban and rural studies programs.

Ranger Rick. See Children section.

2153. *Remote Sensing of Environment: an interdisciplinary journal.* [ISSN: 0034-4257] 1969. 16x/yr. EUR 6292. Ed(s): Emilio Chuvieco, Crystal Schaaf. Elsevier Inc., 230 Park Ave, Ste 800, New York, NY 10169; usinfo-f@elsevier.com; https://www.elsevier.com. Illus., index, adv. Sample. Refereed. Vol. ends: Mar/Dec. *Indexed:* A01, A22, Agr, C45, S25. *Bk. rev.:* Number and length vary. *Aud.:* Ac, Sa.

Remote sensing involves collecting environmental data without coming into physical contact with the environment, via satellite imaging, aerial photography, and radar, among other methods. This interdisciplinary journal "serves the remote sensing community with the publication of results on theory, science, applications and technology of remote sensing of Earth resources and environment." It includes peer-reviewed articles, and is recommended for academic libraries.

Restoration Ecology (Online). See Ecology section.

■ EUROPE

General/Newspapers

See also Latin America and Spain; and Slavic Studies sections.

Sarah Roberts, Access Services Specialist, Physics Research Library, Harvard University, Cambridge, MA 02138

Cheryl LaGuardia, Research Librarian, Widener Library, Harvard University; claguard@fas.harvard.edu

Introduction

The Europe section covers a range of journals, magazines, and newspapers that focus on Central and Western Europe, with an emphasis on artistic, cultural, historical, and literary themes and topics. Numerous journals contain a comparative structure, and most provide scholarly, refereed articles about regional cultural accomplishments, histories, politics, and literature dating from the Middle Ages to the present day, with many attempting to place their specific country's past and present into a larger, global context. Dutch, French, German, Italian, and Scandinavian regions are especially highlighted in this section. Also included are two international, Western Europe–based newspapers, and several magazines published by Western and Central European cultural societies, both of which offer news, information, and cultural review sections for a broader audience.

The interdisciplinary scope of this section necessitates selectivity and the journals, magazines, and newspapers listed here have been included based on librarian recommendations and their selection for inclusion in earlier editions of *Magazines for Libraries.*

Basic Periodicals

Central European History, The Germanic Review, Irish University Review, Journal of European Studies, Scandinavian Review, Yale French Studies.

Basic Abstracts and Indexes

Arts and Humanities Citation Index, Humanities Index, MLA International Bibliography, PAIS International.

General

2154. *Central European History.* Formerly (until 1968): *Journal of Central European Affairs.* [ISSN: 0008-9389] 1941. q. GBP 220 (print & online eds.)). Ed(s): Andrew I. Port. Cambridge University Press, University Printing House, Shaftesbury Rd, Cambridge, CB2 8BS, United Kingdom; journals@cambridge.org; https://www.cambridge.org/. Illus., index, adv. Refereed. Reprint: PSC. *Indexed:* A01, A22, AmHI, BRI, CBRI, E01, IBSS, MASUSE, MLA-IB. *Bk. rev.:* 20, length varies. *Aud.:* Ac.

This journal is published for the Central European History Society and offers articles, book reviews, and review essays by international scholars on a wide range of topics relating to Austria, Germany, and German-speaking regions of Central Europe. Both scholarly and refereed, this journal covers intellectual, economic, social, cultural, military, political, and diplomatic issues and topics within and related to Central Europe from medieval times to the present, and is recommended for academic research libraries. Currently, in a continued effort to be the primary source of debate and intellectual correspondence among Central Europe scholars, this journal is seeking contributions from both new and less well-represented fields and areas of interest, such as post-1989 history, gender studies, post-WWII histories, Hapsburg lands histories, and medieval topics. This journal is also available electronically, and the publisher's web site allows readers to browse by latest issue, back issues, most-downloaded, or most-cited filters, and articles can be downloaded or purchased depending on readers' membership or institutional affiliation status. The web site also offers sales information, a search widget, and related links, and it allows readers to sign up for content alerts. URL: http://journals.cambridge.org/action/displayJournal?jid=CCC

2155. *Contemporary French Civilization.* [ISSN: 0147-9156] 1976. 4x/yr. GBP 174 (print & online eds.)). Ed(s): Denis M Provencher. Liverpool University Press, 4 Cambridge St, Liverpool, L69 7ZU, United Kingdom; lup@liv.ac.uk; http://liverpooluniversitypress.co.uk/. Illus., adv. Refereed. *Indexed:* A22, AmHI, MLA-IB. *Bk. rev.:* Number and length vary. *Aud.:* Ac.

Contemporary French Civilization publishes book reviews, notes, essays, articles, and artistic and cultural information in both French and English on topics related to French culture, civilization, and language, and about the Francophone world in general. This refereed journal aims to serve as a forum of discussion for a diverse audience by providing broad, interdisciplinary content inclusive of all French and Francophone cultures worldwide. It is informative and insightful, and highlights include interviews with artists, scholars, and authors; research articles; annotated bibliographies; and book reviews. This journal is recommended for any academic library that supports French Studies, and is also available as an e-journal. The publisher's web site allows readers to search for content by subject, author, ISBN, or keyword, submit articles, acquire subscription information, sign up for TOC alerts, and download or purchase articles depending on membership or subscription status. URL: http://online.liverpooluniversitypress.co.uk/loi/cfc

Deutschland. See *Magazin-Deutschland.de* in International Magazines section.

2156. *Dutch Crossing: journal of low countries studies.* [ISSN: 0309-6564] 1977. 3x/yr. GBP 282 (print & online eds.)). Routledge, 4 Park Sq, Milton Park, Abingdon, OX14 4RN, United Kingdom; subscriptions@tandf.co.uk; http://www.tandfonline.com. Illus., index. Sample. Refereed. Reprint: PSC. *Indexed:* A01, A22, MLA-IB, P61. *Bk. rev.:* 12, length varies. *Aud.:* Ac.

This multidisciplinary, scholarly, and peer-reviewed journal is published on behalf of the Association for Low Countries Studies. Entries include research reports, book reviews, conference papers, and English translations of Dutch literary works, with a focus on the Dutch language, literature, history, and art of the Low Counties through all periods. Also covered are politics, Dutch as a foreign language, Flemish, Dutch and Afrikaans cultural studies, and transnational and intercultural studies. This journal strives to encourage scholarship among young and established researchers in order to "enhance the profile of Low Countries Studies and of Dutch and Flemish culture in the English-speaking world," and to act as an intellectual exchange for ideas such as Anglo–Dutch relations, Frisian culture, and landscape painting. Areas of topical coverage include Belgium, the Netherlands, and parts of the Americas, Southeast Asia, and Southern Africa, where Dutch has historically had an impact. All articles are written in English. *Dutch Crossing* is available electronically and in print, and is recommended for academic libraries that support research in European Studies and the Low Countries. The publisher's web site offers authors' resources, search functions, and news and alerts. URL: www.maneyonline.com/loi/dtc

The Economist. See Economics section.

2157. *Edinburgh Review.* Formerly (until 1985): *New Edinburgh Review.* [ISSN: 0267-6672] 1969. 3x/yr. GBP 35 (Individuals, GBP 20; GBP 7.99 per issue). Edinburgh Review, 22A Buccleuch Pl, Edinburgh, EH8 9LN, United Kingdom. Illus., adv. Refereed. Microform: PMC; PQC. *Indexed:* MLA-IB. *Bk. rev.:* Number and length vary. *Aud.:* Ga, Ac.

Founded in 1802 and considered the leading journal of ideas from Scotland, Edinburgh's oldest literary journal the *Edinburgh Review* became one of the nineteenth century's most influential British magazines, and is still beloved today. Publication ceased in 1929 but resumed in 1969 with a new title, *New Edinburgh Review,* only to return to its earlier title, *Edinburgh Review,* in 1985. Throughout the course of this history, the review has published the works, reviews, and critiques of such influential literary figures as Carlyle, Gladstone, Macaulay, and Scott, among many others. Balancing international coverage of intellectual debate with its focus on the Scottish perspective and mindset, *Edinburgh Review* offers reviews, poetry, and short fiction, and is considered to have contributed greatly to the development of modern standards of literary criticism and the development of the modern periodical. Online access to this periodical allows readers to browse extracts, subscribe, read featured articles, learn about upcoming events, and submit articles and reviews. Recommended for general and academic audiences. This periodical also offers a presence on Facebook and Twitter. URL: http://edinburgh-review.com

Elsevier. See International Magazines section.

L'Espresso. See International Magazines section.

2158. *L'Esprit Createur.* [ISSN: 0014-0767] 1961. q. USD 110. Ed(s): Maria Minich Brewer, Daniel Brewer. The Johns Hopkins University Press, 2715 N Charles St, Baltimore, MD 21218; http://www.press.jhu.edu. Illus., adv. Sample. Refereed. Reprint: PSC. *Indexed:* A22, AmHI, BRI, CBRI, E01, MLA-IB. *Bk. rev.:* Number and length vary. *Aud.:* Ac.

L'Esprit Createur is a scholarly, peer-reviewed journal that offers critical essays and reviews on Francophone literature, thought, and culture. This American publication, with articles in both English and French, "has been analyzing and documenting contemporary French and Francophone Studies for half a century." With a host of eminent past and present contributors representing a variety of critical approaches and methodologies, *L'Esprit Createur* examines such topics as culture, film, and literature, and ranks among the premier literary and critical publications of its kind. Also available electronically, this journal is highly recommended for all academic research libraries. Access, subscription, and submission information is available on the publisher's web site. URL: www.press.jhu.edu/journals/lesprit_createur/

2159. *European History Quarterly.* Formerly (until 1984): *European Studies Review.* [ISSN: 0265-6914] 1971. q. USD 1291 (print & online eds.)). Ed(s): Julian Swann. Sage Publications Ltd., 1 Oliver's Yard, 55 City Rd, London, EC1Y 1SP, United Kingdom; info@sagepub.com; https://www.sagepub.com/. Illus., index, adv. Sample. Refereed. Reprint: PSC. *Indexed:* A01, A22, AmHI, BRI, E01, IBSS, P61, SSA. *Bk. rev.:* 8-10, length varies. *Aud.:* Ac.

European History Quarterly is a peer-reviewed, scholarly journal published quarterly, with an "international reputation as an essential resource on European history." This title contains articles on a variety of topics associated with European history and political social and thought from the late Middle Ages to the present day, and submissions have been written by prominent scholars from across Europe and North America. Recently published topics have included titles such as "Worker Youth and Everyday Violence in the Post-Stalin Soviet Union (Tsipursky)" and "Becoming Dangerous: Everyday Violence in the Industrial Milieu of Late-Socialist Romania (Morar-Vulcu)," for example. Issues generally contain about six scholarly contributions and an extensive book review section, with occasional historiographical essays and feature review articles. This journal is recommended for all academic libraries, and is also available electronically. Podcasts, indexes, an RSS feed, e-mail alerts, and submission and subscription access can be found on the publisher's web site. URL: http://ehq.sagepub.com/

2160. *Eurozine: the netmagazine.* [ISSN: 1684-4637] 1998. irreg. Ed(s): Carl Henrik Fredriksson. eurozine, Rembrandtstr 31/10, Vienna, 1020, Austria. *Aud.:* Ga, Ac.

Eurozine is both a clearinghouse for European cultural journals and a "netmagazine," run by a nonprofit company and published with the support of the European Union. *Eurozine* is designed to function as an "independent cultural platform" whose purpose is to promote European journal publications; foster communication between countries, cultures, languages, and journals; and provide a critical space for transnational debate. This platform aims to spread and promote cultural, political, and philosophical thought between European languages "[b]y providing a Europe-wide overview of current themes and discussions," and offering "a rich source of information for an international readership," while facilitating "communication and exchange between the journals themselves." Linking "up more than 80 partner journals and just as many associated magazines and institutions from nearly all European countries," with articles translated into at least one major European language, *Eurozine* provides access to such titles as *Kritika & Kontext, Mittelweg36, Ord & Bild, Revista Critica, Samtiden, Transit,* and *Wespennest,* with original articles also offered. The site is well organized with all articles, including some from archival issues, searchable by keyword and able to be downloaded into html or pdf format. There are biographies of contributors and an impressive list of European cultural journals, with links to their web sites, in addition to headlines from the news, editorials, and a strong social media presence, including Twitter and Facebook presences, an RSS feed, and a blog. This netmagazine (and portal) is recommended for general or academic audiences that wish to stay abreast of the current cultural debate in Europe. URL: www.eurozine.com

L'Express. See International Magazines section.

2161. *Forum Italicum: a journal of Italian studies.* [ISSN: 0014-5858] 1967. s-a. USD 353 (print & online eds.)). Ed(s): Mario B Mignone. Sage Publications, Inc., 2455 Teller Rd, Thousand Oaks, CA 91320; info@sagepub.com; http://www.sagepub.com. Illus. Sample. Refereed. Reprint: PSC. *Indexed:* A22, BRI, MLA-IB. *Bk. rev.:* 15-20, length varies. *Aud.:* Ac.

Forum Italicum, published in the United States by the State University of New York at Stony Brook, is a journal of peer-reviewed, scholarly articles that focus on Italian Studies topics such as Italian culture, language, and literature, and how other countries interact with and relate to Italy and Italian culture. This title is intended as a meeting-place for students, critics, scholars, and teachers, and issues typically contain five or six scholarly articles in addition to notes, reviews, poetry, prose, and literary translations. Students and young scholars are encouraged to contribute. The publisher's web site offers a search function, e-mail alerts, subscription information, and back issues. This journal is also available electronically and is highly recommended for academic libraries that support Italian and European Studies. URL: http://foi.sagepub.com

2162. *France.* [ISSN: 0958-8213] 1990. m. GBP 23.99 domestic; GBP 38.70 in Europe; GBP 40.70 elsewhere. Ed(s): Carolyn Boyd. Archant Life Ltd., Archant House, 3 Oriel Rd, Cheltenham, GL50 1BB, United Kingdom; http://www.archantlife.co.uk. Illus., adv. *Aud.:* Ga.

France magazine is marketed to readers as "the next best thing to being there!" and strives to bring readers the "very best of France." Filled with glossy photos, articles about weekend getaways, a food and wine section, holiday destination ideas, articles about France's culture and history, and interviews with A-list French stars, this magazine is "the ultimate way to indulge your love of l'Hexagone between visits." Additional topics include insider tips for travelers, a monthly language section designed to help improve one's spoken French, and film reviews and interviews. The magazine's web site includes a number of useful links such as information about traveling to France, French real estate, French food, special offers and contests, access to the digital version of the magazine (and other French magazines), and a blog. Published for British Francophiles, the web site and magazine are nevertheless helpful for Americans who may wish to steep themselves in French (tourist) culture. Recommended for a general audience. URL: www.completefrance.com/magazines/france-magazine

2163. *French Historical Studies.* [ISSN: 0016-1071] 1958. q. USD 356. Ed(s): Laura Foxworth, Carol E. Harrison. Duke University Press, 905 W Main St, Durham, NC 27701; orders@dukeupress.edu; https://www.dukeupress.edu. Illus., index, adv. Refereed. Reprint: PSC. *Indexed:* A01, A22, AmHI, BRI, E01, MLA-IB. *Bk. rev.:* Essays. *Aud.:* Ac.

French Historical Studies, the official journal of the Society for French Historical Studies, is "the leading journal on the history of France," and publishes articles, commentaries, and research notes about French history from the Middles Ages to the present. This journal also offers a diverse format consisting of review essays, bilingual abstracts of the articles presented in each issue, special issues, forums for scholarly discussion and debate, and bibliographies of dissertations and recent French history article publications. Primarily of interest to French historians and scholars, this journal is recommended for academic libraries. Occasional special issues are supervised by guest editors, and the journal is also available electronically. The publisher's web site provides society news and links to special/back issues, submission and access information, and a link to the journal's own YouTube channel, where one can view related author and book videos. URL: https://www.dukeupress.edu/french-historical-studies

2164. *French History.* [ISSN: 0269-1191] 1987. q. EUR 499. Ed(s): Julian Wright. Oxford University Press, Great Clarendon St, Oxford, OX2 6DP, United Kingdom; onlinequeries.uk@oup.com; http://global.oup.com. Illus., adv. Sample. Refereed. Reprint: PSC. *Indexed:* A22, E01, P61. *Bk. rev.:* 20, length varies. *Aud.:* Ac.

French History is published on behalf of the U.K. Society for the Study of French History, and is a peer-reviewed journal that provides a "broad perspective on contemporary debates from an international range of scholars, and covers the entire chronological range of French history from the early Middle Ages to the twentieth century." The editorial board is composed of international scholars who support the journal's goal of offering an international forum for anyone interested in the latest research on French history. Issues contain research articles covering a range of French history-related topics across historical time periods and encompassing the arts and social sciences, and also "a book reviews section that is essential reference for any serious student of French history." The web site at Oxford University Press provides tables of contents and full text (for subscribers only) from the first volume (1987) to the present, a reader services section, links to free articles and prize information, links to related publications, and submission and subscription information. Recommended for academic libraries, this title is also available as an ejournal. URL: http://fh.oxfordjournals.org/

2165. *The French Review.* [ISSN: 0016-111X] 1927. q. Free to members; Non-members, USD 55. Ed(s): Edward Ousselin, Nathalie Degroult. American Association of Teachers of French, 302 N. Granite St, Marion, IL 62959-2346; aatf@frenchteachers.org; https://www.frenchteachers.org/hq/. Adv. Refereed. Microform: PMC; PQC. *Indexed:* A22, AmHI, BRI, CBRI, MLA-IB. *Bk. rev.:* 75. *Aud.:* Ac.

The *French Review* is the official journal of the American Association of Teachers of French (AATF), and is published four times a year. Each year approximately 50 articles and 300 reviews are published in this journal, in both French and English. According to the journal's web site, the *French Review* has "the largest circulation of any scholarly journal of French and Francophone studies in the world." Each issue contains articles and reviews on French and Francophone literature, linguistics, society and culture, cinema, technology, and pedagogy. There are occasional special issues that cover French-focused topics such as Quebec and French cinema, in addition to compilations of Ph.D. dissertation titles from graduate programs in North America, which are published in order to publicize the scope of scholarship taking place in the field. The web site is informational and contains tables of contents for issues dating back to 2005, society announcements, and a guide for authors, and is recommended for academic libraries. URL: http://frenchreview.frenchteachers.org/

2166. *German Life and Letters.* [ISSN: 0016-8777] 1936. q. GBP 638. Wiley-Blackwell Publishing Ltd., The Atrium, Southern Gate, Chichester, PO19 8QG, United Kingdom; cs-journals@wiley.com; http://onlinelibrary.wiley.com/. Illus., index, adv. Sample. Refereed. Reprint: PSC. *Indexed:* A01, A22, AmHI, E01, MLA-IB. *Aud.:* Ac.

German Life and Letters has long been considered a leading journal in British German Studies, offering a variety of English- and German-language "articles dealing with literary and non-literary concerns in the German-speaking world." This title covers "German thought and culture from the Middle Ages to the present," and topics include politics, social history, language, literature, and the visual arts, with an overall goal of providing an interdisciplinary and international forum for the scholarly analysis of German culture. Special thematic issues are published irregularly but cover interesting topics, such as "Flaschenpost: German Poetry and the Long Twentieth Century." In addition, occasional virtual issues are published. The journal's web site provides access to all articles, depending on institutional subscriptions; a special features section with virtual issues and content-alert sign-up information; and other general information about the journal. This journal is recommended for academic libraries that support research in German Studies, and is also available as an ejournal. URL: http://onlinelibrary.wiley.com/journal/10.1111/%28ISSN%291468-0483

2167. *The German Quarterly.* [ISSN: 0016-8831] 1928. q. GBP 210 (print & online eds.)). Ed(s): Robert E Norton. Wiley-Blackwell Publishing, Inc., 111 River St, Hoboken, NJ 07030; http://onlinelibrary.wiley.com. Index, adv. Sample. Refereed. Microform: PMC; PQC. Reprint: PSC. *Indexed:* A01, A22, AmHI, BRI, CBRI, E01, MLA-IB. *Bk. rev.:* 35, length varies. *Aud.:* Ac.

The German Quarterly is a refereed journal published on behalf of the American Association of Teachers of German (AATG), whose aim is to serve "as a forum for all sorts of scholarly debates-topical, ideological, methodological, [and] theoretical, as well as debates on recent developments in the profession." Along with scholarly articles on German culture, history, language, and literature throughout history, the journal provides special reports and extensive book reviews of academic publications, and encourages essays "addressing new theoretical or methodological approaches, recent developments in the field, and subjects that have recently been underrepresented," in addition to interdisciplinary and comparative articles relevant to German studies. The publisher's journal web site provides access to all back issues dependent on your institution's subscription, in addition to informational resources. The *German Quarterly* should be included in any academic library that supports German Studies, and is also available as an ejournal. URL: www.germanquarterly.aatg.org; or http://onlinelibrary.wiley.com/journal/10.1111/%28ISSN%291756-1183

2168. *German Studies Review.* [ISSN: 0149-7952] 1978. 3x/yr. USD 90. Ed(s): Sabine Hake. The Johns Hopkins University Press, 2715 N Charles St, Baltimore, MD 21218; http://www.press.jhu.edu. Illus., adv. Sample. Refereed. Reprint: PSC. *Indexed:* A01, A22, AmHI, BRI, IBSS, MLA-IB. *Bk. rev.:* 60. *Aud.:* Ac.

German Studies Review is the peer-reviewed, scholarly journal of the "German Studies Association (GSA), the world's largest academic association devoted to the interdisciplinary and multidisciplinary study of the German-speaking countries." This journal features articles on such topics as culture studies, history, literature, and politics relating primarily, though not exclusively, to German-speaking areas of Europe, including Germany, Austria, and Switzerland. Issues generally contain at least six articles and a large section (60+) of reviews of academic book publications. Recent issues have covered such topics as Krupp housing estates in the Ruhr Valley, and the popularity of German gangsta rap. This journal is also available electronically, and the publisher's journal web site includes tables of contents and abstracts for current issues, along with pricing, submission, subscription, and indexing/abstracting information. Recommended for academic libraries that support research in German Studies. URL: www.press.jhu.edu/journals/german_studies_review/; or https://www.thegsa.org/publications/gsr.html

2169. *The Germanic Review: literature, culture, theory.* [ISSN: 0016-8890] 1925. q. GBP 240 (print & online eds.)). Ed(s): Willi Goetschel. Taylor & Francis Inc., 711 3rd Ave, 8th Fl, New York, NY 10017; support@tandfonline.com; http://www.tandfonline.com. Illus., index, adv. Sample. Refereed. Microform: PQC. Reprint: PSC. *Indexed:* A01, A22, AmHI, BRI, E01, MLA-IB. *Bk. rev.:* 3-9, length varies. *Aud.:* Ac.

The Germanic Review is a refereed scholarly journal that features contributors from leading research institutes in the U.S., Canada, the U.K., France, Australia, and Germany, and offers "the best of international scholarship in German studies." Articles cover topics such as German culture, historical memory, identity, literature, and literary theory, as well as reviews of recent German Studies publications. Most articles are written in English, but German-language articles are occasionally published. Recent issues have discussed Werner Herzog, Walter Benjamin, and "the politics of German identity and historical memory." This journal is also available as an ejournal, and the publisher's journal web site includes access to articles depending on institutional subscription, a search feature that can filter by most-read and most-cited articles, and submission and subscription information. Published since 1925, *The Germanic Review* is an important title for libraries that support German Studies, and is recommended for academic libraries. URL: www.tandfonline.com/loi/vger20#.VZFnQ6PKI9k

Iceland Review. See International Magazines section.

2170. ***Irish University Review: a journal of irish studies.*** Formerly (until 1970): *University Review.* [ISSN: 0021-1427] 1954. s-a. GBP 62 (print & online eds.)). Ed(s): Emilie Pine. Edinburgh University Press Ltd., The Tun, Holyrood Rd, 12 (2f) Jackson's Entry, Edinburgh, EH8 8PJ, United Kingdom; journals@eup.ed.ac.uk; http://www.euppublishing.com. Illus., adv. Sample. Refereed. *Indexed:* A22, BRI, MLA-IB. *Bk. rev.:* 10, length varies. *Aud.:* Ac.

The *Irish University Review* was founded in 1970 at University College Dublin "as a journal of Irish literary criticism," and is affiliated with the International Association for the Study of Irish Literature (IASIL). It has since become the leading global Irish Literary Studies journal. With an emphasis on contemporary Irish literature, this refereed, scholarly, literary journal consists of literary essays, poetry, short fiction, a large section of book reviews, and interviews with authors, poets, and playwrights. The bi-annual issues are regularly devoted to Irish authors or themes, "particularly submissions which expand the range of authors and texts to receive critical treatment," and the book reviews enable readers to stay abreast of current Irish literary trends. This journal is recommended for academic libraries and is also available as an ejournal. The publisher's journal web site provides tables of contents for recent issues, submission and subscription information, links to most-downloaded articles, and a link where readers can sign up for table-of-contents e-mail alerts. URL: www.euppublishing.com/journal/iur

2171. ***Italica.*** Formerly (until 1926): *American Association of Teachers of Italian. Bulletin.* [ISSN: 0021-3020] 1924. q. Free to members. Ed(s): Michael Lettieri. American Association of Teachers of Italian (A A T I), c/o Colleen M. Ryan, Indiana University, Bloomington, IN 47405; aati@utoronto.ca; http://www.aati-online.org/. Adv. Refereed. Microform: PQC. *Indexed:* A22, BRI, MLA-IB. *Bk. rev.:* Number and length vary. *Aud.:* Ac.

The journal *Italica* publishes interdisciplinary and comparative studies-based scholarly articles on all aspects of Italian culture, including cinema, linguistics, literature, history, and politics, and is the official journal of the American Association of Teachers of Italian (AATI). Issues include "a section devoted to translations of Italian major works/authors, cultural debates, and interviews," and encourages and welcomes all theoretical perspectives and scholarly methods. Authors are generally from North America, as contributing preference is given to AATI members. The web site of the AATI provides a variety of information related to the teaching of Italian, and its section on *Italica* is mostly informational, with the tables of contents of some volumes available. Archival issues may be accessed through JSTOR. This journal is also available electronically, and is recommended for academic libraries. URL: www.aati-online.org/

2172. ***Journal of European Studies (Chalfont Saint Giles).*** [ISSN: 0047-2441] 1971. q. USD 1422 (print & online eds.)). Ed(s): John Flower. Sage Publications Ltd., 1 Oliver's Yard, 55 City Rd, London, EC1Y 1SP, United Kingdom; info@sagepub.com; https://www.sagepub.com/. Illus., index. Sample. Refereed. Microform: PQC. Reprint: PSC. *Indexed:* A01, A22, AmHI, BRI, E01, MLA-IB. *Bk. rev.:* 30, length varies. *Aud.:* Ac.

The *Journal of European Studies* is an interdisciplinary and peer-reviewed journal whose focus is on the "literature and cultural history of Europe since the Renaissance." Published quarterly since 1971, *JES* is led by an international editorial board, and publishes most articles in English, with occasional contributions in French or German, and provides review essays and notices that offer "a wide and informed coverage of many books that are published on European cultural themes." The web site at Sage Publications offers access to tables of contents for all issues, with full-text access provided to users with subscription access, in addition to an index of special issues, a note from the editor, and subscription and submission information. This journal is also available electronically, and is recommended for all research libraries. URL: http://jes.sagepub.com/

Knack. See International Magazines section.

2173. ***New German Critique.*** [ISSN: 0094-033X] 1973. 3x/yr. USD 315. Ed(s): Lara Kelingos, Andreas Huyssen. Duke University Press, 905 W Main St, Durham, NC 27701; orders@dukeupress.edu; https://www.dukeupress.edu. Illus., index, adv. Reprint: PSC. *Indexed:* A01, A22, AmHI, MLA-IB. *Aud.:* Ac.

The *New German Critique* is an interdisciplinary journal that covers twentieth and twenty-first century German Studies subjects, "including literature, mass culture, film, and other visual media film; literary theory and cultural studies; Holocaust studies; art and architecture; political and social theory; and philosophy." Issues are theme-oriented and generally include up to eight lengthy scholarly articles. Since its establishment in 1970, *New German Critique* has played a strong role in introducing readers in the U.S. to the Frankfurt School while acting as a forum for debate in the social sciences and humanities fields. This journal is available electronically, and the publisher's web site provides tables of contents for back issues as well as special issues, a robust search feature, an RSS feed, and subscription and submission information. This journal is highly recommended for all academic libraries, in particular those that support collections in contemporary criticism, philosophy, German Studies, and comparative literature. URL: http://ngc.dukejournals.org/

2174. ***Nineteenth Century French Studies.*** [ISSN: 0146-7891] 1972. s-a. USD 134. Ed(s): Seth Whidden. University of Nebraska Press, 1111 Lincoln Mall, Lincoln, NE 68588; journals@unl.edu; https://www.nebraskapress.unl.edu. Illus., index, adv. Refereed. *Indexed:* A01, A22, AmHI, BRI, E01, MLA-IB. *Bk. rev.:* 10, length varies. *Aud.:* Ac.

Nineteenth Century French Studies is an independent, peer-reviewed, scholarly journal that covers all aspects of nineteenth-century French literature and criticism. This journal examines new trends, publishes reviews of promising new research findings in a variety of related disciplines, and strives to acquaint readers with "professional developments in nineteenth-century French studies." This title is also available electronically, and the publisher's web site provides information about submissions, guidelines, and subscriptions, as well as access to an archive of abstracts of articles published since the journal's inception. The site also includes reviews and special projects sections and a search feature. The journal is available in full text online through Project Muse. A premier resource for nineteenth-century French literary scholarship, this journal is highly recommended for academic libraries that support research in French literature. URL: www.ncfs-journal.org/

Norseman. See *Norwegians Worldwide* in International Magazines section.

Le Point. See International Magazines section.

2175. ***Il Politico: rivista italiana di scienze politiche.*** Formerly (until 1941): *Annali di Scienze Politiche.* [ISSN: 0032-325X] 1928. 3x/yr. Rubbettino Editore, Viale Rosario Rubbettino 10, Soveria Mannelli, 88049, Italy; segreteria@rubettino.it; http://www.rubbettino.it. Illus., index, adv. Sample. *Indexed:* A22, BAS, IBSS, P61. *Aud.:* Ac.

Published in Italian and English as a continuation of *Annali di Scienze Politiche* (*Annals of Political Sciences*), *Il Politico* is generally recognized as one of the more important periodicals in the field of Italian Studies, with an emphasis on political theory. *Il Politico* is renowned for the quality of its articles, written by internationally renowned authors, and for its wealth of research notes and reviews. The essays include brief summaries in English. Its web site is in Italian and provides an archive going back to 1950, and a search function for issues and articles from 1996 to 2014. This journal is recommended for academic and research libraries that support Italian studies. URL: www-3.unipv.it/ilpolitico/

2176. *Revue des Deux Mondes: litterature, histoire, arts et sciences.* Former titles (until 1982): *Nouvelle Revue des Deux Mondes;* (until 1972): *Revue des Deux Mondes.* [ISSN: 0750-9278] 1829. 9x/yr. Individuals, EUR 89 print & online eds; Students, EUR 65 print & online eds. Societe de la Revue des Deux Mondes, 97 Rue de Lille, Paris, 75007, France. Illus., index, adv. Circ: 15000. Reprint: PSC. *Indexed:* A01, A22, BAS, MLA-IB. *Bk. rev.:* 2, length varies. *Aud.:* Ga, Ac.

The *Revue des Deux Mondes,* which translates into English as the *Review of Two Worlds,* was first published in 1829 with the objective of welcoming "ideas related to France and the world emanating from other European countries," and promoting the universal right to vote. Truly multidisciplinary and with a focus on promoting exchanges of ideas between Europe, the Americas, and Asia, this title covers a variety of world issues such as the promotion of literary and artistic creations, economics, important political debates, travel tales, social progress, and science. Providing commentary and analysis on world events, the journal has accumulated an impressive list of contributors over the years, including Balzac, Baudelaire, Hugo, Fenimore Cooper, Heine, and Tocqueville. "Following the 20th century, with all its forms of totalitarianism, there is a felt need for places dedicated to freedom of thought. The *Revue des Deux Mondes* offers just that." The web site is in French, though some parts can be translated into English, and is largely informational with accessible archives, news, boutique, and theme sections. The *Revue des Deux Mondes* is one of few publications worldwide that may rightly claim to be a cultural institution, and is thus an essential title for large public libraries and research libraries. URL: www.revuedesdeuxmondes.fr/

2177. *Rivista di Letterature Moderne e Comparate.* Formerly (until 1954): *Rivista di Letterature Moderne.* [ISSN: 0391-2108] 1946. q. Ed(s): A Pizzorusso. Pacini Editore SpA, Via A Gherardesca 1, Ospedaletto, 56121, Italy; pacini.editore@pacinieditore.it; http://www.pacinimedicina.it. Illus., adv. Sample. *Indexed:* A22, MLA-IB. *Bk. rev.:* 13, length varies. *Aud.:* Ac.

Established by Carlo Pellegrini and Vittorio Santoli in 1946, *Rivista di Letterature Moderne e Comparate,* which translates into English as *The Journal of Modern Comparative Literature,* is an academic journal whose scope covers the entire spectrum of Western literature since the Renaissance. The focus of this journal is to analyze literary texts from a comparative perspective, while offering a forum for cultural debate between Italian and international scholars. Articles are written in English, French, German, and Italian, and each issue contains about six scholarly articles and numerous book reviews that cover cultural topics with a focus on European works, traditions, and perspectives. Every December issue contains an index for the entire previous year. The publisher's journal web site is in Italian and is mainly informational, with links to related journals and items of interest. This journal is recommended for academic libraries that support programs in comparative literature and Italian Studies. URL: www.pacinieditore.it/?p=1295

2178. *Scandinavian Journal of History.* Incorporates (1955-1980): *Excerpta Historica Nordica.* [ISSN: 0346-8755] 1976. 5x/yr. GBP 411 (print & online eds.)). Ed(s): Guomundur Halfdanarson. Routledge, 4 Park Sq, Milton Park, Abingdon, OX14 4RN, United Kingdom; subscriptions@tandf.co.uk; http://www.tandfonline.com. Illus., adv. Sample. Refereed. Reprint: PSC. *Indexed:* A01, A22, AmHI, E01, IBSS. *Bk. rev.:* Number and length vary. *Aud.:* Ac.

The *Scandinavian Journal of History* is published for the Historical Associations of Denmark, Finland, Iceland, Norway, and Sweden, and the Scandinavian subcommittees of the International Committee of Historical Sciences. The journal "presents articles on Scandinavian history and review essays surveying themes in recent Scandinavian historical research," and although most authors are Scandinavian, all articles and reviews are published in English. Long-term and short-term regional developments in culture and society, and "perspectives of national historical particularities" are a primary focus, and articles comparing Scandinavian phenomena, culture, and processes to those in other parts of Europe and the world are of particular interest. This journal also contains a books-reviewed section at the back of each issue, and welcomes polemical communications and review essay proposals. Available as an ejournal as well as in print, this journal is recommended for academic libraries that support Scandinavian Studies. The publisher's journal web site provides abstracts and tables of contents, submission and subscription information, most-read and most-cited article links, and other general publication news. URL: www.tandfonline.com/loi/shis

2179. *Scandinavian Review.* Formerly (until 1975): *The American-Scandinavian Review.* [ISSN: 0098-857X] 1913. 3x/yr. Free to members. American-Scandinavian Foundation, 58 Park Ave, 38th St, New York, NY 10016; info@amscan.org; http://www.amscan.org/. Illus., adv. Sample. *Indexed:* A01, A22, ENW, MLA-IB. *Bk. rev.:* 2-5, 450 words. *Aud.:* Hs, Ga, Ac.

The *Scandinavian Review* is published by the American Scandinavian Foundation (ASF), whose mission is to promote an "international understanding through educational and cultural exchange between the United States and Denmark, Finland, Iceland, Norway, and Sweden." The magazine is issued to members of ASF, but is also available by subscription and in ejournal format. This magazine covers all aspects of contemporary life in Scandinavia, with an "emphasis on areas in which Scandinavian achievement is renowned: art and design, industrial development, commercial, political, economic and social innovation." The primary goal is ultimately to provide information, news, and insights about Scandinavia that are rarely read about or seen in American media, in order to help make Scandinavia better known and understood. Regular features include articles on particular themes or persons, cultural and historical informational articles, and reviews of Nordic books. Submissions are authored by leading journalists and writers from Scandinavia, North America, and other European countries, and subscription information and samples of articles can be found on the ASF web site. Because this magazine offers information rarely found in American media about Nordic countries and Scandinavian culture, it would be an excellent addition to any collection that supports European Studies. URL: www.amscan.org

Der Spiegel. See International Magazines section.

Suomen Kuvalehti. See International Magazines section.

2180. *Yale French Studies.* [ISSN: 0044-0078] 1948. s-a. Ed(s): Alyson Waters. Yale University Press, PO Box 209040, New Haven, CT 06520; customer.care@triliteral.org; http://yalepress.yale.edu/home.asp. Illus., adv. Microform: PQC. Reprint: PSC. *Indexed:* A01, A22, AmHI, MLA-IB. *Aud.:* Ac.

Yale French Studies is one of the premier journals on French literature, thought, and civilization in the English language, and is "the oldest English-language journal in the United States devoted to French and Francophone literature and culture." Each volume is distinct and focuses on a single theme or author, while also being conceived and written by a guest editor(s). Although essays are mostly contributed by North American scholars, articles by the most well-known contemporary French authors and critics have also been included. This journal, which is also available as an ejournal, provides a multidisciplinary approach to literature that includes French-speaking cultures outside of France, and has covered such topics as "Crime Fiction; Surrealism; Contemporary Writing for the Stage; and Memory in Postwar French and Francophone Culture." Full-text articles are accessible through JSTOR with a two-year wall, and the publisher's journal web site is mainly informational. This journal is necessary for any academic library that supports the study of French culture. URL: http://french.yale.edu/yale-french-studies

Newspapers

Newspapers are popular among Europeans. To stay competitive in an electronic-delivery news market that is evolving, rapidly growing, and 24/7 online, newspaper publishers have created user-friendly and continuously updated web versions of their products, while also adding more color and innovative designs to their print editions. This subsection may be brief, but it presents two newspapers whose scope is international; both of them boast high local and expatriate European readership, and both are globally known and popular, while also offering strong and trusted European reporting and perspectives.

See also the "Newspapers" section, and check the index for specific titles not included here.

The Guardian. See Newspapers/General section.

2181. *The Irish Times (Special Edition).* Incorporates (19??-2003): *The Irish Times (City Edition);* Supersedes in part (in 19??): *The Irish Times.* [ISSN: 1393-3515] 1859. d. EUR 2 newsstand/cover; GBP 1.25 newsstand/cover in Northern Ireland. Irish Times Ltd., 24-28 Tara St, PO Box 74, Dublin, 2, Ireland; enquiries@irishtimes.com. Illus., adv. Microform: PQC. *Aud.:* Ga, Ac.

Published since 1859, *The Irish Times* established itself as Ireland's premier independent newspaper in 1974 when it was transferred from private ownership to ownership by the charitable Irish Times Trust, which was created to keep the newspaper free "from any form of personal or party, political, commercial, religious or other sectional control." Correspondents report from all over the world, with the paper covering national and international news, cultural issues, economics, politics, technology, sports, the arts, and any other issue of general interest. The paper's companion web site provides access to selected articles in full text, blogs, editorials, social media links, podcasts, videos, and galleries. This newspaper is recommended for research and large public libraries or those catering to a large Irish community. URL: www.irishtimes.com

2182. *The New York Times (International Edition): the global edition of the New York Times.* Former titles (until 2016): *International New York Times;* (until 2013): *International Herald Tribune.* [ISSN: 2474-7149] 1967. 6x/w. International New York Times, 6 bis, rue des Graviers, Neuilly-sur-Seine, 92521, France. Illus. Microform: PQC. *Indexed:* B03, BRI. *Aud.:* Ga, Ac.

The *International New York Times* is an English-language international newspaper that is printed at 38 sites around the world, is for sale in 160 countries and territories, and combines "the resources of its own correspondents with those of the *New York Times*." Now part of the New York Times Company, this newspaper has been based in Paris since 1887, and was published as the *International Herald Tribune* from 1967 until 2013. Edited from offices in Hong Kong, London, New York, and Paris, the newspaper aims to cover and report on all kinds of relevant cultural, political, social, artistic, and general-interest international journalism stories. The well-organized web site version presents the news with different emphases depending on the selected region of interest, and provides blog entries, editorials, puzzles, weather forecasts, and classifieds, in addition to social media links and interactive videos and newsfeeds. The world's most international paper, the *International New York Times* presents a unique summary of world news. Recommended for general-reader audiences. URL: http://international.nytimes.com/

TLS: the Times literary supplement. See Books and Book Reviews section.

■ FAMILY

See also Lesbian, Gay, Bisexual, and Transgender; Marriage and Divorce; Parenting; Psychology; and Sociology and Social Work sections.

Erin K. McCaffrey, Digital Initiatives & Preservation Librarian, Regis University, 3333 Regis Blvd., D-20, Denver, CO 80221; emccaffr@regis.edu

Introduction

The current family studies literature presents a broad portrayal of what constitutes "family"; it is tough to define a single kind of family. The literature addresses parent-child relationships, family therapy processes, multigenerational families, gender fluidity, military families, LGBTQ families, couple therapy, substance abuse, gender issues, cross-cultural examinations of the family, finances and the family, family caregivers, and family violence. Family therapy and treatment, as well as family therapy training and supervision, continue to receive attention. Here, periodicals that address the broad definition of the contemporary family, as well as family studies and family therapy, are the focus.

The *America's Children: Key National Indicators of Well-Being, 2017* report on ChildStats.gov indicates a continual shift over time in family composition. Single-parent households are more commonplace and the percentage of children living with two married parents has decreased. The percentage of children who had at least one parent working year round remained stable. A variety of intimate and partner relationship structures represent the modern family, in addition to traditional representations of the family. According to the Pew Research Center report *7 facts about U.S. moms* (May 10, 2018), both motherhood and family size are increasing. Mothers and fathers are spending more time on child care. *8 facts about love and marriage in America* (Pew Research Center, February 13, 2018) reports increased public support for same-sex marriage, as well as an increase in intermarriage. The number of American adults cohabiting also continues to increase as does the share of unmarried parents that are cohabiting.

Family studies periodicals in the scholarly category are devoting greater coverage to outside influences on the family. Research on contemporary LGBTQ families continues to increase and is reflected in the titles presented here. Reflective of current population characteristics, there has also been an increase in content addressing multigenerational families, military deployment and its effects on the family, race and ethnicity, and economic factors and their impact on families. Of the scholarly journals represented here, content ranges from theory and research to practice and application. The popular magazines in family studies concentrate on practical self-help for families. Many of the periodicals in this category offer table of contents information and select full text on their websites.

Periodicals related to family and marriage are included in other sections of this volume, such as "Gender Studies," "Gay, Lesbian, Bisexual, and Transgender," "Marriage and Divorce," "Parenting," "Psychology," and "Sociology and Social Work."

Basic Periodicals

Ac: *Family Process, Family Relations, Journal of Comparative Family Studies, Journal of Family Issues, Journal of Family Psychology;* Sa: *Journal of Marital and Family Therapy.*

Basic Abstracts and Indexes

Family Studies Abstracts, PsycINFO, Social Sciences Citation Index, Social Work Abstracts, Sociological Abstracts.

2183. *The American Journal of Family Therapy.* Former titles (until 1979): *International Journal of Family Counseling;* (until 1977): *Journal of Family Counseling.* [ISSN: 0192-6187] 1973. 5x/yr. GBP 359 (print & online eds.)). Ed(s): Len Sperry, Elizabeth Kelsey. Routledge, 530 Walnut St, Ste 850, Philadelphia, PA 19106; enquiries@tandfonline.com; http://www.tandfonline.com. Illus., index, adv. Sample. Refereed. Vol. ends: Winter. Microform: PQC. Reprint: PSC. *Indexed:* A01, A22, BRI, E01, SSA. *Bk. rev.:* 0-4, 600-1,200 words. *Aud.:* Ac, Sa.

The *American Journal of Family Therapy* intends to be "the incisive, authoritative, independent voice" in family therapy and publishes five issues per year. The journal is interdisciplinary in scope and its readership includes marriage and family therapists, counselors, allied health practitioners, clinical social workers, psychiatrists, psychologists, physicians, nurses, and clergy. Book and media reviews are regularly included. Recent topics represent the changing field of family therapy and encompass the impacts of unplugging from technology, correlations between frequency of family mealtimes and family communication, body dissatisfaction and mental health across ethnic/racial groups, and an introduction to global family therapy. This journal is highly recommended for academic libraries seeking more than one scholarly family therapy journal.

2184. *Child & Family Behavior Therapy.* Formerly (until 1982): *Child Behavior Therapy.* [ISSN: 0731-7107] 1978. q. GBP 1149 (print & online eds.)). Ed(s): Charles Diament. Routledge, 530 Walnut St, Ste 850, Philadelphia, PA 19106; enquiries@tandfonline.com; http://www.tandfonline.com. Illus., adv. Sample. Refereed. Circ: 387 Paid. Vol. ends: No. 4. Microform: PQC. Reprint: PSC. *Indexed:* A01, A22, E01, ERIC, SSA. *Bk. rev.:* 1-4, 600-2,200 words. *Aud.:* Ac, Sa.

Child & Family Behavior Therapy is intended for family therapists, counselors, child psychologists, teachers, social workers, researchers, and others interested in utilizing behavior therapy techniques when working with difficult children and adolescents. Published quarterly, each issue of this peer-reviewed journal contains three to four articles, as well as occasional case studies and brief reports. Researchers will find the considerable book reviews helpful. Articles are lengthy and scientific, yet practical in approach, and include original research, clinical applications, and case studies. Recent articles include "Reaching Latino Families Through Pediatric Primary Care: Outcomes of the CANNE Parent Training Program," "Efficacy of Parent-Child Interaction Therapy with Parents with Intellectual Disability," "Deconstructing the Time-Out: What Do Mothers Understand About a Common Disciplinary Procedure?" and "Program for the Education and Enrichment of Relational Skills: Parental Outcomes With an ADHD Sample." Recommended for academic libraries.

Child & Family Social Work. See Sociology and Social Work/Social Work and Social Welfare section.

2185. *Contemporary Family Therapy: an international journal.* Formerly (until 1986): *International Journal of Family Therapy.* [ISSN: 0892-2764] 1979. q. EUR 1180 (print & online eds.)). Ed(s): Russell Crane. Springer New York LLC, 233 Spring St, New York, NY 10013; customerservice@springer.com; http://www.springer.com. Adv. Refereed. Reprint: PSC. *Indexed:* A01, A22, ASSIA, BRI, E01, SSA. *Aud.:* Ac.

Contemporary Family Therapy offers current developments in family therapy practice, theory, and research. The interactions among family systems, society, and individuals are examined, investigating fundamental factors such as family value systems, ethnicity, race, religious background, and social class. Recent topics include promoting marriage and family therapy master's programs to potential applicants, implementing family based music interventions in family therapy, adolescent mothers in foster care, infidelity and attachment, and video game therapy. Recent special issues focus on virtual relationships and systemic practices in the digital era. Published quarterly and international in scope, the editorial board includes broad geographic representation and international advisory editors. This journal is recommended for academic libraries supporting family therapy and sociology programs.

2186. *Couple & Family Psychology: Research and Practice.* [ISSN: 2160-4096] 2012. q. USD 656 (Individuals, USD 151; Members, USD 82). Ed(s): Thomas Sexton. American Psychological Association, 750 First St, NE, Washington, DC 20002; journals@apa.org; http://www.apa.org. Adv. Sample. Refereed. Circ: 900. *Aud.:* Ac.

Couple and Family Psychology: Research and Practice is the official journal of the Society for Family Psychology (APA Division 43) and its first issue was published in 2012. The journal publishes scholarly articles that address both "the science and practice of working with individuals, couples and families from a family systems perspective in general." Many issues focus on specialty themes around emerging issues in the field. "Distant horizons: Marital expectations may be dampened by economic circumstances," "A review of the effects of parental PTSD: A focus on military children," "The mediating effects of stress on the relationship between mindfulness and parental responsiveness," and "Family skills: A naturalistic pilot study of a family-oriented dialectical behavior therapy program" are some recent articles. A special section on "Parenting and Step-Parenting" was published in 2017. Recommended for academic libraries.

2187. *Exceptional Parent (Online).* [ISSN: 2373-2881] 2009. m. Ed(s): Rick Rader, Vanessa B Ira. EP World, Inc., 6 Pickwick Ln, Woodcliff Lake, NJ 07677; HMaher@eparent.com; http://www.eparent.com/. Adv. *Bk. rev.:* Number and length vary. *Aud.:* Ga, Sa.

Exceptional Parent focuses on making life easier for those with disabilities, serving individuals with disabilities as well as their families and caregivers, in addition to physicians, educators, and therapists. Informative articles cover themes related to mobility, diet and nutrition, financial planning, and schools, camps, and residences. Recent articles address aging out of the autism system, caring for a child with a feeding tube, youth empowerment groups and self-advocacy, and housing for loved ones with psychiatric disabilities. Book reviews are also included. In addition, *Exceptional Parent* publishes an annual resource guide for navigating special needs resources and additional news and resources are available on its web site. It is published in a digital format. Recommended for large public libraries. URL: www.eparent.com/

Families in Society. See Sociology and Social Work/Social Work and Social Welfare section.

2188. *Family & Consumer Sciences Research Journal.* Formerly (until 1994): *Home Economics Research Journal;* Which incorporates (1962-1991): *Titles of Dissertations and Theses Completed in Home Economics.* [ISSN: 1077-727X] 1972. q. GBP 597. Ed(s): Sharon A DeVaney. John Wiley & Sons, Inc., 111 River St, Hoboken, NJ 07030; cs-journals@wiley.com; http://onlinelibrary.wiley.com. Illus., adv. Refereed. Microform: PQC. Reprint: PSC. *Indexed:* A&ATA, A22, Agr, B01, BRI, E01. *Aud.:* Ac.

An official publication of the American Association of Family and Consumer Sciences, *Family & Consumer Sciences Research Journal* presents theory, research, and philosophy of family and consumer sciences. Published quarterly, the journal provides scholarly peer-reviewed articles, as well as specialized research and occasional theme issues. Research areas include family economics and management, child and family studies, education, human development, and teacher education. Recent articles include "Continued Barriers Affecting Hispanic Families' Dietary Patterns," "Training Younger Volunteers to Promote Technology Use Among Older Adults," "Age Differences in the Effects of Frugality and Materialism on Subjective Well-Being in Korea," "A Qualitative Evaluation of a Fitness and Nutrition-Focused Wellness Program," and "The Examination of Psychological Factors and Social Norms Affecting Body Satisfaction and Self-Esteem for College Students." The journal also publishes virtual issues, highlighting a selection of articles on a particular topic from prior issues. Content is aimed at professionals, scholars, researchers, and students of family and consumer sciences. Recommended for academic libraries.

The Family Handyman. See Do-It-Yourself/Makers section.

2189. *The Family Journal: counseling and therapy for couples and families.* [ISSN: 1066-4807] 1993. q. USD 1315 (print & online eds.)). Ed(s): Stephen Southern. Sage Publications, Inc., 2455 Teller Rd, Thousand Oaks, CA 91320; info@sagepub.com; http://www.sagepub.com. Adv. Sample. Refereed. Reprint: PSC. *Indexed:* A01, A22, ASSIA, CJPI, E01, ERIC, SSA. *Bk. rev.:* Number and length vary. *Aud.:* Ac, Sa.

The Family Journal: Counseling and Therapy for Couples and Families is the official journal of the International Association of Marriage and Family Counselors. The journal presents an assortment of practice, research, and theory in each issue and this blend of coverage, from a family systems perspective, serves practitioners, educators, and researchers involved with couple and family counseling and therapy. In addition to articles, regular sections include ethics, sex therapy, counselor training, techniques to share, case consultation, literature reviews, and book reviews, as well as the student contribution section. Interviews with leaders in family therapy are also published here. "Predictive Associations Between Family System Characteristics and Emergent Protective Factors," "Examination of Relational Resilience With Couple Burnout and Spousal Support in Families with a Disabled Child," "When Family Gets in the Way of Recovery: Motivational Interviewing with Families," and "A Family Systems Approach to the Understanding and Treatment of Internet Gaming Disorder" are some recent features. A recent special issue focused on Asian and intercultural influences. Recommended for academic libraries.

2190. *Family Process.* [ISSN: 0014-7370] 1962. q. GBP 612 (print & online eds.)). Ed(s): Jay Lebow. Wiley-Blackwell Publishing, Inc., 350 Main St, Malden, MA 02148; http://onlinelibrary.wiley.com. Illus., index, adv. Sample. Refereed. Vol. ends: Dec. Reprint: PSC. *Indexed:* A01, A22, E01, SSA. *Aud.:* Ac, Sa.

Family Process began publication when the field of family therapy was in its infancy. A major resource for more than 55 years and widely indexed, mental health and social service professionals will find research and clinical ideas on a wide range of psychological and behavioral problems. The journal publishes original research articles on topics related to couples, families, treatment, clinical practice, parenting, discursive analysis, families and psychopathology, supervision, culture in family intervention, couple and family intervention, relationship education, mentalizing family violence, and autoethnographic exploration. Recent special sections focus on step-families and family resilience, while a special issue addresses empirically supported treatments in couple and family therapy. This journal is highly recommended for academic libraries that support family therapy, social work, psychiatry, and psychology programs.

2191. ***Family Relations: interdisciplinary journal of applied family studies.*** Former titles (until 1980): *Family Coordinator;* (until 1968): *Family Life Coordinator;* (until 1959): *The Coordinator.* [ISSN: 0197-6664] 1952. 5x/yr. USD 1353 (print or online ed.) Individuals, USD 161 (print & online eds.)). Ed(s): Jason Hans. Wiley-Blackwell Publishing, Inc., 350 Main St, Malden, MA 02148; http://onlinelibrary.wiley.com. Illus., index, adv. Sample. Refereed. Microform: PQC. Reprint: PSC. *Indexed:* A01, A22, AgeL, Agr, BRI, CBRI, Chicano, E01, ERIC, IBSS, SSA. *Bk. rev.:* 7-18, 500-800 words. *Aud.:* Ac, Sa.

Family Relations, one of three journals published by the National Council on Family Relations (NCFR), publishes empirical studies, conceptual analysis, and literature reviews emphasizing "family research with implications for intervention, education, and public policy." It is an applied scholarly journal, focusing on diverse families and family issues. Articles are interdisciplinary in scope and focus on a wide range of family issues, including parent-child engagement and socialization, vulnerable individuals and circumstances, couples, at-risk families, parenting, romantic and marital relations, family stress, couples and money, and family systems. Recent special issues address intersectional variations in the experiences of queer families, translational family science, and feminist framings of sexual violence on college campuses. Readers are scholars and practitioners, including researchers, marriage and family therapists, educators, and family practitioners. NCFR members can access full-text articles through the NCFR web site. *Family Relations* is an excellent resource that is routinely cited. It is highly recommended for academic libraries with programs addressing psychology, family studies and family research, or social work.

FamilyFun. See Parenting section.

2192. ***Journal of Child and Family Studies.*** [ISSN: 1062-1024] 1992. m. EUR 2038 (print & online eds.)). Ed(s): Nirbhay N Singh. Springer New York LLC, 233 Spring St, New York, NY 10013; customerservice@springer.com; http://www.springer.com. Adv. Refereed. Reprint: PSC. *Indexed:* A01, A22, ASSIA, BRI, C45, CJPI, E01, ERIC, IBSS, SSA. *Bk. rev.:* Number and length vary. *Aud.:* Ac, Sa.

The *Journal of Child and Family Studies* addresses all aspects of emotional disorders pertaining to children and adolescents, including diagnosis, rehabilitation, treatment, prevention, and their effects on families. Book reviews are included. International in scope, healthcare practitioners and clinicians will find the basic and applied research, policy issues, and program evaluation useful. Recent articles include "How do Relationship Stability and Quality Affect Wellbeing?: Romantic Relationship Trajectories, Depressive Symptoms, and Life Satisfaction across 30 Years," "Parental Health and Children's Functioning in Immigrant Families: Family Roles and Perceived Treatment at School," "Parents' Understanding of Adopted Children's Ways of Being, Belonging, and Becoming," "The Longitudinal Impact of a Family-Based Communication Intervention on Observational and Self-Reports of Sexual Communication," "When and How Do Race/Ethnicity Relate to Dysfunctional Discipline Practices?" and "Exhausted Parents: Sociodemographic, Child-Related, Parent-Related, Parenting and Family-Functioning Correlates of Parental Burnout." This journal is recommended for academic libraries, particularly those that support programs related to child and adolescent mental health.

2193. ***Journal of Comparative Family Studies.*** [ISSN: 0047-2328] 1970. bi-m. USD 525 (Individuals, USD 275). Ed(s): George Kurian, James White. University of Calgary, Department of Sociology, 2500 University Dr N W, Calgary, AB T2N 1N4, Canada; http://soci.ucalgary.ca/. Illus., index, adv. Refereed. Vol. ends: No. 4. Microform: PQC. *Indexed:* A01, A22, BAS, BRI, C37, CJPI, Chicano, IBSS, SSA. *Bk. rev.:* 0-10, 400-1,300. *Aud.:* Ac.

Aimed at family counselors, social psychologists, anthropologists, and sociologists, the *Journal of Comparative Family Studies* "provides a unique cross-cultural perspective on the study of the family." The editorial board and authors are international in representation and abstracts are provided in English, French, and Spanish. Recent articles include "Context, Opportunity, and Demands: Satisfaction with Work-Life Balance in 26 Countries," "Positive Parenting and Parenting Stress Among Working Mothers in Finland, the UK and the Netherlands: Do Working Time Patterns Matter?" " A Cross-Cultural Mate Selection Study of Chinese and U.S. Men and Women," and "Understanding Happiness and Psychological Wellbeing Among Young Married Women in Rural India." The journal publishes articles, book reviews, and research notes, as well as periodic special issues on selected themes, such as families, citizenship, and human rights in a global era. Highly recommended for academic libraries that serve social psychology, sociology, multicultural studies, or anthropology programs.

Journal of Divorce & Remarriage. See Marriage and Divorce section.

2194. ***Journal of Family and Economic Issues.*** Former titles (until 1991): *Lifestyles;* (until 1984): *Alternative Lifestyles.* [ISSN: 1058-0476] 1978. q. EUR 1258 (print & online eds.)). Ed(s): Elizabeth M Dolan. Springer New York LLC, 233 Spring St, New York, NY 10013; customerservice@springer.com; http://www.springer.com. Illus., adv. Refereed. Vol. ends: Winter. Reprint: PSC. *Indexed:* A22, Agr, BRI, CJPI, E01, EconLit, IBSS, SSA. *Bk. rev.:* Number and length vary. *Aud.:* Ac, Sa.

The *Journal of Family and Economic Issues* presents interdisciplinary research, integrative theoretical articles, and critical reviews addressing the family and its economic environment. International in scope, articles investigate family economic issues in developing and transition economies. Book reviews are included. The journal publishes occasional special sections or issues, recently covering ethnic minorities in America. Current topics include financial hardship on single parents, multigenerational regrets on teaching children about money, effects of children's health on mothers' employment, undergraduate student mothers' experiences, cohabitation transitions among low-income parents, college students financial stress, money matters in military couples' marriages, intergenerational transmission of attitudes, and inheritances and bequest planning. Many articles explore the relationship between work and family life and family financial management. Recommended for academic libraries.

2195. ***Journal of Family Communication.*** [ISSN: 1526-7431] 2001. q. GBP 462 (print & online eds.)). Ed(s): Jordan Soliz. Routledge, 530 Walnut St, Ste 850, Philadelphia, PA 19106; enquiries@tandfonline.com; http://www.tandfonline.com. Adv. Sample. Refereed. Reprint: PSC. *Indexed:* A01, A22, E01. *Aud.:* Ac..

The *Journal of Family Communication* examines all aspects of communication in the family. These aspects include "the intersection between families, communication, and social systems, such as mass media, education, health care, and law & policy." The journal presents articles related to family communication pedagogy and applied family communication, empirical reports, and theoretical and review essays. Special issues are occasionally published such as "A Family Communication Perspective on Substance Use Prevention, Intervention, and Coping." Current articles address topics around positive adult stepchild-stepparent relationships, birth family relationships in open adoption, ethnic-racial inclusion and global diversity in family communication, transracial families, refugee parents' communication and relations with their children, and communication within family businesses. The journal's readership includes family therapists, counselors, communication researchers, social psychologists, and sociologists. Recommended for academic libraries.

2196. *Journal of Family History: studies in family, kinship, gender, and demography.* Supersedes in part (in 1976): *The Family in Historical Perspective.* [ISSN: 0363-1990] 1972. q. USD 1309 (print & online eds.)). Ed(s): Roderick Phillips. Sage Publications, Inc., 2455 Teller Rd, Thousand Oaks, CA 91320; info@sagepub.com; http://www.sagepub.com. Illus., index, adv. Sample. Refereed. Vol. ends: Oct. Reprint: PSC. *Indexed:* A01, A22, AmHI, BRI, E01, IBSS, SSA. *Bk. rev.:* 4-8, 800-1,200 words. *Aud.:* Ac.

Interdisciplinary in scope and published in association with the National Council on Family Relations, this journal publishes contributions representing the international perspective of historically based research on family, kinship, and population. Scholarly research articles present viewpoints in relation to culture, gender, race, class, and sexuality. Recent articles include "The Ties That Bind: Materiality, Identity, and the Life Course in the 'Things' Families Keep," "The Battle for Divorce in Italy and Opposition from the Catholic World (1861-1974)," "Existential Perspective of Biography-related Reflection in the Intergenerational Narrative Messages," and "Exploring the Challenges of Divorce on Saudi Women." "Contemporary Godparenthood in Central and Eastern Europe" is the theme of a special issue published in 2018. Review essays, debates, book reviews, research notes, and thematic symposia are regular features. Recommended for academic libraries.

2197. *Journal of Family Issues.* [ISSN: 0192-513X] 1980. 16x/yr. USD 2684 (print & online eds.)). Ed(s): Constance Shehan. Sage Publications, Inc., 2455 Teller Rd, Thousand Oaks, CA 91320; info@sagepub.com; http://www.sagepub.com. Illus., index, adv. Sample. Refereed. Vol. ends: Nov. Microform: WSH; PMC. Reprint: PSC. *Indexed:* A01, A22, Agr, Chicano, E01, ERIC, SSA. *Aud.:* Ac, Sa.

Published 16 times per year, the *Journal of Family Issues* publishes current research, analyses, and theory from an interdisciplinary perspective, exploring the institutional and social forces influencing marriage and families today. Articles and advocacy pieces represent any topic related to modern family issues and marriage. Recent articles address ultraorthodox Jewish fathers in Israel, sibling relationship in foster care, employment for mothers of children with disabilities, being a parent to an adult child with drug problems, child marriage in Zimbabwe, parent-adolescent closeness, religion and relationships, life satisfaction and relationship dynamics in same-sex and mixed-sex couples in the Netherlands, and meanings of wifehood in a postfeminist era. The journal published several special collections of articles in 2017 on topics including cohabitation, fathers and fathering, mothers and mothering, family relationships and influences, divorce, work and family, and economic influences on family life, among others. This scholarly journal is highly recommended for academic libraries.

2198. *Journal of Family Psychology.* [ISSN: 0893-3200] 1987. 8x/yr. USD 935 (Individuals, USD 271; Members, USD 131). Ed(s): Barbara H. Fiese. American Psychological Association, 750 First St, NE, Washington, DC 20002; journals@apa.org; http://www.apa.org. Illus., index, adv. Sample. Refereed. Circ: 400. Vol. ends: Feb. Reprint: PSC. *Indexed:* A01, A22, ASSIA, SSA. *Aud.:* Ac, Sa.

The *Journal of Family Psychology* provides original scholarly articles devoted to the study of the family system from multiple influences including systems, developmental, and cultural perspectives, and current practice. Published eight times per year by the American Psychological Association, it is regarded as an important journal in family research. The journal addresses such topics as linkages between relationship perceptions and couple conflict behaviors, family communication with adolescents, intimate partner aggression, psychosocial dimensions of childbirth, ethnic differences in mother qualities and its relation to academic achievement, military children's difficulty with reintegration after deployment, parental differences toward infant sleep, father-adolescent engagement in shared activities, relational aggression and marriage quality, and child behavior and sibling relationship quality. Occasionally, the journal publishes literature reviews, case studies, or theoretical articles, but the focus of the journal is empirical research addressing behavioral, biological, cognitive, emotional, and social variables. Recent issues include special sections addressing "Recent Advances in Understanding of Relationship Communication During Military Deployment" and "Advances in Methods and Measurement in Family Psychology." Widely indexed, this journal is highly recommended for academic libraries.

2199. *Journal of Family Psychotherapy: the official journal of the International Family Therapy Association.* Formerly (until 1988): *Journal of Psychotherapy and the Family.* [ISSN: 0897-5353] 1985. q. GBP 863 (print & online eds.)). Ed(s): Dr. Terry S Trepper. Routledge, 530 Walnut St, Ste 850, Philadelphia, PA 19106; enquiries@tandfonline.com; http://www.tandfonline.com. Adv. Sample. Refereed. Circ: 272 Paid. Microform: PQC. Reprint: PSC. *Indexed:* A01, A22, E01, SSA. *Bk. rev.:* Number and length vary. *Aud.:* Ac, Sa.

The *Journal of Family Psychotherapy* is the official journal of the International Family Therapy Association. Case studies, strategies currently in clinical practice, empirical studies, and program reports are written by clinicians for practicing clinicians. The journal is divided into sections that include Family Therapy Around the World, Intervention Interchange, Clinical Reflections, and Media Reviews. Thematic issues are occasionally published, providing in-depth coverage of a current topic such as "The Person of the Therapist Training (POTT) model: Theory, training, and therapist personhood" and "The Intervention Interchange." Recent articles address online financial therapy, practicing and teaching reframing, obsessive-compulsive disorder's impact on partner relationships, therapists' perceptions and experiences of premature dropout from therapy, humor in family therapy, emerging technologies and families, and parents' personal growth. This journal is recommended for academic libraries supporting marriage and family therapy programs.

2200. *Journal of Family Theory & Review (Online).* [ISSN: 1756-2589] 2009. q. Ed(s): Libby Balter Blume, Robert Milardo. John Wiley & Sons, Inc., 111 River St, Hoboken, NJ 07030; cs-journals@wiley.com; http://onlinelibrary.wiley.com. Adv. *Bk. rev.:* Number and length vary. *Aud.:* Ac.

The *Journal of Family Theory & Review* is one of three publications of the National Council on Family Relations. Multidisciplinary and international in scope, the journal "publishes original contributions in all areas of family theory, including new advances in theory development, reviews of existing theory, and analyses of the interface of theory and method." Families are defined broadly and inclusively. Recent articles include "Developmental Pedagogy in Marriage and Family Therapy Education: Preparing Students to Work Across Epistemologies," "Work and Family Research and Theory: Review and Analysis from an Ecological Perspective," "Immigrant Family Resilience in Context: Using a Community-Based Approach to Build a New Conceptual Model," and "The Evolving Nature and Process of Foster Family Communication: An Application and Adaptation of the Family Adoption Communication Model." Special issues are frequently published; recent issues focus on revisioning family theories; family theory: past, present, future; and a special collection on interpersonal acceptance-rejection theory. Book reviews as well as integrative and theory-based reviews of content areas are included. Recommended for academic libraries.

2201. *Journal of Family Therapy.* [ISSN: 0163-4445] 1979. q. GBP 494. Ed(s): Reenee Singh. Wiley-Blackwell Publishing Ltd., The Atrium, Southern Gate, Chichester, PO19 8QG, United Kingdom; cs-journals@wiley.com; http://onlinelibrary.wiley.com. Illus., index, adv. Sample. Refereed. Vol. ends: Nov. Reprint: PSC. *Indexed:* A01, A22, ASSIA, BRI, C42, E01, SSA. *Bk. rev.:* 1-4, 500-1,200 words. *Aud.:* Ac, Sa.

Published on behalf of the Association for Family Therapy and Systemic Practice in the United Kingdom, the *Journal of Family Therapy* seeks to advance "the understanding and treatment of human relationships constituted in systems such as couples, families, professional networks, and wider groups." International contributions to each issue include research papers, training articles, systemic reviews, case examples, and book reviews, and represent all schools of thought within family therapy. Recent papers include "Multi-stressed families, child violence and the larger system: an adaptation of the nonviolent model," "The role of relationships and families in healing from trauma," "Therapist implementation and parent experiences of the three phases of Functional Family Therapy," "Family-based outpatient treatments: a viable alternative to hospitalization for suicidal adolescents," and "Clinical implications from research exploring parent and family perspectives of the August 2011 London riots." Special issues devoted to culture and reflexivity, couple relationships, and Asian Chinese families and multisystemic therapy were published in 2017 and 2018. Recommended for academic libraries that call for original research in family therapy.

2202. *Journal of Family Violence.* [ISSN: 0885-7482] 1986. 8x/yr. EUR 1710 (print & online eds.)). Ed(s): Robert Geffner. Springer New York LLC, 233 Spring St, New York, NY 10013; customerservice@springer.com; http://www.springer.com. Illus., index, adv. Refereed. Vol. ends: Dec. Microform: PQC. Reprint: PSC. *Indexed:* A01, A22, ASSIA, BRI, CJPI, Chicano, E01, IBSS, N13, SSA. *Bk. rev.:* 0-4, 300-1,000 words. *Aud.:* Ac, Sa.

Interdisciplinary in scope, this journal addresses "the broad categories of child abuse and maltreatment, dating violence, domestic and partner violence, and elder abuse." Case studies, systematic reviews, papers, and theoretical discussions are included. Its clinical and research reports draw from clinical and counseling psychology, criminology, marital counseling, psychiatry, public health, law, social work, and sociology. Intimate partner violence in Thailand, needs of American Indian women who sought shelter, reducing intimate partner violence among Latinas, Mexican culture and lower rates of family violence, victim safety planning, youth to parent aggression and violence, mental health of youth in foster care, risk factors of violence against women in Peru, and intergenerational impacts of intimate partner violence are just a few topics recently addressed. Recommended for academic libraries, especially those that support counseling, criminology, or social work programs.

2203. *Journal of G L B T Family Studies.* [ISSN: 1550-428X] 2005. 5x/yr. GBP 862 (print & online eds.)). Ed(s): M Paz Galupo. Routledge, 530 Walnut St, Ste 850, Philadelphia, PA 19106; enquiries@tandfonline.com; http://www.tandfonline.com. Refereed. Reprint: PSC. *Indexed:* A01, A22, E01, GW, IBSS, SSA. *Bk. rev.:* Number and length vary. *Aud.:* Ac, Sa.

The *Journal of GLBT Family Studies* publishes original research covering "the impact of sexual orientation and gender identity on all aspects of family experience - including family structure, relationships, communication, therapy, and functioning." Content is interdisciplinary in scope and is directed to practitioners, researchers and academics in family therapy, social work, human services, psychology, and counseling. Recent articles include "Confiding in the GLBT Community about Problems in Marriage and Long-Term Committed Relationships: A Comparative Analysis," "Donor-Insemination Motherhood: How Three Types of Mothers Make Sense of Genes and Donors," "Stress Spillover and Crossover in Same-Sex Couples: Concurrent and Lagged Daily Effects," "Partner Violence in Transgender Communities: What Helping Professionals Need to Know," and "The Comparison of Grandparents', Parents', and Young People's Attitudes Toward Lesbians and Gay Men in Turkey." Occasionally special issues are published, such as "2016 U.S. Presidential Election and the LGBTQ Community." Book reviews are included. Recommended for academic libraries.

2204. *Journal of Marital and Family Therapy.* Formerly (until 1979): *Journal of Marriage and Family Counseling.* [ISSN: 0194-472X] 1975. q. GBP 435 (print & online eds.)). Wiley-Blackwell Publishing, Inc., 350 Main St, Malden, MA 02148; http://onlinelibrary.wiley.com. Illus., index, adv. Sample. Refereed. Vol. ends: Oct. Microform: PQC. Reprint: PSC. *Indexed:* A01, A22, ASSIA, BRI, E01, ERIC, SSA. *Bk. rev.:* 3-10, 300-1,000 words, signed. *Aud.:* Ac, Sa.

As the leading family therapy journal, this widely circulated journal "publishes articles on research, theory, clinical practice, and training in marital and family therapy." Published quarterly by the American Association for Marriage and Family Therapy, the practical articles are directed to marriage and family therapists and focused on clinical topics. Recent articles include "Transnational Intersectionality in Family Therapy with Resettled Refugees," "Treatment for Suicidal Thoughts and Behavior: A Review of Family-Based Interventions," "Exploring Partner Intimacy Among Couples Raising Children on the Autism Spectrum: A Grounded Theory Investigation," "Integrating Social Justice into the Practice of CBFT: A Critical Look at Family Schemas," "An Interpretive Phenomenological Inquiry of Family and Friend Reactions to Suicide Disclosure," and "Global Mental Health in Action: Reducing Disparities One Community at a Time." The journal publishes virtual issues, collecting previously published material under a theme. Topics related to clinical techniques and marriage and family therapy practice are often included. This title is essential for academic libraries that support programs in marriage and family therapy.

Parents. See Parenting section.

2205. *Psychotherapy Networker.* Former titles (until 2001): *Family Therapy Networker;* (until 1982): *Family Therapy Network Newsletter;* (until 197?): *Family Therapy Practice Network Newsletter; Family Shtick.* [ISSN: 1535-573X] 19??. bi-m. USD 18 domestic; USD 30 foreign. Ed(s): Livia Kent, Richard Simon. Psychotherapy Networker, 5135 MacArthur Blvd NW, Washington, DC 20016. Illus., adv. *Indexed:* A22, MLA-IB. *Bk. rev.:* Number and length vary. *Aud.:* Ac, Sa.

Family therapy is a significant topic addressed in *Psychotherapy Networker.* A trade publication aimed at therapists, its mission is to inspire therapists and to connect therapists with their colleagues. Feature articles, case studies, clinical methods, and career information, as well as regular columns addressing family matters, the business of therapy, consultation, and networking provide practical information for therapists. Reviews are also included. The articles, while written for therapists, are also likely to appeal to general readers interested in psychology and many articles are accessible for free through the publication's web site. Recent issues examine men and #MeToo, challenges and new possibilities of aging, meeting the needs of today's clients, couplehood, and psychotherapy's role in the wider world. Reviews of self-help and therapy books are included, as well as current popular film reviews written from a therapist's perspective. Because of its broad appeal, *Psychotherapy Networker* is recommended for academic and special libraries.

Sexual and Relationship Therapy. See Sexuality section.

Studies in Family Planning. See Family Planning section.

■ FAMILY PLANNING

See also Family, Population Studies, Medicine, Pregnancy, and Sexuality sections.

Skye Bickett, Assistant Director of Library Services, Philadelphia College of Osteopathic Medicine, Suwanee, GA 30024; skyebi@pcom.edu

Stephanie Ferretti, Chief Library Services Officer, Philadelphia College of Osteopathic Medicine, Philadelphia, PA 19131; stephaniefe@pcom.edu

Introduction

Family planning and reproductive health conceptually imply that individuals and couples can make informed choices about their sexual health and the desired number of children, as well as the spacing and timing of their births. Family planning is sometimes used as a synonym for the use of birth control; however, it often includes a wide variety of methods and practices that are *not* birth control. The latter is achieved through use of contraceptive methods and the treatment of involuntary infertility. Meanwhile, a woman's ability to space and limit her pregnancies has a direct impact on her health and well-being, as well as on the outcome of each pregnancy.

The first attempts to offer family planning services began with private groups and often aroused strong opposition. Activists such as Margaret Sanger in the United States, Marie Stopes in England, and Dhanvanthis Rama Rau in India, eventually succeeded in establishing clinics for family planning and related health care. Today, many countries have established national policies and encourage the use of public family services.

The World Health Organization (WHO) has taken a lead on this topic with its Department of Reproductive Health and Research, which sponsors programs to help individuals in this decision-making process, including a resource library on reproductive health. The world's largest international source of funding for population and reproductive health programs is the United Nations Population Fund (UNFPA).

Basic Periodicals

Contraception, Studies in Family Planning.

Basic Abstracts and Indexes

Academic OneFile; Academic Search Premier; CINAHL; PubMed.

2206. ***B M J Sexual & Reproductive Health.*** Former titles (until 2018): *Journal of Family Planning and Reproductive Health Care;* (until 2001): *British Journal of Family Planning;* (until 1977): *Journal of Family Planning Doctors.* [ISSN: 2515-1991] 1974. q. Individuals, GBP 160 (print & online eds.)). Ed(s): Sandy Goldbeck-Wood. B M J Group, BMA House, Tavistock Sq, London, WC1H 9JR, United Kingdom; info.adc@bmj.com; http://www.bmj.com/. Illus., adv. Sample. Refereed. *Indexed:* C45. *Bk. rev.:* 2, length varies. *Aud.:* Ac.

From the Royal College of Obstetricians and Gynecologists in Great Britain, the *Journal of Family Planning and Reproductive Health Care* offers an interesting mix of research, news, and opinion on reproductive health and family planning. Issues include regular research articles, columns such as the "Personal View," and the "History of Contraception," in addition to editorials and reviews on everything from fiction books to nonfiction books, journal articles, and blogs. Recommended for academic libraries.

2207. ***Contraception.*** [ISSN: 0010-7824] 1970. m. USD 2554. Ed(s): Carolyn Westhoff. Elsevier Inc., 1600 John F Kennedy Blvd, Philadelphia, PA 19103; journalscustomerservice-usa@elsevier.com; https://www.elsevier.com. Illus., adv. Sample. Refereed. Microform: PQC. *Indexed:* A01, A22, C45. *Aud.:* Ac.

Contraception is an internationally recognized, monthly, peer-reviewed title that serves as the official journal for the Association of Reproductive Health Professionals (ARHP) and the Society of Family Planning (SFP). The journal contains articles that relate to contraception, family planning, and abortion. Original articles are the key content, but one or two commentaries and reviews are featured in each issue, as well as occasional case reports and clinical guidelines. *Contraception* includes meeting abstracts for the ARHP and SFP. Recommended for academic and special libraries.

2208. ***Contraceptive Technology Update: the trusted source for contraceptive and STI news and research for more than three decades.*** Incorporates (1993-1999): *Women's Health Center Management;* (1989-1991): *Reproductive Technology Update.* [ISSN: 0274-726X] 1980. m. Ed(s): Rebecca Bowers. A H C Media, 950 E Paces Ferry Rd, NE, Ste 2850, Atlanta, GA 30326; customerservice@ahcmedia.com; http://www.ahcmedia.com/. Sample. Microform: PQC. *Indexed:* BRI. *Aud.:* Ac.

Contraceptive Technology Update is a practical publication intended for health care professionals. It provides information about current and emerging contraceptive techniques and reproductive services, discusses how these techniques and services impact patient care, offers continuing medical education credits in each issue, and has free patient handouts. This publication would be most useful for academic and hospital libraries.

2209. ***The European Journal of Contraception and Reproductive Health Care.*** [ISSN: 1362-5187] 1996. bi-m. GBP 1247 (print & online eds.)). Taylor & Francis, 2, 3 & 4 Park Sq, Milton Park, Abingdon, OX14 4RN, United Kingdom; subscriptions@tandf.co.uk; https://www.tandfonline.com. Adv. Refereed. Reprint: PSC. *Indexed:* A01, A22, E01. *Bk. rev.:* 1. *Aud.:* Ac, Sa.

Although most of the articles for this peer-reviewed journal deal with topics and research specific to European Union citizens, it also includes research from Africa, the Middle East, and more. *The European Journal of Contraception and Reproductive Health Care* primarily includes research articles, at least one editorial, and occasional case reports or review articles. Recommended for academic libraries.

Fertility Today See Pregnancy section.

2210. ***Journal of Human Reproductive Sciences.*** [ISSN: 0974-1208] 2008. q. INR 2700. Ed(s): Madhuri Patil. Wolters Kluwer - Medknow Publications and Media Pvt. Ltd., A-202, 2nd Flr, The Qube, CTS No 1498A/2, Mumbai, 400 059, India; publishing@medknow.com; http://www.lww.com/. Adv. Refereed. *Indexed:* A01, C42, C45. *Bk. rev.:* 1. *Aud.:* Ac.

This title, from the Indian Society of Assisted Reproduction, is a quarterly, peer-reviewed journal that is ideal for physicians, researchers, or faculty interested in assisted reproductive techniques. It covers andrology, gynecology, embryology, and all aspects of assisted conception. Each issue primarily contains original articles, but also includes two or three reviews and case reports, as well as occasional commentaries. Recommended for academic and special libraries.

2211. ***Perspectives on Sexual and Reproductive Health (Online).*** Formerly (until 2002): *Family Planning Perspectives (Online).* [ISSN: 1931-2393] 1969. q. GBP 234. Ed(s): Cynthia Summers. Wiley-Blackwell Publishing, Inc., 111 River St, Hoboken, NJ 07030; http://onlinelibrary.wiley.com. Refereed. *Bk. rev.:* 1. *Aud.:* Ac, Sa.

This title should be part of any academic or research collection that supports public health, nursing/medicine, family studies, or social work/counseling programs. It is a peer-reviewed journal, which includes both quantitative and qualitative research in areas such as fertility, adolescent pregnancy, abortion, sexual behavior, sexually transmitted disease, family planning, and reproductive health. Each issue also features an awareness column called "FYI," which includes news briefs with at least one associated citation for further reading. It is co-published by the Guttmacher Institute, a World Health Organization Collaborating Centre, and Wiley-Blackwell.

2212. ***Reproductive Health.*** [ISSN: 1742-4755] 2004. irreg. Free. Ed(s): Jose M Belizan. BioMed Central Ltd., Fl 6, 236 Gray's Inn Rd, London, WC1X 8HB, United Kingdom; info@biomedcentral.com; https://www.biomedcentral.com. Adv. Refereed. *Indexed:* A01, C42, C45. *Aud.:* Ac.

Reproductive Health is an open-access, peer-reviewed journal in BioMed Central that is intended for an international audience. The journal publishes commentaries, research, reviews, and study protocols that discuss all facets of human reproduction, including family planning and the reproductive-health issues faced by men and women. Recommended for academic libraries.

2213. ***Studies in Family Planning.*** Incorporates (1969-19??): *Current Publications in Family Planning.* [ISSN: 0039-3665] 1963. q. GBP 262 (print & online eds.)). Wiley-Blackwell Publishing, Inc., 350 Main St, Malden, MA 02148; http://onlinelibrary.wiley.com. Illus., index, adv. Sample. Refereed. Vol. ends: Dec. Microform: PQC. Reprint: PSC. *Indexed:* A01, A22, ASSIA, BAS, BRI, C42, C45, Chicano, E01, EIP, EconLit, IBSS, SSA. *Bk. rev.:* 3-4. *Aud.:* Ac, Sa.

A peer-reviewed quarterly with an international focus on developing countries, *Studies in Family Planning* publishes original research and reports, commentary, and book reviews. It also routinely includes snapshots of survey data on at least two countries from the Demographic and Health Surveys. Highly recommended for academic and research libraries, particularly those with programs related to population studies and global public health.

■ FASHION AND LIFESTYLE

Amber Paranick, Library of Congress; ampa@loc.gov

Introduction

The modern-day "fashion and lifestyle" magazine began in 1909 when *Vogue* magazine was purchased by young publicist Conde Montrose Nast. His intention was to make *Vogue* the most fabulous magazine of style and culture anywhere. Now known to be the preeminent resource of fashion and lifestyle and a longstanding icon in its own right, *Vogue* magazine has throughout its history made a lasting impression on fashion and popular culture. Though many magazines have published fashion and lifestyle sections in monthly and weekly issues, it was not until the mid-twentieth century that magazines of this type truly proliferated and stood on their own.

Fashion periodicals are transitioning from the analog (print) publications to the world of digital communications, and at present, an increasing number of fashion and lifestyle magazines are only published in a digital format. As publishers adapt to the changing needs of the modern-day fashion magazine reader, many now offer electronic versions of their magazine to current print subscribers or separately through a digital subscription.

Some fashion and lifestyle magazines will no longer be available in print format, such as publisher Conde Nast's *Self, Details*, and *Lucky* magazines. Recently, Meredith's *Siempre Mujer* dropped its print edition, opting to focus on its digital offerings and though *People* magazine's *StyleWatch* was discontinued as a standalone title, it still exists in the popular "PeopleStyle" section in the weekly edition of *People*. Digital-only enterprises such as *Who What Wear, Women's Wear Daily, Refinery29,* and *POPSUGAR* are go-to destinations for fashion, lifestyle, and wellness information.

Many print titles have a strong social media presence, allowing readers to interact with each other and comment on shared digital content. In order to stay in vogue with the changing landscape of print literature, it is best to consider your audience in selecting fashion and lifestyle magazines for your library. Such publications exist for nearly every demographic, and many of the major publications offer a separate publication for younger readers.

Basic Periodicals

Cosmopolitan, Elle, Essence, Glamour, Marie Claire, Maxim, Redbook, Vogue.

Basic Abstracts and Indexes

Berg Fashion Library, Design and Applied Arts Index, MasterFILE Premier, Readers' Guide to Periodical Literature.

2214. *Allure.* [ISSN: 1054-7711] 1991. 11x/yr. USD 8 combined subscription. Conde Nast Publications, Inc., 1 World Trade Center, New York, NY 10007; communications@condenast.com; http://www.condenast.com. Illus., adv. Vol. ends: Feb. Microform: PQC. *Indexed:* BRI. *Aud.:* Ga.

Allure, "The Beauty Expert," provides readers with a thorough guide to beauty advice on hair and skin care, cosmetics and beauty products, and appearance trends. The magazine's "Best of Beauty Awards" are given to products voted upon by readers and editors alike and easily distinguishable by a winner's seal logo. Issues include sections on "News & Trends," "Beauty Reporter," "Beauty by Numbers," celebrity photo shoots, and more features on hair, makeup, and styles. *Allure* is well connected with its web site, social networks, and a digital access subscription. URL: www.allure.com/

2215. *Cosmopolitan.* Supersedes in part (in 1952): *Hearst's International Combined with Cosmopolitan;* Which was formed by the merger of (1921-1925): *Hearst's International;* Which was formerly (until 1921): *Hearst's;* (until 1914): *Hearst's Magazine;* (until 1912): *Hearst's Magazine, the World To-day;* (until 1912): *World To-day;* (1886-1925): *The Cosmopolitan.* [ISSN: 0010-9541] 1886. m. Hearst Magazines, 300 W 57th St, 28th Fl, New York, NY 10019; HearstMagazines@hearst.com; http://www.hearstcorp.com/magazines/. Illus., adv. Vol. ends: Dec. Microform: PQC. *Indexed:* A22, BRI, C37. *Bk. rev.:* 4-6, brief, 500 words. *Aud.:* Ga, Ac.

Cosmopolitan, or *Cosmo*, carries on the sexual revolution of feminist editor Helen Gurley Brown, whose tenure was 1965-1997. Candid columns, articles, and surveys discuss modern sexual relationships. The magazine remains the young career woman's lifestyle guide on fashion and beauty; health and fitness; popular culture and entertainment; and relationships and romance. *Cosmopolitan* is published in 32 languages and 63 editions, and is distributed globally. The fully integrated web site and social media networks provide advice for the socially active *Cosmo* girl. The online component features a "Cosmo Latina" section. Sister publications include *Allure, Elle,* and *Glamour* magazines. *Cosmopolitan*'s United States, Spanish, and French editions are highly recommended for academic and public libraries. Available in print and digital editions. URL: www.cosmopolitan.com/

2216. *Country Woman.* Former titles (until 1987): *Farm Woman;* (until 198?): *Farm Woman News;* (until 1985): *Farm Wife News.* [ISSN: 0892-8525] 1970. bi-m. USD 10; USD 3.99 newsstand/cover. R D A Enthusiast Brands, LLC, 1610 N 2nd St, Ste 102, Milwaukee, WI 53212; customercare@rd.com; http://www.rda.com/. Illus., adv. Sample. Vol. ends: Dec. *Aud.:* Hs, Ga.

Country Woman celebrates the North American rural lifestyle. Many of the articles are written by country women, and topics include country cooking and entertaining; fiction and poetry; gardening and decorating; crafts and hobbies; rural businesses and volunteering; and reader remembrances and profiles. The title's web site provides contest entry forms, home and gardening ideas, and a section devoted to food and entertaining. Recommended for select high school and public libraries. URL: www.countrywomanmagazine.com/

2217. *Elle (New York).* [ISSN: 0888-0808] 1985. m. Hearst Magazines, 300 W 57th St, 28th Fl, New York, NY 10019; HearstMagazines@hearst.com; http://www.hearst.com. Illus., adv. Vol. ends: Aug. *Indexed:* A22, BRI, C37. *Bk. rev.:* 8-12, brief. *Aud.:* Hs, Ga.

Elle magazine is a global publication marketed to the affluent and career-driven woman. The American edition of *Elle* began publication in 1985, 40 years after the first French edition. Magazine topics include beauty and health-product ratings; celebrity and popular culture features; horoscope and trend analyses; and designer and fashion runway reviews. *Elle*'s ability to connect with women's whole lives and the well-balanced editorial approach of personal style and personal power is the key to the publication's success. The companion web site and social media networks, digital editions, and iPad app provides access to topical guides and updates. Recommended for public and select academic and special libraries.

2218. *Essence (New York).* [ISSN: 0014-0880] 1970. m. USD 10; USD 3.99 per issue. Essence Communications Inc., 225 Liberty St, 9th Fl, New York, NY 10048; webmaster@essence.com. Illus., adv. Vol. ends: Dec. Microform: PQC. *Indexed:* A01, A22, BRI, C37, CBRI, ENW, MASUSE, MLA-IB. *Bk. rev.:* 4-5, 75 words. *Aud.:* Hs, Ac, Sa.

Essence, "The Magazine for Today's Black Woman" has been published since 1970 and is one of the major publications of its kind. Celebrity lives, beauty tips, and fashion news now comprise the magazine's major feature articles and columns. African American culture, politics, spirituality, and social issues occasionally appear as news items and articles. *Essence* reflects marketing trends of other fashion and lifestyle magazines by focusing on personalities, careers, clothing, consumption, finance, healthy living, and family. The companion web site ("Essence: fierce, fun and fabulous") is a networked portal to social media and digital apps. Recommended for academic, high school, and public libraries. URL: www.essence.com/

G Q. See General Interest section.

2219. *Glamour (New York).* Incorporates (1935-2001): *Mademoiselle;* (in 1959): *Charm;* Formerly (until 1941): *Glamour of Hollywood.* [ISSN: 0017-0747] 1935. 11x/yr. USD 14.99; USD 19.99 combined subscription (print & online eds.); USD 1.25 per issue). Conde Nast Publications, Inc., 225 Vesey St, New York, NY 10282; communications@condenast.com; http://www.glamour.com. Illus., adv. Microform: PQC. *Indexed:* A22, BRI, C37. *Bk. rev.:* 5, 75 words. *Aud.:* Hs, Ga, Ac.

Glamour magazine provides real-world personal care and style guides for today's American woman. The magazine publishes information on trends in beauty, dating, diet, fashion, health, money, and shopping. The companion web site, digital edition, and iPad app furnish sections on fashion and beauty; youth and weddings; do's and don'ts; blogs and videos; health and fitness; and sex, love, and life. Recommended for public libraries. URL: www.glamour.com/

2220. *Harper's Bazaar.* [ISSN: 0017-7873] 1867. 10x/yr. USD 30; USD 5.99 newsstand/cover. Ed(s): Glenda Bailey. Hearst Magazines, 300 W 57th St, 28th Fl, New York, NY 10019; HearstMagazines@hearst.com; http://www.hearstcorp.com/magazines/. Illus., adv. Vol. ends: Dec. Microform: NBI; PMC; PQC. *Indexed:* A22, BRI, C37, MASUSE, MLA-IB. *Bk. rev.:* Number and length vary. *Aud.:* Hs, Ga, Ac.

Harper's Bazaar, America's first fashion magazine, targets the affluent American woman. The magazine's rich visual past includes the photography by Richard Avedon, Peter Lindbergh, Man Ray, and Solve Sundsbo, as well as illustrations by Erte and Andy Warhol. *Harper's Bazaar*'s motto, "Where Fashion Gets Personal," reflects the sophisticated taste of readers in their purchasing the best from the best, from casual to couture. Each issue features articles and photographic spreads of provocative stylists and renowned designers. The convergent web site, social media networks, digital edition, and iPad app provide readers with up-to-date information on the world of beauty and fashion. Recommended for public libraries. URL: www.harpersbazaar.com/

2221. ***InStyle.*** [ISSN: 1076-0830] 1994. m. USD 15 domestic; USD 20 combined subscription domestic. Ed(s): Laura Brown. Time Inc., 225 Liberty St, New York, NY 10281; information@timeinc.com; http://www.timeinc.com. Illus., adv. *Indexed:* BRI, C37, MASUSE. *Aud.:* Ga.

InStyle, a newsstand beauty magazine, targets active women who want immediate information to tips and step-by-step guides to cosmetic products; skin care techniques; make-up applications; hair styling; shopping deals; and wardrobe assembly. The magazine features celebrity interviews; style-setter photo shoots; and tours of homes of the rich and famous. The companion web site, social media, and iPad app provide quick access to celebrity spottings, fashion news, and shopping deals. URL: www.instyle.com

2222. ***Marie Claire.*** [ISSN: 1081-8626] 1994. m. USD 10; USD 4.99 newsstand/cover. Ed(s): Newell Turner. Hearst Magazines, 300 W 57th St, 28th Fl, New York, NY 10019; HearstMagazines@hearst.com; http://www.hearst.com. Illus., adv. *Indexed:* BRI. *Bk. rev.:* 2-3, 25 words. *Aud.:* Hs, Ga.

Marie Claire magazine offers advice to the modern woman on celebrity and stylist interviews; fashion and pop culture trends; hair and skin care; health and fitness; sex and romance; and careers and wardrobe. There are also occasional features on women's social and political issues. The web site is a portal to "Games & Giveaways," "Sex & Relationships," "Horoscopes," "Fashion, Hair & Beauty," "Virtual Hairstyle and Makeup Makeover," "Health & Fitness," and the "Sex and the Single Guy Blog." It also leads to the digital magazine edition; social media networks; and the iPad app. Recommended for public libraries.

2223. ***Maxim (Print).*** [ISSN: 1092-9789] 1997. bi-m. USD 19.99 combined subscription (print & online eds.); USD 6.99 newsstand/cover). Maxim, Inc, 415 Madison Ave, New York, NY 10017; mlegal@maxim.com; https://www.maxim.com/. Illus., adv. *Bk. rev.:* 5, 200 words, signed. *Aud.:* Ga.

Maxim has found its way onto some library periodical racks, although it's usually found on magazine newsstands. It is a slick, good-looking magazine that will attract male readers. The provocative cover does the trick, but there's as much meat as cheesecake within. Health, holidays, sports, technology, investing, fashion, and sex are all grist for the *Maxim* mill. All types of media are reviewed. A fascination with the slightly offbeat is also apparent. Inquisitive librarians and readers may check out the title through its full-text web site. URL: www.maxim.com/

2224. ***Men's Journal.*** [ISSN: 1063-4657] 1992. m. American Media, Inc, 4 New York Plaza, New York, NY 10004. Illus., adv. *Indexed:* BRI. *Bk. rev.:* 4, 200 words, signed. *Aud.:* Hs, Ga.

A publication for the active male, *Men's Journal* consists of about equal parts sports, action, and travel reading, with a hint of savoring the good life. Known for its outstanding photography and exceptional writing, it is aimed at the active man who wants to get the most out of life. An article about American heroes may stand side-by-side with one about climbing Mt. Everest. There are also columns on the latest innovations in digital and other equipment, sports, fashion trends, health, grooming, sex, cars, books, and music. URL: www.mensjournal.com/

2225. ***Nylon.*** [ISSN: 1524-1750] 1999. 10x/yr. USD 19.95 domestic. Ed(s): Marvin Scott Jarrett. Nylon Holding Inc., 110 Greene St, Ste 607, New York, NY 10012. Illus., adv. *Aud.:* Ga, Ac.

Co-founded by super-model Helena Christensen and editors from the rock-and-roll magazine *Ray-Gun, Nylon* is strictly for the hip and fashion-forward set. The magazine places a high emphasis on film, art, pop culture, music, and of course, up-to-the minute trends in fashion, as it combines equal parts runway and street style. True to its goal of remaining current and unique, *Nylon* is usually the first to feature new models, performers, and actors on its cover. Regularly published issues include the annual "Young Hollywood" and "Music" issues. *Nylon Guys,* the bimonthly, male-targeted companion to *Nylon,* published its last issue April/May 2015. Recommended for public and academic libraries.

O: The Oprah Magazine. See General Interest section.

2226. ***Redbook.*** Incorporates (1928-1978): *American Home.* [ISSN: 0034-2106] 1903. m. USD 8; USD 3.99 newsstand/cover. Ed(s): Meredith Rollins. Hearst Magazines, 300 W 57th St, 28th Fl, New York, NY 10019; HearstMagazines@hearst.com; http://www.hearst.com. Illus., index, adv. Microform: NBI; PQC. *Indexed:* A22, BRI, C37, MASUSE. *Aud.:* Ga, Ac.

Redbook targets readers who have married and outgrown *Cosmo* but do not yet place themselves among the readership of more traditional titles such as *Ladies' Home Journal* and *Good Housekeeping.* The magazine offers great tips on fashion, clothing, gifts, sex, makeup, and shopping. Most of the articles are not just about how you look, but also about how to take care of yourself emotionally and physically. The web site is similar in content but focuses a bit more on sex and marriage. Reader polls, chat, and advice columns complete the site. URL: www.redbookmag.com/

2227. ***Vogue.*** Incorporates (in 1914): *Vanity Fair;* Which was formerly (until 1914): *Dress & Vanity Fair.* [ISSN: 0042-8000] 1892. m. USD 19.99 domestic; USD 50 combined subscription Canada (print & online eds.); USD 70 combined subscription elsewhere (print & online eds.)). Conde Nast Publications, Inc., 225 Vesey St, New York, NY 10282; communications@condenast.com; http://www.condenast.com. Illus., adv. Microform: PQC. *Indexed:* A22, BRI, C37, C42, MLA-IB. *Bk. rev.:* 3-4, 100-200 words. *Aud.:* Ga, Ac.

Vogue started as a society paper in 1892, and since then has become an elite women's lifestyle and fashion magazine. Its layout is beautiful and glossy, as with most expensive fashion magazines, and its advertising content is extremely prolific. In fact, *Vogue* is one of the most advertised-in magazines in the world. Every conceivable tie-in to the fashion industry is included: clothing, footwear, accessories, jewelry, makeup, cosmetics, and medications to make one look and feel younger. The magazine is sectioned into four parts that include articles on haute couture, designers, makeup, and hair trends. It also covers current events such as museum openings and book and film reviews. A core fashion title for public libraries. URL: www.vogue.com/

2228. ***W.*** Incorporates (in Jan.2007): *Jewelry W;* (1987-1988): *Scene.* [ISSN: 0162-9115] 1971. 8x/yr. USD 12 combined subscription domestic (print & online eds.); USD 50 combined subscription Canada (print & online eds.); USD 85 combined subscription elsewhere (print & online eds.)). Ed(s): Stefano Tonchi. Fairchild Publications, Inc., 750 Third Ave, #7, New York, NY 10017. Illus., adv. *Indexed:* BRI. *Aud.:* Ga.

The over-sized *W* is filled with photography and photographic essays that cover all areas of fashion, from designers to current collections. It is divided into sections that highlight trends in cosmetics, accessories, beauty, and interior design. In addition to fashion coverage, a large part of the magazine is devoted to the doings of various people involved in high society. The year 2016 was a special one in the title's history, as it marked the magazine's 45th year.

■ FICTION: GENERAL/MYSTERY AND DETECTIVE

General/Mystery and Detective

Theodore Bergfelt, Humanities Librarian, Gumberg Library, Duquesne University, Pittsburgh, PA 15282; bergfeltt@duq.edu

Introduction

The magazines in this section mainly publish short fiction by new and established writers. Content varies from literary and experimental writing to fiction in all mystery and detective sub-genres. While these publications mainly present short fiction, many include poetry, essays, and other nonfiction, book reviews, author interviews, and additional features of interest to fans and fiction writers alike.

The publishers of these magazines range from small independents, to university departments or presses, to commercial publishers. While the majority of these periodicals are still print-based, most have a website that presents related content, which is often multimedia in nature. Some are hybrids that publish most content online, but then present it at the end of the year in an annual printed volume, and a small number have moved to an online-only format.

Basic Periodicals

GENERAL. Ga, Ac: *Fiction, Fiction International, Narrative Magazine, Zoetrope.*

MYSTERY AND DETECTIVE. Ga, Ac: *Alfred Hitchcock's Mystery Magazine, Mystery Scene, The Strand Magazine.*

Basic Abstracts and Indexes

MLA International Bibliography.

General

These magazines represent a wide range of approaches to publishing high-quality fiction and prose, with some also including poetry, features, book reviews, and author interviews. Some of these magazines feature relatively accessible fiction with broad appeal, while others favor literary experimentation. All of these magazines have relatively small circulations and cater to a committed readership. Many of the print publications offer high-quality art and design to compliment the fiction they publish. Magazines that specialize in romance fiction are also included in this section. The romance fiction magazines mainly provide reviews of romance fiction, rather than works of fiction themselves.

Like many print periodicals in other fields, most of the publications included in this subsection have adapted to the world of digital publication. The web presences of many of these publications provide extensive additional information and content, including blogs, links to social media, additional reviews, and digital audio and video. A few of these periodicals present most of their content online, and then release an occasional printed volume. A small number have become digital-only publications.

2229. *Affaire de Coeur.* [ISSN: 0739-3881] 1979. bi-m. USD 26 combined subscription print & online eds. Ed(s): Louise B Snead. Snead, Inc., 3976 Oak Hill Rd, Oakland, CA 94605. *Bk. rev.:* Number and length vary. *Aud.:* Ga.

For 40 years, *Affaire de Coeur* magazine has been serving fans of all the sub-genres of romance fiction. This title is available in print or online as a pdf. Each issue contains feature articles on the romance genre, writing and publication advice, author interviews, news, trivia, contests, and of course, reviews of the latest books in romance fiction. The book reviews are broken down into the following categories: contemporary, historical, young adult, erotica, and paranormal. Audiobooks are also reviewed. This publication will be of interest to avid romance readers, and will be useful for librarians in public libraries that provide readers' assistance. The website features subscription information, author interviews, a blog, information on romance conventions, and much more. URL: http://www.affairedecoeur.com/

American Short Fiction. See Literary Reviews section.

The Antioch Review. See Literary Reviews section.

2230. *Fiction.* [ISSN: 0046-3736] 1972. bi-m. USD 67. Ed(s): Mark Jay Mirsky. Fiction Inc., c/o City College of NY, Department of English, New York, NY 10031. Illus., index. Microform: PQC. *Indexed:* A22, AmHI. *Aud.:* Ga, Ac.

Published at the City University of New York, *Fiction* features an impressive array of stories by notable and emerging writers. Not favoring any particular school of fiction, the magazine nonetheless aims "to bring the experimental to a broader audience, and to bring new voices to the forefront." Each issue features a range of high-quality stories, including new short fiction, previously published stories, works in translation, and book excerpts. Through the years new writers have seen their works published alongside those of luminaries of modern literature such as Samuel Beckett, Donald Barthelme, Marguerite Duras, and Joyce Carol Oates, to name only a few. *Fiction* is an excellent addition for large public and academic libraries. The website includes submission guidelines, subscription information, an archive of stories previously published in *Fiction,* and a column from the editor. URL: http://www.fictioninc.com/

2231. *Fiction International.* [ISSN: 0092-1912] 1973. a. USD 20 per issue. Ed(s): Harold Jaffe. San Diego State University Press, 5500 Campanile Dr, San Diego, CA 92182; http://sdsupress.sdsu.edu/. Illus. Microform: PQC. *Indexed:* A22, AmHI, BRI, CBRI, MLA-IB. *Aud.:* Ga, Ac.

An annual publication, *Fiction International* features a unique blend of fiction, nonfiction, and art that emphasizes "formal innovation and social activism." Each issue contains fiction, nonfiction, and visual art by established and emerging writers and artists from around the world. Each issue explores a specific theme, past examples of which include "World in Pain," "Fluids," and "Phobia/Philia." Well-known past contributors have included William Burroughs, Robert Coover, Kathy Acker, and Allen Ginsberg. This journal is recommended for academic and large public libraries with an interest in collecting contemporary experimental fiction. The website contains subscription information, submission guidelines, a blog, and selected articles from the current and past issues. URL: http://fictioninternational.sdsu.edu/wordpress/

Glimmer Train. See Little Magazines section.

Granta. See Literary Reviews section.

Kenyon Review. See Literary Reviews section.

2232. *Narrative Magazine.* 2003. irreg. Free. Ed(s): Tom Jenks, Carol Edgarian. Narrative Magazine, tom@tomjenks.com. *Aud.:* Ga, Ac.

Founded in 2003 as a non-profit organization, *Narrative* is dedicated to "advancing literary arts in the digital age by supporting the finest writing talent and encouraging readership across generations, in schools, and around the globe." Although primarily an online publication, *Narrative* occasionally publishes a print issue for sale. This online magazine features an impressive library of free stories, poems, and nonfiction. Recently, *Narrative* has published material by well-known writers like T.C. Boyle, Joyce Carol Oates, Sherman Alexie, and Robert Stone. Each week *Narrative* highlights a poem and a story of the week. It also presents other online content such as art, photography, cartoons, and a page of writer's resources. To access the online content, users need to register for a free account. For a small donation readers can access a section called "Narrative Backstage," which features audio and video files of author readings, unpublished works-in-progress, and discussions on writing. URL: http://www.narrativemagazine.com/

2233. *Painted Bride Quarterly.* [ISSN: 0362-7969] 1973. a. Ed(s): Kathleen V Miller, Marion Wrenn. Drexel University, Department of English and Philosophy, 3141 Chestnut St, Philadelphia, PA 19104. Adv. Circ: 1000 Paid. *Aud.:* Ga.

Published since 1973 by the Department of English and Philosophy at Drexel University, *Painted Bride Quarterly* is one of the longest-running American literary magazines. *Painted Bride Quarterly* publishes short fiction, poetry, and prose by emerging and established authors. Each quarterly issue is published online, then at the end of the year, that year's content is published in a handsome paperback volume that is available for purchase. All content back to the very start of the magazine is available online for free. Quarterly issues often feature a theme, past examples of which include "Humor," "Displacement," and "Costume." Along with the quarterly content, the website provides submission information and news. URL: http://pbqmag.org/

Paris Review. See Literary Reviews section.

2234. ***Ploughshares.*** [ISSN: 0048-4474] 1971. 4x/yr. USD 40. Ed(s): Ladette Randolph. Emerson College, 120 Boylston St, Boston, MA 02116-4624; http://www.emerson.edu. Illus., index, adv. Circ: 6500. Vol. ends: Dec. Microform: PQC. *Indexed:* A01, A22, AmHI, BRI, MLA-IB. *Aud.:* Ga, Ac.

Since 1971, the mission of *Ploughshares* has been to "publish exceptional work by emerging and established writers that pushes the boundaries of what is possible in art." This literary journal publishes four print issues a year. Two issues are guest edited by prominent authors, the third is a mix of prose and poetry, and the fourth is an omnibus volume collecting "Solos," longer stories and prose works that have been published on the website throughout the year. Past guest editors have included Alice Hoffman, Terrance Hayes, Patricia Hampl, and Major Jackson. This title is highly recommended for academic and public libraries. The website gives information on submission, subscription, a blog, and access (for a fee) to the "Ploughshares Solos" mentioned above. The tables of contents for all published issues are also provided. URL: http://www.pshares.org/

Prairie Schooner. See Literary Reviews section.

2235. ***Thema.*** [ISSN: 1041-4851] 1988. 3x/yr. USD 30 domestic (Free to members). Ed(s): Virginia Howard. Thema Literary Society, P O Box 8747, Metairie, LA 70011. Sample. *Indexed:* AmHI. *Aud.:* Ga.

Thema aims to provide a forum for established and emerging literary and visual artists, to serve as a source of material for creative writing teachers, and to entertain readers with a uniquely eclectic selection of fiction, poetry, photography, and art. Each issue is devoted to a different theme and all the literary and artistic work in that issue takes up the theme. Some of the themes from past issues have been "Paper Tigers," "Lost in Translation," and "Where's the Food Truck?" The website includes subscription and submission information, as well as the tables of contents of all published issues. URL: http://themaliterarysociety.com

Mystery and Detective

Magazines in this subsection are devoted to mystery and detective fiction, covering a wide range of subgenres, including suspense fiction, thrillers, whodunits, and hard-boiled crime fiction. Many of these periodicals publish original short fiction, as well as literary criticism, author interviews, book reviews, and other information of interest to readers and writers in the mystery genre. Some do not publish mystery fiction, but rather keep the reader abreast of developments in the mystery and detective publishing world. Most have accompanying websites that supply additional content. Although some publications feature scholarly analysis and may be of interest to academics, the publications in this subsection are mainly directed at a general audience.

2236. ***Alfred Hitchcock's Mystery Magazine.*** [ISSN: 0002-5224] 1956. bi-m. USD 34.97 domestic; USD 46.97 elsewhere. Ed(s): Linda Landrigan. Penny Publications LLP, 6 Prowitt St, Norwalk, CT 06855; customerservice@pennypublications.com; http://www.pennypublications.com. Illus., adv. Vol. ends: Dec. *Bk. rev.:* 300-500 words. *Aud.:* Ga.

This digest-sized, long-running magazine is one of the industry stalwarts. It features short mystery stories from every mystery and crime subgenre. Founded in 1956, *Alfred Hitchcock's Mystery Magazine* continues to publish mystery fiction by new writers as well as best-selling authors such as Martin Limon, Jane K. Cleland, Loren Estleman, Rhys Bowen, and Kristine Kathryn Rusch. Stories vary in length from "short-shorts to novellas." While the emphasis is on new, original stories, issues occasionally feature "mystery classics" from the past. Each issue includes short stories, book reviews, puzzles, and story contests. The website provides submission guidelines, links to a podcast series of author readings and interviews, information on the current issue, excerpts from stories in the current issue, as well as subscription information. An essential subscription for libraries serving a mystery reading public. URL: http:///www.alfredhitchcockmysterymagazine.com

2237. ***Baker Street Journal: an irregular quarterly of sherlockiana.*** [ISSN: 0005-4070] 1946. q. USD 41.95 domestic; USD 55 elsewhere. Ed(s): Steven Rothman. The Sheridan Press, 144 East Grinnell St, Sheridan, WY 82801; http://www.thesheridanpress.com. Illus., index, adv. Microform: PQC. *Indexed:* A22, AmHI, MLA-IB. *Bk. rev.:* 1-10, 30-90 words. *Aud.:* Ga.

The *Baker Street Journal* is the official publication of the Baker Street Irregulars, the major Sherlock Holmes fan association in the United States. The organization's website describes the journal as "the premiere publication of scholarship about Sherlock Holmes." It features scholarly articles and lighter fare devoted to Holmes and Watson and the world of the original stories, and treatments of the characters and stories in film, television, graphic novels, and other popular culture media. In addition to the scholarly articles, each issue features reports on Holmes-related events, book news, and reviews. The website has subscription information, submission guidelines, the table of contents for the most recent issue, selected articles from the print editions, and links to a calendar of events related to Sherlock Holmes. URL: bakerstreetirregulars.com/the-baker-street-journal/

2238. ***Clues: a journal of detection.*** [ISSN: 0742-4248] 1980. s-a. USD 120 (Individuals, USD 40). Ed(s): Elizabeth Foxwell. McFarland & Company, Inc., Box 611, Jefferson, NC 28640; journals@mcfarlandpub.com; http://www.mcfarlandpub.com. Illus. Refereed. *Indexed:* A22, AmHI, MLA-IB. *Bk. rev.:* 0-60, 40-300 words. *Aud.:* Ac.

Clues is the only scholarly journal devoted to mystery and detective fiction, whether in print, on radio, in film, or on television, from the earliest days of the genre to today. Published for almost 40 years, each issue contains literary criticism, essays, and book reviews of recent scholarly work. Special issues focus on particular themes related to mystery fiction, past and present. Recent special issues have focused on global crime fiction, paranormal fiction, and the theme of "reappropriating Agatha Christie." *Clues* is an essential title for academics and students interested in the mystery and detective genre. The website provides submission, publication, and subscription information. URL: http://mcfarlandbooks.com/customers/how-to-buy-journals/clues-a-journal-of-detection/

2239. ***Crimespree Magazine.*** [ISSN: 1551-5826] 2004. bi-m. USD 38 domestic; USD 60 elsewhere. Ed(s): Ruth Jordan, Jon Jordan. Crimespree Magazine, 536 S 5th St, Ste 1 A, Milwaukee, WI 53204. *Bk. rev.:* Number and length vary. *Aud.:* Ga.

Crimespree is an award-winning print magazine "that covers all aspects of crime fiction, including books, movies, DVDs, comics, and more." Each issue features author interviews and other features on mystery writing, short crime fiction, book and media reviews, news on mystery fiction and film, and even crime-fiction-related recipes. The companion website provides additional news, features, and giveaways. URL: http://crimespreemag.com

2240. ***Ellery Queen's Mystery Magazine: the world's leading mystery magazine.*** Former titles (until 1988): *Ellery Queen;* (until 1981): *Ellery Queen's Mystery Magazine.* [ISSN: 1054-8122] 1941. bi-m. USD 34.97 domestic; USD 46.97 elsewhere. Ed(s): Janet Hutchings. Penny Publications LLP, 6 Prowitt St, Norwalk, CT 06855; customerservice@pennypublications.com; http://www.pennypublications.com. Illus., adv. *Bk. rev.:* 8-12, 30-70 words. *Aud.:* Ga, Ac.

Ellery Queen's Mystery Magazine is the oldest magazine of its type. First published in 1941, this digest-sized publication "is credited with setting the standard for the modern crime and mystery short story." It presents short mystery fiction, often by leading writers in the genre, book reviews, occasional poetry, mystery-themed crossword puzzles, and a "department of first stories" section that features the first published work by talented new writers. *Ellery Queen's Mystery Magazine* is recommended for public libraries and academic libraries that support creative writing programs. The website features reviews, subscription information, submission guidelines, an index of stories from recent volumes, and podcasts that feature readings and dramatizations of stories that appear in the magazine. URL: http://www.elleryqueenmysterymagazine.com

2241. *Mystery Readers Journal.* Former titles (until 1989): *M R A Journal;* (until 198?): *Mystery Readers of America Journal.* [ISSN: 1043-3473] 1985. q. Free to members. Ed(s): Janet A. Rudolph. Mystery Readers International, PO Box 8116, Berkeley, CA 94707; http://www.mysteryreaders.org. *Aud.:* Ga, Ac.

Mystery Readers Journal is the official publication of Mystery Readers International, the largest mystery fan organization in the world. This magazine is published quarterly in printed form, each issue of which is on a particular theme. Themes covered recently include "Gardening Mysteries," "Spies and Secret Agents," and "Mysteries in the American South, Parts I and II." This magazine publishes essays by working mystery writers on the theme of the issue, rather than short mystery fiction. Each issue also includes reviews, special columns, a calendar of events, and other mystery-related materials. The accompanying website provides tables of contents for all issues, subscription information, a list of holiday mysteries, as well as a list of mystery book groups from around the country. URL: http://mysteryreaders.org/

2242. *Mystery Scene.* [ISSN: 1087-674X] 1985. 5x/yr. USD 32 domestic; USD 42 Canada; USD 65 elsewhere. Ed(s): Kate Stine. Mystery Scene Magazine, Radio City Station, PO Box 2200, New York, NY 10101; info@mysteryscenemag.com. Illus., adv. Circ: 23000. *Indexed:* MLA-IB. *Bk. rev.:* 10-15, 45-80 words. *Aud.:* Ga, Sa.

Mystery Scene calls itself "your guide to the best in mystery, crime, & suspense." It is glossy, colorful, and fun to read. It does not present works of fiction, but helps its audience keep up with the latest in the trade of mystery, crime, suspense, and detective fiction. This magazine is aimed at authors, booksellers, fans, librarians, or anyone who wants to stay abreast of developments in the field. Profusely illustrated, each issue presents articles on and by major authors in the genre, such as Lee Childs, Lawrence Block, and Ed Gorman, as well as information on award winners, and numerous reviews of new works in mystery and detective fiction. The reviews are arranged in the categories of independents, paperback originals, audiobooks, reference works, and short story collections. The companion website features the table of contents for the current issue, selected previously published articles, reviews, a blog, subscription information, games, and a searchable database of book reviews. URL: http://mysteryscenemag.com

2243. *The Sherlock Holmes Journal.* [ISSN: 0037-3621] 1952. s-a. Free to members. Ed(s): Roger Johnson. Sherlock Holmes Society of London, c/o Roger Johnson, Mole End, 41 Sandford Rd, Chelmsford, CM2 6DE, United Kingdom; rojerjohnson@yahoo.co.uk; http://www.sherlock-holmes.org.uk/. Illus. *Bk. rev.:* 5-10, 80-700 words. *Aud.:* Ga.

The Sherlock Holmes Journal is the official voice of the Sherlock Holmes Society of London, a literary and social organization devoted to Holmes, Dr. Watson, and their times. The journal publishes critical and historical articles and news related to the great detective, as well as reviews of books, both fiction and nonfiction, plays, television shows, audiobooks, and films featuring Holmes. The journal also publishes articles on meetings, banquets, excursions, and other activities of the Sherlock Holmes Society. The society's website provides subscription information, the current issue's table of contents, a calendar of events, the latest society newsletter, and podcasts of dramatizations of canonical and original Sherlock Holmes tales. URL: www.sherlock-holmes.org.uk/category/journal/

2244. *The Strand Magazine (Birmingham).* Supersedes (1891-1950): *The Strand Magazine (Monthly).* [ISSN: 1523-8709] 1891. q. USD 24.99. Ed(s): Andrew F Gulli. Strand Magazine (Birmingham), PO Box 1418, Birmingham, MI 48012. Adv. *Bk. rev.:* 5-10, 300-500. *Aud.:* Ga.

The current *Strand Magazine* traces its origins back to the late Victorian periodical of the same name that published so many of the original Sherlock Holmes stories. The modern *Strand Magazine* features stories representing many different types of mystery and detective fiction "reminiscent of the Golden Age of crime writing." Each quarterly issue features short fiction by well-known contemporary crime and mystery writers like Jeffrey Deaver, Alexander McCall Smith, and Faye Kellerman, as well as previously unpublished stories by greats of the past such as Agatha Christie, Dashiell Hammett, and Graham Greene. This glossy, handsome magazine also publishes in-depth author interviews and reviews of crime and mystery books, audiobooks, and films. The companion website gives subscription information, access to a blog, sample articles from past issues, interviews with mystery writers, and reviews. URL: http://strandmag.com

■ FICTION: SCIENCE FICTION, FANTASY, AND HORROR

Emily Krug, Instructional Services Librarian, King University, Bristol, TN

Devin Phelps, Director of Technical Services, Somerset Community College, Somerset, KY

Introduction

Science fiction, fantasy, and horror fiction have long been relegated to the fringes of mainstream fiction for adults; however, recent trends in popular culture, such as the success of *The Lord of the Rings* and *The Hobbit* movies, television shows such as *Dr. Who,* and novels by Neil Gaiman, have brought the speculative into the mainstream. Although the worlds of film, television, and literature have crossovers, the scope of this section is specifically magazines and journals that publish fiction within the genre and the critical analysis of that fiction. While some still may view the writing that falls under the speculative fiction umbrella as a niche market, we find that it is a rich area of literature that deserves a place in libraries' fiction collections.

Choosing the best titles for a collection of fiction magazines of any genre presents a unique challenge, because the appeal of fiction is largely subjective. Who are we to judge whether our patrons will enjoy one story more than another? Because the nature of serialized fiction is that the stories are ever-changing, deciding which subscriptions to purchase and which to forgo is a particular challenge.

Fortunately, there are some outstanding magazines that publish speculative fiction that should be considered essential titles. Both *Asimov's Science Fiction* and *Analog Science Fiction and Fact* are excellent titles that should be included in any collection. *Dead Reckonings* does not publish fiction, but its reviews of horror fiction are insightful and useful for the library looking to purchase longer fiction works. *Daily Science Fiction* is unique because patrons can freely subscribe to have a short story sent to them each week day.

For critical analysis of speculative fiction, we recommend *Science Fiction Studies.* For the 25th edition of *MFL,* we found no new titles to add. However, we are removing one title, *Polluto,* which has ceased publication.

Basic Periodicals

Analog Science Fiction & Fact, Asimov's Science Fiction, Daily Science Fiction, Dead Reckonings, Fantasy & Science Fiction, Science Fiction Studies.

Basic Abstracts and Indexes

Arts & Humanities Citation Index, Book Review Index, MLA International Bibliography, PIO: Periodicals Index Online.

2245. *Albedo One.* Formerly (until 1991): *F T L.* [ISSN: 0791-8534] 1993. irreg. EUR 25 domestic; EUR 32 foreign; EUR 4 per issue. Albedo One, 8 Bachelor's Walk, Dublin, , Ireland; http://www.albedo1.com/. *Bk. rev.:* 5-10, 200-1,000 words. *Aud.:* Ga, Sa.

Albedo One primarily publishes short stories, including the winners of the Aeon Award, which is administered by the magazine. In addition to short stories, the magazine publishes interviews with science fiction authors, as well as five to ten book reviews per issue. The stories included in this title are generally entertaining and enjoyable. Despite efforts to make all issues available in e-book format in 2014, the magazine's web site does not include recently published issues. However, *Albedo One* would be a welcome print addition to any general collection of speculative fiction.

2246. *Analog Science Fiction & Fact.* Former titles (until 1991): *Analog Science Fiction Science Fact;* (until 1965): *Analog Science Fact - Science Fiction;* (until 1961): *Astounding Science Fiction;* (until 19??): *Astounding Science Fact & Fiction;* (until 1960): *Astounding Science-Fiction;* (until 1938): *Astounding Stories;* (until 19??): *Astounding Stories of Super-Science;* (until 1932): *Astounding Stories;* (until 1931): *Astounding Stories of Super-Science.* [ISSN: 1059-2113] 1930. 12x/yr. USD 34.97 domestic (print or online ed.); USD 49.97 foreign (print or online ed.)). Ed(s): Trevor Quachri. Dell Magazines, 44 Wall St, Ste 904, New York, NY 10005-2401; analog@dellmagazines.com; http://dellmagazines.com. Illus., index, adv. Sample. Vol. ends: Dec. Microform: PQC. *Indexed:* A22, BRI, CBRI. *Bk. rev.:* 3-5, 200-1,000 words. *Aud.:* Hs, Ga, Ac.

Analog Science Fiction and Fact (hereafter, *Analog*) stands firmly in the realm of hard science fiction and maintains its position as one of the essential titles for any serious science fiction collection. *Analog* is concerned with fiction that deals with the real possibilities of actual science rather than "aliens for the sake of aliens." Additionally, the magazine's lengthy history keeps it in good standing in the science fiction community. The magazine is available in print as well as in several e-reader formats; however, *Analog* does not seem to have articles or stories available on its web site as of this writing. By providing an even balance between well-researched articles on scientific facts and well-written science fiction stories, novelettes, and poetry, *Analog* is appropriate for both the scientist and the sci-fi fan.

2247. *Andromeda Spaceways Inflight Magazine.* [ISSN: 1446-781X] 2002. q. AUD 14.95 newsstand/cover. Andromeda Spaceways Publishing Co-Op, PO Box 7311, Kaleen, ACT 2617, Australia. Adv. *Bk. rev.:* 5-10, 100-500 words. *Aud.:* Hs, Ga.

Andromeda Spaceways is an award-winning magazine from Australia. In it, the reader will find imaginative stories, poetry, scholarly essays, and reviews that are rooted in Australia's classic storytelling history. This title should appeal to a wide variety of readers; however, due to the language and some adult themes, it would not be appropriate for a young audience. An electronic version of the magazine is now available by subscription. There are additional benefits to the web site as well, including podcasts, letters, and forums that allow fans of the magazine to interact at a more intensive level. URL: www.andromedaspaceways.com

2248. *Apex Magazine: science fiction, fantasy, and horror.* [ISSN: 2157-1406] 2009. m. USD 19.95; USD 2.99 newsstand/cover per issue. Ed(s): Jason Sizemore, Lesley Conner. Apex Publications, PO Box 24323, Lexington, KY 40524; http://www.apexbookcompany.com. Illus., adv. *Aud.:* Ga.

Apex Magazine is a fully-electronic magazine of short fiction, poetry, and nonfiction in the speculative genre. This title includes podcast fiction in addition to prose. Most content in the magazine is available for free; however, some fiction and poetry are available only to subscribers or for purchase of individual issues. *Apex Magazine*'s easily navigable web site lends itself to easy browsing of current and past issues. The fiction tends to be excellently written and enjoyable. Because of its easy accessibility and quality content, this magazine would be appropriate for general audiences.

2249. *Asimov's Science Fiction.* Former titles (until 1992): *Isaac Asimov's Science Fiction Magazine;* (until 1990): *Isaac Asimov's Science Fiction;* (until 1986): *Isaac Asimov's Science Fiction Magazine.* [ISSN: 1065-2698] 1977. m. USD 34.97 domestic; USD 49.97 foreign. Ed(s): Sheila Williams. Dell Magazines, 6 Prowitt St, Norwalk, CT 06855; customerservice@pennypublications.com; http://www.pennydellpuzzles.com. Illus. Vol. ends: Dec. Microform: PQC. *Bk. rev.:* 5-8, 200-1,000 words. *Aud.:* Ga, Ac.

Asimov's Science Fiction has been an important magazine in the genre for 35 years. It has won the Locus Award for Best Magazine of the Year a total of 15 times. Not only does it provide its readers with short stories, novellas, and novelettes of the highest quality, it also provides book reviews, thought-provoking articles, poetry, and regular features including a whimsical item written by the prolific Robert Silverberg. The quality of *Asimov's Science Fiction* is paramount, and it is the essential magazine of science fiction writing that every library should own.

2250. *Bards and Sages Quarterly.* [ISSN: 1944-4699] 2009. q. USD 10.49 per issue. Ed(s): Julie A Dawson. Bards and Sages Publishing, .201 Leed Ave, Bellmawr, NJ 08031; admin@bardsandsages.com; http://www.bardsandsages.com/. Adv. *Aud.:* Ga, Sa.

Bards and Sages Quarterly is primarily a short story magazine, although it features an occasional author interview. According to its web site, the magazine strives to be "the most inclusive collection of speculative fiction available." Stories in the magazine vary in length and quality; however, this relatively new title has the potential to become a mainstay in speculative fiction publishing. The magazine is published in print as well as electronically. ;Bards and Sages Quarterly would be most appropriate for general audiences as well as academic collections.

2251. *Black Static.* Formerly (until 2007): *The Third Alternative.* [ISSN: 1753-0709] 1994. bi-m. GBP 24 domestic; GBP 27 in Europe; GBP 30 elsewhere. Ed(s): Andy Cox. T T A Press, 5 Martins Ln, Witcham, Ely, CB6 2LB, United Kingdom; info@ttapress.demon.co.uk; http://ttapress.com. Illus., adv. *Bk. rev.:* 15-25, 500-1,000 words. *Aud.:* Ga, Ac.

Black Static is a well-constructed horror and weird-fiction magazine published in the United Kingdom. The "Comment" section is particularly interesting and provides insightful critiques of the perceptions of horror as well as enlightening discussion of films, stories, and novels in the genre. Although the full text of this title is not available electronically, the web site includes teasers for all articles and fiction in each issue, as well as a bibliography of reviewed titles. Featuring op-ed pieces as well as new fiction and reviews of both films and books, this title would be appropriate for both general and academic collections. *Black Static* is published by the same publisher as *Interzone*, which is also included in this section.

2252. *Cemetery Dance: the magazine of horror and suspense.* [ISSN: 1047-7675] 1988. bi-m. USD 27 domestic; USD 35 Canada; USD 50 elsewhere. Cemetery Dance Publications, 132 B Industry Ln, Unit 7, Forest Hill, MD 21050; http://www.cemeterydance.com. Illus., adv. Vol. ends: Winter. *Bk. rev.:* 20-40, 200-5,000 words. *Aud.:* Ga.

This long-standing, award-winning publication includes essays, short stories, and artwork, as well as news and reviews. With a long history in horror, this title has a good combination of established and up-and-coming writers. Readers of horror will appreciate the six to eight original stories published in each issue and the in-depth interviews with the authors, while fans of the broader genre of science fiction will have an interest in this journal's news articles, interviews, and reviews of movies, software, and recent books. Not for the faint of heart, this title is best in general collections, but an academic collection with a horror section should have this on its shelves.

2253. *Clarkesworld Magazine.* [ISSN: 1937-7843] 2006. m. USD 35.88; USD 2.99 per issue. Ed(s): Neil Clarke, Sean Wallace. Wyrm Publishing, PO Box 172, Stirling, NJ 07980; http://www.wyrmpublishing.com/. Adv. *Aud.:* Hs, Ga, Ac.

Clarkesworld is published monthly as a webzine, or you can download the ebook form through Amazon (.mobi) or Weightless books (.epub or .mobi). Each month, the reader can expect at least two original short stories, a number of nonfiction pieces, original art, editorials, and podcasts. The quality of writing is stellar, with some articles incorporating videos or podcasts to enhance the discussion. *Clarkesworld* is a must for anyone who is interested in reading reviews about the broader science fiction, fantasy, and horror world. One of the joys of webzine publishing is the ability to promote forums, and this title is no exception. Having received several awards and nominations, this is a publication not to be missed. URL: http://clarkesworldmagazine.com/

2254. *Daily Science Fiction.* 2010. d. Free. Daily Science Fiction, info@dailysciencefiction.com; http://dailysciencefiction.com/. *Aud.:* Hs, Ga.

Daily Science Fiction uses a refreshingly unique approach to short story publication. The web magazine's title is self-explanatory; subscribers sign up for a daily e-mail of short science fiction. In addition to the e-mail subscription, stories may be read on *Daily Science Fiction*'s web site, which also includes an archive of all published stories. The best thing about this title is that it is available for free. Including a link to *Daily Science Fiction* in a reader's advisory page or on a library's web site would be an excellent way to encourage library patrons to explore short science fiction at no cost to a library's budget. This title is recommended for public or academic libraries, or any library with an interest in science fiction and fantasy.

2255. *Dead Reckonings.* [ISSN: 1935-6110] 2007. s-a. USD 15; USD 7.50 per issue. Ed(s): Michael J Abolafia, Alex Houstoun. Hippocampus Press, PO Box 641, New York, NY 10156; http://www.hippocampuspress.com/. *Bk. rev.:* Number and length vary. *Aud.:* Hs, Ga, Ac.

Dead Reckonings is different from most other titles included in this section because its primary focus is reviews of horror fiction rather than publishing new fiction or literary criticism of the speculative genre. Most reviews are essay-length, and the journal features one or two opinion essays on varying topics related to the genre. All reviews are signed, and the journal includes a brief biography for each contributor. This title is essential for libraries interested in developing horror and speculative fiction collections.

2256. *The Edgar Allan Poe Review.* Former titles (until 2000): *P S A Newsletter (Poe Studies Association);* (until 1978): *Poe Studies Association. Newsletter.* [ISSN: 2150-0428] 1973. s-a. USD 245 (print & online eds.)). Ed(s): Barbara Cantalupo. Pennsylvania State University Press, 820 N University Dr, University Support Bldg 1, Ste C, University Park, PA 16802; info@psupress.org; http://www.psupress.org. Illus., adv. Refereed. Reprint: PSC. *Indexed:* AmHI, MLA-IB. *Bk. rev.:* Number and length vary. *Aud.:* Hs, Ga, Ac.

The Edgar Allan Poe Review is an academic journal devoted to the life and writings of Edgar Allan Poe. This publication recently entered into its fourth year of being published by Pennsylvania State University Press. It features essays, reviews, and features that are well-written and peer-reviewed. Though all articles are about Poe, *The Edgar Allan Poe Review*'s authors from around the globe cover a great variety of topics to keep the reader interested. Not only does it conform to the highest standards of scholarly writing, but it is an aesthetically pleasing journal as well. Unfortunately, due to its niche subject matter, many libraries will forgo this journal, but any academic libraries that support a program that emphasizes Edgar Allan Poe would be greatly benefited by this journal.

2257. *Extrapolation.* [ISSN: 0014-5483] 1959. 3x/yr. GBP 66 (print & online eds.) Free to members). Ed(s): Andrew M Butler, Benjamin J Robertson. Liverpool University Press, 4 Cambridge St, Liverpool, L69 7ZU, United Kingdom; lup@liv.ac.uk; http://liverpooluniversitypress.co.uk/. Index, adv. Sample. Refereed. Vol. ends: Dec. *Indexed:* A01, A22, AmHI, BRI, CBRI, MLA-IB. *Bk. rev.:* 8-10, essay length. *Aud.:* Ga, Ac.

This is an international, peer-reviewed journal that publishes articles and book reviews on science fiction and speculative fiction. With a 50-year history, *Extrapolation* is one of the first peer-reviewed journals that has contained well-written pieces that cover a wide variety of topics within the genre. Its reviews include print, film, television, comics, and videogames. It would be appropriate for any higher education library with an interest in the genres of speculative fiction or science fiction. *Extrapolation* would also be relevant to a public library's science fiction collection.

2258. *Fangoria.* [ISSN: 0164-2111] 1978. 10x/yr. The Brooklyn Company, 138 Union St #1B, Brooklyn, NY 11231; joe@brooklynhomecompany.com; http://www.thebrooklynhomecompany.com. Illus., adv. Circ: 150000. *Bk. rev.:* Number and length vary. *Aud.:* Ga.

A horrific horror magazine for the masses. Fans of the genre will appreciate the gory indulgence of its glossy pages and full-color illustrations. Reviewing movies, plays, film, and occasionally classic-horror history, *Fangoria* will appeal to those interested in new movies and in books that represent the mainstream media more than the alternative experiments of the genre. Some adult content is included, so it would not be recommended for young audiences.

2259. *Fantasy & Science Fiction.* Formerly (until 1987): *The Magazine of Fantasy and Science Fiction;* Incorporates: *Venture Science Fiction.* [ISSN: 1095-8258] 1949. bi-m. USD 36.97 domestic; USD 50.97 foreign. Ed(s): Gordon Van Gelder. Spilogale, Inc., P O Box 3447, Hoboken, NJ 07030. Illus., adv. Sample. Microform: PQC. *Indexed:* A01, AmHI, BRI, C37, CBRI, F01, MASUSE, MLA-IB. *Bk. rev.:* 5-10, 200-1,000 words. *Aud.:* Hs, Ga, Ac.

For over 65 years, *Fantasy & Science Fiction* continues has been a central title for any collection of science fiction, fantasy, and horror journals. Founded in 1949, this essential title has published not only upcoming authors but also many of the giants of speculative fiction, including Stephen King, Ray Bradbury, Ursula K. Le Guin, and others. *Fantasy & Science Fiction* also includes book and movie reviews, and frequently investigates scientific topics of interest to the speculative fiction audience. Back issues of *Fantasy & Science Fiction* are indexed to 1998 on the web site, and readers can access articles and editorials from "Departments," from 1999 to the current issue. Both in print and on the web, *Fantasy & Science Fiction* maintains a clean publication design; the reader is not overwhelmed by flashy advertisements or extraneous information. In addition to the print and web site versions, this title is available for Kindle and Kindle reading apps. *Fantasy & Science Fiction* would be a welcome addition to libraries interested in speculative fiction.

2260. *Femspec: an interdisciplinary feminist journal dedicated to science fiction fantasy,magical realism,surrealism,myth,folklore and other supernatural genres.* [ISSN: 1523-4002] 1999. s-a. USD 110 (Individuals, USD 55). Ed(s): Batya Weinbaum. Femspec, 1610 Rydalmount Rd, Cleveland Heights, OH 44118; http://www.femspec.org/. Adv. Refereed. *Indexed:* AmHI, BRI, FemPer, GW, MLA-IB. *Bk. rev.:* 2-3, essay length, signed. *Aud.:* Ga, Ac.

Femspec purports to be "an interdisciplinary journal dedicated to science fiction, fantasy, magical realism, surrealism, myth, folklore and other supernatural genres." Although most of the stories and articles fit this broad scope, recent issues seem to have strayed from the speculative in favor of the purely feminist. While the critical articles are, in general, well-written and well-researched, the other sections of the journal are inconsistent. Each issue includes at least two or three essay-length book, art, or music reviews, but most of the materials reviewed were published more than two years prior to the journal publication date. Additionally, *Femspec*'s web site is difficult to navigate and does not follow web design conventions. Despite its inconsistencies, *Femspec* would be suitable for academic libraries that specialize in women's studies; however, it is not an essential title.

2261. *Focus (London, 1979).* [ISSN: 0144-560X] 1979. s-a. Free to members. Ed(s): Martin McGrath. British Science Fiction Association Ltd., 61 Ivycroft Rd, Warton, Tamworth, B79 0JJ, United Kingdom; bsfamembership@yahoo.co.uk; http://www.bsfa.co.uk. Sample. *Aud.:* Ga, Ac.

This is the membership magazine of the British Science Fiction Association Ltd. Its focus is on improving writing for the genre. The articles all involve information about the art and craft of storytelling. Its broad content discusses everything from horror to sex, from crafting strange new worlds to patterns of speech. If you are interested in professional opinion on science fiction writing, this would be a good title to check out. It would be appropriate for collections with writing departments, science fiction, or horror collections.

2262. *Foundation: the international review of science fiction.* [ISSN: 0306-4964] 1972. 3x/yr. GBP 22 (Students, GBP 15). Ed(s): Paul March-Russell. Science Fiction Foundation, University of Reading, Department of History, Faculty of Letters and Social Science, Reading, RG1 5PT, United Kingdom; http://www.sf-foundation.org/. Illus., index. Refereed. Vol. ends: Dec. *Indexed:* MLA-IB. *Bk. rev.:* 10-15, 500-2,500 words. *Aud.:* Ga, Ac.

Foundation: The International Review of Science Fiction is a peer-reviewed journal dedicated to scholarship in science fiction. Articles include thorough research in the field of science fiction, and the journal includes lengthy book reviews and occasionally bibliographies and conference proceedings. Because of its specialized field of study, this title would be most appropriate for academic collections, particularly those with a focus on research and theory in literature.

2263. ***Interzone: science fiction and fantasy.*** Incorporates (in 1994): *Nexus;* (1991-1993): *Million.* [ISSN: 0264-3596] 1982. bi-m. GBP 24 domestic; EUR 27 in Europe; USD 30 elsewhere. Ed(s): Andy Cox. T T A Press, 5 Martins Ln, Witcham, Ely, CB6 2LB, United Kingdom; info@ttapress.demon.co.uk; http://ttapress.com. Illus., adv. Sample. *Bk. rev.:* 7-10, 100-500 words. *Aud.:* Ga, Ac.

Interzone is TTA Press's companion publication to *Black Static*. While *Black Static* focuses on horror and weird fiction, *Interzone* is rooted firmly in the science fiction genre. Founded in 1982, this magazine continues to publish excellent fiction and includes beautiful illustrations. As with its companion publication, *Interzone*'s web site features teasers for its published fiction as well as a bibliography of reviewed films and fiction. This award-winning title would be welcome in general and academic collections with a science fiction focus.

2264. ***Lady Churchill's Rosebud Wristlet.*** [ISSN: 1544-7782] 1996. q. USD 20 in US & Canada; USD 36 elsewhere; USD 5 per issue in US & Canada. Ed(s): Kelly Link, Gavin J Grant. Small Beer Press, 150 Pleasant St #306, Easthampton, MA 01027; info@smallbeerpress.com; http://smallbeerpress.com/. Adv. Circ: 1000. *Indexed:* AmHI. *Bk. rev.:* Number and length vary. *Aud.:* Ga, Ac.

This small press title has a fanciful name to go with its eclectic contents. Each issue contains short comics, short fiction, and poetry, as well as a humorous advice column. The stories share a certain dark poignancy, ranging from the suspenseful to the humorous, and never forgetting the fantastical. It is published biannually by Small Beer Press. *LCRW* would be appropriate for any academic collection that has an interest in writing and creative expression. However, its small size and infrequent publication makes it a journal many libraries may wish to forgo.

2265. ***Lightspeed: science fiction and fantasy.*** Incorporates (2005-2012): *Fantasy Magazine.* [ISSN: 2160-4282] 2010. m. USD 35.88; USD 3.99 per issue. Ed(s): John Joseph Adams, Wendy N Wagner. Prime Books, http://www.prime-books.com. Adv. *Aud.:* Ga, Ac.

A hefty magazine that weighs in at 400-plus pages per month, *Lightspeed* is a short-fiction magazine of science fiction and fantasy that provides both original material and reprinted stories. It has recently merged with its sister magazine *Fantasy* and claims to provide an equal amount of science fiction and fantasy, but the issues submitted for review seemed to contain mostly science fiction. The writing throughout the magazine is of good quality, and makes for an enjoyable read. In addition to fiction, author interviews and author spotlights are also included. Issues are available to read for free on the magazine's web site, but subscription copies contain additional content not found online. *Lightspeed* is only available in electronic formats. If your library's collection development plan emphasizes maximizing your good story per dollar spent, then *Lightspeed* would be a good addition to your collection.

2266. ***Locus (Oakland): the magazine of the science fiction and fantasy field.*** [ISSN: 0047-4959] 1968. m. USD 79 (print & online eds.) Individuals, USD 75 (print & online eds.)). Ed(s): Liza Groen Trombi, Kirsten Gong-Wong. Locus Publications, 34 Ridgewood Ln, Oakland, CA 94611. Illus., index, adv. Sample. Circ: 6000. Vol. ends: Dec. *Indexed:* BRI, CBRI, MLA-IB. *Bk. rev.:* 15-30, 200-1,000 words. *Aud.:* Ga, Ac.

Locus is a monthly magazine delivering news for the science fiction, fantasy, and horror field. It leans toward being a trade magazine with publishing information and news. Even the articles are written for an audience of authors, book groups, and publishers. However, *Locus* does offer extensive reviews of books, magazines, and web sites in the science fiction, fantasy, and horror field. This might make it a good magazine for collection development in libraries with extensive collections in this genre. Although an important magazine, *Locus* is so specialized that most library patrons will not benefit from it, and only the most specialized of collections dealing with this genre should subscribe to this magazine.

2267. ***Lovecraft Annual.*** [ISSN: 1935-6102] 2007. a. USD 15. Ed(s): S.T Joshi. Hippocampus Press, PO Box 641, New York, NY 10156; http://www.hippocampuspress.com/. *Indexed:* MLA-IB. *Bk. rev.:* Number and length vary. *Aud.:* Hs, Ga, Ac.

The *Lovecraft Annual* is a yearly publication devoted to literary criticism of the works of H. P. Lovecraft. A fairly new journal, it was started in 2007 and is printed by Hippocampus Press, a small publisher specializing in classic horror and science fiction with an emphasis on Lovecraft and pulp writers of the 1920s and 1930s. While the articles are lengthy and well-written, there are many parts of the journal that fail to measure up to academic-journal standards. Author information is not included, and references are sporadic. The journal offers some reviews of new works, but mainly specializes in critical writing and scholarship. Due to the lack of journals that specialize in this area, academic libraries with programs that emphasize the works of Lovecraft might benefit from this journal, but most libraries simply do not have the patron demand for the *Lovecraft Annual*'s offerings.

2268. ***Mythlore.*** Incorporates (1965-1972): *Tolkien Journal.* [ISSN: 0146-9339] 1969. s-a. Members, USD 35; Non-members, USD 43; USD 15 per issue. Ed(s): Janet Brennan Croft. Mythopoeic Society, PO Box 6707, Altadena, CA 91003; http://www.mythsoc.org. Index, adv. Sample. Refereed. *Indexed:* A22, AmHI, BRI, MLA-IB. *Bk. rev.:* 3-10, 100-300 words. *Aud.:* Hs, Ga, Ac.

Mythlore is published by the Mythopoeic Society, an organization for the study, discussion, and enjoyment of fantasy and mythic literature, especially the works of J.R.R. Tolkien, C. S. Lewis, and Charles Williams. It is an academic journal of impeccable scholarly standards with high-quality articles. This journal is a must-have for any academic library with a collection or program that emphasizes this genre.

2269. ***Nightmare: horror & dark phantasy.*** 2012. m. USD 24.99 Formats: ePub, Mobi (Kindle-compatible), or PDF). Ed(s): John Joseph Adams. Nightmare, http://www.nightmare-magazine.com. *Aud.:* Ga, Ac.

Nightmare is a new monthly fiction magazine that started as an offshoot of *Lightspeed* magazine to showcase its horror and dark fantasy short stories. As such, it is very similar to *Lightspeed* magazine in format and tone. Unfortunately, *Nightmare* is not quite up to its sister magazine's standard, with wildly inconsistent story quality. However, this might not (and possibly should not) dissuade some libraries from pursuing this title. The writing is very representative of the genre as a whole, and may find eager readers in the hands of fans. Public libraries in particular might find this magazine very popular with their patrons. *Nightmare* is only available in electronic format.

2270. ***On Spec: the Canadian magazine of the fantastic.*** [ISSN: 0843-476X] 1989. q. CAD 24 domestic; USD 25 United States; USD 35 elsewhere. Ed(s): Diane Walton. Copper Pig Writers' Society, PO Box 4727, Edmonton, AB T6E 5G6, Canada. Illus., index, adv. Sample. *Aud.:* Ga, Ac.

Created as a venue for English-speaking Canadian science fiction writers to explore their genre, *On Spec* has a wonderful editorial team to help new writers develop their craft. It supports fantastical literature from a Canadian point of view. For over 20 years, *On Spec* has been helping readers suspend their disbelief through fantastical and speculative fiction. This title contains award-winning science fiction, fantasy, horror, and poetry. Now available electronically as well as in print. Appropriate for a variety of audiences.

2271. ***Science Fiction Studies.*** [ISSN: 0091-7729] 1973. 3x/yr. USD 65. Ed(s): Joan Gordon, Istvan Csicsery-Ronay. S F - T H Inc., c/o Arthur B. Evans, Department of Modern Languages, Greencastle, IN 46135; aevans@depauw.edu. Illus. Refereed. Vol. ends: Dec. *Indexed:* A01, A22, AmHI, BRI, C37, CBRI, F01, MLA-IB. *Bk. rev.:* 10-20, 500-3,000 words. *Aud.:* Ac.

Science Fiction Studies is one of the few academic journals entirely devoted to the literary criticism of science fiction. Its articles and reviews are of the utmost scholarly quality. The contents of each article explore the vast field of science fiction literature and, thus, fills this highly specialized niche. Because of the specialized content of its articles, *Science Fiction Studies* will not be a journal that is in most libraries' collections. However, for any academic library that supports a program that focuses on science fiction, this journal is essential.

2272. ***Shimmer Magazine.*** [ISSN: 1933-8864] 2005. bi-m. USD 14.99 per issue. Ed(s): Nicola Belte. Shimmer Magazine, PO Box 58591, Salt Lake City, UT 84158-0591; http://www.shimmerzine.com. *Aud.:* Ga.

Shimmer is an independently published and distributed-monthly magazine of "contemporary fantasy short stories," with some stories leaning toward science fiction and horror. Its authors, who come from the United States and the United Kingdom, are predominantly amateurs, with some small-press and independently published authors. Recently, it changed to an electronic format distributed six times a year. Several stories have been reprinted in *Best American Fantasy* and Rich Horton's *Year's Best Fantasy and Science Fiction.* This title is well worth a look, but may not be appropriate for younger audiences.

2273. ***Space and Time.*** [ISSN: 0271-2512] 1966. 3x/yr. USD 19.99 in US & Canada. Ed(s): Hildy Silverman. Space and Time, 1308 Centennial Ave, Ste 101, Piscataway, NJ 08854. Illus., adv. Sample. *Bk. rev.:* Number and length vary. *Aud.:* Hs, Ga.

Space and Time, a small-press, quarterly magazine, is one of the true speculative fiction magazines, offering stories in fantasy, horror, science fiction, and the "wacky blends thereof." Its multitude of different styles will allow any reader with even a passing interest in this genre to find something to enjoy. In addition to its quality short fiction, *Space and Time* devotes equal amounts of space to poetry, articles, and interviews. The articles are not scholarly in nature, but very well written and enjoyable. *Space and Time* is available in both print and electronic format. Although the magazine has recently moved from a quarterly schedule to publishing three times a year, this title is of good enough quality to ensure that it has a long life. It would be a welcome to addition to any library.

2274. ***Strange Horizons.*** 2000. w. Free. Ed(s): Niall Harrison. Strange Horizons, . Adv. *Bk. rev.:* 15-20. *Aud.:* Ga, Ac.

Strange Horizons is a weekly online title, publishing articles, art, reviews, and poetry that are speculative in nature. It focuses on investigating the underlying meaning or message within science fiction and fantasy works. Extremely well-written for a free online publication, the content is relevant and timely. *Strange Horizons* has made a name for itself with numerous reprints in other printed collections of stories and articles. It is fully archived, allowing new readers to explore past and present articles. URL: www.strangehorizons.com

2275. ***Tangent Online: the genre's premiere review magazine for short sf & fantasy since 1993.*** Formerly (until 1997): *Tangent (Print).* 1993. bi-m. Ed(s): David A Truesdale. Tangent, http://www.tangentonline.com. *Bk. rev.:* 60-75, 500-2,000 words. *Aud.:* Hs, Ga, Ac.

For the critical reader, *Tangent Online* is an invaluable web site that reviews most of the short fiction, magazines, and journals in the field. With an impressive history in reviewing the best of science fiction and fantasy, this title has garnered four Hugo awards and multiple nominations for its reviews and interviews. If you would like to know more about the publications and authors in the field, this is one of the first places to look. Readers can access the site without a subscription. URL: www.tangentonline.com

2276. ***Vector.*** Incorporates (1980-1992): *Paperback Inferno;* Which was formerly (until 1980): *Paperback Parlour.* [ISSN: 0505-0448] 1958. bi-m. Free to members. British Science Fiction Association Ltd., 61 Ivycroft Rd, Warton, Tamworth, B79 0JJ, United Kingdom; bsfamembership@yahoo.co.uk; http://www.bsfa.co.uk. Illus. Refereed. Vol. ends: Dec. *Bk. rev.:* 15-25, 200-1,000 words. *Aud.:* Hs, Ga, Ac.

Vector is the publication of the British Science Fiction Association that aims to encourage science fiction in every form. It is defined as leaning toward the academic style for those readers who are interested in this genre, but it keeps itself from becoming too serious. It is composed of articles and reviews. Its articles, while not academic in nature, are thought-provoking and well-written. References are given, though no author information is provided. In addition to its articles, *Vector* offers extensive reviews for newly published works, the majority of which are fiction. It is an important magazine for the British side of this genre, and should be purchased by all libraries with patrons devoted to this genre.

■ FILMS

John Raymond, Access Services & Technology Librarian at Siena College, Loudonville, NY, jraymond@siena.edu

Introduction

Films released within the past couple of years offer perspectives on such topics as the currently volatile American political landscape, civil rights, gender studies and the #metoo movement, masculinity, LGBT, and environmental issues. Film critics and scholars identify these topics and evaluate the artistry of cinema. Film studies, as curriculum, creativity, or hobby, is valuable to nearly any library patron population due to the sheer popularity of the movies. The range of magazines and journals listed here suits scholars, film buffs, critics, and those studying film, looking to make films, or write screenplays. Some of the titles are available in print, both print and electronic, or digital only. Many magazine/journal websites offer supplementary material such as blogs, news, and advertising relevant to the intended reader of the publication. The visual medium of film influences the style of these publications, especially that of the digital counterpart, as most of them are quite attractive and feature film stills with an aesthetically considerate composition, and often links to supplementary video content for direct viewing. As streaming services such as Netflix continue to advance in popularity and ubiquity, access to home cinema will serve audiences and students of all kinds, and further develop critical discussion, both for scholars and the film aficionado. Netflix, a pioneer in film streaming, is encountering uncharted waters as studios and corporations such as Disney and AT&T (the parent company of Warner Media and HBO) pull their content from Netflix and begin to release their own dedicated streaming services.

Basic Periodicals

Hs: *Animation Magazine, Film Comment, Film Quarterly;* Ga: *Cineaste, Film Comment, Film Quarterly, Sight and Sound;* Ac: *Cineaste, Film Comment, Film Quarterly, Journal of Film and Video, Sight and Sound.*

Basic Abstracts and Indexes

Film & Television Literature Index, International Index to Film Periodicals.

2277. ***Alphaville: journal of film and screen media.*** [ISSN: 2009-4078] 2011. . Free. Ed(s): Laura Rascaroli. University College Cork, Film Studies at UCC, O'Rahilly Bldg G28, Cork, , Ireland; http://www.ucc.ie. Refereed. *Aud.:* Ac.

This new, fully online, and open-access journal seeks to be "a dynamic international forum open to the discussion of all aspects of film history, theory and criticism through multiple research methodologies and perspectives. *Alphaville* aims to cultivate inspiring, cutting-edge research, and particularly welcomes work produced by early career researchers in Film and Screen Media." This is a beautifully designed online publication, and its presentation is, well, cool! The articles are far-reaching and international in nature. Some recent article titles are "Exercising Radical Democracy: The Crisis of Representation and Interactive Documentary as an Agent of Change" and "The Poetics and Politics of Polyphony: Towards a Research Method for Interactive Documentary." The best audience for this fascinating publication will be serious film studies programs. URL: www.alphavillejournal.com

2278. ***American Cinematographer: the international journal of motion imaging.*** [ISSN: 0002-7928] 1920. m. USD 29.95. A S C Holding Corporation, PO Box 2230, Hollywood, CA 90078; office@theasc.com; http://www.ascmag.com/. Illus., index, adv. Vol. ends: Dec. Microform: PQC. *Indexed:* A06, A22, F01, IIPA. *Bk. rev.:* 5-6, 150 words. *Aud.:* Sa.

This monthly publication of the American Society of Cinematographers not only provides current industry information, but also provides lots of interviews with cinematographers of current releases and a behind-the-scenes look at the technical details used to achieve a particular shot. Working cameramen can get reviews of new equipment on the market, and film buffs and burgeoning cinematographers can get detailed information about their new favorite films. Book and DVD reviews, classified ads, and an ad index are in each issue. The title of a recent article is "Game of Thrones; David Franco, Fabian Wagner, ASC, BSC, Jonathan Freeman, ASC Conclude the Epic Saga." This journal is for collections that address the needs of film studies programs and filmmakers.

2279. ***Animation Magazine: the business, technology & art of animation and VFX.*** Formerly (until 1987): *Animation News.* [ISSN: 1041-617X] 19??. m. USD 60 domestic. Ed(s): Ramin Zahed. Terry Thoren Publications, D B A Animation Magazine, 30941 W. Agoura Rd., Ste 102, Westlake Village, CA 91361; sales@animationmagazine.net. Illus., adv. *Indexed:* F01. *Bk. rev.:* 1-2, 300-500 words. *Aud.:* Ga, Sa.

Although this claims to be a fan magazine, the level of technical detail and technical ads indicate that it is as much an industry magazine. Not too surprisingly for a magazine about a visual art form, it is a gorgeous and fun publication, with wonderful glossy illustrations that have wide appeal. It contains articles on animation's use in feature films, games, and television. There are copious ads, film reviews, and regular articles on industry business and conferences. There is also an annual section on animation academic programs. A titles of a recent feature article is "Pixar's Toy Story 4: New Friends, Villains and Oddities." Any academic library with a strong, varied art program should consider purchasing this title, as well as any special or academic library that services a film production population.

2280. ***Black Camera: an international film journal.*** [ISSN: 1536-3155] 1985. s-a. USD 130.90 (print & online eds.)). Ed(s): Michael T Martin. Indiana University Press, Office of Scholarly Publishing, Herman B Wells Library 350, Bloomington, IN 47405; iuporder@indiana.edu; http://iupress.indiana.edu/. Illus., adv. Refereed. Reprint: PSC. *Indexed:* A22, E01, F01, IIPA, MLA-IB. *Bk. rev.:* 3-4, 500-1,000 words. *Aud.:* Ac.

The original *Black Camera* was a newsletter, predominantly focused on American Black film. This new series has turned the title into a glossy, substantive, peer-reviewed academic journal. It covers all Black film, from African film to sites of the African diaspora. It is an excellent journal, filling a niche that had been empty after the death of its first iteration. The included articles are rich and diverse. Some titles of recent articles include "Re-Reading Birth of a Nation: European Contexts and the War Film" and "Strictly a Laughing Matter?: The Significance of the Blaxploitation Movement and Black Dynamite as Parody." There are excellent interviews and book reviews, which are, like the rest of the journal, directed at an academic audience. For any academic library that addresses a film or African American or African Studies departments.

2281. ***Boxoffice Pro: the business of movies.*** Formerly (until 2011): *Boxoffice;* Which incorporated (1920-1977): *Boxoffice (Eastern Edition);* (19??-1977): *Boxoffice (Southeast Edition);* (19??-1977): *Boxoffice (Southwest Edition);* (1932-1977): *Boxoffice (National Executive Edition);* (19??-1977): *Boxoffice (New England Edition).* [ISSN: 2325-1492] 1920. m. USD 59.95 domestic; USD 74.95 in Canada & Mexico; USD 135 elsewhere. Ed(s): Ken Bacon. Boxoffice Media, LLC., 230 Park Ave., Ste. 1000, New York, NY 10169. Illus., adv. Vol. ends: Dec. *Indexed:* BRI, F01, IIPA. *Aud.:* Sa.

For nearly one hundred years, *Boxoffice Pro* has been required reading for every serious player in the industry, from theater owners to studio executives. There is coverage of industry news (national and international), box office grosses, production data on new Hollywood releases, and financial information on the major studios. Also included are numerous reviews of new Hollywood feature films; interviews with filmmakers, screenwriters, executives, actors, producers, and directors; and up-to-date festival information. Although it covers all areas of the film industry, it is definitely skewed toward, as its current subtitle says, the business of movies. It lists current and upcoming studio release charts by month. There are short reviews with "exploitips," a guide to new products, and news on concessions. The magazine is also now promising certain types of timely information (such as financials) directly via e-mail. A title of a recent article is "Swedish Connection: B-Reel Films Looks to Cross Over with Midsommar and King Fury 2." Highly recommended for libraries that need complete coverage of the Hollywood film industry.

2282. ***Bright Lights (Online): film journal.*** Formerly (until 1995): *Bright Lights (Print).* [ISSN: 2376-8290] 1974. q. Free. Ed(s): Gary Morris. Bright Lights, 35200 Cathedral Canyon Dr, No 143, Cathedral City, CA 92234; brightlightswriters@gmail.com; http://www.brightlightsfilm.com. Illus., adv. *Bk. rev.:* Number and length vary. *Aud.:* Ga, Ac.

"A popular-academic hybrid of movie analysis, history and commentary, looking at classical and commercial, independent, exploitation, and international film from a wide range of vantage points from the aesthetic to the political. A prime area of focus is on the connection between capitalist society and the images that reflect, support, or subvert it—movies as propaganda." I admit, I love this site more every time I look at it. It gets broader, edgier, and more interesting! Included on this site are some highly unusual genres, such as "tranny cinema." It has feature articles, film reviews, book reviews, filmmaker interviews, and film festival coverage. Unlike some online film journals, this publication has also caught onto the power of its web-based format, and includes not only stills, but clips from films. Titles of recent articles include "Donald Trump: Lynchian Monster" and "Sexual Politics: On Olivier Assayas's Non-Fiction." Any library with serious filmgoing patrons should consider linking to this edgy, interesting journal.

2283. ***Camera Obscura: feminism, culture, and media studies.*** [ISSN: 0270-5346] 1976. 3x/yr. USD 267. Ed(s): Lalitha Gopalan, Homay King. Duke University Press, 905 W Main St, Durham, NC 27701; orders@dukeupress.edu; https://www.dukeupress.edu. Illus., adv. Refereed. Vol. ends: Sep. Reprint: PSC. *Indexed:* A01, A22, A51, AmHI, BAS, C42, E01, F01, FemPer, GW, IIPA, MLA-IB. *Bk. rev.:* Number and length vary. *Aud.:* Ac.

This title "seeks to provide a forum for dialogue and debate on media, culture, and politics. Specifically, the journal encourages contributions in the following areas: analyses of the conjunctions among gender, race, class, sexuality, and nation, as these are articulated in film, television, popular culture, and media criticism and theory; new histories of film, television, popular culture, and media criticism and theory, as well as contemporary interventions in these fields; [and] politically engaged approaches to visual culture, media production, and contemporary constructions of feminism—inside the academy and in popular culture." Articles are well documented and accompanied by detailed notes. Titles of some recent articles include "Hanging Out Yonkers: A Photographic Record" and "With Chantal in New York in the 1970s: An Interview with Babette Mangolte." A recommended addition to academic film collections.

2284. ***Cineaction!: a magazine of radical film criticism & theory.*** [ISSN: 0826-9866] 1985. 3x/yr. Cineaction!, 40 Alexander St, Ste 705, Toronto, ON M4Y 1B5, Canada. Illus., index. Sample. *Indexed:* BRI, C37, F01, IIPA, MLA-IB. *Bk. rev.:* Number and length vary. *Aud.:* Ac.

This title examines film from various viewpoints. Each issue focuses on a central theme, and forthcoming themes are announced, encouraging the submission of articles. In addition to scholarly articles on film theory, there are interviews with filmmakers, film reviews, book reviews, and reports from international film festivals. Some recent article titles include "Excrement, Garbage, and the City: an Ideological Battlefront in Canadian Apocalypse Cinema" and "All Work and No Play: The Madness of Meaning in Stanley Kubrick's The Shining." For library collections that address the needs of serious students of film and filmmakers.

2285. ***Cineaste: America's leading magazine on the art and politics of the cinema.*** [ISSN: 0009-7004] 1967. q. USD 44 (Individuals, USD 24; USD 8 newsstand/cover domestic). Ed(s): Gary Crowdus. Cineaste Publishers, Inc., 708 Third Ave, 5th Fl, New York, NY 10017; http://www.cineaste.com. Illus., index, adv. Vol. ends: Fall. Microform: PQC. *Indexed:* A01, A22, BRI, C37, Chicano, F01, IIPA, MASUSE, MLA-IB. *Bk. rev.:* Number and length vary. *Aud.:* Ga, Ac.

This publication bills itself as "America's leading magazine on the art and politics of the cinema." It provides interviews with actors and filmmakers, as well as film, home video, and book reviews. Recent article titles include "Film, TV, Streaming, and the Transformation of Narrative" and "Uncovering the True Story of France's Continental Films During the German Occupation." For serious film studies collections.

2286. ***Cinefex: the journal of cinematic illusions.*** [ISSN: 0198-1056] 1980. bi-m. USD 49 (print & online eds.); USD 12.50 newsstand/cover domestic; USD 15 newsstand/cover Canada). Cinefex, PO Box 20027, Riverside, CA 92516. Illus., adv. Vol. ends: Dec. *Indexed:* F01, IIPA. *Aud.:* Sa.

"*Cinefex* is a bimonthly magazine devoted to motion picture special effects. Since 1980 it has been a bible to professionals and enthusiasts, covering the field like no other publication. Profusely illustrated in color, with as many as 180 pages per issue, *Cinefex* offers a captivating look at the technologies and techniques behind many of our most popular and enduring movies." For the professional, there is a profusion of ads for services and products related to special visual effects. And not too surprisingly, this journal has an astounding website! A title of a recent articles is "Game of Thrones Final Season." For any library that serves the needs of a film studies program.

2287. ***Cinema Scope: expanding the frame on international cinema.*** [ISSN: 1488-7002] 1999. q. USD 40 CAD 21.40 domestic. Ed(s): Andrew Tracy, Mark Peranson. Cinema Scope Publishing, 465 Lytton Blvd, Toronto, ON M5N 1S5, Canada. Illus., adv. *Indexed:* F01, MLA-IB. *Bk. rev.:* Number and length vary. *Aud.:* Ac, Sa.

"An independently published quarterly jam-packed with interviews, features, and essays on film and video, *CS* is geared to cinephiles looking for an intelligent forum on world cinema. With unparalleled depth and breadth, *CS* is a real alternative in today's Canadian film scene." This title includes DVD reviews, book reviews, and film festival reviews. Titles of recent articles include "The Meeting of Two Queens: Doris Wishman and Peggy Ahwesh" and "Come on Feel the Noise: The Films of Andres Duque." For any film journal collection that addresses the needs of serious film aficionados and students.

2288. ***Cinemontage: journal of the Motion Pictures Editors Guild.*** Former titles (until 2012): *Editors Guild Magazine;* (until 2000): *Editors Guild Newsletter;* (until 1979): *The Leader.* [ISSN: 2165-3526] 1943. bi-m. Free to members. Ed(s): Tomm Carroll. Motion Picture Editors Guild, 7715 Sunset Blvd, Ste 200, Hollywood, CA 90046; http://www.editorsguild.com/index.shtml. Adv. Vol. ends: Nov/Dec. *Aud.:* Sa.

Next to directors, editors play the single biggest role in the formation of the final paths that films take to completion. Motion picture editors have their own guild, and it produces an official magazine, now entitled *CineMontage* (formerly *The Editors Guild Magazine*). This publication is fully available online. It covers industry events and changes that impact guild members. There are interviews with editors and assessments of new equipment and technologies. Recent articles include "When Editing Began: The Cut that Launched a Filmmaking Craft" and "La 'Vida' Familiar: A Latinx Homecoming." The magazine is fun and glossy, but will be most appropriate for libraries with serious film studies programs, and film industry libraries.

2289. ***Documentary (Los Angeles).*** Formerly (until 2006): *International Documentary.* [ISSN: 1559-1034] 1986. q. Free to members; Non-members, USD 45. Ed(s): Thomas White. International Documentary Association, 3470 Wilshire Blvd Ste 980, Los Angeles, CA 90010; http://www.documentary.org/. Illus., adv. Sample. *Indexed:* F01. *Aud.:* Ac, Sa.

This publication of the International Documentary Association intends to "promote nonfiction film and video and to support the efforts of documentary makers around the world." It provides membership news and reports on festivals. Feature articles on aspects of the documentary filmmaking process are published with the doc filmmaker in mind. Ads for pre- and post-production services, festivals, and classes in documentary filmmaking are included. Columns formerly included in each issue, but now available on the website, are North American broadcast and cable premieres, events and screenings, calls for entries, funding, and jobs and opportunities. Examples of some recent articles include "Beyond Inclusion: Building Narratives of Liberation" and "A (Revised!) Introduction to Documentary Budgeting." Libraries that address either film studies or television journalism should consider this title.

2290. ***Film Comment: because we all need to talk about movies.*** Formerly (until 1962): *Vision.* [ISSN: 0015-119X] 1962. bi-m. USD 29.95 domestic; USD 40 in Canada & Mexico; USD 60 elsewhere. Ed(s): Nicolas Rapold. Film Society of Lincoln Center, 70 Lincoln Center Plz, New York, NY 10023; filminfo@filmlinc.com; http://www.filmlinc.com. Illus., index, adv. Vol. ends: Nov/Dec. *Indexed:* A01, A06, A22, AmHI, BRI, C37, CBRI, F01, IIPA, MASUSE, MLA-IB. *Bk. rev.:* Number and length vary. *Aud.:* Hs, Ga, Ac.

This publication by the Film Society of Lincoln Center gives excellent coverage of filmmaking in the United States and abroad (although, if you don't live in New York City, this publication will make you want to move there!). It contains feature articles, reviews, screenings, and the like. Some examples of recent articles are "Interview: Jim Jarmusch" and "Ossie Davis and Ruby Dee." For academic collections and public libraries that address the needs of serious film buffs.

2291. ***Film Criticism (Online).*** Formerly (until 2016): *Film Criticism (Print).* [ISSN: 2471-4364] 1976. 3x/yr. Free. Ed(s): Joe Tompkins. Michigan Publishing, 839 Greene St, Ann Arbor, MI 48104; mpublishing@umich.edu; http://www.publishing.umich.edu/. Illus., adv. Sample. Refereed. Vol. ends: Spring. *Indexed:* A01, A22, AmHI, BRI, CBRI, F01, IIPA, MLA-IB. *Bk. rev.:* Number and length vary. *Aud.:* Ac.

This journal celebrates its status as the third oldest film magazine in the country. This refereed journal publishes articles that examine and re-examine films from a variety of critical, political, and aesthetic viewpoints. Unusual aspects of films and symbolism are discussed in great detail. Occasionally, the body of work of a specific filmmaker is analyzed. Recent titles include "The Gentrification of John Waters" and "Repressing the Male Gaze? Sidney J. Furie's The Leather Boys and the Growing Pains of Post-War British Masculinity." There are book reviews in most issues. For academic libraries that serve film studies programs.

2292. ***Film History: an international journal.*** [ISSN: 0892-2160] 1987. q. USD 307.45 (print & online eds.)). Ed(s): Julie Lavelle, Gregory Waller. Indiana University Press, Office of Scholarly Publishing, Herman B Wells Library 350, Bloomington, IN 47405; iuporder@indiana.edu; http://iupress.indiana.edu/. Illus., index, adv. Refereed. Vol. ends: Dec. Reprint: PSC. *Indexed:* A01, A22, BRI, E01, F01, IIMP, IIPA, MLA-IB. *Bk. rev.:* Number and length vary. *Aud.:* Ac.

"The subject of *Film History* is the historical development of the motion picture, and the social, technological and economic context in which this has occurred. Its areas of interest range from the technical and entrepreneurial innovations of early and pre-cinema experiments, through all aspects of the production, distribution, exhibition and reception of commercial and non-commercial motion pictures. In addition to original research in these areas, the journal will survey the paper and film holdings of archives and libraries worldwide, publish selected examples of primary documentation (such as early film scenarios) and report on current publications, exhibitions, conferences and research in progress. Most future issues will be devoted to comprehensive studies of single themes." Titles of recent articles include "What Is This Thing? Framing and Unframing the Science-Fiction Film" and "Old Corporate Films and Former Factory Workers: Film Reception as Social Memory." For academic libraries with film studies collections.

2293. ***Film Quarterly.*** Former titles (until 1958): *The Quarterly of Film, Radio and Television;* (until 1951): *The Hollywood Quarterly.* [ISSN: 0015-1386] 1945. q. USD 343 (print & online eds.)). Ed(s): B. Ruby Rich. University of California Press, Journals Division, 155 Grand Avenue, Ste 400, Oakland, CA 94612-3764; http://www.ucpress.edu/journals.php. Illus., index, adv. Sample. Refereed. Circ: 3591. Vol. ends: Oct. Microform: PQC. *Indexed:* A01, A06, A22, AmHI, BRI, CBRI, E01, F01, IIPA, MLA-IB. *Bk. rev.:* Number and length vary. *Aud.:* Ga, Ac.

"International in coverage and reputation, *Film Quarterly* offers lively and penetrating articles covering the entire field of film studies. Articles include interviews with innovative film- and videomakers, writers, editors and cinematographers; readable discussion of issues in contemporary film theory; definitive, thoughtful reviews of international, avant garde, national cinemas, and documentaries; and important approaches to film history." Now also available online. Recent titles include "Free Solo, Transit, Never Look Away" and "Julie Dash's Televisual Legacy." For academic libraries that serve film studies programs.

2294. ***Film Score Monthly (Online): your soundtrack source since 1990.*** Formerly (until 2004): *Film Score Monthly (Print).* [ISSN: 1939-974X] 1990. bi-m. USD 36.95 domestic; USD 42.95 in Canada & Mexico; USD 50 elsewhere. Ed(s): Tim Curran. Film Score Monthly, 6311 Romaine St, Ste 7109, Hollywood, CA 90038; lukas@filmscoremonthly.com; http://www.filmscoremonthly.com. Illus. Sample. *Indexed:* F01, IIMP, IIPA. *Aud.:* Sa.

Film Score Monthly provides information for those interested in what is happening in the film music industry: current news, record label updates on releases, upcoming assignments (who's scoring what for whom), and CD reviews. There are feature articles on composers and behind-the-scenes looks at film music production. Some recent titles include "Dies Irae, Moaning Woman, Braaam!" and "When They See Us: Kris Bowers and the Central Park Five." For libraries that serve serious film studies programs or communities.

2295. *Filmmaker: the magazine of independent film.* Formed by the 1992 merger of: *Off-Hollywood Report; Montage.* [ISSN: 1063-8954] 1992. q. USD 40 (print & online eds.) Individuals, USD 18 (print & online eds.)). Ed(s): Scott Macaulay, Vadim Rizov. Filmmaker, c/o Made in NY Media Center by IFP, 30 John St, Brooklyn, NY 11201; advertise@ifp.org. Illus., adv. Sample. Circ: 60000. *Indexed:* F01, IIPA. *Bk. rev.:* Number and length vary. *Aud.:* Sa.

This title is directed toward those interested in independent, smaller-budgeted films and filmmaking. Lesser-known films currently being released are profiled in each issue, along with independent filmmaker interviews and current film festival news. There are advertisements for film products, pre- and postproduction services, and film festivals, plus a handy advertisers' index. Some recent articles are "Remembering Ben Barenholtz, 1935- 2019" and "The 24 Films (More or Less) Shot on 35mm Released in 2018." This is a nice addition to any collection that supports a film program.

2296. *Journal of Cinema and Media Studies.* Former titles (until 2018): *Cinema Journal;* (until 1967): *Society of Cinematologists. Journal.* [ISSN: 2578-4900] 1961. q. USD 264. Ed(s): Caetlin Benson-Allott. University of Texas Press, Journals Division, PO Box 7819, Austin, TX 78713; journals@utpress.utexas.edu; https://utpress.utexas.edu. Illus., index, adv. Refereed. Vol. ends: Aug. *Indexed:* A01, A22, BRI, E01, F01, IIPA, MLA-IB. *Bk. rev.:* Number and length vary. *Aud.:* Ac.

From their website, this "journal was renamed (from Cinema Journal) in October 2018. JCMS's basic mission is to foster engaged debate and rigorous thinking among humanities scholars of film, television, digital media, and other audiovisual technologies. We are committed to the aesthetic, political, and cultural interpretation of these media and their production, circulation, and reception." The journal publishes essays on a wide variety of subjects from diverse methodological perspectives. A Professional Notes section informs readers about upcoming events, research applications, and the "Transnational Science Fiction at the End of the World: Consensus, Conflict, and the Politics of Climate Change" and "A Dark Exilic Vision of 1960s Britain: Gothic Horror and Film Noir Pervading Losey and Pinter's The Servant." For all film collections that address the needs of film studies programs.

2297. *Journal of Film and Video.* Former titles (until 1984): *University Film and Video Association. Journal;* (until 1982): *University Film Association. Journal;* (until 1968): *University Film Producers Association. Journal.* [ISSN: 0742-4671] 1949. q. USD 95 (print & online eds.)). University of Illinois Press, 1325 S Oak St, MC-566, Champaign, IL 61820; uipress@uillinois.edu; http://www.press.uillinois.edu. Illus., index, adv. Refereed. Microform: PQC. *Indexed:* A01, A22, BRI, E01, F01, IIPA, MLA-IB. *Aud.:* Ac.

This refereed journal "focuses on scholarship in the fields of film and video production, history, theory, criticism, and aesthetics." It is the official publication of the University Film and Video Association. In its call for papers, it requests "articles about film and related media, problems of education in these fields and the function of film and video in society." Some recent titles include "Reverend Billy Goes to Main Street: Free Speech, Trespassing, and Activist Documentary Film" and "Dreaming of Cinema: Spectatorship, Surrealism, and the Age of Digital Media." For academic audiences.

2298. *Journal of Popular Film and Television.* Formerly (until 1978): *The Journal of Popular Film.* [ISSN: 0195-6051] 1972. q. GBP 186 (print & online eds.)). Ed(s): Michael T Marsden, Gary R Edgerton. Routledge, 530 Walnut St, Ste 850, Philadelphia, PA 19106; enquiries@tandfonline.com; http://www.tandfonline.com. Illus., index, adv. Refereed. Reprint: PSC. *Indexed:* A01, A06, A22, AmHI, BRI, C42, CBRI, E01, F01, IIPA, MLA-IB. *Bk. rev.:* Number and length vary. *Aud.:* Ga, Ac.

This title "is dedicated to popular film and television in the broadest sense. Concentration is upon commercial cinema and television: stars, directors, producers, studios, networks, genres, series, the audience, etc." Articles are accompanied by acknowledgements, with notes and works cited. Recent article titles include "Perceptual Realism and Digital VFXs in the Korean Blockbuster of the 2010s: The Admiral: Roaring Currents and Ode to My Father" and "Gender Politics in Food Escape: Korean Masculinity in TV Cooking Shows in South Korea." Book reviews are also included. For serious film and communications libraries.

2299. *Journal of Religion and Film.* [ISSN: 1092-1311] 1997. s-a. Free. Ed(s): John C Lyden. University of Nebraska at Omaha, Department of Philosophy and Religion, 60th & Dodge Streets, Omaha, NE 68182; unophilosophy@unomaha.edu; http://www.unomaha.edu/college-of-arts-and-sciences/philosophy/. Adv. Refereed. *Indexed:* BRI, F01, IIPA, MLA-IB. *Aud.:* Ga, Ac.

The *Journal of Religion and Film* "examines the description, critique, and embodiment of religion in film." The editors "invite articles and discussion on a variety of film types, commercial and academic, foreign and documentary, classic and contemporary." Peer-reviewed and open-access articles and analyses of films that stress spiritual aspects are presented. Some recent articles include "The Representation of Turkish Women in James Bond Films" and "Touched by Grace? A Look at Grace in Bergman's Winter Light and Martin Luther's Writings." For academic collections.

2300. *Jump Cut: a review of contemporary media.* [ISSN: 0146-5546] 1974. a. Free. Ed(s): John Hess, Julia Lesage. Jump Cut Associates, PO Box 865, Berkeley, CA 94701; http://www.ejumpcut.org. Illus. Refereed. Microform: PQC. *Bk. rev.:* 4-5, 500-1,000 words. *Aud.:* Ga, Ac, Sa.

This journal has a definite editorial viewpoint: as its byline says, its editors have been "looking at media in its social and political context. Pioneers since 1974, analyzing media in relation to class, race, and gender." And that certainly describes its content. Its articles often take a radical, thought-provoking perspective on media in general and on film in particular. Recent articles include "From off-brand to franchise: Watchmen as advertisement" and "Shadow films: picturing the environmental crisis." Ever interesting, ever edgy, this should be considered by libraries with large film studies collections.

2301. *MovieMaker: the art and business of making movies.* Formerly (until 200?): *Movie Maker Magazine.* 1993. bi-m. USD 19.95 domestic. Ed(s): Timothy E Rhys, Jennifer M Wood. Moviemaker Pub., 174 Fifth Ave, Ste 300, New York, NY 10010. Illus., adv. *Aud.:* Ac, Sa.

This title features articles on producers, actors, and directors. It also covers independent film industry issues, such as copyright, technical instruction, festivals, shorts, and documentaries. There are ads for film equipment and services, with an advertisers index. Recent articles include "Festival Beat: International Auteur Works and Surreal Live Performances at Kustendorf Film and Music Festival 2019" and "Production Diaries: Trial by Fire Director Edward Zwick and Crew Started Their Shoot by Lighting an On-Screen Inferno." This is a good title for collections that support a film studies program.

2302. *Quarterly Review of Film and Video.* Formerly (until 1989): *Quarterly Review of Film Studies.* [ISSN: 1050-9208] 1976. 8x/yr. GBP 1336 (print & online eds.)). Ed(s): David Sterritt. Routledge, 530 Walnut St, Ste 850, Philadelphia, PA 19106; enquiries@tandfonline.com; http://www.tandfonline.com. Illus., index, adv. Sample. Refereed. Reprint: PSC. *Indexed:* A01, A22, AmHI, BRI, CBRI, E01, F01, MLA-IB. *Bk. rev.:* Number and length vary. *Aud.:* Ac.

This refereed journal is international and interdisciplinary in scope. It publishes "critical, historical, and theoretical essays, book reviews, and interviews in the area of moving image studies including film, video, and digital image studies." Titles of recent feature articles include "Man-Candy, Hot Body, and an Army of Skanks: Mean Girls as Revisionist Text and the Teen Film Genre" and "You Ain't Gonna Get Away Wit' This, Django: Fantasy, Fiction and Subversion in Quentin Tarantino's, Django Unchained." For academic libraries.

2303. ***Script (Calabasas): a division of writer's digest.*** [ISSN: 1092-2016] 1995. bi-m. Active Interest Media, 2520 55th St, Ste 210, Boulder, CO 80301; HR@aimmedia.com; http://www.aimmedia.com/. Illus., adv. *Indexed:* F01. *Aud.:* Sa.

This publication is for those who are beyond asking for examples of the standard script format. Interviews and articles are included of/by writers of currently released films as well, which makes it a source of practical information for both established and burgeoning screenwriters. For film studies and writing center collections.

2304. ***Senses of Cinema.*** [ISSN: 1443-4059] 1999. q. Free. Senses of Cinema Inc., c/o AFI Research Collection, School of Media and Communication, RMIT University, GPO Box 2476V, Melbourne, VIC 3001, Australia; admin@sensesofcinema.com. Adv. Refereed. *Indexed:* F01, MLA-IB. *Bk. rev.:* Number and length vary. *Aud.:* Ac, Sa.

Senses of Cinema is "an online film journal devoted to the serious and eclectic discussion of cinema." It receives financial assistance from the Australian Film Commission, and it has a slight (increasingly slight) down-under, Aussie bias (the "Festivals" section is divided into "international festivals" and "Australian festivals"), and also accept donations. The journal is building up a "Great Directors" database, with a critical essay on each director along with a filmography, bibliography, and web resources. It includes book and DVD reviews. Some titles of recent feature articles include "The Tender Force of Valerie Massadian" and "The Body is a Fact." An excellent choice for film studies collections. URL: www.sensesofcinema.com

2305. ***Sight and Sound: the international film magazine.*** Incorporates (1934-1991): *Monthly Film Bulletin;* (1948-1949): *Monthly Film Strip Review.* [ISSN: 0037-4806] 1932. m. GBP 45 combined subscription domestic (print & online eds.); GBP 68 combined subscription foreign (print & online eds.); GBP 4.50 newsstand/cover). British Film Institute, 21 Stephen St, London, W1T 1LN, United Kingdom; publishing@bfi.org.uk; http://www.bfi.org.uk. Illus., adv. Vol. ends: Dec. Microform: MIM; PQC; WMP. *Indexed:* A01, A06, A22, AmHI, BRI, CBRI, F01, IIPA, MLA-IB. *Bk. rev.:* Number and length vary. *Aud.:* Ga, Ac.

This journal is published under the auspices of the eminent British Film Institute. It is particularly good in the area of film reviews and credits; it consistently gives the most complete credit listings of any film periodical. Coverage includes major film festivals and filmmakers, American and foreign. It also publishes detailed articles and interviews with directors who are not usually found in popular movie magazines. Some recent article titles include "Deep Focus: the Golden Age of Mexican Cinema" and "Let the Footage Speak for Itself: Todd Douglas Miller on Apollo 11." For all academic film studies programs, and for public libraries with serious filmgoing populations.

2306. ***The Velvet Light Trap.*** [ISSN: 0149-1830] 1971. s-a. USD 162. University of Texas Press, Journals Division, PO Box 7819, Austin, TX 78713; journals@utpress.utexas.edu; https://utpress.utexas.edu. Illus., index. Refereed. Vol. ends: Sep. *Indexed:* A01, A22, AmHI, BRI, E01, F01, IIPA, MLA-IB. *Bk. rev.:* Number and length vary. *Aud.:* Ac.

This journal just gets better and better! It is "devoted to investigating historical questions that illuminate the understanding of film and other media." Issues often have a single theme; for example, "Censorship and Regulation" or "Comedy." Articles and interviews are of a scholarly nature and include notes. The content is edited by graduate students in film studies from Austin and Madison. A recent article is "Not Very Attractive: How the Interstate Highway System Reconfigured Cinematic Space and Made the Rural Horrifying." Book reviews are provided in each issue. Recommended for academic collections.

2307. ***Written By: the journal of the Writers Guild of America.*** Former titles (until 1997): *Writers Guild of America, West. Journal;* (until 1988): *W G A West Newsletter.* [ISSN: 1092-468X] 1965. bi-m. Ed(s): Richard Stayton. Writers Guild of America, West, 7000 W Third St, Los Angeles, CA 90048; http://www.wga.org/. Illus. *Indexed:* F01, IIPA. *Aud.:* Sa.

The official publication of the Writers Guild of America West, this title "actively seeks material from Guild members and other writers." It covers current events and creative issues that affect screen and television writers, and offers biographical articles on writers and analyses of current films. Some recent titles of articles Include "The Chuck Lorre Method" and "Not With a Whimper." A good title for libraries that support a screenwriting program.

■ FIRE PROTECTION

Lian Ruan, Director/Head Librarian, Illinois Fire Service Institute Library, University of Illinois at Urbana–Champaign, 11 Gerty Drive, Champaign, IL 61820; lruan@illinois.edu

Diane Richardson, Reference and Training Librarian, Illinois Fire Service Institute Library, University of Illinois at Urbana–Champaign, 11 Gerty Drive, Champaign, IL 61820; dlrichar@illinois.edu

David Ehrenhart, Assistant Director for Library Operations, Illinois Fire Service Institute Library, University of Illinois at Urbana–Champaign, 11 Gerty Drive, Champaign, IL 61820; ehrenha1@illinois.edu

Introduction

Today's firefighters respond to a wide range of emergencies in areas including firefighting, emergency medical care, hazardous materials incidents, rescue operations, terrorism, and other emergency situations. The increasing complexity of the fire service requires firefighters to continuously hone their skills and improve their knowledge through training. Fire protection journals covered in this section are critical resources for firefighter training, teaching, and learning. The targeted primary audience includes firefighters, emergency responders, and fire service administrators.

Fire service titles cover a variety of topics, such as firefighter training, firefighting operations, fire safety, hazardous materials, fire management, leadership, incidents, rescue, and news, among others. The format is similar in most fire service magazines, including featured articles, columns, and news, so each magazine is both familiar and informative. Peer-reviewed and scholarly journals that are highly regarded in the international fire service community were also selected. Both target fire science and fire safety engineering researchers and academic programs.

Basic Periodicals

Ac: *Fire Engineering, Fire Technology, N F P A Journal;* Sa: *Fire Engineering, Wildfire, Fire Technology, Firehouse, Industrial Fire World, N F P A Journal.*

Basic Abstracts and Indexes

Chemical Abstracts, Engineering Index.

2308. ***Fire Engineering.*** Incorporates (1920-1925): *Fire Protection;* Supersedes in part (in 1926): *Fire and Water Engineering;* Which was formerly (until 1903): *Fire and Water.* [ISSN: 0015-2587] 1877. m. USD 44 domestic; USD 57 Canada; USD 79 elsewhere. Ed(s): Bobby Halton. PennWell Corporation, 21-00 Rte 208 S, Fair Lawn, NJ 07410; http://www.pennwell.com. Illus., index, adv. Sample. Microform: PQC. *Indexed:* A01, A22, B03. *Aud.:* Ac, Sa.

With a history that dates back more than 140 years, *Fire Engineering* is a monthly periodical that provides fire and emergency service professionals worldwide with training, education, and management information written by experts in the fire service. Feature articles focus on "lessons learned" from a wide variety of situations that a fire or emergency services professional might encounter, including vehicle extrication, structural collapse rescue, or hazardous materials operations. In addition to the feature articles, regular sections are devoted to emergency medical services, volunteer firefighters, and wildland urban interfaces. The online version of the magazine provides frequently updated content, including daily news, podcasts, webcasts, and articles from the current print issue. *Fire Engineering* is highly recommended for fire service personnel and fire departments, as well as public, academic, and special libraries that serve fire protection and prevention professionals. Available both in print and online. URL: www.fireengineering.com/index.html

2309. ***Fire Technology.*** [ISSN: 0015-2684] 1965. q. EUR 1113 (print & online eds.)). Ed(s): Guillermo M Rein, Jr. Springer New York LLC, 233 Spring St, New York, NY 10013; customerservice@springer.com; http://www.springer.com. Illus., index, adv. Sample. Refereed. Vol. ends: Oct (No. 4). Microform: PQC. Reprint: PSC. *Indexed:* A01, A22, Agr, BRI, E01. *Bk. rev.:* 1, 250-500 words. *Aud.:* Ac, Sa.

Published quarterly in conjunction with the National Fire Protection Association (NFPA) and the Society of Fire Protection Engineers (SFPE), *Fire Technology* is a peer-reviewed journal with both an interdisciplinary and international scope that focuses on fire safety science and engineering. Issues of *Fire Technology* are composed of original papers, both theoretical and empirical, addressing engineering issues and fire safety science in subjects such as materials testing, fire modeling, human behavior in fires, fire suppression, wildfires, structures, fire risk analysis, and fire detection. Issues may also include review articles, letters to the editor, technical communications, and book reviews. Many years one or more special issues address facets of a single topic. Past special issues have been devoted to advances in evacuation modeling, probabilistic methods in fire safety engineering, wildland-urban interface fires, large fires in tunnels, and wildland fires in fire safety engineering. The "Online First Articles" section of the digital edition of the magazine features articles that have not been assigned to a print issue. *Fire Technology* is highly recommended for academic libraries that support fire safety and engineering disciplines and for special libraries that support fire prevention and protection training programs. Available both in print and online. URL: www.springer.com/engineering/civil+engineering/journal/10694

2310. ***Firehouse (Fort Atkinson).*** [ISSN: 0145-4064] 1976. m. USD 24.95 domestic; USD 34.95 Canada. SouthComm Communications, Inc., 1233 Janesville Ave., PO Box 803, Fort Atkinson, WI 53538; info@southcomm.com; https://www.southcomm.com/. Illus., adv. Circ: 76139. Vol. ends: Dec. *Indexed:* BRI. *Aud.:* Sa.

Firehouse provides fire and emergency service professionals with information on training, current news stories, and events relevant to their profession. Monthly issues contain features that detail significant fires and emergencies, training tips for many different functional areas within the fire service, and developments in fire service higher education. Regular columns discuss politics, emergency medical service issues, close calls encountered by firefighters, and professional development topics for fire officers. The online version contains up-to-date news articles and line-of-duty deaths, blogs, forums, webcasts, and training drills that can be utilized by fire departments. *Firehouse* is highly recommended for fire service personnel and fire departments, as well as public, academic, and special libraries that serve fire protection and prevention professionals. Available both in print and online. URL: www.firehouse.com/

2311. ***Industrial Fire World.*** [ISSN: 0749-890X] 1985. q. USD 20 combined subscription domestic print & online eds.; USD 40 combined subscription elsewhere print & online eds. Ed(s): Anton Riecher. Industrial Fire World, PO Box 9161, College Station, TX 77842. Adv. Sample. *Aud.:* Sa.

Industrial Fire World, published quarterly, provides personnel in the industrial fire protection field with the latest information on techniques and technology related to all aspects of industrial emergency response. Regular columns are devoted to emergency medical response, hazardous materials, risk assessment, training, and storage tanks. Each issue also provides a log of a sampling of international industrial incidents, including injury and fatality reports. Feature articles by leaders in the field address the most up-to-date technological and equipment innovations in industrial fire fighting, changes in governmental regulations affecting firefighters, along with training practices and opportunities. A digital copy of the current issue and some articles are made available at the journal's website. *Industrial Fire World* is highly recommended for special libraries supporting industrial emergency response teams and training programs. Available both in print and online. URL: www.fireworld.com

2312. ***N F P A Journal.*** Formed by the merger of (1984-1991): *Fire Command;* Which was formerly (until 1984): *Fire Service Today;* (until 1981): *Fire Command;* (until 1970): *Firemen;* (until 1946): *Volunteer Firemen;* (1965-1991): *Fire Journal;* Which was formerly (until 1965): *Quarterly of the National Fire Protection Association.* [ISSN: 1054-8793] 1991. bi-m. Free to members. Ed(s): Scott Sutherland. National Fire Protection Association, 1 Batterymarch Park, Quincy, MA 02269; custserv@nfpa.org; http://www.nfpa.org. Illus., index, adv. Sample. Circ: 82871 Controlled. Vol. ends: Nov/Dec. Microform: PQC. *Indexed:* A22. *Aud.:* Ac, Sa.

NFPA Journal is the bimonthly membership magazine of the National Fire Protection Agency (NFPA), a nonprofit organization that produces codes and standards accepted as professional guidelines related to fire, electrical, and life safety. Regular columns and feature articles address overviews of recent reports issued by the Fire Analysis and Research Division of NFPA, short summaries of recent significant or fatal fires, reviews of noteworthy historical disasters, and issues related to NFPA's advocacy endeavors, educational enterprises, and development of codes and standards. Statistical reports of United States fire loss, large-loss fires, multiple death fires, and firefighter injuries and fatalities are published annually. The journal is available both online and as a digital edition at NFPA.org. The online version of the magazine includes the following regular columns: First Responder, International, Outreach, Research, and Wildfire. *NFPA Journal* is highly recommended for academic and special libraries that support fire prevention and protection training programs, and for fire service leaders and public administrators. Available both in print and online. URL: https://www.nfpa.org/News-and-Research/Publications-and-media/NFPA-Journal/

2313. ***Wildfire (Chicago).*** Formerly (until 1994): *Hotsheet.* [ISSN: 1073-5658] 1992. bi-m. USD 36 domestic (Free to qualified personnel). Ed(s): Kevin Daniels. Penton, 330 N Wabash Ave, Ste 2300, Chicago, IL 60611; information@penton.com; http://www.penton.com. Adv. Circ: 3000 Paid. *Indexed:* B01. *Aud.:* Sa.

The bimonthly publication *Wildfire* is an official publication of the International Association of Wildland Fire. Feature articles examine specific issues in wildland fire fighting from a global perspective. Topics covered include information on large or notable fires, new technologies being used in the field, and general trends in wildfires worldwide. In addition to the articles, recurring sections include messages from the president of the International Association of Wildland Fire, fire science updates, and leadership articles. The online version of the magazine provides access to articles from the print version. *Wildfire* is recommended for special and academic libraries that support fire protection and prevention training programs and public libraries in areas prone to wildfires. Available both in print and online. URL: www.wildfiremagazine.org/

■ FISH, FISHERIES, AND AQUACULTURE

Kelly MacWatters, Coordinator of Reference and Electronic Resources, Standish Library, Siena College, Loudonville, NY 12211; kmacwatters@siena.edu

Introduction

This section covers the aquaculture industry, fish and fisheries science, research, and practice. *Aquaculture* refers to the breeding and harvesting of plants and animals in marine, brackish, or fresh waters. It is one of the fastest-growing food-producing sectors in the world, and is also playing an important role in the restoration of wild populations.

The titles included here are geared toward researchers, academics, and industry members. There are titles that focus on all aspects of fisheries, some that are devoted solely to fish farming, while others focus on specific research areas such as nutrition or disease. Species covered include finfishes, mollusks, crustaceans, amphibians and reptiles, aquatic invertebrates, and marine and freshwater algae. Recent trends and topics covered include sustainable and responsible practices, conservation and restoration, economic opportunities, health and nutrition, aquaculture systems technologies and design.

Marine and freshwater fisheries and aquaculture are covered, and many titles are international in scope. Types of publications vary, including trade magazines, scholarly, and peer-reviewed journals. Types of articles include original research, review articles, technical papers, and short communications. Many of the titles include an open-access publishing option. Several titles are available only as an online subscription; however, most have print and online availability.

The fisheries and aquaculture industry has many stakeholders and requires an understanding of a variety of sciences. These titles may appeal to students, researchers, and practitioners in many related fields, including biology, biochemistry, ecology, economics, engineering, genetics, health, and social sciences.

Basic Periodicals

Ac, Sa: *American Fisheries Society. Transactions, Aquaculture Research, Fish and Fisheries, Fishery Bulletin, Journal of Applied Aquaculture, Marine Fisheries Review, North American Journal of Fisheries Management, Reviews in Fisheries Science & Aquaculture.*

Basic Abstracts and Indexes

Aquatic Sciences and Fisheries Abstracts (ASFA), Biological Abstracts.

2314. ***American Fisheries Society. Transactions.*** Former titles (until 1900): *American Fisheries Society. Proceedings;* (until 1899): *American Fisheries Society. Minutes;* (until 1897): *American Fisheries Society. Transactions;* (until 1895): *American Fish-Cultural Association. Transactions;* (until 1878): *American Fish Culturists' Association. Transactions;* (until 1876): *American Fish Culturists' Association. Proceedings.* [ISSN: 0002-8487] 1872. bi-m. GBP 1913 print & online eds. Ed(s): Churchill B Grimes, Richard J Beamish. John Wiley & Sons Ltd., . Illus., index. Refereed. Vol. ends: No. 6. Reprint: PSC. *Indexed:* A22, C45, S25. *Bk. rev.:* Number and length vary. *Aud.:* Ac, Sa.

Published bimonthly by the American Fisheries Society, this journal publishes papers on all aspects of fisheries science, including, but not limited to, biology, ecology, genetics, health, psychology, population genetics, economics, and culture. It covers marine and freshwater fish, exploitable shellfish, and their respective fisheries. Each issue includes refereed original research papers, making it an important journal for those studying aquaculture. URL: http://www.tandfonline.com/toc/utaf20/current

2315. ***Aquacultural Engineering.*** [ISSN: 0144-8609] 1982. 6x/yr. EUR 1732. Ed(s): Dr. J van Rijn, J Colt. Elsevier BV, Radarweg 29, Amsterdam, 1043 NX, Netherlands; info@elsevier.com; https://www.elsevier.com/. Illus., index, adv. Refereed. Vol. ends: No. 6. Microform: PQC. *Indexed:* A01, A22, Agr, C45, S25. *Aud.:* Ac, Sa.

Aquacultural Engineering is the official journal of the Aquacultural Engineering Society. This journal publishes original research papers, review articles, and short communications related to the design and development of aquacultural systems for both freshwater and marine facilities. The journal aims to apply the knowledge gained from basic research that potentially can be translated into commercial operations. Topics covered include construction experiences and techniques, engineering and design of aquacultural facilities, and materials selection and their uses. This publication is recommended for libraries that support fisheries and aquaculture programs. URL: https://www.journals.elsevier.com/aquacultural-engineering

2316. ***Aquaculture.*** Incorporates (1990-1996): *Annual Review of Fish Diseases.* [ISSN: 0044-8486] 1972. 16x/yr. EUR 9030. Ed(s): B Austin, G Hulata. Elsevier BV, Radarweg 29, Amsterdam, 1043 NX, Netherlands; info@elsevier.com; https://www.elsevier.com/. Illus., index, adv. Refereed. Microform: PQC. *Indexed:* A01, A22, Agr, C45, S25. *Bk. rev.:* Number and length vary. *Aud.:* Ac, Sa.

Published semi-monthly, *Aquaculture* is an international journal for freshwater and marine researchers interested in the exploration, improvement, and management of all aquatic food resources. Types of articles include original research papers, review articles, technical papers, and short communications. This journal covers all aspects of aquaculture, including diseases, genetics, nutrition, physiology and endocrinology, production science, and sustainability and society. It carries articles that are international in scope. The journal is aimed at aquaculturists and scientists who desire a better understanding of the issues facing those in the field. URL: https://www.journals.elsevier.com/aquaculture

2317. ***Aquaculture Economics & Management.*** [ISSN: 1365-7305] 1997. q. GBP 532 (print & online eds.)). Ed(s): Carole R Engle. Taylor & Francis, 2, 3 & 4 Park Sq, Milton Park, Abingdon, OX14 4RN, United Kingdom; subscriptions@tandf.co.uk; https://www.tandfonline.com. Adv. Sample. Refereed. Reprint: PSC. *Indexed:* A01, A22, Agr, B01, C45, E01, EconLit, S25. *Aud.:* Ac, Sa.

Aquaculture Economics & Management is the official journal of the International Association of Aquaculture Economics and Management. Published quarterly, this journal includes peer-reviewed papers that address the economic issues related to aquaculture in both the public and private sectors. Topics covered include farm management, consumer behavior, pricing, and government policy. Unlike other titles in this section, this journal does not cover the biological or ecological aspects of aquaculture. It would be useful for those studying business, economics, or public policy, as these fields relate to the field of aquaculture. URL:http://www.tandfonline.com/loi/uaqm20

2318. ***Aquaculture Environment Interactions (Online).*** [ISSN: 1869-7534] 2010. 3x/yr. Free. Ed(s): Marianne Holmer, Tim Dempster. Inter-Research, Nordbuente 23, Oldendorf, 21385, Germany; ir@int-res.com; https://www.int-res.com. Refereed. *Aud.:* Ac, Sa.

Aquaculture Environment Interactions is an interdisciplinary international journal that analyzes the environmental effects of aquaculture and vice-versa. Types of articles include original research, reviews, opinion pieces, discussions, and themed sections that address key research areas. This journal is fully open access and provides a unique forum for those interested in aquaculture, environmental, and ecosystem studies. URL: http://www.int-res.com/journals/aei/aei-home/

2319. ***Aquaculture Nutrition (Online).*** [ISSN: 1365-2095] 1995. bi-m. GBP 1067. Ed(s): Marit Espe. Wiley-Blackwell Publishing Ltd., The Atrium, Southern Gate, Chichester, PO19 8QG, United Kingdom; cs-journals@wiley.com; http://onlinelibrary.wiley.com. Refereed. *Aud.:* Ac, Sa.

Published bimonthly, this international journal provides a global perspective on the nutrition of all cultivated aquatic animals. Topics range from extensive aquaculture to laboratory studies of nutritional biochemistry and physiology. The articles included in the journal are technical and the focus of the journal is narrow, so it would be of most value to those researchers who are studying nutritional aspects of aquaculture. URL: http://onlinelibrary.wiley.com/journal/10.1111/

2320. ***Aquaculture Research.*** Former titles (until 1995): *Aquaculture and Fisheries Management;* (until 1985): *Fisheries Management.* [ISSN: 1355-557X] 1970. m. GBP 3554. Ed(s): Marc Verdegem. Wiley-Blackwell Publishing Ltd., The Atrium, Southern Gate, Chichester, PO19 8QG, United Kingdom; cs-journals@wiley.com; http://onlinelibrary.wiley.com/. Illus., index, adv. Sample. Refereed. Vol. ends: No. 12. Microform: PQC. Reprint: PSC. *Indexed:* A01, A22, Agr, C45, E01. *Bk. rev.:* Number and length vary. *Aud.:* Ac, Sa.

Aquaculture Research publishes hypothesis-driven papers on applied or scientific research that is relevant to freshwater aquaculture, brackish-water aquaculture, and marine aquaculture. With an international scope, this journal covers both faunistic and floristic aquatic organisms and includes review articles, reports on original research, short communications, technical papers, and book reviews. The journal invites young scientists to submit short communications based on their own research. As a journal with a global perspective and wide range of coverage, it is recommended for people seeking a broad understanding of aquaculture. URL: http://onlinelibrary.wiley.com/journal/10.1111/

Aquatic Conservation (Online). See Marine Science and Technology/Marine Biology section.

2321. ***Canadian Journal of Fisheries and Aquatic Sciences.*** Former titles (until 1980): *Fisheries Research Board of Canada. Journal;* (until 1937): *Biological Board of Canada. Journal;* (until 1934): *Contributions to Canadian Biology and Fisheries; Contributions to Canadian Biology.* [ISSN: 0706-652X] 1901. m. CAD 2135 (print & online eds.)). Ed(s):

Keith Tierney, Yong Chen. Canadian Science Publishing, 65 Auriga Dr, Ste 203, Ottawa, ON K2E 7W6, Canada; pubs@cdnsciencepub.com; http://www.nrcresearchpress.com. Illus., index, adv. Refereed. Vol. ends: No. 12. *Indexed:* A01, A22, C37, C45, E01, S25. *Aud.:* Ac, Sa.

Published since 1901, *Canadian Journal of Fisheries and Aquatic Sciences* is considered a core publication for those studying the multidisciplinary field of aquatic sciences. This journal is published monthly, and each issue includes articles, perspectives, discussions, and rapid communication relating to current research. Subjects covered include current research on cells, organisms, populations, ecosystems, or processes that affect aquatic systems. This journal is highly recommended for libraries supporting fisheries and aquaculture programs. URL: http://www.nrcresearchpress.com/journal/cjfas

2322. *Diseases of Aquatic Organisms.* [ISSN: 0177-5103] 1985. 15x/yr. EUR 1245 combined subscription (print & online eds.)). Ed(s): Stephen W Feist. Inter-Research, Nordbuente 23, Oldendorf, 21385, Germany; ir@int-res.com; https://www.int-res.com. Refereed. *Indexed:* A22, C45. *Aud.:* Ac, Sa.

Diseases of Aquatic Organisms is a leading journal in its field. It is international and interdisciplinary, including information about animals, plants, and microorganisms in marine, limnetic, and brackish habitats. It covers diseases that affect all facets of life-at the cell, tissue, organ, individual, population, and ecosystem level. It is an indispensable source of information for all who are concerned with health of humans, animals, plants and microorganisms, environmental protection, resource management, ecosystem health, conservation of organisms and habitats, and aquafood production. Those who will find this journal useful include physicians, veterinarians, environmental biologists, fishery biologists and ecologists, aquaculturalists, pathologists, parasitologists, microbiologists, botanists, and zoologists. URL: http://www.int-res.com/journals/dao/index.html

2323. *Ecology of Freshwater Fish (Online).* [ISSN: 1600-0633] 1992. q. GBP 811. Ed(s): David C Heins. Wiley-Blackwell Publishing, Inc., 350 Main St, Malden, MA 02148; cs-journals@wiley.com; http://onlinelibrary.wiley.com. Refereed. *Bk. rev.:* Number and length vary. *Aud.:* Ac, Sa.

Published quarterly, *Ecology of Freshwater Fish* presents original articles on all aspects of fish ecology and fishery sciences in lakes, rivers, and estuaries. This journal publishes reports of studies, research papers, theoretical papers and studies, articles, letters, reviews, and proceedings of papers. Subjects include issues related to ecologically oriented studies of behavior, genetics, and physiology and the conservation, development, and management of recreational and commercial fisheries. As many journals related to aquaculture deal primarily with oceanic fish life, this journal serves as a useful addition to the collections of researchers looking for information beyond the ecology of oceanic fish life. URL: http://onlinelibrary.wiley.com/journal/10.1111/

2324. *Environmental Biology of Fishes.* [ISSN: 0378-1909] 1976. m. EUR 4566 (print & online eds.)). Ed(s): David L G Noakes. Springer Netherlands, Van Godewijckstraat 30, Dordrecht, 3311 GX, Netherlands; http://www.springer.com. Adv. Refereed. Microform: PQC. Reprint: PSC. *Indexed:* A22, Agr, BRI, C45, E01, S25. *Bk. rev.:* Number and length vary. *Aud.:* Ac, Sa.

This international journal covers a large variety of topics in fishery biology including freshwater and marine ecology, zoology, taxonomy, environment, conservation, and more. Types of articles include original research, review papers, brief communications, editorials, book reviews and special issues. This journal is recommended for libraries supporting fisheries and aquaculture programs. URL: https://link.springer.com/journal/10641

2325. *Fish and Fisheries.* [ISSN: 1467-2960] 2000. q. GBP 895. Ed(s): Gary Carvalho, Paul J B Hart. Wiley-Blackwell Publishing Ltd., The Atrium, Southern Gate, Chichester, PO19 8QG, United Kingdom; cs-journals@wiley.com; http://onlinelibrary.wiley.com/. Adv. Sample. Refereed. Reprint: PSC. *Indexed:* A01, A22, Agr, BRI, C45, E01. *Aud.:* Ac, Sa.

Taking an interdisciplinary approach to the subject of fish and fisheries, *Fish and Fisheries* provides critical synthesis of major physiological, molecular, ecological, and evolutionary issues relating to the interdisciplinary study of fish. It publishes discussion papers, review papers, commentaries, and letters that cover a wide range of research. Published quarterly, this journal aims to appeal to a wide range of people involved in all aspects of the study and conservation of fish, with coverage that is both interdisciplinary and global. *Fish and Fisheries* is a must-have for all of those interested in the biology, conservation, and exploitation of fish. URL: http://onlinelibrary.wiley.com/journal/10.1111/

2326. *Fish Physiology & Biochemistry.* [ISSN: 0920-1742] 1986. 6x/yr. EUR 1216 (print & online eds.)). Ed(s): Patrick Kestemont. Springer Netherlands, Van Godewijckstraat 30, Dordrecht, 3311 GX, Netherlands; http://www.springer.com. Illus., index. Refereed. Vol. ends: No. 4. Reprint: PSC. *Indexed:* A22, Agr, C45, E01, S25. *Aud.:* Ac, Sa.

Fish Physiology & Biochemistry publishes original research papers in all aspects of the physiology and biochemistry of fishes. Contents covered include experimental work in biochemistry and structure of organisms, organs, tissues, and cells; nutritional, osmotic, ionic, respiratory, and excretory homeostasis; and more. It contains papers, brief communications, reviews, editorials, and announcements, and has an international audience. Additionally, this journal includes both invited and unsolicited reviews. With its international focus and its in-depth study of fish, this publication is recommended for researchers interested in the physiology and biochemistry aspects of fish. URL: https://link.springer.com/journal/10695

2327. *Fisheries.* Supersedes (in 1976): *American Fisheries Society. Newsletter.* [ISSN: 0363-2415] 1948. m. GBP 1913 print & online eds. Ed(s): Jeff Schaeffer. John Wiley & Sons Ltd., EMEA Institutional Sales, 9600 Garsington Rd, Oxford, OX4 2DQ, United Kingdom; cs-journals@wiley.com; http://onlinelibrary.wiley.com. Illus., index. Refereed. Vol. ends: No. 12. Reprint: PSC. *Indexed:* A01, A22, BRI, C45, S25. *Bk. rev.:* Number varies. *Aud.:* Ac, Sa.

Fisheries is the official trade magazine of the American Fisheries Society. It features peer-reviewed technical articles on all aspects of aquatic resource-related subjects. It focuses more on professional issues, new ideas and approaches, education, economics, administration, and law. Issues also contain AFS news, current events, book reviews, editorials, letters, job notices, chapter activities, and a calendar of events. This title has more advertisements than other publications in this section. *Fisheries* offers an overview of the fisheries industry, but it is not focused on aquaculture research. URL: http://www.tandfonline.com/loi/ufsh20

2328. *Fisheries Management and Ecology.* [ISSN: 0969-997X] 1994. bi-m. GBP 1135. Ed(s): Hal Schramm, Ian G Cowx. Wiley-Blackwell Publishing Ltd., The Atrium, Southern Gate, Chichester, PO19 8QG, United Kingdom; cs-journals@wiley.com; http://onlinelibrary.wiley.com/. Illus., index, adv. Sample. Refereed. Vol. ends: No. 4. Reprint: PSC. *Indexed:* A01, A22, Agr, C45, E01, S25. *Bk. rev.:* Number and length vary. *Aud.:* Ac, Sa.

With an international perspective, *Fisheries Management and Ecology* presents papers that cover all aspects of the management, ecology, and conservation of inland, estuarine, and coastal fisheries. Published bimonthly, this journal presents full research papers as well as management and ecological notes. It is best suited for people interested in fish conservation or those working with, or interested in working with, the management side of fisheries. URL: http://onlinelibrary.wiley.com/journal/10.1111/

2329. *Fisheries Research.* [ISSN: 0165-7836] 1982. 12x/yr. EUR 4520. Ed(s): G A Rose. Elsevier BV, Radarweg 29, Amsterdam, 1043 NX, Netherlands; info@elsevier.com; https://www.elsevier.com/. Illus., index, adv. Refereed. *Indexed:* A01, A22, C45, S25. *Bk. rev.:* Number and length vary. *Aud.:* Ac, Sa.

Fisheries Research takes a multidisciplinary approach to the study of fish. It publishes papers in the areas of fisheries science, fishing technology, fisheries management, and relevant socioeconomics. It includes theoretical and practical papers, as well as reviews and viewpoint articles. This publication is an important resource for fisheries scientists, biological oceanographers, gear technologists, economists, managers, administrators, policy makers, and legislators. URL: http://www.sciencedirect.com/science/journal/01657836

2330. ***Fisheries Science.*** [ISSN: 0919-9268] 1994. bi-m. EUR 1036 (print & online eds.)). Ed(s): Shuichi Satoh. Springer Japan KK, No 2 Funato Bldg, 1-11-11 Kudan-kita, Tokyo, 102-0073, Japan; orders@springer.jp; http://www.springer.jp. Sample. Refereed. Reprint: PSC. *Indexed:* A01, A22, Agr, C45, E01. *Aud.:* Ac, Sa.

Fisheries Science, a bimonthly journal, is the official publication of the Japanese Society of Fisheries Science. With a focus on Asia, and an emphasis on Japan, this journal covers the entire field of fisheries science. It includes original articles, short papers, and review articles on subjects like fisheries, biology, aquaculture, environment, chemistry and biochemistry, and food science and technology. It includes on average more than 180 articles per volume. Though it has a narrow geographical focus, the breadth of topics covered makes this journal an important publication in the field of aquaculture. URL: https://link.springer.com/journal/12562

2331. ***Fishery Bulletin.*** Former titles (until 1971): *Fishery Bulletin of the Fish and Wildlife Service;* (until 1941): *Bureau of Fisheries. Bulletin;* (until 1904): *United States Fish Commission. Bulletin.* [ISSN: 0090-0656] 1881. q. USD 32 domestic; USD 44.80 foreign. Ed(s): Sharyn Matriotti. U.S. National Marine Fisheries Service, Scientific Publications Office, 7600 Sand Point Way, N E, Bin C15700, Seattle, WA 98115; http://spo.nwr.noaa.gov/. Illus. Refereed. Vol. ends: No. 4. Microform: PQC; NTI. *Indexed:* A01, A22, C45, S25. *Aud.:* Ac, Sa.

Published quarterly by the National Oceanic and Atmospheric Administration (NOAA), *Fishery Bulletin* has existed since 1881. It is an official publication of the U.S. government, under various titles, and is the U.S. counterpart to other highly regarded governmental fisheries-science publications. Though it includes articles and notes about other countries, this journal has a decidedly American point of view. The journal features both articles that reflect original research and interpretative articles for all interdisciplinary fields that bear on marine fisheries and marine mammal science. This is the most general of the fisheries-related journals published by NOAA, and it would be good for those interested in fisheries science in the United States. URL: http://fishbull.noaa.gov/index.html

2332. ***Journal of Applied Aquaculture.*** [ISSN: 1045-4438] 1992. q. GBP 695 (print & online eds.)). Ed(s): Rodrigue Yossa. Taylor & Francis Inc., 711 3rd Ave, 8th Fl, New York, NY 10017; support@tandfonline.com; http://www.tandfonline.com. Illus., adv. Sample. Refereed. Circ: 181 Paid. Vol. ends: No. 4. Reprint: PSC. *Indexed:* A01, A22, Agr, C45, E01. *Aud.:* Ac, Sa.

Published quarterly, this journal is a platform for the sharing of practical information needed by researchers to meet the needs of investors, farm managers, extension agents, and policy makers working to adapt aquaculture theory to achieve economic and food-security objectives in the real world. This journal contains both original research papers and process papers, and it occasionally publishes issues focused on a single subject. Examples of topics included in this journal are practical diet formulation and food conversion efficiencies, feed manufacturing, techniques to minimize stress, and techniques for the management of genetic quality in broodstock. This publication is more accessible to farmers and non-specialists (in addition to professional aquaculture researchers), because technical jargon is kept to a minimum, and tables and figures that facilitate comprehension are encouraged. URL: http://www.tandfonline.com/loi/wjaa20

2333. ***Journal of Applied Ichthyology (Online).*** [ISSN: 1439-0426] bi-m. GBP 1096. Ed(s): Christian Wolter. Wiley-Blackwell Verlag GmbH, Rotherstr 21, Berlin, 10245, Germany; blackwell-verlag@wiley.com; http://www.wiley.com/WileyCDA/Brand/id-35.html. *Bk. rev.:* Number and length vary. *Aud.:* Ac, Sa.

Journal of Applied Ichthyology publishes papers that are oriented toward practical application rather than pure research. Topics covered include development and management of fisheries resources, ecotoxicology, genetics, and fisheries in developing countries. Emphasis is placed on the application of scientific research findings, while special consideration is given to ichthyological problems occurring in developing countries. Article formats include original articles, review articles, short communications, technical reports, and book reviews. With its international coverage and focus on the practical applications of aquaculture research, this journal would be good for people working in fisheries or those interested in learning about the practical side of aquaculture and fisheries. URL: http://onlinelibrary.wiley.com/journal/10.1111/

2334. ***Journal of Aquatic Animal Health.*** [ISSN: 0899-7659] 1989. q. GBP 482 print & online eds. Ed(s): Jeffrey C Wolf, Patricia S Gaunt. John Wiley & Sons Ltd., EMEA Institutional Sales, 9600 Garsington Rd, Oxford, OX4 2DQ, United Kingdom; cs-journals@wiley.com; http://onlinelibrary.wiley.com. Illus., adv. Refereed. Reprint: PSC. *Indexed:* A22, C45, S25. *Aud.:* Ac, Sa.

Journal of Aquatic Animal Health is a publication of the American Fisheries Society. It carries research papers on the causes, effects, treatments, and prevention of diseases of marine and freshwater organisms, particularly fish and shellfish. Published quarterly, it also examines the environmental and pathogenic aspects of fish and shellfish health. An important resource for those studying ichthyology. http://afs.tandfonline.com/loi/uahh20

2335. ***Journal of Fish and Wildlife Management.*** [ISSN: 1944-687X] 2010. s-a. Free. Ed(s): Dr. John Wenburg. U.S. Department of the Interior, Fish and Wildlife Service, Dept of the Interior, 1849 C St N W, Washington, DC 20240; fisheries@fws.gov; http://www.fws.gov. *Aud.:* Ac, Sa.

Journal of Fish and Wildlife Management is produced by the U.S. Fish and Wildlife Service. It is a freely accessible journal that covers the practical application and integration of science to conservation and management of native North American fish, wildlife, plants, and their habitats. Article types include articles, notes, surveys, and issues and perspectives. This journal would be of interest to those working in the practical aspects of fish and wildlife. URL: http://fwspubs.org/?code=ufws-site

2336. ***Journal of Fish Biology.*** [ISSN: 0022-1112] 1969. 20x/yr. GBP 3759. Ed(s): J F Craig, H J Craig. Wiley-Blackwell Publishing Ltd., The Atrium, Southern Gate, Chichester, PO19 8QG, United Kingdom; cs-journals@wiley.com; http://onlinelibrary.wiley.com. Illus., index, adv. Sample. Refereed. Reprint: PSC. *Indexed:* A01, A22, BRI, C45, E01. *Bk. rev.:* Number and length vary. *Aud.:* Ac, Sa.

Journal of Fish Biology, the official journal of the Fisheries Society of the British Isles, seeks to cover all aspects of fish biology research. This journal includes review articles and book reviews, and seeks papers of interest to those studying fish around the world. Topics covered include behavior, ecology, genetics, physiology, population studies, and toxicology. With its international scope and breadth of coverage, this journal is recommended for those engaged in research in nearly every area of aquaculture. URL: http://onlinelibrary.wiley.com/journal/10.1111/

2337. ***Journal of Fish Diseases.*** [ISSN: 0140-7775] 1978. m. GBP 2246. Ed(s): David J Speare. Wiley-Blackwell Publishing Ltd., The Atrium, Southern Gate, Chichester, PO19 8QG, United Kingdom; cs-journals@wiley.com; http://onlinelibrary.wiley.com. Illus., index, adv. Sample. Refereed. Vol. ends: No. 9. Microform: PQC. Reprint: PSC. *Indexed:* A01, A22, Agr, BRI, C45, E01. *Bk. rev.:* Number and length vary. *Aud.:* Ac, Sa.

Journal of Fish Diseases is the premier journal dedicated to the diseases of fish and shellfish. This journal is international in its coverage of disease in wild and cultured fish and shellfish. Published monthly, *Journal of Fish Diseases* includes review articles, short communications, scientific papers, and book reviews. Areas of interest regularly covered by the journal include host-pathogen relationships, studies of fish pathogens, pathophysiology, diagnostic methods, therapy, epidemiology, and descriptions of new diseases. This title would be useful to environmental researchers or fish pathologists. http://onlinelibrary.wiley.com/journal/10.1111/

2338. ***The Journal of Shellfish Research.*** Formerly (until 1981): *National Shellfisheries Association. Proceedings;* Which superseded (in 1954): *National Shellfisheries Association. Papers Delivered at the Convention;* Which was formerly (until 1953): *National Shellfisheries Association. Addresses Delivered at the Convention;* (until 1947): *National Association of Fisheries Commissioners. Minutes of the ... Annual Convention.* [ISSN: 0730-8000] 1981. 3x/yr. USD 530 Free to members. Ed(s): Sandra E Shumway. National Shellfisheries Association, Inc., PO Box 465, Hanover, PA 17331; pubsvc@tsp.sheridan.com; http://www.shellfish.org/. Illus., index. Refereed. *Indexed:* A22, C45. *Aud.:* Ac, Sa.

As the title implies, *The Journal of Shellfish Research* focuses solely on research related to shellfish. It is the official publication of the National Shellfisheries Association. Areas of research covered in this journal include aquaculture, biology, ecology, and management. Published three times per year, with an occasional special issue, this journal often includes abstracts of technical papers presented at conferences related to shellfish research. This title targets individuals interested in basic research, commercial production, and resource management. URL: http://www.shellfish.org/jsr-public

2339. ***Marine Fisheries Review.*** Former titles (until 1972): *Commercial Fisheries Review;* (until 1946): *Fishery Market News.* [ISSN: 0090-1830] 1939. q. USD 25 domestic; USD 35 foreign; USD 9.50 per issue domestic. U.S. National Marine Fisheries Service, Scientific Publications Office, 7600 Sand Point Way, N E, Bin C15700, Seattle, WA 98115; http://spo.nwr.noaa.gov/. Illus., index. Refereed. Vol. ends: No. 4. Microform: CIS; NTI. *Indexed:* A01, A22, B01, BRI, C42, S25. *Aud.:* Ac, Sa.

An official publication of the U.S. government since 1939, *Marine Fisheries Review* focuses on applied aspects of marine fisheries. It publishes review articles, research reports, significant progress reports, technical notes, and news articles on fisheries science, engineering and economics, commercial and recreational fisheries, marine mammal studies, aquaculture, and U.S. and foreign fisheries developments. Emphasis, however, is on in-depth review articles and practical or applied aspects of marine fisheries, rather than pure research. This journal is focused on practical application as opposed to pure research, and would be a good resource for anyone interested in marine fisheries, marine biology, or oceanography. URL: http://spo.nwr.noaa.gov/mfr.htm

2340. ***North American Journal of Aquaculture.*** Formerly (until 1999): *Progressive Fish-Culturist;* Which incorporated (1935-1937): *Fish Culture.* [ISSN: 1522-2055] 1934. q. GBP 482 print & online eds. Ed(s): Reginal M Harrell, Christopher C Kohler. John Wiley & Sons Ltd., . Illus., index, adv. Refereed. Vol. ends: No. 4. Microform: PQC. Reprint: PSC. *Indexed:* A22, C45, S25. *Bk. rev.:* Number and length vary. *Aud.:* Ac, Sa.

The North American Journal of Aquaculture is a quarterly journal that publishes research in all areas of fish culture. This international journal carries papers on all areas of fish and other aquatic organisms. It covers a wide range of topics, including nutrition and feeding, broodstock selection and spawning, drugs and chemicals, and health and water quality. This journal is an excellent resource for researchers interested in aquaculture in North America and the global aquaculture community. URL: http://www.tandfonline.com/loi/unaj20

2341. ***North American Journal of Fisheries Management.*** [ISSN: 0275-5947] 1981. bi-m. GBP 1913 print & online eds. Ed(s): Daniel J Daugherty, Geraldine Vander Haegen. John Wiley & Sons Ltd., . Illus., index, adv. Refereed. Vol. ends: No. 4. Reprint: PSC. *Indexed:* A22, C45, S25. *Aud.:* Ac, Sa.

North American Journal of Fisheries Management is published bimonthly to promote communication between managers of both marine and freshwater fisheries. An official journal of the American Fisheries Society, this title covers the maintenance, enhancement, and allocation of fisheries resources. It documents successes and failures of fisheries programs, and explores ways in which fisheries can be managed to best protect fish and fisheries resources. It helps convey practical management experience to others. With a focus on fishery best practices, it will appeal to those involved in fisheries management. URL: http://afs.tandfonline.com/toc/ujfm20/current

2342. ***Reviews in Aquaculture (Online).*** [ISSN: 1753-5131] 2009. q. GBP 2488. Ed(s): Albert Tacon, Sena De Silva. John Wiley & Sons, Inc., 111 River St, Hoboken, NJ 07030; cs-journals@wiley.com; http://onlinelibrary.wiley.com. Adv. Refereed. *Aud.:* Ac, Sa.

Published quarterly, *Reviews in Aquaculture* contains peer-reviewed articles that relate to all aspects of aquaculture. Subjects covered include market trends, genetics and aquaculture, aquaculture practices, biology and culture of species, health management, and policy development. Though it is limited in the types of material it publishes, this journal attempts to be comprehensive in its coverage of the field of aquaculture. *Reviews in Aquaculture* would be most useful to scientists and aquaculturalists interested in keeping current on the latest research developments in the field. URL: http://onlinelibrary.wiley.com/journal/10.1111/

2343. ***Reviews in Fish Biology and Fisheries.*** [ISSN: 0960-3166] q. EUR 1136 (print & online eds.)). Ed(s): Gretta T Peci. Springer Netherlands, Van Godewijckstraat 30, Dordrecht, 3311 GX, Netherlands; http://www.springer.com. Adv. Refereed. Reprint: PSC. *Indexed:* A01, A22, Agr, BRI, C45, E01. *Bk. rev.:* Number and length vary. *Aud.:* Ac, Sa.

Of all the academic journals in this section, this may be the most accessible. Published quarterly, *Reviews in Fish Biology and Fisheries* is an international journal that publishes review articles on varied aspects of fish and fisheries biology. It also includes book reviews, correspondence, and accounts of relevant papers delivered at conferences. Topics include evolutionary biology, taxonomy, stock identification, genetics, functional morphology, fisheries development, and exploitation and conservation. This journal's audience is those in the field of aquaculture and those with an interest in biology but not necessarily aquaculture. This journal would be useful to a wide range of people, from the general population to the seasoned academic researcher. URL: http://link.springer.com/journal/11160

2344. ***Reviews in Fisheries Science & Aquaculture.*** Formerly (until 2014): *Reviews in Fisheries Science.* [ISSN: 2330-8249] 1993. q. GBP 1149 (print & online eds.)). Ed(s): Sandra E Shumway. Taylor & Francis Inc., 711 3rd Ave, 8th Fl, New York, NY 10017; support@tandfonline.com; http://www.taylorandfrancis.com. Illus., index. Sample. Refereed. Vol. ends: No. 4. Reprint: PSC. *Indexed:* A01, A22, C45, E01. *Bk. rev.:* Number and length vary. *Aud.:* Ac, Sa.

Published quarterly, *Reviews in Fisheries Science & Aquaculture* covers nearly every aspect of aquaculture. It provides an important forum for the publication of up-to-date reviews that cover the broad range of subject areas in fisheries science. These areas include management, aquaculture, taxonomy, behavior, stock identification, genetics, nutrition, and physiology. This publication includes reviews, historical articles, and original research. Because of its broad scope and its commitment to covering the current issues of interest to those studying aquaculture, this publication is essential for serious researchers in the field, as well as those interested in learning more about aquaculture. URL:http://www.tandfonline.com/loi/brfs20

Tropical Fish Hobbyist. See Pets section.

2345. ***World Aquaculture Society. Journal.*** Former titles (until 1986): *World Mariculture Society. Journal;* (until 1981): *World Mariculture Society. Proceedings;* (until 1974): *World Mariculture Society. Proceedings of the Annual Meeting;* (until 19??): *World Mariculture Society. Proceedings of the Annual Workshop.* [ISSN: 0893-8849] 1986. bi-m. Ed(s): Carole Engle. Wiley-Blackwell Publishing, Inc., 111 River St, Hoboken, NJ 07030; http://onlinelibrary.wiley.com. Illus., adv. Sample. Refereed. Vol. ends: No. 4. Reprint: PSC. *Indexed:* A22, Agr, C45, E01. *Aud.:* Ac, Sa.

This is the official journal of the World Aquaculture Society, an international organization with more than 2,500 members in more than 80 countries. The journal contains review and research articles, communications, and research notes all focused on the culture of aquatic plants and animals. Topics covered include nutrition, disease, genetics and breeding, physiology, environmental quality, culture systems engineering, husbandry practices, and economics and marketing, as well as a number of other topics related to the culture of aquatic organisms. Though the articles in this journal are aimed at academics, the broad range of topics covered and the global coverage make it accessible to those wishing to get a big-picture understanding of the field of aquaculture. URL: http://onlinelibrary.wiley.com/journal/10.1111/

■ FISHING

Kelly S. MacWatters, Coordinator of Reference and E-Resources of the J. Spencer and Patricia Standish Library of Siena College, 515 Loudon Road, Loudonville, NY 12211

Introduction

Whether you are a novice or experienced fisher, looking for angling tips, shopping for the latest gear, or planning a fishing adventure, there is a fishing magazine to meet your needs. In general, this section describes titles for the recreational fisher and sport fishing enthusiast.

Fishing magazines can be grouped under a variety of categories. General sporting magazines include titles such as *Field & Stream, Outdoor Life,* and *Gray's Sporting Journal.* There are titles devoted to specific families of fish such as *Trout Magazine* and *Musky Hunter,* while other magazines cover particular geographic areas, such as *Northwest Fly Fishing.* Lastly, there are titles that focus solely on technique and instruction, such as *Fly Tyer.*

Given the picturesque setting of most fishing destinations, spectacular photography is a common theme among publications. Most titles offer a digital subscription option, which greatly enhances the reader experience with slideshows, videos, and interactive features. Many titles have companion television shows, and all have a web presence that provides useful content such as current stream conditions, fishing regulations, photo galleries, online forums, and links to social media sites.

The titles listed in this section are recommended for public libraries or for personal subscription. Many titles have a strong conservation and management focus, and therefore are appropriate for academic libraries that support fisheries programs.

Basic Periodicals

American Fly Fisher, Fly Fisherman, Gray's Sporting Journal.

Basic Abstracts and Indexes

MasterFILE Premier.

2346. *American Angler: the fly fishing authority.* Former titles (until 1991): *American Angler and Fly Tyer;* (until 1988): *Fly Tyer.* [ISSN: 1055-6737] 1978. bi-m. USD 21.95 combined subscription domestic (print & online eds); USD 41.95 combined subscription in Canada & Mexico (print & online eds); USD 61.95 combined subscription elsewhere (print & online eds)). Ed(s): Greg Thomas. MCC Magazines, LCC, 725 Broad St, Augusta, GA 30901. Adv. *Bk. rev.:* Number and length vary. *Aud.:* Hs, Sa.

Anyone wishing to become a fly fisher, or those expert in the field, will encounter *American Angler.* Dedicated to fly fishers and fly tyers of all levels, the magazine focuses on coldwater fly fishing for trout and salmon. There are occasionally articles on warm water and saltwater species. Regular contributors are fly fishing authorities. Features and departments cover every aspect of fly fishing, the newest gear, conservation, and news. Where and how to fish are features in every issue. Articles are well written, enjoyable, and accompanied by fine photo illustrations. A must-have for all libraries that serve a fly fishing population. URL: www.americanangler.com/

2347. *American Fly Fisher.* [ISSN: 0884-3562] 1974. q. Free. Ed(s): Kate Achor. The American Museum of Fly Fishing, 4104 Main St, Manchester, VT 05254; amff@amff.com; http://www.amff.com/. *Bk. rev.:* Number and length vary. *Aud.:* Hs, Ga, Ac, Sa.

American Fly Fisher is a magazine published by the American Museum of Fly Fishing in Manchester, Vermont. Each issue contains three or four in-depth articles, museum news, and information about events, projects, and collections. The magazine presents the history of fly fishing, rod building, fly tying, club histories, and fisher biographies. The articles are well written and are usually illustrated with period images. Current issues are sent to museum members and past issues are available online for everyone to read. Recommended for libraries that support history and fly fishers. URL: http://www.amff.org/the-journal/

2348. *Bassmaster Magazine.* [ISSN: 0199-3291] 1968. 9x/yr. USD 15. Ed(s): James Hall. E S P N Publishing, Inc., PO Box 10000, Lake Buena Vista, FL 32830. Illus., adv. *Aud.:* Hs, Ga.

Bassmaster focuses on all aspects of bass fishing. Boats, rods, tackle, and tournaments are given in-depth coverage. Regular departments present tackle tips, fishing strategies, advice from fishing professionals, and best spots to fish. In addition to publishing the magazine, B.A.S.S. produces *The Bassmasters,* a weekly television program. Recommended for libraries that support sport fishing enthusiasts. URL: www.bassmaster.com/

Field & Stream. See Hunting and Guns section.

2349. *Fly Fisherman.* [ISSN: 0015-4741] 1969. 5x/yr. USD 10 combined subscription domestic (print & online eds.)). Ed(s): Ross Purnell. Outdoor Sportsman Group, Inc., 1040 Sixth Ave, 12th Fl, New York, NY 10018; customerservice@imoutdoors.com; http://www.imoutdoorsmedia.com. Illus., adv. Sample. Vol. ends: Nov. *Indexed:* A22, BRI, C37. *Bk. rev.:* Number and length vary. *Aud.:* Hs, Ga.

Fly Fisherman offers a wide range of useful information for the beginner or the experienced fly fisher. Each issue features four well-written articles with colorful photographs. The articles cover fresh and saltwater destinations and a variety of species. Departments cover fly fishing techniques, fly tying, fishing legislation and regulation, restoration projects, book and film reviews, and much more. The web site provides information on gear, fly tying, conservation, destinations, and a fly fisherman forum. Recommended for libraries that support fly fishers. URL: www.flyfisherman.com/

2350. *Fly Fusion: North America's fly-fishing authority.* [ISSN: 1916-1034] 2004. q. CAD 24.95 domestic; USD 23.85 United States; USD 35.95 elsewhere. Ed(s): Derek Bird. Fly Fusion Ltd., RPO Tamarack Hall, PO Box 20029, Cranbrook, BC V1C 6J5, Canada; subscribe@flyfusionmag.com; http://www.flyfusionmag.com/. Adv. *Aud.:* Ga, Ac, Sa.

Dedicated to fly fishers and fly tyers of all levels, *Fly Fusion* provides well-written articles accompanied by fine photography. Many fishing magazines feature destination areas, while *Fly Fusion* is designed to enhance the reader's angling skills. Issues regularly include topics such as fly patterns, tying techniques, casting tips, and species information. Also included are fisher profiles, product reviews, and conservation efforts. This Canadian publication provides a unique look from across the border. Two additional issues are published annually on the *Fly Fusion Mobi Magazine* platform. URL: www.flyfusionmag.com/

2351. *Fly Tyer.* [ISSN: 1082-1309] 1995. q. USD 19.95 domestic; USD 39.95 Canada; USD 59.95 elsewhere. Ed(s): David Klausmeyer. Morris Communications Co., LLC., 725 Broad St, Augusta, GA 30901; http://www.morris.com. Adv. Vol. ends: Nov. *Aud.:* Hs, Ga, Sa.

Fly Tyer focuses exclusively on the art of fly tying. Features provide in-depth information on fly patterns, materials, and methods. The detailed instructions, with accompanying photographs, serve as a valuable guide to the reader. This publication appeals to both novice and experienced fly tyers. The web site offers hundreds of fly recipes, multimedia content, and a fly tyer forum. A digital subscription is available. Recommended for libraries that support fly fishers. URL: http://flytyer.com/

2352. *The Flyfish Journal.* [ISSN: 1947-4539] 2009. q. USD 39.99 domestic; USD 55.59 per issue Canada; USD 89.99 per issue elsewhere. Ed(s): Kirk Deetor. Funny Feelings, LLC, PO Box 2806, Bellingham, WA 98227; http://www.funnyfeelingsllc.com. Illus., adv. *Aud.:* Hs, Ga.

A great addition to any fly fisher's collection, indeed any fisher's collection, this title is for anyone learning the sport, from those looking for the next exotic place to land that unusual fish, to the armchair angler interested in a fictional respite.

The Flyfish Journal is beautiful! Have it on your shelves for the avid fly fisher or for the general public. Articles cover all species of fish from the traditional trout and salmon, to the exotic peacock bass or Manchurian trout. Each issue begins with five to seven gorgeous photographs, and continues throughout with high-quality images and text that inform and entertain the reader. Well worth the yearly subscription. URL: www.theflyfishjournal.com/

2353. *Gray's Sporting Journal.* [ISSN: 0273-6691] 1976. 7x/yr. USD 39.95 domestic; USD 59.95 Canada; USD 79.95 elsewhere. Ed(s): Steve Walburn, James R Babb. Morris Communications Co., LLC., 725 Broad St, Augusta, GA 30901; http://www.morris.com. Illus., adv. Sample. *Aud.:* Ac, Sa.

Gray's Sporting Journal is a unique magazine that contains stories about sporting life and adventure. The articles are well-written, informative, and complemented with beautiful photography, paintings, and original sporting art. On occasion, an artist's work is featured in the magazine. Each issue contains "The Listing," with information about outfitters, guides, lodges, and charters across the country. Selected articles are featured online, along with an art gallery, photographic journals, poetry, and trip planning. URL: www.grayssportingjournal.com/

2354. *In-Fisherman.* [ISSN: 0276-9905] 1979. 8x/yr. USD 10 domestic; USD 23 Canada; USD 25 elsewhere. Ed(s): Doug Stange, Steve Quinn. Outdoor Sportsman Group, Inc., 1040 Sixth Ave, 12th Fl, New York, NY 10018; customerservice@imoutdoors.com; http://www.imoutdoorsmedia.com. Illus., adv. Sample. Vol. ends: Nov. *Indexed:* BRI. *Aud.:* Ga.

In-Fisherman covers a wide range of freshwater and near-shore coastal waters species although core species include bass, walleyes, pike, muskies, catfish, panfish, trout, and salmon. Magazine sections include ice fishing, custom rods, boating safety, midwest finesse, and biology. One double issue is published, which counts as two of the eight issues in an annual subscription. *In-Fisherman* also publishes a series of annual guides and produces a companion television series. Articles are well written and contributors include fisheries scientists, educators, and expert anglers. URL: http://www.in-fisherman.com/

2355. *Musky Hunter.* Formerly (until 19??): *Musky Hunter Magazine.* [ISSN: 1079-3402] 1989. bi-m. USD 23.95 domestic; USD 25.95 foreign; USD 7 per issue. Ed(s): Steve Heiting, Jim Saric. Esox Promotions, Inc, 7978 Hwy 70 E, PO Box 340, St Germain, WI 54558. Adv. *Aud.:* Hs, Sa.

Devoted to the musky-fishing enthusiast, this specialized title focuses on fishing for the elusive Muskellunge. Containing eight to ten feature articles and multiple departments, each issue informs the fisher about fishing methods, new gear, and tournament catches, and includes larger-than-life pictures. "Musky Matters" and "Joe Bucher's Moon Secrets" are two sections that provide fishing information for just this species. Since this fish is found in northern areas of the United States or in Canada, these areas are the title's primary market. Recommended for libraries near the northern waters and down the Mississippi and Ohio River valleys, wherever the Muskellunge are found. URL: www.muskyhunter.com/

2356. *Northwest Fly Fishing.* [ISSN: 1527-8255] 1999. bi-m. USD 34.95. Ed(s): John Shewey. Northwest Fly Fishing, LLC., PO Box 12275, Salem, OR 97309; http://nwflyfishing.net. Adv. Sample. *Aud.:* Hs, Ga, Sa.

Northwest Fly Fishing is a valuable reference for readers who live or fish in the northwestern United States; the Canadian provinces of Alberta, British Columbia, and Yukon; and Alaska. Two companion titles, *Southwestern Fly Fishing* and *Eastern Fly Fishing,* are included in this family of publications. *Eastern Fly Fishing* covers the northeastern, southeastern, and midwestern United States. *Southwest Fly Fishing* covers the southwestern United States, Mexico, and Central America. Each issue features four to six angling destinations. Each feature article contains practical and useful travel information including maps, local fly shops and guides, site accessibility, necessary gear, and useful fly patterns. The articles are well written and filled with interesting facts and history about the location and associated fish populations. "Conservation," "Fish Food," and "Pioneers and Legends" are just a few of the departments included in each issue. These titles are recommended for libraries located in the specified geographic regions. URL: www.matchthehatch.com

Outdoor Life. See Hiking, Climbing, and Outdoor Recreation section.

2357. *Sport Fishing: the magazine of saltwater fishing.* [ISSN: 0896-7369] 1986. 9x/yr. USD 9.97 combined subscription domestic (print & ipad eds.); USD 23.97 combined subscription Canada (print & ipad eds.); USD 37.97 combined subscription elsewhere (print & ipad eds.)). Ed(s): Doug Olander. Bonnier Corp., 460 N Orlando Ave, Ste 200, Orlando, FL 32789; SFHcustserv@cdsfulfillment.com; http://www.bonniercorp.com. Illus., adv. *Indexed:* BRI. *Aud.:* Ga.

Sport Fishing Magazine is an excellent source of information for saltwater fishing enthusiasts. Fishing techniques, location, gear, and conservation are popular topics. Regular features include hands-on techniques for improving inshore and offshore fishing performance, reviews of boats and engines; marine electronics, the latest in fishing gear, location scouting for top sport fishing waters, and reports on salt water marine life. Articles are current, interesting, and well researched. URL: http://www.sportfishingmag.com

2358. *Trout.* [ISSN: 0041-3364] 1959. q. Free to members. Ed(s): Kirk Deeter. Trout Unlimited, 1300 N 17th St, Ste 500, Arlington, VA 22209; trout@tu.org; http://www.tu.org/. Illus., adv. *Bk. rev.:* 3. *Aud.:* Hs, Ga, Ac, Sa.

Trout Magazine is a publication of Trout Unlimited, an organization devoted to coldwater fisheries conservation. Each issue includes six featured stories that are educational, entertaining, and packed full of interesting information on every aspect of trout, salmon, and coldwater fisheries. Regular columns include "Watersheds" and "Blue Lines," and contributors include well-known fishing authors and great fishers. The articles are very well written and include high-quality images. Recommended for any coldwater fishing enthusiast. URL: www.tu.org/media/trout-magazine

■ FOLKLORE

Amanda Brooks, Instructional Media Center Technician, FH Green Library, West Chester University of Pennsylvania, West Chester, PA 19383

Introduction

According to The American Folklore Society, "Folklore is the traditional art, literature, knowledge, and practice that is disseminated largely through oral communication and behavior." Because it encompasses such a diverse range of topics across regions and time, folklore has a wide appeal to both the general reader and the serious scholar; from the curiosity of someone just learning their genealogy to a PhD candidate studying the impact of social media. Included here are titles that attempt to encompass a range of interests.

As is the case in all areas, many resources are now available online; most societies and many individual folklorists have their own web page. As a result, many regional societies are no longer issuing formal publications. Some of the journals can be found in e-format but require a paid subscription. Open Folklore (www.openfolklore.org) continues to be an invaluable source of both free and fee-based journals and related online components.

Basic Periodicals

Ga: *Journal of American Culture;* Ac: *Folklore, Journal of American Folklore, Journal of Folklore Research.*

Basic Abstracts and Indexes

America: History and Life, Historical Abstracts, Humanities Index, MLA International Bibliography.

2359. ***Asian Ethnology.*** Former titles (until 200?): *Asian Folklore Studies;* (until 1963): *Folklore Studies.* [ISSN: 1882-6865] 1942. s-a. JPY 5000. Ed(s): Frank J. Korom, Benjamin Dorman. Nanzan Daigaku Jinruigaku Kenkyujo, 18 Yamazato-cho, Showa-ku, Nagoya, 466-8673, Japan; ai-nu@ic.nanzan-u.ac.jp; http://www.ic.nanzan-u.ac.jp/JINRUIKEN/index.html. Illus., adv. Refereed. Circ: 350. Vol. ends: No. 2. Microform: IDC. *Indexed:* A01, A22, A47, AmHI, BAS, BRI, ENW, IBSS, MLA-IB. *Bk. rev.:* 30, 1,000 words. *Aud.:* Ac.

This journal, now available full-text online, publishes scholarly research on the folklore of Asian nations, including literary works and the oral tradition; it also discusses folkloric aspects of belief, cultural customs, and art. The journal includes scholarly articles, research materials, communications, and lengthy book reviews. Some of the articles are purely descriptive accounts or retellings of folk tales; others are more analytical, based on research, including surveys and textual analysis or comparative study. Recent topics cover the Lion Dance and Chinese diasporic identity; observations of the Mishmis in India and China; how daily and weekly rhythms are maintained in rural Pakistan; and a discussion of Xiangsheng (cross talk) performer Guo Degang. Abstracts are included. Back issues are accessible online from the journal's web site. Recommended for academic libraries with an interest in Asian literature or arts, folklore, or children's literature.

2360. ***Cultural Analysis: an interdisciplinary forum on folklore and popular culture.*** [ISSN: 1537-7873] 2000. irreg. Free. Cultural Analysis, c/o Anthony Bak Buccitelli, Co-Editor, American Studies Program, The Pennsylvania State University, Middletown, PA 1705. Refereed. *Indexed:* BRI. *Aud.:* Ac.

This e-journal is an "interdisciplinary, peer-reviewed journal dedicated to investigating expressive and everyday culture." The journal includes research articles, notes, reviews, and responses. It is designed to be cross-disciplinary and international in scope, with approximately one volume per year. Available free on the web, the journal is produced in both html and pdf formats. Some feature articles are followed by critics' responses. Articles cover topics from many world cultures. Each article is abstracted. Reviews average 1,500 to 2,000 words. Some issues are thematic. One of the strengths of this publication is its diversity of authorship and focus on modernity. Recent issues include articles on the relationship between geo-cache gaming and cultural heritage; "Time, Functionality and Intimacy in Spotify's Featured Playlists"; and the Moroccan diaspora in Istanbul as experienced through social media. This journal seems to have developed a solid foundation for web access. Recommended for academic libraries with cultural studies programs.

2361. ***Folklore.*** Formed by the merger of (1888-1890): *Archaeological Review;* (1883-1890): *The Folk-Lore Journal;* Which was formerly (1878-1883): *The Folk-Lore Record.* [ISSN: 0015-587X] 1890. 3x/yr. GBP 640 (print & online eds.)). Ed(s): Dr. Jessica Hemming. Routledge, 4 Park Sq, Milton Park, Abingdon, OX14 4RN, United Kingdom; subscriptions@tandf.co.uk; http://www.tandfonline.com. Illus., adv. Sample. Refereed. Microform: PMC. Reprint: PSC. *Indexed:* A01, A22, A47, AmHI, BRI, E01, IBSS, MLA-IB. *Bk. rev.:* 20, 500-700 words. *Aud.:* Ac.

A British publication, this scholarly journal considers itself a forum for European folk studies and culture, but also includes some articles on American folklore. Topics in recent issues include: a popular Irish tale of smuggling, the "reconstruction of women's narrative traditions in Iceland," and the evolution of the Aladdin tale. In addition to articles, some issues include papers from meetings of the Folklore Society. Bibliographies, articles about recipients of awards in the field, and book reviews may also be included. This journal is for libraries that provide research materials in the area of folk studies.

2362. ***Folklore.*** [ISSN: 1406-0949] 1996. q. 3 times per year until 2016. Free. Ed(s): Andres Kuperjanov, Mare Koiva. Eesti Kirjandusmuuseum, Vanemuise St 42-235, Tartu, 51003, Estonia; kirmus@kirmus.ee; http://www.kirmus.ee/. Illus. Refereed. *Indexed:* MLA-IB. *Bk. rev.:* Number and length vary. *Aud.:* Ga, Ac.

This journal is the publication of the Folklore Department of the Institute of the Estonian Language and is not to be confused with the British Folklore Society's journal of the same name. Articles cover a wide variety of topics, and some issues are thematic. Books reviews and news items may also be included. There is a special emphasis on Estonia and neighboring regions. Articles are done as pdf files to provide illustrations as well as text. There is online access to both current and back issues. An editorial note welcomes contributors from all countries and contributions on all aspects of folklore. This is a worthy journal and one of the better ones with full online access. It has a strong record of continuing publication. Recommended for academic and general adult readers.

The Foxfire Magazine. See Teenagers section.

2363. ***International Journal of Intangible Heritage.*** [ISSN: 1975-3586] a. Ed(s): Alissandra Cummins. National Folk Museum of Korea, 1-1 Sejongno, Jongno-gu, Seoul, 110-820, Korea, Republic of. Refereed. *Indexed:* C45, IBSS, MLA-IB. *Bk. rev.:* Number and length vary. *Aud.:* Ac.

Published by the National Folk Museum of Korea, this scholarly journal is "dedicated to the promotion of the understanding of all aspects of intangible heritage worldwide, and to the communication of research and examples of good professional practice." Each issue has eight or nine articles, several book reviews, and short biographies of authors. Topics and authors are worldwide. Subjects covered in recent issues have included deities of Igbo Society; Traditional methods of soil and water conservation in Cebu, the Philippines; traditional knowledge of Korean fishermen; and the ceremonial pilgrimages of the southern Paiutes in the United States. Articles often included photographs and/or illustrations. The text is available in English or Korean. Recommended for institutions that serve programs in folklore studies or Asian studies, or put a strong emphasis on preserving local and national heritage.

2364. ***Journal of American Culture.*** Former titles (until 2003): *Journal of American and Comparative Culture;* (until 2000): *Journal of American Culture.* [ISSN: 1542-7331] 1978. q. GBP 300. Ed(s): Kathy Merlock Jackson. Wiley-Blackwell Publishing, Inc., 350 Main St, Malden, MA 02148; http://onlinelibrary.wiley.com. Illus., adv. Sample. Refereed. Vol. ends: No. 4. Microform: PQC. Reprint: PSC. *Indexed:* A01, A22, AmHI, BRI, CBRI, E01, F01, IIMP, IIPA, MLA-IB. *Bk. rev.:* 20-30, 300-500 words. *Aud.:* Ga, Ac.

As the official journal of the American Cultural Association, this publication intends to "promote and facilitate American culture in its broadest sense." Articles are a mix of historic and present-day material that covers traditional folklore themes and pop culture. Topics in recent issues include the role of social media and phenomena of "Fake News"; dancehalls in the early twentieth century; and 1930's "Horrors of War" bubble gum cards. Some issues are thematic, for example, LGBT, music and sound, and mental health issues. Most issues include a few essays and numerous short book reviews. With its wide variety of topics and accessible writing style, this title will be of interest to the general reader and the student of folklore or popular culture.

2365. ***Journal of American Folklore.*** [ISSN: 0021-8715] 1888. q. USD 193 (print & online eds.)). Ed(s): Ann K Ferrell. University of Illinois Press, 1325 S Oak St, MC-566, Champaign, IL 61820; uipress@uillinois.edu; http://www.press.uillinois.edu. Illus., index, adv. Refereed. Vol. ends: No. 4. Microform: MIM; PMC; PQC. *Indexed:* A01, A22, AmHI, BRI, CBRI, Chicano, E01, IIMP, IIPA, MLA-IB. *Bk. rev.:* 10, 500-700 words. *Aud.:* Ga, Ac.

As the official publication of the American Folklore Society, this title contains an emphasis on the United States. However, the scope of this journal is worldwide and varied. Topics in recent issues include an examination of a traditional Chinese folk drama; an interview with retiring American Folklore Society Executive Director Tim Lloyd; and the recordings of the Hammons family of West Virginia. Reviews are lengthy and cover both books and media; there is also a section titled creative writing that features original works. One of journal's goals is to "push the boundaries, explore the borders, and expand the parameters of folklore." Academic libraries should select this title for their basic collection, and large public libraries will also want to consider it.

2366. ***Journal of Cultural Geography.*** [ISSN: 0887-3631] 1980. 3x/yr. GBP 193 (print & online eds.)). Ed(s): Alyson L Greiner. Routledge, 530 Walnut St, Ste 850, Philadelphia, PA 19106; enquiries@tandfonline.com; http://www.tandfonline.com. Illus., adv. Sample. Refereed. Vol. ends: No. 2. Reprint: PSC. *Indexed:* A01, A22, BAS, BRI, C45, E01, IBSS, MLA-IB. *Bk. rev.:* 12, 400-500 words. *Aud.:* Ac.

This journal's articles discuss the influences of culture on the physical world. Topics vary widely, from the historic to current pop culture. Recent issues include street artists in Austin, Texas; ethnic identity in northwest China; and mental maps. Some issues are thematic. Most contributors are professors or graduate students. In addition to articles, there are book reviews and occasional annotated bibliographies. This title should appeal to a wide variety of readers. A good pick for academic libraries and larger public libraries.

2367. ***Journal of Folklore Research: an international journal of folklore and ethnomusicology.*** Formerly (until 1983): *Folklore Institute. Journal;* Which superseded in part (in 1964): *Midwest Folklore;* Which superseded in part (in 1951): *Hoosier Folklore;* Which was formerly (until 1946): *Hoosier Folklore Bulletin.* [ISSN: 0737-7037] 1942. 3x/yr. USD 99.85 (print & online eds.)). Ed(s): Kristina Downs, Ray Cashman. Indiana University Press, Office of Scholarly Publishing, Herman B Wells Library 350, Bloomington, IN 47405; iuporder@indiana.edu; http://www.iupress.indiana.edu/. Illus., adv. Refereed. Vol. ends: No. 3. Microform: PQC. Reprint: PSC. *Indexed:* A01, A22, A47, AmHI, BRI, E01, IBSS, IIMP, IIPA, MLA-IB. *Bk. rev.:* Number and length vary. *Aud.:* Ac.

"Devoted to the study of the world's traditional creative and expressive forms, the *Journal of Folklore Research* provides an international forum for current theory and research among scholars of folklore and related fields." International in scope, the journal covers a wide variety of topics, including folk music of Inner Mongolia; scrapbooking at the turn of the twenty-first century; and Mayan hip-hop of Guatemalan youth. Theme issues are also published; the most recent of which focuses on an examination of human-animal relationship. Most issues include reviews of books, media, and museum exhibits. Access is available by subscription or fee-based databases. This title is important for libraries that serve academic folklore research and folklore programs.

2368. ***Louisiana Folklore Miscellany.*** [ISSN: 0090-9769] 1958. a. Free to members. Ed(s): Keagan Lejeune. Louisiana Folklore Society, PO Box 44149, Lafayette, LA 70504; http://www.louisianafolklore.org/. *Indexed:* MLA-IB. *Aud.:* Ga, Ac.

Published under the auspices of the Louisiana Folklore Society, this is described on the society's web site as a publication of "articles, notes, and commentaries on all aspects of Louisiana folklore and folklife." While often focusing on Cajun and Creole social life and customs, the publication does offer a variety of articles relating to Southern culture. Issues have included such topics as the emerging Mardi Gras traditions; the importance of the fishboat to the Atchafalaya Basin people; and Yoruba-Cuban folk medicine. The society's web site offers full text of some articles. This is an entertaining publication for general readers and folklore researchers interested in the traditions of the South.

2369. ***Marvels & Tales: journal of fairy-tale studies.*** Formerly (until 1996): *Merveilles et Contes.* [ISSN: 1521-4281] 1987. s-a. USD 145 (print & online eds.)). Ed(s): Anne F Duggan, Cristina Bacchilega. Wayne State University Press, The Leonard N Simons Bldg, 4809 Woodward Ave, Detroit, MI 48201; bookorders@wayne.edu ; http://wsupress.wayne.edu/. Illus., adv. Refereed. *Indexed:* A01, A22, AmHI, BRI, E01, IBSS, MLA-IB. *Bk. rev.:* Number and length vary. *Aud.:* Ac.

According to its editorial statement, this journal is "committed to promoting advances in fairy-tale studies." This title covers a wide variety of cultural groups and disciplines, and it contains up to five lengthy articles, plus translations of tales and numerous reviews covering both print and media. Articles encompass a wide variety of scholarship on fairy tales. Some issues are organized by themes. A scholarly journal for academic folklore programs or strong children's literature programs.

2370. ***New Directions in Folklore.*** Formerly (until 1997): *Impromptu Journal.* [ISSN: 2161-9964] 19??. s-a. Free. Ed(s): David J Puglia. New Directions in Folklore, c/o David J. Puglia, 2155 University Ave, Bronx, NY 10453. Refereed. *Indexed:* MLA-IB. *Bk. rev.:* Number and length vary. *Aud.:* Ac.

In partnership with the American Folklore Society, Indiana University Libraries, and IUScholarWorks, this title covers a wide variety of topics, often looking at contemporary culture. Some issues are thematic. Articles are peer reviewed. Each issue is a mix of articles and book reviews. Recent editions cover a variety of topics including Anonymous as a trickster figure; Zombies on Flickr; and a Star Wars themed issue. This title is for libraries that support folklore or pop cultural programs. Publication is lagging a bit, with 2016 being the most recent.

2371. ***Now & Then (Johnson City): the Appalachian magazine.*** [ISSN: 0896-2693] 1984. 2x/yr. USD 25 (Individuals, USD 15). Ed(s): Randy Sanders, Fred Sauceman. East Tennessee State University, Center for Appalachian Studies and Services, PO Box 70556, Johnson City, TN 37614-0556. Circ: 1500. *Indexed:* MLA-IB. *Bk. rev.:* 5, 500 words. *Aud.:* Ga.

Sponsored by the Center for Appalachian Studies and Services, this journal is probably the best source of folk culture relating to Appalachia. It is a nice mix of articles, essays, poetry, interviews, and photographs that cover views of past and present folk life. Reviews are limited, but additional titles are listed under "Books in Brief" and "Music in Brief." Most issues are loosely based on a theme, such as cultivating Appalachia or justice in Appalachia. An excellent title that covers Appalachian-related folklore, it is recommended for libraries of the region and others that support interest in its folk culture. There are two issues per year.

2372. ***Oral Tradition (Online).*** [ISSN: 1542-4308] 1986. irreg. Free. Ed(s): Vicki Polansky. Slavica Publishers, Inc., Indiana University, 2611 E 10th St, Bloomington, IN 47408; slavica@indiana.edu; https://slavica.indiana.edu/. *Aud.:* Ac.

As one of the few publications devoted to oral traditions, this journal describes its purpose as a "comparative and interdisciplinary focus for studies of oral literature and related fields by publishing research and scholarship on the creation, transmission, and interpretation of all forms of oral tradition expression." Articles are worldwide in scope, with subjects ranging from ancient epics and religious texts to modern drama and e-texts. Some issues are thematic. The issues are available in full text in pdf or html on the journal's web site. This scholarly title is for academic libraries that support folk literature programs.

2373. ***Tennessee Folklore Society Bulletin.*** Formerly (until 1937): *Tennessee Folklore Society. Bulletin.* [ISSN: 0040-3253] 1935. s-a. Free to members. Ed(s): Brent Cantrell. Tennessee Folklore Society, c/o Jubilee Community Arts, 1538 Laurel Ave, Knoxville, TN 37916; info@tennesseefolklore.org; http://www.tennesseefolklore.org. Illus., index. Refereed. Vol. ends: No. 2. *Indexed:* IIMP, IIPA, MLA-IB. *Bk. rev.:* 2-3, 600 words. *Aud.:* Ga, Ac.

Most of the articles in this journal pertain to folk culture in Tennessee and neighboring states. However, there are occasional pieces on folklore outside the United States, and some issues are thematic. In addition to articles, there are reviews of books and media, and a section listing coming events. Issues also usually contain a section listing publications available from the Tennessee Folklore Society. The journal is available through subscription and does not allow open access online. This journal is a good source for Tennessee and the surrounding geographic region.

2374. ***Voices (Schenectady): the journal of New York folklore.*** Formed by the merger of (1982-1999): *New York Folklore Newsletter;* (1975-1999): *New York Folklore;* Which was formerly (until 1975): *New York Folklore Quarterly.* [ISSN: 1551-7268] 1999. s-a. Free to members. New York Folklore Society, 129 Jay St, Schenectady, NY 12305; nyfs@nyfolklore.org; http://www.nyfolklore.org. Adv. Refereed. *Indexed:* BRI, IIMP, IIPA, MLA-IB. *Aud.:* Ga, Ac.

Published by the New York Folklore Society, *Voices* covers New York State and surrounding regions. Most issues include feature articles, columns, interviews, poetry, art, reviews, and all things related to folklore. The scope of the publication covers a wide variety of topics from pressing cider in the Finger Lakes to the performance technique of a storyteller. The editors view the journal as publishing "peer-reviewed, research-based articles, written in an accessible style, on topics related to traditional art and life, including ethnic culture." Issues are previewed online through the society's web page. However, full access is membership-based. For libraries that are interested in Northeastern folklore, this is a good title.

2375. *Western Folklore.* Formerly (until 1947): *California Folklore Quarterly.* [ISSN: 0043-373X] 1942. q. Western States Folklore Society, c/o Elliott Oring, PO Box 3557, Long Beach, CA 90803; http://www.westernfolklore.org. Refereed. *Indexed:* A01, A22, AmHI, BRI, CBRI, Chicano, IIMP, IIPA, MLA-IB. *Bk. rev.:* Number and length vary. *Aud.:* Ga, Ac.

This title's geographic scope includes California and neighboring regions. Most issues are composed of articles and reviews. Some may have a thematic approach. Topics cover all aspects of folklore, taking a wide interpretation of the subject. Reviews are numerous and vary in length from several paragraphs to several pages, and are available on the society's web site. This journal is a good addition for both academics and the sophisticated general reader.

■ FOOD AND NUTRITION

Diane T. Sands, Collection Development Librarian, California Academy of Sciences, San Francisco, CA 94118

Introduction

Academic programs in food, nutrition, and wellness studies teach people about the role of food in health, wellness, and development, as well as the relationship between eating and health. Libraries with collections supporting research in the health sciences are the target audience for these food and nutrition titles. Some of the publications herein are appropriate for well-versed general audiences. Libraries that support researchers in nutrition or health professionals will best benefit from these titles and their range of content. Articles may include information on health policy; food supply safety; healthy eating behaviors; food allergies; obesity; new treatments; medications and their effects; technical discussions of cutting-edge research in nutrition; and lighter articles describing general issues in the nutrition and health fields.

Basic Periodicals

Ga: *Nutrition Today;* Ac: *American Journal of Clinical Nutrition, Annals of Nutrition and Metabolism, The British Journal of Nutrition, The Journal of Nutrition, Nutrition Reviews.*

Basic Abstracts and Indexes

Biological Abstracts, CAB Abstracts, Current Contents/Life Sciences, MEDLINE, Nutrition Abstracts and Reviews.

2376. *Academy of Nutrition and Dietetics. Journal.* Former titles (until 2012): *American Dietetic Association. Journal;* (until 1925): *American Dietetic Association. Bulletin.* [ISSN: 2212-2672] 1925. 12x/yr. USD 865. Ed(s): Dr. Linda Snetselaar. Elsevier Inc., 230 Park Ave, Ste 800, New York, NY 10169; journalscustomerservice-usa@elsevier.com; https://www.elsevier.com. Illus., index, adv. Sample. Refereed. *Indexed:* A01, A22, Agr, BRI, C45, Chicano, H&TI, SD. *Bk. rev.:* Number and length vary. *Aud.:* Ac, Sa.

Formerly titled *The American Dietetic Association Journal,* this is the publication of the world's largest organization of food and nutrition professionals. Aimed at professional nutritionists and dietitians, the refereed reports include original research on diet therapy, community nutrition, and education and training; reports of association activities and conferences; columns that focus on professional advice; and articles approved for continuing-education credits (codes are provided). Access to the full text of this official association journal is available to ADA members and professional subscribers at the journal's web site; tables of contents and abstracts are free to all. Appropriate for collections that support professional or research populations in the health sciences.

2377. *American College of Nutrition. Journal.* [ISSN: 0731-5724] 1982. bi-m. GBP 432 (print & online eds.)). Ed(s): John J Cunningham. American College of Nutrition, 300 S Duncan Ave, Ste 225, Clearwater, FL 33755; office@amcollnutr.org; http://www.am-coll-nutr.org/jacn/jacn.htm. Illus., adv. Refereed. Reprint: PSC. *Indexed:* A22, Agr, C45, SD. *Bk. rev.:* Number and length vary. *Aud.:* Ac, Sa.

This official journal of the American College of Nutrition focuses on original and innovative research in nutrition, with useful application for researchers, physicians, and other health professionals. Professionals and investigators focused on current nutrition research will find scholarly articles that describe clinical and laboratory reports, as well as critical reviews on pertinent nutrition topics that highlight key teaching points. Tables of contents and article abstracts can be found at no charge online, along with full-text articles available to subscribers.

2378. *The American Journal of Clinical Nutrition.* Formerly (until 1954): *Journal of Clinical Nutrition;* Incorporates (1950-1958): *National Vitamin Foundation, Nutrition Symposium Series.* [ISSN: 0002-9165] 1952. m. EUR 672 (print & online eds.)). Ed(s): Dennis M Bier, Darren T Early. Oxford University Press, 198 Madison Ave, New York, NY 10016. Illus., index, adv. Refereed. Circ: 2081. Microform: PMC; PQC. *Indexed:* A22, Agr, BRI, C45, Chicano. *Bk. rev.:* 1-4, 500-1,000 words. *Aud.:* Ac, Sa.

The American Society for Clinical Nutrition has as its primary focus the publication of basic and clinical studies relevant to human nutrition. Articles are often grouped into subject areas such as obesity and eating disorders, aging, or cardiovascular disease risk. The web site provides access to tables of contents and abstracts. Subscribers have full access to editorials, book reviews, and full-text articles, as well as access to articles in press (published weekly). Supplements to *AJCN* are published on occasion, and these contain proceedings from internationally recognized conferences on clinical nutrition. The web site provides access to tables of contents and abstracts. Subscribers have full access to editorials, book reviews, and full-text articles, as well as access to articles in press (published weekly). This journal is appropriate for health science collections that support professional or research populations.

2379. *Annals of Nutrition and Metabolism: European journal of nutrition, metabolic diseases and dietetics.* Formed by the merger of (1947-1981): *Annales de la Nutrition et de l'Alimentation;* (1970-1981): *Nutrition and Metabolism;* Which was formerly (1959-1969): *Nutritio et Dieta.* [ISSN: 0250-6807] 1981. 6x/yr. CHF 4055. Ed(s): B Koletzko. S. Karger AG, Allschwilerstr 10, Basel, 4055, Switzerland; karger@karger.com; https://www.karger.com. Illus., index, adv. Sample. Refereed. *Indexed:* A01, A22, Agr, C45, E01. *Aud.:* Ac, Sa.

Basic and clinical reports that offer new information relating to human nutrition and metabolic diseases (including molecular genetics) are the focus of this peer-reviewed publication. Papers present original findings that deal with problems such as the consequences of specific diets and dietary supplements, and nutritional factors in the etiology of metabolic and gastrointestinal disorders. All articles are published electronically ahead of print copies, with full text available online to subscribers. The web site also includes free access to tables of contents, abstracts, and full text of selected "must-read" articles. Health science collections that support research populations will benefit from access to this journal.

2380. *The British Journal of Nutrition: an international journal of nutritional science.* [ISSN: 0007-1145] 1947. 24x/yr. GBP 1550 (print & online eds.)). Ed(s): G C Burdge. Cambridge University Press, University Printing House, Shaftesbury Rd, Cambridge, CB2 8BS, United Kingdom; journals@cambridge.org; https://www.cambridge.org/. Illus., index, adv. Refereed. Circ: 2230. Microform: SWZ; PMC; PQC. Reprint: PSC. *Indexed:* A22, Agr, C45, E01. *Bk. rev.:* 1-2, 500 words, signed. *Aud.:* Ac, Sa.

This international, peer-reviewed journal focuses on clinical nutrition research, animal nutrition, and basic science as applied to nutrition. It addresses the multidisciplinary nature of nutritional science, and includes material from all of the specialties involved in nutrition research, including molecular and cell biology and the emerging area of nutritional genomics. Tables of contents and abstracts are freely available on the web site. This journal is appropriate for health science collections that support professional or research populations.

2381. *European Journal of Clinical Nutrition.* Formerly (until 1988): *Human Nutrition. Clinical Nutrition;* Which superseded in part (in 1982): *Journal of Human Nutrition;* Which was formerly (until 1976): *Nutrition;* (until 1951): *Nutrition, Dietetics, Catering.* [ISSN: 0954-3007] 1947. m. EUR 1968. Ed(s): Manfred J Muller. Nature Publishing Group, The MacMillan Bldg, 4 Crinan St, London, N1 9XW, United Kingdom; nature@nature.com; https://www.nature.com. Illus., adv. Sample. Refereed. *Indexed:* A01, A22, Agr, BRI, C45, E01. *Bk. rev.:* 1-3, length varies, signed. *Aud.:* Ac, Sa.

EJCN is an international, peer-reviewed journal that publishes articles about human nutrition. The scope of the journal includes original articles, short communications, and case reports based on clinical, metabolic, and epidemiological studies that describe methodologies, mechanisms, relationships, and benefits of nutritional interventions for disease and health promotion. The web site provides one free issue, selected free articles and reviews, and weekly online advance publications that are available to subscribers. This journal is appropriate for health science collections that support professional or research populations.

2382. *The Journal of Nutrition.* [ISSN: 0022-3166] 1928. m. EUR 903 (print & online eds.)). Ed(s): Teresa A Davis. Oxford University Press, 198 Madison Ave, New York, NY 10016; custserv.us@oup.com; https://academic.oup.com/journals. Illus., index, adv. Refereed. Circ: 1137. Vol. ends: Dec. Microform: PMC; PQC. *Indexed:* A01, A22, Agr, BRI, C45. *Bk. rev.:* Number and length vary. *Aud.:* Ac, Sa.

This is the first scientific journal created solely for the publication of nutrition research, and its contents range from peer-reviewed research reports on all aspects of experimental nutrition, critical reviews, and commentaries, to symposia and workshop proceedings. Original research in nutrition is the focus of this scholarly journal, with articles geared toward research professionals. The web site contains access to articles in press (updated weekly) and full text for subscribers; tables of contents and abstracts are available to all. Supplements are frequently published to provide additional discussion of topics of special interest.

2383. *Journal of Nutrition Education and Behavior.* Formerly (until 2002): *Journal of Nutrition Education.* [ISSN: 1499-4046] 1969. 10x/yr. USD 710. Ed(s): Karen Chapman-Novakofski. Elsevier Inc., 230 Park Ave, Ste 800, New York, NY 10169; usinfo-f@elsevier.com; https://www.elsevier.com. Illus., index, adv. Sample. Refereed. *Indexed:* A01, A22, Agr, BRI, C37, C45, ERIC, H&TI, MLA-IB, SD. *Aud.:* Ac, Sa.

This official journal of the Society for Nutrition Education (SNE) is a refereed scientific periodical aimed at all professionals with an interest in nutrition education and dietary/physical activity behaviors. Articles cover original research on emerging issues and practices that are relevant to worldwide nutrition education and behavior. Access is available via the web site to full-text articles from 2006 to the present for subscribers and SNE members; access to abstracts is complimentary, as are certain open-access articles.

2384. *The Journal of Nutritional Biochemistry.* Supersedes (in 1990): *Nutrition Reports International.* [ISSN: 0955-2863] 1970. 12x/yr. USD 3713. Ed(s): Dr. Bernhard Hennig. Elsevier Inc., 230 Park Ave, Ste 800, New York, NY 10169; usinfo-f@elsevier.com; https://www.elsevier.com. Illus., index, adv. Sample. Refereed. Vol. ends: Dec. Microform: PQC. *Indexed:* A01, A22, Agr, C45. *Aud.:* Ac, Sa.

Health science collections that support professionals and researchers will find this to be a good selection. Devoted to advancements in nutritional science, *The Journal of Nutritional Biochemistry* presents experimental nutrition research as it relates to biochemistry, neurochemistry, molecular biology, toxicology, physiology, and pharmacology. It periodically publishes on emerging issues, conference summaries, experimental methods, symposium reports, metabolic pathways, and short communications. Authors can choose to publish their papers using an open-access option.

2385. *Nutrition: an international journal of applied and basic nutritional science.* Formerly (until 1987): *Nutrition International.* [ISSN: 0899-9007] 1985. 12x/yr. USD 2117. Ed(s): Dr. Michael M Meguid. Elsevier Inc., 230 Park Ave, Ste 800, New York, NY 10169; usinfo-f@elsevier.com; https://www.elsevier.com. Adv. Sample. Refereed. Vol. ends: No. 17. *Indexed:* A01, A22, Agr, C45. *Aud.:* Ac, Sa.

Articles in this scholarly journal focus on advances in nutrition research and science; new and advancing technologies in clinical nutrition practice; encouraging the application of the techniques of outcomes research; and meta-analyses of problems in patient-related nutrition. Many issues are available online, with open-access articles published regularly. Tables of contents and indexes can be accessed without a subscription. This journal is appropriate for health science collections that support professional or research populations.

2386. *Nutrition Research: an international publication for nutrition to advance food and life science research.* Incorporates (1975-1993): *Progress in Food and Nutrition Science;* Which was formerly: *International Encyclopedia of Food and Nutrition.* [ISSN: 0271-5317] 1981. 12x/yr. USD 3428. Ed(s): Bruce A Watkins. Elsevier Inc., 230 Park Ave, Ste 800, New York, NY 10169; usinfo-f@elsevier.com; https://www.elsevier.com. Illus., index, adv. Sample. Refereed. Vol. ends: Dec (No. 21). *Indexed:* A01, A22, Agr, C45. *Aud.:* Ac, Sa.

Academic or health science libraries that support nutrition research will find this title valuable. The journal's principal focus is on publishing research that advances the understanding of nutrients in food for improving the human condition. This is a scholarly journal for global communication of nutrition and life sciences research on food and health. Articles cover the study of nutrients during growth; reproduction; athletic performance; and aging and disease. Abstracts, tables of contents, and one sample issue are available to all online; subscribers can access full text. Some open-access articles can also be found within.

2387. *Nutrition Reviews.* [ISSN: 0029-6643] 1942. m. EUR 595 (print & online eds.)). Ed(s): Naomi Fukagawa. Oxford University Press, 2001 Evans Rd, Cary, NC 27513; custserv.us@oup.com; https://academic.oup.com/journals. Illus., index. Sample. Refereed. Microform: PQC. Reprint: PSC. *Indexed:* A01, A22, Agr, BRI, C45, E01, H&TI, SD. *Aud.:* Ac, Sa.

This title offers in-depth coverage of nutrition topics, including experimental and clinical nutrition research, food science, food and nutrition legislation, and policy as developed by national and international bodies. Supplements contain proceedings from the World Congress of Public Health Nutrition. Abstracts, tables of contents, and free sample issues are available online to all. While this monthly scholarly journal is appropriate for libraries that support research in the health sciences, the writing is accessible to knowledgeable consumers as well.

2388. *Nutrition Today.* [ISSN: 0029-666X] 1966. bi-m. USD 464. Ed(s): Johanna T Dwyer, Randi Konikoff Beranbaum. Lippincott Williams & Wilkins, Two Commerce Sq, 2001 Market St, Philadelphia, PA 19103; customerservice@lww.com; http://www.lww.com. Illus., index, adv. Refereed. *Indexed:* A01, A22, Agr, BRI, C45. *Aud.:* Ga, Ac, Sa.

An official partner publication of the American Society for Nutrition (ASN) since 2011, this title is appropriate for all health science collections and is accessible to an educated general audience. Informative articles cover topics such as the role of bioactive food ingredients in chronic diseases, sports nutrition, the food business, communicating nutrition, the politics of food, food in culture, and articles approved for continuing-education credits (codes are provided). The web site has links to all CE-credit articles published in *Nutrition Today* under one tab.

2389. *World Review of Nutrition and Dietetics.* [ISSN: 0084-2230] 1964. irreg. Ed(s): B Koletzko. S. Karger AG, Allschwilerstr 10, Basel, 4055, Switzerland; karger@karger.com; https://www.karger.com. Refereed. *Indexed:* A22, Agr. *Aud.:* Ac, Sa.

Volumes in this series consist of exceptionally thorough reviews on single specific topics, which are selected as either fundamental to improved understanding of human and animal nutrition, or relevant to problems of social and preventive medicine. Tables of contents and indexes are available online without a subscription, along with many free article excerpts. Filled with comprehensive reviews of topics related to nutrition, this is a good addition to academic or health science collections.

■ FOOD INDUSTRY

Beer, Wine, and Spirits; Cooking and Cookery; Food and Nutrition; and Hospitality/Restaurant sections.

Margaret E. (Bess) Robinson, Associate Professor, University of Memphis Libraries, University of Memphis, Memphis, TN 38152; merobnsn@memphis.edu

Introduction

While food nourishes our bodies, evokes powerful memories, and is an expression of cultural identity, the food industry drives a significant percentage of our national economy. Advances in food-related sciences; disruptive technologies; and changes in regulation (like the legalization of cannabis) continue to evolve to meet customers' seemingly insatiable demand for healthy food, new flavors, transparency, and sustainability.

Of the thousands of industry-related publications, the trade magazines and refereed journals selected for inclusion here primarily target industry professionals, but could also be relevant to researchers, educators, and students interested in the latest innovations. The trade magazines offer analysis of industry, market, consumer, and regulation trends; highlight new products and technologies; profile principals; and track upcoming industry events.

The refereed journals offer scientific research, trends, and analysis on diet and nutrition, food engineering and science, laws and regulations, developing products and processes, and food safety and protection.

Each entry includes a brief description of the range of additional related information available on publishers' websites.

Please see the Beer, Wine, and Spirits, Cooking and Cookery, Food and Nutrition, and Hospitality/Restaurant chapters of *Magazines for Libraries* for additional food- and beverage-related entries.

Basic Periodicals

Ac: *Critical Reviews in Food Science and Nutrition, Food Engineering, Food Protection Trends, Food Technology;* Sa: *Beverage Industry, Critical Reviews in Food Science and Nutrition, Dairy Foods, Food Engineering, Food Technology, Journal of Food Law & Policy, Journal of Food Protection, The National Provisioner, Prepared Foods, Refrigerated and Frozen Foods.*

Basic Abstracts and Indexes

ABI/INFORM, Business Source Premier, CINAHL, Science Citation Index.

2390. *Beverage Industry: trends, technology & products shaping the marketplace.* Former titles (until 1972): *Soft Drink Industry;* (until 1966): *Bottling Industry;* Incorporates (in 199?): *Beverage Industry Annual Manual;* Which was formerly (until 1973): *Soft Drink Industry Annual Manual.* [ISSN: 0148-6187] 1946. m. Free to qualified personnel (print or online ed.)). Ed(s): Barbara Harfmann, Jessica Jacobsen. B N P Media II, LLC., 155 N Pfingsten Rd, Ste 205, Deerfield, IL 60015; http://www.bnpmedia.com. Illus., index, adv. Microform: PQC. *Indexed:* A22, B01, B03, BRI, H&TI. *Aud.:* Ac, Sa.

Beverage Industry is a supersized (10" x 13"!) presentation of industry issues, selected categories of beverages, new products, channel strategies, packaging, research and development, ingredients, and the distribution, operations, marketing, and retail behind just about every conceivable potable liquid in North America. This monthly trade magazine profiles companies and plants, analyzes trends, and reports on new technology, manufacturing, and warehousing. Industry-related event information, a supplier's marketplace, a classified network section, and an advertisers index round out each issue. A subscription to the publication is free to those who qualify; visitors to the publisher's website (bevindustry.com/) may see titles, authors, and selected content from issues back to November 2007 and search for stories by keyword.

2391. *Candy Industry.* Former titles (until 1982): *Candy and Snack Industry;* (until 1971): *Candy and Baked Snack Industry;* (until Jan.1971): *Candy Industry;* (until 1968): *Candy Industry and Confectioner's Journal;* Which was formed by the merger of (1944-1956): *Candy Industry;* (1874-1956): *Confectioners Journal.* [ISSN: 0745-1032] 1956. m. Free to qualified personnel (print or online ed.)). Ed(s): Bernard Pacyniak. B N P Media II, LLC., 155 N Pfingsten Rd, Ste 205, Deerfield, IL 60015; http://www.bnpmedia.com. Illus., index, adv. Sample. Microform: PQC. *Indexed:* A22, B01, B03, BRI, C42. *Aud.:* Ac, Sa.

The monthly trade publication *Candy Industry* magazine provides news and analysis on all aspects of the global confectionery market. Colorful, easy-to-read issues deliver the latest in consumer, market, and industry trends (notably cannabis confections); technologies related to ingredients, processing, manufacturing, and packaging; new products; and retail. In addition to manufacturer and company descriptions and interviews with industry leaders, issues cover related international conferences and trade shows and include a classified network section and an ad index. There's an annual "State of the Industry" issue—and a "Gold Book" that highlights products and suppliers. The publisher's website (candyindustry.com) includes digitized versions of issues back to March 2008, selected content of most issues back to November 2007, and the ability to search available content by keyword.

2392. *Cereal Foods World.* Formerly (until 1975): *Cereal Science Today.* [ISSN: 2576-1056] 1956. bi-m. USD 465; USD 549. A A C C International, 3340 Pilot Knob Rd, St. Paul, MN 55121; aacc@scisoc.org; http://www.aaccnet.org. Illus., index, adv. Refereed. Vol. ends: Dec. Microform: PQC. *Indexed:* A22, Agr, C45. *Aud.:* Ac, Sa.

Cereal Foods World, the online bimonthly publication of the AACC (American Association of Cereal Chemists) International, focuses on global research, trends, and analysis of grains and grain-based products. Each themed issue (Global Food Systems/Analytical; Safety & Security; Health & Nutrition; Processing/Pre-Annual Meeting; Cereal Foods; Product Development & Innovation) contains peer-reviewed and referenced articles and technical reports by food industry professionals worldwide, profiles of institutions and members, association and member news, a calendar of events, and an advertisers index. Recent issues cover food analysis and the regulatory institutions in the United States and the European Union. Contains technical language and figures. The publisher's website provides the tables of contents, abstracts, and selected content from past issues back to January/February 2006, and a keyword search box. URL: aaccnet.org/publications/cfw/Pages/CerealFoodsWorld.aspx

2393. *Critical Reviews in Food Science and Nutrition.* Former titles: *C R C Critical Reviews in Food Science and Nutrition; C R C Critical Reviews in Food Technology.* [ISSN: 1040-8398] 1970. 22x/yr. GBP 5310 (print & online eds.)). Ed(s): Fergus M Clydesdale. Taylor & Francis Inc., 711 3rd Ave, 8th Fl, New York, NY 10017; support@tandfonline.com; http://www.tandfonline.com. Illus., index. Refereed. Vol. ends: Dec. Reprint: PSC. *Indexed:* A01, A22, Agr, C45, E01, SD. *Aud.:* Ac, Sa.

With a five-year Impact Factor of 7.037 (2018 Journal Citation Reports), *Critical Reviews in Food Science and Nutrition* is written by and for food scientists, nutritionists, and health professionals worldwide. Available online and/or in print (22 issues/year), this authoritative publication addresses topics as varied as the relationship between diet and disease, health, and behavior; allergens and toxins; flavor chemistry; innovations in food products, ingredients, and technologies; food processing and labeling; federal regulations and policies; and food safety. Peer-reviewed articles in this scientific journal comprise technical language and supporting figures and tables. The publisher's website lists the journal's most-read and most-cited articles (offering the full text of those that are Open Access), and searchable tables of contents and abstracts of articles back to the inaugural issue in 1970. URL: tandfonline.com/toc/bfsn20/current)

2394. *Dairy Foods: innovative ideas for dairy processors.* Incorporates (in 2007): *Dairy Field;* Which was formerly (until 1991): *Dairy Field Today;* (until 1990): *Dairy Field;* (until 1979): *Dairy & Ice Cream Field;* (1965-1967): *Ice Cream Field & Ice Cream Trade Journal;* Which was formed by the merger of (1922-1965): *Ice Cream Field;* (1905-1965): *Ice Cream Trade Journal;* Dairy & Ice Cream Field incorporated (1917-1968): *Ice Cream Review;* (1911-1968): *Milk Dealer;* Which incorporated (in 1967): *Manufactured Milk Products Journal;* Which was formerly (until 1962): *The Milk Products Journal;* (until 1953): *The Butter, Cheese and Milk Products Journal;* (1932-1950): *National Butter & Cheese Journal;* Which was formed by the merger of (1930-1932): *National Cheese Journal;* (1930-1932): *Concentrated Milk Industries;* (1930-1932): *National Butter Journal;* All three of which superseded in part: *Butter and Cheese Journal;* Which incorporated (1927-1928): *World's Butter Review;* Butter and Cheese Journal was formerly (1910-1928): *Butter Cheese and Egg Journal;* Dairy Foods was formerly (until 1986): *Dairy Record;* Which incorporated (1890-1950): *Creamery Journal;* (in 1981): *American Dairy Review;* Which was formerly (until 1965): *American Milk Review;* (until 1960): *American Milk Review and Milk Plant Monthly;* Which was formed by the merger of (1930-1958): *Milk Plant Monthly;* Which was formerly (until 1930): *Creamery and Milk Plant Monthly;* (1939-1958): *American Milk Review (Year);* Which superseded in part (in 1939): *American Produce Review;* Which was formerly (until 1937): *American Creamery & Poultry Produce Review;* (1897-1930): *New York Produce Review and American Creamery.* [ISSN: 0888-0050] 1958. m. Free to qualified personnel (print or online ed.)). Ed(s): Kathie Canning. B N P Media II, LLC., 155 N Pfingsten Rd, Ste 205, Deerfield, IL 60015; http://www.bnpmedia.com. Illus., index, adv. Vol. ends: Dec. Microform: PQC. *Indexed:* A22, B01, B03, BRI. *Aud.:* Ac, Sa.

The monthly trade publication *Dairy Foods* delivers information on every category of milk and milk-related products. Clear, well-illustrated articles written by experts in the field provide news and analysis of industry, market, consumer, and regulation trends and issues. Regular columns focus on new products, ingredient technologies and R&D, processing, operations, packaging, marketing, and distribution. Cover stories often profile processors and describe their plants' history, operation, safety measures, equipment, and technology. Promotions of upcoming industry events, supplier news, a classifieds section, and an index to the extensive advertisements complete each issue. Links to major content of most issues back to January 2003 and keyword searching for articles are available from the website (dairyfoods.com). Subscriptions are free to qualified individuals.

2395. ***Emerging Food R & D Report.*** [ISSN: 1050-2688] 1990. m. USD 365. Food Technology Intelligence, Inc., 215 Godwin Ave, PO Box 322, Midland Park, NJ 07432; ftiinfo@ftipub.com; http://www.ftipub.com. Adv. Sample. *Indexed:* B01. *Aud.:* Ac, Sa.

Concise descriptions and analysis of the latest food technologies being developed by food researchers in government, academic, and corporate labs worldwide pack the eight pages of the monthly newsletter *Emerging Food R&D Report.* Examples of new processes and products in recent issues include "Determine beef trim safety using microbial profiling," "Machine vision helps determine sensory quality of fish," "Eliminate bacteria in bagged leafy greens with natural approaches," and news about NaturCEASE Dry, an innovative new meat packaging product developed by Kemin Industries. Such processes and products could be developed for commercial use; for potential collaborators, each of an issue's 10-12 developments includes the names and contact information of the researchers whose findings are highlighted. A sample issue is available online; subscribers may choose to receive issues in print or electronically. URL: http://www.ftipub.com/food/emergingfood

2396. ***Food Engineering: the magazine for operations and manufacturing management.*** Former titles (until 1998): *Chilton's Food Engineering;* (until 1977): *Food Engineering;* (until 1951): *Food Industries.* [ISSN: 1522-2292] 1928. m. Free to qualified personnel (print or online ed.)). Ed(s): Casey Laughman, Rose Shilling. B N P Media II, LLC., 2401 W Big Beaver Rd, Ste 700, Troy, MI 48084; http://www.bnpmedia.com. Illus., index, adv. Vol. ends: Dec. Microform: CIS; PQC. *Indexed:* A22, B01, B03, BRI, H&TI. *Aud.:* Ac, Sa.

Published since 1928, *Food Engineering* targets manufacturing, operations, and engineering executives in the food and beverage industry in North America. This monthly trade magazine covers innovations in manufacturing, food packaging, products, engineering research and development, processing, and upcoming national and international events, and includes a classified section and index of advertisers. Issues are packed with the latest developments in facilities, technology, automation, food safety, traceability, sustainability, staffing challenges, and the influence of consumer trends. The language is reasonably technical; the publication is well-illustrated. Cover-to-cover access to most issues back to December 2010 is available on the publication's website, as are selected cover stories, articles, and departments from most issues back to January 1999—and the option to search for articles by keyword. URL: foodengineeringmag.com

2397. ***Food Protection Trends: science and news from the International Association for Food Protection.*** Former titles (until 2003): *Dairy, Food and Environmental Sanitation;* (until 1989): *Dairy and Food Sanitation; Food and Fieldmen.* [ISSN: 1541-9576] 1980. bi-m. International Association for Food Protection, 6200 Aurora Ave, Ste 200W, Des Moines, IA 50322-2864. Illus., adv. Microform: PQC. *Indexed:* A22, Agr, B01, C45. *Bk. rev.:* Number and length vary. *Aud.:* Ac, Sa.

Published for members of the International Association for Food Protection (IAFP), *Food Protection Trends* targets food safety industry employees, regulators, teachers, and those researching or who are interested in food safety and protection. Each bi-monthly issue (available in print and online) includes peer-reviewed papers on applied research; practical technical articles; a profile of an IAFP member; reports on various IAFP Professional Groups (e.g., Fruit and Vegetable Safety and Quality; Food Chemical Hazards and Food Allergy); industry, association, and member news; general interest/review papers; government regulations; new product announcements; and a calendar of upcoming events worldwide. The association's website provides links to a digitized sample issue and to a keyword- or author-searchable archive of abstracts and complete bibliographic information of most articles back to 1981. URL: foodprotection.org/publications/food-protection-trends/

2398. ***Food Technology: advancing food & health through sound science.*** [ISSN: 0015-6639] 1947. m. Ed(s): Bob Swientek, Mary Ellen Kuhn. Institute of Food Technologists, 525 W Van Buren, Ste 1000, Chicago, IL 60607; http://www.ift.org. Illus., index, adv. Vol. ends: Dec. Microform: PQC. *Indexed:* A01, A22, Agr, BRI, C45, H&TI. *Aud.:* Ac, Sa.

Through articles written in "feature" rather than "scientific research" style, *Food Technology* magazine, the monthly publication of the Institute of Food Technologists, covers all aspects of the food industry. Topics include science-based analysis, research and development to new food products, production, and distribution; regulation; education; marketing; consumption; and sustainability. Regular columns explore "Consumer Trends," "Inside Academia," "Food, Medicine & Health," "Nutraceuticals," "Food Safety & Quality," "Ingredients," "Processing," and "Packaging." Issues include eye-catching photos and effective graphics, news about upcoming events, a classified section, and an advertisers index. The publisher's website provides the table of contents and access to selected material in current and past issues, and keyword-searchable content of issues back to January 2000. URL: ift.org/food-technology.aspx

2399. ***Journal of Food Law & Policy.*** [ISSN: 1942-9762] 2005. 2x/yr. Ed(s): Jordan Broyles, Andrew Tarvin. University of Arkansas, School of Law, 1045 W. Maple St, Waterman Hall University of Arkansas, Fayetteville, AR 72701; http://media.law.uark.edu/. *Indexed:* A01, BRI, L14. *Aud.:* Ac, Sa.

Since 2005, the *Journal of Food Law & Policy* has focused on "food law and its impact on society." This biannual publication is the first of its kind edited by students in the University of Arkansas School of Law (recognized for agricultural and food law education and research). Scholarly, analytical articles address food labeling, safety, security, and assistance; food policy of interest to consumers; how food production affects the environment; nutrition policy; animal welfare; and regulation of food-related technologies. Recent issues explore how non-profit organizations are influencing food law and corporate responsibility; how the FDA's Food Safety and Inspection Service assumed responsibility for inspecting catfish; the consequences of the failure of the Endangered Species Act to protect bees from "inadvertent pesticide poisoning"; and the 2018 Farm Bill and food policy.

2400. ***Journal of Food Protection.*** Former titles (until 1977): *Journal of Milk and Food Technology;* (until 1947): *Journal of Milk Technology.* [ISSN: 0362-028X] 1937. m. International Association for Food Protection, 6200 Aurora Ave, Ste 200W, Des Moines, IA 50322-2864; info@foodprotection.org; http://www.foodprotection.org. Illus., index, adv. Refereed. Microform: PMC; PQC. *Indexed:* A01, A22, Agr, C45, H&TI. *Aud.:* Ac, Sa.

Journal of Food Protection, the monthly publication of the International Association for Food Protection (IAFP), comprises research, review, and general-interest articles written by and for food science and safety professionals all over the world interested in protecting the safety and quality of food. Refereed papers examine food-related hazards; microbiological food quality; food fermentation, spoilage, and preservation; safe food handling from pre-harvest through consumption; risk assessment and economic impact of food-related hazards; and food fraud, authentication, and defense. Academic/scholarly in nature, this scientific journal (available in print and online) uses technical language and supporting figures and tables. The "Available Issues" link on the publisher's website leads to the tables of contents and abstracts of articles published since October 1937, and full access to selected articles. URL: foodprotection.org/publications/journal-of-food-protection

2401. *The National Provisioner: 128 years of editorial leadership in the meat & poultry industry.* [ISSN: 0027-996X] 1891. m. Free to qualified personnel (print or online ed.)). Ed(s): Andy Hanacek. B N P Media II, LLC., 2401 W Big Beaver Rd, Ste 700, Troy, MI 48084; http://www.bnpmedia.com. Illus. Sample. *Indexed:* A22, B01, B03, C42. *Aud.:* Ac, Sa.

The National Provisioner covers all aspects of the meat, poultry, pork, and seafood processing industry. This monthly trade publication delivers updates on food safety; regulations and legislation; and technology related to ingredients, processing, food safety, and packaging. Readers discover industry trends and news and successful business, marketing, and operations strategies. Interviews with principals in the industry, new products, supplier news, announcements of upcoming industry events, classified ads, and an advertisers index round out each issue. Some issues include special reports ("Seafood," "Annual Food Safety Report," "State of the Industry"); the April issue features an "Annual Buyer's Guide for Meat and Poultry Processors." Subscribers may request *Independent Processor*—a separate publication that targets small and mid-sized processors of meat, poultry, and game. The publisher's website (provisioneronline.com) offers access to digitized issues back to February 2010 and selected content from most issues back to April 2008.

2402. *Prepared Foods.* Incorporates (in 1986): *Food Plant Equipment;* Former titles (until 1984): *Processed Prepared Foods;* Which Incorporated (in 1981): *Food Development;* Which was formerly (until 19??): *Food Product Development;* (until 1977): *Canner Packer.* [ISSN: 0747-2536] 1895. m. Free to qualified personnel (print or online ed.)). Ed(s): Bob Garrison. B N P Media II, LLC., 2401 W Big Beaver Rd, Ste 700, Troy, MI 48084; http://www.bnpmedia.com. Illus., index, adv. Sample. Vol. ends: Dec. Microform: PQC. *Indexed:* A22, B01, B03, H&TI. *Aud.:* Ac, Sa.

Focusing on the development and introduction of new food and beverage products, the trade magazine *Prepared Foods* marries mouthwatering photographs with up-to-date information on industry, market, and consumer trends; research and development; new products; functional foods; and ingredient formulation and effects. July and August issues cover trends and developments in the retail and foodservice channels, respectively; the December issue, on the influences predicted to shape the industry in the coming year. News of upcoming industry events, a classified section, and an advertisers index complete each issue. The publisher's website (preparedfoods.com) offers access to digitized issues back to May 2010 and selected content from most issues back to January 2001. New in fall 2018 was *Cannabis Products*, a supplement to *Prepared Foods* that reports on the development of legal cannabis edibles and beverages.

2403. *Refrigerated & Frozen Foods: cold supply chain solutions & technologies.* Formerly (until 19??): *Dairy and Frozen Foods.* [ISSN: 1061-6152] 1990. 7x/yr. Free to qualified personnel (print or online ed.)). Ed(s): Marina Mayer. B N P Media II, LLC., 155 N Pfingsten Rd, Ste 205, Deerfield, IL 60015; portfolio@bnpmedia.com; http://www.bnpmedia.com. Illus., adv. Sample. *Indexed:* B03. *Aud.:* Ac, Sa.

Cold food safety, supply chain and logistics, energy management, and packaging are just the tip of the iceberg for *Refrigerated & Frozen Foods* (rffmag.com). In seven issues a year, this trade publication reports on cutting-edge trends and innovative technologies and products; features interviews with professionals from various category sectors; and provides show previews and advertisements related to temperature-sensitive food. Cover stories focus on the state of the industry, industry leaders, and cutting-edge technologies in manufacturing plants. An eighth issue comprises a comprehensive listing of refrigerated and frozen foods warehouses; a ninth is a directory of companies specializing in cold storage construction. The publisher's website provides access to digitized issues back to August/September 2010; and keyword-searchable selected content of most issues back to February 2008.

2404. *Snack Food & Wholesale Bakery: the preferred source for bakers and snack producers.* Former titles (until Jul.1997): *Snack & Bakery Foods;* (until Jan.1997): *Snack Food;* (until 1968): *Biscuit and Cracker Baker;* (until 1950): *The Cracker Baker.* [ISSN: 1096-4835] 1912. m. Free to qualified personnel (print or online ed.)). Ed(s): Douglas J Peckenpaugh. B N P Media II, LLC., 2401 W Big Beaver Rd, Ste 700, Troy, MI 48084; http://www.bnpmedia.com. Illus., index, adv. Sample. Vol. ends: Dec. *Indexed:* B03, BRI. *Aud.:* Ac, Sa.

In May 2019, *Snack Food & Wholesale Bakery* became *SF&WB: Snack Food & Wholesale Bakery*! This easy-to-read, richly illustrated trade magazine reports on trends and innovations in the snack and baked goods industry. In addition to profiling companies and their plants, the monthly publication (available in print and online) covers logistics, market intelligence, consumer trends; ingredients, processing, packaging, sanitation, food safety, clean label, efficiency, supplier news, new products, equipment, and industry-related events. The June and July issues review the "State of the Industry: Bakery" and "State of the Industry: Snacks" respectively; the October issue is the annual Buyer's Guide. Selected content of most issues back to January 2008 and the means to search online content by keyword are available at the publisher's website. URL: snackandbakery.com

■ FORENSICS

Kelly MacWatters, Coordinator of Reference and Electronic Resources, Standish Library, Siena College, Loudonville, NY 12211; kmacwatters@siena.edu

Introduction

Forensic science is the study and application of science to law and encompasses a wide range of disciplines within the criminal justice system. Forensic scientists and practitioners work in a variety of settings, including crime scenes, laboratories, classrooms, hospitals, and morgues. Some of the more common specializations within forensics include anthropology, digital and multimedia forensics, document examiner, engineering, odontology, pathology, psychology, and toxicology.

The majority of titles reviewed in this section are peer reviewed and international in scope, and cover the full spectrum of forensic studies.

Basic Periodicals

American Journal of Forensics Medicine and Pathology, Digital Investigation, Forensic Magazine, Forensic Science International, Forensic Science, Medicine and Pathology, International Journal of Legal Medicine, Journal of Forensic and Legal Medicine; The Journal of Forensic Practice; Medicine, Science and the Law, Science and Justice.

Basic Abstracts and Indexes

BIOSIS Previews; Criminal Justice Abstracts; Criminal Justice Periodical Index; EMBASE; MEDLINE; Science Citation Index; Scopus.

2405. *The American Journal of Forensic Medicine and Pathology.* [ISSN: 0195-7910] 1980. q. USD 1356. Ed(s): Dr. Vincent J M Dimaio. Lippincott Williams & Wilkins, Two Commerce Sq, 2001 Market St, Philadelphia, PA 19103; customerservice@lww.com; http://www.lww.com. Illus., adv. Refereed. *Indexed:* A22. *Aud.:* Ac, Sa.

The American Journal of Forensic Medicine and Pathology covers a wide array of topics in forensic medicine. Each issue contains original articles and multiple reports detailing unusual and peculiar cases. Research articles focus on forensic pathology and offer the reader valuable insight into the examination and documentation process and other techniques associated with the investigation of unexpected or violent death. URL: www.amjforensicmedicine.com

2406. ***Digital Investigation: the international journal of digital forensics & incident response.*** [ISSN: 1742-2876] 2004. q. EUR 1339. Ed(s): Eoghan Casey. Elsevier Advanced Technology, The Blvd, Langford Ln, Kidlington, OX5 1GB, United Kingdom; http://www.elsevier.com. Adv. Sample. Refereed. *Indexed:* CJPI. *Aud.:* Ac, Sa.

Digital Investigation covers current challenges, techniques, and the latest technologies associated with digital forensics. Recent topics in this rapidly developing field include cloud security, payment card fraud, child pornography, multimedia forensics, spam, and malware analysis. Contributors are affiliated with corporations, military institutions, and universities from around the world. This journal is relevant to researchers and practitioners, and is recommended for academic libraries with computer science, information science, criminal justice, and engineering programs. URL: www.journals.elsevier.com/digital-investigation/

2407. ***Forensic Magazine.*** [ISSN: 1553-6262] 2004. bi-m. USD 120 in US & Canada (Free to qualified personnel). Ed(s): Chris Janson. Vicon Publishing, Inc., 4 Limbo Ln, Amherst, NH 03031; http://www.viconpublishing.com. Adv. *Indexed:* CJPI. *Aud.:* Hs, Ga, Ac, Sa.

Forensic Magazine provides the latest news and information on products, trends, and technologies in all areas of forensic science. Each issue contains information applicable to both forensic lab and field work. Articles cover a wide range of topics, such as evidence collection and analysis, digital forensics, and cybersecurity. This magazine is written for forensic professionals; however, the content would be of interest to college students studying in forensics, criminal justice, and related programs, as well as to the general public. Free subscriptions for those who qualify. URL: www.forensicmag.com

2408. ***Forensic Science International: an international journal dedicated to the applications of genetics in the administration of justice.*** Formerly (until 1978): *Forensic Science;* Which was formed by the merger of (1953-1972): *Journal of Forensic Medicine;* part of (1956-1972): *Journal of Forensic Sciences;* Which was formerly (until 1956): *American Academy of Forensic Sciences. Proceedings.* [ISSN: 0379-0738] 1972. m. EUR 6033. Ed(s): P Saukko. Elsevier Ireland Ltd., Elsevier House, Brookvale Plz, E Park, Shannon, , Ireland; JournalsCustomerServiceemea@elsevier.com; http://www.elsevier.com/. Illus., adv. Sample. Refereed. Microform: PQC. *Indexed:* A01, A22, BRI, C45, CJPI, HRIS, L14. *Bk. rev.:* 0-3. *Aud.:* Ac, Sa.

Forensic Science International covers the many different branches of forensic science. Types of articles include original research papers, literature review articles, and case reports on the legal aspects of general forensics disciplines. It also features investigations of value to public health in its broadest sense, and the important area where science and medicine interact with the law. Examples of topics include bite-mark evidence; ballistics; projectiles and wounds; fingerprints and identification; tool marks; and poisoning. Medical forensics coverage in this journal requires a strong medical or science background on the part of the reader. URL: www.fsijournal.org/

2409. ***Forensic Science, Medicine, and Pathology.*** [ISSN: 1547-769X] 2005. q. EUR 1009 (print & online eds.)). Springer, Tiergartenstr 17, Heidelberg, 69121, Germany; subscriptions@springer.com; https://www.springer.com. Refereed. Reprint: PSC. *Indexed:* A01, A22, BRI, E01. *Aud.:* Ac, Sa.

Forensic Science, Medicine, and Pathology is broad in scope and covers trending and current topics in pathology, forensic medicine, and criminology. Contents include research articles, short communications, meeting proceedings, and case reports. This journal will appeal to a wide range of readers and is recommended for academic libraries supporting forensic science, criminal justice, and health science programs. https://link.springer.com/journal/12024

2410. ***International Journal of Legal Medicine (Print).*** Former titles (until 1990): *Zeitschrift fuer Rechtsmedizin - Journal of Legal Medicine;* (until 1989): *Deutsche Zeitschrift fuer die Gesamte Gerichtliche Medizin;* (until 1921): *Vierteljahresschrift fuer Gerichtliche Medizin und Offentliches Sanitatswesen;* (until 1875): *Vierteljahresschrift fuer die Gerichtliche und Offentliche Medizin.* [ISSN: 0937-9827] 1922. bi-m. EUR 3751 (print & online eds.)). Ed(s): T Bajanowski, H Pfeiffer. Springer, Tiergartenstr 17, Heidelberg, 69121, Germany. Illus., adv. Refereed. Reprint: PSC. *Indexed:* A01, A22, BRI, CJPI, E01. *Bk. rev.:* 0-3. *Aud.:* Ac, Sa.

The *Journal of Forensic and Legal Medicine* provides a forum for rapid publication of research related to the clinical aspects of forensic medicine. Topics are broad in scope, and the journal has an international perspective. Types of articles include reviews, original research, case reports, personal views, and learning points. This journal is appropriate for practitioners and students studying forensic science. URL: www.journals.elsevier.com/journal-of-forensic-and-legal-medicine/

2411. ***The Journal of Forensic Practice: research relating to criminology, psychology and evidence-based practice across all forensic settings.*** Former titles (until 2013): *The British Journal of Forensic Practice;* (until 1999): *Psychiatric Care.* [ISSN: 2050-8794] 1994. q. EUR 676 (print & online eds.) (excluding UK)). Ed(s): Carol A Ireland, Neil Gredecki. Emerald Publishing Limited, Howard House, Wagon Ln, Bingley, BD16 1WA, United Kingdom; emerald@emeraldinsight.com; http://www.emeraldgrouppublishing.com. Sample. Refereed. Reprint: PSC. *Indexed:* CJPI. *Aud.:* Ac, Sa.

The Journal of Forensic Practice covers a wide range of research, with a strong focus on forensic psychology. Topics include but are not limited to mental health, witness testimony and memory, expert witnesses, prisons, the legal system, and the assessment and treatment of criminals. Research articles focus on practical application of theory across numerous disciplines, with an emphasis on qualitative methods. This journal is essential for the practitioner and will support research in forensics and related fields. URL: www.emeraldinsight.com/loi/jfp

2412. ***Journal of Forensic Sciences.*** Formerly (until 1956): *The American Academy of Forensic Sciences. Proceedings.* [ISSN: 0022-1198] 1956. bi-m. Ed(s): Michael A Peat. Wiley-Blackwell Publishing, Inc., 111 River St, Hoboken, NJ 07030; http://onlinelibrary.wiley.com. Illus., index, adv. Refereed. Reprint: PSC. *Indexed:* A&ATA, A01, A22, BRI, C45, CJPI, E01, HRIS, L14, N13. *Bk. rev.:* 0-3. *Aud.:* Ac, Sa.

The *Journal of Forensic Sciences* is the official publication of the American Academy of Forensic Sciences (AAFS). Journal content spans a broad range of studies including biology, pathology, odontology, engineering, psychiatry, and criminalistics. Published materials include research papers; technical notes that measure the effectiveness of techniques used in forensic practice; and case reports, often accompanied by crime scene and autopsy photographs. University professors, forensic practitioners, and medical and law enforcement professionals are among the content contributors. This journal is recommended for researchers and students of the various branches of forensic science. URL: http://onlinelibrary.wiley.com/journal/10.1111/(ISSN)1556-4029

2413. ***Medicine, Science and the Law.*** [ISSN: 0025-8024] 1960. q. USD 669 (print & online eds.)). Ed(s): Bob Peckitt. Sage Publications Ltd., 1 Oliver's Yard, 55 City Rd, London, EC1Y 1SP, United Kingdom; info@sagepub.com; https://www.sagepub.com/. Adv. Sample. Refereed. Reprint: PSC. *Indexed:* A22, B01, BRI, HRIS, L14. *Bk. rev.:* 0-2. *Aud.:* Ac, Sa.

Medicine, Science and the Law covers a wide variety of forensic subjects and aims to inform readers on the relationship between the forensic disciplines. Types of articles include viewpoints, case reports, technical reports, original research, and cover a wide range of medicolegal topics. Occasional book reviews are included. This journal is recommended for academic libraries that support forensic disciplines that focus on medical jurisprudence and legal medicine. URL: http://msl.sagepub.com/

2414. ***Science and Justice.*** Formerly (until 1995): *Forensic Science Society. Journal.* [ISSN: 1355-0306] 1960. bi-m. q. until 2014. EUR 488. Ed(s): T Thompson. Elsevier Ltd, 125 London Wall, London, EC2Y 5AS, United Kingdom; corporate.sales@elsevier.com; http://www.elsevier.com. Illus., index, adv. Sample. Refereed. *Indexed:* A22, BRI, CJPI, L14. *Bk. rev.:* 0-3. *Aud.:* Ac, Sa.

Science and Justice publishes formal scientific and technical articles on all aspects of forensic science. The journal is international in scope and aims to promote communication and debate within forensic science and criminal justice communities. Position papers on issues that impact forensic practice are a common feature of this journal. Popular topics include fingerprint evaluation, DNA profiling, likelihood ratios, forensic entomology, and mass spectrometry application in forensic cases. This journal is best suited for the practicing forensic scientist and is appropriate for academic libraries that support forensic and criminal justice programs. URL: www.journals.elsevier.com/science-and-justice

■ FORESTRY

Kari Anderson, Environmental and Forest Sciences Librarian, University of Washington, Suzzallo Library, Box 352900, Seattle, WA 98195-2900; karia@uw.edu

Introduction

Forestry, like many subjects related to the natural environment, is becoming increasingly interdisciplinary. Included within the discipline are all aspects of the forest ecosystem: trees and other plants, soils, water, insects, wildlife, and their interaction, as well as the commercial products derived from that environment. Beyond the study and management of trees, forestry includes managing developed forest stands, cultivating and using forest products sustainably, managing recreational uses of forest lands, and providing careful stewardship of the natural environment.

The forestry literature represents all of these aspects: oversight and management, product development and trade, and scientific research. This is reflected in the types of forestry publications produced, including government resources, trade and technical publications, and scholarly journals.

Government agencies and international non-governmental organizations, such as the U.S. Forest Service and the Food and Agriculture Organization (FAO) Forestry Sector, have established strong print collections that are available at larger, depository libraries. Newer materials are provided free of charge online. The U.S. Forest Service publications are searchable from the Service's Treesearch database: www.treesearch.fs.fed.us/. Canadian governmental publications are available on the National Resource Council Canada site: http://nparc.nrc-cnrc.gc.ca/eng/home/. FAO's site includes databases, information resources, and statistical information with an international focus: http://www.fao.org/forestry/publications/en/. These materials are not included in this list of publications, as they are in the public domain and are easily accessible.

While some trade and technical publications are included here, the focus is mostly on scholarly and academic journals. Academic subjects in forestry reflect the intersection between science, applied technology, and the social sciences when studying the natural world. Some current areas of focus include forest ecology, urban forestry, the effects of climate change on forest ecosystems, forest soils, bioresource science and engineering, restoration ecology, sustainable resource management, and wildlife science. Because humans interact with the forest environment, social sciences such as recreational use and conservation must also be considered. Related subject areas include agriculture, biology, chemistry, engineering, landscape architecture, and land use and planning.

The list here is limited in scope to basic titles in forest sciences, and while international in scope, titles are mostly in English. The classic *Literature of Forestry and Agroforestry,* published by Cornell University Press in 1996, continues to serve as a solid introduction to the literature of forestry and a place to start for building a forestry collection.

Basic Periodicals

Hs: *American Forests, Journal of Forestry, Unasylva;* Ga: *American Forests, Eastern Native Tree Society Bulletin, Journal of Forestry, National Woodlands, Unasylva;* Ac, Sa: *Agricultural and Forest Meteorology, Agroforestry Systems, Arboriculture and Urban Forestry, Arborist News, Canadian Journal of Forest Research, Fire Ecology, Forest Ecology and Management, Forest Policy and Economics, Forest Products Journal, Forest Science, Forest Systems, Forestry Chronicle, iForest, International Forestry Review, International Journal of Forestry Research, IAWA Journal, International Journal of Forest Engineering, International Journal of Wildland Fire, Journal of Forestry, Journal of Sustainable Forestry, New Forests, Revista Arvore, Silva Fennica, Small-Scale Forestry, Tree Physiology, Wood Material Science and Engineering.*

Basic Abstracts and Indexes

Academic Search Complete, AGRICOLA, Biological and Agricultural Index Plus, CAB Direct, Environmental Science Collection, Forest Science Database, Google Scholar, Environmental Science Collection.

2415. *Agricultural and Forest Meteorology: an international journal.* Formerly (until 1984): *Agricultural Meteorology.* [ISSN: 0168-1923] 1964. 16x/yr. EUR 5885. Ed(s): X Lee. Elsevier BV, Radarweg 29, Amsterdam, 1043 NX, Netherlands; info@elsevier.com; https://www.elsevier.com/. Illus., index, adv. Sample. Refereed. Microform: PQC. *Indexed:* A01, A22, Agr, C45, S25. *Bk. rev.:* 1-3, 500-800 words. *Aud.:* Ac, Sa.

This international journal covers the interrelationship between forestry, meteorology, agriculture, and natural ecosystems. Articles emphasize research relevant to the practical problems of plant and soil sciences, and ecology and biogeochemistry as affected by the weather, as well as climate variability and change. Topics include the effect of weather on forests, soils, crops, water use, and forest fires; the effect of vegetation on climate and weather; and canopy micrometeorology. This journal is heavily used by specialists working in these areas and, as a result, it has a high impact factor. Beginning in 2014, 16 volumes appear annually, each comprising a single issue. While this is an expensive journal, a number of thematic, special issues are available for purchase as monographs. Options for online access are available through Elsevier's online platform ScienceDirect. This journal offers authors two choices to publish their research: subscription or open access. The open-access publication fee for this journal is USD 3700.

2416. *Agroforestry Systems.* Incorporates (1972-1999): *Agroforestry Forum;* Which was formerly (until 1992): *Agroforestry in the U K.* [ISSN: 0167-4366] 1982. 6x/yr. EUR 3398 (print & online eds.)). Ed(s): Shibu Jose. Springer Netherlands, Van Godewijckstraat 30, Dordrecht, 3311 GX, Netherlands; http://www.springer.com. Adv. Refereed. Microform: PQC. Reprint: PSC. *Indexed:* A22, Agr, BRI, C45, E01, GardL, S25. *Bk. rev.:* Occasional, 500-1,500 words. *Aud.:* Ac, Sa.

Agroforestry Systems is an international scientific journal that focuses on any aspect of agroforestry, which is agriculture incorporating the cultivation and conservation of trees. Papers deal with both biophysical and socioeconomic aspects. These may include results of investigations of integrated systems that involve trees and crops and/or livestock. To be acceptable for publication, the information presented must be relevant to a context wider than the specific location where the study was undertaken, and provide new insight or make a significant contribution to the agroforestry knowledge base. The journal publishes one volume with six issues every year. This title would complement collections that support agriculture and environmental studies as well as forestry, particularly those with an international development focus. Online access is available via SpringerLink. Authors may publish open access through Springer's Open Choice option. Publishing Open Choice involves an open-access publication fee of USD 3000.

2417. *American Forests.* Incorporates (1990-1995): *Urban Forests;* Which was formerly (until 1990): *Urban Forest Forum;* (until 1988): *National Urban Forest Forum;* (until 1986): *National Urban and Community Forestry Forum;* Former titles (until 1931): *American Forests and Forest Life;* (until 1924): *American Forestry;* (until 1910): *Conservation;* (until 1908): *Forestry & Irrigation;* Which was formed by the merger of (1900-1902): *National Irrigation;* Which was formerly (until 1900): *The National Advocate;* (1895-1902): *The Forester;* Which was formerly (until 1985): *New Jersey Forester.* [ISSN: 0002-8541] 1895. 3x/yr. Free to members. Ed(s): Susan Laszewski. American Forests, 1220 L St NW, Ste 750, Washington, DC 20005; info@americanforests.org; http://www.americanforests.org. Illus., index. Vol. ends: Winter. Microform: PQC. *Indexed:* A01, A22, Agr, B01, BRI, C37, CBRI, GardL, MASUSE. *Aud.:* Hs, Ga, Ac.

This magazine, issued three times per year, features forestry information for a general audience from environmentalists to outdoor enthusiasts. American Forests, one of the oldest conservation organizations in the United States, has been publishing this journal since 1895. It is also made available free via the publisher's web site. Typical of this magazine's well-illustrated and easily read features include articles on the role of urban forests in urban planning and on wildfire recovery efforts in the Southwest. The organization's programs include "Global ReLeaf," "Endangered Western Forests," and "Urban Forests." They also maintain the "National Register of Big Trees." Editorial emphasis is placed on coverage of forests and trees located "on land where people live, work, and relax." Further explanation of sponsored programs and memberships is available on the organization's web site, as is an archive of many of the magazine's articles. Authors retain copyright of their works in this publication. URL: https://www.americanforests.org/

2418. *Arboriculture & Urban Forestry.* Formerly (until 2006): *Journal of Arboriculture;* Which was formed by the merger of (1935-1975): *Arborist's News;* (1929-1975): *International Shade Tree Conference. Annual Meeting. Proceedings.* [ISSN: 1935-5297] 1975. bi-m. Free to members; Non-members, USD 160. Ed(s): Jason C Grabosky, Aaron Bynum. International Society of Arboriculture, PO Box 3129, Champaign, IL 61826; isa@isa-arbor.com; http://www.isa-arbor.com. Illus., adv. Refereed. *Indexed:* A01, A22, Agr, C45, GardL. *Aud.:* Ac, Sa.

This bimonthly journal (formerly, *Journal of Arboriculture*) is published by the International Society of Arboriculture (ISA) and is focused on the science and art of planting and caring for trees in the urban environment. Each issue includes four to six research papers intended for the practitioner. Although scientific in nature, articles are accessible to the interested layperson. While the focus is on arboricultural research, related topics include urban forestry, entomology, and horticulture. Authors of articles published in this journal retain all rights to reproduce their work for internal or academic purposes. Articles are available in a free, open-access back file from 1975 forward.

2419. *Arborist News.* [ISSN: 1542-2399] 1992. bi-m. Free to members. International Society of Arboriculture, PO Box 3129, Champaign, IL 61826; isa@isa-arbor.com; http://www.isa-arbor.com. Adv. Circ: 22000. *Indexed:* C45. *Aud.:* Hs, Ga, Ac, Sa.

This is a bimonthly publication from the International Society of Arboriculture. Covering the latest in arboricultural news and education, it will be of interest to the tree-care professional as well as the general homeowner interested in tree care. Regular features include the "Tree Industry Calendar"; professional profiles; summaries of articles published in the journal *Arboriculture & Urban Forestry*; the "Climbers Corner"; and "European News." Continuing-education articles feature general tree care, current tree-health problems, and business aspects of arboriculture. Selected articles are available in full text on the society's web site, as is membership information needed for subscribing. This publication is suitable for a general collection or public library. The most recent issue of *Arborist News* and those dating back to February 2002 are now available online on the ISA web site. Additional back issues are being added to its digital archive on an ongoing basis.

2420. *Canadian Forest Industries.* Incorporates (1992-2010): *Canadian Wood Products;* and was formed by the merger of (1940-1964): *Timber of Canada;* (1921-1964): *Canada Lumberman;* Which was formerly (until 1921): *Canada Lumberman and Woodworker;* (1880-1905): *Canada Lumberman.* [ISSN: 0318-4277] 1881. bi-m. Ed(s): Andrew Snook. Annex Business Media, 105 Donly Dr. S., PO Box 530, Simcoe, ON N3Y 4N5, Canada; http://www.annexweb.com/. Illus., adv. Vol. ends: Dec. Microform: PQC. *Indexed:* A22. *Aud.:* Ac, Sa.

Canadian Forest Industries, a trade publication, is Canada's leading national logging and solid wood products magazine since 1881. It covers breaking news in the forest sector, new technology in harvesting and wood processing, issues affecting the sector, growth opportunities, efficiency tips, case studies, and more. The title is published six times per year, and the digital edition is available on the Woodbusiness.ca web site. Sister publications include *Canadian Biomass* and *Operations Forestieres.*

2421. *Canadian Journal of Forest Research.* [ISSN: 0045-5067] 1970. m. CAD 2017 (print & online eds.)). Canadian Science Publishing, 65 Auriga Dr, Ste 203, Ottawa, ON K2E 7W6, Canada; pubs@cdnsciencepub.com; http://www.nrcresearchpress.com. Illus., index, adv. Sample. Refereed. Vol. ends: Dec. *Indexed:* A01, A22, Agr, C37, C45, E01, S25. *Aud.:* Ac, Sa.

Consistently in the top ten forestry journal rankings as issued by the Institute for Scientific Information (ISI), this refereed journal should be a core title for any research collection in forest sciences. It is international in scope, and articles are in English with French summaries. They report on primary research that addresses an array of questions; they are also accompanied by extensive bibliographies. This monthly journal features articles, reviews, notes, and commentaries on all aspects of forest science, including biometrics and mensuration, conservation, disturbance, ecology, economics, entomology, fire, genetics, management, operations, pathology, physiology, policy, remote sensing, social science, soil, silviculture, wildlife, and wood science, contributed by internationally respected scientists. Back issues (1971-1995) are available on the web site of the National Research Council of Canada (NRC). As of 2009, copyright in all articles among the NRC Research Press journals remains with the authors, who may archive their accepted manuscripts, but not use the publisher's version.

2422. *Eastern Native Tree Society. Bulletin.* [ISSN: 1933-799X] 2006. s-a. Free. Ed(s): Dr. Don Bragg. Eastern Native Tree Society, c/o Don C Bragg, Eic, USDA Forest Service-SRS, Monticello, AR 71656; http://www.nativetreesociety.org/. *Aud.:* Ga, Ac.

This friendly journal is available free from the Eastern Native Tree Society (ENTS) web site. ENTS originated in 1996 to make record of the tallest trees, historical trees, and ancient trees of North America. The society is now a "cyberspace interest group devoted to the documentation and celebration of trees and forests of North America and around the world." It also serves as an archive of information on specific trees and stands of trees, and as an arbiter of "big tree disputes." In 2011, the group changed its name to the Native Tree Society (NTS), but it maintains two formal chapters to serve regional interests within the United States - the ENTS (eastern) and WNTS (western). The *Bulletin* typically includes announcements, one to three feature articles, prose or poetry, a field report, one to three pieces on "notable trees and forests," and an editorial. Articles are illustrated with fine photography. This publication serves as a good representative of citizen scientist groups that both public and academic libraries might include to promote local knowledge and interests. URL: www.nativetreesociety.org/

2423. *Fire Ecology.* [ISSN: 1933-9747] 2005. . Free. Ed(s): James K Agee. SpringerOpen, The Campus, 4 Crinan St, London, N1 9XW, United Kingdom; info@springeropen.com; https://www.springeropen.com/. Refereed. *Indexed:* Agr. *Bk. rev.:* Occasional. *Aud.:* Ac, Sa.

Fire Ecology, now published by SpringerOpen, is the international scientific journal supported by the Association for Fire Ecology. The journal contains peer-reviewed articles, opinion pieces, responses, and book reviews, as well as occasional reprints of "classic" fire ecology articles. The journal has more than 42 associate editors representing scientists on five continents. Issues are published three times per year: April, August, and December. Coverage includes the role of fire in forests and natural settings; historical fires and their impact on landscape and ecology; and the roles and effects of prescribed fires and fuel breaks in fire ecology. Topics cover research, education, management, and policy. The geographic scope is largely North America.

2424. *Forest Ecology and Management.* [ISSN: 0378-1127] 1977. 24x/yr. EUR 8588. Ed(s): M Adams, T S Fredericksen. Elsevier BV, Radarweg 29, Amsterdam, 1043 NX, Netherlands; info@elsevier.com; https://www.elsevier.com/. Illus., index, adv. Sample. Refereed. Microform: PQC. *Indexed:* A22, Agr, C45, S25. *Aud.:* Ac, Sa.

The scope of *Forest Ecology and Management* includes all forest ecosystems of the world. This peer-reviewed journal features scientific articles that link forest ecology with forest management, focusing on the application of biological, ecological, and social knowledge to the management and conservation of plantations and natural forests. Volumes are often thematic. Typical articles report on research related to tree growth, nutrient cycling, landscape ecology, the forest as habitat, the effect of logging practices, and numerous other subjects. This Elsevier title is available online through ScienceDirect. This journal offers authors a subscription or open-access publishing model, with an open-access fee of USD 3600.

2425. *Forest Ecosystems.* Former titles (until 2014): *Forest Science and Practice;* (until 2013): *Forestry Studies in China;* (until 1999): *Beijing Forestry University. Journal.* [ISSN: 2095-6355] 1992. q. Ed(s): Klaus V Gadow, Weilun Yin. Springer, Tiergartenstr 17, Heidelberg, 69121, Germany. Refereed. Reprint: PSC. *Indexed:* A22, E01. *Aud.:* Ac, Sa.

Forest Ecosystems is an international open-access journal that publishes scientific communications from any discipline, and that can provide interesting contributions about the structure and dynamics of "natural" and "domesticated" forest ecosystems, and their services to people. Academic in focus, this title covers both theoretical and applied ecology and forestry. Journal issues are composed of studies of protected and managed forest ecosystems, including peer-reviewed original articles, reviews, and short communications. It is a high-quality journal with an international scope, originally initiated and published by the Beijing Forestry University in collaboration with Springer. *Forest Ecosystems* is a fully open-access journal, with all volumes and issues freely available online. URL: http://forestecosyst.springeropen.com/

2426. *Forest Policy and Economics.* [ISSN: 1389-9341] 2000. 12x/yr. EUR 1017. Ed(s): Lukas Giessen. Elsevier BV, Radarweg 29, Amsterdam, 1043 NX, Netherlands; info@elsevier.com; https://www.elsevier.com. Refereed. *Indexed:* A22, Agr, B01, C45. *Aud.:* Ac, Sa.

Forest Policy and Economics has grown into a well-established and recognized academic journal, which publishes peer-reviewed political and economic research relating to forests and forest-related industries. It also welcomes contributions from other social science and humanities perspectives including, but not limited to, planning, sociology, anthropology, history, jurisprudence, and psychology research on forests. As a moderately priced, scholarly forestry title, it will be an important addition to research collections, but may also be useful for large public library collections in locations where forestry is an important part of the economy. Online access is available through Elsevier's ScienceDirect platform. Authors may choose an open-access or subscription model for publication. The open-access publication fee for this journal is USD 2500.

2427. *Forest Products Journal.* Formerly (until 1955): *Forest Products Research Society. Journal;* Which superseded in part (in 1951): *Forest Products Research Society. Proceedings of the National Annual Meeting.* [ISSN: 0015-7473] 1947. 8x/yr. USD 400 (print & online eds., for non-members) Free to members). Forest Products Society, 15 Technology Pky S, Ste 115, Peachtree Corners, GA 30092; mary@forestprod.org; http://www.forestprod.org. Illus., adv. Refereed. Microform: PMC; PQC. *Indexed:* A&ATA, A22, Agr, B01, BRI, C42, C45. *Bk. rev.:* 0-1, 1,000-2,000 words. *Aud.:* Ac, Sa.

Sponsored by the Forest Products Society and published eight times a year, this refereed journal is well respected for its technical coverage of research in wood science and technology. The *Forest Products Journal* features technical research findings at the applied or practical level that reflect the current state of wood science and technology. Articles headed as "Technical Notes" are brief notes that describe new or improved equipment or techniques. There are also reports on findings produced as byproducts of major studies; or articles outlining progress to date on long-term projects. Although this journal is a technical publication, many of its articles would be useful to engineers, economists, and those wishing to keep abreast of the forest products industry. This journal is offered free of charge in print and online to members. Nonmember individual and institutional subscriptions are now available.

2428. *Forest Science: a bimonthly journal of research and technical progress.* Incorporates (1977-2013): *Southern Journal of Applied Forestry;* (1986-2013): *Western Journal of Applied Forestry;* (1984-2013): *Northern Journal of Applied Forestry.* [ISSN: 0015-749X] 1955. bi-m. GBP 1080. Ed(s): W Keith Moser. Oxford University Press, Great Clarendon St, Oxford, OX2 6DP, United Kingdom; jnls.cust.serv@oup.com; https://academic.oup.com/journals. Illus., index, adv. Sample. Refereed. Vol. ends: Dec. Microform: PQC. *Indexed:* A22, Agr, C45, S25. *Bk. rev.:* 2-3, 1,000 words. *Aud.:* Ac, Sa.

Now offered online via the Oxford Academic platform, *Forest Science* is a peer-reviewed journal that publishes fundamental and applied research exploring all aspects of natural and social sciences as they apply to the function and management of the forested ecosystems of the world. Topics include silviculture, forest management, biometrics, economics, entomology and pathology, fire and fuels management, forest ecology, genetics and tree improvement, geospatial technologies, harvesting and utilization, landscape ecology, operations research, forest policy, physiology, recreation, social sciences, soils and hydrology, and wildlife management. All journals published by the Society of American Foresters (SAF) allow authors to post the accepted, pre-print version of their manuscript on the author's personal web site or deposit the article into any institutional repository maintained by the author's employer. SAF also offers a gold open-access option for USD 2800.

2429. *Forest Systems.* Former titles (until 2009): *Investigacion Agraria. Sistemas y Recursos Forestales;* (until 1985): *Instituto Nacional de Investigaciones Agrarias. Anales. Serie Forestal;* (until 1980): *Instituto Nacional de Investigaciones Agrarias. Anales. Serie Recursos Naturales;* Which superseded in part (1952-1970): *Instituto Nacional de Investigaciones Agronomicas. Anales.* [ISSN: 2171-5068] 1974. 3x/yr. Free. Ed(s): Ricardo Alia. Instituto Nacional de Investigacion y Tecnologia Agraria y Alimentaria (I N I A), Carretera de la Coruna km. 7.5, Madrid, 28040, Spain. Refereed. *Indexed:* C45. *Aud.:* Ac, Sa.

This peer-reviewed journal, published three times per year, aims to integrate multidisciplinary research with forest management in complex systems with different social and ecological backgrounds. Preference is given to papers that bring together two or more approaches or disciplines. All aspects of forestry are covered, including genetics, ecology, silviculture, management and policy, and wood and non-wood forest products. Articles are in either English or Spanish, with abstracts in both languages. Articles cover topics from a vast international scope. *Forest Systems* became an electronic-only journal with no print equivalent in 2015. This is a fee-free, open-access journal.

2430. *The Forestry Chronicle.* Incorporates (19??-1967): *Canadian Institute of Forestry. Annual Report.* [ISSN: 0015-7546] 1925. bi-m. Ed(s): Ron Ayling. Canadian Institute of Forestry, c/o The Canadian Ecology Centre, 6905 Hwy, 17 West, PO Box 430, Mattawa, ON P0H 1V0, Canada; admin@cif-ifc.org; http://www.cif-ifc.org. Illus., adv. Vol. ends: Nov/Dec. *Indexed:* A22, Agr, C45. *Bk. rev.:* 1-10, 500-1,500 words. *Aud.:* Ac, Sa.

The Forestry Chronicle, first published in 1925, is the official journal of the Canadian Institute of Forestry/Institut forestier du Canada. This refereed journal includes both peer-reviewed articles and membership news. Bimonthly issues include articles in English and, less frequently, in French with English summaries. In recent issues, the ratio of "Professional Papers" to "Scientific and Technical Papers" is two to one. Online access to this publication is available with a subscription and includes an archive back to 1925. The intended audience for this journal is the professional forester; however, given its modest price, it is an accessible publication for collections that serve undergraduates and the general public. Authors may deposit their accepted manuscript (post-peer review) on their personal or institutional server six months after publication, but must acknowledge the published source, must link to the journal homepage, and not use the publisher's pdf version.

2431. *I A W A Journal.* Former titles (until 1993): *I A W A Bulletin;* (until 1970): *I A W A Publications.* [ISSN: 0928-1541] 1931. q. EUR 314. Ed(s): Pieter Baas, Marcelo R Pace. Brill, PO Box 9000, Leiden, 2300 PA, Netherlands; marketing@brill.com; https://brill.com. Adv. Refereed. Reprint: PSC. *Indexed:* A01, A22, C45. *Bk. rev.:* 2-3, 500-1,000 words. *Aud.:* Ac, Sa.

The *International Association of Wood Anatomists* [IAWA] *Journal* covers topics in wood anatomy such as the micro-structure of wood, bark, and related plant products, including bamboo, rattan, and palms. It is published quarterly by Brill Publishers. Each issue is more than 400 pages and comprises eight to ten well-documented, illustrated articles on the anatomy and properties of a variety of species. It also includes association news, announcements of conferences and workshops, and two or three book reviews. An open-access back file of issues is available with a two-year lag from the association's web site. For specialized and research collections, this highly cited journal is an important and inexpensive addition. There are no page charges for authors, except for color plates.

2432. ***iForest: biogeosciences and forestry.*** [ISSN: 1971-7458] 2007. bi-m. Free. Ed(s): Marco Borghetti. Societa Italiana di Selvicoltura ed Ecologia Forestale (S I S E F), Dipartimento di Produzione Vegetale, Via dell'Ateneo Lucano 10, Potenza, 85100, Italy; https://www.sisef.org/society/. Refereed. *Indexed:* A01, C45. *Aud.:* Ac, Sa.

iForest is an open-access, peer-reviewed online journal published by the Italian Society of Silviculture and Forest Ecology (SISEF). The scope is broad and includes forest ecology, biodiversity and genetics, ecophysiology, silviculture, forest inventory and planning, forest protection and monitoring, forest harvesting, landscape ecology, forest history, and wood technology. Of particular interest is research on sustainable management of forest ecosystems. Although the journal is published in Italy, articles are in English, and include reports of original research; reviews; short communications or brief reporting of research findings; progress reports by individual authors on specific topics; and commentaries on recently published research results. This bi-monthly journal is fully open access, and no article-processing charge is applied.

2433. ***The International Forestry Review.*** Former titles (until 1999): *Commonwealth Forestry Review;* (until 1962): *Empire Forestry Review;* (until 1946): *Empire Forestry Journal;* (until 1923): *Empire Forestry.* [ISSN: 1465-5489] 1922. q. Free to members. Ed(s): Alan Pottinger. Commonwealth Forestry Association, The Crib, Dinchope, Craven Arms, SY7 9JJ, United Kingdom; cfa@cfa-international.org; http://www.cfa-international.org. Illus., adv. Refereed. *Indexed:* A22, BRI, C45. *Bk. rev.:* 5-7, 300-500 words. *Aud.:* Ga, Ac, Sa.

Formerly the *Commonwealth Forestry Review,* this refereed journal is published quarterly by the Commonwealth Forestry Association (CFA). *The International Forestry Review* is a peer-reviewed scholarly journal that publishes original research and review papers on forest policy and science, with an emphasis on issues of transnational significance. It is published four times per year, in March, June, September, and December. Special issues are a regular feature and have covered such topics as climate change and forestry in Africa, illegal logging, and gender in agroforestry. The Commonwealth Forestry Association joined BioOne in 2010 in order to broaden the usage and impact of *The International Forestry Review.* BioOne coverage of *IFR* is from volume 6 (2004) to the present. The option of open-access publishing is available to authors at the special introductory rate of USD 850.

2434. ***International Journal of Forest Engineering.*** Formerly (until 2000): *Journal of Forest Engineering.* [ISSN: 1494-2119] 1989. 3x/yr. GBP 296 (print & online eds.)). Ed(s): Charlie Blinn. Taylor & Francis Inc., 711 3rd Ave, 8th Fl, New York, NY 10017; support@tandfonline.com; http://www.taylorandfrancis.com. Illus. Sample. Refereed. Vol. ends: Jul. *Indexed:* Agr, C45. *Aud.:* Ac, Sa.

Although articles on forest engineering appear in other forestry journals, this journal is unique in being devoted to the research aspects of this field. An important role of the *IJFE* is to report on existing practices and innovations in forest engineering by scientists and professionals from around the world, in order to promote environmentally sound forestry practices and contribute to sustainable forest management. Topics covered include tree harvesting, processing, and transportation; stand establishment, protection, and tending; operations planning and control; machine design, management, and evaluation; forest-access planning and construction; human factors engineering; and education and training. Nonmember individuals and all institutional subscriptions are ordered from the publisher Taylor & Francis. Modestly priced, this is an important addition to library collections that support practitioners and researchers in forest operations. Authors can choose to publish either gold or green open access, with a gold OA charge of USD 2950 per article.

2435. ***International Journal of Forestry Research.*** [ISSN: 1687-9368] 2008. . USD 295. Hindawi Publishing Corporation, 315 Madison Ave, 3rd Fl, Ste 3070, New York, NY 10017; info@hindawi.com; https://www.hindawi.com. Refereed. *Indexed:* C45, S25. *Aud.:* Ac, Sa.

International Journal of Forestry Research is a peer-reviewed, open-access journal that publishes original research articles as well as review articles in all areas of forestry research. This journal is a reasonably priced option for students and faculty. When the home institution becomes a member of Hindawi, the author fees are waived. Recent calls for papers in special issues include "Forest Biomass Utilization for Biofuels and Bioproducts" and "Eucalyptus beyond Its Native Range: Environmental Issues in Exotic Bioenergy Plantations." The journal uses a Creative Commons attribution license, assuring authors the right to archive the published version of their articles when they are properly cited.

2436. ***International Journal of Wildland Fire.*** [ISSN: 1049-8001] 1991. m. Ed(s): Stefan Doerr, Susan G Conard. C S I R O Publishing, Locked Bag 10, Clayton, VIC 3169, Australia; publishing@csiro.au; http://www.publish.csiro.au/home.htm. Adv. Sample. Refereed. *Indexed:* A22, Agr, C45, E01. *Aud.:* Ac, Sa.

This peer-reviewed journal is published commercially by the Commonwealth Scientific and International Research Organisation Australia (CSIRO). It is presented under the auspices of the International Association of Wildland Fire and has an editorial board representative of North America, Australia, and Europe. The scope is extremely international and regularly covers basic and applied research of wildland fires in areas of fire ecology, fire behavior, and fire management systems, as well as modeling of fire in relation to history, climate, landscape, and ecosystems. The journal is well indexed. The increased and sustained interest in fire management in relation to forested lands makes this publication a desirable addition to both specialized forestry collections and academic collections. Relative to other journals in this field, it is modestly priced. All institutional subscriptions include access to full-text archives from volume 1. Authors may choose open-access publishing for a fee of USD 2700.

2437. ***Journal of Ecosystems and Management.*** Formerly (until 2012): *B C Journal of Ecosystems and Management.* [ISSN: 2293-3328] 2001. 3x/yr. Ed(s): Marilyn Bittman, Don Gayton. FORREX Forest Research Extension Society, FORREX Forum for Research and Extension in Natural Resources, Site 400, 235 1st Ave, Kamloops, BC V2C 3J4, Canada; http://www.forrex.org. Refereed. *Indexed:* C45. *Aud.:* Ac, Sa.

The *Journal of Ecosystems and Management* (*JEM*) is a peer-reviewed electronic journal that covers natural resource and ecosystem management issues relevant to British Columbia, Canada. In addition to scientific articles, *JEM* provides a forum for commentary on current natural resource challenges. *JEM*'s broad readership includes natural resource practitioners, professionals, policymakers, and researchers. The journal extends research results, indigenous knowledge, management applications, socio-economic analyses, and scholarly opinions. *JEM* is an open-source journal, freely available to the public. URL: www.jem-online.org

2438. ***Journal of Forestry.*** Formed by the merger of (1902-1916): *Forestry Quarterly;* (1905-1916): *Society of American Foresters. Proceedings.* [ISSN: 0022-1201] 1902. bi-m. GBP 491. Ed(s): Keith Blatner. Oxford University Press, Great Clarendon St, Oxford, OX2 6DP, United Kingdom; jnls.cust.serv@oup.com; https://academic.oup.com/journals. Illus., index, adv. Sample. Refereed. Vol. ends: Dec. Microform: PMC; PQC. *Indexed:* A22, Agr, C45, GardL, HRIS, S25. *Bk. rev.:* 5-10, 100 words; 0-1, lengthy. *Aud.:* Hs, Ga, Ac.

Now available online via the Oxford Academic platform, the *Journal of Forestry* is the most widely circulated scholarly forestry journal in the world. In print since 1902, the journal has received several national awards for excellence. Feature articles undergo peer review, but they are written for a broad audience in areas of technology, practice, and the teaching of professional forestry. This title covers topics of economics, education and communication, entomology and pathology, fire, forest ecology, geospatial technologies, history, international forestry, measurements, policy, recreation, silviculture, social sciences, soils and hydrology, urban and community forestry, utilization and engineering, and wildlife management. Regular columns include pieces on legislation and society, opinions, and news updates. Issues are often thematic, with an annual "Professional Resource Guide" included. Past themes include ethics, GIS, fire, and sustainable development. Regular features include member "Commentary"; "Discussion"; and "Departments," which include "Forest Health," "Research in Review," and "Forestry Reports," which are useful for librarians wishing to keep up with the literature of forestry. Both the writing and range of topics covered make this an important addition to public and college libraries, as well as collections that serve the professional forester and researcher. This journal could also be a useful addition to a secondary school library. The gold open-access article-processing charge is USD 2800.

2439. ***Journal of Sustainable Forestry.*** [ISSN: 1054-9811] 1993. 8x/yr. GBP 1138 (print & online eds.)). Ed(s): Graeme P Berlyn, Uromi M Goodale. Taylor & Francis Inc., 711 3rd Ave, 8th Fl, New York, NY 10017; support@tandfonline.com; http://www.taylorandfrancis.com. Illus., index, adv. Sample. Refereed. Microform: PQC. Reprint: PSC. *Indexed:* A01, A22, Agr, C45, E01, GardL, S25. *Bk. rev.:* Occasional, brief. *Aud.:* Ac, Sa.

The scope of the *Journal of Sustainable Forestry* is broad. While the emphasis is on sustainable use of forest products and services, the journal covers a wide range of topics from the underlying biology and ecology of forests to the social, economic, and policy aspects of forestry. The *Journal of Sustainable Forestry* provides an international forum for dialogue between research scientists, forest managers, economists, and policy and decision makers who share the common vision of sustainable use of natural resources. This imprint is now owned by Taylor & Francis. Taylor & Francis Open Select provides authors or their research sponsors and funders with the option of paying a publishing fee for open access. The standard charge for gold open access is USD 2950.

2440. ***National Woodlands.*** Formerly (until 1979): *National Woodlands Magazine.* [ISSN: 0279-9812] 1978. q. Membership, USD 35. Ed(s): Eric A Johnson. National Woodland Owners Association, 374 Maple Ave E, Ste 310, Vienna, VA 22180; info@woodlandowners.org; http://www.woodlandowners.org. Illus., adv. Vol. ends: Oct. *Aud.:* Ga.

This quarterly magazine serves the membership of the National Woodland Owners Association. This association monitors government activities related to its membership, and works with nonprofit groups and professional societies to communicate the concerns and interests of nonindustrial, private woodlot owners. Each issue includes three to five feature articles on such topics as income tax and carbon credits, forest ownership patterns, and restoration projects, as well as regular political-news columns and insert reports from both the United States and Canada. Regular departments include "Non-industrial Forestry Commentary," "Conservation News Digest," "National Historic Lookout Register," and updates to the "National Directory of Consulting Foresters." The magazine has a broad geographic focus within the United States and Canada. An inexpensive addition to a general collection, it serves to represent the point of view of the nonindustrial forest landowner. Membership and subscription information is available from the association's web site, as is the full text of articles from 2002 to 2016.

2441. ***New Forests: international journal on the biology, biotechnology, and management of afforestation and reforestation.*** [ISSN: 0169-4286] 1986. bi-m. EUR 1551 (print & online eds.)). Ed(s): Douglass F Jacobs. Springer Netherlands, Van Godewijckstraat 30, Dordrecht, 3311 GX, Netherlands; http://www.springer.com. Illus., index, adv. Sample. Refereed. Microform: PQC. Reprint: PSC. *Indexed:* A22, Agr, C45, E01. *Aud.:* Ac, Sa.

This refereed journal is international in scope and is intended for an audience of scientists and practitioners. Six issues appear annually. Each contains eight to ten papers that report on the findings of original research. "New forests" refers to the reproduction of trees and forests by reforestation or afforestation, whether for the purposes of resource protection, timber production, or agroforestry. Topics included are silviculture, plant physiology, genetics, biotechnology, propagation methods and nursery practices, ecology, economics, and forest protection. This journal should be considered a core title for a research collection. Archival full-text access to issues is available via SpringerLink for an additional fee through the publisher's web site. Springer also provides an alternative publishing option, Springer Open Choice. Open Choice allows authors to publish open access in the majority of Springer's subscription-based journals for a publication fee of USD 3000.

Northern Journal of Applied Forestry. See *Forest Science.*

2442. ***Revista Arvore.*** [ISSN: 0100-6762] 1977. bi-m. Universidade Federal de Vicosa, Campus Universitario, Vicosa, 36570-000, Brazil; reitoria@mail.ufv.br; http://www.ufv.br. *Indexed:* C45. *Aud.:* Ac, Sa.

This well-indexed technical and scientific journal is published bimonthly by the Sociedade de Investigacoes Florestais (SIF) in Brazil. It contains original papers on all aspects of forestry and forest products including silviculture, forest management, technology and use of forest products, environment, and conservation. Among other things, this journal offers a local perspective on issues related to the fate of tropical forests, particularly in the Brazilian Amazon. The text of most articles is in Portuguese; however, informative abstracts are available in English. This journal is freely available online through SciELO, Scientific Electronic Library Online, an electronic library that covers a selected collection of Brazilian scientific journals. The journal uses Creative Commons attribution licensing, so authors retain the right to archive the published version of their articles.

2443. ***Silva Fennica (Online).*** [ISSN: 2242-4075] 1998. . Free. Ed(s): Eeva Korpilahti. Suomen Metsatieteellinen Seura, PO Box 18, Helsinki, 01301, Finland. Refereed. *Bk. rev.:* Occasional. *Aud.:* Ac, Sa.

Silva Fennica is a classic, international, peer-reviewed forestry journal. It is a scientific online journal, published in five issues per volume, by the Finnish Society of Forest Science. New articles are posted online as soon as they are in their final form. All aspects of forestry are covered, with a special interest in the boreal forests. Special issues have focused on wood quality, uneven-aged forest management, disturbance dynamics, climate change, and biodiversity. On the *Silva Fennica* web site, you have access to tables of contents, abstracts, and full-text articles in pdf or html format. Full-text pdf files are available from 1998 on, and full-text articles in html from 2013 on. From the very beginning of its online presence, *Silva Fennica* has adhered to the principle of open access. This means that access to all abstracts and full-text articles is free. *Silva Fennica* has an article-processing charge of USD 935 per published article.

2444. ***Small-Scale Forestry.*** Formerly (until 2007): *Small-Scale Forest Economics, Management and Policy.* [ISSN: 1873-7617] 2002. q. EUR 576 (print & online eds.)). Ed(s): Brett J Butler. Springer Netherlands, Van Godewijckstraat 30, Dordrecht, 3311 GX, Netherlands; http://www.springer.com. Refereed. Reprint: PSC. *Indexed:* A22, BRI, C45, E01. *Bk. rev.:* 2-3, substantive. *Aud.:* Ga, Ac, Sa.

This peer-reviewed journal began in 2002 from discussions within the Small-Scale Forestry group of the International Union of Forest Research Organizations (IUFRO). Its aim is to provide an international forum for publishing high-quality, peer-reviewed papers on pure and applied research into small-scale forestry. The range of topics extends from the role of small-scale forestry in rural development, to financial modeling and decision-support systems, to wood harvesting and processing and beyond. The result is a thorough examination of the social, economic, and technical dimensions of farm, family, non-industrial, and community forestry. With international coverage and a very modest subscription cost, this journal is a welcome addition to academic collections. It should also be of use to general collections where management of private woodlots plays a role in the local economy. Authors may choose to publish open access with a publication fee of USD 3000. You may view all open-access articles for this journal through SpringerLink.

Southern Journal of Applied Forestry. See *Forest Science.*

2445. ***Tree Physiology: an international botanical journal.*** [ISSN: 0829-318X] 1986. m. Ed(s): Ram Oren, Sari Palmroth. Oxford University Press, Great Clarendon St, Oxford, OX2 6DP, United Kingdom; onlinequeries.uk@oup.com; http://global.oup.com. Illus., index, adv. Sample. Refereed. Reprint: PSC. *Indexed:* A01, A22, Agr, C45, GardL. *Bk. rev.:* 0-3, 300-500 words. *Aud.:* Ac, Sa.

Published by Oxford University Press, this online-only refereed journal is international in scope and distribution. It is a medium for disseminating theoretical and experimental research results as well as occasional review articles. Each issue consists of eight to ten papers that deal with an array of topics related to tree physiology, including genetics, reproduction, nutrition, and environmental adaptation, as well as those relevant to environmental management, biotechnology, and the economic use of trees. Research of non-tree woody and arborescent species such as shrubs, vines, tree ferns, palms, and bamboo is also included. This is an important journal for forest science and botany collections. Through Oxford Open, authors of accepted papers are given the option of paying an open-access publication charge to make their paper freely available online immediately via the journal web site. The open-access charge for this journal is USD 3060.

2446. ***Trees: structure and function.*** [ISSN: 0931-1890] 1987. bi-m. EUR 3686 (print & online eds.)). Ed(s): Ulrich E Luettge, Robert D Guy. Springer, Tiergartenstr 17, Heidelberg, 69121, Germany. Illus., index, adv. Sample. Refereed. Vol. ends: Sep. Reprint: PSC. *Indexed:* A22, Agr, C45, E01. *Aud.:* Ac, Sa.

This international, refereed journal publishes original articles on the physiology, biochemistry, functional anatomy, structure, and ecology of trees and other woody plants. Also presented are articles concerned with pathology and technological problems, when they contribute to the basic understanding of structure and function of trees. All volumes and issues of this journal are available on the publisher's web site, SpringerLink. Authors may publish open access through Springer's Open Choice option. Publishing Open Choice involves an open-access publication fee of USD 3000.

2447. ***Unasylva (English Edition): international journal of forestry and forest products.*** [ISSN: 0041-6436] 1947. q. Food and Agriculture Organization of the United Nations (F A O), Viale delle Terme di Caracalla, Rome, 00153, Italy; publications-sales@fao.org; http://www.fao.org. Illus., index. Sample. Vol. ends: Dec. Microform: CIS. *Indexed:* A22, BAS, C45, S25. *Bk. rev.:* 2-5, 300 words. *Aud.:* Hs, Ga, Ac.

Available in French, Spanish, and English editions, this international journal is published by the Food and Agriculture Organization (FAO) of the United Nations to promote better understanding of issues in international forestry. The journal covers all aspects of forestry: policy and planning; conservation and management; rural socioeconomic development; species improvement; industrial development; international trade; and the effects of environmental change on forestry. As FAO membership has grown, the emphasis within *Unasylva* has changed from wood production and wood technology to sustainability and the social role of forestry. Articles are well illustrated and readable, and would appeal to students, policymakers, and professional foresters. This would be a good addition to general, high school, and college libraries as well as research collections. The full text of articles in each issue of the journal since 1947 is available on the FAO web site. Payment is no longer required. Free subscriptions can be obtained by sending an e-mail to Unasylva@fao.org.

Western Journal of Applied Forestry. See *Forest Science.*

2448. ***Wood and Fiber Science.*** Formed by the merger of (1969-1983): *Wood and Fiber;* (1968-1983): *Wood Science.* [ISSN: 0735-6161] 1968. q. Free to members; Non-members, USD 300. Ed(s): Frank C Beall. Society of Wood Science and Technology, PO Box 6155, Monona, WI 53716; http://www.swst.org. Illus., index, adv. Sample. Refereed. Vol. ends: Oct. *Indexed:* A22, C45. *Bk. rev.:* 1-3, 400-600 words. *Aud.:* Ac, Sa.

This refereed journal is the product of the Society of Wood Science and Technology (SWST) and covers the science, processing, and manufacture of renewable biomaterials such as wood or fiber of lignocellulosic origin. Typical of the range of subjects covered by articles in each issue are biomaterials; timber structures and engineering; natural fiber composites; adhesives and bioresins; and operations research, plus one or two book reviews. This journal is modestly priced and highly regarded by wood scientists and wood technologists. This journal is recommended for comprehensive research collections and for collections that need an economical representative title in this area. For subscribers, the full run of this journal (1969 to date) is available electronically. Authors do not retain the right to archive any version of their articles published in this journal.

2449. ***Wood Material Science and Engineering.*** [ISSN: 1748-0272] 2006. bi-m. 5/yr. until 2019; q. until 2016. GBP 372 (print & online eds.)). Ed(s): Dr. Dick Sandberg. Taylor & Francis, 2, 3 & 4 Park Sq, Milton Park, Abingdon, OX14 4RN, United Kingdom; subscriptions@tandf.co.uk; http://www.tandf.co.uk. Adv. Sample. Refereed. Reprint: PSC. *Indexed:* A22, C45, E01. *Aud.:* Ac, Sa.

Wood Material Science and Engineering is a multidisciplinary and international journal that focuses on the wood science and technology field, particularly the science and engineering associated with wood as a sustainable building material. It is devoted to the application of wood for construction purposes and as products; the development of engineered wood products; and eco-efficient design and production. Issues generally include an editorial of broader interest, and four to six articles that report either original research or a review of current research. This is a Taylor & Francis imprint. Authors may pay a charge to make their article freely available online upon publication via the Open Select program, with a charge of USD 2950.

■ GAMES AND GAMING

See also Computers and Information Technology; and Sports sections.

David S. Carter, Video Game Archivist & Reference Librarian, University of Michigan Library, 2281 Bonisteel Blvd., Ann Arbor, MI, USA, 48109-2094; superman@umich.edu

Introduction

Game playing is a fundamental human activity. Evidence of board games have been found in archeological sites that date as far back as 3500 BCE. Modern games take on many forms, from board and card games to modern electronic and video games; as would be expected, magazines covering the area of games and gaming reflect this diversity.

In the video game space, the shift away from printed publications has continued as many players and consumers turn to online sources for information. Magazines devoted to a particular gaming platform are now more or less extinct; as *Nintendo Power* and *Playstation: The Official Magazine* have been joined by *Official Xbox Magazine* on the cancellation heap leaving no official magazines devoted to a single gaming platform. Several general purpose video game magazines such as *Game Informer Magazine* still remain and have branched out beyond platforms and handhelds to also include areas such as mobile and online gaming.

The past several years have also shown a dramatic rise in the interest of games as a subject of serious study in the academy. Academic publications such as *Journal of Gaming & Virtual Worlds*, *Games and Culture: A Journal of Interactive Media*, and *Simulation & Gaming* offer papers on research, criticism and commentary on aspects of game design, game theory, and relation of games to society.

Traditional games such as chess and bridge continue to enjoy devoted followings, and publications such as *Chess Life* and *Bridge Bulletin* cater to those games' serious devotees.

Basic Periodicals

Ga: *The Bridge World, Chess Life, Game Informer Magazine, PC Gamer.*

Basic Abstracts and Indexes

Academic Search Premier, MasterFILE Premier.

2450. ***A C F Bulletin.*** [ISSN: 1045-8034] 1952. bi-m. Free to members. Ed(s): Jim Loy. American Checker Federation, PO Box 1, Belpre, OH 45714; http://www.usacheckers.com. Illus. *Aud.:* Ems, Hs, Ga, Ac.

The *ACF Bulletin* is the bimonthly newsletter of the American Checker Federation (ACF) and is available through membership in the ACF. Notifications of upcoming and events and tournaments, obituaries, player standings, a marketplace, and game transcripts make this publication a one-stop shop for the serious checker player. Sample issues and archived game analysis, strategy, and transcripts are available on the Federation's web site at http://usacheckers.com.

2451. *Battlefleet.* 19??. q. Free to members. Naval Wargames Society, c/o Peter Colbeck, Down House, 76, Church Rd, Bristol, BS36 1BY, United Kingdom; http://www.navalwargamessociety.org. *Aud.:* Hs, Ga.

Battlefleet: The Journal of the Naval Wargames Society is published quarterly and contains naval wargaming scenarios, reviews, and notices of interest to wargame consumers and members of the Society. This publication would be of interest to public libraries with active wargamers, particularly in the United Kingdom.

2452. *The Bridge Bulletin.* Former titles: *American Contract Bridge League. Bulletin;* (until 1993): *Contract Bridge Bulletin.* [ISSN: 1089-6376] 1935. m. Free to members. Ed(s): Brent Manley. American Contract Bridge League, 2990 Airways Blvd, Memphis, TN 38116; service@acbl.org; http://www.acbl.org. Illus., adv. Sample. Circ: 150000 Paid. *Bk. rev.:* 3, 50 words. *Aud.:* Ga.

Published by the American Contract Bridge League, *The Bridge Bulletin* contains regular columns, feature articles, player profiles, tournament listings, and game-play scenarios and advice for contract and duplicated bridge. Definitely worth considering, especially for public libraries in North America.

2453. *Bridge Magazine.* Incorporates (1980-200?): *International Popular Bridge Monthly;* Which was formerly (until 1980): *Popular Bridge Monthly;* Former titles (until 1993): *Bridge (Sutton Coldfield);* (until 1989): *Bridge International;* (until 1984): *Bridge Magazine;* (until 1930): *Auction Bridge Magazine;* Bridge Magazine incorporated: *British Bridge World.* [ISSN: 1351-4261] 1926. m. GBP 44.95 domestic; GBP 54.95 in Europe; GBP 60 in US & Canada. Ed(s): Mark Horton. Chess & Bridge Ltd., 369 Euston Rd, London, NW1 3AR, United Kingdom; info@chess.co.uk; http://www.chess.co.uk. Illus., adv. *Bk. rev.:* Number and length vary. *Aud.:* Ga, Ac, Sa.

Bridge Magazine is well laid out and easy to read. Featuring strategy and game analysis, player profiles, and tournament listings, this magazine is aimed at intermediate and advanced-level players. Recommended for public libraries that serve established bridge clubs or players. The journal's web site is worth a look, and features a variety of bridge-related items for sale. URL: www.bridgeshop.com

2454. *The Bridge World.* [ISSN: 0006-9876] 1929. m. USD 99. Ed(s): Jeff Rubens. Bridge World Magazine Inc., PO Box 299, Scarsdale, NY 10583; mail@bridgeworld.com; http://www.bridgeworld.com. Illus., adv. Circ: 7800. *Bk. rev.:* Number and length vary. *Aud.:* Ga.

Tournament reports, book reviews, articles on strategy and defense, and player standings combine to make *The Bridge World* an excellent resource. Practice exercises, humor, and feature articles round out the content to make this publication the must-have bridge magazine. The web site has subscription information, a glossary, and an excellent introduction to the game. URL: www.bridgeworld.com

2455. *Card Player: the power authority.* [ISSN: 1089-2044] 1988. 26x/yr. USD 39.95 domestic; USD 59.95 Canada; USD 75.95 elsewhere. Shulman, Barry and Jeff, PO Box 434, Congers, NY 10920-0434; https://www.cardplayer.com/. Illus., adv. *Aud.:* Ga.

Though a little ad-heavy, *Card Player* is a worthwhile purchase. This biweekly glossy will appeal to both amateur and serious card players. It contains European and North American poker news, industry happenings, player profiles and interviews, poker strategy and analysis, and tournament information. Rich online content supplements the print magazine. URL: www.cardplayer.com

2456. *Chess Life.* Formerly (until 1980): *Chess Life and Review.* [ISSN: 0197-260X] 1969. m. Free to members. Ed(s): Daniel Lucas. United States Chess Federation, PO Box 3967, Crossville, TN 38557; feedback@uschess.org; http://main.uschess.org/. Illus., index, adv. Vol. ends: Dec. Microform: PQC. *Indexed:* A22, MLA-IB. *Bk. rev.:* 2-3, 250 words. *Aud.:* Hs, Ga, Ac.

The most polished and professional-looking of the chess magazines reviewed here, *Chess Life* bills itself as the world's most widely read chess magazine. Published by the United States Chess Federation, this magazine is a worthy purchase with its feature articles, game analysis, player profiles, and tournament listings. *Chess Life for Kids,* launched in 2006, is also worth considering. URL: www.uschess.org

2457. *Chess Life for Kids.* [ISSN: 1932-5894] 2006. m. Free to members. Ed(s): Glenn Peterson. United States Chess Federation, PO Box 3967, Crossville, TN 38557; feedback@uschess.org; http://main.uschess.org/. *Aud.:* Ems, Hs.

Published by the United States Chess Federation (the publishers of *Chess Life*), *Chess Life for Kids* is a colorful, fun magazine aimed at children 12 and under. Featuring many of the same elements included in *Chess Life,* the kids' version has tournament listings, game analysis, feature articles, and player profiles. A worthy addition to public library collections.

2458. *The Citizens' Companion: the voice of civilian reenacting.* [ISSN: 1075-9344] 1993. bi-m. Lakeway Publishers, Inc., http://www.lakewaypublishers.com/. Adv. *Aud.:* Hs, Ga.

This companion publication to *Camp Chase Gazette* focuses on civilian reenactors of the Civil War instead of on their military counterparts. Interesting historical articles on topics such as fashion and food will likely intrigue those interested in this period of history. Some articles and news items are posted on the web site. URL: www.citizenscompanion.com

2459. *Game Informer Magazine.* [ISSN: 1067-6392] 1991. m. USD 19.98. Ed(s): Andy McNamara, Matt Bertz. Game Informer Magazine, 724 N 1st St,3rd Fl, Minneapolis, MN 55401; customerservice@gameinformer.com; http://www.gameinformer.com. Adv. *Aud.:* Hs, Ga.

Billing itself as "The World's #1 Video Game Magazine," *Game Informer Magazine* is a solid choice for most public library collections. This heavily illustrated magazine focuses primarily on issues related to console gaming and announcements of upcoming systems and games. It contains the expected content in terms of previews, reviews, and articles on how the games are made, but it also provides feature articles on topics such as gender in gaming and on the history of popular gaming franchises, such as The Sims. It also includes interviews with industry leaders. Beyond console gaming, interesting forays are also made into PC gaming, Internet games, and mobile gaming such as Bejeweled Blitz and Farmville, that are attracting casual gamers in droves.

2460. *Games and Culture: a journal of interactive media.* [ISSN: 1555-4120] 2006. bi-m. USD 1214 (print & online eds.)). Ed(s): Tanya Krzywinska. Sage Publications, Inc., 2455 Teller Rd, Thousand Oaks, CA 91320; info@sagepub.com; http://www.sagepub.com. Adv. Sample. Refereed. Reprint: PSC. *Indexed:* A22, E01. *Aud.:* Ac, Sa.

The academic journal *Games and Culture* takes a more theoretical approach to gaming than the other periodicals reviewed here. This quality publication cuts across disciplines to examine issues such as race, gender, and community in the gaming context. Too academic for most public libraries, but a worthy purchase for college or university library collections.

2461. *Journal of Gaming & Virtual Worlds.* [ISSN: 1757-191X] 2009. 3x/yr. GBP 250 (print & online eds.)). Ed(s): Eben Muse. Intellect Ltd., The Mill, Parnall Rd, Fishponds, Bristol, BS16 3JG, United Kingdom; info@intellectbooks.com; http://www.intellectbooks.co.uk/. Adv. Sample. Refereed. Reprint: PSC. *Bk. rev.:* Number and length vary. *Aud.:* Ac.

A worthy addition to the scholarly literature on games and gaming, the peer-reviewed *Journal of Gaming & Virtual Worlds* contains substantial book and game reviews, conference reports, interviews, and interesting articles on a wide range of topics such as sex and gender in virtual worlds, narrative modes, the use of different video game genres, and in-game suicide. Recommended for college and university libraries, because many articles transcend the world of gaming and virtual worlds and would appeal to scholars in many other disciplines.

2462. ***Miniature Wargames.*** [ISSN: 0266-3228] 1983. m. Pireme Publishing Ltd., 1 Carrara House, Cemetery Rd, Nottingham, NG9 8AP, United Kingdom. Illus., index, adv. *Bk. rev.:* Number and length vary. *Aud.:* Hs, Ga.

A respected publication that covers miniature wargaming in the United Kingdom, *Miniature Wargames* is packed with colorful illustrations and modeling advice for collectors of military miniatures. The articles cover all historical periods, and naval modeling is also covered in detail. This magazine has something for everyone who might be interested in miniatures. The journal's web site has links to editorials, reviews, and information on vendors of miniatures. URL: www.wargames.co.uk

2463. ***New in Chess Magazine.*** Supersedes in part (in 1984): *Schaakbulletin (Amsterdam).* [ISSN: 0168-8782] 1968. 8x/yr. EUR 76.50 in the European Union; GBP 64.50 United Kingdom; USD 98 in North America. Interchess B.V., PO Box 1093, Alkmaar, 1810 KB, Netherlands; nic@newinchess.com; http://www.newinchess.com/. Illus., adv. Sample. Vol. ends: Jan. *Bk. rev.:* 3, 100 words. *Aud.:* Hs, Ga, Ac.

More European in focus than the other chess magazines reviewed here, *New in Chess* is well balanced with extensive game reviews and analysis, well-written feature articles, columns by the big names in chess, and chess news and trends. The magazine's web site has valuable content, including a large database of free online chess games and an extensive online store. URL: www.newinchess.com

2464. ***P C Gamer.*** Former titles (until May 1994): *Game Player's P C Entertainment;* (until 1992): *Game Player's P C Strategy Guide;* (until 19??): *Game Player's M S - D O S Strategy Guide;* (until 1988): *Game Player's Guide to M S - D O S Computer Games.* [ISSN: 1080-4471] 1988. m. USD 8.99 newsstand/cover. Ed(s): Evan Lahti, Tim Clark. Future U S, Inc., 1390 Market St, Ste 200, San Francisco, CA 94102; http://www.futureus.com. Adv. *Aud.:* Hs, Ga, Ac.

Focusing on games for the personal computer, *PC Gamer* contains game previews, sneak peaks, ratings, and feature articles. Game hints and cheats are also included, but you will find much more of that type of content at the magazine's web site. Recommended for public libraries. URL: www.gamesradar.com

2465. ***Simulation & Gaming: an international journal of theory, design and research.*** Formerly (until 1990): *Simulation and Games.* [ISSN: 1046-8781] 1970. bi-m. Ed(s): David Crookall. Sage Publications, Inc., 2455 Teller Rd, Thousand Oaks, CA 91320; info@sagepub.com; http://www.sagepub.com. Illus., index, adv. Sample. Refereed. Vol. ends: Dec. Microform: PQC. Reprint: PSC. *Indexed:* A01, A22, B01, BRI, CompLI, E01, ERIC, IBSS, P61. *Aud.:* Ac.

An official journal of the Association for Business Simulation and Experiential Learning, *Simulation & Gaming* serves as a multidisciplinary journal exploring simulation and gaming methodologies used in education, training, consultation and research. Topics such as virtual reality, educational games, video games and industrial simulators are considered. Issues include theoretical and applied articles, conceptual papers, empirical studies, game reviews, news and notes.

■ GARDENING

See also Agriculture; and Home sections.

Rex J. Krajewski, Head of Library Information Services, Simmons College, 300 The Fenway, Boston, MA 02115; krajewsk@simmons.edu

Introduction

While interest in gardening continues to grow, the number and diversity of consumer publications on the topic has not. Perhaps strong, long-standing local and informal communication networks, such as gardening clubs, blogs, and online message boards mitigate the need for more magazines and journals on the topic, but the fact remains that little has changed on this list since 2007, when gardening participation began its strong and steady growth.

What has changed about consumer gardening publications over this same time period has been their contents and design. Increased readership for publications with specific social or political agendas like *Soiled & Seeded, The Heirloom Gardener,* and *Organic Gardening* demonstrate a continued interest in the role individuals play in stewarding the environment. Articles in all garden magazines on topics such as GMOs, school gardens, and water use further demonstrate the activist perspective that many gardeners are assuming.

Similarly, according to the NGA, food gardening is the fastest-growing among all categories, and it recently topped flower gardening as the most popular form of gardening. Publications are responding to the desire that more folks have to grow their own food with more coverage of not only vegetable and herb gardening, but also topics like home fruit and nut production, backyard chickens, and the integration of edibles into ornamental gardens.

Magazines about gardening may focus on a single aspect or may integrate multiple aspects. Specific topics of magazines might be defined by species, as in *The Rose*; by region, as in *Northern Gardener*; by environment, as in *Rock Gardener*; or by purpose, as in *Garden Design.* Even multidisciplinary, or generalist, titles tend to espouse a perspective. So, for example, *Organic Gardening* deals with many different kinds of gardening, including ornamentals, vegetables, and water gardening, but it does so on the assumption that all will be done using organic techniques and principles.

When choosing magazines on gardening, readers are likely to be attracted to the angle and focus. Libraries should be aware of the interests of gardeners in their user population and choose accordingly. In addition to titles that cater to local interests, libraries should have generalist gardening titles from a number of different perspectives to satisfy diverse needs and interests. Provided here is just such a list of core generalist titles.

Please note that region-specific titles, those that deal with the growing needs and conditions of a particular area, have been left off this list. Consider such titles based on the region where your library patrons live. It should be noted, though, that increasingly, general gardening magazines are treating relevant topics from a number of different regional perspectives, rendering regionally specific titles less unique.

There are very few strictly electronic journals in the realm of gardening magazines; in fact, one long-standing online-only presence, *HortIdeas,* ceased publishing new content in December 2013, after going online and growing up with the Internet since 1995! It should also be noted that most print garden magazines have some kind of online presence. These might take the form of selected articles and content available to everyone for free, or all articles and content available to subscribers for free. Another variation would be extra content available online to subscribers, such as guides, reader communities or blogs, free offers, and reference material. As well, garden magazines are increasingly active in social networks such as Twitter and Facebook, so readers can find additional information and more regular updates via social media. Most magazines are now producing digital editions for e-readers, tablets, smartphones, and other mobile devices. It is worthwhile for libraries to investigate what garden magazines of interest offer information online, and consider linking to these online resources via library catalogs, subject guides, or other resource-finding vehicles for patrons.

One surprising thing is that there have not been many new serial magazines published on the topic of gardening. Instead, publishers have produced irregular "special publications," such as *The Edible Gardener,* from the publishers of *The English Garden*; *Dream Garden Rooms,* from Meredith Publishers; or *Garden Doctor,* from Better Homes and Gardens. Libraries are unlikely to collect titles such as these, as they are not readily available from subscription services or book jobbers.

Basic Periodicals

Ga: *The American Gardener, The Garden, Horticulture.*

Basic Abstracts and Indexes

Garden, Landscape & Horticulture Index.

2466. ***The American Gardener.*** Former titles (until 1996): *American Horticulturist;* (until 1972): *American Horticultural Magazine;* (until 1960): *National Horticultural Magazine.* [ISSN: 1087-9978] 1922. bi-m. Free to members. Ed(s): Mary Yee, David J Ellis. American Horticultural Society, 7931 E Boulevard Dr, Alexandria, VA 22308; http://www.ahs.org. Illus., index, adv. Circ: 22000 Paid. Vol. ends: Nov/Dec. Microform: PQC. *Indexed:* A01, A22, BRI, GardL, MASUSE. *Bk. rev.:* 3, 500 words. *Aud.:* Ga, Ac.

The American Gardener is the official publication of the American Horticultural Society. It includes regular features on such topics as design, regional issues, conservation, and habitat gardening. Reviews, regional calendars, and vibrant photography round out this mainstay among gardening magazines. A unique perspective offered by *The American Gardener* is the attention paid to gardening for children and families. The magazine is designed for serious gardeners, so topics are treated in great detail, and articles provide sound information.

2467. ***B B C Gardeners' World.*** [ISSN: 0961-7477] 1991. m. GBP 47.90; GBP 4.99 newsstand/cover. Ed(s): Lucy Hall. Immediate Media Co. Ltd., Media Ctr, 201 Wood Ln, London, W12 7TQ, United Kingdom; enquiries@immediatemedia.co.uk; http://www.immediate.co.uk. Illus., index, adv. Sample. Vol. ends: Feb. *Indexed:* GardL. *Aud.:* Ga.

BBC Gardeners' World Magazine is part of a multimedia gardening experience from the British media outlet BBC. Because the magazine is so closely aligned with television, the Internet, and radio, it features celebrity contributors like "Ground Force" alum Alan Titchmarsh. This magazine is aimed at a broad market, and articles cover a wide range of gardening topics. Regular features include the "Fresh Ideas" section, which offers "creative projects, garden design tips, new plants[,] and great shopping ideas for a brighter and better garden"; "What to Do Now," which offers a planting and project schedule for Britain's gardening season; and "Problem Solving," a forum for readers to submit questions and receive expert advice.

2468. ***Best of Country Gardens.*** Former titles (until 2013): *Country Gardens;* (until 2003): *Country Home Country Gardens.* [ISSN: 2325-9876] 1992. a. USD 6 per issue. Meredith National Media Group, 1716 Locust St, Des Moines, IA 50309; http://www.meredith.com. Illus. *Indexed:* GardL. *Bk. rev.:* 500 words. *Aud.:* Hs, Ga, Ac.

Best of Country Gardens is a product of the well-known mainstream publisher of *Better Homes and Gardens.* With an emphasis on successful personal experiences, this magazine would inspire and motivate even novice gardeners. Tips and projects are basic enough to be tackled by anyone. A more advanced gardener might go to another source for more cutting-edge or sophisticated information, but everyone would enjoy the lush photography and illustrations. Another universally appealing feature is that advertisements are limited to a separate section in the back of the magazine.

2469. ***Birds & Blooms: beauty in your own backyard.*** [ISSN: 1084-5305] 1995. bi-m. USD 10; USD 3.99 newsstand/cover. R D A Enthusiast Brands, LLC, 1610 N 2nd St, Ste 102, Milwaukee, WI 53212; customercare@rd.com; http://www.rda.com/. Illus., adv. *Indexed:* GardL. *Aud.:* Ga.

Through the lens of creating landscapes that are hospitable to animals - especially birds - this magazine will satisfy many of today's ornamental gardeners, as well as wildlife enthusiasts and eco-conscious homeowners. *Birds & Blooms* is similar to other gardening magazines, though its emphasis on native plants, pesticide- and petrochemical-free additives, and non-destructive maintenance techniques is not a new editorial priority for this publication. Setting this magazine apart from other gardening magazines is the bird and wildlife information and features. With useful information, creative ideas, and amazing pictures, *Birds & Blooms* is an important part of any gardening magazine collection.

2470. ***The English Garden.*** [ISSN: 1361-2840] 1997. bi-m. GBP 44.95; GBP 4.50 newsstand/cover. Ed(s): Clare Foggett. Chelsea Magazine Company Ltd., Jubilee House, 2 Jubilee Pl, London, SW3 3TQ, United Kingdom; info@chelseamagazines.com; https://www.chelseamagazines.com. Adv. *Indexed:* GardL. *Aud.:* Hs, Ga, Ac.

As its subtitle says, *The English Garden* is "for everyone who loves beautiful gardens," and the content is relevant to gardeners all over the world. Filled with the requisite tips and ideas, this magazine excels in offering information on enjoying gardens, such as ideas on gardens to visit and descriptions of storied estates. Indeed, regardless of whether or not the style of garden you enjoy is "English," this publication will inspire you with its beautiful, breathtaking images.

2471. ***The Garden.*** Former titles (until 1975): *Royal Horticultural Society. Journal;* (until 1866): *Horticultural Society of London. Journal;* Which superseded (1838-1843): *Royal Horticultural Society. Proceedings.* [ISSN: 0308-5457] 1804. m. Free to members. Ed(s): Chris Young. Royal Horticultural Society, 80 Vincent Sq, London, SW1P 2PE, United Kingdom; http://www.rhs.org.uk. Illus., index. Sample. Vol. ends: Dec. *Indexed:* A22, GardL. *Aud.:* Ga.

By far the oldest, longest-running publication on this list, *The Garden* is the flagship publication of the Royal Horticultural Society (RHS). Each issue is beautifully illustrated with full-color photographs. It contains original articles on a diversity of topics including plant varieties, garden design, horticultural history, garden techniques and tools, and a variety of other topics that are entertaining and informative for readers, "whatever their gardening interest." In service to Society membership, it includes information about shows, trials, research, and RHS charitable work. While the focus is on U.K. growing and gardens, this title is a must for any periodical collection that serves gardeners in temperate climates everywhere.

2472. ***Garden Gate.*** [ISSN: 1083-8295] 1995. bi-m. USD 20 domestic; CAD 46 Canada. August Home Publishing Co., 2200 Grand Ave, Des Moines, IA 50312; orders@augusthome.com; http://www.augusthome.com. Illus. Sample. *Indexed:* GardL. *Aud.:* Hs, Ga, Ac.

The unique feature of this general gardening magazine is that it does not include advertisements. Therefore, it appears smaller than other comparable magazines, but, in fact, it contains just as much information in each issue. Articles tend to be practical in nature, including a lot of how-to narratives supported by color photographs and sketches. Although *Garden Gate* may not provide as sophisticated or cutting-edge content as some other magazines of its type, it is a good, basic gardening periodical.

2473. ***Garden History.*** Formed by the merger of (1971-1972): *Garden History Society. Newsletter;* Which was formerly (until 1971): *Garden History Society. Quarterly Newsletter;* (1969-1972): *Garden History Society. Occasional Paper.* [ISSN: 0307-1243] 1972. s-a. Free to members. Ed(s): Dr. Barbara Simms. Garden History Society, 70 Cowcross St, London, ECIM 6EJ, United Kingdom; enquiries@gardenhistorysociety.org; http://www.gardenhistorysociety.org. Illus., index. Refereed. Vol. ends: Winter. *Indexed:* GardL. *Aud.:* Ga, Ac.

Another British title, *Garden History* is unique among most gardening titles in two ways. First, it is a journal; content is refereed and produced primarily for a scholarly audience. Second, its focus is not on gardening techniques but on the history of gardening. Despite these distinctions, or perhaps because of the them, this publication is sure to interest most garden enthusiasts. It is the official journal of the Garden History Society, and its purpose is to provide "support to the society's promotion of the study of garden history, landscape gardening[,] and horticulture." Articles cover such important and broadly appealing topics as historical gardens, conservation, regional garden issues, and the intersection of other scholarship with gardens and garden history.

2474. ***Gardening How-To.*** [ISSN: 1087-0083] 1996. bi-m. North American Media Group, Inc., 12301 Whitewater Dr, Minnetonka, MN 55343; NAMGhq@namginc.com; http://www.northamericanmediagroup.com/. *Indexed:* GardL. *Bk. rev.:* Number and length vary. *Aud.:* Ga.

Gardening How-To is the official magazine of the National Gardening Club, which is a paid-membership association of home gardening enthusiasts. In many ways, this title is not unlike other general consumer magazines, but it has more reader-contributed content, including book and product reviews. The how-to and science of horticulture information are more basic than in some other gardening magazines, but where this publication really shines is in its inclusion of "good ideas," i.e., helpful tips and strategies for more effective and efficient gardening. Much of this advice comes from other club members, so content is being generated by the audience. This publication recently changed to a quarterly publishing format, so individual issues include more content.

2475. *Gardens Illustrated.* [ISSN: 0968-8927] 1993. m. GBP 40.95. Ed(s): Juliet Roberts. Immediate Media Co. Ltd., Tower House, Fairfax St, Bristol, BS1 3BN, United Kingdom; enquiries@immediatemedia.co.uk; http://www.immediate.co.uk. Adv. *Indexed:* GardL. *Aud.:* Hs, Ga, Ac, Sa.

As its name implies, *Gardens Illustrated*'s specialty is its visual depiction of gardens and gardening. While the photography in the magazine is exceptional, the narrative is every bit as worthwhile as the pictures. Gardens from all over the world provide a backdrop for inspiration and information. Regular features include plant profiles, news, product reviews, and recipes.

2476. *Green Prints: the weeder's digest.* [ISSN: 1064-0118] 1990. q. USD 19.97 (print or online ed.); USD 6 newsstand/cover). Ed(s): Pat Stone. Green Prints, PO Box 1355, Fairview, NC 28730. Illus. *Indexed:* GardL. *Aud.:* Ems, Hs, Ga, Ac.

Green Prints: The Weeder's Digest is a title that fulfills a unique role among gardening magazines. Rather than being a how-to publication or one that inspires primarily with stunning imagery, this magazine offers a collection of personal narratives on the topic of gardening. Essays, stories, quotations, relevant ads, and black-and-white illustrations all serve to provide the perfect companion to readers who can't get enough of all things having to do with gardening.

2477. *The Heirloom Gardener Magazine.* [ISSN: 1548-1085] 2003. q. USD 24.95 domestic; USD 35 Canada; USD 39 elsewhere. Ogden Publications, Inc., 1503 SW 42nd St, Topeka, KS 66609; http://www.ogdenpubs.com. Adv. *Indexed:* GardL. *Aud.:* Hs, Ga, Ac.

Since 2003, *The Heirloom Gardener* has been a magazine dedicated to home heirloom gardeners. Interest in heirloom gardening is steadily growing as people become more aware of issues like native heritage and garden history. Also, as concern grows about genetically modified plants, heirloom species have garnered more attention. This magazine's appeal continues to grow. Covering topics listed above, as well as related concerns like organic gardening and preservation, *The Heirloom Gardener* would be a nice addition to a generalist gardening magazine collection, because it views the topic through a somewhat alternative lens. The magazine includes charming illustrations reminiscent of old-time seed catalogs. An interesting note: The magazine does not accept advertising from the tobacco, chemical, or automobile industries, or others it sees as countering its view on responsible citizenship and sustainability.

2478. *Hobby Greenhouse.* Formerly (until 1986): *The Planter.* [ISSN: 1040-6212] 1975. q. Free to members. Hobby Greenhouse Association, c/o Richard Schreiber, 922 Norwood Dr, Norwalk, IA 50211; http://www.hobbygreenhouse.org. Illus., index. *Indexed:* GardL. *Aud.:* Ga, Sa.

This publication is the membership magazine of the Hobby Greenhouse Association, and as such, it covers topics like greenhouse management, operations, and maintenance, and is a source of information and inspiration for hobby greenhouse gardeners. While greenhouse growing is a niche among gardeners, many gardeners incorporate some greenhouse growing techniques into their overall gardening strategy, such as through-season extension and houseplant cultivation. Thus, this magazine will meet the needs of most gardeners in that it provides plenty of information on growing plants in greenhouses, cold frames, and houseplants, as written by experts and member hobbyists.

2479. *Horticulture: the art and science of smart gardening.* [ISSN: 0018-5329] 1904. bi-m. USD 29.95 United States; USD 39.95 Canada; USD 5.99 per issue. Ed(s): Meghan Shinn. F + W Media Inc., 1140 Broadway, 14th Fl, New York, NY 10001; contact_us@fwmedia.com; http://www.fwcommunity.com/. Illus., adv. Circ: 73168 Paid. *Indexed:* A01, A22, BRI, C37, CBRI, GardL, MASUSE. *Bk. rev.:* 3, 500 words. *Aud.:* Ga, Ac.

Horticulture is one of the oldest titles in this list, and it could serve as a representative archetype of gardening magazines. While it is beautifully illustrated with inspiring color photographs, the strength of this title is as an information source. Reading this magazine makes one feel like a smarter, better-informed gardener with a scientific understanding, artistic knowledge, and technical savvy. Regular features include "Pest Watch," "Plant Index and Pronunciation Guide," and product reviews. *Horticulture* has long defined standards for gardening magazines, and is leading the way in addressing regional needs with content that is specific to major growing regions in the United States.

2480. *Hortus: a gardening journal.* [ISSN: 0950-1657] 1987. q. GBP 38; GBP 9.50 per issue. The Bryansground Press, Bryan's Ground, Stapleton, Presteigne, LD8 2LP, United Kingdom. Illus., index, adv. Sample. Vol. ends: Winter. *Indexed:* GardL. *Bk. rev.:* Varying number; 1,000 words. *Aud.:* Ga, Ac.

Hortus is a publication that is inspired by and indulges in the artistic side of gardening. Itself a beautiful specimen, the journal is in black-and-white on ochre-colored paper. While topics such as historical and notable gardens, plant introductions, gardeners of note, and ideas worth sharing are included, much of the content comes from the "place" where gardens intersect with art. For example, books about how to garden are reviewed, but so is fiction that features gardens. *Hortus* is for those who believe gardening is a high art, but also for those who only occasionally enjoy losing themselves in the beauty of gardens.

2481. *National Gardener.* Formerly (until 1948): *National Council of State Garden Clubs. Bulletin.* [ISSN: 0027-9331] 1930. q. USD 8 domestic; USD 18 foreign; USD 2 per issue. Ed(s): Patricia Binder. National Garden Club, Inc., 4401 Magnolia Ave, St. Louis, MO 63110; headquarters@gardenclub.org; http://www.gardenclub.org. Illus., adv. *Indexed:* GardL. *Bk. rev.:* Number and length vary. *Aud.:* Ga.

National Gardener is a publication of the National Gardening Association (NGA), which "is a nonprofit leader in plant-based education." The magazine includes an exceptional collection of articles that provide useful strategies for growing flowers, fruits, vegetables, and herbs. It also offers advice on landscaping, basic garden care like pest control, and home and health issues like cooking and crafts. Articles are straightforward and practical, and photographs are inspirational because they come from real gardens of home-growers. Many of the articles, plus additional useful features, can be found on the NGA web site, www.gardenclub.org. Overall, the magazine successfully fulfills the parent organization's mission "to connect people to gardening in five core fields: plant-based education, health and wellness, environmental stewardship, community development, and responsible home gardening."

2482. *Rodale's Organic Life.* Former titles (until 2015): *Organic Gardening;* (until 2003): *O G;* (until 2001): *Organic Gardening;* (until 1988): *Rodale's Organic Gardening;* (until 1985): *Organic Gardening;* (until 1978): *Organic Gardening and Farming;* Which was formed by the merger of (1949-1953): *The Organic Farmer;* (1943-1953): *Organic Gardening;* Which was formerly (until 1943): *Organic Farming and Gardening.* [ISSN: 2377-2778] 1953. bi-m. USD 18 for 2 yrs. Rodale, Inc., 400 S Tenth St, Emmaus, PA 18098; info@rodale.com; http://www.rodaleinc.com. Illus., index, adv. Vol. ends: Dec. Microform: NBI; PQC. *Indexed:* A01, A22, Agr, BRI, C37, GardL, MASUSE. *Aud.:* Ga.

While its focus is on organic gardening techniques, all gardeners will find something to like in this magazine. *Organic Gardening* recently reworked its image to keep up with its growing readership. Color sketches and gorgeous photographs serve the very practical purpose of illustrating the narrative. The articles are thorough and informative, and often provide reference to a source for more information on a topic. *Organic Gardening* harkens back to its roots as a vehicle for communication and education provided by J.I. Rodale, the early advocate of organic agriculture and sustainability; and it also covers political and social topics that impact these areas. If you are an organic gardener, *Organic Gardening* is a must; it treats gardening naturally and organically from every angle. If you are a gardener of any sort, it is a great read that offers new ideas and inspiration.

2483. ***Soiled & Seeded: cultivating a garden culture.*** [ISSN: 1925-0452] 2010. q. Ed(s): Barbara Ozimec. Soiled And Seeded Natural Heritage Explorations, 2084 Pen St, Oakville, ON L6H 3L3, Canada; donate@soiledandseeded.com. Adv. *Aud.:* Ga.

Soiled & Seeded is a unique title among the selections in this section. It is the most overtly political magazine, aimed mainly at urban gardeners. Its stated purpose-in a manifesto-shows its intent: "to expand the conventional approach to gardens and the practice of gardening." Published in Canada, *Soiled & Seeded* is international in scope, highlighting horticultural projects and topics from all over the world. This publication focuses less on how-to and science, and more on can-do and community. Stories discuss people reclaiming front lawns for food production, individuals starting community gardens, and villages celebrating native crops. Again, in the words of the manifesto, *Soiled & Seeded* is "cultivating a garden culture not based on decorative, hi-gloss scenarios, but rather one that restores our connection to the natural world and redefines our relationship to plants."

2484. ***Studies in the History of Gardens & Designed Landscapes: an international quarterly.*** Formerly (until 1998): *The Journal of Garden History.* [ISSN: 1460-1176] 1981. q. GBP 1017 (print & online eds.)). Ed(s): John Dixon Hunt. Routledge, 4 Park Sq, Milton Park, Abingdon, OX14 4RN, United Kingdom; subscriptions@tandf.co.uk; http://www.tandfonline.com. Illus., index, adv. Sample. Refereed. Vol. ends: Winter. Reprint: PSC. *Indexed:* A&ATA, A01, A22, GardL, MLA-IB. *Bk. rev.:* Number and length vary. *Aud.:* Ac.

Studies in the History of Gardens & Designed Landscapes is a scholarly journal on garden history. Readers of this publication are almost exclusively scholars in garden history or related topics such as art, architecture, design, or other histories. The journal's "main emphasis is on documentation of individual gardens in all parts of the world," although it includes other topics such as design, horticulture, technique, and conservation. Also, it is well known for its book reviews. Photography and other illustration are included.

2485. ***Taunton's Fine Gardening.*** Formerly (until 19??): *Fine Gardening.* 1988. bi-m. USD 29.95 combined subscription (print & online eds.)). The Taunton Press, Inc., 63 South Main St, PO Box 5506, Newtown, CT 06470; publicrelations@taunton.com; http://www.taunton.com. Illus., index, adv. *Indexed:* BRI, CBRI, GardL. *Bk. rev.:* 4, 250 words. *Aud.:* Ga.

Don't be fooled by the descriptive adjective in the title of *Fine Gardening.* As far as this publication is concerned, *all* gardening is "fine." Most articles are practical-for example, providing information about plants, step-by-step directions on projects, and techniques for effective gardening. While there are a lot of ads in this magazine, they are appropriate to the content. The publication is sleek in appearance-the color photographs and illustrations are stunning, design ideas are hip, and product features are trendy. However, the content is well written and the information is sound, so this general gardening magazine lives up to its own hype.

■ GENDER STUDIES

See also LGBT+; and Sexuality sections.

Chloe Pascual, Archivist and Special Collections Librarian, California State University, Long Beach, CA; Chloe.Pascual@csulb.edu

Introduction

Gender studies is an interdisciplinary field in the social sciences focused on the study of gender identity and representation. This includes women's studies, men's studies, and queer studies. The field examines gender identity and expression through a variety of academic disciplines, and in turn interprets those disciplines through the lens of gender. Those disciplines can include political science, psychology, history, economics, literature, art, and popular culture. The study of gender tends to be intersectional as well, and looks at the connections among gender, sexuality, socio-economic status, race, and other overlapping identities.

Three major databases in this field include *GenderWatch, Women's Studies Archive: Women's Issue and Identities,* and *Archives of Sexuality and Gender.* Selectors should keep in mind the interdisciplinary nature of gender studies, which has influenced many other disciplines. Accordingly, many interdisciplinary databases and databases outside the field will have material related to gender studies.

As representations of gender can vary greatly from culture to culture, the resources represented here include many international titles. The majority of titles focus on women's studies and feminism, which reflects the discipline's roots in women's suffrage and women's liberation movements. However, there are several titles represented that examine men and masculinity as an academic discipline. For resources related to sexuality and transgender issues, please see LGBT+; and Sexuality sections.

The resources below would be relevant to any academic library, especially those that have a gender studies department. General-interest publications such as *Bitch, Bust,* and *Ms.* reflect the wider popular interest in gender studies and are appropriate for public libraries as well. Librarians may also want to acquaint themselves with popular web resources such as *Feministing* and *Everyday Feminism,* in order to keep abreast of the myriad conversations about gender that happen online every day.

Basic Periodicals

Hs: *Ms., Feminist Formations.* Ga: *Bust, Frontiers, Herizons, Voice Male, XY: men, masculinities, and gender politics.* Ac: *Feminist Formations, Feminist Studies, Frontiers, Gender and Education, Gender and History, Gender Issues, Hypatia, Journal of Men's Studies, Journal of Women's History, Men and Masculinities, Psychology of Men and Masculinity, Signs, Violence Against Women, Women & Health, Women's Studies Quarterly, Psychology of Women Quarterly.*

Basic Abstracts and Indexes

Ac: *Archives of Sexuality and Gender, Contemporary Women's Issues, Feminist Periodicals, GenderWatch, Studies on Women and Gender Abstracts, Violence & Abuse Abstracts, Women Studies Abstracts, Women's Studies International, Women's Studies Archive: Women's Issue and Identities.*

2486. ***Affilia: journal of women and social work.*** [ISSN: 0886-1099] 1986. q. USD 1115 (print & online eds.)). Ed(s): Yoosun Park. Sage Publications, Inc., 2455 Teller Rd, Thousand Oaks, CA 91320; info@sagepub.com; http://www.sagepub.com. Illus., adv. Sample. Refereed. Vol. ends: Nov. Reprint: PSC. *Indexed:* A01, A22, BRI, CJPI, E01, FemPer, SSA, WSA. *Bk. rev.:* 7-14, 350-900 words, signed. *Aud.:* Ac, Sa.

This scholarly journal addresses the concerns of social work and its clients from a feminist perspective. It aims to provide the knowledge and tools needed to improve the delivery of social services through research reports, empirical articles, opinion pieces, and book reviews. Issues also include news updates and literary works. Recent topics include gender-sensitive therapy, a social work curriculum, experiences of cancer survivors, and women in the military.

The Aging Male. See Geriatrics and Gerontological Studies section.

2487. ***Asian Journal of Women's Studies.*** [ISSN: 1225-9276] 1995. 4x/yr. GBP 347 (print & online eds.)). Ed(s): Kim Eun-Shil. Taylor & Francis, 2, 3 & 4 Park Sq, Milton Park, Abingdon, OX14 4RN, United Kingdom; subscriptions@tandf.co.uk; https://www.tandfonline.com. Adv. Sample. Refereed. Circ: 700 Paid and controlled. Reprint: PSC. *Indexed:* FemPer, GW, MLA-IB. *Bk. rev.:* 2, 800-3,000 words, signed. *Aud.:* Ac.

This multidisciplinary, international journal from the Asian Center for Women's Studies provides a feminist perspective on women's issues in Asia and throughout the world. It aims to communicate scholarly ideas and "to develop women's studies in Asia and expand the horizon of Western-centered women's studies." It includes scholarly articles, country reports, notes on teaching and research, and book reviews. A new section, "Special Corner: Voices from Asian Feminist Activism," presents narratives by activists and young scholars on their individual and collective experiences. Print and online.

2488. ***Atlantis.*** [ISSN: 0702-7818] 1975. s-a. Ed(s): Krista Montelpare. Mount Saint Vincent University, Institute for the Study of Women, 166 Bedford Highway, Halifax, NS B3M 2J6, Canada; http://www.msvu.ca/en/home/community/communityservices/instituteforthestudyofwomen.aspx. Illus., index. Refereed. Vol. ends: Spring/Summer. *Indexed:* A22, BRI, C37, FemPer, MLA-IB, WSA. *Bk. rev.:* 8, length varies, signed. *Aud.:* Ac.

Atlantis is an established Canadian journal that provides scholarly, critical, and creative writing in English and French about women and women's studies. Publication alternates between general, open, and special issues. Recent topics include identity politics, transgender children, motherhood, and sexuality. Its perspective is international and interdisciplinary. Contributors are academics, artists, and feminists. The content of current and archived issues can be accessed through Open Journal Systems.

2489. ***Australian Feminist Studies.*** [ISSN: 0816-4649] 1985. q. GBP 884 (print & online eds.)). Ed(s): Maryanne Dever, Lisa Adkins. Routledge, Level 2, 11 Queens Rd, Melbourne, VIC 3004, Australia; books@tandf.com.au; http://www.routledge.com. Adv. Sample. Refereed. Reprint: PSC. *Indexed:* A01, A22, AmHI, E01, F01, FemPer, IBSS, P61, SSA. *Bk. rev.:* 6-8, 1,500 words, essay length, signed. *Aud.:* Ac.

This international, interdisciplinary journal focuses on feminist scholarship, teaching, and practice. Its contents include research articles, reviews, critiques, and correspondence, as well as news, conference reports, and discussions of feminist pedagogy. Some articles fall within familiar disciplinary boundaries, while others are interdisciplinary. Others offer interesting insights into women's studies and feminist issues in Australia. A recent issue features an article on "The Logic of Life: Thinking Suicide through Somatechnics." A free contents-alerting service is available from the publisher.

Bitch: the feminist response to pop culture. See News and Opinion section.

2490. ***Boyhood Studies.*** Formerly (until 2015): *Thymos.* [ISSN: 2375-9240] 2007. s-a. USD 234 combined subscription print & online eds. Ed(s): Diederik F Janssen. Berghahn Books Inc., 20 Jay St, Ste 512, Brooklyn, NY 11201; journals@berghahnbooks.com; http://www.berghahnbooks.com. Refereed. Reprint: PSC. *Indexed:* GW. *Bk. rev.:* 1,500 words. *Aud.:* Ac, Sa.

Boyhood Studies publishes theoretical and empirical contributions to the discussion of boyhood, young masculinities, and boys' lives. Articles are from a variety of research fields, including the social and psychological sciences, historical and cultural studies, philosophy, and social, legal, and health studies. Recent contents include an article on "Restricted access Boarding School for First-Grade Black Boys."

2491. ***Bust.*** [ISSN: 1089-4713] 1993. bi-m. USD 29.95 combined subscription print & online eds. Ed(s): Debbie Stoller. Bust, Inc., 18 W 27th St, 9th Fl, New York, NY 10001. Illus., adv. *Indexed:* FemPer. *Bk. rev.:* 150-250 words. *Aud.:* Hs, Ga.

Bust is a women's lifestyle magazine with a feminist and intelligent take on current events, gender, and sexuality. It also includes articles on crafting, fashion, and music and book reviews. It is "a cheeky celebration of all things female."

Camera Obscura. See Films section.

2492. ***Canadian Woman Studies.*** Formerly (until 1981): *Canadian Women's Studies.* [ISSN: 0713-3235] 1978. q. CAD 75 print & online eds. Ed(s): Luciana Ricciutelli. Inanna Publications and Education Inc., 210 Founders College, York University, 4700 Keele St, North York, ON M3J 1P3, Canada; http://www.yorku.ca/inanna/about.html. Illus., adv. Refereed. Vol. ends: Winter (No. 4). Microform: PQC. *Indexed:* AmHI, BRI, C37, C42, FemPer, GW, MLA-IB, WSA. *Bk. rev.:* 7, 600-750 words, signed. *Aud.:* Ac, Sa.

This bilingual feminist quarterly "was founded with the goal of making current writing and research on a wide variety of feminist topics accessible to the largest possible community of women." Issues are theme-based and include scholarly and experiential articles, art, creative writing, and book reviews. Coverage is international. The editors encourage submissions that deal with the diverse lives of "women of color, Aboriginal women, immigrant women, working class women, women with disabilities, lesbians, and other marginalized women."

2493. ***Differences: a journal of feminist cultural studies.*** [ISSN: 1040-7391] 1989. 3x/yr. USD 280. Ed(s): Denise Davis, Ellen Rooney. Duke University Press, 905 W Main St, Durham, NC 27701; orders@dukeupress.edu; https://www.dukeupress.edu. Illus., adv. Refereed. Vol. ends: Fall. Reprint: PSC. *Indexed:* A01, A22, AmHI, BRI, C42, E01, FemPer, GW, IBSS, MLA-IB, P61, SSA, WSA. *Aud.:* Ac.

This scholarly journal focuses on how concepts and categories of "difference" are produced and operate within culture and over time. The main, but not exclusive, focus is women and gender. Articles are interdisciplinary and often theoretical. Special issues have included "Queer Theory without Antinormativity" and "Other Genders, Other Sexualities." Some issues include "Critical Exchanges" between scholars on key issues. Open access is available after a one-year embargo.

2494. ***European Journal of Women's Studies.*** [ISSN: 1350-5068] 1994. q. USD 1507 (print & online eds.)). Ed(s): Hazel Johnstone, Dubravka Zarkov. Sage Publications Ltd., 1 Oliver's Yard, 55 City Rd, London, EC1Y 1SP, United Kingdom; info@sagepub.com; https://www.sagepub.com/. Illus., adv. Sample. Refereed. Vol. ends: Nov. Reprint: PSC. *Indexed:* A01, A22, AmHI, E01, FemPer, GW, IBSS, MLA-IB, P61, SSA, WSA. *Bk. rev.:* 2-10, 1,000-1,500 words, signed. *Aud.:* Ac.

This interdisciplinary, academic journal publishes theoretical and thematic articles as well as open letters, book reviews, and conference reports that deal with women and feminism in the European context. Some issues focus on specific issues such as gender and transnationalism, race and ethnicity, and religion and politics. Articles are published in English, but Dutch, French, German, Italian, and Spanish articles are also refereed and may be published in translation.

2495. ***Feminist Economics.*** [ISSN: 1354-5701] 1995. q. GBP 546 (print & online eds.)). Ed(s): Diana Strassmann, Gunseli Berik. Routledge, 4 Park Sq, Milton Park, Abingdon, OX14 4RN, United Kingdom; subscriptions@tandf.co.uk; http://www.tandfonline.com. Illus., adv. Sample. Refereed. Vol. ends: No. 3. Reprint: PSC. *Indexed:* A01, A22, AmHI, B01, BAS, C42, E01, EconLit, FemPer, IBSS, P61, SSA. *Bk. rev.:* Number and length vary. *Aud.:* Ac.

This journal offers feminist insights into the relationship between gender and power in the economy and in the discipline of economics. Its goals are "not just to develop illuminating theories but to improve the conditions of living for all children, women, and men," and to provide "an open forum for dialogue and debate about feminist economic perspectives." Coverage is cross-cultural and global. Book reviews are also included. Recommended for academic and research libraries.

2496. ***Feminist Formations.*** Formerly (until 2010): *National Women's Studies Association. Journal.* [ISSN: 2151-7363] 1988. 3x/yr. USD 195 (print or online ed.)). Ed(s): Patti Duncan. The Johns Hopkins University Press, 2715 N Charles St, Baltimore, MD 21218; http://www.press.jhu.edu. Illus., adv. Sample. Refereed. Reprint: PSC. *Indexed:* A01, A22, AmHI, BRI, C42, CBRI, Chicano, E01, FemPer, GW, MLA-IB, WSA. *Bk. rev.:* 9-12, up to 1,500 words, signed. *Aud.:* Ac.

This is the journal of the National Women's Studies Association, formerly *NWSA Journal.* It publishes interdisciplinary, multicultural scholarship in women's studies. It seeks to connect feminist scholarship and theory with activism and teaching. In addition to research articles, its contents include articles about the theory and teaching of women's studies, and it includes reviews of books, teaching materials, and films. Covers now feature "politically charged feminist artwork." Tables of contents updates are available via e-mail and RSS feed through Project Muse.

Feminist Media Studies. See Television, Video, and Radio section.

2497. ***Feminist Review.*** [ISSN: 0141-7789] 1979. 3x/yr. USD 923. Sage Publications Ltd., 1 Oliver's Yard, 55 City Rd, London, EC1Y 1SP, United Kingdom; info@sagepub.com; https://www.sagepub.com. Illus., adv. Sample. Refereed. Reprint: PSC. *Indexed:* A01, A22, AmHI, BRI, C42, E01, FemPer, GW, IBSS, MLA-IB, P61, SSA. *Bk. rev.:* 4-17, length varies, signed; online only. *Aud.:* Ga, Ac.

This is a key feminist journal, published in Great Britain, that seeks "to unite research and theory with political practice, and contribute to the development of both." It publishes academic articles, feminist analysis, dialogues, review essays, interviews, creative writing, and book reviews on issues related to gender, sexuality, race, and class. Its perspective is international and interdisciplinary. A recent special issue focuses on feminism and the politics of austerity. Contents pages and a contents-alerting service are available from the publisher's website. Book reviews are now published only in the online edition, and are available for free along with articles selected from the journal archives by the Feminist Review Collective.

2498. ***Feminist Studies.*** [ISSN: 0046-3663] 1972. 3x/yr. USD 410 (print & online eds.)). Ed(s): Karla Mantilla. Feminist Studies, Inc., 4137 Susquehanna Hall, 4200 Lehigh Rd, College Park, MD 20742; info@feministstudies.org. Illus., index, adv. Refereed. Vol. ends: Fall (No. 3). Microform: PQC. Reprint: PSC. *Indexed:* A01, A22, ASSIA, AmHI, BAS, BRI, C42, Chicano, FemPer, GW, IBSS, MASUSE, MLA-IB, P61, WSA. *Bk. rev.:* 0-1, essay length, signed. *Aud.:* Ac.

Feminist Studies seeks to promote discussion among feminist scholars, activists, and writers, to develop an interdisciplinary body of knowledge and theory, and to change women's condition. It is both scholarly and political in its coverage. Contents include scholarly research from all disciplines, essays, interviews, commentaries, creative writing, full-color art works, and book reviews. Published by an editorial collective in association with the University of Maryland's Women's Studies Program, this is a core resource for women's studies programs. Contents pages are available from the publisher's website.

2499. ***Feminist Theology.*** [ISSN: 0966-7350] 1992. 3x/yr. USD 1663 (print & online eds.)). Sage Publications Ltd., 1 Oliver's Yard, 55 City Rd, London, EC1Y 1SP, United Kingdom; info@sagepub.com; https://www.sagepub.com/. Adv. Sample. Refereed. Reprint: PSC. *Indexed:* A01, A22, E01, R&TA. *Bk. rev.:* 6-8, length varies, signed. *Aud.:* Ac, Sa.

Feminist Theology provides an interdisciplinary and feminist perspective on theology, biblical studies, and the sociology of religion. It is a refereed, academic journal that aims to be accessible to a wide range of readers. Contents include articles and conference papers on various aspects of theology and practice. While its main focus is on Christianity, coverage includes Judaism, Islam, and Buddhism as well.

2500. ***Feminist Theory: an international interdisciplinary journal.*** [ISSN: 1464-7001] 2000. 3x/yr. USD 1045 (print & online eds.)). Sage Publications Ltd., 1 Oliver's Yard, 55 City Rd, London, EC1Y 1SP, United Kingdom; info@sagepub.com; https://www.sagepub.com/. Illus., index, adv. Sample. Refereed. Vol. ends: Dec. Reprint: PSC. *Indexed:* A22, E01, FemPer, IBSS, MLA-IB, P61, SSA. *Bk. rev.:* Number and length vary, signed. *Aud.:* Ac.

This international journal focuses on the critical examination and discussion of diverse feminist theoretical and political positions across the humanities and social sciences. Written by feminists from around the world, its contents include articles, interchanges between theorists, and book reviews.

2501. ***Frontiers (Lincoln): a journal of women studies.*** [ISSN: 0160-9009] 1975. 3x/yr. USD 198.80 (print & online eds.)). Ed(s): Wanda S Pillow, Cindy Cruz. University of Nebraska Press, 1111 Lincoln Mall, Lincoln, NE 68588; journals@unl.edu; https://www.nebraskapress.unl.edu. Illus., index, adv. Refereed. *Indexed:* A01, A22, AmHI, BAS, BRI, C42, Chicano, E01, FemPer, GW, MLA-IB, WSA. *Aud.:* Ac.

This multicultural, cross-disciplinary journal is a mix of scholarly work, personal essays, and creative works that examine "relationships among place, region, and topics of longstanding concern to feminist scholars: gender, race, ethnicity, class, dis/ability, and sexuality." This well-known journal has published a number of landmark articles throughout its history, and has now expanded its geographic and comparative focus.

2502. ***Gender and Development.*** Formerly (until 1995): *Focus on Gender.* [ISSN: 1355-2074] 1993. 3x/yr. GBP 431 (print & online eds.)). Ed(s): Caroline Sweetman. Routledge, 4 Park Sq, Milton Park, Abingdon, OX14 4RN, United Kingdom; subscriptions@tandf.co.uk; http://www.tandfonline.com. Adv. Sample. Reprint: PSC. *Indexed:* A01, A22, C45, E01, FemPer, IBSS, P61, SSA. *Bk. rev.:* 800-1,000 words. *Aud.:* Ac, Sa.

This Oxfam journal aims to "promote, inspire, and support development policy and practice, which furthers the goal of equality between women and men." Issues are thematic and include articles, case studies, conference reports, interviews, resources, and book reviews. Articles are directed toward development practitioners, policy makers, and academics. A "Resources" section provides an annotated listing of relevant publications. A "Views, Events, and Debates" section features interviews, organizational profiles, reports of events, and responses from readers.

2503. ***Gender and Education.*** [ISSN: 0954-0253] 1989. 7x/yr. GBP 2384 (print & online eds.)). Ed(s): Gabrielle Ivinson, Jo-Anne Dillabough. Routledge, 4 Park Sq, Milton Park, Abingdon, OX14 4RN, United Kingdom; subscriptions@tandf.co.uk; http://www.tandfonline.com. Illus., adv. Sample. Refereed. Vol. ends: Dec (No. 4). Reprint: PSC. *Indexed:* A01, A22, ASSIA, C42, E01, ERIC, FemPer, IBSS, SSA. *Bk. rev.:* 9-15, 500-1,000 words, signed. *Aud.:* Ac.

Gender and Education is an international journal that publishes multidisciplinary educational research with global perspectives on education, gender, and culture. It is committed to promoting international feminist scholarship and practice on formal and informal education at all levels.

2504. ***Gender and History.*** [ISSN: 0953-5233] 1989. 3x/yr. GBP 720. Wiley-Blackwell Publishing Ltd., The Atrium, Southern Gate, Chichester, PO19 8QG, United Kingdom; cs-journals@wiley.com; http://onlinelibrary.wiley.com/. Illus., adv. Sample. Refereed. Vol. ends: Nov. Reprint: PSC. *Indexed:* A01, A22, AmHI, BRI, E01, FemPer, IBSS, MLA-IB, P61, SSA, WSA. *Bk. rev.:* Number varies, essay length, signed. *Aud.:* Ac.

This peer-reviewed journal offers "research and writing on the history of femininity and masculinity and of gender relations." It has a broad chronological and geographical scope and reflects a variety of perspectives. It covers both specific episodes in gender history and broader methodological questions. It provides review essays and extensive book reviews. Articles are rigorous and readable.

2505. ***Gender & Society.*** [ISSN: 0891-2432] 1987. bi-m. USD 1272 (print & online eds.)). Ed(s): Joya Misra. Sage Publications, Inc., 2455 Teller Rd, Thousand Oaks, CA 91320; info@sagepub.com; http://www.sagepub.com. Illus. Sample. Refereed. Vol. ends: Dec. Reprint: PSC. *Indexed:* A22, BRI, C42, Chicano, E01, FemPer, IBSS, MLA-IB, P61, SSA, WSA. *Bk. rev.:* Number varies, essay length, signed. *Aud.:* Ac.

This official publication of Sociologists for Women in Society is a top-ranked journal in both sociology and women's studies. It publishes articles that "analyze gender and gendered processes in interactions, organizations, societies, and global and transnational spaces." This peer-reviewed journal publishes qualitative, quantitative, and comparative-historical research articles. It also includes book reviews and occasionally presents a "book review symposium" that features critical evaluations of the same or thematically related works.

2506. ***Gender Issues.*** Formerly (until 1998): *Feminist Issues.* [ISSN: 1098-092X] 1980. q. EUR 471 (print & online eds.)). Ed(s): J M Simons-Rudolph, A P Simons-Rudolph. Springer New York LLC, 233 Spring St, New York, NY 10013; customerservice@springer.com; http://www.springer.com. Illus. Refereed. Vol. ends: Fall. Microform: PQC. Reprint: PSC. *Indexed:* A01, A22, BRI, C37, C42, E01, FemPer, GW, MASUSE, MLA-IB, SSA, WSA. *Bk. rev.:* 2, essay length, signed. *Aud.:* Ac.

Gender Issues publishes basic and applied research that examines gender relationships as well as the impact of economic, legal, political, and social forces on those relationships. Contributors come from the social sciences and coverage is interdisciplinary and international.

Gender, Place and Culture. See Geography section.

2507. *Gender, Technology & Development.* [ISSN: 0971-8524] 1997. q. GBP 418 print & online eds. Taylor & Francis, 2, 3 & 4 Park Sq, Milton Park, Abingdon, OX14 4RN, United Kingdom; enquiries@taylorandfrancis.com; https://www.tandfonline.com. Illus., index. Sample. Refereed. Vol. ends: Nov. Reprint: PSC. *Indexed:* A22, E01, FemPer, IBSS, P61, SSA. *Bk. rev.:* 4, length varies, signed. *Aud.:* Ac.

This international, refereed journal explores how changing gender relations and technologies are linked in developing societies. It mainly focuses on the Asian region, but includes dialogues along East-West and North-South lines. Its intended audience is educators, researchers, graduate students, policy makers, and practitioners. In addition to scholarly articles, it includes book reviews, research notes, and conference reports. A "News and Events" section provides information on current issues.

2508. *Gender, Work and Organization.* [ISSN: 0968-6673] 1994. bi-m. GBP 1138. Ed(s): Deborah Kerfoot, David Knights. Wiley-Blackwell Publishing Ltd., The Atrium, Southern Gate, Chichester, PO19 8QG, United Kingdom; cs-journals@wiley.com; http://onlinelibrary.wiley.com/. Illus., adv. Sample. Refereed. Vol. ends: No. 4. Reprint: PSC. *Indexed:* A01, A22, B01, E01, ErgAb, FemPer, IBSS, SSA. *Bk. rev.:* Number and length vary, signed. *Aud.:* Ac.

This interdisciplinary journal is dedicated to "debate and analysis of gender relations, the organization of gender and the gendering of organizations." It publishes theory-driven or empirical papers, and its focus is international and it includes coverage of new technologies.

2509. *Hawwa: journal of women of the Middle East and the Islamic world.* [ISSN: 1569-2078] 2003. 3x/yr. EUR 369. Ed(s): Randi Deguilhem, Rogaia Abusharaf. Brill, PO Box 9000, Leiden, 2300 PA, Netherlands; marketing@brill.com; https://brill.com. Adv. Refereed. Reprint: PSC. *Indexed:* A22, A47, E01, FemPer, MLA-IB. *Bk. rev.:* Number and length vary. *Aud.:* Ac.

This peer-reviewed journal publishes theoretical, methodological, and topical articles from all disciplinary and comparative perspectives that concern women and gender issues in the Middle East and the Islamic world. Its main focus is on the contemporary era, but about one third of the submissions deal with the pre-modern era.

2510. *Herizons: women's news & feminist views.* Formerly (until 1981): *Manitoba Women's Newspaper.* [ISSN: 0711-7485] 1980. q. CAD 27.14 combined subscription domestic print & online eds.; CAD 36 combined subscription foreign print & online eds. Ed(s): Penni Mitchell. Herizons, PO Box 128, Winnipeg, MB R3C 2G1, Canada. Illus., adv. Circ: 4200. *Indexed:* A01, BRI, C37, C42, FemPer, GW, MASUSE. *Bk. rev.:* 4, 325 words, signed. *Aud.:* Ga, Ac.

This popular Canadian feminist magazine covers topics of interest to feminists worldwide. Different sections cover news, opinion, art, music, literature, health, and sexuality. Selected articles are available on the magazine's website.

2511. *Hypatia: a journal of feminist philosophy.* Supersedes in part (in 1986): *Women's Studies International Forum;* Which was formerly (until 1982): *Women's Studies International Quarterly.* [ISSN: 0887-5367] 1978. q. Cambridge University Press, 1 Liberty Plaza, Fl 20, New York, NY 10004; online@cambridge.org; https://www.cambridge.org/. Illus., adv. Sample. Refereed. Vol. ends: Fall. Reprint: PSC. *Indexed:* A01, A22, AmHI, BRI, E01, FemPer, GW, MLA-IB, P61, SSA, WSA. *Bk. rev.:* 3-5, 1,500-2,500 words, signed. *Aud.:* Ac.

This peer-reviewed journal publishes scholarly research in feminist philosophy and provides a perspective not available in many women's studies journals. It draws on traditions and methods within the discipline but is also interdisciplinary in outlook. It seeks to promote feminist discourse in philosophy and to represent the work of women philosophers, while it also serves "as a resource for the wider women's studies community, for philosophers generally, and for all those interested in philosophical issues raised by feminism." The journal also includes book reviews and "Musings" on controversial issues.

2512. *International Feminist Journal of Politics.* [ISSN: 1461-6742] 1999. 5x/yr. GBP 840 (print & online eds.)). Ed(s): Catherine Jean, Laura Sjoberg. Routledge, 4 Park Sq, Milton Park, Abingdon, OX14 4RN, United Kingdom; subscriptions@tandf.co.uk; http://www.tandfonline.com. Adv. Sample. Refereed. Reprint: PSC. *Indexed:* A01, A22, E01, FemPer, IBSS, P61. *Bk. rev.:* Number and length vary. *Aud.:* Ac.

This peer-reviewed journal publishes "research at the intersection of politics, international relations, and women's studies." Articles by feminist scholars from across the world investigate issues of women, gender, and sexuality in the context of international relations, globalization, development, politics, and culture. Articles may be disciplinary or interdisciplinary in focus. The journal's "Conversations" section seeks to promote dialogue and debate. The publication also includes first-person narratives, interviews, letters, photographs, conference reports, and media reviews. The book review section contains review articles as well as reviews of individual works. Recent articles include "Mothers, Mammaries, and the Military," "The Political Economy of 'Transnational Business Feminism,'" and "The (In)Visibility of Gender in Scandinavian Climate Policy-Making." This is a good choice for larger gender studies collections.

2513. *International Journal of Gender, Science and Technology.* [ISSN: 2040-0748] 2009. 3x/yr. Free. Ed(s): Clem Herman. Open University, Walton Hall, Milton Keynes, MK7 6AA, United Kingdom; http://www.open.ac.uk. Refereed. *Indexed:* FemPer. *Bk. rev.:* Number and length vary. *Aud.:* Ga, Ac, Sa.

This online, open-access journal from the United Kingdom's Open University Press focuses on gender issues in science and technology and on "the intersections of policy, practice and research." Science and technology are broadly defined to include engineering, construction, and the built environment. Coverage is international in scope. Contents include research and theoretical papers, case studies, "perspectives" essays, book reviews, and podcasts. Recent articles include "Reviews of Women in Engineering" and "Spotting the Science Culture: Integrating Gender Perspectives into Science Courses." This publication is of particular interest for science educators and others concerned with developing gender equality and diversity in the sciences. URL: http://genderandset.open.ac.uk/index.php/genderandset/

International Journal of Women's Health. See Health and Fitness/Journals and Magazines section.

Journal of Feminist Studies in Religion. See Religion section.

2514. *Journal of Gender Studies.* [ISSN: 0958-9236] 1991. bi-m. GBP 1125 (print & online eds.)). Ed(s): Blu Tirohl, John Mercer. Routledge, 4 Park Sq, Milton Park, Abingdon, OX14 4RN, United Kingdom; subscriptions@tandf.co.uk; http://www.tandfonline.com. Illus., index, adv. Sample. Refereed. Vol. ends: Nov. Reprint: PSC. *Indexed:* A01, A22, AmHI, BRI, C42, E01, FemPer, IBSS, MLA-IB, P61, SSA. *Bk. rev.:* 8-33, 300-1,500 words, signed. *Aud.:* Ac.

This peer-reviewed, interdisciplinary, feminist journal uses gender as a framework for analysis in the natural, social, and health sciences, the arts, humanities, literature, and popular culture. Research articles come from around the world. They provide a variety of perspectives on social and cultural definitions of gender and gender relations. Book reviews, and a "Forum" that features interviews, debates, or responses to articles, are also included.

2515. *Journal of International Women's Studies.* [ISSN: 1539-8706] 1999. s-a. Free. Bridgewater State College, 131 Summer St, Bridgewater, MA 02325; http://www.bridgew.edu. Refereed. *Indexed:* C42, GW. *Bk. rev.:* 0-2, 1,000-2,500 words, signed. *Aud.:* Ac.

This open-access, peer-reviewed journal provides an opportunity for scholars, activists, and students to bridge "across the conventional divides of scholarship and activism; 'western' and 'third world' feminisms; professionals and students; [and] men and women." Contents grow out of conferences and activist meetings and include research articles, essays, and film and book reviews. In addition, the journal publishes multi-media submissions through streaming-audio capability, embedded video, and links to video sites to display short films and other visual materials. One special issue each year features new writings in feminist and women's studies from the Feminist and Women's Studies Association's essay competition. URL: http://vc.bridgew.edu/jiws

2516. *The Journal of Men's Studies: a scholarly journal about men and masculinities.* [ISSN: 1060-8265] 1992. 3x/yr. USD 459 (print & online eds.)). Ed(s): James Doyle. Sage Publications, Inc., 2455 Teller Rd, Thousand Oaks, CA 91320; info@sagepub.com; http://www.sagepub.com. Illus., adv. Sample. Refereed. Circ: 390 Paid. Vol. ends: May. Reprint: PSC. *Indexed:* A01, A22, AmHI, BRI, C42, GW, MLA-IB, SD. *Bk. rev.:* 4, 800 words. *Aud.:* Ac, Sa.

This peer-reviewed journal publishes theoretical and empirical research on the varied influences of class, culture, race, and sexual orientation on men's experiences. Its approach is interdisciplinary and cross-cultural. Substantial book reviews are also included. This is a leading academic journal in the field and belongs in academic and research libraries.

2517. *Journal of Women, Politics & Policy: a quarterly journal of research & policy studies.* Formerly (until 2005): *Women & Politics.* [ISSN: 1554-477X] 1980. q. GBP 847 (print & online eds.)). Ed(s): Heidi Hartmann. Routledge, 530 Walnut St, Ste 850, Philadelphia, PA 19106; enquiries@tandfonline.com; http://www.tandfonline.com. Illus., adv. Sample. Refereed. Circ: 566 Paid. Vol. ends: No. 4. Microform: PQC. Reprint: PSC. *Indexed:* A01, A22, BRI, C42, Chicano, E01, FemPer, GW, IBSS, P61, WSA. *Bk. rev.:* 5-14, 600 words, essay length, signed. *Aud.:* Ac, Sa.

This peer-reviewed journal "explores women and their roles in the political process, covering voters, activists, and leaders in interest groups and political parties." Its approach is multidisciplinary and international. It takes special interest in "the intersection of gender, race/ethnicity, class, and other dimensions of women's experiences." Contents include research and theoretical articles by social scientists and public policy experts, as well as book reviews.

2518. *Journal of Women's History.* [ISSN: 1042-7961] 1989. q. USD 170. Ed(s): Chelsea Gibson, Elisa Camiscioli. The Johns Hopkins University Press, 2715 N Charles St, Baltimore, MD 21218; http://www.press.jhu.edu. Illus., adv. Refereed. Vol. ends: Winter. Reprint: PSC. *Indexed:* A01, A22, AmHI, BRI, C42, E01, FemPer, GW, IBSS, MLA-IB, P61, SSA, WSA. *Bk. rev.:* 2-4, essay length; 23-120 brief abstracts. *Aud.:* Ac.

This journal features articles based on original empirical research as well as reflections on conceptual, theoretical, and methodological issues in women's history. It is committed to "expanding the boundaries of women's and gender history to insure geographic diversity and comparative perspectives." It also publishes commentary, review essays, and book reviews. This is an important journal for historical collections.

Media Report to Women. See Television, Video, and Radio section.

2519. *Men and Masculinities (Online).* [ISSN: 1552-6828] 1998. 5x/yr. USD 983. Ed(s): Michael S Kimmel. Sage Publications, Inc., 2455 Teller Rd, Thousand Oaks, CA 91320; info@sagepub.com; http://www.sagepub.com. Adv. Refereed. *Bk. rev.:* 6, 1,500 words;, signed. *Aud.:* Ac, Sa.

Men and Masculinities publishes interdisciplinary research in men's and masculinities studies. Contents include articles, essays, research notes, and book reviews. Theoretical and empirical articles included in this publication include research from a variety of academic fields such as criminology, psychology, sociology, ethnic studies, and more. This title provides the comprehensive coverage of men's studies that is essential for academic and research library collections.

2520. *Meridians (Bloomington): feminism, race, transnationalism.* [ISSN: 1536-6936] 2000. s-a. USD 116. Ed(s): Ginetta Candelario. Duke University Press, 905 W. Main St, Durham, NC 27701; orders@dukeupress.edu; https://www.dukeupress.edu. Adv. Refereed. Reprint: PSC. *Indexed:* A01, A22, AmHI, BRI, C42, E01, FemPer, GW, MLA-IB, P61. *Aud.:* Ga, Ac.

This interdisciplinary journal publishes scholarship and creative work by and about women of color in the United States and international contexts; its goal is to make scholarship by and about women of color central to contemporary definitions of feminism. It also examines the interplay between feminism, race, and transnationalism. Contents include articles, essays, discussions of topical issues, interviews, reports, creative works, and media reviews.

Ms. See News and Opinion section.

2521. *N O R A: nordic journal of feminist and gender research.* [ISSN: 0803-8740] 1993. q. GBP 209 (print & online eds.)). Ed(s): Paula K Sandberg, Tiina Suopajarvi. Taylor & Francis Scandinavia, PO Box 3255, Stockholm, 10365, Sweden; victoria.babbit@se.tandf.no; http://www.tandf.co.uk/journals/scandinavia/index.asp. Illus., adv. Sample. Refereed. Reprint: PSC. *Indexed:* A01, A22, ASSIA, E01, FemPer, GW, IBSS, MLA-IB. *Bk. rev.:* 6, up to 2,000 words, signed. *Aud.:* Ac.

This journal publishes works on gender and women's studies, focusing on Nordic positions of feminist research, but it also "acknowledges the need to speak across borders, challenging academic, linguistic and national limits and boundaries." Its approach is interdisciplinary and international. Content includes research articles, review essays, and short communications. Review essays and book reviews provide access to works published in Nordic languages as well as in English.

2522. *Nashim: a journal of Jewish women's studies and gender issues.* [ISSN: 0793-8934] 1998. s-a. USD 95.15 (print & online eds.)). Ed(s): Deborah Greniman, Renee Levine Melammed. Indiana University Press, Office of Scholarly Publishing, Herman B Wells Library 350, Bloomington, IN 47405; iuporder@indiana.edu; http://iupress.indiana.edu/ . Adv. Refereed. Reprint: PSC. *Indexed:* A01, A22, AmHI, BRI, C42, E01, ENW, FemPer, GW, MLA-IB. *Bk. rev.:* Number and length vary. *Aud.:* Ac.

This journal "provides an international, interdisciplinary, and scholarly forum in Jewish women's and gender studies." Each issue is based on a theme such as "Feminist Interpretations of the Talmud" or "Gender and The Holocaust." Contents include articles, review essays, and book and literary pieces relating to women/feminism/gender and Judaism. Academic articles predominate. *Nashim* is published by the Hadassah-Brandeis Institute at Brandeis University, the Schechter Institute of Jewish Studies in Jerusalem, and Indiana University Press.

2523. *New Male Studies.* [ISSN: 1839-7816] 2012. 3x/yr. Free. Ed(s): Miles Groth. Australian Institute of Male Health and Studies, PO Box 512, St Peters, SA 5069, Australia; http://aimhs.com.au. Refereed. *Indexed:* A01. *Bk. rev.:* Number and length vary. *Aud.:* Ac, Sa.

New Male Studies is an open-access, peer-reviewed journal that publishes quantitative and qualitative research, essays, opinion pieces, interviews, podcasts, and book reviews. Its approach is multidisciplinary and global. Topics of particular concern and interest include education for adolescent males; parenting and the father role; health disparities between men and women; puberty and the development processes; masculinity; and how gender roles that are promoted through cultural, occupational, and familial systems affect boys and men. Contributors are scholars and writers in the areas of anthropology, biology, economics, education, history, law, literature, medicine, psychology, and sociology. Not yet indexed by the leading academic-article databases, this resource provides an interesting, global perspective on men, masculinity, and gender.

New Moon Girls. See Children section.

2524. ***Outskirts (Online): feminisms along the edge.*** Formerly (until Nov.1996): *Outskirts (Print).* [ISSN: 1445-0445] 1996. s-a. Free. Ed(s): Alison Bartlett. University of Western Australia, Centre for Women's Studies, Arts Building, The University of Western Australia, Crawley, W.A. 6009, Australia; general.enquiries@uwa.edu.au; https://www.uwa.edu.au/. Sample. Refereed. *Indexed:* GW. *Bk. rev.:* Number and length vary. *Aud.:* Ac.

This is an open-access, refereed, feminist cultural-studies e-journal issued from the English Department of the University of Western Australia. Its focus is on a broad range of issues. Contents include research articles, commentaries, conference reports, and reviews of performances and books. This publication is also a useful resource for information on teaching women's studies in Australia. Full text is available online from 1996 forward. URL: www.outskirts.arts.uwa.edu.au/

2525. ***Politics & Gender.*** [ISSN: 1743-923X] 2005. q. GBP 260. Ed(s): Cindy Simon Rosenthal, Jill A. Irvine. Cambridge University Press, University Printing House, Shaftesbury Rd, Cambridge, CB2 8BS, United Kingdom; journals@cambridge.org; https://www.cambridge.org/. Adv. Refereed. Reprint: PSC. *Indexed:* A22, E01, FemPer, GW, IBSS, P61. *Bk. rev.:* Number and length vary. *Aud.:* Ac.

Published by Cambridge University Press for the Women and Politics Research section of the American Political Science Association, this journal "aims to represent the full range of questions, issues, and approaches on gender and women across the major subfields of political science, including comparative politics, international relations, political theory, and U.S. politics." Most issues include book reviews.

2526. ***Psychology of Men & Masculinities.*** [ISSN: 1524-9220] 2000. q. USD 735 (Individuals, USD 151; Members, USD 82). Ed(s): William Ming Liu. American Psychological Association, 750 First St, NE, Washington, DC 20002; journals@apa.org; http://www.apa.org. Adv. Sample. Refereed. Vol. ends: Dec. Reprint: PSC. *Indexed:* A01, ASSIA. *Aud.:* Ac, Sa.

This American Psychological Association Society journal disseminates research, theory, and clinical scholarship that advances the psychology of men and masculinity. Articles address issues relating to male gender role socialization, identity, development, mental health, behavior, interpersonal relationships, sexuality, and sexual orientation. Rigorously peer-reviewed, this journal is important for libraries that support research and study in psychology and/or gender studies.

2527. ***Religion and Gender.*** [ISSN: 2589-8051] 2019. s-a. EUR 218. Ed(s): Nella van den Brandt, Sarah Bracke. Brill, PO Box 9000, Leiden, 2300 PA, Netherlands; marketing@brill.com; https://brill.com. Adv. Refereed. *Bk. rev.:* Number and length vary. *Aud.:* Ac, Sa.

Religion and Gender is a refereed, open-access journal situated in Europe that addresses international issues. It looks at multiple manifestations of religion in varied contexts, with particular attention to contemporary or emerging issues. Its outlook is postmodern, postcolonial, and post-secular. Issues are themed, and have included "Pussy Riot as Litmus Paper: Political Protest and Religious Culture" and "Religion, Gender and Postcoloniality." Contents include high-quality research articles in the humanities and social sciences, invited keynote articles by outstanding scholars, and critical book reviews. The rigorous peer-review process and high editorial standards make this an important journal for academic libraries that support research in gender and religion. URL: www.religionandgender.org/index.php/rg

2528. ***Resources for Gender and Women's Studies: a feminist review.*** Formerly (until 2018): *Feminist Collections.* [ISSN: 2576-0750] 1980. q. USD 75. Ed(s): Phyllis Holman Weisbard, JoAnne Lehman. University of Wisconsin at Madison, Women's Studies Librarian, Memorial Library, Rm.430, 728 State St., Madison, WI 53706; wiswsl@library.wisc.edu; http://womenst.library.wisc.edu/. Illus., adv. Vol. ends: Summer. *Indexed:* A01, A22, BRI, C42, GW, MLA-IB, WSA. *Bk. rev.:* Number varies, essay length, signed. *Aud.:* Ac, Sa.

Resources for Gender and Women's Studies is a key resource for research and teaching in women's studies. It provides reviews of books, periodicals, audiovisuals, and online resources. Regular features include "New Reference Works in Women's Studies"; "E-Sources on Women and Gender," which provides notices of new websites, blogs, and other digital or online resources; while "Periodical Notes" provides information about new publications, special issues, and ceased publications. A print subscription includes *Feminist Periodicals,* an online current-contents listing service, and *New Books on Women & Feminism.* Back issues are available in the University of Wisconsin repository.

Sex Roles. See Sociology and Social Work/General section.

2529. ***Signs: journal of women in culture and society.*** [ISSN: 0097-9740] 1975. q. USD 490. Ed(s): Suzanna Danuta Walters. University of Chicago Press, 1427 E 60th St, Chicago, IL 60637; subscriptions@press.uchicago.edu; http://www.journals.uchicago.edu. Illus., index, adv. Sample. Refereed. Vol. ends: Summer. Reprint: PSC. *Indexed:* A01, A22, AmHI, BAS, BRI, CBRI, Chicano, F01, FemPer, IBSS, MLA-IB, P61, SSA, WSA. *Bk. rev.:* 2-12, 1,200-2,000 words, signed. *Aud.:* Ac.

This leading journal from the University of Chicago Press publishes path-breaking interdisciplinary articles on gender, sexuality, race, class, ethnicity, and nationality. It publishes articles that express different, often contradictory, viewpoints. Contents include research articles, review essays, comparative perspectives symposia, reviews, letters/comments, editorials, primary documents, and notes. The journal's online blog offers announcements, links to open-access content, and other resources that supplement and extend the print edition.

2530. ***Social Politics: international studies in gender, state, and society.*** [ISSN: 1072-4745] 1994. q. EUR 373. Ed(s): Rianne Mahon, Aleksandra Kanjuo-Mrcela. Oxford University Press, Great Clarendon St, Oxford, OX2 6DP, United Kingdom; onlinequeries.uk@oup.com; http://global.oup.com. Illus., index, adv. Sample. Refereed. Vol. ends: No. 3. Microform: PQC. Reprint: PSC. *Indexed:* A22, E01, FemPer, GW, IBSS, P61, SSA. *Bk. rev.:* Number varies, essay length, signed. *Aud.:* Ac, Sa.

This multidisciplinary journal addresses "the critical emerging issues of our age: globalization, transnationality and citizenship, migration, diversity and its intersections, the restructuring of capitalisms and states." Contents include research articles as well as articles on policy perspectives. Issues are often themed. The publisher's website provides advance access to some articles, tables of contents, article abstracts, and a contents-alerting service.

2531. ***Spectrum: a journal on Black men.*** [ISSN: 2162-3244] 2012. s-a. USD 108.35 (print & online eds.)). Ed(s): Molly Reinhoudt, Judson L Jeffries. Indiana University Press, Office of Scholarly Publishing, Herman B Wells Library 350, Bloomington, IN 47405; iuporder@indiana.edu; http://iupress.indiana.edu/. Adv. Refereed. *Bk. rev.:* 1-2, up to 1,500 words, signed. *Aud.:* Ac, Sa.

Spectrum is a peer-reviewed multidisciplinary research journal from Indiana University Press. It examines "the social, political, economic, and historical factors that influence the life chances and experiences of men of Black descent." Contents include empirical research, theoretical analysis, literary criticism, essays, review essays, and book reviews. It is of particular interest for the perspective on Black masculinities that it brings to academic libraries that support African American and gender studies programs.

2532. ***Studies in Gender and Sexuality.*** [ISSN: 1524-0657] 2000. q. GBP 298 (print & online eds.)). Ed(s): Muriel Dimen. Routledge, 530 Walnut St, Ste 850, Philadelphia, PA 19106; enquiries@tandfonline.com; http://www.tandfonline.com. Adv. Sample. Refereed. Reprint: PSC. *Indexed:* A01, A22, E01, FemPer, GW, MLA-IB. *Aud.:* Ac.

This journal looks at gender and sexuality from the perspectives of feminism, psychoanalytic theory, developmental research, and cultural studies. It is directed toward promoting interdisciplinary dialogue among academic researchers and scholars, clinicians, and practitioners. It publishes work across the arts, humanities, and the social and natural sciences. Contents represent a variety of theoretical, clinical, and methodological approaches. Some issues offer roundtable discussions and sets of papers on topics such as dressing in drag, self-image, or shame. Contents pages and e-mail or RSS feed tables-of-contents notifications are available on the publisher's website.

2533. ***Violence Against Women: an international and interdisciplinary journal.*** [ISSN: 1077-8012] 1995. m. USD 2170 (print & online eds.)). Ed(s): Claire M Renzetti. Sage Publications, Inc., 2455 Teller Rd, Thousand Oaks, CA 91320; info@sagepub.com; http://www.sagepub.com. Illus., adv. Sample. Refereed. Vol. ends: Dec. Reprint: PSC. *Indexed:* A01, A22, BRI, CJPI, E01, FemPer, IBSS, N13, SSA. *Bk. rev.:* 2, essay length, signed. *Aud.:* Ga, Ac, Sa.

This journal publishes empirical research and cross-cultural and historical analyses of all aspects of the problem of violence against women. It is concerned with both well-known and lesser-known forms of violence, and seeks to promote dialogue among people of diverse backgrounds working in various fields and disciplines. Contents include research articles, review essays, and clinical, legal, and research notes, as well as book reviews. The journal's website offers forthcoming articles that are published online ahead of print, and podcasts that feature discussions between selected authors and the journal editor.

2534. ***Voice Male.*** Formerly (until 1998): *Valley Men.* [ISSN: 1522-5585] 1986. q. USD 45 (Individuals, USD 30). Ed(s): Rob Okun. Voice Male Magazine, PO Box 1246, Amherst, MA 01004. Illus., adv. *Indexed:* GW. *Bk. rev.:* Number and length vary. *Aud.:* Ga, Sa.

Voice Male is "a magazine exploring critical issues relevant to men's growth and health while cataloguing the damaging effects of men's isolation and violence." It publishes men's experiences in learning about their inner lives, overcoming violence, and surviving abuse. It is a forum for men's voices from around the world on topics that affect them, such as war, violence in sports, and depiction of men in pornography. Contributors to the magazine include men of all ages, trans men, and women. A good resource for a public or high school library, especially alongside *Bitch* or *Bust.*

2535. ***Women: a cultural review.*** [ISSN: 0957-4042] 1990. 4x/yr. GBP 581 (print & online eds.)). Ed(s): Helen Carr, Isobel Armstrong. Routledge, 4 Park Sq, Milton Park, Abingdon, OX14 4RN, United Kingdom; subscriptions@tandf.co.uk; http://www.tandfonline.com. Adv. Sample. Refereed. Reprint: PSC. *Indexed:* A01, A22, AmHI, BRI, C42, E01, FemPer, GW, IBSS, MLA-IB. *Bk. rev.:* Number and length vary. *Aud.:* Ac.

This journal focuses on "the role and representation of gender and sexuality in the arts and culture, with a particular focus on the contemporary world." It looks at literature, the media, history, education, law, philosophy, psychoanalysis, and the performing and visual arts. Contents include research articles, essays, review essays, interviews, book reviews, and a listing of new titles in the study of gender and culture. Two issues per year are devoted to special topics, such as "Reassessing Barbara Pym" and "The Politics of New Materialism." The publisher's website provides tables of contents and an article-alert service.

Women and Music. See Music/General section.

Women & Therapy. See Psychology section.

2536. ***Women, Gender, and Families of Color.*** [ISSN: 2326-0939] 2013. s-a. USD 103 (print & online eds.)). Ed(s): Jennifer Hamer. University of Illinois Press, 1325 S Oak St, MC-566, Champaign, IL 61820; uipress@uillinois.edu; http://www.press.uillinois.edu. Adv. Refereed. *Indexed:* BRI. *Aud.:* Ga, Ac.

This multidisciplinary, peer-reviewed journal is important for its explorations of the intersections of race, gender, and class. It publishes comparative and transnational research and analyses of social, political, economic, and cultural policies and practices in the United States. Research comes from the fields of history, the social and behavioral sciences, and humanities. Recommended for academic libraries that support a program in race and ethnicity or women's or gender studies, and for larger public libraries.

2537. ***Women's History Review.*** [ISSN: 0961-2025] 1992. 6x/yr. GBP 843 (print & online eds.)). Ed(s): June Purvis. Routledge, 4 Park Sq, Milton Park, Abingdon, OX14 4RN, United Kingdom; subscriptions@tandf.co.uk; http://www.tandfonline.com. Illus., index, adv. Sample. Refereed. Vol. ends: Dec. Reprint: PSC. *Indexed:* A01, A22, AmHI, BRI, E01, FemPer, MLA-IB, P61, SSA. *Bk. rev.:* 5-8, length varies, signed. *Aud.:* Ac.

This British journal provides an interdisciplinary feminist perspective on women and gender relations in history. Coverage is international and emphasizes the nineteenth, twentieth, and twenty-first centuries. The journal publishes research articles, viewpoint essays, review essays, and book reviews from a range of disciplines.

2538. ***Women's Studies: an interdisciplinary journal.*** [ISSN: 0049-7878] 1972. 8x/yr. GBP 1278 (print & online eds.)). Ed(s): Wendy Martin. Taylor & Francis Inc., 711 3rd Ave, 8th Fl, New York, NY 10017; support@tandfonline.com; http://www.tandfonline.com. Illus., adv. Sample. Refereed. Microform: MIM. Reprint: PSC. *Indexed:* A01, A22, AmHI, BRI, E01, F01, FemPer, GW, IBSS, MLA-IB, WSA. *Bk. rev.:* Number and length vary. *Aud.:* Ac.

This journal publishes research articles, critical essays, and book reviews that focus largely on women in literature, history, art, sociology, law, political science, economics, anthropology, and the sciences. Contents also include poetry, short stories, and film and book reviews. Occasional issues focus on special topics such as "Irish Women's Writing and Experience" and "Anne Bradstreet." Tables of contents and a contents-alerting service are available on the publisher's website.

2539. ***Women's Studies International Forum.*** Formerly (until 1982): *Women's Studies International Quarterly;* Incorporates (1982-1986): *Feminist Forum;* Which was formerly (until 1982): *Women's Studies International Quarterly Forum.* [ISSN: 0277-5395] 1978. bi-m. EUR 1536. Ed(s): Kalwant Bhopal. Pergamon Press, The Blvd, Langford Ln, E Park, Kidlington, OX5 1GB, United Kingdom; JournalsCustomerServiceEMEA@elsevier.com; http://www.elsevier.com. Illus., adv. Sample. Refereed. Microform: PQC. *Indexed:* A01, A22, AmHI, BAS, BRI, FemPer, IBSS, MLA-IB, P61, SSA, WSA. *Bk. rev.:* 6-10, length varies, signed. *Aud.:* Ac.

This expensive journal offers truly global coverage of feminist research in women's studies and other disciplines. It publishes research and theoretical articles, review essays, and book reviews. The publisher's website offers tables of contents, abstracts, and a contents-alerting service.

2540. ***Women's Studies Quarterly.*** Formerly (until 1981): *Women's Studies Newsletter.* [ISSN: 0732-1562] 1972. s-a. USD 85 (Individuals, USD 60). Ed(s): Julia Berner-Tobin. Feminist Press, CUNY, 365 5th Ave, Ste 5406, New York, NY 10016; info@feministpress.org; http://www.feministpress.org. Illus., adv. Sample. Refereed. Vol. ends: Fall/Winter (No. 3 - No. 4). Reprint: PSC. *Indexed:* A01, A22, BRI, Chicano, E01, F01, FemPer, GW, MLA-IB, P61, SSA, WSA. *Bk. rev.:* 0-5, 1,000-1,800 words, signed. *Aud.:* Ga, Ac.

This journal from Feminist Press provides an international and cross-cultural perspective on women, gender, and sexuality. Its contents, aimed at both popular and academic readers, include research articles from psychoanalytic, legal, queer, cultural, technological, and historical fields. Articles provide diverse viewpoints and in-depth coverage of contemporary feminist topics. The journal also includes fiction and creative nonfiction, poetry, book reviews, and the visual arts. Some issues are theme-based.

2541. ***X Y: Men, Masculinities and Gender Politics.*** 1990. irreg. Free. X Y: Men, Masculinities and Gender Politcs, PO Box 473, Blackwood, SA 5051, Australia. *Bk. rev.:* 1, 200 words, signed. *Aud.:* Ga, Ac.

Originally a print journal published between 1990 and 1998 in Canberra, Australia, *XY* continues as a nonprofit website on issues such as fathering, men's health, domestic violence, and relationships between masculinity, class, race, and sexuality. It also includes 60 of the best articles from the print journal. *XY* functions as a forum for debate and discussion and as a clearinghouse for reports, articles, and other information. It also hosts several blogs on men, masculinities, and gender issues. Content reflects a variety of feminist positions and is of interest to readers and contributors around the world. The style is accessible to lay readers.

■ GENEALOGY

General Interest Periodicals/Specialized Periodicals

See also Canada; Europe; and History sections.

Roberta Sittel, Government Information Librarian, University of North Texas

Introduction

In recent years, the growth in genealogy's popularity opened the field beyond professionals and scholars to include novice researchers and hobbyists. The proliferation of digitized records and other historical documents brought the discipline out of local genealogical societies, libraries, and dark archives, mobilizing volunteers around the world on crowd-sourced indexing projects to make materials more discoverable. The greater discoverability of records as well as increased access to personal and family histories allows professional and amateur genealogists to more easily span boundaries and create new connections. Additionally, as materials become more discoverable, the field is becoming accessible and inclusive to previously marginalized and underrepresented ethnically and racially diverse populations.

Genealogy periodicals are reflective of the broadening popularity of the field. Long-standing journals continue the tradition of well-documented and researched family histories, while others find a balance providing research methodologies, book reviews, resource highlights, and feature articles exploring a variety of historical and genealogical subjects. Genealogy publications may have a national focus while many focus more narrowly on geographies, ethnicities, or time periods. The field also offers consumer publications that appeal to a broad audience offering tips, tricks, and deeper dives in a colloquial way.

In accordance with editorial policy, periodicals with a local or state focus have been excluded from this edition; though patrons should be encouraged to explore state and local historical and genealogical societies for additional resources. Similarly, blogs, online newsletters, podcasts, and websites offer tools and other information on the latest developments in genealogy.

Publications featured in this section aim to present a basic core list of genealogy periodicals to appeal to users of every library type. As used herein, the term "scholarly" designates journals that properly footnote each genealogically significant event to a primary source, so that readers may go directly to that source.

Basic Abstracts and Indexes

MasterFILE Premier; MLA International Bibliography; PIO: Periodicals Index Online.

General Interest Periodicals

2542. *American Ancestors.* Formerly (until 2010): *New England Ancestors;* Which was formed by the merger of (1996-2000): *Nexus;* Which was formerly (until 1996): *N E H G S Nexus;* (1994-2000): *The New England Computer Genealogist;* Which was formerly (until 1994): *Nerug News.* [ISSN: 2154-6533] 19??. q. Free to members. Ed(s): Lynn Betlock. New England Historic Genealogical Society, 101 Newbury St, Boston, MA 02116-3007; membership@nehgs.org; http://www.newenglandancestors.org. Illus., index, adv. Vol. ends: Dec. *Indexed:* MLA-IB. *Aud.:* Ga.

This quarterly, full-color magazine from the New England Historic Genealogical Society (NEHGS) publishes articles with mostly a New England focus, though issues have included occasional articles of a more general nature, such as an interview with Henry Louis Gates, Jr., and a general article on writing your family history. Also includes regular columns on topics such as genetics and genealogy, manuscripts, and New York genealogy, along with news and announcements of the society's activities. The NEHGS also publishes the more scholarly *The New England Historical and Genealogical Register*. Members of the society have access to a variety of online databases.

2543. *Family Tree.* [ISSN: 0267-1131] 1984. 13x/yr. GBP 70. Warners Group Publications Plc., Fifth Fl, 31-32 Park Row, Leeds, LS1 5JD, United Kingdom; wgpsubs@warnersgroup.co.uk; http://www.warnersgroup.co.uk/. Illus., adv. *Bk. rev.:* Number and length vary. *Aud.:* Ga.

Full-color consumer magazine published in the United Kingdom. This title explains methods of research, highlights various kinds of sources, and helps readers to explore their family history by offering answers to their questions and providing an advertising section of companies that can help. Regular features include a Q&A section and reviews. Although this magazine is heavily U.K.-centric, it has enough worthwhile information for North American researchers to be worthy of consideration by libraries in Canada and the United States.

2544. *Federation of Genealogical Societies Forum.* Formerly (until 1989): *Federation of Genealogical Societies Newsletter.* [ISSN: 1531-720X] 1976. q. Non-members, USD 15. Ed(s): Julie Tarr. Federation of Genealogical Societies, PO Box 200940, Austin, TX 78720-0940; forum@fgs.org; http://www.fgs.org. Illus., adv. Vol. ends: Winter. *Bk. rev.:* Number and length vary. *Aud.:* Ga, Sa.

This online-only journal provides society news, upcoming events, software reviews, book reviews, and more, to its constituent audience: genealogical societies, libraries, and archives. Some methodology articles appear. Regular features include book reviews and a family associations update. An archive of all issues is available in a "Members-Only" part of the website. Of interest for genealogical researchers of all types.

2545. *The Genealogist.* [ISSN: 0197-1468] 1980. s-a. USD 25 domestic; USD 43 foreign; USD 15 per issue. Ed(s): Gale Ion Harris, Charles M Hansen. American Society of Genealogists, c/o Jane Fletcher Fiske, 44 Stonecleave Rd, Boxford, MA 01921; asg.sec@gmail.com; http://www.fasg.org/. Index. Sample. Refereed. Vol. ends: Fall. *Aud.:* Ac, Sa.

This is a highly respected scholarly journal dealing with European origins, royal and medieval ancestry, difficult genealogical problems, complete descendant genealogies, and related studies that are considered too lengthy by other scholarly journals in the field. Founded in 1980 as a private enterprise with an irregular publishing schedule, it became the official journal of the American Society of Genealogists (ASG) in 1997 (volume 11). Under the aegis of ASG, it has consistently maintained its semi-annual publication as well as its longstanding quality. Tables of contents for all issues are available online at fasg.org/the-genealogist. This is a journal for all academic libraries and public libraries with a major focus in genealogy.

2546. *Internet Genealogy.* [ISSN: 1718-0414] 2006. bi-m. USD 27.95. Ed(s): Edward Zapletal. Moorshead Magazines Ltd., PO Box 194, Niagara Falls, NY 14304; http://www.moorshead.com. Illus., adv. *Aud.:* Ga.

This magazine, aimed at a general audience, covers numerous topics relating to online genealogy, though it "will also tell you what to do if you cannot find the records you need and how to confirm your findings" (from website). Articles include "Yesterday's Weather for Today's Genealogists," "Online Photo Editing Solutions," "Cloud Storage and Your Genealogy," and "Reduce Your Digital Clutter." This title also includes reviews of software and hardware, case studies, information on databases, and more.

2547. *N G S Magazine.* Former titles (until 2008): *N G S News Magazine;* (until 1999): *N G S Newsletter;* (until 1987): *National Genealogical Society. Newsletter.* [ISSN: 2472-4661] 1975. q. Free to members. Ed(s): Deb Cyprych. National Genealogical Society, 6400 Arlington Blvd,Ste 810, Falls Church, VA 22042; ngs@ngsgenealogy.org; http://www.ngsgenealogy.org. Illus., adv. *Bk. rev.:* Number and length vary. *Aud.:* Ga.

This quarterly publication from the National Genealogical Society (NGS) contains informative, well-documented articles that "show and tell" readers how to do effective genealogical research. Issues have contained articles on educational opportunities in genealogy, tips on using *FamilySearch* to solve problems, background information on the waves of German migrations in the eighteenth and nineteenth centuries, and other very useful topics. Regular columns cover the National Archives, the "Reference desk," genetic genealogy, and technology. Membership in the NGS includes subscriptions to both this title and to the *National Genealogical Society Quarterly*.

2548. ***National Genealogical Society Quarterly: a journal for today's family historian.*** [ISSN: 0027-934X] 1912. q. Free to members. Ed(s): Allen R Peterson, Nancy A Peters. National Genealogical Society, 3108 Columbia Pike, Ste 300, Arlington, VA 22204-4370; ngs@ngsgenealogy.org; http://www.ngsgenealogy.org. Illus., index, adv. Refereed. Vol. ends: Dec. Microform: PMC. *Indexed:* A22, BRI, CBRI. *Bk. rev.:* Number and length vary. *Aud.:* Ga, Ac.

This quarterly scholarly journal, published since 1912, includes articles that run the gamut of American genealogy: all regions, ethnic groups, and time periods, including the twentieth century. Types of articles include compiled genealogies, case studies, essays on new methodology and little-known resources, critical reviews of current books, and previously unpublished source materials. Review essays and regular book reviews are in each issue. A free online index covers the entire run of the journal. URL: www.ngsgenealogy.org/cs/publications

2549. ***Your Genealogy Today.*** Formerly (until 2015): *Family Chronicle;* Which incorporates (2008-2010): *Discovering Family History.* 199?. bi-m. USD 27.95. Ed(s): Edward Zapletal. Moorshead Magazines Ltd., PO Box 194, Niagara Falls, NY 14304; http://www.moorshead.com. Illus., adv. Sample. *Indexed:* BRI, C37. *Aud.:* Ga.

This popular magazine, previously called *Family Chronicle,* is perfect for general public library collections. It's aimed at the genealogy beginner but includes enough substance to interest the expert researcher as well. Articles in recent issues have covered topics such as writing family histories, organizing and caring for old photos, watches and clocks as family history and heirlooms, specific family stories, and much more. Regular columns cover topics such as genealogy tourism, DNA and genealogy, advice from the pros, and more. There's something for just about every genealogical researcher here.

Specialized Periodicals

2550. ***Afro-American Historical and Genealogical Society. Journal.*** [ISSN: 0272-1937] 1980. a. Free to members. Ed(s): Paula W Matabane. Afro-American Historical and Genealogical Society, PO Box 73067, Washington, DC 20056; publications@aahgs.org; http://www.aahgs.org. Illus., index. *Indexed:* A01. *Bk. rev.:* 10 per yr. *Aud.:* Ac, Sa.

This scholarly journal is "committed to documenting and preserving the African and African American experience by publishing historical and genealogical subject matter of interest to the African American family researcher, and facilitating the dissemination of historical and genealogical resources that will assist the African American family researcher" (from the journal website www.aahgs.org). Content discusses detailed methodologies for African American ancestry research, and includes depository materials, reports of archives, and family genealogies. Primary source transcriptions, along with their data analysis, are also included. Includes brief "Book Notes." Annual indexes for most years from 1990 to 2008 and a cumulative index for 1980-1990 are available in print. Recommended for all public libraries.

2551. ***American-Canadian Genealogist.*** Formerly (until 1991): *The Genealogist.* [ISSN: 1076-3902] 1975. q. USD 50 (Individual members, USD 35). Ed(s): Pauline Cusson. American-Canadian Genealogical Society, PO Box 6478, Manchester, NH 03108-6478; editor@acgs.org; http://acgs.org/. *Bk. rev.:* Number and length vary. *Aud.:* Ga.

The *American-Canadian Genealogist* is the official quarterly journal of the American-Canadian Genealogical Society and is sent to all society members. Material focuses on Acadian, French-Canadian, and Franco-American family history and genealogy, and the editorial board encourages all members to submit articles for publication. Regular sections include letters to the editor, messages from the president and the editor, book reviews, material "From Other Publications," "Queries," "New Members," "Etoile d'Acadie," and a "Readers' Forum."

2552. ***The American Genealogist.*** Former titles (until 1937): *American Genealogist and New Haven Genealogical Magazine;* (until 1932): *New Haven Genealogical Magazine.* [ISSN: 0002-8592] 1922. q. USD 40. Ed(s): Nathaniel Lane Taylor, Joseph C Anderson, III. American Genealogist, PO Box 11, Barrington, RI 02806-0011. Illus., index. Refereed. Vol. ends: Oct. Microform: PQC. *Indexed:* A22, BRI, CBRI. *Bk. rev.:* 40 per yr. *Aud.:* Ac, Sa.

Founded in 1922, this independent scholarly journal is "dedicated to the elevation of genealogical scholarship through carefully documented analyses of genealogical problems and through short compiled genealogies" (from the journal website at americangenealogist.com). This journal focuses primarily on colonial American families and genealogical methodology. A few articles go further afield geographically and temporally to include medieval and royal articles and European origins. Includes book reviews. Tables of contents for all issues from 1932 (vol 9) to date are available at the journal's website. Appropriate for both public and academic libraries.

2553. ***Association of Professional Genealogists. Quarterly.*** Formerly (until 1991): *A P G Quarterly;* Which was formed by the merger of (19?? -1986): *A P G Green Sheet;* (19??-1986): *A P G News;* (19??-1986): *A P G Books for Professionals;* (1979-1986): *A P G Newsletter;* Which was formerly (until 1979): *Professional Genealogists News Bulletin.* [ISSN: 1056-6732] 1986. q. Free to members. Association of Professional Genealogists, PO Box 535, Wheat Ridge, CO 80034; editor@apgen.org; http://www.apgen.org. Illus., adv. Sample. Vol. ends: Dec. *Bk. rev.:* 25 per yr. *Aud.:* Ga, Sa.

Although many articles in this journal are aimed at the professional genealogist, others are of potential interest to any serious researcher. Articles of general interest include "Geographic Information Systems for Genealogists," "Evernote Image Capture," "The Julian Calendar: And Why We Need to Know About It," "What is the Value of Your Genealogy Research Collection?" and "DNA and the GPS." The journal website includes an "Article Index" from 1979 to the present. The parent site for the association (www.apgen.org) includes an index for finding a professional genealogist by name, location, research specialty, and geographic specialty. URL: www.apgen.org/publications/index.html#Quarterly

2554. ***Avotaynu: the international review of Jewish genealogy.*** [ISSN: 0882-6501] 1985. q. USD 38 in North America; USD 46 elsewhere. Ed(s): Sallyann Amdur Sack-Pikus. Avotaynu Inc., 794 Edgewood Ave, New Haven, CT 06515; info@avotaynu.com; http://www.avotaynu.com. Illus., adv. Vol. ends: Winter. *Bk. rev.:* 15 per yr. *Aud.:* Ga, Sa.

A scholarly journal devoted to Jewish genealogy, *Avotaynu* publishes 300+ pages annually to aid researchers. Methodology suggestions, queries (known as "Ask the Experts"), book reviews, and Internet help are common features. Contributing editors from 15 countries around the world regularly gather the information that appears here, and the editors maintain strong ties to officials at institutions that contain genealogical data throughout the world, including the YIVO Institute, American Jewish Archives, American Jewish Historical Society, U.S. National Archives, U.S. Library of Congress, U.S. Holocaust Memorial Museum, Leo Baeck Institute, U.S. Holocaust Museum, Yad Vashem, and Central Archives for the History of the Jewish People. The journal is complemented by an e-zine entitled *Nu? What's Nu?* There is also an online archive of all 2,900+ articles from 1985 to 2011 available as a separate subscription. An index to the first 24 volumes is available for major articles. URL: www.avotaynu.com/indexsum.htm

2555. ***Germanic Genealogy Journal.*** [ISSN: 1548-3150] q. Free to members. Ed(s): Warren Mitchell. Germanic Genealogy Society, P. O. Box 16312, St. Paul, MN 55116-0312; journal@ggsmn.org; http://www.ggsmn.org/. Illus. *Aud.:* Ga.

A quarterly journal that provides a wide range of articles of practical interest to those doing research on German ancestors. Written by Germanic Genealogy Society members. Articles include titles such as "Finding the Person Behind the

Facts," "Spotlight on Hesse [*Hessen*]," "Personal Names in German Catholic Records," and "German Marriage Laws and Customs." Individual issues are short; each issue examined contained 32 pages. Worthwhile for libraries that serve people doing research on German ancestry.

2556. ***Irish Roots: family history magazine.*** [ISSN: 0791-6329] 1992. q. EUR 25 domestic; USD 42 United States; GBP 30 United Kingdom. Ed(s): Maureen Phibbs. Irish Roots Media Ltd., Blackrock, Blessington, , Ireland; editor@irishrootsmagazine.com; http://www.irishrootsmedia.com. Illus., adv. *Bk. rev.:* Number and length vary. *Aud.:* Ga.

Irish Roots, available in print, online, and via various apps (iOS, Google, Kindle, to name a few), is a publication well suited for its intended audience: people interested in researching their Irish genealogy. Articles address a range of topics, including researching specific record types and places in Ireland and regular articles on the use of DNA for genealogy research. Short features include book reviews, a Q&A with an Irish genealogy expert, and letters to the editor. The website offers a blog featuring articles similar to those in the magazine: https://www.irishrootsmedia.com/. *Irish Roots* is an excellent magazine for libraries that serve patrons interested in genealogy, especially in communities with many Irish-Americans.

2557. ***New England Historical and Genealogical Register.*** Former titles (until 1874): *New England Historical & Genealogical Register and Antiquarian Journal;* (until 1853): *New England Historical & Genealogical Register;* (until 1847): *New Hampshire Repository.* [ISSN: 0028-4785] 1845. q. Free to members. Ed(s): Henry Hoff. New England Historic Genealogical Society, 101 Newbury St, Boston, MA 02116-3007; membership@nehgs.org; http://www.newenglandancestors.org. Illus., index, adv. Vol. ends: Oct. Microform: PQC. *Indexed:* MLA-IB. *Bk. rev.:* 50 per yr. *Aud.:* Ga, Ac.

Published quarterly by the New England Historic and Genealogical Society since 1845, the *Register* is the oldest American genealogical periodical in existence. Its primary focus has been on New England, New York State, and out-migration from New England. As of the Winter 2015 issue, however, the editorial focus changed to include content of a more national and international scope. Most articles fall into one of four categories: (1) immigrant origins with a genealogical summary, (2) problem-solving articles with a genealogical summary, (3) genealogical accounts of families, especially families for which no genealogy now exists, and (4) source material. There is an online digital archive for recent years. Earlier volumes, through 1923, are available at the Internet archive. Recommended for both academic and public libraries.

2558. ***The Scottish Genealogist.*** [ISSN: 0300-337X] 1954. q. Free to members. Ed(s): Caroline Gerard. Scottish Genealogy Society, 15 Victoria Terr, Edinburgh, EH1 2JL, United Kingdom; enquiries@scotsgenealogy.com; http://www.scotsgenealogy.com/. Illus., index. Vol. ends: Dec. *Aud.:* Ga.

Each issue of this quarterly publication from the Scottish Genealogy Society contains several articles relating to Scottish history and family history. A small number of articles are focused on methods and sources. Many articles include black-and-white photos. Articles include "Identity and Fate of Capt. John Dalzell," "Prisoners in Edinburgh Castle," and "The Franklin Expedition." Free downloadable indexes to the entire run of the journal are available at the website. Worthwhile for libraries that serve people doing research on Scottish ancestry. URL: www.scotsgenealogy.com

2559. ***Swedish American Genealogist: a quarterly journal devoted to Swedish American biography, genealogy and personal history.*** [ISSN: 0275-9314] 1981. q. Members, USD 20; Non-members, USD 30. Ed(s): Mrs. Elisabeth Thorsell. Swenson Swedish Immigration Research Center, Augustana College, 639 38th St, Rock Island, IL 61201; sag@etgenealogy.se; http://www.etgenealogy.se/sag.htm. Illus., index, adv. Vol. ends: Dec. *Aud.:* Ga.

The slender journal is subtitled "devoted to Swedish American biography, genealogy and personal history," and all these areas are covered. It provides methodology articles and primary source materials on Swedes in both the United States and Sweden. Family genealogies, ancestor tables, and queries are included.

■ GENERAL INTEREST

See also Alternatives; Canada; Europe; and News and Opinion sections.

Amber Paranick, Library of Congress, Washington, DC; ampa@loc.gov

Introduction

"General Interest" implies that the topics will appeal to a broad audience. What is collected here are magazines that cover a wide array of topics that will likely appeal to a large audience. Many of these titles have become staples in American publishing, and are some of the oldest continually published magazines available.

These magazines cover topics such as news, health, beauty, politics, culture, celebrities, arts, and travel, and there is something here for every type of reader. We know that in the current economic environment, decisions on what to keep have become more difficult, and it is our hope that this collection will make those decisions easier.

Within the pages of these publications is information that will keep us abreast of current events in the world, provide information so that we may form opinions, or bring order to our thoughts, lives, and homes. Some titles are starting points of research for students from grade school to college.

Basic Periodicals

Hs: *Smithsonian;* Ga: *The Atlantic Monthly, National Geographic, The New Yorker, Reader's Digest, TV Guide, Vanity Fair;* Ac: *The Atlantic Monthly, Harper's, The New Yorker.*

Basic Abstracts and Indexes

MAS Ultra: School Edition, Research Library (ProQuest), Readers' Guide to Periodical Literature.

2560. ***The Atlantic Monthly.*** Former titles (until 1993): *The Atlantic;* (until 1981): *The Atlantic Monthly;* (until 1971): *The Atlantic;* (until 1932): *The Atlantic Monthly;* Which incorporated (1866-1878): *The Galaxy;* (1909-1910): *Putnam's Magazine;* Which was formerly (until 1909): *Putnam's & the Reader;* (until 1908): *Putnam's Monthly;* (until 1907): *Putnam's Monthly & the Critic;* (until 1906): *The Critic;* Which incorporated (in 1905): *Literary World;* The Critic was formerly (in 1884): *Critic & Good Literature;* Which was formed by the merger of (1881-1884): *Critic;* (1880-1884): *Good Literature.* [ISSN: 1072-7825] 1857. 10x/yr. USD 34.50 combined subscription domestic print & online eds.; USD 54.50 combined subscription elsewhere print & online eds. Ed(s): Jeffrey Goldberg. Atlantic Media Company, 600 New Hampshire Ave, N W, Washington, DC 20037. Illus., index, adv. Circ: 477990. Vol. ends: Jun/Dec. *Indexed:* A01, A06, A22, AmHI, BAS, BRI, C37, C42, CBRI, F01, MASUSE, MLA-IB. *Bk. rev.:* 3-5, 1,000 words. *Aud.:* Hs, Ga, Ac.

The Atlantic Monthly has been published for over 150 years and is a regarded as an American periodical that has truly set the standard for outstanding writing throughout its long publishing history. The magazine contains book reviews, literary critiques, and articles on myriad national and international topics, such as technology, arts, food, travels, religion, politics, and science. You can access even more content through its robust web site and blog, "The Atlantic Wire," which offers the "authoritative guide to the news and ideas that matter most right now." Now with the "Atlantic eReader," you can take a digital version (containing most articles and images found in the print edition of the magazine) auto-delivered wirelessly to your reading device. Older issues from November 1995 to the present are available on the magazine's web site for free, along with notable articles from 1857 to 1995. Its premium archive (1857-present) is available via a third party for a small fee, and a selection of pre-1923 articles can be freely accessed via HathiTrust (http://catalog.hathitrust.org/Record/000597656). A digital edition has just been released for tablet readers. *The Atlantic* is truly a staple for all libraries. URL: www.theatlantic.com

2561. *AudioFile: the magazine for people who love audiobooks.* [ISSN: 1063-0244] 1992. bi-m. USD 19.95 combined subscription print & online eds. Ed(s): Jennifer M Dowell, Robin F Whitten. AudioFile, 37 Silver St, PO Box 109, Portland, ME 04112; info@audiofilemagazine.com. Illus., adv. Sample. *Indexed:* BRI. *Bk. rev.:* 150 per issue. *Aud.:* Hs, Ga, Ac.

The use of audiobooks in today's society has grown tremendously and is evident in every generation. *AudioFile,* a decade-old magazine that caters to those who love audiobooks, provides reviews of audio presentations, awards, interviews of authors and narrators, lists of new releases, and resources for product information. It is important to note that *AudioFile* does not critique the written material. There are various subscription packages available, such as a basic subscription for libraries on a tight budget. Along with a subscription, you gain access to the full web site, archive, and reference guides. *AudioFile* is highly recommended for all libraries that serve audiobooks, but especially for those libraries that have programs that serve audiobooks to the blind and physically handicapped populations. URL: http://audiofilemagazine.com

2562. *Bloomberg Businessweek.* Incorporates (1914-1940): *Annalist;* Supersedes (in 1929): *Magazine of Business.* [ISSN: 0007-7135] 1929. w. USD 70. Bloomberg Finance L.P., 731 Lexington Ave, New York, NY 10022; http://www.bloomberg.com. Illus., index, adv. Sample. Circ: 993267 Paid. *Indexed:* A22, AgeL, B01, B03, BRI, C37, C42, CBRI, Chicano, F01. *Aud.:* Ga, Ac.

Not just for the business-minded patron, library users of many types will find value in the content of *Bloomberg Businessweek.* In a recent issue, this title demonstrates that business permeates all aspects of life: from art to fashion to comedic performances, to ice cream delivered to your doorstep. A unique feature of the weekly edition is the alphabetical index to people and companies; and every page is color-coded by subject: "Global Economics," "Companies/Industries," "Politics/Policy," "Technology," "Markets/Finance," etc. URL: www.bloomberg.com/businessweek

Conde Nast Traveler. See Travel and Tourism/General section.

2563. *Consumer Reports.* Incorporates (19??-1947): *Bread & Butter;* Formerly (until 1942): *Consumers Union Reports.* [ISSN: 0010-7174] 1936. m. except s-m. Dec. USD 30. Consumers Union of the United States, Inc., 101 Truman Ave, Yonkers, NY 10703; http://www.consumersunion.org. Illus., index, adv. Vol. ends: Dec. Microform: NBI. *Indexed:* A01, A22, AgeL, Agr, B01, BRI, C37, F01, HRIS. *Aud.:* Hs, Ga, Ac.

Consumer Reports is the go-to publication for reviews on numerous products, from home appliances to health products to electronics to vehicles. The monthly magazine has been making us more informed shoppers since 1936, and its mission is "to work for a fair, just, and safe marketplace for all consumers and to empower consumers to protect themselves." Feature columns and articles include the popular "Up Front," "Special Reports," "Ask the Experts," and "Lab Tests." The magazine's "Auto" issue, published every April, is immensely popular. After you read the reviews and articles, the last page offers a humorous side of the marketplace with advertisement goofs, glitches, and gotchas submitted by readers. You can choose between a print or online subscription. A print subscription contains 13 issues (including the April "Auto" issue and *Annual Buying Guide*) for USD 29.00. *CR*'s free web site offers helpful information; however, only subscribers have full access to exclusive online features that are not available to the general public. URL: www.consumerreports.org

2564. *Daedalus.* Formerly (until 1955): *American Academy of Arts and Sciences. Proceedings.* [ISSN: 0011-5266] 1846. q. USD 219 print & online eds. Ed(s): Phyllis S Bendell. M I T Press, One Rogers St, Cambridge, MA 02142-1209; journals-cs@mit.edu; http://mitpress.mit.edu/. Illus., adv. Refereed. *Indexed:* A01, A22, AmHI, BAS, BRI, CBRI, Chicano, E01, IBSS, MLA-IB. *Aud.:* Ac.

Daedalus was founded by the American Academy of the Arts and Sciences in 1955. The quarterly journal "draws on the enormous intellectual capacity of the American Academy, whose Members are among the nation's most prominent thinkers in the arts, sciences, and the humanities, as well as the full range of professions and public life." Each of its issues addresses a theme such as judicial independence, the global nuclear future, mass incarceration, an aging society, food, health and the environment, the Internet, and race in today's society, with authoritative essays. It's clear from its nondescript cover that this magazine's main focus is on content, and the journal now includes poetry, fiction, interviews, and comments. This journal is geared toward the academic library, but it will also suit the public library's introspective reader and lifelong learner. URL: www.mitpressjournals.org/loi/daed

Discover. See Science and Technology/General section.

2565. *Entertainment Weekly.* [ISSN: 1049-0434] 1990. w. USD 20. Entertainment Weekly Inc., 135 W 50th St, 3rd Fl, New York, NY 10020. Illus., adv. Circ: 56934. *Indexed:* A01, A22, BRI, C37, CBRI, F01, MASUSE. *Bk. rev.:* Number and length vary. *Aud.:* Ga.

For information on the latest television, music, movie, book, and gaming news, look no further than the pages of *Entertainment Weekly.* Fans of all ages have been flipping through the title since it was first published 25 years ago, in February 1990. Regular columns include: "The Must List," "Sound Bites," "News & Notes," and "The Bullseye" (pop culture news that was right on target, and those that that missed the mark). Special editions are published throughout the year, including "The Photo Issue"; "The End-of-the-Year Issue"; and the Academy Awards issue. URL: www.ew.com/

2566. *Esquire.* Former titles (until 1979): *Esquire Fortnightly;* (until 1978): *Esquire.* [ISSN: 0194-9535] 1933. 8x/yr. USD 15. Hearst Magazines, 300 W 57th St, 28th Fl, New York, NY 10019; HearstMagazines@hearst.com; http://www.hearstcorp.com/magazines/. Illus., adv. Vol. ends: Dec. Microform: PQC. *Indexed:* A01, A22, BRI, C37, CBRI, F01, MLA-IB. *Aud.:* Ga, Ac.

Esquire is a refined lifestyle magazine written primarily for the male audience. Living up to its confident motto of "Man at His Best," the magazine delves into an array of topics that would interest the modern and well-informed man, such as art, current events, entertainment, food, fashion, health, politics, sports, and dating. Regular features include "The Cold Open, the e-magazine," made specifically for e-book devices; this allows readers to watch exclusive videos and photos, listen to recommended music, read book reviews, and swipe in 360 degrees around the best new cars, the best new clothes, and so much more. This title's web site boosts a selection of the magazine's feature articles and videos, along with "Politics," "Style," and "Food" blogs. Recommended for all libraries. URL: www.esquire.com

2567. *Fortune.* Incorporates: *Fortune C N E T. Technology Review;* Which was formerly (until 2001): *Fortune. Technology Guide;* (until 2000): *Fortune. Technology Buyer's Guide.* [ISSN: 0015-8259] 1930. 14x/yr. USD 29.98. Time Inc., 225 Liberty St, New York, NY 10281; information@timeinc.com; http://www.timeinc.com. Illus., adv. *Indexed:* A06, A22, ATI, AgeL, Agr, B01, BLI, BRI, C37, CBRI, Chicano, MLA-IB. *Aud.:* Ga.

Not strictly for the business-minded professional or student, *Fortune* magazine's content includes interviews of executives and offers personal finance information and covers social-interest pieces such as social media in health care, environmental issues, and hydraulic fracturing. The highly-anticipated annual April issue includes the Fortune 500 ranking. This title's digital-component features (available from the web and the tablet versions) include information on conferences and leadership opportunities, and lists the top businessperson(s) of the year, the top 100 places to work, and the world's most admired companies.

2568. *G Q (New York): look sharp, live smart.* Former titles (until 1983): *Gentlemen's Quarterly;* (until 1958): *Apparel Arts;* (until 1956): *Esquire's Apparel Arts;* (until 1950): *Apparel Arts.* [ISSN: 0016-6979] 1931. 11x/yr. USD 15 combined subscription print & online eds. Conde Nast Publications, Inc., 1 World Trade Center, New York, NY 10007; communications@condenast.com; http://www.condenast.com. Illus., adv. Microform: PQC. *Indexed:* A22, BRI. *Aud.:* Hs, Ga, Ac.

GQ's advice to its readers is to "Look Sharp, Live Smart." Also known as *Gentleman's Quarterly,* it continues to live up to the standards that it set forth in 1957 when it first began. This title primarily caters to an urban male audience and publishes special issues throughout the year, such as the annual "Style Bible." Readers can connect with the magazine via various social media channels and download the latest issue through devices that handle e-magazines. Not only does it offer readers advice on style and dating, it also provides articles on the best restaurants/bars, entertainment, news, and politics. Regular columns include: "GQ Intelligence," "The GQ Report," "Manual," and "The Style Guy." Highlights on the web site include the increasingly popular up-to-the-minute style advice, as well as must-read feature articles on topics such as stylish couples at Paris Fashion week, athletes, and top female models of the century. There are also sketch comedy videos from the magazine's annual "Comedy Issue."

2569. *Grit: rural American know-how.* Supersedes in part (in 1907): *Pennsylvania Grit;* Which was formerly (until 1887): *Sunday Grit;* (until 1884): *Grit Daily Sun and Banner.* [ISSN: 0017-4289] 1882. bi-m. USD 16.95; USD 22.95 combined subscription print & online eds. Ed(s): Caleb D Regan, Kellsey Trimble. Ogden Publications, Inc., 1503 SW 42nd St, Topeka, KS 66609; http://www.ogdenpubs.com. Illus., adv. Sample. Circ: 235000. *Indexed:* BRI. *Bk. rev.:* Number and length vary. *Aud.:* Ems, Hs, Ga.

Initially started as a newspaper in 1882, *Grit: American Life and Customs* has been publishing content that focuses on rural communities, featuring inspirational thoughts, readers' true stories, book reviews, crafts, recipes, outdoor life, and much more. This magazine is now produced in color, and its feature articles include recipes using local food; do-it-yourself projects; and gardening and farming hints. The magazine's web site contains practical advice on the household, and offers video webinars on a variety of topics such as tool and equipment reviews. User-generated content available on *Grit*'s blogs contain practical advice for the experienced and novice farmer alike. Recommended for rural and public libraries. URL: www.grit.com

2570. *Harper's.* Former titles (until 1976): *Harper's Magazine;* (until 1913): *Harper's Monthly Magazine;* (until 1900): *Harper's New Monthly Magazine;* Which incorporated (1850-1852): *International Magazine of Literature, Art, and Science;* Which was formerly (until Dec.1850): *International Miscellany of Literature, Art, and Science;* (until Oct.1850): *International Weekly Miscellany of Literature, Art, and Science.* [ISSN: 0017-789X] 1850. m. USD 23.99 combined subscription domestic print & online eds.; USD 45.99 combined subscription elsewhere print & online eds. Harpers Magazine, 666 Broadway, 11th Fl, New York, NY 10012; http://www.harpers.org. Illus., adv. Vol. ends: Jun/Dec. Microform: NBI; PMC; PQC. *Indexed:* A01, A22, BRI, C37, CBRI, F01, MASUSE, MLA-IB. *Bk. rev.:* 3-5. *Aud.:* Hs, Ga, Ac.

Harper's is the second-oldest continuously published monthly magazine in the U.S., and is the oldest general-interest monthly in America, featuring works on art, literature, and culture. It's been published since 1850 and continues to offer voices from up-and-coming writers, as well as distinguished authors. Feature articles are thought-provoking and entertaining, such as "The Magic Toilet: Providing sanitation for the world's poor." The magazine offers works of fiction by notable authors, photo essays, book reviews, crossword puzzles, and the infamous "Harper's Index"-a monthly list of ironic factoids. Along with a subscription comes access to the *Harper's* archive. Readers can opt for digital-only subscription. Readers may subscribe to the print edition of *Harper's* and receive access to the magazine's digital archive, or opt for a digital subscription only (without access to the magazine's 163 years of content). Historical articles (those published in pre-1923 issues) may be accessed through the HathiTrust web site: http://catalog.hathitrust.org/Record/000505748

2571. *Money (New York).* [ISSN: 0149-4953] 1972. 11x/yr. USD 14.95. Time Inc., 225 Liberty St, New York, NY 10281; information@timeinc.com; http://www.timeinc.com. Illus., adv. *Indexed:* A01, A22, ATI, AgeL, B01, BLI, BRI, C37, CBRI, MASUSE. *Aud.:* Ga, Ac.

One of the best magazines around for personal finance, *Money* offers us a wide range of investment and money management advice, with a mix of articles, regular columns, and interviews. The use of plain English to explain the terminology used by financial planners makes the complex issues of finance and investment easier to understand. This magazine covers all aspects of money management from retirement planning to how and where to invest, and includes features on "best places to retire" or "best colleges," and even a "small business start up guide" in "Popular Topics." All this adds to the continued popularity of this magazine. With a focus on the casual investor, this is an excellent resource for managing personal finances and is essential for public libraries. Content from the magazine can also be found on the CNN/*Money* web site, which is a service of CNN, *Money,* and *Fortune* magazine. URL: http://money.cnn.com

2572. *Mother Jones.* [ISSN: 0362-8841] 1976. bi-m. USD 12 domestic; USD 24 elsewhere; USD 18 combined subscription domestic. Ed(s): Clara Jeffery, Monika Bauerlein. Foundation for National Progress, 222 Sutter St, Ste 600, San Francisco, CA 94108. Illus., adv. Circ: 200000. Vol. ends: Dec. Microform: NBI; PQC. *Indexed:* A01, A22, BRI, C37, C42, CBRI, Chicano, MASUSE, MLA-IB, WSA. *Aud.:* Hs, Ga, Ac.

The aim of *Mother Jones* is simply stated-"Smart, Fearless Journalism"-as it covers politics, current affairs, environmental issues, health, media, and culture. An organization with both a print and online presence, *Mother Jones* delves into major topics with abandon. The progressive publication, featuring stories not found anywhere else, is a frequent winner of awards from the American Society of Magazine Editors and its regular departments include: "OutFront," "Mixed Media," and "Food + Health." Its publishing frequency is bimonthly, but its web site offers original reporting 24/7. We think it's a good addition for any library, as it will undoubtedly fill the need for an alternative open-minded perspective on the world in which we live. URL: www.motherjones.com

2573. *National Geographic.* Formerly (until 1959): *The National Geographic Magazine.* [ISSN: 0027-9358] 1888. m. USD 19 combined subscription in US & Canada print & online eds.; USD 49 combined subscription elsewhere print & online eds. Ed(s): Susan Goldberg. National Geographic Society, 1145 17th St, NW, Washington, DC 20036; http://www.nationalgeographic.com/. Illus., index, adv. Vol. ends: Jun/Dec. *Indexed:* A&ATA, A01, A22, BRI, C37, F01, MASUSE, MLA-IB. *Aud.:* Ems, Hs, Ga, Ac, Sa.

National Geographic is a magazine that provides us with a closer look at our world. Its motto reads: "inspiring people to care about our planet since 1888." Contributors have fulfilled this promise to us by providing articles on culture, animals, the environment, science, and space. You'll continually browse this title for the award-winning photographs and maps published within that truly bring the subjects to life. *National Geographic* is meant for all age groups, and the magazine's web site, blogs, and social media channels provide up-to-the-minute coverage of daily news stories, videos, user-submitted photographs, and sections on adventure, travel, and the environment. A digital subscription is also available. *National Geographic* is quite possibly one of the most well-known magazines, and is a definite must for all libraries. URL: www.nationalgeographic.com

2574. *New York Magazine.* [ISSN: 0028-7369] 1968. bi-w. 42/yr. until Mar.2014. USD 70 combined subscription domestic print & online eds.; USD 90 combined subscription elsewhere print & online eds. Ed(s): Adam Moss, Ann Clarke. New York Media Holdings, LLC., 75 Varick St, New York, NY 10013. Illus., adv. Circ: 433289 Paid. Vol. ends: Dec. Microform: NBI; PQC. *Indexed:* A01, A22, BRI, CBRI, F01, IIMP, IIPA, MASUSE, MLA-IB. *Aud.:* Ga, Ac.

New York magazine has won more national magazine awards than any other title on the market. Published since 1968 and considered the first to incorporate New Journalism, *New York* is published in New York, though its audience is not limited to New Yorkers. This biweekly title presents readers with eye-opening stories on a variety of relevant topics, all the while maintaining its purpose of providing content for all audiences. NYmag.com holds the fashion site, "The Cut," "Daily Intelligencer," "Grub Street," and "Vulture." URL: http://nymag.com/

2575. *The New Yorker.* [ISSN: 0028-792X] 1925. 47x/yr. USD 149.99 combined subscription print & online eds. Ed(s): David Remnick. Conde Nast Publications, Inc., 4 Times Sq, 6th Fl, New York, NY 10036; http://www.condenast.com. Illus., adv. Vol. ends: Dec. Microform: PQC. *Indexed:* A01, A06, A22, AgeL, BRI, C37, CBRI, Chicano, F01, IIMP, IIPA, MASUSE, MLA-IB. *Bk. rev.:* 5-7, 200-3,000 words. *Aud.:* Hs, Ga, Ac.

The New Yorker has been a premier publication since it began in 1925. Going beyond the events, reviews, and cultural life of New York City, this magazine has built up a global audience. Well known for its illustrated and topical covers, *The New Yorker* continues to provide some of the best cartoons, essays, fiction, and poetry, as well as articles from best-selling authors. Readers of this magazine are sure to find something of interest in each issue. *The New Yorker* also has an online site, with podcasts, videos, puzzles, and a complete archive of articles that are accessible to subscribers and that are also available for purchase. A must for all libraries. Now available for smartphones, tablets (iPad, Kindle Fire, Nook), and an audio edition of selected pieces from audible.com. URL: www.newyorker.com

Newsweek (Online). See News and Opinion section.

2576. ***O: The Oprah Magazine.*** [ISSN: 1531-3247] 2000. m. USD 15. Hearst Magazines, 300 W 57th St, 28th Fl, New York, NY 10019; HearstMagazines@hearst.com; http://www.hearst.com. Illus., adv. *Indexed:* BRI, C37. *Bk. rev.:* 3-5. *Aud.:* Ga.

This magazine from Oprah Winfrey touches on the topics of everyday life that appeal to women. Every issue of *O: The Oprah Magazine* has a section on entertainment, advice, style, health, food, books, and connections. In each issue, readers will find timely articles and updates on upcoming trends and products; a book section that includes book reviews on hot new releases, as well as lists of forthcoming titles; and celebrity picks. The web site ties the magazine into the rest of Oprah's media empire and includes online contests, inspirations, and videos. The new look and feel of the site allow for more user interaction, and allow those that create an online account to save favorites. A great addition for public libraries, and the web site is a nice value-add. URL: www.oprah.com/magazine

2577. ***Pacific Standard.*** Formerly (until 2012): *Miller-McCune.* [ISSN: 2165-5200] 2008. 8x/yr. The Social Justice Foundation, 801 Garden St, Ste 101, Santa Barbara, CA 93101. Illus., adv. Sample. *Indexed:* BRI. *Bk. rev.:* Number and length vary. *Aud.:* Hs, Ga, Ac.

Even though it began in 2008, *Pacific Standard* is still considered a newcomer to the world of magazines in print. Feature articles mostly fall into the political realm, yet this title includes articles on education, health, economy, culture, and science. The magazine sets out to explore academic and research-based solutions to current social issues, in areas including politics, social problems, science, and economics. Regular departments include: "In the Picture," "Subculture," "Five Studies," and "There's a Name for That." Book reviews as well as thoughtful, authoritative essays are included in every bimonthly issue. In 2015, the title was awarded a National Magazine Award in the Public Interest category, which honors magazine journalism that illuminates issues of national importance. URL: www.psmag.com/

2578. ***People (New York).*** Formerly (until 2002): *People Weekly.* [ISSN: 0093-7673] 1974. 54x/yr. USD 89.10 in US & Canada. Time Inc., 225 Liberty St, New York, NY 10281; http://www.timeinc.com. Illus. Sample. *Indexed:* A01, A22, BRI, C37, CBRI, MASUSE. *Aud.:* Ga.

Published weekly since 1974, *People* magazine offers readers of all ages a glimpse into the lives of celebrities and other notable persons. Popular culture stories are published alongside human interest stories. This highly illustrated magazine also publishes weekly movie, music, and television reviews. Regular features include: "SCOOP," "Heroes Among Us," "Stylewatch," "Star Tracks," and the weekly crossword, "Puzzler." Its web site contains celebrity news, photographs, pets, and babies. Special editions include "Style Watch" and "Most Beautiful People." Recommended for all libraries.

2579. ***Popular Mechanics.*** Former titles (until 1959): *Popular Mechanics Magazine;* Which incorporated (in 1923): *Illustrated World;* (in 1931): *Science and Invention;* (until 1913): *Popular Mechanics.* [ISSN: 0032-4558] 1902. 11x/yr. USD 12 domestic; USD 34 elsewhere. Hearst Magazines, 300 W 57th St, 28th Fl, New York, NY 10019; HearstMagazines@hearst.com; http://www.hearst.com. Illus., index, adv. Vol. ends: Dec. Microform: NBI; PQC. *Indexed:* A&ATA, A01, A22, BRI, C37, HRIS, MASUSE. *Aud.:* Hs, Ga.

An excellent source for the "do it yourself" person in all of us, *Popular Mechanics* features sections on automotive, how to (for just about anything), space, science, and technology. The "How To" section is geared to those looking to embark on "do it yourself" projects, so the articles are not cluttered with technical language, and they include photos and diagrams as guides for the reader. *Popular Mechanics*' regular features include sections on "Automotive," "Technology," "Science," and "Space," along with feature articles that touch on recent events and related technology. Since 1902, this magazine has been providing articles in science and technology. The web site features most of the articles from the current issue, as well as user communities, blogs, and videos. An iPad edition is also available. Essential for all public libraries. URL: www.popularmechanics.com

Popular Science. See Science and Technology/General section.

Prologue. See Archives and Manuscripts/General section.

2580. ***Reader's Digest (U.S. Edition).*** [ISSN: 0034-0375] 1922. 10x/yr. USD 10 combined subscription print & online eds. Reader's Digest Association, Inc, Reader's Digest Rd, Pleasantville, NY 10570; letters@rd.com. Illus., index, adv. Sample. Vol. ends: Dec. Microform: PQC. *Indexed:* A22, BRI, C37, HRIS, MASUSE, MLA-IB. *Aud.:* Ems, Hs, Ga.

Reader's Digest has been a favorite of American households since 1922. With regular offerings of amazing and inspirational stories, interviews, and puzzles and quizzes that keep our minds alert, as well as tips on maintaining our health, *Reader's Digest* has become a staple in our homes. This publication provides book excerpts to whet our appetite for upcoming new releases. Available in large-print, iPad, Kindle, B&N Nook, and Android editions. The web site has a similar feel to the magazine, but provides different material with cooking tips, recipes, photos, and games. *Reader's Digest* is essential for all public libraries. URL: www.rd.com

2581. ***Saturday Evening Post.*** Formerly (until 1839): *Atkinson's Evening Post and Philadelphia Saturday News;* Which was formed by the merger of (1836-1838): *Philadelphia Saturday News and Literary Gazette;* (1833-1839): *Atkinson's Saturday Evening Post;* Which was formerly (until 1833): *Atkinson's Saturday Evening Post and Bulletin;* Which was formed by the merger of (1827-1832): *Saturday Bulletin;* (1831-1832): *Atkinson's Saturday Evening Post;* Which was formerly (until 1831): *Saturday Evening Post;* Incorporates (1976-19??): *Country Gentleman;* Which superseded in part (1955-1956): *Farm Journal and Country Gentleman;* Which was formed by the merger of (1898-1955): *Country Gentleman;* Which was formerly (until 1898): *Cultivator & Country Gentleman;* Which was formed by the merger of (1834-1865): *Cultivator;* Which incorporated (1842-1844): *Central New-York Farmer;* (1831-1839): *Genesee Farmer;* (1853-1865): *Country Gentleman;* (1945-1955): *Farm Journal;* Which was formerly (until 1945): *Farm Journal and Farmer's Wife;* Which was formed by the merger of (1877-1939): *Farm Journal;* (1935-1939): *Farmer's Wife Magazine;* Which was formerly (until 1935): *Farmer's Wife.* [ISSN: 0048-9239] 1821. bi-m. USD 15 combined subscription print & online eds. Benjamin Franklin Literary and Medical Society, Inc., 1100 Waterway Blvd, Indianapolis, IN 46202; http://www.saturdayeveningpost.com. Illus., adv. Vol. ends: Dec. *Indexed:* A01, A22, BRI, C37, CBRI, F01, MASUSE, MLA-IB. *Aud.:* Ems, Hs, Ga.

Beginning with Benjamin Franklin's *Pennsylvania Gazette* in 1721, *The Saturday Evening Post* has been taking us through the events and cultural changes that have shaped America. We all recall the famous and endearing covers that were painted by Norman Rockwell or illustrated by J.C. Leyendecker, N.C. Wyeth, Charles Livingston Bull, or John E. Sheridan. *The Saturday Evening Post* has featured short stories and commentary by the likes of F. Scott Fitzgerald, Sinclair Lewis, and Ring Lardner, to name just a few. Early issues tackled political controversy, morality, and various commercial interests. Today the magazine provides readers with articles on art, entertainment, health, family, people, places, trends, and opinions. With an appeal to older Americans for the nostalgia it presents, the magazine also appeals to a younger generation with the fun, games, and cartoons. "The Post

Perspective" is a feature that provides a historical context to current issues and hot topics in the news or of interest today. The web site provides online versions of past articles on a variety of topics. Recommended for public libraries. URL: www.saturdayeveningpost.com

2582. *Smithsonian.* [ISSN: 0037-7333] 1970. m. USD 12 domestic; USD 38 elsewhere. Smithsonian Magazine, 420 Lexington Ave Ste 2335, New York, NY 10170; MagazinePermissions@si.edu. Illus., index, adv. Microform: PQC. *Indexed:* A01, A22, AmHI, BRI, C37, CBRI, Chicano, F01, MASUSE, MLA-IB. *Aud.:* Hs, Ga, Ac.

Putting the reader in touch with "fascinating and intriguing" aspects of history, science, innovation, the arts and culture, and travel, the *Smithsonian Magazine* is always a popular choice. Providing opportunities, through the stunning photography and articles, to travel from our favorite chair, we can explore the latest archaeological dig or travel to places we have only dreamed of visiting. Since 1970, we have enjoyed the thoughtful journalism that is as diverse as the Institute. The web site provides additional content, photos and videos of the day, games to keep our minds entertained, and the archive of past issues. This is a wonderful addition for all libraries. An iPad edition is also available. URL: www.smithsonianmag.com

2583. *T V Guide.* [ISSN: 0039-8543] 1953. bi-w. USD 20. Ed(s): Mickey O Connor. Gemstar - TV Guide International, 135 N Los Robles Ave, Pasadena, CA 91101; http://www.tvguide.com. Illus., index, adv. *Indexed:* A22, BRI. *Aud.:* Ga.

Since 1953, households have been depending on *TV Guide* to keep us informed on what's on television each night. While still providing our nightly television listings, this weekly magazine also provides us with exclusive interviews with the stars of our favorite programs, and keeps us up-to-date with the latest news and behind-the-scenes looks. *TV Guide* not only feeds our television-viewing desires, but it also feeds our mind with the weekly crossword puzzle. The web site provides the information in the weekly guide, and so much more-interviews, a guide for viewing full episodes online, and photos of our favorite stars, complete with red-carpet coverage. With 56 issues a year, this continues to be a must for public libraries. URL: www.tvguide.com

2584. *Town & Country (New York).* Former titles (until 1901): *Home Journal;* (until 1846): *Morris's National Press;* Incorporates (1901-1992): *Connoisseur.* [ISSN: 0040-9952] 1846. 11x/yr. USD 12. Hearst Magazines, 300 W 57th St, 28th Fl, New York, NY 10019; HearstMagazines@hearst.com; http://www.hearst.com. Illus., adv. Vol. ends: Dec. *Indexed:* A06, A22, BAS, BRI, C37, MASUSE, MLA-IB. *Bk. rev.:* Number and length vary. *Aud.:* Ga.

Since 1846, *Town & Country* has been "America's premier lifestyle magazine for the affluent." Known as the "authority on the meaning of modern society, and why it matters," it showcases this seductive world of exceptional people and exclusive places, as well as fashion, travel, design, beauty, health, the arts, and antiques. Over the years *Town & Country* has highlighted the achievements of some of the country's most famous people. Sections include "Style," "Beauty," "Philantropy," and "Weddings," and these are just a few of the spectacular items gracing its pages. Available in both print and digital editions. URL: www.townandcountrymag.com/

2585. *Travel & Leisure.* Former titles (until 1971): *Travel and Camera;* (until 1969): *U.S. Camera & Travel;* (until 1964): *U.S. Camera;* Which incorporated (in 19??): *Travel & Camera;* (until 1941): *U.S. Camera Magazine.* [ISSN: 0041-2007] 1971. m. USD 12. Ed(s): Nancy Novogrod, Laura Teusink. American Express Publishing Corp., 225 Liberty St, New York, NY 10281. Illus., index, adv. Sample. Vol. ends: Dec. Microform: PQC. *Indexed:* A22, BRI, H&TI. *Aud.:* Ga.

Travel magazines have reached an all-time popularity level. Though the content of *Travel & Leisure* is unique, distinguishing it from other popular travel magazines while still being accessible, it is a solid choice for public libraries and academic libraries alike. From the armchair traveler to the frequent flier, this title caters to a general audience and is recommended for all libraries. Each issue procures sound advice on the latest and greatest travel destinations and how to travel in style. URL: www.travelandleisure.com/

2586. *Us Weekly: read us, talk us, trust us.* Formerly (until 2000): *Us.* [ISSN: 1529-7497] 1977. w. USD 51.48. Ed(s): Janice Min, Michael Steele. Wenner Media, Inc., 1290 Ave of Americas, New York, NY 10104. Illus., adv. Circ: 1900000 Paid. Microform: PQC. *Indexed:* A22, BRI. *Aud.:* Ga.

Us Weekly fans have been paging through this weekly magazine since 1977 for all the latest celebrity news and interviews, gossip, and photos. In today's celebrity obsessed culture, this title is the preeminent go-to for the goings-on in Hollywood and beyond. Readers look for the regular columns included in every issue: "Red Carpet" for photos from awards shows; "Loose Talk" for quotes from stars; "The Record" for birthdays, divorces, and other news-worthy items; "Hot Pics!" for celeb style; and "Stars: They're Just Us!" for glimpses into stars' personal lives. The content is juicy from cover to cover, from the opening "Hot Hollywood" to the relentless "Fashion Police" photo gallery to round out the issue. For even more up-to-the-second celebrity news and gossip, photos, red-carpet galleries, readers can visit the magazine's dynamic web site. URL: www.usmagazine.com/

2587. *Utne Reader: understanding the next evolution.* Former titles (until 2006): *Utne;* (until Nov. 2002): *Utne Reader.* 1984. q. USD 40 combined subscription domestic print & online eds.; USD 55 combined subscription elsewhere print & online eds. Ed(s): David Schimke, Keith Goetzman. Ogden Publications, Inc., 1624 Harmon Place, Ste 330, Minneapolis, MN 55403; http://www.ogdenpubs.com. Illus., adv. Circ: 100000 Paid. *Indexed:* A01, A22, BRI, CBRI, IIMP, IIPA, MASUSE, MLA-IB. *Bk. rev.:* Number and length vary. *Aud.:* Hs, Ga, Ac.

For more than 30 years, the *Utne Reader* (now with Utne.com) has been a "[digest] of new ideas and fresh perspectives percolating in arts, culture, politics, and spirituality." *Utne* is most interested in creating a conversation about everything from the environment to the economy, from politics to pop culture. This title provides original content as well as articles gleaned from independent media to locate the most essential stories, interviews, and cultural criticism to present to readers in one handy place. The magazine groups the content in sections such as "Environment," "Mind & Body," "Politics," "Arts," "Media," "Science & Tech," and more. The *Utne Reader* offers writings from sources that do not reach a wide audience, and is a nice supplement to mainstream news magazines. The web site provides access to some of the articles from the print issue, as well as blogs. Now a quarterly publication in print. The digital edition (online) is updated monthly. URL: www.utne.com

2588. *Vanity Fair.* Formerly (until 1914): *Dress & Vanity Fair.* [ISSN: 0733-8899] 1913. m. USD 15 combined subscription print & online eds. Ed(s): Graydon Carter. Conde Nast Publications, Inc., 4 Times Sq, 6th Fl, New York, NY 10036; magpr@condenast.com; http://www.condenast.com. Illus., adv. Sample. Vol. ends: Dec. *Indexed:* A22, BRI, C37, C42, F01. *Aud.:* Ga.

Though it may appear to many as a fashion and celebrity magazine, *Vanity Fair* is so much more. This title provides news on politics, business, and technology as well as offers looks back through history at noteworthy events, all in thought-provoking and informative ways throughout its pages. This title also allows readers to keep up on what's new in literature, film, television, style, and, of course, all manner of culture. Covering current topics that impact us all, this is one publication that has managed to hold its own with more serious magazines and still keep its readers current on cultural issues. Available in print and online, it's a favorite addition to most public libraries. The web site offers exclusive content, trending news, and a nice mix of articles and photographs. A daily newsletter is available, "Vanity Fair's Cocktail Hour"-which provides subscribers with topics to discuss over drinks. This newsletter is free to all, but does require signup on the site. URL: www.vanityfair.com

2589. *The Village Voice (Online).* 1955. . Ed(s): Stephen Mooallem. Village Voice Media, Inc., 80 Maiden Lane, Ste 2105, New York, NY 10038; voice@villagevoice.com; http://www.villagevoice.com/~voice/. Adv. *Aud.:* Ga, Ac.

The Village Voice was founded in 1955 by Dan Wolf, Ed Fancher, and Norman Mailer as showcasing "free-form, high-spirited[,] and passionate journalism [within] the public discourse." This recipient of three Pulitzer prizes, the National Press Foundation Award, and the George Polk Award continues to retain its "no-holds-barred reporting and criticism." The *Voice* has earned a reputation for its groundbreaking investigations of New York City politics; and it is the authoritative source on all that New York has to offer as the premier expert on New York's cultural scene, with its coverage of local and national politics, and its opinionated arts, culture, music, dance, film, and theater reviews; its daily web dispatches; and its comprehensive entertainment listings. The web site, www.villagevoice.com, "has twice been recognized as one of the nation's premier online sites for journalistic quality and local content. The site is a past winner of both the National Press Foundation's Online Journalism Award and the Editor and Publisher Eppy Award for Best Overall [U.S.] Weekly Newspaper Online." *The Village Voice* still maintains a high readership, with over 1 million print readers and 2.5 million unique visitors online. Available in print, online, and microform. Highly recommended for public libraries. URL: www.villagevoice.com

2590. *The Wilson Quarterly (Online): surveying the world of ideas.* [ISSN: 2328-529X] 1978. q. Ed(s): Steven Lagerfeld. Woodrow Wilson International Center for Scholars, 1 Woodrow Wilson Plaza, 1300 Pennsylvania Ave, NW, Washington, DC 20004-3027; http://www.wilsoncenter.org/. Illus. *Bk. rev.:* 5-7 per quarterly issue. *Aud.:* Hs, Ga, Ac.

The Wilson Quarterly "explores our world by examining ideas, culture, news, and the real lives they affect." Within the new digital platform, you will find the writings and thinking of scholars, specialists, and others in an effort to provide analysis, diverse viewpoints, and thought-provoking human stories that help "foster a more informed and engaged conversation on the ideas that matter." The subjects covered by this magazine include politics and policy, culture, religion, science, and others that impact our everyday lives. *Wilson Quarterly* launched a new digital platform in 2014 and is now free to all. Offerings include a "Quarterly" feature that provides content from different perspectives on a single topic. The "Current" content, updated regularly, allows the reader to obtain stories as they are published, or the reader may see what is available by topic or location. *WQ* welcomes submissions in all subject areas. There are guidelines, and if you are interested in submitting content, please review the information on their "About" page. URL: www.wilsonquarterly.com/

Wired. See World Wide Web section.

■ GEOGRAPHY

See also Cartography, GIS, and Imagery; Globalization; Population Studies; and Travel and Tourism sections.

Fred Burchsted, Research Librarian, Services for Academic Programs, Widener Library, Harvard University, Cambridge, MA 02138; burchst@fas.harvard.edu

Introduction

Geographers study the surface of the earth, its physical processes and human interactions, including cultural, political, economic, historical and other aspects. Those geographers studying physical processes have long been allied to the earth sciences, those studying human interactions to the humanities and social sciences.

Recently, much interest has focused on global processes and problems, including climate and land use change, globalization, human migration, epidemics, and other matters. This trend offers an opportunity for unification in a historically disparate discipline.

The diversity within the discipline is reflected in its journal literature. In this section I try to include journals reflecting the whole range of geographical points of view, as well as providing worldwide geographical coverage. Technical aspects of geography, cartography, GIS, and so on, are treated in a separate section of this volume ("Cartography, GIS, and Imagery").

Geo-Guide (Gottingen State and University Library; http://geo-leo.de/e-zeitschriften/geographie/) offers a list of electronic journals in geography and cartography.

Since 1938, the American Geographical Society Library at the University of Wisconsin–Milwaukee listed publications received—including books, periodical articles, pamphlets, maps and atlases, and government documents—in *Current Geographical Publications* (http://guides.library.uwm.edu/c.php?g=56532). The print version ceased with the December 2003 issue. It currently exists as a list of links to tables of contents of current issues of geographical journals.

The GEOBASE database (http://www.elsevier.com/solutions/engineering-village/content#id03) covers the literature of human and physical geography, as well as ecology, oceanography, and earth science. It includes *Geographical Abstracts: Physical Geography* and *Geographical Abstracts: Human Geography*, both 1989 going forward.

Basic Periodicals

Hs: *Geographical;* Ga: *Explorers Journal, Geographical;* Ac: *American Association of Geographers. Annals, Geographical Review, Institute of British Geographers. Transactions, The Professional Geographer.*

Basic Abstracts and Indexes

GEOBASE.

2591. *Acme: an international e-journal for critical geographies.* [ISSN: 1492-9732] 2002. s-a. Free. Ed(s): Simon Springer. ACME Geography Editorial Collective, c/o University of Northern British Columbia, 3333 University Way, Prince George, BC V2N 4Z9, Canada; acmegeography@gmail.com; https://acme-journal.org. Adv. Refereed. *Indexed:* A01, IBSS. *Aud.:* Ac.

A journal of radical approaches to spatial relationships involved in inequality and social justice. Coverage is aimed at fostering social and political change. Articles approach geography from anarchist, anti-racist, environmentalist, feminist, Marxist, postcolonial, queer, and other perspectives. The articles are largely in English, but may be in French, Italian, German, or Spanish. Frequent special issues are on particular themes. The editorial board is international, with a Canadian emphasis. Of interest to any library that supports a geography department with a political or social orientation.

African Geographical Review. See Africa section.

2592. *American Association of Geographers. Annals.* Formerly (until 2016): *Association of American Geographers. Annals.* [ISSN: 2469-4452] 1911. bi-m. USD 3291 (print & online eds.)). Ed(s): Jennifer Cassidento. Routledge, 530 Walnut St, Ste 850, Philadelphia, PA 19106; enquiries@tandfonline.com; http://www.tandfonline.com. Illus., index, adv. Sample. Refereed. Vol. ends: Dec. Microform: PQC. Reprint: PSC. *Indexed:* A01, A22, Agr, BAS, BRI, C45, CBRI, E01, IBSS, MLA-IB, S25. *Bk. rev.:* 10-20, 750-2,000 words, signed. *Aud.:* Ac.

The *Annals* is often considered the leading American research journal in geography. Covering all areas of geography worldwide, it offers research articles, commentaries on published articles, book review forums, and occasional review articles and map supplements. The emphasis is on integrative and cross-disciplinary papers. The editorship/authorship is largely American, with some international editors and contributors. Important for all academic and large public libraries.

2593. *Antipode: a radical journal of geography.* [ISSN: 0066-4812] 1969. 5x/yr. GBP 860. Ed(s): Sharad Chari, Tariq Jazeel. Wiley-Blackwell Publishing Ltd., The Atrium, Southern Gate, Chichester, PO19 8QG, United Kingdom; cs-journals@wiley.com; http://onlinelibrary.wiley.com/. Illus., index, adv. Sample. Refereed. Vol. ends: Oct. Reprint: PSC. *Indexed:* A01, A22, E01, IBSS, P61, SSA. *Bk. rev.:* 3-6, 1,200-2,400 words, signed. *Aud.:* Ac.

Antipode publishes articles from a variety of radical ideological positions, offering dissenting perspectives on environmentalism, feminism, postcolonialism, postmodernism, race, urbanism, war, and other topics. Most issues include focused groups of papers. This journal is devoted to fostering social and political change through activist scholarship and free discussion. Editors and authors are American and British, with an international editorial board. *Antipode Online*, the journal's new website, offers several features, including some free content, interviews and book reviews, and links to left-wing journals and organizations. This journal is important for academic libraries that support geography and political science departments. URL: www.antipode-online.net

2594. ***Applied Geography: putting the world's human and physical resource problems in a geographical perspective.*** [ISSN: 0143-6228] 1981. m. EUR 1570. Elsevier Ltd, The Boulevard, Langford Lane, Oxford, OX5 1GB, United Kingdom; customerserviceau@elsevier.com; http://www.elsevier.com. Illus., adv. Sample. Refereed. Microform: PQC. *Indexed:* A01, A22, C45, S25. *Aud.:* Ac, Sa.

Applied Geography focuses geographical thought and methods on human problems that have a spatial component, by fostering an understanding of the underlying systems, whether human or physical. Coverage includes resource management, environmental problems, agriculture, and urban and regional planning. The target audience is planners and policymakers, as well as academics. The editorship is British, with a British/American/international editorial board. Authorship is international, with a British emphasis. Important for libraries that support academic geography departments or agencies concerned with policy and planning.

2595. ***Arab World Geographer.*** [ISSN: 1480-6800] 1998. q. USD 215 (Individuals, USD 52; USD 60 per issue). Ed(s): Ghazi-Walid Falah, Virginie Mamadouh. A W G PUBLISHING, 1215 Stonesthrow Way, Wadsworth, OH 44281; tawg@uakron.edu. Refereed. *Indexed:* C45, IBSS. *Aud.:* Ac, Sa.

Arab World Geographer publishes articles on geographical research, both theoretical and applied, on all aspects, cultural and physical, of the human environment in the Arab countries. There is an emphasis on application of research to policy and on the publication of work by Arab geographers. The editorship is American, with an international editorial board. Authorship is international. Important for academic libraries that support geography departments or Middle Eastern Area Studies programs.

2596. ***Area.*** [ISSN: 0004-0894] 1969. q. GBP 321. Ed(s): Kavita Datta, Paul Wood. Wiley-Blackwell Publishing Ltd., The Atrium, Southern Gate, Chichester, PO19 8QG, United Kingdom; cs-journals@wiley.com; http://onlinelibrary.wiley.com/. Illus., adv. Sample. Refereed. Vol. ends: Dec. Reprint: PSC. *Indexed:* A01, A22, BAS, BRI, C45, E01, IBSS, SD. *Bk. rev.:* 6-20, 1,000-2,000 words, signed. *Aud.:* Ac.

Published on behalf of the Royal Geographical Society, *Area* is a scholarly journal that features short research and discussion articles on topics of current professional interest and expressions of opinion by geographers on public questions—largely human geography, but some physical. Groups of several articles that focus on special subjects are often published. The "Observation" section features short reviews and opinion pieces on subjects of current debate. This journal aims at a free discussion of geographical ideas, results, and methodology. Authorship and editorship are British. Important for libraries that support a geography department.

2597. ***Australian Geographer.*** [ISSN: 0004-9182] 1928. q. GBP 622 (print & online eds.)). Ed(s): Chris Gibson. Routledge, Level 2, 11 Queens Rd, Melbourne, VIC 3004, Australia; books@tandf.com.au; http://www.routledge.com. Illus., index, adv. Sample. Refereed. Vol. ends: Nov. Reprint: PSC. *Indexed:* A01, A22, BAS, C45, E01, IBSS, MLA-IB, S25. *Aud.:* Ac.

Published under the auspices of the Geographical Society of New South Wales, *Australian Geographer* offers research articles on human and physical geography, focusing on environmental studies. There is a strong Australian concentration, but with articles on the broader Asia-Pacific and Antarctic regions. Occasional special issues on focused topics are published. Editorship/authorship is largely Australian. Important for academic libraries that support geography departments, and environmental or area studies programs with Australasian interests.

Cartographic Perspectives. See Cartography, GIS, and Imagery section.

Cartography and Geographic Information Science. See Cartography, GIS, and Imagery section.

2598. ***Chinese Geographical Science.*** [ISSN: 1002-0063] 1991. bi-m. EUR 1180 (print & online eds.)). Ed(s): Bojie Fu. Kexue Chubanshe, 16 Donghuang Cheng Genbei Jie, Beijing, 100717, China; http://www.sciencep.com/. Refereed. Reprint: PSC. *Indexed:* A01, A22, BRI, C45, E01. *Aud.:* Ac, Sa.

Chinese Geographical Science covers all aspects of geography with the purpose of making Chinese geographical research available worldwide. It emphasizes geographical work on China and on major world issues: population, natural resources, environmental problems, globalization, regional development, and so on. It publishes original research papers and review articles. It is sponsored by Northeast Institute of Geography and Agroecology, Chinese Academy of Sciences, and Geographical Society of China.

2599. ***Cultural Geographies: a journal of cultural geographies.*** Formerly (until 2002): *Ecumene.* [ISSN: 1474-4740] 1994. q. USD 1424 (print & online eds.)). Ed(s): Dydia DeLyser, Tim J Cresswell. Sage Publications Ltd., 1 Oliver's Yard, 55 City Rd, London, EC1Y 1SP, United Kingdom; info@sagepub.com; https://www.sagepub.com/. Illus., index, adv. Sample. Refereed. Vol. ends: Oct. Reprint: PSC. *Indexed:* A01, A22, AmHI, C45, E01, IBSS, MLA-IB, P61. *Bk. rev.:* 4-8, 700-1,300 words, signed. *Aud.:* Ac.

Drawing on contributors from a wide range of disciplines, *Cultural Geographies* explores thought on the perception, representation, and interpretation of the Earth and on "the cultural appropriation of nature, landscape, and environment." Interest in these themes comes from a variety of artistic, humanistic, environmental, and geographical communities. The section "Cultural Geographies in Practice" offers critical reflections from practitioners and academics on how civic, policy, and artistic practices relate to cultural geography. The editorship is American and British, with international editorial/advisory boards. The authorship is international, with the United States, Canada, and the United Kingdom most heavily represented. Important for libraries that support geography departments, and for environmental and cultural studies programs.

2600. ***CyberGEO: revue europeenne de geographie/European journal of geography.*** [ISSN: 1278-3366] 1996. irreg. Free. Ed(s): Christine Kosmopoulos. CyberGeo, 13 rue du Four, Paris, 75006, France. *Bk. rev.:* 10-20/year, 200-800 words, signed. *Aud.:* Ac.

This is a free online journal that publishes articles on the whole range of geography. It offers authors quick publication and immediate reader feedback. The results of reader feedback may be incorporated into or added to articles. There is an associated discussion mailing list. The website has an English version. Articles have English summaries and are in French, English, and other languages. The editorial board is European, largely French. Of interest to any library that supports a geography department, especially with theoretical or European interests.

2601. ***Dialogues in Human Geography.*** [ISSN: 2043-8206] 2011. 3x/yr. USD 586 (print & online eds.)). Ed(s): Rob Kitchin. Sage Publications Ltd., 1 Oliver's Yard, 55 City Rd, London, EC1Y 1SP, United Kingdom; info@sagepub.com; https://www.sagepub.com/. Adv. Sample. Refereed. Reprint: PSC. *Bk. rev.:* Number and length vary. *Aud.:* Ac, Sa.

The goal of *Dialogues in Human Geography* is to foster debate on the foundations of geographic thought and practice. Each issue has one or more article forums that feature an article and several responses, together with book review forums with several reviews of one book. There is an international editorial board. This title offers entry for nonspecialists (as well as for geographers) to current debates in geography. Important for any academic library.

2602. ***Diversity and Distributions: a journal of conservation biogeography.*** Formerly (until 1998): *Biodiversity Letters.* [ISSN: 1366-9516] 1993. bi-m. Ed(s): Janet Franklin. Wiley-Blackwell Publishing Ltd., The Atrium, Southern Gate, Chichester, PO19 8QG, United Kingdom; cs-journals@wiley.com; http://onlinelibrary.wiley.com. Illus., adv. Sample. Refereed. Reprint: PSC. *Indexed:* A01, A22, Agr, C45, E01. *Aud.:* Ac, Sa.

Although more closely tied to ecology, the spatial distribution of plants and animals has longstanding connections with geographical thought. *Diversity and Distributions*' particular mission is the application of biogeographical theories and methods to conservation problems. Editors are American and British; the editorial board is international. Sister journals are the *Journal of Biogeography*, which publishes articles in all areas of the field, and *Global Ecology and Biogeography* (see Ecology section), which focuses on macroecology.

Earth Interactions. See Atmospheric Sciences section.

Earth Surface Processes and Landforms. See Earth Sciences and Geology section.

2603. ***Economic Geography.*** [ISSN: 0013-0095] 1925. q. GBP 412 (print & online eds.)). Ed(s): James T Murphy. Taylor & Francis Inc., 530 Walnut St, Ste 850, Philadelphia, PA 19106; support@tandfonline.com; http://www.tandfonline.com. Illus., index, adv. Sample. Refereed. Vol. ends: Oct. Microform: PMC; PQC. Reprint: PSC. *Indexed:* A01, A22, B01, BAS, BRI, C45, CBRI, E01, EconLit, HRIS, IBSS, P61. *Bk. rev.:* 5-10, 800-1,800 words, signed. *Aud.:* Ac.

Economic Geography publishes theoretical articles and empirical papers that make a contribution to theory. Topics include geopolitics, international finance, land use, agriculture, and urban and regional development, with an emphasis on recent approaches that involve gender, environmental issues, and industrial change. The editors wish to make *EG* a focus for debate on the current diversity of theories in economic geography. The editorship and authorship are largely American/British/Commonwealth. Important for libraries that support academic geography and economics departments, or urban and regional planning programs.

2604. ***Ethics, Policy & Environment.*** Formerly (until Jan. 2011): *Ethics, Place and Environment;* Incorporates (1997-2005): *Philosophy and Geography.* [ISSN: 2155-0085] 1998. 3x/yr. GBP 502 (print & online eds.)). Ed(s): Robert C Thomas, Benjamin Hale. Routledge, 4 Park Sq, Milton Park, Abingdon, OX14 4RN, United Kingdom; subscriptions@tandf.co.uk; http://www.tandfonline.com. Illus., index. Sample. Refereed. Vol. ends: Oct. Reprint: PSC. *Indexed:* A22, E01, GardL, SSA. *Bk. rev.:* 4-8, 600-2,000 words, signed. *Aud.:* Ac.

This scholarly journal of geographical and environmental ethics is concerned with human behavior in social/cultural and physical/biological environments. Emphases are on ethical problems of geographical and environmental research, ethical implications of environmental legislation, and business ethics from a geographical/environmental perspective. Both research and review articles are published, together with sets of short communications on special topics, including debates, conference reports, commentaries on published papers, opinions, and book reviews. This publication absorbed the journal *Philosophy & Geography* in 2005. The editorial board and authors are largely American/British/Commonwealth, with some broader international representation. Important for academic libraries that support geography or philosophy departments, and for any library that supports an environmental studies program.

2605. ***European Journal of Geography.*** [ISSN: 1792-1341] 2010. 3x/yr. Free. Ed(s): Kostis C. Koutsopoulos. European Association of Geographers (EUROGEO), 3 Sint Blasiusstraat, Wardamme, 8020, Belgium; http://www.eurogeography.eu. Illus. Refereed. *Aud.:* Ac, Sa.

The *European Journal of Geography*, produced by the European Association of Geographers, is a peer-reviewed, open-access journal that publishes theoretical and empirical articles that foster research, teaching, and application of geographical work with a European dimension. It aims at a unified approach to European geographical studies. Edited in Greece, with a Europe-wide editorial board.

2606. ***Explorers Journal.*** [ISSN: 0014-5025] 1921. q. Ed(s): Angela M H Schuster. Explorers Club, 46 E 70th St, New York, NY 10021; president@explorers.org; http://www.explorers.org/. Illus., index, adv. Refereed. Vol. ends: Dec. Microform: PQC. *Indexed:* A22. *Bk. rev.:* 5-7, 100-400 words, signed. *Aud.:* Hs, Ga, Ac.

The Explorers Club, a learned society devoted to the advancement of exploration, promotes all areas of field research by publishing in its journal scholarly articles of high literary and aesthetic quality that communicate the excitement of exploration and field research. The articles are accessible to nonspecialist readers, and feature high-quality color illustrations. Also included are brief notes on new discoveries and news of exploration and explorers. Useful for academic and public libraries, and for libraries of institutions that undertake overseas field research.

2607. ***Gender, Place and Culture: a journal of feminist geography.*** [ISSN: 0966-369X] 1994. 10x/yr. GBP 1986 (print & online eds.)). Ed(s): Pamela Moss. Routledge, 4 Park Sq, Milton Park, Abingdon, OX14 4RN, United Kingdom; subscriptions@tandf.co.uk; http://www.tandfonline.com. Illus., index, adv. Sample. Refereed. Vol. ends: Dec. Reprint: PSC. *Indexed:* A01, A22, AmHI, C42, C45, E01, FemPer, IBSS, MASUSE, SSA. *Bk. rev.:* 5-12, 900-1,500 words, signed. *Aud.:* Ac.

Gender, Place and Culture provides a forum for research and debate concerning the connections of geography and gender issues. Topics include the spatial aspects of gender relations; oppression structures; gender construction and politics; and relations between gender and ethnicity, age, class, and other social categories. Articles are theoretical or empirical, but with implications for theory. The journal emphasizes the relevance of its subject area for feminism and women's studies. The "Viewpoint" feature offers commentaries on published papers, debates, and other short items. Editorship and authorship are largely American, British, and Commonwealth. Important for academic libraries that support geography departments or programs in women's or cultural studies.

2608. ***Geoforum.*** [ISSN: 0016-7185] 1970. 10x/yr. EUR 1820. Ed(s): P Carmody. Pergamon Press, The Blvd, Langford Ln, E Park, Kidlington, OX5 1GB, United Kingdom; JournalsCustomerServiceEMEA@elsevier.com; http://www.elsevier.com. Illus., adv. Sample. Refereed. Microform: PQC. *Indexed:* A22, BAS, C45, IBSS, P61, SSA. *Aud.:* Ac, Sa.

Geoforum addresses the management of the physical and social human environment by focusing on the spatial organization of economic, environmental, political, and social systems on scales from the global to the local. It emphasizes international, interdisciplinary, and integrative approaches and applications to policy. Issues generally focus on special subjects. Appropriate for libraries that support programs in urban/regional planning and environmental programs, as well as in academic geography.

2609. ***Geographical: magazine of the Royal Geographical Society.*** [ISSN: 0016-741X] 1935. m. GBP 35 domestic; GBP 69 in Europe; GBP 78 elsewhere. Ed(s): Geordie Torr. Geographical Magazine Limited, Rm 320, Q W, Great W Rd, London, TW8 0GP, United Kingdom. Illus., adv. Vol. ends: Dec. Microform: WMP. *Indexed:* A01, A22, AmHI, BAS, BRI, C37, H&TI, MASUSE. *Bk. rev.:* 3-5, 150-300 words, signed. *Aud.:* Ga.

The official magazine of the Royal Geographical Society (RGS), *Geographical* publishes colorfully illustrated, popular, but scholarly articles on field research in geography, anthropology, environmental studies, and natural history, and on subjects of geographical interest worldwide. Regular features include brief articles on climate change, photography, items from the RGS collection, interesting destinations, and more. The "I'm a Geographer" section offers interviews. The magazine carries news of the activities of the society. The editorship and authorship are largely from the United Kingdom. Important for academic and public libraries, and for libraries that support overseas field research.

2610. ***Geographical Analysis (Online): an international journal of theoretical geography.*** [ISSN: 1538-4632] 1969. q. GBP 309. Ed(s): Rachel S Franklin. Wiley-Blackwell Publishing, Inc., 350 Main St, Malden, MA 02148; cs-journals@wiley.com; http://onlinelibrary.wiley.com. Sample. Refereed. *Bk. rev.:* Occasional, 700-1,200 words, signed. *Aud.:* Ac.

GEOGRAPHY

Geographical Analysis publishes methodological articles and new applications of mathematical and statistical methods in geography, including spatial data analysis and spatial econometrics. The editorship is largely American and British; authorship is international. Appropriate for college and university libraries with programs in quantitative social science research and in geography.

2611. *The Geographical Journal.* Former titles (until 1893): *Royal Geographical Society and Monthly Record of Geography. Proceedings;* (until 1879): *Royal Geographical Society of London. Proceedings;* Royal Geographical Society of London. Proceedings incorporated (1832-1880): *Royal Geographical Society of London. Journal;* Royal Geographical Society of London. Proceedings incorporated (1874-1878): *Geographical Magazine;* Which was formerly (until 1874): *Ocean Highways;* (1870-1872): *Our Ocean Highways.* [ISSN: 0016-7398] 1857. q. GBP 294. Ed(s): Fiona Nash, Keith Richards. Wiley-Blackwell Publishing Ltd., The Atrium, Southern Gate, Chichester, PO19 8QG, United Kingdom; cs-journals@wiley.com; http://onlinelibrary.wiley.com. Illus., index, adv. Sample. Refereed. Vol. ends: Nov. Microform: PQC. Reprint: PSC. *Indexed:* A01, A22, AmHI, BAS, BRI, C45, CBRI, E01, IBSS, S25. *Bk. rev.:* 1-8, 400-600 words, signed. *Aud.:* Ga, Ac.

This journal of the Royal Geographical Society, *The Geographical Journal,* publishes articles on all aspects of geography, with an emphasis on environment and development. Book reviews, society news, meeting reports, and a substantial section on news of the profession are included. There are frequent topic-focused special issues. Editorship is British; authors are increasingly international. Important for any library that supports geography or area studies departments.

2612. *Geographical Review.* Former titles (until 1916): *American Geographical Society. Bulletin;* (until 1901): *American Geographical Society of New York. Journal;* (until 1872): *American Geographical and Statistical Society. Journal.* [ISSN: 0016-7428] 1859. q. GBP 265. Ed(s): David H Kaplan. John Wiley & Sons, Inc., 111 River St, Hoboken, NJ 07030; cs-journals@wiley.com; http://onlinelibrary.wiley.com. Illus., index, adv. Refereed. Vol. ends: Oct. Reprint: PSC. *Indexed:* A01, A22, BAS, BRI, C45, CBRI, Chicano, E01, IBSS, MLA-IB. *Bk. rev.:* 14-16, 600-2,000 words, signed. *Aud.:* Ga, Ac.

A publication of the American Geographical Society, *Geographical Review* publishes research articles and numerous book reviews. Regular features include "Geographical Record," which comprises short, sharply focused review articles; and "Geographical Field Note," which comprises short, local case studies. This journal is designed to present the results of geographical research to the interested nonprofessional as well as to academics. Authorship is largely American and Canadian. Important for most academic and large public libraries.

2613. *Geography.* Formerly (until 1927): *Geographical Teacher.* [ISSN: 0016-7487] 1901. 3x/yr. Membership, GBP 68. Geographical Association, 160 Solly St, Sheffield, S1 4BF, United Kingdom; info@geography.org.uk; http://www.geography.org.uk. Illus., index, adv. Refereed. Vol. ends: Oct. *Indexed:* A01, A22, AmHI, BAS, BRI, EIP, S25. *Bk. rev.:* 10-15, 250-500 words, signed. *Aud.:* Ac.

This is the major journal of the Geographical Association, the society devoted to the teaching of geography in Britain at the college and secondary levels. Articles present research results with classroom applications, report on ongoing changes in the Earth's human and physical geography, and discuss environmental, policy, and quality issues in geographical education. "This Changing World" features short articles on contemporary issues. A new emphasis began in 2008 on fostering communication among geographical subdisciplines. Relatively new features include "Challenging Assumptions," which is devoted to debunking popular myths, and "Spotlight," which was planned to offer in-depth reviews of educational resources. The editorship and authorship are British. Useful in any library that supports a geography department or teacher education program.

2614. *Geography and Natural Resources.* [ISSN: 1875-3728] 2007. q. EUR 918 (print & online eds.)). Ed(s): Viktor M Plyusnin. Springer, https://www.springer.com. Refereed. Reprint: PSC. *Indexed:* S25. *Aud.:* Ga, Ac.

Geography and Natural Resources emphasizes regional nature management and environmental protection; geographical forecasting; and modeling, mapping, and monitoring approaches. Coverage relates largely to Russia and Central Asia. The editorial board is largely from Russia, Ukraine, and Belarus. English translation is from the Russian version.

2615. *Geography Compass.* [ISSN: 1749-8198] 2007. m. GBP 1120. Ed(s): Michael Bradshaw. Wiley-Blackwell Publishing Ltd., The Atrium, Southern Gate, Chichester, PO19 8QG, United Kingdom; cs-journals@wiley.com; http://onlinelibrary.wiley.com/. Sample. Refereed. *Indexed:* A01, C45, S25. *Aud.:* Ac, Sa.

Geography Compass is an online-only scholarly journal that publishes review articles, or surveys, of current research. It attempts to cover the entire discipline but with emphasis on the human side of geography. The editorial board is mainly United States/United Kingdom, with some worldwide representation. Its review articles offer a broader perspective than the specialized articles in other journals, and thus this title offers useful overviews for nonspecialists. Important for any academic library.

2616. *GeoJournal: spatially integrated social sciences and humanities.* [ISSN: 0343-2521] 1977. bi-m. EUR 3837 (print & online eds.)). Ed(s): Barney Warf. Springer Netherlands, Van Godewijckstraat 30, Dordrecht, 3311 GX, Netherlands; http://www.springer.com. Illus., index, adv. Refereed. Vol. ends: No. 4. Reprint: PSC. *Indexed:* A22, BAS, BRI, C45, E01, H&TI, IBSS, S25. *Bk. rev.:* 0-8, 800-1,000 words, signed. *Aud.:* Ac, Sa.

GeoJournal applies the methods and results of human geography and allied fields to problems of social/environmental change and technological development. Applications to forecasting and planning are emphasized. There are frequent special issues with guest editors and occasional review articles. Letters to the editor discussing published articles are encouraged. The editors and authors are international. Important for libraries that support geographical/environmental research or management/planning with a spatial emphasis.

Imago Mundi. See Cartography, GIS, and Imagery section.

2617. *Indian Geographical Journal.* Formerly (until 1941): *Madras Geographical Association. Journal.* [ISSN: 0019-4824] 1926. s-a. Ed(s): S Subbiah. Indian Geographical Society, c/o Dept. of Geography, University of Madras, Chepauk, Chennai, 600 005, India. Refereed. Microform: IDC. *Indexed:* BAS. *Aud.:* Ac, Sa.

The *Indian Geographical Journal* publishes original research on all aspects of geography and related fields. Largely Indian authorship and subject matter. Articles cover both physical and human geography, and geoinformatics. Issues 2014 to the present are available open-access online.

2618. *Institute of British Geographers. Transactions.* Former titles (until 1965): *Institute of British Geographers. Transactions and Papers;* (until 1946): *Institute of British Geographers. Transactions.* [ISSN: 0020-2754] 1935. q. GBP 555. Ed(s): Adrian Bailey, Simon Naylor. Wiley-Blackwell Publishing Ltd., The Atrium, Southern Gate, Chichester, PO19 8QG, United Kingdom; cs-journals@wiley.com; http://onlinelibrary.wiley.com. Illus., index, adv. Sample. Refereed. Vol. ends: No. 4. Reprint: PSC. *Indexed:* A01, A22, BAS, C45, E01, IBSS. *Bk. rev.:* 4-6, 900-1,200 words, signed. *Aud.:* Ac.

This is the major journal of the leading British research-oriented geographical society, now joined with the Royal Geographical Society, and one of the leading geographical journals. Editorials discuss current trends in geographical research. Although general in scope, this title publishes more human than physical geography. Important for any library that supports a geography department.

2619. *International Journal of Health Geographics.* [ISSN: 1476-072X] 2002. irreg. Free. Ed(s): Maged N Kamel Boulos. BioMed Central Ltd., Fl 6, 236 Gray's Inn Rd, London, WC1X 8HB, United Kingdom; info@biomedcentral.com; https://www.biomedcentral.com. Adv. Refereed. *Indexed:* A01, C45. *Aud.:* Ac, Sa.

The *International Journal of Health Geographics* is an open-access, peer-reviewed online journal on all aspects of geospatial information systems and science applications, with an emphasis on interdisciplinary topics. Editorship is British, with an international editorial board.

2620. *Island Studies Journal.* [ISSN: 1715-2593] 2006. 2x/yr. Free. Ed(s): Adam Grydehoj. University of Prince Edward Island, Institute of Island Studies, 550 University Ave, Charlottetown, PE C1A 4P3, Canada; iis@upei.ca; http://www.upei.ca/~iis/about.htm. Sample. Refereed. *Indexed:* A01, BRI, C37. *Aud.:* Ac, Sa.

Official journal of the International Small Islands Studies Association (ISISA) and of RETI: The Network of Island Universities. Emanating from the University of Prince Edward Island, *Island Studies Journal* is devoted to the interdisciplinary and comparative study of all social/cultural/economic aspects of islands. This journal emphasizes islands as parts of broader patterns, thus focusing on island-island and island-mainland linkages. It includes a strong interest in sustainability and developing sets of best practices. The editorial board is international, with Commonwealth/U.S. emphasis. The website offers a blog on island-related news. Of interest to any library that supports a geography department, or a program in island or coastal studies.

2621. *Journal of Geography.* Formed by the merger of (1897-1902): *The Journal of School Geography (Print);* (1900-1902): *American Bureau of Geography. Bulletin (Print).* [ISSN: 0022-1341] 1902. bi-m. USD 350 (print & online eds.)). Ed(s): Jerry T. Mitchell. Taylor & Francis Inc., 711 3rd Ave, 8th Fl, New York, NY 10017; support@tandfonline.com; http://www.tandfonline.com. Illus., index, adv. Sample. Refereed. Vol. ends: Dec. Microform: PQC. Reprint: PSC. *Indexed:* A22, BAS, E01, ERIC, MLA-IB. *Bk. rev.:* 2-5, 500-600 words, signed. *Aud.:* Ac.

As the official journal of the National Council for Geographic Education, the *Journal of Geography* is concerned with geographical teaching at all levels. It offers articles on teaching methods and strategies, as well as educational policy, and contains teaching resources and news of the profession. The "Teacher's Notebook" section offers K-12 teaching strategies. Occasional special-theme sections are published. The editorship and authorship are largely American. Useful in any library that supports a geography department or teacher education program.

2622. *Journal of Historical Geography.* [ISSN: 0305-7488] 1975. q. EUR 1160. Ed(s): Andrew Sluyter, Miles Ogborn. Elsevier Ltd, 125 London Wall, London, EC2Y 5AS, United Kingdom; corporate.sales@elsevier.com; http://www.elsevier.com. Illus., index, adv. Sample. Refereed. Vol. ends: Oct. Reprint: PSC. *Indexed:* A01, A22, BAS, BRI, CBRI, Chicano, E01. *Bk. rev.:* 15-30, 500-750 words, signed. *Aud.:* Ac.

Journal of Historical Geography publishes research papers, methodological contributions, commentaries on published papers, news of the specialty, and occasional review articles. Subjects treated include reconstruction of past human environments, instances of environmental change, geographical aspects of imagination and culture in the past, and historical methodology. Applications to historic preservation are discussed. The editorship and authorship are American, British, and Commonwealth. Important for academic libraries that support geography or history departments.

2623. *Journal of Latin American Geography.* Former titles (until 2002): *Conference of Latin Americanist Geographers. Yearbook;* (until 1984): *Conference of Latin Americanist Geographers. Proceedings;* (until 197?): *Conference of Latin Americanist Geographers. Publication Series.* [ISSN: 1545-2476] 1971. 3x/yr. USD 120. Ed(s): Christopher Gaffney. University of Texas Press, Journals Division, PO Box 7819, Austin, TX 78713; journals@utpress.utexas.edu; https://utpress.utexas.edu. Illus., adv. Refereed. *Indexed:* A01, A22, BRI, E01. *Bk. rev.:* 5-6, 1,000 words, signed. *Aud.:* Ac.

This journal publishes articles on all aspects of Latin America, but largely human geography, with an emphasis on interdisciplinary approaches. The "Forum" section offers a variety of short articles, including preliminary reports of field or archival work, descriptions of field courses, and seminar or conference reports. There are occasional film reviews, as well as a regular section on website reviews. The awards section profiles recipients of several awards from the Conference of Latin Americanist Geographers.

Journal of Transport Geography. See Transportation section.

National Geographic. See General Interest section.

2624. *Physical Geography.* [ISSN: 0272-3646] 1980. bi-m. GBP 578 (print & online eds.)). Ed(s): Carol Harden. Taylor & Francis, 2, 3 & 4 Park Sq, Milton Park, Abingdon, OX14 4RN, United Kingdom; subscriptions@tandf.co.uk; https://www.tandfonline.com. Illus., index. Refereed. Vol. ends: Dec. Reprint: PSC. *Indexed:* A22, S25. *Aud.:* Ac.

Physical Geography offers research papers on geomorphology, climatology, soil science, biogeography, and related subjects. Coverage is worldwide. Review articles, as well as methodological and discussion papers, are also published. The editors and editorial board are American/Canadian. Important for academic libraries that support geography, geology, or environmental studies departments.

2625. *Polar Geography.* Former titles (until 1995): *Polar Geography and Geology;* (until 1980): *Polar Geography.* [ISSN: 1088-937X] 1977. q. GBP 384 (print & online eds.)). Ed(s): Jessica Graybill. Taylor & Francis Inc., 711 3rd Ave, 8th Fl, New York, NY 10017; support@tandfonline.com; http://www.tandfonline.com. Illus. Sample. Refereed. Reprint: PSC. *Indexed:* A22. *Bk. rev.:* Occasional, 400-600 words, signed. *Aud.:* Ac, Sa.

Polar Geography publishes scholarly research on physical and human geography of the polar regions, with some emphasis on the Russian Arctic. Particular attention is paid to contextualizing results of international research projects and to interactions of the polar regions with the global climate system. Long papers and substantial review articles are welcomed. Some translations of Russian articles and sources are published. The editorship is American, with an international editorial board; authorship is international.

2626. *Political Geography: an interdisciplinary journal for all students of political studies with an interest in the geographical and spatial aspects of politics.* Formerly (until 1992): *Political Geography Quarterly.* [ISSN: 0962-6298] 1982. bi-m. EUR 1734. Ed(s): P Steinberg. Pergamon Press, The Blvd, Langford Ln, E Park, Kidlington, OX5 1GB, United Kingdom; JournalsCustomerServiceEMEA@elsevier.com; http://www.elsevier.com. Illus., adv. Sample. Refereed. Microform: PQC. *Indexed:* A01, A22, BRI, IBSS, P61. *Bk. rev.:* 3-6, 800-1,400 words, signed. *Aud.:* Ac.

This title includes traditional, quantitative, political, economic, poststructuralist, and other approaches. Contributions from nongeographers on spatial aspects of politics are encouraged. Debates on topics of wide interest are published, as are special issues. The "Book Forum" offers multiple reviews of a major new book. The editorship and authorship are largely British and American. Important for academic libraries that support geography, political science, or international relations departments.

2627. *Population, Space and Place.* Formerly (until 2004): *International Journal of Population Geography.* [ISSN: 1544-8444] 1995. 8x/yr. Ed(s): Darren P Smith, Clara H Mulder. John Wiley & Sons Ltd., cs-journals@wiley.com; http://www.wiley.com. Illus., index, adv. Sample. Refereed. Vol. ends: Dec. Reprint: PSC. *Indexed:* BRI, C45, IBSS. *Bk. rev.:* 3-4, 800-1,500 words, signed. *Aud.:* Ac.

Population, Space and Place publishes research and review articles, book reviews, and articles on current debates. Topics covered include migration, the geography of fertility/mortality, population modeling and forecasting, environmental issues, spatial aspects of labor, housing, minority groups, and historical demography. The planning and policy implications of population research are emphasized. Articles originating in allied disciplines are published. The editorship is largely British, with an international advisory board; the authorship is international. Important for any library that supports research in geography or population studies, or in social science generally.

2628. *The Professional Geographer.* [ISSN: 0033-0124] 1949. q. USD 2735 (print & online eds.)). Ed(s): Barney Warf. Routledge, 530 Walnut St, Ste 850, Philadelphia, PA 19106; enquiries@tandfonline.com; http://www.tandfonline.com. Illus., index. Sample. Refereed. Vol. ends: Nov. Microform: PQC. Reprint: PSC. *Indexed:* A01, A22, BAS, BRI, E01, IBSS, S25. *Bk. rev.:* 4-7, 700-1,200 words, signed. *Aud.:* Ac.

A publication of the Association of American Geographers, *The Professional Geographer* publishes short research papers and essays on all aspects of geography. New approaches and alternative perspectives are emphasized. "Focus" is a section for collections of short articles on special topics. The "Commentary" section discusses issues of current interest. Important for all academic and for large public libraries.

2629. *Progress in Human Geography.* Supersedes in part (in 1977): *Progress in Geography.* [ISSN: 0309-1325] 1969. bi-m. USD 1775 (print & online eds.)). Ed(s): Noel Castree. Sage Publications Ltd., 1 Oliver's Yard, 55 City Rd, London, EC1Y 1SP, United Kingdom; info@sagepub.com; https://www.sagepub.com/. Illus., index. Sample. Refereed. Vol. ends: No. 4. Reprint: PSC. *Indexed:* A01, A22, BAS, C45, E01, IBSS, P61, SSA. *Bk. rev.:* 9-21, 700-1,600 words, signed. *Aud.:* Ac.

This journal publishes review articles on trends and developments in human geography and related work in other disciplines. The articles cover the full international literature and discuss possible applications. Editorship and authorship are largely British, Commonwealth, and American, with an international advisory board. This journal is important for academic libraries that support social science research and geography departments, as well as for large public libraries. Sage also issues a similar title, *Progress in Physical Geography* [ISSN: 0309-1333], which is important for libraries that serve geography and geology departments and environmental studies programs.

2630. *Singapore Journal of Tropical Geography (Online).* [ISSN: 1467-9493] 1953. 3x/yr. GBP 338. Ed(s): Lu Xi Xi, Tim Bunnell. Wiley-Blackwell Publishing Asia, 155 Cremorne St, Richmond, VIC 3121, Australia; melbourne@wiley.com; http://onlinelibrary.wiley.com. Illus., adv. Refereed. *Bk. rev.:* 2-6, 400-600 words, signed. *Aud.:* Ac.

Edited at the Department of Geography of the University of Singapore, this journal treats, largely, human geography and spatial aspects of development from an interdisciplinary perspective. Papers from scholars outside of geography are welcome. Authorship is international. Important for academic libraries that support geography departments or area studies programs with interests in the tropics.

Surveying and Land Information Science. See Cartography, GIS, and Imagery section.

2631. *Terrae Incognitae: the journal of the Society for the History of Discoveries.* [ISSN: 0082-2884] 1969. 3x/yr. GBP 286 (print & online eds.)). Ed(s): Lauren Beck. Routledge, 4 Park Sq, Milton Park, Abingdon, OX14 4RN, United Kingdom; subscriptions@tandf.co.uk; http://www.tandfonline.com. Illus., index. Refereed. Reprint: PSC. *Indexed:* A22. *Bk. rev.:* 15-20, 300-1,000 words, signed. *Aud.:* Ac.

This scholarly journal covers the worldwide history of discovery and exploration. It publishes research articles, book reviews, and a bibliography of current literature. Its website hosts a subject index for volumes 1-28 (1969-1996). The editorship is American, Canadian, and British; authorship is international. Important for academic libraries that support geography and history departments.

2632. *Tijdschrift voor Economische en Sociale Geografie.* [ISSN: 0040-747X] 1910. 5x/yr. GBP 458. Ed(s): Manuel B Aalbers. Wiley-Blackwell Publishing Ltd., The Atrium, Southern Gate, Chichester, PO19 8QG, United Kingdom; cs-journals@wiley.com; http://onlinelibrary.wiley.com. Illus., index, adv. Sample. Refereed. Vol. ends: No. 5. Reprint: PSC. *Indexed:* A01, A22, BRI, C45, E01, HRIS, IBSS, MLA-IB, P61. *Bk. rev.:* 2-5, 1,000-1,500 words, signed. *Aud.:* Ac.

Published under the auspices of the Royal Dutch Geographical Society, *TESG* offers scholarly articles and subject-focused issues on human geography, emphasizing new approaches that emanate from both Continental and Anglo-American traditions. Special sections discuss Dutch and European geographical trends. Each issue carries maps that illustrate Netherlands human geography. The editorship is largely Dutch; authorship is international. Important for academic libraries that support geography departments or area studies programs with interests in Western Europe.

2633. *Urban Geography.* [ISSN: 0272-3638] 1980. 8x/yr. GBP 917 (print & online eds.)). Taylor & Francis, 2 & 4 Park Sq., Milton Park, Abingdon, OX14 4RN, United Kingdom; enquiries@taylorandfrancis.com; https://www.tandfonline.com. Illus., index. Sample. Refereed. Vol. ends: No. 8. Reprint: PSC. *Indexed:* A22, BAS, BRI. *Aud.:* Ac, Sa.

Urban Geography focuses on geographical aspects of urban problems and issues, such as ethnicity, historic preservation, housing and services, and economic health and poverty. Includes original papers and review articles. There are occasional special issues on particular topics with a guest editor.

■ GERIATRICS AND GERONTOLOGICAL STUDIES

Michelle Eichelberger, Systems & Electronic Services Librarian at Genesee Community College, Batavia, NY 14020-9704; maeichelberger@genesee.edu

Introduction

Geriatrics is a specialized field of medicine that covers the aging process and the health and medical changes or disorders that affect the elderly. Gerontology is the study of aging and older people. These fields have been growing in order to meet the needs of the growing elderly population and their caregivers and support systems. Interdisciplinary in nature, these fields are addressed by many specialized journals that look at the biological, psychological, sociological, and other aspects of aging.

Many different, subject-specific databases index these journals, although *Abstracts in Social Gerontology* and *AgeLine* are the most targeted indexes for geriatrics and gerontology. Other indexes in the fields of psychology, sociology, social work, medicine, education, women's studies, and others will be useful, depending on the focus of research. The journals that have been selected for this section are only a representative subset of the many quality publications that are available in geriatrics and gerontology. Some of the journals will be of interest to the general public, but most are useful primarily to students, educators, scholars, and practitioners in geriatrics and gerontology.

Basic Periodicals

A A R P: the magazine, Ageing International, Generations, The Gerontologist, International Journal of Aging & Human Development, American Geriatrics Society. Journal, Journals of Gerontology: Series A and B.

Basic Abstracts and Indexes

Abstracts in Social Gerontology, AgeLine.

2634. *A A R P the Magazine.* Formed by the merger of (2001-2003): *My Generation;* (2002-2003): *A A R P Modern Maturity;* Which was formerly (until Mar.2002): *Modern Maturity;* Which incorporated (in 1960): *We;* (1955-1960): *Journal of Lifetime Living;* Which was formerly (1935-1955): *Journal of Living;* (1977-1986): *Dynamic Years;* Which was formerly (1965-1977): *Dynamic Maturity.* [ISSN: 1541-9894] 2003. bi-m. Free to members. Ed(s): Robert Love. American Association of Retired Persons (A A R P), 601 E St, NW, Washington, DC 20049; ageline@aarp.org; http://www.aarp.org. Adv. Sample. *Indexed:* AgeL, BRI. *Aud.:* Ga.

This lifestyle magazine is included with membership in the American Association of Retired Persons (AARP). It covers a wide range of topics from the areas of health, entertainment, personal finance, government and law, and consumer affairs, among others. Regular short columns and sections include "What to Know Now," "The Mail," "AARP & You," "Health," "Family &

Friends," "Just for Fun," "Money," "Between Us," and "Big 5-Oh." Each issue has several longer feature articles as well, with at least one profiling a famous person over 50. Some recent feature articles are "A Guide to Gratuities on the Road," "Melissa McCarthy Will Make You Laugh," "Health Guide for People 50+," and "Families Behind the Badge." Recommended for public libraries. URL: www.aarp.org/magazine/

2635. ***Activities, Adaptation & Aging.*** [ISSN: 0192-4788] 1980. q. GBP 996 (print & online eds.)). Ed(s): Linnea Couture. Routledge, 530 Walnut St, Ste 850, Philadelphia, PA 19106; enquiries@tandfonline.com; http://www.tandfonline.com. Illus. Sample. Refereed. Microform: PQC. Reprint: PSC. *Indexed:* A01, A22, ASSIA, AgeL, C45, E01, SD, SSA. *Bk. rev.:* 5-7, 1-4 pages, signed. *Aud.:* Ac, Sa.

An international journal "for activity directors and all health care professionals concerned with the enhancement of the lives of the aged." Its content includes formal and informal research on a wide variety of topics related to the therapeutic value of activities for the older adult: "such important topics as evidence-based practice, evaluation, assessment of psychosocial history, culture and its influence on meaningful activity, activities and caregivers, volunteerism, and successful aging" in institutional and community settings. Included are research findings, case studies, and program evaluations, plus book and media reviews, announcements, and news. This journal presents information and methodologies from the disciplines of physical therapy, art and music therapy, and recreational and occupational therapy; social work; nursing; psychiatry; and medicine. Recent articles are "Sudoku and Changes in Working Memory Performance for Older Adults and Younger Adults," "The Feasibility of Adopting an Evidence-Informed Tailored Exercise Program within Adult Day Services: The Enhance Mobility Program," "The Experience of Older Adults in a Walking Program at Individual, Interpersonal, and Environmental Levels," "Older Adults Recently Diagnosed with Age-Related Vision Loss: Readjusting to Everyday Life," and "Perceived Competence and Physical Activity in Older Adults." Appropriate for relevant special libraries and academic libraries that support gerontological programs. URL: www.tandfonline.com/loi/waaa20

2636. ***Age and Ageing.*** [ISSN: 0002-0729] 1972. bi-m. EUR 647. Ed(s): David J Scott. Oxford University Press, Great Clarendon St, Oxford, OX2 6DP, United Kingdom; onlinequeries.uk@oup.com; http://global.oup.com. Illus., adv. Sample. Refereed. Reprint: PSC. *Indexed:* A01, A22, ASSIA, AgeL, BRI, C45, E01, ErgAb. *Bk. rev.:* 2-3, 100-400 words, signed. *Aud.:* Ac, Sa.

Associated with the British Geriatrics Society, this international, peer-reviewed journal "includes research on human ageing and clinical, epidemiological, and psychological aspects of later life." It is written for clinicians and other health professionals. Original research articles and commissioned reviews are presented in the following sections: "Research Papers" and "Short Reports" to report original findings; "Reviews" and "Systematic Reviews"; and "Case Reports" and "Clinical Reminders." There are also "Conference Reports," "New Horizons," "Editorials," "Editor's View," "Corrigenda," and "Commentaries." A few recent articles include: "Accurate Identification of Hospital Admissions from Care Homes; Development and Validation of an Automated Algorithm" (a research Book Review), and "Letters to the Editor" (an Examples paper); "Simple Prediction Scores Predict Good and Devastating Outcomes After Stroke More Accurately Than Physicians" (a research paper); "Frailty and Physical Function in Older HIV-Infected Adults" (a short report); and "Interventions for the Prevention and Treatment of Disability Due to Acquired Joint Contractures in Older People: A Systematic Review." Appropriate for medical libraries and any other library that maintains a geriatric medicine collection. URL: ageing.oxfordjournals.org/

2637. ***Ageing and Society.*** [ISSN: 0144-686X] 1981. 12x/yr. GBP 599. Ed(s): Christina R Victor. Cambridge University Press, University Printing House, Shaftesbury Rd, Cambridge, CB2 8BS, United Kingdom; journals@cambridge.org; https://www.cambridge.org. Illus., index, adv. Sample. Refereed. Microform: PQC. Reprint: PSC. *Indexed:* A01, A22, AgeL, BRI, C45, E01, IBSS, P61, SSA. *Bk. rev.:* 4-6, 1-4 pages, signed. *Aud.:* Ac.

Associated with the Centre for Policy on Ageing and the British Society of Gerontology, this international, peer-reviewed journal has an interdisciplinary focus, and thus it "has readers from many academic social science disciplines, and from clinical medicine and the humanities." Emphasis is placed on "the understanding of human ageing and the circumstances of older people in their social and cultural contexts." The journal publishes original articles, book reviews, occasional review articles and special issues. A few examples of recent articles are "Patterns of Changing Residential Preferences During Late Adulthood," "Lost and Unfulfilled Relationships Behind Emotional Loneliness in Old Age," and "Intergenerational Support and Depression Among Chinese Older Adults: Do Gender and Widowhood Make a Difference?" Appropriate for academic libraries that support programs in sociology, global studies, or gerontology. URL: www.cambridge.org/core/journals/ageing-and-society

2638. ***Ageing International: information bulletin of the International Federation on Ageing.*** [ISSN: 0163-5158] 1973. q. EUR 410 (print & online eds.)). Ed(s): S Levkoff. Springer New York LLC, 233 Spring St, New York, NY 10013; customerservice@springer.com; http://link.springer.com. Illus., index, adv. Sample. Refereed. Vol. ends: Winter. Reprint: PSC. *Indexed:* A01, A22, AgeL, BRI, E01, ErgAb, SSA. *Aud.:* Ga, Ac, Sa.

This peer-reviewed journal focuses on improving the lives of older people regionally and globally. It specifically aims to reduce "the implementation gap between good science and effective service, between evidence-based protocol and culturally suitable programs, and between unique innovative solutions and generalizable policies." The range of subject areas is wide: housing, finances, health care, employment and retirement, technology, long-term care, death and dying, culture and aging, and elder abuse and neglect, among other topics. There are occasional special thematic issues, the most recent being "Broadening the Perspective on Long-Term Residential Care." The journal publishes long and short articles that report on original research, program reviews, review articles, and commentaries. Some recent articles are "Skills of Workers in Long-Term Residential Care: Exploring Complexities, Challenges, and Opportunities," "Engaging Nursing Home Residents in Formal Volunteer Activities: A Focus on Strengths," and "Healthy Aging in a Global Context: Comparing Six Countries." Appropriate for large public libraries, special libraries that focus on public and health policy, and academic libraries that support gerontology and public-health programs. URL: link.springer.com/journal/12126

2639. ***Ageing Research Reviews.*** [ISSN: 1568-1637] 2001. 8x/yr. EUR 1473. Ed(s): M P Mattson. Elsevier Ireland Ltd., Elsevier House, Brookvale Plz, E Park, Shannon, , Ireland; JournalsCustomerServiceemea@elsevier.com; http://www.elsevier.com/. Sample. Refereed. *Indexed:* A01, A22. *Aud.:* Ac, Sa.

This journal is written for scientists and scholars interested in the biology of aging. The journal seeks to provide "critical reviews and viewpoints on emerging findings on mechanisms of ageing and age-related disease." Articles focus on the cellular and molecular mechanism of the aging process and age-related diseases or application of research in these areas in medicine. There are special issues, the most recent being "Nutritional Interventions Modulating Aging and Age-Associated Diseases." A few recent articles are: "Prenatal Exposure to Oxidative Phosphorylation Xenobiotics and Late-Onset Parkinson Disease," "Gut Microbiota: A Player in Aging and a Target For Anti-Aging Intervention," "Does Music Therapy Enhance Behavioral and Cognitive Function in Elderly Dementia Patients? A Systematic Review and Meta-Analysis," and "Sex Differences in the Prevalence and Incidence of Mild Cognitive Impairment: A Meta-Analysis." URL: www.journals.elsevier.com/ageing-research-reviews/

2640. ***The Aging Male.*** [ISSN: 1368-5538] 1998. q. GBP 700 (print & online eds.)). Taylor & Francis, 2, 3 & 4 Park Sq, Milton Park, Abingdon, OX14 4RN, United Kingdom; subscriptions@tandf.co.uk; https://www.tandfonline.com. Illus., adv. Sample. Refereed. Reprint: PSC. *Indexed:* A01, A22, AgeL, E01, SD. *Aud.:* Ac, Sa.

The official journal of the International Society for the Study of the Aging Male, this multidisciplinary, peer-reviewed publication covers a broad range of topics related to older men's health, but tends heavily toward biomedical topics. Regular features include editorials, original research articles, review articles, and "other appropriate educational materials," as well as conference paper and poster session abstracts. Titles of a few recent articles: "Metabolic and Hormonal Responses to Different Resistance Training Systems in Elderly Men," "High-Intensity Interval Training (HIIT) Increases Insulin-Like Growth

Factor-I (IGF-I) in Sedentary Aging Men But Not Masters' Athletes: An Observational Study," "Vitamin D Treatment Improves Levels of Sexual Hormones, Metabolic Parameters and Erectile Function in Middle-Aged Vitamin D Deficient Men," and "Could Gonadal and Adrenal Androgen Deficiencies Contribute to the Depressive Symptoms in Men with Systolic Heart Failure?" Appropriate for research and medical libraries, as well as practicing health-care professionals. URL: www.tandfonline.com/loi/itam20

2641. *American Geriatrics Society. Journal.* Incorporates (1900-1952): *American Therapeutic Society. Transactions.* [ISSN: 0002-8614] 1953. m. USD 1353. Ed(s): William B Applegate. Wiley-Blackwell Publishing, Inc., 350 Main St, Malden, MA 02148; http://onlinelibrary.wiley.com. Illus., index, adv. Sample. Refereed. Vol. ends: Dec. Microform: PQC. Reprint: PSC. *Indexed:* A01, A22, AgeL, BRI, C45, E01. *Aud.:* Ac, Sa.

This international, peer-reviewed journal from the American Geriatrics Society is intended primarily for medical practitioners. Its primary goal is "to publish articles that are relevant in the broadest terms to the clinical care of older persons." It addresses a wide range of issues related to biomedical, psychological, and social aspects of aging, in addition to diseases and disorders commonly encountered. The majority of articles included are reports on original clinical investigations ("Clinical Investigations," "Brief Reports," and "Brief Methodological Reports"). Every issue also contains other types of articles, such as reviews, editorials, letters to the editor, and descriptive reports on service, programs, and models of geriatric care. Supplements appear occasionally, usually devoted to papers from conferences or "from projects or initiatives with older adults." Some recent articles: "Whether to Ask: How Valid Are Memory Complaints in Alzheimer's Disease?," "The Effect of Treatment of Anemia with Blood Transfusion on Delirium: A Systematic Review," "Cerebral Amyloid Deposition Is Associated with Gait Parameters in the Mayo Clinic Study of Aging," and "Objective Longitudinal Measures of Physical Activity and Bone Health in Older Japanese: The Nakanojo Study." This is a core journal for geriatrics and gerontology and, therefore, appropriate for medical libraries and academic libraries that support pre-med, gerontology, sociology, and/or psychology programs. URL: onlinelibrary.wiley.com/journal/15325415

2642. *The American Journal of Geriatric Psychiatry.* [ISSN: 1064-7481] 1993. m. USD 2930. Ed(s): Charles F Reynolds. Elsevier Inc., 230 Park Ave, Ste 800, New York, NY 10169; usinfo-f@elsevier.com; https://www.elsevier.com. Illus., index, adv. Sample. Refereed. Microform: PQC. *Indexed:* A22, AgeL. *Bk. rev.:* Number and length vary. *Aud.:* Ac, Sa.

From the American Association for Geriatric Psychiatry, this peer-reviewed journal covers topics such as "the diagnosis and classification of the psychiatric disorders of later life, epidemiological and biological correlates of mental health of older adults, psychopharmacology, and other somatic treatments." Published 12 times a year, the journal contains peer-reviewed articles and occasional editorials. Examples of recent articles are "A Palliative Approach to Falls in Advanced Dementia," "Older Adults with PTSD: Brief State of Research and Evidence-Based Psychotherapy Case Illustration," and "Measurement of Functional Cognition and Complex Everyday Activities in Older Adults with Mild Cognitive Impairment and Mild Dementia: Validity of the Large Allen's Cognitive Level Screen." Appropriate for academic and medical libraries. URL: www.ajgponline.org

2643. *Canadian Journal on Aging.* [ISSN: 0714-9808] 1982. q. GBP 160. Ed(s): Margaret J Penning. Cambridge University Press, University Printing House, Shaftesbury Rd, Cambridge, CB2 8BS, United Kingdom; journals@cambridge.org; https://www.cambridge.org. Illus., adv. Sample. Refereed. Vol. ends: Winter. Reprint: PSC. *Indexed:* A22, AgeL, BRI, C37, E01, ERIC, IBSS, SSA. *Bk. rev.:* Number and length vary. *Aud.:* Ac, Sa.

This international, peer-reviewed journal is associated with the Canadian Association on Gerontology. It "disseminates the latest work of researchers in the social sciences, humanities, health and biological sciences who study the older population of Canada and other countries." The journal is multidisciplinary in approach, so authors are encouraged to highlight in their articles the value of the work for professionals in other fields. Emphasis is on Canadian research, but non-Canadian authors are included, too. Regular features include "Editorials," "Articles," "Research Notes" (long and short reports on original research or theoretical papers), "Policy and Practice Notes" (clinical and policy-related articles), "Corrigendum," and "Book Reviews." Most papers are in English, with one or two in each issue in French. Some recent articles are "Going it Alone: A Scoping Review of Unbefriended Older Adults," "Long-term Evaluation of the 'Get Fit for Active Living' Program," "Aging Filipino Domestic Workers and the (In)Adequacy of Retirement Provisions in Canada," and "Job Satisfaction: Insights from Home Support Care Workers in Three Canadian Jurisdictions." Appropriate for academic libraries for which an emphasis on Canada would be of interest. URL: www.cambridge.org/core/journals/canadian-journal-on-aging-la-revue-canadienne-du-vieillissement

2644. *Clinical Gerontologist (Online).* [ISSN: 1545-2301] 1982. 6x/yr. GBP 1246. Routledge, 530 Walnut St, Ste 850, Philadelphia, PA 19106; enquiries@tandfonline.com; http://www.tandfonline.com. Refereed. *Bk. rev.:* Number and length vary. *Aud.:* Ac, Sa.

This peer-reviewed journal is associated with Psychologists in Long-Term Care, Inc., and is written for "psychologists, physicians, nurses, social workers, and counselors (family, pastoral, and vocational), and other health professionals who address the issues commonly found in later life." The journal's focus is on providing practitioners with current information that is applicable in daily assessment and management of mental disorders in the elderly. It consists of articles that report on original empirically based research, literature reviews, and case studies on a broad range of topics related to the mental health of older people. Typical topics are diversity and aging, spirituality, depression, education and the aged, changing roles and older people, and caregiving. Additional regular features are "Clinical Comments" (brief clinical reports from practitioners), "New and Emerging Professionals" (articles by students, postdoctoral fellows, or new faculty), and reviews of books, media, or software, as well as special issues. An example of a recent special issue is "Cultural Aspects of Dementia." Recent articles include "Helping Hispanic Dementia Caregivers Cope with Stress Using Technology-based Resources," "Psychometric Evaluation of the Saving Inventory-Revised in Older Adults," and "Understanding the Progression from Physical Illness to Suicidal Behavior: A Case Study Based on a Newly Developed Conceptual Model." Appropriate for medical and academic libraries. URL: www.tandfonline.com/loi/wcli20

2645. *Educational Gerontology: an international journal.* [ISSN: 0360-1277] 1976. m. GBP 884 (print & online eds.)). Ed(s): Nieli Langer. Routledge, 530 Walnut St, Ste 850, Philadelphia, PA 19106; enquiries@tandfonline.com; http://www.tandfonline.com. Sample. Refereed. Microform: PQC. Reprint: PSC. *Indexed:* A01, A22, AgeL, E01, ERIC, MLA-IB. *Bk. rev.:* 0-1, 1-2 pages, signed. *Aud.:* Ac, Sa.

Written for "gerontologists, adult educators, behavioral and social scientists, and geriatricians," this international, peer-reviewed journal covers topics in "gerontology, adult education, and the social and behavioral sciences." Specifically, it focuses not on the education of professionals who will work with older people, but on education and the learning process of older people, broadly understood. It publishes reports on current original research, review articles, and reviews of books and other media. Several recent articles are "Participation in an Intergenerational Service Learning Course and Implicit Biases," "Attitudes, Perceptions, and Aging Knowledge of Future Law Enforcement and Recreation Majors," "Gerontological Training Programs Offered by Latin American Universities: Number, Characteristics, and Disciplinary Contents," and "Barriers to Older People's Participation in Local Governance: The Impact of Diversity." Appropriate for academic libraries that support education or gerontology programs. URL: www.tandfonline.com/loi/uedg20

2646. *Generations (San Francisco).* [ISSN: 0738-7806] 1976. q. USD 138 (print & online eds.) Individuals, USD 75). American Society on Aging, 575 Market St, Ste 2100, San Francisco, CA 94105; info@asaging.org; http://www.asaging.org. Illus., adv. Sample. Refereed. Microform: PQC. Reprint: PSC. *Indexed:* A01, A22, AgeL, BRI, CBRI, MLA-IB, SSA. *Aud.:* Ga, Ac, Sa.

This journal from the American Society on Aging is written for "practitioners and researchers in the field of aging" and is devoted to "in-depth research, practical applications, and valuable insights" in subject areas related to aging and public health. Each issue has a prominent scholar as guest editor and focuses on a particular theme; for example: "Gender and Age: A Focus on Women" and "Generation X: From Fiction to Fact, and Still a Mystery." Most articles are literature reviews, overviews of a particular topic, or argumentative papers, not reports on original research. Some recent articles are "Women and the Crisis of Care in the United States," "Aid in Dying: A Consideration of Two Perspectives," and "Hope for Persons with Dementia: Why Comfort Matters." Recommended for academic libraries and public or special libraries that serve professionals, policy makers, or members of the public concerned with aging and public health. URL: asaging.org/generations-journal-american-society-aging

2647. ***The Gerontologist: a journal of the Gerontological Society of America.*** [ISSN: 0016-9013] 1961. bi-m. EUR 558. Ed(s): Rachel Pruchno, Megan McCutcheon. Oxford University Press, 2001 Evans Rd, Cary, NC 27513; orders.us@oup.com; https://global.oup.com. Illus., index, adv. Sample. Refereed. Microform: PQC. Reprint: PSC. *Indexed:* A01, A22, AgeL, BRI, Chicano, ERIC, MLA-IB, SSA. *Bk. rev.:* 2, 2-6 pages, signed. *Aud.:* Ac, Sa.

From the Gerontological Society of America, this peer-reviewed journal presents a "multidisciplinary perspective on human aging through the publication of research and analysis in gerontology, including social policy, program development, and service delivery." There are articles from a wide range of disciplines, such as social sciences, biomedical fields, the humanities, economics, education, and the law. Each issue contains 10 to 14 articles of several types: "Research Articles," "The Forum" (review or viewpoint articles on a hot topic), "Practice Concepts" (on innovative practices or programs), "Policy Studies," "Letters to the Editor," "Book Reviews," "On Film and Digital Media," and "Guest Editorials." It does occasionally have special thematic issues or supplements; for instance, "Aging in Context." Examples of recent articles are "Rationales for Anti-aging Activities in Middle Age: Aging, Health, or Appearance?," "Prior Military Service, Identity Stigma, and Mental Health Among Transgender Older Adults," and "Who Knew? Hospice Is a Business. What that Means for All of Us." A core journal for any library that covers geriatrics or gerontology. URL: academic.oup.com/gerontologist

2648. ***Gerontology: international journal of experimental, clinical, behavioral, regenerative and technical gerontology.*** Formed by the 1976 merger of: *Gerontologia; Gerontologia Clinica.* [ISSN: 0304-324X] 1957. bi-m. CHF 2191. Ed(s): George Wick. S. Karger AG, Allschwilerstr 10, Basel, 4055, Switzerland; karger@karger.com; https://www.karger.com. Index, adv. Refereed. *Indexed:* A01, A22, C45, E01. *Bk. rev.:* 0-1, 1 page. *Aud.:* Ac, Sa.

From the International Association of Gerontology and Geriatrics, this peer-reviewed journal draws "topical contributions from diverse medical, biological, behavioural and technological disciplines" regarding aging in humans and animals. The main body of the journal is divided into several sections: usually "Clinical Section," "Experimental Section," "Behavioural Science Section," and "Regenerative and Technological Section." Within those sections are original papers, short review papers, commentary, opposing-viewpoints papers, and "Short Communication" (brief reports on research). Most articles are reports on original studies, secondary data analyses, or literature reviews. Other regular features are editorials, letters to the editor, book reviews, "Images in Gerontology," and "Announcements." Titles of recent articles include "Predicting Trajectories of Functional Decline in 60- to 70-Year-Old People," "Prevalence of Impaired Kidney Function in the German Elderly: Results from the Berlin Aging Study II (BASE-II)" (original papers), "The Potential of sGC Modulators for the Treatment of Age-Related Fibrosis: A Mini-Review," and "Fragile and Enduring Positive Affect: Implications for Adaptive Aging" (viewpoint). Suitable for research and medical libraries. URL: www.karger.com/Journal/Home/224091

2649. ***Gerontology & Geriatrics Education: the official journal of the Association for Gerontology in Higher Education.*** [ISSN: 0270-1960] 1980. q. GBP 1035 (print & online eds.)). Ed(s): Judith L Howe, Kelly Niles-Yokum. Routledge, 530 Walnut St, Ste 850, Philadelphia, PA 19106; enquiries@tandfonline.com; http://www.tandfonline.com. Illus., index. Sample. Refereed. Reprint: PSC. *Indexed:* A01, A22, AgeL, E01, ERIC, MLA-IB, SSA. *Aud.:* Ac, Sa.

This peer-reviewed journal is from the Association for Gerontology in Higher Education, the educational unit of the Gerontological Society of America. Specifically, it is concerned with the education of gerontologists and other professionals who will work with older people. Its intended audience consists of faculty, students, practitioners, administrators, and policy makers. Included are review articles, articles reporting on original research, editorials, and reports on programs, through which it fosters "the exchange of information related to research, curriculum development, course and program evaluation, classroom and practice innovation, and other topics with educational implications for gerontology and geriatrics." The journal occasionally releases a special issue, such as "Educating a New Generation of Professionals in Aging Worldwide." Some recent articles are "Lessons Learned from Narrative Feedback of Students on a Geriatric Training Program," "The Growth of Gerontology and Geriatrics in Mexico: Past, Present, and Future," "Students Explore Supportive Transportation Needs of Older Adults," and "Empathy in Dentistry: How Attitudes and Interaction with Older Adults Make a Difference." Valuable for research and academic libraries that support academic programs in education, social work, or gerontology. URL: www.tandfonline.com/loi/wgge20

2650. ***iAdvance Senior Care.*** Former titles (until 2016): *Long-Term Living;* (until 2008): *Nursing Homes;* (until 1991): *Nursing Homes and Senior Citizen Care;* (until 1986): *Nursing Homes.* 1950. m. Free to qualified personnel. Ed(s): Pamela Tabar. Vendome Group, LLC, 6 E 32nd St, 8th Fl, New York, NY 10016; info@vendomegrp.com; http://www.vendomegrp.com. Illus., adv. Microform: PQC. *Indexed:* A01, A22, AgeL, B01, BRI, C42. *Aud.:* Sa.

This monthly trade journal is designated specifically for the continuing care professional: "owners, executives, administrators, and directors." The journal seeks to publish articles from long-term managers and supervisors on a wide range of topics related to long-term care - for example, Medicare, new products, law, finance, staffing and training, and innovations in service. It presents five to eight feature articles per issue, plus several brief, timely informational articles, and opinion pieces, organized under regular headings, such as "Field Studies," "Community," "Tech Notes," "Exemplars in LTC," and "Care Management." Some recent articles are "Tech-driven Care Transitions," "10 Ways to Reduce UTIs," "The ACA and Medicaid," and "LTC Care Quality: The Medical Directors' View." Appropriate for libraries that serve long-term care professionals and others concerned with the well-being of people in long-term care facilities. URL: www.iadvanceseniorcare.com/

2651. ***International Journal of Ageing and Later Life.*** [ISSN: 1652-8670] 2006. s-a. Free. Ed(s): Lars Anderson. Linkoeping University Electronic Press, Linkoeping Universitet, Linkoeping, 58183, Sweden; ep@ep.liu.se; http://www.ep.liu.se. Refereed. *Indexed:* SSA. *Bk. rev.:* Number and length vary. *Aud.:* Ac, Sa.

This open-access electronic journal is published with the support of the Swedish Council for Working Life and Social Research. Articles go through a double-blind review process before publication. The journal is intended for an international audience and is focused on "social and cultural aspects of ageing and later life development." It publishes primarily lengthy articles that "aim at advancing the theoretical and conceptual debate on research," but it also prints empirically or methodologically based articles, editorials, and book reviews. There are usually three or four articles and one to three book reviews per issue. A few recent article titles are "Educational Needs of Japan's Dementia Care Workforce: Results of a National Online Survey," "Comparative Analysis of National and Regional Models of the Silver Economy in the European Union," and "'Equally Mixed': Artistic Representations of Old Love." Suitable for relevant special libraries and academic libraries. URL: www.ep.liu.se/ej/ijal

2652. ***The International Journal of Aging & Human Development.*** Formerly (until 1973): *Aging and Human Development.* [ISSN: 0091-4150] 1970. 8x/yr. USD 1008 (print & online eds.)). Ed(s): Julie Hicks Patrick. Sage Publications, Inc., 2455 Teller Rd, Thousand Oaks, CA 91320; info@sagepub.com; http://www.sagepub.com. Illus., index. Sample. Refereed. Reprint: PSC. *Indexed:* A01, A22, AgeL, BAS, BRI, Chicano, ERIC, MLA-IB, SSA. *Aud.:* Ac, Sa.

This peer-reviewed journal emphasizes "psychological and social studies of aging and the aged"; however, its scope is quite broad. The journal also publishes "research that introduces observations from other fields that illuminate the 'human' side of gerontology, or utilizes gerontological observations to illuminate [issues] in other fields." Each issue contains four to six articles, mostly original research, but occasionally secondary analysis or review articles. Examples of recent articles are "Depression, Poverty, and Abuse

Experience in Suicide Ideation Among Older Koreans," "Older Women in New Romantic Relationships," "The Representation of Older People in East Asian Television Advertisements," and "Financial Care for Older Adults with Dementia." This journal is a core journal for academic libraries that support programs in gerontology, psychology, social work, or sociology. URL: journals.sagepub.com/home/ahd

2653. *Journal of Aging and Health: an interdisciplinary research forum.* [ISSN: 0898-2643] 1989. 8x/yr. USD 1315 (print & online eds.)). Ed(s): Kyriakos S Markides. Sage Publications, Inc., 2455 Teller Rd, Thousand Oaks, CA 91320; info@sagepub.com; http://www.sagepub.com. Illus., index, adv. Refereed. Reprint: PSC. *Indexed:* A01, A22, AgeL, C45, E01, SSA. *Aud.:* Ac, Sa.

This international, peer-reviewed journal "explores the complex and dynamic relationship between gerontology and health." For example, diet and nutrition, long-term care, mental health, disease prevention, and health-care services. These topics are examined from the perspective of various disciplines: psychology, medicine, sociology, demography, and social work, to name just a few. Most of the eight or nine articles per issue report on original research (based on newly conducted research or secondary data analysis), but occasional review or methodological articles appear, as well. Recent articles include "Retirement, Leisure Activity Engagement, and Cognition Among Older Adults in the United States," "Mood Disorders in Middle-Aged and Older Veterans With Multimorbidity," and "Factors Associated with Injurious Falls in Residential Care Facilities." This journal provides broad coverage of gerontology and is appropriate for all academic libraries. URL: journals.sagepub.com/home/jah

2654. *Journal of Aging and Physical Activity.* [ISSN: 1063-8652] 1993. bi-m. USD 798. Ed(s): Philip D Chilibeck. Human Kinetics, Inc., PO Box 5076, Champaign, IL 61825; info@hkusa.com; http://journals.humankinetics.com. Illus., adv. Refereed. Vol. ends: Oct. Reprint: PSC. *Indexed:* A22, AgeL, ErgAb, SD. *Aud.:* Ac, Sa.

From the International Coalition for Aging and Physical Activity, this peer-reviewed journal focuses on the relationship between physical activity and the well-being of older people. The focus of the journal is on "articles that can contribute to an understanding of (a) the impact of physical activity on physiological, psychological, and social aspects of older adults and (b) the effect of advancing age or the aging process on physical activity among older adults." The journal has a multidisciplinary approach, presenting "articles from the biological, behavioral, and social sciences, as well as from fields such as medicine, clinical psychology, physical and recreational therapy, health, physical education, and recreation." The vast majority of articles are reports on original research, but occasionally a scholarly review, a case study, or a letter to the editor appears. There are 5 to 12 articles per issue, and supplements and special issues are published intermittently. Recent articles include "Routine Yoga Practice Impacts Whole Body Protein Utilization in Healthy Women," "Social Cognitive Determinants of Physical Activity in Czech Older Adults," "Exercise Test Performance Reveals Evidence of the Cardiorespiratory Fitness Hypothesis," and "Walking Up to One Hour Per Week Maintains Mobility as Older Women Age: Findings from an Australian Longitudinal Study." Appropriate for research libraries, medical libraries, and academic libraries that support programs in physical therapy or physical education. URL: journals.humankinetics.com/journal/japa

2655. *Journal of Aging & Social Policy: a journal devoted to aging & social policy.* [ISSN: 0895-9420] 1989. q. GBP 1026 (print & online eds.)). Ed(s): Robert P Geary, Francis G Caro. Routledge, 530 Walnut St, Ste 850, Philadelphia, PA 19106; enquiries@tandfonline.com; http://www.tandfonline.com. Illus. Sample. Refereed. Microform: PQC. Reprint: PSC. *Indexed:* A01, A22, AgeL, BRI, E01, P61, SSA. *Bk. rev.:* 0-1, 4-6 pages, signed. *Aud.:* Ac, Sa.

This international, peer-reviewed journal is intended for "educators, practitioners, researchers, and administrators, and other readers who work with or are concerned about elders." The journal "examines and analyzes critical phenomena that affect aging and development and implementation of programs for elders from a global perspective." Each issue's five to eight articles cover social policy around the world at all levels of government. It is interdisciplinary in nature and covers a wide variety of policy issues that affect older people, such as housing, retirement, health care, and transportation. Examples of recent articles are "Primary Care Providers' Perspectives on Screening Older Adult Patients for Food Insecurity," "Working Beyond the Traditional Retirement Age: The Influence of Health on Australia's Older Workers," and "The Human Right to Leisure in Old Age: Reinforcement of the Rights of an Aging Population." A core journal for libraries with collections in gerontology, public policy, social work, or sociology. URL: www.tandfonline.com/loi/wasp20

2656. *Journal of Aging Studies.* [ISSN: 0890-4065] 1987. q. EUR 917. Ed(s): J Gubrium. Pergamon Press, The Blvd, Langford Ln, E Park, Kidlington, OX5 1GB, United Kingdom; JournalsCustomerServiceEMEA@elsevier.com; http://www.elsevier.com. Adv. Sample. Refereed. Microform: PQC. Reprint: PSC. *Indexed:* A01, A22, AgeL, MLA-IB, SSA. *Bk. rev.:* Number and length vary. *Aud.:* Ga, Ac, Sa.

This multidisciplinary, peer-reviewed journal covers the subject of aging broadly. "Articles need not deal with the field of aging as a whole, but with any defensibly relevant topic pertinent to the aging experience and related to the broad concerns and subject matter of the social and behavioral sciences and the humanities." Emphasis is on innovation and critique "regardless of theoretical or methodological orientation or academic discipline." The types and number (10-15) of articles vary, but they include empirical, theoretical, and critical analyses, as well as book reviews. There are occasional special sections, such as "Innovative Approaches to International Comparisons." Some recent articles are "A Comparison of Stepgrandchildren's Perceptions of Long-Term and Later-Life Stepgrandparents" and "Sex After 60? You've Got to be Joking! Senior Sexuality in Comedy Film." This journal provides broad coverage of aging and is a core title for all libraries that collect in gerontology, sociology, or psychology. URL: www.journals.elsevier.com/journal-of-aging-studies/

2657. *Journal of Applied Gerontology.* [ISSN: 0733-4648] 1982. 5x/yr. USD 2231 (print & online eds.)). Ed(s): Joseph E Gaugler. Sage Publications, Inc., 2455 Teller Rd, Thousand Oaks, CA 91320; info@sagepub.com; http://www.sagepub.com. Illus., index, adv. Refereed. Vol. ends: Dec. Reprint: PSC. *Indexed:* A22, AgeL, BRI, E01, SSA. *Aud.:* Ac, Sa.

This international, peer-reviewed journal is published in association with the Southern Gerontological Society and features articles "whose findings, conclusions, or suggestions have clear and sometimes immediate applicability to the problems encountered by older persons as well as articles that inform research and the development of interventions." All disciplines of gerontological research, policy, and practice are treated, such as caregiving, physical activity, housing, mental health, ethnicity, and retirement. The concept of applicability is interpreted broadly to include useful information on practice, methodology, theory, and policy. Each issue consists of four to eight articles, almost all reports on original research. The journal does print "Brief Reports" and the occasional editorial. Recent articles include "Relevance of Perpetrator Identity to Reporting Elder Financial and Emotional Mistreatment," "Program Components and Outcomes of Individuals With Dementia: Results From the Replication of an Evidence-Based Program," and "Translating Strong for Life into the Community Care Program: Lessons Learned." Suitable for academic and medical libraries. URL: journals.sagepub.com/home/jag

2658. *Journal of Cross-Cultural Gerontology.* [ISSN: 0169-3816] 1986. q. EUR 798 (print & online eds.)). Ed(s): Margaret A Perkinson. Springer New York LLC, 233 Spring St, New York, NY 10013; customerservice@springer.com; http://www.springer.com. Illus., index, adv. Sample. Refereed. Microform: PQC. Reprint: PSC. *Indexed:* A01, A22, AgeL, BRI, E01, IBSS, SSA. *Aud.:* Ac, Sa.

This international, peer-reviewed journal provides a venue for analysis of the aging process and problems of aging from a global, interdisciplinary perspective. Emphasis is placed on "research findings, theoretical issues, and applied approaches and provides a comparative orientation to the study of aging in cultural contexts." Contributions come from a wide variety of disciplines, such as history, anthropology, sociology, political science, psychology, demography, and health. Each issue of the journal is composed of five or six lengthy research articles, but it may also contain brief reports or editorials. Some recent articles are "Validation of a Social Networks and Support Measurement Tool for Use in International Aging Research: The International

Mobility in Aging Study," "Validation of a Chinese Version of the Geriatric Anxiety Scale Among Community-Dwelling Older Adults in Mainland China," and "Rearing Generations: Lakota Grandparents' Commitment to Family and Community." This is a core title for research and academic libraries with collections in geriatrics and gerontology, and it is also appropriate for libraries that support sociology or global studies curricula. URL: link.springer.com/journal/10823

2659. *Journal of Elder Abuse & Neglect.* [ISSN: 0894-6566] 1988. 5x/yr. GBP 1077 (print & online eds.)). Ed(s): Karen Stein. Routledge, 530 Walnut St, Ste 850, Philadelphia, PA 19106; enquiries@tandfonline.com; http://www.tandfonline.com. Illus., adv. Sample. Refereed. Microform: PQC. Reprint: PSC. *Indexed:* A01, A22, AgeL, BRI, C45, CJPI, E01, N13, SSA. *Bk. rev.:* Number and length vary. *Aud.:* Ac, Sa.

A peer-reviewed journal that "explores the advances in research, policy and practice, and clinical and ethical issues surrounding the abuse and neglect of older people" from an interdisciplinary and international perspective. It is written for an audience of "professionals in social work, nursing, medicine, law, gerontology, adult protective services, criminal justice, sociology, psychology, domestic violence, counseling, ethics, public policy, aging network, research, practitioner, educator, student, and policymakers." The articles published are primarily reports on original research or literature reviews, but may also analyze specific conceptual models and programs related to clinical practice, international issues, public policy, or education and training. Issues may contain book reviews. Specific topics vary widely. Articles may address tools and programs for evaluating, treating, or preventing abuse of older people. Some issues are devoted to a special topic - for example, "Polyvictimization." Examples of recent articles are "The Mistreatment of Older Canadians: Findings from the 2015 National Prevalence Study," "Mortality Among Elder Abuse Victims in Rural Malaysia: A Two-Year Population-Based Descriptive Study," and "Elder Mistreatment Predicts Later Physical and Psychological Health: Results from a National Longitudinal Study." Appropriate for academic, medical, and law libraries. URL: www.tandfonline.com/loi/wean20

2660. *Journal of Geriatric Psychiatry and Neurology.* Formerly (until 1988): *Topics in Geriatrics.* [ISSN: 0891-9887] 1982. q. USD 1166 (print & online eds.)). Ed(s): Alan M Mellow. Sage Publications, Inc., 2455 Teller Rd, Thousand Oaks, CA 91320; info@sagepub.com; http://www.sagepub.com/. Illus., adv. Sample. Refereed. Reprint: PSC. *Indexed:* A01, A22, C37, E01. *Aud.:* Ac, Sa.

This peer-reviewed journal is written for clinicians who care for the elderly and researchers in neurology and/or psychiatry. The journal "brings together original research, clinical reviews, and timely case reports on neuropsychiatric care of aging patients, including age-related biologic, neurologic, and psychiatric illness; psychosocial problems; forensic issues; and family care." Examples of specific topics covered are Alzheimer's disease and other forms of dementia, depression, addiction, sleep disorders, bereavement, evaluative methods, drug therapies, genetics, neuroimaging, caregivers, economics of neuropsychiatric care, and ethics. A typical issue contains seven to nine reports of original research, clinical reviews, case reports, and/or editorials. The approach to topics covered is broad and practical: emphasis is on presenting information from a wide range of the allied sciences that will be useful to the clinician in daily practice. Some recent articles are "Color Vision Impairment Differentiates Alzheimer Dementia from Dementia with Lewy Bodies," "Pharmacological Management of Psychiatric Symptoms in Frontotemporal Dementia: A Systematic Review," and "Diagnostic Accuracy and Confidence in the Clinical Detection of Cognitive Impairment in Early-Stage Parkinson Disease." Appropriate for medical and academic libraries. URL: journals.sagepub.com/home/jgp

2661. *Journal of Gerontological Nursing: for nursing care of older adults.* [ISSN: 0098-9134] 1975. m. USD 379 (Individuals, USD 107). Ed(s): Donna M Fink. Slack, Inc., 6900 Grove Rd, Thorofare, NJ 08086; editor@slackinc.com; http://www.slackinc.com. Illus., index. Sample. Refereed. Vol. ends: Dec. *Indexed:* A22, AgeL, BRI. *Aud.:* Ac, Sa.

This journal is written for gerontological nurses, but is also of interest to researchers and educators in gerontological nursing. Although a peer-reviewed journal, it has a magazine format with many color graphics and sidebars. The focus is "on the practice of gerontological nursing across the continuum of care in a variety of health care settings." The journal is intended to be a complete guide to all aspects of the field, with emphasis on currency and practical value. All articles are required to discuss clinical implications of the information being presented. The journal is divided into sections, including geropharmacology, product news, clinical concepts, diagnosis, dementia, legal issues, public policy, research briefs, feature and Continuing Nursing Education articles, and technology innovations, as well as a Continuing Nursing Education quiz. Some recent articles are "Ask the Right Questions: What Do Non-Caregiving Adult Children Need from Health Care Providers?," "Enhancing the ADMIT Me Tool for Care Transitions for Individuals with Alzheimer's Disease," and "Long-Term Adherence and Effectiveness of a Multicomponent Intervention for Community-Dwelling Overweight Thai Older Adults with Knee Osteoarthritis: 1-Year Follow Up." Appropriate for medical libraries and academic libraries that support nursing programs. URL: www.healio.com/nursing/journals/jgn

2662. *Journal of Gerontological Social Work.* [ISSN: 0163-4372] 1978. 8x/yr. GBP 1808 (print & online eds.)). Ed(s): Dr. Michelle Putnam, Dr. Carmen L Morano. Routledge, 530 Walnut St, Ste 850, Philadelphia, PA 19106; enquiries@tandfonline.com; http://www.tandfonline.com. Illus., adv. Sample. Refereed. Circ: 640 Paid. Microform: PQC. Reprint: PSC. *Indexed:* A01, A22, ASSIA, AgeL, BRI, E01, SSA. *Bk. rev.:* 1, 2-3 pages, signed. *Aud.:* Ac, Sa.

From the Association for Gerontology Education in Social Work, this peer-reviewed journal seeks to present "articles across a wide range of domains and settings of gerontological social work including, but not limited to, theoretical analysis, original research using qualitative, quantitative or mixed methods, clinical interventions, knowledge translation, systematic reviews, scoping reviews, and policy analysis." Its audience consists of social work practitioners, supervisors, administrators, and consultants along the entire range of service settings. Any topic related to social work with older people may be covered, such as mental health services, public welfare coordination of services for the elderly, crisis intervention, substance abuse, diversity, law, public policy, and social work education. Each issue contains four to seven articles: most are reports on original research, but a few are theoretical, review articles, editorials, and book reviews. There are occasional special thematic issues - for example, "Special Section on Older Immigrants and Refugees." Examples of recent articles are "Arriving Old: A Qualitative Study of Elder Refugee Women's Self-Perceptions of the First Year of Resettlement," "Mechanisms of the Effect of Involuntary Retirement on Older Adults' Self-Rated Health and Mental Health," "Silver Alerts: A Notification System for Communities with Missing Adults," and "The Aging Semantic Differential in Mandarin Chinese: Measuring Attitudes toward Older Adults in China." Appropriate for any library with a collection emphasis on gerontology or social work. URL: www.tandfonline.com/loi/wger20

2663. *Journal of Nutrition in Gerontology and Geriatrics.* Formerly (until Jan. 2011): *Journal of Nutrition for the Elderly.* [ISSN: 2155-1197] 1980. q. GBP 1058 (print & online eds.)). Ed(s): Connie Bales. Routledge, 530 Walnut St, Ste 850, Philadelphia, PA 19106; enquiries@tandfonline.com; http://www.tandfonline.com. Illus. Sample. Refereed. Vol. ends: Summer. Microform: PQC. Reprint: PSC. *Indexed:* A22, AgeL, Agr, C45, E01. *Aud.:* Ga, Ac, Sa.

This peer-reviewed journal presents information and analysis related to nutrition and older people in clinical or community settings. Articles included are reports on original research, review articles, editorials, and notes on newly available findings. Nutrition is covered broadly, with articles in areas such as "preventive nutrition, nutritional interventions for chronic disease, aging effects on nutritional requirements, nutritional status and dietary intake behaviors, nutritional frailty and functional status, usefulness of supplements, programmatic interventions, transitions in care and long term care, and community nutrition issues." Some recent articles are "Measuring Nutrition-Related Unmet Needs in Recently Hospital-Discharged Homebound Older Adults," "Does Depressive Affect Mediate the Relationship between Self-Care Capacity and Nutritional Status Among Rural Older Adults?: A Structural Equation Modeling Approach," "Effect of Calcitriol Supplementation on Blood Pressure in Older Adults," and "Modulating Oxidative Stress and Inflammation in Elders: The MOXIE Study." Appropriate for medical libraries and academic libraries that support curricula in gerontology or nutrition. URL: www.tandfonline.com/loi/wjne21

2664. *Journal of Religion, Spirituality & Aging: the interdisciplinary journal of practice, theory & applied research.* Former titles (until 2004): *Journal of Religious Gerontology;* (until vol.7, 1990): *Journal of Religion and Aging.* [ISSN: 1552-8030] 1985. q. GBP 638 (print & online eds.)). Ed(s): James W Ellor. Routledge, 530 Walnut St, Ste 850, Philadelphia, PA 19106; enquiries@tandfonline.com; http://www.tandfonline.com. Illus. Sample. Refereed. Vol. ends: Fall. Reprint: PSC. *Indexed:* A01, A22, ASSIA, AgeL, E01, R&TA. *Bk. rev.:* 0-5, 1-3 pages, signed. *Aud.:* Ga, Ac, Sa.

This interdisciplinary, interfaith, peer-reviewed journal is intended for both religious and secular professionals who work with the elderly and their families, but also for scholars within academic disciplines related to religious studies. In four to six articles per issue, the journal aims to provide discussion of current practices, theory, and information regarding spirituality, religion, and aging through research, clinical, theoretical, and methodological articles, case studies, editorials, and the occasional special double issue. Typical topics addressed are "long-term care for the aging, support systems for families of the aging, retirement, counseling, death, ethical issues, and more." A recent special issue is "Aging in the Jewish World." Some recent articles are "Older Adults in Churches: Differences in Perceptions of Clergy and Older Members," "Retirement Among Members of the Clergy: Findings from a Protestant Fellowship," and "DSM-5: The Intersectionality of Spirituality, Culture, and Aging." This journal is appropriate for theological seminary libraries, academic libraries that support religious studies or social work curricula, and public libraries that serve a large aging population. URL: www.tandfonline.com/loi/wrsa20

2665. *Journal of Women and Aging: the multidisciplinary quarterly of psychosocial practice, theory & research.* [ISSN: 0895-2841] 1989. q. GBP 976 (print & online eds.)). Ed(s): J Dianne Garner. Routledge, 530 Walnut St, Ste 850, Philadelphia, PA 19106; enquiries@tandfonline.com; http://www.tandfonline.com. Illus., adv. Sample. Refereed. Microform: PQC. Reprint: PSC. *Indexed:* A01, A22, AgeL, BRI, C42, E01, FemPer, GW, SSA, WSA. *Bk. rev.:* 1-2, 1-3 pages, signed. *Aud.:* Ga, Ac.

The stated goal of this peer-reviewed journal is to provide "practitioners, educators, researchers, and administrators with a comprehensive guide to the unique challenges facing women in their later years." This journal is multidisciplinary, publishing articles from gerontology, medicine, psychology, sociology, and social work. Articles selected for publication may be research, clinical, or review articles. Sample topics are osteoporosis, domestic violence, hysterectomy and menopause, breast cancer, and terminal illness. Every issue has an editorial, about five articles, and one or two book reviews. Examples of recent articles are "Yoga Stretching for Improving Salivary Immune Function and Mental Stress in Middle-Aged and Older Adults," "Strong, Healthy, Energized: Striving for a Healthy Weight in an Older Lesbian Population," "Can Concern for the Long-Term Care of Older Parents Explain Son Preference at Birth in India?" and "The Experience of High-Frequency Gambling Behavior of Older Adult Females in the United Kingdom: An Interpretative Phenomenological Analysis." Useful for students, educators, researchers, practitioners, and administrators, this journal is appropriate for academic libraries, especially those that desire strong collections in gerontology, women's studies, social work, or sociology. URL: www.tandfonline.com/loi/wjwa20

2666. *Journals of Gerontology. Series A: Biological Sciences & Medical Sciences.* Supersedes in part (in 1995): *Journal of Gerontology.* [ISSN: 1079-5006] 1946. m. EUR 1524. Ed(s): Stephen B Kritchevsky, Rafael de Cato. Oxford University Press, 2001 Evans Rd, Cary, NC 27513; orders.us@oup.com; https://academic.oup.com/journals. Illus., index, adv. Sample. Refereed. Vol. ends: Dec. Microform: PQC. Reprint: PSC. *Indexed:* A01, A22, AgeL, C45, CBRI, ErgAb. *Aud.:* Ac, Sa.

This peer-reviewed journal is designed for "gerontological researchers, educators, and practitioners in biological, medical, behavioral, and social sciences and the humanities." It is divided into two parts (with separate pagination): "Biological Sciences," which is devoted to the biological aspects of aging; and "Medical Sciences," which covers medical aspects of aging. Its mission is "to promote the scientific study of aging, to encourage exchanges among researchers and practitioners from various disciplines related to gerontology, and to foster the use of gerontological research in forming public policy." "Biological Sciences" covers biochemistry, biodemography, cellular and molecular biology, comparative and evolutionary biology, endocrinology, exercise science, genetics, immunology, morphology, neuroscience, nutrition, pathology, pharmacology, and physiology. "Medical Sciences" covers basic medical sciences, clinical epidemiology, clinical research, and health-services research from professions such as medicine, dentistry, allied health sciences, and nursing. The journal contains full and brief reports on original research, but also theoretical or review articles, editorials, letters to the editor, and invited special articles. Some recent articles are "Patterns and Perceived Benefits of Utilizing Seven Major Complementary Health Approaches in U.S. Older Adults," "Heterogeneity of Human Aging and Its Assessment," "A Clinically Relevant Frailty Index for Aging Rats," and "Interrelations Between Mitochondrial DNA Copy Number and Inflammation in Older Adults." A core journal for geriatrics and gerontology. URL: academic.oup.com/biomedgerontology

2667. *Journals of Gerontology. Series B: Psychological Sciences & Social Sciences.* Supersedes in part (in 1995): *Journal of Gerontology.* [ISSN: 1079-5014] 1946. 8x/yr. EUR 695. Ed(s): Rachel Pruchno, Megan McCutcheon. Oxford University Press, 2001 Evans Rd, Cary, NC 27513; orders.us@oup.com; https://global.oup.com. Illus., index. Sample. Refereed. Vol. ends: Nov. Microform: PQC. Reprint: PSC. *Indexed:* A01, A22, ASSIA, AgeL, C45, CBRI, ErgAb, SSA. *Aud.:* Ac, Sa.

This international, peer-reviewed journal is published by the Gerontological Society of America and is the companion journal to *Journals of Gerontology. Series A: Biological Sciences and Medical Sciences.* It also is divided into two parts, each with separate pagination: "Psychological Sciences" and "Social Sciences." "Psychological Sciences" covers applied, clinical, counseling, developmental, experimental, and social psychology related to aging and the elderly. Articles are expected to demonstrate the theoretical or methodological implications of the research results reported. They may also relate psychological aspects of aging to other disciplines. Four types of articles are included: lengthy articles on original research, brief reports on original research, invited reviews and position papers, and articles on theory or methodology. The second section, "Social Sciences," covers topics related to aging in various social science disciplines, such as anthropology, demography, economics, epidemiology, geography, political science, public health, social history, social work, and sociology. The types of articles published in this journal are lengthy articles or brief reports on original research, review articles, articles on theory or methodology, commentary or letters to the editor, and editorials. Examples of recent articles are "Daily Stress Reactivity Across the Lifespan: Longitudinal and Cross-Sectional Effects of Age," "To Love Is to Suffer: Older Adults' Daily Emotional Contagion to Perceived Spousal Suffering," "Health Equity and Aging of Bisexual Older Adults: Pathways of Risk and Resilience," and "Older Gay Men and Their Support Convoys." A core title for geriatrics and gerontology. URL: academic.oup.com/psychsocgerontology

2668. *Kiplinger's Retirement Report: your guide to a richer retirement.* [ISSN: 1075-6671] 1994. m. USD 39.95 combined subscription (print or online ed.)). Ed(s): Rachel L Sheedy, Susan B Garland. Kiplinger Washington Editors, Inc., 1729 H St, NW, Washington, DC 20006; http://www.kiplinger.com. Sample. *Indexed:* ATI, AgeL, B01, BRI. *Aud.:* Ga.

This consumer-oriented newsletter is written for the general public and, therefore, consists of short informational articles with graphics. The newsletter addresses a variety of financial topics as they would interest the older adult: investments, taxes, retirement benefits, and health. Each issue has about ten articles and is divided into sections: "Investing," "Benefits," "Taxes," "Estate Planning," "Retirement Living," "Managing Your Finances," and "Your Health." Other regular features are "Information to Act On" and "Your Questions Answered." Some recent feature articles are "Stop Wasting Money," "Living with Cancer," "Your TV Might Be Spying on You," "Words That Will Help Sell Your Home Fast," and "How Misinformation from Social Security Can Cost You Tens of Thousands of Dollars." Recommended for public libraries or a library that serves a large older population. URL: www.kiplinger.com/fronts/archive/magazine/

2669. *Physical & Occupational Therapy in Geriatrics: current trends in geriatric rehabilitation.* [ISSN: 0270-3181] 1980. q. GBP 1030 (print & online eds.)). Taylor & Francis Inc., 530 Walnut St, Ste 850,

Philadelphia, PA 19106; support@tandfonline.com; http://www.tandfonline.com. Illus., adv. Sample. Refereed. Reprint: PSC. *Indexed:* A01, A22, ASSIA, AgeL, E01, MLA-IB, SD. *Aud.:* Ac, Sa.

This peer-reviewed journal is written for and by allied health professionals. It is intended to provide opportunities to share "information, clinical experience, research, and therapeutic practice." Its scope is broad: "the entire range of problems experienced by the elderly; and the current skills needed for working with older clients." Each issue contains five to eight articles: reports on original research, clinical practice, or review articles. Some recent articles are "Enhancing Interprofessional Rehabilitation Team Competence through Low Vision Continuing Education," "Self-Management Program Participation and Social Support in Parkinson's Disease: Mixed Methods Evaluation," "Awareness of Medicare Regulation Changes: Occupational Therapists' Perceptions and Implications for Practice," and "The Role of the Occupational Therapist in Driver Rehabilitation After Stroke." This journal is valuable for medical libraries and academic libraries with collections in physical therapy, occupational therapy, geriatrics and gerontology, or social work. URL: www.tandfonline.com/loi/ipog

2670. ***Psychology and Aging.*** [ISSN: 0882-7974] 1986. 8x/yr. USD 992 (Individuals, USD 271; Members, USD 131). Ed(s): Ulrich Mayr. American Psychological Association, 750 First St, NE, Washington, DC 20002; journals@apa.org; http://www.apa.org. Illus., index, adv. Sample. Refereed. Circ: 350. Microform: PQC. Reprint: PSC. *Indexed:* A01, A22, ASSIA, AgeL, BRI, ErgAb. *Aud.:* Ac, Sa.

This international, peer-reviewed journal from the American Psychological Association is devoted to the physiological and behavioral aspects of adult development and aging. It includes lengthy articles and brief reports on original research, theoretical analyses, clinical case studies, and editorials. Articles may be written on applied, biobehavioral, clinical, educational, experimental, methodological, and psychosocial research. Some recent articles are "Stability of Genetic and Environmental Influences on Executive Functions in Midlife," "Stereotype Threat as a Trigger of Mind-Wandering in Older Adults," "The Interplay Between Personality and Cognitive Ability Across 12 Years in Middle and Late Adulthood: Evidence for Reciprocal Associations," and "Familiar Real-World Spatial Cues Provide Memory Benefits in Older and Younger Adults." A core title for libraries with collections in geriatrics and gerontology, psychology, or sociology. URL: www.apa.org/pubs/journals/pag/

2671. ***Research on Aging: an international journal.*** [ISSN: 0164-0275] 1979. 10x/yr. USD 1713 (print & online eds.)). Ed(s): Jeffrey A Burr. Sage Publications, Inc., 2455 Teller Rd, Thousand Oaks, CA 91320; info@sagepub.com; http://www.sagepub.com. Illus., index, adv. Sample. Refereed. Reprint: PSC. *Indexed:* A01, A22, AgeL, E01, IBSS, SSA. *Aud.:* Ac, Sa.

A peer-reviewed journal for scholars, researchers, and practitioners. It is interdisciplinary in approach, with articles from sociology, history, psychology, anthropology, economics, social work, political science, criminal justice, geriatrics, and public health. Research and review articles cover topics in all these fields as they relate to aging and the elderly, such as age discrimination, Alzheimer's disease, caretaking, and the aging workforce. The journal publishes full and brief reports on original research, systematic literature reviews, meta-analyses, and editorials. Each issue has five to eight articles. Occasional special issues are published, such as "Aging with Disabilities." Recent articles are "Grandparenting and Self-Rated Health Among Older Korean Women," "Extending the Promise of the Older Americans Act to Persons Aging With Long-Term Disability," and "Two-Wave Dyadic Analysis of Marital Quality and Loneliness in Later Life: Results From the Irish Longitudinal Study on Ageing." A core journal in gerontology, for academic libraries. URL: journals.sagepub.com/home/roa

2672. ***Social Security Bulletin (Online).*** [ISSN: 1937-4666] 1938. q. Free. U.S. Social Security Administration, Office of Research, Evaluation and Statistics, 500 E St, S W, 8th Fl, Washington, DC 20254; ORES.Epidemiological.Requests@ssa.gov; http://www.ssa.gov/policy/about/ORES.html. *Aud.:* Ga, Ac, Sa.

This governmental quarterly is available in open-access online format. It is written "to promote the discussion of research questions and policy issues related to Social Security and the economic well-being of the aged." Its intended audience is broad: government and businesspeople; students, educators, and scholars; and the general public. Most articles are written by researchers and analysts connected with the Social Security Administration, but the "Perspectives" section prints articles from outside the agency. The journal contains articles that describe and analyze the changing aging population and the economic, demographic, social, and medical factors that affect their economic security. Other items assess Social Security programs, as well as other programs and tools that may be of value to aging Americans before and after retirement. All papers are required to be written in accessible, nontechnical language and must have a clearly stated connection to public policy. Sample titles include: "The Incidence and Consequences of Private Sector Job Loss in the Great Recession," "Contributory Retirement Saving Plans: Differences Across Earnings Groups and Implications for Retirement Security," "The Decline in Earnings Prior to Application for Disability Insurance Benefits," and "Supplemental Security Income and Social Security Disability Insurance Beneficiaries with Intellectual Disability." Recommended for all libraries. URL: www.ssa.gov/policy/docs/ssb

2673. ***Topics in Geriatric Rehabilitation.*** [ISSN: 0882-7524] 1985. q. USD 603. Ed(s): Carole B Lewis, Wendy Powers James. Lippincott Williams & Wilkins, Two Commerce Sq, 2001 Market St, Philadelphia, PA 19103; customerservice@lww.com; http://www.lww.com. Illus., adv. Sample. Refereed. *Indexed:* A22, AgeL. *Aud.:* Ac, Sa.

Specifically intended for "the health care professional practicing in the area of geriatric rehabilitation," this peer-reviewed journal may be of interest to other health professionals who work with older people. The journal's general scope is very broad, although most issues focus on a particular subject. Each issue contains six to ten research articles that report the results of "clinical, basic, and applied research," and review articles. Emphasis in each article is placed on the practical value of the information presented, so that the reader can use that information in the daily treatment of elderly clients. The themes of two recent issues are "Thinking about Cognition" and "Thieves' Market." Recent articles include "Efficacy of Elastic Resistance Training Program for the Institutionalized Elderly," "Role of Family in the Process of Rehabilitation of Older Adults Hospitalized in a Nursing Home," "The Effects of Body Mass Index on Balance, Mobility, and Functional Capacity in Older Adults," and "Filling the Breast Cancer Survivor Gap of Care Through Pilates-Based Exercise." Appropriate for medical libraries, research libraries, and academic libraries that support geriatric, gerontology, social work, or physical therapy curricula. URL: journals.lww.com/topicsingeriatricrehabilitation/pages/default.aspx

Travel 50 & Beyond. See Travel and Tourism/General section.

■ GLOBALIZATION

See also Advertising, Marketing, and Public Relations; Africa; Asia and the Pacific; Cultural Studies; Business and Finance-International; Civil Liberties; Economics; Environment and Conservation; Europe; Geography; International Magazines; Latin America and Spain; Latino Studies; Middle East; Multicultural Studies; Peace and Conflict Studies; Political Science-International Relations; Population Studies; Public Health; Slavic and Eurasian Studies; Sociology and Social Work; Travel and Tourism; Urban Studies.

Karen Dearing, Reference & Instruction Librarian, Liaison for Cultural Geography, Global Studies, International Relations, and Political Science, Middle Tennessee State University, Murfreesboro, Tennessee; karen.dearing@mtsu.edu

Introduction

This year an international debate on the definition of nationalists vs. globalists roared to the forefront in the news and political arenas. Emotional wildfires ignited within social and conventional media. Nationalists separated into their tribes fiercely protecting their autonomy, patriotism, and cultural traditions, while globalists continued to shout the benefits of melding cultures, international trade, and minimization of national confrontations. Some of these discussions yielded helpful discussions while others intentionally ignited divisive opinions. In the blink of an eye, a new national discourse surrounding the concept of globalization emerged. As a result, library resources on the topic of globalization are more vital now than ever.

Yes, there are shades of difference between the terms globalist, globalism, and globalization. However, for the sake of peaceful research, those differences are put aside and are instead integrated into one section. While globalization technically refers to the dynamic shrinking of distance on a large scale, the serials recommended in this section will also cover globalist views. In simple terms, globalists exhibit an interest in the world around them. They possess an interest in sorting out how the forces of politics, economics, environment, and culture work together for problem solving. Globalists understand that globalization is not a unified phenomenon that must be adopted wholesale or rejected entirely. It is a mosaic of issues that can and should be addressed separately in order to improve the quality of life for all.

To that end, the content of this globalization section strongly focuses on serials that examine the premises and fallacies of conventional and non-conventional beliefs about the world. There is a fair balance between subscription and non-subscription resources as well as resources written for scholarly and popular audiences. It is my hope that the serials selected in this globalization section provide a guide to understanding the challenges we all face in the global era and what solutions are worth pursuing.

Basic Periodicals

Ga: *Harvard International Review, RAND Review* (online), *The World Today*. Ac, Sa: *Development, Fletcher Forum of World Affairs, Harvard Human Rights Journal, SAIS Review of International Affairs, World Politics Review, Yale Global Online*.

Basic Abstracts and Indexes

ABI/INFORM, Hein Online, International Political Science Abstracts, JSTOR, Political Science Complete, Project Muse, Social Sciences Citation Index, Sociological Abstracts, Worldwide Political Science Abstracts.

2674. *Development (London).* Former titles (until 1978): *Revista del Desarrollo Internacional;* (until 1970): *International Development Review.* [ISSN: 1011-6370] 1957. q. GBP 517. Ed(s): Stefano Prato. Palgrave Macmillan Ltd., Macmillan Building, 4 Crinan St, London, N1 9XW, United Kingdom; onlinesales@palgrave.com; http://www.palgrave.com. Adv. Sample. Reprint: PSC. *Indexed:* A01, A22, C45, E01, EconLit, IBSS, P61, SSA. *Bk. rev.:* Number and length vary. *Aud.:* Ga, Ac, Sa.

Since 1957, *Development* has been the flagship subscription journal published by the Society for International Development. It explores differing perspectives on global societal issues and offers a dialogue platform for researchers, activists, and alternative thinkers. Issues are normally devoted to single subjects and divided into specific sections. The "Upfront and Thematic" section includes essays and articles. The "Book Shelf" section includes recommended readings on the subject of the issue. There are also sections for "Dialogues" and "Book Reviews." As an added bonus, issues contain a "Window on the World" section highlighting websites for international and regionally based organizations involved directly with the selected subject. Online (ISSN 1461-7072) subscribers can create journal alerts and RSS feeds. Non-subscribers can view several open-access articles from each issue and post to social media. Although the content is academic, this journal should also appeal to general audience readers interested in actively participating in solutions for global problems. Highly recommended for academic libraries.

2675. *Ethics & Global Politics.* [ISSN: 1654-4951] 2008. q. Free. Ed(s): Eva Erman. Routledge, 4 Park Sq, Milton Park, Abingdon, OX14 4RN, United Kingdom; subscriptions@tandf.co.uk; http://www.tandfonline.com. Refereed. *Indexed:* IBSS, P61, SSA. *Bk. rev.:* Number and length vary. *Aud.:* Ac, Sa.

Ethics & Global Politics publishes original research that "fosters theoretical contributions to the study of global politics." The issue content varies, but usually includes critical debates, invited editorials, research articles, essays, notes, and book reviews. The journal also publishes one special thematic issue each year. Everything, with the exception of book reviews and editorials, is subjected to a double-blind peer-review process. The online content (ISSN 1654-6369) is open access with searchable archives. Supported by a grant from the Swedish government, *Ethics & Global Politics* "does not favour any theoretical perspective or political problem, but emphasizes the importance of closing the gap between moral and democratic theory, on the one hand, and contemporary empirical problems on the global arena, on the other." This journal is a good balanced research source for academic and specialized audiences within international politics. Recommended for academic libraries.

2676. *Ethics & International Affairs.* [ISSN: 0892-6794] 1987. q. GBP 401 (print & online eds.)). Ed(s): Joel H Rosenthal, Zornitsa Stoyanova-Yerburgh. Cambridge University Press, 1 Liberty Plaza, Fl 20, New York, NY 10004; journals@cambridge.org; https://www.cambridge.org. Adv. Refereed. Circ: 534 Paid. Reprint: PSC. *Indexed:* A01, A22, BRI, E01, IBSS, P61. *Bk. rev.:* Number and length vary. *Aud.:* Ac, Sa.

Ethics & International Affairs publishes original essays that attempt to bring theorists and practitioners closer together by discussing justice and morality when applied to practical global dilemmas. The journal has been published by the Carnegie Council on International Affairs for more than 30 years. Full access is only available through subscription. Issues regularly contain policy briefs, essays, peer-reviewed articles, and book reviews. Online (ISSN 1747-7093) subscribers can create new content alerts and RSS feeds, post to social media, view the most read and cited articles, and use the suggested links for additional articles about similar subjects. Recommended for academic libraries.

2677. *Fletcher Forum of World Affairs.* Formerly (until 1989): *Fletcher Forum.* [ISSN: 1046-1868] 1975. s-a. USD 50 (Individuals, USD 20). The Fletcher School of Law and Diplomacy, Tufts University, 160 Packard Ave, Medford, MA 02155. Illus. Refereed. Vol. ends: No. 2. Microform: WSH. Reprint: WSH. *Indexed:* A22, BAS, BRI, L14. *Aud.:* Ga, Ac, Sa.

Fletcher Forum of World Affairs is a student-managed foreign-policy journal published by the Fletcher School of Law and Diplomacy at Tufts University. Student-managed publications offer unique perspectives and can sometimes provide an opportunity to view the world through the lenses of our young adults, who are essentially our future. *FFWA* tries to provide "a broad, interdisciplinary platform for analysis of legal, political, economic, environmental, and diplomatic issues in international affairs." Print issues have subject themes and contain a mixture of academic articles and conversational articles based on interviews conducted by Fletcher's editors. Authors selected for the journal's print edition are established experts that most often focus on big picture analyses. Fletcher's editors intentionally solicit articles representing conflicting viewpoints to spur discussion among academics, practitioners, and students around the world. Access to print issue content is only available through a subscription fee. However, a few selected articles from various print issues are available for free in the online archives dating back to 1976. Fletcher's online edition (ISSN 1046-1868) is very different from the print edition and offers a youthful breath of fresh air. The online edition is open access and contains short exclusive articles on a variety of current topics written by a wide range of authors, including students. Readers are encouraged to post comments and questions to the authors. The online edition also contains video and photo essays, keyword searchable content, and recent trending articles. Readers can also follow and leave comments on the journal's social media websites. Broad subject coverage and good readability make this journal appropriate for both academic and interested general audiences. Highly recommended for academic libraries and most large public libraries.

2678. *Forced Migration Review (English Edition).* Formerly (until 1998): *Refugee Participation Network.* [ISSN: 1460-9819] 1987. 3x/yr. Free. Ed(s): Maurice Herson, Marion Couldrey. Refugee Studies Centre, Department of International Development, University of Oxford, Oxford, OX1 3TB, United Kingdom; rsc@qeh.ox.ac.uk; http://www.rsc.ox.ac.uk/. *Indexed:* A01, C45, P61. *Aud.:* Ga.

Forced Migration Review has been published for more than 30 years by the Refugee Studies Centre at the Oxford Department of International Development, University of Oxford. This open-access magazine is wholly dependent on reader donations and external funding sources for both publishing and staffing costs. The magazine addresses all aspects of forced migration within all parts of the world. Article topics are broad; but there is a detectable emphasis on topics that address the causes and impacts of forced migration as well as the reflective experiences of migrants. Articles that present research findings and policy debates contain important examples of good practices and, most importantly, recommendations for policy changes and actions. Articles are written by international authors representing academics, practitioners, organizational volunteers, and students. The diversity of author experience and backgrounds provide readers with a variety of perspectives and viewpoints. The print and online (ISSN 2051-3070) versions of the magazine are published in four languages: English, French, Spanish, and Arabic. English-language articles are also available in audio format. Audio files for whole issues are available on the journal's podcasting web page. The expansive issues are devoted to subject themes and typically contain more than 30 articles averaging three pages in length. Some articles are supplemented with quality images; others are text only. To help readers prioritize and access articles, *FMR* produces a digest that contains an expanded contents listing for each issue. The digest is easily scanned and contains quick information about the theme of each issue plus the article titles, authors/affiliations, and direct links to the full text of the articles. Interested readers are encouraged to follow the journal's active social media conversations for updates, useful link recommendations, and interactions with other readers. Articles are interesting, timely, and written for general audience appeal. *Forced Migration Review* is a treasure trove of vital information and reflective conversations concerning one of the most pressing human issues on our planet. Highly recommended for academic, public, and some high school libraries supporting a global studies curriculum.

2679. *Global Discourse: an interdisciplinary journal of current affairs and applied contemporary thought.* [ISSN: 2326-9995] 2010. 4x/yr. Bristol University Press, 1-9 Old Park Hill, Bristol, BS2 8BB, United Kingdom; pp-info@bristol.ac.uk; http://bristoluniversitypress.co.uk. Refereed. Reprint: PSC. *Bk. rev.:* Number and length vary. *Aud.:* Ac, Sa.

Global Discourse is an "interdisciplinary, problem-oriented journal of applied contemporary thought." Content is only available through subscription. Most issues are theme based and cover a very broad and often unusual range of topics. In addition to the broad scope, the journal also has an unusual format design. Peer-reviewed research articles are presented along with professional reader replies. This format encourages discussion and debate and creates conversations that continue across multiple issues. Each issue also contains short essays, discussion pieces, and book reviews. The book review section follows the same discussion format design. Book reviews are presented along with a response from the author of the book being reviewed. Online subscribers (ISSN 2043-7897) can see the most viewed and cited articles, post to social media, link to blogs, and download formatted citations. Online articles also contain links to additional articles by subject and author as well as cross-reference links. This journal will appeal to academics and students who are particularly interested in global discussions from a multidisciplinary perspective. Recommended for academic libraries.

2680. *Global Environmental Politics.* [ISSN: 1526-3800] 2000. q. Ed(s): Steven Bernstein, Erika Weinthal. M I T Press, One Rogers St, Cambridge, MA 02142-1209; journals-cs@mit.edu; http://mitpress.mit.edu/. Adv. Refereed. *Indexed:* A01, A22, B01, E01, EconLit, P61. *Bk. rev.:* Number and length vary. *Aud.:* Ac, Sa.

Global Environmental Politics is an academic subscription-based journal published by MIT Press. Articles examine the relationship between global political forces and environmental change. Articles focus on local-global interactions that affect environmental management and world politics. Contributors come from a variety of disciplines. Each issue contains peer-reviewed research articles, commentary articles for the purpose of debate, and book reviews. The online edition (ISSN 1536-0091) usually contains a few open-access articles. Online subscribers can create article alerts and RSS feeds. Online subscribers can also view forthcoming articles and the journal's most read and most cited articles. In addition, online subscribers have the option to download articles in PDF Plus format which provides hyperlinked reference lists. This journal will appeal to academics interested in subject areas that intersect politics and science. Recommended for academic libraries.

2681. *Global Governance: a review of multilateralism and international organizations.* [ISSN: 1075-2846] 1995. q. USD 173. Ed(s): J Matthew Clarke, Kendall Stiles. Brill, PO Box 9000, Leiden, 2300 PA, Netherlands; marketing@brill.com; https://brill.com. Illus., index, adv. Refereed. Vol. ends: No. 4. Reprint: WSH. *Indexed:* A01, A22, B01, BRI, IBSS, P61, SSA. *Bk. rev.:* Number and length vary. *Aud.:* Ac, Sa.

Global Governance is a joint publication from Lynne Rienner, one of the last remaining independent scholarly publishers, and the Academic Council on the United Nations Systems. Contributors include both scholars and practitioners. The journal attempts to provide a real world view of problems along with the practical and creative solutions occurring globally. Articles focus on international policies, multilateral governance issues, and how international and national agents/organizations cooperate within the international arena. Each issue includes a forum section containing one or more thought-provoking essays, a peer-reviewed articles section, and a book review section. Several issues each year are devoted to specific topics. This journal will be helpful for any researcher interested in learning more about international cooperation between governments and organizations. The practitioner perspectives will be especially helpful for students and anyone interested in working with or for intergovernmental and nongovernmental organizations. Recommended for academic libraries.

2682. *Global Health Action.* [ISSN: 1654-9880] 2008. a. Free. Ed(s): Nawi Ng. Taylor & Francis, 2, 3 & 4 Park Sq, Milton Park, Abingdon, OX14 4RN, United Kingdom; subscriptions@tandf.co.uk; https://www.tandfonline.com. Illus. Sample. Refereed. *Indexed:* IBSS. *Aud.:* Ga, Ac, Sa.

Global Health Action is an open-access journal affiliated with the Centre for Global Health Research at Umea University in Sweden and is associated with the World Health Organization Centre on Epidemiological Surveillance and Public Health Training. This journal sets itself apart from others by focusing on content with hands-on practical approaches and strategies. The published articles and papers present practical implementations of current knowledge and suggestions for strategies where none already exist. "All papers are expected to address a global agenda and include a strong implementation or policy component." Readers can expect to see original articles, short essays, debate articles, study design articles, and PhD reviews. All articles are peer reviewed and posted online immediately when ready for publication. Readers can create journal alerts, search journal contents, see the most read and most viewed articles, and access special issues. Readers can also follow the journal on social media and post comments about article contents and global health issues. The journal is published only once each year; however, the large volume of content should provide something of interest for anyone interested in this new field. Although the content is academic, *Global Health Action* will also appeal to a general audience. Recommended for academic libraries and some public libraries.

2683. *Global Journal of Health Science.* [ISSN: 1916-9736] 2009. s-a. Ed(s): Trisha Dunning. Canadian Center of Science and Education, 1120 Finch Ave W, Ste 701-309, Toronto, ON M3J 3H7, Canada; info@ccsenet.org; http://www.ccsenet.org. Sample. Refereed. Circ: 200 Paid. *Aud.:* Ac, Sa.

There are two interesting and distinguishing factors about *Global Journal of Health Science*. The first factor is the inclusion of equality as a pertinent area of health research. The second factor is the focus on content that explores the sociological impacts made by health services and health professionals around the world. In addition to these two factors, there is some typical content found in most other health journals including empirical research, experimental results, and articles on administration and staffing issues. The journal aims to "encourage and publish research and studies in the fields of public health, community health, environmental health, behavioral health, health policy, health service, health education, health economics, medical ethics, health protection, and equity in health." The online edition (ISSN 1916-9744) offers free open-access content. Articles are peer reviewed, archived, and searchable by issue, author, title, and keyword. Interested readers can also create journal alerts and email notifications with current table of contents listings. *Global Journal of Health Science* is a good choice for academics and professionals looking for articles that cover health sciences within a global sociological context. Recommended for academic libraries.

2684. ***Global Media and Communication.*** [ISSN: 1742-7665] 2005. 3x/yr. USD 1086 (print & online eds.)). Sage Publications Ltd., 1 Oliver's Yard, 55 City Rd, London, EC1Y 1SP, United Kingdom; info@sagepub.com; https://www.sagepub.com/. Adv. Sample. Refereed. Reprint: PSC. *Indexed:* A22, E01, F01, IBSS. *Bk. rev.:* Number and length vary. *Aud.:* Ac, Sa.

Global Media and Communication offers a forum for critical debates and new developments. The peer-reviewed articles cover a wide range of topics within the broader fields of communications and media studies, anthropology, sociology, telecommunications, public policy, migration, diasporic studies, transnational security, and international relations. Issues typically contain research articles, opinion essays, and reviews for books, film, and television. The online edition (ISSN 1742-7673) is accessible only through subscription. This journal is a very good resource for academics, researchers, and students interested in the international debates concerning communication and global policies. Recommended for academic libraries.

2685. ***Global Mental Health.*** [ISSN: 2054-4251] 2015. . Free. Ed(s): Gary Belkin. Cambridge University Press, University Printing House, Shaftesbury Rd, Cambridge, CB2 8BS, United Kingdom; online@cambridge.org; https://www.cambridge.org. Refereed. *Indexed:* A01. *Aud.:* Ga, Ac, Sa.

This is a relatively new peer-reviewed open-access journal from Cambridge University Press. The purpose of *Global Mental Health* is to "publish papers that apply the global point of view to mental health research." Because global mental health is still an emerging discipline, the journal attempts to provide a forum for new perspectives and the resulting paradigms. The journal publishes papers in four subject areas: interventions, etiology, policy and systems, and teaching and learning. Past articles have focused on stigma, advocacy, longstanding treatment gaps, and the disparities in care, access, and capacity. Current and archived articles are available in both PDF and EPUB format for mobile devices. Readers can download articles directly to cloud services; see the most viewed and most downloaded articles; and view the article metrics. *Global Mental Health* covers an important new developing discipline and will be of interest to academic researchers and to a special segment of general audience readers interested in this subject. Recommended for academic libraries and some public libraries.

2686. ***Global Policy.*** [ISSN: 1758-5880] 2010. 4x/yr. Ed(s): David Held. Wiley-Blackwell Publishing Ltd., The Atrium, Southern Gate, Chichester, PO19 8QG, United Kingdom; cs-journals@wiley.com; http://onlinelibrary.wiley.com. Refereed. Reprint: PSC. *Indexed:* A22, E01. *Bk. rev.:* Number and length vary. *Aud.:* Ac, Sa.

Global Policy is published by Durham University. It is aimed at academic researchers, government officials, and practitioners in nongovernmental organizations. Articles analyze public and private solutions to global problems and issues. Past articles have focused on policy challenges with global impact; case studies of policy combined with lessons learned; and how policy responses, politics, and institutions interrelate. The focus of most articles is on understanding global risks and collective-action problems as well as policy issues that have global impacts. Each issue contains five sections: research articles, survey articles, practitioner comments, article responses, and book reviews. The online edition (ISSN 1758-5899) allows subscribers to create new content alerts or RSS feeds; search current and archived articles; and access articles in multiple formats. For interested non-subscribers, the journal provides a few open-access articles within most issues. The content is definitely academic and leans toward the European perspective. Recommended for academic libraries.

Global Social Policy. See Sociology and Social Work/General section.

2687. ***Global Society: journal of interdisciplinary international relations.*** Formerly (until 1996): *Paradigms.* [ISSN: 1360-0826] 1987. q. GBP 790 (print & online eds.)). Ed(s): Andrea den Boer. Routledge, 4 Park Sq, Milton Park, Abingdon, OX14 4RN, United Kingdom; subscriptions@tandf.co.uk; http://www.tandfonline.com. Illus., index, adv. Sample. Refereed. Vol. ends: No. 4. Reprint: PSC. *Indexed:* A01, A22, AmHI, E01, IBSS, P61, SSA. *Bk. rev.:* Number and length vary. *Aud.:* Ac, Sa.

Global Society is an interdisciplinary journal that promotes the analysis of social, economic, and political globalization from a multitude of related disciplines. Articles explore themes related to "global governance, human rights, poverty and development conflict, trade, gender, nationalism, religion, ethnicity, migration, terrorism, genocides, health, and environmental degradation." This quarterly journal publishes two or three issues each year devoted to special topics. Each issue includes approximately seven peer-reviewed articles. The online edition (ISSN 1469-789X) allows subscribers to create journal alerts; see the most read and most cited articles; view article metrics; share through social media; and view related articles. *Global Society* will appeal to special academic audiences and those interested in becoming practitioners within the related disciplines. Recommended for academic libraries.

2688. ***The Globalist: rethinking globalization.*** [ISSN: 1532-5466] 2000. . Free. Ed(s): Stephan Richter. Transatlantic Futures, 927 15th St. NW, Washington, DC 20005. *Bk. rev.:* Number and length vary. *Aud.:* Hs, Ga, Ac.

The Globalist is a free electronic journal publication updated daily by contributors reporting from all continents. The publication's mission statement is to "help audiences everywhere in the world to make up their own mind on the issue of globalization." Content is a mixed bag of factual news reporting, editorials, and book reviews. Graphics, photographs, media links, and further readings supplement every entry. In addition to the main content, *The Globalist* also regularly updates a section on current book recommendations, photo galleries, links to in-depth reports, and links to published work done by *Globalist* contributors for other major publications. *The Globalist* also produces and distributes six columns for international syndication. Interested readers can follow stories, get further information, and link to podcasts via social media. All entries contain highlighted takeaway points for those who prefer to skim before delving into the full content. Email subscribers can select an option to receive headlines three times each week. Overall, this is a good current publication with broad scope editorials representing a diverse range of subjects and viewpoints. The content is thought provoking and good for general readers who want to keep up with events happening in parts of the world that do not normally receive coverage within traditional publications and websites. This could be especially helpful for students and other readers intentionally seeking multiple viewpoints about current events and issues. Recommended for academic, public, and some high school libraries supporting an international curriculum.

2689. ***Globalization and Health.*** [ISSN: 1744-8603] 2004. irreg. Free. Ed(s): Greg Martin. BioMed Central Ltd., Fl 6, 236 Gray's Inn Rd, London, WC1X 8HB, United Kingdom; info@biomedcentral.com; https://www.biomedcentral.com. Adv. Refereed. *Indexed:* A01, C45. *Bk. rev.:* Number and length vary. *Aud.:* Ac, Sa.

This specialized journal focuses on the effects of globalization on health issues. Open access and peer reviewed, *Globalization and Health* is an international forum "for high quality original research, knowledge sharing, and debate on the topic of globalization and its effects on health, both positive and negative." Aiming for a balanced view on global health issues, the journal includes research, book reviews, editorials, and debate and commentary articles. The articles are available in pdf and ePub format, and contain links for finding related articles on Google Scholar and PubMed. There is also a designation for "highly accessed" articles, which tracks the most viewed in the past month to give readers insight into what is currently trending. Readers can also follow the journal's Twitter account for related announcements and to participate in debate concerning article contents. The intended audience includes professionals and academic researchers in the fields of political science, international health, and public safety. Recommended for academic libraries.

2690. ***Globalizations.*** [ISSN: 1474-7731] 2004. 8x/yr. GBP 915 (print & online eds.)). Ed(s): Barry Gills. Routledge, 4 Park Sq, Milton Park, Abingdon, OX14 4RN, United Kingdom; subscriptions@tandf.co.uk; http://www.tandfonline.com. Adv. Sample. Refereed. Reprint: PSC. *Indexed:* A01, A22, E01, IBSS, P61. *Bk. rev.:* Number and length vary. *Aud.:* Ac, Sa.

Globalizations is a peer-reviewed academic journal that attempts to "publish the best work that contributes to constructing new meaning of globalization." The journal aims to bring fresh ideas to the concept of globalization while broadening the scope and shaping future practices. Most issues are devoted to special topics. The wide variety of subjects within each issue make it a perfect choice for serious generalists and allows most everyone to find something of interest. The online edition (ISSN 1474-774X) allows subscribers to view article metrics, related articles by keyword, and a list of the most read and most cited articles. In addition, sharing links for social media are included with each article. Recommended for academic libraries.

2691. ***Glocalism: journal of culture, politics and innovation.*** [ISSN: 2283-7949] 2013. 3x/yr. Free. Ed(s): Piero Bassetti. Globus et Locus, Via Brisa 3, Milan, 20123, Italy; info@globusetlocus. Refereed. *Aud.:* Ac, Sa.

Glocalism is a multidisciplinary peer-reviewed journal published by the Association Globus et Locus in Milan, Italy. The purpose of this open-access journal is to "stimulate increasing awareness and knowledge around the new dynamics that characterise the glocal reality." The strong point of this journal is the emphasis on cultural contributions to globalization. Articles examine major aspects of globalization and their impacts at local levels. In order to elicit online discussion, each issue is devoted to one subject and is composed of related research articles and essays. Readers can view, download, and search for articles. There is also a media gallery for related videos and photographs. In addition, *Glocalism* is indexed in several open-access websites such as Journal Seek, DOAJ, and ROAD and maintains a presence on numerous social media websites. Recommended for academic libraries.

2692. ***Harvard Human Rights Journal.*** Formerly (until 1990): *Harvard Human Rights Yearbook.* [ISSN: 1057-5057] 1988. a. USD 32 domestic; USD 37 foreign. Ed(s): Hannah Belitz, Rebecca Rattner. Harvard University, Law School, Wasserstein Hall Ste 3050, 1585 Massachusetts Ave, Cambridge, MA 02138; http://www.law.harvard.edu/. *Indexed:* A01, A22, BAS, BRI, L14. *Bk. rev.:* Number and length vary; usually in-depth essay format. *Aud.:* Ga, Ac, Sa.

Since 1988, Harvard Law School students have published an annual issue of the *Harvard Human Rights Journal.* The journal contains a wide variety of original research articles about human rights topics deemed to have current relevance both nationally and internationally. Print subscription issues contain research articles, opinion essays, and book reviews. The online edition (ISSN 1057-1057) offers free access to selected articles from the print editions dating back to 2003. The online edition also offers additional interesting content including an interview section with media links and a symposia section with content links. Online readers also have the option of subscribing to journal RSS feeds and following the journal on social media. *HHRJ* presents current human rights topics in an interesting format that will appeal to a wide academic audience and some general audiences. Highly recommended for academic libraries and most large public libraries.

2693. ***Harvard International Review.*** [ISSN: 0739-1854] 1979. q. USD 38 (Individuals, USD 28; USD 7.95 per issue domestic). Ed(s): Basia Rosenbaum, Kevin Xie. Harvard International Relations Council, Inc., 59 Shepard St, Box 205, Cambridge, MA 02138; contact@hir.harvard.edu. Adv. Microform: PQC. *Indexed:* A01, A22, B01, BAS, BRI, C37, MASUSE. *Bk. rev.:* Number and length vary. *Aud.:* Ga, Ac, Sa.

Harvard International Review is published by the Harvard International Relations Council at Harvard University. There are several factors that make this journal different. Rather than "presenting facts previously unreported elsewhere," *HIR* provides an analysis and debate forum for global issues. The journal features "under-appreciated topics" and "novel perspectives on more widely discussed topics." This approach allows the journal to guide public attention to specific topics instead of following existing public attention. Issues contain commentary on global topics, interviews with global leaders, and reviews of books and, occasionally, films. The online edition contains feature articles, analysis articles, interviews, review essays, and blog posts. Online readers can sign up for RSS feeds and a free newsletter. In addition, online readers can follow the journal's social media conversations. *HIR* has an appealing design and an easy-to-use web platform. Readers will find many interesting global topics not found elsewhere. The articles are written for general audiences with a serious interest in global issues. Highly recommended for academic and public libraries.

2694. ***The International Journal of Cultural Policy.*** Formerly (until 1997): *The European Journal of Cultural Policy.* [ISSN: 1028-6632] 1994. 7x/yr. GBP 1279 (print & online eds.)). Ed(s): Oliver Bennett. Routledge, 4 Park Sq, Milton Park, Abingdon, OX14 4RN, United Kingdom; subscriptions@tandf.co.uk; http://www.tandfonline.com. Adv. Sample. Refereed. Reprint: PSC. *Indexed:* A01, A22, A51, C45, E01, IBSS, P61. *Bk. rev.:* Number and length vary. *Aud.:* Ac, Sa.

International Journal of Cultural Policy explores the global "meaning, function and impact of cultural policies" from many relevant disciplines. While the historical range for cultural topics is not limited, the journal primarily focuses on topics that are relevant to the contemporary world. Articles fuse cultural policy topics from both the social sciences and the humanities. The journal considers itself to be independent without any political or economic interests. Each peer-reviewed issue includes approximately six original research articles and two book reviews. Online (ISSN 1477-2833) subscribers can create journal alerts; view the most read and most cited articles; view article metrics; connect to related articles by subject; and post to social media. Recommended for academic libraries.

2695. ***International Journal of Cultural Studies.*** [ISSN: 1367-8779] 1998. bi-m. USD 1894 (print & online eds.)). Ed(s): John Hartley. Sage Publications Ltd., 1 Oliver's Yard, 55 City Rd, London, EC1Y 1SP, United Kingdom; info@sagepub.com; https://www.sagepub.com/. Illus., adv. Sample. Refereed. Reprint: PSC. *Indexed:* A01, A22, A47, AmHI, E01, IBSS, MLA-IB, P61, SSA. *Aud.:* Ac, Sa.

International Journal of Cultural Studies provides a place for academic debate on global issues pertaining to media and culture. Topics reflect "international perspectives on cultural and media developments around the globe" and the "impact of globalization on local cultural practices and media." The journal is labeled as a motivated thinking periodical by the editors. Articles present critical reflections, new ideas, and numerous quirky interpretations and observations not found in any other related publication. Each peer-reviewed issue contains approximately six research articles and a few book reviews from multidisciplinary contributors. Online (ISSN 1460-356X) subscribers can create journal alerts and RSS feeds, view the journal's most read and most cited articles, and post to social media. Recommended for academic libraries.

2696. ***Journal of Global Ethics.*** [ISSN: 1744-9626] 2005. 3x/yr. GBP 420 (print & online eds.)). Ed(s): Sirkku Hellsten, Christien van den Anker. Routledge, 4 Park Sq, Milton Park, Abingdon, OX14 4RN, United Kingdom; subscriptions@tandf.co.uk; http://www.tandfonline.com. Adv. Sample. Refereed. Reprint: PSC. *Indexed:* A22, E01, IBSS, P61. *Bk. rev.:* Number and length vary. *Aud.:* Ac, Sa.

The Journal of Global Ethics explores the meaning, function, and impact of cultural practices and values. The journal focuses on content that is relevant to the modern world and publishes theoretical and practice papers from all relevant disciplines. Issues typically contain a section for peer-reviewed research articles and a small section for book reviews. Online (ISSN 1744-9634) subscribers can view all editorials, articles, and special issues, as well as lists of the most cited and most read articles. Online articles contain links to social media and to related articles by author and subject within other journals from the same publisher. Recommended for academic libraries.

2697. ***Journal of International & Global Studies.*** [ISSN: 2158-0669] 2009. s-a. Free. Ed(s): Raymond Scupin. Lindenwood University, 209 S Kingshighway, St Charles, MO 63303; http://www.lindenwood.edu. *Indexed:* A01, BRI, C42. *Bk. rev.:* Number and length vary. *Aud.:* Ga, Ac, Sa.

The *Journal of International & Global Studies* is an open-access journal published by Lindenwood University. The journal contains academic essays and book reviews. The essays primarily focus on the related topics and consequences of globalization from multidisciplinary perspectives. However, the strength of this journal comes from the extensive book reviews. Each semi-annual issue contains more than a dozen lengthy book reviews from researchers and practitioners around the world. Online archives are searchable from 2009 to the present. Recommended for academic libraries.

2698. ***Journal of Knowledge Globalization.*** [ISSN: 1938-7717] 2008. s-a. Ed(s): Nargis A Mahmud. Knowledge Globalization Institute, 71 Winter St, Lexington, MA 02420; info@kglobal.org; http://www.kglobal.org. Refereed. *Indexed:* B01. *Aud.:* Ac, Sa.

The *Journal of Knowledge Globalization* is published by the Knowledge Globalization Institute and sponsored by the Sawyer Business School at Suffolk University. This open-access journal has a fairly broad scope and purpose. The editors solicit articles addressing multidisciplinary topics that can be applied for practical purposes within developed and underdeveloped countries. In reality, the most recent issues do not contain articles that represent broad multidisciplinary topics; instead, the most recently published articles relate to business, technology, economics, and finance. Contributing authors come from academic, business, government, NGO, and related organizational backgrounds. The searchable archives date back to 2008. Recommended for academic libraries supporting international business programs.

2699. ***Millennium: journal of international studies.*** [ISSN: 0305-8298] 1971. 3x/yr. USD 684 (print & online eds.)). Ed(s): Nick Smicek, Eddie Arghand. Sage Publications Ltd., 1 Oliver's Yard, 55 City Rd, London, EC1Y 1SP, United Kingdom; info@sagepub.com; https://www.sagepub.com/. Sample. Refereed. Reprint: PSC. *Indexed:* A01, A22, AmHI, BAS, E01, IBSS, P61, SSA. *Aud.:* Ac, Sa.

Millennium is a student-run, peer-reviewed journal based at the London School of Economics and Political Science. The journal is edited completely by postgraduate students and encourages submissions from students and young scholars as well as established professionals. The journal aims "to publish critical, theoretical, and boundary-pushing articles from the discipline of International Relations and elsewhere in the social sciences with global dimension." The journal content differs from most academic journals. In addition to the standard peer-reviewed articles and discussion forums, there is a response section that allows readers to counter argue topics from both the forum and review articles sections. Online (ISSN 1477-9021) subscribers can create journal alerts and RSS feeds. Online subscribers can also view article metrics; link to social media; view the most read and most cited articles; and read similar articles by subject from the publisher and Google Scholar. Recommended for academic libraries.

2700. ***National Identities.*** [ISSN: 1460-8944] 1999. 4x/yr. GBP 596 (print & online eds.)). Ed(s): Peter Catterall, Elfie Rembold. Routledge, 4 Park Sq, Milton Park, Abingdon, OX14 4RN, United Kingdom; subscriptions@tandf.co.uk; http://www.tandfonline.com. Adv. Sample. Refereed. Reprint: PSC. *Indexed:* A01, A22, E01, IBSS, MLA-IB, P61, SSA. *Bk. rev.:* Number and length vary. *Aud.:* Ga, Ac, Sa.

National Identities discusses how cultural and political factors contribute to national identity and how these factors have been adapted and changed over time. The peer-reviewed articles primarily focus on the creation of national identities. Contributors come from a wide range of disciplines including literature, history, geography, religion, sociology, architecture, and political science, just to name a few. Each issue contains approximately five research articles and three book reviews. Online (ISSN 1469-9907) subscribers can view article metrics; see lists of the most read and most cited articles; and post to social media. Recommended for academic libraries.

2701. ***The National Interest.*** [ISSN: 0884-9382] 1985. bi-m. USD 29.95 domestic; USD 34.95 Canada; USD 49.95 elsewhere. Ed(s): Robert Golan-Vilella, Zachary Keck. The Nixon Center, 615 L St, Ste 1250, Washington, DC 20036; backissues@nationalinterest.org; http://www.nixoncenter.org/. Illus., adv. Vol. ends: Winter. Microform: PQC. *Indexed:* A01, A22, BRI, IBSS, MLA-IB, P61. *Bk. rev.:* Number and length vary. *Aud.:* Ga, Ac.

The National Interest is a self-proclaimed conservative magazine that publishes articles about American interests in global affairs. The magazine is published by the Nixon Center and is "guided by the belief that nothing will enhance American interests as effectively as the approach to foreign affairs commonly known as realism." Editors intentionally ignite debate by inviting contributors from government, journalism, and academia to discuss the course of American policy. Articles are written for a general audience and discuss a wide range of global and domestic topics. Online (ISSN 1938-1573) subscribers have unlimited access to all articles plus the archives through a digital download option that is mobile compatible. The online subscription also contains free blog articles that allow readers to post open comments and share on social media. The journal also offers some free content on its website; however, most readers will be annoyed by the rotating advertisements on every page. This magazine will be especially helpful for library users intentionally seeking conservative viewpoints on global issues. Recommended for academic and public libraries.

2702. ***New Global Studies.*** [ISSN: 1940-0004] 2007. 3x/yr. EUR 233. Walter de Gruyter GmbH, Genthiner Str 13, Berlin, 10785, Germany; service@degruyter.com; https://www.degruyter.de. Refereed. *Indexed:* P61. *Bk. rev.:* Number and length vary. *Aud.:* Ac, Sa.

Combining anthropology and history, *New Global Studies* takes a unique multidisciplinary approach to globalization by focusing on social patterns that have developed over time and locality. This historical perspective brings something new to the study of globalization, and casts "increasing light on the common history of humankind." This is a subscription-based journal published by De Gruyter, a longstanding independent academic publisher. In contrast to most historical journals, the primary emphasis is on the twentieth and twenty-first centuries. The journal adjusts the content categories to accommodate submissions; however, issues generally include a variation of peer-reviewed articles, commentaries, editor forums, book reviews, documentations, reports, and review essays. Online (ISSN 1940-0004) subscribers can view the most downloaded articles and create journal alerts or RSS feeds. Each article contains options for formatting citations, posting comments, and sharing on social media. Recommended for academic libraries.

2703. ***New Internationalist: people, ideas and action for global justice.*** Formerly (until 1973): *Internationalist.* [ISSN: 0305-9529] 1971. 10x/yr. GBP 70. New Internationalist Publications Ltd., 3 Queensbridge, The Lakes, Northampton, NN4 7BF, United Kingdom; help@newint.org; http://www.newint.org. Illus., index, adv. Sample. *Indexed:* A01, A22, AmHI, BRI, C37, MASUSE. *Bk. rev.:* Number and length vary. *Aud.:* Ga, Ac.

New Internationalist is an activist magazine with a liberal viewpoint. The purpose of the magazine is to "investigate global injustice and expose inequality." The magazine accepts no corporate advertising dollars and operates as an independent non-profit organization funded mainly by donations and subscriptions. The magazine addresses global topics currently in the news and also seeks out stories overlooked by mainstream media. Articles generally fall into the investigative, narrative, and argumentative categories. The in-depth investigative articles are lengthy and include references; however, they are written for general audience appeal. Digital subscribers can access all content from the print editions plus exclusive web-only content. Digital subscribers can also access content through the magazine's mobile app. For non-subscribers, the website provides free access to a few blog articles and links to recommended videos and podcasts. For social media users, the magazine's most recent Twitter activity continually displays on the website along with lists of the most read articles as well as the most recent trending topics. This magazine will be especially useful for library users intentionally seeking liberal viewpoints about global issues. Recommended for academic and public libraries.

2704. ***Perspectives on Politics.*** Supersedes in part (in 2003): *American Political Science Review;* Which incorporated (1904-1906): *American Political Science Association. Proceedings.* [ISSN: 1537-5927] 1904. q. Ed(s): James Moskowitz, Jeffrey C Isaac. Cambridge University Press, University Printing House, Shaftesbury Rd, Cambridge, CB2 8BS, United Kingdom; journals@cambridge.org; https://www.cambridge.org/. Adv. Reprint: PSC. *Indexed:* A22, E01, IBSS, P61. *Bk. rev.:* Number and length vary. *Aud.:* Ac, Sa.

Perspectives on Politics is published on behalf of the American Political Science Association (APSA). Each issue contains research articles, review essays, and book reviews. Articles usually combine political history with current global issues. However, the main purpose of this journal is to serve as the APSA's "official venue for book reviews." The journal publishes approximately 250 book reviews each year. Books selected for review fall primarily into four categories: political theory, American politics, comparative politics, and international relations. Online (ISSN 1541-0986) subscribers can create journal alerts; send articles to mobile devices and cloud services; view article metrics; and post to social media. Recommended for academic libraries.

2705. *Politics & Society.* [ISSN: 0032-3292] 1970. q. USD 1443 (print & online eds.)). Ed(s): Mary-Ann Twist. Sage Publications, Inc., 2455 Teller Rd, Thousand Oaks, CA 91320; info@sagepub.com; http://www.sagepub.com. Illus., index, adv. Refereed. Vol. ends: No. 4. Microform: PQC. Reprint: PSC. *Indexed:* A01, A22, BAS, CJPI, E01, IBSS, P61, SSA. *Aud.:* Ac, Sa.

Politics & Society was established in 1970 as an alternative critical voice of the social sciences. The journal's mission is to "develop Marxist, post-Marxist, and other radical perspectives, in addition to examining some outrageous hypotheses." The peer-reviewed research articles focus on raising questions about "the way the world is organized politically, economically, and socially." Each issue contains approximately five research articles. Online (ISSN 1552-7514) subscribers can create journal alerts and RSS feeds; view the article metrics; view the journal's most read and most cited articles; and post to social media. This journal will be helpful for users intentionally seeking alternative views on political topics, social sciences issues, and historical theories. Recommended for academic libraries.

2706. *Portal: journal of multidisciplinary international studies.* [ISSN: 1449-2490] 2004. s-a. Free. Ed(s): Paul Allatson. U T S ePRESS (University of Technology Sydney), Broadway, PO Box 123, Sydney, NSW 2007, Australia; utsepress@lib.uts.edu.au; http://epress.lib.uts.edu.au/. Sample. Refereed. *Indexed:* A01, MLA-IB, P61. *Bk. rev.:* Irregular. *Aud.:* Ac, Sa.

Portal is a scholarly open-access journal published by the University of Technology in Sydney, Australia. The journal's mission is to provide a publication venue "for practitioners of and dissenters from" international, regional, ethnic, and migration studies. The peer-reviewed articles are primarily in English, but other languages are also included. Issues are theme based and usually contain research articles, general-interest articles, and a variety of cultural pieces such as poetry, prose, and short stories. Contributing authors for cultural pieces are referred to as cultural producers and come from disciplines related to the humanities, the social sciences, and cultural studies. Subject themes are diverse. Readers can create journal alerts, email articles, email authors, and post comments. The articles contain formatted citations and links for finding additional materials by author on Google Scholar. This journal will be helpful for users searching for contemporary cultural pieces created by international authors not widely known. Recommended for academic libraries.

2707. *Rand Review (Online).* 2015. bi-m. Free. Ed(s): Steve Baeck. Rand Corporation, Publications Department, 1776 Main St, PO Box 2138, Santa Monica, CA 90407-2138; order@rand.org; http://www.rand.org. *Aud.:* Ga.

The *Rand Review* is the flagship magazine from the RAND Corporation. It was redesigned and relaunched in online format beginning with the March/April 2015 issue. Readers can download the free issues directly from the RAND website or sign up for the free email notification service. Issues are available in pdf and ePub. Issues are also accessible through the magazine's new iOS and Android apps. The apps contain additional video and interactive features. RAND is a nonprofit and nonpartisan organization that focuses on developing public policy solutions affecting global safety, health, security, and prosperity. Since the magazine's redesign, articles have covered a diverse range of subjects from a global perspective. Although some articles contain references to research results and primary statistical data, all articles are written for general audience appeal. In addition to the online magazine, the *Rand Review* website contains essays, blog posts, and human interest pieces. The design of the online magazine and the supplementary website is modern, visually appealing, and easy to use. Articles include high-quality images. Interested readers can sign up for RSS feeds and participate in social media conversations. Highly recommended for all academic and public libraries as well as some high school libraries supporting a global studies or current events curriculum.

2708. *The S A I S Review of International Affairs.* Former titles (until 2004): *S A I S Review (Paul H. Nitze School of Advanced International Studies)*; (until 1989): *S A I S Review.* [ISSN: 1945-4716] 1956. s-a. USD 125. Ed(s): Michael Cass-Antony, Devan Kerley. The Johns Hopkins University Press, 2715 N Charles St, Baltimore, MD 21218; http://www.press.jhu.edu. Illus., index, adv. Sample. Refereed. Vol. ends: No. 2. Reprint: PSC. *Indexed:* A22, BAS, BRI, E01, IBSS, P61. *Bk. rev.:* Number and length vary. *Aud.:* Ga, Ac, Sa.

SAIS Review is published by the Foreign Policy Institute, the Johns Hopkins School of Advanced International Studies (SAIS), and the Johns Hopkins University Press. The *Review* is a subscription-based peer-reviewed journal that publishes essays on current global political, economic, and security questions. The editors prefer essays that "straddle the boundary between scholarly inquiry and practical experience." Contributing authors for the print edition are established academics and practitioners. Issues are theme based and cover a diverse range of topics from differing perspectives. Online access for the print subscription content is available exclusively through Project Muse. In 2012, *SAIS Review* launched a free supplementary online (ISSN 1088-3142) magazine that serves as a forum for exploring global studies and economics. The free online magazine contains blog posts, interviews, book reviews, and exclusive articles that are short and written for general audience appeal. Although most of the online articles are written by established practitioners and academics, some are written by students who contribute some great content and fresh ideas. Online readers can post article comments, share article links, and follow the magazine's social media conversations. Highly recommended for academic and large public libraries.

The Wilson Quarterly (Online): surveying the world of ideas. See General Interest section.

2709. *World Development: the multi-disciplinary international journal devoted to the study and promotion of world development.* Former titles (until 1973): *New Commonwealth & World Development;* (until 1970): *New Commonwealth Trade & Commerce;* (until 1966): *New Commonwealth;* (until 1950): *The Crown Colonist.* [ISSN: 0305-750X] 1931. m. EUR 4869. Ed(s): Arun Agrawal. Pergamon Press, The Blvd, Langford Ln, E Park, Kidlington, OX5 1GB, United Kingdom; JournalsCustomerServiceEMEA@elsevier.com; http://www.elsevier.com. Illus., adv. Sample. Refereed. Microform: PQC. *Indexed:* A01, A22, Agr, AmHI, B01, BAS, BRI, C45, EconLit, IBSS, P61, SSA. *Aud.:* Ac.

World Development is one of the best academic journals devoted to exploring improvements for the human condition. Article topics primarily focus on subjects that involve potential solutions, constructive problem solving, and lessons learned. Potential solutions usually address problems such as poverty, homelessness, malnutrition, illiteracy, and unemployment. Lessons learned are usually gleaned from the experiences of different nations, societies, and economies. Editors solicit articles that help readers "learn from one another, regardless of nation, culture, income, academic discipline, profession or ideology." The overall purpose of the journal is "to set a modest example of enduring global cooperation through maintaining an international dialogue and dismantling barriers to communication." In theory, the goal and purpose of this journal is inspirational. In reality, there is a sad irony surrounding this journal. The astronomical institutional subscription price prohibits most academic libraries from ever acquiring this title. It is irrational that a journal devoted to the study of poverty and the dismantling of communication barriers is so difficult to access due to cost. Pricing aside, *World Development* adds a great deal of new and interesting information to the research conversations surrounding global development issues. The expansive issues typically contain more than 40 articles with each article averaging 10 pages in length. Online subscribers can create new article RSS feeds, view the article metrics, and share content on social media. Non-subscribers can access a few open-access articles provided in most issues. Due to prohibitive pricing, this journal is only recommended for large academic libraries.

2710. *World Politics Review.* [ISSN: 1944-6284] 2008. d. USD 118. Ed(s): Judah Grunstein. World Politics Review, 1776 I St NW, 9th Fl, Washington, DC 20016; info@worldpoliticsreview.com; http://worldpoliticsreview.com. Adv. *Bk. rev.:* Number and length vary. *Aud.:* Ga, Ac, Sa.

World Politics Review is an online magazine that analyzes current global trends. Library access is provided by EBSCO; but thankfully an institutional subscription also includes full access to the magazine's website, which readers will overwhelmingly prefer. The online magazine is primarily divided into three sections. The daily section contains "multiple five-minute reads" that include briefings on matters of current importance, columns with differing professional perspectives, and trend lines with brief current events and interviews. The in-depth section contains full-length reports focusing on single subjects and country reports. The media roundup section is updated every weekday morning and contains editor links to items in the global English-language press that have the potential to develop into headline news. The magazine's website is visually appealing, easy to use, and mobile friendly. iOS and Android apps are also available for mobile users. Articles include high-quality images. Readers can view trending news stories, watch podcasts, follow the magazine on social media, and subscribe to the free weekly newsletter. *World Politics Review* offers concise, current, and interesting news analyses that should appeal to business, academic, and general audiences. Highly recommended for academic and public libraries.

2711. *The World Today.* Formerly (until 1945): *Bulletin of International News.* [ISSN: 0043-9134] 1925. m. GBP 137 (Individuals, GBP 38; Free to members). Ed(s): Alan Philips. Royal Institute of International Affairs, Chatham House, 10 St James's Sq, London, SW1Y 4LE, United Kingdom; http://www.riia.org. Illus., index, adv. Microform: PQC. *Indexed:* A01, A22, BAS, BRI, IBSS, P61. *Bk. rev.:* Number and length vary. *Aud.:* Ga, Ac, Sa.

The World Today has been published for more than 90 years by the Royal Institute of International Affairs, which is part of the British think tank, Chatham House. The magazine contains current analyses on global topics aimed at both an academic and general audience. Each issue contains a cover story section with several subject-related articles; a features section with short articles on global issues and interviews; and a regulars section with editorials, a retrospective article, and a few film and book reviews. The online edition includes free access to the content of the most recent issue and free access to a searchable video archive. Online access for older content requires a subscription. Online readers can share articles by email and post to social media. Articles are interesting, concise, and supplemented with high-quality images. Highly recommended for academic and public libraries.

2712. *Worldpress.org.* 1997. d. Free. Ed(s): Teri Schure. Worldpress.org, c/o AllMedia Inc., 5601 Democracy Drive Suite 255, Plano, TX 75024. Adv. *Bk. rev.:* Number and length vary. *Aud.:* Hs, Ga, Ac.

Worldpress.org is a free independent online magazine that pulls together news headlines and articles from around the world. The mission of this online magazine is to "foster the international exchange of perspectives and information" by offering a first-hand look at how issues are presented in the world press. *Worldpress.org* originally served as an online magazine supplement to the *World Press Review,* a print publication that ceased in 2004. The online magazine continued to be published independently and retained its website formatting and design, which is now dated but still functional. *Worldpress.org* editors select articles that allow readers to understand "the information that shapes opinions and views in other societies." Articles are a mixture of both original content and republished articles from press outside of the United States. Readers can select articles by front-page news, world headlines, world newspapers, or specific geographic region. The world news headline articles are updated every 15 minutes. There are additional supplementary links for accessing world blog news, entertainment news, think tank/NGO news, maps of the world, and country profiles. Options are available to create email alerts and RSS feeds. All articles contain links for emailing, posting on social media, and contacting the editors and authors. Although there are no pop-ups, some readers may be annoyed by the embedded advertisements. Other readers may not like the dated design of the magazine's website. However, the free content makes *Worldpress.org* a financially attractive option for high school libraries supporting a global studies or journalism curriculum. Recommended for some academic, public, and high school libraries.

2713. *Yale Global Online.* 2002. irreg. Free. Ed(s): Nayan Chanda. Yale University, Center for the Study of Globalization, The Betts House, 393 Prospect St, New Haven, CT 06511; globalization@yale.edu; http://www.ycsg.yale.edu. *Bk. rev.:* Number and length vary. *Aud.:* Ga, Ac, Sa.

Yale Global Online is a free online magazine published by the MacMillan Center for International and Area Studies at Yale University. The magazine recently implemented a design transformation that vastly improved both visual appeal and usability. Articles now contain high-quality images. The purpose of the magazine is to "analyze and promote debate on all aspects of globalization through published original articles and multimedia presentations." The online magazine is searchable by topic, geographic region, and information type such as special reports, essays, book reviews, multimedia, and websites. Within copyright provisions, *Yale Global* also republishes globalization articles from other sources that support further learning and promote debate. Readers can share articles through email and social media. In addition, readers can make public comments concerning article content. Highly recommended for academic and public libraries.

■ GOVERNMENT PERIODICALS—FEDERAL

Rosemary L. Meszaros, Professor and Coordinator, Government Information and Law, Western Kentucky University, Bowling Green, KY 42101; 270-745-6441; rosemary.meszaros@wku.edu

Introduction

The U.S. Government Publishing Office, known by its acronym, GPO, maintains the Federal Depository Library Program, consisting of 1,150 libraries across the country. After more than 150 years of service as the Government Printing Office, its name has been updated to reflect more accurately what it does. GPO's mission remains, as its motto says, "Keeping America Informed."

GPO continues to publish and disseminate federal government reports, studies, testimony, hearings, analyses, and surveys - in short, the very words uttered and written by our federal public servants. The many federal agencies in the executive branch, the Congress and its agencies, and the Supreme Court all offer something for every interest. Law, military, politics, education, environment, business, economics, agriculture, weather, science, demographics, large print, audio and braille bibliographies, consumer information, and statistics - all are represented in the array of magazines and journals that GPO publishes, or distributes (whether in paper form, in microform, or on the Internet), or sells.

Two gateways seek to facilitate access to web-based federal government information: USA.gov, from the General Services Administration, www.usa.gov; and the Library of Congress's web site, http://loc.gov. The Federal Citizen Information Center in Pueblo, Colorado, has been merged with USA.gov. USA.gov incorporates several social media sites: GobiernoUSA.gov is the Spanish-language counterpart, and it includes Blog.USA.gov. USA.gov seeks to create the digital front door for the United States government.

https://bensguide.gpo.gov/ is the federal government's official web site for kids, linking educators, parents, and kids (in grades K-8) with fun and educational activities and lesson plans. For social media in English or Spanish for helpful, up-to-the-minute information, use Twitter, YouTube, Instagram, e-mail alerts, and updates. GPO is continually maintaining its presence in all new technology.

Through digitization and working partnerships with depository libraries, the GPO has made significant progress in keeping the Federal Depository Library Program a vital conduit that provides citizens with access to government information. The GPO's web site, www.gpo.gov/fdsys/ - connected with the Federal Digital System, FDsys (pronounced "fed sis") - is being replaced by govinfo.gov, https://www.govinfo.gov/ - an attractive and informative web site.

Basic Periodicals

Ga: *Congressional Record, Federal Register, Compilation of Presidential Documents;* Ac: *MMWR: Morbidity and Mortality Weekly Report.*

Basic Abstracts and Indexes

LexisNexis, PAIS International.

2714. *A R C R Alcohol Research: Current Reviews.* Former titles (until 2015): *Alcohol Research;* (until 2012): *Alcohol Research & Health;* (until 1999): *Alcohol Health & Research World.* 1973. 3x/yr. USD 21 domestic; USD 29.40 foreign. Ed(s): Troy J Zarcone, Jennifer A Hobin. U.S. National Institute on Alcohol Abuse and Alcoholism, 5635 Fishers Lane, MSC 9304, Bethesda, MD 20892; NIAAAPressOffice@mail.nih.gov; http://www.niaaa.nih.gov. Illus., index. Refereed. Vol. ends: No. 4. *Indexed:* A01, A22, Agr, C42, CJPI, Chicano, HRIS, MASUSE. *Aud.:* Ac, Sa.

Each issue presents an in-depth review of an important area of alcohol research. Topics cover a wide range of disciplines in the biomedical and social sciences. An editorial advisory board meets annually to propose upcoming issue themes and to identify leaders in the field who are invited to contribute articles. Editorial advisory board members also serve as scientific review editors for each issue. This peer-reviewed scientific journal is available in full text from 1994 to date on the web site of the National Institute on Alcohol Abuse and Alcoholism. URL: www.arcr.niaaa.nih.gov/arcr

2715. *Army History.* Formerly (until 1989): *The Army Historian.* [ISSN: 1546-5330] 1983. q. USD 20. Ed(s): William R Scherer. U.S. Army, Center of Military History, 102 4th Ave Bldg 35, Fort McNair, DC 20319; contactcenter@gpo.gov; http://www.history.army.mil/. *Bk. rev.:* Number and length vary. *Aud.:* Ga, Ac, Sa.

First published in fall 1983 as *The Army Historian,* this is a publication of the United States Army Center of Military History. Each issue contains feature articles on some aspect of, or person important to, military history. In addition to the feature articles, there are signed book reviews. All issues are online. A searchable index is at the bottom of the page. URL: www.history.army.mil/armyhistory

The Astronomical Almanac. See Astronomy section.

2716. *Cityscape (Washington, D.C.): a journal of policy development and research.* [ISSN: 1936-007X] 1994. 3x/yr. Free. U.S. Department of Housing and Urban Development, Office of Policy Development and Research, PO Box 23268, Washington, DC 20026; helpdesk@huduser.org; https://www.huduser.gov. Refereed. *Aud.:* Ga, Ac, Sa.

Cityscape: A Journal of Policy Development and Research strives to share HUD-funded and other research on housing and urban policy issues with scholars, government officials, and others who are involved in setting policy and determining the direction of future research. This refereed journal focuses on innovative ideas, policies, and programs that show promise in revitalizing cities and regions, renewing their infrastructure, and creating economic opportunities. A typical issue consists of articles that examine various aspects of a theme of particular interest to its audience, such as the home-equity conversion mortgage or reverse mortgage; personal bankruptcy exemption laws; mortgage availability; housing discrimination; and assisted housing, among others. It has been online since its first issue in August 1994. URL: www.huduser.org/portal/periodicals/cityscape.html

2717. *Compilation of Presidential Documents.* Former titles (until 2016): *Daily Compilation of Presidential Documents;* (until 2009): *Weekly Compilation of Presidential Documents (Online).* 1965. d. Free. National Archives and Records Administration, U.S. Office of the Federal Register, 8601 Adelphi Rd, College Park, MD 20740; http://www.federalregister.gov. Illus., index. Vol. ends: No. 52. *Indexed:* A01, A22, Chicano. *Aud.:* Ga, Ac, Sa.

As of January 29, 2009, the *Weekly Compilation of Presidential Documents* was replaced by the *Daily Compilation of Presidential Documents.* Now it is more often referred to as *Compilation of Presidential Documents.* This is the authoritative source for all presidential communications, including proclamations, executive orders, speeches, press conferences, communications to Congress and federal agencies, statements regarding bill signings and vetoes, appointments, nominations, reorganization plans, resignations, retirements, acts approved by the president, nominations submitted to the Senate, White House announcements, and press releases. It is only in electronic form from the U.S. Government Publishing Office's Federal Digital System (FDsys) web site (https://www.gpo.gov/fdsys/browse/collection.action?collectionCode=CPD). Take a look at http://whitehouse.gov for additional administration doings by the vice president and the first lady, updated daily.

2718. *Congressional Record: proceedings and debates of the Congress.* Former titles (until 1873): *Congressional Globe;* (until 1833): *Register of Debates in Congress;* (until 1824): *United States. Congress. Debates and Proceedings;* (until 1789): *United States. Continental Congress. Journal.* [ISSN: 0363-7239] 1774. d. USD 503 domestic; USD 704.20 foreign. U.S. Government Printing Office, 710 N Capitol St, NW, Washington, DC 20401; http://www.gpo.gov. Illus., index. *Aud.:* Ac, Sa.

The *Congressional Record* is the most widely recognized published account of the debates, proceedings, and activities of the United States Congress. Currently averaging more than 200 pages a day, it is a substantially verbatim account of the proceedings of Congress. It is published daily when either or both houses of Congress are in session. It may be thought of as the world's largest daily newspaper, because it contains an account of everything that is said and done on the floors of the House and Senate, extensive additional reprinting of inserted materials, and, since 1947, a resume of congressional activity (the *Daily Digest*). Available and searchable online through the Government Publishing Office, it has digitized the entire *CR* from 1873 to current. URL: https://www.govinfo.gov/app/collection/crecb/158_crecb/Volume%20001%20(1873)

2719. *Emerging Infectious Diseases (Print).* [ISSN: 1080-6040] 1995. m. Free. Ed(s): D P Drotman. U.S. Department of Health and Human Services, Centers for Disease Control and Prevention, 1600 Clifton Rd, Atlanta, GA 30329; http://www.cdc.gov. Illus. Refereed. Vol. ends: No. 4. *Indexed:* A01, A22, BRI, C45. *Bk. rev.:* Number and length vary. *Aud.:* Ga, Sa.

This is a monthly peer-reviewed journal that tracks and analyzes disease trends. It has a very high citation rate and ranking in its field. In addition to dispatches on the latest epidemiology of infectious diseases, the issues contain research articles, columns, letters, commentary, and book reviews. It is available in full text beginning with its inaugural issue in 1995 from the Centers for Disease Control and Prevention web site. The online-edition articles are expedited ahead of print articles. URL: www.cdc.gov/ncidod/eid/

2720. *Engineer (Fort Leonard Wood): the professional bulletin of Army engineers.* [ISSN: 0046-1989] 1971. 3x/yr. USD 24 domestic; USD 33.60 foreign. Ed(s): Diane K Dean, Cheryl A Nygaard. U.S. Army Maneuver Support Center, Development Support Department, P O Box 979050, St. Louis, MO 63197; leon.engineer@conus.army.mil; http://www.wood.army.mil. *Indexed:* A01, A22, BRI. *Bk. rev.:* Number and length vary. *Aud.:* Sa.

Engineer is a professional-development bulletin designed to provide a forum for exchanging information and ideas within the Army engineer community. Articles are by and about officers, enlisted soldiers, warrant officers, Department of the Army civilian employees, and others. Writers discuss training, current operations and exercises, doctrine, equipment, history, personal viewpoints, or other areas of general interest to engineers. Articles may share good ideas and lessons learned or explore better ways of doing things. In addition to regular columns from the Commandant of the U.S. Army Engineer School and the Command Sergeant Major, and a book review column, there are updates of revisions on Engineer Doctrine. Full-text electronic coverage as of 2003. URL: www.wood.army.mil/engrmag/

2721. *English Teaching Forum.* Former titles (until 2000): *U.S. Department of State. Bureau of International Information Programs. Forum;* (until 1982): *United States. International Communication Agency. Forum;* (until 197?): *United States Information Agency. Forum;* (until 1978): *English Teaching Forum.* [ISSN: 1559-663X] 1963. q. Ed(s): Tom Glass. U.S. Department of State, Bureau of Education and Cultural Affairs, 2201 C St NW, Washington, DC 20520. Illus. *Indexed:* A22, ERIC, MLA-IB. *Bk. rev.:* 4, 1/2 page. *Aud.:* Ga, Ac, Sa.

A quarterly journal published by the U.S. Department of State for teachers of English as a foreign or second language. The journal emphasizes teaching American English (AE). More than 60,000 copies of the magazine are distributed in 100 countries. Most of the authors published in the journal are classroom teachers and regular readers of the journal. Submissions from English-language teachers around the world are welcomed. Book reviews are a half-page in length. Printed copies of the journal may be obtained from the U.S. Superintendent of Documents, at the U.S. Government Publishing Office. Articles from issues of the *Forum* dating back to 1993 are available online at the U.S. Department of State web site. URL: http://americanenglish.state.gov/english-teaching-forum

Environmental Health Perspectives. See Public Health section.

Federal Probation (Online). See Criminology and Law Enforcement section.

2722. *Federal Register.* [ISSN: 0097-6326] 1936. d. (Mon.-Fri.) except federal holiday. National Archives and Records Administration, U.S. Office of the Federal Register, 8601 Adelphi Rd, College Park, MD 20740; fedreg.info@nara.gov; http://www.federalregister.gov. Microform: BHP; WSH; PMC; PQC. *Indexed:* A&ATA, B01. *Aud.:* Ga, Ac, Sa.

The *Federal Register* is the official daily publication for rules, proposed rules, and notices of federal agencies and organizations, as well as executive orders and other presidential documents. It is updated daily by 6 a.m. and is published Monday through Friday, except federal holidays. FDsys contains *Federal Register* volumes from 59 (1994) to the present. URL: https://www.federalregister.gov/. Browse all issues online since March, 1936, through GPO's govinfo.gov. URL: https://www.govinfo.gov/app/collection/fr

2723. *Federal Reserve Bulletin.* [ISSN: 0014-9209] 1914. q. USD 25 domestic; USD 35 foreign. U.S. Federal Reserve System, Board of Governors, 20th St and Constitution Ave, NW, Washington, DC 20551; regs.comments@federalreserve.gov; http://www.federalreserve.gov. Microform: CIS; MIM; PMC; PQC. Reprint: WSH. *Indexed:* A01, A22, B01, BLI, EconLit. *Aud.:* Ac, Sa.

Staff members of the Board of Governors of the Federal Reserve prepare the articles for this publication. In general, they report and analyze economic developments, discuss bank regulatory issues, and present new data. Available in full text online since 1996 on the Federal Reserve Board web site. The quarterly *paper* version of the *Bulletin* is available for sale. The board produces an annual compilation in print for sale. Online access is free. An e-mail notification service alerts subscribers to newly available testimonies, speeches, articles, and reports in the *Federal Reserve Bulletin.* URL: www.federalreserve.gov/pubs/general.htm

Fishery Bulletin. See Fish, Fisheries, and Aquaculture section.

Humanities: the magazine of the national endowment for the humanities. See Cultural Studies section.

Marine Fisheries Review. See Fish, Fisheries, and Aquaculture section.

Mariners Weather Log (Online). See Marine Science and Technology/Ocean Science section.

Military History. See Military section.

Military Review (English Edition). See Military section.

Monthly Labor Review Online, U.S. Bureau of Labor Statistics. See Labor and Industrial Relations section.

2724. *Morbidity and Mortality Weekly Report (Online).* Formerly (until 1976): *Morbidity and Mortality.* [ISSN: 1545-861X] 19??. w. Free. Ed(s): Sonja A Rasmussen, Jacqueline Gindler. U.S. Department of Health and Human Services, Centers for Disease Control and Prevention, 1600 Clifton Rd, Atlanta, GA 30329; cdcinfo@cdc.gov; http://www.cdc.gov. Illus., index. *Aud.:* Ac, Sa.

Often called the voice of CDC (Centers for Disease Control). This title contains data on specific diseases as reported by state and territorial health departments, and reports on infectious and chronic diseases, environmental hazards, natural or human-generated disasters, occupational diseases and injuries, and intentional and unintentional injuries. Also included are reports on topics of international interest and notices of events of interest to the public health community. No longer distributed in paper to federal depository libraries. Available online from 1982, on the Centers for Disease Control's own web site. URL: www.cdc.gov/mmwr/

2725. *N I S T Journal of Research (Online).* Formerly (until 2015): *National Institute of Standards and Technology. Journal of Research (Online).* 1904. . Free. Ed(s): Ron B Goldfarb, Barbara Silcox. U.S. Department of Commerce, National Institute of Standards and Technology, 100 Bureau Dr, Stop 2500, Gaithersburg, MD 20899; inquiries@nist.gov; http://www.nist.gov. Refereed. *Aud.:* Ac, Sa.

This journal reports on National Institute of Standards and Technology (NIST) research and development in metrology and related fields of physical science, engineering, applied mathematics, statistics, biotechnology, and information technology. Papers are peer reviewed and cover a broad range of subjects, with the major emphasis on measurement methodology and the basic technology that underlies standardization. Also included, on occasion, are articles on topics closely related to the institute's technical and scientific program. NIST was formerly the National Bureau of Standards. Full text of all articles since its inception as the *Bulletin of the National Bureau of Standards* in 1904 are available on the NIST web site. Starting in 2012, the journal became an electronic-only publication under a new rapid-publication model - articles are published as soon as they are received. URL: www.nist.gov/nvl/jres.cfm

Occupational Outlook Quarterly. See Occupations and Careers section.

2726. *OnSafety.* Former titles (until 2009): *The Safety Review;* (until 200?): *Consumer Product Safety Review;* (until 1996): *N E I S S Data Highlights;* (until 19??): *N E I S S News.* 1976. q. U.S. Consumer Product Safety Commission, 5 Research Place, Rockville, MD 208550. *Aud.:* Ga, Sa.

With its new title, *OnSafety,* this quarterly journal has become a blog that offers an in-depth look at the latest hazards associated with 15,000 types of consumer products under the agency's jurisdiction, both home and recreational products, as well as the most significant current product recalls. Available from its first issue in summer 1996 to its current issue. Available in English and Spanish. URL: www.cpsc.gov/onsafety/

Parameters. See Military section.

2727. *Peaceworks.* [ISSN: 1946-4517] 1995. irreg. U.S. Institute of Peace, 2301 Constitution Ave NW, Washington, DC 20037; http://www.usip.org. *Aud.:* Ga, Ac, Sa.

This title presents in-depth background and analysis on topics that represent the full range of the work of the United States Institute of Peace (USIP). Its reports explore specific conflicts; offer comparative analysis across conflicts; evaluate peacebuilding efforts; and present new approaches to conflict through a variety of lenses, such as economics, gender, media and technology, religion, rule of law, and reform of the security sector. Searchable by issue, country, and expert. URL: https://www.usip.org/publications

Prologue (Washington). See Archives and Manuscripts section.

Public Health Reports. See Public Health section.

Public Roads. See Transportation section.

2728. *State Magazine (Online).* [ISSN: 1939-3679] 1961. m. Free. Ed(s): Isaac D Pacheco. U.S. Department of State, 2401 E Street NW, Rm H232, Washington, DC 20037; http://www.state.gov/. *Indexed:* A51. *Aud.:* Ga, Sa.

State Magazine is published to facilitate communication between management and employees of the State Department at home and abroad, and to acquaint employees with developments that may affect operations or personnel. The magazine is no longer in print. It is digital only. While the magazine serves the members of the State Department, it contains interesting articles about people and places all over the world. Online since 1998. URL: www.state.gov/m/dghr/statemag

2729. *Treasury Bulletin.* Formerly (until 1945): *Treasury Department. Bulletin;* Incorporates (in 1945): *Financial Condition and Results of the Operations of the Highway Trust Fund. Annual Report;* Which was formerly (until 1982): *Highway Trust Fund. Annual Report.* [ISSN: 0041-2155] 1939. q. USD 51 domestic; USD 64.40 foreign. U.S. Department of the Treasury, Financial Management Service, 3700 E-W Hwy, Hyattsville, MD 20782; http://www.fms.treas.gov. Microform: CIS; PMC. *Indexed:* B01, BLI. *Aud.:* Ga, Sa.

This is a quarterly synopsis of U.S. Department of the Treasury activities, covering financing operations, budget receipts and expenditures, debt operations, cash income and outgo, IRS collections, capital movements, yields of long-term bonds, ownership of federal securities, and other Treasury activities. There are lots of charts and graphs. Regular features include "Profile of the Economy," "Market Yields," "International Statistics," "Capital Movements," "Foreign Currency Positions," and "Federal Debt." Costs of print copies or subscriptions to data reports vary. Online since March 1996. URL: https://www.fiscal.treasury.gov/fsreports/rpt/treasBulletin/treasBulletin_home.htm

■ GOVERNMENT PERIODICALS—STATE AND LOCAL

General/State and Municipal Associations

See also Political Science; and Urban Studies sections.

Rosemary L. Meszaros, Professor and Coordinator, Government Information and Law, Western Kentucky University, Bowling Green, KY 42101; FAX: 270-745-6175; rosemary.meszaros@wku.edu

Introduction

Locally focused are the real conveyers of the wealth of information about their areas. They are hidden treasures. Only one or two maintain a print version exclusively. Open electronic access is the norm. By far, however, most of these publications are digital. Sometimes the electronic access is limited to a membership in the organization that produces the periodical.

Although only six states (California, Florida, Michigan, South Carolina, Texas, and Virginia) maintain a state depository program similar to that of the federal government, searching the Internet yields the web sites of an overwhelming majority of the municipal leagues or state governments that provide the platform for state and local periodicals.

Budgeting, the environment, infrastructure, technology, telecommunications, and health care are common topics. The periodicals are essentially narrowly focused and offer a homegrown coverage that national periodicals do not. Besides these communal concerns, some of the periodicals feature articles on how the policies of the federal government may impact local issues, such as unemployment and health care.

The fears about retention of archives are well founded, because several of the titles in this section have dropped previous years of the publication off their web sites. As librarians, we lament this situation. For those of us who have the history gene, this is a tragedy. It is understandable that tight budgets may mandate a leaner web site, but it is distressing to lose the past.

While some of the periodicals in this section may be of interest primarily to state and local officials, most are of interest to residents of the areas. A companion section in this volume is "Urban Studies."

Basic Periodicals

Ac: *State and Local Government Review, State Legislatures.*

Basic Abstracts and Indexes

LexisNexis, PAIS International, Urban Studies Abstracts, Worldwide Political Science Abstracts.

General

American City & County. See Urban Studies section.

2730. *Capitol Ideas.* Former titles (until 2010): *State News;* (until 2004): *State Government News;* Which incorporated (19??-1978): *Legislative Session Sheet;* (199?-2001): *State Trends;* Which was formerly (until 199?): *State Trends Bulletin;* State Government News incorporated: *States and Nation;* Which was formerly (until 1962): *Washington Bulletin;* (until 1961): *Washington Legislative Bulletin.* [ISSN: 2152-8489] 19??. bi-m. USD 42; USD 7 per issue. Ed(s): Kelley Arnold. Council of State Governments, 2760 Research Park Dr, PO Box 11910, Lexington, KY 40511; info@csg.org; http://www.csg.org/. Illus., adv. Microform: WSH. *Indexed:* A01, A22, BRI. *Aud.:* Ga, Sa.

For more than 50 years, *Capitol Ideas* magazine, formerly titled *State News,* has been a source of nonpartisan information. It offers updates and in-depth analyses of state programs, policies, and trends in the executive, legislative, and judicial branches. It covers areas such as budget shortfalls, health and human services, environment and natural resources, agriculture and rural policy, public safety and justice, education, energy, transportation, telecommunications, digital government, fiscal policy, economic development, state leadership, state management and administration, federalism and intergovernmental relations, interstate relations, election coverage, emergency management, and more. Online since 2007. URL: www.csg.org/pubs/capitolideas/

2731. *County News (Washington).* Formerly (until 1973): *N A C O News and Views.* [ISSN: 0744-9798] 1969. s-m. National Association of Counties, 25 Massachusetts Ave N W, Washington, DC 20001; naco@naco.org; http://www.naco.org. Illus., adv. Vol. ends: Dec. *Aud.:* Sa.

Published by the National Association of Counties (NACo), this journal evaluates issues and policies of interest to county officials nationwide. Sections include: "News from Across the Nation," "Human Services," "Transportation & Infrastructure," "Tax & Finance," "Justice," "Telecommunications & Technology," "Labor & Employment," "Rural Affairs," "Health," "Environment," "Intergovernmental Affairs," "Public Safety," "Elections," and "Profiles in Service" (profiles of county officials). Full text is available online since January 2007 at NACo's web site. URL: http://www.naco.org/news

2732. *P M Magazine.* Former titles (until 19??): *I C M A Public Management Magazine;* (until 2007): *Public Management;* Which incorporated (in 1970): *International City Management Association. Annual Conference. Proceedings;* (until 1926): *City Manager Magazine;* (until 1923): *City Manager Bulletin.* 1919. 11x/yr. Free to members; Non-members, USD 46. Ed(s): Beth Payne. International City/County Management Association, 777 N Capitol St NE, Ste 500, Washington, DC 20002; info@icma.org; http://icma.org/en/icma/home. Illus., adv. Circ: 9500. Vol. ends: Dec. Microform: MIM; PQC. *Indexed:* A22, B01, BRI. *Aud.:* Ga, Sa.

The International City/County Management Association (ICMA) is the publisher of *PM.* ICMA is the professional and educational organization for chief appointed managers, administrators, and assistants in cities, towns, counties, and regional entities throughout the world. It is dedicated exclusively to the public sector practitioner. Feature articles are written from the local government manager's point of view. The intent of the articles is to allow other local government managers to adapt solutions to fit their own situations. Regular sections include letters to the editor, profiles of individual officials and corporate entities, an ethics column, and FYI news briefs. Articles online are passworded, but are available to ICMA members and subscribers to *PM Magazine.* Online since 2003. URL: https://icma.org/public-management-pm-magazine

2733. ***State and Local Government Review: a journal of research and viewpoints on state and local government issues.*** Formerly (until 1976): *Georgia Government Review.* [ISSN: 0160-323X] 1968. q. USD 375 (print & online eds.)). Ed(s): Michael J Scicchitano. Sage Publications, Inc., 2455 Teller Rd, Thousand Oaks, CA 91320; info@sagepub.com; http://www.sagepub.com. Illus., index, adv. Refereed. Vol. ends: Fall. Reprint: PSC. *Indexed:* A22, E01, P61. *Bk. rev.:* 1, 1,000 words. *Aud.:* Ac, Sa.

State and Local Government Review is a peer-reviewed journal that is jointly sponsored by the Carl Vinson Institute of Government of the University of Georgia and the Section on Intergovernmental Administration and Management (SIAM) of the American Society for Public Administration (ASPA). SIAM is the section of ASPA that is dedicated to state and local as well as intergovernmental teaching and research. Membership in SIAM includes a subscription to *State and Local Government Review.* Issues include feature stories and the "Practitioner's Corner," which offers practical advice for government officials on issues such as local government, social equity, sustainability, federalism, telecommunications, utility deregulation, and so on. This is one of the few scholarly journals in this field. Contents and abstracts of articles are available for the most recent issue. Full text is available for previous issues from 1993 forward, through the Carl Vinson Institute of Government. Online for subscribers since 1993. Abstracts only, 1993-1996; abstracts and full text, 1997 to the present. URL: www.sagepub.com/journalsProdDesc.nav?prodId=Journal201992

2734. ***State Legislatures.*** [ISSN: 0147-6041] 1975. 10x/yr. USD 49. Ed(s): Julie Lays. National Conference of State Legislatures, 7700 E First Pl, Denver, CO 80230; http://www.ncsl.org/. Illus., adv. Circ: 18200. Vol. ends: Dec. *Indexed:* A22, BRI. *Aud.:* Ga, Ac.

The trends, issues, solutions, personalities, innovations, and challenges of managing a state - they will all be found in *State Legislatures* magazine, which is published by the National Conference of State Legislatures. This national magazine of state government and policy provides lively, insightful articles that encompass vital information on public policies. From agriculture to cloning to transportation, it covers a wide variety of topics. Only excerpts are available online for nonsubscribers; full access is for government officials, librarians, lobbyists, and university subscribers. URL: www.ncsl.org/magazine

State and Municipal Associations

State and municipal associations are the providers of common ground for local officials to exchange ideas and information in a discussion forum on issues of mutual interest. What shape the content of the periodicals are the common issues of budget shortfalls, legislation, growth, lotteries, crime, traffic, energy, the environment, telecommunications, and leadership. Many of the periodicals contain such helpful features as a calendar of events and a legal advice column. The usual tone is positive, even with consideration of dire issues. The periodicals take a matter-of-fact perspective on confronting and solving problems. The principal audience for these periodicals comprises practitioners and observers of local government.

2735. ***Actionlines Magazine.*** Formerly (until 19??): *Municipal League Review & Hoosier Municipality.* [ISSN: 1092-6259] 19??. a. Free to members. Indiana Association of Cities and Towns, 125 W Market St, Ste 240, Indianapolis, IN 46204; http://www.citiesandtowns.org. Adv. *Aud.:* Ga, Ac, Sa.

Actionlines is the official magazine of the Indiana Association of Cities and Towns. It includes relevant, timely articles about issues that affect Indiana cities and towns and municipal government. It accepts proposals and articles from association members, municipal members, affiliate groups, state agencies, and others. At last *Actionlines* is available online from 2015 at URL: https://issuu.com/indianacitiesandtowns

2736. ***Alabama Municipal Journal.*** Formerly (until 1953): *Alabama Local Government Journal.* [ISSN: 0002-4309] 1935. bi-m. USD 24. Ed(s): Carrie Banks. Alabama League of Municipalities, PO Box 1270, Montgomery, AL 36102; perryr@alalm.org; http://www.alalm.org. Illus., adv. Circ: 4500 Paid and controlled. Vol. ends: Jun. *Aud.:* Sa.

This periodical is from the Alabama League of Municipalities. Its articles highlight the practical issues faced by local governments in Alabama and spotlight common problems, solutions, trends, and legal information. It offers reprints of speeches and articles from other publications from time to time. There is unrestricted Internet access to content since the September 2002 issue. URL: www.alalm.org

2737. ***Cities and Villages.*** Formerly (until 1970): *Ohio Cities and Villages.* [ISSN: 0009-7535] 1953. bi-m. USD 15. Ed(s): Cynthia L Grant. Ohio Municipal League, 175 S 3rd St Ste 510, Columbus, OH 43215; http://www.omlohio.org/. Illus., index, adv. *Aud.:* Ga, Ac, Sa.

The official publication of the Ohio Municipal League, *Cities and Villages* is read by officials who are directly involved in every aspect of municipal management and service. The magazine keeps the leadership of Ohio's cities and villages informed on current developments and the latest techniques for solving municipal problems. Since 2017, this journal has also been posted online. URL: http://omlohio.org/35/Resources

2738. ***City & Town.*** Formerly (until 1977): *Arkansas Municipalities.* [ISSN: 0193-8371] 1947. m. USD 20 (Free to qualified personnel). Ed(s): Andrew Morgan. Arkansas Municipal League, 301 W 2nd St, PO Box 38, North Little Rock, AR 72115; http://www.arml.org. Illus., index, adv. Circ: 7000 Paid and free. Vol. ends: Dec. *Aud.:* Sa.

Designed to provide a forum for municipal officials to exchange ideas and compare notes on accomplishments and problems in Arkansas, *City & Town* is sent to elected officials; city administrators and managers; police chiefs, fire chiefs, and other department heads; and state officials, local newspapers, chambers of commerce, and other offices and persons who are interested in municipal affairs. Employment opportunities and classified ads are spotlighted in the "Municipal Mart" section. Full text, from 2005 on, appears online. URL: www.arml.org/services/publications/city-town

2739. ***CITYScan (Bismarck): connecting cities to solutions.*** Former titles (until 2015): *City Scan;* (until 1996): *North Dakota League of Cities Bulletin.* [ISSN: 1094-5784] 1969. 10x/yr. USD 10. Ed(s): Chelsey Benson. North Dakota League of Cities, 410 E. Front Ave., Bismarck, ND 58504; http://www.ndlc.org/. Illus., adv. *Aud.:* Sa.

Written specifically for city and park district officials and designed to promote best municipal practices, this magazine regularly features information about technology, cost-saving ideas, innovative programs, leadership issues, and products and services that help city leaders increase the efficiency and effectiveness of municipal operations. Selected articles are online only since 2012. URL: www.ndlc.org/index.aspx?NID=159

2740. ***Cityscape (Des Moines).*** Former titles (until 1995): *Iowa Municipalities;* (until 1960): *League of Iowa Municipalities Monthly Magazine.* [ISSN: 1088-5951] 1946. m. Free to members; Non-members, USD 60. Iowa League of Cities, 500 SW 7th St, Ste 101, Des Moines, IA 50309; http://www.iowaleague.org/. Illus., adv. *Aud.:* Sa.

Cityscape is part of the membership benefits of the Iowa League of Cities. The publication contains articles about city government issues in Iowa, and serves as a communication tool for local government officials. Some of the articles featured in *Cityscape* are available online in a Q&A section on the league's web site. Full text is available online only to members. URL: https://www.iowaleague.org/Pages/CityscapeDistribution.aspx

2741. ***Colorado Municipalities.*** [ISSN: 0010-1664] 1925. bi-m. USD 150. Ed(s): Traci Stoffel. Colorado Municipal League, 1144 Sherman St, Denver, CO 80203; cml@cml.org; http://www.cml.org. Illus., adv. *Bk. rev.:* Number and length vary. *Aud.:* Ga, Ac, Sa.

This is the flagship magazine of the Colorado Municipal League. Its target audience is Colorado municipal government officials. Each issue runs to about 30 pages, and is packed with in-depth coverage of the topics and issues important to those officials. The current issue is available free on the web site, but past issues are available online only to members. URL: www.cml.org/magazines/

2742. *CommonWealth: politics, ideas and civic life in Massachusetts.* 1996. q. USD 75. Ed(s): Bruce Mohl. The Massachusetts Institute for a New Common Wealth, 11 Beacon St Ste 500, Boston, MA 02108; http://www.massinc.org. Adv. *Bk. rev.:* Number and length vary. *Aud.:* Ga, Ac, Sa.

The mission of MassINC, publisher of *CommonWealth,* is to develop a public agenda for Massachusetts that promotes the growth and vitality of the middle class. MassINC has four primary initiatives: economic prosperity, lifelong learning, safe neighborhoods, and civic renewal. The publication includes articles, interviews, news, and book reviews. *CommonWealth* calls itself the Bay State's leading political magazine. A *Boston Globe* journalist has called it "snazzy and fair-minded." Web access has been available since summer 1996. Subscribers to the print version are asked for a USD 75 donation to become a friend of MassINC. Online access since 1996. URL: www.massinc.org

2743. *Connecticut Town & City.* 19??. bi-m. Free to members. Ed(s): Kevin Maloney. Connecticut Conference of Municipalities, 900 Chapel St, 9th Fl, New Haven, CT 06510; ccm@ccm-ct.org; http://www.ccm-ct.org. Adv. *Aud.:* Sa.

This journal reports on major intergovernmental issues, new ideas in municipal management, and cost-saving measures by towns. Regular features include "Regional and Intermunicipal Cooperation," "Innovative Ideas for Managing Local Governments," "Civic Amenities" (which includes beautification projects, noise and litter abatement, and other ideas to make communities better places), "Volunteers," "Municipal Ethics Quiz," "What's New," and "Public-Private Cooperation." This is the only periodical devoted exclusively to issues that concern Connecticut's municipal market. This title is no longer in print: it has gone digital. Available online to members only. URL: http://www.ccm-ct.org/ccm-magazine

2744. *Connection (Phoenix).* 2003. m. Free. League of Arizona Cities and Towns, 1820 W Washington St, Phoenix, AZ 85007; league@azleague.org; http://www.azleague.org. *Aud.:* Ga, Ac, Sa.

Through its publication *Connection,* the League of Arizona Cities and Towns, a voluntary membership organization of the incorporated municipalities in Arizona, aims to provide vital services and tools to all its members. It focuses principally on representing the interests of cities and towns before the legislature, and secondarily on providing technical and legal assistance, coordinating shared services, and producing high-quality conference and educational events. All issues are online. URL: www.azleague.org/index.aspx?NID=115

2745. *Creating Quality Cities.* Formerly (until 199?): *City Report.* 19??. 9x/yr. Free to members. Ed(s): GayDawn Oyler. Association of Idaho Cities, 3100 S Vista Ave, Ste 310, Boise, ID 83705; http://www.idahocities.org. Adv. *Aud.:* Ga, Ac, Sa.

This blog is of interest to government officials and citizens alike. Its content includes news; job openings in city government from around Idaho; a calendar of events listing conferences, workshops, and institutes; profiles of city officials; grant opportunities; and a Q&A section on legislative issues. It requires members to register. URL: http://membersidahocities.site-ym.com/blogpost/1235530/AIC-Blog

2746. *Illinois Issues - In Depth.* Formerly (until 2015): *Illinois Issues.* 1975. m. 10/yr. University of Illinois at Springfield, One University Plz, MS HRB 10, Springfield, IL 62703; http://www.uis.edu. Illus., adv. Vol. ends: Dec. *Bk. rev.:* 1, 1,000 words. *Aud.:* Ga, Ac.

Illinois Issues has become more of a blog than a magazine. Stories are online, with comments following. With a special focus on Illinois government and politics, it pays close attention to current trends and legislative issues, and examines the state's quality of life. It also engages its readers in dialogue, enhancing the quality of public discourse in Illinois. As a not-for-profit monthly magazine, it also sponsors and promotes other appropriate public-affairs educational activities. URL: http://nprillinois.org/topic/illinois-issues-0

2747. *Illinois Municipal Review.* [ISSN: 0019-2139] 1922. m. USD 30. Ed(s): Brad Cole. Illinois Municipal League, PO Box 5180, Springfield, IL 62705-5180; gkoch@iml.org; http://www.iml.org. Illus., adv. Circ: 13500 Controlled. Vol. ends: Dec. *Aud.:* Sa.

A legal Q&A, municipal calendar, exchange column, editorials, and a variety of articles of interest to local Illinois government officials make up this long-running magazine. Available online back to 1997. Current issues are at https://www.iml.org/page.cfm?category=3820&cell=10. URL: www.iml.org/

2748. *Kansas Government Journal.* [ISSN: 0022-8613] 1914. m. Members, USD 20; Non-members, USD 40. Ed(s): Kate Cooley, Andrey Ukrazhenko. League of Kansas Municipalities, 300 S W Eighth Ave, Topeka, KS 66603; info@lkm.org; http://www.lkm.org. Illus., index, adv. Circ: 4500. Vol. ends: Dec.

Published since 1914, the Kansas Government Journal (KGJ) is the official monthly magazine of the League of Kansas Municipalities, and is the only statewide publication designed specifically for city, county, and state government officials. The KGJ boasts a monthly circulation of about 4,500, and is distributed to individuals and government officials across Kansas. K.S.A. [Kansas Statutes Annotated] 12-1610a expressly authorizes local governments to purchase annual subscriptions of the KGJ for their officers and employees, and to maintain at least one bound set of issues of this journal in their archives for reference. Archives available online since its first issue, December 1914. URL: www.lkm.org/journal/archive/

2749. *Kentucky City Magazine.* Former titles (until 2009): *City Magazine;* (until 199?): *Kentucky City;* (until 1968): *Kentucky City Bulletin.* 1929. bi-m. USD 18. Innovative Publishing Ink, 10629 Henning Way, Ste 8, Louisville, KY 40241; info@innovativepublishing.com; http://www.innovativepublishing.com/. Illus., adv. Circ: 27100 Controlled. *Aud.:* Sa.

The award-winning *City Magazine* has transitioned to *Kentucky City Magazine* in 2009. In 2011 it was retooled and redesigned. Published by the Kentucky League of Cities, it is Kentucky's only magazine dedicated specifically to city and municipal issues. It covers critical topics; profiles people; and reports on events and innovative initiatives and practices in Kentucky's cities. For example, it reviews significant bills; runs articles on funeral protests; covers current topics such as childhood obesity, workplace violence, and cyber-liability; profiles Kentucky cities; and includes a colorful calendar of events. (See www.klc.org/news/1559/Magazines.) Online since 2014. Prior issues may be requested in electronic format. URL: www.klc.org

2750. *Local Focus.* 19??. m. Free to members; Non-members, USD 96. Ed(s): Kevin Toon. League of Oregon Cities, 1201 Court St, NE, Ste 200, Salem, OR 97301; loc@orcities.org; http://www.orcities.org. *Aud.:* Ga, Ac, Sa.

This journal presents regular updates on state and federal matters. It also includes League of Oregon Cities news; city happenings and best practices; feature articles; a calendar of events; reference to helpful publications; summaries of legal cases; and a list of job openings. Issues since 2006 are available online. URL: www.orcities.org/Publications/Newsletters/tabid/873/Default.aspx

2751. *Louisiana Municipal Review.* [ISSN: 0164-3622] 1938. m. USD 24. Ed(s): Anita Tillman. Louisiana Municipal Association, PO Box 4327, Baton Rouge, LA 70821; lamunicipalassociation@compuserve.com; http://www.lamunis.org. Adv. Circ: 3300 Paid and controlled. *Aud.:* Ga, Ac, Sa.

The official publication of the Louisiana Municipal Association, a statewide league of villages, towns, and cities in Louisiana, *Louisiana Municipal Review* serves as a medium of exchange of ideas and information on municipal affairs for the public officials of Louisiana. It includes news articles, features, obituaries, and a column written by the state's governor. Online for one calendar year. URL: http://www.lma.org/LMA/LMA_Marketplace/Louisiana_Municipal_Review/LMA/LMA_Marketplace/

2752. *M A Co News.* 1971. . Free. Montana Association of Counties, 2715 Skyway Dr, Ste A, Helena, MT 59602; maco@mtcounties.org; http://www.mtcounties.org. *Aud.:* Ga, Ac, Sa.

Online since August 2001, this journal offers news of all Montana counties. In each issue, there is a highlighted article of newsworthy interest. The issues feature interviews with officials, reportage of important trends, and attention to conferences held in the state. Not confining itself exclusively to local news, the journal also covers issues of national importance. Available online. URL: www.mtcounties.org/news

2753. *Maine Policy Review.* [ISSN: 1064-2587] 1991. s-a. Free to qualified personnel. Ed(s): Barbara Harrity, Ann Acheson. Margaret Chase Smith Center for Public Policy, 5784 York Complex, Bldg #4, University of Maine, Orono, ME 04469; mcsc@umit.maine.edu; http://mcspolicycenter.umaine.edu/. Refereed. *Aud.:* Ga, Ac, Sa.

A publication of the Margaret Chase Smith Center for Public Policy at the University of Maine. The majority of articles in *Maine Policy Review* are written by Maine citizens, many of whom are readers of the journal. It publishes independent analyses of public policy issues relevant to Maine by providing accurate information and thoughtful commentary. Issues range from snowmobiling to housing. Most issues since 1991 are on the web site. Starting with the Spring 2017 issue the journal is now available in a new flipbook format for easy reading on your phone or tablet. They have converted issues back to the 2011 Special Issue on Maine's Food System into the new format. To search for and read individual articles in pdf format, visit the Digital Commons site at https://digitalcommons.library.umaine.edu/mpr/. URL: http://mcspolicycenter.umaine.edu/mpr/

2754. *Minnesota Cities.* Formerly (until 1976): *Minnesota Municipalities;* Which superseded in part (in 1916): *League of Minnesota Municipalities. Annual Convention. Proceedings.* [ISSN: 0148-8546] 1913. bi-m. USD 30. Ed(s): Claudia Hoffacker. League of Minnesota Cities, 145 University Ave W, St Paul, MN 55103; http://www.lmnc.org. Illus., adv. Circ: 7000. *Aud.:* Ga, Ac, Sa.

The League of Minnesota Cities' monthly magazine includes articles on a wide range of city-related topics. Each issue is based on a theme - for example, human resources, technology, and winter. One year online. URL: www.lmc.org/magazine

2755. *Mississippi Municipalities.* [ISSN: 0026-6337] 1955. q. Ed(s): Samantha Hil. Mississippi Municipal League, 600 E Amite St, Ste 104, Jackson, MS 39201; info@mmlonline.com; http://www.mmlonline.com. Illus. *Aud.:* Ga, Ac, Sa.

Mississippi Municipalities contains feature articles as well as an auditor's column and a column on tax collections. The second issue is the annual conference issue. Some archived issues are online. URL: http://www.mmlonline.com/

2756. *Missouri Municipal Review.* [ISSN: 0026-6647] 1936. bi-m. Non-members, USD 30. Ed(s): Laura Holloway. Missouri Municipal League, 1727 Southridge Dr, Jefferson City, MO 65109; info@mocities.com; http://www.mocities.com. Illus., index, adv. Circ: 6400. *Aud.:* Ga, Ac, Sa.

Designed to meet the needs and interests of municipal officials in Missouri, this publication features articles on all phases of municipal government and serves as a medium through which member officials can exchange ideas on current issues. Selected articles are available online. Three special issues are published each year: "Economic Development" (January), "Public Works" (May), and "Pre-Conference" (July). Feature articles only are online. Online issues available since 2011. URL: www.mocities.com/?CurrentIssue

2757. *Municipal Advocate.* Formerly (until 1988): *Municipal Forum.* [ISSN: 1046-2422] 1980. q. Massachusetts Municipal Association, One Winthrop Square, Boston, MA 02111; https://www.mma.org/. Adv. *Aud.:* Ga, Ac, Sa.

This publication presents in-depth articles about important and timely municipal issues, such as budgeting, technology, management, infrastructure maintenance, education, and legal issues. An emphasis is placed on innovative solutions and problem-solving strategies. Selected feature articles from the latest two years are available online. URL: https://www.mma.org/municipal-advocate-magazine

2758. *Municipal Maryland.* Supersedes in part (in 1972): *Maryland Municipal News.* [ISSN: 0196-9986] 1948. 9x/yr. USD 40. Ed(s): Karen A Bohlen. Maryland Municipal League, Inc., 1212 W St, Annapolis, MD 21401; mml@mdmunicipal.org; http://www.mdmunicipal.org/. Adv. *Aud.:* Ga, Ac, Sa.

Municipal Maryland features articles on a variety of city/town topics, such as downtown revitalization, public works, financial management, conducting effective council meetings, consensus building, legal and personnel issues, recreation, and public safety. The November issue features articles that summarize the general sessions and most of the workshops from the Maryland Municipal League's annual summer convention. Registration information for the annual convention is published in the March issue; registration information for the league's legislative conference is published in the July/August issue. Selected articles are available online since 2012. URL: www.mdmunicipal.org/index.aspx?NID=421

2759. *Municipal Matters.* Former titles (until 2017): *N Y C O M Municipal Bulletin; Municipal Bulletin.* 1941. q. New York Conference of Mayors and Municipal Officials, 119 Washington Ave, Albany, NY 12210; info@nycom.org; http://www.nycom.org/. Adv. Circ: 7000. *Aud.:* Ga, Ac, Sa.

Municipal Matters is a resource for expanded coverage of NYCOM activities and events. It reports on legislative and other developments at the state and federal levels, and presents in-depth analysis of special issues, affiliate news, and the latest information on the municipal legal front. Available online only to members. URL: www.nycom.org/resource-center/municipal-bulletin.html

2760. *The Municipality.* Formerly (until 1916): *Wisconsin Municipality.* [ISSN: 0027-3597] 1900. m. USD 25; USD 5 per issue. League of Wisconsin Municipalities, 131 W Wilson St, Madison, WI 53703; league@lwm-info.org; http://www.lwm-info.org. Illus., index, adv. Circ: 10000. Vol. ends: Dec. *Aud.:* Sa.

From mosquito control to complex legal matters, this periodical showcases issues of interest to local government officials in Wisconsin. News about local officials, web links of interest, and a calendar are also included. Archived since 2013. Full text of the current edition can be found on the web site under "Resources." URL: http://www.lwm-info.org/828/The-Municipality-Magazine

2761. *N J Municipalities: official publication of the New Jersey state League of municipalities.* 1917. 9x/yr. Members, USD 25 (print or online ed.); Non-members, USD 30 (print or online ed.)). Ed(s): Amy Spiezio, Michael J Darcy. New Jersey State League of Municipalities, 222 W State St, Trenton, NJ 08608; http://www.cityconnections.com/njleag/njlabont.html. Illus., index, adv. *Aud.:* Sa.

Typical lead articles are on such topics as public-private partnerships, energy, and urban sprawl. Columns include "Legal Q&A," "Legislative Update," "Labor Relations," "Washington Watch," job notices, and a calendar. Selected articles since January 2007 are available online. After the first few pages, a subscription is needed to view the rest. URL: www.njslom.org/magazine/

2762. *Nebraska Municipal Review.* [ISSN: 0028-1905] 1930. m. USD 50. Ed(s): Lynn Marienau. League of Nebraska Municipalities, 1335 L St, Lincoln, NE 68508; info@lonm.org; http://www.lonm.org. Illus., adv. Circ: 3400. *Bk. rev.:* Number and length vary. *Aud.:* Ga, Ac, Sa.

This official publication of the League of Nebraska Municipalities features articles on laws and issues that affect local government, government officials, leadership, and training. Not available online. The general web site is at https://www.lonm.org/news/

2763. ***New Hampshire Town and City.*** [ISSN: 0545-171X] 19??. bi-m. Members, USD 25; Non-members, USD 50. Ed(s): Timothy W Fortier. New Hampshire Municipal Association, 25 Triangle Park Dr, PO Box 617, Concord, NH 03301; nhmainfo@nhmunicipal.org; http://www.nhmuicipal.org. Adv. *Aud.:* Ga, Ac, Sa.

Provides local officials and others with 40-60 pages of timely information on legal issues, legislative issues, upcoming programs, and services of the local government center. Selected articles from past issues are available online through topical links, such as "Finance and Taxation," "Land Use," "Liability," and "Governance." Online since 2004. URL: www.nhmunicipal.org/TownAndCity/Issues

2764. ***New Mexico Municipal League. Municipal Reporter.*** [ISSN: 0028-6257] 1959. m. Free. Ed(s): Roger Makin, William F Fulginiti. New Mexico Municipal League, PO Box 846, Santa Fe, NM 87504-0846; http://nmml.org. *Aud.:* Ga, Ac, Sa.

The New Mexico Municipal League has produced this monthly newsletter for many years. There is a link to municipal job openings; and a regular column, "HR Insights," tackles personnel policy and problems in a Q&A format. Online publication begins with the May 2014 issue. As of the July 2016 issue, this monthly publication is in digital format only. URL: http://nmml.org/publications/

2765. ***Pennsylvania Township News.*** [ISSN: 0162-5160] 1948. m. Members, USD 36; Non-members, USD 40. Ed(s): Ginni Linn. Pennsylvania State Association of Township Supervisors, 4855 Woodland Dr, Enola, PA 17025; psatsweb@psats.org; http://www.psats.org. Illus., adv. Circ: 10000 Paid and free. Vol. ends: Dec. *Aud.:* Sa.

Regular features of *Pennsylvania Township News* include "Legislative Update," "Environmental Digest," "Newsworthy Items," "One Source Municipal Training" (a listing and description of courses offered to township officials), and a "Questions & Answers" column. Articles deal with common interests to the more than 1,450 Pennsylvania member townships: stormwater drainage, animal control, recycling, and so on. There are also interviews with top-ranking township officials. Regarding what is freely available to all, the table of contents is online, along with a free feature article. The entire publication is available online to subscribers only. URL: www.psats.org/subpage.php?pageid=TwpNewsMain

2766. ***Quality Cities.*** Formerly (until 1987): *Florida Municipal Record.* [ISSN: 0892-4171] 1928. bi-m. Members, USD 10; Non-members, USD 20. Ed(s): Beth Dolan. Florida League of Cities, Inc., 301 S Bronough St, Ste 300, Tallahassee, FL 32301; http://www.floridaleagueofcities.com/. Illus., adv. Vol. ends: May. *Aud.:* Ga, Sa.

Quality Cities serves as a medium for exchange of ideas and information for Florida's municipal officials. Reporting addresses legislation that affects cities; current municipal issues; and innovative local-government ideas. The two summer issues cover the post-legislative session report and the Florida League of Cities conference. Now available online since 2011 cover to cover. *Quality Cities* is searchable by topic archives back to 2009. URL: www.floridaleagueofcities.com/Publications.aspx?CNID=182

2767. ***The Review (Ann Arbor).*** Formerly (until 2008): *Michigan Municipal Review.* [ISSN: 1941-532X] 1928. 10x/yr. USD 24. Ed(s): Lisa Donovan. Michigan Municipal League, 1675 Green Rd, Ann Arbor, MI 48106; http://www.mml.org. Illus., index, adv. Circ: 11300 Controlled. Vol. ends: Dec. Microform: PQC. *Indexed:* A22. *Aud.:* Sa.

This periodical aims to provide a forum to Michigan officials for the exchange of ideas and information. Municipal officials, consultants, legislators, and staff members of the Michigan Municipal League contribute to the publication. Want ads, a marketplace column, a municipal calendar, and legal spotlights round out the issues. Online since 2007. URL: www.mml.org/resources/publications/mmr/index.html

2768. ***South Dakota Municipalities.*** [ISSN: 0300-6182] 1934. m. Free to members; Non-members, USD 30. Ed(s): Sara M Rankin. South Dakota Municipal League, 208 Island Dr, Ft Pierre, SD 57532; http://www.sdmunicipalleague.org/. Adv. Circ: 3000. *Aud.:* Ga, Ac, Sa.

The magazine contains articles on legislation, court decisions, attorney general opinions, and issues that affect municipal operations on a daily basis. Every issue has a column by the director and the president of the League, as well as a Washington report and risk-sharing news. Available online since 2012. URL: www.sdmunicipalleague.org/index.asp?Type=B_BASIC&SEC=

2769. ***Tennessee Town and City.*** [ISSN: 0040-3415] 1950. s-m. Members, USD 6; Non-members, USD 15; USD 1 per issue. Ed(s): Carole Graves. Tennessee Municipal League, 226 Capitol Blvd, Ste 710, Nashville, TN 37219-1894; gstahl@tml1.org; http://www.tml1.org. Illus., index, adv. Circ: 6250 Controlled. *Aud.:* Ga, Ac, Sa.

Tennessee Town and City looks like a newspaper. It has numerous photographs of the subjects of its news items. There is a classified ad section. In addition to distribution by subscription, free copies of *Tennessee Town and City* can be picked up in various newspaper stands in Nashville in the Legislative Plaza and the State Capitol. Online since 2013. URL: https://www.tml1.org/town-and-city

2770. ***Texas Town & City.*** Former titles (until 1994): *T M L Texas Town & City;* (until 1984): *Texas Town & City;* (until 1959): *Texas Municipalities.* [ISSN: 1084-5356] 1914. 11x/yr. Members, USD 15; Non-members, USD 30. Ed(s): Christina Corrigan. Texas Municipal League, 1821 Rutherford Ln, Ste 400, Austin, TX 78754. Illus., adv. Circ: 11015. *Aud.:* Ga, Ac, Sa.

This is the official publication of the Texas Municipal League, and it sets its sights on alerting member cities to important governmental or private-sector actions or proposed actions that may affect city operations. The magazine has several feature articles, a legal Q&A, and a "Small Cities Corner." A sample issue is online, but no other issues are available online. URL: www.tml.org/pub_ttc

2771. ***V L C T News.*** 2000. 11x/yr. Free to members; Non-members, USD 60. Ed(s): David Gunn. Vermont League of Cities & Towns, 89 Main St, Ste 4, Montpelier, VT 05602-2948; info@vlct.org; http://www.vlct.org. *Aud.:* Sa.

Legal and regulatory info, staff news, job vacancies, and classifieds. Online since January 2000. URL: https://www.vlct.org/resource-type/vlct-newsletter

2772. ***Virginia Town & City.*** [ISSN: 0042-6784] 1966. 10x/yr. Members, USD 8; Non-members, USD 16. Ed(s): Manuel Timbreza. Virginia Municipal League, PO Box 12164, Richmond, VA 23241; e-mail@vml.org; http://www.vml.org/. Illus., adv. *Bk. rev.:* Number and length vary. *Aud.:* Ga, Ac, Sa.

Each issue has about three or four major articles on topics such as the environment, the bailout, the digital divide, terrorism, budgets, urban planning, and records management. Available on the web since 2012. URL: http://www.vml.org/publications/town-and-city

2773. ***W A M News.*** Former titles (until 1979): *W A M News Bulletin;* (until 1961): *News Bulletin.* 19??. 11x/yr. Free to members. Wyoming Association of Municipalities, 315 W 27th St, Cheyenne, WY 82001; http://www.wyomuni.org/. Illus. *Aud.:* Ga, Ac, Sa.

WAM News is the official newsletter of the Wyoming Association of Municipalities, and serves as an exchange of ideas and information for officials of municipalities. It has a broad audience of local and state elected officials, along with state agencies, businesses, and associations involved in local government. In addition to news, there are a calendar of events, a professional directory, and municipal ads, including job vacancies. The last four issues are online. URL: www.wyomuni.org

2774. ***Western City.*** Former titles (until 1976): *Western City Magazine;* (until 1960): *Western City;* (until 1930): *Hydraulic Engineering;* (until 1927): *Modern Irrigation.* [ISSN: 0279-5337] 1925. m. USD 39 domestic; USD 52 foreign. Ed(s): Jude Hudson, Eva Spiegel. League of California Cities, 1400 K St, 4th Fl, Sacramento, CA 95814; http://www.cacities.org. Illus., adv. Circ: 10000. *Aud.:* Sa.

Both practical ideas and bigger-picture policy issues and trends are the twin foci of coverage of *Western City.* The magazine's stated mission is to support and serve elected and appointed city officials (and those interested in local government), and to examine the policy, process, and fiscal issues that affect local government. It does the latter from a number of angles, including individual city success stories, legal analyses, and statewide perspectives. Online since September 2006. URL: www.westerncity.com/

■ HEALTH AND FITNESS

Journals and Magazines/Newsletters

Alison Larsen, M.S.I.S., Serials & Web Resources Librarian, Siena College, 515 Loudon Rd., Loudonville, NY 12211; alarsen@siena.edu

Introduction

Health and fitness is a subject that all people take some interest in, whether they like it or not! And the industry continues to grow year after year. From children to senior citizens, health and fitness issues affect us all and, thus, most of the titles included in this section cover health and fitness for the general population, while some titles included do focus on a specific subsection (men, women, children, seniors), to illustrate the kinds of publications available. There has been a shift toward online environments to deliver health and fitness information where it's easier to watch exercises or see someone cooking versus still pictures. Staples in the industry like *Self* and *Fitness* have ceased print publication and shifted to websites. Overall body and mind health and fitness is trending with mindfulness and mental health increasing in coverage. This area has seen its own growth of magazine titles and are worth checking into. Some of note are *Breathe, Teen Breathe,* and *Mindful.* Because of the large quantity of information and the potentially sensitive subject matter, it is imperative that each library/patron decides what type of information to subscribe to.

In this section, the journals and magazines are separated from the newsletters because of their volume, a phenomenon somewhat unique to this subject area. Most of the publications included are not health-topic specific, and individual sports, with respect to fitness, are not included in this section (see the "Sports" section). The health and fitness publications listed here are a good foundational start to building a health and fitness collection for most libraries and can be enhanced by demographic/health need.

Basic Periodicals

Consumer Reports on Health, The Harvard Health Letter, Health, Prevention, Shape.

Basic Abstracts and Indexes

CINAHL, Health Source: Consumer Edition, MEDLINE.

Journals and Magazines

The journals and magazines listed in the section are just a sampling of the many that are currently available. From double-blind, peer-reviewed scholarly journals to popular magazines, there is something in this section for everyone and for every library interested in health and fitness. Because health and fitness comprise such a universal topic, a single publication can be applicable to a wide variety of libraries, and the recommendations generally reflect this concept.

2775. *American Journal of Men's Health.* [ISSN: 1557-9883] 2007. bi-m. Free. Ed(s): Demetrius J Porche. Sage Publications, Inc., 2455 Teller Rd, Thousand Oaks, CA 91320; info@sagepub.com; http://www.sagepub.com. Adv. Sample. Refereed. Reprint: PSC. *Indexed:* A22, C45, E01. *Aud.:* Ac, Sa.

American Journal of Men's Health is a peer-reviewed journal, published bimonthly, that focuses on men's health and illness. The journal's description claims to publish in all areas that fall within men's health. When you scan various tables of contents, this is evident. The subject scope is expansive, as well as is the geographic coverage area as international studies are frequently published. Special issues are published regularly. The articles are intended for professionals and scholars, but many could be useful for and applicable to the typical undergraduate student. The journal is now open access and is listed in DOAJ and indexed in PubMed. Recommended for medical/health libraries and well as academic libraries.

2776. *Childhood Obesity.* Former titles (until 2010): *Obesity and Weight Management;* (until 2009): *Obesity Management.* [ISSN: 2153-2168] 2005. 8x/yr. USD 972. Ed(s): Tom Baranowski, Elsie M Taveras. Mary Ann Liebert, Inc. Publishers, 140 Huguenot St, 3rd Fl, New Rochelle, NY 10801; info@liebertpub.com; http://www.liebertpub.com. Adv. Sample. Refereed. Reprint: PSC. *Indexed:* A22, BRI, C45, E01. *Aud.:* Ac, Sa.

Childhood Obesity claims to be the only journal "that provides a central forum for exploring effective, actionable strategies for weight management and obesity prevention in children and adolescents." Each issue contains a minimum of five original research articles (review articles are also published), along with various other re-occurring sections, like "The Experts Weigh In," "Brief Reports," and "Case Reports." Theme issues are also published on occasion. The articles themselves tend to focus primarily on the United States, but articles focusing on international research are present. The journal is targeted to a wide range of individuals: those in the medical field, school administrators, and even parents. And though scholarly, many of the articles are applicable to laypeople. The journal is available in print and/or online formats at individual and institutional rates. Recommended for medical/health libraries, academic libraries that support health sciences and childhood/adolescent psychology, and potentially larger public libraries.

2777. *Experience Life.* Formerly (until 2001): *Life Time Fitness Experience.* [ISSN: 1537-6656] 1998. 10x/yr. USD 24.95. Ed(s): Pilar Gerasimo. Life Time Fitness, 2145 Ford Pkwy, Ste 302, Saint Paul, MN 55116; http://clubs.lifetimefitness.com/. Adv. Circ: 630000. *Aud.:* Ga.

With the tag line "the no-gimmicks, no-hype health & fitness magazine," *Experience Life* takes a slightly different approach to health and fitness, in that the magazine spends a lot of time dispelling what other more mainstream health and fitness magazines publish or emphasize. Its mantra of "Being Healthy is a Revolutionary Act," and the mission to "empower people to become their best, healthiest selves, and supporting their enjoyment of a balanced, sustainable, deeply satisfying way of life" is evident in the get-out-there-and-do focused articles. The magazine is published ten times per year, and is accompanied by a very clean, neatly organized website that is highly recommended. With a reasonable subscription price for a popular magazine, this one is worth a try! Recommended for public libraries.

2778. *Health.* Formed by the merger of (1990-1992): *In Health;* (1981-1991): *Health;* Which was formerly (until 1981): *Family Health;* Which incorporated (1950-1976): *Today's Health;* Which was formerly (until 1950): *Hygeia.* [ISSN: 1059-938X] 1992. 10x/yr. USD 12. Ed(s): Theresa Tamkins. Time Inc., 1271 Ave of the Americas, New York, NY 10020; information@timeinc.com; http://www.timeinc.com. Illus., adv. *Indexed:* A01, A22, BRI, C37, MASUSE, MLA-IB, SD. *Aud.:* Ga, Ac, Sa.

Health continues to remain one of the standard health and fitness magazines on the market. Published ten times per year, the magazine is geared toward women over 30 and provides fun and trendy ways to maintain overall health and fitness. Celebrities grace each cover with an interview relating to some aspect of their healthy lifestyle. Recurring columns and cover features hit all aspects of health and fitness through a variety of lenses including: exercise, food, sex, relationships, and beauty. *Health* is glossy, eye-catching, and recognizable. It presents tips and advice in an easy-to-read and possible-to-accomplish tone. The website also mirrors a lot of what is contained in the magazine, but it provides additional stories, tips, recipes, and more at no cost. With such a reasonable subscription price, *Health* is highly recommended for public libraries. It is also recommended for academic and medical/health libraries who desire a strong, well-known consumer-based health magazine.

2779. *Healthy Children.* 2012. . Free. American Academy of Pediatrics, 141 NW Point Blvd, Elk Grove Village, IL 6000; csc@aap.org; http://www.aap.org. *Aud.:* Ga.

Healthy Children is an electronic magazine published by healthychildren.org, a website of the American Association of Pediatrics. The magazine, with no set publication pattern to speak of, is focused on children's health and wellness issues. The magazine offers articles as well as a Q&A with pediatricians; sound, practical advice backed by studies; and official AAP recommendations. It provides a lot of medical knowledge in a way that is comprehensible to the average parent. The publication is freely available to download and is also available on Apple and Android tablets and smartphones. The healthychildren.org website also offers e-newsletters on a monthly basis that each focus on a different topic (April 2018 focused on communication and discipline). While e-magazines and e-newsletters are hard to recommend to libraries, they are the current trend, and it is important for librarians to be aware of their presence to potentially recommend to individual patrons or link to via their sites (LibGuides).

2780. *International Journal of Women's Health.* [ISSN: 1179-1411] 2009. . Free. Ed(s): Elie D Al-Chaer. Dove Medical Press Ltd.(Dovepress), Beechfield House, Winterton Way, Macclesfield, SK11 0JL, United Kingdom; http://www.dovepress.com. Refereed. *Indexed:* A01, C42. *Aud.:* Ac, Sa.

The *International Journal of Women's Health* is an open-access, peer-reviewed journal that publishes one continuous volume per calendar year. In 2017, 101 articles were published. The journal publishes original research, reviews, and case reports, and some articles include video. The geographic coverage of the subject matter is, indeed, international. While the journal claims to cover a wide range of women's health topics, looking at recent articles reflect an emphasis on obstetrics and gynecology. The journal is indexed in a variety of places, including Scopus and PubMed. This journal is recommended for medical/health libraries, particularly those that may focus on women's health, as well as academic libraries.

2781. *Journal of Physical Activity & Health.* [ISSN: 1543-3080] 2004. 12x/yr. USD 1566. Ed(s): Loretta DiPietro. Human Kinetics, Inc., PO Box 5076, Champaign, IL 61825; info@hkusa.com; http://journals.humankinetics.com. Adv. Refereed. *Indexed:* SD. *Aud.:* Ac, Sa.

With a tagline that reads "The official journal of the International Society for Physical Activity and Health," the *Journal of Physical Activity & Health* (*JPAH*) focuses on providing original research for researchers of chronic disease where physical activity may help the treatment, recovery, and longtime prognosis of those suffering from such diseases. The articles cover all age ranges and does include international research. The journal is peer-reviewed and published eight times per year. Each issue publishes a decent number (around 10) of original research articles, with an occasional review and/or commentary included. *JPAH* is available in print and/or online format. The subscription price for an institution is a little higher than that for other journals listed in this section, but the number of articles published needs to be taken into consideration. Highly recommended for medical/health libraries. Recommended for academic libraries with health studies offerings.

2782. *Men's Health: tons of useful stuff.* Formerly (until 1987): *Prevention Magazine's Guide to Men's Health.* [ISSN: 1054-4836] 1986. 10x/yr. USD 12. Ed(s): Matt Bean. Rodale, Inc., 733 Third Ave, 15th Fl, New York, NY 10022; http://www.rodaleinc.com. Illus., adv. Vol. ends: Dec (No. 10). *Indexed:* A01, A22, BRI, C37, GW. *Aud.:* Ga.

Men's Health is probably the most identifiable general-interest health and fitness magazine geared toward men currently on the market. Like its counterpart *Women's Health, Men's Health* looks at health and fitness from an overall lifestyle perspective, and thus includes articles, advice, recipes, and more that target relationships, nutrition, and style/grooming, in addition to its core focus on fitness and health-related issues. The magazine is highly visual and ad heavy, but the content does not suffer. The *Men's Health* website is impressive and publishes e-newsletters, available at no cost, delivered via e-mail. *Men's Health* is highly recommended for public libraries.

2783. *Prevention.* [ISSN: 0032-8006] 1950. m. USD 44 domestic; CAD 65 Canada. Rodale, Inc., 733 Third Ave, 15th Fl, New York, NY 10022; info@rodale.com; http://www.rodaleinc.com. Illus., adv. Sample. Vol. ends: Dec. Microform: PQC. *Indexed:* A01, A22, AgeL, BRI, C37, C42, MASUSE. *Aud.:* Ga.

Prevention magazine remains steadfast in its approach to health and fitness for its readers. Having published for more than 65 years, *Prevention* sports covers that are clean and the content is straightforward. Middle-aged readers will get the most from the magazine, but much of the content is applicable to other age demographics. With such a long-standing publication history, the readership base continues to be loyal. Echoing the size of the physical magazine, many of the articles in each issue are smaller in size, but do incorporate a wide variety of topics. In 2016, the magazine moved to an advertisement-free model, providing readers with more content. While the print magazine is ad-free, the website is full of them, making it difficult to determine headlines from ads. A staple for public libraries.

2784. *Shape.* [ISSN: 0744-5121] 1981. 10x/yr. USD 5.99 domestic; USD 28.97 Canada; USD 6.99 per issue domestic. A M I - Weider Publications, 4 New York Plz, 4th fl, New York, NY 10004; http://www.americanmediainc.com. Illus., adv. Sample. Circ: 1650000 Paid. Vol. ends: Aug. *Indexed:* A22, BRI, C37, C42, SD. *Aud.:* Hs, Ga, Ac.

An eye-catching, glossy, celebrity-covered magazine, *Shape* continues to be a mainstay of health and fitness magazines aimed at women. *Shape* takes a holistic approach to women's health and fitness, and is the most balanced in providing information on fitness as well as lifestyle topics when compared to its counterparts *Fitness* and *Women's Health.* The content caters to young to middle-aged women. There are plenty of photographs to accompany the articles, demonstrations of exercises, and pictures of food items that will make any foodie hungry. The website provides additional content as well as full access to the current print cover story with multimedia extras. Highly recommended for public libraries and academic libraries that have a popular magazine collection.

2785. *Women's Health.* [ISSN: 0884-7355] 2005. 10x/yr. USD 10 combined subscription domestic (print & online eds.) ; CAD 15 combined subscription Canada (print & online eds.)). Ed(s): Michele Promaulayko. Rodale, Inc., PO Box 3064, Harlan, IA 51593; customer_service@rodale.com; http://www.rodaleinc.com. Adv. *Indexed:* BRI. *Aud.:* Ga.

One of the staples of women's health and fitness magazines, *Women's Health* continues to hold steady in providing health and fitness content while increasing the lifestyle health issues (food/nutrition, beauty, sex, relationships, fashion). The magazine covers still emphasize health and fitness, but once the cover is flipped open, you see a total approach to women's health and fitness. The information is fun, informative, and captivating. Celebrities grace each cover issue, and there is an accompanying in-depth expose. The *Women's Health* website provides a great deal of additional content. *Women's Health*'s current lingo and approach is trying to capture a younger generation of readership. Recommended for public libraries.

Newsletters

Probably in no other subject area will you find more newsletters than in health and fitness. With a wide variety of subject matter falling within the broad definition of health and fitness, and with it impacting the entire population, the amount of information available can be overwhelming. What is beneficial about the high volume of newsletters is that the type and detail of information can be tailored to meet the desired need. Newsletters are shorter than a traditional journal/magazine publication and tend to be affordable. In today's world, most newsletter subscriptions include the ability to download electronic versions and offer additional content on the publication's web site. Also, many newsletters send alerts and have created sub-newsletters that allow one to narrow the focus of information one receives. Newsletters are trending to electronic-only formats as well as becoming increasingly more open-access. Included in this section are a sampling of the many newsletters currently available. These are more general health newsletters - but they are recommended if a library serves a population with specific health and fitness needs - to search out more specific content to enhance or supplement the general health and fitness newsletters included here.

2786. *Consumer Reports on Health.* Formerly (until 1991): *Consumer Reports Health Letter.* [ISSN: 1058-0832] 1989. m. USD 24. Consumers Union of the United States, Inc., 101 Truman Ave, Yonkers, NY 10703; http://www.consumersunion.org. Illus., index, adv. Vol. ends: Dec. *Indexed:* A01, A22, B01, C37. *Aud.:* Ga.

Consumer Reports on Health is a newsletter from well-respected *Consumer Reports* magazine that focuses explicitly on health-related issues. Published monthly, the newsletter looks at health issues from a consumer's perspective, to provide advice, debunk myths or stereotypes, and answer questions with the expertise of medical experts. Reviews of trends, procedures, and discoveries are also included. The topics covered are of a general health focus and thus applicable to every demographic. *Consumer Reports On Health* is highly recommended for public libraries.

2787. ***Environmental Nutrition: the newsletter of food, nutrition and health.*** Formerly (until 1986): *Environmental Nutrition Newsletter.* [ISSN: 0893-4452] 1977. m. USD 39 domestic; USD 49 Canada; USD 59 elsewhere. Ed(s): Sharon Palmer. Belvoir Media Group, LLC, PO Box 5656, Norwalk, CT 06856; customer_service@belvoir.com; http://www.belvoir.com. Illus., index. Sample. *Indexed:* A01, A22, Agr, BRI. *Aud.:* Ga.

Since the 1970s, *Environmental Nutrition* has been offering advice and recommendations for nature-based nutrition. The newsletter is published by medical professionals (many registered dieticians) and claims to have no sponsors or advertisers, thus enabling it to provide unbiased advice to readers. The articles, typical in a newsletter, are shorter and written for lay people. All subject matter focuses on adult nutrition. A recent issue included articles about food to soothe stomach issues. Individuals who are focused on nutrition and what they put into their bodies will find this newsletter interesting and informative. The newsletter is published monthly in print, and additional digital options are also available. Recommended for public libraries.

2788. ***The Harvard Health Letter.*** Formerly (until 1990): *Harvard Medical School Health Letter.* [ISSN: 1052-1577] 1975. m. USD 24 combined subscription print & online eds. Ed(s): Gregory Curfman. Harvard Health Publications Group, 10 Shattuck St, 2nd Flr, Boston, MA 02115; info@health.harvard.edu; http://www.health.harvard.edu. Illus., index. Sample. Vol. ends: Oct. *Indexed:* A01, A22, Agr, BRI, C37, MASUSE. *Aud.:* Ga, Sa.

The Harvard Health Letter is a staple among health newsletters. Published monthly, the newsletter provides information on a wide variety of health topics, and answers questions and dispels myths in a clear, concise manner. All information comes via the doctors of Harvard Medical School and focuses on adult health. While this title is still published in print, the subscription cost does provide an online pdf copy of each newsletter. The website provides some free access to parts of previous issues as well as extras. In addition to *The Harvard Health Letter,* the doctors at Harvard Medical School also publish three other newsletters with more specified subject matter: *Harvard Heart Letter, Harvard Men's Health Watch,* and *Harvard Women's Health Watch.* One can also subscribe to Harvard Health Online which provides access to all newsletters plus additional content. This is monthly subscription. A free email subscription called HEALTHbeat is also available. *The Harvard Health Letter* is highly recommended for public libraries, and recommended as well for medical/health libraries. The subject-specific newsletters are also recommended for public and medical/health libraries.

2789. ***Health After 50: health advice from American leading doctors.*** Formerly (until 2015): *Johns Hopkins Medical Letter Health After 50.* 1989. m. Free. University of California, Berkeley, School of Public Health, . Illus. Sample. Vol. ends: Feb. *Indexed:* A22. *Aud.:* Ga, Ac, Sa.

As the title implies, *Health After 50* supplies health information specific to that age demographic. Previously published as the *Johns Hopkins Medical Letter Health after 50,* the title is now being published by the University of California, Berkeley. Taking a general approach to managing your health, *Health After 50* provides practical advice about disease, prevention, medicines, and exercise through the lens of the 50-plus community. Both male- and female-specific health issues are included. The newsletter is published monthly for a very reasonable price. The website contains a lot of additional material, which is either material freely available or items available for purchase. Recommended for public libraries, medical/health libraries, and those libraries that support gerontology programs.

2790. ***N I H News in Health.*** Former titles (until 2005): *N I H Word on Health;* (until 1998): *Healthwise.* [ISSN: 1556-3898] 1996. m. Free. Ed(s): Harrison Wein. National Institutes of Health, NIH Office of Communications, Building 31, Room 5B64, Bethesda, MD 20892-2094; nihinfo@od.nih.gov; http://www.nih.gov. *Aud.:* Ga, Sa.

The *NIH News in Health* is a monthly newsletter from the National Institute of Health, part of the U.S. Department of Health and Human Services. Each newsletter contains two features; recent issues focus on dealing with trauma, eye health, and building social bonds; there are also several "Health Capsules," which are short, concise, yet focused articles. A vast majority of the subject matter covered is focused on adult health. Each article also includes information and resources provided by the NIH, which is a nice feature for those looking for more. Special issues are also published that include a collection of articles previously published in separate issues. One focused on seniors is currently available. The *NIH News in Health* is freely available online for everyone, and is freely available in print to offices, clinics, community centers, and libraries. Recommended for public libraries as well as medical/health libraries.

2791. ***Tufts University Health & Nutrition Letter: your guide to living healthier longer.*** Formerly (until 1997): *Tufts University Diet & Nutrition Letter (Print).* [ISSN: 1526-0143] 1983. m. USD 24 domestic. Tufts University, PO Box 5656, Norwalk, CT 06856. Illus. Sample. Microform: PQC. *Indexed:* A01, Agr, BRI, C42, MASUSE, SD. *Aud.:* Ga, Ac, Sa.

The *Tufts University Health & Nutrition Letter* is published monthly by the Friedman School of Nutrition Science and Food Policy at Tufts University. The newsletter offers articles, news-bites, and reports that provide information, advice, and recommendations on living healthier longer. The newsletter is geared for adults of all ages. Each issue also has a Q&A section where each question is answered by an identified medical professional. The newsletter is available in print via subscription. Additionally, the subscription provides you the option of downloading electronic copies and reading articles via the newsletter's site. The articles are timely, understandable, frank, and informative. Recommended for public libraries. Medical/health and academic libraries that support health sciences and nutrition programs may also find this of use.

2792. ***University of California, Berkeley. Wellness Letter: the newsletter of nutrition, fitness, and stress management.*** [ISSN: 0748-9234] 1984. m. USD 24. Health Letter Associates, Prince St Sta, PO Box 412, New York, NY 10012. Illus. Sample. Vol. ends: Sep. *Indexed:* A01. *Aud.:* Ga.

Articles and news items in the *UC Wellness Letter* (*UCWL*) address a wide range of adult-oriented health topics, including diet and nutrition, fitness, and physical health. Though adult health is the primary focus of the letter, family and children's health is also covered. The expert contributors to *UCWL* evaluate and report recent research using a layperson-friendly approach. Its authors also tackle common health myths, dispense advice, and answer readers' questions. Health-conscious folks from all walks of life will find the expert reporting to be useful and matter-of-fact. The Berkeley Wellness website (www.berkeleywellness.com) is also a wealth of information and is worth checking out. To subscribe, visit the Berkeley Wellness bookstore at https://www.healthandwellnessalerts.berkeley.edu/bookstore/. Recommended for public libraries.

■ HEALTH CARE ADMINISTRATION

See also Health Professions; and Nursing sections.

Shelly Burns, MLIS, AHIP, Health Sciences Librarian; scburns2@gmail.com

Introduction

Health care administration (HCA) is the business of health care and includes the practice of leadership, management, and administration in health-care facilities ranging from single-physician practices to large health-care systems. HCA is considered a multidisciplinary field, due to the variety of health professionals involved, and the literature is equally varied and multi-faceted.

There are two main categories of HCA publications: trade magazines, which tend to feature practical, newsworthy content and trends in an attractive and often easy-to-read format; and refereed journals, which provide content in the form of original research, theory-driven articles, and scholarly discourse. Although most of the titles included in this section will be of interest to both health-care executives and academics, there are some titles that are specifically targeted toward particular groups of administrators, such as nurse managers or private practice physicians.

Hospital libraries will certainly find many of the titles listed to be of particular interest to administrators, executives, and managers, as will academic libraries that support the researchers, faculty, and students of health-related educational programs such as health care administration, and medical, dental, nursing, or public health.

All titles are available in an online format, and most have web sites, which provide access to archived tables of contents, as well as other supplementary materials including blogs, videos, and podcasts. Many of the trade magazines listed provide free access to limited html content, and a few even offer complimentary access to those who register with the site. All refereed journals require a subscription, which may be purchased either through the publisher or a vendor.

Basic Periodicals

Health Care Management Review, Journal of Healthcare Management, Nursing Administration Quarterly, Modern Healthcare.

Basic Abstracts and Indexes

CINAHL, MEDLINE.

2793. *Dental Economics.* Former titles (until 1968): *Oral Hygiene / Dental Economics;* (until 1967): *Oral Hygiene;* Which superseded in part (in 1911): *Dental Headlight.* [ISSN: 0011-8583] 19??. m. USD 132 domestic; USD 179 in Canada & Mexico; USD 248 elsewhere. Ed(s): Chris Salierno, Zachary Kulsrud. PennWell Corporation, 1421 S Sheridan Rd, Tulsa, OK 74112; http://www.pennwell.com. Illus., index, adv. Sample. *Indexed:* A22, ATI. *Aud.:* Ac, Sa.

Dental Economics is a monthly trade magazine, which is freely available to subscribing dental professionals. The magazine touts itself as "the only business journal for the dental profession"; however, the content is not refereed. The web site includes a digital version of the magazine, which is available to subscribers, and provides online archives with tables of contents back to 1995. Older back issues can be purchased through subscription vendors. Due to the nature of the magazine, it includes many advertisements for dental-related products, devices, courses, and services. The publication aims to provide current business and management information specifically for dental practitioners. Recent topics include: dental start-ups, Medicare enrollment, student loan debt, digital dentistry, social media marketing, multipractice ownership, instrument cleaning and sterilization, pediatric dentistry, online reviews, staffing issues, practice transitions, and technology. Each issue includes both a continuing education article and a section titled "Pearls for Your Practice," which provides reviews for dental-related products or devices. *Dental Economics* is geared toward the practicing dental professional and is available in print and online. URL: www.dentaleconomics.com

2794. *Frontiers of Health Services Management.* [ISSN: 0748-8157] 1984. q. USD 135 domestic; USD 145 foreign; USD 35 per issue. Health Administration Press, 1 North Franklin St, Ste 1700, Chicago, IL 60606; hapbooks@ache.org; https://www.ache.org/Publications/. Illus. Sample. Microform: PQC. *Indexed:* A22, B01. *Aud.:* Ac, Sa.

Frontiers of Health Services Management is a scholarly publication produced quarterly by the American College of Healthcare Executives. Each issue is themed and focuses on a single health-care management topic such as trends or issues within the field. This publication offers a unique "bookazine" format, which aims to provide an in-depth understanding of topics in a concise and compact magazine format. All articles are written by experts and include feature articles, editorials, and commentaries. Each issue welcomes informed debate, as well as differing viewpoints. Recent topics include: big data, physician leadership, governance, value-based reimbursement, retail medicine, nursing leadership, health-care facility design and planning, population health management, health disparities, and equitable care. Access to the publication can be obtained by subscription or through professional membership in the American College of Healthcare Executives. This publication is available in print and online. URL: www.ache.org/pubs/frontiers.cfm

2795. *H F M Magazine.* Former titles: *Healthcare Financial Management;* (until 1982): *Hospital Financial Management;* (until 1968): *Hospital Accounting.* 1946. m. USD 150 USD 280 foreign. Ed(s): Eric Reese. Healthcare Financial Management Association, 3 Westbrook Corporate Ctr, Ste 700, Westchester, IL 60154; http://www.hfma.org. Illus., index. Sample. Vol. ends: Dec. Microform: PQC. *Indexed:* A22, ATI, AgeL, B01, B03, BRI. *Bk. rev.:* Number and length vary. *Aud.:* Ac, Sa.

HFM Magazine is the monthly trade publication of the Healthcare Financial Management Association. Issues are themed and follow an editorial calendar of broad topics. The magazine does include advertisements and sponsorships. Articles are generally between 2,000 and 2,500 words, are written by experts in the field, and are practical in nature, typically providing specific tools and examples, as well as action-oriented steps or strategies readers can use to improve performance. Online content includes a video column each month from HFMA's president and CEO. Recent topics include: public-private partnerships, using data to improve patient care, capital planning, risk management, EHR challenges, and tele-health. The target audience is senior and mid-level health-care financial managers working in hospitals or health systems. The most recent three years are archived online, and subscriptions are available through HFMA. This publication is available in print and online. URL: www.hfma.org/hfm

2796. *Health Care Management Review.* [ISSN: 0361-6274] 1976. q. USD 564. Ed(s): L Michele Issel. Lippincott Williams & Wilkins, 16522 Hunters Green Pky, Hagerstown, MD 21740. Illus., adv. Refereed. Microform: PQC. *Indexed:* A22, BRI. *Bk. rev.:* Number and length vary. *Aud.:* Ac, Sa.

Health Care Management Review is a quarterly, peer-reviewed journal, which focuses on theory-driven articles related to health-care management, leadership, and administration. *HCMR* is a multidisciplinary, international journal. Issues include editorials, evidence-based research articles, systematic reviews, and practice recommendations. Each year, *HCMR* publishes one paper selected by the Health Care Administration Division of the Academy of Management as the "Best Theory to Practice" paper. Recent topics include: distributed leadership in health-care teams, high-performance management system, coordination within medical neighborhoods, transitioning between EMRSs, implementation of HIT, workplace injuries, knowledge management, and organizational factors and patient safety. The target audience includes health-care administrators, researchers, and educators. Access to the publication can be obtained by subscription, and it is available in print and online. URL: http://journals.lww.com/hcmrjournal

2797. *The Health Care Manager.* Formerly (until 1999): *The Health Care Supervisor.* [ISSN: 1525-5794] 1982. q. USD 564. Ed(s): Charles R McConnell. Lippincott Williams & Wilkins, Two Commerce Sq, 2001 Market St, Philadelphia, PA 19103; customerservice@lww.com; http://www.lww.com. Illus., adv. Refereed. Vol. ends: Jun. *Indexed:* A22, B01, BRI. *Bk. rev.:* Number and length vary. *Aud.:* Ac, Sa.

The Health Care Manager is a quarterly, refereed publication, which aims to strengthen health-care managers' skills and increase their knowledge of the current health-care environment. It is written for all health-care managers in any setting and provides practical advice and research studies on current issues. Each issue contains a "Case in Health Care Management" feature, allowing readers to analyze the problem presented and come up with a reasonable solution. Recent topics include: cultural diversity training, employee termination, concierge medicine, transformational leadership, patient access, and decision-making. Access to the publication can be obtained by subscription, and it is available in print and online. URL: http://journals.lww.com/healthcaremanagerjournal

2798. *Hospitals & Health Networks.* Incorporates (1999-2003): *Health Forum Journal;* Which was formerly (until 1999): *Healthcare Forum Journal;* (until 1987): *Healthcare Forum;* (until 1985): *Hospital Forum;* Formerly (until 1993): *Hospitals.* [ISSN: 1068-8838] 1936. m. USD 102

domestic (Free to qualified personnel). Ed(s): Bill Santamour. Health Forum, Inc., 155 N Wacker Dr, Ste 400, Chicago, IL 60606; hfcustsvc@healthforum.com; http://www.healthforum.com. Illus., index. Sample. Vol. ends: Dec. Microform: PQC. *Indexed:* A01, A22, B01, B03, BRI, C42. *Bk. rev.:* Number and length vary. *Aud.:* Ga, Ac, Sa.

Hospital & Health Networks, or *H&HN,* is a trade magazine and the flagship publication of the American Hospital Association. It claims to be the most trusted and credible management publication in the field, and it has won more national editorial and design awards than any other health-care management magazine. The articles are consistent with typical trade magazine content and include editorials, profiles, interviews, informational pieces, human-interest stories, and many advertisements. Most articles do not include bibliographies. The publication is available in print and online as a digital magazine. Online content also provides access to videos and podcasts. *H&HN*'s target audience is hospital and system executives. Recent topics include: rethinking women's services, enhancing continuum of care, health reform, community health workers, value-based strategy, health care's interoperability challenge, and palliative care. This publication is available in print and online. Complimentary access to the digital magazine is available online by registering with *H&HN.* Access to the print version can be obtained by subscription. URL: www.hhnmag.com/magazine/magazine-archives.dhtml?nasearch=1010

2799. ***Inquiry (Rochester): the journal of health care organization, provision and financing.*** [ISSN: 0046-9580] 1963. q. Excellus Health Plan, Inc., PO Box 22999, Rochester, NY 14692; https://www.excellusbcbs.com. Illus., index. Sample. Refereed. Vol. ends: Winter. Microform: PQC. Reprint: PSC. *Indexed:* A22, AgeL, B01, BRI, EconLit. *Bk. rev.:* Number and length vary. *Aud.:* Ac, Sa.

Inquiry is a quarterly, refereed journal, which promotes "continuous improvement in the nation's health care system." It is broad in scope and is an excellent venue for scholarly communication and original research. Many of the articles focus on public policy issues, such as health-care reform, Medicare and Medicaid, and other national, system-wide concerns. Most issues include regular features such as the "The View from Here" editorial, as well as book reviews; however, neither of these two were published in the most current issue. Recent topics include: the Affordable Care Act, organizational characteristics, health economics, health inequality, and managed care. Access to the publication can be obtained by subscription, and it is available in print and online. URL: http://inq.sagepub.com/

2800. ***Journal of Healthcare Management.*** Former titles (until 1998): *Hospital and Health Services Administration;* (until 1976): *Hospital Administration.* [ISSN: 1096-9012] 1956. bi-m. Free to members; Non-members, USD 135. Ed(s): Janice Snider, Bita A Kash. Health Administration Press, 1 North Franklin St, Ste 1700, Chicago, IL 60606; contact@ache.org; https://www.ache.org/Publications/. Illus. Sample. Refereed. Microform: PQC. *Indexed:* A01, A22, B01, BRI. *Bk. rev.:* Number and length vary. *Aud.:* Ac, Sa.

Journal of Healthcare Management is the official journal of the American College of Health Executives. It is a scholarly, refereed journal, which is published on a bimonthly basis. Each issue contains expert interviews, original research, and practical information pieces on industry issues and trends. Feature articles include a "Practitioner Application" component, which is written by a practitioner and provides a practical take on the information presented in the article. Recent topics include: physician reimbursement structures, value-based care, succession planning, workflow, organizational justice, and health-care transformation. The target audience includes executives, managers, educators, and researchers. This journal would be an excellent addition to hospital libraries, as well as academic libraries with health-related education and research programs. Access to the publication can be obtained by subscription, and it is available in print and online. URL: www.ache.org/Publications/SubscriptionPurchase.aspx#jhm

2801. ***M G M A Connection.*** Former titles (until 2014): *M G M A Connexion;* (until 2001): *Medical Group Management Journal;* (until 1987): *Medical Group Management;* (until 1960): *National Association of Clinic Managers. Bulletin.* 1953. 10x/yr. Free to members. Medical Group Management Association, 104 Inverness Terr E, Englewood, CO 80112; support@mgma.com; http://www.mgma.com. Illus., index, adv. Vol. ends: Nov/Dec. Microform: PQC. *Indexed:* A22. *Aud.:* Ac, Sa.

MGMA Connection is the monthly trade magazine of the Medical Group Management Association. Each year, MGMA publishes an editorial calendar outlining the focus of each issue, with eight issues dedicated to the body of knowledge domain for medical practice management, which is determined by the American College of Medical Practice Executives (ACMPE). Each themed issue includes at least one feature article and several department articles on the highlighted topic. Although the publication is not refereed, manuscripts are evaluated for acceptance by the MGMA Publications Advisory Panel and the editorial staff. This publication does include advertisements, and the digital magazine version provides some exclusively online content. Recent topics include: meaningful use, advanced care directives, interoperability, cybersecurity, disruptive physicians, and physician-hospital alignment models. This publication looks to provide practical information on the organization and management of medical group practices, and is aimed at administrators and physician executives. Access to the publication can be obtained by subscription or through professional membership in MGMA, and it is available in print and online. URL: www.mgma.com/practice-resources/publications/mgma-connexion/mgma-connection-magazine-members

2802. ***Medical Economics.*** [ISSN: 0025-7206] 1923. s-m. USD 95 domestic; USD 150 foreign; USD 18 per issue domestic. U B M Advanstar Communications, Inc., 131 W 1st St, Duluth, MN 55802; info@advanstar.com; http://ubmadvanstar.com//. Illus., adv. Sample. Circ: 190013 Paid and controlled. Vol. ends: Dec. Microform: RPI; PQC. *Indexed:* A22, B01, BRI. *Aud.:* Ac, Sa.

Medical Economics is a freely available trade magazine, which caters to private-practice physicians and covers a broad spectrum of management issues such as staffing, health-care legislation, financial affairs, and public relations. It is published twice a month and is available in a digital magazine format. As with most trade magazines, it includes a great deal of paid advertising, as well as social media plugs, which readers must wade through in order to locate content. Articles cover trends and current issues, and often provide an update on the latest, selected guidelines. Recent topics include: negotiating narrow networks, billing and coding transitional-care management, population health, HIPAA compliance, the Medicare-overpayment rule, and dealing with high-deductible plans. This publication is available in print and online. URL: www.medicaleconomics.com

2803. ***Modern Healthcare: the newsmagazine for administrators and managers in hospitals, and other healthcare institutions.*** Formed by the merger of (1967-1976): *Modern Healthcare (Long-Term Care);* Which superseded (in 1974): *Modern Nursing Home;* Which was formerly (until 1967): *Modern Nursing Home Administrator;* (until 1966): *Nursing Home Administrator;* (until 1950): *Nursing Home Magazine;* (1913-1976): *Modern Healthcare (Short-Term Care);* Which superseded (in 1974): *Modern Hospital.* [ISSN: 0160-7480] 1976. w. USD 164 domestic; USD 255 Canada; USD 218 elsewhere. Ed(s): Neil McLaughlin, David Burda. Crain Communications, Inc., 150 N Michigan Ave, Chicago, IL 60601; info@crain.com; http://www.crain.com. Illus., index. Sample. Vol. ends: Dec. *Indexed:* A01, A22, AgeL, B01, B03, BRI. *Aud.:* Ga, Ac, Sa.

Modern Healthcare is a weekly newsmagazine aimed at health-care executives, administrators, and managers. It focuses mainly on healthcare-related current events and news coverage, and provides readers with business profiles, product reviews, and regional reports. Content includes feature articles, interviews, columns, and commentaries, as well as special reports, including a yearly outlook on the state of health care. The following sections are recurring: "Outliers," which provides random tidbits of health-related information; "Data Points," which includes a statistical summary of a health-care-related topic; and "Q&A," which discusses important health-care issues through interviews with leading industry experts. Recent topics include: EHR and patient safety, the Affordable Care Act, abortion law, Medicare supplemental-insurance plan issues, and gun control as a public health concern. Access to the publication can be obtained by subscription, and it is available in print and online. URL: www.modernhealthcare.com

2804. ***Nursing Administration Quarterly.*** [ISSN: 0363-9568] 1976. q. USD 583. Ed(s): Kathleen D Sanford. Lippincott Williams & Wilkins, Two Commerce Sq, 2001 Market St, Philadelphia, PA 19103; customerservice@lww.com; http://www.lww.com. Illus., adv. Refereed. Vol. ends: Summer. Microform: PQC. *Indexed:* A22, BRI. *Bk. rev.:* Number and length vary. *Aud.:* Ac, Sa.

Nursing Administration Quarterly is a refereed journal written specifically for the nursing administrator. Each issue deals with a particular theme, allowing for an in-depth look at the most current topics in nursing administration. This scholarly journal aims to provide up-to-date and practical information on effective management and leadership in the field of nursing. Content includes editorials, original research, interviews, book reviews, a nursing informatics column, and a regulatory issues column. Recent topics include: behavioral health, nursing retention, nurse-to-nurse bullying, empowering staff nurses, nursing leadership, interprofessional collaboration, nursing informatics, virtual-case management, and nurse contract negotiations. This is an important journal for both hospital libraries and academic libraries that support nursing programs. Access to the publication can be obtained by subscription, and it is available in print and online. URL: www.naqjournal.com

2805. ***Nursing Economics: the journal for health care leaders.*** [ISSN: 0746-1739] 1983. bi-m. USD 118 (Individuals, USD 86; USD 22 per issue domestic). Ed(s): Kenneth J Thomas, Donna M Nickitas. Jannetti Publications, Inc., E Holly Ave, PO Box 56, Pitman, NJ 08071; contact@ajj.com; http://www.ajj.com/jpi. Illus., index, adv. Sample. Refereed. Vol. ends: Nov. *Indexed:* A01, A22, BRI. *Bk. rev.:* Number and length vary. *Aud.:* Ac, Sa.

Nursing Economics is a scholarly, refereed journal, which is published six times per year. This journal aims to provide content on current and emerging best practices in nursing administration and management, with a focus on economics, policy making, and the future of health care. Each issue contains a number of regular features such as editorials, research articles, CNE series, success stories, interviews, and book reviews, as well as staffing, informatics, and policy columns. Recent topics include: staffing models, readmissions, leadership strategies, nursing-quality measurement, and ambulatory care. This journal is recommended for all hospital libraries and academic libraries that support nursing programs. Access to the publication can be obtained by subscription, and it is available in print and online. URL: www.nursingeconomics.net

■ HEALTH PROFESSIONS

See also Health Care Administration; Medicine; Nursing; and Public Health sections.

Amanda Tarbet, Assistant Director of Library Services, MGH Institute of Health Professions, Boston, MA 02129; atarbet@mghihp.edu

Introduction

The health professions are a diverse set of fields with distinct issues and scopes of practice, but with interlinking missions of providing high-quality patient care. The journals and magazines that support this aim are equally diverse in content, focus, and format. This section includes publications targeted at a variety of professions that reflect the growing health-care industry: nursing, physical therapy, occupational therapy, speech-language pathology, physician assistants, and dentistry.

Interprofessional care (IPC) and education (IPE) continue to be the future of healthcare, meaning journals about IPC and IPE are becoming increasingly important to scholarly communication.

Education is integral to the health professions, and each profession highlighted in this section has at least one journal dedicated to or regularly publishing content on education in that discipline. As expected, interprofessional education is frequently featured even in these discipline-specific journals. Education in the health professions has its own unique challenges - simulation and clinical placements, for example - that need unique and innovative solutions, and these scholarly publications are doing an admirable job of meeting that need.

Providing at least some (if not all) open-access content seems to be a burgeoning priority for health professions journals. In addition to full OA journals seeing vast readership numbers, journals that have been traditionally pay access are expanding their OA options, and this is a trend that will no doubt continue to dominate publishing models.

A thread of innovation weaves together all of these professions and their scholarly output. Whether they are addressing health disparities and social justice, the opioid crisis, or patient engagement, the journals in this section are publishing cutting-edge research and sharing revolutionary methods of practice and education, which is to be expected in such a dynamic industry.

Basic Periodicals

American Journal of Occupational Therapy, American Journal of Speech-Language Pathology, Health Professions Education, JAAPA: Journal of the American Academy of Physician Assistants, American Dental Association. Journal, Nursing Forum, Physical Therapy. See also "Nursing" section, *American Journal of Nursing; International Nursing Review.*

Basic Abstracts and Indexes

CINAHL; MEDLINE; PEDro, the Physiotherapy Evidence Database.

2806. ***American Dental Association. Journal.*** Formerly (until 1939): *The Journal of the American Dental Association and the Dental Cosmos;* Which was formed by the merger of (1859-1937): *The Dental Cosmos;* Which superseded (in 1859): *Dental Newsletter;* (1922-1937): *American Dental Association. Journal;* Which was formerly (until 1922): *National Dental Association. Journal;* (until 1915): *National Dental Association. Official Bulletin.* [ISSN: 0002-8177] 1913. m. USD 358. Ed(s): Dr. Michael Glick. American Dental Association, 211 E Chicago Ave, Lower Level, Chicago, IL 60611; adapub@ada.org; http://www.ada.org. Illus., index, adv. Refereed. Circ: 149132 Paid. Vol. ends: Dec. Microform: PQC. *Indexed:* A01, A22, BRI, MLA-IB. *Aud.:* Ac, Sa.

More than one hundred years old, *JADA* is a peer-reviewed scholarly journal published by the American Dental Association (www.ada.org), which claims that *JADA* is consistently ranked the nation's "best-read" dental journal and that its members say it is one of the most important benefits of belonging to the association. A subscription is included with ADA membership. *JADA* can be accessed in a dedicated mobile app. Like many journals published by professional societies, *JADA* seeks to provide a broad overview of the dental profession, including research studies, opportunities for continuing education, and discussions of professional issues. Readers of *JADA* can expect to find editorials, letters to the editor, "News Updates," "Original Research Studies," "Case Reports," and even "Summaries/Systematic Reviews" to assist in making evidence-based clinical decisions. Furthermore, *JADA* continues to address the role dentists play in prescribing opioids to patients, showing that *JADA* is committed to promoting overall health and to publishing timely articles that address important social and health issues like the opioid crisis. Practicing dentists will also find opportunities for continuing education credits.

American Journal of Nursing. See Nursing section.

2807. ***American Journal of Occupational Therapy.*** Former titles (until 1980): *A J O T: The American Journal of Occupational Therapy;* (until 1977): *The American Journal of Occupational Therapy.* [ISSN: 0272-9490] 1947. bi-m. USD 299 (Individuals, USD 249; Free to members). Ed(s): Lorie Richards. American Occupational Therapy Association, Inc., 4720 Montgomery Ln Ste 200, Bethesda, MD 20814; members@aota.org; http://www.aota.org. Illus., index, adv. Refereed. Vol. ends: Nov/Dec. Microform: PQC. *Indexed:* A22, ASSIA, AgeL, BRI. *Aud.:* Ac, Sa.

The aim of the *American Journal of Occupational Therapy* (*AJOT*), an official publication of the American Occupational Therapy Association, Inc. (www.aota.org), is to publish peer-reviewed research that OT professionals can use to make evidence-based decisions in their clinical practice about instruments and treatment plans. It also provides a forum for professional and ethical issues in the field of occupational therapy, especially those that affect practice, research, and education. Reflecting the breadth of OT practice, readers will find studies on mental health, youth, aging, health policy and participation in the form of case reports, systematic reviews, reliability and validity studies, randomized controlled trials, and more. Conference abstracts and proceedings from the annual AOTA conference can be found in supplementary issues. Recent 2018 content includes a special section on policies and interventions for community-dwelling older adults (aging in place) and sensory integration research. Single issues pick up on trends in the literature, but typically include a wide variety of topics. The AOTA publishes the *AJOT* six times per year, and a subscription is included with an AOTA membership. While not entirely open access, a selected number of articles published are open access or free to the public, and these tend to be at the top of their "Most Read" list on the journal's website.

2808. *American Journal of Physical Medicine and Rehabilitation.* Former titles (until 1988): *American Journal of Physical Medicine;* (until 1952): *Occupational Therapy and Rehabilitation;* (until 1925): *Archives of Occupational Therapy.* [ISSN: 0894-9115] 1921. m. USD 883. Ed(s): Walter R Frontera. Lippincott Williams & Wilkins, Two Commerce Sq, 2001 Market St, Philadelphia, PA 19103; customerservice@lww.com; http://www.lww.com. Illus., adv. Refereed. *Indexed:* A01, A22, ErgAb, SD. *Aud.:* Ac, Sa.

While aimed at practicing physiatrists, the *American Journal of Physical Medicine and Rehabilitation* (*AJPMR*) has cross-disciplinary appeal for physical therapists, occupational therapists, and rehabilitation nurses. The *AJPMR* is the official journal of the Association of Academic Physiatrists, which publishes it monthly, and provides opportunities for readers to earn up to 18 continuing medical education credits annually. Research articles are peer-reviewed, and authors have the option to publish their articles as open access. In addition to original research articles, an issue of *AJPMR* may contain literature reviews, case reports, and letters to the editor. Its "Video Gallery" and "Visual Vignettes" sections, in which multimedia is used to present and discuss procedures or imaging cases, are rare among health sciences journals, and they offer a fresh take on the dissemination of scholarly knowledge. Frequent topics such as stroke, traumatic brain injury, and spinal cord injury have special sections on the journal website that collect all of the articles on the respective topic in one place. Issues published in 2018 have also featured research on muscle stiffness, bilateral patellar tendon tears, and risk factors for falls in older adults. *AJPMR* also makes articles available ahead of print.

2809. *American Journal of Speech - Language Pathology: a journal of clinical practice.* [ISSN: 1058-0360] 1991. q. USD 348 (Individuals, USD 141). Ed(s): Julie Barkmeier-Kraemer. American Speech - Language - Hearing Association, 2200 Research Blvd, Rockville, MD 20850; journals@asha.org; http://www.asha.org. Illus. Refereed. *Indexed:* A01, A22, ERIC, MLA-IB. *Aud.:* Ac.

An official publication of the American Speech-Language-Hearing Association (ASHA), the *American Journal of Speech-Language Pathology* (*AJSLP*) is an indispensable resource for practicing SLP clinicians, as well as students, faculty, and researchers in SLP or Communication Sciences and Disorders programs worldwide. Research articles, which are peer reviewed and clinically oriented, cover all aspects of communication and swallowing disorders, including screening, diagnosis, etiology, and management. In addition to original research, *AJSLP* actively solicits for meta-analyses and critical reviews of previously published papers. As a publication of a professional society, the scope of *AJSLP* is very broad, seeking to cover every area of speech-language pathology and all age groups of patients. *AJSLP* is published exclusively online and takes advantage of the format by including a "Topics" page that groups articles together by content rather than by issue number. Similarly, it is heavily integrated with other ASHA publications. It rarely has articles available for free. *AJSLP* places heavy emphasis on evidence-based practice, so in addition to publishing studies that can be used by practitioners as evidence, there are also articles about why evidence-based practice (EBP) is necessary and how it should be done. *AJSLP* publishes four times per year, provides continuing education activities for readers, and boasts a five-year impact factor of 2.343.

2810. *Global Health Research and Policy.* [ISSN: 2397-0642] 2016. . Free. Ed(s): Youmei Feng. BioMed Central Ltd., Floor 6, 236 Gray's Inn Rd, London, WC1X 8HB, United Kingdom; info@biomedcentral.com; https://www.biomedcentral.com. Refereed. *Aud.:* Ac, Sa.

Global Health Research and Policy is an open-access, peer-reviewed scholarly journal from BioMed Central, in partnership with Wuhan University Global Health Institute, that published its first articles in June 2016. In the two years since its launch, the journal has stayed selective, publishing only a few articles every month, but those few articles have been downloaded more than 50,000 times, suggesting that the journal has wide appeal. Its editors have defined its scope broadly, seeking to cover topics such as global health education and practice, health equity, population health, disease burden and more, in the form of research, methodologies, reviews, case reports, short reports, letters to the editor, and commentary articles. Of note is the fact that it does not charge article processing fees, which is rare among open-access journals. Thus far, content on *Global Health Research and Policy* has placed a strong focus on healthcare delivery to vulnerable regions and populations. Additionally, articles on outbreaks such as Zika and Ebola are some of its most significant and timely contributions to the global health literature.

Health Affairs. See Public Health section.

2811. *Health and Interprofessional Practice.* [ISSN: 2159-1253] 2011. q. Free. Ed(s): Amber V Buhler. Pacific University, 2043 College Way, Forest Grove, OR 97116; http://www.pacificu.edu/. Refereed. *Aud.:* Ac, Sa.

Health and Interprofessional Practice (*HIP*) is an online-only, open-access journal that Pacific University began publishing in 2011. Since then, it has published two complete volumes of four issues each, and recently released the third issue of its third volume. The journal's scope is simultaneously specific and broad. It focuses on interprofessional practice, but as such could include papers from a number of fields as long as they are healthcare-related. *HIP* is one of only a few journals that are dedicated to interprofessional health care and that consistently include articles about interprofessional education. There is an "Educational Strategies" section in nearly every issue, as well as original research and theories, and occasionally commentary. Interprofessional practice, especially in health professions education, is gaining traction. Since interprofessional health care is still a relatively new field, the research published in *HIP* is genuinely cutting-edge and no doubt contributes heavily to the evidence necessary to make informed practice decisions in interprofessional care. Communication between interprofessional care teams is a recurring theme of the research, as are student attitudes toward such teams and their experiences training as part of one. Recent articles also look at competencies and readiness of health sciences students for interprofessional practice, and the use of simulation training, all of which are very hot topics in the field right now. *HIP* does publish infrequently compared to other academic journals.

2812. *Health Professions Education.* [ISSN: 2452-3011] 2015. s-a. Free. Ed(s): Henk Schmidt. Elsevier BV, Radarweg 29, Amsterdam, 1043 NX, Netherlands; info@elsevier.com; https://www.elsevier.com. Refereed. *Aud.:* Ac, Sa.

A fresh face on the health professions education (HPE) scholarly scene is *Health Professions Education* (*HPE*), an open-access and peer-reviewed title from King Saud bin Abdulaziz University for Health Sciences, which is less than three years old. As with many new journals, its presence reflects a growing interest in HPE research, but it will take some time to determine the caliber of this journal and its impact on the scholarly record. While the bulk of the content is still very focused on medical students, it has recently published research on physical therapy, dental, and pharmacy education. Where *HPE* differs from similar journals is in its commitment to supporting new authors, inclusion of articles on the practice of HPE and not just the science of it, and solicitation of papers that replicate landmark studies (to combat the reproducibility crisis) or report non-significant results of interesting hypotheses. *HPE* also actively encourages authors to make their data freely available.

2813. *Healthcare Policy.* [ISSN: 1715-6572] 2005. q. Individuals, CAD 195 (print & Online eds.)). Ed(s): Jennifer Zelmer. Longwoods Publishing Corp., 260 Adelaide St East, P.O. Box 8, Toronto, ON M5A 1N1, Canada; subscribe@longwoods.com; http://www.longwoods.com. Adv. Refereed. *Indexed:* ASSIA. *Aud.:* Ac, Sa.

Healthcare Policy is a genuinely interdisciplinary journal whose content about policy development and decision making will appeal to researchers and students in the health sciences, social sciences, humanities, ethics, law, and management sciences. A peer-reviewed journal with open-access options, *Healthcare Policy* disseminates research papers, knowledge translation case studies, data analysis with policy implications, and evidence-based commentary on significant issues in health-care policy. While not exclusively Canadian, it is published by a

Canadian company and accepts submissions in French. Thus, much of the literature tends to be about Canadian health care, offering readers an in-depth look at policy research in a nation with universal health care. *Healthcare Policy* publishes four times a year.

2814. *International Journal of Speech-Language Pathology.* Formerly (until 2008): *Advances in Speech Language Pathology.* [ISSN: 1754-9507] 1999. bi-m. GBP 819 (print & online eds.)). Ed(s): Anne Whitworth, Kirrie Ballard. Taylor & Francis, 2, 3 & 4 Park Sq, Milton Park, Abingdon, OX14 4RN, United Kingdom; subscriptions@tandf.co.uk; http://www.tandf.co.uk. Adv. Sample. Refereed. Reprint: PSC. *Indexed:* A22, E01. *Aud.:* Ac.

The *International Journal of Speech-Language Pathology* (*IJSLP*) is a bimonthly, peer-reviewed publication of the Speech Pathology Association of Australia. It aims to promote discussion of clinical and theoretical issues in SLP practice by publishing review articles, experimental research of any quantitative or qualitative design, and theoretical discussion papers. *IJSLP* accepts international submissions, although articles appear to be from mostly Australian authors. Differentiating *IJSLP* from similar journals is its option to include video and audio files from studies on the website with the associated paper. The website also includes an altmetric impact factor to show how articles are influencing the field through methods other than citation counts, and it ranks the most-read articles so that readers can easily see which papers are resonating with SLP students and professionals. *IJSLP* provides evidence essential for SLP professionals to continue to advance their individual practice and the SLP field as a whole. *IJSLP* has a 2017 impact factor of 1.441 and authors have the option to publish their article as open access.

International Nursing Review. See Nursing section.

2815. *The Internet Journal of Allied Health Sciences and Practice: a journal dedicated to allied health professional practice and education.* [ISSN: 1540-580X] 2003. q. Free. Ed(s): Cheryl Hill. Nova Southeastern University, 3200 S University Dr, Fort Lauderdale, FL 33328; ron@nsu.nova.edu; http://www.nova.edu. Refereed. *Bk. rev.:* Number and length vary. *Aud.:* Ac, Sa.

The Internet Journal of Allied Health Sciences and Practice (*IJAHSP*) is an open-access publication that is publicly funded - accepting no advertisements - and professionally edited and reviewed. Articles are published from the global allied health community on topics related but not limited to physical therapy, occupational therapy, speech-language pathology, physician assistants, interprofessional care, and more. *IJAHSP* consistently publishes articles from the entire spectrum of health professions in each issue. Emphasis is placed on the research, clinical practice, and education of allied health professionals, but it also publishes commentary and opinion pieces. As the concept of interprofessional care becomes more prevalent in academic and clinical settings, the content of *IJAHSP* will only increase in relevancy and utility. The more than 650 papers published in *IJAHSP* have been downloaded more than 200,000 times across the globe.

2816. *J A A P A.* Formerly (until 1994): *American Academy of Physician Assistants. Journal.* [ISSN: 1547-1896] 1988. m. USD 624. Ed(s): Reamer L Bushardt. Lippincott Williams & Wilkins, Two Commerce Sq, 2001 Market St, Philadelphia, PA 19103; customerservice@lww.com; http://www.lww.com. Illus., adv. Refereed. Microform: PQC. *Indexed:* A22, BRI. *Aud.:* Ac.

JAAPA: Journal of the American Academy of Physician Assistants is an indispensable professional journal for practicing PAs or students in a PA program. *JAAPA* publishes information and research on all aspects of PA clinical practice, such as diagnosis and treatment of conditions, as well as education, health policy, and professional issues. A unique feature is the "Becoming a PA" section, which looks at life as a student and the transition into a professional. Research is peer reviewed. *JAAPA* is released monthly, and a subscription is included with membership to the AAPA, or can be purchased by non-members. Articles published in *JAAPA* may be research studies, guidelines and recommendations, continuing medical education (CME), commentary and editorials, reviews, case reports, and more. *JAAPA* has a robust website with a great deal of supplementary material (including a blog and podcast). Like similar journals, *JAAPA* aids its readers by having a topics page on the website that collects articles by concept, as an alternative to browsing by issue.

2817. *Journal of Communication Disorders.* Incorporates (1991-1994): *Clinics in Communication Disorders.* [ISSN: 0021-9924] 1967. bi-m. EUR 1831. Ed(s): Jean K Gordon. Elsevier Inc., 1600 John F Kennedy Blvd, Philadelphia, PA 19103; journalscustomerservice-usa@elsevier.com; https://www.elsevier.com. Illus., adv. Sample. Refereed. Microform: PQC. *Indexed:* A01, A22, ERIC, MLA-IB. *Aud.:* Ac.

The *Journal of Communication Disorders*, a scholarly, peer-reviewed, bimonthly journal with open-access options, publishes original articles on aspects of speech, language, and hearing disorders. Articles may be experimental or descriptive investigations, theoretical or tutorial papers, case reports, or brief communications to the editor. Special issues focus on the assessment, diagnosis, and treatment of communication disorders, and are intended especially for professionals to support evidence-based practice. Release of individual articles within an issue is staggered. Many of the most recent articles in *Journal of Communication Disorders* have been about disorders in children, although the journal's scope is not specifically pediatric. A wide variety of disorders are discussed in this publication, including but not limited to stuttering, Williams syndrome, cognitive-communicative impairments, social communication in individuals with autism, selective mutism, hearing impairment with and without cochlear implants, specific language impairment, and dysarthria.

2818. *Journal of Continuing Education in the Health Professions.* Formerly (until 1988): *Mobius.* [ISSN: 0894-1912] 1981. q. USD 328 domestic; USD 374 foreign. Ed(s): Simon Kitto. Lippincott Williams & Wilkins, 16522 Hunters Green Pky, Hagerstown, MD 21740; customerservice@lww.com; http://www.lww.com. Illus., adv. Refereed. Reprint: PSC. *Indexed:* A01, A22, BRI, ERIC. *Bk. rev.:* Number and length vary. *Aud.:* Ac.

The Journal of Continuing Education in the Health Professions (*JCEHP*) is the official journal of the Alliance for Continuing Education in the Health Professions, the Association for Hospital Medical Education, and the Society for Academic Continuing Medical Education. Despite changing publishers in spring 2016, it appears that all back issues are now available from its current publisher, Lippincott Williams & Wilkins. *JCEHP* is a quarterly journal with open-access options for authors. It is aimed at an audience of practitioners (those developing and implementing continuing education programs), researchers, and policymakers. As a result, the content is intended to address issues in the theory and practice of CE in the health professions, such as instructional design, learning and behavior change, outcomes assessment, and educational research methods. As with similar journals, the interests of medical physicians are well represented, but much of the content in *JCEHP* has interdisciplinary appeal, and recent articles have looked at occupational therapy, pharmacy, and interprofessional care. In addition to original research studies, literature reviews, book reviews, and commentary, *JCEHP* stands out for welcoming articles on the application of new educational methods for its "Innovations" section.

2819. *Journal of Interprofessional Care.* Former titles (until 1992): *Holistic Medicine;* (until 1986): *British Journal of Holistic Medicine.* [ISSN: 1356-1820] 1984. bi-m. GBP 2807 (print & online eds.)). Ed(s): Scott Reeves. Taylor & Francis, 2, 3 & 4 Park Sq, Milton Park, Abingdon, OX14 4RN, United Kingdom; subscriptions@tandf.co.uk; https://www.tandfonline.com. Adv. Sample. Refereed. Reprint: PSC. *Indexed:* A01, A22, ASSIA, E01, SSA. *Aud.:* Ac.

A bimonthly, peer-reviewed journal with open-access options for authors, the *Journal of Interprofessional Care* publishes original research articles, systematic reviews, and theoretical papers about aspects of interprofessional education or practice, and short reports about research (complete or incomplete) and innovations in the field of interprofessional care. Interprofessional care is not limited to any one health-care setting, and so articles may discuss research or practice in hospitals, community clinics, health education, public health, and even criminal justice and K-12 education. This resource is essential for those who teach interprofessional care or manage interprofessional healthcare teams. Recent issues explore numerous assessment tests and scales, student experiences with interprofessional education, and even patient perspectives of interprofessional care. Individual issues are expansive, well more than one hundred pages in length. The *Journal of Interprofessional Care* keeps its offerings diverse by not focusing heavily on practice over education or vice versa. The *Journal of Interprofessional Care* has a 2017 impact factor of 1.601.

2820. *Journal of Interprofessional Education & Practice.* [ISSN: 2405-4526] 2015. q. EUR 648. Ed(s): Al Rundio, Devin R Nickol. Elsevier Inc., 1600 John F Kennedy Blvd, Philadelphia, PA 19103; journalscustomerservice-usa@elsevier.com; https://www.elsevier.com. Refereed. *Aud.:* Ac.

As health professionals continue to establish interprofessional care as a vital practice in the industry, new journals will appear to meet the scholarly needs of its practitioners and educators. One of the newest such journals is the peer-reviewed, online-only *Journal of Interprofessional Education & Practice (JIEP)*, which began publishing in 2015. *JIEP* is affiliated with University of Nebraska Medical Center and the official journal of National Academies of Practice (NAP). *JIEP* is partially open access, and defines its scope as examining current issues and trends in interprofessional care with an emphasis on innovative ideas and solutions to the challenges that health professionals face regarding interprofessional care. *JIEP* features research studies, literature reviews, abstract-only reports of studies, editorials, and short communications. With a focus on education, many of the innovative ideas found in *JIEP* concern educating future health professionals to work successfully as members of interprofessional teams. Studies tend to favor functional solutions over theoretical ones, reporting on new programs or models of education and practice. Journal output is not limited to North America and several articles concern programs in international locations.

2821. *Journal of Midwifery & Women's Health.* Former titles (2000): *Journal of Nurse - Midwifery;* (until 1973): *American College of Nurse - Midwives. Bulletin;* (until 1969): *American College of Nurse - Midwifery. Bulletin.* [ISSN: 1526-9523] 1955. 6x/yr. GBP 516. Ed(s): Frances E Likis. Wiley-Blackwell Publishing, Inc., 111 River St, Hoboken, NJ 07030; http://onlinelibrary.wiley.com. Illus., index, adv. Sample. Refereed. Vol. ends: Nov/Dec. Microform: PQC. Reprint: PSC. *Indexed:* A22, ASSIA, BRI. *Bk. rev.:* Number and length vary; online. *Aud.:* Ac, Sa.

The *Journal of Midwifery & Women's Health* is the official peer-reviewed journal of the American College of Nurse-Midwives (ACNM), which aims to develop and support the profession of midwifery as practiced by certified midwives and nurse-midwives. Thus, the additional benefit of access to *JMWH*'s continuing education courses will prove valuable to practicing members of the profession. *JMWH* may also be of interest to other women's health nurses, clinicians, and OB/GYNs. The bulk of a typical issue is dedicated to original research and reviews, often featuring reports of international studies and evidenced-based guidelines for practice. There is also research in clinical settings that reflects trends in childbirth and has implications for education of future professionals. Additional content includes resources specifically for clinicians, as well as for evidence-based practice. Other sections include an editorial, commentary, and letters to the editor, the aforementioned CE resources, and patient education materials. This bimonthly publication is both thorough and cutting-edge, and demonstrates the willingness of the profession to evolve in accordance with new evidence. Practitioners will appreciate the ample library of patient education handouts that come with a subscription and the continuing education special issues.

Journal of Orthopaedic and Sports Physical Therapy. See Sports/ Physical Education, Coaching, and Sports Sciences section.

2822. *The Journal of Physician Assistant Education.* Formerly (until 2006): *Perspective on Physician Assistant Education.* [ISSN: 1941-9430] 1989. q. USD 535. Ed(s): David Asprey. Physician Assistant Education Association, 300 N Washington St, Ste 710, Alexandria, VA 22314; info@paeaonline.org; http://www.paeaonline.org. Refereed. *Bk. rev.:* Number and length vary. *Aud.:* Ac.

The *Journal of Physician Assistant Education* (*JPAE*) is published by the Physician Assistant Education Association and is intended to advance the field of PA education by publishing scholarly articles for and by PA educators and providing a forum for the exchange of ideas and innovations. *JPAE* is a quarterly journal with some open-access content. Research articles, letters to the editor, and brief research reports build the bulk of each issue, but *JPAE* also includes book reviews and special feature articles that cover topics like global health, cultural perspectives, ethics, teaching methods and, rare among health-sciences journals, exploring medicine through the arts and humanities. Recent issues have also discussed diversity and discrimination in PA studies, demonstrating that *JPAE* has a commitment to social justice in the profession. *JPAE* may have wide appeal with other health professions as well, based on this title's inclusion of articles on interprofessional care.

2823. *Minority Nurse: the career and education resource for the minority nursing professional.* Former titles (until 1999): *M N;* (until 1998): *Minority Nurse.* 1993. q. Free to qualified personnel. Ed(s): Megan Larkin. Springer Publishing Company, 11 W 42nd St, 15th Fl, New York, NY 10036; http://www.springerpub.com. Adv. *Aud.:* Ga, Ac, Sa.

In every profession, there should be space for career discussion, and especially space dedicated to minority issues within and related to that profession. *Minority Nurse* provides such a space for nursing and does so in magazine format, allowing for less formal discussions in the form of columns and special features. Published four times a year, *Minority Nurse* can be found in many hospitals and health centers as complimentary subscriptions are provided to these locations. Furthermore, the majority of featured articles in each issue are available for free on the magazine's website: https://minoritynurse.com. *Minority Nurse* covers important topics of interest to professional nurses such as an annual salary survey, lists of top nursing employers, the impact of mentoring programs, and achieving professional satisfaction. The website has additional content such as information on scholarships for nursing students, blogs written by working nurses, and an active jobs board.

2824. *Nursing Forum: an independent voice for nursing.* [ISSN: 0029-6473] 1961. q. GBP 255. Ed(s): Patricia S Yoder-Wise. Wiley-Blackwell Publishing, Inc., 111 River St, Hoboken, NJ 07030; http://onlinelibrary.wiley.com. Illus., adv. Sample. Refereed. Microform: PQC. Reprint: PSC. *Indexed:* A01, A22, ASSIA, E01. *Aud.:* Ac, Sa.

Nursing Forum is a quarterly, peer-reviewed publication that explores and reports on issues, trends, and other factors that impact and ultimately shape the nursing profession. The target audience is practicing nurses, but nurse administrators, nurse educators, and student nurses may also be interested in its content. "Concept analysis" is a process often used in the field of nursing, and *Nursing Forum* publishes at least one per issue (usually more than one), providing a publishing platform for such articles that advance the profession and follow an established framework. Recent "concept analysis" topics include intentional learning and patient engagement in prenatal care. The "Creative Controversy" column is another example of novel content. These articles attempt to thoroughly explain controversies that nurses may encounter in a professional setting, helping nurses navigate potentially sensitive situations. A typical issue also includes results of research studies, literature reviews, the occasional systematic review, quality improvement studies, and editorials. The journal's mission explicitly calls for cutting-edge, innovative perspectives and articles with practical implications for the profession.

2825. *P T in Motion.* Formerly (until 2009): *P T - Magazine of Physical Therapy.* [ISSN: 1949-3711] 1993. m. 11/yr. Free to members. Ed(s): Donald N Tepper. American Physical Therapy Association, 1111 N Fairfax St, Alexandria, VA 22314; memberservices@apta.org; http://www.apta.org. Adv. Circ: 82552 Paid. *Indexed:* A01, A22, BRI, SD. *Bk. rev.:* Number and length vary. *Aud.:* Ac, Sa.

PT in Motion is the professional issues magazine (not peer-reviewed) of the American Physical Therapy Association (APTA) and is included with APTA membership. A typical issue features several short news briefs with a few longer feature articles, accompanied by color images. Content addresses issues that practicing physical therapists may face in the workplace, such as language barriers, ethical issues, HIPAA compliance, and new opportunities for the profession to expand. Additional content on the website includes an RSS news feed that provides daily updated news items between monthly issues, and is accessible without a subscription to the magazine. On the website, PTs can also discover new products in the marketplace and subscribe to APTA newsletters.

2826. *Pediatric Physical Therapy.* [ISSN: 0898-5669] 1989. q. USD 539. Ed(s): Linda Fetters. Lippincott Williams & Wilkins, Two Commerce Sq, 2001 Market St, Philadelphia, PA 19103; customerservice@lww.com; http://www.lww.com. Index, adv. Refereed. *Indexed:* A22. *Bk. rev.:* Number and length vary. *Aud.:* Ac.

Unique in its field, *Pediatric Physical Therapy* is a quarterly, international journal with a specific aim of disseminating research on physical therapy for children with movement disorders. It is the official journal of the Academy of Pediatric Physical Therapy. Individual issues consist of several original-research articles, and follow-up commentary on previously published articles discussing the applications and/or limitations of the studies. An issue may also have book reviews or letters to the editor. *Pediatric Physical Therapy* also occasionally includes practice guidelines and systematic reviews, and a podcast accompanies each issue as a medium to discuss its contents. A minimal amount of articles are open access and the list of OA articles is not often updated. Research articles have a heavy focus on the effectiveness of treatments for children of all ages and manner of disorder in a wide variety of clinical settings and global locations. *Pediatric Physical Therapy* also has a YouTube channel where they regularly post informational videos.

Physical & Occupational Therapy in Geriatrics. See Geriatrics and Gerontological Studies section.

2827. *Physical Therapy.* Former titles (until 1964): *American Physical Therapy Association. Journal;* Which superseded in part (in 1962): *The Physical Therapy Review;* Which was formerly (until 1948): *Physiotherapy Review;* (until 1927): *P.T.Review.* [ISSN: 0031-9023] 1921. m. Ed(s): Alan M Jette. Oxford University Press, 2001 Evans Rd, Cary, NC 27513; orders.us@oup.com; https://academic.oup.com/journals. Illus., index. Refereed. Vol. ends: Dec. Microform: PQC. *Indexed:* A01, A22, BRI, SD. *Aud.:* Ac.

Physical Therapy is an essential resource for practicing physical therapists, PT educators, and PT students. Independently published by the American Physical Therapy Association, it boasts a five-year impact factor of 3.343 and is ranked number 12 out of 65 rehabilitation journals. A subscription is included with APTA membership. *Physical Therapy* is international in scope and seeks to cover all aspects of the physical therapy field, including evidence-based practice, health policy, acute care, obesity, neurology, musculoskeletal disorders, measurement tools and scales, and pain management. *Physical Therapy* achieves this primarily in the form of research reports and case reports, with occasional protocols and commentary. Individual issues are substantial in length and released monthly. Supplementary content includes podcasts of interviews with article authors and conference roundtables. *Physical Therapy* publishes with the greater intent of improving patient care throughout the field by providing professionals with the evidence they need to make the best decisions. Readers can subscribe to e-mail alerts on the journal's website.

2828. *Rehabilitation Nursing.* Formerly (until 1981): *A R N Journal.* [ISSN: 0278-4807] 1975. bi-m. GBP 194. Ed(s): Kristen L Mauk. John Wiley & Sons, Inc., 111 River St, Hoboken, NJ 07030; cs-journals@wiley.com; http://onlinelibrary.wiley.com. Illus., adv. Refereed. Microform: PQC. Reprint: PSC. *Indexed:* A22. *Aud.:* Ac.

Rehabilitation Nursing is published by the Association of Rehabilitation Nurses, and access is included with membership. Content such as editorials, continuing education, and features reflects and supports the ARN mission to promote and advance the rehabilitation nursing profession and its more than 6,800 members who work in a variety of practice settings to help people affected by disability and chronic illness. The bulk of each issue comprises original peer-reviewed research articles carrying implications for professional practice. Some content is freely available through the journal website. Subscribers are given early access to some articles from each issue. Features are summarized in a "Key Practice Points" section that demonstrates clinical relevance of the research. Subscribers can also access continuing education modules.

■ HIKING, CLIMBING, AND OUTDOOR RECREATION

See also Boats and Boating; Fishing; Hunting and Guns and Sports sections.

Jennifer Sundheim, Assistant Director, University of Washington Tacoma Library, 1900 Commerce Street, Tacoma, WA 98402; sundheim@uw.edu

Introduction

Nearly half of all Americans participated in an outdoor recreation activity in the past year. The participation rate has remained steady since 2006, according to The Outdoor Foundation, a nonprofit organization that conducts an online survey of over 40,000 Americans each year for their annual *Outdoor Recreation Participation Report.* With such a large percentage of people involved in outdoor recreation, it is important for libraries to provide access to magazines focused on outdoor recreation topics.

The magazines reviewed below are commercial English-language titles published in North America with a focus on hiking, climbing, and general outdoor recreational activities. The magazines are readily available to libraries through stand-alone subscriptions (publications requiring society or club memberships prior to obtaining a subscription are not included); and all titles have a broad geographic scope (smaller regional or local-interest publications were eliminated). Both recreational and competitive/professional-content–level publications are included. Whenever possible, the stated mission and scope of the magazine are quoted so as to make the target audience of the publication clear. Additionally, general retail availability is sometimes provided to give a sense of circulation and the significance of a potential library subscription.

Basic Periodicals

Hs: *Outside* (Santa Fe); Ga: *Backpacker, Climbing, Outside* (Santa Fe), *Rock & Ice.*

Basic Abstracts and Indexes

MasterFILE Premier; Research Library (ProQuest); Readers' Guide to Periodical Literature.

2829. *Alpinist Magazine.* [ISSN: 1540-725X] 2002. q. USD 49.95; USD 14.95 per issue. Ed(s): Katie Ives. Alpinist LLC, 60 Main St, Ste 201, Jeffersonville, VT 05464. Adv. *Aud.:* Sa.

The *Alpinist* significantly describes itself as "an archival-quality, quarterly publication dedicated to world alpinism and adventure climbing. The pages of *Alpinist* capture the art of ascent in its most powerful manifestations, presenting an articulation of climbing and its lifestyle that matches the intensity of the pursuit itself." It is true; the publication is as much an art-level design and photography publication printed on a heavier stock, matte paper as it is a climbing magazine. Each issue contains feature articles, gear reviews, climbing technique write-ups, and interviews. Most online back-issue content is limited to subscribers. An additional "premier monthly electronic newsletter" entitled *High Camp* is also available to subscribers to supplement the print. The publication is rarely available in retail establishments, so the only way individuals can get access to the publication would be through a subscription or library holding, and this publication is best suited to libraries with extensive outdoor recreation collections.

2830. *Backpacker: the outdoor at your doorsteps.* Incorporates (1977 -198?): *Backpacker Footnotes;* (19??-1979): *Wilderness Camping.* [ISSN: 0277-867X] 1973. 9x/yr. USD 12 domestic; USD 21 Canada; USD 34 elsewhere. Active Interest Media, 5720 Flatiron Pkwy, Boulder, CO 80301; http://www.aimmedia.com/. Illus., adv. Sample. Circ: 500000 Paid. Vol. ends: Nov/Dec. Microform: PQC. *Indexed:* A22, BRI, C37, MASUSE, SD. *Aud.:* Hs, Ga, Sa.

The stated mission of *Backpacker* is "We inspire and enable people to enjoy the outdoors by providing the most trusted and engaging information about backcountry adventure in North America." Published since 1973, the magazine is well known in the hiking world and is a staple of outdoor sporting-goods retailers. It is for sale in most airports and can even be found in many grocery stores. Typical issues contain sections on hiking destinations and on skills for backcountry camping; gear reviews; and profiles of people involved in backcountry activities. Special themed issues are also produced. April is the month of the annual "Gear Guide." The web site provides access to the current issue, including featured articles, as well as the content of some past issues, a directory of hikes from across North America, blogs, and videos. Through the Google Magazines project, full-text back issues of the period 1973-2009 are freely available.

2831. ***Climbing.*** [ISSN: 0045-7159] 1970. 9x/yr. USD 14.95 domestic; USD 29.95 Canada; USD 34.95 elsewhere. Active Interest Media, http://www.aimmedia.com/. Illus., adv. Sample. Circ: 38263 Paid. Vol. ends: Dec/Jan. *Indexed:* SD. *Bk. rev.:* 2-3, 200 words. *Aud.:* Ga, Sa.

Climbing stays true to its title, focusing on the activity of climbing in all forms-alpine, bouldering, sport, and traditional climbing. The one dalliance is photography, but any information on photography serves only to enable better climbing pictures. Typical issues contain features on climbing locales, technical climbing tips, equipment write-ups, climber profiles, and brief reviews of climbing books and videos. The "Gear Guide" is released in April and a "Photo Annual" issue comes out in the summer. Access to online issues requires an electronic subscription. Freely available on the web site are climbing news, indexing of past issues, blogs, photography, and a database of climbs.

Field & Stream. See Hunting and Guns section.

2832. ***Gripped: the climbing magazine.*** [ISSN: 1488-0814] 1999. bi-m. USD 25.95. Gripped Publishing Inc., 75 Harbord St, Toronto, ON M5S 1G4, Canada; info@gripped.com; http://gripped.com. Adv. *Bk. rev.:* 2-4, 200-300 words. *Aud.:* Ga, Sa.

Gripped sports the subtitle "The climbing magazine," but sometimes you will find it referred to as "Canada's climbing magazine." Published out of Toronto, *Gripped* features worldwide climbing news, gear reviews, articles on climbing destinations, and issues and reviews on books and media. Their complementary web site to the print magazine is clean and well-organized, providing access to differentiated climbing news, event calendars, routes, gear, climber profiles, and videos. However, the online access to the full magazine requires a subscription or individual issue purchase via iTunes, Press Display, Nook, or Zinnio.

2833. ***Mud & Obstacle.*** 2014. bi-m. Cruz Bay Publishing, PO Box 420235, Palm Coast, FL 32142-0235; http://www.aimmedia.com/. Sample. *Aud.:* Hs, Ga, Sa.

A publication catering to enthusiasts of Tough Mudder events, a type of extreme sport drawn from British military training where teams work to complete a series of 10- to 12-mile-long obstacle courses replete with mud. The events have been growing in such popularity (since their introduction in 2010) that a niche has emerged for a dedicated magazine. With the glossy look and feel of something like *Runner's World,* each issue covers event news and highlights, training techniques and fitness, gear considerations, and athlete profiles. The publication would be of high interest for public libraries looking for something edgy to appeal to young, outdoorsy patrons, or potentially a college-recreational reading periodical collection.

National Geographic Traveler. See Travel and Tourism/General section.

2834. ***Outdoor Life.*** Incorporates: *Fisherman;* (in 1927): *Outdoor Recreation;* Which was formerly (until 1924): *Outer's Recreation;* (until 1919): *Outer's Book-Recreation;* Incorporates (in 1907): *Pacific Sportsman;* Which was formerly (until 1904): *Pacific Coast Sportman.* [ISSN: 0030-7076] 1898. m. USD 10 combined subscription domestic (print & ipad eds.); USD 26 combined subscription Canada (print & ipad eds.); USD 40 combined subscription elsewhere (print & ipad eds.)). Bonnier Corp., 2 Park Ave, 9th Fl, New York, NY 10016; http://www.bonniercorp.com. Illus., adv. Sample. Vol. ends: Dec. Microform: NBI; PQC. *Indexed:* A01, A22, BRI, C37, MASUSE. *Aud.:* Hs, Ga, Sa.

The subtitle of *Outdoor Life* is "The source for hunting and fishing adventure." To that end, each issue has dedicated sections for hunting, fishing, shooting, and gear news. An additional section called "Snap Shots" often details readers' real-life experiences while hunting and fishing. Featured articles cover things such as tactics for giant buck hunting and big-game safaris. A gear issue comes out in late summer. The web site provides access to some of the magazine content and the standard blog and video fare, as well as offers a message board and an additional Q&A.

2835. ***Outside (Santa Fe).*** Formerly (until 1980): *Mariah - Outside;* Which was formed by the merger of (1976-1979): *Mariah;* (1977-1979): *Outside (San Francisco).* [ISSN: 0278-1433] 1979. m. USD 19.95. Ed(s): Scott Rosenfrield. Mariah Media Inc., 400 Market St, Santa Fe, NM 87501; letters@outsidemag.com. Illus., adv. *Indexed:* A01, A22, SD. *Aud.:* Hs, Ga, Ac.

With quality writing and wide coverage on all things athletic, *Outside* has become a standard title in most public libraries. The magazine describes itself as "America's leading active-lifestyle and adventure-travel magazine." It says it is "dedicated to covering the people, activities, gear, art, and politics of the world outside." While its featured topics can be far-ranging, the journalistic coverage is more in-depth than that of most magazines. *Outside* publishes writers such as John Krakauer and Sebastian Junger, and the subjects of articles have often shown up later as full-length books and/or feature films. Special "Buyer's Guide" issues with gear reviews are produced annually. The web site features access to ten years of the magazine's archive, as well as additional article features, blogs, videos, photos, and podcasts.

2836. ***Rock & Ice: the climber's magazine.*** [ISSN: 0885-5722] 1984. 8x/yr. USD 29.95. Ed(s): Duane Raleigh, Jeff Jackson. Big Stone Publishing, 2567 Dolores way, corbondale, CO 81623; http://www.bigstonepub.com. Illus., adv. Vol. ends: Nov/Dec. *Bk. rev.:* 3-6, 300-500 words. *Aud.:* Ac, Sa.

Rock & Ice claims to be "the only climber-owned and operated climbing magazine." The Western Publishers Association voted it the "Best Consumer Outdoor Recreation" magazine in 2005. Each issue has climbing news, photography, gear and book reviews, an accident analysis report, featured climbs, and advice on sports injuries and climbing techniques. It is perhaps because of the standard analysis and review columns that a search of WorldCat shows this publication to be a preferred title for academic libraries if they are going to subscribe to a climbing magazine. As for special issues: once a year in June the magazine puts out *Ascent*-a collection of longer articles on people and events in "the climbing life." The web site provides access to the current issue and archives that range several years back. There are also directories for guides, gear, and gyms.

2837. ***Trail Runner: one dirty magazine.*** [ISSN: 1526-3134] 1999. bi-m. USD 21.95 (print or online eds.)). Ed(s): Michael Benge. Big Stone Publishing, 2567 Dolores way, corbondale, CO 81623; http://www.bigstonepub.com. Adv. *Aud.:* Ac, Sa.

Like the magazine *Rock & Ice, Trail Runner* is a Big Stone Publishing production. And just as *Rock & Ice* establishes its authority with the claim "Built by Climbers," *Trail Runner* states that it is "written by trail runners for trail runners." It also claims to be "the only magazine dedicated to the off-road running community." There is another trail running magazine from the United Kingdom that has been in print for some time called *Trail Running*; however, for North America, this is the publication (the magazine *Runner's World* does a special single issue per year on off-road trail running). Standard content for *Trail Runner* includes information on trail-running skills, nutrition, and injury rehabilitation; runner interviews; gear reviews; and information on trail travel destinations. Special themed issues are produced each year. Between December and January, the big "Race" issue is put out, listing more than 1,000 trail races slated for the coming year. June is when the annual "Gear Guide" appears. The web site provides free access to scanned images of back issues, a calendar of race events, a forum board, and sign-up for a bimonthly e-mail newsletter.

■ HISTORY

American History/World History/Interdisciplinary Interests/General History

Lindsay Brownfield, Reference and Instruction Librarian, University of Nebraska-Kearney, Kearney, NE; brownfieldlj@unk.edu

Introduction

History, as a discipline, relates a broad interest to varied audiences, and it is difficult to single out a few select magazines and journals. Hundreds of titles for both a general and academic audience exist to serve the field. Some are focused on very specific times (*American Colonial History*), places (*Russian History*), or themes (*Journal of the History of Sexuality*). This section presents magazines and journals that cover the field broadly, from an international perspective, or from a focus on a theme, such as economic, social, or gender history.

American libraries will desire a selection of journals devoted to the American historical experience, including journals that cover specific periods. It is noteworthy that there are now journals that cover the diversity of American history. And any library with an adult readership should consider subscribing to titles that cover local and regional history. A list of these follows, arranged by state. There are also some excellent regional periodicals listed at the end.

Alabama Review, Alaska History, Journal of the Southwest [Arizona], *Arkansas Historical Quarterly, California History, Colorado Heritage, Connecticut History, Delaware History, Florida Historical Quarterly, Georgia Historical Quarterly, Idaho Yesterdays, Illinois Heritage, Journal of Illinois History, Illinois State Historical Society Journal, Indiana Magazine of History, Annals of Iowa: a quarterly journal of history, Kansas History: a journal of the central plains, Kentucky Ancestors, Louisiana History, Maine History, Maryland History Magazine, Historical Journal of Massachusetts/Massachusetts Historical Review, Michigan Historical Review, Minnesota History, Journal of Mississippi History, Missouri Historical Review, Montana: the magazine of western history, Nebraska History, Nevada Historical Society Quarterly, New Jersey History (Rutgers), New Mexico Historical Review, New York History: quarterly journal of the New York State Historical Association, North Carolina Historical Review, North Dakota History, Ohio History, Chronicles of Oklahoma, Oregon Historical Quarterly, Pennsylvania History: a journal of Mid-Atlantic States, Rhode Island History, South Carolina Historical Magazine, South Dakota History, Tennessee Historical Quarterly, Southwestern Historical Quarterly* [Texas], *Utah Historical Quarterly, Vermont History, Virginia Magazine of History and Biography, West Virginia History, Wisconsin Magazine of History, Annals of Wyoming.*

REGIONAL

Journal of Southern History, Journal of the West: an illustrated quarterly of Western American history and culture, New England Quarterly, Pacific Historical Review, True West, Western Historical Quarterly.

Basic Periodicals

Ems: *American History* (Leesburg); Hs: *American History, History Today;* Ga: *American History* (Leesburg), *History Today;* Ac: *American Historical Review, English Historical Review, Hispanic American Historical Review, The Historian* (East Lansing), *History, History Today, Journal of American History, Journal of Contemporary History, Journal of Modern History, Journal of Urban History, William and Mary Quarterly.*

Basic Abstracts and Indexes

America: History and Life, Arts and Humanities Citation Index, Historical Abstracts, Research Library (ProQuest).

American History

2838. *American History (Leesburg).* Formerly (until 1995): *American History Illustrated.* [ISSN: 1076-8866] 1966. bi-m. USD 26.95. HistoryNet, 1919 Gallows Rd, Vienna, VA 22182; comments@historynet.com; http://www.historynet.com. Illus., index, adv. *Indexed:* A01, A22, AmHI, BRI, C37, MASUSE. *Bk. rev.:* 2-29, 200-300 words. *Aud.:* Ems, Hs, Ga.

Written for a general audience, *American History* covers a wide range of topics in brief, well-written, and attractively illustrated articles. Each issue has six or so feature articles, plus shorter pieces on news about American history, historic firsts, artifacts, and important encounters. This title also includes short book and media reviews and information on historic sites. Very readable, and balanced in its approach to potentially controversial topics and current political issues. Recommended for public and school libraries.

2839. *Civil War History.* [ISSN: 0009-8078] 1955. q. USD 90 (Individuals, USD 60). Ed(s): Brian Craig Miller. Kent State University Press, 1118 Library, PO Box 5190, Kent, OH 44242; http://www.kentstateuniversitypress.com. Illus., index. Refereed. Microform: MIM; PQC. *Indexed:* A01, A22, AmHI, BRI, E01, MLA-IB. *Bk. rev.:* 7-13, 1-2 pages. *Aud.:* Ga, Ac.

The American Civil War is still of very wide interest to all audiences. *Civil War History* covers "not only the War Between the States but the events leading up to it and the results flowing from it." Each issue includes two to four articles, on topics like "Relevance, Resonance, and Historiography: Interpreting the Lives and Experience of Civil War Soldiers" and "Interpreting Race, Slavery, and United States Colored Troops at Civil War Battlefields." This title also contains in-depth book reviews, mostly of academic books, but also some books for a general audience. Recommended for college libraries.

2840. *Civil War Times.* Formerly (until 2002): *Civil War Times Illustrated;* Which incorporates (1958-1962): *Tradition;* (until 1962): *Civil War Times.* [ISSN: 1546-9980] 1959. bi-m. USD 26.95. HistoryNet, 1600 Tysons Blvd, Ste 1140, Leesburg, VA 22102-4883; comments@historynet.com; http://www.historynet.com. Illus., index, adv. *Indexed:* A01, A22, BRI, MASUSE. *Bk. rev.:* 2-3, length varies. *Aud.:* Hs, Ga.

Civil War publications have a large and loyal readership, and *Civil War Times* is one of the most popular. The extensive use of illustrations supplements this title's coverage of such topics as the use of photography, artillery, and music, although numerous advertisements sometimes make it difficult to follow a story from one part of the magazine to another. Regular features such as "Gallery," "Travel," and "My War," as well as book reviews, enhance the magazine's appeal. Intended primarily for the general reader and Civil War enthusiast, this publication would also be helpful to high school and junior college students beginning research on a Civil War topic.

2841. *Diplomatic History: the journal of the Society for Historians of American Foreign Relations.* [ISSN: 0145-2096] 1977. 5x/yr. EUR 546. Ed(s): Nick Cullather. Oxford University Press, Great Clarendon St, Oxford, OX2 6DP, United Kingdom; onlinequeries.uk@oup.com; https://academic.oup.com/journals/. Illus., adv. Sample. Refereed. Circ: 2267 Paid. Vol. ends: Oct. Reprint: PSC. *Indexed:* A01, A22, AmHI, BAS, BRI, E01, IBSS, P61. *Bk. rev.:* 4-5, 3-8 pages. *Aud.:* Ac, Sa.

Diplomatic History is published by the Society for Historians of American Foreign Relations. It covers U.S. international history, diplomacy, security, and foreign relations, broadly defined. In addition to well-researched articles, there are forums on special topics like "Gender and Sexuality in American Foreign Relations." Some issues include commentary on specific articles or broad themes, often with a response from the author. Each issue also includes book reviews. This title is written for an academic audience, but much of the material is relevant for anyone interested in current U.S. foreign policy.

Ethnohistory. See Multicultural Studies section.

Journal of African American History. See African American section.

2842. *The Journal of American History.* Formerly (until 1964): *The Mississippi Valley Historical Review (Print).* [ISSN: 0021-8723] 1914. q. EUR 320. Oxford University Press, 2001 Evans Rd, Cary, NC 27513; custserv.us@oup.com; https://academic.oup.com/journals. Illus., index, adv. Refereed. Circ: 9000. Vol. ends: Dec. Microform: PMC; PQC. Reprint: PSC. *Indexed:* A01, A22, AmHI, BAS, BRI, CBRI, Chicano, MLA-IB. *Bk. rev.:* 100, 1-5 pages. *Aud.:* Ac, Sa.

JAH is published by the Organization of American Historians and is the leading journal in American history, in contrast to the *American Historical Review,* which covers world history. The OAH includes not only academic historians, but also teachers, public historians, and curators of historic sites and archives; *JAH* also includes not only academic articles that cover American history very broadly, but also essays on pedagogy and the practice of public history. Articles are supplemented by an extensive section of book, museum exhibit, and website reviews. This title is essential for any academic library, and it is especially valuable for colleges preparing future history teachers.

2843. *Journal of the Gilded Age and Progressive Era.* [ISSN: 1537-7814] 2002. q. GBP 143 (print & online eds.)). Ed(s): Robert D Johnston, Benjamin H Johnson. Cambridge University Press, 1 Liberty Plaza, Fl 20, New York, NY 10004; https://www.cambridge.org. Refereed. Reprint: PSC. *Bk. rev.:* Number and length vary. *Aud.:* Ac.

This journal covers "all aspects of U.S. history for the time period from 1865 through 1920." This is a period that tends to fall between journals, so it is welcome to have something that covers this era. Most issues include three or four articles, plus a few in-depth book reviews. There is a companion website with digital material that relates to the articles, which is especially useful for teaching. Suitable for academic libraries.

2844. *Reviews in American History.* [ISSN: 0048-7511] 1973. q. USD 195. Ed(s): Michael Hoppin Read, Thomas P Slaughter. The Johns Hopkins University Press, 2715 N Charles St, Baltimore, MD 21218; http://www.press.jhu.edu. Illus., index, adv. Sample. Refereed. Vol. ends: Dec. Reprint: PSC. *Indexed:* A01, A22, AmHI, BRI, CBRI, E01. *Bk. rev.:* 30-40, lengthy. *Aud.:* Ac, Sa.

RAH specializes in longer high-quality critical book reviews, usually about 20 per issue. The journal covers all areas of American history, including cultural history, intellectual history, political history and philosophy, religion, social history, gender, sexuality, popular culture, law, military history, and economics. The reviews generally place the book(s) in historiographic context, making them useful not only for staying current, but also as starting points for further research. The books reviewed reflect the perspectives of a wide range of subfields in American history. This makes *RAH* a useful supplement to online book review sites such as H-NET. Written for an academic audience; also useful as a collection development resource.

2845. *William and Mary Quarterly.* Former titles (until 1944): *William and Mary College Quarterly Historical Magazine;* (until 1894): *William and Mary College Quarterly Historical Papers.* [ISSN: 0043-5597] 1892. q. USD 185 (print & online eds.)). Ed(s): Margaret T Musselwhite, Joshua Piker. Omohundro Institute of Early American History & Culture, PO Box 8781, Williamsburg, VA 23187; oieahc@wm.edu; http://oieahc.wm.edu. Illus., index, adv. Refereed. Vol. ends: Oct. Microform: PQC. Reprint: PSC. *Indexed:* A01, A22, AmHI, BRI, CBRI, MLA-IB, R&TA. *Bk. rev.:* 13-20, 1,000 words. *Aud.:* Ac, Sa.

WMQ is the oldest and most prestigious journal for scholarship on North America from the colonial period through about 1820. Although it is essentially a journal for historians, it also publishes work from other disciplines, such as material culture, political science, and literature. The quality of the writing and editing is high. The journal also publishes articles on sources and source interpretation, and some articles have online supplements. Each issue also includes book reviews and review essays. Highly recommended for any academic library.

World History

2846. *British Heritage Travel.* Former titles (until 2016): *British Heritage;* (until 1979): *British History Illustrated.* 1974. bi-m. USD 29.95. British Heritage Society, 201 E 87th St, Ste 23C, New York, NY 10128; privacy@britishheritage .com; https://britishheritage.com. Illus., index, adv. *Indexed:* A01, A22, BRI, C37, MASUSE. *Bk. rev.:* 3-4, 300-400 words. *Aud.:* Hs, Ga.

British Heritage is a suited combination of history for a general audience and travel planning advice. Most articles feature historic sites or places, together with information on travel, hotels, and nearby attractions. Anglophile readers and armchair travelers will enjoy the short, well-illustrated articles.

2847. *The English Historical Review.* [ISSN: 0013-8266] 1886. q. EUR 636. Ed(s): Martin Conway, Catherine Holmes. Oxford University Press, Great Clarendon St, Oxford, OX2 6DP, United Kingdom; onlinequeries.uk@oup.com; http://global.oup.com. Illus., index, adv. Sample. Refereed. Vol. ends: Nov. Microform: IDC; PMC; PQC. Reprint: PSC. *Indexed:* A01, A22, AmHI, BAS, BRI, CBRI, E01, MLA-IB, P61. *Bk. rev.:* Number and length vary. *Aud.:* Ac, Sa.

The venerable *EHR* began publication in 1886, making it one of the oldest continuously published history journals. Articles tend to focus on British history, but the journal also covers European history, world history, and the Americas (including U.S. foreign policy, but excluding books on the internal politics of the United States). *EHR* covers history from the early medieval period onward. There are essay reviews, in-depth book reviews, and shorter notices of newly published books. Plus, there is an annual summary of international periodical literature published in the previous 12 months. Authoritative, respected, and essential for libraries at colleges and universities that teach British and European history.

2848. *Hispanic American Historical Review.* [ISSN: 0018-2168] 1918. q. USD 658. Ed(s): Sean Mannion. Duke University Press, 905 W Main St, Durham, NC 27701; orders@dukeupress.edu; https://www.dukeupress.edu. Illus., index, adv. Refereed. Reprint: PSC. *Indexed:* A01, A22, AmHI, BRI, CBRI, E01, IBSS, MLA-IB. *Bk. rev.:* Number and length vary. *Aud.:* Ac.

HAHR is the pioneer and premier journal in the field of Latin American history from the colonial period onward, and covers "every facet of scholarship on Latin American history and culture." There are substantive articles and an extensive section of book reviews, including reviews of books in Spanish. Recommended for academic libraries.

2849. *Historical Journal.* Formerly (until 1958): *Cambridge Historical Journal.* [ISSN: 0018-246X] 1923. q. GBP 505. Ed(s): Phil Withington, Andrew Preston. Cambridge University Press, University Printing House, Shaftesbury Rd, Cambridge, CB2 8BS, United Kingdom; journals@cambridge.org; https://www.cambridge.org/. Illus., index, adv. Refereed. Circ: 1300. Vol. ends: Dec. Microform: PQC. Reprint: PSC. *Indexed:* A01, A22, AmHI, BAS, BRI, E01, IBSS, MLA-IB, P61. *Bk. rev.:* 5-28, lengthy. *Aud.:* Ac, Sa.

This journal's articles cover world history since 1500 broadly, including from political, cultural, and economic perspectives. European history dominates, but there are also articles on topics concerning Africa, Asia, and South America. Many articles reflect an interdisciplinary approach. Rather than publishing book reviews, this title prefers substantive historiographical reviews and essay reviews that cover a number of books on related topics, e.g., "The Peculiarities of German Philhellenism" or "Historicizing Citizenship in Post-War Britain." For an academic audience.

2850. *History: the journal of the Historical Association.* [ISSN: 0018-2648] 1912. q. GBP 683 (print & online eds.)). Ed(s): Emma Griffin. Wiley-Blackwell Publishing Ltd., The Atrium, Southern Gate, Chichester, PO19 8QG, United Kingdom; cs-journals@wiley.com; http://onlinelibrary.wiley.com/. Illus., adv. Sample. Refereed. Vol. ends: Oct. Microform: MIM; IDC; PQC. Reprint: PSC. *Indexed:* A01, A22, AmHI, BAS, BRI, E01, IBSS, MLA-IB. *Aud.:* Ac, Sa.

The mission of the Historical Association, a British society, is to "support the study, teaching and enjoyment of history at all levels." The HA publishes several journals, and *History* is its journal for an academic and scholarly audience. Unsurprisingly, British history accounts for the bulk of the articles, but the journal reflects a wide range of approaches and contributions from social, political, cultural, economic, and ecclesiastical historians. *History* contains review articles, special issues, and essays on records and archives, but no book reviews were found in the most recent issues.

2851. *History Today.* [ISSN: 0018-2753] 1951. m. GBP 49; GBP 74 combined subscription (print & online eds.)). Ed(s): Paul Lay. History Today Ltd., 25 Bedford Ave, London, WC1B 3AT, United Kingdom. Illus., index, adv. Sample. Vol. ends: Dec. Microform: NBI. *Indexed:* A01, A22, AmHI, BAS, BRI, C37, CBRI, MASUSE, MLA-IB. *Bk. rev.:* 3-7, length varies. *Aud.:* Ga, Ac.

This beautifully illustrated popular magazine, published in Britain, is written for a general audience but is also valuable for academic researchers. Each issue includes several substantive articles, which generally cover a wide range of times, places, and topics. Recent issues include articles on "Princes, Profits, and the Prophet," "Richard Nixon's Opening to China and Closing the Gold Window," and "Napoleon: Cutting a Swathe through Europe." There is an emphasis on British history, but world history is also covered. Many of the articles are written by academic historians, and generally include recommended further reading, making this a good resource for undergraduates and high school students. There are also essays, news, reviews (of books, media, and exhibitions), and letters to the editor. The style is exceptionally readable. Recommended for all libraries.

2852. *History Workshop Journal.* Formerly (until 1995): *History Workshop.* [ISSN: 1363-3554] 1976. s-a. EUR 293. Ed(s): Kate Shaw. Oxford University Press, Great Clarendon St, Oxford, OX2 6DP, United Kingdom; onlinequeries.uk@oup.com; http://global.oup.com. Illus., adv. Sample. Refereed. Reprint: PSC. *Indexed:* A22, E01, GW, MLA-IB, P61. *Bk. rev.:* 6. *Aud.:* Ga, Ac, Sa.

HWJ is the flagship journal of the "history workshop" movement, and champions the perspective of "history from below," that is, history from the perspective of ordinary people rather than elites. Articles address a wide range of topics in European history. Beyond the usual academic articles, *HWJ* also publishes essays on research and the writing of history; articles regarding history in social and political context ("History on the Line"); and conference reports, as well as roughly half a dozen book reviews per issue. *HWJ* is academically rigorous, but written for a wider audience, and would be appropriate for most academic libraries.

2853. *The International History Review.* [ISSN: 0707-5332] 1979. 6x/yr. GBP 420 (print & online eds.)). Ed(s): Andrew Williams. Routledge, 4 Park Sq, Milton Park, Abingdon, OX14 4RN, United Kingdom; subscriptions@tandf.co.uk; http://www.tandfonline.com. Illus., adv. Refereed. Reprint: PSC. *Indexed:* A01, A22, AmHI, BAS, BRI, C37, IBSS, MLA-IB. *Bk. rev.:* 70-80, length varies. *Aud.:* Ac.

The editors of the *IHR* seek to create a bridge between historical research and the study of international relations. The journal publishes articles on political and diplomatic history, especially on "the history of current conflicts and conflicts of current interest." The journal also covers the intellectual history of international thought and international relations theory, as well as the history of international organizations. Most issues contain in-depth book reviews or review essays. Much of the content is about the twentieth century, but there are occasional articles on earlier periods. For an academic audience.

The Journal of African History. See Africa section.

2854. *Journal of Contemporary History.* [ISSN: 0022-0094] 1966. q. USD 1511 (print & online eds.)). Ed(s): Stanley Payne, Richard J Evans. Sage Publications Ltd., 1 Oliver's Yard, 55 City Rd, London, EC1Y 1SP, United Kingdom; info@sagepub.com; https://www.sagepub.com/. Illus. Sample. Refereed. Microform: PQC. Reprint: PSC. *Indexed:* A01, A22, AmHI, BAS, BRI, E01, IBSS, MLA-IB, P61. *Bk. rev.:* 6-12. *Aud.:* Ga, Ac.

JCH covers twentieth-century world history after World War I. While most articles are on European political and cultural history, there is an occasional article on America or other parts of the world. In addition to articles, there are also book reviews and review articles. This journal is for an academic audience, but is well-written and intelligible to the non-specialist. Recent articles include "Helen Glew, Gender, Rhetoric, and Regulation: Women's Work in the Civil Service" and "Beyond the War: Nazi Propaganda Aims in Spain during the Second World War."

2855. *Journal of Early Modern History: contacts, comparisons, contrasts.* [ISSN: 1385-3783] 1997. bi-m. EUR 474. Ed(s): Simon Ditchfield. Brill, PO Box 9000, Leiden, 2300 PA, Netherlands; marketing@brill.com; https://brill.com. Adv. Refereed. Reprint: PSC. *Indexed:* A01, A22, E01. *Bk. rev.:* 5-10, length varies. *Aud.:* Ac.

Established in 1997, *JEMH* covers world history from 1300 to 1800, and it is a key journal for this relatively recently established academic field. In general, there are three or four articles in each issue, and in some issues, book reviews supplement the scholarly articles. Some articles are comparative; many address contacts between cultures; and others address specific topics in particular times and places; for example, "Protecting the Mediterranean: Ottoman Responses to Maritime Violence, 1718-1770" or "Philip II of Spain and His Italian Jewish Spy." Special issues cover broader topics, such as Perspectives on Women's Religious Activities.

2856. *Journal of Global History.* [ISSN: 1740-0228] 2005. 3x/yr. GBP 271 (print & online eds.)). Ed(s): William Gervase Clarence-Smith, Merry Wiesner-Hanks. Cambridge University Press, University Printing House, Shaftesbury Rd, Cambridge, CB2 8BS, United Kingdom; journals@cambridge.org; https://www.cambridge.org/. Adv. Refereed. Reprint: PSC. *Indexed:* A22, E01, IBSS. *Bk. rev.:* Number and length vary. *Aud.:* Ac.

This journal covers world history, particularly from the point of view of interactions between peoples, countries, and cultures. The editors are broadly interested in "global change over time, together with the diverse histories of globalization." Recent articles examine Latin American archaeology, fiscal policy, and the United Nations. Each issue includes about eight articles, and some in-depth book reviews. Written for an academic audience.

Journal of Latin American Studies. See Latin America and Spain section.

2857. *Journal of Medieval History.* [ISSN: 0304-4181] 1975. 4x/yr. GBP 932 (print & online eds.)). Ed(s): C M Woolgar. Routledge, 4 Park Sq, Milton Park, Abingdon, OX14 4RN, United Kingdom; subscriptions@tandf.co.uk; http://www.tandfonline.com. Illus., index. Refereed. Microform: PQC. Reprint: PSC. *Indexed:* A01, A22, AmHI, MLA-IB. *Aud.:* Ac, Sa.

The European Middle Ages is well represented in popular culture and mythology, and this is a key journal for the academic study of medieval history. Each issue contains roughly a half-dozen articles on topics that cover the entire span from the fall of Rome to the Renaissance. Topics include political and military history, religion, and social and intellectual history. No book reviews. For an academic audience.

2858. *The Journal of Modern History.* [ISSN: 0022-2801] 1929. q. USD 430. Ed(s): Jan E Goldstein, John W Boyer. University of Chicago Press, 1427 E 60th St, Chicago, IL 60637; subscriptions@press.uchicago.edu; http://www.journals.uchicago.edu. Illus., index, adv. Sample. Refereed. Vol. ends: Dec. Reprint: PSC. *Indexed:* A01, A22, AmHI, BAS, BRI, CBRI, IBSS, MLA-IB, P61. *Bk. rev.:* 40-50, 1-2 pages. *Aud.:* Ac, Sa.

This title covers the history of Europe since the Renaissance, from the varied perspectives of intellectual, cultural, and political history. Some articles concern the history of specific countries or events, and others look at broader topics such as Spanish politics. Recent articles range from "The Motherland Calls: Soft Repatriation of Soviet Citizens from Europe, 1945-1953," "The People's Prince: Popular Politics in Early Modern Venice," and "Global Rules: America, Britain, and a Discovered World." In addition to several articles, close to half of each issue is book reviews. Recommended for an academic audience.

2859. *Journal of World History: official journal of the World History Association.* [ISSN: 1045-6007] 1990. q. USD 160. Ed(s): Fabio Lopez Lazaro. University of Hawai'i Press, 2840 Kolowalu St, Honolulu, HI 96822; uhpjourn@hawaii.edu; http://www.uhpress.hawaii.edu. Illus., adv. Sample. Refereed. *Indexed:* A01, A22, AmHI, BRI, E01, IBSS, MLA-IB, P61, SSA. *Bk. rev.:* 10, 1-4 pages. *Aud.:* Ac, Sa.

Published by the World History Association, this journal covers an exceptionally wide range of geography and time - one recent issue ranges from 1415 to 1978. Many articles are comparative or transnational in focus, discussing a topic across many countries or cultures. Each issue also includes book reviews, both short and long. A good choice for any academic library that serves teaching and research on world history, and an excellent resource for understanding the range of topics addressed by world historians.

2860. ***Past & Present: a journal of historical studies.*** [ISSN: 0031-2746] 1952. q. EUR 441. Ed(s): Matthew Hilton, Alexandra Walsham. Oxford University Press, Great Clarendon St, Oxford, OX2 6DP, United Kingdom; onlinequeries.uk@oup.com; http://global.oup.com. Illus., index, adv. Sample. Refereed. Reprint: PSC. *Indexed:* A01, A22, AmHI, BAS, BRI, E01, IBSS, MLA-IB, P61, SSA. *Bk. rev.:* Occasional review essay. *Aud.:* Ac, Sa.

Past & Present was founded in 1952 by a group of Marxist historians, to focus on social and economic history, in a period when most academic journals primarily addressed political history. It covers historical, social, and cultural change in the widest possible range of times and places. Articles like "Diets, Hunger and Living Standards during the British Industrial Revolution" and "A Grammar of Conquest: The Spanish and Arabic Reorganization of Granada after 1492" indicate the breadth of topics. There are no book reviews, but the journal features an occasional review essay.

Interdisciplinary Interests

2861. ***Comparative Studies in Society and History: an international quarterly.*** [ISSN: 0010-4175] 1958. q. GBP 249 (print & online eds.)). Ed(s): Andrew Shryock. Cambridge University Press, University Printing House, Shaftesbury Rd, Cambridge, CB2 8BS, United Kingdom; journals@cambridge.org; https://www.cambridge.org/. Illus., index, adv. Refereed. Vol. ends: Nov. Microform: PQC. Reprint: PSC. *Indexed:* A01, A22, A47, AmHI, BAS, BRI, C45, E01, IBSS, MLA-IB, P61, SSA. *Bk. rev.:* 0-5, 1 page. *Aud.:* Ac, Sa.

International in scope, *CSSH* is a forum for "interpretation concerning problems of recurrent patterning and change in human societies through time and the contemporary world." Articles are paired in themes like science and religion in Iran and colonial commodities. Most articles incorporate a theoretical or social science perspective, drawing on fields like anthropology, history, political science, and sociology. The result is a stimulating mix of approaches, making this journal appropriate for academic history collections and also for libraries that focus on the social sciences. Each issue also includes a few in-depth book reviews.

2862. ***Environmental History.*** Formed by the merger of (1990-1996): *Environmental History Review;* Which was formerly (until 1990): *Environmental Review;* Which incorporated (1974-198?): *Environmental History Newsletter;* (1990-1996): *Forest and Conservation History;* Which was formerly (until 1990): *Journal of Forest History;* (until 1974): *Forest History.* [ISSN: 1084-5453] 1996. q. EUR 295. Ed(s): Lisa M Brady. Oxford University Press, 2001 Evans Rd, Cary, NC 27513; https://academic.oup.com/journals. Illus., index, adv. Sample. Refereed. Vol. ends: Oct. Microform: PQC. Reprint: PSC. *Indexed:* A22, Agr, C45, GardL, MLA-IB. *Bk. rev.:* Number and length vary. *Aud.:* Ac.

Published jointly by the Forest History Society and the American Society for Environmental History, this is the premier journal in this relatively new field. The focus is on "international articles that portray human interactions with the natural world over time." Recent issues have included articles on whale meat in Japanese culture and the effects of the BP oil spill on Louisiana's shrimping industry. Some issues include a "Gallery" section, with essays on an image. Each issue also includes an extensive section of book reviews, and some issues also include a very valuable listing of "new scholarship" - regarding books, articles, dissertations, and archival sources.

Gender and History. See Gender Studies section.

2863. ***History and Theory: studies in the philosophy of history.*** [ISSN: 0018-2656] 1960. q. GBP 363. Ed(s): Ethan Kleinberg, Julie Perkins. Wiley-Blackwell Publishing, Inc., 111 River St, Hoboken, NJ 07030; http://onlinelibrary.wiley.com. Index, adv. Sample. Refereed. Vol. ends: Dec. Microform: PQC. Reprint: PSC. *Indexed:* A01, A22, AmHI, BAS, BRI, CBRI, E01, IBSS, MLA-IB, P61. *Bk. rev.:* Number varies; essay length. *Aud.:* Ac, Sa.

This journal features articles on theory and philosophy of history, historiography, methodology, time and culture, and related topics. In-depth, article-length review essays go beyond the usual scope of a book review; some issues include a "book forum," which has multiple articles about the same book. Brief book reviews are also included, along with abstracts of articles that originally appeared in Chinese journals. There is an annual themed issue, on a topic such as "Theorizing Histories of Violence." This title is for specialists, not the general reader, but the articles are of very high quality.

Isis. See Science and Technology/History and Philosophy of Science section.

Journal of Interdisciplinary History. See Interdisciplinary Studies section.

2864. ***Journal of Social History.*** [ISSN: 0022-4529] 1967. q. Ed(s): Mathew B Karush. Oxford University Press, 2001 Evans Rd, Cary, NC 27513; custserv.us@oup.com; https://academic.oup.com/journals. Illus., adv. Refereed. Vol. ends: Summer. Microform: MIM; PQC. Reprint: PSC. *Indexed:* A01, A22, AmHI, BAS, BRI, CBRI, E01, IBSS, P61, SSA. *Bk. rev.:* 25-30, lengthy. *Aud.:* Ac, Sa.

JSH covers social history worldwide, including issues of gender, class, and race, but also topics like migration, recreation, and government social policy. The emphasis is on the eighteenth, nineteenth, and twentieth centuries, but occasionally articles on the early modern period are published. In most issues, articles are grouped by topic, and each issue also contains in-depth book reviews. There are also special issues, and an essay competition for graduate students. For an interdisciplinary academic audience, this is an influential journal in this subfield.

2865. ***Journal of the History of Sexuality.*** [ISSN: 1043-4070] 1990. 3x/yr. USD 390. Ed(s): Annette Timm. University of Texas Press, Journals Division, PO Box 7819, Austin, TX 78713; journals@utpress.utexas.edu; https://utpress.utexas.edu. Illus., adv. Refereed. Vol. ends: Nov. *Indexed:* A01, A22, AmHI, BRI, C42, E01, GW, IBSS, MLA-IB. *Bk. rev.:* 11-16, 2-3 pages. *Aud.:* Ac, Sa.

This journal seeks to illuminate sexuality "in all its expressions, recognizing differences of class, culture, gender, race, and sexual preference" within a scope transcending "temporal and geographic boundaries." Articles include studies on "The Sin of Sodom in Late Antiquity" and "The Callous Appetites of Debauched Readers: Edmund Curll and The Potent Ally." The entire content reflects first-rate scholarship. Occasionally, there is a critical commentary or debate relevant to a previous article. The book reviews, book lists, and review essays provide a comprehensive bibliographic source.

2866. ***Journal of Urban History.*** [ISSN: 0096-1442] 1974. bi-m. USD 1806 (print & online eds.)). Ed(s): David R Goldfield. Sage Publications, Inc., 2455 Teller Rd, Thousand Oaks, CA 91320; info@sagepub.com; http://www.sagepub.com. Illus., index, adv. Refereed. Vol. ends: Sep. Reprint: PSC. *Indexed:* A01, A22, AmHI, BAS, BRI, CBRI, E01, IBSS, P61, SSA. *Bk. rev.:* 3-4, essay length. *Aud.:* Ac.

This journal is focused on "the history of cities and urban societies throughout the world." The emphasis is primarily on modern history, post-1800, but the coverage is international. There are book reviews and excellent longer review essays on "new interpretations and developments in urban history." In a largely urbanized America, this journal is appropriate for most academic libraries.

Journal of Women's History. See Gender Studies section.

2867. *Radical History Review.* Former titles (until 1975): *M A R H O Newsletter;* (until 1974): *Mid-Atlantic Radical Historians' Organization. Newsletter;* (until 19??): *Mid-Atlantic Radical Historians' Newsletter.* [ISSN: 0163-6545] 1973. 3x/yr. USD 300. Ed(s): Thomas Harbison. Duke University Press, 905 W Main St, Durham, NC 27701; orders@dukeupress.edu; https://www.dukeupress.edu. Illus., adv. Refereed. Reprint: PSC. *Indexed:* A01, A22, AmHI, BAS, BRI, E01, IBSS, MLA-IB, P61, SSA. *Bk. rev.:* Number and length vary. *Aud.:* Ac.

This journal is managed by an "editorial collective" and is intentionally provocative. Articles address issues of gender, race, sexuality, imperialism, and class, in both Western and non-Western history. Each issue has a theme, like "Premodern History" or "Political Histories of Technoscience." The journal is divided into subsections such as "Interventions" or "Reflections," and a section called "Curated Spaces" often addresses art as a form of recreating history. There are also interviews, book and media reviews, and essays on teaching. The style is sometimes heavy on jargon, but the unusual perspective, links to current events, and the diversity of topics make this title stimulating reading. Appropriate for academic libraries.

General History

2868. *The American Historical Review.* Supersedes in part (in 1995): *Recently Published Articles.* [ISSN: 0002-8762] 1895. 5x/yr. EUR 364. Oxford University Press, 2001 Evans Rd, Cary, NC 27513; orders.us@oup.com; https://academic.oup.com/journals. Illus., index, adv. Sample. Refereed. Vol. ends: Dec. Reprint: PSC. *Indexed:* A01, A22, AmHI, BAS, BRI, CBRI, Chicano, EconLit, F01, IBSS, MASUSE, MLA-IB. *Bk. rev.:* 250-275, 450 words. *Aud.:* Ac, Sa.

AHR is the official publication of the American Historical Association. It is the most prestigious academic history journal in the United States, and covers every field of historical study worldwide. Occasional features bring together a group of articles on related topics with commentary, most recently, "Ending Civil Wars." There is also an annual "conversation" on a topic such as exploring historical change, presenting the views of several historians together. About half of each issue is an exceptional section of book reviews, arranged by subfield, which is very valuable for anyone trying to keep current in this field. Essential for any academic library.

The Economic History Review. See Economics section.

2869. *The Historian (East Lansing): a journal of history.* [ISSN: 0018-2370] 1938. q. GBP 239. Wiley-Blackwell Publishing, Inc., 111 River St, Hoboken, NJ 07030; http://onlinelibrary.wiley.com. Illus., adv. Sample. Refereed. Vol. ends: Aug. Reprint: PSC. *Indexed:* A01, A22, AmHI, BAS, BRI, CBRI, E01, MLA-IB. *Bk. rev.:* 40-60, 400-500 words. *Aud.:* Ga, Ac.

The Historian has four substantive articles in each issue, on a very wide range of topics. The choice of topics is a good match for undergraduate interests, and this journal is recommended for a college audience. Approximately half the articles are about American history. There is also an especially extensive section of book reviews, arranged geographically. The reviews are briefer than in some academic journals, but they provide a good survey of current publishing in the field.

2870. *Historical Research.* Formerly (until 1987): *University of London. Institute of Historical Research. Bulletin.* [ISSN: 0950-3471] 1923. q. GBP 324. Ed(s): Miles Taylor. Wiley-Blackwell Publishing Ltd., The Atrium, Southern Gate, Chichester, PO19 8QG, United Kingdom; cs-journals@wiley.com; http://onlinelibrary.wiley.com/. Illus., adv. Sample. Refereed. Vol. ends: Nov. Microform: IDC. Reprint: PSC. *Indexed:* A01, A22, AmHI, E01, MLA-IB. *Aud.:* Ac, Sa.

Historical Research has been published by the prestigious British Institute for Historical Research since 1923. It covers a broad time span, from medieval to twentieth-century history. Articles reflect a variety of approaches, including of social, political, urban, intellectual, and cultural history. While most articles are on British history, there are some on Europe and other areas of the world, like "Young China in Europe: The Lives and Politics of the May Fourth Youth in France." The online version also offers "virtual special issues" of articles on a particular topic, or themes that have previously been published in the journal. No book reviews.

The History Teacher. See Education/Specific Subjects and Teaching Methods—Social Studies (including History and Economics) section.

2871. *History (Washington): reviews of new books.* [ISSN: 0361-2759] 1972. q. GBP 311 (print & online eds.)). Ed(s): Miriam Aronin, Robin Conner. Routledge, 530 Walnut St, Ste 850, Philadelphia, PA 19106; enquiries@tandfonline.com; http://www.tandfonline.com. Illus., index, adv. Refereed. Reprint: PSC. *Indexed:* A01, A22, BRI, CBRI, Chicano, E01, MASUSE. *Bk. rev.:* Number varies; 450 words. *Aud.:* Hs, Ga, Ac.

This journal is entirely devoted to book reviews, about 35 per issue, and it is a key resource for current awareness and collection development in the field of history. It covers world history in all periods. Most issues also feature essay reviews of several related books, on a theme like the Constitution or environmental history.

The Public Historian. See Archives and Manuscripts/General section.

■ HOME

See also Do-It-Yourself; and Interior Design and Decoration sections.

Sarah Roberts, Access Services Specialist, Physics Research Library, Harvard University, Cambridge, MA 02138

Introduction

Magazines within this section focus on the home as both a physical structure and abstract concept, and the diverse range of topics associated with home life. These topics include, but are not limited to, architecture, arts and crafts, collecting, cooking, domestic life, entertaining, food, gardening, health and wellness, interior decorating and design, relationships, and renovation.

Several magazines contain articles that cover a variety of home-centric topics, such as *Family Circle* and *Good Housekeeping,* which appeal to broad reader audiences, while others primarily focus on more specific topics, styles, or aspects of the home and home life, such as *Cottages and Bungalows, Electronic House: Fast Track to the Connected Lifestyle,* and *Victorian Homes. Home Cultures* offers a scholarly perspective and is a peer-reviewed journal that is international in scope; it explores connections between such disciplines as architecture, gender and cultural studies, social history, art history, and geography, all within a home-cultures framework. All magazines listed in this section, with the exception of the *Home Cultures* journal, have companion web sites that offer additional or related home-oriented articles, photos, videos, blogs, social media links, and DIY guides.

Home Cultures does provide article abstracts and table-of-contents information online, but an electronic subscription is required to obtain electronic full-text articles.

This journal and each magazine provide a dynamic array of material about a wide range of home-life advice, needs, interests, ideas, and skills; and as people continue to build, care for, and have pride in their homes, gardens, and domestic lives, there will continue to be a market for resources that provide information on everything from growing plants to undertaking budget-friendly home renovations, and from cooking healthy meals to choosing paint schemes.

The goal in compiling this list has been to provide a variety of useful resources that cover as many home-themed topics as possible.

Basic Periodicals

Ga: *Better Homes and Gardens, House Beautiful, Martha Stewart Living, Real Simple.*

Basic Abstracts and Indexes

Readers' Guide to Periodical Literature.

2872. *Backwoods Home Magazine: practical ideas for self reliant living.* [ISSN: 1050-9712] 1989. bi-m. USD 26.95; USD 6.95 per issue. Ed(s): Jessie Denning, Dave Duffy. Backwoods Home Magazine, PO Box 712, Gold Beach, OR 97444; customer-service@backwoodshome.com; http://www.backwoodshome.com. Illus., adv. Sample. Vol. ends: Dec. *Indexed:* BRI. *Bk. rev.:* 1, 200 words. *Aud.:* Ga.

Backwoods Home Magazine is an excellent resource for readers interested in a DIY, self-reliant, back-to-the-land lifestyle. This magazine's main focus is providing information on how to live greenly, self-sufficiently, and resourcefully. Examples of covered topics include emergency preparedness, farm and garden projects, economics for those living outside traditional market structures, homeschooling, alternative energy resources, small-town America culture, self-defense, hunting, and food canning and storage advice. Examples of recent articles include "Defending Against Terroristic Mass Murder," "The Adventures of a First Time Homesteader," and "How to Grow Edible Alliums." Though most articles lack an overtly political focus, editorials often highlight relevant current issues in domestic politics while reinforcing *Backwoods Home*'s themes of personal freedom and self-reliance. *Backwoods Home Magazine* is now also available as an e-subscription for the Kindle, and the magazine's companion web site contains links to current and back issues where some articles can be read for free. The web site also contains an article and author index, links to "free stuff," recipes, book links, specials, related blogs, and an online forum. This title can also be found on Facebook, YouTube, and Twitter. This title would be appropriate for general readers in public libraries. URL: www.backwoodshome.com

2873. *Better Homes and Gardens.* Formerly (until 1924): *Fruit, Garden and Home.* [ISSN: 0006-0151] 1922. m. USD 2.51 per issue. Ed(s): Stephen Orr. Meredith National Media Group, 1716 Locust St, Des Moines, IA 50309; http://www.meredith.com. Illus. Vol. ends: No. 12. *Indexed:* A22, BRI, C37, GardL. *Aud.:* Ga.

Better Homes and Gardens is a long-established, home-life-oriented magazine whose main function is to provide inspiration, resources, tips, and instructions about home life to a general-reader audience. Featuring articles and sections on recipes, decorating, home improvement, gardening, entertaining, beauty, holidays, pets, and health, *Better Home and Gardens* strives to motivate and inspire readers to create and maintain their homes and gardens in manageable, practical, and economical ways. The occasional seasonally themed issue may feature appropriate garden-planting guides, decorating tips, and meal ideas. Sample articles include such topics as "How to Freeze Fresh Green Beans," "7 Unexpected Ways to use String Lights," "Our Best Blueberry Desserts," and "14 Summer DIY Projects That Will Brighten Your Home." A companion web site can be found at www.bhg.com, and includes video project instructions, cooking, decorating, holiday, and craft ideas for kids, contests, giveaways, social media links, blogs, and *BHG* shopping links with coupons and savings on purchases made through the web site. *Better Homes and Gardens* is a well-known, trusted, and popular magazine. Appropriate for a general-reader audience in public libraries.

2874. *Cottages & Bungalows.* [ISSN: 1941-4056] 2007. q. USD 14.95; USD 224 combined subscription (print & online eds.)). Engaged Media Inc., 17890 Sky Park Circle, Ste. 250, Irvine, CA 92614; http:// engagedmediamags.com/. Illus., adv. *Aud.:* Ga.

Spotlighting small living areas, *Cottages & Bungalows* is an innovative resource that provides creative ideas and information about vintage materials and vintage-inspired design themes that can be used to create or enhance dynamic, small-space living areas. This magazine is filled with glossy photo spreads, real-life, small-space living and redesign testimonials, remodeling guides, do-it-yourself tutorials, and crafting ideas, and provides valuable information for readers who wish to make their small living areas more dynamic and functional. Articles cover such topics as finding new uses for vintage furniture and fabrics, small home and room makeovers, vintage-inspired paint color schemes, simple weekend projects, seasonal design ideas, arts and crafts, and caring for classic small homes and antique furniture, all with a focus on vintage-inspired simplicity and workmanship. There is an overall theme of doing more with less. There are also excellent product reviews and special features about cottage and bungalow communities, historically sensitive homes, and cottage and bungalow destinations. In addition to the print magazine, there is a companion web site that offers useful information on topics such as interior decorating, entertaining, and renovating old and/or small living spaces, DIY guides, crafts, blogs, and an online forum. There are links to the magazine's Facebook and Pinterest accounts. This web site content is accompanied by photos and how-to videos, and reflects the print magazine's simplistic, DIY approach to making one's small living space useful, functional, and stylish. This magazine would appeal to arts and crafts enthusiasts, small-space dwellers and homeowners, art students, and anyone interested in "retro" and vintage designs and homes. Appropriate for any public library. URL: http:// cottagesandbungalowsmag.com

2875. *Country Living (New York).* Formerly (until 198?): *Good Housekeeping's Country Living.* [ISSN: 0732-2569] 1978. 10x/yr. USD 10; USD 4.99 newsstand/cover. Hearst Magazines, 300 W 57th St, 28th Fl, New York, NY 10019; HearstMagazines@hearst.com; http:// www.hearst.com. Illus., adv. Circ: 1385566 Paid. Vol. ends: Dec. *Indexed:* BRI, C37, GardL, MASUSE. *Aud.:* Ga.

Country Living is a lifestyle magazine that features articles on home decorating, gardening and landscaping, collecting and collectibles, travel, entertaining, crafting, leisure, real estate, and simple healthy recipes, all featured with an overall Americana and country-lifestyle perspective. This magazine is filled with inspirational glossy photographs showcasing country-style decorating ideas, DIY how-tos, budget-friendly home-makeover ideas, and easy-to-follow crafting, gardening, and cooking guides. Sample articles include "Before and After: 9 Shocking Home Exteriors," "20 of the Best Things to Collect," and "How to Turn a Vintage Scarf into a Necklace." *Country Living* is available in a digital format; and there is a robust companion web site, which includes dozens of home-decorating, DIY, food, entertaining, and outdoor-living ideas, in additional to supplemental how-to videos for projects featured in the magazine. There are also promotions, a newsletter, a "free stuff" section, and a marketplace that offers deals and coupons available via the web site. *Country Living* also hosts annual "*Country Living* Fairs" throughout the United States, which are promoted through the magazine and web site. This magazine is appropriate for any public-library audience. URL: www.countryliving.com

2876. *Dwell.* [ISSN: 1530-5309] 2000. 10x/yr. USD 19.95 domestic; USD 34.95 Canada; USD 49.95 elsewhere. Dwell Media, LLC, 901 Battery St, Ste 401, San Francisco, CA 94111; subhelp@dwell.com; http:// www.dwell.com. Illus., adv. *Aud.:* Ga.

Dwell is a modernist architectural and interior-design magazine that features home remodels from around the globe, new designer showcases, "endless ideas for modern living," and articles covering a wide variety of modernist-themed home-centric topics. A sleek and minimalist design aesthetic guides home goods and furniture reviews, with detailed pro-and-con reviews of products located in the magazine's "Product Reviews" section. Other features may include essays that cover such topics as "The Latest in Home Automation, From Carmel to Finland," a "Home Tours" segment, how-to guides for buying modern furniture, and articles featuring "after" photographs of home-renovation projects undertaken by renowned or upcoming architects or designers. Prefabricated homes are a common feature of this magazine, and an annual issue is devoted to innovative design ideas for ready-made homes. Reports from international design shows and events are also featured, including interviews with up-and-coming designers and reviews of show collections and newly released products. The magazine's web site includes slide shows; online interviews; links to pages that feature professional designers and their collections and contact information; and a wide variety of ideas for implementing all aspects of modern design. This magazine is also available in digital formats. *Dwell* is appropriate for public libraries and academic libraries with a design or architecture focus. URL: www.dwell.com/magazine

2877. *Early American Life: traditions, period style, antiques, architecture, history.* Former titles (until 2001): *Early American Homes;* (until 1996): *Early American Life.* [ISSN: 1534-2042] 1970. bi-m. plus special issue. USD 24.36 domestic; USD 36 Canada; USD 6.99 per issue. Firelands Media Group, LLC, PO Box 221228, Shaker Heights, OH 44122; letters@firelandsmedia.com; http://www.firelandsmedia.com. Illus., adv. *Indexed:* A01, A22, AmHI, BRI, MASUSE, MLA-IB. *Aud.:* Ga.

Early American Life is a unique resource that covers such topics as Colonial life, Colonial and early-American memorabilia, historical architecture, antiques, history, and restored homes. Historians and hobbyists will enjoy the magazine's multi-page features on period antiques and artwork, restoration projects, and Colonial-era history and folklore, all accompanied by glossy photographs. Articles are written in an accessible and easy-to-read format, and recent issues cover such topics as "American Painted Weathervanes," "A Wooden Plane Primer," "Make Your Own Colonial Cheese," and "Mapping the Way to Liberty." A companion web site contains subscription information, tables of contents from recent issues, listings of related events and calendars arranged by state, interactive comment tools, and an online version of the "Reader's Exchange," a discontinued feature from the print magazine. *Early American Life* is appropriate for public and some academic libraries. URL: www.ealonline.com

2878. *Electronic House.* [ISSN: 0886-6643] 1986. 8x/yr. E H Publishing, Inc., 111 Speen St, Ste 200, PO Box 989, Framingham, MA 01701; info@ehpub.com; http://www.ehpub.com. Illus., adv. Sample. *Aud.:* Ga, Sa.

Focused on technology within the home, *Electronic House* provides information on home networking, computing, entertainment, lighting, security, energy management, accessories and gadgets, and installation projects. These topics are broad in scope, and feature articles may highlight topics as varied as automated home furnishings, reviews of specific equipment, or how to install modern equipment in historical homes. There is also a focus on implementing new technologies within the home, with product reviews and guides a fundamental aspect of the publication. Many high-end electronic systems are reviewed; and though there are articles aimed at the budget-conscious, the majority of electronic homes and rooms profiled are luxury environments within sports or entertainment venues. The accompanying web site features blogs, links to social media, free downloadable guides, a "Home of the Week" feature, installer listings, editorials, slide shows, product reviews and news, and lots of helpful articles on topics such as energy management, audio, lighting, and gadgets necessary to supporting a cutting-edge, efficient, and exciting new electronic-home environment. Appropriate for public libraries. URL: www.electronichouse.com

Elle Decor. See Interior Design and Decoration section.

2879. *Family Circle.* Former titles (until 1963): *Everywoman's Family Circle;* (until 1958): *The Family Circle;* Which incorporated (in 1958): *Everywoman's.* [ISSN: 0014-7206] 1932. m. USD 5.01 per issue; USD 9.98. Ed(s): Ron Kelly. Meredith National Media Group, 1716 Locust St, Des Moines, IA 50309; http://www.meredith.com. Illus., adv. Sample. Vol. ends: Dec. *Indexed:* A22, BRI. *Aud.:* Ga.

Family Circle is a well-known, popular magazine that features articles, tips, and general information on all things home and family-related. Each issue contains sections on healthy recipes, healthy living, fashion, shopping and ways to save, family matters, and entertaining. Accompanied by a robust suite of online features on its companion web site, *Family Circle* is a great source of tips and tools for busy families. Containing concise articles on home, health, and family fun, this magazine also prominently features advertising for various personal and home products, and it has offers and special deals for magazine readers and monthly "web exclusive" deals on different products on its web site. *Family Circle* also provides access to current and past magazine articles on the web site, in addition to links to social media, videos, and blogs. The highlight of the web site is a "Momster" blog that features advice to/from moms, with a helpful comments-from-readers component. *Family Circle* is appropriate for general audiences in any public library. URL: www.familycircle.com

2880. *Good Housekeeping.* Former titles (until 1919): *Good Housekeeping Magazine;* (until 1909): *Good Housekeeping.* [ISSN: 0017-209X] 1885. m. USD 8; USD 3.99 newsstand/cover. Hearst Magazines, 300 W 57th St, 28th Fl, New York, NY 10019; HearstMagazines@hearst.com; http://www.hearstcorp.com/magazines/. Illus., adv. Vol. ends: Jun/Dec. Microform: NBI; PQC. *Indexed:* A01, A22, BRI, C37, C42, MASUSE, MLA-IB. *Aud.:* Hs, Ga, Ac.

Good Housekeeping magazine has been in existence for over 125 years, and is a trustworthy and renowned source of advice, tips, and recommendations on all topics related to the home and family. Features in the magazine include healthy living and beauty advice, seasonal home and garden projects, home organizing, diet and health information, family and relationship features and advice, celebrity interviews, renovation projects, and self-improvement ideas, among many other related topics. The Good Housekeeping Institute and the Good Housekeeping Seal also provide product evaluations and quality assurance on many household items, and these products are prominently featured throughout the magazine's glossy pages. The print magazine is supported by an extensive online presence on its web site, where readers can learn more about product news and reviews, read articles and features, sign up for and access the *GH* newsletter, find links to social media, access promotions, and enter to win drawings. Appropriate for general audiences in any public library. URL: www.goodhousekeeping.com

2881. *Home Cultures: the journal of architecture, design and domestic space.* [ISSN: 1740-6315] 2004. 3x/yr. GBP 303 (print & online eds.)). Routledge, 4 Park Sq, Milton Park, Abingdon, OX14 4RN, United Kingdom; subscriptions@tandf.co.uk; http://www.tandfonline.com. Adv. Sample. Refereed. Reprint: PSC. *Indexed:* A01, A47, BRI, IBSS, MLA-IB, P61. *Bk. rev.:* Number and length vary. *Aud.:* Ac.

Home Cultures is "an interdisciplinary, peer-reviewed journal dedicated to the critical understanding of the domestic sphere, its artifacts, spaces and relations, across time frames and cultures." International in scope, this journal examines the connections between "home" as a physical space and human culture across time, and brings together such disciplines as history, architecture, anthropology, religious studies, gender and cultural studies, social history, literary studies, art history, and geography, in order to highlight the concept of "home" as a "highly fluid and contested site of human existence that reflects and reifies identities and values." Recent articles have included such titles as "Identity, Consumption and the Home" and "Redefining Kitsch: The Politics of Design." An introductory essay, written by the editors, contextualizes the articles in each issue. Academic libraries that support a diverse social science curriculum would be the most appropriate audience for *Home Cultures*.

2882. *House Beautiful.* Incorporates (in 1902): *Domestic Science Monthly;* (in Jan.1908): *Indoors and Out;* (in 1910): *Modern Homes;* (in Mar.1912): *American Suburbs;* (in Jan.1934): *Home and Field.* [ISSN: 0018-6422] 1896. 10x/yr. USD 10; USD 4.99 newsstand/cover. Ed(s): Newell Turner. Hearst Magazines, 300 W 57th St, 28th Fl, New York, NY 10019; HearstMagazines@hearst.com; http://www.hearstcorp.com/magazines/. Illus., adv. Circ: 812152 Paid. Vol. ends: No. 12. Microform: NBI; PQC. *Indexed:* A22, BRI, C37, GardL, MASUSE. *Aud.:* Ga.

House Beautiful focuses on luxury domestic style with an emphasis on design, home goods, and making aesthetically-pleasing decorating choices, from paint colors to cleaning tips. Interviews with decorators and stylists walk readers though glamorous interior design projects, reviewing in great detail the decoration and furniture in the photographs. "Tablescapes," wallpaper samples, and seasonal color palettes emphasize the design aesthetic of the magazine, while also serving as connections to the entertaining and cooking features in each issue. A popular recurring series in the magazine has been the "Makeover" section, where a complete small house is restyled both indoors and outdoors, with a new space featured each month. A regular "Kitchen of the Month" feature also highlights how to incorporate stylish decor while increasing functionality. The *House Beautiful* web site contains an extensive collection of step-by-step instructions for home decorating and small renovation projects, as well as photo galleries, gift guides, social media links, a marketplace section, giveaways, and organizing tips. Appropriate for general audiences in public libraries. URL: www.housebeautiful.com

2883. *Ladies' Home Journal.* Formerly (until 1889): *Ladies Home Journal and Practical Housekeeper.* [ISSN: 0023-7124] 1883. 3x/yr. Ed(s): Diane Salvator, Marissa Golde. Meredith National Media Group, PO Box 37792, Boone, IA 50037; http://www.meredith.com. Illus. Vol. ends: Dec. *Indexed:* A22, BRI, C37, MASUSE, MLA-IB. *Bk. rev.:* Number and length vary. *Aud.:* Hs, Ga, Ac.

Marketed toward the working woman whose many roles may include mother, daughter, girlfriend, and wife, the newly redesigned *Ladies' Home Journal* maintains a focus on women's lives and interests. Beauty, fashion, health, food, pets, relationships, book reviews, and real-life stories are highlighted in this magazine, with self-improvement/lifestyle topics and home decorating serving as main themes. Celebrity profiles include stories of personal transformations, charitable endeavors, and life lessons. Practical fashion, beauty, and marriage advice are also featured. The accompanying web site contains dozens of freely available stories running on similar themes, but also includes hairstyle tutorials, gift and charity ideas, a personal story section, giveaways, social media links, and a daily beauty blog. Appropriate for a public library audience. URL: www.divinecaroline.com/ladies-home-journal

2884. *Martha Stewart Living.* [ISSN: 1057-5251] 1990. m. USD 19.99. Ed(s): Pilar Guzman. Martha Stewart Living Omnimedia LLC, 601 W 26th St 10th Fl, New York, NY 10001; http://www.marthastewart.com. Illus., adv. Vol. ends: No. 12. *Indexed:* BRI, GardL. *Bk. rev.:* Number and length vary. *Aud.:* Ga.

Martha Stewart Living is a detailed and thorough magazine that overflows with articles on all topics involved with maintaining a stylish, appealing, and organized household. Martha Stewart is synonymous with high-quality, reliable, authoritative advice and instruction on a wide variety of home-centric topics, and *Martha Stewart Living* combines this homemaking knowledge and advice into a valuable resource that covers such topics as gardening, home decorating, cooking, arts and crafts, entertaining, collecting, renovating, health and wellness, and interior design, all with a focus on quality, encouragement, instruction, and a do-it-yourself-better attitude. There are also additional features on weddings, pets, and seasonal recipes and entertaining. The articles are in-depth, with accompanying glossy photo spreads, and many ideas and tips function as do-it-yourself guides. Examples of article topics include garden planting and maintenance tips, party themes and decoration ideas, architectural design, living-space organization, interior and exterior paint-color schemes, etiquette, and seasonal craft projects. The companion web site offers an array of how-to instructional guides, photos, videos, design ideas, landscape guides, entertaining ideas, blogs and blog recommendations, prize giveaways, a digital magazine and mobile apps page, links to social media, book reviews, and links to Martha Stewart television programming and additional Martha Stewart subject-specific magazines. This magazine could be of interest to a wide demographic, from new homeowners to expert hostesses, and would be appropriate for any public library. URL: www.marthastewart.com

2885. *Real Simple.* [ISSN: 1528-1701] 2000. m. USD 2 domestic. Ed(s): Brenda Dargan Levy. Time Inc., 225 Liberty St, New York, NY 10281; information@timeinc.com; http://www.timeinc.com. Illus. Circ: 1975000. *Indexed:* BRI, C37. *Aud.:* Ga.

Real Simple's motto, "Life Made Easier," is demonstrated throughout the magazine's feature articles on time-saving tips for work-life balance and daily routines, and simple home, beauty, decorative, and fashion ideas and "trends worth trying." Cost-conscious product reviews and recommendations, as well as before-and-after room makeovers, maintain the magazine's focus on domestic space design and improvement, while inspirational stories and quotes provide balance and reflection for busy readers drawn to the magazine's articles on beauty and fashion, home organizing, food and recipes, and entertaining. The companion web site includes videos, blogs, social media links, a meal planner tool, and checklists, all of which function to streamline readers' busy lives, in keeping with the magazine's overall goal of making readers' lives more simplified. Readers are encouraged to respond online with product reviews, ideas for decorating, etiquette, and life issue advice. Recommended for public libraries. URL: www.realsimple.com

This Old House. See Do-It-Yourself/Makers section.

2886. *Traditional Home.* [ISSN: 0883-4660] 198?. bi-m. USD 24. Meredith National Media Group, 805 Third Ave, New York, NY 10022; http:// www.meredith.com. Illus. Vol. ends: No. 6. *Aud.:* Ga.

Traditional Home focuses on luxury home goods and interior design, and includes beautifully photographed features on society events, philanthropists, and grand elegantly and lavishly decorated homes. Information on collectibles, updates on design trends, food and wine-pairing guides, and eco-friendly tips for pets and children help to elevate this magazine to one that celebrates a traditional luxury lifestyle. A companion web site features links to different home-design themes, such as "Lakeside Home in Quiet Colors," "Nantucket Home with a Quiet Palette," and "Design Ideas for White Kitchens," in addition to access to "Great Kitchens," a free digital magazine. There is also a newsletter and links to blogs and social media. *Traditional Home* would be appropriate for public libraries whose patrons are interested in interior decorating and design, and luxury lifestyles. URL: www.traditionalhome.com

2887. *Victorian Homes.* [ISSN: 0744-415X] 1982. q. USD 14.95; USD 24 combined subscription (print & online eds.); USD 7.99 per issue). Engaged Media Inc., 17890 Sky Park Circle, Ste. 250, Irvine, CA 92614; http://engagedmediamags.com/. Illus., adv. Vol. ends: No. 6. *Bk. rev.:* Number and length vary. *Aud.:* Ga, Sa.

Victorian Homes is the premier magazine for owners and fans of houses and furnishings from the Victorian period, and is "your go-to guide to the Victorian lifestyle." *Victorian Homes* includes articles on restoration, renovation, vintage-inspired decorating and style, and history. There is also a recurring do-it-yourself theme to most articles, with tips on collecting and how to create your own Victorian-themed party, holiday furnishings, or gifts, in addition to "Great insider tours to beautifully restored historic homes, house museums[,] and bed-and-breakfast inns." Recent articles include "The Victorian Art of Flowers" and "4 Victorian Curb Appeal Basics." The accompanying web site features subscription information and letters from the editor, in addition to social media links and links to articles related to those in the print edition. This niche publication is also available electronically and is suitable for public libraries whose patrons are interested in this topic, or in areas where Victorian architecture is prevalent. URL: www.victorianhomesmag.com

2888. *Woman's Day.* [ISSN: 0043-7336] 1937. m. USD 7.99; USD 2.79 newsstand/cover. Hearst Magazines, 300 W 57th St, 28th Fl, New York, NY 10019; HearstMagazines@hearst.com; http://www.hearst.com. Illus., adv. Vol. ends: Dec. *Indexed:* A01, A22, BRI, C37, MASUSE. *Aud.:* Ga.

With over 75 years in the domestic magazine industry, *Woman's Day*'s motto is to "Live Well Everyday." In keeping with this motto, this popular magazine provides lifestyle, food, health, relationship, and beauty advice to a broad audience. Including a book-of-the-month feature, celebrity-lifestyle interviews, room makeovers, and fun party tips, along with product evaluations and affordable everyday-meal recipes, *Woman's Day* is a staple among supermarket glossy magazines. Feature articles frequently highlight real-life stories related to weight loss, relationships, and family, along with fashion advice, simple crafts projects, and general lifestyle tips. A robust web site supports the print edition with a blog, links to social media, coupons and giveaways, games, and articles and slide shows relevant to the print edition. Digital subscriptions are also available. *Woman's Day* is most suitable for a public library audience. URL: www.womansday.com

■ HOSPITALITY/RESTAURANT

Amy J. Watson, Information Specialist, PPG Industries Inc., GBDC Library, 400 Guys Run Road, Cheswick, PA 15024; amywatson@ppg.com

Introduction

As was the case during preparation of the previous edition of this section, this industry continues to struggle with the global economic downturn, which has impacted the titles available in the field. Several historically key titles either have migrated to online-only versions, or have ceased publication entirely. It is optimistically forecast that the performance of this sector will accelerate. It is a hope that as the economy changes in coming years, new publications will come forth to replace those that have folded, potentially more with international focuses.

The magazines and journals in this section cover both the hotel and restaurant industries with a variety of focuses and depths. There are several refereed journals that offer research and analysis from a high-quality, in-depth perspective. Additionally, the diverse assortment of trade publications keeps those in the industry abreast of cutting-edge information and breaking news. A wide array of information needs are covered, with titles that address such topics as management, human resources, hospitality trends, design and decor, and security issues. The majority of titles listed have accompanying web sites that offer useful additional information and interactive tools.

Basic Periodicals

Ac: *Cornell Hospitality Quarterly, International Journal of Hospitality and Tourism Administration;* Sa: *Restaurant Hospitality, Restaurant Startup & Growth, Restaurant Business.*

Basic Abstracts and Indexes

Hospitality and Tourism Index; Leisure, Recreation and Tourism Abstracts.

2889. ***Catering Magazine: the magazine for catering professionals.*** [ISSN: 1098-089X] bi-m. USD 65 domestic; USD 125 elsewhere. Ed(s): Sara Perez Webber. G P Publishing, 60 E Rio Salado Parkway, Ste 900, Tempe, AZ 85281. Illus., adv. Circ: 20000 Paid and free. *Indexed:* H&TI. *Aud.:* Sa.

This title continues to be a must-have trade journal for catering and special events professionals. Issues balance informative content that is useful to businesses with impressive photography and coverage of cutting-edge trends. Most issues are themed and provide examples of stellar catered special events. At first glance, heavy advertising is present, but even this is lush and interesting. Well recommended.

2890. ***Chef: the magazine for foodservice professional.*** Former titles (until 1994): *Chef Institutional;* (until 1971): *Chef Magazine.* [ISSN: 1087-061X] 1956. 8x/yr. USD 32 domestic. Ed(s): Brent Frei. Talcott Communications Corporation, 233 N Michigan Ave, Ste 1780, Chicago, IL 60601; talcottpub@talcott.com; http://www.talcott.com. Illus., adv. *Indexed:* H&TI. *Aud.:* Sa.

This title packs an informative punch in a slim volume, especially when complemented by exclusive online content. Issues cover regional highlights as well as culinary trends with complimentary recipes. Feature articles cover new technologies in depth as well as well written profiles of culinary pros in a variety of positions. Remains highly recommended as a trade journal for libraries that serve those in the culinary fields.

2891. ***Cornell Hospitality Quarterly: hospitality leadership through learning.*** Formerly (until 2008): *The Cornell Hotel & Restaurant Administration Quarterly.* [ISSN: 1938-9655] 1960. q. USD 802 (print & online eds.)). Ed(s): Michael S LaTour. Sage Publications, Inc., 2455 Teller Rd, Thousand Oaks, CA 91320; info@sagepub.com; http://www.sagepub.com. Illus., index, adv. Sample. Refereed. Vol. ends: Nov/Dec (No. 42). Reprint: PSC. *Indexed:* A22, B01, BAS, BRI, C42, C45, E01, H&TI. *Aud.:* Ac, Sa.

Perhaps the most key scholarly journal in the hospitality field, this title remains a potentially singular subscription for special libraries. Issues cover a variety of themed refereed topics across the broad hospitality field-gaming, food service, hotels-as well as specialty areas such as marketing and HR.

2892. ***Foodservice and Hospitality: Canada's hospitality business magazine.*** Former titles (until 1972): *Foodservice Hospitality Canada;* (until 1971): *C R A Magazine.* [ISSN: 0007-8972] 1968. m. USD 55 per issue domestic; USD 80 per issue United States; USD 100 per issue elsewhere. Ed(s): Rosanna Caira. Kostuch Media Ltd., 101-23 Lesmill Rd, Don Mills, ON M3B 3P6, Canada; http://www.kostuchmedia.com. Illus. *Indexed:* BRI, C37, H&TI. *Aud.:* Sa.

This monthly Canadian trade journal is recommended to school libraries with an international focus on hospitality education. Of the trade titles reviewed in this section, it has the strongest content for the business practitioner, as well as solid editorial and news coverage. Other standout features include venue and professional profiles as well as solid trend coverage.

2893. ***Hospitality Design.*** Former titles (until 1992): *Restaurant - Hotel Design International;* (until 1988): *Restaurant and Hotel Design;* (until 1982): *Restaurant Design.* [ISSN: 1062-9254] 1979. 9x/yr. Ed(s): Michael Adams. Nielsen Business Publications, 770 Broadway, New York, NY 10003; bmcomm@nielsen.com; http://www.nielsenbusinessmedia.com. Illus., adv. Microform: PQC. *Indexed:* A22, BRI, H&TI. *Aud.:* Sa.

Of the titles reviewed in this section, this is the most lushly photographed and a treat for the eyes. It is advertising-heavy, but the ads flow seamlessly through the content, portraying luxury and cutting-edge hospitality design accommodation. Design inspiration is geared toward the high-end consumer, but will inspire all. Recommended for libraries that support either hospitality or design programs.

2894. ***Hospitality Style.*** [ISSN: 1945-6301] 2008. q. USD 48 domestic; USD 70 Canada; USD 92 elsewhere. Ed(s): Mary Scoviak. S T Media Group International, Inc., 11262 Cornell Park Dr, Cincinnati, OH 45242; http://stmediagroupintl.com/. *Aud.:* Sa.

While similar in scope to other design titles reviewed in this section, this title provides a crisper, more streamlined layout and focus. Eye-catching photography and design features balance nicely with more editorial content than is seen in other design titles. Recommended for both design- and hospitality-focused libraries.

2895. ***International Journal of Contemporary Hospitality Management.*** Formerly (until 1990): *Journal of Contemporary Hospitality Management.* [ISSN: 0959-6119] 1989. m. EUR 13739 (print & online eds.) (excluding UK)). Ed(s): Mathilda Van Niekerk, Dr. Fevzi Okumus. Emerald Publishing Limited, Howard House, Wagon Ln, Bingley, BD16 1WA, United Kingdom; emerald@emeraldinsight.com; http://www.emeraldinsight.com. Sample. Refereed. Reprint: PSC. *Indexed:* A22, B01, C45, E01, ErgAb, H&TI. *Aud.:* Ac, Sa.

This is an international scholarly journal that aims to communicate the latest developments on management of hospitality operations worldwide. Subject areas include operations, marketing, and finance. Target market ranges from hospitality managers to educators and researchers. For academic libraries that support hospitality research.

2896. ***International Journal of Hospitality and Tourism Administration.*** Supersedes (in 2000): *Journal of International Hospitality, Leisure and Tourism Management.* [ISSN: 1525-6480] 1997. q. GBP 482. Ed(s): Clayton W Barrows. Routledge, 530 Walnut St, Ste 850, Philadelphia, PA 19106; enquiries@tandfonline.com; http://www.tandfonline.com. Adv. Refereed. Circ: 173 Paid. Microform: PQC. Reprint: PSC. *Indexed:* A01, A22, B01, C45, E01, H&TI. *Aud.:* Ac, Sa.

This peer-reviewed and scholarly title represents a broad, general, yet international focus on a wide variety of hospitality management issues. Articles are in-depth scientific explorations into their fields of research, and are well cited, often with supplementary charts or graphs. Recommended for academic and special libraries that support research in the hospitality fields.

2897. ***International Journal of Hospitality Management.*** [ISSN: 0278-4319] 1982. 8x/yr. EUR 1820. Ed(s): Abraham Pizam. Pergamon Press, The Blvd, Langford Ln, E Park, Kidlington, OX5 1GB, United Kingdom; JournalsCustomerServiceEMEA@elsevier.com; http://www.elsevier.com. Adv. Sample. Refereed. Microform: PQC. *Indexed:* A22, C45, H&TI. *Aud.:* Ac, Sa.

This scholarly research journal discusses trends in a variety of areas relative to the hospitality industry. Analysis and research are well written and reflect current management issues internationally. This journal is unique in application, while it is a research journal first, and it feels approachable to those in general management in the field. Recommended to libraries that support hospitality programs.

2898. ***Journal of Hospitality and Tourism Technology.*** [ISSN: 1757-9880] 2010. 4x/yr. EUR 578 (print & online eds.) (includes UK)). Ed(s): Dr. Cihan Cobanoglu. Emerald Publishing Limited, Howard House, Wagon Ln, Bingley, BD16 1WA, United Kingdom; emerald@emeraldinsight.com; http://www.emeraldinsight.com. Sample. Reprint: PSC. *Indexed:* C45, H&TI. *Aud.:* Ac, Sa.

This relatively new scholarly journal reaches a niche in the hospitality field while addressing the increasing presence of technology in every aspect of our lives. Article topics are broad in scope, but well written and researched. Topics range from e-business to virtual technology, to social media, to end-user technology. While it may appear to be of a limited subject-area interest, as technology continues to invade our lives, the relevance of this title will only increase.

2899. *Journal of Hospitality Marketing and Management.* Formerly (until 2008): *Journal of Hospitality & Leisure Marketing.* [ISSN: 1936-8623] 1992. 8x/yr. GBP 1073 (print & online eds.)). Ed(s): Dogan Gursoy. Routledge, 530 Walnut St, Ste 850, Philadelphia, PA 19106; enquiries@tandfonline.com; http://www.tandfonline.com. Illus., index. Sample. Refereed. Vol. ends: Winter. Microform: PQC. Reprint: PSC. *Indexed:* A01, A22, B01, C45, E01, H&TI. *Bk. rev.:* Number and length vary. *Aud.:* Ac, Sa.

The strength of this scholarly journal may be the special issues and the niche research represented in those issues. While it is not immediately obvious by title, the international scope of this research should also be noted. Content focuses on the relationship between marketing and hospitality, and does so in well-researched scientific publications. Recommended for both marketing and hospitality library collections.

2900. *Lodging Hospitality: ideas for hotel developers & operators.* Former titles: *Hospitality Lodging; Hospitality-Food and Lodging; Hospitality-Restaurant and Lodging; American Motel Magazine.* [ISSN: 0148-0766] 1949. 15x/yr. USD 80 domestic (Free to qualified personnel). Ed(s): Ed Watkins. Penton, 9800 Metcalf Ave, Overland Park, KS 66212-2216; information@penton.com; http://www.penton.com. Illus., index, adv. Sample. Circ: 50976 Controlled. Vol. ends: Dec. Microform: CIS; PQC. *Indexed:* A22, B01, B03, BRI, C42, H&TI. *Aud.:* Sa.

This trade journal is geared toward hotel developers and operators who wish to keep an eye on the trends and innovations in the field. Well balanced between editorial content and advertising, the regular departments (technology, back of house) remain standouts. The online version is a good complement to the print edition.

2901. *Restaurant Business: street smarts for the entrepreneur.* Formerly (until 1974): *Fast Food.* [ISSN: 0097-8043] 1902. m. USD 99 domestic (Free to qualified personnel). Ed(s): Sam Smith. C S P Business Media, LLC, 90 Broad St, New York, NY 10004; cspinquire@cspnet.com; http://www.monkeydish.com/. Illus., adv. Circ: 77000 Controlled. Microform: CIS; PQC. *Indexed:* A22, Agr, B01, BRI, C42, Chicano, H&TI. *Aud.:* Sa.

As trade journals go, this is an excellent resource for the restaurant industry. Very high-quality business articles address current issues and trends to an impressive degree. While this title is new to this section with this edition, we strongly recommend it to libraries that support hospitality programs. Regular columns are reliable in content, but the standout here is the thumb-on-the-pulse content.

2902. *Restaurant Hospitality.* Former titles (until 1976): *Hospitality, Restaurant;* (until 1967): *American Restaurant Hospitality;* (until 1962): *American Restaurant Magazine;* (until 1928): *American Restaurant.* [ISSN: 0147-9989] 1919. m. USD 80 domestic; USD 100 Canada; USD 150 elsewhere. Ed(s): Michael Sanson. Penton, 9800 Metcalf Ave, Overland Park, KS 66212-2216; information@penton.com; http://www.penton.com. Illus., adv. Circ: 119300 Controlled. Vol. ends: Dec. Microform: PQC. *Indexed:* A22, B01, B03, BRI, H&TI. *Bk. rev.:* Number and length vary. *Aud.:* Sa.

This trade journal sets itself apart from others reviewed in this section through the ease and readability of the articles. Also unique to this title is the inclusion of a wide range of recipes, often up to a quarter of the issue. Content includes regular columns on current affairs, rising stars, and equipment selection. Recommended as a key resource, especially in light of the complementing online version.

2903. *Restaurant Startup & Growth: helping restaurants profit and grow.* Formerly (until 2007): *Restaurant Startup & Growth Distributor.* [ISSN: 1552-9746] 2004. m. USD 39.95 domestic. Ed(s): Barry Shuster. Restaurant Startup & Growth LLC, 20235 N. Cave Creek Rd. Ste 104, Phoenix, AZ 85024; info@restaurantowner.com; http://www.restaurantowner.com. *Aud.:* Sa.

While this is technically a trade journal, where this title excels is in how detailed and research-oriented the articles are. More approachable than some of the scholarly, peer-reviewed titles reviewed here, this is a technically focused journal with the aim of helping restaurant owners find success. Strongly recommended.

2904. *Tourism Analysis: an interdisciplinary tourism & hospitality journal.* [ISSN: 1083-5423] 1996. q. USD 720 (print & online eds.)). Ed(s): Ercan Sirakaya-Turk. Cognizant Communication Corporation, 18 Peeksill Hollow Rd, PO Box 37, Putnam Valley, NY 10579; inquiries@cognizantcommunication.com; http://www.cognizantcommunication.com. Adv. Sample. Refereed. *Indexed:* C45, H&TI. *Bk. rev.:* Number and length vary. *Aud.:* Ac, Sa.

This journal is a high-level scholarly resource that aims to be a research forum for the fields of leisure, recreation, tourism, and hospitality, with an international scope. Content leans toward research for researchers more than for everyday practitioners. Recommended for academic institutions with in-depth hospitality collections.

2905. *Tourism, Culture & Communication.* [ISSN: 1098-304X] 1998. q. USD 445 (print & online eds.)). Ed(s): Wantanee Suntikul, Brian King. Cognizant Communication Corporation, 18 Peeksill Hollow Rd, PO Box 37, Putnam Valley, NY 10579; inquiries@cognizantcommunication.com; http://www.cognizantcommunication.com. Sample. Refereed. *Indexed:* C45. *Bk. rev.:* Number and length vary. *Aud.:* Ac, Sa.

This is a scholarly research journal that places no restriction on content or range beyond relation to tourism and hospitality. Topics lean into far-reaching niches that find no home elsewhere, therefore this journal is good for very in-depth research and researchers. Occasional theme issues blend regular subject areas nicely. Recommended for academic libraries with in-depth hospitality collections.

2906. *Tourism in Marine Environments.* [ISSN: 1544-273X] 2004. q. USD 495 (print & online eds.)). Ed(s): Michael Luck. Cognizant Communication Corporation, 18 Peeksill Hollow Rd, PO Box 37, Putnam Valley, NY 10579; inquiries@cognizantcommunication.com; http://www.cognizantcommunication.com. Adv. Sample. Refereed. *Indexed:* C45. *Aud.:* Ac, Sa.

Truly a niche journal, this title aims to cover a variety of hospitality issues as specific to marine settings. Beyond that restriction, its content is broad-ranging across tourism, environmental issues, marketing, economics, and more. An example of a special issue would be the "Scuba Diving Tourism" volume. For academic libraries that have an incredibly in-depth collection to support hospitality issues.

■ HUMAN RESOURCES

Nancy McGuire, Instructional Services Librarian, Mack Library at Bob Jones University, Greenville, SC 29614; ncmcguir@bju.edu

Introduction

In the area of business professionalism the human resources magazines are vitally important across the work world, emphasizing areas that affect the workforce, such as recruiting, hiring models, compensation and incentives, training, employee development, wellness programs including mindfulness and meditation, and legal issues that attract, motivate, and retain employees. Another emphasis is the importance of how employees relate to the customer base and influence the shareholders. Publications that attract and encourage the patrons of our library community who are interested in employee information are essential for a healthy business community.

Basic Periodicals

H R Magazine, People & Strategy, Training, Workspan.

Basic Abstracts and Indexes

Business Source Complete.

2907. *H R Magazine.* Formerly (until 1990): *Personnel Administrator;* Which superseded (in 1956): *Journal for Personnel Administration.* [ISSN: 1047-3149] 1956. 10x/yr. Free to membership. Ed(s): Desda Moss, Nancy M Davis. Society for Human Resource Management, 1800 Duke St, Alexandria, VA 22314-3499; shrm@shrm.org; http://www.shrm.org. Illus., index, adv. Circ: 239832 Paid. Vol. ends: Dec. *Indexed:* A22, AgeL, B01, BRI, CBRI. *Bk. rev.:* 1, 600 words. *Aud.:* Ac, Sa.

H R Magazine is the flagship magazine for the Society for Human Resource Management (SHRM), which has more than 275,000 members. The periodical has well-written articles in a glossy magazine format. Short, timely articles inform the HR community of pertinent changes in their profession and provide information for employees seeking up-to-date news. Many employees and business students interested in the human resource field may appreciate the information contained in this periodical. A typical issue has nearly 25 articles and 40 HR-related advertisements. Recent articles include "Better Policies Create Better Workplaces," "The Blue Collar Drought," "Bright Ideas," and "Give Employees Tools They Will Use." Members of the Society for Human Resource Management have access to more information online. URL: www.shrm.org/HRmagazine

2908. *HR Focus: the hands-on tool for human resources professionals.* Formerly (until 1991): *Personnel.* [ISSN: 1059-6038] 1919. m. USD 521 (print or online ed.)). Ed(s): Anthony A Harris. Bloomberg B N A, 1801 S Bell St, Arlington, VA 22202; http://www.bna.com. Illus., index. Sample. Vol. ends: Dec. *Indexed:* A22, B01, BRI, C42, E01. *Aud.:* Ac, Sa.

HR Focus is a source of the latest news and management advice for HR professionals. This is a trade publication of Bloomberg BNA, Bureau of National Affairs, Inc., and the topics it covers include recruiting and retaining top-flight talent; complying with ever-changing HR laws and regulations; creating fair and effective compensation strategies; putting the latest technology to work for your department; and cultivating leadership. A recent issue contained 16 pages of concise information, with no ads. Articles included "Nike Accused of Systematic Discrimination Against Women," "Prosecutors Treating 'Wage Theft' as a Crime in These States," where some states risk criminal charges for failure to pay minimum wage or overtime when appropriate, "Death of the Salesman: Humans Lose as Computers Close Deals," citing instances where computers are doing what salesmen have done in the past and "Artificial Intelligence Is Coming for Hiring, and It Might Not Be That Bad." The articles are concise and short. The publication would be helpful to those professionals with minimal time to read in depth, but who need the facts. All articles were viewed for this review using an online database.

2909. *Human Resource Management.* Formerly (until 1972): *Management of Personnel Quarterly.* [ISSN: 0090-4848] 1961. bi-m. GBP 880. Ed(s): James Hayton. John Wiley & Sons, Inc., 111 River St, Hoboken, NJ 07030; cs-journals@wiley.com; http://onlinelibrary.wiley.com. Illus., index, adv. Refereed. Microform: PQC. Reprint: PSC. *Indexed:* A22, B01, BRI. *Aud.:* Ac.

Human Resource Management is published six times per year, providing practicing managers and academics with the latest concepts, tools, and information for effective problem solving and decision making. Recent issues have articles including "Workforce analytics: A case study of scholar-practitioner collaboration" where researchers and practitioners work together. Another article explores an analysis of the employees' perception of HR in their role as change agent in "Perceived human resource system strength and employee reactions toward change: Revisiting human resource's remit as change agent." The articles are readable, with the online version an exact replica of the paper journal, making life easier for the researching student who needs to cite the information. I especially appreciate the two-column design of the pages, with the graphs nicely balanced throughout the article, making it convenient to read information quickly. The online version with the Wiley interface provides convenient tools for students. URL: https://onlinelibrary.wiley.com/journal/1099050x

2910. *The Journal of Human Resources.* [ISSN: 0022-166X] 1965. q. USD 411 print & online eds. Ed(s): David N Figlio. University of Wisconsin Press, Journals Division, 1930 Monroe St, 3rd Fl, Madison, WI 53711; journals@uwpress.wisc.edu; http://www.uwpress.org/. Illus., index. Refereed. Circ: 2000. Microform: MIM; PQC. Reprint: PSC. *Indexed:* A22, AgeL, B01, Chicano, ERIC, EconLit, IBSS. *Aud.:* Ac, Sa.

The articles in *The Journal of Human Resources* are intended for scholars, policy makers, and practitioners interested in the data and statistical analysis that support decisions. Each issue has eight to ten articles with data and graphs. Recent issues include "The Effects of Aggregate and Gender-Specific Labor Demand Shocks on Child Health"; "Democracy and Demography: Societal Effects of Fertility Limits on Local Leaders"; "Keeping the Production Line Running: Internal Substitution and Employee Absence"; and "Rise and Shine: The Effect of School Start Times on Academic Performance from Childhood through Puberty." The articles are peer-reviewed and have many references. The article layout is nicely designed, with graphs and charts and a text that is large enough to read with no eye strain. The online view is clear and fully searchable. The web site is helpful, with links to set up alerts and abstracts of articles. URL: http://jhr.uwpress.org/

2911. *People & Strategy.* Formerly (until 2008): *Human Resource Planning.* [ISSN: 1946-4606] 1978. 4x/yr. Free to members; Non-members, USD 150. Ed(s): Mary Barnes, Anna Tavis. Human Resource Planning Society, 1800 Duke St, Alexandra, VA 22314; info@hrps.org; http://www.hrps.org. Illus., index, adv. Vol. ends: No. 4. *Indexed:* A22, B01, BRI. *Bk. rev.:* 4, 1,000 words. *Aud.:* Ac, Sa.

People & Strategy is published quarterly by the nonprofit Human Resource Planning Society. Experts in the field of human resources and academics write articles and publish research studies for this magazine. Communication and growth articles gear themselves to the employees' health and development. Recent articles include "The Basics of Evidence-Based Practice"; "Real-Life EBM: What It Feels Like to Lead Evidence-based HR"; "Perspectives," views of authors on people analytics; "People Analytics as a Form of Evidence-Based Management"; "Linking Theory + Practice"; and "How Organizations Are Using Behavioral Science to Make Better People Decisions." There seems to be minimal advertising. Viewing the pdf version shows that the layout is readable and pleasing to the eye. This journal will be useful in business, academic, and corporate libraries. URL: www.hrps.org/?page=PeopleStrategy

2912. *Public Personnel Management.* Formerly (until 1973): *Personnel Administration and Public Personnel Review;* Which was formed by the merger of (1940-1972): *Public Personnel Review;* (1938-1972): *Personnel Administration.* [ISSN: 0091-0260] 1972. q. USD 392 (print & online eds.)). Ed(s): Edward P French. Sage Publications, Inc., 2455 Teller Rd, Thousand Oaks, CA 91320; info@sagepub.com; http://www.sagepub.com. Illus., index. Refereed. Vol. ends: Winter. Microform: MIM; PQC. Reprint: PSC. *Indexed:* A22, B01, BRI, CBRI. *Aud.:* Ac, Sa.

Research studies and articles comprise the content of *Public Personnel Management,* which concentrates on HR issues. Recent content includes "Job Satisfaction Among Federal Employees: The Role of Employee Interaction With Work Environment"; "Moderators of the Motivational Effects of Performance Management: A Comprehensive Exploration Based on Expectancy Theory"; "Do Trustful Leadership, Organizational Justice, and Motivation Influence Whistle-Blowing Intention? Evidence From Federal Employees"; "Public Service Motivation: A Rationalist Critique"; "Weathering the Storm: The Impact of Cutbacks on Public Employees"; and "An Emergent Taxonomy of Public Personnel Management: Exploring the Task Environment of Human Resource Managers in Spanish Local Government." The first issue of 2019 has five articles contained in 119 pages. Each article has an extensive bibliography. No advertising is in the journal. All articles were viewed using an online database.

2913. *Training: the source for professional development.* Formerly (until 1974): *Training in Business and Industry.* [ISSN: 0095-5892] 1964. 6x/yr. USD 79 combined subscription domestic (print & online eds.); USD 89 combined subscription Canada (print & online eds.); USD 159 combined subscription elsewhere (print & online eds.)). Ed(s): Lorri Freifeld. Lakewood Media Group, 27020 Noble Rd, PO Box 247, Excelsior, MN 55331; http://www.mach1businessmedia.com. Illus., index, adv. Circ: 40585. Vol. ends: Dec. *Indexed:* A22, Agr, B01, BRI, ERIC. *Bk. rev.:* 1-3, 750 words. *Aud.:* Sa.

The online version of *Training* is colorful and easy to navigate. The design is professional and pleasing to the eye. The advertising includes training- specific products in about 18 ad boxes evenly spaced throughout the magazine. The issue reviewed had ten feature articles in 84 pdf pages including articles such as "We're All Leaders. Let's Be Good Ones!," "The First Thing Leaders Need to Do," "Full-Circle Feedback," "Choose the Best Learning Path," "Strategies for Success," and "Profound Learning: Creating The 'Edge Effect'." The glossy, nicely designed magazine can be purchased by libraries for patrons who appreciate reading a paper magazine. The articles are well-designed with highlights and bullets. The magazine has articles for anyone in the world of work, but especially for those who train others to work. The web site is full of information pertaining to training. URL: www.trainingmag.com/

2914. *Workspan.* [ISSN: 1529-9465] m. Membership, USD 350. Ed(s): Michele Kowalski. WorldatWork, 14040 N Northsight Blvd, Scottsdale, AZ 85260; customerrelations@worldatwork.org ; http://www.worldatwork.org/. Illus., index, adv. *Indexed:* ATI. *Aud.:* Ac, Sa.

Workspan, published monthly, has timely, well-written articles from a professional perspective for a readership of more than 70,000 members and others interested in the human resources field. The emphasis on effective communication is vitally important to attract, motivate, and retain members of the workforce. The focus of the World at Work organization, which publishes *Workspan,* is "compensation, benefits, work-life effectiveness, and total rewards; strategies to attract, motivate and retain an engaged and productive workforce." Recent articles include "The Evolution of Salary Structures—Are Broadbands a Thing of the Past?"; "Tossing a Lifeline"; "Eldercare Drain"; "Expect the Unexpected When Implementing Student Loan Repayment Benefits"; and "The Potential Evolution of the Performance Review Process." A compilation of white papers published by World at Work Press are available to members at the website. Even if you are neither in business nor belong to a human resources department, the articles are excellent for those of us still privileged to work. Advertisements are informative and apropos to the field of human resources, with many from their own organization. The World at Work website has many online resources for members of the organization and articles available to the public. URL: www.worldatwork.org/workspan

■ HUMOR

Paul Mascarenas, Associate Professor, Dayton Memorial Library, Regis University, Denver, CO 80221; pmascarena@regis.edu

Introduction

Scholarship in humor bridges parallels between humor and human experience. Humor and comedy are important because they narrate a person's experience through sly and insightful commentary on our beliefs, customs, rituals, and history. Increased interest and research into humor are widely represented in recently published monographs, for example, *Ha!: The Science of When We Laugh and Why* and *The Humor Code: The Search for What Makes Things Funny,* authored by Dr. Peter McGraw, Associate Professor of Marketing and Psychology at University of Colorado, Boulder.

McGraw is also the creator of the Humor Research Lab, which is more fondly known as HuRL. HuRL is "dedicated to the scientific study of humor, its antecedents, and its consequences."

But seriously, folks, the study of humor not only helps us understand what is funny and why, but also the cognitive functions that occur when we hear humorous tales. Publications ranging from *Mad Magazine* to the *Annals of Improbable Research: Research That Makes People LAUGH and then THINK* provide laughs and insight into why we find the chicken crossing the road so hilarious.

Basic Periodicals

Hs: *Mad*; Ga: *Mad*; Ac: *The Annals of Improbable Research.*

Basic Abstracts and Indexes

Reader's Guide to Periodical Literature.

2915. *Annals of Improbable Research (Online).* [ISSN: 1935-6862] 2007. bi-m. USD 25. Annals of Improbable Research, PO Box 380853, Cambridge, MA 02238; info@improbable.com; http://www.improbable.com. *Aud.:* Ac, Sa.

This journal requires detailed perusal - the wit and humor abound if by any indication of the journal's tagline, "Research that makes people Laugh then THINK." For example, the letters to the editor section, or rather "Exhalations from our Readers," is titled "AIR Vents" (acronymic pun intended), and at the end of the magazine reside the enigmatic "Unclassified Ads," with the caveat to "Proceed at your own risk." Colorful, glossy front and back covers relate to the special themes treated in each issue, and the back sports a generally unanswerable "What is this picture?" challenge (with answers, fortunately, in the front). The rest of the publication, running 30 pages, is solely in black-and-white text - likewise the illustrations, diagrams, or photographs; and there is no outside advertising. Serious research is lampooned, and "many of the other articles are genuine, too, but [the editors] don't know which ones." Don't miss the web site, which has a monthly newsletter (mini-AIR), a weekly newspaper column, a blog, and the "Improbable Research TV" series. "Issues not available yet in digital form" range from volume 1 (1995) to volume 16 (2010). Sample articles are viewable in most issues from volume 1 (1995) up to the current issue. This title is excellent for college and large public libraries, and even high school libraries (since the editors encourage copying, sharing, and discussing favorite articles with classes, as advocated in the AIR Teachers' Guide). URL: https://www.improbable.com/

2916. *The Believer.* [ISSN: 1543-6101] 2003. bi-m. USD 48; USD 12 per issue. Ed(s): Joshua Wolf Shenk, Daniel Gumbiner. McSweeney's, 849 Valencia St, San Francisco, CA 94110; custservice@mcsweeneys.net; http://www.mcsweeneys.net. Illus., adv. *Indexed:* MLA-IB. *Bk. rev.:* Currency and length vary. *Aud.:* Ac, Sa.

"*The Believer* is a bimonthly literature and arts, and culture magazine. In each issue, readers will find journalism and essays that are frequently very long, book reviews that are not necessarily timely, and interviews that are intimate, frank, and also very long." This note from the web site succinctly summarizes this title. It includes articles, poems, book reviews, interviews, and columns, with illustrations, photographs, or other art sprinkled throughout; and the two- and three-column text format is elegantly simple, clean, and free of advertising. The tables of contents from the inaugural March 2003 issue to the present are available on the web, with excerpts from almost everything and full text for some things. Contributors cover a broad spectrum of novelists, poets, musicians, actors, and freelancers, and can be searched by issue or name. The editors state that they focus on writers and books they like and give people and books the benefit of the doubt. Its appeal will be for those with literary or artistic interests, in large public or academic libraries. Included on *The Believer* web site is the podcast "The Organist"; this is a biweekly experimental arts-and-culture program from editors of *The Believer* and KCRW. The scope of the podcast reflects that of the print edition. "Pieces from the podcast grow out of stories in the magazine, and vice versa. Weaving together the voices of its contributors, which include the brightest talents in literature and the arts." Other mediums to enjoy more of *The Believer* include connecting with them on Facebook, Instagram, Tumblr, and following them on Twitter. Fans can also subscribe to their newsletter for updates and special offers. URL: www.believermag.com

2917. *Humor Times: the news, cartoon style.* Formerly (until 200?): *Comic Press News.* [ISSN: 1937-299X] 1991. m. USD 24.95 domestic; USD 48.95 Canada; USD 72.95 elsewhere. Ed(s): James Israel. Comic Press News, PO Box 162429, Sacramento, CA 95816; info@humortimes.com; http://www.humortimes.com. Illus., adv. *Aud.:* Hs, Ga, Ac.

According to the *Humor Times* "About Us" page, "We feature the best political cartoons by the world's finest editorial cartoonists, who give their hilariously irreverent take on what's happening on the world stage." This title should be considered for high schools (a few lesson plans are offered using editorial cartoons, and special subscription rates are available for downloadable digital version, or receive $2 off by subscribing online), public libraries, and academic institutions. *Humor Times* publishes different types of cartoons, humor columns, and political observations as well as a "Faux News" section. Humor column contributors include Jim Hightower, Will Durst, and Argus Hamilton. The intended audience includes anyone looking for excellent political and social satire on current events. To receive more from *Humor Times*, readers can subscribe for free Cartoon of the Week and More Newsletter! Subscribe to their RSS feed, visit their Facebook page, or follow them on both LinkedIn and Twitter. URL: www.humortimes.com

2918. ***Journal of Irreproducible Results: the science humor magazine.*** [ISSN: 0022-2038] 1955. bi-m. USD 39 (Individuals, USD 26.95). Ed(s): Norman Sperling. Journal of Irreproducible Results, 2625 Alcatraz Avenue #235, Berkeley, CA 94705. Illus., index, adv. Vol. ends: No. 6. *Indexed:* A22. *Aud.:* Ga, Ac, Sa.

Although 70 percent of *Journal of Irreproducible Results'* readers have doctorates, you don't have to be a rocket scientist to enjoy this magazine. However, since it is subtitled "The Science Humor Magazine," a ready sense of humor and an interest or background in the sciences certainly would not hurt. Colorful covers, black-and-white illustrations (drawings, photos, diagrams, and charts), and the wide-ranging variations in font types inside make for interesting viewing, uncomplicated by little, if any, advertising. Articles in every issue present fresh ideas from worldwide contributors, and these range from such subjects as "The decline and fall of the species *Pasta pasta*" to "How to narrow your search, or 'Oh crap, how can I read 5,000 articles by tomorrow.'" There is also "A taxonomic scale of cluedness in humans" and "Therapeutic benefits of beer for recovery from traumatic injury." *JIR*'s editor, Norman Sperling, states that readers will "get more new ideas, perspectives, and viewpoints per issue from *JIR* than from any other scientific publication. *JIR* can spur new insights into real science." Occasional poems and song parodies are included, as are crossword puzzles and cartoons. Back issues are available for purchase but are not archived online (except for some "Favorites") or indexed on the web site or commercially. *JIR* is both interesting and fun and should be in the collections of college, university, hospital, and research libraries and considered by high school and public libraries as well. URL: www.jir.com

2919. ***Light (Chicago): a journal of light verse since 1992.*** 1992. s-a. Ed(s): Kevin Durkin, Melissa Belmain. The Foundation for Light Verse, http://www.lightquarterly.org. Illus. *Bk. rev.:* Number and length vary. *Aud.:* Ga, Ac.

According to the *Light* web site, this is "...America's oldest and best-known journal of light verse." The original goal of the publication has not changed, even though the format has moved completely online. "The essence of *Light*...has always set it apart from other journals [and] is the same as it's been from the get-go: fun." Even non-poetry lovers can enjoy these light and amusing poems; there is everything from parodies to puns to limericks to haiku and sonnets. Each publication contains poems by the "Featured Poet" for that issue. The subsequent pages contain groups of poems categorized under playful titles such as "Resurrect Resurrection," "Amorous Dings and Pings," "A Parable? Noah Boat," and "Straight Talk to the Pretty Cool Greek Dude." Earlier editions of the journal conclude with "Reviews and Reflections," a section of book reviews and related ruminations, followed by much abbreviated letter and news sections. Advertising is absent, and the web site contains details on how to make a tax deductible contribution because, "$1 helps one person giggle for a day. $100 keeps a family of four guffawing all month. $1000 makes an entire village pee in its pants." Sample excerpts from back issues go back to 1997. This title would be a good selection for an academic library or a large public library. Occasional poems may not be appropriate for all ages. URL: https://lightpoetrymagazine.com/

2920. ***Mad.*** [ISSN: 0024-9319] 1952. q. USD 19.99 domestic; USD 29.99 Canada; USD 31.99 elsewhere. Ed(s): John Ficarra. E.C. Publications, Inc., 1700 Broadway, New York, NY 10019. Illus. Circ: 500000 Paid. *Aud.:* Hs, Ga.

This enduring favorite of the boomer and subsequent generations' adolescents and young adults, and written by "the usual gang of idiots," is now much more contemporary-looking, with graphics delivered in glossy color throughout the magazine, but with an occasional black-and-white nostalgia trip thrown in. Perennial favorites such as the clever fold-in back cover, "Spy vs. Spy," and the "marginals," the tiny cartoon sketches that have one perusing literally every inch of this magazine, continue to amuse. With fun poked at virtually anything from current movies, TV shows, and other pop culture icons, to dating to politics and the surefire parent/child relationships, very little is sacred in the world of *MAD*, enabling it to stay fresh and funny and contemporary. Although this may not look quite like your dad's (or grandad's) *MAD*, some things never change. One thing that has changed, however, is that *MAD* is now bimonthly rather than monthly. There is an online presence, but it's not very heavily populated with "*MAD*ness." Sure to be popular in school and public libraries; the main problem may be keeping a copy around until the next issue. Individual back issues are available for purchase. https://www.madmagazine.com/

2921. ***Studies in American Humor.*** Incorporates (1974-1983): *American Humor.* [ISSN: 0095-280X] 1974. s-a. USD 185 (print & online eds.)). Ed(s): Lawrence Howe. Pennsylvania State University Press, 820 N University Dr, University Support Bldg 1, Ste C, University Park, PA 16802; info@psupress.org; http://www.psupress.org. Illus., index, adv. Refereed. Reprint: PSC. *Indexed:* AmHI, BRI, MLA-IB. *Bk. rev.:* 2-4, 400-600 words. *Aud.:* Ac.

This journal was founded in 1974 by the American Humor Studies Association. *Studies in American Humor* "...publishes essays, review essays, and book reviews on all aspects of American humor." The journal is peer reviewed and is indexed in several literature indexes such as Humanities Index and MLA. It has no advertising, and occasionally has black-and-white cartoons, drawings, or photographs. Representative articles include "Humor after Postmodernism: David Foster Wallace and Proximal Irony," "How to Die Laughing: Kurt Vonnegut's Lessons for Humor," "Pious Policymaking: The Participatory Satires of Stephen Colbert," and "Pornographic Parodies of Situation Comedies: Can Explicit Sex Be Funny?," along with other thoughtful scholarship on the topic of humor in America. "Special Issues" contain topic-specific articles; for example, "Mad Magazine and Its Legacies," and "Funny Girls: Humor and American Women Writers." The subscription rate is very reasonable, and includes membership in the association. Recommended for research, academic, and possibly for larger public libraries. https://studiesinamericanhumor.org/

■ HUNTING AND GUNS

Christine K. Oka, Library Instruction Specialist, Northeastern University Libraries, Boston, MA 02115

Introduction

Stop at any large bookstore or newsstand and prepare to be inundated with periodicals that specialize in a wide range of hunting: for elk, whitetail, wild turkey, and waterfowl, and an even larger selection of titles related to guns: handguns, blackpowder guns, revolvers, muzzle-loaders, and automatic rifles, to name a few. This diversity is a reflection of the deep ties Americans have to their guns. A recent Pew Research Center Report about gun ownership describes the deeply ingrained historical link to early settlers who had guns for hunting to provide food and protection for their families and how this can be an essential part of the character of gun owners and their communities. Many gun owners surveyed in the study saw "owning a gun as very or somewhat important to their overall identity. . . " and many of them had early exposure to guns, living in communities where gun ownership is the social norm. "In stark contrast, among the non-gun owning public, only one in-ten say all or most of their friends own guns." But more than half of members of this group express the opinion they may be open to becoming gun owners in the future.

How does one decide what a library should have when the economic environment and tight budgets require libraries to reduce hours, services, collections, or all three? For this edition of *MFL*, most of the magazines listed were included because they provided overviews of hunting and guns, appealed to a range of readers interested in travel and adventure, conservation, and/or

Second Amendment rights. The magazines contained a range of accessible articles for novices and experts on firearms, technical data and field testing, gun legislation, land management, conservation, adventure hunting, concealed carry, and of course, safety. Many magazines have associated websites and offer selected online access to feature articles as well as many social media platforms, providing an opportunity for library collection managers to preview the content and sometimes, the readership by their blog posts. See individual entries for the relevant URLs. /References

"America's Complex Relationship with Guns: An in-depth look at the attitudes and experiences of U.S. Adults." Pew Research Center, Washington, D.C. (June 2017) http://assets.pewresearch.org/wp-content/uploads/sites/3/2017/06/06151541/Guns-Report-FOR-WEBSITE-PDF-6-21.pdf

Basic Periodicals

Hs, Ga, Ac: *American Hunter, Field & Stream, Guns & Ammo.*

Basic Abstracts and Indexes

Readers' Guide to Periodical Literature.

2922. *American Hunter.* [ISSN: 0092-1068] 1973. m. Membership, USD 35. National Rifle Association of America, 11250 Waples Mill Rd, Fairfax, VA 22030; membership@nrahq.org; http://home.nra.org. Illus. Sample. Vol. ends: Dec. *Indexed:* A22. *Bk. rev.:* 1-4, 500 words. *Aud.:* Hs, Ga, Ac.

According to the National Rifle Association (NRA), *American Hunter,* the official journal of the NRA, is about "tactics, adventure, great places to hunt, the latest hunting gear, and a special emphasis on the guns hunters love; all delivered by experts in the field." This magazine contains information for hunters with bows or with guns and of different types of prey: especially pheasant, turkey, deer, and elk, as well as other big game. It also well serves gun collectors. Departments and columns in each issue include informative articles from choosing the right tent to dealing with the less pleasant aspects of outdoor life. "There are some things in the woods that I truly fear, because they can cause me both pain and illness. Worse, some of them are difficult, if not impossible, to see and can attack from anywhere. I speak of chiggers and ticks, two critters that can make a grown person cringe with horror and hysteria." On the other side of the coin is an encouraging lifestyle article, "Why Conservation and Charity Auctions are Ideal for New Hunters." It was inspiring, as it was addressed to female hunters. The author described this as a positive and empowering experience. In addition to safety information, *American Hunter* also covers news about "Your Rights" with legislative and legal news. Recommended for any hunter and any library that serves novice and expert users with an interest in hunting and guns. Access to some of the feature articles is available at the website, with links to videos, blogs, hunting news, gear reviews, and social media. URL: https://www.americanhunter.org/

2923. *Field & Stream.* Formed by the merger of (1984-2003): *Field & Stream. Northeast Edition;* (1984-2003): *Field & Stream. Far West Edition;* (1984-2003): *Field & Stream. West Edition;* (1984-2003): *Field & Stream. South Edition;* (1984-2003): *Field & Stream. Midwest Edition;* All of which superseded in part (in 1984): *Field & Stream;* Which incorporated: *Living Outdoors;* Which was formerly: *Western Field and Stream;* Which incorporated: *Field and Stream.* [ISSN: 1554-8066] 2003. m. USD 10 combined subscription domestic (print & ipad eds.); USD 26 combined subscription Canada (print & ipad eds.); USD 40 combined subscription elsewhere (print & ipad eds.)). Bonnier Corp., 2 Park Ave, New York, NY 10016; http://www.bonniercorp.com. Adv. *Indexed:* A01, BRI, MASUSE. *Bk. rev.:* 4-6, 200-300 words. *Aud.:* Ems, Hs, Ga.

This is more than a monthly magazine for hunting and fishing enthusiasts. Each issue of *Field & Stream* "celebrates the outdoor experience with great stories, compelling photography, and sound advice, and honors the traditions hunters and fishermen have passed down for generations." If a library must limit its hunting and fishing holdings to one periodical, this is it. Each issue contains departments with well written and accessible information. Columns include "The Latest" equipment reviews; and "Skills," including how to manipulate a thin piece of fish into a thick steak with a knife and "piscatorial origami." A forthright favorite is "Ask Petzal," who writes product reviews and responded to a reader question about positive reviews "bought by the manufacturer." His response was "...we're not afraid to say that we think something is doo-doo, and we have taken our fiscal lumps for that." Other columns cover subjects such as survival, rifles, bow-hunting, fishing, and conservation. More than simply survival, a recent issue included a recipe for preparing spring trout, "one of Hemingway's favorite meals." A surprising, but important topic of discussion in recent issues - dealing with depression and suicide. A number of reader responses to the article were personal stories about suffering from depression or dealing with the suicide of a family member or friend. Highly recommended for public libraries for its broad and practical coverage and safety tips. The website contains selected articles, with blog and other social media links. URL: www.fieldandstream.com/

2924. *Guns & Ammo.* Incorporates (1995-1996): *Performance Shooter.* [ISSN: 0017-5684] 1958. m. USD 14; USD 19 combined subscription (print & online eds.)). Ed(s): Eric R Poole. Outdoor Sportsman Group, Inc., 1040 Sixth Ave, 12th Fl, New York, NY 10018; customerservice@imoutdoors.com; http://www.imoutdoorsmedia.com. Illus., index, adv. Vol. ends: Dec. *Indexed:* A22, BRI. *Aud.:* Hs, Ga, Ac.

Published by Outdoor Sportsman Group, *Guns & Ammo* is celebrating its 60th anniversary covering the practical applications of firearms, along with their safe and proper use. The content is accessible to many different aspects of firearms experience (hunting, collectible guns, education, and competitive shooting). Articles examine the latest specifications and technical design of a wide variety of firearms from handguns to automatic rifles; ammunition and reloading; and securing firearms. All with an emphasis on practicality and safety. While reflecting on the past 60 years, editor Eric R. Poole considers the future and the *G&A* tradition to "always offer objective reviews of firearm products with mass appeal. And we must never harden ourselves to learning." Readers can see the broad scope of this magazine in the departments in each issue, such as "Reader Blowback," and answers in the column, "Gun Room." In addition to articles about the latest types of firearms and everyday carry rig (EDC), such as an ankle holster, a recent issue looked at the features of an early twentieth century pocket pistol, the Walther's PPK, a small double-action semiautomatic, "probably best known to the greater majority of people - even nongun types - as the trusty companion" of Ian Fleming's creation, James Bond. Selected articles are available online at the website, which also offers links to reviews, shooting, and online videos produced by *Guns & Ammo.* Recommended for libraries that serve hunting and gun enthusiasts. URL: www.gunsandammo.com/

Outdoor Life. See Hiking, Climbing, and Outdoor Recreation section.

2925. *Rifle: sporting firearms journal.* Formerly: *Rifle Magazine.* [ISSN: 0162-3583] 1968. bi-m. USD 19.97. Ed(s): Dave Scovill. Wolfe Publishing Co., 2180 Gulfstream, Ste A, Prescott, AZ 86301; wolfepub@riflemag.com. Adv. Sample. Vol. ends: Dec. *Aud.:* Hs, Ga.

Published bi-monthly by the Wolfe Publishing Company, *Rifle* covers everything of interest to hunting and shooting enthusiasts with substantial reviews of rifles, cartridges, shooting gear (such as scopes), and collectible rifles. The focus is on rifles and carbines for hunting and sport shooting. Articles look at the latest firearms as well as examining historical rifles, such as Japanese WWII sniper rifles or the linguistic background of the word "eumatic," which is a way to define handling characteristics in firearms of all kinds. These articles add to the more traditional firearms and adventure hunting content. All are well-written articles by the knowledgeable staff and contributors. While articles are not online, a sampling from the latest issue may be found at the website. Recommended for large public libraries. URL: www.riflemagazine.com

2926. *Shooting Sportsman.* [ISSN: 1050-5717] 1987. bi-m. USD 33; USD 38 combined subscription (print & online eds.)). Ed(s): Ralph Stuart. Down East Enterprise, Outdoor Group Publications, PO Box 1357, Camden, ME 04843. Illus., adv. Sample. *Bk. rev.:* 700-1,000 words. *Aud.:* Sa.

International in scope, *Shooting Sportsman* is a glossy, full-color magazine dedicated to covering "birds, guns, dogs, people and places." Departments in each issue include "From the Editor" and "Letters," along with coverage of specialized topics, such as "Game and Gun Gazette," "Hunting Dogs, "Conservation," and "Fine Gunmaking." Features cover a range of wingshooting, from clays to pheasant, duck, and grouse. Also thoroughly covered is the craftsmanship of shotguns made around the world. Articles are accessible to connoisseurs as well as to the interested general reader. Recent issues include stories about gundogs, and bespoke guns that combine traditional handwork with the latest technology. Articles on gun dogs range from practical tips for "Making Sense of Setters," to a personal story "Lost & Found," starting with "The worst thing that can happen to your dog may depend on what you fear the most." The author's "top horror" was a lost dog. As the title indicates, there was a happy ending to this story. For those interested in gun technology and craftsmanship, "The ACGC's Simson Project" details the artistry and teamwork that can go into the making of guns. The article documents the two-year work of a team of American Custom Gunmaker Guild members to restore a 1950s-vintage Simson 12-gauge donor shotgun. For readers interested in reading about more active pursuits, there are adventure stories, such as traveling to Peru for duck hunting in "new and interesting surroundings." Recommended for large public and special libraries that serve gun enthusiasts and shooters.

2927. *Sports Afield: the premier hunting adventure magazine.* Former titles (until 1940): *Sports Afield with Rod and Gun; Sports Afield.* [ISSN: 0038-8149] 1887. bi-m. Sports Afield, Inc., 15621 Chemical Ln, Bldg B, Huntington Beach, CA 92649; letters@sportsafield.com. Illus., adv. Sample. Circ: 43000. *Indexed:* A01, A22, BRI. *Bk. rev.:* 500-800 words. *Aud.:* Hs, Ga.

Founded in 1887, *Sports Afield* published its first issue in January 1888 with the intent "to help propagate the true spirit of gentle sportsmanship, to encourage indulgence in outdoor recreations and to assist in the dissemination of knowledge regarding natural history, photography, firearms, and kindred subjects." The magazine has evolved over time, looking at conservation issues before they became politically correct. Famous writers who have worked for *Sports Afield* include Zane Grey and mystery writer Earle Stanley Gardner, who became known for his articles on the rights of gun owners and hunters. Today, *Sports Afield* is a high-end, glossy magazine, providing the armchair adventurer and the serious big-game hunter with stories on popular hunting destinations, personal experiences described by readers, and news about the latest gadgets and gear. Departments include the "Conservation Corner," "Rifles," "Shotguns," "Survival," and "The Traveling Hunter." Recent issues feature articles about packhorse hunting in the Rockies, muskox hunting in Alaska, and advice on hunting mule deer: "they aren't easy to find, but they're still out there." Historical articles provide background details about big game hunting and guns with a timeline feature about the life of the African elephant hunter, Walter Dalrymple Maitland Bell, 1880-1954; or the story of custom gunmaker Friedrich R. Adolph, with a close-up look at one of his rare custom rifles. Then there is an amusing fact and fiction article about "Tales of the Baron: The Life and Times of the Real and the Legendary Baron Munchausen, Teller of Hunting's Tallest Tales." All articles are accompanied by illustrations and breathtaking color photography. The magazine web page has teasers to encourage visitors to subscribe to the magazine for the complete content. Truly "the world's premier hunting adventure magazine." Recommended for special libraries and large public libraries. URL: www.sportsafield.com

2928. *Women & Guns Magazine.* [ISSN: 1045-7704] 1989. bi-m. USD 18; USD 3.95 newsstand/cover domestic; USD 5.95 newsstand/cover Canada. Second Amendment Foundation, 12500 NE 10th Pl, Bellevue, WA 98005; AdminForWeb@saf.org; http://www.saf.org. Illus., adv. Sample. Vol. ends: No. 6. *Bk. rev.:* 1, 300 words. *Aud.:* Sa.

Women & Guns is published bimonthly by the Second Amendment Foundation (www.saf.org), a nonprofit, tax-exempt organization that is "dedicated to promoting a better understanding about our Constitutional heritage to privately own and possess firearms." Touted as "the world's first firearms publication for women," the magazine is "written and edited by women, for women, the emphasis is on self-defense and personal protection, including real life encounters, with a large dose of recreational shooting, too." The publication works from a woman's perspective to ensure this is not "just another gun magazine. . . We don't get bogged down in excessively technical jargon." Most issues include articles on guns, gear and training. In a review of "Perfect Size Carry Pistols," the pistols are selected for their size, "which fits a lot of folk's hands," carry plenty of ammunition and are priced not to "break the bank." Testing from the firing range showed both pistols "are reliable and easy to learn." In the "Making a Difference" section of the current issue, there is the unexpected question, "Can we have a conversation?" This was in light of heated debates after recent school shootings. While acknowledging differences of opinions, the author suggests keeping an open mind and "Thinking of the other's arguments allows us to understand the different ways of looking at a particular part of the situation. This gives us a chance of again finding something on which we can agree. Then, we can resume at the new point of agreement and move further forward in the same manner." This is a methodical discussion of an issue, piece by piece, and progressing to points of potential agreement. Content from the current issue is accessible online; past issues may be purchased individually. Check the magazine's website for subscription and purchase options. URL: www.womenshooters.com/

■ INFORMATICS

Khue Duong, Math, Physical Sciences, and Environmental Science & Policy Librarian, California State University, Long Beach, 1250 Bellflower Blvd., Long Beach, CA 90840; khue.duong@csulb.edu

Introduction

Informatics examines computational, cognitive, and communicative aspects of computer systems applied to specific specialties, such as astronomy, business, genetics, healthcare, or law. Combining computer science, information science, mathematics, and statistics with study of the ethical and social facets of information systems, informatics focuses on the design, application, use, and impact of information technology.

By gathering, manipulating, storing, retrieving, and classifying information, informatics practitioners develop human-centered uses for information technology to solve specific problems as diverse as smartphone applications, medical records storage and retrieval, financial market analysis, or disaster preparedness and response. As the need of contextualizing and making sense of data becomes indispensable, the advancement of informatics increasingly impacts the well-being of both individuals and society.

To respond to the field's widespread presence, many universities have developed rigorous undergraduate and graduate informatics programs. As the discipline evolves, specializations arise, focusing on topics such as artificial intelligence, cybersecurity, data mining, deep learning, information architecture, or user-experience research.

Basic Periodicals

BMC Medical Informatics and Decision Making, Computers, Informatics, Nursing (CIN); International Journal of Medical Informatics, Journal of Biomedical Informatics, Journal of Chemical Information and Modeling, Journal of Cheminformatics, American Medical Informatics Association. Journal; (JAMIA); Neuroinformatics, PLOS Computational Biology.

Basic Abstracts and Indexes

BIOBASE, BIOSIS, CINAHL, EMBASE, Information Science and Technology Abstracts, INSPEC, MEDLINE, PsycINFO, PubMed, Science Citation Index, Scopus.

2929. *American Medical Informatics Association. Journal: a scholarly journal of informatics in health and biomedicine.* [ISSN: 1067-5027] 1994. m. Ed(s): Lucila Ohno-Machado. Oxford University Press, Great Clarendon St, Oxford, OX2 6DP, United Kingdom; onlinequeries.uk@oup.com; https://academic.oup.com/journals/. Illus., adv. Sample. Refereed. Reprint: PSC. *Indexed:* A22, CompLI, ErgAb, ISTA. *Bk. rev.:* Number and length vary. *Aud.:* Ac, Sa.

A premier journal in biomedical and health informatics, *JAMIA* is the official journal of the American Medical Informatics Association (AMIA). Emphasizing informatics research and systems that help to advance biomedical science and to promote health, the journal includes articles in the areas of clinical care, clinical research, translational science, implementation science, imaging, education, consumer health, public health, and policy. *JAMIA* articles describe innovative informatics research and systems that help to advance biomedical science and to promote health. In addition, case reports, perspectives, and reviews inform readers about the most important informatics developments in implementation, policy, and education. Topics covered by some of the most downloaded papers include the role of medical bioinformatics in the advancement of clinical and translational medicine; the usability of personal health record (PHR) systems; and secure protocol in protecting personal information and minimizing errors in medical records. All content published in *JAMIA* is deposited with PubMed Central with a 12-month embargo. Authors may pay an open-access fee to make the article free immediately after publication on the *JAMIA* website and PubMed Central. This title is highly recommended for both hospital libraries and health-focused academic libraries. AMIA membership includes subscription to *JAMIA*.

2930. *B M C Medical Informatics and Decision Making.* [ISSN: 1472-6947] 2001. irreg. Free. Ed(s): Diana Marshall. BioMed Central Ltd., Fl 6, 236 Gray's Inn Rd, London, WC1X 8HB, United Kingdom; info@biomedcentral.com; https://www.biomedcentral.com. Illus., index, adv. Refereed. *Indexed:* A01. *Bk. rev.:* Number and length vary. *Aud.:* Ac, Sa.

BMC Medical Informatics and Decision Making is an open-access, peer-reviewed journal publishing original articles in relation to the design, development, implementation, use, and evaluation of health information technologies and decision-making for human health. Large data sets, illustrations, and moving pictures can be included and read directly by other software packages, so as to allow readers to manipulate the data for themselves. The journal also lists the most-viewed articles. Frequently discussed topics include mobile health apps, computerized clinical documentation systems, management of electronic health records, and artificial intelligence in medical informatics.

Bioinformatics. See Biotechnology section.

2931. *Computers, Informatics, Nursing.* Formerly (until 2002): *Computers in Nursing;* Incorporates (1998-2002): *C I N Plus.* [ISSN: 1538-2931] 1983. m. bi-m. until 2016. USD 643. Ed(s): Dr. Leslie H Nicoll. Lippincott Williams & Wilkins, Two Commerce Sq, 2001 Market St, Philadelphia, PA 19103; customerservice@lww.com; http://www.lww.com. Illus., index, adv. Refereed. Microform: PQC. *Indexed:* A22. *Aud.:* Ac, Sa.

CIN: Computers, Informatics, Nursing focuses on the latest developments in nursing informatics, research, education, and administration of health information technology. Whereas new original content is published online each month, *CIN* also continues to publish quarterly print collections of articles grouped by relevant theme. Accepted manuscripts are fast-tracked for online publication ahead of print. In addition, the supplementary section, "CIN Plus," provides quick-access and how-to pieces on practical issues and applications of nursing informatics computing tools. Recent topics of discussion include the role of informatics in nursing education; designing decision-support systems; building patient relationships using smartphone applications; and enhancing oncology care and survivorship through informatics. The journal is an endorsed member benefit of AMIA, HIMSS, and all other member organizations of the Alliance for Nursing Informatics (ANI). Members of the ANI are eligible to receive the journal at a reduced subscription rate.

2932. *International Journal of Medical Informatics.* Formerly (until 1997): *International Journal of Bio-Medical Computing.* [ISSN: 1386-5056] 1970. m. EUR 4868. Ed(s): J Talmon, C Safran. Elsevier Ireland Ltd., Elsevier House, Brookvale Plz, E Park, Shannon, , Ireland; JournalsCustomerServiceemea@elsevier.com; http://www.elsevier.com/. Illus., adv. Sample. Refereed. *Indexed:* A01, A22, C45, CompLI. *Aud.:* Ac, Sa.

The official journal of the European Federation of Medical Informatics (EFMI), *International Journal of Medical Informatics* publishes original results and interpretative reviews, focusing on the evaluation of information systems in health-care settings. Specific coverage of this peer-reviewed journal includes electronic medical-record systems, hospital information systems, computer-aided medical-decision support systems, and educational computer-based programs in medicine, as well as the clinical, ethical, and socioeconomic aspects of information technology (IT) applications in health care. The journal periodically publishes special issues that concentrate on themes such as mining clinical and biomedical text and data; security in health information systems; or human-factors engineering for health-care applications. Potential audience groups include researchers in medicine and those in health policy and administration, and medical educators.

2933. *Journal of Biomedical Informatics.* Formerly (until 2001): *Computers and Biomedical Research.* [ISSN: 1532-0464] 1969. bi-m. EUR 1582. Ed(s): Dr. E H Shortliffe. Academic Press, 3251 Riverport Ln, Maryland Heights, MO 63043; usbkinfo@elsevier.com; http://www.elsevier.com/. Illus., index, adv. Sample. Refereed. *Indexed:* A22, C45, E01. *Bk. rev.:* Irregular. *Aud.:* Ac, Sa.

The *Journal of Biomedical Informatics* publishes high-quality original research papers, reviews, and commentaries in the area of biomedical informatics methodology. Whereas the peer-reviewed articles are motivated by applications in the biomedical sciences (for example, clinical medicine, health care, population health, imaging, and translational bioinformatics), the journal emphasizes reports of new methodologies and techniques with general applicability and those that form the basis for the evolving science of biomedical informatics. The journal periodically produces special-theme issues that highlight topics such as ontologies for clinical and translational research; biomedical complexity and error; and biomedical natural-language processing. The potential audience includes researchers in medicine, bioinformatics, computer science, and professionals in health policy, administration, and management.

2934. *Journal of Chemical Information and Modeling.* Former titles (until 2005): *Journal of Chemical Information and Computer Sciences;* (until 1975): *Journal of Chemical Documentation.* [ISSN: 1549-9596] 1961. m. USD 1197. Ed(s): Kenneth M Merz. American Chemical Society, 1155 16th St NW, Washington, DC 20036; help@acs.org; http://pubs.acs.org. Adv. Sample. Refereed. *Indexed:* A22, Agr, CompLI. *Bk. rev.:* Irregular. *Aud.:* Ac, Sa.

Published by the American Chemical Society Publications, the *Journal of Chemical Information and Modeling* produces peer-reviewed papers that focus on the methodology and applications of chemical informatics and molecular modeling. Specific topics include the representation and searching of chemical databases, molecular modeling, computer-aided molecular design of new materials, catalysts, or ligands, and development of new computational methods or efficient algorithms for chemical software. The coverage also extends to analyses of biological activity and other issues related to drug discovery. The online interface lists the most-read and most-cited articles as well as "Just Accepted" manuscripts. Authors can pay a one-time fee to make their papers freely accessible online. This title is highly ranked in the "Computer Science, Information Systems" category by Journal Citation Reports, and it helps computational chemists, computer scientists, and information specialists stay current with recent developments in this multidisciplinary field.

2935. *Journal of Cheminformatics.* [ISSN: 1758-2946] 2009. . Free. Ed(s): David J Wild, Christoph Steinbeck. Chemistry Central, 236 Gray's Inn Rd, London, WC1X 8HB, United Kingdom; info@chemistrycentral.com; http://www.chemistrycentral.com/. Refereed. *Indexed:* A01. *Bk. rev.:* Irregular. *Aud.:* Ac, Sa.

Established in 2009, the *Journal of Cheminformatics* is an open-access, peer-reviewed, online journal that addresses all aspects of cheminformatics and molecular modeling, including chemical information systems, software, and databases; computer-aided molecular design; chemical-structure representations; and data mining techniques. Published material may include electronic supplementary material such as data sets, spectra, x-ray crystallographic data, or graphical chemical structures. The journal offers different types of articles including primary research; coverage of a database or software feature; and methodology articles that describe a new experimental method, test, or procedure. In addition to RSS feeds and advanced search features, the journal also highlights the most accessed articles. The potential audience includes academic and industrial groups involved in computational chemistry and cheminformatics.

2936. ***Neuroinformatics.*** [ISSN: 1539-2791] 2002. q. EUR 865 (print & online eds.)). Springer, Tiergartenstr 17, Heidelberg, 69121, Germany; subscriptions@springer.com; https://www.springer.com. Illus. Sample. Refereed. Reprint: PSC. *Indexed:* A22, E01. *Aud.:* Ac, Sa.

Neuroinformatics publishes articles and reviews with an emphasis on data structure and software tools related to analysis, modeling, integration, and sharing in all areas of neuroscience research. Per the journal's description, coverage consists of "theory and methodology, including discussions on ontologies, modeling approaches, database design, and meta-analyses; descriptions of developed databases and software tools, and of the methods for their distribution; relevant experimental results, such as reports accompanied by the release of massive data sets; computational simulations of models integrating and organizing complex data; and neuroengineering approaches, including hardware, robotics, and information theory studies." The journal also publishes independent "tests and evaluations" of available neuroscience databases and software tools. Authors can pay an open-access fee to make their articles freely available. Recommended for both hospital libraries and health-focused academic libraries.

2937. ***P L o S Computational Biology (Online).*** [ISSN: 1553-7358] 2005. m. Free. Ed(s): Philip E Bourne. Public Library of Science, 1160 Battery St, Koshland Bldg E, Ste 100, San Francisco, CA 94111; plos@plos.org; http://www.plos.org. Refereed. *Aud.:* Ac, Sa.

PLOS Computational Biology publishes monthly open-access research articles on all aspects of computational biology applied to different and integrated biological scales, from molecules and cells to patient populations and ecosystems. The journal features works that further current understanding of living systems at all scales through the application of computational methods. Research articles are grouped into the following categories: General, Methods, or Software. Software articles form a specific sub-category describing outstanding open source software leading to new biological insights. The journal also includes invited and submitted reviews and perspectives on topics of broad interest to the readership as well as high-quality tutorials (including multimedia presentations) teaching important concepts in the field of computational biology.

■ INTERDISCIPLINARY STUDIES

Courtney L. Young, Head Librarian, Greater Allegheny Campus Library, The Pennsylvania State University, McKeesport, PA 15132; cly11@psu.edu

Introduction

Interdisciplinary studies as a field reflects the continued importance of scholarship that applies multiple approaches, as well as the scholarly conversations taking place across disciplines. This section is a complement to sections that focus on and incorporate diverse fields of study.

While race and gender are often equated with interdisciplinary studies, broader disciplines within the sciences, social sciences, and humanities are also strong collaborators with and contributors to this area. The publications included in this section focus on cross-disciplinary education and the facilitation of conversations among educators in a variety of fields.

The emphasis of the journals included here is on science, approaches to education, and the understanding that one approach is really one strategy among many approaches. A large number of journals include "interdisciplinary" as a subtitle but are better suited for other sections. A challenge in editing this section was the large number of journals with a sporadic publishing history or journals that had simply ceased publishing.

Consider these publications when building and maintaining a collection to support interdisciplinary studies. In addition to the journals recommended, explore the many sections that more directly focus on specific disciplines and types of diversity. Your suggestions for expanding this list are encouraged.

Basic Periodicals

Ac: *Interdisciplinary Studies.*

Basic Abstracts and Indexes

Academic Search Premier, Project MUSE, Research Library (ProQuest).

American Quarterly. See Cultural Studies section.

American Studies. See Cultural Studies section.

Critical Inquiry. See Cultural Studies section.

Discourse. See Education/Comparative Education and International section.

Environmental Ethics. See Environment and Conservation section.

Film History. See Films section.

Inquiry: An Interdisciplinary Journal of Philosophy. See Philosophy section.

2938. ***Interdisciplinary Literary Studies: a journal of criticism and theory.*** [ISSN: 1524-8429] 1999. q. USD 259 (print & online eds.)). Ed(s): Kenneth L Womack. Pennsylvania State University Press, 820 N University Dr, University Support Bldg 1, Ste C, University Park, PA 16802; info@psupress.org; http://www.psupress.org. Adv. Reprint: PSC. *Indexed:* MLA-IB. *Bk. rev.:* Number and length vary; signed. *Aud.:* Ac.

This journal publishes research exploring "the interconnections between literary study and other disciplines, ideologies, and cultural methods of critique." Scholarship focuses on discussions of the "pedagogical possibilities of interdisciplinary literary studies." Also includes book reviews and interviews with key scholars in the field.

2939. ***Interdisciplinary Science Reviews.*** [ISSN: 0308-0188] 1976. q. GBP 905 (print & online eds.)). Ed(s): Willard McCarty. Routledge, 4 Park Sq, Milton Park, Abingdon, OX14 4RN, United Kingdom; subscriptions@tandf.co.uk; http://www.tandfonline.com. Adv. Refereed. Reprint: PSC. *Indexed:* A01, A22, MLA-IB. *Bk. rev.:* Number and length vary; signed. *Aud.:* Ac.

Founded in 1976, *ISR* aims to "foster inclusive pluralistic appreciation and understanding of scientific activity." Submissions by scholars with diverse research interests in the physical and biological sciences, social sciences, and humanities advance that goal. Faculty and researchers from around the world contribute frequently. Special issues are often published, with themes including "Science and Poetry" and "Neuroscience: the humanities and arts." Most issues are heavily illustrated. Book reviews and letters to the editor round out each issue. A fascinating and essential journal for interdisciplinary collections.

2940. ***Interdisciplinary Studies.*** Former titles (until 2015): *Issues in Interdisciplinary Studies;* (until 2012): *Issues in Integrative Studies.* 1982. a. Free to members. Association for Interdisciplinary Studies, Oakland University - Macomb County, 44575 Garfield Road, Clinton Township,, MI 48038. Refereed. *Bk. rev.:* Number and length vary; signed. *Aud.:* Ac.

While other journals take an interdisciplinary approach to the study of disciplines, research in *Interdisciplinary Studies* explores what, exactly, the field of interdisciplinary studies is all about. Each publication examines the challenges of exploring this area of study, including "interdisciplinary theory and methodology; the nature, means, and problems of integrative research, especially on the human experience; and special pedagogical approaches for enhancing interdisciplinary/integrative comprehension, perspectives, knowledge, and utilization." This is an impressive, key journal for institutions with interdisciplinary studies programs. It is equally applicable to institutions with education programs. Issues from 1982 to 2013 are accessible in pdf form online; issues 2014 and on are password-protected.

2941. ***Interdisciplinary Studies in Literature and Environment.*** [ISSN: 1076-0962] 1993. q. EUR 175. Ed(s): Andrew B Ross, Frank Merksamer. Oxford University Press, 198 Madison Ave, New York, NY 10016; https://global.oup.com. Adv. Refereed. Reprint: PSC. *Indexed:* AmHI, MLA-IB. *Bk. rev.:* Number and length vary; signed. *Aud.:* Ac.

Focused on the increasing research and scholarship on the environment, *ISLE* "seeks to bridge the gap between scholars, artists, students, and the public." Published since 1993 by the Association for the Study of Literature and Environment, *ISLE* bridges the gap with scholarship on advertising, poetry, religion, the environment, and representations of nature in literature. Also includes book reviews and an annotated list of recently published books in the field.

2942. ***Journal of Interdisciplinary History.*** [ISSN: 0022-1953] 1969. q. USD 412 (print & online eds.)). Ed(s): Theodore K Rabb, Robert I Rotberg. M I T Press, One Rogers St, Cambridge, MA 02142-1209; http://mitpress.mit.edu/. Illus., adv. Refereed. Reprint: SCH. *Indexed:* A01, A22, AmHI, BAS, BRI, CBRI, E01, IBSS, MLA-IB, P61. *Bk. rev.:* 30-45, 2-3 pages, signed. *Aud.:* Ac, Sa.

Incorporating "contemporary insights on the past," articles in this journal employ a diverse approach to analysis and methodology in historical scholarship. Sample titles of articles, clearly influenced by an interdisciplinary approach to research, include "Reconceptualizing the Republic: Diversity and Education in France, 1945-2008"; "Nutritional Success on the Great Plains: Nineteenth-Century Equestrian Nomads"; and "Weather, Harvests, and Taxes: A Chinese Revolt in Colonial Taiwan." Book reviews, research notes, and review essays continue to be a strength of the journal. While it remains an important journal in the discipline of history, the *Journal of Interdisciplinary History* is a solid contributor to the field of interdisciplinary studies.

Journal of the History of Ideas. See Cultural Studies section.

Philosophy and Literature. See Philosophy section.

Social Theory and Practice. See Cultural Studies section.

■ INTERIOR DESIGN AND DECORATION

See also Home section.

Holly Stec Dankert, Research & Access Services Librarian, John M. Flaxman Library, School of the Art Institute of Chicago, 37 S. Wabash, Chicago, IL 60603; FAX: 312-899-1465; hdankert@saic.edu

Introduction

Shelter magazines listed here are targeted toward two audiences: professional designers and consumers. This section focuses on trade magazines for professionals, but also includes consumer-oriented magazines that play an important role in providing product information and trends to practitioners, while bringing design principles to everyone. Another segment that crosses into interior design is the do-it-yourself magazine. All of these types are important to interior design.

Trade publications serve to inform decorators, designers, and architects of current practices, trends, and new products and services, in both commercial and residential interiors. Most of these trade titles include reader-service information, professional development opportunities, new technology advancements in furnishings and materials, calendars of professional events, and reviews of new publications in interior design. In addition, these publications provide many full-color illustrations of interiors and the materials used for their creation. The field's professional literature is best suited to academic libraries that offer degrees in interior design and public or special libraries that support their local design community.

Consumer-oriented titles target the affluent buyer as well as the professional decorator or designer, and generally devote a great deal more copy space to photography of the featured interiors and to advertisements that highlight furnishings, appliances, wall coverings, textiles, flooring, and interior architecture.

The hallmark of all titles in this section is the extensive use of lush, full-color illustrations. The websites of both the trade and consumer titles provide relevant content to their constituents, though a few only provide subscriber services and some content that augments the print issues. Magazines in this section will appeal to all library users, but are aimed at working designers and a clientele in search of professional design services.

Basic Periodicals

Ga: *Architectural Digest;* Ac: *Architectural Digest, Contract, Interior Design, Interiors and Sources, Journal of Interior Design.*

Basic Abstracts and Indexes

Art Abstracts, Art Index, Avery Index to Architectural Periodicals, Design and Applied Arts Index.

2943. ***Apartamento: an everyday life interiors magazine.*** [ISSN: 2013-0198] 2008. s-a. EUR 18 newsstand/cover. Apartamento Publishing S.L., Bruc 49 3-2, Barcelona, 08009, Spain. *Aud.:* Ac, Sa.

Apartamento is a relative newcomer to the interiors scene, recently celebrating its tenth anniversary, and is quite different in its conception from other interiors magazines. As the editors state, the focus is not on buying and owning things but on showcasing the homes of people they admire and discovering the stories of these people that have had an impact in their lives. Each issue is a substantial booklike format that explodes with color images of the dozen featured living spaces and their owners paired with interviews that delve into the interior spaces and lives of the artists, writers, and other creative folks that are featured. Short stories, comics and snapshot-style images of lived-in spaces give this magazine a greater sense of intimacy and depth with its subjects. Recommended for all libraries, it may be best suited for academic libraries with art and design programs.

2944. ***Architectural Digest.*** [ISSN: 0003-8520] 1925. 11x/yr. USD 15. Ed(s): Amy Astley. Conde Nast Publications, Inc., 1 World Trade Center, New York, NY 10007; communications@condenast.com; http://www.condenast.com. Illus., adv. Vol. ends: Dec. Microform: PQC. *Indexed:* A&ATA, A01, A06, A22, AmHI, BRI, C37, F01, GardL, MASUSE, MLA-IB. *Aud.:* Ga, Ac.

Architectural Digest has long been acknowledged as a mainstay for celebrating international design that features lavish interiors of homes owned by the rich and famous. Each issue showcases residences exquisitely furnished with expensive antiques, objets d'art, and premium designer furniture. Occasional issues are devoted to a theme, such as collecting art, famous fashion industry folks, and (in January) the AD100 issue, featuring the top design talent. *Architectural Digest* is aimed at the well-to-do and cosmopolitan, with its glossy advertising of luxury products; with its showcase for antiques, designer, and collector items; and with its sophisticated international locations. Many readers, regardless of income, will find it appealing. A standard design magazine recommended for all libraries. URL: www.architecturaldigest.com

2945. ***Atomic Ranch: midcentury marvels.*** [ISSN: 1547-3902] 2004. q. USD 19.95; USD 32 combined subscription (print & online eds.); USD 6.99 per issue). Engaged Media Inc., 17890 Sky Park Circle, Ste. 250, Irvine, CA 92614; http://engagedmediamags.com/. Adv. *Aud.:* Ga, Ac, Sa.

Mid-century modern living at its finest: postwar, modern, ranch homes, and their furnishings are the focus of *Atomic Ranch.* This magazine often highlights renovations and makeovers for enthusiasts of mid-century housing with photographic spreads in glorious color. Recent issues include important architects; retro vacation spots; and a robust renovation issue. Departments let readers keep up with modernist furnishings and vendors. Chock-full of advertising for new products and appliances, plus sources for vintage furnishings, *Atomic Ranch* is a great source for mid-twentieth-century residential interiors. Additional information available on their website. Appropriate for all libraries. URL: www.atomic-ranch.com

Azure: design architecture & art. See Architecture section.

2946. *Contract: inspiring commercial design solutions.* Former titles (until 2000): *Contract Design;* (until 1990): *Contract.* [ISSN: 1530-6224] 1960. m. Free to qualified personnel. Ed(s): John Czarnecki, Danine Alati. Nielsen Business Publications, 85 Broad St, New York, NY 10004; ContactCommunications@nielsen.com; http://www.nielsenbusinessmedia.com. Illus., adv. Sample. Vol. ends: Dec. *Indexed:* B01, BRI. *Bk. rev.:* Number and length vary. *Aud.:* Ac, Sa.

Focusing on commercial interiors, *Contract* is an important magazine for industry information aimed at the design professional. Carefully lit, full-color interior photos illustrate trends in corporate, retail, hospitality, health-care, entertainment, government, educational, and institutional design. *Contract* also covers new-product information on floor and wall coverings, textiles, lighting, and furniture. Professional designers will value the wide variety of briefs on current practices, resources, materials, trends, and industry news. An annual source guide/brand report comes out in December of each year. Most useful is the website, which offers current design projects, industry updates, a vendor database, conferences, trade shows, and professional associations. The website offers everything needed to stay current in nonresidential design. Aimed at the architecture and design community, this core title is a must-have for all libraries that serve architects, design professionals, and students. URL: www.contractdesign.com

Cottages & Bungalows. See Home section.

Dwell. See Home section.

2947. *Elle Decor.* [ISSN: 1046-1957] 1989. 10x/yr. USD 10; USD 5.99 newsstand/cover. Ed(s): Michael Boodro, Gyna Soucy. Hearst Magazines, 300 W 57th St, 28th Fl, New York, NY 10019; HearstMagazines@hearst.com; http://www.hearst.com. Illus., adv. Vol. ends: Nov. *Indexed:* A22, C37. *Aud.:* Ga.

Elle Decor is like a fashion magazine for your home. Posh interiors, modern renovations, urban townhomes, and country retreats that are highlighted by colorful photography are the focus of this journal's articles, which feature artists and designers and their young, affluent clients. *Elle Decor* includes an abundance of artful objects, kitchen gadgets, bed-and-bath linens, furniture, and fixtures for the style-conscious individual. Each issue includes trend-setting designs that are inspirational and attainable. Resource contacts and reader services make this title valuable for both professionals and do-it-yourself decorators. The website includes decorating and remodeling tips, celebrity style, and shopping and entertaining advice. Suitable for public libraries, and all libraries that serve design professionals.

2948. *Frame.* [ISSN: 1388-4239] 1997. bi-m. EUR 109 (Students, EUR 89). Frame Publishers, Luchtvaartstraat 4, Amsterdam, 1059 CA, Netherlands; http://www.frameweb.com. Illus., adv. *Bk. rev.:* 5-7, 300 words. *Aud.:* Sa.

A glossy European magazine bursting with full-color photos, *Frame: The Great Indoors* focuses on sleek, ultra-contemporary designed objects and interiors from around the world targeting the commercial market. *Frame* succeeds in looking very different from other professional interiors magazines, and is enhanced with artful advertising for a wide range of international furniture, lighting, and designed objects; and it is targeted to creative professionals. Regular features include an in-depth portrait of new interior designers and architects, a handful of articles on business, retail, healthcare interiors and furnishings, and a multitude of briefs on new industrial designs from mobile homes to bars and museums. The website gives much of the print content at no cost, but with very few illustrations. Recommended for design collections. URL: www.framemag.com

2949. *Interior Design.* Former titles (until 1950): *Interior Design and Decoration;* (until 1937): *The Decorators Digest.* [ISSN: 0020-5508] 1932. m. USD 49.95 domestic; USD 77 Canada; USD 177 elsewhere. Ed(s): Helene Oberman. Sandow Media Corporation, 1271 Ave of the Americas, 17th Fl, New York, NY 10020; sandowinfo@sandowmedia.com; http://www.sandow.com. Illus. *Indexed:* A01, A06, A22, BRI, C37. *Bk. rev.:* 4-5, 150 words. *Aud.:* Ac, Sa.

Interior Design is renowned for its extensive coverage of commercial and residential interior design projects. The print edition offers broadly themed issues with lengthy feature articles on notable projects or design firms with beautifully shot interiors. Regular departments include "Headliners," "Blips," "Market," and the latest innovations in furnishings from international manufacturers. A subscription includes fall and spring "Market Tabloids," which feature new furnishing for home and office. The website serves the professional interior design community with new products, projects, industry giants, events, and a digital library of product source literature. Filled with color illustrations and industry advertising, it is recommended for all libraries and is a must-have for those that support the interior design community. URL: www.interiordesign.net

2950. *Interiors and Sources.* Former titles (until 2004): *I S Magazine;* (until 2002): *Interiors & Sources.* 198?. bi-m. Stamats Business Media, 615 5th St, S E, Cedar Rapids, IA 52401; salesmf@meetingsmedia.com; http://www.stamatscommunications.com/. Illus., index, adv. Sample. Vol. ends: Nov/Dec. *Aud.:* Ac, Sa.

Dedicated to the advancement of the commercial interior design professional, *IS* continues to focus on the newest and best products and designers. Each issue features designers and projects with photo essays on relevant topics for design problems, often thematic; for example, "The Influential Issue," "Art + Fashion" issue, and "Design Charrette." The journal also promotes best practices in professional design services. Regular departments include association forums, product sources, and industry news, all delivering relevant and timely information to design professionals. The journal's website is full of helpful content, from white papers and webinars, to materials resources and archives. Recommended for academic libraries with a design focus, and public libraries that serve the local interior design/architecture community. URL: www.interiorsandsources.com

2951. *Journal of Interior Design.* Formerly (until 1993): *Journal of Interior Design Education and Research.* [ISSN: 1071-7641] 1976. 3x/yr. GBP 481 (print & online eds.)). Ed(s): John C Turpin. Wiley-Blackwell Publishing, Inc., 350 Main St, Malden, MA 02148; cs-journals@wiley.com; http://onlinelibrary.wiley.com. Illus., index, adv. Sample. Refereed. Reprint: PSC. *Indexed:* A22, E01, ErgAb. *Bk. rev.:* 4-5, 500 words. *Aud.:* Ac.

Other academic journals exist with a broad design focus, but *Journal of Interior Design* is one of the few scholarly titles in print devoted to the interior design profession. Published by the Interior Design Educators Council, it focuses on education, practice, research, and theory, providing scholars and teachers with a forum for "scientific applications of design principles," historical research, and design processes in theory and practice. Each issue contains three to five articles that explore a wide variety of topics in interiors, from case studies to historic reviews. The council's website provides annual conference, membership, graduate program, and other information pertinent to design educators. Recommended for all academic collections that serve design programs. URL: www.idec.org

Metropolis: architecture and design at all scales. See Architecture section.

Old-House Journal. See Do-It-Yourself/Makers section.

Wallpaper. See Architecture section.

2952. *The World of Interiors.* Formerly (until 1982): *Interiors.* [ISSN: 0264-083X] 1981. m. GBP 18 for 6 mos. Ed(s): Augusta Pownall. Conde Nast Publications Ltd., Vogue House, Hanover Sq, London, W1S 1JU, United Kingdom; OnlineAdvertisingQueries@condenast.co.uk; http://www.worldofinteriors.co.uk. Illus. Circ: 58008. Vol. ends: Dec. *Indexed:* A22. *Bk. rev.:* 5-6, 500 words. *Aud.:* Ga, Sa.

This lush British monthly offers international coverage of residential interior design. Articles often feature renowned personalities and showcase royal abodes, historic homes, modern penthouses, and gardens from the whimsical to the formal that are located throughout the world, often in the United Kingdom. Fine art and antiques collections are also featured. Regular departments with catchy titles provide design trends, auction and fair dates, merchandise, and suppliers. Aimed at designers in the United Kingdom and their clients, this journal is best suited to large libraries that serve the design community.

■ INTERNATIONAL MAGAZINES

Elizabeth McKeigue, Executive Director of the Library, Salem State University, emckeigue@salemstate.edu

Introduction

This section recommends a list of popular general-interest magazines that represent multiple nations and languages. The primary criterion for selection is the appeal these titles would have in American libraries, either for studying another language, for learning about another culture, or for foreign-born nationals' wanting to stay in touch with news and culture from home.

The languages represented here include those frequently taught in American secondary schools and in universities, including English, Spanish, French, German, and Italian.

Titles included in this section have been chosen because of the high percentage of foreign-born nationals in the United States who speak, in addition to the languages already named, Russian, Arabic, Portuguese, and Serbo-Croatian. I recommend reviewing other sections in *Magazines for Libraries* that focus on a particular geographic area or a specific country (Canada, Africa, Asian American, and others) for references to general-interest periodicals for those areas. For example, most general-interest magazines in Spanish can be found in the "Latin America and Spain" section. Another consideration for selection for the titles in this section is that they are indexed in major American-produced indexes like Factiva, LexisNexis, and Academic Search Complete.

In addition, these magazines have been recommended because they offer robust content on their web sites, often for free, that make generous use of multimedia and utilize the latest tools for sharing links and getting newsfeeds.

Recommendations from experts and natives of foreign countries are welcome, so those may please feel free to contact me.

Basic Periodicals

Ga: *Elsevier* (Netherlands), *L'Espresso* (Italy), *L'Express* (France), *Ogonek* (Russia), *Paris Match* (France), *Der Spiegel* (Germany), *Stern* (Germany).

Basic Abstracts and Indexes

Factiva, IBZ, LexisNexis, Academic Search Complete.

2953. *Ahlan! (Arabic Edition).* [ISSN: 1728-3051] 2003. w. Ed(s): Andre Neveling. I T P Consumer Publishing, PO Box 500024, Dubai, , United Arab Emirates; info@itp.com; http://www.itp.com. *Aud.:* Ga.

In Arabic, from the United Arab Emirates. *Ahlan!* is as similar in scope (as it is in title) to Britain's *Hello!* magazine (*ahlan* means *hello* in Arabic). Offering fashion, royalty, and celebrity news, *Ahlan!* is not available in print in North America, but is accessible online, with full-content available, by subscription. An alternate edition [ISSN: 1727-5431] is also available in English. Recommended for libraries that support an Arabic-speaking population or Arabic-language programs. URL: http://ahlanlive.com

2954. *Bunte.* Incorporates: *Bunte Oesterreich;* Formerly: *Bunte Illustrierte.* [ISSN: 0172-2050] 1948. w. EUR 176.80; EUR 3.40 newsstand/cover. Ed(s): Patricia Riekel. Bunte Entertainment Verlag GmbH, Arabellastr 23, Munich, 81925, Germany; birgit.peters@burda.com; http://www.burda.com. Illus., adv. Sample. Circ: 500648 Paid. *Aud.:* Ga.

In German, from Germany. *Bunte* is the German equivalent of *People* magazine. It gives you entertainment news, style advice, and paparazzi photos of royalty, all with a European focus. It's great for students of German who are looking for some "fun" reading. Although the major focus is on European celebrities and royalty, there are also sections on sports, business, technology, travel, and health. Online, you'll find some of the same features of the print magazine and lots of photos of internationally famous people with their children. The travel advice section online is particularly good. Recommended for libraries that support elementary German-language programs or that cater to a German-speaking population. URL: http://bunte.de

2955. *Caras.* [ISSN: 0104-396X] 1993. w. BRL 400. Editora Abril, S.A., Avenida das Nacoes Unidas 7221, Pinheiros, Sao Paulo, 05425-902, Brazil; abrilsac@abril.com.br; http://www.abril.com.br. Illus., adv. *Bk. rev.:* Number and length vary. *Aud.:* Ga.

In Portuguese, from Brazil. If *Bunte* is Germany's *People* magazine, then *Caras* is the Brazilian *Bunte*! This magazine provides news and general-interest stories. Contents include feature articles and interviews with and photographs of celebrities. While each issue is just as likely as any American "celebrity" magazine to report on the latest Hollywood break-ups, the focus of *Caras* is almost entirely on the entertainment and sport stars of Latin America, particularly Brazil. There are even some stories about ordinary people as celebrities. Rich with advertising, photos, book reviews, film (and some theater) reviews, and music reviews, *Caras* is pretty to look at and great for popular culture news from Brazil. The web site provides a wealth of free content, including videos and news feeds. Recommended for public libraries that serve Brazilian Portuguese-speaking communities and for academic libraries that support Portuguese-language programs. URL: http://caras.uol.com.br

Contenido. See Latin America and Spain section.

2956. *Dani.* [ISSN: 1512-5130] 1992. w. Ed(s): Vildana Selimbegovic. Civitas d.o.o., Skenderija 31A, Sarajevo, 71000, Bosnia & Herzegovina. Illus., adv. *Bk. rev.:* Number and length vary. *Aud.:* Ga.

In Serbo-Croatian, from Bosnia and Herzegovina. *Nezavisni* is a weekly magazine that has been in print since 1992. It is also known by the English translation of its title, *Independent Magazine Dani.* Articles include such content as news (from Bosnia and Herzegovina and beyond); coverage of social issues; interviews; and book, film, music, video, DVD, and television reviews. Recommended for public libraries that serve an immigrant Balkan population and for academic libraries that support Slavic Studies programs.

The Economist. See Economics section.

2957. *Elsevier.* Incorporates (1970-1998): *Elseviers Weekblad;* Formerly (until 1987): *Elseviers Magazine.* [ISSN: 0922-3444] 1944. w. EUR 6 per month. Ed(s): J A S Joustra. ONE Business B.V., Spaklerweg 53, Amsterdam-Duivendrecht, 1114 AE, Netherlands; info@onebusiness.nl; https://www.onebusiness.nl. Illus., adv. *Indexed:* A22. *Aud.:* Ga.

In Dutch, from the Netherlands. A primary newsmagazine in the Netherlands, *Elsevier* is the publication that lent its name to the well-known publishing company. Articles present research and commentary on a variety of social, political, and cultural topics. This glossy magazine is easily browsable and is probably most reminiscent of *Time* or *Newsweek.* Many issues focus on business and the European economy. Another popular topic is American politics, particularly the relationship between the United States and the European Union. *Elsevier* is an excellent resource for Dutch-reading students of Europe and politics. Recommended for research and large academic libraries. URL: http://elsevier.nl

2958. *L'Espresso: settimanale di politica, cultura, economia.* [ISSN: 0423-4243] 1955. w. EUR 59 domestic. Gruppo Editoriale l' Espresso SpA, Via Cristoforo Colombo 149, Rome, 00147, Italy; espresso@espressoedit.it; http://www.espressoedit.it. Illus., adv. Sample. Microform: PQC. *Indexed:* A22. *Aud.:* Ga.

In Italian, from Italy. This newsmagazine provides articles on a variety of general-interest topics, such as politics, culture, business, health, religion, and world news (from an Italian point of view). Although heavy on advertising, this magazine nonetheless provides nice photographic essays, detailed articles, and reviews. The well-designed web site has full text of current issues that are freely available (in both Italian and English) and includes a section of blogs on various topics (in Italian only). The web site also has video and audio files freely available. Strongly recommended for libraries that serve Italian-speaking patrons or students of Italian. URL: http://espresso.repubblica.it/

2959. ***L'Express.*** [ISSN: 0014-5270] 1953. w. Ed(s): Denis Jeambar. Groupe Express-Roularta, 29 Rue de Chateaudun, Paris Cedex 09, 75308, France; http://www.groupe-exp.com. Illus., adv. Sample. Microform: PQC. *Indexed:* BRI, PdeR. *Aud.:* Ga.

In French, from France. In print since 1953, this news and current affairs magazine offers investigative articles and point-of-view pieces on a variety of political and social debates, both in France and the wider world. Specific sections include world news, French issues, society, science and health, media (television and film), sport, and photographic essays. Like its Italian counterpart *L'Espresso, L'Express* has a very good web site, and complete articles from the current edition are available for free. Both the print and the online versions include advertising, and articles are frequently punctuated with photos, graphs, charts, and illustrations. Highly recommended for large public and most academic libraries. URL: www.lexpress.fr

2960. ***Focus (Munich): das moderne Nachrichtenmagazin.*** [ISSN: 0943-7576] 1993. w. EUR 234; EUR 4.50 newsstand/cover. Focus Magazin Verlag GmbH, Arabellastr 23, Munich, 81925, Germany; medialine@focus.de; http://www.focus.de. Illus., adv. Sample. *Indexed:* A22. *Aud.:* Ga, Ac.

In German, from Germany. This newsmagazine includes in-depth reporting on world news (from a German perspective), business, technology, health, culture, and sports. *Focus* also has an annual ranking of the top German universities. Each issue includes many photographs, statistics, charts, and graphs. The letters to the editor give a good idea of current topics of political debate in Germany. The online version includes full text of the current issue for free. The online version also features a blog and video downloads of recent news stories from "Focus Online TV." Recommended primarily for academic and research libraries. Public libraries may want to consider this magazine if they support a user population of German speakers. URL: www.focus.de

2961. ***Iceland Review: the magazine of Iceland.*** Former titles (until 1985): *Atlantica and Iceland Review;* (until 1967): *Iceland Review.* [ISSN: 1670-004X] 1963. q. USD 40. Ed(s): Pall Stefansson. Heimur hf., Borgartuni 23, Reykjavik, 105, Iceland; heimur@heimur.is; http://www.heimur.is. Illus., adv. Sample. Circ: 20000. *Bk. rev.:* Number and length vary. *Aud.:* Ga.

In English, German, and some Icelandic, from Iceland. Articles in *Iceland Review* focus on Icelandic nature, culture, art, literature, and daily life. The online version includes daily news stories. Each issue includes advertising, interviews, classifieds, book reviews, and still, after all these years, at least one mention of Bjork. The primary focus of the magazine is promoting tourism in Iceland. Articles highlight the activities in Iceland that make it a unique travel experience, such as hiking, bathing in outdoor hot springs, or surfing. Recommended for libraries that support a Scandinavian Studies program or libraries that serve a significant population of Scandinavian Americans. URL: www.icelandreview.com

2962. ***Knack.*** [ISSN: 0772-3210] 1971. w. EUR 183. Roularta Media Group, Meiboomlaan 33, Roeselare, 8800, Belgium; info@roularta.be; http://www.roularta.be. Illus., adv. *Bk. rev.:* Number and length vary. *Aud.:* Ga, Ac.

In Dutch, from Belgium. This glossy popular magazine covers news, politics, business, literature, films, celebrity news, and sports in Belgium. Each issue of *Knack* includes lists of the top-selling books, films, and music in Belgium. Those lists and the full text of most articles from the current issue are also found on the web. Sections include news, economy, technology, lifestyle, entertainment, and sport. Recommended for large public libraries and for large academic libraries that support European Studies programs. URL: www.knack.be

Maclean's. See Canada section.

2963. ***Magazin-Deutschland.de (English Edition).*** Former titles (until 2009): *Deutschland (English Edition);* (until 1993): *Scala;* (until 1973): *Scala International.* 1961. bi-m. Ed(s): Peter Hintereder. Frankfurter Societaets-Medien GmbH, Frankenallee 71-81, Frankfurt am Main, 60327, Germany; vertrieb@societaets-verlag.de; https://societaets-verlag.de. Illus., adv. *Indexed:* A22. *Bk. rev.:* Number and length vary. *Aud.:* Ga.

In English, from Germany. This primarily English-language magazine is great way for non-German-speaking Germany lovers to learn about today's Germany. It is published six times a year by Societats-Verlag, Frankfurt am Main, in cooperation with the Federal Foreign Office, Berlin. Articles focus on political, economic, scientific, and cultural events in Germany, and are written by German journalists. The magazine also includes advertising, photos, interesting photographic essays, and book and film reviews. The content-rich online version is available in a variety of languages, including French, Arabic, Spanish, and Portuguese. Highly recommended for large public and all academic libraries. URL: www.deutschland.de/en

2964. ***Al- Majalla.*** Formerly (until 200?): *Al- Majalla (Print).* 1980. w. Saudi Research & Publishing Co., PO Box 478, Riyadh, 11411, Saudi Arabia; editorial@majalla.com; http://www.srpc.com. Illus., adv. Circ: 92860 Paid. *Aud.:* Ga.

In Arabic, from Saudi Arabia. This weekly magazine is available online with all content accessible for free. It covers news, business, culture, and social issues of the Arab world. It is recommended for libraries with an Arabic-speaking population and for libraries that support Arabic language programs. URL: www.majalla.com/ar

2965. ***The Monthly: Australian politics, society and culture.*** [ISSN: 1832-3421] 2005. m. AUD 99.95 combined subscription (print & online eds.); AUD 11.95 newsstand/cover). Ed(s): Nick Feik. The Monthly Pty Ltd, 37-39 Langridge St, Collingwood, VIC 3066, Australia; subscribe@themonthly.com.au. Adv. Circ: 29769. *Bk. rev.:* Number and length vary. *Aud.:* Ga.

In English, from Australia. This news and culture magazine is like a mash-up of *Vanity Fair, The New Yorker,* and *The Atlantic* for Australians. With well-researched and informative articles, *The Monthly* opens a window onto Australian culture, politics, and society that will appeal to native Australians and Australiophiles alike. Regular features include news commentary, book and media reviews (including film and theater), interviews, and essays from regular columnists. Recommended for large public or academic libraries. URL: http://themonthly.com.au

2966. ***Norwegians Worldwide.*** Formerly (until 2012): *Norseman;* Incorporates (1907-1984): *Nordmanns-forbundet.* [ISSN: 1893-0042] 1943. 4x/yr. NOK 450 (Students, NOK 350). Nordmanns-Forbundet, Raadhusgatan 23 B, Oslo, 0158, Norway; info@nww.no; http://www.nww.no. Illus., adv. *Indexed:* MLA-IB. *Bk. rev.:* Number and length vary. *Aud.:* Ga.

In English and some Norwegian, from Norway. Written more for Norwegian Americans than for Norwegians, *Norwegians Worldwide* includes feature articles, interviews, photos, advertising, illustrations, and book reviews. The focus is primarily on cultural and historical issues. It is published by Nordmanns Forbundet under the patronage of His Majesty the King of Norway. Included are letters to the editor, articles on business (particularly shipping), Norway's relationship with the United States and Norwegian Americans, the history of Norway and Scandinavia, travel, and sports. Recommended for libraries that support a population of Scandinavian Americans, or academic libraries that support Scandinavian Studies programs. URL: www.nww.no/

2967. ***Novoe Vremya: ezhenedel'nyi zhurnal.*** [ISSN: 0137-0723] 1943. w. Ed(s): Evginiya Al'bats. Izdatel'stvo Novoe Vremya, Tverskoi bul'var, dom 14, stroenie 1, Moscow, 125009, Russian Federation. Illus., adv. Microform: BHP; EVP; MIM; PQC. *Bk. rev.:* Number and length vary. *Aud.:* Ga.

In Russian, from Russia. This magazine includes news, blogs, and articles on a variety of topics of interest to Russian emigres and to students of the Russian language. It is packed with glossy photos and advertising, as well as charts, illustrations, and book, film, and music reviews. Recommended for public libraries that serve a Russian-speaking population and for academic libraries that support Slavic Studies programs. URL: http://newtimes.ru

2968. ***Oggi.*** [ISSN: 0030-0705] 1945. w. Ed(s): Pino Belleri. R C S Periodici, Via San Marco 21, Milan, 20121, Italy; info@periodici.rcs.it; http://www.rcsmediagroup.it/siti/periodici.php. Illus., adv. *Indexed:* MLA-IB. *Aud.:* Ga.

In Italian, from Italy. This current-affairs journal features articles by some of Italy's top journalists. Published since 1945, *Oggi* is the traditional weekly magazine of the Italian family. As such, it features investigative reports and interviews of interest to most Italians.

2969. ***Ogonek.*** [ISSN: 0131-0097] 1899. w. Izdatel'stvo Ogonek, Bumazhnyi pr 14, Moscow, 101456, Russian Federation. Illus., adv. Vol. ends: Dec. *Indexed:* CDSP, MLA-IB. *Aud.:* Ga, Ac.

In Russian, from Russia. Published since 1899, this weekly magazine features articles on current news events and interviews with people in the news. Highly recommended for libraries that serve a Russian-speaking population, and for most academic libraries.

2970. ***Paris Match.*** Former titles (until 1976): *Nouveau Paris Match;* (until 1972): *Paris Match.* [ISSN: 0397-1635] 1949. w. EUR 96. Ed(s): Didier Rapaud. Hachette Filipacchi Associes S.A., 149/151 Rue Anatole France, Levallois-Perret, 925340, France; segolene.delloye@lagardere-active.com; http://www.lagardere.com. Illus., adv. *Indexed:* MLA-IB, PdeR. *Aud.:* Ga.

In French, from France. *Paris Match* is one of the most widely read magazines in France. With its combination of news, current affairs, celebrity interviews, and great photography, this magazine is also a favorite of Francophones (and Francophiles) all over the world. There is a stylish web site where one can find a number of articles from the current and past issues in full text without a subscription. It is also one of the few commercial web sites with a bare minimum of annoying pop-up advertisements. Highly recommended for public and academic libraries everywhere. URL: www.parismatch.com

2971. ***Le Point.*** [ISSN: 0242-6005] 1972. w. EUR 98 domestic; EUR 139 in Belgium & Luxembourg; EUR 149 in Europe. Ed(s): Jean Schmitt. Le Point, 74 av. du Maine, Paris, 75014, France; cyber@lepoint.tm.fr; http://www.lepoint.fr. Illus. Microform: PQC. *Indexed:* A22, PdeR. *Aud.:* Ga, Ac.

In French, from France. The primary competitor of *L'Express* for the distinction of being France's top newsmagazine, *Le Point* has been covering news and current-interest stories since 1972. Main features include editorials, letters, world news, news from France, society, business, economics, and media/technology. Most issues also include essays on travel, food, wine, cinema, literature, and art. The table of contents can be found online, but one must subscribe to the magazine to receive electronic access to the full text of the current issue. *Le Point* is an important resource for the study of current events and issues in France. Highly recommended for large public libraries and most academic libraries. URL: www.lepoint.fr

Proceso. See Latin America and Spain section.

2972. ***Der Spiegel.*** [ISSN: 0038-7452] 1947. w. EUR 208 domestic; EUR 262.20 per issue in Europe; EUR 340.60 per issue elsewhere. Ed(s): Wolfgang Buechner. Spiegel-Verlag Rudolf Augstein GmbH und Co. KG, Ericusspitze 1, Hamburg, 20457, Germany. Illus., adv. Sample. *Indexed:* A22, BAS. *Aud.:* Ga, Ac.

In German, from Germany. Packed with more than 200 pages of text, this magazine is one of the most popular in Germany. With text entirely in German, each issue includes many articles (both short pieces and longer features) on politics (both German and worldwide), business, current affairs, culture, technology, and sport. Think of this journal as *Time* magazine in German. *Der Spiegel* is known for its superior investigative reporting, especially in the area of German and European politics. The online version is updated daily and includes the full text of the current weekly print issue. If you can purchase just one magazine in German, this should be it. Strongly recommended for academic, research, and public libraries. URL: www.spiegel.de

2973. ***Stern.*** [ISSN: 0039-1239] 1948. w. EUR 244.40; EUR 4.70 newsstand/cover. Ed(s): Christian Krug. Gruner + Jahr GmbH & Co KG, Am Baumwall 11, Hamburg, 20459, Germany; info@gujmedia.de; http://www.guj.de. Illus., adv. Sample. *Aud.:* Ga, Ac.

In German, from Germany. *Stern* is a current-affairs magazine that provides articles on news and culture but seems to focus primarily on lifestyle issues, particularly stories about ordinary Germans faced with extraordinary circumstances. Articles report from both scientific and humanistic points of view. A unique feature of *Stern* is its bestseller list that ranks the week's 20 most popular books, films, DVDs, and music CDs in Germany. The electronic version includes the full text of the current issue and an archive of articles that have appeared in the past six months. As one of the most intellectually accessible magazines in Germany, *Stern* is highly recommended for academic and public libraries. URL: www.stern.de

2974. ***Suomen Kuvalehti.*** [ISSN: 0039-5552] 1916. w. 49/yr. EUR 218. Ed(s): Ville Pernaa, Tapani Ruokanen. Otavamedia Ltd., Maistraatinportti 1, Helsinki, 00015, Finland; asiakaspalvelu@otavamedia.fi; http://www.otavamedia.fi. Illus., adv. Circ: 86786. *Bk. rev.:* Number and length vary. *Aud.:* Ga, Ac.

In Finnish, from Finland. This newsmagazine is the most popular and well-respected in Finland. It is reminiscent of other newsmagazines that are known for their strong current-affairs reporting, such as *Der Spiegel, Time, L'Express,* among others. Most articles focus on politics, economics, and culture, in Finland and abroad. Each issue includes ample advertising, and articles are illustrated with charts, graphs, statistics, and photos. Issues generally include book reviews. The online version provides the full text of articles in all issues since early 2003. Recommended for large public libraries and academic libraries that support Slavic, Scandinavian, or European Studies. URL: www.suomenkuvalehti.fi

■ JOURNALISM AND WRITING

Journalism/Writing/Pedagogy

Caroline M. Kent, Director of Research Support and Instruction, Shain Library, Connecticut College, New London, CT 06320; ckent@conncoll.edu

Introduction

As the Internet and its importance grew, print sources began to struggle, and in many cases, fail. This was particularly true for those sources that contained fleeting, constantly changing information, that is to say, print newspapers. By 2009, major print newspapers began to decrease in number, and local newspapers fared even worse. Online news sources, of course, were flourishing. But the editorial processes, fact-checking, and archiving seemed unimportant to many of their producers. Correspondingly, schools of journalism began to stagger slightly. How to adapt? How to educate? How to survive?

This edition of *Magazines for Libraries* section began to suffer. The smaller journals began to disappear. Opinion and news columns began to reflect the anxiety of the profession.

The traditional ethical imperatives of accuracy and fairness were looking old fashioned to much of the reading public, a public that was already consuming large numbers of dubious tabloids, and, of course, was beginning to consume large amounts of reality TV, a medium that created further ethical chaos. And then, of course, there was the ever-increasing importance of social media in everyone's life. Importance? Well, maybe centrality has been a better word.

Were old, serious, and legitimate print news sources going to survive? Was the profession going to survive? Was the ethos that had traditionally dominated their editorial policies going to survive? Did people care? Did it matter? Traditionalists wrung their hands and struggled, and appeared to be giving up their positions.

Whether or not you agree with the politics of our current presidential administration in Washington, it cannot be disputed that out of this chaos rose Donald Trump. Created by the short business view of high stakes real estate and by reality TV, he brought the promise of "the now." Watch me now, don't worry about what I've done, and our chaos can change the future.

For several years now, the United States has been swimming in this murky pool of "the now": fake news, election interference by the Russians, Twitter storms, the Alt Right phenomena, WikiLeaks. We all read news off of Twitter and FaceBook streams, and our country is now led by someone who happily swims daily in that murky pool, making his own cultural- and political-shattering contributions.

However, as the national murkiness grew, there came a rebirth of legit news and journalism. Fact-checking became a national pastime; ethical arguments against "the now" grew and grew. The swamp was not drained, but people are beginning to step back from it in horror. The newspaper industry has begun to stabilize. Yes, many smaller newspapers disappeared, replaced by dubious, ad-driven online sites. But the big national newspapers strengthened and thrived. Some of this has to do with social and political backlash, but it also has to do with the industry finding new business models. Publications were finding a good balance between online content and print content.

I ended the last edition's essay with: "...traditional mainstream journalists and writers have once again found their footing." Like Gandalf when faced with the Balrog in the movie *The Fellowship of the Rings*, journalists have planted their staffs in front of the chaos and said "You shall not pass!" This is now even truer.

Basic Periodicals

JOURNALISM. Ga: *American Journalism, Columbia Journalism Review, Newspaper Research Journal.*

WRITING. Hs: *Writer's Digest;* Ga: *Poets & Writers Magazine, Writer's Digest;* Ac: *Poets & Writers Magazine.*

PEDAGOGY. Ac: *Assessing Writing, Journalism & Mass Communication Educator.*

Basic Abstracts and Indexes

Communication Abstracts; MLA International Bibliography; Readers' Guide to Periodical Literature.

Journalism

2975. *American Journalism.* [ISSN: 0882-1127] 1983. q. GBP 355 (print & online eds.)). Ed(s): Ford Risley. Taylor & Francis Inc., 711 3rd Ave, 8th Fl, New York, NY 10017; support@tandfonline.com; http://www.taylorandfrancis.com. Adv. Sample. Refereed. Reprint: PSC. *Indexed:* A22, AmHI. *Bk. rev.:* 8-10, 500-1,000 words. *Aud.:* Ac.

This small scholarly journal always seems to be packed with fascinating articles—fascinating not just to media historians, but also to anyone interested in cultural history. It contains excellent book reviews, and now also includes digital media reviews. Some recent article titles include "Journalism Versus the Flying Saucers: Assessing the First Generation of UFO Reportage, 1947-1967," "Stoicism and Courage as Journalistic Values: What Early Journalism Textbooks Taught About Newsroom Ethos," and "Poor Richard Revised: Benjamin Franklin and the Ritual Economy of Copyright in Colonial America." The writing is livelier than that found in many scholarly journals (perhaps because of the journalistic orientation of many of the authors), but this in no way detracts from the serious nature of the publication. Given that its articles cross disciplinary lines, and given that the journal is well indexed, it should be purchased by any academic library with serious history programs and media-history collections.

2976. *Columbia Journalism Review.* Incorporates: *More Magazine; Public Interest Alert; Media and Consumer.* [ISSN: 0010-194X] 1961. bi-m. USD 19.95 domestic; USD 27.95 combined subscription domestic (print & online eds.); USD 35.95 combined subscription foreign (print & online eds.)). Ed(s): Elizabeth Spayd. Columbia University, Graduate School of Journalism, 801 Pulitzer Hall, 2950 Broadway, New York, NY 10027; http://www.journalism.columbia.edu. Illus., adv. Vol. ends: No. 6. Microform: PQC. *Indexed:* A01, A22, AmHI, B01, BRI, CBRI, F01. *Bk. rev.:* 4-6, 100-300 words; 1-2, 1,000-2,000 words. *Aud.:* Hs, Ga, Ac.

This wonderfully accessible, well-edited journal also has an excellent website where many of its articles are archived in full text. Further, there are up-to-date pieces on very current news, of which there is currently a lot to cover! Coverage ranges from journalistic practice to articles of both national and international newsworthiness. It is also one of the publications that is taking on the issues of digital versus print reporting very effectively. Some recent article titles include "What remains of the Turkish press" and "Targeted by Duterte." The book review section is a particularly rich one. Each issue not only contains four to six short (100- to 300-word) book reports, but also one or two extensive, in-depth reviews. Despite its high academic pedigree, this magazine would be a very good choice not only for college and university libraries but also for high school libraries (at an excellent price). Public libraries that serve populations with a high interest in current events should also consider it.

2977. *Digital Journalism.* [ISSN: 2167-0811] 2013. 10x/yr. GBP 465 (print & online eds.)). Ed(s): Oscar Westlund. Routledge, 4 Park Sq, Milton Park, Abingdon, OX14 4RN, United Kingdom; subscriptions@tandf.co.uk; http://www.tandfonline.com. Refereed. *Bk. rev.:* 1-4, varies. *Aud.:* Ac, Sa.

Among this journal's ambitious goals are: "Digital media and the future of journalism; Social media as sources and drivers of news; The changing places and spaces of news production and consumption in the context of digital media; News on the move and mobile telephony; The personalisation of news; Business models for funding digital journalism in the digital economy." The journal succeeds admirably with these goals. Some titles of recent articles include "Who shared it? Deciding what news to trust on social media," and "The paradox of participation versus misinformation: social media, political engagement, and the spread of misinformation." You can look at any one issue and find multiple articles of interest, even if your field is not journalism. But the recommendation would be that academic libraries serving populations of serious journalism and communication programs should consider its purchase, or at least be very aware of it. For the only negative thing about this excellent journal is its price. However, given where it is indexed and the libraries that do own it, access to content and then retrieval of specific articles will be possible.

2978. *International Journal of Press / Politics.* Formerly (until 2008): *The Harvard International Journal of Press / Politics.* [ISSN: 1940-1612] 1996. q. USD 827 (print & online eds.)). Ed(s): Rasmus Kleis Nielsen. Sage Publications, Inc., 2455 Teller Rd, Thousand Oaks, CA 91320; info@sagepub.com; http://www.sagepub.com. Illus., adv. Sample. Refereed. Vol. ends: Fall. Reprint: PSC. *Indexed:* A01, A22, B01, E01, P61, SSA. *Bk. rev.:* 4-6, 100-250 words, signed. *Aud.:* Ac.

This journal strives to address the academic needs of journalists, politicians, and political scientists. It is heavily academic, with well-written, well-referenced, refereed articles. In addition to the feature articles, issues often lead off with a substantive interview with a well-known practitioner. Recent articles include "From Epistemic to Identity Crisis: Perspectives on the 2016 U.S. Presidential Election" and "Protests, Media Coverage, and a Hierarchy of Social Struggle." Academic libraries in colleges or universities with strong political science, communication, or journalism programs will want this title.

2979. *Journal of Mass Communication and Journalism.* [ISSN: 2165-7912] 2011. m. Free. Ed(s): Massimo Cecaro. Omics Publishing Group, 5716 Corsa Ave, Ste 110, Los Angeles, CA 91362; info@omicsonline.org; http://www.omicsonline.org. Refereed. *Aud.:* Ac.

This journal seeks to be "a broad-based journal [that] was founded on two key tenets: To publish the most exciting researches with respect to the subjects of [m]ass communication [and j]ournalism. Secondly, to provide [the most] rapid turn-around time possible for reviewing and publishing, and to disseminate the articles freely for research, teaching and reference purposes." In keeping with these aims, it is, in fact, an open-access journal, only available on the web and freely available. It seeks to contribute an international scope to the issues. Some recent articles are "Coverage of Honor Killing: A Content Analysis of English Language Newspapers of Pakistan" and "Pictorial Communication in Digital Era: Challenges and Prospects." The OMICS website provides metrics, Google Translator, varying available formats, links to Twitter, and Facebook. Is this what all journals may eventually look like? We might say...PLEASE. Recommended for academic libraries with collections for journalism and communications programs.

2980. ***Journal of Media Ethics: exploring questions of media morality.*** Formerly (until 2015): *Journal of Mass Media Ethics.* [ISSN: 2373-6992] 1985. q. GBP 651 (print & online eds.)). Ed(s): Patrick Lee Plaisance. Routledge, 530 Walnut St, Ste 850, Philadelphia, PA 19106; enquiries@tandfonline.com; http://www.tandfonline.com. Illus., adv. Sample. Refereed. Microform: PQC. Reprint: PSC. *Indexed:* A01, A22, AmHI, B01, BRI, E01, F01, P61. *Bk. rev.:* Number and length vary. *Aud.:* Ac.

As we watch the growing confusion between reporting and media experts with government sources, we learn quickly that ethical behavior and moral positioning are critical for our journalists. This academic journal does not take positions, but rather includes articles that articulate conflicts and present and define ethical issues. Some recent articles include "Perceived Ethical Performance of News Media: Regaining Public Trust and Encouraging News Participation" and "Cyberbullies, Trolls, and Stalkers: Students' Perceptions of Ethical Issues in Social Media." It includes a varying number of substantive book reviews, as well as case studies. Appropriate for academic libraries that serve communications and journalism departments.

2981. ***Journalism & Mass Communication Quarterly.*** Former titles (until 1995): *Journalism Quarterly;* (until 1928): *The Journalism Bulletin;* (until 1924): *American Association of Teachers of Journalism. Monthly Newsletter.* [ISSN: 1077-6990] 1915. q. USD 434 (print & online eds.)). Ed(s): Louisa Ha. Sage Publications, Inc., 2455 Teller Rd, Thousand Oaks, CA 91320; info@sagepub.com; http://www.sagepub.com. Illus., adv. Refereed. Vol. ends: Winter. Microform: PQC. Reprint: PSC. *Indexed:* A01, A22, AmHI, B01, BAS, BRI, CBRI, F01, IBSS, MLA-IB, P61. *Bk. rev.:* 12-25, 700-1,200 words. *Aud.:* Ac.

This scholarly publication "strives to be the flagship journal of the Association for Education in Journalism and Mass Communication." Its articles develop theory, introduce new ideas, and work to challenge the boundaries of the existing bodies of research. Its issues often contain themes, such as "Advertising Effects," "Copyright Law," and "Research Methodology." Some recent titles of articles include "Is Facebook Making Us Dumber? Exploring Social Media Use as a Predictor of Political Knowledge" and "The Digital Architectures of Social Media: Comparing Political Campaigning on Facebook, Twitter, Instagram, and Snapchat in the 2016 U.S. Election." This is an interesting journal, filled with thoughtful, well-researched articles. Any library that serves academic programs in communications and journalism should subscribe to it.

2982. ***Journalism Studies.*** [ISSN: 1461-670X] 2000. bi-m. Ed(s): Bob Franklin. Routledge, 4 Park Sq, Milton Park, Abingdon, OX14 4RN, United Kingdom; subscriptions@tandf.co.uk; http://www.tandfonline.com. Adv. Sample. Refereed. Reprint: PSC. *Indexed:* A01, A22, E01. *Bk. rev.:* 8-12, 800-1,200 words. *Aud.:* Ac.

This British journal, published in association with the European Journalism Training Association, is geared to serious journalists and journalism historians. Some recent articles include "Weathering the Storm: Occupational Stress in Journalists Who Covered Hurricane Harvey," "The Rise of a Populist Zeitgeist? A Content Analysis of Populist Media Coverage in Newspapers Published between 1990 and 2017," and "Coping with Audience Hostility. How Journalists' Experiences of Audience Hostility Influence Their Editorial Decisions." It contains regular columns such as "Debate," "Reviews," and "Feature Review." Yes, this *is* a relatively expensive journal—expensive enough that some academic libraries will decide not to purchase it. But for university libraries that serve strong journalism programs, it is invaluable. Full text is available online.

2983. ***Newspaper Research Journal.*** [ISSN: 0739-5329] 1979. q. USD 465 (print & online eds.)). Ed(s): Elinor Kelley Grusin, Sandra H Utt. Sage Publications, Inc., 2455 Teller Rd, Thousand Oaks, CA 91320; info@sagepub.com; http://www.sagepub.com. Illus. Refereed. Vol. ends: Fall. Reprint: PSC. *Indexed:* A01, A22, BRI. *Bk. rev.:* 3-5, 500-750 words. *Aud.:* Ac.

This scholarly journal addresses the needs of both the journalism student and the serious media practitioner. Its articles are well written, interesting, and often practical. Sometimes an entire issue will be dedicated to a particular topic. In others, there is a wide selection of articles, such as "Mediating empathy: The role of news consumption in mitigating attitudes about race and immigration," "News stories framed episodically offer more diversified portrayals of immigrants," and "Civic participation and connectivity with a metro newspaper." Libraries that support serious journalism programs should consider this journal.

2984. ***Nieman Reports.*** [ISSN: 0028-9817] 1947. q. USD 25 domestic; USD 35 foreign. Ed(s): James Geary. Nieman Foundation for Journalism at Harvard, One Francis Ave, Cambridge, MA 02138; http://www.nieman.harvard.edu. Illus., index. Vol. ends: Dec. *Indexed:* A01, A22, B01, BRI. *Bk. rev.:* 3-6, 700-1,500 words, signed. *Aud.:* Ga, Ac.

This title publishes articles intended to be thought-provoking discussions for practitioners on current events and issues surrounding the profession of journalism. The breadth of its articles, however, should give it a much wider audience. Some recent titles include "Why Newsrooms Are Unionizing Now," "Three News Outlets Discover Fresh Collaborators and Audiences in Libraries," and "Journalism and Libraries: Both Exist to Support Strong, Well-informed Communities." It contains excellent book reviews and alumni reports for Harvard's Nieman fellows. This journal should be purchased by academic libraries that serve journalism programs, as well as ones with active public service programs. Public libraries that serve well-read audiences should also consider it.

2985. ***Social Media and Society.*** [ISSN: 2056-3051] 2015. q. Free. Ed(s): Zizi Papacharissi. Sage Publications Ltd., 1 Oliver's Yard, 55 City Rd, London, EC1Y 1SP, United Kingdom; https://www.sagepub.com/. Refereed. *Aud.:* Ac.

Social Media and Society is not strictly, or simply, a journalism publication. It is very interdisciplinary, ranging from ethical, to historical, to social, to political content. But it has a heavy emphasis, clearly, on media, and in particular, social media. In our current climate, you cannot talk about journalism without talking about the issues surrounding social media. Titles of some recent articles include "Analysis of Facebook Meme Groups Used During the 2016 US Presidential Election," "Winning on Social Media: Candidate Social-Mediated Communication and Voting During the 2016 US Presidential Election," and "Breakdown of Democratic Norms? Understanding the 2016 US Presidential Election Through Online Comments." It is a substantive peer-reviewed scholarly journal, which is also open access. As such, it would be well "placed" in the collections of any academic setting.

Writing

2986. ***Mslexia: the magazine for women who write.*** [ISSN: 1473-9399] 1999. q. GBP 25 domestic. Mslexia Publications Ltd., PO Box 656, Newcastle upon Tyne, NE99 1PZ, United Kingdom; postbag@mslexia.co.uk. Illus., adv. *Bk. rev.:* Number and length vary. *Aud.:* Hs, Ga, Ac, Sa.

The term *Mslexia* was coined to express the condition of "women being unable to get into print easily." This interesting journal not only seeks to address this issue, but also to give women a forum so that they can get into print. It includes feature articles, relevant book reviews, new writing, and editorial opinion. It has an obvious British bias, but that should not preclude American libraries from buying it. It talks technology, writing technique, and the art of writing. Its content is thoughtful, sometimes edgy, and always interesting. Some recent articles include "Crime: an exploration into why so many romance writers successfully turn their pens to crime" and "Agenda: a deep dive by Editor

Debbie Taylor into the revolutionary effects of cultural democracy." For academic libraries with good writing programs, and for large public libraries that serve the interests of a writing community.

2987. ***New Writing: the international journal for the practice and theory of creative writing.*** [ISSN: 1479-0726] 2004. 3x/yr. GBP 234 (print & online eds.)). Ed(s): Graeme Harper. Routledge, 4 Park Sq, Milton Park, Abingdon, OX14 4RN, United Kingdom; subscriptions@tandf.co.uk; http://www.tandfonline.com. Adv. Sample. Refereed. Reprint: PSC. *Indexed:* AmHI, MLA-IB. *Aud.:* Ac, Sa.

This journal purports to contain "both critical and creative work—offering a forum for debate, as well as an avenue for the publication of the best stories, poems, works of creative non-fiction or works for the stage or for the screen, in all its contemporary varieties." Though this title had a slow start, the most recent years' content clearly demonstrates its success with its mission. Generally, it is odd that writers, and in particular creative writers, frequently do not seem to write about what they do. There are notable exceptions to that, of course. But many creative writers tend to leave how-we-do-it to literature critics who write how-they-do-it pieces. This British journal has articles from academics teaching writing, literature critics, and creative writers. Some recent titles include "How to do things with words: teaching creative writing as performance" and "Transitioning from soldiers to captives: how New Zealand POWs used poetry to reinterpret their capture experience." In this era when historians are coming to write fictionalized history, and fiction writers are coming to write on only slivers of reality, this journal fits into an interesting niche. Any academic library that serves either a population of creative writers or those teaching creative writing should consider this journal's purchase.

2988. ***Poets & Writers Magazine.*** Formerly (until 1987): *Coda: Poets and Writers Newsletter.* [ISSN: 0891-6136] 1972. bi-m. USD 15.95 combined subscription (print & online eds.)). Ed(s): Kevin Larimer. Poets & Writers, Inc., 90 Broad St, Ste 2100, New York, NY 10004; http://www.pw.org. Illus., adv. *Indexed:* A01, A22, AmHI, BRI, MLA-IB. *Aud.:* Ga, Ac.

The content of this important publication is specifically directed to the interests of poets and writers of serious fiction. Each issue contains interviews with important authors, some venerable, some new. There are articles directed at the creative writing process, although this is not a how-to journal for the uninitiated. Some recent articles have been "Be bold: A profile of Ocean Vuong," "Four lunches and a breakfast: what I learned about the book business while breaking bread with five hungry agents," and "Shape shifter: a profile of Marlon James." Regular departments include "News and Trends," "The Literary Life," and "The Practical Writer." There is an extensive and invaluable "Resources" section that includes grants and awards, conferences and residencies, and classifieds. All academic libraries should subscribe to this journal, and public libraries that serve populations of writers should also have it.

Script (Calabasas): where film begins. See Films section.

2989. ***Technical Communication Quarterly.*** Formerly (until 1992): *Technical Writing Teacher.* [ISSN: 1057-2252] 1973. q. GBP 360 (print & online eds.)). Ed(s): Donna Kain. Routledge, 530 Walnut St, Ste 850, Philadelphia, PA 19106; enquiries@tandfonline.com; http://www.tandfonline.com. Illus., adv. Sample. Refereed. Vol. ends: Fall. Microform: PQC. Reprint: PSC. *Indexed:* A01, A22, B01, E01, MLA-IB. *Bk. rev.:* 1-2, 1,000 words. *Aud.:* Ac, Sa.

This title publishes refereed articles on teaching and research methodologies, historical research, ethics, practical methodologies, digital applications, and so on—all as they relate to technical communication practices. Recent article titles include "Student Perceptions of Diversity in Technical and Professional Communication Academic Programs" and "Communicating Campus Sexual Assault: A Mixed Methods Rhetorical Analysis." Any academic library that supports a technical writing program should have this journal.

2990. ***The Writer.*** [ISSN: 0043-9517] 1887. m. USD 28.95 domestic; USD 38.95 Canada; USD 43.95 elsewhere. Ed(s): Nicki Porter. Madavor Media, Llc., 25 Braintree Hill Office Park, Ste 404, Braintree, MA 02184; http://www.madavor.com. Illus., index, adv. Vol. ends: Dec. *Indexed:* A01, A22, AmHI, BRI, C37, MASUSE, MLA-IB. *Bk. rev.:* Number and length vary. *Aud.:* Hs, Ga, Ac.

This publication has grown in its sophistication and its substance as the years pass. Its website offers greater clarity and good navigation (unlike some of the more well-known ones). The publication itself is well designed and has great appeal. It contains columns of general interest, such as "Dear Writer" and "How I Write." The articles are much more in the how-to vein than those in the more serious literary writing magazines; they have titles such as "A writer's argument for political correctness." There are also book reviews and classified ads of interest to writers. The magazine's primary market is probably more general than some, but not every writer is destined for a Booker Prize! ...in fact, very few are. This publication would be well-placed placed in high school, public, and college libraries.

2991. ***The Writer's Chronicle.*** Former titles (until 1998): *A W P Chronicle;* (until 1989): *A W P Newsletter.* [ISSN: 1529-5443] 197?. quadrennial. Non-members, USD 20. Ed(s): Supriya Bhatnagar. Association of Writers & Writing Programs, George Mason University, 4400 University Dr., Mail Stop 1E3, Fairfax, VA 22030; awp@awpwriter.org; http://www.awpwriter.org. Illus., adv. Sample. Circ: 32000. *Indexed:* AmHI. *Aud.:* Ga, Ac.

The Writer's Chronicle is aimed at a broad audience, with its "information designed to enlighten, inform, and entertain writers, editors, students, and teachers of writing." It contains many interviews and feature articles that have wide appeal, as well as actual fiction and poetry. Some recent articles include "Has the Happy Ending in Fiction Fallen Out of Style?" "On the Motion & Meaning of Humor in Poetry," and "The Vulnerability of Outrage." Academic libraries and any public library that supports a population of creative writers should consider this journal.

2992. ***Writer's Digest.*** Formerly (until 1921): *Successful Writing.* [ISSN: 0043-9525] 1920. 8x/yr. USD 29.96 United States; USD 39.96 Canada; USD 6.99 per issue. Ed(s): Jessica Strawser. F + W Media Inc., 1140 Broadway, 14th Fl, New York, NY 10001; contact_us@fwmedia.com; http://www.fwcommunity.com/. Illus., adv. Circ: 71423 Paid. Microform: MIM; PQC. *Indexed:* A22, BRI. *Aud.:* Hs, Ga, Ac.

If a library can purchase only one writing journal, *Writer's Digest* should be it. It contains a huge amount of information on all types of nontechnical writing, interviews, and feature articles on issues of interest to writers, such as book doctoring and copyright. There is market information, classifieds, and advertisements galore. Its glossy format is newsy and would be interesting even to the non-writer. An example of a recent feature article is "Why Writers Should Embrace Their Weird Side." All public libraries and academic libraries that serve writing programs should have this title.

Written By. See Films section.

Pedagogy

2993. ***Across the Disciplines.*** Formed by the merger of (2000-2004): *Academic Writing;* (1994-2004): *Language and Learning Across the Disciplines.* [ISSN: 1554-8244] 2004. irreg. Free. Ed(s): Michael Pemberton. W A C Clearinghouse, Department of Writing and Linguistics, Georgia Southern University, PO Box 8026, Statesboro, GA 30460; http://wac.colostate.edu/. Refereed. *Indexed:* MLA-IB. *Bk. rev.:* Occasional, 1,000-1,500 words. *Aud.:* Ac.

"*Across the Disciplines,* a refereed journal devoted to language, learning, and academic writing, publishes articles relevant to writing and writing pedagogy in all their intellectual, political, social, and technological complexity." Despite that mouthful of words, this is an excellent web-based publication that is actually now an amalgam of two former e-journals, *Academic Writing* and *Language and Learning Across the Disciplines.* The current issues and the archives of articles are now all held in the open access WAC Clearinghouse. The interesting content includes discussions of both academic writing and pedagogy. It is predominantly a pedagogical publication, but since most academics teach writing in the context of courses, it should have broad appeal. Some titles from recent issues include "Writing in the Disciplines and Student Pre-professional Identity: An Exploratory Study" and "Sprinting toward Genre Knowledge: Scaffolding Graduate Student Communication through 'Sprints' in Finance and Engineering Courses." For those of us who live with the complexities of traditional academic language, and who watch our students and faculty struggle to write between conflicting traditions on interdisciplinary topics, this journal fills a significant gap. Any academic library of merit should consider linking to this title.

2994. *Assessing Writing.* [ISSN: 1075-2935] 1994. q. EUR 621. Elsevier Ltd, The Boulevard, Langford Lane, Oxford, OX5 1GB, United Kingdom; customerserviceau@elsevier.com; http://www.elsevier.com. Adv. Sample. Refereed. Reprint: PSC. *Indexed:* A01, A22, ERIC, MLA-IB. *Bk. rev.:* 1-3, 1,000-2,000 words. *Aud.:* Ac.

This substantive refereed journal strives to publish articles on writing and the teaching of writing from an international perspective. That makes it a somewhat more theoretical journal than a "how-to" publication, but does not detract from its quality. Recent article titles include "Source use in the story continuation writing task," "A validation program for the Self-Beliefs, Writing-Beliefs, and Attitude Survey: A measure of adolescents' motivation toward writing," and "Connecting writing assessment with critical thinking: An exploratory study of alternative rhetorical functions and objects of enquiry in writing prompts." Given the journal's cost, many academic libraries will choose not to purchase it. But for those with strong writing programs, this is a title worth considering.

2995. *Computers and Composition: an international journal.* [ISSN: 8755-4615] 1983. 4x/yr. EUR 760. Ed(s): Kristine L Blair. Elsevier Ltd, 125 London Wall, London, EC2Y 5AS, United Kingdom; corporate.sales@elsevier.com; http://www.elsevier.com. Adv. Sample. Refereed. Vol. ends: No. 18. Reprint: PSC. *Indexed:* A01, A22, CompLI, MLA-IB. *Bk. rev.:* 1-4, 2,500-3,000 words. *Aud.:* Ac.

This journal "is devoted to exploring the use of computers in writing classes, writing programs, and writing research." It looks at these issues from pedagogical, psychological, and social points of view. Articles may discuss legal or ethical issues or interface design. In keeping with the journal's charge, the editors also maintain an excellent website that includes not only a complete archive but also supplementary materials and discussions, including blogs on various issues. Some recent articles include "From Opportunities to Outcomes: The Wikipedia-Based Writing Assignment," "Smartphones, Distraction Narratives, and Flexible Pedagogies: Students' Mobile Technology Practices in Networked Writing Classrooms," and "Resisting 'Let's Eat Grandma': The Rhetorical Potential of Grammar Memes." Any academic library that serves a school of education or writing programs should purchase this title.

2996. *Journal of Writing Assessment.* [ISSN: 1543-043X] 2003. s-a. Ed(s): Peggy O'Neill, Diane Kelly-Riley. Hampton Press, Inc., 307 Seventh Ave, Ste 506, New York, NY 10001; info@hamptonpress.com; http://www.hamptonpress.com. Refereed. Vol. ends: Fall. *Indexed:* MLA-IB. *Bk. rev.:* 1-2, 500-1,000 words. *Aud.:* Ac, Sa.

Although this journal professes to be for all levels of teaching and assessment of writing, K–12 through college, I did not see much content appropriate for any level below upper high school. That being said, this American refereed journal's content is substantive and serious. As with its British cousin journal *Assessing Writing,* many of its articles are theoretical in nature; however, there are more "how-to" articles than are found in its British counterpart. Some titles of recent articles include "Helping Faculty Self-Regulate Emotional Responses in Writing Assessment: Use of an 'Overall Response' Rubric Category," "Argument Essays Written in the 1st and 3rd Years of College: Assessing Differences in Performance," and "Let Them In: Increasing Access, Completion, and Equity in English Placement Policies at a Two-Year College in California." This journal is a good choice for colleges and universities with strong writing programs, or programs that train writing instructors.

2997. *Journalism & Mass Communication Educator.* Formerly (until 1995): *The Journalism Educator.* [ISSN: 1077-6958] 1944. q. USD 300 (print & online eds.)). Ed(s): Maria B Marron. Sage Publications, Inc., 2455 Teller Rd, Thousand Oaks, CA 91320; info@sagepub.com; http://www.sagepub.com. Illus., index, adv. Refereed. Vol. ends: Winter. Microform: CIS; PQC. Reprint: PSC. *Indexed:* A01, A22, BRI, ERIC. *Bk. rev.:* 10-12, 250-500 words. *Aud.:* Ac.

This title focuses on issues of interest to the faculty of communications and journalism programs. Each issue includes research articles and some focused book reviews, often following a theme. Some recent articles include "Undergraduate Students Prefer Learning Text and Broadcast Skills Sequentially Versus Concurrently, But Assessments of Their Final Projects are Mixed" and "Through Reflective Lenses: Enhancing Students' Perceptions of Their Media Writing Skills." Recommended for academic libraries that serve communications and journalism programs.

2998. *Journalism Practice.* [ISSN: 1751-2786] 2007. 10x/yr. GBP 1034 (print & online eds.)). Ed(s): Bonnie Brennen. Routledge, 4 Park Sq, Milton Park, Abingdon, OX14 4RN, United Kingdom; subscriptions@tandf.co.uk; http://www.tandfonline.com. Adv. Sample. Refereed. Reprint: PSC. *Indexed:* A22, E01. *Aud.:* Ac, Sa.

This journal is actually broader than its commitment to provide refereed articles to the education of future writers and journalists. It also seeks to provide materials that are "reflective, critical and research-based studies focused on the professional practice of journalism," which means it has great value for those already in the field. Titles of some recent articles include "Ice Cream is Worse, and Joblessness is Not an Option: Gendered experiences of freelancing," "Tell Me Who Your Sources Are: Perceptions of news credibility on social media," and "Tweeting the Agenda: How print and alternative web-only news organizations use Twitter as a source." Unfortunately, given the cost of this journal, only journalism programs in a university setting will probably be able to afford it.

■ LABOR AND INDUSTRIAL RELATIONS

See also Business; Disabilities; Economics; and Occupations and Careers sections.

Danielle Colbert-Lewis, Head of Research and Instructional Services, James E. Shepard Memorial Library, North Carolina Central University, 1801 Fayetteville Street, P.O. Box 19436, Durham, NC 27707; dcolbert@nccu.edu

Introduction

The central focus of industrial relations is based on the relationship between employees and employers ("Industrial Relations," 2006). Labor is the physical and mental talents people use in producing goods and services (Atkins, 2011). Both of these areas together—"Labor and Industrial Relations," also known as "Industrial and Labor Relations"—comprise the way in which employee and employers function in a work environment while producing goods and services. Central topics include regulation, conflict/dispute resolution, management, employment, unions, collective bargaining, and economics, to name a few. This section will cover resources that present information on both labor and industrial relations.

Interest in the subject of labor and industrial relations in the United States and internationally include, but are not limited to, the following eras in history and essential areas of study: United States and the original 13 colonies; slavery and indentured servants; immigration; inflation; industrialization; manufacturing; automation; unions/unionization; depressions; recessions; labor demand during wartime; exports and imports; trade; direct investment abroad and foreign investment in the United States; technology; and globalization. The aforementioned issues relate directly to the history and the future of labor and industrial relations.

Issues that face labor and industrial relations in the twenty-first century are related to technology in many ways. The impact of technology on labor was felt in the latter part of the twentieth century with jobs being automated and sent overseas (manufacturing industry, consumer goods). Moreover, the economy has played a major role in the twenty-first century, starting with the Great Recession (2007–2009). This recession impacted the workforce and labor dramatically around the globe. Many of the resources listed will describe economic issues that impact labor and industrial relations.

REFERENCES

Atkins, A. (2011). "Labor." In *The American Economy: A Historical Encyclopedia.* Retrieved from http://search.credoreference.com/content/entry/abcamerecon/labor/0

"Industrial Relations" (2006). In *Cambridge Dictionary of Sociology.* Retrieved from http://search.credoreference.com/content/entry/cupsoc/industrial_relations/0

Basic Periodicals

Ga: *Monthly Labor Review;* Ac: *Industrial and Labor Relations Review, Labor History, World of Work;* Sa: *Benefits Quarterly, Employee Relations Law Journal.*

Basic Abstracts and Indexes

ABI/INFORM, America: History and Life, Business Periodicals Index, Econlit, PAIS International, Social Sciences Index, Sociological Abstracts.

2999. ***A F L - C I O Now.*** 2006. w. Free. A F L - C I O, 815 16th St, N W, Washington, DC 20006; http://www.aflcio.org. *Aud.:* Ga, Ac, Sa.

AFL-CIO is an interactive website that highlights various initiatives and political objectives of the AFL-CIO, along with other union movement news. The website covers the following areas: What Unions Do; Form a Union; What We Care About; and Take Action. Moreover, the informative AFL-CIO website also includes a Blog section that covers up-to-date union movements articles and also a Speech section that includes recent speeches from AFL-CIO leadership. AFL-CIO.org does not cover other organizations, but it is a good starting point to learn about current events and the world of labor. URL: https://aflcio.org/

Academy of Management Journal. See Management and Administration section.

3000. ***Benefits Quarterly.*** [ISSN: 8756-1263] 1985. q. Free to members; Non-members, USD 125. Ed(s): Jack L VanDerhei. International Society of Certified Employee Benefit Specialists, Inc., 18700 W Bluemound Rd, PO Box 209, Brookfield, WI 53008; iscebs@iscebs.org; http://www.iscebs.org. Illus., index, adv. Sample. Circ: 13000. Vol. ends: Dec. *Indexed:* A22, AgeL, B01, BRI. *Bk. rev.:* 6-8, 200-500 words. *Aud.:* Sa.

This journal aims to provide a full-service news resource for all practitioners and students studying benefits and compensation. Articles offer a range of in-depth analyses of employee benefits issues. The text features pithy "pull quotes" and is formatted effectively for quick scanning. Articles explore breaking trends and new developments, frequently including case studies or strategic suggestions for practitioners. The editors also analyze legislative developments and court rulings that affect compensation issues. "Legal Update" and "Employee Benefits Bookshelf" features help readers stay current on legal news and new publications.

3001. ***British Journal of Industrial Relations: an international journal of employment relations.*** [ISSN: 0007-1080] 1963. q. GBP 670. Ed(s): John S Heywood. Wiley-Blackwell Publishing Ltd., The Atrium, Southern Gate, Chichester, PO19 8QG, United Kingdom; cs-journals@wiley.com; http://www.wiley.com/. Illus., index, adv. Sample. Refereed. Vol. ends: Dec. Reprint: PSC. *Indexed:* A22, B01, BAS, BRI, E01, EconLit, ErgAb, IBSS, P61. *Aud.:* Ac, Sa.

This journal addresses a broad spectrum of trends in the field of industrial relations, and has changed with the times to reflect the evolving nature of the field. Its articles balance empirical studies and theoretical issues, underscoring the fact that the field is composed of many academic disciplines, chiefly economics, business, and sociology. Journal topics include "differing forms of work and employment, work organisation, employer practices, systems of representation and rights at work, trade unionism, state policies, and international organizations, especially as these topics intersect with emergent social and economic issues, but also as they pertain to more traditional ones." Each issue has substantive articles and several shorter features. Most authors provide extensive tables and charts to support their arguments. This journal is aimed at academics who have an awareness of the deeper issues in industrial relations, and therefore it may not be easily accessible to the casual reader.

3002. ***Daily Labor Report.*** Former titles (until 1948): *Daily Report on Labor-Management Problems;* (until 1946): *Daily Report on Labor Problems, Manpower Control, Wage & Salary Regulation;* (until 1943): *Bureau of National Affairs. Daily Labor Report.* [ISSN: 0418-2693] 1941. d. USD 12328. Ed(s): Susan McGolrick. Bloomberg B N A, 1801 S Bell St, Arlington, VA 22202; blawhelp@bna.com; http://www.bna.com. Sample. *Aud.:* Ac, Sa.

Daily Labor Report is published by Bloomberg BNA. When Bloomberg acquired the Bureau of National Affairs, Inc., it became one of the leading players in labor law publishing. *Daily Labor Report* is a paid subscription online resource. Bloomberg BNA is comprehensive in its coverage of labor relations topics. It is designed to provide labor lawyers, unionists, and government officials with all the information they need about the world of work. The online resource includes the following designated sections: "News," "Insights," and "In Brief." A key feature of Bloomberg BNA is the "Insights" section, which details perspectives on topics of interest in the world of work; for instance, LGBTQ workplace; The Supreme Court; retirement plans; wellness plans. The "In Brief" section includes current labor relations cases. Subscribers can sign up for email updates to stay abreast on the field of labor relations and other topics such as immigration law, employment discrimination, hiring, workplace rules, employee conduct, and more. This publication is essential for lawyers and practitioners, but would also makes a very useful addition to a central reference collection that is heavily used by patrons with legal and employment questions.

3003. ***Dispute Resolution Journal.*** Formerly (until 1993): *Arbitration Journal.* [ISSN: 1074-8105] 1937. q. USD 195 combined subscription domestic (print & online eds.); USD 225 combined subscription foreign (print & online eds.)). Ed(s): Susan Zuckerman. Juris Publishing, Inc., 71 New St, Huntington, NY 11743; http://www.jurispub.com. Illus., index, adv. Vol. ends: Dec. Microform: PQC. *Indexed:* A22, B01, BRI, L14, SD. *Aud.:* Ga, Ac, Sa.

Alternative dispute resolution (ADR) has emerged as a viable legal strategy to apply, instead of starting out with litigation. The workplace generates a hefty percentage of all lawsuits, and therefore ADR is often cast as a better alternative to litigation. *Dispute Resolution Journal* is published by the American Arbitration Association, and highlights new developments in the field as well as creative strategies for keeping litigants out of court. Articles explore negotiation, mediation, final offer arbitration, and any other alternative to impasse. The journal also explores industrial trends, including developments in construction, technology, commerce, and health care. Since federal law allows for public employees to utilize alternative dispute resolution, public-sector issues figure highly in the article mix. Not all contributors are attorneys; expert authors hail from international relations, business, finance, construction, insurance, and technology. The articles are incisive and include good footnotes that facilitate further research. This title would be an important addition for law libraries, business libraries, and general social science collections.

3004. ***Economic and Industrial Democracy: an international journal.*** [ISSN: 0143-831X] 1980. q. USD 1624 (print & online eds.)). Ed(s): Jan Ottosson, Lars Magnusson. Sage Publications Ltd., 1 Oliver's Yard, 55 City Rd, London, EC1Y 1SP, United Kingdom; info@sagepub.com; https://www.sagepub.com/. Index, adv. Sample. Refereed. Reprint: PSC. *Indexed:* A22, B01, BAS, E01, EconLit, IBSS, P61, SSA. *Bk. rev.:* Number and length vary. *Aud.:* Ga, Ac.

This journal has an international scope but also includes substantive articles about U.S. conditions. The prefatory material for each paper includes an abstract and a set of keywords, facilitating a handy, item-level guide. Each issue includes peer-reviewed journal articles, published quarterly. Publication issues focused on large-scale topics "designed to enhance the quality of working life through extending the democratic control of workers over the workplace and the economy." Early researchers are encouraged to submit articles for special featured journals and seasoned research professionals are encouraged to submit articles. The journal has a special emphasis on empirical research methods.

3005. ***The Economic and Labour Relations Review.*** [ISSN: 1035-3046] 1990. s-a. USD 1425 (print & online eds.)). Sage Publications Ltd., 1 Oliver's Yard, 55 City Rd, London, EC1Y 1SP, United Kingdom; info@sagepub.com; https://www.sagepub.com/. Refereed. Reprint: PSC. *Indexed:* BAS, BRI, EconLit. *Aud.:* Ac.

The Economic and Labour Relations Review is a double-blind, peer-reviewed journal that focuses on research topics such as economics, labor relations, and policy questions. This journal encourages articles that challenge viewpoints and brings new models of thinking critically and alternatively at issues. The journal's "About" page states that it leans toward a "post-Keynesian (heterodox) approach to economics," that is, equality or justice-based view of labor relations and social policy (from the publisher).

3006. ***Employee Relations Law Journal.*** Incorporates (2000-2002): *Employee Rights Quarterly.* [ISSN: 0098-8898] 1975. q. USD 695; USD 261 per issue. Ed(s): Steven A Meyerowitz. Aspen Publishers, Inc., 76 Ninth Ave, 7th Fl, New York, NY 10011; customer.service@wolterskluwer.com; http://lrus.wolterskluwer.com. Illus., index. Vol. ends: Spring. *Indexed:* A22, B01, BRI, L14, SD. *Aud.:* Ac, Sa.

This journal targets human resources managers, in-house counsel, and employment law specialists, and offers a comprehensive means for them to keep up with the rapid pace of change in workplace issues. Authors strike an analytical and practical note without sinking too far into technical discourse. Well-known professionals contribute signed, short "Literature Review" essays. The journal covers a wide range of "hot" labor issues, including personnel management techniques, legal compliance, and court cases. Recent articles address such topics as family medical leave, sexual harassment, age discrimination, and alternative dispute resolution. This is the sort of publication that could be consulted for quick reading and "brushing up," although it also offers some real substance for those moments when time allows a more thoughtful perusal. This journal is a top choice for selectors who must make difficult decisions with limited funds.

3007. ***The Employment Situation (Online).*** Formerly (until 2000): *The Employment Situation (Print).* 19??. m. Free. U.S. Department of Labor, Bureau of Labor Statistics, 2 Massachusetts Ave, NE, Washington, DC 20212; blsdata_staff@bls.gov; http://www.bls.gov. Microform: CIS. *Aud.:* Ga, Ac, Sa.

The Employment Situation details the state of employment in the United States of America. It comes in the form of an "Economic News Release" from the Bureau of Labor Statistics. Each publication reports on the previous month's employment status, including the non-payroll employment numbers and the unemployment rate. Each issue of *The Employment Situation* includes details on growth areas of employment and employment by sectors: professional and business services; health care and social assistance; leisure and hospitality; transportation and warehousing; and manufacturing.

3008. ***Hofstra Labor & Employment Law Journal.*** Former titles (until 1997): *Hofstra Labor Law Journal;* (until 1984): *Hofstra Labor Law Forum.* 1982. s-a. Ed(s): Domenick J Pesce. Hofstra University, School of Law, 121 Hofstra University, Hempstead, NY 11549; http://law.hofstra.edu. *Indexed:* A22, BRI, L14. *Aud.:* Ga.

Hofstra Labor & Employment Law Journal contains scholarly articles written by practitioners and scholars and in the field of labor and employment law. Now past its 35th year, this journal publishes Fall and Spring issues. Each issue includes submitted notes and comments written by Hofstra law students. Moreover, the journal's website contains a legal blog that covers current issues relating to the labor and employment law field. Blog entries contain legal reference and footnotes to resources that are related to the issue at hand. The previous issue of *Hofstra Labor & Employment Law Journal* is accessible via the website for the journal under Current Issues, as well as Scholarly Commons and via print subscription.

3009. ***Industrial and Labor Relations Review.*** [ISSN: 0019-7939] 1947. 5x/yr. USD 533 (print & online eds.)). Ed(s): Lawrence M Kahn, Rosemary Batt. Sage Publications, Inc., 2455 Teller Rd, Thousand Oaks, CA 91320; info@sagepub.com; http://www.sagepub.com. Illus., index, adv. Refereed. Vol. ends: Jul. Reprint: PSC; WSH. *Indexed:* A22, B01, BAS, BRI, C42, CBRI, Chicano, EconLit, IBSS, L14, P61, SSA, WSA. *Bk. rev.:* Number and length vary. *Aud.:* Ac, Sa.

This multidisciplinary journal is one of the preeminent scholarly publications in the field of industrial relations. Its empirical studies reflect all aspects of industrial relations, and researchers can rely upon it to guide them to the most important issues of the day. Articles are quantitative, dense, and statistical, which means that a literature search could begin here and move outward to other journal titles. The content is international in scope. Articles reflect "all aspects of the employment relationship, including collective bargaining, labor law, labor markets, social security and protective labor legislation, management and personnel, human resources, worker participation, workplace health and safety, organizational behavior, comparative industrial relations, and labor history." As is the case with all of the most scholarly publications in this field, readers will require a commanding knowledge of statistics and economic theory to follow many of the offerings. The book review section offers in-depth, subject-based literature reviews that track the latest publications in the field. This scholarly journal is required for serious academic collections.

3010. ***Industrial Relations: a journal of economy and society.*** Formerly (until 1961): *Civilian Defense.* [ISSN: 0019-8676] 1942. q. GBP 459. Ed(s): Chris Riddell. Wiley-Blackwell Publishing, Inc., 111 River St, Hoboken, NJ 07030; info@wiley.com; http://onlinelibrary.wiley.com. Illus., index, adv. Sample. Refereed. Vol. ends: Fall. Microform: PQC. Reprint: PSC. *Indexed:* A22, B01, BRI, Chicano, E01, EconLit, ErgAb, IBSS, L14, P61, SSA. *Bk. rev.:* Brief notes. *Aud.:* Ac.

The substantive and wide-ranging articles in this journal deal with all aspects of employee-employer relationships. The publication leans heavily in the direction of economic analysis, and thus requires a deeper knowledge of economic principles in many cases. Many authors address the challenge of how to bring theory into practice, or explore how real-world events may be explained utilizing theory. Each issue has a column on Internet resources and a survey of recent publications. The scope of the articles is international, although most deal with American scenarios. In addition to economics, authors hail from sociology, business administration, psychology, and history. Although the authors are clearly involved in a conversation with each other and not with the average reader, the overall editorial strategy for this publication has balanced "plain English" with complex theory. Therefore, readers can expect to find a substantial amount of accessible scholarship here. This is a valuable journal in the field and should be part of academic collections and large public library collections.

3011. ***Industrial Worker.*** [ISSN: 0019-8870] 1909. 10x/yr. USD 18 domestic; USD 22 foreign. Ed(s): Diane Krauthamer. Industrial Workers of the World, PO Box 180195, Chicago, IL 60618; ghq@iww.org; http://iww.org. Illus., adv. Vol. ends: Dec. Microform: BHP; PQC. *Aud.:* Ga, Ac.

Industrial Worker is a vibrant website and the public voice of the Industrial Workers of the World (IWW). It is unabashedly partisan in its editorial direction. Precisely for this reason, it is closely read by both labor activists and academics. As one of the most radical labor newspapers in print and online, it brings an important ideological perspective to any collection, whatever the politics of the region. World labor news is covered in depth, as is news from local unions in the United States. Authors are very much concerned with organizing strategies, the "strike tool," and other longtime labor strategies. Rank-and-file union members are frequent contributors, and the editor is an elected official with a two-year term.

3012. ***International Labour Review.*** [ISSN: 0020-7780] 1921. q. GBP 363 (print & online eds.)). Ed(s): Mark Lansky. Wiley-Blackwell Publishing Ltd., The Atrium, Southern Gate, Chichester, PO19 8QG, United Kingdom; cs-journals@wiley.com; http://www.wiley.com/. Illus., index, adv. Sample. Refereed. Vol. ends: Nov/Dec. Microform: CIS; PMC; PQC. Reprint: PSC; WSH. *Indexed:* A22, ASSIA, B01, BAS, BRI, C45, CBRI, E01, EIP, EconLit, ErgAb, GW, IBSS, P61, SSA. *Bk. rev.:* Number and length vary. *Aud.:* Ac, Sa.

The International Labour Organization (ILO) is an important publisher that addresses international issues in industrial relations and the trade union movement. The ILO's *Review* focuses heavily on developing countries that do not receive much attention from U.S.- and European-based journals. Contributors include academics, labor leaders, government officials, nongovernmental organization (NGO) leaders, and technical experts. The ILO tracks many controversial issues such as the worldwide incidence of child labor. This publication is often the best place to start a search on issues that span national boundaries. The editors publish a literature review, which is unusual in that it provides a means to find international literature. Tables of contents and article abstracts are online from 1996 to the present, and subscribers to the print edition have full online access as well.

3013. ***Journal of Labor and Society.*** Formerly (until 2017): *Working U S A (Online).* [ISSN: 2471-4607] 1997. q. GBP 362. Ed(s): Immanuel Ness. Wiley-Blackwell Publishing, Inc., 111 River St, Hoboken, NJ 07030; info@wiley.com; http://onlinelibrary.wiley.com. Refereed. *Indexed:* B01. *Bk. rev.:* Number and length vary. *Aud.:* Ga, Ac.

In operation since 1997, this publication has made waves as a publishing venue for a large number of progressive academics and policymakers. It bills itself as an instrument for studying the workplace with the needs and concerns of "working people" in mind, and this is reflected in the topics it covers. In many cases, authors express partisan viewpoints, in contrast to the more arid language typically employed by many scholarly journals. Article topics include organizing temporary workers, labor education's challenges, and home-care worker issues. Authors are careful to write in plain English, yet offer solid scholarship that is footnoted and enhanced with tables and charts. This journal has earned a place as a core title both for industrial relations collections and for general business collections.

3014. ***Journal of Labor Economics.*** [ISSN: 0734-306X] 1983. q. USD 524. Ed(s): Paul Oyer. University of Chicago Press, 1427 E 60th St, Chicago, IL 60637; subscriptions@press.uchicago.edu; http://www.journals.uchicago.edu. Illus., index, adv. Sample. Refereed. Vol. ends: Oct. Reprint: PSC. *Indexed:* A22, B01, EconLit, IBSS. *Bk. rev.:* Number and length vary. *Aud.:* Ac, Sa.

This journal's editors recognize that the interplay between the economy, broad social trends, and private behavior is complex and requires multidisciplinary study. Articles can be either highly theoretical or applied, as authors explore labor market institutions (such as unions, management, and government) from a variety of perspectives. Topics cover a wide range of labor economics issues, varying from changes in the supply and demand of labor services, to the distribution of income, to the impact of public-policy decisions. Not a layperson's sourcebook, this journal requires a working knowledge of economic theory. The quality of the scholarship and the diversity of the material covered make this an excellent addition to academic collections.

3015. ***Journal of Labor Research.*** [ISSN: 0195-3613] 1980. q. EUR 515 (print & online eds.)). Ed(s): Ozkan Eren. Springer New York LLC, 233 Spring St, New York, NY 10013; customerservice@springer.com; http://www.springer.com. Illus., index, adv. Refereed. Reprint: PSC. *Indexed:* A22, B01, BRI, E01, EconLit, IBSS, P61, SD, SSA. *Aud.:* Åc, Sa.

This top-ranked journal takes the challenge of exploring the "employment relationship" very seriously, and offers hard-hitting articles by academics and practitioners. Authors rely heavily on economic theory and statistical analysis, and the lay reader may find this a challenge. Nonetheless, this journal is widely cited and is a necessary addition to the labor library. Most issues feature a symposium that brings together several articles that present a variety of viewpoints on a trend or policy issue. Recent topics include hospital workers, unemployment of older workers, union wage effects in the public sector, gender promotion gap, and family leave.

3016. ***Journal of Workplace Rights.*** Formerly (until 2008): *Journal of Individual Employment Rights.* [ISSN: 1938-4998] 1992. q. Ed(s): Joel Rudin. Sage Publications, Inc., 2455 Teller Rd, Thousand Oaks, CA 91320; info@sagepub.com; https://us.sagepub.com. Sample. Refereed. *Indexed:* A01, B01, BRI, L14. *Aud.:* Ac.

The *Journal of Workplace Rights* is dedicated to the idea that human rights should be upheld in the workplace, which requires input from both management and the workforce itself. Its definition of human rights is based on the Universal Declaration of Human Rights as passed by the United Nations in 1948. Topics of interest to the editors run through the full range of industrial relations issues, including job security, discrimination, living wages, collective bargaining, privacy, workplace democracy, and intellectual property rights. The editors also give special attention to doctoral students and non-tenured faculty members as authors, because they possess fewer rights and privileges than tenured professors do. Recent articles include "A Human Rights Lens on Full Employment and Decent Work in the 2030 Sustainable Development Agenda," "In the Middle of a Family Story: Meaning of Commodification for Child Care Workers," "Workplace Bullying Not a Manager's Right?" and others that relate to human rights issues in the workplace.

3017. ***Labor (Durham): studies in working-class history.*** [ISSN: 1547-6715] 2004. q. USD 505. Ed(s): Patrick Dixon, Leon Fink. Duke University Press, 905 W Main St, Durham, NC 27701; orders@dukeupress.edu; https://www.dukeupress.edu. Adv. Refereed. Reprint: PSC. *Indexed:* MLA-IB, P61. *Aud.:* Ga, Ac, Sa.

Labor: Studies in Working-Class History of the Americas is the official journal for the Labor and Working-Class History Association (LAWCHA). This journal is available for individual subscription, which includes membership to the organization LAWCHA. *Labor* covers issues relating to industrial work, slavery, unpaid and domestic labor, the informal sector, and the professions. This journal pays particular attention to current and historical labor trends and industrial work social movements. Submissions are from academic scholars, journalists, labor educators, poets, and writer-activists.

3018. ***Labor History.*** Incorporates (1967-1968): *Labor Historians Newsletter;* Formerly (1960): *The Labor Historian's Bulletin.* [ISSN: 0023-656X] 1953. 5x/yr. GBP 538 (print & online eds.)). Ed(s): Craig Phelan, Gerald Friedman. Routledge, 4 Park Sq, Milton Park, Abingdon, OX14 4RN, United Kingdom; subscriptions@tandf.co.uk; http://www.tandfonline.com. Illus., adv. Sample. Refereed. Reprint: PSC. *Indexed:* A22, AmHI, B01, BRI, Chicano, E01, EconLit, IBSS, P61, SSA. *Aud.:* Ac, Sa.

This journal publishes original research about the history of work and how it is represented in literature. It also explores the historical record of labor systems, the social production of labor, occupational culture, and folklore. Authors focus primarily on American labor, but the growing interest in transnational movements is showing up as an additional focus for the editors. This journal is the most important venue for scholars who are interested in presenting new ideas about labor history. The journal's reputation is built on its solid scholarly research and writing, yet it avoids limiting itself to a narrow focus. As the standard journal for this area of study, it is a natural fit in large public libraries and academic collections.

3019. ***Labor Notes.*** [ISSN: 0275-4452] 1979. m. USD 50 (Individuals, USD 30). Ed(s): Jenny Brown, Alexandra Bradbury. Labor Education & Research Project, 7435 Michigan Ave, Detroit, MI 48210. Illus. *Indexed:* A22. *Aud.:* Ga, Ac, Sa.

Labor Notes is one of the hardest-hitting titles in labor news coverage, directed by the slogan "Putting the Movement Back in the Labor Movement." It carries news and opinion about rank-and-file struggles that are written by participants and observers, and it has a 40-year history. Contributors freely explore the contradictions and nuances of the different forces involved in labor issues. The publication prides itself on its independence, and is equally critical of failings within unions and management. There is a steady supply of controversial op-ed pieces, guest editorials, and a lively letters section. In addition to the magazine, there is an active blog that offers extensive commentary and additional articles.

3020. ***Labor Studies Journal.*** [ISSN: 0160-449X] 1976. q. USD 579 (print & online eds.)). Ed(s): Robert Bruno. Sage Publications, Inc., 2455 Teller Rd, Thousand Oaks, CA 91320; info@sagepub.com; http://www.sagepub.com. Illus., adv. Sample. Refereed. Vol. ends: Winter. Microform: PQC. Reprint: PSC. *Indexed:* A22, B01, BRI, E01, IBSS, P61, SSA. *Bk. rev.:* 7-12, 400-2,700 words. *Aud.:* Ac, Sa.

This publication successfully acts as a bridge between academic researchers and labor practitioners. *Labor Studies Journal* is also the official journal of the United Association for Labor Education (UALE). Papers presented at the annual UALE conference are published in *LSJ*. It is a multidisciplinary journal that publishes material based on research about work, workers, labor organizations, labor studies, and worker education in the United States and internationally. The content covers diverse research methods, both qualitative and quantitative. The articles are directed at a general audience, including union, university, and community-based labor educators, and labor activists and scholars from across the social sciences and humanities.

3021. *Monthly Labor Review Online.* [ISSN: 1937-4658] m. Ed(s): Michael D Levi, Terry L Schau. U.S. Department of Labor, Bureau of Labor Statistics, Division of Compensation Data Analysis & Planning, Postal Square Bldg., Washington, DC 20212; http://www.bls.gov. *Bk. rev.:* Occasional. *Aud.:* Ga.

Monthly Labor Review Online continues a long tradition of excellence in digital form. This journal is the top scholarly/professional journal of the Bureau of Labor Statistics (BLS), and it attracts prestigious authors. Full-text versions are available in pdf format, both at the article and full-issue levels. Articles include links to related Bureau of Labor Statistics programs and data, and author e-mail links are embedded. "The Editor's Desk," a useful review of new BLS data and research, is updated each business day. The content is informative and neutral, including current labor statistics, book reviews, publications received, and a section called "Labor Month in Review." Content searching is facilitated by an index of articles published in print since 1988, as well as an archive of past issues. URL: www.bls.gov/mlr/

3022. *New Labor Forum: a journal of ideas, analysis and debate.* [ISSN: 1095-7960] 1997. 3x/yr. USD 637 (print & online eds.)). Ed(s): Paula Finn. Sage Publications, Inc., 2455 Teller Rd, Thousand Oaks, CA 91320; info@sagepub.com; http://www.sagepub.com/. Illus., adv. Refereed. Reprint: PSC. *Indexed:* A01, A22, B01, E01, P61, SSA. *Bk. rev.:* Number and length vary. *Aud.:* Ga, Ac.

Bold and provocative, this journal is of the sort that gets locked up for safekeeping and placed on two-hour reserve. Otherwise it manages to "disappear," which is a testament to its popularity. Subtitled "A Journal of Ideas, Analysis and Debate," this publication invites controversy and does not eschew strong rhetoric. Articles from union organizers mingle with those of tenured faculty. Topics such as labor union revitalization and new labor-community coalition building are examples of the controversial issues that the editors take on. Fresh ideas abound, such as approaching high-tech globalized distribution as a union organizing opportunity, or exploring the future of the "strike weapon" as a strategic tool.

3023. *New Technology, Work & Employment.* [ISSN: 0268-1072] 1986. 3x/yr. GBP 509. Ed(s): Philip Taylor, Debra Howcroft. Wiley-Blackwell Publishing Ltd., The Atrium, Southern Gate, Chichester, PO19 8QG, United Kingdom; cs-journals@wiley.com; http://onlinelibrary.wiley.com. Adv. Sample. Refereed. Reprint: PSC. *Indexed:* A22, ASSIA, B01, BRI, CompLI, E01, ErgAb, IBSS. *Aud.:* Ga.

Technology has brought sweeping changes to the way most people work, and this internationally edited, interdisciplinary journal assesses the impact of technology in the workplace. Articles balance solid academic work with readable text. Topics include automation of retail distribution, telecommuting in small- and medium-sized firms, management style and worker autonomy, and teamwork in factory assembly lines.

Occupational Outlook Quarterly. See Occupations and Careers section.

3024. *Perspectives on Work.* [ISSN: 1534-9276] 1997. s-a. Free to members. Labor and Employment Relations Association, 121 Labor & Industrial Relations Bldg, University of Illinois at Urbana-Champaign, Champaign, IL 61820; LERAoffice@ad.uiuc.edu; http://www.lera.uiuc.edu/. Illus., adv. *Aud.:* Ac, Sa.

Perspectives on Work is a magazine of the Labor and Employment Relations Association (LERA). Members of this association are interested in aspects of labor and employee relations that include academic research and education, compensation and benefits, human resources, labor and employment law, labor and management resources, labor markets and economics, public policy, training and development, and union administration and organizing. This publication is practical in nature and informs members on current issues facing the industry. Topics of articles in the magazine include, but are not limited to, health care, labor-management relations, sustainability, collective bargaining, and pensions.

3025. *Union Democracy Review.* Formerly (until 1972): *Union Democracy in Action.* [ISSN: 1077-5080] 1961. bi-m. Free to members; Non-members, USD 30. Ed(s): Herman Benson. Association for Union Democracy, Inc., 104 Montgomery St., Brooklyn, NY 11225; info@uniondemocracy.org; http://www.uniondemocracy.com. Sample. *Aud.:* Ga, Ac, Sa.

The Association for Union Democracy (AUD) is a nonprofit organization dedicated to advancing the principles and practices of democratic trade unionism in the North American labor movement. It is a nonpartisan organization and does not support or endorse candidates for union office or particular policies within unions. Rather, AUD supports actions that strengthen the democratic process, promote membership participation, support free speech, and encourage fair elections so that union members can shape and steer the direction of their union. *Union Democracy Review* is AUD's published voice, and serves as a vital clearinghouse for this movement.

3026. *Work, Employment & Society.* [ISSN: 0950-0170] 1987. bi-m. USD 1051 (print & online eds.)). Ed(s): Mark Stuart, Irena Grugulis. Sage Publications Ltd., 1 Oliver's Yard, 55 City Rd, London, EC1Y 1SP, United Kingdom; market@sagepub.com; https://www.sagepub.com/. Adv. Sample. Refereed. Microform: PQC. Reprint: PSC. *Indexed:* A22, ASSIA, E01, ErgAb, IBSS, P61, SSA. *Bk. rev.:* Number and length vary. *Aud.:* Ac.

This British entry is heavily dominated by the sociological study of work, and this is a value point for labor researchers. It addresses work in the broadest possible sense, and it includes a wide array of articles that explore global and transnational employment trends. This is the sort of journal that citizen-researchers and students may consult to get the big picture, and that academics consult to stay current with their international colleagues. Recent articles explore management trends with significant impact on workers, such as "total quality management," the impact of technology on work, and disabilities in the workplace. For full-service research collections, this journal is a valuable addition.

3027. *Workers' Compensation Outlook.* [ISSN: 1052-6358] 1990. m. USD 297 domestic; USD 373.10 foreign; USD 339 combined subscription domestic (print & online eds.)). Ed(s): Katherine Allnutt Panikian. Standard Publishing Corp., 155 Federal St, 13th Fl, Boston, MA 02110; info@spcpub.com; http://www.spcpub.com. Sample. *Aud.:* Ac, Sa.

Workers' Compensation Outlook is a monthly publication that gives practical commentary on workers' compensation issues. Each issue focuses on a topic related to employment practices, workers' compensation, and legal issues surrounding both. Managers are the target audience for this publication. Issues that are covered in the articles are the aging workforce, alternative dispute resolution, risk management, fraud, claims, and insurance, to name a few. The articles are written in a pragmatic way that detail definitions and directives in order to be clear and concise on matters of workers' compensation.

3028. *Workforce (Chicago): business, strategy and management.* Former titles (until Sept. 2013): *Workforce Management (Print);* (until 2003): *Workforce (Costa Mesa, Print);* (until 1997): *Personnel Journal;* (until 1927): *Journal of Personnel Research.* [ISSN: 2331-2793] 1922. m. Free. Ed(s): Norman B Kamikow, Rick Bell. MediaTec Publishing, Inc., 111 E Wacker, Ste 1290, Chicago, IL 60601; http://www.mediatecpub.com. Illus., index, adv. Vol. ends: Dec. *Indexed:* A01, A22, Agr, B01, BLI, BRI, CBRI. *Aud.:* Ga.

Workforce provides practical information about the impact of current events on human relations. The format is akin to commercial magazine publishing, with rich graphics, pull-text boxes, and a vibrant letters section. One section covers the trends, problem-solving strategies, and resources necessary for action;

another covers legal briefings; and a third distills economic data into a usable form for human resources professionals. Topics covered include employer-provided child care, personnel practices at "big box" retailers, and the impact of changed overtime pay regulations.

3029. *Workplace: a journal for academic labor.* [ISSN: 1715-0094] 1998. s-a. Free. Ed(s): E. Wayne Ross, Stephen Petrina. University of British Columbia, Institute for Critical Education Studies, 2125 Main Mall, Vancouver, BC V6T 1Z4, Canada; ices.ubc@gmail.com; https://ices.library.ubc.ca. Adv. Refereed. *Bk. rev.:* Number and length vary. *Aud.:* Ga, Ac, Sa.

Workplace is an open-access, peer-reviewed journal published by the Institute for Critical Education at the University of British Columbia Faculty of Education. This journal is unique in focus in that it covers the area of academic labor and workplace activism in the higher-education and K-12 labor environment. Each issue critiques a topic that deals with management of educational institutions and systems. Topics include equity, governance, teacher unions, organizing, social policy, and law, to name a few. Book reviews are also included in each issue. Articles are written in personal narratives (firsthand accounts) and in a reflective style, and offer critical analysis of academic labor.

3030. *World of Work: the magazine of the ILO.* Formerly (until 1992): *I L O Information.* [ISSN: 1020-0010] 1965. 3x/yr. Free. Ed(s): Hans von Rohland. I L O, 4 Route des Morillons, Geneva, 1211, Switzerland; ilo@ilo.org; http://www.ilo.org. Illus. Vol. ends: Dec. *Indexed:* A22, B01, BRI, CBRI. *Bk. rev.:* Number and length vary. *Aud.:* Ga.

Although this magazine is published by the International Labour Organization (ILO), a specilized agency of the United Nations, its editorial masthead is careful to note that it is not the ILO's official voice. Nor does it concern itself with the legal status of affairs of any country. It does, however, explore a wide range of topics addressed by the ILO. Each issue includes an extensive cover story ("Working for peace and social justice," or "Migration should be a choice"), numerous general articles, and brief book recommendations. This title is freely available full text online at https://www.ilo.org under Publications or https://www.ilo.org/global/publications/world-of-work-magazine/issues/WCMS_710860/lang—en/index.htm

■ LANDSCAPE ARCHITECTURE

Patrick Tomlin, Art and Architecture Library, Virginia Tech, 100 Cowgill Hall, Blacksburg, VA 24062-9001; tomlinl@vt.edu

Introduction

The literature of landscape architecture is interdisciplinary and diverse in nature, reflective of the profession from which it originates. Although it encompasses elements of architecture and design, is informed by environmental studies and the social sciences, and embraces the challenges presented by new technologies as well as a long-standing commitment to the preservation of the past, landscape architecture is fundamentally shaped by how humans see themselves in relation to the natural world.

Landscape architecture journals cover this wide terrain, and range in scope and subject matter from historical case studies and detailed analyses of contemporary projects to the politics of sustainability and the impact of global warming on the practice of landscape architects. The following journals offer a representative sampling of the periodical literature in this field.

While fewer in number than journals published in architecture or the visual arts, landscape architecture periodicals vary greatly in content and design. Nevertheless, like journals in those disciplines, many landscape architecture publications are as much visual as textual in nature: readers will find that almost all are heavily illustrated with images, drawings, plans, and photographs, as the one fundamentally contributes to the meaning of the other. The majority of landscape architecture journals featured below, moreover, display a discernible international flavor, which reflects the European origins of their publication and the profession's own increasingly global visibility and scale of operation. Accordingly, these journals often publish summaries or entire texts of articles in multiple languages for an international readership.

Professional and scholarly societies publish, or are directly affiliated with, nearly half of the landscape journals reviewed in this section. These include publications with sustained analysis of the history of landscape architecture, such as the monograph *Dumbarton Oaks Papers* from the Colloquium on the History of Landscape Architecture, as well as periodicals that focus on contemporary design and research issues like *Landskab* and the *Journal of Landscape Architecture.* Nevertheless, given the relatively small number of journals in the field, there is little useful distinction between "scholarly" and "non-scholarly" journals. Even those "glossy" titles that are characterized by their sophisticated production levels and high-quality design, and that frequently focus on new and relatively unknown projects rather than architectural history, are usually edited and written by educators and researchers who are also practitioners, firm leaders, and theorists. The audience for these publications will consist primarily of landscape architecture students and faculty, as well as practicing landscape architects. Those working in contiguous fields such as land conservation, urban planning, and environmental science will likely find such publications of interest as well.

Currently, print remains the dominant format for landscape architecture journals, though this appears to be quickly changing, as publishers offer more and more content, including access to older volumes, on the web. The list below will be most useful to libraries that serve academic programs in landscape architecture, architecture, urban design, and environmental studies. Those suitable for a public library with a strong architecture collection or landscape architecture component have been indicated as such.

Basic Periodicals

Ac: *Landscape Architecture, Landscape Journal;* Sa: *Landscape and Urban Planning, Landscape Research, Topos.*

Basic Abstracts and Indexes

Art and Architecture Complete; Avery Index to Architectural Periodicals; Environment Complete; Garden, Landscape and Horticulture Index; ICONDA.

3031. *Anthos: vierteljahres-Zeitschrift fuer Freiraumgestaltung, Gruen und Landschaftsplanung.* [ISSN: 0003-5424] 1962. q. CHF 85 (Students, CHF 45). Ed(s): Stephanie Perrochet. Bund Schweizer Landschaftsarchitekten und Landschaftsarchitektinnen, Rue du Doubs 32, La Chaux-de-Fonds, 2300, Switzerland; bsla@bsla.ch; http://www.bsla.ch. Illus., adv. Circ: 5000. Vol. ends: Dec. *Indexed:* A22, GardL. *Bk. rev.:* 10. *Aud.:* Ac, Sa.

This official publication of the L'Union Suisse des Service des Parc et Promenades provides coverage of current developments in landscape architecture around the globe. The content of each volume of *Anthos* centers on a specific theme or particular aspect of the profession; a recent issue, for example, focuses on environmental design in the Alps. Content also includes articles on individual landscape projects, a book review section, and information about notable competitions, awards, and individual architects. Written in German and French, with portions published in English, *Anthos* represents the Federation Suisse des Architectes Paysagiste (FSAP) and the German Bund Schweizer Landschaftsarchitekten und Landschaftsarchitektinnen (BSLA). Its international perspective makes this publication a valuable contribution to an academic architecture library collection.

3032. *Colloquium on the History of Landscape Architecture. Papers.* 1972. irreg. Dumbarton Oaks, 1703 32nd St, NW, Washington, DC 20007; DoaksBooks@doaks.org; http://www.doaks.org/. Refereed. *Aud.:* Ac, Sa.

This monograph serial gathers papers originally presented at the annual colloquium on landscape architecture organized by Harvard's Dumbarton Oaks in Washington, D.C. Begun in 1971, the series has achieved a reputation for its notable contributors, erudite scholarship, and high-quality production. Essays in each volume address an overarching theme, each usually focusing on one aspect of the history of landscape architecture, but the *Papers* as a whole journal has addressed a striking variety of topics over the past four decades: archaeological evidence from Pompeii, Islamic garden traditions, and individual landscape architects such as Beatrix Jones Farrand. Essays are accompanied by bibliographic matter, illustrations, and information about the contributor. Volumes are relatively small in size, rarely amounting to more than 150 pages, but the series is an essential component for library collections that support a program in landscape architecture. Any landscape architecture or garden history research library should own the complete set.

3033. ***Garten und Landschaft: Zeitschrift fuer Landschaftsarchitektur.*** [ISSN: 0016-4720] 1890. m. EUR 149; EUR 159; EUR 95. Callwey Verlag, Streitfeldstr 35, Muenchen, 81673, Germany; info@callwey.de; http://www.callwey.de. Illus., index, adv. Vol. ends: Dec. *Indexed:* A22, GardL. *Bk. rev.:* 4. *Aud.:* Ac, Sa.

This German-language journal is published by the Deutsche Gesellschaft fuer Gartenkunst und Landschaftskulture (German Society for Garden Design and Landscape Architecture). *Garten und Landschaft* provides information about working landscape architects (principally European) and articles focusing on contemporary landscape design in Germany. Individual articles are devoted to a specific theme such as sustainability, or concentrate on projects within an individual city. Additional features include local news items, book reviews, notices of symposia and job openings, exhibitions, and other special events. Most content is written by landscape architects or recognized scholars in the field. Each issue is substantially illustrated with color and black-and-white reproductions. Some English-language summaries are present. An archive of older issues is available in electronic format for subscribers on the journal's German-language web site. *Garten un Landschaft* is a well-designed and relevant periodical for any library collection with a strong landscape architecture component. URL: www.garten-landschaft.de

3034. ***Green Places: dedicated to improving public space.*** Former titles (until Nov.2003): *Landscape Design;* (until 1971): *Institute of Landscape Architects. Journal;* (until 1946): *Institute of Landscape Architects. War-Time Journal;* (until 1941): *Landscape and Garden.* [ISSN: 1742-3716] 1934. 10x/yr. GBP 65 domestic (Students, GBP 53 in UK). Landscape Design Trust, PO Box 651, Redhill, RH1 9AJ, United Kingdom; info@landscape.co.uk; http://www.landscape.co.uk. Illus., index, adv. Sample. Vol. ends: Jun. *Indexed:* A22, BRI, GardL. *Bk. rev.:* 2-6. *Aud.:* Ga, Ac.

Formerly published by the Landscape Design Trust, *Green Places* is now the product of GreenSpace Forum, a British charity organization whose mission is "to improve parks and green spaces by raising awareness, involving communities[,] and creating skilled professionals." This journal is published ten times a year, and each issue highlights current public landscape projects across the United Kingdom and, on occasion, other European locations. Despite its glossy appearance and numerous photographs, *Green Places* devotes substantial scholarly attention to environmental issues of interest to many landscape architecture researchers, including "green" park design, the ecological impact of tourism, and sustainable urban planning. Other features include book reviews, notices of regional events, and debates between practicing landscape architects or environmental experts on topical concerns. An important publication for academic architecture libraries, *Green Places* would also make a unique contribution to a public library with an emphasis on art and architecture or urban studies materials.

3035. ***Journal of Landscape Architecture.*** [ISSN: 1862-6033] 2006. 3x/yr. GBP 284 (print & online eds.)). Ed(s): Kelly Shannon, Karsten Jorgensen. Routledge, 4 Park Sq, Milton Park, Abingdon, OX14 4RN, United Kingdom; subscriptions@tandf.co.uk; http://www.tandfonline.com. Adv. Refereed. Reprint: PSC. *Bk. rev.:* 6. *Aud.:* Ac, Sa.

Published by the European Council of Architecture Schools, *JoLA* often presents an interdisciplinary range of topics, including cultural landscapes, land conservation, and urban design. Each issue is typically composed of four or five articles, two thematic columns, book reviews, and announcements for conferences and international special events in landscape architecture. Special columns include "Thinking Eye," a visual presentation of a landscape architect's research project; "Under the Sky," an empirical analysis of a constructed landscape; and "JoLA Lab," a lecture or textual criticism by a noted scholar or practitioner. Articles are written primarily by landscape architecture scholars. Well designed and with ample full-color illustrations, drawings, and maps, *JoLA* has quickly assumed a place alongside other highly regard publications in the field, making it an important addition to research library collections that support landscape architecture programs. Its international scope and quality of scholarship make it an important publication in landscape architecture studies.

3036. ***Landscape.*** [ISSN: 1742-2914] 2004. q. GBP 25 domestic; GBP 45 in Europe; GBP 55 elsewhere. Ed(s): Ruth Slavid. Landscape Institute, Charles Darwin House, 12 Roger St, London, WC1N 2JU, United Kingdom; membership@landscapeinstitute.org; http:// www.landscapeinstitute.org. Adv. Circ: 6000. *Aud.:* Ac, Sa.

This quarterly journal, published by the Landscape Institute, focuses principally on events and projects in U.K. landscape architecture. Compact and attractively designed, *Landscape* typically features five or six regular components, including an events diary; "In Design," an examination of new projects; an obituary column; "Elements," a list of leading suppliers of a featured project; and "My Favorite Landscape," a brief ruminative column in which an architect or designer is selected to highlight a site or design of personal importance. The remainder of the magazine consists of four to five articles on various U.K. firms or thematic topics, ranging from the rejuvenation of historic town squares to waterfront design. This title would be desirable for any research collection with an emphasis on landscape architecture.

3037. ***Landscape and Urban Planning.*** Incorporates (in 1988): *Reclamation and Revegetation Research;* (in 1986): *Urban Ecology;* Formerly (until 1986): *Landscape Planning.* [ISSN: 0169-2046] 1974. 12x/yr. EUR 3923. Ed(s): W N Xiang, J I Nassauer. Elsevier BV, Radarweg 29, Amsterdam, 1043 NX, Netherlands; info@elsevier.com; https://www.elsevier.com. Illus., index, adv. Refereed. *Indexed:* A22, C45, GardL, S25. *Bk. rev.:* 2-4. *Aud.:* Ac, Sa.

Landscape and Urban Planning focuses attention on "the interrelated nature of problems posed by nature and human use of land." Interdisciplinary and international in approach, the publication has traditionally presented a diverse array of issues over the years, ranging from landscape ecology in Sweden to landscape planning in Asia and urban design in rural New England. Thematic issues are published on occasion; individual articles frequently include black-and-white maps, charts, and diagrams with infrequent color illustrations. Intended primarily for a specialized academic landscape architecture audience, *Landscape and Urban Planning* would also be of benefit for any research collection that supports urban and environmental studies, geography, or planning. Electronic full-text versions of articles are available with a subscription.

3038. ***Landscape Architecture.*** [ISSN: 0023-8031] 1910. m. USD 118 (Individuals, USD 59; Members, USD 5.50). Ed(s): Lisa Speckhardt, Bradford McKee. American Society of Landscape Architects, 636 Eye St, NW, Washington, DC 20001; info@asla.org; http://www.asla.org. Illus., index, adv. Sample. Vol. ends: Dec. *Indexed:* A06, A22, EIP, GardL. *Bk. rev.:* 4. *Aud.:* Ac, Sa.

Landscape Architecture is the flagship journal of the American Society of Landscape Architects (ASLA). Although its coverage does occasionally extend to international topics and projects, the journal focuses principally on one activity in the United States. Article topics range from individual landscape architecture projects to theoretical issues concerning urban design and planning; many issues concentrate on land conservation and environmental sustainability. Although most articles are fairly brief—few exceed ten pages—the journal is heavily illustrated throughout with color photographs, maps, plans, and drawings. Typical of many society-based publications in the field, book reviews, product analyses, and columns on professional practice round out each volume. One issue per year is devoted to the winners of the ASLA awards in various categories of design, practice, and communication. Aimed at the professional landscape architect, *Landscape Architecture* is an essential publication for an academic library with a research-level collection in the subject.

3039. ***Landscape Architecture Australia.*** Formerly (until 2006): *Landscape Australia.* [ISSN: 1833-4814] 1971. q. AUD 53 in Australia & New Zealand; AUD 88 elsewhere; AUD 16 per issue in Australia & New Zealand. Ed(s): Ricky Ricardo. Architecture Media Pty Ltd., Level 6, 163 Eastern Rd, South Melbourne, VIC 3205, Australia; melbourne@archmedia.com.au; http://architecturemedia.com. Illus., index, adv. Sample. *Indexed:* GardL. *Bk. rev.:* 2. *Aud.:* Ac.

The official journal of the Australian Institute of Landscape Architects (AILA), *Landscape Architecture Australia* addresses current issues within the profession and provides information on the contemporary projects and designs in Australian landscape architecture. It includes multiple illustrated feature articles on practitioners, firms, environmental policies, and more. Regularly appearing sections include book reviews, product reviews, news items, special events, and an annual summary of the AILA National and State Project Awards. Although its scope is necessarily limited to its geographic purview, this journal is recommended for any research library with specialized interests in landscape architecture or a particular focus on Australian culture.

3040. ***Landscape Journal: design, planning, and management of the land.*** [ISSN: 0277-2426] 1982. s-a. USD 307 print & online eds. Ed(s): Brian D. Lee. University of Wisconsin Press, Journals Division, 1930 Monroe St, 3rd Fl, Madison, WI 53711; journals@uwpress.wisc.edu; http://www.uwpress.org/. Illus., index, adv. Sample. Refereed. Microform: PQC. Reprint: PSC. *Indexed:* A22, Agr, B01, E01, GardL. *Bk. rev.:* 8. *Aud.:* Ac.

Landscape Journal is published by the Council of Educators in Landscape Architecture (CELA), an international body composed of scholars and practitioners active in landscape architecture education and research. As its subtitle suggests, the publication's scope encompasses all areas of practice related to landscape architecture. Articles on the theory and practice of design, planning, and management of the environment around the world are staples. *Landscape Journal* is edited by faculty in the University of Minnesota's Department of Landscape Architecture, and published by the University of Wisconsin Press. Each issue consists of four to six articles and a series of brief reviews of books, conferences, and new technology. Articles contain abstracts and black-and-white illustrations, photographs, tabular data, and drawings. The journal's contributors comprise scholars, educators, or practitioners in the field. Unlike many landscape architecture periodicals, *Landscape Journal* frequently includes articles on historical research topics, making it an appropriate selection for an academic architecture library.

3041. ***Landscape Research.*** Formerly (until 1976): *Landscape Research News.* [ISSN: 0142-6397] 1968. 8x/yr. GBP 1279 (print & online eds.)). Ed(s): Dr. Anna Jorgensen. Routledge, 4 Park Sq, Milton Park, Abingdon, OX14 4RN, United Kingdom; subscriptions@tandf.co.uk; http://www.tandfonline.com. Illus., adv. Sample. Refereed. Reprint: PSC. *Indexed:* A22, B01, C45, E01, S25. *Bk. rev.:* 4, 600-800 words. *Aud.:* Ac, Sa.

Published by Routledge, *Landscape Research* combines "original research papers with reflective critiques of landscape practice." International and multidisciplinary, the journal covers a wide variety of scholarly topics related to landscape architecture, including environmental design, ecology and environmental conservation, land survey, behavioral and cultural studies, and archaeology and history. Volumes are occasionally devoted to a single theme, and typically contain four to seven individual research articles or case studies contributed by scholars in the field. A book reviews section, consisting of four or five brief reviews, closes out each issue. *Landscape Research* is available in print and electronic formats, and is ideally suited for an academic library collection with students and faculty active in landscape research.

3042. ***Landscapes.*** Former titles (until 1999): *Landscape Architectural Review;* (until 1980): *Ontario Association of Landscape Architects Review.* [ISSN: 1492-9600] 1975. q. Free to members; Non-members, CAD 175. Ed(s): Laurie Blake. Naylor (Canada), Inc., 1630 Ness Ave, Ste 300, Winnipeg, MB R3J 3X1, Canada; customersupport@naylor.com. Illus., index, adv. Vol. ends: Dec. *Indexed:* A01, GardL. *Bk. rev.:* Number and length vary. *Aud.:* Ac, Sa.

This quarterly, the journal of the Canadian Society of Landscape Architects (CSLA), focuses primarily on contemporary landscape architecture in Canada. Volumes contain discussion and review of thematic topics. Recent issues include forums on "Montreal's Evolving Urban Vision" and "The Residential Landscape" from a Canadian viewpoint. The subjects of the scholarly articles range from landscape design and planning to the environmental sciences and aspects of professional practice, with some attention devoted to landscape and architectural history. Written primarily by academics and practitioners, the journal's content includes case studies, editorials, book reviews, and a list of recent and forthcoming events such as conferences and competitions. Each year, one issue is devoted to winners of the annual CSLA awards. When coupled with the U.S. journal *Landscape Architecture, Landscapes* offers readers an extensive view into contemporary North American landscape architecture (with the exception of Mexican examples, of course), making it a solid resource for an academic audience but also appropriate for general readers and researchers. The text is in French and English; some articles are written in French with summaries in English. All English-language articles are accompanied by French summaries.

3043. ***Landskab: tidsskrift for planlaegning af have og landskab, review for garden and landscape planning.*** Formerly (until 1968): *Havekunst.* [ISSN: 0023-8066] 1920. 8x/yr. DKK 930 domestic; DKK 990 in Europe; DKK 1168 elsewhere. Ed(s): Annemarie Lund. Arkitektens Forlag, Pasteursvej 14,4, Copenhagen V, 1799, Denmark; arkfo@arkfo.dk; http://www.arkfo.dk. Illus., index, adv. Sample. Vol. ends: Dec. *Bk. rev.:* 2-4. *Aud.:* Ac, Sa.

Published by the Association of Danish Landscape Architects, *Landskab* provides readers extensive coverage of current international projects in landscape architecture and urban design. Although texts are written in Danish, most articles are accompanied by summaries in English. Color photographs, drawings, plans, and details appear extensively throughout. Book reviews are included, but do not appear in every issue. *Landskab* is an appealing publication for any researcher or specialist interested in international, but particularly Danish and Scandinavian, landscape architecture.

Studies in the History of Gardens & Designed Landscapes. See Gardening section.

3044. ***Topos: European landscape magazine.*** [ISSN: 0942-752X] 1992. q. EUR 135 domestic (Students, EUR 95). Callwey Verlag, Streitfeldstr 35, Muenchen, 81673, Germany; info@callwey.de; http://www.callwey.de. Illus., index, adv. *Indexed:* A22. *Bk. rev.:* Number and length vary. *Aud.:* Ac, Sa.

A well-designed and amply illustrated publication, *Topos* covers contemporary international landscape architecture and urban design. *Topos* engages a truly striking assortment of geographical regions, from Argentina to Dubai, and from China to Zambia. Individual issues center on an individual theme (recent examples include "Culturescapes," "Crisis Landscapes," and "Making Space"), with several brief articles that explore different aspects of it. Additional features include a news column, competition and awards notices, and book reviews. Multiple individual projects or firms are also discussed in brief (two- or three-page) articles. The publication's robustly international focus, exceptional book reviews, and overall high quality of production make it an essential purchase for any landscape architecture collection, whether general or academic in nature. Although the journal was previously published in German and English, texts now appear solely in English.

■ LATIN AMERICA AND SPAIN

Michael Scott, Bibliographer for Latin American Studies and Iberian Languages, Lauinger Library, Georgetown University, 37th & O Streets, N.W., Washington, DC 20057

Cheryl LaGuardia, Research Librarian, Widener Library, Harvard University; claguard@fas.harvard.edu

Introduction

The entries in this section discuss popular periodicals published in and about Latin America and Spain. Journals and magazines of all kinds continue to thrive in both regions. General-interest magazines are still quite similar to American counterparts; home-decorating, cars, teenage life, and pop culture are common themes, just as in the United States. While there is a still a great deal of economic inequality, especially in Latin America, overall the middle class continues to grow, and this is reflected in the kinds of magazines currently being published.

Print is still dominant in general-interest magazines, although many of the magazines listed here are quite generous with their online content as well. With an ever-growing population of native Spanish- and Portuguese-speakers in the United States, there are plenty of excellent magazines for all.

Many Latin American countries are world leaders in the open-access academic research movement. Indeed, many of the academic journals listed below that are published in Latin America (and several in Spain) are freely available. The two major open-access platforms in Latin America continue to be Scientific Electronic Library Online (www.scielo.br/) from Brazil, and Redalyc (www.redalyc.org) from the Universidad Autonoma del Estado de Mexico. An ever-growing variety of topics continues to be studied in both non-U.S. and U.S. journals; cinema, art, queer studies, and other interdisciplinary topics are all quite common. Indeed, over the past few years, there has been a gradual trend away from traditional literary studies; "reading" has taken many different forms, from experimental film to murals, to more abstract concepts such as space or historical memory.

The journals and magazines in this section are from an enormous territory and are merely a sampling. If you wish to investigate even more titles, have a look at the Academic Journals and Magazines links via the Latin American Network Information Center (LANIC): http://lanic.utexas.edu/subject/media/. Subscriptions are available either directly through the magazine or through many excellent distributors located throughout the region.

Basic Periodicals

Ga: *America Economia, The Americas* (English edition), *Hola, Tu, TV y Novelas, Vanidades*; Ac: *Hispanic Review, Journal of Latin American Studies, Latin American Literary Review, Latin American Research Review.*

Basic Abstracts and Indexes

Hispanic American Periodicals Index (HAPI) (HAPI).

3045. *Alto Nivel.* [ISSN: 1665-7977] m. Ed(s): Ulises Navarro. Iasa Communications, Rosaleda #34, Colonia Lomas Altas, 11950, Mexico; bbracamonte@iasanet.com.mx; http://www.iasanet.com.mx/. Adv. *Aud.:* Ga, Ac.

Alto Nivel deals primarily with Mexican and Latin American business news. Topics within its scope include government business policy, entrepreneurship, the economy within Mexico and abroad, women in business, banking, technology trends, career advice, and biographical profiles of successful businesspeople. Recommended for public libraries that serve large Latino/Chicano populations, as well as academic libraries that support international business programs with a particular focus on Latin America. (MS)

3046. *America Economia.* 1986. s-m. USD 260 United States. AmericaEconomia, Av Apoquinado 4499, Piso 10, Santiago, , Chile; http://www.americaeconomia.com. *Aud.:* Ga, Ac.

America Economia is a renowned business and economics magazine, similar in scope and content to *The Economist.* Besides in-depth economic reporting and analysis, the magazine also covers business education in Latin America, politics, and economic and educational rankings; and includes opinion columns and blogs. Recommended for public libraries that serve populations interested in Latin American business, and academic libraries that serve Latin American-focused international business programs. (MS)

3047. *The Americas: a quarterly review of Latin American history.* [ISSN: 0003-1615] 1944. q. GBP 154 (print & online eds.)). Ed(s): Donald F Stevens, Ben Vinson, III. Cambridge University Press, 1 Liberty Plaza, Fl 20, New York, NY 10004; online@cambridge.org; https://www.cambridge.org/. Illus., index, adv. Refereed. Reprint: PSC. *Indexed:* A01, A22, AmHI, BRI, CBRI, E01, MLA-IB. *Bk. rev.:* 15, 500-700 words. *Aud.:* Ac.

The Americas is a well-respected journal of Latin American History, published by the Academy of American Franciscan History and edited at Drexel University. Each issue usually contains several book reviews and in-depth academic articles, often relating to the indigenous peoples of the region. Other common topics include the history of the Catholic Church, Latin Americans of African descent, and intellectual history. One recent addition is interviews with Latin American historians. Highly recommended for academic libraries that serve Latin American Studies programs, especially those with a strong indigenous focus. The many book reviews are also excellent for Latin American collection development librarians. (MS)

Ancient Mesoamerica. See Archaeology section.

3048. *Automovil Panamericano.* 1995. m. MXN 480. Editorial Motorpress Televisa, Av Vasco de Quiroga 2000, Edif E, Mexico, Col Santa Fe, Mexico City, 01210, Mexico; automovil.panamericano@editorial.televisa.com.mx. Circ: 52700 Paid. *Aud.:* Ga.

Although naturally focused on the Mexican auto industry, *Automovil panamericano* also reviews new cars manufactured around the world. Other topics include Mexican government policy on highways and car travel; car racing; and, on occasion, even general transit issues and automobile insurance. Highly recommended for public libraries that serve large Spanish-speaking populations. (MS)

3049. *Caras.* Formerly (until 1992): *Tal Cual.* [ISSN: 0328-4301] 1980. w. ARS 3744; ARS 72 newsstand/cover. Editorial Perfil S.A., Chacabuco 271, Buenos Aires, 1069, Argentina; perfilcom@perfil.com.ar; http://www.perfil.com. Adv. *Aud.:* Ga.

Caras is an Argentine general-interest magazine, somewhat like the American publication *People.* Celebrities and other famous people take center stage in this magazine, with stories about the various dramatic (and perhaps less-than-dramatic) events in their lives, all accompanied by many color photos. The publication is naturally but not entirely focused on Argentina; successful Latin Americans, Spaniards, and other nationalities from around the world are regularly featured. Articles are in clear and direct Spanish; and given its broad cultural content, this title may be a great primary-source teaching tool in language classrooms. However, it is recommended mostly for public libraries that serve Spanish-speaking populations.

3050. *Caribbean Quarterly.* [ISSN: 0008-6495] 1949. q. GBP 356 (print & online eds.)). Taylor & Francis, 2, 3 & 4 Park Sq, Milton Park, Abingdon, OX14 4RN, United Kingdom; subscriptions@tandf.co.uk; https://www.tandfonline.com. Index, adv. Microform: PQC. Reprint: PSC. *Indexed:* AmHI, BRI, IIPA, MLA-IB. *Bk. rev.:* Number and length vary. *Aud.:* Ga, Ac.

According the journal itself, *Caribbean Quarterly* "publishes scholarly articles, personal and critical essays, public lectures, poetry, short fiction[,] and book reviews." This journal is published by the University of West Indies, and its focus is primarily (but far from exclusively) on the English-speaking Caribbean. A recent issue, for example, included articles mostly about Jamaica and Barbados, yet there were two articles about the Dominican Republic and the Caribbean coast of Colombia. Highly recommended for academic libraries, as well as for public libraries that serve Caribbean or Caribbean-heritage patrons, and the book reviews are excellent for collection development librarians. (MS)

3051. *Chasqui: revista de literatura latinoamericana.* [ISSN: 0145-8973] 1972. s-a. USD 47 (Individuals, USD 32). Ed(s): David William Foster. Chasqui, c/o David William Foster, Arizona State University, Tempe, AZ 85287. Illus. Refereed. *Indexed:* A01, A22, AmHI, BRI, MLA-IB. *Bk. rev.:* 25-30, 500-3,000 words. *Aud.:* Ac.

Chasqui is devoted entirely to Latin American literature of all periods and regions, and articles may be in English, Spanish, or Portuguese. The articles tend to focus on twentieth- and twenty-first-century literature, and deal with postmodernist themes, as well as marginalized populations (queer, indigenous, women, etc.). The journal has an excellent selection of book reviews from both Latin American and U.S. publishers, as well as review essays written in the style of *The New York Review of Books* and similar publications. Highly recommended for academic libraries with strong Latin American literature programs. (MS)

3052. ***Colonial Latin American Review.*** [ISSN: 1060-9164] 1992. 3x/yr. GBP 784 (print & online eds.)). Ed(s): Kris Lane. Routledge, 4 Park Sq, Milton Park, Abingdon, OX14 4RN, United Kingdom; subscriptions@tandf.co.uk; http://www.tandfonline.com. Illus., index, adv. Sample. Refereed. Reprint: PSC. *Indexed:* A01, A22, A47, AmHI, E01, MLA-IB, P61. *Bk. rev.:* Number and length vary. *Aud.:* Ac.

This interdisciplinary academic journal deals primary in the historical and political milieu of colonial Latin America, yet within this context, literature and the arts are treated as well. Each issue also contains at least several book reviews, and articles are written in English, Spanish, or Portuguese. *CLAR* would provide excellent support for Latin American Studies programs/ departments, as well as history, literature, and art history departments that have a strong focus on Latin America. (MS)

3053. ***Contenido.*** [ISSN: 0010-7581] 1963. m. Editorial Contenido S.A., Darwin 101, Nueva Cobertura, Mexico City, 11590, Mexico; ecsa@data.net.mx; http://www.contenido.com.mx. Illus., adv. *Aud.:* Ga, Ac.

This newsmagazine naturally focuses on Mexico, but other topics such as international relations (especially with the United States), health, and science are also covered. It is similar to the American magazines *Time* and *Newsweek,* although-as it is a monthly publication-its articles tend to be more in-depth and analytical. Highly recommended for public libraries that serve Spanish-speaking patrons, especially Mexicans or Mexican-Americans, and also for academic libraries that serve academic programs that have a particularly strong focus on Mexico. (MS)

3054. ***Cuadernos Hispanoamericanos.*** [ISSN: 0011-250X] 1948. m. Agencia Espanola de Cooperacion Internacional (A E C I), Avenida Reyes Catolicos 4, Madrid, 28040, Spain; http://www.aecid.es/es/. Illus. Reprint: PSC. *Indexed:* A22, MLA-IB. *Bk. rev.:* Number and length vary. *Aud.:* Ga, Ac.

Different from many academic publications, *Cuadernos hispanoamericanos* contains original essays, poetry, and fiction, as well as more traditional articles that deal with literary analysis and history, all by leading Latin American writers and academics. For those seeking the region's latest philosophical and literary trends, the journal is hard to surpass. Interviews and themed issues are also common. Highly recommended for academic libraries with strong programs in Latin American studies and literature, and because of the large amount of original content, perhaps also for public libraries that serve Hispanic populations. (MS)

3055. ***Cult.*** [ISSN: 1414-7076] 1997. m. BRL 148 domestic. Ed(s): Daysi Bregantini. Editora Bregantini, Santo Agostinho 70, Paraiso, Sao Paulo, 01533-070, Brazil. Illus. *Aud.:* Ga, Ac.

Cult (short for "Cultura") is a Brazilian general-interest magazine that primarily covers literary and philosophical topics, as well as film and the fine and performing arts. About half of the content has a worldwide focus, and usually it deals with postmodern arts and philosophy. The other half is about the newest trends in Brazilian literature and other arts. For such highbrow themes, this magazine is quite glossy and beautifully made, and readily accessible to any patron who is interested in the latest literary and arts news from Brazil. Recommended for public libraries that have large Portuguese-speaking populations (especially but not exclusively Brazilians and Brazilian-Americans), and also for academic libraries that serve Lusophone-focused departments. (MS)

3056. ***Ene (Madrid).*** [ISSN: 1699-5856] 2005. q. EUR 48. La Fabrica, Calle Veronica 13, Madrid, 28014, Spain; lafabrica@lafabrica.com; http://www.lafabrica.com/es/. *Aud.:* Ga, Ac.

Ene is a literary and arts magazine that focuses on both Iberia and Latin America. Top contemporary writers and artists are featured in each issue, each of which has a particular theme. Most articles are long-form essays about these topics. Up-and-coming writers are also regularly featured in special issues, so the magazine is an excellent place to start to find the latest works by authors from all parts of the Spanish-speaking world. Highly recommended for academic libraries, and also for public libraries that serve Spanish-speaking populations. (MS)

3057. ***Frontera Norte.*** [ISSN: 0187-7372] 1989. s-a. Individuals, MXN 500. Ed(s): Miguel Olmos Aguilera. El Colegio de la Frontra Norte, A.C., Blvd Abelardo L. Rodriguez 2925, Zona del RIo, Tijuana, Baja California, 22010, Mexico; subscribe@colef.mx; http://www.colef.mx/. Illus. Refereed. Circ: 500. *Indexed:* A01, Chicano. *Bk. rev.:* Number and length vary. *Aud.:* Ac.

This academic journal mostly focuses on U.S.-Mexico border issues, although Mexico's relations with other countries are also discussed on occasion. Given recent events in the region, articles currently focus on security and political issues, but there are also others that discuss economics, culture, and historical aspects as well. Vital for academic collections that serve departments that teach and research these same issues (Latin American Studies, security studies, etc.), and also for programs that focus on border studies in general. Patrons of public libraries near the U.S.-Mexican border may also find it of great interest. (MS)

3058. ***Guaraguao: revista de cultura latinoamericana.*** [ISSN: 1137-2354] 1996. 3x/yr. EUR 45 domestic; EUR 53 in Europe; EUR 60 elsewhere. Ed(s): Nela Filimon. Centro de Estudios y Cooperacion para America Latina, Calle Mare de Deu del Port 265, Bajos 2a, Barcelona, 08038, Spain; e.bielsa@socsci.gla.ac.uk. *Indexed:* MLA-IB. *Bk. rev.:* Number and length vary. *Aud.:* Ga, Ac.

Guaraguao covers the latest Latin American literary, cultural, and arts criticism. Each issue has several articles that deals with timely topics, from the U.S.-Mexican border to classic and avant-garde writers, to heady articles on aesthetics. Also included are original stories and poetry, fragments of newly published novels, and many book reviews. Although its themes are generally academically-focused, the language is clear and readily accessible to a variety of audiences. Highly recommended for academic libraries that serve Latin American Studies and literature departments, as well as public libraries that serve Latin American and/or Chicano patrons. (MS)

3059. ***Hispanic Journal (Indiana).*** [ISSN: 0271-0986] 1979. s-a. Ed(s): Vicente Gomis-Izquierdo. Indiana University of Pennsylvania, Department of Foreign Languages, Sutton Hall, Rm 455, Indiana, PA 15705; http://www.iup.edu/spanish/publications/default.aspx. Refereed. *Indexed:* A22, AmHI, MLA-IB. *Bk. rev.:* Number per issue varies; 550-1,750 words. *Aud.:* Ac.

Hispanic Journal covers literary and linguistics topics from both Iberia and Latin America, with a slight emphasis on nineteenth- through twenty-first-century literature. A helpful feature is a bibliography of books and journals that the journal has received recently, which may aid in collection development decisions. Highly recommended for academic libraries. (MS)

Hispanic Journal of Behavioral Sciences. See Psychology section.

3060. ***Hispanic Review.*** [ISSN: 0018-2176] 1933. q. USD 104 (print & online eds.) Individuals, USD 55 (print & online eds)). Ed(s): Linda Grabner. University of Pennsylvania Press, 3905 Spruce St, Philadelphia, PA 19104; journals@pobox.upenn.edu; http://www.upenn.edu/pennpress. Illus., adv. Sample. Refereed. Vol. ends: Fall. *Indexed:* A01, A22, AmHI, BRI, E01, ENW, MASUSE, MLA-IB. *Bk. rev.:* Number and length vary. *Aud.:* Ac.

This is one of the premier academic journals on Hispanic literature and culture. Articles cover all time periods and regions (although balanced about evenly between Spain and Spanish-speaking America), and are either in Spanish or English. Some articles are more general in nature, such as on a literary theory topic or intellectual history. At least a few book reviews are included in each issue. Highly recommended for academic libraries. (MS)

3061. ***Hispanofila: ensayos de literatura.*** [ISSN: 0018-2206] 1957. 3x/yr. USD 55 (Individuals, USD 45). Ed(s): Juan Carlos' Gonzalez-Espitia. University of North Carolina at Chapel Hill, Department of Romance Studies, CB 3170, 238 Day Hall, Chapel Hill, NC 27599; romlpub@unc.edu; http://www.ibiblio.org/. Illus., index, adv. Refereed. Vol. ends: May. Microform: PQC. *Indexed:* A01, A22, AmHI, BRI, MLA-IB. *Bk. rev.:* Number and length vary. *Aud.:* Ac.

This journal publishes academic articles, summaries, and reviews of new titles in the field of Hispanic literatures. Articles are in Spanish or English, and cover all time periods and literary genres. Recommended for academic libraries. (MS)

3062. *Historia Mexicana.* [ISSN: 0185-0172] 1951. 4x/yr. Ed(s): Beatriz Moran Gortari. Colegio de Mexico, A.C., Departamento de Publicaciones, Camino al Ajusco 20, Col. Pedregal Santa Teresa, Mexico City, 10740, Mexico; http://www.colmex.mx. Illus., index, adv. Refereed. Vol. ends: Jun. *Indexed:* A22, A47, AmHI, BAS, Chicano, IBSS, MLA-IB, P61. *Bk. rev.:* 2-8, 500-2,000 words. *Aud.:* Ac.

This Spanish-language journal is published by the Colegio de Mexico, and is one of the "go-to" publications on Mexican history. Occasionally there are themed issues, but usually each number deals with a wide variety of historical topics. Critical essays, book reviews and summaries, bibliographies of received publications, and abstracts of the main articles in both English and Spanish are also often included. Highly recommended for academic libraries, especially those that serve institutions with a strong focus on Mexican history and culture.(MS)

3063. *Hola.* [ISSN: 0214-3895] 1944. w. Empresa Editora Hola, S.A., C. Velazquez, 98 3o., Madrid, 28006, Spain. Illus., adv. Sample. *Aud.:* Ga.

The main focus of *Hola* is celebrity gossip and lifestyles, but each issue also contains information about both men's and women's fashion, food, interior decorating, and even current events and politics. Content is chiefly focused on Spanish celebrities and royalty, but superstars from all corners of the globe are also regularly featured. It is somewhat like a combination of the American magazines *People* and *Time,* with more emphasis on the celebrity side of things. Recommended for public libraries with Spanish-speaking patrons. Both digital and print subscriptions are available. (MS)

3064. *Journal of Latin American Cultural Studies.* Formerly (until 1995): *Travesia.* [ISSN: 1356-9325] 1992. 4x/yr. GBP 1030 (print & online eds.)). Ed(s): Fernando Sdrigotti, Jens Andermann. Routledge, 4 Park Sq, Milton Park, Abingdon, OX14 4RN, United Kingdom; subscriptions@tandf.co.uk; http://www.tandfonline.com. Illus., adv. Sample. Refereed. Reprint: PSC. *Indexed:* A01, A22, AmHI, E01, MLA-IB, P61, SSA. *Bk. rev.:* Varies by issue. *Aud.:* Ac.

Articles in this academic journal often take a multidisciplinary approach; film, popular culture, racial politics, and new ways of looking at canonical works are just a few topics in recent issues. Some issues also contain reprints of earlier articles for rereading, and others contains book reviews or review essays as well. Highly recommended for universities and colleges with Latin American Studies programs, especially those with particular strengths in literary and culture theory, film, literature, and cultural history. (MS)

3065. *Journal of Latin American Studies.* [ISSN: 0022-216X] 1969. q. GBP 413. Ed(s): Gareth A. Jones, Diego Sanchez-Ancochea. Cambridge University Press, University Printing House, Shaftesbury Rd, Cambridge, CB2 8BS, United Kingdom; journals@cambridge.org; https://www.cambridge.org/. Illus. Refereed. Vol. ends: Nov. Microform: PQC. Reprint: PSC. *Indexed:* A01, A22, A47, BRI, C45, Chicano, E01, IBSS, MLA-IB, P61, SSA. *Bk. rev.:* 22-28, 350-2,000 words. *Aud.:* Ga, Ac.

The articles in *JLAS* chiefly focus on the relevant social sciences, history, international relations, politics, and indigenous peoples, as well as specific topics such as colonization/decolonization and land reform. One valuable aspect of the journal is the many book reviews that cover a wide variety of recent publications, as well as the "Books Received" section, which is a brief list of even more recent titles. Highly recommended for academic libraries that serve Latin American Studies programs (especially programs focused on the topics listed above) and, because of its breadth, possibly for public libraries that serve Latino/Chicano populations. (MS)

3066. *Latin American Business Review.* [ISSN: 1097-8526] 1998. q. GBP 500 (print & online eds.)). Ed(s): Lucilia Silva, Carlos Heitor Campani. Routledge, 530 Walnut St, Ste 850, Philadelphia, PA 19106; enquiries@tandfonline.com; http://www.tandfonline.com. Adv. Sample. Refereed. Reprint: PSC. *Indexed:* A01, A22, B01, E01, IBSS. *Aud.:* Ga, Ac.

This journal contains academic articles on Latin American business culture, trends, and practices. A variety of subfields in economics are also covered, including applied and developmental economics. Articles are in English, and cover all parts of Latin America, including non-Spanish-speaking countries. Highly recommended for libraries that serve international business programs in Latin America, and recommended for specialized public library collections. (MS)

3067. *Latin American Indian Literatures Journal.* Formerly (until 1985): *Latin American Indian Literatures.* [ISSN: 0888-5613] 1977. s-a. USD 51 (Individuals, USD 30; USD 30 per issue). Ed(s): Dr. Mary H Preuss. Pennsylvania State University at McKeesport, 4000 University Dr, McKeesport, PA 15132. Illus. Refereed. *Indexed:* A22, A47, AmHI, MLA-IB. *Bk. rev.:* 3-5, 500-1,500 words. *Aud.:* Ac.

This academic journal is about the literature, mythology, and oral tradition of Latin American indigenous peoples. Articles are generally in English, but French, Spanish, and Portuguese appear from time to time as well. It is truly multidisciplinary, with articles by anthropologists, historians, literary scholars, and political scientists. Book reviews and stories or poems in indigenous languages also often make an appearance. Highly recommended for academic libraries that serve Latin American Studies programs and/or Spanish departments with an especially strong focus on indigenous literatures, culture, and history. (MS)

3068. *Latin American Literary Review.* [ISSN: 0047-4134] 1972. s-a. USD 53 (Individuals, USD 30). Latin American Literary Review Press, PO Box 7530, Pittsburgh, PA 15213; http://www.lalrp.org. Illus., index. Refereed. Microform: PQC. *Indexed:* A01, A22, AmHI, BRI, Chicano, MLA-IB. *Bk. rev.:* 4-6, 90-100 words. *Aud.:* Ac.

As one can infer from the title, this prestigious journal chiefly is about Latin American literature, especially from the nineteenth century until the present day. Articles are in English, Spanish, or Portuguese, and excellent book reviews are often included as well. Highly recommended for academic libraries. (MS)

3069. *Latin American Perspectives: a journal on capitalism and socialism.* [ISSN: 0094-582X] 1974. bi-m. USD 963 (print & online eds.)). Ed(s): Ronald H Chilcote. Sage Publications, Inc., 2455 Teller Rd, Thousand Oaks, CA 91320; info@sagepub.com; http://www.sagepub.com. Illus. Refereed. Microform: PQC. Reprint: PSC. *Indexed:* A22, BRI, Chicano, E01, IBSS, MLA-IB, P61. *Bk. rev.:* Number and length vary. *Aud.:* Ga, Ac.

Each issue of *Latin American Perspectives* focuses on a single theme, and articles often deal with topics on the Latin American diaspora, including the United States and other countries. The overall tone is academic, but given its multidisciplinary approach, general readers may enjoy reading about popular culture via hip-hop music, contemporary and experimental film, and other less traditional forms of expression. Articles are in English, but abstracts are in both English and the language of the country considered in the article (Portuguese for Brazil, etc.). Highly recommended for academic libraries that serve highly multidisciplinary programs in Latin American Studies, and for public libraries with patrons that have an interest in the region. (MS)

3070. *Latin American Research Review.* [ISSN: 0023-8791] 1965. 3x/yr. Free to members. Ed(s): Philip Oxhorn. Latin American Studies Association, 315 Bellefield Ave, Pittsburgh, PA 15213; lasa@pitt.edu; http://lasa.international.pitt.edu/. Illus., index, adv. Refereed. *Indexed:* A01, A22, AmHI, B01, BRI, C42, Chicano, E01, IBSS, MLA-IB, P61. *Aud.:* Ga, Ac.

This journal, the official publication of the Latin American Studies Association, deals with a broad range of topics in each issue. Indigenous studies, literary criticism, historical analysis, and sociological quality-of-life studies all have appeared in recent issues. Each issue also includes review essays, in which scholars write about topics using recent publications as the base of discussion. Highly recommended for academic libraries that serve Latin American Studies departments or programs, and also for large public libraries or for public libraries that serve large Latino/Chicano populations. (MS)

3071. ***Latin American Theatre Review.*** [ISSN: 0023-8813] 1967. s-a. Kansas State University, Department of Spanish and Portuguese, 1445 Jayhawk Blvd, Rm 2650, Lawrence, KS 66045; latrsubscription@ku.edu . Illus., index, adv. Sample. Refereed. *Indexed:* A22, Chicano, IIPA, MLA-IB. *Bk. rev.:* Number and length vary. *Aud.:* Ac.

LATR is the premier journal for Latin American theater and performance studies. Each issue contains many academic articles, of course, but interviews, conference and theater reports, and many book reviews also make appearances. Articles treat both contemporary theater and the history of theater in the region, and are chiefly in Spanish. Highly recommended for academic libraries and also larger public libraries, as Latin American theater and performance art continue to grow in popularity in the United States.

3072. ***Letras Femeninas.*** [ISSN: 0277-4356] 1975. s-a. Free to members. Ed(s): Dianna Niebylski. University of Texas at Austin, College of Liberal Arts, 601 S. Morgan Str ((MC 315)), 1722 University Hall, Chicago, IL 60607; https://silc.asu.edu/. Illus. Refereed. *Indexed:* BRI, MLA-IB. *Bk. rev.:* Number and length vary. *Aud.:* Ac.

Articles in *Letras femeninas* look at the gamut of Hispanic literature from a feminist perspective. Each issue covers virtually all regions and time periods, all dealing with women and their relation to literary culture, as well as the field of women's studies in general. Many issues contain summaries and reviews of newly published monographs, as well. Highly recommended for academic libraries that serve Latin American literature or women's studies programs.

3073. ***Letras Libres.*** [ISSN: 1606-5913] 1999. m. MXN 500 domestic; USD 80 in US & Canada; USD 110 elsewhere. Ed(s): Enrique Krauze. Editorial Vuelta, SA de CV, Presidente Carranza 210, Coyoacan, Mexico, D.F., 04000, Mexico. Circ: 30000. *Indexed:* MLA-IB. *Aud.:* Ga, Ac.

Letras libres is a multicolor, glossy publication that is probably most similar to the American publication *The New Yorker.* Its focus is primarily literary, including many summaries and reviews of new titles, but politics, the fine arts, media, and opinion pieces figure prominently as well. The publication mostly covers Mexico or Spain (there are two different editions from these countries), but most issues deal with other Latin American-and even famous non-Spanish-language writers and events. Articles are almost always by the foremost current writers and intellectuals. Highly recommended for public libraries that serve a Spanish-speaking population, and also for academic libraries that serve institutions with strong Spanish-language and comparative literature programs.

3074. ***Luso - Brazilian Review.*** [ISSN: 0024-7413] 1963. s-a. USD 265 print & online eds. Ed(s): Peter M Beattie, Pedro Meira Monteiro. University of Wisconsin Press, Journals Division, 1930 Monroe St, 3rd Fl, Madison, WI 53711; journals@uwpress.wisc.edu; http://www.uwpress.org/. Illus. Refereed. Microform: PQC. Reprint: PSC. *Indexed:* A01, A22, AmHI, E01, MLA-IB, P61. *Bk. rev.:* 5, 700 words. *Aud.:* Ga, Ac.

Luso-Brazilian Review publishes articles (in both English and Portuguese) on Portuguese, Brazilian, and Luso-African literatures, linguistics, and cultures. It is the oldest publication of its kind in the United States. The focus is primarily on literary studies, but issues often contain articles on Lusophone history, politics, or other social sciences. Each issue also contains many book reviews. While it is an academic journal, and therefore best suited to academic libraries that serve Latin American and Lusophone studies, the journal may be popular in public libraries that serve large Luso/Brazilian-American populations. (MS)

3075. ***Mexican Studies.*** [ISSN: 0742-9797] 1985. 3x/yr. USD 240 (print & online eds.)). Ed(s): Ruth Hellier-Tinoco. University of California Press, Journals Division, 155 Grand Avenue, Ste 400, Oakland, CA 94612-3764; http://www.ucpress.edu/journals.php. Illus., index, adv. Refereed. *Indexed:* A01, A22, A47, AmHI, BRI, Chicano, E01, ENW, MLA-IB, P61, SSA. *Bk. rev.:* Number and length vary. *Aud.:* Ga, Ac.

This journal covers the history, economics, politics, and culture of Mexico, with a bit more of an emphasis on the social sciences. Articles are in English or Spanish and cover all regions and historical time periods. Some issues contain book reviews or a bibliography of books received. Highly recommended for academic libraries that serve academic programs with a strong emphasis on Mexico, and for public libraries that serve large Mexican or Mexican-American populations. (MS)

3076. ***Mexico Desconocido.*** [ISSN: 0187-1560] 1976. m. MXN 599 domestic. Ed(s): Beatriz Quintanar. Editorial Mexico Desconocido S.A.de C.V., Rosalea no. 34, Col. Lomas Altas, Mexico, D.F., 11950, Mexico. Illus., index, adv. *Aud.:* Ga.

A lavishly illustrated and carefully designed journal, *Mexico Desconocido* celebrates the lesser-known beauties of Mexico, covering the art, music, culture, and customs of Mexican regions and cultures that generally get little attention from tourists. The color photo essays are stunning, and the articles are written in an informative yet engaging style. The magazine is justly celebrated for its efforts, having received a number of national awards from the Mexican government for its efforts to promote and preserve traditional Mexican arts and folklore. Excerpts from the print magazine are available from the magazine's web site in English and Spanish; however, the reader may be tempted to skip the text and go straight to the beautiful photos. Recommended for public libraries that service Mexican and Mexican-Americans in particular.

3077. ***N A C L A Report on the Americas.*** Former titles (until 1993): *Report on the Americas;* (until 1991): *N A C L A Report on the Americas;* (until 1977): *N A C L A's Latin America and Empire Report;* (until 1971): *N A C L A Newsletter.* [ISSN: 1071-4839] 1967. q. GBP 292 (print & online eds.)). Ed(s): Alejandro Velasco. Routledge, 530 Walnut St, Ste 850, Philadelphia, PA 19106; enquiries@tandfonline.com; http://www.tandfonline.com. Illus., adv. Vol. ends: Jul/Jun. Reprint: PSC. *Indexed:* A01, A22, BRI. *Bk. rev.:* Number and length vary. *Aud.:* Ga, Ac.

After a year of hiatus, this excellent journal is back in print. It is chiefly a political science, history, and current affairs journal, edited by the North American Congress on Latin America but now published by Routledge. Each issue centers on a specific topic, mostly from a social sciences and historical perspective, and articles are often less academic in tone than those of other journals with the same sort of coverage. Issues surrounding racial minorities and women are also often given particular attention, many times with an activist point of view. U.S. and Latin American relations are also a common topic. Recommended for academic libraries that serve Latin American studies programs or departments, and also for public libraries that serve politically active Chicano/Latino populations and their allies. (MS)

3078. ***Problemas del Desarrollo: revista latinoamericana de economia.*** [ISSN: 0301-7036] 1969. q. Universidad Nacional Autonoma de Mexico, Instituto de Investigaciones Economicas, Torre II de Humanidades 5o Piso, Ciudad Universitaria, Mexico City, 04510, Mexico; revprode@servidor.unam.mx; http://probdes.iiec.unam.mx. Illus., index, adv. Refereed. *Indexed:* A01, A22, B01, EconLit, IBSS. *Bk. rev.:* 1-10, 800-1,500 words. *Aud.:* Ac.

As one can guess from its title, this Spanish-language academic journal contains articles about economic development issues, particularly in Latin America. General economics issues are also often discussed, such as the growing relationship between Latin America and China, and the effects of economic uncertainty in the region. This title is vital for libraries that serve Latin American Studies programs that specialize in political economy and economic development, as well as economics departments with a particularly strong focus on Latin America. Issues are also available in English from 2012 onward, and, beginning in 2016, abstracts are available in Mandarin Chinese. (MS)

3079. ***Proceso: semanario de informacion y analisis.*** [ISSN: 0185-1632] 1976. w. MXN 1600 domestic; USD 390 United States; CAD 430 Canada. Ed(s): Rafael Rodriguez Castaneda. Comunicacion e Informacion S.A. de C.V. (CISA), Fresas 13, Col Del Valle, Mexico City, 03100, Mexico; buzon@proceso.com.mx; http://www.proceso.com.mx/. Illus., adv. Sample. *Bk. rev.:* 1, lengthy. *Aud.:* Ga, Ac.

This newsmagazine naturally chiefly focuses on Mexican politics and culture, but international issues and events are treated in depth. Similar to *Time* or *Newsweek, Proceso* is aimed toward a general readership, and articles are highly analytical and in-depth. Highly recommended for public libraries that serve Latino and Chicano populations, and also for academic libraries that serve departments and programs that have a strong focus on Mexico. (MS)

3080. ***Review (New York, 1968): literature and arts of the Americas.*** Formerly (until 1987): *Review - Center for Inter-American Relations.* [ISSN: 0890-5762] 1968. s-a. GBP 313 (print & online eds.)). Ed(s): Daniel Shapiro, Daniel Shapiro. Routledge, 530 Walnut St, Ste 850, Philadelphia, PA 19106; orders@taylorandfrancis.com; http://www.tandfonline.com. Illus., adv. Sample. Refereed. Microform: PQC. Reprint: PSC. *Indexed:* A22, AmHI, E01, MLA-IB. *Bk. rev.:* 9-12, 900-1,200 words. *Aud.:* Ga, Ac, Sa.

This is a leading English-language journal on contemporary arts and literature in the Americas. Each issue focuses on a particular topic, place, and/or time period, and articles tend to be written in a kind of "public scholar" tone. Each issue also contains numerous reviews of recently published monographs. Highly recommended for public, academic, and arts libraries. (MS)

3081. ***Revista Canadiense de Estudios Hispanicos.*** [ISSN: 0384-8167] 1970. 3x/yr. CAD 60. Ed(s): Richard Young. Revista Canadiense de Estudios Hispanicos, Dept of Language, Literatures & Cultures, McGill University, Montreal, QC H3A 3RI, Canada. Illus., index, adv. Refereed. Vol. ends: Spring. *Indexed:* A22, MLA-IB. *Bk. rev.:* 10-15, 500-1,500 words. *Aud.:* Ac.

This prestigious academic journal covers a broad variety of topics (literature, linguistics, cultural studies, etc.) within the field of Hispanic Studies. Issues often focus on a specific event or topic, and are generally in Spanish, although English and other languages appear from time to time as well. All time periods and places are also represented, often even within a single issue. On occasion, there are articles particularly about Canada's relations with the Hispanic world. Highly recommended for academic libraries. (MS)

3082. ***Revista de Critica Literaria Latinoamericana.*** [ISSN: 0252-8843] 1975. s-a. USD 80 (Individuals, USD 50). Latinoamericana Editores, Department of Spanish and Portuguese, 5319 Dwinelle Hall, Berkeley, CA 94720; gspa@berkeley.edu. Refereed. *Indexed:* A01, A22, AmHI, MLA-IB. *Bk. rev.:* Number and length vary. *Aud.:* Ac.

RCLL includes articles and literary criticism summaries of recently published academic books, as well as brief essays on a wide variety of topics. Much of the criticism has a comparative focus; a recent issue, for example, focused on the relations between French philosophy and Latin American literature. Highly recommended for academic libraries that serve academic programs in Latin American and comparative literature. (MS)

3083. ***Revista de Indias.*** [ISSN: 0034-8341] 1940. 3x/yr. EUR 68 domestic; EUR 105 foreign. Ed(s): Consuelo Naranjo Orovio. Consejo Superior de Investigaciones Cientificas (C S I C), Departamento de Publicaciones, Vitruvio 8, Madrid, 28006, Spain; publ@csic.es; http://www.publicaciones.csic.es. Illus., index. *Indexed:* A22, A47, BAS, MLA-IB. *Bk. rev.:* Number and length vary. *Aud.:* Ac.

Published continuously since 1940, *Revista de Indias* publishes articles about the political and cultural history of Latin America, and these often, but not exclusively, focus on colonial- and Independence-era topics. Articles are in Spanish, English, or Portuguese. Many articles also deal with political and cultural relations between Iberia and Latin America. Recommended for academic libraries that have history departments with strong programs in Latin American history, and for multidisciplinary programs in Hispanic studies, especially those that specialize in trans-Atlantic topics. (MS)

3084. ***Revista de Occidente.*** [ISSN: 0034-8635] 1923. m. USD 200 foreign. Ed(s): Jose Varela Ortega. Fundacion Jose Ortega y Gasset, Fortuny 53, Madrid, 28010, Spain; comunicacion@fog.es; http://www.ortegaygasset.edu/. Illus., index, adv. *Indexed:* A22, MLA-IB. *Bk. rev.:* 1-3, 500-1,250 words. *Aud.:* Ga, Ac.

Founded in 1923 by the eminent Spanish philosopher Jose Ortega y Gasset, *Revista de Occidente* contains articles on a variety of cultural topics. Spanish and Latin American literature is discussed, of course, but other features make appearances, too-articles on non-Spanish-language literature and film, author interviews, and general philosophical and cultural essays. It is fairly similar in style and content to *The Paris Review* and comparable publications, although it is perhaps slightly more outright-scholarly. Issues often contain original literary works as well. Highly recommended for academic libraries that serve Hispanic literature, linguistics, and comparative literature programs, and also for public libraries that serve Spanish-speaking populations. (MS)

3085. ***Revista Iberoamericana (Print).*** [ISSN: 0034-9631] 1938. q. USD 195 (print & online eds.)). International Institute of Ibero-American Literature, 1312 Cathedral of Learning, University of Pittsburgh, Pittsburgh, PA 15260. Illus. Refereed. Microform: PQC. Reprint: PSC. *Indexed:* A22, MLA-IB. *Bk. rev.:* 15-20, 500-3,500 words. *Aud.:* Ac.

While many issues of *Revista iberoamericana* cover a range of topics, some issues consider a particular theme or writer in Latin American literature. Articles are chiefly in Spanish, but may appear in Portuguese or English, and often focus on twentieth-century or contemporary literature. The many book reviews and summaries that appear in each issue are also of great use to scholars and librarians alike. The journal's intensely academic tone is especially suited to libraries that serve graduate programs and faculties that research and write on Hispanic-American literature, especially that of past century or so. Highly recommended. (MS)

3086. ***T V y Novelas.*** [ISSN: 0188-0683] 1982. bi-w. USD 12. Editorial Televisa, Vasco de Quiroga 2000, Edificio E, Mexico City, 01210, Mexico; info@editorialtelevisa.com; http://www.esmas.com/editorialtelevisa/. Adv. Circ: 145000 Paid. *Aud.:* Ga.

Falling somewhere in between the American magazines *People* and *Entertainment Weekly, TV y Novelas* (the "Novelas" refers to *telenovelas*) mostly contains celebrity gossip from both the Latin American and Anglo-American regions, as well as TV and film news, and articles and photography on the latest fashion trends. Recommended for public libraries that serve Spanish-speaking populations, and possibly for academic libraries that serve programs with a particular focus on Latin American popular culture. (MS)

3087. ***Tu.*** Former titles: *Tu Internacional; Tu.* 1980. m. MXN 207. Editorial Televisa, Vasco de Quiroga 2000, Edificio E, Mexico City, 01210, Mexico; info@editorialtelevisa.com; http://www.esmas.com/editorialtelevisa/. Illus., adv. Circ: 190000. *Aud.:* Ga.

This teen magazine focuses on both Latino/Chicano and Anglo teen celebrities, as well as providing style tips and advice for its young readers. It is very similar in content and presentation to the American magazine *Tiger Beat,* with very bright graphics, many photographs, and short articles. Recommended for public libraries that serve Spanish-speaking patrons. (MS)

3088. ***Vanidades.*** 1961. bi-w. USD 11. Editorial Televisa, Vasco de Quiroga 2000, Edificio E, Mexico City, 01210, Mexico; info@editorialtelevisa.com; http://www.esmas.com/editorialtelevisa/. Illus., adv. Sample. Circ: 891000 Paid. *Aud.:* Ga.

Vanidades covers a broad range of women's issues, and has been in print for more than 50 years. Each issue contains a great amount of information on beauty, fashion, work, and home life and cooking. Highly recommended for public libraries that serve Spanish-speaking populations. (MS)

3089. ***Veja.*** Formerly: *Veja e Leia.* [ISSN: 0100-7122] 1968. w. BRL 51.30 combined subscription (print & online eds.)). Editora Abril, S.A., Avenida das Nacoes Unidas 7221, Pinheiros, Sao Paulo, 05425-902, Brazil; abrilsac@abril.com.br; http://www.abril.com.br. Illus., adv. Microform: PQC. *Indexed:* B03. *Aud.:* Ga, Ac.

Veja is similar to the American magazines *Time* and *Newsweek.* Each issue focuses on both Brazilian and international politics, and also includes articles on education, history, popular culture, the arts, and opinion pieces as well. Highly recommended for public libraries that serve Brazilian or Brazilian-American patrons, and also academic libraries that serve Latin American Studies programs that have a particular focus on Brazil. (MS)

3090. ***Wadabagei (Online): a journal of the Caribbean and its diasporas.*** [ISSN: 2377-6595] 1998. 3x/yr. Lexington Books, 1150 Carroll St, Room C-315, Brooklyn, NY 11225; caribbeanresearchcenter@gmail.com. Refereed. *Bk. rev.:* Number and length vary. *Aud.:* Ga, Ac.

Wadabagei is an academic journal dedicated to the study of the people of the Caribbean and their diaspora. All languages and nationalities are represented, and articles cover popular, literary, historical, and political culture, all in nearly equal amounts. Each issue contains at least one book review as well. Recommended for academic libraries that serve Latin American programs with a Caribbean focus, and also for other multidisciplinary programs such as migration studies. Also recommended for public libraries that serve Caribbean populations. (MS)

■ LATINO STUDIES

Lisa Gardinier, Latin American & Iberian Studies Librarian, University of Iowa, 100 Main Library, Iowa City, IA 52240; lisa-gardinier@uiowa.edu

Introduction

Like other fields of ethnic and area studies, Latino studies is an inherently interdisciplinary field. Thus, research concerning Latinos is scattered through the mainstream scholarly literature, as well as the specific titles listed here. Some titles, such as *Aztlan* or the *Bilingual Research Journal,* have been around for decades, but many titles are much newer, having appeared within the past 15 years, and they have quickly established strong reputations and academic respect, while allowing for, arguably, a more authentic voice and discussion among peer scholars. As one reviews the list, it is apparent that education and law are well represented, as they reflect major concerns of the Latino population in the United States.

As noted in previous editions of *Magazines for Libraries,* electronic publishing has created an instability that has not yet settled, and the field of Latino studies is no exception, in both popular and scholarly publishing. Electronic publishing is a complex environment with formats that are ever-changing: is it a blog, a web site, an electronic magazine, or a journal? While researching titles included in long-ago editions of *MFL,* I stumbled across *Pocho.com,* the Internet reincarnation of a seminal Chicano zine from the early 1990s. To impose some order, I limited the electronic-only publications that I included in this list to scholarly journals, though that criterion is likely a very inadequate rule.

Latino communities maintain a vibrant set of local news media. I strongly advise public and academic librarians alike to search out their local Latino news outlets, in both English and Spanish, both in the interest of serving Latino patrons and in order to preserve and document the local community through a distinctive perspective. Research for this section found local news publications, both print and online, across the United States, in large urban areas as well as in small population centers.

Basic Periodicals

Aztlan, Journal of Latinos and Education, Latino Studies, People en Espanol.

Basic Abstracts and Indexes

Alternative Press Index, America: History and Life, Chicano Database, Ethnic Newswatch, Hispanic American Periodicals Index (HAPI).

3091. ***The Association of Mexican-American Educators Journal.*** [ISSN: 2377-9160] 1987. 3x/yr. Free. Ed(s): Antonio Camacho, Patricia Sanchez. A M A E Inc., 634 S Spring St, Ste 602, Los Angeles, CA 90014; ExecutiveDirector@amae.org. Refereed. *Bk. rev.:* 1. *Aud.:* Ac, Sa.

The *AMAE Journal* is an open-access, refereed journal published by the Association of Mexican-American Educators and hosted by the Mary Lou Fulton Teachers College at Arizona State University. It is intended to be a forum in which to address research and issues of importance to Mexican-American and Latino children and their families, to inform academia as well as other stakeholders involved in education. Recent articles have addressed undocumented students; professional development of science teachers in immigrant communities; and school finance. Issues also regularly include a book review, a short essay, and/or poetry. URL: http://amaejournal.asu.edu/

3092. ***Aztlan: a journal of Chicano studies.*** [ISSN: 0005-2604] 1970. s-a. USD 225 (print & online eds.) Individuals, USD 30 (print & online eds.)). University of California, Los Angeles, Chicano Studies Research Center Press, 10920 Wilshire Blvd. Ste 900, Los Angeles, CA 90024; csrcinfo@chicano.ucla.edu; http:/www.chicano.ucla.edu. Illus., adv. Refereed. Circ: 700 Paid. Microform: LIB. *Indexed:* A01, A22, AmHI, BRI, CBRI, Chicano, ERIC, MLA-IB, P61. *Bk. rev.:* 1-7, 350-1,000 words. *Aud.:* Ac.

Published since 1970, *Aztlan* is a well-respected journal of refereed scholarly articles from the humanities, social sciences, and arts with a focus on Chicano studies. Each issue includes an "Editor's Commentary," "Essays," "Dossier" (a collection of articles on a similar theme), an "Artist's Communique" by the artist of the cover illustration, and book reviews. Articles examine the intersection of Chicano studies with anthropology, Latino studies, and literature, among other disciplines. Recent topics include Chicana women in politics; immigration; ethnic studies in public schools; Chicano community art initiatives; and Chicano literature. Highly recommended for academic libraries, as it is a core title in its field.

3093. ***Berkeley La Raza Law Journal (Online).*** s-a. Free. Ed(s): Andrea Obando, Joys Choi. University of California, Berkeley, School of Law, 215 Boalt Hall, Berkeley, CA 94720; journalpublications@law.berkeley.edu; https://www.law.berkeley.edu. Reprint: WSH. *Aud.:* Ac, Sa.

As one of the few law reviews in the United States focused on Latino issues, the *Berkeley La Raza Law Journal* declares its mission "to provide an open forum for the analysis of legal issues affecting the Latina/o community; to publish articles written by Latina/o students, scholars, and practitioners; to serve as a legal research resource." It is also of note that the *BLRLJ* has a special interest in encouraging future law students through an undergraduate fellowship. Recent articles include "Erasing Race, Dismissing Class: San Antonio Independent School District v. Rodriguez" and "Improving Legal Aid to Rural Communities in California." Back issues are available on the journal web site. Recommended for academic libraries that support Latino studies collections. URL: www.boalt.org/LRLJ

3094. ***Bilingual Research Journal.*** Former titles (until 1992): *N A B E Journal;* (until 1979): *N A B E.* [ISSN: 1523-5882] 1975. 3x/yr. GBP 246 (print & online eds.)). Ed(s): Maria E Franquiz, Alba Ortiz. Routledge, 530 Walnut St, Ste 850, Philadelphia, PA 19106; enquiries@tandfonline.com; http://www.tandfonline.com. Illus., adv. Refereed. Reprint: PSC. *Indexed:* A01, A22, BRI, Chicano, ERIC, MLA-IB. *Bk. rev.:* 1-2, 800-2200 words. *Aud.:* Ac.

The scope of the *Bilingual Research Journal* goes beyond Latino studies to all language-minority children and youth, but a significant number of the articles concern the education of Latino students. Topics include language politics, pedagogical approaches, and multilingualism. Recent articles include, "Vamos a jugar counters! Learning mathematics through funds of knowledge, play, and the third space" and "The role of bilingual education teachers in preventing inappropriate referrals of ELLs to special education: Implications for response to intervention." *BRJ* is peer-reviewed and publishes three issues per year. Highly recommended for academic libraries.

3095. ***Harvard Journal of Hispanic Policy.*** Former titles (until 1993): *Journal of Hispanic Policy;* (until 1987): *Journal of Hispanic Politics.* [ISSN: 1074-1917] 1985. a. USD 20 per issue. Ed(s): Jeffrey Reynoso. Harvard University, John F. Kennedy School of Government, Harvard Kennedy School, 79 John F. Kennedy Street Box #143, Cambridge, MA 02138; admissions@hks.harvard.edu; http://www.hks.harvard.edu/. Adv. Refereed. *Indexed:* A01, BRI, C42, Chicano, ENW, ERIC. *Bk. rev.:* 1-2. *Aud.:* Ac, Sa.

HJHP is a student-edited annual publication at the Harvard Kennedy School that strives to be a nonpartisan review of politics and policy that affect U.S. Latinos. It publishes a vibrant mix of commentary, interviews, and research articles written by young researchers and graduate students alongside established academics, politicians, and professionals. Recent articles include "Social Security: Strengthening a Vital Safety Net for Latinos," "The Interplay between Prejudice against Latinos and Policy: A Social Psychological Perspective," and "Preserving Latino Heritage: An Interview with Ken Salazar." Back issues are available on the journal web site. Recommended for academic libraries and large public libraries. URL: www.hks.harvard.edu/kssgorg/hjhp/

3096. ***Harvard Latinx Law Review.*** Formerly (until 2018): *Harvard Latino Law Review.* 1994. a. USD 32 domestic; USD 37 foreign. Ed(s): Stephanie Jimenez, Rich Ramirez. Harvard Latino Law Review Committee, c/o Harvard Law School, 1585 Massachusetts Ave WCC 3038, Cambridge, MA 02138. *Indexed:* A01, BRI, L14. *Aud.:* Ac, Sa.

The *Harvard Latino Law Review* is a student-edited law journal that focuses on legal issues of Latinos in the United States. In addition to scholarly articles, *HLLR* publishes conference papers and panel transcripts and occasional interviews. Recent articles have discussed immigration law; accommodations for non-English-speakers; and LatCrit theory. Recommended for academic libraries that support Latino Studies collections.

Hispanic Journal of Behavioral Sciences. See Psychology section.

3097. ***Hispanic Network Magazine: a Latino lifestyle, business and employment magazine.*** [ISSN: 1550-6444] 199?. q. USD 16; USD 4.50 per issue. Ed(s): Beth Fhaner. DiversityComm, Inc., 18 Technology Dr., Ste 170, Irvine, CA 92618; info@hnmagazine.com; http://diversitycomm.net/. Adv. *Aud.:* Hs, Ga.

Hispanic Network is a human resources magazine published by DiversityComm, Inc., which also publishes similar titles focused on the black, veteran, and female workforce. While prominent sponsorships on its web site and advertisements adjacent to articles leave the connection between content and advertising less than transparent, this journal is still of significant value for its short, concise articles about Hispanic impact on and experience in various industries. *HN* also includes a regular section of summaries and photos from recent conferences of Hispanic-oriented professional and advocacy organization, such as the National Council of La Raza and the Society of Mexican Engineers & Scientists. The web site also hosts job listings. Back issues are available on the magazine's web site. Despite the murky policy on advertising and content, *Hispanic Network* would be a valuable addition to public and school libraries that serve a Hispanic population. URL: http://hnmagazine.com/

3098. ***Hispanic Outlook in Higher Education.*** [ISSN: 1054-2337] 1990. bi-w. except Jun. Jul. & Aug. Hispanic Outlook in Higher Education Publishing Company, Inc., 220 Kinderkamack Rd, Westwood, NJ 07675. Illus., adv. Sample. *Indexed:* Chicano, ENW. *Bk. rev.:* Number and length vary. *Aud.:* Sa.

Published since 1990, the *Hispanic Outlook in Higher Education* is a biweekly publication that provides news and analysis on higher education as it impacts Hispanic students, staff, and faculty. Articles are short (one to four pages long) and cover topics specific to Hispanic higher education as well as general higher education trends of interest. There are 11 themed issues each year, including on health professions, graduate education, and women in higher education. It also produces an annual ranking of universities by number of degrees conferred to Hispanic students at bachelor's, master's, and doctoral levels. Recommended for academic libraries that serve education programs and/or Hispanic populations.

3099. ***Journal of Hispanic Higher Education.*** [ISSN: 1538-1927] 2002. q. USD 692 (print & online eds.)). Ed(s): Esther Elena Lopez-Mulnix, Michael William Mulnix. Sage Publications, Inc., 2455 Teller Rd, Thousand Oaks, CA 91320; info@sagepub.com; http://www.sagepub.com. Adv. Sample. Refereed. Reprint: PSC. *Indexed:* A01, A22, Chicano, E01, ERIC, MLA-IB. *Aud.:* Ac.

The *Journal of Hispanic Higher Education* publishes research concerning the entire spectrum of higher education as it relates to Hispanic students and faculty, particularly at Hispanic-serving institutions. It is especially interested in research with a multicultural and interdisciplinary approach. Recent articles have explored service learning, academic achievement, educational leadership training, and student motivation. While articles are in English, abstracts are in both English and Spanish. Recommended for academic libraries.

3100. ***Journal of Latinos and Education.*** [ISSN: 1534-8431] 2002. q. GBP 467 (print & online eds.)). Ed(s): Enrique G Murillo, Jr. Routledge, 530 Walnut St, Ste 850, Philadelphia, PA 19106; enquiries@tandfonline.com; http://www.tandfonline.com. Adv. Sample. Refereed. Reprint: PSC. *Indexed:* A01, A22, E01, ERIC, MLA-IB. *Bk. rev.:* Varies. *Aud.:* Ac.

The *Journal of Latinos and Education* is a quarterly refereed journal focused on creating an interdisciplinary forum for researchers, policymakers, and other stakeholders interested in the education of Latinos, from preschool students to university faculty. The journal solicits articles on policy, practice, and original research, as well as creative works within the overall scope. A recent issue was dedicated to the role and identity of Hispanic-serving institutions in higher education. Other articles have examined de facto segregated schools and research motivation of Latino faculty in STEM disciplines. *JLE* encourages creativity in reoccurring sections such as "Alternative Formats," in which an author recently traced her educational trajectory from Chicago's Little Village to doctoral studies; and "Voces," which recently featured the *testimonio* of working-class Latina scholars. Highly recommended for academic libraries.

3101. ***Latino Leaders: the national magazine of the successful Hispanic American.*** [ISSN: 1529-3998] 1999. bi-m. Ed(s): Wendy Pedrero. Ferraez Publications of America, Corp., Invierno 16, Merced Gomez, 01600, Mexico. Circ: 100000. *Indexed:* BRI. *Aud.:* Ga.

As the title implies, *Latino Leaders* is interested in today's Latino leadership and the cultivation of future Latino leaders. Recent issues have profiled Latino leaders in academia, business, politics, and technology, as well as the primary challenges and opportunities for creating a new generation of leadership. Though much of the subject material comes from the business world, the focus is on the human side of business. *Latino Leaders* is a full-color glossy magazine, published six times per year, and also available in a digital edition. Recommended for public libraries.

3102. ***Latino Policy & Issues Brief.*** [ISSN: 1543-2238] 2002. irreg. Free. University of California, Los Angeles, Chicano Studies Research Center Press, 10920 Wilshire Blvd. Ste 900, Los Angeles, CA 90024; csrcinfo@chicano.ucla.edu; http:/www.chicano.ucla.edu. *Aud.:* Ac.

Latino Policy & Issues Briefs are concise four-page single article research summaries. Recent titles include "Not Quite a Breakthrough: The Oscars and Actors of Color, 2002-2012" and "Undergraduate Student Response to Arizona's Anti-ethnic Studies Bill: Implications for Mental Health." All briefs are available for download online. Recommended for academic libraries. URL: www.chicano.ucla.edu/press/briefs/current.asp

3103. ***Latino Studies.*** [ISSN: 1476-3435] 2003. q. GBP 767. Ed(s): Maria Isabel Ochoa, Lourdes Torres. Palgrave Macmillan Ltd., Macmillan Building, 4 Crinan St, London, N1 9XW, United Kingdom; onlinesales@palgrave.com; http://www.palgrave.com. Illus., adv. Sample. Refereed. Reprint: PSC. *Indexed:* A22, E01, ENW, IBSS, MLA-IB, P61. *Bk. rev.:* 4-9, 750-1,500 words. *Aud.:* Ac.

In just ten years of publication, *Latino Studies* has established itself as a prominent peer-reviewed journal in its interdisciplinary field. Its stated focus is "the lived experience and struggles of Latinas and Latinos for equity, representation, and social justice" in the tradition of activist scholarship. Besides traditional scholarly articles, it also features regular reports from the field, essays on pedagogy and curriculum, and reflections on historical groundbreaking scholarship and events in the context of contemporary Latino scholarship. Also of note, *Latino Studies* publishes the most book reviews of any scholarly journal in the field. Highly recommended for academic libraries.

3104. ***People en Espanol.*** [ISSN: 1096-5750] 1997. m. Time Inc., 1271 Ave of the Americas, New York, NY 10020; information@timeinc.com; http://www.timeinc.com. Adv. *Aud.:* Ga.

Like its weekly English-language sister magazine *People*, this title is focused on celebrity news, human interest stories, fashion, and reviews of beauty supplies and other consumer products, all in Spanish, of course. The celebrities in the pages of *People en Espanol* are familiar to the Latino media, both foreign and U.S. Latinos. *People en Espanol* also runs an annual "Most Beautiful People" issue. Complete issues are by subscription only but a significant number of articles are available on the magazine's web site. Highly recommended for public libraries. URL: www.peopleenespanol.com/

3105. ***Texas Hispanic Journal of Law and Policy.*** Formerly (until 1998): *Hispanic Law Journal.* [ISSN: 1547-4887] 1994. a. USD 30 per issue domestic; USD 40 per issue foreign. Ed(s): Cecilia Bernstein. University of Texas at Austin, School of Law Publications, 727 E Dean Keeton St, Ste 4.134B, Austin, TX 78705; webmaster@law.utexas.edu; https://law.utexas.edu/publications/. Adv. Reprint: WSH. *Indexed:* A01, L14. *Aud.:* Ac, Sa.

This title focuses on the analysis of legal issues and public policy relevant to the Hispanic community and strives to be a neutral forum for such topics. Articles in recent issues have addressed the legal status of Puerto Rico, undocumented migrants, racial profiling, and the legal implications of ESL classrooms. Recommended for academic libraries that support Latino Studies collections.

■ LAW

Austin Martin Williams, Assistant Law Library Director, North Carolina Central University Law Library, Durham, NC 27707

Introduction

There are more than 1,000 English-language legal periodicals published in the United States. That amount alone is enough to overwhelm the average researcher. And yet, this figure doesn't even account for the growing number of international legal periodicals that researchers rely upon to conduct legal research. Due to the number of legal periodicals available, this section will primarily focus on those published in the United States.

While this section does not serve as an exhaustive list of legal periodicals that deserve consideration when building a collection, it does represent the most popular and well-established works of their type. Collection development librarians will find several law journal ranking systems in existence, each with its own criteria and formula for how it determines what it considers to be "the best" legal periodicals. Washington and Lee Law School's "Law Journals: Submissions and Ranking" (managementtools4.wlu.edu/LawJournals/) is by far one of the most dynamic ranking systems. It allows users to filter journals by several characteristics, such as subjects, countries, and language, as well as sort journals by different ranking criterion, such as combined score, journal cites, currency factor, and case cites. While rankings can be helpful, your ultimate consideration should be the needs and interests of your library.

Law schools, commercial entities, and bar associations are the primary publishers of legal periodicals in the United States. While legal periodicals come in a variety of formats, they typically fall within one of the following categories: (1) law reviews, (2) subject-specialty law journals, (3) bar association journals, (4) interdisciplinary journals, (5) news and current awareness journals, and (6) foreign legal periodicals.

Law reviews and journals published by law schools are the most prevalent type of legal scholarship in the United States. Unlike most disciplines, the majority of legal scholarship is edited by student-run journals. Almost every American Bar Association (ABA) accredited law school in the United States supports at least one student-run journal, typically a general-interest law review. There are a number of law schools that support two or more journals. Many journals beyond the general-interest law review are subject-specific, such as *The Journal of Law and Economics*, which is published by the University of Chicago Law School.

Law reviews and journals are generally published as consecutively paginated throughout an entire volume, with each volume encompassing two to eight issues. Depending on the journal, the volume may correspond to an academic year (e.g., 2017-2018) or a calendar year (e.g., 2018). The general format of an issue includes approximately three lead or feature articles, which are written by law professors, legal scholars, and practitioners. In addition, most issues will also include shorter student-written works, typically by members of the journal, in the form of a "comment" or a "note." A comment provides an analysis or a critique of a recent case or legislation. A note discusses and analyzes an original legal issue or problem. Some journals also include book reviews, legislative histories, and summaries of recent court opinions.

The value of law reviews and journals to legal research cannot be overstated. While the articles are academic in nature, their introductory sections provide significant background information on a legal topic. Extensive and thorough footnotes within articles often provide researchers with citations to seminal cases, legislation, and rules that govern the article's topic.

Commercial publishers and bar associations are also great places to find quality legal scholarship. Both are distinguishable from academic law reviews and journals because they include ads, and their articles are generally more practice-focused. Commercial entities tend to publish peer-reviewed, subject-specific journals, and therefore their selection will depend mostly on the needs and interests of your audience. The specific content of bar association journals will vary between associations. Many combine aspects of law journals and magazines to include a mix of scholarly and featured articles, along with general legal news, updates, notices, and other information pertinent to members of that bar association. Bar association journals will not be included in this section because they are generally tailored to a specific geographic region or area of law. Nevertheless, bar association journals are a great source of local and regional information and would add value to a library's collection.

With the evolution of electronic research over the past decade, more researchers have been able to search and access periodicals of all subjects through subscription databases and free online sources. The legal field is no exception. Researchers can access law reviews and journals through the most prevalent academic databases, such as EBSCO, Nexis Uni (formerly LexisNexis Academic), and JSTOR, or through the major legal databases, such as Thomson Reuters Westlaw, Lexis Advance, Bloomberg Law, and HeinOnline. The availability and coverage of the journals will vary depending on the database.

The Open Access movement's impact on the distribution of legal scholarship cannot be understated. Many academic law reviews and journals provide access to current and past issues on their websites for free. Some journals also offer "online companions" or op-ed pieces that supplement their print issues. Moreover, researchers can now find a growing number of journals published exclusively online, without a print counterpart. In conjunction with these developments, law professors and legal scholars are also adding their articles to institutional repositories and uploading their working papers to the Social Science Research Network (SSRN) or LawArXiv. In addition, Law Review Commons (lawreviewcommons.com) provides access to over 300 open-access law reviews and journals.

There is no shortage of legal scholarship available for researchers to explore. At times, there may seem to be too many publications, which makes purchasing decisions increasingly difficult. The key is to find the right balance between print, subscription databases, and freely accessible sources. A suitable collection consists of a few core staples, along with selections that fit your unique needs and interests.

Basic Periodicals

Ga: *A B A Journal, The National Law Journal;* Ac: *A B A Journal, Business Lawyer, Columbia Law Review, Harvard Law Review, Law and Contemporary Problems, The National Law Journal, Yale Law Journal.*

Basic Abstracts and Indexes

Current Law Index; Index to Foreign Legal Periodicals; Index to Legal Periodicals and Books; Index to Legal Periodicals and Books Retrospective; LegalTrac.

3106. *A B A Journal.* Formerly (until 1984): *American Bar Association. Journal;* Which incorporated (1908-1915): *American Bar Association. Comparative Law Bureau. Annual Bulletin.* [ISSN: 0747-0088] 1915. m. USD 75. Ed(s): Molly McDonough, Allen Pusey. American Bar Association, 321 N Clark St, Chicago, IL 60654; service@americanbar.org; http://www.americanbar.org. Illus., index, adv. Sample. Circ: 375045. Vol. ends: Dec. Microform: WSH; PQC. Reprint: WSH. *Indexed:* A01, A22, ATI, B01, BAS, BRI, CBRI, CJPI, Chicano, L14, MLA-IB. *Bk. rev.:* 2-4, 2,000 words. *Aud.:* Ga, Ac, Sa.

The *ABA Journal* is distributed to members of the American Bar Association (ABA), and is designed to be of interest to all segments of the legal profession. Generally, it contains several timely feature articles, along with sections that address various aspects of legal practice, such as "President's Message," where the ABA president expounds on major legal issues; "Supreme Court Report," which discusses pending and recently decided U.S. Supreme Court cases; and "Ethics," which highlights professional responsibility development and ethical issues in the profession. The journal's website also has several useful features, including current news, a list of legal blogs ("blawg"), and podcasts.

3107. *The American Journal of Comparative Law.* [ISSN: 0002-919X] 1952. q. EUR 122. Ed(s): Helge Dedek, Franz Werro. Oxford University Press, 2001 Evans Rd, Cary, NC 27513; orders.us@oup.com; https://academic.oup.com/journals. Illus., index. Refereed. Microform: PQC. Reprint: WSH. *Indexed:* A01, A22, BAS, BRI, IBSS, L14, P61. *Bk. rev.:* 6-10, 1,200-5,000 words. *Aud.:* Ac, Sa.

Comparative law studies the laws of one or more nations and compares them with laws of another, or discusses one jurisdiction's laws in order for the reader to understand how they might differ from the laws of the United States or some other country. *The American Journal of Comparative Law* is a respected, peer-reviewed publication that features articles by major scholars, comments by law students, and book reviews.

3108. *American Journal of International Law.* [ISSN: 0002-9300] 1907. q. GBP 250 (print & online eds.)). Ed(s): Laurence Helfer, Curtis Bradley. Cambridge University Press, University Printing House, Shaftesbury Rd, Cambridge, CB2 8BS, United Kingdom; journals@cambridge.org; https://www.cambridge.org/. Illus., index, adv. Refereed. Vol. ends: Oct. Reprint: PSC; WSH. *Indexed:* A01, A22, BAS, BRI, IBSS, L14, MLA-IB, S25. *Bk. rev.:* 15-20. *Aud.:* Ac, Sa.

The *American Journal of International Law* focuses on all aspects of private and public international law. An annual issue contains discussions on international organizations, foreign-relations law, and international conventions and protocols. A typical issue includes major articles, book reviews, and overviews of recent international decisions. "Contemporary Practice of the United States Relating to International Law," which analyzes international issues by subject, is arranged according to the *Annual Digest of United States Practice in International Law,* which is published by the U.S. Department of State.

3109. *The Business Lawyer.* [ISSN: 0007-6899] 1946. q. Free to members; Non-members, USD 65. Ed(s): Christopher J Rockers. American Bar Association, Section of Business Law, 321 North Clark St, Chicago, IL 60654; service@americanbar.org; http://www.americanbar.org/groups/business_law.html. Illus. Refereed. Microform: MIM; WSH. Reprint: WSH. *Indexed:* A22, B01, BLI, BRI, L14. *Aud.:* Ac, Sa.

The Business Lawyer is highly regarded for its coverage of business law issues, such as commercial law, securities, partnership, and finance law. Focusing on developing trends and case law analysis, the journal often contains special reports, surveys, revisions of model acts, and committee reports from the ABA Business Law Section.

3110. *California Law Review.* [ISSN: 0008-1221] 1912. bi-m. USD 100 (Individuals, USD 85; USD 13 per issue). University of California, Berkeley, School of Law, 40 Boalt Hall, Berkeley, CA 94720; https://www.law.berkeley.edu. Illus., index. Refereed. Vol. ends: Dec. Microform: WSH; PQC. Reprint: WSH. *Indexed:* A01, A22, B01, BRI, CJPI, Chicano, L14. *Bk. rev.:* Occasional, length varies. *Aud.:* Ac, Sa.

The *California Law Review* was the first student-edited law review published west of Illinois, and has included male and female editors since its inception. Each volume includes six issues, and the articles within each issue cover a wide range of topics from business law to tribal sovereignty. The law review also has an online companion called *California Law Review Online.* (californialawreview.org/online/)

Children's Legal Rights Journal. See Sociology and Social Work/General section.

3111. *Columbia Law Review.* [ISSN: 0010-1958] 1901. 8x/yr. Non-members, USD 60. Ed(s): Krystina L Ho. Columbia Law School, 435 W 116th St, New York, NY 10027; Admissions@law.columbia.edu; http://www.law.columbia.edu/. Illus. Refereed. Microform: WSH. Reprint: WSH. *Indexed:* A01, A22, B01, BRI, CBRI, CJPI, IBSS, L14, MLA-IB, P61. *Bk. rev.:* Occasional, essay length. *Aud.:* Ac, Sa.

A prestigious law review from a law school with a long and distinguished history, the *Columbia Law Review* follows the traditional model of publishing lead articles by scholars and professionals, comments and notes by students, and book reviews. The law review publishes eight issues a year, and also has an online companion called *CLR Online.* (columbialawreview.org/content-type/clro/)

Employee Relations Law Journal. See Labor and Industrial Relations section.

Family Law Quarterly. See Marriage and Divorce section.

3112. *The Georgetown Law Journal.* [ISSN: 0016-8092] 1912. bi-m. USD 60 domestic; USD 75 foreign; USD 100 combined subscription domestic (print & online eds.)). Ed(s): Shauna M. Kramer, Greta L. Mattessich. Georgetown University Law Center, 600 New Jersey Ave, NW, Washington, DC 20001; oja@law.georgetown.edu; http://www.law.georgetown.edu. Illus., index. Refereed. Microform: WSH. Reprint: WSH. *Indexed:* A01, A22, B01, BRI, L14, MLA-IB. *Aud.:* Ac, Sa.

The Georgetown Law Journal is the oldest journal published by law schools in the District of Columbia, and has an outstanding reputation for producing traditional legal scholarship. Articles by noted scholars and student research pieces are lengthy, well-documented, and influential. Its "Annual Review of Criminal Procedure" provides a comprehensive survey of all criminal procedure in the federal courts. The journal also has an online companion called *The Georgetown Law Journal Online.* (georgetownlawjournal.org)

Harvard Civil Rights - Civil Liberties Law Review. See Civil Liberties/General section.

3113. *Harvard Journal of Law and Public Policy.* [ISSN: 0193-4872] 1978. 3x/yr. USD 55 domestic; USD 75 foreign. Ed(s): Paul Vanderslice, Jason Shaffer. Harvard Society for Law and Public Policy, Inc., 1585 Massachusetts Ave, Cambridge, MA 02138. Illus. Refereed. Microform: WSH; PMC. Reprint: WSH. *Indexed:* A01, A22, B01, BRI, CJPI, L14. *Bk. rev.:* Occasional. *Aud.:* Ac, Sa.

The *Harvard Journal of Law and Public Policy* is one of the most widely circulated student-edited law journals in the nation. Published by the Harvard Society for Law and Public Policy, a conservative and libertarian student group, this journal primarily publishes symposia issues with articles focusing on a central theme or legal issue. The contributors over the years have included conservative politicians and U.S. Supreme Court justices.

3114. *Harvard Journal on Legislation.* Formerly (until 1964): *Selected Drafts.* [ISSN: 0017-808X] 1958. s-a. USD 42 domestic; USD 52 foreign. Ed(s): Grace Signorelli. Harvard University, Law School, 1563 Massachusetts Ave, Cambridge, MA 02138; http://www.law.harvard.edu/. Illus. Refereed. Reprint: WSH. *Indexed:* A01, A22, B01, BRI, L14, P61. *Bk. rev.:* Occasional. *Aud.:* Ac, Sa.

The *Harvard Journal on Legislation* specializes in the analysis of legislation and the legislative process by focusing on legislative reform and on organizational and procedural factors that affect legislative decision-making. The journal publishes articles that examine a public-policy problem of nationwide significance and propose legislation to resolve it. It also frequently publishes policy essays written by current and former members of Congress.

3115. *Harvard Law Review.* [ISSN: 0017-811X] 1887. 8x/yr. USD 200 (Individuals, USD 60). Harvard Law Review Association, Gannett House, 1511 Massachusetts Ave, Cambridge, MA 02138. Illus. Refereed. Vol. ends: Jun/Nov. Microform: WSH; PQC. Reprint: WSH. *Indexed:* A01, A22, B01, BRI, CBRI, IBSS, L14, MLA-IB, P61. *Bk. rev.:* Occasional, essay length. *Aud.:* Ac, Sa.

Harvard Law School's primary law review is steeped in tradition. Articles published by the *Harvard Law Review* are chosen from an enormous pool of submissions. One highly regarded and useful feature of this law review is its annual "Supreme Court" issue, which provides commentary on and analysis of decisions issued by the U.S. Supreme Court during its most recently completed term, along with tables of relevant statistics. The journal also has an online companion called *Forum.* (harvardlawreview.org/topics/forum/)

Human Rights Law Review. See Civil Liberties/General section.

Journal of Air Law and Commerce. See Transportation section.

3116. *Journal of Civil Law Studies.* [ISSN: 1944-3749] 2008. s-a. Free. Ed(s): Olivier Moreteau, Agustin Parise. Louisiana State University, Paul M. Hebert Law Center, 1 E Campus Dr, Baton Rouge, LA 70803; info@law.lsu.edu; http://www.law.lsu.edu. Refereed. *Indexed:* BRI, L14. *Bk. rev.:* Number and length vary. *Aud.:* Ac, Sa.

As comparative and foreign law becomes more prevalent in the law school curriculum, there is greater demand for articles that deal with different legal systems. The *Journal of Civil Law Studies* is a peer-reviewed, student-edited journal that publishes articles that focus on civil law, mixed jurisdictions that include aspects of civil and common law, and comparative law. Articles may be written in English, French, or Spanish.

Journal of Criminal Justice. See Criminology and Law Enforcement section.

3117. *Journal of Empirical Legal Studies.* [ISSN: 1740-1453] 2004. q. GBP 573. Wiley-Blackwell Publishing, Inc., 350 Main St, Malden, MA 02148; cs-journals@wiley.com; http://onlinelibrary.wiley.com. Adv. Sample. Refereed. Reprint: PSC. *Indexed:* A22, CJPI, E01, L14. *Aud.:* Ac, Sa.

Published on behalf of the Society for Empirical Legal Studies and Cornell Law School, the *Journal of Empirical Legal Studies* is a peer-edited, interdisciplinary journal that focuses on empirical studies of the legal system that would interest scholars in a diverse range of law-related fields. The rise in empirical studies and data analysis in both graduate and undergraduate programs make this journal a logical choice for academic libraries.

3118. *The Journal of Law and Economics.* [ISSN: 0022-2186] 1958. q. USD 178. University of Chicago Press, 1427 E 60th St, Chicago, IL 60637; subscriptions@press.uchicago.edu; http://www.journals.uchicago.edu. Illus., index, adv. Sample. Refereed. Vol. ends: Oct. Reprint: PSC; WSH. *Indexed:* A22, B01, BAS, C45, CJPI, EconLit, IBSS, L14. *Aud.:* Ac, Sa.

The University of Chicago Law School is known for its strong law and economics perspective. Many of the articles published in *The Journal of Law and Economics* are rife with statistical analysis and formulas. Its broad range of topics include economic analysis of regulation and the behavior of regulated firms; the political economy of legislation and the legislative process; law and finance; corporate finance and governance; and industrial organization.

Journal of Law and Religion. See Civil Liberties/Freedom of Thought and Belief section.

Journal of Maritime Law and Commerce. See Transportation section.

Journal of Transportation Law, Logistics and Policy. See Transportation section.

3119. *Law and Contemporary Problems.* [ISSN: 0023-9186] 1933. q. USD 58 domestic; USD 70 foreign. Ed(s): William P Sowers. Duke University, School of Law, 210 Science Dr, Box 90362, Durham, NC 27708; publications@law.duke.edu; http://www.law.duke.edu/. Illus., index, adv. Refereed. Vol. ends: Sep. Reprint: WSH. *Indexed:* A01, A22, BAS, BRI, CJPI, EconLit, IBSS, L14, MLA-IB, P61, SSA. *Aud.:* Ac, Sa.

Many journals have symposium issues, but each issue of *Law and Contemporary Problems* provides a symposium devoted to a timely legal topic. Articles are scholarly, interdisciplinary, and faculty-edited. A special editor for each issue solicits the articles and writes the foreword.

3120. *Law and History Review.* [ISSN: 0738-2480] 1983. q. 3/yr. until 2010. GBP 192 (print & online eds.)). Ed(s): Elizabeth R. Dale. Cambridge University Press, University Printing House, Shaftesbury Rd, Cambridge, CB2 8BS, United Kingdom; journals@cambridge.org; https://www.cambridge.org. Illus., index, adv. Refereed. Microform: WSH; PQC. Reprint: WSH. *Indexed:* A22, BRI, CJPI, L14, MLA-IB, P61. *Bk. rev.:* 10-15, 1,000-2,000 words. *Aud.:* Ac, Sa.

Law and History Review is the official publication of the American Society of Legal History, a membership organization dedicated to further research and writing in the fields of social history of law and the history of its legal ideas and institutions. Articles are scholarly and refereed. Its editorial board consists of preeminent scholars throughout the country. As an interdisciplinary journal, it covers the interplay between law and history.

Law and Human Behavior. See Psychology section.

Law & Inequality: a journal of theory and practice. See Civil Liberties/General section.

3121. *Law and Literature.* Formerly (until 2002): *Cardozo Studies in Law and Literature.* [ISSN: 1535-685X] 1989. 3x/yr. GBP 262 (print & online eds.)). Ed(s): Peter Goodrich. Routledge, 530 Walnut St, Ste 850, Philadelphia, PA 19106; enquiries@tandfonline.com; http://www.tandfonline.com. Illus., index, adv. Refereed. Vol. ends: Winter. Reprint: PSC; WSH. *Indexed:* A22, AmHI, BRI, E01, L14, MLA-IB. *Aud.:* Ga, Ac.

Edited by the faculty at the Benjamin N. Cardozo School of Law and a board of international scholars, *Law and Literature* features contributions by practitioners, scholars, poets, playwrights, artists, and technicians of all kinds. The list of noted contributors is impressive, and the content is a delightful diversion from traditional law review articles.

Law and Philosophy. See Philosophy section.

3122. *Law & Society Review.* Formerly (until 1966): *Law and Society Association. Newsletter.* [ISSN: 0023-9216] 1966. q. GBP 473. Ed(s): Danielle McClellan, Joachim Savelsberg. Wiley-Blackwell Publishing, Inc., 350 Main St, Malden, MA 02148; http://onlinelibrary.wiley.com. Illus., index, adv. Sample. Refereed. Vol. ends: Dec. Microform: WSH. Reprint: PSC; WSH. *Indexed:* A01, A22, BAS, BRI, CJPI, E01, HRIS, IBSS, L14, P61, SSA. *Bk. rev.:* 3-4, essay length. *Aud.:* Ac, Sa.

The Law and Society Association is an international group drawn primarily from the legal and social science professions, whose purpose is the stimulation and support of research and teaching on the cultural, economic, political, psychological, and social aspects of law and legal systems. Contributions to this journal are drawn from law professors, sociologists, and political scientists.

Law Library Journal. See Library and Information Science section.

3123. *Law Practice: the business of practicing law.* Former titles (until 2004): *Law Practice Management;* (until 1990): *Legal Economics;* Which superseded (in 1975): *Legal Economics News.* [ISSN: 1547-9102] 1975. 6x/yr. Free to members; Non-members, USD 64. Ed(s): Daniel E Pinnington, Joan Hamby Feldman. American Bar Association, Law Practice Management Section, 321 N Clark St, Chicago, IL 60610; lpm@abanet.org; http://www.abanet.org/lpm/about/home.shtml. Illus., index, adv. Sample. Vol. ends: Nov. Microform: WSH. *Indexed:* A01, A22, BRI, L14. *Aud.:* Ac, Sa.

The purpose of *Law Practice* is to assist a practicing lawyer in operating and managing a law office in an efficient and economical manner. This magazine provides practical tips and how-to advice on a wide array of topics, such as office management, marketing, file storage, office space design, and technology.

3124. *Michigan Law Review.* [ISSN: 0026-2234] 1902. 8x/yr. USD 60 domestic; USD 70 foreign; USD 10 per issue. Michigan Law Review Association, Hutchins Hall, 625 S State St, Ann Arbor, MI 48109; http://www.law.umich.edu/Pages/default.aspx. Illus., index. Vol. ends: Jun. Microform: WSH. Reprint: WSH. *Indexed:* A01, A22, B01, BRI, EconLit, L14. *Bk. rev.:* Occasional, essay length. *Aud.:* Ac, Sa.

The *Michigan Law Review* is well-known for its high-quality legal scholarship. A typical issue includes articles by legal scholars and notes by law students. The journal also publishes an annual issue devoted to substantive book reviews, which can serve as a useful collection development tool. The law review also has an online companion called *Michigan Law Review Online.* (michiganlawreview.org/category/mlr-online/)

3125. *The National Law Journal.* Former titles (until 20??): *The National Law Journal & Legal Times;* (until 2010): *The National Law Journal.* 1978. w. USD 29.99 combined subscription (print & online eds.)). Ed(s): Beth Frerking. A L M Media, LLC., 120 Broadway, 5th Fl, New York, NY 10271; customercare@alm.com; http://www.alm.com. Illus., index, adv. Vol. ends: Aug. *Indexed:* A22, BRI, Chicano, L14. *Aud.:* Ga, Ac, Sa.

The National Law Journal is one of the most read legal newspapers, and it draws contributors from throughout the United States. This is an excellent source for keeping up with current legal developments. It also offers popular supplements, such as salary surveys and listings of the largest law firms.

3126. *New York University Law Review (New York, 1950).* Former titles (until 1950): *New York University Law Quarterly Review;* (until 1929): *New York University Law Review;* (until 1925): *New York University. Law School. Annual Review.* [ISSN: 0028-7881] 1924. bi-m. USD 50 domestic; USD 56 foreign; USD 16 per issue. New York University School of Law, 40 Washington Sq S, New York, NY 10012; lawlibrary@nyu.edu; http://www.law.nyu.edu. Illus., index, adv. Refereed. Vol. ends: Dec. Microform: WSH. Reprint: WSH. *Indexed:* A01, A22, B01, BRI, HRIS, L14, MLA-IB. *Aud.:* Ac, Sa.

New York University School of Law, founded in 1835, is one of the oldest law schools in the United States. The *New York University Law Review* is a student-edited journal that provides some of the finest legal scholarship from some of the best legal minds in the country. The law review also has an online companion called *N.Y.U. Law Review Online.* (nyulawreview.org/online-features)

News Media and the Law. See Journalism and Writing/Journalism section.

3127. *Preview of United States Supreme Court Cases.* [ISSN: 0363-0048] 1973. 8x/yr. USD 175 (Members, USD 120; Non-members, USD 130). American Bar Association, Public Education Division, 321 N Clark St, Chicago, IL 60654; publiceducation@americanbar.org; http://www.americanbar.org/portals/public_education.html. Illus. Sample. Vol. ends: May. *Indexed:* CJPI. *Aud.:* Ga, Ac, Sa.

Published by the ABA Division for Public Education, *Preview of United States Supreme Court Cases* highlights cases scheduled for oral arguments before the U.S. Supreme Court. Legal professionals with subject matter expertise present the issues, the facts, and their analysis of each case. Unlike issues 1-7, which serve as a preview for each month of the term, issue 8 serves as a review of the entire term, and includes essays and summaries of issued opinions. The journal is an ideal current-awareness tool for a public or academic library.

3128. *Stanford Law Review.* Formerly (until 1948): *Stanford Intramural Law Review.* [ISSN: 0038-9765] 1948. bi-m. USD 60 domestic; USD 75 foreign; USD 22 per issue. Ed(s): Sean Janda, Erica Sollazzo. Stanford University, Stanford Law School, Crown Quadrangle, 559 Nathan Abbott Way, Stanford, CA 94305-8610; communications@law.stanford.edu; https://law.stanford.edu. Illus., index. Refereed. Vol. ends: Jul. Microform: WSH. Reprint: WSH. *Indexed:* A01, A22, ATI, B01, BAS, BRI, L14. *Bk. rev.:* 1-2, 4,000-8,000 words. *Aud.:* Ac, Sa.

The *Stanford Law Review* is a consistently highly ranked journal that can serve as a core source for any law journal collection. Its articles cover a broad range of subjects from constitutional law to corporate governance. Occasionally, essays are published in response to an earlier piece. The law review also has an online companion called *Stanford Law Review Online.* (stanfordlawreview.org/online)

3129. *Student Lawyer (Chicago).* Former titles (until 1972): *Student Lawyer Journal;* (until 1967): *American Bar Association. Student Lawyer Journal;* (until Sep.1967): *American Law Student Association. Student Lawyer Journal;* (until 1964): *Student Lawyer;* (until 1957): *Student Lawyer Journal;* (until 1955): *Student Lawyer.* [ISSN: 0039-274X] 1952. m. Free to members. Ed(s): Barry Malone. American Bar Association, Law Student Division, 321 N Clark St, Chicago, IL 60654; http://www.americanbar.org/groups/law_students.html. Illus. Vol. ends: May. Microform: WSH. *Indexed:* A01, A22, BRI, L14. *Aud.:* Ga, Ac, Sa.

The *Student Lawyer* often contains articles on legal education, social issues, careers, law practice, and news from the ABA Law Student Division. Academic and public libraries should find it to be a worthwhile selection for the insight that it provides on issues that affect students.

3130. *The Supreme Court Review.* [ISSN: 0081-9557] 1960. a. USD 175 (print & online eds.)). Ed(s): David A Strauss, Geoffrey R Stone. University of Chicago Press, 1427 E 60th St, Chicago, IL 60637; subscriptions@press.uchicago.edu; http://www.journals.uchicago.edu. Illus., index. Refereed. Reprint: WSH. *Indexed:* A01, A22, L14. *Aud.:* Ac, Sa.

Since 1960, *The Supreme Court Review* has provided an authoritative survey of the implications of the U.S. Supreme Court's most significant decisions, with an in-depth annual critique of the U.S. Supreme Court and its work. This journal offers an impressive array of authors from a variety of perspectives, including legal academics, judges, political scientists, journalists, historians, economists, policy planners, and sociologists. The editors are respected faculty members at the University of Chicago Law School. This journal is ideal for any academic or public library where patrons research issues related to the U.S. Supreme Court.

3131. *Texas Law Review.* [ISSN: 0040-4411] 1922. 7x/yr. USD 47 domestic; USD 55 foreign; USD 15 per issue. Ed(s): Katherine A Marcom, Casey Mathews. University of Texas at Austin, School of Law Publications, 727 E Dean Keeton St, Ste 4.134B, Austin, TX 78705; webmaster@law.utexas.edu; https://law.utexas.edu/publications/. Illus., index. Refereed. Vol. ends: Jun. Microform: WSH. Reprint: WSH. *Indexed:* A01, A22, B01, BRI, L14, MLA-IB. *Bk. rev.:* Occasional, lengthy. *Aud.:* Ac, Sa.

The University of Texas is considered to have one of the finest law schools and law reviews in the nation. Like other student-edited law school publications, the *Texas Law Review* contains two or three major articles by legal scholars on an array of legal topics, student notes relating to recent legislation or cases, and essay-length book reviews. The law review also has an online companion called *Texas Law Review Online.* (texaslawreview.org/online-edition/)

Transportation Law Journal. See Transportation section.

3132. *University of Pennsylvania. Law Review.* Former titles (until 1945): *University of Pennsylvania. Law Review and American Law Register;* (until 1908): *American Law Register;* (until 1898): *American Law Register and Review;* (until 1892): *American Law Register;* (until 1852): *American Law Journal;* (until 1848): *Pennsylvania Law Journal.* [ISSN: 0041-9907] 1852. 7x/yr. USD 47 domestic; USD 57 foreign; USD 10 per issue. University of Pennsylvania, Law School, 3501 Sansom St, Philadelphia, PA 19104; reg@law.upenn.edu; http://www.law.upenn.edu/. Illus., index, adv. Refereed. Vol. ends: Jun. Reprint: WSH. *Indexed:* A01, A22, B01, BRI, L14, P61. *Bk. rev.:* Occasional, essay length. *Aud.:* Ac, Sa.

Founded in 1852, the *University of Pennsylvania Law Review* is one of the oldest law reviews in the nation. It is influential and highly ranked, traditional in format, diverse in the type of subjects discussed, and edited by a student board of editors with first-rate academic credentials. Articles concentrate mainly on everyday issues such as bankruptcy, constitutional law, intellectual property, and criminal law. The law review also has an online companion called *University of Pennsylvania Law Review Online.* (pennlawreview.com/online/)

3133. *The Yale Law Journal.* [ISSN: 0044-0094] 1891. 8x/yr. USD 55 domestic; USD 87 (in Canada, Western Europe); USD 79 Mexico). Ed(s): Michael Clementre, Elizabeth Ingriselli. Yale Journal Co. Inc., 127 Wall St, PO Box 208215, New Haven, CT 06520; admissions.law@yale.edu; http://www.law.yale.edu. Illus., index. Vol. ends: Jul. Microform: WSH. Reprint: WSH. *Indexed:* A01, A22, B01, BAS, BRI, CBRI, Chicano, EconLit, IBSS, L14. *Bk. rev.:* Occasional, essay length. *Aud.:* Ac, Sa.

One would find *The Yale Law Journal* among the first journals mentioned in any survey or discussion of the most influential law journals. The journal includes major articles, essays, notes, comments, and book reviews. The law journal also has an online companion called *YLJ Forum.* (yalelawjournal.org/forum)

■ LGBT+

Hilary Kline, Manager of Reformatting Support Services, Imaging Services, Harvard Library, Widener Library, Harvard University, Cambridge, MA 02138; kline@fas.harvard.edu

Introduction

It is my goal in this section to select titles that appeal to a broad general audience, rather than to niche readers. The titles that you will not find included here are many of the very narrowly focused scholarly publications like *Journal of LGBT Issues in Counseling, Journal of LGBT Youth,* and *Law & Sexuality.* All of these have a defined place in the literature, but I felt they were too narrow for this section.

Also, not included in this section are titles dealing with travel, such as *Out Traveler* and *Passport.* There is a lot of information available for free on their web sites and many others, thus I felt it was redundant to give them full reviews.

Basic Periodicals

Hs: *The Advocate, Out;* Ga: *The Advocate, Curve, The Gay & Lesbian Review Worldwide, Out;* Ac: *The Advocate, Curve, The Gay & Lesbian Review Worldwide, Journal of Homosexuality.*

Basic Abstracts and Indexes

Alternative Press Index, GenderWatch, LGBT Life.

3134. *The Advocate (Los Angeles, 1967).* Former titles (until 1970): *Los Angeles Advocate;* (until 1967): *P R I D E Newsletter.* [ISSN: 0001-8996] 1966. bi-m. USD 29.95. Here Publishing Inc., PO Box 5236, New York, NY 10185. Illus., adv. *Indexed:* A01, A22, BRI, C42, CBRI, F01, GW, MASUSE, MLA-IB. *Bk. rev.:* 1-5, 50-100 words. *Aud.:* Hs, Ga, Ac.

If your library owns only one GLBT title, this should be it. *The Advocate* is the most important and widely read newsmagazine that focuses on GLBT issues in the United States. A recent issue includes the articles "Battle For the Future" and "Truly Queer TV." You can get a good idea of the magazine's depth and breadth at its web site; topic sections include "Politics," "Commentary," "Transgender," "Crime," and "Youth." A copy should be in every library that serves adults in the United States. It is important to note that the print edition of *The Advocate* is no longer available separately; it must be purchased with the print edition of *Out.* URL: www.advocate.com

3135. *Curve.* Formerly (until 1996): *Deneuve.* [ISSN: 1087-867X] 1991. q. USD 45 combined subscription (print & online eds.)). Ed(s): Merryn Johns. Avalon Media Pty Ltd., P.O. Box 467, New York, NY 10034. Illus., adv. Circ: 48569. *Indexed:* BRI, C42, GW, MLA-IB. *Bk. rev.:* 4-6, 100-400 words. *Aud.:* Hs, Ga, Ac.

Curve is the thinking lesbian's *People.* Yes, it's slick and glossy, but it brings together in one place all the photos, interviews, ads, and inside information about the celebs you want to read about, as well as public figures you might not otherwise hear about. Check out the web site to get the flavor; topic sections include "News," "Events," "Culture," "Lifestyle," "Reviews," "Advice," and "History," but the print publication is still more complete. Recommended for public library collections. URL: www.curvemag.com

3136. *The Gay & Lesbian Review Worldwide.* Formerly (until 2000): *Harvard Gay & Lesbian Review.* [ISSN: 1532-1118] 1994. bi-m. USD 31.50 combined subscription domestic (Print & Online eds.); USD 39 combined subscription Canada (Print & Online eds.); USD 46.50 combined subscription elsewhere (Print & Online eds.)). Ed(s): Richard Schneider. Gay & Lesbian Review Worldwide, PO Box 180300, Boston, MA 02118. Illus., adv. *Indexed:* A01, A22, AmHI, BRI, C42, F01, GW, MLA-IB. *Bk. rev.:* 10-15, 500-1,000 words. *Aud.:* Ga, Ac.

The mission of the *Review* is "to provide a forum for enlightened discussion of issues and ideas of importance to lesbians and gay men; to advance gay and lesbian culture by providing a quality vehicle for its best writers and thinkers; and to educate a broader public on gay and lesbian topics." Regular sections include "Music," "Reviews," "Essays," and "BTW." Each issue is organized on a theme, with essays and book reviews supporting that theme. The recent "Pride" issue included the articles "The 'Virile' Style in American Art" and "Sappho Transfigured." The web site archives the table of contents of the recent printed copies, and includes some full-text articles. The easiest way to describe the *Review* is to say it is *The New Yorker* for gays.

3137. *Journal of Homosexuality (Print).* [ISSN: 0091-8369] 1974. 14x/yr. Ed(s): John Elia. Routledge, 530 Walnut St, Ste 850, Philadelphia, PA 19106; enquiries@tandfonline.com; http://www.tandfonline.com. Illus., adv. Sample. Refereed. Reprint: PSC. *Indexed:* A01, A22, ASSIA, AmHI, BRI, C42, CBRI, E01, GW, IBSS, MLA-IB, SSA, WSA. *Bk. rev.:* 4, 2,000-5,000 words. *Aud.:* Ac, Sa.

This peer-reviewed scholarly publication aims to "publish thought-provoking scholarship by researchers, community activists, and scholars who employ a range of research methodologies and who offer a variety of perspectives to continue shaping knowledge production in the arenas of lesbian, gay, bisexual, [and] transgender (LGBT) studies and queer studies." This journal is generally divided into three major sections: the largest section contains scholarly articles, sometimes encompassing a theme; the second section consists of book reviews; and the third section is an annotated bibliography of references. Two recent articles are "Debating LGBT Workplace Protections in the Bible Belt: Social Identities in Legislative and Media Discourse" and "Investigating the Islamic Perspective on Homosexuality." The audience of this journal is definitely the academic and/or special library sectors.

3138. *Lesbian Connection: the free worldwide forum of news & ideas for, by and about lesbians.* [ISSN: 1081-3217] 1974. bi-m. Free to qualified personnel. Elsie Publishing Institute, PO Box 811, E Lansing, MI 48826; elsiepub@aol.com. Illus., adv. Sample. *Bk. rev.:* 2-4, 200-300 words. *Aud.:* Ga.

This is a bimonthly free publication; however, a suggested donation of $42 per year is always welcome. *Lesbian Connection* is a grassroots lesbian network and readers' forum. Each issue is made up of the letters, responses, articles, reviews, etc., from subscribers. It also includes information and ads for lesbian festivals, events, and businesses; information on lesbian land and retirement communities; and the popular comic strips "Dykes to Watch Out For" by Alison Bechdel. According to the web site, a recent issue includes the topics of "Addiction" and "Girl Scout Stories." *LC* has been publishing since 1974 with the simple goal of connecting the lesbian community worldwide. URL: www.lconline.org

3139. *Lesbian News.* [ISSN: 0739-1803] 1975. m. USD 0.99 per issue. Ed(s): Ella Matthes. L N Publishing Inc., PO Box 55, Torrance, CA 90507. Illus., adv. *Indexed:* A01, MASUSE. *Bk. rev.:* 8-10, 300-500 words. *Aud.:* Ga.

As of August 2014, *LN* was to no longer be a print publication; the publisher has shifted focus to the digital format, and that is where they will continue to concentrate their efforts. Founded in 1975, *LN* is North America's longest-running lesbian publication, serving as the foremost voice for lesbians of all ages. It is published monthly, with sections including "Cover Story," "Lesbians On Location," "Lifestyles," and "Arts & Entertainment." A recent issue included the articles "Sibling Rivalry" and "HELL: What A Year It Has Been?!"

3140. *Out.* [ISSN: 1062-7928] 1992. 10x/yr. USD 19.95 domestic; USD 49.95 foreign. Ed(s): Aaron Hicklin, R Kurt Osenlund. Here Publishing Inc., P.O. Box 241579, Los Angeles, CA 90024. Illus., adv. Microform: PQC. *Indexed:* GW, MLA-IB. *Bk. rev.:* 6-9, 50-400 words. *Aud.:* Hs, Ga, Ac.

Out is published by the same company that publishes *The Advocate,* so you will definitely see the similarities in the two web sites. *Out* is more focused on a young gay male audience, while *The Advocate* is more bipartisan. The sections included in the magazine are "Entertainment," "Fashion," "Lifestyle," "Travel & Nightlife," "Out Exclusives," and "News & Opinion." Music, theater, and the arts, as well as fashion, are showcased. Two recent articles are "The Gay Agenda" and "Wild at Heart."

3141. *Transgender Studies Quarterly.* [ISSN: 2328-9252] 2014. q. USD 278. Ed(s): Abraham B Weil, Susan Stryker. Duke University Press, 905 W Main St, Durham, NC 27701; orders@dukeupress.edu; https://www.dukeupress.edu. Adv. Reprint: PSC. *Aud.:* Ac, Sa.

TSQ aims to provide a "venue for innovative research and scholarship that contest the objectification, pathologization, and exoticization of transgender lives. It publishes interdisciplinary work that explores the diversity of gender, sex, sexuality, embodiment, and identity in ways that have not been adequately addressed by feminist and queer scholarship." Sections included are: "Articles," "Documents," "Interviews," "Fashion," and "Book Reviews." Two recently published articles are "Trans Men Engaging, Reforming, and Resisting Feminisms" and "Looking Back on Queering the Center."

■ LIBRARY AND INFORMATION SCIENCE

See also Archives and Manuscripts; Bibliography; Books and Book Reviews; Printing and Graphic Arts; and Serials sections.

Melissa Bauer, Online Learning Librarian, University of Kent State at Stark, Canton, OH 44313

Introduction

The field of library science is the study and practice of collecting, organizing, preserving, and disseminating information. Library and information professionals will find journals listed in this section useful because the content reflects current library trends and issues, as well as theory and practice. A limited number of the publications focus on general topics of interest to all practitioners, but the majority focus on subject-specific topics. Library science journals listed in this section represent all types of libraries, ranging from academic to public to specialized. These journals are designed to meet the needs of library directors, librarians, researchers, and library science graduate students.

Library journals are an optimal resource for professional communication across the profession. Within the journals' pages, a reader will find best practices, current research, book and product reviews, and opinion pieces. Current topics focus on embedded librarianship, assessment in libraries, and next-generation catalogs.

Library science journals have remained stable over the years, with few additions or deletions. There has been a move over the last several years to switch from print to online format, with some journals becoming open-access titles.

The following section is not a comprehensive listing of the available library and information science journal titles. Local and in-house publications, along with non-English language titles, are excluded. Most journals have been published in the United States.

Basic Periodicals

Ga: *American Libraries, Library Journal;* Ac: *College & Research Libraries, The Journal of Academic Librarianship;* Sa: *Children and Libraries, School Library Journal, School Library Research, Teacher Librarian, Voice of Youth Advocates, Young Adult Library Services.*

Basic Abstracts and Indexes

Information Science and Technology Abstracts, Library Literature and Information Science Index, LISA: Library and Information Science Abstracts.

3142. *A L C T S News.* Former titles (until 2013): *A L C T S Newsletter Online;* (until 1998): *A L C T S Newsletter (Print);* (until 1990): *R T S D Newsletter.* 1976. irreg. Free. American Library Association, 50 E Huron St, Chicago, IL 60611; ala@ala.org; http://www.ala.org. Illus. *Aud.:* Ac, Sa.

The primary goal of this open-access newsletter, published by the Association for Library Collections and Technical Services, is to keep members informed of news and activities of the association. Issues contain conference reports, announcements, information about new publications, calendars, and articles that discuss new standards and best practices. Highly recommended for librarians in technical services and members of ALCTS. URL: www.ala.org/alctsnews/

3143. *Against the Grain: linking publishers, vendors and librarians.* [ISSN: 1043-2094] 1989. bi-m. USD 55 domestic; USD 65 Canada; USD 95 elsewhere. Ed(s): Katina Strauch. Against the Grain, LLC, C/o Katina Strauch, MSC 98, Charleston, SC 29409. Illus. Sample. Refereed. Vol. ends: Dec/Jan. *Indexed:* A22, ISTA, MLA-IB. *Bk. rev.:* 10-20, 100-500 words. *Aud.:* Ga, Ac, Sa.

This bimonthly publication provides information relevant to acquisition and technical services librarians, publishers, vendors, book jobbers, and subscription agents. Each issue contains news, articles, interviews, book reviews, technology issues, legal issues, and current information from the publishing and book selling fields. Recent issues explore trends in health sciences, cultivating scholarship, and electronic resources. This publication is highly recommended for acquisition librarians, publishers, and booksellers.

The American Archivist See Archives and Manuscripts/General section.

3144. *American Libraries.* Supersedes (in 1970): *A L A Bulletin;* Which was formerly (1907-1939): *American Library Association. Bulletin;* Which incorporated (1924-1930): *Adult Education and the Library;* American Library Association. Bulletin incorporated (1947-1956): *Public Libraries.* [ISSN: 0002-9769] 1970. 6x/yr. USD 74 Free to members. Ed(s): Laurie D Borman. American Library Association, 50 E Huron St, Chicago, IL 60611; customerservice@ala.org; http://www.ala.org. Illus., index, adv. Circ: 59000 Paid. Microform: NBI; PMC; PQC. *Indexed:* A01, A22, BRI, C37, CBRI, Chicano, ISTA, MASUSE, MLA-IB. *Aud.:* Ga, Ac, Sa.

This is the official journal of the American Library Association. It reports on the activities, purposes, and goals of the association, as well as broader library-related topics. Regular sections include job postings, national and international library news, continuing education, and information technology. Featured articles cover a broad range of library-related topics and current events. The journal also maintains a strong online presence. This magazine is recommended for all librarians interested in current events, and is highly recommended for all libraries. URL: http://americanlibrariesmagazine.org

3145. ***Ariadne (Online): web magazine for information professionals.*** [ISSN: 1361-3200] 1996. q. Free. U K O L N, c/o The Library, University of Bath, Bath, BA2 7AY, United Kingdom; ukoln@ukoln.ac.uk; http://www.ukoln.ac.uk/. Illus. *Indexed:* ISTA. *Bk. rev.:* 4-5, length varies. *Aud.:* Ac, Sa.

Ariadne is an open-access, quarterly magazine published by UKOLN, and its primary focus is digital library initiatives in the United Kingdom and technological developments in related fields. Each issue contains articles, conference reports, and book reviews. Recent articles address digital archiving, shared repositories, and digital library infrastructure. Highly recommended for professionals interested in digital initiatives in the library, archive, and museum fields. Freely available online. URL: www.ariadne.ac.uk

3146. ***Art Documentation.*** Formerly (until 1982): *A R L I S - N A Newsletter;* Which incorporated in part (in 1974): *College Art Association of America. Visual Resources Committee. Newsletter;* Which was formerly (19??-1973): *C A A Slides & Photographs Newsletter.* [ISSN: 0730-7187] 1972. s-a. USD 361 (print & online eds.)). Ed(s): Judy Dyki. University of Chicago Press, 1427 E 60th St, Chicago, IL 60637; custserv@press.uchicago.edu; http://www.press.uchicago.edu/. Illus., adv. Refereed. Reprint: PSC. *Indexed:* A22, A51. *Bk. rev.:* Number and length vary. *Aud.:* Ga, Ac, Sa.

This peer-reviewed publication is the official bulletin of the Art Libraries Society of North America. Articles discuss recent developments in the field of art librarianship and visual resource curatorship, as well as news and events of the society. Recent article topics include digital archives, collection practices, and academic freedom in relation to library exhibits. Each issue includes book reviews, which are also available online. An essential publication for all art libraries and visual resource centers.

3147. ***Art Libraries Journal.*** Supersedes in part (in 1976): *ARLIS Newsletter.* [ISSN: 0307-4722] 1969. q. GBP 157. Ed(s): Erica Foden-Lenahan. Cambridge University Press, University Printing House, Shaftesbury Rd, Cambridge, CB2 8BS, United Kingdom; journals@cambridge.org; https://www.cambridge.org. Illus., adv. Refereed. Vol. ends: Jan. Reprint: PSC. *Indexed:* A22, A51, ISTA. *Bk. rev.:* Number and length vary. *Aud.:* Ac, Sa.

This international journal covers art libraries and visual resource collections around the world. Although most articles are in English, articles written in German, French, and Spanish are also included, accompanied by an English summary. Recent articles cover specific art library collections, the history and future of art libraries, and digitization. Other content includes book reviews and a bibliography of art librarianship. This publication is essential reading for all art librarians and visual resource curators.

3148. ***Association for Information Science and Technology. Bulletin.*** Former titles (until 2013): *American Society for Information Science and Technology. Bulletin (Online);* (until 2001): *American Society for Information Science. Bulletin (Online).* [ISSN: 2373-9223] 1974. bi-m. Free to members. Association for Information Science and Technology (A S I S & T), 8555 16th St, Ste 850, Silver Spring, MD 20910; asis@asis.org; http://www.asis.org. Reprint: PSC. *Indexed:* A01, B01. *Aud.:* Ga, Ac, Sa.

This open-access publication is the news magazine of the American Society for Information Science and Technology. Its primary purpose is to communicate with society members and other information science professionals. In addition to pragmatic, non-research articles, the publication also contains opinion columns and news regarding the members and events of the society. Recent issues discuss open-access publishing, knowledge management, and standards for archives. This is an important title for information science professionals and other librarians interested in information science. Freely available online. URL: www.asis.org/bulletin.html

3149. ***Association for Information Science and Technology. Journal.*** Former titles (until 2014): *American Society for Information Science and Technology. Journal;* (until 2001): *American Society for Information Science. Journal;* (until 1970): *American Documentation;* (until 1942): *Journal of Documentary Reproduction.* [ISSN: 2330-1635] 1938. m. USD 3005. Ed(s): Javed Mostafa. John Wiley & Sons, Inc., 111 River St, Hoboken, NJ 07030; cs-journals@wiley.com; http://onlinelibrary.wiley.com. Illus., index, adv. Refereed. Microform: PQC. Reprint: PSC. *Indexed:* A01, A22, B01, BRI, CompLI, ErgAb, ISTA, MLA-IB. *Bk. rev.:* Number and length vary. *Aud.:* Ga, Ac, Sa.

As the scholarly journal of the American Society for Information Science and Technology, this fully refereed journal reports new research in the field of information science and technology. Recent article topics include information retrieval; ontologies; metadata quality in digital repositories; and citation analysis software. There is also full-text online access to this content. This publication also includes book reviews, calls for papers, best student papers, and brief communications. Highly recommended for information science and technology professionals and library science collections.

Booklist. See Books and Book Reviews section.

3150. ***The Bottom Line: managing library finances.*** [ISSN: 0888-045X] 1988. q. EUR 2036 (print & online eds.) (excluding UK)). Ed(s): Bang Nguyen. Emerald Publishing Limited, Howard House, Wagon Ln, Bingley, BD16 1WA, United Kingdom; emerald@emeraldinsight.com; http://www.emeraldinsight.com. Sample. Refereed. Reprint: PSC. *Indexed:* A01, A22, ATI, E01. *Bk. rev.:* Number and length vary. *Aud.:* Ga, Ac, Sa.

Focusing on individuals responsible for financial decisions in libraries, this publication discusses library finances and other broad issues regarding library administration. Recent article topics include asset management; policies and procedures; and predicting demand for inter-library loan requests. Issues also include news, opinion columns, and book reviews. Highly recommended for library administrators in all types of libraries.

3151. ***Cataloging & Classification Quarterly.*** [ISSN: 0163-9374] 1980. 8x/yr. GBP 1342 (print & online eds.)). Ed(s): Sandra K Roe. Routledge, 530 Walnut St, Ste 850, Philadelphia, PA 19106; enquiries@tandfonline.com; http://www.tandfonline.com. Illus., adv. Sample. Refereed. Microform: PQC. Reprint: PSC. *Indexed:* A01, A22, E01, ISTA. *Bk. rev.:* Number and length vary. *Aud.:* Ga, Ac, Sa.

This peer-reviewed journal examines all aspects of bibliographic organization from both theoretical and practical points of view. Creation, usability, and findability of records are all examined in the articles included in this publication. Recent articles address taxonomies, RDA, and faceted browsing. This journal is essential reading for all librarians involved in any aspect of cataloging or classification.

3152. ***The Charleston Advisor: critical reviews of Web products for information professionals.*** [ISSN: 1525-4011] 1999. q. USD 295. The Charleston Company, 6180 E Warren Ave, Denver, CO 80222; rlenzini@charlestonco.com; http://www.charlestonco.com. Adv. Sample. Refereed. *Indexed:* ISTA. *Aud.:* Ga, Ac, Sa.

The Charleston Advisor is the leading source of reviews for Internet-accessible electronic resources. Each resource reviewed is rated on content, searchability, price, and contract terms, and all reviews are peer reviewed. Readers can browse all products that have been reviewed in the past in the online edition and view ratings assigned to each resource. In addition to formal reviews, each issue of the publication also contains comparative reviews, articles, press releases, editorials, and news. An essential publication for all librarians responsible for purchasing electronic resources.

3153. ***Children and Libraries.*** Supersedes in part (in 2002): *Journal of Youth Services in Libraries;* Which was formerly (1942-1987): *Top of the News.* [ISSN: 1542-9806] 2003. 4x/yr. Free to members; Non-members, USD 50. Ed(s): Laura Schulte-Cooper, Sharon Verebeten. American Library Association, 50 E Huron St, Chicago, IL 60611; http://www.ala.org. Adv. Refereed. Circ: 4000 Paid. *Indexed:* A01. *Bk. rev.:* Number and length vary. *Aud.:* Ems, Hs.

Children and Libraries is the official publication of the Association for Library Service to Children, a division of the American Library Association. Articles address all aspects of library services for children, including technology, collection development, cataloging, information literacy, and programming. Issues also include book reviews, association news, and recommended titles. An essential title for libraries that provide services to children.

3154. *Collection and Curation.* Formerly (until 2018): *Collection Building.* [ISSN: 2514-9326] 1978. q. EUR 2183 (print & online eds.) (excluding UK)). Ed(s): Steve O'Connor. Emerald Publishing Limited, Howard House, Wagon Ln, Bingley, BD16 1WA, United Kingdom; emerald@emeraldinsight.com; http://www.emeraldinsight.com. Sample. Refereed. Reprint: PSC. *Indexed:* A01, A22, E01, ISTA, MLA-IB. *Bk. rev.:* Number and length vary. *Aud.:* Ems, Hs, Ga, Ac, Sa.

This publication offers practical and theoretical articles that discuss collection development and management. International in scope, the articles discuss academic, public, and school library collections. Recent articles include university press, open-source journals, and citation studies. Issues also include library collection news and trends, book reviews, and editorials. Recommended for librarians responsible for collection development. Online since 2018.

3155. *Collection Management.* Formerly (until 1977): *De-Acquisitions Librarian.* [ISSN: 0146-2679] 1975. q. GBP 454 (print & online eds.)). Ed(s): Karen Fischer. Routledge, 530 Walnut St, Ste 850, Philadelphia, PA 19106; enquiries@tandfonline.com; http://www.tandfonline.com. Illus., adv. Sample. Refereed. Microform: PQC. Reprint: PSC. *Indexed:* A01, A22, E01, ISTA. *Bk. rev.:* Number and length vary. *Aud.:* Ac, Sa.

This peer-reviewed quarterly publication addresses all issues of collection management, including digital collections, staff training, management, consortial agreements, and assessment. Each issue also includes an extended review section. Recent articles address data-driven deselection, storage of print collections, and faculty support for remote storage. Recommended for collection managers and library science students.

3156. *College & Research Libraries News.* Formerly (until 1967): *A C R L News.* [ISSN: 0099-0086] 1966. 11x/yr. Free to members; Non-members, USD 55. Ed(s): David Free. Association of College and Research Libraries, 50 E Huron St, Chicago, IL 60611; acrl@ala.org; http://www.ala.org/acrl. Illus., adv. Sample. Vol. ends: Dec. *Indexed:* A&ATA, A01, A22, MLA-IB. *Bk. rev.:* Number and length vary. *Aud.:* Ac, Sa.

The official open-access newsmagazine and publication of record for the Association of College & Research Libraries, this journal reports current news and trends that affect academic and research libraries. Recent articles address the participatory design in libraries, cataloging backlogs, and collaborating with the writing center. Highly recommended for academic and research libraries. URL: http://crln.acrl.org

3157. *College & Research Libraries (Online).* [ISSN: 2150-6701] 1939. bi-m. Free. Association of College and Research Libraries, 50 E Huron St, Chicago, IL 60611; acrl@ala.org; http://www.ala.org/acrl. *Bk. rev.:* 6 per issue; length varies. *Aud.:* Ac, Sa.

A journal recently made open-access, *College & Research Libraries* is the scholarly research journal of the Association of College and Research Libraries, a division of the American Library Association. Articles discuss trends and developments that impact academic librarians and research libraries. Recent articles cover outcome assessment in library instruction, usability testing, and e-approval plans in research libraries. Articles are supported with tables, figures, and surveys, and each issue includes book reviews. Highly recommended for academic and research libraries. URL: http://crl.acrl.org/

3158. *Communications in Information Literacy.* [ISSN: 1933-5954] 2007. s-a. Free. Ed(s): Stewart Brower, Robert Schroeder. Communications in Information Literacy, c/o Stewart Brower, University of Oklahoma-Tulsa Library, Tulsa, TX 74135. Refereed. *Aud.:* Ga, Ac, Sa.

This peer-reviewed open-access journal focuses on knowledge, theory, and research of information literacy. Recent articles explore moving from the ACRL standards to the new framework, program level assessment, and discipline-specific information literacy skills. An important journal for all information literacy and instruction librarians. Available online. URL: www.comminfolit.org

3159. *D - Lib Magazine: the magazine of digital library research.* [ISSN: 1082-9873] 1995. bi-m. Corporation for National Research Initiatives, 1895 Preston White Dr, Ste 100, Reston, VA 20191; info@cnri.reston.va.us; http://www.cnri.reston.va.us. *Indexed:* ISTA. *Aud.:* Ac, Sa.

This free online journal is an important publication in the digital library community. A primary goal of the journal is timely exchange of information, and articles are published quickly in order to remain relevant to readers and practitioners. Recent articles examine mobile access to digital collections, rights information registries, and repository protocols. Highly recommended for all librarians involved in digital library activities. URL: www.dlib.org

3160. *D T T P (Online).* Formerly (until 1974): *Documents to the People.* [ISSN: 2688-125X] 1972. q. Free. Ed(s): Elizabeth Psyck. American Library Association, 50 E Huron St, Chicago, IL 60611; customerservice@ala org; http://www.ala.org. Illus., adv. Circ: 1350 Paid. Vol. ends: Dec. *Indexed:* A22. *Bk. rev.:* Number and length vary. *Aud.:* Ac, Sa.

This quarterly publication is the official journal of the Government Documents Round Table (GODORT) of the American Library Association. *DttP* covers the news and activities of the roundtable, as well as local, state, national, and international government information and activities. Recent articles cover promoting electronic government documents, the National Archives, and disaster plans. Issues also include book reviews and columns by GODORT officers. An essential publication for government document librarians.

3161. *Digital Library Perspectives.* Former titles (until 2016): *O C L C Systems & Services;* (until 1993): *O C L C Micro.* [ISSN: 2059-5816] 1984. q. EUR 1668 (print & online eds.) (excluding UK)). Ed(s): Anna Maria Tammaro. Emerald Publishing Limited, Howard House, Wagon Ln, Bingley, BD16 1WA, United Kingdom; emerald@emeraldinsight.com; http://www.emeraldinsight.com. Sample. Refereed. Reprint: PSC. *Indexed:* A01, A22, CompLI, E01, ISTA. *Bk. rev.:* Number and length vary. *Aud.:* Ga, Ac, Sa.

This quarterly, peer-reviewed publication covers all aspects of web-based delivery of cultural heritage materials. Article formats include featured articles, case studies, and news and reviews. Recent themed issues examine digital preservation, music information retrieval, and open-source digital tools. Recommended for academic librarians interested in digital projects and services.

3162. *Evidence Based Library and Information Practice.* [ISSN: 1715-720X] 2006. q. Free. Ed(s): Alison Brettle. University of Alberta, Learning Services, Cameron Library, 5th Floor, Edmonton, AB T6G 2J8, Canada; http://www.ls.ualberta.ca. Refereed. *Indexed:* ISTA. *Aud.:* Ga, Ac, Sa.

Evidence Based Library and Information Practice is an open-access, peer-reviewed journal. Articles and other features provide librarians and library administrators with research that may help inform decision- and policy-making. Each issue features peer-reviewed articles and some non-peer-reviewed columns. Highly recommended for all librarians.

First Monday. See World Wide Web section.

3163. *Global Knowledge, Memory and Communication.* Formerly (until 201?): *Library Review.* [ISSN: 2514-9342] 1927. 9x/yr. EUR 14151 (print & online eds.) (excluding UK)). Ed(s): Judith Broady-Preston. Emerald Publishing Limited, Howard House, Wagon Ln, Bingley, BD16 1WA, United Kingdom; emerald@emeraldinsight.com; http://www.emeraldinsight.com. Sample. Refereed. Reprint: PSC. *Indexed:* A22, AmHI, BRI, CBRI, E01, ISTA, MLA-IB. *Bk. rev.:* 2-6, length varies. *Aud.:* Ga, Ac, Sa.

Library Review provides librarians, educators, and researchers with information from libraries around the world. Articles are written by librarians with diverse backgrounds, and recent topics explore information-seeking behavior, social networking sites, and information literacy assessment. Recent themed issues consider knowledge sharing in emerging economies, and open-source software. Each issue also includes reviews of recent library and information science publications. Recommended for all library collections.

3164. ***Government Information Quarterly: an international journal of information technology management, policies, and practices.*** Incorporates (1994-2004): *Journal of Government Information;* Which was formerly (until vol.21, 1994): *Government Publications Review;* Which was formed by the merger of (1980-1981): *Government Publications Review. Part A: Research Articles;* (1980-1981): *Government Publications Review. Part B: Acquisitions Guide to Significant Government Publications at All Levels;* Both of which superseded in part (in 1980): *Government Publications Review.* [ISSN: 0740-624X] 1982. q. EUR 1206. Ed(s): M Janssen, T Janowski. Elsevier Ltd, 125 London Wall, London, EC2Y 5AS, United Kingdom; corporate.sales@elsevier.com; http://www.elsevier.com. Illus., adv. Sample. Refereed. Vol. ends: Oct. Microform: PQC. Reprint: PSC. *Indexed:* A22, B01, ERIC, ISTA, P61. *Bk. rev.:* Number and length vary. *Aud.:* Ac, Sa.

This peer-reviewed journal presents theoretical and practical articles that explore government information-based resources and services. Each issue contains editorials, articles, and reviews. Recent articles address government information portals, Congress as a publisher, and the use of social media in local governments. This publication is recommended for all government document librarians.

3165. ***The Indexer.*** [ISSN: 0019-4131] 1958. q. s-a. until 2008. GBP 257 (Free to members). Ed(s): Mary Coe. Liverpool University Press, 4 Cambridge St, Liverpool, L69 7ZU, United Kingdom; lup@liv.ac.uk; http://liverpooluniversitypress.co.uk/. Illus., adv. Refereed. *Indexed:* A22, BRI, CBRI, ISTA, MLA-IB. *Bk. rev.:* Number and length vary. *Aud.:* Ac, Sa.

Published by the Society of Indexers, this semi-annual peer-reviewed publication informs readers of the trends and developments in the international indexing community. Articles address practical, theoretical, and historical aspects of indexing. Recent article topics address the semantic web, XML indexing, and new technology and indexes. Each issue includes articles that highlight the activities of the society, reviews of books and electronic resources. An essential journal for all indexers and librarians interested in the field of indexing.

3166. ***Information & Culture.*** Former titles (until 2012): *Libraries & the Cultural Record;* (until 2006): *Libraries & Culture;* (until 1988): *The Journal of Library History;* (until 1974): *Journal of Library History, Philosophy, and Comparative Librarianship;* (until 1973): *The Journal of Library History.* [ISSN: 2164-8034] 1966. 3x/yr. USD 230. Ed(s): Ciaran Trace. University of Texas Press, Journals Division, PO Box 7819, Austin, TX 78713; journals@utpress.utexas.edu; https://utpress.utexas.edu. Illus., index, adv. Refereed. Vol. ends: Nov. *Indexed:* A01, A22, AmHI, BRI, CBRI, E01, MLA-IB. *Bk. rev.:* 11-20, 500-1,200 words, signed. *Aud.:* Ac, Sa.

This interdisciplinary journal explores the history of information. The peer-reviewed articles examine the social and cultural context of recorded knowledge and the history of information studies. Recent article topics include the development of public libraries, archival management, and information-seeking behavior. Highly recommended for library and information science collections and others interested in the history of information and recorded knowledge.

3167. ***Information Technology and Libraries (Online).*** [ISSN: 2163-5226] 1968. q. Free. Ed(s): Robert Gerrity. Library and Information Technology Association, 50 E Huron St, Chicago, IL 60611; lita@ala.org; http://www.lita.org/ala/mgrps/divs/lita/index.cfm. Illus., index, adv. Refereed. Vol. ends: Mar. *Aud.:* Ac, Sa.

This open-access publication is the refereed journal of the Library and Information Technology Association, a division of the American Library Association. Articles address all aspects of information technology relevant to libraries, including digital libraries, online catalogs, software engineering, electronic publishing, and metadata. Each issue includes a "President's Message," editorials, and feature articles. Recent article topics include rural public libraries, new media literacy, and discovery tools. Highly recommended for all librarians interested in technology and its use in libraries.

3168. ***Issues in Science and Technology Librarianship.*** [ISSN: 1092-1206] 1991. q. Free. Ed(s): Andrea L Duda. Association of College and Research Libraries, Science and Technology Section, 50 E Huron St, Chicago, IL 60611; acrl@ala.org; http://www.ala.org/acrl/aboutacrl/directoryofleadership/sections/sts/stswebsite. Illus. Refereed. *Indexed:* ERIC, ISTA. *Bk. rev.:* 350-500 words; number varies. *Aud.:* Ac, Sa.

This quarterly, open-access, electronic publication from the Science and Technology section of the Association of College and Research Libraries offers materials of interest to science and technology librarians. Each issue contains themed articles, refereed articles, electronic resource reviews, viewpoints, and book reviews. Recent refereed articles have included instruction, research behaviors of engineers, and print and e-book comparisons.

3169. ***The Journal of Academic Librarianship.*** [ISSN: 0099-1333] 1975. bi-m. EUR 729. Ed(s): E Blakesley. Pergamon Press, The Blvd, Langford Ln, E Park, Kidlington, OX5 1GB, United Kingdom; JournalsCustomerServiceEMEA@elsevier.com; http://www.elsevier.com. Illus., adv. Sample. Refereed. Microform: PQC. Reprint: PSC. *Indexed:* A01, A22, B01, BRI, CBRI, ERIC, ISTA, MLA-IB. *Bk. rev.:* Approx. 500 words, number varies. *Aud.:* Ac, Sa.

The Journal of Academic Librarianship, published six times each year, is a refereed journal with international contributions and readership. Contributors present research findings and case studies, analyze policies and procedures, and review books relevant to the library profession. Recent article topics include social media for information seeking and integrating information literacy into academic curricula. Highly recommended for academic libraries and librarians.

3170. ***The Journal of Creative Library Practice.*** [ISSN: 2330-4227] 2013. irreg. Free. Creative Library Practice, jclp-editors@du.edu; http://creativelibrarypractice.org/. Refereed. *Aud.:* Ga, Ac, Sa.

This open-access journal provides librarians and information professionals a place to share successes and failures of creative ventures in the library. This can include library as place; policies; instruction; and other areas. This journal is written for library and information professionals working in all types of libraries, including academic, public, special, school, and others. Contents include peer-reviewed articles, case studies, editorials, and reviews.

3171. ***Journal of Digital Information.*** [ISSN: 1368-7506] 1997. irreg. Free. Ed(s): Mark McFarland. Texas A & M University Libraries, 5000 TAMU Corner of Spence & Lamar, College Station, TX 77843; http://library.tamu.edu. Refereed. *Indexed:* A01, ISTA. *Aud.:* Ac, Sa.

A peer-reviewed, open-access journal, the *Journal of Digital Information* publishes papers about the management of information in the online environment. All articles fit into three main areas: digital libraries, visual interfaces, and information discovery. Recent article topics include information about repositories; preserving audiovisual content; and OAI-ORE. Highly recommended for librarians involved in digital projects. Freely available online.

3172. ***Journal of Documentation.*** [ISSN: 0022-0418] 1945. bi-m. EUR 1410 (print & online eds.) (excluding UK)). Ed(s): David Bawden. Emerald Publishing Limited, Howard House, Wagon Ln, Bingley, BD16 1WA, United Kingdom; emerald@emeraldinsight.com; http://www.emeraldinsight.com. Illus., index. Sample. Refereed. Reprint: PSC. *Indexed:* A01, A22, BAS, CompLI, E01, ISTA, MLA-IB. *Bk. rev.:* Number and length vary. *Aud.:* Ac, Sa.

This peer-reviewed journal focuses on the theories and philosophies of information science. Each issue includes several research articles and book reviews. Recent article topics include information-seeking and retrieval; story-based image indexing; and knowledge production. Highly recommended for information science scholars and library science collections.

3173. *Journal of East Asian Libraries (Online).* 1995. s-a. Free. Ed(s): Gail King. Association for Asian Studies, Council on East Asian Libraries, 825 Victors Way, Ste 310, Ann Arbor, MI 48108; https://www.asian-studies.org/. Refereed. *Bk. rev.:* Number and length vary. *Aud.:* Ga, Ac, Sa.

The premier journal of the Council on East Asian Libraries. This peer-reviewed journal is issued twice a year, in February and October. The journal includes a selection of peer-reviewed articles, reports, book reviews, and institutional member news. Recent articles explore leadership issues at the University of Hong Kong; and highlights from the Manga Collection at the Ohio State University Library. An important journal for all East Asian librarians.

3174. *Journal of Electronic Resources in Medical Libraries.* [ISSN: 1542-4065] 2004. q. GBP 500 (print & online eds.)). Ed(s): Justin Robertson. Routledge, 530 Walnut St, Ste 850, Philadelphia, PA 19106; enquiries@tandfonline.com; http://www.tandfonline.com. Adv. Sample. Refereed. Reprint: PSC. *Indexed:* A01, A22, E01. *Bk. rev.:* Number and length vary. *Aud.:* Ac, Sa.

This peer-reviewed journal focuses on issues and topics relevant to electronic resource librarians in medical libraries. The topics are designed to complement *Medical Reference Services Quarterly,* which covers the reference and instruction side of electronic resources in libraries. Recent article topics include mobile computing, electronic e-book platforms, and responsive web design. Recommended for medical and health science libraries.

3175. *Journal of Electronic Resources Librarianship.* Formerly (until 2008): *The Acquisitions Librarian.* [ISSN: 1941-126X] 1989. q. GBP 591 (print & online eds.)). Ed(s): Gary M Pitkin. Routledge, 530 Walnut St, Ste 850, Philadelphia, PA 19106; enquiries@tandfonline.com; http://www.tandfonline.com. Illus., index, adv. Sample. Refereed. Circ: 345 Paid. Microform: PQC. Reprint: PSC. *Indexed:* A01, A22, Chicano, E01, ERIC, ISTA, MLA-IB. *Bk. rev.:* Number and length vary. *Aud.:* Ga, Ac, Sa.

This quarterly, peer-reviewed publication addresses collection, acquiring, and creating library resources in the digital environment. Each issue includes editorials, "professional communications," scholarly articles, and book reviews. Recent peer-reviewed article topics include data management; usability testing of discovery layers; and screencasting. Essential reading for all electronic resources librarians.

3176. *Journal of Information Ethics.* [ISSN: 1061-9321] 1992. s-a. USD 120 (Individuals, USD 40). Ed(s): Robert Hauptman. McFarland & Company, Inc., Box 611, Jefferson, NC 28640; info@mcfarlandpub.com; http://www.mcfarlandpub.com. Illus. Refereed. *Indexed:* A22, ISTA, MLA-IB. *Bk. rev.:* Number varies, 800-1,200 words, signed. *Aud.:* Ac, Sa.

This semi-annual publication features articles about ethics and information science. Each issue contains book reviews, web site reviews, and feature articles. Recommended for all library science collections.

3177. *Journal of Information Literacy.* [ISSN: 1750-5968] 2006. s-a. Free. Ed(s): Jane Secker. Information Literacy, c/o Cathie Jackson, Cardiff University, PO Box 430, Wales, CF24 0DE, United Kingdom; cjackson@dinkycrew.com; http://www.informationliteracy.org.uk. Refereed. *Bk. rev.:* Number and length vary. *Aud.:* Ga, Ac, Sa.

This semi-annual, peer-reviewed, open-access publication investigates all aspects of information literacy. Articles address practical, technical, and philosophical aspects of information literacy, and recent article topics include online learning, information literacy, and embedded librarianship. Highly recommended for all librarians and teachers of information literacy.

3178. *Journal of Library Metadata.* Formerly (until 2008): *Journal of Internet Cataloging.* [ISSN: 1938-6389] 1997. q. GBP 339 (print & online eds.)). Ed(s): Jung-ran Park. Routledge, 530 Walnut St, Ste 850, Philadelphia, PA 19106; enquiries@tandfonline.com; http://www.tandfonline.com. Adv. Sample. Refereed. Circ: 556 Paid. Microform: PQC. Reprint: PSC. *Indexed:* A01, A22, E01, ISTA, MLA-IB. *Aud.:* Ga, Ac, Sa.

This peer-reviewed, quarterly journal examines metadata and all applications of metadata in libraries and information management. Recent articles examine Google Books' metadata; government information management; and digital object metadata. Highly recommended for all metadata librarians and digital library practitioners.

3179. *Journal of Web Librarianship.* [ISSN: 1932-2909] 2007. q. GBP 165 (print & online eds.)). Ed(s): Hannah G Rempel. Taylor & Francis Inc., 711 3rd Ave, 8th Fl, New York, NY 10017; support@tandfonline.com; http://www.tandfonline.com. Sample. Refereed. Reprint: PSC. *Indexed:* A22, E01, ERIC. *Bk. rev.:* Number and length vary. *Aud.:* Ga, Ac, Sa.

The Journal of Web Librarianship focuses on the librarianship as practiced on the Internet. Articles address all aspects of online interaction, including user behavior, web interfaces, online project management, and many other related topics. Practical and theoretic topics are examined, and all issues contain peer-reviewed scholarly articles, peer-reviewed practical communications, and reviews. Recent article topics include usability study of a discovery tool, digital library management, and web analytics. Highly recommended for all librarians.

3180. *Journal of Web Semantics: science, services and agents on the world wide web.* [ISSN: 1570-8268] 2003. 6x/yr. EUR 1001. Ed(s): I Horrocks, T Finin. Elsevier BV, Radarweg 29, Amsterdam, 1043 NX, Netherlands; info@elsevier.com; https://www.elsevier.com/. *Aud.:* Ac, Sa.

The Journal of Web Semantics is an interdisciplinary journal with subjects focused on web technologies, linked data, knowledge organization, databases, human-computer interaction, and other similar fields. The journal publishes research papers, survey papers, ontology papers, and systems papers. Recent topics include mapping life sciences data using RDF; using Avalanche; and ontology classification. Highly recommended for information scientists and library science collections.

3181. *Knowledge Organization: international journal devoted to concept theory, classification, indexing, and knowledge representation.* Formerly (until 1992): *International Classification.* [ISSN: 0943-7444] 1974. q. EUR 329; EUR 359 combined subscription (print & online eds.)). Ed(s): Richard P Smiraglia. Ergon Verlag, Waldseestr 3-5, Baden-Baden, 76530, Germany; service@ergon-verlag.de; http://www.ergon-verlag.de. Illus., adv. Refereed. Vol. ends: Fall. *Indexed:* A22, ISTA, MLA-IB. *Bk. rev.:* Number and length vary. *Aud.:* Ac, Sa.

This peer-reviewed, quarterly journal is the official journal of the International Society for Knowledge Organization. Each issue contains scholarly articles, reports on conferences, the society's newsletter, book reviews, and letters to the editor. Recent article topics include the semantic web; semantic relations in knowledge organization systems; and development of metadata elements. Recommended for library science collections and librarians interested in knowledge organization.

3182. *Knowledge Quest.* Supersedes in part (in 1997): *School Library Media Quarterly;* Which was formerly (1972-1981): *School Media Quarterly;* Which superseded (in 1972): *School Libraries;* Which was formerly (1951-1952): *American Association of School Librarians. Newsletter.* [ISSN: 1094-9046] 1951. bi-m. USD 50 domestic (Free to members). Ed(s): Meg Featheringham. American Library Association, 50 E Huron St, Chicago, IL 60611; customerservice@ala.org; http://www.ala.org. Illus., adv. Refereed. Vol. ends: Sep. Microform: PQC. *Indexed:* A01, A22, BRI, CBRI, ERIC. *Bk. rev.:* Number and length vary. *Aud.:* Ems, Hs, Ac.

This bimonthly publication from the American Association of School Librarians, a division of the American Library Association, brings information regarding school libraries and library media services to developers of school library centers and services. Each themed issue is shaped by editorial questions, and feature articles address these questions. Recent themes have included designing activities to foster creativity; creating life-long learners; and library spaces. Essential reading for all school library media specialists.

3183. *L O E X Quarterly.* Formerly (until 2004): *L O E X News.* [ISSN: 1547-0172] 1973. q. Members, USD 80 (print & online eds.)). Ed(s): Chessa Grasso Hickox, Brad Sietz. Eastern Michigan University Library, 203 Halle Library, Eastern Michigan University, Ypsilanti, MI 48197; heather.neff@emich.edu; http://www.emich.edu/public/loex/loex.html. Circ: 1200. *Bk. rev.:* Number and length vary. *Aud.:* Ac.

This quarterly publication, published by LOEX (Library Orientation Exchange), gathers together articles and research about library instruction and information literacy. Recent article topics explore the flipped classroom; Wikipedia as an authentic learning space; and one-shot instruction techniques. Highly recommended for all teaching librarians.

3184. *Law Library Journal.* Incorporates (1927-1937): *Law Library News.* [ISSN: 0023-9283] 1908. q. Free to members; Non-members, USD 110. Ed(s): James E Duggan. American Association of Law Libraries, 105 W Adams St, Ste 3300, Chicago, IL 60603; orders@aall.org; https://www.aallnet.org. Illus., index, adv. Refereed. Vol. ends: Fall. Microform: PMC. Reprint: WSH. *Indexed:* A22, BRI, L14, MLA-IB. *Bk. rev.:* Number and length vary. *Aud.:* Ac, Sa.

The official publication of the American Association of Law Libraries, this quarterly journal communicates news and events of the association, as well as articles related to law, legal materials, and librarianship. Issues include book reviews, proceedings and reports of the association, annotated bibliographies, and obituaries. Recent article topics include mentoring the next generation of law librarians; and law student information literacy. Essential reading for all law librarians and providers of legal reference services.

3185. *Library & Information Science Research.* Formerly (until 1983): *Library Research.* [ISSN: 0740-8188] 1979. q. EUR 891. Ed(s): Candy Schwartz, Peter Hernon. Pergamon Press, The Blvd, Langford Ln, E Park, Kidlington, OX5 1GB, United Kingdom; JournalsCustomerServiceEMEA@elsevier.com; http://www.elsevier.com. Illus., adv. Sample. Refereed. Reprint: PSC. *Indexed:* A01, A22, ISTA. *Bk. rev.:* 4-7; length varies. *Aud.:* Ac, Sa.

This quarterly, refereed journal offers research articles that focus on research in library and information science. Research findings, practical applications, and their significance are presented. Recent articles explore job satisfaction and job performance of university librarians; collaboration in the library; and emotions as motivators for information seeking. Highly recommended for all collections that support library and information science programs.

3186. *Library Collections, Acquisitions, and Technical Services.* Formerly (until 1999): *Library Acquisitions: Practice and Theory.* [ISSN: 1464-9055] 1977. q. GBP 502 (print & online eds.)). Ed(s): W A Shelburne. Taylor & Francis, 2, 3 & 4 Park Sq, Milton Park, Abingdon, OX14 4RN, United Kingdom; subscriptions@tandf.co.uk; https://www.tandfonline.com. Illus., adv. Sample. Refereed. Vol. ends: Winter. Microform: PQC. Reprint: PSC. *Indexed:* A01, A22, ISTA. *Bk. rev.:* Number and length vary. *Aud.:* Ac, Sa.

This quarterly publication brings together ideas from diverse specialties within library technical services, including collections management, acquisitions, cataloging, and document delivery, as well as publishers and vendors. Articles are based on practical experiences, research reports, and theoretical approaches. Recent article topics include patron-driven acquisition of e-books; records and information management; and information literacy instruction. Recommended for all libraries in technical services positions.

3187. *Library Hi Tech.* [ISSN: 0737-8831] 1983. q. EUR 676 (print & online eds.) (excluding UK)). Ed(s): Michelle M Kazmer. Emerald Publishing Limited, Howard House, Wagon Ln, Bingley, BD16 1WA, United Kingdom; emerald@emeraldinsight.com; http://www.emeraldinsight.com. Illus., index. Sample. Refereed. Microform: PQC. Reprint: PSC. *Indexed:* A22, BRI, CBRI, CompLI, E01, ErgAb, ISTA. *Bk. rev.:* Number and length vary. *Aud.:* Ga, Ac, Sa.

Library Hi-Tech is a quarterly, peer-reviewed journal that focuses on all types of technology used in the international library community. The majority of issues focus on specific topics; recent topics include structuring the digital domain, linking open vocabularies, and green libraries. Article formats include case studies, general articles, research papers, technical papers, and conceptual papers. Highly recommended for academic libraries.

3188. *Library Journal.* Incorporates (2002-2008): *Movers & Shakers;* (1999-2008): *Net Connect;* Former titles (until 1976): *L J (Library Journal);* (until 1974): *Library Journal.* [ISSN: 0363-0277] 1876. 20x/yr. USD 101 combined subscription. Ed(s): Bette-Lee Fox. Library Journals, LLC., 123 William St Ste 802, New York, NY 10038; ljinfo@mediasourceinc.com; http://lj.libraryjournal.com. Illus., index, adv. Sample. Vol. ends: Dec. Microform: CIS; NBI; RPI; PMC. *Indexed:* A01, A22, B01, B03, BAS, BRI, C37, C42, CBRI, Chicano, ERIC, MASUSE, MLA-IB. *Bk. rev.:* 175-200 words, number varies. *Aud.:* Ga, Ac, Sa.

Library Journal's mission is to be a "one-stop source" for the information needs of all librarians. Each issue contains letters to the editor, opinion pieces, library news, feature articles, interviews, and reviews of books, DVDs, and software. Recommended for all library professionals. The journal also maintains an active web site. URL: www.libraryjournal.com

3189. *Library Leadership & Management (Online).* [ISSN: 1945-886X] 2009. q. Free. Ed(s): Bradford Lee Eden. American Library Association, 50 E Huron St, Chicago, IL 60611; ala@ala.org; http://www.ala.org. Refereed. *Bk. rev.:* Number and length vary. *Aud.:* Ga, Ac, Sa.

This open-access, peer-reviewed journal is the official publication of the Library Administration and Management Association, a division of the American Library Association. With an audience of library managers at all levels, articles explore issues and methodologies of library management in a practical manner. Articles and columns include case studies, interviews, feature articles, and news of the association. Recent article topics include organizational change through servant leadership, and visual management for libraries. An essential publication for all library administrators and managers.

3190. *Library Management.* Incorporates (1993-1999): *Librarian Career Development.* [ISSN: 0143-5124] 1979. 9x/yr. EUR 16314 (print & online eds.) (excluding UK)). Ed(s): Steve O'Connor. Emerald Publishing Limited, Howard House, Wagon Ln, Bingley, BD16 1WA, United Kingdom; emerald@emeraldinsight.com; http://www.emeraldinsight.com. Sample. Refereed. Reprint: PSC. *Indexed:* A22, E01, ISTA. *Bk. rev.:* Number and length vary. *Aud.:* Ga, Ac, Sa.

This peer-reviewed journal seeks to provide international perspectives on library management issues. Articles provide practical implications of management theories through case studies, research papers, and general papers. Recent articles address ETD repositories; publication trends in information and library science; and library education. Highly recommended for library managers.

3191. *The Library Quarterly.* [ISSN: 0024-2519] 1931. q. USD 294. Ed(s): Paul Jaeger, Natalie Greene Taylor. University of Chicago Press, 1427 E 60th St, Chicago, IL 60637; subscriptions@press.uchicago.edu; http://www.journals.uchicago.edu. Illus., index, adv. Sample. Refereed. Vol. ends: Oct. Reprint: PSC. *Indexed:* A01, A22, B01, BAS, BRI, CBRI, ERIC, MLA-IB. *Bk. rev.:* 4-5, 900-1,300 words. *Aud.:* Ac, Sa.

This refereed quarterly journal seeks to inform its readership on research in all aspects of librarianship. Each issue includes book reviews and articles that discuss topics such as digital libraries, diversity in LIS, information literacy training, and information-seeking behavior. Recent article topics include funding in public libraries; supporting intellectual freedom; and information services to older adults. Recommended for academic and special libraries.

3192. *Library Resources & Technical Services (Online).* [ISSN: 2159-9610] 2012. q. USD 100 (Free to members). Ed(s): Mary Beth Weber. American Library Association, 50 E Huron St, Chicago, IL 60611; customerservice@ala.org; http://www.ala.org. Illus., adv. Refereed. *Bk. rev.:* 4-6; length varies. *Aud.:* Ac, Sa.

This is the official journal of the Association of Library Collections & Technical Services, a division of the American Library Association. Articles in this publication address collection management and development, acquisitions, cataloging and classification, preservation and reformatting, and serials. Articles are subject to a double-blind peer review. A basic publication for all academic library collections.

3193. ***Library Trends.*** [ISSN: 0024-2594] 1952. q. USD 185. Ed(s): Cindy Ashwill. The Johns Hopkins University Press, 2715 N Charles St, Baltimore, MD 21218; http://www.press.jhu.edu. Illus., index, adv. Sample. Refereed. Reprint: PSC. *Indexed:* A01, A22, E01, ISTA, MLA-IB. *Aud.:* Ga, Ac, Sa.

This quarterly publication examines new and emerging trends in the field of library and information science. Each themed issue covers all aspects of a topic and its impact on libraries. Articles address the impact of the topic on all library departments, including reference, technical services, administration, and systems. Recommended reading for all librarians.

3194. ***Medical Library Association. Journal.*** Formerly (until 2002): *Medical Library Association. Bulletin.* [ISSN: 1536-5050] 1911. q. Ed(s): Katherine G Akers. University of Pittsburgh, University Library System, 7500 Thomas Blvd, Pittsburgh, PA 15260; e-journals@mail.pitt.edu; http://www.library.pitt.edu. Adv. Sample. Refereed. Circ: 4000. *Indexed:* A01, A22, BRI, ISTA, MLA-IB. *Bk. rev.:* Number and length vary. *Aud.:* Sa.

This quarterly, peer-reviewed journal is the official publication of the Medical Library Association. Each issues includes papers, case studies, opinions, and book reviews. Recent articles address information-seeking behaviors, journal impact factors, and subject guides. Essential reading for all medical librarians.

3195. ***Medical Reference Services Quarterly.*** [ISSN: 0276-3869] 1982. q. GBP 585 (print & online eds.)). Ed(s): M Sandra Wood. Routledge, 530 Walnut St, Ste 850, Philadelphia, PA 19106; enquiries@tandfonline.com; http://www.tandfonline.com. Illus., adv. Sample. Refereed. Microform: PQC. Reprint: PSC. *Indexed:* A01, A22, E01, ISTA. *Bk. rev.:* 8-12, 500-800 words. *Aud.:* Ac, Sa.

Medical Reference Services Quarterly is a peer-reviewed publication for an audience of medical and health-sciences librarians who provide reference services in the educational, clinical, and research environments. Articles provide practical information on topics such as postgraduate medical training programs, citation formats, guides to medical information resources, and Internet medical resources. Each issue also includes book reviews and reviews of articles in related publications. Essential for all medical and health-sciences reference librarians.

3196. ***Portal: libraries and the academy.*** [ISSN: 1531-2542] 2001. q. USD 230. Ed(s): Sara Dreyfuss, Marianne Ryan. The Johns Hopkins University Press, 2715 N Charles St, Baltimore, MD 21218; http://www.press.jhu.edu. Adv. Sample. Refereed. Reprint: PSC. *Indexed:* A01, A22, B01, E01, ERIC, ISTA, MLA-IB. *Bk. rev.:* Number and length vary. *Aud.:* Ac.

A quarterly, peer-reviewed journal that focuses on the role of academic libraries and librarianship. Recent articles address fair use, social media, and liaison librarians. Recommended for all academic librarians.

3197. ***Progressive Librarian: a journal for critical studies and progressive politics in librarianship.*** [ISSN: 1052-5726] 1990. s-a. USD 40 Free to members. Ed(s): Elaine Harger. Progressive Librarians Guild, Rider University Library, 2083 Lawrenceville Rd, Lawrenceville, NJ 08648; plgwebteam@libr.org; http://libr.org/plg/index.php. *Bk. rev.:* Number and length vary. *Aud.:* Ga.

Progressive Librarian is a peer-reviewed journal about progressive politics in libraries. Recent articles examine the use of space in libraries, copyright, and marketing the library. Recommended for librarians interested in progressive politics and its impact on library services.

3198. ***Public Libraries.*** Former titles (until 1978): *P L A Newsletter;* (until 1970): *Just Between Ourselves.* [ISSN: 0163-5506] 1962. bi-m. USD 65 United States; USD 75 in Canada & Mexico; USD 100 elsewhere. Ed(s): Kathleen M Hughes. Public Library Association, 50 E Huron St, Chicago, IL 60611; pla@ala.org; http://www.ala.org/pla. Illus., index, adv. Microform: PQC. *Indexed:* A22, BRI. *Bk. rev.:* Number and length vary. *Aud.:* Ga, Ac, Sa.

This journal is the official publication of the Public Library Association, a division of the American Library Association. Articles and columns examine industry news, association updates, professional development, literature reviews, and ideas and strategies for providing library services to the public. Recent articles explore preserving obituaries; library services to the homeless; and education programs. Essential reading for all public librarians.

3199. ***Reference and User Services Quarterly (Online).*** [ISSN: 2163-5242] q. Free. Ed(s): Kathleen Kern. American Library Association, 50 E Huron St, Chicago, IL 60611; http://www.ala.org. Refereed. *Bk. rev.:* 18-25; length varies. *Aud.:* Ga, Ac, Sa.

As the official publication of the Reference and User Services Association of the American Library Association, this journal communicates information regarding user-oriented library services to librarians in special, public, and academic libraries. In addition to reference trends and e-resources, articles also address professional development, literature reviews, and news of the association. Annotated bibliographies are also included. Recent articles examine discovery services, text a librarian services, and instruction. A basic title for all library collections.

3200. ***The Reference Librarian.*** [ISSN: 0276-3877] 1981. q. GBP 1406 (print & online eds.)). Ed(s): Lauri Rebar, William Miller. Routledge, 530 Walnut St, Ste 850, Philadelphia, PA 19106; enquiries@tandfonline.com; http://www.tandfonline.com. Illus., index, adv. Sample. Refereed. Circ: 636 Paid. Microform: PQC. Reprint: PSC. *Indexed:* A01, A22, E01, ISTA. *Aud.:* Ac, Sa.

This quarterly publication addresses new trends and developments in the field of reference librarianship. Articles are appropriate for professional librarians and graduate students enrolled in reference and user services courses. Recent articles discuss discovery services, e-books, and distance learners. Recommended reading for all reference librarians.

3201. ***Reference Services Review: reference and instructional services for libraries in the digital age.*** [ISSN: 0090-7324] 1973. q. EUR 676 (print & online eds.) (includes UK)). Ed(s): Sarah Barbara Watstein. Emerald Publishing Limited, Howard House, Wagon Ln, Bingley, BD16 1WA, United Kingdom; emerald@emeraldinsight.com; http://www.emeraldinsight.com. Illus., index. Sample. Refereed. Reprint: PSC. *Indexed:* A22, BRI, CBRI, E01, ISTA. *Aud.:* Ac, Sa.

Reference Services Review is a quarterly, peer-reviewed publication that examines all aspects of reference services. Recent themed issues examine mobile services, learning landscapes, and conference reports. Contents include research papers, viewpoints, case studies, and literature reviews. Recommended for all library collections.

3202. ***School Library Connection.*** Formed by the merger of (2009-2015): *School Library Monthly;* (2003-2015): *Library Media Connection.* [ISSN: 2380-9841] 2015. m. Libraries Unlimited, Inc., 130 Cremona Dr, Santa Barbara, CA 93117; https://www.abc-clio.com/LibrariesUnlimited.aspx. *Bk. rev.:* 25-50 words, number varies. *Aud.:* Ems, Hs.

A professional journal for school library media and technology specialists, *Library Media Connection* provides book reviews and practical professional development articles that focus on three key areas, Organization and Management, Instructional Leadership, and Library in Context. Recent article topics include community involvement and the urban learner. Essential reading for all school library media and technology professionals.

3203. ***School Library Journal.*** Formerly (until 1961): *Junior Libraries.* [ISSN: 0362-8930] 1954. m. USD 136.99. Ed(s): Rebecca T Miller. Media Source Incorporated, 160 Varick St, 11th Fl, New York, NY 10013; http://www.mediasourceinc.com. Illus., index, adv. Sample. Vol. ends: Aug. Microform: NBI; PQC. *Indexed:* A01, A22, BRI, C37, CBRI, Chicano, ERIC, MASUSE. *Bk. rev.:* 50-100 words; number varies. *Aud.:* Ems, Hs, Ga.

This monthly publication contains news, trends, and literature reviews relevant to librarians who provide services for children and young adults. Recent articles discuss collaboration between school and public libraries; access to technology; and encouraging children to read. Each issue also includes book reviews. Essential reading for all young adult and children's librarians.

3204. *School Library Research.* Former titles (until 2007): *School Library Media Research;* (until 1998): *School Library Media Quarterly (Online);* Which superseded in part (in 1997): *School Library Media Quarterly (Print);* Which was formerly (until 1981): *School Media Quarterly;* Which superseded in part (in 1972): *School Libraries;* Which was formerly (until 1952): *American Association of School Librarians. Newsletter.* [ISSN: 2165-1019] 1951. a. Free. Ed(s): Ruth V Small, Mega Subramaniam. American Library Association, 50 E Huron St, Chicago, IL 60611; ala@ala.org; http://www.ala.org. Illus. Refereed. *Indexed:* ERIC. *Aud.:* Ems, Hs.

This open-access journal is a refereed publication of the American Association of School Librarians, a division of the American Library Association. *School Library Research* publishes high-quality research papers concerning the management and utilization of school library media programs. Articles emphasize information literacy, teaching methods, and school library programs. Recent topics cover professional skills development; portrayal of disabilities in young adult graphic novels; and school librarians as health information gatekeepers. A valuable resource for school library media professionals. Available online. URL: www.ala.org/aasl/slr

3205. *Science & Technology Libraries.* [ISSN: 0194-262X] 1980. q. GBP 676 (print & online eds.)). Ed(s): Tony Stankus. Routledge, 530 Walnut St, Ste 850, Philadelphia, PA 19106. Illus., index, adv. Sample. Refereed. Circ: 538 Paid. Microform: PQC. Reprint: PSC. *Indexed:* A01, A22, E01, ISTA. *Aud.:* Ac, Sa.

Science & Technology Libraries is a quarterly, peer-reviewed publication with an audience of librarians in science, engineering, clinical investigation, and agriculture. Each issue focuses on original research, and also includes profiles of prominent scientists and reviews of recent developments in the science fields. Recent article topics include outreach, collection development, and digital repositories. Highly recommended for all science and technology librarians.

3206. *The Serials Librarian: the international journal of continuing print & electronic resources.* [ISSN: 0361-526X] 1976. q. GBP 1138 (print & online eds.)). Ed(s): Louise Penn, Andrew Shroyer. Routledge, 711 3rd Ave, 8th Fl., New York, NY 10017; http://www.routledge.com. Illus., adv. Sample. Refereed. Vol. ends: No. 4. Microform: PQC. Reprint: PSC. *Indexed:* A01, A22, E01, ISTA, MLA-IB. *Bk. rev.:* Number and length vary. *Aud.:* Ac, Sa.

This peer-reviewed journal addresses the complex and changing environment of continuing resources management, including preservation, collection development, acquisitions, and cataloging. Recent article topics address RDA, open-access journals, and sustainable scholarship. Highly recommended for all librarians who work with continuing resources.

3207. *Serials Review.* [ISSN: 0098-7913] 1975. 4x/yr. GBP 536 (print & online eds.)). Ed(s): Maria Collins. Taylor & Francis, 2, 3 & 4 Park Sq, Milton Park, Abingdon, OX14 4RN, United Kingdom; subscriptions@tandf.co.uk; https://www.tandfonline.com. Illus., index, adv. Sample. Refereed. Vol. ends: No. 4. Reprint: PSC. *Indexed:* A01, A22, B01, BRI, CBRI, ISTA, MLA-IB. *Bk. rev.:* Number and length vary. *Aud.:* Ga, Ac, Sa.

This quarterly, peer-reviewed journal focuses on all issues surrounding serials and their management, from practical and theoretical points of view. Recent article topics include pay-per-view transactions, scholarly communication, and discovery layers. Each issue also includes opinion columns, conference reviews, and standards updates. Recommended for all serial and e-resource librarians.

3208. *Teacher Librarian: the journal for school library professionals.* Formerly (until 1998): *Emergency Librarian.* [ISSN: 1481-1782] 1973. 5x/yr. USD 62 combined subscription in US & Canada (print & online eds.); USD 75 combined subscription elsewhere (print & online eds.)). Scarecrow Press, Inc., 16211 Oxford Ct, Bowie, MD 20715; custserv@rowman.com; https://rowman.com/Scarecrow. Illus., adv. Sample. Vol. ends: Jun. *Indexed:* A01, A22, BRI, C37, CBRI, Chicano, ERIC, ISTA. *Bk. rev.:* Number and length vary. *Aud.:* Ems, Hs, Ac.

Published five times a year, *Teacher Librarian* provides information for professional librarians who work with children and young adults. Regular features include reviews of professional literature, Internet resources, and new books for children, as well as articles that discuss information technology and school library management. Highly recommended for school librarians and library media specialists.

3209. *Technical Services Quarterly: new trends in computers, automation & advanced technologies in the technical operation of libraries & information centers.* [ISSN: 0731-7131] 1983. q. GBP 869 (print & online eds.)). Ed(s): Gary M Pitkin. Routledge, 530 Walnut St, Ste 850, Philadelphia, PA 19106; enquiries@tandfonline.com; http://www.tandfonline.com. Illus., index, adv. Sample. Refereed. Circ: 507 Paid. Reprint: PSC. *Indexed:* A22, E01, ISTA. *Bk. rev.:* Number and length vary. *Aud.:* Ac, Sa.

This peer-reviewed publication provides information, current trends, and research regarding the technical operations of libraries. Each issue includes original articles, technical services reports, reviews of tech services on the web, and book reviews. Recent article topics address RDA, e-readers, and identifying emerging technologies. Highly recommended for all librarians in technical services departments.

3210. *Visual Resources: an international journal of documentation.* [ISSN: 0197-3762] 1980. q. GBP 933 (print & online eds.)). Ed(s): Christine Sundt. Routledge, 4 Park Sq, Milton Park, Abingdon, OX14 4RN, United Kingdom; subscriptions@tandf.co.uk; http://www.tandfonline.com. Illus., index, adv. Sample. Refereed. Vol. ends: No. 4. Reprint: PSC. *Indexed:* A01, A22, A51, AmHI, BAS, E01. *Bk. rev.:* Number and length vary. *Aud.:* Ac, Sa.

This referred journal examines images, the use of images, and visual literacy. It explores how visual languages are structured, how meaning is conveyed, and how images are organized, stored, delivered, and preserved. Although art and architecture are the most common uses of images, other subjects using visual information are also explored. Recent articles discuss open-access content; art history research; and the use of digital images in teaching art history. This journal is highly recommended for all information professionals working with visual information.

3211. *Voice of Youth Advocates: the library magazine serving those who serve young adults.* [ISSN: 0160-4201] 1978. bi-m. USD 57. Ed(s): RoseMary Honnold. E L Kurdyla Publishing LLC, PO Box 958, Bowie, MD 20718-0958. Illus., index, adv. Sample. *Indexed:* A22, CBRI, MLA-IB. *Bk. rev.:* Number and length vary. *Aud.:* Ems, Hs, Ga.

This bimonthly publication is intended for professionals who provide information services to teenagers. The guiding principles of the journal state that young adults deserve their own targeted library services and collections, free and equal access to information, advocates for their information needs, and participation in decision-making processes. Each issue includes several well-written articles that address various aspects of young adult librarianship, as well as numerous reviews of young adult fiction and reference books. Recent articles explore library services on a tight budget, and library-classroom partnership. Strongly recommended for all librarians who serve young adults. An active web site is maintained.

3212. *Weave: journal of library user experience.* [ISSN: 2333-3316] 2014. s-a. Free. Ed(s): Rebecca Blakiston. Michigan Publishing, 839 Greene St, Ann Arbor, MI 48104; mpublishing@umich.edu; http://www.publishing.umich.edu/. Refereed. *Aud.:* Ga, Ac, Sa.

This peer-reviewed, open-access journal focuses on user experience design for library professionals. Peer-reviewed articles are theoretical and practical in nature. Recent articles cover improving UX using Query analysis, and performance enhancements for library web sites. Available online.

3213. ***Young Adult Library Services (Online).*** Supersedes in part (in 2002): *Journal of Youth Services in Libraries;* Which was formerly (1942-1987): *Top of the News.* [ISSN: 2374-7706] 2002. q. Free to members; Non-members, USD 70. Ed(s): Linda W Braun. American Library Association, 50 E Huron St, Chicago, IL 60611; http://www.ala.org. Adv. *Indexed:* A01, BRI. *Aud.:* Ems, Hs, Ga.

Young Adult Library Services is the official publication of the Young Adult Library Services Association (YALSA), a division of the American Library Association. This journal publishes news and articles relevant to providers of teen library services. Recent articles explore teens' space in the library, teens and web making, and summer reading. Other features include bibliographies, association news, and announcements of awards. Essential reading for all professionals who provide library services to young adults.

■ LIFE WRITING/BIOGRAPHY

Sandra Hussey, Senior Research/Instruction Librarian & Library Research Instruction Coordinator, Georgetown University Library; husseys@georgetown.edu

Introduction

Two types of publications were reviewed for this section: journals that treat biography and life writing as a genre and those that provide biographical information. While biographical facts may be found on the web, there is still a need for well-researched, factual biographies of people in the news. Several titles providing biographical information have ceased. However, *Current Biography* remains as well as the standard biographical reference sources.

While biography and life writing are long-standing literary forms, in the last 30 years both study of the genre and types of life writing have broadened in several ways. Biographies, autobiographies, memoirs, diaries, travel accounts, slave narratives, and other life writing are of interest to multiple disciplines beyond literature and history. Although celebrities and public figures are obvious candidates for biography, the stories of obscure and hidden lives are being written as well. In the age of social media, it can be argued that we are all writing our autobiographies in real time, episode by episode. In addition, although biographies and autobiographies are usually considered with other types of nonfiction writing, new forms of life writing may be semi-fictional. Theme issues from biography and life writing journals cover such diverse areas as corporate personhood, testimony, oral tradition, and autoethnography. The following publications provide a window into this ever-expanding genre and area of study.

Basic Abstracts and Indexes

Biography Index Past and Present, Biography and Genealogy Master Index, Dictionary of Literary Biography, Biography in Context.

3214. ***Auto/Biography Studies.*** [ISSN: 0898-9575] 1986. 3x/yr. GBP 314 (print & online eds.)). Ed(s): Emily Hipchen, Ricia Anne Chansky. Routledge, 530 Walnut St, Ste 850, Philadelphia, PA 19106; enquiries@tandfonline.com; http://www.tandfonline.com. Illus. Refereed. Vol. ends: Fall (No. 2). Reprint: PSC. *Indexed:* A22, MLA-IB. *Bk. rev.:* Various number and length. *Aud.:* Ac.

A densely packed scholarly journal devoted to the study of all forms of life writing, including autobiography, biography, diaries, letters, and the relationships between these forms and other discourse. Sponsored by the Autobiography Society, this journal covers broad cultural, literary, and historical terrain, with occasional special issues on topics such as contemporary pedagogies of life writing, cross-cultural or intercultural life writing, and autobiography and photography. Each issue provides seven or eight scholarly articles, several lengthy book reviews, and announcements for papers and conferences. The focus is on autobiography, making it a valuable complement to other biography and life writing journals. Membership in the society includes subscription to the journal.

3215. ***Biography (Honolulu): an interdisciplinary quarterly.*** [ISSN: 0162-4962] 1978. q. USD 110. Ed(s): Anjoli Roy. University of Hawai'i Press, 2840 Kolowalu St, Honolulu, HI 96822; uhpjourn@hawaii.edu; http://www.uhpress.hawaii.edu. Illus., index, adv. Sample. Refereed. Vol. ends: Fall (No. 4). *Indexed:* A01, A22, BRI, C37, CBRI, E01, IBSS, MLA-IB. *Bk. rev.:* Various number and length. *Aud.:* Ac.

This scholarly journal publishes lengthy articles on theoretical, generic, historical, and cultural dimensions of life writing, encompassing biography, autobiography, journal writing, and other forms. Each issue provides five to eight articles and four to eight reviews. An annual bibliography of recent biographical writing appears in the fall issue as well as an annual index to the volume. One or two issues per year is devoted to special topics. Recent topics include online lives, verse biography, and life writing and corporate personhood. Recommended for all academic collections, especially those that specialize in literature, history, or life writing. Tables of contents and abstracts back to the Winter 1998 issues are available on the University of Hawaii Press website. Available both in print and online. http://www.uhpress.hawaii.edu/t-biography.aspx

3216. ***Current Biography (Print).*** [ISSN: 0011-3344] 1940. m. USD 199. Grey House Publishing, 4919 Rte 22, Amenia, NY 12501; customerservice@greyhouse.com; https://greyhouse.com/. Illus., index. *Indexed:* A01, C37, F01, IIMP, IIPA, MASUSE, MLA-IB. *Aud.:* Ga, Ac.

Each issue of *Current Biography* provides an eclectic mix of straightforward biographical sketches focusing on prominent living individuals from many different fields, including the arts, politics, science, sports, religion, and business. Coverage is primarily American, with some international entries. Beyond the cover photograph, illustrations are limited to a small black-and-white portrait for each individual. Entries include contact information, selected works, and selected biographical references. Each issue ends with an obituary section that includes a reference to the *Current Biography Yearbook* entry for the deceased. At the end of each year, articles from the monthly issues are cumulated into *Current Biography Yearbook*, available in print and online.

3217. ***European Journal of Life Writing.*** [ISSN: 2211-243X] 2012. . Free. University of Groningen Press, University Library, Postbus 559, Groningen, 9700 AN, Netherlands; ugp@rug.nl; http://www.rug.nl/library/ugp. Refereed. *Bk. rev.:* Various number and length. *Aud.:* Ga, Ac.

The *European Journal of Life Writing* (*EJLW*), founded by the European chapter of the International Auto/Biography Association, is an international, peer-reviewed e-journal, focusing on articles about life writing in or about Europe. Articles are written in English. It is an open-access initiative supported by the Vrije Universiteit Amsterdam's library. The *EJLW* aims to provide a forum for work in the field of all forms of life narratives, with contributions ranging from conceptual to practical and creative work. Articles and reviews may be submitted at any time and are published as soon as they are ready for publication. Article themes include Europe and refugees, teaching life writing texts in Europe, and gender and politics in autobiography. Includes reports from conferences and reviews.

3218. ***Life Writing.*** [ISSN: 1448-4528] 2004. q. GBP 473 (print & online eds.)). Ed(s): Maureen Perkins. Routledge, 4 Park Sq, Milton Park, Abingdon, OX14 4RN, United Kingdom; subscriptions@tandf.co.uk; http://www.tandfonline.com. Adv. Sample. Refereed. Reprint: PSC. *Indexed:* A22, AmHI, E01, MLA-IB. *Bk. rev.:* Various number and length. *Aud.:* Ga, Ac.

Published quarterly, issues include four to six scholarly articles on all forms of biography and life writing as well as critically-informed personal narratives titled "reflections" and two to four reviews. The journal emphasizes that it will provide expert and sympathetic reviewing of interdisciplinary work. In addition, *Life Writing* intends to be international in scope and inclusive of disciplines and perspectives that use biography and autobiography as analytical tools, such as object biography, autoethnography, and autofiction. Recent themes include Romantic and Victorian auto/biography, illness and disability life writing, life writing after empire, and looking at photos in life writing.

■ LINGUISTICS

See also Anthropology; Classical Studies; Education; Literature; Psychology; and Sociology and Social Work sections.

Jillian M. Slater, Librarian/Archivist and Assistant Professor, Marian Library, University of Dayton, Dayton, OH; jslater1@udayton.edu

Introduction

As a whole, linguistics journals cover a broad range of practical, theoretical, technical, and historical perspectives in the systematic study of language and its many subfields. Articles tend to be highly specialized, and much of the content is interdisciplinary. Most journals aim to publish articles grounded in empirical evidence that may help to advance the field through new insights. Some of the major subfields in linguistics include phonetics, phonology, morphology, syntax, semantics, sociolinguistics, psycholinguistics, neurolinguistics, and computational linguistics.

Journals including the *Canadian Journal of Linguistics, Folia Linguistica, Language, Lingua, Linguistic Inquiry,* and *Linguistics: an interdisciplinary journal of the language sciences* comprise some of the core journals in the field. These publications lean toward presenting important research on a range of current linguistics topics.

Some journals focus on research related to one or more of the basic subfields of linguistics. For example, the *Journal of Phonetics, Journal of Semantics, Morphology, Linguistic Review* (which is devoted to syntax), and *Linguistic Analysis* (on phonetics, semantics, morphology, and syntax) focus on publishing research in a specific "core" area. Additionally, a number of linguistics journals focus on corpus linguistics, a method of analysis that relies on *corpora,* or field samples, to study language. Journals in this area include *Corpora, International Journal of Corpus Linguistics,* and the recently founded *Corpus Linguistics and Linguistic Theory.*

Applied linguistics and pragmatics, which investigate and offer solutions to practical or real-world language issues, are primarily covered in *Applied Linguistics* and *Intercultural Pragmatics.*

A number of journals focus on linguistics research as it relates to a specific language. Among top journals reporting on the systematic study of English is the *Journal of the English Language. English World-Wide* covers English learning and use around the world. *American Speech: a quarterly of linguistic usage* focuses specifically on American English, and indigenous languages of the Americas are covered in *International Journal of American Linguistics.* A well-rounded academic collection might also include the *Journal of German Linguistics,* which publishes research on topics relating to Germanic languages, including English up to 1500; and *Probus: International Journal of Latin and Romance Linguistics.* Additionally, *Languages in Contrast* publishes studies contrasting one or more languages.

Because of the nature of the field, linguistics journals tend to include interdisciplinary content. Certain journals, however, are devoted to publishing studies at the intersection of disciplines, including *Anthropological Linguistics, Cognitive Linguistics, Language and Education, Language and Literature,* and *Linguistics and Philosophy.* Along with these established journals, several recent titles including *Laboratory Phonetics, Language Learning and Development,* and *The Mental Lexicon* also report on current interdisciplinary trends.

Also interdisciplinary in nature are linguistics journals with a pedagogical perspective. *English Language Teaching Journal, Modern Language Journal, Studies in Second Language Acquisition,* and *TESOL Quarterly* report on both practical and theoretical issues related to language instruction.

Although other publications report on the development of language throughout history, *Language Variation and Change* focuses (more so than other journals) on historical perspectives in linguistics. *Probus* and *Journal of Latin Linguistics* also include historical perspectives.

Basic Periodicals

Ac: *American Speech, Applied Linguistics, Journal of English Linguistics, Journal of Linguistics, Journal of Phonetics, Language (Washington), Language in Society, Linguistic Inquiry, The Linguistic Review, Linguistics, Modern Language Journal, Natural Language and Linguistic Theory.*

Basic Abstracts and Indexes

Linguistics Abstracts, Linguistics and Language Behavior Abstracts (LLBA), MLA International Bibliography, Social Sciences Citation Index, Sociological Abstracts.

3219. *Advances in English Linguistics.* [ISSN: 2325-2197] 2012. q. Free. World Science Publisher, LLC., worldsciencepublisher@gmail.com; http://worldsciencepublisher.org/. *Aud.:* Ac, Sa.

Founded in 2012, *Advances in English Linguistics* identifies scientists, engineers, students, and professors as its main audience and publishes a range of linguistics research, focusing on English. Two articles from the most recent edition include "Nativist Emergentism in Second Language Acquisition" and "English Grammatical Collocations in Azeri." Recommended supplement for academic collections.

3220. *American Journal of Linguistics.* [ISSN: 2326-0750] 2012. bi-m. USD 50 per issue. Ed(s): Christo Kaftandjiev. Scientific & Academic Publishing Co., 1200 Rosemead Blvd, Ste D #105, Rosemead, CA 91731; feedback@sapub.org; http://www.sapub.org. Refereed. *Aud.:* Ac.

Founded in 2012, *American Journal of Linguistics* is an open-access journal that publishes theoretical articles in all areas of linguistics. The journal lists topics of interest as "[a]pplied, computational, developmental, evolutionary, and historical linguistics, as well as language geography, linguistic typology, psycholinguistics, sociolinguistics, and stylistics." Recent articles include "Why and How the Translator Constantly Makes Decisions about Cultural Meaning" and "Phatic Communication: How English Native Speakers Create Ties of Union." Recommended supplement for academic libraries.

American Journal of Philology. See Classical Studies section.

3221. *American Speech: a quarterly of linguistic usage.* [ISSN: 0003-1283] 1925. q. USD 346. Ed(s): Charles E Carson, Thomas C Purnell. Duke University Press, 905 W Main St, Durham, NC 27701; orders@dukeupress.edu; https://www.dukeupress.edu. Illus., adv. Refereed. Vol. ends: Winter. Reprint: PSC. *Indexed:* A01, A22, AmHI, BRI, E01, MLA-IB. *Bk. rev.:* 1-2, 2-6 pages. *Aud.:* Ga, Ac.

Founded in 1925, this publication of the American Dialect Society reports on English language use in the western hemisphere, linguistic theory, and the influence of other languages by or on English. The journal emphasizes "current usage, dialectology, and the history and structure of English." Recent issues have included articles titled "A Weird (Language) Tale: Variation and Change in the Adjectives of Strangeness" and "Fixin' To: The Emergence of an American Quasi-Modal." The journal also includes book reviews, brief essays, and notes. As a highly cited journal with broad appeal, it is recommended for academic linguistic collections. See also *International Journal of American Linguistics.*

3222. *Anthropological Linguistics.* [ISSN: 0003-5483] 1959. q. USD 184 (Individuals, USD 58). Ed(s): Douglas R Parks. University of Nebraska Press, 1111 Lincoln Mall, Lincoln, NE 68588; journals@unl.edu; https://www.nebraskapress.unl.edu. Illus., index, adv. Refereed. Microform: PQC. *Indexed:* A01, A22, A47, AmHI, BAS, BRI, E01, IBSS, MLA-IB. *Bk. rev.:* 3-4, 2-6 pages. *Aud.:* Ac.

This journal covers a broad range of topics at the intersection of linguistics and anthropology, focusing on cultural, historical, and philological aspects of linguistic study. Articles include analyses of texts and discourse, studies of semantic systems, cultural classification, linguistic prehistory, and onomastics, as well as discussions on archival material and the history of the field. For example, recent articles include "Linguistic Archaeology, Kinship Terms, and Language Contact in Suriname" and "The Historical Linguistics of Uto-

Aztecan Agriculture." The journal is global in scope, although the majority of its analyses is based on the indigenous languages of the Americas. *Anthropological Linguistics* is published jointly by the Department of Anthropology and the American Indian Research Institute at Indiana University. Institutions whose linguistics programs are complemented by programs in anthropology and Native American studies will be most likely to benefit from a subscription to this journal.

3223. *Applied Linguistics.* [ISSN: 0142-6001] 1980. 6x/yr. EUR 671. Ed(s): Anna Mauranen, John Hellermann. Oxford University Press, Great Clarendon St, Oxford, OX2 6DP, United Kingdom; onlinequeries.uk@oup.com; http://global.oup.com. Illus., adv. Sample. Refereed. Reprint: PSC. *Indexed:* A01, A22, E01, ERIC, IBSS, MLA-IB. *Bk. rev.:* 4-5, 1-3 pages. *Aud.:* Ac.

This journal publishes original research and conceptual articles that address "practical issues in linguistics in a principled way by reference to theoretical studies." Articles focus on the relationship between theory and current practice, as well as specific situations in language acquisition and use. *Applied Linguistics* covers a range of topics, including bilingualism and multilingualism; computer-mediated communication; conversation analysis; deaf linguistics; discourse analysis and pragmatics; corpus linguistics; critical discourse analysis; first and additional language learning, teaching, and use; forensic linguistics; language assessment; language planning and policies; languages for special purposes; literacies; multimodal communication; rhetoric and stylistics; and translations. The journals "Forum" section (which includes responses to articles, commentary on practice, and brief research reports) serves to foster debate via efficient turnaround time for shorter pieces. Considered a core journal in the field, *Applied Linguistics* is recommended for academic libraries.

C L A Journal. See African American section.

3224. *Canadian Journal of Linguistics.* Formerly (until 1961): *Canadian Linguistic Association. Journal.* [ISSN: 0008-4131] 1954. 4x/yr. GBP 212 (print & online eds.)). Ed(s): Sarah Cummins. Cambridge University Press, University Printing House, Shaftesbury Rd, Cambridge, CB2 8BS, United Kingdom; journals@cambridge.org; https://www.cambridge.org. Illus., index. Sample. Refereed. Circ: 618. Vol. ends: Nov. Microform: PQC. Reprint: PSC. *Indexed:* A22, BAS, E01, IBSS, MLA-IB. *Bk. rev.:* 5-8, 1,000 words. *Aud.:* Ac.

The *Canadian Journal of Linguistics / Revue Canadienne de Linguistique* publishes original research on a variety of practical and theoretical issues in linguistics. The articles report on linguistic theory; linguistic description of English, French, and a variety of other natural languages; phonetics; phonology; morphology; syntax; semantics; historical linguistics; sociolinguistics; psycholinguistics; and language acquisition. Examples of recent themed issues include "Temporal and Modal Dimensions of Legal Discourses" and "The Syntax of Relative Clauses." A supplementary academic purchase.

3225. *Cognitive Linguistics: an interdisciplinary journal of cognitive science.* [ISSN: 0936-5907] 1989. q. EUR 630. Ed(s): John Newman. De Gruyter Mouton, Genthiner Str 13, Berlin, 10785, Germany; mouton@degruyter.de; https://www.degruyter.com. Illus., index, adv. Sample. Refereed. Reprint: PSC. *Indexed:* A01, A22, BRI, E01, MLA-IB. *Bk. rev.:* 0-5, 5-15 pages. *Aud.:* Ac, Sa.

This journal reports on a variety of research on language and cognition, focusing on language as a tool for organizing, processing, and conveying information. Topics include the functional principles of linguistic organization; conceptual relationships between syntax and semantics; language and thought; and the experiential background of language-in-use. Examples of recent articles include "Nouns and Verbs in Cognitive Grammar: Where is the 'Sound' Evidence?" and "Individual Differences in the Interpretation of Ambiguous Statements about Time." The journal is suitable for academic libraries that support strong linguistic collections.

3226. *Corpora: corpus-based language learning, language processing and linguistics.* [ISSN: 1749-5032] 2006. 3x/yr. GBP 119 (print & online eds.)). Ed(s): Tony McEnery, Randi Reppen. Edinburgh University Press Ltd., The Tun, Holyrood Rd, 12 (2f) Jackson's Entry, Edinburgh, EH8 8PJ, United Kingdom; journals@eup.ed.ac.uk; http://www.euppublishing.com. Adv. Sample. Refereed. *Indexed:* MLA-IB. *Bk. rev.:* 0-2; 3-5 pages. *Aud.:* Ac.

Like the *International Journal of Corpus Linguistics* (below), this journal is devoted to the study of *corpora*, a methodology in contemporary linguistics that allows researchers to discover patterns of authentic language use through analysis of actual usage. *Corpora* publishes articles by a wide range of theorists using corpus data. It actively promotes interdisciplinary perspectives (for example, cultural studies, historical studies, and literary studies) and aims to engage the full range of human languages. Examples of recent articles include "Male and Female Shame: A Corpus-based Study of Emotion" and "Dimensions of Web Registers: An Exploratory Multi-dimensional Comparison." A supplemental purchase for academic libraries.

3227. *Corpus Linguistics and Linguistic Theory.* [ISSN: 1613-7027] 2005. 2x/yr. EUR 275. Ed(s): Stefan Th. Gries. De Gruyter Mouton, Genthiner Str 13, Berlin, 10785, Germany; mouton@degruyter.de; https://www.degruyter.com. Adv. Refereed. Reprint: PSC. *Indexed:* A22, BRI, E01, MLA-IB. *Bk. rev.:* Number and length vary. *Aud.:* Ac.

This relatively new journal (founded in 2005) provides coverage of corpus-based research that focuses on theoretically relevant issues in all core areas of linguistics, including, for example, phonology, morphology, syntax, semantics, and pragmatics. Examples of recent articles include "Complementation of Ditransitive Verbs in South Asian Englishes: A Multifactorial Analysis" and "The Portuguese Inflected Infinitive: An Empirical Approach." The journal also includes "Squibs" (short reports on theoretical issues, interesting data, or responses to articles) and reviews of books and software packages. A good supplementary purchase for research institutions.

3228. *E L T Journal: an international journal for teachers of English to speakers of other languages.* Former titles (until 1981): *English Language Teaching Journal;* (until 1973): *English Language Teaching.* [ISSN: 0951-0893] 1946. q. EUR 338. Ed(s): Alessia Cogo. Oxford University Press, Great Clarendon St, Oxford, OX2 6DP, United Kingdom; onlinequeries.uk@oup.com; http://global.oup.com. Illus., adv. Sample. Refereed. Microform: PQC. Reprint: PSC. *Indexed:* A01, A22, AmHI, BRI, E01, ERIC, MLA-IB. *Bk. rev.:* 2-10, 1-15 pages. *Aud.:* Hs, Ga, Ac.

This quarterly publication is directed toward teachers of English as a second, additional, foreign, or bridge language. Content focuses on linking practical issues "with insights gained from related academic disciplines such as applied linguistics, education, psychology, and sociology." A recent article, "Learning English by Walking Down the Street," explores the potential and practice of English literacy walks in ELT education. In addition to refereed articles, the journal publishes special features including "key concepts in ELT," which provides concise accounts of important concepts in the field, and news from the *International Association of Teachers of English as a Foreign Language.* Recommended for libraries at institutions with ELT programs.

3229. *English World-Wide: a journal of varieties of English.* [ISSN: 0172-8865] 1980. 3x/yr. EUR 379 combined subscription (print & online eds.)). Ed(s): Daniel Schreier, Marianne Hundt. John Benjamins Publishing Co., PO Box 36224, Amsterdam, 1020 ME, Netherlands; subscription@benjamins.nl; http://www.benjamins.com. Illus., adv. Sample. Refereed. *Indexed:* A22, IBSS, MLA-IB. *Bk. rev.:* 3-5, 1-5 pages. *Aud.:* Ac.

This journal publishes research on dialects and social contexts of English-speaking communities, including both native and second-language speakers around the world. Additionally, articles report on general issues in general and historical sociolinguistics, pidgin and creole linguistics, language planning, and multilingualism as they relate to modern varieties of English. For example, recent articles include "An 18th-Century Novel from the Miskito Coast: What was Creolized?" and "Economic Migrants, Social Networks, and the Prospect of Koineization in the United Arab Emirates." Although the journal does not directly address applied linguistics and language teaching, it may provide important background information for teachers of the English language. The journal also features reviews and review essays. Topics should be of interest to linguistics researchers throughout the English-speaking world.

3230. *Folia Linguistica: acta societatis linguisticae Europaeae.* [ISSN: 0165-4004] 1967. 3x/yr. EUR 398. Ed(s): Nikolaus Ritt, Hubert Cuyckens. De Gruyter Mouton, Genthiner Str 13, Berlin, 10785, Germany; mouton@degruyter.de; https://www.degruyter.com. Illus., index, adv. Sample. Refereed. Reprint: SCH. *Indexed:* A01, A22, BAS, E01, MLA-IB. *Bk. rev.:* 0-1, 1,000 words. *Aud.:* Ac, Sa.

This journal is international in scope and published by the Societas Linguistica Europaea. It presents original research grounded in empirical evidence and treats all "non-historical" areas of general linguistics, as well as "sociological, discoursal, computational, and psychological aspects of language and linguistic theory." Recent articles include "Arguing for a Wide Conception of Grammar: The Case of Final Particles in Spoken Discourse" and "Vocabular Clarity Meets Faroese Noun Declensions." A recent issue was devoted to the theme of grammatical gender. The journal also contains reviews, conference reports, and bibliographies. Subscribers also receive an annual supplement, *Folia Linguistica Historica*. Recommended for large academic linguistics collection.

3231. *Functional Linguistics.* [ISSN: 2196-419X] 2014. . Free. Ed(s): Chang Chenguang, Huang Guowen. SpringerOpen, Tiergartenstr 17, Heidelberg, 69121, Germany; info@springeropen.com; http://www.springeropen.com. Refereed. *Aud.:* Ac.

This new, open-access journal, founded in 2014, publishes original research that primarily focuses on systemic functional linguistics. They list topics of interest as "language and context, functional grammar, semantic variation, discourse analysis, multimodality, register and genre analysis, and educational linguistics." Two recent articles include "Teachers and Teacher Aides Initiating Five-Year-Olds into Science" and "An Analysis of Causal Asyndetic Constructions in United States History Textbooks." Recommended supplement for academic collections.

3232. *Indo-European Linguistics.* [ISSN: 2212-5884] 2013. a. EUR 167. Ed(s): Ronald Kim, Joseph F Eska. Brill, PO Box 9000, Leiden, 2300 PA, Netherlands; marketing@brill.com; https://brill.com. Adv. Refereed. *Aud.:* Ac.

Founded in 2013, *Indo-European Linguistics* (*IEL*) is devoted to the study of the ancient and medieval Indo-European languages from the perspective of modern linguistics. With a focus on theoretical and analytical articles, *IEL* publishes studies on a range of topics, including cross-linguistic data, language acquisition, cognitive science, variationist sociolinguistics, and language contact. Examples of articles include "Morphosyntax of Fear and Distance" and "Accent in Thematic Nouns." This new title is a recommended supplement for academic collections.

3233. *Intercultural Pragmatics.* [ISSN: 1612-295X] 2004. q. EUR 286. Ed(s): Istvan Kecskes. De Gruyter Mouton, Genthiner Str 13, Berlin, 10785, Germany; mouton@degruyter.de; https://www.degruyter.com. Adv. Refereed. Reprint: PSC. *Indexed:* A22, BRI, E01, MLA-IB. *Bk. rev.:* 2 reviews; 5-9 pages. *Aud.:* Ac, Sa.

This journal publishes articles on theoretical and applied pragmatics, and aims to promote the development and understanding of pragmatic theory and intercultural competence. In addition, the journal promotes scholarly debate in subfields of pragmatics, including the linguistic, cognitive, social, and interlanguage paradigms. Recent articles include "Corpus Methods in Pragmatics: The Case of English and Russian Emotions" and "Your Kids Are So Stinkin' Cute! :-): Complimenting Behavior on Facebook Among Family and Friends." Additionally, the journal publishes interviews, debates, and research statements. Because of its interdisciplinary, intercultural perspective, articles may be of interest to other disciplines such as anthropology, applied and theoretical linguistics, psychology, sociolinguistics, and communication. Recommended for large academic linguistics collections.

3234. *International Journal of American Linguistics.* [ISSN: 0020-7071] 1917. q. USD 458. Ed(s): David Beck. University of Chicago Press, 1427 E 60th St, Chicago, IL 60637; subscriptions@press.uchicago.edu; http://www.journals.uchicago.edu. Illus., index, adv. Sample. Refereed. Vol. ends: Oct. Reprint: PSC. *Indexed:* A01, A22, A47, AmHI, BRI, MLA-IB. *Bk. rev.:* 2-5, 2-4 pages. *Aud.:* Ac, Sa.

Founded by anthropologist Franz Boas in 1917 and published in association with the Society for the Study of the Indigenous Languages of the Americas, this quarterly publication is devoted to the study of indigenous languages of the Americas. According to its mission statements, *IJAL* "concentrates on the investigation of the linguistic data and on the presentation of grammatical fragments and other documents relevant to the Amerindian languages." The articles deal with the full range of linguistics issues raised by individual indigenous languages. For example, recent articles include "An Introduction to Classical Nahuatl" and "A Grammar of Creek (Muskogee)." Along with *Anthropological Linguistics*, this journal is a recommended resource for academic communities with programs in Native American studies and anthropology. See also *American Speech*.

3235. *International Journal of Corpus Linguistics.* [ISSN: 1384-6655] 1996. 4x/yr. EUR 488 combined subscription (print & online eds.)). Ed(s): Michaela Mahlberg. John Benjamins Publishing Co., PO Box 36224, Amsterdam, 1020 ME, Netherlands; subscription@benjamins.nl; http://www.benjamins.com. Illus., index. Sample. Refereed. *Indexed:* A01, A22, MLA-IB. *Bk. rev.:* 3-5, 3-15 pages. *Aud.:* Ac, Sa.

Corpus linguistics is the branch of the field that uses samples (*corpora*) of "real-world" language to discover patterns and insights in authentic language use. *IJCL* publishes original research in areas such as lexicology, discourse analysis, stylistics, sociolinguistics, contrastive linguistics, applied linguistics, and translation studies. Examples of recent articles include "Adverb Use and Language Proficiency in Young Learners' Writing" and "'Your mum!' Teenagers' Swearing by Mother in English, Spanish and Norwegian." The journal also includes articles relating to the interface between computational and corpus linguistics, and includes book and software reviews. A supplementary purchase for academic linguistics collections. See also *Corpora*.

3236. *Journal of English Linguistics.* [ISSN: 0075-4242] 1967. q. USD 1005 (print & online eds.)). Ed(s): Peter Grund, Matthew Gordon. Sage Publications, Inc., 2455 Teller Rd, Thousand Oaks, CA 91320; info@sagepub.com; http://www.sagepub.com. Illus., index, adv. Sample. Refereed. Vol. ends: Dec. Reprint: PSC. *Indexed:* A01, A22, AmHI, E01, MLA-IB. *Bk. rev.:* 1-5, 4-6 pages. *Aud.:* Ac, Sa.

Published quarterly, *Journal of English Linguistics* is considered a leading journal in the field. *Journal of English Linguistics* publishes original theoretical and methodological pieces focusing on the history of English, English grammar, corpus linguistics, sociolinguistics, and dialectology. For example, topics may include language change, word origins, emerging computer methods and new quantitative methods for the study of English, gender issues in language, and historical and formal studies of Old and Middle English. A recent themed issue was "Diachronic Approaches to Modality in World Englishes." Examples of recent articles include "The Extremes of Insubordination: Exclamatory as if!" and "The Verb-Second Phenomenon in the Old English Bible: The Question of Representativeness." Regular features include interviews with leading scholars, book reviews, reports on trends in the field, and a column "on the profession," in which key issues are discussed. Recommended for academic linguistics collections.

3237. *Journal of Germanic Linguistics.* Formerly (until 2001): *American Journal of Germanic Linguistics and Literatures.* [ISSN: 1470-5427] 1989. q. GBP 264. Ed(s): Tracy Alan Hall. Cambridge University Press, University Printing House, Shaftesbury Rd, Cambridge, CB2 8BS, United Kingdom; journals@cambridge.org; https://www.cambridge.org/. Illus., index, adv. Sample. Refereed. Circ: 350. Reprint: PSC. *Indexed:* A22, E01, MLA-IB. *Bk. rev.:* 1-5, 4-6 pages. *Aud.:* Ac, Sa.

This is the premier journal for the study of the Germanic languages, published for the Society of Germanic Linguistics. Original articles cover Germanic languages and dialects from the earliest phases to the present, including English up to 1500. Topics include formal analyses of phonological, morphological, syntactic, and semantic features of the Germanic languages, and there is coverage of historical development. Examples of recent articles include "The Imperative of Say as a Pragmatic Marker in English and Dutch" and "Language Contact and Morphosyntactic Complexity: Evidence from German." Recommended for academic collections at large research institutions.

3238. *Journal of Latin Linguistics.* Formerly (until 2013): *Papers on Grammar.* [ISSN: 2194-8739] 1980. 2x/yr. EUR 194. Ed(s): Pierluigi Cuzzolin, Gualtiero Calboli. De Gruyter Mouton, Genthiner Str 13, Berlin, 10785, Germany; mouton@degruyter.de; https://www.degruyter.com. Refereed. Reprint: PSC. *Indexed:* BRI. *Aud.:* Ac.

Journal of Latin Linguistics, previously *Papers on Grammar,* is the only journal devoted to Latin in both the synchronic and diachronic perspectives. The journal provides coverage on all phases of Latin-Archaic, Classical, Vulgar, Medieval, Renaissance, and Modern. Examples of recent articles include "Genetiuus and Ablatiuus Pretii in Latin: Concepts, Functions, and Formal Marks" and "Towards a Taxonomy of Latin Cleft Sentences." Because of Latin's influence on modern languages, this title is recommended for large academic collections or those that support strong linguistics programs.

3239. ***Journal of Linguistics.*** [ISSN: 0022-2267] 1965. 3x/yr. GBP 308. Ed(s): S.J. Hannahs, Kersti Boerjars. Cambridge University Press, University Printing House, Shaftesbury Rd, Cambridge, CB2 8BS, United Kingdom; journals@cambridge.org; https://www.cambridge.org/. Illus., index, adv. Sample. Refereed. Circ: 2200. Vol. ends: Nov. Microform: PQC. Reprint: PSC. *Indexed:* A01, A22, AmHI, BAS, BRI, E01, IBSS, MLA-IB. *Bk. rev.:* 10-12, 3-6 pages. *Aud.:* Ac, Sa.

Published for the Linguistics Association of Great Britain (www.lagb.org.uk), this journal covers current, theoretical linguistics research. The journal aims to provide a forum for advances in all branches of theoretical linguistics. Topics covered are syntax, morphology, phonology, phonetics, semantics, and pragmatics, as well as historical, sociological, computational, and psychological aspects of language and linguistic theory. Examples of recent articles include "Soft Labial Conspiracy in Kurpian" and "A Cognitive Grammar Account of the Semantics of the English Present Progressive." Substantial (approximately 30) book reviews are included in every issue. The broad scope of this journal, combined with its emphasis on current linguistics theory, makes it a core selection for academic collections.

3240. ***Journal of Phonetics.*** [ISSN: 0095-4470] 1973. bi-m. EUR 1220. Ed(s): T Cho. Academic Press, 32 Jamestown Rd, Camden, London, NW1 7BY, United Kingdom; corporate.sales@elsevier.com; http://www.elsevier.com/. Adv. Sample. Refereed. Reprint: PSC. *Indexed:* A01, A22, E01, MLA-IB. *Bk. rev.:* 0-3, length varies. *Aud.:* Ac, Sa.

This is a leading journal reporting on the phonetic aspects of language and communication. The journal publishes experimental or theoretical research on topics such as "speech production, acoustics, and perception; phonetic aspects of psycholinguistics; speech synthesis; automatic speech recognition; descriptive phonetics; [and] speech and language." The journal also welcomes articles on "technological and/or pathological topics, or papers of an interdisciplinary nature...provided that linguistic-phonetic principles underlie the work reported." Examples of recent articles include "Laryngeal-Oral Coordination in Mixed-Voicing Clusters" and "Differences in Acoustic Vowel Space and the Perception of Speech Tempo." Recommended for academic linguistic collections.

3241. ***Journal of Semantics.*** [ISSN: 0167-5133] 1982. q. EUR 593. Ed(s): Rick Nouwen. Oxford University Press, Great Clarendon St, Oxford, OX2 6DP, United Kingdom; onlinequeries.uk@oup.com; http://global.oup.com. Adv. Sample. Refereed. Reprint: PSC. *Indexed:* A01, A22, AmHI, E01, IBSS, MLA-IB. *Bk. rev.:* 0-1, length varies. *Aud.:* Ac, Sa.

This quarterly journal publishes formal and experimental research articles relating to the range of topics in the study of meaning. In addition to semantics, articles may address "pragmatics, the syntax/semantics interface, cross-linguistic semantics, experimental studies of meaning (processing, acquisition, neurolinguistics), and semantically informed philosophy of language." Examples of recent articles include "Negative Polarity in German: Some Experimental Results" and "Embedded Scalars and Typicality." Brief empirical or theoretical pieces are published in the "Short Contributions" section. Since semantics is relevant to most linguistics research, this journal is recommended for academic libraries.

Journal of Slavic Linguistics. See Slavic and Eurasian Studies section.

3242. ***Laboratory Phonology (Online).*** [ISSN: 1868-6354] 2010. a. Free. Ed(s): Mirjam Ernestus. Ubiquity Press Ltd., Unit 2N, 6 Osborn St., London, E1 6TD, United Kingdom; support@ubiquitypress.com; https://www.ubiquitypress.com/. Refereed. *Aud.:* Ac.

This journal, published by the Association of Laboratory Phonology, presents original research on the study of the elements of spoken and signed language. The journal's focus is on publishing research grounded in quantitative analysis and empirical data from diverse languages. According to its web site, the journal aims to publish phonology research from "a range of disciplinary perspectives including linguistics, psychology, speech & hearing science, communication science, computer science, electrical & computer engineering, and other related fields." Recent articles include "The Perception of Voice-initiating Gestures" and "Sound Change in the Individual: Effects of Exposure on Cross-Dialect Speech Processing." Because of its interdisciplinary nature and focus on empirical methods, this journal is a recommended purchase for academic libraries.

3243. ***Language and Education.*** [ISSN: 0950-0782] 1987. bi-m. GBP 777 (print & online eds.)). Ed(s): Viv Edwards. Routledge, 4 Park Sq, Milton Park, Abingdon, OX14 4RN, United Kingdom; subscriptions@tandf.co.uk; http://www.tandfonline.com. Illus., adv. Sample. Refereed. Reprint: PSC. *Indexed:* A01, A22, BRI, ERIC, MLA-IB. *Bk. rev.:* 1-4, 2-5 pages, signed. *Aud.:* Ac.

This journal provides a forum for current issues and topics related to teaching language. With an international scope, the journal focuses on practical issues in language education including curriculum, pedagogy, and/or evaluation. Examples of recent articles include "The Learner's Voice: Exploring Bilingual Children's Selective Language Use and Perceptions of Minority Language Competence" and "The Ecology of Language in Classrooms at a University in Eastern Ukraine." This journal is relevant to collections at institutions with strong departments in linguistics and education.

3244. ***Language and Literature.*** [ISSN: 0963-9470] 1992. q. USD 1487 (print & online eds.)). Ed(s): Geoff Hall. Sage Publications Ltd., 1 Oliver's Yard, 55 City Rd, London, EC1Y 1SP, United Kingdom; market@sagepub.com; https://www.sagepub.com/. Adv. Sample. Refereed. Reprint: PSC. *Indexed:* A01, A22, AmHI, E01, MLA-IB. *Bk. rev.:* 1-4, 2-5 pages. *Aud.:* Ac.

With a focus on stylistics and linguistic analysis of literature, this journal is international in scope and focuses on emerging research in the field. It also covers analysis of non-literary texts, connections between stylistics and other theoretical approaches to literature, and the implications of these issues for the teaching of literature to both native and non-native speakers. Recent special issues have included the themes "Narrative" and "Rhetoric and Narratology." Recent articles have considered topics including the portrayal of autistic characters in fiction and sociolinguistic styles in cinema and television. The journal offers book reviews and a "Notes and Comments" section for discussion of current issues. Because of the journal's specialized focus, it may be a supplementary purchase for academic library collections.

3245. ***Language in Society.*** [ISSN: 0047-4045] 1972. 5x/yr. GBP 412. Ed(s): Jenny Cheshire. Cambridge University Press, University Printing House, Shaftesbury Rd, Cambridge, CB2 8BS, United Kingdom; journals@cambridge.org; https://www.cambridge.org/. Illus., adv. Sample. Refereed. Vol. ends: Dec. Microform: PQC. Reprint: PSC. *Indexed:* A01, A22, AmHI, BAS, BRI, CBRI, E01, IBSS, MLA-IB, SSA. *Bk. rev.:* 10-15, 2-4 pages; signed. *Aud.:* Ac.

This is a leading journal in the field of sociolinguistics, the discipline that investigates the social aspects of language and speech. International in scope, this journal includes theoretical, comparative, and methodological articles related to sociolinguistics, social anthropology, and related disciplines. Examples of recent topics include signed languages and sociopolitical formation and Spanish as sociocultural discourse. The journal offers extensive reviews, book notes, and occasional discussion sections on current topics, as well as themed issues. Recommended for academic library collections.

3246. ***Language Learning and Development.*** [ISSN: 1547-5441] 2005. q. GBP 425 (print & online eds.)). Ed(s): Cynthia Fisher. Psychology Press, 530 Walnut St, Philadelphia, PA 19106; orders@taylorandfrancis.com; http://www.psypress.com. Adv. Sample. Refereed. Reprint: PSC. *Indexed:* A22, E01, ERIC, MLA-IB. *Aud.:* Ac.

Published by The Society for Language Development, this interdisciplinary journal covers language learning from a range of current perspectives: linguistic, psychological, cognitive, anthropological, and others. According to the journal's web site, articles employ "experimental, observational, ethnographic, comparative, neuro-scientific, and formal methods of investigation." Articles from a recent issue include "Slowly but Surely: Adverbs Support Verb Learning in 2-Year-Olds" and "Acquiring Word Class Distinctions in American Sign Language: Evidence from Handshape." Recent issues have also included "commentary" and "response" sections. A recommended purchase for any large research collection, especially those that support programs in linguistics and education.

3247. ***Language Variation and Change.*** [ISSN: 0954-3945] 1989. 3x/yr. GBP 222. Ed(s): Rena Torres Cacoullos, William Labov. Cambridge University Press, University Printing House, Shaftesbury Rd, Cambridge, CB2 8BS, United Kingdom; journals@cambridge.org; https://www.cambridge.org/. Illus., adv. Sample. Refereed. Circ: 800. Microform: PQC. Reprint: PSC. *Indexed:* A22, E01, MLA-IB. *Aud.:* Ac.

This journal is devoted to sociolinguistics, specifically focusing on historical and systemic variation in language usage. The articles consider "actual-speech production (or writing)" and develop general theoretical, conceptual, and methodological considerations. Articles cover a broad spectrum of language and linguistic situations, many of them employing quantitative analysis to investigate linguistic features and patterns. Recent articles have included "The Role of African Americans in Philadelphia Sound Change" and "Vowel Variation and Reverse Acquisition in Rural Syrian Child and Adolescent Language." Because of its specialized scope, this journal may be a supplemental purchase for most academic libraries.

3248. ***Language (Washington).*** [ISSN: 0097-8507] 1925. q. USD 180 Free to members. Ed(s): Greg Carlson. Linguistic Society of America, 502 Lattimore Hall, Department of Linguistics, Rochester, NY 14627; lsa@lsadc.org; https://www.linguisticsociety.org. Illus., adv. Sample. Refereed. Vol. ends: Dec. Reprint: PSC. *Indexed:* A01, A22, A47, AmHI, BRI, E01, ERIC, IBSS, MLA-IB. *Bk. rev.:* 5-9, 1-4 pages. *Aud.:* Ac.

Published by the Linguistic Society of America since 1924, this is a leading, authoritative publication in the field. In addition to original research in linguistics, the journal also regularly includes short reports, review articles, book reviews, and book notices. Its special focus is theoretical linguistics, but all aspects of linguistic research are represented here, including historical, sociological, and pragmatic orientations, among others. Examples of recent articles include "The Surface-Compositional Semantics of English Intonation" and "Canadian Raising with Language-Specific Weighted Constraints." At least one author of each article must be a member of the LSA (www.lsadc.org). Highly recommended for academic library collections at all levels.

3249. ***Languages in Contrast: international journal for contrastive linguistics.*** [ISSN: 1387-6759] 1998. s-a. EUR 233 combined subscription (print & online eds.)). Ed(s): Barbara De Cock, Marie-Aude Lefer. John Benjamins Publishing Co., PO Box 36224, Amsterdam, 1020 ME, Netherlands; subscription@benjamins.nl; http://www.benjamins.com. Refereed. *Indexed:* MLA-IB. *Aud.:* Ac, Sa.

This journal's focus is on recent studies that illustrate contrast in two or more languages. Articles may concentrate on "any aspect of language" as well as "sociolinguistics and psycholinguistics," and these in turn may be discussed from a wide range of interdisciplinary approaches, including "translation, lexicography, computational linguistics, language teaching, literary and linguistic computing, [and] literary and cultural studies." *Languages in Contrast* also aims to provide a forum for a consideration of the theoretical place of comparative studies within the larger context of linguistics. A recent special issue of this journal explored genre- and register-related discourse features in contrast. The articles in this journal are specialized, yet the subject covered by the journal as a whole is of broad interest. A recommended purchase for large academic linguistic collections.

3250. ***Lingua.*** [ISSN: 0024-3841] 1947. 16x/yr. EUR 2216. Ed(s): Harry Whitaker. Elsevier BV, Radarweg 29, Amsterdam, 1043 NX, Netherlands; info@elsevier.com; https://www.elsevier.com/. Illus., index, adv. Sample. Refereed. Microform: PQC. *Indexed:* A01, A22, AmHI, BAS, MLA-IB. *Bk. rev.:* 0-3, 5-10 pages. *Aud.:* Ac, Sa.

This journal addresses a variety of topics in the field of linguistics. Individual pieces may be highly specialized, but must have "such general theoretical implications as to be of interest to any linguist." In addition to articles that expound original research, *Lingua* publishes review articles of trends in the field, occasional discussions, and critical book reviews. One forum entitled "Lingua Franca" presents debates on current topics; another, "The Decade In," offers surveys of various topics in linguistics for the non-professional. Also, a special section, "Taking up the Gauntlet," offers a forum for scholarly debate and discourse. A recent theme issue was titled "How Children Learn to Detect and Interpret Agreement Morphology: A Crosslinguistic Perspective." Recommended for academic linguistic collections.

3251. ***Linguistic Analysis.*** [ISSN: 0098-9053] 1975. q. Ed(s): David R Willingham. Linguistic Analysis, PO Box 2237, Vashon Island, WA 98070; info@linguisticanalysis.com; http://www.linguisticanalysis.com/. Illus., index, adv. Refereed. *Indexed:* A22, BAS, MLA-IB. *Aud.:* Ac, Sa.

Founded in 1976, this highly cited linguistics journal publishes new research in formal, core subfields including phonology, morphology, syntax, and semantics. An example of a recent issue focused on the theme "Universal Syntax and Parametric Phonology," and included an article titled "Phasing Out Projection: Considerations From The Syntax-Phonology Interface." Because of its focus on fundamental subfields of linguistics, this journal is recommended for academic library collections.

3252. ***Linguistic Inquiry.*** [ISSN: 0024-3892] 1970. q. USD 761 (print & online eds.)). Ed(s): Samuel Jay Keyser. M I T Press, One Rogers St, Cambridge, MA 02142-1209; http://mitpress.mit.edu/. Illus., adv. Refereed. Reprint: SCH. *Indexed:* A22, BAS, E01, MLA-IB. *Aud.:* Ac.

Considered a leader in the field, *Linguistic Inquiry* publishes articles with a focus on contemporary debate and current trends in linguistics. The journal presents content with a formal approach and international scope. For example, recent articles include "A Syntactic Universal and Its Consequences" and "An Ellipsis Approach to Contrastive Left-Dislocation." In addition to full-length articles, shorter contributions are presented in "Squibs and Discussions," and commentary on current developments are included in "Remarks and Replies." Recommended for academic collections.

3253. ***The Linguistic Review.*** [ISSN: 0167-6318] 1981. q. EUR 447. Ed(s): Nancy A Ritter, Harry van der Hulst. De Gruyter Mouton, Genthiner Str 13, Berlin, 10785, Germany; mouton@degruyter.de; https://www.degruyter.com. Illus., adv. Sample. Refereed. Reprint: PSC. *Indexed:* A01, A22, BAS, BRI, E01, MLA-IB. *Bk. rev.:* 0-1. *Aud.:* Ac.

The Linguistic Review publishes articles that address fundamental linguistics subfields: syntax, semantics, phonology, and morphology. Articles are presented in the framework of Generative Grammar and also focus on cognitive psychology. Examples of recent articles include "The Emergence of the Romanian Subjunctive" and "A Unified Analysis of wh-in-situ in Spanish." The journal also includes letters to the editor, dissertation abstracts, and book reviews. The content of this journal is highly specialized, but because of its coverage of fundamental linguistics subfields, it is a recommended purchase for medium to large academic linguistics collections.

3254. ***Linguistics: an interdisciplinary journal of the language sciences.*** [ISSN: 0024-3949] 1963. bi-m. EUR 747. Ed(s): Johan van der Auwera. De Gruyter Mouton, Genthiner Str 13, Berlin, 10785, Germany; mouton@degruyter.de; https://www.degruyter.com. Illus., adv. Sample. Refereed. Reprint: PSC. *Indexed:* A01, A22, AmHI, BAS, BRI, E01, MLA-IB. *Bk. rev.:* 3-4, 3-7 pages. *Aud.:* Ac.

This journal is devoted to traditional linguistics disciplines, including core areas such as semantics, syntax, morphology, and phonology. The journal occasionally publishes pieces of interest to linguists in other subspecialties. Recent themed issues have addressed topics such as differential object marking and a multifaceted approach to verb classes. A core journal in the field-recommended for academic linguistics collections.

3255. ***Linguistics and Philosophy: a journal of natural language syntax, semantics, logic, pragmatics, and processing.*** [ISSN: 0165-0157] 1977. bi-m. EUR 1325 (print & online eds.)). Ed(s): Graeme Forbes, Thomas E Zimmermann. Springer Netherlands, Van Godewijckstraat 30, Dordrecht, 3311 GX, Netherlands; http://www.springer.com. Illus., index, adv. Sample. Refereed. Vol. ends: No. 6. Microform: PQC. Reprint: PSC. *Indexed:* A22, AmHI, BRI, E01, MLA-IB. *Bk. rev.:* Number and length vary. *Aud.:* Ac, Sa.

This journal deals with topics that fall into the convergence of linguistics and philosophy. As the subtitle suggests, it examines core areas of linguistics, especially as they relate to philosophical theories of meaning and truth, as well as linguistic and psycholinguistic theories of semantic interpretation and related issues. Its other chief interests include "mathematical and logical properties of natural language and general aspects of computational linguistics," as well as "philosophical questions raised by linguistics as a science." Articles, replies, book reviews, and review articles round out the contents of this journal. While *Linguistics and Philosophy* is not considered a core journal in either discipline, it covers the common ground between them, and is thus a recommended purchase for large academic linguistics collections.

3256. ***The Mental Lexicon.*** [ISSN: 1871-1340] 2005. 3x/yr. EUR 354 combined subscription (print & online eds.)). Ed(s): Gary Libben, Gonia Jarema. John Benjamins Publishing Co., PO Box 36224, Amsterdam, 1020 ME, Netherlands; subscription@benjamins.nl; http://www.benjamins.com. Refereed. *Aud.:* Ac.

This relatively recent addition (founded in 2006) publishes research "on the issues of representation and processing of words in the mind and brain." It embraces a variety of approaches in modern linguistics research, including experimental investigations and corpus research that provide new insights into lexical processing, development, and structure. Two recent themed issues illustrate the interdisciplinary focus: "Semantic Considerations of Lexical Processing" and "Phonological and Phonetic Consideration in Lexical Processing." Covering an emerging, interdisciplinary perspective in the science of language and mind, this journal would be an important addition to collections at major research institutions.

3257. ***Modern Language Journal: devoted to research and discussion about the learning and teaching of foreign and second languages.*** [ISSN: 0026-7902] 1916. q. GBP 235. Ed(s): Heidi Byrnes, Charlene Polio. Wiley-Blackwell Publishing, Inc., 350 Main St, Malden, MA 02148; http://onlinelibrary.wiley.com. Illus., index, adv. Sample. Refereed. Vol. ends: Dec. Microform: PMC; PQC. Reprint: PSC. *Indexed:* A01, A22, BRI, CBRI, Chicano, E01, ERIC, MLA-IB. *Bk. rev.:* 20-30, 1-2 pages. *Aud.:* Hs, Ga, Ac.

As the journal of the National Federation of Modern Language Teachers Associations, *Modern Language Journal* (*MFL*) focuses primarily on applied linguistics, and publishes "research and discussion about the learning and teaching of foreign and second languages." The journal is dedicated to scholarly exchange among researchers and teachers, and linking research findings to teaching and learning. Examples of articles from a recent issue include "The Motion of Emotion: Idiodynamic Case Studies of Learners' Foreign Language Anxiety" and "Literate Actions, Reading Attitudes, and Reading Achievement: Interconnections Across Languages for Adolescent Learners of English in Korea." The journal also publishes an array of other types of relevant professional material: response articles, book reviews, reports on new course materials, "News and Notes," an events calendar, a listing of relevant articles published in other journals, and an annual survey of doctoral degrees in all areas concerning foreign and second languages. This highly cited, core journal is highly recommended for academic library collections. See also *TESOL Quarterly, ELT Journal,* and *Studies in Second Language Acquisition.*

3258. ***Morphology.*** Formerly (until 2006): *Yearbook of Morphology.* [ISSN: 1871-5621] 1988. 4x/yr. EUR 355 (print & online eds.)). Ed(s): Ingo Plag, Adam Albright. Springer Netherlands, Van Godewijckstraat 30, Dordrecht, 3311 GX, Netherlands; http://www.springer.com. Refereed. Reprint: PSC. *Indexed:* A22, BRI, E01, MLA-IB. *Aud.:* Ac.

Previously *Yearbook of Morphology, Morphology* publishes articles within the core subfield of linguistics that is concerned with how words are formed within and across languages. The articles engage in empirical investigation of the morphological properties of a particular language, or may do cross-linguistic analysis, and address broader implications of new research. Examples of two recent special issues include "New Theoretical Tools in the Modeling of Morphological Exponence" and "Linking Elements: Origin, Change, and Functionalisation." This is the only journal devoted specifically to morphology, a core area in the field of linguistics. Recommended for medium to large academic linguistics collections.

3259. ***Natural Language and Linguistic Theory.*** [ISSN: 0167-806X] 1983. q. EUR 1539 (print & online eds.)). Ed(s): Julie A Legate. Springer Netherlands, Van Godewijckstraat 30, Dordrecht, 3311 GX, Netherlands; http://www.springer.com. Illus., adv. Sample. Refereed. Vol. ends: Nov. Microform: PQC. Reprint: PSC. *Indexed:* A22, AmHI, BRI, E01, MLA-IB. *Bk. rev.:* 0-1, 5,000 words. *Aud.:* Ac.

This journal aims to bridge the gap between highly theoretical research and empirical data in linguistics. It offers articles that are accessible to linguists unfamiliar with the theoretical framework or language under review. Recent themed issues include "Finiteness in South Asian Languages" and "Phi-feature Inflection and Agreement." The journal facilitates discussion among researchers from different linguistic subfields. In addition to articles reporting on current research, the journal also features surveys of recent theoretical developments "that facilitate accessibility for a graduate student readership"; replies to recent articles; and book reviews. A recommended journal for academic linguistics collections.

3260. ***Probus: international journal of Latin and Romance linguistics.*** [ISSN: 0921-4771] 1989. s-a. EUR 306. Ed(s): W. Leo Wetzels. De Gruyter Mouton, Genthiner Str 13, Berlin, 10785, Germany; mouton@degruyter.de; https://www.degruyter.com. Adv. Refereed. Reprint: PSC. *Indexed:* A01, A22, AmHI, E01, MLA-IB. *Aud.:* Ac.

Probus publishes articles grounded in empirical evidence that report on Latin and Romance languages in the context of core linguistics subfields, including phonology, morphology, and syntax, as well as language acquisition and sociolinguistics. Many articles investigate a linguistic feature of Latin or Romance languages at a point in their historical development, and present findings in the context of broader theoretical implications for the field. Examples of recent articles include "The Acquisition of Coda Consonants by Catalan and Spanish Children: Effects of Prominence and Frequency of Exposure" and "Satellite-framed Latin vs. Verb-framed Romance: A Syntactic Approach." Because of its specific focus, this journal would be a good supplemental purchase for academic linguistics collections.

Slavic and East European Journal. See Slavic and Eurasian Studies section.

3261. ***Studies in Second Language Acquisition.*** [ISSN: 0272-2631] 1977. 5x/yr. GBP 376. Ed(s): Susan Gass, Kimberly L. Geeslin. Cambridge University Press, University Printing House, Shaftesbury Rd, Cambridge, CB2 8BS, United Kingdom; journals@cambridge.org; https://www.cambridge.org/. Illus., adv. Sample. Refereed. Vol. ends: Dec. Microform: PQC. Reprint: PSC. *Indexed:* A22, BAS, E01, ERIC, MLA-IB. *Bk. rev.:* 5-12, 1-2 pages. *Aud.:* Ac.

This journal is devoted to the scientific study of topics related to second and foreign language learning. *Studies in Second Language Acquisition* contains articles of both theoretical and pedagogical nature, as well as reports on qualitative and quantitative data. An example of a recent article is "Second Language Acquisition of Pitch Range in German Learners of English." In addition to research articles, the journal also includes a variety of supplementary material, including a "Notes and Discussion" section, review articles, book reviews, book notices, and a feature entitled "State-of-the-Art," which reports on trends in the field. This journal is recommended for academic collections that also support programs related to the teaching of second and foreign languages. See also *ELT Journal, Modern Language Journal,* and *TESOL Quarterly.*

3262. ***T E S O L Quarterly: a journal for teachers of English to speakers of other languages and of standard English as a second dialect.*** [ISSN: 0039-8322] 1967. q. GBP 318 (print or online ed.)). Ed(s): Meaghan McDonnell. Wiley-Blackwell Publishing, Inc., 350 Main St, Malden, MA 02148; http://onlinelibrary.wiley.com. Illus., adv. Sample. Refereed. Vol. ends: Winter. Microform: PQC. Reprint: PSC. *Indexed:* A22, Chicano, ERIC, MLA-IB. *Bk. rev.:* 4-6, 3-5 pages. *Aud.:* Hs, Ac, Sa.

TESOL Quarterly publishes research that bridges theory and practice in English language teaching and learning. Its primary areas of interest are the study of the psychology and sociology of language learning and teaching, curriculum design, pedagogy, testing and evaluation, professional preparation/standards, language planning, and research methodology. As an interdisciplinary journal, *TESOL* also includes articles that relate to the fields of anthropology, psychology, English education, and a range of linguistics subfields. Examples of recent articles include "The Interaction of Motivation, Self-Regulatory Strategies, and Autonomous Learning Behavior in Different Learner Groups" and "The Impact of Experience Abroad and Language Proficiency on Language Learning Anxiety." In addition to research articles, issues include review articles, book reviews, discussion forum, and brief reports and summaries. According to the *TESOL* web site, readership consists of ESL educators, teacher learners, researchers, and applied linguists, among others. Especially recommended for academic collections at institutions with strong programs related to teaching English as a second or foreign language. See also *ELT Journal, Modern Language Journal,* and *Studies in Second Language Acquisition.*

Visible Language. See Printing and Graphic Arts section.

Yearbook of Morphology. See *Morphology.*

■ LITERARY REVIEWS

See also Fiction; Literature; Little Magazines; and News and Opinion sections.

Susan Gilman, Research Librarian, Harvard College Library, Harvard University; sgilman@fas.harvard.edu.

Reed Lowrie, Manager, Reference and Information Services, Harvard College Library, Harvard University; lowrie@fas.harvard.edu

Introduction

Attempting to choose a small set of top literary reviews is in some cases a frustrating experience, as it's inevitable that worthy titles need to be left out. To focus our endeavor, we've concentrated on titles that print a large number of pieces that are anthologized in yearly collections like *Best American Short Stories*, and the Pushcart Prizes. As in past years we've also put a premium on long-running titles, as this is a publishing area where new titles appear and disappear fairly regularly. There are many web sites dedicated to tracking "the best" literary reviews, usually from the perspective of the aspiring writer. If your library can afford more than the titles we're recommending here, we encourage you to look at some of these lists for more excellent suggestions. In addition, many literary reviews are focused on a tight geographical area, so librarians may wish to explore any local possibilities beyond the more nationally focused titles we cover here.

Our list is only slightly altered from previous editions; we've added a few titles and subtracted a few others. Despite the overall churn in this area, the top titles remain fairly stable. In our last entry we noted the increased attention to an improved online presence by many titles. This has only continued in the past two years with many titles debuting very professional and attractive web sites. More free content seems to generally be available online as well, text-based as well as audio and video. As we noted last time, however, the print editions of most of these titles continue to be produced with great care and attention to detail and make lovely additions to a library collection.

Basic Periodicals

Ga, Ac: *The Antioch Review, Conjunctions, The Georgia Review, Granta, The Hudson Review, The Iowa Review, The Kenyon Review, The Paris Review, Prairie Schooner, The Southern Review, Virginia Quarterly Review, The Yale Review.*

Basic Abstracts and Indexes

Annual Bibliography of English Language and Literature (ABELL), Humanities Index, MLA International Bibliography.

3263. ***Agni.*** Formerly (until 1988): *Agni Review.* [ISSN: 1046-218X] 1972. s-a. USD 25 (Individuals, USD 20). Ed(s): Sven Birkerts. Agni Review, Inc., 236 Bay State Rd, Boston, MA 02215-1403. Adv. *Indexed:* AmHI, MLA-IB. *Aud.:* Ga, Ac.

Agni publishes fiction, nonfiction, essays, art, and poetry, including translations, by writers and artists from around the world. An art feature is also included in each issue, with additional content exclusively available on the frequently updated companion web site. *Agni*'s focus is on work that sees "literature and the arts as part of a broad, *ongoing cultural conversation* that every society needs to remain vibrant and alive. Literature for literature's sake is not what *AGNI* is about." Content includes well-known and rising authors, and is regularly republished in the *Best American,* O. Henry Prize, and Pushcart Prize anthologies. The print version is particularly attractive.

3264. ***Alaska Quarterly Review: a literary magazine of consequence.*** [ISSN: 0737-268X] 1982. s-a. USD 20 domestic; USD 24 Canada; USD 30 elsewhere. Ed(s): Ronald Spatz. University of Alaska at Anchorage, College of Arts and Sciences, 3211 Providence Dr, Anchorage, AK 99508; http://www.uaa.alaska.edu/. Illus. Vol. ends: Fall/Winter. Microform: PQC. *Indexed:* AmHI. *Aud.:* Ga, Ac.

The award-winning *AQR* has been hailed as "one of our best, and most imaginative, literary magazines" (*The New York Review of Books*). It features traditional and innovative fiction, short plays, poetry, photo essays, and literary nonfiction, as well as occasional "Special Features." While work from Alaska is often highlighted - "From the Top of the World," as the title's motto says - content is international in scope. *AQR* has a fairly active presence on Facebook and YouTube, and its content is often included in leading literary anthologies. Archived content is available gratis online, but the print publication is especially attractive, featuring gorgeous color photography from leading photographers.

3265. ***American Short Fiction.*** [ISSN: 1051-4813] 1991. 3x/yr. USD 40. Ed(s): Adeena Reitberger, Rebecca Markovits. American Short Fiction, Inc., PO Box 4152, Austin, TX 78765. Adv. *Aud.:* Ga. Ac.

Begun in the 1990s and revived in 2006, *American Short Fiction* publishes what its title suggests: short stories. The title aims to present "stories that dive into the wreck, that stretch the reader between recognition and surprise, that conjure a particular world with delicate expertise - stories that take a different way home." Featuring less well-known authors than some of the other titles in this section, this magazine nonetheless regularly has stories featured in the major best-story anthologies. The "Online Fiction" section offers a free story every month, which sometimes also includes the author reading the story. The online "Notebook" contains interviews and news items. *ASF* continues to be very active on social media.

3266. ***The Antioch Review (Yellow Springs).*** Incorporates (1957-1966): *Monocle;* Which was formerly (until 1964): *Outsider's Newsletter.* [ISSN: 0003-5769] 1941. q. USD 138. Ed(s): Robert S Fogarty. Antioch Review, Inc., PO Box 148, Yellow Springs, OH 45387-0148; cgabbard@antiochreview.org. Illus., index, adv. Microform: MIM; PMC; PQC. *Indexed:* A01, A22, AmHI, BAS, BRI, CBRI, MLA-IB. *Bk. rev.:* 15-30, 300 words. *Aud.:* Ga, Ac.

Begun in 1941, *The Antioch Review,* "one of the oldest, continuously publishing literary magazines in America," publishes fiction, essays, and poetry by both new and established writers. The review is especially strong in its commitment to the essay as a form. Also of interest is the "From our Archives" feature, which highlights an early work by a now well-known author. Over the years, works from such authors as Ralph Ellison, Sylvia Plath, Joyce Carol Oates, Daniel Ellsberg, T. C. Boyle, Gordon Lish, and Raymond Carver have been featured. An "All Fiction" issue is published annually, and issues are often themed around a particular concern. The website has a fairly active blog, including audio recordings, and the review can be found on multiple social media platforms. Recent issues include more essays on topics of contemporary interest than in past years.

The Atlantic Monthly. See General Interest section.

3267. *Boulevard: journal of contemporary writing.* [ISSN: 0885-9337] 1985. 3x/yr. USD 15 domestic; USD 25 foreign. Ed(s): Jessica Rogen. St. Louis University, 6614 Clayton Rd, Box 325, Richmond Heights, MO 63117. Illus., adv. Sample. *Indexed:* AmHI, MLA-IB. *Aud.:* Ga, Ac.

Now housed at Saint Louis University, *Boulevard* came out of the gates strong in 1985 with heavy hitting authors and hasn't looked back since. The review includes poetry, fiction, and nonfiction by established authors as well as emerging writers. *Boulevard* is widely recognized as one of the leading literary journals for promising young writers to consider. Unlike most of its fellows on this list, digital subscriptions are available for e-readers. The review also has an active blog and social media accounts. There is also a fun section of "super-short reviews" of new fiction, poetry, and nonfiction.

3268. *Conjunctions.* [ISSN: 0278-2324] 1982. s-a. USD 40 (Individuals, USD 18). Ed(s): Micaela Morrissette, Bradford Morrow. Bard College, Publication Department, PO Box 5000, Annandale On Hudson, NY 12504; admission@bard.edu; http://www.bard.edu. *Indexed:* AmHI, MLA-IB. *Aud.:* Ga, Ac.

Begun in the early 1980s, *Conjunctions* publishes innovative fiction, poetry, criticism, drama, art, and interviews by writers whose work "challenge[s] accepted forms and styles, with equal emphasis on groundbreaking experimentation and rigorous quality." Currently edited by Bradford Morrow, most issues are themed; recent themes include preservation, architecture, and bodies. Work by both well-established and lesser-known writers are included. Translated work from international writers is also included. Selected stories are made available online, and an extensive audio vault contains writers reading from work published in the journal. Certain volumes are available in e-book format. Also with an active social media presence, *Conjunctions* is outstanding in its use of both the print and digital formats.

3269. *Crazyhorse: poems stories essays.* [ISSN: 0011-0841] 1960. s-a. USD 20 domestic; USD 34 foreign. Ed(s): Garrett Doherty. College of Charleston, 66 George St, Charleston, SC 29424; http://www.cofc.edu/. Adv. Sample. Refereed. *Indexed:* AmHI, MLA-IB. *Aud.:* Ga, Ac.

Emerging from Los Angeles in 1960, *Crazyhorse* is now housed at the College of Charleston. Over the years it has published an impressive array of authors, including John Updike, Raymond Carver, Jorie Graham, John Ashberry, and many more. A mixture of fiction, poetry, and essays, *Crazyhorse* is attractive both in print and online, with one of the more attractive web sites in the field. The review sponsors prizes in fiction, poetry, and nonfiction judged by distinguished authors, as well as a "short-short fiction" prize called "Crazyshorts!" The online version offers selected content for free.

3270. *The Georgia Review: poetry, art, fiction, essays, reviews.* [ISSN: 0016-8386] 1947. q. USD 40 (print or online ed.); USD 50 combined subscription (print & online eds.)). Ed(s): Stephen Corey. University of Georgia, Georgia Review, 706A Main Library, 320 S Jackson St, The University of Georgia, Athens, GA 30602; http://www.ugd.edu/garev. Illus., index, adv. Vol. ends: Winter. Microform: PQC. *Indexed:* A01, A22, AmHI, BRI, CBRI, MLA-IB. *Bk. rev.:* 4-11, 1-25 pages, signed. *Aud.:* Ga, Ac.

Founded in 1947, the award-winning *Georgia Review* includes short stories, general-interest essays, poems, reviews, and visual art from a variety of contemporary writers, ranging from the unpublished to the Pulitzer Prize-winning. Content in *The Georgia Review* is regularly republished in the annual "best of" anthologies. This acclaimed journal is noteworthy as well for the high quality and visual appeal of the glossy print publication, which regularly wins awards for its design as well as its content. A rich and attractive website contains additional video and audio content, selections from the past 60-plus years of the review, and news and events listings. Digital subscriptions are also available for e-readers.

3271. *The Gettysburg Review.* [ISSN: 0898-4557] 1988. q. USD 35 domestic; USD 50 foreign; USD 50 combined subscription domestic (print & online eds.)). Ed(s): Ellen Hathaway, Peter Stitt. Gettysburg College, 300 N Washington St, Gettysburg, PA 17325; http://www.gettysburg.edu. Illus., index, adv. Vol. ends: Winter. *Indexed:* A01, A22, AmHI, BRI, MLA-IB. *Aud.:* Ga, Ac.

Founded in 1988, *The Gettysburg Review* is committed to "seeking out and publishing the very best contemporary poetry, fiction, essays, essay-reviews, and art...." The highly selective editorial policy has resulted in a publication renowned for its high literary quality and award-winning editing and design. Many works first published in *The Gettysburg Review* have reappeared in well-known prize anthologies. Select content is also available gratis on the very attractive website.

Glimmer Train. See Little Magazines section.

3272. *Granta.* Formerly (until 1979): *The Granta.* [ISSN: 0017-3231] 1889. q. GBP 36 in Europe; USD 48 United States; USD 56 Canada. Granta Publications Ltd., 12 Addison Ave, London, W11 4QR, United Kingdom. Illus., adv. *Indexed:* A01, A22, AmHI, BRI, MLA-IB. *Aud.:* Ga, Ac.

Granta was founded in 1889 by students at the University of Cambridge. In 1979, under the guidance of Bill Buford, it was transformed from a magazine aimed at a local readership to the wide-reaching magazine it is today. Each issue of *Granta* might include fiction, nonfiction, investigative journalism, photography, and poetry, all centered on one theme. Recent themes have included aftermaths, animals, and Canada. The work of emerging writers and well-established writers is showcased in this highly selective publication. Ian McEwan, Salman Rushdie, and Jeffrey Eugenides are some of the authors whose works have appeared in *Granta.* Selected content can be found on the website free of charge. The magazine produces editions in 12 different languages, including Chinese, Spanish, Italian, and even Norwegian.

Harper's. See General Interest section.

3273. *The Harvard Review.* Former titles (until 1992): *Harvard Book Review;* (until 1989): *Erato.* [ISSN: 1077-2901] 1986. s-a. USD 30 (Individuals, USD 20; USD 13 per issue). Ed(s): Christina Thompson. Harvard University, Lamont Library, Harvard University, Cambridge, MA 02138; http://www.harvard.edu. Illus., adv. *Indexed:* AmHI, BRI, MLA-IB. *Bk. rev.:* Number and length vary. *Aud.:* Ga, Ac.

The Harvard Review publishes a selection of fiction, essays, poetry, and visual art from an international and eclectic selection of writers and artists. Contributors have included Arthur Miller, Joyce Carol Oates, Seamus Heaney, Jorie Graham, John Updike, John Ashbery, Alice Hoffman, and Gore Vidal, as well as promising new writers. A monthly online supplement, *Harvard Review Online,* publishes an interesting mix of content. Started in a library in 1986, the review continues to be overseen by a library today.

3274. *The Hudson Review: a magazine of literature and the arts.* [ISSN: 0018-702X] 1948. q. USD 49 (Individuals, USD 40; USD 11 per issue). Ed(s): Ronald Koury, Paula Deitz. Hudson Review, Inc., 33 W 67th St, New York, NY 10023. Illus., adv. Microform: MIM; PQC. *Indexed:* A01, A22, AmHI, BAS, BRI, CBRI, MLA-IB. *Bk. rev.:* 5-7, 2-11 pages, signed. *Aud.:* Ga, Ac.

Since its founding in 1948, *The Hudson Review* "has dealt with the area where literature bears on the intellectual life of the time and on diverse aspects of American culture." Based in New York City and unaffiliated with a university, the journal publishes fiction, poetry, essays, reviews, and literary criticism that represent and explore new developments in these areas. Readers can access quite a bit of content on the review's newly designed website, including an archive of audio recordings of poets reading their work.

3275. *The Idaho Review.* [ISSN: 1520-8389] 1998. a. USD 15 per issue. Ed(s): Brady Udall, Mitch Wieland. Boise State University, 921 S 8th Ave, Stop 8079, Pocatello, ID 83209; http://www.boisestate.edu. Refereed. *Indexed:* AmHI. *Aud.:* Ga, Ac.

The Idaho Review has made an impact on the writing scene since its first issue in 1998, consistently publishing award-winning stories by authors both well-known and more obscure. The title is housed at Boise State University, but features writers from across the globe, including major figures like Ann Beattie, Madison Smartt Bell, and William Kittredge. The review only comes out once a year, but can almost be guaranteed to include stories or poems that will be anthologized in various "best of" volumes. The website is functional but offers little extra content.

3276. ***The Iowa Review.*** [ISSN: 0021-065X] 1970. 3x/yr. USD 20 domestic; USD 8.95 newsstand/cover; CAD 10.95 newsstand/cover. Ed(s): Lynne Nugent. University of Iowa, College of Liberal Arts & Sciences, 308 English-Philosophy Bldg, University of Iowa, Iowa City, IA 52242-1492; clas@uiowa.edu; http://clas.uiowa.edu/. Illus., index, adv. *Indexed:* A01, A22, AmHI, BRI, MLA-IB. *Bk. rev.:* 2, 2-4 pages, signed. *Aud.:* Ga, Ac.

Housed at the University of Iowa, home of the Writers Workshop as well as the oldest M.F.A. program devoted to literary translation in the United States, *The Iowa Review* publishes the work of Iowa writers as well as a mix of poems, stories, and essays by an international selection of authors. Artwork and interviews are also included. The elegant website provides access to additional interviews, selected content from the print edition, and an archive of book reviews. The website also features writing from military veterans and a Human Rights Index that highlights major global issues. The review has an active social media presence as well. An excellent title both in print and online.

3277. ***The Kenyon Review.*** [ISSN: 0163-075X] 1939. bi-m. USD 30 combined subscription domestic; USD 55 combined subscription foreign; USD 10 per issue domestic. Ed(s): Abigail Wadsworth Serfass, David Lynn. Kenyon College, Finn House, 102 W Wiggin St, Gambier, OH 43022; http://www.kenyon.edu/. Illus., index, adv. *Indexed:* A22, BRI, CBRI, MLA-IB. *Bk. rev.:* 1-2, 7-11 pages, signed. *Aud.:* Ga, Ac.

Founded in 1939, *The Kenyon Review* publishes fiction, nonfiction, drama, and poetry. Content includes international writing in translation. A very interactive online supplement gives readers access to forums, podcasts, and a daily blog. Cover photography often highlights the work of an international photographer. The *KR* sponsors annual contests for short fiction and the Patricia Grodd Poetry Prize for Young Writers (high school sophomores and juniors), along with many other workshops and programs.

Lambda Literary Review. See Books and Book Reviews section.

McSweeney's. See Literature section.

3278. ***Michigan Quarterly Review.*** Supersedes in part (in 1962): *Michigan Alumnus.* [ISSN: 0026-2420] 1894. s-a. USD 35 domestic; USD 50 foreign. Ed(s): Khaled Mattawa. University of Michigan, 0576 Rackham Bldg, 915 East Washington St, Ann Arbor, MI 48109-1070. Illus., index. Refereed. Vol. ends: Fall. Microform: PQC. *Indexed:* A22, AmHI, BAS, BRI, CBRI, MLA-IB. *Bk. rev.:* 1-3, 5-16 pages, signed. *Aud.:* Ga, Ac.

The flagship journal of the University of Michigan, the *Michigan Quarterly Review* is an interdisciplinary journal that combines creative writing with critical essays on literary, cultural, social, and political topics. Aiming for an audience both within and beyond the academy, each issue includes a selection of essays, interviews, memoirs, fiction, poetry, and book reviews. *MQR* publishes work by both established and emerging writers, including essayists and scholars. Readers can access selected content online.

3279. ***The Missouri Review.*** [ISSN: 0191-1961] 1978. q. USD 30 domestic; USD 35 foreign. Ed(s): Speer Morgan. University of Missouri at Columbia, 357 McReynolds Hall, Columbia, MO 65211; visitus@missouri.edu; http://www.missouri.edu/. Illus., index, adv. *Indexed:* A22, AmHI, E01, MLA-IB. *Bk. rev.:* 11-18, 1-5 pages, signed. *Aud.:* Ga, Ac.

Founded in 1978, *The Missouri Review* publishes poetry, fiction, and nonfiction of general interest. Content is often selected for inclusion in leading literary anthologies such as *Best American Short Stories* and *The Pushcart Prize*. Some issues include a "Special Feature" such as a historical document of literary significance, or a previously unpublished work by a well-known author of the past. The website provides access to a blog, a "Poem of the Week," and podcasts, including interviews and author readings. An annual Editor's Prize is awarded, and unique to this publication, an audio contest is held each year.

New England Review. See Little Magazines section.

3280. ***New Ohio Review.*** [ISSN: 1935-357X] 2007. s-a. USD 25 (Individuals, USD 16; USD 9 per issue domestic). Ed(s): Patti Wisland, David Wanczyk. Ohio University, Department of English, 360 Ellis Hall, Athens, OH 45701; https://www.ohio.edu/cas/english/#_. *Aud.:* Ac.

Since 2007, the *New Ohio Review* has been published by the Ohio University's Creative Writing Program. Content includes fiction, poetry, and nonfiction, with works appearing in the *Best American* series and the annual *Pushcart* anthology. This magazine also hosts an annual contest. Some content can be accessed online through the archives of the *Review*'s website.

The New Yorker. See General Interest section.

3281. ***Noon.*** [ISSN: 1526-8055] 2000. a. USD 12 domestic; USD 17 foreign. Ed(s): Diane Williams. Noon, Inc., 1324 Lexington Ave, PMB 4, New York, NY 10128; http://www.noonannual.com/. Adv. *Indexed:* AmHI. *Aud.:* Ga.

Founded in 2000 by author Diane Williams, the *Noon* literary journal is published annually. It is an independent journal that is archived at Indiana University. *Noon* includes fiction, essays, illustrations, and interviews. Many of the works that have been included in this title have won Pushcart and O. Henry prizes. The journal is noted for its well-designed and visually stunning layout. While its website is as stunning as its printed editions, it does not contain a large amount of content.

3282. ***The Paris Review.*** [ISSN: 0031-2037] 1953. q. USD 49 domestic; USD 54 Canada; USD 64 elsewhere. Ed(s): Lorin Stein. The Paris Review Foundation, Inc., 544 West 27th St, New York, NY 10001. Illus., index, adv. Microform: PQC. *Indexed:* A01, A22, AmHI, BRI, MLA-IB. *Aud.:* Ga, Ac.

Founded in 1953 by American expatriates in Paris but now operating in New York, *The Paris Review* publishes a variety of creative work, including fiction, poetry, and art "portfolios." Eschewing literary criticism in favor of author interviews, both the print journal and its website provide a wealth of opportunities to either read or listen to writers discussing their life and work. The website also features art, photography, letters, and essays. *The Paris Review* has a very active social media presence across multiple platforms.

Ploughshares. See Fiction: General/Mystery and Detective/General section.

3283. ***Prairie Schooner.*** [ISSN: 0032-6682] 1926. q. USD 28 domestic; USD 38 foreign; USD 9 per issue. Ed(s): Glenna Luschei, Ashley Strosnider. University of Nebraska at Lincoln, 123 Andrews Hall, Lincoln, NE 68588; http://www.unl.edu. Index, adv. Vol. ends: Winter. Microform: PQC. Reprint: PSC. *Indexed:* A01, A22, AmHI, BRI, CBRI, E01, MLA-IB. *Bk. rev.:* 0-7, 1-8 words, signed. *Aud.:* Ga, Ac.

Prairie Schooner has been publishing the work of beginning, mid-career, and established writers for more than 90 years. It is now under the editorship of Kwame Dawes, and its content includes stories, poems, essays, and reviews, including work by Pulitzer Prize-winners, Nobel Laureates, National Endowment for the Arts recipients, and MacArthur and Guggenheim fellows. Supplementing the print publication is a lively website where readers will find a blog, featured archival content, and a podcast called Air Schooner.

3284. ***Shenandoah (Online).*** [ISSN: 2332-8134] 1950. 2x/yr. Ed(s): R T Smith. Washington and Lee University, Shenandoah, 204 W Washington St, Lexington, VA 24450; wlunews@wlu.edu; http://www.wlu.edu/x6.xml. Index. *Bk. rev.:* 0-7, 1-3 pages. *Aud.:* Ga, Ac.

Shenandoah is a digital magazine of poems, stories, essays, and reviews, published biannually. Work from *Shenandoah* appears regularly in leading anthologies. The magazine features a nice array of writers and it estimates that 40 percent of contributors in each issue have never been published in *Shenandoah* before. The magazine's mission statement notes that its interest is in publishing "work which has its sources in acutely observed personal experience but which also aims to bear witness to something larger than the individual."

3285. *The Southern Review.* [ISSN: 0038-4534] 1935. q. USD 90 (Individuals, USD 35). Ed(s): Cara Blue Adams. Louisiana State University Press, Johnston Hall, 3rd Fl, Louisiana State University, Baton Rouge, LA 70803; http://lsupress.org/. Index, adv. Sample. Vol. ends: Oct. Microform: PQC. *Indexed:* A01, A22, AmHI, BRI, CBRI, MLA-IB. *Bk. rev.:* 1, 4-6 pages, signed. *Aud.:* Ga, Ac.

Produced by the Louisiana State University Press, *The Southern Review* publishes poetry, fiction, essays, and visual art. The editors place an emphasis on contemporary writing of a high standard and with clear artistic purpose. This solid history of publishing quality work has earned it a reputation as one of the leading literary quarterlies in the country. The review maintains an active social media presence, and readers can find additional content on the review's blog.

3286. *The Southwest Review.* Formerly (until 1924): *Texas Review;* Incorporates (1921-1925): *The Reviewer;* Which was formerly (until 19??): *Reviewer of Richmond.* [ISSN: 0038-4712] 1915. q. Individuals, USD 24. Ed(s): Willard Spiegelman. Southern Methodist University Press, PO Box 750100, Dallas, TX 75275; http://www.smu.edu. Illus., index. Sample. Microform: PQC. *Indexed:* A01, A22, AmHI, BRI, CBRI, MLA-IB. *Aud.:* Ga, Ac.

Established in 1915 and now housed at Southern Methodist University, *The Southwest Review* publishes fiction and poetry in both traditional and experimental styles. Each issue also includes approximately four substantive articles on a wide range of topics, including contemporary affairs, history, folklore, fiction, poetry, literary criticism, art, music, and theater. *SWR* editors offer annual awards for the best works of fiction, nonfiction, and poetry published in the review. They also sponsor two annual contests, the Marr Poetry Prize and the Meyerson Prize for Fiction.

3287. *The Threepenny Review.* [ISSN: 0275-1410] 1980. q. USD 25 domestic. Ed(s): Wendy Lesser. Threepenny Review, PO Box 9131, Berkeley, CA 94709. Adv. Microform: PQC. *Indexed:* AmHI, BRI, CBRI, MLA-IB. *Bk. rev.:* 0-7. *Aud.:* Ga, Ac.

Based in Berkeley, California, *The Threepenny Review* includes a cosmopolitan array of content including poetry, fiction, memoirs, and symposia. Essay-like book reviews, as well as music, dance, theater, and film reviews, provide readers with a thoughtful and engaging look at the arts. This title's website is very basic and does not contain much additional content aside from "The Lesser Blog," which is written by founding editor Wendy Lesser. Readers can find content that is not available in the print journal on Lesser's blog.

Tin House. See Little Magazines section.

3288. *The Virginia Quarterly Review (Online): a national journal of literature and discussion.* [ISSN: 2154-6932] 1925. q. USD 32. Ed(s): Allison Wright. University of Virginia, 5 Boar's Head Ln, Charlottesville, VA 22904; http://www.virginia.edu. Adv. *Bk. rev.:* 90-100, 40-2,000 words, signed. *Aud.:* Ga, Ac.

The Virginia Quarterly Review was established in 1925. Each themed issue contains essays, poetry, and prose by an international selection of authors. Celebrated writers who have appeared in the journal include H. L. Mencken, Thomas Wolfe, Katherine Anne Porter, Joyce Carol Oates, Robert Penn Warren, Robert Frost, Conrad Aiken, and Marianne Moore. In addition to the written word, this review also includes multimedia pieces, photography, and comics.

3289. *Witness: the modern writer as witness.* [ISSN: 0891-1371] 1987. 3x/yr. USD 10 domestic; USD 14 Canada. Ed(s): Maile Chapman, Joseph Langdon. University of Nevada, Las Vegas, Black Mountain Institute, PO Box 455085, Las Vegas, NV 89154. Illus., adv. Refereed. *Indexed:* AmHI, MLA-IB. *Aud.:* Ga, Ac.

According to their masthead, *Witness* "blends the features of a literary and an issue-oriented magazine to highlight the role of the modern writer as witness to their times." As this description suggests, thematic issues tend to focus on important contemporary and historical issues. Past examples include political oppression, religion, the natural world, crime, aging, civil rights, love, ethnic America, and exile. Of the three issues published each year, two are online-only with free content, and one is print. All issues are a blend of fiction, poetry, nonfiction, and photography.

3290. *The Yale Review.* Formerly (until 1892): *New Englander and Yale Review.* [ISSN: 0044-0124] 1911. q. GBP 199. Ed(s): Susan Bianconi, J D McClatchy. Wiley-Blackwell Publishing, Inc., 111 River St, Hoboken, NJ 07030; http://onlinelibrary.wiley.com. Illus., index, adv. Sample. Vol. ends: Oct. Microform: PMC; PQC. *Indexed:* A01, A22, AmHI, BAS, BRI, CBRI, E01, MLA-IB. *Bk. rev.:* 4-5, 6-22 pages, signed. *Aud.:* Ga, Ac.

The nation's oldest continuously published literary quarterly, *The Yale Review* has featured the work of well-known writers around the world, including Thomas Mann, Henry Adams, Virginia Woolf, George Santayana, Robert Frost, Jose Ortega y Gasset, W. H. Auden, Robert Lowell, Robert Penn Warren, and Katherine Anne Porter, among many others. This journal is committed to new and promising contemporary writers as well, and its content includes a balance of fiction, essays, poetry, and book reviews. *The Yale Review*'s website is very user-friendly and contains a large amount of content.

3291. *Zoetrope: all-story.* [ISSN: 1091-2495] 1997. q. USD 50 domestic; USD 65 in Canada & Mexico; USD 99 elsewhere. Ed(s): Michael Ray. A Z X Publications, 916 Kearny St, San Francisco, CA 94133. Illus., adv. *Aud.:* Ga, Ac.

Zoetrope is a quarterly title that was launched in 1997 by the film director Francis Ford Coppola. Not surprisingly, it is interested in the intersection of film and writing. In addition to publishing new fiction, each issue contains a reprint of a previously published story that inspired a film. Major authors have consistently published in *Zoetrope* including Haruki Murakami, Don DeLillo, Mary Gaitskill, Ha Jin, and others. Special attention is paid to the design of the print issue, with contemporary artists illustrating and designing each issue. Fairly active on social media, the website, part of the larger Coppola "brand," is uninspiring. Best stick to the attractive print version.

Zoetrope: All-Story. See Fiction: General/Mystery and Detective/General section.

3292. *Zyzzyva: the journal of west coast writers & artists.* [ISSN: 8756-5633] 1985. 4x/yr. USD 40. Ed(s): Oscar Villalon, Laura Cogan. Zyzzyva, Inc., 57 Post St, Site 604, San Francisco, CA 94102; editor@zyzzyva.org; http://www.zyzzyva.org. Illus., index, adv. Vol. ends: Winter. *Indexed:* AmHI, MLA-IB. *Aud.:* Ga, Ac.

Zyzzyva is a review based in San Francisco and published since 1985. It publishes fiction, poetry, and nonfiction by leading as well as up and coming authors. The title stresses its relationship to the city where it's based, so libraries in the Bay Area may want to strongly consider it. There is a robust online book review section, a frequently updated blog, and the usual social media accounts. Scattered material from the archive is available online for free.

■ LITERATURE

See also Africa; African American; Classical Studies; Europe; Fiction; Latin America and Spain; LGBT+; Literary Reviews; Little Magazines; and Theater sections.

Brian Flota, Humanities Librarian, James Madison University Libraries and Educational Technologies, Harrisonburg, VA 22801; flotabc@jmu.edu

Introduction

The Literature section of *Magazines for Libraries* includes high quality peer-reviewed journals and magazines that mainly focus their attention on literary criticism. A few entries in this section, such as *McSweeney's*, also feature original creative content. This collection of resources represents a wide range of regional, national, and international literatures (from a variety of genres and literary eras) that are subjected to a broad swath of critical methodologies. In these journals and magazines, we can find pieces ranging from the study of *The Odyssey* and Geoffrey Chaucer to more contemporary voices like Roxane Gay, J.M. Coetzee, and Arundhati Roy.

Though traditional print journals and magazines make up the bulk of the entries in this section, peer-reviewed open-access publications continue to make great headways. Some of the entries in this section have transferred their contents to online-only platforms, especially as they become a more viable and publicly accessible scholarly platform. Most of the journals in this section are filled with essays typically ranging from 10 to 30 pages. These are generally accompanied by shorter notes, reprinted or translated creative works, book reviews, bibliographies, or interviews.

In this section, the contents of each journal, magazine, or e-publication is given a brief description. The scope of each title is described. Entries with quoted contents come directly from the journal or publisher's web page (unless otherwise indicated). An average number of articles, book reviews, and other key features are noted, as well as the typical page length for each. The titles of recent articles and/or special issues are highlighted to give a sense of the coverage contained within that particular journal or magazine. Important or longstanding publications will be accompanied with a brief history, noting details such as the first year of publication, notable founders and current or former members of the editorial staff, awards it has received, or special scholarships it hosts.

Most of the titles in the Literature section are aimed at academic libraries, particularly those with literature-related graduate programs. There are plenty of titles in this section, though, that would be great additions to school or larger public libraries. The journals and magazines in this section speak to broad regional, historic, and stylistic categories. As a result, author-specific literary journals have been excluded from this section, owing to the sheer abundance of these types of publications. For those interested in creative writing, please refer to the Little Magazines and Literary Reviews sections of *Magazines for Libraries*.

Basic Periodicals

Ac: *American Literature, Comparative Literature, Contemporary Literature, Essays in Criticism, Modern Fiction Studies, Nineteenth-Century Literature* (Berkeley), *P M L A, Speculum, Studies in English Literature 1500-1900, Victorian Studies, World Literature Today.*

Basic Abstracts and Indexes

Annual Bibliography of English Language and Literature (ABELL), Arts & Humanities Citation Index, Humanities Index, Literature Online (LION), MLA International Bibliography.

3293. *A N Q: A Quarterly Journal of Short Articles, Notes and Reviews.* Formerly (until 1988): *American Notes and Queries.* [ISSN: 0895-769X] 1962. bi-m. GBP 249 (print & online eds.)). Ed(s): Sandro Jung. Routledge, 530 Walnut St, Ste 850, Philadelphia, PA 19106; enquiries@tandfonline.com; http://www.tandfonline.com. Index, adv. Refereed. Microform: PQC. Reprint: PSC. *Indexed:* A01, A22, AmHI, BRI, CBRI, MLA-IB. *Bk. rev.:* 1-7, 2-4 pages, signed. *Aud.:* Ac.

This journal targets literary scholars of many stripes by publishing brief, focused research articles on "the literature of the English-speaking world and the language of literature." Maintaining a broad chronological scope, *ANQ* flits with unabashed eclecticism from Old English word studies to readings of twenty-first century short stories. Essays generally range from 2 to 12 pages, with 10 to 14 pieces published in each issue. Recent essays include "The Feral Brain: Hemingway and Ted Hughes," "Performative Sherlock Holmes: Male Direction and Female Digression in 'A Scandal in Bohemia,'" and "Sarah Pearson (1767-1833): A Laboring-Class Sheffield Poet's Career and Work." This title is appropriate for academic and large public libraries.

3294. *A R I E L.* Formerly (until 1967): *Review of English Literature.* [ISSN: 0004-1327] 1960. q. USD 110. Ed(s): Faye Halpern, Michael Tavel Clarke. The Johns Hopkins University Press, 2715 N Charles St, Baltimore, MD 21218; http://www.press.jhu.edu. Illus., adv. Sample. Refereed. Vol. ends: Oct. Reprint: PSC. *Indexed:* A01, A22, AmHI, BRI, C37, MLA-IB. *Bk. rev.:* 1-5, 3-5 pages, signed. *Aud.:* Ac.

This journal from Johns Hopkins University Press, "one of the first journals in Commonwealth studies," publishes scholarly articles "focused on the critical and scholarly study of global literatures in English." Recent issues include studies of the politics of food, William Demby, postcolonial capitalism, Tash Aw, Caryl Phillips, and Eileen Chang. The publication's broad scope and good coverage of contemporary international authors make it a valuable addition to any academic library.

3295. *American Imago: psychoanalysis and the human sciences.* [ISSN: 0065-860X] 1939. q. USD 195. Ed(s): Nancy Mandel, Murray Schwartz. The Johns Hopkins University Press, 2715 N Charles St, Baltimore, MD 21218; http://www.press.jhu.edu. Illus., adv. Sample. Refereed. Reprint: PSC. *Indexed:* A01, A22, AmHI, BRI, E01, MLA-IB. *Bk. rev.:* Number and length vary. *Aud.:* Ac.

This journal, published by Johns Hopkins University Press, examines "Freud's legacy across the humanities, arts, and social sciences." According to the publisher's website, the journal was founded by Sigmund Freud and Hans Sachs (it began as *Imago* in 1912 and continued as *American Imago* in 1939). The publication is included in this section because it frequently includes literary topics as they relate to psychoanalysis. Each issue contains several lengthy (20-50 pages) scholarly studies from various disciplines. Recent articles include "Judith and Beatrix: Oedipal Echo-Effects in *Kill Bill,*" and "Baudelaire, Nietzsche, and the Malicious Muse." Reviews of books relevant to Freud studies are occasionally included. Recommended for academic libraries that support graduate programs, especially those interested in psychoanalysis.

3296. *American Literary History.* [ISSN: 0896-7148] 1989. q. EUR 338. Ed(s): Noel Zavala, Gordon Hutner. Oxford University Press, 2001 Evans Rd, Cary, NC 27513; https://academic.oup.com/journals. Illus. Sample. Refereed. Vol. ends: Dec. Reprint: PSC. *Indexed:* A01, A22, AmHI, BRI, E01, MLA-IB. *Bk. rev.:* 3-5, 8-16 pages, signed. *Aud.:* Ac.

Since 1989, this journal has provided a forum for literary inquiry published across a variety of sources in American literature. Publishing essays, commentaries, reviews, and critical exchanges, *American Literary History* accepts articles on theoretical and historical issues as well as those concerned with particular authors and works. A number of essays also analyze the condition and trends of literary scholarship itself. The journal welcomes articles with an interdisciplinary focus, such as "Network Unavailable: Informal Populations and Literary Form." In fact, the frequency with which essays in this journal cross disciplinary boundaries lends with it a strong Americanist flavor that is of potential interest to scholars outside the field of literature. Users of all academic libraries and large public libraries will find value in this publication.

3297. *American Literary Realism.* Formerly (until 1999): *American Literary Realism, 1870-1910.* [ISSN: 1540-3084] 1967. 3x/yr. USD 67 (print & online eds.)). Ed(s): Gary Scharnhorst. University of Illinois Press, 1325 S Oak St, MC-566, Champaign, IL 61820; uipress@uillinois.edu; http://www.press.uillinois.edu. Illus., index, adv. Refereed. *Indexed:* A22, AmHI, BRI, E01, MLA-IB. *Bk. rev.:* 3-7, 1-2 pages, signed. *Aud.:* Ac.

American Literary Realism, published by University of Illinois Press, consists of critical essays on authors and topics in late nineteenth- and early twentieth-century American literature. Essays average 15 to 30 pages in length. Each issue also includes up to eight book reviews, as well as occasional pieces contributed to the "Notes and Documents" section. Recent articles include "Edith Eaton/Sui Sin Far: True 'Westerner?,'" "The Democratic Reconfiguration of History of Mark Twain's *Personal Recollections of Joan of Arc,*" and "Bret Harte's Oscar Wilde Tale." Recommended for academic libraries.

3298. *American Literature.* [ISSN: 0002-9831] 1929. q. USD 538. Ed(s): Lisl Hampton, Matthew A Taylor. Duke University Press, 905 W Main St, Durham, NC 27701; orders@dukeupress.edu; https://www.dukeupress.edu. Illus., adv. Refereed. Vol. ends: Dec. Reprint: PSC. *Indexed:* A01, A22, AmHI, BRI, CBRI, Chicano, E01, MLA-IB. *Bk. rev.:* 25-40, 1-2 pages, signed. *Aud.:* Ac.

This quarterly journal is one of the most recognizable titles in the field of literary studies. Published by Duke University Press in cooperation with the Modern Language Association's American Literature Section, *American Literature* focuses on American authors from colonial to contemporary times. Each issue generally includes six critical essays, ranging in length from 25 to 35 pages, 15 to 30 book reviews, and occasional announcements (updates on conferences, grants, competitions, and publishing opportunities) and brief mentions (citations of new editions, anthologies, collections). Special issues are sometimes published, most recently "Postexceptionalist Puritanism." Other recent essays include "Region, Capitalism, and the Jew in the post-*Tom* Plantation Novel," "A Poetics of Dissociability: Poetry and Punk in Los Angeles, 1976-83," and "The Race of Machines: Blackness and Prosthetics in Early American Science Fiction." *American Literature* is a core title for academic libraries and should be seriously considered for larger public library collections.

3299. ***Appalachian Journal: a regional studies review.*** [ISSN: 0090-3779] 1972. q. USD 48 (Individuals, USD 24). Ed(s): Sandra L Ballard. Appalachian State University, Center for Appalachian Studies, Belk Library, Appalachian State University, PO Box 32026, Boone, NC 28608; appstudies.appstate.edu/. Illus. Refereed. *Indexed:* A22, AmHI, MLA-IB. *Bk. rev.:* 5-10, 1-4 pages. *Aud.:* Hs, Ga, Ac.

This interdisciplinary journal features "field research, interviews, and other scholarly studies" on a variety of topics related to the Appalachian Mountain region. The journal devotes much attention to Appalachian literature and folklore. Recent issues have featured interviews with novelists, poets, and filmmakers. Each issue features scholarly essays as well, with topics ranging from managing Type 2 diabetes in rural Appalachia to fiction about mountaintop removal. A recent special issue focuses on Black Mountain College. The journal publishes a selection of original poetry by regional authors and 10 to 20 book reviews per issue. Longer review essays are often included. A must for any library in the Appalachian region. Also recommended for academic and large public libraries.

3300. ***Arizona Quarterly: a journal of American literature, culture & theory.*** [ISSN: 0004-1610] 1945. q. USD 70 USD 21 per issue. Ed(s): Lynda Zwinger. The Johns Hopkins University Press, http://www.press.jhu.edu. Illus., adv. Sample. Refereed. Vol. ends: Winter. Reprint: PSC. *Indexed:* A22, AmHI, Chicano, E01, MLA-IB. *Aud.:* Ac.

This journal "publishes scholarly essays on American literature, culture, and theory." Recent articles, which are 15 to 30 pages in length, present scholarship on the works of Truman Capote, Marilynne Robinson, Wiliam Faulkner, Frank O'Hara, Caroline Kirkland, Louisa May Alcott, Ralph Ellison, Li-Young Lee, and Sarah Orne Jewett. Recommended for large academic libraries.

Asian American Literature. See Asian American section.

3301. ***Boundary 2: an international journal of literature and culture.*** [ISSN: 0190-3659] 1972. q. USD 486. Ed(s): Margaret A Havran, Paul A Bove. Duke University Press, 905 W Main St, Durham, NC 27701; subscriptions@dukeupress.edu; https://www.dukeupress.edu. Illus., adv. Refereed. Vol. ends: Fall. Reprint: PSC. *Indexed:* A01, A22, AmHI, BRI, E01, MLA-IB, P61. *Bk. rev.:* Number and length vary. *Aud.:* Ac.

Boundary 2, published by Duke University Press, is a journal that expresses commitment to publishing "critical and scholarly materials" about literature "in a manner fully informed by important developments in theory and method." Articles generally number 6 to 11 per issue and run up to 35 pages in length. Themed issues are common, with a recent example being "Critical Space in Contemporary China." Recent articles include "Serious Crises: Rethinking the Neoliberal Subject," "Somapolitics: A Biohermeneutic Paradigm in the Era of Empire," and "The Hegemony of the Local: Taiwanese Multiculturalism and Indigenous Identity Politics." *Boundary 2* is recommended for academic libraries.

C L A Journal. See African American section.

3302. ***The Cambridge Quarterly.*** [ISSN: 0008-199X] 1965. q. EUR 400. Ed(s): Ann Newton, K Boddy. Oxford University Press, Great Clarendon St, Oxford, OX2 6DP, United Kingdom; onlinequeries.uk@oup.com; http://global.oup.com. Illus., index, adv. Sample. Refereed. Reprint: PSC. *Indexed:* A22, AmHI, BRI, E01, MLA-IB. *Bk. rev.:* 4-7, 4-13 pages. *Aud.:* Ac.

While focusing on literary criticism, *The Cambridge Quarterly* also publishes articles that address music, cinema, and the visual arts. At times, the journal aims to be more accessible to a readership beyond the academy. Each issue contains three or four articles, and four to seven reviews. Articles tend to run anywhere from 15 to 30 pages in length. The journal covers a wide variety of authors, periods, and geographic frames. Recent essays include "Bharati Mukherjee and the Politics of the Anthology," "Queer Heritage/Queer Horizons: Disruptive Temporality in the Works of David Wojnarowicz," and "The Empty Centre of Conrad's *Nostromo*: A New Economic Approach." This title is suitable for academic and larger public libraries.

3303. ***College Literature: a journal of critical literary studies.*** [ISSN: 0093-3139] 1974. q. USD 120. Ed(s): Carolyn Sorisio. The Johns Hopkins University Press, 2715 N Charles St, Baltimore, MD 21218; http://www.press.jhu.edu. Illus., adv. Sample. Refereed. Vol. ends: Oct. *Indexed:* A01, A22, AmHI, BRI, CBRI, E01, MLA-IB. *Bk. rev.:* 1-5, 2-4 pages. *Aud.:* Ac.

This journal presents "scholarly research across the various periods, intellectual fields, and geographical locations that comprise the changing discipline of Anglophone and comparative literary studies." The scholarly essays are intended to help college teachers (and others) keep up to date in the field of literary scholarship. Undergraduates may find the material more readable here than in other scholarly journals. The topics in each issue are diverse, and the authors studied range from the medieval period to the twenty-first century. Recent essays include "Christian Conversion to the Model Minority in John Okada's *No-No Boy*," "Of Poodles, Mockingbirds, and Beetles: Gertrude Stein's Zoopoetics," and "Redefining Family in Jennifer Johnston's *Foolish Mortals*." Issues contain three or four relevant book reviews. This journal would be valuable for both college instructors and students, and is recommended for all academic libraries.

3304. ***The Comparatist.*** [ISSN: 0195-7678] 1977. a. USD 65. University of North Carolina Press, 116 S Boundary St, Chapel Hill, NC 27514; uncpress@unc.edu; http://www.uncpress.unc.edu. Refereed. Circ: 200. *Indexed:* A22, AmHI, BRI, E01, MLA-IB. *Bk. rev.:* Number and length vary. *Aud.:* Ac.

The Comparatist is an annual publication from the University of North Carolina Press concerned with literature, culture, and the arts. It applies a comparative approach to the study of European and American texts, as well as "third world, Afro-Caribbean, and Central European literary phenomena." In terms of methodology, the journal displays "a stimulating interplay [of] intertextual and comparative methods, of theoretical-historical analysis, and of critical interpretation." Each issue contains up to 20 articles, including many that are clustered thematically, along with a dozen or more book reviews. Recently, issues of *The Comparatist* have included articles such as "Nobody's Protest Novel: Novelistic Strategies of the Black Lives Matter Movement," "Transnational Collaboration in Yeats' *The Herne's Egg*: The Swami, the Poet & the Play," and "The Waterfall, the Whirlpool, and the Stage: 'Boundaries of Americanness' in Poe's 'A Descent into the Maelstrom.'" Recommended for medium to large academic libraries.

3305. ***Comparative Critical Studies.*** Formed by the merger of (1979-2004): *Comparative Criticism;* (1986-2004): *New Comparison;* Which was formerly (1975-1986): *Comparison.* [ISSN: 1744-1854] 2004. 3x/yr. GBP 101 (print & online eds.)). Edinburgh University Press Ltd., The Tun, Holyrood Rd, 12 (2f) Jackson's Entry, Edinburgh, EH8 8PJ, United Kingdom; journals@eup.ed.ac.uk; http://www.euppublishing.com. Adv. Sample. Refereed. *Indexed:* A22, AmHI, E01, MLA-IB. *Bk. rev.:* 0-9, 2-4 pages. *Aud.:* Ac.

This "house" journal of the British Comparative Literature Association (BCLA) is published by Edinburgh University Press. The journal "seeks to advance methodological (self)reflection on the nature of comparative literature as a discipline." Some issues focus on a theme, such as "Thinking Language with Henri Meschonnic" or "The French Revolution Effect." The journal also publishes winners of the John Dryden Translation Prize, which the BCLA awards "for unpublished literary translations from any language into English" (BCLA website). The peer-reviewed articles are generally 12 to 25 pages long. Some issues contain book reviews. Best for academic libraries that support graduate programs in literature.

3306. ***Comparative Literature.*** [ISSN: 0010-4124] 1949. q. USD 246. Ed(s): Michael Allan, George E Rowe. Duke University Press, 905 W Main St, Durham, NC 27701; orders@dukeupress.edu; https://www.dukeupress.edu. Illus., index, adv. Refereed. Vol. ends: Nov. Reprint: PSC. *Indexed:* A01, A22, AmHI, BAS, BRI, CBRI, MLA-IB. *Bk. rev.:* 3-7, 2-5 pages, signed. *Aud.:* Ac.

Affiliated with the American Comparative Literature Association, this journal dates back to 1949 and claims to be the oldest in the field. It is "owned and directed" by the University of Oregon and published by Duke University Press. The journal "represents a wide-ranging look at the intersections of national literatures, global literary trends, and theoretical discourse." The journal accepts different theoretical perspectives and encourages emerging scholars to submit their manuscripts. Recent articles (approximately 20 pages) include "The Empires Write Back: The Language of Postcolonial Nigerian Literature and the United States of America" and "Verticality and Vertigo: Spatial Effects in Tayeb Salih's *Season of Migration to the North.*" A recent special issue was dedicated to "The Material Turn in Comparative Literature." Some issues feature three to five thorough and scholarly book reviews. The content of this journal is not as undergraduate-friendly as others in its field. Recommended for academic libraries that support graduate programs in literature.

3307. ***Comparative Literature Studies.*** [ISSN: 0010-4132] 1963. q. USD 259 (print & online eds.)). Ed(s): Astrid Meyer, Thomas Oliver Beebee. Pennsylvania State University Press, 820 N University Dr, University Support Bldg 1, Ste C, University Park, PA 16802; info@psupress.org; http://www.psupress.org. Illus., index, adv. Refereed. Reprint: PSC. *Indexed:* A01, A22, AmHI, BAS, BRI, CBRI, E01, MLA-IB. *Bk. rev.:* 4-15, 2-4 pages, signed. *Aud.:* Ac.

Comparative Literature Studies consists of critical scholarly essays that "range across the rich traditions of Africa, Asia, Europe, and North and South America, and that examine the literary relations between East and West, North and South." Essays are generally 15 to 30 pages in length. Many issues are organized thematically. Recent examples include "Ecocriticism in East Asia: Toward a Literary (Re) Construction of Nature and Environment" and "Global Crises and Twenty-First-Century World Literature." *Comparative Literature Studies* also publishes a prize-winning paper written by a graduate student in a comparative literature program. Issues contain a book review section; many of the reviews relate to the topic of the special issue. The diverse selection of articles offers something for literary scholars at every level. Recommended for all academic libraries.

3308. ***Contemporary Literature.*** Formerly (until 1968): *Wisconsin Studies in Contemporary Literature.* [ISSN: 0010-7484] 1959. q. USD 242 print & online eds. Ed(s): Thomas Schaub. University of Wisconsin Press, Journals Division, 1930 Monroe St, 3rd Fl, Madison, WI 53711; journals@uwpress.wisc.edu; http://www.uwpress.org. Illus., index, adv. Refereed. Circ: 2000. Microform: PQC. Reprint: PSC. *Indexed:* A01, A22, AmHI, BRI, E01, MLA-IB. *Bk. rev.:* 2-4, 5-10 pages, signed. *Aud.:* Ac.

This journal is a premier publication in the scholarship of contemporary literature, engaging the works of established and emerging writers of English-language works and striving to cover "the full diversity of critical practices." They claim to have introduced "Kazuo Ishiguro, Eavan Boland, and J.M. Coetzee to American readers." Articles published, ranging in length from 20 to 30 pages, tend to situate discussion of individual works within relevant cultural, historical, and theoretical contexts. Interviews also are an important component of *Contemporary Literature.* Recent issues include interviews with Viet Thanh Nguyen and Charles Yu. Four to six articles generally are included in each issue, along with two to four book reviews. Recent articles include "Islands in the Aether Ocean: Speculative Ecosystems in Science Fiction," "A Leap Out of Our Biology: History, Tautology, and Biomatter in Don DeLillo's Later Fiction," and "Somali Soundscapes: Signal and Noise in Nuruddin Farah's *Crossbones.*"

Critical Inquiry. See Cultural Studies section.

3309. ***Criticism: a quarterly for literature and the arts.*** [ISSN: 0011-1589] 1959. q. USD 220 (print & online eds.)). Ed(s): Jaime Goodrich. Wayne State University Press, The Leonard N Simons Bldg, 4809 Woodward Ave, Detroit, MI 48201; tara.reeser@wayne.edu; http://wsupress.wayne.edu/. Illus., index, adv. Refereed. Microform: PQC. *Indexed:* A01, A22, AmHI, BRI, CBRI, E01, MLA-IB. *Bk. rev.:* 0-4, 2-6 pages, signed. *Aud.:* Ac.

Published by Wayne State University Press, *Criticism* focuses on scholarship in literature, music, media, and visual culture. Self-described as a forum for "rigorous theoretical and critical debate as well as formal and methodological self-reflexivity and experimentation," the journal lives up to its interdisciplinary aspirations by situating literature in a variety of critical contexts. Four to six articles, usually between 20 and 35 pages in length, are included in each issue. Some issues contain interviews and book reviews. Recent articles include "Modernism as Gesture: The Experience of Music, Samuel Beckett, and Performed Bewilderment," "Milton's Panorama: *Paradise Regained* in the Age of Critique," and "Utopian Tremors, or, The Enigmatic Restlessness of the Israeli Literary Soldier." Recommended for academic and larger public libraries.

3310. ***Critique (Washington): studies in contemporary fiction.*** Formerly (until 1956): *Faulkner Studies.* [ISSN: 0011-1619] 1952. 5x/yr. GBP 239 (print & online eds.)). Ed(s): Geoffrey Green, Larry McCaffery. Routledge, 530 Walnut St, Ste 850, Philadelphia, PA 19106; enquiries@tandfonline.com; http://www.tandfonline.com. Illus., index, adv. Refereed. Vol. ends: Fall. Reprint: PSC. *Indexed:* A01, A22, AmHI, BRI, CBRI, E01, MLA-IB. *Aud.:* Ac.

This influential journal focuses on the study of contemporary fiction and prides itself on the identification and analysis of important and emerging writers from the middle of the twentieth century to the present. The geographic scope is broad, and essays on writers are invited from around the globe. Each issue offers five to eight scholarly essays, with lengths between 15 and 25 pages. Recent articles published include "Flooded Futures: The Representation of the Anthropocene in Twenty-First-Century British Flood Fictions," "Ahmed Khaled Towfik: Days of Rage and Horror in Arabic Science Fiction," and "The Poetic Language of David Foster Wallace." Appropriate for most academic and larger public libraries.

3311. ***E L H.*** [ISSN: 0013-8304] 1934. q. USD 255. Ed(s): Sarah Ross, Drew Daniel. The Johns Hopkins University Press, 2715 N Charles St, Baltimore, MD 21218; http://www.press.jhu.edu. Illus., adv. Sample. Refereed. Vol. ends: Winter. Reprint: PSC. *Indexed:* A01, A22, AmHI, BRI, E01, MLA-IB. *Aud.:* Ac.

ELH (*English Literary History*), which dates back to 1934, is published by Johns Hopkins University Press. The journal aim is to "balance historical, critical, and theoretical concerns in seeking to publish the very best work on English-language writing from its beginnings to the present day." Recent articles (around 20 to 30 pages long) examine a range of authors including H.G. Wells, Geoffrey Chaucer, Aphra Behn, Charles Dickens, William Shakespeare, George Eliot, and Frederick Douglass. This core journal is recommended for all academic libraries.

3312. ***Early American Literature.*** Formerly (until 1968): *Early American Literature Newsletter.* [ISSN: 0012-8163] 1966. 3x/yr. USD 75 (Individuals, USD 45). Ed(s): Sandra Gustafson. University of North Carolina Press, 116 S Boundary St, Chapel Hill, NC 27514; uncpress@unc.edu; http://www.uncpress.unc.edu. Illus., index. Sample. Refereed. *Indexed:* A01, A22, AmHI, BRI, E01, MASUSE, MLA-IB. *Bk. rev.:* 3-4, 3-5 pages, signed. *Aud.:* Ac.

Early American Literature, the official publication of the Society of Early Americanists as well as the journal of the Modern Language Association's Division on American Literature to 1830, provides a forum for examining "the scholarship and criticism of American literature through the early national period." The publication particularly invites "work treating Native American traditional expressions, colonial Ibero-American literature from North America, colonial American Francophone writings, Dutch colonial, and German American colonial literature as well as writings in English from British America and the U.S." Each issue contains approximately five to seven critical essays ranging from 15 to 35 pages in length, and includes a mix of 5 to 15 book reviews and review essays. It also occasionally publishes primary documents from the period under consideration. Articles published recently include "Settler Colonial Statistics: Jefferson, Biopolitics, and *Notes on the State of Virginia,*" "Cesar Lyndon's Lists, Letters, and a Pig Roast: A Sundry Account Book," and "Carrying Home the Enemy: Smallpox and Revolution in American Love and Letters, 1775-76." Recommended for academic libraries, particularly those with strong programs in early American literature or American Studies.

3313. ***Early Modern Literary Studies: a journal of sixteenth- and seventeenth-century English literature.*** [ISSN: 1201-2459] 1995. s-a. Free. Ed(s): Annaliese Connolly, Matthew Steggle. Sheffield Hallam University, Department of English, School of Cultural Studies, c/o Matthew Steggle, City Campus, Howard St, Sheffield, S1 1WB, United Kingdom. Illus. Refereed. Vol. ends: Dec. *Indexed:* AmHI, BRI, C37, CBRI, MLA-IB. *Bk. rev.:* 8-11, signed. *Aud.:* Ac.

Articles in this open-access journal center on "English literature, literary culture, and language during the sixteenth and seventeenth centuries." Recent articles include "Shakestats: Writing About Shakespeare Between the Humanities and the Social Sciences," "'High Delights that Satisfy All Appetites': Thomas Traherne and Gender," and "Keeping Boys and Men: Marvelous Pageboys in Romantic Tragicomedy." Special issues have focused on topics such as "European Women in Early Modern Drama" and "John Ford." The presentation of this web-based journal is still strongly wedded to web 1.0 formats and design, though recent articles are being published in a far more readable pdf format. Despite these improvements, the page is rather cumbersome to navigate. However, its articles are well-researched, and issues include book and even theater reviews. Academic libraries should consider adding this to their catalogs or research guides.

3314. ***EHumanista: journal of Iberian studies.*** [ISSN: 1540-5877] 2001. 3x/yr. Free. Ed(s): Antonio Cortijo-Ocana. University Of California, Santa Barbara, Department of Spanish & Portuguese, Phelps Hall 4206, Santa Barbara, CA 93106; http://spanport.wisc.edu. Refereed. *Indexed:* BRI, MLA-IB. *Bk. rev.:* 6-8, signed. *Aud.:* Ac.

This electronic journal is "devoted to the study of the cultures and languages of the Iberian Peninsula." Three volumes are published each year, each including 20 to 30 articles and 5 to 15 reviews and review articles. (Reviews are not included in every volume.) Articles run approximately 15 to 30 pages in length. The journal accepts articles written in Spanish, Portuguese, English, Catalan, Galician, or Euskera. Articles published in recent volumes include "The Other-for-Me: The Construction of Saladin in El conde Lucanor" and "Los comienzos del teatro profesional en la Nueva Espana." Academic libraries may wish to facilitate access to this journal. *EHumanista* also publishes journals in three other journals: *EHumanista IVITRA* (which focuses on "language and literature of the Crown of Aragon"), *EHumanista Cervantes* (devoted scholarship on the author of *Don Quixote*), and *EHumanista Conversos* (which deals with "research on new Christians in the Iberian Peninsula and across the Spanish lands during the 14th-17th centuries.")

3315. ***Eighteenth-Century Fiction.*** [ISSN: 0840-6286] 1988. q. CAD 170. Ed(s): Eugenia Zuroski. University of Toronto Press, Journals Division, 5201 Dufferin St, Toronto, ON M3H 5T8, Canada; journals@utpress.utoronto.ca; http://www.utpjournals.com. Illus., adv. Sample. Refereed. Circ: 385. *Indexed:* A01, A22, AmHI, BRI, C37, E01, MLA-IB. *Bk. rev.:* 10-15, 2-4 pages, signed. *Aud.:* Ac.

Eighteenth-Century Fiction, or *ECF*, is published by the University of Toronto Press. The journal is "devoted to the critical and historical investigation of literature and culture of the period 1660-1832." Most articles are published in English, though some are in French; corresponding translations are not provided. A recent special topic, spread out over two issues, is entitled "Material Fictions." The scholarly articles, which tend to be about 20 to 30 pages long, discuss authors such as Henry Mackenzie, T.S. Surr, Dorothea Banks, Eliza Haywood, and Aphra Behn. Many issues contain 10 to 15 book reviews. Suitable for academic libraries that support graduate programs in literature.

3316. ***English Language Notes.*** [ISSN: 0013-8282] 1962. s-a. USD 138. Ed(s): Caci Pippin. Duke University Press, 905 W Main St, Durham, NC 27701; orders@dukeupress.edu; https://www.dukeupress.edu. Illus., index, adv. Refereed. Vol. ends: Dec. *Indexed:* A01, A22, AmHI, BRI, MLA-IB. *Bk. rev.:* 1-3, 2-3 pages, signed. *Aud.:* Ac.

Each issue of *English Language Notes*, which has been published since 1962, is devoted to a special topic in literary and cultural studies, in support of a mission that seeks to reinvigorate the short note format and encourage "interdisciplinary and collaborative work among literary scholarship and fields as disparate as theology, fine arts, history, geography, philosophy, and science." As part of this raison d'etre, two recent issues have focused on topics such as "Hydro-Criticism" and "Latinx Lives in Hemispheric Context." The number of short articles in each issue can vary widely. Despite the emphasis on shorter notes, many essays run between 10 and 20 pages in length. At times, other content such as poems and interviews is published alongside the critical essays. The occasional review essay is published as well. This innovative and eclectic publication is recommended for academic libraries.

3317. ***English Literary Renaissance.*** [ISSN: 0013-8312] 1971. 3x/yr. USD 343. Ed(s): Arthur F. Kinney. University of Chicago Press, 1427 E 60th St, Chicago, IL 60637; custserv@press.uchicago.edu; http://www.journals.uchicago.edu. Illus., index, adv. Sample. Refereed. Vol. ends: No. 3. *Indexed:* A01, A22, AmHI, E01, MLA-IB. *Aud.:* Ac.

This journal publishes "new research in Tudor and Stuart literature, including the Sidneys, Spenser, Shakespeare, Jonson, Donne, Milton, and their many contemporaries." Articles from recent issues include: "Commodifying the Author: The Mediation of Aretino's Fame in the Harvey-Nashe Pamphlet War" and "The Ring as an Object Lesson in Temporality and Genre in *Romeo and Juliet*." Articles often feature text and illustrations from rare manuscripts, such as broadside ballads and letters. The journal also publishes bibliographic essays that describe "recent studies," which could be on a particular author (Ben Jonson) or topic (reading). The word "recent" is misleading—the bibliographic essays generally cover 20 years' worth of scholarship. Recommended for all academic libraries.

3318. ***English Literature in Transition, 1880-1920.*** Formerly (until 1963): *English Fiction in Transition, 1880-1920.* [ISSN: 0013-8339] 1957. q. USD 67 (Individuals, USD 50). Ed(s): Robert Langenfeld. E L T Press, 1412 Garland Dr, Greensboro, NC 27408. Illus., index, adv. Sample. Refereed. Vol. ends: No. 4. Microform: PQC. *Indexed:* A01, A22, AmHI, BRI, CBRI, E01, MLA-IB. *Bk. rev.:* 5-10, 3-5 pages. *Aud.:* Ac.

This journal from the University of North Carolina Press publishes critical essays "on fiction, poetry, drama, or subjects of cultural interest in the 1880-1920 period of British literature." The focus of the journal is on "less prominent" literary figures of the era or how they relate to major authors. Recent articles include "Flora Annie Steel's Ecological Imagination: Narratives of Empire's Excess" and "The Trick of Modernist Difficulty: Oscar Wilde, G. K. Chesterton and the Essay." Each issue also includes about 8 to 12 scholarly review essays. Recommended for academic libraries that support graduate programs in literature.

3319. ***Essays in Criticism.*** [ISSN: 0014-0856] 1951. q. EUR 379. Ed(s): Dr. Seamus Perry. Oxford University Press, Great Clarendon St, Oxford, OX2 6DP, United Kingdom; onlinequeries.uk@oup.com; http://global.oup.com. Illus., adv. Sample. Refereed. Microform: MIM; PQC. Reprint: PSC. *Indexed:* A01, A22, AmHI, BRI, E01, MLA-IB. *Bk. rev.:* 3-4, 6-8 pages. *Aud.:* Ac.

This respected British journal of literary criticism "covers the whole field of English Literature from the time of Chaucer to the present day." Each issue of *Essays in Criticism* usually includes around five scholarly articles and book reviews. Articles generally are 10 to 25 pages in length. Occasionally, the journal devotes an issue to a special topic. A recent special issue was devoted to "Wordsworth and His Editors." Recent articles include "The Austere Comforts of Barbara Pym," "Leopold Bloom Behaving Badly," and "Jane Austen's Universals." Once every year, the journal publishes the F. W. Bateson Memorial Lecture, an Oxford address named after the journal's founder and delivered by notable scholars in the field. Recommended for all academic and large public libraries.

3320. ***Exemplaria: medieval, early modern, theory.*** [ISSN: 1041-2573] 1989. q. GBP 304 (print & online eds.)). Routledge, 4 Park Sq, Milton Park, Abingdon, OX14 4RN, United Kingdom; subscriptions@tandf.co.uk; http://www.tandfonline.com. Illus., adv. Sample. Refereed. Reprint: PSC. *Indexed:* A22, AmHI, MLA-IB. *Aud.:* Ac.

This journal publishes scholarly essays that address the literature of the Medieval and Renaissance periods and prides itself on the inclusion of pieces that engage "critical theories, or otherwise seeks to sharpen the edges of current intellectual or literary debates." Essays are approximately 20 pages in length. Special issues, such as "Feeling for the Premodern," are published on occasion.

Articles published in recent issues include "Ower Felaws Blake: Blackface, Race, and Muslim Conversion in the Digby *Mary Magdalene*," "Shakespeare in the Capitalocene: *Titus Andronicus, Timon of Athens*, and Early Modern Eco-Theater," and "Networking Froissart's *Florin*." Recommended for academic libraries.

3321. *The Explicator.* [ISSN: 0014-4940] 1942. q. GBP 195 (print & online eds.)). Ed(s): Jonathan Bolton, Catherine Loomis. Routledge, 530 Walnut St, Ste 850, Philadelphia, PA 19106; enquiries@tandfonline.com; http://www.tandfonline.com. Illus., index, adv. Vol. ends: No. 4. Reprint: PSC. *Indexed:* A01, A22, AmHI, E01, MASUSE, MLA-IB. *Aud.:* Hs, Ac.

This journal features short articles (usually around two to four pages) that are "concise notes on passages of prose or poetry." The journal focuses specifically on literature that is "anthologized and studied in college classrooms." Articles, which are generally two to three pages long, examine an aspect or theme of a particular passage or certain excerpts from a work; for example, the transgressive aesthetics of Siri Hustvedt's *The Summer Without Men*; the use of metaphor in the work of Sylvia Plath; or the use of sound in John Updike's "A&P." *The Explicator*, which has been around since 1942, occupies a special niche in literary research. It covers a wide range of authors and their works, and the journal is a great resource for anyone searching for interpretations of a particular poem or work of fiction. Highly recommended for all academic libraries. High school and public libraries should also consider subscribing to this journal.

3322. *The Global South.* [ISSN: 1932-8648] 2007. s-a. Ed(s): Leigh Anne Duck. Indiana University Press, Office of Scholarly Publishing, Herman B Wells Library 350, Bloomington, IN 47405; iuporder@indiana.edu; http://iupress.indiana.edu/. Adv. Reprint: PSC. *Indexed:* A01, A22, E01, MLA-IB. *Aud.:* Ac.

This e-journal focuses on how "world literatures and cultures respond to globalization, particularly how authors, writers, and critics respond to issues of the environment, poverty, immigration, gender, race, hybridity, cultural formation and transformation, colonialism and postcolonialism, modernity and postmodernity, transatlantic encounters, homes, and diasporas, and resistance and counter discourse." Published by Indiana University Press, *The Global South* includes five to ten articles in every issue, ranging in length from 10 to 25 pages. Special issues are the rule, rather than the exception, with recent themes being "Caribbean Transmigration in the Twenty-First Century: Contemporary Reimaginings and Globalizing Conditions" and "The Global South as Subversive Practice." Articles published in recent issues include "Alternative Spatiality and Temporality: Diasporic Mobilities and Queer West Indian Inclusion," "Decolonizing Reproductive Labor: Caribbean Women, Migration, and Domestic Work in the Global Economy," and "Peripheral Aesthetics after Modernism: South Korean Neo-realism and Chang-dong Lee's *Poetry*." Recommended for large academic libraries.

The Horn Book Magazine. See Books and Book Reviews section.

3323. *J E G P.* Former titles (until 1959): *Journal of English and Germanic Philology;* (until 1903): *Journal of Germanic Philology.* [ISSN: 0363-6941] 1897. q. USD 203 (print & online eds.)). Ed(s): Renee R Trilling, Robert J Meyer-Lee. University of Illinois Press, 1325 S Oak St, MC-566, Champaign, IL 61820; uipress@uillinois.edu; http://www.press.uillinois.edu. Adv. Refereed. Microform: MIM; IDC; PMC; PQC. *Indexed:* A01, A22, AmHI, BRI, CBRI, E01, MLA-IB. *Bk. rev.:* 6-7, 1-4 pages. *Aud.:* Ac.

JEGP, also known as the *Journal of English and Germanic Philology*, is a premier journal in its field. First published in 1897, *JEGP* "focuses on Northern European cultures of the Middle Ages, covering Medieval English, Germanic, and Celtic Studies," as well as links between the medieval and subsequent periods, modern incarnations of "medievalism," and the history of Medieval Studies. Each issue offers three to five scholarly essays that range in length from 20 to 35 pages. Ten to 20 book reviews also are included, as well as the occasional review essay. Recent articles include "Constructions of Queenship: Envisioning Women's Sovereignty in *Havelok*," "The Role of Technical Vocabulary in the Construction of the Medieval Romance Text Type," and "Humor and Humoralism: Representing Bodily Experience in the Prologue of the *Siege of Thebes*." Recommended for most academic libraries.

3324. *The Journal of Commonwealth Literature.* [ISSN: 0021-9894] 1965. q. USD 1193 (print & online eds.)). Ed(s): Susan Watkins, Claire Chambers. Sage Publications Ltd., 1 Oliver's Yard, 55 City Rd, London, EC1Y 1SP, United Kingdom; info@sagepub.com; https://www.sagepub.com/. Adv. Sample. Refereed. Reprint: PSC. *Indexed:* A01, A22, AmHI, BAS, BRI, E01, MLA-IB. *Bk. rev.:* Number and length vary. *Aud.:* Ac.

This journal features pieces about literary texts "bound up with colonialism and the English language, the Commonwealth, diaspora, and postcoloniality." Recent articles study literature from South Africa, India, Jamaica, Lebanon, Zimbabwe, and Singapore. Examples of article titles are "The Significance of Magical Realism in the Novels of Elechi Amadi" and "From Indianness to Englishness: The Foreign Selves of Michael Madhusudan Dutt, Nirad C. Chaudhuri, and Salman Rushdie's Salahuddin Chamchawala." There is a recent special issue on "Dalit Literature." Each issue contains book reviews, and the journal features an excellent annual bibliography, which is arranged according to region (e.g., Australia, Canada, The Caribbean, and East and Central Africa). Suitable for academic libraries that support graduate programs in English.

3325. *Journal of Modern Literature.* [ISSN: 0022-281X] 1970. q. USD 219.45 (print & online eds.)). Ed(s): Paula Marantz Cohen, Robert L Caserio. Indiana University Press, Office of Scholarly Publishing, Herman B Wells Library 350, Bloomington, IN 47405; iuporder@indiana.edu; http://iupress.indiana.edu/. Illus., index, adv. Sample. Refereed. Vol. ends: Nov. Microform: PQC. Reprint: PSC. *Indexed:* A01, A22, AmHI, BRI, E01, MLA-IB. *Aud.:* Ac.

For nearly fifty years, *Journal of Modern Literature* has published scholarly articles on literature in all languages while also accepting essays that deal with cultural artifacts and related arts. The chronological scope of the journal is 1900 to the present. The geographic scope is international, with contributors hailing from countries around the world. Content, however, tends to be dominated by studies of English and U.S. authors and works. Special issues are published occasionally. The journal includes approximately 10 to 15 articles per issue, ranging in length from 8 to 25 pages. Recent issues have included articles such as "'Contemplating the Idiot' in Virginia Woolf's *Between the Acts*," "Textual Frustration: The Sonnet and Gender Performance in 'The Love Song of J. Alfred Prufrock,'" and "How Colette Became a Feminist: Selling Colette in the United States 1960-1985." This accessible and respected journal is appropriate for academic and larger public libraries.

3326. *Journal of Narrative Theory.* Formerly (until 1999): *The Journal of Narrative Technique.* [ISSN: 1549-0815] 1971. 3x/yr. Ed(s): Natasa Kovacevic. Eastern Michigan University, Department of English Language and Literature, 612 Pray-Harrold, Ypsilanti, MI 48197; http://www.emich.edu/english. Illus. Sample. Refereed. Microform: PQC. *Indexed:* A22, AmHI, E01, MLA-IB. *Aud.:* Ac.

This journal, published by Eastern Michigan University, "showcases theoretically sophisticated essays that examine narrative in a host of critical, interdisciplinary, or cross-cultural contexts." Recent articles, which are typically 15 to 30 pages long, include studies of Octavia Butler, James Joyce, John Keats, Diane di Prima, and Oscar Wilde. Special issues are published on occasion. With articles such as "'How Do You Not Understand a Word? Language as Contagion and Cure in *Pontypool*." this journal is best suited for scholars and graduate students with a good grasp of narrative theory.

3327. *Kritika Kultura.* [ISSN: 1656-152X] 2002. s-a. Ed(s): Vincenz Serrano. Ateneo de Manila University, Department of English, Loyola Heights, Quezon City, 1108, Philippines; kritikakultura@admu.edu.ph. *Indexed:* AmHI, MLA-IB. *Aud.:* Ac.

This e-journal from Ateneo de Manila University in the Philippines publishes articles on language and literary/cultural studies that address "issues relevant to the 21st century," and it explores the nexus of language, literature, society, and culture. Topics covered by *Kritika Kultura* vary widely and range from the political economy of language to postcolonialism. Recent issues have included between three and seven articles that range widely in length from 7 to 50 pages. (Review essays sometimes are intermixed with critical essays.) The journal also includes other regular sections, which offer columns, interviews, poetry, and a forum for new scholars. Recent essays include "Born of Two Koreas, of Human Blood: Monstrosity and the Discourse of Humanity and Pacifism in the Film Bulgasari" and "Fan Entrepreneurship: Fandom, Agency, and the Marketing of Hallyu in Israel."

Literature and Theology. See Religion section.

3328. *M E L U S.* [ISSN: 0163-755X] 1974. q. EUR 151. Ed(s): Kaylee Jangula Mootz, Gary Totten. Oxford University Press, 2001 Evans Rd, Cary, NC 27513. Illus., index, adv. Refereed. Vol. ends: Winter. Reprint: PSC. *Indexed:* A22, BRI, C42, Chicano, E01, MLA-IB. *Bk. rev.:* 0-7, 2-4 pages, signed. *Aud.:* Ac.

MELUS, published by The Society for the Study of the Multi-Ethnic Literature of the United States in collaboration with Oxford University Press, "endeavors to expand the definition of American literature through the study and teaching of Latina/o American, Native American, African American, Asian and Pacific American, and ethnically specific Euro-American literary works, their authors, and their cultural contexts." Issues tend to be organized thematically, with recent issues focusing on "Twenty-First-Century Perspectives on US Ethnic Literatures" and "Teaching Multi-Ethnic Literatures of the United States: Pedagogy in Anxious Times." Each issue contains 8 to 12 articles and 5 or more book reviews. Interviews with established and emerging authors also may be included. Some articles published recently include "Water Occupation and the Ecology of Arab American Literature," "Speculating on Jim Crow Queerness in African American Lesbian and Gay Life Writing," and "Adopted or Married: Families of Choice in Ann Petry's *The Narrows.*" This important publication is recommended for all academic and large public libraries.

3329. *M L N.* Formerly (until 1962): *Modern Language Notes.* [ISSN: 0026-7910] 1886. 5x/yr. USD 250. The Johns Hopkins University Press, 2715 N Charles St, Baltimore, MD 21218; http://www.press.jhu.edu. Illus., index, adv. Sample. Refereed. Vol. ends: Dec. Reprint: PSC. *Indexed:* A01, A22, AmHI, BRI, CBRI, E01, MLA-IB. *Bk. rev.:* 1-7, 1-3 pages, signed. *Aud.:* Ac.

This long-standing journal, formerly titled *Modern Language Notes*, was first published nearly 135 years ago with a focus on contemporary Continental criticism. Concerned with critical studies in the modern languages and recent work in comparative literature, *MLN* publishes four issues each year on literature in a single language (one issue each for Italian, Spanish, German, and French) and devotes the fifth issue of the year to comparative literature. The comp-lit issue also includes an index to the entire year's volume. Issues contain from 8 to as many as 16 essays that range in length from 8 to 20 pages. Essays often present an interdisciplinary perspective, and sometimes are written in one of the non-English languages under consideration. Five to ten book reviews also are included, as well as occasional notes. Recent articles include "Waking the Dead: Miguel de Cervantes' *Numancia* and the Problem of Golden Age Historical Drama," "Early Modern Media Theory: Comedy and Government in Machiavelli's *Clizia,*" and "Miniaturization: Reading Benjamin in the Digital Age." Highly recommended for academic libraries. It should also be considered by larger public libraries as well.

3330. *M L Q: a journal of literary history.* [ISSN: 0026-7929] 1940. q. USD 446. Ed(s): Marshall Brown. Duke University Press, 905 W Main St, Durham, NC 27701; orders@dukeupress.edu; https://www.dukeupress.edu. Illus., index, adv. Refereed. Vol. ends: Dec. Reprint: PSC. *Indexed:* A22, BRI, E01, MLA-IB. *Bk. rev.:* 5-6, 3-5 pages, signed. *Aud.:* Ac.

This long-standing journal emphasizes the "broader scope of literary history." Each essay focuses on how a topic relates to its place in time. Issues include a range of topics that span time periods, genre, and geography. Articles are typically 20 to 40 pages long. Recent articles include "Elegy's Generation: Muriel Rukeyser, M. L. Rosenthal, and Poetry after the Left," "An Indian It-Narrative and the Problem of Circulation: Reconsidering a Useful Concept for Literary Study," and "Value and Abstraction in Thomas Hardy." Recent special issue topics include "Gender, History, and the Novel: Desire and Domestic Fiction after Thirty Years" and "Chinese Encounters with Western Theories." Each issue contains several three- to five-page book reviews. The articles are probably best for upper-level undergraduates, graduate students, and scholars.

3331. *McSweeney's.* [ISSN: 2325-2588] 1998. q. USD 60. Ed(s): Dave Eggers. McSweeney's, 849 Valencia St, San Francisco, CA 94110; custservice@mcsweeneys.net; http://www.mcsweeneys.net. *Aud.:* Ga, Ac.

Also known as *Timothy McSweeney's Quarterly Concern,* this journal "exists to champion ambitious and inspired new writing, and to challenge conventional expectations about where it's found, how it looks, and who participates." Issues contain fiction by authors such as Chimamanda Ngozi Adichie, Laura van der Berg, and Eskor David Johnson, yet the publisher is also "committed to finding new voices...and promoting the work of gifted but underappreciated writers." The archives on the website include full-text selections from issues dating back to 1998. *McSweeney's* won't be for everyone, but for those liking humor, short fiction pieces, interesting articles, and occasional quarterly surprises with regard to format, this is an obvious choice for large public and academic libraries to consider. URL: http://mcsweeneys.net

3332. *Medium Aevum.* Formerly (until 1932): *Arthuriana.* [ISSN: 0025-8385] 1928. s-a. Ed(s): Sylvia Huot, Nigel F Palmer. Society for the Study of Mediaeval Languages and Literature, The Executive Officer, c/o History Faculty, George St, Oxford, OX1 2RL, United Kingdom; ssmll@history.ox.ac.uk; http://mediumaevum.modhist.ox.ac.uk/. Illus., index. Refereed. Vol. ends: No. 2. *Indexed:* A01, A22, AmHI, BRI, MLA-IB. *Bk. rev.:* 16-82, 1-2 pages, signed. *Aud.:* Ac.

This journal, published since its inception in 1932 by the Society for the Study of Medieval Languages and Literature, is "one of the leading international academic periodicals in medieval studies." Typically, each issue includes six or seven scholarly essays, 15 to 25 pages in length. (Occasionally, longer essays and short notes are published, as well.) In addition, 15 to 30 book reviews and perhaps a review essay are included. Recent article titles include "Bishops Blessing the Bridal Bedchamber in the Early Middle Ages: Reconsidering the Western Evidence," "Imperial Fantasies: Imagining Christian Empire in Three Fourteenth-Century versions of *The Book of Sir John Mandeville*," and "Imitation, Interpretation, and Ascetic Impulse in Medieval English Devotional Culture." Appropriate for research libraries and other academic institutions with a strong Medieval Studies program.

3333. *Middle Eastern Literatures.* Incorporates (1976-2003): *Edebiyat (Print);* Formerly (until 2002): *Arabic and Middle Eastern Literatures (Print).* [ISSN: 1475-262X] 1998. 3x/yr. GBP 538 (print & online eds.)). Ed(s): Wen-Chin Ouyang. Routledge, 4 Park Sq, Milton Park, Abingdon, OX14 4RN, United Kingdom; subscriptions@tandf.co.uk; http://www.tandfonline.com. Adv. Sample. Refereed. Reprint: PSC. *Indexed:* A01, A22, AmHI, E01, MLA-IB. *Bk. rev.:* Number and length vary. *Aud.:* Ac.

This journal is devoted to the study of "all Middle Eastern literatures," both classical and modern, and is endorsed by the Union Europeenne des Arabisants et Islamisants and the Classical Arabic Poetry Symposium. Submissions are accepted in English, German, or French. *Middle Eastern Literatures* publishes articles "of a cross- and multi-linguistic nature that focus on East-West (and/or East-East) relations," as well as those that examine "the relationship of literature with other arts and media." Three to eight essays, book reviews, and an occasional note are generally included in each issue. Special issues are sometimes published. Recent essays include "She is No Desdemona: A Syrian Woman in Samar Attar's Shakespearean Subversions," "Whose War is it Anyway? Multilingual Games as Political Encoding in Rawi Hage's *De Niro's Game*," and "'The True Face of the Work': Sovereignty and Literary Form in Literary Historiography." Appropriate for academic libraries.

3334. *Modern Fiction Studies.* [ISSN: 0026-7724] 1955. q. USD 190. Ed(s): John N Duvall. The Johns Hopkins University Press, 2715 N Charles St, Baltimore, MD 21218; http://www.press.jhu.edu. Illus., adv. Sample. Refereed. Vol. ends: Winter. Reprint: PSC. *Indexed:* A01, A22, AmHI, BRI, CBRI, E01, MLA-IB. *Bk. rev.:* 0-40, 1-3 pages, signed. *Aud.:* Ac.

Modern Fiction Studies, or *MFS,* publishes "theoretically engaged and historically informed articles on modernist and contemporary fiction," with an openness to both canonical and emergent works. A product of the Purdue University English Department and published by the Johns Hopkins University Press, this journal offers two general issues and two special issues each year. The publication is supported by two extensive and distinguished editorial boards. Issues include five to eight scholarly articles that range in length from 20 to 35 pages. General issues also contain approximately 40 book reviews, and occasionally review essays. Recent special issues include "Cripping Modernism" and "Inter-Imperiality: An Introduction." Articles in recent volumes include "Fossils of Tomorrow: Len Lye, J. G. Ballard, and Planetary Futures," "Cultivating America: Colonial History in the Morrisonian Wilderness," and "Dispatches from the Drug Wars: Ishmael Reed, Oscar Zeta Acosta, and the Viet Cong of America." Highly recommended for most academic libraries.

3335. *Modern Language Review.* Supersedes in part: *Modern Language Quarterly.* [ISSN: 0026-7937] 1905. q. USD 383 print & online eds. Modern Humanities Research Association (M H R A), Salisbury House, Station Road, Cambridge, CB1 2LA, United Kingdom; mail@mhra.org.uk; http://www.mhra.org.uk. Illus. Refereed. Circ: 1800. Vol. ends: Oct. *Indexed:* A01, A22, AmHI, BRI, CBRI, F01, MLA-IB. *Bk. rev.:* Approx. 125, 1-4 pages, signed. *Aud.:* Ac.

This "flagship" journal of the Modern Humanities Research Association dates back to 1905. The journal publishes scholarly studies that focus on "medieval and modern literature in the languages of Europe." Recent articles (typically 10 to 20 pages long) study a variety of genres (critical theory, poetry, memoir). Authors studied in recent issues include William Shakespeare, Jonathan Franzen, Dante Gabriel Rossetti, Gabriel Garcia Marquez, Elena Ferrante, Tirso de Molina, and Algernon Swinburne. The wide range of scholarly topics, along with the extensive and diverse book review section, make *Modern Language Review* a staple for every academic library.

3336. *Modern Philology: critical and historical studies in literature, medieval through contemporary.* [ISSN: 0026-8232] 1903. q. USD 323. Ed(s): Timothy Campbell, Ellen MacKay. University of Chicago Press, 1427 E 60th St, Chicago, IL 60637; custserv@press.uchicago.edu; http://www.journals.uchicago.edu. Illus., index, adv. Sample. Refereed. Vol. ends: May. Reprint: PSC. *Indexed:* A01, A22, AmHI, BRI, CBRI, MLA-IB. *Bk. rev.:* 10-15, 2-4 pages, signed. *Aud.:* Ac.

This long-standing journal, published since 1903, is concerned generally with literary scholarship, criticism, and history, from the medieval period to the present. The current editors include scholarship that "encompasses literary works, literary traditions, and literary criticism from, roughly, the time of Charlemagne to the present." While *Modern Philology* continues to focus on literatures written in English or European languages, the journal's scope has expanded to include scholarship on non-European language works, including a marked interest in comparative studies. Issues also include book reviews and review essays, which take part in the publication's expanded geographic scope. A "Notes and Documents" section may contribute research on manuscripts and other archival documents. Special sections sometimes are included. Articles can run from 25 to 40 pages in length. Essays published recently include "The Sounds of Appleton House: Andrew Marvell's Poetic Audioscapes," "The Satanic Sublime in *Paradise Lost*: Tasso, Charisma, Abjection," and "Present, Period, Crisis: Desynchronization and Social Cohesion in Jane Austen." Highly recommended for most academic libraries.

3337. *Mosaic (Winnipeg, 1967): a journal for the interdisciplinary study of literature.* Formerly (until 1978): *Journal for the Comparative Study of Literature and Ideas.* [ISSN: 0027-1276] 1967. q. CAD 55; CAD 24.95 per issue. Ed(s): Dr. Dawne McCance. University of Manitoba, Tier Bldg, Rm 208, Winnipeg, MB R3T 2N2, Canada; http://www.umanitoba.ca. Illus., index. Sample. Refereed. Vol. ends: Fall. Microform: PQC. *Indexed:* A01, A22, AmHI, BAS, BRI, C37, F01, MLA-IB, RILM. *Aud.:* Ac.

This Canadian journal, published under the purview of the University of Manitoba, ties literary topics to other disciplines such as art, history, music, ethics, and film. Topics are wide-ranging and eclectic; the journal "brings insights from a wide variety of disciplines to bear on literary texts, cultural climates, topical issues, divergent art forms and modes of creative activity." Scholarly essays (typically 15 to 20 pages long) from recent issues include "From Peyton Plantation to Peyton Place: Gothic Tropes in Grace Metalious's Infamous New England Novel," "Subalternity and Scale in Arundhati Roy's *The God of Small Things*," and "From Bird Girls to Bat Souls: Joycean Transformations of a Homeric Trope." Though popular culture topics often appear, this journal is academic and highly cerebral. Recommended for academic libraries that support graduate programs in the humanities.

3338. *Narrative.* [ISSN: 1063-3685] 1993. 3x/yr. USD 111 (print or online ed.)). Ed(s): James Phelan. Ohio State University Press, 180 Pressey Hall, 1070 Carmack Rd, Columbus, OH 43210; info@osupress.org; http://www.ohiostatepress.org. Refereed. *Indexed:* A01, A22, AmHI, BRI, E01, MLA-IB. *Aud.:* Ac.

Narrative, the official journal of the International Society for the Study of Narrative, covers a wide range of scholarship focused on the American, English, and European novel, as well as nonfiction narrative, film, and narrative as performance art. Each issue contains five or six essays in criticism ranging from 10 to 25 pages in length. Occasionally, an editor's column is included. The journal explores literature from several periods, with marked strength in contemporary and twentieth-century fiction. Interdisciplinary studies are not uncommon. In recent issues, *Narrative* has published such essays as "The Question of James's Speech: Consensual Talk in *The Ambassadors,*" "What Mary Poppins Knew: Theory of Mind, Children's Literature, History," and "Postcolonial Graphic Lifewriting: *Finding My Way* and the Subaltern Public Sphere." This journal is relevant to scholars in both literature and film studies, and may be of interest to readers outside the academy. Recommended for all academic and medium or large public libraries.

3339. *New Literary History: a journal of theory and interpretation.* [ISSN: 0028-6087] 1969. q. USD 235. Ed(s): Mollie H Washburne, Bruce Holsinger. The Johns Hopkins University Press, 2715 N Charles St, Baltimore, MD 21218; http://www.press.jhu.edu. Illus., index, adv. Sample. Refereed. Vol. ends: Nov. Reprint: PSC. *Indexed:* A01, A22, AmHI, BAS, E01, MLA-IB, P61, SSA. *Aud.:* Ac.

This formidable journal, now in its fiftieth year, is focused on "questions of theory, method, interpretation, and literary history" and strives to spark "debate on the relations between literary and cultural texts and present needs." *New Literary History* is especially interested in scholarship that engages with literary and cultural theory and addresses methodological or theoretical questions of interest to scholars across multiple fields. Special issues are published on occasion, including the more recent "Style, Form, Formalism." The advisory editors of this publication constitute a virtual "Who's Who" of literature criticism, including, but not limited to, Helene Cixous, Jonathan Culler, Toril Moi, Fredric Jameson, Martha Nussbaum, and Hayden White. Articles published recently include "Ralph Cohen on Literary Periods: Afterword as Foreword," "The Arabesque from Kant to Comics," "Audre Lorde, Theodor Adorno, and the Administered Word," and "Making Sense of Eurasia: Reflections on Max Weber and Jack Goody." Highly recommended for academic libraries, especially those that support graduate programs in the study of literature.

3340. *Nineteenth-Century Literature (Berkeley).* Former titles (until 1986): *Nineteenth-Century Fiction;* (until 1949): *The Trollopian.* [ISSN: 0891-9356] 1945. q. USD 304 (print & online eds.)). Ed(s): Saree Makdisi, Jonathan Grossman. University of California Press, Journals Division, 155 Grand Avenue, Ste 400, Oakland, CA 94612-3764; http://www.ucpress.edu/journals.php. Illus., index, adv. Sample. Refereed. Circ: 1446. Vol. ends: Mar. Microform: PQC. *Indexed:* A01, A22, AmHI, BRI, CBRI, E01, MLA-IB. *Bk. rev.:* 8-10, 2-4 pages, signed. *Aud.:* Ac.

This elite journal from the University of California Press examines "transatlantic authors and poets, literary characters, and discourses" of the nineteenth century. Each issue contains three or four articles, and approximately ten book reviews. The 20- to 30-page articles exhibit quality literary scholarship. Authors studied in recent issues include Ann Lister, William Dean Howells, Frances Hodgson Burnett, Rudyard Kipling, Herman Melville, and Charles Chesnutt. The broad coverage of nineteenth-century topics and authors from both sides of the pond makes this a good selection for all academic libraries.

3341. *Notes and Queries: for readers and writers, collectors and librarians.* [ISSN: 0029-3970] 1849. q. EUR 479. Ed(s): L G Black. Oxford University Press, Great Clarendon St, Oxford, OX2 6DP, United Kingdom; onlinequeries.uk@oup.com; http://global.oup.com. Adv. Sample. Refereed. Microform: PMC; PQC. Reprint: PSC. *Indexed:* A01, A22, AmHI, BRI, E01, MLA-IB. *Bk. rev.:* 17-30, 1-2 pages, signed. *Aud.:* Ac, Sa.

This well-respected journal, "devoted principally to English language and literature, lexicography, history, and scholarly antiquarianism," has the principal aim of asking and responding to the questions of readers. Articles tend to be brief examinations (no more than a few pages in length) that explore facts and details about language and literature. The journal's scope encompasses work produced from the Medieval period to the early twentieth century. Each issue also includes 10 to 20 book reviews and sometimes a "Memorabilia" section, offering festschriften or other topical discussion. Recent articles include "*Canterbury Tales* for Children in China," "The Earliest Surviving Homily in English," "Commonplaces, Aristophanes, and Clouds in *Hamlet*," and "The Origin of Longfellow's 'The Warning.'" Suitable for academic and large public libraries.

3342. *Novel: a forum on fiction.* [ISSN: 0029-5132] 1967. 3x/yr. USD 182. Ed(s): Nancy Armstrong. Duke University Press, 905 W Main St, Durham, NC 27701; orders@dukeupress.edu; https://www.dukeupress.edu. Illus., index, adv. Refereed. Vol. ends: Spring. Microform: PQC. Reprint: PSC. *Indexed:* A01, A22, AmHI, BRI, MASUSE, MLA-IB. *Bk. rev.:* 6-9, 2-4 pages, signed. *Aud.:* Ac.

Novel, the official journal of the Society for Novel Studies, is "devoted to the best new criticism and theory in novel studies." Special issues are fairly common, with the most recent example being "The Victorian Novel Now." Issues generally contain five to nine articles, and five to ten book reviews. Articles usually run 15 to 30 pages in length. Recently published articles include "Proust's Genies: *In Search of Lost Time* and Population Biology," "Something Extraordinary Keeps Happening: J. G. Ballard's Enclave World," and "Nella Larsen's Etiquette Lesson: Small Talk, Racial Passing, and the Novel of Manners." Suitable for academic and large public libraries.

3343. *P M L A.* Formerly (until 1888): *Modern Language Association of America. Transactions and Proceedings;* Which was formed by the merger of (1885-1886): *Modern Language Association of America. Transactions;* (1884-1886): *Modern Language Association of America. Proceedings.* [ISSN: 0030-8129] 1886. 5x/yr. Free to members. Ed(s): Kathleen Fitzpatrick, Simon Gikandi. Modern Language Association of America, 85 Broad St, Ste 500, New York, NY 10004; execdirector@mla.org; http://www.mla.org. Illus., index, adv. Sample. Refereed. Vol. ends: Nov. Microform: PQC. Reprint: PSC. *Indexed:* A01, A22, AmHI, MLA-IB. *Aud.:* Ac.

PMLA, the flagship journal of the Modern Language Association of America, publishes "members' essays judged to be of interest to scholars and teachers of language and literature." This core journal publishes five issues a year that offer scholarly essays on language and literature. (The fourth issue in each volume serves as the annual association directory and annual convention program, respectively.) Content represents a broad spectrum of topics, methods, and theoretical perspectives. Some essays are translated from languages other than English prior to publication. Issues focusing on special topics are sometimes published. The journal also publishes "little-known documentary material" that is deemed appropriate; an editor's column; talks from the Modern Language Association's annual convention; and letters to the editor. Special topics are covered frequently. The journal's format also employs recurring sections of content, such as "Theories and Methodologies" and "The Changing Profession." Recent essays include "Pictography, Law, and Earth: Gerald Vizenor, John Borrows, and Louise Erdrich" and "Autofiction Infiltrated: Anne Garreta's *Pas un jour.*" This essential title is recommended for all academic and medium-to-large public libraries.

3344. *Papers on Language and Literature: a journal for scholars and critics of language and literature.* Formerly (until 1966): *Papers on English Language & Literature.* [ISSN: 0031-1294] 1965. q. USD 190. Ed(s): Helena Gurfinkel. Southern Illinois University at Edwardsville, SIUE Campus, Edwardsville, IL 62026-1434; http://www.siue.edu. Illus., index, adv. Refereed. Vol. ends: Fall. *Indexed:* A01, A22, AmHI, BRI, MLA-IB. *Bk. rev.:* 0-3, 4-6 pages, signed. *Aud.:* Ac.

Papers on Language and Literature considers itself a generalist journal and publishes scholarship on "a variety of literatures, languages, and chronological periods," as well as "film, print culture, translation, and digital humanities." Most of the articles, though, tend to examine the works of well-known American and English writers. Each issue contains approximately four articles, with an occasional review sometimes included. Articles run 20 to 30 pages in length. Essays published in recent issues include "'What was It?': The *avant-texte* and the 'Grinding Feeling of Wretchedness' in Katherine Mansfield's 'The Fly'"; "The Crisis of Interpretation in the Allegorical Reading of Iris Murdoch's *The Unicorn*"; and "From Sausages to Hoplites of Ham and Beyond: The Status of Genetically Modified Pigs in Margaret Atwood's *MaddAddam* Trilogy." Recommended for academic and large public libraries.

3345. *Postcolonial Text.* [ISSN: 1705-9100] 2004. s-a. Free. Ed(s): Chantal Zabus. Postcolonial Text, https://www.postcolonial.org/index.php/. Refereed. *Indexed:* MLA-IB. *Bk. rev.:* 0-5, 3-5 pages. *Aud.:* Ac.

This electronic open-access journal "examines the relationship between postcolonial studies, diaspora studies and such newly emerging fields as transnational cultural and globalization studies." Recent scholarly essays, which are typically around 15 pages long, include "Past Meets Present: *Monsoon Wedding* Redux," "Uncovering a Love of Self: Individuality and Coloured Identity in Ntokozo Madlala and Mandisa Haarhoff's *Crush-hopper,*" and "Nation and Censorship: A Reading of Aubrey Menen's *Rama Retold.*" The journal adds value by publishing interviews with writers, book reviews, and postcolonial poetry and fiction. Articles are easy to access thanks to a user-friendly platform. This free peer-reviewed journal is recommended for all academic libraries.

3346. *Postmedieval: a journal of medieval cultural studies.* [ISSN: 2040-5960] 2010. q. GBP 599. Ed(s): Myra Seaman, Eileen Joy. Palgrave Macmillan Ltd., Macmillan Building, 4 Crinan St, London, N1 9XW, United Kingdom; onlinesales@palgrave.com; http://www.palgrave.com. Adv. Sample. Refereed. Reprint: PSC. *Indexed:* A22, E01, MLA-IB. *Aud.:* Ac.

This peer-reviewed journal from Palgrave Macmillan began in 2010 with the aim to encourage "present-minded approach to medieval studies, which inspires new critical investigations of the Middle Ages by examining contemporary events, issues, ideas, problems, objects, and studies." The journal is interdisciplinary, but many articles address literature or film and connect contemporary and medieval topics. Issues, or parts of issues, have themes such as "ecomaterialism," or disability and illness. Though the journal features articles that are relatively short (six to ten pages) and have pithy titles, the essays are very scholarly. Recent articles include "Prophecy and Emendation: Merlin, Chaucer, Lear's Fool," "Vegetal Continuity and the Naming of Species," and "Trans Textuality: Dysphoria in the Depths of Medieval Skin." This journal is most suitable for graduate students and faculty.

3347. *Qui Parle: critical humanities and social sciences.* Formerly (until 1987): *Ca Parle.* [ISSN: 1041-8385] 1985. s-a. USD 132. Ed(s): Patrick Lyons, Lauren Miller. Duke University Press, 905 W Main St, Durham, NC 27701; orders@dukeupress.edu; https://www.dukeupress.edu. Adv. Refereed. *Indexed:* A22, E01, MLA-IB. *Aud.:* Ac.

Qui Parle strives to "start critical conversations and introduce new analytic modes by bringing together diverse scholarly and artistic voices." The journal is innovative and formidable, having published such pioneering scholars as Jacques Derrida, Judith Butler, Peggy Kamuf, and Slavoj Zizek. Occasionally, issues have a "special dossier," most recently on the theme "Friendship: Correspondences." Issues usually contain eight to ten essays that range widely in length from 6 to 60 pages. Recent articles include "Queer Procreation: Reading Kleist Plantwise," "The Politics of Fiction," and "Robert Duncan and the 1960s: Psychoanalysis, Politics, Kitsch." Recommended for academic libraries, especially those with graduate programs in the humanities and social sciences.

3348. *Religion and Literature.* Formerly (until 1984): *Notre Dame English Journal.* [ISSN: 0888-3769] 1961. 3x/yr. Individuals, USD 25. Ed(s): Tyler Gardner, Romana Huk. University of Notre Dame, Department of English, B009F McKenna Hall, Notre Dame, IN 46556; english@nd.edu; http://english.nd.edu/. Adv. Refereed. *Indexed:* A01, A22, AmHI, C26, MLA-IB, R&TA. *Bk. rev.:* 0-10, 3-6 pages, signed. *Aud.:* Ac.

This journal from the University of Notre Dame publishes scholarly articles regarding the relationship between "the religious impulse and the literary forms of any era, place, or language." Recent articles (usually 20 to 30 pages) include

"Comparative Demonologies: Dostoevsky and Ferrante on the Boundaries of the Self" and "Blood on the Wall: Christianity, Colonialism, and Mimetic Conflict in Margaret Atwood's *Cat's Eye*." Occasionally, issues have a special topic. The most recent such issue focused on the work of David Jones. Some issues feature a "Forum" section, which presents shorter essays on a particular topic (e.g., logos). Most issues contain book reviews, which are usually about three pages long. Recommended for academic libraries that support graduate programs in the humanities.

Research in African Literatures. See Africa section.

3349. ***The Review of English Studies: the leading journal of English literature and language.*** [ISSN: 0034-6551] 1925. q. EUR 564. Ed(s): Thomas Keymer. Oxford University Press, Great Clarendon St, Oxford, OX2 6DP, United Kingdom; onlinequeries.uk@oup.com; http://global.oup.com. Illus., index, adv. Sample. Refereed. Microform: PQC. Reprint: PSC. *Indexed:* A01, A22, AmHI, BRI, CBRI, E01, MLA-IB. *Bk. rev.:* 7-22, 2-3 pages, signed. *Aud.:* Ac.

Founded in 1925, this elite journal from Oxford University Press focuses on "literary-historical research in all areas of English literature and the English language from the earliest period to the present." Recent scholarship includes "Spenser in Buskins: *The Shepheardes Calender* and the Tragedians," "Afro-Creole Revelry and Rebellion on the British Stage: Jonkanoo in *Obi; or, Three-Fingered Jack* (1800)," "Self-Fashioning and Poetic Voice: Elizabeth Singer Rowe's Authorial Prerogative," and "At the Jamesian Altar: Commemorating Henry James's Corpus." Each issue also features about 20 two- to three-page reviews. Recommended for academic libraries.

3350. ***Romanticism.*** [ISSN: 1354-991X] 1995. 3x/yr. GBP 159 (print & online eds.)). Ed(s): Nicholas Roe. Edinburgh University Press Ltd., The Tun, Holyrood Rd, 12 (2f) Jackson's Entry, Edinburgh, EH8 8PJ, United Kingdom; journals@eup.ed.ac.uk; http://www.euppublishing.com. Illus., adv. Sample. Refereed. *Indexed:* A01, A22, AmHI, E01, MLA-IB. *Bk. rev.:* 10-15, 2-4 pages, signed. *Aud.:* Ac.

For 25 years, this journal from Edinburgh University Press has featured "critical, historical, textual and bibliographical essays" about the Romantic period, which the journal defines as 1750-1850. Recent articles, which are generally 10 to 15 pages, highlight writers such as Samuel Taylor Coleridge, John Keats, Lord Byron, Charlotte Smith, Jane Austen, Walter Scott, and Mary Tighe. Entire issues are devoted to topics such as "Hydra-Romanticism" or "Exiles." Issues also contain about ten two- to three-page book reviews. Recommended for academic libraries that serve graduate programs in literature.

3351. ***Romanticism on the Net.*** Former titles (until 2017): *Romanticism and Victorianism on the Net;* (until 2007): *Romanticism on the Net.* 1996. 2x/yr. Free. Ed(s): Michael E Sinatra, Julia S Carlson. Universite de Montreal, Succursale Centre-Ville, P O Box 6128, Montreal, QC H3C 3J7, Canada. Refereed. *Indexed:* MLA-IB. *Bk. rev.:* 5-15, signed. *Aud.:* Ac.

This open-access journal, which recently returned to its original appellation, *Romanticism on the Net*, examines Romantic-era British authors. Recent articles study Samuel Taylor Coleridge, Mary Robinson, Ann Yearsley, Richard Southey, and William Wordsworth. A recent special issue examines "Recollecting the Nineteenth-Century Museum." Issues also contain a substantial section of review essays. The redesigned site is easy to navigate and access. Academic libraries and public libraries should consider adding this peer-reviewed journal to their catalogs or research guides. URL: https://ronjournal.org/

3352. ***Speculum: a journal of Medieval studies.*** [ISSN: 0038-7134] 1926. q. USD 324 (print & online eds.)). Ed(s): Sarah Spence. University of Chicago Press, 1427 E 60th St, Chicago, IL 60637; custserv@press.uchicago.edu; http://www.journals.uchicago.edu. Illus., index, adv. Refereed. Vol. ends: Oct. Reprint: PSC. *Indexed:* A01, A06, A22, AmHI, BRI, CBRI, MLA-IB. *Bk. rev.:* 80-90, 2 pages, signed. *Aud.:* Ac.

This multidisciplinary and interdisciplinary journal purports to be "the most widely distributed journal of medieval studies." The contents of each issue represent its broad scope. The journal focuses on Western Europe, although "Arabic, Byzantine, Hebrew, and Slavic studies are included." Roughly half of each issue is devoted to an enormous number (around 50 or 60) of book reviews and brief notices about publications relevant to Medieval Studies. Recent essays, including copious footnotes to the text, have ranged from 25 to 45 pages in length. While articles are written in English, notes often present material in its original language. Recent articles published in *Speculum* include "Masculinity and Prostitution in Late Medieval German Literature," "In the Name of Charlemagne, Roland, and Turpin: Reading the Oxford *Roland* as a Trinitarian Text," and "Piccarda's Weakness: Reflections on Freedom, Force, and Femininity in Dante's *Paradiso*." While this journal includes much content that does not engage literature directly, those articles that deal with literature are important reading for literary scholars studying the period. Highly recommended for academic libraries, especially those that support Medieval Studies programs.

3353. ***Studies in American Fiction.*** [ISSN: 0091-8083] 1973. s-a. USD 93. Ed(s): Paul Thifault, Duncan Faherty. The Johns Hopkins University Press, 2715 N Charles St, Baltimore, MD 21218; http://www.press.jhu.edu. Illus., adv. Sample. Refereed. Vol. ends: Fall. Reprint: PSC. *Indexed:* A01, A22, AmHI, BRI, E01, MLA-IB. *Bk. rev.:* 2-5, 1-2 pages, signed. *Aud.:* Ac.

Studies in American Fiction (*SAF*) publishes scholarship on the prose fiction of the United States with the intent to "feature not only major canonical works by Charles Brockden Brown, Harriet Beecher Stowe, Edith Wharton, and Thomas Pynchon, but scholarly analyses of contemporary Chicano literature and Harlem Renaissance fiction." *SAF* includes approximately six essays in each issue, generally falling in the range of 20 to 25 pages in length. Recently published articles include "Regulating Feeling in the First American Novel: Sympathy, Sensibility, and Sentiment in William Hill Brown's *The Power of Sympathy*," "Unlike the Average Mental Disability as Narrative Form and Social Critique in Morrison's *The Bluest Eye*," and "Temperance, Abolition, and Genre Collision in Whitman's *Franklin Evans*." Recommended for most academic libraries.

3354. ***Studies in English Literature 1500-1900.*** [ISSN: 0039-3657] 1961. q. USD 165. Ed(s): Becky Byron. The Johns Hopkins University Press, 2715 N Charles St, Baltimore, MD 21218; http://www.press.jhu.edu. Illus., adv. Sample. Refereed. Reprint: PSC. *Indexed:* A01, A22, AmHI, BRI, E01, MASUSE, MLA-IB. *Aud.:* Ac.

This quarterly journal from Rice University (and published by Johns Hopkins University Press) devotes one issue a year to the following: the English Renaissance, Tudor and Stuart drama, Restoration and eighteenth-century literature, and the nineteenth century. The journal, also known as *SEL*, publishes "readable papers that contribute significantly to the understanding of British literature from 1500 to 1900." Each issue contains eight or nine scholarly essays (typically 20 to 30 pages long) and concludes with a lengthy review essay of "recent studies" relevant to the issue's literary period. Recent essays include "Pirate Economics in Robert Daborne's *A Christian Turned Turk*," "Andrew Marvell on Renaissance Translation Practice," and "Christianity and Class in Elizabeth Gaskell's *Mary Barton*." With this journal's wide span of scholarship, each volume provides a great overview of the study of literature. A core title for all academic libraries and some larger public libraries.

3355. ***Studies in Philology.*** [ISSN: 0039-3738] 1903. q. University of North Carolina Press, 116 S Boundary St, Chapel Hill, NC 27514; uncpress@unc.edu; http://www.uncpress.unc.edu. Refereed. Microform: MIM; IDC; PMC; PQC. *Indexed:* A01, A22, AmHI, BRI, E01, MLA-IB. *Aud.:* Ac.

This scholarly journal, which was founded in 1903, focuses on "British literature through Romanticism and articles on relations between British literature and works in the classical, Romance, and Germanic languages." Scholarly studies are typically around 20 pages; the journal does not include book reviews. Recently published articles include "Shakespeare's Snuff-Play: Suffocating Figures in *Henry IV*, Parts 1 and 2" and "Vicissitude of Years: Temporal Experience in Donne's *Anniversaries*." This journal is best suited for academic libraries that support graduate programs in literature.

3356. *Studies in Romanticism.* [ISSN: 0039-3762] 1961. q. USD 75 (Individuals, USD 28; USD 7 per issue). Ed(s): Deborah Swedberg, Charles Rzepka. Boston University, Graduate School, 236 Bay State Rd, Boston, MA 02215; http://www.bu.edu/. Illus., index, adv. Refereed. Vol. ends: Winter. Microform: PQC. *Indexed:* A01, A22, AmHI, BRI, MLA-IB. *Bk. rev.:* 3-6, 2-6 pages, signed. *Aud.:* Ac.

Billing itself as "the flagship journal of Romantic literary studies," *Studies in Romanticism* publishes articles on literature, arts, and culture associated with the Romantic movement. The preponderance of essays engages English authors and works, with occasional pieces also addressing other European and U.S. literature. Most issues include six articles, along with three to six book reviews. Articles generally are 15 to 30 pages in length. Recent essays include "Prophetic Poetics and Enthusiasm in Mary Shelley's *Valperga*," "Secret Agents: Agency without Responsibility in *The Mysteries of Udolpho*," "Keats, Ecocriticism, and the Poetics of Place," and "Free Indirect Discourse and the Problem of the Will in Two Novels by William Godwin." This is a leading journal in the study of Romanticism and is recommended for academic libraries.

3357. *Studies in the Novel.* [ISSN: 0039-3827] 1969. q. USD 120. Ed(s): Timothy Boswell, Nora Gilbert. The Johns Hopkins University Press, 2715 N Charles St, Baltimore, MD 21218; http://www.press.jhu.edu. Illus., adv. Sample. Refereed. Vol. ends: No. 4. Reprint: PSC. *Indexed:* A22, BRI, E01, MLA-IB. *Bk. rev.:* 8-10, 1-2 pages, signed. *Aud.:* Ac.

Now in its fiftieth year, *Studies in the Novel* publishes "incisive criticism of the novel across all periods and genres, and from all interpretive approaches." In each issue, readers will find five or six essays in criticism, eight to ten book reviews, and an occasional review essay. The journal publishes an occasional special issue, the most recent one titled "Fifty Years of Studies in the Novel: A Look Back." Examples of articles published most recently are "Sexual Selection and Female Choice in Austen's *Northanger Abbey*," "Joseph Conrad's Atmospheric Modernism: Enveloping Fog, Narrative Frames, and Affective Attunement," and "Chronotope in Moore and Gibbons's *Watchmen*." Recommended for all academic libraries and large public libraries.

3358. *Studies in Twentieth and Twenty-First Century Literature (Online).* [ISSN: 2334-4415] 1976. s-a. Free. Ed(s): Kathleen Antonioli. New Prairie Press, 201 Dickens Hall, Kansas State University, Manhattan, KS 66506; csimser@ksu.edu; http://newprairiepress.org. Refereed. *Bk. rev.:* 0-13, 2-3 pages, signed. *Aud.:* Ac.

This journal is devoted to "articles written in English on post-1900 literature in French, German, and Spanish." It expanded its scope in 2003 to include twenty-first century literature. Essays often are written with an interdisciplinary perspective, including frequent intersections with theater, history, and aspects of popular culture. Issues with a "Special Focus" are published on occasion, including a recent one titled "Set Up and Shut Out: Immigration and Criminality in Contemporary Spanish Fiction." Articles generally run 8 to 12 pages in length. Recent articles include "Cold War Nature: Transforming German Poetry," "Performing Editorial Authority in Ingo Schulze's Epistolary Novel *Neue Leben*," and "Neoliberalism in the Gutter: Latin American Comics and Society since the 1990s." Each issue includes between 4 and 12 book reviews. Recommended for larger academic libraries. URL: http://newprairiepress.org/sttcl/

3359. *Style (University Park).* [ISSN: 0039-4238] 1967. q. USD 240 (print & online eds.)). Ed(s): John V Knapp. Pennsylvania State University Press, 820 N University Dr, University Support Bldg 1, Ste C, University Park, PA 16802; info@psupress.org; http://www.psupress.org. Adv. Refereed. Reprint: PSC. *Indexed:* A22, BRI, MLA-IB. *Bk. rev.:* 0-2, 2-3 pages, signed. *Aud.:* Ac.

Style publishes articles on "questions of style, stylistics, and poetics." Recently, the journal has begun to publish work "employing recent developments in several psychologies—cognition, bioevolutionary psychology, family systems, and human development—as those may relate to the study of literature and the humanities." The essays included cover a broad range of fields, including literary criticism and theory, cognitive linguistics, rhetoric and writing studies, computational linguistics, and the philosophy of language. Reviews and review essays are included in some issues. Articles range in length from 20 to 35 pages. Recently published pieces include "The Pathological Family System in Saul Bellow's *The Adventures of Augie March*," "Late Dickinson: In Praise of Blandness, Agedness, and Oblivion," and "A Reading in Temporal Poetics: Wallace Stevens's 'Domination of Black.'" Recommended for academic libraries.

3360. *Texas Studies in Literature and Language.* Supersedes (in 1959): *Texas Studies in English;* Which was formerly (1911-1957): *University of Texas. Studies in English.* [ISSN: 0040-4691] 1911. q. USD 252. Ed(s): James Cox, Douglas Bruster. University of Texas Press, Journals Division, PO Box 7819, Austin, TX 78713; journals@utpress.utexas.edu; https://utpress.utexas.edu. Illus., index. Refereed. Vol. ends: Winter. *Indexed:* A01, A22, AmHI, BRI, E01, MLA-IB. *Aud.:* Ac.

This journal from the University of Texas Press publishes "substantial essays reflecting a variety of critical approaches and covering all periods of literary history." Subjects of the 20- to 40-page articles are broad in scope; authors studied include Charles Dickens, Robert Lowell, Karen Joy Fowler, Herman Melville, and Norah Lange. The Summer 2019 issue features essays on "The Cause and Effect of Milton's Blindness," "The Politics of Resentment in J. D. Vance's *Hillbilly Elegy,*" and "Opal Whiteley's Spell of Words, among others. Academic libraries should consider adding this journal to their collection.

3361. *Textual Practice.* [ISSN: 0950-236X] 1987. 12x/yr. GBP 1424 (print & online eds.)). Ed(s): Peter Boxall. Routledge, 4 Park Sq, Milton Park, Abingdon, OX14 4RN, United Kingdom; subscriptions@tandf.co.uk; http://www.tandfonline.com. Illus., adv. Sample. Refereed. Vol. ends: Winter. Reprint: PSC. *Indexed:* A01, A22, AmHI, E01, MLA-IB. *Bk. rev.:* 8-15, 3-7 pages, signed. *Aud.:* Ac.

Textual Practice publishes articles that operate "at the turning points of theory with politics, history, and texts," with an emphasis on the historically marginalized. A recent special issue addresses the topic of "Spinoza's Artes." Articles usually run from 20 to 30 pages in length. Recently published essays include "The Politics of Punctuation in *Jacob's Room* and *Between the Acts*," "The New Alchemy: Economic Liberalism, Neoliberalism, and Thomas Pynchon's *Against the Day*," and "Metaffective Fiction: Structuring Feeling in Post-postmodern American Literature." Reviews and review essays are typically included in each issue. Appropriate for larger academic libraries with strong literature programs.

3362. *Tulsa Studies in Women's Literature.* [ISSN: 0732-7730] 1982. s-a. USD 35 (Individuals, USD 26). Ed(s): Laura M Stevens. University of Tulsa, 800 S Tucker Dr, Tulsa, OK 74104; news@utulsa.edu; http://www.utulsa.edu. Illus., index. Refereed. Microform: PQC. *Indexed:* A01, A22, AmHI, BRI, CBRI, E01, FemPer, MLA-IB, WSA. *Bk. rev.:* 7-15, 2-3 pages. *Aud.:* Ac.

Tulsa Studies in Women's Literature, the first journal "devoted solely to women's literature," was founded in 1982. It publishes "articles, notes, research, and reviews of literary, historicist, and theoretical work by established and emerging scholars in the field of women's literature and feminist theory." The scope is not limited to a geographical or chronological place, and articles discuss all issues dealing with women's literature. Recent issues highlight studies of Soledad Acosta, Margaret Atwood, Gertrude Stein, Rita Dove, and Mina Loy. In addition to review essays, there is a section containing several book reviews. The journal sometimes includes an "Archives" section, which features "bibliographies, descriptions of particular archives, or narratives of archival research." It also occasionally features a section called "The Academy," which recently held a discussion of the impact of the #MeToo Movement in academia. Recommended for academic libraries.

3363. *Twentieth Century Literature.* [ISSN: 0041-462X] 1955. q. USD 226. Ed(s): Keith Dallas, Lee Zimmerman. Duke University Press, 905 W Main St, Durham, NC 27701; orders@dukeupress.edu; https://www.dukeupress.edu. Illus., index, adv. Refereed. Vol. ends: No. 4. Reprint: PSC. *Indexed:* A01, A22, AmHI, BRI, MASUSE, MLA-IB. *Bk. rev.:* 3-4, 4-10 pages. *Aud.:* Ac.

As the title suggests, this excellent publication limits its content to studies of literature from the twentieth century. Apart from that constraint, the journal's scope is broad and inclusive. The majority of articles, however, cover American and English writers and works. Each issue typically contains four essays, ranging in length from 20 to 30 pages, followed by three or four book reviews. The journal also publishes the winner of the Andrew J. Kappel Prize in Literary Criticism, awarded each year to "the author (or authors) of a work submitted to the journal during the preceding year that is judged to make the most impressive contribution to our understanding and appreciation of the literature of the twentieth century." Recent articles include "Geopolitical Imaginaries: Croatian Diasporic Writers in North America," "The Queer Afterlife of Gossip: James Merrill's 'Celestial Salon,'" and "Hard Romping: Zora Neale Hurston, White Women, and the Right to Play." This journal should be considered a core title for academic library collections, and is appropriate for larger public libraries as well.

3364. *University of Toronto Quarterly: a Canadian journal of the humanities.* [ISSN: 0042-0247] 1931. q. USD 250. Ed(s): Victor Li. University of Toronto Press, Journals Division, 5201 Dufferin St, Toronto, ON M3H 5T8, Canada; journals@utpress.utoronto.ca; http://www.utpjournals.com. Adv. Sample. Refereed. Circ: 390. Microform: PQC. *Indexed:* A01, A22, AmHI, BRI, C37, E01, IIPA, MLA-IB. *Bk. rev.:* in annual review issue. *Aud.:* Ac.

This journal, which has been around since 1931, "publishes interdisciplinary articles and review essays of international repute." Articles are accepted in both English and French (most articles in recent issues are in English). Though this is an interdisciplinary journal, most issues discuss literary topics; for example, recent articles have examined work by Denis Diderot, W.O. Mitchell, and Jean Rollin. A recent special issue is devoted to "Monster Studies." The annual (bilingual) special issue, "Letters in Canada," reviews a year's work in fiction, poetry, drama, translations, and the humanities. The letters issue includes an index of books reviewed. Recommended for large academic libraries that support relevant programs.

3365. *Victorian Poetry.* [ISSN: 0042-5206] 1963. q. USD 110 (Individuals, USD 50). Ed(s): John B Lamb. West Virginia University Press, Victorian Poetry Office, PO Box 6295, Morgantown, WV 26506; press@mail.wvu.edu; http://www.wvu.edu/. Illus., index. Sample. Refereed. Vol. ends: Winter. Microform: PQC. Reprint: PSC. *Indexed:* A01, A22, AmHI, BRI, E01, MLA-IB. *Aud.:* Ac.

This scholarly journal from West Virginia University Press "publishes articles from a broad range of theoretical and critical angles, including but not confined to new historicism, feminism, and social and cultural issues." Recently, the journal has included studies of William Barnes, Matthew Arnold, Elizabeth Barrett Browning, and Gerard Manley Hopkins; it has also offered an entire issue on poetry published in periodicals from the period. Each year, the journal publishes a "Guide to the Year's Work"—bibliographic essays organized by literary figure (e.g., Thomas Hardy) or broader category (e.g., "Victorian Women Poets," or the Pre-Raphaelites). The readable articles and inclusive scope make this a good choice for any academic library and some larger public libraries.

3366. *Victorian Studies: an interdisciplinary journal of social, political, and cultural studies.* [ISSN: 0042-5222] 1957. q. USD 219.45 (print & online eds.)). Ed(s): Lara Kriegel, Ivan Kreilkamp. Indiana University Press, Office of Scholarly Publishing, Herman B Wells Library 350, Bloomington, IN 47405; iuporder@indiana.edu; http://iupress.indiana.edu/. Illus., index, adv. Refereed. Microform: PQC. Reprint: PSC. *Indexed:* A01, A22, AmHI, BAS, BRI, CBRI, E01, MLA-IB. *Bk. rev.:* 30-35, 1-3 pages, signed. *Aud.:* Ac.

This journal from Indiana University Press is "devoted to the study of British culture of the Victorian age." This journal has an interdisciplinary approach, including articles on "comparative literature, social and political history, and the histories of education, philosophy, fine arts, economics, law, and science"; nevertheless, literary topics are heavily represented. Examples of recent articles include "*New Grub Street*'s Ecologies of Paper," "Industrial Souls: Climate Change, Immorality, and Victorian Anticipations of the Good Anthropocene," and "George Eliot and John Everett Millais: The Ethics and Aesthetics of Realism." The substantial book review section in each issue provides a good survey of recent studies in the discipline. Furthermore, *Victorian Studies* highlights conference papers from the annual conference of the North American Victorian Studies Association along with responses. Recommended for all academic libraries.

3367. *Western American Literature.* [ISSN: 0043-3462] 1966. q. USD 140 domestic; USD 164 foreign. Ed(s): Tom Lynch. University of Nebraska Press, 1111 Lincoln Mall, Lincoln, NE 68588; journals@unl.edu; https://www.nebraskapress.unl.edu. Refereed. *Indexed:* A22, AmHI, BRI, CBRI, Chicano, E01, MLA-IB. *Bk. rev.:* 14-18, 1-2 pages, signed. *Aud.:* Ac, Sa.

Western American Literature publishes literary criticism on any aspect of the literature of the American West, including interdisciplinary pieces with a literary focus. A recent focus of the journal includes "new approaches to literary and cultural studies more broadly, such as our groundbreaking work in ecocriticism and scholarly support for the Hispanic Literary Heritage Recovery Project." Issues generally contain three scholarly essays (ranging in length from 20 to 35 pages), 14 to 18 book reviews, and an occasional review essay. Recently published essays include "Performing the Empty Archive: Feeling and Public Lands in the Bundy Case and Percival Everett's *Grand Canyon, Inc.*," "Sounding Silence in *Sundown*: Survivance Ecology and John Joseph Mathews's Bildungsroman," and "The Indigenous Erotics of Riding Bareback, or, the West Has Always Been Queer." This journal's geographic focus gives it a distinctive niche within library collections. It should be considered for most academic and larger public libraries.

3368. *World Literature Today: your passport to great reading.* Formerly (until 1977): *Books Abroad.* [ISSN: 0196-3570] 1927. bi-m. USD 180 (print & online eds.)). Ed(s): Daniel Simon, Michelle Johnson. University of Oklahoma, 630 Parrington Oval, Ste 110, Norman, OK 73019; ou-pss@ou.edu; http://www.ou.edu/. Illus., index, adv. Refereed. Microform: PQC. Reprint: PSC. *Indexed:* A01, A22, AmHI, BAS, BRI, C37, CBRI, Chicano, MASUSE, MLA-IB. *Bk. rev.:* 150-250, 1/2-1 page, signed. *Aud.:* Ac.

This bimonthly journal published by the University of Oklahoma is concerned with contemporary world literature, and it features a variety of content of potential interest to academics and general readers alike. Issues feature essays on writers who work in several languages, original poetry and fiction, interviews, analysis of transnational issues, book reviews, travel writing, author profiles, and a column on children's literature. The journal welcomes interdisciplinary perspectives and, as a result, it features "coverage of the other arts, culture, and politics as [each] intersects with literature." Special sections are frequent, including a recent one titled "Alien Citizen Field Notes" written by Ladan Osman. This extremely accessible title is recommended for both academic and public libraries.

■ LITTLE MAGAZINES

See also Alternatives; Literary Reviews; and Literature sections.

Helen Georgas, Reference & Instruction Librarian and Assistant Professor, Brooklyn College of the City University of New York (CUNY), New York, NY

Introduction

Both oft-heard voices and voices that may not otherwise be heard continue to have their place in the hundreds of little magazines being published today. All of these little magazines are unified in their commitment to publishing exciting new writers alongside more established ones.

The world of small magazines is an extremely competitive one, however, and promising new publications such as *The American Reader, Cousin Corinne's Reminder,* and *Tweed's* (formerly *The Coffin Factory*), all of them beautifully produced, have recently ceased publication after a few years or only a few issues. This is where online-only publications such as *Two Serious Ladies,* which publishes work written exclusively by women, may have the advantage. Looking at the bright side, the increasing presence and success of online-only little magazines (with lower production costs) affirm that the desire to discover new writers is still thriving, now more than ever.

The titles presented here have proven themselves in the quality of their fiction, nonfiction, poetry, and artwork. The focus is on print publications, although many of these little magazines also feature work online. These little magazines have consistently produced excellent issues, with many of their stories, poems, and essays being reprinted in anthologies such as *Pushcart Prize: Best of the Small Presses, Best American Poetry, Best American Essays, Prize Stories: The O. Henry Awards, Best American Non-Required Reading,* and *Best American Short Stories.*

The aim of this list is to ensure that any library that decides to subscribe to one of the selected little magazines will be adding a valuable title to its collection. Sadly, this list is extremely selective, and there are still many other high-quality little magazines, both new and established, that have not been included. In acknowledging that we live in a time in which library budgets are increasingly limited, the focus is mainly on U.S. publications, with the exception of a handful of Canadian titles. In addition, publications that are more regional in focus, both in terms of the writing they produce and the audience for which they are intended, have largely been excluded.

Basic Periodicals

Ga: *A Public Space, Glimmer Train, Poetry* (Chicago), *Tin House;* Ac: *A Public Space, Glimmer Train, Poetry* (Chicago), *Tin House..*

Basic Abstracts and Indexes

PIO: Periodicals Index Online, Project MUSE; Research Library (ProQuest).

3369. ***A Public Space.*** [ISSN: 1558-965X] 2006. 3x/yr. USD 36 combined subscription domestic print & online eds.; USD 66 combined subscription elsewhere print & online eds. Ed(s): Megan Cummins, Brigid Hughes. A Public Space Literary Projects, Inc, 323 Dean St, Brooklyn, NY 11217; editors@apublicspace.org. Illus., adv. *Aud.:* Ga, Ac.

Founded by Brigid Hughes, a former editor with *The Paris Review, A Public Space* (*APS*) is a quarterly magazine of literature and culture that has published superlative fiction, essays, poetry, and artwork since its inception in 2006. Its aim is "to give voice to the twenty-first century," and it does. *APS* features the work of prominent American and international writers (Etel Adnan, Rae Armantrout, Kimiko Hahn, Kelly Link, Elena Poniatowska) alongside newer but fast-rising voices (Jai Chakrabarti, Katy Lederer). In addition to the excellent writing, each issue of *APS* is highly visual, including essays of images, illustrations, or photographs (in either black-and-white or color), along with additional, beautiful artwork embedded throughout the text, as well as featured on the cover. Recent issues have been themed-e.g., "Chance Encounters" and "The Other Interest"-the latter devoted to artists' work other than that primary to them (the fiction of painter Dorothea Tanning, for example).

Agni. See Literary Reviews section.

Alaska Quarterly Review. See Literary Reviews section.

The Antioch Review. See Literary Reviews section.

3370. ***Black Warrior Review.*** [ISSN: 0193-6301] 1974. s-a. USD 20; USD 12 per issue. Ed(s): Gail Aronson, Bronwyn Valentine. Black Warrior Review, Office of Student Media, The University of Alabama, PO Box 870170, Tuscaloosa, AL 35487. Adv. *Indexed:* AmHI, BRI, CBRI, MLA-IB. *Bk. rev.:* Number and length vary. *Aud.:* Ga, Ac.

Black Warrior Review publishes poetry, fiction, nonfiction, and art by prize-winning authors alongside up-and-coming ones. Each issue includes a chapbook from a nationally known poet, as well as work (via beautiful full-color plates) by a featured artist. Stories and poems that have appeared in *Black Warrior Review* have been reprinted in many of the major anthologies. *Black Warrior Review* is published twice a year by the University of Alabama.

Callaloo. See African American section.

3371. ***The Common.*** [ISSN: 2160-1216] 2011. s-a. USD 24 domestic; USD 40 domestic in AK, HI & Canada; USD 50 foreign. Ed(s): Jennifer Acker, Diana Babineau. The Common Foundation, Frost Library, Amherst College, Amherst, MA 01002; info@thecommononline.org. *Aud.:* Ga, Ac.

The Common publishes fiction, poetry, essays, and artwork that convey a strong sense of place. It is a relatively new journal, now in its fifth year, and is published twice a year (spring/April and fall/October) by Amherst College. Each issue of *The Common* opens with a short prologue (called "The Common Statement") written by the magazine's editor, Jennifer Acker, and the remaining pages are divided into sections: "Fiction," "Images," "Essays," and "Poetry." Some issues also include works in translation from a feature country (China, for example). The writing is uniformly excellent, featuring work by both established and new writers, and each issue is elegantly designed and beautifully produced. Recent established writers and artists who have contributed to *The Common* include Teju Cole, Jonathan Freeman, and Mazen Kerbaj, among others.

Conjunctions. See Literary Reviews section.

3372. ***The Cream City Review.*** [ISSN: 0884-3457] 1975. s-a. USD 22; USD 12 newsstand/cover; CAD 14 newsstand/cover. Ed(s): Mollie Boutell, Loretta McCormick. University of Wisconsin at Milwaukee, English Department, PO Box 413, Milwaukee, WI 53201; http://www4.uwm.edu/letsci/english/. Adv. Refereed. *Indexed:* AmHI, MLA-IB. *Bk. rev.:* 1-3. *Aud.:* Ga, Ac.

Cream City Review was founded in 1975 and recently celebrated its 40th year in print. Each issue features fiction, poetry, creative nonfiction, and (occasionally) comics and full-color artwork, that is both energetic and "pushes the boundaries." With its most recent issue, *Cream City Review* debuted its new "genre," which the editors describe as "text that stretch[es] the boundaries of print-digital hybridity." The magazine also includes reviews of contemporary literature, criticism, and author interviews. *Cream City Review* prides itself on featuring the work of both established and previously unpublished writers, many of whom are M.F.A. candidates or recent M.F.A. graduates. Each issue includes a multi-color glossy cover of original artwork, a feature for which the magazine has become known. *Cream City Review* is published twice a year by graduate students at the University of Wisconsin-Milwaukee.

3373. ***Ecotone.*** [ISSN: 1553-1775] 2005. s-a. USD 39.95 (Individuals, USD 16.95; USD 12.95 per issue). Ed(s): David Gessner, Katie O?Reilly. University of North Carolina at Wilmington, Department of Creative Writing, 601 S College Rd, Wilmington, NC 28403; registrar@uncw.edu; http://uncw.edu/writers/. Refereed. *Indexed:* MLA-IB. *Aud.:* Ga, Ac.

Ecotone is a semiannual journal that "seeks to reimagine place." Each issue contains work that spans the disciplines, ranging from the literary to the scientific. Since its founding in 2005 (the magazine recently celebrated its tenth anniversary), *Ecotone* has quickly established a national reputation for publishing high-quality fiction, nonfiction, poetry, and artwork by both well-known and newer writers and artists. Notable recent contributors have included Steve Almond, Paul Lisicky, Jamie Quatro, and Claire Vaye Watkins. Many of the issues are themed, and recent themes have included "Sound" and "Sustenance." Work in *Ecotone* has been reprinted in *Best American Essays, Best American Short Stories, Best American Poetry, Best American Science and Nature Writing, The Pushcart Prize,* and *The O. Henry Prize Stories. Ecotone* is published at the University of North Carolina-Wilmington.

3374. ***Five Points: a journal of literature & art.*** [ISSN: 1088-8500] 1996. 3x/yr. USD 21; USD 10 per issue. Georgia State University, Department of English, PO Box 3970, Atlanta, GA 30302; engsli@gsu.edu; http://english.gsu.edu. Illus., adv. Refereed. *Indexed:* AmHI, MLA-IB. *Aud.:* Ga, Ac.

Five Points features short stories, poetry, essays, artwork, and interviews, and publishes work by both established and emerging writers. Each issue contains a "Portfolio" section of visual art, with images reprinted on high-quality color pages and, often, a short statement by the artist. Recent notable contributors include Billy Collins, Andre Dubus III, Bobbie Ann Mason, and Sharon Olds. Work featured in *Five Points* is regularly reprinted in anthologies such as *Pushcart Prize: Best of the Small Presses* and *Best American Essays. Five Points* is published three times a year by Georgia State University.

The Georgia Review. See Literary Reviews section.

The Gettysburg Review. See Literary Reviews section.

3375. ***Glimmer Train.*** [ISSN: 1055-7520] 1991. 3x/yr. USD 38 domestic; USD 48 Canada; USD 62 elsewhere. Glimmer Train Press, Inc., PO Box 80430, Portland, OR 97280; http://www.glimmertrain.com. Sample. *Indexed:* AmHI, MLA-IB. *Aud.:* Ga, Ac.

Glimmer Train is a quarterly short story journal founded by two sisters, Susan Burmeister-Brown and Linda B. Swanson Davies, who are known for their commitment to publishing great stories by emerging writers. Since its inception in 1990, *Glimmer Train* has risen to national prominence, yet each issue feels incredibly welcoming and deeply personal. The journal features eight to 12 stories by both "luminaries" and "fresh new voices" selected from unsolicited submissions, and each piece begins with a short author biography, a photograph of the writer as a child, and an endearing caption penned by the author. In addition to the stories, interviews with well-known writers such as Jonathan Lethem, Tom Franklin, and Beth Ann Fennelly, just to name a recent few, are also included, as is "Silenced Voices," an essay about an international author or journalist who has been imprisoned or killed because of his or her writing. Stories published in *Glimmer Train* have been represented in recent editions of *Pushcart Prize: Best of the Small Presses, New Stories from the Midwest, The PEN/O. Henry Prize Stories, New Stories from the South, Best of the West,* and *Best American Short Stories. Glimmer Train* also sponsors a number of fiction prizes throughout the year, and publishes a supplement called "Writers Ask," in which well-respected authors talk about their techniques, their personal and professional challenges, and what they teach their creative-writing students.

3376. ***Guernica.*** 2004. s-m. Ed(s): Riederer Rachel, Hillary Brenhouse. Guernica Magazine, 81 Prospect St, Brooklyn, NY 11201; publisher@guernicamag.com. Adv. *Aud.:* Ga, Ac.

Guernica is a bimonthly online magazine of art and politics that has risen to national prominence since its founding in 2004. Claire Messud has called it "the most important online intellectual and literary journal in America today." Each issue of *Guernica* features reportage, criticism, and first-person narrative (via a "Features" section), along with fiction, poetry, visual art, and interviews. It regularly publishes the work of internationally acclaimed writers such as Chimamanda Ngozi Adichie and Dinaw Mengestu, and includes much work in translation. *Guernica* is also committed to publishing younger writers and launching new voices.

3377. ***Gulf Coast (Houston): a journal of literature and fine arts.*** Formerly (until 198?): *Domestic Crude.* [ISSN: 0896-2251] 1987. s-a. USD 16 domestic; USD 28 foreign; USD 10 per issue domestic. Ed(s): Martin Rock, Adrienne G Perry. University of Houston, Department of English, 3687 Cullen Blvd Rm 205, Houston, TX 77204-3004; http://www.uh.edu/class/english/. Refereed. *Indexed:* AmHI, MLA-IB. *Bk. rev.:* 4-5. *Aud.:* Ga, Ac.

Gulf Coast was founded by Donald Barthelme and Phillip Lopate in 1983 and is published in April and October of each year by the University of Houston's English Department. Each issue features fiction, nonfiction, poetry, and reviews, along with, occasionally, a roundtable with various authors and artists in conversation on topics such as contemporary female writers. *Gulf Coast* is also deeply committed to publishing visual art, and recent issues have included increased art and art criticism content. Thus, each volume now includes a section called "Art Lies," which highlights the work of one or two artists (via stunning full-color images), along with essays and conversations about these and other artists' works. The writing in *Gulf Coast* is uniformly fantastic, and within its pages you'll find the work of authors such as Traci Brimhall, Stuart Dybek, and Anis Shivani. The work of emerging voices is also included (Leslie Jamison and Ocean Vuong, for example). Beautifully produced, this is a journal that is as interesting to look at as it is to read.

The Harvard Review. See Literary Reviews section.

3378. ***Indiana Review.*** Formerly (until 1982): *Indiana Writes.* [ISSN: 0738-386X] 1976. s-a. USD 23 (Individuals, USD 20; USD 12 per issue). Ed(s): Peter Kispert. Indiana Review, Ballantine Hall 465, 1020 E Kirkwood Ave, Indiana University, Bloomington, IN 47405. Illus. Refereed. Microform: PQC. *Indexed:* AmHI, MLA-IB. *Bk. rev.:* 3-10. *Aud.:* Ga, Ac.

Indiana Review is a biannual literary magazine dedicated to publishing "well-crafted and lively" short stories, poetry, and nonfiction by mostly emerging but also established writers. The magazine has featured younger writers such as Halimah Marcus, while also publishing well-known writers such as Amiri Baraka and Patricia Smith. Each issue features six to ten stories, a wealth of poetry, and one or two essays. Recent issues have included a section called "Special Folio," featuring the work of a selection of visual artists or writers on a particular theme ("Graphic Memoir" and "Understanding Readiness" are two recent examples). Past and more recent works by contributors to *Indiana Review* have appeared in all the major anthologies, confirming its long-held reputation as a little magazine of excellence. Now in its 39th year, *Indiana Review* continues to be edited and managed by Indiana University graduate students. *Indiana Review*'s web site also includes a podcast called "The Bluecast," in which writers published in the magazine read their work.

The Iowa Review. See Literary Reviews section.

3379. ***Little Star: a journal of poetry and prose.*** [ISSN: 2151-8637] 2009. a. USD 18.95 per issue domestic; USD 24.95 per issue foreign. Ed(s): Ann Kjellberg. Ann Kjellberg, Ed. & Pub., 107 Bank St, New York, NY 10014; editor@littlestarjournal.com. *Aud.:* Ga, Ac.

Little Star was founded in New York City in 2009 by editors Ann Kjellberg (formerly of *The New York Review of Books* and Farrar, Straus, & Giroux) and Melissa Green, and is an annual journal of poetry and prose. In its short history, it has quickly risen to become one of the most exciting new little magazines in the country. Looking through the list of its contributors will undoubtedly impress: Lydia Davis, Per Petterson, and W. G. Sebald, just to name a recent few. In addition to the print publication, *Little Star* publishes a mobile-mini magazine, *Little Star Weekly,* available as an app. *Little Star Weekly*'s issues have also included work by well-known writers such as Denis Johnson, Jamaica Kincaid, and Joy Williams.

3380. ***The Malahat Review: essential poetry & fiction.*** [ISSN: 0025-1216] 1967. q. CAD 35 domestic; CAD 40 United States; CAD 45 elsewhere. Ed(s): John Barton. University of Victoria, Stn CSC, PO Box 1700, Victoria, BC V8W 2Y2, Canada; http://www.uvic.ca. Illus., adv. Refereed. Microform: PQC. *Indexed:* A22, BAS, C37, MLA-IB. *Bk. rev.:* 5-6. *Aud.:* Ga, Ac.

The Malahat Review was founded in 1967 and is one of Canada's leading literary journals. Its focus is on Canadian and international fiction and poetry, publishing work by established writers right next to work by promising new ones. Issues of *The Malahat Review* regularly include one or two creative nonfiction pieces and reviews of recently published Canadian poetry, fiction, and literary nonfiction. On occasion, *The Malahat Review* also publishes interviews, essays, and issues on a single theme or author. Over the years, many pieces published in *The Malahat Review* have won Canada's Western Magazine Award and National Magazine Award. *The Malahat Review* is published by the University of Victoria, and the cover of each issue features full-color artwork culled from the university's own collection.

Michigan Quarterly Review. See Literary Reviews section.

The Missouri Review. See Literary Reviews section.

3381. ***New England Review.*** Former titles (until 1990): *New England Review and Bread Loaf Quarterly;* (until 1982): *New England Review.* [ISSN: 1053-1297] 1978. q. USD 45. Ed(s): Carolyn Kuebler. Middlebury College, Attn: Orders, Middlebury, VT 05753; http://www.middlebury.edu. Microform: PQC. *Indexed:* A01, A22, AmHI, BRI, CBRI, MLA-IB. *Bk. rev.:* 1. *Aud.:* Ga, Ac.

New England Review (*NER*) prides itself on publishing serious work, and includes both traditional and experimental poetry, fiction, and nonfiction. Regular nonfiction sections include "Literary Lives," "Testimonies," "Revaluations," "Rediscoveries," and "Investigations," among others, which feature works in translation, criticism, and reviews in arts, culture, and literature. Recent contributors include Kim Addonizio, Alex Dimitrov, Ursula Hegi, Brenda Shaughnessy, and G. C. Waldrep. Works from the *NER* continue to be regularly featured in all of the "best of" anthologies, including *Pushcart,*

O. Henry, and *Best American*. *New England Review* was founded in 1978, is published four times per year by Middlebury College, and has a solid history of publishing challenging yet stellar work.

3382. ***One Story.*** 2002. q. USD 21 domestic; USD 23 in Canada & Mexico; USD 27 elsewhere. One Story, 232 3rd St, #A108, Brooklyn, NY 11215. *Aud.:* Ga, Ac.

One Story is a unique literary magazine founded in 2002 by Maribeth Batcha and Hannah Tinti. *One Story* publishes a single story every three weeks, in a simply designed but appealing small-format print issue. In keeping with its name and its quest to seek out and publish exciting new writing, *One Story* only publishes any given writer once. Since 2002, *One Story* has published over 200 writers, and is now one of the largest circulating literary magazines in the country, with over 15,000 readers. Recent notable contributors include Charles Bock, Bonnie Jo Campbell, Joyce Carol Oates, and Victoria Redel. Many *One Story* stories have been awarded Pushcart Prizes, and stories are regularly cited in the various *Best American* and *PEN/O. Henry* anthologies.

3383. ***Pank.*** [ISSN: 1935-7133] 2007. a. USD 12 per issue. Ed(s): John Gosslee, Ashley M Jones. Michigan Technological University, Department of Humanities, 1400 Townsend Dr, Houghton, MI 49931; humanities@mtu.edu; http://www.hu.mtu.edu/hu_dept/undergraduate/stc/stc.php. *Indexed:* AmHI. *Aud.:* Ga, Ac.

Pank magazine was founded in 2006 by then-editors Roxane Gay and M. Bartley Seigel, and publishes twice-yearly issues devoted to emerging and experimental poetry and prose (both fiction and creative nonfiction). Each issue is beautifully designed, with original full-color artwork featured on every cover, and with the interior work printed on high-quality glossy paper. Under the helm of its new editors, John Gosslee, Chris Campanioni, and Ashley M. Jones, *Pank* continues to be one of the most interesting and innovative little magazines in the country today. A valuable addition to any library seeking to expose its patrons to the work of up-and-coming writers.

The Paris Review. See Literary Reviews section.

Ploughshares. See Fiction: General/Mystery and Detective/General section.

3384. ***Poetry (Chicago).*** [ISSN: 0032-2032] 1912. 11x/yr. USD 35 domestic; USD 47 foreign; GBP 3 newsstand/cover United Kingdom. Ed(s): Don Share. The Poetry Foundation, 61 West Superior St, Chicago, IL 60654; info@poetryfoundation.org; http://www.poetrymagazine.org. Adv. Vol. ends: Oct/Sep. Microform: PMC; PQC. *Indexed:* A22, B01, BRI, CBRI, MLA-IB. *Bk. rev.:* 2-11. *Aud.:* Ga, Ac.

Publishing a new issue every month since its founding in 1912, *Poetry* is one of the most important poetry magazines in the country. In its first year of existence, it presented the work of Ezra Pound, William Carlos Williams, and William Butler Yeats. Today, it continues that trend by regularly publishing new work by the most recognized poets, such as Mary Jo Ban, Ben Lerner, and Robert Pinsky, to name a recent few. Nonetheless, its primary commitment "is still to discover new voices," and in keeping with that, it has recently featured the work of up-and-coming poets such as Leah Umansky and Ocean Vuong. In addition to the poetry itself, every issue includes a "Comment" section, featuring essays and book reviews. Other occasional features include a Q & A section (conversations with poets about their work) and "The View from Here" (artists and professionals from outside the poetry world writing about their experience of poetry). The complete 100-year run of the magazine is available online. However, the print publication is superlative and definitely worth subscribing to. In 2014, *Poetry* magazine won the Ellie Award for General Excellence in Literature, Science and Politics.

3385. ***Prairie Fire: a Canadian magazine of new writing.*** Formerly (until 1982): *Writers News Manitoba.* [ISSN: 0821-1124] 1978. q. CAD 30 domestic; CAD 40 United States; CAD 50 elsewhere. Ed(s): Janine Tschuncky, Andris Taskans. Prairie Fire Press, Inc., 423 - 100 Arthur St, Winnipeg, MB R3B 1H3, Canada; prfire@mts.net; http://www.prairiefire.ca/. Adv. *Indexed:* BRI, C37, MLA-IB. *Aud.:* Ga, Ac.

Prairie Fire was founded in 1978, making it one of Canada's oldest literary magazines. It is an award-winning quarterly published in Manitoba, and features writing both regional and national in scope. *Prairie Fire* is known for publishing innovative writing, and includes poetry, short stories, and personal essays. Work in *Prairie Fire* may be by a renowned Canadian author, or by a young new writer being published for the first time, perhaps after having won one of the magazine's three annual writing awards in poetry, fiction, and creative nonfiction. Occasionally, *Prairie Fire* will publish a special issue. For example, the most recent issue was themed "Suffrage 100," and featured short pieces reflecting on the 100th anniversary of (some) Manitoba women getting the vote. The beautiful full-color covers feature work primarily by Manitoba artists. Pieces published in *Prairie Fire* (fiction, poetry, personal journalism) have won Canada's National Magazine Awards.

Prairie Schooner. See Literary Reviews section.

3386. ***Prism International.*** Formerly (until 1964): *Prism.* [ISSN: 0032-8790] 1959. q. USD 35 domestic; USD 40 United States; USD 45 elsewhere. University of British Columbia, Faculty of Arts, Creative Writing Program, A240 1866 Main Mall, Vancouver, BC V6T 1Z1, Canada; http://www.arts.ubc.ca. Adv. Microform: PQC. Reprint: PSC. *Indexed:* A22, MLA-IB. *Aud.:* Ga, Ac.

PRISM International was founded in 1959 and is a quarterly magazine that aims to publish "the best in contemporary writing and translation from Canada and around the world." The focus is on fiction and poetry, but *Prism* also includes, on occasion, creative nonfiction and writing in translation. *PRISM* publishes both new voices and more established writers, and has a solid history as one of Canada's premier literary journals. Writing from *PRISM* has been featured in *Best American Stories, Best American Essays,* and *The Journey Prize Stories,* one of Canada's most prestigious anthologies.

Shenandoah (Online). See Literary Reviews section.

3387. ***Slice Magazine.*** [ISSN: 1938-6923] 2007. s-a. Free to members; Non-members, USD 25. Ed(s): Elizabeth Blachman. Slice Literary, Inc, 920 8th Ave, Ste 1, Brooklyn, NY 11215. Illus. *Aud.:* Ga, Ac.

Slice, a Brooklyn-based magazine, was launched in 2007 by book editors Maria Gagliano and Celia Johnson and has since garnered rave reviews from the literary community. *Slice* "aims to bridge the gap between emerging and established authors by offering a space where both are published side-by-side." In each issue, a specific theme becomes the catalyst for articles and interviews from both renowned writers and lesser-known voices. Recent themes have included "Hope" and "Resistance." Along with these themed pieces, *Slice* publishes fiction and poetry by writers who show promise in becoming tomorrow's literary stars. The magazine is published twice each year, in March and September. The list of recent notable authors either published or interviewed in *Slice* reads like a literary Who's Who: Ron Carlson, Porochista Khakpour, Elissa Schappell, Dani Shapiro, Terese Svoboda, Justin Taylor, and Adele Waldman, just to name a recent few. *Slice* is both beautiful to look at and compelling to read.

The Southern Review. See Literary Reviews section.

The Threepenny Review. See Literary Reviews section.

3388. ***Tin House.*** [ISSN: 1541-521X] 1999. q. USD 34.95 combined subscription domestic (print & online eds.); USD 49.95 combined subscription Canada (print & online eds.); USD 64.95 combined subscription elsewhere (print & online eds.)). Tin House, PO Box 10500, Portland, OR 97296; info@tinhouse.com. Illus., adv. *Indexed:* AmHI. *Bk. rev.:* 1-4. *Aud.:* Ga, Ac.

Tin House is a quarterly literary journal of fiction, nonfiction, and poetry based in Brooklyn, N.Y., and Portland, Oregon. Each issue is themed, and recent themes have included "Faith," "Winter Reading," "Theft," "Summer Reading," and "Rejection." *Tin House* is committed to publishing both established and emerging writers. Recent notable contributors include Dorothy Allison, Ann Carson, Helen Phillips, Marilynne Robinson, Darcey Steinke, Claire Vaye Watkins, and Joy Williams. Within each issue you'll also find a "Lost & Found" section, featuring short essays about little-known or forgotten older published books, or books out of print. Many issues also feature interviews (Emma Komlos-Hrobsky interviewing Louise Erdrich, for example) and "Readable Feast" (an often humorous food-themed essay, followed by a recipe). Since its founding in 1999, *Tin House* has firmly established itself as one of the best literary journals in the country, and its stories, essays, and poems are regularly anthologized in *Pushcart Prizes: Best of the New Presses, Best American Short Stories*, and *The O. Henry Prize Stories*, among others.

The Virginia Quarterly Review (Online). See Literary Reviews section.

3389. *West Branch.* [ISSN: 0149-6441] 1977. 3x/yr. USD 16 (Individuals, USD 10; USD 6 per issue). Ed(s): G C Waldrep. Bucknell University, 701, Moore Ave, Lewisburg, PA 17837; http://www.bucknell.edu. Illus., adv. Refereed. *Indexed:* AmHI, BRI, MLA-IB. *Bk. rev.:* Number and length vary. *Aud.:* Ga, Ac.

West Branch is a thrice-yearly magazine with a focus on poetry and fiction (two or three stories in each issue). It also includes book reviews and, occasionally, essays and works in translation. Founded in 1977, *West Branch* is edited by G. C. Waldrep and published by the Stadler Center for Poetry at Bucknell University. *West Branch* also publishes *West Branch Wired,* a quarterly extension of the print magazine. The poetry, fiction, and creative nonfiction included in *West Branch Wired* are distinct from the print publication and therefore original. Book reviews and columns run in both *WBW* and the print magazine. Each full-color cover of the print publication features compelling original artwork, accompanied by a brief biography and an artist's statement.

3390. *Willow Springs.* [ISSN: 0739-1277] 1977. s-a. USD 18; USD 10 per issue. Ed(s): Megan Rowe, Samuel Ligon. Eastern Washington University, 125 Tawanka Hall, Cheney, WA 99004; https://www.ewu.edu/. Adv. *Indexed:* AmHI. *Aud.:* Ga, Ac.

Willow Springs was founded in 1977 and is published twice yearly, and each issue includes fiction, nonfiction, and poetry, as well as interviews with important contemporary authors such as Kim Addonizio and D. A. Powell. *Willow Springs* also publishes work in translation, giving it an international scope. For over 30 years, *Willow Springs* has sought out and published the best writing by both fresh and established voices. Recent contributors include Hadara Bar-Nadav, James Kimbrell, Genevieve Plunkett, Ed Skoog, and Jess Walter. In addition, each year's covers (for both issues) showcase full-color work by a particular visual artist. For example, the most recent issue features the work of photographer Marta Berens.

The Yale Review. See Literary Reviews section.

Zoetrope: all-story. See Fiction: General/Mystery and Detective/General section.

■ MANAGEMENT AND ADMINISTRATION

See also Business; Finance; Labor and Industrial Relations sections.

Joan Plungis, Reference and Instruction Librarian, University of Dayton

Introduction

According to Peter F. Drucker (1909-2005), a seminal theorist and prolific writer in the field, "management pertains to every human effort that brings together in one organization people of diverse knowledge and skills." Managers in both the for-profit and nonprofit arenas share similar responsibilities, he wrote, "among them defining the right strategies and goals, developing people, measuring performance, and marketing the organization's services." (*The Essential Drucker: The Best of Sixty Years of Peter Drucker's Essential Writings on Management.* New York: HarperCollins, 2001, pp. 7-8.) Planning, organizing, leading, directing, and controlling are functions traditionally ascribed to management, but the field comprises numerous subdisciplines, including management science, organization studies, strategic planning, decision-making, leadership studies, human resource management, cross-cultural and international management, quality management, supply chain management, knowledge management, logistics management, crisis management, product innovation management, management communication, management research, manufacturing and service operations management, and project management.

The selection of management journals and magazines discussed in this section include scholarly, peer-reviewed sources as well as publications intended for practitioners and general readers. They offer a mix of theoretical articles, empirical research reports and pragmatic advice, and article summaries and book reviews that can be easily processed by busy professionals. Most of the publications are now available in both print and online formats. Many journals also offer open-access options to authors, who for an additional fee can make their articles available online to both subscribers and non-subscribers of the journal. Early publication online options are also common, under which the version of record of an article is posted online before appearing in a journal issue.

Basic Periodicals

For academic libraries, a basic collection would include: *Academy of Management Journal, Academy of Management Review, Administrative Science Quarterly, British Journal of Management, Decision Sciences: Information Systems, Operations & Supply Chain Management, International Entrepreneurship and Management Journal, Journal of International Management, Journal of Management, Journal of Management Studies, Journal of Operations Management, Journal of Supply Chain Management, Knowledge Management Research & Practice, Long Range Planning: International Journal of Strategic Management, Management Decision, Management Science, M I T Sloan Management Review, Organization Science, Project Management Journal, Quality Management Journal, Strategic Management Journal.*

For public libraries with more general readers, a basic collection would include: *Academy of Management Perspectives; Business Strategy Review; Ivey Business Journal: improving the practice of management; Interface; Journal of Business Strategy; M I T Sloan Management Review; Organizational Dynamics; S A M Advanced Management Journal; Strategy & Leadership; Strategy + Business.*

Basic Abstracts and Indexes

ABI/INFORM; Business Abstracts with Full Text; Business Source Complete.

Interfaces. See *INFORMS Journal on Applied Analytics.*.

3391. *A P I C S.* Formerly (until 2005): *A P I C S - The Performance Advantage.* [ISSN: 1946-0384] 1991. q. Individuals, USD 93; Members, USD 20. Ed(s): Jennifer Proctor. A P I C S, 8430 West Bryn Mawr Ave, Ste 1000, Chicago, IL 60631; service@apics.org; http://www.apics.org. Illus., index, adv. *Indexed:* A22. *Aud.:* Ac, Sa.

Published and maintained by APICS (originally the American Production and Inventory Control Society), *APICS* magazine is available to members of the trade organization via digital or print subscription and to nonmembers via print subscription. Five articles per month may be downloaded for free on the magazine website. *APICS* is targeted to an audience of busy practitioners in the fields of resource management, manufacturing, production, and inventory control. The publication features short, timely articles written by seasoned, knowledgeable professionals who share successful innovative ideas, along with trends, important changes, events, and news in the field of supply chain and operations management. Topics cover real-world strategies for inventory, materials, production, and supply chain management, planning and scheduling, purchasing, logistics, warehousing, and transportation and logistics. Recommended for academic libraries that support undergraduate business students and public libraries that support supply chain and operations management professionals. URL: http://www.apics.org/apics-for-individuals/apics-magazine-home

3392. ***The Academy of Management Annals.*** [ISSN: 1941-6520] 2008. s-a. USD 230 domestic; USD 260 elsewhere; USD 350 combined subscription domestic (print & online eds.)). Academy of Management, 235 Elm Rd, PO Box 3020, Briarcliff Manor, NY 10510; szaid@pace.edu; http://www.aomonline.org. Adv. Sample. Reprint: PSC. *Indexed:* B01. *Aud.:* Ac.

Highly regarded and ranked, *The Academy of Management Annals* provides critical reviews of the research undertaken and written by leaders in management. Its mission is to summarize studies and concepts, identify potential problems, and advance discussions for further research. This publication is written for academic scholars in management and allied fields, such as the sociology of organizations and organizational psychology. Highly recommended for all academic libraries. URL: http://aom.org/annals/

3393. ***Academy of Management Journal.*** Formerly (until 1963): *The Journal of the Academy of Management.* [ISSN: 0001-4273] 1957. bi-m. USD 230 domestic; USD 260 elsewhere; USD 350 combined subscription domestic (print & online eds.)). Ed(s): Jason D Shaw. Academy of Management, 235 Elm Rd, PO Box 3020, Briarcliff Manor, NY 10510; connect@aom.org; http://annals.aom.org/. Illus., index, adv. Refereed. Vol. ends: Dec. Microform: PQC. *Indexed:* A22, B01, BAS, ErgAb, IBSS. *Aud.:* Ac, Sa.

Published by the Academy of Management, the preeminent organization for management and organization scholars, the peer-reviewed, scholarly articles in the highly cited and highly respected *Academy of Management Journal* provide original empirical research that tests, extends, or builds management theory and contributes to management practice. The research presented in these articles is often cited in *The New York Times, The Economist, The Wall Street Journal,* and *Fortune.* Written by international scholars and academics, the articles cover a broad spectrum of important management areas and are indispensable reading for management scholars, executive leadership, and graduate business students. This bimonthly journal is an essential title for academic libraries; it is also recommended for corporate libraries interested in cutting-edge awareness, and large public libraries. URL: http://aom.org/amj/

3394. ***Academy of Management Learning and Education.*** [ISSN: 1537-260X] 2002. q. USD 180 domestic; USD 210 elsewhere; USD 260 combined subscription domestic print & online eds. Ed(s): William M Foster. Academy of Management, 235 Elm Rd, PO Box 3020, Briarcliff Manor, NY 10510; connect@aom.org; http://annals.aom.org/. Adv. Sample. Refereed. *Indexed:* B01. *Bk. rev.:* 3-5, 1,300-3,000 words, signed. *Aud.:* Ac, Sa.

Focused on the teaching and learning process in management, the frequently cited and well respected *Academy of Management Learning & Education* presents theory, empirical research, reviews, critiques, and other resources. Its scope includes schools and universities as well as businesses and public and non-profit organizations. Each issue comprises four sections: "Research & Reviews"; "Essays & Dialogues"; "Exemplary Contributions"; and "Books & Resource Reviews." The peer-reviewed articles found in the "Research & Reviews" section contain theoretical models and reviews, quantitative and qualitative research, and literature reviews. The "Essays & Dialogues" section contains original essays or critiques of trends or issues in teaching, learning, and management education, and dialogues that respond to previously published research. The "Exemplary Contributions" section contains invited papers from prominent scholars and practitioners. "Books & Resource Reviews" covers materials relevant to individual learning and management education, including books, videos, simulations, and exercises. Article topics range from group and individual learning behaviors to leadership development, to social entrepreneurship education. These interdisciplinary articles would be of interest to scholars, academic educators, deans, directors, and administrators as well as policy-makers, practitioners, and consultants involved in management training and development in the public and private sectors. Published quarterly, this title is essential for academic libraries with business programs and for corporate collections interested in training and development. URL: http://aom.org/AMLE/

3395. ***The Academy of Management Perspectives.*** Former titles (until 2006): *Academy of Management Executive;* (until 1993): *Executive;* (until 1990): *Academy of Management Executive.* [ISSN: 1558-9080] 1987. q. USD 260 combined subscription per issue domestic print & online eds.; USD 290 combined subscription per issue foreign print & online eds. Ed(s): Mike Wright, Phillip H Phan. Academy of Management, 235 Elm Rd, PO Box 3020, Briarcliff Manor, NY 10510; connect@aom.org; http://annals.aom.org/. Illus., adv. Sample. Refereed. *Indexed:* A22, B01, BRI, IBSS. *Aud.:* Ac, Sa.

The need to keep abreast of new knowledge in the specialized sub-fields of management is important. The mission of *The Academy of Management Perspectives* is to "synthesize and translate theoretical and empirical evidence found in specialized sub-fields of management" for the non-specialist. The well-respected and frequently cited peer-reviewed articles, written by experts in the field, consist of (1) reviews of existing knowledge in the field; (2) integration of theories and empirical evidence to present new ideas with provocative perspectives; and (3) integration of management theory and research with advances in other disciplines. The arrangement of articles within the publication follows two formats: a thematic format in the "Symposium" section and individual articles in the "Articles" section, both with well-documented lists of references for further consultation. Articles are written for other academics, executives, consultants, and students, and their language is accessible to non-specialists in the field. Published quarterly, this journal is essential for academic, corporate, and larger public libraries. URL: http://aom.org/amp/

3396. ***Academy of Management Review.*** Supersedes in part (in 1976): *Academy of Management Journal.* [ISSN: 0363-7425] 1963. q. USD 350 combined subscription domestic print & online eds.; USD 380 combined subscription elsewhere print & online eds. Ed(s): Jay Barney. Academy of Management, 235 Elm Rd, PO Box 3020, Briarcliff Manor, NY 10510; connect@aom.org; http://annals.aom.org/. Illus., index, adv. Sample. Refereed. Vol. ends: Oct. Microform: PQC. *Indexed:* A22, B01, BRI, IBSS. *Bk. rev.:* Number and length vary, signed. *Aud.:* Ac, Sa.

The preeminent, highly cited, well-respected *Academy of Management Review* published by the Academy of Management features peer-reviewed, theory-based conceptual papers that advance the understanding of management and organizations. Topics in the "Articles" section challenge conventional wisdom of organizations and their roles in society. The "Dialogue" section responds to previously published research. The recently expanded *AMR* book reviews section, "What Inspires the Academy: Book Reviews and Beyond," features bibliographical essays by leading academic scholars and scholar-practitioners. This quarterly journal is essential for all academic libraries and is recommended for large public libraries. URL: http://aom.org/amr/

3397. ***Administrative Science Quarterly.*** [ISSN: 0001-8392] 1956. q. USD 465 (print & online eds.)). Ed(s): Henrich R Greve. Sage Publications, Inc., 2455 Teller Rd, Thousand Oaks, CA 91320; info@sagepub.com; http://www.sagepub.com. Illus., index, adv. Sample. Refereed. Vol. ends: Dec. Microform: PQC. Reprint: PSC. *Indexed:* A22, B01, BAS, BRI, IBSS, P61, SSA. *Bk. rev.:* 3-5, 500-2,000 words, signed. *Aud.:* Ac, Sa.

Owned and managed by the Samuel Curtis Johnson Graduate School of Management at Cornell University, the highly ranked and frequently cited *Administrative Science Quarterly* makes available empirical investigations and theoretical analysis in the social processes of administration. The peer-reviewed research papers seek to "advance the understanding of management, organizations, and organizing" of teams, organizations, government agencies, and markets. Interdisciplinary in nature, the papers incorporate research from organizational behavior, sociology, psychology, strategic management, economics, industrial relations, and public policy. The journal publishes new and evolving work from the best dissertations, as well as the work of established scholars. It publishes qualitative papers as well as quantitative work and purely theoretical papers. The quarterly publication also provides in-depth book reviews for notable books in the field, as well as a convenient listing of recently published books in the field for current awareness. Represented in a large number of business, academic, and general indexing and abstracting services, this title is highly recommended for academic libraries and large public libraries. URL: www.sagepub.com/journals/Journal202065

3398. ***Asia Pacific Journal of Management.*** [ISSN: 0217-4561] 1983. q. EUR 720 (print & online eds.)). Ed(s): Jane Lu. Springer New York LLC, 233 Spring St, New York, NY 10013; customerservice@springer.com; http://www.springer.com. Adv. Sample. Refereed. Reprint: PSC. *Indexed:* A22, B01, BAS, BRI, E01. *Aud.:* Ac, Sa.

Asia Pacific Journal of Management is the official journal of the Asia Academy of Management. It publishes empirical and conceptual papers written by scholars and researchers on key management and organizational trends in the Asia-Pacific region, including the Pacific Rim countries and mainland Asia. This peer-reviewed journal is published quarterly, with one or more issue each year focused on a single topic; the most recent special issue focuses on the development of dragon multinationals. The journal solicits papers that develop, test, replicate, or refute concepts and theories related to the question, "What determines firm success?" Recent article topics include Chinese investments in Africa; development of human resource management in Vietnam; and the role of trust in institutional distance and knowledge acquisition in international buyer-supplier relationships. The articles in this journal will be of interest to scholars, researchers, students, and practitioners. Highly recommended for academic libraries that support business programs. URL: http://link.springer.com/journal/10490

3399. *Associations Now.* Former titles (until 2005): *Association Management;* Which incorporated (in 1963): *A S A E News;* (in 1963): *Here's How;* (until 1956): *American Trade Association Executives. Journal; American Society of Association Executives. Journal.* [ISSN: 1557-7562] 1949. bi-m. Free to members; Non-members, USD 60. Ed(s): Lisa Junker, Samantha Whitehorne. American Society of Association Executives, 1575 I St, NW, Washington, DC 20005; editorial@asaecenter.org; http://www.asaecenter.org. Illus., index, adv. Vol. ends: Dec. Microform: PQC. *Indexed:* A22, ATI, B01, B03, BRI, C42. *Bk. rev.:* Number and length vary. *Aud.:* Sa.

The professional publication of ASAE: The Center for Association Leadership, *Associations Now* publishes in-depth reporting, quick tips, inspiring stories, case studies, book reviews, and news briefs for executives and professionals managing the work of volunteer associations, individual membership societies, and trade associations. The publication is mailed monthly to individual members of ASAE, but non-members may also subscribe. Articles are written either by the editorial staff of *Associations Now* or by experienced association executives. Well-designed graphics enliven the print edition. Recommended for corporate libraries and public libraries with a business collection. URL: https://associationsnow.com/magazine/

3400. *British Journal of Management: an international forum advancing theory and research.* [ISSN: 1045-3172] 1990. q. USD 2283 (Individuals, USD 194 print & online eds.). Ed(s): Geoffrey Wood, Pawan Budhwar. Wiley-Blackwell Publishing Ltd., The Atrium, Southern Gate, Chichester, PO19 8QG, United Kingdom; cs-journals@wiley.com; http://www.wiley.com/. Adv. Sample. Refereed. Microform: PQC. Reprint: PSC. *Indexed:* A22, B01, BRI, E01, ErgAb, IBSS. *Aud.:* Ac, Sa.

Published in collaboration with the British Academy of Management, the *British Journal of Management* features often-cited, peer-reviewed articles of a multi-disciplinary, interdisciplinary, and international nature that are intended to make a positive social impact. Written by scholars from around the globe, articles in the journal are insightful, empirical, and methodological, on topics such as organizational behavior, equality, diversity and inclusion, business ethics, strategic management, operations management, R&D management, and public sector management. Each issue of the quarterly journal contains seven or eight original articles, about 6,000 words in length, which are targeted to academics and executives interested in cutting-edge, evidence-based management research. Among recent article topics are the power of positive regard at work; entrepreneurial activity among gay men and lesbian women; and how leaders affect followers' work engagement and performance. A "Methodology Corner" section in each issue presents shorter articles on research methods, for example, corporate governance and Tobin's Q as a measure of organizational performance, and methodology-as-technique and the meaning of rigor in globalized management research. The *British Journal of Management* does not include conceptual and review papers, except in its special issues. Referenced extensively in academic indexing and abstracting services, this publication is highly recommended for academic libraries with a business program. URL: https://onlinelibrary.wiley.com/journal/14678551

3401. *Cross Cultural & Strategic Management.* Formerly (until 2016): *Cross Cultural Management.* [ISSN: 2059-5794] 1994. q. EUR 1410 (print & online eds.) (excluding UK)). Ed(s): Rosalie L Tung. Emerald Publishing Limited, Howard House, Wagon Ln, Bingley, BD16 1WA, United Kingdom; emerald@emeraldinsight.com; http://www.emeraldinsight.com. Sample. Refereed. Reprint: PSC. *Indexed:* A22, B01, E01. *Aud.:* Ac, Sa.

The quarterly publication *Cross Cultural & Strategic Management* features peer-reviewed, theoretical/conceptual and empirical papers based on quantitative and qualitative research on issues pertinent to business and management in the global context. Each issue offers lengthy, well documented research articles written by international scholars from a variety of disciplines, including international business, management, anthropology, economics, political science, psychology, and sociology. Topics covered include but are not limited to: strategic issues facing emerging markets of the global economy; management of the multinational enterprise (MNE); innovation in the international context; comparative and international entrepreneurship; corporate governance and social issues of the firm in the global context; global talent management; cross-cultural communication, work motivation, and leadership; and inter- and intra-organizational group, teamwork, and negotiation strategies. Each volume features one or more special issues, with themes such as East Asian wisdom and its impact on business culture and performance in a cross-cultural context, and gender in international business. Academics, researchers, business students, executives, and managers would benefit from the information presented in this journal. Recommended for academic libraries that support a business program and corporate libraries. URL: www.emeraldinsight.com/loi/ccsm

3402. *Decision Sciences (Online): information systems, operations & supply chain management.* [ISSN: 1540-5915] 1970. bi-m. USD 614. Ed(s): Cheri Speier-Pero, Mark Ferguson. Wiley-Blackwell Publishing, Inc., 111 River St, Hoboken, NJ 07030; http://onlinelibrary.wiley.com. Sample. Refereed. *Aud.:* Ac.

Published for the Decision Sciences Institute, the journal *Decision Sciences* publishes peer-reviewed research papers that address contemporary business problems and provide novel managerial and/or theoretical insights in the broad areas of Information Systems, Operations and Supply Chain Management. The journal features theoretical, empirical, and methodological investigations of managerial decisions that drive business productivity and success. Topics of particular interest are analytics as an emerging synthesis of sophisticated methodology and large data systems used to guide managerial decision making in an increasingly complex business environment. This journal became online-only in 2015. Highly recommended for academic libraries that support graduate business programs. URL: https://onlinelibrary.wiley.com/journal/15405915

3403. *Directors & Boards: thought leadership in governance since 1976.* Incorporates (2004-2008): *Boardroom Briefing.* [ISSN: 0364-9156] 1976. q. USD 325 domestic; USD 350 foreign. Ed(s): Eve Tahmincioglu, David Shaw. Directors & Boards, 1845 Walnut St, 9th Fl, Ste 900, Philadelphia, PA 19103. Illus., index, adv. Sample. Vol. ends: Summer. Microform: PQC. *Indexed:* A22, B01, BLI, BRI, L14. *Bk. rev.:* 1-2 signed, 500 words each. *Aud.:* Sa.

Written by and for board chairmen, CEOs, senior management, corporate board members, and board advisers, the quarterly publication *Directors & Boards* publishes short, practical advisories on every aspect of the role of the board in corporate governance. Issues addressed include effective board structure and processes, recruiting the best directors, getting the most value from the board, crisis management, succession planning, and compensation. Each issue contains "Directors Roster," a comprehensive listing of executives elected each quarter to be new board members. Advisory information useful for directors, board members, and students. Recommended for academic libraries that support a business school and public libraries. URL: www.directorsandboards.com

3404. *Global Business and Organizational Excellence: a review of research & best practices.* Former titles (until 2006): *Journal of Organizational Excellence;* (until 2000): *National Productivity Review;* Incorporates (19??-2001): *Competitive Intelligence Review;* Which was formerly (until 1990): *Competitive Intelligencer.* [ISSN: 1932-2054]

1981. bi-m. GBP 660. Ed(s): Mary Ann Castronovo Fusco. John Wiley & Sons, Inc., 111 River St, Hoboken, NJ 07030; cs-journals@wiley.com; http://onlinelibrary.wiley.com. Illus., adv. Vol. ends: Fall. Microform: PQC. Reprint: PSC. *Indexed:* A22, B01, BRI. *Bk. rev.:* 1, signed. *Aud.:* Ac, Sa.

Global Business and Organizational Excellence is a bimonthly publication of applied research and detailed case studies on operational issues in global organizations. Each issue contains six articles between 8 and 20 pages in length. Articles are written for leaders and managers of businesses and other organizations, consultants and advisers to leadership professionals, and educators in leadership studies, and they combine a synthesis and analysis of scholarly research with experience in the field. Topics include change management, employee engagement, organizational culture, restructured work relationships, corporate social responsibility, and process reinvention; many articles provide a global perspective. The articles are written by academics and experienced executives for the practitioner audience. A "Currents" section provides an excerpt from a highlighted book, a topical book review of multiple recent titles, and summary of important research on organizational issues recently published elsewhere. Recommended for academic libraries with an undergraduate business major, corporate libraries, and public libraries. URL: https://onlinelibrary.wiley.com/journal/19322062

3405. ***I N F O R M S Journal on Applied Analytics.*** Former titles (until 2018): *Interfaces (Hanover);* (until 1971): *Institute of Management Sciences. Bulletin.* [ISSN: 2644-0865] 1954. bi-m. USD 638 (print & online eds.)). Ed(s): Michael F Gorman. Institute for Operations Research and the Management Sciences (I N F O R M S), 5521 Research Park Dr, Ste 200, Catonsville, MD 21228; informs@informs.org; https://pubsonline.informs.org/. Illus., index, adv. Sample. Refereed. *Indexed:* A22, B01, BRI, EconLit, IBSS. *Bk. rev.:* 2-4, 450-1,450 words, signed. *Aud.:* Ac, Sa.

The journal *INFORMS Journal on Applied Analytics* is published by the Institute for Operations Research and the Management Sciences (INFORMS), the professional society for operations research, management sciences, and business analytics professionals. *INFORMS Journal on Applied Analytics*, one of INFORMS's 13 journals, publishes peer-reviewed articles that describe the practical applications of operational research (OR) and management sciences (MS) to decisions and policies in today's organizations and industries. Each article provides details of the completed applications, along with the results and impact on the organizations, with supporting references. Articles cover all areas of OR/MS, including operations management, information systems, finance, marketing, education, quality, and strategy. The accessible articles are written by knowledgeable, experienced OR professional leaders and practitioners in the field, as well as academics. Analysts, engineers, managers, students, and educators will find these articles essential and useful. This bimonthly publication is essential for academic libraries that support business management and engineering studies, as well as corporate libraries. URL: http://pubsonline.informs.org/journal/inte

3406. ***The International Entrepreneurship and Management Journal.*** [ISSN: 1554-7191] 2005. q. EUR 839 (print & online eds.)). Ed(s): David B Audretsch, Salvador Roig. Springer New York LLC, 233 Spring St, New York, NY 10013; customerservice@springer.com; http://www.springer.com. Sample. Refereed. Reprint: PSC. *Indexed:* A22, BRI, E01, EconLit. *Bk. rev.:* 1, 1,000 words, signed. *Aud.:* Ac, Sa.

The highly cited *International Entrepreneurship and Management Journal* features peer-reviewed articles on entrepreneurship and the management of entrepreneurial organizations, from new ventures to family owned businesses to large corporations. With articles written by scholars, researchers, consultants, entrepreneurs, businessmen, managers, and practitioners, the journal features both conceptual and empirical research papers that advance the field of entrepreneurship, as well as articles on business corporate strategy and government economic policy. Each issue includes 12-14 original research articles, with recent topics such as the entrepreneurial orientation in work groups, microfranchise emergence and its impact on entrepreneurship, institutional support for female technology entrepreneurs, and entrepreneurial resilience. The journal occasionally features case studies of successful firms or other cases having important practical implications. A few issues per year include a signed book review essay. With the growth of the economy tied to new entrepreneurial activities, the articles in this journal will be of importance to scholars, researchers, students, and entrepreneurs. The journal is essential for academic libraries that support a business program and public libraries that encourage and support new business. URL: http://link.springer.com/journal/11365

3407. ***The International Journal of Logistics Management.*** [ISSN: 0957-4093] 1990. q. EUR 641 (print & online eds.) (excluding UK)). Ed(s): Britta Gammelgaard. Emerald Publishing Limited, Howard House, Wagon Ln, Bingley, BD16 1WA, United Kingdom; emerald@emeraldinsight.com; http://www.emeraldinsight.com. Illus. Sample. Refereed. Vol. ends: No. 2. Reprint: PSC. *Indexed:* A22, B01, E01, HRIS. *Aud.:* Ac, Sa.

The International Journal of Logistics Management features peer-reviewed, scholarly articles on logistics and supply chain management. It puts particular emphasis on quantitative and/or qualitative empirical research. Recent articles have discussed Internet of Things adoption in logistics and supply chain management; optimal levels of decentralization for resilient supply chains; hospital-supplier integration and hospital performance in Saudi Arabia; and organizational design change in multinational supply chain organizations. Each issue contains 16 to 18 research papers, plus a few literature reviews, case studies, and/or conceptual papers. Articles are written by academics and practitioners in the field. This journal is recommended for academic libraries with business and engineering programs, and corporate libraries that are interested in leading-edge logistics information. URL: www.emeraldinsight.com/loi/ijlm

3408. ***International Journal of Management Reviews.*** [ISSN: 1460-8545] 1999. q. GBP 1699 (print & online eds.)). Ed(s): Dermot Breslin, Caroline Gatrell. Wiley-Blackwell Publishing Ltd., The Atrium, Southern Gate, Chichester, PO19 8QG, United Kingdom; cs-journals@wiley.com; http://www.wiley.com/. Adv. Sample. Refereed. Reprint: PSC. *Indexed:* A22, B01, E01. *Aud.:* Ac.

Published on behalf of the British Academy of Management by Wiley, the *International Journal of Management Reviews* (*IJMR*) is the first reviews journal in the field of business and management. It publishes authoritative literature surveys and systematic literature reviews, on all the main management subdisciplines including human resource management; organizational behavior; international and strategic management; operations management; management sciences; information systems and technology management; accounting and finance; and marketing. This title is published quarterly, and each issue includes state-of-the-art literature review articles about 20 to 25 pages in length. One issue each year has a special topic focus. The reviews will be of particular interest to academics, researchers, and doctoral students in business and management. Highly recommended for academic libraries that support business research. URL: https://onlinelibrary.wiley.com/journal/14682370

3409. ***International Journal of Organizational Analysis.*** Former titles (until 2005): *Organizational Analysis;* (until 2004): *The International Journal of Organizational Analysis.* [ISSN: 1934-8835] 1993. 5x/yr. EUR 793 (print & online eds.) (excluding UK)). Ed(s): Peter Stokes. Emerald Publishing Limited, Howard House, Wagon Ln, Bingley, BD16 1WA, United Kingdom; emerald@emeraldinsight.com; http://www.emeraldinsight.com. Illus. Sample. Refereed. Vol. ends: Oct. Reprint: PSC. *Indexed:* A22, B01, E01. *Aud.:* Ga, Ac, Sa.

The *International Journal of Organizational Analysis* features peer-reviewed, critical analyses of the theory of organization and its practical impact in business and society. This title is published five times a year with an occasional special issue on a focused research topic; a recent theme was leading for organizational excellence in the Middle East. Each issue contains eight or nine academic articles written by international scholars and researchers that draw from organizational theory, organizational behavior, organizational development, organizational learning, and human resource management, as well as strategic and change management. A review of recent issues finds topics including the influence of open/closed innovation on employees' performance; authenticity at work; the effect of abusive supervision on employee intention to quit in Indian IT organizations; and organizational opinion leader charisma, role modeling, and relationships. Article types include research, conceptual, literature reviews, and case studies, many of which focus on a particular country or region of the world. With content written for academic scholars, practitioners, and students, this journal is recommended for academic libraries that support business studies, large public libraries that support an active business community, and corporate libraries interested in organizational analysis. URL: www.emeraldinsight.com/loi/ijoa

3410. *Ivey Business Journal (Online): improving the practice of management.* Former titles (until 2002): *Ivey Business Journal (Print);* (until 1999): *Ivey Business Quarterly;* (until 1997): *Business Quarterly;* (until 1950): *Quarterly Review of Commerce.* [ISSN: 1492-7071] 1933. bi-m. Free. Ed(s): Thomas Watson. Ivey Management Services, 179 John St, Ste 501, Toronto, ON M5T 1X4, Canada. Illus., adv. Microform: PQC. *Indexed:* A22, B01, BRI, C37. *Aud.:* Ga, Ac, Sa.

Ivey Business Journal, freely available online, publishes exclusive executive interviews along with feature articles. Feature articles are from 2,000 to 5,000 words in length and deliver practitioner versions of academic articles, productivity-enhancing management advice, and transformative ideas with practical applications. Topics range from issues such as leadership, strategy, and marketing to more recent areas of development and investigation, such as corporate culture, sustainable business, social media, and entrepreneurship. Examples of recent relevant articles include "Paying for CSR is Good Governance," "Reinventing Big Food," and "The Case for Religious Diversity." Another regular section is "IBJ Insights," concise commentaries written by a global cadre of business professionals and thought leaders that offer unique observations or analysis of current events and market trends. This is a trade publication, and its primary target audience comprises executives, corporate directors, managers, and academics. Recommended for academic, corporate, and public libraries. URL: www.iveybusinessjournal.com

3411. *Journal of Business Strategy.* Incorporates (1989-1994): *Journal of European Business;* Which incorporated (1990-1991): *Journal of Pricing Management.* [ISSN: 0275-6668] 1980. bi-m. EUR 727 (print & online eds.) (excluding UK)). Ed(s): Nanci Healy. Emerald Publishing Limited, Howard House, Wagon Ln, Bingley, BD16 1WA, United Kingdom; emerald@emeraldinsight.com; http://www.emeraldgrouppublishing.com. Illus. Sample. Refereed. Vol. ends: Dec. Microform: PQC. Reprint: PSC. *Indexed:* A22, Agr, B01, B03, BRI, C42, E01. *Aud.:* Ac, Sa.

The bimonthly *Journal of Business Strategy* publishes peer-reviewed articles with a practical focus. Each issue presents seven articles drawing from a mixture of conceptual papers, research papers, literature reviews, case studies, and viewpoint articles, which are written by academics, business writers, and consultants. *Journal of Business Strategy* explores topics such as marketing strategy, innovation, developments in the global economy, mergers and acquisition integration, and human resources, in unique and innovative ways. Articles are written in an accessible style, and the audience for *JBS* includes executives and middle and senior managers at companies of all sizes and types; academics; consultants; and undergraduate and graduate business students. Highly recommended for academic libraries that support business programs, large public libraries that support the business community, and corporate libraries. URL: www.emeraldinsight.com/loi/jbs

3412. *Journal of Contingencies and Crisis Management.* [ISSN: 0966-0879] 1993. q. GBP 742. Ed(s): Ira Helsloot. Wiley-Blackwell Publishing Ltd., The Atrium, Southern Gate, Chichester, PO19 8QG, United Kingdom; cs-journals@wiley.com; http://onlinelibrary.wiley.com. Adv. Sample. Refereed. Reprint: PSC. *Indexed:* A01, A22, B01, BRI, E01, P61, SSA. *Bk. rev.:* Number and length vary. *Aud.:* Ac, Sa.

Published in collaboration with the European Crisis Management Academy (ECMA), the *Journal of Contingencies and Crisis Management* features peer-reviewed articles on crisis prevention, crisis planning, recovery, and turnaround management, in both corporate and public sectors. The journal features one or two special issues per year; recent topics have included human-computer interaction and social media in safety-critical systems, and ethical, legal, and social considerations surrounding the use of crisis data and information sharing during a crisis. Contributions come from corporations, governmental agencies, think tanks, and influential academics around the world. The JCCM Forum encourages discussion of fresh and controversial ideas on crisis management policies and practices. Each issue includes 5 to 13 original articles and a forum article, and sometimes research papers, research notes, and a book review or two. URL: https://onlinelibrary.wiley.com/journal/14685973

3413. *Journal of International Management.* [ISSN: 1075-4253] 1995. q. EUR 1269. Ed(s): M Kotabe. Elsevier Inc., 1600 John F Kennedy Blvd, Philadelphia, PA 19103; journalscustomerservice-usa@elsevier.com; https://www.elsevier.com. Adv. Sample. Refereed. Microform: PQC. *Indexed:* A22, B01, IBSS. *Bk. rev.:* 1, signed, 2,100 to 2,300 words. *Aud.:* Ac, Sa.

The frequently cited *Journal of International Management* publishes peer-reviewed theoretical and empirical research relating to international management and strategy issues. Written by international academics and experts, the articles address subdisciplines such as international business strategy; comparative and cross-cultural management; risk management; organizational behavior; and human resource management, among others. *JIM* regularly publishes special issues that emphasize timely topics; recent examples include "Global Innovation Networks' Organizations and People," "Working Across Boundaries: Current and Future Perspectives on Global Virtual Teams," and "Management of Human Resources in MNCs from the BRICS Countries." Published quarterly, the journal is designed to serve an audience of academic researchers and educators, as well as business professionals. Each issue has five to ten original research articles and one lengthy book review. This journal is essential for academic libraries with international business or graduate business programs, as well as corporate libraries with international interests. URL: www.journals.elsevier.com/journal-of-international-management

3414. *Journal of Management.* [ISSN: 0149-2063] 1975. 8x/yr. USD 1502 (print & online eds.)). Ed(s): David G Allen. Sage Publications, Inc., 2455 Teller Rd, Thousand Oaks, CA 91320; info@sagepub.com; http://www.sagepub.com. Illus., index, adv. Sample. Refereed. Vol. ends: No. 6. Microform: PQC. Reprint: PSC. *Indexed:* A22, B01, E01, IBSS. *Aud.:* Ac, Sa.

As the official journal of the Southern Management Association, an affiliate of the Academy of Management, the preeminent, highly cited *Journal of Management* is a leading venue for management scholarship worldwide. It publishes peer-reviewed empirical, theoretical, and review articles that emphasize new ideas and perspectives, written by international scholars. Topic areas covered include business strategy and policy, entrepreneurship, human resource management, organizational behavior, organizational theory, and research methods. This title is published eight times a year, and each issue includes 7 to 12 research articles. The January and July issues are review issues that include widely read and widely cited collections of articles on management topics from a range of academic disciplines, methodologies, and theoretical paradigms, and are considered a major resource for management scholars. Essential for all academic libraries; highly recommended for large public and corporate libraries. URL: http://jom.sagepub.com

3415. *Journal of Management Studies.* [ISSN: 0022-2380] 1964. 8x/yr. GBP 1595. Wiley-Blackwell Publishing Ltd., The Atrium, Southern Gate, Chichester, PO19 8QG, United Kingdom; cs-journals@wiley.com; http://onlinelibrary.wiley.com. Illus., index, adv. Sample. Refereed. Vol. ends: Nov. Reprint: PSC. *Indexed:* A22, B01, BRI, E01, ErgAb, IBSS. *Aud.:* Ac, Sa.

Published for the U.K.-based Society for the Advancement of Management Studies, the *Journal of Management Studies* is a well-respected and highly ranked publication that has been around for more than 50 years. The journal is multidisciplinary and publishes cutting-edge articles on organization theory, strategic management, and human resource management. Written by international scholars and experienced practitioners, the peer-reviewed, academic articles range from empirical studies and theoretical works to practical applications. Eight issues are published per year, some with a special thematic focus; among recent special issue topics have been social and economic inequality: knowledge worker mobility; and the social value of hybrid organizational design. Each issue features four to eight original articles, and some offer issue-based "point-counterpoint" articles and an essay on a selected topic in management theory. International academics, researchers, students, consultants, executives, and managers will find the information contained in this journal useful. Essential for academic libraries that support business programs, and for corporate libraries. URL: https://onlinelibrary.wiley.com/journal/14676486

3416. ***Journal of Managerial Issues.*** [ISSN: 1045-3695] 1989. q. USD 115 (Individuals, USD 95; USD 190 foreign). Ed(s): Eric Harris. Pittsburg State University, Department of Economics, Finance & Banking, 1701 S Broadway St, Pittsburg, KS 66762; econ@pittstate.edu; http://www.pittstate.edu/department/economics/. Illus., index. Refereed. Microform: PQC. *Indexed:* A22, B01. *Aud.:* Ac.

The *Journal of Managerial Issues* features peer-reviewed articles on the theory of organizations and the practice of management. Articles include empirical studies and practical applications, as well as methodological and theoretical developments. The journal disseminates the results of new and original scholarly activity to an audience of university faculty and administrators, business executives, consultants, and governmental managers. Published by the Department of Economics, Finance, and Banking at Pittsburg State University (in Kansas), the journal was established as a bridge between academic research and practice. Recommended for academic libraries. URL: http://www.pittstate.edu/business/journal-of-managerial-issues/

3417. ***Journal of Operations Management.*** [ISSN: 0272-6963] 1980. 8x/yr. EUR 1192. John Wiley & Sons, Inc., 111 River St, Hoboken, NJ 07030; cs-journals@wiley.com; http://www.wiley.com. Illus., index, adv. Sample. Refereed. Vol. ends: Nov. *Indexed:* A22, B01, C42. *Aud.:* Ac, Sa.

The highly cited *Journal of Operations Management* publishes original, empirical operations management research that demonstrates both academic and practical relevance. The four to six peer-reviewed research articles in each issue focus on the management of operations: manufacturing operations, service operations, supply chain operations, and the like, in both for-profit and nonprofit organizations. The journal publishes one or two special thematic issues per year; recent topics have included competitive manufacturing in a high-cost environment; supply chain management in emerging markets; and empirically grounded research in humanitarian operations management. A section called the "JOM Forum," presents invited essays from influential and experienced scholars from both within and outside operations management, intended to provoke and challenge thinking about the discipline. Researchers in operations management and operations managers who are interested in cutting-edge research will want to seek out these articles. Highly recommended for academic libraries that support business, industrial engineering, and project management studies, and for corporate libraries. URL: www.journals.elsevier.com/journal-of-operations-management

3418. ***Journal of Product Innovation Management.*** [ISSN: 0737-6782] 1984. bi-m. GBP 1048. Ed(s): Gloria Barczak. Wiley-Blackwell Publishing, Inc., 111 River St, Hoboken, NJ 07030; http://onlinelibrary.wiley.com. Illus., index, adv. Sample. Refereed. Vol. ends: Nov. Reprint: PSC. *Indexed:* A22, B01, BRI, C42, E01. *Bk. rev.:* Number and length vary. *Aud.:* Ac, Sa.

The *Journal of Product Innovation Management* is affiliated with the Product Development and Management Association (PDMA), the professional organization of corporate practitioners of new product development. It is an interdisciplinary, international, academic journal devoted to the latest research, theory, and practice in new product and service development. The journal publishes original theoretical or empirical research articles that are double-blind peer-reviewed; "From Experience" articles that describe unique perspectives and approaches to improving new product and service development; and "Perspective" articles that do not fit into the category of original research yet provide value to scholars and/or practitioners. The scope of the journal includes organizations of all sizes (start-ups, small-medium enterprises, large), from the consumer, business-to-business, and institutional domains. The journal is a benefit of PDMA membership, but subscriptions are also available directly from the publisher. Published bimonthly with an additional special issue each year, the journal is of interest to scholars, managers, executives, and new-product professionals. It is extensively referenced in business and engineering indexing and abstracting services. Recommended for academic libraries that support business and industrial engineering studies, and corporate libraries that support new-product development. URL: https://onlinelibrary.wiley.com/journal/15405885

3419. ***Journal of Productivity Analysis.*** [ISSN: 0895-562X] 1988. bi-m. EUR 994 (print & online eds.)). Ed(s): William H Greene, Chris O'Donnell. Springer New York LLC, 233 Spring St, New York, NY 10013; customerservice@springer.com; http://www.springer.com. Illus., index, adv. Refereed. Vol. ends: No. 4. Reprint: PSC. *Indexed:* A22, B01, C45, E01, EconLit. *Aud.:* Ac, Sa.

The *Journal of Productivity Analysis* is a bimonthly, peer-reviewed scholarly journal. Its scope covers productivity integrated with research findings from economics, management sciences, operations research, and business and public administration. The journal publishes theoretical and applied research that addresses the measurement, analysis, and improvement of productivity. A partial list of recent topics includes estimation of cost efficiency without cost data; misallocation, productivity and fragmentation of production in Latvia; a cost efficiency analysis of the insurance industry in Mexico; and persistent and transient cost efficiency, as applied to the Swiss hydropower sector. The journal also publishes research on computational methods employed in productivity analysis and empirical research based on data at all levels of aggregation. Articles are written by academics and researchers for an academic audience. This title is recommended for academic libraries that support advanced business programs. URL: www.springer.com/economics/microeconomics/journal/11123

3420. ***Journal of Supply Chain Management: a global review of purchasing and supply.*** Former titles (until 1999): *International Journal of Purchasing & Materials Management;* (until 1991): *Journal of Purchasing and Materials Management;* (until 1974): *Journal of Purchasing.* [ISSN: 1523-2409] 1965. q. GBP 300. Ed(s): Barbara Flynn, Mark Pagell. Wiley-Blackwell Publishing, Inc., 111 River St, Hoboken, NJ 07030; http://onlinelibrary.wiley.com. Illus., index, adv. Sample. Refereed. Vol. ends: Nov (No. 4). Microform: PQC. Reprint: PSC. *Indexed:* A22, B01, BRI, C42, E01. *Aud.:* Ac, Sa.

The *Journal of Supply Chain Management*, published in collaboration with the Institute for Supply Management, provides frequently cited, peer-reviewed papers by thought leaders and top scholars in the field. The journal aims to make a strong contribution to supply chain management theory, as well as provide articles of empirical research, with a connection to practical relevance. Each issue provides four or more articles; some issues include invited papers and guest editorials, along with essays and papers from related disciplines, including marketing channels and strategy, transaction cost economics, strategic management, operations management, and social network analysis. One issue per year features a forum on a focused topic. Recently published articles have explored single-respondent research designs in supply chain management; supply chain management in emerging markets; and supplier switching behavior, among other subjects. Of interest to scholars and supply chain managers, this journal is highly recommended for academic libraries with programs in business management, operations management, engineering project management, or industrial engineering. URL: https://onlinelibrary.wiley.com/journal/1745493x

3421. ***Knowledge Management Research & Practice.*** [ISSN: 1477-8238] 2003. q. GBP 646 (print & online eds.)). Taylor & Francis, 2, 3 & 4 Park Sq, Milton Park, Abingdon, OX14 4RN, United Kingdom; enquiries@taylorandfrancis.com; https://www.tandfonline.com. Adv. Sample. Refereed. Reprint: PSC. *Indexed:* A22, E01. *Aud.:* Ac, Sa.

An official publication of the Operational Research Society, the peer-reviewed journal *Knowledge Management Research & Practice*, publishes articles on all aspects of managing knowledge, organizational learning, intellectual capital, and knowledge economics. Each issue includes eight to ten articles on theoretical and practical aspects of knowledge management, including cross-disciplinary topics and case studies. Recent article topics have included the relation between knowledge transfer and productivity in knowledge work; dealing with knowledge in a product development setting in the automotive industry; and the role of human capital, renewal capital and entrepreneurial capital in innovation performance in high-tech and low-tech firms. Authors include academics as well as practitioners. Highly recommended for academic business libraries, corporate libraries that support managers interested in knowledge management, and large public libraries. URL: https://www.tandfonline.com/toc/tkmr20/current

3422. *The Leadership Quarterly: an international journal of political, social and behavioral science.* [ISSN: 1048-9843] 1990. bi-m. EUR 1248. Ed(s): John Antonakis. Elsevier BV, https://www.elsevier.com. Adv. Sample. Refereed. Microform: PQC. Reprint: PSC. *Indexed:* A22, B01, P61. *Aud.:* Ac, Sa.

The Leadership Quarterly publishes peer-reviewed, multidisciplinary articles on leadership geared toward an international audience of scholars, consultants, managers, executives, administrators, and university faculty members who teach leadership courses. Its purpose is to advance understanding of leadership as a phenomenon, how to study it, and its practical implications. Each issue features 10 to 12 medium-length research and application articles. Recent articles have addressed how CEO narcissism increases firms' vulnerability to lawsuits; investor response to appointment of female CEOs and CFOs; authentic leadership and leaders' mental well-being; and leadership for organizational adaptability. One or two issues per year focus on special themes, such as strategic leadership and strategic management; charismatic leadership; and gender and leadership. A yearly review section highlights theoretical and methodological advances in leadership during the preceding year. This journal is recommended for academic and corporate libraries. URL: www.journals.elsevier.com/the-leadership-quarterly

3423. *London Business School Review.* Formerly (until 2015): *Business Strategy Review (Print).* [ISSN: 2057-1607] 1990. q. GBP 400. Ed(s): Calandra Smith, Julian Birkinshaw. Wiley-Blackwell Publishing Ltd., The Atrium, Southern Gate, Chichester, PO19 8QG, United Kingdom; cs-journals@wiley.com; http://onlinelibrary.wiley.com/. Illus., adv. Sample. Reprint: PSC. *Indexed:* A22, B01, BRI, C42, E01. *Aud.:* Ga, Ac, Sa.

London Business School Review, which changed its title from *Business Strategy Review* in 2015, publishes articles from London Business School faculty and those with a connection to the school. Its format is very much that of a news magazine, with short articles and lots of graphics. Many pieces are written by the researchers themselves, in an accessible style intended to draw in the general, rather than academic, reader. Citations to the original studies are included for those who wish to see the scholarly articles, published elsewhere. Other content includes brief articles written by editorial board members on a broad range of business topics, plus opinion pieces, ideas, and advice from business leaders and consultants. The articles are targeted to executives as well as managers, and are appropriate for undergraduate business students. Recommended for public libraries; appropriate, but optional for academic and corporate libraries. URL: https://onlinelibrary.wiley.com/journal/20571615

3424. *Long Range Planning: international journal of strategic management.* [ISSN: 0024-6301] 1968. bi-m. EUR 2875. Ed(s): Tomi Laamanen. Pergamon Press, The Blvd, Langford Ln, E Park, Kidlington, OX5 1GB, United Kingdom; JournalsCustomerServiceEMEA@elsevier.com; http://www.elsevier.com. Illus., adv. Sample. Refereed. Microform: MIM; PQC. *Indexed:* A22, B01, BRI. *Aud.:* Ac, Sa.

Long Range Planning, a publication of the U.K.-based Strategic Planning Society, is a leading international journal for the field of strategic management. Each issue features 5 to 13 original, peer-reviewed research articles, on topics related to corporate strategy and governance, business strategy, strategies for emerging markets, entrepreneurship, innovation, and corporate social responsibility. A special themed issue is published at least once a year. Among recent themes have been transparency and inclusion in strategy processes; strategic management of dynamic growth; and innovation and sustainability. The journal's target audience includes academic researchers, students in professional programs, and practicing managers. *Long Range Planning* is recommended for academic libraries that support graduate business studies and corporate libraries interested in cutting-edge research. URL: www.journals.elsevier.com/long-range-planning

3425. *M I T Sloan Management Review: MIT's journal of management research and ideas.* Former titles (until 1998): *Sloan Management Review;* (until 1970): *Industrial Management Review.* [ISSN: 1532-9194] 1960. q. USD 289 combined subscription domestic print & online eds.; USD 349 combined subscription elsewhere print & online eds. Ed(s): Paul Michelman. Massachusetts Institute of Technology, 1 Charles Pk, EE20-601, Cambridge, MA 02142; info@mit.edu; http://mit.edu. Illus., index. Refereed. Vol. ends: Summer. Microform: PQC. *Indexed:* A22, B01, BLI, BRI, C42, EconLit. *Aud.:* Ac, Sa.

The *MIT Sloan Management Review* provides innovative, peer-reviewed articles on the intersection of important management research and ideas with practice. Content consists primarily of articles written by researchers, academic scholars, and thought leaders that analyze and interpret original research for application in the business environment. In addition, collaborative "Big Ideas" articles focus on a single, significant, transformative idea in the business environment, such as sustainability, data and analytics, social business, or digital transformation. Shorter articles in the "Frontiers" section present new insights on how technology is transforming the practice of management. Executives and top business managers are the primary audience for the publication, which is also appropriate for undergraduate business students. Essential for academic libraries that support business programs, and corporate and public libraries. URL: http://sloanreview.mit.edu/

3426. *Management Communication Quarterly: an international journal.* [ISSN: 0893-3189] 1987. q. Ed(s): Patricia M Sias. Sage Publications, Inc., 2455 Teller Rd, Thousand Oaks, CA 91320; info@sagepub.com; http://www.sagepub.com. Illus., adv. Sample. Refereed. Vol. ends: May. Reprint: PSC. *Indexed:* A22, B01, E01. *Bk. rev.:* Number, frequency, and length vary. *Aud.:* Ac, Sa.

Management Communication Quarterly (*MCQ*) presents peer-reviewed, conceptual, empirical, and practice-relevant research papers in organizational and management communication. Articles address business communication through the lens of management, organizational studies, organizational behavior and human resource management, organizational theory and strategy, critical management studies, leadership, information systems, knowledge and innovation, globalization and international management, corporate communication, and cultural and intercultural studies. Each issue of *Management Communication Quarterly* features three to five original research articles, plus a regular "Forum" section devoted to provocative essays and commentaries on evolving issues in the field. The journal also publishes research notes on emerging areas of inquiry, empirical explorations, and reviews of current books and texts. A recent review of current issues reveals topics such as how authority figures may unwittingly invite and co-create a team's collective resistance in response to their actions; the crisis communication of meta-organizations; using communication privacy management theory to understand disclosures in the workplace; and photo and video methods in organizational and managerial communication research. Academics, researchers, students, and practitioners will find these articles relevant and useful. Recommended for academic libraries that support business studies and corporate libraries. URL: http://mcq.sagepub.com/

3427. *Management Decision.* Incorporates (1995-2000): *Journal of Management History;* (in 1975): *Management in Action;* Which was formerly (until 1969): *Office Methods and Machines;* Formerly (until 1967): *Scientific Business.* [ISSN: 0025-1747] 1963. m. EUR 16706 (print & online eds.) (excluding UK)). Ed(s): Patrick J Murphy. Emerald Publishing Limited, Howard House, Wagon Ln, Bingley, BD16 1WA, United Kingdom; emerald@emeraldinsight.com; http://www.emeraldinsight.com. Illus. Sample. Refereed. Reprint: PSC. *Indexed:* A22, B01, BRI, E01, MLA-IB. *Aud.:* Ac.

The frequently cited, peer-reviewed journal *Management Decision* is one of the oldest and longest-running scholarly management journals. It presents the research work of leading international scholars and practitioners, covering broad management topics that include operations management and logistics research, corporate social responsibility, financial management, motivation, entrepreneurship, strategic management, organizational behavior, and tactics for turning around company crises. Each issue contains between 11 and 14 articles, including research papers, conceptual papers, viewpoint essays, case studies, and literature reviews. Recent articles have explored the impacts of regulatory focus and institutions on innovation; the importance of communication and trust in building successful franchise partnerships; antecedents and consequences of nurses' burnout; and employee learning in high-contact service industries. One or more special issues per year focus on a theme. Among recent examples are entrepreneurship and innovation management; sustainability and ethical consumerism; intellectual property management; and the human dimension of open innovation. Highly recommended for academic libraries that support business programs. URL: www.emeraldinsight.com/loi/md

3428. *Management Research Review.* Formerly (until 2010): *Management Research News.* [ISSN: 2040-8277] 1978. m. EUR 6838 (print & online eds.) (excluding UK)). Ed(s): Jay J Janney, Lerong He. Emerald Publishing Limited, Howard House, Wagon Ln, Bingley, BD16 1WA, United Kingdom; information@emeraldinsight.com; http://www.emeraldinsight.com. Sample. Refereed. *Indexed:* A22, B01, E01. *Aud.:* Ac, Sa.

Management Research Review publishes a wide variety of articles outlining the latest in general management research. Key issues featured are human resource management, financial management, consumerism, information and knowledge management, marketing, industrial relations, personnel management, organization development, production and operations management, entrepreneurship and small business management, and sustainability including corporate social responsibility and ethics. Each monthly issue contains five or more timely, peer-reviewed research and conceptual papers, literature reviews, and case studies written by international scholars and experienced practitioners. One or more special issues with a thematic focus appear each year. Recent topics include collaborative firms; networks and social media; circular economy and sustainability innovation; innovative research methods in management, spirituality, and religion; and corporate governance. Academics, students, consultants, and executives will find the information of interest. Recommended for corporate libraries and academic libraries that support business programs. URL: http://emeraldgrouppublishing.com/products/journals/journals.htm?id=mrr

3429. *Management Science.* Incorporates (1960-1964): *Management Technology.* [ISSN: 0025-1909] 1954. m. USD 1403 (print & online eds.)). Ed(s): David Simchi-Levi. Institute for Operations Research and the Management Sciences (I N F O R M S), 5521 Research Park Dr, Ste 200, Catonsville, MD 21228; informs@informs.org; https://pubsonline.informs.org/. Illus., index, adv. Refereed. Vol. ends: Dec. *Indexed:* A22, B01, BRI, C42, EconLit, HRIS, IBSS. *Aud.:* Ac, Sa.

Management Science is one of 13 journals published by the Institute for Operations Research and the Management Sciences (INFORMS), the professional society for operations research, management sciences, and business analytics professionals. *Management Science* publishes scholarly, peer-reviewed theoretical, computational, and empirical research on managerial issues in diverse organizations, such as for-profit and nonprofit firms, private and public-sector institutions, and formal and informal networks of individuals. The articles use interdisciplinary tools from fields such as operational research, management sciences, mathematics, statistics, industrial engineering, psychology, sociology, and political science. Management topics explored include business strategy, decision analysis, entrepreneurship, product development, social networks, and supply chains. The in-depth, detailed articles with extensive references, written by academic authors and practitioners, are important sources for other academics, students, and management executives interested in theory and empirical research. To support the scientific process, *Management Science* encourages (but does not require) the disclosure of data associated with the manuscripts published. *Management Science* is essential for academic libraries that support either business or industrial engineering programs. URL: https://pubsonline.informs.org/journal/mnsc

3430. *Manufacturing & Service Operations Management.* [ISSN: 1523-4614] 1999. q. USD 641 (print & online eds.)). Ed(s): Christopher Tang. Institute for Operations Research and the Management Sciences (I N F O R M S), 5521 Research Park Dr, Ste 200, Catonsville, MD 21228; informs@informs.org; https://pubsonline.informs.org/. Illus., adv. Refereed. *Indexed:* A22, B01, EconLit. *Aud.:* Ac, Sa.

Published quarterly by the Institute for Operations Research and the Management Sciences (INFORMS), *Manufacturing & Service Operations Management* (*M&SOM*) is the premier journal for the operations-management research community. It publishes a wide range of research that focuses on the production and operations management of goods and services, with topics including control and improvement, operational decision-making, operations strategy, process design, and supply chain coordination. Written by academic researchers and practitioners, *M&SOM*'s articles help to solve operations management (OM) problems and explore the control, planning, design, and improvement of these OM processes. Each issue includes 7 to 13 research articles, and most issues include a regular "OM Forum" section that offers invited essays on OM research and managerial practice. One or more issues per year focus on a special theme. Recent examples include research at the interface of finance, operations, and risk management (iFORM), and practice-focused research. Academic researchers and practitioners responsible for operation management, as well as graduate students in business schools and industrial engineering, are the audience for *M&SOM*. Highly recommended for academic libraries that support business and engineering studies, and for corporate libraries interested in the improvement of OM processes. URL: http://pubsonline.informs.org/journal/msom

3431. *Organization: the critical journal of organization, theory and society.* [ISSN: 1350-5084] 1994. bi-m. USD 2542 (print & online eds.)). Ed(s): Raza Mir, Yvonne Benschop. Sage Publications Ltd., 1 Oliver's Yard, 55 City Rd, London, EC1Y 1SP, United Kingdom; info@sagepub.com; https://www.sagepub.com/. Sample. Refereed. Reprint: PSC. *Indexed:* A22, B01, E01, IBSS, MLA-IB, P61, SSA. *Bk. rev.:* 2-4, 1,000 words. *Aud.:* Ac.

Organization examines organizations from a wide range of perspectives, addressing significant current and emergent theoretical, meta-theoretical, and substantive developments in the field of organizational studies. It presents peer-reviewed papers and essays that tie together contemporary social problems and the study of organizing. The articles are theory-oriented, international in scope, provocative, imaginative and critical, and interdisciplinary. Each issue contains five to eight articles plus two to four book reviews, with occasional editorials, opinion papers written to challenge contemporary orthodoxies, and review essays. A new feature is "Acting Up," short articles that support relevance, political engagement, resistance, and activism. Several issues per year focus on a specific theme. Recent special topics include "Diversifying the Creative: Creative Work, Creative Industries, Creative Identities," "Post-Capitalistic Politics in the Making: Practices of Alternative Economics," and "Thinking Critically About Affect in Organization Studies." Recommended for academic libraries that serve scholars and students interested in the intersection of organizations, society, and theory. URL: https://us.sagepub.com/en-us/nam/journal/organization

3432. *Organization Management Journal.* [ISSN: 1541-6518] 2004. q. GBP 260. Ed(s): Kerri A Crowne, Priscilla Elsass. Taylor & Francis Inc., 530 Walnut St, Ste 850, Philadelphia, PA 19106. Adv. Refereed. *Indexed:* A22, B01, E01. *Bk. rev.:* Number and length vary. *Aud.:* Ac.

As the official publication of the Eastern Academy of Management, an affiliate of the Academy of Management, the *Organization Management Journal* publishes peer-reviewed articles that intersect theory and practice, address strategies for effective teaching and learning, and "represent the early stages of theorizing about management and organizing in unique and perceptive ways." Each issue provides three to seven peer-reviewed articles on a common theme written by scholars, practitioners, and doctoral students. While the mix of article types is different for each issue, the common theme of the issue is explored through different modes of writing and creating knowledge, including empirical research articles, conceptual articles, analytical essays, case studies, white papers, conference papers, and book reviews. Academic researchers and instructors, as well as business students, will find relevant content in this journal. Highly recommended for academic libraries that support all business management programs. URL: www.tandfonline.com/toc/uomj20/current

3433. *Organization Science.* [ISSN: 1047-7039] 1990. bi-m. USD 702 (print & online eds.)). Ed(s): Gautam Ahuja. Institute for Operations Research and the Management Sciences (I N F O R M S), 5521 Research Park Dr, Ste 200, Catonsville, MD 21228; informs@informs.org; https://pubsonline.informs.org/. Illus. Refereed. Vol. ends: Nov/Dec. *Indexed:* A22, B01, IBSS. *Aud.:* Ac.

Organization Science is one of 13 journals published by the Institute for Operations Research and the Management Sciences (INFORMS), the professional society for operations research, management sciences, and business analytics professionals. One of the top journals in the fields of strategy, management, and organization theory, *Organization Science* publishes original, theoretical, and empirical research about organizations, including their processes, structures, technologies, identities, capabilities, forms, and performance. Each issue includes seven to ten peer-reviewed articles that explore new research applied to organizations from various disciplines such as artificial intelligence, communication theory, economics, information science, psychology, sociology, strategic management, and systems theory. The journal occasionally publishes essays in the "Perspectives" and "Crossroads" sections on new organizational phenomena, redirected lines of research, or debate about current organizations. The articles are written by academics worldwide for students and faculty of business schools. Published bimonthly, this journal is recommended for academic libraries that support business programs. URL: http://pubsonline.informs.org/journal/orsc

3434. *Organizational Dynamics.* [ISSN: 0090-2616] 1972. q. EUR 553. Ed(s): G Latham. Elsevier Ltd, 66 Siward Rd, Bromley, BR2 9JZ, United Kingdom; http://www.elsevier.com. Illus., adv. Sample. Refereed. Microform: PQC. *Indexed:* A22, ASSIA, B01, BRI, C42, E01. *Aud.:* Ac, Sa.

The articles featured in *Organizational Dynamics* focus on the use of research findings to deal more effectively with the dynamics of organizational life. The seven to ten original research articles per issue are written by academics in an accessible style targeted to practicing managers. The analytical articles combine theoretical with practical content. The journal's primary domain is organizational behavior and development, and secondarily, human resources management and strategic management. Articles in recent issues have explored the critical importance of meetings to leader and organizational success; organizational resilience; open innovation in entrepreneurial private family firms in low- and medium-technology industries; addressing complex politically charged transorganizational problems; and how entrepreneurs can benefit from failure management. One or two issues per year are devoted to special themes. Recent examples are employee engagement; enabling career success; and bad behavior. Recommended for corporate libraries and academic libraries that support business programs. URL: www.journals.elsevier.com/organizational-dynamics/

3435. *Organizational Research Methods.* [ISSN: 1094-4281] 1998. q. USD 1549 (print & online eds.)). Ed(s): Paul D Bliese. Sage Publications, Inc., 2455 Teller Rd, Thousand Oaks, CA 91320; info@sagepub.com; http://www.sagepub.com. Adv. Sample. Refereed. Reprint: PSC. *Indexed:* A22, B01, E01. *Aud.:* Ac.

Organizational Research Methods (*ORM*) is sponsored by the Research Methods Division of the Academy of Management and CARMA, the Consortium for the Advancement of Research Methods and Analysis. The journal aims to promote understanding of current and new methodologies as applied in organizational research, for readers with doctoral-level methodological and statistical training in the field. Articles may evaluate the merits of various quantitative and qualitative methods and research designs, or address how new applications of existing methods advance understanding of organizational research, or introduce research techniques from other disciplines to organizational researchers. *ORM* is recommended for academic libraries that support advanced organization and management business and psychology degrees. URL: https://us.sagepub.com/en-us/nam/organizational-research-methods/journal200894

3436. *Production and Operations Management.* [ISSN: 1059-1478] 1992. m. GBP 450. Ed(s): Kalyan Singhal. Wiley-Blackwell Publishing, Inc., 111 River St, Hoboken, NJ 07030; http://onlinelibrary.wiley.com. Illus., adv. Sample. Refereed. Reprint: PSC. *Indexed:* A22, B01, E01, EconLit. *Aud.:* Ac, Sa.

Production and Operations Management is published in collaboration with the Productions and Operations Management Society (POMS), an international professional organization dedicated to the improved understanding and practice of production and operations management. This is the main research journal in operations management in manufacturing and services. The double-blind peer-reviewed articles, written by international academic scholars, present scientific research into the management of products and process design, operations, and supply chains. In January 2014, *Production and Operations Management* became a monthly publication; it was formerly published bimonthly. Each issue includes ten original articles that will be of particular interest to practitioners and academic scholars. Recommended for academic libraries that support advanced business and engineering programs and corporate libraries that support production and operations management. URL: https://onlinelibrary.wiley.com/journal/19375956

3437. *Project Management Journal.* Formerly (until 1984): *Project Management Quarterly.* [ISSN: 8756-9728] 1970. bi-m. USD 891 (print & online eds.)). Ed(s): Gary Klein, Ralf Muller. Sage Publications Ltd., . Adv. Refereed. Vol. ends: Dec. Reprint: PSC. *Indexed:* A22, B01, BRI, C42. *Bk. rev.:* 4 per issue, 600 words, online. *Aud.:* Ac, Sa.

The *Project Management Journal* features academic, peer-reviewed articles on state-of-the-art project management techniques, along with research, theories, and applications. As the professional publication of the Project Management Institute, this bimonthly journal provides a balance of content about research, technique, theory, and practice in project, program, and portfolio management. The journal publishes papers that represent perspectives through the lenses of other disciplines, such as organizational behavior and theory, strategic management, sociology, economics, political science, history, information science, systems theory, communication theory, and psychology. Written by academic scholars and professionals, the six to nine papers in each issue will be of interest to project management practitioners, academics, executives, business leaders, and students. Each issue also includes four book reviews that are available online. One or two special issues per year focus on a theme. In 2018, the journal introduced a new section featuring peer-reviewed teaching cases and their accompanying instructor's manuals. Highly recommended for academic libraries that support business programs and corporate libraries interested in new developments in project management. URL: https://www.pmi.org/learning/publications/project-management-journal

3438. *Quality Management Journal.* [ISSN: 1068-6967] 1993. q. GBP 1297 print & online eds. Ed(s): Thomas Foster, Jr. Taylor & Francis Inc., 530 Walnut St, Ste 850, Philadelphia, PA 19106. Illus., adv. Refereed. Vol. ends: No. 4. *Indexed:* A22, B01. *Bk. rev.:* 4-7, 500-1,000 words. *Aud.:* Ac, Sa.

Quality Management Journal is an official journal of the American Society for Quality (ASQ). Each issue contains three or four peer-reviewed research articles, plus four to seven book reviews. The journal actively seeks to publish new research that scientifically explores the principles of quality management. Empirical and review articles, research case studies, and management theory articles written by academics and quality management practitioners are featured in the publication. The audience for these papers includes quality management professionals, scholars, and students. Essential for academic libraries with business programs and corporate libraries. URL: https://tandfonline.com/toc/uqmj20/current

3439. *Research-Technology Management: international journal of research management.* Formerly (until 1988): *Research Management.* [ISSN: 0895-6308] 1958. bi-m. GBP 284 (print & online eds.)). Ed(s): James Euchner, MaryAnne Gobble. Taylor & Francis Inc., 530 Walnut St, Ste 850, Philadelphia, PA 19106; support@tandfonline.com; http://www.tandfonline.com. Illus., index, adv. Refereed. Vol. ends: Nov/Dec. Microform: PQC. *Indexed:* A22, B01, B03, BRI. *Aud.:* Ac, Sa.

Research-Technology Management, the award-winning journal of the Innovation Research Interchange (formerly the Industrial Research Institute), focuses on the practice of innovation. Each issue features peer-reviewed research articles written by leading academics, executives, managers, and influential thinkers on the entire spectrum of technological innovation, from research and development through product development and marketing. The articles "map the cutting edge in R&D management, illustrate how academic management theory can be applied in the real world, and give R&D leaders the tools to promote innovation throughout their organizations." The "Perspectives" section provides short reports on significant international news of the current research-technology scene. Editorials, interviews, opinion essays, and a forum section for questions and answers from IRI's membership round out each issue. Several special issues per year address a current or emerging issue in innovation management. Recommended for corporate libraries and academic libraries that support business and engineering programs. URL: www.tandfonline.com/loi/urtm20

3440. ***S A M Advanced Management Journal.*** Former titles (until 1984): *Advanced Management Journal;* (until 1974): *S A M Advanced Management Journal;* (until 1969): *Advanced Management Journal;* (until 1963): *Advanced Management-Office Executive;* Which was formed by the merger of (1939-1962): *Advanced Management;* Which was formerly (until 1939): *The Society for the Advancement of Management. Journal;* (1951-1962): *Office Executive;* Which was formerly (until 1951): *The N O M A Forum for the Office Executive.* [ISSN: 0749-7075] 1935. q. Free to members. Ed(s): Moustafa H Abdelsamad. Society for Advancement of Management, 6300 Ocean Dr, Corpus Christi, TX 78412; sam@samnational.org; http://islander.tamucc.edu/~cobweb/sam/. Illus., index, adv. Refereed. Microform: PQC. *Indexed:* A22, B01, BRI. *Bk. rev.:* Approx. 6, 200-400 words. *Aud.:* Ac, Sa.

SAM Advanced Management Journal is published quarterly by the Society for Advancement of Management at Texas A&M University-Corpus Christi. The publication, refereed by an editorial review board, is designed "to provide general managers with knowledge to communicate with specialists without being specialists themselves." Each issue contains five or six articles of medium length, written by academics and business professionals. They cover a variety of management topics, including human resource management and organizational behavior, strategic management, international management, planning, ethics, productivity improvement, time management, health-care management, nonprofit management, sustainability, and computer use in managerial decisions. The emphasis is on new concepts, innovative ideas, and well-written articles that are easy for practicing managers to understand. The audience "is interested in knowing what current terms mean, what new management concepts can do (including their limitations), how to apply them to a particular situation, and what questions should be asked of experts who implement them." This is a recommended source for corporate libraries and academic libraries that support business programs at all levels. URL: http://samnational.org/publications/sam-advanced-management-journal/

3441. ***Strategic Management Journal.*** [ISSN: 0143-2095] 1980. 13x/yr. GBP 2031. Ed(s): Sendil Ethiraj, Constance Helfat. John Wiley & Sons Ltd., EMEA Institutional Sales, 9600 Garsington Rd, Oxford, OX4 2DQ, United Kingdom; cs-journals@wiley.com; http://onlinelibrary.wiley.com. Illus., index, adv. Sample. Refereed. Vol. ends: Dec. Microform: PQC. Reprint: PSC. *Indexed:* A22, B01, BAS, IBSS. *Aud.:* Ac.

Strategic Management Journal is the official publication of the Strategic Management Society, an international organization. Each issue of *SMJ* features from 9 to 19 research articles that develop theories, test them with evidence, and evaluate the methodologies used in strategic management. Major topics include strategic resource allocation; organization structure; leadership; entrepreneurship and organizational purpose; methods and techniques for evaluating and understanding competitive, technological, social, and political environments; planning processes; and strategic decision processes. The content is intended to interest academics, students, and practicing managers. Highly recommended for academic libraries with business programs. URL: https://onlinelibrary.wiley.com/journal/10970266

3442. ***Strategy + Business.*** [ISSN: 1083-706X] 1995. q. USD 38 combined subscription domestic print & online eds.; USD 48 combined subscription foreign print & online eds. PricewaterhouseCoopers LLP, 90 Park Ave, New York, NY 10016; http://www.pwc.com. Adv. Circ: 133501 Paid and controlled. *Indexed:* A22. *Bk. rev.:* 2-5. *Aud.:* Ac, Sa.

Strategy + Business is a newsmagazine available in print and via open access on the web (with new articles added weekly). Lively articles, targeted to decision makers in business and organizations, address timely issues on strategy, marketing, operations, human capital, and governance. The articles are written by business thought-leaders, including executives, corporate leaders, best-selling business thinkers, academics, researchers, practitioners, and journalists. Featured are articles, interviews, and commentaries relevant to large-scale corporations. These are written and published from the perspectives of seasoned consultants and practitioners, for an audience of practitioners, potential clients, and students. Recommended for corporate, public, and academic libraries with a business program. URL: www.strategy-business.com

3443. ***Strategy & Leadership.*** Formerly (until 1996): *Planning Review;* Incorporates (1996-2000): *The Antidote.* [ISSN: 1087-8572] 1972. bi-m. EUR 2121 (print & online eds.) (excluding UK)). Ed(s): Mr. Robert Randall. Emerald Publishing Limited, Howard House, Wagon Ln, Bingley, BD16 1WA, United Kingdom; emerald@emeraldinsight.com; http://www.emeraldinsight.com. Illus. Sample. Refereed. Vol. ends: Nov/Dec. Reprint: PSC. *Indexed:* A01, A22, B01, BRI, C42, E01. *Bk. rev.:* Length and frequency vary. *Aud.:* Ac, Sa.

Strategy & Leadership features peer-reviewed, medium-length articles on significant issues and trends in business leadership, strategy, and planning. The articles focus on identifying the successful strategies of innovative companies. Each issue contains five to eight articles and consists of a mix of research-based articles, conceptual papers, general reviews, case studies, interviews, and opinion pieces. The articles are written in a clear and accessible style by a diverse group of well-respected academics, business thought-leaders, seasoned executives, and other professionals in the field. The target audience is existing and potential leaders, executive leader coaches, leadership trainers, HR strategists and employers, and business students. *Strategy & Leadership* is highly recommended for academic libraries that support business programs and corporate libraries. URL: https://www.emeraldinsight.com/journal/sl

■ MARINE SCIENCE AND TECHNOLOGY

Marine Biology/Marine Policy/Marine Technology/Ocean Science

David Romito; Kenan Science Library, University of North Carolina at Chapel Hill;dromito@email.unc.edu

Introduction

The field of Marine Science and Technology encompasses the study and utilization of the world's ocean environments. It is inherently interdisciplinary, touching on other areas such as environmental science, biology, public policy, geology, meteorology, physics, and chemistry. Marine science research is essential to discussions about climate change and global biodiversity.

Popular magazines for the general public dealing specifically with marine science are few; however, the prominent titles in general science, natural history, and environment, such as *Scientific American*, *Smithsonian* magazine, and *National Wildlife*, cover ocean topics as well as terrestrial. One notable title for children is *Cousteau Kids*, produced by the Cousteau Society. Many academic research institutions dealing with marine science once produced magazines that communicated their work to the public as part of their commitment to outreach but have since developed into blogs that are still valuable resources. Others retain a magazine-type format, even in online form. *Oceanus*, from the Woods Hole Oceanographic Institute, is an excellent example. Many of the research centers in NOAA's National Sea Grant College Program (https://seagrant.noaa.gov/) also produce magazines that are useful for a broad audience; it is worth seeking these out if a Sea Grant institution is located in your area.

The majority of titles in marine science are academic in nature and concentrated in the major science publishers, although a few scholarly societies still self-publish, and many are available through aggregated full-text abstracting and indexing collections. Some titles are completely open access and others offer an open-access option for authors, so articles are becoming increasingly available even to non-subscribers. Most of the titles described below are global or regional in scope; librarians may need to supplement these with more locally focused titles if they are available for their location. Note that researchers doing work in marine sciences will also typically need to venture into other affiliated subjects for comprehensive research; for example, a scientist studying coral reefs will need to consult titles in marine biology, ecology, and environmental science, as well as general science titles. Because of all these factors, it can be challenging to build a relevant collection in marine science and technology, and librarians will need to coordinate their collection development efforts carefully with their users as well as their colleagues both within their institution and with any consortia they are members of.

Because of marine science and technology's breadth the most appropriate abstracting and indexing tool will depend on the researcher's disciplinary approach. Web of Science and Scopus provide good coverage of the field, and multidisciplinary databases such as Academic Search Premier or ProQuest Research Library are good options for institutions with more modest budgets. The National Sea Grant Library is the freely available digital library and archive for the NOAA Sea Grant documents program and is a small but useful resource, providing literature citations and full-text sources on a variety of marine topics. However, other discipline-specific tools will often be better for more focused searches: GeoRef for marine geology and physical oceanography; Aquatic Science and Fisheries Abstracts for fisheries science; BIOSIS or Zoological Record for marine biology; Environmental Sciences and Pollution Management or GreenFILE for environmental topics; and Compendex for marine engineering.

For more insight into library services and collections for marine science and technology, the website of the International Association of Aquatic and Marine Science Libraries and Information Centres http://www.iamslic.org/) provides excellent information.

Basic Periodicals

Hs, Ga: *Oceanus*; Ac: *Advances in Marine Biology, Deep-Sea Research, Parts 1 and 2, Journal of Experimental Marine Biology and Ecology, Journal of Marine Research, Journal of Physical Oceanography, Limnology and Oceanography, Marine Biology, Marine Ecology–Progress Series, Marine Geology, Marine Mammal Science, Oceanography, Oceanography and Marine Biology, Progress in Oceanography.*

Basic Abstracts and Indexes

Aquatic Sciences and Fisheries Abstracts (ASFA), BIOSIS, GeoRef, National Sea Grant Library Database (http://nsgd.gso.uri.edu/), *Scopus, Web of Science*.

Marine Biology

Note that titles dealing specifically with the applied science of fish biology will be in the Fish, Fisheries, and Aquaculture section.

3444. ***Advances in Marine Biology.*** [ISSN: 0065-2881] 1963. irreg. Ed(s): Michael P Lesser, Barbara E Curry. Academic Press, 225 Wyman St, Waltham, MA 02144; JournalCustomerService-usa@elsevier.com; http://store.elsevier.com/Academic-Press/IMP_5/. Index. Refereed. *Indexed:* A01, A22. *Aud.:* Ac.

This publication provides in-depth, timely review articles on a wide range of topics in marine biology, fisheries science, ecology, zoology, and oceanography. One to three volumes are published annually, with some volumes containing three or four review articles on unrelated topics. Others focus on a theme such as aquatic geomicrobiology or biogeography of the oceans.

American Fisheries Society. Transactions. See Fish, Fisheries, and Aquaculture section.

3445. ***Annual Review of Marine Science (Online).*** [ISSN: 1941-0611] 2009. a. USD 287. Ed(s): Stephen J Giovannoni, Craig A Carlson. Annual Reviews, PO Box 10139, Palo Alto, CA 94303; service@annualreviews.org; http://www.annualreviews.org. Refereed. *Aud.:* Ac.

This annual publication provides review articles on a range of emerging marine topics such as ocean physics, biology, chemistry, and geology. Some recent articles focus on topics such as carbon cycling, reef conservation, and research methodology. A good choice for academic libraries that serve marine biology and oceanography programs.

Aquaculture. See Fish, Fisheries, and Aquaculture section.

3446. ***Aquatic Botany.*** [ISSN: 0304-3770] 1975. 8x/yr. EUR 2801. Ed(s): T Wernberg, E M Gross. Elsevier BV, Radarweg 29, Amsterdam, 1043 NX, Netherlands; info@elsevier.com; https://www.elsevier.com. Illus., index, adv. Refereed. Vol. ends: No. 4. Microform: PQC. *Indexed:* A01, A22, C45, S25. *Bk. rev.:* 1-2, 1,000-3,000 words, signed. *Aud.:* Ac, Sa.

This publication focuses on structure, function, dynamics, and classification of aquatic and marine plant communities. Coverage is split between freshwater and salt/brackish water, with a strong interest in various types of wetlands. It is recommended for academic collections that support botany and environmental studies.

3447. ***Aquatic Conservation (Online): marine and freshwater ecosystems.*** [ISSN: 1099-0755] 1991. m. GBP 1223. Ed(s): Philip Boon, John M Baxter. John Wiley & Sons Ltd., EMEA Institutional Sales, 9600 Garsington Rd, Oxford, OX4 2DQ, United Kingdom; cs-journals@wiley.com; http://onlinelibrary.wiley.com. Adv. Sample. Refereed. Reprint: PSC. *Bk. rev.:* 3, 500-1,000 words. *Aud.:* Ac, Sa.

Practical management issues and more basic considerations of the biology and ecology of freshwater, brackish, and saltwater environments are examined. Topics are wide-ranging, for example: the effect of invasive species on habitats; questions of management and resource use; species distribution; and habitat modeling for conservation ends. Special issues appear annually, usually as supplements, and address issues such as wetlands management. Recommended for institutions that serve aquatic, conservation, and resource management interests.

3448. ***Aquatic Living Resources (Online).*** Incorporates: *Revue des Travaux de l'Institut des Peches Maritimes.* [ISSN: 1765-2952] 1999. q. EUR 487 in the European Union; USD 599 United States; EUR 487 elsewhere. E D P Sciences, 17 Ave du Hoggar, Parc d'Activites de Courtaboeuf, Les Ulis, 91944, France; subscribers@edpsciences.org; https://www.edpsciences.org. Refereed. *Aud.:* Ac.

Fisheries science, aquaculture, aquatic botany, and ecology are the primary focus of this title. Coverage is worldwide, with research papers and shorter notes that address resource biology as it relates to management and exploitation of those resources. Typically, one of the four issues per volume is dedicated to a special issue, such as an ecosystem approach to fisheries or fish stock assessments. Appropriate for academic collections with a strong marine and fisheries focus.

3449. ***Aquatic Mammals.*** [ISSN: 0167-5427] 1972. q. USD 439 (Individuals, USD 199). Western Illinois University Regional Center, 3561 60th St, Moline, IL 61265. Illus. Refereed. Vol. ends: No. 3. *Indexed:* A01, A22. *Bk. rev.:* 1, 1,000 words. *Aud.:* Ac, Sa.

The European Association for Aquatic Mammals, the Alliance of Marine Mammals Parks and Aquariums, and the International Marine Animal Trainers' Association share a strong interest in the husbandry, care, and conservation of aquatic mammals. Articles in this journal reflect this interest, covering health issues and human interactions as well as basic life history of various species. They vary in length from brief observations of behavior to in-depth descriptions of diseases. The journal focuses more on medicine and care than does *Marine Mammal Science,* another of the few titles that address marine mammals. This journal is appropriate for academic collections that support veterinary schools and marine mammal research.

3450. ***Botanica Marina.*** [ISSN: 0006-8055] 1957. bi-m. EUR 1853. Ed(s): Matthew Dring. Walter de Gruyter GmbH, Genthiner Str 13, Berlin, 10785, Germany; service@degruyter.com; https://www.degruyter.de. Illus., index, adv. Sample. Refereed. Reprint: PSC. *Indexed:* A01, A22, C45, E01, S25. *Aud.:* Ac, Sa.

This journal is global in scope, covering basic research in marine botany, microbiology, and mycology for scientists at the university level. It includes work on taxonomy and basic biology, as well as on the utilization of marine plants and algae. It differs from *Aquatic Botany,* in that it focuses on marine organisms. *Botanica Marina* is accredited with the International Association for Plant Taxonomy for the registration of new names of algae and fungi (including fossils). Recommended for institutions that support botany or marine ecology research.

3451. ***Bulletin of Marine Science: research from the world's oceans.*** Formerly (until 1965): *Bulletin of Marine Science of the Gulf and Caribbean.* [ISSN: 0007-4977] 1951. q. USD 800 combined subscription (print & online eds)). Ed(s): Rafael J Araujo, Joseph E Serafy. Rosenstiel School of Marine and Atmospheric Science, 4600 Rickenbacker Causeway, Miami, FL 33149; http://www.rsmas.miami.edu. Refereed. *Indexed:* A01, A22, C45, S25. *Bk. rev.:* 3, 300 words, signed. *Aud.:* Ac.

Previously focused on research involving the Gulf of Mexico and Caribbean, this publication of the Rosenstiel School of Marine and Atmospheric Science is now more global in scope. Concentrating on marine biology, it covers all aspects of marine research, including basic and applied science, management, technology, and policy.

Canadian Journal of Fisheries and Aquatic Sciences. See Fish, Fisheries, and Aquaculture section.

3452. ***Coral Reefs.*** Formerly: *International Society for Reef Studies. Journal.* [ISSN: 0722-4028] 1982. 4x/yr. EUR 2234 (print & online eds.)). Ed(s): Howard R Lasker. Springer, Tiergartenstr 17, Heidelberg, 69121, Germany. Adv. Refereed. Reprint: PSC. *Indexed:* A22, Agr, BRI, E01, S25. *Aud.:* Ac, Sa.

This title focuses on all aspects of reef-related research, especially relevant given the importance of coral reefs as indicators of the state of the marine environment. Articles cover broad time scales and geographic range. One aim of the journal is to emphasize the importance of experimentation, modeling, quantification, and applied science in reef studies. This title is key for academic audiences doing research on marine environments.

3453. ***Deep-Sea Research. Part 2: Topical Studies in Oceanography.*** Supersedes in part (in 1993): *Deep-Sea Research. Part A, Oceanographic Research Papers;* Which was formerly (until 1979): *Deep-Sea Research;* (until 1977): *Deep-Sea Research and Oceanographic Abstracts;* (until 1962): *Deep-Sea Research.* [ISSN: 0967-0645] 1993. 12x/yr. EUR 6703. Elsevier Ltd, The Boulevard, Langford Lane, Oxford, OX5 1GB, United Kingdom; customerserviceau@elsevier.com; http://www.elsevier.com. Adv. Sample. Refereed. Microform: PQC. *Indexed:* A01, A22. *Aud.:* Ac, Sa.

Topical issues of this journal include results of international or interdisciplinary projects and collections of conference papers. Recent examples of thematic issues include drifting sea ice and habitats of the Mid-Atlantic Ridge. Along with its companion journal, *Deep-Sea Research, Part 1: Oceanographic Research Papers,* this title is essential for any institution with a marine biology or oceanography program.

Environmental Biology of Fishes. See Fish, Fisheries, and Aquaculture section.

Fish and Fisheries. See Fish, Fisheries, and Aquaculture section.

Fisheries. See Fish, Fisheries, and Aquaculture section.

Fisheries Management and Ecology. See Fish, Fisheries, and Aquaculture section.

3454. ***Fisheries Oceanography.*** [ISSN: 1054-6006] 1992. bi-m. GBP 1155. Ed(s): Steven J Bograd. Wiley-Blackwell Publishing Ltd., The Atrium, Southern Gate, Chichester, PO19 8QG, United Kingdom; cs-journals@wiley.com; http://onlinelibrary.wiley.com/. Adv. Sample. Refereed. Microform: PQC. Reprint: PSC. *Indexed:* A01, A22, E01. *Aud.:* Ac.

This journal, from the Japanese Society of Fisheries Oceanography, is global in scope and offers a forum for the exchange of information among fisheries scientists worldwide. Typical articles may examine entire food chains, recruitment and abundance of fish species, and dynamics of fish populations. This is a highly ranked journal for a field that has gained recognition in the past decade.

Fisheries Research. See Fish, Fisheries, and Aquaculture section.

Fishery Bulletin. See Fish, Fisheries, and Aquaculture section.

3455. ***Harmful Algae.*** [ISSN: 1568-9883] 2002. 10x/yr. EUR 914. Ed(s): Christopher Gobler. Elsevier BV, Radarweg 29, Amsterdam, 1043 NX, Netherlands; info@elsevier.com; https://www.elsevier.com. *Indexed:* A01, C45. *Aud.:* Sa.

This title provides a forum for information on harmful microalgae and cyanobacteria in both fresh and marine waters. It focuses on the life histories, physiology, toxicology, monitoring, and management of blooms, and includes both original research and reviews. This journal is appropriate for libraries that support research in marine science and botany, as well as those that serve an extensive environmental studies, toxicology, or environmental health program.

3456. ***Helgoland Marine Research (Online).*** [ISSN: 1438-3888] . Free. Ed(s): Maarten Boersma. BioMed Central Ltd., The Campus, 4 Crinan St, London, N1 9XW, United Kingdom; info@biomedcentral.com; https://www.biomedcentral.com. Refereed. *Indexed:* C45. *Aud.:* Ac.

This open-access journal covers all aspects of marine and brackish water biology, with a focus on environmental aspects. The official publication of the Alfred Wegener Institute, Helmholtz Centre for Polar and Marine Research, it is international in scope. Articles present original research and reviews on such topics as ecology, physiology, evolution, and taxonomy.

3457. ***I C E S Journal of Marine Science: journal du conseil.*** Incorporates (1991-1995): *I C E S Marine Science Symposia;* Which was formerly (1903-1989): *Conseil Permanent International pour l'Exploration de la Mer. Rapport et Proces-Verbaux des Reunions;* Former titles (until 1991): *Conseil International pour l'Exploration de la Mer. Journal;* (until 1968): *Conseil Permanent International pour l'Exploration de la Mer. Journal;* (until 1926): *Conseil Permanent International pour l'Exploration de la Mer. Publications de Circonstance.* [ISSN: 1054-3139] 1903. 10x/yr. EUR 2002. Ed(s): Howard I Browman. Oxford University Press, Great Clarendon St, Oxford, OX2 6DP, United Kingdom; onlinequeries.uk@oup.com; http://global.oup.com. Adv. Sample. Refereed. Reprint: PSC. *Indexed:* A01, A22, C45, E01. *Aud.:* Ac.

The International Council for the Exploration of the Sea (ICES) coordinates and promotes applied research in the North Atlantic. Its journal is an outlet for that research, as well as for other information contributing to a broad understanding of all marine systems, their resources, and the effects of human activity on both. Articles address management and conservation issues, biology, ecology, fishing, climate change, and changes in technology. Typically, this title includes three issues per year of proceedings from ICES symposia.

Invertebrate Biology. See Zoology/Invertebrates section.

3458. ***The Journal of Cetacean Research and Management.*** Former titles (until 1999): *International Whaling Commission. Report;* (until 1978): *International Commission on Whaling. Report.* [ISSN: 1561-0713] 1950. 3x/yr. GBP 110 (Individuals, GBP 75; GBP 25 per issue). Ed(s): G P Donovan. International Whaling Commission, The Red House,135 Station Rd, Impington, CB24 9NP, United Kingdom; secretariat@iwc.int; http://www.iwc.int. Refereed. *Indexed:* A01. *Aud.:* Ac, Sa.

This title replaces the scientific section of *Reports of the International Whaling Commission* (IWC) and publishes peer-reviewed papers important to the conservation and management of cetaceans. The focus tends toward population abundance and distribution, and the effects of harvest and other human interactions, with occasional notes on unusual sightings or behavior. An annual supplement includes the *Reports of the IWC Scientific Committee,* which contains population trends, discussion of issues and concerns, and management updates. Appropriate for research collections with strong marine mammal and conservation programs.

3459. *Journal of Experimental Marine Biology and Ecology.* [ISSN: 0022-0981] 1967. 12x/yr. EUR 8313. Ed(s): B Konar, P Petraitis. Elsevier BV, Radarweg 29, Amsterdam, 1043 NX, Netherlands; info@elsevier.com; https://www.elsevier.com/. Illus., index, adv. Refereed. Vol. ends: No. 2. Microform: PQC. *Indexed:* A01, A22, C45, S25. *Bk. rev.:* 1,000 words, signed. *Aud.:* Ac.

The focus of this journal is laboratory and field experimental study, and its scope includes biochemistry, physiology, behavior, genetics, ecosystems, and ecological modeling. Of interest to marine ecologists, physiologists, and biochemists, this title is appropriate for academic institutions with marine biology, oceanography, and ecology programs.

Journal of Fish Biology. See Fish, Fisheries, and Aquaculture section.

3460. *Journal of Marine Animals and Their Ecology.* [ISSN: 1911-8929] 2008. q. Free. Ed(s): Dr. Carin Wittnich. Oceanographic Environmental Research Society (O E R S), 12 Burton Ave, Barrie, ON L4N 2R2, Canada; http://www.oers.ca/. *Indexed:* C45. *Aud.:* Ac.

This online, open-access journal attempts to fill a niche in marine biology publications—applied science of marine animals. Its potential strength is the focus on practical research and techniques for handling and rehabilitating marine animals, and an interest in the impact that human activities in the marine environment has on animals. It will be useful for academic programs with veterinary interests and marine mammal programs.

3461. *Journal of Marine Biology.* [ISSN: 1687-9481] 2008. . USD 495. Hindawi Publishing Corporation, 315 Madison Ave, 3rd Fl, Ste 3070, New York, NY 10017; info@hindawi.com; https://www.hindawi.com. Refereed. *Indexed:* C45. *Aud.:* Ac, Sa.

This open-access journal is global in scope and has published original research as well as review articles in all areas of marine biology since 2009. Focus and special issues undertaken to date are titled "Coral Reef Ecosystems" and "Ecosystem-based Management of Pacific Islands." This title is freely available online or in print at a modest price.

3462. *Journal of Marine Research (Online).* [ISSN: 1543-9542] 1973. bi-m. USD 200. Ed(s): Kenneth H Brink. Sears Foundation for Marine Research, Yale University, PO Box 208118, New Haven, CT 06520; http://peabody.yale.edu/scientific-publications/sears-foundation-marine-research-publications. Index. Refereed. *Aud.:* Ac.

The scope of this journal includes physical, biological, and chemical oceanography, and preference is given to articles that report on a combination or interaction of ecological and physical processes. This publication is global in scope and useful for marine science collections.

3463. *Journal of Plankton Research.* [ISSN: 0142-7873] 1979. bi-m. EUR 1708. Ed(s): John R Dolan. Oxford University Press, Great Clarendon St, Oxford, OX2 6DP, United Kingdom; onlinequeries.uk@oup.com; http://global.oup.com. Illus., index, adv. Sample. Refereed. Circ: 300. Vol. ends: No. 3. Reprint: PSC. *Indexed:* A01, A22, C45, E01, S25. *Bk. rev.:* 1, 500 words, signed. *Aud.:* Ac, Sa.

Ecology, physiology, taxonomy, and behavior of plankton are covered in this journal, with a majority of the articles describing marine species. Contributors address these drifting organisms (zooplankton and phytoplankton) with research articles and short communications. Occasional "Horizons" pieces challenge traditional views or review current trends. This is an essential title for biological oceanography research collections.

The Journal of Shellfish Research. See Fish, Fisheries, and Aquaculture section.

3464. *Marine and Coastal Fisheries: dynamics, management, and ecosystem science.* [ISSN: 1942-5120] 2008. a. Free. Ed(s): Debra Murie. Wiley-Blackwell Publishing Ltd., The Atrium, Southern Gate, Chichester, PO19 8QG, United Kingdom; cs-journals@wiley.com; http://onlinelibrary.wiley.com. Refereed. *Indexed:* S25. *Aud.:* Ac.

Launched in 2008, this open-access publication of the American Fisheries Society is a strong addition to the literature of marine biology. This journal presents innovative research on marine, coastal, and estuarine fisheries, and its mission is to improve the conservation and sustainability of fishery resources and ecosystems. It is a good choice for library collections that support a marine biology or fisheries program.

3465. *Marine & Freshwater Research.* Formerly (until 1995): *Australian Journal of Marine and Freshwater Research.* [ISSN: 1323-1650] 1950. m. Ed(s): Max Finlayson. C S I R O Publishing, Locked Bag 10, Clayton, VIC 3169, Australia; publishing@csiro.au; http://www.publish.csiro.au/home.htm. Illus., adv. Sample. Refereed. Vol. ends: No. 8. *Indexed:* A22, Agr, C45, E01, S25. *Aud.:* Ac, Sa.

This journal includes a broad range of interdisciplinary research in ecology, hydrology, biogeochemistry, and oceanography, with the overarching goal of highlighting the interconnectedness of aquatic environments, processes, and management applications. Specific subjects can include fisheries science, biogeochemistry, physiology, genetics, biogeography, and toxicology. Although published in Australia, this journal is global in scope. It is recommended for academic libraries that support marine or aquatic-based programs.

3466. *Marine Biodiversity: international journal of marine science.* Formerly (until 2009): *Senckenbergiana Maritima.* [ISSN: 1867-1616] 1969. 4x/yr. EUR 496 (print & online eds.)). Ed(s): Pedro M Arbizu. Springer, Tiergartenstr 17, Heidelberg, 69121, Germany; subscriptions@springer.com; https://www.springer.com. Adv. Refereed. Reprint: PSC. *Indexed:* A22, E01. *Aud.:* Ac, Sa.

Marine Biodiversity is an international journal containing short notes, original research, and review articles on all aspects of biodiversity in marine ecosystems, including systematics, species interactions, genetic analyses, effects of human populations, and discussions of methodology.

3467. *Marine Biodiversity Records.* Formerly (until 2008): *Marine and Freshwater Biodiversity.* [ISSN: 1755-2672] 19??. . Free. Ed(s): Nova Mieszkowska. BioMed Central Ltd., Floor 6, 236 Gray's Inn Rd, London, WC1X 8HB, United Kingdom; info@biomedcentral.com. Adv. Refereed. *Indexed:* A01, A22, C45, E01. *Aud.:* Ac, Sa.

This open-access title is a companion publication to the *Journal of the Marine Biological Association of the United Kingdom* for rapid communications on changes in geographical location of marine organisms as well as habitat loss. Articles are short and document new species, new locations for organisms, and changes in habitat and behavior.

3468. *Marine Biological Association of the United Kingdom. Journal.* [ISSN: 0025-3154] 1887. bi-m. GBP 1570. Ed(s): Jane Lewis. Cambridge University Press, University Printing House, Shaftesbury Rd, Cambridge, CB2 8BS, United Kingdom; online@cambridge.org; https://www.cambridge.org/. Illus., index, adv. Sample. Refereed. Circ: 1600. Vol. ends: No. 4. Microform: BHP; PQC. Reprint: PSC. *Indexed:* A22, C45, E01. *Aud.:* Ac, Sa.

This journal is international in scope and includes articles on all aspects of marine biology: ecological surveys; population studies of oceanic, coastal, and shore communities; physiology and experimental biology; taxonomy, morphology, and life history of marine animals and plants; and chemical and physical oceanographic work that relates closely to the biological environment. This journal is appropriate for all academic research libraries with a marine biology program.

3469. *Marine Biology: international journal on life in oceans and coastal waters.* [ISSN: 0025-3162] 1967. m. EUR 7688 (print & online eds.)). Ed(s): Ulrich Sommer. Springer, Tiergartenstr 17, Heidelberg, 69121, Germany. Illus., adv. Sample. Refereed. Vol. ends: No. 4. Reprint: PSC. *Indexed:* A01, A22, Agr, C45, E01, S25. *Aud.:* Ac, Sa.

This journal is very broad in scope, and includes articles on a wide variety of topics: all aspects of plankton research; biological and biochemical oceanography; environment-organism interrelationships; experimental biology; metabolic rates and routes; biochemical research on marine organisms;

biosystem research; energy budgets; dynamics and structures of communities; the use of marine resources; anthropogenic influences on marine environments; and evolution, modeling, and scientific apparatus and techniques. This is a core journal for marine biology collections.

3470. ***Marine Biology Research.*** Formed by the merger of (1961-2005): *Sarsia;* (1964-2005): *Ophelia.* [ISSN: 1745-1000] 2005. 10x/yr. GBP 677 (print & online eds.)). Ed(s): Haakon Hop. Taylor & Francis, 2, 3 & 4 Park Sq, Milton Park, Abingdon, OX14 4RN, United Kingdom; subscriptions@tandf.co.uk; https://www.tandfonline.com. Adv. Sample. Refereed. Reprint: PSC. *Indexed:* A01, A22, C45, E01. *Aud.:* Ac, Sa.

This journal came about as a merger of the longstanding core titles *Sarsia* and *Ophelia.* It aims to provide an international forum for all areas of marine biology and oceanography, including ecology, behavior, taxonomy, environment, and evolution. Articles on applied research that contribute to general biological insight are also included. A core title in academic and research institutions with marine biology or oceanography collections.

3471. ***Marine Biotechnology: an international journal focusing on marine genomics, molecular biology and biotechnology.*** Formed by the merger of (1930-1999): *Molecular Marine Biology and Biotechnology;* (1993-1999): *Journal of Marine Biotechnology.* [ISSN: 1436-2228] 1999. bi-m. EUR 1480 (print & online eds.)). Ed(s): J Grant Burgess, Nobuhiro Fusetani. Springer New York LLC, 233 Spring St, New York, NY 10013; customerservice@springer.com; http://www.springer.com. Illus., adv. Sample. Refereed. Vol. ends: No. 4. Reprint: PSC. *Indexed:* A22, Agr, BRI, C45, E01. *Aud.:* Ac, Sa.

This title explores the biotechnological applications of marine organisms. Its scope includes research in genomics, proteomics, biochemistry, cell biology, and novel applications of marine natural products. It is the official journal of the European Society for Marine Biotechnology and the Japanese Society for Marine Biotechnology and is an important title for institutions with both molecular biology and marine science research programs.

3472. ***Marine Ecology - Progress Series.*** [ISSN: 0171-8630] 1979. 23x/yr. EUR 5480 combined subscription (print & online eds.)). Ed(s): Myron Peck. Inter-Research, Nordbuente 23, Oldendorf, 21385, Germany; ir@int-res.com; https://www.int-res.com. Illus., index, adv. Refereed. Vol. ends: No. 3. *Indexed:* A22, C45, S25. *Aud.:* Ac, Sa.

This journal features research articles, reviews, and notes on both fundamental and applied topics in marine ecology. The scope includes botany, zoology, ecological aspects of fisheries and aquaculture, resource management, and ecosystem research. Occasional "theme" sections will synthesize information on a topic by a multi-author team. This is a core title for libraries that support teaching and research in environmental studies and marine biology.

3473. ***Marine Environmental Research.*** Incorporates (in 1991): *Oil and Chemical Pollution;* Which was formerly (until 1986): *Journal of Oil and Petrochemical Pollution.* [ISSN: 0141-1136] 1978. 10x/yr. EUR 3352. Ed(s): F Regoli, I Sokolova. Elsevier Ltd, 125 London Wall, London, EC2Y 5AS, United Kingdom; corporate.sales@elsevier.com; http://www.elsevier.com. Illus., index, adv. Sample. Refereed. Vol. ends: No. 5. Microform: PQC. *Indexed:* A01, A22, C45, S25. *Aud.:* Ac, Sa.

This journal focuses on chemical, physical, and biological interactions within the marine realm. Articles examine processes and environmental change with an eye toward understanding systems to facilitate more informed management. The international scope enhances the sharing of information on marine environmental science. It is useful for extensive marine science collections.

Marine Fisheries Review. See Fish, Fisheries, and Aquaculture section.

3474. ***Marine Mammal Science (Online).*** [ISSN: 1748-7692] 1985. q. GBP 249. Ed(s): Daryl Boness. Wiley-Blackwell Publishing, Inc., 111 River St, Hoboken, NJ 07030; http://onlinelibrary.wiley.com. Refereed. *Bk. rev.:* 3, 2,000 words. *Aud.:* Ac, Sa.

The journal of the Society for Marine Mammalogy, this title covers all aspects of the biology of marine mammals: evolution, systematics, physiology, biochemistry, behavior, ecology, conservation, and genetics. Original research, reviews, notes, opinions, and letters are included. This is a core title for libraries that serve a marine biology program.

3475. ***Oceanography and Marine Biology: an annual review.*** [ISSN: 0078-3218] 1963. a. C R C Press UK, 2 Park Sq, Milton Park, Abingdon, OX14 4RN, United Kingdom; book.orders@tandf.co.uk; http://www.crcpress.com/. *Indexed:* A22. *Aud.:* Ac.

These authoritative review articles, including comprehensive reference lists, are appropriate introductory material for students and are also useful for researchers keeping abreast of topics beyond their own fields of research. Sample topics from a recent issue include global ecology of kelp, diversity in benthic communities, and effects of climate change on marine life. This is an essential element in any library that supports marine biology or environmental studies undergraduate education.

Reviews in Fish Biology and Fisheries. See Fish, Fisheries, and Aquaculture section.

Marine Policy

3476. ***B O E M Ocean Science.*** Former titles (until 2012): *Bureau of Ocean Energy Management, Regulation and Enforcement. Ocean Science;* (until 2010): *Minerals Management Service. Ocean Science;* (until 2004): *Minerals Management Service. Today.* [ISSN: 2328-630X] 1990. q. Free. Ed(s): Melanie Damour. U.S. Department of the Interior, Bureau of Ocean Energy Management, Office of Public Affairs, 1849 C St, NW, Washington, DC 20240; BOEMPublicAffairs@boem.gov; http://www.boem.gov. *Aud.:* Ga, Ac, Sa.

Ocean Science is a quarterly publication of the U.S. Department of the Interior's Bureau of Ocean Energy Management. This freely available online journal addresses science and technology issues related to ocean-based fossil fuel and renewable energy development, as well as policy, history, geology, and marine conservation topics. While academic, government, and marine industry audiences will find it most useful, the articles are accessible and may be of interest to the general public, especially in coastal regions.

3477. ***Coastal Management: an international journal of marine environment, resources, law and society.*** Formerly (until 1987): *Coastal Zone Management Journal.* [ISSN: 0892-0753] 1973. bi-m. GBP 1141 (print & online eds.)). Ed(s): Patrick Christie. Taylor & Francis Inc., 711 3rd Ave, 8th Fl, New York, NY 10017; support@tandfonline.com; http://www.taylorandfrancis.com. Illus., adv. Sample. Refereed. Microform: WSH. Reprint: PSC. *Indexed:* A22, B01, C45, E01, S25. *Aud.:* Ac.

The official journal of The Coastal Society focuses on issues relating to the use of coastal environments and resources. Current topics concern coastal tourism, planning and management of seaports and waterfronts, sea level rise, and ocean policy and planning. International in scope, this publication would be a good addition to any library that supports research in marine policy or law of the sea.

3478. ***Coastal Services (Online): the magazine that links people, resources and information.*** 1998. bi-m. Free. National Oceanic and Atmospheric Administration (N O A A), Coastal Services Center, 2234 S Hobson Ave, Charleston, SC 29405; http://www.csc.noaa.gov/index.html. *Aud.:* Hs, Ga, Ac, Sa.

This free electronic newsletter provides useful information for resource managers and those interested in coastal issues. Produced by the U.S. National Oceanic and Atmospheric Administration's Coastal Services Center, it highlights projects throughout the country and solutions or strategies to address real issues. Appropriate for public and academic collections with an audience interested in coastal issues and policy. It includes useful links to additional resources.

3479. ***Marine Policy.*** [ISSN: 0308-597X] 1977. m. bi-m. until 2014. EUR 2408. Ed(s): H D Smith. Pergamon Press, The Blvd, Langford Ln, E Park, Kidlington, OX5 1GB, United Kingdom; JournalsCustomerServiceEMEA@elsevier.com; http://www.elsevier.com. Illus., adv. Sample. Refereed. Microform: PQC. *Indexed:* A22, IBSS. *Aud.:* Ac, Sa.

The focus of policy formulation and analysis addresses the needs of lawyers, marine resource managers, economists, political scientists, and other social scientists. Recent volumes have an increased focus on fisheries policy, although maritime issues and marine management tools are also covered. Occasionally, issues may contain historical overviews or discussions of emerging trends. This journal is a core title for academic collections with a marine policy or management component.

3480. ***Ocean & Coastal Management.*** Formerly (until 1992): *Ocean and Shoreline Management;* Which was formed by the merger of (1973-1988): *Ocean Management;* (1985-1988): *Journal of Shoreline Management.* [ISSN: 0964-5691] 1988. 16x/yr. EUR 3333. Ed(s): V de Jonge. Elsevier Ltd, 66 Siward Rd, Bromley, BR2 9JZ, United Kingdom; http://www.elsevier.com. Illus., adv. Sample. Refereed. Vol. ends: No. 44. Microform: PQC. *Indexed:* A22, S25. *Bk. rev.:* 1-2, 300-600 words. *Aud.:* Ac, Sa.

This multidisciplinary, international journal covers near-shore and coastal environmental issues. Topics include coastal zone management throughout the world, environmental impacts of ocean use, and resolution of multiple-use conflicts. One or two issues of the 12 annually are dedicated to special topics on coastal management. This is a core title for academic collections with marine policy and management aspects.

3481. ***Ocean Development and International Law.*** Formerly (until 1973): *Ocean Development and International Law Journal.* [ISSN: 0090-8320] 1973. q. GBP 783 (print & online eds.)). Ed(s): Ted L McDorman. Taylor & Francis Inc., 711 3rd Ave, 8th Fl, New York, NY 10017; support@tandfonline.com; http://www.taylorandfrancis.com. Adv. Sample. Refereed. Microform: WSH. Reprint: PSC. *Indexed:* A01, A22, B01, BRI, C45, E01, IBSS, L14, P61. *Aud.:* Sa.

Less specialized than *Marine Policy,* this journal contains articles on law of the sea; comparative domestic ocean law; shipping, ocean engineering, and marine economics; and marine science that will be of interest to those involved in the management or utilization of ocean resources. It is appropriate for libraries that support programs in aquaculture, resource management, and environmental law.

3482. ***The Sandbar: legal reporter of the national sea grant college program.*** [ISSN: 1947-3966] 2002. q. Ed(s): Terra Bowling. Sea Grant Law Center, 256 Kinard Hall, Wing E, PO Box 1848, University, MS 38677; http://nsglc.olemiss.edu. *Indexed:* L14. *Aud.:* Ac, Sa.

Published by the National Sea Grant Law Center at the University of Mississippi, this quarterly publication provides insight on legal issues affecting the coasts and oceans of the United States. The articles are two- to four-page summaries written for an informed but non-legal audience. It serves as a companion to the more legalistic *Sea Grant Law and Policy Journal.* A useful publication for readers interested in coastal and ocean issues from legal and policy perspectives.

3483. ***Sea Grant Law & Policy Journal.*** [ISSN: 1947-3982] 2008. s-a. Ed(s): Stephanie Showalter. University of Mississippi, National Sea Grant Law Center, 256 Kinard Hall, Wing E, University, MS 38677; http://nsglc.olemiss.edu. *Indexed:* L14. *Aud.:* Ac, Sa.

This open-access online journal continues a strong Sea Grant tradition of communicating law and policy information on marine issues. The two issues a year (usually) highlight the National Sea Grant Law Center annual symposium in the summer issue and selected articles from law students and others in the winter. Articles address a variety of topics from the effect of sea-level rise on coastal community planning to territorial sea policy on marine renewable energy. All are written in a law review style, but are briefer and more accessible for the informed reader. *The SandBar* (above in this section) is an online quarterly publication from the center, which presents legal and policy information in a very accessible newsletter format. Both are worthy additions to a marine policy collection, as they tend to focus on more applied research and case studies.

Marine Technology

3484. ***Applied Ocean Research.*** [ISSN: 0141-1187] 1979. 8x/yr. EUR 2064. Elsevier Ltd, The Boulevard, Langford Lane, Oxford, OX5 1GB, United Kingdom; customerserviceau@elsevier.com; http://www.elsevier.com. Adv. Refereed. Microform: PQC. *Indexed:* A01, A22. *Aud.:* Ac, Sa.

This title focuses on ocean engineering and provides solid research articles on topics ranging from mooring systems to wave dynamics. This title is useful for specialized research collections with engineering interests in the marine environment.

3485. ***Coastal Engineering.*** [ISSN: 0378-3839] 1977. 12x/yr. EUR 3432. Ed(s): Inigo J Losada. Elsevier BV, Radarweg 29, Amsterdam, 1043 NX, Netherlands; info@elsevier.com; https://www.elsevier.com. Refereed. Microform: PQC. *Indexed:* A01, A22. *Aud.:* Ac, Sa.

Coastal Engineering focuses on marine and coastal technology, with particular interest in coastal structures (breakwaters and jetties) and the wave dynamics of this environment. One volume annually is usually devoted to special topics, such as coastal video monitoring systems. Relevant for specialized research collections with engineering interests in the marine environment.

3486. ***I E E E Journal of Oceanic Engineering (Online).*** [ISSN: 1558-1691] 1976. q. USD 415. Ed(s): Mandar Chitre. Institute of Electrical and Electronics Engineers, 445 Hoes Ln, Piscataway, NJ 08854; onlinesupport@ieee.org; http://www.ieee.org. Refereed. *Aud.:* Ac, Sa.

The IEEE Oceanic Engineering Society encourages articles and technical communications that apply electrical, electronics, and instrumentation engineering to the marine environment. Topics vary from specific design of new instruments for marine research, such as satellite tags, to investigation of ambient noise. Occasional issues are dedicated to special topics such as sediment acoustic processes. This journal is more important and far more affordable than *Ocean Engineering* to both engineering and oceanographic collections.

3487. ***International Journal of Offshore and Polar Engineering.*** [ISSN: 1053-5381] 1991. q. Free to members; Non-members, USD 170. International Society of Offshore and Polar Engineers, 495 N Whisman Rd, Ste 300, Mountain View, CA 94043; info@isope.org; http://www.isope.org. Index. Refereed. *Aud.:* Ac, Sa.

IJOPE is the journal of the International Society of Offshore and Polar Engineers. It reports technical information and research papers on technologies used in ocean and polar applications, such as fossil fuel pipelines, renewable energy generators, and marine vessels. Most suitable for engineers in an academic or industry setting.

3488. ***Journal of Marine Science and Technology.*** Formerly (until 1995): *Naval Architecture and Ocean Engineering;* (until 1977): *Selected Papers from the Journal of the Society of Naval Architects of Japan.* [ISSN: 0948-4280] 1968. q. EUR 442 (print & online eds.)). Ed(s): Ken Takagi. Springer Japan KK, No 2 Funato Bldg, 1-11-11 Kudan-kita, Tokyo, 102-0073, Japan; http://www.springer.jp. Refereed. Reprint: PSC. *Indexed:* A01, A22, Agr, E01. *Aud.:* Ac, Sa.

This title focuses on issues relating to ocean and marine engineering, and can include articles on naval architecture, hull design, stability modeling, and material strength. It is most appropriate for libraries that support marine engineering studies and applications.

3489. *Journal of Ocean Engineering and Marine Energy.* [ISSN: 2198-6444] 2015. 4x/yr. EUR 251 (print & online eds.)). Ed(s): R. Cengiz Ertekin. Springer, Tiergartenstr 17, Heidelberg, 69121, Germany; subscriptions@springer.com; https://www.springer.com. Refereed. Reprint: PSC. *Aud.:* Ac.

This is a journal of research, short communications, and reviews on various applications of engineering in ocean habitats, with a focus on energy technologies, both fossil fuel and renewable. It covers theoretical models as well as practical applications, and touches on environmental and climate issues.

3490. *Journal of Waterway, Port, Coastal, and Ocean Engineering.* Former titles (until 1983): *American Society of Civil Engineers. Waterway, Port, Coastal and Ocean Division. Journal;* (until 1977): *American Society of Civil Engineers. Waterways, Harbors, and Coastal Engineering Division. Journal;* (until 1970): *American Society of Civil Engineers. Waterways and Harbors Division. Journal;* (until 1956): *American Society of Civil Engineers. Waterways Division. Journal;* (until 1955): *American Society of Civil Engineers. Proceedings.* [ISSN: 0733-950X] 1873. bi-m. USD 900. Ed(s): Ronald H Riggs. American Society of Civil Engineers, 1801 Alexander Bell Dr, Reston, VA 20191; ascelibrary@asce.org; http://www.asce.org. Illus., adv. Refereed. *Indexed:* A01, A22, BRI, HRIS, S25. *Aud.:* Ac, Sa.

This international journal focuses on the applied issues of civil engineering in the aquatic environment, from bridge construction to wave action on breakwaters, to forcing action in open waters. It is sponsored by the American Society of Civil Engineers, and the technical papers, notes, and discussion items address issues of interest globally, while describing local solutions. This journal is essential for engineering collections with an interest in the marine and aquatic environments.

3491. *Marine Geodesy: an international journal of ocean surveys, mapping and sensing.* [ISSN: 0149-0419] 1977. q. . GBP 797 (print & online eds.)). Ed(s): Rongxing Li. Taylor & Francis Inc., 711 3rd Ave, 8th Fl, New York, NY 10017; support@tandfonline.com; http://www.taylorandfrancis.com. Illus., adv. Sample. Refereed. Vol. ends: No. 4. Reprint: PSC. *Indexed:* A01, A22, E01. *Bk. rev.:* 3, 500 words. *Aud.:* Ac, Sa.

This international journal covers the highly specialized science of measuring and monitoring the ocean. Articles describe instrument bias and calibration challenges, boundary datum, and use of remote sensing. This is a relevant addition to research collections that support field-based oceanography programs.

3492. *Marine Georesources & Geotechnology.* Formed by the merger of (1975-1993): *Marine Geotechnology;* (1977-1993): *Marine Mining.* [ISSN: 1064-119X] 1993. 10x/yr. GBP 1024 (print & online eds.)). Ed(s): John C Wiltschire. Taylor & Francis Inc., 711 3rd Ave, 8th Fl, New York, NY 10017; support@tandfonline.com; http://www.taylorandfrancis.com. Illus., index, adv. Sample. Refereed. Vol. ends: No. 4. Microform: PQC. Reprint: PSC. *Indexed:* A01, A22, E01, S25. *Aud.:* Ac, Sa.

A companion title to *Marine Geology,* this journal focuses on applied research relating to seafloor sediments and rocks. Topics range from characterizations of dredged materials to restoration of marine macrofauna, to the effect of nodule mining. It is useful for academic collections with marine engineering and applied geology programs.

3493. *Marine Log.* Former titles (until 1987): *Marine Engineering - Log;* (until 1979): *Marine Engineering - Log International;* (until 1977): *Marine Engineering - Log;* (until 1956): *Marine Engineering;* (until 1953): *Marine Engineering Shipping and Review;* (until 1935): *Marine Engineering & Shipping Age;* (until 1921): *Marine Engineering;* (until 1920): *International Marine Engineering;* (until 1906): *Marine Engineering.* [ISSN: 0897-0491] 1876. m. USD 92 in North America (print or online ed.) (Free to qualified personnel). Ed(s): John R Snyder. Simmons-Boardman Publishing Corp., 55 Broad St., 26th Fl., New York, NY 10004-2580; http://www.simmonsboardman.com. Illus., adv. Circ: 27458. Microform: PQC. *Indexed:* A22, B01, HRIS. *Aud.:* Ga, Sa.

The various trade magazines in marine technology have some overlap, but they target slightly different audiences. *Marine Log* is the oldest U.S. trade magazine, starting as *Marine Engineering* in 1876. Today, it broadly covers the business and technology of shipping and the maritime trades from an American perspective. Aimed at maritime business, it has a slick online presence, with topics of articles ranging from policy concerns to greening the industry.

3494. *Marine News.* [ISSN: 1087-3864] 19??. m. Free to qualified personnel. Ed(s): Joseph Keefe. Maritime Activity Reports Inc., 118 E 25th St, 2nd Fl, New York, NY 10010; http://www.marinelink.com. Adv. *Aud.:* Ga, Sa.

Maritime Activity Reports publishes two magazines for the maritime industry, *Maritime Reporter and Engineering News* and *Marine News*. The latter targets the shallow-draft workboat audience, including owners, operators, and service providers. As a trade magazine, it includes interviews with industry leaders, short articles on timely topics, and advertisements. It is freely available online, making it a useful resource for those that serve a maritime audience.

3495. *Marine Pollution Bulletin: the international journal for marine environmental scientists, engineers, administrators, politicians and lawyers.* [ISSN: 0025-326X] 1970. 24x/yr. EUR 3556. Ed(s): Francois Galgani, Victor Quintino. Elsevier Ltd, 125 London Wall, London, EC2Y 5AS, United Kingdom; corporate.sales@elsevier.com; http://www.elsevier.com. Illus., index, adv. Sample. Refereed. Vol. ends: No. 12. Microform: PQC. *Indexed:* A22, C45, S25. *Bk. rev.:* 2, 500 words. *Aud.:* Ac, Sa.

Using a variety of features, this inclusive and rigorous journal documents conditions, effects of human activity, and responses to pollutants in the marine environment. The editorials and invited reviews offer in-depth insight into marine environmental issues, and briefer news items cover pollution events around the globe. In addition to the monthly issues, special issues focus on conferences or topics such as water quality in a specific geographic region. This is a high-ranked journal that is appropriate for academic and research collections that support environmental science, marine management, and biological oceanography programs.

3496. *Marine Technology Reporter.* [ISSN: 1559-7415] 1994. 9x/yr. Free. Ed(s): Gregory R Trauthwein. New Wave Media, 118 E 18th St 2nd Fl, New York, NY 10010. Adv. Circ: 12825 Controlled. *Aud.:* Ga, Sa.

Marine Technology Reporter competes with *Sea Technology* for the marine techie audience, those buying, installing, and using equipment for marine operations, research, and exploration. Coverage includes salvage, offshore oil and gas, and commercial diving, as well as underwater operations and surveying. Increased focus on scientific support adds dimension. While somewhat North American in focus, it provides solid information on global developments in the field.

3497. *Marine Technology Society Journal.* Formerly (until 1969): *Journal of Ocean Technology.* [ISSN: 0025-3324] 1966. bi-m. USD 155 Free to members. Ed(s): Amy Morgante, Anni Vuorenkoski Dalgleish. Marine Technology Society, 1100 H St N W Ste LL-100, Washington, DC 20005; membership@mtsociety.org; https://www.mtsociety.org/. Illus., index, adv. Sample. Refereed. Vol. ends: No. 4. *Indexed:* A22, C45, HRIS, S25. *Bk. rev.:* 1-3, 500 words. *Aud.:* Ga, Ac, Sa.

This publication addresses all aspects of marine technology—how it works, how to use it in science, how it affects society. Articles are written for a wide audience. Regular issues focus on uses of technology in marine sciences, with articles written by both scientists and industry researchers. Special issues address such topics as acoustic tracking of fish, ocean education, and marine sanctuary management. This is a title for general collections that serve an audience with marine interests, as well as for academic collections that support broad marine programs.

3498. *Maritime Reporter and Engineering News.* Formerly (until 1962): *Maritime Reporter.* [ISSN: 0025-3448] 1939. m. USD 98 elsewhere (Free to qualified personnel). Ed(s): Greg Trauthwein. Maritime Activity Reports Inc., 118 E 25th St, 2nd Fl, New York, NY 10010; http://www.marinelink.com. Illus., adv. *Aud.:* Ga, Sa.

This publication has a broader scope than its sister magazine, *Marine News*. It is more international, covering all aspects of shipping from design and construction to operations and policy, providing wide insight into the industry.

3499. *Ocean Engineering.* [ISSN: 0029-8018] 1968. 18x/yr. EUR 5672. Ed(s): Atilla Incecik. Pergamon Press, The Blvd, Langford Ln, E Park, Kidlington, OX5 1GB, United Kingdom; JournalsCustomerServiceEMEA@elsevier.com; http://www.elsevier.com. Illus., index, adv. Sample. Refereed. Vol. ends: No. 28. Microform: PQC. *Indexed:* A01, A22, S25. *Aud.:* Ac, Sa.

This highly specialized journal covers marine engineering from ships to structures to instrumentation. It is aimed at engineers, and the coverage of its research articles ranges from offshore engineering to naval architecture. Issues may include review articles as well as short communications on recent field work, instrument modeling, and testing. It is appropriate for specialized marine and engineering collections as interest in marine renewable energy increases.

3500. *Ocean News & Technology.* Former titles (until Sep. 1995): *Underwater News and Technology;* (until June 1993): *Waves;* (until Jan. 1991): *Subnotes.* [ISSN: 1082-6106] 1981. bi-m. USD 75 domestic (Free to qualified personnel). Ed(s): Ladd Borne. Technology Systems Corporation, 7897 S W Jack James Dr, Ste A, Ste 130, Stuart, FL 34997; http://www.ocean-news.com. Adv. Circ: 21000 Paid and controlled. *Aud.:* Ga, Sa.

This magazine has articles on news and trends in marine technologies such as underwater vehicles, energy production, imaging, defense, offshore oil and gas, and diving. Includes calendar of events, shows, and conferences. Primarily used by those in marine industries, but may be of interest to a general audience in coastal areas.

3501. *Professional Mariner: journal of the maritime industry.* [ISSN: 1066-2774] 1993. 8x/yr. USD 29.95 domestic; USD 39.95 Canada; USD 44.95 elsewhere. Ed(s): John Gormley. Navigator Publishing LLC., 58 Fore St, Portland, ME 04101; http://www.navigatorpublishing.com. Illus. Sample. Circ: 29000. *Indexed:* HRIS. *Aud.:* Sa.

This maritime trade magazine addresses the concerns and interests of the people who work on the water: safety, current news, new and old working vessels, environmental updates, and more. While *Marine Officer* addresses concerns of those who manage vessels, *Professional Mariner* speaks to the people working on myriad platforms in various positions. An inexpensive print magazine with a digital version included in the price. Most articles are also available on the magazine's website.

Remote Sensing of Environment. See Environment and Conservation section.

3502. *Sea Technology.* Formerly (until 1973): *Undersea Technology and Oceanology International & Offshore Technology;* Which was formed by the merger of (1971-1972): *Oceanology International Offshore Technology;* Which was formed by the merger of (19??-1971): *Offshore Technology;* (1966-1971): *Oceanology International;* Which was formerly (until 1966): *Oceanology;* (1961-1972): *Undersea Technology;* Which was formerly (until 1961): *Underwater Engineering;* (until 1960): *Underwater Engineering News.* [ISSN: 0093-3651] 1972. m. USD 60 domestic (Free to qualified personnel). Ed(s): Aileen Torres-Bennett. Compass Publications, Inc. (Arlington), 1600 Wilson Blvd, Ste 1010, Arlington, VA 22209. Illus., adv. Vol. ends: No. 12. Microform: PQC. *Indexed:* A22, HRIS. *Aud.:* Sa.

This monthly trade journal for marine technology and engineering combines short articles on issues and new developments with product reviews and news from the industry and the U.S. government. Articles address such topics as homeland security, toxicity sensors, and remotely operated vehicles. This journal is appropriate for a general audience with technical and engineering interests.

3503. *Underwater Technology.* Formerly (until 1984): *Society for Underwater Technology. Journal.* [ISSN: 1756-0543] 1975. q. GBP 96 domestic; GBP 102 foreign; GBP 24 per issue domestic. Ed(s): Dr. M D J Sayer. Society for Underwater Technology, 1 Fetter Ln, London, EC4A 1BR, United Kingdom; info@sut.org; http://www.sut.org.uk. Illus., adv. Refereed. *Indexed:* A22. *Aud.:* Ac.

Produced by the Society for Underwater Technology, this open-access journal reports on development in various types of aquatic technologies, including underwater vehicles, diving applications, energy systems, and applications of the physical forces that affect these technologies.

Ocean Science

3504. *Continental Shelf Research.* [ISSN: 0278-4343] 1982. 20x/yr. EUR 4674. Elsevier Ltd, The Boulevard, Langford Lane, Oxford, OX5 1GB, United Kingdom; customerserviceau@elsevier.com; http://www.elsevier.com. Adv. Sample. Refereed. Microform: PQC. *Indexed:* A01, A22, C45, S25. *Aud.:* Ac, Sa.

This journal focuses on the shallow marine environment that is defined as the coast to the continental shelf break. All aspects of marine science are covered, with an emphasis on processes and innovative techniques applied in this environment. Two to four issues every year address special topics, such as physical oceanographic modeling and harmful algal blooms.

3505. *Deep-Sea Research. Part 1: Oceanographic Research Papers.* Supersedes in part (in 1993): *Deep-Sea Research. Part A: Oceanographic Research Papers;* Which was formerly (until 1979): *Deep-Sea Research;* (until 1977): *Deep-Sea Research and Oceanographic Abstracts;* (until 1962): *Deep-Sea Research.* [ISSN: 0967-0637] 1953. m. EUR 5001. Elsevier Ltd, The Boulevard, Langford Lane, Oxford, OX5 1GB, United Kingdom; customerserviceau@elsevier.com; http://www.elsevier.com. Illus., adv. Sample. Refereed. Microform: PQC. *Indexed:* A01, A22, S25. *Aud.:* Ac, Sa.

This journal focuses on geological, physical, chemical, and biological aspects of the ocean beyond the continental shelf, including research on theoretical, instrumentation-related, and methodological problems. Along with its companion journal, *Deep-Sea Research, Part 2: Topical Studies in Oceanography,* this title is essential for any institution with a marine biology or oceanography program.

Dynamics of Atmospheres and Oceans. See Atmospheric Sciences section.

Earth Interactions. See Atmospheric Sciences section.

3506. *Earth System Monitor.* [ISSN: 1068-2678] 1990. q. Free. Ed(s): Andrew Allegra. U.S. National Oceanographic Data Center, NOAA NESDIS E/OC, SSMC3, 4th Fl, Silver Spring, MD 20910; NODC.Services@noaa.gov; http://www.nodc.noaa.gov/. *Indexed:* S25. *Aud.:* Ga, Ac.

National Oceanic and Atmospheric Association research programs, information products, and services are described in this freely available newsletter. Short articles and links to additional information on NOAA environmental data and research programs explain current problems and issues related to the ocean and the atmosphere. Appropriate for general audiences, as well as marine scientists.

3507. *Estuaries and Coasts.* Former titles (until 2006): *Estuaries;* (until 1978): *Chesapeake Science;* (until 1960): *Maryland Tidewater News.* [ISSN: 1559-2723] 19??. bi-m. EUR 705 (print & online eds.)). Ed(s): Charles Simenstad, Wayne S Gardner. Springer New York LLC, 233 Spring St, New York, NY 10013; customerservice@springer.com; http://www.springer.com. Illus., index, adv. Refereed. Vol. ends: No. 4. Microform: MIM; PMC; PQC. Reprint: PSC. *Indexed:* A22, Agr, BRI, C45, E01, S25. *Bk. rev.:* 2, 500 words. *Aud.:* Ac.

Estuaries and Coasts (formerly *Estuaries*) covers research relating to physical, chemical, geological, or biological systems of habitats within the ocean/land interface, such as lagoons, wetlands, tidal rivers, shorelands, and beaches. Original research, reviews, methodology, and management applications are included. Appropriate for academic collections with a near-shore focus or interest in environmental change.

3508. ***Estuarine, Coastal and Shelf Science.*** Formerly (until 1981): *Estuarine and Coastal Marine Science.* [ISSN: 0272-7714] 1973. 16x/yr. EUR 6609. Ed(s): I Valiela, E Wolanski. Academic Press, 32 Jamestown Rd, Camden, London, NW1 7BY, United Kingdom; corporate.sales@elsevier.com; http://www.elsevier.com/. Illus., index, adv. Sample. Refereed. Vol. ends: No. 6. Reprint: PSC. *Indexed:* A01, A22, C45, E01, S25. *Aud.:* Ac.

This title provides a focused forum for dealing with the study of estuaries, coastal zones, and continental shelf seas. It is both international and multidisciplinary, and includes research on the wide range of biological, anthropogenic, physical, and meteorological influences that come to play within estuaries and coasts. This journal is an important part of any marine science collection.

3509. ***Flotsam & Jetsam.*** [ISSN: 1948-0997] 1972. q. Free to members. Ed(s): Howard Dimmick. Massachusetts Marine Educators, Inc., c/o Erin Hobbs, Newburyport High School, Newburyport, MA 01950; mme@massmarineeducators.org; http://www.massmarineeducators.org. *Aud.:* Ga.

Flotsam & Jetsam is an excellent example of a regional marine education publication. Each issue has a theme such as sharks or the intertidal, and then provides a succinct description of the theme, examples of projects, and ideas for conversations. The newsletter also serves as a means of promoting local and national marine education conferences and regional events. The Massachusetts Marine Educators Association produces this free, quarterly newsletter.

3510. ***Frontiers in Marine Science.*** [ISSN: 2296-7745] 2014. . Free. Ed(s): Carlos M Duarte. Frontiers Research Foundation, Avenue du Tribunal Federal 34, Lausanne, 1005, Switzerland; info@frontiersin.org; https://www.frontiersin.org. Refereed. *Aud.:* Ac, Sa.

This publication in an international, interdisciplinary, open-access journal covering all aspects of marine science. The title has numerous specialty sections such as "Aquatic Microbiology," "Environmental Informatics," and "Ocean Engineering, Technology, and Solutions for the Blue Economy." Various article types are published, including original research, reviews, protocols, and general commentary.

G3: Geochemistry, Geophysics, Geosystems: an electronic journal of the earth sciences. See Earth Sciences and Geology section.

Geo-Marine Letters: an international journal of marine geology. See Earth Sciences and Geology section.

Geophysical Research Letters. See Earth Sciences and Geology section.

3511. ***Global and Planetary Change.*** [ISSN: 0921-8181] 1988. 12x/yr. EUR 3502. Ed(s): T M Cronin, S A P L Cloetingh. Elsevier BV, Radarweg 29, Amsterdam, 1043 NX, Netherlands; info@elsevier.com; https://www.elsevier.com/. Illus., index, adv. Refereed. Vol. ends: No. 6. Microform: PQC. *Indexed:* A01, A22, C45, S25. *Aud.:* Ac, Sa.

This journal focuses on the record of change in the Earth's history. Topics include changes in the chemical composition of the oceans and atmosphere, climate change, sea level variations, human geography, global geophysics and tectonics, global ecology, and biogeography. One or two issues annually focus on a special topic or theme. Useful for a wide variety of academic institutions, particularly those with environmental studies and oceanography programs.

3512. ***Global Biogeochemical Cycles: an international journal of global change.*** [ISSN: 0886-6236] 1987. q. GBP 513. Ed(s): Eric Sundquist. Wiley-Blackwell Publishing, Inc., 111 River St, Hoboken, NJ 07030; info@wiley.com; http://onlinelibrary.wiley.com. Illus., adv. Refereed. Vol. ends: No. 4. Reprint: PSC. *Indexed:* A22, Agr, C45, S25. *Aud.:* Ac, Sa.

This journal explores the relationship between oceanography and atmospheric science. Articles examine large-scale interactions in the geosphere and biosphere—changes resulting from marine, hydrologic, atmospheric, extraterrestrial, geologic, and human causes over time-scales large and small. This is a useful title for academic collections that support oceanography and environmental studies programs.

3513. ***International Journal of Marine Science.*** [ISSN: 1927-6648] 2011. . Ed(s): Robert J T Zhu. Sophia Publishing Group, 11388 Stevenston Hwy, Richmond, BC V7A 5J5, Canada. Refereed. *Aud.:* Ac, Sa.

This open-access journal focuses on all facets of marine science, with special attention to the consequences of global issues such as climate change and pollution on the marine environment of developing countries. Topics range from fisheries, oceanography, and ecology to marine spatial planning. The journal provides access to an international perspective on marine science, and encourages authors from outside of North America to submit content.

Journal of Atmospheric and Oceanic Technology. See Atmospheric Sciences section.

3514. ***Journal of Coastal Conservation.*** [ISSN: 1400-0350] 1995. bi-m. EUR 588 (print & online eds.)). Ed(s): David R Green. Springer Netherlands, Van Godewijckstraat 30, Dordrecht, 3311 GX, Netherlands; http://www.springer.com. Adv. Refereed. Reprint: PSC. *Indexed:* A01, A22, BRI, E01, S25. *Aud.:* Ac, Sa.

This research title deals with multidisciplinary and integrated approaches to the management of coastal environments, from both a physical and human approach. It covers physical and biological processes, policies and human development, and data collection technologies.

3515. ***Journal of Coastal Research: an international forum for the littoral sciences.*** Formerly (until 1985): *Litoralia.* [ISSN: 0749-0208] 1984. bi-m. Membership, USD 125 (print & online eds.)). Ed(s): Charles W Finkl, Jr. Coastal Education & Research Foundation, Inc., 5130 NW 54th St, Coconut Creek, FL 33073; cerf.jcr@gmail.com; http://www.cerf-jcr.org. Illus., index. Refereed. Vol. ends: No. 4. *Indexed:* A01, A22, BRI, C45, E01, S25. *Aud.:* Ac, Sa.

JCR is a research journal focusing on the study, protection, and management of marine, brackish, and freshwater environments along coastal regions, though it focuses on the shoreline areas. It addresses the physical, environmental, and biological processes of both natural and engineered habitats.

3516. ***Journal of Geophysical Research: Oceans.*** Supersedes in part (in 2013): *Journal of Geophysical Research;* Which was formerly (until 1949): *Terrestrial Magnetism and Atmospheric Electricity;* (until 1899): *Terrestrial Magnetism.* [ISSN: 2169-9275] 1896. m. Ed(s): Peter G Brewer. Wiley-Blackwell Publishing, Inc., 111 River St, Hoboken, NJ 07030; info@wiley.com; http://onlinelibrary.wiley.com. Illus. Refereed. Reprint: PSC. *Indexed:* S25. *Aud.:* Ac.

This academic research journal focuses on the physical, chemical, biological, and geological processes of the world's oceans. One of the American Geophysical Union's titles, it covers both experimental and theoretical approaches.

3517. ***Journal of Marine Systems.*** [ISSN: 0924-7963] 1990. 12x/yr. EUR 4134. Ed(s): E Hofmann, A Piola. Elsevier BV, Radarweg 29, Amsterdam, 1043 NX, Netherlands; info@elsevier.com; https://www.elsevier.com/. Illus., adv. Refereed. Vol. ends: No. 4. Microform: PQC. *Indexed:* A01, A22. *Aud.:* Ac, Sa.

This journal examines interdisciplinary, system-driven questions in the marine environment. With its coverage ranging in scale from lagoons to ocean basins, its articles focus on how the marine system shapes the biological, chemical, and physical environment. Coverage is international. It is appropriate for research collections, especially those with an emphasis in physical oceanography.

3518. ***Journal of Oceanography.*** Supersedes in part (in 1992): *Oceanographical Society of Japan. Journal.* [ISSN: 0916-8370] 1941. bi-m. EUR 1432 (print & online eds.)). Ed(s): Toshiyuki Hibiya. Springer Netherlands, Van Godewijckstraat 30, Dordrecht, 3311 GX, Netherlands; http://www.springer.com. Illus., adv. Refereed. Reprint: PSC. *Indexed:* A22, Agr, E01. *Aud.:* Ac, Sa.

Originally published as the outlet for the Oceanographic Society of Japan, this journal is primarily focused on the western North Pacific and Asian coastal waters. Relevant topics include current dynamics, chemical fluxes, and biological phenomena. The title is useful mostly for oceanography collections that support research in the Pacific.

3519. ***Journal of Operational Oceanography.*** Formerly (until 2008): *Journal of Marine Science & the Environment.* [ISSN: 1755-876X] 2003. s-a. GBP 467 (print & online eds.)). Ed(s): R Rayner. Taylor & Francis, 2, 3 & 4 Park Sq, Milton Park, Abingdon, OX14 4RN, United Kingdom; subscriptions@tandf.co.uk; https://www.tandfonline.com. Refereed. Reprint: PSC. *Aud.:* Ac, Sa.

Focusing on applied aspects of ocean science, this title includes articles on issues such as climate modeling and weather forecasting, environmental outcomes, public health, and ocean policy. It publishes material related directly to several international networks involved in coordinating environmental data such as the Global Ocean Observing System (GOOS), Global Climate Observing System (GCOS), Global Monitoring for Environment and Security (GMES), and Global Earth Observing System of Systems (GEOSS).

3520. ***Journal of Physical Oceanography.*** [ISSN: 0022-3670] 1971. m. Members, USD 165 (print & online eds.); Non-members, USD 2265 (print & online eds.)). Ed(s): Jerome A Smith. American Meteorological Society, 45 Beacon St, Boston, MA 02108; amsinfo@ametsoc.org; http://www.ametsoc.org. Illus., index. Refereed. Vol. ends: No. 12. *Indexed:* A01, A22, E01, S25. *Aud.:* Ac, Sa.

Contributions to this journal relate to the physics of the ocean and the processes that operate at its boundaries. The primary aim of the journal is to promote understanding of the ocean and its role within the Earth system. Typical articles address surface phenomena, oceanography (large- and small-scale), circulation, and modeling. Produced by the American Meteorological Society, this is an important journal for academic libraries that serve an oceanography program.

3521. ***Journal of Sea Research.*** Formerly (until vol.35, 1996): *Netherlands Journal of Sea Research.* [ISSN: 1385-1101] 1961. 12x/yr. EUR 1385. Ed(s): H W van der Veer. Elsevier BV, Radarweg 29, Amsterdam, 1043 NX, Netherlands; info@elsevier.com; https://www.elsevier.com/. Refereed. *Indexed:* A01, A22, C45. *Aud.:* Ac, Sa.

This title is a multidisciplinary journal that focuses on the functioning of ecosystem processes in coastal and continental shelf areas. Produced in collaboration with Royal NIOZ, the Netherlands Institute for Sea Research, this title has become much more international in scope, previously focusing on the North Atlantic.

3522. ***Limnology and Oceanography.*** [ISSN: 0024-3590] 1956. bi-m. Ed(s): Robert W Howarth. John Wiley & Sons, Inc., 111 River St, Hoboken, NJ 07030; cs-journals@wiley.com; http://www.wiley.com. Illus., index. Refereed. Vol. ends: No. 8. *Indexed:* A01, A22, BRI, C45, S25. *Bk. rev.:* 2, 750 words, signed. *Aud.:* Ac, Sa.

This journal is the main research publication of the Association for the Sciences of Limnology and Oceanography. Global in scope, the focus of this journal is the study of fresh-water and marine ecosystems; it includes original research articles on all aspects of limnology and oceanography. This journal is available as part of a package that also includes the more specialized partner journals *Limnology and Oceanography: Methods* , *Limnology and Oceanography: Fluids and Environments* , and the society's *Bulletin.* A top-ranking journal and essential for any academic institution with a marine biology or oceanography program.

3523. ***Limnology and Oceanography: Fluids and Environments.*** [ISSN: 2157-3689] 2011. irreg. Ed(s): Josef Daniel Ackerman. John Wiley & Sons, Inc., 111 River St, Hoboken, NJ 07030; cs-journals@wiley.com; http://www.wiley.com. Adv. *Indexed:* S25. *Aud.:* Ac, Sa.

Limnology and Oceanography: Fluids and Environments focuses on fluid dynamics and transport processes in biological, chemical, and geological aspects of aquatic environments, from the molecular to global scale. Like *L&O: Methods*, it is available as a package with other publications of the Association for the Sciences of Limnology and Oceanography.

3524. ***Limnology and Oceanography: Methods.*** [ISSN: 1541-5856] 2003. m. Ed(s): Paul F Kemp. John Wiley & Sons, Inc., 111 River St, Hoboken, NJ 07030; cs-journals@wiley.com; http://www.wiley.com. Refereed. *Indexed:* C45, S25. *Aud.:* Ac, Sa.

Developed as a companion to the long-standing *Limnology and Oceanography,* this electronic-only journal of the Association for the Sciences of Limnology and Oceanography is bundled with that as well as with the society's bulletin and the newest title, *Limnology and Oceanography: Fluids and Environments. Methods* provides a mechanism for rapid publication of articles that address problems and solutions in aquatic science methodology.

3525. ***Marine Chemistry.*** [ISSN: 0304-4203] 1972. 10x/yr. EUR 4038. Ed(s): T S Bianchi. Elsevier BV, Radarweg 29, Amsterdam, 1043 NX, Netherlands; info@elsevier.com; https://www.elsevier.com. Illus., adv. Refereed. Vol. ends: No. 4. Microform: PQC. *Indexed:* A01, A22, S25. *Aud.:* Ac, Sa.

This highly ranked journal includes original research and occasional reviews that address the dynamics of chemistry of the marine environment. It is an international forum, and will be of interest to marine chemists, chemical oceanographers, and geochemists. This journal is appropriate for academic collections that support a research program in marine chemistry or oceanography.

3526. ***Marine Geology.*** [ISSN: 0025-3227] 1964. 12x/yr. EUR 6540. Ed(s): E J Anthony, G de Lange. Elsevier BV, Radarweg 29, Amsterdam, 1043 NX, Netherlands; info@elsevier.com; https://www.elsevier.com/. Illus., index, adv. Refereed. Vol. ends: No. 4. Microform: PQC. *Indexed:* A01, A22. *Aud.:* Ac, Sa.

Along with *Journal of Geophysical Research,* this top-ranked title contains articles on marine geology, geochemistry, and geophysics. The focus is on the science of marine geology rather than its management or hydrodynamics. Multiple volumes are published annually, with one or two addressing a special topic such as tidal sedimentation or prodelta systems. This is a core title for geologic oceanography collections.

3527. ***Marine Geophysical Researches: an international journal for the study of the earth beneath the sea.*** [ISSN: 0025-3235] 1970. q. EUR 1022 (print & online eds.)). Ed(s): Shu-Kun Hsu, Roger Urgeles. Springer Netherlands, Van Godewijckstraat 30, Dordrecht, 3311 GX, Netherlands; http://www.springer.com. Illus., adv. Refereed. Microform: PQC. Reprint: PSC. *Indexed:* A01, A22, BRI, E01. *Aud.:* Ac, Sa.

This publication has traditionally dealt with data on the deep ocean basins, but recently has expanded to include the global mid-ocean ridge system and the geophysics of continental margins. Typical articles address techniques and tools for deep-sea-floor imaging and measurement. This title will be of interest to geologists and oceanographers and is recommended for academic and research libraries that support these types of programs.

3528. ***Mariners Weather Log (Online).*** [ISSN: 1554-950X] 3x/yr. Free. Ed(s): Paula Rychtar. National Oceanic and Atmospheric Administration (N O A A), National Weather Service, National Data Buoy Ctr, Bldg 3203, Stennis Space Center, MS 39529-6000; http://www.noaa.gov/. *Aud.:* Ga, Ac, Sa.

This online publication from the National Weather Service (NWS) includes articles addressing weather forecasting, marine weather phenomena, and news from more than 10,000 ships involved in the NWS Voluntary Observing Program. The meteorological content will be of interest to the maritime community, including marine institutions, scientists, and educational and research facilities. This is not a core title, but a nice addition to public, academic, and other libraries.

3529. *Ocean Dynamics: theoretical, computational and observational oceanography.* Formerly (until 2001): *Deutsche Hydrographische Zeitschrift;* Which superseded in part (in 1948): *Annalen der Hydrographie und Maritimen Meteorologie;* Which was formerly (until 1874): *Hydrographische Mitteilungen.* [ISSN: 1616-7341] 1873. bi-m. EUR 1058 (print & online eds.)). Ed(s): Joerg-Olaf Wolff. Springer, Tiergartenstr 17, Heidelberg, 69121, Germany. Illus., index, adv. Sample. Refereed. Reprint: PSC. *Indexed:* A01, A22, Agr, E01, S25. *Aud.:* Ac.

Formerly *Deutsche Hydrographische Zeitschrift,* this is an international, interdisciplinary, academic research journal publishing material on theoretical, computational, and observational aspects of biological, chemical, and physical oceanography.

3530. *Ocean Modelling.* [ISSN: 1463-5003] 1999. 12x/yr. EUR 1327. Ed(s): W A Perrie. Elsevier Inc., 1600 John F Kennedy Blvd, Philadelphia, PA 19103; journalscustomerservice-usa@elsevier.com; https://www.elsevier.com. Adv. Sample. Refereed. Vol. ends: No. 3. *Indexed:* A01, A22. *Aud.:* Ac.

This research journal focuses on rapid communications dealing with ocean modeling, including theoretical, observational, and laboratory studies. It includes work on interactions between physical, biological, geological, and atmospheric processes. Content in the form of primary research papers, reviews, preliminary communications, and discussions is included.

3531. *Ocean Science.* [ISSN: 1812-0784] 2005. 6x/yr. EUR 498; EUR 91.30 newsstand/cover. Ed(s): William Jenkins. Copernicus GmbH, Bahnhofsallee 1e, Goettingen, 37081, Germany; info@copernicus.org; http://www.copernicus.org. Refereed. *Indexed:* S25. *Aud.:* Ac.

Ocean Science is a publication of the European Geosciences Union, open access and international in scope. It publishes experimental, theoretical, and laboratory studies on all aspects of ocean science, although with a focus on physical processes.

3532. *Oceanography: the official magazine of the oceanography society.* [ISSN: 1042-8275] 1988. q. USD 195 (Individuals, USD 40; Free to members). Ed(s): Ellen S Kappel. Oceanography Society, PO Box 1931, Rockville, MD 20849; http://tos.org/. Illus., adv. Refereed. Vol. ends: No. 4. *Indexed:* A01. *Bk. rev.:* 2, 1,000 words, signed. *Aud.:* Ga, Ac, Sa.

This title presents a range of research, technological developments, book reviews, and current events of interest to the broad community of scientists and managers involved with ocean science. Written for an informed and knowledgeable audience, it is highly readable, with strong supporting illustrations. Issues frequently focus on a special topic such as ocean modeling or climate change. Issues are freely available at the Oceanography Society's website, including a recent issue on marine renewable energy. This is an excellent choice for a college or public library for its general science collection.

3533. *Oceanus: reports on research at the Woods Hole Oceanographic Institution.* Incorporates (in 1994): *Woods Hole Oceanographic Institution. Reports on Research.* [ISSN: 0029-8182] 1952. 3x/yr. USD 8 domestic; USD 23 foreign. Woods Hole Oceanographic Institution, 266 Woods Hole Rd, Woods Hole, MA 02543; info@whoi.edu; http://www.whoi.edu. Illus., index, adv. Vol. ends: No. 2. Microform: PQC. *Indexed:* A01, A22, BRI, MASUSE. *Aud.:* Hs, Ga, Ac, Sa.

The Woods Hole Oceanographic Institution (WHOI), one of the world's premier marine research organizations, resumed publication of this title in 2004, both in print and online. Articles by WHOI scientists and science writers report on current research, expeditions, and marine issues. Topics range from intertidal animals to oceanographic instrumentation. Short news items are interspersed with two- or three-page articles. All are profusely illustrated. The online version has additional features such as video and digital photos. This title is very useful for general public collections as well as for high schools and academic institutions.

3534. *Paleoceanography and Paleoclimatology.* Formerly (until 2018): *Paleoceanography.* [ISSN: 2572-4517] 1986. m. Ed(s): Ellen Thomas. Wiley-Blackwell Publishing, Inc., 111 River St, Hoboken, NJ 07030; http://onlinelibrary.wiley.com. Illus., index. Sample. Refereed. Vol. ends: No. 6. *Indexed:* A22. *Aud.:* Ac, Sa.

A publication of the American Geophysical Union, *Paleoceanography* is devoted to research dealing with the history of the earth's oceans, climate, and environmental conditions, and how these processes can help us understand present day and future environmental developments. Its emphasis is global and regional, and deals with all geological ages, Precambrian to Quaternary.

3535. *Progress in Oceanography.* [ISSN: 0079-6611] 1963. 10x/yr. EUR 4948. Ed(s): Nate Mantua, Enrique Curchitser. Pergamon Press, The Blvd, Langford Ln, E Park, Kidlington, OX5 1GB, United Kingdom; JournalsCustomerServiceEMEA@elsevier.com; http://www.elsevier.com. Illus., index, adv. Sample. Refereed. Vol. ends: No. 4. Microform: PQC. *Indexed:* A01, A22, S25. *Aud.:* Ac, Sa.

This core journal in oceanography includes longer, comprehensive articles that review aspects of oceanography or offer a treatise on a developing aspect of oceanographic research. Some volumes include collections of papers and conference proceedings. This title belongs in libraries that support oceanography programs, and will be of interest to physical and chemical oceanographers as well as marine biologists.

Tellus. Series A: Dynamic Meteorology and Oceanography (Online). See Atmospheric Sciences section.

■ MARRIAGE AND DIVORCE

Ann Walsh Long, Head of Research & Digital Collections Librarian and Assistant Professor of Law, Lincoln Memorial University Duncan School of Law, 601 W. Summit Hill Drive, Knoxville, TN 37921; ann.long@lmunet.edu

Introduction

When this reviewer researched magazines for this section, *Ulrichsweb Global Serials Directory* contained 397 active magazine titles under the subject heading of "matrimony." Of these titles, very few actually deal with the subject of both marriage and divorce. The majority of these titles focus on the bliss of wedding planning or on beauty and fashion. Other titles focus on tracking statistics of marriage and/or divorce by geographic area and are not included in this section. Additionally, there are numerous online-only journals related to divorce that appear to be created as a means for advertising services to a specific geographic area or group (such as attorneys or counselors). Scholarly titles aimed at legal professionals working in family law are also not included.

On June 26, 2015, the Supreme Court ruled that the right to marry is a fundamental right that can not be denied to same-sex couples. This decision overturns state laws that previously banned or did not recognize same-sex unions. The Fourteenth Amendment requires states to license a marriage between two people of the same sex and to recognize a marriage between two people of the same sex when their marriage was lawfully licensed and performed out-of-state. Today, state courts are wrestling with related issues, such as the adoption rights of divorced same-sex couples, because many related state statutes still contain non-gender-neutral language.

Basic Periodicals

Divorce Magazine, Journal of Divorce & Remarriage, Marriage & Family Review.

Basic Abstracts and Indexes

Family Studies Abstracts, ProQuest Central, PsycINFO, Social Sciences Abstracts, Social Work Abstracts, Sociological Abstracts, Studies on Women and Gender Abstracts.

Bride's. See Weddings section.

Contemporary Family Therapy: an international journal. See Family section.

3536. ***Divorce Magazine.*** Formerly (until 1998): *Toronto's Divorce Magazine.* [ISSN: 1484-9054] 1996. s-a. CAD 25.99 for 2 yrs. in US & Canada. Ed(s): John Matias. Segue Esprit Inc., 2255B Queen St, E, Ste #1179, Toronto, ON M4E 1G3, Canada; editors@divorcemag.com. Adv. *Aud.:* Ga.

Divorce Magazine is published twice a year and aimed at individuals involved in the divorce process. Articles include feature stories and columns that offer tips, advice, and insights for a successful divorce. A recent issue offered an "essential" divorce guide with suggestions on working with your divorce lawyer and an overview of mediation.

The Family Journal. See Family section.

3537. ***Family Law Quarterly.*** Former titles (until 1967): *American Bar Association. Section of Family Law. Proceedings of the Section;* (until 1964): *American Bar Association. Section of Family Law. Summary of Proceedings.* [ISSN: 0014-729X] 1959. q. Free to members; Non-members, USD 79.95. Ed(s): Linda D Elrod, Deborah Eisel. American Bar Association, 321 N Clark St, 20th Fl, Chicago, IL 60654; service@americanbar.org; http://www.americanbar.org. Illus., index, adv. Refereed. Vol. ends: Winter. Microform: WSH; PMC; PQC. Reprint: WSH. *Indexed:* A01, A22, BRI, CJPI, L14. *Aud.:* Ac, Sa.

The purpose of the American Bar Association's (ABA) Section of Family Law is "to promote the objectives of the American Bar Association by improving the administration of justice in the field of family law by study, conferences, and publication of reports and articles with respect to both legislation and administration." This publication, under the editorship of students at Washburn University School of Law, is one of the principal means toward that end. Issues discuss such topics as divorce, parentage, international custody and support, property rights, artificial reproductive technology, domestic torts, and adoption. The annotated "Summary of the Year in Family Law" is found in the Winter issue. *The Family Advocate,* also published by this ABA section, offers practical advice for attorneys practicing family law.

3538. ***The Family Law Reporter.*** [ISSN: 0148-7922] 1974. w. USD 1494. Ed(s): David B Jackson. Bloomberg B N A, 1801 S Bell St, Arlington, VA 22202; http://www.bna.com. Sample. *Indexed:* CJPI. *Aud.:* Ac, Sa.

The BNA *Family Law Reporter* covers state and federal court decisions on domestic matters and related federal legislative and administrative updates. A well-respected source praised for its thorough and unbiased coverage, the *Family Law Reporter* is a trusted resource for family law attorneys. Recent topics include same-sex marriage and divorce, paternity, and custody issues.

3539. ***Family Therapy Magazine.*** Former titles (until 2002): *Family Therapy News;* (until 198?): *American Association for Marriage and Family Therapy Newsletter.* [ISSN: 1538-9448] 1969. bi-m. Free to members. American Association for Marriage and Family Therapy, 112 S Alfred St, Alexandria, VA 22314; http://www.aamft.org. Adv. *Aud.:* Ac, Sa.

This bi-monthly magazine is produced by the American Association for Marriage and Family Therapy (AAMFT), which is the professional association for the field of marriage and family therapists (MFTs). This magazine is aimed at that audience. Recent issues discuss courtship and mating and delve into how technology affects relationships. Other issues address the impact of U.S. health-care law and emerging ethical and legal trends for MFTs. Each issue includes a calendar of upcoming professional events.

Fathering Magazine. See Parenting section.

Journal of Comparative Family Studies. See Family section.

3540. ***Journal of Divorce & Remarriage: research and clinical studies in family theory, family law, family mediation and family therapy.*** Formerly (until 1990): *Journal of Divorce.* [ISSN: 1050-2556] 1977. 8x/yr. GBP 2087 (print & online eds.)). Ed(s): Craig A Everett. Routledge, 530 Walnut St, Ste 850, Philadelphia, PA 19106; enquiries@tandfonline.com; http://www.tandfonline.com. Illus., index, adv. Sample. Refereed. Circ: 379 Paid. Vol. ends: No. 4. Microform: PQC. Reprint: PSC. *Indexed:* A01, A22, ASSIA, C42, E01, GW, SSA. *Aud.:* Ac, Sa.

The *Journal of Divorce and Remarriage* covers all aspects of divorce, including pre-divorce and family treatment, marital separation and dissolution, children's responses to divorce and separation, single parenting, remarriage, and stepfamilies. The journal is aimed at professionals, such as family therapists, family law attorneys, counselors, and social workers. Three of the most recent cited articles discuss topics such as reasons for divorce, the factors that contribute to quality co-parenting, and forgiveness of an ex-spouse.

Journal of Family Issues. See Family section.

Journal of Marital and Family Therapy. See Family section.

3541. ***Journal of Marriage and Family.*** Former titles (until 1964): *Marriage and Family Living;* (until 1941): *Living.* [ISSN: 0022-2445] 1939. 5x/yr. USD 1522. Ed(s): R Kelly Raley. Wiley-Blackwell Publishing, Inc., 350 Main St, Malden, MA 02148; http://onlinelibrary.wiley.com. Illus., index, adv. Sample. Refereed. Microform: PQC. Reprint: PSC. *Indexed:* A01, A22, AgeL, Agr, BRI, C45, CBRI, Chicano, E01, ERIC, IBSS, MLA-IB, SSA. *Aud.:* Ac.

Journal of Marriage and Family is a publication of the National Council on Family Relations. Articles are scholarly in nature and focus on research and theory, research interpretation and reviews, and critical aspects of all marriage types, close relationships, and marital dissolution. Recent articles discuss stresses to the marital relationship including cultural issues, co-parenting across multiple generations, incarceration, deportation, and LGBTQ (Lesbian, Gay, Bisexual, Transgender, and Queer) relationships.

Journal of Social and Personal Relationships. See Communication section.

3542. ***Marriage & Family Review.*** [ISSN: 0149-4929] 1978. 8x/yr. GBP 2118 (print & online eds.)). Ed(s): Walter R Schumm. Routledge, 530 Walnut St, Ste 850, Philadelphia, PA 19106; enquiries@tandfonline.com; http://www.tandfonline.com. Adv. Sample. Refereed. Circ: 413 Paid. Microform: PQC. Reprint: PSC. *Indexed:* A01, A22, ASSIA, AgeL, Agr, AmHI, BRI, C42, E01, GW, SSA. *Aud.:* Ac, Sa.

Marriage & Family Review is published by the National Council on Family Relations and is considered to be the leading publication in the family field since 1978. It is a peer-reviewed journal that publishes original research and theory, research interpretation and reviews, and critical discussion concerning all aspects of marriage. Every ten years, a "Decade in Review" issue is published that focuses on major research trends over the past decade. The last "Decade in Review" issue was the June 2010 issue, which discussed trends and new developments in the research on divorce.

Sexual and Relationship Therapy. See Sexuality section.

■ MATHEMATICS

General/Research Journals

John J. Meier, Physical and Mathematical Sciences Library, Pennsylvania State University, 201 Davey Lab, University Park, PA 16802; 814-867-1448; FAX: 814-865-2565; meier@psu.edu

Introduction

The mathematics magazines and journals included in this section can be of interest to mathematicians, students, and teachers of mathematics.

Mathematicians create the tools that solve present and future problems in science, engineering, and computation. Even "pure" mathematics, which explores solutions that do not yet have a known problem, can be "applied" in the future in many disciplines. Libraries serving applied fields such as engineering, physics, statistics, and even biology or medicine, should consider mathematics journals and magazines for their users. This section primarily includes research journals with a broad subject coverage, rather than journals in the many specialized sub-fields of mathematics, such as logic or topology.

The "Research Journals" subsection presents original research primarily intended for mathematicians, graduate students in mathematics, and other scientists or researchers. When material suitable for undergraduates in mathematics is included that will be specifically noted. The "General" subsection will also include a number of more general research journals, but primarily consists of magazines that present more accessible mathematics articles. This can include popularizations of mathematics, articles on teaching mathematics, and even puzzles or news. Libraries serving K-12 educators, public libraries, and academic libraries supporting any math or science programs should review these with an eye to their users' needs.

Most mathematics journals are now available in either print, online, or both, but there are notable exceptions as indicated in those entries. Many of the "General" titles are easier to read in print as they have many short articles and features. There have been a few changes in the journal publishing world related to mathematics since the last edition of this book. Current issues of the magazines and journals of the Mathematical Association of America (MAA) moved from JSTOR to the publisher Taylor and Francis in 2018. The non-profit publisher Mathematical Sciences Publishers (MSP) has grown in the past decade from a small organization to offer more than a dozen mathematics journals, including the student research journal *Involve*.

In addition to this book, librarians can consult resources made available by the Physics Astronomy Mathematics (PAM) Division of the Special Library Association (SLA). There are also books on math librarianship that may be useful when considering mathematics journals and magazines, including *Guide to Information Sources in Mathematics and Statistics* by Martha A. Tucker and Nancy D. Anderson; *Using the Mathematics Literature* by Kristine K. Fowler; and the forthcoming *Sudden Selectors in Mathematics* by John J. Meier, Annie Zeidman-Karpinski, and Nastasha Johnson.

Basic Periodicals

Hs: *Mathematics Teacher*; Ga: *Mathematics Magazine*; Ac: *The American Mathematical Monthly, American Mathematical Society. Bulletin. New Series, The Mathematical Intelligencer, SIAM Review.*

Basic Abstracts and Indexes

MathSciNet, arXiv.org.

General

3543. *The American Mathematical Monthly.* [ISSN: 0002-9890] 1894. 10x/yr. GBP 435 (print & online eds.)). Ed(s): Susan Jane Colley. Taylor & Francis Inc., 530 Walnut St, Ste 850, Philadelphia, PA 19106; support@tandfonline.com; http://www.tandfonline.com. Illus., index, adv. Refereed. Vol. ends: No. 10. *Indexed:* A01, A22, BRI, MSN. *Bk. rev.:* 1-4, 1,200-2,000 words, signed. *Aud.:* Hs, Ga, Ac, Sa.

The American Mathematical Monthly is the most notable research publication of the Mathematical Association of America (MAA). Articles of "broad appeal" are encouraged, as the audience is collegiate-level math students in addition to professional mathematicians. Short articles are published as "Notes," along with example math problems and a few long, signed book reviews. Another similar journal from the MAA is *College Mathematics Journal* (not reviewed in this section), which also presents research that may be accessible to undergraduates. The *Journal* has worked problems in "Classroom Capsules," in addition to problems and book reviews similar to those in the *American Mathematical Monthly*. Both journals became available from Taylor and Francis in 2018 (see also *Mathematics Magazine*, below in the General subsection). Although Taylor and Francis has a backfile to volume 1 (1894) available for purchase, the archive from 1894-2017 is also offered by JSTOR. Both are recommended for all academic libraries that serve undergraduate mathematics programs with both print and online. They may also be of interest to some high school or public libraries.

Chance. See Statistics section.

3544. *Journal for Research in Mathematics Education.* [ISSN: 0021-8251] 1970. 5x/yr. USD 385 (print & online eds.)). Ed(s): Jinfa Cai. National Council of Teachers of Mathematics, 1906 Association Dr, Reston, VA 20191; NCTM@nctm.org; http://www.nctm.org. Illus., index, adv. Refereed. Vol. ends: Jul. Microform: PQC. *Indexed:* A01, A22, Chicano, ERIC. *Bk. rev.:* 1-2, 1,500-2,000 words, signed. *Aud.:* Ems, Hs, Ac, Sa.

The National Council of Teachers of Mathematics (NCTM) publishes many journals and magazines of interest to educators at all levels (see also *Mathematics Teacher*, below in this General subsection). The *Journal for Research in Mathematics Education* includes original research articles, commentaries on research, brief reports on theoretical topics, discussions of research topics, and a few book reviews that are lengthy and signed. In particular, articles need to go beyond proofs of pure mathematics and have an implication for teaching methods. There may also be official NCTM reports where the focus is often on college education. In partnership with the Association of Mathematics Teacher Educators (AMTE), the NCTM started an online-only journal in 2012, *Mathematics Teacher Educator* (*MTE*, not reviewed in this section), for research manuscripts that address problems in teacher practice, using evidence. *MTE*, a peer-reviewed journal, is published twice a year and would best benefit those who educate mathematics teachers. Though Taylor and Francis now publishes NCTM journals, JSTOR has volume 1 through 2018 (https://www.jstor.org/publisher/nctm). They are appropriate for academic education libraries and libraries that support professional development for K-12 teachers. URL: www.nctm.org/publications/jrme.aspx

3545. *The Mathematical Gazette.* [ISSN: 0025-5572] 1894. 3x/yr. GBP 146 (print & online eds.)). Ed(s): Gerry Leversha. Cambridge University Press, University Printing House, Shaftesbury Rd, Cambridge, CB2 8BS, United Kingdom; online@cambridge.org; https://www.cambridge.org. Illus., index, adv. Vol. ends: No. 3. Reprint: PSC. *Indexed:* A22, MSN. *Bk. rev.:* 10-25, 200-1,500 words, signed. *Aud.:* Hs, Ac, Sa.

Mathematical Gazette is a publication of the United Kingdom's Mathematical Association (www.m-a.org.uk) that covers the teaching and learning of mathematics with a focus on "the 15-20 age range." It includes news and events of the association, but it primarily comprises expository articles, letters, problems, and extensive book reviews. It is useful for teachers of high school students through college undergraduates. A companion publication by the same association is *Mathematics in School* (not reviewed in this section), which is aimed at teachers of students aged 10-18. This latter title has relatively short articles, worksheets for classroom use, occasionally cartoons or fun facts, and a few short, signed book reviews. It is appropriate for middle school and high school libraries, though it is focused on the curriculum of the United Kingdom, both journals have an online moving archive starting with volume 1 through 2012 on JSTOR (www.jstor.org). The *Mathematical Gazette* is now published online by Cambridge University Press. URL: http://journals.cambridge.org/action/displayJournal?jid=MAG

3546. *The Mathematical Intelligencer.* [ISSN: 0343-6993] 1977. q. EUR 219 (print & online eds.)). Ed(s): Marjorie Senechal. Springer New York LLC, 233 Spring St, New York, NY 10013; customerservice@springer.com; http://www.springer.com. Illus., index, adv. Refereed. Vol. ends: No. 4. Microform: PQC. Reprint: PSC. *Indexed:* A01, A22, BRI, E01, MASUSE, MLA-IB, MSN. *Bk. rev.:* 2-5, 1,000-2,000 words, signed. *Aud.:* Hs, Ga, Ac, Sa.

The Mathematical Intelligencer "informs and entertains a broad audience of mathematicians and the wider intellectual community." There are "articles about mathematics, mathematicians, and the history and culture of mathematics," as well as humor, poetry, puzzles, engaging images, and popular hobbies such as stamps. There are a few lengthy, signed book reviews. It is available online with archives back to volume 1 (1977) and a rare open-access article from author fees. This title is appropriate for a broad audience because of its entertaining treatment of mathematics. It should be considered a basic resource for academic libraries, and should be highly considered for public and high school libraries. URL: www.springerlink.com/content/0343-6993

3547. *Mathematics Magazine.* Incorporates (in 1977): *Delta;* Which was formerly (until 1947): *National Mathematics Magazine;* (until 1934): *Mathematics News Letter.* [ISSN: 0025-570X] 1926. 5x/yr. GBP 273 (print & online eds.)). Ed(s): Walter A Stromquist. Mathematical Association of America, 1529 18th St, NW, P O Box 91112, Washington, DC 20036; maahq@maa.org; http://www.maa.org. Illus., index. Circ: 8400. Microform: PQC. *Indexed:* A01, A22, BRI, MASUSE, MSN. *Bk. rev.:* 6-8, 300-750 words. *Aud.:* Hs, Ga, Ac, Sa.

Mathematics Magazine is published by the Mathematical Association of America (MAA), which is the "largest professional society that focuses on mathematics accessible at the undergraduate level." This title and *Math Horizons* (not reviewed in this section) are general magazines intended to introduce advanced mathematical concepts and proofs to students in interesting ways. It uses the history of mathematics, applied mathematics, or visuals to explain difficult concepts. *Mathematics Magazine* has a small problems section and several medium-length, unsigned book reviews. Though articles are written by college and university faculty, this title is very approachable for undergraduates and advanced high school students. Both journals are available online From Taylor and Francis, along with other MAA journals (see *The American Mathematical Monthly*). JSTOR also has the archives of both journals until 2017. Both are recommended for all academic libraries, and may be of interest to public and high school libraries.

3548. *Mathematics Teacher.* [ISSN: 0025-5769] 1908. 7x/yr. USD 306 (print & online eds.)). Ed(s): Albert Goetz. National Council of Teachers of Mathematics, 1906 Association Dr, Reston, VA 20191; NCTM@nctm.org; http://www.nctm.org. Illus., adv. Refereed. *Indexed:* A01, A22, BRI, CBRI, ERIC. *Bk. rev.:* 3-10, 100-300 words, signed. *Aud.:* Ems, Hs, Ac, Sa.

Mathematics Teacher is the flagship publication of the National Council of Teachers of Mathematics (NCTM; www.nctm.org). The NCTM is the world's largest organization focused solely on the teaching of mathematics, though the membership is primarily in North America. *Mathematics Teacher* offers activities, lesson ideas, teaching strategies, and problems including a "Monthly Calendar" of math problems. Regular columns include teaching with technology, math problems with solutions, and many other practical examples. Each issue has a few short, signed book reviews. The NCTM also publishes *Mathematics Teaching in the Middle School* (not reviewed here) with similar content for middle school educators and *Teaching Children Mathematics* (below in this subsection) for the pre-K to elementary school audience. These also have activities, problems, teaching strategies, and occasionally book reviews. These titles are essential for school libraries and academic libraries that serve education students. All three journals are available online via institutional access through JSTOR. URL: https://www.jstor.org/journal/mathteacher

3549. *Mathematics Teaching.* Incorporates (1985-2005): *Micromath.* [ISSN: 0025-5785] 1955. bi-m. Free to members. Ed(s): Tony Cotton. Association of Teachers of Mathematics, 2A Vernon St Vernon House, Derby, DE1 1FR, United Kingdom; admin@atm.org.uk; http://www.atm.org.uk. Illus., adv. Microform: PQC. *Indexed:* A01, A22, ERIC. *Bk. rev.:* Occasional. *Aud.:* Ems, Hs, Sa.

Mathematics Teaching is a publication of the Association of Teachers of Mathematics (ATM), a society in the United Kingdom that was established in 1950 to "encourage the development of mathematics education such that it is more closely related to the needs of the learner." The primary journal of the association has some official reports and conference news, but consists primarily of reflective articles on teaching. Indeed, the anecdotes and narratives describe teaching mathematics in the classroom from both a student and a teacher perspective, making *Mathematics Teaching* a unique publication. The perspective is strongly British, where the majority of the ATM membership is based. There are occasional book reviews, and some articles and extras are available online to ATM members. Some content is open access on the journal's web site, but the journal now offers libraries online access via IP authentication through institutional membership. Recommended for elementary, middle, and high school libraries. URL: https://www.atm.org.uk/Mathematics-Teaching-Journal-Archive

3550. *Pi Mu Epsilon Journal.* [ISSN: 0031-952X] 1949. s-a. USD 20 for 2 yrs. domestic; USD 25 for 2 yrs. foreign. Ed(s): Brigitte Servatius. Pi Mu Epsilon, Inc, c/o Leo J Schneider, Department of Mathematics and Computer Science, University Heights, OH 44118; LEO@jcu.edu; http://www.pme-math.org. Illus. Refereed. Microform: PQC. *Indexed:* A22, MSN. *Aud.:* Ac, Sa.

The *Pi Mu Epsilon Journal* is the official publication of the Pi Mu Epsilon National Honorary Mathematics Society (PME; www.pme-math.org), which is "dedicated to the promotion of mathematics and recognition of students who successfully pursue mathematical understanding." The journal is written for undergraduates and focuses mostly on pure mathematics. Undergraduate authors are preferred, though most articles seem to be written by graduate students or faculty. There are short biographies for each author, and a large problem section with open access to upcoming problems in the online "Problem Department." There are no book reviews. It has two issues annually. The journal is only available in print, though volumes 1-11 (1949-2004) are available for free online. Recommended for academic libraries that serve mathematics majors. URL: www.pme-math.org/journal/issues.html

3551. *U M A P Journal.* [ISSN: 0197-3622] 1980. q. Free to members. Ed(s): Paul Campbell. Consortium for Mathematics and Its Applications, 175 Middlesex Turnpike, Ste 3B, Bedford, MA 01730; info@comap.com; http://www.comap.com. Illus., index, adv. Vol. ends: No. 4. *Indexed:* A22. *Bk. rev.:* 3-10, 250-1,500 words. *Aud.:* Hs, Ac, Sa.

The *UMAP Journal* is published by the Consortium for Mathematics and Its Applications (COMAP) (www.comap.com), which is a "non-profit organization whose mission is to improve mathematics education for students of all ages," founded in 1980. COMAP also publishes *Consortium,* which focuses on teaching activities (free online since issue 104), and the *International Journal for the History of Mathematics Education,* which is a biannual publication on math teaching over the past millennia (both titles not reviewed in this section). The *UMAP Journal* "focuses on mathematical modeling and applications of mathematics at the undergraduate level." Written at such a general level, it is also approachable for some high school and public library users, though most authors are college and university professors. It has several medium-length, signed book reviews. Online access is only available through a username login. Recommended for academic libraries, and it may be suitable for some high school and public libraries.

Research Journals

3552. *Acta Mathematica.* [ISSN: 0001-5962] 1882. q. 2 vols/yr. USD 746 (print & online eds.)). Ed(s): Tobias Ekholm. International Press, 387 Somerville Ave, PO Box 502, Somerville, MA 02143; http://www.intlpress.com. Illus., index. Refereed. Vol. ends: No. 2. Reprint: PSC. *Indexed:* A01, A22, E01, MSN. *Aud.:* Ac, Sa.

Acta Mathematica is published by the Institut Mittag-Leffler, a research institute of the Royal Swedish Academy of Sciences. The journal (also known as *Acta Mathematica Djursholm*) is well established and publishes lengthy research articles in all areas of mathematics, and all within around 800 pages annually in two volumes of two issues each. There are about 12 to 16 articles total annually, some of which tend to be quite lengthy. There are no book reviews. Springer published this journal from volume 1 (1882) until volume 217 (2016) when the journal moved to the International Press of Boston and became a fully open online journal. Recommended for all academic libraries. URL: https://intlpress.com/

3553. *American Journal of Mathematics.* [ISSN: 0002-9327] 1878. bi-m. USD 455. Ed(s): Christopher Sogge. The Johns Hopkins University Press, 2715 N Charles St, Baltimore, MD 21218; http://www.press.jhu.edu. Illus., adv. Sample. Refereed. Vol. ends: No. 6. Reprint: PSC. *Indexed:* A01, A22, E01, MSN. *Aud.:* Ac, Sa.

The *American Journal of Mathematics* has been in publication since 1878. It is published by the Johns Hopkins University Press and contains "articles of broad appeal covering the major areas of contemporary mathematics." Between 40 and 50 articles are published annually in six issues with more than 1,700 pages. There are no book reviews. The journal is available online through Project Muse, with a historic archive before 1996 available at JSTOR (www.jstor.org). Recommended for academic libraries. URL: http://muse.jhu.edu/journals/american_journal_of_mathematics

3554. *American Mathematical Society. Bulletin. New Series.* Former titles (until 1979): *American Mathematical Society. Bulletin;* (until 1894): *New York Mathematical Society. Bulletin.* [ISSN: 0273-0979] 1891. q. Institutional members, USD 518.40; Corporations, USD 583.20; Non-members, USD 648. Ed(s): Susan J Friedlander. American Mathematical Society, 201 Charles St, Providence, RI 02904; ams@ams.org; http://www.ams.org. Adv. Microform: PMC. *Indexed:* A01, A22, BRI, MSN. *Bk. rev.:* 4-8, 3,000-7,000 words, signed. *Aud.:* Ac, Sa.

The *Bulletin (New Series) of the American Mathematical Society,* published since 1891, is the oldest publication of the American Mathematical Society (AMS). The AMS promotes "mathematical research and its uses, strengthens mathematical education, and fosters awareness and appreciation of mathematics and its connections to other disciplines and to everyday life." It publishes a number of significant journals as well as the index of *Mathematical Reviews* (online as MathSciNet). The *Bulletin* publishes articles written specifically to be accessible to most mathematicians, and contains several very lengthy, signed book reviews. It is available free online, including an archive from volume 1 to the present. More advanced research journals from the AMS are *Transactions of the American Mathematical Society* (not reviewed in this section) for lengthy articles, *Proceedings of the American Mathematics Society* (not reviewed in this section) for shorter articles, and *Journal of the American Mathematical Society* (not reviewed in this section). All are recommended as core for academic libraries, available online with an archive through Project Euclid (http://projecteuclid.org/). URL: www.ams.org/journals/

3555. *Annals of Mathematics.* Formerly (until 1884): *The Analyst.* [ISSN: 0003-486X] 1874. bi-m. USD 630 (print & online eds.)). Princeton University, Department of Mathematics, 311 Fine Hall, Washington Rd, Princeton, NJ 08544; www@math.princeton.edu; http://www.math.princeton.edu/. Illus. Vol. ends: No. 3. *Indexed:* A22, MSN. *Aud.:* Ac, Sa.

Annals of Mathematics is a bimonthly university press journal published by Princeton University in cooperation with the Institute of Advanced Study (IAS) (www.ias.edu). "The Institute exists to encourage and support fundamental research in the sciences and humanities," including mathematics. *Annals* is a respected, highly cited journal that publishes in all areas of mathematics. There are 40 to 60 articles published annually in two volumes totaling about 2,000 pages. There are no book reviews. Current issues are available online. JSTOR now hosts the journal and archive for this publication. This is one of a number of journals that allow authors to submit manuscripts through arXiv.org. Highly recommended for academic libraries. URL: www.jstor.org/journal/annamath

Annals of Probability. See Statistics section.

Annals of Statistics. See Statistics section.

Applied Statistics. See *Royal Statistical Society. Journal. Series C. Applied Statistics* in the Statistics section.

3556. *Cambridge Philosophical Society. Mathematical Proceedings.* Formerly (until 1975): *Cambridge Philosophical Society. Proceedings. Mathematical and Physical Sciences.* [ISSN: 0305-0041] 1866. bi-m. GBP 697. Ed(s): B J Green. Cambridge University Press, University Printing House, Shaftesbury Rd, Cambridge, CB2 8BS, United Kingdom; journals@cambridge.org; https://www.cambridge.org/. Illus., index. Refereed. Vol. ends: No. 3. Microform: PMC; PQC. Reprint: PSC. *Indexed:* A01, A22, E01, MLA-IB, MSN. *Aud.:* Ac, Sa.

Published by Cambridge University Press, the *Mathematical Proceedings of the Cambridge Philosophical Society* is is a very inclusive mathematics journal that publishes bimonthly with research from "the whole range of pure and applied mathematics, theoretical physics and statistics." There are two volumes published per year with about 50 to 80 articles, totaling around 1,000 pages per year. No book reviews are included. No articles are open access, but CUP allows early versions to be posted on arXiv.org or in institutional repositories. The digital archive for the years 1924-1997 is available for purchase, in addition to current electronic issues. Appropriate for academic libraries. URL: http://journals.cambridge.org/action/displayJournal?jid=PSP

3557. *Canadian Journal of Mathematics.* [ISSN: 0008-414X] 1949. bi-m. GBP 816. Ed(s): Eyal Goren, Louigi Addario-Berry. Cambridge University Press, University Printing House, Shaftesbury Rd, Cambridge, CB2 8BS, United Kingdom; journals@cambridge.org; https://www.cambridge.org/. Illus., adv. Refereed. Vol. ends: No. 6. *Indexed:* A22, MSN. *Aud.:* Ac, Sa.

The *Canadian Journal of Mathematics* (also known as *Journal Canadien de Mathematiques*) is one of two research journals published by the Canadian Mathematical Society (CMS). The CMS was originally conceived in June 1945 as the Canadian Mathematical Congress, and works to "share experiences, work on collaborative projects and generally enhance the perception and strengthen the profile of mathematics in Canada"; it has dealt with diverse topics. Lengthy articles (15 pages or more) are published in this journal, and shorter pieces are published in the *Canadian Mathematical Bulletin* (not reviewed in this section). Papers are in English and, rarely, in French. There are about 50 to 60 articles published annually, totaling 1,400 pages. This title is available online, including an archive from volume 1 (1949) with issues published before 2013 freely available. As a hybrid journal, some articles are open access, and an author's fee of $2,000 is charged for open access. Recommended for academic libraries. URL: http://cms.math.ca/cjm/

3558. *Duke Mathematical Journal.* [ISSN: 0012-7094] 1935. 18x/yr. USD 3090. Ed(s): Richard Hain, Jonathan Wahl. Duke University Press, 905 W Main St, Durham, NC 27701; orders@dukeupress.edu; https://www.dukeupress.edu. Illus., adv. Refereed. Vol. ends: No. 3. Reprint: PSC. *Indexed:* A22, MSN. *Aud.:* Ac, Sa.

An important university press title, *Duke Mathematical Journal* (*DMJ*) has been published by Duke University Press since 1935. It is one of the more costly of university press titles (compare to *Indiana University Mathematics Journal*). It is focused primarily on pure mathematics and publishes 18 issues annually with two to five articles each, totaling almost 3,600 pages annually. Volumes 1-100 are available through *DMJ 100*. The journal is hosted at Project Euclid (http://projecteuclid.org/dmj100). Recommended for academic libraries. URL: http://projecteuclid.org/dmj/

3559. *Forum of Mathematics, Pi.* [ISSN: 2050-5086] 2013. . Free. Cambridge University Press, University Printing House, Shaftesbury Rd, Cambridge, CB2 8BS, United Kingdom; journals@cambridge.org; https://www.cambridge.org. Refereed. *Indexed:* A01, MSN. *Aud.:* Ac, Sa.

Forum of Mathematics, Pi and *Forum of Mathematics, Sigma* (not reviewed in this section) editorial boards of the highest standing. *Pi* is intended to be a general mathematics journal accessible to a broad audience of mathematicians, and publishes less than a dozen articles in each annual volume. *Sigma* is a more specialized journal, with groups of editors working around topical areas such as applied mathematics, computation, topology, and many more. *Sigma* can have between five and dozens of articles in each annual volume. URL: http://journals.cambridge.org/action/displayJournal?jid=FMP

3560. *Historia Mathematica.* [ISSN: 0315-0860] 1974. q. EUR 668. Ed(s): Niccolo Guicciardini, Thomas Archibald. Academic Press, 3251 Riverport Ln, Maryland Heights, MO 63043; JournalCustomerService-usa@elsevier.com; http://www.elsevier.com/. Illus., adv. Refereed. *Indexed:* A01, A22, E01, MSN. *Bk. rev.:* 6-8, 500-1,500 words, signed; 18-22 pages of 50- to 100-word abstracts. *Aud.:* Ga, Ac, Sa.

Historia Mathematica "publishes historical scholarship on mathematics and its development in all cultures and time periods." It is published by the International Commission on the History of Mathematics (ICHM; www.unizar.es/ichm). Besides a dozen research articles per year in the 400-500 pages published, in each issue there are 20 or more pages of abstracts from the current literature on the history of mathematics. Each short entry is categorized either by time period or by geographic region and includes cross-references and reference to reviews in *Mathematical Reviews* and *Zentralblatt MATH* (both titles not reviewed in this section). There are several medium-length, signed book reviews. This title is available online starting at volume 1. Recommended for academic libraries, and it may also be suitable for public libraries for its strong bibliographic focus. URL: www.sciencedirect.com/science/journal/03150860

3561. *I M A Journal of Applied Mathematics.* Supersedes in part (in 1981): *Institute of Mathematics and Its Applications. Journal.* [ISSN: 0272-4960] 1965. bi-m. EUR 1317. Ed(s): A Champneys. Oxford University Press, Great Clarendon St, Oxford, OX2 6DP, United Kingdom; onlinequeries.uk@oup.com; http://global.oup.com. Illus., adv. Sample. Refereed. Reprint: PSC. *Indexed:* A01, A22, E01, MSN. *Aud.:* Ac, Sa.

The *IMA Journal of Applied Mathematics* is published by the Institute of Mathematics and its Applications (IMA; www.ima.org.uk). The IMA "exists to support the advancement of mathematical knowledge and its applications and to promote and enhance mathematical culture." The IMA also publishes the *IMA Journal of Numerical Analysis* (not reviewed in this section), which is focused on "analytic and numerical treatments of both physical and non-physical applied mathematical problems." Papers for either journal have applications to more than one field, and occasionally there are surveys "on recent progress in topical fields of mathematics and its applications." There are six issues of the *IMA Journal of Applied Mathematics* per year, with about 40 to 60 articles totaling 1,200-2,000 pages. There are no book reviews. This title is available online, with a digital archive available back to volume 1. Some articles are open access through author fees. Recommended for academic libraries. URL: http://imamat.oxfordjournals.org

3562. *Indiana University Mathematics Journal.* Former titles (until 1970): *Journal of Mathematics and Mechanics;* (until 1956): *Journal of Rational Mechanics and Analysis.* [ISSN: 0022-2518] 1952. bi-m. USD 490 (Individuals, USD 155). Ed(s): Chris Judge. Indiana University, Department of Mathematics, 831 E Third St, Bloomington, IN 47405; http://www.math.indiana.edu/. Illus., index. Refereed. *Indexed:* A22, MSN. *Aud.:* Ac, Sa.

The *Indiana University Mathematics Journal* is a university press title that publishes research on "both pure and applied mathematics," with an emphasis on "significance, originality, lucidity, and expository concision." There are 70 to 100 articles published annually in six issues, totaling more than 2,000 pages. The journal has quite a long backlog of submissions, but dozens of preprints are available on the web site. All issues are available online, with the 1952-1994 digital archive still freely available. Access to volumes 20-63 (1970-2014) is available through JSTOR as well. Highly recommended for academic libraries. URL: www.iumj.indiana.edu

3563. *Inventiones Mathematicae.* [ISSN: 0020-9910] 1966. m. EUR 3339 (print & online eds.)). Ed(s): H Hofer. Springer, Tiergartenstr 17, Heidelberg, 69121, Germany. Illus., adv. Sample. Refereed. Vol. ends: No. 3. Reprint: PSC. *Indexed:* A01, A22, E01, MSN. *Aud.:* Ac, Sa.

Inventiones Mathematicae (also known simply as *Inventiones*) has been published since 1966 by Springer. It has a strong impact in the area of pure mathematics. Articles are mainly in English, with the rare article in French or German. There are four volumes of three issues annually, about 60 to 80 articles per year, that total almost 4,000 pages. This title is available online, and volumes 1-123 are available free from the Archive Gottingen (http://gdz.sub.uni-goettingen.de). Some articles from recent years are available as open access through author fees. Recommended for academic libraries. URL: www.springerlink.com/content/0020-9910

The Journal of Symbolic Logic. See Philosophy section.

3564. *London Mathematical Society. Proceedings.* [ISSN: 0024-6115] 1865. m. GBP 1236 (print & online eds.)). Wiley-Blackwell Publishing Ltd., The Atrium, Southern Gate, Chichester, PO19 8QG, United Kingdom; cs-journals@wiley.com; http://onlinelibrary.wiley.com. Illus., index, adv. Refereed. Vol. ends: No. 3. Reprint: PSC. *Indexed:* A01, A22, E01, MSN. *Aud.:* Ac, Sa.

The *Proceedings of the London Mathematical Society* is the venue for longer papers published by the London Mathematical Society (LMS; www.lms.ac.uk). The LMS also publishes medium-length papers in its *Journal* and short research papers in its *Bulletin* (both not reviewed in this section). The *Proceedings* has been published since 1865, when the society was founded, and "covers a wide range of mathematical topics" in pure and some applied areas of mathematics. *Proceedings* publishes two volumes a year of six issues, with 70 to 90 articles annually totaling almost 2,500 pages. Current issues and an archive are available online from publisher Wiley, though Oxford University Press published the journal until 2016. Some articles are open access through an author fee model. Recommended for academic libraries, along with many of the society's other journal titles. URL: https://academic.oup.com/plms

3565. *S I A M Review.* [ISSN: 0036-1445] 1959. q. USD 582 (print & online eds.)). Ed(s): Desmond Higham. Society for Industrial and Applied Mathematics, 3600 Market St, 6th Fl, Philadelphia, PA 19104; siam@siam.org; http://www.epubs.siam.org. Illus., index, adv. Sample. Refereed. Vol. ends: No. 4. *Indexed:* A01, A22, B01, BRI, CBRI, CompLI, MSN. *Bk. rev.:* 5-15, 300-1,500 words, signed. *Aud.:* Ga, Ac, Sa.

SIAM Review is the flagship publication of the Society for Industrial and Applied Mathematics (SIAM), and it "provides a forum for the exchange of information and ideas among mathematicians, engineers, and scientists." Of the 16 journals published by SIAM, the *Review* has the broadest appeal, since it includes "SIGEST" (digest of a recent paper from one of SIAM's other journals), in addition to review articles and surveys of the literature. This title contains a featured book review and several other medium-length, signed reviews. The entire collection of SIAM journals is available online and should be considered a core resource for academic libraries. Archives for these journals are available either from SIAM through its *Locus* collection or from JSTOR (through 2012; https://www.jstor.org/publisher/siam). The *Review* is also useful for some public and school libraries. URL: www.siam.org/journals/

3566. *Studies in Applied Mathematics (Malden).* Formerly (until 1968): *Journal of Mathematics and Physics.* [ISSN: 0022-2526] 1922. 8x/yr. GBP 1824. Ed(s): Jianke Yang. Wiley-Blackwell Publishing, Inc., 111 River St, Hoboken, NJ 07030; http://onlinelibrary.wiley.com. Illus., adv. Sample. Refereed. Vol. ends: No. 3. Microform: PQC. Reprint: PSC. *Indexed:* A01, A22, B01, E01, MSN. *Aud.:* Ac, Sa.

Studies in Applied Mathematics "explores the interplay between mathematics and the applied disciplines." There are two volumes a year with four issues each, for about 30 to 40 articles published each year in roughly 1,000 pages, but no book reviews. This title is available online with an archive available beginning in 1922 with volume 1. Recommended for some academic libraries. URL: http://onlinelibrary.wiley.com/journal/10.1111/(ISSN)1467-9590

3567. *Symmetry, Integrability and Geometry: Methods and Applications.* [ISSN: 1815-0659] 2005. a. Free. Ed(s): Anatoliy Nikitin. Natsional'na Akademiya Nauk Ukrainy, Instytut Matematyky, vul Tereschenkivska 3, Kyiv, 01601, Ukraine; sam@imath.kiev.ua; http://www.imath.kiev.ua. Refereed. *Indexed:* MSN. *Aud.:* Ac, Sa.

Symmetry, Integrability and Geometry: Methods and Applications (*SIGMA*) is an arXiv.org overlay journal, which means that articles are submitted to the preprint repository as part of the review process. The articles are then reviewed through the arXiv and collected into annual issues. The journal also occasionally creates special issues as a part of each annual volume (www.emis.de/journals/SIGMA/special_issues.html). There are no page limits to articles, and since there is no set number of articles, the first volume had 28 articles and recent volumes average around 100. This title is an open-access journal, financially supported by a number of foundations and libraries. Recommended for academic libraries.

■ MEDIA AND AV

See also Communication; Education; Films; and Television, Video, and Radio sections.

Andrea Reed Rodgers, Reference Librarian, Delaware County Community College, Media, PA 19063; arodgers4@dccc.edu

Introduction

The Media and AV section heavily features publications (17 titles) that focus on the evolving intersection of education and technology. In the past 15 years, there have been incredible changes to the role computers play in how people learn. Therefore, it comes as no surprise that publications reviewed in this section primarily address the theoretical and methodical issues in the field of educational technology.

Overall, these journals are rich in research-oriented content, and articles are written geared to professors, practitioners, and researchers of education and instructional technology design. These titles address a wide range of learning environments from K to 12 to higher education, as well as post-school education. Many are refereed. Common themes throughout the publications include mobile technologies, the online learning environment, performing online assessment and interaction, and the use of interactive learning games. Since this field is becoming increasingly digitized, readers should also consult the other technology-related sections in this volume.

Also included in this section are titles focused on the mass media and audio-visual fields (4 titles) and their educational and cultural impact.

It is worth noting that since the 25th edition of *Magazines for Libraries*, the *International Journal of Learning and Media* and *Media* have ceased publication, and as a result, have not been reviewed for this edition. Six new titles have been reviewed and added to the Media and AV section. Interestingly, out of the reviewed 21 titles, four have begun publication within the past 10 years, 12 started their publication in the past 17 years, and 9 are available as open-access; facts that seem indicative of the growing educational technology field.

Basic Periodicals

Innovations in Education and Teaching International, Journal of Media Literacy Education, TechTrends.

Basic Abstracts and Indexes

Education Abstracts, ERIC.

3568. ***British Journal of Educational Technology.*** Formerly (until 19??): *Journal of Educational Technology.* [ISSN: 0007-1013] 1970. bi-m. GBP 1065. Ed(s): Nick Rushby. Wiley-Blackwell Publishing Ltd., The Atrium, Southern Gate, Chichester, PO19 8QG, United Kingdom; cs-journals@wiley.com; http://onlinelibrary.wiley.com. Illus., index, adv. Sample. Refereed. Vol. ends: Nov. Microform: PQC. Reprint: PSC. *Indexed:* A01, A22, BRI, CompLI, E01, ERIC, ErgAb, MLA-IB. *Bk. rev.:* 10, 150-500 words. *Aud.:* Ac.

One of the many journals that the British Educational Research Association publishes, this title examines the theory, development, application, and current issues relating to educational technology. Each issue contains articles and reviews. This journal's articles are peer-reviewed, are relevant, and are often research studies about worldwide education and technology topics (K-12 and higher education) such as plagiarism, collaborative learning, social technologies, the e-learning environment, and student/teacher technology perceptions. The featured reviews are related to recently published books, or they are literature reviews on a specific topic. In the rapidly growing age of MOOCs and online learning, this title is a great addition to any academic serials collection. Available in print or online.

3569. ***E-Learning and Digital Media.*** Formerly (until 2010): *E-Learning.* [ISSN: 2042-7530] 2004. bi-m. USD 1570. Sage Publications Ltd., 1 Oliver's Yard, 55 City Rd, London, EC1Y 1SP, United Kingdom; info@sagepub.com; https://www.sagepub.com/. Refereed. *Indexed:* ERIC. *Aud.:* Hs, Ac.

With a title change in 2010 from *E-Learning* to *E-learning and Digital Media,* this publication still has a stronger emphasis on e-learning rather than digital media arts/education. It is peer-reviewed, international in scope, and published bimonthly, and on average contains 10 to 15 scholarly articles on mostly e-learning topics like pedagogy, curriculum, and philosophy. The articles tend to be heavily research-based, rather than driven by case studies, which adheres to its desire to publish academic articles, national and international policy reports, and policy research notes. It is similar in content to the *Electronic Journal of E-Learning* (also reviewed in this section), but in this reviewer's opinion it doesn't feel as accessible. Every so often it publishes a themed issue, like the March 2015 issue that was entirely dedicated to digital media production. All educational learning is considered (K-12, higher education, specialized education, workforce training, and so on). Available online.

3570. ***Educational Media International.*** Former titles (until 1986): *Educational Media International;* (until 1971): *Audio-Visual Media.* [ISSN: 0952-3987] 1967. q. GBP 557 (print & online eds.)). Ed(s): Charalambos Vrasidas. Routledge, 4 Park Sq, Milton Park, Abingdon, OX14 4RN, United Kingdom; subscriptions@tandf.co.uk; http://www.tandfonline.com. Illus., adv. Sample. Refereed. Microform: PQC. Reprint: PSC. *Indexed:* A01, A22, E01, ERIC. *Bk. rev.:* 2-3, 500 words. *Aud.:* Ac.

Published four times a year, *Educational Media International* offers the latest innovations in educational and mass media, including educational technologies and open/distance learning. It examines technology's use in all types of educational environments, from preschool to professional development practices, as well as lifelong learning situations. Only containing easily read, peer-reviewed articles, it seeks to inform and provide a forum for its readers on the challenges and successes relating to educational technologies, such as blended learning, social media in the classroom, and online course design. Some of the articles are studies, while others report on case-study findings. Contributors are drawn from academics, educators, and media professionals from around the world. It's worth noting that abstracts of articles published in this journal are available online in multiple languages at http://emi.cardet.org. Available in print or online. Recommended for academic library collections.

Educational Technology Research & Development. See Education/ Specific Subjects and Teaching Methods: Technology section.

3571. ***Electronic Journal of E-Learning.*** [ISSN: 1479-4403] 2003. s-a. Free. Ed(s): Karin Tweddell Levinsen, Rikke Orngreen. Academic Conferences and Publishing International Ltd., Curtis Farm, Kidmore End, Nr Reading, RG4 9AY, United Kingdom; info@academic-conferences.org; http://www.academic-conferences.org. Refereed. *Indexed:* ERIC. *Bk. rev.:* Number and length vary. *Aud.:* Ac.

This open-source e-journal is published by Academic Conferences and Publishing International. It publishes double-blind peer-reviewed papers, empirical research, case studies, action research, theoretical discussions, literature reviews, reports, conference papers, and other work (though it is light in book reviews). This online journal's aim is to provide a perspective on e-learning practices, theories, and development. Published biannually, the *Electronic Journal of E-Learning* (*EJEL*) additionally offers special issues and, as a result, it produces on average three or four issues each year. Compared to other titles in this Media and AV section, *EJEL* takes a broader perspective of e-learning by its inclusion of technology-focused articles relating to educational gaming, e-learning portals, security and confidentiality issues, grading, and the psychological aspects of an e-learning classroom. Publication content comes from authors worldwide. For academic libraries on a tight budget, this is a great, affordable journal to include in a serials collection. URL: www.ejel.org/

3572. ***Innovations in Education and Teaching International (Print).*** Former titles (until 2001): *Innovations in Education and Training International (Print);* (until 1995): *Educational and Training Technology International;* (until 1989): *P L E T. Programmed Learning and*

Educational Technology; (until 1984): *Programmed Learning and Educational Technology;* (until 1967): *Programmed Learning;* (until 1964): *Association for Programmed Learning. Bulletin.* [ISSN: 1470-3297] 1964. bi-m. GBP 721 (print & online eds.)). Ed(s): Gina Wisker. Routledge, 4 Park Sq, Milton Park, Abingdon, OX14 4RN, United Kingdom; subscriptions@tandf.co.uk; http://www.tandfonline.com. Illus., adv. Sample. Refereed. Vol. ends: Nov. Microform: PQC. Reprint: PSC. *Indexed:* A01, A22, E01, ERIC. *Bk. rev.:* 1-2, 750-1,000 words. *Aud.:* Ac.

As the official journal of the Staff and Educational Development Association (SEDA), *Innovations in Education and Teaching International* (*IETI*) promotes innovation and best practices in higher education, through staff and educational development. To this end, it publishes articles about research, experience, scholarship, and evaluation pertaining to educational development in higher and post-school education. On average, each issue contains one book review. *IETI* is not as heavily focused on media and technology in education as other titles reviewed in this section. Rather, it addresses innovative educational technologies and their theories as one aspect within the framework of educational development. The journal's content includes various topics such as pedagogy, blended learning, assessment, student learning support, and technology-supported collaboration. Its contributors are educators from all over the world. Available in print or online.

3573. *International Journal of Instructional Technology and Distance Learning.* [ISSN: 1550-6908] 2004. m. Free. Ed(s): Elizabeth Perrin, Muhammad Betz. International Journal of Instructional Technology and Distance Learning, 1873 Calle Borrego, Thousand Oaks, CA 91360. Refereed. *Aud.:* Ems, Hs, Ac.

A relatively new publication, having published its first issue in 2004, the *International Journal of Instructional Technology and Distance Learning* is freely (and only) available online. As noted in its "Publisher's Declaration," the journal's focus is "to facilitate communication and collaboration among researchers, innovators, practitioners, and administrators of education and training involving innovative technologies and/or distance learning." On average, each issue contains from four to seven articles and one editorial. This title is published monthly. Contributors and topics tackle a global perspective of instructional technology and distance learning, as indicated in the journal's title. This peer-reviewed journal does not shy away from addressing far-reaching topics pertaining to instructional technology and distance learning within K-12 schools as well as within higher education, and as a result, it offers a unique perspective. Subjects include how instructional technology lends itself to an institution's brand, use of mobile devices in the classroom, how to foster a strong presence in the online classroom, and case studies focusing on specific technologies (i.e., Twitter, Webquests, digital game resources, and so on). The breadth of topics featured in this publication makes it a compelling title to include in either the academic or the school library setting. URL: www.itdl.org/

3574. *International Journal of Social Media and Interactive Learning Environments.* [ISSN: 2050-3954] 2013. q. USD 790 (print or online ed.)). Ed(s): Dr. Qiyun Wang, Zhiting Zhu. Inderscience Publishers, PO Box 735, Olney, MK46 5WB, United Kingdom; info@inderscience.com; https://www.inderscience.com/index.php. Sample. Refereed. *Aud.:* Ems, Hs, Ac.

As the title indicates, this journal focuses on the use of social media for teaching and formal/informal learning. This title is published quarterly, and each issue contains about six or seven articles written by practitioners and researchers, and includes original research papers, case studies, and conceptual papers. The articles don't particularly place an emphasis on media literacy, but rather seek to inform readers about collaborative and engaging uses of social media and Web 2.0 within K-12, higher-education, and adult-learning educational contexts. Sometimes issues are dedicated to a special topic, such as the "Flipped Classroom with Technology" and "Using Facebook as an Educational Tool," which allows for an in-depth analysis and discussion of issue's topic. In general, the *International Journal of Social Media and Interactive Learning Environments* aims to inform on ways of designing interactive and collaborative educational environments in which social media tools are important. There is an international emphasis on the content, so that a more complete picture of social media usage in different cultural and educational contexts is addressed. Because of its wide appeal to professionals, academics, researchers, and teachers, this journal is recommended for school libraries and academic libraries.

3575. *International Journal of Technology in Teaching and Learning.* [ISSN: 1937-5204] 2005. s-a. Ed(s): Leping Liu, Aaron S Richmond. Society of International Chinese in Educational Technology, Dept of Technology Education, McLemore Hall Rm 157, Hattiesburg, MS 39406; wuprofessor@gmail.com; http://www.sicet.org. Refereed. *Aud.:* Ems, Hs, Ac.

A semi-annual peer-reviewed journal, its main scope is broad, seeking original research on methods of integrating technology into teaching and learning on all related topics. True to its title, the journal publishes five articles per issue that focus on aspects of educational technology, such as theoretical foundations, successful applications, and/or potential international avenues for advancing technology integration. In evaluating the journal's website, it appears articles from the current issue and past issues (dating back to 2005) are freely available in pdf format. Topics are published with a global audience in mind and cover the pedagogy of teaching with technology, online teaching and learning, new technology tools and innovations, and development of technology-based curriculum, among others. Since it publishes articles addressing all educational levels, this journal is recommended for academic and school libraries. URL: https://sicet.org/main/journals/ijttl/

3576. *Journal of Educational Media, Memory, and Society.* Former titles (until 2009): *Contexts;* (until 2008): *Internationale Schulbuchforschung;* (until 1979): *Internationales Jahrbuch fur Geschichts- und Geographie-Unterricht;* (until 1967): *Internationales Jahrbuch fur Geschichtsunterricht.* [ISSN: 2041-6938] 1951. s-a. USD 248 combined subscription (print & online eds.)). Ed(s): Eckhardt Fuchs. Berghahn Books Ltd., 3 Newtec Pl, Magdalen Rd, Oxford, OX4 1RE, United Kingdom; journals@berghahnbooks.com; http://journals.berghahnbooks.com/. Adv. Sample. Refereed. Reprint: PSC. *Indexed:* A22, MLA-IB. *Aud.:* Sa.

The *Journal of Educational Media, Memory and Society* is a print/online publication of the George Eckert Institute for International Textbook Research. International in scope, it aims to publish interdisciplinary empirical, theoretical, and/or methodological articles that discuss perceptions of society as examined primarily through text-based educational media. The journal defines educational media as textbooks/curriculum, museums, memorials, and film. This title is published semi-annually, and each issue contains about four to six articles (with accompanying illustrations). It is common for at least one article in an issue to discuss the effects of textbooks on a certain historical or societal issue. At this time, it does not publish book reviews. Since the use of technology in education is such a driving force within the field, it seems like a missed opportunity to exclude it from the journal's scope. Because of its specific focus, this journal is recommended only for special libraries.

3577. *Journal of Educational Technology Systems.* Formerly (until 199?): *Journal of Educational Instrumentation.* [ISSN: 0047-2395] 1972. q. USD 721 (print & online eds.)). Ed(s): Lori L Scarlatos, Thomas T Liao. Sage Publications, Inc., 2455 Teller Rd, Thousand Oaks, CA 91320; info@sagepub.com; http://www.sagepub.com. Illus., index, adv. Sample. Refereed. Reprint: PSC. *Indexed:* A22, CompLI, ERIC. *Bk. rev.:* Number and length vary. *Aud.:* Ac.

Published with all levels of education as well as commercial and training organizations in mind, the *Journal of Educational Technology Systems* (*JETS*) is a peer-reviewed publication with a primary interest in applications of technology that enable or improve learning. It contains papers from academia and industry, and addresses topics pertaining to educational systems (hardware and software) that improve or evaluate instruction. There is a special emphasis on papers that address computers and web-based instruction as an important component of the education system. Another area of interest to *JETS* is the design and development of interactive, computer-based systems that can be linked to other instructional technologies. It seeks papers that explore techniques that utilize technology and that are curriculum-applied, and/or experimented with, in actual classroom practices. Alternative models of distance learning are also a focus. Each issue includes about six to eight papers, an editorial overview, and book reviews. Available in print or online.

3578. *Journal of Interactive Online Learning.* [ISSN: 1541-4914] 2002. 3x/yr. Free. Ed(s): Jason T Abbitt, Cynthia S Sunal. National Center for Online Learning Research, c/o Vivian H. Wright, Executive Editor, University of Alabama, College of Education, Tuscaloosa, AL 35401; http://www.ncolr.org. Refereed. *Indexed:* ERIC. *Aud.:* Ac.

The *Journal of Interactive Online Learning* aims to provide its readers with theory, research and practical application of online education. Scholarly in tone, it is freely published two to four times a year. Issues contain a collection of three to four peer-reviewed articles and reviews that delve into topics relating to online learning and its utilities, such as gamification, security concerns, classroom blogs, collaborative communities, MOOCs, and asynchronous discussion forums. Authors worldwide contribute to its focus on online learning in higher education. Its smaller issue size is a drawback, especially for those looking to save time while researching. Similar titles such as the *Electronic Journal of E-Learning* and the *International Journal of Instructional Technology and Distance Learning* provide comparable research articles and more of them in their issues. URL: http://www.ncolr.org/

3579. *The Journal of Literacy and Technology: an international online academic journal.* [ISSN: 1535-0975] 2000. 3x/yr. Free. Ed(s): Noemi Marin. Florida Atlantic University, Department of Communication, 777 Glades Rd, Boca Raton, FL 33431; http://www.fau.edu/. Refereed. *Aud.:* Ems, Hs, Ac.

Whereas a number of the titles reviewed in this section focus on the broad scope of technology in education, the *Journal of Literacy and Technology* focuses specifically on the role technology plays in teaching reading, writing, digital, and other literacies. It is an open-access, peer-reviewed journal featuring contributions from around the world that address the use of technology in literacy pedagogy in educational, workplace, public, and individual settings. This academic journal is published two to three times a year. Recent issues address diverse topics such as e-book reading, college students' Internet search strategies, digital poetry instruction to secondary education distance students, online commerce as a digital literacy, and literacy and technology studies focusing on specific nationalities and age groups. Given its important focus on literacy within the technological landscape, this journal is recommended for school, public, and academic libraries. URL: http://www.literacyandtechnology.org/

3580. *The Journal of Media Literacy: a publication of the National Telemedia Council.* Former titles (until 2006): *Telemedium;* (until 1984): *Better Broadcasts News; Better Broadcasts Newsletter.* [ISSN: 1944-4982] 1953. 3x/yr. USD 80 (Individuals, USD 40). Ed(s): Marieli Rowe. National Telemedia Council, Inc., 1922 University Ave, Madison, WI 53705; ntelemedia@aol.com; http://www.nationaltelemediacouncil.org/. Illus. Sample. *Aud.:* Ems, Hs.

The official publication of the National Telemedia Council, the *Journal of Media Literacy* is published three times a year. This non-refereed periodical produces its issues based on a theme. Each issue contains about 15 to 20 articles, curated by a guest editor, that discuss various media literacy aspects and practices pertaining to the issues' theme. Past issues explored media literacy's role in cultural diversity, K-12 learning in the digital age, and civic engagement. The current issue and two past issues are freely available online in html format. To access the journal's past issues online, you must become a member of the National Telemedia Council. *The Journal of Media Literacy*'s primary readership is K-12 teachers, teacher educators, professors, community activists, and media professionals. Recommended for K-12 school libraries.

3581. *The Journal of Media Literacy Education.* [ISSN: 2167-8715] 2009. s-a. Free. Ed(s): Renee Hobbs, Vanessa Domine. National Association for Media Literacy Education, The Harrington School of Communication and Media, University of Rhode Island, Kingston, RI 02881. Refereed. *Indexed:* ERIC. *Bk. rev.:* 4-6. *Aud.:* Ems, Hs, Ac.

This open-access publication is produced by the National Association for Media Literacy Education (NAMLE) and hosted in The University of Rhode Island's DigitalCommons@URI repository. This journal is generally published twice a year, and its aim is to foster development in media literacy education research, scholarship, and pedagogy for the digestion of scholars, media professions, and educational practitioners. Through its research and scholarship articles, practitioner-focused essays, and reviews, *The Journal of Media Literacy Education* encourages the development and application of media literacy and critical-thinking skills in educating students within the context of the digital age. Content-wise, this journal covers a breadth of educational topics and their relationship to media literacy. Each issue contains four or five research articles and four to six reviews. The reviews examine newly published books in this field, as well as curriculum materials and multimedia and online resources. Issues also include a section entitled "Voices from the Field," which contain two or three essays written by emerging scholars, media professionals, and educational practitioners. Recommended for K-12 school libraries and academic libraries. URL: http://digitalcommons.uri.edu/jmle/

3582. *Journal of Media Practice.* [ISSN: 1468-2753] 2000. 3x/yr. GBP 317 (print & online eds.)). Ed(s): Julian McDougall. Routledge, 4 Park Sq, Milton Park, Abingdon, OX14 4RN, United Kingdom; subscriptions@tandf.co.uk; http://www.tandfonline.com. Adv. Sample. Refereed. Reprint: PSC. *Indexed:* A01, A22, A51, E01, F01, MLA-IB. *Bk. rev.:* 1-3, 700-900 words. *Aud.:* Ac.

As identified in its aims and scope, the *Journal of Media Practice* has a "particular emphasis on creative projects that integrate issues of scholarly interest." The title is published three times a year, and each issue contains approximately four or five peer-reviewed articles and an editorial piece. Newer issues feature an average of three book reviews, while older issues contain one review. The articles tend to focus on current media topics pertaining to journalism; media industries like film, radio, and television; social media; and the use of archives in media production. There isn't a strong emphasis on media education, but rather the journal presents scholarly perspectives on present-day media practices. Despite this journal's being published out of the United Kingdom, its content and contributing authors possess a global mindset toward the subject matter. Available in print or online. Recommended for academic libraries that support strong media arts programs.

3583. *Journal of Special Education Technology.* [ISSN: 0162-6434] 1978. q. USD 341 (print & online eds.)). Sage Publications, Inc., 2455 Teller Rd, Thousand Oaks, CA 91320; info@sagepub.com; http://www.sagepub.com. Illus., adv. Refereed. *Indexed:* A22, ERIC. *Aud.:* Ems, Hs, Ac.

Published quarterly, the *Journal of Special Education Technology* presents current information and opinions about issues, research, policy, and practice related to the use of technology in the field of special education. Each year it publishes three non-topical issues and one topical issue. Issues mostly contain five experimental or applied research articles with an occasional article on an applied practice in the field. The journal addresses a broad range of technology applications within the special education field. Examples of technology discussed include online learning for learners with disabilities, tablet-based instruction for autistic children, use of vocabulary videos for students with language impairments, and teaching online social skills to students with emotional and behavioral disorders. Though not exclusively geared toward K-12 educators, the majority of the journal's articles are studies from this academic setting. Given the importance of special education in elementary and grade schools, this journal is recommended for school libraries and academic libraries that support special education training programs.

3584. *Journal of Teaching and Learning with Technology.* [ISSN: 2165-2554] 2012. s-a. Ed(s): Robin K Morgan. Indiana University, 755 W Michigan St, UL 1180D, Indianapolis, IN 46202; http://www.indiana.edu/. Refereed. *Aud.:* Ac.

The *Journal of Teaching and Learning with Technology,* is a relatively new, open-source, peer-reviewed journal that focuses on enhancing student learning at the university level through technology. It began publication in 2012 and is published semi-annually. Each issue contains four to six qualitative or quantitative evidence-based articles and one to four "quick hits," which are brief contributions describing practical innovative procedures, courses, or materials involving technology. While the journal's scope indicates its acceptance of book reviews, only one was included in the issues reviewed here. Examples of topics addressed in recent issues include using video to enhance learning and discussion, online education pedagogy, social media usage and the classroom, screencasting, and the flipped classroom approach. Because of its focus on higher education and its mixture of empirical content along side of practitioner insights, this journal is highly recommended for academic libraries. URL: http://jotlt.indiana.edu/

Learning, Media & Technology (Online). See Education/Specific Subjects and Teaching Methods: Communication Arts section.

3585. ***Media Education Research Journal.*** [ISSN: 2040-4530] 2010. s-a. GBP 60 (print & online eds.) Individuals, GBP 30). Ed(s): Julian McDougall, Richard Berger. Auteur Publishing, The Old Surgery, 9 Pulford Rd, Leighton Buzzard, LU7 1NP, United Kingdom; info@auteur.co.uk; http://www.auteur.co.uk/. Refereed. *Bk. rev.:* 2-4, 700-1,200 words. *Aud.:* Ems, Hs, Ac.

Media Education Research Journal publishes issues twice a year. A typical issue features two to four book reviews, four or five full articles, one or two research reports, and an editorial piece. The journal's peer-reviewed content focuses on the use of media in the classroom (both in K-12 and higher education), as well as media arts education (how to create media; how to use it). Common topics written about include gaming, web design, digital filmmaking, social media, and media literacy. This title is published for an international audience. Articles are current and tap into the latest trends in media creation, production, and classroom use. Available to individuals in print, and to institutions in print and as a pdf file. Recommended for academic and school libraries.

3586. ***Media History Monographs: an online journal of media history.*** [ISSN: 1940-8862] 1997. s-a. Free. Ed(s): David Copeland. Elon University, c/o David Copeland, School of Communications, Elon, NC 27244; http://www.elon.edu. Refereed. *Aud.:* Ac.

Only available online, *Media History Monographs* (*MHM*) is a freely available scholarly journal that publishes essays and papers on the history of journalism and mass communication. Submissions that are too long for regular journals, but too short to be published as a book, are perfect candidates for publication in *MHM*. This title is affiliated with the American Journalism Historians Association and sponsored by the School of Communications at Elon University. Generally, the journal is published twice a year, and typically features one article per issue. Most of the content comes from American institutions of higher education, though a few European colleges and universities are represented. Recommended for academic libraries. URL: http://facstaff.elon.edu/dcopeland/mhm/mhm.htm

3587. ***Research in Learning Technology.*** Formerly (until 2011): *A L T - J / Association for Learning Technology Journal.* [ISSN: 2156-7069] 1993. a. Free. Routledge, 4 Park Sq, Milton Park, Abingdon, OX14 4RN, United Kingdom; subscriptions@tandf.co.uk; http://www.tandfonline.com. Sample. Refereed. Reprint: PSC. *Indexed:* A22, E01, ERIC. *Aud.:* Ac.

Research in Learning Technology is an open-access journal. Until recently, it was published three times a year. Starting in 2013, the journal contains one issue with articles added to it throughout the year. Like the *International Journal of Technology in Teaching and Learning*, *Research in Learning* seeks articles on a broad range of educational technology topics, ranging from wearable technologies, simulation, and learning environments to online learning, pedagogy, and open educational practice. Each issue contains 15 to 20 high-quality evidence-based research articles from researchers, practitioners, and policy makers. Like its broad scope, *Research in Learning Technology* also addresses a broad readership from any level of education-from formal primary, secondary, further and higher education, to professional learning and informal learning. While some articles will be useful in a primary or secondary school library setting, much of the content focuses on higher education from around the world. Recommended for academic libraries. URL: http://www.tandfonline.com/toc/zrlt20/current

School Library Media Research. See *School Library Research* in Library and Information Science section.

3588. ***TechTrends: linking research and practice to improve learning.*** Former titles (until 1985): *Instructional Innovator; Audiovisual Instruction with Instructional Resources; Audiovisual Instruction.* [ISSN: 8756-3894] 1956. bi-m. EUR 260 (print & online eds.)). Ed(s): Charles B Hodges. Springer New York LLC, 233 Spring St, New York, NY 10013; customerservice@springer.com; http://www.springer.com. Illus., index, adv. Refereed. Vol. ends: Nov. Reprint: PSC. *Indexed:* A01, A22, BRI, E01, ERIC. *Aud.:* Ems, Hs, Ac.

This bimonthly, peer-reviewed journal is aimed at professionals within the educational communication and technology field. Produced by the Association for Educational Communications and Technology (AECT), this title examines new technologies in education and training that occurs in K-12 schools, colleges and universities, and private industry. *TechTrends* differs from many of the journals reviewed in this section, since each issue is primarily composed of articles on the latest trends and practices, and it is not as reliant on scholarly research as other titles listed in this section. Therefore, it is a complementary title to include in any academic-periodicals collection. General topics of interest to the journal include management of media and programs, and the application of educational technology principles and techniques to instructional programs. Most issues begin with a note from the editor, include AECT news, and include about 10 to 15 articles, which have a conversational style and are easy to follow.

■ MEDICINE

See also Family Planning; Health and Fitness; Health Care Administration; Health Professions; Nursing; and Public Health sections.

Cynthia J. Beeler, Preston Medical Library, University of Tennessee Graduate School of Medicine, Knoxville, TN 37920; cvaughn@utmck.edu

Introduction

Health information is everywhere: on the Internet, on TV, as the subject of movies and documentaries, and in active debates in politics. As part of the Affordable Care Act, patients and their families are encouraged to be an active participant in their health care, which means that they are often turning to libraries for information. Some health sciences and public libraries carry "consumer health" magazines, written for the lay public. These help to demystify conditions in order that patients can more fully participate in the management of their own health.

In addition, doctors, nurses, and physician assistants are required to keep up with the latest research. Their patients may query them about a study they heard about on a morning talk show, or show them print outs from a web site. Medical journal collections offer physicians, medical administrators, nurses, residents, students, and the interested public the most current information in the various specialties and sub-specialties of medicine. The journals have peer-reviewed information from randomized controlled trials, reviews, case reports, and other updates from the medical field. These trials can change practice, such as types of drugs administered and other therapies prescribed.

In this section, journals and magazines have been evaluated for their place in various types of libraries. Naturally, health sciences libraries will have a much broader collection than the journals described here, and some public and academic libraries will have a smaller collection, depending on the population they serve. Most journals and magazines have online content available as well as a print journal, and most are indexed in databases such as MEDLINE and CINAHL.

Basic Periodicals

J A M A: The Journal of the American Medical Association, The Lancet (North American Edition), *The New England Journal of Medicine.*

Basic Abstracts and Indexes

CINAHL, EMBASE, MEDLINE, Scopus.

3589. ***AIDS Patient Care and S T Ds.*** Incorporates (1990-1997): *Pediatric AIDS and HIV Infection;* Formerly (until 1996): *AIDS Patient Care.* [ISSN: 1087-2914] 1987. m. USD 1830. Ed(s): Jeffrey Laurence. Mary Ann Liebert, Inc. Publishers, 140 Huguenot St, 3rd Fl, New Rochelle, NY 10801; info@liebertpub.com; http://www.liebertpub.com. Illus., adv. Sample. Refereed. Vol. ends: Dec. Reprint: PSC. *Indexed:* A01, A22, BRI, C45, E01. *Aud.:* Ac, Sa.

This peer-reviewed scholarly journal publishes original articles on HIV/AIDS as well as on other STDs. It has an international scope for its articles, and it also publishes case reports, letters to the editor, and current drug development news. Articles deal with diagnosis, treatment, patient care, epidemiology, education, prevention, policy issues, and psychological issues. This journal is appropriate for all health sciences libraries, as HIV/AIDS is a global concern. Some other academic libraries may consider it as well for their medical and allied health programs.

3590. ***American Family Physician.*** Formerly (until Dec.1970): *American Family Physician - G P;* Which was formed by the merger of (1962-Jan.1970): *American Family Physician;* (1950-Jan.1970): *G P.* [ISSN: 0002-838X] 1970. 24x/yr. USD 340 (print & online eds.) Individuals, USD 199 (print & online eds.); Free to members). Ed(s): Jay Siwek. American Academy of Family Physicians, PO Box 11210, Shawnee Mission, KS 66207; contactcenter@aafp.org; http://www.aafp.org. Illus., index, adv. Sample. Refereed. Circ: 178338 Paid and controlled. Vol. ends: Dec. Microform: PMC; PQC. *Indexed:* A22, BRI, C45. *Aud.:* Ac, Sa.

Published by the American Academy of Family Physicians, this peer-reviewed, scholarly journal provides several topic reviews per issue. In addition to the reviews, rounding out the journal are practice guidelines, CME opportunities, "Cochrane for Physicians," and editorials. Articles are filled with tables and charts that physicians can easily refer to when needed. The web site offers RSS feeds, e-mail alerts, "Point-of-Care Guides," and free online access to articles after about one year. Recommended for health sciences libraries especially; some academic and larger public libraries may find it useful as well. URL: www.aafp.org/journals/afp.html

3591. ***American Journal of Health Behavior (Online).*** [ISSN: 1945-7359] 2009. bi-m. USD 262 (Individuals, USD 142). Ed(s): Elbert D Glover. P N G Publications, 2205-K Oak Ridge Rd, #115, Oak Ridge, NC 27310. Illus. Refereed. *Aud.:* Ac, Sa.

This is the official publication of the American Academy of Health Behavior. All types of health behaviors are analyzed, often within specific populations. Examples are: adolescent weight tied to substance abuse; dental services barriers for older adults; and self-management in older women. Besides diet, exercise, smoking, and screenings, articles in this journal deal with issues such as health literacy and spirituality. Also of note is that this journal is online only. This peer-reviewed, scholarly journal is recommended for any collection of social science materials, as well as health sciences libraries.

3592. ***The American Journal of Medicine.*** [ISSN: 0002-9343] 1946. m. USD 2214. Ed(s): Joseph Alpert. Elsevier Inc., 230 Park Ave, Ste 800, New York, NY 10169; journalscustomerservice-usa@elsevier.com. Illus., adv. Refereed. *Indexed:* A01, A22, BRI, C45, Chicano. *Aud.:* Ac, Sa.

This is the official journal of the Alliance for Academic Internal Medicine, and its mission is "to lead academic internal medicine, specifically in the education, research, and patient care arenas." Each issue has "Clinical Research Studies," "Images" articles, "Reviews," and "Perspectives." In addition, it features topics pertaining to clinical effectiveness and medical humanities. This peer-reviewed, scholarly journal is for both private-practice physicians and those in academic medicine. Recommended for health sciences libraries, especially academic medical libraries.

3593. ***CA: a cancer journal for clinicians.*** [ISSN: 0007-9235] 1950. bi-m. GBP 72. Ed(s): Otis Webb Brawley. John Wiley & Sons, Inc., 111 River St, Hoboken, NJ 07030; cs-journals@wiley.com; http://www.wiley.com/. Illus., adv. Refereed. Microform: PQC. Reprint: PSC. *Indexed:* A22, BRI. *Aud.:* Ac, Sa.

This peer-reviewed, scholarly journal is published by the American Cancer Society for all physicians, not just oncologists. Each issue has original articles and reviews on various types of cancer, as well as current news and commentary. Because cancer is a disease state that can affect any part of the body, this journal is a valuable supplement to general medical journals. Recommended for all health sciences libraries, and academic libraries with any health programs.

3594. ***Coping with Cancer.*** Formerly (until 199?): *Coping.* [ISSN: 1544-5488] 1986. bi-m. USD 19 domestic; USD 35 foreign. Media America, Inc., PO Box 682268, Franklin, TN 37068; info@copingmag.com; http://www.copingmag.com. Illus. Vol. ends: Dec. *Aud.:* Ga, Sa.

According to its web site, this magazine is primarily found in the waiting rooms of doctors' offices. However, it has a place in consumer health collections of health sciences libraries and public libraries. *Coping with Cancer* is filled with upbeat tales of survivorship and "assumes that everyone diagnosed with cancer has a chance to beat the odds." Also of note is that *Coping with Cancer* is not affiliated with any particular treatment center and does not accept advertising in order to remain free of bias. Also, the editorial guidelines state that articles must be written for the lay public, with attention given to short sentences and paragraphs. URL: http://copingmag.com/cwc/index.php

3595. ***Cure: for patients, survivors & their caregivers.*** [ISSN: 1534-7664] 2002. q. Ed(s): Debu Tripathy, Beth Incollingo. Cure Media Group, LP., 2 Clarke Dr, Ste 100, Cranbury, NJ 08512. Adv. Circ: 300000. *Aud.:* Ga.

CURE Magazine strives to "make cancer understandable." Each issue is filled with the latest cancer treatment news, various special reports, and inspiration written by cancer survivors. The web site offers additional news, blogs, and an online community. Recommended for public libraries, especially those with a consumer health collection. URL: www.curetoday.com

3596. ***Diabetes Care.*** Incorporates (1993-1999): *Diabetes Reviews.* [ISSN: 0149-5992] 1978. m. USD 790 (print & online eds.) Individuals, USD 395 (print & online eds.); Members, USD 187 (print & online eds.)). Ed(s): William T Cefalu. American Diabetes Association, 2451 Crystal Dr, Ste 900, Arlington, VA 22202; askada@diabetes.org; http://www.diabetes.org. Illus., adv. Refereed. Microform: PQC. *Indexed:* A01, A22, Agr, BRI, C45, Chicano. *Aud.:* Ac, Sa.

Diabetes Care is published by the American Diabetes Association (ADA), and focuses on all types of diabetes research. The original articles are divided into various categories, including "Meta-analysis," "Complications," and "Epidemiology." In addition to original articles, reviews and ADA statements fill out this peer-reviewed, scholarly journal. As diabetes is well-studied and affects all body systems, *Diabetes Care* is recommended for all health sciences libraries.

3597. ***Diabetes Forecast: the healthy living magazine.*** Formerly (until 1974): *A D A Forecast.* [ISSN: 0095-8301] 1948. m. USD 12 combined subscription domestic (print & online eds.); USD 68 combined subscription Mexico (print & online eds.); USD 71.40 combined subscription Canada (print & online eds.)). Ed(s): Paris Roach, John C Warren. American Diabetes Association, 2451 Crystal Dr, Ste 900, Arlington, VA 22202; askada@diabetes.org; http://www.diabetes.org. Illus., adv. Vol. ends: Dec. *Indexed:* A01, A22, Agr, BRI. *Aud.:* Hs, Ga, Ac, Sa.

Since 1948, the American Diabetes Association has been publishing *Diabetes Forecast* for people with either type 1 or type 2 diabetes. In addition to practical articles, advocacy is a theme that runs throughout the magazine. The magazine is filled with management tips, recipes, and articles about new treatments. This magazine is recommended reading for anyone with diabetes, and is recommended for public libraries and health sciences libraries with a consumer health collection. URL: www.diabetesforecast.org/

3598. ***Diabetes Self-Management.*** [ISSN: 0741-6253] 1983. bi-m. USD 14.97 domestic; USD 24.97 Canada. Ed(s): Aubrey Everett. R.A. Rapaport Publishing, Inc., 25 Braintree Hill Office Park Ste 404, Braintree, MA 02184. Illus., adv. Vol. ends: Nov/Dec. *Indexed:* A22. *Aud.:* Hs, Ga, Sa.

This magazine features stories on the latest diabetes research, as well as several self-care articles that cover the basics of caring for diabetes, such as glucose monitoring and diet. The web site states that this magazine offers "up-to-date, practical 'how-to' information on nutrition, exercise, new drugs, medical advances, self-help, and the many other topics people need to know about to stay healthy." Recommended for public libraries and health sciences libraries with a consumer health collection. URL: www.diabetesselfmanagement.com

Harvard Men's Health Watch. See *The Harvard Health Letter* in Health and Fitness/Newsletters section.

Health Affairs. See Public Health section.

Health Care Management Review. See Health Care Administration section.

3599. ***J A M A: The Journal of the American Medical Association.*** Formerly (until 1960): *American Medical Association. Journal;* Which superseded (1848-1883): *American Medical Association. Transactions.* [ISSN: 0098-7484] 1883. w. 48/yr. USD 1490. Ed(s): Howard Bauchner, Stacy L Christiansen. American Medical Association, AMA Plz, 30 N Wabash Ave, Ste 39300, Chicago, IL 60611; sales@jamanetwork.com; http://www.ama-assn.org. Illus., index, adv. Sample. Refereed. *Indexed:* A01, A22, AgeL, Agr, BRI, C45, Chicano, MLA-IB. *Bk. rev.:* Number and length vary. *Aud.:* Ac, Sa.

JAMA is one of the most frequently cited publications in medicine. It is known for having artwork on the cover of each issue, and *JAMA*'s mission is to "promote the science and art of medicine and the betterment of the public health." This peer-reviewed weekly journal publishes original contributions, book reviews, editorials, and correspondence as expected. It also has a "Poetry and Medicine" column for medical poets, as well as a detailed article about the current week's cover art selection. Because many of the published articles are summarized in national news sources, it is an essential journal for all health sciences libraries, and strongly recommended for academic and public libraries.

3600. ***Journal of Alternative & Complementary Medicine: paradigm ,practice, and policy advancing integrative health.*** [ISSN: 1075-5535] 1995. m. USD 1892. Ed(s): John Weeks, Susan K Jensen. Mary Ann Liebert, Inc. Publishers, 140 Huguenot St, 3rd Fl, New Rochelle, NY 10801; info@liebertpub.com; http://www.liebertpub.com. Adv. Sample. Refereed. Vol. ends: Dec. Reprint: PSC. *Indexed:* A01, A22, C45, E01. *Aud.:* Ac, Sa.

This journal is the "the premier peer-reviewed journal of scientific work for healthcare professionals, practitioners, and scientists seeking to evaluate and integrate Complementary and Alternative Medicine (CAM) into mainstream practice." More and more practitioners are faced with questions about alternative and complementary medicine from their patients, and this journal features studies that use scientific methods to test these treatments. Recommended for health sciences libraries, as well as academic libraries with health sciences programs.

3601. ***The Lancet (North American Edition).*** [ISSN: 0099-5355] 1966. w. USD 1919. Ed(s): Dr. Richard Horton. The Lancet Publishing Group, 32 Jamestown Rd, London, NW1 7BY, United Kingdom; custserv@lancet.com; http://www.thelancet.com. Illus., index, adv. Sample. Refereed. Vol. ends: Jun/Dec. Microform: PQC. *Indexed:* A01, Agr, B01, ErgAb. *Bk. rev.:* Number and length vary. *Aud.:* Ac, Sa.

This peer-reviewed British weekly is the "world's leading independent general medical journal." Each issue provides new research articles, commentary, reviews, seminars, and perspectives. Unlike many medical journals, *The Lancet* is completely independent; it is not affiliated with any scientific or medical society. It is one of the "big three" medical journals that are frequently cited in the popular news media, and *The Lancet* is recommended for all health sciences libraries. Academic and public libraries should consider subscribing as well.

3602. ***Mayo Clinic Proceedings.*** Formerly (until 1964): *Mayo Clinic. Staff Meetings. Proceedings.* [ISSN: 0025-6196] 1926. m. USD 1142. Ed(s): William L Lanier. Elsevier Inc., 230 Park Ave, Ste 800, New York, NY 10169; usinfo-f@elsevier.com; https://www.elsevier.com. Illus., adv. Refereed. Microform: PMC. *Indexed:* A01, A22, BRI, C42, C45. *Aud.:* Ac, Sa.

As the title of this peer-reviewed scholarly journal indicates, *Mayo Clinic Proceedings* is sponsored by the Mayo Clinic. Since 1926, this journal has published "original articles dealing with clinical and laboratory medicine, clinical research, basic science research, and clinical epidemiology." The focus is internal medicine; however, many specialties will benefit from the reviews, images, and original articles. Recommended for all health sciences libraries.

3603. ***Medical Care Research and Review.*** Former titles (until 1995): *Medical Care Review;* (until 1967): *Public Health Economics and Medical Care Abstracts;* (until 1964): *Public Health Economics.* [ISSN: 1077-5587] 1944. bi-m. USD 1664 (print & online eds.)). Ed(s): Thomas A D'Aunno. Sage Publications, Inc., 2455 Teller Rd, Thousand Oaks, CA 91320; info@sagepub.com; http://www.sagepub.com. Illus., adv. Sample. Refereed. Vol. ends: Dec. Microform: PQC. Reprint: PSC. *Indexed:* A01, ASSIA. *Bk. rev.:* 2-3, 200-300 words. *Aud.:* Ac, Sa.

Medical Care Research and Review focuses on the area of medicine known as health services research. Reviews are the heart of this journal; these are syntheses of previously published literature. Patient safety indicators, nursing homes, comparative effectiveness, technology, health-care plans, screenings, and quality of care are themes that run throughout. These are the types of studies that administrators of hospitals, nursing homes, health systems, and insurance companies frequently request. Academic, special, and public libraries with business collections should have this publication.

3604. ***N I H Medline Plus.*** [ISSN: 1935-956X] 2006. q. Ed(s): Emily Poe. Strategic Communications, 24 Prime Pky, Ste 103, Natick, MA 01760g. *Aud.:* Ga, Sa.

A spinoff of the popular MedlinePlus web site (www.medlineplus.gov), this free publication is packed with stories that center on all types of medicine. Many articles are updates from the NIH on research progress on various conditions. Patient stories about overcoming diseases, history of medicine articles, and seasonal health information are found in this glossy magazine. One of the goals of the MedlinePlus web site is to provide quality information (at appropriate reading levels) for the lay public, and this magazine strives to do the same. Recommended for all public libraries and medical libraries that are open to the public. URL: www.nlm.nih.gov/medlineplus/magazine/

3605. ***National Medical Association. Journal.*** [ISSN: 0027-9684] 1909. q. USD 388. Ed(s): William E Lawson. Elsevier Inc., 230 Park Ave, Ste 800, New York, NY 10169; journalscustomerservice-usa@elsevier.com; https://www.elsevier.com. Illus., index, adv. Sample. Refereed. Vol. ends: Dec. *Indexed:* A22, C45, Chicano. *Aud.:* Ac, Sa.

Called "the nation's leading journal on minority health," this peer-reviewed scholarly journal focuses on issues of minority health, in particular within the African-American population. The journal consists primarily of original reports, and it includes case reports, editorials, correspondence, and relevant recent "InfoPOEMs" (reviews of pertinent clinical trials). Recommended for any health sciences library, particularly those that serve a significant African-American population.

3606. ***The New England Journal of Medicine.*** Formerly (until 1928): *Boston Medical and Surgical Journal;* Which was formed by the merger of (1823-1828): *Boston Medical Intelligencer;* (1827-1828): *The New England Medical Review and Journal;* Which was formerly (until 182?): *The New England Journal of Medicine and Surgery, and the Collateral Branches of Science.* [ISSN: 0028-4793] 1828. w. Individuals, USD 189 (print & online eds.)). Ed(s): Dr. Jeffrey M Drazen, Stephen Morrissey. Massachusetts Medical Society, 860 Winter St, Waltham Woods Corporate Center, Waltham, MA 02451; nejmcust@mms.org; http://www.nejm.org/. Illus., index, adv. Sample. Refereed. Vol. ends: Jun/Dec. *Indexed:* A01, A22, AgeL, Agr, BRI, C45, Chicano, MLA-IB. *Bk. rev.:* Number and length vary. *Aud.:* Ga, Ac, Sa.

Established in 1812, *The New England Journal of Medicine* is one of the most highly regarded and highly cited peer-reviewed scholarly journals in the medical field. Articles published in the weekly journal frequently become news items on national news programs and publicly discussed. In addition to original articles, the journal contains regular features such as images, book reviews, editorials, and reviews. The web site offers free access to articles after six months, as well as a free table of contents service, e-mail alerts, podcasts, and RSS feeds. This journal is essential for any type of health sciences library, and highly recommended for academic and public libraries.

3607. *Obstetrics & Gynecology.* [ISSN: 0029-7844] 1953. m. USD 1250. Ed(s): Nancy C Chescheir, Rebecca S Benner. Lippincott Williams & Wilkins, Two Commerce Sq, 2001 Market St, Philadelphia, PA 19103; customerservice@lww.com; http://www.lww.com. Illus., adv. Refereed. Vol. ends: No. 97 - No. 98. *Indexed:* A01, A22, C45. *Aud.:* Ac, Sa.

Known as the "green journal" among Ob/Gyns, this is the official publication of the American College of Obstetricians and Gynecologists (ACOG) and has been published since 1952. Most peer-reviewed articles are original research, but one reason libraries like to keep this journal around is for the frequently-requested ACOG publications. The "Practice Bulletins" and "Committee Opinions" are found at the back of each issue as they are released. In addition, updates on Cochrane articles in the Ob/Gyn field, editorials, and correspondence are published in this monthly journal. Recommended for all health sciences libraries and academic libraries with health-related programs.

3608. *Pediatrics (English Edition).* [ISSN: 0031-4005] 1948. m. Free to members; Non-members, USD 769 (print & online eds.)). Ed(s): Kate Larson, Lewis R First. American Academy of Pediatrics, 141 NW Point Blvd, Elk Grove Village, IL 6000; csc@aap.org; http://www.aap.org. Illus., adv. Refereed. *Indexed:* A01, A22, Agr, BRI, C45, Chicano. *Aud.:* Ac, Sa.

The premier peer-reviewed scholarly journal in the field of pediatrics, this is the official publication of the American Academy of Pediatrics (AAP), and has been published continuously since its founding in 1948. The journal publishes mostly original articles within all areas of pediatrics practice, including but not limited to "nutrition, surgery, dentistry, public health, child health services, human genetics, basic sciences, psychology, psychiatry, education, sociology, and nursing." Issues also contain reviews, AAP statements, historical articles, and commentaries. Recommended for all health sciences libraries and academic libraries with health-related programs.

3609. *Quest (Tucson).* Former titles (until 1994): *M D A Reports;* (until 1992): *M D A Newsmagazine;* (until 1984): *M D A News - Muscular Dystrophy Association;* (until 1975): *Muscular Dystrophy News.* [ISSN: 1087-1578] 1950. q. USD 15 domestic (Free to qualified personnel). Muscular Dystrophy Association, Inc., 3300 E Sunrise Dr, Tucson, AZ 85718; publications@mdausa.org; http://www.mda.org. Illus., adv. Sample. Vol. ends: Fall. *Indexed:* BRI. *Bk. rev.:* 1-2, 150 words. *Aud.:* Ga, Sa.

Quest is published by the Muscular Dystrophy Association, and provides "articles on all aspects of living with a neuromuscular disease, and updates on research findings." Reports on clinical trials, celebrity interviews, personal stories, and technology reports fill this glossy magazine. *Quest* is free online and is available at low cost in print format. Recommended for consumer health collections of health sciences libraries and public libraries. URL: www.mda.org/quest

■ MENOPAUSE/ANDROPAUSE

Miriam Leigh, MLS, Information Systems Manager for Faculty Affairs, Harvard Law School, Cambridge, MA 02138; mleigh@law.harvard.edu

Introduction

In recent years, our society has become increasingly concerned with the aging process. What does it mean to age, particularly in respect to changes in our bodies brought on by menopause and andropause (the latter, a drop in testosterone in older men)? Researchers and journalists are exploring topics such as the effects of menopause on mental functions, traditional and alternative symptom treatments, and changes in relationships as a result of menopause.

The publications listed in this section are scholarly journals, primarily directed toward researchers and physicians, and all are published under the purview of medical societies.

Basic Periodicals

Ac, Sa: *Maturitas.*

Basic Abstracts and Indexes

Current Contents/Clinical Medicine, EMBASE, GenderWatch, MEDLINE, Science Citation Index, ScienceDirect.

The Aging Male. See Geriatrics and Gerontological Studies section.

3610. *Climacteric.* [ISSN: 1369-7137] 1998. bi-m. GBP 630 (print & online eds.)). Ed(s): Dr. Anna J Fenton, Mr. Nick Panay. Taylor & Francis, 2, 3 & 4 Park Sq, Milton Park, Abingdon, OX14 4RN, United Kingdom; subscriptions@tandf.co.uk; https://www.tandfonline.com. Illus., index, adv. Refereed. Circ: 725 Paid. Vol. ends: Dec (No. 4). Reprint: PSC. *Indexed:* A01, A22, E01. *Aud.:* Ac, Sa.

Climacteric is published six times annually, plus supplementary issues, as the mouthpiece of the International Menopause Society. It offers literature reviews, editorials, letters to the editor, and society meeting details, in addition to peer-reviewed original research articles. *Climacteric* reports on "all aspects of aging women." The content covers "underlying endocrinological changes, treatment of the symptoms of the menopause and other age-related changes, hormone replacement therapies, alternative therapies, effective life-style modifications, non-hormonal midlife changes, and the counselling and education of perimenopausal and postmenopausal patients." Its articles are largely technical in nature, though there are many that would also appeal to practicing physicians. Recent articles have critiqued custom compounded bioidentical hormones; investigated rates of osteoporosis and fragility fractures; and explored the rate of pelvic floor disorder in women in Bangladesh. Recommended for academic and medical libraries.

3611. *Maturitas.* Incorporates (1994-1998): *European Menopause Journal.* [ISSN: 0378-5122] 1978. 12x/yr. EUR 3083. Ed(s): Margaret Rees. Elsevier Ireland Ltd., Elsevier House, Brookvale Plz, E Park, Shannon, , Ireland; JournalsCustomerServiceemea@elsevier.com; http://www.elsevier.com/. Adv. Sample. Refereed. Microform: PQC. *Indexed:* A01, A22, C45. *Bk. rev.:* Number and length vary. *Aud.:* Ac, Sa.

Maturitas, a peer-reviewed monthly journal, is published as the official journal of the European Menopause and Andropause Society, and is affiliated with the Australasian Menopause Society. Thus, it does not merely focus on midlife changes for women, but rather on "all aspects of postreproductive health" for both men and women, "ranging from basic science to health and social care." It is international in scope, and comprises primarily original research articles, although it does also feature book reviews, letters to the editor, review articles, and case studies as appropriate. Articles published fall into the following categories: "Predictors, effects and management of chronic diseases[;] Sex steroid deficiency in both genders[;] Epidemiology, health and social care[;] Therapeutic advances[; and] Complementary and alternative medicines." The journal also publishes notices of conferences and other announcements. In addition, *Maturitas* provides "fast track" publishing for ground-breaking research that demands rapid dissemination. Recent articles have explored such topics as screening approaches for secondary osteoporosis; the use of wearable technology in gait assessment in older adults; and urinary tract infection prevention without antibiotics. This technical periodical would be a good fit for an academic or medical research library, although there are a number of more accessible articles that would be of interest to the practicing physician.

3612. ***Menopause.*** [ISSN: 1072-3714] 1994. m. USD 1153. Ed(s): Isaac Schiff, Diane K Barker. Lippincott Williams & Wilkins, Two Commerce Sq, 2001 Market St, Philadelphia, PA 19103; customerservice@lww.com; http://www.lww.com. Illus., adv. Refereed. Microform: PQC. *Indexed:* A22, C45. *Aud.:* Ac, Sa.

Menopause, launched in 1994, is a peer-reviewed journal geared to providing "a forum for new research, applied basic science, and clinical guidelines on all aspects of menopause." It includes a variety of article formats, including editorials, original research articles, clinical articles, review articles, meeting abstracts, case studies, and letters to the editor. *Menopause* encompasses far more than simply the immediate gynecological aspects of menopause. It explores cancer risk, the effects of menopause on the whole body, treatment trends, cognitive concerns, sleep disorders, alternative therapies, and more. Doctors looking for continuing medical education credits will be pleased to find opportunities offered in selected issues. Published for the North American Menopause Society (NAMS), this journal is also used as a forum for NAMS to explore its role in the menopause research community. Recent issues have included topics such as the link between anxiety and quality of life impairment in post-menopausal women; telomere length in women with late maternal age; and sexual functioning over the menopause transition. Because over 60 percent of *Menopause* subscribers have an office-based clinical practice, this publication would be appropriate for academic and research libraries that support practicing physicians and medical researchers.

3613. ***Post Reproductive Health.*** Former titles (until Mar.2014): *Menopause International;* (until 2007): *British Menopause Society. Journal.* [ISSN: 2053-3691] 1995. q. USD 696 (print & online eds.)). Ed(s): Heather Currie, Edward Morris. Sage Publications Ltd., 1 Oliver's Yard, 55 City Rd, London, EC1Y 1SP, United Kingdom; info@sagepub.com; https://www.sagepub.com/. Adv. Sample. Refereed. Reprint: PSC. *Indexed:* A22, E01. *Bk. rev.:* Number and length vary. *Aud.:* Ac, Sa.

This readable journal, formerly ;Menopause International published quarterly, focuses heavily on subjects that are most relevant to practicing doctors. *Post Reproductive Health* is aimed at "all those involved in the study and treatment of menopausal conditions across the world." This journal has a broad scope, and in addition to research articles, it offers editorials, news briefs, practice notes, British Menopause Society reports and meeting proceedings, book reviews, and literature reviews of relevant articles in other journals. Recent topics have included cognitive behavioral therapy for menopausal symptoms; a study of the use and discontinuation of hormone replacement therapy; and the influence of attitudes on menopause treatment decisions. This journal would be most appropriate in a library that supports practicing physicians.

■ MIDDLE EAST

Joshua Parker, Harvard Divinity School and Watertown Free Public Library

Introduction

The Middle East spans Asia Minor, the Levant, the Arabian Peninsula, Iraq, Iran, and in some contexts, North Africa. Since antiquity, the region has played an influential role in culture, politics, and world history. The area is home to a diverse array of ethnicities, cultures, languages, and religions. The Middle East is the birthplace of the monotheistic religious traditions of Judaism, Christianity, and Islam, and the region remains an important center for all three faiths.

In addition to the dominant Arabic, Iranian, Turkish, and Israeli cultural traditions of the region, there are numerous minority ethnic and linguistic communities. The Middle East's history and diversity contribute to a complex contemporary social, cultural, and political situation, and developments in the region can often have a far-reaching influence on global affairs.

The journals selected for review in this section include publications that cover the full range of Middle East Studies, as well as those focused on the study of specific regions or communities. All of the publications reviewed here are available both online and in print.

Basic Periodicals

British Journal of Middle Eastern Studies, International Journal of Middle East Studies, Middle East Policy, Middle East Report.

Basic Abstracts and Indexes

ATLA Religion Index, Historical Abstracts, Index Islamicus, Index to Jewish Periodicals, PAIS International.

3614. ***British Journal of Middle Eastern Studies.*** Formerly (until 1991): *British Society for Middle Eastern Studies. Bulletin.* [ISSN: 1353-0194] 1974. 4x/yr. GBP 820 (print & online eds.)). Ed(s): Lloyd Ridgeon. Routledge, 4 Park Sq, Milton Park, Abingdon, OX14 4RN, United Kingdom; subscriptions@tandf.co.uk; http://www.routledge.com. Adv. Sample. Refereed. Reprint: PSC. *Indexed:* A01, A22, A47, BRI, E01, IBSS, MLA-IB, P61. *Bk. rev.:* Number and length vary. *Aud.:* Ac.

The *British Journal of Middle Eastern Studies* is an academic, peer-reviewed journal published four times a year by the British Society for Middle Eastern Studies. The journal aims to "maintain a balance...between the modern social sciences and the more traditional disciplines associated with Middle Eastern and Islamic studies." Articles cover all aspects of the Middle East "from the end of classical antiquity and the rise of Islam [to the present day]," with a focus on cultural, political, and religious history. The journal occasionally publishes special issues devoted to a particular topic. Each issue includes a book review section. The *British Journal of Middle Eastern Studies* is recommended for academic collections with a focus on the Middle East.

3615. ***International Journal of Middle East Studies.*** [ISSN: 0020-7438] 1970. q. plus two bulletins. GBP 336. Ed(s): Akram Khater. Cambridge University Press, University Printing House, Shaftesbury Rd, Cambridge, CB2 8BS, United Kingdom; journals@cambridge.org; https://www.cambridge.org/. Illus., adv. Refereed. Vol. ends: Spring. Microform: PQC. Reprint: PSC. *Indexed:* A01, A22, BRI, E01, IBSS, MLA-IB, P61, SSA. *Bk. rev.:* Number and length vary. *Aud.:* Ac.

The *International Journal of Middle East Studies* is a peer-reviewed journal published quarterly under the auspices of the Middle East Studies Association of North America. The publication covers "the Arab world, Iran, Turkey, the Caucasus, Afghanistan, Israel, Transoxiana, and Muslim South Asia from the seventh century to the present." Topics include a broad range of subjects, including cultural and political history, literature, anthropology, and sociology of the region. Each issue of the journal also includes an extensive book review section. The *International Journal of Middle East Studies* is recommended for academic collections with materials related to the Middle East and Central/South Asia.

3616. ***Iranian Studies.*** [ISSN: 0021-0862] 1967. bi-m. GBP 557 (print & online eds.)). Ed(s): Homa Katouzian. Routledge, 4 Park Sq, Milton Park, Abingdon, OX14 4RN, United Kingdom; subscriptions@tandf.co.uk; http://www.tandfonline.com. Illus., index, adv. Sample. Refereed. Reprint: PSC. *Indexed:* A01, A22, AmHI, BRI, E01, MLA-IB, P61, SSA. *Bk. rev.:* Number and length vary. *Aud.:* Ac.

Iranian Studies is published six times a year by the International Society for Iranian Studies. It is a peer-reviewed, academic journal, featuring articles on the history, literature, and culture of "all areas of the world with a Persian or Iranian legacy, especially Iran, Afghanistan, Central Asia and the Caucasus, and northern India." The journal occasionally publishes special issues devoted to a particular topic. Each issue includes a book review section. This journal will be most interesting to scholars studying Persian and Iranian culture, literature, and politics, and is recommended for academic collections with materials related to Persian Studies and the Middle East generally.

3617. ***Israel Affairs.*** [ISSN: 1353-7121] 1994. q. GBP 823 (print & online eds.)). Ed(s): Efraim Karsh. Routledge, 4 Park Sq, Milton Park, Abingdon, OX14 4RN, United Kingdom; subscriptions@tandf.co.uk; http://www.tandfonline.com. Adv. Sample. Refereed. Reprint: PSC. *Indexed:* A01, A22, E01, IBSS, P61, SSA. *Bk. rev.:* Occasional. *Aud.:* Ac.

Israel Affairs is a quarterly, peer-reviewed journal that covers modern Israeli history, politics, and culture, as well as related topics involving the broader Middle East region. Articles examine a broad variety of historical and contemporary topics and will be of interest to scholars across a range of disciplines. *Israel Affairs* is recommended for collections that deal with modern Israeli and Middle Eastern history, politics, and strategic affairs.

3618. *Israel Studies.* [ISSN: 1084-9513] 1996. 3x/yr. USD 168.30 (print & online eds.)). Ed(s): Natan Aridan, Ilan Troen. Indiana University Press, Office of Scholarly Publishing, Herman B Wells Library 350, Bloomington, IN 47405; iuporder@indiana.edu; http://www.iupress.indiana.edu/. Adv. Refereed. Reprint: PSC. *Indexed:* A01, A22, BRI, E01, ENW, IBSS, MLA-IB, P61. *Bk. rev.:* Occasional. *Aud.:* Ac.

Israel Studies is an academic, peer-reviewed journal published three times a year with a focus on scholarship related to Israeli history, society, and politics. Although primarily concerned with the modern Israel, the journal also publishes material related to events preceding the foundation of the state. Content covers a wide span of modern Israeli society and encompasses a range of political and scholarly perspectives. *Israel Studies* is recommended for collections that deal with modern Israeli and Middle Eastern history, society, and politics.

3619. *Israel Studies Review: an interdisciplinary journal.* Former titles (until 2011): *Israel Studies Forum;* (until 2001): *Israel Studies Bulletin;* (until 1992): *Association for Israel Studies. Newsletter.* [ISSN: 2159-0370] 198?. s-a. USD 336 combined subscription (print & online eds.)). Ed(s): Yoram Peri. Berghahn Books Inc., 20 Jay St, Ste 512, Brooklyn, NY 11201; journals@berghahnbooks.com; http://www.berghahnbooks.com. Adv. Sample. Refereed. Reprint: PSC. *Indexed:* A01, BRI, MLA-IB, P61. *Bk. rev.:* 5-8. *Aud.:* Ac.

Israel Studies Review is a semi-annual, peer-reviewed academic journal started in 2011 as a continuation of the journal *Israel Studies Forum.* Explicitly interdisciplinary in its approach, the *Review* "explores modern and contemporary Israel from the perspective of the social sciences, history, the humanities, and cultural studies." The journal explicitly seeks to expose and discuss controversy, with each issue prominently featuring a "Forum" section in which scholars of varying perspectives discuss a subject. Each issue also features an extensive book review section and at least one review article that discusses a related set of recently published works. *Israel Studies Review* is recommended for collections with materials related to Middle Eastern and Israeli culture, politics, history, and sociology.

3620. *The Jerusalem Report.* [ISSN: 0792-6049] 1990. m. Ed(s): Eeta Prince-Gibson. Jerusalem Post, The Jerusalem Post Building, PO Box 81, Jerusalem, 91000, Israel. Illus., adv. *Bk. rev.:* 2. *Aud.:* Ga.

Published by the *Jerusalem Post,* the editorially independent *Jerusalem Report* is a biweekly magazine that covers news from "Israel, the Middle East, and the Jewish World." Primarily focused on current affairs, the magazine regularly features articles on Israeli and Palestinian politics, and Israeli foreign relations, culture, and business. Each issue also features book reviews, opinion pieces, and occasional fiction. The *Jerusalem Report* offers a useful perspective on news from Israel and the Middle East, and is recommended for collections that cover international current events.

3621. *Jewish Review of Books.* [ISSN: 2153-1978] 2010. q. USD 39.95 domestic; USD 49.95 foreign. Ed(s): Abraham Socher. Bee.Ideas, LLC, 3091 Mayfield Rd, Ste 412, Cleveland Heights, OH 44118; pgetz@jewishreviewofbooks.com. Adv. *Indexed:* MLA-IB. *Bk. rev.:* Number and length vary. *Aud.:* Ga, Ac.

The *Jewish Review of Books* is a quarterly book review publication. The *Review* publishes reviews of books, films, and other works related to Jewish religion, culture, identity, and political life. Each issue also includes original essays on subjects relevant to the Jewish world. Describing itself as "committed to the ideal of the thoughtful essay that illuminates as it entertains," the *Review* is oriented toward an intellectual audience, though not an exclusively academic one. The publication features occasional symposiums that collect brief discussions by several contributors focused on a specific topic. This title is recommended for collections with a focus on Jewish culture and intellectual life, Judaism, Jewish history, and the contemporary politics of the Middle East and Jewish identity.

3622. *The Journal of Israeli History: politics, society, culture.* Formerly (until 1994): *Studies in Zionism;* Which superseded (in 1982): *Zionism: Studies in the History of the Zionist Movement and of the Jews in Palestine - Ha-Tsiyonut.* [ISSN: 1353-1042] 1980. s-a. GBP 382 (print & online eds.)). Ed(s): Derek J Penslar, Anita Shapira. Routledge, 4 Park Sq, Milton Park, Abingdon, OX14 4RN, United Kingdom; subscriptions@tandf.co.uk; http://www.tandfonline.com. Illus., adv. Sample. Refereed. Vol. ends: Fall. Reprint: PSC. *Indexed:* A22, AmHI, E01, MLA-IB, P61, R&TA. *Bk. rev.:* 3-6. *Aud.:* Ac.

The Journal of Israeli History is a scholarly, peer-reviewed journal published twice yearly that focuses on modern Israeli history from the period of the British Mandate to the present. Articles cover a wide range of subjects relevant to scholars of Israeli and Middle East history, and each issue includes a book review section. *The Journal of Israeli History* is recommended for academic collections with a concentration in Israeli and Middle Eastern history.

3623. *Journal of Middle East Women's Studies.* [ISSN: 1552-5864] 2005. 3x/yr. USD 245. Ed(s): Soha Bayoumi, Ellen McLarney. Duke University Press, 905 W Main St, Durham, NC 27701; orders@dukeupress.edu; https://www.dukeupress.edu. Adv. Refereed. Reprint: PSC. *Indexed:* A01, A22, AmHI, BRI, E01, FemPer, GW, IBSS, MLA-IB, P61. *Bk. rev.:* Number and length vary. *Aud.:* Ac.

The *Journal of Middle East Women's Studies* is a peer-reviewed, academic journal published three times a year by the Association of Middle East Women's Studies. It aims to "advance the fields of Middle East women's studies, gender studies and Middle East studies through contributions across disciplines in the social sciences and humanities." Issues include book reviews and occasional film reviews. The *Journal* takes an explicitly interdisciplinary and transnational approach to gender studies and the Middle East. Some special issues bring together several contributors on a single topic. The *Journal* is recommended for academic collections with a focus on the Middle East and women's studies.

3624. *Journal of Palestine Studies.* [ISSN: 0377-919X] 1971. q. USD 326 (print & online eds.)). Ed(s): Rashid I Khalidi. University of California Press, Journals Division, 155 Grand Avenue, Ste 400, Oakland, CA 94612-3764; http://www.ucpress.edu/journals.php. Illus., index, adv. Refereed. Microform: PQC. *Indexed:* A01, A22, BRI, E01, ENW, IBSS, MLA-IB, P61, SSA. *Bk. rev.:* Number and length vary. *Aud.:* Ac, Sa.

The *Journal of Palestine Studies* is a quarterly, peer-reviewed, academic journal published by the University of California Press on behalf of the Institute for Palestine Studies. It is "devoted exclusively to Palestinian affairs and the Arab-Israeli conflict." The *Journal*'s regular content includes articles, essays, and book reviews, as well as several special features. This title is recommended for collections with a focus on Palestinian Studies, the Palestinian-Israeli conflict, and the contemporary Middle East more generally.

3625. *Middle East Journal.* [ISSN: 0026-3141] 1947. q. Free to members. Ed(s): Michael Collins Dunn. Middle East Institute, 1761 N St N W, Washington, DC 20036; information@mei.edu; http://www.mei.edu. Illus., adv. Refereed. Vol. ends: Fall. Microform: PQC. *Indexed:* A01, A22, BAS, BRI, CBRI, E01, IBSS, MLA-IB, P61. *Bk. rev.:* Number and length vary. *Aud.:* Ga, Ac.

The *Middle East Journal* is a peer-reviewed, quarterly journal published by the Middle East Institute that covers the "post World War II Middle East including Pakistan, the Caucasus, and Central Asia." Articles cover a range of topics related to political, social, and economic developments in the Middle East. A chronology section, continuous since 1947, is organized by subject and country and lists significant events from the past quarter. The book review section includes in-depth reviews of books divided by country and subject, as well as brief descriptions of recent publications. The *Journal* is recommended for collections with a focus on the Middle East and Central Asia.

3626. ***Middle East Policy.*** Formerly (until 1992): *American Arab Affairs.* [ISSN: 1061-1924] 1981. q. GBP 321. Ed(s): Anne Joyce. Wiley-Blackwell Publishing, Inc., 350 Main St, Malden, MA 02148; cs-journals@wiley.com; http://onlinelibrary.wiley.com. Illus., index, adv. Sample. Refereed. Vol. ends: Spring/Winter. Reprint: PSC. *Indexed:* A01, A22, BRI, CBRI, E01, ENW, IBSS, P61. *Bk. rev.:* Number and length vary. *Aud.:* Ga, Ac.

Middle East Policy is an academic, peer-reviewed journal published quarterly by the Middle East Policy Council. It focuses on the Middle East as it relates to international affairs. It provides a "forum for a wide range of views on U.S. interests in the region and the value of the policies that are supposed to promote them." The journal includes book and film reviews, and occasionally book excerpts. *Middle East Policy* is recommended for collections with concentrations on the Middle East and contemporary political affairs.

3627. ***The Middle East Quarterly.*** [ISSN: 1073-9467] 1994. q. Ed(s): Judy Goodrobb, Efraim Karsh. Middle East Forum, 1650 Market St #3600, Philadelphia, PA 19103; info@meforum,org; http://www.meforum.org. Illus. *Indexed:* A01, A22, BRI, C42, CBRI, IBSS, P61. *Bk. rev.:* Number varies. *Aud.:* Ga, Ac.

A publication of the Middle East Forum, *Middle East Quarterly* presents reporting, analysis, and policy recommendations intended to help "define and promote American interests in the Middle East." Content is fully available online at the journal's web site, with the exception of material in the most recently published issue. *Middle East Quarterly* should be considered for inclusion in collections that cover the Middle East, international affairs, and U.S. foreign policy.

3628. ***Middle East Report.*** Former titles (until 1988): *M E R I P Middle East Report;* (until 1986): *M E R I P Reports;* Which incorporated (1970-1973): *Pakistan Forum.* [ISSN: 0899-2851] 1970. q. USD 180 (Individuals, USD 42; USD 10 per issue in North America). Middle East Research & Information Project, 1344 T St N W #1, Washington, DC 20009; http://www.merip.org. Illus., index, adv. Microform: PQC. *Indexed:* A22, E01, IBSS, P61. *Bk. rev.:* Number and length vary. *Aud.:* Ac.

The *Middle East Report* is a quarterly, peer-reviewed academic journal published by the Middle East Research and Information Project. It focuses on the "political economy of the contemporary Middle East and popular struggles there." Most issues are thematic, focusing on a topic or region, with articles that address "a broad range of social, political, and cultural issues." Issues include a book review section, as well as an "Editor's Picks" section that addresses recent publications relating to the Middle East. *Middle East Report* is recommended for collections with a focus on the contemporary Middle East and political affairs.

Middle Eastern Literatures. See Literature section.

3629. ***Middle Eastern Studies.*** [ISSN: 0026-3206] 1964. bi-m. GBP 917 (print & online eds.)). Ed(s): Sylvia Kedourie. Routledge, 4 Park Sq, Milton Park, Abingdon, OX14 4RN, United Kingdom; subscriptions@tandf.co.uk; http://www.tandfonline.com. Illus., adv. Sample. Refereed. Microform: PQC. Reprint: PSC. *Indexed:* A01, A22, AmHI, BRI, E01, IBSS, MLA-IB, P61, SSA. *Bk. rev.:* Number and length vary. *Aud.:* Ac, Sa.

Middle Eastern Studies is a peer-reviewed, academic journal published six times a year. It offers "academic research on the history and politics of the Arabic-speaking countries in the Middle East and North Africa as well as on Turkey, Iran and Israel." Articles cover a broad range of historical and contemporary topics from across the region, and each issue includes a book review section. *Middle Eastern Studies* is recommended for academic collections with a focus on the Middle East.

3630. ***Turkish Studies.*** [ISSN: 1468-3849] 2000. q. GBP 507 (print & online eds.)). Ed(s): Paul Kubicek. Routledge, 4 Park Sq, Milton Park, Abingdon, OX14 4RN, United Kingdom; subscriptions@tandf.co.uk; http://www.tandfonline.com. Adv. Sample. Refereed. Reprint: PSC. *Indexed:* A01, A22, E01, IBSS, MLA-IB, P61. *Bk. rev.:* Number and length vary. *Aud.:* Ac.

Turkish Studies is a quarterly, peer-reviewed journal published by the Global Research in International Affairs Center. It features articles on "the history of the Turkish republic from the 1920s to the present, including political, social and intellectual issues; Turkish politics; [g]overnment policies and programs; and Turkish international relations and foreign policy." Occasional special issues focus on a single topic. Most issues include a book review section that addresses books about Turkey. Recommended for academic collections covering Turkey.

■ MILITARY

Joseph E. Straw, Head of Instruction, Humanities Bibliographer, Marietta College Library, Marietta, OH 45750; js001@marietta.edu

Introduction

The world today is haunted by the specter of armed conflict. For the United States, national security concerns have been fed by the ongoing War on Terror, the ISIS threat in the Middle East, instability on the Korean peninsula, and the growing conventional military pressure exerted by Russia and China. In facing these challenges, clearly the role of the military will be in sharp focus for the foreseeable future.

Both in the United States and internationally, those looking to explore military affairs face a staggering number of choices. The available information has long since reached the point of saturation. In navigating this vast universe, problems are clearly involved in finding information that's free of distortion or outright bias. Any informed look at this area must take into account more nuanced information that's only a minority of the available whole.

The military or defense periodical is a way that information in this field can be focused and managed. This type of resource can often provide an interesting window into this complex, somewhat perplexing world. Magazines, journals, and trade publications are one of the key avenues in which ideas are communicated to both military professionals or civilian policy makers. Around the world, a wide variety of periodicals report on strategy, tactics, training, logistics, military history, and general defense policy. In the case of the United States, just about every area of the defense community has a periodical that covers its particular niche.

Throughout most of their history, military periodicals served a very limited audience of practitioners. They were mainly found in special library collections that served military posts, war colleges, or government agencies. In the past few decades, interest in the military has peaked among the public, with relevant publications now being found in libraries that serve more general audiences. Scholarly interest in this area has grown, and academic libraries are aggressively acquiring resources of this type to supplement collections in a wide variety of fields. Public libraries are also seeking to build periodical collections to support user interests in such topics as unconventional war, defense policy, and military hardware.

With interest in the military growing in libraries of all types, this section will profile core military periodicals, with a particular emphasis on the United States Armed Forces. Selected publications that cover foreign militaries or defense affairs will also be profiled. Two types of periodicals will be covered as part of this section: (1) professional military periodicals that focus on problems in contemporary armed forces or current defense policies; and (2) military history periodicals that deal with past wars. For all the listed periodicals, those that are geared to trade, general, and academic audiences will be covered.

Professional military periodicals are used to communicate news, innovations, and doctrine for application in contemporary militaries. Serving officers and defense officials often consult such publications to discover what's cutting-edge in their areas of expertise. They also serve as a forum for like-minded professionals to sort out institutional parameters and clarify common goals.

The professional military periodical has a long history of authorship that comes from military personnel or civilian experts active in the defense community. In recent years, however, contributions from people outside the security establishment have grown in importance as the number of academically oriented journals has increased. Much of this comes from social science disciplines that recognize the interdependency of multiple factors in impacting the success of potential military missions. The insights of sociologists, anthropologists, political scientists, and psychologists are now seen as providing important benefits for military or civilian planners in thinking about future defense contingencies.

Military history periodicals cover the things in the past that deal with war and conflict. Some of the areas of military history would include battles, soldier life, military thought, leadership, technology, and the development of weapons. Contributions to military history are made by an eclectic group of people that would include journalists, generals, common soldiers, creative writers, military enthusiasts, genealogists, and trained historians. Military history is popular for the general reading public, but it also takes on an added importance because of the pedagogical role that it plays for many militaries today. By considering history, current operational performance can be improved by appreciating parallels that can be drawn from the past.

The field of military history is dynamic and continues to evolve. For many years, the dominant historiographical tradition focused on detailed battle narratives, and biographical studies. This tradition is strongly retained in periodicals that are geared more to hobbyist, amateur, and general audiences. Recently, however, scholarly interest in military history has grown, with social history increasingly setting the interpretive framework. A number of academic journals have emerged that focus almost exclusively on the social context of war. Connecting past conflict with forces like race, religion, politics, and gender is now commonplace, helping to establish military history as a respected subfield within the broader discipline of history.

Obtaining and providing access to military periodicals incur both challenges and opportunities for libraries. Many periodicals of this type are highly specialized, and knowledge of appropriate titles can easily escape the attention of the uninitiated. Electronic publishing is growing rapidly in this field, but the potential benefits are often mitigated by a traditional revenue and distribution model that relies on individual subscriptions, institutional membership, and association dues. Far too many military-oriented titles escape coverage by indexing and abstracting tools, with access to the digital versions further complicated by their limited penetration through electronic subscription services like JSTOR, ProQuest, and EBSCO.

Despite these problems, the costs of these publications are not prohibitive and can fall within the budgeting of most libraries. Many of these periodicals also come from government agencies that are increasingly using free digital platforms to disseminate publications, making it easier for libraries to provide direct links to relevant material from their electronic resources pages. Subject knowledge, careful consideration of the needs of users, and the extent to which any title will add to or supplement existing resources, must be taken into account by libraries that collect military periodicals.

Basic Periodicals

Hs: *Aviation History, Soldiers;* Ga: *Air Force Magazine, Armed Forces Journal, Army, Aviation History, Leatherneck, Military History, National Guard, Naval History, World War II;* Ac: *The Air & Space Power Journal, AirForces Monthly, Armed Forces and Society, Armed Forces Journal, Army, Joint Force Quarterly, Journal of Military History, The Journal of Strategic Studies, Military Review, Naval War College Review, Survival* (Abingdon), *U S Naval Institute. Proceedings.*

Basic Abstracts and Indexes

Air University Library Index to Military Periodicals.

3631. *A P S Diplomat Strategic Balance in the Middle East.* [ISSN: 1986-2024] 1972. m. Arab Press Service, PO Box 23896, Nicosia, , Cyprus; apsnews@spidernet.com.cy. *Aud.:* Ac.

This English-language publication from the Arab Press Service (APS) offers intelligence on the military and strategic picture in the Middle East. Military analysis and surveys are provided for the Arab nations, Israel, Iran, Russia, and the United States. APS news reports and updates on defense-related issues in the region are also included as part of the monthly issues. Taken together, the content of this publication gives an important perspective on security questions from an Arab point of view. Given the focus, this publication would best support specialized academic libraries that collect heavily in Middle Eastern Studies.

3632. *The Air & Space Power Journal.* Former titles (until 2002): *The Aerospace Power Journal;* (until 1999): *Airpower Journal;* (until 1987): *Air University Review;* (until 1963): *Air University Quarterly Review.* [ISSN: 1555-385X] 1947. bi-m. Ed(s): Richard T Harrison. U.S. Air Force, Air University, 155 N Twining St, Maxwell, AL 36112. Illus., index. Sample. Refereed. Vol. ends: Nov/Dec. Microform: PQC. *Indexed:* A01, A22, BAS, BRI, MLA-IB. *Bk. rev.:* Number varies; 200-500 words. *Aud.:* Ac, Sa.

The Air & Space Power Journal is the official publication of Air University, which serves as the U.S. Air Force's (USAF) center for professional military education. This journal seeks to present current thinking on issues relating to the employment of air and space forces in the scheme of national defense. A recent issue contains articles that explore joint air liaison officer promotions, developing field grade officers, and the role of big data in structuring the future of USAF intelligence. The articles are heavily researched and are written mostly by serving USAF officers. A real strength of this publication is the large list of book reviews that cover titles related to national defense, air power, foreign relations, and the history of military aviation. This journal has companion international versions that are published in French, Spanish, and Chinese. These sister publications are edited by native speakers and provide articles targeted to regions like Asia, Latin America, Europe, Africa, and the Caribbean. *The Air & Space Power Journal* can be viewed freely online from the Air University website. Given the professional focus, this publication would be highly recommended for inclusion on the electronic resources pages of special and academic libraries

3633. *Air Force Magazine.* Former titles (until 1972): *Air Force and Space Digest;* (until 1959): *Air Force;* (until 1942): *Air Forces Newsletter;* (until 1941): *Air Corps Newsletter.* [ISSN: 0730-6784] 1927. m. Free to members; Non-members, USD 10. Ed(s): Juliette Kelsey Chagnon, Adam J Hebert. Air Force Association, 1501 Lee Hwy, Arlington, VA 22209; letters@afa.org; http://www.afa.org. Illus., adv. Vol. ends: Dec. *Indexed:* A22, BRI. *Bk. rev.:* 5, 150-200 words. *Aud.:* Ga, Ac.

Air Force Magazine is one of the most respected and oldest publications dealing with air power in the United States. Published by the Air Force Association, it is geared to serving military personnel and the general public. Print and digital versions of the magazine are made available for free to members of the association. This magazine is a good source of news and current events regarding issues that affect the U.S. Air Force. Feature articles deal with current operations, doctrine, aviation history, and biographical information on key personnel. A particularly useful annual "Almanac" is published in May, which provides an authoritative statistical overview of the Air Force. Much of the content is drawn from serving officers, freelance journalists, and academic researchers. Given both the news and analytical content, this publication would be of potential interest to libraries of all types.

3634. *AirForces Monthly: the world's leading military aviation magazine.* [ISSN: 0955-7091] 1988. m. GBP 47 in UK & USA; GBP 57 elsewhere. Key Publishing Ltd., PO Box 100, Stamford, PE9 1XQ, United Kingdom; orders@keypublishing.com; http://www.keypublishing.com. Illus., adv. *Aud.:* Ga, Ac.

This British publication covers military aviation from an international perspective. Aviation news is reported from around the world and would include the United Kingdom, Europe, North America, Latin America, Africa, the Middle East, Asia/Pacific, Russia, and Australasia. The feature articles cover technology, conflicts, doctrine, and of course the latest in military aircraft. The articles are by the editorial staff, freelance journalists, and serving air force officers. Attractive photographs greatly add to the overall appeal of the magazine. *AirForces Monthly*'s glossy format, international focus, and light analysis make it a suitable purchase for libraries of all types.

3635. *The American Legion.* Former titles (until 1981): *American Legion Magazine;* (until 1937): *The American Legion Monthly;* (until 1926): *The American Legion Weekly.* [ISSN: 0886-1234] 1920. m. Free to members; Non-members, USD 15. The American Legion, 700 N Pennsylvania St, PO Box 1055, Indianapolis, IN 46204; http://www.legion.org. Illus., adv. Circ: 18000. Vol. ends: Jun/Dec. *Indexed:* A22, BRI, HRIS. *Aud.:* Ga.

The American Legion is one of the most respected publications dealing with American veterans' affairs. It openly advocates for veterans on issues such as health care, employment, pensions, education, and homelessness. Excellent coverage of current legislation that impacts veterans and currently serving military personnel is provided. One of the other themes of *The American Legion* is promotion of "Americanism," patriotism, service, citizenship, and a strong national defense. This would be a good general-interest publication for veterans or any part of the general public interested in issues related to military service. Highly recommended for public library collections.

3636. *Ancient Warfare.* [ISSN: 1874-7019] 2007. bi-m. EUR 38.95; USD 43.68. Ed(s): Jasper Oorthuys, Josho Broiwers. Karwansaray BV, PO Box 1110, Rotterdam, 3000 BC, Netherlands. Adv. *Aud.:* Ga, Ac.

Ancient Warfare is a military history periodical that covers warfare in antiquity. The time period includes the origins of recorded history in the Mesopotamian city-states (3100 B.C.E.) to the end of the classical period (600 C.E.). Most of the issues focus on a particular theme, such as a battle or an abstract topic like sieges, swords, or logistics. Thematic issues will usually start off with a topical introduction, an article about a relevant primary source (like an ancient chronicle), a historical narrative, or a significant group of archaeological objects. The theme is further developed in articles by specialists that deal with battles, personalities, or social history related to the topic of the issue. This publication is greatly enhanced by illustrations consisting of maps, artifact photographs, and original artwork from noted historical artists. *Ancient Warfare*'s contributors are largely scholars, but the aim is to make the writing accessible to general audiences. The readability and scholarship of the articles make this a publication of potential interest to libraries of all types.

3637. *Armed Forces and Society.* [ISSN: 0095-327X] 1972. q. USD 825 (print & online eds.)). Ed(s): Patricia M Shields. Sage Publications, Inc., 2455 Teller Rd, Thousand Oaks, CA 91320; info@sagepub.com; http://www.sagepub.com. Illus., index, adv. Sample. Refereed. Vol. ends: Summer. Microform: PQC. Reprint: PSC. *Indexed:* A01, A22, BAS, BRI, CBRI, E01, IBSS, P61, SSA. *Bk. rev.:* 5-10, 300-500 words. *Aud.:* Ac.

Armed Forces and Society is one of the premier scholarly publications focusing on the military. This is the official journal of the Inter-University Seminar on Armed Forces and Society that provides an international forum for current topics like military organization, recruitment, family issues, conflict resolution, and defense policy. Most of the articles are written by academics with strong disciplinary orientations toward sociology and the behavioral sciences. Given the academic and research emphasis, this journal is an obvious candidate for academic library collections.

3638. *Armed Forces Journal (Online).* Former titles (until 2013): *Armed Forces Journal (Print);* (until 2002): *Armed Forces Journal International;* (until 1973): *Armed Forces Journal;* (until 1968): *The Journal of the Armed Forces;* (until 1964): *Army, Navy, Air Force Journal & Register;* Which was formed by the merger of (1950-1962): *Army, Navy, Air Force Journal;* Which was formerly (until 1950): *Army and Navy Journal;* (until 1924): *The American Army and Navy Journal and Gazette of the Regular, National Guard, and Reserve Forces;* (until 1921): *National Service;* Which incorporated (1915-1918): *International Military Digest;* (1961-1962): *Army-Navy-Air Force Register;* Which was formerly (until 1961): *Army-Navy-Air Force Register & Defense Times;* (until 1959): *The Army-Navy-Air Force Register;* (1879-1949): *Army and Navy Register;* Which incorporated (1949-1956): *The R O T C Journal.* [ISSN: 1930-8698] 1962. m. Sightline Media Group, 1919 Gallows Rd, Vienna, VA 22182; cust-svc@sightlinemg.com; http://sightlinemediagroup.com/. Illus., adv. *Indexed:* A01, A22. *Aud.:* Ga, Ac.

Armed Forces Journal is a respected American monthly publication geared to senior military officers and civilian defense executives. First published in 1863 as the *Army and Navy Journal,* this periodical is one of the oldest military-oriented publications in the world. Articles are generally short but provide useful coverage of the defense industry, tactics, strategy, procurement, and public administration. Serving officers from all military branches, and civilian defense officials provide most of the content. Despite the orientation to government insiders, the accessibility of the articles might well appeal to a broader general public with interests in national security. *Armed Forces Journal* can be highly recommended for libraries of all types.

3639. *Armor.* Former titles (until 1950): *Armored Cavalry Journal;* (until 1946): *The Cavalry Journal;* (until 1920): *United States Cavalry Association. Journal.* [ISSN: 0004-2420] 1888. q. Free to qualified personnel. Ed(s): Lisa Alley. U.S. Army, Armor School, McGinnis-Wickam Hall, Ste W-142, 1 Karker St, Fort Benning, GA 31905. Illus., index. *Indexed:* A22, BRI. *Bk. rev.:* 5-9, 500-1,000 words. *Aud.:* Ac.

This is one of the oldest publications dealing with a military specialty in the U.S. Armed Forces. *Armor* can trace its origins to the *Journal of the United States Cavalry Association,* which first appeared in 1888. The original journal provided a forum for horse cavalry officers who were posted at widely separated frontier posts, to exchange ideas about tactics, equipment, and doctrine. As the Army turned in its horses for armored vehicles, *Armor* became the official organ for the U.S. Army Armor School. One of the aims is to connect doctrine with practical operational experience. Articles about equipment, training, and tactics are featured, particularly if they can be connected to the Army's current missions. The contributors are exclusively serving officers and enlisted personnel, and many of the articles have a strong training or pedagogical focus. The issues are illustrated with color photographs, charts, and high-quality map images that add to the publication's visual appeal. As this is an official United States Government publication, pdf versions of the current issue and back issues can be freely viewed by the general public from the Armor School website. While aimed at a professional military audience, this journal might be of interest to enthusiasts of armored warfare among the general public, and therefore can be recommended for the electronic resources pages of libraries of all types.

3640. *Army.* Former titles (until 1956): *The Army Combat Forces Journal;* Which incorporated (1948-1954): *Antiaircraft Journal;* Which was formerly (until 1948): *The Coast Artillery Journal;* (until 1922): *Journal of the United States Artillery;* TheÅrmy Combat Forces Journal was formerly (until 1954): *United States Army Combat Forces Journal;* Which was formed by the merger of (1910-1950): *Infantry Journal;* Which was formerly (1904-1910): *United States Infantry Association. Journal;* (1911-1950): *The Field Artillery Journal.* [ISSN: 0004-2455] 1950. m. Free to members. Ed(s): Liz Rathburn, Rick Maze. Association of the U.S. Army, 2425 Wilson Blvd, Arlington, VA 22201; ausa-info@ausa.org; http://www.ausa.org. Illus., adv. Vol. ends: Dec. *Indexed:* A01, A22, BRI. *Bk. rev.:* 2-3, 500 words. *Aud.:* Ga, Ac.

A very appealing, glossy, and profusely illustrated publication that provides news and analysis of issues that impact the U.S. Army. Put out by the Association of the U.S. Army, this periodical is free to members of the association in both its print and digital formats. Feature articles deal with recent operational experience, new weapons, logistics, and possible future trends in land warfare. The magazine also offers a yearly "Green Book" that provides status reports on the functional areas of the Army. Most of the articles are written by serving officers, civilian defense officials, and regular contributing editors. *Army* is geared to anyone that would have an interest in the Army and the role that it plays in national defense. This publication can be recommended to libraries of all types.

3641. *Army Times.* [ISSN: 0004-2595] 1940. w. Mon. USD 55; USD 3.25 newsstand/cover. Ed(s): Tobias Naegele, Chuck Vinch. Gannett Government Media Corp., 6883 Commercial Dr, Springfield, VA 22159; cust-svc@atpco.com; http://www.gannett.com/about/map/armytimes.htm. Illus., adv. Circ: 107171 Paid. Microform: PQC. *Indexed:* A22. *Aud.:* Ga.

Army Times is the oldest and perhaps the flagship of the weekly newspapers that cover the main uniformed branches of the U.S. military. This independent publication provides news for active duty, reserve, and retired army personnel. The topics covered are pay, benefits, promotion, housing, and transitioning out of the military. Reporting and light analysis are also offered for public policy issues that impact the Army or the defense posture of the United States. This publication is put out by Sightline Media Group, which also publishes *Air Force Times, Marine Corps Times,* and *Navy Times* newspapers that cover much of the same ground for these other service branches. Popular and highly circulating among service members, these weeklies belong in public or special library collections that serve a military clientele.

3642. *Australian Defence Force Journal: journal of the Australian profession of arms.* Former titles (until 1991): *Defence Force Journal;* (until 1976): *Army Journal;* (until 1968): *Australian Army Journal.*

[ISSN: 1320-2545] 1976. 3x/yr. Free. Ed(s): Dr. Bob Ormston. Australia. Department of Defence, PO Box 488, Kensington Park, SA 5068, Australia; dsc@defence.gov.au; http://www.defence.gov.au. Illus., index. Refereed. *Bk. rev.:* 6-10, 500-1,000. *Aud.:* Ac, Sa.

Australian Defence Force Journal (*ADFJ*)is the official journal of all the branches of the Australian Defence Forces (ADF). Content focuses on strategy, tactics, logistics, and all facets of national defense. Many articles also look at the broader security contingencies in the Indian Ocean and South Pacific regions. Authors are serving officers in the ADF, academics, and civilian experts from the Department of Defence. This publication is an official Australian government publication, and pdf versions of all issues can be freely accessed off the *ADFJ* website. Given Australia's status as a key U.S. ally, the audience for *ADFJ* would potentially be broad, and libraries of all types should consider linking to this publication from their electronic resources pages.

3643. *Aviation History.* Former titles (until 1994): *Aviation;* (until 1993): *Aviation Heritage.* [ISSN: 1076-8858] 1990. bi-m. USD 26.95; USD 29.95 combined subscription print & online eds. HistoryNet, 1919 Gallows Rd, Vienna, VA 22182; comments@historynet.com; http://www.historynet.com. Illus., adv. *Indexed:* A01, BRI, C37, MASUSE. *Bk. rev.:* 2-5, 500-750 words. *Aud.:* Ga.

Aviation History is a magazine that deals with the history of manned flight. Articles cover all areas of aviation including commercial, high-performance, and space flight, and of course military aviation. Recent articles that focus on military aviation include "Giving the Machine Guns Wings" and "Saburo Sakai: Samurai of the Air." Biographical pieces on aviation pioneers, military aces, and other famous pilots are often featured. *Aviation History* is profusely illustrated with photographs and aviation art that greatly add to its appeal to general audiences, thus making it a strong candidate for public library collections.

3644. *Canadian Military Journal (Ottawa).* [ISSN: 1492-465X] 2000. q. Ed(s): David L Bashow. Minister of National Defence, Canadian Military Journal/Canadian Defence Academy, Station Forces, PO Box 17000, Kingston, ON K7K 7B4, Canada; http://www.forces.gc.ca/. *Bk. rev.:* 6-10, 300-500. *Aud.:* Ac, Sa.

Canadian Military Journal/Revue Militaire Canadienne is the bilingual official publication of the Canadian Armed Forces and the civilian Department of National Defense. This publication gears content to broad issues of interest across the Canadian defense establishment. Contributors are serving officers, academics, and civilian experts. Articles from a recent issue include "Scholars and Soldiers: Some Reflections on Military Academe," "Canadian Search and Rescue Puzzle: The Missing Pieces," and "Modelling Command from a Balanced Perspective." This is an official publication of the Canadian government, and all of the editions have been made available to the public from the Department of National Defense website. *Canadian Military Journal* is potentially of interest to a wide audience, and should be prominently linked to the electronic resources pages of libraries of all types.

3645. *Civil Wars.* [ISSN: 1369-8249] 1998. q. GBP 457 (print & online eds.)). Ed(s): Jonathan Fisher, Paul Jackson. Routledge, 4 Park Sq, Milton Park, Abingdon, OX14 4RN, United Kingdom; subscriptions@tandf.co.uk; http://www.tandfonline.com. Illus., index, adv. Sample. Refereed. Vol. ends: Winter. Reprint: PSC. *Indexed:* A01, A22, E01, IBSS, P61. *Aud.:* Ac.

In the contemporary world, civil wars have emerged as a dangerous source of tension and instability. *Civil Wars* is a quarterly academic journal that looks at the causes, conduct, and ending of civil wars. This journal invites contributions from scholars across a broad array of disciplines, covering topics such as nation building, ethnic conflict, religious strife, and the politics of intervention. Some articles from a recent issue include "Violence and Order: The February 2016 Cease-fire and the Development of Rebel Governance Institutions in Southern Syria," "Buying Peace? Civil War Peace Duration and Private Military & Security Companies," and "Uncultured: Civil War and Cultural Policy." The interdisciplinary focus and policy-relevant material make this journal of interest to those in academia, government, and the military. *Civil Wars* can be strongly recommended for academic library collections with particular interests in political science and international relations.

3646. *Defence Journal.* [ISSN: 0257-2141] 1975. m. USD 11 domestic; USD 80 foreign. Ed(s): M Ikram Sehgal. Pathfinder Fountain, 2-C Zamazama Boulevard, Clifton, Karachi, 75000, Pakistan. Illus., adv. *Indexed:* A01, BAS. *Bk. rev.:* Number and length vary. *Aud.:* Ga, Ac, Sa.

In recent years, Pakistan has emerged as a key ally of the United States in the War on Terror. The Pakistani military plays an important political role in its own country and influences security affairs in neighboring Afghanistan. *Defence Journal* is a key periodical that reports on the military and defense establishment in Pakistan. This publication combines opinion, news, and analysis on issues that impact Pakistani defense and the broader security of the Central and South Asian regions. Contributors are journalists, academics, military officers, and policymakers. Appealing to a potentially broad audience, *Defence Journal* would be an important addition for libraries of all types.

3647. *Defense News.* [ISSN: 0884-139X] 1986. w. Mon. Sightline Media Group, 1919 Gallows Rd, Vienna, VA 22182; cust-svc@sightlinemg.com; http://sightlinemediagroup.com/. Adv. *Indexed:* A22, B03. *Aud.:* Ac, Sa.

Defense News is a weekly trade publication that reports on defense issues from an international perspective. The general news section is divided into land, naval, air warfare, space, and cyber sections. International news is regionally divided with sections for the Americas, Europe, Asia/Pacific, and the Middle East/Africa. The articles focus heavily on the business and procurement side of the defense industry. The pages of this publication have frequent full-color ads for the latest military hardware from around the world. This publication can currently be subscribed to in both print and online versions. Civilian contractors, executives in the defense industry, and military officers concerned with supply would find this publication useful. *Defense News* can be recommended to all libraries that would have an interest in military or defense affairs.

3648. *European Security.* [ISSN: 0966-2839] 1992. q. GBP 570 (print & online eds.)). Ed(s): Jocelyn Mawdsley, Laura Chappell. Routledge, 4 Park Sq, Milton Park, Abingdon, OX14 4RN, United Kingdom; subscriptions@tandf.co.uk; http://www.tandfonline.com. Adv. Sample. Refereed. Reprint: PSC. *Indexed:* A01, A22, CJPI, E01, IBSS, P61. *Bk. rev.:* Number varies. *Aud.:* Ac.

Can any current European state be considered a world power? How is Europe facing the new Russian threat? Does migration pose new security problems for the European Union (EU)? *European Security* potentially tackles these questions and others that relate to the defense issues that impact the continent. While having a clear regional focus, this periodical attempts to frame discussions in a global context. Some articles in a recent issue would include "Transatlantic cooperation on terrorism and Islamist radicalisation in Africa: the Franco-American axis," "Identity and anxiety: Germany's struggle to lead," and "The military dimension of Russia's connection with Europe." Contributors are mainly scholars in political science, international relations, and security affairs. Clearly oriented to an audience of academics, this publication is best recommended for academic library collections.

3649. *Homeland Security Affairs.* [ISSN: 1558-643X] 2005. q. Free. Ed(s): Stephen Twing, David O'Keeffe. U.S. Naval Postgraduate School, Center for Homeland Defense and Security, I University Circle, Monterey, CA 93943-5001; http://www.chds.us/. Refereed. *Indexed:* CJPI. *Aud.:* Ac.

Homeland Security Affairs is the official peer-reviewed publication of the Naval Postgraduate School Center for Homeland Defense and Security (CHDS). This online open-access publication provides an active forum for insightful analysis of all dimensions of U.S. internal security. Articles are contributed by academics, policymakers, government officials, military officers, and CHDS faculty. Articles in recent issues include "SCADA Fusion with Commercial Fission," "Defected from ISIS or Simply Returned, and for How Long? - Challenges for the West in Dealing with Returning Foreign Fighters," and "Improving Maritime Transportation Security in Response to Industry Consolidation." Geared to an audience of scholars and practitioners, *Homeland Security Affairs* would be an appropriate link for the electronic resources pages of large academic libraries.

3650. *Indian Defence Review.* [ISSN: 0970-2512] 1986. q. INR 1000 domestic; USD 80 foreign. Ed(s): J S Bajwa. Lancer Publishers & Distributors, 56 Gautam Nagar, New Delhi, 110 049, India; http://www.lancerpublishers.com/. Adv. Refereed. *Bk. rev.:* Number varies, 200-500 words. *Aud.:* Ac, Sa.

Indian Defence Review is a respected periodical that deals with national security issues in India. This publication offers news and analysis on the Indian military and broader security affairs for the South Asian region. Contributors are high-ranking military officers, academics, and journalists. The emergence of India as a regional power, its growing problem of domestic terrorism, and its ongoing conflict with Pakistan give this periodical a potentially wide audience. Libraries of all types should consider obtaining this publication.

3651. *Infantry: a professional bulletin for the U.S. Army infantryman.* Former titles (until 1957): *Infantry School Quarterly;* (until 1947): *The Infantry School Mailing List;* (until 1934): *Infantry School. Mailing List.* [ISSN: 0019-9532] 1930. q. Ed(s): Russell A Eno. U.S. Army Infantry School, 1 Karker St, McGinnis-Wickam Hall, Fort Benning, GA 31905; http://www.infantry.army.mil/infantry/index.asp. Microform: PQC. *Indexed:* A22, BRI. *Bk. rev.:* 2 per issue. *Aud.:* Ac, Sa.

Often called the "Queen of Battle," the infantry carries the fight to the enemy and is the primary way the Army completes its mission of taking and holding ground. *Infantry* is the bulletin of the U.S. Army Infantry School at Fort Benning, Georgia. This is one of the older professional publications in the U.S. military, with a publishing history that goes back to 1930. The articles are heavily focused on training and pedagogy, with a strong emphasis on current experience. Contributors are overwhelmingly serving company-grade officers or senior enlisted personnel. Current and back issues to 1982 are available to the public in pdf from the Infantry School website. While certainly geared to serving infantrymen, *Infantry* may find an audience among general readers with an interest in the Army or land warfare. This publication can certainly be recommended for the electronic resources pages of libraries of all types.

3652. *International Journal of Intelligence and Counterintelligence.* [ISSN: 0885-0607] 1986. q. GBP 366 (print & online eds.)). Ed(s): Richard R Valcourt. Taylor & Francis Inc., 711 3rd Ave, 8th Fl, New York, NY 10017; support@tandfonline.com; http://www.taylorandfrancis.com. Illus., adv. Sample. Refereed. Reprint: PSC. *Indexed:* A22, CJPI, E01, P61. *Bk. rev.:* 4 per issue. *Aud.:* Ac, Sa.

Intelligence is the pivot on which military and national security decisions are often made. This peer-reviewed journal serves as a forum for scholars and professionals to exchange ideas on intelligence. Its emphasis is clearly on contemporary experience, but it can also be a good resource for the historical uses of intelligence. The articles are interdisciplinary reflecting a wide range of approaches and opinions. This title would be best for large academic research collections, particularly those that support programs in national security studies or international relations.

3653. *Jane's Defence Weekly.* Former titles (until 2017): *I H S Jane's Defence Weekly;* (until 2012): *Jane's Defence Weekly;* (until 1984): *Jane's Defence Review.* [ISSN: 2399-8334] 1980. w. GBP 430. Ed(s): Peter Felstead. Jane's by I H S Markit, 163 Brighton Rd, Coulsdon, CR5 2YH, United Kingdom; orders.ihs@dsbnet.co.uk; https://ihsmarkit.com/industry/aerospace-defense-security.html. Illus., adv. *Indexed:* A22, B03, C42. *Aud.:* Ga, Ac, Sa.

Jane's Defence Weekly is one of the more respected publications that reports on defense and national security from an international perspective. News and analysis are combined to cover key elements of the contemporary military scene. A large bulk of the news content is divided by region, which includes the Americas, Europe, Asia/Pacific, and Middle East/Africa. "Armed Forces," "Network-Centric Warfare," "Homeland Security," "Business," and "Analysis" are some of the sections that have regular features. Illustrations and other visual material enhance the text, making the publication glossy and visually appealing in both its print and digital formats. While it certainly strives to be authoritative, this publication's emphasis is often on military technology, and the related specialized terminology may very well baffle readers who come to it without a strong military background. *Jane's Defence Weekly* is potentially a core resource for academic libraries, particularly those that support programs in political science or international relations. Despite the specialized content, some public or special libraries may also find this publication useful in serving users with an interest in defense affairs and technology.

3654. *Jiefangjun Huabao.* [ISSN: 0009-3823] 1951. s-m. USD 144. Jiefangjun Baoshe, 34, Fuwei Dajie, Beijing, 100832, China. Illus. *Aud.:* Ga, Ac, Sa.

The People's Liberation Army (PLA) is the title for the unified armed forces of The People's Republic of China, which consists of the army, navy, air force, strategic missile forces, and militia. The PLA is the largest military force in the world, with more than two million active members and millions more in reserve components. *Jiefangjun Huabao* is a Chinese-language semi-monthly that reports on all branches of the military. Combining news with light analysis, this periodical provides an interesting perspective on current Chinese military thinking. A major strength of *Jiefangjun Huabao* is the glossy illustrations of personnel and hardware that come with each issue. Potential users need to keep in mind that this is a government publication, and the content still reflects the official Marxism of most Chinese governing institutions. Given the language and area of focus, this publication would be best suited for larger academic libraries, particularly those that have collections that support Chinese or Asian Studies programs.

3655. *Joint Force Quarterly.* [ISSN: 1070-0692] 1993. q. Ed(s): William T Eliason, Jeffrey D Smotherman. National Defense University, Fort Lesley J McNair, 260 Fifth Ave. Bldg 64, Washington, DC 20319; NDUPress@ndu.edu; http://www.ndu.edu. Illus., index. Sample. *Indexed:* A01, A22, BRI. *Bk. rev.:* 4, 500 words. *Aud.:* Ac.

Joint Force Quarterly (*JFQ*) discusses the use of air, land, space, and sea forces in an integrated operational environment. This publication also focuses on the complexities of coalition warfare, inter-service coordination, and organizing unified commands. Prepared for the Joint Chiefs of Staff by the Institute for National Strategic Studies, National Defense University, *JFQ* can be regarded as an important official organ for American strategic military doctrine. Articles from a recent edition include "Climate Change and Urbanization: Challenges to Global Security and Stability" and "Structuring Airpower to Win in 2030: Designing a Joint Division of Labor Between Land- and Sea-Based Combat Aviation." Most of the contributors are high-ranking officers from all branches of the armed services, many of them involved in high-level planning or in leadership positions in unified commands. *JFQ* is an official U.S. government publication, with current and back issues available freely in pdf form from the National Defense University website. This journal would make a useful link from the electronic resources pages of academic libraries particularly those that support programs in defense studies, public administration, or political science.

3656. *Journal of Military History.* Former titles (until 1989): *Military Affairs;* (until 1941): *American Military Institute. Journal;* (until 1939): *American Military History Foundation. Journal.* [ISSN: 0899-3718] 1937. q. Free to members. Ed(s): Roberta Wiener, Bruce Vandervort. Society for Military History, George C Marshall Library, Virginia Military Institute, Lexington, VA 24450; JMHSMH@vmi.edu; http://www.smh-hq.org. Illus., index, adv. Sample. Refereed. Vol. ends: Oct. Microform: PQC. *Indexed:* A01, A22, AmHI, BAS, BRI, CBRI, E01, MLA-IB. *Bk. rev.:* Number varies, 200-300 words. *Aud.:* Ga, Ac.

This publication is one of the most scholarly and respected titles for general military history. At the heart of every quarterly issue are highly researched articles that can potentially cover any area of historic conflict regardless of period or geography. Most of the articles are written by historians, with some contributions by academics in other social science or humanities fields. One of the strengths of this journal is the 50-60 book reviews that appear in each issue and cover a wide range of military history titles. The *Journal of Military History* is published by the Society for Military History, with print and electronic versions of the journal free to members. Many libraries can get complete electronic access through their subscriptions to any of the EBSCOhost databases that index the journal. The academic and research focus of this publication makes it an obvious choice for college and university libraries.

3657. *The Journal of Slavic Military Studies.* Formerly (until 1993): *Journal of Soviet Military Studies.* [ISSN: 1351-8046] 1988. q. GBP 667 (print & online eds.)). Ed(s): David M Glantz, Christopher Donnelly. Routledge, 4 Park Sq, Milton Park, Abingdon, OX14 4RN, United Kingdom; subscriptions@tandf.co.uk; http://www.tandfonline.com. Illus., adv. Sample. Refereed. Reprint: PSC. *Indexed:* A01, A22, E01, IBSS, P61. *Bk. rev.:* 50-60, 200-600 words. *Aud.:* Ac.

The Journal of Slavic Military Studies is a peer-reviewed academic journal that examines military affairs in Central and Eastern Europe. While it covers security issues for the whole region, the emphasis is clearly on Russia. This journal combines views of the contemporary scene with historical perspectives. The contributors are academics drawn from a wide variety of social science fields. Some articles from a recent issue include "Tools of Future Wars: Russia is Entering the Precision-Strike Regime," "Russian Airpower's Success in Syria: Assessing Evolution in Kinetic Counterinsurgency," and "Russia's National Security Strategy: Analysis of Conceptual Evolution." Clearly oriented to a specialized audience, this publication would be best suited to academic library collections that support collections in Russian or Eastern European studies.

3658. *The Journal of Strategic Studies.* [ISSN: 0140-2390] 1978. 7x/yr. GBP 987 (print & online eds.)). Ed(s): Joe A Maiolo, Thomas G Mahnken. Routledge, 4 Park Sq, Milton Park, Abingdon, OX14 4RN, United Kingdom; subscriptions@tandf.co.uk; http://www.tandfonline.com. Illus., index, adv. Sample. Refereed. Microform: PQC. Reprint: PSC. *Indexed:* A01, A22, AmHI, BAS, E01, IBSS, P61. *Bk. rev.:* 3-4, 500 words. *Aud.:* Ac.

The Journal of Strategic Studies is a scholarly publication that seeks to combine theoretical and historical approaches to strategy, defense policy, and warfare. Articles are heavily researched written by academics from a wide range of disciplines and methodological perspectives. Some articles in a recent issue include "Think again - supplying war: reappraising military logistics and its centrality to strategy and war" and "Beyond the Double Game: Lessons from Pakistan's Approach to Islamist Militancy." The heavy research tone of this journal would make it highly suitable to most academic library collections.

3659. *The Korean Journal of Defense Analysis.* [ISSN: 1016-3271] 1989. q. KRW 35000. Ed(s): Tak S Han. Korea Institute for Defense Analyses, 37 Hoegiro, Dongdaemun-gu, Seoul, 130-871, Korea, Republic of; wklee@kida.re.kr; http://www.kida.re.kr/. Refereed. Reprint: PSC. *Indexed:* BAS, P61. *Bk. rev.:* Number varies, 300-600 words. *Aud.:* Ac.

This scholarly publication provides analysis of defense issues for the Korean peninsula and the Northeast Asian region. *The Korean Journal of Defense Analysis* pays particular attention to the security and military posture of South Korea (ROK). Much of this treatment looks at South Korea as a regional military power and key geopolitical player for the entire Pacific Rim. Authors are primarily academics, with some contributions coming from high-ranking military officers and civilian policymakers. While paid subscriptions are still available for the print version, free electronic access is provided for the full run of the journal. This publication would be best suited to academic libraries that support programs in Asian Studies, but given the current visibility of the topic many special and public libraries might also have interested readers.

3660. *Leatherneck: magazine of the marines.* Formerly (until 19??): *The Quantico Leatherneck.* [ISSN: 0023-981X] 1917. m. Free to members. Ed(s): Col Mary Reinwald. Marine Corps Association, 715 Broadway St, PO Box 1775, Quantico, VA 22134; mcaf@mca-marines.org; http://www.mcafdn.org/. Illus., index, adv. Sample. Circ: 77085 Paid. Vol. ends: Dec. Microform: PQC. *Indexed:* A22. *Bk. rev.:* 5, 200 words. *Aud.:* Ga.

Leatherneck aims to be "the magazine of Marines yesterday, today, and tomorrow." Put out by the Marine Corps Association, this publication is one of the older service-oriented publications, with origins going back to 1917. The magazine mostly covers current news of specific interest to Marines, including reports on new weapons, technology, and current conflicts. Articles about general Marine Corps history and personal stories from past wars are also featured. Many of the contributors are serving or retired Marines, both officers and enlisted. Free print and online access to the magazine comes with paid membership in the Marine Corps Association. The general tone of this publication makes it an ideal choice for public or special libraries that would serve a military clientele.

3661. *M H Q: the quarterly journal of military history.* [ISSN: 1040-5992] 1988. q. USD 49.95. HistoryNet, 1919 Gallows Rd, Vienna, VA 22182; comments@historynet.com; http://www.historynet.com. Illus., index, adv. Vol. ends: Summer. *Indexed:* BRI, MLA-IB. *Bk. rev.:* 2-4, 200-300 words. *Aud.:* Hs, Ga.

MHQ is a highly respected military history publication aimed at a general audience. The articles cover all eras and are highly accessible. Some feature articles that appear in recent issues include "Holding the Farm at Waterloo" and "King William's War: New England's Mournful Decade." The contributors are historians, military experts, freelance writers, and the staff of *MHQ.* A column that looks at the origins of military jargon, a book review section, and a regular article on war art are some of the special features of the magazine. This glossy publication is profusely illustrated, which greatly enhances the overall appeal. *MHQ* would be a suitable choice for any public library collection.

3662. *Marine Corps Gazette: professional journal of U.S. marines.* [ISSN: 0025-3170] 1916. m. Free to members. Ed(s): Christopher Woodbridge. Marine Corps Association, 715 Broadway St, PO Box 1775, Quantico, VA 22134; mcaf@mca-marines.org; http://www.mca-marines.org. Illus., index, adv. Sample. Circ: 465 Free. Vol. ends: Dec. Microform: PQC. *Indexed:* A22, BRI, CBRI. *Bk. rev.:* 6, 300-750 words. *Aud.:* Ga, Ac.

Known as "the *Gazette,*" this publication is the professional journal for the Marine Corps. Like its news magazine counterpart *Leatherneck,* this is one of the older publications dealing with a military branch, dating back to 1916. The *Gazette* shares with other professional military publications a desire to link theory with practical experience. Articles in a recent issue include "Counternarcotics Expertise in the Marine Corps" and "A Leadership Taxonomy for the Marine Corps." The articles are overwhelmingly written by serving Marine officers, with some contribution from senior enlisted personnel. Published by the Marine Corps Association, the *Gazette* comes free with paid membership to the association. This publication would contain much of interest for audiences in libraries of all types.

3663. *Medieval Warfare.* [ISSN: 2211-5129] 2011. bi-m. EUR 38.95; USD 43.68. Ed(s): Peter Konieczny. Karwansaray BV, PO Box 1110, Rotterdam, 3000 BC, Netherlands; http://www.karwansaraypublishers.com. Adv. *Aud.:* Ga, Ac.

Medieval Warfare is a military history periodical that covers warfare in the period 500 C.E.-1500 C.E. This is a sister publication to *Ancient Warfare* and is organized in a similar thematic pattern. Some themes for recent issues would include Edward I's invasion of Wales, the Battle of Hastings, and the War of Bouvines. Very colorful illustrations consisting of maps, photographs, drawings, and original art grace the pages of this publication. Most of the content is contributed by specialists in the medieval period that are drawn from many different disciplines. Despite credible scholarship, most of the articles are written for a general audience making *Medieval Warfare* a potential candidate for libraries of all types.

3664. *Militaergeschichtliche Zeitschrift.* Formerly (until 2000): *Militaergeschichtliche Mitteilungen.* [ISSN: 2193-2336] 1967. s-a. EUR 46. Ed(s): Michael Epkenhans, Hans-Hubertus Mack. De Gruyter Oldenbourg, Rosenheimer Str 145, Muenchen, 81671, Germany; service@degruyter.com; https://www.degruyter.com. Illus., adv. Refereed. Reprint: SCH. *Aud.:* Ac, Sa.

This German-language publication is a respected European periodical that deals with general military history. Reflecting a wide range of topics drawn from all periods of history, *Militaergeschichtliche Zeitschrift* seeks to view the changing interaction between conflict, culture, society, and the military. This publication is strongly academic, welcoming a variety of disciplinary and methodological approaches. Authors are historians or other academics largely drawn from social science fields. The strong research orientation of this journal should make it a candidate for specialized academic library collections.

3665. *Military.* Formerly: *Military History Review.* [ISSN: 1046-2511] 1985. m. USD 21 domestic; USD 40 in Canada & Mexico; USD 64 elsewhere. Ed(s): John Shank. M H R Publishing Corp., 2116 28 St, Sacramento, CA 95818. Illus., adv. Sample. *Bk. rev.:* 8-10, 200-600 words. *Aud.:* Ga.

This publication is unique in that it seeks to use its subscribers as its base of writers. The editors actively invite accounts from former servicemen and women that span all of America's recent wars, from World War II to the present. The intent seems to be to reverse the trend in writing about military history that makes it an exclusive club for academics, statesman, and high-ranking military officers. The feature articles are mostly oral histories of military service written by active subscribers. Readers can also contribute book reviews and offer opinions in the magazine's regular sections "Sound Off" and "Intercom." It must be noted that the bulk of the editorial content is openly pro-defense and strongly conservative. The firsthand accounts would make this publication attractive to a wide audience, and this magazine deserves consideration by public libraries of all sizes.

3666. ***Military Collector & Historian.*** [ISSN: 0026-3966] 1949. q. Free to members. Company of Military Historians, PO Box 910, Rutland, MA 01543; cmhhq@aol.com; http://www.military-historians.org. Illus., adv. Microform: PQC. *Indexed:* A22. *Bk. rev.:* 3-6, 250-750 words. *Aud.:* Ac, Sa.

This is one of the principal periodicals dealing with the history of uniforms, colors, standards, traditions, and weapons of all branches of the United States military. *Military Collector & Historian* also covers the armed forces of other nations that have served in the western hemisphere at different times in the past. Published by The Company of Military Historians, this magazine comes with membership and reports on the activities of the organization and provides a forum for members. Contributors are very eclectic and include historians, collectors, archivists, antiquarians, museum people, and members of the military. Beautiful color and black-and-white plates appear in every issue and contribute greatly to the quality and overall appeal of the magazine. Recommended for libraries of all types.

3667. ***Military History.*** [ISSN: 0889-7328] 1984. bi-m. USD 26.95. HistoryNet, 1919 Gallows Rd, Vienna, VA 22182; comments@historynet.com; http://www.historynet.com. Adv. *Indexed:* A01, A22, BRI, MASUSE. *Bk. rev.:* 3-5, 250-700 words. *Aud.:* Ga.

Military History is one of the most popular periodicals devoted to military history. All types of warfare from antiquity to the present day are covered in this publication. Contributors are historians, journalists, military enthusiasts, and freelance writers. The feature articles are very traditional, mostly focusing on great battles or noted people. Recent articles include "Murder in Vietnam," "Jihad in the Age of Victoria," and "The Siege of Kut." Personality profiles, espionage, weaponry, and firsthand interviews are regular features of the magazine. Frequent and high-quality illustrations grace the pages of *Military History,* making it very attractive to general audiences. This publication would be appropriate for public library collections of all sizes.

3668. ***Military Review (English Edition): the professional journal of the United States Army.*** Former titles (until 1939): *The Command and General Staff School Quarterly;* (until 1936): *Review of Military Literature;* (until 1933): *Quarterly Review of Military Literature;* (until 1932): *Review of Current Military Literature;* (until 1931): *Review of Current Military Writings;* (until 1925): *Instructor's Summary of Military Articles.* [ISSN: 0026-4148] 1922. bi-m. Ed(s): Anna R Friederich-Maggard. U.S. Army Combined Arms Center, Truesdale Hall, 290 Stimson Ave, Unit 2, Fort Leavenworth, KS 66027; leav-milrevweb@conus.army.mil; http://usacac.army.mil/CAC2/. Illus., index, adv. Sample. Vol. ends: Dec. Microform: PQC. *Indexed:* A01, A22, BAS, BRI. *Bk. rev.:* 6-11, 200-300 words. *Aud.:* Ga, Ac.

This publication is the professional journal of the U.S. Army. The purpose of *Military Review* is to provide a forum for exchanging ideas and innovations about doctrine, mostly on the tactical level. The content is mostly geared to the Army's current missions and operational environments. A number of historical articles appear that may have particular lessons for current preparedness or potential combat operations. Articles are mostly contributed by serving Army officers or credentialed scholars. This title has substantial book reviews that cover military history or national security titles. The audience is highly geared to field-grade officers that are in many cases commanding troops in active commands. *Military Review* is also published in Spanish and Portuguese-language editions that offer articles on military affairs in Latin America. The current and back editions of this journal are now available for free online from the Army University Press website. Both academic, special, and public libraries should consider linking to this title from their electronic resources pages.

3669. ***Military Thought: a Russian journal of military theory and strategy.*** [ISSN: 0869-5636] 1918. q. USD 1305. Ed(s): S Rodikov. East View Information Services, 10601 Wayzata Blvd, Hopkins, MN 55305; info@eastview.com; http://www.eastview.com/. Adv. Sample. Refereed. Microform: EVP. *Indexed:* A01, BRI, P61. *Aud.:* Ac.

Military Thought is the English-language version of *Voennaia Mysl,* one of the official theoretical organs of the Russian Defense Ministry. This publication is one of the oldest military publications in the world with origins going back to the beginnings of the Soviet era in 1918. Since 1992, East View Press has offered a translation of this journal to present a unique view of military affairs from a key U.S. adversary. Contributors are high ranking military officers, academics, and civilian defense officials. The content is dense, mostly focusing on advanced strategic and operational problems. Some articles from a recent issue include "The Battle of Mosul in Iraq as a Mirror of U.S. City Capturing Tactics," "Methodological Recommendations for Analyzing Results of Combat Actions Simulation," and "Auto-Technical Support for Automated Command and Control Systems." The technical and specialized content of *Military Thought* would make it a good choice for academic library collections, particularly those that support programs in political science, international relations, and Russian studies.

3670. ***N A T O Review (Online).*** [ISSN: 1608-7569] 1991. q. Free. Ed(s): Vicki Nielson. North Atlantic Treaty Organization (N A T O), Office of Information and Press, Blvd Leopold III, Brussels, 1110, Belgium; natodoc@hq.nato.int; http://www.nato.int. *Aud.:* Ga, Ac, Sa.

NATO Review is the official periodical of the North Atlantic Treaty Organization (NATO). The current incarnation of this publication is the digital successor to a print periodical that ceased in 2003. Access to the online version is free, and has links to earlier issues going back to 2000. *NATO Review* provides both news and analysis on the state of the organization, and the projection of the alliance outside of Europe. Contributors are academics, senior policy makers, alliance officials, and military officers from member states. Given the renewed interest in European security, this publication might appeal to a more general audience and could be recommended for the electronic resources pages of libraries of all types.

3671. ***National Guard.*** Former titles (until 1978): *Guardsman;* (until 1975): *The National Guardsman.* [ISSN: 0163-3945] 1947. m. Free to members; Non-members, USD 25. Ed(s): John Goheen. National Guard Association of the United States, One Massachusetts Ave N W, Washington, DC 20001; ngaus@ngaus.org; http://www.ngaus.org. Illus., adv. Vol. ends: Dec. Microform: PQC. *Indexed:* A01, A22. *Aud.:* Ga.

National Guard highlights the role that both the Army and Air National Guard play in the overall structure of national defense. Articles are newsy and often focus on the political and budgetary climate that the Guard faces in both Washington and the states. Contributors are journalists, freelance writers, and current members of the Guard. Published by the National Guard Association of the United States, this magazine is distributed free for members. Given the role the Guard has played in the wars in both Iraq and Afghanistan, this publication may be of interest to a broader audience and can be recommended to libraries of all types.

3672. ***Naval History.*** [ISSN: 1042-1920] 1987. bi-m. Free to members; Non-members, USD 35. U S Naval Institute, 291 Wood Rd, Annapolis, MD 21402; customer@usni.org; http://www.usni.org. Illus., adv. *Indexed:* A01. *Bk. rev.:* 1-2, 250-500 words. *Aud.:* Ga, Ac.

This title deals with the general naval history of the United States and the world. Published by the U.S. Naval Institute, *Naval History* is profusely illustrated and provides high-quality feature articles for a general audience. Many of the articles are oral histories of participants in past conflicts, profiles of historic vessels, and detailed descriptions of important naval actions. Some of the articles in a recent issue include "A POW's Secret Diary of Captivity," "Citizen Sailors in Naval Service," and "Remembering the Pueblo." The articles are written by historians, independent scholars, freelance writers, and both active-duty and retired military. This publication would be a good addition to any public library collection.

3673. ***Naval War College Review.*** [ISSN: 0028-1484] 1948. q. Ed(s): Carnes Lord. U.S. Naval War College, 686 Cushing Rd, Newport, RI 02841; PAO@usnwc.edu; http://www.nwc.navy.mil. Illus., index. Microform: BHP; MIM; PQC. *Indexed:* A01, A22, BAS, BRI, CBRI, P61. *Bk. rev.:* 20-25, 300-500 words. *Aud.:* Ac.

This title is the official research journal of the U.S. Naval War College. The content reflects the interests and mission of the War College as the primary training ground for the Navy's senior leadership. Articles generally focus on current naval affairs, but considerable attention is also given to public-policy issues related to national defense. Contributors are senior naval officers, civilian policy-makers, and leading scholars. Essay-length book reviews generally include naval and general military titles. Beautifully illustrated naval art and photographs appear on the cover of each issue. The current and back issues from 1981 are available online for free off the Naval War College website. Given its research content, *Naval War College Review* would most appropriately be suited to the electronic resource pages of academic or special libraries that would serve a military clientele.

3674. ***Parameters (Carlisle).*** [ISSN: 0031-1723] 1971. q. USD 26 domestic (Free to qualified personnel). Ed(s): Antulio J Echevarria. U.S. Army, War College, Attn: Parameters, 47 Asburn Drive, Carlisle, PA 17013-5238; carl_atwc-cpa@conus.army.mil. Illus., index. Sample. Refereed. Vol. ends: Winter. Microform: PQC. *Indexed:* A01, A22, BRI, CBRI, P61. *Bk. rev.:* 4-13, 500-1,000 words. *Aud.:* Ac.

Parameters is the professional publication of the U.S. Army War College and seeks to encourage reflection on the strategic dimensions of warfare on land. The audience comprises senior army officers and civilian policy-makers concerned with national security. Several feature articles appear in each issue and a recent issue includes "Clausewitz's Theory of War and Victory in Contemporary Conflict," "Lessons Unlearned: Army Transformation and Low-Intensity Conflict," and "Expansibility and Army Special Operations Forces." The articles are written by army officers, outside scholars, and the faculty of the college. In each issue, nearly essay-length book reviews will cover 10 to 20 titles all on different military topics. This is clearly an important core publication, and it should find its way into academic or special libraries that would serve a military clientele.

3675. ***R U S I Journal.*** Former titles (until 1972): *Royal United Services Institute for Defence Studies. Journal;* (until 1971): *Royal United Service Institution. Journal;* (until 1860): *United Service Institution. Journal.* [ISSN: 0307-1847] 1857. 7x/yr. USD 1679 (print & online eds.)). Ed(s): Emma De Angelis. Routledge, 4 Park Sq, Milton Park, Abingdon, OX14 4RN, United Kingdom; subscriptions@tandf.co.uk; http://www.tandfonline.com. Illus., adv. Sample. Vol. ends: Dec. Microform: PQC. Reprint: PSC. *Indexed:* A22, E01. *Bk. rev.:* Number varies. *Aud.:* Ac.

The *RUSI Journal* is the official publication of the Royal United Services Institute and provides an interesting mirror on British thinking on military and security affairs. First published in 1857, this publication is the oldest unified military and defense periodical in the world. Every bimonthly issue contains articles on contemporary national defense affairs, regular features on military history, and a substantial book review section. Contributors are high-ranking military officers, currently serving government ministers, academics, and "defense insiders." Despite the journal's high price tag, the articles are of exceptional quality, providing a valuable perspective from a key American ally. The *RUSI Journal* should be strongly considered for library collections of all types.

3676. ***Revue Defense Nationale.*** Former titles (until 2010): *Defense Nationale et Securite Collective;* (until 2005): *Defense Nationale;* (until 1973): *Revue de Defense Nationale.* [ISSN: 2105-7508] 1939. m. EUR 150. Ed(s): Jerome Pellistrandi. Comite d'Etudes de Defense Nationale, BP 8607, Paris, 75325 Cedex 07, France; cednrevu@worldnet.fr. *Indexed:* A22, BAS, P61. *Aud.:* Ac, Sa.

Revue Defense Nationale is a French-language periodical that addresses military, strategic, and defense issues as they relate to France. It also publishes articles that deal with broader European security, the NATO alliance, international peacekeeping, and stability in the developing world. Authors are academics, policymakers, defense officials, and military officers. Given the professional and specialized focus, this periodical would be recommended for academic libraries, particularly those that support collections in French or European Studies.

3677. ***Sea Power.*** Formerly (until 1971): *Navy;* (until 1958): *Now Hear This.* [ISSN: 0199-1337] 1949. m. USD 58 domestic (Free to members). Ed(s): Danielle Lucey, Rick Burgess. Navy League of the United States, 2300 Wilson Blvd, Ste 200, Arlington, VA 22201; http://www.navyleague.org. Illus., adv. Microform: PQC. *Indexed:* A01, A22, BRI. *Aud.:* Ga, Ac.

Sea Power is the voice of the Navy League, a group of citizens that support a strong maritime defense for the United States. Articles cover topics like technology, satellite reconnaissance, coastal defense, shipping lanes, port security, and future projection of sea power. Subscribers also receive an annual almanac issue that profiles the mission and organizational structure of the principal maritime services, including the Coast Guard, Navy, Marine Corps, and the Merchant Marine. The main audience comprises members of the military and those of the general public who have an interest in the Navy or maritime security. *Sea Power* can be recommended for library collections of all types.

3678. ***Small Wars and Insurgencies.*** Incorporates (1992-2005): *Low Intensity Conflict & Law Enforcement.* [ISSN: 0959-2318] 1990. 8x/yr. GBP 991 (print & online eds.)). Ed(s): Paul B Rich. Routledge, 4 Park Sq, Milton Park, Abingdon, OX14 4RN, United Kingdom; subscriptions@tandf.co.uk; http://www.routledge.com. Index, adv. Sample. Refereed. Reprint: PSC. *Indexed:* A22, BAS, E01, IBSS, P61. *Bk. rev.:* Number varies. *Aud.:* Ac.

Terrorism, insurgency, and civil wars are increasingly competing with state-on-state conflict as the face of war in the contemporary world. *Small Wars and Insurgencies* is an interesting academic journal that addresses the political, social, and psychological implications of conflict at this level. It is clearly designed as a forum for academics, military professionals, policymakers, and law enforcement officials to air out many of the concerns of preparing and engaging in current or future low-level threats. Many of the issues are thematic, with some recent themes tackling insurgents in Syria, and the impact of Jihadists on the Internet. Academic libraries would benefit the most from having this publication, but given the relevance of the topic, many public or special libraries might also consider this journal for their collections.

3679. ***Soldiers.*** Former titles (until 1971): *Army Digest;* (until 1966): *Army Information Digest;* (until 1946): *I & E Digest.* [ISSN: 0093-8440] 1946. a. U.S. Department of the Army, 6700 Taylor Ave, Ste E155-17, Fort Meade, MD 20755; APDFCMP@conus.army.mil; http://www.army.mil. Illus., index. Microform: PQC. *Indexed:* A22, BAS, BRI. *Aud.:* Ga, Ac, Sa.

Soldiers is the official publication of the U.S. Army. It features reports on recruitment, training, substance abuse, health benefits, and current news about what's happening within the Army community. The content is generally short, and much of it is practical advice for enlisted soldiers for managing their careers or exiting the military. The main audience consists of current soldiers, but the focus is broad enough to appeal to the general public or young people thinking of enlisting in the Army. *Soldiers* is an official publication of the Department of Defense and current issues of the magazine are available to the public for free online. This publication would be most appropriately linked to via the electronic resources pages of public or special libraries serving a military clientele.

3680. ***Special Warfare: the professional bulletin of Army Special Operations.*** [ISSN: 1058-0123] 1988. q. Ed(s): Janice Burton. U.S. Army, John F. Kennedy Special Warfare Center and School, AOJK-DTD-MP, USAJFKSWCS; Attn: AOJK-PAO, Ft. Bragg, NC 28310. *Indexed:* BRI. *Bk. rev.:* 2, 750-1,000 words. *Aud.:* Ac, Sa.

The Green Berets, Delta Force, and Airborne Rangers are parts of the U.S. Army's special-operations community. The roles of special-ops are broad, with missions that include commando operations, intelligence gathering, reconnaissance, and civil affairs activities. *Special Warfare* is the official publication of the John F. Kennedy Special Warfare Center and School (SWCS) at Fort Bragg, North Carolina. Articles focus on current experience covering topics like small-unit tactics, training, insertion techniques, equipment, and new weapons. Much of the content is written by currently serving members of Army special-ops units supplemented by contributions by civilian policy-makers and academic researchers. *Special Warfare* is an official government publication with current and back issues freely available in pdf format off the SWCS website. The primary audience would be members of this elite community, but the popular mystique that surrounds special forces would give this title a wider civilian readership. Libraries of all types should consider linking to this publication from their electronic resources pages.

3681. ***Strategic Assessment.*** [ISSN: 0793-8942] 1998. q. Ed(s): Amos Yadlin, Moshe Grundman. Institute for National Security Studies, 40 Haim Levanon St, Tel Aviv, 61398, Israel; info@inss.org.il; http://www.inss.org.il.

Strategic Assessment is one of the principal theoretical publications dealing with the defense posture of the State of Israel. This English-language quarterly journal is published by the Institute for National Security Studies (INSS), a think tank affiliated with Tel Aviv University. *Strategic Assessment* serves as a forum for the latest in operational practice for the Israel Defense Forces (IDF), and also covers security issues dealing with the broader Middle East, Europe, and the Mediterranean basin. Contributors are serving IDF officers, academics, and civilian policymakers. The content of the journal is an important mirror into the thinking of a major strategic player in the Middle East and key U.S. ally. Both current and back runs of the journal are available as free open-source documents off the INSS website. Geared for an audience of specialists, this resource would be a great candidate for the electronic resources pages of academic libraries particularly those that support programs in Jewish or Middle Eastern Studies.

3682. ***Survival (Abingdon): global politics and strategy.*** [ISSN: 0039-6338] 1959. bi-m. GBP 585 (print & online eds.)). Ed(s): Dana Allin. Routledge, 4 Park Sq, Milton Park, Abingdon, OX14 4RN, United Kingdom; subscriptions@tandf.co.uk; http://www.tandfonline.com. Adv. Sample. Refereed. Microform: PQC. Reprint: PSC. *Indexed:* A01, A22, BAS, BRI, E01, IBSS, P61. *Bk. rev.:* 1-5 per issue. *Aud.:* Ac.

Published by the International Institute for Strategic Studies, *Survival* provides a scholarly forum for discussion of defense and strategic affairs. Content is contributed mainly by scholars in the areas of political science, defense studies, history, law, and international relations. Articles from the current issue include "China's Innovation Trajectories," "Reaching an Understanding on Baltic Security," and "European Defence: Give PESCO a Chance." The articles are well written, encouraging a reasoned forum for current issues that may potentially be driving conflicts around the world. Given its research focus, *Survival* can be recommended for academic library collections of all types.

3683. ***U S Naval Institute. Proceedings.*** Incorporates (1963-1969): *Naval Review;* Formerly (until 1879): *United States Naval Institute. Record.* [ISSN: 0041-798X] 1874. m. Free to members. U S Naval Institute, 291 Wood Rd, Annapolis, MD 21402; customer@usni.org; http://www.usni.org. Illus., index, adv. Vol. ends: Dec. Microform: PQC. *Indexed:* A01, A22, BAS, MLA-IB. *Bk. rev.:* 3, 500-1,000 words. *Aud.:* Ga, Ac.

Another title published by the United States Naval Institute, *Proceedings* focuses on contemporary maritime security issues as they relate to the U.S. Navy, Coast Guard, and Marines. With origins going back to 1874, this is one of the oldest periodicals that deals with naval affairs. *Proceedings* provides a rigorous space for refining doctrine, appraising technology, assessing current practices, and critically debating maritime security. Articles in a recent issue include "Visualize Chinese Sea Power," "Framing Marine Corps Culture," and "Give a Cyber Edge to the Warfighters." Contributors are serving military officers, civilian experts, and credentialed scholars. This publication is geared to audiences who are directly involved with national security, or to members of the general public who are interested in naval thinking and practice. Highly recommended for library collections of all types.

3684. ***Vietnam.*** [ISSN: 1046-2902] 1988. bi-m. USD 26.95. HistoryNet, 1919 Gallows Rd, Vienna, VA 22182; comments@historynet.com; http://www.historynet.com. Illus., adv. Sample. *Indexed:* A22, BRI. *Bk. rev.:* Number varies, 250-600 words. *Aud.:* Ga.

This publication covers the military history of the Vietnam War. Content is strongly oriented to the military dimension of the war, and less attention is given to the societal aspects of the conflict. Articles will generally look at a particular battle, weapons, or an important personality. Photographs and profuse illustrations are an attractive part of each issue. Contributors are military historians, veterans, and freelance writers. Aimed at general audiences, this title would be of interest to public library collections of all types.

3685. ***War & Society.*** [ISSN: 0729-2473] 1983. 3x/yr. GBP 328 (print & online eds.)). Ed(s): Eleanor Hancock. Routledge, 4 Park Sq, Milton Park, Abingdon, OX14 4RN, United Kingdom; subscriptions@tandf.co.uk; http://www.tandfonline.com. Refereed. Reprint: PSC. *Indexed:* A22, BAS, MLA-IB. *Aud.:* Ac.

This respected periodical publishes articles on the social impacts of past wars and conflicts. *War & Society* encourages a broad range of methodological approaches in coming to new and innovative understandings of socially driven topics that are drawn from all periods of military history. Authors are mostly historians, with other contributors coming from related social science fields. Articles in a recent issue tackled the "The Politics of Provisioning: Feeding South Asian Prisoners During the First World War," "The Road to the Chaco War: Bolivia's Modernization in the 1920s," and "Sensory Stress and Personal Agency: Emotional Casualty Rates amongst USAAF Heavy Bomber Crews over Europe during the Second World War." The content of this publication is heavily geared to historians or other academics that have an interest in war. The scholarly thrust of this publication makes it an ideal candidate for academic library collections.

3686. ***War in History.*** [ISSN: 0968-3445] 1994. q. USD 985 (print & online eds.)). Ed(s): Simon Ball, Phillips O'Brien. Sage Publications Ltd., 1 Oliver's Yard, 55 City Rd, London, EC1Y 1SP, United Kingdom; market@sagepub.com; https://www.sagepub.com/. Illus., adv. Sample. Refereed. Reprint: PSC. *Indexed:* A01, A22, AmHI, E01. *Bk. rev.:* 15-35 per issue. *Aud.:* Ac.

War in History attempts to put military history in a broader context that accounts for political, economic, and social factors. This peer-reviewed publication looks for innovative approaches that can contribute new interpretations to all periods of warfare. Contributors are mostly historians, with some content coming from academics in related disciplines. Recent articles explore "Generating distrust through intelligence work: Psychological terror and the Dutch security services in Indonesia, 1945-1949," "Colonial Containment? Repression of Pro-Independence Street Demonstrations in Algiers, Casablanca and Paris, 1945-1962," and "'Devils that suck the blood of the Malayan People': The Case for Post-Revisionist Analysis of Counter-insurgency Violence." An extensive book review section covers 10 to 35 titles an issue, greatly adding to the utility and scholarly quality of this journal. This publication is highly recommended for academic library collections.

3687. ***World War II (Leesburg).*** [ISSN: 0898-4204] 1986. bi-m. USD 26.95. HistoryNet, 1919 Gallows Rd, Vienna, VA 22182; comments@historynet.com; http://www.historynet.com. Adv. *Indexed:* A01, A22, BRI, C37, MASUSE. *Bk. rev.:* Number and length vary. *Aud.:* Ga.

This magazine provides interesting and entertaining articles on the events of World War II. The articles generally detail an important battle or profile a particular individual. Recent articles include "A Surprising Encounter at Rapido" and "The Unloved, Unlovely, yet Indispensable LST." Most of the contributions are made by journalists, military historians, and freelance authors. The content is overwhelmingly oriented to the military dimension of the conflict, and very limited attention is given to the war's political and social impacts. Photographs, drawings, maps, charts, and other illustrations are liberally spread throughout every issue. Aimed at general audiences, this publication would be of interest for most public library collections.

3688. ***Y: Magazin der Bundeswehr.*** [ISSN: 1617-5212] 2001. m. EUR 37. Ed(s): Dieter Buchholtz. Frankfurter Societaets-Medien GmbH, Frankenallee 71-81, Frankfurt am Main, 60327, Germany; vertrieb@societaets-verlag.de; https://societaets-verlag.de. Adv. Circ: 73500 Paid and controlled. *Aud.:* Ac.

This German-language publication provides news and light analysis of the Bundeswehr, the unified armed forces of the Federal Republic of Germany. *Y* reports on recruitment, training, weapons, general force readiness, and stories of interest to members of the armed forces. Overseas deployments as peacekeepers, or in operations as part of the NATO alliance, are also given extensive coverage. This is an official government publication, and a good deal of content can be viewed freely from the Bundeswehr military portal called "Y-Punkt.de." A print edition and more extensive electronic access can be obtained by a paid subscription. The language and focused content would make this a suitable choice for large academic collections particularly those that support programs related to NATO or German Studies.

■ MINDFULNESS

Ann Vogl, Reference and Distance Learning Librarian, University of Wisconsin-Stout, Menomonie, WI 54751; voglan@uwstout.edu

Introduction

Mindfulness meditation can be defined as "the awareness that arises from paying attention, on purpose, in the present moment and non-judgmentally." Jon Kabat-Zinn brought this definition and mindfulness into the secular realm in 1979 through an eight-week mindfulness-based stress reduction course. Research in this field continues to grow and has found this practice of paying attention and being aware can reduce rumination, reduce stress, boost working memory and focus, reduce emotional reactivity, and increase cognitive flexibility. Surprisingly, academic and research journals dedicated to this idea are limited. However, there are a growing number of online and print well-being magazines that include some mindfulness practices and ideas that libraries should consider.

In this subject area we need to realize that mindfulness has its roots in Buddhism as part of the Noble Eightfold Path. It is part of a practice to allow insight to arise and brings an end to suffering/dissatisfaction in daily life. Thus the magazines in this section range from general well-being to Buddhist periodicals.

There are magazines and websites that have a general well-being focus, but include mindfulness in their values and principles. *Mindful* and *Breathe: and make time for yourself,* from the United States, and *Teen Breathe,* out of the United Kingdom, have print magazines that fit this category. *In the Moment, Project Calm,* and *Flow* are other European mindful/well-being magazines that are expensive and subscriptions are more difficult to obtain, but libraries with very large budgets might consider adding them to their collections. *The Mindful Word* and *Greater Good* provide much web-only content on mindfulness along with other ways to improve life.

Research on the topic of mindfulness is evolving and relatively new. Journals such as *Mindfulness* and *Contemporary Buddhism* are publishing articles in this emerging field. *Mindfulness and Performance* is a new open-access journal for academic libraries with performing arts programs.

Those wishing to explore the Buddhist practice of mindfulness should focus on periodicals such as *The Mindfulness Bell, Tricycle, Lion's Roar,* and *Mountain Record.*

A few Buddhist online periodicals that publish content sporadically that librarians should keep in mind are, *The Joy of Living Magazine, New Chan Forum, Primary Point* (Kwan Um School of Zen), and *Turning Wheel Media* (Buddhist Peace Fellowship).

Basic Periodicals

Ga: *Mindful*; Ac: *Contemporary Buddhism, Mindfulness.*

Basic Abstracts and Indexes

ABI/INFORM, Academic OneFile, Academic Search Complete, PsycINFO, Web of Science.

3689. *Breathe: and make time for yourself.* [ISSN: 2397-9747] 2016. bi-m. EUR 35.94 domestic; EUR 50.32 foreign. G M C Publications Ltd., 86 High St, Lewes, BN71XN, United Kingdom; mags@thegmcgroup.com; http://www.thegmcgroup.com/. *Aud.:* Ga.

Breathe is a bimonthly magazine, out of the United Kingdom that focuses on readers' well-being. Each full color, 120-page issue includes five sections: well-being, living, mindfulness, creativity, and escaping. The issues include articles on mental health and well-being with a focus toward mindfulness, as well as art and craft projects, food and drink recipes, and travel tips. This magazine will appeal to a general audience interested in projects and information to bring a sense of calm and relaxation to their lives. Many past articles are also available on their website. Recommended for public libraries. URL: https://breathemagazine.com

3690. *Contemporary Buddhism: an interdisciplinary journal.* [ISSN: 1463-9947] 2000. s-a. GBP 312 (print & online eds.)). Ed(s): Kate Crosby, Andrew Skilton. Routledge, 4 Park Sq, Milton Park, Abingdon, OX14 4RN, United Kingdom; subscriptions@tandf.co.uk; http://www.tandfonline.com. Adv. Refereed. Reprint: PSC. *Indexed:* A01, A22, E01, R&TA. *Aud.:* Ac.

Contemporary Buddhism is an international, peer-reviewed journal that "publishes articles on the current state and influence of Buddhism." The journal should appeal to scholars in many disciplines, ranging from psychologists to teachers. Recent articles include, "Awareness Versus Un-Clinging: Which Matters in Mindfulness?," "Counselor Self-care and Mindfulness," and "Spacious Awareness in Mahayana Buddhism and Its Role in the Modern Mindfulness Movement." Recommended for academic libraries. URL: http://www.tandfonline.com/loi/rcbh20

3691. *Greater Good: magazine of the center for the development of peace and well-being.* [ISSN: 1553-3239] 2004. s-a. Free. Ed(s): Jason Marsh, Dacher Keltner. Greater Good Science Center, 2425 Atherton St. #6070, UCB, Berkeley, CA 94720-6070; greater@berkeley.edu; http://www.greatergoodscience.org/. *Aud.:* Ga, Ac.

Greater Good magazine "turns scientific research into stories, tips, and tools for a happier life and a more compassionate society." This online-only magazine provides content on a range of topics, such as education, mind and body, parenting and relationships, workplace, and more. The content should appeal to a general audience as well as scholars who are looking for ways to improve their lives. The website can be searched to find mindfulness content. URL: https://greatergood.berkeley.edu/

Lion's Roar. See Religion section.

3692. *Mindful: healthy mind, healthy life.* [ISSN: 2169-5733] 2013. bi-m. USD 24; USD 29 combined subscription print & online eds. Ed(s): Barry Boyce. Foundation for a Mindful Society, 228 Park Ave South #91043, New York, NY 10003-1502; http://www.mindful.org/. Adv. *Aud.:* Ga, Ac.

Mindful, published six times a year, in full color, by the Foundation for a Mindful Society, "celebrates mindfulness, awareness, and compassion in all aspects of life." Recent articles include "Optimism in Action: How to be Positive and Still Keep it Real," "Mindfulness Made Simple," and "Can Meditation Change Your Brain?" The website also includes information to help readers start a mindfulness practice, with articles on living mindfully, the connection between mind and body, meditation practice, and mindfulness at work. Essential for public and academic libraries that want to introduce their communities to mindfulness. URL: https://www.mindful.org/magazine/

3693. *The Mindful Word.* 2007. . Free. The Mindful Word, contact@themindfulword.org contact@themindfulword.org; https://www.themindfulword.org. *Aud.:* Ga.

Volunteer writers for *The Mindful Word* contribute "articles on a range of engaged living topics, such as mindfulness, personal growth, voluntary simplicity, wholistic health and community building." This volunteer collective started in 2007 to create a print magazine and website. It is completely digital now. The content should appeal to a general audience that is new to mindfulness and interested in ways to integrate mindfulness into their lives. Readers can sign up for the newsletter to receive articles as they are published, or recent articles can be accessed on the website. URL: https://www.themindfulword.org/

3694. ***Mindfulness.*** [ISSN: 1868-8527] 2010. 4x/yr. EUR 961 (print & online eds.)). Ed(s): Nirbhay Singh. Springer New York LLC, 233 Spring St, New York, NY 10013; customerservice@springer.com; http://www.springer.com. Refereed. Reprint: PSC. *Indexed:* BRI. *Aud.:* Ac.

Mindfulness is an interdisciplinary journal that publishes peer-reviewed papers on the "latest research findings and best practices in mindfulness." And "it explores the nature and foundations of mindfulness, its mechanisms of actions, and its use across cultures." This journal provides information on the mindful provision of services, aimed at clinicians, teachers, parents, and industry personnel. Recent articles include "Leader Mindfulness and Employee Well-Being: The Mediating Role of Transformational Leadership," "Building Blocks of Emotional Flexibility: Trait Mindfulness and Self-Compassion Are Associated with Positive and Negative Mood Shifts," and within the "Mindfulness in Practice" section "Working with People in Prison." Essential for all academic libraries with psychology programs. URL: https://link.springer.com/journal/12671

3695. ***The Mindfulness Bell.*** 1990. 3x/yr. USD 30; USD 40 combined subscription print & online eds. Unified Buddhist Church, PO Box 38325, Charlotte, NC 28278; http://www.mindfulnessbell.org/. Adv. *Aud.:* Ga, Ac.

The Mindfulness Bell is a Buddhist magazine aimed at those who wish to practice mindfulness in their daily lives. Each of the three black-and-white and approximately 50-page issues contains a teaching from Vietnamese Zen Master Thich Nhat Hahn. Also included are teachings, advice, and stories that "emphasize simple and successful ways to transform the difficulties and limitations in our lives." The website includes an archive of some of the past issues, as well as a mindfulness section with articles providing information on meditation, mindful eating, and being mindful online. Recommended for public and academic libraries that serve mindfulness practitioners. URL: https://www.mindfulnessbell.org

Mountain Record. See Religion section.

3696. ***Teen Breathe.*** [ISSN: 2514-930X] 2017. bi-m. EUR 23.94 domestic; EUR 33.52 foreign. G M C Publications Ltd., 86 High St, Lewes, BN71XN, United Kingdom; mags@thegmcgroup.com; http://www.thegmcgroup.com/. *Aud.:* Hs.

Teen Breathe is a bimonthly magazine, out of the United Kingdom, that focuses on teenage girls' well-being. Each full-color, 64-page issue inspires teens to be inspired, be brave, be kind, and be yourself. The issues include self-help articles with a subtle nod toward mindfulness, as well as creative projects, and eating tips and recipes. This magazine will appeal to girls interested in ways to boost self-esteem. As this magazine comes out of Great Britain, readers will need to adjust to some of the British English words and slang. Recommended for high school libraries that have a budget for self-help magazines. URL: https://www.teenbreathe.co.uk/

Tricycle. See Religion section.

■ MODEL MAKING

General/Model Railroads/Model Aircraft/Model Automobiles

Jennifer Fairall, Coordinator of Cataloging & Metadata Services, Siena College, Standish Library, 515 Loudon Rd., Loudonville, NY 12211; jfairall@siena.edu

Introduction

Model making as a hobby involves the creation of models from kits or from materials and components acquired by the builder. Model making encompasses a wide range of subjects in a variety of different genres, formats, specialties, and skill levels. There are specialty magazines devoted to the construction of model railroads, model aircraft, model automobiles, and model ships.

Models may be static or operational, simple or highly detailed, large or small. Some hobbyists create realistic commercial replicas, carrying military or historical themes, while others create models of ships and vehicles from science fiction or fantasy worlds. Models are made of various materials, including wood, plastic, carbon fiber, resin, and metal.

In general, this section focuses on the building and collecting of models, with helpful tips and best practices for varying skill levels. Collecting of antique and modern dolls, miniatures, figurines, and toys will not be covered in this section, as those activities fall outside its scope.

This section is not intended to be an exhaustive or comprehensive list of all the periodicals that touch on modeling as a hobby. Instead, it focuses on purchase recommendations for library collections, taking into account such factors as usefulness, readability, affordable pricing, electronic availability, and popularity. Most of the magazines listed here are aimed at an adult audience, and are also suitable for young adults. These publications were selected as a representative cross-section of the best of what is commercially available and appealing to a diverse audience of varying skill levels.

Basic Periodicals

Ga: *FineScale Modeler, Model Railroader, Model Airplane News, Scale Auto.*

Basic Abstracts and Indexes

Readers' Guide to Periodical Literature.

General

3697. ***FineScale Modeler.*** [ISSN: 0277-979X] 1981. 10x/yr. USD 39.95 domestic; USD 47.95 Canada; USD 51.95 elsewhere. Ed(s): Mark Savage. Kalmbach Publishing Co., 21027 Crossroads Circle, PO Box 1612, Waukesha, WI 53187; customerservice@kalmbach.com; http://www.kalmbach.com. Illus., index, adv. Sample. Vol. ends: Dec. *Indexed:* BRI. *Aud.:* Hs, Ga.

FineScale Modeler, or *FSM,* targets the serious model builder and is the best-known of the plastic scale modeling magazines. All types of plastic scale models are included, such as planes, armored vehicles, ships, figures, automobiles, sci-fi spaceships, and real space vehicles, with a focus on historically accurate models. Each issue features how-to articles on model assembly and finishing techniques submitted by experts, as well as reader-submitted photos and tips. Extensive product reviews and directories are also provided. The annual "Great Scale Modeling" issue features a selection of the world's best models from various shows. URL: www.finescale.com

Model Railroads

3698. ***Great Model Railroads.*** [ISSN: 1048-8685] 1991. a. USD 9.99 domestic; USD 11.99 foreign. Kalmbach Publishing Co., 21027 Crossroads Circle, PO Box 1612, Waukesha, WI 53187; customerservice@kalmbach.com; http://www.kalmbach.com. *Aud.:* Hs, Ga.

Great Model Railroads is an annual publication from the publishers of *Model Railroader* that concentrates on model railroad layouts. It offers step-by-step instructions, photographs, insights, track plans, and practical advice. Prior issues are available for purchase on the publisher's web site. URL: www.mrr.trains.com

3699. ***Model Railroad Hobbyist Magazine.*** [ISSN: 2152-7423] 2009. m. Free. Ed(s): Joe D Fugate. Model Railroad Hobbyist, 515 Willow Ave, Woodburn, OR 97071. Illus., index, adv. *Aud.:* Hs, Ga.

Model Railroad Hobbyist Magazine is a free online digital publication. It is available in pdf and other formats for viewing on electronic devices and is interactive with links to videos and other online content. The publication is monthly, and the content is extensive. It features clickable indexes for both advertisements and topics covered in the issue. Articles focus on realistic train, track, and landscape layouts and design, featuring color photographs and highly detailed illustrations. This online publication provides very practical tips for model railroad hobbyists. URL: http://model-railroad-hobbyist.com

3700. ***Model Railroader.*** [ISSN: 0026-7341] 1934. m. USD 42.95 domestic; USD 55.95 Canada; USD 62.95 elsewhere. Ed(s): Neil Besougloff. Kalmbach Publishing Co., 21027 Crossroads Circle, PO Box 1612, Waukesha, WI 53187; customerservice@kalmbach.com; http://www.kalmbach.com. Illus., index, adv. Sample. Vol. ends: Dec. *Indexed:* A22, BRI, C37, CBRI, MASUSE. *Bk. rev.:* 100-400 words. *Aud.:* Hs, Ga.

Model Railroader boasts the highest circulation among model railroad enthusiast magazines. The focus is on creating realistic railroad layouts for operating model trains. Regular columns include industry news, event coverage, step-by-step projects, and expert advice. Articles feature special projects, complete with instructions. This attractive, full-color publication includes an advertising index and a directory of retailers by state, as well as buyers' guides and product reviews. *MR* appeals to a general audience of enthusiasts regardless of skill level. URL: www.modelrailroader.com

3701. ***N M R A Magazine.*** Former titles (until 2010): *Scale Rails;* (until 2003): *National Model Railroad Association. Bulletin.* [ISSN: 2156-5120] 1935. m. Free to members; Non-members, USD 22. Ed(s): Stephen M Priest. National Model Railroad Association, Inc, PO Box 1328, Soddy Daisy, TN 37384; http://www.nmra.org. Illus., adv. Microform: PQC. *Indexed:* A22. *Aud.:* Hs, Ga.

NMRA Magazine (formerly *Scale Rails*) is the official monthly publication of the National Model Railroad Association. The issues include full-color photographs of model railroads and tips for model building, model upgrading, kit busting, scratchbuilding, and other interests of the membership. Written submissions, photographs, and drawings of layout designs from readers are highly encouraged and welcomed. URL: www.nmra.org/nmra-magazine

3702. ***Railroad Model Craftsman.*** Former titles (19??): *Model Railroad Craftsman;* (until 1949): *Model Craftsman.* [ISSN: 0033-877X] 1933. m. USD 47.95 combined subscription domestic (print & online eds.); USD 60 combined subscription Canada (print & online eds.); USD 68 combined subscription elsewhere (print & online eds.)). Ed(s): Stephen Priest. White River Productions, PO Box 48, Bucklin, MO 64631; info@whiteriverproductions.com; http://whiteriverproductions.com. Illus., index, adv. Sample. Vol. ends: May. *Bk. rev.:* 100-400 words. *Aud.:* Hs, Ga.

Railroad Model Craftsman is a leading magazine in the railroad hobby industry geared toward a more advanced skill level than *Model Railroader. RMC* features high-quality articles, photographs, prototype drawings, and critical product reviews, as well as reviews of new books and DVDs on the topic of model railroading. This full-color, glossy magazine includes outstanding projects, how-to articles, and an events calendar. URL: www.rrmodelcraftsman.com

Model Aircraft

3703. ***Electric Flight.*** Formerly (until 2011): *Backyard Flyer.* [ISSN: 2159-0672] 2001. bi-m. USD 19.95 combined subscription domestic (print & online eds.); USD 25.95 combined subscription Canada (print & online eds.); USD 31.95 combined subscription elsewhere (print & online eds.)). Ed(s): Debra Cleghorn. Air Age Media, 88 Danbury Rd, Rte 7, Wilton, CT 06897; sales@airage.com; http://www.airage.com. Illus. *Indexed:* MASUSE. *Aud.:* Ems, Hs, Ga.

Electric Flight covers new developments and product innovations in electric aircraft: radio-control planes, helicopters, jets, and associated accessories. Small-electric and park-flyer technology has made RC more accessible to hobbyists, and *Electric Flight* is appropriate for beginners as well as enthusiasts. The magazine includes tips for proper plane assembly, first-flight success, and troubleshooting. Articles feature product reviews and a buyers' guide to the best ready-to-fly aircraft. URL: www.modelairplanenews.com

3704. ***Model Airplane News.*** Former titles (until 1935): *Universal Model Airplane News;* (until 1932): *Model Airplane News and Junior Mechanics; Junior Mechanics and Model Airplane News; Model Airplane News.* [ISSN: 0026-7295] 1929. m. USD 24.95 combined subscription domestic (print & online eds.); USD 36.95 combined subscription Canada (print & online eds.); USD 48.95 combined subscription elsewhere (print & online eds.)). Ed(s): Debra Cleghorn. Air Age Media, 88 Danbury Rd, Rte 7, Wilton, CT 06897; sales@airage.com; http://www.airage.com. Illus., adv. Sample. Circ: 61552 Paid. Vol. ends: Dec. Microform: PQC. *Indexed:* A22, BRI, C37, MASUSE. *Aud.:* Hs, Ga.

Model Airplane News is a popular magazine dedicated to the building and flying of radio-control airplanes. Regular content focuses on the construction of planes and engines, flight tests, product reviews, project descriptions, and tips and advice for beginners. Monthly issues feature various themes such as model helicopters or jets. This attractive, full-color title is the model-airplane magazine of choice for most public libraries. URL: www.modelairplanenews.com

3705. ***Model Aviation.*** Incorporates (in 1937): *Air Youth Horizons.* [ISSN: 0744-5059] 1975. m. USD 16 (Individuals, USD 36; Free to members). Ed(s): Jay Smith. Academy of Model Aeronautics, 5161 E Memorial Dr, Muncie, IN 47302; http://www.modelaircraft.org/Intro.htm. Illus., index, adv. Vol. ends: Dec. *Aud.:* Ga, Sa.

Model Aviation, the official publication of the Academy of Model Aeronautics (AMA), covers the whole arena of model aeronautics: control line, free flight, and radio control. Appearing in each highly structured issue are regular columns including "how-to" articles, plans builds, product reviews, AMA news, features, and event coverage relating to aeromodeling. Content includes articles on model airplane construction, reports from national and regional offices, and an extensive calendar of events. This publication not only supports its membership, but is also highly regarded in the model aviation field. URL: www.modelaviation.com

3706. ***Rotor Drone Pro.*** Formerly (until 2019): *Rotor Drone.* 2014. bi-m. Individuals, USD 19.95 (print & online eds.)). Ed(s): Debra Cleghorn. Air Age Media, 88 Danbury Rd, Rte 7, Wilton, CT 06897; sales@airage.com; http://www.airage.com. *Aud.:* Hs, Ga.

Rotor Drone captures the explosive growth of unmanned aerial vehicles (UAVs), quadcopters, and multirotor drones. This title covers ready-to-fly models and also includes modification tips. It contains relevant information on upcoming products, and new regulations relating to drones. Appearing in each full-color issue are "Features," "Air Support," and "Expert Tech." Appropriate for experienced pilots as well those just thinking about getting into the hobby. URL: http://rotordronemag.com

Model Automobiles

3707. ***Model Cars Magazine.*** Formerly (until 1998): *Plastic Fanatic.* [ISSN: 1527-4608] 1985. bi-m. USD 23 domestic; USD 45 foreign. Model Cars Magazine, 89530, Honolulu, HI 96830; http://www.modelcarsmag.com/. Illus., adv. *Bk. rev.:* Number and length vary. *Aud.:* Hs, Ga, Sa.

Model Cars Magazine is dedicated to the building and customizing of static scale models of automobiles from kits. Tips on scratchbuilding and scratchbashing (combining scratchbuilding and kit parts) are also provided. Issues feature reviews of kits and new products. How-to articles are clearly illustrated with step-by-step color photographs. Regular columns also cover resin, model trucks, coming events, and a collector's showcase. URL: www.modelcarsmag.com/

3708. ***Scale Auto.*** Formerly (until 2002): *Scale Auto Enthusiast.* [ISSN: 1550-5251] 1979. bi-m. USD 29.95 domestic; USD 36.95 foreign; USD 35.95 combined subscription domestic. Ed(s): Mark Savage, Jim Haught. Kalmbach Publishing Co., 21027 Crossroads Circle, PO Box 1612, Waukesha, WI 53187; customerservice@kalmbach.com; http://www.kalmbach.com. Illus., adv. Sample. Vol. ends: Apr. *Aud.:* Hs, Ga.

Scale Auto is the leading publication on building and collecting static (non-operating) automotive models, including classic muscle cars, modern stock cars, street rods, customs, tuners, trucks, and more. Regular columns highlight industry news and product and kit reviews, as well as coverage of events. Articles feature readers' outstanding projects, including kit construction, super-detailing, modification, and painting, complete with full-color photographs. If a library can afford only one automotive modeling magazine, this is the one to buy. URL: www.scaleautomag.com

■ MULTICULTURAL STUDIES

Jessica Zieman, Social Sciences Librarian, Morris Library, Southern Illinois University–Carbondale, Carbondale, IL 62901; jessica.zieman@lib.siu.edu

Introduction

There are countless journals devoted to the study of a particular ethnic or religious group, but most multicultural journals seek to broadly examine issues that affect minority peoples around the world. The vast majority of journals in this section are multi- or interdisciplinary, and examine issues of ethnicity, race, and culture from a variety of academic perspectives and frameworks. Most focus on social and political topics, but many also delve into explorations of the music, art, film, and literature of minority, indigenous, or ethnic groups. As the world continues to globalize at a rapid rate, many of the titles in this list emphasize immigration, migration, and related topics.

This section contains scholarly journals, yearbooks, and trade journals. Additional related journals can be found in the "African American," "Asian American," "Native Americans," and "Latino Studies" sections. When purchasing periodicals, public, research, and academic libraries must consider the needs and interests of their own constituency when faced with ever-shrinking budgets. Many of the titles in this section may be a good choice for many institutions because of their multidisciplinary focus.

Basic Periodicals

Ga, Ac: *Annual Editions: Race & Ethnic Relations;* Ac: *Multicultural Education.*

Basic Abstracts and Indexes

America: History and Life, Ethnic NewsWatch, Historical Abstracts, Humanities International Index, Race Relations Abstracts, Social Sciences Index, Sociological Abstracts, SocINDEX.

3709. ***Afro-Hispanic Review.*** [ISSN: 0278-8969] 1982. s-a. USD 90 (Individuals, USD 50; USD 30 per issue domestic). Ed(s): William Luis. Vanderbilt University, Department of Spanish and Portuguese, The Bishop Joseph Johnson Black Cultural Ctr, Vanderbilt University PMB 351666, Nashville, TN 37235; admin@afrohispanicreview.com; http://www.vanderbilt.edu. Illus., adv. Sample. Refereed. *Indexed:* A01, A22, AmHI, BRI, ENW, MLA-IB. *Bk. rev.:* Number and length vary. *Aud.:* Ga, Ac.

Afro-Hispanic Review was founded in 1982 at Howard University by Ian Smart, Henry Richards, and the late Stanley Cyrus. The journal was founded to explore "the richness of Afro-Hispanic culture, the considerable body of Afro-Hispanic literature, [and] the diverse contributions of Spanish-speaking Blacks to the creation and development of the nations of Latin America and elsewhere." Celebrating its tenth year as a publication of Vanderbilt University, this multilingual, peer-reviewed journal continues to explore the literature, history, and culture of persons of African descent in the Hispanic world. Contents include research articles, signed book and film reviews, interviews, creative works, and translations and the cover contains art that expresses "blackness or representations of blackness." A recent special issue explores Hispaniola, the island containing Haiti and the Dominican Republic. Recommended for academic and research libraries.

3710. ***Annual Editions: Multicultural Education.*** [ISSN: 1092-924X] 1993. a. USD 53.67. Ed(s): Nancy Gallavan. McGraw-Hill, Contemporary Learning Series, 1221 Ave of the Americas, New York, NY 10020; customer.service@mcgraw-hill.com; http://www.mcgraw-hill.com. Illus. *Aud.:* Ga, Ac.

This publication focuses on developments in multicultural education, and provides convenient, inexpensive access to a wide range of accessible, current articles previously published in public press magazines, newspapers, and journals. Most articles from recent years focus on education in the United States. Topics explored in the most recent issue include methods of teaching about Martin Luther King, Jr.; biracial students; immigrant student experiences; and teaching global competence. Articles are divided into thematic units, and each issue also contains a general introduction, an annotated bibliography, a topic guide, an annotated list of Internet sources, and an overview for each unit. Each issue is also accompanied by an online "Instructor's Resource Guide" with testing materials. Highly recommended for academic and research libraries, and for a general audience.

3711. ***Annual Editions: Race & Ethnic Relations.*** [ISSN: 1075-5195] 1991. a. USD 61.33 per issue. Ed(s): John A Kromkowski. McGraw-Hill, Contemporary Learning Series, 1221 Ave of the Americas, New York, NY 10020; customer.service@mcgraw-hill.com; http://www.mhhe.com/cls/index.mhtml. Illus. *Aud.:* Ga, Ac.

Every issue of *Annual Editions: Race & Ethnic Relations* contains an accessible collection of articles that explore race and ethnicity in the United States and elsewhere. Articles are selected from among 300 periodical sources, including magazines, journals, and newspapers, and are divided into thematic units. In addition to articles, each issue includes a general introduction, an annotated bibliography, a topic guide, an annotated list of Internet sources, an overview for each unit, and a topical index. An online "Instructor's Resource Guide" with testing materials also accompanies each issue. Highly recommended for academic and research libraries, as well as for general audiences.

3712. ***E C M I Journal on Ethnopolitics and Minority Issues in Europe.*** [ISSN: 1617-5247] 2001. s-a. Ed(s): Andreea Carstocea. European Centre for Minority Issues, Schiffbruecke 12, Flensburg, 24939, Germany; info@ecmi.de; http://www.ecmi.de. Refereed. Reprint: WSH. *Indexed:* IBSS, P61. *Bk. rev.:* Number and length vary. *Aud.:* Ga, Ac.

The flagship publication of the European Centre for Minority Issues, the *Journal on Ethnopolitics and Minority Issues in Europe* (*JEMIE*) is a multi-disciplinary, open-access journal devoted to comparative analyses of developments in minority-majority relations in Europe. It explores European minority issues including conflict management, minority rights, democratization, ethnopolitics, good governance, and participation, as well as related policies and developments in European institutions and countries. Recent special issues include "Minority Participation in Estonia and Latvia" and "Distribution of Financial Support to Organizations Representing National Minorities." This title contains articles and book reviews, and frequent special issues include substantive introductions. Recommended for academic and research libraries. URL: www.ecmi.de/publications/jemie/

3713. ***Ethnic and Racial Studies.*** [ISSN: 0141-9870] 1978. 14x/yr. GBP 1126 (print & online eds.)). Ed(s): John Solomos, Martin Bulmer. Routledge, 4 Park Sq, Milton Park, Abingdon, OX14 4RN, United Kingdom; subscriptions@tandf.co.uk; http://www.tandfonline.com. Illus., index, adv. Sample. Refereed. Vol. ends: Oct. Reprint: PSC. *Indexed:* A01, A22, A47, BAS, BRI, C42, CBRI, CJPI, Chicano, E01, IBSS, P61, SSA. *Bk. rev.:* Number varies; 500-1,000 words. *Aud.:* Ac.

Ethnic and Racial Studies contains interdisciplinary works on theory and research related to ethnicity, nationalism, and race from emerging theoretical and empirical perspectives. Beginning in 2015, three issues a year have been devoted to reviews of books in English and other languages, conferences reviews, and discussion articles. Several issues a year are devoted to special topics with guest editors. Highly recommended for academic and research libraries. Available both in print and online.

3714. ***Ethnic Studies Review.*** Formed by the merger of (1978-1996): *Explorations in Ethnic Studies;* (1981-1996): *Explorations in Sights and Sounds.* [ISSN: 1555-1881] 1996. s-a. USD 379. Ed(s): Ron Scapp.

University of California Press, Journals Division, 155 Grand Avenue, Ste 400, Oakland, CA 94612-3764; customerservice@ucpressjournals.com; http://www.ucpress.edu. Refereed. *Indexed:* BAS, BRI, Chicano, ENW, MLA-IB. *Bk. rev.:* Number and length vary. *Aud.:* Ac.

Published by the National Association for Ethnic Studies (NAES), this journal provides an international, interdisciplinary perspective on ethnicity, culture, and inter-group relations through articles, essays, research notes, and book reviews. It also seeks to promote activities and scholarship in the field of ethnic studies. Recommended for academic libraries and scholarly research centers.

3715. *Ethnohistory.* [ISSN: 0014-1801] 1954. q. USD 306. Ed(s): John F Schwaller, Robbie L Ethridge. Duke University Press, 905 W Main St, Durham, NC 27701; orders@dukeupress.edu; https://www.dukeupress.edu. Illus., adv. Refereed. Vol. ends: Fall. Reprint: PSC. *Indexed:* A01, A22, A47, AmHI, BAS, BRI, Chicano, E01, IBSS, MLA-IB, P61, SSA. *Bk. rev.:* 10-15, 800-1,200 words. *Aud.:* Ac.

The official publication of the American Society for Ethnohistory, this journal explores "anthropological and historical approaches to the human condition" and seeks to illuminate the identities, organization, and experiences of indigenous, diasporic, and minority peoples throughout the world. Past issues have explored the human condition through the lenses of history, anthropology, geography, literature, and sociology; and there has been focus primarily on indigenous peoples of the Americas. This title includes periodic special issues with guest editors. A recent special issue is entitled "Colonial Mesoamerican Literacy." All issues contain research articles and several signed book reviews, and some issues also include review essays. Available in print and online. Recommended for academic libraries.

3716. *I Z A : Journal of Migration.* [ISSN: 2193-9039] 2012. . Free. Ed(s): Tommaso Colussi, Denis Fougere. SpringerOpen, Tiergartenstr 17, Heidelberg, 69121, Germany; info@springeropen.com; http://www.springeropen.com. *Indexed:* A01, EconLit. *Aud.:* Ac, Sa.

The Institute for the Study of Labor, or IZA, is an independent economic research institute in Germany that studies world labor markets and publishes a suite of economics journals. *IZA: Journal of Migration* focuses on the socioeconomics of migration and ethnicity worldwide, and seeks to foster international debate on migration. Further, it aspires to provide research-based insight to policymakers. Research and theoretical articles explore topics such as immigrants' occupational choices; the assimilation of immigrants' children; and immigrants' social networks. Recently published articles examine the impact of cultural diversity on wages in Australia; the relationship between income, amenities, and attitudes; and increasing emigration in Spain. Available online only.

3717. *Identities: global studies in culture and power.* Formerly (until 1994): *Ethnic Groups;* Incorporates (1970-1975): *Afro-American Studies.* [ISSN: 1070-289X] 1976. bi-m. GBP 515 (print & online eds.)). Ed(s): Claire Alexander. Routledge, 4 Park Sq, Milton Park, Abingdon, OX14 4RN, United Kingdom; subscriptions@tandf.co.uk; http://www.tandfonline.com. Illus., adv. Sample. Refereed. Reprint: PSC. *Indexed:* A01, A22, BRI, C45, E01, IBSS, MLA-IB, P61, SD, SSA. *Bk. rev.:* Number and length vary. *Aud.:* Ac.

Identities is an international and interdisciplinary journal devoted to empirical research on, and critical analyses of, the formation and transformation of "racial, ethnic, national, transnational, and postcolonial identities in the contemporary world." Article authors are established and emerging scholars primarily from U.S. and European institutions. Articles draw on perspectives from anthropology, social psychology, sociology, cultural studies, political science, social policy, and cultural geography. This title includes special issues several times a year; the most recent special issue is entitled "Aesthetics of Arrival: Spectacle, Capital, Novelty in Post-reform India." Recommended for academic libraries. Available both in print and online.

3718. *Journal of American Ethnic History.* [ISSN: 0278-5927] 1981. q. USD 335 (print & online eds.)). Ed(s): SUZANNE M SINKE. University of Illinois Press, 1325 S Oak St, MC-566, Champaign, IL 61820; uipress@uillinois.edu; http://www.press.uillinois.edu. Illus., index, adv. Sample. Refereed. Vol. ends: Summer (No. 4). Microform: PQC. *Indexed:* A01, A22, AmHI, BAS, BRI, Chicano, E01, P61, SSA. *Bk. rev.:* Number and length vary. *Aud.:* Ac, Sa.

The official publication of the Immigration & Ethnic History Society, this journal examines American immigration, past and present; race; and ethnicity. The editors encourage submissions on the processes of migration, adjustment and assimilation, group relations, mobility, politics, culture, and group identity. Each issue includes articles, review essays, book reviews, and short biographical essays about the contributors. Select issue also contain scholarly forums; "Research Comments," which are short essays on key issues in the field, guides to further research, or important historical items to stimulate further conversation and research; and "Teaching and Outreach" essays that describe innovative teaching methods or outreach efforts. Highly recommended for academic and research libraries. Available both in print and online.

3719. *Journal of Ethnic and Migration Studies.* Former titles (until 1998): *New Community;* (until 1971): *Community.* [ISSN: 1369-183X] 1970. 12x/yr. GBP 2515 (print & online eds.)). Ed(s): Jenny Money, Paul Statham. Routledge, 4 Park Sq, Milton Park, Abingdon, OX14 4RN, United Kingdom; subscriptions@tandf.co.uk; http://www.tandfonline.com. Adv. Sample. Refereed. Reprint: PSC. *Indexed:* A01, A22, AmHI, BRI, E01, IBSS, P61, SSA. *Bk. rev.:* Number and length vary. *Aud.:* Ac.

The fully refereed *Journal of Ethnic and Migration Studies,* or *JEMS,* publishes 15 issues a year, featuring articles on migration and its effects around the world. Related topics, including ethnic conflict, discrimination and racism, nationalism, policy, and citizenship, are also explored; and the journal puts a particular emphasis on comparative analyses. Recent special issues include "Regulation of Speech in Multicultural Societies" and "International Organisations and the Politics of Migration." Previous issues included several signed book reviews each, but with a recent change in editorship, future issues will contain multiple short pieces that examine fewer books. Highly recommended for research and academic libraries. Available both in print and online.

3720. *Journal of Intercultural Studies.* Formerly (until 1980): *Ethnic Studies.* [ISSN: 0725-6868] 1977. bi-m. GBP 1243 (print & online eds.)). Ed(s): Vince Marotta, Fethi Mansouri. Routledge, Level 2, 11 Queens Rd, Melbourne, VIC 3004, Australia; books@tandf.com.au; http://www.routledge.com. Illus., adv. Sample. Refereed. Reprint: PSC. *Indexed:* A01, A22, BRI, E01, IBSS, MLA-IB, P61, SSA. *Bk. rev.:* Number and length vary. *Aud.:* Ac.

This journal is sponsored by the Centre for Citizenship and Globalisation at Deakin University, and it addresses "emerging cultural formations, intercultural negotiations, and contemporary challenges to cultures and identities" around the world. Interdisciplinary and with international contributors, the journal encourages innovative examination of topics such as nationhood, citizenship, diaspora, post-colonialism, cross-cultural knowledge, and more. It includes articles, review essays, and book reviews. Recent special issues include "End-of-Life Care and Rituals in Contexts of Post-Migration Diversity in Europe" (volume 37, issue 2, 2016) and "National Identity in an Age of Migration: The US Experience" (volume 36, issue 5, 2015), and these include substantive introductions. General issues often contain reports of studies on particular topics-for instance, "Studies in Mixed Marriages and Migration"-or commentary. Highly recommended for academic libraries. Available both in print and online.

3721. *Migration News.* [ISSN: 1081-9908] 1994. q. University of California, Davis, Department of Agricultural Economics, One Shields Ave, Davis, CA 95616; http://migration.ucdavis.edu. Illus. *Aud.:* Ga, Ac.

Migration News is produced with the support of the German Marshall Fund of the United States and the University of California-Berkeley Center for German and European Studies, and it summarizes and examines immigration and integration developments from the preceding quarter. Articles are grouped into four geographic regions: "The Americas," "Europe," "Asia," and "Other." This title is recommended for academic and public libraries. It is available in print, online, and as an e-mail subscription; the version available both online and via e-mail is significantly longer. Recommended for academic and public libraries. URL: http://migration.ucdavis.edu

3722. *Multicultural Education.* [ISSN: 1068-3844] 1993. q. USD 100 (Individuals, USD 50). Ed(s): Heather L Hazuka, Alan H Jones. Caddo Gap Press, 3145 Geary Blvd, PMB 275, San Francisco, CA 94118; info@caddogap.com; http://www.caddogap.com. Illus. *Indexed:* BRI, C42, ERIC. *Bk. rev.:* Number and length vary. *Aud.:* Hs, Ac.

Published quarterly, by the progressive education publishers Caddo Gap Press, this journal focuses on advances and new perspectives in the field of multicultural education. Authors include scholars and practitioners at all levels. Contents include feature articles; research articles; promising practices; opinion pieces; book and other educational material reviews; and news and announcements related to multicultural education. Recent issues contain works on preparing teachers for urban indigenous communities, and the diversity of authors in the first-grade core reading series, among other topics. Recommended for school and academic libraries.

Multicultural Perspectives. See Education/General, K-12 section.

3723. *Patterns of Prejudice.* [ISSN: 0031-322X] 1967. 5x/yr. GBP 999 (print & online eds.)). Ed(s): David Cesarani, Dan Stone. Routledge, 4 Park Sq, Milton Park, Abingdon, OX14 4RN, United Kingdom; subscriptions@tandf.co.uk; http://www.tandfonline.com. Adv. Sample. Refereed. Microform: PQC. Reprint: PSC. *Indexed:* A01, A22, E01, IBSS, P61, SSA. *Bk. rev.:* Number and length vary. *Aud.:* Ac, Sa.

Published five times a year, this peer-reviewed journal examines the historical roots and contemporary varieties of social exclusion, race, ethnicity, and ethnic conflicts. Articles explore topics such as race and capitalism, the history of anti-Semitism, and identities. While maintaining a global perspective, articles focus primarily on the history of intolerance and chauvinism in the United States and Europe. One or two special issues are published each year. Recommended for academic and research libraries. Available both in print and online.

■ MUSIC

General/Popular

See also Music Reviews section.

Sheridan (Sheri) Stormes, Performing and Fine Arts Librarian, Butler University, 4600 Sunset Ave., Indianapolis, IN 46208; sstormes@butler.edu (General subsection)

Bill Lamb, About.com, Top40/Pop; http://top40.about.com (Popular subsection)

Introduction

Libraries serving music patrons in today's technology-driven society are under growing pressure to provide resources in digital formats. Users place an increasingly high premium on convenience, ease-of-use, and accessibility. Under the circumstances, it would seem more practical to recommend core databases that provide online access to full-text music journals rather than to try to identify and recommend individual titles. However, these databases often come with moderate to high subscription fees. Since the intended audience of *Magazines for Libraries* is small- to medium-sized libraries whose budgets may not allow them to purchase all the recommended databases, the list of recommended music journals that follows has been chosen to assist these libraries in making conscientious (if also difficult) choices among databases and individual journal subscriptions.

Because of the daunting number of quality publications related to classical music available, the list suggested here is not intended to be comprehensive, neither is it designed for use by research libraries or doctorate-granting institutions. Rather, it has been created as a representative core list for school music programs, public library patrons, small- to medium-sized academic music programs (including those offering Master's level curricula), and adult music practitioners. It is not expected that any one institution will necessarily provide access to all of these titles, but libraries are encouraged to make available a reasonable number of the titles recommended for their specific type of library, bearing in mind the particular needs of the clientele they serve.

The contributor has applied several parameters in determining the selection of these titles. All have been judged to be of high quality, reliable frequency, and affordable cost. While some trade journals are included, most of the recommended titles are of a scholarly nature and are included in major music indexing sources. The titles principally address the fields of music history, music theory and composition, music education, and/or applied music. Academic titles serving more limited, specialized audiences, such as *Fontes Artis Musicae* and *Acta Musicologica* are not included.

It should be noted that while representative titles serving vocal study and some more widely studied instruments are included, it is assumed that students majoring in music study at the collegiate level and professional musicians will maintain personal subscriptions to key titles related to their specific instruments. Therefore, respected journals such as *The Horn Call, The Double Reed, ITG* (International Trumpet Guild) *Journal,* and *Saxophone Symposium* among others, have not been included in this list.

Due to increasing emphasis on open educational resources in academia, a deliberate attempt has been made to include some online, open-access titles of quality. Users are cautioned that there continue to be some concerns with these publications (e.g., bad links, security risk messages on certain browsers, and irregularities either with frequency of publication or content itself). Finally, due to a growing interest in interdisciplinary studies and social justice issues involving music, a representative group of titles supporting such studies also appears.

Recognizing the previously mentioned patron preference for online access as well as the space constraints of libraries, institutions serving music patrons are strongly encouraged to subscribe to the following databases that provide excellent full-text coverage as well as indexing of core music magazines and journals: *Academic Search Premier, JSTOR* (especially "Arts & Sciences III Collection"), *Project MUSE,* and *Music Periodicals Database* (ProQuest).

Basic Periodicals

GENERAL. Hs: *American Music Teacher, Choral Journal, Instrumentalist, Music Educators Journal;* Ga: *American Music, Ethnomusicology, The Musical Quarterly, Opera News;* Ac: *American Musicological Society. Journal, Music Theory Spectrum, Journal of Research in Music Education.*

POPULAR. Hs, Ga, Ac: *Rolling Stone.*

Basic Abstracts and Indexes

Music Periodicals Database, Music Index, RILM Abstracts of Music Literature.

General

Libraries serving music patrons in today's technology-driven society are under growing pressure to provide resources in digital formats. Users place an increasingly high premium on convenience, ease-of-use, and accessibility. Under the circumstances, it would seem more practical to recommend core databases that provide online access to full-text music journals rather than to try to identify and recommend individual titles. However, these databases often come with moderate to high subscription fees. Since the intended audience of *Magazines for Libraries* is small- to medium-sized libraries whose budgets may not allow them to purchase all the recommended databases, the list of recommended music journals that follows has been chosen to assist them in making conscientious (if also difficult) choices among databases and individual journal subscriptions.

Because of the availability of a large number of quality publications related to classical music, the list suggested here is neither intended to be comprehensive, nor is it designed for use by research libraries or doctorate-granting institutions. Rather, this chapter presents a representative core list for school music programs, public library patrons, small- to medium-sized academic music programs (including those offering Master's level curricula), and adult music practitioners. No one institution will necessarily provide access to all of these titles, but libraries should make available a reasonable number of the recommended titles for their specific type of library, bearing in mind the particular needs of the clientele they serve.

This contributor has applied several parameters in determining the selection of these titles, all of which have been judged to be of high quality, having a (reasonably) regular publication schedule and affordable cost. While some trade journals are included, most of the recommended titles are of a scholarly nature and are included in major music indexing sources. The titles principally address the fields of music history, music theory and composition, music education, and/ or applied music. Academic titles serving more limited, specialized audiences are not included. While representative titles serving vocal study and more widely studied instruments are included, the author presumes students majoring in music at the collegiate level and professional musicians will maintain personal subscriptions to key titles related to their specific instruments. Therefore, respected journals such as *The Horn Call, The Double Reed, ITG* (International Trumpet Guild) *Journal,* and *Saxophone Symposium* among others, do not appear on this list.

Due to increasing emphasis on open educational resources in academia, some high quality online open-access titles are included. The reader should be aware that there continue to be some concerns with these publications (e.g., bad links, security risk messages on certain browsers, and irregularities either with frequency of publication or content itself). Finally, due to a growing interest in interdisciplinary studies and social justice issues involving music, a representative group of titles supporting such studies also appears.

Recognizing the earlier-mentioned preferences for online access as well as the space constraints of many libraries, institutions serving music patrons are strongly encouraged to subscribe to the following databases which provide excellent full-text coverage as well as indexing of core music magazines and journals: *Academic Search Premier, JSTOR* (especially "Arts & Sciences III Collection"), *Project MUSE,* and *Music Periodicals Database* (ProQuest).

3724. *19th Century Music.* [ISSN: 0148-2076] 1977. 3x/yr. USD 347 (print & online eds.)). Ed(s): Lawrence Kramer. University of California Press, Journals Division, 155 Grand Avenue, Ste 400, Oakland, CA 94612-3764; http://www.ucpress.edu/journals.php. Illus., index, adv. Refereed. Vol. ends: Spring. *Indexed:* A01, A22, AmHI, BRI, E01, IIMP, MLA-IB, RILM. *Bk. rev.:* 1, 4,000 words, signed. *Aud.:* Ac, Sa.

19th Century Music seeks to publish "far-reaching investigations at the leading edge of musical and multidisciplinary scholarship" on all aspects of western art music created and produced from approximately 1780 to 1930. Topics of articles published in this journal include, but are not limited to, composers and their compositional styles, specific compositions, performances, historical watersheds, cultural developments that either affected or were affected by nineteenth-century music, analyses, aesthetics, and musical institutions. Articles published are substantial (often in excess of 15 pages) and written principally by academicians. Published in print and electronic formats. Recommended for academic libraries. URL: http://ncm.ucpress.edu/

3725. *Acta Musicologica.* Formerly (until 1931): *Internationale Gesellschaft fuer Musikwissenschaft. Mitteilungen.* [ISSN: 0001-6241] 1928. 2x/yr. EUR 98; EUR 48.95 newsstand/cover. Ed(s): Philip V Bohlman, Federico Celestini. Baerenreiter Verlag, Heinrich-Schuetz-Allee 35, Kassel, 34131, Germany; order@baerenreiter.com; http://www.baerenreiter.com. Illus., index. Refereed. Vol. ends: Dec. *Indexed:* A22, IIMP, MLA-IB, RILM. *Aud.:* Ac.

The official journal of the International Musicological Society (IMS), *Acta Musicologica* contains articles reflecting important musicological research of worldwide interest. The journal is published semiannually. Up to 14 articles appear per year in one of five languages (English, French, German, Italian, and Spanish). The scope of the publication is broad, including various sub-divisions of musicology, ethnomusicology, and inter-disciplinary topics. Biographies of contributors and abstracts of articles including keyword assignations appear at the end of each issue. This journal is committed to open access and offers its authors a green open-access policy. A subscription is included with IMS membership. Nonmember subscriptions are offered. Available in print and digital formats. URL: http://www.acta-musicologica.net/

3726. *American Music.* [ISSN: 0734-4392] 1983. q. USD 157 (print & online eds.)). University of Illinois Press, 1325 S Oak St, MC-566, Champaign, IL 61820; uipress@uillinois.edu; http://www.press.uillinois.edu. Illus., adv. Refereed. Microform: PQC. *Indexed:* A01, A22, AmHI, BRI, CBRI, E01, IIMP, MLA-IB, RILM. *Bk. rev.:* 1-2, 1,000 words, signed. *Aud.:* Ga, Ac, Sa.

Published quarterly, *American Music* is an independent, peer-reviewed journal dedicated to American music both historical and contemporary and including musical practices of North, South, and Central America. Article content ranges from features on individual performers, composers, publishers, work, and collections, to discussions about American musical institutions, events, and the music industry. Genres covered include classical, popular, blues, musical theater, folk, and jazz. Recent issues have included four feature articles plus reviews on books, recordings, and multimedia. Issues devoted to special topics (e.g., "Silent Film Music") appear occasionally. Of interest to both scholars and performers alike, this is a necessary title for academic and public libraries with any focus on American music. Available in both print and online formats. URL: http://www.press.uillinois.edu/journals/am.html

3727. *American Music Teacher.* Former titles (until 1951): *Music Teachers National Association. Bulletin;* (until 1938): *Advisory Council Bulletin.* [ISSN: 0003-0112] 19??. bi-m. USD 36. Music Teachers National Association, 1 W. 4th St., Ste. 1550, Cincinnati, OH 45202; mtnanet@mtna.org; http://www.mtna.org. Illus., adv. Refereed. Vol. ends: Jun/Jul. *Indexed:* A01, A22, BRI, CBRI, IIMP. *Bk. rev.:* 5-7, 500 words, signed. *Aud.:* Ems, Hs, Ga, Ac, Sa.

American Music Teacher is the official publication of the Music Teachers National Association (MTNA). The publication exists "to provide articles, reviews and regular columns that inform, educate and challenge music teachers and foster excellence in the music teaching profession." Each issue includes several feature articles that cover topics related to pedagogy and wellness as well as several regular columns. Also included are shorter articles relaying news about MTNA competitions, conferences, and workshops. In addition, this title provides reviews of books, pedagogical materials, and DVDs as well as advertisements for teaching tools, new repertoire, and relevant publications. Useful to music teachers at all levels, this publication is recommended for school, academic, and large public libraries. Available in both print and online formats. URL: http://www.mtnafoundation.net/publications/american-music-teacher/

3728. *American Musicological Society. Journal.* Former titles (until 1948): *American Musicological Society. Bulletin;* (until 1936): *New York Musicological Society. Bulletin.* [ISSN: 0003-0139] 1931. 3x/yr. USD 247 (print & online eds.)). Ed(s): Kevin C Karnes, Joy H Calico. University of California Press, Journals Division, 155 Grand Avenue, Ste 400, Oakland, CA 94612-3764; http://www.ucpress.edu/journals.php. Illus., index, adv. Refereed. *Indexed:* A01, A22, AmHI, BAS, BRI, E01, IIMP, MLA-IB, RILM. *Bk. rev.:* 3-5, 3,000 words, signed. *Aud.:* Ac, Sa.

The Journal of the American Musicological Society (JAMS) is renowned for its well-documented, refereed articles. *JAMS* makes available "scholarship from a broad array of musical inquiry: from historical musicology, critical theory, music analysis, iconography and organology, to pedagogy, performance practice, aesthetics and hermeneutics, ethnomusicology, gender and sexuality, popular music, and cultural studies." In addition to several extensive articles, each issue includes book reviews and communications. *JAMS* is published three times per year and is available in both print and electronic formats. Highly recommended for academic libraries; necessary for music libraries that support research programs. URL: https://jams.ucpress.edu/

3729. *British Journal of Music Education.* [ISSN: 0265-0517] 1984. 3x/yr. GBP 282 (print & online eds.)). Ed(s): Ally Daubney, Martin Fautley. Cambridge University Press, University Printing House, Shaftesbury Rd, Cambridge, CB2 8BS, United Kingdom; journals@cambridge.org; https://www.cambridge.org/. Adv. Refereed. Circ: 1750. Microform: PQC. Reprint: PSC. *Indexed:* A01, A22, E01, ERIC, IIMP, RILM. *Aud.:* Ems, Hs, Ac, Sa.

Refereed and international in scope, *British Journal of Music Education* (*BJME*) provides insightful articles on topics of interest to music teachers providing musical instruction in virtually all formal and informal contexts, including private lessons, grade school instruction, higher education, and community choral and instrumental organizations. The journal's stated aim is "to strengthen connections between research and practice, so enhancing professional development and improving practice within the field of music education." *BJME* is published three times a year in both print and online formats. Each issue contains several lengthy research articles followed by a number of reviews of resources relating to music teaching. This title is recommended for music teachers at all levels. URL: https://www.cambridge.org/core/journals/british-journal-of-music-education

3730. ***Choral Journal.*** Incorporates (1959-1964): *Texas Choirmaster.* [ISSN: 0009-5028] 1959. m. Except for July. Free to members. Ed(s): Amanda Bumgarner. American Choral Directors Association, 545 Couch Dr, Oklahoma, OK 73102; membership@acda.org; http://acda.org. Illus., index, adv. Refereed. Vol. ends: Jun. Microform: PQC. *Indexed:* A01, A22, IIMP, RILM. *Bk. rev.:* 3-5, 200-500 words, signed. *Aud.:* Hs, Ga, Ac, Sa.

Choral Journal is the refereed international publication of the American Choral Directors Association (ACDA). It is relevant for choral directors and educators who work with singers at any level. In addition to current news about the association and information on the annual ACDA convention, this journal seeks "to provide practical and scholarly information about choral music and its performance." Each issue contains "three scholarly articles, anonymously peer-reviewed by the editorial board; editorials from association leadership and the *Choral Journal* editor; reviews of books, recorded sound, and choral works by choral experts; and columns of practical advice and ideas for choral conductors." It is available in both print and online formats. Recommended for academic, public, and high school libraries. URL: https://acda.org/ACDA/Publications/Choral_Journal/ACDA/Publications-Root/Choral_Journal/Choral_Journal.aspx

3731. ***The Choral Scholar.*** [ISSN: 1948-3058] 2009. s-a. Free. Ed(s): Sean Burton. National Collegiate Choral Organization, c/o Bonnie Borshay Sneed, 100 Campus Dr, Weatherford, OK 73096-3098; the_choral_scholar@ncco-usa.org; http://www.ncco-usa.org. Adv. Refereed. *Indexed:* A01, IIMP, RILM. *Bk. rev.:* Number and length vary. *Aud.:* Ac, Sa.

The Choral Scholar: The Online Journal of the National Collegiate Choral Organization is an anonymously peer-reviewed journal, the primary focus of which is music research relating to choral music. Most contributors are academic music professionals or independent music scholars. However, contributions are welcomed from experts in other fields whose research relates to the study of choral music. Each issue includes several well foot-noted feature articles as well as reviews of books, recordings, and/or musical scores relating to choral music repertoire, composers, and/or performance. Feature articles range from approximately 4,000 to 10,000 words in length and may concern themselves with issues such as choral vocal techniques, analyses and/or histories of specific choral works, and discussions of repertoire considerations. Recommended for academic libraries. URL: https://www.ncco-usa.org/pubs/tcs/

3732. ***Classical Singer.*** Formerly (until 1998): *New York Opera Newsletter.* [ISSN: 1534-276X] 1988. m. 10/yr. USD 58 combined subscription domestic (print & online eds.); USD 78 combined subscription Canada (print & online eds.); USD 88 combined subscription elsewhere (print & online eds.)). Ed(s): Sara Thomas. Classical Singer Corporation, PO Box 1710, Draper, UT 84020; http://www.classicalsinger.com. Adv. *Aud.:* Ac, Sa.

Begun in 1988 as the *New York Opera Newsletter, Classical Singer Magazine* has expanded over the years to include a vast array of information about the opera and singing scene across the nation. Useful to aspiring and established singers, voice teachers, and coaches, the magazine is packed with practical information relating to care of the voice and the development of a professional singing career. Articles are written by singers, voice teachers, doctors, and freelance writers and cover such topics as singers' diction, audition preparation, repertoire, care of the voice, development and maintenance of a successful singing career, and creation of a healthy work/life balance. Other articles feature interviews with singers and provide information about apprentice programs and vocal competitions. The back pages of each issue are devoted to listings of auditions and job postings for various operatic, concert, choral, and church/temple positions. The magazine's accompanying website provides online directories to coaches and accompanists, singers' websites, summer programs, university vocal programs, voice teachers, and young artist programs and includes audition and competition listings and alerts. Available in both print and online formats. (The print subscription includes access to the website.) Highly recommended for large public and academic libraries. URL: https://www.classicalsinger.com/

3733. ***Computer Music Journal.*** [ISSN: 0148-9267] 1977. q. USD 402 (print & online eds.)). Ed(s): Douglas Keislar. M I T Press, One Rogers St, Cambridge, MA 02142-1209; journals-cs@mit.edu; http://mitpress.mit.edu/. Illus., adv. Refereed. *Indexed:* A01, A22, BRI, CompLI, E01, IIMP, RILM. *Bk. rev.:* 2-3, 1,500 words, signed. *Aud.:* Ac, Sa.

Computer Music Journal (*CMJ*) is dedicated to the exploration of "digital sound technology and all musical applications of computers." Engineers, computer scientists, composers, performers, and anyone studying or interested in electroacoustic music will find a wide range of relevant topics and current information on both technical and aesthetic issues. Edited by experts in the field, content includes feature articles on technologies, aesthetics, tutorials, surveys, interviews with leading composers of computer music, product reports, and reviews of recent events and new products and publications. Subscriptions to the quarterly journal include an "annual sound and video anthology containing curated music." This journal is also available online. Recommended for academic libraries; highly recommended for those who serve music programs with an emphasis on digital technology. URL: https://www.mitpressjournals.org/loi/comj

3734. ***Contributions to Music Education.*** [ISSN: 0190-4922] 1972. a. USD 40 (Individuals, USD 25; Free to members). Ed(s): Craig Resta. Ohio Music Education Association, PO Box 1067, Massillon, OH 44648; https://www.omea-ohio2.org. Refereed. *Indexed:* A22, ERIC, IIMP, RILM. *Aud.:* Ac.

A publication of the Ohio Music Education Association, *Contributions to Music Education* is a peer-reviewed journal concerned with demonstrating the "importance of social science research in guiding educational practice." In publication since 1972, its articles detail the results of philosophical, historical, and scientific research "that contribute to an understanding of music teaching and learning." Some issues include comprehensive research literature reviews covering unique aspects of music education. Recent issues have included articles on "Keeping Our Doors Open: Diversity, Equity, and Inclusion in Music Education for 2019" and "Assessing the Educational Value of You Tube Videos for Beginning Instrumental Music." This journal is currently produced on an annual basis in both print and electronic format. Highly recommended for academic libraries supporting music education study. URL:https://www.omea-ohio.org/cme.a5w.

3735. ***Council for Research in Music Education. Bulletin.*** [ISSN: 0010-9894] 1963. q. USD 136 (print & online eds.)). Ed(s): Janet R. Barrett. University of Illinois Press, 1325 S Oak St, MC-566, Champaign, IL 61820; uipress@uillinois.edu; http://www.press.uillinois.edu. Illus., index, adv. Refereed. Microform: PQC. *Indexed:* A22, IIMP, MLA-IB, RILM. *Bk. rev.:* 5-10, 750-1,000 words, signed. *Aud.:* Ac, Sa.

The Bulletin of the Council for Research in Music Education (*CRME*) has international appeal and provides a forum where contemporary research of timely and significant topics and reviews of relevant books are made accessible to all with interest in music education. Its scholarly articles address various aspects of teaching, learning, and experiencing music. Recent issues have presented research on such topics as competition in high school bands, the use of music listening apps to engage students, and Chinese-American adolescent identity in a children's choir. Relevant to music educators with students at all levels, this publication is recommended for academic and large public libraries and is available in both print and electronic formats. URL: http://bcrme.press.illinois.edu/

3736. ***Early Music.*** [ISSN: 0306-1078] 1973. q. EUR 382. Ed(s): Helen Deeming, Stephen Rose. Oxford University Press, Great Clarendon St, Oxford, OX2 6DP, United Kingdom; onlinequeries.uk@oup.com; http://global.oup.com. Illus., adv. Sample. Refereed. Microform: PQC. Reprint: PSC. *Indexed:* A01, A22, AmHI, BRI, E01, IIMP, MLA-IB, RILM. *Bk. rev.:* 2-4, 750-1,000 words, signed. *Aud.:* Ac, Sa.

Founded in 1973, *Early Music* looks at all facets of the study of early music and how it is being interpreted and performed today. The topics presented include matters pertaining to repertoire, interpretation, notation, iconography, performance practice, period instruments, and both historical and analytical perspectives of specific composers and performers. Recent issues have included articles on "Mozart and the Moravians," "Notation as a Transformative

Technology: Orality, Literacy, and Early Modern Instrumentalists," and "Tallis's Epitaph Revisited." In addition to scholarly articles replete with rich illustrations, a typical issue includes reviews of books, new editions of printed music, recordings, and online resources, as well as current workshop and festival listings. This journal will be of great use to anyone interested in early music and is highly recommended for academic libraries that support programs in historical musicology. Available in both print and online formats. URL: https://academic.oup.com/em

3737. ***Early Music History: studies in medieval and early modern music.*** [ISSN: 0261-1279] 1982. a. GBP 213. Ed(s): Iain Fenlon. Cambridge University Press, University Printing House, Shaftesbury Rd, Cambridge, CB2 8BS, United Kingdom; journals@cambridge.org; https://www.cambridge.org/. Illus., adv. Refereed. Circ: 550. Microform: PQC. Reprint: PSC. *Indexed:* A22, AmHI, E01, IIMP, RILM. *Bk. rev.:* 2, 2,500 words, signed. *Aud.:* Ac, Sa.

Early Music History presents the scholarship of researchers specializing in European and American music from the early Middle Ages through the end of the seventeenth century. The journal is peer reviewed. Accepted papers tend to reflect novel approaches in their methodologies and explore interdisciplinary possibilities. Topics such as manuscripts and texts, iconography, music within society, and the relationship between words and music are discussed from both historical and analytic perspectives. Highly recommended for academic libraries, especially those that support early music studies or musicology. Also available in online format. URL: https://www.cambridge.org/core/journals/early-music-history

3738. ***Eighteenth-Century Music.*** [ISSN: 1478-5706] 2004. s-a. GBP 166 (print & online eds.)). Ed(s): David R Irving, W D Sutcliffe. Cambridge University Press, University Printing House, Shaftesbury Rd, Cambridge, CB2 8BS, United Kingdom; journals@cambridge.org; https://www.cambridge.org/. Adv. Refereed. Reprint: PSC. *Indexed:* A22, E01, IIMP, MLA-IB, RILM. *Bk. rev.:* Number and length vary. *Aud.:* Ac, Sa.

Eighteenth-Century Music provides a forum for research and discussion of all aspects of eighteenth-century music (ca. 1660-1830). Content is contributed by scholars and focuses on topics ranging from musical analyses of compositions, analyses of performance practices, and critiques, to interdisciplinary studies of the music in its cultural and social contexts. Issues also include many book, music, and recording reviews and reports of conferences and related current events. Available in both print and electronic formats. Recommended for academic collections. URL: https://www.cambridge.org/core/journals/eighteenth-century-music

3739. ***Electronic Musician.*** Incorporates (1990-2011): *E Q (New York);* Formerly (until 1985): *Polyphony.* [ISSN: 0884-4720] 1976. m. USD 29.97 combined subscription domestic (print & online eds.); USD 36 combined subscription Canada (print & online eds.); USD 56 combined subscription elsewhere (print & online eds.)). Ed(s): Simon Truss. NewBay Media, LLC, 1111 Bayhill Dr, Ste 125, San Bruno, CA 94066; customerservice@nbmedia.com; http://www.nbmedia.com. Adv. *Indexed:* A01, A22, C37, C42, IIMP. *Aud.:* Ac, Sa.

Published monthly, *Electronic Musician* seeks to cover all aspects of music production, including performance, recording, and technology. Feature articles, which tend to run three to seven pages in length, include profiles of influential music makers, reviews and analyses of the latest recording equipment and applications, and techniques and tips to enhance music production and live performances. In addition, the publication addresses such career-related concerns as promotion, marketing, publishing, and social media. Also available as an online subscription. Recommended for large public and academic libraries, especially those that support programs in electronic music composition and recording industry studies. URL: http://www.emusician.com/

3740. ***Ethnomusicology.*** [ISSN: 0014-1836] 1953. 3x/yr. USD 206 (print & online eds.)). Ed(s): Frank Gunderson. University of Illinois Press, 1325 S Oak St, MC-566, Champaign, IL 61820; uipress@uillinois.edu; http://www.press.uillinois.edu. Illus., index, adv. Refereed. Vol. ends: Fall. *Indexed:* A01, A22, A47, AmHI, BAS, BRI, IBSS, IIMP, MLA-IB, RILM. *Bk. rev.:* 6-8, 500-1,000 words, signed. *Aud.:* Ac, Sa.

Ethnomusicology is an international, peer-reviewed journal published by the Society for Ethnomusicology. It presents theoretical perspectives plus research and analysis of various subjects from within the field of ethnomusicology. Its contents include aspects of musicology, sociology, cultural anthropology, and other disciplines. Some articles look at the general field of ethnomusicology, while others focus on research done on the music and practices of specific cultures, religions, geographic areas, and the like. Each issue contains substantial reviews of books, recordings, and multimedia. Scholars from a wide variety of fields will find information of relevance. Also available in electronic format. Recommended for academic and large public libraries, and essential for those that support research in ethnomusicology. URL: https://www.press.uillinois.edu/journals/ethno.html

3741. ***Indiana Theory Review.*** [ISSN: 0271-8022] 1977. s-a. USD 102.85 (print & online eds.)). Ed(s): David Geary. Indiana University Press, Office of Scholarly Publishing, Herman B Wells Library 350, Bloomington, IN 47405; iuporder@indiana.edu; http://iupress.indiana.edu/. Adv. Reprint: PSC. *Indexed:* IIMP, RILM. *Bk. rev.:* Number and length vary. *Aud.:* Ga, Ac.

Produced by the graduate students of the Department of Music Theory at Indiana University's Jacobs School of Music since its founding in 1977, *Indiana Theory Review* is a peer-reviewed journal publishing scholarly articles and reviews covering "all facets of music theory and analysis." All submissions are subjected to a double-blind review process. Contributors include both established and emerging theory scholars. The publication also occasionally includes commissioned articles from eminent scholars in the field. Each issue usually contains three to six feature articles and at least one review. Highly recommended for academic libraries. Available in print and electronic formats. URL: http://music.indiana.edu/ITR/

3742. ***The Instrumentalist.*** [ISSN: 0020-4331] 1946. m. Except June/July. Ed(s): Dan Blaufuss. The Instrumentalist Publishing Co., 1838 Techny Ct, Northbrook, IL 60062; advertising@instrumentalistmagazine.com. Illus., index, adv. Vol. ends: Jul. *Indexed:* A22, IIMP. *Aud.:* Hs, Ga, Ac.

The Instrumentalist focuses on the interests and needs of band, marching band, and orchestra directors at the primary, secondary, and higher education levels. It offers practical advice and discussions on pedagogy, repertoire, conducting, instrument care, and running rehearsals. A typical issue also contains interviews with directors and composers of note, reviews of music scores and audio recordings, and listings of workshops and festivals. The website contains additional features, such as links to historical articles, a camp directory, advertisers, and past and current music reviews. Recommended for high school, academic, and public libraries. URL: https://theinstrumentalist.com/

3743. ***Integral (Online).*** [ISSN: 2168-8419] 1987. a. Free. Eastman School of Music, 26 Gibbs St, Rochester, NY 14604; https://www.esm.rochester.edu/. Refereed. *Indexed:* A01, IIMP, RILM. *Aud.:* Ga, Ac.

Published annually by the graduate students of music theory at Eastman School of Music, *Integral* is a peer-reviewed journal mandated to "explore and exploit the increasing pluralism of the music-theoretic field." Articles appearing in this publication address topics relating to music theory, analysis, and criticism. Issues contain between four and ten extended articles, some of which exceed 50 pages in length, and select book reviews. Recent issues have included discussions of Corelli's tonal and rhythmic models and Rachmaninoff's harmony. With volume 33, *Integral* will become an online, open-access journal. This publication is recommended for academic libraries. URL: https://www.esm.rochester.edu/theory/integral/

3744. ***International Musician.*** [ISSN: 0020-8051] 1901. m. Ed(s): Jason Emerson. American Federation of Musicians of the United States and Canada, 120 Walton St., Ste 300, Syracuse, NY 13202; http://www.afm.org. Illus., adv. Circ: 94886 Paid. Vol. ends: Jun. Microform: PQC. *Indexed:* A01, A22, IIMP. *Bk. rev.:* 4, 100 words, unsigned. *Aud.:* Ga, Ac, Sa.

International Musician is the official journal of the American Federation of Musicians of the United States and Canada. Its content focuses on the interests and concerns of its more than 80,000 members, most of whom are professional musicians and music educators. Each issue features union and legislative news, interviews, advice on self-promotion, information and reviews of relevant resources and products for the working musician, and recognition of member achievements across the gamut of musical styles. Included in each publication is a feature article on an accomplished professional musician, ensemble, or organization as well as editorials, orchestra and local chapter news, and classifieds listing auditions, equipment for sale, training opportunities, and stolen instrument notices. Available in both print and electronic formats. Recommended for public and academic libraries. URL: https://internationalmusician.org/

3745. ***Journal of Band Research.*** [ISSN: 0021-9207] 1964. s-a. Ed(s): John R Locke. Journal of Band Research, c/o Dr. John R. Locke, Editor, UNCG School of Music, P O Box 26170, Greensboro, NC 27402-6170; dernsberger@troy.edu. Illus. Circ: 1000 Paid. Microform: PQC. *Indexed:* A01, A22, IIMP, RILM. *Aud.:* Ac, Sa.

The official publication of The American Bandmasters Association, the *Journal of Band Research* is a peer-reviewed journal published in the fall and spring of each year. The four or five feature articles in each issue are lengthy and scholarly in nature and cover research that relates to various types of bands and wind ensembles. Among the topics addressed are repertoire and repertoire analysis, programming considerations, band ensemble histories, pedagogy, and band recruitment. The final pages of each issue provide brief biographies of the contributors. Available as a print journal only. Back issues from 1964 to 2005 are available for purchase on CD-ROM. Recommended for large public and academic libraries. URL: http://www.journalofbandresearch.org/

3746. ***Journal of Music Theory Pedagogy.*** [ISSN: 0891-7639] 1987. a. Ed(s): Steven Laitz. Appalachian State University, Hayes School of Music, Broyhill Music Center, Rm.111, 813 Rivers St., Boone, NC 28608; music@appstate.edu; https://music.appstate.edu/. Refereed. *Indexed:* IIMP, RILM. *Aud.:* Ga, Ac, Sa.

The *Journal of Music Theory Pedagogy* is given "philosophical direction and financial support" by the Gail Boyd de Stwolinski Center for Music Theory Pedagogy. The center seeks "to provide a national clearinghouse for the collection and dissemination of information concerning the teaching and learning of music theory." Articles submitted for publication in this journal are reviewed by an editorial board and chosen for their "originality, relevance, interest to a diverse audience, and clarity of writing." The scope of the journal embraces all aspects of teaching and learning music theory, including analysis, pedagogical trends, historical analyses, and theory software. Reviews of theory books and texts are included. All *JMTP* articles can be accessed from the *Music Theory Pedagogy Online* site at no charge. Strongly recommended for academic libraries. URL: https://jmtp.appstate.edu/.

3747. ***Journal of Music Therapy.*** Supersedes (in 1964): *National Association for Music Therapy. Bulletin.* [ISSN: 0022-2917] 1962. q. EUR 278. Ed(s): A B LaGasse. Oxford University Press, 2001 Evans Rd, Cary, NC 27513; orders.us@oup.com; https://academic.oup.com/journals. Illus., index, adv. Refereed. Vol. ends: Winter. Microform: PQC. Reprint: PSC. *Indexed:* A22, IIMP, RILM. *Aud.:* Ac, Sa.

The *Journal of Music Therapy,* published by the American Music Therapy Association, seeks to promote scholarly activity in music therapy and to foster the development and understanding of music therapy and music-based interventions. The publication disseminates articles that present a variety of research methods on topics concerning the psychology of music, applied music therapy techniques, perception of music, and effects of music on human behavior. Aspects of music therapy education and problems for students in the field are also considered. Submissions undergo an anonymous peer review. Each issue contains two to five articles of approximately 20 to 30 pages in length. Articles include abstracts and references. An index appears in the last issue of each volume. This title is available in print and online formats. Recommended for academic libraries and libraries that serve the health sciences. URL: https://academic.oup.com/jmt

3748. ***The Journal of Musicology: a quarterly review of music history, criticism, analysis, and performance practice.*** [ISSN: 0277-9269] 1982. q. USD 343 (print & online eds.)). Ed(s): Jesse Rodin, Elaine Kelly. University of California Press, Journals Division, 155 Grand Avenue, Ste 400, Oakland, CA 94612-3764; http://www.ucpress.edu/journals.php. Illus., adv. Refereed. Circ: 878. Microform: PQC. *Indexed:* A01, A22, AmHI, BRI, E01, IIMP, MLA-IB, RILM. *Aud.:* Ac, Sa.

The Journal of Musicology provides a forum for peer-reviewed articles on topics in all areas of musical scholarship, including analysis, criticism, history, performance, research, and theory. This journal's very accessible and well-documented articles and review essays treat music from a variety of perspectives and make it appealing to both practicing musicians and music scholars. Issues contain four to five articles with abstracts appearing at the end of each article. Recent issues have included discussions of genealogies of performance in Italian baroque opera, comic irony in *Harold in Italy,* and musical theatre in the Third Reich. Available in print and online formats. Recommended for academic and large public libraries. URL: https://jm.ucpress.edu/

3749. ***Journal of Research in Music Education.*** [ISSN: 0022-4294] 1953. q. USD 345 (print & online eds.)). Ed(s): Steven J Morrison. Sage Publications, Inc., 2455 Teller Rd, Thousand Oaks, CA 91320; info@sagepub.com; http://www.sagepub.com. Illus., adv. Sample. Refereed. Vol. ends: Winter. Microform: PQC. Reprint: PSC. *Indexed:* A01, A22, E01, ERIC, IIMP, MLA-IB, RILM. *Aud.:* Hs, Ac, Sa.

The *Journal of Research in Music Education* (*JRME*), published quarterly for the National Association for Music Education, presents original research on a broad range of topics, including "various aspects of music pedagogy, history, and philosophy." Articles published also address "vocal, instrumental, and general music at all levels, from early childhood through adult." Contents are peer reviewed by an editorial committee of scholars and intended for researchers and music teachers in all settings. Each issue contains six to ten articles written by professional educators, and announcements, including calls for papers. Articles in recent issues address such topics as the effect of conductor expressivity on the evaluation of rehearsal instruction, university environmental factors affecting the well-being of LGBTQ music and art students, and the enhancement of musical performance through the adoption of an external point of focus. Available in print and online subscriptions. Recommended for academic, high school, and large public libraries. URL: https://journals.sagepub.com/home/jrm

3750. ***Journal of Singing.*** Former titles (until Sep.1995): *N A T S Journal;* (until May1985): *N A T S Bulletin;* (until 1962): *National Association of Teachers of Singing. Bulletin.* [ISSN: 1086-7732] 1944. bi-m. Except July/August. Ed(s): Richard Dale Sjoerdsma. National Association of Teachers of Singing (N A T S), 9957 Moorings Dr, Ste 401, Jacksonville, FL 32257; info@nats.org; http://www.nats.org. Illus., index, adv. Refereed. Microform: PQC. *Indexed:* A22, IIMP, RILM. *Bk. rev.:* 1-2, 300-500 words, signed. *Aud.:* Ac, Sa.

Published by the National Association of Teachers of Singing (*NATS*), The *Journal of Singing* offers practical information on a variety of topics related to vocal study for its worldwide membership. In addition to information about the organization, each issue contains feature articles on such topics as career overviews of noteworthy singers and teachers of voice, vocal pedagogy and techniques, diction, repertoire, medical issues, and music history. The publication also lists upcoming workshops appropriate for students and/or teachers of voice, and other relevant events. A section of each issue is devoted to critical reviews of new books, scores, and multimedia items. Of interest to singers, private voice instructors, vocal coaches, and choral conductors, this title is recommended for academic and large public libraries. URL: https://www.nats.org/cgi/page.cgi/about_journal_singing.html

3751. ***Latin American Music Review.*** Former titles (until 1980): *Anuario Interamericano de Investigacion Musical;* (until 1970): *Anuario - Tulane University. Inter-American Institute for Musical Research.* [ISSN: 0163-0350] 1965. s-a. USD 174 domestic; USD 194 Canada; USD 201 elsewhere. Ed(s): Robin Moore. University of Texas Press, Journals Division, PO Box 7819, Austin, TX 78713; journals@utpress.utexas.edu; https://utpress.utexas.edu. Illus., index, adv. Refereed. *Indexed:* A01, A22, BRI, E01, IIMP, MLA-IB, RILM. *Aud.:* Ac, Sa.

Latin American Music Review (*LAMR*) "explores the historical, ethnographic, and socio-cultural dimensions of Latin American music in Latin American social groups, including the Puerto Rican, Mexican, Cuban, and Portuguese populations in the United States." It is a scholarly publication. Each issue contains three to four feature articles written in English, Spanish, and Portuguese. Interdisciplinary in nature, *LAMR* is of primary interest to musicologists, ethnomusicologists, sociologists, and anthropologists. Issues include extensive book, film, video, and recording reviews of English and non-English works. Announcements about upcoming conferences and other related events appear at the end of each issue. Available in print and electronic formats. Recommended for large public and academic libraries. URL: https://utpress.utexas.edu/journals/latin-american-music-review

3752. ***Medical Problems of Performing Artists.*** [ISSN: 0885-1158] 1986. q. Ed(s): Bronwen Ackermann. Science & Medicine, PO Box 313, Narberth, PA 19072. Illus., index, adv. Refereed. *Indexed:* A22, BRI, ErgAb, IIMP, IIPA, RILM. *Bk. rev.:* 1, 250 words, signed. *Aud.:* Ga, Ac, Sa.

Medical Problems of Performing Artists publishes peer-reviewed articles that focus on the origins, diagnoses, and treatments of medical problems encountered by performing artists, including muscular and neurological disorders, anxieties, stress, voice and hearing disorders, repetitive stress injuries, and substance abuse. As the official journal of the Performing Arts Medical Association (PAMA), the Dutch Performing Arts Medicine Association (NVDMG), and the Australian Society for Performing Arts Healthcare (ASPAH), this publication serves as a worldwide forum for medical and academic professionals to communicate their research findings and practices. Each issue contains approximately six to ten articles with abstracts, abstracts of relevant articles in other journals, and occasional book reviews. Tables of contents, abstracts, and full text are available for back issues on the website. Available in print and digital formats. Recommended for academic, medical, and large public libraries. URL: https://www.sciandmed.com/mppa/

3753. ***Music and Arts in Action.*** [ISSN: 1754-7105] 2008. irreg. 1-3/yr. Free. Ed(s): Pedro S Boia. University of Exeter, Department of Sociology, Philosophy and Anthropology, Amory Bldg, Rennes Dr, Exeter, EX4 4RJ, United Kingdom; socphil@exeter.ac.uk; https://socialsciences.exeter.ac.uk. Refereed. *Indexed:* IIMP, IIPA, RILM. *Aud.:* Ga, Ac, Sa.

Music and Arts in Action (*MAiA*) is an online, open-access, peer-reviewed journal that publishes articles that explore issues relating to the interplay of music and arts in society. In an effort to present a broad, inclusive forum for discussion of the issues, this journal includes contributions from not only researchers and educators but also from journalists, art historians, artists, practitioners, cultural professionals, and others. The contents of some issues revolve around a specific theme, while others contain articles on a wide variety of topics. Contributions may take the form of academic writings, case studies, interviews, and documents of the proceedings of meetings and conferences. Recent issues have included discussions of "the development and uses of audio biographical cues to support people living with dementia and other long-term conditions" and "music and peacebuilding." *MAiA*'s articles often include images, sound, and video embedded in the text. Recommended for academic and large public libraries. URL: http://www.musicandartsinaction.net/index.php/maia/index

3754. ***Music and Letters.*** [ISSN: 0027-4224] 1920. q. EUR 371. Ed(s): Rebecca Herrisone, Sam Barrett. Oxford University Press, Great Clarendon St, Oxford, OX2 6DP, United Kingdom; onlinequeries.uk@oup.com; http://global.oup.com. Illus., index, adv. Sample. Refereed. Vol. ends: Nov. Microform: PQC. Reprint: PSC. *Indexed:* A01, A22, AmHI, E01, IIMP, MLA-IB, RILM. *Bk. rev.:* 25, 500-1,000 words, signed. *Aud.:* Ac, Sa.

Music and Letters is an international, refereed journal that publishes articles of any length on aspects of historical, analytical, and critical musicology of any musical period and of musics from classical, popular, and world traditions. Emphasis is often on dialog between musicology and other disciplines. Article topics can be letters, documents, reminiscences, and other written records that relate to musical performers and composers and their compositions; e.g., "Manuel De Falla's Music in Letters." A typical issue contains three or four articles and a large number of book reviews as well as occasional music reviews. The journal's website contains tables of contents back to 1920. Searching capability by author, article title, volume, and keyword is provided. Available in print and electronic formats. Recommended for academic libraries. URL: https://academic.oup.com/ml

3755. ***Music and Politics.*** [ISSN: 1938-7687] 2007. s-a. Free. Ed(s): Gabriela Cruz. Michigan Publishing, 839 Greene St, Ann Arbor, MI 48104; mpublishing@umich.edu; http://www.publishing.umich.edu/. Refereed. *Indexed:* IIMP, RILM. *Aud.:* Ac, Sa.

Music and Politics is a peer-reviewed, open-access journal published twice a year. First published in 2007, this publication contains articles that explore the interaction of music and politics. Articles address such issues as the impact of politics on the lives of musicians, music as a form of political discourse, and the influences of ideology on musical historiography. Contributing scholars represent a variety of fields, including ethnomusicology, film studies, musicology, political science, and sociology. All articles are published in English, but individual issues often include translations of relevant articles previously published in foreign-language journals. Most issues contain a list of recent books that cover topics related to music and politics. Recommended for academic libraries. URL: https://quod.lib.umich.edu/m/mp/

3756. ***Music Educators Journal.*** Former titles (until 1934): *Music Supervisors' Journal;* (until 1915): *Music Supervisors' Bulletin.* [ISSN: 0027-4321] 1914. q. USD 377 (print & online eds.)). Ed(s): Ella Wilcox. Sage Publications, Inc., 2455 Teller Rd, Thousand Oaks, CA 91320; info@sagepub.com; http://www.sagepub.com. Illus., index. Refereed. Vol. ends: May. Microform: PQC. Reprint: PSC. *Indexed:* A01, A22, BAS, BRI, CBRI, E01, ERIC, IIMP, MLA-IB, RILM. *Bk. rev.:* 8, 150-200 words, signed. *Aud.:* Ems, Hs, Ga, Ac, Sa.

A publication of the National Association for Music Education (NAfME), *Music Educators Journal* seeks to provide "articles on music teaching approaches and philosophies, instructional techniques, current trends and issues in music education in schools and communities and the latest in products and services." Articles are peer-reviewed, scholarly, and practical in nature. Topics addressed in recent issues include using music to help students with autism and the impact of commissioned works and composer residencies on student growth. Each issue contains five to eight feature articles and several regular columns. Issues also include brief reviews of books, videos, and technology resources. Available in print and electronic formats. Recommended for all libraries and music teachers. URL: https://journals.sagepub.com/home/mej

3757. ***Music Library Association. Notes.*** [ISSN: 0027-4380] 1934. q. USD 100 Free to members. Ed(s): Deborah Campana. Music Library Association, 1600 Aspen Commons, Ste 100, Middleton, WI 53562; http://www.musiclibraryassoc.org. Illus., index, adv. Refereed. Vol. ends: Jun. Microform: PQC. *Indexed:* A01, A22, AmHI, BRI, CBRI, E01, IIMP, MLA-IB, RILM. *Bk. rev.:* 40-50, 250-500 words, signed. *Aud.:* Ac, Sa.

Notes, the quarterly journal of the Music Library Association (MLA), publishes articles on contemporary and historical issues in music librarianship, music bibliography and discography, and particular aspects of music history. Each issue contains two to four feature articles, but the main body of the journal is an extensive section of signed reviews of books that cover a wide range of music-related topics and genres, including publications on music librarianship and research. Issues also contain reviews of scores, sound recordings, digital media, and software; a long list of books recently published; and lists of music scores and music publishers' catalogs received. Highly recommended for all music librarians and bibliographers. URL: https://www.musiclibraryassoc.org/page/Notes

3758. ***Music Perception.*** [ISSN: 0730-7829] 1983. 5x/yr. USD 674 (print & online eds.)). Ed(s): Catherine Stevens. University of California Press, Journals Division, 155 Grand Avenue, Ste 400, Oakland, CA 94612-3764; http://www.ucpress.edu/journals.php. Illus., index, adv. Refereed. Circ: 640. Vol. ends: Summer. Microform: PQC. *Indexed:* A01, A22, BRI, E01, IIMP, MLA-IB, RILM. *Bk. rev.:* 2, 2,000-3,500 words, signed. *Aud.:* Ac, Sa.

Music Perception publishes refereed articles on studies about how music is experienced and interpreted. Contributors include scientists and musicians using critical, methodological, theoretical, and empirical approaches from disciplines such as psychology, neurology, linguistics, acoustics, and artificial intelligence. Topics covered in recent issues include "Distortion and Rock Guitar Harmony" and "Psychological and Musical Factors Underlying

Engagement with Unfamiliar Music." Contains some book reviews and announcements of future conferences and meetings. Recommended for academic libraries. URL: http://mp.ucpress.edu/

3759. ***Music Performance Research.*** [ISSN: 1755-9219] 2007. a. Ed(s): Dr. Jane Ginsborg. Royal Northern College of Music, 124 Oxford Rd, Manchester, M13 9RD, United Kingdom; info@rncm.ac.uk; http://www.rncm.ac.uk/. Refereed. *Indexed:* A01, IIMP, RILM. *Aud.:* Ac, Sa.

Music Performance Research is an open-access, peer-reviewed journal that aims "to disseminate theoretical and empirical research on the performance of music." International in scope, the journal is published once or twice yearly. The editorial board includes members from a wide range of backgrounds and geographic areas. Contributing researchers represent various disciplines relevant to music performance. Recent articles have addressed "Music performance anxiety and self-efficacy in young musicians" and "Successful approaches to mental practice." Contents can be downloaded, copied, and distributed free of charge. Recommended for academic libraries. URL: http://mpronline.net/.

3760. ***Music Reference Services Quarterly.*** [ISSN: 1058-8167] 1993. q. GBP 229 (print & online eds.)). Ed(s): Rachel E Scott, Ana Dubnjakovic. Routledge, 530 Walnut St, Ste 850, Philadelphia, PA 19106; enquiries@tandfonline.com; http://www.tandfonline.com. Adv. Sample. Refereed. Microform: PQC. Reprint: PSC. *Indexed:* A01, A22, E01, IIMP, RILM. *Aud.:* Ac.

Begun in 1993, *Music Reference Services Quarterly* seeks to cover "all aspects of the management and use of music collections and services" in the wide variety of libraries, archives, and museums charged with handling music-related materials. Its contents focus on "research related to administration and management, bibliographic instruction, collection development, digital audio delivery, electronic resources, facilities, music librarianship, education, preservation of music materials, reference services, cataloging, and bibliographies relating to printed music and audio-visual materials." Article published in this journal have undergone editorial screening and anonymous double-blind peer review. Topics covered in recent issues include "Creating a Welcoming and Inclusive Environment for Transgender and Gender Fluid Music Library Users" and "Patron-Driven Acquisition of Print Monographs and Music Scores." Subscriptions available for online only or combined print and online access. Recommended for academic and special libraries. URL: https://www.tandfonline.com/loi/wmus20.

3761. ***Music Theory Online.*** [ISSN: 1067-3040] 1993. q. Free. Ed(s): Brent Yorgason, Jeff Perry. Society for Music Theory, University of Chicago, Department of Music, 1010 E 59th St, Chicago, IL 60637; vlong@uchicago.edu; http://societymusictheory.org/. Illus. Refereed. *Indexed:* A01, IIMP, RILM. *Aud.:* Ga, Ac.

Published four times a year, *Music Theory Online* (*MTO*) is a refereed open-access electronic journal of the Society for Music Theory. *MTO* provides its readers with articles and essays reflecting scholarly research, criticisms, and commentary covering a wide variety of topics relating to music theory and its related disciplines. Recent issues address such subjects as "Harmony in Elliott Carter's Late Music," and "Music Theory as Social Justice: Pedagogical Applications of Kendrick Lamar's *To Pimp a Butterfly.* Feature articles include keywords, abstracts, and references. Some issues also include reviews of scholarly books and texts and conference reports. Recommended for academic libraries and professional musicians. URL: http://www.mtosmt.org/index.php.

3762. ***Music Theory Spectrum.*** [ISSN: 0195-6167] 1979. s-a. EUR 177. Ed(s): Marianne Wheeldon. Oxford University Press, 2001 Evans Rd, Cary, NC 27513; custserv.us@oup.com; https://academic.oup.com/journals. Adv. Refereed. Reprint: PSC. *Indexed:* A01, A22, E01, IIMP, RILM. *Bk. rev.:* Number and length vary. *Aud.:* Ac.

An official publication of the Society for Music Theory, *Music Theory Spectrum* publishes well-documented articles "on a wide range of topics in music theory and analysis, including aesthetics, critical theory and hermeneutics, history of theory, post-tonal theory, Schenkerian analysis, musical form, rhythm, music cognition, and the analysis of popular musics." Interdisciplinary articles that intersect with fields such as ethnomusicology, mathematics, musicology, philosophy, psychology, and performance are also included. Each issue generally contains six to eight articles and extensive book reviews. Print and/or online subscriptions are available. Recommended for academic libraries. URL: https://academic.oup.com/mts/.

3763. ***Musica Disciplina.*** Formerly (until 1948): *Journal of Renaissance and Baroque Music.* [ISSN: 0077-2461] 1946. a. Ed(s): Inga M Groote. American Institute of Musicology, 1600 Aspen Commons, Ste 100, Middleton, WI 53562; orders@corpusmusicae.comers@corpusmusicae.com ; http://www.corpusmusicae.com. Refereed. *Indexed:* IIMP, MLA-IB, RILM. *Aud.:* Ga, Ac.

Musica Disciplina focuses on the scholarly exploration of early music. The publication presents research on music written principally from the Medieval and Renaissance periods but its issues often include submissions on music of the seventeenth century. The yearbook's double-blind reviewed articles concern source studies, editions, aesthetics and criticism, analyses, cultural and contextual studies, and other musicological issues. Submissions are accepted in English, French, German, Spanish, or Italian. Recommended for academic libraries. URL: http://www.corpusmusicae.com/md.htm.

3764. ***The Musical Quarterly.*** [ISSN: 0027-4631] 1915. q. EUR 264. Ed(s): Irene Zedlacher, Leon Botstein. Oxford University Press, 2001 Evans Rd, Cary, NC 27513; https://global.oup.com. Illus., index. Sample. Refereed. Vol. ends: Winter. Microform: PMC; PQC. Reprint: PSC. *Indexed:* A01, A22, AmHI, BRI, CBRI, E01, IIMP, MLA-IB, RILM. *Aud.:* Ga, Ac.

The Musical Quarterly, founded in 1915 by Oscar Sonneck, publishes peer-reviewed articles that focus on the contemporary study of music from the perspective of, and in combination with, other scholarly disciplines. Regularly occurring section headings include "American Musics," "Music and Culture," "Institutions, Industries, Technologies," "Texts and Contexts," and "Primary Sources." Most issues contain two to six feature articles with notes. Issues also may include review essays about new books and recordings and recent performances of note. The website contains links to tables of contents of issues from 1915 forward and search functions by author, title, citation, and keyword. Print, online, or package subscriptions options are available. Recommended for public and academic libraries. URL: https://academic.oup.com/mq.

3765. ***The Musical Times.*** Formerly (until 1903): *Musical Times and Singing Class Circular.* [ISSN: 0027-4666] 1844. q. Ed(s): Antony Bye. Musical Times Publications Ltd., Unit 8, The Old Silk Mill, Brook St., Tring, , United Kingdom. Microform: PQC; WMP. *Indexed:* A01, A22, AmHI, BRI, IIMP, MLA-IB, RILM. *Bk. rev.:* Number and length vary. *Aud.:* Ga, Ac, Sa.

Begun in 1844 and still published quarterly in the United Kingdom, *Musical Times* boasts it is "the world's oldest continuously publishing classical music journal." Contributors are established musical scholars and performers. Most issues contain several heavily footnoted feature articles that cover a "wide variety of subjects pertaining to classical music" and that are of potential interest to both scholars and general readers. The featured articles are followed by several book reviews. Available in print and online editions. Recommended for large public and academic libraries. URL: https://shop.exacteditions.com/the-musical-times.

3766. ***Opera News.*** [ISSN: 0030-3607] 1936. m. USD 24.99 domestic. Ed(s): F. Paul Driscoll. Metropolitan Opera Guild, Inc., 70 Lincoln Center Plaza, New York, NY 10023; http://www.metguild.org/. Illus., index. Vol. ends: Jun/Jun. Microform: PQC. *Indexed:* A01, A22, AmHI, BRI, C37, CBRI, IIMP, IIPA, MASUSE, MLA-IB, RILM. *Bk. rev.:* 1-3, 500 words, signed. *Aud.:* Ga, Ac.

Published by the Metropolitan Opera Guild, *Opera News* provides fans with the latest news and information about the Metropolitan Opera Company and opera around the world. Each glossy issue contains approximately three to six feature articles that provide history and analysis of selected works and profiles of singers, conductors, directors, designers, and so on. Readers are referred to online links for broadcast operas' stories and background information as well as suggestions for further reading and listening. Also included in each print issue are the latest opera-related news and concert reviews arranged by countries and cities. (Additional reviews can be found in the online version.) Reviews of CDs, videos, and books and lists of upcoming performances worldwide occupy several pages at the back of each issue. Online access to current contents and archives is available with a subscription. Recommended for public and academic libraries. URL: https://www.operanews.com/.

3767. *The Opera Quarterly.* [ISSN: 0736-0053] 1983. q. EUR 320. Ed(s): Ann Lewis, Arman Schwartz. Oxford University Press, 2001 Evans Rd, Cary, NC 27513; https://global.oup.com. Illus. Sample. Refereed. Vol. ends: Fall. Reprint: PSC. *Indexed:* A01, A22, AmHI, BRI, E01, IIMP, IIPA, MLA-IB, RILM. *Bk. rev.:* 4-5, 1,000-1,500 words, signed. *Aud.:* Ga, Ac.

The Opera Quarterly publishes scholarly articles and essays on opera and opera production, performers, opera history, and analyses of historical and contemporary works as well as interviews and remembrances of major vocalists. At least one issue of each volume is usually devoted to a specific theme; for example, operetta, vocal organologies and philologies, and the like. Each issue contains approximately three to six feature articles with illustrations and/or musical examples. Performance reviews and occasionally book, CD, and video reviews also appear. Tables of contents from 1983 to the present are available at the journal's website. Subscription includes online access. Recommended for large public and academic libraries. URL: https://academic.oup.com/oq.

3768. *Percussive Notes.* Incorporates (in 1983): *Percussive Notes. Research Edition;* Which was formerly (until 1982): *Percussive Notes. Research Edition, Percussionist;* Which superseded in part (in 1980): *Percussionist;* Which incorporated: *Percussionist and Percussive Notes.* [ISSN: 0553-6502] 1961. 5x/yr. Ed(s): Rick Mattingly. Percussive Arts Society, Inc., 110 W Washington St, Ste A, Indianapolis, IN 46204; percarts@pas.org; http://www.pas.org. Illus., adv. *Indexed:* A22, IIMP, RILM. *Bk. rev.:* Number and length vary. *Aud.:* Hs, Ga, Ac.

Published five times a year, *Percussive Notes* is the journal of the Percussive Arts Society, the aim of which is "to inspire, educate, and support percussionists and drummers throughout the world." The publication's intended audience is professional and student percussionists. Among the journal's contributors are professors, graduate and doctoral students, performers, composers, and private teachers. Articles focus on percussion instruments, their history, and various aspects of performing with them. Regular headings found in the journal include "Career Development," "Drumset," "Education," "Health and Wellness," "Research," "Technology," and various genre headings (e.g., "Keyboard," "Symphonic," "Marching"). There are generally one or two articles under each major heading. The journal also includes three regular columns, one of which includes reviews of new books, scores, and recordings. Three subscription levels are available. Published in print and online. Recommended for large public and academic libraries. URL: https://www.pas.org/publications/percussive-notes.

3769. *Performance Practice Review (Online).* Formerly (until 1997): *Performance Practice Review.* 1988. a. Free. Ed(s): Robert Zappulla. Claremont Graduate University, Claremont Colleges Library, 150 E 10th St, Claremont, CA 91711; http://www.cgu.edu. Refereed. *Indexed:* IIMP, RILM. *Bk. rev.:* Number and length vary. *Aud.:* Ga, Ac, Sa.

Published continuously online since 2006, *Performance Practice Review (PPR)* is a "blind, peer-reviewed, open access journal devoted to the study of Western musical performance practices." (From 1988 to 1997, it was published biannually in print format; all issues of this title are available from the website.) Articles are a minimum of 3,000 words and may cover performance practices from any historical period. The online format facilitates the inclusion of audio-visual examples as well as musical examples and illustrations. Articles may appear in languages other than English (including Dutch, French, German, Italian, and Spanish). Many issues include book reviews and correspondence that responds to previously published articles and reviews. Recommended for academic and large public libraries. URL: https://scholarship.claremont.edu/ppr/

3770. *Perspectives of New Music.* [ISSN: 0031-6016] 1962. s-a. USD 160 (print & online eds.)). Ed(s): Benjamin Boretz, Robert Morris. Perspectives of New Music, Inc., 1107 NE 45th St, Ste 424, Seattle, WA 98105. Illus., index, adv. Refereed. Circ: 1350 Paid. Vol. ends: Summer. *Indexed:* A01, A22, AmHI, BRI, IIMP, MLA-IB, RILM. *Aud.:* Ac, Sa.

Perspectives of New Music publishes articles on musicians and developments in contemporary music and is aimed at composers, performers, and scholars. Articles contain research and analyses of new music theory and composition, sociological and philosophical studies, interviews, reviews, and occasional excerpts from musical scores. Current issues explore such topics as "Sound Installation and Time: Becoming, Place, and the Case for Performance" and "Me, Myself, and I: Aesthetics and Self-Presentation in Stockhausen's 'Trans.'" Some issues or parts of issues are devoted to a specific contemporary composer or part of the world. Issues generally contain seven to nine articles with musical diagrams and notation. Tables of contents of issues back to Summer 2006 can be viewed on the journal's website. Print and/or electronic subscriptions are available. Recommended for academic libraries. URL: http://www.perspectivesofnewmusic.org/

3771. *The Piano Magazine.* Formerly (until 2019): *Clavier Companion;* Which was formed by the merger of (1990-2009): *Keyboard Companion;* (1966-2009): *Clavier;* Which was formerly (1962-1966): *Piano Teacher.* [ISSN: 2643-0673] 2009. q. USD 36 combined subscription print & online eds. Ed(s): Pamela Pike. Frances Clark Center for Keyboard Pedagogy, PO Box 651, Kingston, NJ 08528; exdir@francesclarkcenter.org; http://www.francesclarkcenter.org. Illus., index, adv. Vol. ends: Dec. *Indexed:* A01, A22, IIMP, RILM. *Aud.:* Ga, Ac.

The Piano Magazine, formerly *Clavier Companion* purports to be "the only publication devoted exclusively to piano teaching, learning and performing." Published quarterly by the Frances Clark Center for Keyboard Pedagogy, it seeks to provide practical articles for its readers. The publication is geared toward teachers of piano students at all skill levels but is also of interest to students, performers, and non-specialist music educators. Each issue features contents under the categories of "Exploring," "Learning," "Teaching," "Playing," "Reflecting," and "Discovering." Issues contain practical advice on teaching techniques; recommendations and reviews of new repertoire, editions, and software; and feature articles on successful teachers, performers, and composers. Listings for workshops, festivals, camps, and competitions for both teachers and students can be found in each issue. A "digital only" subscription also is available. Recommended for academic and large public libraries. URL: https://www.claviercompanion.com/

3772. *R I M E.* [ISSN: 1532-8090] 2003. a. Free. Ed(s): Dr. Bruce Gleason. Research and Issues in Music Education, 2115 Summit Ave, LOR 103, St. Paul, MN 55105. Refereed. *Indexed:* BRI, ERIC, IIMP, RILM. *Aud.:* Hs, Ac.

RIME (*Research and Issues in Music Education*) is an online, open-access journal published annually. Its stated purpose is "to provide a forum devoted to thorough research and commentary that energizes, informs, advances, and reforms the practice and pedagogy of music teaching." This privately funded, peer-reviewed research publication is international in scope. Articles focus on various levels and aspects of music education and are preceded by abstracts. Recent articles address such topics as "A Content Analysis of Recommended Composers in Repertoire Lists for Band," "Student Perspectives and Learning Outcomes from Self-Guided Ensemble Rehearsal," and "Children's Musical Empowerment in Two Composition Task Designs." Recommended for academic libraries and some high school libraries. URL: http://ir.stthomas.edu/rime/

The Source. See African American section.

3773. *The Strad: a monthly journal for professionals and amateurs of all stringed instruments played with the bow.* Incorporates (1996-2008): *The Double Bassist.* [ISSN: 0039-2049] 1890. m. GBP 59.95 domestic. Ed(s): Christian Lloyd, Charlotte Smith. Newsquest Specialist Media Ltd., 4th Floor, 120 Leman St., London, E1 8EU, United Kingdom; info@newsquestspecialistmedia.com; http://www.newsquestspecialistmedia.com. Illus., adv. Sample. Microform: PQC; WMP. *Indexed:* A01, A22, AmHI, IIMP. *Bk. rev.:* 3-5, length varies. *Aud.:* Ac, Sa.

The Strad seeks to provide content relating to "all issues of interest to string teachers, players, students, instrument makers and enthusiasts." Topics of articles include profiles of orchestras, soloist-conductors, ensembles, performers, luthiers, and famous string teachers and their methods. Regular columns have such headings as "Trade Secrets," "Making Matters," "Masterclass," and "Technique." Issues also contain book, CD, and concert reviews. This magazine has a well-designed website that includes job postings, a listing of services and course offerings, reviews, and other useful information. Subscriptions are available in print and digital formats. Recommended for public and academic libraries. URL: https://www.thestrad.com/contact-us/

3774. ***Strings: for players of violin, viola, cello, bass, and fiddle.*** [ISSN: 0888-3106] 1986. bi-m. USD 42 domestic; USD 54 Canada; USD 72 elsewhere. Ed(s): Stephanie Powell, Megan Westberg. String Letter Publishing, 501 Canal Blvd., Suite J, Richmond, CA 94804-3505. Adv. *Indexed:* A22, IIMP, RILM. *Bk. rev.:* Number and length vary. *Aud.:* Ac, Sa.

Strings is a magazine devoted to all aspects of stringed instruments played with a bow, including violin, viola, violoncello, double bass, and fiddle. It explores "all musical genres where string players are active." Articles feature topics such as instrument care and repair, repertoire, performance issues, interviews with players and composers, and information about various violin makers and materials used in creating stringed instruments. Occasionally, issues have a special focus (e.g., "Contemporary Instruments & Bows"). Issues also provide reviews of books, recordings, and scores. Subscriptions include 24/7 web access to the enhanced, interactive current edition of this publication. The online version provides information about and links to related events, newsletters, an online store, and social media. Of interest to string players, teachers, and stringed-instruments makers and repair persons, this title is recommended for academic and public libraries. URL: https://stringsmagazine.com.

3775. ***Symphony (New York).*** Former titles (until 1989): *Symphony Magazine;* (until 1980): *Symphony News.* [ISSN: 1046-3232] 1948. q. USD 25. Ed(s): Robert Sandla, Jennifer Melick. League of American Orchestras, 33 W 60th St, New York, NY 10023; http://www.americanorchestras.org. Illus., adv. *Indexed:* A22, IIMP. *Aud.:* Ga, Ac.

Published quarterly by the League of American Orchestras, *Symphony* reports on the critical issues, trends, personalities, and developments of the orchestra world. The publication includes in-depth articles on topics of interest to anyone employed by or interested in the orchestra industry and related fields. The publication includes news, essays, and current research related to orchestras of all types. Recent issues have included articles about the future of opera in America, the effect of organizational culture on maintaining an effective workforce, and the centennial celebration of the L.A. Philharmonic. Announcements of orchestra personnel changes are also posted. Issues from January 2010 forward are available free of charge on the league's website, "*Symphony* Online." The online edition includes additional features, among them direct web links, interactivity, and enhanced multimedia. For large public and academic libraries. URL: http://www.americanorchestras.org/symphony-magazine.html

3776. ***Twentieth Century Music.*** [ISSN: 1478-5722] 2004. s-a. GBP 199 (print & online eds.)). Ed(s): Alejandro Madrid, Pauline Fairclough. Cambridge University Press, University Printing House, Shaftesbury Rd, Cambridge, CB2 8BS, United Kingdom; journals@cambridge.org; https://www.cambridge.org/. Adv. Refereed. Reprint: PSC. *Indexed:* A22, E01, IIMP, RILM. *Bk. rev.:* Number and length vary. *Aud.:* Ac.

Twentieth Century Music publishes articles examining all aspects of music from the late nineteenth century to the present. Taking into account past research, writers and editors strive to present new views and analyses of past and current studies of modern music. Articles cover topics related to music from Western and non-Western traditions, as well as popular music, jazz, improvised music, and film music. Recent issues have included contributions that address "Why the Next Song Matters: Streaming, Recommendation, Scarcity," and "'There Is Music in It, But It Is Not Music': A Reception History of Musique Concrete in Britain." Occasionally, special issues appear devoted to aspects of a single topic, such as "Music and Socialism." Each issue includes several extensive book reviews. Print and online subscriptions are available. Recommended for academic libraries. URL: https://www.cambridge.org/core/journals/twentieth-century-music

3777. ***The Voice.*** Former titles: *The Voice of Chorus America;* (until 1999): *Voice.* 1978. q. USD 95 (print & online eds.); Includes subscr. to: American Choral Review, and Research Memorandum Series Free to individual members). Ed(s): Liza W Beth. Chorus America, 1156 15th St, NW, Ste 310, Washington, DC 20005; service@chorusamerica.org; http://www.chorusamerica.org. Illus., adv. Vol. ends: Summer. *Indexed:* A01, IIMP. *Aud.:* Ac, Sa.

Chorus America's *The Voice* publishes articles of practical use to anyone involved in directing and/or running a successful choral organization. Articles address topics such as marketing strategies, vocal music trends, technology tools, hiring soloists, fundraising strategies, and touring tips. Each issue also highlights member news pertaining to world premieres, chorus anniversaries, awards and grants received, recording releases, and staff appointments. *The Voice* is published in spring, summer, fall, and winter. Libraries can subscribe to a package that includes a print copy and online access to *The Voice* as well as online access to *American Choral Review*, a journal that explores choral repertoire and performance practice issues, and the *Research Memorandum Series*, a bibliographic journal designed to provide programming ideas and assist in locating repertoire. Recommended for public and academic libraries. URL: https://www.chorusamerica.org/publications/voice

3778. ***Voices: a world forum for music therapy.*** [ISSN: 1504-1611] 2001. 3x/yr. Free. Ed(s): Rune Rolvsjord. Uni Health, The Grieg Academy Music Therapy Research Centre, c/o Grieg Academy, PO Box 7810, Bergen, 5020, Norway; http://helse.uni.no/Default.aspx?site=4&lg=2. Refereed. *Indexed:* IIMP, RILM. *Bk. rev.:* Number and length vary. *Aud.:* Ac, Sa.

Voices: A World Forum for Music Therapy is an online publication of international scope that "values inclusiveness and socio-cultural awareness." Its aim is to foster "dialogue and discussion about music, health, and social change." The publication especially seeks to encourage the growth of music therapy in developing countries. Contributions that reflect the cultural influences of a particular region on music and music therapy are encouraged. Articles accepted for publication generally fall into one of the following categories: research, book reviews, columns, essays, interviews, position papers, reflections on practice, or reports. Submissions are solicited from every continent. Recommended for academic, large public, and hospital libraries. URL: https://voices.no/index.php/voices.

3779. ***Women and Music: a journal of gender and culture.*** [ISSN: 1090-7505] 1997. a. USD 90. Ed(s): Emily Wilbourne. University of Nebraska Press, 1111 Lincoln Mall, Lincoln, NE 68588; journals@unl.edu; https://www.nebraskapress.unl.edu. Adv. Refereed. *Indexed:* A22, BRI, C42, E01, FemPer, GW, IIMP, MLA-IB, RILM. *Bk. rev.:* 10, essay length, signed. *Aud.:* Ac, Sa.

Women and Music began as an annual publication of the International Alliance for Women in Music (IAWM). This affiliation ended in 2008. Coverage since then is available via Project MUSE and the University of Nebraska is the current publisher. Articles in this refereed scholarly journal report on the interrelationships of music, gender, and culture with emphasis on the concerns of women. Topics addressed are international in scope. The articles analyze cultures, works, and historical periods from the perspective of a variety of disciplines; or they may discuss issues relating to women composers, performers, teachers, and so on. This journal contains review essays and book reviews. Recommended for academic collections. URL: https://nebraskapressjournals.unl.edu/search/?keyword=women+and+music

3780. ***The World of Music.*** [ISSN: 0043-8774] 1959. 2x/yr. EUR 54 domestic; EUR 60 foreign; EUR 28 newsstand/cover. Ed(s): Birgit Abels. V W B - Verlag fuer Wissenschaft und Bildung, Postfach 110368, Berlin, 10833, Germany; info@vwb-verlag.com; http://www.vwb-verlag.com. Illus., adv. Refereed. *Indexed:* A22, A47, BAS, IBSS, IIMP, MLA-IB, RILM. *Bk. rev.:* 5, 750-1,000 words, signed. *Aud.:* Ac, Sa.

Begun in 2009, *The World of Music (New Series)* is a continuation of the journal *The World of Music* as previously edited by Jonathan Stock. It is an international, peer-reviewed journal that seeks to publish the results of ethnomusicological research into music and dance practices and traditions around the world. Representing a variety of theoretical perspectives and approaches, the articles of this journal reflect a shared goal of "understanding the musics of the world, their histories, and their manifold contexts." Each issue focuses on a musical topic or a cultural or geographic region. A typical issue contains six to eight articles and several book and recording reviews. Articles vary in length from five to twenty pages with notes and bibliographies. Photographs and musical examples are often included. The journal's site displays abstracts of articles from 1997 to the present, as well as a bibliography arranged alphabetically by author. This title is available only in print format. Recommended for academic libraries. URL: http://www.journaltheworldofmusic.com/

Popular

Competition from online popular music resources, such as blogs and information provided by online retailers of music, has caused a significant reduction in relevant magazines in the past decade. Primary popular music genres such as rock, jazz, and blues maintain key publications that provide in-depth information for fans and professionals alike. The publications included here are selected as stable, core resources for those looking for periodicals that provide both quality writing and timely information on the current state of popular music.

3781. ***Alternative Press.*** [ISSN: 1065-1667] 1985. m. USD 14.95 domestic; USD 29.95 Canada; USD 39.95 elsewhere. Ed(s): Jason Pettigrew. Alternative Press Magazine, Inc., 1305 W 80th St, Ste 2 F, Cleveland, OH 44102-1996; http://www.altpress.com. Illus., adv. *Indexed:* IIMP. *Aud.:* Ga.

This publication began in 1985 as a fanzine devoted to underground music. It has grown to become a key resource covering punk and alternative pop and rock music. It includes tour reviews and profiles of top bands. The publication began hosting its own awards ceremony in 2014.

3782. ***Billboard (New York): the international newsweekly of music, video, and home entertainment.*** Formerly: *Billboard Music Week.* [ISSN: 0006-2510] 1894. w. USD 199 combined subscription domestic (print & online eds.); USD 299 combined subscription foreign (print & online eds.)). Ed(s): M Tye Comer. Prometheus Global Media, 770 Broadway, 7th Fl, New York, NY 10003; http://www.prometheusgm.com. Illus., adv. *Indexed:* A01, A22, B01, B03, BRI, C37, C42, CBRI, Chicano, F01, IIMP, IIPA, MASUSE. *Aud.:* Ga.

Billboard remains the most trusted resource in charting the popularity of music in all forms, from pop to country, R&B, Latin, and classical. The coverage of genres is extensive and always growing. The publication continues to extend efforts to chart the impact of social media and Internet streaming on popular music. Among these efforts is a joint real-time chart with social media giant Twitter. The publication publishes reviews that focus primarily on describing the songs or albums and their prospects for commercial success. Upcoming trends and artists are documented thoroughly, as well as the latest news affecting the music industry. The publication's web site covers the same material, as well as adding access to voluminous historical archives of music charts from the past. URL: http://Billboard.com

3783. ***D J Times: the international magazine for the professional mobile & club DJ.*** [ISSN: 1045-9693] 1988. m. USD 14.85. Ed(s): Jim Tremayne. Testa Communications, Inc., 25 Willowdale Ave, Port Washington, NY 11050. Illus., adv. *Indexed:* IIMP. *Aud.:* Ga.

This trade publication for the disc jockey market was the first in the United States specifically targeted to the disc jockey industry. Influence in popular music has grown with the emergence of electronic dance music as a key popular music genre. The publication provides charts of the most popular songs currently played in dance clubs, an authoritative annual poll on the most popular disc jockey in the United States, and an annual influential trade show.

3784. ***DownBeat.*** [ISSN: 0012-5768] 1934. m. USD 27.99 combined subscription domestic (print & online eds); USD 39.99 combined subscription Canada (print & online eds); USD 51.99 combined subscription foreign (print & online eds)). Maher Publications, 102 North Haven Rd, Elmhurst, IL 60126; editor@downbeat.com. Illus., adv. Microform: PQC. *Indexed:* A01, A22, AmHI, BRI, CBRI, Chicano, IIMP, MASUSE, RILM. *Bk. rev.:* 25-35, 500-1,000 words. *Aud.:* Ga.

This publication is one of the oldest and most respected periodicals in any popular music genre. Coverage centers on jazz, but this title also provides extensive material on blues and related music. Readers' polls on the year's best music have been published since the 1930s, and critics' polls since the 1950s. The results of these polls are archived on the publication's web site. Extensive reviews of current music are provided. Profiles of current artists and in-depth interviews help provide an even richer view of the current world of jazz and blues music. A unique feature of the periodical is "The Blindfold Test," in which a current musician is asked to listen to tracks and discuss the relevance of the music heard. This publication is an outstanding introduction to current jazz and blues music for a general audience, as well as being an essential resource for academic audiences.

3785. ***JazzTimes: America's jazz magazine.*** Supersedes: *Radio Free Jazz.* [ISSN: 0272-572X] 1972. 10x/yr. USD 29.99 domestic; USD 39.99 Canada; USD 44.99 elsewhere. Madavor Media, Llc., 25 Braintree Hill Office Park, Ste 404, Braintree, MA 02184; customerservice@madavor.com; http://www.madavor.com. Illus., adv. Circ: 100000 Paid. Microform: PQC. *Indexed:* A22, IIMP, RILM. *Bk. rev.:* Number and length vary. *Aud.:* Ga.

This publication provides a very thorough examination of the current state of jazz music for an audience ranging from casual fans to music professionals. Many of the contributors have received awards for being among the best in jazz journalism. The reviews cover not only recorded music, but also books, concerts, audio equipment, and even instruments. Regular columns provide examinations of key artists, interviews, and previews of upcoming events. Extensive directories of record labels, festivals, and artists are provided as a useful reference resource. The publication provides extensive annual critics and readers' polls to give a snapshot of the current state of jazz music. These are archived on the publication's web site. The stylish look of this publication and the quality of the photography included make it very pleasing to read and browse.

3786. ***Living Blues: the magazine of the African American blues tradition.*** Incorporates: *Living Bluesletter.* [ISSN: 0024-5232] 1970. bi-m. USD 29.95 domestic; USD 39.95 Canada; USD 47.95 elsewhere. Ed(s): Brett Bonner. University of Mississippi, Center for the Study of Southern Culture, 1111 Jackson Ave W, PO Box 1848, University, MS 38677; mark@livingblues.com; http://www.olemiss.edu/depts/south/. Illus., adv. Microform: PQC. *Indexed:* A22, IIMP, MLA-IB, RILM. *Aud.:* Ga, Ac.

This publication sets the standard for magazines that cover the blues scene. The magazine not only provides in-depth coverage of the music with profiles of artists, reviews of new music, and radio charts, but it also helps sponsor events that preserve the blues tradition, including annual music awards that have been presented each year since 1993. The approach and style of the magazine are suitably laid-back, to match the music itself. For general to academic audiences, this publication is a first choice for coverage of blues music. URL: www.livingblues.com

3787. ***Popular Music.*** [ISSN: 0261-1430] 1981. 3x/yr. GBP 441. Ed(s): Allan Moore, Sarah Hill. Cambridge University Press, University Printing House, Shaftesbury Rd, Cambridge, CB2 8BS, United Kingdom; journals@cambridge.org; https://www.cambridge.org/. Illus., index, adv. Refereed. Microform: PQC. Reprint: PSC. *Indexed:* A01, A22, AmHI, BRI, E01, IIMP, MLA-IB, RILM. *Aud.:* Ac.

A triannual publication of Cambridge University Press, *Popular Music* presents peer-reviewed articles of international and interdisciplinary scope, grounded in a core of musicological and ethnomusicological analysis. Feature scholarly articles are inventive in their originality, tremendously inclusive, and remarkably conscious of both mainstream popular acts (for example, Led Zeppelin, Korn, and The Beatles) and broader topics (New Zealand popular music and cultural identity, policy and performance in the Caribbean, to name a few). Meanwhile, these articles sacrifice none of the discipline and analytical rigor expected of a high-quality academic publication. The "Middle Eight" section provides one or two pieces of polemical interest, including but not limited to conference reviews and special case studies. Special issues are intermittently published, with recent examples presenting on such topics as Dance and Italian Popular Music. Highly recommended for academic libraries. (Osik, Jason J.)

3788. *Popular Music & Society.* [ISSN: 0300-7766] 1972. 5x/yr. GBP 305 (print & online eds.) Individuals, USD 149). Ed(s): Thomas M Kitts, Gary Burns. Routledge, 4 Park Sq, Milton Park, Abingdon, OX14 4RN, United Kingdom; subscriptions@tandf.co.uk; http://www.tandfonline.com. Illus., index, adv. Sample. Refereed. Microform: PQC. Reprint: PSC. *Indexed:* A01, A22, AmHI, BRI, CBRI, E01, IBSS, IIMP, MLA-IB, RILM. *Aud.:* Ac.

A peer-reviewed scholarly journal of broad interdisciplinary scope, accepting historical, theoretical, critical, sociological, and cultural perspectives on a similarly broad range of popular music in scholarly articles and in relevant book, audio, and media reviews. Academic contributors offer original and authoritative views on music as it interfaces with culture at large. Special-topic issues are presented (typically every other release), with recent and upcoming issues addressing such topics as New Orleans music legacy and survival, record charts, music as torture, krautrock, popular music in the post-Soviet space, and Bob Dylan. The book reviews, at lengths similar to those of the regular articles, represent a substantial resource for further reading and research. The editorial staff clearly understands the value of these reviews, as they often constitute a large fraction of a typical issue, at nearly half the total volume on average. Full text is available to online subscription. (Osik, Jason J.)

3789. *Rolling Stone.* [ISSN: 0035-791X] 1967. 26x/yr. USD 29.95 domestic; USD 38 Canada; USD 85 elsewhere. Ed(s): Jann S Wenner. Rolling Stone LLC, 1290 Ave. of the Americas, 2nd Fl, New York, NY 10104; letters@rollingstone.com. Illus., adv. Circ: 1469213 Paid. Microform: PQC. *Indexed:* A01, A22, BRI, C37, CBRI, Chicano, F01, IIMP, IIPA, MASUSE. *Bk. rev.:* Number and length vary. *Aud.:* Ga.

This publication continues to be a cornerstone of popular music criticism and news in the United States. The periodical's rock leanings are not as prominent as in the past. There have been changes in coverage, as the relative size of rock in the commercial marketplace has shrunk. Politics and movies continue to be areas in which the publication reaches beyond simple coverage of music. Quality feature writing continues to be a hallmark of the magazine. Its album reviews, graded with a five-star system, are influential in the industry. The publication's web site has a very extensive and well-organized archive of material from the past. Subscribers have complete access to all past issues of the publication, while extensive material remains available for free browsing. URL: www.rollingstone.com/

3790. *Sing Out!: folk music - folk songs.* [ISSN: 0037-5624] 1950. q. Free to members; Non-members, USD 60. Ed(s): Mark D Moss. Sing Out Corp., 512 E Fourth St, PO Box 5460, Bethlehem, PA 18015; http://www.singout.org. Illus., adv. *Indexed:* A01, A22, BRI, IIMP, MLA-IB, RILM. *Bk. rev.:* Number and length vary. *Aud.:* Ga.

This magazine is a quarterly publication issued by an organization of the same name that is dedicated to supporting and preserving traditional and contemporary folk music. A centerpiece of the print publication remains complete lead sheets on ten folk songs, accompanied by a CD with performances by the original artists. In addition, the magazine provides articles, news, and reviews. The definition of folk music is broad and ranges from blues to bluegrass, Celtic, and Cajun music. Festivals and awards dedicated to folk music are covered. The web site for the publication provides access to a weekly streaming radio magazine, as well as folk music directories. URL: www.singout.org/magazine.html

■ MUSIC REVIEWS

General/Audio Equipment

Scott Pfitzinger, Multimedia Librarian, Maag Library, Youngstown State University, One University Plaza, Youngstown, OH 44555; sgpfitzinger@ysu.edu

Introduction

There are many options for consumers to stream music in the twenty-first century. Libraries and even individuals must, therefore, be increasingly judicious about their purchases of physical recordings of music. This section contains resources to help make those decisions easier. The focus is on magazines published in the United States and United Kingdom that contain reviews of classical and jazz music recordings and audio equipment. For other genres of music, see the "Music/Popular" section. All listed magazines have online versions, as well as print.

While there are still a few magazines that offer reviews of music recordings and audio equipment, more of these resources are moving to online-only formats, allowing them to share reviews much more frequently and in a more timely manner. Because of their importance in this subject area, some recommended web sites are listed below.

CLASSICAL MUSIC RECORDINGS

Classical CD Review: A Site for the Serious Record Collector. URL: http://classicalcdreview.com—CD and DVD reviews and more, updated "at least every two weeks."

Classical.net: The Internet's Premier Classical Music Source. URL: http://classical.net—Reviews and articles, information on composers, repertoire lists, and more. Updated frequently.

Classics Today: Your Online Guide to Classical Music. URL: www.classicstoday.com—News and reviews updated daily. Enhanced "Insider Reviews" ($49/year) provide enhanced search features, weekly emails, reviews with audio, and more.

JAZZ MUSIC RECORDINGS

All About Jazz. URL: www.allaboutjazz.com—Information and opinion about jazz from the past, present, and future for both the curious listener and the jazz aficionado. Updated daily.

Jazz Review. URL: www.jazzreview.com—CD and concert reviews, interviews, photos, and more.

Pitchfork. URL: http://pitchfork.com—News, reviews, and articles about jazz and independent music, updated daily.

AUDIO EQUIPMENT

AudioReview.com. URL: www.audioreview.com—Product information, user reviews, community discussion boards, and shopping for all kinds of audio equipment. Updated frequently.

SoundStage Network. URL: www.soundstagenetwork.com—News, reviews, buying guides, and a measurements library. With daily updates.

Basic Periodicals

Ga: *The Absolute Sound, American Record Guide, Fanfare* (Tenafly), *Gramophone;* Ac: *The Absolute Sound, American Record Guide, Fanfare* (Tenafly), *Gramophone.*

Basic Abstracts and Indexes

International Index to Music Periodicals, Music Index, RILM Abstracts of Music Literature.

General

3791. *American Record Guide.* Former titles (until 1944): *Listener's Record Guide;* (until Sep.1944): *The American Music Lover;* (until 1935): *Music Lover's Guide.* [ISSN: 0003-0716] 1932. bi-m. USD 48 domestic (print or online ed.); USD 75 foreign; USD 7 per issue). Ed(s): Donald R Vroon. Record Guide Productions, 4412 Braddock St, Cincinnati, OH 45204; subs@americanrecordguide.com. Illus., index, adv. Sample. Vol. ends: Dec. *Indexed:* A01, A22, BRI, C37, CBRI, IIMP, MASUSE. *Bk. rev.:* Number and length vary. *Aud.:* Ga, Ac.

American Record Guide, "America's oldest classical music review magazine," aims to remain free of advertiser influence. This results in a high-quality, robust magazine with few ads and over 150 pages of straightforward, critical recording reviews. The reviews often begin with a history of the composer, performer, or work to place the recording in context, and most end with a recommendation. All aspects of the recording are considered, including vocal and instrumental performance, listenability, interpretation of classics, song selection in collections, recording quality, and even CD packaging with regard to liner notes and accompanying texts. Most issues contain an "Overview" article that provides an extensive review of recordings on a specific topic-for example, focusing on one composer or one area of the repertoire, such as Russian music. The magazine also includes reviews of videos and live performances, as well as articles on current events in the classical music world. An annual index is published in the November/December or January/February issue. The web site provides an index to the overviews, current contents, brief biographies of reviewers, and a searchable index for subscribers only. The large number of reviews makes this an excellent magazine for public and academic libraries. URL: www.americanrecordguide.com

DownBeat. See Music/Popular section.

3792. *Fanfare (Tenafly): the magazine for serious record collectors.* [ISSN: 0148-9364] 1977. bi-m. USD 60 combined subscription domestic (print & online eds.); USD 100 combined subscription foreign (print & online eds.)). Fanfare, Inc., 17 Lancaster Rd, PO Box 17, Tenafly, NJ 07670. Illus., adv. Sample. Vol. ends: Jul/Aug. *Indexed:* A01, A22, BRI, CBRI, IIMP. *Bk. rev.:* Number and length vary. *Aud.:* Ga, Ac.

Since its inception, *Fanfare* was intended to provide informative reviews without being "stuffy and academic," and this is still the case. Each issue includes over 250 reviews written in an easy-to-read, descriptive, and informal style. The "Classical Recordings" section includes CD and DVD reviews arranged by composer. The "Collections" section is divided into vocal, choral, early music, instrumental, ensemble, and orchestral. Extensive reviews often cover the background of the composer, artist, or work; performance quality; sound quality; and comparisons with other recordings. Additional review columns include "Jazz," "Classical Hall of Fame," and "Book Reviews." The magazine also includes articles, interviews, and label profiles. The web site includes tables of contents and a selection of recently published articles and reviews. Subscribers can access full articles and reviews in the archive. With numerous and lengthy reviews, this magazine is highly recommended for public and academic libraries. URL: www.fanfaremag.com

3793. *Gramophone.* Incorporates (in 1923): *Vox; Radio Critic; Broadcast Review; Cassettes and Cartridges.* [ISSN: 0017-310X] 19??. 13x/yr. GBP 59.80 domestic; GBP 74.80 in Europe; USD 87 United States. Haymarket Publishing Ltd., Bridge House, 69 London Rd, Twickenham, TW1 3SP, United Kingdom; info@haymarket.com; http://www.haymarket.com. Illus., index, adv. Vol. ends: May. *Indexed:* A22, IIMP. *Bk. rev.:* Occasional. *Aud.:* Ga, Ac.

Gramophone, "the world's best classical music reviews," provides articles, news, and reviews from a global perspective. The entertaining, informative, and easy-to-read reviews cover orchestral, chamber, vocal, and instrumental music, and opera. While the performance and music are the focus of the review, there is often discussion of the performer and history of the works. Issues also include profiles, interviews, news, obituaries, book and DVD reviews, and a small product-review section. The web site includes news, blogs, forums, feature articles, a festival guide, awards, and their "Gramophone Hall of Fame," which has categories of conductors, singers, pianists, string/brass/woodwind players, vocal and instrumental ensembles, and producers/engineers/record label executives. A digital archive app can be purchased to view the entire contents of every issue back to 1923. Recommended for both neophytes and classical aficionados. URL: www.gramophone.co.uk

JazzTimes. See Music/Popular section.

Sound & Vision. See Television, Video, and Radio/Home Entertainment section.

Audio Equipment

3794. *The Absolute Sound.* [ISSN: 0097-1138] 1973. m. USD 14.95. Ed(s): Robert Harley, Julie Mullins. NextScreen, LLC, 2500 McHale Ct Ste A, Austin, TX 78758; http://www.nextscreen.com/. Illus., index, adv. Sample. Vol. ends: Dec/Jan. *Aud.:* Ga, Ac.

The Absolute Sound "explores music and the reproduction of music in the home" by providing columns, reports, and reviews of audio equipment and music recordings. Equipment reports are easy to read and include physical attributes, performance quality, comparisons to similar products, and discussion of the testing process and recordings used. A sidebar highlights specifications, manufacturer information, and a list of associated equipment, when appropriate. The music review section is divided by genre and includes rock, classical, and jazz, with an average of five reviews in each category. Ratings are provided for music and sonics based on a scale of one to five, with one being poor and five extraordinary. Reviews generally begin with a brief background of the artist, group, or album, followed by discussion of music quality; they wrap up with comment on production quality. Further listening recommendations of albums by other groups are also included. *The Absolute Sound*'s online version is part of AVguide.com, which also includes reviews from *Playback, Perfect Vision,* and *Hifi Plus.* Reviews, "Buyers' Guides," news, blogs, and forums round out the site. With well-written reviews and extensive content, this magazine and web site are highly recommended for public and academic libraries. URL: www.theabsolutesound.com

Stereophile. See Television, Video, and Radio/Home Entertainment section.

■ NATIVE AMERICANS

Law/Education

Berlin Loa, Museum/Archives Technician; berlinloa@gmail.com

Introduction

The Native American collection of publications includes scholarly works and popular magazines relating to Native American cultures, law, art, and general interest subjects. The journals included here include those targeted to academic and public library audiences.

Basic Periodicals

Hs: *American Indian Law Review, Winds of Change;* Ac: *American Indian Culture and Research Journal, Wicazo Sa Review.*

Basic Abstracts and Indexes

Abstracts in Anthropology, Alternative Press Index, America: History and Life, Anthropological Literature, Ethnic NewsWatch, Historical Abstracts, Project MUSE.

3795. *American Indian Culture and Research Journal.* Formerly (until 1974): *American Indian Culture Center. Journal.* [ISSN: 0161-6463] 1971. q. USD 110 (Individuals, USD 60; USD 15 per issue). Ed(s): Duane Champagne. University of California, Los Angeles, American Indian Studies Center, 3220 Campbell Hall, PO Box 951548, Los Angeles, CA 90095-1548; sales@aisc.ucla.edu; http://www.books.aisc.ucla.edu. Illus., adv. Refereed. *Indexed:* A01, A22, A47, AmHI, BRI, CBRI, ERIC, MLA-IB, P61, SSA. *Bk. rev.:* 20-21, 400-800 words. *Aud.:* Ac, Sa.

The contents of the *American Indian Culture and Research Journal* represent a spectrum of the Native American experience and cultures. This journal contains articles, book reviews, and features regarding culture, film, arts, rights issues and activism, education, and cultural resource management and research. It invites academic articles, poetry, and commentary; it covers the fields of history, anthropology, geography, sociology, health, law, literature, education, and the arts. Recommended for academic libraries. Specifically recommended for institutions with cultural studies programs, including Native American Studies, anthropology, literature, and interdisciplinary cultural-resource studies.

3796. ***Etudes Inuit Studies.*** [ISSN: 0701-1008] 1977. s-a. CAD 225 (print & online eds.) Individuals, CAD 50 (print & online eds.)). Ed(s): Murielle Nagy. Inuksiutiit Katimajiit Association, Inc., Universite Laval, 0450 Pavillon Charles de Konink, Quebec, QC G1V 0A6, Canada; http://www.fss.ulaval.ca/etudes-inuit-studies/. Adv. Refereed. *Indexed:* A47, IBSS, MLA-IB, PdeR, SSA. *Bk. rev.:* Number and length vary. *Aud.:* Ac, Sa.

Etudes/Inuit/Studies is an academic journal that features articles and research papers, as well as book reviews and dissertation reviews. Issues are thematic and contents relate primarily to traditional and contemporary Inuit ethnology, history, politics, cultures, and Inuit-related global issues. Additionally, issues may include conference call-for-papers, research notes, memorials, and recognition of scholars contributing to Inuit studies. The journal is published semi-annually and is multilingual in English and French, with a limited use of the Inuit language in the form of Inuktitut syllabics. Articles are refereed. This journal is recommended for academic and research libraries-specifically for those serving studies in ethnology, politics, archaeology, linguistics, and history pertaining to indigenous cultures, Native American Studies, and First Nations.

3797. ***Indigenous Woman.*** [ISSN: 1070-1400] 1991. a. Indigenous Women's Network, 13621 FM 2769, Austin, TX 78726; almademujer@igc.org; http://www.honorearth.com/iwn/. Illus. *Aud.:* Hs, Ga, Ac, Sa.

Indigenous Woman Magazine is a publication of the Indigenous Women's Network. Issues contain articles, essays, and features regarding legal, ethical, health, and cultural concerns of indigenous peoples. Items in this journal are written and published by women activists and artists. Recommended for public and academic libraries, specifically for those with Gender Studies, Women's Studies, or Native American Studies programs.

3798. ***Whispering Wind: American Indian: past & present.*** [ISSN: 0300-6565] 1967. bi-m. USD 25 domestic; USD 43 foreign; USD 4.50 per issue. Jack Heriard, Ed. & Pub., PO Box 1390, Folsom, LA 70437. Illus., index, adv. Sample. Vol. ends: No. 6. *Indexed:* A47, BRI, C42, ENW. *Bk. rev.:* 4-6, 300-500 words. *Aud.:* Hs, Ga, Sa.

Whispering Wind is a bimonthly magazine dedicated to the review of Native American material culture, traditions, and arts. The magazine features book and music reviews, articles regarding dance, music, traditional and modern arts, clothing and traditions, and advertisements for craft materials. A calendar of events is available on the web site, and a list of events is included in the print copy. Recommended for public or school libraries.

3799. ***Wicazo Sa Review: a journal of native American studies.*** [ISSN: 0749-6427] 1985. s-a. USD 87 (print & online eds.)). Ed(s): James Riding. University of Minnesota Press, 111 Third Avenue South, Ste 290, Minneapolis, MN 55401; http://www.upress.umn.edu. Illus., adv. Refereed. Vol. ends: No. 2. *Indexed:* A01, A22, A47, AmHI, BRI, E01, MLA-IB. *Bk. rev.:* 1-2, 800 words. *Aud.:* Ac, Sa.

Wicazo Sa Review is a journal developed with the goal of assisting indigenous peoples in intellectual and creative endeavors. Published semi-annually, the journal includes articles, interviews, reviews, and research primarily regarding cultural, religious, legal, and historical issues. The journal also includes book reviews, literature and poetry reviews, and essays. Recommended for academic libraries, this journal is essential to those that offer Native American Studies, but is also recommended for public libraries that serve Native American populations or within regions with an interest in Native American cultures.

3800. ***Winds of Change: empowering opportunities for American Indians, Alaska natives, and native Hawaiians.*** [ISSN: 0888-8612] 1986. 5x/yr. Free to members. Ed(s): Amy Norcross, Karen English. A I S E S Publishing, 2305 Renard Place, Ste 200, Albuquerque, NM 87106; info@aises.org; http://www.aises.org. Illus., index, adv. Sample. Vol. ends: Fall. *Bk. rev.:* 2-10, 250-600 words. *Aud.:* Hs, Ga, Ac, Sa.

Winds of Change is a full-color, quarterly magazine focused on career and educational opportunities for Native American and Alaska Native peoples. The journal is primarily business-related and STEM-related ("STEM" means "science, technology, engineering, or mathematics"). It includes contents related to business, universities, health and well-being, and Native cultures from both tribal and non-tribal resources. Issues contain articles related to career development, educational opportunities and strategies, book reviews, and advertisements. The journal also publishes an annual "College Issue" for students and recruiters. Recommended for school, public, and academic libraries.

3801. ***Yellow Medicine Review: a journal of indigenous literature, art, and thought.*** [ISSN: 1939-4624] 2007. s-a. USD 21.50 domestic; USD 30 foreign; USD 15 per issue foreign. Southwest Minnesota State University, 1501 State St, Marshall, MN 56258; http://www.smsu.edu/. *Aud.:* Hs, Ga, Ac, Sa.

Yellow Medicine Review is published as a place for new artists, writers, and scholars to present new work, and is published through the Difficult Dialogues Initiative of Southwest Minnesota State University. The journal invites poetry, essays, art, memoir, drama, and fiction of indigenous perspectives. The journal defines indigenous "universally as representative of all pre-colonial peoples." Subscriptions are available via the journal's web site; single current and past issues are available via the journal web site and on Amazon.

Law

3802. ***American Indian Law Review.*** [ISSN: 0094-002X] 1973. s-a. USD 30. Ed(s): Mallory Irwinsky, Abbi Slaton. University of Oklahoma, College of Law, Andrew M Coats Hall, 300 Timberdell Rd, Norman, OK 73019; law@law.ou.edu; http://www.law.ou.edu. Refereed. Microform: WSH; PMC. Reprint: WSH. *Indexed:* BRI, L14. *Aud.:* Ac, Sa.

American Indian Law Review is a scholarly journal published semi-annually, and features articles and expository essays by legal scholars and practitioners. The *Law Review* also includes commentary from students and editorial board members. Contents of the journal pertain to legislation and legal issues that affect Native Americans and indigenous peoples throughout the U.S. and internationally. Submissions are double-blind peer-reviewed. The journal is recommended for academic libraries and is essential to those that offer studies in Native American cultures and U.S. law. Reprints and subscription information are available on the web site, but full-text articles are only available in print.

3803. ***N A R F Legal Review.*** Formerly (until 1983): *Native American Rights Fund. Announcements.* [ISSN: 0739-862X] 1972. s-a. Free. Ed(s): Ray Ramirez. Native American Rights Fund, 1506 Broadway, Boulder, CO 80302; pubrequest@narf.org; http://www.narf.org. *Aud.:* Ga, Ac, Sa.

The *Native American Rights Fund Legal Review* provides information on current law topics and updates on NARF cases. The review is free, but contributions are suggested, which would support NARF. Recommended for academic libraries, specifically those with a Native American Studies program and for public libraries that serve Native American populations.

Education

3804. ***Financial Aid for Native Americans.*** Supersedes in part (in 1999): *Directory of Financial Aids for Minorities.* [ISSN: 1099-9116] 1985. biennial. USD 45 per issue. Ed(s): R David Weber, Gail A Schlachter. Reference Service Press, 5000 Windplay Dr, Ste 4, El Dorado Hills, CA 95762; info@rspfunding.com; http://www.rspfunding.com. *Aud.:* Hs, Ga, Ac.

Financial Aid for Native Americans is a reference list of scholarships, grants, fellowships, and other financial sources for Native American students. The journal is published a part of a series of financial aid guides for minorities. A preview of the current issue is available on the web site. Recommended for public, school, and academic libraries that serve Native American students.

3805. ***Journal of American Indian Education.*** [ISSN: 0021-8731] 1961. 3x/yr. USD 130 (print & online eds.)). Ed(s): Bryan McKinley Jones Brayboy, K Tsianina Lomawaima. University of Minnesota Press, 111 Third Avenue South, Ste 290, Minneapolis, MN 55401. Illus., index, adv. Refereed. Vol. ends: Spring (No. 3). Microform: PQC. *Indexed:* A22, C42, ERIC, MLA-IB. *Bk. rev.:* Number and length vary. *Aud.:* Ac, Sa.

Journal of American Indian Education is published three times per year by the Arizona State University Center for Indian Education. Contents include articles, book reviews, research papers, and field report features related to educational issues and innovations that affect Native American, First Nations, and other indigenous cultures. This journal is recommended for academic and research libraries that support studies in education and Native American cultures.

■ NEWS AND OPINION

See also General Interest; and Newspapers sections.

Lorena O'English, Social Sciences Librarian, Washington State University, Pullman, WA 99164; oenglish@wsu.edu

Erica Carlson Nicol, Humanities & Social Sciences Librarian, Washington State University, Pullman, WA 99164; eacarlson@wsu.edu

Introduction

Americans are living in a time where they are constantly bombarded with news, from television, newspapers, the web, news apps, and more. Current events keep the feed flowing, but what often generates interest, response, and debate—as well as policy making—are the informative and or provocative feature articles that are originally published in news and opinion magazines. These articles provide awareness of the wide range of supporting and opposing viewpoints on the issues of the day. Newsmagazines provide information and analysis around contemporary events; and opinion and ideas journals provide different perspectives across political, ideological, and issue spectrums. News and opinion journals serve an even more important function in the modern misinformation/disinformation era, generally providing solid reporting and punditry backed up by known writers and journal reputations, as well as (usually) fact-checking and legal departments.

Keeping up with current events and public affairs via news and opinion magazines is a fine American tradition. Like many magazines these days, however, the space around news and opinion publications is in flux; a function of political, economic, and technological changes. Some magazines that were available in print only a few years ago are now online-only, have completely changed direction, or have gone out of business completely. *The Weekly Standard* is an interesting example. A neoconservative magazine that started publication in 1995, the *The Weekly Standard*'s circulation and political impact was diminishing, and the publication was shuttered by its publisher in late 2018, with its subscriber list moving over to its publisher's other political magazine, *The Washington Examiner*, a Beltway publication trying to go national. In the wake of these events, a number of the "Never Trump" writers from the *The Weekly Standard* have started a new political website, *The Bulwark*.

Opinion and news publications are also keeping themselves in the conversation via blogs, podcasts, video, and e-newsletters that can be sent out quickly to keep up with the 24/7 news cycle. Virtually every print publication has an extensive web presence, with multiple options for sharing article links across social media, and subscription and newsstand purchases now include digital versions for smartphone or tablet mobile access via in-app purchases on iOS, Android, and other app store markets, in addition to traditional print issues. Increasingly, news articles from current events publications are being integrated directly into devices (i.e., Apple's News and News Plus apps for iOS) and platforms (Facebook and Twitter, and the like). The result is that there are two major and complementary forces that affect how Americans get articles from news and opinion magazines: the impact of disintermediation and aggregation, and the increasing use of mobile devices as a means of getting and reading information about current events.

Disintermediation means that many articles are read independently of their initial publication source, disassociated from the cues that readers were previously able to obtain from the magazine cover and other articles in the issue. Readers are as likely to read an article because they saw referral link to it in their social media feeds—or had an article pushed to their tablet or smartphone via aggregated magazine apps such as Flipboard or Google News as they are to read it directly from the magazine itself (whether in print or digital format). They may even curate their own current events magazine on the fly, using "read it later" services such as Instapaper or Pocket, as they come across interesting articles over time. This separation—and the increased existence of manipulated misinformation and "fake news"—increases the importance of critical evaluation of content, authorship, purpose, and the perspective, or bias, in which articles are framed; that is, it usually matters that an article comes from the *National Review* versus coming from the *Nation*, versus coming from DailyBuzzLive.

A casual observer may note that the airport and bookstore magazine racks that used to host multiple news and opinion publications now hold considerably fewer. Library patrons may be exposed to a publication's articles through a blog they follow, coming to their local library to investigate the publication further, and librarians may find that they need to have an awareness of the publications that are likely to be asked about. Thus libraries still need to provide reliable access to current and back issues for their patrons for a wide range of publications across the ideological spectrum. In addition to print subscriptions and article access through aggregators, libraries may be able to provide online access to digital issues through digital magazine distribution vendors such as RBdigital and Overdrive's Libby app, or digital archives such as OpinionArchives or Exact Editions.

Basic Periodicals

The Nation, National Review, The New Republic, Newsweek, Time.

Basic Abstracts and Indexes

Academic OneFile, Alt-Press Watch, PAIS International.

3806. *The American Conservative: the magazine for thinking conservatives.* [ISSN: 1540-966X] 2002. bi-m. USD 59.95 combined subscription domestic print & online eds.; USD 79.95 combined subscription elsewhere print & online eds. American Conservative LLC, PO Box 9030, Maple Shade, NJ 08052. Adv. *Indexed:* A01, BRI. *Bk. rev.:* 1,500-2,000 words; signed. *Aud.:* Ga, Ac.

The American Conservative, a non-profit publication, was founded in 2002 by Pat Buchanan and others to provide a space for conservative opposition to the Iraq War and other Bush administration policies. Almost two decades later it considers itself to be a "Main Street" conservativism publication that is against unchecked government and corporate power, and in favor of "vibrant markets and free people," and a foreign policy grounded in America's national interests. The magazine's motto is "Ideas over Ideology, Principles over Party," and a reader might find a wide range of ideas and voices in its pages, with political commentary joining cultural commentary and book review essays. Its website includes free links to selected articles from print issues as well as extensive web-only articles and blog content. Recommended for academic libraries and public libraries.

3807. *The American Spectator (Online).* 1967. . The American Spectator, 1611 N Kent St, Ste 901, Arlington, VA 22209; editor@spectator.org; http://www.spectator.org. *Bk. rev.:* 3-4, 1,500 words; signed. *Aud.:* Ga, Ac.

The American Spectator provides articles on political issues as well as social and cultural articles, commentary and reviews, all from a conservative perspective. The layout of the magazine's website is eye-catching and fairly easy to navigate, although for some users "advertorial" web advertisements may be difficult to distinguish from actual *American Spectator* articles. Often humorous, the magazine showcases numerous political cartoons, mostly lambasting liberal politicians, on its site. As with many publications with a particular political lens, the writing fluctuates between opinion-driven journalism and sheer opinion. Its often-satirical right-wing perspective is not unique among the constellation of online publications, but it is of better quality than much else that is available, and *The American Spectator* is a known venue for prominent conservative pundits such as Ben Stein and Paul Kengore. This makes it a worthwhile purchase for public and academic libraries that serve more conservative communities, or those interested in representing the full political spectrum in their collections.

3808. ***Bitch: the feminist response to pop culture.*** [ISSN: 1524-5314] 1996. q. USD 24.95 domestic; USD 34.95 Canada; USD 47.95 elsewhere. Ed(s): Andi Zeisler. B - Word Worldwise, 4930 NE 29th Ave, Portland, OR 97211. Illus., adv. *Indexed:* A01, F01, FemPer, GW. *Bk. rev.:* Number and length vary. *Aud.:* Hs, Ga, Ac.

Bitch provides reporting, critical essays, opinion pieces, and interviews from a feminist viewpoint. Each issue contains several feature articles as well as opinion columns; reviews of movies, music, and books; and a cartoon spread that addresses a person or event important to feminist history. *Bitch* prides itself on offering a smart, fresh approach to women's and gender issues in social and popular culture, and its writing is geared toward modern feminists. Writing featured in *Bitch* tends to look at issues complexly, paying attention to the intersections of gender, race, policy, and culture. More traditional feminist viewpoints and post-feminist views are often both represented and sometimes interrogated. The magazine offers print and online subscriptions. Supplementary content, including a blog, a regular "Feminist News Roundup," and two regular podcasts, is available from the "Bitch Media" website. *Bitch* is a good addition to the collections of academic libraries where popular culture and women's and gender studies are taught, and also to public libraries serving populations of young adults and young professionals.

3809. ***Commentary.*** Formerly (until 1945): *Contemporary Jewish Record.* [ISSN: 0010-2601] 1938. m. except Jul./Aug. combined. USD 29.99 combined subscription (print & online eds.); USD 5.95 per issue domestic; USD 7 per issue Canada). Ed(s): John Podhoretz. American Jewish Committee, 165 E 56th St, New York, NY 10022; PR@ajc.org; http://www.ajc.org. Index, adv. Sample. Circ: 26000 Paid. Vol. ends: Jun/Dec. *Indexed:* A01, A22, AmHI, BAS, BRI, C37, C42, CBRI, MASUSE, MLA-IB. *Bk. rev.:* 1,500-2,000 words; signed. *Aud.:* Ga, Ac.

Commentary, a neoconservative news monthly, was originally published by the American Jewish Committee but went independent in 2007. The magazine has a history of publishing provocative and influential articles; areas of interest include anti-totalitarianism, security, the preservation of high culture, Israel, and American and worldwide Judaism. Each issue includes an "Articles" section with feature articles; a "Monthly Commentaries" section including a usually lively letters page, often with responses from article authors; and "Politics and Ideas" and "Culture and Civilization" sections that include shorter articles and reviews. The magazine also occasionally publishes short fiction. The online edition includes timely articles and podcasts by *Commentary* writers and contributors, and provides users with a number of free articles a month before requiring a subscription. Individual subscriptions include full access to the website and its online archive. Online articles have commenting and social sharing options, and the magazine has a social media presence, including on Twitter (@Commentary and some individual writers) and Facebook. This title is appropriate for academic and public libraries.

Commonweal. See Religion section.

3810. ***Dissent (New York).*** [ISSN: 0012-3846] 1954. q. USD 69.95 (print & online eds.) Individuals, USD 29.95 (print & online eds.)). Ed(s): Michael Kazin. Foundation for the Study of Independent Social Ideas, Inc., 120 Wall St, Fl 31, New York, NY 10005. Illus., index, adv. Sample. Vol. ends: Fall (No. 4). Microform: PQC. *Indexed:* A01, A22, AmHI, BAS, BRI, CBRI, E01, MLA-IB, P61, SSA. *Bk. rev.:* 5, 2,000 words; signed. *Aud.:* Ga, Ac.

Dissent, founded in 1954 with the clear intent of providing a voice to socialist and radically leftist ideas and journalism, retains a strong progressive perspective to this day. While most of the magazine is devoted to coverage of the United States, each issue also contains significant international coverage. The magazine also publishes substantial book reviews, essays on culture, and the occasional piece of fiction. This magazine is published quarterly, and its strength is not of breaking news but of the in-depth and intellectual discussion of social and political events. While being accessible to a general audience, pieces published in the magazine often contain significant historical background and the discussion of political and social theory, unsurprising in a publication that once included Hannah Arendt as a contributor. Current contributors to the magazine include academic authors as well as journalists and activists. This publication's intellectual and leftist outlook is unique; while its perspective may be off-putting to more conservative readers, it is strongly recommended for both academic and public libraries interested in providing news and opinion magazines from a variety of perspectives.

The Economist. See Economics section.

Foreign Affairs. See Political Science/International Relations section.

Foreign Policy (Washington). See Political Science/International Relations section.

3811. ***Human Events (Online): powerful conservative voices.*** 20??. . Free. Ed(s): Raheem Kassam. Eagle Publishing, Inc., 300 New Jersey Ave, NW, Ste 500, Washington, DC 20001; humanresources@eaglepub.com; http://www.eaglepub.com. Adv. *Bk. rev.:* Number and length vary; signed. *Aud.:* Ga, Ac.

Human Events went online-only in 2013 after almost 70 years in print. Originally a publication that presented a traditional conservative perspective, *Human Events* was sold and relaunched in 2019; its new owners have positioned it as "Real news and MAGA views," framed around "Trump as a philosophy, not Trump the man." Areas of interest include U.S. politics, foreign affairs, technology, and culture. Articles are freely available, however paid members get additional access. Articles have social sharing options, and the magazine supports a social media presence on Facebook and Twitter. *Human Events* is recommended for academic and public libraries.

3812. ***In These Times.*** [ISSN: 0160-5992] 1976. m. USD 19.95 combined subscription domestic (print & online eds.); USD 34.95 combined subscription Canada (print & online eds.); USD 40.95 combined subscription elsewhere (print & online eds.)). Ed(s): Joel Bleifuss. Institute for Public Affairs, PO Box 6347, Harlan, IA 51593. Illus., adv. Vol. ends: Nov. Microform: PQC. *Indexed:* A22, Chicano, MLA-IB. *Bk. rev.:* Number and length vary. *Aud.:* Ga, Ac.

In These Times has a strong socialist history and provides a progressive, democratic socialist perspective on current news. Opinion pieces can be especially critical of far-right standard bearers and policies, but the magazine publishes occasional pieces critical of the left as well. *In These Times* provides a useful table of contents for each monthly issue where investigative news pieces, opinion pieces, and pieces on culture are clearly delineated, making it easy to separate opinion pieces from the more serious news reporting. A unique feature of this magazine is the "Act Locally" section, which features articles on activism. While the magazine reports on major news issues, many of the stories it covers, of both national and international scope, are not reported widely by other media sources. This is a good choice for academic libraries looking for titles that speak to news reporting outside of the mainstream, and for both public and academic libraries with collections that present a balance of conservative and liberal media perspectives.

3813. ***Monthly Review.*** [ISSN: 0027-0520] 1949. m. Individuals, USD 29; USD 6 per issue. Ed(s): John Bellamy Foster. Monthly Review Foundation, 146 W 29th St, Ste 6W, New York, NY 10001. Illus., index, adv. Refereed. Vol. ends: Dec. Microform: PQC. *Indexed:* A01, A22, BAS, BRI, MLA-IB, P61, SSA. *Bk. rev.:* Number and length vary; signed. *Aud.:* Ga, Ac, Sa.

The *Monthly Review* has been publishing articles from an independent socialist perspective since 1949. Areas of interest include the environment, anti-imperialism, feminism, labor, inequality, and framing current issues from the perspective of the propertyless; often through a Marxist lens. The publication has an international scope, including articles in translation, and a scholarly-yet-readable tone (including citations and end notes), which is not surprising given how many of its writers are also academics; however, it also occasionally publishes poetry. The *Monthly Review* values dialogue, and each issue will often include at least one response to an earlier essay, and sometimes a response to that from the original author. Most issues include at least one long book review essay. Most articles published since 1999, and some older articles, are freely available online as HTML documents for the benefit of those limited by finances and/or geography. Individual and institutional subscribers have access to more complete archives with better searching and browsing options. There is also two companion sites, "MR Online," which is updated daily with articles, reviews, and commentary (including some re-posted from other sites), and the environment-focused "Climate and Capitalism." The magazine has a social media presence, including Twitter (@Monthly_Review) and Facebook. The *Monthly Review* is recommended for academic libraries and larger, more research-intensive public libraries.

Mother Jones. See General Interest section.

3814. *Ms.* [ISSN: 0047-8318] 1972. q. Ed(s): Katherine Spillar. Liberty Media for Women, L.L.C., 1600 Wilson Blvd, Ste 801, Arlington, VA 22209. Illus. Vol. ends: Nov/Dec. Microform: PQC. *Indexed:* A01, A22, BRI, C37, C42, CBRI, Chicano, F01, FemPer, GW, MASUSE, MLA-IB, WSA. *Bk. rev.:* 8, 124-300 words; signed. *Aud.:* Hs, Ga, Ac.

Founded by Gloria Steinem and Dorothy Pitman Hughes in 1971, *Ms.* magazine continues to address a wide range of social, political, environmental, economic, and cultural issues from a feminist perspective, earning its ongoing reputation as the foremost feminist print journalism publication in the United States. Each issue contains sections of both national and global news, as well as feature articles; it also includes shorter pieces on money, reviews of books and media, and opinion columns. Although published quarterly, the magazine's coverage of women's issues often precedes more mainstream news attention, making it a valuable source for readers who are interested in news about women and gender. The magazine is available in print and digitally, and its online form offers supplementary material with "Feminist Daily News." A key publication for many researchers working with women's and gender studies, *Ms.* is highly recommended for academic libraries. It is also a good choice for public libraries interested in adding a feminist perspective to their magazine collections.

3815. *The Nation.* [ISSN: 0027-8378] 1865. 34x/yr. USD 39.95 combined subscription (print & online eds.)). Ed(s): Katrina vanden Heuvel. The Nation Company, L.P., 520 Eighth Ave, New York, NY 10018; permissions@thenation.com; http://www.thenation.com. Illus., adv. Vol. ends: Jun/Dec. Microform: PMC; PQC. *Indexed:* A01, A22, BRI, C37, C42, CBRI, Chicano, F01, MASUSE, MLA-IB. *Bk. rev.:* 4, 1,000 words, signed. *Aud.:* Ga, Ac.

The Nation is a strongly leftist publication that includes original in-depth reporting as well as significant editorial and opinion content. With a venerable history (the magazine was founded in 1865), this weekly publication currently provides up-to-date coverage of national and global politics, social issues, and economic topics. Each issue contains poems and a crossword puzzle, as well as book and film reviews. Feature journalism is accessible and well-researched, and editorial content is often biting and irreverent. *The Nation*'s website offers some free access to articles from the current issue as well as a supplementary blog, video, podcast, and news content. The magazine is recommended for any public or academic library looking to include a magazine with a solid liberal perspective in its collection.

The National Interest. See Globalization section.

3816. *National Review.* [ISSN: 0028-0038] 1955. m. USD 19.95 domestic; USD 31.95 Canada; USD 43.95 elsewhere. National Review, Inc., 19 West 44th St, Ste 1701, New York, NY 10036. Illus., index, adv. Vol. ends: No. 25. *Indexed:* A01, A22, BAS, BRI, C37, C42, CBRI, Chicano, F01, MASUSE, MLA-IB. *Bk. rev.:* 1,000 words, signed. *Aud.:* Hs, Ga, Ac.

National Review was founded in 1955 by the noted author and pundit William F. Buckley, and still retains his imprint of exceptional prose and a sense of humor. It is generally considered to be the premier mainstream conservative publication. Areas of interest include limited government, anti-communism, and domestic affairs including education, legal affairs, and cultural criticism. The *National Review* comes out twice a month in print, and each issue includes news, opinion, and commentary, generally framed by longer feature articles, shorter pieces and columns, a humor column, and a "Books, Arts and Manners" section that includes book and movie reviews, poetry, art criticism, and more. Notable columnists include Mona Charen, Jonah Goldberg, Larry Kudlow, Ben Shapiro, and others. The "National Review Online" (NRO) is its daily web presence, and includes articles, blogs, and e-newsletters, such as the group blog, "The Corner." The website also includes photo essays and podcasts, and articles include commenting and sharing options. A subscription is necessary to access print magazine content archives, but all other content is freely available. The *National Review*'s social media presence includes Twitter (@NRO) as well as Facebook. The *National Review* is recommended for all libraries regardless of type.

3817. *The New American (Appleton).* Formed by the merger of (1958-1985): *American Opinion;* Which was formed by the 1958 merger of: *One Man's Opinion; Hubert Kregeloh Comments;* (1965-1985): *Review of the News;* Which was formerly (until 1965): *Correction, Please;* Review of the News incorporated (1956-1971): *Dan Smoot Report;* Which was formerly (until 1956): *Dan Smoot Speaks.* 1985. bi-w. USD 49 domestic; USD 58 Canada; USD 76 elsewhere. Ed(s): Gary Benoit. American Opinion Publishing Inc., PO Box 8040, Appleton, WI 54912. Illus., adv. Sample. Vol. ends: Dec. Microform: PQC. *Indexed:* A22. *Bk. rev.:* Number and length vary, signed. *Aud.:* Ga, Ac.

The New American is a hard-right magazine (usually further to the right than *The National Review*), published by the John Birch Society in one form or another since the 1950s. Its motto is "That freedom shall not perish," and areas of interest include civil liberties, constitutional principles, limited government, avoiding foreign entanglements, free-enterprise economics, and culture and history; the magazine covers domestic and international issues. Each print issue includes a cover story; features that include articles on politics, culture, and religion; and sections with short pieces, such as the "Exercising the Right" column about people using guns in self-defense. There is also a column calling out articles from other publications, called "Correction, Please!" Each issue of the magazine also includes book reviews and an article looking back at a historical event of note. The website includes a print magazine section that provides the first paragraphs of articles from each print issue with prompts to purchase the full issue or subscribe, but also includes extensive free content that is distinct from the magazine and that goes back many years. It is on Twitter (@NewAmericanMag) and Facebook. *The New American* is recommended for academic libraries and larger public libraries.

New Criterion. See Art/General section.

3818. *New Perspectives Quarterly: a journal of social and political thought.* Formerly (until 1986): *Center for the Study of Democratic Institutions. Center Magazine;* (until 1967): *Center for the Study of Democratic Institutions. Center Diary.* [ISSN: 0893-7850] 1963. q. GBP 523. Ed(s): Nathan Gardels. Wiley-Blackwell Publishing, Inc., 111 River St, Hoboken, NJ 07030; http://onlinelibrary.wiley.com. Illus., adv. Sample. Refereed. Vol. ends: No. 5. Microform: PQC. Reprint: PSC. *Indexed:* A01, A22, B01, BAS, BRI, E01, MASUSE, P61. *Bk. rev.:* Number and length vary. *Aud.:* Hs, Ga, Ac.

New Perspectives Quarterly covers politics and social issues as well as some culture and literature. While the magazine's editors stand to the political left, the publication features writing from a variety of political perspectives. Each issue is organized thematically, with significant coverage of international, as well as domestic, issues and events. Articles published are not overly lengthy, and are written to be accessible to a general audience, and the publication doesn't implement peer review in the way of academic journals. However, its layout and content aspires to a more serious and academic tone than many other news and opinion magazines. Contributors include well-known journalists, scholars, and public figures, many from countries outside the United States. The magazine's website provides access to current issues and to some archival content as well. This is a recommended title for academic and public libraries interested in providing multinational perspectives in their collections.

3819. *The New Republic: a journal of politics and the arts.* [ISSN: 0028-6583] 1914. 20x/yr. USD 19.97 domestic; USD 54.97 Canada; USD 79.97 elsewhere. Ed(s): Chris Highes. New Republic, 1400 K St, NW, Ste 1200, Washington, DC 20005. Illus., index, adv. Vol. ends: Jun/Dec. Microform: NBI; PMC; PQC. *Indexed:* A01, A22, B01, BAS, BRI, C37, CBRI, Chicano, F01, MASUSE, MLA-IB. *Bk. rev.:* Number and length vary. *Aud.:* Ga, Ac.

Although *The New Republic* claims to be an objective publication, much of its content is liberal-leaning. Having undergone an organizational upheaval in late 2014 that suspended publication, the magazine resumed print publication in 2015. Coverage includes politics, social issues, and culture, with a focus on national issues and events, although there is some international reporting as well. Each issue contains sections on books and the arts, as well as brief news pieces and more lengthy features of in-depth journalism. Articles are well-written and suitable for a general audience, and while the magazine includes several photos and makes use of striking graphics, its layout is clean and very readable, with few advertisements to distract the eye. The magazine is available in print and digitally, and its website offers a clearly organized selection of freely available content. This is a recommended title for most public and academic libraries.

3820. *Newsweek (Online).* [ISSN: 1069-840X] 1993. . USD 99. Newsweek Daily Beast Company, 7 Hanover Sq, New York, NY 10004. *Bk. rev.:* 500-1,300 words; signed. *Aud.:* Ems, Hs, Ga, Ac.

Newsweek is a general-interest news weekly, providing news and analysis of current events. It went digital-only in 2013 but returned to print under new ownership in 2014 and became independent in 2018. *Newsweek* emphasizes photography and graphic design, and includes more international content than in the past. Articles cover news, culture, technology, international affairs, and politics, as well as book, music, and movie reviews, from a mainstream perspective. In recent years *Newsweek*'s reputation has taken a bit of a hit, with internal scandals and prominent retractions, but it has taken on a media ethics advisor and still remains a major news publication. The online version emphasizes recent content, with a magazine archive going back to May 2013 (providing free access to a few articles from each issue), but the site includes links to issues going back at least ten years. The website includes video content. *Newsweek* has a presence on social media, including Twitter (@Newsweek) and Facebook. *Newsweek* is recommended for all libraries, regardless of type.

3821. *The Progressive (Madison).* Supersedes (in 1929): *La Follette's Magazine;* Which was formerly (until 1914): *La Follette's Weekly;* (until 1913): *La Follette's Weekly Magazine.* [ISSN: 0033-0736] 1909. m. USD 12 combined subscription domestic (print & online eds.); USD 25 combined subscription Canada (print & online eds.); USD 30 combined subscription elsewhere (print & online eds.)). Ed(s): Bill Lueders. The Progressive, Inc., 30 W. Mifflin St, Ste 703, Madison, WI 53703; info@progressive.org; http://www.progressive.org. Illus., index, adv. Sample. Microform: PQC. *Indexed:* A01, A22, BAS, BRI, C37, C42, CBRI, Chicano, MASUSE, MLA-IB. *Bk. rev.:* 2, 1,200 words, signed. *Aud.:* Ga, Ac.

The Progressive is one of the best-known liberal magazines in the United States, and has published articles by such notable progressive figures as Jane Addams, Martin Luther King, Jr., Howard Zinn, Molly Ivins, Barbara Ehrenreich, and Bernie Sanders. Covering politics and social issues, the magazine provides feature articles with in-depth reporting as well as editorial and opinion content, poems, book reviews, and political cartoons. Each issue includes several articles devoted to a theme, along with content that varies from that theme. Published monthly, the magazine has a noted history of pacifism and of addressing issues of social justice, and its content often critiques military policy and engagement. *The Progressive* is available in print and digitally, and its website offers some freely available content from current and past issues. The title is recommended for public and academic libraries with an interest in including an often pacifist, liberal viewpoint in their collections.

Reason. See Civil Liberties/Political-Economic Rights section.

3822. *Slate (Online).* [ISSN: 1091-2339] 1996. d. The/Slate Group, LLC, 95 Morton St, 4th Fl, New York, NY 10014; slateoffice@slate.com. Illus., adv. *Aud.:* Ga, Ac.

Slate is a freely available online magazine, updated daily. It provides commentary and analysis of politics, culture, news, and business as well as the popular "Dear Prudence" advice column. The publication focuses on entertaining and often provocatively written content and doesn't claim to focus on breaking news, but it often serves as a source of news on current events. The site is heavily illustrated with photos and graphic images, promoting most popular and most recent articles at the top of the site. While this makes sense for a publication with a keen interest in promoting the sharing of online content, it can make it difficult to tell at first glance what kind of article a reader is looking at. Some scrolling down will eventually bring a reader to a more traditionally organized section of the site, where one can find articles categorized as "Culture," "Technology," "News & Politics," and the like. The magazine includes some clearly labeled sponsored content and significant advertising content as well. As a freely available online resource, the publication is recommended for academic and public libraries as a popular and current news and opinion magazine.

3823. *Time.* Incorporates (in 1937): *Literary Digest;* Which was formerly (1890-1937): *Digest;* Which incorporated (in 1937): *Review of Reviews;* Which was formerly (until 1935): *Review of Reviews and World's Work;* (until 1932): *Review of Reviews;* (until 1929): *American Review of Reviews;* Literary Digest incorporated (1912-1925): *Current Opinion;* Which was formerly (Jul.1888-Dec.1912): *Current Literature;* Which incorporated: *Current History and Modern Culture;* Current Opinion incorporated: *Democracy.* [ISSN: 0040-781X] 1923. 52x/yr. USD 30 domestic. Ed(s): Ratu Kamlani, Edward Felsenthal. Time Inc., 225 Liberty St, New York, NY 10281; http://www.timeinc.com. Illus., index, adv. Vol. ends: Jun. *Indexed:* A01, A06, A22, AgeL, B01, BRI, C37, CBRI, Chicano, F01, IIPA, MASUSE, MLA-IB. *Bk. rev.:* Number and length vary; signed. *Aud.:* Ems, Hs, Ga, Ac.

Time is a general-interest newsweekly, with something for everyone. It covers domestic and international events, politics, religion, technology, culture (including reviews), medicine, sports, education, and other topics of the day, providing an overview that will bring a reader up to date with the basic issues. Articles are usually short, with a few longer feature pieces, including the cover article. Infographic-like inserts often provide data to supplement text. The "Lightbox" section showcases photography. *Time* includes some opinion commentary, focusing on the economy and politics. *Time*'s website has three sections: "The Latest" provides updated content; "The Magazine" includes the most recent issue, with free access without a subscription to selected articles (users can also select three international editions) ; and a video section. *Time* is recommended for all libraries, regardless of type.

3824. *U.S. News & World Report (Online).* Formed by the merger of (1946-1948): *World Report;* (1933-1948): *The United States News;* Which was formerly (until 1933): *The United States Daily.* [ISSN: 2169-9283] 1948. w. Ed(s): Brian Kelly. U.S. News & World Report, L.P., 1050 Thomas Jefferson St, NW, 4th Fl, Washington, DC 20007. Adv. *Aud.:* Hs, Ga, Ac.

U.S. News & World Report is one of the best-known national news and opinion magazines, in spite of a history of hard times leading it to become an online-only publication since 2010. The magazine is known not only for its news and opinion coverage, but also for its rankings, most notably of colleges and universities, as well as of health services, cars, and other subjects. The magazine strives for objective news reporting, not espousing a strong leftist or conservative bent for its content. Opinion pieces are published from both moderately conservative and moderately liberal viewpoints. News and opinion content includes politics, economy, health, finance, and world news. The site is not difficult to navigate, but can feel somewhat cluttered, and at times the lines between news and rankings feels blurred. The magazine is a good choice for collections of public and academic libraries looking for moderate news perspectives.

3825. *The Washington Monthly.* [ISSN: 0043-0633] 1969. 5x/yr. Ed(s): Paul Glastris, Amy M Stackhouse. Washington Monthly LLC, 1200 18th St NW Ste 330, Washington, DC 20036. Illus., adv. Vol. ends: Feb. Microform: PQC. *Indexed:* A01, A22, B01, BRI, CBRI, MASUSE. *Bk. rev.:* 800-1000 words; signed. *Aud.:* Ga, Ac.

The Washington Monthly is a glossy independent magazine that provides high-quality journalism with a perspective that is center to slightly liberal. Areas of interest include politics and government, diplomacy, the general Washington Beltway policy scene, higher education and K-12 education, and health care. The magazine is nonprofit, and functions with heavy foundation support, including the Bill and Melinda Gates Foundation and the Lumina Foundation. *The Washington Monthly* provides full online archives of the magazine back to

2011 on its website; older issues are available for a fee via links to OpinionArchives.com. The website also includes some web-exclusive content. *The Washington Monthly* is recommended for academic libraries and larger public libraries.

■ NUMISMATICS

David Hill, Librarian, Harry W. Bass, Jr. Library, American Numismatic Society, 75 Varick Street, Floor 11, New York, NY 10013; library@numismatics.org

Introduction

The term *numismatics,* in the strictest sense, refers to the scientific study of coins, paper money, and other circulating media of exchange. Though this was the term's original meaning, it has, over time, come to be applied both to non-scientific activities, such as coin collecting and coin sales, and to items that don't qualify as coins or money but are similar to them, such as medals and tokens.

In the United States, there are two national organizations, each of which, broadly stated, represents one side of the scientific and non-scientific divide. Though there is great overlap in the interests of membership and the mission of each organization, it can be said generally that the American Numismatic Association (ANA) caters mainly to the hobbyist collector, while the American Numismatic Society (ANS) takes a more scholarly approach. Each organization produces a general-interest magazine for their members, the *Numismatist* (for the ANA) and *ANS Magazine,* both of which cover a broad spectrum of topics within the field. The ANS also publishes an academic journal annually.

Interest in numismatics is a worldwide phenomenon. The International Numismatic Council has more than 150 institutional members from all over the world: numismatic societies, coin cabinets, museums, and clubs, many of which publish magazines and journals. Some have a fairly narrow focus, discussing only ancient coinage or modern medals, for example. In fact, some can be quite specific in their coverage, dealing only with, say, those tokens issued during the American Civil War. While periodicals with such a narrow focus may not be suitable for most libraries, there are some whose coverage includes a broader range of numismatic topics and may be considered to be of use to collectors or scholars interested in the field. In addition to the *Numismatist* and *ANS Magazine,* other general-interest publications relating to numismatics are *Coin World, COINage, Coins Magazine,* and *Numismatic News.*

Librarians seeking a single periodical subscription to represent numismatics might consider *Coin World,* which has been publishing respected content for more than 50 years.

Basic Periodicals

American Numismatic Society Magazine, Coin World, COINage, Coins, Numismatic News, Numismatist.

3826. *American Numismatic Society Magazine.* Former titles (until 2002): *American Numismatic Society Newsletter;* (until 199?): *A N S Newsletter.* [ISSN: 2167-2547] 1955. q. Free to members. Ed(s): Peter van Alfen. American Numismatic Society, 75 Varick St 11th Fl, New York, NY 10013; orders@numismatics.org; http://www.numismatics.org. Illus., adv. *Aud.:* Ga, Ac.

This is the member magazine of the American Numismatic Society. It covers a broad range of numismatics, and is aimed at both a scholarly and general-interest audience.

3827. *Bank Note Reporter.* [ISSN: 0164-0828] 1973. m. USD 39.98 domestic; USD 55.98 Canada. Ed(s): Bob Van Ryzin. F + W Media Inc., 1140 Broadway, 14th Fl, New York, NY 10001; contact_us@fwmedia.com; http://www.fwcommunity.com/. Illus., adv. Circ: 4427 Paid. *Bk. rev.:* Occasional, 200-400 words. *Aud.:* Ga, Sa.

Broadly covering the collecting of all forms of paper money and related items, this publication focuses primarily on U.S. currency, while still having representative material on international currency. Its news content often addresses current trends and developments in paper money collecting, as well as the present condition of the marketplace for paper currency. This is a pricing and value aid, with (as a standard feature) its lengthy price guide that lists approximate retail prices for most U.S. paper money issued since 1861. Feature material is interesting and informative, is often comprehensive, and is typically well written. These articles usually center on a specific piece or type of currency, and frequently provide historical background events relating to that currency. This is a solid and reliable resource for collectors of U.S. paper money.

3828. *Coin World.* [ISSN: 0010-0447] 1960. w. USD 69.99 combined subscription domestic (print & online eds.); USD 169.99 combined subscription Canada (print & online eds.); USD 224.99 combined subscription elsewhere (print & online eds.)). Ed(s): wiiliam T Gibbs. Amos Publishing, Hobby, PO Box 926, Sidney, OH 45365; http://www.amospress.com. Illus., adv. Vol. ends: Dec. *Indexed:* A22, B01, BRI. *Bk. rev.:* 1-3, 200-400 words. *Aud.:* Hs, Ga.

This is one of the most highly respected and widely read of all numismatic publications. Issued weekly, it covers a broad range of numismatic interests and topics, effectively mixing current news items with feature material. Regular articles and contributed features are typically written by specialists or acknowledged experts in their field, most of whom are well-versed within numismatics. Coverage extends to virtually all areas of numismatics, and includes a considerable amount of material that can be very useful for collectors in enhancing their knowledge and collecting skills. Special monthly editions feature an extensive and comprehensive retail price guide for all U.S. coins, as well as sections devoted to paper money and world coins. This is an informative, instructional, and comprehensive publication, with quality features and departments, and it should be a primary resource for most libraries.

3829. *COINage.* [ISSN: 0010-0455] 1964. m. USD 32. Beckett Media, LLC., 4635 McEwen Rd, Dallas, TX 75244; customerservice@beckett.com; http://www.beckett.com. Illus., adv. Sample. Vol. ends: Dec. Microform: PQC. *Indexed:* A22. *Bk. rev.:* Occasional, 500-600 words. *Aud.:* Ga.

This is a very sound general-interest magazine that covers a wide array of numismatic topics. Feature articles are informative and can be extensive, focusing most often on currently significant numismatic topics. Articles frequently include historically based content as well as material that addresses collecting techniques or the condition of the coin marketplace. An interesting and sometimes educational regular feature is "Coin Capsule," which highlights the coinage or significant numismatic events of a selected year, and sets these events in the perspective of that year's noteworthy historical, political, and cultural events. The magazine has solid writing, is well produced, and has attractive close-up color photos of coins and paper money. The magazine's general content and broad coverage have potential appeal to both beginning and experienced collectors, and should be strongly considered as an integral part of a basic numismatic literature collection.

3830. *Coins.* Former titles (until 1962): *Coin Press Magazine;* (until 196?): *Coin News Magazine.* [ISSN: 0010-0471] 1955. m. USD 39.98 domestic; USD 54.98 Canada. Ed(s): Bob Van Ryzin. F + W Media Inc., 1140 Broadway, 14th Fl, New York, NY 10001; contact_us@fwmedia.com; http://www.fwcommunity.com/. Illus., adv. Circ: 20934 Paid. *Indexed:* A22. *Bk. rev.:* Occasional, 600-800 words. *Aud.:* Hs, Ga.

This is a general-purpose magazine that has long been popular in the field. It covers most areas of numismatics and has enough breadth that it has potential appeal and usefulness to a variety of collectors. Each issue is usually built around a specific collecting theme, such as silver dollars, and has several feature articles devoted to that topic. It is then rounded out with additional shorter features, news items, and regularly appearing columns. A regular feature, one that makes up over half of each issue, is an extensive price guide that approximates retail values for all regularly issued U.S. coins. This is supplemented periodically by issues that have price guides for other popular numismatic areas, such as paper money or Canadian coins. Because of its general nature, this magazine can be used either as part of a basic collection or as a complement to one.

3831. *CoinWeek.* Incorporates (1995-2012): *CoinLink.* 2011. . Free. CoinWeek LLC., PO Box 916909, Longwood, FL 32791-6903; news@CoinWeek.com; http://www.coinweek.com. Adv. *Aud.:* Ga.

This numismatic web site is an impressive resource of both current and archived information covering almost every sector of numismatic interest. It is updated daily, with an extensive selection of rare coin news, commentary, and opinion on U.S. coins, ancient coins, world coins, modern coins, paper money, and bullion products, centered on current numismatic events, collector tips, and trends within the rare coin marketplace. Information on specialty and niche areas of numismatics is abundant. Within the site are more than 2,500 videos and podcasts containing interviews and features on famous collectors, dealers, and numismatic items. The archived content of the site is voluminous, with more than 11,500 articles, each with custom graphics, extending back to 2010. The site is fully keyword-searchable, making this comprehensive repository a great resource for anyone who has an interest in the history of coinage and the current numismatic market.

3832. *Numismatic News.* Formerly (until 19??): *Numismatic News Weekly.* [ISSN: 0029-604X] 1952. 52x/yr. USD 79.99 domestic; USD 144.99 Canada. Ed(s): Dave Harper. F + W Media Inc., 1140 Broadway, 14th Fl, New York, NY 10001; contact_us@fwmedia.com; http://www.fwcommunity.com/. Illus., adv. Circ: 30265 Paid. *Bk. rev.:* Occasional, 100-300 words. *Aud.:* Ga.

This weekly newspaper covers a broad range of numismatic topics and is primarily a source of current news and events, especially those affecting the coin market. Its regular columns and features are frequently aimed at improving collector knowledge and skills, and are sometimes augmented with longer historically oriented pieces. Articles may feature lesser-known and less popular areas of collecting, which can serve as good introductions to those fields. Successive issues contain retail price guides that highlight several different areas of the U.S. coin market. As a general numismatics resource, this may serve to supplement a basic collection.

3833. *The Numismatist: for collectors of coins, medals, tokens and paper money.* Former titles (until 1893): *The Numismatist and Year Book;* (until 1891): *Numismatist.* [ISSN: 0029-6090] 1888. m. Free to members. Ed(s): Barbara Gregory. American Numismatic Association, 818 N Cascade Ave, Colorado Springs, CO 80903; ana@money.org; http://www.money.org. Illus., index, adv. Sample. Vol. ends: Dec. *Indexed:* A06. *Bk. rev.:* 1-3, 50-200 words. *Aud.:* Ga, Ac.

This is the membership publication of the American Numismatic Association, one of the premier collecting and leadership societies in numismatics. It is the oldest continuously published magazine in the field and is a wide-ranging resource that combines news and informational articles with comprehensive feature material. Articles and features are consistently well written and are typically interesting and informative, touching on almost any numismatic topic. A continuing editorial focus is providing material that collectors can use to enhance their numismatic knowledge and to sharpen their awareness of key issues in numismatics. This is a very inclusive publication that is potentially interesting to a wide range of collectors, and it should be considered as a part of almost any basic collection.

3834. *Paper Money.* 1962. bi-m. Free to members. Ed(s): Benny Bolin. Society of Paper Money Collectors, Inc., c/o Jeff Brueggeman Secretary, SPMC, 711 Signal Mtn. Rd. #197, Chattanooga, TN 37405; http://www.spmc.org/. Illus., index, adv. Vol. ends: Nov/Dec. *Bk. rev.:* 1, 250 words. *Aud.:* Ga, Sa.

This is the membership journal of the Society of Paper Money Collectors, and it provides usually lengthy, interesting, and informative articles about all forms of paper money and related fiscal paper. Feature articles are typically historical treatments of specific currency issues or monetary events, with the added perspective of such things as national economic situations or significant bank or banking events. Articles are frequently contributed by acknowledged paper money experts, and are usually well researched and scholarly in approach. Some articles are very extensive, perhaps offering more thoroughness and depth than those in any other numismatic publication. The material is enhanced by high-quality visuals and photography. This should have strong appeal for readers interested in the historical context of paper money, and may also be useful academically for programs in American Studies or American History.

3835. *World Coin News.* [ISSN: 0145-9090] 1973. m. USD 39.99 domestic; USD 54.99 Canada. Ed(s): Dave Harper. F + W Media Inc., 1140 Broadway, 14th Fl, New York, NY 10001; contact_us@fwmedia.com; http://www.fwcommunity.com/. Illus., adv. Circ: 3918. *Aud.:* Ga.

Dealing exclusively with international coinage, this publication mixes current news articles with feature material on coins and occasionally paper money. Feature material is usually informative, often including the historical or political context of the described coins or monetary events. Article content ranges from current coinage to that of centuries earlier, and can include any money-issuing country or municipality. Some content is aimed at keeping collectors apprised of trends within the coin marketplace, as well as aiding them in developing or refining their collecting knowledge and skills. As a general resource that covers the vast expanse of international coinage, this is a useful periodical that can serve as a nice supplement to core numismatic titles.

■ NURSING

See also Health Care Administration; and Medicine sections.

Michelle DeMars, Health Sciences & Nursing Librarian, California State University, Long Beach, 1250 Bellflower Blvd., Long Beach, CA 90840; Michelle.DeMars@csulb.edu

Introduction

Keeping up with recent research can be challenging in the ever-evolving discipline of Nursing. The nursing profession is distinctive in that no matter if someone is a nursing assistant, registered nurse, nurse manager or anyone in between these individuals, act simultaneously as both independent caregivers and members of a health care team. They may act as patient advocates, develop and manage nursing care plans, and educate patients and communities. Nurses of every level provide highly personalized hands-on care and keeping up with current literature is a crucial part of that effort. The literature to support the nursing profession must not only support a wide range of professional levels but it also must include a variety of specialties.

The periodicals selected for inclusion represent both clinical and professional elements of nursing and encompass: nursing practice, nursing specialties, international nursing, nursing education, nursing profession, and nursing management. The titles selected are not meant to cover every aspect of this multifaceted discipline but will instead provide a glimpse of a variety of aspects appealing to a specific audience. Given the specialized audience that these selections are geared toward, these titles are most relevant to special and academic libraries especially those supporting nursing programs.

Basic Periodicals

Hs: *Imprint (New York);* Ac: *American Journal of Nursing, International Nursing Review;* Sa: *The Nurse Practitioner, Nursing (Year).*

Basic Abstracts and Indexes

CINAHL, Health Source: Nursing/Academic; Nursing Resource Center; ProQuest Nursing and Allied Health Database (ProQuest).

3836. *American Association of Nurse Practitioners. Journal.* Formerly (until 2012): *American Academy of Nurse Practitioners. Journal (Print).* [ISSN: 2327-6886] 1988. m. USD 642. Ed(s): Charon Pierson. Wolters Kluwer Health, 530 Walnut St, Philadelphia, PA 19106; info@wolterskluwer.com; http://www.wkhealth.com. Sample. Refereed. Reprint: PSC. *Indexed:* A01, A22, E01. *Aud.:* Ac, Sa.

The official publication of the American Association of Nurse Practitioners (AANP) is a peer-reviewed, professional journal that contains articles of original clinical research, reviews, case studies, professional news, and continuing education credit on an array of topics. The journal focuses on "serving the needs of nurse practitioners...who have a major interest in primary, acute and/or long-term health care." Recent articles include "Improving perceptions of patient safety through standardizing handoffs from the emergency department to the inpatient setting: a systematic review,"

"Adolescent obesity in the past decade: A systematic review of genetics and determinants of food choice," and "The hands that cradle: A pilot study of parent adverse childhood experience scores." There is access to selected content and samples of the tables of contents of all issues available online. This journal is recommended for academic libraries with graduate nursing programs, and for large medical libraries. URL: http://onlinelibrary.wiley.com/journal/10.1002/(ISSN)2327-6924

3837. *American Journal of Nursing.* [ISSN: 0002-936X] 1900. m. USD 770. Ed(s): Kim Curry. Lippincott Williams & Wilkins, Two Commerce Sq, 2001 Market St, Philadelphia, PA 19103; customerservice@lww.com; http://www.lww.com. Illus., index, adv. Sample. Refereed. Vol. ends: Dec. Microform: PMC; PQC. *Indexed:* A01, A22, ASSIA, AgeL, BRI, CBRI, Chicano. *Aud.:* Ac, Sa.

This professional journal, simply known as *AJN*, is the official journal of the American Nurses Association (ANA), and is a staple in every medical library and academic library that supports a nursing program. Articles focus on evidence-based clinical practice, continuing education credit opportunities, professional news, and some peer-reviewed original research. Recent titles include "Rising to the Challenge Re-Embracing the Wald Model of Nursing," "Helping Health Care Providers and Staff Process Grief Through a Hospital-Based Program," and "Understanding the Complications of Sickle Cell Disease." The journal's website provides tables of contents of past volumes and free full-text access to several of the current volume's articles, including continuing education credit articles. This small, readable periodical is of value to every nursing student and practicing registered nurse, and should be in every academic or clinical library that supports nursing programs and nurses. URL: http://journals.lww.com/ajnonline/paages/default.aspx

3838. *Heart & Lung: the journal of acute and critical care.* [ISSN: 0147-9563] 1972. bi-m. USD 910. Elsevier Inc., 1600 John F Kennedy Blvd, Philadelphia, PA 19103; usinfo-f@elsevier.com; https://www.elsevier.com. Illus., adv. Sample. Refereed. Microform: PQC. *Indexed:* A22, E01. *Aud.:* Ac, Sa.

The official journal of the American Association of Heart Failure Nurses features scholarly, peer-reviewed articles on acute and critical care of heart and respiratory failure patients. The regularly occurring sections "Care of Patients with Pulmonary Disorders," "Care of Patients with Cardiovascular Disorders," and "Care of Patients with Comorbid Disorders" focus on advances, innovations, and research observations primarily in an acute and critical care nursing setting. Patient education, pharmacotherapy, and infection control are regularly occurring topics of articles. Recent articles include "Metabolic effects of beta-blockers in critically ill patients: A retrospective cohort study" and "The role of illness uncertainty in the relationship between disease knowledge and patient-reported outcomes among adolescents and adults with congenital heart disease." Tables of contents of current and archived issues are available at the website. This journal is essential for all critical care nurses, and nursing students studying critical care in undergraduate or graduate courses. This outstanding journal is recommended for all academic libraries that support nursing programs and clinical settings that support critical care. URL: www.heartandlung.org

3839. *Home Healthcare Now.* Formerly (until 2015): *Home Healthcare Nurse;* Which incorporated (1979-1983): *Nephrology Nurse.* [ISSN: 2374-4529] 1983. 10x/yr. USD 496. Ed(s): Maureen Anthony. Lippincott Williams & Wilkins, Two Commerce Sq, 2001 Market St, Philadelphia, PA 19103; customerservice@lww.com; http://www.lww.com. Illus., adv. Sample. Refereed. *Indexed:* A22, Chicano. *Bk. rev.:* Number and length vary. *Aud.:* Ac, Sa.

This is the official journal of the Home Healthcare Nurses Association, an affiliate professional nursing organization of the National Association for Home Care & Hospice. Peer-reviewed articles focus primarily on the clinical and operational aspects of this nursing specialty, which includes hospice nursing. There are two or three continuing education (CE) credit articles per issue, with free online access to the current issue's CE articles at the website. Tables of contents for current and back issues are also available at the website. Recent articles include "The Value of Home Health Physical Therapy" and "Home Healthcare Visits Following Hospital Discharge: Does the Timing of Visits Affect 30-Day Hospital Readmission Rates for Heart Failure Patients?" Regular sections include "Hospice and Palliative Care" and "VNAA's Voice" (Visiting Nurse Associations of America). As the U.S. population ages, the need for this type of nursing publication will increase greatly. Recommended for hospice, home health agencies, libraries that serve clinical practice, and consumer health collections. URL: www.homehealthcarenurseonline.com

3840. *Imprint (New York).* Former titles (until 1968): *N S N A Newsletter;* (until 1965): *National Student Nurses' Association. Newsletter.* [ISSN: 0019-3062] 1954. 5x/yr. USD 36 (Individuals, USD 18; Members, USD 3). Ed(s): Jonathan Buttrick, Alison Faust. National Student Nurses' Association, 45 Main St, Ste 606, Brooklyn, NY 11201; nsna@nsna.org; http://www.nsna.org. Illus., index, adv. Sample. Circ: 51000. Vol. ends: Dec/Jan. *Indexed:* A22. *Aud.:* Hs, Ac.

The official publication of the National Student Nurses Association (NSNA), this title contains focused articles specifically for high school students interested in nursing; nursing or pre-nursing and college students; recent nursing graduates; and nursing and pre-nursing educators. The title is heavy with advertisements, but that can be overlooked when one considers free access online to the current issue and archives at the website. Regular departments and columns include "Editorial" and "News." Recent articles include "Modernizing Nursing Roles through the Use of Telehealth" and "Conquering Test Anxiety (and How Not to Let it Conquer You)." This periodical is an excellent resource and is recommended for high school libraries, especially those supporting health career vocational programs, and academic libraries that support nursing programs. Additionally, hospitals that provide clinical experience for the students mentioned above should have this title in their library's collection. URL: www.nsna.org/Publications.aspx

3841. *International Nursing Review.* Incorporates (1968-1971): *I C N Calling;* Former titles (until 1954): *International Nursing Bulletin;* (until 1945): *International Nursing Review;* (until 1930): *The I C N.* [ISSN: 0020-8132] 1926. q. GBP 345. Ed(s): Sue Turale. Wiley-Blackwell Publishing Ltd., The Atrium, Southern Gate, Chichester, PO19 8QG, United Kingdom; cs-journals@wiley.com; http://onlinelibrary.wiley.com. Illus., adv. Sample. Refereed. Vol. ends: Nov/Dec. Microform: PQC. Reprint: PSC. *Indexed:* A01, A22, ASSIA, E01. *Bk. rev.:* Number and length vary. *Aud.:* Ac, Sa.

As the official journal of the International Council of Nurses, this journal provides U.S. nurses with a glimpse into the profession worldwide and into global health issues. There are sections such as "International Perspectives" and "Nursing and Health Policy Perspectives," along with review and peer-reviewed research articles. Articles focus on topics such as governmental impact on nursing, ethics, technology, innovations in practice, and much more. Some of the most recent articles include "The effect of peer education on health beliefs about breast cancer screening," "Self-efficacy and organizational commitment among Spanish nurses: the role of work engagement," and "Systems leadership doctor of nursing practice: global relevance." The tables of contents and full-text access are available online. This title is a nice counterpoint to U.S. nursing titles and is recommended for all academic libraries that support nursing programs, and any other nursing collections. URL: www.wiley.com/bw/journal.asp?ref=0020-8132

3842. *Journal of Professional Nursing.* [ISSN: 8755-7223] 1985. 6x/yr. USD 960. Elsevier Inc., 1600 John F Kennedy Blvd, Philadelphia, PA 19103; usinfo-f@elsevier.com; https://www.elsevier.com. Adv. Refereed. *Indexed:* A22, ASSIA, E01. *Aud.:* Ac, Sa.

This scholarly, peer-reviewed journal is the official publication of the American Association of Colleges of Nursing and aims to address "the practice, research, and policy roles of nurses with baccalaureate and undergraduate degrees, the education and management concerns of the universities in which they are educated, and the settings in which they practice." Examples of recent articles are "An Evidence-based Approach to Measuring Affective Domain Development," "Mentoring Nurse Faculty: Outcomes of a Three-Year Clinical Track Faculty Initiative," and "Research Prescription for Undergraduate Students: Research Mentoring in a Small Liberal Arts University." The website provides the tables of contents from 1995 to the most current issue with limited full text for free. This is a very valuable resource to all professional nurses, and specifically to the faculty in nursing programs leading to baccalaureate and graduate degrees. Highly recommended for all academic libraries that support baccalaureate and graduate degree nursing programs. URL: www.professionalnursing.org/

3843. ***M C N: The American Journal of Maternal / Child Nursing.*** [ISSN: 0361-929X] 1976. bi-m. USD 450. Ed(s): Kathleen Rice Simpson. Lippincott Williams & Wilkins, Two Commerce Sq, 2001 Market St, Philadelphia, PA 19103; customerservice@lww.com; http://www.lww.com. Illus., index, adv. Sample. Refereed. Vol. ends: Nov/Dec. Microform: PQC. *Indexed:* A22. *Bk. rev.:* Number and length vary. *Aud.:* Ac, Sa.

This scholarly, peer-reviewed journal focuses on the nursing issues of women's health, particularly childbearing women, and prenatal and neonatal infants. Featured are research articles, continuing education credit articles, and ongoing columns. Recent research articles discuss miscarriage, bereavement alliances, and pediatric quality of life. The ongoing columns such as "Toward Evidence-based Practice," "Nutrition for the Family," and "Global Health and Nursing" are clinically relevant. Recent articles include: "Oxytocin Guidelines Associated with Compliance to National Standards," "Predictors of HIV Risk Reduction in Adolescent Girls," and "Nurses' Views on Using Pasteurized Donor Human Milk for Hypoglycemic Term Infants." The tables of contents for current and previous issues are available online at the website, but very little is available for free. This journal is indispensable for nurses in maternal/child care, and nursing students studying maternal/child care at either the undergraduate or graduate level. Highly recommended for all academic libraries that support nursing programs, and clinical collections of large institutions with a focus on maternal/child health and care. URL: www.mcnjournal.com

Minority Nurse. See Health Professions section.

3844. ***The Nurse Practitioner: the American journal of primary healthcare.*** [ISSN: 0361-1817] 1975. m. USD 615. Ed(s): Jamesetta A Newland, Erika Fedell. Lippincott Williams & Wilkins, Two Commerce Sq, 2001 Market St, Philadelphia, PA 19103; customerservice@lww.com; http://www.lww.com. Illus., index, adv. Sample. Refereed. Vol. ends: Dec. Microform: PQC. *Indexed:* A01, A22, BRI. *Bk. rev.:* Number and length vary. *Aud.:* Ac, Sa.

This journal is targeted at the advanced practice nursing specialty of nurse practitioners. This useful journal has peer-reviewed feature articles and regularly occurring departments. Articles in a recent issue include "Pediatric metabolic syndrome" and "NPs' use of guidelines to diagnose and treat childhood ADHD." Limited free access to articles, along with the tables of contents of recent and archival issues, are available at the website. This journal is a must for all academic libraries that serve graduate nurse practitioner programs, and institutional clinical collections where nurse practitioners are actively practicing. URL: http://journals.lww.com/tnpj/pages/default.aspx

3845. ***Nursing Education Perspectives.*** Former titles (until 2002): *Nursing and Health Care Perspectives;* (until 1997): *N and H C Perspectives on Community;* (until 1995): *Nursing and Health Care;* (until 1980): *N L N News.* [ISSN: 1536-5026] 1952. bi-m. USD 275. Ed(s): Joyce Fitzpatrick. National League for Nursing, 61 Broadway, 33rd Fl, New York, NY 10006; generalinfo@nln.org; http://www.nln.org. Illus. Sample. Refereed. *Indexed:* A01, A22, BRI, MLA-IB. *Bk. rev.:* 0-7, length varies. *Aud.:* Ac, Sa.

This periodical is the official research publication of the National League for Nursing (NLN). This peer-reviewed journal centers on nursing education and educators. There is a section, "Emerging Technologies Center," that highlights the latest in technological innovations to enhance instruction, especially in clinical simulation and distance learning. Other sections and departments address best practices in education and curriculum; news from the NLN; book reviews; and career opportunities for nursing educators. Articles in a recent issue include "Where Do You Think You Are? A Grounded Theory Study of the Critical Factors Triggering the Existence and Fueling the Persistence of Incivility in Nursing," "Student and Faculty Experiences in the Flipped Learning Environment in Undergraduate Nursing," and "A Systematic Review of the Use of Standardized Patients as a Simulation Modality in Nursing Education." Current and archival issues, with tables of contents and some free access, are available at the website. This is a valuable resource for nursing educators in all types of nursing programs, from associate degree to baccalaureate to graduate level, and should be in every academic library that supports a nursing program. URL: www.nlnjournal.org/

Nursing Forum. See Health Professions section.

3846. ***Nursing Management.*** Formerly (until 1981): *Supervisor Nurse;* Incorporates (1994-1999): *Recruitment, Retention & Restructuring Report;* Which was formerly (1988-1994): *Recruitment & Retention Report.* [ISSN: 0744-6314] 1970. m. USD 568. Ed(s): Rosanne Raso, Coleen M F Stern. Lippincott Williams & Wilkins, Two Commerce Sq, 2001 Market St, Philadelphia, PA 19103; customerservice@lww.com; http://www.lww.com. Illus., adv. Sample. Refereed. Vol. ends: Dec. Microform: PQC. *Indexed:* A01, A22, B01, BRI. *Bk. rev.:* 0-2, length varies. *Aud.:* Ac, Sa.

This valuable publication focuses on the needs and interests of nurses who are in management, leadership, or supervisory positions within the profession of nursing. Recently featured articles include "Managing interpersonal conflict: Steps for success," "Can laughter yoga provide stress relief for clinical nurses?," and "A guide to fostering an LGBTQ-inclusive workplace." There are also articles that provide continuing education (CE) credit, and others that address management issues such as leadership, critical thinking, and quality improvement. There are regularly occurring departments presenting articles on "Information Technology," "Evidence-based Nursing," "Team Concepts," and "Regulatory Readiness," as well as other topics of interest to managers. Online access provides current and archived tables of contents and limited free full-text access to selected articles. Recommended for all academic libraries that support nursing programs, and all clinical collections that support nurses and nurse managers. URL: www.nursingmanagement.com

3847. ***Nursing (Year): the voice and vision of nursing.*** Incorporates (1981-1988): *Nursing Life;* (1970-1976): *Nursing Update.* [ISSN: 0360-4039] 1971. m. USD 671. Ed(s): Linda Laskowski-Jones, Cynthia A Laufenberg. Lippincott Williams & Wilkins, Two Commerce Sq, 2001 Market St, Philadelphia, PA 19103; customerservice@lww.com; http://www.lww.com. Illus., index. Sample. Refereed. Vol. ends: Dec. Microform: PQC. *Indexed:* A01, A22, BRI. *Bk. rev.:* Number and length vary, some signed. *Aud.:* Ac, Sa.

This periodical is an excellent resource for all nurses. It contains practical, hands-on, and how-to articles, as well as continuing education credit articles, updates on the latest techniques, and legal issues. Recent articles include "Interventions for children with reactive attachment disorder," "Using health coaching to improve patients' BP management," and free continuing education credit articles, such as "Increasing cultural competence with LGBTQ patients." Regular departments include "Ethical Problems," "Drug News," and "Medication Errors," to mention only a few. The magazine is available online, and the website provides access to tables of contents back to 1971, with limited free full-text access to selected articles. This long-lasting periodical continues to be a popular resource for practicing nurses, both vocational and registered, across North America. Recommended for all academic libraries that support nursing programs, and all institutional and clinical collections where nurses practice. URL: http://journals.lww.com/nursing/pages/default.aspx

■ OCCUPATIONS AND CAREERS

See also Education; and Labor and Industrial Relations sections.

Kate Irwin-Smiler, Reference Librarian, Wake Forest University Professional Center Library, Winston-Salem, NC 27106; kate.irwin.jd@gmail.com

Introduction

Most people seeking career or job opportunity information do so only when necessary: when they are in need of a job, when they are dissatisfied with their career or lack thereof, or when a new career or job opportunity presents itself. It is unlikely that library patrons subscribe to career periodicals on a regular basis, and they are likely to rely on a library for access to these publications. Academic researchers, of course, often do not maintain a sufficient collection even of periodicals they subscribe to, so they must rely on their supporting research library.

Periodicals that focus on careers and occupations fall into a few basic categories: job listings, career development, and academic research. While these categories sometimes overlap in a single periodical, most titles are primarily one of these. Both the job listing and career development periodicals often specialize in a subject area or industry; in other cases, they specialize in terms of their projected audience. Many career periodicals are aimed at college students or people considering additional training.

Academic journals publish research in the career development or recruiting processes, with articles authored by career services personnel, psychologists, or education specialists. Such research is not generally directed toward job seekers, but rather toward educators, fellow researchers, or career services personnel.

Particularly in regard to career development publications, some publishers may produce highly specialized periodicals in several overlapping areas. While each title may be appropriate for some audiences, it is unlikely that all titles would be appropriate for any one library, due to duplication and minute variations. Some specialized publications aimed at job seekers offer free or very low-cost subscriptions.

Many career-development and most job-listing periodicals have accompanying web sites that expand on the material that is already published. Links to advertising employers are common on these pages. In addition, some job listing sites include more information online for each listing, or more listings than are included in the print publication.

National job listing web sites, not associated with any print publications, are plentiful and can be extremely useful to library patrons who are using job-listing periodicals. Indeed.com, Monster.com, CareerBuilder.com, and JobBankUSA.com are but a few examples of broadly-based sites that post jobs in many geographical and employment areas. RegionalHelpWanted.com maintains scores of local job-listing sites in the United States and Canada, listing jobs available by city and employment category. Specialized online sites such as HigherEdJobs.com or TheLadders.com provide listings in a particular industry, or those meeting particular criteria. Professional associations often list available jobs on a web site or discussion list, although these listings may be restricted to members of the association. Social networks such as LinkedIn.com are also increasingly being used as sources of job leads; and creating personalized connections using these sites may be more advantageous in some industries than using job search sites and published sources of job listings.

Basic Periodicals

Hs: *Occupational Outlook Quarterly;* Ga: *Federal Jobs Digest, Insight into Diversity, Occupational Outlook Quarterly;* Ac: *Occupational Outlook Quarterly;* Sa: *Careers and the Disabled.*

Basic Abstracts and Indexes

ERIC, Research Library (ProQuest), PsycINFO.

3848. ***African-American Career World: the diversity employment magazine.*** 2001. s-a. USD 18 (Free to qualified personnel). Ed(s): Barbara Capella Loehr. Equal Opportunity Publications, Inc., 445 Broad Hollow Rd, Ste 425, Melville, NY 11747; info@eop.com; http://www.eop.com. Adv. *Bk. rev.:* 3-6. *Aud.:* Ga.

This magazine profiles industries via descriptions of three to four successful African Americans in a variety of related occupations. Practical tips emphasize the importance of workplace diversity and encourage career success; and reviews of general career and occupations books highlight diversity issues. Employer advertisements throughout the magazine are indexed in each issue.

Black Enterprise. See African American section.

3849. ***Careers and the Disabled.*** Formerly (until 1986): *Careers and the Handicapped.* [ISSN: 1056-277X] 1986. q. Ed(s): James Schneider. Equal Opportunity Publications, Inc., 445 Broad Hollow Rd, Ste 425, Melville, NY 11747; info@eop.com; http://www.eop.com. Illus., adv. Sample. *Indexed:* BRI. *Bk. rev.:* 3-5, 150 words. *Aud.:* Ga, Sa.

This magazine profiles careers, industries, and companies that are friendly to employees with disabilities of various kinds, as well as successful professionals with various disabilities. Job-hunting advice includes suggestions for handling visible and invisible disabilities during the job search process, as well as more generalized concerns about disabilities in the workforce. Disabilities discussed include impaired vision, hearing, and mobility, as well as learning and developmental disabilities. A few pages of Braille text are included in each issue. Advertisements for employers are scattered throughout but indexed in each issue; these employers are committed to hiring people with disabilities.

The Chronicle of Higher Education. See Education/Higher Education section.

Entrepreneur. See Business and Finance/Small Business section.

3850. ***Federal Jobs Digest.*** [ISSN: 0739-1684] 1977. 25x/yr. USD 125. Ed(s): Young S Kim. HYR LLC, PO Box 89, Edgemont, PA 19028. Illus., adv. *Aud.:* Ga, Ac.

This biweekly newsletter provides job listings for the federal government. Each issue lists several thousand jobs, organized regionally and listed by General Schedule code and grade level. An index by federal job title and General Schedule code indicates what jobs are listed in each issue, but not how to find the listings, making this publication most useful to someone job hunting in one geographical region. Separate lists include overseas jobs, Veterans Affairs jobs, Senior Executive Service jobs, and Postal Exams. Job listings include the title, grade, closing date for applications, location, term of employment, salary range, contact information, and announcement number. A key to the listings is available to interpret this information, which is presented in a brief format and very small type. Information about the federal resume requirements and application process is also provided. Brief news articles highlight trends and upcoming opportunities in federal agencies. Web sites listing agency job vacancies are listed.

3851. ***Hispanic Career World: the diversity employment magazine.*** 2001. s-a. USD 18 (Free to qualified personnel). Ed(s): Barbara Capella Loehr. Equal Opportunity Publications, Inc., 445 Broad Hollow Rd, Ste 425, Melville, NY 11747; info@eop.com; http://www.eop.com. *Aud.:* Ga.

This magazine provides career and industry profiles that focus on interviews with professionals of Hispanic extraction-who discuss their career paths, obstacles they faced, and how they overcame them, and offer their advice for job seekers. Articles about careers and industries highlight diversity initiatives in training and hiring, as well as jobs with an international aspect or where language ability is important, and areas in which there are programs designed to increase Hispanic presence in a field. Notes in the top margin identify the field or industry in each article and make for easy skimming. Columns provide new developments in the employment of Hispanics, including profiles of employers. While the table of contents headings are presented in English and Spanish, content is exclusively English. Advertising employers are indexed in each issue.

3852. ***Insight into Diversity.*** Formerly (until 2009): *Affirmative Action Register.* [ISSN: 2154-0349] 1974. m. except July. Free. Ed(s): Michael Rainey. Potomac Publishing, Inc, 225 S Meramec Ave Ste 400, St. Louis, MO 63105; http://www.potomacpub.com/. Illus., adv. Sample. Vol. ends: Feb/Aug. *Indexed:* B01. *Aud.:* Ga, Ac.

This magazine is aimed at the college-and-university-diversity professional community. Diversity is broadly conceived, including religious diversity and paying special attention to veterans. Diversity in on-campus activity and post-graduation life are considered in the articles. The magazine includes job listings for professionals in academic settings. Most advertisements are display ads, generally taking up a quarter to a half-page, with full descriptions and application information included. Up-to-date listings are available on the web site, and news updates are available by RSS feed and on Twitter (@INSIGHT_News), and a free app is available for both Apple and Android devices. URL: www.insightintodiversity.com

Monthly Labor Review Online. See Labor and Industrial Relations section.

3853. *Occupational Outlook Quarterly.* Formerly (until 1958): *The Occupational Outlook.* [ISSN: 0199-4786] 1957. q. Sep.-June. Ed(s): Kathleen Green. U.S. Department of Labor, Bureau of Labor Statistics, 2 Massachusetts Ave, NE, Washington, DC 20212; blsdata_staff@bls.gov; http://www.bls.gov. Illus., index. Sample. Vol. ends: Winter. Microform: CIS; NBI; PQC. *Indexed:* A01, A22, B01, BRI, C37, ERIC, MASUSE. *Aud.:* Ems, Hs, Ga, Ac.

This publication uses statistics from the federal government to supplement a narrative profile and often forecast projected labor markets for careers and industries. Job duties, education background and training, and earnings data are all provided, as well as sources of more information for interested readers. Other occupational trends are also outlined, such as opportunities for telecommuting. Occupational news such as information about reports, scholarships, and other material are reported in brief. The *Occupational Outlook Quarterly* updates the biennial *Occupational Outlook Handbook*, a standard reference work. This duo forms a valuable resource for those researching careers, whether they are students in search of a first career or adults looking for a change. A biennial "Job Outlook in brief" offers projections for hundreds of career fields from the *Occupational Outlook Handbook.* Online access is available, including an index back to 1999. URL: www.bls.gov/opub/ooq/home.htm

Techniques. See Education/Specific Subjects and Teaching Methods: Technology section.

Work and Occupations. See Sociology and Social Work/General section.

■ PALEONTOLOGY

See also Biological Sciences; and Earth Sciences sections.

Hilary Kline, Manager of Reformatting Support Services, Imaging Services, Harvard Library, Widener Library, Harvard University, Cambridge, MA 02138; kline@fas.harvard.edu

Introduction

When most people hear the word *paleontology,* they probably think of the skeleton of a dinosaur that they see at the natural history museum. In fact, there is much more to the study of prehistoric life than just dinosaur bones. Fossils are the keys to understanding the history of life on our planet; without them, we would know little of past climate change, and virtually nothing of evolution and extinction.

Not surprisingly, the field of paleontology is closely related to archaeology, but it also has a connection to biology, geology, ecology, and climatology. Due to the overlapping nature of the field, there are many journals from which to choose.

Two of the titles included for review are free open-access publications, so there is nothing to lose by taking a look at *Acta Palaeontologica Polonica* and *Palaeontologia Electronica.* Another good web site to look at is the University of Kansas's Paleontological Institute page, http://paleo.ku.edu, which has both an open-access publication and print ones for purchase, as well as some basic paleontology information.

It should also be noted that all of the reviews in this section have been done by looking at the online versions of the journals.

Basic Periodicals

Journal of Paleontology, Journal of Vertebrate Paleontology, Lethaia, Palaeontologia Electronica, Palaeontology, Palaios, Paleobiology.

Basic Abstracts and Indexes

BioOne Complete (www.bioone.org/), *BIOSIS, GeoRef, Zoological Record.*

3854. *Acta Palaeontologica Polonica.* [ISSN: 0567-7920] 1956. q. EUR 78.75. Ed(s): Andrzej Kaim. Polska Akademia Nauk, Instytut Paleobiologii, ul Twarda 51-55, Warsaw, 00-818, Poland; paleo@twarda.pan.pl ; http://www.paleo.pan.pl. Illus., adv. Refereed. Circ: 500. *Indexed:* A01, A22, BRI. *Bk. rev.:* 0-1, 500-1,200 words. *Aud.:* Ac, Sa.

Acta Palaeontologica Polonica is a quarterly, open-access journal that publishes original research papers from all areas of paleontology, especially those rooted in biologically-oriented paleontology. Areas covered in the journal include fossils, ancient organisms, vertebrates, and evidence of evolution of the biosphere and its ecosystems. Two recent articles include "New Miocene sulid birds from Peru and considerations on their Neogene fossil record in the Eastern Pacific Ocean" and "Fossil population structure and mortality analysis of the cave bears from Ursilor Cave, northwestern Romania." URL: www.app.pan.pl

Cretaceous Research. See Earth Sciences and Geology section.

3855. *International Journal of Paleopathology.* [ISSN: 1879-9817] 2011. q. EUR 394. Ed(s): Jane Buikstra. Elsevier Ltd, The Boulevard, Langford Lane, Oxford, OX5 1GB, United Kingdom; journalscustomerserviceemea@elsevier.com; http://www.elsevier.com. Refereed. *Aud.:* Ac, Sa.

This quarterly journal focuses on the study and application of methods and techniques for investigating diseases and related conditions from skeletal and soft-tissue remains. It is the official journal of the Paleopathology Association, and issues may include research articles, case studies, technical notes, brief communications, reviews, and invited commentaries. There are a limited numbered of articles that are open access, just one of 17 in a recent issue. Two recent inclusions are "An exploration of interpersonal violence among Holocene foragers of Southern Africa" (which is open access) and "First probable case of scurvy in ancient Egypt at Nag el-Qarmila, Aswan."

3856. *Journal of Paleontology.* [ISSN: 0022-3360] 1927. bi-m. GBP 422 (print & online eds.)). Ed(s): Sara Marcus, Brenda Hunda. Cambridge University Press, 1 Liberty Plaza, Fl 20, New York, NY 10004; online@cambridge.org; https://www.cambridge.org/. Illus., index, adv. Refereed. Vol. ends: Nov (No. 6). Microform: PQC. Reprint: PSC. *Indexed:* A01, A22, E01. *Bk. rev.:* 4, 500 words. *Aud.:* Ac, Sa.

Published by The Paleontological Society, the *Journal of Paleontology* publishes original articles and notes on the systematics, phylogeny, paleoecology, paleogeography, and evolution of fossil organisms. It emphasizes specimen-based research and features high-quality illustrations. All taxonomic groups are treated, including invertebrates, microfossils, plants, vertebrates, and ichnofossils. Recent articles include "Requirements and limits of anatomy-based predictions of locomotion in terrestrial arthropods with emphasis on arachnids" and "A new Eocene genus of ant-like stone beetles sheds new light on the evolution of Mastigini." A very limited number of articles are open access.

Journal of Quaternary Science. See Earth Sciences and Geology section.

3857. *Journal of Vertebrate Paleontology.* [ISSN: 0272-4634] 1980. bi-m. GBP 501 (print & online eds.)). Ed(s): Jason Anderson, Lars Werdelin. Taylor & Francis Inc., 711 3rd Ave, 8th Fl, New York, NY 10017; support@tandfonline.com; http://www.tandfonline.com. Illus., index, adv. Refereed. Vol. ends: Dec (No. 4). Reprint: PSC. *Indexed:* A01, A22, E01. *Bk. rev.:* 0-4, 1,000-2,000 words. *Aud.:* Ac, Sa.

This journal is produced six times a year on behalf of the Society of Vertebrate Paleontology, with original contributions on all aspects of vertebrate paleontology, including evolution, functional morphology, taxonomy, phylogeny, biostratigraphy, paleoecology, and paleobiogeography. The contributions include an invited article, articles, short communications, and book reviews. A recent issue contains the two articles, "A juvenile sauropod dinosaur from the Late Jurassic of Utah, U.S.A., presents further evidence of an avian style air-sac system" and "A new therapsid from the Permian Madumabisa Mudstone Formation (Mid-Zambezi Basin) of southern Zambia." A few articles are open access.

3858. ***Lethaia: an international journal of palaeontology and stratigraphy.*** [ISSN: 0024-1164] 1968. q. GBP 429 (print & online eds.)). Ed(s): Peter Doyle. Wiley-Blackwell Publishing Ltd., The Atrium, Southern Gate, Chichester, PO19 8QG, United Kingdom; cs-journals@wiley.com; http://onlinelibrary.wiley.com. Illus., index, adv. Sample. Refereed. Vol. ends: No. 4. Microform: PQC. Reprint: PSC. *Indexed:* A01, A22, E01. *Bk. rev.:* 1,700 words. *Aud.:* Ac, Sa.

This journal is the formal publication for the International Palaeontological Association (IPA) and the International Commission on Stratigraphy (ICS). It emphasizes new developments and discoveries in paleobiological and biostratigraphical research and is published quarterly. The publication aims to "concentrate on the development of new ideas and methods and descriptions of new features of wide significance rather than routine descriptions." Two recent articles are "Late Mississippian vertebrate palaeoecology and taphonomy, Buffalo Wallow Formation, western Kentucky, USA" and "Leftover prey remains: a new taphonomic mode from the Late Miocene Cerro Azul Formation of Central Argentina." Some articles are open access.

3859. ***Palaeontologia Electronica.*** [ISSN: 1935-3952] 1997. s-a. Ed(s): Jennifer Pattison Rumford. Coquina Press, PO Box 577, Columbia, CA 95310; coquinapress@mac.com; http://www.coquinapress.com. Refereed. *Bk. rev.:* 0-3, 1,000-1,500 words. *Aud.:* Ac, Sa.

The sponsors of and contributors to *Palaeontologia Electronica* are the Palaeontological Association, the Paleontological Society, the Society of Vertebrate Paleontology, and the Western Interior Paleontological Society. This title deals with all aspects of paleontology and is the longest-running open-access, peer-reviewed electronic journal. One recent article is "Upper Pleistocene blow flies (Diptera: Calliphoridae) trapped in fossilized crania of large mammals discovered from gravel pits in the Rhine rift valley from Hesse (Germany)." One recent commentary that is available is "Amateur paleontological societies and fossil clubs, interactions with professional paleontologists, and social paleontology in the United States." URL: http://palaeo-electronica.org

3860. ***Palaeontology (Online).*** [ISSN: 1475-4983] 1957. bi-m. GBP 836. Ed(s): Dr. Andrew B Smith. Wiley-Blackwell Publishing Ltd., The Atrium, Southern Gate, Chichester, PO19 8QG, United Kingdom; cs-journals@wiley.com; http://onlinelibrary.wiley.com. *Aud.:* Ac, Sa.

This journal of the Palaeontological Association has a very broad scope and publishes a variety of research that aims to significantly advance our understanding of the history of life on Earth. The scope includes paleozoology, paleobotany, systematic studies, paleoecology, micropaleontology, paleobiogeography, functional morphology, stratigraphy, taxonomy, taphonomy, paleoenvironmental reconstruction, paleoclimate analysis, and biomineralization studies. Sections include original articles, rapid communications, reviews, discussions, and technical reports. Two recent articles are "A new Upper Cretaceous titanosaur nesting site from La Rioja (NW Argentina), with implications for titanosaur nesting strategies" and "Endothermic mosasaurs? Possible thermoregulation of Late Cretaceous mosasaurs (Reptilia, Squamata) indicated by stable oxygen isotopes in fossil bioapatite in comparison with coeval marine fish and pelagic seabirds." Some articles are open access.

3861. ***Palaios: emphasizing the impact of life on earth's history.*** [ISSN: 0883-1351] 1986. bi-m. Free to members. Ed(s): Kathleen Huber. Society for Sedimentary Geology (S E P M), 4111 S Darlington, Ste 100, Tulsa, OK 74135; foundation@sepm.org; http://www.sepm.org. Illus., index, adv. Refereed. Vol. ends: No. 6. *Indexed:* A22, E01. *Bk. rev.:* 1-3, 300-800 words. *Aud.:* Ac, Sa.

This journal is published monthly by the Society for Sedimentary Geology to disseminate information to geologists and biologists who are interested in a broad range of topics, including biogeochemistry, ichnology, paleoclimatology, paleoecology, paleoceanography, sedimentology, stratigraphy, geomicrobiology, paleobiogeochemistry, and astrobiology. The articles published in *Palaios* emphasize the impact of life on Earth's history as recorded in the paleontological and sedimentological records. Two recently published articles include "Preservation of fossil microbes and biofilm in cave pool carbonates and comparison to other microbrial carbonate environments" and "Late Triassic durophagy and the origin of the Mesozoic marine revolution."

3862. ***Paleobiology.*** [ISSN: 0094-8373] 1975. q. GBP 229 (print & online eds.)). Ed(s): Sara Marcus, Michal Kowalewski. Cambridge University Press, 1 Liberty Plaza, Fl 20, New York, NY 10004; online@cambridge.org; https://www.cambridge.org/. Illus., index, adv. Refereed. Vol. ends: Fall (No. 4). Microform: PQC. Reprint: PSC. *Indexed:* A22, C45, E01. *Bk. rev.:* 1, 1,500-2,000 words. *Aud.:* Ac, Sa.

Paleobiology is published quarterly by The Paleontologicial Society, with an emphasis on biological or paleobiological processes and patterns, including macroevolution, extinction, diversification, speciation, functional morphology, bio-geography, phylogeny, paleoecology, molecular paleontology, taphonomy, natural selection and patterns of variation, abundance, and distribution in space and time. Two recent articles are "Climate-mediated changes in predator-prey interactions in the fossil record: a case study using shell-drilling gastropods from the Pleistocene Japan Sea" and "Compositional turnover and ecological changes related to the waxing and waning of glaciers during the late Paleozoic ice age in ice-proximal regions (Pennsylvanian, western Argentina)."

■ PARANORMAL

Christianne Casper, Librarian, Broward College

Cheryl LaGuardia, Research Librarian, Widener Library, Harvard University

Introduction

The Urban Dictionary's top definition of Paranormal at this writing is: "Anything unexplainable by science. Anything supposedly thought to be the figment of imagination which cannot be proved by scientific means. Extraterrestrials and ghosts fit into this category. There is no proof that either do not exist. If you have ever seen anything you can't explain scientifically, then that is paranormal by definition." This encompassing definition serves this chapter well—we're not going to try to convince you of anything except that these are the journals we consider to be essential to provide in library collections serving paranormal researchers.

Basic Periodicals

American Society for Psychical Research. Journal, Society for Psychical Research. Journal.

Basic Abstracts and Indexes

Academic Search Premier; ATLA Religion Database; Philosopher's Index.

3863. ***American Society for Psychical Research. Journal.*** Former titles (until 1932): *Psychic Research;* (until 1928): *American Society for Psychical Research. Journal.* [ISSN: 0003-1070] 1907. q. Free to members. American Society for Psychical Research, Inc., 5 W 73rd St, New York, NY 10023; aspr@aspr.com; http://www.aspr.com. Illus., index. Sample. Refereed. Microform: PQC. *Indexed:* A22. *Aud.:* Ga, Ac, Sa.

The American Society for Psychical Research was founded in 1885 and is the oldest psychic research organization in the United States. This core journal is known for its informative, scholarly coverage of topics including, but not limited to, ESP, precognition, psychokinesis, and psychic healing. The journal includes scholarly reports, research, and field studies that focus on firsthand reports of paranormal phenomena. Issues average about four articles, with tables/graphs, footnotes, and references. Some issues include a correspondence column and a book review section. The society's website includes sample articles. URL: http://www.aspr.com/jaspr.htm

3864. ***Fortean Times.*** Formerly (until 1976): *News.* [ISSN: 0308-5899] 1973. m. GBP 55. Dennis Publishing Ltd., 30 Cleveland St, London, W1T 4JD, United Kingdom; reception@dennis.co.uk; http://www.dennis.co.uk/. Illus., adv. *Aud.:* Ga, Ac, Sa.

Fortean Times was founded to continue the investigative research of Charles Fort (1874-1932), one of the first UFOlogists and a skeptical investigator of the bizarre and unusual. This publication provides news; reviews; research on strange phenomena, psychic experiences, and prodigies; and portents from around the world. While the publication maintains a humorous air, its goal is to provide thought-provoking, educational information. The articles provide resources that usually include recommended readings, web-surfings, and/or notes. In addition to articles, each issue includes book and media reviews, "Strange Days," and "Forum." The online edition includes the table of contents for the current issue, brief book and media reviews, archives, a community board to share information, breaking news, and exclusive features.

3865. ***The Journal for Spiritual and Consciousness Studies.*** Former titles (until 2012): *The Journal of Spirituality and Paranormal Studies;* (until 2006): *The Journal of Religion & Psychical Research;* (until 1981): *Academy of Religion and Psychical Research. Journal.* [ISSN: 2325-8780] 197?. q. Free to members. Ed(s): Michael E Tymn, Boyce Batey. Academy of Spirituality and Paranormal Studies, Inc., PO Box 614, Bloomfield, CT 06002; http://ascsi.org/. Index. Sample. *Indexed:* A01. *Aud.:* Ac, Sa.

This journal was established to provide a forum among clergy, academics, and researchers concerning religion, philosophy, and psychical research. There are about five articles in each issue, some with references. In addition, there are research proposals, abstracts of completed research, views and comments, book reviews, and correspondence. Recommended for religion or parapsychology collections. An index to the publishing organization's journals and journal articles are available online. URL: http://www.ascsi.org/ASCS/Publications/publications.shtml#journal

3866. ***Journal of Parapsychology.*** [ISSN: 0022-3387] 1937. s-a. Individuals, USD 65; Free to members. Ed(s): Dave Roberts, John A. Palmer. Rhine Research Center, 2741 Campus Walk Ave, Bldg 500, Durham, NC 27705; http://www.rhine.org/. Illus., index. Refereed. Vol. ends: Dec. Microform: PQC. *Indexed:* A01, A22, BRI, CBRI. *Aud.:* Ac, Sa.

The Journal of Parapsychology, founded by J. B. Rhine, was one of the first scholarly parapsychology journals published. Its primary focus is to provide a professional forum for original research reports on experimental parapsychology. In addition to the technical experimental reports, the journal averages six to eight articles and includes surveys of literature, book reviews, and correspondence. Now available only online. URL: http://www.parapsych.org/section/17/journal_of_parapsychology.aspx

3867. ***Skeptic.*** [ISSN: 1063-9330] 1992. q. USD 30 domestic; USD 40 in Canada & Mexico; USD 50 elsewhere. Ed(s): Michael Shermer. Millenium Press, 570 Silver St, Agawam, MA 01001; http://www.millenniumpress.com/. Illus., adv. *Indexed:* A01, AmHI, BRI, CBRI, MLA-IB. *Aud.:* Ac, Ga.

Skeptic promotes scientific and critical thinking while investigating claims made on a variety of topics, including pseudoscience, the paranormal, superstition, fringe claims, and revolutionary science. The features included in every issue are "Articles," "News," "Forum," "Reviews," and "Junior Skeptic." Some issues of Skeptic also include movie and audio reviews. The online version provides issues of the "eSkeptic" newsletter, archives, a reading room, forum, "Junior Skeptic," and podcasts. URL: http://www.skeptic.com

3868. ***Skeptical Inquirer: the magazine for science and reason.*** Formerly (until 1978): *The Zetetic.* [ISSN: 0194-6730] 1976. bi-m. USD 19.95; USD 5 per issue. Ed(s): Kendrick Frazier. Committee for the Scientific Investigation of Claims of the Paranormal, PO Box 703, Buffalo, NY 14226; info@csicop.org; http://www.csicop.org. Illus. *Indexed:* A22, BRI, MLA-IB. *Aud.:* Ga, Ac, Sa.

Skeptical Inquirer focuses on what the scientific community knows about claims of the paranormal as opposed to media sensationalism. The journal promotes scientific research, critical thinking, and science education. Standard features include "News and Comment," "Notes on a Strange World," "Science Watch," "Articles," and "Book Reviews," as well as "Investigative Files," "Skeptical Inquiree," "Psychic Vibrations," "Science of Medicine," and "Thinking @ Science." In addition to parapsychology, topics investigated include UFOs, alternative therapy, psychic claims, astrology, skepticism in general, and other paranormal experiences. Online at www.csicop.org/si includes an archive, resources, special articles, and "Skeptical Briefs." URL: ttp://www.csicop.org/si

3869. ***Society for Psychical Research. Journal.*** [ISSN: 0037-9751] 1884. q. Free to members; Non-members, GBP 40. Ed(s): David Vernon. Society for Psychical Research, 1 Vernon Mews, London, W14 0RL, United Kingdom; secretary@spr.ac.uk; http://www.spr.ac.uk/. Illus., index. Sample. Refereed. Vol. ends: Oct. *Indexed:* A01, A22. *Aud.:* Ac, Sa.

The Journal of the Society for Psychical Research is one of the oldest parapsychological publications. It aims to objectively examine paranormal experiences and reports that appear to be otherwise inexplicable. The journal publishes field and case studies, experimental reports, book reviews, a correspondence section, and historical, theoretical, and methodological papers from the field of parapsychology. There are approximately five articles per issue, complete with tables, graphs, and references. The contents of approximately 120 years' worth of journals and proceedings, and abstracts from 2000 onward, are available online to society members only. URL: https://www.spr.ac.uk/publications/journal-society-psychical-research

■ PARENTING

Caroline M. Kent, Director of Research Support and Instruction, Charles E. Shain Library, Connecticut College, New London, CT 06320

Introduction

Are there publications that can actually help a new (or even experienced) parent?! It is certainly the case that new parents are always desperate for information and help, and that there is, therefore, a market for such publications. This is particularly so in this era when many parenting individuals are separated from the older generations of their families—generations that carry parenting wisdom and experience.

It is also arguable that parenting is now more complicated in this era of dual-career families, single and divorced parents, and alternative families of all sorts. Even those families who are practicing a more traditional family form, with a stay-at-home mom, may find the lack of neighborhoods and extended family daunting. The modern reality is that there aren't too many parents who don't feel that they need all the help they can get! One significant addition to this section is the new title *Life and the Single Parent,* an excellent publication that is the first commercial publication seeking to legitimize that family experience.

Commercial parenting magazines really fall neatly into two categories: magazines that are general enough to contain articles of interest to a wide range of families; and magazines that contain articles interesting to particular parents, such as adoptive or single parents. Social computing on the web also is taking a front seat for communities of people (like parents of all sorts) that need fast information and community support.

An increasing number of former magazines, both print and online, are becoming pure blogging sites, and those are not included here. There are moments when I have wondered if blogging and web sites will actually, someday, fully replace print journals in this subject area. "Mommy blogging" and, for that matter, "Daddy blogging" provide powerful writing as well as new-product reviewing. Unfortunately, many blogging sites drift off; and an increasing number of more ephemeral parent publications are taking the same route. So print magazines have stabilized, and remain an important format.

Another note on format: This section necessarily must be more tolerant of the newsletter format, since parents often have little time for prolonged reading. There are some very thoughtful newsletters that address a niche need, and these should be evaluated carefully.

New this year are two titles that are really academic in nature, *Adoption and Fostering* and *Gifted Child Quarterly*. Although this section has traditionally been more personal and commercial in nature, these two important journals are not reviewed elsewhere.

In addition to the titles listed here, there are a large number of excellent local parenting magazines (such as *Boston Parents' Paper* and *Black Parenting Today: Information and Resources for Greater Philadelphia Families*). Public libraries should identify such publications for their areas and include them in current collections.

Basic Periodicals

Ga: *American Baby, FamilyFun, Parent & Child, Parents.*

Basic Abstracts and Indexes

ERIC, PsycINFO, Readers' Guide to Periodical Literature, SocINDEX.

3870. *Adoption and Fostering.* Formerly (until 1976): *Child Adoption.* [ISSN: 0308-5759] 1952. q. USD 686 (print & online eds.)). Ed(s): Roger Bullock. Sage Publications Ltd., 1 Oliver's Yard, 55 City Rd, London, EC1Y 1SP, United Kingdom; info@sagepub.com; https://www.sagepub.com/. Sample. Refereed. Reprint: PSC. *Indexed:* A22, ASSIA, BRI, C42, SSA. *Bk. rev.:* 2-3, 700-1000 words. *Aud.:* Ac, Sa.

Adoption and Fostering is a 50-year-old, peer-reviewed journal that is "dedicated to adoption and fostering issues, providing an international forum for a wide range of professionals: academics and practitioners in social work, psychology, law, medicine, education, [and] training and caring for children and young people." It must be noted that this journal is from the United Kingdom, and as such, it contains some local information that is not relevant to American libraries (such as its "Legal Notes" section). However, there are many excellent articles on the practice, psychology, and social consequences of adoption and fostering that are relevant to any social work practitioner anywhere. Some titles of recent articles include "Preventing exploitation, promoting equity: findings from the International Forum on Intercountry Adoption and Global Surrogacy 2014," "How I care: foster fathers recount their experiences of caring for children," and "Global commercial surrogacy and international adoption: parallels and differences." Given the price of this journal, it would be best placed in the collections of universities that support professional schools of social work.

3871. *Adoption Today (Online).* Former titles (until 200?): *Adoption Today (Print);* (until 2000): *Chosen Child.* 1998. m. Free. Ed(s): Christie Renick, Kim Phagan-Hansel. Fostering Media Connections, 412 W. 6th St, Ste. 925, Los Angeles, CA 90014; info@fosteringmediaconnections.org; http://www.fosteringmediaconnections.org/. *Bk. rev.:* 3-4, 50-100 words. *Aud.:* Ga, Sa.

Unlike the softer, more adoptive parent-oriented *Adoptive Families, Adoption Today* pulls few punches. It more clearly represents all voices in adoption, that is, the voices of adoptees, birth parents, and adoption professionals, as well as those of adoptive parents. The result is an interesting magazine that seeks to illuminate those adoption issues that are often hard to face. A new and very interesting aspect is that the magazine now advertises itself as being "The only magazine dedicated to International and Transracial Adoption." Its articles and editorials are edgy and interesting, often authored by controversial adoption advocates. Some recent articles include "Embryo Adoption," "Reconnecting Ethiopian Adoptees," and "Self-Determination and Self-Advocacy as a Part of an Individual Transitional Plan for Internationally Adopted Children." Any public library that serves a large adoption community should consider its purchase, as well as any academic or special library that serves the needs of social work students or adoption professionals.

3872. *Adoptive Families.* Former titles (until 1994): *Ours (Minneapolis);* (until 1969): *News of Ours.* [ISSN: 1076-1020] 1967. bi-m. USD 24.95 domestic; USD 32.95 Canada; USD 44.95 elsewhere. Ed(s): Susan Caughman. Adoptive Families Magazine, 39 W 37th Str, 15th fl, New York, NY 10018. Illus., adv. Sample. Circ: 25000. *Bk. rev.:* 3-8, 50 words. *Aud.:* Ga, Sa.

This glossy, family-oriented magazine is considered the standard publication by the adoptive family community. The editor, Susan Caughman, has done much to broaden the editorial perspective from the magazine's earlier version: there are now regular columns contributed by birth parents, adoption lawyers, doctors, and adoption experts, such as Lois Melina, etc. The magazine still maintains its family orientation, with pictures of subscribing families and feature articles of general interest. Recent examples of articles include "Adoptees on Open Adoption: 'I Have All My Pieces'" and "To the White Parents of My Black Son's Friends." *Adoptive Families* has a slightly softer, more cheerful take on adoption than the harder *Adoption Today,* but it remains a central and important magazine for the adoption community. American adoption has become less secret and more of a topic for public discussion. For that reason, any public library that serves growing families should consider purchasing this magazine, as should academic or special collections that serve adoption professionals.

3873. *American Baby: healthy pregnancy, healthy baby.* Formerly: *Mothers-to-Be - American Baby.* [ISSN: 0044-7544] 1940. m. Meredith National Media Group, 125 Park Ave, 25th Fl, New York, NY 10017; http://www.meredith.com. Illus., adv. Sample. *Indexed:* A22, Agr, BRI. *Aud.:* Ga.

There aren't too many American families with young children who don't read or at least receive issues of this magazine. Expectant parents can get it free for several months. It is the oldest and most reliable of the commercial baby-parenting magazines, containing a wide range of short, easy-to-read articles on baby and parent health issues, developmental discussions, baby care, and family issues. In addition to the huge number of advertisements for baby-related products, this magazine also contains discussion and reviews of new products. There are advice columns that cover everything from behavior to health and nutrition. The magazine seems to have taken a slight turn toward celebrating celebrity pregnancies, but maybe that is just fine. Glowing, healthy, happy celebrity women showing off their baby bumps is probably a good thing. The magazine also has a healthy and well-maintained web site that is updated frequently with articles and videos. All public libraries should invest in this.

3874. *Brain, Child: the magazine for thinking mothers.* [ISSN: 1528-5170] 2000. q. Ed(s): Marcelle Soviero. March Press, LLC, PO Box 714, Lexington, VA 24450. Vol. ends: Winter. *Bk. rev.:* 2-4. *Aud.:* Ga, Ac.

How can we resist a journal that says in its mission statement that "motherhood is worthy of literature"? Or that this "isn't your typical magazine. We couldn't cupcake-decorate our way out of a paper bag." This journal is totally irresistible! Each issue contains a mix of intriguing essays, feature articles, humor, fiction, and art-some of which has some powerful names attached, such as Barbara Kingsolver, Perri Klass, Mary Gordon, and Alice Hoffman (all mothers themselves). This isn't a how-to magazine; rather, it is a why-do-we-do-it-at-all magazine. Recent essays include "Yearning for Superhero Status," "When Baby Has No Name," and finally "Blended, Stepfamilies with Young Children Are on the Rise." There's a great humor column ("MotherWit") and a book review section that is thoughtful without taking itself too seriously. Funny, thought-provoking, and full of terrific reads, this magazine should be considered by any college library with a writing program and any public library with the right constituency. And although it helps to be a mother when reading this, it is not necessary!

Child & Family Behavior Therapy. See Family section.

3875. *Digital Parenting.* [ISSN: 2051-1221] 2010. irreg. Vodafone Group Plc, Vodafone House, The Connection, Newbury, RG14 2FN, United Kingdom; http://www.vodafone.com. Adv. *Aud.:* Ga.

Digital Parenting fits an important niche. In this world of ever-changing technologies, social media, and ever-increasing web content, parents are often at a loss as to how to protect their children, how to teach them to use social media responsibly, and how to evaluate the web-based materials that their children find. This magazine seeks to assist in solving many of those puzzles. It is British, so there are times that the content is geographically irrelevant to American parents. But most of the content is interesting, up-to-date, and very useful for American audiences. Some recent articles include "What Parents

Should Really Do About Internet Safety," "Me, My Selfie, and I," and "Are Online Games Damaging Your child?" Any public library should consider this publication, as well as any teacher resource collection.

Exceptional Parent (Online). See Family section.

3876. *FamilyFun.* [ISSN: 1056-6333] 1991. 8x/yr. USD 5.99 domestic; USD 22 Canada. Meredith Corporation, 1716 Locust St., Des Moines, IA 50309; http://www.meredith.com/. Illus., adv. *Bk. rev.:* 5-6, 75-100 words. *Aud.:* Ga.

This magazine has moved in and out of different ownerships, and now it is owned by the *Parents Magazine* network. This publication is full of, well, fun ideas. The format is nice, with great photographs of kids and their families-all having fun! There are craft activities, rainy-day-fun ideas, traveling-with-the-kids ideas, and party ideas of all kinds, as well as reviews of toys and games, books, and videos. This is actually a wonderful magazine, jam-packed with ideas for even the most creative of parents. It is really the only magazine that has family activities as its total focus; therefore, it is an invaluable addition to any parenting magazine collection. Any public library not located in a retirement home should purchase this. Very highly recommended.

3877. *Fathering Magazine.* [ISSN: 1091-5516] 1995. m. Free. Ed(s): John Gill. Fathering Enterprises, Inc., PO Box 231891, Houston, TX 77223. Illus., adv. *Indexed:* BRI. *Aud.:* Ga, Sa.

This substantive online journal is intended for teachers, students, and practitioners, as well as dads themselves. It includes research and practice-based articles on all aspects of fatherhood and males in the role of parent. Issues covered include parenting, father/child relationships, divorce, stepfathers, child custody, and more. Recent articles include "The War on Boys," and autism. There are copious links, and Twitter feeds. *Fathering Magazine* is a title that academic and research librarians should be aware of and recommend when appropriate. All public libraries should consider it.

3878. *Fostering Families Today.* [ISSN: 1531-409X] 2001. bi-m. USD 24.95. Ed(s): Christie Renick, Kim Phagan-Hansel. Fostering Media Connections, 412 W. 6th St, Ste. 925, Los Angeles, CA 90014; info@fosteringmediaconnections.org; http://www.fosteringmediaconnections.org/. *Aud.:* Ga, Sa.

The foster-parent community clearly deals with many of the same issues as do adoptive parents and people parenting their birth children; but there is a deep range of social, legal, medical, and psychological issues that are particular to their interests. This glossy magazine strives to service those interests, and it includes recent articles such as "Life After Adoption Through Foster Care," "Co-Parenting with Birth Family," and "Hope and Possibility: A Toolbox of Possibilities for Struggling Families." There are also regular columns, such as "Washington Beat" and "Family Talk," which keep an eye on important legislative and medical issues relevant to fostering. Given the number of children in foster care in the United States, any medium-to-large public library should purchase this magazine. In addition, any special or academic library that serves social workers or social work students should consider its purchase.

3879. *Gay Parent.* [ISSN: 1545-6714] 1998. bi-m. USD 22 domestic; USD 30 foreign; USD 3.50 per issue. Ed(s): Angeline Acain. Gay Parent, PO Box 750852, Forest Hills, NY 11375. Adv. Sample. *Bk. rev.:* 1, 150 words; signed. *Aud.:* Ga.

With legal same-sex marriage now widespread, and with more members of the LGBT community finding easier paths to parenting, journals like this one will become increasingly important. Beyond its obvious audience, *Gay Parent* is one of the more thoughtful parenting magazines in print. It assumes that its readership is interested in substantive interviews, and legislative information. It periodically publishes lists of gay-friendly private schools and camps, and articles on adoption and foster care. Some recent articles include "Six Camps Specifically for LGBT Families" and "No Drama Mama, Parenting and Relationship Advice." Subscribers may elect to get the full text of the magazine online for a reduced subscription rate. This magazine will be well placed in any public library with a parent population interested in diverse family structures.

3880. *Gifted Child Quarterly.* Formerly (until 1958): *The Gifted Child Newsletter.* [ISSN: 0016-9862] 1957. q. USD 565 (print & online eds.)). Ed(s): D Betsy McCoach, Del Siegle. Sage Publications, Inc., 2455 Teller Rd, Thousand Oaks, CA 91320; info@sagepub.com; http://www.sagepub.com. Illus., adv. Sample. Refereed. Vol. ends: Fall. Microform: PQC. Reprint: PSC. *Indexed:* A01, A22, BRI, E01, ERIC, MLA-IB. *Bk. rev.:* 2-3, 500-1000 words. *Aud.:* Ac, Sa.

The next entry, *Gifted Child Today,* is intended for parents raising exceptional children. *Gifted Child Quarterly,* however, is very much a professional journal directed at educators. It is peer-reviewed, and is "the official journal of the National Association for Gifted Children. As a leading journal in the field, *GCQ* publishes original scholarly reviews of the literature and quantitative or qualitative research studies." Some of the recent titles of articles include "Life in the Fast Lane: Effects of Early Grade Acceleration on High School and College Outcomes" and "Equity and Excellence: Proactive Efforts in the Identification of Underrepresented Students for Gifted and Talented Services." This journal would be best placed in colleges and universities with well-developed education programs.

3881. *Gifted Child Today.* Former titles (until 1993): *The Gifted Child Today;* (until 1986): *G C T (Gifted, Creative, Talented Children).* [ISSN: 1076-2175] 1978. q. USD 162 (print & online eds.)). Ed(s): Susan K Johnsen. Sage Publications, Inc., 2455 Teller Rd, Thousand Oaks, CA 91320; info@sagepub.com; http://www.sagepub.com. Illus. Sample. Refereed. Reprint: PSC. *Indexed:* A22, BRI, ERIC. *Bk. rev.:* 3-5, 100 words. *Aud.:* Ga, Sa.

This magazine is intended to support both teachers and parents of gifted children, but is increasingly focused on the former. It is full of articles not only on the educational theory of the teaching of the gifted but also on ideas for both curriculum development and learning plans for home. Some recent article titles include "Pedagogy for Early Childhood Gifted Education" and "Boushieness and Helping Others: The Life of a Gifted Female African American Student." Recommended for school libraries, academic libraries that support education programs, and large public libraries.

3882. *Kiwi: growing families the natural and organic way.* [ISSN: 1933-2920] 2006. bi-m. May Media Group, Llc., 104 Centre Blvd, Ste A, Marlton, NJ 08053. Adv. *Bk. rev.:* 3-4, 100-200 words. *Aud.:* Ga.

It is notable that retail grocers such as Whole Foods and Wild Oats feature this journal at their checkout stands! The editors of the magazine state as their mission that *Kiwi* "is dedicated to helping parents raise their children the healthiest way possible." There are columns on food, nutrition, eco-crafts, and book reviews of both adult and children's selections, as well as feature articles. A few recent article titles include "Your Dream Kitchen, Eco-Friendly and Gorgeous" and "Smart Foods." Public libraries with environmentally-minded parent groups should consider purchasing this title.

3883. *Life and the Single Parent: helping single parents thrive in today's world.* 2014. q. USD 17.50. Ed(s): Katherine Hope. Y W S Publishing, PO Box 30122, Palm Beach Gardens, FL 33420; info@lifeandthesingleparent.com; Htto://www.lifeandthesingleparent.com. *Bk. rev.:* 1-2, 300 words. *Aud.:* Ga.

According to the Pew Research Center, in 2014 fewer than half of the minor children in the United States lived in a two-parent home. Until the publication of *Life and the Single Parent,* there was no substantive commercial publication that addressed the particular needs of those homes. This excellent, new publication is published in Southern Florida, but beyond some community content, its focus is absolutely national in nature. Its content strives to address all family members, with columns such as "Teens Talk," "Community," "Healthy Living," and "Parent Corner." It has coloring pages and puzzles for the youngest, and interviews with teens. Some recent article titles include "Teach Your Children Well, Helping Kids Honor the Other Parent" and "Single Parenting With Chronic Illness." Its content is thoughtful, generous, and very positive. Any public library that addresses the needs of families should be purchasing this title.

3884. *Parent & Child: raising smarter, happier families.* [ISSN: 1070-0552] 1993. q. Ed(s): Jane Isabel Nussbaum. Scholastic Inc., 557 Broadway, New York, NY 10012; http://www.scholastic.com. Adv. *Indexed:* A01. *Bk. rev.:* 3-4, 25 words. *Aud.:* Ga, Sa.

Parent & Child has an interesting life: first, it is a printed magazine that covers learning issues from birth to about six years, happening to be part of Scholastic's larger web presence, which includes not only this magazine's content. But also, it takes the reader further through middle school. Not surprisingly, Scholastic has collected an advisory board for the magazine that includes several national early-childhood experts. The articles are short and informative, and are intended to bridge a child's preschool learning experience with his or her learning life at home. The magazine presents learning and health issues, behavioral and developmental information, and lots of activities for parents to use at home. All public libraries should consider this magazine; also, learning resource centers at schools that train early-childhood staff should purchase it.

3885. ***Parents.*** Former titles (until 1993): *Parents' Magazine;* (until 1985): *Parents;* Which incorporated (in 1981): *Parents Home;* Which was formerly (until 19??): *Handy Andy Magazine;* (until 1978): *Parents' Magazine;* (until 1977): *Parents' Magazine and Better Homemaking; Parents' & Better Family Living;* (until 1973): *Parents' Magazine and Better Family Living;* (until 1968): *Parents' Magazine & Better Homemaking;* (until 1959): *Parents' Magazine & Family Home Guide;* (until 1953): *Parents' Magazine; Children; Mother's Magazine; Mother's Activities.* [ISSN: 1083-6373] 1926. m. USD 6 per issue. Ed(s): Dana Points. Meredith National Media Group, 1716 Locust St, Des Moines, IA 50309; patrick.taylor@meredith.com; http://www.meredith.com. Illus., adv. Sample. *Indexed:* A22, BRI, C37, CBRI, PdeR. *Bk. rev.:* 4-5, 50 words. *Aud.:* Ga.

Parents has in many ways become the industry standard for parenting magazines. As with many others, its focus tends to be on early-childhood development and health topics rather than on issues associated with older children. There are many regular columns on child development and health, and on maternal and parental health-which are often focused on readers' questions. Feature articles include many short pieces on family life, home style, fun time, and health and safety, to name just a few departments. Highly recommended for any public library that addresses the needs of families.

3886. ***Twins (Online): the magazine for multiples.*** 1984. bi-m. Free. Ed(s): Laura Cunningham. Panoptic Media, 142 Mariner Blvd #510, Spring Hill, FL 34609; http://www.panoptic-media.com/. Adv. Sample. *Bk. rev.:* 2-3, 50 words. *Aud.:* Ga.

Oh, my. Double the joy-and double the trials of parenthood! Although there probably isn't a parent of twins (or triplets) who would have it any other way, there's no question that there are particular issues, both logistical and psychological, of handling the children of multiple birth. With fertility technologies increasing in use and sophistication, twinning (and beyond!) is much more common than it once was, so a cheerful, helpful magazine like *Twins* is welcome. It contains product reviews, feature articles, developmental discussions, and more. Articles are thoughtful, often highly personal discussions of issues and successes. Some recent titles include "The Best of Both Worlds, How Parents of Multiples Run Successful Home-Based Businesses" and "Double Talk, Do Your Twins Speak a Secret Language." Recommended for public libraries.

■ PEACE AND CONFLICT STUDIES

Julia Frankosky, Government Information and Political Science Librarian, Michigan State University, 366 W. Circle Dr., East Lansing, MI 48824; frankosk@msu.edu

Introduction

Peace and conflict studies is a relatively new field that grew out of the devastating violence of the First World War and gained traction in academia in the decades following World War II. President Woodrow Wilson's Fourteen Points for peacemaking in 1918 laid out many of the same principles for peace that are still accepted by peace scholars to this day, such as disarmament and free trade. With the end of the Second World War and the creation of the United Nations, it became evident to scholars that in order for the United Nations to maintain its mission of promoting international cooperation and peace, rigorous research needed to be done in the areas of peace and conflict resolution.

In 1948, Manchester University in Indiana created the first undergraduate academic program in peace studies in the United States. Similar programs and related courses became more widespread throughout the 1960s due to the Vietnam War and the desire of anti-war undergraduate students to pursue peaceful solutions to violent conflicts. By the 1980s, as the prospect of nuclear apocalypse seemed almost imminent, the number of peace studies courses available at universities worldwide increased dramatically. With the end of the Cold War, peace and conflict studies remained widespread throughout university curricula, but the focus shifted from pre-Cold War emphasis on international conflict to a more comprehensive focus on peace and conflict as it relates to the human condition with a growth in interest related to human rights, gender inequality, human security, democratization, as well as the more traditional aspects related to security issues and conflicts.

While peace and conflict studies grew in academic curricula, peace-related research institutes were founded. The Peace Research Institute Oslo (PRIO) was the first to be created in 1959 and with it, the creation of the first peace and conflict-focused journal: the *Journal of Peace Research.* Many other peace research centers were created, such as the Peace Science Society (which publishes the journals *Journal of Conflict Resolution* and *Conflict Management and Peace Science*), the International Peace Research Association, and the Peace and Justice Studies Association (which publishes the journal *Peace and Change: A Journal of Peace Research*), just to name a few.

Peace and conflict studies encompasses a variety of disciplines including international relations, political science, philosophy, gender studies, religious studies, economics, geography, history, anthropology, and psychology. It is also multicultural and examines conflict and relationships at all levels, from interpersonal to international in scope. Researchers apply both theoretical and empirical methods to analyze conflicts and propose peaceful resolutions, while also examining issues related to human rights, marginalization, and ecological degradation, with the goal of promoting sustainable world peace.

This topic is of interest to scholars and laypeople alike and as such, there is a variety of literature available for all levels of expertise. From grassroots organization newsletters to peer-reviewed scholarly articles written by leading experts in the field, there is no shortage of resources for peace and conflict studies and the publications highlighted in this section represent the top resources on this spectrum. These resources provide the latest insights and research in the multifaceted area of peace and conflict studies for researchers, activists, scholars, and policy makers.

Basic Periodicals

Hs: *Arms Control Today, Fellowship, Peace Review;* Ac: *Arms Control Today, Bulletin of the Atomic Scientists, Conflict Management and Peace Science, Journal of Conflict Resolution, Journal of Peace Research, Peace & Change, Peace Review.*

Basic Abstracts and Indexes

Alternative Press Index, Peace Research Abstracts.

3887. ***Arms Control Today.*** Formerly (until 1974): *A C A Newsletter.* [ISSN: 0196-125X] 1971. 10x/yr. USD 85 print & online eds. Free to members. Ed(s): Terry Atlas. Arms Control Association, 1313 L St, NW, Ste 130, Washington, DC 20005; aca@armscontrol.org; http://www.armscontrol.org. Illus., index, adv. Vol. ends: Dec. Microform: PQC. *Indexed:* A22, BRI. *Bk. rev.:* 1, 800-1,200 words. *Aud.:* Ac.

The Arms Control Association, which publishes *Arms Control Today*, was founded in 1971 and is a national nonpartisan membership organization dedicated to promoting public understanding and support for arms control policies. It helps provide policy makers, the press, and the public with authoritative information, analysis, and commentary on arms control proposals, treaties, negotiations, agreements, and other national security-related issues. This magazine is dedicated to promoting a better understanding of arms control subjects and offers comprehensive data and intelligence on national security issues. Each issue begins with a "Focus" essay that highlights an important issue related to arms control: for instance, an article in the latest issue talks about "Freezing and Reversing North Korea's Nuclear Advances." Other feature articles include "Papal Condemnation of Nuclear Deterrence and What Is Next," and "Improving U.S. Ballistic Missile Defense Policy." Interviews with important decision makers in the arms control arena are also conducted and well documented in the Q&A section, such as the article "Ambassador Adam Bugajski: 'The NPT is still strong and alive,'' in which Poland's permanent representative to the U.N. office discusses the Nonproliferation Treaty. The "News" section has articles such as "Chemical Attack Kills Dozens in Douma" and "'Denuclearization' Poses Summit Challenge." A bibliography with citations to current literature on topics relevant to the subject being discussed is found in each issue. This is an excellent resource for academic libraries and research centers.

3888. ***Bulletin of the Atomic Scientists (Online).*** [ISSN: 1938-3282] 1945. bi-m. GBP 233. Ed(s): John Mecklin. Routledge, 530 Walnut St, Ste 850, Philadelphia, PA 19106; enquiries@tandfonline.com; http://www.tandfonline.com. Adv. Sample. Refereed. *Bk. rev.:* Number and length vary. *Aud.:* Ga, Ac, Sa.

Founded by a former physicist who worked on the Manhattan Project, the *Bulletin of the Atomic Scientists* aims to increase the public's interest in regard to atomic energy and its risks. Since 1945, the *Bulletin* has stuck to its mission of educating citizens about the dangers of nuclear weapons, and in 1947, the *Bulletin* created the Doomsday Clock, which has become the universal symbol of the various threats to humanity, including weapons of mass destruction, climate change, and other disruptive technologies. Featured articles cover such topics as climate change and rising sea levels, nuclear proliferation, and cybersecurity. The "Nuclear Notebook" column has been published since 1987 and provides an overview of a different country's nuclear capabilities. In the "Global Forum" section of a recent issue, there is an article "Ban the bomb by... banning the bomb?" in which authors from three countries, Joelien Pretorius of South Africa, Polina Sinovets of Ukraine, and Mustafa Kibaroglu of Turkey, discuss what aspects the prospective U.N. treaty that would outright ban nuclear weapons should include and debate whether such a treaty would actually speed up the disarmament process. Issues often have a theme that shapes the content. Recent themes include "The wages of climate inaction: Ever-rising seas," "Resilience and the climate threat," and "How dangerous is hybrid war?" The *Bulletin* provides refereed articles about nuclear weapons, global security issues, and threats to humanity that are written in an accessible manner for the general public, policy makers, scientists, scholars, and journalists.

3889. ***Conflict Management and Peace Science.*** Formerly (until 1980): *Journal of Peace Science.* [ISSN: 0738-8942] 1973. 6x/yr. USD 836 (print & online eds.)). Ed(s): Caroline Hartzell. Sage Publications Ltd., 1 Oliver's Yard, 55 City Rd, London, EC1Y 1SP, United Kingdom; market@sagepub.com; https://www.sagepub.com/. Illus., adv. Sample. Refereed. Vol. ends: No. 2. Reprint: PSC. *Indexed:* A22, E01, EconLit, IBSS, P61. *Bk. rev.:* 1, 1,200 words. *Aud.:* Ac.

Conflict Management and Peace Science is a peer-reviewed journal published in association with the Peace Science Society (International) at Pennsylvania State University. It contains scientific papers on topics such as international conflict, arms races, the effect of international trade on political interactions, foreign policy decision making, international mediation, and game theoretic approaches to conflict and cooperation. A current issue includes articles such as "Anger, legacies of violence, and group conflict: An experiment in post-riot Acre, Israel" and "Economic sanctions and the dynamics of terrorist campaigns." This journal occasionally has special issues with all the articles focused on a particular topic. Previous special issue topics include "Gendered participation, well-being, and representations in political violence" and "Managing territorial conflict." These articles are primarily written for a scholarly audience and would be most useful in academic and research library collections.

3890. ***Fellowship.*** [ISSN: 0014-9810] 1918. q. USD 40 in North America; USD 75 elsewhere. Ed(s): Ethan Vesely-Flad. Fellowship of Reconciliation, 521 N Broadway, PO Box 271, Nyack, NY 10960; for@forusa.org; http://forusa.org/. Illus., adv. Microform: PQC. *Indexed:* A22. *Bk. rev.:* 6, 350 words. *Aud.:* Hs, Ga, Ac.

Fellowship is the oldest continuously published multi-faith, multi-cultural peace journal in the United States. Published quarterly by the Fellowship of Reconciliation since 1935, it follows its predecessor, *The World Tomorrow*, which began in 1918. *Fellowship* publishes analytical insights, spiritual visions, and personal journeys to aid people of all faiths commit themselves to a nonviolent world of justice, peace, and freedom. A recent issue features articles such as "This is an Uprising: How Nonviolent Revolt is Shaping the Twenty-First Century" and "Christianity is Not the Enemy." In addition to articles on both current and historical events, *Fellowship* also provides interviews, poems, and news briefs to round out its thoughtful approach to encourage conflict resolution through peaceful efforts by all individuals. This publication would be useful in both public and academic libraries.

3891. ***Global Change, Peace & Security (Print).*** Former titles (until 2003): *Pacifica Review: Peace, Security & Global Change (Print);* (until 1994): *Interdisciplinary Peace Research (Print).* [ISSN: 1478-1158] 1989. 3x/yr. GBP 653 (print & online eds.)). Ed(s): Aran Martin. Routledge, 4 Park Sq, Milton Park, Abingdon, OX14 4RN, United Kingdom; subscriptions@tandf.co.uk; http://www.tandfonline.com. Index, adv. Sample. Refereed. Reprint: PSC. *Indexed:* A22, CJPI, E01, IBSS, P61, SSA. *Bk. rev.:* Number and length vary. *Aud.:* Ac.

This international, double-blind, peer-reviewed journal addresses complex practical and theoretical questions related to rapid globalization and its consequences. Taking a multidisciplinary and multifaceted approach, this scholarly journal strives to analyze geopolitics, human security, violence and insecurity, peacekeeping and peacebuilding, as well as ethno-nationalism, environmental degradation, and explore issues related to the contradictions of an increasingly integrated world that is at the same time becoming more fragmented. Articles from recent issues include "Obstacles to understanding the emergence and significance of the treaty on the prohibition of nuclear weapons," "When conquest would have paid: domestic mobilization and political constraints in the Thai-Cambodian border conflict 2008-2011," and "The Ankara consensus: the significance of Turkey's engagement in sub-Saharan Africa." This journal is a good resource for academic libraries and research centers.

3892. ***International Journal on World Peace.*** [ISSN: 0742-3640] 1984. q. USD 40 (Individuals, USD 30). Professors World Peace Academy, 3600 Labore Rd, Site 1, Saint Paul, MN 55001; http://www.pwpa.org. Illus., index. Sample. Refereed. Vol. ends: Dec. Microform: PQC. *Indexed:* A01, A22, BRI, C42, P61, SSA. *Bk. rev.:* 6, 150-1,100 words. *Aud.:* Ga, Ac.

International Journal on World Peace is an academic journal that has multidisciplinary articles that focus on all aspects of peace. This journal was founded by scholars gathered in Virginia for a Professors World Peace Academy Conference in 1983 and began its quarterly publication with the September 1984 issue. Its editorial board consists of members from 17 countries such as France, Sri Lanka, Russia, Kenya, New Zealand, the United States, and the Czech Republic. Recent articles include "Moving from reactive to proactive Islam," "Just war theory: North Korea and the United States," and "Religion, NGOs, and the United Nations: visible and invisible actors in power." In addition to refereed articles written by international scholars with diverse backgrounds and specialties, this journal also includes a news section and book reviews. While scholarly in nature, the content would appeal to patrons at both academic and public libraries.

3893. ***International Peacekeeping.*** [ISSN: 1353-3312] 1994. 5x/yr. GBP 700 (print & online eds.)). Ed(s): Philip Cunliffe. Taylor & Francis, 2, 3 & 4 Park Sq, Milton Park, Abingdon, OX14 4RN, United Kingdom; subscriptions@tandf.co.uk; https://www.tandfonline.com. Illus., adv. Sample. Refereed. Vol. ends: Winter. Reprint: PSC. *Indexed:* A01, A22, E01, IBSS, P61. *Bk. rev.:* 4-6. *Aud.:* Ac.

Founded in 1994, *International Peacekeeping* was the first scholarly journal to focus on examining peacekeeping activities following the end of the Cold War. This international peer-reviewed journal examines the theory, practice, outcomes, and consequences of peacekeeping operations throughout the world. With an expansive scope, this journal provides analysis and debates regarding peacebuilding and monitoring activities, humanitarian intervention, preventative deployments, sanctions, international policing, and the complex relationships between peacekeepers, civilians, NGOs, rival factions, and state authorities. Articles from a recent issue include "Social Capital Made Explicit: The Role of Norms, Networks, and Trust in Reintegrating Ex-combatants and Peacebuilding in Liberia," "The Spatial Concentration of Peacekeeping Personnel and Public Health During Intrastate Conflicts," and "Information

Processing Challenges in Peacekeeping Operations: A Case Study on Peacekeeping Information Collection Efforts in Mali." In addition to scholarly articles, this journal also includes book reviews. This journal is a valuable resource for scholars at academic research institutions who study international relations, peace and conflict, and security and strategic studies.

3894. ***International Security.*** [ISSN: 0162-2889] 1976. q. USD 338 (print & online eds.)). Ed(s): Steven E Miller, Owen R Cote. M I T Press, One Rogers St, Cambridge, MA 02142-1209; journals-cs@mit.edu; http://mitpress.mit.edu/. Illus., adv. Refereed. *Indexed:* A01, A22, BAS, BRI, CJPI, E01, IBSS, P61. *Aud.:* Ac.

International Security has been a peer-reviewed journal with a focus on international security and peacekeeping activities since 1978. Edited at Harvard University's Belfer Center for Science and International Affairs, it provides well-researched analysis of current, theoretical, and historical security issues. Articles provide coherent and timely analysis on topics such as the causes and prevention of war; U.S.-China relations; ethnic conflict and internal war; terrorism and insurgency; Asian, European, and regional security; U.S. foreign and defense policy; nuclear proliferation; international relations theory; diplomatic and military history; and cybersecurity. Articles from the most recent issue include "Do U.S. Drone Strikes Cause Blowback? Evidence from Pakistan and Beyond" and "U.S.-China Rivalry in Southeast Asia: Power Shift or Competitive Coexistence?" In addition to research articles, a "Correspondence" section allows international relations scholars to share their thoughts and expert opinions with recent "Correspondence" articles on "Arms, Alliances, and Patron-Client Relationships" and "Debating Drone Proliferation." This journal is vital for academic libraries and research centers that focus on international studies and peace.

3895. ***The Journal of Conflict Resolution.*** Formerly (until 1957): *Conflict Resolution.* [ISSN: 0022-0027] 195?. 10x/yr. USD 2242 (print & online eds.)). Ed(s): Paul Huth. Sage Publications, Inc., 2455 Teller Rd, Thousand Oaks, CA 91320; info@sagepub.com; http://www.sagepub.com. Illus., index, adv. Refereed. Vol. ends: Dec. Microform: PQC. Reprint: PSC. *Indexed:* A01, A22, B01, BAS, BRI, E01, ERIC, EconLit, IBSS, P61, SSA. *Aud.:* Ac.

This scholarly, interdisciplinary journal focuses primarily on international conflict, while also exploring intergroup conflict and conflict between nations, to help advance the comprehension of issues related to war and peace. Articles frequently come from such disciplines as political science, law, economics, sociology, international relations, history, psychology, anthropology, and methodology to analyze the causes, prevention, and solution of international, domestic, and interpersonal conflicts. This journal is the official publication for the Peace Science Society (International) and has an editorial board made up of scholars from academic institutions around the world. Each journal consists of 6 to 10 articles that focus on solid measurable facts and lucid arguments to provide scholars and researchers with the latest ideas, approaches, and processes in conflict resolution. In a recent issue, articles included "Why Do People Join Backlash Protests? Lessons from Turkey," "The Determinants of Religious Radicalization: Evidence from Kenya," "Distributive Outcomes in Contested Maritime Areas: The Role of Inside Options in Settling Competing Claims," and "Identities in between Political Conflict and Ethnonational Identities in Multicultural States." In addition to research articles, there is a "Data Set Feature" that provides a review for a new, relevant dataset that would be useful to researchers interested in conflict studies. These reviews highlight the dataset's major features, describe patterns and new trends that can be uncovered, as well as explain the utility for the data set. A recent "Data Set Feature" was "Disputes over the Divine: Introducing the Religion and Armed Conflict (RELAC) Data, 1975 to 2015." This journal is an exceptional addition to academic libraries that have a collection focus on peace studies.

3896. ***Journal of Peace Education.*** [ISSN: 1740-0201] 2004. 3x/yr. GBP 411 (print & online eds.)). Ed(s): Jeannie Lum. Routledge, 4 Park Sq, Milton Park, Abingdon, OX14 4RN, United Kingdom; subscriptions@tandf.co.uk; http://www.tandfonline.com. Adv. Sample. Refereed. Reprint: PSC. *Indexed:* A01, A22, E01, ERIC. *Bk. rev.:* Number and length vary. *Aud.:* Ga, Ac.

The *Journal of Peace Education* is a peer-reviewed, multidisciplinary and intercultural journal sponsored by the Peace Education Commission of the International Peace Research Association. This journal aims to promote discourse related to all aspects of peace education, including theory, curriculum, and pedagogy. Topics published in this journal include education regarding disarmament, environmental care, cultural diversity, conflict resolution, ecological sustainability, and educational social movements. Articles in a recent issue include "Con-/divergences between postcolonial and critical peace education: towards pedagogies of decolonization in peace education"; "Shining light into dark shadows of violence and learned helplessness: peace education in South Korean schools"; "Peace education, militarism and neo-liberalism: conceptual reflections with empirical findings from the UK"; and "Cross-cultural conflicts within sports teams." In addition to original articles, this publication also includes book reviews. This journal is a useful resource in peace and conflict studies academic and research libraries.

3897. ***Journal of Peace Research.*** [ISSN: 0022-3433] 1964. q. USD 2255 (print & online eds.)). Ed(s): Gudrun Ostby. Sage Publications Ltd., 1 Oliver's Yard, 55 City Rd, London, EC1Y 1SP, United Kingdom; market@sagepub.com; https://www.sagepub.com/. Illus., index, adv. Sample. Refereed. Vol. ends: Nov. Microform: PQC. Reprint: PSC. *Indexed:* A01, A22, AmHI, BRI, CBRI, E01, EconLit, IBSS, P61, SSA. *Bk. rev.:* 15-20, 150-450 words. *Aud.:* Ga, Ac.

This quarterly, interdisciplinary and international journal is peer-reviewed and published by the International Peace Research Association. This publication is a member of the Committee on Publication Ethics (COPE) and edited at the Peace Research Institute OSLO (PRIO) by an international editorial committee. First published in 1964 and with authors from more than 50 countries, the *Journal of Peace Research* primarily focuses on the causes of violence and conflict resolution from a global perspective. Recent articles include "Which groups fight? Customary institutions and communal conflicts in Africa"; "The build-up of coercive capacities: Arms imports and the outbreak of violent intrastate conflicts"; "Backdoor peacekeeping: Does participation in UN peacekeeping reduce coups at home?"; and "Refugees, xenophobia, and domestic conflict: Evidence from a survey experiment in Turkey." In addition to the original articles, this journal also includes a "Special Data Feature" section in which scholars review new data sets, as well as data sets that have been updated. Two reviews from the most recent issue consulted are "Organized violence, 1989-2017" and "Days of rage: Introducing the NAVCO 3.0 dataset." The timely articles in this journal provide peace researchers with the latest developments in the field of peace studies and is a useful resource for academic libraries and research centers.

3898. ***Peace & Change: a journal of peace research.*** [ISSN: 0149-0508] 1972. q. GBP 476. Ed(s): Heather Fryer. Wiley-Blackwell Publishing, Inc., 350 Main St, Malden, MA 02148; http://onlinelibrary.wiley.com. Illus., index, adv. Sample. Refereed. Vol. ends: Oct. Reprint: PSC. *Indexed:* A01, A22, BRI, E01, P61. *Bk. rev.:* 3-4, essay length. *Aud.:* Ga, Ac.

This peer-reviewed, international and interdisciplinary-focused journal is published on behalf of the Peace History Society and the Peace and Justice Association. Articles in this journal aim to connect peace research, education, and activism and focus on a wide variety of peace-related topics such as peace movements and activism, conflict resolution, nonviolence, internationalism, race and gender issues, cross-cultural studies, economic development, the legacy of imperialism, and the post-Cold War upheaval. Recent articles include "The End of the Armed Conflict in Colombia: A Multiple Causal Factor Explanation," "New Rebels in Postconflict Settings: The Principal-Agent Dilemma of Peacebuilding," and "Effective Mediative Diplomacy and Its Seven Virtues: The Case of the European Union." Following the original research articles are five to six book reviews and a notes section that includes biographical information for the authors. This journal would be useful in an academic library or peace research center.

3899. ***Peace and Conflict: journal of peace psychology.*** [ISSN: 1078-1919] 1995. q. USD 983 (Individuals, USD 151; Members, USD 82). Ed(s): Fathali M Moghaddam. American Psychological Association, 750 First St, NE, Washington, DC 20002; journals@apa.org; http://www.apa.org. Illus., index, adv. Sample. Refereed. Circ: 430. Vol. ends: Dec. Reprint: PSC. *Indexed:* A01, A22, E01, IBSS, P61, SSA. *Bk. rev.:* 4, 500-600 words. *Aud.:* Ac.

Peace and Conflict: Journal of Peace Psychology publishes empirical, theoretical, clinical, and historical scholarly articles on topics related to peace, conflict, and their interaction at all levels, such as in a community, nationally, and internationally. This journal is published by the American Psychological Association's Division of Peace Psychology and encourages the submission of articles from psychologists and scholars in related disciplines that would help support the ideals of the Division of Peace Psychology while advancing psychological knowledge related to peacebuilding. Articles from the most recent issue include "Trauma as a collective disease and root cause of protracted social conflict," "Nationhood as a social representation: Making sense of the Kurdish opening in Turkey," "Still not one people: Implicit ethnic perception of Tutsis in Rwanda," and "The Israeli-Palestinian and the Russian-Ukrainian conflict: Perception and conflict-resolution strategies." Thematic special issues on timely topics are occasionally published, with the last special issue being "Social Movements and Political and Social Transformation." In addition to the research-oriented original articles, book reviews are also included in this publication. This journal would be a useful addition to peace research centers and academic libraries.

3900. ***Peace Magazine.*** Formerly (until 1985): *Peace Calendar.* [ISSN: 0826-9521] 1983. q. CAD 18.90 domestic; CAD 23 United States; CAD 30 elsewhere. Ed(s): Metta Spencer. Canadian Disarmament Information Service (CANDIS), PO Box 248, Toronto, ON M5S 2S7, Canada; http://candis-peace.org/. Illus., index, adv. Sample. Vol. ends: Nov/Dec. Microform: PQC. *Indexed:* A01, BRI, C37. *Bk. rev.:* 3-4, 250-600 words. *Aud.:* Hs, Ga, Ac.

Peace Magazine is published by the Canadian Disarmament Information Service, a group committed to educating the public on all aspects of peace. Published quarterly, this magazine consists of articles, news stories, interviews, reviews of films and books, and letters. Their online site also includes a weekly video stream from the magazine's editor called "Talk about saving the world." The magazine's focus includes peace, disarmament, human rights abuses, weapons of mass destruction, conflict resolution, and political or military affairs. Authors include scholars, journalists, and activists. Articles are written in an approachable manner and can be easily understood by laypersons. Recent articles include "Cyberpeacekeeping: The Challenge," "Nuclear Disarmament: Universalizing the Treaty," and "Your Dharma is to Make the World Better: A Conversation with Larry Brilliant." This magazine is available both online and in print, but full content is not always available online until after the publication year has ended. This is a good magazine for high school libraries, as well as public and academic libraries.

3901. ***Peace Research: the Canadian journal of peace and conflict studies.*** [ISSN: 0008-4697] 1969. s-a. CAD 105 (Individuals, CAD 65). Ed(s): Anna Snyder, Neil Funk-Unrau. Menno Simons College, 210-102 Portage Ave, Winnipeg, MB R3C 0G2, Canada; http://www.brandonu.ca/. Illus., index. Sample. Refereed. Vol. ends: Nov. Microform: PQC. *Indexed:* A01, A22, BRI, C37, MLA-IB. *Bk. rev.:* 1-2, 500-1,000 words. *Aud.:* Ga, Ac.

Continuously published since 1969, *Peace Research: the Canadian Journal of Peace and Conflict Studies* is Canada's oldest peace-related scholarly journal. Published twice a year, this journal focuses on issues of conflict, violence, disarmament, poverty, just peace, and human well-being, with an emphasis toward encouraging peaceful methods for conflict resolution. Articles from the most recent issue include "The Legacy of Colonialism Among Indigenous Peoples: Destructive Outcomes, Healing and Reconciliatory Potentials," "'Deviously Ingenious': British Colonialism in Jamaica," and "The Three Rs: Resistance, Resilience, and Reconciliation in Canada and Ireland." This publication is a valuable addition to peace research centers and academic libraries.

3902. ***Peace Review: a journal of social justice.*** [ISSN: 1040-2659] 1989. q. GBP 727 (print & online eds.)). Ed(s): Robert Elias. Routledge, 4 Park Sq, Milton Park, Abingdon, OX14 4RN, United Kingdom; subscriptions@tandf.co.uk; http://www.tandfonline.com. Illus., adv. Sample. Refereed. Reprint: PSC. *Indexed:* A01, A22, E01, MLA-IB, P61, SSA. *Bk. rev.:* 2-3, 1,000-1,500 words. *Aud.:* Ga, Ac.

This quarterly journal is a multidisciplinary, international publication that focuses on current issues that affect the pursuit of a peaceful world. *Peace Review* explores peace in a broad sense to include aspects related to human rights, development, ecology, culture, and conflict resolution. Issues tend to revolve around a central theme, such as teaching peace education, though articles outside of this topic may also be published in the same issue. Articles in the most recent issue focused on capitalism, with an emphasis on disaster capitalism, with articles including "Violence and Disaster Capitalism in Post-Haiyan Philippines," "Living with Disaster Capitalism after Fukushima," and "Making Money from Misery." This publication also includes book reviews and a recommended films section. This journal is a good addition to collections in peace research centers and academic libraries.

3903. ***Security Dialogue.*** Formerly (until 1992): *Bulletin of Peace Proposals.* [ISSN: 0967-0106] 1970. bi-m. USD 1781 (print & online eds.)). Ed(s): Mark B Salter. Sage Publications Ltd., 1 Oliver's Yard, 55 City Rd, London, EC1Y 1SP, United Kingdom; market@sagepub.com; https://www.sagepub.com/. Illus., index, adv. Sample. Refereed. Microform: PQC. Reprint: PSC. *Indexed:* A01, A22, BAS, E01, IBSS, P61. *Aud.:* Ac.

This bi-monthly, peer-reviewed international journal focuses on global peace and security. Articles that present provocative new theories and insights based on empirical findings on topics like new and traditional security issues, such as globalization, nationalism, ethnic conflict and civil war, information technology, biological and chemical warfare, resource conflicts, pandemics, global terrorism, non-state actors and environmental and human security are encouraged in this publication. Multidisciplinary in its scope, this journal publishes articles by scholars from disciplines such as international studies, gender studies, political sociology, political economy, geography, cultural studies, political theory, anthropology, development studies, postcolonial studies, and peace and conflict studies. Recent articles include "Resistance beyond sovereign politics: Petty sovereigns' disappearance into the world of fiction in post-Fukushima Japan," "Crowd surveillance: The (in)securitization of the urban body," and "From protection to coordinated preparedness: A genealogy of critical infrastructure in Canada." This is a leading journal for scholars interested in security studies and would be a valuable addition to academic libraries and research centers.

■ PETS

Associations

See also Animal Welfare; Birds; Horses; Sports; and Veterinary Science sections.

Camille McCutcheon, Assistant Dean of the Library, Coordinator of Collection Management, University of South Carolina Upstate, 800 University Way, Spartanburg, SC 29303; CMcCutcheon@uscupstate.edu

Introduction

Articles concerning health, wellness, nutrition, care, welfare, behavior, communication, grooming, training, advocacy and rescue, and the human-animal bond, as well as heartwarming stories of actual animals, are commonly featured in many of the magazines in this section.

Most pet magazines, such as *The Bark, Catster Magazine, Reptiles,* and *Tropical Fish Hobbyist,* focus exclusively on either dogs, cats, reptiles, or fish. *Pets Magazine,* however, contains articles on both cats and dogs.

During the past several years, there has been an increase in the number of titles that publish articles on natural care, nutrition, and holistic medicine. The focus of *Animal Wellness Magazine* and *The Whole Dog Journal* is on natural health care. Other publications provide medical information for pet owners. The Cummings School of Veterinary Medicine at Tufts University publishes *Catnip* and *Your Dog,* and the Cornell University College of Veterinary Medicine publishes *CatWatch* and *DogWatch,* which are newsletters that provide medical, health, and behavioral information on cats and dogs.

Titles that are part lifestyle magazine and part pet publication continue to be popular. Many of these magazines, such as *The Bark, Fido Friendly, Modern Cat,* and *Modern Dog,* contain articles on fashion, travel, and social and activism issues, as well as profiles of and interviews with celebrity pet owners.

Many of the publications noted in this section actively engage their readers using social media and Facebook. Most have web sites where visitors can locate subscription information, scan the tables of contents, and view photographs of the covers of the current issues. Other sites are more extensive and allow visitors to read selected articles from current and previous issues, participate in online forums, and pose questions to veterinarians and other pet experts.

Basic Periodicals

Hs: *Catster Magazine, Dogster Magazine;* Ga: *AFA Watchbird, AKC Family Dog, The Bark, Best Friends, Catster Magazine, Dogster Magazine, Modern Cat, Modern Dog, Pets Magazine, Reptiles, Tropical Fish Hobbyist;* Ac: *Amazonas, Anthrozoos, Coral.*

Basic Abstracts and Indexes

Readers' Guide to Periodical Literature.

3904. ***A F A Watchbird: journal of the American Federation of Aviculture.*** [ISSN: 0199-543X] 1974. 3x/yr. Free to members. American Federation of Aviculture, PO Box 91717, Austin, TX 78709; afaoffice@earthlink.net; http://www.afabirds.org/. Illus., adv. Vol. ends: Nov/Dec. *Aud.:* Hs, Ga, Ac.

AFA Watchbird is the official publication of the American Federation of Aviculture. The AFA is dedicated to "represent[ing] all aspects of aviculture and to educat[ing] the public about keeping and breeding birds in captivity." The magazine's color photography is beautiful. The articles are detailed and informative, and some of them contain a list of references. Contributors include aviculturists, veterinarians, avian scientists, and avian biologists. Featured are profiles of bird species, as well as articles on conservation, bird breeding, the health and welfare of birds, legislative issues that affect aviculture and aviculturists, and the activities of the AFA. The web site for the American Federation of Aviculture contains general information about *AFA Watchbird,* including the table of contents and a photograph of the cover of the current issue. Recommended for academic and large public library collections. URL: www.afabirds.org

3905. ***A K C Family Dog.*** [ISSN: 1559-5072] 2003. bi-m. USD 24.95 domestic. American Kennel Club, Inc., 260 Madison Ave, New York, NY 10016; ejm@akc.org; http://www.akc.org. Illus., adv. Sample. *Aud.:* Ga.

AKC Family Dog is an informative lifestyle magazine for dog enthusiasts. Each issue contains feature articles, columns, and departments on topics such as health, behavior, training, and grooming. Contributors include veterinarians, professional dog trainers, and authors of books on dogs. The American Kennel Club web site is extensive and includes general information about the magazine, along with the table of contents and a photograph of the cover of the current issue. Information about breeds, breeders, AKC events, and an online store are all available on the web site. Recommended for public library collections. URL: www.akc.org

3906. ***Amazonas: freshwater aquariums & tropical discovery.*** [ISSN: 2166-3106] 2012. bi-m. USD 44 domestic; USD 53.80 Canada. Ed(s): Hans-Georg Evers, James M Lawrence. Reef to Rainforest Media, Llc., 140 Webster Rd, PO Box 490, Shelburne, VT 05482; http://www.reef2rainforest.com/. Adv. *Aud.:* Ga, Ac, Sa.

Lavishly illustrated, *Amazonas* caters to serious freshwater aquarists and tropical fish enthusiasts. The color photography is beautiful, the layout is very attractive, and the articles are well written. Some of the articles even contain a list of references. There are feature articles on fishes, invertebrates, aquatic plants, husbandry and breeding, and field trips to tropical locales. The web site for *Amazonas* contains general information about the magazine. Recommended for academic and large public library collections. URL: www.amazonasmagazine.com

3907. ***Animal Wellness: for a long, healthy life!*** Formerly (until 2001): *Animal.* [ISSN: 1710-1190] 1999. bi-m. USD 39 domestic; USD 33 Canada. Ed(s): Dana Cox. Redstone Media Group Inc., 160 Charlotte St #202, Peterborough, ON K9J 2T8, Canada; http://redstonemediagroup.com/. Adv. *Bk. rev.:* 2, 150-200 words. *Aud.:* Hs, Ga.

The purpose of *Animal Wellness* is to provide owners of companion animals with the information needed to improve the quality of life for their animals. It is an attractive publication that has many color photographs and well-written and interesting articles. It offers information on holistic and natural alternatives to Western medicine. There are also feature articles on nutrition, health, behavior, and social and activism issues. Contributors include veterinarians who practice holistic veterinary medicine, psychologists, authors of books on holistic and natural medicine for animals, animal behaviorists, professional groomers, and veterinary naturopaths. Regularly featured columns and departments include a wellness resource guide, pet products endorsed by *Animal Wellness,* book reviews that average 150 words in length, and a classified ads section. The web site for the magazine provides additional content. Recommended for large public library collections. URL: www.animalwellnessmagazine.com

3908. ***Anthrozoos: a multidisciplinary journal of the interactions of people and animals.*** Formerly (until 1987): *Delta Society. Journal.* [ISSN: 0892-7936] 1987. q. GBP 459 (print & online eds.)). Ed(s): Anthony L Podberscek. Taylor & Francis Inc., 530 Walnut St, Ste 850, Philadelphia, PA 19106; subscriptions@tandf.co.uk; http://www.taylorandfrancis.com. Illus., adv. Sample. Refereed. Vol. ends: No. 4. Reprint: PSC. *Indexed:* A01, A22, Agr, BRI, C45. *Bk. rev.:* 1-4, 1,000 to 2,000 words. *Aud.:* Ac.

Anthrozoos is the official journal of the International Society for Anthrozoology. It is a multidisciplinary, refereed journal that would appeal to individuals interested in human-animal interactions. Some of the fields covered include psychology, anthropology, ethology, medicine, zoology, and veterinary medicine. One of the primary components of this publication is the "Reviews and Research Reports" section, which includes research articles on human-animal interactions. There are conference announcements and in-depth book reviews. The web site contains general information about *Anthrozoos,* including the tables of contents of issues dating back to 1987, when the journal was launched. Recommended for academic and large public library collections. URL: www.tandfonline.com/toc/rfan20/current

3909. ***The Bark.*** [ISSN: 1535-1734] 1997. q. USD 28 domestic. Ed(s): Claudia Kawczynska. The Bark, Inc., 2810 8th St, Berkeley, CA 94710; customerservice@thebark.com. Illus., adv. Sample. *Bk. rev.:* 1-4, 500 words. *Aud.:* Ga.

The Bark is an upscale and intelligent publication about dog culture. The magazine's motto is "Dog is my co-pilot." The layout is very attractive, and the color photography is impressive. Focusing on the human-canine bond, *The Bark* offers a variety of interesting and well-written articles on behavior, health, wellness, art, literature, travel, recreation, and social and activism issues. There are also interviews, stories, poetry, and book reviews. *The Bark*'s web site provides additional content. Recommended for large public library collections. URL: www.thebark.com

3910. ***Best Friends (Kanab): together, we can save them all.*** Formerly (until 1992): *Best Friends Magazine.* [ISSN: 1949-0259] 19??. bi-m. Ed(s): Mary-Jo Dionne, Mary Girouard. Best Friends Animal Society, 5001 Angel Canyon Rd, Kanab, UT 84741; info@bestfriends.org; http://www.bestfriends.org. Illus., adv. *Bk. rev.:* 3-5, 100-200 words. *Aud.:* Hs, Ga.

Best Friends is the official publication of the Best Friends Animal Society, which runs the largest sanctuary in the United States for abused and abandoned animals. It is a perfect magazine for people who love animals. Some of the magazine's highlights include news and articles about animals, information about pet health and behavior, and profiles of animals that reside at the Best Friends Animal Sanctuary. There are also book reviews that average 100-200 words in length. The web site for *Best Friends* is attractive, easy to navigate, and provides additional content. Recommended for public library collections. URL: www.bestfriends.org

3911. *Cat Talk (Alliance): a publication of the Cat Fanciers' Association.* 2011. bi-m. USD 49 domestic; USD 59 Canada. Ed(s): Teresa Keiger. The Cat Fanciers' Association, Inc., 260 E Main St, Alliance, OH 44601; http://www.cfa.org. *Bk. rev.:* Number and length vary. *Aud.:* Hs, Ga, Sa.

Cat Talk is a publication of the Cat Fanciers' Association. The CFA is dedicated to "promoting the welfare of all cats through progressive actions[,] which range from legislative advocacy to the support of feline research and providing breeder assistance." The magazine's color photography is beautiful, the layout is very attractive, and the articles are well written. There are feature articles on health, cats in popular culture, and social, activist, and legislative issues. Cat art, interviews with authors of books on cats, and information concerning news, activities, and the history of the CFA are also included. The web site for *Cat Talk* contains general information about the magazine. Recommended for large public library collections. URL: www.cfa.org

3912. *Cat World.* Formerly (until 1982): *Cat World Weekly.* [ISSN: 0952-2875] 1981. m. GBP 59.99; GBP 4.99 newsstand/cover. Ashdown Broadcasting, PO Box 2258, Pulborough, RH20 9BA, United Kingdom; support@ashdown.co.uk; http://www.ashdown.co.uk. Illus., adv. Sample. *Bk. rev.:* Number and length vary. *Aud.:* Hs, Ga.

Published in the United Kingdom, *Cat World* is a terrific resource for cat owners and enthusiasts. The magazine's layout is very attractive and contains many color photographs. The articles are informative and practical, with topics ranging from personality, health, behavior, and social and activist issues to the human-feline bond. Other regular features include cats in the news, a breed profile, a question-and-answer section where readers can pose questions to experts, a breeder directory, and a classified ads section. The web site is attractive, easy to navigate, and provides general content about *Cat World.* Recommended for large public library collections. URL: www.catworld.co.uk

3913. *Catnip: the newsletter for caring cat owners.* [ISSN: 1069-6687] 1993. m. USD 50. Ed(s): John Berg. Belvoir Media Group, LLC, 535 Connecticut Ave, Norwalk, CT 06856; http://www.belvoir.com. Illus., adv. Sample. *Aud.:* Ga.

Catnip is a monthly newsletter published by the Cummings School of Veterinary Medicine at Tufts University. Sixteen pages in length, *Catnip* provides medical and behavioral information and does not accept commercial advertising. This newsletter contains numerous black-and-white photographs. The articles are informative and would be of interest to cat owners. *Catnip* has articles on cat medicine, health, behavior, and feline diseases, and a question-and-answer section. *Catnip*'s web site provides general information about the newsletter. Recommended for large public library collections. URL: www.tuftscatnip.com

3914. *Catster Magazine.* Formerly (until 2015): *Cat Fancy;* Which superseded (in 1986): *International Cat Fancy.* [ISSN: 2376-8258] 1965. bi-m. USD 31.95 domestic. Ed(s): Melissa L Kauffman. Belvoir Media Group, LLC, 535 Connecticut Ave, Norwalk, CT 06856; customer_service@belvoir.com; http://www.belvoir.com. Illus., index, adv. Vol. ends: Dec. *Indexed:* A22. *Bk. rev.:* Number varies, 20-50 words. *Aud.:* Hs, Ga.

Catster Magazine is an excellent publication for cat lovers. The magazine's motto is "Live with Cattitude." The layout is attractive, and the color photography is impressive. Some of its contributors include veterinarians, master certified pet first-aid instructors, and certified animal behavior consultants. The articles are practical and informative, with topics ranging from stories of actual cats to profiles of breeds to features on cat care, health, behavior, grooming, training, advocacy, rescue, and living with cats. Also included in *Catster Magazine* are new products, a breeder directory, a classified ads section, and cat photographs that have been submitted by readers. Some issues have brief book reviews. The web site for *Catster Magazine* provides additional content. Recommended for public library collections. URL: www.catster.com

3915. *CatWatch.* Supersedes in part (in 1997): *Animal Health Newsletter.* [ISSN: 1095-9092] 1997. m. USD 47 combined subscription in US & Canada (print & online eds.); USD 62 combined subscription elsewhere (print & online eds.)). Ed(s): Bruce G Kornreich. Belvoir Media Group, LLC, 535 Connecticut Ave, Norwalk, CT 06856; http://www.belvoir.com. Sample. *Aud.:* Ga.

CatWatch is a monthly newsletter published by the Cornell University College of Veterinary Medicine Feline Health Center. The articles are informative and would be of interest to cat owners. Eight pages in length, this newsletter contains numerous black-and-white photographs and does not accept commercial advertising. *CatWatch* has articles on medicine, behavior, health, nutrition, first aid, and parasites, as well as information on cats in the news and a question-and-answer section. *CatWatch*'s web site provides general information about the newsletter. Recommended for large public library collections. URL: www.catwatchnewsletter.com

3916. *Coral: the reef & marine aquarium magazine.* [ISSN: 1556-5769] 2004. bi-m. USD 42 combined subscription (print & online eds.)). Ed(s): James M Lawrence. Reef and Rainforest Media, 140 Webster Road, Shelburne, VT 05482; customerservice@coralmagazineservice.com; http://www.reef2rainforest.com. *Aud.:* Ga, Ac, Sa.

Coral caters to serious marine aquarists. The color photography is beautiful, the layout is very attractive, and the articles are well written. Some of the articles even contain a list of references. There are fish and invertebrate species profiles, tips for beginning marine aquarists, news, interviews, technology updates, and information on aquarium systems. Departments such as "Species Spotlight," "Reefkeeping 101," and "Reef Stewardship" are included in each issue. *Coral*'s web site contains general information about the magazine. Recommended for academic and large public library collections. URL: www.coralmagazineus.com

3917. *Dogster Magazine.* Former titles (until 2015): *Dog Fancy;* (until 1986): *International Dog Fancy;* (until 198?): *Dog Fancy.* [ISSN: 2376-8266] 1970. bi-m. USD 31.95. Ed(s): Melissa L Kauffman. Belvoir Media Group, LLC, 535 Connecticut Ave, Norwalk, CT 06856; customer_service@belvoir.com; http://www.belvoir.com. Illus., index, adv. *Indexed:* BRI. *Bk. rev.:* Number varies, 20-50 words. *Aud.:* Hs, Ga.

Dogster Magazine is a terrific publication for dog lovers. The magazine's motto is "For the Love of Dog." The layout is attractive, and the color photography is impressive. Some of its contributors include veterinarians, master certified pet first-aid instructors, dog trainers, and pet nutrition consultants. The articles are practical and informative, with topics ranging from stories of actual dogs to profiles of breeds, to features on dog care, health, behavior, grooming, training, advocacy, rescue, and living with dogs. Also included in *Dogster Magazine* are new products, a breeder directory, a classified ads section, and dog photographs that have been submitted by readers. Some issues contain brief book reviews. The web site for *Dogster Magazine* provides additional content. Recommended for public library collections. URL: www.dogster.com

3918. *DogWatch.* [ISSN: 1098-2639] 1997. m. USD 50 in US & Canada. Ed(s): William H Miller. Belvoir Media Group, LLC, PO Box 5656, Norwalk, CT 06856; http://www.belvoir.com. Sample. *Aud.:* Ga.

DogWatch is a monthly newsletter published by the Cornell University College of Veterinary Medicine. The articles are informative and would be of interest to dog owners. Eight pages in length, this newsletter contains numerous black-and-white photographs and does not accept commercial advertising. *DogWatch* has articles on medicine, behavior, and health, as well as information on dogs in the news and a question-and-answer section. The *DogWatch* web site provides general information about the newsletter. Recommended for large public library collections. URL: www.dogwatchnewsletter.com

3919. *Fido Friendly.* [ISSN: 1945-5828] 2001. 3x/yr. USD 25. Fido Friendly, PO Box 160, Marsing, ID 83639. Illus., adv. Sample. *Aud.:* Hs, Ga.

Fido Friendly is an upscale lifestyle magazine for dogs and their owners, and its motto is "Leave no dog behind." This publication has articles on travel, health, wellness, nutrition, and social and activism issues, and it is also a guide to dog-friendly accommodations in the United States. It provides tips for traveling with dogs and has departments such as "Crate & Garden," "Bowser on a Budget," and "The Tropical Dog." The web site for *Fido Friendly* provides additional content. Recommended for large public library collections. URL: www.fidofriendly.com

3920. ***Modern Cat: the lifestyle magazine for modern cats and their companions.*** [ISSN: 1929-3933] 2012. s-a. USD 18 for 2 yrs. in US & Canada; USD 45 for 2 yrs. elsewhere. Ed(s): Connie Wilson. Modern Cat, Inc., 343 Railway St, Ste 202, Vancouver, BC V6A 1A4, Canada; info@moderncat.com; http://moderncat.com/. *Bk. rev.:* Number and length vary. *Aud.:* Hs, Ga.

Published in Canada, *Modern Cat* is a glossy magazine that is an excellent resource for cats and their companions. The articles are extremely informative and well written. The magazine's layout is very attractive and contains many color photographs. *Modern Cat* has breed profiles, information on cats in the news, new products and toys, cat art, interviews with celebrity cat owners, and cat photographs submitted by readers. There are profiles of actual cats and feature articles on feline communication, behavior, health, nutrition, and training. The web site for *Modern Cat* provides additional content. Recommended for public library collections. URL: http://moderncat.com

3921. ***Modern Dog: the lifestyle magazine for modern dogs and their companions.*** [ISSN: 1703-812X] 2002. q. USD 27. Ed(s): Connie Wilson. Modern Dog, 343 Railway St, Ste 202, Vancouver, BC V6A 1A4, Canada; info@moderndogmagazine.com; http://www.moderndogmagazine.com. Illus., adv. Sample. *Bk. rev.:* Number and length vary. *Aud.:* Ga.

Published in Canada, *Modern Dog* is a glossy publication that is an excellent resource for dogs and their companions. The articles are extremely informative and well written. The magazine's layout is very attractive and contains many color photographs. *Modern Dog* includes a breed profile; a guide to new products; dog art; interviews with celebrity dog owners; grooming and training tips; and articles on health, behavior, and nutrition. The web site for the magazine provides additional content. Recommended for public library collections. URL: www.moderndogmagazine.com

3922. ***Pets Magazine.*** Former titles (until 1985): *Pets;* (until 1983): *Pets Magazine.* [ISSN: 0831-2621] 1983. bi-m. USD 42. Ed(s): Brad Hussey. Dorman Sales & Marketing Ltd., 100 Belliveau Beach Rd, Pointe-du-Chene, Pointe-du-Chene, NB E4P 3W6, Canada; http://www.dormansales.com. Illus., adv. Sample. *Indexed:* C37. *Aud.:* Hs, Ga.

The Canadian publication *Pets Magazine* explores the bond between humans and animals. The articles are informative and well written, and the format is very attractive. Many of the contributors are veterinarians. This excellent resource has the latest pet news; information on pet health; and feature articles on caring for puppies, dogs, kittens, cats, and older pets. Published bimonthly, *Pets Magazine* has a different theme for each issue. These themes are puppies and kittens, rescuing pets, preventive health care, cat care, dog care, and senior pets. The web site for *Pets Magazine* provides additional content. Recommended for public library collections. URL: www.petsmagazine.ca

3923. ***Practical Fishkeeping.*** Former titles (until 1978): *P F M: Practical Fishkeeping Monthly;* (until 1976): *Petfish Monthly.* [ISSN: 0262-5806] 19??. 13x/yr. GBP 52 combined subscription domestic (print & online eds.); USD 73.49 combined subscription United States (print & online eds.)). Ed(s): Ben Hawkins. H. Bauer Publishing Ltd., Media House, Lynchwood, Peterborough, PE2 6EA, United Kingdom; http://www.bauermedia.co.uk. Illus., adv. *Aud.:* Ga, Sa.

Published in the United Kingdom, *Practical Fishkeeping* is a terrific resource for fishkeeping enthusiasts. The articles are well written and extremely informative. The magazine's layout is very attractive and contains lots of color photographs. It has fish news, new product evaluations, and feature articles on topics ranging from marine fish, tropical fish, and marine invertebrates, to fish husbandry, aquatic plants, and aquascaping, to water quality, lighting, and aquarium set-ups. One of the features of *Practical Fishkeeping* is a question-and-answer section where readers can pose questions to a panel of experts. The magazine's web site is attractive, easy to navigate, and provides additional content. Recommended for large public library collections. URL: www.practicalfishkeeping.co.uk

3924. ***Reptiles: the world's leading reptile magazine.*** Incorporates (1988-2000): *The Vivarium.* [ISSN: 1068-1965] 1993. bi-m. USD 14.99. Pet360 Media, Inc., 60 E 42nd St, New York, NY 10165; http://www.pet360.com. Illus., index, adv. Vol. ends: Dec. *Aud.:* Ga.

Loaded with stunning photographs, *Reptiles* contains feature articles on both reptiles and amphibians. These in-depth articles are well written and informative, and the magazine's layout is very attractive. Some of the departments featured in each issue of *Reptiles* include "Herpers' Most Wanted," which profiles a reptile or amphibian species; "Herp Queries," a question-and-answer section; and "Herp Happenings," a listing of reptile events. The web site for *Reptiles* is extensive and filled with useful information about reptiles and amphibians, including the latest reptile news, subscription information, photo and video galleries, and species profiles. Recommended for public library collections. URL: www.reptilesmagazine.com

3925. ***Tropical Fish Hobbyist.*** [ISSN: 0041-3259] 1953. bi-m. USD 28 domestic; USD 48 Canada. Ed(s): Glen S Axelrod. T.F.H. Publications, Inc., 85 W Sylvania Ave, Neptune, NJ 07753; http://www.tfh.com. Illus., index, adv. Sample. Vol. ends: Aug. *Indexed:* BRI. *Aud.:* Ga, Sa.

Tropical Fish Hobbyist is an excellent resource for the tropical fish enthusiast. The color photography is beautiful, the layout is attractive, and the in-depth articles are well written. Some of the articles even have a list of references. Contributors include biologists; veterinarians; aquarium hobbyists; breeders; freshwater, marine, and reef aquarists; and authors of books on marine aquariums. There are several question-and-answer sections where readers can submit questions and problems related to freshwater and saltwater aquariums. Columns such as "Bottom of the Tank," "Cichlid World," and "Reef and Coral Corner" are included in each issue. *TFH*'s web site is informative, easy to navigate, and provides additional content. Recommended for public library collections. URL: www.tfhmagazine.com

3926. ***The Whole Dog Journal: your complete guide to natural dog care and training.*** [ISSN: 1097-5322] 1998. m. USD 20 combined subscription domestic (print & online eds.); CAD 26 combined subscription Canada (print & online eds.); USD 39 combined subscription elsewhere (print & online eds.)). Ed(s): Nancy Kerns. Belvoir Media Group, LLC, 535 Connecticut Ave, Norwalk, CT 06856; http://www.belvoir.com. Illus. Vol. ends: Dec. *Indexed:* BRI. *Aud.:* Ga, Sa.

Whole Dog Journal offers dog owners "well-researched, in-depth articles about all aspects of dog care and training." There are feature articles on herbal remedies, adoption, neutering, behavior, training, health, diet, and care, as well as information on complementary therapies such as chiropractic care, massage, acupuncture, and homeopathy. There are also product reviews. *Whole Dog Journal* does not accept commercial advertising and conducts its own tests, reviews, and evaluation of products. The web site for this publication provides additional content. Recommended for large public library collections. URL: www.whole-dog-journal.com

3927. ***Your Cat.*** [ISSN: 1353-260X] 1994. m. USD 154.63 domestic; USD 154.63 Canada. Ed(s): Sarah Wright. Warners Group Publications Plc., The Maltings, West St, Bourne, PE10 9PH, United Kingdom; http://www.warnersgroup.co.uk/. Illus., adv. Sample. *Bk. rev.:* Number and length vary. *Aud.:* Hs, Ga.

Published in the United Kingdom, *Your Cat* is a terrific resource for cat owners and enthusiasts. The articles are well written and extremely informative. The magazine's layout is very attractive and contains many color photographs. Contributors include veterinarians, professional pet groomers, pet behaviorists, counseling psychologists, and authors of books on cats. Topics of articles range from health and welfare, to personality and behavior, to profiles of breeds, to the human-feline bond. One of the features of *Your Cat* is a question-and-answer section where readers pose questions to a panel of experts. Overall topics of these Q&A sections include general cat care, health, behavior, veterinary, and nutrition. Other regular features include fictional stories about cats, cats in the news, a breeder directory, a preview of the upcoming issue of the magazine, cat photographs submitted by readers, book reviews, and a classified ads section. The web site is attractive, easy to navigate, and provides additional content. Recommended for large public library collections. URL: www.yourcat.co.uk

3928. ***Your Dog.*** [ISSN: 1355-7386] 1994. m. USD 151.75 domestic; USD 151.75 Canada. Warners Group Publications Plc., The Maltings, West St, Bourne, PE10 9PH, United Kingdom; http://www.warnersgroup.co.uk/. Illus., adv. Sample. *Aud.:* Ga.

Published in the United Kingdom, *Your Dog* is a terrific resource for dog owners and enthusiasts. The articles are well written and extremely informative. The magazine's layout is very attractive and contains lots of color photographs. Contributors include veterinarians, breeds experts, show judges, professional groomers, canine behaviorists, animal nutritionists, trainers, homeopathic veterinarians, and authors of books on dogs. Topics of articles range from health and welfare to personality and behavior, to breed profiles, to the human-canine bond. One of the features of *Your Dog* is a question-and-answer section where readers pose questions to a panel of experts. Other regular features include dog news, dog photographs submitted by readers, and a classified ads section. The web site is attractive, easy to navigate, and provides additional content. Recommended for large public library collections. URL: www.yourdog.co.uk

3929. ***Your Dog: the newsletter for caring dog owners.*** [ISSN: 1078-0343] 1994. m. USD 50 in US & Canada. Belvoir Media Group, LLC, PO Box 5656, Norwalk, CT 06856; http://www.belvoir.com. Illus., adv. Sample. *Aud.:* Ga.

Your Dog is a monthly newsletter published by the Cummings School of Veterinary Medicine at Tufts University. Sixteen pages in length, *Your Dog* provides medical and behavioral information on canines. The articles are informative and would be of interest to dog owners. This newsletter contains information on canine behavior, medicine, health, nutrition, welfare, training, and grooming. The *Your Dog* web site provides general information about the newsletter. Recommended for large public library collections. URL: www.tuftsyourdog.com

Associations

American Cat Fanciers Association, P.O. Box 1949, Nixa, MO 65714-1949; www.acfacat.com, acfa@aol.com.

American Cichlid Association, 530 Los Angeles Ave., Suite 115-243, Moorpark, CA 93021; https://cichlid.org.

American Federation of Aviculture, P.O. Box 91717, Austin, TX 78709-1717; www.afabirds.org, afaoffice@afabirds.org.

American Fancy Rat and Mouse Association, 9230 64th Street, Riverside, CA 92509-5924; www.afrma.org.

American Ferret Association, Box 554, Frederick, MD 21705-0554; www.ferret.org, afa@ferret.org.

American Gerbil Society, c/o Amy Paben, 2283 Barker Court NE, Albany, OR 97321-9507; http://us.agsgerbils.org.

American Kennel Club, 260 Madison Avenue, New York, NY 10016; www.akc.org.

American Society for the Prevention of Cruelty to Animals, 424 E. 92nd Street, New York, NY 10128-6804; www.aspca.org.

Avicultural Society of America, P.O. Box 3161, San Dimas, CA 91773; http://asabirds.org, info@asabirds.org.

Canadian Cat Association, 5045 Orbitor Drive, Building 12, Suite 102, Mississauga, ON L4W 4Y4; www.cca-afc.com.

Canadian Kennel Club, 200 Ronson Drive, Suite 400, Etobicoke, ON M9W 5Z9; https://www.ckc.ca/en, information@ckc.ca.

Cat Fanciers' Association, 260 East Main Street, Alliance, OH 44601; http://cfa.org.

House Rabbit Society, 148 Broadway, Richmond, CA 94804; https://rabbit.org, rabbit-center@rabbit.org.

Humane Society of the United States, 1255 23rd Street, NW, Suite 450, Washington, DC 20037; www.humanesociety.org.

■ PHILATELY

Tara Murray, Director of Information Services/Librarian, American Philatelic Research Library, 100 Match Factory Place, Bellefonte, PA 16823

Introduction

Philately, or stamp collecting, is one of the world's most popular hobbies, and is nearly as old as the postage stamp itself.

The first adhesive postage stamp, the Penny Black, was issued by Great Britain in 1840. Other countries soon followed suit, and the first U.S. postage stamps, the 5 cent Franklin and the 10 cent Washington, were issued in 1847.

Literature related to stamp collecting began to appear in the 1860s. The first issue of *The Stamp-Collector's Magazine* was published in England in February 1863, and M. Georges Herpin coined the term "philately" in *Le Collectionneur de Timbres-Poste* in 1864. The American Philatelic Society, the national organization for philatelists in the U.S., was founded in 1886, and the first issue of its journal appeared in 1887.

While some rare stamp errors, such as the Inverted Jenny (the famous "upside-down airplane" stamp), are extremely valuable, anyone can start a stamp collection for a small amount of money at a local hobby shop or stamp show, by ordering through advertisements in philatelic magazines, or simply by removing stamps from envelopes received in the mail. Some philatelists don't collect anything at all, choosing to study stamps and postal history without acquiring the items themselves. In some cases, the objects of their study may be available only in museum collections.

In the early days of philately, it was possible to assemble a worldwide collection, but today even the most advanced collectors specialize—by geography, type of material (e.g., postal stationery or air mail stamps), or topic (e.g., baseball on stamps).

Philatelists are prolific writers, contributing to magazines and journals published all over the world, covering just about every specialty imaginable. The titles selected for inclusion here have broad appeal, and most have worldwide coverage with a focus on U.S., Canadian, or British stamps.

Basic Periodicals

Ga: *American Philatelist, Linn's Stamp News*; Ac: *Philatelic Literature Review, Postal History Journal.*

3930. ***American Philatelist.*** [ISSN: 0003-0473] 1887. m. Ed(s): Jay Bigalke. American Philatelic Society, Inc., 100 Match Factory Pl, Bellefonte, PA 16823; flsente@stamps.org; http://www.philately.com/philately/aps.htm. Illus., index, adv. Sample. Circ: 35000. Vol. ends: Dec. *Indexed:* BRI, CBRI, MLA-IB. *Bk. rev.:* 100-300 words. *Aud.:* Ga, Ac.

The American Philatelist is the official publication of the American Philatelic Society (APS), the leading philatelic organization in the United States. The journal covers worldwide stamps and postal history, as well as news about the hobby and the society in a glossy magazine format. Articles range from collecting tips ("How to Collect by Year of Issue") to detailed discussions of individual stamp issues ("The Legacy of the Penny Black") and nuggets of postal history ("America's Smallest Post Office"). Regular features include a calendar of stamp shows and society events, a list of U.S. new issues, book reviews, and classified ads. Recommended for all general collections.

3931. ***Canadian Philatelist.*** [ISSN: 0045-5253] 1950. bi-m. Free to members; Non-members, CAD 30. Ed(s): Tony Shaman. Philaprint Ltd., 10 Summerhill Ave, Toronto, ON M4T 1AB, Canada. Illus., index, adv. Vol. ends: Nov/Dec. Microform: PQC. *Bk. rev.:* 5-10, 300-500 words. *Aud.:* Ga, Ac.

The Canadian Philatelist (*Le Philateliste canadien*) is the official publication of the Royal Philatelic Society of Canada. Articles cover worldwide stamps and postal history, with color illustrations. Most articles are in English, but a few are in French, and news items and other short pieces are usually in both languages. Each issue includes society news, an events calendar, a list of philatelic web sites, book reviews, and classified ads. The society's web site (www.rpsc.org/tcp) provides a searchable index of articles and pdf images of issues from 1950 to the current period, excluding the most recent five years.

3932. ***Gibbons Stamp Monthly.*** Formerly (until 1977): *Stamp Monthly.* [ISSN: 0954-8084] 1890. m. GBP 46.20 domestic; GBP 95 foreign. Ed(s): Dean Shepherd. Stanley Gibbons Ltd., 7 Parkside, Christchurch Rd, Ringwood, BH24 3SH, United Kingdom; info@stanleygibbons.co.uk; http://www.stanleygibbons.com. Illus., index, adv. Sample. Vol. ends: May. *Bk. rev.:* 3-5, 300-700 words. *Aud.:* Ga.

Published by the same company that produces Great Britain's most popular stamp catalog, *Gibbons Stamp Monthly* appeals to both the novice collector and the serious philatelist. It includes a section on British stamps and a monthly supplement to the *Stanley Gibbons Catalogue,* as well as articles on stamps from around the world with plentiful color illustrations. Regular features include society and auction house news, a column for the new collector, book reviews, and classified ads.

3933. *Linn's Stamp News.* Formerly: *Linn's Weekly Stamp News.* [ISSN: 0161-6234] 1928. w. Ed(s): Donna Houseman. Amos Media, PO Box 4129, Sidney, OH 45365; cuserv@amospress.com; http://www.amospress.com. Illus., adv. Sample. Vol. ends: Dec. Microform: PQC. *Indexed:* A22. *Bk. rev.:* Occasional. *Aud.:* Ga.

Linn's, as most collectors refer to the stamp news weekly, is one of the most widely read philatelic publications in the world, and essential for those who buy and sell stamps. It covers new issues, the stamp market, auctions, shows, societies, and awards, and includes several pages of classified ads. *Linn's* began as a newspaper but now appears in a full-color magazine format. In 2010, *Scott Stamp Monthly* merged with *Linn's.* As a result, one issue of *Linn's* each month appears in a larger, glossier format and includes content from *Scott Stamp Monthly,* most notably a new-issues update to the *Scott Stamp Catalogue,* the most popular stamp catalog in the U.S. Recommended for all general collections.

3934. *Mekeel's and Stamps Magazine.* Formerly (until 1997): *Mekeel's Weekly and Stamps;* Which was formed by the merger of (1932-1996): *Stamps;* (1891-1996): *Mekeel's Weekly Stamp News;* Which incorporated (in 1891): *Weekly Philatetic Era.* [ISSN: 1095-0443] 1996. s-m. USD 46.50. Stamp News Publishing, Inc., 42 Sentry Way, Merrimack, NH 03054; jd@stampnewsnow.com; http://www.stampnewsnow.com. Illus., adv. Sample. *Bk. rev.:* Occasional. *Aud.:* Ga.

This weekly magazine, printed on newsprint, includes news and short articles, as well as numerous display and classified ads. The primary focus is on the U.S., although there is some worldwide coverage. Each issue contains a show calendar, an auction calendar, a list of pictorial postmarks, and U.S. stamp issues. Some issues also contain book reviews and reprints of older articles from other philatelic magazines. The cover and some illustrations are printed in color.

3935. *Philatelic Literature Review.* [ISSN: 0270-1707] 1942. q. Free to members. Ed(s): Jay Bigalke. American Philatelic Research Library, 100 Match Factory Pl, Bellefonte, PA 16823; plr@stamps.org; http://www.stamps.org. Illus., index, adv. Sample. Vol. ends: Dec. *Indexed:* BRI, CBRI. *Bk. rev.:* 10-20, 100-750 words. *Aud.:* Ac, Sa.

This journal focuses on the extensive literature of philately and is aimed at bibliophiles, researchers, and librarians. It began its life as a publication of the Philatelic Literature Association, and is now the official journal of the American Philatelic Research Library (APRL). Feature articles discuss the history of philately and research resources and techniques. The journal also includes original bibliographies and indexes on all aspects of philately, in-depth book reviews, news from the APRL and other philatelic libraries, and a literature clearinghouse and dealer directory. It is illustrated in black and white. A companion blog (http://blog.stamplibrary.org) provides updates and short articles between quarterly issues. Recommended for all collections that support philatelic or postal history research.

3936. *Postal History Journal.* [ISSN: 0032-5341] 1957. 3x/yr. USD 35 domestic (Free to members). Ed(s): Diane F DeBlois, Robert Dalton Harris. Postal History Society, Inc., PO Box 482, East Schodack, NY 12063; http://www.postalhistorysociety.org. Illus., index, adv. Vol. ends: Oct. Microform: PQC. *Indexed:* A22. *Bk. rev.:* 2-5, 500 words. *Aud.:* Ac, Sa.

Published by the Postal History Society, this journal features research articles on all aspects of postal history and the development of communication and transportation systems related to the mail. Articles are thorough and include numerous references and color illustrations. Each issue also includes a bibliography of postal history articles in other journals, in-depth book reviews by subject experts, and news for society members. Recommended for all collections that support philatelic or postal history research.

Scott Stamp Monthly. See *Linn's Stamp News.*

3937. *Topical Time.* [ISSN: 0040-9332] 1949. bi-m. Free to members. Ed(s): Wayne Youngblood. American Topical Association, Inc., PO Box 8, Carterville, IL 62918; americantopical@msn.com; http://americantopicalassn.org/. Illus., index, adv. *Aud.:* Ga, Sa.

Topical stamp collecting, or collecting based on the subject depicted rather than on geography or type of philatelic material, is very popular. *Topical Time* features articles on a wide variety of topics, with numerous color illustrations. As the official journal of the American Topical Association, it includes news from the society and its many chapters and study units. The latter help topical collectors connect with others who share their interest (e.g., sports on stamps, or cats on stamps).

■ PHILOSOPHY

Peggy Keeran, Arts & Humanities Librarian, University of Denver Libraries, Denver, CO 80208; peggy.keeran@du.edu

Introduction

The philosophical journals in this chapter reflect the broad range of discussions and interests of philosophers, as well as individuals interested in philosophical questions related to their fields of study or professions. Although philosophy departments at academic institutions tend to be small, the impact of philosophic conversations reverberate across the disciplines, such as those that examine how nature (sexuality, reproduction, gender), events (war, terrorist attacks, natural disasters), policies (incarceration, climate change, professional ethics), and technology (artificial intelligence, robotics) impact human life and value, and affect our understanding of our world.

The journals offer a variety of approaches to philosophical discussions, from those publications that focus more exclusively on an era or a school of thought, such as ancient, analytic, or Continental philosophies, to those that delve deeply into a subdiscipline, such as logic or phenomenology, or a philosopher, such as Kant or Hume, or those that offer forums for engaging in the diverse conversations of philosophical thought. Both general philosophical publications and periodicals that examine the intersections of philosophy with other fields of study provide insight into historic and contemporary concerns. Many of the journals offer special issues that focus on specific questions or debates, such as contemporary issues related to social justice, animal rights, and ethics and future generations. Although the majority of the journals in this chapter are exclusively in English, editors welcome and encourage articles from the international community, in order to generate conversations and debates that provide a diverse array of global viewpoints. To broaden a journal's appeal, some editors explicitly ask that articles be readable and jargon limited, while important yet highly technical journals are intended for specialists in the field. The aim of *Philosophy Now*, the only non-academic, non-peer reviewed journal in this chapter, is to make philosophy more accessible for the educated layperson.

Basic Periodicals

Ac: *American Philosophical Quarterly, Ethics, European Journal of Philosophy, Inquiry, Journal of Philosophy, Journal of the History of Philosophy, Mind, Nous, Philosophical Review, Philosophical Studies, Philosophy, Philosophy of Science*; Sa: *The Journal of Symbolic Logic*; Ga: *Philosophy Now.*

Basic Abstracts and Indexes

L'Annee Philologique, Arts and Humanities Citation Index, International Philosophical Bibliography, Philosopher's Index, PhilPapers: Online Research in Philosophy.

3938. ***Acta Analytica.*** [ISSN: 0353-5150] 1986. q. EUR 378 (print & online eds.)). Ed(s): Danilo Suster. Springer Netherlands, Van Godewijckstraat 30, Dordrecht, 3311 GX, Netherlands; http://www.springer.com. Adv. Reprint: PSC. *Indexed:* A01, A22, BRI, E01. *Aud.:* Ac.

Acta Analytica is an important English-language Slovenian journal that publishes articles by authors internationally in the analytic tradition on topics, primarily involving philosophical logic, metaphysics, epistemology, philosophy of science, philosophy of mind, cognitive science, and metaethics, with special attention given to cognitive science.

3939. ***American Philosophical Association. Journal.*** [ISSN: 2053-4477] 2015. q. GBP 445 (print & online eds.)). Ed(s): John Heil. Cambridge University Press, 1 Liberty Plaza, Fl 20, New York, NY 10004; journals@cambridge.org; https://www.cambridge.org. Refereed. *Aud.:* Ac.

In the editorial piece for the inaugural issue of this general philosophy journal, the editors explain why this publication matters: "the world needs a philosophy journal that serves philosophers by providing a venue for trendsetting—as distinguished from trendy-papers." The journal seeks to effect change within the scholarly publishing world of philosophy by purposefully soliciting and publishing articles from both new and established scholars in all areas that transform philosophical discussions, and they have added specialists and consultants who can be called upon to review research that takes risks. Thus far, a mixture of articles address contemporary questions, from the analytic tradition in the areas of metaphysics, ethics, philosophy of language, philosophy of mind, as well as issues related to other approaches and traditions, such as the history of philosophy, philosophical psychology, critical race theory, and German idealism. The journal won the 2017 PROSE Award for Best New Journal in the Humanities and Social Sciences.

3940. ***American Philosophical Quarterly.*** [ISSN: 0003-0481] 1964. q. USD 343 (print or online ed.)). Ed(s): John Greco. University of Illinois Press, 1325 S Oak St, MC-566, Champaign, IL 61820; uipress@uillinois.edu; http://www.press.uillinois.edu. Illus., index, adv. Sample. Refereed. *Indexed:* A01, A22, AmHI, IBSS. *Aud.:* Ac.

American Philosophical Quarterly is a wide-ranging philosophy journal that covers particular issues and problems in metaphysics, epistemology, philosophy of mind, ethics, philosophy of language, and action theory. Articles in recent issues have ranged from theory of knowledge to nihilism to thought and thinking related to blame, perception, and cognitive phenomenology. Essays that focus on recent areas of inquiry, such as on truth or on naive realism, are offered occasionally. An excellent general philosophical journal for all collections.

3941. ***Analysis.*** [ISSN: 0003-2638] 1933. q. EUR 285. Ed(s): David Liggins. Oxford University Press, Great Clarendon St, Oxford, OX2 6DP, United Kingdom; https://academic.oup.com/journals/. Illus., index, adv. Sample. Refereed. Vol. ends: No. 4. Reprint: PSC. *Indexed:* A01, A22, AmHI, E01, MLA-IB, MSN. *Bk. rev.:* Number varies, 1,000-2,500 words, signed. *Aud.:* Ac.

Analysis offers short articles that further or critique positions or arguments on topics concerning contemporary analytical philosophy, primarily in metaphysics, philosophical logic, philosophy of language, philosophy of mind, epistemology, and ethics. The publication also includes the "Analysis Reviews," which provides book symposia, critical notices, and book reviews of recent work in analytical philosophy. Highly recommended for collections that support work in contemporary analytic philosophy.

3942. ***Analytic Philosophy.*** Formerly (until 2011): *Philosophical Books.* [ISSN: 2153-9596] 1960. q. GBP 476. Ed(s): David Sosa. Wiley-Blackwell Publishing Ltd., The Atrium, Southern Gate, Chichester, PO19 8QG, United Kingdom; cs-journals@wiley.com; http://www.wiley.com/. Illus., index, adv. Sample. Refereed. Circ: 310 Paid. Vol. ends: No. 4. Reprint: PSC. *Indexed:* A01, A22, E01. *Aud.:* Ac.

Analytic Philosophy, out of the philosophy department at the University of Texas, publishes substantive articles of original research in all areas of philosophy. It regularly publishes discussion essays that critique and/or respond to a philosophical question or issue. Formerly *Philosophical Books*.

3943. ***Ancient Philosophy: a journal devoted to ancient Greek and Roman philosophy and science.*** [ISSN: 0740-2007] 1980. s-a. USD 78. Ed(s): Ronald Polansky. Philosophy Documentation Center, PO Box 7147, Charlottesville, VA 22906; order@pdcnet.org. Illus. Refereed. Vol. ends: No. 2. Reprint: PSC. *Indexed:* A22, AmHI, BRI. *Bk. rev.:* Number varies, 1,000-2,000 words, signed. *Aud.:* Ac.

Although most peer-reviewed articles in this journal focus on Plato and Aristotle, other philosophers, such as Thales and Socrates, Presocratics such as Parmenides, Neoplatonists such as Damascius and Porphyry, and Roman Stoics such as Epictetus are discussed. Substantive book reviews are included. A good supplement to *Phronesis* (below in this section), for collections with strong emphasis on ancient philosophy.

3944. ***Apeiron: a journal for ancient philosophy and science.*** [ISSN: 0003-6390] 1966. q. EUR 225. Ed(s): Benjamin Morison, Christian Wildberg. Walter de Gruyter GmbH, Genthiner Str 13, Berlin, 10785, Germany; service@degruyter.com; https://www.degruyter.de. Adv. Refereed. Reprint: PSC. *Indexed:* A22. *Aud.:* Ac.

Apeiron, a key journal and one of the important journals on ancient philosophy published in North America, is dedicated to the study of ancient philosophy, of ancient science, and, in particular, of problems that concern both fields. The journal publishes research concerning ancient Greco-Roman intellectual history and the reception of ancient philosophical and scientific ideas in the later western tradition. Aristotle and Plato are well represented, although recent issues also offered discussions on Socrates, Galen, and Democritus. Articles address issues in the philosophical areas of metaphysics, ethics, mind, political philosophy, virtue, and more, and scientific concepts in fields such as biology, cognition, physics, astronomy, cosmology, mathematics, and medicine.

3945. ***Aristotelian Society. Proceedings. Supplementary Volume.*** [ISSN: 0309-7013] 1918. a. GBP 155. Ed(s): Guy Longworth. Oxford University Press, Great Clarendon St, Oxford, OX2 6DP, United Kingdom; onlinequeries.uk@oup.com; https://academic.oup.com/journals/. Illus., adv. Refereed. Reprint: PSC. *Indexed:* A22, E01. *Aud.:* Ac.

The Aristotelian Society is a preeminent organization for Anglo-American philosophers, and the supplementary volume of its proceedings, published in June, contains commissioned papers that are to be read at the annual joint sessions of the Aristotelian Society and the Mind Association, with the first article being the presidential address. The papers, by notable philosophers in the English-speaking world, cover all topics and historical figures. Recent volumes offer articles addressing topics such as racial justice; benevolence; Augustine on perception; the idea of Europe; and facts and factivity. This superior publication is highly recommended for all collections.

3946. ***The Australasian Journal of Logic.*** [ISSN: 1448-5052] 2003. a. Free. Ed(s): Edwin Mares. Australasian Association for Logic, c/o The University of Melbourne, School of Philosophy, Carlton, VIC 3010, Australia; aal-info@unimelb.edu.au; http://aal.ltumathstats.com/. Refereed. *Indexed:* MSN. *Aud.:* Ac, Sa.

Sponsored by the Australasian Association for Logic and the Centre for Logic, Language and Computation at Victoria University, this open-access online journal publishes articles of interest to those working in logic, both pure logic (i.e., theory) and applied logic (i.e., logic as it relates to mathematics, computer science, linguistics, and philosophy). URL: http://ojs.victoria.ac.nz/ajl/index

3947. ***Australasian Journal of Philosophy.*** Formerly (until 1947): *Australasian Journal of Psychology and Philosophy.* [ISSN: 0004-8402] 1923. q. GBP 190 (print & online eds.)). Ed(s): Stephen Hetherington. Routledge, 4 Park Sq, Milton Park, Abingdon, OX14 4RN, United Kingdom; subscriptions@tandf.co.uk; http://www.tandfonline.com. Illus., index, adv. Sample. Refereed. Vol. ends: No. 4. Microform: MIM. Reprint: PSC. *Indexed:* A22, AmHI, E01, MLA-IB. *Bk. rev.:* 5-10, 1,000-2,000 words, signed. *Aud.:* Ac.

Sponsored by the Australasian Association of Philosophy, this highly respected international journal is Australia's oldest continuously published philosophy journal. It includes original articles concerned with contemporary issues in metaphysics, epistemology, philosophy of science, and ethics. The journal also contains discussion notes that critique recent publications, longer book reviews, and shorter book notes. Recommended for larger collections.

Bioethics. See Civil Liberties/Bioethics: Reproductive Rights, Right-to-Life, and Right-to-Die section.

3948. *British Journal for the History of Philosophy.* [ISSN: 0960-8788] 1993. bi-m. GBP 815 (print & online eds.)). Ed(s): Michael Beaney. Routledge, 4 Park Sq, Milton Park, Abingdon, OX14 4RN, United Kingdom; subscriptions@tandf.co.uk; http://www.tandfonline.com. Illus., index, adv. Sample. Refereed. Vol. ends: No. 3. Reprint: PSC. *Indexed:* A01, A22, AmHI, E01. *Bk. rev.:* Number varies, 1,000-2,000 words, signed. *Aud.:* Ac.

Sponsored by the British Society for the History of Philosophy, this journal primarily publishes articles on the history of Western philosophy from the ancient world to the end of the twentieth century. Articles seek to contextualize a philosophical figure, theory, or text within the intellectual and cultural environment of the time. In addition, articles that focus on lesser-known figures or on neglected relationships and influences, or that explore connections to other traditions, are offered as well. The journal also publishes discussions, review articles, book reviews, and books received.

3949. *The British Journal for the Philosophy of Science.* [ISSN: 0007-0882] 1950. q. EUR 351. Ed(s): Steven French, Wendy Parker. Oxford University Press, Great Clarendon St, Oxford, OX2 6DP, United Kingdom; onlinequeries.uk@oup.com; http://global.oup.com. Illus., index, adv. Sample. Refereed. Vol. ends: No. 4. Reprint: PSC. *Indexed:* A01, A22, AmHI, BRI, E01, MLA-IB, MSN. *Aud.:* Ac.

Under the direction of the British Society for the Philosophy of Science, this core journal publishes articles that explore traditional and cutting-edge intersections between philosophy and science, including logic, methods, and ideas related to issues in the physical, life, and social sciences. Some recent articles explore topics on social effects on social cognition, risk aversion, and scientific realism. Book reviews are now published in *BJPS Review of Books*: URL: https://bjpsbooks.wordpress.com

3950. *British Journal of Aesthetics.* [ISSN: 0007-0904] 1960. q. EUR 408. Ed(s): John Hyman, Elisabeth Schellekens. Oxford University Press, Great Clarendon St, Oxford, OX2 6DP, United Kingdom; onlinequeries.uk@oup.com; http://global.oup.com. Illus., adv. Sample. Refereed. Microform: PQC. Reprint: PSC. *Indexed:* A01, A06, A22, A51, AmHI, BRI, E01, MLA-IB. *Bk. rev.:* 4-6, 1,500-2,500 words, signed. *Aud.:* Ac.

Published by the British Society of Aesthetics, the journal is a forum for discussions on philosophical aesthetics and the philosophy of art. Article topics range from the nature of aesthetic judgement and the principles of art criticism to foundational issues concerning the visual arts, architecture, literature, music, dance, film, and theater. Substantive book reviews are included in each issue. A useful journal for collections that support teaching and theory of the fine arts.

3951. *Canadian Journal of Philosophy.* [ISSN: 0045-5091] 1971. 8x/yr. GBP 280 (print & online eds.)). Taylor & Francis, 2, 3 & 4 Park Sq, Milton Park, Abingdon, OX14 4RN, United Kingdom; subscriptions@tandf.co.uk; http://www.tandf.co.uk. Illus., index. Refereed. Vol. ends: No. 4. Microform: PQC. Reprint: PSC. *Indexed:* A01, A22, AmHI, BRI, C37, E01, IBSS, MLA-IB. *Aud.:* Ac.

This leading Canadian journal of philosophy publishes articles, primarily in English although occasionally in French, that provide original contributions on any philosophical debate, such as those related to ethics, social and political philosophy, epistemology, and the history of philosophy.

3952. *Charles S. Peirce Society. Transactions: a quarterly journal in American philosophy.* [ISSN: 0009-1774] 1965. q. USD 124.30 (print & online eds.)). Ed(s): Cornelis de Waal, Dwayne Tunstall. Indiana University Press, Office of Scholarly Publishing, Herman B Wells Library 350, Bloomington, IN 47405; iuporder@indiana.edu; http://iupress.indiana.edu/. Adv. Refereed. Reprint: PSC. *Indexed:* A01, A22, AmHI, BRI, E01, MLA-IB. *Bk. rev.:* 2-4, 1,500-2,000 words, signed. *Aud.:* Ac.

The official publication of the Charles S. Peirce Society, this journal specializes in the history of American philosophy, and, although the general focus is on the founder of American pragmatism and pragmatism in general, articles on other American philosophers, schools, and periods are published as well. Substantive reviews of scholarly books on the history of American philosophy are included. Important for the history of American philosophy and intellectual history.

Criminal Justice Ethics. See Criminology and Law Enforcement section.

3953. *Dialogue: Canadian philosophical review/revue Canadienne de philosophie.* [ISSN: 0012-2173] 1962. q. GBP 192 (print & online eds.)). Ed(s): Dr. Luc Langlois, Dr. Susan Dimock. Cambridge University Press, University Printing House, Shaftesbury Rd, Cambridge, CB2 8BS, United Kingdom; journals@cambridge.org; https://www.cambridge.org/. Illus. Sample. Refereed. *Indexed:* A22, AmHI, BRI, C37, CBRI, MLA-IB. *Bk. rev.:* 10-15, 500-2,500 words, signed. *Aud.:* Ac.

Dialogue is the official journal of the Canadian Philosophical Association, and publishes English and French articles in all branches of philosophy, including the history of philosophy, metaphysics, epistemology, logic, philosophy of science, political philosophy, ethics, and the philosophy of religion. It also publishes book symposia, critical notices, and book reviews.

Environmental Ethics. See Environment and Conservation section.

3954. *Erkenntnis: an international journal of scientific philosophy.* Former titles (until 1975): *Journal of Unified Science;* (until 1939): *Erkenntnis;* (until 1930): *Annalen der Philosophie und Philosophischen Kritik;* (until 1924): *Annalen der Philosophie.* [ISSN: 0165-0106] 1919. bi-m. EUR 1649 (print & online eds.)). Ed(s): Hannes Leitgeb. Springer Netherlands, Van Godewijckstraat 30, Dordrecht, 3311 GX, Netherlands; http://www.springer.com. Illus., index, adv. Sample. Refereed. Vol. ends: No. 3. Microform: PQC. Reprint: PSC. *Indexed:* A22, AmHI, BRI, E01, MSN. *Bk. rev.:* Occasional, 1-2, 1,500-2,500 words, signed. *Aud.:* Ac.

Erkenntnis is a top-tier international journal in analytic philosophy that publishes technical systematic papers and original research in epistemology, philosophy of science, mathematics, logic, philosophy of language, philosophy of psychology, metaphysics and ontology, and practical philosophy (e.g., ethics, philosophy of action, philosophy of law). A core title for graduate-level collections.

3955. *Essays in Philosophy.* [ISSN: 1526-0569] 2000. s-a. Free. Ed(s): Ramona Ilea. Pacific University, 2043 College Way, Forest Grove, OR 97116; http://www.pacificu.edu/. *Indexed:* AmHI, MLA-IB. *Bk. rev.:* Number varies, 1,000-6,000 words, signed. *Aud.:* Ac.

Each issue of this freely available philosophical e-journal is devoted to a theme-specific issue, which is coordinated by a guest editor. Subjects such as philosophical methodology, or interdisciplinary concerns related to political science, public policy, psychology, aesthetics, language, science, and so on, are explored. Recent special issues examine topics related to the morality of procreation, Latin American feminist philosophy, and the philosophy of memory. Each issue contains several substantive book reviews. URL: http://commons.pacificu.edu/eip/

3956. *Ethical Theory and Moral Practice: an international forum.* [ISSN: 1386-2820] 1998. 5x/yr. EUR 1210 (print & online eds.)). Ed(s): Marcus Duewell, T Schramme. Springer Netherlands, Van Godewijckstraat 30, Dordrecht, 3311 GX, Netherlands; http://www.springer.com. Illus., adv. Sample. Refereed. Reprint: PSC. *Indexed:* A01, A22, AmHI, BRI, E01, IBSS. *Bk. rev.:* 5-10, 1,000-2,000 words, signed. *Aud.:* Ac, Sa.

This international journal focuses on all fields of ethics, with the aim to promote interdisciplinary cooperation between ethics, theology, and empirical disciplines such as medicine, economics, sociology, psychology, and law, in order to break down artificial distinctions between theory and practice. Recent special issues cover topics on dimensions of responsibility, risk and moral theory, and practical rationality and evil action. The journal also has a substantive book review section, including books in languages other than English. For collections with comprehensive holdings in ethics.

3957. ***Ethics: an international journal of social, political, and legal philosophy.*** Former titles (until 1938): *International Journal of Ethics;* (until 1890): *The Ethical Record.* [ISSN: 0014-1704] 1888. q. USD 339. Ed(s): Connie S. Rosati, Julia L. Driver. University of Chicago Press, 1427 E 60th St, Chicago, IL 60637; subscriptions@press.uchicago.edu; http://www.journals.uchicago.edu. Illus., adv. Sample. Refereed. Vol. ends: Jul. Reprint: PSC. *Indexed:* A01, A22, AmHI, BRI, CBRI, IBSS, L14, MLA-IB, P61, SSA. *Bk. rev.:* 7-10, 2,500-3,500 words, signed. *Aud.:* Ac.

Ethics is a leading philosophy journal in social, political, and legal ethics. It publishes articles on traditional and contemporary issues related to moral philosophy, philosophy of law, public policy issues, religious ethics, normative economics, international law, and choice theory, as well as symposia centered on themes or theories, discussions, review articles, and book reviews. Highly recommended for academic collections.

3958. ***Ethics & Behavior.*** [ISSN: 1050-8422] 1991. bi-m. GBP 1131 (print & online eds.)). Ed(s): Thomas Hadjistavropoulos. Routledge, 530 Walnut St, Ste 850, Philadelphia, PA 19106; enquiries@tandfonline.com; http://www.tandfonline.com. Illus., adv. Sample. Refereed. Vol. ends: No. 4. Reprint: PSC. *Indexed:* A01, A22, ASSIA, E01. *Aud.:* Ac.

This journal publishes articles, case analyses, and brief summaries of problem cases on a range of topics related to moral issues and conduct, in disciplines such as law, medicine, pediatrics, psychiatry, psychology, public health, sociology, and theology. Topics include social and ethical responsibilities in human behavior, ethical dilemmas and misconduct in health and human services, ethical research using human and animal participants, fraudulence in scientific research, and ethics in public policy. Contributors are largely from the social sciences, in disciplines such as psychology, social work, education, and business. An excellent addition to collections supporting research and studies in applied ethics.

3959. ***European Journal of Philosophy.*** [ISSN: 0966-8373] 1993. q. GBP 685. Ed(s): Joseph K Schear. Wiley-Blackwell Publishing Ltd., The Atrium, Southern Gate, Chichester, PO19 8QG, United Kingdom; cs-journals@wiley.com; http://onlinelibrary.wiley.com/. Illus., index, adv. Sample. Refereed. Vol. ends: No. 3. Reprint: PSC. *Indexed:* A01, A22, AmHI, BRI, E01, IBSS. *Bk. rev.:* Number varies, 2,000-3,000 words, signed. *Aud.:* Ac.

This journal aims to overcome the insularity of philosophical discussions in European schools by providing a forum for philosophers, both within and outside of Europe, in order to engage with the diversity and variety of analytic and Continental traditions. The goal is to spark exchanges of ideas and connections between traditions, while making contributions to the tradition in which the philosopher works. The journal publishes original articles, symposia, review articles, book reviews, and the annual Mark Sacks lecture, named in honor of the journal's founder. Recommended for collections that focus broadly on European philosophy.

3960. ***Faith and Philosophy.*** [ISSN: 0739-7046] 1984. q. USD 79. Ed(s): Mark C Murphy. Philosophy Documentation Center, PO Box 7147, Charlottesville, VA 22906; order@pdcnet.org; http://www.pdcnet.org. Illus., index. Refereed. Microform: PQC. *Indexed:* A22, R&TA. *Bk. rev.:* 3-5, 1,500-3,000 words, signed. *Aud.:* Ac.

Faith and Philosophy publishes articles that aim to examine philosophical issues, questions, and foundations from a Christian perspective in ways that hold up to rigorous scrutiny by both those who share the faith and those who don't. Both established and relatively new scholars, primarily in philosophy of religion, contribute. There are also reviews of recent books in the field. For libraries that support work in philosophy of religion and religious studies.

3961. ***History and Philosophy of Logic.*** [ISSN: 0144-5340] 1980. q. GBP 838 (print & online eds.)). Ed(s): Volker Peckhaus. Taylor & Francis, 2, 3 & 4 Park Sq, Milton Park, Abingdon, OX14 4RN, United Kingdom; subscriptions@tandf.co.uk; https://www.tandfonline.com. Illus., adv. Sample. Refereed. Vol. ends: No. 4. Reprint: PSC. *Indexed:* A01, A22, BRI, E01, MSN. *Bk. rev.:* Number varies, 1,000-1,500 words, signed. *Aud.:* Ac.

This important journal publishes articles, notes, and book reviews dealing with the general history and philosophy of logic around the world, from ancient times to this century. Very recent work on a topic or specialized studies in philosophical logic are excluded. Logic is defined as knowledge that was regarded as logic at the time in question. Topics include the existential and ontological aspects of logic, the relationship between classical and nonclassical logic, and the application of logic to mathematics, economics, science, and linguistics.

3962. ***History of Philosophy Quarterly.*** [ISSN: 0740-0675] 1984. q. USD 346 (print or online ed.)). Ed(s): Aaron Garrett. University of Illinois Press, 1325 S Oak St, MC-566, Champaign, IL 61820; uipress@uillinois.edu; http://www.press.uillinois.edu. Illus., index, adv. Sample. Refereed. Vol. ends: No. 4. *Indexed:* A22. *Aud.:* Ac.

History of Philosophy Quarterly publishes articles that explore primarily well-known philosophers, texts, and historical topics from antiquity to the present, emphasizing the value and relevance of historical studies for ongoing philosophical concerns. Along with the *Journal of the History of Philosophy* (below in this section), this is a core history of philosophy publication.

3963. ***Human Studies: a journal for philosophy and the social sciences.*** [ISSN: 0163-8548] 1978. q. EUR 1111 (print & online eds.)). Ed(s): Martin Endress. Springer Netherlands, Van Godewijckstraat 30, Dordrecht, 3311 GX, Netherlands; http://www.springer.com. Illus., index, adv. Sample. Refereed. Vol. ends: No. 4. Microform: PQC. Reprint: PSC. *Indexed:* A01, A22, BRI, E01, IBSS, MLA-IB, P61, SSA. *Bk. rev.:* 1-2, 1,000-3,000 words, signed. *Aud.:* Ac.

Human Studies, the official journal of the Society for Phenomenology and the Human Sciences, publishes empirical and theoretical philosophical articles in the social sciences, primarily from phenomenological perspectives. Theoretical studies largely involve Continental philosophers, such as Merleau-Ponty, Husserl, Nietzsche, and Heidegger, while recent empirical studies investigate topics such as a phenomenological account of living with death in rehabilitation and a study of record-keeping practices at the museum. Contributors are primarily from philosophy and the social sciences. Some issues have book reviews.

3964. ***Hume Studies.*** [ISSN: 0319-7336] 1975. s-a. USD 60 Free to members. Ed(s): PJ E Kail, Angela M Coventry. Hume Society, . Illus. Refereed. Vol. ends: No. 2. Microform: PQC. Reprint: PSC. *Indexed:* A22, BRI, E01. *Bk. rev.:* 1-2, 1,000-1,500 words, signed. *Aud.:* Ac.

Published by the Hume Society, this interdisciplinary journal publishes articles that contribute to the understanding of Hume's thought and all aspects of his philosophy (metaphysics, epistemology, philosophy of mind, ethics, political philosophy, and philosophy of religion), as well as essays that analyze Hume in relation to the ideas of his predecessors and contemporaries. This journal is useful for collections that support research in early modern philosophy and British philosophy.

3965. ***Husserl Studies.*** [ISSN: 0167-9848] 1984. 3x/yr. EUR 693 (print & online eds.)). Ed(s): Sonia Rinofner, Steven Crowell. Springer Netherlands, Van Godewijckstraat 30, Dordrecht, 3311 GX, Netherlands; http://www.springer.com. Illus., index, adv. Sample. Refereed. Microform: PQC. Reprint: PSC. *Indexed:* A22, AmHI, BRI, E01. *Bk. rev.:* 1-3, 3,000-4,000 words, signed. *Aud.:* Ac.

Husserl Studies publishes articles that offer historical, interpretive, and comparative studies of Husserl's philosophy, including systematic investigations into sub-areas of phenomenological research (e.g., theory of intentionality, theory of meaning, ethics, and action theory) that are concerned with the development, adaptation, or criticism of Husserlian phenomenology. The journal also publishes work on phenomenology in relation to hermeneutics, critical theory, and the various modes of analytic philosophy. The journal aims to be a forum for close textual analysis of Husserl's writings and for historical, systematic, and problem-oriented phenomenological inquiry. Articles are in English and German.

Hypatia. See Gender Studies section.

3966. ***Idealistic Studies: an interdisciplinary journal of philosophy.*** [ISSN: 0046-8541] 1971. 3x/yr. USD 64. Ed(s): Jennifer Bates. Philosophy Documentation Center, PO Box 7147, Charlottesville, VA 22906; order@pdcnet.org; http://www.pdcnet.org. Illus., adv. Sample. Refereed. Vol. ends: No. 3. Reprint: PSC. *Indexed:* A01, A22, AmHI, MLA-IB. *Aud.:* Ac.

This journal is a forum for themes and topics related to the tradition and legacy of idealism, including American personalism, post-Kantian idealism, and movements that share idealism in their development: phenomenology, neo-Kantianism, historicism, hermeneutics, life philosophy, the Frankfurt School, existentialism, and pragmatism. A good source for scholarly critiques on British and German idealist philosophers and broader issues related to idealism.

3967. ***Inquiry: an interdisciplinary journal of philosophy.*** [ISSN: 0020-174X] 1958. 10x/yr. GBP 663 (print & online eds.)). Ed(s): Herman Cappelen. Routledge, 4 Park Sq, Milton Park, Abingdon, OX14 4RN, United Kingdom; subscriptions@tandf.co.uk; http://www.tandfonline.com. Illus., index, adv. Sample. Refereed. Vol. ends: No. 4. Microform: PQC. Reprint: PSC. *Indexed:* A01, A22, AmHI, B01, BAS, BRI, E01, IBSS, MLA-IB, P61. *Aud.:* Ac.

Inquiry is an interdisciplinary journal that publishes articles primarily in the areas of metaphysics, epistemology, philosophy of mind, ethics, aesthetics, social and political philosophy, and Continental philosophy. Issues frequently contain lengthy symposia in which commentators respond to an author's paper. Regular special issues feature invited authors to discuss a philosophical question or theme. An important journal for all collections.

International Journal for Philosophy of Religion. See Religion section.

3968. ***International Journal of Philosophical Studies.*** Formerly (until 1993): *Philosophical Studies (Print).* [ISSN: 0967-2559] 1951. 5x/yr. GBP 896 (print & online eds.)). Ed(s): Rowland Stout. Routledge, 4 Park Sq, Milton Park, Abingdon, OX14 4RN, United Kingdom; subscriptions@tandf.co.uk; http://www.tandfonline.com. Illus., adv. Sample. Refereed. Reprint: PSC. *Indexed:* A01, A22, AmHI, C26, E01, IBSS. *Bk. rev.:* 3-6, 2,000-4,500 words, signed. *Aud.:* Ac.

This journal publishes articles from different traditions and areas, including philosophy of mind and action, epistemology, metaphysics, philosophy of language, ethics, and aesthetics. The journal aims to encourage discussion and comprehension between the analytic and Continental styles, and to offer articles on the history of philosophy that provide insights into current conversations alongside those examining contemporary problems. The recent Robert Papazian Prize Special Issue focused on topics related to trust. Issues may offer book reviews, discussions, or symposia. A good addition for general collections.

3969. ***International Philosophical Quarterly.*** [ISSN: 0019-0365] 1961. q. USD 40 Latin America, Africa (excluding S. Africa), Middle East, India, Asia (excluding Japan)). Ed(s): Joseph W Koterski. Philosophy Documentation Center, PO Box 7147, Charlottesville, VA 22906; order@pdcnet.org; http://www.pdcnet.org. Illus., index. Sample. Refereed. Vol. ends: No. 4. Microform: PQC. Reprint: PSC. *Indexed:* A01, A22, AmHI, BAS, BRI, CBRI, MLA-IB. *Bk. rev.:* 5-6, 1,000-2,000 words, signed. *Aud.:* Ac.

This journal, a joint collaboration between Fordham University and the Universie de Namur in Belgium, publishes articles in English and provides an international forum for the exchange of basic philosophical ideas that offer either discussions of contemporary issues or historical studies. Intercultural articles in the tradition of theistic and personalist humanism are of special interest. Each issue concludes with several short book reviews and a list of books received.

The Journal of Aesthetics and Art Criticism. See Cultural Studies section.

3970. ***The Journal of Ethics: an international philosophical review.*** [ISSN: 1382-4554] 1997. q. EUR 892 (print & online eds.)). Ed(s): J Angelo Corlett. Springer Netherlands, Van Godewijckstraat 30, Dordrecht, 3311 GX, Netherlands; http://www.springer.com. Illus., adv. Sample. Refereed. Vol. ends: No. 4. Reprint: PSC. *Indexed:* A01, A22, BRI, E01. *Aud.:* Ac.

This journal publishes articles on topics that address historical and contemporary issues in ethics, philosophically construed, including ethical theory and moral, social, political, and legal philosophy. Although primarily for philosophical research, the topics are intended to be of interest to other disciplines and fields also concerned with issues of ethics. A core journal, along with *Ethics* (above in this section) and *Journal of Moral Philosophy* (below in this section).

3971. ***Journal of Ethics & Social Philosophy: journal of moral, political and legal philosophy.*** [ISSN: 1559-3061] 2005. irreg. Free. Ed(s): Mark Schroeder. University of Southern California, Gould School of Law, University Park, Los Angeles, CA 90089; academicsupport@law.usc.edu; http://gould.usc.edu/. Refereed. *Indexed:* AmHI, L14. *Aud.:* Ac.

Published by the University of Southern California, this online open-access journal contains peer-reviewed articles in moral, political, and legal philosophy related to contemporary ethical issues. The journal also publishes discussion notes throughout the year. For collections that support programs and research in ethics and social philosophy. URL: http://www.jesp.org/

3972. ***Journal of Indian Philosophy.*** [ISSN: 0022-1791] 1970. 5x/yr. EUR 1479 (print & online eds.)). Ed(s): Diwakar Acharya. Springer Netherlands, Van Godewijckstraat 30, Dordrecht, 3311 GX, Netherlands; http://www.springer.com. Illus., index, adv. Sample. Refereed. Microform: PQC. Reprint: PSC. *Indexed:* A22, AmHI, BAS, BRI, E01, IBSS, MLA-IB. *Aud.:* Sa.

This specialized journal is intended for scholars knowledgeable about classical and modern philosophical thought and religions of the Indian subcontinent and Tibet, especially Hinduism, Buddhism, and Jainism. Scholars of philosophy, religious studies, and Indian/Asian studies offer close textual analysis of works, annotated translations of texts, and speculative discussions of issues based upon close readings of primary sources, providing critical analysis and explication of traditional and contemporary philosophical issues related to language, ethics, religion, logic, metaphysics, and epistemology. A graduate-level journal for collections that support the study of Eastern philosophy and religion.

3973. ***Journal of Moral Philosophy.*** [ISSN: 1740-4681] 2004. bi-m. EUR 661. Ed(s): Tom Weterings, S Matthew Liao. Brill, PO Box 9000, Leiden, 2300 PA, Netherlands; marketing@brill.com; https://brill.com. Adv. Refereed. Reprint: PSC. *Indexed:* A01, A22, E01, P61. *Aud.:* Ac.

This international journal publishes articles in all areas of normative philosophy that address historical and contemporary moral, political, and legal issues. The journal encourages readable yet academically sound contributions, from both established and newer scholars, intended for those in the field and from the wider community. One thematic issue is published each year. Along with *Ethics* and *The Journal of Ethics* (both discussed above in this section), an important title for academic collections.

3974. ***Journal of Nietzsche Studies.*** [ISSN: 0968-8005] 1991. s-a. USD 212 (print & online eds.)). Ed(s): Jessica Berry. Pennsylvania State University Press, 820 N University Dr, University Support Bldg 1, Ste C, University Park, PA 16802; info@psupress.org; http://www.psupress.org. Adv. Refereed. Reprint: PSC. *Indexed:* A01, A22, AmHI, E01, MLA-IB. *Bk. rev.:* 7-10, 1,500-2,500 words, signed. *Aud.:* Ac.

Originally founded by the Friedrich Nietzsche Society in 1991, this publication is now owned by Penn State University Press. The journal publishes research about and related to Nietzsche's thought, his relevance to contemporary philosophical problems, and philology. Articles and reviews are in English, although monographs published in other languages are reviewed. Collections that support philosophy (especially twentieth-century Continental philosophy) and German intellectual history will want to subscribe to it.

3975. ***Journal of Philosophical Logic.*** [ISSN: 0022-3611] 1972. bi-m. EUR 1224 (print & online eds.)). Springer Netherlands, Van Godewijckstraat 30, Dordrecht, 3311 GX, Netherlands; http://www.springer.com. Illus., index, adv. Sample. Refereed. Microform: PQC. Reprint: PSC. *Indexed:* A01, A22, AmHI, E01, MLA-IB, MSN. *Aud.:* Sa.

This journal publishes articles, from the conceptual to the technical, that cross in all areas of philosophy and logic and across all eras. Topics cover logic in the traditional areas of philosophical logic and those that use formal logic, as well as applications of logic to new areas and in other disciplines, such as computer science, artificial intelligence, linguistics, law, and social sciences. For advanced collections, a leading journal for research in and the study of philosophical logic and related fields.

3976. ***The Journal of Philosophy.*** Formerly (until 1921): *The Journal of Philosophy, Psychology and Scientific Methods.* [ISSN: 0022-362X] 1904. m. USD 150. Ed(s): Alyssa Timin. Journal of Philosophy, Inc., Columbia University, Heyman Center for the Humanities B-200, New York, NY 10027. Illus., adv. Refereed. Microform: PMC. *Indexed:* A01, A22, AmHI, BRI, CBRI, IBSS, MLA-IB. *Bk. rev.:* 1-2, 1,000-3,000 words, signed. *Aud.:* Ac.

A prominent American philosophy journal, this publication typically publishes two articles and a list of new books in each monthly issue. Issues and problems examined are generally of interest to American philosophers, and fall within the areas of metaphysics, epistemology, philosophy of mind, philosophy of language, philosophical logic, social and political philosophy, ethics, action theory, and aesthetics. Short responses are occasionally published in "Comments and Criticism." A core journal.

Journal of Philosophy of Education. See Education/Comparative Education and International section.

3977. ***Journal of Speculative Philosophy.*** [ISSN: 0891-625X] 1867. q. USD 245 (print & online eds.)). Ed(s): John J Stuhr. Pennsylvania State University Press, 820 N University Dr, University Support Bldg 1, Ste C, University Park, PA 16802; info@psupress.org; http://www.psupress.org. Illus., index, adv. Refereed. Vol. ends: No. 4. Reprint: PSC. *Indexed:* A01, A22, AmHI, E01, MLA-IB. *Aud.:* Ac.

This journal, originally published in the nineteenth century and the first primarily philosophical journal published in the United States, was a forum for classical American philosophers such as Peirce, Dewey, James, Hall, and Morris. It was revived in 1987, and publishes systematic and interpretive articles about basic philosophical questions that examine productive interactions between Continental and American philosophy, as well as unique and relevant ways in which the philosophical thoughts of past philosophers are being applied today. At times the journal will publish discussions of art, religion, and literature that are not strictly or narrowly philosophical. For collections that support research and programs in the history of American philosophy, American intellectual history, and Continental philosophy.

3978. ***The Journal of Symbolic Logic.*** [ISSN: 0022-4812] 1936. q. Cambridge University Press, 1 Liberty Plaza, Fl 20, New York, NY 10004; journals@cambridge.org; https://www.cambridge.org/. Illus., index. Refereed. Vol. ends: No. 4. Microform: PMC; PQC. *Indexed:* A22, AmHI, BRI, MLA-IB, MSN. *Aud.:* Sa.

This well-established and reputable leading journal, sponsored by the Association for Symbolic Logic, publishes highly technical articles in mathematical logic and its applications. Papers are expected to be of interest to a broad audience, including philosophers of logic, logicians, and mathematicians. The journal is distributed with *The Bulletin of Symbolic Logic.* A core title for graduate-level collections.

Journal of the History of Ideas. See Cultural Studies section.

3979. ***Journal of the History of Philosophy.*** [ISSN: 0022-5053] 1963. q. USD 155. Ed(s): Alan McLuckie, Jack Zupko. The Johns Hopkins University Press, 2715 N Charles St, Baltimore, MD 21218; http://www.press.jhu.edu. Illus., adv. Sample. Refereed. Vol. ends: No. 4. Reprint: PSC. *Indexed:* A01, A22, AmHI, BRI, E01, IBSS, MLA-IB. *Bk. rev.:* 10-20, 750-1,000 words, signed. *Aud.:* Ac.

This core journal in the history of Western philosophy publishes articles primarily on major philosophical figures and movements from antiquity through the twentieth century, although articles on lesser-known figures are occasionally offered. Each issue has book reviews and books received sections, and includes symposia and announcements on an irregular basis. An essential journal for all general philosophy collections.

3980. ***The Journal of Value Inquiry.*** [ISSN: 0022-5363] 1967. q. EUR 1217 (print & online eds.)). Ed(s): John Hacker-Wright. Springer Netherlands, Van Godewijckstraat 30, Dordrecht, 3311 GX, Netherlands; http://www.springer.com. Illus., index, adv. Sample. Refereed. Vol. ends: Oct/Dec. Microform: PQC. Reprint: PSC. *Indexed:* A22, AmHI, BRI, E01, MLA-IB. *Bk. rev.:* 1-5, 1,000-2,000 words, signed. *Aud.:* Ac.

This international, interdisciplinary journal is an important title devoted to value theory, or axiology. It offers articles that explore the nature, origin, experiences, and scope of value across a broad range of contexts and disciplines, from ethics to aesthetics, religion to law, and education to the sciences.

3981. ***Kant Studien: philosophische Zeitschrift der Kant-Gesellschaft.*** [ISSN: 0022-8877] 1896. q. EUR 255. Ed(s): Bernd Dorflinger, Manfred Baum. Walter de Gruyter GmbH, Genthiner Str 13, Berlin, 10785, Germany; service@degruyter.com; https://www.degruyter.de. Illus., index, adv. Refereed. Vol. ends: No. 4. Reprint: SCH. *Indexed:* A22, AmHI, BRI, E01, MLA-IB. *Bk. rev.:* 5-10, 750-1,500 words, signed. *Aud.:* Ac.

This journal publishes articles that contribute to the interpretation, history, and editorial questions of Kant, inquiries into the philosophers that influenced him as well as the effects of his legacy, and debates that fall within the scope of transcendental philosophy. Articles are in German, English, and French, with English abstracts. Discussions and book reviews are published regularly, and a useful annual bibliography published in the fourth issue provides an extensive annual list of Kant studies. Given the importance of Kant, a good selection for general collections and those that emphasize the modern period.

3982. ***Law and Philosophy: an international journal for jurisprudence and legal philosophy.*** [ISSN: 0167-5249] 1982. bi-m. EUR 866 (print & online eds.)). Ed(s): John Oberdiek, Kimberly Kessler Ferzan. Springer Netherlands, Van Godewijckstraat 30, Dordrecht, 3311 GX, Netherlands; http://www.springer.com. Illus., index, adv. Sample. Refereed. Microform: WSH; PQC. Reprint: PSC. *Indexed:* A22, BRI, E01, IBSS, L14, P61, SSA. *Bk. rev.:* Number and length varies, signed. *Aud.:* Ac.

A valuable journal for those academics and professionals who are invested in the philosophical issues related to law, including justice, rights, liberty, punishment, moral and criminal responsibility, ethics, legal positivism, and legal reasoning and interpretation. Contributors are largely from the fields of philosophy and law. A solid choice for philosophy, law, and criminology collections.

Linguistics and Philosophy. See Linguistics section.

3983. ***Metaphilosophy.*** [ISSN: 0026-1068] 1970. q. GBP 708. Ed(s): Armen T Marsoobian, Otto Bohlmann. Wiley-Blackwell Publishing Ltd., The Atrium, Southern Gate, Chichester, PO19 8QG, United Kingdom; cs-journals@wiley.com; http://onlinelibrary.wiley.com. Illus., adv. Sample. Refereed. Vol. ends: No. 4. Reprint: PSC. *Indexed:* A01, A22, AmHI, BRI, E01, MLA-IB. *Bk. rev.:* Occasional, 2,000-3,000 words, signed. *Aud.:* Ac.

This journal publishes articles that address issues concerning philosophy broadly, with particular interest for the foundation, scope, function, and direction of philosophy, justification for its methods and arguments, the relationships between schools or fields of philosophy, and teaching. Studies also investigate the relationship of philosophy to other disciplines and relevance for social and political action. *Metaphilosophy* has consistently been on the leading edge for publishing work on new trends in philosophy. A core journal.

3984. *Midwest Studies in Philosophy.* [ISSN: 0363-6550] 1976. a. USD 751. Ed(s): Howard K Wettstein, Peter A French. Wiley-Blackwell Publishing, Inc., 111 River St, Hoboken, NJ 07030; info@wiley.com; http://www.wiley.com/. Adv. Sample. Reprint: PSC. *Indexed:* A01, A22, AmHI, E01. *Aud.:* Ac.

Each volume of this annual publication is devoted to a philosophical area, theme, philosopher, or historical period, with articles written by experts in fields related to the topic. Topics range widely, with recent issues focused on moral responsibility and the financial crisis; phenomenology of affective life; ethics and climate change; and philosophy and science fiction. An important, core journal for all philosophy collections.

3985. *Mind: a quarterly review of philosophy.* [ISSN: 0026-4423] 1876. q. EUR 336. Ed(s): Lucy O'Brien, A W Moore. Oxford University Press, Great Clarendon St, Oxford, OX2 6DP, United Kingdom; onlinequeries.uk@oup.com; http://global.oup.com. Illus., index, adv. Sample. Refereed. Vol. ends: No. 4. Microform: PMC; PQC. Reprint: PSC. *Indexed:* A01, A22, AmHI, BRI, E01, MLA-IB, MSN. *Bk. rev.:* 5-10, 1,500-2,000 words, signed. *Aud.:* Ac.

Published on behalf of the Mind Association, *Mind* is one of the foremost British philosophy journals. Founded in 1876, editors G. K. Stout, G. E. Moore, and Gilbert Ryle helped establish its reputation by publishing many articles now considered classics. In 2016 the new editors stated that they seek to continue the high level of quality of articles the journal has always known, but also to expand the breadth of content, to publish articles that address significant trends in the history of philosophy, and to map connections and divisions between different philosophical traditions. Alongside the practice of publishing articles on epistemology, metaphysics, philosophy of language, philosophy of logic, and philosophy of mind, they plan to expand to include mainstream topics they believe are currently underrepresented in the journal, such as ethics, political philosophy, and the history of philosophy. For the book review section, the editors made the decision to publish substantive book reviews that "vie with articles in terms of impact and potential for setting agendas," thus shrinking the number included. Despite being somewhat in transition, this remains a core journal for all collections.

3986. *The Monist: an international journal of general philosophical inquiry.* [ISSN: 0026-9662] 1888. q. EUR 106. Ed(s): Fraser MacBride. Oxford University Press, 2001 Evans Rd, Cary, NC 27513; custserv.us@oup.com; https://academic.oup.com/journals. Illus. Refereed. Vol. ends: No. 4. Reprint: PSC. *Indexed:* A01, A22, AmHI, BRI, MLA-IB, P61. *Aud.:* Ac.

The Monist publishes quarterly thematic issues on specific philosophical topics. Topics are broad in scope, and can encompass a range of philosophical questions related to ethics, the history of philosophy, politics, literature, and more. Most recently, topics covered issues related to collective responsibility and social ontology, climate complicity and individual accountability, and Carnap's metaphilosophy. An important journal for all philosophy collections.

3987. *Notre Dame Journal of Formal Logic.* [ISSN: 0029-4527] 1960. q. USD 426. Ed(s): Anand Pillay, Michael Detlefsen. Duke University Press, 905 W Main St, Durham, NC 27701; orders@dukeupress.edu; https://www.dukeupress.edu. Illus., index, adv. Refereed. Vol. ends: No. 4. Reprint: PSC. *Indexed:* A22, MSN. *Aud.:* Ac, Sa.

An important, specialized journal covering philosophical and mathematical logic, including philosophy, history, and foundations of logic and mathematics. Articles are very technical, with substantive formulas that inform the arguments. Contributors are primarily philosophers of logic or mathematicians. For graduate-level collections that support advanced work in logic.

3988. *Nous.* [ISSN: 0029-4624] 1967. q. USD 1046 (print or online ed.) Individuals, USD 152 (print & online eds.)). Ed(s): Ernest Sosa. Wiley-Blackwell Publishing, Inc., 350 Main St, Malden, MA 02148; http://onlinelibrary.wiley.com. Illus., index, adv. Sample. Refereed. Vol. ends: No. 4. Microform: PQC. Reprint: PSC. *Indexed:* A01, A22, AmHI, E01, MSN. *Aud.:* Ac.

This high-quality journal publishes articles on topics in a broad range of philosophical fields, chiefly in metaphysics, epistemology, philosophical logic, philosophy of religion, ethics, and the history of philosophy. Subscribers also receive at no extra cost the annual publications *Philosophical Issues* and *Philosophical Perspectives.* A core journal for philosophy collections.

3989. *Oxford Studies in Ancient Philosophy.* [ISSN: 0265-7651] 1983. irreg. 2-4/yr. Ed(s): Victor Caston. Oxford University Press, Great Clarendon St, Oxford, OX2 6DP, United Kingdom; onlinequeries.uk@oup.com; http://global.oup.com. Illus. Refereed. *Aud.:* Ac.

This journal publishes scholarly articles on ancient Greek and Roman philosophical themes and problems, from its origins up until the middle ages. Each volume typically contains one or more articles related to Plato and Aristotle, while others may focus on individual thinkers or topics concerning Stoicism, Epicureanism, or Neoplatonism. Essays are lengthy and substantive, and quotations in Greek and Latin are provided with English translations. Each volume concludes with an *Index Locorum.* Recent volumes are available on Oxford Scholarship Online.

3990. *Pacific Philosophical Quarterly.* Formerly (until Jan.1980): *Personalist.* [ISSN: 0279-0750] 1920. q. GBP 443. Ed(s): Rima Basu. Wiley-Blackwell Publishing Ltd., The Atrium, Southern Gate, Chichester, PO19 8QG, United Kingdom; cs-journals@wiley.com; http://onlinelibrary.wiley.com. Illus., index, adv. Sample. Refereed. Vol. ends: No. 4. Microform: PQC. Reprint: PSC. *Indexed:* A01, A22, AmHI, E01, MLA-IB. *Aud.:* Ac.

Edited by the faculty of the School of Philosophy, University of Southern California, this journal publishes a mix of articles in areas of analytic philosophy (e.g., philosophy of language, philosophy of mind, metaphysics, epistemology, ethics, philosophy of action, philosophy of law, political philosophy, aesthetics) and in the history of philosophy. Occasional special thematic issues are published. An important analytic philosophy journal for comprehensive contemporary Anglo-American philosophy collections.

3991. *Philosophers' Imprint.* [ISSN: 1533-628X] 2001. q. Free. University of Michigan, Library, 818 Hatcher Graduate Library South, 913 S University Ave, Ann Arbor, MI 48109; http://www.lib.umich.edu/. Refereed. *Aud.:* Ac.

An early participant in the open-access movement, *Philosophers' Imprint* is a peer-reviewed journal published by Michigan Publishing at the University of Michigan, with papers posted on an irregular basis. Although the journal is edited by analytically trained philosophers, articles are not restricted by any field or school and include work in metaphysics, epistemology, ethics, perception, logic, and the history of philosophy. Traditional and contemporary issues are explored. The journal has demonstrated its relevance through its longevity, surviving suspicions about open access, and has shown its value to philosophers and philosophical research. URL: http://www.philosophersimprint.org/

3992. *The Philosophical Forum.* [ISSN: 0031-806X] 1942. q. GBP 417. Ed(s): Alan W Grose, Douglas Lackey. Wiley-Blackwell Publishing, Inc., 350 Main St, Malden, MA 02148; http://onlinelibrary.wiley.com. Illus., index, adv. Sample. Refereed. Vol. ends: No. 4. Reprint: PSC. *Indexed:* A01, A22, AmHI, BRI, E01, MLA-IB, P61. *Aud.:* Ac.

This journal publishes articles on diverse approaches and viewpoints about contemporary philosophers, philosophical inquiry, and discussions that bridge gaps between analytical and Continental scholarship. It is a journal of interest to those curious about looking at philosophical topics and historical figures from perspectives that may be at the fringes or outside of the contemporary mainstream analytic world, especially in the areas of ethics, social and political philosophy, aesthetics, feminist philosophy, and Continental philosophy.

3993. *Philosophical Investigations.* [ISSN: 0190-0536] 1978. q. GBP 535. Ed(s): H O Mounce. Wiley-Blackwell Publishing Ltd., The Atrium, Southern Gate, Chichester, PO19 8QG, United Kingdom; cs-journals@wiley.com; http://onlinelibrary.wiley.com. Illus., index, adv. Sample. Refereed. Vol. ends: No. 4. Reprint: PSC. *Indexed:* A01, A22, AmHI, BRI, E01. *Bk. rev.:* 1-5, 2,000-3,000 words, signed. *Aud.:* Ac.

Named for his work, *Philosophical Investigations* primarily publishes critical studies related to the philosopher Ludwig Wittgenstein, and, at times, selections from his unpublished writings and lectures. Although he is the principal focus, articles on a range of topics in contemporary analytic philosophy are also published. Good for collections that support work in twentieth-century analytic philosophy and Wittgenstein scholars.

3994. *Philosophical Practice.* [ISSN: 1742-8173] 2005. 3x/yr. USD 180 (Individuals, USD 72; Members, USD 36). Ed(s): Lou Marinoff. American Philosophical Practitioners Association, The City College of New York, 160 Convent Ave, New York, NY 10031; admin@appa.edu; http://www.appa.edu/. Index, adv. Sample. Refereed. Reprint: PSC. *Indexed:* A01, A22, E01. *Bk. rev.:* 2-4, 1,000-1,500 words, signed. *Aud.:* Ac, Sa.

Published by the American Philosophical Practitioners Association, this journal offers theoretical, empirical, and review articles on the professional, ethical, legal, sociological, and political aspects of philosophical practice in the areas of client counseling, group facilitation, and organizational consulting. The work being done in this area may be of interest to philosophers, and practitioners in counseling and human services fields. Each issue includes book reviews.

3995. *The Philosophical Quarterly.* [ISSN: 0031-8094] 1950. q. GBP 343. Ed(s): Sarah Broadie. Oxford University Press, Great Clarendon St, Oxford, OX2 6DP, United Kingdom; onlinequeries.uk@oup.com; https://academic.oup.com/journals. Illus., index, adv. Sample. Refereed. Microform: PQC. Reprint: PSC. *Indexed:* A01, A22, AmHI, BRI, E01, MLA-IB. *Bk. rev.:* 10-20, 1,000-2,000 words, signed. *Aud.:* Ac.

This British journal, sponsored by the Scots Philosophical Club and the University of St. Andrews, is a superior journal in the analytic tradition, publishing articles primarily on subjects related to metaphysics, epistemology, ethics, philosophy of language, and philosophy of logic. Topics range widely, from traditional to contemporary matters. Each issue offers book reviews, and discussions are published occasionally.

3996. *Philosophical Review.* [ISSN: 0031-8108] 1892. q. USD 264. Ed(s): Michelle Kosch, Nicholas Silins. Duke University Press, 905 W Main St, Durham, NC 27701; orders@dukeupress.edu; https://www.dukeupress.edu. Illus., index, adv. Refereed. Vol. ends: No. 4. Reprint: PSC. *Indexed:* A01, A22, AmHI, BAS, BRI, CBRI, MLA-IB. *Bk. rev.:* 4-6, 1,000-2,500 words, signed. *Aud.:* Ac.

Established in 1892, this prestigious American academic philosophy journal publishes articles in all areas of philosophy, with an emphasis on metaphysics, epistemology, philosophy of mind, ethics, the history of philosophy, and other areas of contemporary philosophical interest. It offers high-quality articles, and, in the postwar era, published essays now considered classics, such as those by Quine, Nagel, and Rawls. Includes book reviews. A core journal for all collections.

3997. *Philosophical Studies: an international journal for philosophy in the analytic tradition.* [ISSN: 0031-8116] 1950. m. EUR 3404 (print & online eds.)). Ed(s): Stewart Cohen. Springer Netherlands, Van Godewijckstraat 30, Dordrecht, 3311 GX, Netherlands; http://www.springer.com. Illus., index, adv. Sample. Refereed. Vol. ends: No. 3. Microform: PQC. Reprint: PSC. *Indexed:* A01, A22, AmHI, BRI, E01, MLA-IB, MSN. *Aud.:* Ac.

Philosophical Studies was founded in 1950 by Herbert Feigl and Wilfrid Sellars, and is one of the leading journals for analytic philosophy. The journal publishes original works in analytic philosophy on traditional problems analyzed from new perspectives and on contemporary issues, particularly in the areas of metaphysics, epistemology, philosophy of mind, philosophical logic, philosophy of science, action theory, and ethics. Each volume contains several special issues, some devoted to specific topics and others selected papers from the American Philosophical Association's annual Pacific Division meetings, the Bellingham Summer Philosophy Conference, and the Oberlin Colloquium in Philosophy. The journal also offers regular symposia on recently published books. In spite of its cost, it is a core journal for philosophy collections.

3998. *Philosophical Topics.* Formerly (until 1981): *Southwestern Journal of Philosophy.* [ISSN: 0276-2080] 1970. s-a. USD 70 (Individuals, USD 35). Ed(s): Jack Lyons, Edward Minar. University of Arkansas Press, 105 N McIlroy Ave, Fayetteville, AR 72701; http://www.uapress.com. Illus., adv. Refereed. Vol. ends: No. 2. *Indexed:* A22, MLA-IB. *Aud.:* Ac.

Each issue of *Philosophical Topics* is a special issue, in which exclusively invited articles, many by leading scholars on an international level, are published on a specific topic, philosopher, or historical period. The Department of Philosophy at the University of Arkansas has oversight of the publication. Recent topics include "Can Beliefs Be Wrong," "Philosophy of Language," "Epistemology and Cognition," and "New Directions in the Philosophy of Perception."

3999. *Philosophy.* Formerly (until 1931): *Journal of Philosophical Studies.* [ISSN: 0031-8191] 1926. q. plus two supplements. GBP 356 (print & online eds.)). Ed(s): Anthony O'Hear. Cambridge University Press, University Printing House, Shaftesbury Rd, Cambridge, CB2 8BS, United Kingdom; journals@cambridge.org; https://www.cambridge.org/. Illus., index, adv. Refereed. Circ: 2000. Vol. ends: No. 4. Microform: PQC. Reprint: PSC. *Indexed:* A01, A22, AmHI, BAS, BRI, E01, MLA-IB. *Bk. rev.:* 4-6, 1,000-2,500 words, signed. *Aud.:* Ac.

The official journal of the Royal Institute of Philosophy, its focus and contributors are, for the most part, British. This publication offers articles on all branches of philosophy, but with the aim of providing an academic platform that meets the needs of philosophers and the philosophical interests of specialists in other fields (law, medicine, humanities, social sciences) and of non-specialists in the wider educated public. Therefore, authors are required "to avoid needless technicality of language and presentation." Each issue also presents an editorial on a topic of philosophical or public interest, book reviews, and book notes. The April issue offers the winner and commended essays of the *Philosophy* prize essay competition. A core journal.

4000. *Philosophy and Literature.* [ISSN: 0190-0013] 1976. s-a. USD 140. Ed(s): Cynthia Werthamer, Garry L Hagberg. The Johns Hopkins University Press, 2715 N Charles St, Baltimore, MD 21218; http://www.press.jhu.edu. Illus., index, adv. Sample. Refereed. Vol. ends: No. 2. Reprint: PSC. *Indexed:* A01, A22, AmHI, BRI, CBRI, E01, MLA-IB. *Bk. rev.:* 2-4, 750-1,500 words, signed. *Aud.:* Ac.

Sponsored by Bard College, this interdisciplinary journal is a forum for discussions that explore intersections between philosophy and literature in British, American, and Continental literature, including literary aesthetics, theory of criticism, philosophical interpretations of literature, and literary treatment of philosophy. Issues also contain shorter papers in the "Notes and Fragments" section, and occasionally symposia are included. Recommended for both literature and philosophy collections.

4001. *Philosophy and Phenomenological Research.* [ISSN: 0031-8205] 1940. bi-m. Ed(s): Ernest Sosa. Wiley-Blackwell Publishing, Inc., 111 River St, Hoboken, NJ 07030; http://onlinelibrary.wiley.com. Illus., adv. Sample. Refereed. Reprint: PSC. *Indexed:* A01, A22, AmHI, BRI, E01, MLA-IB. *Aud.:* Ac.

Philosophy and Phenomenological Research publishes articles with no specific methodology or philosophical orientation required. Although it originated as the publication of the International Phenomenological Society, articles on a broad range of subjects are offered. Emphasis is on metaphysics, epistemology, philosophy of mind, ethics, and issues in the history of philosophy, when relevant to contemporary problems. Symposia, frequently focusing on recent books, are a regular feature. A core journal for philosophy collections.

4002. *Philosophy and Public Affairs.* [ISSN: 0048-3915] 1971. q. GBP 205. Ed(s): Meaghan McDonnell, Debra Satz. Wiley-Blackwell Publishing, Inc., 350 Main St, Malden, MA 02148; http://onlinelibrary.wiley.com. Illus., index, adv. Sample. Refereed. Microform: PQC. Reprint: PSC. *Indexed:* A22, AmHI, BRI, CJPI, E01, IBSS, P61, SSA. *Aud.:* Ac.

This journal publishes roughly a dozen high-quality articles a year that investigate the philosophical dimensions of public concerns in the areas of contemporary ethical, political, social, legal, and public policy. Authors either interrogate broad concepts such as privacy, republicanism, colonialism, and altruism, or focus on specific sociopolitical issues such as campaign finance reform, homelessness, war, and experimental animals. An important journal for philosophy, law, and political science collections.

4003. ***Philosophy and Rhetoric.*** [ISSN: 0031-8213] 1968. q. USD 240 (print & online eds.)). Ed(s): Erik Doxtader. Pennsylvania State University Press, 820 N University Dr, University Support Bldg 1, Ste C, University Park, PA 16802; info@psupress.org; http://www.psupress.org. Illus., index, adv. Refereed. Reprint: PSC. *Indexed:* A22, AmHI, E01, MLA-IB. *Bk. rev.:* 1-3, 1,500-2,500 words, signed. *Aud.:* Ac.

Articles in *Philosophy and Rhetoric* explore the relationship between the two disciplines through topics such as: connections between logic and rhetoric; the philosophical aspects of argumentation and argumentation in philosophy itself; rhetorical views held by historical philosophic figures and during historical eras; psychological and sociological philosophical studies of rhetoric; and philosophical analyses between rhetoric and other areas of human culture and thought, political theory, and law. The fourth issue is a special issue dedicated to a topic. Book reviews are published irregularly. Recommended for philosophy, rhetoric, and many social sciences collections.

4004. ***Philosophy & Social Criticism: an international, interdisciplinary journal.*** Formerly (until 1978): *Cultural Hermeneutics.* [ISSN: 0191-4537] 1973. 9x/yr. USD 3467 (print & online eds.)). Ed(s): David Rasmussen. Sage Publications Ltd., 1 Oliver's Yard, 55 City Rd, London, EC1Y 1SP, United Kingdom; market@sagepub.com; https://www.sagepub.com/. Illus., index, adv. Sample. Refereed. Vol. ends: No. 6. Reprint: PSC. *Indexed:* A01, A22, E01, IBSS, MLA-IB, P61, SSA. *Aud.:* Ac.

This interdisciplinary journal publishes research that critiques contemporary societies—in terms of political philosophy, neoliberalism, social theory, critical theory, ethics, feminism, aesthetics, modernity, and more—from a Continental perspective, and generally with a political slant. Recent special issues focus on toleration, exemplarity and normativity, a tribute to Charles Taylor, and populist upsurge and the decline of diversity capital. Those interested in the works of Adorno, Arendt, Derrida, Habermas, Foucault, and others, will find this publication valuable.

4005. ***Philosophy East and West: a quarterly of comparative philosophy.*** [ISSN: 0031-8221] 1951. q. USD 160 (Individuals, USD 50). Ed(s): Franklin Perkins. University of Hawai'i Press, 2840 Kolowalu St, Honolulu, HI 96822; uhpjourn@hawaii.edu; http://www.uhpress.hawaii.edu. Illus., index, adv. Sample. Refereed. Vol. ends: No. 4. Microform: PQC. *Indexed:* A01, A22, AmHI, BAS, BRI, E01, IBSS, MLA-IB, R&TA. *Bk. rev.:* 8-12, 1,000-2,500 words, signed. *Aud.:* Ac.

This journal aims to increase knowledge about non-Western traditions of philosophy by publishing studies that focus on specifics of Asian philosophies, as well as intercultural articles that compare philosophical traditions of the East and West that reveal the relevance of philosophy for the art, literature, science, and social practice of Asian civilizations. The general scope of this publication is broader than that of the *Journal of Indian Philosophy* (above in this section). This journal will benefit both philosophy and Asian Studies collections.

4006. ***Philosophy Now: a magazine of ideas.*** [ISSN: 0961-5970] 1991. 6x/yr. USD 55. Ed(s): Rick Lewis. Philosophy Documentation Center, . Illus., adv. *Indexed:* AmHI. *Bk. rev.:* 3-5, 750-1,500 words, signed. *Aud.:* Ga.

Philosophy Now is the only non-academic, non-peer-reviewed publication in this chapter. This popular British periodical aims to make philosophy more accessible to the educated layperson. Engaging articles, without jargon or footnotes but generally accompanied by photographs, cartoons, or caricatures, address contemporary social, political, scientific, and medical problems and issues from philosophical perspectives, such as free will, new realism, human rights, and bioethics. In addition, philosophical traditions are examined for contemporary relevance, such as existentialism and metaphysics. *Philosophy Now* is best for public libraries where *The Humanist, Skeptical Inquirer*, and related publications are popular. It will also be of interest for libraries that offer collections that engage their communities with philosophical conversations at all levels.

4007. ***Philosophy of Science.*** Incorporates (1970-1994): *P S A.* [ISSN: 0031-8248] 1934. 5x/yr. USD 352. Ed(s): Andrea Woody. University of Chicago Press, 1427 E 60th St, Chicago, IL 60637; subscriptions@press.uchicago.edu; http://www.journals.uchicago.edu. Illus., index, adv. Sample. Refereed. Vol. ends: Dec. Reprint: PSC. *Indexed:* A01, A22, AmHI, BRI, IBSS, MLA-IB, MSN. *Bk. rev.:* 2-4, 2,000-3,000 words, signed. *Aud.:* Ac.

The official journal of the Philosophy of Science Association, this publication offers articles that are concerned with fundamental issues in the philosophy of science, such as: the logic of deductive, nomological, and statistical explanations; the nature of scientific laws and theories; and scientific methods involving observation, evidence, confirmation, induction, probability, and causality. Contributors also analyze philosophic issues that emerge from the physical, biological, cognitive, and social sciences, as well as mathematics, on topics that range from time reversal myths to human genetics to evolutionary psychology and racism to manipulative behavior. The December issue contains the contributed or symposia papers of the biennial meetings of the Philosophy of Science Association. A core journal for all academic libraries.

4008. ***Philosophy of the Social Sciences.*** [ISSN: 0048-3931] 1971. 6x/yr. USD 1098 (print & online eds.)). Ed(s): Ian C Jarvie. Sage Publications, Inc., 2455 Teller Rd, Thousand Oaks, CA 91320; info@sagepub.com; http://www.sagepub.com. Illus., index, adv. Sample. Refereed. Vol. ends: No. 4. Reprint: PSC. *Indexed:* A01, A22, BRI, C37, E01, IBSS, P61, SSA. *Bk. rev.:* 1-2, 1,000-5,000 words, signed. *Aud.:* Ac.

This international, interdisciplinary journal publishes articles, discussions, review essays, and book reviews related to the philosophical foundations across the social sciences, reflecting current research, theory, and debate. The journal solicits articles that offer analysis of issues concerned with general methodology (explaining, theorizing, testing), the application of philosophy (individualism over holism preferred), the nature of rationality, and the history of theories and concepts. The journal includes the *Roundtable on Philosophy of the Social Sciences* as an annual special issue. Important for philosophers and social scientists, especially economists, linguists, political scientists, psychologists, and sociologists.

4009. ***Philosophy, Psychiatry & Psychology.*** [ISSN: 1071-6076] 1994. q. USD 220. Ed(s): John Z Sadler, Sebastien Arviset. The Johns Hopkins University Press, 2715 N Charles St, Baltimore, MD 21218; http://www.press.jhu.edu. Illus., adv. Sample. Refereed. Vol. ends: No. 4. Reprint: PSC. *Indexed:* A01, A22, CJPI, E01. *Aud.:* Ac.

The official journal of the Association for the Advancement of Philosophy and Psychiatry and cosponsored in conjunction with the Royal College of Psychiatrists Philosophy Group, *Philosophy, Psychiatry & Psychology* focuses on topics on philosophical issues concerned with psychiatry and abnormal psychology, as well as philosophical problems in clinical theory and methodology related to metaphysics, epistemology, and ethics. Special issues offer articles on "target" topics (currently important clinical or research topics), most recently on diagnosis and practice, schizophrenia psychopathology, and philosophy and psychoanalysis, which are followed by commentaries and responses. Although contributors are largely from psychiatry and psychology, they are also from many other disciplines, including medicine, neuroscience, literary studies, philosophy, ethics, and religion. The journal also regularly features a "Concurrent Contents" section listing recent publications and an "International News and Notes" section.

4010. ***Philosophy Today: an international journal of contemporary philosophy.*** [ISSN: 0031-8256] 1957. q. USD 65. Ed(s): Peg Birmingham. Philosophy Documentation Center, order@pdcnet.org; http://www.pdcnet.org. Illus., adv. Refereed. Vol. ends: No. 4. Microform: PQC. Reprint: PSC. *Indexed:* A01, A22, AmHI, BRI, C26, MLA-IB. *Aud.:* Ac.

This journal, under the auspices of DePaul University's Department of Philosophy, publishes articles on current interdisciplinary topics from a Continental philosophical perspective and frequently on phenomenology and existentialism, where philosophy, political theory, comparative literature, and cultural studies overlap. Important for Continental philosophy and theology collections.

4011. ***Phronesis: a journal for ancient philosophy.*** [ISSN: 0031-8868] 1955. q. EUR 463. Ed(s): Ursula Coope, George Boys-Stones. Brill, PO Box 9000, Leiden, 2300 PA, Netherlands; marketing@brill.com; https://brill.com. Illus., adv. Refereed. Reprint: PSC. *Indexed:* A01, A22, AmHI, E01. *Bk. rev.:* 1-2, 3,000-6,000 words, signed. *Aud.:* Ac.

The journal specializes in the study of ancient Greek and Roman thought from its origins to the end of the sixth century A.D., including ancient philosophy, metaphysics, epistemology, logic, and philosophy of science and medicine. Although most contributors offer critical analysis of Aristotle and Plato's texts that provide new insights or revisit neglected issues, others cover broader historical approaches, or are concerned with earlier or later philosophers, texts, or movements. Articles are primarily in English. An important addition for collections that support classical studies and ancient philosophy, and for general comprehensive collections.

4012. ***Ratio: an international journal of analytic philosophy.*** [ISSN: 0034-0006] 1958. q. GBP 698. Ed(s): David S Oderberg. Wiley-Blackwell Publishing Ltd., The Atrium, Southern Gate, Chichester, PO19 8QG, United Kingdom; cs-journals@wiley.com; http://onlinelibrary.wiley.com. Illus., adv. Sample. Refereed. Vol. ends: No. 4. Reprint: PSC. *Indexed:* A01, A22, AmHI, BRI, E01, MLA-IB. *Bk. rev.:* 1-2, 1,000-2,500 words, signed. *Aud.:* Ac.

As indicated by its subtitle, articles are primarily in the analytic tradition, although others are welcome. Articles analyze contemporary issues in metaphysics, epistemology, philosophical logic, and ethics. The core of the special issue published in December consists of papers given at the one-day conference organized by the Philosophy Department at the University of Reading, most recently on mind and language, experimental philosophy, and indeterminacy in ethics. An important journal for general collections and philosophy collections.

4013. ***The Review of Metaphysics.*** [ISSN: 0034-6632] 1947. q. Ed(s): John C McCarthy. Philosophy Education Society, Inc., 223 Aquinas Hall, Catholic University of America, Washington, DC 20064; mail@reviewofmetaphysics.com; http://www.reviewofmetaphysics.org. Illus., index, adv. Refereed. Vol. ends: No. 4. Microform: PQC. *Indexed:* A01, A22, AmHI, BRI, CBRI, MLA-IB. *Bk. rev.:* 15-20, 500-1,000 words, signed. *Aud.:* Ac.

Articles primarily focus on issues in metaphysics, philosophy of mind, phenomenology and existentialism, ethics, and the history of philosophy, although they also investigate the history and philosophy of science, philosophy of religion, hermeneutics, aesthetics, epistemology, and political philosophy. Each issue contains book reviews, as well as abstracts from articles written in other philosophy journals—a charming holdover in this day of RSS feeds and tables of contents email delivery, yet a convenient way for subscribers to keep up with current scholarship.

4014. ***Review of Philosophy and Psychology.*** [ISSN: 1878-5158] 2010. q. Ed(s): Paul Egre. Springer Netherlands, Van Godewijckstraat 30, Dordrecht, 3311 GX, Netherlands; http://www.springer.com. Refereed. Reprint: PSC. *Aud.:* Ac.

Hosted by the Institut Jean Nicod, a research center of the French Centre National de la Recherche Scientifique, this interdisciplinary journal is a forum for philosophical and scientific discussions of the mind. It publishes empirical studies that explore topics related to the mind, such as consciousness, mental illness, thought, language, perception, memory, and the like, at the borders of philosophy, psychology, and cognitive science, including neural, behavioral, and social sciences. Recent themed special issues examined topics such as current approaches to teaching as a cognitive ability, key topics in philosophy of language and mind, and consciousness and inner awareness.

4015. ***Review of Symbolic Logic.*** [ISSN: 1755-0203] 2008. q. GBP 740. Ed(s): Andrew Arana. Cambridge University Press, University Printing House, Shaftesbury Rd, Cambridge, CB2 8BS, United Kingdom; journals@cambridge.org; https://www.cambridge.org/. Adv. Refereed. Reprint: PSC. *Indexed:* A01, A22, E01, MSN. *Aud.:* Ac, Sa.

An interdisciplinary journal that promotes research that engages with logic, philosophy, and the sciences. Articles, for example, address topics within the general study of logical systems (non-classic and algebraic), philosophical logic and formal epistemology (including how these relate to decision theory and game theory), the history of philosophy of logic and mathematics, and applications of logic in such areas as computer science, cognitive science, and linguistics. Along with *The Journal of Symbolic Logic* (above in this section), this is another important journal sponsored by the Association for Symbolic Logic. For collections that support advanced work in logic.

4016. ***Social Epistemology: a journal of knowledge, culture and policy.*** [ISSN: 0269-1728] 1987. q. GBP 986 (print & online eds.)). Ed(s): James H Collier. Routledge, 4 Park Sq, Milton Park, Abingdon, OX14 4RN, United Kingdom; subscriptions@tandf.co.uk; http://www.tandfonline.com. Illus., index, adv. Sample. Refereed. Vol. ends: No. 4. Reprint: PSC. *Indexed:* A01, A22, E01, IBSS, MLA-IB, P61, SSA. *Aud.:* Ac.

A collaboration between the Society for Social Studies of Science and the European Association for the Study of Science and Technology, *Social Epistemology* is concerned with philosophical and social scientific investigations into the production, assessment, and validation of knowledge. The journal publishes both empirical studies on the origins and transmission of knowledge and the risk analysis when such research is implemented. Exchanges discussing articles are posted on *Social Epistemology Review and Reply Collective* at https://social-epistemology.com. A good choice for philosophy and social science collections.

4017. ***Social Philosophy and Policy.*** [ISSN: 0265-0525] 1983. s-a. GBP 250. Ed(s): David Schmidtz. Cambridge University Press, University Printing House, Shaftesbury Rd, Cambridge, CB2 8BS, United Kingdom; journals@cambridge.org; https://www.cambridge.org/. Illus., adv. Refereed. Circ: 1000. Vol. ends: No. 2. Reprint: PSC. *Indexed:* A22, E01, IBSS, P61, SSA. *Aud.:* Ac.

An interdisciplinary journal that focuses on the philosophical foundations of contemporary social policy debates, each issue offers articles related to a single theme. Contributors representing a diversity of viewpoints are from many disciplines, especially philosophy, economics, political science, and law. While articles are primarily theoretical, each issue does include articles that connect theory with practice. Recent topics include corruption; norms; progress; and philosophy, politics, and economics.

4018. ***The Southern Journal of Philosophy.*** [ISSN: 0038-4283] 1963. q. GBP 239 (print & online eds.)). Ed(s): Stephan Blatti. John Wiley & Sons, Inc., 111 River St, Hoboken, NJ 07030; cs-journals@wiley.com; http://onlinelibrary.wiley.com. Illus. Refereed. Vol. ends: No. 4. Microform: PQC. Reprint: PSC. *Indexed:* A01, A22, AmHI, E01, MLA-IB. *Aud.:* Ac.

This solid journal, committed to philosophical pluralism, publishes articles from the analytic and Continental traditions as well as from the history of philosophy. In 2018 "The State of the Question" was re-introduced as a new series, offering a snapshot of the literature on a specific topic or figure in each issue, with the first article focused on the study of Plato. Authors of these articles will critically review the literature over the past two decades, and evaluate where trends in research are heading and where they should be heading. A supplementary issue, the Spindel Supplement, features the invited papers and commentaries presented at the annual Spindel Conference. A core journal.

4019. ***Studia Logica: an international journal for symbolic logic.*** [ISSN: 0039-3215] 1953. 6x/yr. EUR 1814 (print & online eds.)). Ed(s): Jacek Malinowski. Springer Netherlands, Van Godewijckstraat 30, Dordrecht, 3311 GX, Netherlands; http://www.springer.com. Illus., index, adv. Sample. Refereed. Vol. ends: No. 3. Microform: PQC. Reprint: PSC. *Indexed:* A22, BRI, E01, MLA-IB, MSN. *Bk. rev.:* 1-2, 1,000-2,000 words, signed. *Aud.:* Sa.

An English-language journal that publishes articles on technical issues in symbolic and philosophical logic that employ methods of contemporary formal logic, such as those of algebra, model theory, proof theory, and others. It is most interested in topics in general logic and applications of logic to other branches of knowledge, such as philosophy, the methodology of science, or linguistics. Book reviews are occasionally included. Important for graduate-level collections.

Studies in History and Philosophy of Modern Physics. See *Studies in History and Philosophy of Science Part B: Studies in History and Philosophy of Modern Physics* in the Physics section.

4020. ***Studies in History and Philosophy of Science Part A.*** [ISSN: 0039-3681] 1970. bi-m. q. until 2015. EUR 1159. Ed(s): Anjan Chakravartty. Pergamon Press, The Blvd, Langford Ln, E Park, Kidlington, OX5 1GB, United Kingdom; JournalsCustomerServiceEMEA@elsevier.com; http://www.elsevier.com. Illus., adv. Sample. Refereed. Microform: PQC. *Indexed:* A01, A22, AmHI, BRI, IBSS, MLA-IB. *Bk. rev.:* Occasional. *Aud.:* Ac.

The editors aim to publish articles that are international in scope and that address the history, philosophy, and sociology of the sciences, including scientific issues related to gender, culture, society, and the arts. International contributors, primarily from philosophy, history, and the history of science, focus on individual philosophers or scientists across history, or on philosophical issues and concerns in the history of science. Special issues, discussions, and book reviews are published on an irregular basis. A high-quality journal for collections that emphasize the history and philosophy of science.

4021. ***Synthese: an international journal for epistemology, methodology and philosophy of science.*** [ISSN: 0039-7857] 1936. m. EUR 4420 (print & online eds.)). Ed(s): Otavio Bueno, Catarina D Novaes. Springer Netherlands, Van Godewijckstraat 30, Dordrecht, 3311 GX, Netherlands; http://www.springer.com. Illus., index, adv. Sample. Refereed. Vol. ends: No. 3. Microform: PQC. Reprint: PSC. *Indexed:* A22, AmHI, E01, MLA-IB, MSN. *Aud.:* Ac, Sa.

Synthese has long been a top-tier analytic philosophy journal, focusing on contemporary issues in epistemology, methodology, and philosophy of science; the foundations of logic and mathematics; formal methods of philosophy (including those connecting it to other fields); and ethical and historical logical, mathematical, and scientific issues that have contemporary relevance. Contributors include philosophers, mathematicians, scientists, and economists, among others. There are several special issues a year, including an irregular issue dedicated to "Neuroscience and Its Philosophy" that continues the scholarly tradition of the ceased Kluwer journal *Brain and Mind*. *Synthese* is a highly technical and very costly journal; nonetheless, given its prominence and quality, it is recommended for graduate-level collections.

4022. ***Theory and Decision: an international journal for multidisciplinary advances in decision sciences.*** [ISSN: 0040-5833] 1970. 8x/yr. EUR 1176 (print & online eds.)). Ed(s): Mohammed Abdellaoui. Springer New York LLC, 233 Spring St, New York, NY 10013; customerservice@springer.com; http://www.springer.com. Illus., index, adv. Sample. Refereed. Vol. ends: No. 4. Microform: PQC. Reprint: PSC. *Indexed:* A22, BRI, E01, EconLit, IBSS, MSN, P61, SSA. *Aud.:* Ac, Sa.

This interdisciplinary journal publishes highly technical research on all aspects of decision making, including models (mathematical and computer science; preference and uncertainty modeling); social science philosophies and methodologies; types of decision making and choices (multicriteria, social, negotiation, group); and processes (rationality, cognitive, and interactive). The journal attracts international contributors from, and has relevance for, the fields of psychology, management science, economics, game theory, statistics and operations management, artificial intelligence, cognitive science, and analytic philosophy. For graduate-level collections.

4023. ***Utilitas.*** Formed by the merger of (1978-1988): *Bentham Newsletter;* (1965-1988): *Mill News Letter.* [ISSN: 0953-8208] 1989. q. GBP 334. Ed(s): Dale E Miller. Cambridge University Press, University Printing House, Shaftesbury Rd, Cambridge, CB2 8BS, United Kingdom; journals@cambridge.org; https://www.cambridge.org/. Illus., adv. Sample. Refereed. Vol. ends: No. 3. Reprint: PSC. *Indexed:* A01, A22, AmHI, E01, IBSS. *Bk. rev.:* 1-2, 1,500-2,000 words, signed. *Aud.:* Ac.

The journal for the International Society for Utilitarian Studies, which originated as newsletters devoted to Bentham and Mill, now goes beyond those two important advocates and publishes articles in all areas where utilitarian, or more generally consequentialist, thought has made contributions, including its historical development and its detractors, and contemporary utilitarian ideas in philosophy, ethics, intellectual history, politics, economics, law, public policy, and literature. Book reviews and debates on topics or philosophers are published irregularly. An important addition for collections that focus on historical and contemporary ethics, political philosophy, and intellectual history.

■ PHOTOGRAPHY

Berlin Loa, Museum/Archives Technician; berlinloa@gmail.com

Introduction

The periodicals selected here are considered basic to any library collection and include those targeted to general audiences, as well as those targeted to more experienced photographers.

Basic Periodicals

Hs: *Popular Photography;* Ga: *Afterimage, Aperture, Popular Photography, Shutterbug;* Ac: *Aperture, Popular Photography.*

Basic Abstracts and Indexes

Academic Search Premier, Reader's Guide to Periodical Literature.

4024. ***Afterimage (Online).*** [ISSN: 2578-8531] q. Free. Ed(s): Karen vanMeenen. University of California Press, Journals Division, 155 Grand Avenue, Ste 400, Oakland, CA 94612-3764; customerservice@ucpressjournals.com; http://www.ucpress.edu. Refereed. *Bk. rev.:* 2-3, 1,500 words. *Aud.:* Hs, Ga, Ac.

Afterimage is a full-color journal that contains articles, book and film reviews, exhibit reviews, and cultural features that cover photography as well as multimedia arts. Issues also include notices regarding exhibits, screenings, events, jobs, and opportunities for freelance work. The web site contains highlights from current issues and a searchable "article archive." Recommended for academic as well as public libraries.

4025. ***Aperture (New York).*** [ISSN: 0003-6420] 1952. q. USD 75 combined subscription domestic (print & online eds.); USD 95 combined subscription Canada (print & online eds.); USD 105 combined subscription elsewhere (print & online eds.)). Ed(s): Brendan Wattenberg, Michael Famighetti. Aperture Foundation, Inc., 547 W 27th St, 4th Fl, New York, NY 10001; http://www.aperture.org. Illus., adv. Microform: PQC. *Indexed:* A06, A22, A51, AmHI, BRI. *Aud.:* Hs, Ga, Ac.

Aperture is a full-color publication developed by renowned photographers and writers under the auspices of the Aperture nonprofit foundation for photography. Contents include articles, scholarly essays, exhibit reviews, artist profiles, advertisements, and an extensive display of photography from a wide range of international contributors. The web site offers an index of the current issue, as well as feature images. Back issues are available for purchase directly from the web site. Recommended for academic and public libraries.

4026. ***Black & White.*** Formerly (until 2012): *B & W + Color;* Which was formed by the merger of (1999-2011): *B & W;* (2009-2011): *Color.* [ISSN: 2168-6688] 2011. bi-m. USD 35 domestic; USD 50 Canada; USD 60 elsewhere. Ross Periodicals, Inc., PO Box 1529, Ross, CA 94957; rosspub@pacbell.net. Adv. Sample. *Bk. rev.:* Number and length vary. *Aud.:* Ga, Ac, Sa.

Black & White + Color is the journal for those with experience or a developed interest in black-and-white photography. Issues contain essays, feature articles, and book reviews. The magazine is known for its extensive display of photographic works submitted by professional and amateur artists in both traditional and digital formats. Special color issues are published periodically.

Fee-based back issues and no-fee sample issues are available on the web site. A limited selection of full-text articles are also available on the web site, from back issues. Recommended primarily for academic and public libraries, the journal is also appropriate for school libraries with an arts or humanities focus.

4027. ***European Photography.*** [ISSN: 0172-7028] 1980. s-a. EUR 72 for 2 yrs. in Europe; EUR 92 for 2 yrs. elsewhere. Ed(s): Andreas Mueller-Pohle. European Photography, Postfach 080227, Berlin, 10002, Germany; http://equivalence.com. Illus., index, adv. Vol. ends: Fall. *Indexed:* A51. *Aud.:* Ga, Ac, Sa.

This international magazine features contemporary digital and traditional photography and visual media. The journal is published bilingually in English/German, and offers in-depth articles, artist profiles, book and exhibit reviews, and technical equipment articles from throughout Europe. Recommended for academic libraries. *European Photography* also publishes the *European Photography Guide*, a sourcebook for photographers, journalists, curators, and collectors who are interested in European photography and visual artists.

4028. ***Exposure (Cleveland).*** [ISSN: 0098-8863] 1963. s-a. USD 35 Free to members; (Non-members, USD 15). Ed(s): Stacey McCarroll Cutshaw. Society for Photographic Education, 2530 Superior Ave, #403, Cleveland, OH 44114; membership@spenational.org; http://www.spenational.org/. Illus., adv. Refereed. *Indexed:* A22, A51. *Bk. rev.:* Number and length vary. *Aud.:* Ac, Sa.

The Society for Photographic Education has published *Exposure* since 1973. The journal is published biannually and includes content on traditional and digital photography as well as related visual media. Issues include scholarly articles, essays, interviews, reviews, and images from a range of contributors that include photographers, writers, critics, students, and educators. *Exposure* seeks to highlight the work of photographers and artists working in visual media. Recommended primarily for academic libraries.

4029. ***Nueva Luz: photographic journal.*** Incorporates (in 1997): *Critical Mass.* [ISSN: 0887-5855] 1984. 3x/yr. En Foco, Inc, 1738 Hone Ave, Bronx, NY 10461; info@enfoco.org; http://www.enfoco.org. Illus., adv. *Aud.:* Ems, Hs, Ga, Ac, Sa.

Nueva Luz is an award-winning journal published by En Foco, Inc., a nonprofit group dedicated to cultural diversity in the photographic arts. The journal is bilingual (English/Spanish), and features specifically Latino, African, Asian, Pacific Islander, and Native American artists, but it is open to all ethnicities. Issues include artist portfolios, photographic essays, commentary, interviews, and minimal advertising. It also contains notifications regarding grants, exhibits, and awards. Photo features are professionally selected and high-quality, and beautifully represent multicultural American experiences. Highly recommended for any library collection.

4030. ***Outdoor Photographer: scenic, wildlife, travel, sports.*** [ISSN: 0890-5304] 1985. 11x/yr. USD 15.97 domestic; USD 25.97 Canada; USD 30.97 elsewhere. Madavor Media, Llc., 25 Braintree Hill Office Park, Ste 404, Braintree, MA 02184; customerservice@madavor.com; http://www.madavor.com. Illus., adv. Sample. *Aud.:* Ga.

Outdoor Photographer content is targeted to the outdoor photography enthusiast. Issues include articles, essays, and tips for the travel, sports, plant, and wildlife photographer. Features include product reviews, site tips and recommendations, profiles, and news primarily related to digital photography techniques and equipment. The web site offers limited access to articles, a blog, and multiple links to additional sources. Recommended for public libraries.

4031. ***Photo District News.*** Supersedes in part (in 198?): *Photo District News;* Which was formerly: *New York Photo District News.* [ISSN: 1045-8158] 1980. m. USD 65 combined subscription domestic (print & online eds.); USD 105 combined subscription Canada (print & online eds.); USD 125 combined subscription elsewhere (print & online eds.)). Ed(s): Holly Hughes. Nielsen Business Publications, 770 Broadway, New York, NY 10003; ContactCommunications@nielsen.com; http://www.nielsenbusinessmedia.com. *Indexed:* A22, BRI. *Bk. rev.:* Number and length vary. *Aud.:* Ac, Sa.

Photo District News contains product reviews, industry news, interviews, artist portfolios, an events calendar, and essays. Issues are often theme-based and include industry-related content specific to professionals such as intellectual property rights, photography markets, and digital manipulation; there are also reviews of both digital and analog equipment and techniques. The web site offers access to selected feature articles, links to popular photography blogs, and links to additional resources for professional and new photographers. Recommended for academic and public libraries.

4032. ***Popular Photography: the image of today.*** Former titles (until 2008): *Popular Photography & Imaging;* (until 2003): *Popular Photography;* (until 1955): *Photography;* Popular Photography was incorporated (1949-1989): *Modern Photography;* Which was formerly (until 1950): *Minicam Photography;* (until 1941): *Minicam.* [ISSN: 1944-0510] 1937. m. USD 14 domestic; USD 22 foreign. Bonnier Corp., 2 Park Ave, 9th Fl, New York, NY 10016; http://www.bonniercorp.com. Illus., index, adv. Sample. Circ: 457132 Paid. Vol. ends: Dec. *Indexed:* A&ATA, A01, A22, BRI, C37, CBRI, MASUSE. *Bk. rev.:* Number and length vary. *Aud.:* Hs, Ga, Ac, Sa.

Popular Photography is widely known and popular with photographers of all levels for its buyer's guides, product reviews, tips, and tricks. Content includes illustrated how-to articles, feature images, techniques, and tips for the beginning and experienced photographer, and special-interest sections. Content covers both digital and traditional photography in language accessible to professionals and amateurs. Extensive advertisements also make this journal available for a lighter read. Recommended primarily for public libraries and school libraries, but can be popular for academic libraries as well.

4033. ***Shutterbug.*** Former titles (until 198?): *Shutterbug Ads Photographic News;* (until 19??): *Shutterbug Ads.* [ISSN: 0895-321X] 1971. m. USD 17.95 domestic; USD 29.95 Canada; USD 41.95 foreign. TEN: The Enthusiast Network, 831 South Douglas St, El Segundo, CA 90245; info@enthusiastnetwork.com; http://www.enthusiastnetwork.com. Illus. *Aud.:* Hs, Ga.

Shutterbug is targeted to both amateur and professional photographers, as well as photo enthusiasts. Issues contains articles, product test reports, equipment reviews, and photographer profiles. The magazine is popular for reviews, a Q&A section, and articles written for the general public; however, the magazine also contains a large number of product and service advertisements. Content addresses both digital and traditional photography and the layout makes it appealing for browsing. Recommended primarily for public libraries.

■ PHYSICS

Kiyomi Deards, Librarian for Chemistry, Biochemistry, Forensic Science, Physics and Astronomy, University of Nebraska–Lincoln

Barbara Williams, MIT Libraries

Introduction

Physics is often described as the fundamental science that underpins all other sciences; its most ardent fans assert, it is pure science, with a capital P. Hailed as the science that explains how things work, physics helps us understand many scientific breakthroughs. From technology that detected gravitational waves emanating from a collision between two black holes over 1.3 billion years ago; to the most mundane, how to get the last of the ketchup out of its container without banging on its bottom.

It is rumored that in their daily work lives, physicists encounter more mathematics than other scientists. Understanding the language of mathematics is essential to describe the work of physicists, and necessitates at least a college level mathematical vocabulary. Physicists typically have good analytical and critical thinking skills. According to the *Why Study Physics?* website at Cornell University, physicists secure more top management and policy positions than other technical professionals. Physicists specialize in subjects such as astronomy; atmospheric physics; atomic, molecular, and optical physics; computational physics; condensed matter physics; cryogenics; dynamics; electromagnetism; homeokinetics; materials physic; mechanics; nuclear physics; optics; particle physics; plasma physics; polymer physics; quantum physics; relativity; statics; solid state physics and theoretical physics. Examples of interdisciplinary fields physicists work in are astrophysics; biophysics; chemical physics; econophysics; engineering physics; geophysics; mathematical physics; medical physics; physical chemistry; and quantum computing.

Although physicists use math on a daily basis they are less likely to cite articles that contain lots of mathematics according to a 2016 study in the *New Journal of Physics*. Apparently, the placement and usage of math equations in articles can influence whether an article is read. Some publishers urge authors to put their mathematical equations in the appendix and use the body of the text to explain what the equations represent. There is an ongoing effort by publishers to expand their readership to non-physicists. To increase the readability of its specialized journals, the American Institute of Physics advises authors to summarize their research findings so general audiences can understand their abstracts. There are more articles about physics published in interdisciplinary journals than in the core physics journals.

American Institute of Physics, European Professional Physics organizations, and the Institute for Physics are all prestigious publishers of some of the most recognizable journal titles in physics. The above three physics associations produce over a third of the titles reviewed on this list. While Elsevier and Springer publish the most commercial titles on the list. On the rise is the number of physics journals that allow authors to deposit the original versions of their articles that incorporate changes made during the peer review process but prior to the publisher brand marks via edits, typesetting etc. All of the titles on this list are appropriate for institutions that support major physics research initiatives.

Physicist tend to concentrate on specific aspects of a topic, in so doing, new research topics may emerge. New areas of study give rise to the proliferation of specialized journals. These journals are meant to inform, update and galvanize communities of practice around a particular topic. These specialized journals can be expensive while the communities they serve may be few in numbers. A library builds its journal collection to align with the areas of research at its institution, when it can afford to. If it cannot afford to purchase subscriptions on demand, and who can? It can rely on the interlibrary loan system to fulfill users' requests, and in the process document need.

Once a library has exceeded the number of articles it can borrow from a journal in a calendar year, that title can be added to a wish list. Meanwhile until items on the wish list can be subscribed to, the following journals can help researchers stay abreast of articles on emerging trends: *Reviews of Modern Physics, Physics Reports, Reports on Progress in Physics, Physical Review X, Physical Review Letters* and *Physics Today*. Additionally, INSPIRE and arXiv.org are specialized repositories heavily used by the physics community to stay up-to-date on new topics too.

The physics community was an early adopter in the use of preprints as a means to speed up the dissemination of scientific communications. arXiv.org pronounced archive.org is the premier open access platform for scientists in physics and other science disciplines. It is a repository of scientific papers comprised of electronic preprints known as e-prints. The content in the arXiv is not peer reviewed, rather subject moderators are the gatekeepers tasked with submission reviews. Early versions of a paper in its development stage can be found on the arXiv server. A new subject category called *Applied Physics* was added in 2017, which focuses on applications of physics to new technology. The server is hosted by Cornell University Library. The arXiv also includes transcripts, lectures, talks, and other such content, which may never be published but nevertheless may provide inspiration.

INSPIRE, the high energy literature free database previously known as SPIRES is another database favored by the physics community and also able to search the full-text of all of the arXiv content. Most high school students who take physics courses are exposed to arXiv.org, which means they are accustom to a one-stop-shopping search box. The allure of a Google like search experience has given rise to discovery tools that have the capacity to search the holdings of a given library via a single search box.

Many undergraduates never have to go beyond the most prominent search box at their library to find the information they need. Discovery tools have changed the way undergraduates and some graduate students discover articles. Physics undergraduates who have access to these discovery tools can usually find relevant articles, which exceed their information needs. Moreover, arXiv.org is accessible via these discovery platforms as is most of the titles on this list. A search that combines arXiv.org with academic general databases will quickly overwhelm the average undergraduate with lots of relevant information.

Yet, there may be unintended consequences that need to be contemplated when discovery tools become the virtual point of entry into libraries. One misguided perception is that the single search box searches the entire digital collection of a library. It is not always easily discernable what is in the container the single search box is searching for. Are full text journals in the search container because the library subscribes to them or are they included with a particular database on a trial basis? How do we ensure that the journals we subscribe to are discoverable when their license prevent inclusion in discovery tools? Might the use of discovery tools minimize the need for specialized journals not accessible via the discovery tool?

Futhermore if a user finds one or more relevant articles on a hard to find topic from a non-physics peer reviewed journal via a discovery tool does that end their search? In all likelihood, it will. It is possible for physics majors to get through four years of college without direct exposure to core physics journals in a meaningful way. Unfortunately, it is also why a large number of undergraduates have no incentive to intentionally interact with the majority of journal titles on this list.

Finally, all public libraries should subscribe to *Physics Today* the ultimate browsable journal. If acquiring both formats are not viable opt for the print as the digital copy is accessible via many general databases. Five free informative online resources, which provide information on physics aimed at the general public and undergraduates are: *Physics, Physical Review Focus, Physics News, the Planetary society blog,* and *Galileo's Pendulum*. In a concerted effort to increase public access to their journals, the American Physical Society makes available to U.S. public libraries and high schools, free access to all their online journals. Public libraries should publicize this opportunity to their communities.

Basic Periodicals

Hs: *American Journal of Physics, Physics, Physics Education, The Physics Teacher, Physics Today;* Ga: *Physics, Physics Today;* Ac: *American Journal of Physics, Applied Physics Letters, Journal of Applied Physics, Journal of Physics, Nature Physics, Physical Review, Physics, Physics Letters, Physics Today.*

Basic Abstracts and Indexes

arXiv; High-Energy Physics Literature Database (INSPIRE); Physics Abstracts.

4034. ***A I P Advances.*** [ISSN: 2158-3226] 2011. m. Free. A I P Publishing LLC, 1305 Walt Whitman Rd, Melville, NY 20740; aipinfo@aip.org; http://www.aip.org. Illus., adv. Refereed. *Indexed:* A01. *Aud.:* Ac, Sa.

AIP Advances is a peer-reviewed, open-access online multidisciplinary journal that covers all areas of the experimental, theoretical, and applied physical sciences. It publishes original research papers in topics such as superconductors, condensed matter, nanotechnology, quantum mechanics, computational physics, plasma physics, and ultrafast science. To create communication and discussion of the papers published, readers are allowed to comment on any article in a blog-like fashion. As a free, open-access title with creative commons licensing (CC-BY), this journal should become part of any physics research collection.

4035. ***A P L Materials.*** [ISSN: 2166-532X] 2013. m. Free. Ed(s): Judith L MacManus-Driscoll. A I P Publishing LLC, 1305 Walt Whitman Rd, Melville, NY 11747; aipinfo@aip.org; http://www.aip.org. Refereed. *Aud.:* Ac, Sa.

APL Materials is an open-access, online-only journal that covers original experimental research on significant topical issues within the field of materials science. Experimental research is emphasized. This title publishes original research papers on topics such as nanostructures; advanced microscopy; amorphous materials; batteries; bioinspired materials; biological materials; carbon materials; catalytic materials; colloids; drug delivery; energy and environment materials; ferroic and multiferroic materials; first-principles calculations alongside experimental data; first-principles calculations of wide interest and impact on experimental materials research; hierarchical materials; interfaces; magnetic materials; metal organic framework materials; metamaterials; multiscale (molecular, mesoscopic, macroscopic) modeling of materials in combination with experiment; nanobiotechnology;

nanocomposites; nitride materials; photocatalytic materials; photonic materials; photovoltaics; polymers; quantum effects in materials; semiconductors; solar cells; supercapacitors; superconductors; thermoelectrics; thin films; and tissue engineering. As a free, open-access title with creative commons licensing, this journal should become part of any physics research collection.

4036. ***Acoustical Society of America. Journal.*** [ISSN: 0001-4966] 1929. m. USD 2570 (print & online eds.)). A I P Publishing LLC, 1305 Walt Whitman Rd, Melville, NY 11747; aipinfo@aip.org; http://www.aip.org. Illus., index, adv. Sample. Refereed. *Indexed:* A01, A22, ErgAb, HRIS, MLA-IB. *Bk. rev.:* 1-3 per issue. *Aud.:* Ac, Sa.

Available in print and online. The *Journal of the Acoustical Society of America* is the leading source of theoretical and experimental research results in the broad interdisciplinary subject of sound. It is designed to serve physical scientists, life scientists, engineers, psychologists, physiologists, architects, musicians, and speech communication specialists. Subject coverage includes linear and nonlinear acoustics; aeroacoustics, underwater sound, and acoustical oceanography; ultrasonics and quantum acoustics; architectural and structural acoustics and vibration; speech, music, and noise; psychology and physiology of hearing; engineering acoustics, sound transducers, and measurements; and bioacoustics, animal bioacoustics, and bioresponse to vibration. In addition to full-length research papers, the *Journal* contains news items of interest to acoustical scientists, book reviews, references to contemporary papers in acoustics, reviews of acoustical patents, and news on the development of standards. The "JASA Express Letters" section provides rapid dissemination of important new research results and technical information. "JASA Express Letters" are published online as accepted. *Letters* are included in journal volumes as they are published. In the online version, some articles include multimedia components such as video or sound recordings. As the most comprehensive journal in the world on this branch of physics, this title belongs in every physics collection.

4037. ***Acoustics Today.*** [ISSN: 1557-0215] 2005. q. Free to members. Acoustical Society of America, Ste 300, 1305 Walt Whitman Rd, Melville, NY 11747; asa@acousticalsociety.org; http://acousticalsociety.org/. Adv. *Aud.:* Ga, Ac, Sa.

Acoustics Today was created as a means for disseminating interesting research and developments in the study of sound to a wide audience. Authors strive to present their articles in a manner that readers will find interesting, understandable (regardless of their own acoustic discipline), and most importantly, worth reading. It contains tutorials, technical articles about and related to acoustics, and articles that expand upon conference presentations. Some articles contain multimedia components, which is very appropriate in a field of study based on sound. In addition, it also provides news of developments in the field, notices of events and meetings and new publications, news about researchers in the field of acoustics, and the work of the committees of the Acoustical Society of America. Although the journal is a benefit to members of the society, it is also freely available to everyone on the web. More than simply a newsletter, this journal belongs in any collection that supports research or study in the field of acoustics.

4038. ***Advanced Science.*** [ISSN: 2198-3844] 2014. s-m. Free. Ed(s): Kirsten Severing. Wiley - V C H Verlag GmbH & Co. KGaA, Postfach 101161, Weinheim, 69451, Germany; cs-germany@wiley.com; http://onlinelibrary.wiley.com. Refereed. *Aud.:* Ac, Sa.

Available online only. This open-access journal is an interdisciplinary premium title that covers fundamental and applied research in materials science, physics and chemistry, and medical and life sciences, as well as engineering. All *Advanced Science* articles are published under the terms of the Creative Commons Attribution (CC-BY) License, which permits use, distribution, and reproduction in any medium, provided the original work is properly cited. This journal is targeted at researchers in materials science, chemistry, physics, engineering, and biology. Research papers are generally six or seven pages in length and fall into the following categories: "Communications," which provide short reports of novel findings; "Reviews," which give a general overview of a particular field; "Progress Reports," which present recent progress in an important research field; "Feature Articles," which are invited articles summarizing recent developments in a research field; "Research News," written for nonspecialists and covers recent developments in science and technology; "Essays," which allow contributors to present opinions, or report news of national and international interest; and "Correspondences," which are comments on articles previously published in the journal. Articles are published as completed, and grouped into quarterly issues. Citations and download statistics are available for each article. This open-access journal belongs in all collections that support research in physics and the physical sciences.

4039. ***Advances in Optics and Photonics.*** [ISSN: 1943-8206] 2009. q. USD 602. Ed(s): Govind Agrawal. Optical Society of America, 2010 Massachusetts Ave, NW, Washington, DC 20036; info@osa.org; http://www.osapublishing.org. Refereed. *Aud.:* Ac, Sa.

Available online only. Published by the Optical Society of America, this journal is designed to provide review articles and tutorials to assist researchers in the field of optics. It also includes peer-reviewed letters to the editor and replies to published review articles and multimedia tutorials appropriate for students, researchers, faculty, business professionals, and engineers. It covers fundamental and experimental optics, along with applications of optics and photonics technology, including fiber optics and optical communications; quantum optics; ultrafast optics; lasers and laser optics; nonlinear optics; and optical devices. All of the articles emphasize multimedia content and applications. To maximize their reach, tutorials feature interactive components such as animation and video. Each article has navigational links and external reference-linking for easy sourcing and enhanced learning. In addition, the journal also links to review articles in recent issues of other journals published by the society. Articles are published as completed and grouped into quarterly issues. Citations and download statistics are available for each article. This journal belongs in all collections that support research in optics.

4040. ***Advances in Physics.*** [ISSN: 0001-8732] 1952. bi-m. GBP 4861 (print & online eds.)). Ed(s): David Sherrington. Taylor & Francis, 2, 3 & 4 Park Sq, Milton Park, Abingdon, OX14 4RN, United Kingdom; subscriptions@tandf.co.uk; https://www.tandfonline.com. Illus., adv. Sample. Refereed. Vol. ends: Nov/Dec. Reprint: PSC. *Indexed:* A01, A22, E01. *Aud.:* Ac, Sa.

Available in print and online. *Advances in Physics* publishes authoritative critical reviews by experts on topics of interest and importance in condensed-matter physics and statistical mechanics-broadly defined to include the overlap with quantum information, cold atoms, soft-matter physics, and biophysics. These reviews present the current state of knowledge within this highly specialized subfield of physics, and serve as benchmarks in our knowledge of the physical universe. They are written for readers with a basic knowledge of condensed-matter physics who want to learn more about specific research areas within that field. Because of the comprehensiveness of the research, most papers in this journal are very long, often more than 100 pages. Most issues consist of a single article that essentially serves as a monograph on the topic under review. One of the key features of each article is its bibliography, which lists all the important past research on the topic under consideration. The "Perspectives" section is occasionally included to present shorter provocative articles that are intended to be controversial and to promote debate. *Annals of Physics, Contemporary Physics,* and *Reports on Progress in Physics* (all below in this section) also publish review articles, but these journals are all aimed at the nonspecialist. *Advances in Physics* is written for the specialized researcher or student of condensed matter, and will only be of marginal value to the nonspecialist or to scientists working in other disciplines.

4041. ***American Journal of Physics.*** Formerly (until 1940): *American Physics Teacher.* [ISSN: 0002-9505] 1933. m. USD 1366 (print & online eds.)). Ed(s): David P Jackson. A I P Publishing LLC, 1305 Walt Whitman Rd, Melville, NY 11747; aipinfo@aip.org; http://www.aip.org. Illus., index, adv. Sample. Refereed. *Indexed:* A01, A22, BRI, MLA-IB. *Bk. rev.:* Number and length vary. *Aud.:* Hs, Ga, Ac.

Available in print and online. While most physics journals serve solely as archives of original research results, the *American Journal of Physics* exists to help teachers do a better job of instructing students about physics. As the official journal of the American Association of Physics Teachers, this title is devoted to the instructional and cultural aspects of the physical sciences. Rather than concentrating on new research results, this journal focuses on methods of teaching physics to students at the university and college level. Articles provide a deeper understanding of physics topics taught at the undergraduate and graduate level; insight into current research in physics and related areas; suggestions for instructional laboratory equipment and demonstrations; insight into and proven suggestions for better teaching methodologies; insight into how college students learn physics; and information on the historical, philosophical, and cultural aspects of physics. In addition to full-length papers, the journal also publishes letters, notes, book reviews, information on laboratory equipment, and editorials. Occasional articles that discuss research in physics education are also included. All libraries that support college physics courses should subscribe to this title.

4042. *Annalen der Physik.* Former titles (until 1799): *Neues Journal der Physik;* (until 1795): *Journal der Physik.* [ISSN: 0003-3804] 1790. 10x/yr. Ed(s): Stefan Hildebrandt. Wiley - V C H Verlag GmbH & Co. KGaA, Postfach 101161, Weinheim, 69451, Germany; service@wiley-vch.de; http://www.wiley-vch.de. Illus., index. Sample. Refereed. Reprint: PSC. *Indexed:* A01, A22, MSN. *Bk. rev.:* Occasional. *Aud.:* Ac, Sa.

Available in print and online. As the oldest continuously published German physics journal, *Annalen der Physik* occupies a historic place in the physics literature. This journal publishes original papers in the areas of experimental, theoretical, applied, and mathematical physics, and related areas. Throughout its long history, it has published some of the most important papers in the field, including the original work of Planck, Roentgen, and Einstein. This title covers a broad range of topics including condensed matter, solid state, materials, optics, photonics, quantum information, cosmology, gravitation, relativity, high energy, particles, nuclear, biophysics, biological and medical application, geo, climate, and environment physics. It still publishes peer-reviewed original papers in the areas of experimental, theoretical, applied, and mathematical physics and related areas. In addition to original research papers and review articles, the journal welcomes "Rapid Research Letters" ("RRLs"). The "Physics Forum" articles report about current highlights in *AdP* and about the historic relation of recent and ongoing research efforts in physics. Even though it is a German journal, all of the articles are now published in English. It supports video abstracts and additional online materials to supplement articles. Although it has been surpassed in prestige by several other prominent physics journals such as *Journal of Physics* and the *Physical Review* (see below in this section), *Annalen der Physik* is still an important component of any comprehensive physics collection.

4043. *Annals of Physics.* [ISSN: 0003-4916] 1957. m. EUR 4335. Ed(s): V Gurarie. Academic Press, 3251 Riverport Ln, Maryland Heights, MO 63043; JournalCustomerService-usa@elsevier.com; http://www.elsevier.com/. Illus., index, adv. Sample. Refereed. *Indexed:* A01, A22, E01, MSN. *Aud.:* Ac, Sa.

Available in print and online. Unlike most physics research journals, which publish brief reports of original research aimed at the specialist in the field, *Annals of Physics* presents original work in all areas of basic physics research. The journal publishes papers on topics spanning theory, methodology, and applications. It emphasizes clarity and intelligibility in the articles it publishes, thus making them more accessible to the reader than in many other journals. Researchers familiar with recent developments in the field are provided with sufficient detail and background to follow the arguments and understand their significance. Because of the emphasis on extensive background material, the articles in this journal can be very long, sometimes consisting of 50 or more pages. *Contemporary Physics, Reports on Progress in Physics,* and *Reviews of Modern Physics* (all below in this section) all serve the same general purpose as *Annals of Physics,* and each is useful for a college-level physics collection.

4044. *Applied Optics.* Formed by the merger of (1990-2003): *Applied Optics. Information Processing;* (1995-2003): *Applied Optics. Optical Technology and Biomedical Optics;* (1990-2003): *Applied Optics. Lasers, Photonics, and Environmental Optics;* All of which superseded (1962-1989): *Applied Optics.* [ISSN: 1559-128X] 2004. 3x/m. USD 6134 print & online eds. Ed(s): Ronald N Driggers. Optical Society of America, 2010 Massachusetts Ave, NW, Washington, DC 20036; info@osa.org; http://www.osapublishing.org. Illus., index, adv. Refereed. *Indexed:* A22, BRI. *Aud.:* Ac, Sa.

Available in print and online. Along with the *Journal of the Optical Society of America* and *Optics Letters* (see below in this section), *Applied Optics* is one of the official journals of the Optical Society of America. While the other two titles publish reports of original research, this journal concentrates on the applications of optical principles and methods. Thus, it is the most widely read journal in the field of optics. Articles are published online as accepted and gathered in three issues per month. Articles cover a wide variety of topics including optical technology, photonics, lasers, information processing, sensing, and environmental optics. In addition to full-length papers, the journal provides occasional review articles and comments, and engineering and laboratory notes on equipment and methodologies (brief articles devoted to the design, analysis, fabrication, integration, alignment, and measurement techniques used when creating optical components and systems). This is one of the core journals in the field of optics, and it belongs in any physics or engineering research collection.

4045. *Applied Physics A: materials science & processing.* Former titles: *Applied Physics A: Solids and Surfaces;* Supersedes in part (in 1981): *Applied Physics;* Which superseded: *Zeitschrift fuer Angewandte Physik.* [ISSN: 0947-8396] 1973. m. EUR 8770 (print & online eds.)). Ed(s): Michael Stuke. Springer, Tiergartenstr 17, Heidelberg, 69121, Germany. Illus., adv. Refereed. Reprint: PSC. *Indexed:* A01, A22, E01. *Aud.:* Ac, Sa.

Available in print and online. *Applied Physics A* is a monthly journal for the rapid publication of experimental and theoretical investigations in applied research. It primarily covers the condensed phase, including nanostructured materials and their applications. Surfaces, thin films, advanced processing, and characterization techniques are also explored. This title publishes full-length articles and short, rapid communications. It also features invited reviews. Many of the issues are devoted to papers on a single topic, often presenting the proceedings of relevant conferences or festschriften. This journal jointly sponsors the Julius Springer Prize for Applied Physics, which is awarded annually to a researcher who has made outstanding and innovative contributions to the field of applied physics. For libraries that seek a comprehensive physics collection, this journal will serve as a European complement to the *Journal of Applied Physics.*

4046. *Applied Physics B: lasers and optics.* Formerly: *Applied Physics. B: Photophysics and Laser Chemistry;* Supersedes in part (in 1981): *Applied Physics.* [ISSN: 0946-2171] 16x/yr. EUR 7020 (print & online eds.)). Ed(s): Dieter Meschede. Springer, Tiergartenstr 17, Heidelberg, 69121, Germany. Adv. Refereed. Reprint: PSC. *Indexed:* A01, A22, E01. *Aud.:* Ac, Sa.

Available online and in print. *Applied Physics B* is a journal for the rapid publication of laser and optical experimental and theoretical research. This research includes the applications of laser radiation in chemistry and biochemistry. The journal publishes both full-length articles and short, rapid communications. Occasional issues present the proceedings of relevant conferences or festschriften. This journal is published in cooperation with the German Physical Society and was originally published under its German title, *Zeitschrift fur Angewandte Physik.* Much of the research reported in this title is still conducted in German universities and research centers. However, all of the papers accepted are published in English. For libraries that seek a comprehensive physics collection, this journal will serve as a European complement to the *Journal of Applied Physics.*

4047. *Applied Physics Letters.* [ISSN: 0003-6951] 1962. w. Ed(s): Reuben T Collins. A I P Publishing LLC, 1305 Walt Whitman Rd, Melville, NY 11747; aipinfo@aip.org; http://www.aip.org. Illus., index, adv. Sample. Refereed. *Indexed:* A01, A22. *Aud.:* Ac, Sa.

Available in print and online. This title serves as the letters section of the *Journal of Applied Physics* (below in this section). It is the most highly cited journal in applied physics. Thus, it provides for the rapid dissemination of key data and physical insights, including new experimental and theoretical findings on the applications of physics to all branches of science, engineering, and technology. Topics covered by this journal include photonics and optoelectronics; surfaces and interfaces; structural, mechanical, optical, and thermodynamic properties of advanced materials; semiconductors; magnetics and spintronics; superconductivity and superconducting electronics; dielectrics, ferroelectrics, and multiferroics; nanoscale science and technology; organic electronics and photonics; device physics; biophysics and bio-inspired systems; energy conversion and storage; and interdisciplinary and general physics research. Because all of the papers accepted are letters, they are extremely brief, with none longer than five printed pages. Content is published online daily, then collected into weekly online and printed issues. In addition to original research results, each issue also includes comments on previously published material. The comments can result in lively debate over the accuracy and interpretation of experimental results. This title is the most heavily cited journal in the field of applied physics. It is one of the core journals in physics and belongs in any physics research collection.

4048. ***Applied Physics Research.*** [ISSN: 1916-9639] 2009. s-a. Ed(s): Riccardo Bartolini. Canadian Center of Science and Education, 1120 Finch Ave W, Ste 701-309, Toronto, ON M3J 3H7, Canada; info@ccsenet.org; http://www.ccsenet.org. Sample. Refereed. *Aud.:* Ac, Sa.

Available in print and online. *Applied Physics Research* is an open-access journal that publishes original research reports in all areas of physics. Topics covered include acoustics; astrophysics and geophysics; biophysics; computational physics; condensed-matter physics; engineering physics; free electron physics; laser and quantum electronics; medical physics; optics; semiconductor physics and devices; solid state physics, space physics. Because the articles are reports of original research, they tend to be highly technical in nature and readable only by other experts in the field. The journal is available in both print and electronic formats. With free open access to the online version, it is unlikely that many libraries will choose to spend $20 plus shipping per issue for the print equivalent. Because it is a free open-access title, the online edition of this journal should be included in all physics research collections. URL: www.ccsenet.org/journal/index.php/apr

Biophysical Journal. See Biology/Biochemistry and Biophysics section.

4049. ***Canadian Journal of Physics.*** [ISSN: 0008-4204] 1929. m. CAD 1332 (print & online eds.)). Ed(s): Michael Steinitz. Canadian Science Publishing, 65 Auriga Dr, Ste 203, Ottawa, ON K2E 7W6, Canada; pubs@cdnsciencepub.com; http://www.nrcresearchpress.com. Illus., index, adv. Refereed. Vol. ends: Dec. *Indexed:* A01, A22, C37, E01. *Aud.:* Ac, Sa.

Available in print and online. As an official publication of the National Research Council of Canada, the *Canadian Journal of Physics* is the premier physics publication emanating from that nation. It covers all branches of physics, including atomic and molecular physics, condensed matter, elementary particles and nuclear physics, gases, fluid dynamics and plasmas, electromagnetism and optics, mathematical physics, and interdisciplinary, classical, and applied physics. It also covers relativity and cosmology; physics education research; statistical mechanics and thermodynamics; quantum physics and quantum computing; gravitation and string theory; biophysics; aeronomy and space physics; and astrophysics. Most of the articles are published in English, although French-language articles are also accepted. In addition to full research reports, shorter rapid communications and research notes are also accepted. The journal also occasionally publishes review articles and tutorials that bring together and explain previously published research results. Supplemental data and other accompanying materials are available to subscribers on the journal website. Although this journal is an official publication of the Canadian government, it is not restricted to Canadian authors, and it attracts research reports from around the world. As the major Canadian journal in physics, it should be part of any comprehensive physics research collection.

4050. ***Chaos: an interdisciplinary journal of nonlinear science.*** [ISSN: 1054-1500] 1991. q. Ed(s): Jurgen Kurths. A I P Publishing LLC, 1305 Walt Whitman Rd, Melville, NY 11747; aipinfo@aip.org; http://www.aip.org. Adv. Sample. Refereed. *Indexed:* A01, A22, MSN. *Aud.:* Ac, Sa.

Available in print and online. While most of physics seeks to describe the universe in an orderly fashion, some processes and systems simply do not fit in an orderly model. Chaos theory is a discipline that tries to understand such behaviors. The journal *Chaos* is devoted to research of such nonlinear systems. This journal covers the most recent developments in nonlinear science, including contributions from physics, mathematics, chemistry, biology, engineering, economics, and social sciences, as well as other disciplines in which inherently nonlinear phenomena are of interest and importance. Examples of topics covered include classical deterministic chaos; quantum and wave chaos; solitons and coherent structures; pattern formation and competition; and adaptive and evolving systems networks. In addition to full-length peer-reviewed articles, this title also includes letters, brief reports, and technical reviews. Every other issue is a special-focus issue, which is intended to provide a critical introduction and overview of a particular topic, suitable as an introduction to nonspecialists but also of value to experts in the area. In addition, occasional articles that are aimed at the teaching of chaos theory are provided. The online version of the journal also features select multimedia content. This journal covers an interesting and unique subdiscipline of physics, and it belongs in any collection that supports research in this area.

4051. ***Communications in Mathematical Physics.*** [ISSN: 0010-3616] 1965. 24x/yr. EUR 5268 (print & online eds.)). Ed(s): Horng-Tzer Yau. Springer, Tiergartenstr 17, Heidelberg, 69121, Germany. Illus., index, adv. Sample. Refereed. Reprint: PSC. *Indexed:* A01, A22, E01, MSN. *Aud.:* Ac, Sa.

Available in print and online. The field of physics relies heavily on high-level mathematics as a tool for developing new theories and in explaining experimental results. Whether defining the motion of an apple, exploring the heavens, or analyzing the nature of fundamental particles, physicists always attempt to explain natural phenomena in terms of mathematical functions. *Communications in Mathematical Physics* was developed in order to present physicists with a source for learning new mathematical techniques as well as for presenting new research findings. It also attempts to generate, among mathematicians, an increased awareness of and appreciation for the current problems in physics. All branches of physics are covered, although particular emphasis is placed on statistical physics, quantum theory, string theory, dynamical systems, atomic physics, relativity, and disordered systems. The common thread among all the papers is the strong mathematical approach to the problem. This journal complements the *Journal of Mathematical Physics* (see below in this section), and belongs in comprehensive physics collections.

4052. ***Computer Physics Communications.*** [ISSN: 0010-4655] 1969. 12x/yr. EUR 5539. Elsevier BV, Radarweg 29, Amsterdam, 1043 NX, Netherlands; info@elsevier.com; https://www.elsevier.com/. Illus., index, adv. Sample. Refereed. *Indexed:* A01, A22, CompLI, MSN. *Aud.:* Ac, Sa.

Available in print and online. *Computer Physics Communications* deals with the applications of computing to physics and physical chemistry. Unlike most scientific research journals, the focus is on computational methods and techniques rather than the experimental results. Specific topics covered include computational models in physics and physical chemistry; computer programs in physics and physical chemistry; computational models and programs associated with the design, control, and analysis of experiments; numerical methods and algorithms; algebraic computation; the impact of advanced computer architecture and special-purpose computers on computing in the physical sciences; and software topics related to the physical sciences. In addition, subscribers have access to a website that contains a program library of actual computer software that may be used for these purposes. Most of the older programs in the library were written in FORTRAN for mainframe systems, while newer entries tend to be PC-based and run under Windows, UNIX, or Linux. Some are available in other scientific programming languages, including Maple and Mathematica. When new versions of existing programs are developed, announcements are included in this journal. With the program library, researchers are able to duplicate or modify experiments that would be otherwise difficult to conduct. More than 2,200 programs are currently available in the CPC program library. Each issue of the journal is evenly divided between articles and program descriptions. This journal is unique in providing not only original research articles, but also the research tools used in compiling the information.

4053. ***Contemporary Physics.*** [ISSN: 0010-7514] 1959. q. GBP 1324 (print & online eds.)). Ed(s): Peter L Knight. Taylor & Francis, 2, 3 & 4 Park Sq, Milton Park, Abingdon, OX14 4RN, United Kingdom; subscriptions@tandf.co.uk; https://www.tandfonline.com. Illus., index, adv. Sample. Refereed. Vol. ends: Nov/Dec. Microform: MIM; PMC. Reprint: PSC. *Indexed:* A01, A22, BRI, E01. *Bk. rev.:* 5-15 per issue, varying length. *Aud.:* Ac, Sa.

Available in print and online. *Contemporary Physics* has a unique place in the spectrum of physics journals. Although written primarily for physicists, the articles appearing in this journal have more background material and are more accessible to a wider scientific audience than articles in most physics journals. Each article attempts to explain the essential physical concepts of the topic and to relate those concepts to more familiar aspects of physics that are accessible to a broader range of readers. Because of this emphasis, students and scientists in other scientific disciplines can use this journal to learn about important developments in the field of physics. *Contemporary Physics* is of particular use to undergraduates, teachers, and lecturers, and those starting postgraduate studies. A feature of interest to librarians is that in addition to the review articles, the journal publishes dozens of reviews of books and essays in physics and related fields. *Contemporary Physics* is the most readable of all of the physics review journals, and belongs in every college-level physics collection.

4054. *Cryogenics.* [ISSN: 0011-2275] 1960. 8x/yr. EUR 4105. Elsevier Ltd,

Illus., adv. Sample. Refereed. Microform: PQC. *Indexed:* A01, A22. *Bk. rev.:* Number and length vary. *Aud.:* Ac, Sa.

Available in print and online. *Cryogenics* is the world's leading journal that focuses on all aspects of cryoengineering and cryogenics. Papers published in this journal cover a wide variety of subjects in low-temperature engineering and research, including the applications of superconductivity in magnets, electronics, and other devices; superconductors and their properties; properties of materials; new applications of cryogenic technology; refrigeration and liquefaction technology; thermodynamics; fluid properties and fluid mechanics; heat transfer; thermometry and measurement science; cryogenics in medicine; and cryoelectronics. The majority of the publication consists of full-length research papers, although review articles, research notes, and technical notes are also included. Conference papers are published on an occasional basis, in addition to book reviews, news features, and a calendar of events relevant to the field. As the premier journal for low-temperature studies, this journal belongs in any physics or engineering collection that supports research in this field.

4055. *European Journal of Physics.* [ISSN: 0143-0807] 1980. bi-m. USD 1760 (print & online eds.)). Ed(s): M Vollmer. Institute of Physics Publishing Ltd., Temple Circus, Temple Way, Bristol, BS1 6HG, United Kingdom; custserv@iop.org; http://iopscience.iop.org. Illus., adv. Sample. Refereed. Vol. ends: Nov. *Indexed:* A01, A22, ERIC. *Aud.:* Ga, Ac, Sa.

Available in print and online. The primary mission of the *European Journal of Physics* is to assist in maintaining and improving the standard of physics teaching in universities and other institutes of higher education. It publishes articles on topics relating to the fundamentals of physics education; papers on laboratory exercises that illustrate novel techniques; original insights into the derivation of results; reports on new developments in physics curricula and the techniques of teaching physics; and papers describing the cultural, historical, and technological aspects of physics. It is a place for teachers, instructors, and professors to exchange their views on teaching physics at the university level and share their experiences. Because the papers are intended to aid in the teaching of the subject rather than to present original research results, the editors encourage authors to avoid high-level mathematics, thus making the papers more accessible to a general audience. Although this is a European journal, almost every article published is in English. Full papers and letters are accepted, along with comments on previously published works. Some articles have accompanying multimedia content that is available through the website. Occasional special issues follow specific themes. In order to reach the widest possible audience in the physics education community, all articles from the current month are provided free for the first 30 days after publication. This title is the European equivalent of the *American Journal of Physics* (above in this section) and is a useful supplement to any college or university physics collection.

4056. *European Physical Journal A. Hadrons and Nuclei.* Incorporates (2004-2006): *Acta Physica Hungarica. B. Quantum Electronics;* (1951-2006): *Acta Physica Hungarica. A. Heavy Ion Physics;* Which was formerly (until 1994): *Acta Physica Hungarica;* (until 1982): *Acta Physica Academiae Scientiarum Hungaricae;* (until 1949): *Hungarica Acta Physica;* Incorporated in part (1903-2000): *Anales de Fisica;* (1855-1999): *Societa Italiana di Fisica. Nuovo Cimento. A. Nuclei, Particles and Fields;* Which was formerly (until 1982): *Societa Italiana di Fisica. Nuovo Cimento A;* (until 1971): *Nuovo Cimento A;* Which superseded in part (in 1965): *Nuovo Cimento;* Former titles (until 1997): *Zeitschrift fuer Physik A. Hadrons and Nuclei;* (until 1991): *Zeitschrift fuer Physik. Section A. Atomic Nuclei;* (until 1986): *Zeitschrift fuer Physik. Section A: Atoms and Nuclei; Zeitschrift fuer Physik.* [ISSN: 1434-6001] 1920. m. EUR 5792 (print & online eds.)). Ed(s): T S Biro, N Alamanos. Springer, Tiergartenstr 17, Heidelberg, 69121, Germany. Illus., adv. Refereed. Reprint: PSC. *Indexed:* A01, A22, E01. *Aud.:* Ac, Sa.

Available in print and online. In 1998, the German, French, and Italian Physical Societies decided to merge all of their specialized national physics journals into a single publication. The *European Physical Journal* in all six of its parts is the result of that merger. Over the past decade, national physics societies in more than 40 nations have joined in to expand this effort. *Part A* directly replaces the former *Zeitschrift fuer Physik A* and *Il Nuovo Cimento A*. It covers the specialized subfield of high-energy physics relating to hadrons and nuclei, including nuclear structure; nuclear reactions; heavy-ion physics; quark matter; weak interactions; heavy-ion physics; hypernuclei; radioactive beams; nuclear astrophysics; and related interdisciplinary topics. The common framework of these systems is that they are few- and many-body systems bound by strong interactions. This section is complemented by *Part C,* which emphasizes the elementary aspects of particles and fields. Articles that present experimental results, including methods and instruments, are published in addition to theoretical papers. Full-length research papers, review articles, short research notes, and letters are all included. Although this is a European journal, all of the articles are in English. The *European Physical Journal* is now the premier physics journal published on the continent, and it belongs in all physics research collections.

4057. *European Physical Journal B. Condensed Matter and Complex Systems.* Incorporates in part (1903-2000): *Anales de Fisica;* Formed by the merger of (1963-1998): *Journal de Physique I;* Which was formerly (until 1991): *Journal de Physique;* (until 1962): *Journal de Physique et le Radium;* (1963-1998): *Zeitschrift fuer Physik B: Condensed Matter;* Which was formerly (until 1980): *Zeitschrift fuer Physik B (Condensed Matter and Quanta);* (until 1973): *Physik der Kondensierten Materie - Physique de la Matiere Condensee - Physics of Condensed Matter;* (1771-1998): *Societa Italiana di Fisica. Nuovo Cimento D;* Which superseded in part (in 1982): *Nuovo Cimento;* Which was formerly (until 1885): *Il Cimento;* (until 1843): *Miscellanee di Chimica, Fisica e Storia Naturale;* Which superseded in part (in 1843): *Giornale Toscano di Scienze Mediche Fisiche e Naturali;* Which was formerly (until 1840): *Nuovo Giornale dei Letterati;* (until 1822): *Accademia Italiana di Scienze Lettere ed Arti. Giornale Scientifico e Letterario;* (until 1810): *Giornale Pisano di Letteratura, Scienze ed Arti;* (until 1807): *Giornale Pisano dei Letterati;* (until 1806): *Nuovo Giornale dei Letterati;* (until 1820): *Giornale dei Letterati.* [ISSN: 1434-6028] 1998. s-m. EUR 7356 (print & online eds.)). Ed(s): A Rubio. Springer, Tiergartenstr 17, Heidelberg, 69121, Germany. Illus., index, adv. Refereed. Reprint: PSC. *Indexed:* A01, A22, E01, MSN. *Aud.:* Ac, Sa.

Available in print and online. *Part B* of the *European Physical Journal* concentrates on solid-state physics, condensed matter, and complex systems. Topics covered include solid state and materials; mesoscopic and nanoscale systems; computational methods; statistical and nonlinear physics; and interdisciplinary physics. The majority of the articles published are full-length research reports, although some colloquia papers are also included. Colloquia papers describe the development of new areas of research or the impact of new and promising experimental or theoretical methods in the field. While not as extensive and complete as reviews in the usual sense, they are intended to suitably introduce new research directions and techniques in their early stages of development, and to a wider audience. All of the articles are published in English. In order to speed publication, many of the articles are published in the *Online First* electronic delivery service before appearing in print. As the official publication of more than 40 different European physics societies, this title belongs in any comprehensive physics collection.

4058. *European Physical Journal C. Particles and Fields.* Incorporates in part (1903-2000): *Anales de Fisica;* (1855-1999): *Societa Italiana di Fisica. Nuovo Cimento. A. Nuclei, Paticles and Fields;* Which was formerly (until 1982): *Societa Italiana di Fisica. Nuovo Cimento. A;* (until 1971): *Nuovo Cimento A;* Which superseded in part (in 1965): *Nuovo Cimento;* Formerly (until 1997): *Zeitschrift fuer Physik C. Particles and Fields.* [ISSN: 1434-6044] 1979. 20x/yr. Ed(s): I Antoniadis, G Isidori. Springer, Tiergartenstr 17, Heidelberg, 69121, Germany. Illus., index, adv. Sample. Refereed. Microform: PMC; PQC. Reprint: PSC. *Indexed:* A01, A22, E01. *Aud.:* Ac, Sa.

Available in print and online. *Part C* of the *European Physical Journal* covers theoretical and experimental physics research. It emphasizes the elementary aspects of particles and fields, and specializes in reporting research results from the world's leading laboratories, including CERN, Fermilab, and KEK. Topics covered include, but are not limited to: phenomenology of the standard model; quantum chromodynamics; heavy-ion physics; astroparticle physics; hadron and lepton collisions; high-energy nuclear reactions; neutrino physics; high-energy cosmic rays; computational methods and analysis tools; gravitation, astroparticle physics, and cosmology; general aspects of quantum field theories, and alternatives; and dark matter. This section of the journal is the continuation of *Il Nuovo Cimento A* and *Zeitschrift fuer Physik C.* Full-length articles, rapid notes, reviews, notes on new experimental tools and devices, and letters are all included. Occasional issues contain the proceedings of relevant conferences. Although this is a European journal, all of the articles are published in English. This is the premier journal for European research in particle physics, and it belongs in comprehensive physics collections.

4059. *European Physical Journal D. Atomic, Molecular, Optical and Plasma Physics.* Incorporates (1951-2007): *Czechoslovak Journal of Physics;* Incorporates in part (1903-2000): *Anales de Fisica;* Formed by the merger of (1991-1998): *Journal de Physique II;* (1986-1998): *Zeitschrift fuer Physik D. Atoms, Molecules and Clusters;* Supersedes in part (1982-1999): *Societa Italiana di Fisica. Nuovo Cimento D;* Which incorporated in part (1855-1965): *Nuovo Cimento;* Which superseded (1843-1847): *Cimento; Miscellanee de Chimica, Fisica e Storia Naturale;* Which superseded in part (in 1843): *Giornale Toscano di Scienze Mediche Fisiche e Naturali;* (until 1840): *Nuovo Giornale dei Letterati;* Which superseded (in 1822): *Accademia Italiana di Scienze Lettere ed Arti. Giornale Scientifico e Letterario;* (until 1809): *Giornale Pisano di Letteratura, Scienze ed Arti;* (until 1807): *Giornale Pisano dei Letterati;* (1802-1806): *Nuovo Giornale dei Letterati;* Which superseded (1771-1796): *Giornale dei Letterati.* [ISSN: 1434-6060] 1998. 15x/yr. EUR 3994 (print & online eds.)). Ed(s): Vladimir Buzek, Andrey Solov'yov. Springer, Tiergartenstr 17, Heidelberg, 69121, Germany. Illus., index, adv. Refereed. Reprint: PSC. *Indexed:* A01, A22, E01. *Aud.:* Ac, Sa.

Available in print and online. The fourth section of the *European Physical Journal* is devoted to atomic, molecular, nanostructures, nonlinear dynamics, quantum information, ultraintense and ultrashort laser fields, plasma, cold matter and quantum gases, and optical physics. This journal was formed through the combination of three similar journals: *Il Nuovo Cimento D, Journal de Physique,* and *Zeitschrift fuer Physik D.* Topics in this section include atomic physics; molecular physics; chemical physics; atomic and molecular collisions; clusters and nanostructures; plasma physics; laser cooling and quantum gas; nonlinear dynamics; optical physics; quantum optics and quantum information; and ultraintense and ultrashort laser fields. In addition to full-length research articles, the journal publishes occasional colloquia papers that describe the development of new areas of research or the impact of new and promising experimental or theoretical methods in the fields that are within the spectrum of topics covered by the respective journals. Some of the issues present the papers from conferences in the disciplines represented by the journal. All of the papers are published in English, even though they represent the results of European research. Recommended for comprehensive physics collections.

4060. *European Physical Journal E. Soft Matter.* Formed by the merger of part of (1998-2000): *European Physical Journal. B. Condensed Matter Physics;* part of (1992-2000): *Anales de Fisica;* Which was formed by the merger of (1903-1992): *Anales de Fisica. Serie A: Fenomenos e Interacciones;* (1903-1992): *Anales de Fisica. Serie B: Aplicaciones, Metodos e Instrumentos;* Both of which superseded in part (in 1981): *Anales de Fisica;* Which was formerly (until 1968): *Real Sociedad Espanola de Fisica y Quimica. Anales. Serie A: Fisica;* Which superseded in part (in 1948): *Anales de Fisica y Quimica;* Which was formerly (until 1941): *Sociedad Espanola de Fisica y Quimica. Anales.* [ISSN: 1292-8941] 2000. m. EUR 3599 (print & online eds.)). Ed(s): Jean-Marc Di Meglio, Francesco Sciortino. Springer, Haber Str 7, Heidelberg, 69126, Germany. Adv. Sample. Refereed. Reprint: PSC. *Indexed:* A01, A22, BRI, E01. *Aud.:* Ac, Sa.

Available in print and online. The fifth section of the *European Physical Journal* covers the fields of soft matter, flowing matter, and living systems. Soft matter is a term for a large group of condensed, often heterogeneous systems that display a large response to weak external perturbations and that possess properties governed by slow internal dynamics. Flowing matter examines liquids and complex fluids, granular materials, interfacial phenomena, and nonlinear physics. Physics that emerges from novel insights into the properties and behaviors of living systems can examine biological networks, multicellular systems, cellular processes, biomimetic systems, structure and function, and biological matter. Full-length research articles and instructional colloquia papers are both included. As in each of the other sections of this journal, all of the articles are published in English. Recommended only for comprehensive physics collections.

4061. *European Physical Journal H: historical perspectives on contemporary physics.* Formerly (until 2009): *Annales de Physique;* Which superseded in part (in 1914): *Annales de Chimie et de Physique.* [ISSN: 2102-6459] 1816. q. EUR 692 (print & online eds.)). Ed(s): Francesco Guerra, Wolf Beiglboeck. Springer, Tiergartenstr 17, Heidelberg, 69121, Germany; https://www.springer.com. Illus. Refereed. *Indexed:* A01, A22. *Aud.:* Ac, Sa.

Available in print and online. Most physics journals publish current research results, but this is not the purpose of this new section of the *European Physical Journal.* This journal focuses on the history of modern physics, presenting papers that discuss how current concepts in the field were identified and developed. The purpose of this title is to catalyze, foster, and disseminate an awareness and understanding of the historical development of ideas in contemporary physics, and more generally, ideas about "how Nature works." The journal specifically encourages contributions that address the history of physics and of physical ideas and concepts; the interplay of physics and mathematics, as well as with the natural sciences; and the history and philosophy of sciences, together with discussions of experimental ideas and designs-inasmuch as they clearly relate, and preferably add, to the understanding of modern physics. In addition, this journal also seeks articles that discuss past mistakes and abandoned ideas in physics, providing a historical perspective on the rise and failure of those concepts. In addition to papers about the history of physics, the journal also reproduces key historical articles from the field, and publishes personal recollections by people who shaped modern physics. This journal belongs in any collection that supports research into the history of physics.

4062. *The European Physical Journal. Special Topics.* Former titles (until 2007): *Journal de Physique IV;* (until 1991): *Journal de Physique. Colloque.* [ISSN: 1951-6355] 1966. 14x/yr. EUR 3035 (print & online eds.)). Springer, Tiergartenstr 17, Heidelberg, 69121, Germany; subscriptions@springer.com. Refereed. Reprint: PSC. *Indexed:* A01, A22, E01. *Aud.:* Ac, Sa.

Available in print and online. The newest section of the *European Physical Journal* publishes topical issues that are collections of review-type articles or extensive, detailed progress reports. This publication is devoted to the rapid and timely publication of complete topical issues in all fields pertaining to the pure and applied physical sciences. This explicitly includes related fields such as complex systems, physical biology, and chemistry, as well as materials sciences. Each issue is focused on a specific subject matter of topical interest. The journal scope covers the whole spectrum of pure and applied physics, including related subjects such as materials science, physical biology, physical chemistry, and complex systems. Individual articles are only accepted if they are of such length to fill a full-length publication. The journal offers a new feature in the form of "Discussion and Debate" issues. The aim of such topical issues is to provide balanced critical presentation of specific unsolved problems, controversial topics, rival theories, alternative methodologies, and negative results of interest at the cutting edge of scientific and technological development. Formerly published as part IV of the *Journal de Physique,* this title will be a source for highly specialized research in a wide range of fields within physics.

4063. *Europhysics Letters (Online): a letters journal exploring the frontiers of physics.* Formerly (until 2018): *Europhysics Letters (Print);* Which was formed by the merger of (1974-1986): *Journal de Physique. Lettres;* (1971-1986): *Societa Italiana di Fisica. Lettere al Nuovo Cimento;* Which was formerly (1969-1970): *Lettere al Nuovo Cimento.* [ISSN: 1286-4854] 1986. m. USD 4070. Institute of Physics Publishing Ltd., Temple Circus, Temple Way, Bristol, BS1 6HG, United Kingdom; custserv@iop.org; http://iopscience.iop.org. Sample. Refereed. *Indexed:* A22. *Aud.:* Ac, Sa.

Available in print and online. *EPL* serves as the letters-to-the-editor journal for all of the sections of the *European Physical Journal.* It publishes short, rapid communications of important research results. Letters published in *EPL* contain new research results, ideas, concepts, experimental methods, and theoretical treatments of broad interest and importance to one or several sections of the physics community, including those with application potential. Articles are written for the specialist, yet remain understandable to the researchers in other fields. Topics are covered in all areas of physics, from condensed matter and interdisciplinary research to astrophysics and plasma science. For a fee, authors may elect to have their article available as an open-access article. Although the journal is European, all of the articles are published in English. This title belongs in research-level physics collections.

4064. *Foundations of Physics: an international journal devoted to the conceptual bases and fundamental theories of modern physics.* Incorporates (1988-2006): *Foundations of Physics Letters.* [ISSN: 0015-9018] 1970. m. EUR 2730 (print & online eds.)). Ed(s): Gerard 't Hooft. Springer New York LLC, 233 Spring St, New York, NY 10013; customerservice@springer.com; http://www.springer.com. Illus., index, adv. Refereed. Vol. ends: Dec. Microform: PQC. Reprint: PSC. *Indexed:* A01, A22, BRI, E01, MSN. *Bk. rev.:* Number and length vary. *Aud.:* Ac, Sa.

Available in print and online. One of the major objectives of modern physics research is to develop a single unified theory that can explain all physical properties, effects, and interactions. Ever since Einstein proposed that researchers work toward a single theory of the universe, scientists have approached this problem from a number of angles. *Foundations of Physics* emphasizes the logical, methodological, and philosophical premises of modern physical theories and procedures. Much of the material covers cosmology, quantum mechanics, quantum field theory, thermodynamics and statistical mechanics, and special and general relativity. The editors also accept contributions in the areas of quantum gravity, quantum information, string theory, M-theory, and brane cosmology. Articles tend to be speculative in nature and often question existing theoretical concepts. This journal is somewhat unusual in the field of physics in that it stresses theory rather than experimental results. Full-length papers and letters to the editor are accepted. Because of its focus on one of the single most important questions in physics today, this title is a useful addition to comprehensive collections in theoretical physics.

4065. *General Relativity and Gravitation.* Formerly (until 1970): *Bulletin on General Relativity and Gravitation.* [ISSN: 0001-7701] 1962. m. Ed(s): R Maartens, A Ashtekar. Springer New York LLC, 233 Spring St, New York, NY 10013; customerservice@springer.com; http://www.springer.com. Illus., index, adv. Refereed. Vol. ends: Dec. Microform: PQC. Reprint: PSC. *Indexed:* A01, A22, BRI, E01, MSN. *Bk. rev.:* Number and length vary. *Aud.:* Ac, Sa.

Available in print and online. Einstein spent much of his professional life working on the theories of gravity and relativity. This journal was developed to continue that research. Coverage includes extensions of general relativity; numerical relativity; astrophysical applications of relativistic gravity; experimental gravitational physics, in particular experimental tests of general relativity; gravitational wave data analysis and phenomenology; theoretical and observational cosmology; quantum field theory in curved space-time; supergravity and gravitational aspects of string theory and its extensions; quantum gravity and cosmology; and the teaching, public understanding, and history of general relativity and gravitation. Although this title primarily publishes research papers on the theoretical and experimental aspects of these areas, it occasionally includes letters, review articles, book reviews, conference programs, historical articles, and news items. Most of the articles are of a highly theoretical nature, which is inherent in the subject matter. As the official publication of the International Society on General Relativity and Gravitation, this journal serves as the premier source for research on and discussion of the two topics in its title. It was founded by some of the most prominent researchers in twentieth-century physics, and it maintains those high standards today. *General Relativity and Gravitation* is an important title in any comprehensive collection on theoretical physics.

4066. *International Journal of Theoretical Physics.* [ISSN: 0020-7748] 1968. m. EUR 4202 (print & online eds.)). Ed(s): Heinrich Saller. Springer New York LLC, 233 Spring St, New York, NY 10013; customerservice@springer.com; http://www.springer.com. Illus., index, adv. Sample. Refereed. Vol. ends: Dec. Microform: PQC. Reprint: PSC. *Indexed:* A01, A22, E01, MSN. *Aud.:* Ac, Sa.

Available in print and online. One of the major goals of modern physics is to develop a grand unification theory that links all known physical forces. Dedicated to the unification of the latest physics research, the *International Journal of Theoretical Physics* seeks to map the direction of future research by presenting original work in traditional physics such as related to general relativity; via quantum theory with relativistic quantum field theory; and by fresh inquiry into quantum measurement theory, and other similarly fundamental areas, among them quantum geometry and quantum logic, and others. Only full-length research papers are accepted. Occasional special issues contain the proceedings of conferences related to unification theory. *Foundations of Physics* (see above in this section) serves a similar objective and contains very similar material. With the continuing search for a grand unification theory, both of these journals will remain important for comprehensive physics collections.

4067. *J C P: Biochemical Physics.* [ISSN: 1931-9223] 2007. m. Ed(s): Marsha I Lester. A I P Publishing LLC, 1305 Walt Whitman Rd, Melville, NY 20740; aipinfo@aip.org; http://www.aip.org. *Aud.:* Ac, Sa.

Available online only. As interest in biochemical processes has grown, the editors of the *Journal of Chemical Physics* created a spin-off online journal dedicated specifically to biophysics. This title includes the subset of articles from the *Journal of Chemical Physics* that directly deal with or have important implications for biologically related systems. All articles included in this journal are also published in the *Journal of Chemical Physics,* but those interested only in the biological section may purchase this title separately. Articles appear online on a daily basis and are compiled into monthly issues. Like its parent title, this journal publishes primarily full-length research articles, but it also includes brief communications and letters to the editor. Libraries that specialize in biological research and not physics may wish to purchase only this section of the *Journal of Chemical Physics.*

4068. *Japanese Journal of Applied Physics.* Supersedes (in 2008): *Japanese Journal of Applied Physics: Part 1. Regular Papers & Short Notes;* Which superseded in part (in 1981): *Japanese Journal of Applied Physics.* [ISSN: 0021-4922] 1962. m. 18 special issues. USD 2915 (print & online eds.)). Institute of Physics Publishing Ltd., Temple Circus, Temple Way, Bristol, BS1 6HG, United Kingdom; custserv@iop.org; http://iopscience.iop.org. Illus. Refereed. *Indexed:* A&ATA. *Aud.:* Ac, Sa.

Available in print and online. The *Japanese Journal of Applied Physics* is an international journal, and is the primary publication outlet for Japanese research in all fields of applied physics. This title publishes articles that deal with the applications of physical principles as well as articles that concern the understanding of physics that have particular applications in mind. Topics covered by this journal include semiconductors, dielectrics, and organic materials; photonics, quantum electronics, optics, and spectroscopy; spintronics, superconductivity, and strongly correlated materials; device physics; nanoscale science and technology; crystal growth, surfaces, interfaces, thin films, and bulk materials; plasmas, applied atomic and molecular physics, and applied nuclear physics; device processing, fabrication and measurement technologies, and instrumentation; and cross-disciplinary areas. The journal publishes research papers, rapid communications, brief notes, and reviews. Letters are published in the sister journal *Applied Physics Express.* Although the journal is Japanese, all of the articles are published in English. Articles in this journal are free to any registered user for 90 days, after which time a subscription is required to retrieve them. As one of the major journals that cover Japanese research, this title is essential to providing balanced coverage of worldwide physics research.

4069. ***Journal of Applied Physics.*** Formerly (until 1937): *Physics;* Which incorporated (1929-1932): *Journal of Rheology.* [ISSN: 0021-8979] 1929. 48x/yr. Ed(s): Andre Anders. A I P Publishing LLC, 1305 Walt Whitman Rd, Melville, NY 11747; aipinfo@aip.org; http://www.aip.org. Illus., index, adv. Sample. Refereed. *Indexed:* A01, A22, BRI. *Aud.:* Ac, Sa.

Available in print and online. The *Journal of Applied Physics* is a primary journal for the publication of applications-centered research in optics, photonics, imaging, and sensing. As opposed to most other physics journals, which concentrate on theoretical or experimental advances, this journal specializes in the application of physical concepts to industrial processes and to other scientific disciplines. Its articles emphasize the understanding of the physics that underlies modern technology, but distinguished from technology on the one side and pure physics on the other. Topics include applied biophysics; dielectrics, ferroelectrics, and multiferrorics; electrical discharges; plasmas and plasma-surface interactions; electrical and thermal transport; energy conservation and storage; magnetism; spintronics; superconductivity; organic–inorganic systems; organic electronics; photonics; plasmonics; lasers' optical phenomena; physics of devices and sensors, matter under extreme conditions, nanoscale, mesoscale, and low-dimensional systems, and semiconductors; thin films; interfaces; surfaces; and applied, emerging, and interdisciplinary physics. The common thread is that the articles clearly describe the uses and applications of a physical concept rather than its theoretical foundations. Full papers and brief communications are included in each issue. Some articles include multimedia components to enhance the text. This journal is the single most highly cited archival research journal in the area of applied physics. Letters are published in the sister publication *Applied Physics Letters* (see above in this section). This title belongs in every physics research collection.

4070. ***The Journal of Chemical Physics.*** [ISSN: 0021-9606] 1933. 48x/yr. Ed(s): Marsha I Lester. A I P Publishing LLC, 1305 Walt Whitman Rd, Melville, NY 11747; aipinfo@aip.org; http://www.aip.org. Illus., index, adv. Sample. Refereed. *Indexed:* A01, A22. *Aud.:* Ac, Sa.

Available in print and online. The purpose of the *Journal of Chemical Physics* is to bridge the gap in scholarly research journals between physics and chemistry. As the boundary between these two disciplines continues to narrow, there are more and more researchers working on issues related to both fields of study. This journal publishes quantitative research based on physical principles and techniques as applied to chemical systems. It covers topics such as spectroscopy, kinetics, statistical mechanics, and quantum mechanics. In addition, newer areas such as polymers, materials, surfaces/interfaces, information theory, and systems of biological relevance are of increasing importance. Most of this journal consists of full-length research reports, although brief communications, letters, and notes are also occasionally included. This title belongs in any research collection devoted to either physics or chemistry.

4071. ***Journal of Computational Physics.*** [ISSN: 0021-9991] 1966. 24x/yr. EUR 9284. Ed(s): R Abgrall. Academic Press, 3251 Riverport Ln, Maryland Heights, MO 63043; JournalCustomerService-usa@elsevier.com; http://www.elsevier.com/. Illus., index, adv. Refereed. *Indexed:* A01, A22, E01, MSN. *Aud.:* Ac, Sa.

Available in print and online. The *Journal of Computational Physics* thoroughly treats the computational aspects of physical problems, as it presents techniques for the numerical solution of mathematical equations arising in all areas of physics. The journal seeks to emphasize methods that cross disciplinary boundaries. Most of the papers deal with the development and application of algorithms for the solution of physical problems. The articles do not contain new research findings, but provide scientists with the methodology for conducting and refining the research process using mathematical processes. Papers dealing solely with hardware or software are excluded; each article must discuss the applications of computing to a physical or mathematical problem. Full-length research reports, short notes, and letters to the editor are all accepted. Occasional themed issues deal with special topics. Supplemental material such as audio, video, animation, images, or data are included in the online version of this journal along with the article. This journal supplements other physics research titles and belongs in comprehensive collections.

4072. ***Journal of Magnetism and Magnetic Materials.*** [ISSN: 0304-8853] 1975. 24x/yr. EUR 10315. Ed(s): S D Bader. Elsevier BV, North-Holland, Postbus 211, Amsterdam, 1000 AE, Netherlands; JournalsCustomerServiceEMEA@elsevier.com; http://www.elsevier.com. Illus., index, adv. Sample. Refereed. Microform: PQC. *Indexed:* A01, A22. *Aud.:* Ac, Sa.

Available in print and online. As one of the basic forces of physics, magnetism is a property that has been widely studied for centuries. The *Journal of Magnetism and Magnetic Materials* provides an important forum for the disclosure and discussion of original contributions that cover the whole spectrum of topics, from basic magnetism to the technology and applications of magnetic materials and magnetic recording. The journal encourages greater interaction between the basic and applied subdisciplines of magnetism. Theoretical, experimental, and applied-research papers are all included. The journal also publishes letters to the editor, short communications, and occasional review articles. Some issues contain the proceedings of conferences relating to magnetism or magnetic materials. This journal belongs in any library that supports research in this field.

4073. ***Journal of Mathematical Physics.*** [ISSN: 0022-2488] 1960. m. Ed(s): Bruno L Z Nachtergaele. A I P Publishing LLC, 1305 Walt Whitman Rd, Melville, NY 11747; aipinfo@aip.org; http://www.aip.org. Illus., index, adv. Sample. Refereed. *Indexed:* A01, A22, MSN. *Aud.:* Ac, Sa.

Available in print and online. The purpose of this journal is to provide a place for the publication of articles that deal with the application of mathematics to problems in modern physics. It also covers the development of mathematical techniques and research methods and the application of mathematics to physical theories. Specific topics cover the entire range of the field of physics, including: classical mechanics, kinetic theory, dynamical systems, quantum mechanics, scattering theory, particles and fields, relativity, gravitation, string theory, statistical mechanics, dynamical systems, and quantum information and computation. New articles are published online every day, then collected into monthly online and print issues. An annual special issue provides in-depth analysis of one specific aspect of mathematical physics. The editors request that the mathematics be presented in such a way as to be understandable by a wide audience within the physics community. Even so, most of the articles will require a graduate-level understanding of mathematics and physics in order to completely comprehend the material. An important addition to any graduate physics collection.

4074. ***Journal of Physics A: Mathematical and Theoretical.*** Formerly (until 2007): *Journal of Physics A: Mathematical and General;* Which superseded in part (in 1975): *Journal of Physics A: Mathematical Nuclear and General;* Which was formerly (until 1973): *Journal of Physics. A, Physical Society. Proceedings. General;* Which superseded in part (in 1968): *Physical Society. Proceedings;* Which was formed by the merger of (1949-1958): *Physical Society. Proceedings. Section A;* (1949-1958): *Physical Society. Proceedings. Section B;* Both of which superseded in part (in 1949): *Physical Society. Proceedings;* (until 1926): *Physical Society of London. Proceedings;* Physical Society. Proceedings incorporated (1900-1932): *Optical Society. Transactions.* [ISSN: 1751-8113] 1958. 50x/yr. USD 12660 (print & online eds.)). Institute of Physics Publishing Ltd., Temple Circus, Temple Way, Bristol, BS1 6HG, United Kingdom; custserv@iop.org; http://iopscience.iop.org. Illus. Sample. Refereed. *Indexed:* A01, A22, MSN. *Aud.:* Ac, Sa.

Available in print and online. As the British counterpart to the *Physical Review* (see below in this section), the *Journal of Physics* is one of the two most prominent collections of physics research journals published anywhere the world. It is also one of the most heavily cited sources in the field and is highly respected by researchers worldwide. Like the *Physical Review,* this journal is issued in many parts that cover the various subdisciplines of physics. *Part A* covers mathematical and statistical physics. Thus, it is primarily concerned with the mathematical structures that describe fundamental processes of the physical world and on the analytical, computational, and numerical methods for exploring these structures. It is divided into six subsections, covering the fields of statistical physics; chaotic and complex systems; mathematical physics; quantum mechanics and quantum information theory; field theory and string theory; and fluid and plasma theory. Both full-length research papers and letters to the editor are included, along with short corrections to previously published material. Review articles appear occasionally, and sometimes special issues are devoted to specific topics. This title belongs in every physics research collection.

4075. *Journal of Physics and Chemistry of Solids: an international journal.* Formerly (until 1963): *Physics and Chemistry of Solids.* [ISSN: 0022-3697] 1956. m. EUR 4071. Ed(s): M Azuma, K Prassides. Pergamon Press, The Blvd, Langford Ln, E Park, Kidlington, OX5 1GB, United Kingdom; JournalsCustomerServiceEMEA@elsevier.com; http://www.elsevier.com. Illus., adv. Sample. Refereed. Microform: MIM; PQC. *Indexed:* A01, A22. *Aud.:* Ac, Sa.

Available in print and online. The *Journal of Physics and Chemistry of Solids* publishes original research in condensed-matter physics and materials science. General areas of interest are the electronic, spectroscopic, and structural properties of solids; the statistical mechanics and thermodynamics of condensed systems, including perfect and defect lattices; surfaces, interfaces, thin films, and multilayers; amorphous materials and nanostructures; and layered and low-dimensional structures. Specific topics covered include the preparation and structural characterization of novel and advanced materials, especially in relation to the measurement and interpretation of their electrical, magnetic, optical, thermal, and mechanical properties; phase transitions, electronic structure, and defect properties; and the application of appropriate experimental and theoretical techniques in these studies. Also covered is the application of appropriate experimental and theoretical techniques used in these studies. From time to time, special issues of the journal are published that contain invited articles devoted to topical or rapidly developing fields. Only full-length articles are accepted, with letters published in the related *Solid State Communications* (see below in this section). For comprehensive physics research collections.

4076. *Journal of Physics B: Atomic, Molecular and Optical Physics.* Incorporates (in 1999): *Journal of Optics B: Quantum and Semiclassical Optics;* Which was formerly (until 1999): *Quantum and Semiclassical Optics;* (until 1995): *Quantum Optics;* Former titles (until 1988): *Journal of Physics B: Atomic and Molecular Physics;* (until 1969): *Journal of Physics B: Physical Society. Proceedings. Atomic and Molecular Physics;* Which superseded in part (in 1968): *Physical Society. Proceedings;* Which was formed by the merger of (1949-1958): *Physical Society. Proceedings. Section A;* (1949-1958): *Physical Society. Proceedings. Section B;* Both of which superseded in part (in 1949): *Physical Society. Proceedings;* Which was formerly (until 1926): *Physical Society of London. Proceedings;* Physical Society. Proceedings incorporated (1900-1932): *Optical Society. Transactions.* [ISSN: 0953-4075] 1958. s-m. USD 9085 (print & online eds.)). Institute of Physics Publishing Ltd., Temple Circus, Temple Way, Bristol, BS1 6HG, United Kingdom; custserv@iop.org; http://iopscience.iop.org. Illus. Sample. Refereed. *Indexed:* A01, A22. *Aud.:* Ac, Sa.

Available in print and online. As part of the *Journal of Physics* collection of titles, this is one of the most prominent physics journals published worldwide. This section covers atoms, ions, molecules and clusters, and their structure and interactions with particles, photons, or fields. It also covers those aspects of spectroscopy, quantum optics and non-linear optics, laser physics, astrophysics, plasma physics, chemical physics, optical cooling and trapping, and other investigations where the objects of study are the elementary atomic, ionic, or molecular properties of processes. In addition to publishing full-length research reports, this title also publishes invited papers, review articles, fast-track communications, and Ph.D. tutorials. The Ph.D. tutorials guide newcomers into rapidly developing fields, and the "Fast Track" papers take the place of the former letters to the editor. This journal is similar in coverage and scope to *Part B* of the *Physical Review* (see below in this section). Occasional special issues are devoted to a single topic. This is one of the most respected journals in the field, and it belongs in every physics research collection.

4077. *Journal of Physics: Condensed Matter.* Formed by the merger of (1971-1989): *Journal of Physics F: Metal Physics;* Which superseded in part (in 1971): *Metal Physics;* (1968-1989): *Journal of Physics C: Solid State Physics;* Which was formerly (until 1968): *Journal of Physics C: Physical Society. Proceedings. Solid State Physics;* Which superseded in part (in 1968): *Physical Society. Proceedings;* Which was formed by the merger of (1949-1958): *Physical Society. Proceedings. Section A;* (1949-1958): *Physical Society. Proceedings. Section B;* Both of which superseded in part (in 1949): *Physical Society. Proceedings;* Which was formerly (until 1926): *Physical Society of London. Proceedings;* Physical Society. Proceedings incorporated (1900-1932): *Optical Society. Transactions.* [ISSN: 0953-8984] 1958. 50x/yr. USD 18290 (print & online eds.)). Institute of Physics Publishing Ltd., Temple Circus, Temple Way, Bristol, BS1 6HG, United Kingdom; custserv@iop.org; http://iopscience.iop.org. Illus., adv. Sample. Refereed. *Indexed:* A22. *Aud.:* Ac, Sa.

Available in print and online. Another journal in the important *Journal of Physics* collection, this title is devoted to articles on experimental and theoretical studies of the structural, thermal, mechanical, electrical, magnetic, optical, and surface properties of condensed matter. Specific topics include surface, interface, and atomic-scale science; liquids, soft matter, and biological physics; nanostructures and nanoelectronics; solid structure and lattice dynamics; electronic structure; correlated electrons; superconductors and metals; semiconductors; dielectrics and ferroelectrics; computational and experimental methods; and magnetism and magnetic materials. Most articles are full research papers, although the journal also publishes topical review articles. "Fast Track Communications" takes the place of letters to the editor and publishes short, important research findings. The journal provides free open access to articles that the editors consider to be outstanding. As part of the *Journal of Physics,* this title belongs in all physics research collections.

4078. *Journal of Physics: Conference Series (Online).* [ISSN: 1742-6596] 2004. a. Free. Institute of Physics Publishing Ltd., Temple Circus, Temple Way, Bristol, BS1 6HG, United Kingdom; custserv@iop.org; http://iopscience.iop.org. *Aud.:* Ac, Sa.

Available online only. This section of the *Journal of Physics* was established as an open-access journal for the publication of the proceedings of conferences, workshops, and institutes on topics throughout the field of physics. Since it is freely available online, it allows for publication within three months of the event and provides long-term archiving of the papers. All papers are printed in pdf format, with accompanying multimedia materials where appropriate. As it has become an established publication outlet, it has recruited more and more conferences to participate. In 2010, the papers from 61 different conferences were published through this journal. Because the papers are presented at meetings for specialists in the field, they are highly specific in content and not for the casual reader. This journal makes conference proceedings available to a worldwide audience at no cost. It belongs in every physics research collection.

4079. *Journal of Physics D: Applied Physics.* Former titles (until 1970): *British Journal of Applied Physics. Journal of Physics D;* (until 1968): *British Journal of Applied Physics.* [ISSN: 0022-3727] 1950. 50x/yr. USD 7915 (print & online eds.)). Ed(s): J Morante. Institute of Physics Publishing Ltd., Temple Circus, Temple Way, Bristol, BS1 6HG, United Kingdom; custserv@iop.org; http://iopscience.iop.org. Illus. Sample. Refereed. *Indexed:* A01, A22. *Aud.:* Ac, Sa.

Available in print and online. The *Journal of Physics D* is concerned with all aspects of applied-physics research. The editors welcome experimental, computational (including simulation and modeling), and theoretical studies of applied physics, and also studies in physics-related areas of biomedical and life sciences. Specific areas of interest include applied magnetism and magnetic materials; semiconductors and photonics materials and device physics; low-temperature plasmas and plasma-surface interactions; applied surfaces and interfaces; the structure and properties of matter; condensed matter, interfaces, and related nanostructures; and biological applications of physics. The editors are particularly interested in publishing articles on novel effects and new materials. It publishes full-length research papers, as well as "Fast Track Communications," which are short, timely articles of high impact; and occasional topical reviews. This title is the British equivalent of the *Journal of Applied Physics* (see above in this section), and is an essential component of all physics research collections.

4080. *Journal of Physics G: Nuclear and Particle Physics.* Formerly (until 1989): *Journal of Physics G: Nuclear Physics;* Which superseded in part (in 1975): *Journal of Physics A: Mathematical Nuclear and General;* Which was formerly (until 1973): *Journal of Physics A: Physical Society. Proceedings. General;* Which superseded in part (in 1968): *Physical Society. Proceedings;* Which was formed by the merger of (1949-1958): *Physical Society. Proceedings. Section A;* (1949-1958): *Physical Society. Proceedings. Section B;* Both of which superseded in part (in 1949): *Physical Society. Proceedings;* Which was formerly (until 1926): *Physical Society of London. Proceedings;* Physical Society. Proceedings incorporated (1900-1932): *Optical Society. Transactions.* [ISSN: 0954-3899] 1989. m. USD 5285 (print & online eds.)). Ed(s): Jacek Dobaczewski. Institute of Physics Publishing Ltd., Temple Circus, Temple Way, Bristol, BS1 6HG, United Kingdom; custserv@iop.org; http://iopscience.iop.org. Illus. Sample. Refereed. Vol. ends: Dec. *Indexed:* A01, A22. *Aud.:* Ac, Sa.

Available in print and online. As another section of the *Journal of Physics* collection, *Part G* covers theoretical and experimental topics in the physics of elementary particles and fields, intermediate-energy physics, and nuclear physics. The particle astrophysics section includes all aspects of experimental and theoretical research into cosmic rays, nuclear and particle astrophysics, gamma-ray astronomy, and neutrino astrophysics and dark matter. Full-length research papers, review articles, and research notes are all included, with full-length papers predominating. Tutorials are review articles that define standards or procedures and/or proposes rules or benchmarks, with a goal of focusing and unifying a diverse scientific activity in a given domain of physics. They are original works published by invitation or recommendation of the editorial board. One volume each year consists of the annual *Review of Particle Physics.* This journal is the British equivalent of *Physical Review Sections C* and *D* (see below in this section), and it belongs in any physics research collection.

4081. *Journal of Plasma Physics.* [ISSN: 0022-3778] 1967. bi-m. Ed(s): Bill Dorland. Cambridge University Press, University Printing House, Shaftesbury Rd, Cambridge, CB2 8BS, United Kingdom; journals@cambridge.org; https://www.cambridge.org/. Illus., index, adv. Refereed. Microform: PQC. Reprint: PSC. *Indexed:* A01, A22, E01. *Aud.:* Ac, Sa.

Available in print and online. Plasma physics is a branch of physics that has applications in a wide variety of fields, including astrophysics, fluids, and nuclear physics. This specialized journal publishes original-research reports on laboratory plasmas, space physics, and plasma astrophysics, and hence it takes advantage of the rapid ongoing progress in instrumentation and computing to advance fundamental understanding of multiscale plasma physics. Basic topics include the fundamental physics of plasmas; ionization; kinetic theory; particle orbits; stochastic dynamics; wave propagation; solitons; stability; shock waves; transport; heating; and diagnostics. Applications include fusion; laboratory plasmas; communications devices; laser plasmas; technological plasmas; space physics; and astrophysics. Both theoretical and experimental results are presented, along with applications of plasma science in other fields. Full research papers, reviews, and letters to the editor are included. Occasionally, special themed issues are published. This journal belongs in specialized and comprehensive physics collections. Of note, preprints submitted to arXiv are linked to the final version of record when published.

4082. *Measurement Science and Technology.* Former titles (until 1990): *Journal of Physics E: Scientific Instruments;* (until 1970): *Journal of Physics. E, Journal of Scientific Instruments;* (until 1968): *Journal of Scientific Instruments;* (until 1950): *Journal of Scientific Instruments and of Physics in Industry;* (until 1948): *Journal of Scientific Instruments.* [ISSN: 0957-0233] 1922. m. USD 3540 (print & online eds.)). Ed(s): K T Christensen. Institute of Physics Publishing Ltd., Temple Circus, Temple Way, Bristol, BS1 6HG, United Kingdom; custserv@iop.org; http://iopscience.iop.org. Illus. Sample. Refereed. Vol. ends: Dec. *Indexed:* A22, MLA-IB. *Aud.:* Ac, Sa.

Available in print and online. Experimental research in physics relies a great deal on specialized equipment and precise instrumentation. This journal is devoted to the theory, practice, and application of measurement in physics, chemistry, engineering, and the environmental and life sciences. Topics of interest include measurement theory and practical developments; sensors and sensor systems; optical and laser-based techniques; measurement methods for fluids; imaging techniques; spectroscopy; techniques for materials and materials processing evaluation; measurement techniques for biological, medical, and life-science applications; instrumentation for environmental and atmospheric measurements; and novel instrumentation. Full-length research papers, review articles, and technical design notes are all included. Special issues and featured articles are also commissioned by the editorial board. This title is part of the *Journal of Physics* collection and is the British equivalent of the *Review of Scientific Instruments* (see below in this section). It belongs in any physics research collection.

4083. *Nanotechnology.* [ISSN: 0957-4484] 1990. 50x/yr. USD 7625 (print & online eds.)). Institute of Physics Publishing Ltd., Temple Circus, Temple Way, Bristol, BS1 6HG, United Kingdom; custserv@iop.org; http://iopscience.iop.org. Sample. Refereed. *Indexed:* A01, A22. *Aud.:* Ac, Sa.

Available in print and online. Nanotechnology is the study of phenomena in extremely small dimensions, usually on the order of the size of a hydrogen atom. In this journal, nanotechnology is taken to include the ability to individually address, control, and modify structures, materials, and devices with nanometer precision, and the synthesis of such structures into systems. It encompasses the understanding of the fundamental physics, chemistry, biology, and technology of nanometer-scale objects and how such objects can be used in the areas of computation, sensors, nanostructured materials, and nano-biotechnology. *Nanotechnology* is the official publication of the Institute of Physics that is dedicated to this area of research. It publishes papers that present original research in the field, as well as review articles and tutorials. Articles are grouped into seven sections: biology and medicine; electronics and photonics; patterning and nanofabrication; energy at the nanoscale; sensing and actuating; materials (synthesis or self-assembly); and materials (properties, characterization, or tools). Some articles have supplemental multimedia files that are available alongside the text in the online version of the journal. A related website, http://nanotechweb.org, provides links to news, conferences, employment opportunities, and key papers on nanotechnology from other scientific journals. As the premier journal that covers this branch of physics, this title belongs in every collection that supports research in the field.

4084. *Nature Physics.* [ISSN: 1745-2473] 2005. m. EUR 6648. Ed(s): Alison Wright. Nature Publishing Group, The MacMillan Bldg, 4 Crinan St, London, N1 9XW, United Kingdom; nature@nature.com; https://www.nature.com. Adv. Sample. Refereed. *Indexed:* A01. *Bk. rev.:* 1-3, 500 words. *Aud.:* Ga, Ac, Sa.

Available in print and online. For many years, *Nature* has been one of the two most prestigious science journals published anywhere in the world (the other is *Science*). In order to expand its ability to publish significant research, the editors of *Nature* have created a series of subject-specific spinoff journals that cover the entire range of science and medicine. *Nature Physics* is the title that is devoted to research in physics. The journal content reflects core physics disciplines, but is also open to a broad range of topics whose central theme falls within the bounds of physics. Theoretical physics, particularly where it is pertinent to experiment, also is featured. Research areas covered in the journal include quantum physics; atomic and molecular physics; statistical physics, thermodynamics, and nonlinear dynamics; condensed-matter physics; fluid dynamics; optical physics; chemical physics; information theory and computation; electronics, photonics, and device physics; nanotechnology; nuclear physics; plasma physics; high-energy particle physics; astrophysics and cosmology; biophysics; and geophysics. The main body of the journal consists of original research papers and letters to the editor. Although the most outstanding findings in the field are still published in the general journal *Nature*, the papers published in *Nature Physics* are still considered to be highly prestigious. In addition to research papers, the journal also contains review articles, news from the field, information on conferences and workshops, job ads, and book reviews. Although a derivative of the general journal *Nature*, this title publishes original material and belongs in all physics research collections.

4085. *New Journal of Physics: the open access journal at the forefront of physics.* [ISSN: 1367-2630] 1998. m. Free to institutions. Ed(s): Barry Sanders. Institute of Physics Publishing Ltd., Temple Circus, Temple Way, Bristol, BS1 6HG, United Kingdom; custserv@iop.org; http://iopscience.iop.org. Illus. Sample. Refereed. *Indexed:* A01, MSN. *Aud.:* Ac, Sa.

Available online only. The *New Journal of Physics* is an open-access title supported by author publication charges. The scope of the journal extends across the whole of physics, encompassing pure, applied, theoretical, and experimental research, as well as interdisciplinary topics. Research areas covered by the journal include quantum physics (including quantum information); atomic and molecular physics; optics; condensed matter; surface science; nanoscale science; photonics and device physics; soft matter and polymers; chemical physics; statistical mechanics, thermodynamics, and nonlinear systems; fluid dynamics; plasmas; nuclear physics; high-energy particle physics; cosmology and astrophysics; biological and medical physics; and earth science and geophysics. By publishing only in electronic format, the journal allows for rapid distribution of articles of any length. All articles are subject to the standard peer-review process, but they are not limited by the space and distribution considerations of the print format. Journal coverage extends across the entire range of the discipline of physics, encompassing pure, applied, theoretical, and experimental research, as well as interdisciplinary topics. The journal's online format allows it to be made available to readers at no cost. It is funded by article charges paid by the authors, which is similar to the page charges of print journals. Key articles on hot topics in physics are grouped together to form "Focus" issues. Because of its electronic-only format, many of the articles have accompanying multimedia files. With its no-cost pricing model and the ease of electronic access, this journal should be available in all college libraries. URL: www.iop.org/EJ/journal/1367-2630

4086. *Optica.* [ISSN: 2334-2536] 2014. m. Free. Ed(s): Alex Gaeta. Optical Society of America, 2010 Massachusetts Ave, NW, Washington, DC 20036; info@osa.org; http://www.osapublishing.org. Refereed. *Aud.:* Ac, Sa.

Available online only. Published by the Optical Society of America, this open-access journal is dedicated to the rapid dissemination of high-impact peer-reviewed research across the entire spectrum of optics and photonics. *Optica* provides a forum for pioneering research to be swiftly accessed by the international community, whether that research is theoretical or experimental, fundamental or applied. Published articles are included for their significance, potential impact, originality, technical quality, integrity, scientific rigor, readability, and interest to the broader optics and scientific communities. *Optica* consists of four types of publications, including research letters of four pages or less, research articles of six to eight pages, and mini-reviews of eight to 12 pages. Comments and replies are also included at the editors' discretion. Articles are published as completed and grouped into monthly issues. Citations statistics are available for each article. This journal belongs in all collections that support research in optics.

4087. *Optical Society of America. Journal A: Optics, Image Science, and Vision.* Formerly (until 1993): *Optical Society of America. Journal A, Optics and Image Science;* Which superseded in part (in 1983): *Optical Society of America. Journal;* Which superseded in part (in 1929): *Optical Society of America. Journal. Review of Scientific Instruments;* Which was formerly (until 1922): *Optical Society of America. Journal.* [ISSN: 1084-7529] 1984. m. USD 3233 combined subscription domestic print & online eds.; USD 3223 combined subscription in Canada & Mexico print & online eds.; USD 3413 combined subscription elsewhere print & online eds. Ed(s): Scott Carney. Optical Society of America, 2010 Massachusetts Ave, NW, Washington, DC 20036; info@osa.org; http://www.osapublishing.org. Illus., index, adv. Refereed. Vol. ends: Dec. *Indexed:* A22. *Aud.:* Ac, Sa.

Available in print and online. As one-half of the official journal of the Optical Society of America, this title is the premier publication outlet for research in the field of optics. *Part A* covers classical optics, image science, and vision. Topics include atmospheric optics; clinical vision; coherence and statistical optics; color; diffraction and gratings; image processing; machine vision; physiological optics; polarization; scattering; signal processing; thin films; and visual optics. The publication includes full-length research articles, tutorials, discussion papers, feature issue contributions, and comments on published articles. Letters to the editor are published in the sister journal *Optics Letters* (see below). Articles are published online as they are accepted and collected in monthly volumes. Along with the *Journal of the Optical Society of America B* (below), this title forms the core of the optics literature and belongs in all physics research collections.

4088. *Optical Society of America. Journal B: Optical Physics.* Supersedes in part (in 1983): *Optical Society of America. Journal;* Which superseded in part (in 1929): *Optical Society of America. Journal. Review of Scientific Instruments;* Which was formerly (until 1922): *Optical Society of America. Journal.* [ISSN: 0740-3224] 1984. m. USD 3233 combined subscription domestic print & online eds.; USD 3323 combined subscription in Canada & Mexico print & online eds.; USD 3413 combined subscription elsewhere print & online eds. Ed(s): Grover Swartzlander. Optical Society of America, 2010 Massachusetts Ave, NW, Washington, DC 20036; info@osa.org; http://www.osapublishing.org. Illus., index, adv. Refereed. *Indexed:* A22. *Aud.:* Ac, Sa.

Available in print and online. As the second half of the official journal of the Optical Society of America, this title comprises part of the core literature in the field of optics. *Part B* covers research on the fundamentals of the interaction of light with matter such as quantum optics, nonlinear optics, and laser physics. It includes such topical areas as atom optics and cold atoms, integrated and fiber optics, metamaterials, nanophotonics, photonic crystals, photorefractive optics and holography, physics of optical materials, spectroscopy, THz optics, ultrafast phenomena, and other related subjects. Like its sister section the *Journal of the Optical Society of America [Part] A*, it publishes research articles, feature issue contributions, invited reviews, and comments on published articles. Letters are published in the related *Optics Letters* (see below). Articles are published online as accepted and collected in monthly volumes. As major journals in one of the most prominent branches of physics, *Part A* and *Part B* belong in all physics research collections.

4089. *Optics Express.* [ISSN: 1094-4087] 1997. bi-w. Free. Ed(s): Andrew Weiner. Optical Society of America, 2010 Massachusetts Ave, NW, Washington, DC 20036; info@osa.org; http://www.osapublishing.org. Refereed. *Aud.:* Ac, Sa.

Available online. *Optics Express* is an open-access journal. It publishes original, peer-reviewed articles that report new developments of interest to the optics community in all fields of optical science and technology. The "Energy Express" supplement reports research on the science and engineering of light and its impact on sustainable energy development, the environment, and green technologies. All subfields of optics are covered, including atmospheric and oceanic optics; detectors; diffraction and gratings; fiber optics and optical communications; holography; image processing; imaging systems; instrumentation, measurement, and metrology; integrated optics; laser micromachining; lasers and laser optics; medical optics and biotechnology; metamaterials; microscopy; nonlinear optics; optical design and fabrication; optical devices; optical trapping and manipulation; optics at surfaces; optoelectronics; photonic crystal fibers; photonic crystals; physical optics; quantum optics; remote sensing and sensors; scattering; thin films; ultrafast optics; and coherence and statistical optics. Occasional focus issues cover specific topics of interest in the field of optics. Because it is available to all individuals at no charge, this journal belongs in all physics collections. URL: www.opticsexpress.org

4090. *Optics Letters.* [ISSN: 0146-9592] 1977. s-m. USD 3541 print & online eds. Ed(s): Xi-Cheng E Zhang. Optical Society of America, 2010 Massachusetts Ave, NW, Washington, DC 20036; info@osa.org; http://www.osapublishing.org. Illus., index. Refereed. Vol. ends: Jan/Dec. *Indexed:* A22. *Aud.:* Ac, Sa.

Available in print and online. *Optics Letters* serves as the letters-to-the-editor section for both *Applied Optics* and the *Journal of the Optical Society of America* (see above in this section). It covers the latest research in all areas of optics and photonics, including optical measurements; optical components and devices; atmospheric optics; biomedical optics; Fourier optics; integrated optics; optical processing; optoelectronics; lasers; nonlinear optics; optical storage and holography; optical coherence; polarization; quantum electronics; ultrafast optical phenomena; photonic crystals; and fiber optics. Criteria used in the selection of contributions include newsworthiness to a substantial part of the optics community and the effect of rapid publication on the research of others. All articles are short, usually three pages or less. This is a core journal in the field of optics, and it belongs in any collection that supports research in this field.

4091. ***Physical Review A: covering atomic, molecular, and optical physics and quantum information.*** Former titles (until 2016): *Physical Review A (Atomic, Molecular and Optical Physics);* (until 1990): *Physical Review A (General Physics);* Which superseded in part (in 1970): *Physical Review.* [ISSN: 2469-9926] 1893. m. Ed(s): Thomas Pattard, Gordon W.F. Drake. American Physical Society, One Physics Ellipse, College Park, MD 20740; help@aps.org; http://www.aps.org. Illus., index. Refereed. Vol. ends: Jun/Dec. *Indexed:* A22. *Aud.:* Ac, Sa.

Available in print and online. The *Physical Review* collection of journals is the most prestigious set of physics journals published in the world. Along with its British counterpart, the *Journal of Physics* collection (see above in this section), the various components of the *Physical Review* comprise the core research literature of the field. Like many other journals in the sciences, the *Physical Review* has been subdivided into a number of sections that cover specific branches and subdisciplines of physics. *Section A* covers the area of atomic, molecular, and optical physics and related fundamental concepts. Specific subjects found in this title include quantum mechanics; quantum information theory; atomic and molecular structure and dynamics; collisions and interactions (including interactions with surfaces and solids); clusters (including fullerenes); atomic and molecular processes in external fields; matter waves (including Bose-Einstein condensation); and quantum optics. Full-length articles, brief reports, comments, and short rapid communications are all included. Letters are published in the related *Physical Review Letters* (see below). As in all of the sections of the *Physical Review,* the number of articles and pages published is tremendous, with more than 2,500 articles and 20,000 pages per year. However, the refereeing process is highly selective, rejecting more than half of all articles submitted. The large number of papers published has led to a paper/page system, instead of consecutively numbered pages. Color images are not published in the print edition, but are included in the web version of appropriate papers. As one section of the most important journal in the field, this title belongs in every physics research collection.

4092. ***Physical Review Accelerators and Beams.*** Formerly (until 2015): *Physical Review Special Topics - Accelerators and Beams.* [ISSN: 2469-9888] 1998. m. Free. Ed(s): Frank Zimmermann. American Physical Society, One Physics Ellipse, College Park, MD 20740; help@aps.org; http://www.aps.org. Refereed. *Aud.:* Ac, Sa.

Available online only. *Physical Review Accelerators and Beams* is a peer-reviewed, open-access journal distributed without charge to readers, and funded by sponsors from national and international laboratories and other partners. The articles are published by the American Physical Society under the terms of the Creative Commons Attribution 3.0 License. It covers the full range of accelerator science and technology: subsystem and component technologies; beam dynamics; accelerator applications; and design, operation, and improvement of accelerators used in science and industry. This includes accelerators for high-energy and nuclear physics, synchrotron radiation production, spallation neutron sources, medical therapy, and intense beam applications. Papers may present new research results; review the state of the art of accelerator research or technology; propose new experiments; review active areas of research; or expand upon previously published research. Because of its electronic nature, there is no limit to the number of pages or illustrations that can be included in any given article. Although not as large as other sections of the *Physical Review,* this journal publishes hundreds of articles and thousands of pages each year. Another important feature of the electronic nature of this publication is that most articles are freely available, without restriction, to any reader. In addition to the original research articles, the journal links to relevant papers published in other sections of the *Physical Review* and *Physical Review Letters.* Recommended for any library that supports specialized research in this area. URL: http://prst-ab.aps.org

4093. ***Physical Review B: covering condensed matter and materials physics.*** Former titles (until 2016): *Physical Review B (Condensed Matter and Materials Physics);* (until 1998): *Physical Review B (Condensed Matter);* (until 1978): *Physical Review B (Solid State);* Which superseded in part (in 1970): *Physical Review.* [ISSN: 2469-9950] 1893. 48x/yr. Ed(s): Laurens W Molenkamp. American Physical Society, One Physics Ellipse, College Park, MD 20740; help@aps.org; http://www.aps.org. Illus., index. Refereed. *Indexed:* A01, A22. *Aud.:* Ac, Sa.

Available in print and online. The second section of the *Physical Review* is devoted to condensed-matter and materials science. It is published monthly in two sections, B1 and B15. Topics covered in B1 include structure, phase transitions, ferroelectrics, nonordered systems, liquids, quantum solids, magnetism, superconductivity, and superfluidity. B15 covers electronic structure, photonic crystals, semiconductors, mesoscopic systems, surfaces, clusters, fullerenes, graphene, and nanoscience. Full-length papers predominate, but short, rapid communications are also accepted. Accompanying color images are included only in the online version of the journal. Letters to the editor are published in the related *Physical Review Letters* (see below in this section). This is the most frequently cited journal in the world devoted to condensed-matter physics. Like all sections of the *Physical Review,* this section is not for the casual reader. It publishes close to 50,000 pages of primary research results of a highly technical nature each year. The large number of papers published has led to a paper/page system, instead of consecutively numbered pages. Along with the *Journal of Physics: Condensed Matter* (see above in this section), *Part B* of the *Physical Review* presents the most important research in the field. Like all of the sections of the *Physical Review,* it belongs in every physics research collection.

4094. ***Physical Review C: covering nuclear physics.*** Formerly (until 2016): *Physical Review C (Nuclear Physics);* Supersedes in part (1893-1969): *Physical Review.* [ISSN: 2469-9985] 1970. m. Ed(s): Benjamin F. Gibson. American Physical Society, One Physics Ellipse, College Park, MD 20740; help@aps.org; http://www.aps.org. Illus., index. Refereed. Vol. ends: Jun/Dec. *Indexed:* A01, A22. *Aud.:* Ac, Sa.

Available in print and online. *Part C* of the *Physical Review* covers experimental and theoretical research results in all aspects of nuclear physics, including the nucleon-nucleon interaction, few-body systems, nuclear structure, nuclear reactions, relativistic nuclear collisions, hadronic physics and QCD, electroweak interaction, symmetries, and nuclear astrophysics. Both full-length research papers and brief reports are included, along with comments on previously published research. Letters to the editor are published in the separate *Physical Review Letters* (see below in this section). Like all of the sections of the *Physical Review,* this section is the most prestigious journal published in its branch of physics. *Physical Review* publishes more than 1,000 articles per year. The large number of papers published has led to a paper/page system, instead of consecutively numbered pages. Along with the *Journal of Physics G* (see above in this section), this title represents the core literature of nuclear physics and belongs in any physics research collection.

4095. ***Physical Review D: covering particles, fields, gravitation, and cosmology.*** Former titles (until 2016): *Physical Review D (Particles, Fields, Gravitation and Cosmology);* (until 2004): *Physical Review D (Particles and Fields);* Which superseded in part (in 1970): *Physical Review.* [ISSN: 2470-0010] 1893. s-m. Ed(s): Urs M Heller, Erick J. Weinberg. American Physical Society, One Physics Ellipse, College Park, MD 20740; help@aps.org; http://www.aps.org. Illus., index. Refereed. *Indexed:* A01, A22, MSN. *Aud.:* Ac, Sa.

Available in print and online. This section of the *Physical Review* covers particles, field theory, gravitation, and cosmology. The first issue of each month, D1, is devoted to experimental high-energy physics, phenomenologically oriented theory of particles and fields, cosmic-ray physics, electroweak interactions, applications of QCD, and lattice gauge theory. The second issue of the month, D2, covers general relativity, the quantum theory of gravitation, cosmology, particle astrophysics, formal aspects of theory of particles and fields, general and formal development in gauge field theories, and string theory. Issues consist primarily of full-length research reports, and some (short) rapid communications. Review articles also appear on an irregular basis. Letters appear in the related *Physical Review Letters* (see below). Almost 3,000 articles are published per year, filling well more than 30,000 pages. As with the other sections of the *Physical Review,* the editors have abandoned sequential page-numbering in favor of an article/page system. Along with all the other parts of the journal, *Part D* is the premier journal in the world that covers its branch of physics, and it belongs in every physics research library.

4096. ***Physical Review E: covering statistical, nonlinear, biological, and soft matter physics.*** Former titles (until 2016): *Physical Review E (Statistical, Nonlinear, and Soft Matter Physics);* (until 2001): *Physical Review E (Statistical Physics, Plasmas, Fluids, and Related*

Interdisciplinary Topics); Which superseded in part (in 1993): *Physical Review A (Atomic, Molecular and Optical Physics);* Which was formerly (until 1990): *Physical Review A (General Physics);* Which superseded in part (in 1970): *Physical Review.* [ISSN: 2470-0045] 1893. m. Ed(s): Eli Ben-Naim. American Physical Society, One Physics Ellipse, College Park, MD 20740; help@aps.org; http://www.aps.org. Illus., index. Refereed. Vol. ends: Jun/Dec. *Indexed:* A01, A22, MSN. *Aud.:* Ac, Sa.

Available in print and online. *Physical Review E* is broad and interdisciplinary in scope. It focuses on collective phenomena of many-body systems, with statistical physics and nonlinear dynamics as the central themes of the journal. It publishes recent developments in biological and soft-matter physics, including granular materials, colloids, complex fluids, liquid crystals, fluid dynamics and plasma physics, polymers, and computational and interdisciplinary physics. The journal is very large, with more than 20,000 pages published annually. Full articles, brief research reports, and rapid communications of important findings are all accepted, along with comments on previously published material. Letters are published in the related *Physical Review Letters* (see below). As with all other sections of the *Physical Review,* the editors reject more than half of all papers submitted. The journal uses an article/page numbering system, instead of page numbering. *Part E,* as one part of the most prestigious physics journal in the world, belongs in any physics research collection.

4097. *Physical Review Letters.* Supersedes in part (in 1958): *Physical Review.* [ISSN: 0031-9007] 1893. w. Ed(s): Robert Garisto, Reinhardt B Schuhmann. American Physical Society, One Physics Ellipse, College Park, MD 20740; help@aps.org; http://www.aps.org. Illus., index. Refereed. *Indexed:* A01, A22, MSN. *Aud.:* Ac, Sa.

Available in print and online. This title is the letters-to-the-editor section for all parts of the *Physical Review* (see above). It publishes brief reports of important discoveries in any branch of physics. Topical sections are devoted to general physics (including statistical and quantum mechanics), gravitation, and astrophysics; elementary particles and fields; nuclear physics; atomic, molecular, and optical physics; nonlinear dynamics, fluid dynamics, and classical optics; plasma and beam physics; condensed matter; and soft-matter, biological, and interdisciplinary physics. All articles published are very brief, with a maximum length of five pages. Like its parent journal, *Physical Review Letters* is one of the most respected and most cited journals in all of physics. Comments on letters and replies to those comments may also be printed. It was one of the very first letters-only journals and maintains the high editorial standards of the *Physical Review.* Even though hundreds of pages are published each week, the editors reject more than half of all papers submitted. *Physical Review Letters* is the single most prestigious journal of its kind and belongs in every physics research collection.

4098. *Physical Review Physics Education Research.* Formerly (until 2015): *Physical Review Special Topics - Physics Education Research.* [ISSN: 2469-9896] s-a. Free. Ed(s): Charles Henderson. American Physical Society, One Physics Ellipse, College Park, MD 20740; help@aps.org; http://www.aps.org. Refereed. *Indexed:* ERIC. *Aud.:* Ga, Ac, Sa.

Available online only. *Physical Review Physics Education Research* is a peer-reviewed, open-access journal sponsored by the American Physical Society (APS), the American Association of Physics Teachers (AAPT), and the APS Forum on Education (APS FEd). The articles are published by the American Physical Society under the terms of the Creative Commons Attribution 3.0 License. The journal covers the full range of experimental and theoretical research on the teaching and/or learning of physics. Contents consist of review articles, replication studies, descriptions of the development and use of new assessment tools, presentation of research techniques, and methodology comparisons/critiques. Because of its high standards and free availability, it is recommended for any college or university that has a physics program.

4099. *Physical Review X.* [ISSN: 2160-3308] 2011. q. Free. Ed(s): Jean-Michel Raimond, M Cristina Marchetti. American Physical Society, One Physics Ellipse, College Park, MD 20740; help@aps.org; http://www.aps.org. Refereed. *Aud.:* Ac, Sa.

Available online only. *Physical Review X* is a peer-reviewed, open-access journal funded by open-access charges to authors or their institutions. The articles are published by the American Physical Society under the terms of the Creative Commons Attribution 3.0 License. It is a highly selective, peer-reviewed journal that aims to publish, as timely as possible, exceptional original research papers from all areas of pure, applied, and interdisciplinary physics. *PRX*'s mission is to disseminate innovative results, which are apt to have impact, to the broad science and engineering communities from all areas of pure, applied, and interdisciplinary physics. Because of its electronic nature, there is no limit to the number of pages or illustrations that can be included in any given article. Another important feature of this publication is that all articles are freely available, without restriction, to any reader. Recommended for any library that supports a physics research program. URL: http://prx.aps.org

4100. *Physical Society of Japan. Journal.* Formerly: *Physico-Mathematical Society of Japan. Proceedings.* [ISSN: 0031-9015] 1946. m. Ed(s): Tsuneya Ando. Institute of Pure and Applied Physics, Toyokaiji Bldg, no.12, 6-9-6 Shinbashi, Minato-ku, Tokyo, 105-0004, Japan; subscription@ipap.jp; http://www.ipap.jp. Illus., index. Refereed. Vol. ends: Dec. *Indexed:* A22. *Aud.:* Ac, Sa.

Available in print and online. This title is the official journal of the Physical Society of Japan, publishing some of the most significant physics research conducted in Japan and Asia. It is devoted to the rapid dissemination of important research results in all fields of physics, from condensed-matter physics to particle physics. All of the subdisciplines of physics are covered, including elementary particles and fields; nuclear physics; atomic and molecular physics; fluid dynamics; plasma physics; condensed matter; metal, superconductor, semiconductor, magnetic materials, and dielectric materials; physics of nanoscale materials; optics and quantum electronics; physics of complex systems; mathematical physics; chemical physics; biophysics; geophysics; and astrophysics. Despite the broad nature of its scope, this journal publishes more articles on condensed-matter physics than on any other topic. Although the journal is published in Japan, all of the articles are written in English, making them accessible to the wider scientific community. Full-length scientific papers, short notes (on recent research breakthroughs), comments, addenda, errata, and letters to the editor are all included. This title is the Japanese equivalent of the other national journals included here, and it belongs in comprehensive physics research collections.

4101. *Physics.* [ISSN: 1943-2879] 2008. d. Free. Ed(s): Jessica Thomas. American Physical Society, One Physics Ellipse, College Park, MD 20740; help@aps.org; http://www.aps.org. Refereed. *Aud.:* Ac, Sa.

It takes a little audacity to name your publication after the field of study, but *Physics* lives up to that burden. Published online by the American Physical Society, this open-access title highlights key articles from all of the sections of the *Physical Review* (see above). Rather than reproduce or link to the original research paper, *Physics* contains viewpoints (commentaries by prominent experts at the college physics level); focus stories (written by a journalist for general audiences); and synopses (written by editors and journalists at the college physics level). Thus, the articles in this journal are accessible to a wider audience than that of the original research reports. In addition, select notes from the editor are included, in order to share brief tidbits of information on topics of interest from *Physical Review* and the American Physical Society national meetings. All subfields within physics are covered. The goal of this journal is to provide a guide to the best research in physics. Given the quality of the source material, *Physics* is able to achieve that goal. This title belongs in any collection that serves researchers, and students, in the field of physics.

4102. *Physics Education.* [ISSN: 0031-9120] 1966. bi-m. USD 885 (print & online eds.)). Ed(s): Gary Williams. Institute of Physics Publishing Ltd., Temple Circus, Temple Way, Bristol, BS1 6HG, United Kingdom; custserv@iop.org; http://iopscience.iop.org. Illus. Sample. Refereed. Vol. ends: Nov. *Indexed:* A01, A22, ERIC. *Bk. rev.:* Number and length vary. *Aud.:* Hs, Ga, Ac.

Available in print and online. *Physics Education* is a British journal for teaching physics to students from the age of 11 to beginning undergraduate college levels. As such, it is one of the few physics journals that can be read by a general audience. The editors seek to provide teachers with a forum for practicing teachers to make an active contribution to the teaching and learning of physics; the examining and assessment of physics; new approaches to the general presentation and application of physics in the classroom; classroom experiments and demonstrations; investigations; equipment, practical work, and ways of teaching difficult topics in physics; news; the schools and the personalities who have made an impact in physics education or, equally importantly, in industry, finance, the media or technology; and curriculum developments around the world. In addition, resource reviews, letters, and end results are also included. All of the articles are written for the nonspecialist and avoid much of the higher-level mathematics inherent in most physics research publications. The goals of the journal are (1) to cover the wide range of topics included in the field of physics, (2) to enhance the standards and quality of teaching, (3) to make physics more attractive to students and teachers, (4) to keep teachers up to date on new developments in the field, and (5) to provide a forum for the sharing of ideas about teaching physics. Each issue contains articles on new developments in physics, ideas for teaching physical concepts, profiles of prominent scientists, reviews of resources that can be used by physics teachers, news from the field, and even a little humor. Articles in the electronic version are supplemented by multimedia content such as worksheets, spreadsheets, programs, audio and video clips, and video abstracts (when available). This journal is the British equivalent of *The Physics Teacher* (see below in this section), and it is an excellent choice for those libraries that seek to add a general physics journal to their collections.

4103. *Physics Letters. Section A: General, Atomic and Solid State Physics.* Supersedes in part (in 1967): *Physics Letters.* [ISSN: 0375-9601] 1962. 48x/yr. EUR 8092. Ed(s): C R Doering, A Eisfeld. Elsevier BV, North-Holland, Postbus 211, Amsterdam, 1000 AE, Netherlands; JournalsCustomerServiceEMEA@elsevier.com; http://www.elsevier.com. Illus., index. Sample. Refereed. Vol. ends: No. 278 - No. 291. Microform: PQC. *Indexed:* A01, A22, MSN. *Aud.:* Ac, Sa.

Available in print and online. *Physics Letters* is a publication outlet for rapid communication of significant, original, and timely research results. Articles tend to be very brief, with longer review articles printed in the related journal *Physics Reports* (see below in this section). *Section A* of this journal is the general physics portion, covering all branches of physics except high-energy nuclear and particle physics. Topics usually include condensed matter physics; theoretical physics; nonlinear science; statistical physics; mathematical and computational physics; general and cross-disciplinary physics; atomic, molecular, and cluster physics; plasma and fluid physics; optical physics; biological physics; and nanoscience. Articles are accepted for publication based on the originality of the research, desirability for speedy publication, and the clarity of the presentation. This journal publishes an incredible number of articles, producing close to 5,000 pages per volume. Along with the *Physical Review Letters* (see above), it is one of the most cited and most prominent letters journals in the field. This title belongs in any physics research collection.

4104. *Physics Letters. Section B: Nuclear, Elementary Particle and High-Energy Physics.* Supersedes in part (in 1967): *Physics Letters.* [ISSN: 0370-2693] 1962. 12x/yr. EUR 659. Ed(s): M Doser, W D Schlatter. Elsevier BV, North-Holland, Postbus 211, Amsterdam, 1000 AE, Netherlands; JournalsCustomerServiceEMEA@elsevier.com; http://www.elsevier.com. Illus., index. Sample. Refereed. Vol. ends: No. 497 - No. 523. Microform: PQC. *Indexed:* A01, A22, MSN. *Aud.:* Ac, Sa.

Available in print and online. *Physics Letters B* is the second part of the Physics Letters series. It covers the three areas excluded from *Part A*: particle physics, nuclear physics, and cosmology. Despite its more limited subject scope, this section is the larger of the two journals, reflecting the vast amount of research published in nuclear and particle physics and cosmology. There can be as many as 5,000 pages printed in this journal in a single year. Each issue is divided into four sections: astrophysics and cosmology; experiments; phenomenology; and theory. Because of the specialized nature of the field, separate editors are assigned to the areas of experimental nuclear physics, theoretical nuclear physics, experimental high-energy physics, theoretical high-energy physics, and astrophysics. As with most physics research journals, each article must be the result of original research and must not have appeared in print before. This journal is frequently used to determine precedent in scientific discoveries in its fields of interest. Both sections of *Physics Letters* should be a part of any serious physics research collection.

4105. *Physics of Fluids.* Formerly (until 1994): *Physics of Fluids A: Fluid Dynamics;* Which superseded in part (in 1988): *Physics of Fluids.* [ISSN: 1070-6631] 1958. m. Ed(s): A Jeffrey Giacomin. A I P Publishing LLC, 1305 Walt Whitman Rd, Melville, NY 11747; aipinfo@aip.org; http://www.aip.org. Illus., index, adv. Sample. Refereed. *Indexed:* A01, A22, S25. *Aud.:* Ac, Sa.

Available in print and online. This journal is the official publication of the Division of Fluid Dynamics of the American Physical Society. It is devoted to the publication of original research in the field of fluid dynamics, as well as dynamics of gases, liquids, and complex or multiphase fluids. Theoretical, experimental, and computational studies are all included. Specific areas covered include kinetic theory, fluid dynamics, wave phenomena, hypersonic physics, hydrodynamics, compressible fluids, boundary layers, conduction, and chaotic phenomena. Material on plasmas and plasma physics is published in the related *Physics of Plasmas* (see below), which can be purchased in combination with this title at a reduced rate. Full papers, brief reports, and letters are all accepted. Comments on previously published papers are also included, sometimes leading to interesting scientific debate. A few of the articles include multimedia components that contribute to the understanding of the underlying physics discussed in the text. The annual "Gallery of Fluid Motion" presents visual representations of fluid flow and fluid problems. The editors also invite award-winning speakers at the annual conference of the Division of Fluid Dynamics to write expanded papers for the journal. This is the primary journal for research in fluids and belongs in any comprehensive physics collection.

4106. *Physics of Plasmas.* Formerly (until 1994): *Physics of Fluids B: Plasma Physics;* Which superseded in part (in 1989): *Physics of Fluids.* [ISSN: 1070-664X] 1958. m. Ed(s): Ronald C Davidson. A I P Publishing LLC, 1305 Walt Whitman Rd, Melville, NY 11747; aipinfo@aip.org; http://www.aip.org. Illus., index, adv. Sample. Refereed. *Indexed:* A01, A22. *Aud.:* Ac, Sa.

Available in print and online. As the official publication of the Division of Plasmas of the American Institute of Physics, *Physics of Plasmas* is devoted to original experimental and theoretical contributions, and in-depth reviews of, the physics of plasmas, including equilibria, linear waves, and instabilities; nonlinear behavior (including turbulent and stochastic phenomena and associated transport) and solitons and shock waves; plasma physics of lasers and particle beams and charged-particle acceleration and transport; radiation generation, transport, propagation, and interaction with plasmas; low-temperature plasmas; plasma chemistry and processing; geophysical, planetary, solar, and astrophysical plasmas; plasma confinement by magnetic fields; inertial confinement physics; physics of high-energy density plasmas or matter under extreme conditions; and dusty plasmas. Articles are published online on a daily basis, and are then compiled into online and print monthly issues. This journal formerly was published with *Physics of Fluids,* but the two journals were divided in 1994. Full-length articles, brief reports, and letters to the editor are all included. This journal is the most highly cited publication in this branch of physics, and it belongs in any collection that supports research in this area.

4107. *Physics Reports.* Incorporates (1983-1991): *Computer Physics Reports;* (1972-1975): *Case Studies in Atomic Physics.* [ISSN: 0370-1573] 1971. 60x/yr. EUR 9450. Ed(s): Marc Kamionkowsi. Elsevier BV, North-Holland, Postbus 211, Amsterdam, 1000 AE, Netherlands; JournalsCustomerServiceEMEA@elsevier.com; http://www.elsevier.com. Illus., index. Sample. Refereed. Vol. ends: No. 338 - No. 353. Microform: PQC. *Indexed:* A01, A22, MSN. *Aud.:* Ac, Sa.

Available in print and online. In contrast to its sister publications *Physics Letters A* and *B* (see above), both of which publish large numbers of brief papers that present new research findings, *Physics Reports* publishes lengthy articles designed to provide state-of-the-art reviews that benchmark research throughout the field of physics. Each issue contains a single article, which is usually somewhat longer than a literature review but shorter than a monograph. The published reviews are specialist in nature, but contain enough background and introductory material to be understandable to physicists who are working in other subdisciplines. In addition to identifying significant developments and trends, the extensive literature reviews serve as indexes to the topic being discussed. Subjects can be from any field of physics, and the editorial board consists of specialists in a variety of fields who are able to judge the quality and accuracy of the manuscripts. Submissions to this journal are by invitation only.

This title is similar in scope to *Contemporary Physics* (above in this section) and *Reports on Progress in Physics* (below), although *Physics Reports* is written at the highest level of the three. All three of these journals are useful additions to a physics research collection.

4108. *The Physics Teacher.* [ISSN: 0031-921X] 1963. 9x/yr. USD 892 (print & online eds.)). Ed(s): Pamela R Aycock, Gary White. A I P Publishing LLC, 1305 Walt Whitman Rd, Melville, NY 11747; aipinfo@aip.org; http://www.aip.org. Illus., index, adv. Sample. Refereed. *Indexed:* A01, A22, BRI, ERIC. *Bk. rev.:* Number and length vary. *Aud.:* Hs, Ga, Ac.

Available in print and online. *The Physics Teacher* publishes papers on the teaching of physics, and on topics such as contemporary physics, applied physics, and the history of physics-all aimed at the introductory-level teacher. It is the primary journal that supports high school physics teachers. Articles are written for the nonspecialist and present physics principles without the higher-level mathematics that are usually included in physics research journals. Papers cover topics of interest to students and to the general public, often focusing on the applications of physical principles to everyday life. In addition to full articles, the journal also publishes ideas for new teaching methods; notes on interesting applications and phenomena; information on equipment and apparatus for teaching physics; and editorials, websites, and book reviews. Every month, the journal publishes several problems for readers to solve, and follows this up in the next issue with solutions and the names of the people who answer correctly. Other features include tips for new teachers, web resources, reviews of YouTube videos that can be used in the classroom, and "Fermi questions," where readers use physics to estimate answers to everyday problems. A few featured articles are free to all readers, although a subscription is required to see all content. This journal is similar to its British equivalent, *Physics Education* (see above). *The Physics Teacher* is a very readable journal and one of the few that is approachable by both the specialist and non-scientist. It is one of the few physics journals that should be considered for general library collections.

4109. *Physics Today.* [ISSN: 0031-9228] 1948. m. Ed(s): Charles Day, Richard J Fitzgerald. A I P Publishing LLC, 1305 Walt Whitman Rd, Melville, NY 11747; aipinfo@aip.org; http://www.aip.org. Illus., index. Sample. Refereed. *Indexed:* A&ATA, A01, A22, BRI, C37, CBRI, MASUSE. *Bk. rev.:* 7-10. *Aud.:* Hs, Ga, Ac.

Available in print and online. If a library subscribes to just one physics journal, this should be it. *Physics Today* is the only true general-interest physics journal currently being published. It is the flagship publication of the American Institute of Physics and is intended to keep readers informed on new research in physics and its impact on society. In addition to providing full-length articles on interesting areas throughout the discipline of physics, this journal serves as a news source for anyone interested in the field, including scientists, teachers, students, and the general public. Its wide appeal is evidenced by the fact that it is the only physics journal to be indexed in the *Readers' Guide to Periodical Literature.* Articles are written specifically for the nonspecialist and present advanced physical concepts without burdening the reader with advanced mathematics. With color photographs, well-written prose, and timely and engaging subject matter, this is the only physics journal that consistently could be considered for newsstand distribution. Each issue provides feature articles, news of recent discoveries, conference updates, editorials, book reviews, new-product announcements, and obituaries. The daily online version also provides news, editorials, policy and politics updates, the editor's blog, and links to original research in other journals published by the American Institute of Physics. *Physics Today* is essential for any college or university library, and should be considered by public and school libraries as well. Unless a library supports a physics research program, this title is the only subscription physics journal that should be included in its journal collection.

4110. *Reports on Progress in Physics.* [ISSN: 0034-4885] 1934. m. USD 5035 (print & online eds.)). Ed(s): Gordon Baym. Institute of Physics Publishing Ltd., Temple Circus, Temple Way, Bristol, BS1 6HG, United Kingdom; custserv@iop.org; http://iopscience.iop.org. Illus. Sample. Refereed. *Indexed:* A&ATA, A01, A22, MSN. *Aud.:* Ac, Sa.

Available in print and online. *Reports on Progress in Physics* publishes review articles in all subdisciplines of physics. Articles combine a critical evaluation of the field with a reliable and accessible introduction to the topic, making the articles accessible to a wider scientific community. As with all review journals, its articles tend to be very long, often more than 100 pages. Topics include condensed matter and materials; soft matter and biological physics; atomic molecular and optical physics; astrophysics and cosmology; nuclear and particle physics; earth science; and general physics. In addition to full-length review articles, the journal also publishes two types of more speculative articles. The section "Reports on Progress" provides an accurate and well-organized presentation of the present status of research results, even if these results and their interpretation are not in universal accord. "Key Issues Reviews" highlights critical questions in a line of physics research that continues to develop, where important advances are widely acknowledged, but whose ultimate significance and goals have not yet been realized or are in dispute. This journal does not review papers submitted by potential authors; rather, most articles are invited by the editors from distinguished researchers in the field. Researchers may also submit proposals to write review articles. This journal is similar in scope to *Contemporary Physics* and *Physics Reports* (see above in this section). College libraries should subscribe to at least one of these titles, and research libraries will probably wish to get all three.

4111. *Review of Scientific Instruments.* Supersedes in part (in 1930): *Optical Society of America and Review of Scientific Instruments. Journal;* Which was formerly (until 1922): *Optical Society of America. Journal.* [ISSN: 0034-6748] 1917. m. Ed(s): Richard C Pardo. A I P Publishing LLC, 1305 Walt Whitman Rd, Melville, NY 11747; aipinfo@aip.org; http://www.aip.org. Illus., index, adv. Sample. Refereed. *Indexed:* A01, A22, MLA-IB. *Aud.:* Ac, Sa.

Available in print and online. Modern physics research relies heavily on sophisticated instrumentation to make measurements, conduct experiments, analyze data, and test current theories. *Review of Scientific Instruments* is a specialized journal whose role is to evaluate equipment, apparatus, experimental techniques, and mathematical analysis of results. This journal publishes original research articles and literature reviews on instrumentation in physics, chemistry, and the life sciences. The editors interpret the concept of instrumentation very widely and include all of the tools used by the modern scientist. Topics typically covered include optics; atoms and molecules; spectroscopy; particle sources; microscopy; nuclear physics, fusion, and plasmas; condensed matter; chemistry; biology and medicine; electronics and thermometry; and acoustics. In addition to full articles, the journal also provides notes on new instruments and materials, letters to the editor, and occasional conference proceedings from relevant meetings. Online versions of articles may include multimedia components. Because of its focus on instrumentation, many manufacturers also advertise their products in this journal. This title is similar in scope to the British *Measurement Science and Technology* (see above in this section). North American libraries that serve scientific researchers will want to subscribe to *Review of Scientific Instruments,* and comprehensive physics and scientific research libraries will probably need both titles.

4112. *Reviews of Modern Physics.* Formerly (until 1930): *Physical Review, Supplement.* [ISSN: 0034-6861] 1929. q. Ed(s): Achim Richter. American Physical Society, One Physics Ellipse, College Park, MD 20740; help@aps.org; http://www.aps.org. Illus., index. Refereed. *Indexed:* A01, A22, MSN. *Aud.:* Ac, Sa.

Available in print and online. *Reviews of Modern Physics* enhances communication among physicists by publishing comprehensive scholarly reviews and tutorials on significant topics in modern physics. As with *Contemporary Physics, Physics Reports,* and *Reports on Progress in Physics* (all above in this section), the articles do not contain results of original research but collect and synthesize existing research on topics of current interest. Research from any branch or subdiscipline of physics is included, although articles from newly developing fields are given preference. Its review articles offer in-depth treatment of a research area, surveying recent work and providing an introduction that is aimed at physics graduate students and nonspecialists. These reviews also feature bibliographies that are of great value to the specialist. In addition to lengthy review articles, some shorter colloquia articles are also included. The colloquia articles describe recent work of interest to all physicists, especially work at the frontiers of physics, which may have an impact on several different subfields. Each year, *Reviews of Modern Physics* also publishes the Nobel lecture from the Nobel Prize-winner in physics. This title is especially useful for helping physics teachers and graduate students keep abreast of recent developments. To enhance this role, the journal also accepts occasional tutorial articles aimed primarily at students or those new to the field. *Reviews of Modern Physics* is the most cited of all physics journals, and belongs in most physics research collections.

4113. ***Solid State Communications.*** [ISSN: 0038-1098] 1963. s-m. EUR 4447. Ed(s): A Pinczuk. Pergamon Press, The Blvd, Langford Ln, E Park, Kidlington, OX5 1GB, United Kingdom; JournalsCustomerServiceEMEA@elsevier.com; http://www.elsevier.com. Illus., adv. Sample. Refereed. Microform: MIM; PQC. *Indexed:* A01, A22. *Aud.:* Ac, Sa.

This journal serves as the letters section of the *Journal of Physics and Chemistry of Solids* (see above in this section). *Solid State Communications* publishes original experimental and theoretical research on the physical and chemical properties of solids and other condensed systems, and also on their preparation. It also publishes original research on the basic physics of materials science and devices, as well as of state-of-the-art microstructures and nanostructures. The emphasis is on brevity, with papers usually four or five pages in length. A coherent quantitative treatment that emphasizes new physics is expected, rather than a simple accumulation of experimental data. The "Fast-Track" section allows for very rapid publication of short communications on significant developments in condensed-matter science. The goal is to offer, to the broad condensed-matter community, quick and immediate ability to publish recently completed papers in research areas that are rapidly evolving and in which there are developments with great potential impact. Like its parent title, *Solid State Communications* belongs in graduate research physics collections.

4114. ***Spotlight on Optics: highlighted articles from O S A journals.*** 2009. m. Free. Ed(s): Miguel A Alonso. Optical Society of America, 2010 Massachusetts Ave, NW, Washington, DC 20036; info@osa.org; http://www.osapublishing.org. Vol. ends: Dec. *Aud.:* Ac, Sa.

Spotlight on Optics features articles nominated by The Optical Society of America's Topical and Associate Editors to show the breadth and quality of OSA content from the six major technical divisions: "Information Acquisitions, Processing, and Display"; "Light-Matter Interactions"; "Optical Design and Instrumentation"; "Optics in Biology"; "Optoelectronics"; and "Vision and Color." Journal editors identify articles for *Spotlight* that have excellent scientific quality, are representative of the level of work taking place in a specific area, and put other work in perspective. Readers may post comments to the website, creating the potential for dialogue. In addition to the research paper, each article is summarized in more general terms, making it accessible to those who are not experts in optics. Four types of commentaries are included: "An Explanation" of the content, the foremost purpose being a description of the research that makes it understandable to the nonspecialist; a "Viewpoint" piece that presents a subjective evaluation of the research; an "Application" perspective that connects and/or introduces this work to a discipline other than its stated category; and/or a "Review/Synopsis" of the research, with perspective points as applicable. This free online journal will serve as a useful tool for researchers, students, and scientists in other fields who are interested in reading about the most significant current research in optics.

4115. ***Studies in History and Philosophy of Science Part B: Studies in History and Philosophy of Modern Physics.*** [ISSN: 1355-2198] 1995. q. EUR 1033. Ed(s): James Ladyman, Wayne Myrvold. Pergamon Press, The Blvd, Langford Ln, E Park, Kidlington, OX5 1GB, United Kingdom; JournalsCustomerServiceEMEA@elsevier.com; http://www.elsevier.com. Illus., adv. Sample. Refereed. Microform: PQC. *Indexed:* A01, A22, MSN. *Bk. rev.:* 0-5, 1,000-2,000 words. *Aud.:* Ac, Sa.

Available in print and online. As scientists make new discoveries and develop new theories, they also change the ways in which we understand and approach our world. One result of this has been a rise in the study of the history of science, with particular emphasis on the history of modern physics, including astronomy, chemistry, and other non-biological sciences. This journal focuses on those areas. The primary emphasis is on research from the mid- to late nineteenth century to the present, the period of emergence of the kind of theoretical physics that came to dominate in the twentieth century. In each issue, original articles and review essays are published. About one issue each year is devoted to a special theme, such as quantum field theory or mathematical modeling. Because the focus is on the history of ideas, many of the articles are approachable by a wider audience. This journal belongs in any collection dealing with the history of science.

■ PHYSIOLOGY

See also Biology; Botany; Medicine; Sports; and Zoology sections.

Kristine Nowak, Assistant Professor, Instruction and Foundational Experience Librarian, Morgan Library, Colorado State University, Fort Collins, CO 80538-1019

Introduction

Physiology is the study of living systems. It includes everything from the study of viruses and cells to the study of complex living organisms. As such, it has a great deal of overlap with other fields of study, including biology, medicine, exercise science, zoology, and many others. Although physiology is distinct from the medical sciences, many of its findings also have important implications for medical practice.

The majority of key physiology journals are peer-reviewed academic journals that focus on reporting new research findings and best practices. Most are written primarily for an audience of researchers, although some articles may be appropriate for upper-division and graduate student readers. The titles highlighted in this section are highly ranked peer-reviewed journals with high expectations and citation ratings. Many offer free online access to articles after one year.

Basic Periodicals

American Journal of Physiology (Consolidated), Annual Review of Physiology, Journal of Applied Physiology, Journal of General Physiology, The Journal of Physiology, Physiological Reviews.

Basic Abstracts and Indexes

Biological Abstracts, Biological Abstracts/RRM, Biological and Agricultural Index, BIOSIS, Current Contents/Life Sciences, MEDLINE, PubMed, SPORTDiscus, Web of Science.

4116. ***American Journal of Physiology (Consolidated).*** [ISSN: 0002-9513] 1898. m. USD 7820 Free to members. American Physiological Society, 6120 Executive Blvd, Ste 600, Rockville, MD 20852-4906; subscriptions@the-aps.org; http://www.the-aps.org. Illus., adv. Refereed. *Indexed:* A01, A22, Agr, MLA-IB. *Aud.:* Ac, Sa.

This journal consolidates content of seven individual journals published by the American Physiological Society: *AJP-Cell Physiology, AJP-Endocrinology and Metabolism, AJP-Gastrointestinal and Liver Physiology, AJP-Lung Cellular and Molecular Physiology, AJP-Heart and Circulatory Physiology, AJP-Regulatory, Integrative and Comparative Physiology,* and *AJP-Renal Physiology.* Each monthly issue is a hefty volume printed in two parts. Each of the seven journals has its own index and yearly pagination by volume. In the combined print volumes, the page numbers are proceeded by a letter that signifies the topic and journal, for example, C1264 in the "Cell Physiology" section and F1719 in the "Renal Physiology" section. Most articles are recent, peer-reviewed research studies. In addition to the research articles, there are smaller components such as "Themes," "Editorials," "Reviews," and "Innovative Methodology." In general, this is a highly technical journal that is best suited for an audience of other researchers, although there are a few articles that could appeal to a wider audience. Both black-and-white and color illustrations accompany the articles. Articles are available online after 12 months, and are searchable through Google as well as major indexes such as PubMed and Web of Science. The broad scope of coverage and content of seven prominent journals in a single subscription make this an important publication for libraries that support biological science and human physiology programs.

4117. *Annual Review of Physiology.* [ISSN: 0066-4278] 1939. a. USD 431 (print & online eds.)). Ed(s): Kenneth Walsh, Mark T Nelson. Annual Reviews, PO Box 10139, Palo Alto, CA 94303; service@annualreviews.org; http://www.annualreviews.org. Refereed. Reprint: PSC. *Indexed:* A01, A22, Agr, C45. *Aud.:* Ac, Sa.

This annual publication contains invited articles on physiology research in the fields of cardiovascular physiology; cell physiology; ecological, evolutionary, and comparative physiology; endocrinology; gastrointestinal physiology; neurophysiology; renal and electrolyte physiology; and respiratory physiology. In addition, each volume contains several articles on a "Special Topic." Accompanied by high-quality color illustrations, the articles are generally written for the scientific community, although some could be accessible and of interest to a wider audience. The articles are published first online as "Review in Advance." Individual articles may be purchased through the web site. Overall, this is a valuable resource because it provides high-quality synthesized information regarding key developments in the field.

4118. *Journal of Applied Physiology.* Former titles (until 1985): *Journal of Applied Physiology: Respiratory, Environmental and Exercise Physiology;* (until 1977): *Journal of Applied Physiology.* [ISSN: 8750-7587] 1948. m. USD 2490 Free to members. Ed(s): Sue Bodine. American Physiological Society, 6120 Executive Blvd, Ste 600, Rockville, MD 20852-4906; subscriptions@the-aps.org; http://www.the-aps.org. Illus., adv. Refereed. *Indexed:* A22, C45, ErgAb, SD. *Aud.:* Ac, Sa.

The *Journal of Applied Physiology* publishes peer-reviewed articles that cover a broad range of physiological research, with a preference for those employing "cutting-edge techniques" and innovative methods. The vast majority of content in this journal is peer-reviewed articles reporting current research, but the journal also publishes several other key article types. "Review Articles," one of the more common, are typically invited and present a synthesis of current knowledge on a particular topic. Another key article type is "Innovative Methodology," in which researchers describe and evaluate new methodological practices. While this journal is clearly written by and for researchers, some articles would be accessible to a motivated lay reader. Illustrations, generally black-and-white figures with some color photographs, accompany the articles. There are a few ads per issue, such as for conferences or professional societies. New articles are published first on the website as "Articles in Press," and the print journal is published monthly. The online archive is free after one year, but content prior to 1996 is only available on a pay-per-view or subscription basis. This journal specifically recognizes the interdisciplinary nature of physiology, including the relevance of research findings to applied medical practice. As such, this journal is not only useful for physiology collections, but may also be of interest to biology, medicine, and other related collections. URL: http://jap.physiology.org

4119. *Journal of General Physiology.* [ISSN: 0022-1295] 1918. m. USD 2800 (print & online eds.)). Ed(s): Sharona E Gordon. Rockefeller University Press, 950 Third Ave., 2nd Fl, New York, NY 10022; subs@rockefeller.edu; http://jgp.rupress.org. Illus., index. Refereed. *Indexed:* A01, A22. *Aud.:* Ac, Sa.

The *Journal of General Physiology* publishes quality peer-reviewed articles focused on elucidating the basic mechanisms of living organisms. Although it covers all areas of general physiology, the journal has a strong focus on the cellular and molecular level. Articles are detailed scientific reports, accompanied by sparse illustrations, charts, or photographs, and written for an audience of fellow researchers. In addition to the research articles, the journal also contains reviews, commentaries, and research news items. Each print issue has 100-150 pages, with two or three advertisements, often for lab equipment or supplies. This journal also allows authors to retain copyright of their published articles, although the publisher does retain exclusive rights for the first six months. New articles are first published online and made available to subscribers, but the journal's archives from 1918 through current issues (six months after publication) are freely available on the *JGP* website. URL: http://jgp.rupress.org and in PubMed Central.

4120. *The Journal of Physiology.* [ISSN: 0022-3751] 1878. s-m. plus proceedings 5/yr. GBP 5184. Ed(s): Kim E Barrett. Wiley-Blackwell Publishing Ltd., The Atrium, Southern Gate, Chichester, PO19 8QG, United Kingdom; cs-journals@wiley.com; http://onlinelibrary.wiley.com. Illus., index, adv. Sample. Refereed. Microform: PMC; PQC. Reprint: PSC. *Indexed:* A01, A22, C45, E01. *Aud.:* Ac, Sa.

This journal covers all topics within physiology and pathophysiology, but has a particular focus on research with clinical applications. It also focuses on the physiology of more complex organisms, mainly humans and other mammals, but does include informative research on other organisms. The content is mainly peer-reviewed research articles, but does include some special article categories, including topical and symposium reviews, reports on developments in research techniques, and letters to the editor. Some issues include a "Crosstalk" section, in which two experts debate a controversial subject in the field. Also included in some issues is the "Journal Club" section, which is an opportunity for "training-level scientists" to submit reviews of recent research. Some key articles are highlighted as "Editor's Choice." The research articles are most useful to professionals and graduate students, but many sections are accessible to a wider audience. It is published twice a month and some issues have a special focus or topic. Members of the Physiological Society have immediate access to all society publications, but articles are available on the website and in PubMed Central after one year. The free website archives go back to 1878. There are no paid advertisements, but the journal will occasionally print information on upcoming events or similar organizations. Overall, this is a valuable, highly cited journal that would be of interest to both physiology and biomedical collections.

4121. *Physiological Reviews.* [ISSN: 0031-9333] 1921. q. USD 935 Free to members. Ed(s): Sadis Matalon. American Physiological Society, 6120 Executive Blvd, Ste 600, Rockville, MD 20852-4906; subscriptions@the-aps.org; http://www.the-aps.org. Illus., adv. Refereed. *Indexed:* A01, A22, C45. *Aud.:* Ac, Sa.

Physiological Reviews is one of the most cited journals in the field. It is an excellent resource for physiology researchers and students looking for a thorough overview of the current knowledge on a topic. Each quarterly issue consists of invited, peer-reviewed reviews. Each of the reviews is a synthesis of the literature in a specific area, typically divided into major themes within that field of interest. Each review covers hundreds (500+ is common) of research studies, and provides suggestions for further research. The reviews are technical, and intended for an audience of researchers, although many would be accessible to upper-level undergraduate or graduate students. There are color illustrations and full-color cover art. The website includes free access to tables of contents and abstracts, and articles older than one year are freely available. Overall, this is one of the most highly respected and highly cited journals in physiology, and would also be of interest for biomedical collections.

4122. *Physiology.* Formerly (until 2004): *News in Physiological Sciences.* [ISSN: 1548-9213] 1986. bi-m. USD 595 Free to members. Ed(s): Gary C Sieck. American Physiological Society, 6120 Executive Blvd, Ste 600, Rockville, MD 20852-4906; info@the-aps.org. Illus., adv. Refereed. *Indexed:* A01, A22, SD. *Aud.:* Ac, Sa.

This journal is a joint venture of the American Physiological Society and the International Union of Physiological Sciences. It presents expert reviews of current research, highlighting significant advances in the various fields of physiology and identifying opportunities for further research. The editorial board selects the topics and invites leading researchers to write short-form reviews, which are peer-reviewed. Review articles are generally less than ten pages, excluding references, and are accompanied by high-quality illustrations created by a professional artist. There are six issues per year, and each contains a few ads, often for professional societies or laboratory equipment. After one year, the reviews are made publicly available on the website. Overall, this is a high-quality resource for concise reviews, and would be particularly useful for researchers looking for synthesized information.

■ POLITICAL SCIENCE

General and Political Theory/Comparative and American Politics/International Relations

Hilary Bussell, Political Science, Economics, & Communication Librarian, Ohio State University Libraries, Columbus, OH; 614-292-9437; bussell.21@osu.edu

Introduction

This section provides a list of prominent English-language periodicals that focus on political issues. While this list is rooted in the discipline of political science, many of the titles feature multidisciplinary perspectives on politics from scholars in related fields such as economics and psychology. The periodicals feature a range of content including original research, analysis, commentary, and debates on contemporary and historical political issues. Although the section is not meant to be exhaustive, effort was made to create a list of core titles that take a range of methodological and theoretical approaches and that are written with a variety of audiences in mind.

Each title is categorized under one of three subsections: "General and Political Theory," "Comparative and American Politics," and "International Relations." Entries contain information about a periodical's aims and scope, the type of content it publishes (e.g., original research, literature reviews, commentary, book reviews, and so on), topics covered in recent issues, and intended audience.

Basic Periodicals

Hs: *Current History, Foreign Affairs, The Washington Quarterly;* Ga: *American Political Science Review, CQ Magazine, Current History, Foreign Affairs, Foreign Policy, Governance, International Affairs, Journal of Democracy, Political Research Quarterly, PS: Political Science, Presidential Studies Quarterly, The Washington Quarterly, World Affairs;* Ac: *American Political Science Review, CQ Magazine, Current History, Electoral Studies, Foreign Affairs, Foreign Policy, Governance, International Affairs, International Organization, International Studies Quarterly, Journal of Democracy, The Journal of Politics, National Journal, Policy Studies Journal, Political Analysis, Political Communication, Political Research Quarterly, PS: Political Science, Political Theory, Presidential Studies Quarterly, Quarterly Journal of Political Science, Review of International Studies, The Washington Quarterly, World Affairs.*

Basic Abstracts and Indexes

International Political Science Abstracts, PAIS International, Social Sciences Citation Index, Worldwide Political Science Abstracts.

Perspectives on Politics. See Globalization section.

Politics & Gender. See Gender Studies section.

Politics & Society. See Globalization section.

General and Political Theory

The periodicals in this subsection provide broad coverage of contemporary scholarship in political science, including political philosophy as well as the theoretical foundations and analytical methodologies that are used in political science research.

4123. ***American Academy of Political and Social Science. Annals.*** [ISSN: 0002-7162] 1889. bi-m. USD 2676 (print & online eds.)). Ed(s): Thomas A Kecskemethy. Sage Publications, Inc., 2455 Teller Rd, Thousand Oaks, CA 91320; info@sagepub.com; http://www.sagepub.com. Illus., adv. Sample. Refereed. Vol. ends: Nov. Microform: PMC; PQC. Reprint: PSC. *Indexed:* A22, AgeL, BAS, BRI, CBRI, CJPI, Chicano, E01, EconLit, IBSS, MLA-IB, P61, SSA. *Aud.:* Ga, Ac, Sa.

The *Annals* are published in thematic issues, individually edited with essays that offer multidisciplinary approaches to a wide range of topics in the social sciences. Each issue is designed to "promote the use of the social sciences to inform public opinion and improve public policy." The *Annals* publishes on contemporary social issues in the United States and in other regions of the world. Recent thematic issues focus on migrant smuggling, developing secure and accessible data for policy and scholarship, inequality in educational opportunities, rural-urban boundaries, and student debt. Because of the broad social issues covered, the *Annals* will appeal to a wide variety of academics, professionals, and students of the social sciences. Recommended for academic and public libraries.

4124. ***American Political Science Review: the leading journal of political science research.*** Incorporates (1904-1914): *American Political Science Association. Proceedings.* [ISSN: 0003-0554] 1906. q. Ed(s): Steven Forde, Marijke Breuning. Cambridge University Press, University Printing House, Shaftesbury Rd, Cambridge, CB2 8BS, United Kingdom; journals@cambridge.org; https://www.cambridge.org/. Illus., index, adv. Sample. Refereed. Circ: 16000. Vol. ends: No. 4. Microform: MIM; PMC; PQC. Reprint: PSC. *Indexed:* A01, A22, B01, BAS, BRI, CBRI, Chicano, E01, EconLit, IBSS, MLA-IB, P61. *Aud.:* Ac, Sa.

APSR is sponsored by the American Political Science Association and has been published continuously since 1906. It presents new research in all areas of political science, including political theory, American politics, public policy, public administration, comparative politics, and international relations. Recent articles focus on decision making of elected politicians; using machine learning to predict armed conflict; mass political effects of the Medicaid expansion; impact of secular party rule on religious violence in Pakistan; and H.G. Wells' pragmatist political thought. Recommended for academic and public libraries.

4125. ***Annual Review of Political Science (Online).*** [ISSN: 1545-1577] 1998. a. USD 273. Ed(s): Nancy Rosenblum, Margaret Levi. Annual Reviews, PO Box 10139, Palo Alto, CA 94303; service@annualreviews.org; http://www.annualreviews.org. Refereed. *Aud.:* Ac.

Covering all areas of political science, this publication's annual volumes provide comprehensive critical reviews of the literature on broad topics in "political theory and philosophy, international relations, political economy, political behavior, American and comparative politics, public administration and policy, and methodology." The articles provide historical context for scholarship on a topic, present the current state of knowledge and the direction of research in recent years, and identify issues for future work. Recent articles focus on research in foreign aid, radicalization, institutional corruption, political trust in the United States, and just war theory. Recommended for academic libraries.

4126. ***British Journal of Political Science.*** [ISSN: 0007-1234] 1971. q. GBP 461. Ed(s): Robert E. Goodin, Shaun Bowler. Cambridge University Press, University Printing House, Shaftesbury Rd, Cambridge, CB2 8BS, United Kingdom; journals@cambridge.org; https://www.cambridge.org/. Illus., index. Refereed. Circ: 1350. Vol. ends: Oct. Microform: PQC. Reprint: PSC. *Indexed:* A01, A22, B01, BAS, BRI, E01, IBSS, P61, SSA. *Aud.:* Ac.

This journal covers "developments across a wide range of countries," with research from all areas of political science, "including political theory, political behaviour, public policy and international relations," and related disciplines such as "sociology, social psychology, economics and philosophy." Each issue has research articles; some issues have essays under the heading of "Notes and Comments" and review articles on the literature of a topic of research. Recent articles are on the effects of social diversity on democracy; the gender gap in voting for Radical Right Parties in Europe; the impact of election violence on incumbent victory and post-election dynamics; and the connection between voter mobilization and political information. Recommended for academic libraries.

4127. ***Journal of Political Philosophy.*** [ISSN: 0963-8016] 1993. q. GBP 941. Ed(s): Robert E Goodin. Wiley-Blackwell Publishing Ltd., The Atrium, Southern Gate, Chichester, PO19 8QG, United Kingdom; cs-journals@wiley.com; http://onlinelibrary.wiley.com. Illus., adv. Sample. Refereed. Microform: PQC. Reprint: PSC. *Indexed:* A01, A22, E01, IBSS, P61. *Aud.:* Ac.

International in scope, the *Journal of Political Philosophy* focuses on "the study of theoretical issues arising out of moral, legal and political life." It publishes across a range of disciplines including "philosophy, sociology, history, economics and political science." Each issue contains original articles; some issues also contain survey articles, symposiums, and debates. Recent issues have included articles on the challenge to political liberalism presented by the rise of right-wing populism; anonymity in political deliberation; the impact of political marketing on citizen autonomy; and an analysis of the political concept of privilege. Recommended for academic libraries.

4128. *The Journal of Politics.* Supersedes (in 1939): *Southern Political Science Association. Annual Session. Proceedings.* [ISSN: 0022-3816] 1933. q. USD 880. Ed(s): Jeffrey A Jenkins. University of Chicago Press, 1427 E 60th St, Chicago, IL 60637; custserv@press.uchicago.edu; http://www.press.uchicago.edu. Illus., index, adv. Refereed. Vol. ends: Nov. Reprint: PSC. *Indexed:* A01, A22, B01, BAS, CBRI, Chicano, E01. *Bk. rev.:* 5+ per issue. *Aud.:* Ac.

The Journal of Politics is published for the Southern Political Science Association. The journal offers "theoretically innovative and methodologically diverse" research in "American politics, comparative politics, formal theory, international relations, methodology, political theory, public administration and public policy." Recent articles are on South African electoral politics; the impact of changes in personal financial circumstances on voting behavior and attitudes; attempts to reduce affective polarization between supporters of U.S. political parties; and the connection between droughts and rebel violence in developing countries. Book reviews appear in each issue. Recommended for academic libraries.

4129. *P S: Political Science & Politics.* Incorporates (1988-1990): *Political Science Teacher;* Which was formerly (until 1988): *News for Teachers of Political Science;* (until 1978): *D E A News;* Formerly (until 1988): *Political Science;* Which superseded in part (in 1968): *American Political Science Review;* Which incorporated (1904-1906): *American Political Science Association. Proceedings.* [ISSN: 1049-0965] 1904. q. Ed(s): Paul Gronke, Phillip Ardoin. Cambridge University Press, University Printing House, Shaftesbury Rd, Cambridge, CB2 8BS, United Kingdom; journals@cambridge.org; https://www.cambridge.org/. Illus., index, adv. Refereed. Circ: 16000. Vol. ends: No. 4. Microform: PQC. Reprint: PSC. *Indexed:* A22, BRI, Chicano, E01, ERIC, P61. *Aud.:* Ga, Ac, Sa.

PS, published by the American Political Science Association, is the organization's "journal of record for the discipline of political science." It is a peer-reviewed journal "reporting on research, teaching, and professional development" and offers a mix of research articles, news about the profession, activities of members, and memorials. Articles range broadly in the field and offer "critical analyses of contemporary political phenomena" for scholars, students, and general readers. Articles may examine big data and politics; using Wikipedia in the classroom; evidence of gender bias in student evaluations; scholarly communication; and election studies. *PS* offers thematic symposiums, such as "Latinos, Immigration, and the 2016 Presidential Election," "Advancing Philanthropic Scholarship: The Implications of Transformation," and "Contentious Politics in the United States: What Role for Political Scientists?" Recommended for academic and public libraries.

4130. *Political Analysis.* Formerly (until 1985): *Political Methodology.* [ISSN: 1047-1987] 1974. q. GBP 464. Ed(s): Jeff Gill. Cambridge University Press, University Printing House, Shaftesbury Rd, Cambridge, CB2 8BS, United Kingdom; online@cambridge.org; https://www.cambridge.org. Adv. Refereed. Reprint: PSC. *Indexed:* A22, E01, P61. *Aud.:* Ac.

This journal, published on behalf of the Society for Political Methodology and the Political Methodology Section of the American Political Science Association, is at the forefront of communicating the use of quantitative and qualitative methodologies in political science research. The research incorporates empirical analysis and seeks to be consistent with the rules and terminology of mathematics, probability, and statistics in offering greater understanding of political phenomena. This analytical approach is applied to issues such as voting and elections, political campaigns, decision-making, public policy evaluation, budgets, relations between nations, analysis of political regimes such as democracy, and public support for political parties. The journal publishes two types of articles: research articles, which "focus on the development, implementation, or analysis of new methodologies," and letters, which are "short reports of original research focused on important methodological or empirical contributions." Recommended for academic libraries.

4131. *Political Behavior.* [ISSN: 0190-9320] 1979. q. EUR 1421 (print & online eds.)). Ed(s): David A Peterson. Springer New York LLC, 233 Spring St, New York, NY 10013; customerservice@springer.com; http://www.springer.com. Adv. Sample. Refereed. Microform: PQC. Reprint: PSC. *Indexed:* A01, A22, E01, P61, SSA. *Aud.:* Ac.

Political Behavior, which is affiliated with the Elections, Public Opinion, and Voting Behavior section of the American Political Science Association, publishes research on "conventional and unconventional political behavior of individuals or small groups, and of large organizations that participate in the political process such as parties, interest groups, political action committees, governmental agencies, and mass media." The journal publishes articles with a variety of theoretical and empirical approaches and is interdisciplinary in scope, drawing from fields including economics, psychology, and sociology, in addition to political science. Recent issues have articles on challenges for Republican women candidates running in U.S. general elections; the causal connection between educational attainment and political participation; the use of moral appeals in political advertising; support for gay rights in EU member states; citizen support for vigilante justice in Mexico; and intervention strategies to reduce racist harassment on Twitter. Recommended for academic libraries.

4132. *Political Research Quarterly.* Formerly (until 1993): *The Western Political Quarterly.* [ISSN: 1065-9129] 1948. q. USD 472 (print & online eds.)). Ed(s): Jeanette Mendez, J S Maloy. Sage Publications, Inc., 2455 Teller Rd, Thousand Oaks, CA 91320; info@sagepub.com; http://www.sagepub.com. Illus., index, adv. Sample. Refereed. Vol. ends: No. 4. Reprint: PSC. *Indexed:* A01, A22, BAS, BRI, CBRI, Chicano, E01, IBSS, MLA-IB, P61. *Aud.:* Ga, Ac.

Sponsored by the Western Political Science Association, *Political Research Quarterly* features "pluralistic and intellectually innovative research" in all areas of political science. The journal publishes articles by international scholars working across a range of subfields, methodological approaches, and theoretical orientations. The editors seek work that is "problem-driven" and that addresses "major political problems or puzzles" through diverse methods and theoretical approaches. In addition to original research, *PRQ* publishes occasional symposiums issues in which authors discuss or debate a specific theme, such as anarchist feminism. Recent issues feature articles on the effect of female political leadership on women's political leadership in East and Southeast Asia, punishment by labor unions of congressional Democrats who vote for free-trade legislation, the influence of dehumanizing language against immigrants on public opinion, the place of racial injustice in the work of John Rawls, social identity polarization and anti-deliberative attitudes, and a social network theory of co-voting among legislators. Recommended for public and academic libraries.

4133. *Political Theory: an international journal of political philosophy.* [ISSN: 0090-5917] 1973. bi-m. USD 1794 (print & online eds.)). Ed(s): Lawrie Balfour. Sage Publications, Inc., 2455 Teller Rd, Thousand Oaks, CA 91320; info@sagepub.com; http://www.sagepub.com. Illus., index. Refereed. Vol. ends: No. 6. Microform: PQC. Reprint: PSC. *Indexed:* A01, A22, BRI, E01, IBSS, P61, SSA. *Bk. rev.:* 2-3 review essays; 2-4 shorter reviews. *Aud.:* Ac.

This journal focuses on "political philosophy from every philosophical, ideological and methodological perspective," and particularly welcomes work "that addresses pressing political and ethical issues or events." Recent articles are on themes such as settler-colonial politics, freedom of thought, the body politic, just war theory, liberal multiculturalism, the politics of yoga, and analyses of ideas from one or more political philosophers such as Plato, Hobbes, Rousseau, and Foucault. Issues may have multi book review essays, individual reviews of books, critical response, and special-topic symposiums, such as the moral foundations of women's rights. Recommended for academic libraries.

4134. ***Quarterly Journal of Political Science.*** [ISSN: 1554-0626] 2006. q. USD 560 in the Americas; EUR 560 elsewhere; USD 660 combined subscription in the Americas (print & online eds.)). Ed(s): Joshua D Clinton, Scott Ashworth. Now Publishers Inc., PO Box 1024, Hanover, MA 02339; journal.admin@nowpublishers.com; https://www.nowpublishers.com. Sample. Refereed. *Indexed:* EconLit, P61. *Aud.:* Ac.

This journal emphasizes quality research in "positive political science and contemporary political economy." Editors encourage submissions that use scientific method to test empirical implications of positive political theories. The journal publishes "cutting-edge research on any aspect of private, local, national, comparative, or international politics" from political science as well as scholars in economics, business, and law. Recent articles deal with the causal effect of divided government on legislative delay; the "ideological migration" of moderates in the U.S. Congress to more extreme positions; how cell phones affect protests; the impact of newspaper op-eds on public opinion; and the role of social identity in conditioning voter attitudes and behavior regarding incumbents. Recommended for academic libraries.

Comparative and American Politics

Periodicals in this subsection focus either on (1) research in politics or contemporary policy in the United States, or (2) the subfield of political science that is known as comparative politics. The latter uses research methodologies of the social sciences and sciences to draw causal inferences about political issues in multiple countries or regions.

4135. ***American Journal of Political Science.*** Formerly (until 1973): *Midwest Journal of Political Science.* [ISSN: 0092-5853] 1950. q. GBP 922. Ed(s): Jennifer L Lawless, Kathleen Dolan. Wiley-Blackwell Publishing, Inc., 111 River St, Hoboken, NJ 07030; http://onlinelibrary.wiley.com. Illus. Sample. Refereed. Vol. ends: No. 4. Microform: PQC. Reprint: PSC. *Indexed:* A01, A22, B01, BAS, E01, IBSS, P61, SSA. *Aud.:* Ac.

Sponsored by the Midwest Political Science Association, *AJPS* publishes research that makes "outstanding contributions to scholarly knowledge about notable theoretical concerns, puzzles or controversies in any subfield of political science." Recent papers consider the gender gap in political knowledge, how the media influences popular attitudes about austerity, the role of high-profile female politicians in motivating women to run for office, and how the impact of partisan media sources is extended through interpersonal discussions. Most issues have an "AJPS Workshop" section featuring one or two articles that focus on research methodologies, such as using a computer-assisted statistical approach to select keywords for analyzing large textual corpora. Recommended for academic libraries.

4136. ***American Politics Research.*** Formerly (until 2001): *American Politics Quarterly.* [ISSN: 1532-673X] 1973. bi-m. USD 1833 (print & online eds.)). Ed(s): Brian J Gaines. Sage Publications, Inc., 2455 Teller Rd, Thousand Oaks, CA 91320; info@sagepub.com; http://www.sagepub.com. Illus., index, adv. Sample. Refereed. Vol. ends: No. 4. Reprint: PSC. *Indexed:* A01, A22, E01, IBSS, P61, SSA. *Aud.:* Ac.

APR is dedicated to the "dissemination of the latest theory, research and analysis in all areas of American politics, including local, state, and national." It offers scholarly articles on a wide variety of topics related to political institutions, leadership, elections, and social influences on politics. Recent articles have covered beliefs about voter fraud in the U.S. electorate; causal mechanisms between entertainment media and political attitudes; legislative redistricting formulas; the impact of social capital and racial diversity on health care inequality; and the effects of campaign advertising on political polarization. Recommended for academic and public libraries.

4137. ***C Q Magazine.*** Former titles (until 2016): *C Q Weekly;* (until 1998): *Congressional Quarterly Weekly Report.* [ISSN: 2472-419X] 1945. w. 48/yr. C Q Press, 1255, 22nd St, N.W., Washington, DC 20037; customerservice@cq.com; http://www.cqpress.com/. Illus., index, adv. Sample. Vol. ends: No. 52. *Indexed:* A01, A22, B01, BRI, C37, Chicano, MASUSE. *Aud.:* Hs, Ac, Sa.

Each issue of *CQ Magazine* provides current information about legislative and political activities happening in the United States Congress. It includes feature and brief articles on key issues and persons who work in or with the government; it covers the "status of bills in play, behind-the-scenes maneuvering, committee and floor activity, debates, and all roll-call votes." Recent issues have articles on the threat of North Korea's chemical and biological weapons; the expansion of college savings plans under the 2018 tax reform legislation; congressional midterm ads; and Congressional committee activities. Recommended for academic, public, and school libraries.

4138. ***Comparative Political Studies.*** [ISSN: 0010-4140] 1968. 14x/yr. USD 2440 (print & online eds.)). Ed(s): Benjamin W Ansell, David J Samuels. Sage Publications, Inc., 2455 Teller Rd, Thousand Oaks, CA 91320; info@sagepub.com; http://www.sagepub.com. Illus., index, adv. Sample. Refereed. Vol. ends: No. 14. Microform: PQC. Reprint: PSC. *Indexed:* A01, A22, BAS, BRI, E01, IBSS, P61, SSA. *Aud.:* Ac.

CPS is a scholarly journal that publishes theoretical and empirical research articles, with a focus "on comparative politics at both the cross-national and intra-national levels." Recent articles have been on drug cartels in Mexico; the effect of social diversity on party fragmentation; transnational labor activism; and the adoption of welfare systems by autocratic governments. Recommended for academic libraries.

4139. ***Electoral Studies: an international journal on voting and electoral systems and strategy.*** [ISSN: 0261-3794] 1982. q. EUR 1793. Elsevier Ltd, The Boulevard, Langford Lane, Oxford, OX5 1GB, United Kingdom; customerserviceau@elsevier.com; http://www.elsevier.com. Illus., adv. Sample. Refereed. Microform: PQC. Reprint: PSC. *Indexed:* A01, A22, IBSS, P61. *Aud.:* Ga, Ac, Sa.

Electoral Studies provides a forum for a variety of social science scholars who are interested in empirical and theoretical research on all aspects of elections and voting throughout the world. Readers can find articles on voting processes, voter behavior, electoral systems, turnout, campaigns, and examinations of research methodologies. Recent articles are on the European far right; suspicion among citizens about election integrity; ethnic heterogeneity and electoral turnout by neighborhood; the impact of the Scottish independence referendum on the Labour party; and decentralization and democratic participation in Latin America and the Caribbean. The journal offers special issues on topics such as electoral integrity and the intersection of economics and elections. This journal will appeal to scholars, students, and practitioners.

4140. ***European Journal of Political Research.*** [ISSN: 0304-4130] 1973. q. GBP 971 print & online eds. Ed(s): Emiliano Grossman, Cas Mudde. Wiley-Blackwell Publishing Ltd., The Atrium, Southern Gate, Chichester, PO19 8QG, United Kingdom; cs-journals@wiley.com; http://onlinelibrary.wiley.com. Illus., index, adv. Sample. Refereed. Circ: 900. Microform: PQC. Reprint: PSC. *Indexed:* A01, A22, E01, IBSS, P61, SSA. *Aud.:* Ga, Ac.

EJPR, published for the European Consortium of Political Research, offers research based on theoretical and methodological studies that utilize either qualitative or quantitative approaches. Articles present "conceptual and comparative perspectives in political science." Recent studies focus on lobbying regulation in the European Union; partisan effects on morality policy outputs; dissenting votes among European party members; the effect of populist attitudes on populist party support; and the impact of mass media on political agenda settings. A subscription to *EJPR* includes the *European Journal of Political Research Political Data Yearbook,* which was formerly published as a double issue of *EJPR* but now appears annually in December in print and at the Wiley web page for the title. The yearbook "documents election results, national referendum[s], changes in government, and institutional reforms in all EU member states plus Australia, Canada, Iceland, Israel, Japan, New Zealand, Norway, Switzerland, and the United States." Commentators write on the "principal issues in national politics during the year." Associated with the yearbook is a free interactive resource (www.politicaldatayearbook.com), which has graphic representations of data on each country. Recommended for academic and public libraries.

4141. ***Governance (Online): an international journal of policy, administration, and institutions.*** [ISSN: 1468-0491] 1987. q. GBP 869. Ed(s): Adam Sheingate, Paolo Graziano. Wiley-Blackwell Publishing, Inc., 350 Main St, Malden, MA 02148; cs-journals@wiley.com; http://onlinelibrary.wiley.com. Adv. Sample. Refereed. *Bk. rev.:* 5-6 per issue. *Aud.:* Ga, Ac, Sa.

Sponsored by the International Political Science Association's Research Committee on the Structure and Organization of Government, this journal offers a "theoretical and practical discussion of executive politics, public policy, administration, and the organization of the state," with a focus on international and comparative approaches. Each issue includes research articles and book reviews, and some issues have topical symposiums and commentary. Authors may be policy practitioners and analysts, political scientists, and public administration scholars. Recent articles are on issue prioritization among interest groups; elite management in Chinese government; educational policy in India; the influence of religious groups on state governance approaches; the role of gender in reducing distrust of police; municipal debt policy in Mexico; and collective action against governmental corruption. Recommended for academic, public, and special libraries.

4142. ***Journal of Democracy.*** [ISSN: 1045-5736] 1990. q. USD 185. Ed(s): Marc F Plattner. The Johns Hopkins University Press, 2715 N Charles St, Baltimore, MD 21218; http://www.press.jhu.edu. Illus., index, adv. Sample. Refereed. Vol. ends: No. 4. Reprint: PSC. *Indexed:* A01, A22, BRI, E01, IBSS, P61, SSA. *Bk. rev.:* 1+ per issue. *Aud.:* Ga, Ac, Sa.

The *Journal of Democracy* web site says that the journal is an "influential international forum for scholarly analysis and competing democratic viewpoints." It "monitors and analyzes democratic regimes and movements around the world" and publishes news and information on activism for democracy and election results. Each issue includes book reviews or review essays, news and election updates, and selected primary source documents, such as an excerpt from a national leader's speech or the text of a European Union document. Recent articles have focused on China under Xi Jinping's leadership; Iran's 2017 election; the rise of kleptocratic rule around the globe; and the proliferation of referendum votes. Recommended for academic and public libraries.

4143. ***Policy Studies Journal (Online).*** [ISSN: 1541-0072] 1972. q. GBP 1742. Ed(s): Chris Weible, Peter deLeon. Wiley-Blackwell Publishing, Inc., 111 River St, Hoboken, NJ 07030; info@wiley.com; http://www.wiley.com/. Refereed. *Aud.:* Ac, Sa.

Policy Studies Journal is sponsored by the Public Policy Section of the American Political Science Association and the Policy Studies Organization. It offers "theoretically and empirically grounded research on policy process and policy analysis." The journal seeks articles in which the methods of data collection and analysis are clearly stated and that clearly articulate how their findings advances the literature of the field. Recent articles focus on collaborative governance; the policy impact of interest groups; medical marijuana laws; environmental justice; advocacy groups' use of social media to advance policy agendas; the connection between public opinion and social policy; and theories of incremental institutional change. *PSJ* also publishes a supplementary issue that highlights and links to the Policy Studies Journal's *Public Policy Yearbook* (www.psjyearbook.com/). The supplementary issue introduces the yearbook and provides topical review articles. Recommended for academic libraries.

4144. ***Political Communication: an international journal.*** Formerly (until 1992): *Political Communication and Persuasion.* [ISSN: 1058-4609] 1980. 6x/yr. GBP 774 (print & online eds.)). Ed(s): Claes H de Vreese. Taylor & Francis Inc., 711 3rd Ave, 8th Fl, New York, NY 10017; support@tandfonline.com; http://www.tandfonline.com. Illus., adv. Sample. Refereed. Vol. ends: No. 4. Reprint: PSC. *Indexed:* A01, A22, BRI, E01, IBSS, P61, SSA. *Bk. rev.:* 3-4 per issue. *Aud.:* Ac, Sa.

This journal is sponsored by the Political Communications divisions of the American Political Science Association and the International Communication Association. It seeks "cutting-edge theory-driven empirical research at the intersection of politics and communication, broadly conceived." The journal publishes literature using a variety of research methods and analytic approaches to explore the practice, process, and policy implications of political communication. Recent issues follow media coverage of the U.S. Supreme Court; constituent responses to English- and Spanish-language candidate advertisements; use of Facebook and Twitter in a German federal election campaign; influence of media platforms on perception of incivility in media content; use of social media for protests; and how types of political TV ads affect the viewer's memory of candidate issue positions. Book reviews and symposium issues on a particular topic also appear. Recommended for academic and public libraries.

4145. ***Presidential Studies Quarterly.*** Formerly (until 1974): *Center House Bulletin.* [ISSN: 0360-4918] 1972. q. Ed(s): Marissa Madsen, George C Edwards, III. Wiley-Blackwell Publishing, Inc., 111 River St, Hoboken, NJ 07030; http://onlinelibrary.wiley.com. Illus., index, adv. Sample. Refereed. Vol. ends: No. 4. Reprint: PSC. *Indexed:* A01, A22, BRI, CBRI, E01, IBSS, P61. *Bk. rev.:* 3-18 per issue. *Aud.:* Ga, Ac, Sa.

Presidential Studies Quarterly is a journal about the United States presidency from historical and contemporary perspectives on a broad range of topics, such as elections, campaigns, voters, foreign policy, decision making, and relationships with Congress, federal courts, the press, and the public. Scholars and professionals in history, political science, and communications contribute articles for an interdisciplinary journal that appeals to a broad audience of scholars, students, and political professionals. Recent articles focus on the role of the president in the polarization of the U.S. electorate; the invocation of American exceptionalism by the president in different global contexts; the rhetoric of the Bush administration's justification for the 2003 Iraq war; Republican congressional candidates' positions on Trump during the 2016 election; and spatial metaphors used by Nixon before, during, and after his visit to the People's Republic of China. Issues include book reviews and special feature essays. Recommended for academic, public, and special libraries.

4146. ***Publius: the journal of federalism.*** [ISSN: 0048-5950] 1971. q. EUR 579. Ed(s): John S Dinan. Oxford University Press, Great Clarendon St, Oxford, OX2 6DP, United Kingdom; onlinequeries.uk@oup.com; https://academic.oup.com/journals/. Illus., index, adv. Sample. Refereed. Vol. ends: No. 4. Microform: PQC. Reprint: PSC. *Indexed:* A01, A22, BRI, E01, IBSS, P61, SSA. *Bk. rev.:* 0-10 per issue. *Aud.:* Ac, Sa.

Publius is sponsored by the Section on Federalism and Intergovernmental Relations of the American Political Science Association. It focuses on "the latest research from around the world on the federalism theory and practice; the dynamics of federal systems; intergovernmental relations and administration; regional, state and provincial governance; and comparative federalism." It seeks articles from many disciplines that illustrate the intergovernmental impact of policy changes. In addition to articles and book reviews, issues may include literature reviews and research notes. *Publius* publishes special issues on topics such as gender and federalism and an "Annual Review of American Federalism" that covers the preceding year. Recent articles focus on the impact of fiscal federalism on secessionist movements; judicial federalism in the United States; federalism in Nepal, Myanmar, and Sri Lanka; and climate change policy in Canada. Recommended for academic libraries.

4147. ***State Politics & Policy Quarterly.*** [ISSN: 1532-4400] 2000. q. USD 430 (print & online eds.)). Ed(s): Chris Bonneau. Sage Publications, Inc., 2455 Teller Rd, Thousand Oaks, CA 91320; info@sagepub.com; http://www.sagepub.com. Adv. Refereed. Reprint: PSC. *Indexed:* A01, IBSS, P61. *Aud.:* Ac.

This journal is the official publication of the State Politics and Policy Section of the American Political Science Association. It seeks articles "that develop and test general hypotheses of political behavior and policy making, exploiting the unique advantages of the states." This aim includes cross-national and comparative studies on subnational governments. Issues may include field review essays, research notes, papers on methods and data used to study states, and replication or extension papers. Examples of recent research topics are the role of organized labor in limiting economic inequality; how local media coverage of voter fraud influences viewer perceptions; a comparison of U.S. and Mexican policies on legal rights for same-sex couples; and the development of a "gender equality mood" measure of variation in attitudes toward gender roles. Recommended for academic libraries.

International Relations

This subsection has periodicals that focus on research and analysis of contemporary issues related to international relations theory, relations between nation states, international organizations, multinational corporations, and political economy. These journals may also cover international security and peace studies, but journals dedicated to these subjects are found in the "Peace and Conflict Studies" section of this volume.

4148. ***Current History: a journal of contemporary world affairs.*** Formed by the merger of (1940-1941): *Current History & Forum;* (1937-1941): *Events;* Incorporates (1940-1941): *Key to Contemporary Affairs;* (1945-1950): *Forum;* Which was formerly (until 1945): *Forum and Column Review;* (until 1943): *Column Review and Editorial Digest;* (until 1939): *Column Review.* [ISSN: 0011-3530] 1914. 9x/yr. USD 39.95 domestic (print or online ed.); USD 55.95 foreign; USD 49.95 combined subscription domestic (print & online eds.)). Ed(s): Joshua Lustig. Current History, Inc., 4225 Main St, Philadelphia, PA 19127. Illus., index, adv. Vol. ends: Dec. Microform: NBI; PQC. *Indexed:* A22, BAS, BRI, C37, CBRI, E01, IBSS, MLA-IB, P61. *Bk. rev.:* 1+ essays per issue. *Aud.:* Hs, Ga, Ac, Sa.

This long-running periodical, the "oldest US publication devoted exclusively to world affairs," provides analysis by contributors who range from academic scholars and government and diplomatic leaders, to politicians with expertise. Each issue has either a regional or topical focus. There are annual issues on China and East Asia; Russia and Eurasia; the Middle East; Latin America; South Asia; Europe; Africa; and Global Trends. Occasionally, there is a special issue on a topic, such as the November 2016 issue on diasporas. In addition to articles, each issue includes a book review section and the "Month in Review," with a chronology of important events organized by region and country. Recommended for academic, public, and school libraries.

4149. ***European Journal of International Relations.*** [ISSN: 1354-0661] 1995. q. USD 2016 (print & online eds.)). Ed(s): Geoffrey Underhill. Sage Publications Ltd., 1 Oliver's Yard, 55 City Rd, London, EC1Y 1SP, United Kingdom; info@sagepub.com; https://www.sagepub.com/. Illus., index, adv. Sample. Refereed. Vol. ends: No. 4. Reprint: PSC. *Indexed:* A01, A22, B01, E01, EconLit, IBSS, P61, SSA. *Aud.:* Ac.

Published for the European Consortium for Political Research, this journal offers research on all aspects of international relations worldwide. It is open to all methodologies and theoretical approaches in international relations (IR), and "aims to achieve a representative balance across the diversity of the field and to promote deeper understanding of the rapidly-changing world around us." Recent articles focus on the Islamic State's public displays of violence; debates on the Iran Nuclear Deal in the U.S. Congress; ableism in IR scholarship's use of disability metaphors; welfare internationalism; and the biopolitics of the Anthropocene. Recommended for academic libraries.

4150. ***Foreign Affairs.*** Former titles (until 1922): *The Journal of International Relations;* (until 1919): *The Journal of Race Development.* [ISSN: 0015-7120] 1910. bi-m. USD 34.95 domestic; USD 46.95 Canada; USD 69.95 elsewhere. Ed(s): Gideon Rose. Council on Foreign Relations, Inc., PO Box 60001, Tampa, FL 33662; communications@cfr.org; http://www.cfr.org. Illus., index, adv. Vol. ends: No. 6. Microform: WSH; PMC; PQC. Reprint: WSH. *Indexed:* A01, A22, B01, BAS, BRI, C37, CBRI, EconLit, IBSS, MASUSE, MLA-IB, P61. *Bk. rev.:* 1-3 essays per issue; usually 35-50 short reviews. *Aud.:* Hs, Ga, Ac, Sa.

Foreign Affairs is published by the Council on Foreign Relations (CFR), a nonpartisan organization that is "dedicated to improving the understanding of United States foreign policy and international affairs through the free exchange of ideas." The CFR publishes articles that are written by academics, foreign affairs practitioners, journalists, and other informed writers. The magazine covers a broad range of issues in contemporary international affairs from political, historical, legal, and economic perspectives. Articles include illustrations and maps, and bimonthly issues include topical essays and book reviews. Recent articles focus on xenophobic populist movements in the West; recent political reform in China; the opioid epidemic in the United States; Trump's international trade policy; Mugabe's political career; and different perspectives on American exceptionalism. Recommended for academic, public, and school libraries.

4151. ***Foreign Policy (Washington): the magazine of global politics, economics and ideas.*** [ISSN: 0015-7228] 1971. bi-m. USD 47.99 combined subscription print & online eds. Ed(s): Jonathan Tepperman. F P Group, 11 Dupont Circle, Ste 600, Washington, DC 20036; fp@cambeywest.com; http://foreignpolicy.com. Illus., index, adv. *Indexed:* A01, A22, B01, BRI, C37, IBSS, MASUSE, P61. *Bk. rev.:* 1-3 essays per issue. *Aud.:* Ga, Ac, Sa.

Foreign Policy is an international source for global news and analysis. The magazine offers information on contemporary politics and economics in the context of foreign policy-making worldwide. Notable academics, policy makers, and journalists contribute to a resource that is accessible to both specialists and a general audience seeking current information and ideas from a nonpartisan source. Recent issues include articles on women's rights in Russia; education in Tunisia; Brexit; the Afghan military after U.S. troop withdrawal; and human smuggling in Europe. Recommended for academic, public, and school libraries.

4152. ***International Affairs (London).*** Former titles (until 1944): *International Affairs Review Supplement;* (until 1940): *International Affairs;* (until 1931): *Royal Institute of International Affairs. Journal;* (until 1926): *British Institute of International Affairs. Journal.* [ISSN: 0020-5850] 1922. bi-m. GBP 482. Ed(s): Heidi Pettersson, Andrew Dorman. Wiley-Blackwell Publishing Ltd., The Atrium, Southern Gate, Chichester, PO19 8QG, United Kingdom; cs-journals@wiley.com; http://onlinelibrary.wiley.com. Illus., index, adv. Sample. Refereed. Microform: PMC. Reprint: PSC. *Indexed:* A01, A22, AmHI, B01, BAS, BRI, E01, IBSS, P61. *Bk. rev.:* 1-3 topical review essays; 40+ reviews per issue. *Aud.:* Hs, Ac, Sa.

Published for more than 95 years on behalf of Chatham House, the Royal Institute of International Affairs in London, *International Affairs* is "one of the world's leading journals of international relations," with an emphasis on scholars and practitioners of international relations. Articles offer "critical thinking on the key issues shaping today's world." Each issue includes topic review essays of multiple books as well as individual reviews of books. Recent issues have articles on China's position on North Korea; differing security conceptions among Gulf Cooperation Council countries; covert action and plausible deniability in state intervention; United Nations' attempts to prevent violence extremism; counter-insurgency in Somalia; and liberal internationalism. Recommended for academic and public libraries.

4153. ***International Organization.*** [ISSN: 0020-8183] 1947. q. GBP 228. Ed(s): Erik Voeten. Cambridge University Press, University Printing House, Shaftesbury Rd, Cambridge, CB2 8BS, United Kingdom; journals@cambridge.org; https://www.cambridge.org/. Illus., index, adv. Refereed. Circ: 1700. Vol. ends: No. 4. Microform: PQC. Reprint: PSC. *Indexed:* A22, B01, BAS, BRI, E01, EconLit, IBSS, L14, P61, SSA. *Bk. rev.:* 0-1 thematic reviews of multiple books. *Aud.:* Ac, Sa.

International Organization is published on behalf of the International Organization Foundation. It covers all aspects of international affairs, including "foreign policies, international relations, international and comparative political economy, security policies, environmental disputes and resolutions, regional integration, alliance patterns and war, bargaining and conflict resolution, economic development and adjustment, and international capital movements." Some issues contain a "research note" section highlighting specific topics and "review essays" focusing on developments and future research needs in a particular field of study. Recent articles examine human trafficking; forum isolation in international law; ethnic stratification in post-colonial states; use of force in U.N. peacekeeping efforts; foreign aid; and the effects of international trade on U.S. presidential elections. Recommended for academic libraries.

International Security. See Peace and Conflict Studies section.

4154. ***International Studies Quarterly.*** Former titles (until 1967): *Background;* (until 1962): *Background on World Politics.* [ISSN: 0020-8833] 1957. q. GBP 1730. Ed(s): Daniel H Nexon. Oxford University Press, 2001 Evans Rd, Cary, NC 27513; custserv.us@oup.com; https://academic.oup.com/journals. Illus., index, adv. Sample. Refereed. Circ: 4154 Paid. Vol. ends: No. 4. Microform: PQC. Reprint: PSC. *Indexed:* A01, A22, AmHI, B01, BAS, BRI, E01, IBSS, P61. *Aud.:* Ga, Ac, Sa.

International Studies Quarterly, published for the International Studies Association, focuses on "political, economic, social, or cultural processes that cross the borders of states." It is a journal that will appeal to a general audience that includes scholars, writers, and persons in leadership positions who may benefit from studies of contemporary international issues and controversies. Features include sections for "research notes," "theory notes," and debates. Recent issues cover data transparency in international finance; Soviet-Japanese-U.S. triangular diplomacy in the 1950s; use of social media by world leaders; the cross-national influence of governing parties; global climate governance; and the application of Social Identity Theory to understand status-seeking among states. Recommended for academic and public libraries.

The Journal of Conflict Resolution. See Peace and Conflict Studies section.

4155. ***Political Science Quarterly: the journal of public and international affairs.*** [ISSN: 0032-3195] 1886. q. GBP 584 (print & online eds.)). Ed(s): Marylena Mantas, James Demetrios Caraley. Wiley-Blackwell Publishing, Inc., 111 River St, Hoboken, NJ 07030; info@wiley.com; http://onlinelibrary.wiley.com. Illus., index, adv. Refereed. Circ: 8000 Paid. Vol. ends: No. 4. Microform: PMC; PQC. Reprint: PSC. *Indexed:* A01, A22, BAS, BRI, CBRI, EconLit, IBSS, MLA-IB, P61, SSA. *Bk. rev.:* 25-30. *Aud.:* Ga, Ac, Sa.

Published since 1886 by the Academy of Political Science, this is a nonpartisan, scholarly journal that covers government, politics, and public policy. Its intended audience is political scientists and general readers interested in politics and foreign affairs. Written by leading scholars, its articles often include a historical perspective on domestic and international issues. Recent articles are on energy security in China; an analysis of the 2014 midterm election in the United States; relations between the United States and Central America in the 1980s; higher education and the "American Dream"; political engagement by wealthy Americans; and authoritarianism and democracy in Muslim countries. The book review section is extensive, with approximately 30 reviews in an issue. Recommended for academic and public libraries.

4156. ***Review of International Studies.*** Formerly (until 1981): *British Journal of International Studies.* [ISSN: 0260-2105] 1975. q. plus one supplement. GBP 424. Ed(s): Ruth Blakeley, Sophie Harman. Cambridge University Press, University Printing House, Shaftesbury Rd, Cambridge, CB2 8BS, United Kingdom; journals@cambridge.org; https://www.cambridge.org/. Illus., index, adv. Refereed. Circ: 1700. Vol. ends: No. 4. Reprint: PSC. *Indexed:* A01, A22, AmHI, E01, EconLit, IBSS, P61. *Aud.:* Ac.

Review of International Studies, the official journal of the British International Studies Association, publishes articles related to contemporary and historical issues in global politics. Recent articles focus on norms around autonomous weapon systems; security governance; feminist international relations (IR) scholarship between World Wars I and II; and the application of just war theory to cyber warfare. Occasionally, *RIS* publishes literature reviews, forums, and interviews with important scholars. Recommended for academic libraries.

4157. ***Third World Quarterly.*** [ISSN: 0143-6597] 1979. m. GBP 1735 (print & online eds.) Individuals, USD 590). Ed(s): Shahid Qadir. Routledge, 4 Park Sq, Milton Park, Abingdon, OX14 4RN, United Kingdom; subscriptions@tandf.co.uk; http://www.tandfonline.com. Illus., index, adv. Sample. Refereed. Vol. ends: No. 10. Reprint: PSC. *Indexed:* A01, A22, AmHI, B01, BAS, BRI, C45, E01, IBSS, P61, SSA. *Bk. rev.:* 0-1 thematic review articles on multiple books. *Aud.:* Ac, Sa.

This interdisciplinary journal offers "analysis of micro-economic and grassroots efforts of development practitioners and planners." The focus is on political, social, and economic structures and policy studies in Asia, Africa, Latin America, and the Middle East. Editors welcome "provocative and exploratory articles" to encourage debate. Special issues are published frequently on topics such as developmental states; interdisciplinary drug scholarship; and an examination of the concept of imperialism in light of neoliberal globalization. Recent articles examine Brazil's oil-based industrial policy; Japan's practice of economic diplomacy in the Arctic; the impact of liberalization on the political economy in the Democratic Republic of Congo; and the interactions between the drug trade and the state in post-transition Bolivia. Recommended for academic and special libraries.

4158. ***The Washington Quarterly.*** Formerly (until 1978): *The Washington Review of Strategic and International Studies.* [ISSN: 0163-660X] 1978. q. GBP 420 (print & online eds.)). Ed(s): Alexander T J Lennon. Routledge, 711 3rd Ave, 8th Fl., New York, NY 10017; enquiries@tandfonline.com; http://www.tandfonline.com. Illus., index, adv. Refereed. Vol. ends: No. 4. Microform: PQC. Reprint: PSC. *Indexed:* A01, A22, BAS, BRI, E01, IBSS, MASUSE, MLA-IB, P61. *Aud.:* Hs, Ga, Ac, Sa.

This journal of international affairs, hosted by the Elliott School of International Affairs at George Washington University, offers analyses of "strategic changes, trends, and relations around the world and their public policy implications." The articles it publishes are "authoritative yet written for the global affairs generalist." Recent issues have articles on U.S. foreign policy under Trump; China's conflict management strategies; the 2020 Nuclear Proliferation Treaty; Boko Haram and modern insurgency; and U.S. and Iranian efforts to battle ISIS. Recommended for academic, public, school, and special libraries.

4159. ***World Affairs (Washington): a journal of ideas and debate.*** Former titles (until 1932): *Advocate of Peace Through Justice;* (until 1920): *The Advocate of Peace;* (until 1894): *The American Advocate of Peace and Arbitration;* (until 1892): *American Advocate of Peace;* (until 1847): *Advocate of Peace;* (until 1846): *The Advocate of Peace and Universal Brotherhood; The Advocate of Peace;* (until 1837): *American Advocate of Peace;* Which incorporates (1831-1835): *The Calumet;* Which was formerly (1828-1831): *Harbinger of Peace.* [ISSN: 0043-8200] 1837. q. USD 410 (print & online eds.)). Ed(s): Emma Norman. Sage Publications, Inc., 2455 Teller Rd, Thousand Oaks, CA 91320; info@sagepub.com; http://www.sagepub.com. Illus., index, adv. Refereed. Vol. ends: Summer. Reprint: PSC. *Indexed:* A01, A22, BAS, BRI, MASUSE, P61. *Bk. rev.:* 1+ essays per issue. *Aud.:* Hs, Ga, Ac.

World Affairs was founded in 1837 as part of the peace literature of the 1830s-1930s. It is now published as an academic journal by the World Affairs Institute, which is dedicated to promoting "public education and awareness on international issues related to war and peace." The journal presents a wide range of perspectives and opinions through articles that "bridge the academic and public spheres and promote stimulating conversation between them." Each issue includes essays and book reviews written for a wide range of readers. Recent issues have articles on the origins of U.S. policy toward Russia in Woodrow Wilson's administration; Sweden's soft power diplomacy on human rights issues; Trump's "America First" doctrine; and an examination of public policy rhetoric around Syrian refugee relocation. Recommended for academic, public, and school libraries.

4160. ***World Politics: a quarterly journal of international relations.*** [ISSN: 0043-8871] 1948. q. GBP 246. Ed(s): Deborah Yashar. Cambridge University Press, University Printing House, Shaftesbury Rd, Cambridge, CB2 8BS, United Kingdom; journals@cambridge.org; https://www.cambridge.org/. Illus., index, adv. Refereed. Vol. ends: No. 4. Microform: PQC. *Indexed:* A01, A22, B01, BRI, CBRI, E01, IBSS, P61, SSA. *Aud.:* Ac.

This journal is published on behalf of the Princeton Institute for International and Regional Studies at Princeton University. Editors seek "research articles that make theoretical and empirical contributions to the literature, and review articles bearing on problems in international relations and comparative politics." Recent issues have articles on the impact of economic treaties on trade; the connection between the strength of political parties and economic growth; ideational salience and judicial decision making; and social welfare claims in rural India. Recommended for academic libraries.

■ POPULATION STUDIES

ı *Megan Townley, Circulation, Bob Jones University, Greenville, SC*

Introduction

As a field, population studies pulls from a wide assortment of academic disciplines; the periodicals listed here reflect the interdisciplinarity of the area. All of the publications stress that the articles come from multiple disciplines, including, but not limited to, demography; sociology; public policy; political science; economics; history; statistics; geography; biology; and health. Due to the nature of the area of study, most publications have a global scope of coverage. The titles listed here also reflect the relatively academic and professional nature of the field, with most having target audiences of scholars, professionals, and policy makers. However, a couple titles address topics in population studies for a general audience.

Basic Periodicals

Ga: *Population Bulletin;* Ac: *Demography, European Journal of Population, Population and Development Review, Population Research and Policy Review.*

Basic Abstracts and Indexes

ABI/INFORM, AgeLine, LexisNexis, MEDLINE, PAIS International.

4161. *Demography.* [ISSN: 0070-3370] 1964. q. EUR 296 (print & online eds.)). Ed(s): Pamela J Smock. Springer New York LLC, 233 Spring St, New York, NY 10013; customerservice@springer.com; http://www.springer.com. Illus., adv. Refereed. Vol. ends: No. 4. Reprint: PSC. *Indexed:* A01, A22, AgeL, B01, BAS, BRI, C45, Chicano, E01, EconLit, IBSS, SSA. *Aud.:* Ac.

Published by the Population Association of America (PAA) since 1964, this bimonthly, peer-reviewed publication comes out every February, April, June, August, October, and December. The PAA "is a non-profit, scientific professional organization that promotes research on population issues." Articles in *Demography* present research from multiple disciplines, including the social sciences, geography, history, biology, statistics, epidemiology, and public health. As indicated by the definition on the cover, "n. the statistical study of human populations," the journal features many statistically based, quantitative research articles on population studies. Geographical coverage of this publication is global, covering both the developed and developing world and related population issues. Recent issues included articles on a variety of issues in infant mortality, adult mortality, life expectancy, racial diversity, and immigration policy impacts. Recommended for academic libraries.

Ethnic and Racial Studies. See Multicultural Studies section.

4162. *European Journal of Population.* Formerly (until 1983): *European Demographic Information Bulletin.* [ISSN: 0168-6577] 1970. q. EUR 1191 (print & online eds.)). Ed(s): Helga A G de Valk. Springer Netherlands, Van Godewijckstraat 30, Dordrecht, 3311 GX, Netherlands; http://www.springer.com. Illus., adv. Refereed. Vol. ends: No. 4. Reprint: PSC. *Indexed:* A22, BRI, C45, E01, EconLit, IBSS, SSA. *Bk. rev.:* 2-3, 1,000-1,200 words. *Aud.:* Ac.

This quarterly, peer-reviewed publication also goes by its French title *Revue Europeenne de Demographie.* The journal is published under the auspices of the European Association for Population Studies (EAPS). It seeks to improve "understanding of population phenomena, fostering development of theory and method." The *European Journal of Population* covers the intersection of demography and a wide range of social science disciplines and the health sciences. Its stated geographic coverage includes European and non-European countries. This title will occasionally have special, thematic issues. Issues typically have a few research articles and a couple book reviews. Articles in recent issues have covered topics ranging from fertility, cohabitation and marital habits, and childbearing. Despite the stated global scope, recent articles focused on European countries. Recommended for academic libraries.

4163. *International Migration Review: a quarterly studying sociological, demographic, economic, historical, and legislative aspects of human migration movements and ethnic group relations.* Formerly (until 1966): *International Migration Digest;* Which incorporated (in 1973): *International Newsletter on Migration;* Which was formerly (1971-1972): *International Migration Newsletter.* [ISSN: 0197-9183] 1964. q. USD 517. Sage Publications, Inc., 2455 Teller Rd, Thousand Oaks, CA 91320; info@sagepub.com; http://www.sagepub.com. Illus., index, adv. Sample. Refereed. Vol. ends: Winter. Reprint: PSC. *Indexed:* A01, A22, A47, ASSIA, BAS, BRI, C45, Chicano, E01, IBSS, P61, SSA. *Bk. rev.:* 3-6; 350-700 words. *Aud.:* Ac.

The Center for Migration Studies of New York (CMS) puts out the *International Migration Review,* which embraces an interdisciplinary approach to the study of population movement. This peer-reviewed publication focuses on the population movement aspect of population studies. Global in scope, it addresses all aspects of the title topic, including socio-demographic, historical, economic, political, legislative, and pastoral dimensions of human mobility. Article topics generally focus on migration, immigration, and refugees. A typical issue will include six to seven research articles and three signed book reviews. Recent issues of the *International Migration Review* included articles on the following topics: illegal immigration; Group Conflict Theory; and migrant domestic work. Recommended for academic and research libraries.

Journal of Ethnic and Migration Studies. See Multicultural Studies section.

Journal of Family History. See Family section.

Perspectives on Sexual and Reproductive Health. See Family Planning section.

4164. *Population and Development Review.* [ISSN: 0098-7921] 1975. q. GBP 277 (print & online eds.)). Ed(s): Geoffrey McNicoll. Wiley-Blackwell Publishing, Inc., 111 River St, Hoboken, NJ 07030; http://onlinelibrary.wiley.com. Illus., adv. Sample. Refereed. Vol. ends: No. 4. Microform: PQC. *Indexed:* A01, A22, ASSIA, B01, BAS, BRI, C42, C45, Chicano, E01, EIP, EconLit, IBSS, P61, SSA. *Bk. rev.:* 10-12. *Aud.:* Ac.

Published by Wiley-Blackwell on behalf of the Population Council, this journal focuses on the relationship between population studies and development. The journal's stated scope is the interplay between population and social, economic, and environmental change, as well as related public policy issues. Geographic coverage includes both the developed and developing world and come from across a variety of academic disciplines. The journal welcomes theoretically focused articles and empirical analysis, but strives to maintain readability by publishing articles that present ideas and insights instead of highly analytical work. Time period coverage of articles spans both current and historical topics. Document types include articles, commentaries, review essays, book reviews, and relevant excerpts from past writings. Recent issues included articles on fertility in the developed world; adult mortality in the developing world; and Alexis de Tocqueville's influence. Recommended for academic and research libraries. URL: www.popcouncil.org/publications/pdr.asp

4165. *Population Bulletin.* [ISSN: 0032-468X] 1945. q. Free to qualified personnel. Ed(s): Marlene Lee. Population Reference Bureau, Inc., 1875 Connecticut Ave, NW, Ste 520, Washington, DC 20009; popref@prb.org; http://www.prb.org. Illus. *Indexed:* A01, A22, BAS, C45, EIP, EconLit, MASUSE. *Aud.:* Ga, Ac.

This is one of the major publications of the Population Reference Bureau (PBR). Issues of the *Population Bulletin* are highly regarded by academics and professionals alike. The PBR "informs people around the world about population, health, and the environment, and empowers them to use that information to advance the well-being of current and future generations." The journal presents trends in population studies on both a domestic and international level. Topic areas of editions of the *Population Bulletin* are the core themes of the PBR's work: aging; education; environment; gender; health/nutrition; HIV/AIDS; immigration/migration; income/poverty; marriage/family; population basics; race/ethnicity; reproductive health; U.S. Census 2010 & ACS; and youth. Written by experts in the field for a general audience, the *Population Bulletins* present their topics in thematic issues with clear text and colorful graphics. Target audiences of the publication include university classes, population professionals, and the media. Themes of recent issues included: "Achieving a Demographic Dividend"; "Household Change in the United States"; and "A Post-Recession Update on U.S. Social and Economic Trends." Highly recommended for academic, research, and public libraries. URL: www.prb.org/Publications/PopulationBulletins.aspx

4166. *Population Connection.* Former titles (until 2014): *Population Connection. The Reporter;* (until 2003): *Zero Population Growth Reporter;* (until 1979): *Zero Population Growth National Reporter.* [ISSN: 2331-0529] 1969. q. Free to members; Non-members, USD 25. Ed(s): Marian Starkey. Population Connection, 2120 L St, NW, Ste 500, Washington, DC 20037; info@populationconnection.org; http://www.population connection.org. *Bk. rev.:* 1-2. *Aud.:* Ga.

The Population Connection, formerly known as Zero Population Growth, is an organization that advocates for population stabilization. The organization publishes *The Reporter* quarterly. Geared toward a general audience, the publication reports on population news and demographic trends with approachable language and colorful graphics. Each thematic issue includes a few feature articles on the theme, book reviews, an "Editor's Note," "Letters to the Editor," "Pop Facts," "In the News," "The President's Circle," "Washington View," "Field & Outreach," "PopEd," a cartoon, and "Editorial Excerpts." *The Reporter* covers global issues, but recent issues have focused on the United States. Themes of recent issues included: the teen birth rate in the United States; "Population Aging and the U.S. Economy"; and "Congressional Report Card." Recommended for all readers. URL: www.populationconnection.org/site/PageServer?pagename=news_publications_reporter

4167. *Population Research and Policy Review.* [ISSN: 0167-5923] 1980. bi-m. EUR 1382 (print & online eds.)). Ed(s): Lloyd B Potter, Jennifer Glick. Springer Netherlands, Van Godewijckstraat 30, Dordrecht, 3311 GX, Netherlands; http://www.springer.com. Illus., adv. Refereed. Microform: PQC. Reprint: PSC. *Indexed:* A22, Agr, C45, E01, EconLit, IBSS, P61, SSA. *Bk. rev.:* 3, 400-500 words. *Aud.:* Ac.

The flagship journal of the Southern Demographic Association (SDA), this peer-reviewed publication presents interdisciplinary work on population studies, as well as implications for policy and program development of such studies. With a relatively practical focus, the articles in this journal frequently present the related policy issues with demographic research. Subject coverage includes the fields of demography, economics, politics, and health studies. The journal includes work utilizing all methodological approaches, including ethnographic studies, comparative-historical studies, and discourse analysis. Recent issues include articles on mortality in the United States, immigrants in Swedish schools, population aging in Europe, and survival rates of diabetics. Recommended for academic and research libraries.

4168. *Population Review (Online).* [ISSN: 1549-0955] 2003. s-a. Ed(s): Archibald O Haller. Population Review Publications, 3522 2nd fl. rm.2 AL 11B, Lardproa Rd., Klongchang Bangkapi, Bangkok, 10240, Thailand. Refereed. *Bk. rev.:* Number and length vary. *Aud.:* Ac, Sa.

This is a longstanding journal published since 1957. Articles in *Population Review* tend to focus on sociological demography, but may come from an array of social science fields. The journal prioritizes articles that present empirical research in population studies. Content includes international coverage from both the developed and developing world. Content types include original articles and book reviews. A recent issue presented a series of articles on population issues for Southern Europe, mostly Italy and Spain. Issues do not necessarily have such a geographic or thematic focus; other recent articles cover topics such as historical Czech marriage trends and land conflict in Brazil. Recommended for academic and research libraries. URL: http://populationreview.com/

Population, Space and Place (Online). See Geography section.

4169. *Population Studies: a journal of demography.* [ISSN: 0032-4728] 1947. 3x/yr. GBP 270 (print & online eds.)). Ed(s): John Simons. Routledge, 4 Park Sq, Milton Park, Abingdon, OX14 4RN, United Kingdom; subscriptions@tandf.co.uk; http://www.tandfonline.com. Illus., adv. Sample. Refereed. Reprint: PSC. *Indexed:* A01, A22, A47, B01, BAS, BRI, C45, E01, EconLit, IBSS, P61, SSA. *Bk. rev.:* 4-6; 800-1,200 words. *Aud.:* Ac.

A peer-reviewed journal published since 1947, *Population Studies* has a long history of publishing demography research, and covers all aspects of the field comprehensively: "applications in developed and developing countries; historical and contemporary studies; quantitative and qualitative studies; analytical essays and reviews. The Population Investigation Committee (PIC)[,] based at the London School of Economics (LSE)[,] produces this journal. The subjects of papers range from classical concerns, such as the determinants and consequences of population change, to such topics as family demography and evolutionary and genetic influences on demographic behaviour [*sic*]. Often the Journal's papers have had the effect of extending the boundaries of its field." This title includes articles on a variety of methods and theories of demographic analyses, as well as practical applications of theories and methods. An issue typically includes six or seven research articles, as well as several book reviews. Recent issues addressed topics pertaining to fertility in India, divorce and mortality in Belarus, and migration within and from China. Recommended for academic and research libraries.

Studies in Family Planning. See Family Planning section.

■ PREGNANCY

Sheryl Walters, Reference and Electronic Resources Librarian, Logan University, Chesterfield, MO 63017; sheryl.walters@logan.edu

Introduction

No other life event can compare to the time of pregnancy. It brings with it a great deal of excitement, but at the same time, much uncertainty. Creating another human life is a wonder in itself and entails an abundance of new knowledge to acquire. Women who are contemplating pregnancy, those who are dealing with infertility, those who are pregnant, and the men who support them, may turn to reading materials to help guide them through their unique journey. Everyone's story is different and we learn more by sharing with one another. Therefore, periodicals can be a great resource, as they contain a wealth of information compiled by others who have taken the journey themselves, or are experts in the field.

A great duty is placed on physicians and health practitioners who work with fertility, fetal development, and pregnancy. These professionals also share expertise through trade publications and academic journals. It is essential to promote and support research that further meets the needs of women's health.

Included in this pregnancy section are magazines for consumers, such as *Pregnancy and Newborn* or *Parents*, and peer-reviewed literature through journals like *The American Journal of Obstetrics & Gynecology* or *Midwifery*. Also reviewed is a trade publication for professionals entitled *ACOG Clinical Review*. Through these periodicals, a wide range of knowledge is ready to be gained.

Basic Periodicals

American Journal of Obstetrics & Gynecology, Fertility Today, Midwifery Today, Obstetrics & Gynecology, Pregnancy, Pregnancy and Newborn.

Basic Abstracts and Indexes

CINAHL, *Family Health Index, Maternity and Infant Care,* MEDLINE.

4170. ***A C O G Clinical Review.*** Supersedes (in 1996): *A C O G Current Journal Review.* [ISSN: 1085-6862] 1987. bi-m. Free to members. Ed(s): Nancy Rowe, Morton A Stenchever. American College of Obstetricians and Gynecologists, PO Box 70620, Washington, DC 20024; publication@acog.org; http://www.acog.org. Sample. Refereed. Microform: PQC. *Aud.:* Ga, Ac, Sa.

ACOG Clinical Review is a newsletter from the American College of Obstetrics and Gynecology (ACOG), which is only available through an ACOG membership. ACOG is a non-profit organization with professional membership belonging to physicians practicing in obstetrics and gynecology (OB/GYN), or students enrolled in relevant programs in an allopathic or osteopathic medical school. The website of the ACOG is available only to those with a membership. The ACOG is dedicated to the improvement of women's health and esteems safe access to quality healthcare, professionalism in membership, scholarship through health research and education, and advocacy for women. The newsletter provides synopses of relevant journal articles in the fields of obstetrics, gynecology, oncology, and infertility. This periodical, aimed at conveying research information in a review format for physicians, is best suited for a medical library, or a library within a hospital system.

4171. ***American Journal of Obstetrics & Gynecology.*** Formerly (until 1920): *The American Journal of Obstetrics and Diseases of Women and Children.* [ISSN: 0002-9378] 1868. m. USD 2229. Ed(s): Dr. Roberto Romero, Dr. Ingrid Nygaard. Mosby, Inc., 1600 John F. Kennedy Blvd, Ste 1800, Philadelphia, PA 19103; elspcs@elsevier.com; http://www.us.elsevierhealth.com. Illus., adv. Sample. Refereed. Microform: PMC; PQC. *Indexed:* A22, BRI, C45, E01. *Aud.:* Ac, Sa.

The *American Journal of Obstetrics & Gynecology* (*AJOG*) is also referred to as the "The Gray Journal." *AJOG* is devoted to obstetrics, gynecology, fetuses, the placenta, and the newborn. It is aimed at professionals in the field of obstetrics and gynecology (OB/GYN) and the language is written in a scholarly context. The periodical's concentration is on publishing original research, reviews, opinions, video clips, podcasts, and interviews that will have an impact on the understanding of health and disease pertaining to the practice of women's health care. The periodical is a leading peer-reviewed publication that is well respected in the medical community. Additionally, it is the official journal of several leading societies and organizations in the purview of OB/GYN, and contains papers from their meetings. *AJOG* is a suitable addition to any medical or health sciences library, as well as a library within a hospital system.

4172. ***Fertility Today.*** [ISSN: 1559-8888] 2005. bi-m. USD 27.80 domestic; USD 34 Canada; USD 42 elsewhere. Fertility Today, PO Box 117, Laurel, MD 20725. Adv. *Bk. rev.:* Number and length vary. *Aud.:* Ga.

Fertility Today is a magazine written by fertility professionals for the general consumer. The periodical is available in print by subscription, and their website also offers free overview materials. The print magazine contains a broad range of topics and expertise aimed at supporting couples coping with infertility concerns. Many of the individual magazine issues contain a story from a celebrity who shares her own experience of going through processes due to reproductive obstacles. Stories like these, and others that are written for the layperson, may be comforting for couples experiencing the same reproductive struggles. Information contained within is done by highly qualified physicians in reproductive medicine and other related professional experts. It is arranged in a very colorful and easy to digest format. The topic of infertility is relevant to many consumers, with the abundance of couples currently dealing with issues of infertility, which is about 10 percent of women (6.1 million) in the United States ages 15-44, according to the Centers for Disease Control. Therefore, this periodical is an appropriate addition to any public library. URL: http://www.fertilitytoday.org

Journal of Midwifery & Women's Health. See Health Professions section.

M C N: The American Journal of Maternal / Child Nursing. See Nursing section.

4173. ***Midwifery.*** [ISSN: 0266-6138] 1985. m. EUR 1379. Ed(s): Debra Bick. Churchill Livingstone, 32 Jamestown Rd, London, NW1 7BY, United Kingdom; corporate.sales@elsevier.com; http://www.elsevier.com/. Adv. Sample. Refereed. *Indexed:* A22, ASSIA, E01. *Aud.:* Ac, Sa.

Midwifery is an academic journal that publishes peer-reviewed research to illuminate the scope of pregnancy, birth, and maternity care for childbearing women, their babies, and families. More specifically, this periodical provides support and knowledge for midwives and maternity care providers. In addition, it is officially recognized by the European Midwives Association. It is an international and interdisciplinary resource that furthers discourse of advances and strife in midwifery. The periodical is appropriate for any health science or medical library that supports programs within obstetrics and gynecology, and also those that include programs in integrative health care.

4174. ***Midwifery Today: the heart and science of birth.*** Formerly (until 1997): *Midwifery Today and Childbirth Education with International Midwife;* Which was formed by the merger of (1987-1996): *Midwifery Today;* (1995-1996): *International Midwife.* [ISSN: 1551-8892] 1996. q. USD 55 domestic; USD 68 Canada; USD 75 elsewhere. Ed(s): Jan Tritten. Midwifery Today with International Midwife, PO Box 2672, Eugene, OR 97402. Illus., adv. Sample. *Indexed:* BRI, C42, FemPer, GW. *Aud.:* Ga.

Midwifery Today is a magazine for birth practitioners, although the language is written for any educated reader. The periodical seeks to share information between practitioners and families and fosters communication to promote natural childbirth and child rearing. It is quite colorful and contains many artistic images of midwives, doulas, babies, and mothers. Many of the articles are anecdotal in nature, and the magazine welcomes materials that contain the emotion of personal experiences from birth practitioners, which is unearthed in the articles very translucently. However, sophistication is still maintained throughout the publication. Some content is available online, but the majority of information is viewable by subscription only. The magazine promotes professionalism through balancing scientific and technical material with philosophy and personal accounts. This makes *Midwifery Today* appropriate for a public library audience, but it also has great value for an academic library that meets the needs of health science programs that value complementary and integrative health. URL: https://midwiferytoday.com/magazine/

4175. ***Pregnancy.*** [ISSN: 1540-8485] 2001. m. USD 14.99; USD 2.99 per issue. Ed(s): Kendra Smith. Future U S, Inc., 4000 Shoreline Ct, Ste 400, South San Francisco, CA 94080; http://www.futureus.com. Adv. Sample. *Aud.:* Ga.

Pregnancy is a digital magazine available by subscription. First-time mothers will benefit the most from its content. A subscription includes special issues on the first, second, and third trimesters, the big day, and an issue for the pregnant dad. It also includes a buyer's guide to help parents with product selections. Content in the regular issues covers pregnancy, labor and delivery, baby, and breastfeeding. Many parts of the website may be accessed without a subscription, and it offers several free educative articles. Articles on the site, and in each issue, are easy to read and contain an abundance of images. There is also a plethora of ads. This magazine is a very informative resource with content that may be quickly browsed and digested by anyone. It is highly recommended for all public libraries. URL: http://www.pregnancymagazine.com/

4176. ***Pregnancy and Newborn.*** [ISSN: 2324-741X] 2006. 8x/yr. USD 16 domestic; USD 24 Canada; USD 28 foreign. Halcyon Media, LLC, 200 Galleria Pkwy SE, Ste 920, Atlanta, GA 30339. Adv. *Aud.:* Ga.

Pregnancy and Newborn is a print magazine for pregnant women and new mothers. It also has a well-organized website that offers an abundance of freely available information through an online community. The audience for this magazine includes those at any stage of pregnancy or childbirth, and often includes information for fathers. Each issue has a pregnant woman on the cover and numerous taglines to hint at article content. Many of the covers dote a celebrity and/or promote maternity fashion. Content is straightforward and very catchy. Any reader will easily comprehend the content with little effort. It contains ads in the usual manner of a resplendent magazine. This monthly publication is recommended for public libraries. URL: http://www.pnmag.com/

■ PRINTING AND GRAPHIC ARTS

Donna B. Smith, Digital Collections Librarian, W. Frank Steely Library, Northern Kentucky University, Highland Heights, KY 41099.

Wendy Wood, Metadata and Collections Maintenance Librarian, W. Frank Steely Library, Northern Kentucky University, Highland Heights, KY 41099

Introduction

Communicating the message visually is the job of the graphic designer and the printer. Designers and printers work with innovation and persuasion in order to inform, entertain, and impress visually inundated and discriminating audiences. Clients look to these groups for marketing, technical, and high-impact graphic support. Competition is stiff as customers increasingly demand better service, more innovative products, and faster cycle times. Successful professionals need to be active in the marketing of their skills, as well as identify new markets for their products.

Recent years have witnessed major changes in the graphic design services and printing industries, including the rise of desktop publishing, the Internet, 3D printing, and digital technology. Technological advances have allowed designers to become closer to the production process and allowed them to reach their audiences at a more rapid pace. The use of digital print technology will increase in an environment of shorter runs and on-demand production demands. Designers and printers make use of new technology to create images that are more visually active than in the past. The industry has transformed into an imaging business that feeds a variety of media, only one of which is print. It is expected that print will continue in an expanded role that enhances the emerging interactive non-print alternatives.

As in most industries today, graphic designers and printers must remain current with the latest technology and marketing innovations. Rapid changes in design software require timely reports of their new capabilities. The printing industry continues to expand beyond print media publishing into such areas as packaging and labeling. Additionally, printers are offering more ancillary services to maintain their competitiveness within the industry. Many now offer variable-data printing (personalization), short-run printing, and warehousing. Profitability for individual companies also depends on decreasing costs via the introduction of new workflow efficiencies and growing new revenue sources. To remain relevant and successful, professionals must monitor emerging technologies such as security printing, 3D printing, nanotechnology, and printed electronics. Some printers are even positioning themselves to be complete communications services providers by offering graphic design, web site creation and maintenance, marketing services, and distribution services.

Therefore, the majority of publications recommended here are trade publications that provide necessary and timely information to practitioners, managers, suppliers, and anyone else interested in visual communications. They may cover the entire graphic communication industry or target specific segments, such as gravure printers, paper producers, or screen printers. Most magazines provide practical how-to information, and many profile artists, design studios, and printing firms. Some provide a showcase of leading designs in the industry by sponsoring competitions and displaying the winners in special issues. The trade publications also address the business side of the industry: legal concerns, environmental regulations, economic trends, marketing and sales, and management issues. Scholarly publications focus on the history of printing, the impact of visual phenomena, and new research in the field.

Colorful glossy journals dominate the resources for the graphic designers. Strictly electronic publications are not yet prevalent in this field. Although some publications are available online, these versions complement or coexist with the print issues. Some publishers' web sites do offer additional resources and articles not available in the print versions. The professional organizations tend to provide electronic publications such as newsletters for members. However, these may be delivered via e-mail and are not often archived.

Basic Periodicals

Ga: *Communication Arts, Print;* Ac: *Communication Arts, Design Issues, Print, Printing History, Visible Language;* Sa: *Communication Arts, Graphic Design USA, Print, The Seybold Report.*

Basic Abstracts and Indexes

Abstract Bulletin of Paper Science and Technology, Art Index, Design and Applied Arts Index, Scopus.

4177. ***Acta Graphica: journal of printing science and graphic communications.*** [ISSN: 0353-4707] 1989. q. Ed(s): Damir Modric, Miroslav Mikota. Acta Graphica Publishers, Getaldiceva 2, PO Box 225, Zagreb, 41001, Croatia; acta.graphica@grf.hr. Refereed. *Aud.:* Ac.

This English-language, international journal is published quarterly by the Faculty of Graphic Arts at the University of Zagreb, Croatia. It is scholarly, double-blind peer-reviewed, and open access. Scientific research and technical papers from the fields of graphic technology, printing and engineering, and graphical communication and design are featured in this journal. Each article is preceded by an abstract, a list of keywords, and a "how to cite item" clickable button, followed by the full-text pdf. Readers register and receive by e-mail the table of contents for each new issue of the journal. Librarians are encouraged to list this journal among their library's electronic journal holdings. As a respected open-access journal, it is indexed in the Directory of Open Access Journals and EBSCO's collection of open-access journals.

4178. ***Baseline (East Malling).*** [ISSN: 0954-9226] 1979. q. Ed(s): Hans Dieter Reichert. Bradburne Publishing Ltd., Bradbourne House, East Malling, ME19 6DZ, United Kingdom; info@baselinemagazine.com. Adv. *Bk. rev.:* Number and length vary. *Aud.:* Ac, Sa.

Baseline is an award-winning international typographic magazine devoted to typography, book arts, and graphic design. Launched in 1979, it is the authoritative magazine about type and typography. Contributors are from the academic as well as the practicing graphic design fields. Renowned for its high production standards, each issue is a large format, full-color illustrated magazine featuring seven to twelve articles. Topics include the history of graphic design, overviews of graphic design academic programs, presentations of student projects, and profiles of international designers. Book reviews are also offered. An issue index is offered on the website. This magazine is considered one of the top resources for the typographical community. URL: www.baselinemagazine.com

4179. ***Communication Arts.*** Former titles (until 1969): *C A Magazine;* (until 1967): *C A;* (until 1959): *Annual Exhibition of Communication Art.* [ISSN: 0010-3519] 19??. bi-m. USD 53 combined subscription domestic (print & online eds.); USD 70 combined subscription Canada (print & online eds.); USD 110 combined subscription elsewhere (print & online eds.)). Ed(s): Tad Crawford. Communication Arts, 110 Constitution Dr, Menlo Park, CA 94025. Illus., adv. *Indexed:* A01, A06, A22, BRI, F01. *Bk. rev.:* 2, 100-200 words, signed. *Aud.:* Ga, Ac, Sa.

Communication Arts is a high-quality trade publication for commercial artists. Issues serve as juried showcases for leading work in advertising, design, illustration, interactive design, typography, and photography. Included are feature articles that may profile design studios and artists, or highlight special advertising and design projects. Informative columns cover typography, design trends, advertising, business advice, and new books. Additional features are available online. This title is an important addition to any graphic arts collection. URL: https://www.commarts.com/

4180. ***Design Issues.*** [ISSN: 0747-9360] 1984. q. USD 610 (print & online eds.)). M I T Press, One Rogers St, Cambridge, MA 02142-1209; journals-cs@mit.edu; http://mitpress.mit.edu/. Illus., adv. Refereed. *Indexed:* A01, A22, AmHI, B01, E01, MLA-IB. *Bk. rev.:* Number and length vary. *Aud.:* Ac, Sa.

This scholarly journal focuses on the history, criticism, and theory of design. Regular issues offer six to eight articles on diverse perspectives of past and present design issues. Some issues feature special guest editors. Themed issues present broad topics such as design research and practices in various countries, artificial intelligence, and the state of design education throughout the world. The journal provides an international forum in which to explore the various dimensions of design, not only as a professional practice, but also as an economic force and a form of cultural art. This journal is an important addition to academic libraries that support a design program.

4181. ***Early Book Society. Journal: for the study of manuscripts and printing history.*** [ISSN: 1525-6790] 1997. a. USD 40 per issue. Ed(s): Martha W Driver. Pace University Press, 41 Park Row, Rm 1510, New York, NY 10038; PaceUP@Pace.Edu. Illus. *Indexed:* MLA-IB. *Bk. rev.:* 10-20, 500-1,500 words. *Aud.:* Ac, Sa.

This peer-reviewed journal focuses on the history of the book, emphasizing the period of transition from manuscript to print. Early English and continental works produced from 1350 to 1550 are explored. Each volume contains ten to fourteen substantial essays that cover such topics as book culture, traveling libraries, and the reception of early printed books. In addition, brief notes in the journal offer diverse new perspectives on works of the period, as well as updates on libraries and special collections. Book reviews are also featured. A useful addition to printing history collections.

4182. ***Elephant.*** Formerly (until 2009): *Graphic Magazine.* [ISSN: 1879-3835] 2003. q. Ed(s): Marc Valli. Frame Publishers, Laan der Hesperiden 68, Amsterdam, 1076 DX, Netherlands. Adv. *Indexed:* A51. *Bk. rev.:* Various number and length. *Aud.:* Ac, Sa.

Art, graphic arts, and printing are all the subjects of this beautiful magazine designed by London studio Kellenberger-White, and printed on four different paper stocks. Interviews with artists, which include reproductions of their works, provide the main content of the journal, along with book reviews and reviews of exhibitions. *Elephant* is is a continuation of *Graphic Magazine,* but encompasses so much more. This eye-opening serial is a multidisciplinary survey of the international art scene, and as such is perfect for college and special art libraries. *Elephant* is published in March, June, October, and December. Student discounts are available.

4183. ***Eye (London, 1990).*** [ISSN: 0960-779X] 1990. q. GBP 100 domestic. Ed(s): John L Walters. Haymarket Publishing Ltd., Studio 6, The Lux Bldg, 2-4 Hoxton Sq, London, N1 6NU, United Kingdom; info@haymarket.com; http://www.haymarket.com. Illus., adv. *Indexed:* A22, BRI. *Bk. rev.:* 10-15, 200-600 words. *Aud.:* Ac, Sa.

Noted for its articles combined with extraordinary visual material, this journal is an important addition to any graphic design collection. It focuses on typography, history, art direction, and graphic design for multimedia, advertising, publishing, and the web. Features include interviews with international designers, overviews of new trends in graphic design, and profiles of design studios. Regular columns provide critiques and book reviews. Article extracts from past issues are available online. URL: www.eyemagazine.com

4184. ***Flexo: the flexographic technology source.*** Formerly (until 1984): *Flexographic Technical Journal.* [ISSN: 1051-7324] 1976. m. Ed(s): Chris Bonawandt. Foundation of Flexographic Technical Association, 900 Marconi Ave, Ronkonkoma, NY 11779; memberinfo@flexography.org; http://www.flexography.org. Illus., adv. Sample. Vol. ends: Dec. *Indexed:* A22. *Aud.:* Ac, Sa.

Flexo is the official journal of the Flexographic Technical Association, which is devoted to advancing flexographic technology. This relief printing process is especially popular in the packaging and newspaper industries. Although *Flexo* is mainly a trade publication directed toward managers and technicians, its audience includes anyone who is interested in learning more about the technical aspects of flexography. Articles include such topics as designing packaging, comparing flexo presses, improving color quality, and examining printing techniques. The articles are written by practitioners, so they are informative and practical. Regular columns highlight new products, events, and association news. One issue features an annual buyer's guide. Issues are archived on the web site.

4185. ***Graphic Design: U S A.*** Formerly: *Graphics: U S A;* Incorporates: *Graphics: New York.* [ISSN: 0274-7499] 1965. 10x/yr. Free to qualified personnel. Kaye Publishing Corporation, 89 5th Ave, Ste 901, New York, NY 10003; http://www.gdusa.com. Illus., adv. *Aud.:* Ac, Sa.

This trade publication provides news and information for and about the professional design community, including graphic design firms, corporate and publishing in-house departments, advertising agencies, and nonprofit organizations. Popular features consist of people in the industry to watch, color forecasts, logo trends, and top design schools. Each issue provides news, events, and updates on people in the field. The magazine also sponsors national design competitions in 25 categories from annual reports to motion graphics.

4186. ***How.*** [ISSN: 0886-0483] 1985. bi-m. USD 40 United States; USD 55 Canada; USD 16.95 per issue. Ed(s): Andrew Gibbs. F + W Media Inc., 1140 Broadway, 14th Fl, New York, NY 10001; contact_us@fwmedia.com; http://www.fwcommunity.com/. Illus., adv. Circ: 15561 Paid. *Indexed:* A22. *Aud.:* Ac, Sa.

This is an instructional trade magazine that addresses the ideas and techniques that graphic design professionals use to create their work. Directed toward practitioners and design firm managers, it provides hands-on advice on making a design studio more profitable and more professional, and increasing its profile. Special issues focus on international design, in-house design, self-promotion, and creativity. Feature articles may include advice on managing a freelance business, tips for building a design portfolio, details on award-winning design projects, or comparisons of fonts. Regular columns profile design firms, report on new technology, and provide general industry news.

4187. ***The Imaging Channel: the business and people of managed print.*** [ISSN: 2153-375X] 2010. q. Free to qualified personnel. Ed(s): Patricia Ames. BPO Media, 840 S. Rancho Dr., Ste 4-558, Las Vegas, NV 89106; info@bpomedia.com; https://bpomediablog.wordpress.com. Adv. *Aud.:* Sa.

The managed-print industry is the focus of this quarterly magazine that brings together vendors, distributors, manufacturers, and resellers to report on the latest trends. The popular "Channel Chat" feature covers interviews with prominent industry executives on current industry topics. Profiles of independent dealers are included, as are accounts of how their corporations are structured to support managed-service offerings. An editorial column offers commentary on the latest industry happenings, as well as makes suggestions for transforming recent events into practical applications for dealerships. This magazine provides case studies, vertical market profiles, and hardware information for managed-print industry professionals.

4188. ***In-Plant Graphics.*** Former titles (until 1996): *In-Plant Reproductions;* (until 1988): *In-Plant Reproductions and Electronic Publishing;* (until 1985): *In-Plant Productions;* (until 1979): *Reproductions Review and Methods; Graphic Arts Supplier News; Reproductions Methods; Reproductions Review.* [ISSN: 1087-2817] 1951. m. Free to qualified personnel. Ed(s): Bob Neubauer. North American Publishing Co., 1500 Spring Garden St., 12th Fl, Philadelphia, PA 19130; magazinecs@napco.com; http://www.napco.com. Illus., adv. *Indexed:* A22, B03. *Aud.:* Sa.

In-plant printing operations include the printing departments in corporations, government agencies, and institutions. This journal targets the special needs of the managers, graphic artists, and technical personnel that work in these shops. Articles offer tips to managers on increasing productivity and controlling costs, profiles of successful in-plant shops, the latest graphic arts equipment and software, industry news, and conference information. Special reports cover a variety of topics, such as analysis of shops in specific industries and tips for expansion into marketing services.

4189. ***Information Design Journal.*** Formerly (until 2006): *Information Design Journal + Document Design;* Which was formed by the merger of (1979-2002): *Information Design Journal;* (1999-2003): *Document Design.* [ISSN: 1876-486X] 2003. 3x/yr. EUR 260 (print & online eds.)). Ed(s): Carla G Spinillo. John Benjamins Publishing Co., PO Box 36224, Amsterdam, 1020 ME, Netherlands; subscription@benjamins.nl; http://www.benjamins.com. Refereed. *Indexed:* ErgAb. *Bk. rev.:* Number and length vary. *Aud.:* Ac.

This international, English-language journal focuses on graphic design, typography, written language, and how these impact and aid different segments of society. Peer-reviewed and scholarly in nature, *Information Design Journal* publishes research papers, case studies, book reviews, and critiques of information design and related theory. Illustrative material is highly prized for inclusion in article submissions. This title's intended audience is multidisciplinary, from fields such as communication design, writing, typography, applied linguistics, discourse studies, instructional design, and graphic design.

4190. ***Ink World: covering the printing inks, coatings and allied industries.*** [ISSN: 1093-328X] 1995. bi-m. Free to qualified personnel. Ed(s): David Savastano. Rodman Media, 25 Philips Pkwy, Montvale, NJ 07645; label@rodpub.com; http://rodmanmedia.com/. Adv. Sample. *Indexed:* B01, B03, C42. *Aud.:* Ac, Sa.

This trade magazine provides ink industry professionals with in-depth information on the development, manufacture, and sale of all lithographic, flexographic, gravure, radiation-cured, letterpress, and specialty inks, coatings, and allied products. Developments affecting printers and suppliers of ink companies are discussed. Annual features include top North American companies, top international companies, buyers' guides, a U.S. ink directory, a packaging inks report, and an industry review of the previous year.

4191. ***The New Bookbinder: journal of designer bookbinders.*** Formerly (until 1981): *Designer Bookbinders Review.* [ISSN: 0261-5363] 1973. a. Free to members. Designer Bookbinders Publications Ltd., c/o Wendy Hood, Secretary, 24 Junction Rd, Bath, BA2 3NH, United Kingdom; secretary@designerbookbinders.org.uk; http://www.designerbookbinders.org.uk. Illus. Refereed. *Bk. rev.:* Number and length vary. *Aud.:* Ac, Sa.

Bookbinding is considered a skilled and unique craft in the printing industry. As the journal of the Designer Bookbinders, this refereed, scholarly publication covers all aspects of bookbinding. Six to ten articles in each issue address binding design and techniques; contemporary and historical methods; and profiles of binders worldwide. Work examples and explanatory sketches highlight many of the articles. Topics may include longstitch binding techniques, leather binding methods, reviews of book and small presses, and profiles of preservation departments in libraries. Listed in each issue are the winners of the Man Booker Prize for Fiction award, who are rewarded with a copy of their book bound by the Designer Bookbinders. This is a prominent journal for the specialized bookbinding industry.

4192. ***PackagePrinting: the package printer's leading resource for business solutions.*** Former titles (until 1999): *Package Printing & Converting;* (until 1987): *Package Printing;* (until Mar. 1978): *Package Printing and Diecutting;* Which was formed by the merger of: *Diemaking, Diecutting and Converting; Gravure; Flexography Printing and Converting.* [ISSN: 1536-1039] 1974. m. Free to qualified personnel. Ed(s): Noel Ward. North American Publishing Co., 1500 Spring Garden St., 12th Fl, Philadelphia, PA 19130; magazinecs@napco.com; http://www.napco.com. Illus., index, adv. Vol. ends: Dec. *Indexed:* A22, B03. *Aud.:* Sa.

This trade publication targets the industry of container and package design and production. Diemaking/diecutting, tags, labels, and tape, as well as flexible packaging, folding cartons, and corrugated containers are all this industry's focus. Articles included each month discuss innovations in the equipment needed to manufacture these containers and labels. Inks and printing techniques, suppliers, and management issues are also discussed. Also available online.

4193. ***Paper 360 Degrees: around the industry, around the world.*** Incorporates (1959-2015): *Pulp & Paper International;* Formerly (until 2006): *Solutions;* Which was formed by the merger of (1982-2001): *T A P P I Journal;* Which was formerly (until 1982): *T A P P I;* (until 1949): *Technical Association Papers;* (until 1920): *Technical Papers and Addresses;* (1997-2001): *P I M A's Papermaker;* Which was formed by the merger of (1986-1996): *P I M A Magazine;* (1991-1996): *American Papermaker;* (1992-1996): *Canadian Papermaker.* [ISSN: 1933-3684] 2001. bi-m. Free to members. Naylor, LLC., 5950 NW 1st Pl, Gainesville, FL 32607; http://www.naylor.com. Illus., index, adv. Sample. Vol. ends: Dec. *Indexed:* A&ATA, A22, Agr, B01. *Aud.:* Ac, Sa.

A very comprehensive journal of the paper industry, *Paper360* combines journalistic articles with peer-reviewed papers. Every aspect of paper production is discussed, including finances and industry trends. Its readership is largely members of the Technical Association of the Pulp and Paper Industry, so each issue includes information about the association and its conferences.

4194. ***Print.*** Incorporates (1911-1950): *Print Collectors' Quarterly;* (1938-1941): *Printing Art;* Which was formerly (until 1938): *Printing Art Quarterly;* (until 1935): *Printed Salesmanship;* (until 1925): *Printing Art.* [ISSN: 0032-8510] 1940. bi-m. USD 57 United States; USD 72 Canada; USD 29.95 per issue. Ed(s): Zachary Petit. F + W Media Inc., 1140 Broadway, 14th Fl, New York, NY 10001; contact_us@fwmedia.com; http://www.fwcommunity.com/. Illus., adv. Circ: 147900 Paid. Vol. ends: No. 6. *Indexed:* A01, A06, A22, A51, B01, BRI, F01, MLA-IB. *Aud.:* Ga, Ac, Sa.

The purpose of this high-quality journal is to provide thorough and wide-ranging coverage of the graphic design field. Directed mainly at practitioners, it provides in-depth articles on pertinent topics. Half of the six issues published each year are devoted to juried showcases of leading work in graphic design. The annual "Regional Design" issue organizes artists' work by geographic region. Highly aware of the development of digital technology, *Print* offers a "Digital Design and Illustration" issue that explores the effects of computers on design. This title is an important addition to any graphic design collection. Also available online.

4195. ***Print and Promo: business strategies for the distributor sales professional.*** Former titles (until 2012): *Print Professional;* (until 2007): *Business Forms, Labels and Systems;* (until 198?): *Business Forms and Systems;* (until 1982): *Business Forms Reporter.* [ISSN: 2168-5266] 1963. m. Free to qualified personnel. North American Publishing Co., 1500 Spring Garden St., 12th Fl, Philadelphia, PA 19130; magazinecs@napco.com; http://www.napco.com. Adv. *Indexed:* A22. *Aud.:* Sa.

This monthly trade publication targets executives and owners in the printing and promotional product industries. Each issue offers five to seven feature articles that cover such topics as sales strategies, management issues, manufacturing, safety regulations, and product trends. Regular columns cover new products, industry news, executive perspectives, and classified ads. Available in print or as a digital edition, the magazine is offered free to individuals who meet pre-established demographic criteria.

4196. ***Print Business.*** [ISSN: 1746-5117] 2005. m. Free to members. Ed(s): Gareth Ward. Print Business Media Ltd., 3 Zion Cottages, Ranters Lane, Goudhurst, Cranbrook, TN17 1HR, United Kingdom; printbusiness@me.com; http://www.printbusinessmedia.co.uk. Adv. *Aud.:* Sa.

This British publication, offered both in print and online, is aimed at the print professional focused on the future of the craft and the ability to bring cutting-edge techniques to print and an ever-expanding audience. Each issue offers features and case studies that highlight innovations and sometimes their resulting problems. The archive for past issues goes back to January 2013. *Print Business* is free to those in the profession. Interested professionals may upgrade to *Print Business Premium* and receive "Business Briefing," a quarterly supplement, "Bespoke Reports," "Instant Analysis," "Drupa Updates," and the digital magazine a week before the print edition appears.

4197. ***Print Solutions Magazine.*** Formerly (until 2001): *Form.* [ISSN: 1535-9727] 1962. m. Free to members; Non-members, USD 99. Print Services & Distribution Association, 330 N Wabash Ave Ste 2000, Chicago, IL 60611; psda@psda.org; http://www.psda.org. Illus., adv. *Aud.:* Sa.

This award-winning magazine addresses issues of importance to professionals involved in printing, document distribution, promotional products, bar coding, security documents, commercial printing, and on-demand printing. Each issue is devoted to a current topic that is central to the printing industry. Some articles are available in podcast format. In every issue there is an industry events calendar, industry news, and a profile of a successful innovator or entrepreneur in the field. A subscription includes the award-winning "Buyer's Guide," an annual 500-page directory of industry sources of supply published in October. The annual Print Solutions Conference and Expo is exclusively focused on the independent print distribution channel. The web site for the magazine includes a career center where employers can search resumes and job seekers can find opportunities. Available online.

4198. ***Printing Historical Society. Journal.*** Formerly (until 1965): *The Black Art;* Incorporates (1980-2000): *Printing Historical Society. Bulletin;* Which was formerly (until 1980): *Printing Historical Society. Newsletter.* [ISSN: 0079-5321] 1962. a. Free to members. Ed(s): Paul W Nash. Printing Historical Society, The Secretary, St Bride Institute, Bride Ln, Fleet St, London, EC4Y 8EE, United Kingdom; secretary@printinghistoricalsociety.org.uk; http://www.printinghistoricalsociety.org.uk/. Adv. Refereed. *Indexed:* MLA-IB. *Bk. rev.:* 6-9, 200-300 words, signed. *Aud.:* Ac, Sa.

This journal is published by the Printing Historical Society. All aspects of printing history and the preservation of equipment and printed materials are examined. Contributors include practitioners and researchers in the printing field. Three or four articles are featured and are scholarly in nature. Shorter articles and book reviews are found in the society's *Bulletin,* which appears as part of the journal. Historically important typefaces that have been revived are also reviewed. The *Bulletin* features society news and a list of antiquarian book catalogs. Both publications are free to society members.

4199. ***Printing History.*** [ISSN: 0192-9275] 1979. s-a. Free to members. Ed(s): William T La Moy. American Printing History Association, Grand Central Sta, PO Box 4519, New York, NY 10163; publications@printinghistory.org; http://printinghistory.org. Illus., adv. Sample. Refereed. *Indexed:* BRI, C42, MLA-IB. *Bk. rev.:* 3, 500-600 words, signed. *Aud.:* Ga, Ac.

This scholarly publication offers five or six research articles on topics that may range from profiles of leaders in the field to fifteenth-century papermaking. Its main focus is on American printing history, but its actual range is much broader and includes international developments that influenced the industry. Contributors are researchers in the field. This journal is only available through membership in the association. It is a useful addition to any printing history collection. Also available on the American Printing History Association's web site.

4200. ***Printing Impressions.*** Incorporates (1970-197?): *Printing Management;* Which superseded in part (1958-1970): *Printing Production;* Which was formerly (1930-1958): *Printing Equipment Engineer.* [ISSN: 0032-860X] 1958. 12x/yr. Free to qualified personnel. Ed(s): Mark T Michelson, Erik Cagle. North American Publishing Co., 1500 Spring Garden St., 12th Fl, Philadelphia, PA 19130; magazinecs@napco.com; http://www.napco.com. Illus., adv. Sample. *Indexed:* A22, C42. *Aud.:* Ac, Sa.

This trade publication offers commercial printers, graphic artists, and newspaper publishers up-to-date information in the areas of printing, marketing, finance, and technology. Each issue includes profiles of successful businesses, how-to reports on recent technological advances, management advice, and a calendar of events. New products are reviewed. News about important people in the printing industry is a prominent feature. Also available online.

4201. ***Quaerendo: a journal devoted to manuscripts and printed books.*** Former titles (until 1971): *Het Boek (Antwerpen);* (until 1912): *Tijdschrift voor Boek- en Bibliotheekwezen.* [ISSN: 0014-9527] 1971. q. EUR 356. Ed(s): Lisa Kuitert. Brill, PO Box 9000, Leiden, 2300 PA, Netherlands; marketing@brill.com; https://brill.com. Illus., adv. Refereed. Vol. ends: No. 4. Reprint: PSC. *Indexed:* A01, A22, AmHI, E01, MLA-IB. *Bk. rev.:* Number and length vary. *Aud.:* Ac.

Devoted to the history of printing and books, this peer-reviewed journal presents scholarly articles in English, French, and German. Important manuscripts, collections, and recent discoveries are highlighted. The subjects of codicology and palaeography, printing from around 1500 until present times, humanism, book publishers and libraries, typography, bibliophily, and book binding receive special attention. Book reviews and information about upcoming exhibits and conferences are provided. *Quaerendo* is delightful reading for anyone who loves books. Also available online.

4202. ***S G I A Journal.*** [ISSN: 1546-4431] 1997. bi-m. Free to members. Specialty Graphic Imaging Association, 10015 Main St, Fairfax, VA 22031; sgia@sgia.org; http://www.sgia.org. *Aud.:* Ac, Sa.

This journal is a publication of the Specialty Graphic Imaging Association and is free to its members. Screen printing, digital printing, embroidery, sublimation, and pad printing are the imaging technologies covered. The journal features new products, production techniques, best business practices, and market trends. Readers are provided with the latest news shaping the industry, including emerging markets, government regulations, and technological developments.

4203. ***Screen Printing.*** Former titles (until 1984): *Screen Printing Technology and Management;* (until 1982): *Screen Printing;* (until 19??): *Screen Printing Magazine;* (until 1968): *Screen Process Magazine;* (until 1956): *Screen Process.* [ISSN: 1932-4944] 1953. m. Individuals, USD 46; Free to qualified personnel. Ed(s): Gregory Sharpless. S T Media Group International, Inc., PO Box 1060, Skokie, IL 60076; SPTG@halldata.com; http://stmediagroupintl.com/. Illus., index, adv. Sample. Vol. ends: Dec. *Indexed:* A&ATA, A22, B01. *Aud.:* Ac, Sa.

This journal reflects its artistic focus by providing readers with clear instructions for a polished end-product. Included also is technical information about screen printing systems, care and maintenance of screen printing equipment, and industry trends. New products are also highlighted. *Screen Printing* is the foremost journal in the screen printing industry. Also available online.

4204. ***The Seybold Report.*** Formed by the merger of (1982-2001): *The Seybold Report on Publishing Systems;* Which was formerly (until 1982): *The Seybold Report;* (1996-2001): *Seybold Report on Internet Publishing;* Which was formerly (until 1996): *The Seybold Report on Desktop Publishing.* [ISSN: 1533-9211] 2001. s-m. USD 499 combined subscription (print & online eds.)). Ed(s): Molly Joss. Seybold Publications, PO Box 682, Gilbertsville, PA 19525; http://www.seyboldpublications.com/. Illus., index. Sample. *Indexed:* A01, B01, B03, BRI, C42, CompLI. *Aud.:* Ac, Sa.

This international journal is very clearly organized so that the publishing professional can see at a glance the important issues and developments in the electronic prepress industry. Information about new technologies and capabilities is combined with financial reports and discussions about legal implications. Overviews of conference proceedings are provided. This is essential reading for anyone in the publishing industry or anyone selecting a publishing system. Available online.

4205. ***Sign & Digital Graphics.*** Formed by the merger of (1997-2009): *Digital Graphics Magazine;* (1986-2009): *Sign Business.* [ISSN: 2158-1533] 2009. m. USD 45. Ed(s): Ken Mergentime. National Business Media, Inc., PO Box 1416, Broomfield, CO 80038; rpmpublisher@nbm.com; http://www.nbm.com. Adv. *Aud.:* Sa.

This trade publication updates the visual communications professional on the latest trends and technologies in the industry. This title is available both in print and electronically, and topics covered include commercial signage, wide-format commercial printing, electric signs and letters, architectural signage, electronic displays, and vehicle wraps and graphics. Each issue includes latest industry news and product reviews. A preview of the next issue's topics is offered, as well as highlights from the previous month.

4206. ***Visible Language.*** Formerly (until 1971): *Journal of Typographic Research.* [ISSN: 0022-2224] 1967. 3x/yr. USD 65 (Individuals, USD 35). Ed(s): Mike Zender. Rhode Island School of Design, Graphic Design Department, PO Box 210016, Cincinnati, OH 45221; http://www.risd.edu. Illus., index. Refereed. Vol. ends: Sep. Microform: PQC. *Indexed:* A22, A51, BAS, ERIC, ErgAb, MLA-IB. *Aud.:* Ac.

This scholarly journal is concerned with written language (as opposed to verbal language) and its impact on humanity and civilization. Literacy is a frequent topic, but there are also many others, including typography, the effect of computer technology on the written word, and semantics. Many issues are devoted to a specific topic. *Visible Language* is important reading for language scholars and researchers.

4207. ***Visual Communication.*** [ISSN: 1470-3572] 2002. q. USD 1309 (print & online eds.)). Ed(s): Elisabetta Adami. Sage Publications Ltd., 1 Oliver's Yard, 55 City Rd, London, EC1Y 1SP, United Kingdom; market@sagepub.com; https://www.sagepub.com/. Adv. Sample. Refereed. Reprint: PSC. *Indexed:* A22, A51, E01, F01, IBSS, MLA-IB. *Aud.:* Ac.

This scholarly journal appeals to a wide audience in the humanities, social sciences, linguistics, and graphic arts academic communities. Its purpose is to bring together interrelated but diverse disciplines in a discussion of how the visual (in general) impacts these disciplines and society at large. Articles accepted in the journal include academic papers, visual essays, and reflective papers by practitioners on aspects of their work. All welcomed in this international forum are works on still and moving images; on graphic design and typography; on the role of the visual in language, music, sound, and action; and on visual phenomena such as fashion, posture, and professional vision. Available online and in print.

4208. ***Visual Communications Journal.*** [ISSN: 0507-1658] 1965. s-a. Free to members. Ed(s): Dan Wilson. International Graphic Arts Education Association, c/o William Delgado, Cuyahoga Valley Career Center, Twinsberg, OH 44087; http://www.igaea.org. Refereed. *Aud.:* Ac.

This refereed journal is the official publication of the Graphic Communications Education Association. Its mission is to provide a link between educators and personnel in the fields of design, presentation, management, and reproduction of graphic forms of communication. Articles are by students, educators, and industry professionals. All manuscripts submitted for publication are subject to peer review by the association. Topics include theories, principles, techniques, and processes relating to graphic communications and imaging technology. The web site provides information about the association's annual conferences, student chapters, awards, and scholarships for graphic arts teachers.

■ PSYCHOLOGY

See also Education; Medicine; Multicultural Studies; and Sociology sections.

Marie I. Rose, Information Services Librarian, The Citadel, The Military College of South Carolina, Daniel Library, 171 Moultrie Street, Charleston, SC 29409; mrose5@citadel.edu

Introduction

Psychology, in the simplest of terms, is the study of behavior in both humans and nonhumans. It is a field of study that is dynamic, diverse, and attractive to people from all walks of life with an interest in why we act the way we do. This is reflected in the sheer volume of journals, magazines, and databases devoted to this discipline. Many of the journals listed here are peer-reviewed and scholarly publications that cater to established professionals, both academic researchers and clinical practitioners. Though these resources can be highly technical at times, students just beginning their academic careers should find them useful for their coursework.

The titles selected for this chapter range from broad psychological research to the very specific ways in which psychology is applied to our society through counseling, education, and various subfields. These subfields include abnormal psychology, child psychology, clinical psychology, cognitive psychology, counseling psychology, neuropsychology, social psychology, and a number of other subfields—some just emerging and taking shape.

The American Psychological Association (APA) is the most influential professional organization for psychologists and, as such, they publish a number of the databases and peer-reviewed journals highlighted in this section. It would be highly advisable that libraries that support psychologists and psychology programs subscribe to some of these publications as they are often cited and well regarded. This can be accomplished by purchasing a subscription to PsycINFO, APA's core abstracting and indexing database. At the time of this writing PsycINFO currently covers 2,435 journals with more than 4.2 million records. PsycINFO is available from a number of vendors such as EBSCO and ProQuest, or directly from the APA on its own platform.

Libraries may want to also take a look at some of the APA's other databases, namely PsycARTICLES, PsycBOOKS, and PsycTESTS, which provide full-text journal articles, e-books, and psychological tests respectively. In particular, PsycARTICLES covers 110 journals, with 201,332 full-text articles currently available. Other multidisciplinary database vendors, such as EBSCO, PubMed, and JSTOR, can provide access to a number of the journals listed here.

It is also worth noting that psychology related resources extend beyond journals and databases. Many organizations and vendors have created streaming video databases, which is an especially useful resource for those supporting clinical psychology programs. APA has PsycTHERAPY, which demonstrates therapy approaches and sessions. Alexander Street Press produces Counseling and Therapy in Video Series. Psychotherapy.net has been producing training videos since 1995 and now provides a streaming video collection for purchase. This can be purchased independently or as an add-on through Alexander Street Press.

Journals relating to psychology are not confined to the parameters of this chapter. Libraries should consider investigating additional titles described in other sections of this book, as well as using *Ulrich's Periodicals Directory*. Those selecting publications for their institution can also look to other categories such as "Education," "Medicine," "Multicultural Studies," and "Sociology" to round out their collections.

Basic Periodicals

The American Journal of Psychiatry, American Psychologist, Annual Review of Psychology, Behavioral and Brain Sciences, PsycCritiques, Psychological Bulletin, Psychological Review, Psychology Today.

Basic Abstracts and Indexes

Communication Abstracts, ERIC, Linguistics and Language Behavior Abstracts (LLBA), PsycArticles, PsycInfo, PubMed, Social Sciences Citation Index, Social Services Abstracts, Social Work Abstracts, Sociological Abstracts.

4209. ***A P S Observer.*** [ISSN: 1050-4672] 1988. 10x/yr. Free to members. Ed(s): Sarah Brookhart, Ann Conkle. Association for Psychological Science, 1133 15th St, NW, Ste 1000, Washington, DC 20005; member@psychologicalscience.org; http://www.psychologicalscience.org. Illus., adv. *Indexed:* A01. *Aud.:* Ga, Ac.

APS Observer is a free online publication from the American Psychological Society. APS is a nonprofit organization dedicated to the advancement of scientific psychology, and has approximately 33,000 members. Recent articles from the *Observer* include cognitive biology, how children perceive play, and the shift in emotion science. This publication is student friendly, and will appeal to all levels of researchers.

4210. ***Acta Psychologica: international journal of psychonomics.*** [ISSN: 0001-6918] 1941. 9x/yr. EUR 2277. Ed(s): W Notebaert. Elsevier BV, Radarweg 29, Amsterdam, 1043 NX, Netherlands; info@elsevier.com; https://www.elsevier.com/. Illus., index, adv. Sample. Refereed. Microform: PQC. *Indexed:* A01, A22, ErgAb, MLA-IB. *Bk. rev.:* 0-3, 1,000-2,500 words. *Aud.:* Ac, Sa.

Acta Psychologica publishes studies and articles in the field of experimental psychology, with an emphasis on human behavior and cognition. Much of the research focuses on perception, memory, and various forms of cognition. Recent articles from *Acta Psychologica* include the effects of depression on information integration, and the comparisons between forced and free choice tasks. This publication is highly recommended for institutions supporting experimental research in psychology.

4211. *Addiction.* Former titles (until 1993): *British Journal of Addiction;* (until 1980): *British Journal of Addiction to Alcohol and Other Drugs;* (until 1947): *British Journal of Inebriety;* (until 1903): *Society for the Study and Cure of Inebriety. Proceedings.* [ISSN: 0965-2140] 1884. m. GBP 2241. Ed(s): Robert West. Wiley-Blackwell Publishing Ltd., The Atrium, Southern Gate, Chichester, PO19 8QG, United Kingdom; cs-journals@wiley.com; http://onlinelibrary.wiley.com/. Illus., adv. Sample. Refereed. Reprint: PSC. *Indexed:* A01, A22, BRI, C45, CJPI, Chicano, E01, IBSS, P61, SD, SSA. *Bk. rev.:* Number and length vary. *Aud.:* Ac.

Addiction is a peer-reviewed journal published on behalf of the Society for the Study of Addiction to Alcohol and other Drugs (SAA). It contains editorials, commentaries, interviews, and books reviews in the field of addiction. Recent articles from *Addiction* cover 12-step behavior programs, methamphetamine related psychosis, and the European viewpoint on Alcoholics Anonymous. This publication is a must have for those with a program in clinical counseling and/or psychology.

4212. *Aggressive Behavior.* [ISSN: 0096-140X] 1975. bi-m. GBP 2548. Ed(s): John Archer. John Wiley & Sons, Inc., 111 River St, Hoboken, NJ 07030; cs-journals@wiley.com; http://onlinelibrary.wiley.com. Illus., index, adv. Refereed. Vol. ends: No. 6. Microform: PQC. Reprint: PSC. *Indexed:* A01, A22, ASSIA, BRI, C45, CJPI. *Bk. rev.:* 0-3, 800-1,000 words. *Aud.:* Ac, Sa.

Aggressive Behavior is the official journal of the International Society for Research on Aggression. Articles in this publication mainly focus on overt or implied conflict behaviors in humans and animals. This multidisciplinary journal will appeal to a wide variety of professions, including anthropologists, behavioral scientists, psychologists, and zoologists. Recent articles from *Aggressive Behavior* include the role of dominance in the confluence model, peer-nominated aggression, and violent behavior among military reservists. This journal is recommended for libraries supporting a variety of fields, including zoology, and behavioral sciences.

4213. *American Academy of Child and Adolescent Psychiatry. Journal.* Formerly (until 1986): *American Academy of Child Psychiatry. Journal.* [ISSN: 0890-8567] 1962. m. USD 1470. Ed(s): Dr. Andres Martin, Mary K Billingsley. Elsevier BV, Radarweg 29, Amsterdam, 1043 NX, Netherlands; info@elsevier.com; https://www.elsevier.com/. Illus., index, adv. Refereed. Vol. ends: Nov/Dec. *Indexed:* A01, A22, ASSIA, BRI, ERIC, MLA-IB, N13. *Aud.:* Ac, Sa.

The *Journal of the American Academy of Child and Adolescent Psychiatry* focuses on providing original research and scientific papers dedicated to the psychiatric research and treatment of children and adolescents. Subscribers can also take advantage of other media provided by this publication, namely podcast interviews with authors in the field. Recent articles from this publication include providing culturally informed care to Muslim adolescents, family based interventions for childhood depression, and the male-to-female ratio in the Autism Spectrum Disorder. This high-impact journal is recommended for those with clinical counseling programs.

4214. *American Behavioral Scientist.* Formerly (until 1960): *Political Research, Organization and Design.* [ISSN: 0002-7642] 1957. m. USD 3585 (print & online eds.)). Ed(s): Laura Lawrie. Sage Publications, Inc., 2455 Teller Rd, Thousand Oaks, CA 91320; info@sagepub.com; http://www.sagepub.com. Adv. Sample. Refereed. Microform: PQC. Reprint: PSC. *Indexed:* A01, A22, B01, BAS, BRI, C45, Chicano, E01, EIP, IBSS, MLA-IB, P61, SSA. *Aud.:* Ac.

American Behavioral Scientist is a peer-reviewed journal providing high frequency, high quality research in the social and behavioral sciences. Each issue focuses on a single topic, allowing it to be explored from a variety of perspectives. Recent topics include the 2016 U.S. presidential election, children and politics, and the understanding of social and community stigma. This multidisciplinary, student friendly journal is a must have for those with social sciences programs.

4215. *American Journal of Community Psychology.* [ISSN: 0091-0562] 1973. q. GBP 1434. Ed(s): Jacob Kraemer Tebes. John Wiley & Sons, Inc., 111 River St, Hoboken, NJ 07030; cs-journals@wiley.com; http://onlinelibrary.wiley.com. Illus., index, adv. Sample. Refereed. Vol. ends: Dec. Reprint: PSC. *Indexed:* A01, A22, Chicano, E01, SSA. *Aud.:* Ac, Sa.

The *American Journal of Community Psychology* is a publication of the Society for Community Research and Action: The Division of Community Psychology of the American Psychological Association, and as of January 2016, switched from publisher Springer to Wiley. This publication features original research, theoretical papers, reviews, reports from programs and policies, and first-person accounts in the far ranging field of community psychology, to include individual, family, peer, and community mental health, social welfare, human rights, and more. Recent articles include trends in volunteer mentoring, college students' helpseeking decisions after sexual assault, and predictors of early community involvement. This multidisciplinary journal is a must have for academic libraries supporting psychology, social science, and/or public health programs.

4216. *American Journal of Drug and Alcohol Abuse.* [ISSN: 0095-2990] 1975. bi-m. GBP 2561 (print & online eds.)). Taylor & Francis Inc., 530 Walnut St, Ste 850, Philadelphia, PA 19106; support@tandfonline.com; http://www.tandfonline.com. Illus., adv. Sample. Refereed. Microform: RPI. Reprint: PSC. *Indexed:* A01, A22, ASSIA, C45, CJPI, Chicano, E01, HRIS, SD, SSA. *Aud.:* Ac.

The *American Journal of Drug and Alcohol Abuse* publishes articles and reviews in the field of public policy, epidemiology, neurobiology, and the treatment of addictive disorders. Recent articles include topics such as marijuana use among young people in an era of policy change, the prevalence of adolescent opioid misuse in Ohio, and electronic cigarette initiation among minority youth in the United States. This journal is recommended for libraries supporting clinical counseling, pharmacology, and public health programs.

4217. *American Journal of Orthopsychiatry: mental health & social justice.* [ISSN: 0002-9432] 1930. bi-m. USD 639 (Individuals, USD 151; Members, USD 101). Ed(s): Jill D. McLeigh, William Spaulding. American Psychological Association, 750 First St, NE, Washington, DC 20002; journals@apa.org; http://www.apa.org. Illus., index, adv. Sample. Refereed. Circ: 350. Vol. ends: Oct. Reprint: PSC. *Indexed:* A01, A22, Chicano, E01, SSA. *Aud.:* Ac, Sa.

The *American Journal of Orthopsychiatry* is the principal publication of the Global Alliance for Behavioral Health and Social Justice. This interdisciplinary journal covers anthropology, criminology, law, nursing, psychiatry, psychology, social work, sociology, public administration, public health, and other fields related to behavioral health and social justice. Recent articles cover topics like adult women survivors of intrafamilial child sexual abuse, what children think about their rights, and reintegration for military service personnel. This important journal is recommended for libraries supporting a range of programs, including social science, psychology, public health, and criminology.

4218. *The American Journal of Psychiatry.* Formerly (until 1921): *The American Journal of Insanity.* [ISSN: 0002-953X] 1844. m. USD 527 combined subscription domestic (print & online eds.); USD 702 combined subscription foreign (print & online eds.)). Ed(s): Dr. Ned Kalin. American Psychiatric Association Publishing, Inc., 800 Maine Ave, SW, Ste 900, Washington, DC 20024; institutions@psych.org; https://www.appi.org. Illus., index, adv. Refereed. Vol. ends: Dec. *Indexed:* A01, A22, AgeL, BAS, BRI, C45, CBRI, Chicano, HRIS, MLA-IB. *Bk. rev.:* 10-15, 250-1,000 words. *Aud.:* Ac, Sa.

The American Journal of Psychiatry is the official journal of the American Psychiatric Association, and covers the full spectrum of mental health diagnoses and treatment. Features include original research, editorials, case vignettes, with relevant research literature, book reviews, letters to the editor, and an audio component called AJP Audio that highlights sections of the journal. Recent articles include topics such as psychodynamic therapy, premenstrual dysphoric disorder symptoms, and low intensity transcranial current stimulation. This high- impact journal is a must have for libraries supporting mental health professionals, students, and researchers.

4219. *The American Journal of Psychoanalysis.* [ISSN: 0002-9548] 1941. q. GBP 579. Ed(s): Giselle Galdi. Palgrave Macmillan Ltd., Macmillan Building, 4 Crinan St, London, N1 9XW, United Kingdom; onlinesales@palgrave.com; http://www.palgrave.com. Index, adv. Sample. Refereed. Reprint: PSC. *Indexed:* A01, A22, BRI, E01, MLA-IB. *Bk. rev.:* Number and length vary. *Aud.:* Ac, Sa.

The American Journal of Psychoanalysis is affiliated with the Association for the Advancement of Psychoanalysis. This peer-review journal covers contemporary clinical and theoretical concepts of psychoanalysis. It publishes original articles, special issues dedicated to a single topic, book reviews, film reviews, reports on the activities of the Karen Horney Psychoanalytic Center, and comments. Recent topics have included trauma and contemporary forms of subjectivity, melancholia, narcissism, and depression, and motivation of young Muslim men to join the Islamic State. This journal is recommended for academic and medical libraries supporting psychology and mental health programs.

4220. *American Journal of Psychology.* [ISSN: 0002-9556] 1887. q. USD 355 (print & online eds.)). Ed(s): Robert W. Proctor. University of Illinois Press, 1325 S Oak St, MC-566, Champaign, IL 61820; uipress@uillinois.edu; http://www.press.uillinois.edu. Illus., index, adv. Refereed. Microform: MIM; PMC; PQC. *Indexed:* A01, A22, ASSIA, BRI, CBRI, ErgAb, MLA-IB. *Bk. rev.:* 4-6, 450-3,000 words. *Aud.:* Ac, Sa.

The American Journal of Psychology is a long-standing, peer-reviewed publication founded in 1887 by G. Stanley Hall. It covers experimental psychology, theoretical presentations, and historical commentaries through original research, reports, and book reviews. Recent topics have included alexithymia, and mood, reading aloud to children, and texting and iPod dependence. This journal is recommended for libraries supporting psychology researchers and programs.

4221. *American Journal of Psychotherapy.* Incorporates (1992-2001): *The Journal of Psychotherapy Practice and Research.* [ISSN: 0002-9564] 1946. q. Ed(s): Dr. Holly Schwartz. American Psychiatric Association Publishing, Inc., 800 Maine Ave, SW, Ste 900, Washington, DC 20024; https://psychiatryonline.org. Refereed. *Indexed:* A01, A22, ASSIA, BAS, BRI, Chicano, MLA-IB, SSA. *Aud.:* Ac.

The *American Journal of Psychotherapy* is the official journal of the Association for the Advancement of Psychotherapy. It offers articles on psychotherapies from a number of different perspectives, serving a "conceptual bridge using the developmental process to reconcile major psychotherapeutic paradigms of the past and present." This publication also publishes special one topic issues from time to time. Recent articles have covered psychotherapy techniques for patients diagnosed with schizophrenia, cognitive-behavioral therapy for olfactory hallucinations, and an introduction to using the Method of Levels (MOL) therapy to work with people experiencing psychosis.

4222. *American Psychologist.* [ISSN: 0003-066X] 1946. 9x/yr. USD 1635 (Individuals, USD 472; Members, USD 12). Ed(s): Dr. Anne E Kazak. American Psychological Association, 750 First St, NE, Washington, DC 20002; journals@apa.org; http://www.apa.org. Illus., adv. Sample. Refereed. Circ: 84000. Microform: PMC; PQC. Reprint: PSC. *Indexed:* A01, A22, ASSIA, B01, CJPI, Chicano, ERIC, IBSS, MLA-IB. *Aud.:* Ga, Ac, Sa.

The *American Psychologist* is the official peer-reviewed journal of the American Psychological Association. This journal publishes empirical reports, meta-analyses, and scholarly reviews on a broad range of topics, including science, practice, education, and policy. This publication is written for practitioners and students alike. Recent articles have covered topics such as evolutionary psychology, healthy cognitive aging, and the psychology of terrorism. This a core title that libraries supporting psychology programs will want to have.

4223. *Annals of General Psychiatry.* Formerly (until 2004): *Annals of General Hospital Psychiatry.* [ISSN: 1744-859X] 2002. irreg. Free. Ed(s): Konstantinos Fountoulakis. BioMed Central Ltd., Fl 6, 236 Gray's Inn Rd, London, WC1X 8HB, United Kingdom; info@biomedcentral.com; https://www.biomedcentral.com. Adv. Refereed. *Indexed:* A01, Agr. *Aud.:* Ac, Sa.

The *Annals of General Psychiatry* is an open- access journal that focuses on psychiatry, to include neuroscience and psychological medicine. They emphasize a biopsychosocial approach to illness and health and support the principles of evidence-based medicine. It publishes case reports, reviews, and primary research. Recent articles have covered treating modalities for patients with gambling disorders, suicidal ideation in children, and research on screening Wilson's disease in a psychiatric population. This publication is indexed via a variety of vendors, such as PsycINFO, PubMed, and Scopus.

4224. *Annual Review of Neuroscience.* [ISSN: 0147-006X] 1978. a. USD 431 (print & online eds.)). Ed(s): Huda Y Zoghbi, Botond Roska. Annual Reviews, PO Box 10139, Palo Alto, CA 94303; service@annualreviews.org; http://www.annualreviews.org. Refereed. Reprint: PSC. *Indexed:* A01, A22, Agr, C45. *Aud.:* Ac.

The *Annual Review of Neuroscience* is a peer-reviewed journal that publishes articles in the field of neuroscience, to include molecular and cellular neuroscience, neurogenetics, development, plasticity and repair, systems neuroscience, cognitive neuroscience, behavior, and neurobiology of disease. Recent topics include inhibitory plasticity, neural circuitry of reward prediction error, and nerve growth factor and pain mechanisms. This publication is recommended for libraries supporting neuroscientists and related disciplines.

4225. *Annual Review of Psychology.* [ISSN: 0066-4308] 1950. a. USD 431 (print & online eds.)). Ed(s): Susan T Fiske. Annual Reviews, PO Box 10139, Palo Alto, CA 94303; service@annualreviews.org; http://www.annualreviews.org. Illus. Refereed. Reprint: PSC. *Indexed:* A01, A22, B01, BAS, MLA-IB. *Aud.:* Ga, Ac, Sa.

The *Annual Review of Psychology* publishes articles covering significant developments in the field of psychology, to include behavior, cognitive processes, animal learning and behavior, human development, clinical and counseling psychology, personality, community psychology, and other subfields. Recent articles talk about prefrontal cortex and neurological impairments of active thought, a bio-psycho-social model for the next generation of preventive interventions, and language processing. This annual review is a core title that academic libraries should provide access to.

4226. *Anxiety, Stress and Coping: an international journal.* Formerly (until 1992): *Anxiety Research.* [ISSN: 1061-5806] 1988. 6x/yr. GBP 1625 (print & online eds.)). Ed(s): Aleksandra Luszczynska, Mark A Ellenbogen. Routledge, 4 Park Sq, Milton Park, Abingdon, OX14 4RN, United Kingdom; subscriptions@tandf.co.uk; http://www.tandfonline.com. Illus., adv. Sample. Refereed. Reprint: PSC. *Indexed:* A01, A22, E01, ErgAb, SD. *Aud.:* Ac.

Anxiety, Stress, & Coping publishes articles and reviews on anxiety, stress, and coping processes, as well as the antecedents and consequences of stress exposure. Recent articles cover the role of stress mindset in shaping cognitive, emotional, and physiological responses to challenging and threatening stress, PTSD symptoms among tsunami-exposed mothers in Sri Lanka, and a meta-analysis of the relationship between anxiety and telomere length. Libraries supporting clinical counseling programs will benefit from this journal.

4227. *Applied Psychological Measurement.* [ISSN: 0146-6216] 1976. 8x/yr. USD 1609 (print & online eds.)). Ed(s): Hua-Hua Chang. Sage Publications, Inc., 2455 Teller Rd, Thousand Oaks, CA 91320; info@sagepub.com; http://www.sagepub.com. Illus., index, adv. Sample. Refereed. Vol. ends: Dec. Microform: PQC. Reprint: PSC. *Indexed:* A01, A22, B01, E01, ERIC. *Bk. rev.:* 1-2, 500-1,000 words. *Aud.:* Ac, Sa.

Applied Psychological Measurement publishes empirical research, reports, and reviews about psychological measurement and methodologies. It also regularly publishes special issues, such as polytomous item response theory and optimal test assembly. Recent topics explore item response theory, reliability theory and methods, and differential item functioning. Libraries that support psychological and behavioral science research will absolutely want to subscribe to this journal.

4228. *Applied Psychophysiology and Biofeedback.* Formerly (until 1997): *Biofeedback and Self Regulation.* [ISSN: 1090-0586] 1975. q. EUR 1625 (print & online eds.)). Ed(s): Frank Andrasik. Springer New York LLC, 233 Spring St, New York, NY 10013; customerservice@springer.com; http://www.springer.com. Illus., index, adv. Refereed. Circ: 1950. Vol. ends: Dec. Microform: PQC. Reprint: PSC. *Indexed:* A01, A22, E01, ErgAb, SD. *Bk. rev.:* Number and length vary. *Aud.:* Ac, Sa.

Applied Psychophysiology and Biofeedback is the official publication of the Association for Applied Psychophysiology and Biofeedback. It is an interdisciplinary journal that explores physiological systems, cognition, social and environmental parameters, and health. It features case studies, clinical replication series, treatment protocols, clinical notes, original research, letters to the editor, and book reviews. Recent articles have been written about the effects of mental stress induction on heart rate variability in patients with panic disorders, effects of partial absence of visual feedback information on gait symmetry, and biofeedback training in crisis managers. This publication is recommended for medical libraries and those supporting clinical psychology programs.

4229. *Archives of Sexual Behavior.* [ISSN: 0004-0002] 1971. bi-m. EUR 3294 (print & online eds.)). Ed(s): Kenneth J Zucker. Springer New York LLC, 233 Spring St, New York, NY 10013; customerservice@springer.com; http://www.springer.com. Illus., adv. Sample. Refereed. Vol. ends: Dec. Reprint: PSC. *Indexed:* A01, A22, BRI, C45, Chicano, E01, SSA. *Bk. rev.:* 3-6, 1,000 words. *Aud.:* Ac, Sa.

Archives of Sexual Behavior is the official publication of the International Academy of Sex Research, and explores the field of sexual science. Features include quantitative and qualitative research, theoretical reviews and essays, clinical case reports, letters to the editor, and book reviews. Recent topics cover preschool gender-typed play behavior, effects of geography on mental health disparities on sexual minorities in New York City, and the perceived devaluation and STI testing uptake. This publication is recommended for libraries supporting sexual health and behavior programs, as well as medical libraries.

4230. *Behavior Modification.* Formerly (until 1977): *Behavior Modification Quarterly.* [ISSN: 0145-4455] 19??. bi-m. USD 1801 (print & online eds.)). Ed(s): Alan S Bellack. Sage Publications, Inc., 2455 Teller Rd, Thousand Oaks, CA 91320; info@sagepub.com; http://www.sagepub.com. Illus., index, adv. Sample. Refereed. Vol. ends: Oct. Reprint: PSC. *Indexed:* A01, A22, E01, ERIC, SSA. *Bk. rev.:* 0-1, 400 words. *Aud.:* Ac, Sa.

Behavior Modification is a peer-reviewed journal that focuses on applied behavior modification. It features original research, reports, and reviews. Topics include anxiety, phobias, child abuse, divorce and children, eating disorders, female assertiveness, gender role stress, and learning disabilities. This journal occasionally publishes special issues, which has featured topics like environmental risk factors in the development of psychopathology, and current research on social behavior. This publication is recommended for libraries supporting psychology programs.

4231. *Behavioral and Brain Sciences: an international journal of current research and theory with open peer commentary.* [ISSN: 0140-525X] 1978. bi-m. Ed(s): Paul Bloom, Barbara L Finlay. Cambridge University Press, University Printing House, Shaftesbury Rd, Cambridge, CB2 8BS, United Kingdom; journals@cambridge.org; https://www.cambridge.org/. Illus., index, adv. Sample. Refereed. Circ: 2100. Vol. ends: Dec. Microform: PQC. Reprint: PSC. *Indexed:* A01, A22, BRI, E01, MLA-IB. *Bk. rev.:* 0-30, 500-2,000 words. *Aud.:* Ac, Sa.

Behavioral and Brain Sciences is an international journal that publishes articles in the fields of psychology, neuroscience, behavioral biology, and cognitive science. It uses the format Open Peer Commentary, in which 20 to 40 commentaries are solicited from specialists, with the author's response to them. Recent topics include a broader perspective on determinants of obesity, attention and memory benefits for physical attractiveness, and the role of adolescence in geographic variation in violent aggression. This unique journal is appropriate for libraries supporting a wide range of programs, including psychology, cognitive science, and the social sciences.

4232. *Behavioral Neuroscience.* Supersedes in part (in 1983): *Journal of Comparative and Physiological Psychology;* Which was formerly (until 1947): *Journal of Comparative Psychology;* Which was formed by the merger of (1917-1921): *Psychobiology;* (1911-1921): *Journal of Animal Behavior.* [ISSN: 0735-7044] 1921. bi-m. USD 2098 (Individuals, USD 488; Members, USD 200). Ed(s): Rebecca D Burwell. American Psychological Association, 750 First St, NE, Washington, DC 20002; journals@apa.org; http://www.apa.org. Illus., index, adv. Sample. Refereed. Circ: 250. Vol. ends: Jan. Microform: PMC; PQC. Reprint: PSC. *Indexed:* A01, A22, Agr, C45. *Aud.:* Ac, Sa.

Behavioral Neuroscience publishes peer-reviewed research and reviews in the field of neural bases of behavior. Topics include learning and memory, perception, spatial cognition, human and non-human animal cognition and emotion, and motivation, reward, homeostasis, and biorhythms. From time to time, special issues are published, and have covered the behavioral neuroscience of sleep and the circadian rhythms in behavioral neuroscience. This publication is recommended for libraries supporting psychological research.

4233. *Behaviour Research and Therapy.* Incorporates (1977-1994): *Advances in Behaviour Research and Therapy;* (1979-1992): *Behavioral Assessment.* [ISSN: 0005-7967] 1963. m. EUR 3501. Ed(s): G T Wilson. Elsevier Ltd, 125 London Wall, London, EC2Y 5AS, United Kingdom; corporate.sales@elsevier.com; http://www.elsevier.com. Illus., index, adv. Sample. Refereed. Vol. ends: No. 12. Microform: MIM; PQC. *Indexed:* A01, A22, ASSIA, Agr, BRI, MLA-IB. *Aud.:* Ac, Sa.

Behaviour Research and Therapy is an international, multidisciplinary journal focusing on an experimental psychopathology approach to understanding emotional and behavioral disorders, as well as their prevention and treatment. Recent articles have covered the behavioral economics of social anxiety disorders, working with parents to treat anxiety-disordered children, and a randomized controlled trial of guided Internet-based CBT for perfectionism. This journal is recommended for libraries supporting clinical counseling and psychology programs.

4234. *Biological Psychology.* [ISSN: 0301-0511] 1974. 9x/yr. EUR 3290. Ed(s): O V Lipp. Elsevier BV, Radarweg 29, Amsterdam, 1043 NX, Netherlands; info@elsevier.com; https://www.elsevier.com/. Adv. Refereed. Microform: PQC. *Indexed:* A01, A22, ErgAb. *Aud.:* Ac.

Biological Psychology publishes original papers on the biological aspects of psychological states and processes, to include electrophysiology and biochemical assessments. This journal also looks at psychological investigations based on biological theories. It features original articles, review articles, and special issues. Recent articles have covered topics like endorphin-mediated synchrony effects on cooperation, sleep and the heart, and the effects of oxytocin on reward motivation in social anxiety disorders. Research and medical institutions supporting research of this nature will benefit from this journal.

4235. *British Journal of Psychiatry.* Former titles (until 1963): *Journal of Mental Science;* (until 1858): *Asylum Journal of Psychiatry.* [ISSN: 0007-1250] 1853. m. GBP 567 (print & online eds.)). Ed(s): Kamaldeep Bhui. Cambridge University Press, University Printing House, Shaftesbury Rd, Cambridge, CB2 8BS, United Kingdom; journals@cambridge.org; https://www.cambridge.org/. Illus., index, adv. Sample. Refereed. Vol. ends: No. 6. *Indexed:* A22, ASSIA, AgeL, C45. *Bk. rev.:* 6-20, 300 words. *Aud.:* Ac, Sa.

The *British Journal of Psychiatry* is a peer-reviewed, monthly journal published by The Royal College of Psychiatrists. This far-ranging publication covers all aspects of psychiatry, particularly from a clinical aspect. It features original research, editorials, review articles, commentaries, reports, book reviews, and a correspondence column. All content from January 2000 is online and is made freely available one year after publication. Recent articles include the disruptive mood dysregulation disorder in offspring of parents with depression and bipolar disorder, Ketamine as the anesthetic for electroconvulsive therapy, and the predictive accuracy of risk scales following self harm. Academic and medical libraries supporting clinical counselors and psychologists will benefit from this core journal.

4236. *British Journal of Psychology.* Formerly (until 1953): *British Journal of Psychology. General Section;* Which superseded in part (in 1920): *British Journal of Psychology.* [ISSN: 0007-1269] 1904. q. GBP 672 (print & online eds.)). Ed(s): Stefan R Schweinberger. John Wiley & Sons Ltd., EMEA Institutional Sales, 9600 Garsington Rd, Oxford, OX4

2DQ, United Kingdom; cs-journals@wiley.com; http://onlinelibrary.wiley.com. Illus., index. Sample. Refereed. Vol. ends: Nov. Microform: PQC. Reprint: PSC. *Indexed:* A01, A22, ASSIA, B01, BRI, E01, ErgAb, IBSS, MLA-IB, SSA. *Bk. rev.:* 0-5, 500-1,000 words. *Aud.:* Ac, Sa.

The *British Journal of Psychology* is published by Wiley on behalf of the British Psychological Society. This international journal focuses on original research on all aspects of general psychology, to include cognition, health and clinical psychology, developmental, social, and occupational psychology. Recent articles cover the attention capture in driving displays, cultural differences in visual attention, and peer influenced risk-taking behavior in young adults. This is a must have journal for libraries supporting psychology programs.

Canadian Journal of Human Sexuality. See Sexuality section.

4237. ***Child Development.*** [ISSN: 0009-3920] 1930. bi-m. USD 872 (print or online ed.)). Ed(s): Cynthia Garcia Coll, Adam Martin. Wiley-Blackwell Publishing, Inc., 111 River St, Hoboken, NJ 07030; info@wiley.com; http://onlinelibrary.wiley.com. Illus., index, adv. Sample. Refereed. Circ: 8712 Paid. Vol. ends: Dec. Microform: PQC. Reprint: PSC. *Indexed:* A01, A22, ASSIA, Agr, BAS, C45, CBRI, Chicano, E01, ERIC, IBSS, MLA-IB. *Aud.:* Ac.

Child Development is published by Wiley on behalf of the Society for Research in Child Development. This journal publishes articles, essays, reviews, and tutorials in the area of child development. Recent articles cover the ethnic-racial identity and friendships in early adolescence, ecological factors in human development, and promoting strengths and resilience in single-mother families. This journal will appeal to libraries supporting child psychiatrists, as well as psychiatric social workers and others in the psychiatric field.

4238. ***Clinical Psychology (Online): science and practice.*** [ISSN: 1468-2850] 1994. 4x/yr. GBP 437. Ed(s): Timothy R Elliot. Wiley-Blackwell Publishing, Inc., 350 Main St, Malden, MA 02148; http://onlinelibrary.wiley.com. Refereed. *Bk. rev.:* 1, 1,200-2,000 words. *Aud.:* Ac, Sa.

Clinical Psychology: Science and Practice is published on behalf of the Society of Clinical Psychology, Division 12 of the American Psychological Association. This journal covers developments in the science and practice of clinical psychology, and publishes research, theory, assessment, intervention, service delivery, and professional issues. Recent topics feature the long-term effects of childhood adversity and trauma, sexual traumatic event exposure, and PTSD and alcohol associations among trauma-exposed women. Those with clinical counseling and psychology programs will benefit from this title.

4239. ***Clinical Psychology Review.*** [ISSN: 0272-7358] 1981. 8x/yr. EUR 3066. Elsevier Ltd, The Boulevard, Langford Lane, Oxford, OX5 1GB, United Kingdom; customerserviceau@elsevier.com; http://www.elsevier.com. Illus., adv. Sample. Refereed. Microform: PQC. *Indexed:* A01, A22. *Bk. rev.:* 0-4, 300 words. *Aud.:* Ac, Sa.

Clinical Psychology Review publishes articles about clinical psychology, to include psychopathology, psychotherapy, behavior therapy, cognition and cognitive therapies, behavioral medicine, community mental health assessment, and child development. Recent articles look at the effectiveness of psychoeducational interventions for careers of people with psychosis, gender differences in social anxiety disorders, and parental ADHS symptoms and parenting behaviors. Libraries supporting clinical psychology are recommended to carry this title.

4240. ***Cognition.*** [ISSN: 0010-0277] 1972. 12x/yr. EUR 3452. Ed(s): Steven Sloman. Elsevier BV, Radarweg 29, Amsterdam, 1043 NX, Netherlands; info@elsevier.com; https://www.elsevier.com/. Illus., index, adv. Sample. Refereed. Vol. ends: Dec. Microform: PQC. *Indexed:* A01, A22, ERIC, IBSS, MLA-IB. *Aud.:* Ac.

Cognition is an international, multidisciplinary journal publishing theoretical and experimental papers on the study of the mind. Contributions come from the varying fields of psychology, neuroscience, linguistics, computer science, mathematics, ethology, and philosophy. Occasional special issues are published focusing on one topic. Readers will find original research, brief articles, discussions, and book reviews. Recent articles look at predicting actions from subtle preparatory movements, signal dimensionality and the emergence of combinatorial structure, and phonological and orthographic coding in deaf skilled readers. This title will appeal to libraries supporting a variety of programs, including psychology, neuroscience, and mathematics.

4241. ***Cognitive Development.*** [ISSN: 0885-2014] 1986. 4x/yr. EUR 847. Ed(s): M Sabbagh. Elsevier Ltd, 125 London Wall, London, EC2Y 5AS, United Kingdom; corporate.sales@elsevier.com; http://www.elsevier.com. Illus., index, adv. Sample. Refereed. Vol. ends: No. 4. Reprint: PSC. *Indexed:* A01, A22, ERIC. *Bk. rev.:* 1, 3,000 words. *Aud.:* Ac, Sa.

Cognitive Development publishes empirical and theoretical articles on the topics of perception, memory, language, concepts, thinking, problem solving, metacognition, and social cognition. Recent articles examine the effects of working memory training on improving fluid intelligence of children during early childhood, exploring links between infants, object manipulation and verbal input, and an assessment of social cognition from adolescence to adulthood. This journal is recommended for academic libraries supporting psychology and education programs.

4242. ***Cognitive Neuropsychology.*** [ISSN: 0264-3294] 1984. 8x/yr. GBP 1860 (print & online eds.)). Ed(s): Brenda Rapp. Routledge, 4 Park Sq, Milton Park, Abingdon, OX14 4RN, United Kingdom; subscriptions@tandf.co.uk; http://www.tandfonline.com. Illus., index, adv. Sample. Refereed. Reprint: PSC. *Indexed:* A01, A22, ASSIA, E01, MLA-IB. *Bk. rev.:* 0-1, 1,500 words. *Aud.:* Ac, Sa.

Cognitive Neuropsychology explores the relationship between human cognition, and neuropsychological methods, including brain pathology, recording, stimulation, brain imaging, and the study of developmental deficits. It claims that it is the only journal that focuses on the investigation of human cognition informed by neural data. Recent articles have looked at the impact of central sparing on the word-length effect in hemianopia, decoding task and stimulus representations in face-response cortex, and social perception in synaesthesia for color. This journal is recommended for researchers studying cognition and neuropsychology.

4243. ***Cognitive Psychology.*** [ISSN: 0010-0285] 1970. 8x/yr. EUR 2023. Ed(s): Dr. G D Logan. Academic Press, 3251 Riverport Ln, Maryland Heights, MO 63043; JournalCustomerService-usa@elsevier.com; http://www.elsevier.com/. Illus., adv. Refereed. *Indexed:* A01, A22, ASSIA, B01, E01, ERIC, ErgAb, MLA-IB. *Aud.:* Ac.

Cognitive Psychology studies attention, memory, language processing, perception, problem solving, and thinking. This peer-reviewed journal focuses on cognitive theory and new theoretical advances in that field. Topics include artificial intelligence, developmental psychology, linguistics, neurophysiology, and social psychology. Recent articles include the parallel interactive retrieval of item and associative information from event memory, an associative account of the development of word learning, and diagnostic causal reasoning with verbal information. This journal is recommended for academic libraries supporting psychology programs.

4244. ***Cognitive Science (Online): a multidisciplinary journal.*** Incorporates (in 1984): *Cognition and Brain Theory;* Which was formerly (until 1980): *The S I STM Quarterly Incorporating the Brain Theory Newsletter;* Which was formed by the merger of (1975-1978): *Brain Theory Newsletter;* (1977-1978): *S I S T M Quarterly.* [ISSN: 1551-6709] 1977. m. USD 1439. Ed(s): Arthur B Markman, Caroline Verdier. Wiley-Blackwell Publishing, Inc., 111 River St, Hoboken, NJ 07030; info@wiley.com; http://www.wiley.com/. Illus., index. Sample. Refereed. Vol. ends: Oct/Dec. Reprint: PSC. *Indexed:* A01, A22, B01, E01, ERIC, ErgAb, MLA-IB. *Aud.:* Ac, Sa.

This journal, published by Wiley, addresses all areas of cognitive science, including knowledge representation, inference, memory processing, learning, problem solving, planning, perception, connectionism, brain theory, motor control, intentional systems, and a wide variety of other topics. Recent articles have studied the spatial grounding of syntax, a corpus-based analysis of online tutoring software, and vocabulary, grammar, sex, and aging. This title is recommended for libraries supporting researchers in the cognitive science field, to include anthropologists, educators, psychologists, philosophers, linguists, and neuroscientists.

4245. *Cognitive Therapy and Research.* [ISSN: 0147-5916] 1977. bi-m. EUR 2167 (print & online eds.)). Ed(s): Stefan G. Hofmann. Springer New York LLC, 233 Spring St, New York, NY 10013; customerservice@springer.com; http://www.springer.com. Illus., index, adv. Sample. Refereed. Vol. ends: Dec. Microform: PQC. Reprint: PSC. *Indexed:* A01, A22, E01. *Aud.:* Ac, Sa.

Cognitive Therapy and Research examines a variety of fields, to include clinical, cognitive, counseling, developmental, experiential, learning, personality, and social psychology. It publishes experimental studies, theoretical, reviews, technical, and methodological articles, case studies, and brief reports. Recent topics include psychological problems, affective disorders, anxiety disorders, schizophrenia, eating disorders, substance abuse, disorders of childhood and adolescence, psychological dysfunction in aging, and personality. This title is recommended for libraries supporting psychology, cognitive psychology, and clinical counseling programs.

4246. *Community Mental Health Journal.* [ISSN: 0010-3853] 1965. bi-m. EUR 2518 (print & online eds.)). Ed(s): Jacqueline M Feldman. Springer New York LLC, 233 Spring St, New York, NY 10013; customerservice@springer.com; http://www.springer.com. Illus., adv. Sample. Refereed. Microform: PQC. Reprint: PSC. *Indexed:* A01, A22, ASSIA, BRI, Chicano, E01, SSA. *Aud.:* Ac.

Community Mental Health Journal, on the Springer platform, focuses on the improvement of public sector services for people who are affected by or at risk of severe mental disorders, serious emotional disturbances, and/or addictions. The journal includes articles about nationally representative epidemiologic projects as well as intervention research that involves benefit-and-risk comparisons between service programs. The areas of behavioral health evaluation and methodology may also appear. Recent issues address the implementation of a weight loss program for Latino outpatients with severe mental illness; the effects of a complete smoking ban on inpatients at an intermediate to long-term psychiatric facility; epidemiology of problem gambling in a Canadian community; the impact of self-stigma and mutual help programs on the quality of life of people with serious mental illness; how underserved women in a women's health clinic describe their experiences of depressive symptoms and why they have low uptake of psychotherapy; evaluation of a suicide prevention training program for mental health services staff; and therapeutic horseback riding for ACT patients with schizophrenia.

4247. *The Counseling Psychologist.* [ISSN: 0011-0000] 1969. 8x/yr. USD 1568 (print & online eds.)). Ed(s): Lydia P Buki. Sage Publications, Inc., 2455 Teller Rd, Thousand Oaks, CA 91320; info@sagepub.com; http://www.sagepub.com. Illus., adv. Sample. Refereed. Microform: PQC. Reprint: PSC. *Indexed:* A22, ASSIA, E01, ERIC. *Aud.:* Ac, Sa.

The Counseling Psychologist, published by Sage, is the official publication of the Society of Counseling Psychology of the American Psychological Association. It focuses on the areas of multiculturalism, prevention, and intervention, research methods, vocational psychology, assessment, international counseling, health, social justice, training, and supervision. This multidisciplinary publication has published on topics such as acculturation, discrimination, ethics, gender issues, health disparities, mechanisms of coping, sexual orientation, and ethnicity and race. This core title is highly recommended for academic and medical libraries supporting psychology and clinical psychology programs.

4248. *Current Psychology: a journal for diverse perspectives on diverse psychological issues.* Formerly (until 1988): *Current Psychological Research and Reviews;* Which was formed by the merger of (1981-1984): *Current Psychological Research;* (1981-1984): *Current Psychological Reviews.* [ISSN: 1046-1310] 1984. q. EUR 1770 (print & online eds.)). Ed(s): F R Ferraro. Springer New York LLC, 233 Spring St, New York, NY 10013; customerservice@springer.com; http://www.springer.com. Adv. Sample. Refereed. Reprint: PSC. *Indexed:* A22, B01, BRI, E01, HRIS. *Aud.:* Ac, Sa.

The journal *Current Psychology*, on the Springer platform, is an international forum for papers on issues at the cutting edge of psychology. It includes empirical articles from the areas of social psychology; small groups and personality; human development; sensation, perception, and cognition; clinical and abnormal psychology; and methodology and field research. Recent issues address the intermingling of social and evolutionary psychology influences on hair-color preferences; sex differences in relationships between verbal fluency and personality; rating of intensity of emotions across auditory, visual, and auditory-visual sensory domains; sports participation and loneliness in adolescents and the mediating role of perceived social competence; children's understanding of real vs. pretend emotions; experiences of touch avoidance; identifying cognitive style and cognitive complexity in reflective personality; the effect of high-anxiety situations on conspiracy thinking; the effect of immorally acquiring money on its spending; and assessing vindictiveness and the psychological aspects by a reliability and validity study of the Vengeance Scale in the Italian context. This is an important journal for studies in comparative psychology.

4249. *Current Research in Social Psychology.* [ISSN: 1088-7423] 1995. irreg. Free. Ed(s): Shane Soboroff, Michael J Lovaglia. University of Iowa, Department of Sociology, 140 Seashore Hall W, Iowa City, IA 52242; sociology@uiowa.edu; http://clas.uiowa.edu/sociology/. Illus. Refereed. *Indexed:* ERIC, IBSS, SSA. *Aud.:* Ac.

This is a publication of the Center for the Study of Group Processes at the University of Iowa. The journal is peer-reviewed and published only in electronic format, with free access to its contents. Articles cover a broad range of social psychology issues and reflect empirical, analytical, and theoretical studies. Recent issues address laboratory evidence of plea bargaining's innocence problem; the moral identity and group affiliation; threat, prejudice, and stereotyping in the context of Japanese, North Korean, and South Korean intergroup relations; how priming ability-relevant social categories improves intellectual test performance; how ambivalence toward the in-group underlies individual identity management strategies; the relative influence of values and identities on academic dishonesty; mitigating damage following scandals-when the personal becomes political; and self-enhancement through group and individual social judgments. Academic libraries that support programs in social psychology should provide an easily found link in their digital interfaces and catalogs to this accessible scholarly journal.

Death Studies. See Death and Dying section.

4250. *Developmental Psychology.* [ISSN: 0012-1649] 1969. m. USD 1837 (Individuals, USD 595; Members, USD 212). Ed(s): Eric F Dubow. American Psychological Association, 750 First St, NE, Washington, DC 20002; journals@apa.org; http://www.apa.org. Illus., adv. Sample. Refereed. Circ: 750. Vol. ends: Dec. Microform: PQC. Reprint: PSC. *Indexed:* A01, A22, ASSIA, C45, CJPI, Chicano, ERIC, IBSS, MLA-IB. *Aud.:* Ac, Sa.

This publication from the American Psychological Association studies the knowledge and theory about development across the lifespan. It publishes single manuscripts, proposed sections, and short reports. Recent articles have examined the spatial exploration and changes in infant-mother dyads around transitions in infant locomotion, heterogeneity in externalizing problems at age three, and predicting growth in English and French vocabulary. This journal is recommended for libraries supporting psychology, education, sociology, and linguistic programs.

4251. *Educational and Psychological Measurement: a bimonthly journal devoted to the development and application of measures of individual differences.* [ISSN: 0013-1644] 1941. bi-m. USD 1732 (print & online eds.)). Ed(s): George A Marcoulides. Sage Publications, Inc., 2455 Teller Rd, Thousand Oaks, CA 91320; info@sagepub.com; http://www.sagepub.com. Adv. Sample. Refereed. Microform: PQC. Reprint: PSC. *Indexed:* A01, A22, B01, BRI, Chicano, E01, ERIC, MLA-IB. *Aud.:* Ac.

Educational and Psychological Measurement, a Sage journal, publishes articles in the field of measurement. Articles are based on both current data and theoretical issues. Studies concern education, psychology, government, and industry testing. Every issue contains short studies that deal with the validity of tests and scales. Recent issues address a new method for analyzing content-validity data using multidimensional scaling; the search for value in the case of complex school effects; a Monte Carlo comparison study of the power of the analysis of co-variance, simple difference, and residual change scores in testing two-wave data; item selection for the development of parallel forms from an IRT-based seed test using a sampling and classification approach; an analysis of the predictive validity of the General-Decision-making Style Inventory; investigating ESL students' performance on outcomes assessments in higher education; and balancing flexible constraints and measurement precision in computerized adaptive testing. Research, academic, and professional educators and psychologists will rely on this valuable journal.

4252. ***Educational Psychologist.*** [ISSN: 0046-1520] 1963. q. GBP 671 (print & online eds.)). Ed(s): Clark A Chinn. Routledge, 530 Walnut St, Ste 850, Philadelphia, PA 19106; enquiries@tandfonline.com; http://www.tandfonline.com. Illus., adv. Sample. Refereed. Vol. ends: Fall. Microform: PQC. Reprint: PSC. *Indexed:* A01, A22, E01, ERIC. *Aud.:* Ac, Sa.

This Taylor & Francis publication presents scholarly essays, reviews, critiques, and theoretical and conceptual articles on all aspects of educational psychology. Articles explore both new and accepted practices. Topics range from meta-analyses of teaching effectiveness to historical examination of textbooks. Empirical studies are not included. Recent issues look at a meta-analytic review of learning through case comparisons; team effectiveness and team development in computer-supported collaborative learning; the strength of the relation between performance-approach and performance-avoidance goal orientations; seeing deep structure from the interactions of surface features; teaching the conceptual structure of mathematics; rethinking formalisms in formal education; and what university admissions tests should predict. Educational psychologists, researchers, teachers, administrators, and policy makers will want access to this title.

Educational Psychology Review. See Education/Educational Psychology and Measurement, Special Education, Counseling section.

4253. ***Environment and Behavior.*** [ISSN: 0013-9165] 1969. 10x/yr. USD 2201 (print & online eds.)). Ed(s): Barbara Brown. Sage Publications, Inc., 2455 Teller Rd, Thousand Oaks, CA 91320; info@sagepub.com; http://www.sagepub.com. Illus., index, adv. Sample. Refereed. Vol. ends: Nov. Microform: PQC. Reprint: PSC. *Indexed:* A01, A22, ASSIA, Agr, BRI, CJPI, E01, ERIC, GardL, HRIS, IBSS, P61, S25, SSA. *Bk. rev.:* 2, 600 words. *Aud.:* Ac, Sa.

This Sage publication presents current research and theoretical articles that concern the influence of environment on individuals, groups, and institutions. The journal includes feature articles, discussions, and book reviews. Topics covered include values and attitudes of people toward various environments; the effectiveness of environmental designs; transportation issues; recreation issues; interrelationships between human environments and behavior; and planning, policy, and political issues. The journal is interdisciplinary, with articles from specialists in anthropology, architecture, design, education, geography, political science, psychology, sociology, and urban planning. Special supplements are sometimes published to highlight leading scholars and significant issues such as litter control, public participation in evaluation of designs, and museum design. Recent issues address a cross-cultural study of environmental values and their effect on the environmental behavior of children; an examination of the effect of perceived risk on preparedness behavior; factors influencing homeowner support for protecting local urban trees; linking personal values to energy-efficient behaviors in the home; preference and tranquility for houses of worship; the influence of social class and cultural variables on environmental behaviors; linking lighting appraisals to work behaviors; the presence of a pleasant ambient scent in a fashion store and the moderating role of shopping motivation and affect intensity; and way-finding and spatial reorientation by Nova Scotia deer hunters. This interdisciplinary journal is important for libraries that serve humanities, social sciences, and science undergraduate and graduate programs.

4254. ***Exceptional Children.*** Former titles (until 1951): *Journal of Exceptional Children;* (until 1935): *Council Review;* (until 1934): *Council Newsletter.* [ISSN: 0014-4029] 1934. q. USD 483 (print & online eds.)). Sage Publications, Inc., 2455 Teller Rd, Thousand Oaks, CA 91320; info@sagepub.com; http://www.sagepub.com. Illus., adv. Refereed. Vol. ends: Summer. Microform: PQC. Reprint: PSC. *Indexed:* A01, A22, BRI, Chicano, ERIC, MLA-IB. *Bk. rev.:* Number and length vary. *Aud.:* Ac.

Exceptional Children publishes research, research reviews, methodological reviews of literature, data-bases position papers, and policy analyses about the education and development of exceptional infants, toddlers, children, youth, and adults. Recent issues look at the critique of the national evaluation of response to intervention, the effects of early writing intervention delivered within a data-based instruction framework, and exploring the involvement of bullying among students with disabilities over time. Libraries supporting special education researchers and programs will want this publication for their collection.

Family Process. See Family section.

4255. ***Health Psychology.*** [ISSN: 0278-6133] 1982. m. USD 1377 (Individuals, USD 328; Members, USD 146). Ed(s): Dr. Anne E Kazak. American Psychological Association, 750 First St, NE, Washington, DC 20002; journals@apa.org; http://www.apa.org. Illus., adv. Sample. Refereed. Circ: 3300. Vol. ends: Dec (No. 6). Reprint: PSC. *Indexed:* A22, ASSIA. *Bk. rev.:* 0-1, 1,500 words. *Aud.:* Ac, Sa.

This is an APA peer-reviewed, scholarly journal concerning behavioral and physical health. Most articles present empirical, theoretical, or practically based research. Studies may focus on cross-cultural and interdisciplinary issues. Topics may include the "role of environmental, psychosocial, or socio-cultural factors that may contribute to disease or its prevention; behavioral methods used in the diagnosis, treatment, or rehabilitation of individuals having physical disorders; and techniques that could reduce disease risk by modifying health beliefs, attitudes, or behaviors[,] including decisions about using professional services. Interventions used may be at the individual, group, multicenter, or community level." Recent issues cover physical activity and the reduced risk of depression; daily analysis of physical activity and satisfaction with life in emerging adults; changes in health-risk behaviors for males and females from early adolescence through early adulthood; affective science and health and the importance of emotion and emotion regulation; the associations between personality, diet, and body mass index in older people; predicting adult physical illness from infant attachment; racial identification, racial composition, and substance-use vulnerability among African American adolescents and young adults; and insomnia symptoms and well-being. This journal should be in libraries that serve clinical psychology and human performance programs.

4256. ***Hispanic Journal of Behavioral Sciences.*** [ISSN: 0739-9863] 1979. q. USD 1339 (print & online eds.)). Ed(s): Dr. Amado M Padilla. Sage Publications, Inc., 2455 Teller Rd, Thousand Oaks, CA 91320; info@sagepub.com; http://www.sagepub.com. Illus., adv. Sample. Refereed. Vol. ends: Nov. Microform: PQC. Reprint: PSC. *Indexed:* A01, A22, BRI, C45, CJPI, Chicano, E01, ERIC, SSA. *Bk. rev.:* 0-1, 400-800 words. *Aud.:* Ac.

This Sage publication is a multidisciplinary behavioral sciences journal that publishes research and analyses on Hispanic issues. Scholarly articles provide theoretical, empirical, and analytical studies from leading experts in Hispanic Studies. Topics include cultural assimilation, communication barriers, intergroup relations, employment discrimination, substance abuse, AIDS prevention, family dynamics, and minority poverty. Recent issues present work on Latina teen suicide and bullying; assessing gender differences in the relationship between negative interaction with the clergy and health among older Mexican Americans; individual, family, and community influences on the migration decision-making among Mexican youth; the relation between maternal and child depression in Mexican American families; the role of family cohesion and family discord in anxiety disorders in Latinos; an ecological perspective on U.S. Latinos' health communication behaviors, access, and outcomes; how Latino economic and citizenship status impact health; the impact of health care and immigration reform on Latino support for President Obama and Congress; and the role of skin color on Hispanic women's perceptions of attractiveness. Researchers and professionals in the fields of psychology, sociology, anthropology, education, linguistics, public health, economics, and political science will find this title important to their work.

4257. *History of Psychology.* [ISSN: 1093-4510] 1998. q. USD 735 (Individuals, USD 151; Members, USD 82). Ed(s): Nadine Weidman. American Psychological Association, 750 First St, NE, Washington, DC 20002; journals@apa.org; http://www.apa.org. Illus., adv. Sample. Refereed. Circ: 500. Vol. ends: Jan. Reprint: PSC. *Indexed:* A01, A22. *Aud.:* Ga, Ac.

The *History of Psychology* examines all aspects of psychology's past, to include the history of consciousness and behavior, psychohistory, theory in psychology as it pertains to history, historiography, biography, and autobiography, teaching the history of psychology, and data mining regarding the history of psychology. Recent articles look at historiography, affect, and the neurosciences, classicism and idealism to scientific naturalism, and how the launch of a new journal in 1904 may have changed the relationship between psychology and philosophy. This journal will appeal to libraries supporting psychology, education, and history programs.

4258. *International Journal of Eating Disorders.* [ISSN: 0276-3478] 1981. 8x/yr. GBP 2397. Ed(s): Ruth Striegel Weissman. John Wiley & Sons, Inc., 111 River St, Hoboken, NJ 07030; cs-journals@wiley.com; http://onlinelibrary.wiley.com. Adv. Refereed. Reprint: PSC. *Indexed:* A01, A22, Agr, BRI, C45. *Aud.:* Ac, Sa.

This Wiley journal and official publication of the Academy of Eating Disorders publishes scholarly clinical and theoretical research. Articles concern several aspects of anorexia nervosa, bulimia, obesity, and atypical patterns of eating behavior and body weight regulation. Clinical and nonclinical populations are the subjects of investigation. The journal includes reviews, brief reports, case studies, literature reviews, and forums for addressing psychological, biological, psychodymamic, socio-cultural, epidemiological, or therapeutic issues. Recent issues have looked at avoidant restrictive food-intake disorder; a cost-effectiveness analysis of stepped care treatment for bulimia nervosa; increased emergency department use by adolescents and young adults with eating disorders; the role of state anxiety in the executive function in eating disorders; the role of eating and emotion in binge eating disorder and loss-of-control eating; an empirical study of diagnostic subtypes with respect to feeding disorders of early childhood; links between psychopathological symptoms and disordered eating behaviors in overweight/obese youths; childbearing and mortality among women with anorexia nervosa; evaluation of appetite-awareness training in the treatment of childhood overweight and obesity; how recovery from anorexia nervosa includes neural compensation for negative body image; and the patient's perspective on preferred therapist characteristics in treatment of anorexia nervosa. Behavioral scientists, psychologists, psychiatrists, neurologists, sociologists, health-care and mental health professionals, neuropsychiatrists, and anthropologists will benefit from access to this title through their libraries.

4259. *International Journal of Group Psychotherapy.* [ISSN: 0020-7284] 1951. q. GBP 676 (print & online eds.)). Routledge, 530 Walnut St, Ste 850, Philadelphia, PA 19106; enquiries@tandfonline.com; http://www.tandfonline.com. Illus., index, adv. Sample. Refereed. Circ: 3500 Paid. Vol. ends: Oct. Reprint: PSC. *Indexed:* A22, ASSIA, BRI, Chicano, E01, SSA. *Bk. rev.:* 5, 750 words. *Aud.:* Ac, Sa.

This Routledge publication and official journal of the American Group Psychotherapy Association focuses on all aspects of group therapy and treatment, including theory, practice, and research. Recent issues have looked at applying systems-centered theory and methods in organizational contexts; interpersonal and social rhythm group therapy for patients with bipolar disorder; attachment style changes following intensive short-term group psychotherapy; a synthesis of psychodynamic and cognitive-behavioral group treatments in integrating empirically supported therapies for treating personality disorders; passion, containment, and commitment as essential elements of groups across the lifespan in Bruce Springsteen's work; long-term improvement in coping skills following multimodal treatment in war veterans with chronic PTSD; and the development and content of an interpersonal psychotherapy group for postnatal depression. Clinicians, researchers, and mental health administrators will want their libraries to have this leading journal in their field.

4260. *Journal of Abnormal Child Psychology.* [ISSN: 0091-0627] 1973. 8x/yr. EUR 2878 (print & online eds.)). Ed(s): Charlotte E Johnston. Springer New York LLC, 233 Spring St, New York, NY 10013; customerservice@springer.com; http://www.springer.com. Illus., adv. Refereed. Vol. ends: Dec. Microform: PQC. Reprint: PSC. *Indexed:* A01, A22, ASSIA, Chicano, E01, ERIC. *Aud.:* Ac, Sa.

This journal, available on the Springer platform, is the official publication of the International Society for Research in Child and Adolescent Psychopathology. The journal, available online, publishes primarily empirical research on the major childhood disorders. Papers focus on epidemiology, etiology, assessment, treatment, prognosis, follow-up, risk factors, prevention, and the development of child and adolescent disorders. Topics include the major childhood disorders, including disruptive behavior, depression, anxiety, and pervasive developmental disorders. Recent issues have looked at intergenerational continuity in maltreatment; examining the validity of ADHD as a diagnosis for adolescents with intellectual disabilities; sex and age differences in the risk threshold for delinquency; goal internalization and outcome expectancy in adolescent anxiety; transactional relationships among cognitive vulnerabilities, stressors, and depressive symptoms in adolescence; etiological contributions to the covariation between children's perceptions of the inter-parental conflict and child behavioral problems; how early childhood assessments of community pediatric professionals predict autism-spectrum and attention deficit hyperactivity problems; trajectories of social anxiety during adolescence and relations with cognition, social competence, and temperament; and the effects of parenting and deviant peers on early to mid-adolescent conduct problems. This is an important journal for clinical, research, medical, behavioral, and social science libraries.

4261. *Journal of Abnormal Psychology.* Supersedes in part (in 1965): *Journal of Abnormal and Social Psychology;* Which was formerly (until 1925): *Journal of Abnormal Psychology and Social Psychology;* (until 1921): *Journal of Abnormal Psychology.* [ISSN: 0021-843X] 1906. 8x/yr. USD 1050 (Individuals, USD 282; Members, USD 131). Ed(s): Angus MacDonald, III. American Psychological Association, 750 First St, NE, Washington, DC 20002; journals@apa.org; http://www.apa.org. Illus., adv. Sample. Refereed. Circ: 700. Vol. ends: Jan. Microform: PMC; PQC. Reprint: PSC. *Indexed:* A01, A22, ASSIA, CJPI, Chicano, MLA-IB. *Aud.:* Ac, Sa.

This journal, from the American Psychological Association, publishes articles on abnormal behavior, its determinants, and its correlates. Articles may be based on empirical and/or experimental research, on case studies, or on theory. Studies dealing with diagnosis or treatment are not included. The journal focuses on several topics, including psychopathology (its etiology, development, and symptomatology); normal processes in abnormal individuals; pathological or atypical behavior of normal persons; disordered emotional behavior or pathology; socio-cultural effects on pathological processes; gender and ethnic issues; and tests of theories. Recent issues look at predictors of first lifetime onset of major depressive disorder in young adulthood; information-seeking bias in social anxiety disorder; sleep and affect coupling in interepisode bipolar disorder; the latent structure of posttraumatic stress disorder as distinguishing different models and different populations; eye-contact perception in schizophrenia and the relationship with symptoms and socioemotional functioning; *DSM-5* personality traits and *DSM-IV* personality disorder; shame regulation in personality disorders; interpretation bias in preschool children at risk for anxiety; and gene-environment interplay in the association between pubertal timing and delinquency in adolescent girls. With its theoretical aim, this scholarly journal belongs in academic libraries that support advanced degrees in psychological research.

4262. *Journal of Anxiety Disorders.* [ISSN: 0887-6185] 1987. 8x/yr. EUR 1810. Ed(s): Gordon J G Asmundson. Pergamon Press, The Blvd, Langford Ln, E Park, Kidlington, OX5 1GB, United Kingdom; JournalsCustomerServiceEMEA@elsevier.com; http://www.elsevier.com. Illus., adv. Sample. Refereed. Microform: PQC. *Indexed:* A01, A22, ASSIA. *Bk. rev.:* Number and length vary. *Aud.:* Ac, Sa.

This publication from Elsevier is an interdisciplinary journal that deals with all aspects of anxiety disorders for all age groups. The *Journal of Anxiety Disorders* covers topics such as traditional, behavioral, cognitive, and biological assessment, diagnosis, and classification, psychosocial and psychopharmacological treatment, genetics, and prevention. Recent articles examine the anxiety sensitivity as a mediator of the association between PTSD symptoms and suicide risk among women firefighters, the impact of attentional and emotional demands on memory performance in obsessive-compulsive disorder, and facial emotion processing in pediatric social anxiety disorder. This journal will benefit academic libraries supporting anxiety disorder research, as well as clinical counseling programs.

4263. ***Journal of Applied Behavior Analysis.*** [ISSN: 0021-8855] 1968. q. GBP 132 (print & online eds.)). Ed(s): Gregory P Hanley. Wiley-Blackwell Publishing, Inc., 111 River St, Hoboken, NJ 07030; http://onlinelibrary.wiley.com. Illus., adv. Refereed. Reprint: PSC. *Indexed:* A01, A22, B01, BRI, CJPI, ERIC, MLA-IB. *Aud.:* Ac, Sa.

This publication of the Society for the Experimental Analysis of Behavior is part of the Wiley Online Library. Tables of contents are available online. The journal publishes research on the application of analyses of behavior to current social issues. Recent issues have addressed research on the functional analysis of problem behavior; comparing the teaching interaction procedure to social stories for people with autism; analysis of variables that affect self-control with aversive events; a computer-based program to teach braille reading to sighted individuals; acquisition of social referencing via discrimination training in infants; generalized instruction following with pictorial prompts; evaluation of strengthening precursors to increase preschooler compliance; disruptive effects of contingent food on high-probability behavior; a comparison of two flash-card methods for improving sight-word reading; and comparison of a stimulus equivalence protocol and traditional lecture for teaching single-subject designs. Access to the behavioral analyses and intervention techniques in this journal is important for students, researchers, and professionals in psychology and social sciences.

4264. ***Journal of Applied Psychology.*** [ISSN: 0021-9010] 1917. m. USD 1519 (Individuals, USD 562; Members, USD 175). Ed(s): Gilad Chen. American Psychological Association, 750 First St, NE, Washington, DC 20002; journals@apa.org; http://www.apa.org. Illus., adv. Sample. Refereed. Circ: 1000. Vol. ends: Jan. Microform: PMC; PQC. Reprint: PSC. *Indexed:* A22, ASSIA, B01, Chicano, ERIC, ErgAb, IBSS, MLA-IB. *Aud.:* Ac, Sa.

This APA journal publishes articles that represent new investigations that seek knowledge in the field of applied psychology. The journal considers research that concerns the psychological and behavioral phenomena of individuals, groups, or organizations in institutional settings such as education, business, government, or health care. Articles are empirical, theoretical, or conceptual, but not clinical, applied experimental, or treatment-based. Topical themes include personnel issues, leadership, job performance and attitudes, addiction, training, organizational design, the impact of technology, and cross-cultural differences. Recent issues look at the impact of furloughs on emotional exhaustion, self-rated performance, and recovery experiences; reciprocal effects of work stressors and counterproductive work behavior; turnover rates and organizational performance; the role of mindfulness in emotion regulation, emotional exhaustion, and job satisfaction; how team personality composition and task conflict interact to improve performance; the importance and outcomes of work-family support policies; employees' behavioral reactions to supervisor aggression; leader identity as an antecedent of the frequency and consistency of transformational, consideration, and abusive leadership behaviors; and how employees pay cognitive costs when customers exhibit verbal aggression. Libraries that support programs in behavioral and organizational psychology will want to have this journal.

4265. ***Journal of Behavioral Health Services and Research.*** Formerly (until 1998): *Journal of Mental Health Administration.* [ISSN: 1094-3412] 1972. q. EUR 601 (print & online eds.)). Ed(s): Bruce Lubotsky Levin. Springer New York LLC, 233 Spring St, New York, NY 10013; customerservice@springer.com; http://www.springer.com. Illus., adv. Sample. Refereed. Circ: 2000 Paid. Microform: PQC. Reprint: PSC. *Indexed:* A01, A22, ASSIA, B01, BRI, CJPI, E01. *Bk. rev.:* Number and length vary. *Aud.:* Ac.

The *Journal of Behavioral Health Services & Research,* on the Springer platform, is the official publication of the National Council for Community Behavioral Healthcare and the Association of Behavioral Healthcare Management. It covers the organization, financing, delivery, and outcomes of behavioral health services, and provides the results of empirical studies. Issues include overviews of contemporary topics, policy perspectives, commentaries, brief reports, and book reviews, as well as scholarly research studies. Recent issues address improving implementation of mental health services for trauma in multicultural elementary schools; characteristics and severity of psychological distress after abortion among university students; successful treatment outcomes among urban American Indians/Alaska Natives and the role of social environment; caregiver participation in community-based mental health services for children receiving outpatient care; hospital readmission among Medicaid patients with an index hospital for mental and/or substance-use disorder; mental health communications-skills training for medical assistants in pediatric primary care; common mental health disorders in developing countries, with insights from urban Ghana; and the quality of communication between primary health care and mental health care.

4266. ***Journal of Child Psychology and Psychiatry.*** [ISSN: 0021-9630] 1960. m. GBP 761. Ed(s): Edmund Sonuga-Barke. Wiley-Blackwell Publishing Ltd., The Atrium, Southern Gate, Chichester, PO19 8QG, United Kingdom; cs-journals@wiley.com; http://onlinelibrary.wiley.com. Illus., index, adv. Sample. Refereed. Vol. ends: Nov. Microform: PQC. Reprint: PSC. *Indexed:* A01, A22, ASSIA, BRI, E01, ERIC. *Bk. rev.:* 2-12, 350-2,000 words. *Aud.:* Ac, Sa.

This is a publication of the Association for Child and Adolescent Mental Health, and it is available on the Wiley online platform. The journal is internationally recognized as a leader in the field of child and adolescent psychology and psychiatry. Contents feature empirical research, clinical studies, and reviews. Articles represent both experimental and developmental studies. Special topic issues appear yearly. Recent issues address attention deficit hyperactivity disorder, tic disorder, and allergy; facial emotional-expression recognition by children at familial risk for depression, and high-risk boys' oversensitivity to sadness; the relationship between large cavum septum pellucidum and antisocial behavior, callous-unemotional traits, and psychopathy in adolescents; efficacy of language intervention in the early years; the effects of juvenile court exposure on crime in young adulthood; diagnosis of autism spectrum disorders in two-year-olds; the impact of maternal depression on young children's executive function; the impact of early father-infant interactions on the onset of externalizing behaviors in young children; brain structure abnormalities in adolescent girls with conduct disorder; child and adolescent predictors of male intimate-partner violence; and dimensions of oppositional defiant disorder in three-year-old preschoolers. Libraries that support education and behavioral and social science researchers, students, and clinicians will want to have this title.

4267. ***Journal of Clinical Child and Adolescent Psychology.*** Formerly (until 2001): *Journal of Clinical Child Psychology.* [ISSN: 1537-4416] 1972. bi-m. GBP 805 (print & online eds.) Individuals, USD 138 (print & online eds.)). Ed(s): Mitchell J Prinstein. Routledge, 530 Walnut St, Ste 850, Philadelphia, PA 19106; enquiries@tandfonline.com; http://www.tandfonline.com. Illus., index, adv. Sample. Refereed. Vol. ends: Dec. Reprint: PSC. *Indexed:* A01, A22, ASSIA, BRI, E01, ERIC. *Bk. rev.:* 0-2, 100-200 words. *Aud.:* Ac, Sa.

This is the official publication of the American Psychological Association's Society of Clinical Child and Adolescent Psychology (Division 53), available on the Taylor & Francis platform. The journal publishes empirical research and scholarly articles, including those focusing on theoretical and methodological issues. Topics include assessment and intervention techniques; development and maintenance of clinical child and adolescent problems; cross-cultural and sociodemographic issues; training and professional practice; and child advocacy. Recent issues address borderline personality features and implicit shame-prone self-concept in middle childhood and early adolescence; potential pathways from stigmatization and externalizing behavior to anger and dating aggression in sexually abused youth; motorsports involvement among adolescents and young adults with childhood ADHD; the reciprocal relationship between alliance and symptom improvement across the treatment of childhood anxiety; perceived barriers to help-seeking among parents of at-risk kindergarteners in rural communities; disentangling the temporal relationship between parental depressive symptoms and early child-behavior problems; and an inventory of callous-unemotional traits in a community sample of preschoolers. Libraries that support clinical psychology, education, and social science research will want to collect this title.

4268. *Journal of Clinical Psychology.* Incorporates (1995-1998): *In Session: Psychotherapy in Practice.* [ISSN: 0021-9762] 1945. m. GBP 893. Ed(s): Timothy R Elliott. John Wiley & Sons, Inc., 111 River St, Hoboken, NJ 07030; cs-journals@wiley.com; http://onlinelibrary.wiley.com. Adv. Refereed. Reprint: PSC. *Indexed:* A01, A22, AgeL, Chicano. *Aud.:* Ac.

The *Journal of Clinical Psychology* publishes articles on the research, assessment, and practice of clinical psychology. It features research studies, articles on professional issues, single case research, brief reports, notes from the field, news, and notes. Special features are sporadically published from time to time. Recent articles look at the mediators of outcome in complicated grief treatment, therapist and client interactions in motivational interviewing for social anxiety disorder, and self-compassion online. This core journal is highly recommended for libraries supporting clinical counseling and psychology programs.

4269. *Journal of Cognitive Neuroscience.* [ISSN: 1530-8898] 1989. m. USD 1262. Ed(s): Mark D'Esposito. M I T Press, One Rogers St, Cambridge, MA 02142-1209; journals-cs@mit.edu; http://mitpress.mit.edu/. Adv. Sample. Refereed. *Aud.:* Ac.

This is an MIT Press journal published with the Cognitive Neuroscience Institute. The journal seeks to promote communication among researchers in the mind sciences, including neuroscience, neuropsychology, cognitive psychology, neurobiology, linguistics, computer science, and philosophy. Articles selected for publication investigate brain behavior interaction and provide descriptions of brain function and underlying brain events. Recent issues look at spatial frequency tuning reveals interactions between the dorsal and ventral visual systems; how contextual processing of abstract concepts reveals neural representations of non-linguistic semantic content; how implicit and explicit second-language training recruits common neural mechanisms for syntactic processing; building blocks of visual working memory with respect to objects or Boolean maps; how the biology of linguistic expression impacts neural correlates for spatial language; dopamine receptor modulation of human response-inhibition and error awareness; the representation of audiovisual regularities in the human brain; and neurocognitive buffers of adolescent risk-taking in the context of meaningful family relationships. Students and researchers in neuroscience, cognition, and neuropsychology will want access to this title through their libraries.

4270. *Journal of Comparative Psychology.* Supersedes in part (in 1983): *Journal of Comparative and Physiological Psychology;* Which was formerly (until 1947): *Journal of Comparative Psychology;* Which was formed by the merger of (1917-1921): *Psychobiology;* (1911-1921): *Journal of Animal Behavior.* [ISSN: 0735-7036] 1921. q. USD 702 (Individuals, USD 164; Members, USD 71). Ed(s): Dorothy M Fragaszy. American Psychological Association, 750 First St, NE, Washington, DC 20002; journals@apa.org; http://www.apa.org. Illus., index, adv. Sample. Refereed. Circ: 150. Vol. ends: Feb. Microform: PQC. Reprint: PSC. *Indexed:* A01, A22, C45. *Aud.:* Ac.

This American Psychological Association journal publishes comparative research studies on the behavior, cognition, social relationships, and perception of diverse species. Articles may reflect original empirical or theoretical research and be descriptive or experimental. Studies conducted both in the field and in captivity are included. The journal covers several topics, such as behavior genetics, behavioral rhythms, communication, comparative cognition, the behavioral biology of conservation and animal welfare, development, endocrine behavior interactions, evolutionary psychology, methodology, phylogenetic comparisons, orientation and navigation, sensory and perceptual processes, social behavior, and social cognition. Recent issues more specifically address turtle vocalizations as the first evidence of portthatching parental care in chelonians; extinction of food-reinforced instrumental behavior in Japanese quail; salmon fishing by bears and the dawn of cooperative predation; effects of overtraining on extinction in newts; choice behavior in pigeons, college students, and preschool children in the Monty Hall dilemma; how wild female African elephants exhibit personality traits of leadership and social integration; inferential reasoning by exclusion in *Homo sapiens* children; characteristics of serial-order learning in common marmosets; outcome-based observational learning in human infants; how imitation, pretend play, and childhood may be essential elements in the evolution of human culture; and explaining both selectivity and fidelity in children's copying behavior with respect to social learning. Libraries that support experimental research should have this title.

4271. *Journal of Consulting and Clinical Psychology.* Formerly (until 1968): *Journal of Consulting Psychology.* [ISSN: 0022-006X] 1937. m. USD 1635 (Individuals, USD 406; Members, USD 175). Ed(s): Joanna Davila. American Psychological Association, 750 First St, NE, Washington, DC 20002; journals@apa.org; http://www.apa.org. Illus., index, adv. Sample. Refereed. Circ: 800. Vol. ends: Jan. Microform: PMC; PQC. Reprint: PSC. *Indexed:* A01, A22, ASSIA, Chicano, ERIC, MLA-IB. *Aud.:* Ac, Sa.

This journal, from the American Psychological Association, publishes original research that deals with clinical diagnosis, treatment, and prevention issues. Its primary audience is the community of clinical practitioners who treat humans with mental illness, clinical dysfunction, and behavioral disorders. Articles concern a variety of populations, including medical patients, ethnic groups, and persons with serious mental illness, regardless of place in the human lifespan. Studies of personality assessment; cross-cultural, gender, or sexual orientation issues; and psychosocial issues of health behaviors are covered. The journal publishes case studies, empirical research, and theoretical manuscripts that investigate change or the effectiveness of treatments. Topics covered include epidemiology; the use of psychological services; health-care economics for behavioral disorders; and critical analyses and meta-analyses of treatment approaches. Recent issues address cultural integration for health research and intervention with respect to religiousness/spirituality, cardiovascular disease, and cancer; treating depressed and anxious smokers in smoking cessation programs; mechanisms in psychosocial interventions for adults living with cancer; the effect of a significant other on client change talk in motivational interviewing; telephone-based physical-activity counseling for major depression in people with multiple sclerosis; the effect of mindfulness-based therapy on symptoms of anxiety and depression in adult cancer patients and survivors; behavioral economic predictors of overweight children's weight loss; the influences of delay and severity of intellectual disability on event memory in children; and maternal depressive symptoms as a predictor of alcohol-use onset and heavy episodic drinking in youths. This is a journal for clinicians and the libraries that support their practice and training.

4272. *Journal of Counseling Psychology.* [ISSN: 0022-0167] 1954. bi-m. USD 760 (Individuals, USD 223; Members, USD 98). Ed(s): Dennis M Kivlighan, Jr. American Psychological Association, 750 First St, NE, Washington, DC 20002; journals@apa.org; http://www.apa.org. Illus., index, adv. Sample. Refereed. Circ: 900. Vol. ends: Dec. Microform: PQC. Reprint: PSC. *Indexed:* A01, A22, ASSIA, B01, BRI, CBRI, Chicano, ERIC. *Aud.:* Ac, Sa.

The *Journal of Counseling Psychology* primarily publishes empirical research in the various areas of counseling psychology, such as counseling activities, career and educational development, diversity and underrepresented populations in relation to counseling activities, the development of new measures, and professional issues in counseling psychology. Recent articles address enhancing the psychotherapy process with common factors feedback, depressive symptoms moderating the association between emotion and communal behavior, and racism in the digital era. This title is recommended for libraries supporting clinical counseling and related psychology programs.

4273. *Journal of Cross-Cultural Psychology.* [ISSN: 0022-0221] 1970. 8x/yr. USD 2029 (print & online eds.)). Ed(s): Deborah L Best. Sage Publications, Inc., 2455 Teller Rd, Thousand Oaks, CA 91320; info@sagepub.com; http://www.sagepub.com. Illus., index, adv. Sample. Refereed. Microform: PQC. Reprint: PSC. *Indexed:* A22, ASSIA, BAS, BRI, Chicano, E01, IBSS, MLA-IB, SSA. *Bk. rev.:* 0-5, 300-500 words. *Aud.:* Ac, Sa.

This Sage online journal is published in association with the International Association for Cross-Cultural Psychology and the Center for Cross-Cultural Research, Department of Psychology, Western Washington University. The journal serves as an "interdisciplinary forum for psychologists, sociologists and educators who study how cultural differences in developmental, social and educational experiences affect individual behavior." Articles address a wide range of topics, such as individualism, self-enhancement, acculturation, family values, ethnic group comparisons, and gender differences and personality. Regular features include empirical and theoretical research, reviews, and book reviews. Special thematic issues appear occasionally. Recent issues look at how the experience of extreme hardship predicts religious meaning-making; a cross-cultural comparison of shared parenting, parental effort, and life-history strategy; similarities and differences in implicit personality concepts across ethnocultural groups in South Africa; changes in pronoun use in American books and the rise of individualism from 1960 to 2008; the relationship between life satisfaction and emotional experience in 21 European countries; a study of 70 nations with respect to consanguinity as a major predictor of levels of democracy; machismo and marital satisfaction in Mexican-American couples; self-enhancement and self-protection strategies in China; and how culture, age, and manual dominance affect directionality in drawing side view objects. Libraries that support programs in cross-cultural studies, as well as general psychology and behavioral and social sciences, will want this title.

Journal of Educational Psychology. See Education/Educational Psychology and Measurement, Special Education, Counseling section.

4274. *Journal of Experimental Child Psychology.* [ISSN: 0022-0965] 1964. 12x/yr. EUR 3851. Ed(s): D F Bjorklund. Academic Press, 3251 Riverport Ln, Maryland Heights, MO 63043; JournalCustomerService-usa@elsevier.com; http://www.elsevier.com/. Illus., index, adv. Refereed. Vol. ends: Dec. *Indexed:* A01, A22, E01, ERIC, MLA-IB. *Aud.:* Ac, Sa.

This is an Academic Press journal, on the Elsevier Science Direct platform, with a focus on child development. It publishes empirical, theoretical, methodological, and analytical studies on child development that span infancy through adolescence and include cognitive, social, and physical aspects. Features include a "Reflections" forum in which scholars discuss issues raised in an initial paper, and a brief notes section. Special-topic supplements appear periodically. Recent research addresses the influence of averageness on children's judgments of facial attractiveness; gender influences on children's selective trust of adult testimony; anger and selective attention to reward and punishment in children; working memory and social functioning in children; young children's fast mapping and generalization of words, facts, and pictograms; investigation of color constancy in 4.5-month-old infants under a strict control of luminance contrast for individual participants; word comprehension and production asymmetries in children and adults; the role of relational memory in thinking about the future early in life; the approximate number system and its relation to early math achievement as evidenced from preschool years; and the development of social learning in interactive and observational contexts. This is an important title for libraries that support students and researchers in psychology and education.

4275. *Journal of Experimental Psychology: Animal Learning and Cognition.* Formerly (until 2014): *Journal of Experimental Psychology: Animal Behavior Processes;* Which superseded in part (in 1975): *Journal of Experimental Psychology.* [ISSN: 2329-8456] 1916. q. USD 710 (Individuals, USD 164; Members, USD 71). Ed(s): Ralph R Miller. American Psychological Association, 750 First St, NE, Washington, DC 20002; journals@apa.org; http://www.apa.org. Illus., index, adv. Sample. Refereed. Circ: 200. Vol. ends: Dec. Microform: PQC. Reprint: PSC. *Indexed:* A01, A22, C45. *Aud.:* Ac, Sa.

This American Psychological Association journal publishes articles based on empirical, theoretical, or experimental studies. Any aspect of animal behavior, including associative, non-associative, cognitive, perceptual, and motivational processes, may be the subject of investigation. Relevant specialized reviews and brief communications on novel experiments are also published. Recent issues look at perceptual learning with complex visual stimuli based on location, rather than content, of discriminating features; a further assessment of the Hall-Rodriguez theory of latent inhibition; contextual control of attentional allocation in human discrimination learning; the influence of excitatory and inhibitory landmarks on choice in environments with a distinctive shape; two ways to deepen extinction and the difference between them; how pigeons make errors as a result of interval timing in a visual, but not visual-spatial, midsession reversal task; changes in attention to relevant and irrelevant stimuli during spatial learning; and human sensitivity to the magnitude and probability of a continuous causal relation in a videogame. This journal is particularly appropriate for libraries that support researchers in experimental psychology.

4276. *Journal of Experimental Psychology: Applied.* [ISSN: 1076-898X] 1995. q. USD 710 (Individuals, USD 164; Members, USD 71). Ed(s): Daniel G Morrow. American Psychological Association, 750 First St, NE, Washington, DC 20002; journals@apa.org; http://www.apa.org. Adv. Sample. Refereed. Circ: 350. Vol. ends: Feb. Reprint: PSC. *Indexed:* A22, B01, ERIC, ErgAb. *Aud.:* Ac, Sa.

This APA journal publishes empirical investigations that bridge practically oriented problems and psychological theory. It also publishes relevant review articles and research studies that concern "models of cognitive processing or behavior in applied situations, including laboratory and field settings." Topics covered may include "applications of perception, attention, decision making, reasoning, information processing, learning, and performance." Studies may have been conducted in industrial, academic, or consumer-oriented settings. Recent issues look at how feedback reduces the metacognitive benefits of tests; implicit approach-avoidance associations for craved-food cues; the influence of affective states on the process of lie detection; extracting the truth from conflicting eyewitness reports; how the effectiveness of test-enhanced learning depends on trait test-anxiety and working-memory capacity; an eye-movement analysis of the spatial contiguity effect in multimedia learning; specificity of postural sway to the demands of a precision task at sea; how humor breaks resistance to influence; and how caffeine enhances real-world language processing as evidenced from a proofreading task. Libraries that support programs in experimental research will find this title important.

4277. *Journal of Experimental Psychology: General.* Supersedes in part (in 1975): *Journal of Experimental Psychology.* [ISSN: 0096-3445] 1916. m. USD 2091 (Individuals, USD 445; Members, USD 175). Ed(s): Nelson Cowan. American Psychological Association, 750 First St, NE, Washington, DC 20002; journals@apa.org; http://www.apa.org. Illus., adv. Sample. Refereed. Circ: 400. Vol. ends: Feb. Microform: PQC. Reprint: PSC. *Indexed:* A01, A22, ERIC, ErgAb, MLA-IB. *Aud.:* Ac.

This APA journal publishes empirical research that bridges two or more communities of psychology. Such issues may concern combinations of work in applied, animal, learning and memory, and human performance experimental research. The journal also publishes articles on other psychological topics, including social processes, developmental processes, psychopathology, neuroscience, or computational modeling. Recent issues contain articles concerning listening to the heart and when false somatic feedback shapes moral behavior; a subjective time-perception account of sexual-cue effects on impatience; the role of first impression in operant learning; how eye movements to audiovisual scenes reveal expectations of a just world; the modular nature of trustworthiness detection; sex differences in the spatial representation of number; the physical burdens of secrecy; fluid movement and creativity; the interplay between nonsymbolic number and its continuous visual properties; stability and change in markets of core numerical competencies; how eye movements reveal sustained implicit processing of others' mental states; the gendering of numbers; the sensorimotor contributions to implicit memory, familiarity, and recollection; and the effect of mental progression on mood. Appropriate for libraries that support experimental psychology programs.

4278. *Journal of Experimental Psychology: Human Perception and Performance.* Supersedes in part (in 1975): *Journal of Experimental Psychology.* [ISSN: 0096-1523] 1916. m. USD 2091 (Individuals, USD 562; Members, USD 212). Ed(s): Isabel Gauthier. American Psychological Association, 750 First St, NE, Washington, DC 20002; journals@apa.org; http://www.apa.org. Adv. Sample. Refereed. Circ: 300. Vol. ends: Jan. Microform: PQC. Reprint: PSC. *Indexed:* A01, A22, ASSIA, B01, ERIC, ErgAb, MLA-IB. *Aud.:* Ac, Sa.

This APA journal publishes primarily empirical research on perception, language processing, human action, and related cognitive processes, and covers all sensory modalities and motor systems. The journal seeks to increase theoretical understanding of human perception and performance and encourages studies with a neuroscientific perspective. Articles concerning machine and animal studies that reflect on human capabilities may also appear. Nonempirical reports, including theoretical notes, commentary, or criticism on pertinent topics are also published. Recent issues have addressed: matching voice and face identity from static images; collective enumeration; divergent effects of cognitive load on quiet stance and task-linked postural coordination; the hue of shapes; rapid acquisition but slow extinction of an attentional bias in space; variants of independence in the perception of facial identity and expression; how eye movements reveal how task difficulty molds visual search; the contributions of facial shape, skin texture, and viewing angle in signals of personality and health; how an archer's perceived form scales the "hit-ableness" of archery targets; rapid activation of motor responses by illusory contours; and the gradual, practice-dependent, and hierarchically organized top-down control of attention. Researchers concerned with human physical performance will want to find this title in their library's collection.

4279. *Journal of Experimental Psychology: Learning, Memory, and Cognition.* Formerly (until 1982): *Journal of Experimental Psychology: Human Learning and Memory;* Which superseded in part (in 1975): *Journal of Experimental Psychology.* [ISSN: 0278-7393] 1916. m. USD 2091 (Individuals, USD 562; Members, USD 212). Ed(s): Robert L Greene. American Psychological Association, 750 First St, NE, Washington, DC 20002; journals@apa.org; http://www.apa.org. Adv. Sample. Refereed. Circ: 400. Vol. ends: Dec. Microform: PQC. Reprint: PSC. *Indexed:* A01, A22, B01, ERIC, ErgAb, MLA-IB. *Aud.:* Ac, Sa.

The *Journal of Experimental Psychology: Learning, Memory, and Cognition* publishes empirical and experimental research on cognition, learning, memory, imagery, concept formation, problem solving, decision making, thinking, reading, and language processing. Specialized reviews and other non-empirical theoretical notes, commentary, or criticism on pertinent topics are also included. Recent issues include articles on experimentally evoking nonbelieved memories for childhood events; the effects of emotional valence and arousal on recollective and nonrecollective recall; the role of rehearsal on the output order of immediate free recall of short and long lists; the processing advantage and disadvantage for homophones in lexical decision tasks; visual statistical learning based on the perceptual and semantic information of objects; the auditory memory-distortion for spoken prose; and the effects of prior knowledge on incidental category learning. Researchers interested in cognition, organizational psychology, or educational psychology will want to find this title in their library's collection.

4280. *Journal of Experimental Social Psychology.* [ISSN: 0022-1031] 1965. bi-m. EUR 3088. Ed(s): R Giner-Sorolla. Academic Press, 3251 Riverport Ln, Maryland Heights, MO 63043; JournalCustomerService-usa@elsevier.com; http://www.elsevier.com/. Illus., adv. Sample. Refereed. Vol. ends: Nov. *Indexed:* A01, A22, E01, IBSS. *Aud.:* Ac.

The *Journal of Experimental Social Psychology* is a peer-reviewed journal focused on social psychology, and specifically reports of research that use experimental or quasi-experimental methods. Recent articles look at the synergistic benefits of valuing diversity and merit, the weighting of positive vs. negative valence, and converging evidence that subliminal social comparison affects self-evaluation. Academic and research libraries supporting psychology programs, and psychologists, will benefit from this journal.

4281. *The Journal of General Psychology: experimental, physiological, and comparative psychology.* [ISSN: 0022-1309] 1927. q. GBP 316 (print & online eds.)). Ed(s): Andrea M Karkowski, Paula Goolkasian. Routledge, 530 Walnut St, Ste 850, Philadelphia, PA 19106; enquiries@tandfonline.com; http://www.tandfonline.com. Adv. Refereed. Reprint: PSC. *Indexed:* A01, A22, B01, BRI, Chicano, E01, ErgAb, MLA-IB. *Aud.:* Ac, Sa.

The Journal of General Psychology, on the Taylor & Francis platform, is devoted to experimental, physiological, and comparative psychology. Articles emphasize functional relationships, involve a series of integrated studies, or present new theoretical insights. Human and animal studies, mathematical and other theoretical investigations, and technological reports are included. Recent issues address hemispheric differences in the processing of words learned early vs. later in childhood; relations among children's coping strategies and anxiety; the effect of a final exam on long-term retention; the relationship between basic psychological needs satisfaction and aggression in late adolescents; recognition memory for faces and scenes; the relationship between language use and depression, and illuminating the importance of self-regulation, self-rumination, and the need for absolute truth; the influence of personal traits on lawyer selection among British adults; and the examination of personality characteristics in a Turkish sample and the development of Basic Personality Traits Inventory.

4282. *Journal of Humanistic Psychology.* [ISSN: 0022-1678] 1961. q. USD 1463 (print & online eds.)). Ed(s): Shawn Rubin. Sage Publications, Inc., 2455 Teller Rd, Thousand Oaks, CA 91320; info@sagepub.com; http://www.sagepub.com. Illus., index, adv. Sample. Refereed. Vol. ends: Fall. Microform: PQC. Reprint: PSC. *Indexed:* A01, A22, ASSIA, BRI, E01. *Aud.:* Ac, Sa.

The *Journal of Humanistic Psychology* is an interdisciplinary journal published by Sage that looks at humanistic psychology. Topics include personal growth, interpersonal encounters, social problems, and philosophical issues, spiritual development, confluent education, and a wide variety of other issues. Recent articles address humanistic psychology, psychedelics, and the transpersonal vision, patient experiences of psilocybin-assisted psychotherapy, and exploring characteristic profiles of heroes using Q-method. This journal is recommended for libraries supporting social science programs, such as psychology and philosophy.

Journal of Learning Disabilities. See Education/Educational Psychology and Measurement, Special Education, Counseling section.

4283. *Journal of Mathematical Psychology.* [ISSN: 0022-2496] 1964. bi-m. EUR 1924. Ed(s): Philip l Smith. Academic Press, 3251 Riverport Ln, Maryland Heights, MO 63043; JournalCustomerService-usa@elsevier.com; http://www.elsevier.com/. Illus., index, adv. Sample. Refereed. Vol. ends: Dec. *Indexed:* A01, A22, E01, MSN. *Bk. rev.:* 1-5, 100-3,000 words. *Aud.:* Ac.

This Elsevier title is a publication of the Society for Mathematical Psychology. The journal publishes empirical and theoretical articles, monographs and reviews, notes and commentaries, and book reviews in the field of mathematical psychology. Topics covered include fundamental measurement and psychological process models; models for sensation and perception, and learning and memory; neural modeling and networks; neuropsychological theories; psycholinguistics; animal behavior; psychometric theory; problem solving, judgment, and decision making; and motivation. Recent issues address using logarithmic derivative functions for assessing the risky weighting function for binary gambles; modeling geometric-optical illusions with a variational approach; information-sharing and aggregation models for interacting minds; connections among decisional field-theory models of cognition; a neural computation model for decision-making times; statistical measures for workload capacity analysis; intractability and approximation of optimization theories of cognition; quantum-like generalization of the Bayesian updating scheme for objective and subjective mental uncertainties; a lexicographic semiorder polytope and probabilistic representations of choice; and a probabilistic study of the psychology of inferring conditionals from disjunctions. Libraries that support quantitative and scientific psychology researchers and students will want this title.

4284. *The Journal of Mind and Behavior.* [ISSN: 0271-0137] 1980. q. USD 185 (Individuals, USD 46). Ed(s): Dr. Raymond C Russ. Institute of Mind & Behavior, Village Sta, PO Box 522, New York, NY 10014. Illus., index, adv. Sample. Refereed. *Indexed:* A01, A22, MLA-IB, SSA. *Bk. rev.:* 0-4, 300-2,000 words. *Aud.:* Ac.

This publication of the Institute of Mind and Behavior at the University of Maine is not yet available online; however, its tables of contents are. The journal is interdisciplinary in that it focuses on the relationship of mind and behavior. Contents reflect the publishing of scholarly work that is experimental, theoretical, empirical, or methodological. Subjects of interest include relationships among psychology, philosophy, sociology, and the scientific method; the mind/body problem in social sciences, medicine, and physical science; the philosophical impact of a mind/body epistemology on psychology and its theories of consciousness; ethical studies of cognition, self-awareness, and higher functions of consciousness in non-humans; and historical perspectives in psychology. While it seeks experimental research, the journal also recognizes "the need to propagate ideas and speculations as well as the need to form empirical situations for testing them." With its emphasis on theory, this is a core journal for libraries with advanced psychology and social-science programs and research collections. Recent issues address the equilibration of the self and the sense of sublation; spirituality in thought, music, and meditation; a theory of hemispheric specialization based on cortical columns; a qualitative perspective on deja vu; counterfactuals, belief, and inquiry by thought experiment; and physiological sources, biological functions, and psychological implications of dreaming.

4285. *Journal of Occupational and Organizational Psychology.* Former titles (until 1992): *Journal of Occupational Psychology;* (until 1975): *Occupational Psychology;* (until 1938): *Human Factors;* (until 1932): *National Institute of Industrial Psychology. Journal.* [ISSN: 0963-1798] 1922. q. GBP 477 (print & online eds.)). Ed(s): George Halbesleben. John Wiley & Sons Ltd., EMEA Institutional Sales, 9600 Garsington Rd, Oxford, OX4 2DQ, United Kingdom; cs-journals@wiley.com; http://onlinelibrary.wiley.com. Illus., index, adv. Sample. Refereed. Vol. ends: Dec. Reprint: PSC. *Indexed:* A01, A22, ASSIA, B01, BRI, E01, ErgAb, IBSS. *Bk. rev.:* 3, 500-1,000 words. *Aud.:* Ac, Sa.

This publication of the British Psychological Society, on the Wiley platform, provides empirical and theoretical articles concerning people and organizations at work. Papers address issues in industrial, organizational, vocational, and personnel psychology, and consider behavioral concerns in industrial relations, ergonomics, and industrial sociology. Recent issues look at the underpinnings of a positive climate for diversity; how ruminative thinking exacerbates the negative effects of workplace violence; affective reactions to a pay-system reform and their impact on employee behavior; understanding the mediating role of toxic emotional experiences in the relationship between negative emotions and adverse outcomes; perceived value congruence and team innovation; investigating the effect of collective organizational commitment on unit-level performance and absence; how being in one's chosen job determines pre-training attitudes and training outcomes; the contradictory influence of perception of organizational politics on organizational citizenship behavior; and age-related differences in work motivation. Libraries that support studies in organizational psychology, industrial relations, and business will want this title.

4286. *Journal of Organizational Behavior.* Formerly (until 1988): *Journal of Occupational Behaviour.* [ISSN: 0894-3796] 1980. 8x/yr. GBP 2077. Ed(s): Suzanne S Masterson. John Wiley & Sons Ltd., EMEA Institutional Sales, 9600 Garsington Rd, Oxford, OX4 2DQ, United Kingdom; cs-journals@wiley.com; http://onlinelibrary.wiley.com. Illus., adv. Sample. Refereed. Microform: PQC. Reprint: PSC. *Indexed:* A22, ASSIA, B01, BRI, CJPI, ErgAb. *Aud.:* Ac, Sa.

The *Journal of Organizational Behavior,* a Wiley publication, publishes empirical reports and theoretical reviews of research in organizational behavior and about the workplace. Topics include all levels of individual, group, and organization, as well as across levels. Articles may discuss personality, motivation, commitment, career behavior, leadership, politics, goal-setting, change management, decision making, turnover, or absenteeism. Recent issues address employee silence motives; pay satisfaction and work-family conflict across time; the role of positive affectivity in team effectiveness during crises; the effects of leadership consideration and structure on employee perceptions of justice and counterproductive work behavior; the dark side of organizational citizenship behavior; an empirical analysis of surface acting in intra-organizational relationships; trust in supervisor and individual performance; increasing the effectiveness of workplace interventions in creating pro-environmental behavior change; and high-performer turnover and firm performance and the moderating role of human capital investment and firm reputation. This journal is important for clinical psychologists, human resources managers, and researchers in occupational psychology.

4287. *Journal of Pediatric Psychology.* Formerly: *Pediatric Psychology.* [ISSN: 0146-8693] 1976. 10x/yr. EUR 1484. Ed(s): Tonya M Palermo. Oxford University Press, Great Clarendon St, Oxford, OX2 6DP, United Kingdom; onlinequeries.uk@oup.com; http://global.oup.com. Illus., index, adv. Sample. Refereed. Circ: 2000. Microform: PQC. Reprint: PSC. *Indexed:* A22, E01. *Bk. rev.:* 5-8, 150-3,000 words. *Aud.:* Ac, Sa.

This Oxford title is the official journal of the Society of Pediatric Psychology, Division 54, of the American Psychological Association. This interdisciplinary journal publishes theoretical papers, empirical research, and professional-practice articles concerning pediatric psychology. Features include analytical reviews, brief reports, and case studies. Articles focus on preventive health and treatment issues, as well as the training of pediatric psychologists. Recent issues look at parenting stress in the Infant Aphasia Treatment Study; trauma reactions in mothers and fathers after their infant's cardiac surgery; body mass index (BMI) differences and psychosocial adjustment among early adolescent girls; the relationship between camp attendance and self-perceptions in children with chronic health conditions; impulse control, diabetes-specific self-efficacy, and diabetes management among emerging adults with type 1 diabetes; how videogame distraction reduces behavioral distress in a preschool-aged child undergoing repeated burn-dressing changes; how stigmatization predicts psychological adjustment and quality of life in children and adolescents with a facial difference; and abdominal pain and health-related quality of life in pediatric inflammatory bowel disease. Clinical child psychologists, medical and health-care professionals who work with children, and researchers pursuing studies related to children's medicine and psychology will want access to this title.

4288. *Journal of Personality.* Formerly (until 1945): *Character and Personality.* [ISSN: 0022-3506] 1932. bi-m. GBP 1564. Ed(s): Howard Tennen. Wiley-Blackwell Publishing, Inc., 111 River St, Hoboken, NJ 07030; http://onlinelibrary.wiley.com. Illus., index, adv. Sample. Refereed. Vol. ends: Dec. Reprint: PSC. *Indexed:* A01, A22, ASSIA, E01, IBSS, MLA-IB. *Aud.:* Ac, Sa.

The *Journal of Personality* focuses on the field of personality, such as behavior dynamics, personality development, and the individual differences in the cognitive, affective, and interpersonal domains. Recent articles explore the lay conceptions of volitional personality change, dispositional anxiety and frontal-midline theta, and the temporal doppler effect and future orientation. Libraries supporting research relating to personality will want this journal in their collection.

4289. *Journal of Personality and Social Psychology.* Supersedes in part (in 1965): *Journal of Abnormal and Social Psychology;* Which was formerly (until 1925): *The Journal of Abnormal Psychology and Social Psychology;* (until 1921): *The Journal of Abnormal Psychology.* [ISSN: 0022-3514] 1906. m. USD 3109 (Individuals, USD 831; Members, USD 297). Ed(s): Kerry Kawakami, Shinobu Kitayama. American Psychological Association, 750 First St, NE, Washington, DC 20002; journals@apa.org; http://www.apa.org. Illus., index, adv. Sample. Refereed. Circ: 900. Vol. ends: Dec. Microform: PQC. Reprint: PSC. *Indexed:* A01, A22, ASSIA, B01, BAS, Chicano, IBSS, MLA-IB, SSA. *Aud.:* Ac, Sa.

This APA online journal publishes empirical, specialized theoretical, methodological, and review articles in all areas of personality and social psychology. It has three sections: "Attitudes and Social Cognition," "Interpersonal Relations and Group Processes," and "Personality Processes and Individual Differences." "Attitudes and Social Cognition" focuses on cognition and social behavior and covers such topics as attitudes, attributions, stereotypes, person memory, self-regulation, the origins and consequences of moods and emotions, the effect of cognition on persuasion, communication, prejudice, social development, and cultural trends. "Interpersonal Relations and Group Processes" addresses psychological interaction and covers such topics as interpersonal attraction, communication, emotion, relationship development, social influence, group decision-making and task performance, intergroup relations, aggression, and pro-social behavior. "Personality Processes and Individual Differences" covers all aspects of personality psychology. Topics may include behavior, emotions, coping, health, motivation, personality structure, personality development, personality assessment, interplay of culture and personality, and personality in everyday life. Recent issues have looked at: promoting cooperative behavior through imagined group discussion; a theoretical framework for personality traits related to intellectual achievements; trust and biased memory of transgressions in romantic relationships; the relationship between age, acceptance, and negative affect; the diverging effects of clean versus dirty money on attitudes, values, and interpersonal behavior; the dynamic interplay between perceived true self-knowledge and decision satisfaction; rising income and the subjective well-being of nations; and an examination of the latent structure of gender. This journal is basic to any psychology collection.

4290. ***Journal of Personality Assessment.*** Former titles (until 1971): *Journal of Projective Techniques and Personality Assessment;* (until 1963): *Journal of Projective Techniques;* (until 1950): *Rorschach Research Exchange and Journal of Projective Techniques;* (until 1947): *Rorschach Research Exchange.* [ISSN: 0022-3891] 1936. bi-m. GBP 876 (print & online eds.)). Ed(s): Steven K Huprich. Routledge, 530 Walnut St, Ste 850, Philadelphia, PA 19106; enquiries@tandfonline.com; http://www.tandfonline.com. Illus., index, adv. Sample. Refereed. Vol. ends: Winter. Microform: PQC. Reprint: PSC. *Indexed:* A01, A22, ASSIA, B01, Chicano, E01, SD. *Aud.:* Ac, Sa.

This Taylor & Francis title is the official publication of the Society for Personality Assessment. The journal publishes articles "dealing with the development, evaluation, refinement, and application of personality assessment methods." Papers may concern the empirical, theoretical, instructional, or professional aspects of using tests, data, or an applied clinical assessment process. The journal seeks to advance the use of personality-assessment methods in clinical, counseling, forensic, and health environments. Articles involve both normal and abnormal subjects. Areas where research is minimal are especially sought by this journal, such as "(a) systematic reviews or meta-analyses that summarize a body of evidence, (b) the effective integration of nomothetic empirical findings with the idiographic requirements of practice in which the assessor reasons through test and extra-test information to make individualized judgments and provide assessment feedback, and (c) the practical value of the clinical assessment process on the individuals receiving services and/or those who refer them for evaluation." Recent issues address verbal expressive testing with older adults after 25 years; using cognitive interviewing for the semantic enhancement of multilingual versions of personality questionnaires; a social-relations analysis of the interpersonal perception of pathological narcissism; the effects of exposure to Internet information about Rorschach on selected comprehensive system variables; gender differences on the MMPI across American and Korean adult and adolescent normative samples; examining the Interpersonal Reactivity Index (IRI) among early and late adolescents and their mothers; measuring positive and negative affect and physiological hyperarousal among Serbian youth; the IIS-32-a brief Inventory of Interpersonal Strengths; and treatment of a woman diagnosed with metastatic cancer and attachment trauma. In addition to researchers and students taking advanced courses in assessment, those who will find this material useful include professionals in clinical, counseling, forensic, community, cross-cultural, education, and health psychology settings.

4291. ***The Journal of Psychology: interdisciplinary and applied.*** [ISSN: 0022-3980] 1935. 8x/yr. GBP 493 (print & online eds.)). Ed(s): Ami Rokach, Ronald G Downey. Routledge, 530 Walnut St, Ste 850, Philadelphia, PA 19106; enquiries@tandfonline.com; http://www.tandfonline.com. Adv. Refereed. Reprint: PSC. *Indexed:* A01, A22, ASSIA, B01, Chicano, E01, ErgAb, IBSS, MLA-IB, SD. *Aud.:* Ac.

The Journal of Psychology is an interdisciplinary journal that publishes empirical research and theoretical articles in all aspects of applied areas of psychology. It includes interdisciplinary research that integrates psychology and other fields (e.g., psychology and law, psychology and consumer behavior, psychology and religion). In addition to publishing manuscripts that have a clearly applied focus, the journal publishes interdisciplinary research that integrates literatures from psychology with other related fields (e.g., occupational health, consumer behavior, law, religion, communication, and political science). The journal encourages critical analysis of all issues. Recent issues address the effects of material and experiential discretionary purchases on consumer happiness; the role of self-compassion in physical and psychological well-being; achievement goals and emotions; exploring the relationship between identity status development and alcohol consumption among Italian adolescents; a team motivation approach to collective autonomy and absenteeism within work teams; negative affectivity and educational attainment as predictors of newlyweds' problem-solving communication and marital quality; processes through which adolescents believe romantic relationships influence friendship quality; and how company norms affect which traits are preferred in job candidates and may cause employment discrimination.

4292. ***Journal of School Psychology.*** [ISSN: 0022-4405] 1963. bi-m. EUR 801. Ed(s): M Demaray. Pergamon Press, The Blvd, Langford Ln, E Park, Kidlington, OX5 1GB, United Kingdom; JournalsCustomerServiceEMEA@elsevier.com; http://www.elsevier.com. Illus., adv. Sample. Refereed. Microform: PQC. *Indexed:* A01, A22, ASSIA, Chicano, ERIC. *Aud.:* Ac, Sa.

The *Journal of School Psychology* focuses on original empirical articles and critical reviews on research and practices relevant to psychological and behavioral processes in school settings. The journal has featured topics like intervention mechanisms, and approaches, schooling effects of the development of social, cognitive, mental-health and achievement-related outcomes, assessment, and consultation. Recent articles explore social, emotional, and behavioral screenings, teacher-child relationships, and school engagement trajectories in adolescence. This journal will be important for libraries supporting education and school psychology programs.

Journal of Sex Research. See Sociology and Social Work/General section.

4293. ***The Journal of Social Psychology.*** Incorporates (1985-2006): *Genetic, Social, and General Psychology Monographs;* Which was formerly (1926-1984): *Genetic Psychology Monographs.* [ISSN: 0022-4545] 1929. bi-m. GBP 381 (print & online eds.)). Psychology Press, 530 Walnut St, Philadelphia, PA 19106; subscriptions@tandf.co.uk; http://www.tandf.co.uk/journals/. Illus. Refereed. Microform: PQC. Reprint: PSC. *Indexed:* A01, A22, ASSIA, B01, BAS, BRI, C42, Chicano, E01, IBSS, MLA-IB, P61, SD, SSA. *Aud.:* Ac, Sa.

This Taylor & Francis online journal was founded in 1929 by John Dewey and Carl Murchison. It publishes empirical research in basic and applied social psychology. The core areas of social and organizational psychology, attribution theory, attitudes, social influence, consumer behavior, decision making, groups and teams, stereotypes and discrimination, interpersonal attraction, pro-social behavior, aggression, organizational behavior, leadership, and cross-cultural studies are all reflected in the journal's selection of articles. Recent articles cover gender and gender-role differences in self- and other-estimates of multiple intelligences; effects of playing videogames on perceptions of one's humanity; customers' emotional regulation in service interactions; portrayals of gender and ethnicity in television advertisements; partner discrepancies in distressed marriages; an investigation of abusive supervision, vicarious abusive supervision, and their joint impacts; cultural stereotypes and personal beliefs about individuals with dwarfism; the impact of the 2008 Mumbai attacks on British and Indian students and the role of revenge, denial, and terrorism distress in restoring just world beliefs; how the voluntariness of apologies affects actual and hypothetical victims' perceptions of the offender; how ego depletion increases risk-taking; and attitudes toward cosmetic surgery patients. An important journal for academic behavioral and social science collections.

4294. ***Journal of Youth and Adolescence: a multidisciplinary research publication.*** [ISSN: 0047-2891] 1972. m. EUR 3016 (print & online eds.)). Ed(s): Roger J R Levesque. Springer New York LLC, 233 Spring St, New York, NY 10013; customerservice@springer.com; http://www.springer.com. Illus., adv. Refereed. Vol. ends: Dec. Microform: PQC. Reprint: PSC. *Indexed:* A01, A22, Agr, BRI, CJPI, Chicano, E01, ERIC, N13, SSA. *Aud.:* Ac, Sa.

This Springer multidisciplinary journal publishes empirical, experimental, and theoretical research and review articles in the fields of psychology, sociology, psychiatry, criminology, and education. The journal focuses especially on papers that address social policies or have policy implications with respect to society's response to youth and adolescence. Recent issues address how parents' participation in a work-based anti-poverty program can enhance their children's future orientation; how the age-crime curve in adolescence and early adulthood is not due to age differences in economic status; associations of neighborhood and family factors with trajectories of physical and social aggression during adolescence; social influences on cyberbullying behaviors among middle and high school students; individual and family predictors of the perpetration of dating violence and victimization in late adolescence; motives for using Facebook, patterns of Facebook activities, and late adolescents' social adjustment to college; adolescent neglect, juvenile delinquency, and the risk of recidivism; thriving in context-findings from the 4-H study of positive youth development; sexual attraction, sexual identity, and psychosocial well-being in a national sample of young women during emerging adulthood; and religiosity profiles of American youth in relation to substance use, violence, and delinquency. Clinical psychologists, social science researchers, educators, and health-care and legal professionals will have interest in this journal.

4295. *Law and Human Behavior.* [ISSN: 0147-7307] 1977. bi-m. USD 2303 (Individuals, USD 158; Members, USD 96). Ed(s): Margaret Bull Kovera. American Psychological Association, 750 First St, NE, Washington, DC 20002; journals@apa.org; http://www.apa.org. Illus., adv. Sample. Refereed. Circ: 3100. Vol. ends: Dec. Microform: PQC. Reprint: PSC. *Indexed:* A01, A22, B01, BRI, CJPI, E01, L14, P61, SSA. *Aud.:* Ac, Sa.

This journal is the official publication of the American Psychology-Law Society. *Law and Human Behavior* looks at the relationship between human behavior, the law, the legal system, and the legal process. It publishes original research, reviews, and theoretical studies. Recent articles address police reports of mock suspect interrogations, a framework of SAVRY and the YLS/CMI, and violent offending among juveniles. This multidisciplinary journal will appeal to libraries supporting a variety of programs, to include psychology, criminal justice, law, political science, and other related areas.

4296. *Media Psychology.* [ISSN: 1521-3269] 1999. 6x/yr. GBP 908 (print & online eds.)). Ed(s): Eun-Ju Lee, Silvia Knobloch-Westerwick. Routledge, 530 Walnut St, Ste 850, Philadelphia, PA 19106; enquiries@tandfonline.com; http://www.tandfonline.com. Adv. Sample. Refereed. Reprint: PSC. *Indexed:* A01, A22, E01, F01. *Aud.:* Ac, Sa.

This interdisciplinary, scholarly journal, on the Taylor & Francis platform, publishes research concerning the intersection of psychology and communication media. Empirical studies, theoretical papers, state-of-the-art reviews, and meta-analyses appear regularly in its contents. The effects, uses, and processes of media as they relate to psychology are primary topics. Various forms of communication, including mass media, television, telecommunications, computer networks, personal media, and multi-media are represented in the journal's articles. Recent issues look at effects of Facebook self-presentation on implicit self-esteem and cognitive task performance; videogames, immersion, and cognitive aggression and whether the controller matters; gaming addiction, gaming engagement, and psychological health complaints among Norwegian adolescents; the influence of moral intuitions on decisions in videogames; narrative persuasion, transportation, and the role of need for cognition in online viewing of fantastical films; pessimism and anxiety and the effects of "tween" sitcoms on expectations and feeling about peer relationships in school; gender disparity in videogame usage; and the role of emotional involvement and trait absorption in the formation of spatial presence. Libraries that support research and studies in communication and media, psychology, education, human development, and related social sciences will want this title.

4297. *Memory and Cognition.* Supersedes in part (in 1973): *Psychonomic Science.* [ISSN: 0090-502X] 1964. 8x/yr. EUR 768 (print & online eds.)). Ed(s): Neil Mulligan. Springer New York LLC, 233 Spring St, New York, NY 10013; customerservice@springer.com; http://www.springer.com. Illus., adv. Refereed. Circ: 1700. Microform: PQC. Reprint: PSC. *Indexed:* A01, A22, B01, E01, MLA-IB. *Aud.:* Ac.

Memory & Cognition is a publication of the Psychonomic Society, published on the Springer platform. Its coverage is broad, including topics such as human memory, learning, conceptual processes, decision making, skilled performance, computer simulation, information processing, mathematical psychology, developmental psychology, and experimental social psychology. Recent issues cover research on how divided attention selectively impairs memory for self-relevant information; the effects of working-memory training in young and old adults; concreteness and word production; discrepancy-plus-search processes in prospective memory retrieval; the effects of sleep on problem solving; cognitive abilities and the production of figurative language; how peripheral vision benefits spatial learning by guiding eye movements; the role of verbal memory in regressions during reading; and how appearance-based interferences bias source memory. Psychology research libraries will want to add this title.

4298. *Neuropsychology.* [ISSN: 0894-4105] 1987. 8x/yr. USD 817 (Individuals, USD 271; Members, USD 131). Ed(s): Gregory G Brown. American Psychological Association, 750 First St, NE, Washington, DC 20002; journals@apa.org; http://www.apa.org. Illus., adv. Sample. Refereed. Circ: 550. Vol. ends: Dec. Reprint: PSC. *Indexed:* A22, AgeL, MLA-IB. *Aud.:* Ac, Sa.

Neuropsychology explores the relation between brain and human cognition, emotional, and behavioral function. Topics include experimental cognitive, behavioral, and neuroimaging research, to include neuropsychological theory, research, and practice. Recent articles have talked about long-term classroom functioning and its association with neuropsychological and academic performance following traumatic brain injury during early childhood, the relation of white-matter microstructure to reading ability and disability in beginning readers, and emotion processing in early blind and sighted individuals. This journal is recommended for libraries supporting neuropsychology research.

4299. *Organizational Behavior and Human Decision Processes.* Formerly (until 1985): *Organizational Behavior and Human Performance.* [ISSN: 0749-5978] 1966. bi-m. EUR 4072. Ed(s): Xiao-Ping Chen. Academic Press, 3251 Riverport Ln, Maryland Heights, MO 63043; JournalCustomerService-usa@elsevier.com; http://www.elsevier.com/. Illus., index, adv. Sample. Refereed. *Indexed:* A01, A22, ASSIA, B01, E01, ERIC, ErgAb, IBSS. *Aud.:* Ac, Sa.

This Elsevier title publishes research in organizational psychology and behavior, and human cognition, judgment, and decision making. Features include empirical research, theoretical papers, literature reviews, and methodological articles. Among the topics found in its contents are cognition, perception, attitudes, emotion, well-being, motivation, choice, and performance. Individuals and variations of social groups are the subjects of these studies. Recent issues look at the impact of learning and performance goals on process and performance; anchoring in sequential judgments; the psychological costs of knowledge specialization in groups, and how unique expertise leaves you out of the loop; the role of moral identity in the aftermath of dishonesty; how past decisions affect future choices; the influence of motivated reasoning on saving and spending decisions; encouraging employees to report unethical conduct internally; social dilemmas between individuals and groups; ostracism and prosocial behavior; self-other decision-making and loss aversion; and the effects of kin density within family owned businesses. Libraries that support programs in organizational and industrial psychology, education, and related social sciences will want to collect this title.

4300. *Perceptual and Motor Skills.* Former titles (until 1955): *Perceptual and Motor Skills Research Exchange;* (until 19??): *Motor Skills Research Exchange.* [ISSN: 0031-5125] 1949. bi-m. USD 1663 (print & online eds.)). Ed(s): J D Ball. Sage Publications, Inc., 2455 Teller Rd, Thousand Oaks, CA 91320; info@sagepub.com; http://www.sagepub.com. Illus., index. Sample. Refereed. *Indexed:* A01, A22, AgeL, BRI, Chicano, ErgAb, HRIS, MLA-IB, SD. *Bk. rev.:* 2-6, 120 words. *Aud.:* Ac, Sa.

Perceptual and Motor Skills is a peer-reviewed journal that publishes in the fields of perception, learning, and motor skills. It publishes in three major sections: "Human Development," "Clinical Problems," and "Peak Performance." Recent articles cover the effects of youth participation in extracurricular sport programs on perceived self-efficacy, predicting factors of zone 4 attack in volleyball, and object-spatial imagery and verbal cognitive styles in high school students. Libraries supporting neuropsychology researchers, as well as health, exercise, and sport science programs will benefit from this title.

4301. *Personality and Social Psychology Bulletin.* Formerly (until 1975): *American Psychological Association. Division of Personality and Social Psychology. Proceedings.* [ISSN: 0146-1672] 19??. m. USD 2493 (print & online eds.)). Ed(s): Duane T Wegener. Sage Publications, Inc., 2455 Teller Rd, Thousand Oaks, CA 91320; info@sagepub.com; http://www.sagepub.com. Illus. Refereed. Microform: PQC. Reprint: PSC. *Indexed:* A22, ASSIA, Chicano, E01, P61, SSA. *Aud.:* Ac, Sa.

This Sage publication is the official publication of the Society for Personality and Social Psychology. The bulletin provides an international forum for research in all areas of personality and social psychology. Articles reflect many schools of thought and new developments in the field. Based primarily on empirical research, papers on a variety of topics appear, including communication, gender and age stereotypes, interpersonal relationships, group psychology, prejudice, and self-consciousness. Special theme issues are periodically published. Themes have included motivational determinants of self-evaluation; autobiographical narratives; publication trends in the field; meta-analysis in personality and social psychology; and principles of psychology. Recent issues address how mastering goals promotes challenge and success despite social identity threat; concepts of happiness across time and cultures; exclusion as self-protection and the function of subtypes for ingroup members; optimism following a tornado disaster; the situational affordance of anger and shame in the United States and Japan; how self-affirmation underlies Facebook use; psychological and sexual costs of income comparison in marriage; how perceived power moderates the effect of stereotype threat on women's math performance; the self-dehumanizing consequences of social ostracism; the differential value of perspective-taking vs. empathy in competitive interactions; and cultural variation in the effectiveness of solicited and unsolicited social support. Libraries that support behavioral and social sciences, education, and industrial psychology will want to have this title.

4302. ***Professional Psychology: Research and Practice.*** Formerly (until 1983): *Professional Psychology.* [ISSN: 0735-7028] 1969. bi-m. USD 879 (Individuals, USD 223; Members, USD 71). Ed(s): Kathi A. Borden. American Psychological Association, 750 First St, NE, Washington, DC 20002; journals@apa.org; http://www.apa.org. Illus., index, adv. Sample. Refereed. Circ: 1600. Vol. ends: Jan. Microform: PQC. Reprint: PSC. *Indexed:* A01, A22, ASSIA, Chicano. *Aud.:* Ac, Sa.

This APA journal publishes theoretical and empirical articles for the clinician on applied psychology. Scientific and evidence-based articles on assessment, treatment, and practice implications are stressed. The journal includes literature reviews, case studies, standards-based practice articles, public policy research, and general research of interest to clinical psychologists. Current topics include health psychology, community psychology, psychology of women, clinical neuropsychology, family psychology, psychology of ethnicity and culture, and forensic psychology. Brief reports also appear. Recent issues look at the impact of continuing education mandates on participation in continuing professional development activities; psychological factors in college students' attitudes toward seeking professional psychological help; perceived organizational support, motivation, and engagement among police officers; neuroscience applications to practice in child and adolescent psychology; predictors of career satisfaction among practicing psychologists; crisis intervention with children of illegal migrant workers threatened with deportation; and multicultural office design. This is a core journal for clinical psychologists in practice, research, and training, and for the libraries that support them.

4303. ***PsycCRITIQUES (Online).*** Formerly (until 2005): *Contemporary Psychology: A P A Review of Books (Print).* [ISSN: 1554-0138] 1956. w. Members, USD 65; Non-members, USD 130. American Psychological Association, 750 First St, NE, Washington, DC 20002; journals@apa.org; http://www.apa.org. Illus., index, adv. Reprint: PSC. *Indexed:* A22, BRI, CBRI, Chicano. *Bk. rev.:* 50-60, 100-1,500 words. *Aud.:* Ga, Ac, Sa.

This American Psychological Association product is more than a journal. It is a searchable electronic database of book reviews in psychology that was formerly published in print as the journal *Contemporary Psychology: APA Review of Books.* In its new electronic format, *PsycCRITIQUES* provides access to current reviews and back files from 1956 forward. Each weekly release delivers approximately 18,220 reviews of current psychological books. Also included are reviews of popular films and videos from a psychological perspective, comparative reviews, and occasional retrospective reviews. Faculty, librarians, students, and practitioners will benefit by having easy access to this database, in order to identify literature for research, course studies, and collection development, and to stay up to date with the latest psychological thinking.

4304. ***Psychological Assessment.*** Supersedes in part (in 1989): *Journal of Consulting and Clinical Psychology;* Which was formerly (1937-1968): *Journal of Consulting Psychology.* [ISSN: 1040-3590] 1937. m. USD 848 (Individuals, USD 328; Members, USD 175). Ed(s): Yossef S. Ben-Porath. American Psychological Association, 750 First St, NE, Washington, DC 20002; journals@apa.org; http://www.apa.org. Illus., adv. Sample. Refereed. Circ: 700. Vol. ends: Feb. Reprint: PSC. *Indexed:* A01, A22, ERIC. *Aud.:* Ac, Sa.

This APA online journal publishes empirical research on measurement and evaluation relevant to the practice of clinical psychology. Articles concern such topics as assessment processes and methods; decision-making models; personality; social psychology; biological psychology; validation; application of assessment instruments; assessment of personality; psychopathological symptoms; cognitive and neuropsychological processes; and interpersonal behavior. The journal focuses on diagnosis, evaluation, and effective interventions. Case studies, reviews, and theoretical articles relevant to assessment and clinical settings are included. Recent issues look at mastery of negative affect and a hierarchical model of emotional self-efficacy beliefs; internal structure of the Reflective Functioning Scale; measuring beliefs about suffering and development of the Views of Suffering Scale; evaluating the properties of the Evidence-Based Practice Attitude Scale in health care; how proportionate responses to life events influence clinicians' judgments of psychological abnormality; convergent validity of and bias in maternal reports of child emotion; and The Positivity Scale. This journal is one to make available to clinical psychology researchers, students, and practitioners.

4305. ***Psychological Bulletin.*** [ISSN: 0033-2909] 1904. m. USD 1401 (Individuals, USD 328; Members, USD 175). Ed(s): Dolores Albarracin. American Psychological Association, 750 First St, NE, Washington, DC 20002; journals@apa.org; http://www.apa.org. Illus., index, adv. Sample. Refereed. Circ: 700. Vol. ends: Dec. Microform: PMC; PQC. Reprint: PSC. *Indexed:* A01, A22, ASSIA, B01, ERIC, ErgAb, IBSS, MLA-IB. *Aud.:* Ac, Sa.

Psychological Bulletin from the American Psychological Association examines the evaluative and integrative research reviews and interpretations of issues in scientific psychology. Recent articles study the interpersonal dysfunction in personality disorders, the three-second subjective present, and the short-term effects of violent games on affect and behavior. This core title is student friendly, and recommended for libraries supporting psychology programs. See *Psychological Methods* for methodological articles, and *Psychological Review* for original theoretical articles.

4306. ***Psychological Inquiry: an international journal of peer commentary and review.*** [ISSN: 1047-840X] 1990. q. GBP 796 (print & online eds.)). Ed(s): Ronnie Janoff-Bulman. Psychology Press, 530 Walnut St, Philadelphia, PA 19106; orders@taylorandfrancis.com; http://www.psypress.com. Illus., adv. Sample. Refereed. Vol. ends: No. 4. Reprint: PSC. *Indexed:* A01, A22, B01, E01. *Aud.:* Ac, Sa.

This international journal provides a forum for discussion in the fields of social psychology and personality. Articles discuss theoretical and meta-theoretical concerns. Issues are theme-oriented, containing a primary article followed by peer commentaries and the author's response. Recent articles include cultural neuroscience; finding meaning in the theories of sense-making; scientific utopia-opening scientific communication; how mind perception is the essence of morality; how social projection can solve social dilemmas; reintegrating the study of accuracy into social cognition research; understanding well-being and optimal functioning with the Multilevel Personal in Context Model; and intuition and "thin slice" judgments. Libraries that support psychology programs will want this title for patrons who perform in-depth topical study.

4307. ***Psychological Review.*** [ISSN: 0033-295X] 1894. bi-m. USD 1149 (Individuals, USD 271; Members, USD 113). Ed(s): Keith J. Holyoak. American Psychological Association, 750 First St, NE, Washington, DC 20002; journals@apa.org; http://www.apa.org. Illus., index, adv. Sample. Refereed. Circ: 700. Vol. ends: Dec. Microform: PMC; PQC. Reprint: PSC. *Indexed:* A01, A22, ERIC, ErgAb, IBSS, MLA-IB. *Aud.:* Ac, Sa.

The focus of this APA online journal is scientific psychology. Its articles present both significant contributions that advance theory and systematic evaluations of alternative theories. Literature reviews, articles regarding methodology and research design, and empirical reports are not included. Theoretical notes and commentary on scientific psychology are part of the contents. Notes may be discussions of earlier articles. Comments may apply to theoretical models in a given domain, may be critiques of alternative theories, or may be meta-theoretical commentary on theory testing. Recent issues look at the co-evolution of knowledge and event memory; how rational temporal predictions can underlie apparent failures to delay gratification; why most dieters fail but some succeed, looking at a goal-conflict model of eating behavior; separating the contributions and unwanted cues in psychophysical studies; when group membership gets personal and a theory of identity fusion; models of verbal working-memory capacity; social class, solipsism, and contextualism-how the rich are different from the poor; and behavioral variability of choices versus structural inconsistency of preferences. This is a basic resource for academic psychology collections.

4308. *Psychological Science.* [ISSN: 0956-7976] 1990. 27x/yr. USD 8968. Ed(s): Robert V Kail. Sage Publications, Inc., 2455 Teller Rd, Thousand Oaks, CA 91320; info@sagepub.com; http://www.sagepub.com. Illus., adv. Sample. Refereed. Reprint: PSC. *Indexed:* A01, A22, B01, BRI, E01, ErgAb, IBSS, SD. *Aud.:* Ac, Sa.

This Sage journal is the official journal of the Association for Psychological Science. It publishes empirical, theoretical, and applied psychology articles, papers concerning psychological issues related to government and public affairs, and reports that summarize recent research developments. Subject areas include brain and behavior, clinical science, cognition, learning and memory, social psychology, and developmental psychology. Recent issues address how lip movements affect infants' audiovisual speech perception; how attention is spontaneously biased toward regularities; how increasing recognition of happiness in ambiguous facial expressions reduces anger and aggressive behavior; detection of audiovisual speech correspondences without visual awareness; sleep consolidation of interfering auditory memories in starlings; the interpersonal legacy of a positive family climate in adolescence; learning, memory, and synesthesia; how the experience of power and authenticity enhances subjective well-being; and how responses to resource scarcity, as when the economy falters, depends on childhood environments. Libraries that support general and advanced psychology programs will benefit from having this title.

4309. *Psychology & Health.* [ISSN: 0887-0446] 1987. m. GBP 1687 (print & online eds.)). Ed(s): Mark Conner, Daryl O'Connor. Routledge, 4 Park Sq, Milton Park, Abingdon, OX14 4RN, United Kingdom; subscriptions@tandf.co.uk; http://www.tandfonline.com. Illus., adv. Sample. Refereed. Reprint: PSC. *Indexed:* A01, A22, C45, E01, SD. *Bk. rev.:* 0-3, 300. *Aud.:* Ac, Sa.

This Taylor & Francis international journal is a publication of the European Health Psychology Society. The journal focuses on the psychological approaches to health and illness. Subjects covered include psychological aspects of physical illness; treatment and recovery; psychosocial factors of physical illnesses; health attitudes; health behavior; preventive health; and health-care systems. The journal publishes empirical research; papers that present new psychological approaches and interventions; reviews; and short reports. Recent issues look at a qualitative study of people with cancer and intimate partners; closing the intention-behavior gap for sunscreen use and sun-protection behaviors; patient and spouse illness beliefs and quality of life in prostate cancer patients; illness perception of migraineurs from the general population; religious involvement and physical and emotional functioning among African Americans-the mediating role of religious support; the effects of (un)employment on young couples' health and life satisfaction; how, when, and why young women use nutrition information on food labels; and the effect of implementation intentions on physical activity among obese older adults. Libraries that serve researchers and students of public health, psychology, and medicine will want to have this title.

4310. *Psychology of Women Quarterly.* [ISSN: 0361-6843] 1976. q. USD 634 (print & online eds.)). Ed(s): Janice D Yoder. Sage Publications, Inc., 2455 Teller Rd, Thousand Oaks, CA 91320; info@sagepub.com; http://www.sagepub.com. Illus., index, adv. Sample. Refereed. Vol. ends: Dec. Microform: PQC. Reprint: PSC. *Indexed:* A01, A22, ASSIA, BRI, C45, Chicano, E01, ERIC, FemPer, IBSS, SSA, WSA. *Bk. rev.:* 4-10, 500-1,000 words. *Aud.:* Ga, Ac, Sa.

Psychology of Women Quarterly is a peer-reviewed journal publishing on topics such as feminist approaches, methodologies, and critiques, body image and objectification, sexism, discrimination, lifespan development and change, physical and mental well-being, therapeutic interventions, and career development. Recent articles have addressed secondary two-year outcomes of a sexual assault resistance program for university women, negotiating femininity, and using video to increase gender bias literacy toward women in science. This title will appeal to libraries supporting psychology disciplines, as well as women's studies, and ethnic and multicultural studies.

4311. *Psychology Today.* Incorporates (in 1969): *Careers Today.* [ISSN: 0033-3107] 1967. bi-m. USD 19.97 domestic; USD 23.97 Canada; USD 29.99 elsewhere. Ed(s): Kaja Perina. Sussex Publishers Inc., 115 E 23rd St, 9th Fl, New York, NY 10010. Illus., adv. Microform: NBI. *Indexed:* A01, A22, B01, BRI, C37, C42, CBRI, Chicano, MASUSE, MLA-IB. *Aud.:* Hs, Ga, Ac.

Psychology Today is a popular magazine that publishes a wide variety of articles related to psychology. Topics have included micro-management, controlling people, management styles, elements of trust, addiction, child development, therapy, sex, relationships, evolutionary psychology, ethics, morality, psychiatry, and more. This is recommended for public, academic, and medical libraries wanting to carry a psychology publication that will appeal to the general population.

4312. *Psychophysiology: an international journal.* Formerly: *Psychophysiology Newsletter.* [ISSN: 0048-5772] 1964. m. Ed(s): Monica Fabiani. Wiley-Blackwell Publishing, Inc., 111 River St, Hoboken, NJ 07030; info@wiley.com; http://onlinelibrary.wiley.com. Illus., index, adv. Sample. Refereed. Vol. ends: Nov. Reprint: PSC. *Indexed:* A01, A22, E01, ErgAb, SD. *Bk. rev.:* Number and length vary. *Aud.:* Ac, Sa.

Psychophysiology is published on behalf of the Society for Psychophysiological Research by Wiley. This journal explores human neuroscience, covering research on the interrelationships between the physiological and psychological aspects of brain and behavior. It publishes theoretical papers, reviews, empirical papers, and methodological papers. Recent articles cover testing food-related inhibitory control to high and low calorie food stimuli, comparing the error-related negativity across groups, and ERP evidence for conflict in contingency learning. This title will benefit libraries supporting psychophysiology and neuroscience programs.

Psychotherapy Networker. See Family section.

4313. *School Psychology Review (Online).* [ISSN: 2372-966X] 1972. q. Free to members. Ed(s): Amy Reschly. National Association of School Psychologists, 4340 East West Hwy, Ste 402, Bethesda, MD 20814; https://www.nasponline.org. Adv. Refereed. *Aud.:* Ac, Sa.

The *School Psychology Review* is a refereed journal published quarterly by the National Association of School Psychologists. It focuses on research, training, and practice in relation to psychology, education, and school psychology. Recent articles examine conflict, closeness, and academic skills, teacher-child relationships, and training the next generation of school psychologists. This is recommended for libraries supporting clinical psychology, child psychology, and education programs.

4314. *Sexual Abuse: a journal of research and treatment.* Formerly (until 1995): *Annals of Sex Research.* [ISSN: 1079-0632] 1988. bi-m. USD 1668 (print & online eds.)). Ed(s): Michael Seto. Sage Publications, Inc., 2455 Teller Rd, Thousand Oaks, CA 91320; info@sagepub.com; http://www.sagepub.com. Illus., adv. Refereed. Reprint: PSC. *Indexed:* A22, C42, CJPI, E01, SSA. *Aud.:* Ac, Sa.

Published by Sage, this is the official journal of the Association for the Treatment of Sexual Abusers. This journal focuses on sexual abuse, and its etiology, consequences, prevention, treatment, and management strategies. Recent articles cover offender mobility during the crime, enhancing the reproducibility of research findings, and youths arrested for trading sex and the relationship between rate of childhood adversity. This journal will be important for libraries supporting psychologists, psychiatrists, social workers, therapists, as well as those in the criminal justice field.

4315. *Women & Therapy: a feminist quarterly.* Formerly: *Women - Counseling Therapy and Mental Health Services.* [ISSN: 0270-3149] 1982. q. GBP 1117 (print & online eds.)). Ed(s): Ellyn Kaschak. Routledge, 530 Walnut St, Ste 850, Philadelphia, PA 19106; enquiries@tandfonline.com; http://www.tandfonline.com. Illus., adv. Sample. Refereed. Circ: 433 Paid. Vol. ends: No. 4. Microform: PQC. Reprint: PSC. *Indexed:* A01, A22, BRI, C42, E01, FemPer, GW, SSA, WSA. *Bk. rev.:* 0-7, 900 words; signed. *Aud.:* Ac, Sa.

Women & Therapy is a peer-reviewed journal that focuses on the interrelationship between women and the therapeutic experience. Topics include the process of therapy with female clients, problems in living that affect women in greater proportion than men, such as depression, eating disorders, and agoraphobia, as well as women's traditional and nontraditional roles in society. Libraries supporting clinical counseling, as well as women's and gender studies programs will benefit from this title.

■ PUBLIC HEALTH

Elaine R. Hicks, M.S., M.P.H., MCHES, Public Health Librarian, Rudolph Matas Library of the Health Sciences, Tulane University; ehicks2@tulane.edu

Introduction

The core disciplines of the study and practice of public health are Behavioral and Social Science, Biostatistics/Bioinformatics, Community Health, Environmental Health, Epidemiology, Global Health, Health Management and Policy, Health Promotion and Communication, Maternal and Child Health, and Minority Health and Health Disparities. It fills the information needs of faculty, researchers, and practitioners for both peer-reviewed and grey literature.

The titles selected for this edition are those that faculty, researchers, and practitioners recommend most frequently for their area of practice. Each is peer-reviewed. Annotations contain information about the audience, scope, content types (i.e., Systematic Reviews and conference papers) and format, including Open Access. Other components are statements regarding publishing ethics, the 2018 Journal Impact Factor, if it is available in low-resourced countries through the Research4Life Hinari program and the Twitter handle. Descriptor terms are found in the MESH database, *Ulrich's Periodicals Directory,* and Journal Citation Reports.

Basic Periodicals

American Journal of Public Health, American Journal of Epidemiology, World Health Organization. Bulletin, Environmental Health Perspectives, Emerging Infectious Diseases, Health Affairs.

Basic Abstracts and Indexes

Abstracts on Hygiene and Communicable Diseases; CAB Abstracts; Nutrition and Food Sciences Database; Plant Protection Database; PubMed; Rural Development Abstracts; Scopus.

4316. *American Journal of Epidemiology.* Formerly (until 1965): *American Journal of Hygiene.* [ISSN: 0002-9262] 1921. m. USD 1181. Ed(s): Dr. Moyses Szklo. Oxford University Press, 2001 Evans Rd, Cary, NC 27513; orders.us@oup.com; https://academic.oup.com/journals. Illus., adv. Sample. Refereed. Reprint: PSC. *Indexed:* A01, A22, BAS, BRI, C45, Chicano, E01. *Bk. rev.:* Number and length vary. *Aud.:* Ac, Sa.

The *American Journal of Epidemiology* (*AJE*) is the official and monthly journal of the Society for Epidemiologic Research. In it, you will find empirical research findings, opinion pieces, reports, and methodological developments in the field of epidemiological research. The journal subscribes to the criteria for authorship detailed in Uniform Requirements for Manuscripts Submitted to Biomedical Journals (Vancouver Guidelines) by the International Committee of Medical Journal Editors (ICMJE Recommendations) and is a member of the Committee on Publication Ethics (COPE). Content is available to researchers in developing countries through the Research4Life Hinari program. Throughout the year, readers and the editors nominate papers they feel represent the very best of the *AJE* and, by extension, the field of epidemiology. New beginning in 2018, authors can submit articles in their preferred reference style and they have the option to publish their paper under the Oxford Open Initiative. On their website you will find the latest tweets, editor's choice, most read, and latest articles.

4317. *American Journal of Preventive Medicine.* [ISSN: 0749-3797] 1984. bi-m. USD 1532. Ed(s): Matthew L. Boulton. Elsevier Inc., 230 Park Ave, Ste 800, New York, NY 10169; usinfo-f@elsevier.com; https://www.elsevier.com. Illus., adv. Sample. Refereed. *Indexed:* A01, A22, ASSIA, C45, Chicano. *Aud.:* Ac, Sa.

The *American Journal of Preventive Medicine* is the official journal of the American College of Preventive Medicine (ACPM) and the Association for Prevention Teaching and Research (APTR). In it, you will find papers that address the primary and secondary prevention of important clinical, behavioral, and public health issues. The journal's scope includes educational initiatives, papers on health services research, official policy statements, guidelines, review articles, media reviews, and editorials. It supports the policies of the International Committee of Medical Journal Editors (ICJME), follows the guidance on editorial independence produced by the World Association of Medical Editors (WAME), subscribes to the tenets of reporting guidelines established by the EQUATOR network, and is a member of the Committee on Publication Ethics (COPE). Content is available to researchers in developing countries through the Research4Life Hinari program. In it, you will find supplements and special theme issues are devoted to areas of current interest to the prevention community. Authors can choose to publish as open access. Download the free mobile app.

4318. *American Journal of Public Health.* Supersedes in part (in 1971): *American Journal of Public Health and the Nation's Health;* Which was formed by the merger of (1921-1928): *Nation's Health;* (until 1919): *Interstate Medical Journal;* (until 1899): *Tristate Medical Journal and Practitioner;* Interstate Medical Journal Incorporated (1881-1907): *St. Louis Courier of Medicine;* Which was formerly (1879-1881): *Saint Louis Courier of Medicine and Collateral Sciences;* (1912-1928): *American Journal of Public Health;* Which was formerly (until 1912): *American Public Health Association. Journal;* (until 1911): *American Journal of Public Hygiene;* (until 1907): *American Journal of Public Hygiene and Journal of the Massachusetts Association of Boards of Health;* (until 1904): *Massachusetts Association of Boards of Health. Journal;* American Journal of Public Health Incorporated (1873-1912): *Public Health Papers and Reports.* [ISSN: 0090-0036] 1911. m. USD 557 domestic; USD 48 per issue domestic; USD 53 per issue foreign. Ed(s): Alfredo E Morabia. American Public Health Association, 800 I St, NW, Washington, DC 20001; APHA@subscriptionoffice.com; http://www.apha.org. Illus., index, adv. Sample. Refereed. Vol. ends: Dec. Microform: PMC; PQC. *Indexed:* A01, A22, AgeL, Agr, B01, BRI, C45, Chicano, ErgAb, HRIS, S25, SD. *Bk. rev.:* Number and length vary. *Aud.:* Ac, Sa.

The mission of the *American Journal of Public Health* (*AJPH*) is to advance public health research, policy, practice, and education by publishing original work in research, research methods, and program evaluation in the field of public health. Publication types include Systematic Reviews and MetaAnalyses, in addition to some grey literature (i.e., guidelines, proceedings) and media reviews. A 2019 special section on "Science and Public Health Conscience" includes research and perspectives on the public health hazards of talc and glyphosate, relations between science and industry, how EPA policies impact public health, as well as a series of perspective pieces about U.S. Food and Nutrition Policy. *AJPH* adheres to the Principles of the Ethical Practice of Public Health of the American Public Health Association (APHA). On the website, you can read articles ahead of print plus the most read and cited articles. Other website features are podcasts and Twitter feeds.

4319. *American Journal of Tropical Medicine and Hygiene.* Formed by the merger of (1921-1952): *The American Journal of Tropical Medicine;* Which was formerly (1904-1921): *Papers Read Before the Society and Published Under its Auspices;* (1942-1952): *National Malaria Society. Journal.* [ISSN: 0002-9637] 1952. m. Free to members. Ed(s): Philip J

Rosenthal, Cathi B Siegel. American Society of Tropical Medicine and Hygiene, 111 Deer Lake Rd, Ste 100, Deerfield, IL 60015; info@astmh.org; http://www.astmh.org/. Illus., adv. Refereed. *Indexed:* A22, Agr, C45. *Bk. rev.:* Number and length vary. *Aud.:* Ac, Sa.

The American Society of Tropical Medicine and Hygiene publishes the *American Journal of Tropical Medicine and Hygiene* monthly. Select it if your patrons are epidemiologists, parasitologists, virologists, clinicians, entomologists, and public health officials concerned with health issues of the tropics, developing nations, and emerging infectious diseases. The journal emphasizes a variety of sciences such as population, clinical and laboratory science, and the application of technology in the fields of tropical medicine, parasitology, immunology, infectious diseases, epidemiology, basic and molecular biology, virology, and international medicine. More than half of the document types are meeting abstracts, followed by a variety of article types, such as peer-reviewed manuscripts, reviews, images, case studies, book reports, prevention and control methodologies, new testing methods, and equipment and guidelines. New are Stories from the Field, descriptive personal stories about practicing clinical tropical medicine, performing tropical medicine research, taking part in international health education, and/or delivering global health services. Authors can select two types of open access. On the website, you can find manuscripts dating back to 1998, articles ahead of print, and many ways to share content.

4320. *Emerging Infectious Diseases (Online).* [ISSN: 1080-6059] 1995. m. Free. Ed(s): D Peter Drotman. U.S. Department of Health and Human Services, Centers for Disease Control and Prevention, 1600 Clifton Rd, Atlanta, GA 30329; http://www.cdc.gov. Refereed. *Bk. rev.:* Number and length vary. *Aud.:* Ac, Sa.

Emerging Infectious Diseases is an open-access peer-reviewed journal published monthly by the U.S. Department of Health and Human Services Centers for Disease Control and Prevention (CDC). It is a tool to promote the recognition of new and reemerging infectious diseases around the world and improve the understanding of factors involved in disease emergence, prevention, and elimination. Its audience includes professionals in infectious diseases and all those who need the most recent updates about infectious disease trends, research factors that influence disease emergence, laboratory and epidemiologic findings and developments in antimicrobial drugs, vaccines, and the prevention or elimination programs. Reviewers are experts who are usually not part of its editorial staff. Types of articles include clinical studies, case reports, systematic, and other review types. Also, it has a variety of grey literature: conference summaries, reports, and media-related content. It is available in developing countries through the Research4Life Hinari program. Recent topics have been coccidioidomycosis diagnosis candida auris in Germany, a review of the book *Infections of Leisure, Fifth Edition,* and the online report, 'Implementation and Evaluation of a Decision Tool for Herpes B.' The website has expedited ahead-of-print articles and podcasts. As a CDC product, it records the page created, updated, and reviewed dates. The journal supports the policies of the International Committee of Medical Journal Editors. Some articles qualify as Medscape CME activities.

4321. *Environmental Health Perspectives.* Incorporates (in 2003): *E H P Toxicogenomics.* [ISSN: 0091-6765] 1972. m. Ed(s): James G Burkhart. U.S. Department of Health and Human Services, National Institute of Environmental Health Sciences, 111 TW Alexander Dr, Research Triangle Park, NC 27709; http://ehp03.niehs.nih.gov/. Illus., adv. Refereed. Vol. ends: Dec (No. 12). *Indexed:* A01, A22, Agr, BRI, C45, S25. *Aud.:* Ac, Sa.

Environmental Health Perspectives (*EHP*) is a monthly open-access journal produced by the U.S. Department of Health and Human Services, National Institute of Environmental Health Sciences. The mission of *EHP* is to make reliable and useful environmental health information freely accessible across the globe as evidenced by their articles frequently mentioned by media outlets worldwide. The Chinese edition is on the website. While the environmental health sciences include a broad array of disciplines, *EHP* original research articles and commentaries typically come from experimental toxicology, epidemiology, exposure science, and risk assessment. Two topics in recent issues are exposure to air pollution and outcomes of in-vitro fertilization and particulate matter exposure and depression. An original bimonthly podcast series, "The Researcher's Perspective," is a forum for researchers across the disciplines to offer insights into the motivation and vision driving their work and explore the implications of their findings for human health. It recently featured a discussion with an *EHP* author about the role that diet plays in arsenic metabolism and diabetogenicity. Find it on the website. *EHP* is a member of the Committee on Publication Ethics (COPE). and is available in developing countries through Research4Life Hinari program.

4322. *Health Affairs.* [ISSN: 0278-2715] 1981. m. USD 175 (print & online eds.)). Ed(s): Alan Weil. Project HOPE, 7500 Old Georgetown Rd, Ste 600, Bethesda, MD 20814-6133; hope@projecthope.org; http://www.projhope.org. Adv. Refereed. Microform: PQC. *Indexed:* A01, A22, AgeL, B01, C45, E01, P61, SSA. *Bk. rev.:* Number and length vary. *Aud.:* Ga, Ac, Sa.

Health Affairs is a multidisciplinary, peer-reviewed journal dedicated to the serious exploration of major domestic and international health policy issues. Its mission is to serve as a high-level, nonpartisan forum to promote analysis and discussion on improving health and health care, and to address such issues as cost, quality, and access. The unique goal of *Health Affairs* is to incorporate in one publication the diverse viewpoints and perspectives of the health sphere—industry, labor, government, and academe—in a way that benefits everyone who reads it. Health policy briefs examine questions currently being debated in health policy. U.S. Supreme Court Chief Justice John Roberts cited the journal in his decision regarding the Affordable Care Act. In addition, *Health Affairs* is frequently cited by national media, including the *Washington Post, New York Times, Wall Street Journal,* network television and radio, and NPR. Three features sections in a recent issue included Determinants of Health: health systems investing in affordable housing; The Practice of Medicine: physicians' well-being; Disparities: social risk factors in dialysis facility ratings. A series of policy briefs is also focused on the social determinants of health. Several publish-ahead-of-print articles are available monthly in print and online. It is available in developing countries through Research4Life Hinari program.

4323. *Health Education & Behavior.* Former titles (until 1997): *Health Education Quarterly;* (until 1980): *Health Education Monographs.* [ISSN: 1090-1981] 1957. bi-m. USD 2117. Ed(s): Jesus Ramirez-Valles. Sage Publications, Inc., 2455 Teller Rd, Thousand Oaks, CA 91320; info@sagepub.com; http://www.sagepub.com. Illus., index, adv. Sample. Refereed. Vol. ends: Nov/Dec. Microform: PQC. Reprint: PSC. *Indexed:* A22, ASSIA, Agr, C45, Chicano, E01, ERIC, SD. *Bk. rev.:* Number and length vary. *Aud.:* Ac, Sa.

Health Education & Behavior (*HE&B*) is a peer-reviewed bimonthly journal that provides empirical research, case studies, program evaluations, literature reviews, discussions of theories of health behavior and health status, and strategies to improve social and behavioral health. Audience members are researchers and practitioners in health behavior and health education. The journal also examines the processes of planning, implementing, managing, and assessing health education and social-behavioral interventions. Content type includes empirical research using qualitative or quantitative methods; formative, process, and outcome evaluations; and systematic reviews. Also included are conference papers, case studies, and discussions of theories of health behavior and health status and strategies to improve social and behavioral health. Each issue features two self-study articles worth 2.0 continuing education contact hours (CECH). Recent issue topics have been in the categories of Policy, Environmental, and Structural Approaches; Physical Activity: Life Events, Diet, and Gamification; Health Disparities in Diverse Populations; Vaccine Information from Health Care Providers; and Social Media and Health Communication. The journal is sold to the librarian community with the society's other journal, *Pedagogy in Health Promotion*, as a package. The journal supports the policies and recommendations for the Conduct, Reporting, Editing and Publication of Scholarly Work in Medical Journals of the International Committee of Medical Journal Editors (ICMJE), is a member of Committee of Publication Ethics (COPE), complies with ethical principles that are contained in the American Psychological Association Ethical Guidelines for Research with Human Subjects, applies the Declaration of Helsinki Ethical Principles for Medical Research Involving Human Subjects, and the Unified Code of Ethics for the Health Education Professionals.

J A M A: The Journal of the American Medical Association. See Medicine section.

4324. *Journal of Community Health: the publication for health promotion and disease prevention.* [ISSN: 0094-5145] 1975. bi-m. EUR 2243 (print & online eds.)). Ed(s): Pascal Imperato. Springer New York LLC, 233 Spring St, New York, NY 10013; customerservice@springer.com; http://www.springer.com. Adv. Sample. Refereed. Microform: PQC. Reprint: PSC. *Indexed:* A01, A22, AgeL, Agr, BRI, C45, Chicano, E01, SSA. *Bk. rev.:* Number and length vary. *Aud.:* Ac, Sa.

The Journal of Community Health is an open-access and global journal that features articles on projects that make a significant impact on the education of health personnel. Topics feature preventive medicine, new forms of health manpower, analysis of environmental factors, delivery of health care services, and the study of health maintenance and health insurance programs. Its audience are those interested in biotechnology, pharma, and public health. In it you will find a variety of study types including participatory research, questionnaires, interviews, and practice guidelines. Three recent original articles have been about health promotion and disease prevention, community and environmental psychology and ethics. It is a member of Committee of Publication Ethics (COPE).

Journal of Safety Research. See Safety section.

The Lancet. See Medicine section.

M M W R. See *Morbidity and Mortality Weekly Report (Online)* in the Government Periodicals—Federal section.

N I H Medline Plus. See Medicine section.

The New England Journal of Medicine. See Medicine section.

4325. *Public Health Reports.* Former titles (until 1974): *Health Services Report;* (until 1973): *H S M H A Health Reports;* (until 1971): *Public Health Reports;* (until 1896): *Abstract of Sanitary Reports;* (until 1890): *Weekly Abstract of Sanitary Reports;* (until 1887): *United States. Marine Hospital Service.;Bulletins of the Public Health;* Public Health Reports incorporated (1945-1951): *Journal of Venereal Disease Information;* Which was formerly (until 1945): *Venereal Disease Information;* (until 1922): *Abstracts from Recent Medical and Public Health Papers;* (1946-1951): *C D C Bulletin.* [ISSN: 0033-3549] 1878. bi-m. USD 635 (print & online eds.)). Ed(s): Frederic E Shaw. Sage Publications, Inc., 2455 Teller Rd, Thousand Oaks, CA 91320; info@sagepub.com; http://www.sagepub.com/. Illus., index, adv. Refereed. Vol. ends: Nov/Dec. Microform: CIS; PMC; PQC. Reprint: PSC. *Indexed:* A01, A22, Agr, BRI, C37, C45, Chicano, E01, S25. *Aud.:* Hs, Ga, Ac, Sa.

Public Health Reports, the journal, follows the history of the study and practice of public health in the United States. It was first published in 1878 as *Bulletins of the Public Health,* issued by the Supervising Surgeon General, United States Marine Health Service, under the National Quarantine Act of April 29, 1878. In 141 years of publication, it has had ten names that reflect the evolution of our understanding of public health in America, from the infectious diseases that arrived in port cities (served by Marine hospitals) to sanitation, venereal diseases, and now its more general present name. Since 1999, it has been a publication of the Association of Schools and Programs of Public Health. The peer-reviewed journal seeks to positively affect the health and wellness of the American public. A "Schools and Programs of Public Health" section is a forum for issues relevant to schools and programs of public health and a "Law and the Public's Health" column raises issues of high importance to public health policy and practice. Through the website, readers can earn Certified in Public Health continuing education credits. In addition, the journal publishes evaluations of public health programs and services, proceedings papers, describes new or proposed applications of epidemiologic or other scientific methods to public health problems, case studies of innovative public health program(s) and initiatives, brief reports of preliminary or exploratory results of original research, reports, and recommendations for public health policy or practice. Recent issue topics have included economic disparities and syphilis incidence in Massachusetts between 2001 and 2013, evaluation of diagnostic codes in morbidity and mortality data sources for heat-related illness surveillance, the structure of policy networks for injury and violence prevention in 15 U.S. cities, and legal authority for mosquito control and pesticide use in the United States. Electronic access to the current volume is available with a valid online subscription or other qualifying subscription. Issues from previous volumes are made available free of charge on PubMed Central and PHR Archives one year after the original publication date. *Public Health Reports* is available to researchers in developing countries from volume 116 (2001) to the present issue through the Research4Life HINARI program. URL: http://www.publichealthreports.org/

4326. *World Health Organization. Bulletin.* Incorporates (1980-1988): *World Health Forum;* Formed by the merger of (1937-1947): *League of Nations. Health Organization. Bulletin;* Which was formerly (1932-1936): *Health Organisation of the League of Nations. Quarterly Bulletin;* (1909-1947): *Office International d'Hygiene Publique. Bulletin Mensuel.* [ISSN: 0042-9686] 1947. m. CHF 331; USD 397.20. World Health Organization, Avenue Appia 20, Geneva, 1211, Switzerland; publications@who.int; http://www.who.int. Illus. Sample. Refereed. *Indexed:* A01, A22, BAS, BRI, C42, C45, IBSS, S25. *Bk. rev.:* Number and length vary. *Aud.:* Ac, Sa.

This is the flagship, peer-reviewed public health journal of the World Health Organization (WHO) with a special focus on developing countries, giving it unrivalled global scope and authority. It is essential reading for all public health decision-makers and researchers. Content includes research, well-informed opinions, news, systematic reviews, guidelines, book reviews, evaluation studies, case reports, and grey literature (conference papers and abstracts). *The Bulletin* is a fully open-access journal with no article-processing charges. The website has Arabic, Chinese, English, French, Russian, and Spanish content and is available in developing countries through Research4Life Hinari program. A recent issue included several review papers (i.e., health worker strikes in low-income countries); a systematic review about antibiotic resistance from a type of Enterobacteriaceae in pediatric patients; and a policy recommendation to support appropriate interventions to reduce the caesarean delivery rate in Mexico. The website provides downloads in multiple eReader formats. *The Bulletin* supports the policies and recommendations for the Conduct, Reporting, Editing and Publication of Scholarly Work in Medical Journals of the International Committee of Medical Journal Editors (ICMJE); and is a member of Committee of Publication Ethics (COPE).

■ REAL ESTATE

See also Architecture; Building and Construction; and Home sections.

Scott St. Martin, Reference Services Supervisor, New York University Libraries, New York, NY 10036; scott.stmartin@nyu.edu

Introduction

Real estate as a subject area can be equally intriguing and infuriating, as it entangles itself into many different disciplines, ranging from economics to public policy, from finance to the environment, or across property types, from housing to hospitality to retail to industrial. The periodical literature focusing on real estate consists mainly of trade publications and specialized academic journals.

Because real estate spans where we live and where we work, as well as where we shop, travel, or visit medical professionals, numerous publications exist within particular niches, both specific to geographies and property types. As such, libraries will need to be aware of the specialized interests of their audiences, especially in academic settings. Retail-focused collections should look to titles like *Shopping Centers Today,* whereas local publications like New York's *The Real Deal* will be less urgently needed outside of that market area.

A number of titles have moved entirely online in recent years, including the trade publication *Commercial Property Executive,* and the more academically focused title, *Real Estate Issues.* Other titles have scaled back publication frequency, in line with larger publishing trends, but also in the face of more readily available services that deliver email roundups of real estate reporting.

The publications listed here are representative of many different publications on the subject, and are appropriate for specialized collections in an academic or business library that supports the study of real estate. These titles cover real estate market analysis, economics, legal issues, taxation, and valuation. While a few titles in this section cover housing, many more journals exist on various aspects of housing construction and design, public policies and planning, mortgage markets and financing, and other housing-related topics.

Basic Periodicals

Ac, Sa: *National Real Estate Investor, Real Estate Economics, Real Estate Forum, Realtor Magazine.*

Basic Abstracts and Indexes

ABI/INFORM, Business Periodicals Index, Business Source Complete.

4327. *The Appraisal Journal.* Incorporates (in 1992): *The Real Estate Appraiser;* Which was formerly (until 1991): *The Real Estate Appraiser and Analyst;* (until 1978): *The Real Estate Appraiser;* (until 1963): *The Residential Appraiser;* (until 1956): *Society of Real Estate Appraisers. Review;* (until 1936): *Residential Appraisers' Review;* Formerly (until 1939): *American Institute of Real Estate Appraisers of the National Association of Real Estate Boards. Journal.* [ISSN: 0003-7087] 1932. q. USD 100 Free to members; (Non-members, USD 48). Ed(s): Nancy Bannon. Appraisal Institute, 200 W Madison, Ste 1500, Chicago, IL 60606; info@appraisalinstitute.org; http://www.appraisalinstitute.org. Illus., index, adv. Refereed. Circ: 21000. Vol. ends: Oct. *Indexed:* A22, ATI, B01, BLI, BRI, C42, H&TI. *Bk. rev.:* 1-3, 500-700 words. *Aud.:* Ac, Sa.

The Appraisal Institute, an international association of professional real estate appraisers, has published the *Appraisal Journal* since it was organized in 1932. This is a quarterly peer-reviewed journal written mostly by appraisal professionals, and each issue provides current news, research articles, and book reviews of interest to institute members, professional appraisers, and others engaged in the real estate industry, such as real estate attorneys and bankers. Strongly recommended for special and academic libraries with collections related to real estate and related subjects.

4328. *Building Operating Management.* Formerly (until 1969): *Building Maintenance and Modernization.* [ISSN: 0007-3490] 1954. m. Free. Ed(s): Naomi Millan, Edward Sullivan. Trade Press Publishing Corp., 2100 W Florist Ave, Milwaukee, WI 53209; info@tradepress.com; http://www.tradepress.com. Illus., index, adv. Circ: 73054. Vol. ends: Dec. *Indexed:* A22. *Aud.:* Ac, Sa.

Building Operating Management (BOM) serves as a leading trade publication for building owners and facilities executives, with monthly issues covering property management, technology, operation, design, and construction. With a focus on commercial and institutional real estate, including data centers and health care facilities, *BOM* contains many articles on sustainability and environmental issues, as well as coverage of specific building technologies related to security, roofing and flooring, HVAC, and more. Practical advice, in articles like "5 Steps on the Road to Smart Buildings," is clearly and plainly written for a wide audience of experts and readers new to facilities management. URL: www.facilitiesnet.com

4329. *Commercial Investment Real Estate.* Former titles (until 1999): *Commercial Investment Real Estate Journal;* (until 1986): *Commercial Investment Journal.* [ISSN: 1524-3249] 1982. bi-m. Free to members; Non-members, USD 45. Ed(s): Nicholas Leidere. C C I M Institute, 430 N Michigan Ave, Ste 800, Chicago, IL 60611; info@ccim.com; http://www.ccim.com. Illus., index, adv. Circ: 20546. *Indexed:* A22, B01. *Aud.:* Ac, Sa.

A trade publication published by the Certified Commercial Investment Members (CCIM) Institute, *Commercial Investment Real Estate* covers trends, forecasting, and important topics in the field. The CCIM designation is conferred on successful real estate professionals, and the institute is a recognized and influential professional organization. The core audience of the publication consists of CCIM members, and the articles discuss topics important to professionals working in brokerage, banking, property management, and real estate law, among other specialties. Regular columns cover specific property types and trending markets, as well as government policies and technological issues like blockchain and e-commerce impacts on retail. This title is strongly recommended for academic and special libraries.

4330. *Development (Herndon).* Formerly: *N A I O P News.* [ISSN: 0888-6067] 1969. q. USD 35. Ed(s): Jennifer LeFurgy. National Association of Industrial and Office Properties, 2355 Dulles Corner Blvd., Suite 750, Herndon, VA 20171; http://www.naiop.org. Adv. *Aud.:* Ac, Sa.

Published by the NAIOP, the Commercial Real Estate Development Association, *Development* is a trade publication with articles on broad trends and specific development cases in commercial real estate, including office, industrial, retail, and mixed-used properties. Most content is available free online, and the inexpensive quarterly print magazine contains articles covering government regulations, technology and sustainability, commercial tenant relations, and finance and investment problems and opportunities. NAIOP is both an advocacy and educational organization, and as such the magazine is a useful read for anyone interested in learning about the business of commercial real estate.

4331. *Journal of Corporate Real Estate.* [ISSN: 1463-001X] 1998. q. EUR 925 (print & online eds.) (excluding UK)). Ed(s): Chris Heywood, Rianne Appel-Meulenbroek. Emerald Publishing Limited, Howard House, Wagon Ln, Bingley, BD16 1WA, United Kingdom; emerald@emeraldinsight.com; http://www.emeraldinsight.com. Sample. Refereed. Reprint: PSC. *Indexed:* A22, B01, E01. *Aud.:* Ac, Sa.

The *Journal of Corporate Real Estate* is a peer-reviewed journal covering corporate real estate (CRE), a specialty focusing on property acquisition, operations, and disposal of workspaces. The articles are written by both academics and professionals, and contain both practical advice and comprehensive research on a number of issues important to the field, including strategic planning, portfolio management, productivity and workplace design, and finance and accounting. Subjects for recent articles include social network analysis, integrated workplace management systems, productivity, and efficiency. Clearly written and topical, articles both inform business practices and add to academic debates. This journal is recommended for academic and special libraries.

4332. *Journal of Housing Economics.* [ISSN: 1051-1377] 1991. q. EUR 1153. Ed(s): Henry O Pollakowski. Academic Press, 3251 Riverport Ln, Maryland Heights, MO 63043; JournalCustomerService-usa@elsevier.com; http://www.elsevier.com/. Adv. Sample. Refereed. *Indexed:* A01, A22, B01, E01, EconLit, IBSS. *Aud.:* Ac, Sa.

An academic, peer-reviewed publication, the *Journal of Housing Economics* provides articles on economic research related to housing. It encourages papers that bring to bear careful analytical technique on important housing-related questions, covering public policy, demographics, spatial modeling, and regulatory issues.

4333. *Journal of Housing Research.* [ISSN: 1052-7001] 1990. s-a. Individuals, USD 200; Free to members; USD 30 per issue. Ed(s): Kimberly Goodwin, Ken H Johnson. American Real Estate Society, Clemson University, 300 Sirrine Hall, Clemson, SC 29634; equarle@clemson.edu; http://www.aresnet.org. Illus., adv. Refereed. *Indexed:* A01, A22, EconLit, IBSS. *Aud.:* Ac, Sa.

This title is one of several published by the American Real Estate Society (ARES), and available free online to its members. The *Journal of Housing Research* publishes a handful of lengthy, well-researched articles in each semi-annual issue, covering topics such as housing economics, home financing and mortgage markets, quantitative price modeling, and international housing issues. This title is appropriate for academic libraries.

4334. *Journal of Property Management: the official publication of the Institute of Real Estate Management.* Incorporates: *Operating Techniques and Products Bulletin;* Former titles (until 1941): *Journal of Certified Property Managers;* (until 1938): *Journal of Real Estate Management.* [ISSN: 0022-3905] 1934. bi-m. USD 62.95 domestic; USD

72.32 Canada; USD 100.99 elsewhere. Institute of Real Estate Management, 430 N Michigan Ave, Chicago, IL 60611; custserv@irem.org; http://www.irem.org. Illus., index, adv. Sample. Circ: 23750 Paid and free. Vol. ends: Nov/Dec. *Indexed:* A22, B01, BRI. *Aud.:* Ac, Sa.

Published since 1934, this long-running trade publication from the Institute of Real Estate Management (IREM) provides comprehensive coverage of the real estate management industry. As a professional organization providing career development support and training, IREM publishes the journal to provide guidance to accredited members, and both young and veteran professionals working in property management. Most articles are concise and informative, with statistics and infographics interspersed throughout, covering industry trends, executive interviews, and case studies. Each issue contains featured articles on current topics, as well as regular columns on policy issues, technology, and the environment. With a growing focus on diversity and talent acquisition in the profession, the *Journal of Property Management* provides useful insights into the profession for all readers, and is recommended for academic and special libraries.

4335. *Journal of Real Estate Finance and Economics.* [ISSN: 0895-5638] 1988. 8x/yr. EUR 2119 (print & online eds.)). Ed(s): Steven R Grenadier, C F Sirmans. Springer New York LLC, 233 Spring St, New York, NY 10013; customerservice@springer.com; http://www.springer.com. Illus., adv. Sample. Refereed. Microform: PQC. Reprint: PSC. *Indexed:* A22, B01, BLI, E01, EconLit, IBSS. *Aud.:* Ac, Sa.

This is a scholarly, peer-reviewed journal created to publish empirical and theoretical research on real estate using the methodologies of finance and economics. The subject areas include urban economics, housing, and public policy. Recent articles look at the impact of public policies, environmental hazards, and educational performance on real estate prices. Complicated issues relating to capital markets, lender relations, and price modeling are regularly covered from an international perspective. Most authors are drawn from academia. This journal is best suited for academic or special libraries.

4336. *Journal of Real Estate Literature.* [ISSN: 0927-7544] 1993. s-a. Free to members. Ed(s): Mauricio Rodriguez, David M Harrison. Florida International University, Hollo School of Real Estate, 1101 Brickell Ave, Ste 1100S, Miami, FL 33131; msire@fiu.edu. Illus., index. Sample. Refereed. Microform: PQC. *Indexed:* A22, B01, BRI, E01, EconLit, IBSS. *Bk. rev.:* 1-2, 1,000-1,500 words, signed. *Aud.:* Ac, Sa.

The peer-reviewed *Journal of Real Estate Literature* is an official publication of the American Real Estate Society. It publishes research of interest to real estate academics and practitioners. Each issue contains articles that provide in-depth insights into trends and topical matters relating to real estate, such as recent articles that provide expansive literature reviews on the impact of big data on real estate investment, and broad trends in the hospitality and lodging industries. The *Journal of Real Estate Literature* publishes rankings of Real Estate Academic Leadership (REAL), assessing academic contributions to real estate research. Like other ARES titles, this is an important title for academic and special libraries supporting real estate programs.

4337. *The Journal of Real Estate Portfolio Management.* [ISSN: 1083-5547] 1995. q. Individuals, USD 300; Free to members; USD 30 per issue. Ed(s): Peng Liu, Simon Stevenson. American Real Estate Society, Clemson University, 300 Sirrine Hall, Clemson, SC 29634; equarle@clemson.edu; http://www.aresnet.org. Illus., adv. Refereed. *Indexed:* A22, B01, EconLit, IBSS. *Aud.:* Ac, Sa.

This journal, published by the American Real Estate Society, presents peer-reviewed academic articles covering topics that include real estate investment, risk analysis, asset allocation, and acquisitions. Recent articles focus on institutional real estate, with research on REITs (Real Estate Investment Trusts) and investment funds holding large portfolios. As an academic publication with a focus on financial analysis and complex business decision-making, this publication is intended for a specific audience, and would be useful for academic and special libraries supporting business and finance research.

4338. *Journal of Real Estate Practice and Education.* [ISSN: 1521-4842] 1998. s-a. Individuals, USD 200; Free to members; USD 30 per issue. American Real Estate Society, Clemson University, 300 Sirrine Hall, Clemson, SC 29634; equarle@clemson.edu; http://www.aresnet.org. Refereed. *Indexed:* ATI, EconLit. *Aud.:* Ac, Sa.

This academic journal, one of six published by the American Real Estate Society (ARES), aims to combine insights from practicing professionals with educators and academic researchers. International in scope, the journal publishes a small number of in-depth articles in each issue, covering a wide range of topics related to real estate education, including real estate licensing, trends in higher education, and broader issues and trends impacting the teaching and practice of real estate. This title is recommended for academic libraries supporting real estate programs.

4339. *Journal of Real Estate Research.* [ISSN: 0896-5803] 1986. q. Ed(s): Ko Wang. American Real Estate Society, Clemson University, 300 Sirrine Hall, Clemson, SC 29634; equarle@clemson.edu; http://www.aresnet.org. Adv. Refereed. *Indexed:* A22, B01, EconLit, IBSS. *Aud.:* Ac, Sa.

The *Journal of Real Estate Research* is the flagship publication of the American Real Estate Society (ARES), dedicated to providing "insights in real estate for practitioners and academics alike." Topic covered include real estate development, finance, management, and market analysis, and each quarterly issue contains a small number of lengthy, peer-reviewed articles that contain detailed financial calculations, statistical analysis, and maps, charts, and other graphics. Recent articles cover uncertainty in real estate and macroeconomic forecasting, the impact of artificial neural networks on property value prediction, and real estate negotiations and behavioral economics. Free for ARES members, this journal is available to non-members as a stand-alone subscription or can be bundled with other ARES titles. Tables of contents and abstracts are available free online. Highly recommended for academic libraries.

4340. *Journal of Sustainable Real Estate.* [ISSN: 1949-8276] 2009. a. USD 30 per issue. Ed(s): Amelia S Caldwell, Robert A Simons. American Real Estate Society, c/o Diane Quarles, Clemson University, PO Box 341323, Clemson, SC 29634; equarle@clemson.edu; http://www.aresnet.org. Refereed. *Indexed:* EconLit. *Aud.:* Ac, Sa.

Published annually by the American Real Estate Society (ARES) since 2009, the *Journal of Sustainable Real Estate* aims to publish peer-reviewed research on sustainability, green building, energy efficiency, productivity, and healthier buildings. Recent articles cover topics that include green rent premiums in commercial real estate, impacts of environmental disasters on pricing, and tax incentives and other policy initiatives for greening real estate and new developments. While many other publications focus on green building from a construction or design perspective, this journal looks at sustainability from a real estate practitioner perspective, with articles authored by owners, managers, investors, and developers.

4341. *National Real Estate Investor.* [ISSN: 0027-9994] 1958. m. plus a. Directory. USD 59 domestic (Free to qualified personnel). Ed(s): David Bodamer. Penton, 6190 Powers Ferry Rd, Ste 320, Atlanta, GA 30339; information@penton.com; http://www.penton.com. Illus., index, adv. Circ: 33708. Vol. ends: Dec. Microform: PQC. *Indexed:* A22, B01, BRI. *Aud.:* Ac, Sa.

National Real Estate Investor is a long-running and popular trade publication containing insights on real estate news, trends, and significant topics. Most articles are brief and easily digestible, and infographics and data visualizations are found throughout every issue. Each issue contains columns on standard property types, such as office, industrial, retail, hotel, and multifamily, as well as less common topics like medical offices, modular construction, and regulatory concerns. Print issues have slimmed down in recent years, but much of the content is also available free online. A number of annual lists, surveys, and outlooks are popular among industry professionals, making this publication a highly recommended one for all libraries where real estate is of interest.

4342. *Real Estate Economics.* Former titles (until 1995): *American Real Estate and Urban Economics Association. Journal;* (until 1988): *A R E U A Journal;* (until 1977): *American Real Estate and Urban Economics Association. Journal.* [ISSN: 1080-8620] 1973. q. GBP 612. Ed(s): Brent W Ambrose, Sumit Agarwal. Wiley-Blackwell Publishing, Inc., 111 River St, Hoboken, NJ 07030; http://onlinelibrary.wiley.com. Illus., index, adv. Sample. Refereed. Vol. ends: Winter. Microform: PQC. *Indexed:* A22, B01, BRI, E01, EconLit. *Aud.:* Ac, Sa.

As the official journal of the American Real Estate and Urban Economics Association, this scholarly journal covers a broad range of real estate topics, including corporate real estate, housing and urban economics, and financial issues surrounding development and investment. Articles in this journal are well-researched, and targeted toward an audience of academics or well-versed professionals. While many articles are either theoretical or analytical, covering legal or economic topics at length, there are also more practical articles on mortgage markets, leasing concerns, corporate relocation decisions, and risk assessment.

4343. *Real Estate Forum.* Incorporates (2002-2004): *Real Estate Mid-America.* [ISSN: 0034-0707] 1946. 8x/yr. Ed(s): Natalie Dolce. A L M Media Properties, LLC, 120 Broadway, Fl 5, New York, NY 10271; https://www.alm.com. Illus., adv. Vol. ends: Dec. *Aud.:* Ac, Sa.

Published since 1946, *Real Estate Forum* is a well-regarded trade publication with insightful articles on the commercial real estate industry. With a focus on practical applications and applied theory, this journal regularly covers major property types and markets, as well as keeping up with new and emerging topics in the industry. Many articles are written by executives and analysts working at significant national firms, combined with in-house articles providing overviews of major transactions and developments. Special issues cover retail, leadership, REITs, and more, including profiles of prominent businesses and executives, and regular columns cover capital markets, corporate leadership, and regulatory issues. Issues feature property-sector and geographic market reports as well as company profiles, interviews with real estate leaders, and reader surveys on various issues impacting the industry. Highly recommended for libraries with commercial real estate collections.

4344. *Real Estate Investment Today.* Former titles (until 2010): *Real Estate Portfolio;* (until 1999): *The R E I T Report;* Which was formed by the 1981 merger of: *R E I T Industry Monthly Review; R E I T Industry Investment Review; Trustee; What If; N A R E I T Clippings.* [ISSN: 2159-1849] 1981. bi-m. Free to members. National Association of Real Estate Investment Trusts, Inc., 1875 I St, NW, Ste 600, Washington, DC 20006; http://www.reit.com. Adv. *Aud.:* Ac, Sa.

Real Estate Investment Today, also known as *REIT Magazine,* is published by the National Association of Real Estate Investment Trusts (NAREIT), a large trade association representing and advocating for its institutional members. The trade journal covers economic issues and regulatory concerns impacting REITs, as well as more general real estate investment and capital markets. Each issue contains profiles of REITs and their executives, as well as statistical analyses of the REIT markets. These "By the Numbers" columns are a snapshot of the larger data and reporting available on the NAREIT website, and while some reporting is restricted to members, much of the website content, including the archived and current issues of this magazine, are publicly available for free. The print magazine is also available free upon request, and is recommended for academic and special libraries, especially those supporting finance programs or researchers interested in REITs and institutional real estate.

4345. *Real Estate Law Journal.* [ISSN: 0048-6868] 1972. q. USD 1668 base vol(s).). Thomson West, 610 Opperman Dr, Eagan, MN 55123; west.customer.service@thomson.com; http://legalsolutions.thomsonreuters.com. Microform: PQC. *Indexed:* A22, BLI, BRI, C42, L14. *Aud.:* Ac, Sa.

This journal presents articles written by practicing real estate attorneys, tax professionals, and academics, covering real estate law, as well as financial and business topics. Some articles cover international legal matters, and each issue contains several longer, topical articles paired with regular columns. The columns regularly cover recent cases, tax law, environmental issues, and zoning and land use planning. For law libraries with real estate practitioners, this could be a useful title. Academic and special libraries outside of law schools or private firms might consider less expensive alternatives that cover legal issues and public policy concerns.

4346. *Real Estate Review.* [ISSN: 0034-0790] 1971. q. USD 996. Thomson West, 610 Opperman Dr, Eagan, MN 55123; west.customer.service@thomson.com; http://legalsolutions.thomsonreuters.com. Illus., index, adv. Circ: 7000 Paid. Microform: PQC. *Indexed:* A22, ATI, B01, BLI, BRI, C42. *Aud.:* Ac, Sa.

Published since 1971, *Real Estate Review* addresses real estate development from many different perspectives, from legal and regulatory issues to planning and finance topics. Articles are typically authored by a combination of academic scholars and legal professionals, with each print issue presenting a fairly small number of in-depth articles on real estate trends, taxation, technology, and more. Recent topics covered include conservation easements, opportunity zones, blockchain technology, contemporary real estate investment strategies, and economic impacts of tax reform.

4347. *Real Estate Taxation.* Formerly (until 2001): *Journal of Real Estate Taxation.* [ISSN: 1538-3792] 1973. 1 Base Vol(s) q. USD 275; USD 335; USD 435 combined subscription (print & online eds.)). Ed(s): Paul D Carman, Robert J Murdich. R I A, PO Box 6159, Carol Stream, IL 60197; ria@thomson.com; http://ria.thomsonreuters.com. Adv. Microform: PQC. *Indexed:* A22, ATI, BRI, C42, L14. *Aud.:* Ac, Sa.

This trade publication from Thomson Reuters covers tax planning, estate issues, leasing, and more, with articles written by attorneys, legal professionals, accountants, and other real estate experts. A wide range of topics can be found throughout the course of each year's quarterly issues, ranging from real estate taxation, partnerships, development, and depreciation. Each issue contains articles on current topics, as well as editorial statements and columns that address recent cases or updates to tax law or regulatory concerns.

4348. *Realtor Magazine.* Former titles (until 1998): *Today's Realtor;* (until 1996): *Real Estate Today;* Which incorporated (in 1968): *Realtor Reviews.* [ISSN: 1522-0842] 1968. m. Free to members; Non-members, USD 56. Ed(s): Stacey Moncrieff, Wendy Cole. National Association of Realtors (Chicago), 430 N Michigan Ave, Chicago, IL 60611; narpubs@realtors.org; http://www.realtor.org. Illus., adv. Sample. Microform: PQC. *Indexed:* A22, B01, BRI. *Aud.:* Ac, Sa.

Realtor Magazine is the flagship publication of the National Association of Realtors (NAR), a leading trade association for over a million real estate professionals, including brokers, salespeople, appraisers, managers, and others. Articles are concise and often conversational, aimed at both educating members on trends and best practices, as well as informing a wider audience of insights into real estate practices and strategies. While every issue contains articles on topics related to homeownership and the housing market, there are columns discussing technology trends, regulatory issues, and both legal and economic concerns. Because NAR is an advocate for its members, issues often include interviews and provide lists of prominent or accomplished professionals. With useful statistical charts and infographics, and promotional materials for new tools and services, this trade journal is recommended for all libraries serving users interested in real estate and housing issues.

4349. *S I O R Report.* Former titles (until 2016): *Society of Industrial and Office Realtors. Professional Report;* (until 1992): *Professional Report of Industrial and Office Real Estate;* (until 1991): *S I O R Reports;* (until 198?): *S I R Reports.* [ISSN: 2472-3436] 19??. q. Free to members; Non-members, USD 45. Ed(s): Tom McCormick, Courtney Williams. Society of Industrial and Office Realtors, 1201 New York Ave NW, Ste 350, Washington, DC 20005; admin@sior.com; http://www.sior.com. Adv. *Aud.:* Ac, Sa.

SIOR Report is a trade journal published by the Society of Industrial and Office Realtors, the commercial and industrial real estate professionals group affiliated with the larger National Association of Realtors. As such, this quarterly publication covers commercial real estate concerns, with many articles written by practicing professional members. Given the specialization of this professional organization, the articles cover topics such as technology's impact on real estate asset and portfolio management, logistics and infrastructure, and leasing and negotiations, among others. There are also profiles of members and companies, as well as highlighted transactions and deals. Special issues entirely dedicated to topics like coworking and evolving tenant demands highlight current concerns for the profession. The print magazine is affordable and the online version provides free access to many articles. It is a recommended title for academic libraries supporting real estate programs focused on commercial real estate.

■ RELIGION

Stephen Bales, Humanities and Social Sciences Librarian, Evans Library, Texas A & M University, College Station, TX 77843; sbales@library.tamu.edu

Introduction

Whether one believes in the existence of a god or gods or not, one must acknowledge that religion is a fundamental aspect of human social existence. Every culture maintains its own beliefs and traditions—and sometimes exports them, resulting in a dialectical process of cultural communication and transformation. It is no surprise, therefore, that the periodical literature relating to religion and spirituality is quite extensive. There are many thousands of serial publications currently in print and more publications appearing, or falling by the wayside, every day.

The popular magazines, newspapers, and scholarly academic journals presented in this section of *Magazines for Libraries* cover a wide range of religious and spiritual ideologies, organizations, concepts, and phenomena. While publications devoted to the Abrahamic religions, e.g., *Studies in World Christianity, Modern Judaism*, and *Muslim World*, are well represented, so are the eastern religions, e.g., *International Journal of Hindu Studies, Lion's Roar* (Buddhism), and *The Empty Vessel* (Taoism). Also reviewed are publications that take a disciplinary, interdisciplinary, or cross-disciplinary approach to the examination of religion, whether it be of a particular religious tradition or of religion more broadly conceived, such as *Sociology of Religion* and the *Journal of Religious Ethics*.

The revolution in digital technology has resulted in a spike in the number of religion-related magazines and journals, owing to the creation of the World Wide Web and the ease of publication that the new electronic formats allow. These advances in modern technologies have also led to new possibilities for information distribution, resulting in a radical increase in interreligious and cross-cultural idea sharing and dialogue. Upon browsing the 76 entries that follow, one will notice that for many of these publications, print versions, when they exist, seem almost vestigial (which is somewhat ironic when one considers the cache that many religions place in the printed word qua spiritual artefact). More and more religion-related materials are born digital. Beyond the obvious advantages that this increased accessibility provides are the benefits that digital publications bring in terms of services that only the web can provide. These value-added features may include easily updatable news feeds and social networking capabilities. The rapid expansion in number of open-access journals has also been a boon to libraries and other information institutions, particularly those with limited budgets for subscriptions. Some religion publications, such as the *Japanese Journal of Religious Studies* and *Methodist Review* are completely free online, while others like *The Journal of the Evangelical Theological Society* might not make the current issue free, but provide open access to much (or all) of their archives. Such a transformation of how we perceive and use religion-related literature is snowballing, making these exciting times for study and scholarship.

Basic Periodicals

America, American Academy of Religion. Journal, Church History, The Humanist, Journal of Biblical Literature, Journal of Ecclesiastical History, The Journal of Religion, Journal of Theological Studies, Muslim World, Religious Studies Review, Theology Today.

Basic Abstracts and Indexes

ATLA Religion Index, Catholic Periodical and Literature Index, New Testament Abstracts, Old Testament Abstracts.

4350. *America: the Jesuit review.* Former titles (until 1909): *The Messenger;* (until 1902): *The Messenger of the Sacred Heart of Jesus.* [ISSN: 0002-7049] 1866. w. USD 60 domestic; USD 75 Canada; USD 125 elsewhere. Ed(s): Matt Malone. America Press Inc., 1212 Sixth Ave, 11th Fl, New York, NY 10036. Illus., index, adv. Sample. Vol. ends: Jun/Dec. Microform: PQC. *Indexed:* A01, A22, AmHI, BAS, BRI, C26, C37, CBRI, Chicano, F01, MASUSE, MLA-IB. *Bk. rev.:* 2-3, 1,000-1,300 words; signed. *Aud.:* Ga, Ac.

America is a weekly news and opinion magazine and one of the largest Catholic print publications in the United States. Each issue contains editorials that center on faith and politics, political dispatches, analyses of culture, media, and art, and original poetry. Media and book reviews are also included in every issue. The magazine's website offers news on politics & society, faith, and arts & culture, as well as opinion pieces by regular bloggers, as well as opportunities for social networking. The website also provides free access to articles found in current and previous issues of the print edition, with subscriptions providing access to additional, web only content. This consumer magazine is recommended for public libraries that serve Catholic communities. URL: https://www.americamagazine.org/.

4351. *American Academy of Religion. Journal.* Former titles (until 1967): *Journal of Bible and Religion;* (until 1937): *National Association of Biblical Instructors. Journal;* Supersedes in part (in 1933): *Christian Education;* Which was formerly (until 1919): *American College. Bulletin.* [ISSN: 0002-7189] 1918. q. EUR 293. Ed(s): Cynthia Eller. Oxford University Press, 2001 Evans Rd, Cary, NC 27513; orders.us@oup.com; https://academic.oup.com/journals. Illus., index, adv. Sample. Refereed. Vol. ends: Winter. Microform: PQC. Reprint: PSC. *Indexed:* A01, A22, AmHI, BAS, BRI, CBRI, E01, MLA-IB, P61, R&TA, SSA. *Bk. rev.:* 15-20, 900-2,000 words; signed. *Aud.:* Ac.

Anglican Theological Review is a peer-reviewed academic journal that serves as a forum for the discussion of Anglican and Episcopalian theology, history, culture, art, and literature. Each issue includes research articles, those that report on praxis, and poetry. There are also two types of book reviews included, "Reviews in Depth," which are critical and scholarly articles that are often heavily footnoted, as well as shorter book reviews. The journal's webpage provides a searchable index to every issue published since it began in 1918. The site also provides a "Conversations" page that gives free, full-text access to a number of important articles from previous issues in categories such as "Anglican Women at Prayer," "Leadership and the Church Today," and "Homosexuality, Ethics, and the Church." Recommended for those libraries, both public and academic, that support Anglican or Episcopal church communities as well as seminary libraries. URL: http://anglicantheologicalreview.org/

4352. *American Baptist Quarterly.* Formerly (until 1982): *Foundations;* Which superseded (in 1958): *Chronicle.* [ISSN: 0745-3698] 1938. q. USD 50 domestic; USD 66 foreign; USD 15 per issue domestic. Ed(s): Deborah Van Broekhoven, Curtin Freeman. American Baptist Historical Society, 3001 Mercer University Dr, Atlanta, GA 30341; http://abhsarchives.org. Illus., index. Sample. Refereed. Microform: PQC. *Indexed:* A22, R&TA. *Bk. rev.:* 0-1, 500-1,400 words; signed. *Aud.:* Ga, Ac, Sa.

This refereed publication of the American Baptist Historical Society publishes themed issues that consider the history and culture of the American Baptist church from historical perspectives. Recent issues have focused on the topics "Baptists and Conscience," "John Bunyan and the Baptist Academy," and "Baptists and American Culture." Academics, clergy members, and general readers will all find this journal to be accessible and informative. Recommended for church libraries, public libraries that serve Baptist communities, and academic libraries that serve Baptist communities and/or build their collections to support programs in history or religious studies.

4353. *American Journal of Theology & Philosophy.* [ISSN: 0194-3448] 1980. 3x/yr. USD 129 (print & online eds.)). Ed(s): Michael S. Hogue. University of Illinois Press, 1325 S Oak St, MC-566, Champaign, IL 61820; uipress@uillinois.edu; http://www.press.uillinois.edu. Adv. Refereed. *Indexed:* A22, BRI, E01, R&TA. *Bk. rev.:* 1 or more, 150-500; signed. *Aud.:* Ac, Sa.

According to its editors, this journal is "a forum for discussions in the following areas: 1) the interface between theology and philosophy, especially as shaped by American empiricist, naturalist, process, and pragmatist tradition; 2) the development of liberal religious thought in America." Issues are published thrice yearly and articles apply the thought of important philosophers like Rawls, Peirce, and Kant. While the articles explore deeply theoretical issues such as metaphysics and ontology, many are of timely concern, with recent articles treating issues like climate change and cross-cultural understanding. Issues are also occasionally themed, with subjects such as "global politics." There are approximately five books reviewed per issue. Recommended for academic libraries, particularly those that support research and study in religious studies, theology, and/or philosophy.

4354. *Anglican Theological Review.* [ISSN: 0003-3286] 1918. q. USD 65 (Individuals, USD 45). Ed(s): Ellen K Wondra, Jacqueline B Winter. Anglican Theological Review, Inc., 8765 W Higgins Rd, Ste 650, Chicago, IL 60631. Illus., index, adv. Sample. Refereed. Vol. ends: No. 4. Microform: PQC. *Indexed:* A01, A22, AmHI, MLA-IB, R&TA. *Bk. rev.:* 25-30, 600-1,400 words; signed. *Aud.:* Ac, Sa.

The *Anglican Theological Review* is a quarterly journal devoted to exploring the theology of the Anglican Church. Articles include both research papers and "Practicing Theology" papers that deal with the application of belief. Poetry is also included, as are multiple book reviews (often more than 20 per issue). Sample articles are available on the journal's website. Recommended for academic libraries and particularly those libraries that serve programs in divinity and/or theology. URL: http://anglicantheologicalreview.org/

4355. *Baptist History and Heritage.* [ISSN: 0005-5719] 1965. 3x/yr. Free to members. Ed(s): Bruce T Gourley. Baptist History & Heritage Society, 151 Braodleaf Dr, Macon, GA 31210; bhhs@baptisthistory.org; http://www.baptisthistory.org. Illus., index, adv. Refereed. Vol. ends: Oct. *Indexed:* A22, BRI, R&TA. *Bk. rev.:* 3, 250-300 words; signed. *Aud.:* Ga, Ac.

A publication of the Baptist History & Heritage Society, this scholarly journal includes around six articles per issue that all consider a common theme such as "Modern Baptists in Thought and Action," "Baptists on the Margins: Minorities, Borders and Controversies," and "Faith, Freedom, Forgiveness: Religion and the Civil War, Emancipation and Reconciliation in Our Time." Frequently issues are festschrifts dedicated to notable scholars in the field. Recommended for academic library history and religious studies collections.

4356. *The Bible Today.* [ISSN: 0006-0836] 1962. bi-m. USD 44 domestic (print & online eds.); USD 61.95 Canada (print & online eds.); USD 59 elsewhere (print & online eds.)). Ed(s): Linda M Maloney, Rev. Donald Senior. Liturgical Press, 2950 Saint John's Rd, P O Box 7500, Collegeville, MN 56321. Illus., index, adv. Sample. Vol. ends: Nov. Microform: PQC. *Indexed:* A01, A22, C26. *Bk. rev.:* 35-40, 50-200 words; signed. *Aud.:* Ga, Ac.

This Roman Catholic journal covers a lot of ground, looking at scripture through many different vantage points, including the historical, archaeological, theological, and literary. Articles are illustrated with photographs and artwork. In addition to the essays and research articles are multiple (25+) short book reviews, as well as announcements. Scholars, clergy, and interested laypeople will all find something here. Also, readers outside of the Catholic Church will find that this journal contains valuable information concerning the Bible and other documents of the early Christian church. Recommended for church, public, and academic libraries.

Biblical Archaeology Review. See Archaeology section.

4357. *B'nai B'rith Magazine.* Former titles (until 2003): *The B'nai B'rith I J M;* (until 2001): *The B'nai B'rith International Jewish Monthly;* (until 1981): *The National Jewish Monthly;* (until 1939): *B'nai B'rith National Jewish Monthly;* (until 1934): *B'nai B'rith Magazine;* (until 1924): *B'nai B'rith News.* [ISSN: 1549-4799] 1886. q. Free to members. Ed(s): Eugene L Meyer. B'nai B'rith International, 1120 20th St NW, Ste 300 N, Washington, DC 20036; info@bnaibrith.org; http://www.bnaibrith.org. Illus., index, adv. Vol. ends: Jun/Jul. *Indexed:* A22. *Aud.:* Ga, Ac.

B'nai B'rith Magazine is a long-lived (founded in 1886) consumer magazine dedicated to reporting on Jewish culture, history, and religion from an international perspective. Each full-color quarterly contains approximately four feature articles, with recent articles focusing on topics like social media, the history of Jewish immigration to the USA, and Jewish intermarriage with other faiths. There are also regular departments that deal with issues of importance to Jewish senior citizens, planned giving, and the activities of the sponsoring organization, B'nai B'rith International. The magazine's website provides free access to a digital version of the magazine from 2009 to the present, as well as free digital-only content. Recommended for synagogue libraries and public libraries that support Jewish communities. URL: http://www.bnaibrith.org/bnai-brith-magazine.html

4358. *Buddhist - Christian Studies.* [ISSN: 0882-0945] 1981. a. USD 60 (Individuals, USD 30). Ed(s): Carol Anderson. University of Hawai'i Press, 2840 Kolowalu St, Honolulu, HI 96822; uhpjourn@hawaii.edu; http://www.uhpress.hawaii.edu. Illus., adv. Sample. Refereed. *Indexed:* A01, A22, AmHI, BRI, E01, R&TA. *Bk. rev.:* 10-15, 800-1,000; signed. *Aud.:* Ac, Sa.

Buddhism and Christianity share a long history of cultural and theoretical exchange, dialogue, and sometimes conflict. The articles in *Buddhist-Christian Studies* attempt to account for this history while pointing to the future. The journal, published annually, collects writing organized around several broad thematic areas, e.g., "Old Buddhist Texts: New Womanist Thought," "Liberation Theology and Engaged Buddhism," and "Comparative Theology." In addition to the approximately 200 pages of research articles and essays is a "News and Views" section and several in-depth book reviews. For scholars of Christianity, scholars of Buddhism, and scholars of comparative religion. Recommended for academic libraries.

4359. *C C A R Journal: the reform Jewish quarterly.* Former titles (until 1991): *Journal of Reform Judaism;* (until 1978): *C C A R Journal.* [ISSN: 1058-8760] 1953. s-a. Free to members; Non-members, USD 125. C C A R Press, PO Box 418185, Boston, MA 02241; ccarpress@ccarnet.org; http://www.ccarnet.org. Illus., adv. Vol. ends: Spring. Microform: PQC. *Indexed:* A22, R&TA. *Bk. rev.:* 3-4, 800-1,200 words; signed. *Aud.:* Ga, Ac, Sa.

CCAR Journal has been published by the Central Conference of American Rabbis since 1953. Focusing on reform Judaism, each biannual issue contains essays that cluster around broad thematic areas, some of which reappear semi-regularly, such as "On Being a Rabbi." Often primary source material and poetry is also included, as well as occasional book reviews. This is an important resource for Jewish studies scholars as well as rabbis. Recommended for academic and synagogue libraries.

4360. *Catholic Biblical Quarterly.* [ISSN: 0008-7912] 1939. q. USD 75. Ed(s): Leslie J Hoppe. Catholic University of America Press, 620 Michigan Ave NE, Washington, DC 20064; jrnlcirc@press.jhu.edu; http://cuapress.cua.edu. Illus., index, adv. Refereed. Vol. ends: Oct. *Indexed:* A01, A22, AmHI, BRI, C26, MLA-IB, R&TA. *Bk. rev.:* 60-65, 400-1,100 words; signed. *Aud.:* Ac, Sa.

Published by the Catholic Biblical Association of America, the *Catholic Biblical Quarterly* is of great value to biblical scholars, theologians, and historians. It includes Old and New Testament biblical exegesis, with articles focusing on particular scripture, e.g., "Mad" Rhoda in Acts 12:12-17: Disciple Exemplar," "A Narrative Analysis of the Baptist's Nativity in Luke 1," or engaging with broader concepts or phenomena in the biblical and classical literature and history, e.g., "Banquet Ceremonies Involving Wine in the Greco-Roman World and Early Christianity." There are multiple book reviews provided in every issue (sometimes 25 or more). Recommended for academic libraries.

4361. *The Christian Century: thinking critically. living faithfully.* Incorporates (1918-1934): *The World Tomorrow;* (in 1926): *The Christian Work;* Which was formerly (until 1914): *Christian Work and the Evangelist;* Which superseded in part (in 1909): *The Arena.* [ISSN: 0009-5281] 1886. bi-w. USD 49.95 combined subscription (print & online eds.)). Christian Century Foundation, 104 S Michigan Ave, Ste 1100, Chicago, IL 60603; letters@christiancentury.org; http://www.christiancentury.org. Illus., index, adv. Vol. ends: Dec. Microform: NBI; PQC. *Indexed:* A01, A22, AmHI, BAS, BRI, C37, CBRI, F01, MASUSE, MLA-IB, R&TA. *Bk. rev.:* 1-3, 1,000-3,000 words; signed. *Aud.:* Ga.

Starting in 1886 as *The Arena*, *Christian Century* is one of the oldest mass market consumer Christian magazines aimed at mainstream American Christians. Articles investigate issues relating to theology, community, culture, health, and a host of other issues of interest to the lay reader. The editorials and columns leans toward progressive viewpoints. Also included is current news, media and art reviews, and poetry. The magazine's website provides free access to a limited number of articles (both current and archived), with paid subscribers receiving unlimited access. The website also includes freely accessible (no subscription required) blog posts, news stories, and reviews. This magazine is recommended for all libraries. URL: https://www.christiancentury.org/

4362. *Christianity and Literature.* Former titles (until 1973): *Conference on Christianity and Literature. Newsletter;* (until 1956): *Christian Teachers of College English. Newsletter.* [ISSN: 0148-3331] 1951. q. USD 247 (print & online eds.)). Ed(s): Mark Eaton. The Johns Hopkins University Press, 2715 N Charles St, Baltimore, MD 21218; webmaster@jhupress.jhu.edu; http://www.press.jhu.edu. Illus., adv. Sample. Refereed. Vol. ends: Summer (No. 4). Reprint: PSC. *Indexed:* A01, A22, AmHI, BRI, MLA-IB, R&TA. *Bk. rev.:* 9-12, 1,200-2,500 words; signed. *Aud.:* Ga, Ac, Sa.

Published by the Conference on Christianity & Literature, this quarterly journal investigates Christian themes in literature. Research articles tend to focus (but not always) on modern prose and poetry, and many concern the work of renowned authors such as Flannery O'Connor, A.S. Byatt, and Federico Garcia Lorca. Occasional special issues are devoted to the work of a single author, form, or genre. Every issue contains original poetry, announcements, and multiple book reviews. This journal is recommended for academic libraries that support programs in religious studies and/or language and literature.

4363. *Christianity Today.* Incorporates (1997-200?): *Christianity Online;* Which was formerly (1997-1999): *Computing Today.* [ISSN: 0009-5753] 1956. m. USD 24.99 combined subscription (print & online eds.)). Ed(s): Mark Galli. Christianity Today International, 465 Gundersen Dr, Carol Stream, IL 60188; http://www.christianitytoday.com. Illus., index, adv. Circ: 140000. Vol. ends: Dec. Microform: PQC. *Indexed:* A01, A22, BAS, BRI, C37, C42, CBRI, Chicano, F01, MASUSE, MLA-IB, R&TA. *Bk. rev.:* 5-6, 600-1,000 words; signed. *Aud.:* Ga.

Evangelist minister Billy Graham started *Christianity Today* in 1956, and today it is one of the most widely circulated Christian consumer magazines. Coming out monthly, each issue contains news and opinions relating to areas of interest to evangelical Christians, as well as feature articles. Recent articles have covered a diverse range of topics including Christian activism, child rearing, and the persecution of Indian Christians. There are also personal testimonies and essays discussing biblical questions. Every issue contains several book reviews. The *Christianity Today* website provides unique web content, full-text access to select articles for non-subscribers, and full access to all digital content for subscribers. Academic and public libraries will both want subscriptions, and particularly those libraries serving communities of evangelist Christians. URL: http://www.christianitytoday.org/

4364. *Church History: studies in Christianity and culture.* [ISSN: 0009-6407] 1932. q. GBP 188. Ed(s): Amanda Porterfield, John Corrigan. Cambridge University Press, University Printing House, Shaftesbury Rd, Cambridge, CB2 8BS, United Kingdom; journals@cambridge.org; https://www.cambridge.org/. Illus., index, adv. Refereed. Circ: 3400. Vol. ends: Dec. Reprint: PSC. *Indexed:* A01, A22, AmHI, BRI, CBRI, E01, MLA-IB, R&TA. *Bk. rev.:* 30-50, 250-1,200 words; signed. *Aud.:* Ac, Sa.

This quarterly academic journal collects historical research on the Christian Church from its early beginnings to the present day. Both Catholic and Protestant denominations are considered. One recent issue displays this breadth of historical coverage with articles about Catholicism in early America, cloistered life in the tenth century, and rock 'n roll and Pentecostalism. Readers will find this to be a useful resource not only for research religious history, but also for situating that history within a larger historical narrative. There are multiple book reviews, sometimes in excess of 30 in an issue. Religion, history, and cultural studies scholars will all find something of value here, but the articles are also accessible to the educated lay reader. Highly recommended for academic libraries that support history and/or religion collections.

Commentary. See News and Opinion section.

4365. *Commonweal: a review of religion, politics & culture.* [ISSN: 0010-3330] 1924. 20x/yr. USD 65 combined subscription domestic (print & online eds.); USD 70 combined subscription Canada (print & online eds.); USD 75 combined subscription elsewhere (print & online eds.)). Commonweal Foundation, 475 Riverside Dr, Rm 405, New York, NY 10115; commonwealads@gmail.com; http://www.commonwealmagazine.org. Illus., index, adv. Microform: MIM; PMC; PQC. *Indexed:* A01, A22, BAS, BRI, C26, C37, CBRI, F01, MASUSE, MLA-IB. *Bk. rev.:* 3-4, 900-1,900 words; signed. *Aud.:* Ga.

Founded in 1924, *Commonweal* is a progressive Catholic magazine, published 20 times a year, that contains opinion, essays, articles, book and media reviews, and poetry. The essays and articles relate faith to a variety of issues, including politics, history, culture, and literature. The magazine's website offers additional news and opinion free, as well as networking tools for finding *Commonweal* reading groups. This magazine is recommended for public and academic libraries that support Roman Catholic communities. URL: https://www.commonwealmagazine.org/

4366. *Cross Currents (New York).* Incorporates (1983-1990): *Religion and Intellectual Life;* Which was formerly (1976-1983): *The N I C M Journal for Jews and Christians in Higher Education.* [ISSN: 0011-1953] 1950. q. GBP 164 (print & online eds.)). Ed(s): Charles Henderson. Wiley-Blackwell Publishing, Inc., 350 Main St, Malden, MA 02148; cs-journals@wiley.com; http://onlinelibrary.wiley.com. Illus., index, adv. Sample. Refereed. Vol. ends: Winter. Reprint: PSC. *Indexed:* A01, A22, AmHI, BAS, BRI, C26, E01, MLA-IB, R&TA. *Bk. rev.:* 6-8, 400-2,000 words; signed. *Aud.:* Ac, Sa.

This journal publishes articles that explore Christian scripture, with articles typically focusing on particular parts of scripture or tackling broader themes that appear in the biblical literature. Issues contain approximately five scholarly articles, with recent pieces including "the Rabbinic God and Mediaeval Judaism," "Mapping the Vineyard: Main Lines of Investigation Regarding the Parable of the Tenants in the Synoptics and *Thomas*," and "Trauma Theory and Biblical Studies." Reviews articles that survey current research on particular subject, e.g., the concept of exile in Judaism or phonological patterns in the Bible, also appear quite frequently, making this journal a useful current-awareness tool not only for biblical scholars, but also for academic library subject selectors. Recommended for academic libraries that support biblical studies programs.

4367. *Currents in Biblical Research.* Formerly (until 2002): *Currents in Research: Biblical Studies.* [ISSN: 1476-993X] 1993. 3x/yr. USD 1320 (print & online eds.)). Ed(s): Scot McKnight, Jonathan Klawens. Sage Publications Ltd., 1 Oliver's Yard, 55 City Rd, London, EC1Y 1SP, United Kingdom; info@sagepub.com; https://www.sagepub.com/. Adv. Sample. Reprint: PSC. *Indexed:* A01, A22, E01, R&TA. *Aud.:* Ac.

Currents in Biblical Research offers summary essays on a wide range of topics related to biblical research that, according to its editors, "cover specific biblical books or clusters of books, ancillary ancient literature, archaeology, [and] historical studies, as well as new and developing areas of study." Issues typically contain five or so such articles. One recent article, "Recent Research on Ancient Israelite Education: A Bibliographic Essay," is fairly representative of the journal's content, providing short critical reviews of multiple books on the topic of interest, as well as suggestions for future research. This journal is of value to both biblical studies researchers and religious studies subject selectors. Recommended for both church and academic libraries.

4368. *Dialogue (Salt Lake City): a journal of Mormon thought.* [ISSN: 0012-2157] 1966. q. USD 50 combined subscription domestic (print & online eds.); USD 70 combined subscription foreign (print & online eds.)). Ed(s): Kristine L Haglund. Dialogue Foundation, PO Box 381209, Cambridge, MA 02238; businessoffice@dialoguejournal.com. Illus., adv. Refereed. Microform: PQC. *Indexed:* A01, A22, MLA-IB. *Bk. rev.:* 2-3, 250-750 words; signed. *Aud.:* Sa.

Dialogue is a quarterly journal devoted to the scholarly analysis of Mormon religious thought as well as the presentation of Mormon culture through creative writing. Issues typically contain three articles and essays, multiple poems and short works of fiction, as well as original works of graphic art. In addition, there are book reviews, some of which are quite extensive and themselves scholarly in nature. A regular feature, "From the Pulpit," presents the text of sermons and devotionals previously presented at church services, conferences, and symposia. The journals website provides free access to digital versions of older issues. The audience for this journal is rather narrow, Mormon researchers, clergy, and interested lay people, but these constituencies will find this publication invaluable for their work. Recommended for both public and academic libraries that serve Mormon communities.

4369. ***Ecclesiology: the journal for ministry, mission and unity.*** [ISSN: 1744-1366] 2004. 3x/yr. EUR 276. Ed(s): Paul Avis. Brill, PO Box 9000, Leiden, 2300 PA, Netherlands; marketing@brill.com; https://brill.com. Adv. Refereed. Reprint: PSC. *Indexed:* A01, A22, E01, R&TA. *Bk. rev.:* Number and length vary. *Aud.:* Ac, Sa.

Ecclesiology is a peer-reviewed journal dedicated to the study of the structure, culture, and doctrinal beliefs of the Christian church broadly considered. Every issue contains three to five scholarly articles, with recent articles including "Priest in the Inner City: Subjecting the Ecclesiology of John Milbank and Rowan Williams to Empirical Scrutiny" and "Authority in the New Testament and the New Testament's Authority. Issues also contain multiple book reviews. Recommended for academic libraries that support divinity and/or religious studies programs.

4370. ***The Ecumenical Review.*** Incorporates (1935-1948): *Christendom;* Which superseded (in 1935): *Christian Union Quarterly.* [ISSN: 0013-0796] 19??. q. GBP 240. Ed(s): Theodore Gill. Wiley-Blackwell Publishing Ltd., The Atrium, Southern Gate, Chichester, PO19 8QG, United Kingdom; cs-journals@wiley.com; http://onlinelibrary.wiley.com. Illus., index, adv. Microform: PQC. Reprint: PSC. *Indexed:* A01, A22, AmHI, BRI, CBRI, E01, MLA-IB, R&TA. *Bk. rev.:* 3-5, 800-1,000 words; signed. *Aud.:* Ac, Sa.

The *Ecumenical Review* collects scholarly articles that explore Christian Ecumenism from multiple perspectives, including the theological, philosophical, educational, and social science perspectives. Research articles tend to be grouped by theme (e.g., "Religion and Development") with issues typically, but not necessarily, sticking to one theme. Book reviews are occasionally included, as are news, announcements, and documents of interest to religion scholars. This resource is recommended for both scholars and practitioners. Recommended for academic libraries.

4371. ***The Empty Vessel: the journal of taoist philosophy and practice.*** [ISSN: 1073-7480] 1993. q. USD 5.95 newsstand/cover domestic; USD 6.95 newsstand/cover Canada. The Abode of the Eternal Tao, 1991 Garfield St, Eugene, OR 97405; http://www.abodetao.com. Illus. *Bk. rev.:* Number and length vary. *Aud.:* Ga, Ac, Sa.

Published by the Abode of the Eternal Tao, *The Empty Vessel* is one of very few magazines aimed at practitioners of Taoism. Each full-color, quarterly issue is approximately forty pages long and contains articles that explore Taoist philosophy, history, culture, and practice in a way that will appeal to both longtime practitioners and scholars as well as to beginners. The magazine regularly includes interviews with renowned Taoist thinkers and practitioners, as well as a page of brief book reviews and a directory of services of interest to Taoists. The magazine's website also provides free qigong lessons, audio downloads, and a blog. Practicing Taoists will want to seek out this magazine, as will anybody with a research or general interest in Eastern spirituality. Recommended for both public and academic libraries. URL: http://abodetao.com/

4372. ***Evangelical Quarterly: an international review of Bible and theology.*** [ISSN: 0014-3367] 1929. q. GBP 69.35 (print or online ed.)). The Paternoster Press, c/o Aplhagraphics, 3.2 Clarendon Park, Nottingham, NG5 1AH, United Kingdom; periodicals@alphagraphics.co.uk; http://www.paternosterperiodicals.com. Illus., index, adv. Microform: PQC. *Indexed:* A01, A22, MLA-IB, R&TA. *Bk. rev.:* 8-20, 800-1,600; signed. *Aud.:* Ac.

Since 1929, *Evangelical Quarterly* has provided research articles on theology from a Christian evangelical perspective. Published four times yearly, recent articles include examinations of the morality of God's actions, the process involved in writing the Gospels, and Paul the apostle's use of psalms. Readers outside of the evangelical tradition will also find this valuable for its discussions of topics of relevance to most contemporary Christians. Theologians, biblical scholars, and clergy will all find this to be a useful resource. Recommended for academic libraries that support programs in theology or biblical studies. Also recommended for public libraries that serve evangelical Christian communities.

4373. ***Evangelical Theological Society. Journal.*** Formerly (until 1969): *E T S Bulletin.* [ISSN: 0360-8808] 1958. q. USD 30 (Free to members). Ed(s): Andreas Kostenberger. Evangelical Theological Society, 2825 Lexington Rd, PO Box 927, Louisville, KY 40280; http://www.etsjets.org. Illus., index, adv. Refereed. Circ: 5000. Vol. ends: Dec. *Indexed:* A01, A22, R&TA. *Bk. rev.:* 16-20, 600-2,000 words; signed. *Aud.:* Ac, Sa.

The Evangelical Theological Society is, according to their website, "a professional academic society of biblical theological scholars, pastors, students [who] serve Jesus Christ and his church by fostering conservative, biblical scholarship." One tool for accomplishing this task is the Society's academic journal. This peer-reviewed, quarterly publication includes articles relating to Evangelical theology and biblical analysis. In addition to the research articles, issues include approximately 70 pages of book reviews as well as books received. The society has made freely available an archive of past issues, from the journal's first issue up to two years prior to the present. Recommended for church libraries as well as academic libraries that support theological research. URL: http://www.etsjets.org/

Feminist Theology. See Gender Studies section.

4374. ***First Things: a monthly journal of religion and public life.*** [ISSN: 1047-5141] 1990. m. USD 39 domestic; USD 49 Canada; USD 57 elsewhere. Ed(s): Lauren Wilson, R R Reno. Institute on Religion and Public Life, 35 E 21st St, 6th Fl, New York, NY 10010; ft@firstthings.com; http://www.firstthings.com. Index, adv. *Indexed:* A01, A22, AmHI, BRI, C26, R&TA. *Bk. rev.:* 4-5, 250-500 words; signed. *Aud.:* Ga.

This monthly journal was started by Catholic priest Richard John Neuhaus in 1990. The essays and opinion pieces approach political, legal, and cultural issues from typically conservative Catholic perspectives, and the authors are well known in their respective fields. Recent articles have concerned radical Islam and the rise of modern populist movements. Every issue contains multiple book reviews of books aimed at both scholarly and popular audiences. Poetry is interspersed throughout each issue. The First Things website includes web-only content including video and podcasts. The magazine is marked by a high level of discourse and is recommended for inclusion in public libraries and academic libraries that serve Christian communities. URL: https://www.firstthings.com/

4375. ***Harvard Theological Review.*** [ISSN: 0017-8160] 1908. q. GBP 221. Ed(s): Jon D Levenson. Cambridge University Press, University Printing House, Shaftesbury Rd, Cambridge, CB2 8BS, United Kingdom; journals@cambridge.org; https://www.cambridge.org/. Illus., index, adv. Sample. Refereed. Circ: 1600. Vol. ends: Oct. *Indexed:* A01, A22, AmHI, BRI, E01, MLA-IB, R&TA. *Bk. rev.:* Number and length vary. *Aud.:* Ac.

Since 1908, the *Harvard Theological Review* has been a premier scholarly journal for the theological analysis of the Judaism, Christianity, their major texts, and their respective historical and ethical traditions. Recent articles display the eclectic nature of the journal, with titles including "Christian Magicians, Jewish Magical Idioms, and the Shared Magical Culture of Late Antiquity" and "Kierkegaard as Socratic Street Preacher? Reimagining the Dialectic of Direct and Indirect Communication for Christian Proclamation." Each issue contains an in-depth, critical review essay of a notable new book in the field, as well as a list of books received. This journal is a vital tool for the study of Christianity and Judaism, and should be included in the collections of any academic library that caters to research and pedagogy in these areas.

4376. *History of Religions.* [ISSN: 0018-2710] 1961. q. USD 310. Ed(s): Matthew Kapstein, Christian K Wedemeyer. University of Chicago Press, 1427 E 60th St, Chicago, IL 60637; subscriptions@press.uchicago.edu; http://www.journals.uchicago.edu. Illus., index, adv. Sample. Refereed. Vol. ends: May. Reprint: PSC. *Indexed:* A01, A22, A47, AmHI, BAS, BRI, MLA-IB, R&TA. *Bk. rev.:* 0-15, 400-1,800 words; signed. *Aud.:* Ac.

This historical journal covers the history of world religions, large and small. Recent articles have provided histories of Hinduism ("God Depends on the Lowest Devotees": Gender, Performance, and Transformation in the Tale of a Female Hindu Renouncer in Rajasthan"), Buddhism ("The Love Letters of a Buddhist Tantric Couple: Reflections on Poetic Style and Epistolary Intimacy"), and Judaism ("Substitutes for Mysticism: A General Model for the Theological Development of Hasidism in the Nineteenth Century"). Book reviews are included in every issue. Recommended for scholars in the areas of religious studies and history. Appropriate for academic libraries.

4377. *Horizons (Villanova).* Formerly (until 19??): *21st Century Genetics Cooperative.* [ISSN: 0360-9669] 1974. s-a. GBP 136 (print & online eds.)). Ed(s): Anthony J Godzieba. Cambridge University Press, 1 Liberty Plaza, Fl 20, New York, NY 10004; journals@cambridge.org; https://www.cambridge.org. Illus. Refereed. Microform: PQC. Reprint: PSC. *Indexed:* A22, C26. *Bk. rev.:* 25-30, 400-1,600 words; signed. *Aud.:* Ac.

Produced semi-annually by the College Theology Society (a sub-organization of the American Academy of Religion, *Horizons* is a scholarly journal of Roman Catholic theology. Articles approach theological questions from theological and cognate scholarly approaches such as women and genders studies, and literary studies. Besides the research articles and essays, a semi-regular feature is the "Theological Roundtable," where articles revolve around a given topic such as "Deconversion and Disaffiliation in Contemporary Catholicism." The collected papers of conferences and symposia also appear often, as do review essays. Every issue also contains multiple book reviews as well as a list of books received. Recommended for theologians and clergy members. Academic libraries that support programs in Catholic theology and/or religious studies should consider adding this journal to their collections.

4378. *The Humanist: a magazine of critical inquiry and social concern.* Supersedes (in 1941): *The Humanist Bulletin;* Which superseded (in 1938): *The New Humanist;* Incorporates (1965-1969): *The Ethical Forum;* Which was formerly (until 1965): *Ethical Culture Today;* (until 1964): *The Ethical Outlook;* (until 1956): *The Standard;* (until 1914): *Ethical Addresses and Ethical Record;* Which was formed by the merger of (1899-1904): *Ethical Record;* (18??-1904): *Ethical Addresses.* [ISSN: 0018-7399] 1941. bi-m. USD 24.95; USD 5.25 per issue domestic; USD 6.25 per issue Canada. Ed(s): Peter Bjork, Jennifer Bardi. American Humanist Association, 1777 T St, NW, Washington, DC 20009; aha@americanhumanist.org; http://www.americanhumanist.org/index.html. Illus., adv. Sample. Vol. ends: Dec. *Indexed:* A01, A22, AmHI, BRI, C37, CBRI, MASUSE, MLA-IB. *Bk. rev.:* 0-3, 600-1,200 words; signed. *Aud.:* Ga, Ac.

This bi-monthly consumer magazine is targeted at secular humanists, atheists, and free thinkers. Every issue contains four to six feature articles, regular columns, book reviews, and poetry. Recent feature articles have included "An Action List for the (Un)Faithful," "Ask What You Can Do for Your Climate," and "Fundamentalism on Trial: How Twelve Claims of the Christian Right Fail under Strict Secular Scrutiny." The magazine's website contains free access to news articles, blogs, and articles not found in print, and regular podcasts. This magazine is recommended for all public and academic libraries. URL: https://thehumanist.com/

4379. *International Journal for Philosophy of Religion.* [ISSN: 0020-7047] 1970. bi-m. EUR 900 (print & online eds.)). Ed(s): Ronald L Hall. Springer Netherlands, Van Godewijckstraat 30, Dordrecht, 3311 GX, Netherlands; http://www.springer.com. Illus., index, adv. Refereed. Vol. ends: Jun/Dec. Microform: PQC. Reprint: PSC. *Indexed:* A01, A22, AmHI, BRI, E01, IBSS, R&TA. *Bk. rev.:* 0-4, 600-1,000 words; signed. *Aud.:* Ac.

The *International Journal for Philosophy of Religion* publishes two volumes per year, with three issues comprising each volume. The journal applies philosophical analyses to religions questions. It is also non-sectarian, inviting articles concerning any religion or religious viewpoint, although Christianity and Judaism are especially well represented. Recent articles include "The Nature of Faith in Analytic Theistic Philosophy of Religion," "Berkeley on the 'Twofold State of Things,'" and "Difficulties in Defining the Concept of God: Kierkegaard in Dialogue with Levinas, Buber, and Rosenzweig." The audience for this book are philosophers and religious studies researchers. Recommended for academic libraries.

4380. *The International Journal for the Psychology of Religion.* [ISSN: 1050-8619] 1991. q. GBP 655 (print & online eds.)). Ed(s): Raymond F Paloutzian. Routledge, 530 Walnut St, Ste 850, Philadelphia, PA 19106; enquiries@tandfonline.com; http://www.tandfonline.com. Illus., adv. Sample. Refereed. Vol. ends: No. 4. Reprint: PSC. *Indexed:* A01, A22, ASSIA, BRI, E01, R&TA. *Bk. rev.:* 1-2, 500-1,500 words; signed. *Aud.:* Ac, Sa.

This is a quarterly journal dedicated to the scholarly examination of psychological concepts and phenomena as they relate to religion and spirituality. All types of religious experience, as well as agnosticism and atheism, are topics of discussion. Both quantitative and qualitative methods are employed, and recent articles include "Does a Religious Transformation Buffer the Effects of Lifetime Trauma on Happiness," "Effect of Religious Day on Prosocial Behavior: A Field Study," and "The Relation between God Concept and Prayer Style Among Male Religious Israeli Jews." This journal has a wide potential audience, and researchers in religious studies, psychology, and sociology will all find it of interest. Recommended for academic libraries that support programs in the social sciences.

4381. *International Journal of Hindu Studies.* [ISSN: 1022-4556] 1997. 3x/yr. EUR 562 (print & online eds.)). Ed(s): Sushil Mittal. Springer Netherlands, Van Godewijckstraat 30, Dordrecht, 3311 GX, Netherlands; http://www.springer-sbm.de. Illus., index, adv. Sample. Refereed. Vol. ends: Dec. Reprint: PSC. *Indexed:* A22, AmHI, BAS, BRI, E01. *Bk. rev.:* 0-1. *Aud.:* Ac, Sa.

This is one of few English-language scholarly journals devoted entirely to the study of religion on the subcontinent of India as well as the Indian diaspora. Although the bulk of the research articles do focus on Hinduism and its many variations and expressions, other religions are considered in the Indian context, including Christianity, Islam, and Jainism, as well as the interplay of religion, history, and culture. Occasionally, special issues are dedicated to topics like "Stotra, Hymns of Praise in Indian Literature." Book reviews appear in some (not all) issues, as well as longer review essays. This journal provides great support for the academic study of Eastern religions, Asian history and culture, and comparative religion. It is recommended for academic libraries that support these pursuits.

4382. *International Journal of Philosophy and Theology.* Former titles (until 2013): *Bijdragen;* (until 1945): *Philosophische en Theologische Faculteiten der Nederlandsche Jezuieten. Bijdragen.* [ISSN: 2169-2327] 1938. 5x/yr. GBP 384 (print & online eds.)). Ed(s): Walter Van Herck. Routledge, 4 Park Sq, Milton Park, Abingdon, OX14 4RN, United Kingdom; subscriptions@tandf.co.uk; http://www.tandfonline.com. Adv. Refereed. Reprint: PSC. *Indexed:* A22, MLA-IB, R&TA. *Aud.:* Ac.

The editors for this journal invite submission of articles, research notes, and scholarly literature surveys that "concern the intersection between philosophy and theology." The type of philosophical and theological inquiry presented is not limited to any particular approach or school, and articles concerning political philosophy and the Christian Bible have appeared alongside historical and ethical analyses. Books reviews appear in some issues. Recommended for inclusion in academic libraries that support researchers in religion, philosophy, and philosophy of religion. URL: http://www.tandfonline.com/toc/rjpt20/current

4383. *International Review of Mission.* [ISSN: 0020-8582] 1911. s-a. GBP 240. Ed(s): Benjamin Simon. Wiley-Blackwell Publishing Ltd., The Atrium, Southern Gate, Chichester, PO19 8QG, United Kingdom; cs-journals@wiley.com; http://onlinelibrary.wiley.com. Illus., index, adv. Vol. ends: Oct. Microform: PQC. Reprint: PSC. *Indexed:* A01, A22, A47, AmHI, BAS, BRI, Chicano, E01, MLA-IB, R&TA. *Bk. rev.:* 0-5, 200-1,000 words; signed. *Aud.:* Ac, Sa.

Published by the World Council of Churches, this journal is a resource for missiology, the academic study of the methods, purposes, and activities of, in this case, Christian missions. Articles discuss the fruit of mission work in both hemispheres. One recent issue, for example, had an article on mission work in Korea as well as one on mission education in Matanzas, Cuba. While the *International Review of Mission* is a useful resource for scholarly study, it is also valuable to the practitioners, the missionaries, with many articles providing practical information from the field. There are also a number of shorter book reviews in every issue (occasionally more than 30). Recommended for academic libraries, as well as libraries serving institutions the engage directly in mission work, or train missionaries.

4384. ***Interpretation: a journal of bible and theology.*** Former titles (until 1947): *The Union Seminary Review;* (until 1913): *Union Seminary Magazine.* [ISSN: 0020-9643] 1889. q. USD 707 (print & online eds.)). Ed(s): Sam Adams, John Carroll. Sage Publications Ltd., 1 Oliver's Yard, 55 City Rd, London, EC1Y 1SP, United Kingdom; info@sagepub.com; https://www.sagepub.com/. Illus., adv. Refereed. Vol. ends: Oct. Microform: PQC. Reprint: PSC. *Indexed:* A01, A22, AmHI, BRI, CBRI, R&TA. *Bk. rev.:* Number and length vary. *Aud.:* Ga, Ac.

Published by Union Presbyterian Seminary, *Interpretation* is a quarterly journal useful to both Bible scholars and pastors. Every issue of the journal focuses on a specific book of the Bible and divides into three primary parts, articles, "Between Text and Sermon," and book reviews. The research articles are dedicated to both Old and New Testament books and include different methodological approaches such as hermeneutical and historical. "Between Text and Sermon" presents several articles meant to aid pastors in drafting their sermons. There are two types of book reviews. Major reviews are extended pieces that go into great depth concerning a newly issued book. There are also multiple (sometimes more than 30 per issue) shorter reviews. Recommended for academic libraries that support theology, biblical studies, and pastoring programs.

4385. ***Japanese Journal of Religious Studies.*** Formerly (until 1974): *Contemporary Religions in Japan.* [ISSN: 0304-1042] 1960. s-a. JPY 5000. Ed(s): Paul L Swanson. Nanzan Shukyo Bunka Kenkyujo, 18 Yamazato-cho, Showa-ku, Nagoya, 466-8673, Japan; nirc-office@ic.nanzan-u.ac.jp; http://www.nanzan-u.ac.jp/SHUBUNKEN/index.htm. Illus., index, adv. Refereed. *Indexed:* A01, A22, BAS, BRI, MLA-IB, R&TA. *Bk. rev.:* 0-15, 1,000-3,000 words; signed. *Aud.:* Ac, Sa.

Many different religious traditions flourish in Japan, including the indigenous (e.g., Shintoism) and the imported (e.g., Buddhism, Christianity). The island nation is also a hotbed for new religious movements (e.g., Soka Gakkai, Happy Science). The *Japanese Journal of Religious Studies* is an open-access journal that publishes scholarly articles on the wide range of religious expression happening in Japan's past and present, with recent articles including "Imagining Rahula in Medieval Japan," "Sacred Forests, Sacred Nation: The Shinto Environmentalist Paradigm and the Rediscovery of Chinju no Mori," and "Nichirenism, Utopianism and Modernity: Rethinking Ishiwara kanji's East Asia League." Two or three in-depth book reviews are also included. Every issue is freely available on the journal's website, stretching back to the first issue in 1960. Academic library subject selectors for religious studies, Asian studies, and history should include links to this journal on their subject guides, as it is an invaluable resource. URL: http://nirc.nanzan-u.ac.jp/en/publications/jjrs/

4386. ***Journal for the Scientific Study of Religion.*** [ISSN: 0021-8294] 1961. q. GBP 222. Ed(s): Laura R Olson. Wiley-Blackwell Publishing, Inc., 111 River St, Hoboken, NJ 07030; http://onlinelibrary.wiley.com. Illus., index, adv. Sample. Refereed. Vol. ends: Dec. Microform: PQC. Reprint: PSC. *Indexed:* A01, A22, AmHI, BAS, BRI, E01, IBSS, MLA-IB, P61, R&TA, SSA. *Bk. rev.:* 4-8, 600-1,500 words; signed. *Aud.:* Ac.

This journal publishes social science research into world religion using a variety of lenses including sociology, anthropology, political science, and psychology. A variety of quantitative and qualitative methods appear in the journal's pages. Besides the research articles, shorter research notes are included, as well book reviews. This is a rigorously peer-reviewed academic journal with a very low (10%) acceptance rate aimed at researchers (its editors write that it "does not publish review articles or articles geared toward clinical or other practitioner audiences." Highly recommended for academic libraries that support the study of religion. This journal would also be an important addition to most any social science-oriented collection.

4387. ***Journal for the Study of the Historical Jesus.*** [ISSN: 1476-8690] 2003. 3x/yr. EUR 338. Brill, PO Box 9000, Leiden, 2300 PA, Netherlands; marketing@brill.com; https://brill.com. Adv. Refereed. Reprint: PSC. *Indexed:* A01, A22, E01. *Bk. rev.:* 4-8, 100-400 words; signed. *Aud.:* Ac.

This academic journal publishes not only historiographies and archaeological research papers relating to the person of Jesus, but also relating to the general time (i.e., extending into the history of the early Christian Church) and culture within which he lived. Also appearing are articles that deal with theoretical and methodological issues of importance to this particular area of study, such as "Fake News and the Jesus Historian," and "Has Jonathan Bernier Rescued Critical Realism?" Articles contain rigorous scholarly apparatuses. Because of the interdisciplinary nature of this journal (history, archaeology, biblical studies, religious studies, and other fields in social sciences and humanities), academic libraries that support research collections in a number of disciplinary areas should consider adding this to their collections.

4388. ***Journal for the Study of the New Testament.*** [ISSN: 0142-064X] 1978. 5x/yr. USD 2231 (print & online eds.)). Ed(s): Dr. Catrin H Williams. Sage Publications Ltd., 1 Oliver's Yard, 55 City Rd, London, EC1Y 1SP, United Kingdom; info@sagepub.com; https://www.sagepub.com/. Illus., index. Sample. Refereed. Vol. ends: Jun. Reprint: PSC. *Indexed:* A01, A22, E01, R&TA. *Bk. rev.:* 2-7, 300-400 words; signed. *Aud.:* Ac.

The *Journal for the Study of the New Testament* is a forum for discussion of New Testament scripture and related literature (e.g., apocryphal texts, early Christian writings, and contemporaneous literature) from various scholarly vantage points including theological, literary, critical/cultural studies, and social science. Each issue contains approximately five research articles, with recent articles including "Beyond the Fourfold Gospel: A Critical Reading of Francis Watson's *Gospel Writing: A Canonical Perspective* and "Accepting Prophecy: Paul's Response to Agabus with insights from Valerius Maximus and Joseph." Book reviews are not included. This resource is useful to the Biblical studies and religious studies researcher. Recommended for academic libraries that support the research of many disciplines including history, theology, literature, religious studies, and philosophy.

4389. ***Journal for the Study of the Old Testament.*** [ISSN: 0309-0892] 1976. 5x/yr. USD 2231 (print & online eds.)). Ed(s): Yvonne Sherwood, John Jarick. Sage Publications Ltd., 1 Oliver's Yard, 55 City Rd, London, EC1Y 1SP, United Kingdom; info@sagepub.com; https://www.sagepub.com/. Illus. Sample. Refereed. Vol. ends: No. 5. Reprint: PSC. *Indexed:* A01, A22, E01, MLA-IB, R&TA. *Bk. rev.:* 100-700 words; signed. *Aud.:* Ac.

The sister volume to Sage's *Journal for the Study of the New Testament*, the *Journal for the Study of the Old Testament* is a scholarly journal, published five times per year that presents research regarding the books of the Old Testament/Jewish Tanakh and related literatures. Articles tend to focus on specific books or portions of Old Testament books, or on concepts or phenomena (e.g., prostration, rape, war) that appear in multiple places in these texts. Useful for those studying the Bible from either Jewish or Christian perspectives. Recommended for academic libraries.

4390. ***Journal of Biblical Literature.*** Formerly (until 1890): *Society of Biblical Literature and Exegesis. Journal.* [ISSN: 0021-9231] 1881. q. USD 310 (print & online eds.)). Society of Biblical Literature, The Luce Ctr, 825 Houston Mill Rd, Atlanta, GA 30329; sblexec@sbl-site.org; http://www.sbl-site.org. Illus., index, adv. Refereed. Vol. ends: Winter. Microform: PMC; PQC. *Indexed:* A01, A22, AmHI, BRI, CBRI, MLA-IB, R&TA. *Bk. rev.:* 20-25, 900-1,500 words; signed. *Aud.:* Ac.

Founded in 1881 by the Society of Biblical Literature, the *Journal of Biblical Literature* is a quarterly peer-reviewed academic journal that critically reviews Biblical texts. Issues contain approximately ten research articles about Old and

New Testament subjects, with recent articles including "Walk, Don't Run: Jesus's Water Walking is Unparalleled in Greco-Roman Mythology" and "Different Dreams: Two Models of Interpretation for Three Pairs of Dreams (Genesis 37-50)." Aimed at specialists, many of the articles contain extracts from the original languages such as Greek and Latin. Recommended for those academic libraries that collect in the areas of Christian theology and Biblical studies.

4391. ***Journal of Church and State.*** [ISSN: 0021-969X] 1959. q. EUR 205. Ed(s): Patricia Cornett, Jerold Waltman. Oxford University Press, 2001 Evans Rd, Cary, NC 27513; https://global.oup.com. Index, adv. Sample. Refereed. Vol. ends: Fall. Microform: WSH; PMC; PQC. Reprint: PSC; WSH. *Indexed:* A01, A22, AmHI, BAS, BRI, CBRI, IBSS, L14, R&TA. *Bk. rev.:* 35-40, 300-800 words; signed. *Aud.:* Ac, Sa.

This quarterly journal publishes articles investigating the relationship between religion and the political state. Issues contain approximately five research articles, and recent articles have included questions about religion and Constitutional law ("Your Land is Holy to Me: The Constitutional Battle to Access Sacred Sites on Public Lands") and historical studies ("John Adams Confronts Quakers and Baptists during the Revolution: A Paradox of the Quest for Liberty"). There are multiple book reviews in each issue, sometimes 20 or more, as well as a list of books received. Regular features also include "Notes on Church-State Affairs," which provides news relating to the separation (or not) of church and state in countries around the world, as well as a "Calendar of Events of Interest in Church and State." This journal is a valuable addition to academic library collections that support research and pedagogy relating to religious studies and/or political science. Law librarians should also consider acquiring the *Journal of Church and State* for their institutions' collections.

4392. ***Journal of Early Christian Studies.*** Formerly (until 1993): *The Second Century;* Incorporates (1972-1993): *Patristics.* [ISSN: 1067-6341] 1981. q. USD 195. Ed(s): Stephen Shoemaker. The Johns Hopkins University Press, 2715 N Charles St, Baltimore, MD 21218. Illus., adv. Sample. Refereed. Vol. ends: Winter. Reprint: PSC. *Indexed:* A01, A22, AmHI, E01, MLA-IB, R&TA. *Bk. rev.:* 10-20, 400-1,000 words; signed. *Aud.:* Ac.

Published by Johns Hopkins University Press, the *Journal of Early Christian Studies* covers the history, culture, archaeology, thought, and literature of the early Christian Church. Each quarterly issue contains five or more research articles. Recent articles have included "Bed, Bath, and Burial: NCE 156 Revisited," "How Greek is Ephrem's Syriac?: Ephrem's *Commentary on Genesis as a Case Study*," and "Evergetism among the Bishops of Hispania between the Sixth and Seventh Centuries: A Dialogue between Archaeological and Documentary Sources." Book reviews and a list of books received are included in every issue. Although this journal is a must-read for all scholars of early Christianity, it is also of great value to those that study and research the history of the Middle East. Recommended for academic libraries that support such researchers.

4393. ***Journal of Ecclesiastical History.*** [ISSN: 0022-0469] 1950. q. GBP 508. Ed(s): James Carleton Paget, Alec Ryrie. Cambridge University Press, University Printing House, Shaftesbury Rd, Cambridge, CB2 8BS, United Kingdom; journals@cambridge.org; https://www.cambridge.org/. Illus., adv. Sample. Refereed. Circ: 1900. Vol. ends: Oct. Microform: PQC. Reprint: PSC. *Indexed:* A01, A22, AmHI, BRI, E01, MLA-IB, R&TA. *Bk. rev.:* 60-75, 300-700 words; signed. *Aud.:* Ac.

Containing historical research on the Christian Church and clergy from the ancient world to the present, the *Journal of Ecclesiastical History* is a forum for well-researched, rigorously documented articles. The majority of articles deal with church history in the west and cover the wide range of Christian sects and denominations. The journal is also notable for its extensive number of book reviews, with some issues presenting 70 or more, as well as a list of books received. This journal is essential for scholars of religious history. Recommended for academic libraries that support academic programs in religious studies, biblical studies, and history.

4394. ***Journal of Feminist Studies in Religion.*** [ISSN: 8755-4178] 1985. s-a. USD 100.65 (print & online eds.)). Ed(s): Abtsam Saleh, Elizabeth Pritchard. Indiana University Press, Office of Scholarly Publishing, Herman B Wells Library 350, Bloomington, IN 47405; journals@indiana.edu; http://iupress.indiana.edu/. Illus., adv. Refereed. Reprint: PSC. *Indexed:* A01, A22, AmHI, BRI, C42, E01, FemPer, MLA-IB, R&TA, WSA. *Bk. rev.:* Essay length; signed. *Aud.:* Ac, Sa.

Contains critical analysis of world religions from feminist, interdisciplinary perspectives. The majority of articles published focus on Christianity and Judaism, although other religions are represented. Special sections, forums, and roundtables are given over to particular topics such as "Catholic Feminism," and "Feminism and Islam: Exploring the Boundaries of Critique." For feminist and critical/cultural studies of religion. Recommended for academic libraries.

4395. ***Journal of Jewish Studies.*** [ISSN: 0022-2097] 1948. s-a. GBP 130 (Individuals, GBP 60). Ed(s): Sarah Pearce, Dr. Sacha Stern. Oxford Centre for Hebrew and Jewish Studies, The Clarendon Institute, Walton St, Oxford, OX1 2HG, United Kingdom; enquiries@ochjs.ac.uk; http://www.ochjs.ac.uk. Illus., adv. Sample. Refereed. Vol. ends: Oct. Microform: PQC. Reprint: PSC. *Indexed:* A01, A22, AmHI, IBSS, MLA-IB, R&TA. *Bk. rev.:* 25-30, 400-3,000 words; signed. *Aud.:* Ac, Sa.

This journal is "one of the leading forums in the world for new findings and discussions of Jewish history, literature and culture from Biblical times to the present day." Besides research articles, there are extended review articles and book reviews. The journal also publishes supplements under the *Journal of Jewish Studies* moniker including monographs and conference proceedings. A subscription gets one full access to digital content online, and the website gives access to a number of open-access articles as well. Recommended for scholars in the areas of Jewish Studies, biblical studies, and history. Recommended for academic libraries that collect in these areas. URL: http://www.jjs-online.net/

4396. ***Journal of Pentecostal Theology.*** [ISSN: 0966-7369] 1992. s-a. EUR 278. Ed(s): John Christopher Thomas, Lee Roy Martin. Brill, PO Box 9000, Leiden, 2300 PA, Netherlands; marketing@brill.com; https://brill.com. Adv. Reprint: PSC. *Indexed:* A01, A22, E01, R&TA. *Bk. rev.:* Number and length vary. *Aud.:* Ac.

This international journal is published by the Centre for Pentecostal Theology of the Pentecostal Theological Seminary, Cleveland. Each issue contains ten or so peer-reviewed articles, as well as invited articles from renowned Pentecostal theologians. This a valuable place to go in order to find information and discussion of important and cutting-edge questions in Pentecostal theology such as transformation theology or the impact of social justice thought on the Christian Church. This journal is of particular value for researchers and students of Pentecostal theology, although anyone interested in Protestant theology is likely to find something of interest. Recommended for academic and seminary libraries that have collections in Christian theology.

4397. ***Journal of Presbyterian History.*** Former titles (until 1997): *American Presbyterians;* (until 1985): *Journal of Presbyterian History;* (until 1962): *Presbyterian Historical Society. Journal;* (until 1943): *Presbyterian Historical Society. Department of History. Journal;* (until 1930): *Presbyterian Historical Society. Journal.* [ISSN: 1521-9216] 1901. s-a. Free to members; Non-members, USD 110. Presbyterian Historical Society, 425 Lombard St, Philadelphia, PA 19147; refdesk@history.pcusa.org; http://www.history.pcusa.org/. Illus., index. Sample. Refereed. Vol. ends: Winter. *Indexed:* A22, BAS, R&TA. *Bk. rev.:* 5-10, 400-600 words; signed. *Aud.:* Ac, Sa.

The *Journal of Presbyterian History* chronicles the stories of the Presbyterian and reformed Presbyterian churches and their congregations. The historical articles are heavily and rigorously researched and every issue contains an article on "Our Documentary Heritage," that is heavily illustrated with contemporaneous photographs and artwork. Book reviews present the latest publications on Church- related history. The content is easily accessible to both historians and laypersons. Recommended for academic libraries and public libraries that support Presbyterian communities or historical research into the history of the Presbyterian Church and mainline Protestantism.

4398. ***Journal of Psychology & Theology: an evangelical forum for the integration of psychology and theology.*** [ISSN: 0091-6471] 1973. q. USD 316 (print & online eds.)). Sage Publications, Inc., 2455 Teller Rd, Thousand Oaks, CA 91320; info@sagepub.com; http://www.sagepub.com. Illus., index, adv. Refereed. *Indexed:* A01, A22, AmHI, MLA-IB, R&TA. *Bk. rev.:* 4-6, 750-1,000 words; signed. *Aud.:* Ac.

Coming out of Biola University, a private evangelical Christian university near Los Angeles, this journal applies psychological research methods to theological and biblical studies questions. Many recent research articles are empirical studies such as "Perspectives Regarding Motivations for Adoption by Christian Adoptive Parents: A Qualitative Study" and "Calvinism, Gender Ideology, and Relational Spirituality: An Empirical Investigation of Worldview Differences." Recommended for academic libraries that support both theological and psychological research.

4399. *The Journal of Religion.* Formed by the merger of (1897-1921): *American Journal of Theology;* (1893-1921): *The Biblical World;* Which was formerly (until 1893): *The Old and New Testament Student;* (until 1889): *The Old Testament Student;* (until 1883): *The Hebrew Student.* [ISSN: 0022-4189] 1921. q. USD 288. Ed(s): James T. Robinson, Richard A. Rosengarten. University of Chicago Press, 1427 E 60th St, Chicago, IL 60637; subscriptions@press.uchicago.edu; http://www.journals.uchicago.edu. Illus., index, adv. Sample. Refereed. Vol. ends: Oct. Reprint: PSC. *Indexed:* A01, A22, AmHI, BAS, BRI, CBRI, MLA-IB, R&TA. *Bk. rev.:* 50-60, 750-1,500 words; signed. *Aud.:* Ac.

Published by the University of Chicago Press, *The Journal of Religion* is a forum for discussing the variety of religious expression and its related institutions from multiple different vantage points including the theological, philosophical, and social sciences. Each quarterly issue contains four or five research articles and essays as well as an extensive number of book reviews (as well as the occasional extended review essay). The broad scope of this publication, as well as the high quality of the articles published within it, make it a necessary addition for academic library collections that support the study and teaching of religious studies, philosophy, and sociology.

4400. *Journal of Religion and Health.* [ISSN: 0022-4197] 1961. q. EUR 2002 (print & online eds.)). Ed(s): Curtis W Hart. Springer New York LLC, 233 Spring St, New York, NY 10013; customerservice@springer.com; http://www.springer.com. Illus., index, adv. Refereed. Vol. ends: Winter. Microform: PQC. Reprint: PSC. *Indexed:* A01, A22, BRI, E01, R&TA. *Bk. rev.:* 15-20, 300-800 words; signed. *Aud.:* Ga, Ac.

This quarterly journal looks at the connection between religion and physical and mental health, with the majority of papers taking social science approaches. Many of the articles look at health in their broader social context, such as smoking behavior of university students in Malaysia or religion and the spread of HIV. There is a lot to read in each issue, with 20-plus original papers as well as book reviews and special articles such as biographical pieces and "psychological explorations." Researchers in religious studies, the health sciences, and health communication will all find the articles here useful. Recommended for academic and medical libraries.

4401. *Journal of Religious Ethics.* [ISSN: 0384-9694] 1973. q. GBP 373 (print & online eds.)). Ed(s): Martin Kawka, Akine Kalbian. Wiley-Blackwell Publishing, Inc., 111 River St, Hoboken, NJ 07030; http://onlinelibrary.wiley.com. Illus., adv. Sample. Refereed. Vol. ends: Fall. Microform: PQC. Reprint: PSC. *Indexed:* A01, A22, AmHI, BRI, E01, MLA-IB, R&TA. *Bk. rev.:* Number varies. *Aud.:* Ac, Sa.

Connects major schools of thought in the philosophical study of ethics to the world's religious traditions. Recent articles include "*Elaborating* Faith: Labor and Interfaith Resistance to Economic Inequality" and "Two Rival Interpretations of Xunzi's Views on the Basis of Morality." There are not book reviews per se, but there are occasional "Book Discussions," which provide detailed critical analysis of works of literature. Recommended for philosophers, religious studies researchers, and those that take an interdisciplinary approach to these areas.

4402. *Journal of Theological Studies.* [ISSN: 0022-5185] 1899. s-a. EUR 552. Ed(s): Katharine Dell, Graham Gould. Oxford University Press, Great Clarendon St, Oxford, OX2 6DP, United Kingdom; onlinequeries.uk@oup.com; http://global.oup.com. Illus., index, adv. Sample. Refereed. Vol. ends: Oct. Microform: PQC. Reprint: PSC. *Indexed:* A01, A22, AmHI, BRI, E01, MLA-IB, R&TA. *Bk. rev.:* 180-200, 400-2,500 words; signed. *Aud.:* Ac, Sa.

The *Journal of Theological Studies* started in 1899 and remains an outlet for all sorts of academic studies relating to Christian theology. There are approximately ten research articles per issue, with each article typically dealing with a particular book of the Bible or the works of an early church father or important Christian theologian. Recent articles include "Gregory of Nyssa's Change of Mind about the Heart," "Jesus' Heavenly Sacrifice in Early Christian Reception of Hebrews: A Survey," and "Intellect Ordered: An Allusion to Plato in *Dialogue* with *Trypho* and its Significance for Justin's Christian Epistemology." Each biannual issue contains many (sometimes more the 100) quite extensive book reviews, making this a valuable resource for collection development purposes. This is an invaluable resource for theologians and biblical studies scholars. Recommended for academic and seminary libraries that collect in the areas of theology, biblical studies, and the history of the early Church.

4403. *Lion's Roar: Buddhist wisdom for our time.* Former titles (until 2016): *Shambhala Sun;* (until Apr. 1992): *Vajradhatu Sun.* [ISSN: 2369-7997] 1978. bi-m. Ed(s): Melvin McLeod. Lion's Roar Foundation, 1660 Hollis St Ste 701, Halifax, NS B3J 1V7, Canada; info@lionsroar.com; https://www.lionsroar.com. Illus., adv. *Bk. rev.:* Number and length vary. *Aud.:* Ga.

Formerly known as *Shambhala Sun*, *Lion's Roar* is a bi-monthly consumer magazine aimed at practicing Buddhists. Articles cover Buddhist teaching and practice and relate the religion to living in the modern world. Many of the articles are written by renowned spiritual leaders and authors like Thich Nhat Hanh. The magazine's website contains much free content, including blog posts relating spirituality to the areas of "Arts & Culture," "Current Events," "Love & Relationships," "Practice in Everyday Life," "Reviews," "Wellness & Psychology," and "Wisdom for Difficult Times." Recommended for public and academic libraries that serve Buddhist patrons. URL: https://www.lionsroar.com/

4404. *Literature and Theology.* Formerly (until 1987): *National Conference of Literature and Religion. Newsletter.* [ISSN: 0269-1205] 1983. q. EUR 453. Ed(s): Dr. Heather Walton. Oxford University Press, Great Clarendon St, Oxford, OX2 6DP, United Kingdom; onlinequeries.uk@oup.com; http://global.oup.com. Illus., adv. Sample. Refereed. Vol. ends: Dec. Reprint: PSC. *Indexed:* A01, A22, AmHI, E01, MLA-IB, R&TA. *Bk. rev.:* 5-10, 400-1,000 words; signed. *Aud.:* Ac, Sa.

Published by Oxford University Press, *Literature and Theology* looks to both modern and earlier works of literature for the purpose of Christian theological analysis and criticism. The interdisciplinary nature of this journal becomes evident when looking at recent article titles: "EarthSong and Desert Art: Painted Literature from Sacred Ground," "Music's Multilayered Subversion of the Word," and "Infant Voices: Embryonic and Neonatal Personhood in Two Recent French Catholic Novels." Also included are book reviews, corrigenda, and notices and reports, the last of which announces upcoming conferences and other meetings as well as other important events. Subscribers have access to advance articles via the journal's website. Scholars in both theology, literary arts, and even the fine arts will find valuable material here. Recommended for academic libraries that support programs in theology, religious studies, and English language and literature. URL: https://academic.oup.com/litthe

4405. *Mennonite Quarterly Review: a quarterly journal devoted to Anabaptist-Mennonite history, thought, life and affairs.* Supersedes (in 1927): *Goshen College Record. Review Supplement.* [ISSN: 0025-9373] 1926. q. USD 35 in US & Canada; USD 45 elsewhere; USD 10 per issue. Ed(s): John D Roth. Goshen College, 1700 S Main St, Goshen, IN 46526; info@goshen.edu; http://www.goshen.edu. Illus., index. Sample. Refereed. Vol. ends: Oct. *Indexed:* A22, BRI, MLA-IB, R&TA. *Bk. rev.:* 5-10, 100-600 words; signed. *Aud.:* Ac, Sa.

Published by Goshen College, this is one of few academic journals that focuses on the Anabaptist Mennonite, Hutterite, and Amish Christian denominations. Recent articles include "Amish Youth and Social Media: A Phase or a Fatal Error?" "The Church that Never Fell: Reconsidering the Narrative of the Church, 100-400 EC," and "The Right Kind of Education and Perhaps Re-education: C. Henry Smith, Mennonite Schooling, and the Lessons of a Usable Past." There are five to ten book reviews provided per issue. Recommended for academic libraries.

4406. *Methodist History.* Supersedes in part (in 1962): *World Parish.* [ISSN: 0026-1238] 1948. q. USD 25 domestic; USD 30 Canada; USD 40 elsewhere. United Methodist Church, General Commission on Archives & History, 36 Madison Avenue, PO Box 127, Madison, NJ 07940; gcah@gcah.org; http://www.gcah.org. Illus. Refereed. Microform: PQC. *Indexed:* A22, BAS, BRI, MLA-IB, R&TA. *Bk. rev.:* 1-5, 50-500 words; signed. *Aud.:* Ac, Sa.

Methodist History is a quarterly publication of the General Commission on Archives and History. Articles relate the history of the Methodist church as an institution as well as the history of Methodist culture. The period covered ranges from the days of the early movement in the eighteenth century through the twenty-first century. There are occasional special issues devoted to general topics, such as the role of women in Methodism, or important historical figures such as John Wesley. Book reviews are also included. The print version of the journal is available to paid subscribers, but the journal is made freely available on the *Methodist History*'s website, which collects the full text from 1971 to the present. Both professional historians and interested laypeople will find this journal useful. Recommended for academic libraries that maintain history and/or religious studies collections, as well as those academic and public libraries that serve Methodist communities. URL: http://www.gcah.org/research/methodist-history-journal

4407. *Methodist Review: a journal of Wesleyan and Methodist studies.* [ISSN: 1946-5254] 2009. a. Emory University, Candler School of Theology, c/o Candler School of Theology, Emory University, Atlanta, GA 30322; candler@emory.edu; http://www.candler.emory.edu/. Refereed. *Indexed:* A01. *Aud.:* Ga, Ac.

This open-access, peer-reviewed online journal gives free access to research articles about the Methodist Church. This is a valuable resource for the ecclesiastical and historical study of Methodism in the United States and internationally. Articles are added as they are accepted, with recent titles including "The Wesleyan Religion Pectorum in Relation to Brazilian 'Cordial' Religion," "Methodist Episcopal Church, South, 1880-1930." In addition to the research articles is a quarterly *Methodist Review Newsletter* that lists news for various Methodist scholarly societies, upcoming academic events, scholarly opportunities, recent scholarly publications and other resources such as archival collections, and job postings. A free user login is required to access some content. Both academic and public librarians will want to link this journal to their religion and theology subject guides. URL: https://www.methodistreview.org/index.php/mr/user

4408. *Modern Judaism: a journal of Jewish ideas and experience.* [ISSN: 0276-1114] 1981. 3x/yr. EUR 255. Ed(s): Dr. Steven T Katz. Oxford University Press, Great Clarendon St, Oxford, OX2 6DP, United Kingdom; onlinequeries.uk@oup.com; http://global.oup.com. Illus., index, adv. Sample. Refereed. Reprint: PSC. *Indexed:* A22, AmHI, BRI, E01, ENW, MLA-IB, R&TA. *Bk. rev.:* 1-3, 2,000-3,000 words. *Aud.:* Ac, Sa.

According to its website, *Modern Judaism* focuses on "topics pertinent to the understanding of Jewish life today and the forces that have shaped that experience." Issues are published three times a year, and they cover academic topics from Jewish history, to philosophy, to rabbinical studies. Recent articles include "Chaim Weizmann: Scientist, Statesman and Architect of Science Policy," "From Social Norm to Legal Claim: How American Orthodox Feminism Changed Orthodoxy in Israel," and "How *Vaterlandsliebe* Shaped Neo-Orthodox Halach: The Case of Rabbi David Zvi Hoffman." Issues typically contain one in-depth critical book review as well as a list of books received in topics relevant to readers. Recommended for researchers and teachers of Jewish studies and for inclusion in academic libraries that support this discipline. URL: https://academic.oup.com/mj

4409. *Mountain Record: the Zen practitioner's journal.* [ISSN: 0896-8942] 1981. q. USD 36 combined subscription domestic (print & online eds.); USD 46 combined subscription Canada (print & online eds.); USD 56 combined subscription elsewhere (print & online eds.)). Dharma Communications, Inc., PO Box 156, Mt. Tremper, NY 12457; support@dharma.net; http://www.dharma.net/dchome.html. Adv. *Bk. rev.:* Number and length vary. *Aud.:* Ga, Ac, Sa.

This is a quarterly magazine aimed at practitioners of Zen Buddhism, but other Buddhist denominations, as well as non-Buddhists, will find the material here to be inspiring. Issues contain Buddhist scripture, short teachings by renowned practitioners, essays, and poetry. *Mountain Record* also boasts an impressive amount of directory and classified information including notifications of retreats and residency opportunities, an affiliate directory, and lists of resources and services. Recommended for public libraries and academic libraries that support programs in religious studies.

4410. *The Muslim World.* Formerly (until 1948): *The Moslem World.* [ISSN: 0027-4909] 1911. q. GBP 308. Ed(s): Yahya M Michot. Wiley-Blackwell Publishing, Inc., 111 River St, Hoboken, NJ 07030; http://onlinelibrary.wiley.com. Illus., index, adv. Sample. Refereed. Vol. ends: Oct. Microform: PQC. Reprint: PSC. *Indexed:* A01, A22, AmHI, BAS, BRI, E01, MLA-IB, P61, R&TA. *Bk. rev.:* 2-3, 500-2,000 words; signed. *Aud.:* Ac, Sa.

The Muslim World is a long lived (founded 1911) quarterly academic journal that publishes on all aspects of Islam as a religion, and as a focal point for community and culture. Articles also frequently provide valuable insight into the relationships between Islam and other religious groups. More often than not, issues are themed, e.g., "Judaism and Islam in America" or "Shifting Boundaries: The Study of Islam in the Humanities." Issues contain approximately ten research articles as well five or so book reviews. This is an important resource for Islamic and Asian studies researchers, but it should also be included in any collection aiming to provide a comprehensive view of world religions. Recommended for academic libraries.

4411. *National Catholic Reporter: the independent news source.* [ISSN: 0027-8939] 1964. 26x/yr. USD 52.95 combined subscription domestic (print & online eds.); USD 92.95 combined subscription foreign (print & online eds.)). Ed(s): Stephanie Yeagle, Dennis Coday. National Catholic Reporter Publishing Co., 115 E Armour Blvd, Kansas City, MO 64111-1203; ncrsub@ncronline.org; http://ncronline.org. Illus., adv. Sample. Microform: PQC. *Indexed:* A01, A22, BRI, C26, Chicano. *Bk. rev.:* 1-2, 700-1,000 words; signed. *Aud.:* Ga, Ac.

The *National Catholic Reporter* is a biweekly independent Catholic newspaper (on actual newsprint) with a broadly liberal editorial policy. News and opinion columns address national and international events of interest to Catholics. The reporting on international politics is particularly strong and this international scope differentiates the *National Catholic Reporter* from the many provincial U.S. papers. The newspaper's website provides regularly updated, free content organized in the categories "Accountability," "Books," "Justice," "Media," "Parish," "People," "Politics," "Spirituality," "Theology," "Vatican," and "World." Both Catholics and non-Catholics will find this resource of interest. Recommended for public libraries. URL: https://www.ncronline.org/

4412. *New Oxford Review.* Former titles (until 1977): *American Church News;* (until 1959): *A C U News.* [ISSN: 0149-4244] 1940. m. USD 24 domestic; USD 38 combined subscription domestic (print & online eds.); USD 4.25 per issue domestic). Ed(s): Elena M Vree, Pieter Vree. New Oxford Review, Inc., 1069 Kains Ave, Berkeley, CA 94706. Illus. Vol. ends: Dec. Microform: PQC. *Indexed:* A01, A22, C26, MLA-IB. *Bk. rev.:* Number and length vary. *Aud.:* Ga, Ac.

The *New Oxford Review* is a politically and culturally conservative magazine that, according to its website, "was founded in 1977 as an Anglo-Catholic magazine in the Anglican tradition, taking its name from the 19th-century Oxford Movement." Articles look at the challenges to modern society, with recent articles including "No Enemies to the Left-Still! and "A New Age of Faith, Even for Atheists." The essays are bookended by brief news stories and book reviews. The magazine's website includes free access to news stories, as well as electronic access to digital versions of the magazine for subscribers. Recommended for public and academic libraries. URL: http://www.newoxfordreview.org/

4413. *Religion.* [ISSN: 0048-721X] 1971. q. GBP 457 (print & online eds.)). Ed(s): Michael Stausberg, Steven Engler. Taylor & Francis, 2, 3 & 4 Park Sq, Milton Park, Abingdon, OX14 4RN, United Kingdom; subscriptions@tandf.co.uk; https://www.tandfonline.com. Illus., adv. Sample. Refereed. Vol. ends: Oct. Reprint: PSC. *Indexed:* A01, A22, AmHI, BAS, BRI, E01, IBSS. *Bk. rev.:* 7-10, 1,000-1,700 words; signed. *Aud.:* Ac, Sa.

The articles in *Religion* are examinations of religion from many different humanities and social sciences fields such as history, archaeology, psychology, political science, and many others. Each issue contains approximately three to five research articles on world religions. Some issues may follow these articles with a "Review Symposium" section where authors contribute review essays concerning an important book. In religious studies such as "Review Symposium on Craig Martin's Capitalizing Religion." Sometimes, the entire issue is themed. The twelve or more book reviews are detailed in nature. Because of the cross-disciplinary and interdisciplinary nature of this journal, researchers and students from many different academic fields will find this journal useful. Recommended for academic libraries that collect for the humanities and social sciences.

4414. *Religion and American Culture: a journal of interpretation.* [ISSN: 1052-1151] 1991. 3x/yr. GBP 210 (print & online eds.)). Ed(s): Tracy Fessenden. Cambridge University Press, University Printing House, Shaftesbury Rd, Cambridge, CB2 8BS, United Kingdom; journals@cambridge.org; https://www.cambridge.org/. Illus., adv. Refereed. Circ: 575. *Indexed:* A01, A22, AmHI, BRI, E01, MLA-IB, P61, R&TA, SSA. *Aud.:* Ac, Sa.

The scholarship in this academic journal explores the interconnections, as well as the conflicts between religion and (primarily U.S.) American culture. The articles published here cover a lot of historical ground, examining the interplay between religion and culture from the colonial period to the present. Recent articles like "'Declension Comes Home': Cotton Mather, Male Youth Rebellion, and the Hope of Providential Affliction in Puritan New England" and "From Sputnik to Spaceship Earth: American Catholics and the Space Age" illustrate this broad scope. Book reviews are not included. Religious studies, cultural and critical studies, history, and sociology scholars will all find this valuable. Recommended for academic libraries that support collections in social sciences and humanities.

4415. *Religious Studies: an international journal for the philosophy of religion.* [ISSN: 0034-4125] 1965. q. GBP 399. Ed(s): Robin Le Poidevin. Cambridge University Press, University Printing House, Shaftesbury Rd, Cambridge, CB2 8BS, United Kingdom; journals@cambridge.org; https://www.cambridge.org/. Illus., index, adv. Sample. Refereed. Circ: 1200. Vol. ends: Dec. Microform: PQC. Reprint: PSC. *Indexed:* A22, AmHI, BAS, BRI, CBRI, E01, MLA-IB, R&TA. *Bk. rev.:* Number and length vary. *Aud.:* Ac, Sa.

Religious Studies is a quarterly journal published by Cambridge University Press that considers the philosophy of religion. The seven to ten articles per issue engage with world religion from a variety of philosophical perspectives, covering questions like the existence of free will, evolution, and creation, and the problem of evil. There are approximately two in-depth book reviews. Recommended for academic libraries that support research philosophy and religious studies.

4416. *Religious Studies Review: a quarterly review of publications in the field of religion and related disciplines.* [ISSN: 0319-485X] 1975. q. GBP 257 (print & online eds.)). Ed(s): Elias Bongmba, Jeremy Biles. Wiley-Blackwell Publishing, Inc., 111 River St, Hoboken, NJ 07030; http://onlinelibrary.wiley.com. Illus., index, adv. Sample. Refereed. Vol. ends: Oct. Reprint: PSC. *Indexed:* A01, A22, AmHI, BRI, CBRI, E01, R&TA. *Bk. rev.:* 1,000 plus annually; signed. *Aud.:* Ac, Sa.

Religious Studies Review is a quarterly journal that collects review articles about new publications in religion as well as related concepts and philosophies. Each issue contains extended bibliographic essays of either individual works or multiple texts that share similar topics. Each issue also contains many brief "Notes on Recent Publications," approximately 30 pages of book reviews (usually around 120 total) that are categorized by topic and geographic location. This is an important resource for religion scholars to keep abreast of new publications in a variety of religious studies areas. It is also a valuable collection development tool for library subject selectors in religious studies and theology. Recommended for academic libraries.

4417. *Review and Expositor: an international Baptist journal.* Formerly (until 1906): *The Baptist Review and Expositor.* [ISSN: 0034-6373] 1904. q. USD 911 (print & online eds.)). Ed(s): Mark E Biddle. Sage Publications, Inc., 2455 Teller Rd, Thousand Oaks, CA 91320; http://www.sagepub.com. Illus., index, adv. Vol. ends: Fall. Microform: PQC. Reprint: PSC. *Indexed:* A22, MLA-IB, R&TA. *Bk. rev.:* 30-50, 300-700 words; signed. *Aud.:* Ga, Sa.

This Baptist theological journal publishes articles on, according to its editors, "The Church's mission in the contemporary world." The article topics are wide-ranging, covering both New and Old Testament theology, and recent article titles include "The Aesthetic Integrity of the Book of Job: Job's Literary Integrity," "Cut from the Same Cloth: A Study of Female Patrons in Luke-Acts and the Roman Empire," and "What is Truth? The Complicated Characterization of Pontius Pilate in the Fourth Gospel." In addition to the research articles, a significant portion of the journal-titled "Expository Words-is devoted to the examination and discussion of specific Bible verses. Every issue also contains multiple book reviews divided among three categories: "Biblical studies," "Historical-theological studies," and "Ministerial studies." This is a useful journal for scholars and practitioners alike, and not only those from Baptist denominations; mainline Protestants and Catholics will also find much here of use. Recommended for both public and academic libraries, and particularly for those academic libraries that support the study of Christian theology.

4418. *Scottish Journal of Theology.* [ISSN: 0036-9306] 1948. q. GBP 212. Ed(s): Ian Torrance, Bryan Spinks. Cambridge University Press, University Printing House, Shaftesbury Rd, Cambridge, CB2 8BS, United Kingdom; journals@cambridge.org; https://www.cambridge.org/. Illus., index, adv. Sample. Refereed. Circ: 1200. Vol. ends: No. 4. Reprint: PSC. *Indexed:* A22, AmHI, BRI, E01, MLA-IB, R&TA. *Bk. rev.:* 10-15, 500-1,000 words; signed. *Aud.:* Ac, Sa.

This journal presents research articles that incorporate a variety of different scholarly approaches and maintaining an expansive and ecumenical approach to the study of theology. Every issue contains a copious amount of book reviews. This is an excellent resource for academic and seminary libraries.

4419. *Sociology of Religion: a quarterly review.* Former titles (until 1993): *S A. Sociological Analysis;* (until 1973): *Sociological Analysis;* (until 1964): *The American Catholic Sociological Review.* [ISSN: 1069-4404] 1940. q. EUR 189. Ed(s): Scott Schieman. Oxford University Press, 2001 Evans Rd, Cary, NC 27513; https://academic.oup.com/journals. Illus., index, adv. Refereed. Vol. ends: Winter. Microform: PQC. Reprint: PSC. *Indexed:* A01, A22, BRI, Chicano, IBSS, P61, R&TA, SSA. *Bk. rev.:* 10-12, 600-1,000 words; signed. *Aud.:* Ac.

Applying the theory and methods of sociology to all nature of religious phenomena, is this quarterly journal. Both quantitative and qualitative sociological approaches appear, and recent articles include "Religious Practices and Beliefs among Religious Stayers and Religious Switchers in Israeli Judaism" and "Beyond Conversion: Socio-Mental Flexibility and Multiple Religious Participation in African-Derived Lukumi and Ifa." Book reviews are included in every issue, as well as the latest news from the Association for the Sociology of Religion. Both sociologists and religious studies researchers may make good use of this publication. Recommended for academic libraries.

4420. *Sophia: international journal of philosophy and traditions.* [ISSN: 0038-1527] 1962. 4x/yr. EUR 577 (print & online eds.)). Ed(s): Jay Garfield, Patrick Hutchings. Springer Netherlands, Van Godewijckstraat 30, Dordrecht, 3311 GX, Netherlands; http://www.springer.com. Adv. Refereed. Microform: PQC. Reprint: PSC. *Indexed:* A22, AmHI, BRI, E01, MLA-IB. *Aud.:* Ac, Sa.

This philosophy of religion journal approaches the large variety of religious experience and phenomena through different philosophical lenses. One recent issue, for instance, employed to the thought of great thinkers such Kant, Badiou, and Derrida to better understand how religion deals with questions about existence and ethics. Every so often issues are dedicated to special topics such as "Philosophy, Violence and Metaphor" or "Biblical Philosophy." Each issue also includes three or four book reviews. Both philosophers and scholars of religion will find this journal useful. Recommended for academic libraries.

4421. *Studies in World Christianity: the Edinburgh review of theology and religion.* Formerly (until 1995): *Edinburgh Review of Theology and Religion.* [ISSN: 1354-9901] 1995. 3x/yr. GBP 167 (print & online eds.)).

Ed(s): Emma Wild-Wood, Alexander Chow. Edinburgh University Press Ltd., The Tun, Holyrood Rd, 12 (2f) Jackson's Entry, Edinburgh, EH8 8PJ, United Kingdom; journals@eup.ed.ac.uk; http://www.euppublishing.com. Illus., adv. Sample. Refereed. Vol. ends: No. 2. *Indexed:* A01, A22, AmHI, E01, R&TA. *Bk. rev.:* 15-20, 250-1,200 words; signed. *Aud.:* Ac.

This interdisciplinary journal publishes articles on Christianity across the world, in the west and well beyond. It explores the religion and its adherents in many countries where it is making inroads like China, India, and the Sudan. *Studies in World Christianity* offers fascinating insight into the dialectical interaction of Christianity and culture, with recent articles including "Buddhist Monks and Christian Friars: Religious and Cultural Exchange in the Making of Buddhism" and "Images of Islam: American Missionary and Arab Perspectives." There are also book reviews that, in the spirit of the journal, look at new material representing a wide range of peoples and cultures. Recommended for academic libraries that support religious studies programs, although this journal will be useful to many humanities and social science researchers and should therefore be considered for inclusion in collections in cognate areas like history and international studies.

4422. ***Theological Studies.*** [ISSN: 0040-5639] 1940. q. USD 650 (print & online eds.)). Ed(s): David G Schultenover. Sage Publications, Inc., 2455 Teller Rd, Thousand Oaks, CA 91320; http://www.sagepub.com. Illus., index. Sample. Refereed. Vol. ends: Dec. Microform: PQC. Reprint: PSC. *Indexed:* A01, A22, AmHI, BRI, C26, CBRI, MLA-IB, R&TA. *Bk. rev.:* Number and length vary. *Aud.:* Ac, Sa.

Founded by the Society of Jesus in 1940, *Theological Studies* is a quarterly journal dedicated to presenting the most current Christian theology by important scholars in the field. There is a lot of information packed into every issue, including peer-reviewed articles (sometimes divided into theme-related sections), research notes, multiple book reviews, and a list of books received. Recent articles include "Return of the Golden Calf: Economy, Idolatry, and Secularization since Gaudium et spes" and "Catholic Doctrine on Divorce and Remarriage: A Practical Theological Examination." Recommended for academic libraries and seminary libraries with collections that support research and study in Catholic theology.

4423. ***Theology Today.*** [ISSN: 0040-5736] 1944. q. USD 1054 (print & online eds.)). Ed(s): Gordon S Mikoski. Sage Publications, Inc., 2455 Teller Rd, Thousand Oaks, CA 91320; info@sagepub.com; http://www.sagepub.com/. Illus., index, adv. Sample. Refereed. Vol. ends: Jan. Microform: MIM; PQC. Reprint: PSC. *Indexed:* A01, A22, AmHI, BRI, CBRI, MLA-IB, R&TA. *Bk. rev.:* 15-30, 200-1,500 words; signed. *Aud.:* Ga, Ac.

A publication of Princeton Theological Seminary, *Theology Today* is a high-quality academic journal that prints articles covering a wide spectrum of theological topics relating to Christianity seeking to, as the editors state on the journal's website, "foster intellectual encounters between Christianity and the other Abrahamic faiths." Book reviews as well as the occasional review essay accompany journal issues. If an academic library can afford only one journal subscription relating to theology, this would be an excellent choice. URL: http://journals.sagepub.com/home/ttj

Tikkun Magazine. See News and Opinion section.

4424. ***Tricycle: the Buddhist review.*** [ISSN: 1055-484X] 1991. q. USD 40 combined subscription domestic (print & online eds.); USD 45 combined subscription Canada (print & online eds.); USD 55 combined subscription elsewhere (print & online eds.)). Ed(s): James Shaheen. The Tricycle Foundation, PO BOX 327, Congers, NY 10920; http://www.tricycle.com. Illus., adv. Vol. ends: Summer. *Indexed:* BRI, CBRI. *Bk. rev.:* 4-6, 400-1,000 words; signed. *Aud.:* Ga.

Tricycle is a mainstream Buddhist magazine aimed at practitioners. Each quarterly, full color, and approximately 90-page issue contains news, advice, and spiritual guidance (much of which comes from renowned Theraveda and Mahayana teachers) as well as brief teachings and reviews of books and other media aimed at popular audiences. Individual online subscribers have access to archival content, streaming movies related to Buddhism, and an e-book library. Recommended for public libraries of any size, and particularly for those that serve Buddhist communities. URL: https://tricycle.org/

4425. ***Worship.*** Formerly (until 1951): *Orate Fratres.* [ISSN: 0043-941X] 1926. bi-m. USD 160 Free to qualified personnel; USD 60 domestic. Liturgical Press, 2950 Saint John's Rd, P O Box 7500, Collegeville, MN 56321; sales@litpress.org; http://www.litpress.org. Illus., index. Sample. Refereed. Circ: 2604. Vol. ends: Nov. Microform: PQC. *Indexed:* A22, C26, MLA-IB, R&TA. *Bk. rev.:* 1-10, 500-1,200 words; signed. *Aud.:* Ac, Sa.

Worship is a venerable scholarly and academic journal(founded in 1926) dedicated to the study and renewal of Christian liturgy, i.e., prescribed public worship ritual, observances, and ceremony. Although the publication is Roman Catholic in origin and maintains a focus in this area, the editors state on the webpage that it aims at ecumenism. Issues contain approximately five essays, with recent articles including "Imagining the Liturgical Past through Literature" and "And the Two Become One Text: Rethinking the Mutual Influence between Monastic and Cathedral Liturgy." Besides the essays, there are book reviews and a regular feature, the "Amen Corner." *Worship* is also notable for its beautiful cover art and illustrations. Recommended for both scholars and practitioners such as clergy members. Appropriate for collection by academic libraries that support programs in liturgical, theological, and religious studies, as well as for inclusion into individual church library collections. URL: http://journalworship.org/Home/Index

4426. ***Zygon: journal of religion and science.*** [ISSN: 0591-2385] 1966. q. GBP 362. Ed(s): Willem B Drees. Wiley-Blackwell Publishing, Inc., 111 River St, Hoboken, NJ 07030; http://onlinelibrary.wiley.com. Illus., index, adv. Sample. Refereed. Vol. ends: Dec. Microform: PQC. Reprint: PSC. *Indexed:* A01, A22, AmHI, BRI, CBRI, E01, R&TA. *Bk. rev.:* 0-5, 1,300-3,000 words; signed. *Aud.:* Ac.

This quarterly academic journal connects science (both the hard and social sciences) with the study of religion. The variety of different scientific lenses applied to religious concepts makes for fascinating reading. Recent articles have looked at psychology and religious experience, modern Islam and technology, and science's relationship with theodicy. Besides the research articles, there are reflective pieces and the occasional discussion forum surrounding cutting edge and influential works. Book reviews are included in each issue. This journal will appeal to researchers in both religious studies and the health sciences, and it is recommended for academic libraries that support programs in both of these areas, as well as for medical libraries.

■ ROBOTICS

Kristan Majors Chilcoat, Science Librarian, Emory University, Woodruff Library, 540 Asbury Circle, Atlanta, GA 30322; kmajors@emory.edu

Introduction

Robotics is a reality throughout our world beyond toys, movies, and our imaginations. While they do not look like C-3PO or Robby, we can find robots in hospitals, academia, industries, government labs, and even our homes. Today's robots are wearable sensors, surgical robotic systems for minimally invasive surgery, planetary rovers, anthropomorphic manipulators for manufacturing, and self-driving cars.

The majority of the journals in this chapter support scientists actively involved in robotics research primarily in mechanical engineering and computer science fields. There is no one ideal collection for robotics, rather one developed around your local researchers' specializations and interests. Librarians should expect to subscribe to a combination of the following: (1) a selection of robotics journals; (2) core journals from the researchers' primary fields (usually mechanical engineering or computer science); and (3) journals in fields relevant to the specific robots they are developing, such as manufacturing, oceanic, aerospace, or medical fields. Thus, a collection supporting biomedical engineers using robotics for designing better prosthetics will be very different from one for computer scientists programming controllers for rescue robots.

Robotics is a growing research field and we are seeing new peer-reviewed journals released in recent years including open access and subscription publications. Researchers should evaluate any new journals to determine the research fields of the authors, the reputation of the journal, and the acceptance of the robotics community to the journal. Librarians should also consider subscription price and if the journal's scope meets your collection plan.

To best support advanced robotics researchers, libraries must have both journal and conference proceedings from the leading professional associations: the Institute of Electrical and Electronics Engineers (IEEE), the Association for Computing Machinery (ACM), and the American Society of Mechanical Engineers (ASME).

Fortunately, a public or college library can support their researchers and hobbyists without the expense of a specialized robotics collection. Because robotics crosses over so many industries and scientific disciplines having a variety of popular science magazines, trade publications, and multidisciplinary science journals, librarians can support most local researchers. Consumer magazines are best for amateurs, makers, and hobbyists who are interested in robot supplies, competitions, and DIY projects. Also add these titles to support school robotics clubs and local robotics competitions.

Librarians can answer many reference questions using *robot* or *robotics* as the keywords. Additional keywords are *manipulators, autonomous vehicles,* and *microbots.* Related fields include artificial intelligence (AI), electrical engineering, automation and control systems, human and computer interactions (HCI), cybernetics, mechatronics, and biomedical engineering.

Basic Periodicals

Hs: *Servo;* Ga: *IEEE Robotics and Automation Magazine;* Ac: *IEEE Transactions on Robotics, International Journal of Robotics Research.*

Basic Abstracts and Indexes

Academic Search Complete; Business Source Complete; IEEE Xplore; INSPEC; PubMed; Web of Science.

4427. ***A C M Transactions on Human - Robot Interaction.*** Formerly (until 2017): *Journal of Human - Robot Interaction.* [ISSN: 2573-9522] 2012. q. Free. Ed(s): Selma Sabanovic, Odest Jenkins. Association for Computing Machinery, 2 Penn Plaza, Ste 701, New York, NY 10121; usacm@acm.org; https://www.acm.org. Refereed. *Aud.:* Ac.

This open-access journal was started in 2012 as *Journal of Human-Robot Interaction* as a part of the ACM/IEEE Human-Robot Interaction (HRI) conference. In 2018 the journal was renamed. It currently is listed as an emerging title in Web of Science and does not have an impact factor yet. Three issues a year are published with about five articles in varying length per issue. The articles are written by psychologists, computer scientists, engineers, and lawyers. Articles are written for and by HRI scholars but are accessible to others, including undergraduates. Recent topics include a robot tutor for language lessons and personal assistive robots. This is a nice addition to any robotics collection.

4428. ***Autonomous Robots.*** [ISSN: 0929-5593] 1994. bi-m. EUR 2941 (print & online eds.)). Ed(s): Gaurav S Sukhatme. Springer New York LLC, 233 Spring St, New York, NY 10013; customerservice@springer.com; http://www.springer.com. Adv. Refereed. Reprint: PSC. *Indexed:* A22, CompLI, E01. *Aud.:* Ac, Sa.

As the title indicates, this journal specializes in papers on robots that are self-sufficient, which is defined as capable of performing in real-world environments. These robots acquire data through sensors, process it, perform their tasks, and are often mobile (legged, tracked, and even finned). Each issue comprises a dozen lengthy articles of 15 or more pages, often illustrated with color (in the tables and graphs as well as the photos), includes some multimedia, and numerous references. The authorship is international, from academia and industrial-research laboratories and often with collaboration from both. The subscription price will likely limit this journal to academic and industrial collections with researchers specializing in autonomous systems.

4429. ***Bioinspiration & Biomimetics: learning from nature.*** [ISSN: 1748-3182] 2006. q. Ed(s): R J Fuller. Institute of Physics Publishing Ltd., Temple Circus, Temple Way, Bristol, BS1 6HG, United Kingdom; custserv@iop.org; http://iopscience.iop.org. Sample. Refereed. *Aud.:* Ac, Sa.

The scope of the journal is broader than robotics, covering all branches of engineering. The basic concept is to apply functions and designs adapted from biological systems to technology. Obvious examples are bird flight to aircraft design, but recent articles have discussed taking inspiration from living cells to build artificial ultra-thin films for microrobots and a water-walking robot mimicking a water strider insect. This journal publishes every two months, and its issues are generally composed of a dozen or so articles, but also include reviews. The time between submission and publication is swift, often under six months. Suitable for programs in engineering design, biomedical engineering, materials science, and robotics.

4430. ***Frontiers in Neurorobotics.*** [ISSN: 1662-5218] 2007. . Free. Ed(s): Florian Roehrbein, Alois Knoll. Frontiers Research Foundation, Avenue du Tribunal Federal 34, Lausanne, 1005, Switzerland; info@frontiersin.org; https://www.frontiersin.org. Refereed. *Indexed:* A01. *Aud.:* Ac.

A specialized journal that focuses on neural systems in robots, machines, and artificial software and hardware. This open-access journal began in 2007 and was first given a journal impact factor in 2015. A recent research article in the journal compares using a joystick versus a glove designed as a wearable robot to help drive a wheelchair for the elderly. *Frontiers* publishes a variety of articles, many based on special topics, known as research topics. Articles vary in length and include color photographs, figures, and algorithms. Written mostly by engineers and roboticists, this journal is cited by biomedical engineers and neuroscientists too. Recommend for robotics and biomedical engineering research collections.

4431. ***I E E E Robotics and Automation Letters.*** [ISSN: 2377-3766] 2016. q. USD 715. Ed(s): Allison Okamura. Institute of Electrical and Electronics Engineers, 445 Hoes Ln, Piscataway, NJ 08854; customer.service@ieee.org; http://www.ieee.org. Refereed. *Aud.:* Ac.

A new journal started in 2016 by the IEEE Robotics and Automation Society. This peer-reviewed journal seeks to stand out by providing timely (papers published within six months of submission) and concise (six to eight pages maximum) articles. Despite the brevity, each article includes the flow charts, algorithms, color diagrams, and references one expects with robotics articles. Recent articles include path planning in unknown environments for bipedal robots and moving large objects with a multi-arm robot. Most authors are engineers from universities. The subscription price is reasonable. This a great addition to any collection supporting robotics researchers.

4432. ***I E E E Robotics and Automation Magazine.*** [ISSN: 1070-9932] 1994. q. USD 525. Ed(s): Bram Vanderborght. Institute of Electrical and Electronics Engineers, 445 Hoes Ln, Piscataway, NJ 08854; contactcenter@ieee.org; http://www.ieee.org. Illus., index. Refereed. Vol. ends: No. 4. *Indexed:* A22. *Bk. rev.:* 1, 500 words. *Aud.:* Ga, Ac, Sa.

This magazine, from the IEEE Robotics and Automation Society, publishes the more practical material not suitable for its *Transactions.* Not really a glossy magazine, it is still attractive, with many color photographs and relatively short, well-illustrated articles designed for both engineers and academia. Each issue includes several peer-reviewed research papers plus short sections on society business, columns (such as "women in engineering"), industry news, tutorials, and the like. The content level is quite approachable by undergraduates and lay readers and the price is modest (for a professional journal), making this a suitable selection for most academic libraries, as well as libraries that serve active robotics industries.

4433. ***I E E E Transactions on Robotics.*** Supersedes in part (in 2004): *I E E E Transactions on Robotics and Automation;* Which was formerly (until 1989): *I E E E Journal of Robotics and Automation.* [ISSN: 1552-3098] 1985. bi-m. USD 1450. Ed(s): Kevin Lynch. Institute of Electrical and Electronics Engineers, 445 Hoes Ln, Piscataway, NJ 08854; contactcenter@ieee.org; http://www.ieee.org. Illus., index, adv. Refereed. Vol. ends: No. 6. *Indexed:* A01, A22, B01. *Aud.:* Ac, Sa.

IEEE Transactions on Robotics (*T-RO*) is a core robotics title. It is highly ranked in the Journal Citation Reports (JCR) and is published by the IEEE Robotics and Automation Society. Articles in *T-RO* are written by and for computer scientists, engineers, mathematicians, roboticists, and industry professionals in related fields. Topics focus on applications of robots in industries such as medical, space, agriculture, and military. Article keywords include *mobile robots, navigation, robot kinematics, grasping, aerospace electronics, intelligent machines,* and *graph theory.* This title is published six times a year, and each issue includes 20 to 30 articles consisting of 15-page regular papers and 10-page short papers. Color images, graphs, and mathematical equations are included in most articles, along with some multimedia in a few articles. Extensive references are provided in each article.

4434. *Intelligent Service Robotics.* [ISSN: 1861-2776] 2006. 4x/yr. Ed(s): Wan K Chung. Springer, Tiergartenstr 17, Heidelberg, 69121, Germany; subscriptions@springer.com; https://www.springer.com. Refereed. Reprint: PSC. *Indexed:* A22, E01. *Aud.:* Ac, Sa.

Intelligent Service Robotics focuses on new technologies for intelligent robots that can assist and support humans. Written for and by engineers and computer scientists, this title can be of interest to those in artificial intelligence and biomedical engineering. Recent articles include development of controls for rehabilitation robots and autonomous drone technologies. Published quarterly, issues include research papers with algorithms and figures. This journal is ranked in the *Journal Citation Reports* for robotics, but because of the journal's specialized focus it is not necessary for all robotics collections. The journal should be considered for collections supporting researchers focusing on service robots and human-robot interactions.

4435. *International Journal of Advanced Robotic Systems.* Incorporates (2004-2012): *Journal of Humanoids.* [ISSN: 1729-8814] 2004. . Free. Sage Publications Ltd., 1 Oliver's Yard, 55 City Rd, London, EC1Y 1SP, United Kingdom; https://www.sagepub.com/. Illus., adv. Sample. Refereed. *Aud.:* Ac.

A peer-reviewed, open-access journal that "focuses on the full spectrum of robotics." The authors are internationally diverse consisting of mostly academic computer scientists and engineers. Published online continuously, each issue includes more than 20 research articles, editorials, and reviews. The articles are often about control systems or algorithms and include schematics and figures. Special themes are common with recent topics including 3D vision and robot path planning. This journal changed publishers, so worth watching to see if the impact factor increases and if robotics researchers begin to cite it more frequently.

4436. *International Journal of Medical Robotics and Computer Assisted Surgery (Online).* [ISSN: 1478-596X] 2004. q. GBP 689. Ed(s): Mehran Anvari. John Wiley & Sons Ltd., EMEA Institutional Sales, 9600 Garsington Rd, Oxford, OX4 2DQ, United Kingdom; cs-journals@wiley.com; http://onlinelibrary.wiley.com. Illus. Refereed. *Aud.:* Ac, Sa.

This peer-reviewed journal seeks to provide a cross-disciplinary platform for researchers in robotics, engineering, and surgeons. It is the official journal for the Clinical Robotic Surgery Association. The authors of many of the articles are co-authored by engineers and physicians. The topics focus on the enhancements and developments of the technology for medical imaging and robot assisted surgery. The title is highly specialized and expensive so likely best for libraries supporting biomedical engineering and medical robotics programs. Both the surgeons and the engineers tend to publish in their primary fields, so most other libraries can rely upon their primary collections.

4437. *The International Journal of Robotics Research.* [ISSN: 0278-3649] 1982. 14x/yr. USD 3498 (print & online eds.)). Ed(s): John M Hollerbach. Sage Publications Ltd., 1 Oliver's Yard, 55 City Rd, London, EC1Y 1SP, United Kingdom; info@sagepub.com; https://www.sagepub.com/. Illus., index. Sample. Refereed. Vol. ends: Dec. Microform: PQC. Reprint: PSC. *Indexed:* A01, A22, B01, CompLI, E01, ErgAb. *Aud.:* Ac, Sa.

Billing itself as the first scholarly publication in robotics, it has one of the highest Impact Factors in the field. The articles are relatively lengthy, and the treatment is highly mathematical. A multidisciplinary journal with common topics including navigation, motion planning, and mapping. Multimedia, datasets, code, and images are included in the articles, as are extensive reference lists. This is an excellent title and essential for any robotics research collection as very often this is the title that authors publish in and cite.

4438. *International Journal of Social Robotics.* [ISSN: 1875-4805] 2009. 6x/yr. EUR 736. Ed(s): Shuzhi Sam Ge. Springer Netherlands, Van Godewijckstraat 30, Dordrecht, 3311 GX, Netherlands; http://www.springer.com. Refereed. *Aud.:* Ga, Ac, Sa.

Social robotics is defined by the journal as the study of robots that are able to communicate and interact with humans, the environment, and other robots. This has caught the attention of a multidisciplinary audience in psychology, sociology, computer science, and engineering. Authors often include a mix of industry and academic teams ranging from the entertainment industry to pediatrics. Themed issues are common and have included therapy and artificial empathy. Recent article titles are "collaborative play of the humanoid robot with children with autism" and "people's attitudes to robots in caring for the elderly." Articles are often 10 to 15 pages, include many color figures and diagrams, and extensive references. The journal seeks to be a resource for students, engineers, and researchers either new to or established in the Social Robotics field and indeed the articles are very much accessible for undergraduates and likely even AP high school students. A great addition to a robotics collection and worth further review for psychology and engineering collections.

4439. *Journal of Field Robotics.* Formerly (until 2006): *Journal of Robotic Systems.* [ISSN: 1556-4959] 1984. bi-m. GBP 3202. Ed(s): Sanjiv Singh, Sanae Urano Minick. John Wiley & Sons, Inc., 111 River St, Hoboken, NJ 07030; cs-journals@wiley.com; http://onlinelibrary.wiley.com. Illus., index, adv. Sample. Refereed. Vol. ends: Dec. Microform: PQC. Reprint: PSC. *Indexed:* A22, CompLI. *Aud.:* Ac, Sa.

The *Journal of Field Robotics* specializes in robots that work in unstructured environments (the "field"). Almost every article features an actual robot rather than a theoretical concept. Color and photographs add to the usual graphs, computer models, equations, and flowcharts. Recent articles include vision-guided autonomous vehicles and underwater robotic mapping. Thematic issues include agricultural robotics and the DARPA Challenge. A quality research journal cited by computer scientists, engineers, and roboticists and ranked highly in JCR for robotics, yet this is one of the most expensive publications in the robotics area. Therefore, best for academic and corporate libraries supporting robotics or engineering departments specializing in related areas, such as aerospace, mining, and automotive.

4440. *Journal of Intelligent and Robotic Systems: with a special section devoted to unmanned systems.* Incorporates (in 1994): *Mechatronic Systems Engineering.* [ISSN: 0921-0296] 1988. 16x/yr. EUR 3705 (print & online eds.)). Ed(s): Kimon P Valavanis. Springer Netherlands, Van Godewijckstraat 30, Dordrecht, 3311 GX, Netherlands; http://www.springer.com. Illus., index, adv. Sample. Refereed. Vol. ends: No. 4. Microform: PQC. Reprint: PSC. *Indexed:* A22, BRI, E01, ErgAb. *Aud.:* Ac, Sa.

The mission of this journal is to "bridge the gap between theory and practice in all areas of intelligent systems and robotics." Autonomous systems are emphasized and terms "UAV" often appears in the article titles. Recent work discusses unmanned aircraft and parcel delivery by drones. Authorship is international, with most researchers from academia, but there is a fair percentage with industrial collaboration. Authors explore the theoretical via simulation or modeling, whereas others create case studies and prototypes. This is a core titles, so a must for supporting robotics collections for both mechanical engineers and computer scientists.

4441. *Journal of Mechanisms and Robotics.* [ISSN: 1942-4302] 2009. bi-m. USD 914; USD 1099 combined subscription (print & online eds.)). Ed(s): Venkat Krovi. The American Society of Mechanical Engineers, Two Park Ave, New York, NY 10016; CustomerCare@asme.org; http://www.asme.org. Sample. Refereed. *Aud.:* Ac, Sa.

Also known as JME and the *Journal of Mechanisms and Robotics-Transactions of the ASME* (American Society of Mechanical Engineers), this journal focuses on theoretical and applied articles about the movement of robots and mechanisms, including manipulators and haptic devices. The journal also includes annually a special issue with selected papers from an ASME conference. Authors are internationally diverse and are mainly from academia and national labs. Recent articles, which are primarily cited by mechanical engineers and robotics researchers, discuss propulsion systems for spherical robots, using origami designs for a solar tracking system, and designing redundantly actuated parallel manipulators. Highly mathematical, this journal is best for those advanced researchers specializing in kinematics of robotics and mechanisms.

4442. *Journal of Robotic Surgery.* [ISSN: 1863-2483] 2007. bi-m. Ed(s): David . Albala. Springer U K, 236 Gray's Inn Rd, Fl 6, London, WC1X 8HB, United Kingdom; derk.haank@springer.com; http://www.springer.com/. Adv. Refereed. Reprint: PSC. *Indexed:* A22, E01. *Aud.:* Sa.

Robotic surgery is now commonplace, but there are few publications that emphasize the theory and practice of minimally invasive surgery (see the *International Journal of Medical Robotics and Computer Assisted Surgery,* above in this section). This journal features short (average of five to ten pages) color-illustrated articles, most of which describe in detail the use of robotic instruments and techniques in specific types of surgery. Occasionally, supplementary material (usually videos) accompany the articles. Surgeons and medical school faculty are the primary audience and authors. This title is too specialized for any but medical collections or corporations that produce medical instruments.

4443. *Robotica.* [ISSN: 0263-5747] 1983. 7x/yr. Ed(s): G S Chirikjian. Cambridge University Press, University Printing House, Shaftesbury Rd, Cambridge, CB2 8BS, United Kingdom; journals@cambridge.org; https://www.cambridge.org/. Illus., index, adv. Sample. Refereed. Circ: 600. Vol. ends: No. 6. Reprint: PSC. *Indexed:* A01, A22, BRI, CBRI, CompLI, E01, ErgAb. *Aud.:* Ac, Sa.

One of the earliest professional journals on robotics. Papers are research level with a focus on "sound theory and realistic applications in robotics." The articles are 15 to 20 pages in length. Articles tend to have a mathematical focus with algorithms and theorems provided. Recent titles include an algorithm for mobile robot navigation and robot manipulators using differential equations. Authors are primarily engineers and roboticists from universities worldwide. A good journal for robotics collections in academia.

4444. *Robotics and Autonomous Systems.* Formerly (until 1988): *Robotics.* [ISSN: 0921-8890] 1985. 12x/yr. EUR 2687. Elsevier BV, Radarweg 29, Amsterdam, 1043 NX, Netherlands; info@elsevier.com; https://www.elsevier.com. Illus., index, adv. Sample. Refereed. Vol. ends: No. 4. *Indexed:* A01, A22, BRI, CompLI. *Aud.:* Ac, Sa.

Autonomous systems are getting a lot of attention these days, with autonomous vehicles being the hot topic. Yet, this journal has been publishing since 1985 and is affiliated with the Intelligent Autonomous Systems Society since shortly after it was founded in the 1990s. Topics can range from the theoretical to experimental and focus primarily on robot control and learning of autonomous systems in industry, outdoor environments, or outer space. Articles average 10 to 15 pages in length. While articles are often written by a team of authors from a variety of fields based on expertise and topic, the majority of the authors are engineers and computer scientists from national and international research labs and universities. There are several thematic issues per year on such topics as multimodal robot control and human-like locomotion. Heavily cited by other robotics journals, this is a good addition for industry or academic robotics collections.

4445. *Robotics and Computer-Integrated Manufacturing: an international journal of manufacturing, product and process development.* Incorporates (1988-1998): *Computer Integrated Manufacturing Systems;* (1988-1991): *Advanced Manufacturing Engineering.* [ISSN: 0736-5845] 1984. bi-m. EUR 2688. Ed(s): A Sharon. Pergamon Press, The Blvd, Langford Ln, E Park, Kidlington, OX5 1GB, United Kingdom; JournalsCustomerServiceEMEA@elsevier.com; http://www.elsevier.nl. Illus., adv. Sample. Refereed. Microform: PQC. *Indexed:* A22, B01, CompLI, ErgAb. *Aud.:* Ac.

Focusing on "new or improved industrial robots and unique manufacturing technologies," this journal is an interdisciplinary one that seeks to avoid overly mathematical or theoretical papers. Topics include cloud-based manufacturing, medical robotics, human-robot collaborations, and mechatronics. Most authors are mechanical engineers working in universities. Articles average 10 pages in length but occasionally are up to 20 pages. Illustrations include high resolution photographs, flow charts, figures, and screen images. Articles are well referenced. This journal cites both robotics and manufacturing journals but is primarily cited by manufacturing engineering journals. Good for industrial robotics collections.

4446. *Science Robotics.* [ISSN: 2470-9476] 2016. m. Free to members. American Association for the Advancement of Science (A A A S), 1200 New York Ave, NW, Washington, DC 20005; membership@aaas.org. Refereed. *Bk. rev.:* No. *Aud.:* Ac, Sa.

The journal started in 2016 and the scope is "broad, addressing both theoretical advances and practical applications." The editors intend to appeal to "both researchers and general stakeholders," but readers do need some advanced knowledge in robotics. While too new for an impact factor, authors are not shying away from publishing here. Authors are mostly academic with some collaborators from national labs and hospitals. Published monthly with five research articles about ten pages each, a few editorials, brief focus papers, and reviews. Given the audience and subscription price, this journal is best for academic or special libraries supporting robotics departments.

4447. *Servo.* [ISSN: 1546-0592] 2003. m. USD 26.95 domestic; USD 33.95 Canada; USD 44.95 foreign. T & L Publications, Inc., 430 Princeland Ct, Corona, CA 92879. Adv. Sample. *Aud.:* Hs, Ga, Ac.

This little magazine is for the amateur robot enthusiasts, but "amateur" does not mean "untrained." The readership is technology-savvy and the articles (and blog posts) reflect this. The magazine covers robot construction, software, circuits, sensors, batteries, and more for hobbyists. The magazine includes a "then and now" column, combat zone, new product highlights, and various feature DIY articles. The articles are deliberately short and well-illustrated. There is an impediment to online library subscriptions in that a password is required and proxy authentication is not allowed, but fortunately, the paper copy is inexpensive. This is an excellent title for any library supporting hobbyists and robotics clubs including public libraries and high school libraries.

4448. *Soft Robotics.* [ISSN: 2169-5172] 2013. bi-m. USD 3105. Ed(s): Barry Trimmer, Craig Ryan. Mary Ann Liebert, Inc. Publishers, 140 Huguenot St, 3rd Fl, New Rochelle, NY 10801; info@liebertpub.com; http://www.liebertpub.com. Adv. Sample. Refereed. Reprint: PSC. *Aud.:* Ac, Sa.

This journal focuses on robots that can interact safely with living systems for use in industries such as healthcare and aeronautics. Recent articles include controls for a robotic catheter and pneumatic artificial muscles. The editorial board consists of an international mix of engineers, biologists, and computer scientists from academia. It is published four to six times a year with about ten original research articles in every issue. Authors are mostly engineers and robotics researchers from universities, but some co-authors include national labs and industry researchers. An essential title now for libraries supporting soft robotics labs and recommended for extensive academic collections in robotics and biomedical engineering.

■ SAFETY

See also Medicine; and Public Health sections.

Christine K. Oka, Library Instruction Coordinator, Snell Library, Northeastern University, Boston, MA 02115; c.oka@northeastern.edu

Introduction

Safety covers a broad range of topics, ranging from regulations and policy, industrial safety and hygiene, injury and accident prevention, to occupational health and safety training programs and crime prevention. It is a challenge to avoid "mission creep" as the subject of safety is so interdisciplinary. A number of the listed subscription-based publications are available online and may be of interest to a general audience. Other more specialized titles are appropriate for special or academic library collections, or practitioners.

During these tough budgetary times, many publishers have chosen not to send samples of print issues for review, or direct reviewers to "sample issues" on their journal web page. Sometimes the online samples are older issues and may not be representative of the publication today. This section comprises a combination of subscription and open-access titles from a variety of publishers. Many of the openly accessible resources allow libraries, and their readers, to connect to safety information. Organizations such as the National Safety Council have a web page linking to articles, news, and advisories on safety issues in a number of venues: work, the home, and on the road. Governmental agencies, such as OSHA (Occupational Safety and Health Administration), CDC (Centers for Disease Control) and Federal Emergency Management Agency (FEMA) also are excellent sources for safety information.

Basic Periodicals

Ga: *Campus Safety Magazine, Industrial Safety and Hygiene News, Professional Safety;* Ac, Sa: *Accident Analysis & Prevention, Campus Safety Magazine, EHS Today, Industrial Safety and Hygiene News, New Solutions.*

Basic Abstracts and Indexes

Health and Safety Science Abstracts, Risk Abstracts, SafetyLit.org

4449. *Accident Analysis & Prevention.* [ISSN: 0001-4575] 1969. m. bi-m. until 2013. EUR 3794. Ed(s): M Abdel-Aty. Elsevier Ltd, The Boulevard, Langford Lane, Oxford, OX5 1GB, United Kingdom; http://www.elsevier.com. Illus., index, adv. Sample. Refereed. Vol. ends: Oct. Microform: PQC. *Indexed:* A01, A22, B01, ErgAb, HRIS. *Aud.:* Ac, Sa.

Affiliated with the Association for the Advancement of Automotive Medicine (AAAM), *Accident Analysis & Prevention* "provides wide coverage of the general areas relating to accidental injury and damage, including the pre-injury and immediate post-injury phases. Published papers deal with medical, legal, economic, educational, behavioral, theoretical or empirical aspects of transportation accidents, as well as with accidents at other sites." The multidisciplinary scope makes this journal of interest to "regional planners, research scientists, civil engineers, trauma physicians, psychologists, [and] public health planners." The original research articles are international in scope. Occasionally, special thematic issues are published, such as research examining the effect of fatigue on "safety, wellness and effectiveness" in driving, the workplace, scheduling, and efficiency. The articles may be of interest to a general audience reading about the relationship of accidents to fatigue, scheduling (one example was the relationship of early morning classes and teenage vehicle crashes), distracted driving and texting while walking. Online articles on the Elsevier ScienceDirect platform are accompanied with links to "Recommended Articles" and "Citing Articles." Recommended for large public libraries, special, and academic libraries.

American Journal of Public Health. See Public Health section.

4450. *Campus Safety Magazine.* 1993. 9x/yr. USD 30 domestic; USD 60 foreign. Ed(s): Robin Hattersley Gray. E H Publishing, Inc., 111 Speen St, Ste 200, PO Box 989, Framingham, MA 01701; info@ehpub.com; http://www.ehpub.com. Adv. Circ: 29693. *Aud.:* Ac, Sa.

Founded in 1993, *Campus Safety Magazine* is described as "the only publication that reaches public safety and security decisionmakers in hospitals, K-12 schools, and universities." *Campus Safety Magazine* is available in print and accessible online with added-value content in webinars, e-newsletters, social media, and other online content. The magazine's homepage is packed with news, product information, research, a blog, photos, video, podcasts, webcasts, and downloads. Magazine topics focus on safety and security within campus environments, such as schools, universities, and hospital settings. Broad subjects under discussion range from Clery/Title IX, school safety, hospital and university security, sexual and other types of harassment, along with security technology, emergency management, and disaster response whether from violence, weather, or other natural disasters. Recent topics covered the U.S. Department of Health and Human Services (HHS) report, 2019-2022 National Health Security Strategy (released every four years), and more general discussions of concealed carry laws by state and cybersecurity. One cybersecurity article named social media companies fined for violating the Child's Online Privacy Protection Act (COPPA). Regular departments in each issue includes updates "From the Editor's Desk," "News Watch," and "Tools of the Trade." While the mission of *Campus Safety Magazine* is "to serve campus police chiefs, security directors, IT personnel and executive administrators" involved in public safety and security, the articles are accessible to a general audience as well as campus staff members and parents. Recommended for academic and special libraries and public libraries. Individuals may register for free access to content and e-mail updates at https://www.campussafetymagazine.com/.

4451. *E H S Today: the magazine of safety, health and loss prevention.* Formerly (until 2008): *Occupational Hazards.* [ISSN: 1945-9599] 1938. m. USD 69 domestic (Free to qualified personnel). Ed(s): Sandy Smith. Penton, 1100 Superior Ave., Cleveland, OH 44114; information@penton.com; http://www.penton.com. Illus., index, adv. Sample. Circ: 65000 Paid and controlled. Vol. ends: Dec. Microform: PQC. *Indexed:* A22, B01, BRI, C42. *Aud.:* Ga, Ac, Sa.

This trade publication contains "news on industrial safety, occupational health, environmental control, insurance, first aid, medical care, [and] hazardous material control," and articles examining risk in the workplace. Updates on EPA, NIOSH, and OSHA compliance requirements, as well as articles about improving safety and industrial hygiene programs, make this a valuable resource for safety, human resources, business, and industry professionals. The magazine has an online presence with tabs for safe information on environment, health, safety, standards, construction, PPE (personal protection equipment), training, emergency management, industrial hygiene, and leadership. Articles cover big issues, such as ergonomics, mental illness in the workplace, safety in confined spaces, and planning for environmental compliance. But there are smaller, important topics as well. Recent issues discussed employee health promotion, such as how hand washing can reduce absenteeism, ergonomic awareness in the workplace to reduce overuse injuries, or employee training for timely response to workplace violence. A regular feature in each issue are the safety equipment product reviews. The publisher's website provides up-to-date information and links to news articles. There is extensive online information accessible through the *EHS Today* webpage, the online magazine, and through social media. Readers may subscribe by email to a weekly update newsletter. Recommended for special and academic libraries. Public libraries can link to the website, as the information is relevant in most environments, jargon-free and accessible. URL: www.ehstoday.com

4452. *Indoor Air (Online): international journal of indoor environment and health.* [ISSN: 1600-0668] 1991. bi-m. GBP 787. Ed(s): Yuguo Li. Wiley-Blackwell Publishing, Inc., 111 River St, Hoboken, NJ 07030; http://onlinelibrary.wiley.com. Refereed. *Aud.:* Ac, Sa.

One reads about dangerous or unhealthy air quality in mines and factories, but there are similar safety and public health issues indoors. *Indoor Air,* the official journal of the International Society of Indoor Air Quality and Climate, provides a forum for the sharing of original research "in the broad area defined by the indoor environment of non-industrial buildings." The journal is multidisciplinary and international in scope, with peer-reviewed articles on broad subjects in this field, such as thermal comfort, monitoring and modeling, ventilation, and other environmental control techniques to present information for "designers, building owners, and operators to provide a healthy and comfortable environment for building occupants, as well as giving medical practitioners information on how to deal with illnesses related to the indoor environment. The journal is published on the Wiley Online Library platform with a link to Video Abstracts. The video abstracts option is offered to all accepted authors of the journal. The service is managed by Wiley in partnership with Research Square which makes "a professionally and custom-produced video abstract to accompany their article. This audio-visual content helps others to quickly understand the research and makes the findings accessible to a much broader audience." Selected research information is now available in a multimedia format on vimeo. Recommended for special and academic libraries as well as larger public libraries.

4453. *Industrial Safety & Hygiene News.* Former titles (until 199?): *Chilton's Industrial Safety and Hygiene News;* (until 1982): *Industrial Safety and Hygiene News;* (until 1981): *Industrial Safety Product News;* (until 1978): *Safety Products News.* [ISSN: 2328-9147] 1967. m. Free to qualified personnel (print or online ed.)). Ed(s): Benita Mehta, Dave Johnson. B N P Media II, LLC., 2401 W Big Beaver Rd, Ste 700, Troy, MI 48084; portfolio@bnpmedia.com; http://www.bnpmedia.com. Illus., adv. Sample. Microform: PQC. *Indexed:* B01, B03, BRI. *Aud.:* Ga, Ac, Sa.

Touted by the publisher, BNP Media, as "The market's only monthly tabloid-sized publication, *Industrial Safety & Hygiene News* (*ISHN*) is consistently ranked as the most useful media brand serving environmental health and safety professionals." This trade journal focuses on news and products related to health and safety in the work environment and contains information on OSHA and EPA regulations, as well as practical safety and health-management news for managers at manufacturing facilities of all sizes. Articles in recent issues reflect some of the risks in these high-hazard environments, such as training workers to identify hazards and report them, using virtual reality (VR) safely for training, protective clothing and equipment, the importance of assessing risks and having a culture of safety in the workplace. The *ISHN* website provides access to current and archived issues; you can sign in for free access to articles. The site has added value with links to the latest headlines, the "ISHN Blog," "Featured Stories," and an events calendar for safety professionals. Highly recommended. URL: www.ishn.com/

4454. *Journal of Patient Safety.* [ISSN: 1549-8417] 2005. q. USD 1061. Ed(s): David Westfall Bates. Lippincott Williams & Wilkins, Two Commerce Sq, 2001 Market St, Philadelphia, PA 19103; customerservice@lww.com; http://www.lww.com. Adv. Refereed. *Aud.:* Ga, Ac, Sa.

International in scope, the *Journal of Patient Safety* is the official journal of the National Patient Safety Foundation (NPSF) and the Institute for Healthcare Improvement (IHI). Working as one organization since 2017 and "committed to using its combined knowledge and resources to focus and energize the patient safety agenda in order to build systems of safety across the continuum of care." The journal is an academic, peer-reviewed publication dedicated "to both rigorous research and field application articles" on all areas of patient safety and quality health care. Recent issues contain a mix of research as well as real-world findings. The research included analysis of the literature regarding medication errors and adverse effects, or a study of the challenges of multiteam systems in emergency medical services and what can be done to improve patient safety. Some real-world articles included a description of a six-month pilot project for patient safety rounds (PSR) "to examine the provider perspective of patient safety and to educate personnel about national patient safety goals at clinics associated with a large research and education institution." The article topics truly range "from bench to bedside," presenting "research advanced and field application in every area of patient safety... articles describing near-miss opportunities, system modifications" that prevent error makes this publication highly recommended for academic and special libraries serving medical researchers and practitioners.

4455. *Journal of Safety Research: a safety and health research forum.* [ISSN: 0022-4375] 1969. q. bi-m. until 2013. EUR 1592. Ed(s): Thomas Planek. Pergamon Press, The Blvd, Langford Ln, E Park, Kidlington, OX5 1GB, United Kingdom; JournalsCustomerServiceEMEA@elsevier.com; http://www.elsevier.com. Illus., adv. Sample. Refereed. Microform: PQC. *Indexed:* A01, A22, BRI, ErgAb, HRIS. *Aud.:* Ac, Sa.

Jointly published by the National Safety Council (www.nsc.org) and Elsevier, the *Journal of Safety Research* provides a multidisciplinary forum for the "exchange of scientific evidence in all areas of safety and health, including traffic, workplace, home and community." The focus here is on "basic and applied research in unintentional injury and illness prevention...to engage the global scientific community including academic researchers, engineers, government agencies, policy makers, corporate decision makers, safety professionals and practitioners, psychologists, social scientists, and public health professionals." Recent articles have included a cost analysis of falls and the need for fall prevention, the connection between belief and behavior in wearing a seat belt while in the car, or the evaluation of a parent education program on recognizing and managing sport-related concussion injuries of their child. *Journal of Safety Research* supports open access and provides a search filter to locate open-access articles. The range of highly focused research topics contained in each issue of the journal provides something of interest to scholars and safety practitioners. Recommended for academic, special libraries, and large public libraries.

Journal of Transportation Safety & Security. See Transportation section.

4456. *New Solutions: a journal of environmental and occupational health policy.* [ISSN: 1048-2911] 1990. q. USD 413 (print & online eds.)). Ed(s): Craig Slatin. Sage Publications, Inc., 2455 Teller Rd, Thousand Oaks, CA 91320; info@sagepub.com; http://www.sagepub.com. Adv. Sample. Refereed. Reprint: PSC. *Indexed:* ErgAb, SSA. *Aud.:* Ga, Ac, Sa.

This peer-reviewed journal attempts "to both define the issues and offer perspective for change" with the interconnected issues of health, work, and the environment. Their contributors are "scientists and policy-makers in academia and government, unionists on the shop floor, environmentalists in their many habitats, and advocates and activists on the streets, all well placed to see what works and what doesn't in policies for sustainable development." Recent articles evaluate the effectiveness of the California Safer Consumer Products Program ten years after implementation, or studied the effects of violence on long-term care staff, "the most common type of workplace violence in the healthcare setting." Thematic, special issues are published, such as one about "BP Oil Spill and Community Sustainability." Published by SAGE Publications, the journal "investigates problems of occupational and environmental health with the people at risk—the workers and the community—uppermost in mind." Writing is accessible for general readers. Highly recommended for academic, special, and public libraries.

4457. *Professional Safety.* Former titles (until 1970): *A S S E Journal;* (until 1969): *American Society of Safety Engineers. Journal.* [ISSN: 0099-0027] 1956. m. USD 51 (Individuals, USD 60). Ed(s): Sue Trebswether. American Society of Safety Engineers, 520 N, Northwest Hwy, Park Ridge, IL 60068; customerservice@asse.org; http://www.asse.org. Illus., index, adv. Sample. Refereed. Circ: 30500 Paid. Vol. ends: Dec. *Indexed:* A01, A22, B01, ErgAb. *Bk. rev.:* 2, 150-250 words, signed. *Aud.:* Ga, Ac, Sa.

The American Society of Safety Professionals (ASSP), formerly known as the American Society of Safety Engineers, is "the oldest professional safety organization," and publishes the peer-reviewed journal, *Professional Safety.* The journal shares the latest technical knowledge and "information on developments in the research and technology of accident prevention, safety management and program development." Each issue provides practical advice, techniques, and suggestions for safety professionals to "identify hazards, protect people, prevent injuries, improve work environment and educate management that investing in safety is a sound business strategy." Recent articles cover that intersection of safety and sound business with a discussion of contractor safety prequalification to limit loss rates; best practices with creating value-driven workplace wellness initiative; and "Understanding, Working With and Retaining Young Professionals." Some of this material is accessible through the American Society of Safety Professionals webpage, which includes a tab linking to technical publications, standards, and *Professional Safety.* Recommended for academic, special, and public libraries.

4458. *Safety.* [ISSN: 2313-576X] 2015. q. Free. M D P I AG, St. Alban-Anlage 66, Basel, 4052, Switzerland; info@mdpi.com; http://www.mdpi.org. Refereed. *Aud.:* Ac, Sa.

Accessible through DOAJ, *Safety* is a peer-reviewed journal on industrial and human health safety. It is one of the over 200 open access journals published by MDPI, (Multidisciplinary Digital Publishing Institute). *Safety* is searchable on the MDPI publication platform by title/keyword, journal title (plus volume, number, issue), author, article type (dropdown menu options) or by the special issue title. Recent articles covered hazardous occupations, such as forest logging, firefighting, petroleum industry and agriculture all over the world. Not all research was industry-based, other studies included a study of heavy episodic drinking (HED) among young adults in Northern Italy, evaluating the effectiveness of a road safety program for higher secondary school students in Belgium, a literature review of the effectiveness of respiratory masks with a nanostructure. There is something for almost every type of safety research. Recommended for academic and special libraries.

■ SCIENCE AND TECHNOLOGY

General/History and Philosophy of Science/Science and Technology Education

Laura Robinson Hanlan, Research and Instruction Librarian, and Bijan Esfahani, Assistant Director for Research and Instruction, George C. Gordon Library, Worcester Polytechnic Institute, Worcester, MA 01609

Introduction

Almost everything we do in modern society, from growing food, reading books, and building roads, to communicating with family and colleagues, and teaching the world's children, is dependent on complex and interconnected technologies based on science across disciplines. The world faces incredible challenges in areas of global importance, including energy, food, and water. Maintaining an understanding of the science and technologies impacting our world is a critical literacy in 2014.

At the same time, global citizens with access to the Internet are overwhelmed with the deluge of information and big data flowing all around them. Most people seeking information rely on robust search tools available through any number of connected devices, but these search tools already know quite a bit about who the searcher is: where she lives, her online search habits, and some level of personal preferences; this creates a scenario that can obscure one's ability to stumble upon information sources beyond what a search tool may deem interesting to a searcher. Publications such as the 30-plus titles annotated here for the reader can play an important role in raising awareness of science and technology issues that impact all of our lives, and can also help encourage people at all levels and ages to pursue further education in science, technology, engineering, and mathematics (STEM).

Reviewed in this section are titles from a diverse group of publishers, representing general science and technology, history and philosophy of science (including social aspects of science and technology), and science and technology education. Scholarly, popular, and trade/professional titles are covered, with some falling into multiple categories (e.g., *Science*). Each annotation provides brief a statement of purpose and highlights features of a typical issue. Publications that assign Digital Object Identifiers (DOIs) are noted as well. COUNTER compliance is reported from the list of compliant vendors on the Project COUNTER web site (www.projectcounter.org/compliantvendors.html), current as of June 2014.

The importance of STEM education became a highlighted part of the U.S. national agenda in 2009 when the White House released the following statement: "President Obama today launched the Educate to Innovate campaign, a nationwide effort to help reach the administration's goal of moving American students from the middle to the top of the pack in science and math achievement over the next decade." This was in response to concerns raised by those in the scientific and education communities about the United States' ability to keep up with the rest of the world with regard to technological innovation. The Trends in International Mathematics and Science Study (TIMSS), begun by the International Association for the Evaluation of Educational Achievement in 1995, tracks performance of fourth- and eighth-grade students from participating countries every four years. The 2007 results show the average science score of United States eighth-graders below that of ten other nations (http://nces.ed.gov/timss/table07_3.asp). The 2011 results of TIMSS, reported in 2012, indicate that since 2007, the United States has gained ground in this area but that work is still needed to raise its rank in relation to some other developed countries. The American Association for the Advancement of Science (AAAS) Project 2061, founded in 1985 to "to help all Americans become literate in science, mathematics, and technology," emphasizes "the connections among ideas in the natural and social sciences, mathematics, and technology." The role of school and public librarians in science and technology literacy for students and citizens is critical, if implicit in national discussions.

In addition to the annotated titles intended to support science educators, many titles reviewed are appropriate for students and general audiences. Also, free online content is common and noted, especially as open access (OA) in some academic publishing (discussed below) gains ground, and may include supplementary content not available in the print counterpart. Knowledge of these titles and their web site offerings can help librarians help their communities of users, even if subscriptions to the titles may be cost prohibitive and out of reach. However, it is important to note that in some developing countries, librarians may be able to negotiate for access to subscriptions at rates far below the list price. Additional current awareness sources are freely available online, among them *ScienceDaily* (www.sciencedaily.com/), a web portal that "is best known for showcasing the top science news stories from the world's leading universities and research organizations. These stories are selected from among dozens of press releases and other materials submitted to ScienceDaily every day, and then edited to ensure high quality and relevance."

A major trend impacting academic and peer-reviewed science and technology publications is the open access movement. A 2006 article by Karen M. Albert in the *Journal of the Medical Library Association* gives a useful history of the beginning and common definitions of open access, and is available through PubMedCentral at www.ncbi.nlm.nih.gov/pmc/articles/PMC1525322/. In 2014 a popular model for making articles open access and available to all through a web browser is the author-pays model. This is popular in STEM disciplines, but questions about who pays open access fees is still an issue, with only some institutions paying publisher fees for open access to their institution's work. This can raise concerns over what research gains more readership and potentially more influence within disciplines. An increasing proportion of new titles are OA since 2000, from about 17 percent of 2000 titles, to about 40 percent of the titles beginning publication in 2010. In 2009, Jeffery Beall published his first review of OA publishers in *The Charleston Advisor*. In 2010, he posted the first annual list of "Predatory Open Access Publishers" to his blog. The current list includes a watch list in addition to the publishers designated predatory. Ongoing reviews and news are available from Beall's blog, *Scholarly Open Access* (http://scholarlyoa.com/). While there has been debate about his reviews, Beall's blog provides current awareness of publishers and practices. An excellent resource for information on OA scholarly publishers is the Open Access Scholarly Publishers Association, established in 2008 (http://oaspa.org).

Another development with the potential for long-term transformative impact on scholarly publishing in the sciences comprises data management, sharing, and preservation requirements for federally funded research. Early in 2011, the National Science Foundation began requiring data management plans for all grant proposals. This followed similar requirements from the National Institutes of Health, with other U.S. federal agencies having implemented similar requirements. The new requirements offered opportunities for librarians to promote institutional and disciplinary repositories for data curation. Products for discovery and dissemination of literature have been held up as models for data management and sharing services.

In reviewing the titles within this section, it is important to note that *Ulrich's* shows a trend of increasing numbers of new multidisciplinary and general science and technology titles per year; the number of new titles was near or well below 50 titles between 2000 and 2008, but for 2009 through 2011, the average number of new titles per year was 71. Similarly, the number of titles reviewed by *Journal Citation Reports* (*JCR*) and categorized as "multidisciplinary sciences" has increased, by about 40 percent from a recent low of 42 in 2008 to 56 in 2012. The most common countries of publication for 2008 to mid-2012 new titles in *Ulrich's* are the United States (64 titles), India (62 titles), United Kingdom (33 titles), and Pakistan (10 titles). Publication countries of origin span the globe, but the regions from which most titles emanate are Asia, North America, and Western Europe (in that order), which, combined, account for more than 80 percent of the titles.

Basic Periodicals

Ems: *Current Science;* (see also titles in "Children" section); Hs: *Discover, Scientific American;* Ga: *Discover, Popular Science, Science, Scientific American, The Scientist;* Ac: *American Scientist, Discover, National Academy of Sciences. Proceedings, Nature, New Scientist, Science, Science News, Scientific American.*

Basic Abstracts and Indexes

Applied Science and Technology Index.

General

4459. *Advanced Science Letters.* [ISSN: 1936-6612] 2008. m. USD 3600. Ed(s): Hari Singh Nalwa. American Scientific Publishers, 26650 The Old Rd, Ste 208, Valencia, CA 91381; order@aspbs.com; http://www.aspbs.com. Adv. Refereed. *Bk. rev.:* Number and length vary. *Aud.:* Ac, Sa.

Advanced Science Letters began publication in 2008, with a varying number of issues and volumes per year. In 2013, the publication was issued as one volume with one issue per month, for a total of 12 issues per year, most with over 500 pages per issue. Issues contain peer-reviewed articles from across science and technology disciplines, with occasional news, commentary, book reviews, job postings, and more, at the discretion of the editors. Policy and education research related to science and technology are also within this publication's scope. Some issues contain selected conference publications. The editorial board is broad, from across disciplines and from around the globe, with the main office in California, U.S.A. DOIs are assigned.

4460. *American Scientist.* Formerly (until 1942): *Sigma XI Quarterly.* [ISSN: 0003-0996] 1913. bi-m. Individuals, USD 36; Free to members. Ed(s): Fenella Saunders. Sigma XI, Scientific Research Society, 3106 East NC Highway 54, PO Box 13975, Research Triangle Park, NC 27709; info@sigmaxi.org; http://www.sigmaxi.org/. Illus., index, adv. Vol. ends: Dec. Microform: PMC; PQC. *Indexed:* A01, A22, Agr, BRI, CBRI, HRIS, MASUSE, MLA-IB, S25. *Bk. rev.:* 250-2,200 words, signed. *Aud.:* Hs, Ga, Ac.

Published by Sigma Xi, the Scientific Research Society, since 1913, *American Scientist* is a general, illustrated magazine on science, engineering, and technology, published bimonthly and including features by prominent scientists and engineers on topics from molecular biology to computer engineering, to the history and practice of science. Feature articles are technical but accessible, and include lists of references. In addition to features, the publication includes brief articles, letters, and a "Scientists' Nightstand" section of book reviews. Strongly recommended for academic, public, and high school libraries. Limited content is available for free through the web site. DOIs are assigned.

4461. *Current Science: a fortnightly journal of research.* [ISSN: 0011-3891] 1932. fortn. USD 300 Free to members. Ed(s): S K Satheesh, R Srinivasan. Scientific Publishers, 5 A, New Pali Rd, Jodhpur, 342 001, India; info@scientificpub.com; http://www.scientificpub.com. Illus., adv. Refereed. Microform: PQC. *Indexed:* A01, A22, C45, S25. *Bk. rev.:* Number and length vary; signed. *Aud.:* Ac, Sa.

Founded in 1932 and published by the Current Science Association in collaboration with the Indian Academy of Sciences. *Current Science* is "intended as a medium for communication and discussion of important issues that concern science and scientific activity." Science and technology are broadly covered, including agriculture, biology, chemistry, Earth sciences, engineering, medicine, and physics. Content includes general research articles, reviews of research trends, articles on administration and policy, rapid communications, research news, and commentary/opinions. Special themed sections are published frequently. Recent examples include the theory of computation, Earth sciences, and microscopy in biology. Several signed book reviews are published in every issue. Detailed tables are accepted and published online as supplementary material. Free full text is online.

4462. *Discover: science, technology and the future.* [ISSN: 0274-7529] 1980. 10x/yr. USD 19.95 domestic; USD 25.95 Canada; USD 38.95 elsewhere. Ed(s): Becky Lang, Kathi Kube. Kalmbach Publishing Co., 21027 Crossroads Circle, PO Box 1612, Waukesha, WI 53187; customerservice@kalmbach.com; http://www.kalmbach.com. Illus., adv. Vol. ends: Dec. Microform: PQC. *Indexed:* A01, A22, Agr, BRI, C37, MASUSE. *Aud.:* Hs, Ga, Ac.

A leading popular science magazine, *Discover* offers accessible articles for a lay audience on recent advances in science, health and medicine, technology, and more. The magazine is currently published in ten regular issues. Special issues include "Medical Mysteries" (2014) and "Einstein's Universe" (2013). Other regular features include "Big Idea, Vital Signs," "Mind Over Matter," and "20 Things You Didn't Know About..." (recent examples include play, animal senses, and hoaxes). The combined January/February issue details the top 100 science developments of the prior year. *Discover* is visually attractive and features compelling photos and illustrations, and tends to offer more coverage of basic research (as opposed to invention and applications) than the publication *Popular Science.* Recommended for high school, public, and academic libraries. Online access to full text is available through third-party vendors and content aggregators. Free access to some content is available through the magazine's web site. URL: http://discovermagazine.com

4463. *Journal of the Royal Society. Interface.* [ISSN: 1742-5689] 2004. m. GBP 2201. Ed(s): Richard Cogdell. The Royal Society Publishing, 6-9 Carlton House Terr, London, SW1Y 5AG, United Kingdom; publishing@royalsociety.org; http://royalsociety.org/journals. Sample. Refereed. *Indexed:* A22, C45, E01. *Aud.:* Ac, Sa.

A cross-disciplinary publication for "research at the interface of the physical and life sciences," this journal includes "research applying chemistry, engineering, materials science, mathematics[,] and physics to the biological and medical sciences," as well as "discoveries in the life sciences that allow advances in the physical sciences." This title is published by The Royal Society, the national academy of science of the U.K. and the Commonwealth. Topics include biocomplexity, bioengineering, bioinformatics, biomaterials, biomechanics, bionanoscience, biophysics, chemical biology, computer applications in life science, medical physics, synthetic biology, systems biology, theoretical biology, and tissue engineering. Original research articles, shorter reports of preliminary research, and invited reviews are published. This title ranked fifth of 56 titles in the 2012 Journal Citation Reports Multidisciplinary Sciences category. Recommended for academic and special libraries that support research programs in physical, life sciences, or biomedical sciences. Online access, via Highwire Press, includes accepted articles. Free online access is available to all review articles; there is a one-year embargo on other content. Also, the society offers an author-pays option for open access. DOIs assigned. Publisher is partially COUNTER-compliant.

4464. *M I T Technology Review.* Former titles (until 1998): *M I T's Technology Review;* (until 1997): *Technology Review;* Which incorporated (1930-1931): *Massachusetts Institute of Technology. Alumni News Report.* [ISSN: 1099-274X] 1899. bi-m. USD 55.95; USD 79.95 combined subscription (print & online eds.)). Ed(s): Gideon Lichfield, David Rotman. Technology Review, One Main St Fl 13, Cambridge, MA 02143; mitalum@mit.edu. Illus., index, adv. Vol. ends: Nov/Dec. *Indexed:* A01, A22, Agr, B01, BRI, C37, CBRI, CompLI, F01, MASUSE. *Bk. rev.:* Number and length vary; signed. *Aud.:* Hs, Ga, Ac, Sa.

Founded in 1899 and naming itself the world's oldest technology magazine, *Technology Review* embraces the mission "to identify important new technologies-deciphering their practical impact and revealing how they will change our lives." It is produced by a global media company owned by the Massachusetts Institute of Technology (MIT). Its content is broad-based and not limited to MIT's research and development environment. Content for sections on features, views, multimedia, and discussions are regularly published. News and analysis includes sections on biomedicine, business, communications, computing, energy, and the web. The annual "10 Breakthrough Technologies" cites ten milestone technologies. Technologies making the list in 2014 included agricultural drones, genome editing, and agile robots. Highly recommended for academic libraries and libraries that serve adult and young-adult populations.

4465. *N A S A Tech Briefs: engineering solutions for design and manufacturing.* Formerly (until 1976): *N A S A Tech Brief.* [ISSN: 0145-319X] 1963. m. USD 75 domestic includes Puerto Rico (Free to qualified personnel). Ed(s): Ted Selinsky. Tech Briefs Media Group, 261 5th Ave, Ste 1901, New York, NY 10016; https://www.techbriefsmediagroup.com. Adv. Sample. Circ: 190200. *Indexed:* A22. *Aud.:* Ac, Sa.

A publication of the National Aeronautics and Space Administration's Innovative Partnerships Program, *NASA Tech Briefs* highlights new developments in electronics and computing, biomed, materials, manufacturing, and other areas of engineering and applied science. This title helps fulfill the legislative mandate from 1958 for NASA to "report to industry any new, commercially-significant technologies developed in the course of their R&D...." The briefs are "exclusive reports of innovations developed by NASA and its industry partners/contractors that can be applied to develop new/improved products and solve engineering or manufacturing problems," and most include supplemental materials, including white papers on the publication's web site. In addition to articles, regular features include "Who's Who at NASA" and "Products," "Application Briefs," and "NASA Tech Needs." Recommended for academic libraries that support engineering and industrial/manufacturing programs. Public and high school libraries may also benefit from this free publication.

4466. ***The National Academies In Focus.*** Former titles (until 2001): *The National Academies News Report;* (until 1999): *National Research Council. News Report.* [ISSN: 1534-8334] 1951. 3x/yr. USD 10 domestic; USD 12 foreign. Ed(s): Valerie Chase. National Academy of Sciences, 500 Fifth St NW, NAS 340, Washington, DC 20001; http://www.nationalacademies.org. Illus. Microform: PQC. *Indexed:* A22, Agr. *Aud.:* Hs, Ga, Ac, Sa.

The National Academy of Sciences, National Research Council, National Academy of Engineering, and Institute of Medicine, collectively called The National Academies, "serve as independent advisers to the federal government on scientific and technical questions of national importance." *In Focus*, published by the National Academies' Office of News and Public Information, highlights the activities of these bodies and makes them accessible to the general public through one- or two-page articles on topics of general interest such as health, energy, the environment, general technology, and psychology. Also included are brief reports on the activities and events of the National Academies. This title is recommended for high school, public, academic, and sci-tech special libraries in the United States. It is freely available online (html and pdf available) back to the first issue (2001), and a back file of the preceding title, *NewsReport*, is available to 1999. Print subscriptions of one to three years are available at a nominal cost. URL: http://infocusmagazine.org

National Academy of Sciences. Proceedings. See Biology/General section.

4467. ***Natural History.*** Formerly (until 1919): *The American Museum Journal;* Incorporates (1923-1959): *Nature Magazine;* Which was formerly (until 1923): *Nature-Study Review.* [ISSN: 0028-0712] 1900. 10x/yr. USD 25 in US & Canada; USD 37 foreign. Natural History Magazine, Inc., PO Box 110623, Research Triangle Park, NC 27709; http://www.naturalhistorymag.com/. Illus., index, adv. Vol. ends: Dec. Microform: PQC. *Indexed:* A01, A22, Agr, BRI, C37, CBRI, GardL, MASUSE, MLA-IB. *Bk. rev.:* 2-3, 500-750 words, signed. *Aud.:* Hs, Ga, Ac.

Natural History is an attractive, accessible magazine that covers nature in the broadest sense, with a mission "to promote understanding and appreciation of the world around us." Long affiliated with the American Museum of Natural History, the publication now has affiliations with nine additional U.S. museums and science centers. Features, two per issue, are written for a general audience by research scientists or professional naturalists about their own work. Feature topics typically relate to the life sciences. "Samplings" are short reports on recent research findings. Regular columnists include astrophysicist Neil deGrasse Tyson and plant biologist Robert H. Mohlenbrock. "Bookshelf" offers two or three book reviews each issue. Stunning graphic content includes the work of award-winning photographers. "The Natural Moment" is a photographic feature in each issue. Recommended for high school, public, and academic libraries. Some content from each issue is freely available via the publisher web site, along with supplementary content and highlights from affiliated museums.

Nature. See Biology/General section.

4468. ***Popular Science.*** 1872. m. USD 12 combined subscription domestic (print & ipad eds.); USD 18 combined subscription Canada (print & ipad eds.); USD 24 combined subscription elsewhere (print & ipad eds.)). Ed(s): Joe Brown, Ken Gawrych. Bonnier Corp., 2 Park Ave, 9th Fl, New York, NY 10016; http://www.bonniercorp.com. Illus., index, adv. Microform: NBI; PMC; PQC. *Indexed:* A22. *Aud.:* Hs, Ga, Ac.

Popular Science covers the latest scientific and technological developments for a lay audience. The print magazine was founded in 1872; the web site was established in 1999. Emphasis is on applications, inventions, and consumer products and services, although basic research is not excluded. Feature authors usually have some experience or expertise with the feature subject matter, but are not themselves researchers. Regular sections include "Gadgets" and "DIY" projects. "FYI" answers questions sent by readers. The January issue profiles the coming year in science, offering projected developments in science and technology, with a graphic month-by-month timeline. The June issue announces the annual Invention Awards bestowed by the magazine; the December issue offers a "Best of What's New" for the year. Some issues are themed; for example, the June 2014 issue focuses on water topics. Recommended for high school, public, and academic libraries. Institutional online access is available through aggregators. Some content is freely available online, and supplementary online content includes book reviews. The entire archive was digitized in a collaboration with Google in 2009, and an innovative text explorer allows readers to see the frequency of topics, and retrieve and read entire issues from the digitized archive.

4469. ***R & D Magazine: where innovation begins.*** Former titles (until Jul. 1995): *Research & Development;* (until 1984): *Industrial Research and Development;* Which was formed by the merger of (1959-1978): *Industrial Research;* (1950-1978): *Research - Development;* Which was formerly (until 1960): *Industrial Laboratories.* 1978. m. Free to qualified personnel. Ed(s): Lindsay Hock, Paul Livingstone. Advantage Business Media, 100 Enterprise Dr, Ste 600, PO Box 912, Rockaway, NJ 07886; AdvantageCommunications@advantagemedia.com; http://www.advantagebusinessmedia.com. Illus., index. Vol. ends: Dec. Microform: CIS. *Indexed:* A22, B01, B03, BRI, C42. *Aud.:* Ac, Sa.

"The high technology journal of applied research and development," this is intended for "lab, R&D and project managers across all industries, government[,] and universities." This title's content is written for a multidisciplinary audience whose work involves physics, chemistry, materials science, biology, and engineering, and is meant to be accessible to readers from all disciplines and specialties. Areas of focus are "state-of-the-art scientific and technical advances, how the latest R&D instruments and techniques help researchers work more productively, and important trends in research management, funding, and policy." Issues regularly cover informatics, materials science, microscopy, nanotechnology, photonics, and software, including product reviews. Regular sections include "New to market," which highlights the latest products featuring technological innovations, and "Tools and technology," which covers innovations that facilitate research. The publisher issues the R&D 100 awards, which recognize technologically significant new products, as well as Laboratory, Scientist, Corporation, and Innovator of the Year awards. Recommended for libraries in technical industrial settings, and for academic libraries that support engineering and industrial technology programs. Free print or electronic subscriptions are currently available to qualified applicants. The web site includes supplementary information, including a collection of industry white papers. Recommended for academic and special libraries that serve industrial technology and engineering programs.

4470. ***Royal Society of London. Philosophical Transactions A. Mathematical, Physical and Engineering Sciences.*** Former titles (until 1996): *Royal Society of London. Philosophical Transactions. Physical Sciences and Engineering;* (until 1990): *Royal Society of London. Philosophical Transactions. Series A. Mathematical and Physical Sciences;* (until 1933): *Royal Society of London. Philosophical Transactions. Series A. Containing Papers of a Mathematical or Physical Character;* (until 1897): *Royal Society of London. Philosophical Transactions A;* Which superseded in part (in 1887): *Royal Society of London. Philosophical Transactions;* Which was formerly (until 1776): *Royal Society of London. Philosophical Transactions;* (until 1682): *Royal Society of London. Philosophical Collections;* (until 1679): *Royal Society* *of London. Philosophical Transactions.* [ISSN: 1364-503X] 1665. bi-w. GBP 2663. Ed(s): John Dainton. The Royal Society Publishing, 6-9 Carlton House Terr, London, SW1Y 5AG, United Kingdom; publishing@royalsociety.org; http://royalsociety.org/journals. Sample. Refereed. Microform: IDC; PMC. Reprint: PSC. *Indexed:* A01, A22, C45, E01, MSN. *Aud.:* Ac, Sa.

The "[w]orld's longest running scientific journal," *Philosophical Transactions* began in 1665, with sections A (Life Sciences) and B diverging in 1887. Themed issues cover an advancing research frontier in math, physical science, or engineering, and typically contain 12 research articles, headed by a general review. Global warming, biosensors, and the "dialectic of materials and information" are topics recently covered. Several discussion-meeting issues per year cover the proceedings of Society meetings, and are also devoted to a specific topical area. This journal is intended for mathematicians, physicists, engineers, and other physical scientists. The publication frequency increased from monthly to every two weeks in 2008. Online access comes via Highwire Press. A complete back file to 1665 is available. DOIs are assigned; cited references are linked.

4471. ***Science.*** Incorporates (1915 -1957): *The Scientific Monthly.* [ISSN: 0036-8075] 1880. w. American Association for the Advancement of Science (A A A S), 1200 New York Ave, NW, Washington, DC 20005; membership@aaas.org; http://www.scienceonline.org. Illus., index, adv. Sample. Refereed. *Indexed:* A&ATA, A01, A22, Agr, BRI, C45, CBRI, CompLI, MASUSE, MLA-IB, MSN, S25. *Bk. rev.:* 2-3, 2,500 words, signed. *Aud.:* Hs, Ga, Ac, Sa.

Science is a venue for "significant original scientific research, plus reviews and analyses of current research and science policy," published by the American Association for the Advancement of Science. According to the publisher, *Science* has the largest paid circulation of any peer-reviewed general science journal. Full research papers (usually one per issue) and shorter reports (about a dozen per issue) present original research from a full spectrum of disciplines. Editor-commissioned pieces feature "broadly accessible commentary," including "Perspectives," which relates to specific research or reports in the issue. This is a core resource for current awareness; regular sections cover science news, including briefs in "News of the Week," and one-page write-ups in "News and Analysis" and longer pieces in "News Focus." Signed book reviews are published weekly. Frequent thematic special issues are published. E-mail alerts and RSS feeds are available for the entire contents, or just portions (for example, position postings). Substantial supplementary online content includes podcasts, streaming, and video. "Science Express" - previews of upcoming articles that comprise potentially high-demand content - are not included with the basic online license. Strongly recommended for all college, university, and research libraries, as well as for public and high school libraries where budgets allow. DOIs assigned; open URL linking is at the article level; partially COUNTER-compliant.

Science News. See Classroom Magazines/Science section.

4472. ***Science Progress: a review journal of current scientific advance.*** Former titles (until 1916): *Science Progress in the Twentieth Century;* (until 1906): *Science Progress.* [ISSN: 0036-8504] 1894. q. Sage Publications Ltd., 1 Oliver's Yard, 55 City Rd, London, EC1Y 1SP, United Kingdom; info@sagepub.com; https://www.sagepub.com. Illus., index. Refereed. *Indexed:* A22, BRI. *Bk. rev.:* Occasional, brief, unsigned. *Aud.:* Ac.

Science Progress presents reviews intended to inform non-specialists in academia and industry of new developments in science, technology, and medicine. Articles are written on commission by researchers who write about their own area of expertise for those in other disciplines. The "Commentaries" section, introduced in 2011, offers "shorter articles focusing on developments in fields that have undergone major conceptual change in the last 2 to 3 years." Brief, unsigned book reviews and retrospective excerpts from 100-year-old issues have also been added. Topical coverage is wide-ranging, including cell and molecular biology, biomedicine, physics, chemistry, energy, and environmental remediation. Recommended for academic libraries. Online access is offered via IngentaConnect and some aggregator databases. Some free and open-access content is available on IngentaConnect. DOIs assigned.

4473. ***Scientific American.*** Incorporates (1920-1921): *Scientific American Monthly;* Which superseded (in 1920): *Scientific American Supplement;* (1853-1854): *People's Journal.* [ISSN: 0036-8733] 1845. m. USD 419. Ed(s): Mariette DiChristina. Nature Publishing Group, 75 Varick St, 9th Fl, New York, NY 10013; subscriptions@nature.com; http://www.nature.com. Illus., index. Vol. ends: Dec. *Indexed:* A01, A22, Agr, B01, BAS, BRI, C37, CBRI, MASUSE, MLA-IB. *Bk. rev.:* Number and length vary. *Aud.:* Hs, Ga, Ac, Sa.

Categorized by major topical area, from animal behavior to space science, eight to ten features per issue offer in-depth, authoritative, accessible, and timely information. These may be authored by researchers or science writers. Brief author profiles and short lists of related research papers are included. The substantial "Advances" section keeps readers current in research news across scientific disciplines. Brief book reviews are published in each issue, along with a list of "notable" books that are not reviewed. Special editions are published, and include an annual "World Changing Ideas" issue. Recommended for high school, public, academic, and research libraries. An institutional online license is available; recent acquisition of the title by *Nature* was accompanied by large price increases for institutional license. Content is also available via aggregators. Some content from monthly issues, plus supplementary content, is freely available on the publisher web site. Publisher is partially COUNTER-compliant.

4474. ***Scientific Reports.*** [ISSN: 2045-2322] 2011. irreg. Free. Nature Publishing Group, The MacMillan Bldg, 4 Crinan St, London, N1 9XW, United Kingdom; NatureReviews@nature.com; https://www.nature.com. Refereed. *Indexed:* A01, C45. *Aud.:* Ac, Sa.

An online-only, open-access title from Nature Publishing Group, *Scientific Reports* offers "original research papers of interest to specialists" across a broad range of scientific disciplines. Emphasis is on rapid review and publication of submissions. Articles are published as they are accepted. Users can search for articles or browse by date or discipline. This journal follows an author-pays open-access model, and "all expenses, including peer review, production, and online hosting and archiving, are recovered via an article-processing charge (APC)," which is payable on acceptance; the current fee is USD 1,350. Note that *Nature Communications,* launched in 2010 by Nature Publishing Group, has a similar focus, and is also appropriate for academic and special libraries, but is not a wholly open-access title. Articles are then published under a Creative Commons license, and authors may post published pdfs to their web sites and deposit in an institutional repository. DOIs assigned. Publisher is partially COUNTER-compliant.

4475. ***The Scientist: magazine of the life sciences.*** [ISSN: 0890-3670] 1986. m. USD 400. Ed(s): Mary Beth Aberlin. LabX Media Group, 478 Bay St, Midland, ON L4R 1K9, Canada; help@labx.com; http://www.labx.com. Illus., adv. *Indexed:* A22, Agr, BRI. *Aud.:* Ac, Sa.

The Scientist offers life scientists "the latest scientific discoveries, trends in research, innovative techniques, new technology, business, and careers," with articles written by both scientists and professional journalists. It targets active researchers, but is accessible to a broader audience, including undergraduates and the general public. Founded by Eugene Garfield, the title was acquired from ScienceNow, Inc., by LabX Media in 2011, which also publishes *LabX* and *Lab Manager Magazine.* In each issue are profiles (of an established researcher, a "scientist to watch," and/or a business); highlights from the literature; a "Notebook" section on research methodologies; coverage of careers and business; and "Foundations," which describes early work of historical significance. The "Lab Tools" column features cutting-edge developments. Recommended for academic and research libraries. Content from each issue is offered free online; and the web site offers some supplemental multimedia content, and users may subscribe to a daily news update.

Skeptical Inquirer. See Parapsychology section.

History and Philosophy of Science

4476. ***British Journal for the History of Science.*** Formerly (until 1962): *British Society for the History of Science. Bulletin.* [ISSN: 0007-0874] 1949. q. GBP 237. Ed(s): Charlotte Sleigh. Cambridge University Press, University Printing House, Shaftesbury Rd, Cambridge, CB2 8BS, United

Kingdom; journals@cambridge.org; https://www.cambridge.org/. Illus., adv. Refereed. Vol. ends: Dec. Microform: PQC. Reprint: PSC. *Indexed:* A01, A22, AmHI, BRI, E01, IBSS, MLA-IB. *Bk. rev.:* Number varies; 2-3 pages, signed. *Aud.:* Ac, Sa.

BJHS publishes "scholarly papers and review articles on all aspects of the history of science," including medicine, technology, and social studies of science. Recent research articles cover a wide array of topics, such as development of vaccines, theories of heredity, Victorian science, and Aristotle. Themed special issues are published; a recent example has been "states of secrecy," which addresses secrecy in corporate- and state-sponsored scientific research. Typically, more than a dozen signed book reviews are in each issue, and these plus an extensive "books received" list offer excellent current awareness of new books in the field. Recommended for academic libraries. Institutional subscriptions are available, online-only or online-plus-print. The most recent issue is freely available through the journal's web site. A digital archive is available as a separate purchase and covers 1962-1996 of *BJHS* and 1949-1961 of the preceding title, *Bulletin of the British Society for the History of Science*. Individual articles may be purchased for USD 30 or rented for 24 hours for USD 5.99. DOIs are assigned; cited and citing references are linked when possible. Publisher is partially COUNTER-compliant.

The British Journal for the Philosophy of Science. See Philosophy section.

4477. *Bulletin of Science, Technology & Society.* [ISSN: 0270-4676] 1981. bi-m. Ed(s): Willem H Vanderburg. Sage Publications, Inc., 2455 Teller Rd, Thousand Oaks, CA 91320; info@sagepub.com; http://www.sagepub.com. Illus., index, adv. Sample. Refereed. Vol. ends: No. 6. Microform: MIM; PQC. Reprint: PSC. *Indexed:* A01, A22, C45, E01, ERIC, P61, SSA. *Bk. rev.:* Occasional, length varies. *Aud.:* Ac, Sa.

Bulletin of Science, Technology & Society aims "to provide a means of communication within as wide of a spectrum of the STS community as possible." The intended audience includes researchers, educators, and students across disciplines, policy makers, journalists, and the general public. Topics include the place of science and technology in society, policy issues related to science and technology, technology assessment, the impact of technology on human values, and public understanding of technology and science. Special thematic issues are published; a recent example is "Commoditization." Issues may include news and correspondence. Recommended for academic libraries. Online access is available with print or alone; a back file can be leased or purchased. Early-view articles are available with online access. Publication appears to lag behind dates on issues; as of June 2014, no 2014 issues have been published, but some articles from 2014 are published online ahead of print, through the journal web site. DOIs are assigned and publisher is partially COUNTER-compliant.

4478. *Endeavour: a quarterly magazine reviewing the history and philosophy of science in the service of mankind.* [ISSN: 0160-9327] 1942. q. some issues combined. EUR 865. Ed(s): J Martin, R Bellon. Elsevier Ltd., Trends Journals, 84 Theobald's Rd, London, WC1X 8RR, United Kingdom; JournalsCustomerServiceEMEA@elsevier.com; http://www.elsevier.com. Illus., index, adv. Sample. Refereed. Microform: MIM; PQC. *Indexed:* A&ATA, A01, A22, BRI, C45, HRIS, MLA-IB. *Bk. rev.:* 20-30 per year, 800-1,000 words, signed. *Aud.:* Ac.

"*Endeavour* publishes brief articles that review the history and philosophy of science," serving as a "critical forum for the inter-disciplinary exploration and evaluation of specific subjects or people that have affected the development of the scientific discipline throughout history." All science disciplines are covered, with a strong focus on life science, technology, and medicine. This title is intended to be accessible to general readers, but is appropriate for historians and practicing scientists. Recent feature articles include such titles as "Genome: twisting stories with DNA" and "How bright planets became dim stars: planetary speculations in John Herschel's double star astronomy." Reviews, opinions, and book reviews are also published. A recent themed issue covered polar exploration. Recommended for academic libraries. Online access is available with or without print. There is free access to content from the latest issue is provided through the publication's web site. DOIs are assigned, and the publisher is partially COUNTER-compliant.

Gender, Technology & Development. See Gender Studies section.

4479. *International Journal of Technoethics.* [ISSN: 1947-3451] 2010. s-a. USD 840. Ed(s): Rocci Luppicini. I G I Global, 701 E Chocolate Ave, Ste 200, Hershey, PA 17033; eresources@igi-global.com; http://www.igi-global.com. Refereed. *Indexed:* BRI. *Bk. rev.:* 1-2 per year, signed. *Aud.:* Ac, Sa.

An official publication of the Information Resource Management Association, and having begun publication in 2010, *International Journal of Technoethics* (*IJT*) aims "to evolve technological relationships of humans with a focus on ethical implications for human life, social norms and values, education, work, and ecological impacts." It publishes empirical research, theoretical studies, innovative methodologies, practical applications, case studies, and book reviews. Themed issues are published; recent examples are military technoethics, and cyborgs and robotics. Published article topics have included biometrics, cyberactivism, surveillance, nuclear waste, piracy, cyberweapons, and nanotechnology. DOIs assigned. Publisher is partially COUNTER-compliant.

4480. *Isis: international review devoted to the history of science and its cultural influences.* [ISSN: 0021-1753] 1913. q. USD 676. Ed(s): Matthew Lavine, Alexandra Hui. University of Chicago Press, 1427 E 60th St, Chicago, IL 60637; subscriptions@press.uchicago.edu; http://www.journals.uchicago.edu. Illus., index, adv. Sample. Refereed. Vol. ends: Dec. Reprint: PSC. *Indexed:* A01, A22, AmHI, BRI, CBRI, IBSS, MLA-IB, MSN, P61, SSA. *Bk. rev.:* 50 or more, signed. *Aud.:* Ac, Sa.

Isis began publication in 1913, making it the first English-language journal dedicated to the history of science. As the official publication of the History of Science Society, it remains a core journal in this area and contains peer-reviewed articles, notes and commentary, and extensive signed book reviews. Each volume year contains four issues plus an annual bibliography that lists journals, articles, and books specific to subdisciplines within the history of science. Issues are between 200 and 300 pages and are organized by article type. Book reviews take a considerable portion of each issue and are organized as follows: "General," "Antiquity," "Middle Ages and Renaissance," "Early Modern (Seventeenth and Eighteenth Centuries)," "Recent (1950-)," and "Sociology and Philosophy of Science." Each article in assigned a DOI, and usage statistics may be obtained through JSTOR.

4481. *Issues in Science and Technology.* [ISSN: 0748-5492] 1984. q. USD 140 (Individuals, USD 48; USD 12 per issue domestic). Ed(s): Kevin Finneran. University of Texas at Dallas, Cecil and Ida Green Center for the Study of Science and Society, 800 W Campbell Rd, Richardson, TX 75080-3021; http://www.utdallas.edu. Illus., index, adv. Sample. Refereed. Vol. ends: Summer (No. 4). Microform: PQC. *Indexed:* A01, A22, Agr, BRI, C37, HRIS, MASUSE, S25. *Bk. rev.:* 2-4 per issue, 2-3 pages, signed. *Aud.:* Hs, Ga, Ac, Sa.

Published jointly by the National Academies, the University of Texas at Dallas, and Arizona State University, *Issues in Science & Technology* is a "forum for discussion of public policy related to science, engineering, and medicine," including science policy as well as science that informs policy. Intended as a venue for researchers, policy-makers, and industry representatives, this publication is accessible to lay readers and "offers authorities an opportunity to share their insights directly with a broad audience." Topical article clusters are published; recent features include "Breaking the Climate Deadlock" and "Is U.S. Science in Decline?" Contributors are national political figures, administrators at research institutions and federal agencies, and industry leaders, and are selected by the editor based on their expertise. Content includes feature articles, legislative updates, an extensive reader forum section, opinion pieces, news, and two or more signed, critical book reviews per issue. This title is recommended especially for college and university libraries, but is appropriate for public and school libraries as well. Online access (html only) is free; back issues to 1996 can be searched or browsed. Some articles are available online in advance of print. E-mail contents alerts are available.

Philosophy of Science. See Philosophy section.

4482. ***Science and Engineering Ethics.*** [ISSN: 1353-3452] 1995. q. EUR 610 (print & online eds.)). Ed(s): R Spier, S J Bird. Springer New York LLC, 233 Spring St, New York, NY 10013; customerservice@springer.com; http://www.springer.com. Illus., adv. Refereed. Reprint: PSC. *Indexed:* A01, A22, AmHI, BRI, E01. *Bk. rev.:* 1 per year; 700 words; signed. *Aud.:* Ac.

"*Science and Engineering Ethics* is [a] multi-disciplinary journal that explores ethical issues of direct concern to scientists and engineers," including "professional education, standards[,] and ethics in research and practice, extending to the effects of innovation on society at large." It covers both conduct of science and application of new technologies. It is relevant to practicing researchers in the sciences and social sciences, and to science educators. Medicine, agricultural biotechnology, environmental science, science education, intellectual property, and animal and human subjects in research are covered. Original papers, educational forums, reviews, commentary, and occasional book reviews are published. Themed issues are published; recent themes were public engagement and responsible data management. Highly recommended for academic libraries. Institutional online access and back file to volume 1 (1995) are available. Some open-access content is available via Springer's author-pays "Open Choice" option. DOIs assigned; cited references are linked. Publisher is partially COUNTER-compliant.

4483. ***Science, Technology & Human Values.*** Former titles (until 1978): *Science, Technology & Human Values. Newsletter;* (until 1976): *Program on Public Conceptions of Science. Newsletter;* Incorporated (in 1988): *Science and Technology Studies;* Which was formerly (until 1986): *4S Review;* (until 1983): *4S. Society for Social Studies of Science;* (until 1976): *SSSS. Newsletter of the Society for Social Studies of Science.* [ISSN: 0162-2439] 1972. bi-m. USD 1237 (print & online eds.)). Ed(s): Edward J Hackett. Sage Publications, Inc., 2455 Teller Rd, Thousand Oaks, CA 91320; info@sagepub.com; http://www.sagepub.com. Illus. Refereed. Reprint: PSC. *Indexed:* A01, A22, B01, BRI, E01, IBSS, P61. *Bk. rev.:* 6 per year, signed. *Aud.:* Ac, Sa.

Published by Sage for the Society for Social Studies of Science, *STHV* offers "research, analyses and commentary on the development and dynamics of science and technology, including their relationship to politics, society and culture." Represented disciplines include political science, sociology, environmental studies, anthropology, literature, history, economics, and philosophy. Articles and commentary are published. Occasional special sections may be published; a recent theme was the cause and implications of research policies emphasizing material outputs. Signed book reviews (3,000 words) are published intermittently. Recommended for academic and research libraries. Online access and a back file to 1976 are available. DOIs assigned; cited references are linked. Publisher is partially COUNTER-compliant.

4484. ***Social Studies of Science: an international review of research in the social dimensions of science and technology.*** Formerly (until 1975): *Science Studies.* [ISSN: 0306-3127] 1971. bi-m. USD 2717 (print & online eds.)). Ed(s): Sergio Sismondo. Sage Publications Ltd., 1 Oliver's Yard, 55 City Rd, London, EC1Y 1SP, United Kingdom; info@sagepub.com; https://www.sagepub.com/. Illus., index. Sample. Refereed. Vol. ends: Dec. Reprint: PSC. *Indexed:* A01, A22, B01, C45, E01, IBSS, P61, SSA. *Bk. rev.:* 1 per year, 3,000 words, signed. *Aud.:* Ac.

Social Studies of Science publishes original research on science, technology, and medicine, covering political science, sociology, economics, history, philosophy, psychology, social anthropology, law, and education. Research articles and shorter research notes are published, as well as review essays (book reviews) and discussion papers. Special sections are published; recent topics were Thomas Kuhn (marking the 50th anniversary of the publication of *The Structure of Scientific Revolutions*) and ethnomethodological studies of science. Recommended for academic libraries. Institutional online access is available with or without print. DOIs assigned; cited references are linked. Publisher is partially COUNTER-compliant.

4485. ***Technology and Culture.*** [ISSN: 0040-165X] 1959. q. USD 220. Ed(s): Suzanne Moon, Peter Soppelsa. The Johns Hopkins University Press, 2715 N Charles St, Baltimore, MD 21218; http://www.press.jhu.edu. Illus., adv. Sample. Refereed. Vol. ends: Oct (No. 4). Reprint: PSC. *Indexed:* A&ATA, A01, A22, BAS, BRI, CBRI, CompLI, E01, IBSS, MLA-IB, SSA. *Bk. rev.:* 30-40 reviews per issue, 500-1,000 words; signed. *Aud.:* Ac.

The quarterly journal of the Society for the History of Technology, *Technology and Culture* is billed as the "preeminent journal for the history of technology." It offers scholarly articles and critical reviews on the history of technology, with broadly interdisciplinary subject coverage. This title is intended for a broad audience of scientists, social scientists, and nonprofessionals. Recommended for academic libraries. It includes an extensive book review section, with 30-40 critical reviews per issue. Occasional special issues may be published. Recent themes for the special issues include biomedical technology, patents and inventions, and engineering in the twentieth century. Reviews of new museum exhibits are also included. Institutional online access to full-text is available via Project MUSE. Free sample issue available online. Online platform is partially COUNTER-compliant.

Science and Technology Education

4486. ***Journal of College Science Teaching.*** [ISSN: 0047-231X] 1971. bi-m. Free to members. Ed(s): Caroline Barnes, Ann Cutler. National Science Teachers Association, 1840 Wilson Blvd, Arlington, VA 22201; nstapress@nsta.org; http://www.nsta.org/. Illus., index, adv. Sample. Refereed. Circ: 5000. Vol. ends: May. Microform: PQC. *Indexed:* A01, A22, BRI, ERIC. *Aud.:* Hs, Ac.

The mission of the NSTA is to "promote excellence and innovation in science teaching and learning for all." The *Journal of College Science Teaching* offers "a forum for the exchange of ideas on and experiences with undergraduate science courses." Innovative materials, methods, and assessment are covered, as are suggestions for improving science instruction and descriptions of disciplinary science teaching with relevance across disciplines. About six features are published per issue; recent feature topics include undergraduate research collaboratives, integrated STEM instruction, authentic research-based versus cookbook lab courses, and concept maps. Brief synopses from the research literature are offered in "Headline Science." "Case studies" demonstrate the application of the scientific method in a current research area; a recent case-study example is "The Mystery of the Seven Deaths: A Case Study in Cellular Respiration." Editorials and point-of-view articles are published. This title is intended for college-level educators and students of science education, but high school science teachers could also benefit. Recommended for academic libraries, including community college libraries. Although there is an online archive of all articles available to individual members via the NSTA web site, institutional online access is via aggregators.

4487. ***Journal of Research in Science Teaching.*** [ISSN: 0022-4308] 1963. 10x/yr. GBP 1559. Ed(s): Elizabeth C Niswander, Fouad Abd-El-Khalick. John Wiley & Sons, Inc., 111 River St, Hoboken, NJ 07030; cs-journals@wiley.com; http://onlinelibrary.wiley.com. Illus., adv. Sample. Refereed. Vol. ends: Dec. Microform: PQC. Reprint: PSC. *Indexed:* A22, ASSIA, ERIC. *Aud.:* Ac.

The *Journal of Research in Science Teaching* "publishes reports for science education researchers and practitioners on issues of science teaching and learning and science education policy," and research "investigations employing qualitative, ethnographic, historical, survey, philosophical, or case study research approaches." This title is published by Wiley on behalf of the National Association for Research in Science Teaching. Position papers, policy perspectives, critical reviews, and comments and criticism are also accepted. Themed issues are published; a recent themed issue focuses on disciplines-centered, postsecondary science education. Recommended for academic libraries. Institutional online access is available. Supplementary information for research articles and "early view" articles may be posted online. RSS and e-mail alerts of new content are available. DOIs assigned. Publisher is partially COUNTER-compliant.

4488. ***School Science and Mathematics.*** Formerly (until 1905): *School Science.* [ISSN: 0036-6803] 1901. 8x/yr. GBP 254. Ed(s): Shelly Harkness, Carla C Johnson. John Wiley & Sons, Inc., 111 River St, Hoboken, NJ 07030; cs-journals@wiley.com; http://onlinelibrary.wiley.com. Illus., index, adv. Sample. Refereed. Vol. ends: May. Microform: PMC; PQC. Reprint: PSC. *Indexed:* A01, A22, BRI, E01, ERIC, MLA-IB. *Aud.:* Ac.

School Science and Mathematics is the journal of the School Science and Mathematics Association. It publishes research papers on "science, mathematics, and connections between science and mathematics for grades K-graduate and teacher education." Areas of focus are assessment, attitudes, beliefs, curriculum, equity, research, translating research into practice, learning theory, alternative conceptions, philosophy and history of science, sociocultural issues, special populations, technology, nontraditional forms of instruction, and science/technology/society. This title typically includes five or six research articles per issue, a letter from the editor, and a "problems section" in which readers can "exchange interesting mathematical problems and solutions." Recommended for academic libraries that support science and mathematics education programs. Online access is via Wiley, which is partially COUNTER-compliant; DOIs assigned.

Science and Children. See Classroom Magazines/Teacher and Professional section.

4489. ***Science Education.*** Incorporates (1973-1976): *A Summary of Research in Science Education;* Formerly (until 1929): *General Science Quarterly.* [ISSN: 0036-8326] 1916. bi-m. GBP 1389. Ed(s): John L Rudolph. John Wiley & Sons, Inc., 111 River St, Hoboken, NJ 07030; cs-journals@wiley.com; http://onlinelibrary.wiley.com. Illus., adv. Refereed. Vol. ends: Nov. Microform: PQC. Reprint: PSC. *Indexed:* A01, A22, BAS, BRI, ERIC. *Bk. rev.:* Number and length vary. *Aud.:* Hs, Ac.

Science Education publishes "original articles on the latest issues and trends occurring internationally in science curriculum, instruction, learning, policy[,] and preparation of science teachers[,] with the aim to advance our knowledge of science education theory and practice." Three to five general research articles and two signed, full book reviews are published in each issue. Semi-regular topical sections, including "Issues and Trends," "Learning," "Science Education Policy," and "Science Teacher Education," offer one or more research articles or reviews. "Comments and Criticism" offers a forum for dialogue or differing interpretations of research. The intended audience includes science educators, science education researchers, and administrators, and the focus is on primary and secondary grades. Online access is available via Wiley; a back file to 1916 is available. RSS and e-mail alerts of new content are available. DOIs assigned; cited references are linked. Publisher is partially COUNTER-compliant.

Science Scope. See Classroom Magazines/Teacher and Professional section.

■ SEXUALITY

See also Gay, Lesbian, Bisexual, and Transgender section.

Daniel C. Tsang, Langson Library, University of California, P.O. Box 19557, Irvine, CA 92623-9557; 949-824-4978; dtsang@uci.edu

Introduction

Sex, although widely practiced, still appears to be a taboo topic for library shelves. The more scholarly collections may contain such titles as the *Journal of Homosexuality,* the *Journal of Sex Research,* or *Archives of Sexual Behavior,* but for titles that veer beyond academia into more-explicit depictions of the phenomenon, their absence from libraries is quite apparent and, from this reviewer's point of view, this needs to be rectified.

Sexually explicit periodicals, often termed "adult magazines," proliferate in American society; even the corner drugstore may stock a few. DVDs have now largely given place to online versions. These sexual videos are mass-marketed all over the United States (in some states more discreetly than in others), and their publishers and editors proclaim themselves to be advocates of sexual liberation and free speech. They may shock some people, since much of the output appears to arouse and stimulate only certain areas of the body; only a few publications attempt to reach the mind.

The proliferation of erotic videos has also spawned a related publishing trend: what a *New York Times* essayist called meta-porn, or porn-on-porn, with review publications that attempt to document, critique, or promote that scene. The prolific migration of erotic content to the electronic world has made such imagery and text almost ubiquitous and unavoidable, making any web surfer a potential instant critic.

The proliferation of independently produced, noncommercial zines with some erotic content brings a new dimension to the sex scene. There is perhaps more attempt at analysis, deconstruction, and intellectual stimulation in these publications. Like their profit-making and market-oriented contemporaries, these zines also may shock the sexually inhibited.

Taken together, these publications reflect contemporary popular culture and society's obsession with matters sexual. Libraries can ill afford to ignore these publications, even if acquiring even one of them may challenge the hardiest librarian to see how far he or she is willing to uphold the Library Bill of Rights.

If libraries are to better serve their communities, we might consider doing more than letting just the corner drug store, liquor store, or adult bookstore satisfy the public's demand for erotica. Some titles have managed to penetrate library walls, as evidenced by the few catalogued under the subject heading "Erotic Literature—Periodicals." Other more scholarly titles have also managed to enter the hallowed halls of academia, given the HIV/AIDS crisis and the moral panic over often-taboo sexual expressions.

In this supposedly liberated era, patrons are unlikely to heed the advice that used to be found in many card catalogs: "For sex, see librarian," a relic of an era when certain such books were not cataloged or were kept in locked cases. Today, patrons want to find it themselves, often by going online. With even the U.S. Supreme Court endorsing formerly taboo sexual behavior, and the right to same-sex marriage, libraries have no excuse not to collect at least some of this material.

Here are some blogs or web sites with otherwise difficult-to-find sex ed, or erotic literature or lifestyle content: *Clean Sheets,* www.cleansheets.com/toc.shtml; *Good Vibes,* http://goodvibesblog.com/, a blog from Good Vibrations bookstore; *Nerve,* www.nerve.com/, with fiction and more; *Nifty Erotic Stories Archive,* www.nifty.org/nifty/, which offers queer adult fiction; and especially for teens, *Scarleteen: sex ed for the real world* and *Sex, etc,* http://sexetc.org/, sex ed by and for teens.

Note, however, that some of the sites listed are for adults only.

Basic Periodicals

Ga: *Penthouse; Playboy; Sexualities;* Ac: *Culture, Health & Sexuality; Penthouse; Playboy; Sexuality and Culture; Sexualities.*

Basic Abstracts and Indexes

Academic Search Complete, LGBT Life, PsycINFO, Sociological Abstracts, Women's Studies International.

4490. ***Adult Video News: the adult entertainment monthly.*** [ISSN: 0883-7090] 1982. m. A V N Publications Inc., 9414 Eton Ave, Chatsworth, CA 91311; erik@avn.com. Illus., adv. Sample. Circ: 45000 Paid. *Bk. rev.:* Number and length vary. *Aud.:* Ga, Ac.

The flagship publication of the adult video industry-which rakes in several billion dollars a year-*AVN,* or *Adult Video News,* which was founded with $900 by several college students, is today the bible of the porn industry, subtitled *The Business of Pleasure,* and is akin to what *Billboard* is to the music industry. Even with erotica now freely available online, there are still thousands of hardcore videos entering the commercial market each year. *AVN* manages to highlight the most marketable, especially to online viewers. There are feature articles on specific new films and videos, and legal advice to porn retailers. But the bulk of the now-free online magazine (with separate print subscription) is devoted to profiles of fresh adult performers, and capsule reviews of new erotic films, videos, and DVDs, as well as reviews of hardware (e.g., vibrators or latex pants). While it is still predominantly heterosexual in its approach, this title now has made an effort to include some gay porn industry news. The magazine is profusely illustrated with explicit color photos and ads from the industry. Many of the news items deal with confrontations by state and church. A serious essay might address zoning laws, while a "Who's Who" section might feature an obituary of a noted anti-censorship lawyer or an aspiring porn star. There are also charts of top video sellers or rentals. Aimed at retailers, it is nonetheless highly recommended for the serious collector. Note that with VOD (video on demand), one can actually view sexually explicit clips online or choose to pay to watch the entire video, gay or straight. Current and back issues are all available for free viewing online or downloadable as pdfs, but one can still subscribe to the hard copy. (DT)

4491. ***Canadian Journal of Human Sexuality.*** Former titles (until 1992): *S I E C C A N Journal;* (until 1986): *Journal - S I E C C A N.* [ISSN: 1188-4517] 1986. q. CAD 85 domestic; USD 105 foreign; CAD 100 combined subscription domestic (print & online eds.)). Ed(s): Terry Humphreys. University of Toronto Press, Journals Division, 5201 Dufferin St, Toronto, ON M3H 5T8, Canada; journals@utpress.utoronto.ca; http://www.utpjournals.com. Refereed. *Indexed:* A01, ASSIA, BRI, C37, C42, IBSS. *Aud.:* Ac.

The only peer-reviewed, interdisciplinary journal to focus on Canadian sex research and sex education, *CJHS* is published by SIECCAN, the Sex Information and Education Council of Canada. Articles cover such topics as Canadian undergraduates' "friends with benefits" relationships; drug use and HIV risk among East Asian and Southeast Asian men who have sex with men in Toronto; Canadian attitudes toward female topless behavior; teen sexual initiation and perception of parental disapproval; sexual compatibility and sexual functioning in intimate relationships; and sexual health education in the schools. Socio-medical aspects of sexuality are addressed; a 2015 commentary asked for expanding research on the transgendered women to encompass those not undergoing surgery or hormonal treatment. Facilitating scholarly communication, detailed English-language abstracts of each article from 1997 are freely posted online at www.sieccan.org/cjhs_abstracts.html. Selected full-text articles are also posted free online at www.sieccan.org/resources.html. Recommended for major collections. (DT)

4492. ***Culture, Health and Sexuality (Online).*** [ISSN: 1464-5351] m. GBP 1196. Routledge, 4 Park Sq, Milton Park, Abingdon, OX14 4RN, United Kingdom; subscriptions@tandf.co.uk; http://www.tandfonline.com. Refereed. *Aud.:* Ac, Sa.

This is a cutting-edge research journal that invites practitioners of sexuality studies to discuss policy implications and outcomes of applied sex research. Its strong point is its refreshing international coverage, especially from developing countries, reflecting its editorial stance. It has garnered one of the highest impact factors for a journal. It covers not just HIV/AIDS research but also other health-related studies. According to the publisher, the focus is not just on methodological concerns but also on empirical and conceptual issues as well. It "offers a forum for debates on policy and practice and adopts a practitioner focus where appropriate." For example, it has researched the issue of how gay men negotiate love and HIV serostatus in actual relationships. An occasional supplement provides abstracts of papers from the Conference of the International Association for the Study of Sexuality, Culture and Society (IASSCS). Members of IASSCS can subscribe at a reduced rate. For residents from least-developed countries, there is also a reduced rate. An excellent source for scholarly debates about international policies related to reproductive and sexual health research and applications in particular. Available in print and online versions. (DT)

4493. ***International Journal of Sexual Health (Print).*** Formerly (until 2007): *Journal of Psychology & Human Sexuality.* [ISSN: 1931-7611] 1988. q. GBP 940 (print & online eds.)). Ed(s): Eli Coleman. Routledge, 530 Walnut St, Ste 850, Philadelphia, PA 19106; enquiries@tandfonline.com; http://www.tandfonline.com. Adv. Sample. Refereed. Circ: 251 Paid. Microform: PQC. Reprint: PSC. *Indexed:* A01, A22, C45, E01, GW. *Aud.:* Ac, Sa.

As the official journal for the World Association for Sexual Health, this title "promotes sexual health as a state of physical, emotional, mental, and social well-being through a positive approach to sexuality and sexual rights. The journal publishes peer-reviewed scientific papers, editorials, and reviews, using quantitative and qualitative methods, descriptive and critical analysis, instrument development, surveys, and case studies to examine the essential elements of this broad concept. Leading experts from around the world present original work that covers a variety of disciplines, including sexology, biology, medicine, psychology, sociology, anthropology, history, and religion." It "is dedicated to the basic understanding that sexual health is not merely the absence of disease, dysfunction, and infirmity, but also the presence of pleasurable and safe sexual enjoyment and satisfaction, free of coercion, discrimination, and violence. The journal examines sexual attitudes, beliefs, and behaviors, public policies and legislative issues, and a variety of sexual health problems, including the assessment and treatment of sexual dysfunctions and disorders, sexual abuse and violence, and sexually transmitted infections." Edited by prominent transgender studies sexologist Eli Coleman, this journal is a source for path-breaking research studies on a broad range of sexual health issues. Recent issues have covered job satisfaction of female sex workers in Australia; femininity and sexuality among young females; and the role of androphilia in the psychosexual development of boys. The most cited articles include "The Role of Androphilia in the Psychosexual Development of Boys," "Gender Differences in Receptivity to Sexual Offers," "DSM-IV-TR and the Paraphilias," and "Top/Bottom Self-Label, Anal Sex Practices, HIV Risk[,] and Gender Role Identity in Gay Men in New York City." Highly recommended for its international coverage, with a long advisory board membership from across the globe. (DT)

Journal of Homosexuality. See Gay, Lesbian, Bisexual, and Transgender section.

Journal of Sex Research. See Sociology and Social Work/General section.

4494. ***Journal of Sexual Medicine: basic research and clinical studies in male and female sexual function and dysfunction.*** [ISSN: 1743-6095] 2004. m. Ed(s): John P Mulhall. Elsevier Ltd, The Boulevard, Langford Lane, Oxford, OX5 1GB, United Kingdom; journalscustomerserviceemea@elsevier.com; http://www.elsevier.com. Adv. Sample. Refereed. *Indexed:* A01, A22, E01. *Aud.:* Ac, Sa.

"Publishing original research in both basic science and clinical investigations, *The Journal of Sexual Medicine* also features review articles, educational papers, editorials highlighting original research, and meeting information. Special topics include symposia proceedings and the official guidelines from the Second International Consultation on Sexual Dysfunctions in Men and Women." The journal is the official publication of the International Society for Sexual Medicine and the International Society for the Study of Women's Sexual Health (ISSWSH). It ranks high among journals in Urology and Nephrology in ISI Journal Citation Reports. It offers research in the following fields: biochemistry, endocrinology, gynecology, neurology, pathophysiology, pharmacology, physiology, physiology, psychiatry, psychology, sex therapy, and surgery. Special issues include conference proceedings. Research articles may cover such topics as premature ejaculation and erectile dysfunction. Literature reviews are provided for specific topics. An editorial gave voice to patient concerns by quoting a woman who managed to overcome sexual pain and make love again. This title is not aimed at the lay reader. Two other journals have spun-off from this title. One is *Sexual Medicine Reviews,* which covers current research monographs. The other is an exciting open-access journal, *Sexual Medicine,* http://onlinelibrary.wiley.com/journal/10.1002/(ISSN)2050-1161, which uses non-commercial Creative Commons license to freely distribute content faster and more accessibly, for which Wiley Online Library is to be commended. Recommended for medical collections. (DT)

Journal of the History of Sexuality. See History/Interdisciplinary Interests section.

4495. ***Penthouse (Online).*** m. USD 19.39. FriendFinder Networks Inc., 910 E. Hamilton Ave, 6th Fl., Campbell, CA 95008. *Aud.:* Ga, Ac.

This long-standing heterosexual erotica magazine continues to be a strong proponent of sexual freedom and free speech. It is decidedly on the side of those who fight state repression. In addition to explicit photography (more private parts showing in the female than the male), the magazine offers strong investigative reportage and analysis of national and international issues by the likes of Joe Conason, Alan Dershowitz, and Nat Hentoff. For more than two decades, until his death in 2001, journalist Tad Szulc's writings graced its pages. Some may dislike how women are depicted in its fiction, news clips, or full-page color layouts, but one cannot dismiss its outstanding contribution by alerting readers to the latest threats to our liberties, such as an article on "Whose Homeland Security?" Regular departments include "Online Humor," "Technomania," "Politics in the Military," "Men's Health & Fitness," and "Ribald Rimes." Selected articles and sections are free online, including "Auto Focus," which has covered automotive art. For the intelligent person's collection. URL: http://penthousemagazine.com/ (DT)

Perspectives on Sexual and Reproductive Health. See Family Planning section.

4496. ***Playboy: entertainment for men.*** [ISSN: 0032-1478] 1953. m. USD 29.97 domestic; USD 47.05 Canada; USD 45 elsewhere. Ed(s): Hugh Hefner, Kevin Buckley. Playboy Enterprises, Inc., 680 N Lake Shore Dr, Chicago, IL 60611; http://www.playboy.com. Illus., adv. Sample. Circ: 3150000 Paid. Vol. ends: No. 12. Microform: BHP; PQC. *Indexed:* A22, BRI, MLA-IB. *Bk. rev.:* 6-9, 200 words, signed. *Aud.:* Ga, Ac.

America's best-selling men's magazine for over half a century, *Playboy* continues to publish excellent, high-quality fiction and nonfiction, along with its well-regarded "Playboy Interview" with notable subjects, including (recently) Chinese dissident Ai Weiwei. The "Playmate of the Month" centerfold is still offered. Readers definitely have to wade through pages of color nudes (mainly of women), but if the photographs don't interest a reader, the text offerings are definitely the "meat" of the magazine. Now it also highlights a "DVD of the month" and includes what's available online on its web site. There has also been a "20Q" column, where politicians or other notables are asked 20 questions; it's a shorter and more concise version of the "Playboy Interview." Reviews cover films, music, games, DVDs, and books. Sexual liberation may be commonplace in many regions, and its message of "entertainment for men" may sound dated and limited, but the audience is still there for this magazine. It now boasts multiple international editions from Brazil to Japan. A digital version is also available, geared for use with a "Playboy App" for iPhone and Android. (DT)

4497. ***Porn Studies.*** [ISSN: 2326-8743] 2014. 4x/yr. GBP 368 (print & online eds.)). Ed(s): Clarissa Smith, Feona Attwood. Routledge, 4 Park Sq, Milton Park, Abingdon, OX14 4RN, United Kingdom; subscriptions@tandf.co.uk; http://www.tandfonline.com. Refereed. *Bk. rev.:* 1-2, 2-3 pages. *Aud.:* Ac, Sa.

In its first issue in 2014, the editors explain the rationale for such a publication as this, which covers the study of pornography: "Pornography is now of interest for academics working across a range of disciplines. Historians and art and literary scholars turned their attention to sexually explicit works during the 1960s. The late 1970s and 1980s saw the publication of groundbreaking work such as film scholar Linda Williams' (1989) *Hard Core: Power, Pleasure, and the "Frenzy of the Visible."* By the time the second edition of her book was published in 1999, she could point to pornography studies as an emergent field; the beginning of critical academic discussion about pornography, moving away from a 'porn debate[,]' centered on disagreements about pornography's harmfulness." The articles in *Porn Studies* focus largely on an analysis of the western discourse on pornography, although more and more coverage is being given to regions outside Europe and the North America. Notable is an article by a porn studies scholar, Katrien Jacobs, at the Chinese University of Hong Kong, which advocates "[I]nternationalizing porn studies." University of California-Berkeley's Linda Williams also writes a self-critical analysis: "Pornography, porno, porn: thoughts on a weedy field." As this is the first academic journal on the topic, it is highly recommended. (DT)

4498. ***Sex Education: sexuality, society and learning.*** [ISSN: 1468-1811] 2001. bi-m. GBP 515 (print & online eds.)). Ed(s): Peter Aggleton. Routledge, 4 Park Sq, Milton Park, Abingdon, OX14 4RN, United Kingdom; subscriptions@tandf.co.uk; http://www.tandfonline.com. Adv. Sample. Refereed. Reprint: PSC. *Indexed:* A01, A22, E01, ERIC, GW. *Aud.:* Ac, Sa.

This journal focuses on sex education (or the lack thereof) within schools and the family as well as society, but its scope is not limited to the United States or Europe. An article in an early issue, for example, covered sex education about AIDS in selected countries in Asia and the Pacific-it delineated the heterosexual bias in some of the government-sponsored programs. Another article more recently argues that sexual pleasure is ignored in evaluating the success of sex education programs in schools. Other articles address the difficulties in teaching sex education to boys; puberty or sex education of primary school students; or the limits of abstinence-only sex education. This journal's editorial board includes members from around the globe. It notes that it "does not assume that sex education takes place only in educational institutions and the family. Contributions are therefore welcomed which, for example, analyse [*sic*] the impacts of media and other vehicles of culture on sexual behaviour [*sic*] and attitudes." The journal is accessible: "Medical and epidemiological papers (e.g., of trends in the incidences of sexually transmitted infections) will not be accepted unless their educational implications are discussed adequately." This title is highly recommended for coverage of a topic often ignored or politicized. (DT)

Sexual Abuse. See Psychology section.

4499. ***Sexual Addiction & Compulsivity: the journal of treatment and prevention.*** [ISSN: 1072-0162] 1994. q. GBP 325 (print & online eds.)). Ed(s): Charles Samenow. Routledge, 530 Walnut St, Ste 850, Philadelphia, PA 19106; enquiries@tandfonline.com; http://www.tandfonline.com. Sample. Refereed. Reprint: PSC. *Indexed:* A01, A22, ASSIA, CJPI, E01. *Aud.:* Ac, Sa.

This journal of the National Council on Sexual Addiction and Compulsivity focuses on all aspects of sexual addiction, described as a "growth phenomenon." Article topics include coming out and sexual compulsivity among gays; addiction among lesbians; seropositive men who have sex with men; ephebophiles; and priests, as well as fraternity males and pornography. A special issue addressed "hypersexual disorder." This title offers continuing education material for professionals. Articles seek to provide guidance to working sex therapists for relating to clients. An editorial concedes that "addiction" may not always be the best description to apply to a particular set of behaviors. (DT)

Sexual and Marital Therapy. See *Sexual and Relationship Therapy.*

4500. ***Sexual and Relationship Therapy.*** Formerly (until 2000): *Sexual and Marital Therapy.* [ISSN: 1468-1994] 1986. q. GBP 778 (print & online eds.)). Ed(s): Dr. Alessandra Iantaffi. Routledge, 4 Park Sq, Milton Park, Abingdon, OX14 4RN, United Kingdom; subscriptions@tandf.co.uk; http://www.tandfonline.com. Illus., index, adv. Sample. Refereed. Vol. ends: Nov. Reprint: PSC. *Indexed:* A01, A22, ASSIA, BAS, E01. *Aud.:* Ac, Sa.

With an applied orientation for professionals in psychology, medical, and marriage-counseling fields, this established journal from the British Association for Sexual and Relationship Therapy had earlier changed its title to better embrace its clientele, thus including couples who are not in traditional marriages. Articles give advice to general practitioners about discussing sex-life issues with coronary heart patients; and they also address such issues as sexual boundaries between clinicians and clients; the connection between induced abortion and sexual attitudes; the impact of sexual assault on one's life; and exercise-induced orgasm among women. While it deals with sexual crises, the journal also provides hope, for example, in an article on women over 65: "still doing it." It has also published editorials such as one paying tribute to martyred Ugandan gay activist David Kato. Recommended for collections that cater to marriage and relationship counseling. (DT)

4501. ***Sexual Health (Online).*** [ISSN: 1449-8987] 2004. bi-m. USD 848. Ed(s): Roy Chan, Christopher Fairley. C S I R O Publishing, Locked Bag 10, Clayton, VIC 3169, Australia; publishing@csiro.au; http://www.publish.csiro.au/home.htm. Adv. Sample. Refereed. *Aud.:* Ac, Sa.

According to its scope note, "*Sexual Health* publishes original and significant contributions to the fields of sexual health[,] including HIV/AIDS, sexually transmissible infections, issues of sexuality[,] and relevant areas of reproductive health. This journal is directed towards those working in sexual health as clinicians, public health practitioners, or researchers in behavioural [*sic*], clinical, laboratory, [or] public health[,] or social sciences. The journal publishes peer-reviewed original research, editorials, review articles, topical debates, case reports[,] and critical correspondence." This is the official journal of the International Union against Sexually Transmitted Infections (IUSTI), Asia-Pacific, and the Asia-Oceanian Federation for Sexology. It is also "officially sponsored" by the Australasian Chapter of Sexual Health Medicine of the Royal Australasian College of Physicians and the Sexual Health Society of Queensland. Special issues include one on HIV in Australia, but articles cover sexual practices from Vietnam to Nigeria. Articles have found "Internet sex-seeking is inconsistently linked with sexual risk in men who have sex with men" and analyzed "Condom Use Errors Among Sexually Unfaithful and Consensually Nonmonogamous Individuals." The journal's focus is more on informing practitioners and researchers than on reaching the general public. A key feature is editorial involvement by sexuality professionals in the region, including in Australia, Singapore, Thailand, Indonesia, India, Taiwan, Hong Kong, and China. Its article on the influence of traditional Vietnamese culture on young Vietnamese Australian women's utilization of sexual health services is among its most accessed articles. Highly recommended. (DT)

4502. ***Sexual Intelligence.*** 200?. m. Free. Ed(s): Marty Klein. Sexual Intelligence, c/o Dr. Marty Klein, 2439 Birch St. #2, Palo Alto, CA 94306; mklein@sexed.org; http://www.sexualintelligence.org. *Aud.:* Ga, Ac.

Sex therapist and marriage counselor Marty Klein steadfastly analyzes current sexuality-related topics in this provocative, online monthly. Topics include "Ten Things Humanists Need to Know About Sex," "National Masturbation Day," "Why Bruce/Caitlyn Jenner Matters to Straight People," and "Reagan's Legacy: World AIDS." The pithy newsletter analyzes news on sexuality from a sex-positive perspective, dismissing as faddish and ideological the popular concept of "sexual addiction," calling it a myth. Another brief item: "F-Word a WMD?" (whether the four-letter word is a weapon of mass destruction). Klein brilliantly skewers sex-negativity, while keeping his analysis concise and pointed. Even earlier issues, all posted on the web site, are worth re-reading to remind us how precarious sexual liberty remains in the United States. His annual Sexual Intelligence Awards, profiled in the newsletter, honor those who manage to overcome such assaults on personal sexual freedom. Favorite targets are the federal government's crackdown on sex research and the religious right's self-righteousness on moral issues. URL: www.sexualintelligence.org/. A related blog is located here: http://sexualintelligence.wordpress.com/ (DT)

4503. ***Sexualidades.*** [ISSN: 1938-6419] 2007. irreg. Free. Ed(s): Eliane Borges Berutti, Maria Mercedes Gomez. City University of New York, Center for Lesbian and Gay Studies, 365 Fifth Ave, Rm 7-115, New York, NY 16016; clags@gc.cuny.edu; http://web.gc.cuny.edu/clags. *Aud.:* Ac, Sa.

This e-journal, which is a working-paper series on Latin American and Caribbean sexualities, aims to reach sexuality practitioners and researchers, especially in areas where Spanish and/or Portuguese are read. The paper is published in three languages, English, Spanish, and Portuguese. Topics have ranged from low-income transvestites' masculine identity in the Chilean army to television representation of prostitution in Argentina. Issues now appear more or less annually. The publisher, International Research Network, self-identifies as a "global community of teachers and researchers sharing knowledge about sexualities," and is funded by the Ford Foundation. Highly recommended for special collections. URL: www.irnweb.org/journal/sexualidades/

4504. ***Sexualities: studies in culture and society.*** [ISSN: 1363-4607] 1998. 8x/yr. USD 2100 (print & online eds.)). Ed(s): Ken Plummer. Sage Publications Ltd., 1 Oliver's Yard, 55 City Rd, London, EC1Y 1SP, United Kingdom; info@sagepub.com; https://www.sagepub.com/. Illus., index. Sample. Refereed. Vol. ends: Nov. Reprint: PSC. *Indexed:* A01, A22, E01, IBSS, MLA-IB, SSA. *Bk. rev.:* 1-2, 2-3 pages. *Aud.:* Ga, Ac.

The very title of this journal implies a social constructionist view of sexualities-not sexuality (singular) but sexualities (plural). Thus the publication has covered sexual mores and identities from across the sexual spectrum. As it itself proclaims on its web site: "[This title] covers a vast array of interdisciplinary topics[,] including the stratification of sexualities by class, race, gender and age and Queer theory and lesbian and gay studies. Its broad scope combines sexualized identities, globalization, pornography and mass media communication." Most-read articles include ones on fellatio, the fag discourse, and sex work for the middle classes. The most cited article was titled, "Girls Want Sex, Boys Want Love: Resisting Dominant Discourses of (Hetero) Sexuality." It dares to address controversial issues even among the sexually liberated. A 2015 special issue, for example, was themed, "Bareback Sex and Queer Theory Across Three National Contexts (France, UK, US)." Highly readable and written in non-technical language, the journal attempts to reach academics and the lay public alike. Highly recommended. (DT)

4505. ***Sexuality and Culture.*** [ISSN: 1095-5143] 1997. q. EUR 742 (print & online eds.)). Ed(s): Roberto Refinetti. Springer New York LLC, 233 Spring St, New York, NY 10013; customerservice@springer.com; http://www.springer.com. Adv. Sample. Refereed. Reprint: PSC. *Indexed:* A01, A22, AmHI, BRI, C42, E01, GW, SSA. *Aud.:* Ga, Ac.

Originally an annual, this journal emerged out of concern about "sexual correctness" (or political correctness involving sexualities), especially in the face of sexual harassment policies in academia. It now covers a broader range of issues, and it plays less of an advocacy role, becoming more research-oriented. The journal states that it "offers an international forum for analysis of ethical, cultural, psychological, social, and political issues related to sexual relationships and sexual behavior. Coverage extends to sexual consent and sexual responsibility; harassment and freedom of speech; privacy; censorship and pornography; impact of film and literature on sexual relationships; and university and governmental regulation of intimate relationships, such as interracial relationships and student-professor relationships." Its pages critically explore affirmative action and child sexual-abuse research, with covered topics including "sexting" and infidelity in cyberspace. Its editorial board includes some of the big names in sex research, even as it takes on the daunting task of critiquing established norms. Look here for past and current sex debates that are often missing from more mainstream journals. The publisher is no longer Transaction; Springer has been publishing it since 2010. (DT)

4506. ***Sexuality Research and Social Policy.*** [ISSN: 1553-6610] 2004. q. EUR 389. Ed(s): Jeffrey T Parsons. Springer New York LLC, 233 Spring St, New York, NY 10013; journals-ny@springer.com; http://link.springer.com. Refereed. Reprint: PSC. *Indexed:* A22, E01. *Bk. rev.:* 2, 500 words. *Aud.:* Ga, Ac.

This online journal, from the Ford Foundation-funded National Sexuality Resource Center (based at San Francisco State University), boasts an impressively multinational editorial board of major scholars doing sexuality studies and public health. It is a platform that "[p]resents state-of-the-art research on sexuality, along with theoretical and methodological discussions; [d]iscusses the implications of new research for worldwide policies on sexual health, sexuality education, and sexual rights; [p]ublishes brief research and conference reports, white papers, and special topical issues; [and] [p]ublishes research from a wide spectrum of disciplines." Topics cover online adult sexting; teen sexuality; youth viewing sexually explicit material online; HIV/AIDS; circumcision; marriage denial and mental health and sexual citizenship; and governmental attacks on sexuality research, from across the globe. Also of new interest are research and policy on the transgendered. The style is less dense than usual for academic journals, for the journal is aimed at the non-academic reader as well as the scholar. The policy articles often take an advocacy stance while grounded in empirical research. In 2010, the publisher changed from University of California Press to Springer. Highly recommended for all major collections. (DT)

Studies in Gender and Sexuality. See Gender Studies section.

4507. ***Theology and Sexuality.*** [ISSN: 1355-8358] 1994. 3x/yr. GBP 345 (print & online eds.)). Routledge, 4 Park Sq, Milton Park, Abingdon, OX14 4RN, United Kingdom; subscriptions@tandf.co.uk; http://www.tandfonline.com. Adv. Refereed. Reprint: PSC. *Indexed:* A01, GW, R&TA. *Aud.:* Ac, Sa.

This journal describes itself as "the primary vehicle for those undertaking theological studies of sexuality and gender issues" that also aims to be accessible to counselors. Themes addressed include "deconstructive and reconstructive approaches to traditional Christian (and other traditions) teaching on sexuality, sexuality and violence and oppression, and the ethics of personal relationships." Members of the Centre for the Study of Christianity and Sexuality receive the journal as part of their annual membership. A liberal take on Christian issues relating to sexuality, it was previously (2008 and before) published by Sage, and subsequently by Equinox before migrating to Maney Publishing. One article advocated for why faith communities should support homosexual relationships, while another was on "The Rainbow Connection: Bridging Asian[-]American and Queer Theologies." It has also addressed queer theology and lesbians in South Africa. Recommended. (DT)

■ SLAVIC AND EURASIAN STUDIES

See also Asia; Europe; and Middle East sections.

Hugh K. Truslow, Librarian for the Fung Library and Davis Center for Russian and Eurasian Studies Collection, Fung Library, Harvard University, 1737 Cambridge St., Cambridge, MA 02138; truslow@fas.harvard.edu

Introduction

This latest edition of *Magazines for Libraries* retains the updated section title, introduced in the 23rd edition, that added "Eurasian" to reflect better the full scope of the geographic range covered and to come more in line with general practice in the field.

The geopolitical tensions in the region following Russia's annexation of Crimea in February 2014, combined with the ongoing crisis in eastern Ukraine, have kept Russia and what is sometimes called the "post-Soviet space" very much in the headlines and on the minds of policymakers. Russia's intervention in Syria and anxiety in NATO countries that were once part of the Soviet sphere of influence over Russian assertiveness are two other dynamics keeping this region, and its complex interrelationships and tangled histories, in continuing relevance.

The titles represented here, however, range far more broadly than history and politics, covering the worlds of literature, culture, economics, religion, sociology, anthropology, law, and many other areas, with much to challenge, edify, and intrigue general readers and scholarly specialists alike.

Basic Periodicals

Hs: *Russian Life;* Ga: *Current Digest of the Russian Press;* Ac: *The Russian Review, Slavic Review, Studies in East European Thought.*

Basic Abstracts and Indexes

American Bibliography of Slavic and Eastern European Studies (ABSEES), Historical Abstracts, MLA International Bibliography, PAIS International.

4508. *Anthropology and Archeology of Eurasia: a journal of translations.* Formerly (until 1992): *Soviet Anthropology and Archeology.* [ISSN: 1061-1959] 1962. q. GBP 1017 (print & online eds.)). Ed(s): Marjorie Mandelstam Balzer. Routledge, 530 Walnut St, Ste 850, Philadelphia, PA 19106; enquiries@tandfonline.com; http://www.tandfonline.com. Illus., index, adv. Sample. Refereed. Vol. ends: Spring (No. 4). Reprint: PSC. *Indexed:* A01, A22, A47, BAS, E01, MLA-IB. *Aud.:* Ac, Sa.

This journal "presents scholarship from Russia, Siberia, the Caucasus, and Central Asia, the vast region that stretches from the Baltic to the Black Sea and from Lake Baikal to the Bering Strait." Each issue has a particular theme, with an introduction by the editor, and includes "translated and annotated manuscripts, articles, and book excerpts reporting fieldwork from every part of the region and theoretical studies on topics of special interest." The articles include complete citations to the original version, and editors' notes when applicable, and they specify the translators. For academic and special libraries that support programs in anthropology, archaeology, and ethnology - as well as Slavic Studies - this publication is highly recommended. It has particular value for researchers in these disciplines who do not have a reading knowledge of Russian.

4509. *Baltic Horizons.* Formerly (until 2004): *Monthly Survey of Baltic and Post-Soviet Politics.* [ISSN: 1736-1834] 1990. q. Euroakadeemia, Mustamae tee 4, Tallinn, 10621, Estonia; euro@euroakadeemia.ee; http://euroakadeemia.ee. Circ: 300. *Aud.:* Ac, Sa.

Based at Euroacademy in Tallinn, Estonia, this multidisciplinary, peer-reviewed journal "publishes original research and review papers in English" on the Baltic states and the region. Each issue is dedicated to one of the following subject areas: translation or interpreting; international relations; environmental science; business management; and art and design. Recommended for academic and special libraries that support programs in Baltic Studies, and for public libraries with user populations interested in Baltic affairs.

4510. *Canadian - American Slavic Studies.* Formerly (until 1972): *Canadian Slavic Studies.* [ISSN: 0090-8290] 1967. q. EUR 256. Ed(s): Russell E Martin. Brill, PO Box 9000, Leiden, 2300 PA, Netherlands; marketing@brill.com; https://brill.com. Illus., index, adv. Refereed. Vol. ends: Winter (No. 4). Reprint: PSC. *Indexed:* A22, E01, MLA-IB. *Bk. rev.:* 20-30, 300-1,000 words, signed. *Aud.:* Ac, Sa.

The scope of this peer-reviewed scholarly journal is "Slavic and East European (including Albania, Hungary and Romania) culture, past and present." It publishes articles, documents, translations, and book reviews in English, French, German, Russian, and Ukrainian. While the focus is largely on history and literature, the journal "welcomes contributions in all areas of the humanities and social sciences." It also publishes special topical issues with guest editors. For librarians with collection-development responsibilities, the lists of books received are useful for selecting materials. Recommended as a significant title for academic and research libraries that support Slavic Studies.

4511. *Canadian Slavonic Papers: an interdisciplinary journal devoted to Central and Eastern Europe.* [ISSN: 0008-5006] 1956. q. GBP 278 (print & online eds.)). Ed(s): Heather J Coleman. Routledge, 530 Walnut St, Ste 850, Philadelphia, PA 19106; enquiries@tandfonline.com; http://www.tandfonline.com. Illus., index. Refereed. Reprint: PSC. *Indexed:* A01, A22, BRI, C37, IBSS, MLA-IB. *Bk. rev.:* 35-40, 300-500 words, signed. *Aud.:* Ac, Sa.

From the Canadian Association of Slavists, this interdisciplinary journal serves as "a forum for scholars from a range of disciplines: language and linguistics, literature, history, political science, sociology, economics, anthropology, geography and the arts." Articles are in English and French. The book reviews and review essays are of high quality, with coverage of materials from Canada and Europe as well, and can be valuable for librarians in collection development. Recommended as a major title for academic and research libraries that support Slavic Studies.

4512. *Central Asian Affairs.* [ISSN: 2214-2282] 2014. q. EUR 284. Ed(s): Marlene Laruelle, Sebastien Peyrouse. Brill, PO Box 9000, Leiden, 2300 PA, Netherlands; marketing@brill.com. Adv. Reprint: PSC. *Bk. rev.:* 1 or so; 1,000-2,000 words, signed. *Aud.:* Ac, Sa.

This relatively new title, with a distinguished editorial committee and board, has the stated aim to inform both scholarly discourse and policy discussions on the region by engaging experts from across the policy and academic arenas. Its subject coverage spans a range of disciplines, including "political science, sociology, anthropology, economics, development studies, and security studies." Its geographic coverage is to include Central Asia, Afghanistan, and the Caucasus, as well as China's Xinjiang region, Kashmir, and the neighboring powers of China, Iran, Pakistan, India, Russia, and Turkey. It will also address "the role of leading international powers and donors in this region." Recommended for academic and research libraries, as well as special libraries that support policy-oriented research on the region.

4513. *Central Asian Survey.* [ISSN: 0263-4937] 1982. q. GBP 1073 (print & online eds.)). Ed(s): Raphael Jacquet, Deniz Kandiyoti. Routledge, 4 Park Sq, Milton Park, Abingdon, OX14 4RN, United Kingdom; subscriptions@tandf.co.uk; http://www.tandfonline.com. Illus., index, adv. Sample. Refereed. Reprint: PSC. *Indexed:* A01, A22, A47, AmHI, E01, IBSS, MLA-IB, P61, SSA. *Bk. rev.:* 5-7, 1,000-1,300 words, signed. *Aud.:* Ac, Sa.

Published since 1982, this established, multi-disciplinary journal covers the "history, politics, cultures, religions and economies of the Central Asian and Caucasian regions," with coverage also extending to the Xinjiang region in China as well as Mongolia, Afghanistan, Iran, and Turkey. Its chief aim, the editors say, "is to reflect and promote advances in area-based scholarship in the social sciences and humanities and [to] enhance understanding of processes of local and regional change that make Central Asia and the Caucasus an area of significant contemporary interest." Recent special issues have dealt with "Urban Spaces and Lifestyles in Central Asia and Beyond" and "Reflections on Post-Soviet Development in Central Asia: A Multi-disciplinary Perspective." Recommended for academic and research libraries, especially those that support programs in area studies.

4514. *Communist and Post-Communist Studies.* Former titles (until 1993): *Studies in Comparative Communism;* (until 1968): *Communist Affairs.* [ISSN: 0967-067X] 1962. q. EUR 730. Elsevier Ltd, The Boulevard, Langford Lane, Oxford, OX5 1GB, United Kingdom; customerserviceau@elsevier.com; http://www.elsevier.com. Illus., adv. Sample. Refereed. *Indexed:* A01, A22, BAS, BRI, IBSS, MLA-IB, P61. *Aud.:* Ac, Sa.

This "is an international journal covering all communist and post-communist states and communist movements, including both their domestic policies and their international relations." Analytical focus is on "historical as well as current developments in the communist and post-communist world, including ideology, economy, and society." The journal also invites "comments of a comparative character from scholars specializing in the same subject matter but in different countries." Beyond "the traditional disciplines of history, political science, economics, and international relations, the editors encourage the submission of articles in less developed fields of social sciences and humanities, such as cultural anthropology, education, geography, religion, and sociology." Most articles published focus on the countries of the former Soviet Union and the Soviet bloc, while countries such as China, Cuba, and North Korea are treated less frequently. Recommended for academic and research libraries; may be of interest to larger public libraries that serve patrons interested in the politics, economics, and contemporary society of the former Soviet sphere of influence.

4515. *Current Digest of the Russian Press.* Former titles (until 2011): *Current Digest of the Post-Soviet Press;* (until 1992): *Current Digest of the Soviet Press;* Which incorporated (1968-1970): *Current Abstracts of the Soviet Press.* [ISSN: 2159-3612] 1949. w. USD 2495 (Individuals, USD 200). Ed(s): Xenia Grushetsky. East View Information Services, 10601 Wayzata Blvd, Hopkins, MN 55305; info@eastview.com; http://www.eastview.com/. Illus., index. Sample. Vol. ends: No. 52. *Indexed:* A01, A22, BAS, BRI, CDSP, MLA-IB. *Aud.:* Hs, Ga, Ac.

This weekly digest, published since 1949, offers a selection of articles from the Russian-language press translated into English for use in teaching and research. Its mission is "to provide the reader with a broad picture of the news presented to the Russian public," and it "strives to ensure that the articles included reflect multiple perspectives, incorporating articles from a number of independent newspapers with diverse editorial stances." Articles on important events are grouped under the heading "Featured News Stories," with additional items, often shorter, appearing under the sections "The Russian Federation," "Other Post-Soviet States," and "International Affairs." Each article includes a citation to the original publication and an indication of whether the text is complete or has been condensed. This is a valuable compilation source for current events in Russia, and is of particular use for readers without a reading knowledge of Russian. Recommended for all libraries, academic or public, with readers interested in the current political scene in Russia.

4516. *Demokratizatsiya: the journal of post-soviet democratization.* [ISSN: 1074-6846] 1992. q. USD 175 (print or online ed.) Individuals, USD 65 (print & online eds.)). Ed(s): Alexander Schmemann. George Washington University, Institute for European, Russian and Eurasian Studies, 1957 E St, NW, Ste 412, Washington, DC 20052; http://www.gwu.edu/~ieresgwu/ . Adv. Refereed. Reprint: PSC. *Indexed:* A01, BRI, P61. *Bk. rev.:* Varies, 500-600 words, signed. *Aud.:* Ac, Sa.

Beginning with *perestroika,* and covering the Yeltsin era through the current era of "managed democracy" under Putin, this is the leading international journal on democratization in post-Soviet countries. "It focuses on the end of the Soviet Union and the contemporary transformation of its successor states," and aims to be "a tool for building institutions from the ashes of the USSR and communism." The subject coverage focuses on "politics, economics, social issues, legal systems, nationalities, international relations, and human rights." Recommended highly for academic and research libraries that support the study of the former Soviet Union and the former Soviet bloc.

4517. *East European Jewish Affairs.* Former titles (until 1992): *Soviet Jewish Affairs;* (until 1971): *Bulletin on Soviet and East European Jewish Affairs.* [ISSN: 1350-1674] 19??. 3x/yr. GBP 355 (print & online eds.)). Ed(s): Anna Shternshis, David Shneer. Routledge, 4 Park Sq, Milton Park, Abingdon, OX14 4RN, United Kingdom; subscriptions@tandf.co.uk; http://www.tandfonline.com. Illus., index, adv. Sample. Refereed. Vol. ends: Winter (No. 2). Microform: PQC. Reprint: PSC. *Indexed:* A22, AmHI, E01, IBSS, MLA-IB. *Bk. rev.:* 5-10, 300-500 words, signed. *Aud.:* Ac, Sa.

This interdisciplinary journal seeks to provide an "understanding of the position and prospects of Jews in the former Soviet Union and the countries of East-Central Europe. It deals with issues in historical perspective and in the context of general, social, economic, political, and cultural developments in the region. The journal includes analytical, in-depth articles; review articles; archival documents; conference notes; and annotated books." The quality and selection of the articles is excellent, as are the book reviews and the review articles when included. The lists of books received for review are of great value for scholars, as well as for collection development librarians. Recommended highly for academic and research libraries, and for larger public libraries with reader populations interested in Jewish affairs of the region.

4518. *East European Politics.* Former titles (until 2011): *Journal of Communist Studies and Transition Politics;* (until 1994): *Journal of Communist Studies;* (until 1985): *Communist Affairs;* (until 1982): *Documents in Communist Affairs.* [ISSN: 2159-9165] 1977. q. GBP 589 (print & online eds.)). Ed(s): Dr. Petr Kopecky, Dr. Adam Fagan. Routledge, 4 Park Sq, Milton Park, Abingdon, OX14 4RN, United Kingdom; subscriptions@tandf.co.uk; http://www.tandfonline.com. Illus., index. Sample. Refereed. Vol. ends: No. 4. Microform: PQC. Reprint: PSC. *Indexed:* A22, E01, IBSS, P61. *Bk. rev.:* Varies, 500-800 words, signed. *Aud.:* Ac, Sa.

More recently known as the *Journal of Communist Studies and Transition Politics,* this scholarly journal addresses "the government, politics[,] and international relations of the post-communist space." Geographic coverage is for "the entire post-communist region, including East Central and South Eastern Europe, Russia[,] and all the other countries of the former Soviet Union." The articles cover "political developments in individual countries, together with cross-country comparative analyses and studies of the relations between post-communist regions and other parts of the world, including internationally based organizations." In addition to a substantial book review section, the journal also publishes thematic special issues, symposium sections, and "review articles devoted to briefer analysis of particular events, political issues[,] and important theoretical and conceptual developments." The journal's editors say that "although the journal aims for a relatively broad methodological coverage, including quantitative and qualitative approaches, and comparative or single country studies," it will also "prioritize empirical scholarship." Recommended for academic and special libraries that support Slavic Studies, and for larger public libraries with user populations interested in the topic.

4519. *East European Politics & Societies.* [ISSN: 0888-3254] 1987. q. USD 625 (print & online eds.)). Ed(s): Wendy Bracewell, Krzysztof Jasiewicz. Sage Publications, Inc., 2455 Teller Rd, Thousand Oaks, CA 91320; info@sagepub.com; http://www.sagepub.com. Illus., adv. Sample. Refereed. Vol. ends: No. 3. Microform: PQC. Reprint: PSC. *Indexed:* A01, A22, BRI, E01, IBSS, MLA-IB, P61. *Aud.:* Ac, Sa.

This journal "covers issues in Eastern Europe from social, political, and humanities perspectives" with the aim of "expanding readers' understanding of past events and current developments in countries from Greece to the Baltics." The publisher writes that the journal "maintains a tradition of imaginative and erudite vision, uniting the cutting-edge social research and political analysis of leading area specialists, historians, sociologists, political scientists[,] and anthropologists from around the world." The coverage is broad and engaging, and the articles are of consistently high quality. This title is published in association with the American Council of Learned Societies. Recommended for academic and research libraries that support Slavic Studies generally, and in particular those with a focus on East Central European Studies.

4520. *Eastern European Economics.* [ISSN: 0012-8775] 1962. bi-m. GBP 1462 (print & online eds.)). Ed(s): Josef C Brada. Routledge, 530 Walnut St, Ste 850, Philadelphia, PA 19106; orders@taylorandfrancis.com; http://www.tandfonline.com. Illus., index, adv. Sample. Refereed. Vol. ends: Nov/Dec (No. 6). Reprint: PSC. *Indexed:* A22, B01, E01, EconLit. *Aud.:* Ac, Sa.

This journal "publishes original research on the newly emerging economies of Central and Eastern Europe, with coverage of the ongoing processes of transition to market economics in different countries, their integration into the broader European and global economies, and the ramifications of the 2008-9 financial crisis." Recent issues have tended to include around five articles, and all feature an introduction by the journal's editor to add "context and expert insights on the articles presented." Themes of some recent issues have included "Economic Complexity, Inflation, and Monetary Policy in Enlarged Europe" and "Patterns of Economic and Financial Development in Poland and the Baltic States." Recommended highly for academic and research libraries that support Slavic Studies as well as the economics and business of the region.

4521. *Eurasian Geography and Economics.* Former titles (until 2002): *Post-Soviet Geography and Economics;* (until 1996): *Post-Soviet Geography;* (until 1992): *Soviet Geography;* (until 19??): *Soviet Geography - Review and Translation.* [ISSN: 1538-7216] 1960. bi-m. GBP 761 (print & online eds.)). Ed(s): John O'Loughlin. Taylor & Francis, 2, 3 & 4 Park Sq, Milton Park, Abingdon, OX14 4RN, United Kingdom; subscriptions@tandf.co.uk; https://www.tandfonline.com. Illus., index. Refereed. Vol. ends: No. 8. Reprint: PSC. *Indexed:* A01, A22, B01, BAS, BRI, C42, EconLit. *Aud.:* Ac, Sa.

This journal "features original papers by leading specialists and scholars on salient geographic and economic issues in China, Russia, India, [the] European Union, and other regions within the Eurasian realm. Included in all issues are symposia on topics of worldwide significance, review papers, and empirical research focused on analysis of recent economic and geographic developments." Though the scope of recent issues has focused on China and India as much as on countries within the former Soviet realm, this expansive regional approach - as in a recent group of articles on water issues, for example - will be welcomed by some scholars. Recommended for academic and research libraries with Slavic Studies programs, as well as geography programs and researchers studying in the non-Slavic Eurasian countries. Also recommended for larger public libraries with readers interested in the spatial aspects of Eurasia and its economies.

4522. *Europe - Asia Studies.* Formerly (until 1993): *Soviet Studies.* [ISSN: 0966-8136] 1949. 10x/yr. GBP 2019 (print & online eds.)). Ed(s): Terry Cox. Routledge, 4 Park Sq, Milton Park, Abingdon, OX14 4RN, United Kingdom; subscriptions@tandf.co.uk; http://www.tandfonline.com. Illus., index, adv. Sample. Refereed. Vol. ends: Dec (No. 8). Reprint: PSC. *Indexed:* A01, A22, AmHI, B01, BAS, BRI, E01, EconLit, IBSS, MASUSE, MLA-IB, P61, SSA. *Bk. rev.:* 20-25, 500-1,000 words, signed. *Aud.:* Ac, Sa.

According to the publishers, this title is "the principal academic journal in the world focusing on the history and current political, social and economic affairs of the countries of the former 'communist bloc' of the Soviet Union, Eastern Europe and Asia. At the same time, the journal explores the economic, political and social transformation of these countries and the changing character of their relationships with the rest of Europe and Asia." Some recent special issues have dealt with "The Ukrainian Crisis and the Post-Post-Cold War Europe" and "Russian Modernisation-Structures and Agencies." The journal is published on behalf of the Central and East European Studies program at the School of Social and Political Sciences at the University of Glasgow. In addition to a well-selected array of book reviews, the list of books received will be helpful to collection-development librarians. Recommended highly for academic, research, and special libraries that support research in Slavic Studies.

Folklore (ISSN 1406-0949). See Folklore section.

4523. *Journal of Baltic Studies.* Formerly (until 1972): *Bulletin of Baltic Studies.* [ISSN: 0162-9778] 1970. q. GBP 520 (print & online eds.)). Ed(s): Terry Clark. Routledge, 530 Walnut St, Ste 850, Philadelphia, PA 19106; enquiries@tandfonline.com; http://www.tandfonline.com. Illus., index, adv. Sample. Refereed. Circ: 1300. Vol. ends: Winter (No. 4). Microform: PQC. Reprint: PSC. *Indexed:* A22, E01, IBSS, MLA-IB. *Bk. rev.:* 5-10, 300-500 words, signed. *Aud.:* Ac, Sa.

This journal is a "peer-reviewed multidisciplinary journal dedicated to advancing knowledge about all aspects of the Baltic Sea Region's political, social, economic, and cultural life, past and present." It is the journal of the Association for the Advancement of Baltic Studies. Most articles are in English. The book reviews and lists of books received may be useful to collection-development librarians with responsibilities for the Baltic region. Recommended for all academic and research libraries with Baltic and Slavic Studies programs, and for those public libraries that have readers interested in Baltic affairs.

4524. *The Journal of Eurasian Studies (Online).* [ISSN: 1879-3673] 2010. s-a. Ed(s): S. White, G. H. Eom. Sage Publications Ltd., 1 Oliver's Yard, 55 City Rd, London, EC1Y 1SP, United Kingdom; info@sagepub.com; https://www.sagepub.com. Refereed. *Bk. rev.:* 2 per issue, 450-1100 words, in recent issues. *Aud.:* Ac, Sa.

According to the publisher, "Eurasian countries are among the most rapidly and drastically changing places since the collapse of the former Soviet Union," and the journal attempts to content with that, with a particular focus on six issues: national identity; political and economic transition; democratization and marketization; migration; energy problems; and international development and ODA (official development assistance). The engaging range of articles and high quality of scholarship in recent issues make good on the editors' claim that the journal "internationalizes local concerns within Eurasian communities and beyond the various Asian civilizations in more cross-regional perspectives." Published on behalf of Hanyang University in Seoul, South Korea, the journal has a distinguished editorial board. Recommended for academic and research libraries with programs that cover the region.

4525. *Journal of Russian and East European Psychology.* Formerly (until 1992): *Soviet Psychology;* Which superseded in part (in 1966): *Soviet Psychology and Psychiatry.* [ISSN: 1061-0405] 1962. bi-m. GBP 1307 (print & online eds.)). Ed(s): Pentti Hakkarainen. Routledge, 530 Walnut St, Ste 850, Philadelphia, PA 19106; enquiries@tandfonline.com; http://www.tandfonline.com. Illus., index, adv. Sample. Refereed. Vol. ends: Nov/Dec (No. 6). Reprint: PSC. *Indexed:* A01, A22, B01, E01. *Aud.:* Ac, Sa.

This journal "publishes thematic issues with translations of original submissions as well as articles published in scholarly journals on a variety of topics from child development to creativity to memory to post-traumatic stress." Another element of the journal's editorial mission is to publish translated works by preeminent Russian scholars in psychology "in excellent translations with helpful bibliographic information, [and with] contributions by peers and proteges," as the publishers write. The articles include complete citations to the original publication and the name of translator. Aimed at specialists in psychology, this journal will be of particular interest to those scholars without Russian-language reading abilities. Recommended for academic and research libraries that support study and research in psychology as well as Slavic Studies.

4526. *Journal of Slavic Linguistics.* [ISSN: 1068-2090] 1993. s-a. Free to members; Non-members, USD 24. Ed(s): Steven Franks, Vicki Polansky. Slavica Publishers, Inc., 1430 N Willis Dr, Bloomington, IN 47404; slavica@indiana.edu; https://slavica.indiana.edu/. Illus. Refereed. Vol. ends: No. 2. *Indexed:* A22, AmHI, BRI, E01, MLA-IB. *Bk. rev.:* 1-3, 500-1,000 words, signed. *Aud.:* Ac, Sa.

This publication, which is the official journal of the Slavic Linguistics Society (www.slaviclinguistics.org), "is intended to address issues in description and analysis of Slavic languages of general interest to linguists, regardless of theoretical orientation." It publishes "papers dealing with any aspect of synchronic or diachronic Slavic phonetics, phonology, morphology, syntax, semantics[,] and pragmatics, as long as they raise substantive problems of broad theoretical concern or propose significant descriptive generalization." Special emphasis is placed on "comparative studies and formal analysis." Each issue is about 150-200 pages in length. The journal is aimed at specialists in the field and should be acquired by academic and research libraries that support Slavic Studies and general linguistic programs.

4527. *Journal of Southeast European and Black Sea Studies.* [ISSN: 1468-3857] 2001. q. GBP 585 (print & online eds.)). Ed(s): Ioannis Armakolas. Routledge, 4 Park Sq, Milton Park, Abingdon, OX14 4RN, United Kingdom; subscriptions@tandf.co.uk; http://www.tandfonline.com. Adv. Sample. Refereed. Reprint: PSC. *Indexed:* A01, A22, AmHI, E01, IBSS, P61. *Bk. rev.:* Varies; 1,000-1,500 words; signed. *Aud.:* Ac, Sa.

Associated with ELIAMEP, the Hellenic Foundation for European and Foreign Policy, the journal includes "cross-country comparative analyses and new research on individual countries within the Southeast European and Black Sea regions," and "invites submissions with innovative new research establishing analytical connections and comparisons between the two regions." Coverage also includes articles on Russian relations with neighboring states, as well as on "Turkey and its policy towards individual countries and entire regions." The specific disciplines reflected are "political science and international relations, political economy, political anthropology[,] and late modern and contemporary history," with an eye to "providing a forum for both academic and original policy-oriented articles." Recent thematic issues have dealt with the Ukraine crisis in terms of sub-state and non-state actors, as well as its global and regional repercussions. Recommended for academic and research libraries that support Slavic and Balkan Studies programs.

4528. *Lituanus.* [ISSN: 0024-5089] 1954. q. USD 40 (Individuals, USD 30). Lituanus Foundation, Inc., 47 W Polk St, Ste 100-300, Chicago, IL 60605; admin@lituanus.org. Illus., index. Sample. Refereed. Vol. ends: Winter (No. 4). Microform: PQC. *Indexed:* A22, MLA-IB. *Bk. rev.:* 3-4, 500-1,000 words, signed. *Aud.:* Ac, Sa.

This English-language journal is "dedicated to Lithuanian and Baltic art, history, language, literature[,] and related cultural topics." The focus is predominantly on Lithuania, though articles on the other Baltic countries and East Central Europe are occasionally featured. The issues generally include scholarly research articles as well as poetry, memoirs, essays, and book reviews. The publisher is working to make the back issues of the journal available online, with the full text of issues for 1954-1957 and 1963-2016 currently available. Recommended for any academic and public library with readers interested in Lithuania and the other Baltic states. URL: www.lituanus.org

4529. *Nationalities Papers: the journal of nationalism and ethnicity.* [ISSN: 0090-5992] 1972. bi-m. GBP 1071 (print & online eds.)). Ed(s): Harris Mylonas. Cambridge University Press, University Printing House, Shaftesbury Rd, Cambridge, CB2 8BS, United Kingdom; journals@cambridge.org; https://www.cambridge.org/. Illus., adv. Sample. Refereed. Reprint: PSC. *Indexed:* A01, A22, AmHI, E01, IBSS, MLA-IB, P61, SSA. *Bk. rev.:* 15-25, 500-800 words, signed. *Aud.:* Ac, Sa.

According to the publisher, this "is the leading journal on nationalism, ethnicity, ethnic conflict[,] and national identity in Central Europe, the Balkans, the former Soviet Union, the Caucasus, the Turkic world and Central Eurasia." From the Association for the Study of Nationalities, the journal also publishes articles "on theories of nationalism, comparative studies of nationalism, and trans- and supranational aspects of interethnic relations and national identity." Disciplines represented include history, political science, sociology, anthropology, and literature. The book reviews are of high quality and can assist collection-development librarians with selection. Recommended highly for academic and research libraries with programs in Slavic as well as European Studies programs, and also for all libraries where patrons may have an interest in the minorities of the former Soviet space and East Central Europe.

4530. *Polish Review.* [ISSN: 0032-2970] 1956. q. USD 155 (print & online eds.)). Ed(s): Neal Pease. University of Illinois Press, 1325 S Oak St, MC-566, Champaign, IL 61820; uipress@uillinois.edu. Illus., index, adv. Refereed. Vol. ends: Dec (No. 4). *Indexed:* A22, AmHI, BRI, MLA-IB. *Bk. rev.:* 4-5, 300-1,000 words, signed. *Aud.:* Ac, Sa.

According to the editors, this publication is a "peer-edited scholarly quarterly, published without pause since 1956 by the Polish Institute of Arts and Sciences of America." The journal publishes "scholarly articles dealing with all aspects of Polish culture, as well as, on occasion, translations of important Polish literature." Articles encompass Polish arts, linguistics, history, sociology, ethnography, and Polish Americana. For collection development librarians, the book reviews, lists of books received, and review articles will be of value. Recommended for academic and research libraries that support Slavic Studies programs, and also for those public libraries with readers interested in Polish history and culture.

4531. *Post-Communist Economies.* Former titles (until 1999): *Communist Economies and Economic Transformation;* (until 1991): *Communist Economies.* [ISSN: 1463-1377] 1989. 8x/yr. GBP 1720 (print & online eds.)). Ed(s): Roger Clarke. Routledge, 4 Park Sq, Milton Park, Abingdon, OX14 4RN, United Kingdom; subscriptions@tandf.co.uk; http://www.tandfonline.com. Illus., adv. Sample. Refereed. Reprint: PSC. *Indexed:* A22, B01, BAS, E01, EconLit, IBSS. *Aud.:* Ac, Sa.

This journal "publishes key research and policy articles in the analysis of post-communist economies." The editors contend that these economies "still form a clearly identifiable group, distinguished by the impact of the years of communist rule," and that they "still present distinctive problems that make them a particular focus of research." Hence, the editors see there to be a need to address issues of "further stabilization, liberalization[,] and privatization" as well as the "fundamental problems of low efficiency, productivity[,] and income" before the countries can catch up to "long-established market economies" and the "much richer countries of the European Union." There are around eight articles in each issue, and the geographic and subject coverage ranges fairly evenly across the economies of all of the post-communist countries. Recommended highly for academic and research libraries with programs in Slavic or Central Asian Studies, as well as those with international economics programs.

4532. *Post-Soviet Affairs.* Formerly (until 1992): *Soviet Economy.* [ISSN: 1060-586X] 1985. 6x/yr. GBP 481 (print & online eds.)). Ed(s): George W Breslauer. Routledge, 530 Walnut St, Ste 850, Philadelphia, PA 19106; enquiries@tandfonline.com; http://www.tandfonline.com. Illus., index. Refereed. Vol. ends: Dec (No. 4). Reprint: PSC. *Indexed:* A01, A22, B01, BRI, EconLit, IBSS, P61. *Aud.:* Ac, Sa.

This journal "features the work of prominent Western scholars on the republics of the former Soviet Union, providing exclusive, up-to-the minute analyses of the state of the economy and society, progress toward economic and political reform, and linkages between political and social changes and economic developments." The editorial board features many prominent scholars in the field of Slavic Studies. The four or so articles in each issue are characterized by high standards of scholarship, with a focus, as the title implies, on the successor states of the former Soviet Union, and in particular on Russia. Recommended highly for any academic and research libraries with programs in Slavic Studies.

4533. *Problems of Economic Transition.* Formerly (until 1992): *Problems in Economics.* [ISSN: 1061-1991] 1958. m. GBP 1514 (print & online eds.)). Routledge, 530 Walnut St, Ste 850, Philadelphia, PA 19106; enquiries@tandfonline.com; http://www.tandfonline.com. Illus., index, adv. Sample. Refereed. Vol. ends: Apr (No. 12). Reprint: PSC. *Indexed:* A22, B01, E01, EconLit, IBSS. *Aud.:* Ac, Sa.

According to the publisher, this journal "enables English-language readers to follow the principal theoretical and policy issues that constitute the core of post-Soviet economic discourse in various regions of the former USSR." The journal's coverage includes "the most recent research papers, policy studies, and analytical reports of articles in leading professional journals." Frequently addressed topics include "reform policy; natural resource economics; foreign economic relations and the impact of the global financial crisis on the transition economies; industrial reorganization; labor economics and social policy; and regional economic development." The articles include complete citations to the original publication and the name of the translator. This journal will be of particular interest to interested scholars without Russian-language reading abilities. Most articles are drawn from the most important Russian economic journals. Recommended for academic and research libraries that support programs in Slavic Studies as well as international economics.

4534. ***Problems of Post-Communism.*** Formerly (until Jan.1995): *Problems of Communism.* [ISSN: 1075-8216] 1951. bi-m. GBP 414 (print & online eds.)). Ed(s): Dmitry Gorenburg. Routledge, 530 Walnut St, Ste 850, Philadelphia, PA 19106; enquiries@tandfonline.com; http://www.tandfonline.com. Illus., index, adv. Sample. Refereed. Vol. ends: Nov/Dec (No. 6). Microform: PQC. Reprint: PSC. *Indexed:* A01, A22, BAS, BRI, E01, MLA-IB, P61. *Aud.:* Ac, Sa.

This venerable journal places emphasis "on timely research covering current economic, political, security, and international developments and trends in Russia and China, Central Europe and Central Asia, Latin America, and Southeast Asia." The editors note that "clarity and readability make the articles fully accessible to researchers, policy makers, and students alike." Each issue includes five or so articles that focus on current issues in the Soviet successor states and those in East Central Europe that were once part of the Soviet bloc. Recommended for academic and research libraries, and also for large public libraries.

4535. ***Region (Indiana): regional studies of Russia, Eastern Europe and Central Asia.*** [ISSN: 2166-4307] 2012. s-a. USD 60 (Individuals, USD 40; Students, USD 20). Ed(s): Lewis Siegelbaum, Wan-Suk Hong. Slavica Publishers, Inc., 1430 N Willis Dr, Bloomington, IN 47404; slavica@indiana.edu; https://slavica.indiana.edu/. Refereed. *Indexed:* A01. *Bk. rev.:* 1 or so; 750-1,000 words, signed. *Aud.:* Ac, Sa.

This is a promising and relatively new title on the "history and current political, economic, and social affairs of the entire former Soviet bloc." Its particular focus is on "various facets of transformation at the local and national levels in the aforementioned regions, as well as the changing character of their relationships with the rest of the world in the context of glocalization [*sic*]." This neologism, as characterized by the co-editor in his preface to the first issue, "stresses both local adaptation to global phenomena and that adaptation's transnational or even global significance." To this end, the editors say the journal "regularly gives a certain portion of space to articles on concrete local issues written by local Eurasianist scholars." Recommended for academic and research libraries.

4536. ***Religion, State and Society.*** Formerly (until 1992): *Religion in Communist Lands.* [ISSN: 0963-7494] 1973. 5x/yr. GBP 1236 (print & online eds.)). Ed(s): Dr. Philip Walters. Routledge, 4 Park Sq, Milton Park, Abingdon, OX14 4RN, United Kingdom; subscriptions@tandf.co.uk; http://www.tandfonline.com. Adv. Sample. Refereed. Microform: PQC. Reprint: PSC. *Indexed:* A01, A22, E01, IBSS, P61, R&TA, SSA. *Bk. rev.:* 3-5, 400-800 words, signed. *Aud.:* Ac, Sa.

According to the publisher, this journal "has a long-established reputation as the leading English-language academic publication focusing on communist and formerly communist countries throughout the world, and the legacy of the encounter between religion and communism." Coverage has since expanded "to include religious developments in countries which have not experienced communist rule, and to treat wider themes in a more systematic way." A comparative approach is encouraged "where appropriate, with the aim of revealing similarities and differences in the historical and current experience of countries, regions and religions, in stability or in transition." Most issues include a selection of book reviews. Recent issues have contained special sections on "Religion and Territorial Politics In Southern Europe" and "Muslim Military Chaplaincy." Recommended for academic and research libraries with Slavic Studies or religious studies programs, and for larger public libraries with reader populations interested in the topic.

4537. ***Revolutionary Russia.*** Former titles (until 1988): *Sbornik;* (until 1975): *Study Group on the Russian Revolution. Newsletter.* [ISSN: 0954-6545] 19??. s-a. GBP 377 (print & online eds.)). Ed(s): Aaron Retish, Sarah Badcock. Routledge, 4 Park Sq, Milton Park, Abingdon, OX14 4RN, United Kingdom; subscriptions@tandf.co.uk; http://www.tandfonline.com. Adv. Sample. Refereed. Reprint: PSC. *Indexed:* A22, E01, P61. *Bk. rev.:* 10-12, 800-1,000 words, signed. *Aud.:* Ac, Sa.

This is the journal of the Study Group on the Russian Revolution, and according to the publisher, it is "the only English-language journal to concentrate on the revolutionary period of Russian history, from c. 1880-c. 1932." The journal is "interdisciplinary and international in approach, publishing original research, documentary sources, book reviews[,] and review articles in the fields of history, politics, economics, sociology, art history[,] and literary and intellectual history from scholars across the world, including Russia and other countries of the former Soviet Union." Each issue includes three or four scholarly articles and a very high-quality book review section, which is of great interest both to scholars and to librarians working in collection development. Recommended highly for academic and research libraries with programs in Slavic Studies programs, or history at the advanced level.

4538. ***Russian Education and Society.*** Formerly (until 1992): *Soviet Education.* [ISSN: 1060-9393] 1958. m. GBP 1491 (print & online eds.)). Routledge, 711 3rd Ave, 8th Fl., New York, NY 10017; enquiries@tandfonline.com; http://www.routledge.com. Illus., index, adv. Sample. Refereed. Vol. ends: Dec (No. 12). Reprint: PSC. *Indexed:* A01, A22, E01, ERIC, MLA-IB. *Aud.:* Ac, Sa.

This journal features selected "material for translation from the Russian-language professional literature on education and socialization," and it covers "preschool, primary, secondary, vocational, and higher education; curricula and methods; and socialization issues related to family life, ethnic and religious identity formation, youth culture, addiction[,] and other behavioral and health problems; [and] professional training and employment." The journal's scope "extends beyond Russia proper to provide coverage of all the former Soviet states as well as international educational issues." Each issue includes five to eight articles, each with a complete citation to the original publication source, and the names of translators. Aimed at specialists in education, this journal will be of particular interest those to scholars without Russian-language reading abilities. Recommended for academic and research libraries that support Slavic Studies programs as well as advanced study in education.

4539. ***Russian History.*** [ISSN: 0094-288X] 1974. q. EUR 307. Brill, PO Box 9000, Leiden, 2300 PA, Netherlands; marketing@brill.com; https://brill.com. Illus., adv. Refereed. Vol. ends: Winter (No. 4). Reprint: PSC. *Indexed:* A22, E01, MLA-IB. *Aud.:* Ac, Sa.

This scholarly journal's "mission is the publication of original articles on the history of Russia through the centuries, [o]n the assumption that all past experiences are inter-related." The journal "seeks to discover, analyze, and understand the most interesting experiences and relationships and elucidate their causes and consequences." The journal's contributors come "from different perspectives: intellectual, economic[,] and military history[;] domestic, social[,] and class relations[;] relations with non-Russian peoples[;] nutrition and health[; and] all possible events that had an influence on Russia." Each issue contains a varying number of articles, generally written in English, and occasional review articles. The journal has an impressive list of prominent scholars on its editorial board. Highly recommended for academic and research libraries that support Slavic Studies programs or advanced study in history.

4540. ***Russian Life.*** Former titles (until 1993): *Soviet Life;* (until 1965): *U S S R.* [ISSN: 1066-999X] 1956. bi-m. USD 39 domestic; USD 54 foreign. Ed(s): Maria Antonova, Paul E Richardson. Russian Life, PO Box 567, Montpelier, VT 05601. Illus., adv. Sample. Vol. ends: Dec (No. 12). Microform: PQC. *Indexed:* A01, A22, BRI, ENW. *Bk. rev.:* Number and length vary. *Aud.:* Ga, Ac.

Published bimonthly, this "is a colorful, insightful look at life as it is lived in Russia today. Featuring quality journalism, amazing photography[,] and a breadth and depth of coverage no other publication can match, *Russian Life* is a bimonthly trip into the heart of Russian reality, past and present." The editor also notes that the journal is "100 percent independent of the Russian government." Although geared toward the nonspecialist, this journal does an excellent job of providing an overview of current events, with an emphasis on culture. It also provides the Russian perspective on world events. Each issue is richly illustrated with color photographs and includes book reviews. The web site includes articles that are not found in the print edition. Highly recommended for all public, academic, and research libraries. URL: www.russianlife.com

4541. ***Russian Linguistics: international journal for the study of Russian and other Slavic languages.*** [ISSN: 0304-3487] 1974. 3x/yr. EUR 1134 (print & online eds.)). Ed(s): Ulrich Schweier. Springer Netherlands, Van Godewijckstraat 30, Dordrecht, 3311 GX, Netherlands; http://www.springer.com. Illus., index, adv. Sample. Refereed. Vol. ends: Nov (No. 3). Microform: PQC. Reprint: PSC. *Indexed:* A22, AmHI, BRI, E01, MLA-IB. *Bk. rev.:* Varies, 800-1,500 words, signed. *Aud.:* Ac, Sa.

This journal "is an international forum for all scholars working in the field of Slavic linguistics (Russian and other Slavic languages) and its manifold diversity, ranging from phonetics and phonology to syntax and the linguistic analysis of texts (text grammar), including both diachronic and synchronic problems." The journal "publishes original articles and reviews as well as surveys of current scholarly writings from other periodicals." Coverage includes: "Traditional-structuralist as well as generative-transformational and other modern approaches to questions of synchronic and diachronic grammar; phonetics and phonology, morphology, syntax, pragmatics[,] and semantics of Russian and other Slavic languages (synchronic and diachronic); philological problems of Russian/Old-Russian texts as well as texts in other Slavic languages; grammar of Russian and other Slavic languages in their relation to linguistic universals; history of Russian and other Slavic literary languages; [and] Slavic dialectology." While highly specialized, this is a very high-quality journal and essential for those in the field. Articles are mostly in English with some in Russian. Book reviews are occasionally published. Recommended for academic and research libraries that support programs in Russian linguistics, language, and literature.

4542. *Russian Literature.* [ISSN: 0304-3479] 1973. 8x/yr. EUR 1378. Ed(s): E Rutten. Elsevier BV, Radarweg 29, Amsterdam, 1043 NX, Netherlands; info@elsevier.com; https://www.elsevier.com/. Illus., index. Sample. Refereed. Vol. ends: No. 4 - No. 8. Microform: PQC. *Indexed:* A22, MLA-IB. *Aud.:* Ac, Sa.

This journal "combines issues devoted to special topics of Russian literature with contributions on related subjects in Croatian, Serbian, Czech, Slovak and Polish literatures. Moreover, several issues each year contain articles on heterogeneous subjects concerning Russian literature. All methods and viewpoints are welcomed, provided they contribute something new, original[,] or challenging to our understanding of Russian and other Slavic literatures." The journal "regularly publishes special issues devoted to: the historical avant-garde in Russian literature and in the other Slavic literatures; [and] the development of descriptive and theoretical poetics in Russian studies and in studies of other Slavic fields." Most articles in this high-quality, rather specialized journal are published in Russian, and quotations often appear in the vernacular language, even when the main text is in English. Recommended for academic and research libraries that support Russian language and literature programs.

4543. *Russian Politics and Law.* Formerly (until 1992): *Soviet Law and Government.* [ISSN: 1061-1940] 1962. bi-m. GBP 1341 (print & online eds.)). Ed(s): Dmitry Gorenburg. Routledge, 530 Walnut St, Ste 850, Philadelphia, PA 19106; enquiries@tandfonline.com; http://www.tandfonline.com. Illus., index, adv. Sample. Refereed. Vol. ends: Nov/Dec (No. 6). Microform: WSH; PMC. Reprint: PSC. *Indexed:* A01, A22, E01, IBSS, L14, P61. *Aud.:* Ac, Sa.

This journal "publishes thematic issues featuring translations of some of the most important political science articles by authors working in the Soviet successor states." The selections are "drawn from both print and electronic sources, as well as from previously unpublished work" and "include both articles examining the politics of the region and theoretical works of interest to the field as a whole." For each issue, an expert chief or guest editor provides a "substantive introduction" to the particular theme. As with the other M.E. Sharpe journals of translation, full citations to the original publication source are given, and so are the original end notes and the name of the translator. Scholars in the fields covered who do not have reading knowledge of Russian will find this a very useful source. Recommended for academic and research libraries with programs in Slavic Studies, international politics, and international law.

4544. *The Russian Review: an American quarterly devoted to Russia past and present.* [ISSN: 0036-0341] 1941. q. GBP 306. Ed(s): Kurt S Schultz, Eve Levin. Wiley-Blackwell Publishing, Inc., 350 Main St, Malden, MA 02148; http://onlinelibrary.wiley.com. Illus., index, adv. Sample. Refereed. Vol. ends: Oct (No. 4). Microform: PQC. Reprint: PSC. *Indexed:* A01, A22, AmHI, BRI, CBRI, E01, IBSS, MLA-IB, P61. *Bk. rev.:* 25-40, 300-1,000 words, signed. *Aud.:* Ac, Sa.

The editors of this venerable journal describe its mission as "the presentation of a broad panorama of the Russian scene, both past and present." It contains "articles and book reviews on a variety of aspects of Russia's history, literature, culture, film, fine arts, society, and politics." The journal's scope "includes not only the Russian nationality, but all the peoples of the Russian Empire, Soviet Union, and contemporary Russian Federation. Topics of particular interest at this time include nationality policy, civil society, identity, gender, religion, modern literature and literary figures, and cultural studies." Scholars and collection development librarians will find the extensive book review sections essential for keeping up with a broad range of current scholarship. The lists within the publications-received section are also valuable for librarians. Recommended highly as an essential title for any academic or research library with a program in Slavic Studies, and it will also be of interest to larger public libraries with interested user populations.

4545. *Russian Social Science Review.* Formerly (until 1992): *Soviet Review;* Which superseded (in 1960): *Soviet Highlights.* [ISSN: 1061-1428] 1959. bi-m. GBP 398 (print & online eds.)). Ed(s): Patricia Kolb. Routledge, 530 Walnut St, Ste 850, Philadelphia, PA 19106. Illus., index, adv. Sample. Refereed. Vol. ends: Nov/Dec (No. 6). Microform: PQC. Reprint: PSC. *Indexed:* A01, A22, BRI, E01, MLA-IB, P61. *Aud.:* Ac, Sa.

This journal "publishes thematic collections of articles that have been carefully selected from Russian scholarly sources for translation into English," drawn "from many disciplines and sources." Issues cover topics such as "youth culture and student life; family relations; social change and inequality; political behavior and ideological beliefs; sex and gender; love and marriage; ethnic relations; and religious attitudes." Full citations to the original publication source are given, as are the original end notes and the name of the translator. Scholars in the fields reflected here who do not have reading knowledge of Russian will find it a worthwhile source. Recommended for academic and research libraries, and also for larger public libraries with readers interested in Russian scholarly advances in the broad topical coverage.

4546. *Russian Studies in History.* Formerly (until 1992): *Soviet Studies in History.* [ISSN: 1061-1983] 1962. q. GBP 958 (print & online eds.)). Ed(s): Christine Ruane, Joseph Bradley. Routledge, 530 Walnut St, Ste 850, Philadelphia, PA 19106; enquiries@tandfonline.com; http://www.tandfonline.com. Illus., index, adv. Sample. Refereed. Vol. ends: Spring (No. 4). Reprint: PSC. *Indexed:* A01, A22, BAS, E01. *Aud.:* Ac, Sa.

This journal "publishes thematic issues featuring translations of scholarly articles selected from diverse Russian sources and introduced by an expert guest editor." These topics can range "over all periods and subfields of Russian and Soviet history[,] as well as more general theoretical and historiographical questions of interest to historians of many specialties." Articles are drawn from the major historical journals, and include the footnotes from the original article as well as complete citations to the original publication. Translators' names are also given. This journal would be of use for students and scholars who do not have a reading knowledge of Russian, and for any historian with even a passing interest in Russia. Recent thematic issues on "Sergei Witte: A Century After His Death," "The Stock Exchange in Tsarist Russia," and "Russian Colonization in North America" contain insights that would otherwise remain hidden to non-specialist readers. Recommended for all academic and research libraries with programs in Russian and international history.

4547. *Russian Studies in Literature.* Formerly (until 1992): *Soviet Studies in Literature.* [ISSN: 1061-1975] 1964. q. GBP 1015 (print & online eds.)). Routledge, 711 3rd Ave, 8th Fl., New York, NY 10017; http://www.routledge.com. Illus., index, adv. Sample. Refereed. Vol. ends: Fall (No. 4). Reprint: PSC. *Indexed:* A01, A22, AmHI, BRI, E01, MLA-IB. *Aud.:* Ac, Sa.

This journal "publishes high-quality, annotated translations of Russian literary criticism and scholarship on contemporary works and popular cultural topics as well as the classics." The "selections are drawn from the leading literary periodicals," and an "editorial introduction to every issue provides context and insight that will be helpful for English-language readers." Articles include all the footnotes in the original article, as well as complete citations to the original publication source. Translators' names are also given. This journal would be of value to students and scholars without reading knowledge of Russian. Recent thematic issues covering "New Directions in Russian Literature," "Orthodox Literature: Shakespeare in Russian Culture Redux," "Tatyana Tolstaya, Mikhail Bulgakov," and "Dostoevsky; Herzen Versus Chernyshevsky" could be of interest to a broad, non-specialist readership. Recommended for academic and research libraries that support comparative literature programs.

4548. ***Russian Studies in Philosophy.*** Formerly (until 1992): *Soviet Studies in Philosophy.* [ISSN: 1061-1967] 1962. q. GBP 1081 (print & online eds.)). Ed(s): Marina F Bykova. Routledge, 530 Walnut St, Ste 850, Philadelphia, PA 19106; enquiries@tandfonline.com; http://www.tandfonline.com. Illus., index, adv. Sample. Refereed. Vol. ends: Spring (No. 4). Reprint: PSC. *Indexed:* A01, A22, AmHI, E01, MLA-IB. *Aud.:* Ac, Sa.

This journal "publishes thematic issues featuring selected scholarly papers from conferences and joint research projects as well as from the leading Russian-language journals in philosophy." The journal's "thematic coverage ranges over significant theoretical topics as well as topics in the history of philosophy, both European and Russian, including issues focused on institutions, schools, and figures such as Bakhtin, Fedorov, Il'enkov, Leont'ev, Losev, Mamardashvili, Rozanov, Solov'ev, and Zino'vev." Articles include all the footnotes in the original article, as well as complete citations to the original publication source. Translators' names are also given. Besides articles, the journal sometimes includes translated book excerpts. This journal would be of value to students and scholars without reading knowledge of Russian. The themes of recent issues have included "Nikolai Berdyaev," "Man, Education, Science: Contemporary Issues," "Contemporary Russian Philosophers: Vyacheslav S. Stepin," and "Contemporary Aesthetics in Russia." Recommended for any academic and research libraries that support programs in philosophy.

4549. ***Sarmatian Review.*** Formerly (until 1988): *The Houston Sarmatian.* [ISSN: 1059-5872] 1981. 3x/yr. Ed(s): Ewa M Thompson. Polish Institute of Houston, PO Box 79119, Houston, TX 77279. Illus. Refereed. *Indexed:* AmHI, BRI. *Bk. rev.:* Number and length vary. *Aud.:* Ac.

This "is a scholarly journal on the history, culture, and society of Central and Eastern Europe, with strong attention to Poland, the post-Soviet period, and American ethnic issues. Recent issues have covered religion and state, the mass media, higher education, literature, inter-ethnic relations, government and politics." The journal's editors write that they also "specialize in the translation of documents." Issues often include works of poetry as well. The book reviews and lists of books received may be useful for collection development librarians. Also, "an abbreviated web edition appears six to ten weeks after the print edition." The journal's web site includes an archive of issues back to April 1992. Recommended for academic and public libraries that serve interested user populations. URL: www.ruf.rice.edu/~sarmatia

4550. ***Slavic & East European Information Resources.*** [ISSN: 1522-8886] 2000. q. GBP 360 (print & online eds.)). Ed(s): Dr. Karen Rondestvedt. Routledge, 530 Walnut St, Ste 850, Philadelphia, PA 19106; enquiries@tandfonline.com; http://www.tandfonline.com. Illus., adv. Sample. Refereed. Reprint: PSC. *Indexed:* A01, A22, E01, ISTA. *Bk. rev.:* 10-14, 300-1,200 words, signed. *Aud.:* Ac, Sa.

This journal's central purpose "is to serve as a focal point for the international exchange of information in the field of Slavic librarianship." Its scope ranges across "news of the profession, technical developments, reviews of the literature, original research, indeed everything that touches on the practice of Slavic librarianship in North America, the countries covered[,] and elsewhere in the world." In addition to featured articles, there are book reviews, an Internet column, a section called "In Our Libraries," and occasional columns by vendors of Slavic material. Double issues, often thematic, delve into specific topics. The emphasis is on "the current, concrete[,] and practical sides of Slavic librarianship." While the journal's primary audience is professional librarians with responsibilities for Slavic collections, it has substantial, and overlooked, potential value for scholars working in the various Slavic Studies disciplines. Recommended highly for academic and research libraries with the relevant kinds of collections.

4551. ***Slavic and East European Journal.*** Former titles (until 1957): *A A T S E E L Journal;* (until 1954): *American Association of Teachers of Slavic and East European Languages. Bulletin;* (until 1947): *American Association of Teachers of Slavonic and East European Languages. Bulletin;* (until 1945): *American Association of Teachers of Slavonic and East European Languages. News Bulletin.* [ISSN: 0037-6752] 1943. q. USD 80. Ed(s): Irene Delic. American Association of Teachers of Slavic and East European Languages, c/o Professor Irene Delic, Room 321, Dey Hall, CB # 3160, Chapel Hill, CA 27599; aatseel@usc.edu; http://www.aatseel.org. Illus., index, adv. Refereed. Vol. ends: No. 4. Microform: PQC. *Indexed:* A01, A22, AmHI, BRI, MLA-IB. *Bk. rev.:* 25-30, 250-500 words, signed. *Aud.:* Ac, Sa.

This journal "publishes research studies in all areas of Slavic languages, literatures, and cultures," and articles "on non-Slavic East European subjects of interest to Slavicists may also be considered." The journal is published quarterly by the American Association of Teachers of Slavic and East European Languages, or AATSEEL. "Pedagogical articles report the results of serious research, experimentation, and evaluation," but the scope does not include "original fiction or translations of literary works." Articles are well documented and of consistently high quality. The occasional review articles, a first-rate selection of book reviews, and lists of publications received will be useful to scholars and librarians alike. Recommended highly as essential for academic and research libraries that support Slavic Studies programs.

4552. ***Slavic Review: interdisciplinary quarterly of Russian, Eurasian, and East European studies.*** Former titles (until 1961): *American Slavic and East European Review;* (until 1945): *Slavonic and East European Review. American Series;* (until 1943): *Slavonic Year-Book. American Series;* (until 1940): *The Slavonic and East European Review;* (until 1928): *The Slavonic Review;* (until 1922): *Anglo-Russian Literary Society. Proceedings.* [ISSN: 0037-6779] 1893. q. GBP 215. Ed(s): Dimitry Tartakovsky, Harriet L Murav. Cambridge University Press, 1 Liberty Plaza, Fl 20, New York, NY 10004; online@cambridge.org; https://www.cambridge.org/. Illus. Refereed. Reprint: PSC. *Indexed:* A01, A22, AmHI, BRI, CBRI, IBSS, MLA-IB, P61. *Bk. rev.:* 55-60, 300-1,000 words, signed. *Aud.:* Ac, Sa.

This is the membership journal of the Association for Slavic, East European, and Eurasian Studies, or ASEEES (known for many years as AAASS). One of the leading publications in the field, it is "an international[,] interdisciplinary journal devoted to the study of eastern Europe, Russia, the Caucasus, and Central Asia, past and present." The journal aims to publish "articles of original and significant research and interpretation, reviews of scholarly books and films, and topical review essays and discussion forums," and the editors welcome contributions "from all disciplines and perspectives." Moreover, they state that a "primary purpose of the journal is to encourage dialogue among different scholarly approaches." Articles are, without exception, of the highest quality of scholarship and documentation. The extensive book reviews and lists of publications received by the journal are essential for collection development librarians, and are highly valuable for scholars as well. A special feature of particular interest is the thematically divided annual list of all dissertations in Slavic Studies granted by U.S. institutions. Recommended highly as essential for academic and research libraries, as well as larger public libraries with any degree of interest in Slavic Studies.

4553. ***Slavonic and East European Review.*** [ISSN: 0037-6795] 1922. q. USD 505 print & online eds. Modern Humanities Research Association (M H R A), Salisbury House, Station Road, Cambridge, CB1 2LA, United Kingdom; mail@mhra.org.uk; http://www.mhra.org.uk. Illus., index. Refereed. Vol. ends: Oct (No. 4). *Indexed:* A01, A22, AmHI, BRI, IBSS, MLA-IB, P61. *Bk. rev.:* 50-60, 300-750 words, signed. *Aud.:* Ac, Sa.

This is the journal of the School of Slavonic and East European Studies, University College London, and is published by the Modern Humanities Research Association. In existence since 1928, it is one of the premier journals in Slavic Studies, publishing "scholarly articles on all subjects related to Russia, Central and Eastern Europe-languages [and] linguistics, literature, art, cinema, theatre, music, history, politics, social sciences, economics, [and] anthropology-as well as reviews of new books in the field." The lists of publications received will also be of use to both scholars and librarians in collection development. Recommended highly for all academic and research libraries, and for larger public libraries with even a passing interest in Slavic Studies.

4554. *Social Sciences: a quarterly journal of the Russian Academy of Sciences.* [ISSN: 0134-5486] 1970. q. USD 595 (Individuals, USD 90). Ed(s): A Guseynov. East View Information Services, 10601 Wayzata Blvd, Hopkins, MN 55305; info@eastview.com; http://www.eastview.com/. Index. Sample. Refereed. *Indexed:* A01, A22, EIP, EconLit, IBSS, P61, SSA. *Bk. rev.:* 3-5, 100-1,000 words, signed. *Aud.:* Ac, Sa.

This journal "presents the most prominent papers and studies appearing in more than 30 journals of the Russian Academy of Sciences," with coverage of "the most pressing issues of Russia's social and economic development." The journal "includes articles on philosophy, history, economics, politics, sociology, law, philology, psychology, ethnography, archeology, literature and culture." In addition to book reviews grouped by discipline, it also prints listings of the contents from many other periodicals of the Russian Academy of Sciences. Articles indicate the original publication source, along with short biographical information on the author. Names of translators are given following the end notes. Scholars and students without a reading knowledge of Russian will find this a valuable title. Recommended for academic and research libraries.

4555. *Sociological Research.* Formerly (until 1992): *Soviet Sociology.* [ISSN: 1061-0154] 1962. bi-m. GBP 1341 (print & online eds.)). Ed(s): Anthony Jones. Routledge, 530 Walnut St, Ste 850, Philadelphia, PA 19106; enquiries@tandfonline.com; http://www.tandfonline.com. Illus., index, adv. Sample. Refereed. Vol. ends: Nov/Dec (No. 6). Reprint: PSC. *Indexed:* A01, A22, B01, E01, P61. *Aud.:* Ac, Sa.

This journal "features unabridged translations of articles that have been selected to reflect trends in the sociological literature and to be of value to researchers interested in the region and the study of societies in transition." The published materials "are drawn from the major Russian-language scholarly journals," as well as from "other relevant sources." Topical coverage is broad, encompassing a range of areas in sociology, and articles are well chosen. Each article includes a complete citation to the original publication and the end notes from the original article, and specifies the name of the translator. For scholars without reading knowledge of Russian, this journal will hold particular interest, but it is of value to a range of scholars working in the field. Recommended for academic and research libraries that support programs in sociology and Slavic Studies.

4556. *Statutes and Decisions: the laws of the U S S R & Its successor states.* Formerly (until 1992): *Soviet Statutes and Decisions.* [ISSN: 1061-0014] 1964. bi-m. GBP 1626 (print & online eds.)). Ed(s): Alexei Trochev. Routledge, 530 Walnut St, Ste 850, Philadelphia, PA 19106; enquiries@tandfonline.com; http://www.tandfonline.com. Illus., index, adv. Sample. Refereed. Microform: WSH; PMC. Reprint: PSC. *Indexed:* A01, A22, E01. *Aud.:* Ac, Sa.

This journal aims to document "the evolving legal regimes of the post-Soviet states." It "publishes thematic series providing comprehensive coverage of a body of law, or of legal or judicial practice, in high-quality translations with expert introductions." The topic of one recent series was "Kazakhstan's New Criminal Procedure: Responsibilities and Oversight in Pretrial Investigation." Earlier issues have examined police reform in Russia; the Ukrainian Constitutional Court; Ukrainian judges; the Russian Federation Law on Extremist Activity; professional ethics for attorneys in Russia; legal regulation of NGOs; and the Code of the Russian Federation on Administrative Violations, among other topics. The materials chosen are of interest to those scholars and students engaged with "the laws and court decisions of the Russian Federation" at a serious level; for them, it will be highly useful, even indispensable. For those without reading knowledge of Russian who wish to study these areas, it will also be of great value, despite the specialized and at times technical nature of its contents. Recommended primarily for law libraries, especially those with a comparative international law program, as well as academic and research libraries that support programs in Slavic Studies.

4557. *Studies in East European Thought.* Formerly (until 1992): *Studies in Soviet Thought.* [ISSN: 0925-9392] 1961. q. EUR 1079 (print & online eds.)). Ed(s): Edward M Swiderski. Springer Netherlands, Van Godewijckstraat 30, Dordrecht, 3311 GX, Netherlands; http://www.springer.com. Illus., index, adv. Sample. Refereed. Vol. ends: Dec (No. 4). Microform: PQC. Reprint: PSC. *Indexed:* A01, A22, AmHI, BAS, BRI, E01, IBSS, P61. *Bk. rev.:* Varies, 500-2,000 words, signed. *Aud.:* Ac, Sa.

This journal "provides a forum for Western-language writings on philosophy and philosophers who identify with the history and cultures of East and Central Europe, including Russia, Ukraine, and the Baltic States." Its "contents include descriptive, critical, comparative, and historical studies of individuals, schools, currents, and institutions whose work and influence are widely regarded in their own environments to be philosophical or provide insight into the socio-cultural conditions of philosophical life in Eastern Europe," says the publisher. Coverage ranges widely, including "concepts of the social, the cultural and the political, following the demise of Marxism-Leninism; foundational questions in metaphysics and epistemology; the standing of 'culture theory' (i.e., Russian 'kul'turologiia'); the reception of Western theories and methods as well as intellectual traditions; the reassessment of 'local' intellectual traditions; ethics, moral theory, theology and religious studies, and much more." The articles are mostly in English but occasionally in German. Issues are often thematic; recent special issues or sections have covered "The philosophy and legacy of Kazimierz Ajdukiewicz (1890-1963)," "The Bakhtin Circle in Its Time and Ours," and "Marxist Roots of Science Studies." Recommended for academic and research libraries that support programs in Slavic Studies and advanced work in philosophy.

4558. *Transitions Online.* [ISSN: 1214-1615] 1999. d. USD 239 public libraries (Individuals, USD 49). Ed(s): Jeremy Druker. Transitions Online, Baranova 33, Prague, 13000, Czech Republic. *Indexed:* A01. *Bk. rev.:* Number and length vary. *Aud.:* Ga, Ac.

This online magazine and web resource "covers political, social, cultural, and economic issues in the former communist countries of Europe and Central Asia," with a "strong network of local contributors, who provide valuable insight into events in the region's 29 countries." The editors say they are "interested in illustrating underlying issues and the process of change in the countries and regions that we cover." The intended audience is "well-informed and intelligent" readers who are not specialists in the field. Besides country-specific pages and country reports, the web site has sections covering: arts and culture; books; conflict and diplomacy; economy and business; education; environment; media; opinion; people; politics; and society. Access to the full online contents, as well as the back file of the current magazine and its predecessors, is by subscription. Articles are also available through Factiva, Academic Search Premier, and Central and Eastern European Online Library (or CEEOL). Recommended for all libraries with patrons interested in the current events and political developments in the countries of the former Soviet bloc. URL: www.tol.org

■ SOCIAL MEDIA

Rebecca Kohn, Associate Librarian, San Jose State University, One Washington Square, San Jose, CA 95112

Introduction

Social media is a phrase used for communication technology platforms, such as Twitter and Facebook, as well as types of activities, like blogging and commenting. Emerging platforms like Pinterest, Vine, and Instagram are used for posting images and short videos. A defining attribute of social media is individual engagement with online communities, but the type of engagement ranges from aspects of pop culture like celebrity sightings and "selfies" to politically charged scenes of police violence. This section describes academic journals that focus on or include discussion of social media and emphasize theoretical analysis of its use.

While some existing communications and media studies journals have broadened their scope to include information communication technologies, new journals to specifically study the emergence of social media on mobile devices have also been created.

Basic Periodicals

Ac: *Information, Communication and Society, The Journal of Social Media in Society, New Media & Society.*

Basic Abstracts and Indexes

Academic Search Premier, Business Source Complete, Communication Abstracts, Communication & Mass Media Complete.

4559. *Continuum: journal of media & cultural studies.* [ISSN: 1030-4312] 1987. bi-m. GBP 1075 (print & online eds.)). Ed(s): John Tebbutt. Routledge, Level 2, 11 Queens Rd, Melbourne, VIC 3004, Australia; books@tandf.com.au; http://www.routledge.com. Adv. Sample. Refereed. Reprint: PSC. *Indexed:* A01, A22, BRI, E01, F01, IBSS, IIMP, MLA-IB. *Bk. rev.:* Number and length vary. *Aud.:* Ac.

Continuum is affiliated with the Cultural Studies Association of Australasia, and provides readers with insight into how social media is being used and viewed from a global perspective. Articles range from case studies of specific platforms in a particular country to theoretical discussions of the role of individual voices in virtual participation. Articles on social media are included as part of the journal's study of media and culture, examining social media uses as part of journalistic patterns. This journal is an important resource for libraries that support cross-cultural research.

4560. *Convergence: the international journal of research into new media technologies.* [ISSN: 1354-8565] 1995. q. USD 1198 (print & online eds.)). Ed(s): Alexis Weedon, Julia Knight. Sage Publications Ltd., 1 Oliver's Yard, 55 City Rd, London, EC1Y 1SP, United Kingdom; info@sagepub.com; https://www.sagepub.com/. Adv. Sample. Refereed. Reprint: PSC. *Indexed:* A22, E01, F01. *Bk. rev.:* Number and length vary. *Aud.:* Ac.

The research agenda of *Convergence* makes this journal an important publication in the area of social media. It publishes the results of studies by researchers on social media platforms and activities. Mobile aspects of social media are frequently discussed in this quarterly.

4561. *Information, Communication and Society.* [ISSN: 1369-118X] 1998. 14x/yr. GBP 1096 (print & online eds.)). Ed(s): William H Dutton, Brian D Loader. Routledge, 4 Park Sq, Milton Park, Abingdon, OX14 4RN, United Kingdom; subscriptions@tandf.co.uk; http://www.tandfonline.com. Adv. Sample. Refereed. Reprint: PSC. *Indexed:* A01, A22, B01, BRI, CompLI, E01, IBSS, P61, SSA. *Aud.:* Ac.

Social media continues to be part of the journal's scope, with a 2011 special issue titled "Networking Democracy?: Social media innovations and participatory politics," and a 2013 special issue titled, "Social Media and Election Campaigns: Key Tendencies and Ways Forward." Libraries that support programs that study political communication will find this a valuable resource for its global perspective.

4562. *The Journal of Social Media in Society.* [ISSN: 2328-3599] 2012. s-a. Free. Ed(s): Dr. Credence Baker, Dr. Sarah Maben. Tarleton State University, Texas Social Media Research Institute, PO Box T-0230, Stephenville, TX 76402; http://www.tarleton.edu/tsmri/index.html. Refereed. *Bk. rev.:* Number and length vary. *Aud.:* Ac.

This research-based journal provides scholarship and commentary on social media and its impact on society. Research topics discussed include all aspects of social media and its various platforms. This open-access journal is hosted by the Texas Social Media Research Institute, which focuses on communication technology and social media for K-12 education, higher education, businesses, and nonprofit organizations.

4563. *Media, Culture & Society.* [ISSN: 0163-4437] 1979. 8x/yr. USD 2930 (print & online eds.)). Sage Publications Ltd., 1 Oliver's Yard, 55 City Rd, London, EC1Y 1SP, United Kingdom; info@sagepub.com; https://www.sagepub.com/. Illus. Sample. Refereed. Reprint: PSC. *Indexed:* A01, A22, BRI, E01, F01, IBSS, MLA-IB, P61, SSA. *Bk. rev.:* Number and length vary. *Aud.:* Ac.

Media, Culture & Society examines information communication technologies from social-science perspectives. Through in-depth research articles and scholarly commentaries, this journal contextualizes investigations into identity, political agency, and language use as manifested in social media platforms and larger media systems. This journal is useful for journalism and mass media studies, as well as broader history and sociology programs.

4564. *New Media & Society.* [ISSN: 1461-4448] 1999. m. USD 3262 (print & online eds.)). Ed(s): Steve Jones. Sage Publications Ltd., 1 Oliver's Yard, 55 City Rd, London, EC1Y 1SP, United Kingdom; info@sagepub.com; https://www.sagepub.com/. Sample. Refereed. Reprint: PSC. *Indexed:* A01, A22, E01, F01, IBSS, MLA-IB, P61. *Bk. rev.:* Number and length vary. *Aud.:* Ac.

This journal takes a multidisciplinary approach to its discussion of "global and local dimensions of the relationship between media and social change." It provides in-depth research articles on how people around the world negotiate with, view, and engage in information communication technologies; in particular, it frequently covers social media. Recent special-issue themes include "The state of online campaigning in politics" in February 2013, and "Scholarly publishing and the Internet" in May 2013.

■ SOCIOLOGY AND SOCIAL WORK

General/Social Work and Social Welfare

See also Criminology and Law Enforcement; Cultural Studies; Ethnic Studies; Family; Law; Marriage and Divorce; and Population Studies sections.

Kelly MacWatters, Coordinator of Reference and Electronic Resources, Standish Library, Siena College, Loudonville, NY 12211; kmacwatters@siena.edu

Introduction

The disciplines of sociology and social work are highly interconnected, and therefore the journals for them are treated together in this volume. Consider the definitions of each field: *sociology* may be defined as the study of relationships between individuals and groups, organizations, cultures, society, and other individuals. It is a science that uses a methodological approach to study and explore these relationships and processes, both in historical and postmodern contexts. *Social work,* on the other hand, is a profession dedicated to advancing individual and societal well-being. The scholarship in this field exists to support and inform professional practice, including clinical practice, management, and policymaking.

The journals listed in this section cross interdisciplinary lines, drawing from (and complementing) fields in the social sciences such as anthropology, political science, economics, psychology, and public administration, and well as religion, history, and law.

In preparing this section, each journal's web site and the contents of several recent issues of each title were thoroughly examined. While several essential or "must-have" titles are noted, each library must decide what to carry in consideration of its own budgets, holdings, and research needs (or gaps). An effective way to increase the quantity and quality of a library's holdings in times of flat budgets may be to add open-access (read *free*) journals. Most of them, as noted in this section, are refereed and indexed in major databases.

Basic Periodicals

GENERAL. Ga: *Annual Review of Sociology, Journal of Social Issues, Social Forces, Social Problems;* Ac: *American Journal of Sociology, American Sociological Review, Annual Review of Sociology, British Journal of Sociology, Current Sociology, International Sociology, Journal of Social Issues, Sex Roles, Social Forces, Social Policy, Social Problems, Social Psychology Quarterly, Social Research, The Sociological Review.*

SOCIAL WORK AND SOCIAL WELFARE. Ga: *Child Welfare, Children & Schools;* Ac: *Advances in Social Work, The British Journal of Social Work, Child Welfare, Children & Schools, Children and Youth Services Review, Clinical Social Work Journal, Families in Society, International Social Work, Research on Social Work Practice, Social Service Review, Social Work, Social Work with Groups.*

Basic Abstracts and Indexes

ASSIA: Applied Social Sciences Index and Abstracts, Social Sciences Citation Index, Social Services Abstracts, Social Work Abstracts, Sociological Abstracts.

General

4565. *Acta Sociologica.* [ISSN: 0001-6993] 1955. q. USD 790 (print & online eds.)). Ed(s): Sigrun Olafsdottir, Jon G Bernburg. Sage Publications Ltd., 1 Oliver's Yard, 55 City Rd, London, EC1Y 1SP, United Kingdom; info@sagepub.com; https://www.sagepub.com/. Illus., index, adv. Sample. Refereed. Microform: SWZ; PQC. Reprint: PSC. *Indexed:* A01, A22, B01, BRI, E01, IBSS, MLA-IB, P61, SSA. *Bk. rev.:* 0-5, signed. *Aud.:* Ac.

Acta Sociologica, the official journal of the Nordic Sociological Association, publishes theoretical and empirical papers on a wide range of sociological and cultural studies issues. Although this journal is published in English, the majority of authors are from Scandinavian and other European countries. Content includes full-length articles, review articles, commentaries, and signed book reviews. Recommended for support of upper-division, graduate, and international sociological research.

Amerasia Journal. See Asian American section.

4566. *American Journal of Sociology.* [ISSN: 0002-9602] 1895. bi-m. USD 630. Ed(s): Elisabeth S Clemens. University of Chicago Press, 1427 E 60th St, Chicago, IL 60637; subscriptions@press.uchicago.edu; http://www.journals.uchicago.edu. Illus., index, adv. Sample. Refereed. Vol. ends: May. Reprint: PSC. *Indexed:* A01, A22, A47, B01, BAS, BRI, CBRI, CJPI, Chicano, F01, IBSS, MLA-IB, P61, SSA. *Bk. rev.:* 20-40, signed. *Aud.:* Ga, Ac, Sa.

AJS was established in 1895 and was the first scholarly sociological journal. Published by the University of Chicago Press, it stands as the core title in the field. The journal boasts cutting-edge work from all aspects of sociology, with emphasis on theory-building, social analysis, and innovative methods. An impressive book review section in each issue presents 20 or more signed reviews of the most prominent works by social scientists. An essential title for all academic libraries, and highly recommended for public libraries and for special libraries involved in social research.

4567. *American Sociological Review.* [ISSN: 0003-1224] 1936. bi-m. USD 781 (print & online eds.)). Ed(s): Larry Isaac, Holly J McCammon. Sage Publications, Inc., 2455 Teller Rd, Thousand Oaks, CA 91320; info@sagepub.com; http://www.sagepub.com/. Illus., index, adv. Sample. Refereed. Vol. ends: Dec. Microform: MIM; PQC. Reprint: PSC. *Indexed:* A01, A22, B01, BAS, BRI, C45, CBRI, Chicano, E01, ERIC, IBSS, MLA-IB, P61, SSA. *Aud.:* Ga, Ac.

Founded in 1936 by the American Sociological Association, the *ASR* is considered the "flagship" journal of the ASA. The journal today remains true to the association's mission of publishing original research that employs innovative methodology, results in advances in better understanding of social processes, and advances the public good. Articles cover all aspects of sociology, with emphasis on topics of general interest. Book reviews are not published in *ASR.* Essential for all academic libraries, and highly recommended for public libraries and for special libraries involved in social research.

4568. *The American Sociologist.* [ISSN: 0003-1232] 1965. 3x/yr. EUR 482 (print & online eds.)). Ed(s): Lawrence T Nichols. Springer New York LLC, 233 Spring St, New York, NY 10013; customerservice@springer.com; http://www.springer.com. Illus. Sample. Refereed. Vol. ends: Winter. Microform: PQC. Reprint: PSC. *Indexed:* A01, A22, Chicano, E01, ERIC, IBSS, P61, SSA. *Bk. rev.:* 1-2, length varies. *Aud.:* Ga, Ac.

This journal publishes papers, essays, and commentaries specific to the intellectual, practical, social, and ethical topics that concern sociologists. Research articles explore the ways in which sociological skills and perspectives relate to issues of broad public concern. Topics include applications of sociological methods and knowledge in a variety of settings, making it ideal for someone considering a career in the field. Recommended for academic libraries and for public libraries that support research.

4569. *Annual Review of Sociology.* [ISSN: 0360-0572] 1975. a. USD 431 (print & online eds.)). Ed(s): Douglas S Massey, Karen S Cook. Annual Reviews, PO Box 10139, Palo Alto, CA 94303; service@annualreviews.org; http://www.annualreviews.org. Refereed. Reprint: PSC. *Indexed:* A01, A22, B01, BRI, CJPI, IBSS, P61, SSA. *Aud.:* Ga, Ac, Sa.

Annual Reviews publishes yearly volumes that cover significant developments in physical, life, and social sciences. The *Annual Review of Sociology* includes current research in the discipline as well as major theoretical and methodological developments in the field. Chapters in a typical issue cover social processes, institutions and culture, individuals and society, social policy, demography, urban and rural sociology, and major sociological developments in other areas of the world. Highly recommended for academic libraries that support sociology.

4570. *Archives Europeennes de Sociologie.* [ISSN: 0003-9756] 1960. 3x/yr. GBP 254. Cambridge University Press, University Printing House, Shaftesbury Rd, Cambridge, CB2 8BS, United Kingdom; journals@cambridge.org; https://www.cambridge.org/. Illus., index, adv. Refereed. Circ: 1750. Vol. ends: Nov. Microform: PQC. Reprint: PSC. *Indexed:* A22, BAS, E01, IBSS, P61, SSA. *Bk. rev.:* Number and length vary. *Aud.:* Ac.

The focus of this journal is historical and comparative sociology from an international perspective. Special attention is paid to the transition from totalitarianism to democracy and multiple citizenship; authors include well-known and emerging scholars. Some issues include review essays and an extensive list of book reviews. Abstracts are in English, French, and German. Recommended for academic libraries that support doctoral programs in sociology.

Armed Forces and Society. See Military section.

4571. *British Journal of Sociology.* [ISSN: 0007-1315] 1950. q. GBP 548. Ed(s): Nigel Dodd. Wiley-Blackwell Publishing Ltd., The Atrium, Southern Gate, Chichester, PO19 8QG, United Kingdom; cs-journals@wiley.com; http://onlinelibrary.wiley.com/. Illus., index, adv. Sample. Refereed. Vol. ends: Dec. Microform: WMP. Reprint: PSC. *Indexed:* A01, A22, A47, BAS, BRI, CJPI, E01, IBSS, MLA-IB, P61, SSA. *Bk. rev.:* 4-10, signed. *Aud.:* Ac.

Housed at the London School of Economics and Political Science, the *British Journal of Sociology* is a mainstay in presenting sociological thinking, concepts, and research. International in scope, it covers all aspects of the discipline. Recent topics have included generational differences, institutions, social class, higher education, sports, economics, crime, climate change, and identity. Issues may include a debate section. Most issues include an extensive selection of book reviews. Highly recommended for academic libraries.

4572. ***Canadian Journal of Sociology (Online).*** [ISSN: 1710-1123] q. Ed(s): Kevin Haggerty. University of Alberta Libraries, B7 Rutherford S, Edmonton, AB T6G 2J4, Canada; leahv@ualberta.ca; http://www.library.ualberta.ca. Refereed. *Bk. rev.:* Number and length vary. *Aud.:* Ac.

This is an online, open-access journal published by the Department of Sociology at the University of Alberta. It publishes research and theoretical articles by social scientists on issues in Canada and around the globe. Regular features include review essays, a debate/commentary section, a "Notes on Society" section that addresses topic issues, and a "Notes on the Discipline" section for discussion on the field of sociology. Each issue includes signed book reviews. A good addition to the online collections of academic libraries that support graduate programs in sociology or Canadian studies.

4573. ***Canadian Review of Sociology (Online).*** [ISSN: 1755-618X] 2008. q. GBP 216. Ed(s): Karen Stanbridge. Wiley-Blackwell Publishing, Inc., 111 River St, Hoboken, NJ 07030; cs-journals@wiley.com; http://www.wiley.com/. Refereed. *Bk. rev.:* 0-8; signed. *Aud.:* Ac.

Published on behalf of the Canadian Sociological Association, this journal features theoretical and research articles primarily focused on Canada. A recent special issue on security and surveillance looked into the implications for society and evolution of the country's social policies. Abstracts are in both French and English; the article itself is in one or the other. Recommended for academic libraries that support graduate programs in sociology.

4574. ***Child Abuse & Neglect: the international journal.*** [ISSN: 0145-2134] 1977. m. EUR 3529. Ed(s): Christine Wekerle. Elsevier Ltd, The Boulevard, Langford Lane, Oxford, OX5 1GB, United Kingdom; http://www.elsevier.com. Illus., index, adv. Sample. Refereed. *Indexed:* A01, A22, ASSIA, BRI, CJPI, ERIC, N13, SSA. *Aud.:* Ac, Sa.

As the official publication of the International Society for Prevention of Child Abuse and Neglect, this journal covers all aspects of child abuse, with prevention and treatment. This title is multidisciplinary in scope, and contributors' fields that are represented include psychology, social work, medicine, law enforcement and legislation, education, and anthropology. Articles are intended for educators, policymakers, scholars, and professional practitioners. Highly recommended for academic, public, and special libraries that serve these fields, social services, and child-oriented advocacy organizations.

4575. ***Child and Youth Care Forum: journal of research and practice in children's services.*** Former titles (until 1991): *Child and Youth Care Quarterly;* (until 1987): *Child Care Quarterly.* [ISSN: 1053-1890] 1971. bi-m. EUR 1710 (print & online eds.)). Ed(s): Carl F Weems. Springer New York LLC, 233 Spring St, New York, NY 10013; customerservice@springer.com; http://www.springer.com. Illus., index, adv. Sample. Refereed. Vol. ends: Dec. Microform: PQC. Reprint: PSC. *Indexed:* A01, A22, ASSIA, Agr, BRI, E01, ERIC, SSA. *Aud.:* Ga, Ac, Sa.

The intent of this journal is to bridge the "research-to-practice gap" between empirical and theoretical research and children's intervention and services - that is, identifying problems and proposing strategies for interventions and services. Contributors include practitioners, researchers, and clinicians in child psychology, early childhood education, pediatrics, psychiatry, public policy, social work, and sociology. Recommended for academic libraries that support social work programs and libraries used by social services that work with children, youth, and families.

4576. ***Child Maltreatment.*** [ISSN: 1077-5595] 1996. q. USD 1148 (print & online eds.)). Ed(s): Daniel J Whitaker. Sage Publications, Inc., 2455 Teller Rd, Thousand Oaks, CA 91320; info@sagepub.com; http://www.sagepub.com. Illus., index, adv. Sample. Refereed. Vol. ends: Nov. Reprint: PSC. *Indexed:* A01, A22, ASSIA, CJPI, E01, N13, SSA. *Aud.:* Ac, Sa.

This journal is the official publication of the American Professional Society on the Abuse of Children. It promotes practice and policy perspectives based on sound empirical evidence. Articles are intended to be useful to practitioners and researchers from mental health, child protection, legal and law enforcement, and medicine. Highly recommended for academic libraries that support social work programs and libraries that support social service agencies.

4577. ***Children's Legal Rights Journal (Online).*** 1979. 3x/yr. Free. Ed(s): Rashal Baz, Caitlin Cevenka. Loyola University of Chicago, School of Law, 25 East Pearson St, Chicago, IL 60611; http://www.luc.edu. Refereed. *Bk. rev.:* 1-2; signed. *Aud.:* Ac, Sa.

This journal is published in association with the National Association of Counsel for Children as a practice resource for professionals in social work, child welfare, juvenile justice and law enforcement, education, health care and mental health, and family law. It covers many aspects of law as it relates to children, such as child abuse, foster care, child custody and adoption, and children's rights. Recent articles have included interviews with practitioners, global perspectives on issues, and reviews of books and films. Recommended for law libraries and academic libraries that support social work and social service programs.

4578. ***Chinese Sociological Review.*** Formerly (until 2011): *Chinese Sociology and Anthropology.* [ISSN: 2162-0555] 1968. 5x/yr. GBP 1309 (print & online eds.)). Ed(s): Xiaogang Wu. Routledge, 530 Walnut St, Ste 850, Philadelphia, PA 19106; orders@taylorandfrancis.com; http://www.tandfonline.com. Illus., index, adv. Sample. Refereed. Vol. ends: Summer. Reprint: PSC. *Indexed:* A01, A22, A47, BAS, E01, IBSS, MLA-IB. *Aud.:* Ac.

Intended for an international audience, this "journal of translations" contains articles by sociologists and other social scientists in mainland China, Taiwan, and abroad. Its mission is to advance the understanding of contemporary Chinese society and to provide a forum for Chinese sociologists to contribute to the global discussion of sociology. Recent topics have included religion, gender, migration patterns, education inequality, social stratification, property rights, and social change in China. Recommended for academic libraries that support graduate programs in sociology, anthropology, or Chinese studies.

4579. ***Contemporary Sociology: a journal of reviews.*** [ISSN: 0094-3061] 1972. bi-m. USD 622 (print & online eds.)). Ed(s): Michael Sauder. Sage Publications, Inc., 2455 Teller Rd, Thousand Oaks, CA 91320; info@sagepub.com; http://www.sagepub.com. Illus., index, adv. Sample. Refereed. Vol. ends: Nov. Microform: PQC. Reprint: PSC. *Indexed:* A22, BRI, CBRI, Chicano, E01, P61, SSA. *Bk. rev.:* 50-60; signed. *Aud.:* Ac.

A journal of the American Sociological Association, this title publishes reviews of recent works in sociology and related disciplines. Reviews are extensive (4-12 pages) and include those of individual works, paired essays, and commentaries and responses to reviews. The books reviewed are selected so as to reflect the most important trends and issues in the field. Highly recommended as a collection development tool for academic libraries.

4580. ***Critical Social Work.*** [ISSN: 1543-9372] 2000. s-a. Free. Ed(s): Brent Angell, Amy M Alberton. University of Windsor, School of Social Work, 401 Sunset Ave, Ontario, ON N9B 3P4, Canada. Refereed. *Aud.:* Ac, Sa.

Critical Social Work is a peer-reviewed, open-access journal hosted by the School of Social Work at the University of Winsor (Ontario). International in scope, the journal offers an opportunity to explore concepts of social justice in the field of social work and anti-oppressive practice. Research articles by scholars, practitioners, and graduate students deal with legal, moral, and economic issues faced by individuals, groups, and institutions. Topics are varied, and approaches include various theoretical, methodological, and analytical approaches and practice applications. Recommended for the electronic holdings of academic libraries that support social work programs and for libraries used by social workers and social service professionals.

4581. ***Critical Sociology.*** Formerly (until 1988): *Insurgent Sociologist.* [ISSN: 0896-9205] 1969. 8x/yr. USD 1673 (print & online eds.)). Ed(s): David Fasenfest. Sage Publications Ltd., 1 Oliver's Yard, 55 City Rd, London, EC1Y 1SP, United Kingdom; info@sagepub.com; https://www.sagepub.com/. Illus., adv. Sample. Refereed. Microform: PQC. Reprint: PSC. *Indexed:* A01, A22, BAS, CJPI, E01, IBSS, P61, SSA. *Bk. rev.:* 4-6; signed. *Aud.:* Ac.

Reflecting its roots in the Association for Critical Sociology, the goal of this journal is to engage and promote critical or radical social science. Research focuses on work that delves into and seeks to understand race, gender, and class using postmodern, feminist, Marxist, and other radical perspectives. It boasts being one of the few "alternative" journals with widespread recognition and respect among social science scholarship. Extensive review essays further explore contemporary thought and scholarship. Recommended for academic libraries that support sociology and political science programs.

Cultural Sociology. See Cultural Studies section.

4582. ***Current Sociology.*** [ISSN: 0011-3921] 1952. 7x/yr. USD 2267 (print & online eds.)). Ed(s): Eloisa Martin. Sage Publications Ltd., 1 Oliver's Yard, 55 City Rd, London, EC1Y 1SP, United Kingdom; info@sagepub.com; https://www.sagepub.com/. Illus., adv. Sample. Refereed. Reprint: PSC. *Indexed:* A01, A22, BRI, E01, IBSS, P61, SSA. *Bk. rev.:* Number and length vary. *Aud.:* Ac.

This is the official journal of the International Sociological Association and has been published since 1952. Articles contain original research, theories, methods, concepts, and critical commentary on current debates within the field, as well as those reviewing emergent and challenging issues. This title is international in focus, and issues also include national/regional developments and controversial sociological topics. Occasional special issues or special sections within a single issue. Recommended for academic libraries that support sociology departments and faculty research.

4583. ***Deviant Behavior: an interdisciplinary journal.*** [ISSN: 0163-9625] 1979. m. GBP 1673 (print & online eds.)). Ed(s): Clifton D Bryant, Dr. Craig J Forsyth. Taylor & Francis Inc., 711 3rd Ave, 8th Fl, New York, NY 10017; support@tandfonline.com; http://www.tandfonline.com. Illus., adv. Sample. Refereed. Microform: PQC. Reprint: PSC. *Indexed:* A01, A22, CJPI, E01, SSA. *Aud.:* Ac.

This journal is international and interdisciplinary, and is the only one that focuses exclusively on social deviance. It publishes theoretical, descriptive, methodological, and applied research on all aspects of deviance, including crime, juvenile delinquency, substance abuse and addiction, sexual behaviors, societal reaction to handicap and disfigurement, mental illness, and socially inappropriate behavior. Recommended for academic libraries that support programs in sociology, psychology, social work, or criminal justice.

4584. ***Economy and Society.*** [ISSN: 0308-5147] 1972. q. GBP 578 (print & online eds.)). Ed(s): Fran Tonkiss. Routledge, 4 Park Sq, Milton Park, Abingdon, OX14 4RN, United Kingdom; subscriptions@tandf.co.uk; http://www.tandfonline.com. Illus., index, adv. Sample. Refereed. Vol. ends: Nov. Microform: PQC. Reprint: PSC. *Indexed:* A22, B01, BAS, BRI, C42, E01, EconLit, IBSS, P61, SSA. *Aud.:* Ac.

This is an international, interdisciplinary journal of radical theory and politics, published since 1972. It promotes and explores new debates and social thought in areas of sociology, anthropology, political science, legal theory, philosophy, economy, and other related social science areas. Most issues contain an extensive review article; each volume includes one special theme issue. Recommended for academic libraries that support graduate programs in the social sciences.

Ethnic and Racial Studies. See Multicultural Studies section.

4585. ***European Journal of Social Theory.*** [ISSN: 1368-4310] 1998. q. USD 1699 (print & online eds.)). Ed(s): Gerard Delanty. Sage Publications Ltd., 1 Oliver's Yard, 55 City Rd, London, EC1Y 1SP, United Kingdom; info@sagepub.com; https://www.sagepub.com/. Illus., index, adv. Sample. Refereed. Vol. ends: Nov. Reprint: PSC. *Indexed:* A01, A22, B01, E01, IBSS, P61, SSA. *Bk. rev.:* 2-4, signed. *Aud.:* Ac.

This journal publishes international and interdisciplinary articles on the broadly defined topic of social theory. Included are the theoretical traditions within the social sciences, critical social analysis from a variety of perspectives, and debates within the philosophy of social science. Research articles explore the theoretical contexts related to social transformations; also included are viewpoint essays, book reviews, and review essays. Recommended for academic libraries that support graduate programs in sociology, political science, and international studies.

4586. ***European Societies.*** [ISSN: 1461-6696] 1999. 5x/yr. GBP 656 (print & online eds.)). Ed(s): Goran Therborn. Routledge, 4 Park Sq, Milton Park, Abingdon, OX14 4RN, United Kingdom; subscriptions@tandf.co.uk; http://www.tandfonline.com. Adv. Sample. Refereed. Reprint: PSC. *Indexed:* A01, A22, E01, IBSS, P61. *Bk. rev.:* Number and length vary. *Aud.:* Ac.

European Societies was developed by the European Sociological Association as an international platform for sociological research and discourse on Europe. It covers social theory and analysis on Europe itself, comparative research on Europe, and Europe in international perspective, with themes that reflect recent changes in Europe from cross-disciplinary viewpoints. Recommended for academic libraries that support graduate programs in sociology, economy, political science, or European studies.

4587. ***European Sociological Review.*** [ISSN: 0266-7215] 1985. bi-m. . EUR 930. Ed(s): Markus Gangl. Oxford University Press, Great Clarendon St, Oxford, OX2 6DP, United Kingdom; onlinequeries.uk@oup.com; http://global.oup.com. Illus., adv. Sample. Refereed. Reprint: PSC. *Indexed:* A22, E01, IBSS, P61, SSA. *Bk. rev.:* Number and length vary. *Aud.:* Ac.

This journal contains articles on all aspects of sociology, ranging from shorter research notes to major reports. Topics include all areas of sociology; recent articles have included migration, xenophobia, gender, labor, religion, families, and children. All articles are in English, with a strong emphasis on Western European countries. Recommended for academic libraries that support graduate programs in sociology.

4588. ***Evaluation: the international journal of theory, research and practice.*** [ISSN: 1356-3890] 1995. q. USD 1626 (print & online eds.)). Ed(s): Elliot Stern. Sage Publications Ltd., 1 Oliver's Yard, 55 City Rd, London, EC1Y 1SP, United Kingdom; info@sagepub.com; https://www.sagepub.com/. Illus., index, adv. Sample. Refereed. Vol. ends: Oct. Reprint: PSC. *Indexed:* A01, A22, ASSIA, E01, IBSS, P61, SSA. *Bk. rev.:* 1-2; signed. *Aud.:* Ac.

This journal is published in association with the Tavistock Institute of Human Relations, which is engaged in evaluation and action research in organizations. *Evaluation* provides an international and interdisciplinary forum for dialogue on evaluation in the social sciences, including the areas of politics, economics, public administration, psychology, sociology, anthropology, health, education, law, and information technology. Includes occasional special issues, book reviews, practice articles, and a section for debate and opinion. Recommended for academic libraries that support programs in sociology, political science, economics, or public administration.

4589. ***Evaluation Review: a journal of applied social research.*** Formerly (until Feb.1980): *Evaluation Quarterly.* [ISSN: 0193-841X] 1977. bi-m. USD 1699 (print & online eds.)). Ed(s): Jacob Klerman. Sage Publications, Inc., 2455 Teller Rd, Thousand Oaks, CA 91320; info@sagepub.com; http://www.sagepub.com. Illus., index, adv. Sample. Refereed. Vol. ends: Dec. Microform: PQC. Reprint: PSC. *Indexed:* A01, A22, E01, ERIC, HRIS, IBSS, L14, N13, SSA. *Aud.:* Ac.

Evaluation Review serves as an interdisciplinary forum in the social sciences for the work of researchers, planners, and policy makers. It presents the latest applied evaluation methods in areas such as homelessness, education, domestic violence, public health, substance abuse, and criminal justice. In addition to extensive research articles, included are review essays, reports on innovative evaluative applications, and research briefs of ongoing studies. Recommended for academic libraries that support social work, sociology, criminal justice, or public administration.

4590. ***Forum Qualitative Sozialforschung.*** [ISSN: 1438-5627] 1999. 3x/yr. Free. Ed(s): Katja Mruck. Freie Universitaet Berlin, Institut fuer Qualitative Forschung, Guerickestr 27, Berlin, 10587, Germany; info@qualitative-forschung.de; http://www.qualitative-forschung.de. Refereed. *Indexed:* IBSS, P61, SSA. *Aud.:* Ac.

This is a multilingual, online, open-access journal that presents qualitative studies on various topics in the social sciences, as well as articles on theory, methods, and application of qualitative research. Features of the journal include review articles, conference reports, and interviews. Articles may be in English, German, or Spanish. Academic libraries that support the social sciences may find this a useful addition to electronic holdings.

4591. ***Global Social Policy: an interdisciplinary journal of public policy and social development.*** [ISSN: 1468-0181] 2001. 3x/yr. USD 1043 (print & online eds.)). Ed(s): Gerard Boychuk, Stephen McBride. Sage Publications Ltd., 1 Oliver's Yard, 55 City Rd, London, EC1Y 1SP, United Kingdom; info@sagepub.com; https://www.sagepub.com/. Adv. Sample. Refereed. Reprint: PSC. *Indexed:* A01, A22, E01, EconLit, IBSS, P61. *Bk. rev.:* 6-8; signed. *Aud.:* Ac, Sa.

GSP is an international and interdisciplinary journal that exists to advance discourse and understanding of the impact of globalization on social policy, social development, social health and governance, gender, poverty, social welfare, education, and food. Included are scholarly research articles as well as policy-oriented discourse that is intended to advocate for global welfare policies and programs. Recommended for academic libraries that support programs in sociology, economics, social work, public administration, political science, or criminal justice.

4592. ***International Journal of Comparative Sociology.*** [ISSN: 0020-7152] 1960. bi-m. USD 1442 (print & online eds.)). Ed(s): David A Smith. Sage Publications Ltd., 1 Oliver's Yard, 55 City Rd, London, EC1Y 1SP, United Kingdom; info@sagepub.com; https://www.sagepub.com/. Illus., adv. Sample. Refereed. Microform: SWZ. Reprint: PSC. *Indexed:* A01, A22, A47, BAS, BRI, Chicano, E01, IBSS, P61. *Aud.:* Ac.

This journal offers research that is international in scope and comparative in method, with contributions from sociologists worldwide. Articles present competing perspectives; topics are drawn from scholars in sociology other social sciences. Each issue has six to eight signed book reviews. Recommended for academic libraries that support programs in sociology.

4593. ***International Sociology.*** [ISSN: 0268-5809] 1986. bi-m. USD 1627 (print & online eds.)). Ed(s): Christine Inglis. Sage Publications Ltd., 1 Oliver's Yard, 55 City Rd, London, EC1Y 1SP, United Kingdom; info@sagepub.com; https://www.sagepub.com/. Illus., index. Sample. Refereed. Vol. ends: Dec. Reprint: PSC. *Indexed:* A01, A22, B01, BAS, E01, IBSS, P61, SSA. *Bk. rev.:* 2-4; signed. *Aud.:* Ac.

This journal was established in 1986 by the International Sociological Association, and as such, it was one of the first publications to invite the research and perspectives of the international community of sociologists. Articles present innovative theory and empirical approaches to key sociological issues, using comparative, quantitative, and qualitative methods. Several issues per year contain extensive (20+) book reviews. Recommended for academic libraries that support graduate programs in sociology.

4594. ***Journal of Applied Social Science.*** Formed by the merger of (1999-2007): *Sociological Practice;* (1984 2007): *Journal of Applied Sociology.* [ISSN: 1936-7244] 2007. s-a. USD 542 (print & online eds.)). Ed(s): Jammie Price. Sage Publications, Inc., 2455 Teller Rd, Thousand Oaks, CA 91320; info@sagepub.com; http://www.sagepub.com/. Refereed. Reprint: PSC. *Indexed:* ASSIA. *Bk. rev.:* 0-3. *Aud.:* Ac.

This online publication is the official publication of the Association for Applied and Clinical Sociology, and the amalgamated successor of previously-published journals: the *Journal of Applied Sociology* and the *Journal of Sociological Practice.* It publishes research articles, essays, research reports, teaching notes, and book reviews on topics of interest to sociological practitioners. Articles apply social science theories or method, critically reflect on the application of social science, or improve the teaching of social science. Recommended for academic libraries that support graduate programs in sociology and other social sciences.

4595. ***Journal of Children and Media.*** [ISSN: 1748-2798] 2007. q. GBP 478 (print & online eds.)). Ed(s): Dafna Lemish, Amy Jordan. Routledge, 4 Park Sq, Milton Park, Abingdon, OX14 4RN, United Kingdom; subscriptions@tandf.co.uk; http://www.tandfonline.com. Adv. Sample. Refereed. Reprint: PSC. *Indexed:* A22, E01. *Bk. rev.:* Number and length vary. *Aud.:* Ac.

The purpose of this journal is to provide a space for the interdisciplinary discussion and examination of the study of the role of media in the lives of children and youth. Written by scholars and professionals from around the globe, research articles focus on the role and effect of media on children, especially in regard to three complementary areas: children as media consumers, portrayals of children in media, and media organizations and productions that are for and by children. Topics of articles are quite varied, including the interaction of children and media, diversity issues, violence, video games, and advertising. Includes occasional reviews of books and other resources. Recommended for academic and public research libraries.

4596. ***Journal of Classical Sociology.*** [ISSN: 1468-795X] 2001. 3x/yr. USD 1631 (print & online eds.)). Ed(s): Simon Susen, Bryan S Turner. Sage Publications Ltd., 1 Oliver's Yard, 55 City Rd, London, EC1Y 1SP, United Kingdom; info@sagepub.com; https://www.sagepub.com/. Sample. Refereed. Reprint: PSC. *Indexed:* A01, A22, E01, IBSS, P61. *Bk. rev.:* Number & length vary. *Aud.:* Ac.

Articles in the *Journal of Classical Sociology* focus on the origins of society and the ways in which classical traditions and thought are reflected in contemporary sociological thinking and research. Research areas include concepts, theory, institutions, ideologies, traditions, methods, and values. Many issues are thematic, often focusing on a single topic or theorist; recent special issues have included Georg Simmel and David Frisby, Durkheim, John Holloway, and natural law. Review essays and book reviews are also included. Recommended for academic libraries that support graduate and faculty-research sociology.

Journal of Comparative Family Studies. See Family section.

Journal of Divorce & Remarriage. See Marriage and Divorce section.

4597. ***Journal of European Social Policy.*** [ISSN: 0958-9287] 1991. 5x/yr. USD 1772 (print & online eds.)). Ed(s): Traute Meyer, Jochen Clasen. Sage Publications Ltd., 1 Oliver's Yard, 55 City Rd, London, EC1Y 1SP, United Kingdom; info@sagepub.com; https://www.sagepub.com/. Sample. Refereed. Reprint: PSC. *Indexed:* A01, A22, E01, IBSS, P61, SSA. *Bk. rev.:* 4-6, signed. *Aud.:* Ac.

This interdisciplinary journal features articles on all aspects of social policy in Europe. Research focuses on innovative insights and empirical analysis that addresses policy-making in the European Union and elsewhere, cross-national comparative studies, and comparisons outside of Europe. Social policy topics have included aging, pensions and social security, poverty and social exclusion, education, work and training, families, health and social services, migration, privatization, and globalization. Other features include reflections on social policy issues, a section called "European Brief" that summarizes trends and legislation in Europe, and book reviews. Recommended for academic libraries supporting programs in sociology, public administration, or European studies.

Journal of Family Issues. See Family section.

4598. ***Journal of Historical Sociology.*** [ISSN: 0952-1909] 1988. q. GBP 709. Ed(s): Yoke-Sum Wong, Derek Sayer. Wiley-Blackwell Publishing Ltd., The Atrium, Southern Gate, Chichester, PO19 8QG, United Kingdom; cs-journals@wiley.com; http://onlinelibrary.wiley.com. Adv. Sample. Refereed. Reprint: PSC. *Indexed:* A01, A22, A47, AmHI, BRI, E01, IBSS, P61, SSA. *Aud.:* Ac.

The focus of this journal is the interdisciplinary exchange of ideas and perspectives with regard to history and social studies. Editors include historians, anthropologists, geographers, and sociologists from the U.S., Canada, and Europe. In addition to scholarly articles, the journal contains review essays and commentary in its "Issues and Agendas" section intended to provoke discussion and debate. Recommended for academic libraries that support programs in the social sciences.

Journal of Homosexuality. See Gay, Lesbian, Bisexual, and Transgender section.

The Journal of Human Resources. See Labor and Industrial Relations section.

4599. *Journal of Leisure Research.* [ISSN: 0022-2216] 1968. 5x/yr. GBP 434 print & online eds. Ed(s): Ingrid Schneider. Taylor & Francis, . Illus., index, adv. Refereed. Microform: PQC. Reprint: PSC. *Indexed:* A22, ASSIA, Agr, BRI, C45, SD. *Bk. rev.:* Number and length vary. *Aud.:* Ac.

This journal is the official publication of the National Recreation and Park Association, and is published in cooperation with the University of Illinois and Sagamore. It contains empirical reports, theoretical and methodological studies, commentaries, and review papers on subjects in sports and leisure studies. Recent articles have focused on outdoor recreation areas, wilderness experiences, sports and other leisure activities, gender, and community management. Recommended for academic libraries that support research in sociology or public administration.

Journal of Marriage and Family. See Family section.

4600. *Journal of Mathematical Sociology.* [ISSN: 0022-250X] 1971. q. GBP 2399 (print & online eds.)). Ed(s): Phillip Bonacich. Taylor & Francis Inc., 711 3rd Ave, 8th Fl, New York, NY 10017; support@tandfonline.com; http://www.tandfonline.com. Illus., index. Sample. Refereed. Reprint: PSC. *Indexed:* A01, A22, BRI, E01, IBSS, MSN, SSA. *Bk. rev.:* Occasional. *Aud.:* Ac.

This is an interdisciplinary journal that publishes papers of interest to social and behavioral scientists. It is oriented toward the mathematical understanding of emergent social structures, networks, groups, organizations, and global systems rather than on individual behavior. Also included are reviews of new and developing areas of mathematics and mathematical modeling with applications in sociology. Recommended for academic libraries that support doctoral programs in sociology.

4601. *Journal of Public and Professional Sociology.* [ISSN: 2154-8935] 2005. s-a. Free. Ed(s): Melvyn L Fein, Linda Treiber. Kennesaw State University, 1000 Chastain Rd, English Bldg. #27/Ste 220, Kennesaw, GA 30144; http://www.kennesaw.edu/. *Aud.:* Ga, Ac, Sa.

This open-access online publication serves as the official journal of the Georgia Sociological Association. It contains research and theory articles intended to inform public debate about the social, political, and moral issues related to sociological scientific expertise. Preference is shown for articles that are professional, scientifically sound, relevant, readable, and innovative. Also included are debates, papers by students, research and teaching notes, and occasional reviews. Academic libraries with graduate programs in sociology may wish to add this to their electronic holdings.

4602. *Journal of Sex Research.* Incorporates (in 2007): *Annual Review of Sex Research;* Formerly (until 196?): *Advances in Sex Research.* [ISSN: 0022-4499] 1965. 9x/yr. GBP 640 (print & online eds.)). Ed(s): Cynthia Graham. Routledge, 530 Walnut St, Ste 850, Philadelphia, PA 19106; enquiries@tandfonline.com; http://www.tandfonline.com. Illus., adv. Refereed. Vol. ends: Nov. Microform: PQC. Reprint: PSC. *Indexed:* A01, A22, ASSIA, BAS, BRI, C45, Chicano, E01, MLA-IB. *Bk. rev.:* Occasional. *Aud.:* Ac, Sa.

As the official publication of the Society for the Scientific Study of Sexuality, this journal provides a forum for research and the promotion of an interdisciplinary understanding of contemporary sexual science. Articles include empirical studies, brief reports, theoretical essays, literature reviews, historical articles, book reviews, and letters to the editor. The audience includes researchers and practitioners in psychology, sociology, education, psychiatry, communication, and allied health. Recommended for academic and research libraries with programs in the fields listed here.

4603. *Journal of Social Issues.* [ISSN: 0022-4537] 1944. q. USD 1092 (print or online ed.)). Ed(s): Ann Bettencourt. Wiley-Blackwell Publishing, Inc., 111 River St, Hoboken, NJ 07030; info@wiley.com; http://onlinelibrary.wiley.com. Illus., adv. Sample. Refereed. Vol. ends: Winter. Microform: PMC; PQC. Reprint: PSC. *Indexed:* A01, A22, BAS, CJPI, Chicano, E01, IBSS, MLA-IB, P61, SSA. *Aud.:* Ac.

This journal is published for the Society for the Psychological Study of Social Issues. It contains articles that employ behavioral and social scientific theory, empirical evidence, and practice in order to study human and social problems. Each issue focuses on a single topic; recent themes have included genocide, globalization, racism in the United States, poverty, youth and violence, and career sustainability. Recommended for academic and research libraries.

4604. *Journal of Social Work Education.* Formerly (until 1985): *Journal of Education for Social Work.* [ISSN: 1043-7797] 1965. q. GBP 428 (print & online eds.)). Ed(s): Susan Robbins. Routledge, 530 Walnut St, Ste 850, Philadelphia, PA 19106; enquiries@tandfonline.com; http://www.tandfonline.com. Adv. Refereed. Reprint: PSC. *Indexed:* A01, A22, ASSIA, BRI, ERIC, SSA. *Aud.:* Ac.

As the official publication of the Council on Social Work Education, this journal covers all aspects of education in social work and social welfare. It serves as a forum for the creative exchange of trends, innovations, and problems with respect to social work education at all levels. Its audience includes educators, students, and practitioners. Topics of research articles in recent issues have included professional socialization, financial literacy for social work students, development of professional skills, measuring learning outcomes, field learning, and evidence-based practice. Other features include research notes and teaching notes. Recommended for academic libraries that support programs in social work at all levels.

4605. *Journal of Social Work Practice: psychotherapeutic approaches in health, welfare and the community.* [ISSN: 0265-0533] 1983. q. GBP 1100 (print & online eds.)). Ed(s): Malcolm Golightley, Gillian Ruch. Routledge, 4 Park Sq, Milton Park, Abingdon, OX14 4RN, United Kingdom; subscriptions@tandf.co.uk; http://www.tandfonline.com. Adv. Sample. Refereed. Reprint: PSC. *Indexed:* A01, A22, ASSIA, E01, IBSS, SSA. *Aud.:* Ac, Sa.

This is the journal of the Group for the Advancement of Psychodynamics and Psychotherapy in Social Work. It publishes articles that explore and analyze practice in social welfare and allied health professions from psychodynamic and systemic perspectives. This may include counseling, social care planning, education and training, research, institutional life, management and organization, or policy making. The scope is international and intercultural. Recommended for academic libraries that support graduate social work programs and for libraries used by social work and social service professionals.

4606. *Journal of Social Work Values & Ethics.* [ISSN: 1553-6947] 2004. q. Ed(s): Stephen M Marson, Donna DeAngelis. Association of Social Work Boards, 400 Southridge Pky, Ste B, Culpeper, VA 22701; http://www.aswb.org/. Refereed. *Indexed:* A01, SSA. *Bk. rev.:* Number and length vary. *Aud.:* Ac, Sa.

This is an open-access, peer-reviewed journal published by the Association of Social Work Boards. It publishes articles that examine ethical and values issues that inform social work practice, research, education, and theory development. Areas studied include models for analyzing and resolving ethical conflicts, discussions of ethical dilemmas, ethical decision-making in social work practice, and examples of good practice with respect to ethical and value considerations. Features also include book reviews. Recommended for the electronic holdings of academic libraries that support social work programs, and for libraries used by social work and social service professionals.

4607. ***Nonprofit and Voluntary Sector Quarterly.*** Formerly (until 1989): *Journal of Voluntary Action Research.* [ISSN: 0899-7640] 1972. bi-m. USD 1201 (print & online eds.)). Ed(s): Jeffery L Brudney, Lucas Meijs. Sage Publications, Inc., 2455 Teller Rd, Thousand Oaks, CA 91320; info@sagepub.com; http://www.sagepub.com. Illus., index, adv. Sample. Refereed. Vol. ends: Dec. Microform: PQC. Reprint: PSC. *Indexed:* A01, A22, ASSIA, E01, EconLit, P61, SSA. *Bk. rev.:* 4-6; signed. *Aud.:* Ga, Ac.

This is an international, interdisciplinary journal that provides research, discussion, and analysis in the nonprofit sector. The focus is on research within nonprofit organization, philanthropy, and volunteerism for an audience of practitioners, administrators, and policymakers. All aspects of the social sciences are represented, including sociology, social work, anthropology, arts and humanities, economics, education, health, history, law, political science, public administration, and urban affairs. Includes book reviews in each issue. Recommended for academic libraries that support programs in sociology or social work and for public research libraries.

4608. ***Qualitative Sociology.*** [ISSN: 0162-0436] 1978. q. EUR 1609 (print & online eds.)). Ed(s): David Smilde. Springer New York LLC, 233 Spring St, New York, NY 10013; customerservice@springer.com; http://www.springer.com. Illus., index, adv. Sample. Refereed. Microform: PQC. Reprint: PSC. *Indexed:* A01, A22, BRI, E01, IBSS, P61, SSA. *Bk. rev.:* 6-8; signed. *Aud.:* Ac.

Qualitative Sociology contains articles that employ qualitative research methods in the interpretation and analysis of social life. Articles demonstrate both theoretical and analytical research based on methods such as interviewing, observation, ethnography, and historical and content analysis. A recent issue included articles on rituals of a Jewish Orthodox congregation, public monuments, and youth violence. Recommended for academic libraries that support sociology programs.

4609. ***Qualitative Sociology Review.*** [ISSN: 1733-8077] 2005. 4x/yr. Free. Ed(s): Krzysztof Tomasz Konecki. Uniwersytet Lodzki, Wydzial Ekonomiczno-Socjologiczny, Instytut Socjologii, ul Rewolucji 1905 r. nr 41/43, Lodz, 90214, Poland. *Indexed:* IBSS. *Bk. rev.:* Number and length vary. *Aud.:* Ac.

This is an open-access, international scientific journal sponsored by Lodz University, Poland. It publishes empirical, theoretical, and methodological articles applicable to all aspects and specializations within sociology. Topics of recent articles included migration, homeless people, and motherhood and addiction. Book reviews are also included. Recommended for academic libraries that support sociology programs.

4610. ***Quality and Quantity: international journal of methodology.*** [ISSN: 0033-5177] 1967. 6x/yr. EUR 2789 (print & online eds.)). Ed(s): Vittorio Capecchi. Springer Netherlands, Van Godewijckstraat 30, Dordrecht, 3311 GX, Netherlands; http://www.springer.com. Illus., adv. Sample. Refereed. Microform: PQC. Reprint: PSC. *Indexed:* A22, E01, IBSS, P61, SSA. *Aud.:* Ac.

This is an interdisciplinary, international journal that contains articles that correlate disciplines such as mathematics and statistics with sociology, economics, social psychology, and other social sciences. Its coverage includes models, methods, and applications of classifications; qualitative and feminist methodologies; discussions on the general logic of empirical research; and similar topics. Recommended for academic libraries that support doctoral programs in sociology.

4611. ***Rural Sociology: devoted to scientific study of rural and community life.*** [ISSN: 0036-0112] 1937. q. GBP 328. Ed(s): Stephen Sapp. Rural Sociological Society, 2040 JFSB, Brigham Young University, Provo, UT 84602; http://www.ruralsociology.org. Illus., index, adv. Refereed. Vol. ends: Winter. Microform: PQC. Reprint: PSC. *Indexed:* A01, A22, Agr, BRI, C45, Chicano, E01, ERIC, IBSS, MLA-IB, P61, SSA. *Bk. rev.:* 4-6; signed. *Aud.:* Ac.

Rural Sociology is the journal of the Rural Sociological Society. It uses sociological and interdisciplinary approaches to focus on emerging and recurring issues, policy discussions, and changes in local and global systems that affect rural people and places. The scope is international. Specific issues may include community revitalization, rural demography changes, rural poverty, natural resource conflicts, environmental impacts, and food and agricultural production. Recommended for academic libraries that support programs in sociology, agriculture, or environmental studies.

4612. ***School Social Work Journal.*** [ISSN: 0161-5653] 1976. s-a. USD 60 (Individuals, USD 30). David Follmer Group, 5758 S Blackstone Ave, Chicago, IL 60637; info@thedavidfollmergroup.com; https://thedavidfollmergroup.com/. Refereed. *Indexed:* A22, B01, BRI, ERIC, SSA. *Aud.:* Ac, Sa.

This journal focuses on the improvement of social work practice in the schools. Articles include reports on research, integrative and comprehensive reviews, conceptual and practical positions, effective assessment and intervention methodologies, and model service delivery programs. Topics in a recent issue included youth in foster care, school violence, homeless children, youth with disabilities, evaluating school social work service, mental health interventions, and working with kids with autism. Recommended for academic libraries that support social work programs and special libraries that serve social services.

4613. ***Sex Roles: a journal of research.*** [ISSN: 0360-0025] 1975. m. EUR 2637 (print & online eds.)). Ed(s): Irene Hanson Frieze. Springer New York LLC, 233 Spring St, New York, NY 10013; customerservice@springer.com; http://www.springer.com. Illus., index, adv. Sample. Refereed. Vol. ends: Jul/Dec. Microform: PQC. Reprint: PSC. *Indexed:* A01, A22, BRI, Chicano, E01, FemPer, MLA-IB, P61, SSA, WSA. *Bk. rev.:* 2-4; signed. *Aud.:* Ac.

Sex Roles publishes interdisciplinary research and review articles in the behavioral sciences from a feminist perspective, primarily focusing on gender issues and perceptions. Topics of recent articles have included gender roles and socialization, gender stereotypes in the family, feminist identity, marriage, patterns of intimacy, women and math education, role models, body image, eating issues, and mothering. Each issue includes extensive reviews of books and often of media that address gender-related topics. As this title is heavily used in undergraduate research, it is essential for academic libraries.

4614. ***Smith College Studies in Social Work.*** [ISSN: 0037-7317] 1930. q. GBP 278 (print & online eds.)). Ed(s): Kathryn Basham, Carolyn Jacobs. Routledge, 530 Walnut St, Ste 850, Philadelphia, PA 19106; enquiries@tandfonline.com; http://www.tandfonline.com. Refereed. Circ: 2000 Paid. Reprint: PSC. *Indexed:* A01, A22, ASSIA, E01, SSA. *Bk. rev.:* Number and length vary. *Aud.:* Ac, Sa.

This is a refereed journal intended for social work and social service practitioners. It features articles that advance theoretical understanding of psychological and social functioning, present clinically relevant research, and promote excellence in clinical practice. Issues addressed include mental health, therapeutic process, trauma and recovery, racial and cultural diversity, community and evidence-based practice, and clinical services to specific populations of psychologically and socially vulnerable clients. Some issues include book reviews. Recommended for academic libraries that support social work programs and special libraries that serve social service programs.

4615. ***Social Change.*** [ISSN: 0049-0857] 1971. q. USD 404 (print & online eds.)). Ed(s): Manoranjan Mohanty. Sage Publications India Pvt. Ltd., B-1/I-1 Mohan Cooperative, Industrial Estate, Post Bag 7, New Delhi, 110 044, India; info@sagepub.in; http://www.sagepub.in. Sample. Refereed. Reprint: PSC. *Indexed:* A22, BAS, C45, E01, P61. *Bk. rev.:* 4-6, signed. *Aud.:* Ac.

Social Change is a multidisciplinary journal that publishes empirical research, analytic reports, theoretical essays, and policy discussions in the field of social change and development. The language is as non-technical as possible, appealing to a wide readership in academia, social movements, NGOs, and policy-making sectors. Features include book reviews and columns that present various perspectives and commentaries. This title is published in India, and many of the articles are written by scholars in that country. Recommended for academic libraries that support sociology programs.

4616. *Social Compass: international review of sociology of religion.* [ISSN: 0037-7686] 1953. q. USD 980 (print & online eds.)). Ed(s): Bernard Charlier. Sage Publications Ltd., 1 Oliver's Yard, 55 City Rd, London, EC1Y 1SP, United Kingdom; info@sagepub.com; https://www.sagepub.com/. Illus., index, adv. Sample. Refereed. Vol. ends: Dec. Reprint: PSC. *Indexed:* A01, A22, BAS, CJPI, E01, IBSS, MLA-IB, P61, R&TA, SSA. *Bk. rev.:* 1-2; signed. *Aud.:* Ac.

Social Compass is an international journal that provides a forum for research and review articles on the sociology of religion. Each issue features articles on a theme as well as those on any topic of religion in contemporary societies. Articles are published in English or French, with abstracts in both languages. Recommended for academic libraries that support graduate programs in sociology or religious studies.

4617. *Social Forces.* Formerly (until 1925): *The Journal of Social Forces.* [ISSN: 0037-7732] 1922. q. EUR 364. Ed(s): Arne L Kalleberg. Oxford University Press, 2001 Evans Rd, Cary, NC 27513; custserv.us@oup.com; https://academic.oup.com/journals. Illus., index. Refereed. Vol. ends: Jun. Microform: MIM; PMC; PQC. Reprint: PSC; WSH. *Indexed:* A01, A22, B01, BAS, BRI, CBRI, CJPI, Chicano, E01, ERIC, IBSS, MLA-IB, P61, SSA. *Bk. rev.:* 2-6; signed. *Aud.:* Ac.

Social Forces is published in association with the Department of Sociology at the University of North Carolina, Chapel Hill. Research articles explore all aspects of sociological inquiry and of other social sciences, including psychology, anthropology, political science, history, and economics. Recent issues have included articles on stratification, immigration, family, health, race, civic and political participation, and unemployment. An extensive list of book reviews in previous volumes has been replaced by shorter book review essays. Recommended for academic libraries that support social science programs.

4618. *Social Indicators Research: an international and interdisciplinary journal for quality-of-life measurement.* [ISSN: 0303-8300] 1974. 15x/yr. EUR 5299 (print & online eds.)). Ed(s): Filomena Maggino. Springer Netherlands, Van Godewijckstraat 30, Dordrecht, 3311 GX, Netherlands; http://www.springer.com. Illus., index, adv. Sample. Refereed. Vol. ends: Dec. Microform: PQC. Reprint: PSC. *Indexed:* A01, A22, Agr, B01, BAS, BRI, C45, E01, ERIC, EconLit, IBSS, P61, SSA. *Bk. rev.:* 2-3; signed. *Aud.:* Ac.

Social Indicators Research is a journal that publishes research on the quality of life. It presents empirical, philosophical, and methodological studies on all aspects of society, such as individual, public, and private organizations, and local, country, national, and international systems. Topics include health, social customs, law enforcement, politics, economics, poverty and welfare, education, science and technology, and the media and arts. Recommended for academic libraries that support graduate programs in the social sciences.

4619. *Social Networks: an international journal of structural analysis.* [ISSN: 0378-8733] 1979. 4x/yr. EUR 1101. Ed(s): P Doreian, M Everett. Elsevier BV, Radarweg 29, Amsterdam, 1043 NX, Netherlands; info@elsevier.com; https://www.elsevier.com/. Illus., index, adv. Sample. Refereed. Microform: PQC. *Indexed:* A22, A47, IBSS, SSA. *Bk. rev.:* Number and length vary. *Aud.:* Ac.

Social Networks is an international and interdisciplinary journal that publishes studies of the empirical structure of social relations, structure, and networks. Topics represented include anthropology, sociology, history, social psychology, economics, communication studies, and others in the social sciences. Included are theoretical and substantive papers, critical reviews of major theoretical or methodological approaches, and occasional book reviews. Recommended for academic libraries that support graduate programs in the social sciences.

4620. *Social Problems.* [ISSN: 0037-7791] 1953. q. EUR 312. Ed(s): Nilda Flores-Gonzalez, Pamela Quiroz. Oxford University Press, 2001 Evans Rd, Cary, NC 27513; custserv.us@oup.com; https://academic.oup.com/journals. Illus., index, adv. Sample. Refereed. Microform: PQC. Reprint: PSC; WSH. *Indexed:* A01, A22, BAS, BRI, CJPI, Chicano, E01, IBSS, P61, SSA. *Aud.:* Ga, Ac.

As the journal for the Society for the Study of Social Problems, this title focuses on influential sociological findings and theories in an array of areas, such as conflict, crime, juvenile delinquency, drugs, health and mental health, poverty and class, sexual behavior, and aging. As one of the most enduring, widely-read, and respected journals in the social sciences, *Social Problems* is essential for academic and research libraries.

4621. *Social Psychology Quarterly.* Former titles (until 1979): *Social Psychology;* (until 1978): *Sociometry.* [ISSN: 0190-2725] 1937. q. USD 553 (print & online eds.)). Ed(s): Richard T Serpe, Jan E Stets. Sage Publications, Inc., 2455 Teller Rd, Thousand Oaks, CA 91320; info@sagepub.com; http://www.sagepub.com. Illus. Refereed. Vol. ends: Dec. Microform: MIM; PQC. Reprint: PSC. *Indexed:* A01, A22, ASSIA, BRI, Chicano, E01, ERIC, IBSS, MLA-IB, P61, SSA. *Aud.:* Ac.

Published in association with the American Sociological Association, this journal publishes theoretical and empirical papers that link individuals to each other and to groups, collectivities, and institutions. The journal is interdisciplinary and publishes work by both sociologists and psychologists. Recommended for academic libraries that support programs in sociology and psychology.

4622. *Social Research: an international quarterly.* [ISSN: 0037-783X] 1934. q. USD 205. Ed(s): Cara Schlesinger, Arien Mack. The Johns Hopkins University Press, 2715 N Charles St, Baltimore, MD 21218; http://www.press.jhu.edu. Illus., adv. Sample. Refereed. Vol. ends: Dec. Reprint: PSC. *Indexed:* A01, A22, B01, BAS, BRI, CBRI, EconLit, MLA-IB, P61, SSA. *Aud.:* Ac.

This journal has been published since 1934 by the New School for Social Research, which offers postgraduate degrees in the social sciences. International in scope, the journal features research by scholars, writers, and experts from a variety of disciplines on topics of political, cultural, and economic concern. Most issues are thematic; recent themes have included giving, politics and comedy, Egypt in transition, the future of higher education, and India. Recommended for academic libraries that support programs in sociology and political science.

4623. *Social Science Computer Review.* Former titles (until 1988): *Social Science Microcomputer Review;* (until 1985): *Social Science Micro Review;* Which incorporated (1985-1986): *Computers and the Social Sciences;* (until 1983): *Political Science Micro Review.* [ISSN: 0894-4393] 1982. bi-m. USD 1329 (print & online eds.)). Ed(s): G David Garson. Sage Publications, Inc., 2455 Teller Rd, Thousand Oaks, CA 91320; info@sagepub.com; http://www.sagepub.com. Illus., index, adv. Sample. Refereed. Vol. ends: Nov. Reprint: PSC. *Indexed:* A01, A22, BRI, CBRI, CompLI, E01, P61, SSA. *Bk. rev.:* 2-4; signed. *Aud.:* Ac.

This journal serves as the official publication of the Social Science Computing Association. It is an interdisciplinary journal that covers computer applications in social science instruction and research. Topics include artificial intelligence, business, computational social science theory, computer-assisted survey research and qualitative analysis, computer simulation, the social impacts of computing and telecommunications, and software evaluation. Features also include brief updates, Web resources for social scientists, book reviews, and sections that examine certain themes. Recommended for academic libraries that support graduate programs in the social sciences.

The Social Science Journal. See Cultural Studies section.

Social Science Research. See Cultural Studies section.

4624. *Social Work and Christianity.* Formerly (until 1979): *The Paraclete.* [ISSN: 0737-5778] 1974. a. USD 140 Free to members. Ed(s): David Sherwood. North American Association of Christians in Social Work, PO Box 121, Botsford, CT 06404; info@nacsw.org; http://www.nacsw.org. Sample. Refereed. *Indexed:* A01, SSA. *Bk. rev.:* Number and length vary. *Aud.:* Ac, Sa.

This is a refereed journal published by the North American Association of Christians in Social Work (NACSW). Its purpose is to support and encourage social workers in the ethical integration of professional practice and Christian faith. Examples of recent articles include faith-based social services, professional values, youth programs, and the experiences of Christian students in social work education. A recent special issue focused on HIV/AIDS and a Christian social work response. Included are articles reporting on qualitative and quantitative research, shorter articles such as practice or teaching notes, reviews of books regarding Christian social work practice, and descriptions of new publications from the NACSW. While the NACSW asks a subscription fee, all content of the journal is freely available online. Recommended for academic libraries that support social work programs (especially programs offered by Christian schools) and for libraries that support faith-based social services.

4625. *Social Work in Health Care.* [ISSN: 0098-1389] 1975. 10x/yr. GBP 1719 (print & online eds.)). Ed(s): Andrew Weissman, Gary Rosenberg. Routledge, 530 Walnut St, Ste 850, Philadelphia, PA 19106; enquiries@tandfonline.com; http://www.tandfonline.com. Illus., adv. Sample. Refereed. Microform: PQC. Reprint: PSC. *Indexed:* A01, A22, ASSIA, AgeL, Chicano, E01, SSA. *Bk. rev.:* Number and length vary. *Aud.:* Ac, Sa.

This journal contains articles on social work theory, practice, and administration for and by professionals working in health-care settings. Themes include research on leadership, clinical practice, management, education, policy, and ethical issues. Issues occasionally include book reviews. Recommended for academic libraries that support social work, health-care, and social service programs.

4626. *Sociation Today.* [ISSN: 1542-6300] 2003. s-a. Free. North Carolina Sociological Association, c/o Beth Davison, Treasurer, Appalachian State University, Department of Sociology, Boone, NC 28608; ncsa@list.appstate.edu; http://www.ncsociology.org/new/index.html. Refereed. *Bk. rev.:* Number and length vary. *Aud.:* Ga, Ac, Sa.

Sponsored by the North Carolina Sociological Association, this is a peer-reviewed, open-access online journal. It publishes research articles of core sociological interest (immigration, inequality, urban life, aging, and so on) written by regional and national authors. A recent issue featured the work of student researchers. Recommended for the electronic collections of academic libraries that support sociology programs.

4627. *Sociological Forum: official journal of the Eastern Sociological Society.* [ISSN: 0884-8971] 1986. q. GBP 815 (print & online eds.)). Ed(s): Jason Torkelson, Karen A Cerulo. Wiley-Blackwell Publishing, Inc., 111 River St, Hoboken, NJ 07030; http://onlinelibrary.wiley.com. Illus., index, adv. Sample. Refereed. Microform: PQC. Reprint: PSC. *Indexed:* A01, A22, BRI, E01, IBSS, MLA-IB, P61, SSA. *Bk. rev.:* 4-6; signed. *Aud.:* Ac.

This title is the published for the Eastern Sociological Society, a nonprofit founded in 1930 to promote excellence in sociological scholarship and instruction. It features empirical articles, as well as those that develop theories, concepts, and methodological strategies. Topics cover all areas of sociology and related fields. Includes book reviews in each issue. Recommended for academic libraries that support programs in sociology.

4628. *Sociological Inquiry.* [ISSN: 0038-0245] 1930. q. GBP 266. Ed(s): Peter B Wood. Wiley-Blackwell Publishing, Inc., 111 River St, Hoboken, NJ 07030; http://onlinelibrary.wiley.com. Illus., index, adv. Sample. Refereed. Microform: PQC. Reprint: PSC. *Indexed:* A01, A22, BRI, CJPI, E01, MLA-IB, P61, SSA. *Bk. rev.:* . *Aud.:* Ac.

Published in one form or another since 1928, this publication is the official journal of Alpha Kappa Delta, the International Sociology Honor Society. As such, it exists to stimulate scholarship among sociology students, and features both theoretical and empirical studies in all aspects of social and cultural life. Recommended for academic libraries that support programs in sociology.

4629. *Sociological Methodology.* [ISSN: 0081-1750] 1969. a. USD 553 (print & online eds.)). Ed(s): Tim Futing Liao. Sage Publications, Inc., 2455 Teller Rd, Thousand Oaks, CA 91320; info@sagepub.com; http://www.sagepub.com/. Adv. Sample. Refereed. Microform: PQC. Reprint: PSC. *Indexed:* A01, A22, E01, IBSS, P61, SSA. *Aud.:* Ac.

Sociological Methodology is published on behalf of the American Sociological Association as an annual edited, hardbound volume. It features a diversity of methodological problems faced in the social sciences, including conceptualization, data analysis and collection, measurement, modeling, and research design. From the journal's web site: "The journal provides a forum for engaging the philosophical issues that underpin sociological research design." Recommended for academic libraries that support programs in sociology.

4630. *Sociological Perspectives.* Formerly (until 1983): *Pacific Sociological Review.* [ISSN: 0731-1214] 1957. bi-m. USD 696 (print & online eds.)). Ed(s): James Elliott, Robert O'Brien. Sage Publications, Inc., 2455 Teller Rd, Thousand Oaks, CA 91320; info@sagepub.com; http://www.sagepub.com. Illus., index, adv. Sample. Refereed. Vol. ends: Sep. Microform: PQC. Reprint: PSC. *Indexed:* A01, A22, B01, BAS, BRI, Chicano, E01, IBSS, P61, SSA. *Aud.:* Ac.

This journal was founded in 1957 and is published for the Pacific Sociological Association. It contains research about social problems related to economic, political, anthropological, and historical issues. Topics of recent articles have included immigration, criminal justice, race, cultural transmission, community, parenting, suicide rates, gender, mental health, families, work and employment, and societal inequality. Recommended for academic libraries with programs in sociology.

4631. *The Sociological Quarterly.* Formerly (until 1960): *Midwest Sociologist.* [ISSN: 0038-0253] 1960. q. GBP 581 (print & online eds.)). Ed(s): Keith Smith, Chris Moloney. Routledge, 530 Walnut St, Ste 850, Philadelphia, PA 19106; enquiries@tandfonline.com; http://www.tandfonline.com. Illus., index, adv. Sample. Refereed. Vol. ends: Nov. Reprint: PSC. *Indexed:* A01, A22, B01, BAS, BRI, CJPI, Chicano, E01, IBSS, MLA-IB, P61, SSA. *Aud.:* Ac.

This journal features cutting-edge research and theory in all areas of sociology; especially favored are articles that advance the field and appeal to a wide audience. It focuses on theoretically informed empirical sociology. Features include an occasional special issue or special section; recent special sections included nature and culture, Latinos and skin color, and first-person ethnography. Recommended for academic libraries with programs in sociology.

Sociological Research. See Slavic Studies section.

4632. *Sociological Research Online.* [ISSN: 1360-7804] 1996. q. USD 433. Ed(s): Paul Hodkinson, Rachel Brooks. Sage Publications Ltd., 1 Oliver's Yard, 55 City Rd, London, EC1Y 1SP, United Kingdom; info@sagepub.com; https://www.sagepub.com. Illus. Refereed. *Indexed:* IBSS, SSA. *Bk. rev.:* 3-10; signed. *Aud.:* Ac.

This online-only journal is jointly published by the University of Surrey, the University of Stirling, the British Sociological Association, and Sage Publications Ltd.. Thus, most of its contributors are from the U.K., and its focus is international. It contains theoretical, empirical, and methodological research and debate on current political, cultural, and intellectual topics. The journal features book reviews, "rapid response" articles, letters to the editors, and special topical sections. Recent topics have included modern girlhoods and the Olympics. Recommended for academic libraries that support programs in sociology. URL: www.socresonline.org.uk

4633. *The Sociological Review.* Formerly (until 1908): *Sociological Papers.* [ISSN: 0038-0261] 1904. q. USD 953 (print & online eds.)). Sage Publications Ltd., 1 Oliver's Yard, 55 City Rd, London, EC1Y 1SP, United Kingdom; info@sagepub.com; https://www.sagepub.com/. Illus., index, adv. Sample. Refereed. Vol. ends: Nov. Microform: PQC. Reprint: PSC. *Indexed:* A01, A22, A47, BRI, C45, CBRI, CJPI, E01, IBSS, MLA-IB, P61, SSA. *Bk. rev.:* 10-12; signed. *Aud.:* Ac.

For over 100 years, *The Sociological Review* has published high-quality, innovative research articles geared toward the general sociological reader. The scope covers all aspects of sociology, including criminology, education, gender, medicine, social policy, women's studies, and social organization. Research orientations vary, and may be anthropological, philosophical, analytical, or ethnographic. Includes book reviews, and there are several special issues per year. Supplemental issues are published as monographs. Recommended for academic libraries.

4634. ***Sociological Spectrum.*** Formed by the merger of (1968-1980): *Sociological Symposium;* (1978-1980): *Sociological Forum.* [ISSN: 0273-2173] 1981. bi-m. GBP 783 (print & online eds.)). Ed(s): Brian P Hinote, Kenin D Breault. Taylor & Francis Inc., 711 3rd Ave, 8th Fl, New York, NY 10017; support@tandfonline.com; http://www.tandfonline.com. Illus., index, adv. Sample. Refereed. Vol. ends: Oct/Dec. Reprint: PSC. *Indexed:* A01, A22, CJPI, E01, IBSS, N13, P61, SSA. *Aud.:* Ac.

As the official journal of the Mid-South Sociological Association, this journal publishes theoretical, methodological, quantitative, and qualitative research. Topics cover all areas of sociology, social psychology, anthropology, and political science. Recent articles have been on caregiving, race, gender, work, wages, cyberbullying, health care, and homelessness. Recommended for academic libraries with graduate programs in sociology.

4635. ***Sociological Theory.*** [ISSN: 0735-2751] 1983. q. USD 553 (print & online eds.)). Ed(s): Neil Gross. Sage Publications, Inc., 2455 Teller Rd, Thousand Oaks, CA 91320; info@sagepub.com; http://www.sagepub.com/. Sample. Refereed. Reprint: PSC. *Indexed:* A01, A22, E01, IBSS, SSA. *Aud.:* Ac.

Published in association with the American Sociological Association, this journal is international and interdisciplinary in scope. It contains research in all areas of theory, metatheory, ethnomethodology, and world systems analysis from authors of varied disciplines and disciplinary orientations. Recommended for academic libraries that support graduate programs in sociology.

4636. ***Sociology.*** [ISSN: 0038-0385] 1967. bi-m. USD 927.32. Sage Publications Ltd., 1 Oliver's Yard, 55 City Rd, London, EC1Y 1SP, United Kingdom; info@sagepub.com; https://www.sagepub.com/. Illus., index. Sample. Refereed. Vol. ends: Nov. Microform: PQC. Reprint: PSC. *Indexed:* A01, A22, B01, BAS, BRI, C45, E01, IBSS, P61, SSA. *Bk. rev.:* 10- 20, signed. *Aud.:* Ac.

This is the "flagship" journal of the British Sociological Association and is the premier sociology journal in the United Kingdom. It contains reports on empirical research, and articles that challenge current concepts or propose innovative conceptual or methodological approaches and solutions to problems. Other features include "Research Notes," which provides brief reports on recent or ongoing studies, and an extensive book review section in each issue. Highly recommended for academic libraries that support sociology programs.

4637. ***Sociology of Education.*** Formerly (until 1963): *The Journal of Educational Sociology.* [ISSN: 0038-0407] 1927. q. USD 553 (print & online eds.)). Ed(s): John Robert Warren. Sage Publications, Inc., 2455 Teller Rd, Thousand Oaks, CA 91320; info@sagepub.com; http://www.sagepub.com/. Illus., index. Refereed. Vol. ends: Oct. Microform: PMC; PQC. Reprint: PSC. *Indexed:* A01, A22, ASSIA, Chicano, E01, ERIC, SSA. *Aud.:* Ac.

This journal is published in association with the American Sociological Association. It contains studies that examine social institutions, individuals' experiences within these institutions, and how educational processes and social development are affected. Recommended for academic libraries that support programs in sociology and education.

4638. ***Sociology of Health and Illness: a journal of medical sociology.*** Incorporates (1995-1999): *Sociology of Health and Illness Monograph Series.* [ISSN: 0141-9889] 1979. 7x/yr. GBP 860. Ed(s): Gareth Williams. Wiley-Blackwell Publishing Ltd., The Atrium, Southern Gate, Chichester, PO19 8QG, United Kingdom; cs-journals@wiley.com; http://onlinelibrary.wiley.com. Illus., index, adv. Sample. Refereed. Vol. ends: Nov. Reprint: PSC. *Indexed:* A01, A22, BRI, C45, E01, IBSS, P61, SSA. *Bk. rev.:* 8-12, signed. *Aud.:* Ac.

This journal publishes sociological articles that address all aspects of health, illness, medicine, mental health, and health care. International in scope, it includes empirical and theoretical research reports and review articles. Although published bimonthly, it publishes an additional special issue each year on a topic of important and current interest. Recommended for academic libraries that support programs in sociology, health sciences, or social work.

Sociology of Religion. See Religion section.

4639. ***Teaching Sociology.*** Incorporates (1979-1985): *Teaching Newsletter;* Which was formerly (197?-1979): *On Teaching Undergraduate Sociology Newsletter.* [ISSN: 0092-055X] 1973. q. USD 553 (print & online eds.)). Ed(s): Stephen A Sweet. Sage Publications, Inc., 2455 Teller Rd, Thousand Oaks, CA 91320; info@sagepub.com; http://www.sagepub.com. Illus. Refereed. Vol. ends: Oct. Reprint: PSC. *Indexed:* A22, ASSIA, E01, ERIC, MLA-IB, SSA. *Bk. rev.:* 2-6; signed. *Aud.:* Ac.

The content of *Teaching Sociology* is intended to be of interest to sociology professors. It publishes full articles, shorter notes, review essays, and reviews of books, films, and the occasional Web or computer resource. Topics include pedagogical issues, curriculum development, course design, writing in the discipline, online teaching, and teaching strategies. Recommended for academic libraries that support postgraduate programs in sociology or education.

Theory and Decision. See Philosophy section.

4640. ***Theory and Society: renewal and critique in social theory.*** [ISSN: 0304-2421] 1974. bi-m. EUR 1472 (print & online eds.)). Ed(s): Janet Gouldner, Karen G Lucas. Springer Netherlands, Van Godewijckstraat 30, Dordrecht, 3311 GX, Netherlands; http://www.springer.com. Illus., index, adv. Sample. Refereed. Vol. ends: Nov. Microform: PQC. Reprint: PSC. *Indexed:* A01, A22, BAS, BRI, E01, IBSS, P61, SSA. *Bk. rev.:* 2-4; signed. *Aud.:* Ac.

This is an international journal that publishes theoretical research articles on social processes and analysis. Topics cover a broad landscape across history, from prehistory to the contemporary; treatment blends theory, methodological critique, criticism, and observation. Recommended for academic libraries that support graduate programs in sociology.

4641. ***Theory, Culture & Society: explorations in critical social science.*** [ISSN: 0263-2764] 1982. 8x/yr. USD 2474 (print & online eds.)). Ed(s): Mike Featherstone. Sage Publications Ltd., 1 Oliver's Yard, 55 City Rd, London, EC1Y 1SP, United Kingdom; info@sagepub.com; https://www.sagepub.com/. Illus., index. Sample. Refereed. Vol. ends: Nov. Reprint: PSC. *Indexed:* A01, A22, A47, BRI, E01, IBSS, MLA-IB, P61, SSA. *Bk. rev.:* 1-2, signed. *Aud.:* Ac.

This journal publishes research and review articles in the social and cultural sciences. International and interdisciplinary in scope, articles present cutting-edge developments in social and cultural theory. Features include research articles, commentaries, interviews, review articles, and book reviews. Recommended for academic libraries that support graduate programs in the social sciences.

Violence Against Women. See Gender Studies section.

4642. ***Work and Occupations: an international sociological journal.*** Formerly (until 1982): *Sociology of Work and Occupations.* [ISSN: 0730-8884] 1974. q. USD 1443 (print & online eds.)). Ed(s): Daniel B Cornfield. Sage Publications, Inc., 2455 Teller Rd, Thousand Oaks, CA 91320; info@sagepub.com; http://www.sagepub.com. Illus., index, adv. Sample. Refereed. Vol. ends: Nov. Microform: PQC. Reprint: PSC. *Indexed:* A01, A22, B01, BRI, E01, ErgAb, IBSS, SSA. *Bk. rev.:* 4-6; signed. *Aud.:* Ac.

This journal publishes social science research on the dynamics of the workplace, employment, and society. It is international in scope and includes the interdisciplinary perspectives of sociology, anthropology, education, history, industrial relations, management, and psychology. Topics addressed in recent articles have included job insecurity and inequality, disability accommodations, gender, immigration policy, workplace diversity, globalization, and work and family. Features also include research notes, review essays, and book reviews. Recommended for academic libraries that support graduate programs in sociology or labor relations.

4643. ***Youth & Society.*** [ISSN: 0044-118X] 1969. 8x/yr. USD 1511 (print & online eds.)). Ed(s): Mark Zimmerman. Sage Publications, Inc., 2455 Teller Rd, Thousand Oaks, CA 91320; info@sagepub.com; http://www.sagepub.com. Illus., index, adv. Sample. Refereed. Vol. ends: Jun. Microform: PQC. Reprint: PSC. *Indexed:* A01, A22, ASSIA, Agr, Chicano, E01, ERIC, P61, SSA. *Aud.:* Ac, Sa.

This is an international journal that focuses on issues faced by adolescents and young adults. Subject coverage is interdisciplinary and includes aspects of sociology, psychology, public health, education, social work, criminology, anthropology, and political science. Topics are of interest to researchers, educators, counselors, policy makers, and others who study and work with adolescents. Articles in recent issues have focused on school culture, youth violence, peer pressure, parenting, tobacco and drug use, and suicide. There are occasional special-theme issues or sections. Highly recommended for academic libraries.

Social Work and Social Welfare

4644. ***Adoption Quarterly.*** [ISSN: 1092-6755] 1997. q. GBP 500 (print & online eds.)). Ed(s): Scott Ryan. Routledge, 530 Walnut St, Ste 850, Philadelphia, PA 19106; enquiries@tandfonline.com; http://www.tandfonline.com. Sample. Refereed. Circ: 305 Paid. Reprint: PSC. *Indexed:* A01, A22, E01, SSA. *Bk. rev.:* Number and length vary. *Aud.:* Ac, Sa.

Adoption Quarterly is an international and multidisciplinary journal that examines issues around adoption and foster care from the ethical, financial, legal, policy, and social perspectives. Recent articles also explored adoptive family relationships, infertility and reproductive technologies, and trends in adoption. This title features conceptual and empirical works focusing on race, culture, and social trends in adoption, as well as commentaries, systematic reviews, and signed book and film reviews that will be relevant to adoption practitioners and researchers. Recommended for academic libraries with social work programs and agencies that serve children and families.

4645. ***Advances in Social Work (Online).*** [ISSN: 2331-4125] s-a. Free. Ed(s): William Barton. Indiana University, School of Social Work, 902 W New York St, Indianapolis, IN 46202; iussw@iupui.edu; http://socialwork.iu.edu/. Refereed. *Aud.:* Ga, Ac.

Advances in Social Work is an online, open-access journal published by the Indiana University School of Social Work. It features original material on social work practice and research, as it addresses issues, challenges, and thought relevant to practitioners and social work educators. Journal topics and discussion encourage the development of innovation in the field, as well as providing a forum for scholarly exchange of research findings and ideas. Recent special issue topics have included global problems and military social work. This journal is an important addition to the online collections of academic libraries that support social work programs and special libraries that serve social services.

4646. ***The British Journal of Social Work.*** Formed by the merger of (1947-1970): *British Journal of Psychiatric Social Work;* (1939-1970): *Social Work.* [ISSN: 0045-3102] 1971. 9x/yr. EUR 1421. Ed(s): Malcolm Golightley, Margaret Halloway. Oxford University Press, Great Clarendon St, Oxford, OX2 6DP, United Kingdom; onlinequeries.uk@oup.com; http://global.oup.com. Illus., adv. Sample. Refereed. Microform: PQC. Reprint: PSC. *Indexed:* A22, ASSIA, BRI, E01, IBSS, SSA. *Bk. rev.:* 7-10, signed. *Aud.:* Ac.

This journal is published by the British Association of Social Workers, and as such, it is the U.K.'s leading social work journal. Covering every aspect of social work, articles include research on various aspects of practice, principles, and theory. Special issues have included death and dying, the political challenges of social work, and practice innovations. The journal's audience includes social work educators, researchers, practitioners, and managers. Issues include signed book reviews. Recommended for academic libraries that support graduate social work programs.

4647. ***Child and Adolescent Social Work Journal.*** Former titles (until 1982): *Family and Child Mental Health Journal;* (until 1980): *Issues in Child Mental Health;* (until vol.5, 1977): *Psychosocial Process.* [ISSN: 0738-0151] 1970. bi-m. EUR 2156 (print & online eds.)). Ed(s): B A Thyer, L S Schelbe. Springer New York LLC, 233 Spring St, New York, NY 10013; customerservice@springer.com; http://www.springer.com. Illus., adv. Sample. Refereed. Reprint: PSC. *Indexed:* A01, A22, ASSIA, Agr, BRI, E01, SSA. *Bk. rev.:* 1-3; signed. *Aud.:* Ga, Ac, Sa.

This journal features research focused on clinical social work practice with children, youth, and families. Articles address problems and current issues in social work as drawn from theory, direct practice, research, and social policy. Examples of recent articles include foster care, juvenile justice, mental health in urban youth, and parenting. Recommended for academic libraries that support social work programs and social services that work with children, youth, and families.

4648. ***Child & Family Social Work.*** [ISSN: 1356-7500] 1996. q. GBP 730. Ed(s): Michelle Lefevre. Wiley-Blackwell Publishing Ltd., The Atrium, Southern Gate, Chichester, PO19 8QG, United Kingdom; cs-journals@wiley.com; http://onlinelibrary.wiley.com/. Adv. Sample. Refereed. Reprint: PSC. *Indexed:* A01, A22, BRI, E01, IBSS, SSA. *Bk. rev.:* 5-8; signed. *Aud.:* Ac, Sa.

Child & Family Social Work publishes original articles by social work practitioners, researchers, policymakers, and administrators. It "is dedicated to advancing the wellbeing and welfare of children and their families throughout the world." It is international in scope; recent articles include orphans in Botswana, adoption in South Africa, and grandparents raising their grandchildren in Australia. The 2011 ISI Journal Citation Reports rank was 14 out of 41 in Social Work and 26 out of 38 in Family Studies. Recommended for academic libraries that support social work programs and other libraries that support social service professionals.

4649. ***Child Welfare: journal of policy, practice and program.*** Formerly (until 1948): *Child Welfare League of America. Bulletin.* [ISSN: 0009-4021] 1921. bi-m. Ed(s): Rachel Adams. Child Welfare League of America, Inc., 2345 Crystal Dr, Ste 250, Arlington, VA 22202; cwla@cwla.org; http://www.cwla.org. Illus., index, adv. Sample. Refereed. Vol. ends: Nov/Dec. Microform: PQC. *Indexed:* A01, A22, Agr, BRI, C42, CJPI, Chicano, ERIC, IBSS, SSA. *Aud.:* Ac, Sa.

Child Welfare is published by the Child Welfare League of America in order to advocate for the welfare of children and youth who are homeless, abused, disabled, or new to the country. Additional topics include traumatic stress, children's rights, residential care, mental health, adoption, protective services and welfare, and parenting, and public policy. One or two issues per volume are thematic. Highly recommended for academic libraries that support social work programs and those that support child welfare professionals.

4650. ***Children & Schools: a journal of social work practice.*** Formerly (until 2000): *Social Work in Education.* [ISSN: 1532-8759] 1978. q. EUR 179. Ed(s): Martell L Teasley. Oxford University Press, 2001 Evans Rd, Cary, NC 27513; orders.us@oup.com; https://academic.oup.com/journals. Illus., index. Vol. ends: Oct. Microform: PQC. Reprint: PSC. *Indexed:* A01, A22, ASSIA, ERIC, SSA. *Aud.:* Ac, Sa.

Children & Schools is published by the National Association of Social Workers. It publishes research articles and commentary that focus on trends in professional school social work and interdisciplinary practice, program evaluation, policy, and planning. Recent topics have included bullying, trauma and violence, multiculturalism, early intervention, needs assessment, and ADHD. A vital "practice-to-practitioner" resource; highly recommended for academic and special libraries that support social work programs and education.

4651. ***Children and Youth Services Review: an international multidisciplinary review of the welfare of young people.*** [ISSN: 0190-7409] 1979. m. EUR 2908. Elsevier Ltd, The Boulevard, Langford Lane, Oxford, OX5 1GB, United Kingdom; customerserviceau@elsevier.com; http://www.elsevier.com. Illus., adv. Sample. Refereed. Microform: PQC. *Indexed:* A01, A22, ASSIA, BRI, SSA. *Bk. rev.:* 0-4, signed. *Aud.:* Ac.

This journal publishes articles that present research and policy discussions that assess social service programs and services for children and youth worldwide. Article topics have included interventions, practice, mental health services, residential placement, case management, and other issues that affect children from early childhood to high school. Book reviews are occasionally included. Recommended for academic libraries that support social work, child psychology, or social service programs.

4652. ***Clinical Social Work Journal.*** [ISSN: 0091-1674] 1973. q. EUR 1488 (print & online eds.)). Ed(s): Carol Tosone. Springer New York LLC, 233 Spring St, New York, NY 10013; customerservice@springer.com; http://www.springer.com. Illus., adv. Sample. Refereed. Vol. ends: Winter. Microform: PQC. Reprint: PSC. *Indexed:* A01, A22, BRI, E01, SSA. *Bk. rev.:* 1-4; signed. *Aud.:* Ac, Sa.

This journal serves as an international forum for the advancement of clinical knowledge and insight of practitioners, educators, researchers, and policymakers. Founded in 1973, journal presents articles relevant to contemporary clinical practice with individuals, couples, families, and groups. Emphasis is placed on innovations in theoretical and practice- and evidence-based clinical research as well as on interdisciplinary approaches. This title features frequent special-topic issues; there are occasional book reviews. Highly recommended for academic libraries that support social work programs and for public and special libraries that serve social service professionals.

4653. ***Critical Social Policy: a journal of theory and practice in social welfare.*** [ISSN: 0261-0183] 1981. q. USD 1060 (print & online eds.)). Sage Publications Ltd., 1 Oliver's Yard, 55 City Rd, London, EC1Y 1SP, United Kingdom; info@sagepub.com; https://www.sagepub.com/. Illus., adv. Sample. Refereed. Reprint: PSC. *Indexed:* A01, A22, E01, IBSS, P61, SSA. *Bk. rev.:* 5-6 signed. *Aud.:* Ac, Sa.

This journal seeks to provide an international forum for advocacy, analysis, and debate on social policy on issues of importance to social welfare. Research is presented from socialist, feminist, anti-racist, and radical perspectives, giving voice to inequalities, injustices, and oppressed individuals and communities. Recent special-theme issues focused on housing and on inequality. Commentaries advocate and provoke debate on social policy issues. Each issue contains signed book reviews. Recommended for academic libraries that support social work, sociology, or political science.

4654. ***Ethics and Social Welfare.*** [ISSN: 1749-6535] 2007. 4x/yr. GBP 428 (print & online eds.)). Ed(s): Derek Clifford, Marian Barnes. Routledge, 4 Park Sq, Milton Park, Abingdon, OX14 4RN, United Kingdom; subscriptions@tandf.co.uk; http://www.tandfonline.com. Adv. Sample. Refereed. Reprint: PSC. *Indexed:* A22, E01, SSA. *Bk. rev.:* Number and length vary. *Aud.:* Ac.

This journal publishes critical and reflective articles concerned with ethical issues in social work and social welfare practice and policy. It focuses on social work practice with individuals, families and groups, social care, youth and community work, and other related professional areas. Contributors include academics, field practitioners, voluntary workers, service users, and others of diverse perspectives. Case studies and a section on ethical issues in practice present problems and dilemmas, as well as reflections on ethics, values, and policy. Recommended for academic libraries that support social work programs.

4655. ***Families in Society: the journal of contemporary social services.*** Former titles (until Jan.1990): *Social Casework;* (until 1950): *Journal of Social Casework;* (until 1946): *The Family.* [ISSN: 1044-3894] 1920. q. USD 358 (print & online eds.)). Sage Publications, Inc., 2455 Teller Rd, Thousand Oaks, CA 91320; info@sagepub.com; http://www.sagepub.com/. Illus., index, adv. Refereed. Vol. ends: Dec. Microform: PQC. *Indexed:* A01, A22, BRI, C37, CBRI, Chicano, SSA. *Bk. rev.:* 2-4; signed. *Aud.:* Ac.

Families in Society was founded in 1920 and is published by the Alliance for Children and Families. It is the oldest and one of the most highly regarded professional journals in North America on social work and social services. Its wide-ranging content appeals to practitioners, educators, and others in the human services. Articles focus on major trends and techniques, research, theory, direct-practice issues, and the delivery and management of services. Book reviews (six to eight) are offered in each issue of the online version only. An essential and standard title for academic libraries with programs in sociology and social work.

Family Process. See Family section.

Family Relations. See Family section.

4656. ***Health & Social Work.*** [ISSN: 0360-7283] 1976. q. EUR 179. Ed(s): Stephen Gorin. Oxford University Press, 2001 Evans Rd, Cary, NC 27513; orders.us@oup.com; https://academic.oup.com/journals. Illus., index, adv. Refereed. Vol. ends: Nov. Microform: PQC. Reprint: PSC. *Indexed:* A01, A22, AgeL, BRI, Chicano, ERIC, IBSS, SSA. *Bk. rev.:* 5-6; signed. *Aud.:* Ga, Ac, Sa.

Published by the National Association of Social Workers Press, this journal covers research, policy, specialized services, quality assurance, and other subjects related to the delivery of health-care service. Health-related topics have included aging, clinical work, oncology, substance abuse, depression, maternal health, and a variety of physical, mental health, and social and cultural issues. Special features include articles on practice, social policy and planning, and legislative issues; and there are occasional book reviews on subjects of interest to professionals in this field. Recommended for academic libraries that support social work, nursing, and social service programs.

4657. ***Human Services Organizations Management, Leadership & Governance.*** Formerly (until 2014): *Administration in Social Work.* [ISSN: 2330-3131] 1977. 5x/yr. GBP 1213 (print & online eds.)). Ed(s): Richard L Edwards. Routledge, 530 Walnut St, Ste 850, Philadelphia, PA 19106; enquiries@tandfonline.com; http://www.tandfonline.com. Illus., adv. Sample. Refereed. Circ: 972 Paid. Vol. ends: Winter. Microform: PQC. Reprint: PSC. *Indexed:* A01, A22, B01, BRI, C42, E01, SSA. *Bk. rev.:* Number and length vary. *Aud.:* Ac.

This journal is the official publication of the National Network of Social Work Managers. It provides articles on theory, practice, and research for human services administrators, managers, and educators, focusing on social service administration and social policy planning. Key issues include program development, employment and professional practices, budgeting and finances, and assessment and quality control. Recent articles have had international origins, and special thematic issues are also published. Recommended for academic libraries with graduate programs in social work, and for social service agencies.

4658. ***International Journal of Child, Youth and Family Studies.*** [ISSN: 1920-7298] 2010. irreg. Free. Ed(s): Sibylle Artz. University of Victoria, School of Child and Youth Care, PO Box 1700, Victoria, BC V8W 2Y2, Canada. Refereed. *Aud.:* Ga, Ac, Sa.

This is an open-access, interdisciplinary journal published by the School of Child and Youth Care at the University of Victoria, British Columbia. Articles include practice issues and research regarding services for children, youth, families, and their communities. Although much of the focus is on Canada, the scope includes other countries as well. Academic libraries that support sociology and social work will find this a useful addition to their electronic holdings.

4659. ***International Social Work.*** Formerly (until 1958): *Social Welfare in South-East-Asia.* [ISSN: 0020-8728] 1959. bi-m. USD 2032 (print & online eds.)). Ed(s): Vasilios Ioakimidis, Lena Dominelli. Sage Publications Ltd., 1 Oliver's Yard, 55 City Rd, London, EC1Y 1SP, United Kingdom; info@sagepub.com; https://www.sagepub.com/. Illus., index. Sample. Refereed. Vol. ends: Oct. Microform: PQC. Reprint: PSC. *Indexed:* A01, A22, BRI, E01, IBSS, SSA. *Bk. rev.:* 2-4; signed. *Aud.:* Ac, Sa.

This journal is published in association with the International Association of Schools of Social Work, the International Counsel on Social Welfare, and the International Federation of Social Workers. Scholarly research in the journal focuses on issues regarding the delivery of services, the functions of social work professionals, and the education of social workers. Emphasis is placed on comparative analysis and cross-national research. Recent theme issues have included religion and spirituality, child rights in Africa, and social work in Latin America. Recommended for academic libraries that support social work programs and those that serve social service programs.

4660. *Journal of Family Social Work.* Formerly (until 1995): *Journal of Social Work and Human Sexuality.* [ISSN: 1052-2158] 1981. 5x/yr. GBP 462 (print & online eds.)). Ed(s): Judith Siegel. Routledge, 530 Walnut St, Ste 850, Philadelphia, PA 19106; enquiries@tandfonline.com; http://www.tandfonline.com. Adv. Sample. Refereed. Circ: 408 Paid. Microform: PQC. Reprint: PSC. *Indexed:* A01, A22, ASSIA, E01, ERIC, SSA. *Bk. rev.:* Number and length vary. *Aud.:* Ac, Sa.

This journal disseminates information related to families through research articles and conceptual, practical, and creative works devoted to practice subjects and ecosystemic theory. The intent is to advance practitioners' abilities to integrate research, policy, theory, and wisdom into their service to families. Approaches include social work, family therapy and studies, sociology, health and mental health, and child welfare. Highly recommended for academic libraries that support social work programs and for public and special libraries that serve social service professionals.

Journal of Gerontological Social Work. See Geriatrics and Gerontological Studies section.

4661. *Journal of Immigrant & Refugee Studies.* Formerly (until 2006): *Journal of Immigrant & Refugee Services.* [ISSN: 1556-2948] 2002. q. GBP 665 (print & online eds.)). Ed(s): Anna Triandafyllidou. Routledge, 530 Walnut St, Ste 850, Philadelphia, PA 19106; enquiries@tandfonline.com; http://www.tandfonline.com. Adv. Refereed. Circ: 53 Paid. Reprint: PSC. *Indexed:* A01, A22, C45, E01, IBSS, SSA. *Bk. rev.:* Number and length vary. *Aud.:* Ac.

This journal focuses on the effects of worldwide migration. It is international and interdisciplinary in scope, and issues include immigration policy, the health and mental health of immigrants, sociological and economic implications, business and service programs and implications, and other related topics. Issues have included the effects of the trauma of war, hate crimes, human trafficking, identity, gender roles, assimilation, and many other challenges faced by displaced people. Recommended for academic libraries that support programs in the social sciences.

4662. *Journal of International and Comparative Social Policy.* Former titles (until 2013): *Journal of Comparative Social Welfare;* (until 2006): *New Global Development;* (until 1995): *Journal of International and Comparative Social Welfare.* [ISSN: 2169-9763] 1984. 3x/yr. GBP 395 (print & online eds.)). Ed(s): Dr. Kevin Farnsworth, Dr. Zoe Irving. Routledge, 4 Park Sq, Milton Park, Abingdon, OX14 4RN, United Kingdom; subscriptions@tandf.co.uk; http://www.tandfonline.com. Adv. Sample. Refereed. Reprint: PSC. *Indexed:* A22, E01, IBSS, P61, SSA. *Bk. rev.:* Number and length vary. *Aud.:* Ac.

As implied by the title, the articles in this journal are comparative and/or international in scope and focus on national, regional, or global social policies. Themes included are country case studies, policy processes, welfare outcomes, and the provision of services. Issues have included the financial crisis in Europe, income inequality, social work practice, adoption, human trafficking, and aging and the elderly. Recommended for academic libraries that support graduate programs in social work, sociology, political science, international studies, and public administration.

Journal of Marital and Family Therapy. See Family section.

4663. *Journal of Social Service Research.* [ISSN: 0148-8376] 1977. 5x/yr. GBP 1234 (print & online eds.)). Ed(s): Sophia F Dziegielewski, Barbara Maisevich. Routledge, 530 Walnut St, Ste 850, Philadelphia, PA 19106; enquiries@tandfonline.com; http://www.tandfonline.com. Illus., adv. Sample. Refereed. Circ: 435 Paid. Microform: PQC. Reprint: PSC. *Indexed:* A01, A22, ASSIA, E01, SSA. *Aud.:* Ac.

The focus of this journal is outcomes-based empirical research and practice, and applications to the design, delivery, and management of social services. Different types of methodologies and funded and non-funded research are featured. Contributors are from a variety national and international social service areas, and include researchers, practitioners, policymakers, and administrators. Recommended for academic libraries that support programs in social work and social services.

4664. *Journal of Social Work.* [ISSN: 1468-0173] 2001. bi-m. USD 1499 (print & online eds.)). Ed(s): Steven M Shardlow. Sage Publications Ltd., 1 Oliver's Yard, 55 City Rd, London, EC1Y 1SP, United Kingdom; info@sagepub.com; https://www.sagepub.com/. Sample. Refereed. Reprint: PSC. *Indexed:* A01, A22, E01, IBSS, SSA. *Bk. rev.:* 6-8; signed. *Aud.:* Ac.

The *Journal of Social Work* is an international journal that presents and debates key research and ideas in social work. Empirical and theoretical articles analyze and advance theoretical understanding, shape policy, and inform practice. The scope is international and topics reflect the diversity of the social work profession. In addition to longer research articles, the "Critical Forum" section includes shorter commentaries, reports of research in progress, and analysis of current trends. Extensive, signed book reviews are included in each issue. ISI Journal Citation Reports ranked it 11 out of 41 in Social Work. Recommended for academic libraries that support programs in social work.

4665. *Journal of Social Work Practice in the Addictions.* [ISSN: 1533-256X] 2001. q. GBP 432 (print & online eds.)). Ed(s): Shulamith Lala Ashenberg Straussner. Routledge, 530 Walnut St, Ste 850, Philadelphia, PA 19106; enquiries@tandfonline.com; http://www.tandfonline.com. Adv. Sample. Refereed. Reprint: PSC. *Indexed:* A01, A22, E01, N13, SSA. *Bk. rev.:* Number and length vary. *Aud.:* Ga, Ac, Sa.

This is a refereed journal intended to inform social work practitioners about the latest developments in the field of addictions. Articles focus on innovative individual, family, and group work, and community practice in the treatment and prevention of substance abuse and other addictions in diverse populations and ages. Journal coverage includes research findings, health care, social policies, and program administration that affects social work practice in addictions. Features include interviews with experts, books reviews, commentaries, and the occasional special-theme issue. Recommended for academic libraries that support graduate social work programs, and public or special libraries that support social services that work with addiction issues.

4666. *Journal of Sociology and Social Welfare.* [ISSN: 0191-5096] 1973. q. USD 86 (print & online eds.) Individuals, USD 52 (print & online eds.)). Ed(s): Gary Mathews, Robert D Leighninger. Western Michigan University, School of Social Work, 1903 W Michigan Ave, Kalamazoo, MI 49008; http://www.wmich.edu. Illus., index. Refereed. Vol. ends: Dec. Microform: PQC. *Indexed:* A22, BRI, C42, SSA. *Bk. rev.:* 5-7; signed. *Aud.:* Ac, Sa.

This online journal is sponsored and hosted by the School of Social Work, Western Michigan University. Its purpose is the promotion of social welfare through the application of social science, methodology, and technology to problems involving social policy, politics, and social services. It contains research articles on topics such as social change, gender, race, migration, social inequality, homelessness, social welfare history, cultural diversity, and health and mental health. International issues are also discussed. Each issue contains signed book reviews. One issue per year is thematic; the topic of the most recent was race. Recommended for academic libraries that support social work and sociology programs.

4667. *Professional Social Work.* [ISSN: 1352-3112] 1994. m. GBP 39.50 domestic (Free to members). Ed(s): Joseph Devo. British Association of Social Workers, 16 Kent St, Birmingham, B5 6RD, United Kingdom; publishing@basw.co.uk; http://www.basw.co.uk. Adv. Circ: 10000 Paid. *Bk. rev.:* Number and length vary. *Aud.:* Ga, Ac.

This magazine for social work practitioners is published by the British Association of Social Workers. It contains news and analysis, feature articles, opinions and letters, brief book reviews, and reports on professional issues in countries of the U.K. The current issue is available to BASW members; past issues are free to the public. Academic or public libraries used by social work programs or social workers may wish to link to this magazine.

4668. ***Psychoanalytic Social Work.*** Former titles (until 1999): *Journal of Analytic Social Work;* (until 1992): *Journal of Independent Social Work.* [ISSN: 1522-8878] 1987. s-a. GBP 686 (print & online eds.)). Ed(s): Jerrold R Brandell. Routledge, 530 Walnut St, Ste 850, Philadelphia, PA 19106; enquiries@tandfonline.com; http://www.tandfonline.com. Illus., adv. Sample. Refereed. Circ: 164 Paid. Vol. ends: Winter. Reprint: PSC. *Indexed:* A01, A22, E01, SSA. *Bk. rev.:* 2-4; signed. *Aud.:* Ac, Sa.

This journal focuses exclusively on the important clinical themes and dilemmas that occur in psychoanalytic social work. It provides research articles relevant to practice with individual clients, including case studies; approaches to special populations, minorities, and the underserved; specialized and innovative techniques and methods in a clinical setting; and clinical approaches to psychoanalytic issues. This title provides clinical social workers with contemporary perspectives, theories, clinical methods, and techniques to enhance knowledge of psychoanalytic practice. Recommended for academic libraries that support graduate social work programs, and for special libraries that serve social work professionals.

4669. ***Qualitative Social Work: research and practice.*** [ISSN: 1473-3250] 2002. bi-m. USD 1473 (print & online eds.)). Ed(s): Karen M Staller, Karen Broadhurst. Sage Publications Ltd., 1 Oliver's Yard, 55 City Rd, London, EC1Y 1SP, United Kingdom; info@sagepub.com; https://www.sagepub.com/. Sample. Refereed. Reprint: PSC. *Indexed:* A01, A22, E01, SSA. *Bk. rev.:* 1-2; signed. *Aud.:* Ac.

This journal contains articles that report on qualitative research and evaluation and qualitative approaches to social work practice. It promotes dialogue on the role of critical perspectives within social work, reflective inquiry and practice, emerging applications for research within the field, and the potential of social constructionist and narrative approaches to research and practice. In addition to full-length research articles, regular and special features of the journal include responses to past articles and commentaries on current research and practice; accounts and reflections on the methodology and practice of qualitative social work; a "New Voices" section from practitioners and new researchers; and signed book reviews. Recommended for academic libraries that support social work programs.

4670. ***Research on Social Work Practice.*** [ISSN: 1049-7315] 1990. 7x/yr. USD 1683 (print & online eds.)). Ed(s): Bruce A Thyer. Sage Publications, Inc., 2455 Teller Rd, Thousand Oaks, CA 91320; info@sagepub.com; http://www.sagepub.com. Illus., index. Sample. Refereed. Vol. ends: Nov. Reprint: PSC. *Indexed:* A01, A22, ASSIA, BRI, E01, ERIC, SSA. *Bk. rev.:* 2-4, signed. *Aud.:* Ac.

This journal publishes empirical research reporting on assessment methods and evidence-based outcomes of social work practice. Interventions may include behavior analysis and therapy, psychotherapy or counseling, case management, education, supervision, practice with couples, families or small group, organizational management, community practice, and policy evaluation. Features include special issues or sections, systematic reviews, a section on new methods of assessment, and book reviews. Recommended for academic libraries that support social work programs.

4671. ***Social Development Issues.*** Supersedes (in 1977): *Iowa Journal of Social Work.* [ISSN: 0147-1473] 1968. 3x/yr. USD 105 (print & online eds.)). Ed(s): Vijayan Pillai. David Follmer Group, 5758 S Blackstone Ave, Chicago, IL 60637; info@thedavidfollmergroup.com; https://thedavidfollmergroup.com/. Refereed. *Indexed:* A22, BRI, IBSS, SSA. *Bk. rev.:* Number and length vary. *Aud.:* Ac.

This journal is sponsored by the International Consortium for Social Development. It serves as an interdisciplinary, scholarly forum to promote issues that affect social justice and advancement of social, cultural, political, and economic theories, policy, and practice within a global context. Topics in recent issues have included women's reproductive health, sustainable development, globalization, and relief services for refugees. Each issue contains book reviews. Recommended for academic libraries that support graduate programs in sociology, social work, political science, and international studies.

4672. ***Social Service Review.*** [ISSN: 0037-7961] 1927. q. USD 347. Ed(s): Mark E Courtney. University of Chicago Press, 1427 E 60th St, Chicago, IL 60637; subscriptions@press.uchicago.edu; http://www.journals.uchicago.edu. Illus., index, adv. Sample. Refereed. Vol. ends: Dec. Reprint: PSC. *Indexed:* A01, A22, ASSIA, B01, BRI, CBRI, Chicano, EconLit, IBSS, P61, SSA. *Bk. rev.:* 5-7; signed. *Aud.:* Ga, Ac.

Since 1927, this journal has published original research that examines and evaluates social welfare policy, organization, theory, and practice from multicultural and multidisciplinary perspectives. Emphasis is placed on the presentation of long-range solutions to critical problems. Points of view from scholars and practitioners in various disciplines are represented, including social service, social policy, sociology, public administration, history, economics, and political science. Each issue includes critical books reviews. Essential title for academic, public, and special libraries that serve social service professionals.

4673. ***Social Work.*** Former titles (until 1956): *Social Work Journal;* (until 1948): *The Compass.* [ISSN: 0037-8046] 1920. q. EUR 182. Ed(s): Tricia B Bent-Goodley. Oxford University Press, 2001 Evans Rd, Cary, NC 27513; orders.us@oup.com; https://academic.oup.com/journals. Illus., index, adv. Refereed. Vol. ends: Nov. Microform: PQC. Reprint: PSC. *Indexed:* A01, A22, ASSIA, AgeL, BRI, CBRI, CJPI, Chicano, ERIC, MASUSE, SSA. *Bk. rev.:* 1-2; signed. *Aud.:* Ac, Sa.

As the official journal of the National Association of Social Workers, *Social Work* is considered the premier journal of the social work profession. It is dedicated to improving practice and advancing knowledge in the profession and in social welfare, and thus it is widely read by practitioners, social work educators, and students. Articles center on new insights into established practices, as well as trends and techniques within the profession, and examine social problems with an emphasis on social policy and a solution to human problems. An essential, must-have title for academic libraries and others that support social work, nursing, and social services professionals.

4674. ***Social Work and Society.*** [ISSN: 1613-8953] 2003. 2x/yr. Free. Ed(s): Fabian Kessl. Di P P - N R W, Juelicher Str 6, Cologne, 50674, Germany; dipp@hbz-nrw.de; http://www.dipp.nrw.de. Refereed. *Indexed:* SSA. *Bk. rev.:* Number and length vary. *Aud.:* Ga, Ac.

Sponsored by the Center for Social Work and Social Policy, this journal is an early pioneer in open-access publishing. This is an international journal that serves as a forum for innovative theories and views about the interrelationships of social work, social policy, government, and the economy. Features include special issues, research articles, essays and debates, historical portraits, and book reviews. Academic libraries that serve social work programs will want to add this to their electronic holdings.

4675. ***Social Work Education: the international journal.*** Incorporates (1981-1999): *Issues in Social Work Education.* [ISSN: 0261-5479] 1981. 8x/yr. GBP 1501 (print & online eds.)). Ed(s): Hugh McLaughlin. Routledge, 4 Park Sq, Milton Park, Abingdon, OX14 4RN, United Kingdom; subscriptions@tandf.co.uk; http://www.tandfonline.com. Adv. Sample. Refereed. Reprint: PSC. *Indexed:* A01, A22, ASSIA, E01, SSA. *Bk. rev.:* Number and length vary. *Aud.:* Ac.

This journal publishes critical and reflective articles concerned with the theory and practice of social work education. Through international coverage and debate, the journal serves as a forum for new and emerging ideas and proposals on all aspects of social work education, training, development, and field work. Themes of recent special issues have included field education and disability studies. Book reviews are also included. An essential title for academic libraries that support social work programs.

4676. *Social Work Research.* Supersedes in part (in 1994): *Social Work Research and Abstracts;* Which was formerly (until 1977): *Abstracts for Social Workers.* [ISSN: 1070-5309] 1977. q. EUR 179. Ed(s): James Herbert Williams. Oxford University Press, 2001 Evans Rd, Cary, NC 27513; orders.us@oup.com; https://academic.oup.com/journals. Illus., index, adv. Refereed. Vol. ends: Dec. Microform: PQC. Reprint: PSC. *Indexed:* A01, A22, ASSIA, ERIC, SSA. *Aud.:* Ac, Sa.

This journal is published on behalf of the National Association of Social Workers. It contains research articles that contribute to and inform social work practice, including review and theoretical articles, evaluation studies, and diverse research pertaining to social work issues and problems. Recent issues have included case management, mental health, poverty, children and families, and challenges to recent immigrants. An essential title for academic libraries that support social work programs and for libraries that serve social work professionals.

4677. *Social Work Today.* [ISSN: 1540-420X] 2001. bi-m. USD 14.99. Ed(s): Marianne Mallon. Great Valley Publishing Co., Inc., 3801 Schuylkill Rd, Spring City, PA 19475; Sales@gvpub.com; http://www.gvpub.com. Adv. Sample. *Bk. rev.:* Number and length vary. *Aud.:* Ga, Sa.

Social Work Today is a professional development vehicle for social workers to keep abreast of their field. Topics covered are mental health, addictions, children and families, aging, professional practice, and ethics. Recent articles have focused on the needs of returning veterans, child protection work, and legalized gambling. Features include research reviews, government briefs, book and media reviews, and a jobs bank. Print and electronic access are by subscription; however, most features are freely available online. Recommended for libraries that support social work practitioners.

4678. *Social Work with Groups: a journal of community and clinical practice.* [ISSN: 0160-9513] 1978. q. GBP 973 (print & online eds.)). Ed(s): Andrew Malekoff. Routledge, 530 Walnut St, Ste 850, Philadelphia, PA 19106; enquiries@tandfonline.com; http://www.tandfonline.com. Illus., adv. Sample. Refereed. Microform: PQC. Reprint: PSC. *Indexed:* A01, A22, ASSIA, BRI, E01, SSA. *Bk. rev.:* Number & length vary. *Aud.:* Ac, Sa.

This journal is unique in that it focuses on practice involving small groups and social work professionals in varied roles and settings. Research articles include issues of group work in clinical and community practice; mental health, and rehabilitative and general social service agencies; crisis, youth, health care, and private practice; and all manner of community and human services departments. Recommended for social services agencies and libraries that support social work practitioners.

4679. *Society for Social Work and Research. Journal.* [ISSN: 2334-2315] 2009. q. USD 275. University of Chicago Press, 1427 E 60th St, Chicago, IL 60637; custserv@press.uchicago.edu; http://www.press.uchicago.edu. Refereed. *Aud.:* Ac.

This peer-reviewed, open-access journal is the official publication of the Society for Social Work Research, an organization founded in 1994 to advance social work research. It publishes research reports, systematic reviews, and methodological studies on social problems, programs, and policies. Special emphasis is placed on research examining the effectiveness of social and health services. The journal is intended for practitioners, administrators, educators, and policy makers interested in social and health problems. A worthwhile addition to the electronic holdings in academic, research, and special libraries that support social work and social services programs, education, and practice.

Suicide and Life-Threatening Behavior. See Death and Dying section.

■ SPIRITUALITY AND WELL-BEING

Deborah Abston; deborah.abston@asu.edu

Introduction

The publications in the Spirituality and Well Being section cover well-being from the viewpoint of modern, non-religious spirituality and non-traditional religions.

The instruction provided for various aspects and concepts of non-religious spirituality, spiritual development, and self-actualization may include: physical activity (various forms of exercise) and mental activity (mindfulness and meditation), which assist with physical and emotional well-being.

Also included are publications that may refer to alternative religious practices that include shamanic, Wiccan, pantheistic, and Modern Paganism. Instruction on a variety of practices include: Tarot card reading, rune readings, channeling, and work with crystal energy.

Basic Periodicals

Kindred Spirit: Sharing Spiritual Wisdom for Over 25 Years; Light of Consciousness: Journal of Spiritual Awakening; Parabola: Where Spiritual Traditions Meet; Pilgrimage; Sedona Journal of Emergence; Spirituality & Health: The Soul and Body Connection; Witches & Pagans.

Basic Abstracts and Indexes

Academic Search Premier, Research Library (ProQuest), Reader's Guide to Periodical Literature.

4680. *Kindred Spirit.* [ISSN: 0955-7067] 1987. bi-m. GBP 23 domestic; GBP 29 in North America & Europe; GBP 38 elsewhere. Ed(s): Claire Gilman. Kindred Spirit Magazine, 19 Cecil Court, London, WC2N 4EZ, United Kingdom; ads.kindred@gmail.com; http://www.kindredspirit.co.uk. Adv. *Aud.:* Ga.

Produced in the United Kingdom, *Kindred Spirit* appeals to readers interested in using spirituality to create positive change on the individual, community, and global levels. Substantive articles within each issue cover a range of diverse subjects such as spiritual growth, personal development, mental health, complementary therapies, travel, native shamanism, I Ching, and rune reading, as well as environmental and medical approaches like cryotherapy, crystal energies, and metamorphic technique. Websites related to topics or authors are included with most articles; these expand the content for readers and help to bridge the geographical gap for United States and Canadian subscribers. Regular features include letters, news briefs, astrology, travel, yoga, cosmic gardening, and arts and entertainment reviews. Recommended for public libraries where there is interest in alternative spirituality and health practices. Available in electronic format. URL: www.kindredspirit.co.uk/

4681. *Light of Consciousness: journal of spiritual awakening.* Formerly (until vol.1, no.1, 1988): *Truth Consciousness Journal.* [ISSN: 1040-7448] 1988. q. USD 17.99 domestic; USD 27.99 Canada; USD 32.99 elsewhere. Ed(s): Sita Stuhlmiller. Truth Consciousness at Desert Ashram, 3403 W Sweetwater Dr, Tucson, AZ 85745-9301; ads@light-of-consciousness.org; http://truthconsciousness.org/. Illus., adv. *Bk. rev.:* Number and length vary. *Aud.:* Ga, Sa.

Published quarterly by the nonprofit organization Truth Consciousness, *Light of Consciousness* highlights the unifying principles that underlie divergent faiths and religious practices and explores the intersection of science and spirituality. Issues examine the transformative power of meditation and contain both philosophical theory and practical instruction in myriad types of meditation. Regular features include a "Satsang" (spiritual discourse) written by Swami Amar Jyoti, the focus of which reflects each issue's theme and content; "Insight," an introduction written by editor Sita Stuhlmiller; and book reviews. Visually striking cover photography as well as abundant photographs and illustrations purposefully enhance the text. Inspirational articles explore ways to deepen spirituality and attain peace of mind, use meditation to retrain the brain for greater happiness, and incorporate mindfulness and the power of prayer in daily life. Experienced practitioners and scholars contribute essays that explore the practice of self-reflection, meditative self-discovery, and spiritual-centeredness. In 2010, the print edition became a greener publication by using 30 percent post-consumer recycled paper, and a digital online edition is available. Recommended for public, academic, and subject-related special libraries or where subject interest exists. URL: http://light-of-consciousness.org/

4682. ***Parabola.*** [ISSN: 0362-1596] 1976. q. USD 39.95; USD 64.95 combined subscription print & online eds. Ed(s): Jeff Zaleski, Dale Fuller. Society for the Study of Myth and Tradition, 20 West 20th St, 2nd Fl, New York, NY 10011; info@parabola.org; http://www.parabola.org. Illus., index, adv. Sample. Circ: 41000 Paid. Vol. ends: Winter. Microform: PQC. *Indexed:* A22, AmHI, BRI, CBRI, MLA-IB, R&TA. *Bk. rev.:* Varies, 600-1,200 words. *Aud.:* Ga, Ac, Sa.

Published by the Society for the Study of Myth and Tradition, *Parabola* emphasizes common themes in world religions and spiritual traditions, and includes scholarly articles that explore varied spiritual traditions. Thematic issues explore the role of spirit in the larger world. *Parabola* regularly includes articles written by well-known literary or historical figures such as Julia Alvarez or James Joyce. Some issues incorporate first-person reflections, such as instructions from a Buddhist monk on how to cultivate love and compassion. Illustrations are placed artfully, enriching the text and drawing in the reader. Many issues include theme-related stories or parables from world traditions. Advertisements are few and consigned to sections at the end of the issue. *Parabola* is also available as an e-journal from its website. It is recommended for its eclectic and unbiased approach to religious traditions and its coverage of mythology and symbolism. It is for general academic libraries, special libraries with related collections, and public libraries where there is subject interest. Available in electronic format. URL: www.parabola.org

4683. ***Pilgrimage.*** [ISSN: 0361-0802] 1972. 3x/yr. USD 44 (Individuals, USD 22). Ed(s): Juan Morales. Pilgrimage Press, Inc., Colorado State University-Pueblo, Department of English and Foreign Languages, Pueblo, CO 81001; info@pilgrimagepress.org; http://www.pilgrimagepress.org. Microform: PQC. *Indexed:* A22. *Aud.:* Ga, Ac, Sa.

A small publication living the big questions, *Pilgrimage Magazine: Story, Witness, Spirit, Place* is a literary magazine that features the work of writers and artists whose work explores various spiritual paths. Issues, published three times a year in Colorado, emphasize themes of place, spirit, peace, and justice, in and beyond the Greater Southwest. Articles, essays, poems, and artwork reflect an eclectic community of readers, writers, artists, and naturalists. The magazine's layout, clear typography, undecorated page margins, and lack of advertisements allow the reader to absorb the contents without distraction. The black-and-white publication is physically sized for the hand, while the poetry, essays, and autobiographical stories within each issue aim "to illuminate the world's great wisdom traditions," and offer to transport the reader into new spiritual insights. While contributing authors are primarily located in the Southwest United States, the publication explores universal themes. This title is highly recommended for both its literary quality and spiritual centeredness across religious backgrounds, to academic, public, and special libraries where there is subject interest. URL: www.pilgrimagepress.org/

4684. ***Sedona Journal of Emergence.*** Formerly (until 199?): *Emergence (Sedona).* [ISSN: 1530-3365] 1989. m. USD 43 domestic; USD 83 Canada; USD 154 elsewhere. Ed(s): Melody O'Ryin Swanson. Light Technology Publishing, PO Box 3870, Flagstaff, AZ 86003; publishing@lighttechnology.net; http://www.lighttechnology.com/. *Bk. rev.:* Number and length vary. *Aud.:* Ga.

Published by Light Technology Publishing, *Sedona* seeks to "provide a forum for those who wish to speak to us from other dimensions and realities." Writings discuss topics such as fifth-dimensional awareness, alchemy, planetary interventions, auric fields, and biorelativity. Regular features include "Channeling," "Predictions," "Tools for Conscious Living," "Inspired Guidance," and "Features," which vary in topic according to each issue's theme. Text is primarily black and white, with photographs of authors and minimal illustration. Advertising is mainly relegated to an end section, and an advertiser index is included. The magazine covers are colorful and imaginative. Readership is limited by the special nature of the magazine's content, but it is appropriate for public libraries where there is interest. Available in electronic format. URL: http://sedonajournal.com

4685. ***Spirituality & Health: the soul body connection.*** [ISSN: 1520-5444] 1998. bi-m. USD 24.95 domestic; USD 36.95 Canada; USD 154 elsewhere. Ed(s): Stephen Kiesling. Spirituality & Health Media, 123 W Front St, Traverse City, MI 49684; editors@spiritualityhealth.com. Adv. *Indexed:* BRI, C42. *Bk. rev.:* Number and length vary. *Aud.:* Ga.

Published bimonthly, *Spirituality & Health* examines the connection between spirituality and personal well-being in its broadest sense. Articles focus on various aspects of spiritual and physical well-being, including Eastern philosophy, meditation, and mainstream religion; nutrition, wellness, yoga, and holistic medicine; creativity, the inner life, social justice, and issues of conscience; and public health, the human body, and the environment. Feature essays often highlight the experience or perspective of a celebrity, such as Susan Sarandon; they also provide practical resources for individual exploration and practice. Focusing on integrating spirituality with everyday life, articles may examine aspects of Buddhism, Christianity, Zen, or other belief systems. Brief articles focus on personal spiritual perspectives, practical life issues, and environmental concerns such as yogic breathing, chakras, allergies, and native plant gardening. Letters of advice columns and news items similarly deal with topics of health and wellness, emphasizing holistic living and spiritual commonality. Numerous thoughtful reviews of books, music, and film are included in each issue. Use of color, paragraph arrangement, and plentiful illustrations give the magazine an enticing popular appeal. Recommended for public libraries, special libraries, and where there is interest. Available in electronic format. URL: http://spiritualityhealth.com/

4686. ***Witches & Pagans.*** Formed by the merger of (2002-2009): *NewWitch;* (1997-2009): *PanGaia;* Which was formerly (until 1997): *The Green Man.* [ISSN: 2153-0467] 2009. q. USD 24 domestic; USD 36 Canada; USD 41 elsewhere. Ed(s): Anne Newkirk Niven. B B I Media, Inc., PO Box 687, Forest Grove, OR 97116; editor2@bbimedia.com; http://www.bbimedia.com. Illus., adv. *Bk. rev.:* Number and length vary. *Aud.:* Ga, Ac, Sa.

Witches and Pagans features and is written by Witches, Wiccans, neo-Pagans, and other Earth-based, ethnic, pre-Christian, shamanic, and magical practitioners. Thematic issues contain substantial content in various literary forms, including fiction, poetry, and experiential writings. Issues regularly feature practical advice, referenced nonfiction, and interviews with practitioners. Artwork enhances the text while advertisements are relegated to pages with shorter articles. Letters, book reviews, and regular columns complete the magazine, which is recommended for public, academic, or special libraries where there is an interest in alternative spirituality. Available in electronic format. URL: www.witchesandpagans.com/

■ SPORTS

General/Extreme Sports/Physical Education, Coaching, and Sports Sciences/Specific Sports

See also Boats and Boating; Environment and Conservation; Fishing; Hiking, Climbing, and Outdoor Recreation; and Hunting and Guns sections.

Betsy Park, Assistant to the Dean, The University of Memphis Libraries, 126 Ned R. McWherter Library, Memphis, TN 38152; ehpark@memphis.edu

Introduction

The President's Council on Fitness, Sports & Nutrition urges us to be physically active. Sports franchises continue to be big business. Universities offer programs that focus on research and the fundamentals of health, exercise, leisure, physical activity, nutrition, and sport. Sports medicine is a medical specialty. Journals and magazines play an important role as they strive to keep us informed and engaged.

Ulrich's Serials Directory lists thousands of serial entries for sports, challenging us to choose specific titles. With dwindling budgets, selectors must carefully examine and justify each purchase to maximize the value and use of each title. In an effort to aid in the decision-making process, I have reviewed several categories of sports magazines: general; extreme; specific sports; and physical education, coaching, and sports sciences.

Basic Periodicals

GENERAL. All levels: *ESPN The Magazine, Sports Illustrated.*

PHYSICAL EDUCATION, COACHING, AND SPORTS SCIENCES. Ems: *Strategies;* Hs: *Coach and Athletic Director; Journal of Physical Education, Recreation and Dance;* Ac: *American Journal of Sports Medicine, British Journal of Sports Medicine, Journal of Teaching in Physical Education, Quest* (Champaign), *Research Quarterly for Exercise and Sport.*

SPECIFIC SPORTS. All levels: *Baseball America, Bicycling, Golf Magazine, The Hockey News, International Figure Skating, Runner's World, Ski, Soccer America, Tennis, VolleyballUSA.*

Basic Abstracts and Indexes

Academic Search Complete, Physical Education Index, SPORTDiscus with Full Text.

General

4687. *Aethlon: the journal of sport literature.* Formerly (until 1988): *Arete.* [ISSN: 1048-3756] 1983. s-a. Free to members. Ed(s): Mark Baumgartner. Sports Literature Association, East Tennessee State University, PO Box 70270, Johnson City, TN 37614; http://www.uta.edu/english/sla/. Illus. Refereed. *Indexed:* AmHI, BRI, CBRI, MLA-IB, SD. *Bk. rev.:* 20, 500 to 2,000 words. *Aud.:* Ac.

Since the 1980s, *Aethlon: The Journal of Sport Literature,* which is "designed to celebrate the marriage of serious, interpretive literature with the world of play, games, and sport," has been published by the Sport Literature Association at East Tennessee State University. It includes critical articles, poetry, fiction, nonfiction, drama, and book reviews, plus reviews and commentary on drama and films. University professors, novelists, short story writers, poets, and dramatists contribute both serious and humorous entries. A particularly suitable purchase for academic libraries, although public libraries may also want to consider it.

4688. *E S P N The Magazine.* [ISSN: 1097-1998] 1998. bi-w. USD 29.95. E S P N The Magazine, Inc., 19 E 34th St, New York, NY 10016. Illus., adv. *Indexed:* SD. *Aud.:* Hs, Ga, Ac.

Published since 1998, *ESPN, the Magazine* is an oversized (12" x 10"), showy, general-interest sports tabloid, published in print and online. Each biweekly issue contains numerous photographs and advertisements. Regular features include double-page spreads of sporting events, short articles of current interest, and profiles of athletes. Since 2009, the magazine has published a "Body Issue," possibly in competition with the "Swimsuit Issue" of another sports magazine. The writing style is informal, sometimes humorous, and will appeal to an 18-to-40-year-old male audience. Sports enthusiasts at academic and public libraries will enjoy this publication.

4689. *The International Journal of the History of Sport.* Incorporates (1999-2003): *The European Sports History Review;* Which was formerly (until 1987): *British Journal of Sports History.* [ISSN: 0952-3367] 1984. 18x/yr. GBP 2130 (print & online eds.)). Ed(s): Rob Hess. Routledge, 4 Park Sq, Milton Park, Abingdon, OX14 4RN, United Kingdom; subscriptions@tandf.co.uk; http://www.tandfonline.com. Illus., index, adv. Sample. Refereed. Microform: PQC. Reprint: PSC. *Indexed:* A22, AmHI, BRI, C45, E01, IBSS, SD. *Bk. rev.:* 15-20, 800 words. *Aud.:* Ac.

As an international refereed journal providing global coverage of the history of sport, *The International Journal of the History of Sport* will be of interest to anthropologists, sociologists, and historians, among others. Each of the 18 annual issues contains 200 or more pages with anywhere from eight to 20 articles. Most issues are theme-based and the journal regularly offers regionally focused issues, including on the Americas, Africa, Asia, Australasia and the Pacific, Europe, and (since 2012) the Middle East. As the title of this peer-reviewed journal implies, articles are written by an international, multidisciplinary group of scholars. Most appropriate for academic libraries.

4690. *Sports Illustrated.* [ISSN: 0038-822X] 1954. w. Sports Illustrated Group, 135 W 50th St, 4th Fl, New York, NY 10020; http://sportsillustrated.cnn.com/. Illus., index, adv. Microform: PQC. *Indexed:* A01, A22, BRI, C37, CBRI, MASUSE, MLA-IB, SD. *Aud.:* Ems, Hs, Ga, Ac.

As the most popular and influential of the general sports magazines, *Sports Illustrated,* an award-winning publication, covers all the popular sports-basketball, baseball, football, golf, racing, wrestling, and others. It includes articles about players, celebrities, teams, sports, and society. Issues are filled with beautiful photography and well-written articles. Each 70- to 80-page issue contains letters to the editor, one or two longer features, shorter articles, analysis, commentary and predictions, and insights; and each issue concludes with a lengthy item known as the "bonus piece." The annual swimsuit issue is legendary. The digitized archives of the magazine's complete collection from 1954 to date may be found at the SIVault (http://sportsillustrated.cnn.com/vault/cover/home/index.htm). A mobile version for tablets, smartphones, and online is currently available. Recommended for public, high school, and academic libraries.

Sports Illustrated for Kids. See Children section.

Extreme Sports

4691. *Hang Gliding and Paragliding.* Formerly (until 2007): *U S H P A. Aero;* (until 200?): *Hang Gliding & Paragliding;* Which was formed by the Merger of (1970-2003): *Hang Gliding;* (19??-2003): *Paragliding.* [ISSN: 1936-2552] 2003. m. Free to members; USD 6.95 newsstand/cover. Ed(s): Nick Greece. U.S. Hang Gliding Association, Inc., PO Box 1330, Colorado Springs, CO 80901; info@ushpa.org; http://www.ushga.org. Adv. *Indexed:* SD. *Aud.:* Ga, Sa.

Hang Gliding and Paragliding is the official publication of the U.S. Hang Gliding and Paragliding Association, an affiliate of the National Aeronautic Association. The content is member-driven. The editor "welcomes editorial submissions from our members and readers...looking for well-written articles, photos[,] and quality artwork." The magazine contains entertaining features on free flight, as well as news and information about the association and its activities. Lead articles may include technical details on improving the flight or entertaining articles that speak to the adventure of ultraflight. A consideration for public libraries.

4692. *Surfer.* [ISSN: 0039-6036] 1960. 8x/yr. USD 24.99 domestic; USD 32.99 Canada; USD 40.99 elsewhere. TEN: Action Outdoor Group, 2052 Corte Del Nogal, Ste 100, Carlsbad, CA 92011; GAoun@enthusiastnetwork.com; http://www.enthusiastnetwork.com. Adv. *Indexed:* A22, BRI, SD. *Aud.:* Ga.

One of the oldest in its class (begun in 1960) with a mission "to bring our readers a slice of the entire surfing world," *Surfer Magazine* is filled with dramatic adventure photography, informative articles, interviews, coverage of amateur and professional competitions, and travel. It covers not only the sport of surfing, but the surfing lifestyle and mindset. Annual issues include an oversized "Collector's" issue, the "Buyer's Guide," and the "Hot 100" (best new surfers). The web site provides selected articles, a photograph gallery, video clips, merchandise, and a chat feature. An appropriate selection for public libraries. URL: www.surfermag.com

4693. *Thrasher.* Formerly (until 1984): *Thrasher Skateboard Magazine.* [ISSN: 0889-0692] 1981. m. USD 17.95 domestic; USD 48 Canada; USD 75 elsewhere. High Speed Productions, Inc., 1303 Underwood Ave, San Francisco, CA 94124. Adv. *Indexed:* BRI. *Aud.:* Hs, Ga.

For over 25 years, *Thrasher* has been read and enjoyed by enthusiasts of skateboarding and its music and lifestyle. Like its readers, the magazine is fast-paced, with interviews, action photography, comics, contests, competitions, and fashion and insider industry gossip. The "The Lunatic Fringe" column indicates the general thrust of this publication. At the magazine's web site, readers can view videos of stunts and competitions, and sign up for RSS feeds, a newsletter, and podcasts. Available in print and digital editions. An appropriate selection for public libraries. URL: www.thrashermagazine.com/

4694. ***Transworld Snowboarding.*** [ISSN: 1046-4611] 1986. q. Ed(s): Taylor Boyd. TEN: Action Outdoor Group, 2052 Corte Del Nogal, Ste 100, Carlsbad, CA 92011; http://www.enthusiastnetwork.com. Illus. *Indexed:* BRI, SD. *Aud.:* Hs, Ga.

Snowboard enthusiasts and those simply curious about the sport will enjoy this glossy publication. The over-200-page issues are filled with dramatic action photographs of amazing stunts and beautiful places. Feature articles are written in a conversational style and highlight the current season, preview upcoming events, examine snow areas, and profile professional snowboarders. Columns include letters to the editor, a question-and-answer section, competitions, instructional tips, product reviews, and the like. The magazine's web site includes several articles, but readers will love the print version for its full-color, dramatic photography. The annual photo issue offers truly amazing photos. Appropriate for public libraries. URL: http://snowboarding.transworld.net

4695. ***Triathlete.*** Formerly (until 1986): *Triathlon.* [ISSN: 0898-3410] 1983. m. USD 29.95 domestic; USD 14 Canada; USD 35 elsewhere. Ed(s): Erin Beresini. Pocket Outdoor Media, 3002 Sterling Cir, Ste 100, Boulder, CO 80301; http://pocketoutdoormedia.com/. Illus., adv. Circ: 33000. *Indexed:* SD. *Aud.:* Ga, Ac.

Published since 1986, this glossy magazine follows a regular format with columns and departments. Departments include editorials, letters, and news. There is a large section devoted to training, while other sections focus on fitness, nutrition, speed, equipment and product reviews (bikes and shoes), techniques, tests, and new developments. Annually the magazine publishes a guide to the top races in North America. Buyer's guides are also regularly published. Appropriate for public libraries.

4696. ***UltraRunning.*** [ISSN: 0744-3609] 1981. 10x/yr. USD 39.99 domestic; USD 59 in Canada & Mexico; USD 69 elsewhere. UltraRunning Magazine, PO Box 6509, Bend, OR 97708. *Indexed:* SD. *Aud.:* Ga.

As the name implies, an ultrarun or ultra marathon is a run that covers distances greater than the 26+ miles of a marathon. Races may be timed (e.g., how far can you run in six hours, 24 hours, etc.) or distance-based (e.g., 50 or 100 kilometers, 50 or 100 miles, etc.), and a run can last several days. Devotees are committed to their sport and will appreciate this magazine that covers all aspects of ultraruns. Typically the publication contains interviews and profiles of runners, adventure running (running in Monument Valley is featured in a recent issue), nutrition advice, injury prevention, training, a philosophical look at runners, and information on clubs and feature races. The magazine seeks to grow the sport. When not running, ultrarunners would enjoy this publication at their public library.

4697. ***WakeBoarding.*** Former titles (until 2014): *TransWorld WakeBoarding;* (until 201?): *WakeBoarding.* [ISSN: 2372-0573] 1993. 8x/yr. USD 14.97 combined subscription domestic (print & ipad eds.); USD 28.97 combined subscription Canada (print & ipad eds.); USD 42.97 combined subscription elsewhere (print & ipad eds.)). Ed(s): Shawn Perry. World Publications LLC, 460 N Orlando Ave, Ste 200, Winter Park, FL 32789; info@worldpub.net; http://www.bonniercorp.com. Illus., adv. Sample. *Indexed:* BRI. *Aud.:* Ga.

Wakeboarding, a combination of waterskiing and snowboarding, is well chronicled in *WakeBoarding Magazine*. This glossy publication is filled with step-by-step instruction, photos, long interviews, the latest product news, tournament updates, and feature articles. As the instruction column "Higher Learning" indicates, this is not a magazine for the novice. This title is published eight times a year. Like others of its kind, it is available for mobile devices and online. Since wakeboarding is growing in popularity, public libraries in appropriate areas might want to consider adding this publication to their collections. URL: www.wakeboardingmag.com/

Physical Education, Coaching, and Sports Sciences

Adapted Physical Activity Quarterly. See Disabilities section.

4698. ***The American Journal of Sports Medicine.*** Formerly (until 1976): *Journal of Sports Medicine.* [ISSN: 0363-5465] 1972. 14x/yr. USD 1291 subscr. includes Sports Health: A Multidisciplinary Approach (Individuals, USD 222 (print & online eds.)). Ed(s): Dr. Bruce Reider. Sage Publications, Inc., 2455 Teller Rd, Thousand Oaks, CA 91320; info@sagepub.com; http://www.sagepub.com/. Illus., index, adv. Sample. Refereed. Vol. ends: Nov/Dec. Microform: PQC. Reprint: PSC. *Indexed:* A01, A22, BRI, C45, E01, SD. *Aud.:* Ac, Sa.

The official publication of the American Orthopaedic Society for Sports Medicine is a monthly peer-reviewed scientific journal published since 1972. The journal's mission is to act "as an important forum for independent orthopaedic sports medicine research and education, allowing clinical practitioners the ability to make decisions based on sound scientific information." Articles include original research and case studies that examine sports injuries, their treatment and frequency of occurrence, rehabilitation and training. Issues of over 200 pages contain 20-40 articles classified into sections ("Knee," "Hip and Thigh," "Shoulder," and the like). Institutional subscriptions may be or print with e-access. The audience for this journal includes orthopaedic surgeons specializing in sports medicine, physicians, team physicians, athletic trainers, physical therapists, and anyone else specializing in sports medicine. This title is appropriate for academic and health science libraries. URL: www.ajsm.org

4699. ***Applied Physiology, Nutrition and Metabolism.*** Former titles (until 2006): *Canadian Journal of Applied Physiology;* (until 1993): *Canadian Journal of Sport Sciences;* (until 1987): *Canadian Journal of Applied Sport Science.* [ISSN: 1715-5312] 1976. m. CAD 1093 (print & online eds.)). Ed(s): Dr. Terry Graham. Canadian Science Publishing, 65 Auriga Dr, Ste 203, Ottawa, ON K2E 7W6, Canada; pubs@cdnsciencepub.com; http://www.nrcresearchpress.com. Illus., index, adv. Refereed. Vol. ends: Dec. *Indexed:* A01, A22, BRI, C45, ErgAb, SD. *Bk. rev.:* 2, 350 words. *Aud.:* Ac, Sa.

The monthly *Applied Physiology, Nutrition, and Metabolism,* formerly the *Canadian Journal of Sports Sciences,* then the *Canadian Journal of Applied Physiology,* is a peer-reviewed, interdisciplinary publication with articles that apply physiology, nutrition, and metabolism to the study of health, physical activity, and fitness. Issues average over 200 pages. A recent issue included articles entitled, "Do older adults experience greater thermal strain during heat waves[?]," "The effects of dietary fish oil on exercising skeletal muscle[:] vascular and metabolic control in chronic heart[-]failure rats," and "Serum S100B level increases after running but not cycling exercise." Since it is a Canadian journal, articles may be written in English or French, with abstracts in both languages. This publication will be of interest to exercise physiologists, physical fitness and exercise rehabilitation specialists, and public health and health-care professionals, as well as basic and applied physiologists, nutritionists, and biochemists. The technical language of this journal makes it of primary interest to medical and academic libraries.

4700. ***Athletic Business: the leading resource for athletic, fitness & recreation professionals.*** Formerly (until 1984): *Athletic Purchasing and Facilities.* [ISSN: 0747-315X] 1977. m. Free to qualified personnel. Ed(s): Dennis Van Milligen, Emily Attwood. Athletic Business Publications, Inc., 22 E Mifflin St, Ste 910, Madison, WI 53703. Illus., adv. Circ: 41250. *Indexed:* A22, SD. *Aud.:* Ac, Sa.

For over 35 years, the monthly trade journal *Athletic Business* has covered the business of sports and athletics, including equipment, programming, facility planning, marketing, management, and design. An annual "Buyer's Guide" is published in February or March (updated daily in the digital edition). Copies are distributed to qualified professionals, including operators and directors of sports, recreation, and fitness facilities. Feature articles are supplemented by columns on sports law, college and high school programs, the recreation industry, and profit-making enterprises. The web site features articles, up-to-date announcements, and news. In January 2011, the magazine began publishing a daily e-newsletter to keep subscribers informed. Suitable for academic libraries at institutions with business sports programs. URL: www.athleticbusiness.com

4701. *British Journal of Sports Medicine.* Formerly (until 1968): *British Association of Sport and Medicine. Bulletin.* [ISSN: 0306-3674] 1965. 24x/yr. GBP 804. Ed(s): Karim Khan. B M J Group, BMA House, Tavistock Sq, London, WC1H 9JR, United Kingdom; http://www.bmj.com/. Illus., adv. Sample. Refereed. Vol. ends: Dec. Microform: PQC. *Indexed:* A01, A22, BRI, C45, E01, ErgAb, SD. *Bk. rev.:* Number and length vary. *Aud.:* Ac, Sa.

Since 1965, the official publication of the British Association of Sport and Exercise Medicine, *BJSM,* has been a well-respected journal in the field. It describes itself as a "a multimedia portal for authoritative original research, critical reviews[,] and timely debate in sport and exercise medicine (SEM)." There are 22 issues per year-the bimonthly *BJSM* and a quarterly special *BJSM* "Injury Prevention and Health Protection" issue, which is devoted to research and education related to injury prevention for the amateur and professional athlete. Although there is no indication that issues are themed, topics do seem to be grouped-e.g., several articles on the patellofemoral joint in one issue, on walking and running in another, and on concussions in still another. Issues contain editorials, peer-reviewed articles, in-depth reviews, and "Head to Head" reviews of a hot clinical topic. Physicians, physiotherapists, exercise scientists, and researchers comprise the audience for the journal. Highly recommended for medical libraries and academic libraries with programs in health or sports sciences. URL: http://bjsm.bmj.com

4702. *Clinical Journal of Sport Medicine.* Former titles (until 1991): *Canadian Academy of Sport Medicine. Review;* (until 1986): *Canadian Academy of Sport Medicine. Newsletter;* (until 1980): *Canadian Academy of Sport Medicine. Journal.* [ISSN: 1050-642X] 1972. bi-m. USD 1023. Ed(s): Christopher Hughes, Jonathan Kemmerer-Scovner. Lippincott Williams & Wilkins, Two Commerce Sq, 2001 Market St, Philadelphia, PA 19103; customerservice@lww.com; http://www.lww.com. Illus., adv. Refereed. Vol. ends: Oct. *Indexed:* A01, A22, SD. *Aud.:* Ac, Sa.

The *Clinical Journal of Sport Medicine* is a bimonthly, international, refereed journal for clinicians specializing in sport medicine. It publishes research, reviews, and case reports concerning "diagnostics, therapeutics, and rehabilitation in healthy and physically challenged individuals of all ages and levels of sport and exercise participation." It is the official journal of the American Medical Society for Sports Medicine, the American Osteopathic Academy of Sports Medicine, the Australasian College of Sports Physicians, and the Canadian Academy of Sport and Exercise Medicine. A typical issue might include a reconsideration of a consensus statement; original articles on strategies to reduce ALC injuries in female soccer players; a case report on vertebral artery dissection caused by a golf swing; and short reports of sports medicine articles published elsewhere. Appropriate for academic and medical libraries.

4703. *Coach and Athletic Director: your resource for building powerful sports programs.* Former titles (until 2010): *Successful Coach and Athletic Director;* (until 2009): *Coach and Athletic Director;* (until 1995): *Scholastic Coach and Athletic Director;* (until 1994): *Scholastic Coach;* Which incorporated (1953-1982): *Coach & Athlete;* (1921-1987): *Athletic Journal.* [ISSN: 2159-6573] 1931. 8x/yr. USD 19.95 domestic (print & online eds.); USD 39 foreign (print & online eds.)). Lessiter Media, Inc., PO Box 624, Brookfield, WI 53008-0624; info@lessitermedia.com; http://lessitermedia.com/. Illus., index, adv. Sample. *Indexed:* A01, A22, BRI, SD. *Bk. rev.:* Number and length vary. *Aud.:* Hs, Ga, Ac.

Published since 1931 as a monthly during the school year, with a combined issue in the summer, this is the professional magazine for high school and collegiate coaches. The non-technical articles include news, information, and advice on different sports (including baseball, basketball, football, softball, and soccer), strength training, and administrative activities. Issues include book and equipment reviews, and an annual buyer's guide for facilities and equipment. Appropriate for high school and academic libraries.

4704. *European Journal of Sport Science.* [ISSN: 1746-1391] 2001. 8x/yr. GBP 1236 (print & online eds.)). Ed(s): Andrew M Jones. Taylor & Francis, 2, 3 & 4 Park Sq, Milton Park, Abingdon, OX14 4RN, United Kingdom; subscriptions@tandf.co.uk; https://www.tandfonline.com. Adv. Sample. Refereed. Reprint: PSC. *Indexed:* A01, A22, C45, E01, ErgAb, SD. *Aud.:* Ac.

This peer-reviewed publication of the European College of Sport Science (ECSS) publishes original research and review articles that cover all types of sport and exercise. For the purposes of this journal, sports are "all forms of human movement that aim to maintain or improve physical and mental well-being, create or improve social relationships, or obtain results in competition at all levels." It is published six times per year and includes original research articles as well as ECSS "Position Statements." Free access to a few articles on the web site provides readers with the flavor of the publication. Suitable for academic libraries. URL: www.tandfonline.com/toc/tejs20/current#.UysLGxCHO1g

4705. *Gridiron Strategies.* [ISSN: 1533-1652] 2001. bi-m. Ed(s): Rex Lardner. Gridiron Strategies, PO Box 14007, North Palm Beach, FL 33408. Adv. *Aud.:* Hs, Ga, Ac.

Published since 2001, *Gridiron Strategies* is a magazine written by football coaches for football coaches at all levels of competition. Each issue offers advice on strategy, play, offense, defense, strength and conditioning, and coaching and management. Occasionally, a famous coach may be featured, but the magazine's focus is on competition and strategy. The web site provides excerpts from articles that may be read by subscribers. An annual subscription includes six issues plus online access to current and archived issues. Coaches would appreciate reading this at a school or public library. URL: www.gridironstrategies.com/

4706. *International Journal of Sport Nutrition & Exercise Metabolism.* Formerly (until 2000): *International Journal of Sport Nutrition.* [ISSN: 1526-484X] 1991. bi-m. USD 974. Ed(s): Ronald J Maughan. Human Kinetics, Inc., PO Box 5076, Champaign, IL 61825; info@hkusa.com; http://journals.humankinetics.com. Illus., index, adv. Refereed. Vol. ends: Dec. Reprint: PSC. *Indexed:* A01, A22, Agr, BRI, C45, SD. *Aud.:* Ac, Sa.

This is a highly technical, peer-reviewed journal drawing from the disciplines of biochemistry, physiology, psychology, and sport and exercise science as they relate to the study of sport nutrition and exercise biochemistry. The journal focuses on original research and scholarly reviews, but also includes applied research. It may also cover systematic case studies and clinical applications when appropriate. A recent issue included an article on beer as a sports drink and the effect of caffeine on the anaerobic performance of wrestlers. This bimonthly publication is indexed by all the major services. Appropriate for academic and medical libraries that support programs in sport medicine and sport sciences.

4707. *International Journal of Sports Physiology and Performance.* [ISSN: 1555-0265] 2006. 10x/yr. USD 1202. Ed(s): Jos de Koning. Human Kinetics, Inc., PO Box 5076, Champaign, IL 61825; info@hkusa.com; http://journals.humankinetics.com. Adv. Refereed. *Indexed:* ErgAb, SD. *Aud.:* Ac.

As its name implies, this peer-reviewed research journal will be of interest to sport and exercise physiologists, sports-performance researchers, and other sport scientists. The journal emphasizes original research, but also publishes practical articles, invited reviews, technical reports, case studies, and an editorial. The journal covers team sports, individual sports, performance aspects of environmental physiology, applied sports nutrition, strength and conditioning, biomedical science, and applications of sport technology. Typical articles examine the effect of cold-water immersion on swimmers' heart rates; hyponatremia in an endurance run; and the effect of heat on the hydration of adolescent judo athletes. Academic libraries will want to consider this title.

4708. *International Journal of Sports Science & Coaching.* [ISSN: 1747-9541] 2006. bi-m. USD 1137 (print & online eds.)). Sage Publications Ltd., 1 Oliver's Yard, 55 City Rd, London, EC1Y 1SP, United Kingdom; info@sagepub.com; https://www.sagepub.com. Sample. Refereed. Reprint: PSC. *Indexed:* C45, SD. *Bk. rev.:* Number and length vary. *Aud.:* Ac.

Launched in 2006, the *International Journal of Sports Science and Coaching* is a relatively new entry in the field. This peer-reviewed academic journal endeavors to bridge the gap between coaching and the sports sciences. Articles are written by an international group of academics and researchers who "integrate theory and practice in sports science, promote critical reflection of coaching practice, and evaluate commonly accepted beliefs about coaching effectiveness and performance enhancement." Articles that reflect collaboration between coaches and sports scientists are encouraged. Typical subjects include a discussion of a two-time Olympic judo champion; an analysis of future coaches' feelings toward social justice; and training profiles of youth soccer players. The journal's web site provides detailed information and links to article abstracts. A suitable purchase for academic libraries.

Journal of Aging and Physical Activity. See Geriatrics and Gerontological Studies section.

Journal of Applied Physiology. See Physiology section.

4709. *Journal of Athletic Training.* Former titles (until 1992): *Athletic Training;* (until 1972): *National Athletic Trainers Association. Journal.* [ISSN: 1062-6050] 1956. m. USD 267 (Individuals, USD 178). Ed(s): Craig R Denegar, Leslie E Neistadt. National Athletic Trainers Association, nata@allenpress.com; http://www.nata.org/. Illus., index, adv. Refereed. Vol. ends: Oct/Dec. Microform: PQC. *Indexed:* A01, A22, BRI, E01, SD. *Bk. rev.:* 4, 350 words. *Aud.:* Ac, Sa.

The official publication of the National Athletic Trainers' Association (NATA), the *Journal of Athletic Training* is a quarterly, peer-reviewed journal (acceptance rate, 45 percent) with the mission of enhancing "communication among professionals interested in the quality of health care for the physically active through education and research in prevention, evaluation, management, and rehabilitation of injuries." Each issue of 120-150 pages is generally subdivided into sections: clinical studies, position statements, case studies, and a literature review. Following a 12-month embargo, articles are freely available through PubMed Central. A suggested acquisition for health sciences libraries and academic institutions with sport sciences and physical education programs.

4710. *Journal of Orthopaedic and Sports Physical Therapy.* [ISSN: 0190-6011] 1979. m. USD 775 (print & online eds.) Individuals, USD 335 (print & online eds.)). Ed(s): Clare Adern. American Physical Therapy Association, Orthopedic Section, 1111 N Fairfax St, Ste 100, Alexandria, VA 22314; tdeflorian@orthopt.org; https://www.orthopt.org. Illus., index, adv. Refereed. *Indexed:* A22. *Bk. rev.:* 4, 300 words. *Aud.:* Ac, Sa.

The official publication of the Orthopaedic Section and the Sports Physical Therapy Section of the American Physical Therapy Association is a scholarly, peer-reviewed, international journal, of interest to physical therapists, others in the health-care community, graduate students, and researchers. The journal's mission is "to publish scientifically rigorous, clinically relevant content to advance musculoskeletal and sports-related practice." Each monthly issue contains editorials, research reports, clinical commentaries, product and book reviews, and the like. Videos are available for readers of the online edition. A suggested purchase for medical and academic libraries. URL: http://jospt.org

4711. *Journal of Physical Education, Recreation and Dance.* Former titles (until 1981): *Journal of Physical Education and Recreation;* (until 1975): *Journal of Health, Physical Education, Recreation;* (until 1954): *American Association for Health, Physical Education, Recreation. Journal;* (until 1950): *The Journal of Health and Physical Education;* Which was formed by the merger of (1928-1930): *Pentathlon;* (1896-1930): *American Physical Education Review;* Which was formerly (until 1896): *American Association for the Advancement of Physical Education. Report of the ... Annual Meeting;* (until 1894): *American Association for the Advancement of Physical Education. Annual Meeting. Proceedings;* (until 1886): *Association for the Advancement of Physical Education. Organization. Proceedings.* [ISSN: 0730-3084] 1930. 9x/yr. GBP 275 (print & online eds.)). Ed(s): Tom Lawson. Routledge, 530 Walnut St, Ste 850, Philadelphia, PA 19106; enquiries@tandfonline.com; http://www.tandfonline.com. Illus., index, adv. Refereed. Circ: 12000. Vol. ends: Dec. Microform: PMC; PQC. *Indexed:* A01, A22, BRI, C45, ERIC, IIPA, SD. *Aud.:* Hs, Ga, Ac.

Published nine times a year by SHAPE America (acronym is for Society of Health and Physical Educators; the group is formerly the American Alliance for Health, Physical Education, Recreation and Dance), the *Journal of Physical Education, Recreation, and Dance* (*JOPERD*) has been in existence since 1896. Its peer-reviewed articles are directly relevant to educators at all levels and cover "teaching strategies, fitness, legal issues, assessment, dancing, teacher education, adapted physical education, leisure for older adults, the use of technology, and ethics and gender equity in sports and physical education." The journal layout has recently been modernized and includes numerous color photographs. Recent issues have included articles on age-appropriate activities in physical education, instruction and assessment activities, teaching self-defense to junior high school students, and promoting work/life balance among coaches. Academic libraries are the most appropriate subscribers.

4712. *Journal of Sports Science and Medicine.* [ISSN: 1303-2968] 2002. q. Free. Ed(s): Dr. Hakan Gur. Journal of Sports Science and Medicine, c/o Hakan Gur, MD, PhD, Department of Sports Medicine, Bursa, 16059, Turkey; hakan@uludag.edu.tr. Refereed. *Indexed:* A01, BRI, SD. *Bk. rev.:* Number and length vary. *Aud.:* Ac, Sa.

Since 2002, the mission of this scientific journal is to "to present easy access to the scientific knowledge for sport-conscious individuals using contemporary methods." It publishes research and review articles, case studies, and book reviews in all areas of the sports sciences and medicine. This journal takes advantage of the electronic medium to publish articles more quickly and to encourage discussion among researchers. The editors encourage the inclusion of multimedia; however, most entries appear to be strictly pdf files. Each quarterly issue may contain 20 or more articles. The journal provides an avenue for open and scholarly communication of research, and the editors should be complimented for their efforts. Of interest to medical and academic libraries. URL: www.jssm.org/index.php

4713. *Journal of Strength and Conditioning Research.* Formerly (until 1993): *The Journal of Applied Sport Science Research.* [ISSN: 1064-8011] 1987. m. USD 833. Ed(s): William J Kraemer. Lippincott Williams & Wilkins, Two Commerce Sq, 2001 Market St, Philadelphia, PA 19103; customerservice@lww.com; http://www.lww.com. Illus., index, adv. Refereed. Vol. ends: Dec. *Indexed:* A01, A22, E01, SD. *Bk. rev.:* Number and length vary. *Aud.:* Ac, Sa.

This peer-reviewed publication has moved from a quarterly to a monthly format for faster dissemination of information. It features "original investigations, reviews, symposia, research notes, and technical and methodological reports contributing to the knowledge about strength and conditioning in sport and exercise." It reports research with practical application, and articles conclude with a "practical applications" section. The audience is the user-strength and conditioning specialists, coaches, athletic trainers, and athletes. Articles are written in English by an international group of scholars. An appropriate purchase for medical and academic libraries. URL: http://journals.lww.com/nsca-jscr/

4714. *Journal of Teaching in Physical Education.* [ISSN: 0273-5024] 1981. q. USD 715. Ed(s): Bryan McCullick. Human Kinetics, Inc., PO Box 5076, Champaign, IL 61825; info@hkusa.com; http://journals.humankinetics.com. Illus., index, adv. Refereed. Vol. ends: Jul. Reprint: PSC. *Indexed:* A22, C45, ERIC, SD. *Aud.:* Ems, Hs, Ac.

This quarterly journal features empirical research and integrative reviews and analyses, descriptive surveys, summary and review articles, and discussions of current topics of interest to physical education teachers at all levels. Each issue contains six or seven articles of approximately 15-20 pages. As a peer-reviewed journal that focuses on research rather than practice, it uses the more technical language of the social sciences and is most appropriate for academic libraries.

4715. *Motor Control.* [ISSN: 1087-1640] 1997. q. USD 822. Ed(s): Mindy Levin. Human Kinetics, Inc., PO Box 5076, Champaign, IL 61825; info@hkusa.com; http://journals.humankinetics.com. Illus., adv. Refereed. Reprint: PSC. *Indexed:* A22, ErgAb, SD. *Bk. rev.:* Number and length vary. *Aud.:* Ac, Sa.

This official journal of the International Society of Motor Control is a quarterly peer-reviewed publication that provides "multidisciplinary examination of human movement across the lifespan." Editors and authors are academicians from international universities and research institutions, representing a variety of disciplines including kinesiology, neurophysiology, neuroscience, psychology, rehabilitation, and physical medicine. Each issue of approximately 100 pages contains five to ten articles. In addition to original research, the journal occasionally accepts review articles, book reviews, commentaries, and quick communications. Occasionally an entire issue may be devoted to a single topic. Suitable for medical and academic libraries.

Palaestra. See Disabilities section.

4716. *Pediatric Exercise Science.* [ISSN: 0899-8493] 1989. q. USD 776. Ed(s): Bareket Falk. Human Kinetics, Inc., PO Box 5076, Champaign, IL 61825; info@hkusa.com; http://journals.humankinetics.com. Illus., adv. Refereed. Vol. ends: Nov. Reprint: PSC. *Indexed:* A22, SD. *Bk. rev.:* Occasional. *Aud.:* Ac, Sa.

Published since 1989, *Pediatric Exercise Science,* the official publication of the North American Society of Pediatric Exercise Medicine, is a peer-reviewed quarterly that focuses on research about exercise in childhood and adolescence. In addition to original research, the journal publishes review articles, abstracts from other journals, book reviews, and editorials. Since this type of research is multidisciplinary, the journal aims to provide a single avenue for its dissemination. The journal's scope is international, and authors include clinicians and academic researchers. Most appropriate for academic and medical libraries.

4717. *Quest (Champaign).* Incorporates (1984-1992): *American Academy of Physical Education Papers;* Which was formerly (1967-1984): *Academy Papers;* (1979-1985): *National Association for Physical Education in Higher Education. Annual Conference. Proceedings;* Which was formerly (until 1979): *N A P E C W / N C P E A M National Conference. Proceedings.* [ISSN: 0033-6297] 1949. q. GBP 253 (print & online eds.)). Ed(s): Mike W Metzler. Routledge, 530 Walnut St, Ste 850, Philadelphia, PA 19106; enquiries@tandfonline.com; http://www.tandfonline.com. Illus. Sample. Refereed. Vol. ends: Nov. Microform: PQC. Reprint: PSC. *Indexed:* A22, C45, ERIC, SD. *Bk. rev.:* Number and length vary. *Aud.:* Ac.

Quest is the official publication of the National Association for Kinesiology in Higher Education. Rather than focusing on original research, the journal seeks articles that are based on, complement, or review scholarly work related to kinesiology and physical education in higher education. Both theoretical and practice-based articles are considered. The journal's audience includes academicians, teachers, and administrators. Articles vary in length from 10 to 20 pages, and issues may include as few as five or as many as ten articles. Appropriate for colleges or universities with strong physical education programs.

4718. *Referee (Franksville).* [ISSN: 0733-1436] 1976. m. USD 46.95 domestic; USD 81.95 foreign. Ed(s): Brent Killackey. Referee Enterprises, Inc., 2017 Lathrop Ave, Racine, WI 53405. Illus., adv. Sample. *Indexed:* SD. *Aud.:* Ga, Ac.

Since 1975, this monthly has published information for the sports referee from youth to the professional levels. Issues contain the latest officiating and industry news, as well as articles on rules and interpretation; there are also special issues on topics such as training and game management. This title also contains interviews with, and profiles of, outstanding officials (e.g., Kari Seitz in a recent issue), columns on specific sports (softball, baseball, soccer, etc.); and articles on officiating, mechanics, skills, psychology, and the like. A "Test Yourself" column provides situations with possible answers; "Caseplays" couples plays with their rulings. Both public and academic libraries might consider this as a purchase.

4719. *Research Quarterly for Exercise and Sport.* Incorporates (1965-1974): *Abstracts of Research Papers;* Former titles (until 1980): *American Alliance for Health, Physical Education, Recreation and Dance. Research Quarterly;* (until 1979): *American Alliance for Health, Physical Education, and Recreation. Research Quarterly;* (until 1974): *American Association for Health, Physical Education, and Recreation. Research Quarterly;* (until 1939): *American Association for Health and Physical Education. Research Quarterly;* (until 1937): *American Physical Education Association. Research Quarterly.* [ISSN: 0270-1367] 1930. q. GBP 348 (print & online eds.)). Ed(s): Weimo Zhu, Linda Topper. Routledge, 530 Walnut St, Ste 850, Philadelphia, PA 19106; enquiries@tandfonline.com; http://www.tandfonline.com. Illus., index, adv. Refereed. Vol. ends: Dec. Microform: PMC; PQC. Reprint: PSC. *Indexed:* A01, A22, BRI, C45, ERIC, ErgAb, SD. *Aud.:* Ac.

Research Quarterly for Exercise and Sport (RQES), from the American Alliance for Health, Physical Education, Recreation and Dance (AAHPERD), has been published since 1930. Its mission is to "publish refereed research articles on the art and science of human movement, which contribute to the knowledge and development of theory, either as new information, substantiation[,] or contraction of previous findings, or application of new or improved techniques." *RQES* publishes more than 50 articles a year and includes an annual supplement with abstracts of presentations from the Research Consortium program at the AAHPERD National Convention. Issues are divided into "Special Reports," "Articles," and "Research Notes" sections. Recommended for academic libraries that support sports and exercise science programs.

Shape. See Health and Fitness/Journals and Magazines section.

4720. *Sociology of Sport Journal.* [ISSN: 0741-1235] 1984. q. USD 715. Ed(s): Michael D Giardina. Human Kinetics, Inc., PO Box 5076, Champaign, IL 61825; info@hkusa.com; http://journals.humankinetics.com. Illus., index, adv. Refereed. Vol. ends: Dec. Reprint: PSC. *Indexed:* A01, A22, BRI, C37, C45, SD, SSA. *Bk. rev.:* 1, 750 words. *Aud.:* Ac.

This official journal of the North American Society for the Sociology of Sport publishes "original research, framed by social theory, on exercise, sport, physical culture, and the (physically active) body." This quarterly journal provides an international perspective and features empirical research, theoretical articles, position papers, and book reviews. The editors encourage a multidisciplinary approach. Abstracts in English and French precede the articles. The intended audience includes sport sociologists, sport psychologists, and coaches. An appropriate consideration for academic libraries.

4721. *Strategies (Philadelphia): a journal for physical and sport educators.* [ISSN: 0892-4562] 1987. bi-m. GBP 163 (print & online eds.)). Ed(s): Tom Lawson. Routledge, 530 Walnut St, Ste 850, Philadelphia, PA 19106; enquiries@tandfonline.com; http://www.tandfonline.com. Illus., adv. Refereed. Reprint: PSC. *Indexed:* A22, ERIC, SD. *Aud.:* Ems, Hs, Ac.

The official publication of SHAPE America (formerly the National Association for Sport and Physical Education), *Strategies* is a peer-reviewed journal published six times a year for physical education teachers and coaches at all levels. It seeks practical articles for sport and physical education educators, particularly ones that "identify a problem and offer concrete, step-by-step solutions, or describe best practices for typical coach or teacher activities or responsibilities." Each 30- to 35-page issue contains 10 to 12 articles. Typical articles include health-related fitness models; the importance of fitness for overall wellness; and dealing with sudden cardiac arrest. Each issue contains a theory-into-practice column. The journal is written in a conversational tone, using non-technical language, making this professional magazine appropriate for large public and school, as well as academic, libraries.

4722. *Strength and Conditioning Journal.* Former titles (until 1999): *Strength and Conditioning;* (until 1994): *N S C A Journal;* (until 1993): *National Strength & Conditioning Association Journal;* (until 1981): *National Strength Coaches Association Journal.* [ISSN: 1524-1602] 1979. bi-m. USD 281. Ed(s): T Jeff Chandler, Britt Chandler. Lippincott Williams & Wilkins, Two Commerce Sq, 2001 Market St, Philadelphia, PA 19103; customerservice@lww.com; http://www.lww.com. Illus., index, adv. Refereed. *Indexed:* A22, E01, SD. *Bk. rev.:* 3, 100-250 words. *Aud.:* Ac, Sa.

This professional journal of the National Strength and Conditioning Association (NSCA) publishes peer-reviewed articles that report practical information from research studies and knowledge from experienced professionals. Each bimonthly issue contains approximately five feature articles and several columns. Articles may include supplemental digital content with links to video files. The target audience is strength coaches, personal trainers, physical therapists, athletic trainers, and other strength and conditioning professionals. Recommended for academic libraries. URL: www.nsca-lift.org

Specific Sports

4723. *American Fencing.* Supersedes (in 1949): *Amateur Fencers League of America. Secretary's Newsletter;* (in 1949): *Amateur Fencers League of America. Riposte.* [ISSN: 0002-8436] 1949. q. Free to members. United States Fencing Association, Inc., 4065 Sinton Rd, Ste 140, Colorado Springs, CO 80907; http://www.usfencing.org. Illus. Microform: PQC. *Indexed:* A22, SD. *Aud.:* Hs, Ga, Ac.

The official publication of the United States Fencing Association, this magazine reports the news, people, tournaments, rankings, rules, training, techniques, and equipment of the sport of fencing. This quarterly publication features articles and essays about fencing and issues surrounding the sport. Regular features include player profiles, sports medicine, fencing psychology, rules, tournament news, and product reviews. Membership in the association includes a subscription to the magazine. High school and collegiate fencers will enjoy this publication.

4724. *Baseball America.* Formerly (until 1982): *All-America Baseball News.* [ISSN: 0745-5372] 1981. bi-w. USD 89.97 combined subscription domestic (print & online eds.); USD 102.97 combined subscription Canada (print & online eds.); USD 115.97 combined subscription elsewhere (print & online eds.)). Baseball America, Inc., 4319 S Alston Ave, Ste 103, Durham, NC 27713; letters@baseballamerica.com; http://www.baseballamerica.com. Illus. *Aud.:* Ga, Ac.

This biweekly newsprint provides comprehensive coverage of baseball from the international, major, minor, collegiate Division I, and high school teams, and both the minor and the major leagues. Articles highlight teams, players, coaches, prospects, leagues, statistics, and averages. The web site publishes weekly rankings of the top 25 college teams, as well as draft and season previews. Recommended for public, high school, and academic libraries.

4725. *Baseball Digest.* [ISSN: 0005-609X] 1942. bi-m. USD 38.95 domestic; USD 48.95 Canada; USD 53.95 elsewhere. Grandstand Publishing, Llc, 990 Grove St, Ste 400, Evanston, IL 60201. Illus., adv. Microform: PQC. *Indexed:* A22, BRI, C37, MASUSE, SD. *Aud.:* Hs, Ga.

Calling itself "a publication for the true baseball fan," *Baseball Digest* was launched in 1942 and focuses purely on major league play. Available as a print or digital subscription, it features articles, interviews, statistics, charts, and rosters of major league baseball. It highlights major league history and current stars. Special features include a "Fans Speak Out" section, a crossword puzzle, quizzes, a review of rules, and extensive statistics, previews, and player profiles. In 2012, the editors began including scouting reports, coverage of amateur games, a youth section, and tips for batters, basemen, fielders, and pitchers. It is published six times a year-with National and American League schedules, directories, and pre-season rosters. The magazine's "Player and Pitcher of the Year" reads like a list of baseball greats. A suitable purchase for high school and public libraries.

4726. *Bicycling.* Incorporates (1990-200?): *Mountain Bike;* (1972-1980): *Bike World;* Formerly (until 1968): *American Cycling.* [ISSN: 0006-2073] 1962. 10x/yr. USD 11. Rodale, Inc., 400 S Tenth St, Emmaus, PA 18098; info@rodale.com; http://www.rodaleinc.com. Illus., adv. Microform: NBI; PQC. *Indexed:* A22, BRI, C37, MASUSE, SD. *Aud.:* Hs, Ga, Ac.

This glossy magazine for the serious cyclist is published 11 times a year, in both a print and an online version. It contains news, training and nutrition, bike repair, road maps, and other information of interest to cyclists. It incorporated the popular *Mountain Bike* magazine in the 1990s. The magazine publishes an annual "Buyers' Guide." The web site includes links to bicycling blogs, videos, bicycling gear, and the like. Readers may also sign up for a free newsletter. Suitable for public libraries. URL: www.bicycling.com

4727. *Black Belt Magazine.* Former titles (until 2005): *Karate - Kung Fu Illustrated;* (until 1991): *Karate Illustrated.* [ISSN: 0277-3066] 1961. bi-m. USD 27.99 domestic; USD 39.99 Canada; USD 51.99 elsewhere. Ed(s): Robert Young. Black Belt Communications, Inc., 24900 Anza Dr, Unit E, Valencia, CA 91355. Adv. *Indexed:* BRI, SD. *Aud.:* Ga.

Billed as the "world's leading magazine of self-defense" and having been published since the early 1960s, *Black Belt* covers more than 15 different martial arts. Topics include techniques, training (traditional, self-defense, and mixed martial arts), masters, weapons, fitness, entertainment, history, and philosophy. Typical articles might be how to be get some Nanchaku training; martial arts injury recovery; cinematic portrayal of Hapkido; and an interview with the kickboxing legend Benny "the Jet" Urquidez. This journal is appropriate for high school, public, and academic library collections.

Climbing. See Hiking, Climbing, and Outdoor Recreation section.

4728. *Collegiate Baseball.* Formerly (until 1959): *Collegiate Baseball Digest.* [ISSN: 0530-9751] 1957. 14x/yr. Individuals, USD 28; USD 4 newsstand/cover. Ed(s): Lou Pavlovich. Collegiate Baseball Newspaper, Inc., PO Box 50566, Tucson, AZ 85703. Illus., adv. Microform: PQC. *Indexed:* A22. *Aud.:* Hs, Ac.

Since 1957, this newspaper has featured up-to-date information about collegiate and high school baseball. It comes out twice a month during the season (monthly June, July, September, and October) and contains editorials, letters to the editor, baseball news, rules and regulations, training and game improvement tips, profiles of outstanding players, and statistics and standings for all college divisions and high school teams. It publishes polls for all the NCCA, NAIA, NJCAA, and California and Pacific Association divisions, as well as high school divisions. The audience includes high school and college coaches and players. An appropriate purchase for high school and academic libraries.

4729. *Cross Country Skier.* Formerly (until 1981): *Nordic Skiing.* [ISSN: 0278-9213] 1976. s-a. USD 12.99 domestic; USD 19.99 Canada; USD 24.99 elsewhere. Cross Country Skier, LLC, PO Box 550, Cable, WI 54821; info@crosscountryskier.com; http://www.crosscountryskier.com/. Illus., adv. Sample. Circ: 7000. *Indexed:* A22, BRI, SD. *Aud.:* Ga.

Cross Country Skier: The Journal of Nordic Skiing will appeal to all who practice the sport. Published twice a year (November/December and January/February), it includes regular columns on training and technique, snow conditions, skiing destinations, and lifestyle. A recent issue featured an equipment preview, an article on one man's solo voyage through the Northwest Passage, a feature on a Michigan ski club, a profile of a ski event in Colorado, and the like. Additional information on cross country skiing is posted at the web site. This would be a consideration for novice and experienced skiers at public libraries. URL: www.crosscountryskier.com/

4730. *Golf Digest.* Formerly (until 1950): *Arrowhead Golf Digest.* [ISSN: 0017-176X] 1950. m. USD 21.97 Canada; USD 59.97 elsewhere. The Golf Digest Companies, 20 Westport Rd, Wilton, CT 06897. Illus., adv. Microform: PQC. *Indexed:* A22, BRI, C37, MASUSE, SD. *Aud.:* Hs, Ga, Ac.

There is nothing short about the monthly issues of *Golf Digest,* each of which is over 200 pages. Articles on game improvement, instruction, equipment, courses, and players fill the magazine. Detailed articles are written by and about famous golfers. Occasional features focus on golf history, golf courses, country clubs, and interviews with major players. It aims to be the number 1 golf publication, and covers recreational and competitive men's and women's golf. A subscription will delight players at public and academic libraries.

4731. *Golf Magazine.* Former titles (until 1991): *Golf;* (until 1986): *Golf Magazine.* [ISSN: 1056-5493] 1959. m. USD 10 combined subscription (print & online eds.)). Time Inc., 225 Liberty St, New York, NY 10281; information@timeinc.com; http://www.timeinc.com. Illus., adv. *Indexed:* A01, A22, BRI, C37, MASUSE, SD. *Aud.:* Hs, Ga, Ac.

The glossy *Golf Magazine* contains articles on equipment, rules, instruction, courses, events, courses and travel, and interviews with golfers. Regular columns include golf events, questions and answers, rules, and questions for tour players. "Private Lessons" provides tips for the beginning, the experienced, and the senior golfer. The magazine is filled with beautiful photography. Subscribers to the print also receive access to the digital edition. Although this title is similar to *Golf Digest,* the two publications complement one another. A suitable purchase for public libraries. URL: www.golf.com

4732. *Handball.* Formerly (until 1971): *Ace.* [ISSN: 0046-6778] 1950. bi-m. Free to members. U.S. Handball Association, 2333 N Tucson Blvd, Tucson, AZ 85716; http://ushandball.org. Illus., adv. Microform: PQC. *Indexed:* A22, SD. *Aud.:* Hs, Ga, Ac.

As the official voice of the U.S. Handball Association (USHA), this magazine will interest all recreational handball players as well as association members. Each quarterly issue contains instructional articles for beginning and advanced players, tournament information and entry forms, tips from the best players, health advice, photographs and stories from major tournaments, and announcements of specials on handball equipment and gear. Handball is an Olympic sport and is popular in many areas of the country. Public and academic libraries may want to consider making this a part of their collection.

4733. *The Hockey News: the international hockey weekly.* [ISSN: 0018-3016] 1947. w. CAD 52.95. T C Media, 25 Sheppard Ave, Ste 100, Toronto, ON M2N 6S7, Canada; http://tctranscontinental.com/. Illus., adv. Microform: PQC. *Indexed:* A22, C37. *Aud.:* Ga.

Published since 1947, *The Hockey News* provides information about North American hockey. Thirty-four issues a year contain editorials, letters to the editor, news in brief, player profiles and interviews, statistics, standings, schedules, rosters, and the like. Special issues include "Season Opener," "People of Power and Influence," "Future Watch," "Draft Preview," "Season in Review," and the "Yearbook." The magazine, printed on newsprint, is richly illustrated. Conference teams receive in-depth coverage in every issue. Less detail is provided for teams in the minor pro, junior, and collegiate leagues. This title is an appropriate consideration for school and public libraries with hockey fans. URL: www.thehockeynews.com

4734. *Hockey Player Magazine (Online).* Formerly (until 1998): *Hockey Player Magazine (Print).* 1991. m. Hockey Player Magazine L.P., http://www.hockeyplayer.com. Illus. *Aud.:* Ga.

Published as a print magazine from 1991 to 1997, *Hockey Player Magazine* became an online-only publication in 1998. Aimed at the recreational ice, roller, and street hockey player, the magazine contains interviews, columns, departments, equipment news, drills, and instruction. The more than 500 online articles are fully searchable and/or browsed by section. Typical sections include "Behind the Bench" (coaching), defense, essays and humor, offense, power skating, profiles, and youth. Hockey fans and players will enjoy this magazine. URL: www.hockeyplayer.com

4735. *International Figure Skating.* [ISSN: 1070-9568] 1994. bi-m. USD 29.99 domestic; USD 34.99 Canada; USD 54.99 elsewhere. Madavor Media, Llc., 25 Braintree Hill Office Park, Ste 404, Braintree, MA 02184; custsvc_ifskate@fulcoinc.com; http://www.madavor.com. Illus., adv. *Indexed:* SD. *Aud.:* Hs, Ga.

International Figure Skating reports the news, business, and personalities of figure skating, covering U.S. and international skaters and competitions. Although based in the U.S., the magazine has correspondents in Canada, Europe, Hong Kong, and the U.K., making it a truly international publication. Each issue profiles famous competitors such as the partnership of Tatiana Volosozhar and Maxim Trankov. The magazine includes beautiful glossy photographs that will appeal to skaters and would-be skaters alike. Most suitable for public libraries. URL: www.ifsmagazine.com/

4736. *International Gymnast.* Former titles (until 1986): *International Gymnast Magazine;* (until 1982): *International Gymnast;* (until 1981): *International Gymnast Magazine;* (until 1979): *International Gymnast;* (until 1976): *Gymnast;* Which was formed by the merger of (1966-1971): *Mademoiselle Gymnast;* (1956-1971): *Modern Gymnast.* [ISSN: 0891-6616] 1971. 10x/yr. USD 30 combined subscription. Paul Ziert & Associates, Inc., 3214 Bart Conner Dr, Norman, OK 73072; http://www.intlgymnast.com. Illus., adv. Circ: 10000. Microform: PQC. *Indexed:* A22, SD. *Aud.:* Hs, Ga.

Since 1956, this magazine under various titles has focused on the individuals that compete in the sport. Published monthly (with combined issues for January/February and July/August), this title includes biographical profiles and coverage of international events and teams. Articles are lavishly illustrated and supplemented by columns on new products, instruction and tips, drills, warm-up exercises, and the like. Appropriate for public and school libraries. URL: www.intlgymnast.com

4737. *Nine: a journal of baseball history & culture.* [ISSN: 1188-9330] 1992. s-a. USD 110. Ed(s): Trey Strecker. University of Nebraska Press, 1111 Lincoln Mall, Lincoln, NE 68588; journals@unl.edu; https://www.nebraskapress.unl.edu. Illus., adv. Refereed. *Indexed:* A01, A22, BRI, E01, MLA-IB, SD. *Bk. rev.:* Number and length vary. *Aud.:* Ac.

Since 1992, this academic peer-reviewed journal has promoted "the study of all historical aspects of baseball and the cultural implications of the game[,] wherever in the world baseball is played." Two issues are published per year and include articles, essays, book reviews, biographies, oral histories, and short fiction. Recent issues included articles on youth baseball and colonial identity in Taiwan; the Wisconsin Badger Nine trip to Japan in 1909; the Cannon Street All Stars and the 1955 Little League World Series; and interviews and book reviews. The journal is available from 2000 to date in Project MUSE. Suitable for academic libraries. URL: http://nine.iweb.bsu.edu/

4738. *Pool & Billiard Magazine.* Incorporates (in 1982): *Games and Leisure Inc.* [ISSN: 1049-2852] 1983. m. USD 39.95 domestic; USD 44.95 in Canada & Mexico; USD 74.95 elsewhere. Ed(s): Thomas C Shaw. Pool & Billiard Magazine, 115 S Main St, Summerville, SC 29483. Adv. *Aud.:* Ga, Sa.

Since 1983, this monthly has covered the sport of pool and billiards, including tournaments, players, rankings, and equipment. Each issue has a number of articles focusing on instruction, with detailed diagrams of shots and tips on game improvement. This magazine was originally founded by a pool hall operator and his daughter, who continue to be involved in its production. Several staff and writers are members of the BCA (Billiard Congress of America) Hall of Fame. Fans, players, owners, and people involved in the business will be avid readers of this publication. A consideration for public libraries.

4739. *Runner's World.* Former titles (until 1987): *Rodale's Runner's World;* Which incorporated (1978-1987): *The Runner;* (until 1985): *Runner's World;* (until 1970): *Distance Running News.* [ISSN: 0897-1706] 1970. 11x/yr. USD 19.97; USD 4.99 per issue. Rodale, Inc., 400 S Tenth St, Emmaus, PA 18098; info@rodale.com; http://www.rodaleinc.com. Illus., index, adv. Circ: 665376 Paid. Microform: PQC. *Indexed:* A22, BRI, C37, MASUSE, SD. *Aud.:* Ga, Ac.

Serious and recreational runners will enjoy the monthly *Runner's World.* Columns and departments include rave run (great places to run), letters, nutrition, gear, motivation, injury prevention, training advice, product reviews, vacation tips, racing reports, and more. The magazine's web site contains breaking news, videos, selected articles, links to relevant sites, and an offer for free online newsletters. Suitable for academic and public libraries. URL: www.runnersworld.com

4740. *Scuba Diving.* Formerly (until 2004): *Rodale's Scuba Diving.* [ISSN: 1553-7919] 1992. bi-m. USD 16 domestic; USD 23.97 Canada; USD 34 elsewhere. Ed(s): Patricia Wuest, Ashley Annin. F + W Media Inc., 1140 Broadway, 14th Fl, New York, NY 10001; http://www.fwcommunity.com/. Illus., adv. *Indexed:* BRI. *Aud.:* Ga.

Scuba divers interested in information on travel, dive deals, the latest photography and scuba gear and technology, the marine environment, training, health and safety, and the like will enjoy this magazine. It contains beautiful underwater photography that can be enjoyed by almost anyone. The training section is extensive and covers everything from using a new camera, to what to do if you are left behind, and diving with kids. Recommended for public libraries.

4741. *Ski.* Incorporates (195?-1961): *Ski Life;* Formed by the merger of (1945-1948): *Western Skiing;* (1938-1948): *Ski News;* (1936-1948): *Ski Illustrated;* (19??-1948): *Ski Sheet.* [ISSN: 0037-6159] 1948. bi-m. USD 10 domestic; USD 20 Canada; USD 30 elsewhere. Bonnier Corp., 5720 Flatiron Pky, Boulder, CO 80301; http://www.bonniercorp.com. Illus., adv. Microform: PQC. *Indexed:* A22, BRI, C37, MASUSE, SD. *Aud.:* Ga, Ac.

With its beautiful photography, travel, equipment, and resort information, *Ski* will attract almost all recreational skiers. The 100+-page issues regularly include instruction, tips for injury prevention, training, interviews, and lifestyle articles. Since skiing is seasonal, articles on the more general aspects of outdoor life are included in the off-season. The magazine's web site contains selected articles, a buyer's guide, snow reports, a calendar of events, a discussion forum, videos, and more. Suitable for public libraries. URL: www.skinet.com/

4742. *Ski Trax: North America's nordic ski magazine.* [ISSN: 1191-2677] 1990. q. CAD 13.95 domestic; USD 14.95 United States; USD 19.95 elsewhere. Ski Trax, 260 Spadina Ave, Ste 200, Toronto, ON M5T 2E4 , Canada; news@skitrax.com. Illus. *Indexed:* SD. *Aud.:* Ga.

Enthusiasts of Nordic skiing will welcome *Ski Trax,* the official publication of the Ski and Snowboard Association (USSA), which is the national governing body of Olympic skiing and snowboarding. Covering all forms of Nordic events (skiing, snowshoeing, snowboarding, biathlons, and the like), the magazine contains beautiful photographs, information on skiing and snowshoeing locations, equipment and product reviews, competition (Olympic, national and international), profiles of coaches and athletes, an annual directory of the best in cross-country skiing and snowshoeing, and a buyer's guide. It is published four times during the ski season. Public libraries in ski areas may consider adding this magazine to their collection.

4743. *Soccer America.* Supersedes in part (in 1972): *Soccer West.* [ISSN: 0163-4070] 1971. q. Ed(s): Paul Kennedy. Soccer America Communications LLC, 145 Pipers Hill Rd, Wilton, CT 06897; feedback@socceramerica.com. Illus., adv. Microform: PQC. *Indexed:* A22. *Bk. rev.:* 1, 800 words. *Aud.:* Ga.

Soccer, one of the world's most popular sports, is quickly gaining fans and players in the United States. For over 40 years, this monthly has published news, statistics, scores, reports and analysis of U.S. and international soccer, including youth, the MLS, and collegiate teams. Players are highlighted in informative articles. Issues contain a "Tournament Calendar," with a comprehensive listing of tournaments in the U.S. and abroad. Editorial columns provide insights into the world of soccer. The publication's web site provides access to selected articles, news, and links of interest to the soccer fan. Recommended for public, high school, and academic libraries. URL: www.socceramerica.com

4744. *Soccer and Society.* [ISSN: 1466-0970] 2000. bi-m. GBP 775 (print & online eds.)). Ed(s): Boria Majumdar. Routledge, 4 Park Sq, Milton Park, Abingdon, OX14 4RN, United Kingdom; subscriptions@tandf.co.uk; http://www.tandfonline.com. Index, adv. Sample. Refereed. Reprint: PSC. *Indexed:* A01, A22, C45, E01, SD. *Aud.:* Ac.

This international peer-reviewed journal writes about the world's most popular game from anthropological, cultural, economic, historical, political, and sociological perspectives. Issues are theme-based. A recent issue examined soccer jersey manufacturers; the political role of football in the Arab world; football and the community; and the like. Academic libraries might want to consider this publication for inclusion in their collections.

Sports 'n Spokes. See Disabilities section.

4745. *Tennis.* [ISSN: 0040-3423] 1965. 10x/yr. USD 10. Tennis Media Co., 814 S Westgate, Ste 100, Los Angeles, CA 90049. Illus., index, adv. Microform: PQC. *Indexed:* A22, BRI, C37, MASUSE, SD. *Aud.:* Hs, Ga, Ac.

For over 40 years, *Tennis* has delighted the novice and advanced player. Instruction is supplemented with profiles of professional players, coverage of major tournaments, equipment and gear reviews, and information on nutrition, health, and fitness for the tennis player. This title contains excellent photographs. The web site contains videos. It is the most popular magazine in the sport. Members of the United States Tennis Association receive free subscriptions. Ten issues are published annually. Almost all of its approximately-100-page issues are devoted to content rather than advertising, which is unusual among the more popular single-sport magazines. Appropriate for school, public, and academic libraries. URL: www.tennis.com/

4746. *Track & Field News: all the best in running, jumping & throwing.* [ISSN: 0041-0284] 1948. m. USD 43.95. Ed(s): Sieg Lindstrom, E Garry Hill. Track & Field News, 2570 El Camino Real, Ste 220, Mountain View, CA 94040; http://www.trackandfieldnews.com. Illus., adv. Sample. Microform: PQC. *Indexed:* A22, SD. *Aud.:* Hs, Ga, Ac.

Calling itself the "Bible of the sport since 1948," *Track and Field News* provides detailed information on high school, college, and professional competition. International coverage includes the European circuit, the Olympics, and world championships. Feature articles are brief and supplemented by meet schedules, lists of records, editorials, statistics, letters, and brief biographical notes. It is published 12 times a year and includes the "Annual Edition," which summarizes the year with world rankings and top 40 lists. This magazine is a good choice for the collections of large public libraries and high schools and academic institutions with track and field programs. URL: www.trackandfieldnews.com/

4747. *U S A Hockey Magazine.* Former titles (until 200?): *American Hockey Magazine;* (until 198?): *American Hockey and Arena;* (until 19??): *United States Hockey and Arena Biz.* [ISSN: 1551-6741] 1973. 10x/yr. Free to members; Non-members, USD 15; USD 4 per issue. Ed(s): Harry Thompson. U S A Hockey, 1775 Bob Johnson Dr, Colorado Springs, CO 80906; http://www.usahockey.com. Illus., adv. *Aud.:* Hs, Ga, Ac.

As the official publication of USA Hockey and USA Hockey Inline, *USA Hockey* covers all aspects of the sport, with articles of interest to fans, players, and coaches alike. Recent issues contained a preview of the U.S. Sled Team and an article on the U.S. Woman's team regrouping after the 2014 Olympics. The regular departments feature biographies of new and historic hockey players, tips from the pros, equipment reviews, and a question-and-answer section. Suitable for public libraries.

4748. *U S A Table Tennis Magazine.* Former titles (until 199?): *Table Tennis Today;* (until 1993): *Table Tennis Topics;* (until 1986): *Spin Magazine.* [ISSN: 1089-1870] 1933. bi-m. Ed(s): Marie Hopkins, Steve Hopkins. U.S.A. Table Tennis, 4065 Sinton Rd Ste 120, Colorado Springs, CO 80907; admin@usatt.org. Illus. *Aud.:* Hs, Ga.

Dubbing itself the "official USA table tennis magazine," this publication has been in existence since 1970. The magazine is divided into a "Features" section (including a report on the progress of the USA Junior team), "Coaching," "Tournaments" (the editors try to include coverage of all tournaments), and "News" (including a "Senior Corner"). Content emphasizes the United States, but international events may be covered if relevant. The magazine is included in a membership to the USA Table Tennis Association.

4749. *U S A Today Sports Weekly.* Formerly (until 2002): *U S A Today Baseball Weekly.* [ISSN: 1541-5228] 1991. w. USD 72; USD 3 newsstand/cover. Ed(s): David Meeks. U S A Today, 8700-k Red Oak Blvd, Charlotte, NC 28217; http://www.usatoday.com. Illus., adv. *Indexed:* A22. *Aud.:* Ga.

Although this title sounds like a general sports magazine, it focuses solely on baseball and football. Issues include fantasy baseball and football reports, with award-winning statistics, analysis, tips, and strategies. There are feature stories that provide a unique insider's view of baseball and professional football; and there are comprehensive major team notes. For the baseball enthusiast, there is an annual "All Star" preview issue, while football enthusiasts can gain information from the annual special NFL preview issue. Fantasy baseball and football are also covered. This would be a popular addition to public libraries.

4750. *VolleyballUSA.* Former titles (until 1992): *Inside U S A Volleyball; Volleyball U S A.* 1972. q. Free to members; Non-members, USD 10. U S A Volleyball, 4065 Sinton Rd, Ste 200, Colorado Springs, CO 80907; http://www.teamusa.org/usa-volleyball/. Illus., adv. *Bk. rev.:* 2, 250 words. *Aud.:* Hs, Ga.

As the official publication of United States Volleyball Association, *Volleyball USA* provides current information on all types of volleyball in the United States (indoor, park, and beach volleyball, and national, junior, collegiate, and disabled teams). In addition to association activities, this quarterly contains tournament and competition news as well as articles about players, coaches and coaching, nutrition, weight training, and camp guides. This glossy magazine will appeal to readers in public and high school libraries where volleyball is popular.

4751. *The Water Skier: having fun today - building champions for tomorrow.* [ISSN: 0049-7002] 1951. 7x/yr. U S A Water Ski, 1251 Holy Cow Rd, Polk City, FL 33868; memberservices@usawaterski.org; http://usawaterski.org. Illus., index. *Aud.:* Ga, Ac.

Since 1952, *The Water Skier,* the official publication of USA Water Ski, has published articles for athletes and fans of all types of competitive water skiing (traditional, show, wakeboard, collegiate, kneeboard, barefoot, hydrofoil, racing, and disabled). Issues contain instructional articles, tournament reports, profiles of teams and athletes, water skiing safety, equipment reviews, and listings of ski camps and schools. An annual issue contains a comprehensive listing of tournaments throughout the nation, including entry forms and in-depth information on each event. The magazine is published six times a year. Recommended for public and academic libraries. URL: www.usawaterski.org

4752. *Women's Running.* Former titles (until 2009): *Her Sports + Fitness;* (until 2006): *Her Sports.* [ISSN: 2165-7106] 2004. 10x/yr. USD 19.95 (print or online ed.); USD 24.95 combined subscription (print & online eds.)). Ed(s): Rebecca Warren. Pocket Outdoor Media, 3002 Sterling Cir, Ste 100, Boulder, CO 80301; http://pocketoutdoormedia.com/. Adv. Circ: 40000. *Aud.:* Hs, Ga, Ac.

This glossy bimonthly targets the active, athletic woman. As the only running magazine specifically for women, it covers all aspects of the sport from beauty tips to nutrition to training. Several columns are written by experts, including physicians, nutritionists, and coaches. A recent issue included articles on coping with disappointment, getting rid of blisters, and gifts for Mother's Day. Women sports and fitness enthusiasts will appreciate reading this magazine at their public libraries. URL: http:// womensrunning.competitor.com

4753. *Wrestling U S A (Missoula).* Formerly (until 1980): *Scholastic Wrestling News.* [ISSN: 0199-6258] 1964. m. USD 35. Ed(s): Lanny Bryant, Cody Bryant. Wrestling U.S.A. Magazine, c/o Cody Bryant, 109 Apple House Ln, Missoula, MT 59802. Illus. Sample. *Indexed:* SD. *Aud.:* Hs, Ac.

As the "National Voice of Wrestling," *Wrestling USA* publishes articles about amateur wrestling at the youth, high school, and college level. Regular features include news, training, injury prevention, sports medicine, nutrition, coaching tips, events and tournaments, and teams. The audience for this magazine is the athlete, not the coach, fan, or parent. It is published 12 times a year-twice a month during October, March, and May, and once a month during September, November, December, January, February, and April. The journal's web site provides access to a cover gallery and article previews from 1965 to the present. Subscribers have the option of print only, print plus online, or online only. Appropriate for high school and academic libraries. URL: www.wrestlingusa.com/

■ STATISTICS

Daniel S. Dotson, Associate Professor, 155 South Oval Mall, 180E Orton Hall, The Ohio State University Libraries, Columbus, OH 43210; 614-688-0053; dotson.77@osu.edu

Introduction

Statistics seems to be widely used in nearly every field to seek answers, test for relationships, predict outcomes, or to simply have a better understanding. Statistics courses are found in some high schools and at most colleges and universities. Some programs are large enough to have an entirely separate statistics department and even have interdisciplinary statistics programs such as biostatistics.

It seems as if statistics is used within nearly every discipline and on nearly any topic imaginable. Some degree programs in the sciences and social sciences may have requirements for students to take a statistics course, potentially one specifically tailored to their discipline. It would not be hard to find in the media the use (and sometimes misuse) of statistics.

This section includes 40 titles, many of which are of use for libraries that serve a college or university with a statistics program or programs that rely heavily on the use of statistics in their research. Several titles focus on applications in specific disciplines.

A few titles can trace their origins back as far as the mid-1800s, showing the longevity of the study of statistics. Most began in the mid- to late 1900s, with a few premiering in the current century. Many have content available online back to their first volume via JSTOR, Project Euclid, or their publisher's site.

In addition to commercially published titles, many statistical societies are represented, including the American Statistical Association, the Royal Statistical Society, the Institute for Mathematical Statistics, the Statistical Society of Australia, the New Zealand Statistical Association, the Statistical Science Association of Canada, and the Statistical Society of Canada.

Beyond the basic abstracts and indexes, several titles may be included in appropriate subject databases for specific science and social science disciplines. Citation indexes *Web of Science* and *Scopus* also cover many of these titles.

Those wishing to view free content are encouraged to check out arXiv.org for preprints/eprints and to look for open-access journals at the *Directory of Open Access Journals.* Some titles in this list provide select open-access content. Several open-access peer-reviewed journals (such as *Journal of Statistical Software, Bayesian Analysis, Electronic Journal of Statistics,* and *Electronic Journal of Probability*) are excellent sources of information.

Basic Periodicals

Hs: *Chance (Philadelphia, 1988);* Ga: *Chance (Philadelphia, 1988); Statistical Science;* Ac: *Advances in Applied Probability; American Statistical Association. Journal(JASA); The American Statistician; Annals of Applied Probability; Annals of Applied Statistics; Annals of Probability; Annals of Statistics; Canadian Journal of Statistics: La Revue Canadienne de Statistique; Computational Statistics; International Statistical Review; Royal Statistical Society. Journal. Series C: Applied Statistics;* Sa: *Advances in Applied Probability; American Statistical Association. Journal; Annals of Applied Probability; Annals of Probability; Annals of Statistics; Computational Statistics; Royal Statistical Society. Journal. Series C: Applied Statistics.*

Basic Abstracts and Indexes

MathSciNet, zbMATH.

4754. *Advances in Applied Probability.* [ISSN: 0001-8678] 1969. 5x/yr. GBP 298 (print & online eds.)). Cambridge University Press, University Printing House, Shaftesbury Rd, Cambridge, CB2 8BS, United Kingdom; journals@cambridge.org; https://www.cambridge.org/. Illus. Refereed. Reprint: PSC. *Indexed:* A22, B01, C45, MSN. *Aud.:* Ac, Sa.

Advances in Applied Probability publishes reviews and expository papers on topics in applied probability and related topics of interest. A special section on stochastic geometry and statistical applications are also included. Articles are typically in the 15- to 30-page range, with issues usually around 325 pages. Recent topics include the Mabinogion urn model. randomly connected neural networks, spatially explicit economical systems, ultrametric spaces, ARMA processes, and a special issue on branching and applied probability. This title is hosted by Cambridge University Press, and it is in JSTOR with a three-year moving wall. Recommended for libraries that serve colleges or universities with a statistics program.

4755. *American Statistical Association. Journal.* Former titles (until 1922): *American Statistical Association. Quarterly Publications;* (until 1912): *American Statistical Association. Publications.* [ISSN: 0162-1459] 1888. q. GBP 558 (print & online eds.)). American Statistical Association, 732

N Washington St, Alexandria, VA 22314; asainfo@amstat.org; http://www.amstat.org. Illus., index, adv. Refereed. Circ: 12000. Vol. ends: Dec. Microform: PMC; PQC. Reprint: PSC. *Indexed:* A22, B01, BRI, EconLit, IBSS, MSN. *Bk. rev.:* 10-20, 500-1,000 words. *Aud.:* Ac, Sa.

The *Journal of the American Statistical Association* dates back to 1888 and has published more than 500 issues. Articles are typically in the 10- to 25-page range, with issues usually around 450 pages. In addition to more theoretical or methodological articles, a wide range of applied topics are also covered. Recent topics include mobile health, U.S. wind gusts, optimal individualized treatment rules, vaccine sieve effects, and gene set enrichment analysis. Recommended for libraries that serve colleges or universities with a statistics program.

4756. *The American Statistician.* Formerly (until 1947): *American Statistical Association. Bulletin.* [ISSN: 0003-1305] 1947. q. GBP 170 (print & online eds.)). Ed(s): Dan Jeske. American Statistical Association, 732 N Washington St, Alexandria, VA 22314; asainfo@amstat.org; http://www.amstat.org. Illus., adv. Refereed. Vol. ends: Nov. Reprint: PSC. *Indexed:* A01, A22, B01, BRI, C45, MSN. *Bk. rev.:* 4-5, 800-1,200 words. *Aud.:* Ac, Sa.

Dating back to 1947, *The American Statistician* is divided into these sections: "Statistical Practice," "General," "Teacher's Corner," "Statistical Computing and Graphics," "History Corner," "Interdisciplinary," "Letters to the Editor," and sections dedicated to reviews of books, teaching materials, and software. Most articles tend to be under ten pages, with most issues totaling under 100. Older issues are in JSTOR with a five-year moving wall. Recent topics include multiple items on p-values, multiple items on expert knowledge, an interactive trivia-based classroom activity used to teach confidence intervals, teaching ethics in a statistics curriculum, and guns and suicides. Recommended for libraries that serve colleges or universities with a statistics program. Teachers of statistics may find this title of special use.

4757. *Annals of Applied Probability.* [ISSN: 1050-5164] 1991. bi-m. USD 589 (print & online eds.)). Ed(s): Michael Phelan, Timo Seppalainen. Institute of Mathematical Statistics, PO Box 22718, Beachwood, OH 44122; ims@imstat.org; http://www.imstat.org. Illus., index. Refereed. Vol. ends: Dec. *Indexed:* A22, B01, MSN. *Aud.:* Ac, Sa.

Annals of Applied Probability publishes papers with a special focus on originality and importance. Content is hosted at Project Euclid, with content at JSTOR with a three-year moving wall. Issues average about 650 pages, with articles usually more than 20 pages, with some significantly longer. Recent topics include trace reconstruction, super-replication, chemical reaction networks, Walsh Brownian motion, and Knudsen gas. Recommended for libraries that serve colleges or universities with a statistics program.

4758. *The Annals of Applied Statistics.* [ISSN: 1932-6157] 2007. q. USD 589 (print & online eds.)). Ed(s): Tilmann Gneiting. Institute of Mathematical Statistics, 3163 Somerset Dr, Shaker Heights, OH 44122; ims@imstat.org; http://www.imstat.org. Illus. Refereed. *Indexed:* MSN. *Aud.:* Ac, Sa.

The Annals of Applied Statistics publishes papers on a wide range of applied statistics topics. Content is hosted at Project Euclid, with content in JSTOR with a three-year moving wall. Issues average around 675 pages, with articles typically in the 15- to 40-page range. Recent topics include ground-level ozone, summer reading intervention, structure of brain networks, race-independent recidivism prediction, and online ratings data. Recommended for libraries that serve colleges or universities with a statistics program. Some articles may be of interest to those studying statistics within other subject disciplines.

4759. *Annals of Probability.* Supersedes in part (in 1973): *Annals of Mathematical Statistics.* [ISSN: 0091-1798] 1930. bi-m. USD 589 (print & online eds.) Free to members). Ed(s): Maria Eulalia Vares. Institute of Mathematical Statistics, 3163 Somerset Dr, Shaker Heights, OH 44122; ims@imstat.org; http://www.imstat.org. Illus. Refereed. *Indexed:* A22, MSN. *Aud.:* Ac, Sa.

Annals of Probability focuses on topics in probability, including applications to various areas of the sciences, with an emphasis on importance, interest, and originality. Content is hosted at Project Euclid and has a three-year moving wall at JSTOR. Articles are typically more than 20 pages, some significantly longer. Issues average around 600 pages. Recent topics include interacting particle systems, random spherical harmonics, Renyi divergence, coupling in the Heisenberg group, and generalized Orlicz balls. Recommended for libraries that serve colleges or universities with a statistics program.

4760. *Annals of Statistics.* Supersedes in part (in 1973): *Annals of Mathematical Statistics.* [ISSN: 0090-5364] 1930. bi-m. USD 589 (print & online eds.) Free to members). Ed(s): Tailen Hsing, Edward I George. Institute of Mathematical Statistics, 3163 Somerset Dr, Shaker Heights, OH 44122; ims@imstat.org; http://www.imstat.org. Illus. Refereed. *Indexed:* A22, MSN. *Aud.:* Ac, Sa.

Annals of Statistics publishes high-quality papers on various topics in statistics, with importance and originality emphasized. Hosted at Project Euclid, it also has a three-year moving wall at JSTOR. Issues average about 650 pages, with articles in the 20- to 50-page range. Recent topics include Bayesian analysis of big data, cyclic arrival rates. high-frequency data, definitive screening designs, and the Stiefel manifold. Recommended for libraries that serve colleges or universities with a statistics program.

4761. *Australian & New Zealand Journal of Statistics.* Formed by the merger of (1966-1998): *New Zealand Statistician;* (1959-1998): *Australian Journal of Statistics;* Which was formerly (until 1959): *Statistical Society of New South Wales. Bulletin.* [ISSN: 1369-1473] 1998. q. GBP 323. Ed(s): James Curran. Wiley-Blackwell Publishing Asia, 155 Cremorne St, Richmond, VIC 3121, Australia; melbourne@wiley.com; http://onlinelibrary.wiley.com. Illus., index, adv. Sample. Refereed. Vol. ends: Dec. Reprint: PSC. *Indexed:* A01, A22, BRI, E01, MSN. *Bk. rev.:* 3-6, 300-1,000 words. *Aud.:* Ac, Sa.

The *Australian & New Zealand Journal of Statistics* is divided into two main sections: "Applications and Theory" and "Methods." Recent topics include bias correction of estimated proportions, constructing narrower confidence intervals, modeling spatial dependence in a network, orthogonal designs, and modeling seismicity. Issues end with book reviews and a list of forthcoming papers. Issues average around 125 pages, with articles typically in the 10- to 20-page range. Recommended for libraries that serve colleges or universities with a statistics program.

4762. *Bernoulli: a journal of mathematical statistics and probability.* [ISSN: 1350-7265] 1995. q. USD 589 (print & online eds.)). Ed(s): Richard A Davis. International Statistical Institute, PO Box 24070, The Hague, 2490 AB, Netherlands; isi@cbs.nl; http://www.cbs.nl/. Illus. Refereed. *Indexed:* A22, E01, MSN. *Aud.:* Ac, Sa.

Published by the Bernoulli Society in conjunction with the Institute of Mathematical Statistics, *Bernoulli* publishes papers on theoretical and applied topics in probability and statistics. Content is hosted at Project Euclid, with older content at JSTOR with a five-year moving wall. Issues average about one thousand pages, with articles usually running 20 to 40 pages. Recent topics include nonparametric testing, high-dimensional prediction, locally stationary Hawkes processes, Thurstonian choice models, and spectral matrix measures. Recommended for libraries that serve colleges or universities with a statistics program.

4763. *Biometrical Journal: journal of mathematical methods in biosciences.* Formerly (until 1977): *Biometrische Zeitschrift.* [ISSN: 0323-3847] 1959. bi-m. GBP 1951. Ed(s): Dankmar Bohning, Marco Alfo. Wiley - V C H Verlag GmbH & Co. KGaA, Postfach 101161, Weinheim, 69451, Germany; cs-germany@wiley.com; http://www.vchgroup.de. Illus., adv. Sample. Refereed. Reprint: PSC. *Indexed:* A22, BRI, MSN. *Bk. rev.:* Occasional, 400-800 words. *Aud.:* Ac, Sa.

Biometrical Journal publishes statistical topics relevant to the life sciences. Case studies, review articles, and letters to the editors are welcome, but purely theoretical statistical papers are not accepted. Issues average around 200 pages, with articles usually in the 10- to 25-page range. Recent topics include chronic prostatitis/chronic pelvic pain syndrome, voice disorder risks, haplotype association studies, cause of death, and cancer phase I trial design. Recommended for libraries that serve colleges and universities with statistics or medical programs. Biostatistics programs would find this journal highly useful.

4764. *Biometrics.* Formerly (until 1947): *Biometrics Bulletin.* [ISSN: 0006-341X] 1945. q. GBP 451. Ed(s): Yi-Hau Chen. Wiley-Blackwell Publishing Ltd., The Atrium, Southern Gate, Chichester, PO19 8QG, United Kingdom; cs-journals@wiley.com; http://onlinelibrary.wiley.com/. Illus., index, adv. Sample. Refereed. Vol. ends: Dec. Microform: BHP; PMC; PQC. Reprint: PSC. *Indexed:* A01, A22, Agr, BRI, C45, E01, MSN, SD. *Bk. rev.:* 10-20, 200-1,000 words. *Aud.:* Ac, Sa.

Biometrics publishes papers in statistical or mathematical topics in the biosciences. Older issues are in JSTOR with a five-year moving wall. Issues average about 375 pages, with articles generally in the 5- to 20-page range. Recent topics include instrumental variable studies, high dimensional confounding adjustment, interval-censored data with informative dropout, brain activation and connectivity in fMRI data, and the Aalen-Johansen estimator. Recommended for libraries that serve colleges or universities with a statistics program. Medical and biology programs may also find it useful, while biostatistics programs will find it highly useful.

4765. *Biometrika.* [ISSN: 0006-3444] 1901. q. EUR 211. Ed(s): A C Davison. Oxford University Press, Great Clarendon St, Oxford, OX2 6DP, United Kingdom; onlinequeries.uk@oup.com; http://global.oup.com. Illus., adv. Sample. Refereed. Microform: PMC; PQC. Reprint: PSC. *Indexed:* A01, A22, C45, E01, MSN. *Aud.:* Ac, Sa.

Biometrika publishes papers on original theoretical contributions of value in applications; papers in bordering fields are occasionally accepted. Older issues are in JSTOR with a five-year moving wall. Issues average about 250 pages, with articles in the 10- to 20-page range. Recent topics include extremal behavior of aggregated data, classification of functional fragments, a mixture cure model, cumulative hazard estimates, and scanning statistics. Recommended for libraries that serve colleges or universities with a statistics program. Medical and biology programs will also find it useful, while biostatistics programs will find it highly useful.

4766. *Biostatistics.* [ISSN: 1465-4644] 2000. q. EUR 904. Ed(s): Dimitris Rizopoulos. Oxford University Press, Great Clarendon St, Oxford, OX2 6DP, United Kingdom; onlinequeries.uk@oup.com; http://global.oup.com. Illus., adv. Sample. Refereed. Reprint: PSC. *Indexed:* A01, A22, C45, E01. *Aud.:* Ac, Sa.

Biostatistics publishes papers on statistical topics related to human health and disease. The year's last issue includes an index. Issues average around 150 pages, with articles usually ranging 10 to 20 pages. Select articles are followed by commentaries or discussion. Recent topics include the rate of HIV testing, medical imaging analysis, professional soccer players, genetic pleiotropy, and asthma sufferers. Recommended for libraries that serve colleges or universities with a statistics program. Medical and biology programs will find it useful, while biostatistics programs will find it highly useful.

4767. *Canadian Journal of Statistics (Online).* [ISSN: 1708-945X] 1973. q. GBP 279. Ed(s): David A Stephens, Roman Viveros-Aguilera. John Wiley & Sons, Inc., 111 River St, Hoboken, NJ 07030; cs-journals@wiley.com; http://onlinelibrary.wiley.com. Refereed. *Aud.:* Ac, Sa.

Canadian Journal of Statistics publishes papers that are broad in scope and of interest to many readers. Older issues are in JSTOR with a three-year moving wall. Issues average around 175 pages, with articles usually 10 to 30 pages. Recent topics include the Bay of Fundy sea scallop fishery, storm cell modeling, imaging genetics, multivariate survival data, and response adaptive designs. Recommended for libraries that serve colleges or universities with a statistics program.

4768. *Chance (Philadelphia, 1988).* [ISSN: 0933-2480] 1987. q. GBP 100. Taylor & Francis Inc., 530 Walnut St, Ste 850, Philadelphia, PA 19106; support@tandfonline.com; http://www.tandfonline.com. Illus., index, adv. Vol. ends: No. 4. Microform: PQC. Reprint: PSC. *Indexed:* A01, A22, BRI, E01. *Aud.:* Hs, Ga.

Chance is a magazine meant for anyone interested in statistics, and it covers statistics topics in all science and social sciences areas. It is meant to entertain and inform. Issues are typically under 75 pages, with articles usually under ten (and often under five) pages. Recent topics include graduate student admissions, teaching statistics in the health sciences, crowdsourcing and big data, falsity of research publication findings, and length of The Beatles' songs. This title is good for most libraries, including college, university, and high school libraries that serve schools that teach statistics.

4769. *Computational Statistics.* Formerly (until 1992): *C S Q - Computational Statistics Quarterly.* [ISSN: 0943-4062] 1982. q. EUR 1120 (print & online eds.)). Ed(s): Yuichi Mori. Springer, Tiergartenstr 17, Heidelberg, 69121, Germany; subscriptions@springer.com; https://www.springer.com. Illus. Refereed. Vol. ends: No. 4. Reprint: PSC. *Indexed:* A01, A22, BRI, E01, MSN. *Bk. rev.:* 1, 700-800 words. *Aud.:* Ac, Sa.

Computational Statistics publishes papers on applied and methodological research topics in computational statistics. Issues average around 500 pages. Articles are usually in the 15- to 30-page range. Recent topics include AIDS studies, population heterogeneity in growth trajectories, simulation of Student-Levy processes, weighted Kendall correlation, and single diamond grinding. Recommended for libraries that serve colleges or universities with a statistics program. Certain computer science programs may also find it of interest.

4770. *Computational Statistics & Data Analysis.* Incorporates (1975-1991): *Statistical Software Newsletter.* [ISSN: 0167-9473] 1983. 12x/yr. EUR 3502. Ed(s): A M Colubi, J C Lee. Elsevier BV, Radarweg 29, Amsterdam, 1043 NX, Netherlands; info@elsevier.com; https://www.elsevier.com/. Illus., index, adv. Sample. Refereed. Vol. ends: No. 35 - No. 37. Microform: PQC. *Indexed:* A01, A22, MSN. *Aud.:* Ac, Sa.

Computational Statistics & Data Analysis is the official journal of the International Association of Statistical Computing. Issue average around 200 pages. Articles are usually in the 10- to 20-page range. Recent topics include variation in stochastic textured surfaces, in-sample forecasting methods, bivariate empirical copulas, conditional Kendall's tau, and robust subspace estimators. Libraries that serve colleges and universities with statistics programs will find this title useful. Some computer science programs may also find the title of use.

4771. *Econometrica.* [ISSN: 0012-9682] 1933. bi-m. GBP 350 (print & online eds.)). Ed(s): Geri Mattson, Daron Acemoglu. Wiley-Blackwell Publishing Ltd., The Atrium, Southern Gate, Chichester, PO19 8QG, United Kingdom; cs-journals@wiley.com; http://www.wiley.com/. Illus., index, adv. Sample. Refereed. Vol. ends: Nov. Microform: PMC; PQC. Reprint: PSC. *Indexed:* A22, B01, BAS, C45, E01, EconLit, IBSS, MSN. *Aud.:* Ac, Sa.

Econometrica publishes papers on all economics topics. The papers often have a statistical bent. In addition to articles, issues may contain announcements, reports, and a list of forthcoming papers. Older issues are in JSTOR with a two-year moving wall. Issues average around 375 pages. Articles are usually in the 15 to 50 pages range, with many articles on the higher end. Recent topics include post-disaster neighborhood rebuilding, multivalued treatments, women's labor supply, economic development in Vietnam, and healthcare costs. This title is recommended for libraries that serve colleges and universities with a statistics program, and it would be of high value to those with business or economics programs that highly emphasize statistical methods.

4772. *International Statistical Review.* Incorporates (1980-2007): *Short Book Reviews;* Former titles (until 1972): *International Statistical Institute Review (Print);* (until 1933): *Institut International de Statistique. Office Permanent. Bulletin Mensuel.* [ISSN: 0306-7734] 1920. 3x/yr. GBP 426 (print & online eds.)). Ed(s): Vijay Nair, Marc Hallin. Wiley-Blackwell Publishing Ltd., The Atrium, Southern Gate, Chichester, PO19 8QG, United Kingdom; cs-journals@wiley.com; http://onlinelibrary.wiley.com. Illus., index, adv. Sample. Refereed. Reprint: PSC. *Indexed:* A01, A22, BRI, E01, MSN. *Bk. rev.:* 10-30 per issue, 100-400 words. *Aud.:* Ac, Sa.

International Statistical Review is the flagship journal of the International Statistical Institute and publishes articles on general-interest topics in probability and statistics. Types of articles published include reviews, expository papers, tutorials, historical topics, interviews, and book reviews. Issues typically have more than a dozen short book reviews. Older issues are in

JSTOR with a five-year moving wall. Issues average about 200 pages, with most scholarly articles under 25 pages. Recent topics include panel count data, medical fraud assessment, non-ignorable non-response, small area estimation, and microdata release. This title fits libraries that serve colleges and universities with statistics programs, and would be of interest to those with science or social science programs that emphasize the use of statistics.

4773. *Journal of Computational and Graphical Statistics.* [ISSN: 1061-8600] 1992. q. GBP 292 (print & online eds.)). Ed(s): Thomas C M Lee. Taylor & Francis Inc., 711 3rd Ave, 8th Fl, New York, NY 10017; support@tandfonline.com; http://www.tandfonline.com. Adv. Refereed. Circ: 1600. Reprint: PSC. *Indexed:* A01, A22, B01, C45, CompLI, MSN. *Aud.:* Ac, Sa.

Journal of Computational and Graphical Statistics publishes articles on computational and graphical methods in statistics and data analysis. The journal recommends that articles be written for those with expertise in statistics, but not necessarily in computing. Older issues are in JSTOR with a five-year moving wall. Issues average about 225 pages, with articles usually between 10 to 30 pages. Recent topics include iterative proportional scaling, irregular experimental regions, supervised statistical learning, pair-copula constructions, and network motif detection. Recommended for libraries that serve colleges and universities with a statistics program.

4774. *Journal of Multivariate Analysis.* [ISSN: 0047-259X] 1971. 10x/yr. EUR 3087. Ed(s): C Genest. Academic Press, 3251 Riverport Ln, Maryland Heights, MO 63043; JournalCustomerService-usa@elsevier.com; http://www.elsevier.com/. Adv. Sample. Refereed. *Indexed:* A01, A22, C45, E01, MSN. *Aud.:* Ac, Sa.

Journal of Multivariate Analysis publishes papers on topics in theoretical methods—and applications to new theoretical methods—in multivariate (and occasionally, univariate) analysis. Issues average around 275 pages, with articles usually numbering 10 to 25 pages. Recent topics include case-control studies for gene-environment independent models, financial distress, mutual fund flows, multiple functional data analysis topics, and a high-dimensional Ornstein-Uhlenbeck process. Recommended for libraries that serve colleges and universities with a statistics program.

4775. *Journal of Statistical Planning and Inference.* [ISSN: 0378-3758] 1977. 12x/yr. EUR 2912. Elsevier BV, North-Holland, Postbus 211, Amsterdam, 1000 AE, Netherlands; JournalsCustomerServiceEMEA@elsevier.com; http://www.elsevier.com. Illus. Refereed. Microform: PQC. *Indexed:* A01, A22, CompLI, MSN. *Aud.:* Ac, Sa.

Journal of Statistical Planning and Inference aims to cover how to collect (planning) and analyze (inference) data. It publishes both research and survey articles. Issues average around 150 pages. Articles are generally between 10 and 20 pages. Recent topics include regression discontinuity designs, Gaussian graphical model selection, checking proportional hazards model assumption, time series of counts, and population bioequivalence. Recommended for libraries that serve colleges and universities with a statistics program.

4776. *Journal of Theoretical Probability.* [ISSN: 0894-9840] 1988. q. EUR 1497 (print & online eds.)). Ed(s): James Allen Fill. Springer New York LLC, 233 Spring St, New York, NY 10013; customerservice@springer.com; http://www.springer.com. Illus., adv. Sample. Refereed. Microform: PQC. Reprint: PSC. *Indexed:* A22, E01, MSN. *Aud.:* Ac, Sa.

Journal of Theoretical Probability covers topics in all areas of probability theory. Issues average around 625 pages, with articles typically in the 15- to 40-page range. Recent topics include competing Brownian particles, Feynman-Kac semigroups, heavy-tailed random variables, rank-one inhomogeneous random graphs, and Markov death-process equations. Recommended for libraries that serve colleges and universities with a statistics program.

4777. *Journal of Time Series Analysis.* [ISSN: 0143-9782] 1980. bi-m. GBP 1775. Ed(s): Robert Taylor. Wiley-Blackwell Publishing Ltd., The Atrium, Southern Gate, Chichester, PO19 8QG, United Kingdom; cs-journals@wiley.com; http://onlinelibrary.wiley.com. Illus., adv. Sample. Refereed. Reprint: PSC. *Indexed:* A01, A22, BRI, E01, IBSS, MSN. *Bk. rev.:* One per issue, 400-600 words. *Aud.:* Ac, Sa.

Journal of Time Series Analysis publishes papers on both fundamental theory and applications on topics in time series analysis. Short communications on theoretical developments and book reviews are sometimes included. Occasionally, issues are dedicated to a specific topic. Issues average about 175 pages, with articles usually in the 10- to 30-page range. Recent topics include spatio-temporal methodology, Arctic sea ice, daily wind speed, DSGE models, and explosive financial bubbles. Recommended for libraries that serve colleges and universities with a statistics program.

4778. *Lifetime Data Analysis: an international journal devoted to the methods and applications of reliability and survival analysis.* [ISSN: 1380-7870] 1995. q. EUR 1147 (print & online eds.)). Ed(s): Mei-Ling Ting Lee. Springer New York LLC, 233 Spring St, New York, NY 10013; customerservice@springer.com; http://www.springer.com. Illus., adv. Refereed. Reprint: PSC. *Indexed:* A22, B01, C45, E01, MSN. *Aud.:* Ac, Sa.

Lifetime Data Analysis is dedicated to statistical methods and applications in lifetime data analysis. It covers a broad range of lifetime data topics in the sciences and social sciences. Issues average around 200 pages, with articles usually 10 to 25 pages. Recent topics include HIV vaccine studies, survival-out-of-hospital, clinical prediction models, multivariate Nelson-Aalen estimators, and quadrivariate udder infection times. Libraries that serve colleges and universities with statistics or medical programs will find this title of use. Biostatistics programs will find it highly useful.

4779. *Multivariate Behavioral Research.* [ISSN: 0027-3171] 1966. bi-m. GBP 858 (print & online eds.)). Ed(s): Keith Widaman. Psychology Press, 530 Walnut St, Philadelphia, PA 19106; orders@taylorandfrancis.com; http://www.psypress.com. Illus., adv. Sample. Refereed. Microform: PQC. Reprint: PSC. *Indexed:* A01, A22, B01, E01, ERIC. *Aud.:* Ac, Sa.

Multivariate Behavioral Research publishes substantive, methodological, and theoretical papers with a multivariate research angle in all areas of the social sciences. Pedagogical and historical topics are also welcome. Issues may be dedicated to a specific topic. Issues average about 150 pages, with articles usually 10 to 25 pages. Recent topics include the COGITO Project (multiple articles), interviewer effects on nonresponse, correcting for sampling error and measurement error, structural equation modeling of social networks, and dyadic interactions. Recommended for libraries that serve colleges or universities with statistics programs, or programs that highly emphasize the use of advanced statistics in behavioral research.

4780. *Probability Theory and Related Fields.* Formerly (until 1985): *Zeitschrift fuer Wahrscheinlichkeitstheorie und Verwandte Gebiete.* [ISSN: 0178-8051] 1962. q. EUR 1824 (print & online eds.)). Ed(s): F. Martinelli, M. Ledoux. Springer, Tiergartenstr 17, Heidelberg, 69121, Germany. Illus., adv. Sample. Refereed. Reprint: PSC. *Indexed:* A01, A22, B01, E01, MSN. *Aud.:* Ac, Sa.

Probability Theory and Related Fields publishes in probability theory and its relations to analysis, geometry, and other areas of mathematics or other, applied fields. Survey papers on emerging areas of importance are also published. Combined double issues average around 575 pages, with articles typically more than 20 pages. Recent topics include the Wiener sausage in dimension four, Liouville quantum gravity, sparse Markov chains, population genetics, and cut-off for lamplighter chains on tori. Recommended for libraries that serve colleges and universities with a statistics program.

4781. *Royal Statistical Society. Journal. Series A: Statistics in Society.* Incorporates in part (1962-2004): *Royal Statistical Society. Journal. Series D: The Statistician;* Which was formerly (1950-1961): *Incorporated Statistician;* Former titles (until 1988): *Royal Statistical Society. Journal. Series A: General;* (until 1948): *Royal Statistical*

Society. Journal; (until 1886): *Statistical Society. Journal;* (until 1838): *Statistical Society of London. Proceedings.* [ISSN: 0964-1998] 1834. q. GBP 417 (print or online ed.)). Wiley-Blackwell Publishing Ltd., The Atrium, Southern Gate, Chichester, PO19 8QG, United Kingdom; cs-journals@wiley.com; http://onlinelibrary.wiley.com. Illus., adv. Sample. Refereed. Microform: BHP. Reprint: PSC. *Indexed:* A22, Agr, B01, BRI, C45, E01, EconLit, IBSS, MLA-IB, MSN. *Bk. rev.:* 5-15 per issue, 300-500 words. *Aud.:* Ac, Sa.

Journal of the Royal Statistical Society. Series A: Statistics in Society publishes papers on statistical topics that are applicable to the real world. Papers should be clearly written, quantitative approaches to topics rather than technically detailed. This journal covers statistics as applied to a wide range of science and social science topics. Welcome are papers on popular or contentious statistical issues, reviews of topics, historical topics, professional issues, biographies, discussions of data collection methods, and ethical issues. Book reviews and obituaries may be found toward the end of an issue. This journal, along with Parts B and C, can trace its origins back to the 1838 premiere of *Journal of the Statistical Society of London.* Older issues, including its predecessor titles, are in JSTOR with a four-year moving wall. Issues average about 325 pages, with articles generally 15 to 30 pages. Recent topics include the Dutch 2017 election, measuring material deprivation, Brexit, property insurance, childhood poverty, and contraceptive behavior in India. Highly recommended for libraries that serve colleges and universities with a statistics program, or those with courses in the social sciences and sciences that heavily emphasize statistics.

4782. ***Royal Statistical Society. Journal. Series B: Statistical Methodology.*** Former titles (until 1998): *Royal Statistical Society. Journal. Series B: Methodological;* (until 1948): *Royal Statistical Society. Journal. Supplement.* [ISSN: 1369-7412] 1934. 5x/yr. GBP 397. Ed(s): I Van Keilegom. Wiley-Blackwell Publishing Ltd., The Atrium, Southern Gate, Chichester, PO19 8QG, United Kingdom; cs-journals@wiley.com; http://onlinelibrary.wiley.com. Illus., index, adv. Sample. Refereed. Vol. ends: No. 4. Reprint: PSC. *Indexed:* A22, Agr, B01, C45, E01, IBSS, MSN. *Aud.:* Ac, Sa.

Journal of the Royal Statistical Society. Series B: Statistical Methodology publishes papers on statistical topics that are at the leading edge of methodological development and that are relevant to statistical practice. This journal, along with Parts A and C, can trace origins back to the 1838 premiere of *Journal of the Statistical Society of London.* Older issues, including its predecessor titles, are in JSTOR with a four-year moving wall. Issues average about 225 pages, although longer issues are sometimes published. Articles are typically 15 to 30 pages, with occasionally much lengthier ones. Some articles may be followed by comments. Recent topics include clustering functional data into groups, hypoelliptic diffusions, sparse reduced rank regression, time series models with conditional heteroscedasticity, and finely stratified experiments. Highly recommended for libraries that serve colleges and universities with a statistics program, or those with courses in the social sciences and sciences that heavily emphasize statistics.

4783. ***Royal Statistical Society. Journal. Series C: Applied Statistics.*** Incorporates in part (in 2004): *Royal Statistical Society. Journal. Series D. The Statistician;* Which was formerly (1950-1961): *Incorporated Statistician.* [ISSN: 0035-9254] 1952. 5x/yr. GBP 373. Ed(s): N Stallard, P W F Smith. Wiley-Blackwell Publishing Ltd., The Atrium, Southern Gate, Chichester, PO19 8QG, United Kingdom; cs-journals@wiley.com; http://onlinelibrary.wiley.com. Illus., index, adv. Sample. Refereed. Vol. ends: No. 4. Reprint: PSC. *Indexed:* A22, Agr, B01, C45, E01, IBSS, MSN. *Aud.:* Ac, Sa.

Journal of the Royal Statistical Society, Series C: Applied Statistics publishes papers that apply statistics to real-life problems in many areas of science and social science. This journal, along with Parts A and B, can trace its origins back to the 1838 premiere of *Journal of the Statistical Society of London.* Older issues, including its predecessor titles, are in JSTOR with a four-year moving wall. Issues average around 300 pages, with articles generally in the 15- to 30-page range. Recent topics include functional magnetic resonance imaging data, Log-Gaussian Cox point processes, count fertility data, multiple items on early phase clinical trial design methodology, and projecting UK mortality. Highly recommended for libraries that serve colleges and universities with a statistics program, or those with courses in the social sciences and sciences that heavily emphasize statistics.

4784. ***Scandinavian Journal of Statistics: theory and applications.*** [ISSN: 0303-6898] 1974. q. GBP 240. Ed(s): Niels Richard Hansen, Peter Dalgaard. Wiley-Blackwell Publishing Ltd., The Atrium, Southern Gate, Chichester, PO19 8QG, United Kingdom; cs-journals@wiley.com; http://onlinelibrary.wiley.com. Illus., index, adv. Sample. Refereed. Vol. ends: Dec. Reprint: PSC. *Indexed:* A01, A22, B01, E01, MSN. *Aud.:* Ac, Sa.

Scandinavian Journal of Statistics: Theory and Applications publishes significant and innovative original contributions on applied and theoretical topics in statistical methodology. Older issues are in JSTOR with a five-year moving wall. Issues average about 275 pages, with articles usually 10 to 30 pages. Recent topics include nonparametric AR-ARCH models, Rosen's fibrous composites experiments, ZIP-distributed data, linear factor copula models, and covariate-varying heterogeneity. Recommended for libraries that serve colleges and universities with a statistics program.

4785. ***Statistica Sinica.*** [ISSN: 1017-0405] 1991. q. USD 255. Ed(s): P Hall, K-Y Liang. Academia Sinica, Institute of Statistical Science, 128, Sec 2 Yen-chiu-Yuan Rd, Taipei, 115, Taiwan, Republic of China; http://www.stat.sinica.edu.tw/. Illus. Refereed. *Indexed:* A22, MSN. *Aud.:* Ac, Sa.

Statistica Sinica focuses on articles that promote the principled use of statistics. Issues may be dedicated to a specific topic or may be dedicated to general topics or discussion. Issues are freely available after one year. Issues average around 725 pages, with articles usually 10 to 30 pages. It is in JSTOR with a one-year moving wall. Recent topics include distributed monitoring large-scale data streams, additive mean residual life model, nearly unstable processes, and dimensional analysis. Recommended for libraries that serve colleges and universities with a statistics program.

4786. ***Statistical Methods in Medical Research.*** [ISSN: 0962-2802] 1992. bi-m. USD 1914 (print & online eds.)). Ed(s): Brian Everitt. Sage Publications Ltd., 1 Oliver's Yard, 55 City Rd, London, EC1Y 1SP, United Kingdom; info@sagepub.com; https://www.sagepub.com/. Illus. Sample. Refereed. Reprint: PSC. *Indexed:* A01, A22, ASSIA, C45, E01, MSN. *Aud.:* Ac, Sa.

Statistical Methods in Medical Research publishes papers on topics in medical statistics and aims to inform medical professionals on the latest available statistical techniques in medicine. Issue length averages around 325 pages, with articles usually 10 to 25 pages. Recent topics include imaging biomarker quantification methods, food-borne disease outbreaks, placebo effects, single-arm clinical-trial data, and epilepsy trials. While libraries that serve colleges and universities with a statistics program may find this title useful, biostatistics or medical programs will find this title even more useful.

4787. ***Statistical Science.*** [ISSN: 0883-4237] 1986. q. USD 335 (print & online eds.)). Ed(s): Peter Green. Institute of Mathematical Statistics, 3163 Somerset Dr, Shaker Heights, OH 44122; ims@imstat.org; http://www.imstat.org. Illus., index. Refereed. Vol. ends: Nov. *Indexed:* A22, MSN. *Aud.:* Ac, Sa.

Statistical Science publishes papers on important statistics topics with a wide range of interest, with casual readers being the main target audience. The interview articles contained in most issues are popular among readers. Older issues are in JSTOR with a three-year moving wall. Issues average about 175 pages, with articles usually in the 10- to 30-page range. Recent topics include probabilistic integration, multiple topics on nonparametric inference under shape constraints, self-exciting spatio-temporal point processes, continuous-time Monte Carlo, and conversations with multiple statisticians. Recommended for libraries that serve colleges and universities with a statistics program, or those with programs that emphasize statistical methods in science or social science research.

4788. ***Statistics: a journal of theoretical and applied statistics.*** Formerly (until 1985): *Series Statistics;* Which superseded in part (in 1977): *Mathematische Operationsforschung und Statistik.* [ISSN: 0233-1888] 1970. bi-m. GBP 2722 (print & online eds.)). Ed(s): Roland Fried,

Markus Reiss. Taylor & Francis, 2, 3 & 4 Park Sq, Milton Park, Abingdon, OX14 4RN, United Kingdom; subscriptions@tandf.co.uk; https://www.tandfonline.com. Illus., adv. Sample. Refereed. Reprint: PSC. *Indexed:* A01, A22, E01, MSN. *Aud.:* Ac, Sa.

Statistics: A Journal of Theoretical and Applied Statistics publishes papers on interesting and novel contributions to theoretical and applied statistics. Occasionally, conference proceedings and related announcements are included. Issues average about 250 pages, with most articles 10 to 25 pages. Recent topics include Bernstein-type inequalities, the generalized Gudermannian distribution, estimating the rare sensitive parameter under Poisson distribution, quantile regression for large-scale data, and ranked set sampling. Recommended for libraries that serve colleges and universities with a statistics program.

4789. ***Statistics and Computing.*** [ISSN: 0960-3174] 1991. q. EUR 1450 (print & online eds.)). Ed(s): Mark Girolami. Springer New York LLC, 233 Spring St, New York, NY 10013; customerservice@springer.com; http://www.springer.com. Illus., adv. Sample. Refereed. Reprint: PSC. *Indexed:* A22, BRI, E01, MSN. *Bk. rev.:* Occasional. *Aud.:* Ac, Sa.

Statistics and Computing covers topics related to the use of statistics in computer science and the use of computers in data analysis. Included are original research reports, authoritative topic reviews, paper discussions, and occasional book or software reviews. Special issues on a topic or relevant conference papers occasionally appear. Issues average around 200 pages, with articles typically 10 to 25 pages. Recent topics include complex-valued time series, tempered Levy processes, the Horseshoe Probit model, Langevin diffusions on the torus, and Bayesian analysis of big data. Recommended for libraries that serve colleges and universities with statistics programs. Some computer science programs may find it of use as well.

4790. ***Stochastic Processes and Their Applications.*** [ISSN: 0304-4149] 1973. 12x/yr. EUR 1891. Ed(s): H Dehling. Elsevier BV, North-Holland, Postbus 211, Amsterdam, 1000 AE, Netherlands; JournalsCustomerServiceEMEA@elsevier.com; http://www.elsevier.com. Illus., index. Refereed. Vol. ends: No. 2. Microform: PQC. *Indexed:* A01, A22, C45, MSN. *Aud.:* Ac, Sa.

Stochastic Processes and Their Applications publishes articles on theoretical or applied stochastic processes topics in mathematics, science, and engineering. Issues average around 350 pages, with articles typically 15 to 50 pages. Recent topics include exceptional rare events of ergodic maps, two dimensional stochastic Navier-Stokes equations, stochastic invariance of closed sets, stochastic particle systems, and biased bootstrap random walks. Recommended for libraries that serve colleges and universities with statistics programs.

4791. ***Technometrics: a journal of statistics for the physical, chemical and engineering sciences.*** [ISSN: 0040-1706] 1959. 4x/yr. GBP 160 (print & online eds.)). Ed(s): Hugh A Chipman. American Statistical Association, 732 N Washington St, Alexandria, VA 22314; asainfo@amstat.org; http://www.amstat.org. Illus., index. Refereed. Vol. ends: Nov. Microform: PQC. Reprint: PSC. *Indexed:* A01, A22, B01, BRI, MSN. *Bk. rev.:* 30-40, 300-2,000 words. *Aud.:* Ac, Sa.

Technometrics publishes papers on statistical methods in the physical and chemical sciences and in engineering. The journal expresses a desire to address issues related to huge data sets in industry. Book reviews are included in some issues, and the year's last issue contains an index. Occasionally, a paper will be followed by comments and a rejoinder. Some papers contain supplementary information online. Older issues are in JSTOR with a five-year moving wall. Issues average about 150 pages, with articles typically running 10 to 20 pages. Recent topics include stochastic simulation experiments, fractional factorial designs, optimal alignment of carbon nanotubes, massive spatial datasets, and accelerated life tests. Recommended for libraries that serve colleges and universities with statistics programs, or those with chemical/physical science programs that emphasize advanced statistics.

4792. ***Test.*** Formerly (until 1992): *Trabajos de Estadistica;* Which superseded in part (in 1986): *Trabajos de Estadistica e Investigacion Operativa;* Which was formerly (until 1963): *Trabajos de Estadistica.* [ISSN: 1133-0686] 1950. 3x/yr. EUR 446 (print & online eds.)). Ed(s): Ana F Militino, Alfonso Gordaliza. Springer, Tiergartenstr 17, Heidelberg, 69121, Germany; subscriptions@springer.com; https://www.springer.com. Illus., adv. Refereed. Reprint: PSC. *Indexed:* A22, E01, EconLit, MSN. *Aud.:* Ac, Sa.

Test focuses on publishing papers on original contributions to statistics or operations research that have, or may have, potential applications. Issues average around 250 pages, with articles usually running 15 to 40 pages. Recent topics include microarray data, accelerated life tests, single-index multiplicative models elevation data maps, and coca cultivation in Peru. Recommended for libraries that serve colleges and universities with a statistics program.

4793. ***Theory of Probability and Its Applications.*** [ISSN: 0040-585X] 1956. q. USD 1190 (print & online eds.)). Ed(s): A N Shiryaev. Society for Industrial and Applied Mathematics, 3600 Market St, 6th Fl, Philadelphia, PA 19104; siam@siam.org; http://www.siam.org. Illus., adv. Sample. Refereed. Vol. ends: Dec. *Indexed:* A01, A22, MSN. *Aud.:* Ac, Sa.

Theory of Probability and Its Applications is a translation of the Russian *Teoriya Veroyatnostei i ee Primeneniya.* The journal publishes papers on theoretical and applied topics in probability, statistics, and stochastic processes. News items are also included. Issues average about 175 pages, with articles generally running 5 to 25 pages. Recent topics include stability conditions for queueing systems, probability distributions on discrete Abelian groups, de Finetti's Theorem, discontinuous densities, and tails of Weibull-type distributions. Recommended for libraries that serve colleges and universities with a statistics program.

■ TEENAGERS

See also Children; Humor; Music; and Sports sections.

Amy Sprung, Librarian, Belmont Day School, 55 Day School Lane, Belmont, MA 02478; asprung@belmontday.org

Introduction

The most recent casualty in the dwindling print teen magazine landscape is *Seventeen,* which has turned to offering primarily digital content after 74 years in print. *Seventeen* will offer an email newsletter subscription, and plans to print four special editions annually that will be available at newsstands. This news follows *Teen Vogue* moving exclusively online at the end of 2017. *Teen Vogue* continues to provide online content including two newsletters: one fashion and beauty focused, and one focused on politics and news. *Rookie,* which was a refreshing alternative to a lot of standard teen fare, ceased operations at the end of 2018.

If you have teens who are looking to get published, *Teen Ink* remains a good bet. *Cicada* used to be standard for teens interested in poetry and fiction, but it has now ceased publication.

With the small field of teen magazines remaining, the best bet for collection development is interest and hobby based. Find out from your patrons what they are interested in and consult the sections of this publication that best support those interests. Some sections worth checking out depending on the interests of the teens you serve include "Cooking and Cookery," "Computers and Information Technology," "Dance," "Do-It-Yourself/Makers," "Sports," and "Music."

Basic Periodicals

Ga: *J-14.*

Basic Abstracts and Indexes

Readers' Guide to Periodical Literature.

Dance Spirit. See Dance section.

Essence. See Fashion and Lifestyle section.

4794. ***The Foxfire Magazine.*** Formerly (until 1992): *Foxfire.* [ISSN: 1084-5321] 1967. s-a. USD 12.95. Foxfire Fund, Inc., PO Box 541, Mountain City, GA 30562; foxfire@foxfire.org; http://www.foxfire.org. Illus., adv. Sample. Microform: PQC. *Indexed:* A22, MLA-IB. *Aud.:* Ems, Hs.

Originally created by high school students in Southern Appalachia in 1966 as a means of capturing and preserving their culture and the lives of senior citizens from their community, *The Foxfire Magazine* is still going strong. In addition to offering profiles of local elders, it is chock-full of photos, recipes, and other tidbits from local history. The students who work on the magazine do a fantastic job of capturing the voice of their subjects with love and humor. It's clear that a lot of work goes into each issue, which starts out with an editorial statement from one of the senior student editors. Highly recommended for area school and public libraries.

Game Informer Magazine. See Games and Gaming section.

4795. ***Girls' Life.*** [ISSN: 1078-3326] 1994. bi-m. USD 19.95. Ed(s): Karen Bokram. Girls' Life Acquisitions Corp., 4529 Harford Rd, Baltimore, MD 21214. Illus., adv. *Indexed:* BRI, C37, C42, GW, MASUSE, P01. *Bk. rev.:* Number and length vary. *Aud.:* Ems, Hs, Ga.

This wholesome teen magazine, geared toward young teenage girls, features your standard array of beauty, fashion, advice, star profiles, and quizzes. Many of the featured starlets, who often grace the cover, tend to be in their teens, and while there's not much sex talk, there is plenty of boy talk. Giveaways include fashion must-haves and beach reads. Issue-oriented features talk about topics like anxiety and homework.

4796. ***J-14.*** [ISSN: 1522-1989] 1999. 10x/yr. USD 14.97 domestic; USD 20.97 Canada; USD 26.97 elsewhere. Bauer Publishing Group, 270 Sylvan Ave, Englewood Cliffs, NJ 07632; info@bauerpublishing.com; http://www.bauerpublishing.com. Adv. *Aud.:* Ems, Hs, Ga.

This colorful, glossy teen magazine focuses on younger stars, many of Disney and Nick fame, as well as YouTubers, pop artists like Taylor Swift, and heartthrobs of the moment. It's just the fix for star-crazy young teens itching for the latest information about their favorite performers. *J-14,* also known as *Just for Teens* (get it?), is just one of just a few remaining print celeb worship choices. My local library's copies of *J-14* were falling apart, but it's unclear if that was from poor staple quality or excessive love. Check with your teens to see what they enjoy. Recommended for public libraries.

Mad. See Humor section.

Otaku USA. See Anime, Comics, Graphic Novels, and Manga section.

People. See General Interest section.

4797. ***Pro Wrestling Illustrated.*** [ISSN: 1043-7576] 1979. bi-m. USD 20.97 domestic; USD 37.47 foreign; USD 6.99 newsstand/cover. Kappa Publishing Group, Inc., 6198 Butler Pike, Ste 200, Blue Bell, PA 19422; http://www.kappapublishing.com. Illus., adv. *Aud.:* Hs, Ga.

As the title would imply, this publication is chock-full of images, which doesn't mean that there isn't plenty of commentary to go along with them. It includes lots of blood-splattered, full-color pictures. The content is geared solely toward professional wrestling fans, so if you serve teens who are interested in that, this title would be a great addition to your collection. Issues contain profiles of wrestlers, commentary on various personalities in that universe, and coverage of recent and historic matches. The writing is similar to that of other sports journalism.

Rolling Stone. See Music/Popular section.

4798. ***Seventeen (Online).*** Formerly (until 1944): *Stardom.* 1944. 5x/yr. Ed(s): Alison Sheffer Jurado. Hearst Magazines, 300 W 57th St, 28th Fl, New York, NY 10019; HearstMagazines@hearst.com; http://www.hearst.com. Illus., adv. Sample. Microform: NBI; PQC. *Indexed:* A22, BRI, C37. *Aud.:* Hs, Ga.

Now exclusively online, *Seventeen* is geared toward the older end of the teenage spectrum, with a polished look and some mature content. The following sections are featured in the menu on their site: celebrity, fashion, beauty, life, and LGBTQ. Online content has a strong entertainment and celebrity focus. Some recent features include awards for beauty products, shopping deals, and dorm room decor.

Sports Illustrated. See Sports/General section.

4799. ***Teen Ink.*** Formerly (until 2000): *The 21st Century.* [ISSN: 1545-1283] 1989. 10x/yr. USD 45 domestic. Ed(s): Cindy W Spertner, Natasza Gawlick. Young Authors Foundation, 2556 Apple Valley Rd NE #250, Atlanta, GA 30319; http://www.teenink.com. Adv. *Indexed:* MASUSE. *Bk. rev.:* Number and length vary. *Aud.:* Ems, Hs, Ga.

This magazine, with an updated look and logo, contains a variety of short fiction, poetry, reviews, opinion pieces, sports stories, nonfiction, and art created exclusively by teens. There is a healthy serving of teen angst and a wide range of quality. Reviews of music, movies, and books (both recent and classics) abound. Submitting to *Teen Ink* is a great option for teens hoping to get published, and if you have teens who contribute, it's a plus to carry the magazine so they can see their work in the library.

4800. ***Teen Vogue (Online).*** . Free. Conde Nast Publications, Inc., 1 World Trade Center, New York, NY 10007. *Aud.:* Hs, Ga, Ac.

Now exclusively online, *Teen Vogue* features political reporting with a feminist bent alongside fashion and beauty reporting. The online magazine features a more diverse group of teens than other options, and as a result, adults have been flocking to the publication as well. The production value is high, and the content can be edgy.

Thrasher. See Sports/Extreme Sports section.

Tu. See Latin America and Spain section.

■ TELEVISION, VIDEO, AND RADIO

Home Entertainment

See also Electronics; Films; and Media and AV sections.

Paul M. Worster, Multimodal Learning Librarian, Lamont Library–Harvard Yard, Harvard University, Cambridge, MA 02138; FAX: 617-496-3692; worster@fas.harvard.edu

Introduction

Is broadcast media dead, or is it the golden age of content? TV, at least? Did the death of television happen, yet? Television, video, and radio continue to evolve and thrive, and most of the lines that divide the media are continuing to blur. Broadcasters, networks, content producers, and aggregators are still experimenting with different online-distribution models, and so are our library patrons.

As may be expected, almost every title listed also has a significant online presence. Equipment reviews, technical challenges, interactive data models, and buyer's guides may be more easily accessed at the journal's website. Additionally, commercial broadcasting titles often have extensive online news updates.

This section attempts to address the needs of Communications and Media Studies departments, radio enthusiasts, film buffs, AV geeks, and anyone with a camera and an opinion. Some crossover with other sections, especially communications and film, is inescapable.

Those with an interest in broadcasting should check *Broadcast and Cable* and *Radio Ink.* Academic departments should also consider *Feminist Media Studies, Journal of Broadcasting and Electronic Media, Journal of Radio & Audio Media,* and *Media Report to Women.* Radio hobbyists may want to scan *QST* and possibly *QEX* or *NCJ.*

Basic Periodicals

Ac: *Broadcasting & Cable;* Sa: *Broadcasting & Cable; Radio Ink.*

Basic Abstracts and Indexes

Academic Search Premier, Film & Television Literature Index, Research Library (ProQuest).

Afterimage. See Photography section.

4801. *Broadcasting & Cable.* Former titles (until 1993): *Broadcasting (Washington);* (until 1957): *Broadcasting Telecasting;* (until 1948): *Broadcasting - The News Magazine of the Fifth Estate;* Incorporated (in 1961): *Television;* (in 1953): *Telecast;* (in 1933): *Broadcast Reporter; Broadcast Advertising.* [ISSN: 1068-6827] 1931. w. USD 249 combined subscription domestic (print & online eds.); USD 299 combined subscription Canada (print & online eds.); USD 349 combined subscription elsewhere (print & online eds.)). Ed(s): Mark Robichaux. NewBay Media, LLC, 28 E 28th St, 12th Fl, New York, NY 10016; customerservice@nbmedia.com; http://www.nbmedia.com. Illus., adv. Sample. Vol. ends: Dec. *Indexed:* A22, B01, B03, BRI, C42, Chicano, F01, IIPA. *Aud.:* Ac, Sa.

This title seeks to reach and inform corporate broadcast staff and the cable TV professional at an accessible level that's half industry news and half *TV Guide* coverage of broadcast shows and network stars. Article topics include national programming, city stations, new cable channels, advertising clients, industry leaders, and the future of broadcasting. Articles are generally short and plentiful. Subscribers get access to all online content for the journal. Non-subscribers can see archives from 2000 to the previous quarter. For more coverage of streaming TV and telecommunications business topics (and identical advertizer and stickiness ratings content), try *Multichannel News.* For more technical coverage, try *TVTechnology.*

4802. *Feminist Media Studies.* [ISSN: 1468-0777] 2001. 8x/yr. GBP 1160 (print & online eds.)). Ed(s): Radha S Hegde, Cynthia Carter. Routledge, 4 Park Sq, Milton Park, Abingdon, OX14 4RN, United Kingdom; subscriptions@tandf.co.uk; http://www.tandfonline.com. Sample. Refereed. Reprint: PSC. *Indexed:* A01, A22, E01, FemPer, GW, IBSS, MLA-IB. *Bk. rev.:* Number and length vary. *Aud.:* Ac.

Feminist Media Studies provides a transdisciplinary forum for readers pursuing feminist approaches to the field of media and communication studies. The journal examines "historical, philosophical, cultural, social, political, and economic dimensions" of these issues, and analyzes print, film, the arts, and electronic media. Articles are peer-reviewed by an editor and by at least two scholars. Articles have grown slightly shorter but more plentiful. For each of eight issues per year, readers should expect about nine article-papers of about 15 pages each. There are also small sections for book reviews and "Commentary and Criticism" pieces of one to three pages each. Authors for this title come from a range of disciplines, and have a more global focus than that of many feminist media journals.

Journal of Popular Film and Television. See Films section.

4803. *Media Report to Women.* [ISSN: 0145-9651] 1972. q. USD 70 (Individuals, USD 40). Ed(s): Sheila Gibbons. Communication Research Associates, Inc., 11988 Tramway Dr, Cincinnati, OH 45241; http://www.commres.com. Illus., index. Vol. ends: Fall (No. 4). *Indexed:* A01, A22, BRI, F01, FemPer, GW, WSA. *Bk. rev.:* 3-5, 50-90 words. *Aud.:* Hs, Ga, Ac, Sa.

Media Report to Women has information on several types of media—television, cable, film, radio, newspapers, magazines, newsletters, the Internet, and the advertisements featured in those media—and the way in which they depict women and issues of interest to women. Each issue is 24 pages of low-frills, minimal pictures, focused research. The sources listed in the bibliography alone may be worth the price of admission. Also included in most issues are field news, news briefs, book reviews, and/or movie reviews.

4804. *Radio Ink.* Former titles (until 1992): *Pulse of Radio;* (until 1989): *Pulse of Broadcasting.* [ISSN: 1064-587X] 1986. fortn. Ed(s): Brida Connolly, Wendy Bernstein. Streamline Publishing, Inc., 224 Datura St, Ste 1015, W. Palm Beach, FL 33401; comments@radioink.com. Illus., adv. Sample. Vol. ends: No. 26. *Aud.:* Sa.

Radio Ink is tightly pitched to broadcast radio managers and marketing staff. As such, it can be an interesting study of that small area for job-seekers or outside observers. Articles vary from inspiration to education, with plenty of marketing advice in between. Frequent topics include advertising, personnel moves, obituaries, and the future of radio. The journal also contains lists of award winners and interviews with leaders in the field; combine this with its annual "Most Powerful People in Radio" issue, and it's somewhat of a *Who's Who* resource for radio.

TV Guide. See General Interest section.

4805. *Videomaker: your guide to creating and publishing great video.* Former titles (until 2005): *Digital Videomaker;* (until 2004): *Computer Videomaker;* (until 1999): *Videomaker.* 1986. m. USD 19.97 domestic; USD 29.97 Canada; USD 44.97 elsewhere. Ed(s): Matthew York. York Publishing, 1350 E 9th St, Chico, CA 95928. Illus., index, adv. Sample. Vol. ends: Dec. *Indexed:* BRI, F01. *Aud.:* Hs, Ac, Sa.

Videomaker is for recently initiated video makers who are looking to understand more and improve on their skills. *Videomaker* covers useful tips and tricks, as well as some product reviews. The how-to articles are an excellent starting point for those new or moderately familiar with video software and production. The equipment reviews are an approachable level of technical but short, so readers may want to check other sources before buying. An article generally contains a very short introduction to six or seven parts of a topic (or software titles, and the like), so this journal is a great place to start or get general exposure to the field. Highly recommended for schools with video production classes and for patrons looking to improve their video skills.

Home Entertainment

4806. *Sound & Vision.* Incorporates (1996-2013): *Home Theater;* Which was formerly (199?-1996): *CurtCo's Home Theater;* (1994-199?): *Curtco's Home Theater Technology;* Formerly (until 2001): *Stereo Review's Sound and Vision;* Which was formed by the merger of (1987-1999): *Video Magazine;* Which was formerly (1978-1987): *Video (New York);* (1968-1999): *Stereo Review;* Which was formerly (1960-1968): *HiFi Stereo Review;* Stereo Review incorporated (1959-1989): *High Fidelity;* Which was formerly (until 1959): *High Fidelity & Audiocraft;* Which was formed by the merger of (1957-1958): *Audiocraft for the Hi-Fi Hobbyist;* (1951-1958): *High Fidelity.* [ISSN: 1537-5838] 1999. 10x/yr. USD 12.97 domestic; USD 22.97 Canada; USD 32.97 elsewhere. TEN: The Enthusiast Network, 1212 6th Ave, 18th Fl, New York, NY 10036; info@enthusiastnetwork.com; http://www.enthusiastnetwork.com. Illus., index, adv. Vol. ends: Dec. *Indexed:* A01, A22, BRI, C37, CBRI, F01, IIMP, MASUSE, RILM. *Aud.:* Ga.

While many other home theater titles have ceased, *Sound & Vision* carries on. All of the expected gear reviews, how-to guides, and component combination and connection advice columns are present, along with music and DVD reviews. Multiple Q&A departments help address the concerns of those interested in legacy equipment, setup, or new formats. Gear reviews have plenty of pro-consumer-level detail in 500-800 words each. Yearly "best of" lists also contain helpful information on several runner-ups and picks based on value for the cost.

4807. *Stereophile.* [ISSN: 0585-2544] 1962. m. USD 12.97 domestic; USD 24.97 Canada; USD 36.97 elsewhere. TEN: The Enthusiast Network, 1212 6th Ave, 18th Fl, New York, NY 10036; info@enthusiastnetwork.com; http://www.enthusiastnetwork.com. Illus., index, adv. Sample. Vol. ends: Dec. *Aud.:* Ga, Sa.

Stereophile is for the knowledgeable home-audio fanatic. This highly technical journal consistently features several scientific charts (e.g., frequency response, "THD+N(%) vs. freq," and circuit maps) in its many gear-review articles. The journal has now fully embraced current technology along with the analog and focuses a fair amount of time on the art of listening in addition to the science. Two added printed niceties are the calendar of industry events and the manufacturers' responses to gear reviews.

■ THEATER

Elizabeth McKeigue, Executive Director of the Library, Salem State University, Salem, MA 01970; emckeigue@salemstate.edu

Introduction

This section highlights the core scholarly journals, magazines, and free websites for theater performance and the study of drama. The majority of titles are appropriate for public as well as for academic library collections. A number of the academic titles cover criticism, performance, dramaturgy, and comparative drama. The popular magazine and website titles focus mostly on performance reviews.

All of the scholarly journals and magazines are indexed, in total or in part, in the major indexes in the field, such as the *MLA International Bibliography* and the *International Index to the Performing Arts*. Additionally, many of them offer some percentage of their content freely online, and all provide some amount of full-text content through the major online aggregated databases.

Basic Periodicals

Hs: *American Theatre, Dramatics, Theater* (Durham); Ga: *American Theatre, Modern Drama, Theater* (Durham); Ac: *American Theatre, Canadian Theatre Review, Modern Drama, P A J, Theater* (Durham), *Theatre Journal* (Baltimore).

Basic Abstracts and Indexes

Academic Search Premier, Humanities Index, International Bibliography of Theatre and Dance, International Index to the Performing Arts, MLA International Bibliography.

4808. ***American Theatre.*** Former titles (until 1984): *Theatre Communications;* (until 1979): *Theatre Communications Group Newsletter.* [ISSN: 8750-3255] 1973. 10x/yr. Free to members. Ed(s): Rob Weinert-Kendt, Russell M Dembin. Theatre Communications Group, Inc., 520 Eighth Ave, 24th Fl, New York, NY 10018; http://www.tcg.org. Illus., adv. Vol. ends: Dec. Microform: PQC. *Indexed:* A01, A22, AmHI, BRI, C37, CBRI, Chicano, IIPA, MASUSE, MLA-IB. *Bk. rev.:* Number varies, 400-1,200 words. *Aud.:* Ga, Ac.

This well-illustrated publication would appeal to academics as well as those who are interested in the theater. Each issue includes articles, book reviews, and production reviews. They frequently feature the text of new plays in their entirety. Occasionally, they will include interviews. A recent issue featured an interview with Beth Henley. The website of its publisher, Theatre Communications Group, offers the full text of all the feature articles in the current issue. This journal is an important title for any college or university library, as well as any large public library that addresses the needs of dedicated theatergoers.

4809. ***Asian Theatre Journal.*** Supersedes: *Asian Theatre Reports.* [ISSN: 0742-5457] 1984. s-a. USD 160 (Individuals, USD 40). Ed(s): Siyuan Liu. University of Hawai'i Press, 2840 Kolowalu St, Honolulu, HI 96822; uhpjourn@hawaii.edu; http://www.uhpress.hawaii.edu. Illus. Sample. Refereed. Vol. ends: Fall. *Indexed:* A01, A22, AmHI, BAS, BRI, E01, IIPA, MLA-IB. *Bk. rev.:* 4-6, 1,000-1,500 words. *Aud.:* Ac.

This English-language journal focuses on contemporary and historical Asian theater through scholarly articles, original plays, play translations, and reviews. Back issues from its inception through 2005 are in JSTOR, and more current issues (1999 to the present) are available through ProjectMUSE. The journal is elegantly illustrated with both color and black-and-white photographs. Academic research libraries that support drama or East Asian literature programs should seriously consider owning this publication.

4810. ***Canadian Theatre Review.*** [ISSN: 0315-0836] 1974. q. USD 164. Ed(s): Laura Levin. University of Toronto Press, Journals Division, 5201 Dufferin St, Toronto, ON M3H 5T8, Canada; journals@utpress.utoronto.ca; http://www.utpjournals.com. Illus., index, adv. Sample. Refereed. Microform: PQC. *Indexed:* A01, A22, AmHI, BAS, BRI, C37, E01, IIPA, MLA-IB. *Bk. rev.:* 2-4, 800-1,200 words. *Aud.:* Ac.

This journal focuses mainly on contemporary and often avant-garde theater productions in Canada. Each issue is organized around a theme, and included in each issue is at least one complete play related to the issue's theme, articles, and reviews. Recent themes include "Digital Performance," "Alternative Globalizations," and "Burlesque." This interesting journal is well illustrated with production photographs. It is strongly recommended for any academic or research collection that focuses on contemporary theater and drama.

Choreographic Practices. See Dance section.

4811. ***Comparative Drama.*** [ISSN: 0010-4078] 1967. q. Ed(s): Elizabeth Bradburn. Western Michigan University, Department of English, 1903 W Michigan Ave, Kalamazoo, MI 49008; http://www.wmich.edu. Illus., index. Sample. Refereed. Vol. ends: Winter. Microform: PQC. *Indexed:* A01, A22, AmHI, BAS, BRI, CBRI, E01, IIPA, MLA-IB. *Aud.:* Ac.

This quarterly journal from Western Michigan University focuses on drama and theater from a literary point of view. Scholarly in nature, it gives equal treatment to various genres (ancient, medieval, Renaissance, and modern) and themes. Its coverage is broad in terms of time period and geography. The website includes an index of the articles from every issue. Shakespeare is covered so frequently that there is a separate "sub-index" for those articles. The journal's website also features abstracts of every article since 2000. It is an important scholarly journal for college or university library collections.

4812. ***CurtainUp: the internet theater magazine of reviews, features.*** 1996. 3x/w. Free. CurtainUp, PO Box 751133, Forest Hills, NY 11375; esommer@pipeline.com; http://www.curtainup.com. *Aud.:* Ga, Ac, Sa.

This is a great source for reviews and information about current (and recent) theatrical productions. Its richest areas are in the New York and Berkshire productions, reflecting the main editor's location, but there are several well-known contributing editors, so regular reports for productions in Toronto, London, and Washington, D.C., also appear. The site's organization is very navigable and user-friendly. There is also a subscription service through which individual readers will be notified of changes to the site. Despite its text-heavy website, this is among the best of online-only theater magazines. Any public or academic library with a theatergoing clientele should include this on its list of websites. URL: www.curtainup.com

4813. ***Dramatics: the magazine for students and teachers of theatre.*** Formerly (until 1944): *High School Thespian;* Incorporates (in 1944): *Dramatics-Dramatic Curtain.* [ISSN: 0012-5989] 1929. bi-m. Free to members; Non-members, USD 38. Ed(s): Gregory Bossler, Caroline Brock. Educational Theatre Association, 2343 Auburn Ave, Cincinnati, OH 45219; info@edta.org; http://www.edta.org. Illus., index, adv. Sample. Vol. ends: May. Microform: PQC. *Indexed:* A22, IIPA. *Aud.:* Hs, Ac.

This is one of the few publications specifically directed at the interests of high school drama students, but is relevant for collegiate programs as well. It presents articles that provide practical information on acting, directing, and design that will be of use to drama students and educators. Content ranges from technique articles, such as advice on auditioning from casting directors, to the full text of short plays. In addition, there is a great deal of information on internships, summer employment, collegiate and institute dramatic programs, and auditions. This is an important journal for colleges and universities that support drama programs. Secondary schools with active drama programs should also consider this title.

4814. ***The Dramatist: the voice of American theater.*** Incorporates (1982-1998): *Dramatists Guild. Newsletter;* Former titles (until 1998): *Dramatists Guild Quarterly;* (until 1964): *Dramatists Bulletin.* [ISSN: 1551-7683] 1960. bi-m. Free to members; Non-members, USD 25. Dramatists Guild, Inc., 1501 Broadway, Ste 701, New York, NY 10036; http://www.dramatistsguild.com. Illus., adv. Sample. Circ: 5752. Vol. ends: Winter. *Indexed:* AmHI. *Aud.:* Ac, Sa.

This is the official publication of The Dramatists Guild of America, the professional association of playwrights, composers, and lyricists. It usually contains eight to ten articles; these articles may contain discussions of some aspect of playwriting, interviews with well-known playwrights, the political and social opinions of playwrights as they affect their writings, or discussions of theatrical companies. There is also a "Dramatists Diary," which lists plays in production around the country, newly published plays and recordings, and recently published books by guild members. This title has great value for any library that supports the needs of a playwriting, music, or creative writing program.

4815. *Modern Drama: world drama from 1850 to the present.* [ISSN: 0026-7694] 1958. q. CAD 136. Ed(s): Darren Gobert. University of Toronto Press, Journals Division, 5201 Dufferin St, Toronto, ON M3H 5T8, Canada; journals@utpress.utoronto.ca; http://www.utpjournals.com. Illus., index, adv. Sample. Refereed. Circ: 1212. Vol. ends: Winter. Microform: PQC. *Indexed:* A01, A22, AmHI, BRI, C37, E01, IIPA, MLA-IB. *Bk. rev.:* 8-12, 500-1,000 words. *Aud.:* Ac.

One of the oldest scholarly modern theater journals, *Modern Drama* has been published quarterly by the University of Toronto since 1958. There are also eight to ten extensive and interesting book reviews in each issue, and an annual bibliography in the summer issue. This journal would be well placed in any academic library collection that supports contemporary drama and literature programs.

4816. *N T Q. New Theatre Quarterly.* Formerly (until 1985): *T Q. Theatre Quarterly.* [ISSN: 0266-464X] 1971. q. GBP 236. Ed(s): Maria Shevtsova, Simon Trussler. Cambridge University Press, University Printing House, Shaftesbury Rd, Cambridge, CB2 8BS, United Kingdom; journals@cambridge.org; https://www.cambridge.org/. Illus., adv. Sample. Refereed. Circ: 1000. Vol. ends: Nov. Microform: PQC. Reprint: PSC. *Indexed:* A01, A22, AmHI, BRI, E01, IIPA, MLA-IB. *Bk. rev.:* Number and length vary. *Aud.:* Ac.

This journal addresses issues of modern performance and dramaturgy. It also claims to provide a forum "where prevailing dramatic assumptions can be subjected to vigorous critical questioning." Its prose style is interesting and eye-catching and therefore more widely accessible than that of some academic journals. *NTQ* usually contains eight to ten scholarly articles that are international in coverage. Book reviews are generally shorter than those of other academic journals, but there are a good number of them. Recommended for academic libraries and special libraries that address modern performance issues.

4817. *New York Theatre Guide.* 2003. d. Free. Ed(s): Alan Bird. New York Theatre Guide, 12 E 86th St, New York, NY 10028. Adv. *Aud.:* Ga.

This site provides everything you need to know about the current New York theater scene. Features include the latest casting and upcoming productions news, links to reviews of both Broadway and off-Broadway productions, production plot synopses, seating plans of major theaters, maps of New York, and, of course, links to sites for purchasing tickets. It is similar to *CurtainUp*, but it has a better site design; moreover, a search box at the top makes it easy to search for reviews. URL: www.newyorktheatreguide.com

4818. *P A J: a journal of performance and art.* Formerly (until 1998): *Performing Arts Journal.* [ISSN: 1520-281X] 1976. 3x/yr. USD 171 (print & online eds.)). Ed(s): Bonnie Marranca. M I T Press, One Rogers St, Cambridge, MA 02142-1209; journals-cs@mit.edu; http://mitpress.mit.edu/. Illus., adv. Refereed. *Indexed:* A01, A22, A51, AmHI, BRI, CBRI, E01, F01, IIPA, MLA-IB. *Bk. rev.:* Occasional. *Aud.:* Ac, Sa.

This journal covers contemporary international performance: dance, theater, and performance art. Each issue contains eight to ten articles, performance reviews, and opinion pieces. Sometimes an issue may have a theme. The journal often contains reviews of new works in theater, dance, film, and opera, and occasionally book reviews. Its illustrations are extensive and fascinating. Issues of *PAJ* from 1996 to the present are available online via ProjectMUSE. The journal's website includes interesting podcasts to which anyone can subscribe for free. Recommended for academic or research libraries where contemporary and avant-garde performance artistry is studied.

Performance Research. See Dance section.

4819. *Playbill On-Line.* 1994. d. Ed(s): Mark Peikert. Playbill Inc, 729 Seventh Ave, 4th Fl, New York, NY 10019. Adv. *Aud.:* Ga.

Anyone who has been in an American commercial theater is familiar with the *Playbill* program, which provides the cast, the number of acts, intermissions, and background on the play. The coverage in the website is not dramatically different, except that it is all in one place, and therefore a very useful tool for planning for visits to New York City. There is some non-New York coverage, including a little international, but that coverage is spotty, and only the New York coverage can be depended on for completeness. There are also feature articles, gossip, a chat room, casting calls, and links to purchase tickets. This website is a must for New York theatergoers, particularly for the up-to-date schedules. URL: www.playbill.com/index.php

4820. *Plays: the drama magazine for young people.* Incorporates (1937-1942): *One Act Play Magazine and Radio-Drama Review.* [ISSN: 0032-1540] 1940. m. Oct-May; except Jan.-Feb. combined. USD 44. Ed(s): Liz Preston. Plays Magazine, PO Box 600160, Newton, MA 02460; customerservice@playsmagazine.com; http://www.playsmag.com/. Illus., index. Sample. Vol. ends: Dec. Microform: PQC. *Indexed:* A01, A22, BRI, C37, MASUSE, P01. *Bk. rev.:* 10-15, 50-100 words. *Aud.:* Ems, Hs, Ga.

The classic magazine *Plays* continues to provide an essential resource to school drama programs everywhere. It contains between 9 and 12 short plays, with subjects ranging from historic to holidays, to skits and comedies, to dramatized classics. Plays are arranged by general grade level, and each contains production notes that include casting and staging suggestions. The plays are not copyright-free, but any current subscriber may produce copies for the cast and produce the play royalty-free. This magazine should be included in the library of any school with a drama program or club. It should also be included in public libraries' children's collections.

4821. *Stage Directions.* [ISSN: 1047-1901] 1988. m. Free. Ed(s): Jacob Coakley. DanceMedia, LLC., 333 7th Ave, New York, NY 10001; http://dancemedia.com. Illus., adv. Sample. *Indexed:* IIPA, MASUSE. *Bk. rev.:* 2-3, 400 words. *Aud.:* Ga, Ac.

This publication addresses the specific technical needs of "regional, academic, and community" theaters, although the best audience would probably be community and small academic theater groups. Each issue has six to ten articles on such technical aspects of performance production as cost-saving ideas, dramatic effects and techniques, and computer control issues. There is also supplier information, articles describing particular theaters and their companies, columns on computers and networked resources, and book reviews. This magazine's online version includes the tables of contents for each issue published since 1988, and links to selected articles online. It is a useful resource for any public library with an active community theater or any academic library that supports a drama program.

4822. *T D R.* Former titles (until 1988): *The Drama Review;* (until 1968): *T D R;* (until 1967): *Tulane Drama Review;* (until 1957): *The Carleton Drama Review;* (until 1956): *Carleton Drama Bulletin.* [ISSN: 1054-2043] 1949. q. USD 254 (print & online eds.)). Ed(s): Richard Schechner. M I T Press, One Rogers St, Cambridge, MA 02142-1209; journals-cs@mit.edu; http://mitpress.mit.edu/. Illus., index, adv. Sample. *Indexed:* A01, A22, AmHI, BAS, BRI, CBRI, E01, IIPA, MLA-IB. *Aud.:* Ac.

MIT Press for the Tisch School at New York University publishes this important publication on theater production, history, and criticism. Each quarterly issue offers articles on a broad range of topics. There are extensive reviews and descriptions of contemporary and often avant-garde performances with photographic illustrations. This journal should be included in any library that addresses the needs of theater studies and/or contemporary performance art.

4823. *Theater (Durham).* Formerly (until 1977): *Yale - Theatre.* [ISSN: 0161-0775] 1968. 3x/yr. USD 257. Ed(s): Michael Breslin, Molly FitzMaurice. Duke University Press, 905 W Main St, Durham, NC 27701; orders@dukeupress.edu; https://www.dukeupress.edu. Illus., index, adv. Refereed. Reprint: PSC. *Indexed:* A01, A22, AmHI, BRI, E01, IIPA, MLA-IB. *Bk. rev.:* 2-3, 600-1,800 words. *Aud.:* Ac.

Edited and produced by the venerable Yale School of Drama and published by Duke University Press, this title offers articles that reflect the social politics of contemporary theater thinkers, artistic directors, and writers. Each issue contains four to six articles, usually organized around a theme. The editors try to include at least one new "pathbreaking" play per issue, and some issues contain several. The articles are often illustrated with what are sometimes breathtaking production photographs. The Duke University Press site offers free searchable access to its contents and links to the full text via subscription. This magazine is an invaluable part of any significant academic theater journal collection, and is also recommended for academic libraries and special libraries that address modern performance issues.

4824. ***Theatre Journal (Baltimore).*** Formerly (until 1979): *Educational Theatre Journal.* [ISSN: 0192-2882] 1949. q. USD 185. Ed(s): Bob Kowkabany, Jennifer Parker-Starbuck. The Johns Hopkins University Press, 2715 N Charles St, Baltimore, MD 21218; http://www.press.jhu.edu. Illus., adv. Sample. Refereed. Vol. ends: Dec. Reprint: PSC. *Indexed:* A01, A22, AmHI, BAS, BRI, CBRI, E01, IIPA, MLA-IB. *Bk. rev.:* 8-12, 1,000-1,800 words. *Aud.:* Ac.

This scholarly journal features historical studies, production reviews, and theoretical inquiries that analyze dramatic texts and production. Each issue contains approximately six articles, a performance review section, and book reviews. The articles are substantial and refereed. They may cover topics from a social or historical point of view, or they may analyze text. Occasionally, the articles will be organized around a central theme. The performance review section contains reviews of American theater productions, although some foreign productions do appear. Regional theaters and repertory company productions are well covered. College and university libraries with drama or comparative literature programs should seriously consider subscribing to this journal.

4825. ***Women & Performance: a journal of feminist theory.*** [ISSN: 0740-770X] 1983. 3x/yr. GBP 186 (print & online eds.)). Ed(s): Summer Kim Lee. Routledge, 530 Walnut St, Ste 850, Philadelphia, PA 19106; enquiries@tandfonline.com; http://www.tandfonline.com. Illus., adv. Sample. Refereed. Circ: 1300 Paid. Reprint: PSC. *Indexed:* A22, E01, F01, FemPer, GW, IIPA, MLA-IB. *Aud.:* Ac.

Founded in 1983 by graduate students in the Department of Performance Studies at New York University's Tisch School of the Arts, this journal includes essays on performance, dance, film, new media, and the performance of everyday life from interdisciplinary feminist perspectives. The journal offers a section that promises "artists' statements, polemics, review essays, performance texts, manifestoes, feminist and queer takes on current events and debates, and other modes of intellectual production that are too wily to conform to the standard model of academic publishing." Recommended for academic and research libraries.

■ TRANSPORTATION

See also Aeronautics and Space Science; Automobiles and Motorcycles; Marine Science and Technology; Safety; and Travel and Tourism sections.

Rachel Martin Cole, Public Services Librarian, Transportation Library, Northwestern University Library, 1970 Campus Dr., Evanston, IL 60208-2300

Introduction

Transportation connects people, goods, and information; it goes everywhere - underground, across continents and oceans, to space - touches all of us, and encompasses myriad ways to travel: from the most ancient of modes through pedestrian travel, ranging to the most complex systems that enable space travel. The journals included in this section likewise cover a wide range of subjects, encompassing trade magazines, popular literature, and scholarly journals alike, and reflecting a diverse readership of transportation enthusiasts, scholars, and professionals.

The current moment in transportation has been referred to as a revolution in mobility. The Internet, the sharing economy, and technological advances in autonomous vehicles, have created new avenues for the movement of people and goods, and for the planning and modeling of this movement. Meanwhile, a growing understanding of the need for environmentally sustainable transportation, along with improvements in electric and alternative fuel technology, has expanded the market for sustainable transportation alternatives. There has been an increasing public demand for active transportation infrastructure and expanded access to public transit in cities. This all amounts to more choices for transportation consumers and an expansion in research in a wide breadth of transportation subjects.

This section reflects the current state of transportation and research toward the development of future transportation systems through trade literature. The literature is geared toward the business of transportation and the professional working in the industry, as well as scholarly journals that publish original, often technical, research on the multitude of topics related to the wide world of transportation. Historical aspects of transportation, particularly rail transportation, are addressed as well.

Because transportation is such an interdisciplinary subject, librarians may also consult sections related to the various modes of transportation such as Aeronautics and Space Science, Automobiles and Motorcycles, and Boats and Boating, as well as other related subjects including Business and Finance, Engineering and Technology, Science and Technology, and Travel and Tourism.

Basic Periodicals

Journal of Transport Economics and Policy, Journal of Transportation Engineering, Transport Reviews, Transportation Research. Parts A-F, Transportation Research Record.

Basic Abstracts and Indexes

Compendex, Engineering Index.

4826. ***Air Cargo World: the source for airfreight logistics.*** Former titles (until 1983): *Air Cargo Magazine;* (until 1976): *Cargo Airlift; Air Transportation.* [ISSN: 0745-5100] 1910. m. USD 80 domestic; USD 120 elsewhere. Ed(s): Randy Woods. Royal Media Group, 8 West 38th St, Ste 901, New York, NY 10018-6229; info@royalmedia.com; http://www.royalmedia.com. Illus., index, adv. Circ: 41000 Controlled. Vol. ends: Dec. Microform: PQC. *Indexed:* B01, C42, HRIS. *Aud.:* Sa.

Published for logistics professionals, *Air Cargo World* provides coverage of air cargo services, carriers, facilities, equipment, and industry trends throughout the world. Regular features include articles, columns surveying news from regions around the world, updates on people in the industry, at-a-glance industry statistical indicators, and upcoming events. Suitable for large academic collections and special libraries. URL: www.aircargoworld.com

Air Transport World. See Aeronautics and Space Science section.

4827. ***Airfinance Journal.*** [ISSN: 0143-2257] 1980. 6x/yr. GBP 1195 combined subscription (print & online eds.); USD 2040 combined subscription (print & online eds.); EUR 1610 combined subscription (print & online eds.)). Ed(s): Jack Dutton. Euromoney Institutional Investor Plc., 8 Bouverie St, London, EC4Y 8AX, United Kingdom; customerservices@euromoneyplc.com; http://www.euromoneyplc.com/. Adv. Sample. *Indexed:* A22, B01, B03, BRI, HRIS. *Aud.:* Sa.

This trade journal is geared toward both the air transportation professional and the researcher in the area of air transportation and finance. It includes feature articles, industry news, analysis, and important market statistics and data; its coverage is international. Appropriate for large academic collections and special libraries. URL: www.airfinancejournal.com

4828. ***Airlines International.*** Supersedes (in 1994): *I A T A Review;* Which was formerly (until 1975): *I A T A News Review.* 1966. bi-m. Free. Ed(s): Graham Newton. Redactive Media Group, 78 Chamber St, London, E1 8BL, United Kingdom; info@redactive.co.uk; http://www.redactive.co.uk. Circ: 8000. *Aud.:* Sa.

A publication of the International Aviation Transport Association (IATA), this title is aimed at specialists in the business of commercial aviation. In addition to industry updates, topics covered include airline and airport management, cargo, environment, security, regulations, and economics. Recommended for special libraries and large academic and business collections. URL: http://airlines.iata.org/

4829. *Airport World.* Formerly (until 1996): *Airlines International.* [ISSN: 1360-4341] 1995. bi-m. Free to members; Non-members, GBP 100. Aviation Media Inc, 448, Feltham, TW139EA, United Kingdom; contactus@aviationmedia.aero; http://aviationmedia.aero/. Illus., adv. *Indexed:* B01, HRIS. *Aud.:* Sa.

Geared to the airport management professional, *Airport World* focuses on current issues in airport management including industry news and events, technology, safety, automation, the environment, legislation, regulations, planning, and finance. Each issue includes concise articles, a calendar of events, airport traffic data and other statistics, project briefs, a section highlighting a specific airport, and a global airport news section. Appropriate for special libraries and large academic or business collections. URL: www.airport-world.com/

4830. *Airports International Magazine.* Former titles (until 1971): *Airports International Directory;* (until 1968): *Airports International.* 1968. 9x/yr. GBP 95 (Free to qualified personnel). Ed(s): Tom Allett. Key Publishing Ltd., PO Box 300, Stamford, PE9 1NA, United Kingdom; info@keypublishing.com; http://www.keypublishing.com. Adv. Sample. *Indexed:* B01, B03, BRI, C42, HRIS. *Aud.:* Sa.

This publication is international in coverage and is geared to the airport management professional. It addresses current airport trends, news and events, economics, and technology. An annotated table of contents for the current and archived issues is available online. This magazine is appropriate for special libraries and large business and academic collections. URL: www.airportsinternational.co.uk

4831. *American Shipper: global trade & logistics.* Former titles (until 1991): *American Shipper International;* (until 1990): *American Shipper Magazine;* (until 1976): *Florida Journal of Commerce - American Shipper;* (until 1974): *Florida Journal of Commerce.* [ISSN: 1074-8350] 1959. m. USD 40 domestic; USD 120 elsewhere. Ed(s): Benjamin Meyer. Howard Publications, 1016 Oak St, Jacksonville, FL 32204; publisher@shippers.com; http://www.howardpub.com. Illus., adv. Vol. ends: Dec. Microform: PQC. *Indexed:* A22, B03, BRI, C42, HRIS. *Aud.:* Sa.

Published monthly, *American Shipper* is a trade publication that targets shipping and logistics industry executives. It is international in coverage. Each issue addresses subjects of interest to shipping professionals: logistics, forwarding, integrated transport, ocean transport, land transport, NVOs, and ports. There are also sections on shippers' case law and corporate appointments. Appropriate for special libraries and large academic and business collections. URL: www.americanshipper.com

Aviation Week & Space Technology. See Aeronautics and Space Science section.

4832. *Bridge Design & Engineering.* [ISSN: 1359-7493] 1995. q. GBP 105 combined subscription (print & online eds.); EUR 168 combined subscription (print & online eds.); USD 216 combined subscription (print & online eds.)). Ed(s): Helena Russell. Hemming Information Services Ltd., 32 Vauxhall Bridge Rd, London, SW1V 2SS, United Kingdom; info@hgluk.com; http://www.hgluk.com. Illus., adv. *Indexed:* BRI, C42, HRIS. *Bk. rev.:* 2-4, 150-250 words. *Aud.:* Ac, Sa.

This journal targets civil engineers, designers, and those working in the bridge construction industry. It is international in coverage and covers bridge aesthetics, design, construction, and management. It includes feature articles, industry news, product information, a calendar of events, and listings of conferences and competitions. Appropriate for special libraries and large academic and engineering collections. URL: www.bridgeweb.com

4833. *Business and Commercial Aviation.* Incorporates (in 2004): *A C Flyer;* Formerly (until 1966): *Business and Commercial Aviation.* 1958. m. USD 59 domestic; USD 79 foreign. Ed(s): William Garvey. Informa Media, Mortimer House, 37-41 Mortimer St, London, W1T 3JH, United Kingdom; media.enquiries@informa.com; http://www.informa.com. Illus., adv. Circ: 50720 Paid. Microform: PQC. *Indexed:* A22, B01, B03, BRI, HRIS. *Aud.:* Sa.

A trade journal directed toward those working in business and commercial aviation, *Business and Commercial Aviation* addresses the concerns of the industry with a decided emphasis on business flying. Its coverage is international. Each issue includes industry news and events, business intelligence, concise feature articles, statistics, commentary, product reviews, classifieds, a resale marketplace, and a section devoted to the causes of accidents. Appropriate for special libraries and large academic and business collections. URL: www.AviationWeek.com/bca

4834. *BUSRide.* [ISSN: 0192-8902] 1965. 8x/yr. Ed(s): Richard Tackett. The Producers, Inc., 4742 N 24th St, Ste 340, Phoenix, AZ 85016. Illus., adv. Sample. Circ: 16000. *Indexed:* B01, HRIS. *Aud.:* Sa.

BUSRide addresses the transit bus and motorcoach industries of the United States and Canada and is meant for bus and transit professionals. It includes current industry news and events, legislative and regulatory information, product reviews, and feature articles on the passenger bus industry. Appropriate for special libraries. URL: www.busride.com

4835. *Case Studies on Transport Policy.* [ISSN: 2213-624X] 2013. 4x/yr. EUR 356. Ed(s): R Macario. Elsevier BV, Radarweg 29, Amsterdam, 1043 NX, Netherlands; info@elsevier.com; https://www.elsevier.com/. Refereed. *Aud.:* Ac, Sa.

With the aim of supporting teaching and transferability of experiences in transport policy and research, this multidisciplinary journal presents case studies on a wide range of transportation research that encompasses engineering, economics, sociology, and law. Case studies included in this journal cover the wide world of transportation, with original research articles on all modes of transportation around the globe. Case studies serve as an effective tool for academic teaching and research, and provide professionals working with transportation policy with analysis and investigations of projects that serve as tools for their own research and practice. This is an important journal for academic and special libraries. URL: https://www.sciencedirect.com/journal/case-studies-on-transport-policy

4836. *Commercial Carrier Journal.* Incorporates (in 1999): *Trucking Company;* Former titles (until 1999): *Commercial Carrier Journal for Professional Fleet Managers;* (until 1997): *Chilton's Commercial Carrier Journal for Professional Fleet Managers;* (until 1990): *Commercial Carrier Journal for Professional Fleet Managers;* (until 1989): *Chilton's C C J;* (until 1984): *Chilton's Commercial Carrier Journal;* (until 1982): *Chilton's C C J;* (until 1977): *Commercial Car Journal.* [ISSN: 1533-7502] 1911. m. USD 48 domestic (Free to qualified personnel). Ed(s): Jeff Crissey. Randall-Reilly Publishing Company, 3200 Rice Mine Rd NE, Tuscaloosa, AL 35406; http://www.randallpub.com. Illus., index, adv. Circ: 96500. Vol. ends: Dec. Microform: CIS; PQC. *Indexed:* A22, B01, B03, BRI, C42, HRIS. *Aud.:* Sa.

An important trade journal in the truck fleet-management industry, *Commercial Carrier Journal* is targeted to professionals within the freight transport business including fleet executives and managers. *CCJ* contains articles on operations, technology, equipment, management, regulations, and safety. Regular features include road tests of vehicles, industry news, events, and editorials. Also published is the Top 250: the top for-hire trucking companies, ranked by *CCJ.* Appropriate for special libraries and large academic and business collections. URL: www.ccjdigital.com/magazine/

4837. *Containerisation International: the box benchmark.* Incorporates (2009-2010): *Reefer International;* Which was formerly (2006-2009): *R Q;* (1994-2010): *Cargo Systems;* Which was formerly (1973-1994): *Cargo Systems International;* (until 1973): *I C H C A Monthly Journal;* Which was formed by the merger of: *International Cargo Handling Coordination; I C H C A Quarterly Journal.* [ISSN: 0010-7379] 1967. m.

GBP 1845 combined subscription domestic print & online eds.; EUR 2280 combined subscription in Europe print & online eds.; USD 3250 combined subscription elsewhere print & online eds. Ed(s): James Baker. Informa Cargo Information, Christchurch Ct, 10-15 Newgate St, London, EC1A 7AZ, United Kingdom; informacargo@informa.com; http://www.informacargo.com. Illus., adv. Circ: 10000. Vol. ends: Dec. *Indexed:* A22, HRIS. *Aud.:* Sa.

This publication covers the worldwide containerization business, with news, analysis, and market intelligence aimed at container industry professionals. Topics include management and policy issues for a variety of transportation modes, but with an emphasis on shipping and ports. Each issue contains a briefing on the state of the industry worldwide, as well as articles covering business, technology, ports and logistics, trade, and statistics on key industry indicators. Yearly features include rankings of the top 100 container ports, and the Power List of the industry's top 25 most influential people and companies. Appropriate for special libraries and large academic and business collections. URL: www.containershipping.com

4838. ***Fairplay.*** Former titles (until 2017): *I H S Fairplay;* (until 2016): *I H S Maritime Fairplay;* (until 2014): *I H S Fairplay;* (until 2011): *Fairplay;* (until 1992): *Fairplay International;* (until 1989): *Fairplay International Shipping Weekly;* (until 1974): *Fairplay International Shipping Journal;* (until 1966): *Fairplay Shipping Journal;* (until 1962): *Fairplay Weekly Shipping Journal.* [ISSN: 2514-4057] 1883. bi-w. GBP 795 domestic; USD 1425 United States; USD 1830 elsewhere. Ed(s): Nicola Wood. I H S Global Limited, Viewpoint One Willoughby Rd, Bracknell, RG12 8FB, United Kingdom; https://www.ihs.com/index.html. Illus., adv. Sample. Vol. ends: Apr/Dec. *Indexed:* HRIS. *Aud.:* Sa.

Published continually since its launch in 1883, *Fairplay* is a bi-weekly resource for shipping decision makers in the maritime industry and a core journal covering the business of maritime shipping. Content includes news, commentary, and analysis on every aspect of the maritime and trade industry, including such areas as insurance, ports, supply chain, markets, commerce, and technology. In addition to its broad coverage of the industry worldwide, each issue features a regional focus section, examining the market, regulations, and industry performance in a chosen region in more detail. Appropriate for a large business, academic, and special libraries. URL: https://fairplay.ihs.com/

4839. ***Fleet Owner.*** Formerly: *Fleet Owner: Big Fleet Edition;* Superseded in part: *Fleet Owner.* [ISSN: 1070-194X] 1928. m. USD 75 domestic (Free to qualified personnel). Ed(s): Neil Abt. Penton, 8109 Greeley Blvd, Springfield, VA 22152; information@penton.com; http://penton.com. Illus., adv. Circ: 105000 Controlled. Vol. ends: Dec. Microform: PQC. *Indexed:* A22, B01, B03, BRI, HRIS. *Aud.:* Sa.

Targeted toward industry professionals involved in the management of commercial trucking fleets, *Fleet Owner* publishes monthly coverage of news, trends, analysis, and research on industry issues. Each issue has sections focusing on equipment, management, and technology. Within these categories, articles cover a range of topics of interest to the fleet industry professional, such as automated driving, safety, EVs, and environmental concerns. Appropriate for libraries that collect in transportation and logistics. URL: http://fleetowner.com

4840. ***Flight Airline Business.*** Formerly (until 2016): *Airline Business.* [ISSN: 2514-0604] 1985. m. Individuals, GBP 124; Free to qualified personnel. Ed(s): Mark Pilling. Reed Business Information Ltd., Quadrant House, The Quadrant, Sutton, SM2 5AS, United Kingdom; rbi.subscriptions@quadrantsubs.com; http://www.reedbusiness.com/. Illus., adv. Circ: 22999. Vol. ends: Dec. *Indexed:* A22, B01, B03, C42, H&TI, HRIS. *Aud.:* Sa.

Produced by FlightGlobal, a key source for aviation intelligence, *Flight Airline Business* is a trade journal covering the business of the airline industry worldwide. Sections include news briefings, analysis, and a monthly "Special Report" feature that focuses on one segment of the industry such as marketing and services or aircraft and engines, offering a deep dive into a topic with several articles centered on a theme. Annual features include the "Airline Business 100" and "Airports Review." The primary audience is airline managers. Appropriate for academic and special libraries that collect on aviation management. URL: www.flightglobal.com/airlines

Flight International. See Aeronautics and Space Science section.

4841. ***Heavy Duty Trucking: the fleet business authority.*** Former titles (until 2012): *Newport's Heavy Duty Trucking;* (until 1999): *Heavy Duty Trucking;* (until 1968): *Western Trucking and Motor Transportation;* (until 1959): *Western Trucking and Motor Transportation in the West;* (until 195?): *Motor Transportation;* (until 1951): *Motor Transportation of the West;* (until 1949): *Motor Transportation.* 1925. m. USD 90 domestic; USD 190 in Canada & Mexico; USD 280 elsewhere. Ed(s): Deborah Lockridge, Stephane Babcock. Bobit Business Media, 3520 Challenger St, Torrance, CA 90503; order@bobit.com; http://www.bobitbusinessmedia.com. Illus., adv. Vol. ends: Dec. *Indexed:* HRIS. *Aud.:* Sa.

Heavy Duty Trucking is published for commercial fleet owners who operate heavy trucks: those within classes one through eight. It covers the heavy trucking fleet industry and includes industry news and events, reports, legislation, safety, technology, and equipment. Regular departments include "Washington Watch," which covers current government concerns in the industry, "Safety and Compliance," "Future Fleet," on new and disruptive technologies, "Fuel Smarts," with information on real-world cases in which companies reduced the carbon footprint of their fleets, "Aftermarket Insight," and product updates. Buyers' guides, offered several times annually, are a significant supplement to the journal. Appropriate for large academic and special libraries with collections on freight and logistics. URL: www.truckinginfo.com

4842. ***I E E E Transactions on Intelligent Transportation Systems.*** [ISSN: 1524-9050] 2000. m. Ed(s): Azim Eskandarian. Institute of Electrical and Electronics Engineers, 445 Hoes Ln, Piscataway, NJ 08854; contactcenter@ieee.org; http://www.ieee.org. Adv. Refereed. *Indexed:* A22, HRIS. *Aud.:* Ac, Sa.

This scholarly publication focuses on the application of information technology to systems across all modes of transportation, including coverage of theoretical, experimental, and operational aspects, making it an important journal for current technical research in transportation systems and engineering. Some of the topics it considers include communications, sensors, human/machine interfaces, decision systems, controls, simulation, reliability, and standards. Frequently, issues of the journal focus on a specific subject. URL: http://ieeexplore.ieee.org/xpl/mostRecentIssue.jsp?punumber=6979

4843. ***I T E Journal.*** Former titles (until 1978): *Transportation Engineering;* (until 1977): *Traffic Engineering;* (until 1937): *Traffic Digest.* [ISSN: 0162-8178] 1930. m. Individuals, USD 80; Free to members. Ed(s): Michelle S Birdsall. Institute of Transportation Engineers, 1627 Eye St, NW, Ste 600, Washington, DC 20006; ite_staff@ite.org; http://www.ite.org/. Illus., adv. Refereed. Vol. ends: Dec. Microform: PQC. *Indexed:* A22, HRIS. *Aud.:* Ac, Sa.

A monthly publication from the Institute of Transportation Engineers, *ITE Journal* is written by and for transportation engineers, planners, and other professionals concerned with the movement of people and goods. This refereed journal thoroughly covers the field of surface transportation, with articles on transit, bicycle and pedestrian transportation, smart cities, technology, street design, tolling, and other topics of interest to today's transportation professional. It focuses largely on North America, particularly the United States, but occasionally includes features from other parts of the world. Regular features include news on people, projects, places, and research, as well as resources available; a calendar of events and meetings; and positions available. Recommended for academic and special libraries. URL: http://www.ite.org/itejournal/

4844. ***I T S International: advanced technology for traffic management and urban mobility.*** Formerly (until 1996): *I T S (Intelligent Transport Systems).* [ISSN: 1463-6344] 1995. bi-m. Free to qualified personnel. Ed(s): Colin Snowman. Route One Publishing Ltd., Waterbridge Ct, 50, Spital St, Kent, DA1 2DT, United Kingdom; media@ropl.com; http://www.ropl.com. Illus. Sample. *Indexed:* HRIS. *Aud.:* Sa.

ITS International covers the intelligent transportation systems (ITS) industry for traffic management and urban mobility planners, engineers, policymakers, and other professionals. Its focus includes ITS industry news and events, technology, product analysis and reviews, and feature articles on ITS issues such as charging and tolling, enforcement, urban traffic control, networking and communication systems, travel information, data collection, GIS and mapping, location-based systems, smart cities, connected vehicles, and parking and access control. Each issue includes a current events section, updates on associations and conferences, and a listing of appointments and promotions within the field. Appropriate for engineering and transportation collections. URL: www.itsinternational.com

4845. *Inbound Logistics: the magazine for demand-driven logistics.* Former titles (until 1990): *Thomas Register's Inbound Logistics;* (until 1985): *Inbound Traffic Guide;* (until 1983): *Thomas Register's Inbound Traffic Guide for Industrial Buyers & Specifiers.* 1981. m. USD 95 in North America (Free to qualified personnel). Ed(s): Felecia J Stratton. Thomas Publishing Company (New York), Five Penn Plz, New York, NY 10001; contact@thomaspublishing.com; http://www.thomaspublishing.com. Illus., adv. Sample. Circ: 60000. Vol. ends: Dec. *Indexed:* HRIS. *Aud.:* Sa.

With news and coverage of supply chain and logistics topics including infrastructure, education, technology, and transportation policy, *Inbound Logistics* is a leading provider of information for professionals working in the industry. Each issue includes an InSight section, with brief articles covering topics like leadership, IT, 3PL, and tips from industry leaders. In-depth features in each issue focus on a broad range of topics of interest to the supply chain professional ranging from automation in the industry to global trade management solutions. An annual 3PL issue offers a deep dive into news, developments, and current issues surrounding third-party logistics. Appropriate for libraries with collections on logistics, shipping, and transportation. URL: http://www.inboundlogistics.com

4846. *International Journal of Automotive Technology and Management.* [ISSN: 1470-9511] 2001. q. USD 790 (print or online ed.)). Ed(s): Giuseppe Giulio Calabrese. Inderscience Publishers, PO Box 735, Olney, MK46 5WB, United Kingdom; info@inderscience.com; https://www.inderscience.com/index.php. Illus. Sample. Refereed. *Indexed:* B01, BRI, ErgAb. *Bk. rev.:* Number and length vary. *Aud.:* Ac, Sa.

The *International Journal of Automotive Technology and Management* is a quarterly academic journal focused on the automotive technology and management industry for an audience of academic experts in the field, as well as policymakers and executives in the automotive industry. The journal publishes original, refereed articles on subjects that include innovation management, economics, manufacturing, policy, information technology, human resources, and supply chain management. Recommended for academic and special libraries with collections on automotive engineering and management. URL: http://www.inderscience.com/jhome.php?jcode=ijatm

4847. *International Journal of Logistics Research and Applications: a leading journal of supply chain management.* Formerly (until 201?): *International Journal of Logistics (Print).* 1998. bi-m. GBP 999 (print & online eds.)). Ed(s): Andrew Lyons, Ming Lim. Taylor & Francis, 2, 3 & 4 Park Sq, Milton Park, Abingdon, OX14 4RN, United Kingdom; subscriptions@tandf.co.uk; https://www.tandfonline.com. Illus., adv. Sample. Refereed. Vol. ends: Nov. Reprint: PSC. *Indexed:* A22, B01, E01, HRIS. *Aud.:* Ac, Sa.

With a focus on logistics and supply chain research and its applications in the business world, the *International Journal of Logistics Research and Applications* is directed toward academics as well as logistics professionals. Subjects covered include the processes and flows that make up the supply chain, 3PL, modeling and simulation of processes and systems, customer relationship management, training and education issues, case studies, and decision support tools. The journal invites contributions from those working in academia as well as the business world. Recommended for academic and special libraries that serve researchers and practitioners in logistics and supply chain management. URL: www.tandfonline.com/CJOL

4848. *International Journal of Physical Distribution & Logistics Management.* Former titles (until 1990): *International Journal of Physical Distribution and Materials Management;* (until 1977): *International Journal of Physical Distribution;* Which incorporated (in 1975): *International Journal of Physical Distribution Monograph;* Which was formerly (1970-1975): *P D M. Physical Distribution Monograph.* [ISSN: 0960-0035] 1970. 10x/yr. EUR 17828 print & online eds. (excluding UK)). Emerald Publishing Limited, Howard House, Wagon Ln, Bingley, BD16 1WA, United Kingdom; emerald@emeraldinsight.com; http://www.emeraldinsight.com. Illus. Sample. Refereed. Reprint: PSC. *Indexed:* A22, B01, BRI, C42, E01. *Aud.:* Ac, Sa.

This journal provides an international platform for new research on current topics in the business of logistics management, directed at academics and professionals working in the fields of transportation, supply chain management, and logistics. With a focus on theoretically grounded original research studies rather than mathematical and modeling research papers, this journal publishes on a wide range of topics of interest to researchers and practitioners, including but not limited to risk management, personnel issues, inventory management, process implementation, network complexity, knowledge management, and sustainability. Appropriate for academic and special libraries that collect on transportation and logistics. URL: http://www.emeraldgrouppublishing.com/ijpdlm.htm

4849. *International Journal of Sustainable Transportation.* [ISSN: 1556-8318] 2007. m. GBP 722 (print & online eds.)). Ed(s): S C Wong, Keechoo Choi. Taylor & Francis, 2, 3 & 4 Park Sq, Milton Park, Abingdon, OX14 4RN, United Kingdom; subscriptions@tandf.co.uk; https://www.tandfonline.com. Adv. Sample. Refereed. Reprint: PSC. *Indexed:* A01, A22, E01, HRIS. *Aud.:* Ac, Sa.

Examining the processes and policies that enable the movement of people, goods, and information around the world is at the core of transportation studies; the environmental impact of that movement on the world is central to this journal, which seeks to provide a discussion forum for information and innovative thinking on sustainable transportation systems. While there is coverage of this topic in other journals, there are few that collect research on sustainable transportation in one resource, as the *International Journal of Sustainable Transportation* does, making it an important part of transportation collections. It presents research of interest not only to transportation researchers, but also to those working in environmental science and policy, and a range of other disciplines. Coverage is global, and includes all modes of transportation. Recommended for academic libraries. URL: https://www.tandfonline.com/toc/ujst20/current

4850. *International Journal of Transport Economics.* [ISSN: 0303-5247] 1974. q. EUR 1095 print & online eds. Ed(s): Enrico Musso. Fabrizio Serra Editore, c/o Accademia Editoriale, Via Santa Bibbiana 28, Pisa, 56127, Italy; accademiaeditoriale@accademiaeditoriale.it; http://www.libraweb.net. Illus., index, adv. Refereed. Vol. ends: Oct. *Indexed:* A22, HRIS. *Bk. rev.:* Occasional. *Aud.:* Ac, Sa.

This journal, published in Italy but with a worldwide focus, brings together current research in transport economics, uniting theoretical and applied approaches to the subject. Occasional special issues are devoted to a single topic, conference proceedings, or the International Journal of Transport Economics Prize: selected papers on transport economics submitted by young researchers. The editorial board and the authors of the articles come from around the world. The journal is published in English, with some supporting information also included in Italian. Appropriate for collections that support transportation research. URL: http://www.ijte.org/

4851. *International Railway Journal.* Former titles (until 2001): *International Railway Journal and Rapid Transit Review;* (until 1979): *International Railway Journal.* [ISSN: 2161-7376] 1960. m. Free. Ed(s): Luther S Miller. Simmons-Boardman Publishing Corp., 55 Broad St., 26th Fl., New York, NY 10004-2580; http://www.simmonsboardman.com. Illus., index. Sample. Vol. ends: Dec. *Indexed:* B01, C42, HRIS. *Aud.:* Ac, Sa.

This trade journal covers the international light-track and heavy-track railroad industries. It is the international version of its sister periodicals for North America, *Railway Age* and *Railway Track and Structures*. Each issue includes sections on industry news, finance, and analysis, with worldwide coverage. These sections include world market reports, feature articles, and a list of conferences and seminars. Of interest to both the academician and the practitioner, it is appropriate for large academic collections and special libraries that focus on transportation. URL: www.railjournal.com

4852. ***Jane's Airport Review.*** Former titles (until 2017): *I H S Jane's Airport Review;* (until 2011): *Jane's Airport Review.* [ISSN: 2514-0418] 1988. m. GBP 235. Ed(s): Ben Vogel. Jane's by I H S Markit, 163 Brighton Rd, Coulsdon, CR5 2YH, United Kingdom; orders.ihs@dsbnet.co.uk; http://www.janes.com. Illus. Vol. ends: Nov/Dec. *Indexed:* HRIS. *Aud.:* Ac, Sa.

This trade journal covers the airport business for airport management professionals, with international coverage of market intelligence and strategic planning. Regular features include sections on news, air traffic control, terminal and ground support equipment, security, environment, and interviews with leading industry professionals. Appropriate for special libraries and large academic and business collections. URL: www.ihs.com/products/janes/transport/airport-review.aspx

4853. ***Journal of Advanced Transportation (Print).*** Formerly (until vol.12, 1979): *High Speed Ground Transportation Journal.* [ISSN: 0197-6729] 1967. q. USD 795. Ed(s): S Chan Wirasinghe, William H K Lam. John Wiley & Sons, Inc., 111 River St, Hoboken, NJ 07030; cs-journals@wiley.com; http://onlinelibrary.wiley.com. Illus., index. Refereed. Circ: 300 Paid. Vol. ends: Winter. *Indexed:* A01, A22, C42, HRIS. *Bk. rev.:* Occasional. *Aud.:* Ac, Sa.

This scholarly journal covers all modes of transportation. The focus is on the engineering and technology behind the analysis, design, economics, operations, and planning of transportation networks. The journal focuses on multi-modal transportation networks, urban rail and bus systems, pedestrian studies, traffic flow theory and control, intelligent transportation systems (ITS), and automated and/or connected vehicles. Occasionally, issues may include review articles that provide an overall survey of an aspect of the field. All articles as of January 2017 are available freely on the journal's website. Appropriate for special libraries. URL: http://onlinelibrary.wiley.com/journal/10.1002/%28ISSN%292042-3195

4854. ***Journal of Air Law and Commerce.*** Formerly (until 1939): *The Journal of Air Law.* [ISSN: 0021-8642] 1930. q. USD 43 domestic; USD 50 foreign; USD 16 per issue. Ed(s): Chase Cobran, Lindsey Altmeyer. Southern Methodist University, S M U Law Review Association, Southern Methodist University, Dedman School of Law, P O Box 750116, Dallas, TX 75275; browning@smu.edu; http://www.smu.edu. Illus., index. Refereed. Vol. ends: Fall. Microform: WSH; PMC; PQC. Reprint: WSH. *Indexed:* A22, BRI, HRIS, L14. *Bk. rev.:* Occasional. *Aud.:* Ac, Sa.

This scholarly publication covers the legal and economic aspects of the airline industry, private aviation, and space. The journal is managed by a student board of editors in association with the *Southern Methodist University Law Review* and overseen by an advisory board of attorneys and experts in the field. The issues include comprehensive articles, case notes, and student commentaries on topical issues. Articles are written by lawyers, economists, government officials, and scholars. Open access is provided to the journal's contents on its website. Appropriate for special, legal, and academic libraries. URL: https://scholar.smu.edu/jalc/

4855. ***Journal of Air Transport Management: an international journal of research, policy and practice.*** [ISSN: 0969-6997] 1994. 9x/yr. EUR 1546. Ed(s): R Merkert, Sveinn V Gudmundsson. Pergamon Press, The Blvd, Langford Ln, E Park, Kidlington, OX5 1GB, United Kingdom; JournalsCustomerServiceEMEA@elsevier.com; http://www.elsevier.com. Illus., adv. Sample. Refereed. Microform: PQC. *Indexed:* ErgAb, H&TI, HRIS. *Aud.:* Ac, Sa.

Published by Elsevier Science, this refereed journal is of interest to both the academician and the practitioner. It addresses theory and application relative to all aspects of the international air transportation industry, including airlines, infrastructure, airports, traffic control, management, policy, operations, marketing, and sustainability, with an international scope. The journal has been issued only in electronic format since 2003 and must be accessed online by subscribers. Appropriate for special and academic collections. URL: https://www.journals.elsevier.com/journal-of-air-transport-management

The Journal of Commerce. See Business and Finance/Scholarly section.

4856. ***Journal of Maritime Law and Commerce.*** [ISSN: 0022-2410] 1969. q. USD 360 domestic; USD 390 elsewhere. Ed(s): Kevin G O'Donovan. Jefferson Law Book Co., 2100 Huntingdon Ave, Baltimore, MD 21211; jefflaw1@juno.com; http://www.jmlc.org. Illus., index, adv. Refereed. Reprint: WSH. *Indexed:* A01, A22, BRI, HRIS, L14, S25. *Bk. rev.:* Occasional, signed. *Aud.:* Ac, Sa.

This scholarly journal is dedicated to coverage of all aspects of admiralty and maritime law. It targets the professional and the academician. Its contents concentrate on topics of current interest, but the editorial board also includes historical or theoretical treatments of the field. Special issues on single topics are often published; the journal also occasionally publishes case analyses, review articles, and book reviews. Appropriate for law libraries and special libraries that collect on maritime transportation. URL: www.jmlc.org

4857. ***Journal of Public Transportation (Online).*** [ISSN: 2375-0901] 1996. q. Free. Ed(s): Robert L Bertini. University of South Florida, Center for Urban Transportation Research, 4202 E. Fowler Ave, CUT100, Tampa, FL 33620-5375; webmaster@cutr.usf.edu; http://www.cutr.usf.edu/. Refereed. *Aud.:* Ac, Sa.

Presenting new case studies and original research, the *Journal of Public Transportation* covers public transportation modes and related policies from all over the world, and makes them available online as an open-access journal. The journal aims to present papers with innovative solutions; approaches can come from any number of disciplines, including engineering, planning, public policy, political science, management, and others. Appropriate for special libraries and academic collections that support transportation research. URL: http://scholarcommons.usf.edu/jpt/

4858. ***Journal of Transport & Health.*** [ISSN: 2214-1405] 2014. q. EUR 637. Ed(s): J Mindell. Elsevier BV, Radarweg 29, Amsterdam, 1043 NX, Netherlands; info@elsevier.com; https://www.elsevier.com/. Refereed. *Aud.:* Ac, Sa.

Bridging the intersections of transportation and health, this journal examines the impacts of transportation systems and processes on public health and inequality. This includes very direct impacts such as road traffic injuries, potential health benefits derived from active transportation, and the impact of systems on users and non-users alike as in the case of air pollution generated by road, air, and rail transport. One of the journal's aims is to promote dialog between the transportation and public health communities, and it publishes articles written by both transportation and health researchers, appealing to an audience of readers working in both fields. Recommended for academic, transportation, and health sciences collections. URL: https://www.journals.elsevier.com/journal-of-transport-and-health

4859. ***Journal of Transport and Land Use.*** [ISSN: 1938-7849] 2008. . Free. Ed(s): David Levinson. University of Minnesota, Center for Transportation Studies, 200 Transportation & Safety Bldg, 511 Washington Ave, SE, Minneapolis, MN 55455; cts@umn.edu; http://www.cts.umn.edu. Refereed. *Aud.:* Ac, Sa.

The official journal of the World Society for Transport and Land Use Research, this journal publishes original interdisciplinary research on the intersection of transportation and land use. The impact of transportation on land use, and vice versa, is examined in contexts throughout the world and across all modes of transportation, not limited to urban planning but including also ports, bicycle lanes, transit-oriented development, campus commuting, and a broad range of other areas globally. This journal will be of interest not only to transportation planners but also to those studying urbanization, planning, public health, and a wide range of other disciplines. Housed at the University of Minnesota and sponsored by the Center for Transportation and the World Society for Transport and Land Use Research, this journal is available freely through an open-access model. Recommended for academic, planning, and transportation collections. URL: https://jtlu.org/index.php/jtlu/index

4860. ***Journal of Transport Economics and Policy.*** [ISSN: 0022-5258] 1967. q. GBP 196 print & online eds. (Individuals, GBP 55 print & online eds.). Ed(s): Steven A Morrison, D N Starkie. University of Bath, Claverton Down, Bath, BA2 7AY, United Kingdom; education@bath.ac.uk; http://www.bath.ac.uk. Illus. Refereed. Reprint: PSC. *Indexed:* A22, AmHI, B01, BAS, BRI, C42, EIP, EconLit, HRIS, IBSS. *Aud.:* Ac, Sa.

This scholarly journal focuses on research on economics and policy for intercity and urban transportation. Topics covered include passenger and freight transport, shipping, aviation, infrastructure, environmental issues, and more. The editorial board, the authors, and the topics they present are international in scope. Occasionally, issues of the journal cover a single topic in depth. Appropriate for academic and special libraries that support transportation research. URL: http://www.jtep.org/

4861. ***Journal of Transport Geography: the international journal focusing on transport and spatial change.*** [ISSN: 0966-6923] 1993. 8x/yr. EUR 1265. Ed(s): Frank Witlox. Pergamon Press, The Blvd, Langford Ln, E Park, Kidlington, OX5 1GB, United Kingdom; JournalsCustomerServiceEMEA@elsevier.com; http://www.elsevier.com. Illus., adv. Sample. Refereed. Microform: PQC. *Indexed:* A01, A22, B01, H&TI, HRIS. *Bk. rev.:* 1-5, 500-1,500 words, signed. *Aud.:* Ac, Sa.

This scholarly, interdisciplinary journal addresses topics related to the geographical, spatial, and land use dimensions of transportation, travel, and mobility. Topics include policies, infrastructure, operations, and transport networks. Occasional special issues are devoted to single themes that have included climate change, accessibility, rail transit, and a variety of other topics. The coverage is international and geared toward the professional and the academician. Appropriate for academic and special libraries. URL: www.sciencedirect.com/science/journal/09666923

4862. ***Journal of Transportation Engineering, Part A: Systems.*** Supersedes in part (in 2017): *Journal of Transportation Engineering;* Which was formerly (until 1983): *American Society of Civil Engineers. Transportation Engineering Journal;* Which was formed by the merger of (1962-1969): *American Society of Civil Engineers. Aero-Space Transport Division. Journal;* Which was formerly (until 1962): *American Society of Civil Engineers. Air Transport Division. Journal;* (1956-1969): *American Society of Civil Engineers. Highway Division. Journal;* (1957-1969): *American Society of Civil Engineers. Pipeline Division. Journal;* All of which superseded in part (1873-1956): *American Society of Civil Engineers. Proceedings.* [ISSN: 2473-2907] 1969. m. USD 1735. Ed(s): Chris T Hendrickson. American Society of Civil Engineers, 1801 Alexander Bell Dr, Reston, VA 20191; ascelibrary@asce.org; http://www.asce.org. Illus., index, adv. Refereed. Vol. ends: Nov/Dec. *Indexed:* A01, A22, BRI, HRIS. *Aud.:* Ac, Sa.

The *Journal of Transportation Engineering, Part A: Systems* is published by the American Society of Civil Engineers. The journal addresses all transportation modes, with a focus on professional engineering and technical literature. It covers the planning, design, construction, and maintenance of highway, air, rail, and urban transportation systems and infrastructure; traffic management; business management; technology; and transportation economics. Other topics include intelligent transportation systems, the impacts of connected and automated vehicles, and the environmental impacts of transportation. Each issue includes articles with detailed references. Appropriate for academic libraries and special libraries with collections on transportation or civil engineering. URL: http://ascelibrary.org/teo

4863. ***Journal of Transportation Law, Logistics and Policy.*** Former titles (until 1994): *Transportation Practitioners Journal;* (until 1984): *I C C Practitioners' Journal;* (until 1933): *Practitioners' Journal;* (until 19??): *Association of Practitioners Before the Interstate Commerce Commission;* (until 1931): *I C C Practitioners' Quarterly Bulletin.* [ISSN: 1078-5906] 19??. q. Free to members. Ed(s): Michael F McBride. Association of Transportation Law Professionals, 5407, Annapolis, MD 21403; info@atlp.org; http://www.atlp.org. Illus., index, adv. Vol. ends: Summer. Microform: WSH; PMC. *Indexed:* A22, B01, BRI, HRIS, L14. *Bk. rev.:* Occasional, 1,200-2,000 words, signed. *Aud.:* Ac, Sa.

Published by the Association for Transportation Law, Logistics, and Policy (ATLLP), this scholarly, peer-reviewed journal includes articles on transportation law, practice, legislation, regulation, history, theory, logistics, economics, and statistics. It is of interest to academic and legal experts, practicing attorneys, and government officials. Coverage is focused on North America, but occasionally articles on other areas of the world are included. Every issue includes updates on recent administrative and regulatory developments. Alternate issues contain book reviews and the ATLLP schedule of events. Appropriate for special and law libraries with collections on transportation and logistics.

4864. ***Journal of Transportation Safety & Security.*** [ISSN: 1943-9962] 2009. 10x/yr. GBP 518 (print & online eds.)). Ed(s): Dr. Stephen H Richards. Taylor & Francis Inc., 711 3rd Ave, 8th Fl, New York, NY 10017; support@tandfonline.com; http://www.tandfonline.com. Sample. Refereed. Reprint: PSC. *Indexed:* A01. *Aud.:* Ac, Sa.

With a focus on transportation safety and security across all modes, the *Journal of Transportation Safety & Security* is unique in the field with an academic concentration on the topics of transportation safety and security. This includes travel by road, transit, pedestrian, bicycle, air, water, and rail, with a global scope. Articles cover a wide range of aspects of transportation safety, including but not limited to, infrastructure design, human factors, crash data collection and analysis, policies and planning, and emergency planning and incident response. This journal is a valuable resource to academics and professionals interested in transportation safety. Recommended for academic and transportation collections. URL: https://www.tandfonline.com/toc/utss20/current

Journal of Travel Research. See Travel and Tourism/Research section.

4865. ***Logistics Management.*** Formerly (until Jun.2002): *Logistics Management & Distribution Report;* Which was formed by the merger (1996-1997): *Logistics Management;* Which was formerly (until 1996): *Traffic Management;* (1992-1997): *Distribution;* Which was formerly (until 1992): *Chilton's Distribution;* (until 1986): *Chilton's Distribution for Traffic and Transportation Decision Makers;* (until 1980): *Chilton's Distribution;* (until 1979): *Chilton's Distribution Worldwide;* (until 1977): *Distribution Worldwide;* (until 1972): *Chilton's Distribution Worldwide;* (until 1970): *Distribution Worldwide;* (until 1969): *Distribution Manager;* (until 1967): *Physical Distribution Manager;* (until 1966): *Distribution Age;* (until 1945): *D and W;* (until 1937): *Distribution & Warehousing;* (until 1920): *Transfer & Storage;* (until 1915): *Team Owners Review.* [ISSN: 1540-3890] 1997. m. Plus annual directory. Free to qualified personnel. E H Publishing, Inc., 111 Speen St, Ste 200, PO Box 989, Framingham, MA 01701; info@ehpub.com; http://www.ehpub.com. Illus., adv. Circ: 74060. Microform: PQC. *Indexed:* A22, B01, B03, BRI, C42, HRIS. *Aud.:* Ac, Sa.

This trade journal provides strong coverage in the areas of transportation operations and policy. Although the focus is on the United States, some coverage is provided on export-import and overseas shipments. Feature articles include company case studies, multipart articles, impacts of government policies and actions, economic analysis, new services, and innovative business practices. The journal includes a large array of monthly columns on various aspects of the industry; for example, acquisitions, express carriers, railroads, air freight, regulation, and so on. It also includes news summaries, economic indicators, and product and equipment notices, as well as an annual salary survey. Other regular annual features include polls and buyers' guides. Appropriate for academic, business, and special libraries that collect on logistics. URL: www.logisticsmgmt.com

4866. ***Maritime Policy and Management: the flagship journal of international shipping and port research.*** Formerly (until 1976): *Maritime Studies and Management.* [ISSN: 0308-8839] 1973. 8x/yr. GBP 2537 (print & online eds.)). Ed(s): Kevin Li, Heather Leggate

McLaughlin. Routledge, 4 Park Sq, Milton Park, Abingdon, OX14 4RN, United Kingdom; subscriptions@tandf.co.uk; http://www.tandfonline.com. Illus., adv. Sample. Refereed. Reprint: PSC. *Indexed:* A01, A22, B01, E01, EconLit, HRIS. *Aud.:* Ga, Sa.

Aimed at researchers, managers, and policymakers, *Maritime Policy and Management* publishes peer-reviewed articles on topics related to the maritime industry worldwide, with an emphasis on business and management concerns. Coverage of the industry is broad, covering topics that might include emergency management, human factors, concessions and competition policy, assessment of economic aspects, development, and more, while addressing issues at port, community, shipping company, and shipboard levels. Recommended for academic and special libraries with transportation, business, and maritime collections. URL: https://www.tandfonline.com/toc/tmpm20/current

4867. ***Mass Transit: best practices for better public transportation.*** [ISSN: 0364-3484] 1974. 8x/yr. USD 37 domestic (Free to qualified personnel). Ed(s): Leah Harnack. SouthComm Communications, Inc., 1233 Janesville Ave., PO Box 803, Fort Atkinson, WI 53538; info@southcomm.com; https://www.southcomm.com/. Illus., adv. Circ: 21206. Vol. ends: Nov/Dec. *Indexed:* A22, B03, BRI, C42, EIP, HRIS. *Aud.:* Sa.

Mass Transit addresses current events, technology solutions, and industry news surrounding mass transportation, with a particular focus on transit systems in the United States, although there is some international coverage. Recent feature article topics include disruptive technologies, ridership data, emergency response and security, and public-private partnerships. Each issue also includes sections on best practices for transit operators, reports from the field, and a section highlighting social media posts from transit agencies around the web. Appropriate for special libraries and large general and academic collections. URL: www.masstransitmag.com

4868. ***Metro Magazine: for transit & motorcoach business.*** Former titles (until 19??): *Metro (Torrance);* (until 1994): *Metro Magazine;* (until 1985): *Metro;* (until 1974): *Metropolitan.* 1904. m. USD 40 domestic; USD 60 Canada; USD 100 foreign. Ed(s): Alex Roman. Bobit Business Media, 3520 Challenger St, Torrance, CA 90503; order@bobit.com; http://www.bobitbusinessmedia.com. Illus., adv. Vol. ends: Nov/Dec. *Indexed:* BRI, HRIS. *Aud.:* Sa.

This trade journal covers national and international urban and interurban transportation systems for the transit and motorcoach business. It addresses urban transportation systems including bus and rail transit, intercity motorcoaches, and paratransit. Topics include technology, equipment, high-speed rail, management, finance, and legislation. Each issue includes industry news and events, feature articles, editorials, product and innovation showcases, a calendar of events, and an industry personnel section. Yearly special features include a tear-out calendar that highlights dates of industry interest, and an annual "Top 50 Motorcoach Fleets" list. Appropriate for special libraries with transportation collections. URL: www.metro-magazine.com

4869. ***Mobilities.*** [ISSN: 1745-0101] 2006. 5x/yr. GBP 487 print & online eds. (Individuals, USD 151). Ed(s): Kevin Hannam, John Urry. Routledge, 4 Park Sq, Milton Park, Abingdon, OX14 4RN, United Kingdom; subscriptions@tandf.co.uk; http://www.tandfonline.com. Adv. Sample. Refereed. Reprint: PSC. *Indexed:* A01, A22, E01, HRIS, MLA-IB. *Aud.:* Ac.

Mobilities is unique among transportation journals in its scope of theoretically informed research on transportation encompassing a broad range of fields of study that includes transportation, the social sciences, humanities, and STEM fields. This includes the processes and policies that inform the movement of people, goods, and information around the world, as well as critical examination of new infrastructures for that movement. Papers cover topics including mobile rights and risks, mobile spatiality and temporality, migration and diasporas framed in terms of wider mobilities theory, climate change and transportation energy, and immobilities and social exclusions, among other topics. Recommended for academic libraries. URL: https://www.tandfonline.com/toc/rmob20/current

4870. ***The Motor Ship.*** Former titles (until 1957): *The British Motor Ship;* (until 19??): *Motor Ship.* [ISSN: 0027-2000] 1920. m. 11/yr. GBP 133.50 (Free to qualified personnel). Ed(s): Bill Thomson. Mercator Media Ltd., The Old Mill, Lower Quay, Fareham, PO16 0RA, United Kingdom; corporate@mercatormedia.com; http://www.mercatormedia.com. Illus., index, adv. Circ: 7124. Vol. ends: Dec. *Indexed:* A22, B03, BRI, C42, HRIS. *Aud.:* Sa.

This trade journal provides news and in-depth coverage of all aspects of marine technology for industry professionals. Feature coverage includes ship technology, environmental concerns, alternative fuels, and propulsion systems. Regular columns cover news on markets, industry challenges, ships, and ship repair, as well as equipment, updates on movers and shakers, and industry news. Appropriate for special libraries with transportation collections. URL: www.motorship.com

4871. ***N R H S Bulletin.*** Former titles (until 2005): *National Railway Bulletin;* (until 1976): *National Railway Historical Society. Bulletin.* [ISSN: 1940-3615] 1935. q. Free to members. Ed(s): Jeffrey S Smith. National Railway Historical Society, 100 N 20th St, Ste 400, Philadelphia, PA 19103; info@nrhs.com; http://www.nrhs.com. Illus. Vol. ends: No. 6. *Indexed:* A01, HRIS. *Bk. rev.:* 200-750 words, signed. *Aud.:* Ga, Sa.

Published by the National Railway Historical Society, the *NRHS Bulletin* is targeted at the society's membership. Rail fans will enjoy the richly illustrated articles on history and current events in the railroad industry. Although many articles focus on passenger transport, there is also historical coverage of freight trains and services. One issue per year is devoted to the activities of the society, with an annual report as well as section-by-section state-of-the-chapter reports. Every issue contains feature articles and book reviews. Appropriate for large general collections and special libraries. URL: www.nrhs.com/publications

4872. ***Overdrive: the voice of the American trucker.*** Incorporates (1970-2001): *Owner Operator.* [ISSN: 0030-7394] 1961. m. USD 34.97 domestic (Free to qualified personnel). Ed(s): Jack Roberts, Lucinda Coulter. Randall-Reilly Publishing Company, 3200 Rice Mine Rd NE, Tuscaloosa, AL 35406; http://www.randallpub.com. Illus., adv. Circ: 90000. Vol. ends: Dec. *Indexed:* B01, BRI, HRIS. *Aud.:* Sa.

With content focused on the concerns of the truck driver, *Overdrive* includes industry news and articles on legislation, regulations, safety, technology, management, personnel issues, and other topics related to the North American trucking industry. Each issue includes feature articles, fleet news, an opinion section, equipment and gear reviews, and a focus on readers' custom rigs. Appropriate for special libraries and large general collections. URL: www.overdriveonline.com

4873. ***Passenger Transport: the source for public transportation news and analysis.*** [ISSN: 0364-345X] 1943. bi-w. USD 75 in North America; USD 87 elsewhere. American Public Transportation Association, 1666 K St, NW Ste 1100, Washington, DC 20006; statistics@apta.com; http://www.apta.com. Illus., index, adv. Vol. ends: Dec. *Indexed:* HRIS. *Aud.:* Sa.

This glossy, newspaper-format bi-weekly publication is targeted to North American transit officials and members of the American Public Transportation Association (APTA), the magazine's publisher. There is significant coverage of people involved in the industry, providing interviews and much space to news items about the movement of people in the field. In addition to providing current news on the subject, regular features include industry briefs, international news, classifieds, and regular columns. In conjunction with APTA conferences, special issues are published that focus on city-by-city transit operations. The online version of the journal and archived articles can be accessed. Appropriate for special libraries. URL: www.apta.com/passengertransport/Pages/LatestIssue.aspx

4874. ***Progressive Railroading.*** [ISSN: 0033-0817] 1958. m. Free to qualified personnel. Ed(s): Jeff Stagl, Patrick Foran. Trade Press Publishing Corp., 2100 W Florist Ave, Milwaukee, WI 53209; info@tradepress.com; http://www.tradepress.com. Illus., adv. Circ: 25059. Vol. ends: Dec. *Indexed:* A22, HRIS. *Aud.:* Ac, Sa.

As a major trade journal in the North American railroad industry, *Progressive Railroading* focuses on operations and equipment used in freight and passenger services, including urban transit. The feature articles provide profiles of key companies, articles on safety, alliances, and more. Regular features are extensive, including industry and regional news and analysis, statistics, events, commentary, and equipment information. This magazine publishes many annual guides to the industry on the subjects of cars, locomotives, and track, finance, and leasing. Appropriate for special libraries and large academic collections. URL: www.progressiverailroading.com

4875. *Public Roads.* [ISSN: 0033-3735] 1918. q. USD 21 domestic; USD 29.40 elsewhere. Ed(s): Maria Romstedt, John J Sullivan. U.S. Federal Highway Administration, 1200 New Jersey Ave, SE, Washington, DC 20590; http://www.fhwa.dot.gov. Illus. Microform: CIS; PQC. *Indexed:* A01, A22, HRIS. *Aud.:* Ga, Sa.

Published by the Federal Highway Administration of the U.S. Department of Transportation, *Public Roads* covers federal highway policies, programs, research, and development. While its primary audience is transportation officials, researchers, field technicians, and engineers, the journal's content could also be used by a general audience wishing to stay informed on transportation issues and progress. Each issue includes features on new research and developments, recent publications, news in the industry, opinion pieces, and online tools. Appropriate for large general collections and special libraries. URL: https://www.fhwa.dot.gov/publications/publicroads/index.cfm

4876. *Public Transport International (French Edition).* Supersedes in part (in 1997): *Public Transport International (Multilingual Edition);* Which was formerly (until 1990): *U I T P Revue; International Union of Tramways, Light Railways and Motor Omnibuses. Review.* [ISSN: 1029-1261] 1952. bi-m. Ed(s): Sylvie Cappaert-Blondelle. International Union of Public Transport, Rue Sainte-Marie 6, Brussels, 1080, Belgium; http://www.uitp.org. Illus., adv. Circ: 3000. Vol. ends: Nov/Dec. *Indexed:* HRIS. *Aud.:* Ac, Sa.

Published by the International Association of Public Transport, *Public Transport International* provides coverage of issues related to urban mobility worldwide. Each issue consists of feature articles on topics like industry trends and innovations, network planning, urban regeneration, light rail, security, and current projects under development. Technological, socioeconomic, and political aspects of public transportation are also covered. *Public Transport International* is directed at public transportation professionals and policymakers, but would also be of interest to readers seeking to understand the state of public transportation worldwide. Appropriate for academic and special libraries. URL: http://www.uitp.org/pti

4877. *Railfan & Railroad.* Formed by the merger of (1974-1979): *Railfan;* (1937-1979): *Railroad Magazine;* Which was formerly (until 1937): *Railroad Stories;* (until 1932): *Railroad Man's Magazine.* 1979. m. USD 42 domestic; USD 57 Canada; USD 67 elsewhere. Ed(s): E S Barry. White River Productions, PO Box 48, Bucklin, MO 64631; info@whiteriverproductions.com; http://whiteriverproductions.com. Illus., adv. Vol. ends: Dec. *Indexed:* HRIS. *Bk. rev.:* Number and length vary. *Aud.:* Ga, Sa.

Published for fans of railroading and railroad history, *Railfan & Railroad* includes articles on current railroad topics as well as rail history, with coverage of passenger and freight rail as well as occasional features and news on public transportation. Contents include feature articles lavishly illustrated with full-color photographs showing trains and equipment in the field. Also covered are news and events; product reviews; preservation information; sections devoted to railway dining, museums, and tour schedules; and product and hobby reviews. A pull-out index for the previous year is published each spring. Appropriate for large general collections and transportation collections. http://railfan.com/

4878. *Railroad History.* Formerly (until 1972): *Railway and Locomotive Historical Society. Bulletin (Print).* [ISSN: 0090-7847] 1921. s-a. Members, USD 7.50; Non-members, USD 15. Ed(s): Peter A Hansen. Railway & Locomotive Historical Society, c/o Peter A. Hansen, 15621 W 87th St, PO Box 152, Lenexa, KS 66219; http://rlhs.org. Illus., index. Refereed. *Indexed:* HRIS. *Bk. rev.:* 20-30, up to 1,500 words, signed. *Aud.:* Ac, Sa.

Published by the Railway and Locomotive Historical Society, *Railroad History* is geared to railroad historians and the enthusiast community. With feature-length articles on railroading's past, the journal covers a range of topics including planning, legislation, company history, accidents, and more, all while placing railroads in a larger historical context. The journal has an impressive book review section and a section on recommended articles from the non-railroad press for additional reading. Articles are beautifully illustrated with photography and, occasionally, archival materials such as timetables and maps. Each issue includes information on preservation and on locomotives, a discussion forum, and a photography section. There is a yearly bonus issue devoted to a specific topic. A cumulative index from 1921 forward and the current issue can be accessed online. Appropriate for large general collections and special libraries. URL: www.rlhs.org/Publications/History/

4879. *Railway Age: serving the railway industry since 1856.* Incorporates (1982-1991): *Modern Railroads;* Which was formerly (until 1982): *Modern Railroads - Rail Transit;* (until 1977): *Modern Railroads; Railway Locomotives and Cars;* Former titles (until 1918): *Railway Age Gazette;* (until 1910): *Railroad Age Gazette;* Which was formed by the merger of (1870-1908): *Railroad Gazette;* Which was formerly (until 1870): *Western Railroad Gazette;* (1900-1908): *Railway Age;* Which was formerly (until 1900): *Railway Age and Northwestern Railroads;* Which was formed by the merger of (1876-1891): *Railway Age;* (1887-1891): *Northwestern Railroads.* [ISSN: 0033-8826] 1876. m. Free to qualified personnel. Ed(s): Douglas John Bowen, William C Vantuono. Simmons-Boardman Publishing Corp., 55 Broad St., 26th Fl., New York, NY 10004-2580; http://www.simmonsboardman.com. Illus., adv. Vol. ends: Dec. Microform: CIS; PQC. *Indexed:* A22, B01, BRI, HRIS. *Aud.:* Ac, Sa.

As one of the major North American railroad trade journals, *Railway Age* covers all aspects of the railroad industry. The journal addresses both freight and passenger service, encompassing commuter, rapid, and light-rail transit, as well as the equipment and supply industry, management, finance, and operational considerations. Annual special issues include such topics as buyers' guides, planners' guides, and year-end outlooks. Regular features include at-a-glance industry indicators and outlooks, railroader of the year, meeting information, company indexes, professional directories, classifieds, and commentary on a variety of aspects of the industry. The focus of the latter manifestation of the journal is on business rather than technical aspects of the industry. Appropriate for large general collections and transportation collections. URL: www.railwayage.com

4880. *Railway Gazette International: a journal of management, engineering and operation.* Former titles (until 1971): *International Railway Gazette;* (until 19??): *Railway Gazette;* Which incorporated (1880-1935): *Railway Engineer; Railway News; Railway Times; Transport and Railroad Center.* [ISSN: 0373-5346] 1835. m. GBP 100 domestic; USD 292 elsewhere. Ed(s): Nick Kingsley. Railway Gazette Group, 7th Fl, Chancery House, St Nicholas Way, Sutton, SM1 1JB, United Kingdom; editor@metro-report.com; http://www.metro-report.com. Illus., index, adv. *Indexed:* A22, B01, BRI, HRIS. *Bk. rev.:* Number and length vary. *Aud.:* Sa.

With coverage of railroad business, industry, and technology news, *Railway Gazette International* covers every aspect of railroads with content of interest to industry practitioners, executives, and policy officials, as well as those studying the international rail industry. Articles encompass heavy and light rail and both freight and passenger services. Each issue contains feature articles on topics including industry intelligence, research, high-speed rail, and urban growth. A different world region is highlighted in each issue. Also included in each issue is a forum with professional updates, information on research and skills, book reviews, and an industry calendar. Appropriate for large academic collections, special libraries, and business collections. URL: www.railwaygazette.com

4881. *Research in Transportation Business and Management.* [ISSN: 2210-5395] 2011. q. EUR 476. Ed(s): S Ison, M R Brooks. Elsevier BV, Radarweg 29, Amsterdam, 1043 NX, Netherlands; info@elsevier.com; https://www.elsevier.com/. Refereed. *Aud.:* Ac, Sa.

A cross-disciplinary journal, *Research in Transportation Business and Management* publishes research on the business and management aspects of transportation, and will be of interest to academics and professionals working in the transportation and business sectors alike. Articles cover such topics as business strategy, risk management, communications, sustainability, law, logistics, privatization and commercialization, across all modes of transportation worldwide. Issues are focused around subjects that might include a single mode or topic, such as the global transport of commodity products, or sustainable efficiency and management in urban goods transport. Recommended for academic, business, and special libraries with collections on business or transportation. URL: https://www.journals.elsevier.com/research-in-transportation-business-and-management

4882. ***Roads & Bridges.*** Former titles (until 1985): *Roads;* (until 1983): *R U R: Rural and Urban Roads;* Which was formed by the merger of (1954-1963): *Rural Roads;* (1956-1963): *Street Engineering.* [ISSN: 8750-9229] 1963. m. USD 45 domestic; USD 65 Canada; USD 95 elsewhere. Ed(s): Allen Zeyher. Scranton Gillette Communications, Inc., 3030 W Salt Creek Ln, Ste 201, Arlington Heights, IL 60005; hgillette@sgcmail.com; http://www.scrantongillette.com. Illus., adv. Microform: PQC. *Indexed:* A01, A22, HRIS. *Aud.:* Sa.

With a focus on the construction and design of roads and bridges in the United States and Canada, *Roads & Bridges* is targeted at engineers, contractors, and government officials with an interest in the transportation construction and maintenance industry. Coverage includes news and events, technology, legislation, safety and regulation, construction materials, construction machinery, products, and equipment. Each issue includes feature articles, a legal section, product and equipment reviews, and sections devoted to technical innovations and construction vehicles. Appropriate for academic and special libraries with collections on transportation and civil engineering. URL: https://www.roadsbridges.com/

4883. ***Supply Chain Management Review.*** [ISSN: 1521-9747] 1997. 7x/yr. USD 199 combined subscription in US & Canada print & online eds.; USD 241 combined subscription elsewhere print & online eds. Ed(s): Bob Trebilcock. E H Publishing, Inc., 111 Speen St, Ste 200, PO Box 989, Framingham, MA 01701; info@ehpub.com; http://www.ehpub.com. Adv. Circ: 12000. Vol. ends: Feb. *Indexed:* B01, BRI, C42, HRIS. *Bk. rev.:* 3-5, 250-750 words. *Aud.:* Ac, Sa.

Supply Chain Management Review is published with the goal of providing thought leadership around best practices in supply chain fundamentals. With an advisory board comprising industry executives, analysts, and academics, the journal's audience is made up of both supply chain professionals and industry scholars. Coverage includes logistics, supply chain management, procurement, technology, e-commerce, warehousing, management, training, and information flow. Each issue includes feature articles, commentary, and special reports. Special reports focus on current industry topics like 3PLs, risk management, finance, and certifications. There is at least one subject-specific supplement issued per year. Appropriate for large academic collections and special collections. URL: www.scmr.com

4884. ***T R News.*** Former titles (until 1983): *Transportation Research News;* (until 1974): *Highway Research News.* [ISSN: 0738-6826] 1963. bi-m. USD 60 domestic; USD 85 foreign; USD 12 per issue. Ed(s): Javy Awan. U.S. National Research Council, Transportation Research Board, The National Academies of Sciences, Engineering, and Medicine, 500 Fifth St, NW, Washington, DC 20001; http://www.trb.org. Illus. Vol. ends: Nov/Dec. *Indexed:* A01, A22, HRIS. *Bk. rev.:* 4-8, up to 150 words. *Aud.:* Ac, Sa.

As the bi-monthly publication of the Transportation Research Board (TRB), *TR News* covers research and innovations in all modes of transportation with a particular focus on U.S.-based initiatives and TRB activities. Article contributions come from academics and professionals in the industry. In addition to feature articles, each issue contains profiles of members, news briefs and TRB highlights, an events calendar, a listing of new TRB publications with abstracts, and book reviews. Following each year's annual TRB meeting, a large section is devoted to meeting highlights. Appropriate for large academic collections and special libraries with transportation collections. URL: http://www.trb.org/Publications/PubsTRNewsMagazine.aspx

4885. ***Traffic Technology International.*** [ISSN: 1356-9252] 1994. bi-m. Free. Ed(s): Nick Bradley. U K & International Press, Abinger House, Church St, Dorking, RH4 1DF, United Kingdom; info@ukintpress.com; http://www.ukipme.com. Adv. *Indexed:* HRIS. *Aud.:* Sa.

Traffic Technology International covers issues of traffic safety and traffic control for a global audience of transportation professionals. Coverage includes industry news and events, intelligent transportation systems, traffic control devices, traffic safety devices, regulations, legislation, traffic systems operations, research, personnel, management, and training. Each issue includes feature articles, transportation news from around the world, a section on the future of transportation communications, and technology profiles. The journal includes a yearly supplement titled "Tolltrans" that addresses every aspect of highway tolls. Appropriate for large academic collections and special libraries with transportation collections. URL: www.traffictechnologytoday.com

4886. ***Trains.*** Formerly: *Trains & Travel.* [ISSN: 0041-0934] 1940. m. USD 42.95 domestic; USD 54.95 Canada; USD 57.95 elsewhere. Ed(s): Jim Wrinn. Kalmbach Publishing Co., 21027 Crossroads Circle, PO Box 1612, Waukesha, WI 53187; customerservice@kalmbach.com; http://www.kalmbach.com. Illus., index, adv. Vol. ends: Dec. *Indexed:* A22, BRI, HRIS, MASUSE. *Bk. rev.:* 3-5, 250-750 words, signed. *Aud.:* Ga, Sa.

Combining current railroad news with an eye on the history of railroading, *Trains* will be primarily of interest to rail enthusiasts, but industry professionals may find some interest in news and industry coverage. *Trains* covers both the light and heavy rail industries of the United States and Canada, with occasional international news. Feature articles are lushly illustrated with color photography and a focus on topics including short line and regional railroads, high-speed rail, safety, and personal essays recollecting memories of railroading. Each issue also features a Map of the Month, which might include trains to be found in a city or a region. In addition, the magazine features a regular section on preservation and a gallery of railroad photography; it also sponsors an annual photography contest for readers. Special issues, published regularly, are devoted to a single issue like train wrecks, locomotives, and train watching. Appropriate for large public library collections, academic collections, and special libraries with transportation collections. URL: http://trn.trains.com/

4887. ***Tramways & Urban Transit: international light rail magazine.*** Former titles (until 1997): *Light Rail and Modern Tramway;* (until 1992): *Modern Tramway and Light Rail Transit;* (until 1980): *Modern Tramway and Rapid Transit;* (until 1977): *Modern Tramway and Light Railway Review.* [ISSN: 1460-8324] 1938. m. Free to members. Ed(s): Simon Johnston. Light Rail Transit Association, LRTA, c/o 138 Radnor Ave, Welling, DA16 2BY, United Kingdom; office@lrta.org; http://www.lrta.org. Illus., adv. *Indexed:* HRIS. *Aud.:* Sa.

Published by the Light Rail Transit Association, this journal has been in continuous publication since 1938. It addresses the global light-rail and urban transport industry and is geared to industry professionals. *Tramways & Urban Transit* covers industry news and events, technology, funding, legislation, safety, management, and personnel. Each issue includes feature articles on developments, innovations, and mobility solutions around the world, a spotlight on a single transit system, a comprehensive review section with brief updates and news on tramway and urban transit systems around the world, as well as commentary, a calendar of events, and a product review section. Appropriate for academic and special libraries with transportation collections. URL: http://tautonline.com/

4888. ***Transport Policy.*** [ISSN: 0967-070X] 1993. 8x/yr. EUR 1339. Ed(s): Tae H Oum. Pergamon Press, The Blvd, Langford Ln, E Park, Kidlington, OX5 1GB, United Kingdom; JournalsCustomerServiceEMEA@elsevier.com; http://www.elsevier.com. Illus., adv. Sample. Refereed. Microform: PQC. *Indexed:* A01, A22, B01, HRIS. *Aud.:* Ac, Sa.

The official publication of the World Conference on Transport Research Society, *Transport Policy* aims to bridge the theoretical and practical aspects of transportation policy, strategy, and administration across all transportation modes. It targets transportation professionals, policymakers, and academics. Some issues focus on a single aspect of transport policy. In addition to scholarly articles, each issue includes a section on the activities of the World Conference on Transport Research Society. Appropriate for academic libraries and special libraries with transportation collections. https://www.journals.elsevier.com/transport-policy

4889. ***Transport Reviews.*** [ISSN: 0144-1647] 1981. bi-m. GBP 1338 (print & online eds.)). Ed(s): David Banister. Routledge, 4 Park Sq, Milton Park, Abingdon, OX14 4RN, United Kingdom; subscriptions@tandf.co.uk; http://www.tandfonline.com. Illus., index, adv. Sample. Refereed. Vol. ends: Oct/Dec. Reprint: PSC. *Indexed:* A01, A22, B01, E01, ErgAb, HRIS. *Bk. rev.:* 1-3, 350-750 words, signed. *Aud.:* Ac, Sa.

A review journal covering all aspects of transportation, *Transport Reviews* is a core title for academic libraries with transportation collections, and is a valuable resource for undergraduates, graduate students, and faculty alike. Peer-reviewed articles cover all modes of transportation and a range of disciplinary subject areas including engineering, social science, and economics, and are global in scope. Due to the wide scope of the journal's content, it is of interest for those who work in transportation research as well as those approaching the subject from different backgrounds. Occasional issues are organized around a specific topic. Appropriate for academic libraries and transportation collections. URL: https://www.tandfonline.com/toc/ttrv20/current

4890. ***Transport Topics: national newspaper of the trucking industry.*** Formerly (until 19??): *A T A News Bulletin.* [ISSN: 0041-1558] 1935. w. Mon. USD 109 domestic (Free to members). Ed(s): Joe Howard. American Trucking Associations, Inc., 950 N Glebe Rd, Ste 210, Alexandria, VA 22203; orders@trucking.org; http://www.truckline.com. Illus., adv. Circ: 28666 Paid. Microform: PQC. *Indexed:* A22, HRIS. *Aud.:* Ga, Sa.

A weekly tabloid-format trade journal, *Transport Topics* covers the trucking and freight transportation industry and is published by the American Trucking Association. It is geared toward trucking and freight professionals, and is composed mostly of short articles concerning all aspects of trucking, but especially state and federal regulations, management, policy analysis, finance, operations, equipment, and events. Issues often include special sections on a single topic. Regular features include state news, a weekly business review, fuel prices, products, people news, a calendar of events, job listings, real estate, and equipment. Appropriate for large general collections or special libraries with transportation collections. URL: http://www.ttnews.com

4891. ***Transportation.*** [ISSN: 0049-4488] 1972. 5x/yr. EUR 2212 (print & online eds.)). Ed(s): Kay Axhausen. Springer New York LLC, 233 Spring St, New York, NY 10013; customerservice@springer.com; http://www.springer.com. Illus., index, adv. Refereed. Vol. ends: No. 4. Microform: PQC. Reprint: PSC. *Indexed:* A22, C45, E01, EconLit, HRIS, IBSS. *Aud.:* Ac, Sa.

This scholarly journal covers transportation planning, policy, research, and practice across all modes of transportation around the world and includes industrialized, newly industrialized, and developing nations. The audience is policymakers, transportation professionals, and academics. Articles are generally focused on technical subjects and include topics like forecasting, data mining, and mode choice. Appropriate for special libraries with transportation collections. URL: https://link.springer.com/journal/11116

4892. ***Transportation Journal.*** [ISSN: 0041-1612] 1961. q. USD 185 (print & online eds.)). Ed(s): David Swanson, Yoshinori Suzuki. Pennsylvania State University Press, 820 N University Dr, University Support Bldg 1, Ste C, University Park, PA 16802; info@psupress.org; http://www.psupress.org. Illus., index, adv. Refereed. Reprint: PSC. *Indexed:* A01, A22, B01, BRI, C42, H&TI, HRIS. *Bk. rev.:* Occasional. *Aud.:* Ac, Sa.

Transportation Journal, a journal of APICS Supply Chain council, publishes articles related to all aspects of the supply chain, transportation, and logistics industries. This scholarly journal includes articles on air transport, international transport, logistics/physical distribution/supply chain management, management information systems and computer applications, motor transport, rail transport, regulation/law, traffic and transport management, transport policy, and water transport. Special-theme issues are published regularly. There are occasional book reviews. Appropriate for special and academic libraries with transportation collections. URL: http://www.psupress.org/Journals/jnls_transportation_journal.html

4893. ***Transportation Law Journal: industry leader in multi-modal law, economics & policy.*** [ISSN: 0049-450X] 1969. s-a. USD 38 domestic; USD 46 foreign; USD 20 per issue domestic. Ed(s): Patricia Thwaites, Meghan Leemon. University of Denver, Sturm College of Law, 2255 E Evans Ave, Ste 448, Denver, CO 80208; mlattimer@law.du.edu; http://www.law.du.edu. Illus., index. Refereed. Vol. ends: Spring. Microform: WSH; PMC. Reprint: WSH. *Indexed:* A01, A22, BRI, HRIS, L14. *Aud.:* Ac, Sa.

Published by the University of Denver, Sturm College of Law, this scholarly journal addresses the international transportation industry and is geared toward the legal, government, and academic communities. It covers transportation law, regulations, economic, and political aspects of all transportation modes. Each issue includes significant research articles with abundant footnotes. Appropriate for law, academic, and special libraries. URL: www.law.du.edu/index.php/transportation-law-journal/issues

4894. ***Transportation Management & Engineering.*** Formerly (until 2001): *I T S World.* [ISSN: 1537-0259] 1996. q. USD 95 foreign (Free to qualified personnel). Scranton Gillette Communications, Inc., 3030 W Salt Creek Ln, Ste 201, Arlington Heights, IL 60005; hgillette@sgcmail.com; http://www.scrantongillette.com. Illus., index, adv. *Indexed:* HRIS. *Aud.:* Sa.

Transportation Management & Engineering is a trade journal focused on the interests of traffic system planners, designers, engineers, and managers. Coverage includes a variety of topics related to transportation management and engineering across all modes: among them, intelligent transportation systems, traffic safety, bus rapid transit, and the future of transportation. It provides transportation professionals with coverage of transportation news and events, feature articles, a product portfolio, editorials, and industry highlights. Appropriate for large academic libraries and special libraries with transportation collections. URL: www.roadsbridges.com/traffic-management

4895. ***Transportation Planning and Technology.*** Incorporates (1982-1991): *Specialized Transportation Planning and Practice.* [ISSN: 0308-1060] 1972. 8x/yr. GBP 3838 (print & online eds.)). Ed(s): David Gillingwater. Taylor & Francis, 2, 3 & 4 Park Sq, Milton Park, Abingdon, OX14 4RN, United Kingdom; subscriptions@tandf.co.uk; https://www.tandfonline.com. Adv. Sample. Refereed. Reprint: PSC. *Indexed:* A01, A22, B01, E01, HRIS. *Aud.:* Ga, Sa.

This multi-disciplinary journal publishes original, scholarly research on the intersections of transportation, technology, planning, urban form, and economics. Based in Europe and with global coverage, *Transportation Planning and Technology* covers such topics as systems technology, urban transport planning, environmental aspects, demand and land use forecasting, and the economic evaluation of these and other subjects with a scientific and technical focus. URL: https://www.tandfonline.com/loi/gtpt20

4896. ***Transportation Research. Parts A-F.*** 46x/yr. Pergamon Press, The Blvd, Langford Ln, E Park, Kidlington, OX5 1GB, United Kingdom; http://www.elsevier.com. *Bk. rev.:* Occasional, 600-2,500 words. *Aud.:* Ac, Sa.

This six-part set of journals covers the gamut of transportation research occurring around the world and is an essential set for transportation collections. Each part can be purchased separately.

A: ***Policy & Practice*** [ISSN: 0965-8564] 10/yr. USD 3,248. J. de D. Ortuzar and J.M. Rose . Vol. ends: Dec. Focuses on general-interest articles, particularly on planning and policy and their interaction with political, socioeconomic, and environmental systems.

B: ***Methodological*** [ISSN: 0191-2615] 10/yr. USD 3,201. Hai Yang. Vol. ends: Apr. Concentrates on the creation, analysis, and performance of models for the movement of freight and people.

C: ***Emerging Technologies*** [ISSN: 0968-090X] bi-m. USD 2,161. Yafeng Yin. Vol. ends: Dec. Discusses implications and applications of new technologies in the field of transportation.

D: ***Transport and Environment*** [ISSN: 1361-9209] bi-m. USD 2,205. R.B. Noland and J.X. Cao. Covers environmental impacts of transportation, policy issues surrounding that impact, and implications for the design and implementation of transportation systems.

E: ***Logistics and Transportation Review*** [ISSN: 1366-5545] bi-m. USD 2,213. J. Sheu. Vol. ends: Dec. Features articles on logistics including economics, cost, and production functions; capacity; demand; infrastructure; models; and supply chain topics.

F: ***Traffic Psychology and Behaviour*** [ISSN: 1369-8478] q. USD 1,538. S. Charlton. Focuses on the behavioral and psychological aspects of traffic and transport.

These journals are geared toward academics and professionals working in transportation. Appropriate for academic and special libraries with transportation collections.

4897. ***Transportation Research Record.*** Former titles (until 1974): *Highway Research Record;* Which incorporated (1927-1963): *Highway Research Board. Annual Meeting. Proceedings;* Which was formerly (until 1927): *Annual Meeting. Proceedings;* (until 1963): *Highway Research Board. Bulletin.* [ISSN: 0361-1981] 1963. m. Sage Publications, Inc., 2455 Teller Rd, Thousand Oaks, CA 91320; http://www.sagepub.com. Illus. Refereed. *Indexed:* A22, C45, HRIS. *Aud.:* Ac, Sa.

Each issue of *Transportation Research Record* contains papers prepared for presentation at Transportation Research Board (TRB) annual meetings, conferences, and workshops. The journal publishes peer-reviewed articles covering all modes of both passenger and freight transportation, and on topics including planning, engineering, design, economics, maintenance, safety, administration, and many more. Issues are focused around a common theme. Approximately 70 issues are published annually. Authors and topics come from all over the world. Along with other TRB publications, this is an essential series for any transportation collection. Appropriate for large academic collections and special libraries with transportation collections. http://journals.sagepub.com/home/trr

4898. ***Transportation Science.*** [ISSN: 0041-1655] 1967. q. USD 648 (print & online eds.)). Ed(s): Martin Savelsbergh. Institute for Operations Research and the Management Sciences (I N F O R M S), 5521 Research Park Dr, Ste 200, Catonsville, MD 21228; informs@informs.org; https://pubsonline.informs.org/. Illus., index. Refereed. Vol. ends: Nov. *Indexed:* A01, A22, B01, HRIS, IBSS. *Bk. rev.:* Occasional, 500-1,500 words. *Aud.:* Ac, Sa.

Published by the Institute for Operations Research and Management Sciences (INFORMS), this refereed, scholarly journal is the flagship journal of the Transportation Science and Logistics Society of INFORMS. It contains articles on all modes of transportation regarding operational management, such as planning and economic and social design. The mission of the journal is to advance analytical, experimental, and observational tools in the study of transportation. The journal contains research articles, critical-review articles, technical notes, letters to the editor, and book reviews. Annually, dissertation abstracts submitted for the Transportation Science Section Prize are published. Appropriate for special libraries and large academic collections. https://pubsonline.informs.org/journal/trsc

4899. ***Transportmetrica A: Transport Science.*** Formerly (until 2013): *Transportmetrica.* [ISSN: 2324-9935] 2005. 10x/yr. GBP 741 print & online eds. Ed(s): William Lam, S C Wong. Taylor & Francis, 2, 3 & 4 Park Sq, Milton Park, Abingdon, OX14 4RN, United Kingdom; subscriptions@tandf.co.uk; https://www.tandfonline.com. Refereed. Reprint: PSC. *Indexed:* HRIS. *Aud.:* Ac, Sa.

Bringing a scientific approach to transportation research, *Transportmetrica A: Transportation Science* aims to provide a forum for original discourse on the science of all aspects and modes of transportation. Recent articles cover such topics as traffic flow modeling, freight transportation planning, analysis of air transportation networks, and a classification of public transit users based on smart card data. This journal is of interest to researchers and practitioners in transportation science, including civil engineers and planners. Appropriate for academic and special libraries that collect in transportation and civil engineering. URL: https://www.tandfonline.com/toc/tmpm20/current

4900. ***Transportmetrica B: Transport Dynamics.*** Supersedes in part (in 2013): *Transportmetrica.* [ISSN: 2168-0566] 2013. 3x/yr. GBP 601 (print & online eds.)). Ed(s): Agachi Sumalee, Hong K Lo. Taylor & Francis, 2, 3 & 4 Park Sq, Milton Park, Abingdon, OX14 4RN, United Kingdom; subscriptions@tandf.co.uk; https://www.tandfonline.com. Refereed. Reprint: PSC. *Aud.:* Ac, Sa.

Focusing on the dynamic aspects of transportation networks and behavior, *Transportmetrica B: Transport Dynamics* seeks to bring together articles on the theoretical and practical aspects of the dynamic movement of people and goods. This might include such topics as activity-based modeling, land use and transport dynamics, time-series analyses of transport data and demand, and traffic emission modeling. Coverage is global in scope and with a scientific approach that will be of interest to researchers and practitioners in transportation science, including civil engineers and planners. Appropriate for academic and special libraries that collect in transportation and civil engineering. URL: https://www.tandfonline.com/action/journalInformation?show=aimsScope&journalCode=ttrb20

Ward's AutoWorld (Online). See Automobiles and Motorcycles section.

4901. ***Waterways Journal.*** [ISSN: 0043-1524] 1887. w. USD 39 domestic; USD 104 in Canada & Mexico. Ed(s): John Shoulberg. Waterways Journal, Inc., 319 N 4th St, Ste 650, St. Louis, MO 63102. Illus. Vol. ends: No. 52. *Indexed:* HRIS. *Bk. rev.:* Occasional. *Aud.:* Sa.

This U.S.-focused, tabloid-format publication covers all aspects of inland waterways, water transportation, and ports. Written for anyone with an interest in inland water transportation, including enthusiasts, its articles cover news, history, and data, among others. Annual features include a combined yearbook-and-directory that provides a chronological listing of the year's important news. Appropriate for special libraries with transportation collections. URL: www.waterwaysjournal.net

4902. ***WorkBoat.*** Incorporates (1954-1959): *Offshore Drilling; Southern Marine Review.* [ISSN: 0043-8014] 1943. m. Free to qualified personnel. Ed(s): David Krapf. Diversified Business Communications, 121 Free St, Portland, ME 04101; custserv@divcom.com; http://www.divbusiness.com. Illus., adv. Circ: 25563. Vol. ends: Dec. *Indexed:* BRI, HRIS. *Aud.:* Sa.

WorkBoat is a trade magazine for the North American workboat industry, which includes but is not limited to tugboats, barges, salvage vessels, crewboats, utility boats, excursion vessels, freighters, tankers, patrol craft, fire boats, and research vessels. It is geared to workboat professionals and covers industry news and events, legislation, regulation, safety, technology, vessel construction and maintenance, marine personnel, equipment, and product news. Each issue includes feature articles, a calendar of events, a classified section, a product showcase, and a section highlighting a specific port. Appropriate for special libraries with transportation collections. URL: https://www.workboat.com/

4903. ***World Highways (London, 1991).*** Formed by the merger of (1950-1991): *World Highways (Washington, 1950);* (1964-1991): *Routes du Monde.* [ISSN: 0964-4598] 1991. 10x/yr. Free to qualified personnel. Route One Publishing Ltd., Waterbridge Ct, 50, Spital St, Kent, DA1 2DT, United Kingdom; media@ropl.com; http://www.ropl.com. Illus., adv. Sample. *Indexed:* HRIS. *Aud.:* Sa.

This journal addresses the international road and highway construction and maintenance industries and targets industry professionals. It covers news and events, technology, materials, signage, lighting, equipment, technology, the environment and weather, maintenance, traffic, and safety. Each issue includes feature articles, a calendar of events, guides to products and services, relevant web sites, and a highlighted construction site. Appropriate for special libraries. URL: www.worldhighways.com

■ TRAVEL AND TOURISM

General/Newsletters/Research

See also Canada section.

Natasha Arguello, Head of Research and Education Services, University of Texas at San Antonio Libraries, San Antonio, TX; Natasha.Arguello@utsa.edu

Introduction

Both domestic and international travel and tourism are on the rise in the United States and worldwide. The traditional travel magazine, geared toward inspiring would-be travelers to dream and plan, is increasingly supplanted by Internet sites and travel apps.

Public library patrons who are planning their own travel will likely turn to web sources for the details of their trips, but may continue to use a general travel and tourism collection to inspire, inform, and excite themselves about world destinations and their travel options.

Academic library patrons rely on journals for high quality research on the current trends and issues in travel and tourism, as well as best practices in developing, promoting, enhancing, and sustaining tourism services. These journals will meet the research and professional needs of students, researchers, educators, and practitioners across multiple disciplines, not just those interested in tourism, travel, and hospitality studies.

There are quite literally hundreds of magazines and journals that focus on specific types of tourism. The periodicals that follow were chosen very carefully to give a solid, broad base to your travel and tourism collection. The magazines and journals included are international in scope and touch on a wide array of travel and tourism topics.

Basic Periodicals

Ga: *National Geographic Traveler;* Ac: *Annals of Tourism Research, Journal of Sustainable Tourism, Tourism Management.*

Basic Abstracts and Indexes

Hospitality and Tourism Index; Leisure, Recreation and Tourism Abstracts; Leisure Tourism Database; Readers' Guide to Periodical Literature.

General

Backpacker: the outdoor at your doorsteps. See Hiking, Climbing, and Outdoor Recreation section.

4904. *Conde Nast Traveler.* Incorporates (1985-1992): *European Travel & Life;* Formerly (until 1987): *Signature.* [ISSN: 0893-9683] 1966. 8x/yr. USD 10 domestic; USD 19.97 Canada; USD 39.97 elsewhere. Ed(s): Melinda Stevens. Conde Nast Publications, Inc., 1 World Trade Center, New York, NY 10007; communications@condenast.com; http://. www.condenast.com. Illus., adv. Vol. ends: Dec (No. 12). Microform: PQC. *Indexed:* A22, BRI, C37, H&TI. *Aud.:* Ga.

Conde Nast Traveler mixes luxury travel destinations and travel advice with exquisite imagery in a magazine synonymous with high class. This title is not for the budget conscious, but in it, readers will find guides to spas, resorts, and exclusive travel destinations, with deals thrown in to appeal to a broader audience. Complementary website offers beautiful photography and a newsletter. Recommended for public libraries. URL: https://www.cntraveler.com/

4905. *Cruise Travel.* [ISSN: 0199-5111] 1979. bi-m. USD 38.95 domestic; USD 48.95 Canada; USD 53.95 foreign. Lakeside Publishing Company, LLC, 990 Grove St, Ste 400, Evanston, IL 60201. Illus., adv. Vol. ends: May/Jun. *Indexed:* A22, BRI, C37, H&TI. *Aud.:* Ga.

Cruise travel has posted some of the biggest gains in the tourism industry over the last few decades, and *Cruise Travel* is the leading consumer magazine for those choosing to travel the seas. International in scope, it covers all aspects of cruising, with particular focus on highlighting ships, ports, and cruises of the month. Because many cruises stop in ports for a limited time, travelers need to make the most of the little time they have. *Cruise Travel* provides one-day itineraries for ports of call and tips for shopping specifically to meet this need. Recommended for public libraries.

Explorers Journal. See Geography section.

Fido Friendly. See Pets section.

4906. *Lonely Planet Traveller.* Formerly (until 2012): *Lonely Planet Magazine.* [ISSN: 2050-635X] 200?. m. GBP 36.50. Ed(s): Peter Grunert. Immediate Media Co. Ltd., Media Ctr, 201 Wood Ln, London, W12 7TQ, United Kingdom; enquiries@immediatemedia.co.uk; http://www.immediate.co.uk. Adv. Sample. *Bk. rev.:* Number and length vary. *Aud.:* Ga.

Lonely Planet Traveller is known for its thorough and practical travel guides, and this magazine showcases its expertise in the field. Each issue includes a mix of short dispatches, as well as in-depth destination guides that offer options from budget to luxury, and essay-length travel narratives. As well, each issue covers several major destinations in detail, with maps of locations and major tourist sites. Content also includes easy trips in Europe, historical destinations, travel book and TV show reviews, and removable single-theme mini-travel guides to places like the bistros of Paris or the canals of Amsterdam. This magazine reflects the years of experience in providing high-quality travel information, and mixes it with stunning photography and practical travel advice. Recommended for public libraries.

4907. *National Geographic Traveler.* [ISSN: 0747-0932] 1984. 8x/yr. USD 10; USD 18 combined subscription (print & online eds.); USD 4.99 newsstand/cover domestic). Ed(s): Keith Bellows. National Geographic Society, PO Box 98199, Washington, DC 20090; askngs@nationalgeographic.com; http://www.nationalgeographic.com/. Illus., index, adv. Sample. Vol. ends: Nov/Dec. *Indexed:* A01, A22, BRI, C37, H&TI, MASUSE. *Aud.:* Ga.

Known for its beautiful photographs and its focus on nature and culture, this magazine inspires readers to learn about the world and dream of travel rather than look for the luxury resort with all the bells and whistles. With a mix of short articles and feature-length essays, this title covers all kinds of travel (for example, sustainable and adventure travel), locales (urban, rural, and wilderness), and budgets. It includes regular features on green travel, travel with kids, two-day city guides, and road trips. Readers will find articles that, according to the National Geographic Society, "inspire narratives that make readers take trips," and they will find "solid service information to help them plan those trips." Recommended for public libraries.

Outside (Santa Fe). See Hiking, Climbing, and Outdoor Recreation section.

4908. *Taste & Travel International.* [ISSN: 1925-6841] 2011. q. USD 25. Taste and Travel Publishing International, Inc., 8289 Boland St # 481, Metcalfe, ON K0A 2P0, Canada; info@TasteandTravelInternational.com; http://www.tasteandtravelinternational.com. *Bk. rev.:* Number and length vary. *Aud.:* Ga.

This food-lover's guide to travel opens up the world of culinary tourism. Each issue covers one U.S. and at least five worldwide destinations in lengthy food-destination articles that are packed with regional recipes. Readers will discover authentic places to eat, and information on local foods, dishes, restaurants, chefs, and growers. In addition, it includes articles on culinary vacations and classes, food tours, and vineyards. Each issue includes the history and use of a different spice; regional cookbook reviews; and dispatches covering a city's culinary highlights. Recommended for public libraries.

4909. ***Travel 50 & Beyond.*** [ISSN: 1049-6211] 1990. q. USD 14. Vacation Publications, Inc., 5851 San Felipe St, Ste 500, Houston, TX 77057; service@Travel50andBeyond.com. Illus., adv. Sample. Circ: 115000. Vol. ends: Fall (No. 4). *Indexed:* AgeL. *Aud.:* Ga.

As the only magazine written specifically for the 50-plus traveler, this magazine covers worldwide travel destinations for those seeking experiences from "soft adventure to slow meanderings." It provides information to those wanting high-quality, enriching travel experiences, and it includes information on train, cruise, and RV travel. Articles are written with older travelers in mind, and include the humorous, poignant, and romantic aspects of travel. Recommended for public libraries, and academic libraries with a gerontology collection.

Newsletters

4910. ***International Travel News.*** [ISSN: 0191-8761] 1976. m. USD 26 combined subscription domestic (print & online eds.); USD 43 combined subscription Canada (print & online eds.); USD 53 combined subscription elsewhere (print & online eds.)). Ed(s): David Tykol. Martin Publications Inc., 2120 28th St, Sacramento, CA 95818. Illus., adv. Sample. *Indexed:* BRI. *Bk. rev.:* 1, 750 words. *Aud.:* Ga.

Aimed at Americans who travel frequently outside the United States, this newsletter is primarily written by other travelers. With its pieces in the form of reviews, travel tips, first-person travel essays, and travel guides, its readers get real travel reports from real travelers. Each issue includes a focus on archaeology and travel alerts, as well as rewarding readers who have met travel challenges with relevant bits of travel humor. The website complements the print publication with color photos, up-to-date news, and message boards to facilitate communication between readers, but full digital access requires a subscription. Recommended for public libraries.

Research

4911. ***Annals of Tourism Research: a social sciences journal.*** [ISSN: 0160-7383] 1973. bi-m. EUR 1837. Elsevier Ltd, The Boulevard, Langford Lane, Oxford, OX5 1GB, United Kingdom; customerserviceau@elsevier.com; http://www.elsevier.com. Illus., adv. Sample. Refereed. Vol. ends: Oct. Microform: PQC. *Indexed:* A22, C45, H&TI, SD. *Bk. rev.:* 8, 750 words. *Aud.:* Ac.

With an intended audience of researchers and scholars, this publication focuses on both theoretical and practical applications of research in tourism and related fields. The focus of the publication is the "academic perspective" of the subject, and its content represents both domestic and international issues. Recommended for academic libraries, especially those with travel, tourism, hospitality, and recreation and leisure collections.

4912. ***Current Issues in Tourism.*** [ISSN: 1368-3500] 1998. s-m. GBP 1960 (print & online eds.)). Ed(s): Chris Cooper, C Michael Hall. Routledge, 4 Park Sq, Milton Park, Abingdon, OX14 4RN, United Kingdom; subscriptions@tandf.co.uk; http://www.tandfonline.com. Adv. Sample. Refereed. Reprint: PSC. *Indexed:* C45, H&TI. *Aud.:* Ac.

This peer-reviewed journal, aimed at tourism researchers, is designed to foster discussion of key tourism issues and encourage debate and critique. Covering a wide range of tourism topics, including international issues, this journal contains applied and theoretical articles from a variety of scholarly fields. Different sections allow for recent highly relevant content to be included quickly and to foster extended discussion of the topics raised in the journal. Recommended for academic libraries, especially those with travel, tourism, hospitality, or recreation and leisure collections.

4913. ***International Journal of Tourism Anthropology.*** [ISSN: 1759-0442] 2010. q. USD 790 (print or online ed.)). Ed(s): Dr. Li Cheng. Inderscience Publishers, PO Box 735, Olney, MK46 5WB, United Kingdom; info@inderscience.com; https://www.inderscience.com/index.php. Illus. Sample. Refereed. *Indexed:* C45. *Aud.:* Ac.

This peer-reviewed international journal looks at tourism through the lens of ethnography, sociology, psychology, archaeology, art, linguistics, economics, ethics, politics, history, philosophy, geography, and ecology. Topics vary widely and include gender, identity, terrorism, pilgrimages, ecology, and folk arts, among many others. The wide range of topics covered offers perspectives on tourism that other, more popularly oriented tourism journals overlook. This journal also publishes open-access articles. Recommended for academic libraries with travel and tourism programs.

4914. ***International Journal of Tourism Research.*** Formerly (until 1999): *Progress in Tourism and Hospitality Research.* [ISSN: 1099-2340] 1995. bi-m. GBP 802. Ed(s): John Fletcher. John Wiley & Sons Ltd., EMEA Institutional Sales, 9600 Garsington Rd, Oxford, OX4 2DQ, United Kingdom; cs-journals@wiley.com; http://onlinelibrary.wiley.com. Adv. Sample. Refereed. Microform: PQC. Reprint: PSC. *Indexed:* A22, B01, C45, H&TI. *Bk. rev.:* 5, 1,000 words. *Aud.:* Ac.

A peer-reviewed journal that is dedicated to research in international tourism and related fields of economics, marketing, sociology, and statistics. Not limited merely to research findings, it also focuses on new methodologies in, and approaches to, tourism research as well as new areas of exploration in research. Geared toward researchers, this title is appropriate for academic libraries with a strong research community focused on hospitality, tourism, or travel.

4915. ***Journal of Outdoor Recreation and Tourism.*** [ISSN: 2213-0780] 2013. q. EUR 494. Ed(s): Pascal Haegeli, Ulrike Proebstl-Haider. Elsevier BV, Radarweg 29, Amsterdam, 1043 NX, Netherlands; info@elsevier.com; https://www.elsevier.com/. Refereed. *Indexed:* C45. *Bk. rev.:* Number and length vary. *Aud.:* Ac.

This international in scope peer-reviewed journal focuses on all aspects of outdoor recreation planning and management from an interdisciplinary perspective. From hiking trail assessments and land use issues to park usage rates and tourist behavior, this journal looks at issues where outdoor recreation and tourism intersect. Both urban and wilderness settings are covered, as well as specific sports (for example, kayaking and rock climbing) and issues (for instance, timber harvesting and environmental attitudes). Case studies are included, in addition to research articles and the occasional book review. Recommended for academic libraries with tourism, outdoor recreation, or leisure studies programs.

4916. ***Journal of Sustainable Tourism.*** [ISSN: 0966-9582] 1993. 10x/yr. GBP 1227 (print & online eds.)). Ed(s): Graham Miller, James Higham. Routledge, 4 Park Sq, Milton Park, Abingdon, OX14 4RN, United Kingdom; subscriptions@tandf.co.uk; http://www.tandfonline.com. Illus., adv. Sample. Refereed. Reprint: PSC. *Indexed:* A01, A22, B01, C45, H&TI. *Bk. rev.:* 3, 1,000 words. *Aud.:* Ac.

A critical understanding of the relationship between sustainable development and tourism is the focus of this peer-reviewed journal. Containing both theoretical and research articles, it attempts to present an interdisciplinary and holistic view of the interrelated economic, social, cultural, political, and environmental issues of tourism. This title also includes book reviews and occasional opinion pieces. Recommended for academic libraries, especially those with travel, tourism, and recreation and leisure collections.

4917. ***Journal of Travel Research.*** Formerly: *Travel Research Bulletin.* [ISSN: 0047-2875] 1962. 8x/yr. USD 1265 (print & online eds.)). Ed(s): Geoffrey I Crouch. Sage Publications, Inc., 2455 Teller Rd, Thousand Oaks, CA 91320; info@sagepub.com; http://www.sagepub.com. Adv. Refereed. Reprint: PSC. *Indexed:* A01, A22, B01, BRI, C45, E01, H&TI, HRIS. *Bk. rev.:* 2, 750 words. *Aud.:* Ac.

This high-impact peer-reviewed journal from the Travel and Tourism Research Association focuses on the business of travel and tourism development, management, marketing, economics, and behavior. This highly selective journal publishes research on trends and issues in tourism and travel, along with best practices in development and management. The articles are multidisciplinary and international in scope, and are intended for scholars, educators, and practitioners. Recommended for academic libraries with travel, tourism, or hospitality collections.

4918. ***Tourism Management: research, policies, practice.*** Formerly (until 1982): *International Journal of Tourism Management.* [ISSN: 0261-5177] 1980. bi-m. EUR 3128. Ed(s): Chris Ryan. Pergamon Press, The Blvd, Langford Ln, E Park, Kidlington, OX5 1GB, United Kingdom; JournalsCustomerServiceEMEA@elsevier.com; http://www.elsevier.com. Illus., adv. Sample. Refereed. Microform: PQC. *Indexed:* A22, C45, H&TI. *Bk. rev.:* Number and length vary. *Aud.:* Ac.

International, national, and regional tourism management, policy, and planning are the focus of this high-impact peer-reviewed journal. Containing research articles, case studies, discussion of current issues, and book reviews, this title takes an interdisciplinary approach to tourism topics that is relevant to both academics and practitioners. Articles range from primary research to case studies, reports, and discussion of current issues. Recommended for academic libraries with programs in hospitality, travel, and tourism.

■ URBAN STUDIES

Alison Larsen, Serials Librarian, Siena College, 515 Loudon Rd., Loudonville, NY 12189; alarsen@siena.edu

Introduction

Space is finite and what we do with it matters. And those choices affect everything and everyone around it. The study of these choices and their impact is at the heart of urban studies. Just like an urban area is a mixing pot of people and cultures, so is the study of the urban community. It is inherently interdisciplinary and this trait is illustrated by the wide depth and breadth of resources included in this chapter and their contents. Recent trends in urban studies have focused on the debate and impact of gentrification, sustainability efforts and issues, as well as social justice issues. The choice of living in an urban area is relatively new along the timeline of human population habitat choices, but it is clear that this shift has impacted life as we know, regardless of where one lives.

This section will include some newer titles in the urban studies landscape, as well as the core titles that anchor the academic field. As you build your collection, or look for a single title to add, know that this section takes a broad approach, geographically speaking, to urban studies because of the sheer number of publications. A little digging may uncover some really fine publications that focus much more specifically on your geographic area and may be more appropriate for your collection, or at least give it some added depth. Most of the reviewed publications are scholarly in nature, but many of them can be understood and appreciated by an interested layperson.

Publications in this section are all written in English (while some article abstracts are also published in other languages). The reviews are written and recommendations are made with libraries in the United States as the potential subscribers. When a recommendation is made for an academic library, it is on the assumption that the library is supporting an urban studies program. If a publication is recommended for the general collection, it is stated in the review. Other recommendations are self-explanatory.

Basic Periodicals

Ga: *American City & County, Planning, Urban Land;* Ac: *American Planning Association. Journal, Cities, Environment and Planning A, International Journal of Urban and Regional Research, Journal of Planning Literature, Journal of Urban Affairs, Journal of Urban Design, Urban History, Urban Studies.*

Basic Abstracts and Indexes

ABI/INFORM, Avery Index to Architectural Periodicals, Business Source Premier, Index to Current Urban Documents, PAIS International, Sociological Abstracts, Urban Studies Abstracts.

4919. ***American City & County.*** Formerly (until 1975): *American City;* Incorporates (1924-1991): *American City & County Municipal Index.* [ISSN: 0149-337X] 1909. m. Ed(s): Bill Wolpin. Informa PLC, 5 Howick Pl., London, SW1P1WG, United Kingdom; media@informa.com; https://informa.com/. Illus., index, adv. Microform: PQC. *Indexed:* A01, A22, B01, BRI, CBRI, HRIS, MASUSE. *Bk. rev.:* Number and length vary. *Aud.:* Ga, Ac, Sa.

American City & County is a magazine dedicated to "serving government leaders." Published since 1909, it is one of the core trade titles in this subject area. It is published monthly and contains a variety of feature articles as well as recurrent topical categories ("Smart Cities," "Issues & Trends"). The application of green technology, data usage, and municipal staffing are popular topics of late. The website provides access to much of the magazine content organized by subject area (e.g., technology, public safety, sustainability) and also provides access to all digital issues of the magazine back to 2009 at no cost. The website is robust and worth visiting. A subscription includes access to the digital edition and the journal's "Municipal Index," a purchasing guide for government officials of necessary equipment and services. This magazine fills a niche area, is a core title, and is highly recommended for public or special libraries that serve local government agencies, and for academic libraries. URL: http://americancityandcounty.com

4920. ***American Planning Association. Journal.*** Former titles (until 1979): *American Institute of Planners. Journal;* (until 1944): *The Planners' Journal.* [ISSN: 0194-4363] 1935. 4x/yr. GBP 381 (print & online eds.)). Ed(s): Sandi Rosenbloom. Routledge, 530 Walnut St, Ste 850, Philadelphia, PA 19106; enquiries@tandfonline.com; http://www.tandfonline.com. Illus., adv. Sample. Refereed. Vol. ends: Oct. Microform: PQC. Reprint: PSC. *Indexed:* A01, A06, A22, B01, BAS, BRI, E01, EIP, GardL, HRIS, MLA-IB. *Bk. rev.:* 5-7, 500-1,000 words, signed. *Aud.:* Ac, Sa.

The official scholarly journal of the American Planning Association, the *Journal of the American Planning Association* (*JAPA*) publishes original research and analysis in four issues per year. The type of research published by *JAPA* includes methodology of planning practice and implementation, policy formulation and implementation, and explanations of empirical relationships related to planning. This research examines "the historical or contemporary planning experience, broadly defined, in domestic or global contexts." Each issue contains an average of six to eight original research articles and a solid book review section. A themed issue is published on occasion and several, of late, have paid tribute to those visionaries the field has lost. Research articles focus heavily on North America but do include some international coverage, predominantly in comparative research articles. Members of the American Planning Association (APA) receive a discount on the subscription cost to the journal. Subscribers can download articles for free from the online archive. Taylor & Francis hosts this title at www.tandfonline.com/toc/rjpa20. Highly regarded in the field, *JAPA* is a core title and is highly recommended for academic libraries.

4921. ***Built Environment.*** Former titles (until 1978): *Built Environment Quarterly;* (until 1975): *Built Environment;* (until 1972): *O A P;* (until 1971): *Official Architecture and Planning;* Which incorporated (1955-1970): *Modular Quarterly;* (until 1955): *Official Architect and Planning Review.* [ISSN: 0263-7960] 19??. q. GBP 355 (print & online eds.) Individuals, GBP 130 (print & online eds.)). Ed(s): David Banister, Stephen Marshall. Alexandrine Press, 1 The Farthings, Marcham, OX13 6QD, United Kingdom; info@alexandrinepress.co.uk; http://www.alexandrinepress.co.uk. Illus. Sample. Refereed. *Indexed:* A22, HRIS. *Bk. rev.:* 2-4, 500 words. *Aud.:* Ac, Sa.

Built Environment is a peer-reviewed journal that emphasizes cross-disciplinary boundaries with a global perspective. This title is published four times a year, and each issue has a specific theme chosen by the editor. Each issue begins with an introductory overview article written by guest editor(s), an international expert(s) in the theme area. The article's intent is to enhance the professionalism, relevance, and academic integrity of the issue. Recent themes have included "Cognition and the City: An Introduction" and "Branded Landscapes in Contemporary Cities." The articles, as well as the members of the editorial board, are international in coverage. Each issue contains publication reviews, and online subscriptions include access to articles from 2003 to the present. *Built Environment* is published by Alexandrine Press and is hosted by IngentaConnect. Recommended for academic libraries.

4922. *Cities: the international journal of urban policy and planning.* [ISSN: 0264-2751] 1983. 10x/yr. EUR 2124. Elsevier Ltd, The Boulevard, Langford Lane, Oxford, OX5 1GB, United Kingdom; customerserviceau@elsevier.com; http://www.elsevier.com. Illus., index, adv. Sample. Refereed. Microform: PQC. *Indexed:* A01, A22, B01, EIP, IBSS, P61, SSA. *Bk. rev.:* Occasional. *Aud.:* Ac.

An international and interdisciplinary title, *Cities: The International Journal of Urban Policy and Planning* has the primary aims "to analyze and assess past and present urban development and management as a reflection of effective, ineffective and non-existent planning policies; and the promotion of the implementation of appropriate urban policies in both the developed and the developing world." This is truly an all-encompassing journal in that it covers topics in the developed and undeveloped world that include housing, homelessness, urban management, public-private sector cooperation, Third World development and planning problems, urban regeneration, urban conservation and design, technological innovation and urban planning, and urban transportation. Volumes (no numbered issues) are published throughout the year, typically every month, but variations in the publication frequency exist. Individual volumes of *Cities* present varying amounts of original research articles (anywhere from eight to 30 plus). Volumes can feature a city profile (recent cities profiled include Santiago, Chile, Wroclaw, Poland, and Jaipur, India) that details the historical development and the contemporary conditions and problems of the city, as well as a critique of current policy and any responses. A "Viewpoints" section is also published occasionally. The journal also supports the Forests, Land and Housing Division of the United Nations Economic Commission for Europe (UNECE). Though this title is expensive, the increase in the number of articles published per volume and their quality make *Cities* fairly easy to highly recommend for academic libraries and general academic collections.

4923. *City: analysis of urban trends, culture, theory, policy, action.* Formerly (until 1995): *Regenerating Cities.* [ISSN: 1360-4813] 1992. 6x/yr. GBP 752 (print & online eds.)). Ed(s): Bob Catterall. Routledge, 4 Park Sq, Milton Park, Abingdon, OX14 4RN, United Kingdom; subscriptions@tandf.co.uk; http://www.tandfonline.com. Adv. Sample. Refereed. Reprint: PSC. *Indexed:* A01, A22, E01, IBSS. *Bk. rev.:* 1-3, signed. *Aud.:* Ac.

City: analysis of urban trends, culture, theory, policy, action "is a journal of provocative, cutting-edge and committed insights into, analysis of, and commentary on the contemporary urban world." Focused on the future of cities, *City* aims to provide a multidisciplinary vantage point to a wide variety of subjects that affect cities, including "information and digital revolutions, war and imperialism, neoliberalism and gentrification, environment and sustainability, resistance and social movements, regeneration, resurgence and revanchism, race, class and gender, multi-culturalism and post-colonialism." *City* claims it is published six times per year but recently has seen combined issues and has only one issue published through May of 2019. An issue contains original research articles, sometimes grouped into themes, recurring sections, and one to three substantial book reviews. *City* has long striven to provide a platform that reaches more than academics, and so in the pursuit of its goal of reaching "intelligent life outside," *City* now maintains a website beyond the journal's site that is well worth taking a look at: www.city-analysis.net/. As *City* focuses on the future of cities, it fulfills a valuable role in the totality of the literature on urban areas and is thus highly recommended for academic libraries.

4924. *City & Community.* [ISSN: 1535-6841] q. GBP 460. Ed(s): Deirdre A Oakley. Wiley-Blackwell Publishing, Inc., 350 Main St, Malden, MA 02148; cs-journals@wiley.com; http://onlinelibrary.wiley.com. Adv. Sample. Refereed. Reprint: PSC. *Indexed:* A01, A22, BRI, E01. *Bk. rev.:* 3-5, 500-1,200 words, signed. *Aud.:* Ac, Sa.

Published quarterly, *City & Community* (*C&C*) is the journal of the Community and Urban Sociology Section of the American Sociological Association. Looking to "advance urban sociological theory" and "encourage sociological perspectives on urban policy," *C&C* publishes articles that are theoretical, as well as qualitative and quantitative case studies. A typical issue includes minimally five research articles and three to five substantial book reviews. Many issues also contain a Symposium section in which scholars on a given topic respond to an accompanying article. Recent topics include the uses of census data and community and crime. The journal has increased its international coverage over the years and now encourages "manuscripts exploring the interface of global and local issues" and nicely balances international and U.S. coverage. Articles are published online in advance of the print edition and the website includes video article abstracts for a handful of articles. It also has a Twitter account: @CiCoJournal. This title is recommended for academic libraries. *C&C* may also be relevant to academic libraries that support comprehensive sociology programs.

4925. *Community Development Journal: an international forum.* Former titles (until 1966): *Community Development Bulletin;* (until 1951): *Mass Education Bulletin.* [ISSN: 0010-3802] 1949. q. EUR 509. Ed(s): Orla O'Donovan, Rosie Mead. Oxford University Press, Great Clarendon St, Oxford, OX2 6DP, United Kingdom; onlinequeries.uk@oup.com; http://global.oup.com. Illus., adv. Sample. Refereed. Microform: PQC. Reprint: PSC. *Indexed:* A01, A22, ASSIA, BAS, C45, E01, EconLit, IBSS, MLA-IB, P61, SSA. *Bk. rev.:* 2-4, 1,000 words, signed. *Aud.:* Ac.

Community Development Journal "provides an international forum for political, economic and social programmes, which link the activities of people with institutions and government." This title offers geographic coverage that is truly international. It includes topics such as community action; village, town, and regional planning; community studies; and rural development. It is a scholarly journal, published quarterly, every article contains an abstract, and book reviews are always present. Special issues are published occasionally. Editorials published in the journal are now freely available online. "Reflections" and "Case Reports" continue to be published occasionally. The journal's website was redone since last review and is worth looking at. Collections of themed articles and special issues are freely available as is an additional website full of information and resources relevant to the journal content. *Community Development Journal* is recommended for academic libraries that support a comprehensive Urban Studies collection. URL: http://www.oxfordjournals.org/cdjc/

4926. *Computers, Environment and Urban Systems.* Former titles (until 1980): *Urban Systems;* (until 1977): *Computers and Urban Society.* [ISSN: 0198-9715] 1975. bi-m. EUR 2483. Elsevier Ltd, The Boulevard, Langford Lane, Oxford, OX5 1GB, United Kingdom; customerserviceau@elsevier.com; http://www.elsevier.com. Illus., index, adv. Sample. Refereed. Vol. ends: No. 25. Microform: PQC. *Indexed:* A01, A22, CompLI, S25. *Aud.:* Ac.

A highly technical journal, *Computers, Environment and Urban Systems* publishes "cutting-edge and innovative computer-based research on urban systems that privileges the geospatial perspective." One of the aims of the journal is to demonstrate how computer-based research can help explain and enhance the totality of urban and environmental systems. Publishing applied, theoretical, and technical articles, the journal encourages using methodological approaches such as geographic information systems (heavy emphasis), geocomputation, and spatial statistical analysis, and applying them to such areas as environmental analysis, modeling and management, emergency response and hazards, land and resource management, infrastructure and facilities management, transportation, business, and service planning. The journal is published six times a year with articles added to a volume as they are ready for publication. Themed volumes are occasionally published, and open access, articles in press, and new virtual issues are available on the journal's website. Due to its highly technical nature and cost, this journal is recommended for larger academic libraries that support a technological component to their urban studies or planning programs. Information technology programs may find this title relevant, as well. For a less technical and costly title, see *Environment and Planning B: Planning & Design.* (below in this section) URL: www.sciencedirect.com/science/journal/01989715/

Economic Geography. See Geography section.

Environment and Behavior. See Psychology section.

4927. *Environment and Planning A: Economy and Space.* Supersedes in part (in 1974): *Environment and Planning.* [ISSN: 0308-518X] 1969. 8x/yr. Ed(s): Jamie Peck. Sage Publications Ltd., 1 Oliver's Yard, 55 City Rd, London, EC1Y 1SP, United Kingdom; info@sagepub.com; https://www.sagepub.com. Illus. Refereed. Reprint: PSC. *Indexed:* A01, A22, BRI, EconLit, HRIS, IBSS, S25. *Aud.:* Ac.

The flagship journal in the *Environment and Planning* family of journals, *Environment and Planning A* (*EPA*) is peer-reviewed and interdisciplinary in nature. *EPA* is published eight times per year and focuses on "contemporary issues at the interface of human geography, environmental studies, and urban and regional research." Issues can contain commentaries (non-refereed), editorials, a featured graphic, and at least ten articles. Occasionally, an issue will have a theme and a guest editor. Geographic coverage of the content is international. New in 2018, EPA is published in conjunction with a new journal in the Environment and Planning suite: *Environment and Planning E: Nature and Space. EPE* is published four times per year making the combination of the two twelve issues per year. A subscription is only available for them together as one, not individually. A very creative approach to launching and supporting a new title! Though the subscription cost is high, taking into account the publication frequency and the number of articles published per issue is important when considering this journal but as this subscription model has recently changed one should pay attention to the details. *EPA* is highly recommended for academic libraries. Sociology, philosophy, and multicultural studies programs may also benefit from this journal.

4928. *Environment and Planning B: Urban Analytics and City Science.* Former titles (until 2017): *Environment and Planning B: Planning & Design;* (until 1983): *Environment & Planning. B;* Which superseded in part (in 1974): *Environment & Planning.* [ISSN: 2399-8083] 1969. bi-m. USD 1851 (print & online eds.)). Ed(s): Mike Batty. Sage Publications Ltd., 1 Oliver's Yard, 55 City Rd, London, EC1Y 1SP, United Kingdom; info@sagepub.com; https://www.sagepub.com. Refereed. Reprint: PSC. *Indexed:* A01, A22, HRIS, IBSS. *Bk. rev.:* Sporadic; 500 words, signed. *Aud.:* Ac.

Environment and Planning B: Urban Analytics and City Space is one of the now five journals that make up the *Environment and Planning* family. The focus of *EPB* is addressing spatial problems of the built environment, particularly "how formal models can be used to explore how cities and their elements behave, reproduce, evolve, or impact upon urban forms and functions, and on the livability, equality and sustainability of cities." This title is published six times a year, and each issue produces between eight and ten research articles and book reviews that vary in number from issue to issue. Issues often contain commentary and/or editorial pieces from the editor or a guest. *EPB* is recommended for academic libraries, specifically those with a technology component in the program. Information technology or computer science programs may also find this title useful. For a more technical (and expensive) title on the same theme, see *Computers, Environment and Urban Systems* (above in this section).

4929. *Environment and Planning D: Society and Space.* [ISSN: 0263-7758] 1983. bi-m. USD 1810 (print & online eds.)). Ed(s): Natalie Oswin. Sage Publications Ltd., 1 Oliver's Yard, 55 City Rd, London, EC1Y 1SP, United Kingdom; info@sagepub.com; https://www.sagepub.com. Refereed. Reprint: PSC. *Indexed:* A01, A22, BRI, IBSS, MLA-IB. *Aud.:* Ac.

Published six times a year, *Environment and Planning D* (*EPD*) is one of five journals in the *Environment and Planning* family, and it focuses on the "contingent and possible relations between the social and the spatial." This is a scholarly journal, and its articles are interdisciplinary and international in coverage. Like the other journals in the *Environment and Planning* family, *EPD* publishes thematic issues on occasion, which includes a guest editor and editorial. *EPD*'s issues include articles and, at times, review essays. The journal also has a companion website to the journal that is maintained by the editors. The site is clean, well organized, and worth some of your time. Sociology and philosophy scholars may also find this title of interest. For academic libraries. URL: http://societyandspace.org/

4930. *Environment & Urbanization.* [ISSN: 0956-2478] 1989. s-a. USD 1363 (print & online eds.)). Ed(s): David Satterthwaite, Diana Mitlin. Sage Publications Ltd., 1 Oliver's Yard, 55 City Rd, London, EC1Y 1SP, United Kingdom; market@sagepub.com; https://www.sagepub.com/. Illus., index, adv. Sample. Refereed. Vol. ends: No. 2. Reprint: PSC. *Indexed:* A22, C45, E01, EIP, IBSS, P61, SSA. *Bk. rev.:* online only. *Aud.:* Ac.

Environment & Urbanization is a scholarly journal focused on seeking "to advance a more socially just and environmentally sustainable urban world through the provision of knowledge." This title has a geographic emphasis on the Global South: Asia, Latin America, and Africa, and is published in association with the International Institute for Environment and Development. It also encourages authorship and readership for NGOs. The journal publishes two issues per year, each focusing on one specific theme. Recent themes include inclusive climate change adaptation and "Local Finance for Local Development." Each issue includes between 7 and 12 articles, all relating to the chosen theme, as well as articles in the recurring sections ("Feedback," "Climate Change in Cities"). Issues also contain a "Book Notes" section that briefly summarizes new books on the market (freely available on the website: https://www.environmentandurbanization.org/book-notes) and a "Summaries of Articles" section that is published at the end of each issue, with summaries in English, French, and Spanish. *Environment & Urbanization* is highly recommended for academic libraries, and also highly recommended for those with environmental studies and/or globalization programs.

4931. *European Planning Studies.* [ISSN: 0965-4313] 1993. m. GBP 3214 (print & online eds.)). Ed(s): Philip Cooke, Louis Albrechts. Routledge, 4 Park Sq, Milton Park, Abingdon, OX14 4RN, United Kingdom; subscriptions@tandf.co.uk; http://www.tandfonline.com. Adv. Sample. Refereed. Reprint: PSC. *Indexed:* A01, A22, B01, C45, E01, IBSS, P61, SSA. *Bk. rev.:* Occasional; number and length vary. *Aud.:* Ac.

Published in cooperation with the Association of European Schools of Planning (AESOP), an independent group of European planning educators, *European Planning Studies* looks to publish original, scholarly research on "spatial development processes and policies in Europe." This title places an emphasis on "infrastructure, communications, environmental quality, design, cultural, social welfare, recreational, housing, [and] industrial and employment concerns of planning at whatever spatial scale." This journal is published monthly, and each issue includes several original research articles. A special themed issue is sometimes published. Other sections—"European Briefing," "Research Briefing," and "Book Reviews"—occasionally appear. The institutional subscription cost is on the higher end, but if you look at the publication frequency, the cost per article does bring it into comparison with a similar title, *European Urban and Regional Studies* (below in this section). Recommended for academic libraries that maintain a comprehensive collection or have a European focus in the program.

4932. *European Urban and Regional Studies.* [ISSN: 0969-7764] 1994. q. USD 1494 (print & online eds.)). Ed(s): Nick Henry. Sage Publications Ltd., 1 Oliver's Yard, 55 City Rd, London, EC1Y 1SP, United Kingdom; info@sagepub.com; https://www.sagepub.com/. Adv. Sample. Refereed. Reprint: PSC. *Indexed:* A01, A22, B01, C45, E01, IBSS, P61. *Aud.:* Ac.

A scholarly journal, *European Urban and Regional Studies* aims to provide a forum for debate between the different processes of urban and regional development. As the name implies, the journal focuses solely on European development, but puts this development into a broader global context and makes connections from the local to global level. The journal is published quarterly. Issues generally include between six and eight articles, each containing an abstract. Special themed issues are published on occasion. A section entitled "Euro-Commentary" appears sporadically as well. A similar title (with a significantly higher subscription cost), *European Planning Studies* (above in this section), is published more frequently and may also be an option for those looking for a European-focused publication. Highly recommended for academic libraries that maintain comprehensive collections or those with a European focus.

4933. *Growth and Change: a journal of urban and regional policy.* [ISSN: 0017-4815] 1970. q. Ed(s): Dan Rickman, Barney Warf. Wiley-Blackwell Publishing, Inc., 111 River St, Hoboken, NJ 07030; info@wiley.com; http://www.wiley.com/. Illus., index, adv. Sample. Refereed. Vol. ends: No. 4. Reprint: PSC. *Indexed:* A01, A22, Agr, B01, BAS, BRI, C45, E01, EconLit, IBSS, P61, S25. *Bk. rev.:* Number varies, 1,000-2,000 words, signed. *Aud.:* Ac, Sa.

Published quarterly, *Growth and Change* is a peer-reviewed, international journal with an interdisciplinary approach to urban studies. The journal encourages manuscript submissions from "scholars and professionals in all disciplines and specialties" that take a multidisciplinary approach to the addressed problem(s). Articles in *Growth and Change* do tend to focus more on economic aspects as compared with other disciplines. Issues tend to contain at least eight articles per issue. Some issues contain a "Perspective" piece, intended as a thought and discussion provoker, and possibly book reviews. Themed issues are occasionally published with guest editors. Because *Growth and Change* tends to focus on economic issues, it is recommended for academic libraries with a comprehensive urban studies collection. Programs with strong economics programs may also find this title of interest.

4934. *Housing Policy Debate.* [ISSN: 1051-1482] 1990. bi-m. GBP 587 (print & online eds.)). Ed(s): Thomas W Sanchez. Routledge, 530 Walnut St, Ste 850, Philadelphia, PA 19106; enquiries@tandfonline.com; http://www.tandfonline.com. Illus. Refereed. Microform: PQC. Reprint: PSC. *Indexed:* A22, EconLit, IBSS. *Aud.:* Ga, Ac, Sa.

Housing Policy Debate (*HPD*) is a scholarly publication dedicated to the study of U.S. housing policy. Topics of research covered include "affordable housing, neighborhood revitalization, housing related poverty alleviation and integration strategies, and metropolitan development trends." Issues of *HPD* can include some of the following sections: "Forum," "Articles," and "Outlook." The "Forum" section focuses on an issue of current debate; a central article is presented with responding commentary (articles are peer-reviewed). The "Articles" section presents original research that has undergone the double-blind, peer-review process. The "Outlook" section presents a current topic and subsequent commentary by the editors or expert guest writers. Thematic issues are published. *HPD* is published six times per year by Taylor & Francis on behalf of Virginia Polytechnic Institute and State University. *HPD* is highly recommended for academic libraries and large public libraries that may support government agencies. Public policy and political science programs may also find it relevant.

4935. *Housing Studies.* [ISSN: 0267-3037] 1986. 10x/yr. GBP 1366 (print & online eds.)). Ed(s): Ed Ferrari, Hal Pawson. Routledge, 4 Park Sq, Milton Park, Abingdon, OX14 4RN, United Kingdom; subscriptions@tandf.co.uk; http://www.tandfonline.com. Illus., index, adv. Sample. Refereed. Reprint: PSC. *Indexed:* A01, A22, ASSIA, B01, BAS, E01, EconLit, IBSS, P61, SSA. *Bk. rev.:* 3-5, 500-2,000 words, signed. *Aud.:* Ac, Sa.

As the title implies, *Housing Studies* publishes on all aspects of housing issues. A scholarly journal, it claims to be "the leading international journal and a major forum for theoretical and analytical developments in the housing field." The journal is now published ten times a year (new for 2019 and up from eight) and includes original articles and three to five book reviews per issue. The geographic coverage is international. *Housing Studies* is interdisciplinary in its approach to the study of urban areas and welcomes articles with a similar approach. Virtual special issues are available on the journal's webpage. It does offer a nice mix of content that appeals to academics and practitioners, and some even for the interested reader. Recommended for academic libraries. Public policy programs may also want to consider this title.

4936. *International Journal of Urban and Regional Research.* [ISSN: 0309-1317] 1976. 6x/yr. GBP 705. Ed(s): Matthew Gandy, Mustafa Dikec. Wiley-Blackwell Publishing Ltd., The Atrium, Southern Gate, Chichester, PO19 8QG, United Kingdom; cs-journals@wiley.com; http://onlinelibrary.wiley.com. Illus., index, adv. Sample. Refereed. Vol. ends: Dec. Reprint: PSC. *Indexed:* A01, A22, BAS, BRI, E01, EconLit, IBSS, P61, SSA. *Bk. rev.:* Number and length vary, signed. *Aud.:* Ac.

Highly regarded in the field of urban studies, the *International Journal of Urban and Regional Research* publishes articles that are critical of existing policies and theories by "linking theoretical development and empirical research." In addition to the average of seven to nine research articles, *IJURR* also publishes articles in other sections ("Debates," "Symposia," and "Book Reviews"). Usually three of the four sections are published in each issue. As the title implies, the journal is international in its coverage of urban and regional studies. *IJURR* offers an app (iTunes) for accessing content and has a Twitter handle: @IJURResearch. Additional special features are also provided at no cost, including the journal's SUSC Book Series and the IJURR Lecture Series. *IJURR* is highly recommended for academic libraries.

4937. *International Journal of Urban Sustainable Development.* Formerly (until 2009): *Journal of the Urban Environment.* [ISSN: 1756-5723] 2010. 3x/yr. GBP 257 (print & online eds.)). Ed(s): Ramin Keivani. Taylor & Francis, 2, 3 & 4 Park Sq, Milton Park, Abingdon, OX14 4RN, United Kingdom; https://www.tandfonline.com. Adv. Sample. Refereed. Reprint: PSC. *Bk. rev.:* Occasional, signed. *Aud.:* Ac, Sa.

The creation of the *International Journal of Urban Sustainable Development* (*IJUSD*) is a response to the trending concept of sustainability that has dominated the urban studies landscape for years. This journal originated in 2010 and is published three times per year, up from two times at last review. It aims to "enhance knowledge and understanding of the two-way interactions between urbanization processes and patterns and environmental changes at the local, regional, and global scales." Each issue includes original research articles with an occasional editorial or review article. *IJUSD* is international in its coverage, with an emphasis on non-Western countries. The content is timely and will probably gain more readership as the topic of sustainability continues to be one of dominance and focus throughout the world. Open-access articles are available. Also by the same publisher is a similar journal, slightly more established, the *Journal of Urbanism,* (below in this section) which may be worth investigating as well. *IJUSD* is recommended for academic libraries.

4938. *International Planning Studies.* [ISSN: 1356-3475] 1996. q. GBP 638 (print & online eds.)). Ed(s): Shin Lee, Scott Orford. Routledge, 4 Park Sq, Milton Park, Abingdon, OX14 4RN, United Kingdom; subscriptions@tandf.co.uk; http://www.tandfonline.com. Illus., index, adv. Sample. Refereed. Reprint: PSC. *Indexed:* A01, A22, B01, E01, IBSS. *Bk. rev.:* Occasional, 3-5, 500 words, signed. *Aud.:* Ac, Sa.

International Planning Studies examines emerging planning changes and challenges that result from the impact of globalization-related growth at the urban, regional, national, and international levels. Published quarterly, *IPS* looks to fill the "gap between the more specialist theoretical and empirical journals in planning and urban-regional studies." Issues contain six to eight original research papers and an occasional review paper or book review section. Additionally, some issues contain introductory or editorial pieces. Each article includes an abstract, and the geographic coverage of the articles is international, as is the editorial board. *IPS* is available as an optional member benefit to those in the Regional Studies Association. Recommended for academic libraries, and highly recommended for libraries that support planning programs. Libraries may also want to investigate any available local planning resources for added relevance.

4939. *Journal of Architectural and Planning Research.* Former titles (until 1984): *Journal of Architectural Research;* (until 1974): *Architectural Research and Teaching.* [ISSN: 0738-0895] 1970. q. USD 607 (Individuals, USD 155). Ed(s): Andrew D Seidel. Locke Science Publishing Company, Inc., 332 S Michigan Ave Ste 1032 #L221, Chicago, IL 60604; customercare@lockescience.com; http://www.lockescience.com/. Illus. Sample. Refereed. *Indexed:* A22. *Bk. rev.:* Occasional, 1-3, length varies. *Aud.:* Ac, Sa.

Published quarterly, the *Journal of Architectural and Planning Research* (*JAPR*) aims to keep readers informed on the most up-to-date research in the disciplines of architecture, planning, and design, within the context of four broad areas (architectural and design research, urban planning research, and architectural, interior, and urban design). A scholarly journal published for academics and practitioners in the field, it is international in coverage. Each issue contains an average of five research articles, and occasionally a book review or position paper. Making the connection between architecture and urban planning is the source of this journal's uniqueness. *JAPR* is only available in print, but the website does have sample articles available, as well as listings of all previous tables of contents. The journal is available via several JSTOR archival collections. The subscription cost is somewhat high, but a slight discount is given if the title is acquired via a subscription agency. Recommended for academic libraries; highly recommended for those libraries that support programs with a city planning or an architecture component. General architecture and planning programs should also consider this title.

4940. ***Journal of Planning Education and Research.*** [ISSN: 0739-456X] 1981. q. USD 611 (print & online eds.)). Ed(s): Karen Lowrie. Sage Publications, Inc., 2455 Teller Rd, Thousand Oaks, CA 91320; info@sagepub.com; http://www.sagepub.com. Adv. Sample. Refereed. Reprint: PSC. *Indexed:* A22, E01, P61. *Bk. rev.:* 6-8 signed, length varies. *Aud.:* Ac, Sa.

The *Journal of Planning Education and Research* is the scholarly journal of the Association of Collegiate Schools of Planning (ACSP). The ACSP is a consortium of universities that offer credentials in urban and regional planning and that are committed to understanding and improving the versatility of urban and regional development and subsequently to improve education on the subject matter. Published quarterly, the *Journal of Planning Education and Research* includes six to eight articles per issue. Each article contains an abstract. Articles are a mix of case studies, theory, and pedagogy that focus on the United States with recent global inclusion. Issues also include upwards of eight book reviews. Boasting the highest percentage increase of citations in social sciences, this journal is a core title and highly recommended for academic libraries, specifically those with planning programs as well as appropriate special libraries. Economics and political science disciplines may also find this title of note.

4941. ***Journal of Planning Literature: incorporating the C P L bibliographies.*** Incorporates (1979-1995): *C P L Bibliography.* [ISSN: 0885-4122] 1979. q. USD 1936 (print & online eds.)). Ed(s): Gulsah Akar. Sage Publications, Inc., 2455 Teller Rd, Thousand Oaks, CA 91320; info@sagepub.com; http://www.sagepub.com. Adv. Sample. Refereed. Microform: PQC. Reprint: PSC. *Indexed:* A01, A22, E01, HRIS, IBSS, P61. *Bk. rev.:* Number and length vary, signed. *Aud.:* Ac, Sa.

The *Journal of Planning Literature* is an international, scholarly journal composed of review articles and abstracts that focus on recent publications in the regional planning and design field. Published quarterly, the *JPL* "aims to give the reader an understanding of the state of knowledge of the field for use in research or professional practice." Each issue includes an average of three review articles, a Council of Planning Librarians (CPL) bibliography, hundreds of abstracts from journal articles and dissertations, and an author and subject index of entries. Three broad subject headings are used to organize the citations: "History/Theory/Administration," "Methodology/Quantitative/Economic/Qualitative," and "Physical/Environmental." Some issues contain book reviews. The journal's website (published by Sage) does provide the ability to search the journal in its entirety, which is a nice feature given the aim and format of the journal. An excellent resource for practitioners, scholars, and students, and a core title for urban studies programs, *JPL* is highly recommended for academic libraries and appropriate special libraries.

4942. ***Journal of Urban Affairs.*** Formed by the merger of (1979-1981): *Urban Affairs Papers;* (1977-1981): *Urban Interest Journal.* [ISSN: 0735-2166] 1976. 8x/yr. GBP 1259 (print & online eds.)). Ed(s): Igor Vojnovic. Taylor & Francis Inc., 530 Walnut St, Ste 850, Philadelphia, PA 19106; enquiries@taylorandfrancis.com; http://www.taylorandfrancis.com. Illus., adv. Sample. Refereed. Microform: PQC. Reprint: PSC. *Indexed:* A01, A22, BRI, E01, EconLit, P61, SSA. *Bk. rev.:* 4-6, 500-1,000 words, signed. *Aud.:* Ga, Ac, Sa.

The *Journal of Urban Affairs* is the journal of the Urban Affairs Association (UAA), an international organization that "encourages the dissemination of information and research findings about urbanism and urbanization." The journal is a member benefit. *JUA* is published eight times per year. Each issue publishes from five to eight articles. The articles are predominantly focused on North America, but international coverage is included. The nature of the articles ranges from theoretical to case studies, and each article contains an abstract; most are understandable to the average reader. An average of four book reviews accompanies each issue as well. This title's web presence includes a really clean, informative blog. The journal also has a social media presence with a Twitter handle: @JUAurban and a Facebook page. The *Journal of Urban Affairs* is very similar in scope and geographic coverage to *Urban Affairs Review* (below in this section) and now publishing more issues per year might give it the edge over *UAR.* Highly recommended for academic libraries and for public libraries in urban settings.

4943. ***Journal of Urban Design.*** [ISSN: 1357-4809] 1996. 6x/yr. GBP 864 (print & online eds.)). Ed(s): Taner Oc. Routledge, 4 Park Sq, Milton Park, Abingdon, OX14 4RN, United Kingdom; subscriptions@tandf.co.uk; http://www.tandfonline.com. Illus., adv. Sample. Refereed. Reprint: PSC. *Indexed:* A01, A22, AmHI, E01, IBSS. *Bk. rev.:* Number varies, 500-1,000 words, signed. *Aud.:* Ac, Sa.

A scholarly journal, the *Journal of Urban Design* publishes articles relating to all aspects of urban design, considered a core knowledge component of a planning education. Some subject areas within urban design that are covered include urban aesthetics and townscape, sustainable development, preservation and conservation, local and regional identity, and urban regeneration. The journal occasionally publishes special issues. Recent special issues include "Becoming Local" and "Design Review in the UK." Each issue produces an average of five to seven original articles, highly international in coverage, and each containing an abstract as well as a varying number of book reviews. Editorials as well as commentary pieces are published occasionally. This journal is an optional member benefit for those in the Regional Studies Association. The *Journal of Urban Design* is highly recommended for academic libraries. Architecture programs should also find this title relevant.

Journal of Urban History. See History/Interdisciplinary Interests section.

4944. ***Journal of Urbanism: international research on placemaking and urban sustainability.*** [ISSN: 1754-9175] 2008. 4x/yr. GBP 515 (print & online eds.)). Ed(s): Emily Talen, Matthew Hardy. Routledge, 4 Park Sq, Milton Park, Abingdon, OX14 4RN, United Kingdom; subscriptions@tandf.co.uk; http://www.tandfonline.com. Adv. Sample. Refereed. Reprint: PSC. *Indexed:* A01, A22, E01, IBSS. *Bk. rev.:* 1-2, signed. *Aud.:* Ac.

The *Journal of Urbanism: International Research on Placemaking and Urban Sustainability* publishes four issues per year aiming to look at "human settlement and its relation to the idea of sustainability, social justice, and cultural understanding." International in coverage, this journal presents original research articles, one or two book reviews, and a "Viewpoint" piece from a player in the field in each issue. Articles include present and historic research and analysis. The *Journal of Urbanism* is somewhat costly, but may be worth the price as the conversation surrounding sustainability remains at the national and international forefront. Recommended for libraries with comprehensive collections.

Landscape and Urban Planning. See Landscape Architecture section.

4945. ***Planetizen Newswire.*** [ISSN: 1536-0547] 2000. s-w. Free. Ed(s): Chris Steins, Abhijeet Chavan. Urban Insight, Inc., 3700 Wilshire Blvd., Ste 570, Los Angeles, CA 90010; info@urbaninsight.com; http://www.urbaninsight.com. Adv. *Bk. rev.:* Number and length vary; on Plantizen.com. *Aud.:* Ga, Ac, Sa.

Published twice weekly (Monday and Thursday) via e-mail, *Planetizen Newswire* is a free electronic publication produced and distributed by Planetizen. Planetizen is a public-interest information exchange provided by Urban Insight. The newsletter begins with featured articles or blog posts written by experts in the field with a link back to the website for the full story. Each newsletter also delivers what the publishers consider the top 20 to 30 news headlines from the previous three or four days, each represented with the title and source. The title is hyperlinked back to Planetizen, where more of the story is presented with a link to the original source. The news stories are pulled predominantly from newspapers and magazines around the United States, thus written with the general public in mind. The newsletter also has an announcement section and links back to the website, which includes jobs, blogs, educational resources, op-eds, and organizational information. The website contains a wealth of information and resources and is really well done. While the subject matter of this newsletter makes it relevant for students, scholars, and practitioners, the general scope enables the newsletter to be utilized by the public. To receive the *Planetizen Newswire,* you must register on the website. Recommended for the general collection of public and academic libraries. URLs: www.planetizen.com/; www.planetizen.com/newswire

4946. ***Planning.*** Former titles (until 1969): *A S P O Newsletter;* (until 1951): *American Society of Planning Officials. Newsletter;* Incorporates (1976-1979): *Practicing Planner;* Which was formerly (until 1976): *Planner's Notebook.* [ISSN: 0001-2610] 1935. 11x/yr. Free to members; Non-members, USD 85. Ed(s): Sylvia Lewis. American Planning Association, 205 N Michigan Ave, Ste 1200, Chicago, IL 60601; customerservice@planning.org; http://www.planning.org. Illus., index, adv. Vol. ends: Dec. Microform: PQC. *Indexed:* A01, A22, B01, BRI, HRIS. *Bk. rev.:* Number and length vary. *Aud.:* Ga, Ac, Sa.

The professional magazine of the American Planning Association (APA), *Planning* is published 11 times a year and is a membership benefit. Members of the APA also receive access to the online edition of *Planning.* This title is geared to those in the field, but the articles are written so that the general public can understand and appreciate the subject matter. Color photos are prevalent throughout each issue; issues also include five to seven articles, in addition to the recurring sections. Book reviews are included in the "Planners Library" section and vary in number from issue to issue. Geographic coverage is predominantly the United States, and some issues are thematic. *Planning* is now additionally offered in a digital format, with a mobile app available. With a reasonable subscription price, *Planning* is highly recommended for general academic and public library collections, especially those that support urban planning programs or are located in heavily urban areas.

4947. ***Planning Perspectives: an international journal of history, planning and the environment.*** Incorporates (1988-2006): *Planning History;* Which was formerly (until 1988): *Planning History Bulletin;* (until 1979): *Planning History Group. Newsletter.* [ISSN: 0266-5433] 1986. bi-m. q. until 2019. GBP 1753 (print & online eds.)). Ed(s): Margaret Gold, John R Gold. Routledge, 4 Park Sq, Milton Park, Abingdon, OX14 4RN, United Kingdom; subscriptions@tandf.co.uk; http://www.tandfonline.com. Illus., adv. Sample. Refereed. Reprint: PSC. *Indexed:* A01, A22, B01, BRI, E01. *Bk. rev.:* 6-10, 500 words, signed. *Aud.:* Ac, Sa.

Planning Perspectives is an interdisciplinary, peer-reviewed journal publishing now six times a year, claiming to be the "premier international journal of history, planning and the environment." Each issue contains research articles, a section devoted to the IPHS (International Planning Historical Society), and an extensive book review section (between six and ten reviews). Book reviews are focused on North American, U.K., and European literature, but the articles and IPHS sections are international in coverage. Members of the IPHS receive *Planning Perspectives* as a membership benefit. For institutions, the price seems a little on the high side if you look at the publication frequency and the number of original research articles per issue. Because of its interdisciplinary nature, this journal is recommended for academic libraries and for libraries that maintain extensive history collections.

4948. ***Planning Practice and Research.*** [ISSN: 0269-7459] 1986. 5x/yr. GBP 923 (print & online eds.)). Ed(s): Vincent Nadin. Routledge, 4 Park Sq, Milton Park, Abingdon, OX14 4RN, United Kingdom; subscriptions@tandf.co.uk; http://www.tandfonline.com. Illus., adv. Sample. Refereed. Reprint: PSC. *Indexed:* A01, A22, B01, C45, E01, IBSS. *Aud.:* Ac, Sa.

A scholarly journal published five times a year, *Planning Practice and Research* claims to have "established itself as the source for information on current research in planning practice. It is intended for reflective, critical academics, professionals and students who are concerned to keep abreast of and challenge current thinking." The journal is committed to creating links between the research, practice, and education of planning, presenting analytical research, and fostering a place of dialogue for these topics. Each issue includes four to six research articles, and themed issues are occasionally published. The coverage is international, with an emphasis on European countries. *Planning Practice and Research* can be chosen as a benefit by members of the Regional Studies Association. Several planning-themed journals are included in this Urban Studies section, so pay close attention to their sometimes subtle differences to determine appropriate publications, especially with respect to price vs. article output. This title is recommended for U.S. academic libraries with a comprehensive collection.

4949. ***Regional Studies.*** [ISSN: 0034-3404] 1967. m. USD 5095 print & online eds. Ed(s): David Bailey. Routledge, 4 Park Sq, Milton Park, Abingdon, OX14 4RN, United Kingdom; subscriptions@tandf.co.uk; http://www.tandfonline.com. Illus., adv. Sample. Refereed. Microform: PQC. Reprint: PSC. *Indexed:* A22, B01, BAS, BRI, C45, E01, EconLit, IBSS, P61, SSA. *Bk..rev.:* 1-3, 500-1,000 words, signed. *Aud.:* Ac.

Publishing for more than fifty years, *Regional Studies* is the official journal of the Regional Studies Association. *Regional Studies* is a scholarly publication with an emphasis on "the development of theories and concepts, empirical analysis and policy debate in the field of regional studies." This title is published 12 times a year, and an issue of *Regional Studies* is composed of seven to nine original research articles, one to three book reviews, and occasionally an "Urban and Regional Horizon" and/or "Policy Debates" section. Each article contains an abstract published in five different languages. The geographic coverage is international, and themed issues are published regularly. Members of the Regional Studies Association receive the journal as a membership benefit. Though broader in geographic coverage than traditional urban studies journals, *Regional Studies* provides an important subnational view that explores the same concepts as those in the urban context. *Regional Studies* is recommended for academic libraries. Geography, environmental studies, and economics programs may also find this title of interest.

4950. ***Regional Studies, Regional Science.*** [ISSN: 2168-1376] 2014. a. Free. Ed(s): Stephen Hincks, Alasdair Rae. Routledge, 4 Park Sq, Milton Park, Abingdon, OX14 4RN, United Kingdom; subscriptions@tandf.co.uk; http://www.tandfonline.com. Illus. Sample. Refereed. *Aud.:* Ac, Sa.

New to the urban studies scene is the open-access title *Regional Studies, Regional Science.* This journal began publication in 2014 and publishes one issue per year. However, don't let the limited frequency fool you! The issues contain a plethora of articles added throughout the course of the calendar year. Types of articles include original articles, short articles, "Regional Graphics," review articles, and editorials. The geographic coverage is international and emphasizes "regional issues on geography, economics, planning, and political science." *Regional Studies, Regional Science* is the open-access journal of the Regional Studies Association, published by Taylor & Francis. It is listed in the Directory of Open Access Journals (DOAJ), has been accepted into Scopus, and is included in many aggregate databases. It is worth taking a look at, keeping your eye on, and knowing about. Recommended for academic libraries.

4951. ***Spacing.*** [ISSN: 1708-5799] 2003. 4x/yr. CAD 22. Ed(s): Michael Blackett. Spacing Media, 401 Richmond St, W, Ste B-02, Toronto, ON M5V 3AS, Canada; contact@spacing.ca; http://spacing.ca/. Adv. *Aud.:* Ga, Sa.

Spacing has been publishing since 2003. The impetus for establishing the magazine came from "a group of young journalists and public space advocates who felt that Toronto needed a publication that would bring together a number of key urban issues that were not being discussed by the local media." *Spacing* publishes four issues per year, two focused on Toronto, and two focused nationally on Canadian cities. "Toronto 2033" is a book project by *Spacing* that was designed to help celebrate the magazine's 15th anniversary (2018) by looking 15 years into the future. The winter 2018-19 edition of *Spacing* marked the magazine's 15th anniversary issue. Subscriptions are available in a variety of options and for a very reasonable price. Back issues are also available for purchase. The website is fantastic, with a blog section that includes an individual blog for six of Canada's large cities. Though this magazine is focused on a specific city, it is so well done that it can serve as inspiration to other cities. Highly recommended for Canadian libraries, and essential for those in Toronto.

Topos: European landscape magazine. See Landscape Architecture section.

4952. ***Town Planning Review.*** [ISSN: 0041-0020] 1910. bi-m. GBP 847 (print & online eds.)). Ed(s): Dave Shaw, Daniel Hess. Liverpool University Press, 4 Cambridge St, Liverpool, L69 7ZU, United Kingdom; lup@liv.ac.uk; http://liverpooluniversitypress.co.uk/. Illus., index, adv. Refereed. Vol. ends: Oct. Reprint: PSC. *Indexed:* A06, A22, AmHI, BAS, BRI, IBSS. *Bk. rev.:* Occasional, 1,000-2,000 words, signed. *Aud.:* Ac, Sa.

Founded more than one hundred years ago, *Town Planning Review* contributes to "the advancement of town and regional planning research in highly developed economies and in emerging industrial states." In addition to the roughly six research articles, issues can include short "Viewpoints" on a given subject presented by a single contributor; a "Commentary" section that provides an outlet for longer pieces of a similar nature; conference reports; review papers; and book reviews. The sections included in each issue vary. A scholarly journal, *TPR* is published six times a year, and the articles are heavily focused on European countries, but some international coverage has recently been included. The basic subscription price includes electronic access from 2002 to the present; a premium option is also available that includes access from 1910 onward. Recommended for academic libraries; highly recommended for academic, special, and larger urban public libraries in Europe.

4953. *Urban Affairs Review.* Formerly (until 1995): *Urban Affairs Quarterly.* [ISSN: 1078-0874] 1965. bi-m. USD 1741 (print & online eds.)). Ed(s): Peter Burns, Jered Carr. Sage Publications, Inc., 2455 Teller Rd, Thousand Oaks, CA 91320; info@sagepub.com; http://www.sagepub.com. Illus., index, adv. Sample. Refereed. Vol. ends: Jun. Microform: PQC. Reprint: PSC. *Indexed:* A01, A22, BRI, Chicano, E01, EIP, EconLit, IBSS, P61, SSA. *Aud.:* Ac, Sa.

Published bimonthly, *Urban Affairs Review* is a multidisciplinary, scholarly journal in the field of urban studies. Affiliated with the Urban Politics section of the American Political Science Association and the UIC College of Urban Planning and Public Affairs, this journal publishes original research articles of timely empirical analysis and research on the programs and policies that affect cities. Each issue contains minimally five research articles. Occasionally other articles are published in their Mini-Symposiums. The geographic coverage tends to focus predominantly on the United States, but the journal does incorporate some international coverage. Articles are published online first, then make their way to an issue. A subscription includes the online-first articles. *UAR* has a complementary website/blog, "Urban Affairs Forum," which is still running but the link is somewhat hidden in the journals description page. The address for the Forum is http://urbanaffairsreview.com. Similar in scope and geographic coverage to the *Journal of Urban Affairs* (above in this section), *Urban Affairs Review* costs more and now publishes less issues per year than *JUA*. A very solid journal in its own right, *UAR* is highly recommended for academic collections, but given the prevalence of budget restraints, only one of the two journals is likely needed. Political science programs may also find this title relevant.

4954. *Urban Ecosystems.* [ISSN: 1083-8155] 1997. q. EUR 1345 (print & online eds.)). Ed(s): Glenn R Guntenspergen, Charles Nilon. Springer New York LLC, 233 Spring St, New York, NY 10013; customerservice@springer.com; http://www.springer.com. Adv. Sample. Refereed. Reprint: PSC. *Indexed:* A22, Agr, C45, E01. *Aud.:* Ac, Sa.

Urban Ecosystems focuses on "scientific investigations of urban environments and the relationships between socioeconomic and ecological structures and processes in urban environments." Since 2013 it is the flagship publication of the Society of Urban Ecology (SURE). *Urban Ecosystems* is scholarly, publishes four times a year, but each issue contains around 20 original research articles. The scope of the journal is broad and international in geographic coverage. Filling a needed gap, *Urban Ecosystems* examines the living aspects of urban areas and the impact the man-made community has had, and is an important component of urban studies. *Urban Ecosystems* is recommended for academic libraries.

4955. *Urban History.* Formerly (until 1992): *Urban History Yearbook;* Which superseded (in 1974): *Urban History Newsletter.* [ISSN: 0963-9268] 1963. 4x/yr. GBP 318. Ed(s): Rosemary Sweet, Simon Gunn. Cambridge University Press, University Printing House, Shaftesbury Rd, Cambridge, CB2 8BS, United Kingdom; online@cambridge.org; https://www.cambridge.org/. Adv. Sample. Refereed. Reprint: PSC. *Indexed:* A22, BAS, E01, P61, SSA. *Bk. rev.:* Number varies, 500-1,000 words, signed. *Aud.:* Ac.

Published four times per year, *Urban History* is a scholarly journal that claims to hold a "central place in historical scholarship." Interdisciplinary in its coverage, *Urban History* publishes research articles "covering social, economic, political and cultural aspects of the history of towns and cities." The geographic coverage of the articles focuses on Europe. In addition to the five to seven articles published, each issue also contains a substantial book review section, as well as an occasional review of a periodical article. Special issues are sometimes published. Published in Part 4 of every issue is a bibliography of more than one thousand publications including periodicals, monographs, and collections from the urban history field, which is a very valuable tool for scholars and students. An index of cities and towns covered by *Urban History* during the previous year is also included in this part. Subscribers have online access to their comprehensive bibliography as well. *Urban History* has also started to include multimedia companions to the journal as a response demand by this interdisciplinary field. They are worth checking out on their website: https://www.cambridge.org/core/journals/urban-history/information/multimedia-companions Because of its focus on European cities and towns, *Urban History* is highly recommended for academic libraries that support international and/or comprehensive urban studies programs.

4956. *Urban Land.* Incorporates (1998-2008): *Multifamily Trends;* Former titles (until 1944): *Urban Land Institute Bulletin;* (until 1942): *Urban Land Institute. News Bulletin.* [ISSN: 0042-0891] 1941. q. Free to members. Ed(s): Elizabeth Razzi. The Urban Land Institute, 2001 L St NW, Washington, DC 20036; customerservice@uli.org; http://www.uli.org. Illus., index, adv. Microform: PQC. *Indexed:* A22, HRIS. *Bk. rev.:* 2-4, 200-300 words, signed. *Aud.:* Ga, Ac, Sa.

Included as a member benefit from the Urban Land Institute (ULI), *Urban Land* is published four times a year and is available to members in print as well as electronically. Members also have electronic access to the archive going back to 1992. The general public can see articles dating back to 2010 at no charge. The online magazine contains additional content posted daily, and many of the articles are placed online within two weeks of the print copies being mailed. The site for the online magazine is well developed and manageable. Apps for the Apple and Android products are available to members. *Urban Land* publishes articles that reflect the mission of the ULI, which is to work together (from landowners to lawyers to librarians) to create and promote best practices in, and sustainability of, community development. *Urban Land* focuses predominantly on North America, but has seen expansion to European and Asia Pacific region. The magazine publishes several feature articles and a number of pieces in recurrent segments such as "ULX," which provides ten items on a given topic (multi-family housing, holistic health design); a "Policy Perspective"; and a "Case Study." Color photographs accompany most of the articles. *Urban Land* includes book reviews in the "In Print" section. Although written for ULI members, this title is understandable and appropriate for the general public as well. Subscriptions are only available through a ULI membership, and those are somewhat expensive. On the whole, it is an enjoyable publication and is recommended for large public libraries as well as academic libraries.

4957. *Urban Morphology.* [ISSN: 1027-4278] 1997. s-a. GBP 50 (Individuals, GBP 25). Ed(s): Jeremy Whitehand. International Seminar on Urban Form, c/o Dr Michael Barke, Division of Geography, Newcastle upon Tyne, NE1 8ST, United Kingdom; http://www.urbanform.org/. Illus., adv. Refereed. Circ: 500 Paid. *Bk. rev.:* 4-6, signed. *Aud.:* Ac.

Originating in 1997, *Urban Morphology* is the journal of the International Seminar on Urban Form (ISUF). Urban morphology is the study of human settlements and the change that these settlements go through over time. Published twice a year, in April and October, *Urban Morphology* contains three to five research articles and a book review section. Reports from various meetings and seminars are also included, as well as a "Viewpoints" section that offers shorter opinion pieces on urban morphology topics. The ISUF offers research articles from 1997 to 2007 in pdf format, freely available on its website. Articles are international in coverage. Membership to the ISUF is the only way to subscribe to this journal, and the membership cost is very reasonable. Recommended for academic libraries.

4958. *Urban Studies: an international journal for research in urban studies.* [ISSN: 0042-0980] 1964. 16x/yr. USD 4931. Ed(s): Tony O'Sullivan. Sage Publications Ltd., 1 Oliver's Yard, 55 City Rd, London, EC1Y 1SP, United Kingdom; info@sagepub.com; https://www.sagepub.com/. Illus., index, adv. Sample. Refereed. Vol. ends: Dec. Reprint: PSC. *Indexed:* A01, A22, AmHI, B01, BAS, BRI, E01, EconLit, HRIS, IBSS, P61, SSA. *Bk. rev.:* 4-6, 500 words, signed. *Aud.:* Ac.

Published since 1964, *Urban Studies* is one of the core journals recommended to support an urban studies program. The journal publishes articles on any urban or regional problem associated with the social sciences. A scholarly journal, *Urban Studies* publishes 16 issues a year. Each issue contains at least ten original articles with abstracts and a handful of book reviews. Some issues have a theme, and in these themed issues there are no book reviews. The articles are international in coverage, with a slight bias toward Europe and the Americas. Articles are available online ahead of print, which is a nice feature, and the website has improved since the last review and includes a separate Urban Studies Online site that hosts a blog and other multimedia. They are also putting effort into publishing abstracts, online resources, and some articles in Chinese. *Urban Studies* is expensive for libraries in either print or electronic format, but note that this publication produces a high number of articles per issue; and the number of issues published per volume is higher than most publications in the field. It also may be relevant for environmental studies and/or sociology programs, which also could help justify the cost. As a core title, essential for academic libraries.

■ VETERINARY SCIENCE

Ana Ugaz, Collection Development and Strategic Initiatives Coordinator, Medical Sciences Library, Texas A&M University, 4462 TAMU, College Station, TX 77843; augaz@tamu.edu

Introduction

The core journals in veterinary science have remained generally consistent over the past few years. Several changes have occurred with a few journals in terms of their scope and online accessibility. As a co-author of the article, "Basic list of veterinary medical serials" (3rd edition), the current author of this section helped identify a core group of veterinary serials, which provides a more expanded foundational list of veterinary journals ranked for library collection development (DOI: 10.3163/1536-5050.98.4.004). Given the relative stability of veterinary science serials, titles in this section received a thorough review in terms of aim, scope, article content, print and online features, and extent of accessibility to determine where updated annotations were needed.

Libraries may wish to supplement the titles identified in this section depending on the needs and interests of the clientele they serve, whether that be with additional research or clinical journals, journals in the basic sciences, materials aimed at pet owners or another client-based audience, or industry journals. All of the titles listed are solid choices for a veterinary collection, while a few of the titles are appropriate for human medicine collections that have a research focus or for libraries with collections in animal science. A select few are fitting for more specialized collections, such as for a diagnostic laboratory or a zoo, or in support of an equestrian program. A range of journals are included that represent publications of non-specialty veterinary associations; journals from some of the major veterinary specialty organizations; research journals; clinical journals; and trade publications. Journals reviewed reflect the international perspective that is necessary for the varied practice situations, and also the broad range of species seen in veterinary medicine.

Journals that are completely open-access are noted, as well as journals where publishers offer fee options for authors to ensure their article is freely available.

Standard features of many of the online journals include the option to adjust font size or the size of accompanying images, choice of viewing articles as either html full text or a pdf version more suitable for printing, establishing alerts when new issues are available, exporting citations into a citation manager database, and the ability to share article abstracts via e-mail. In addition, many journal sites include a sidebar with a ranking of the most frequently accessed and most cited articles.

Other features offered by publishers in the online environment include a secondary presentation of an article that eliminates the extra banners around the edges of the screen; easy methods for downloading figures into slide presentations; pre-publication for the early release of articles online before they appear in the print issues; and responsive design so the content is optimized whether the viewing is done on a desktop computer, tablet, or mobile phone.

Basic Periodicals

Ga: *D V M360*; Ac: *American Animal Hospital Association. Journal, American Journal of Veterinary Research, American Veterinary Medical Association. Journal, Equine Veterinary Journal, Journal of Veterinary Internal Medicine, Veterinary Clinics of North America: Equine Practice, Veterinary Clinics of North America: Exotic Animal Practice, Veterinary Clinics of North America: Food Animal Practice, Veterinary Clinics of North America: Small Animal Practice, The Veterinary Journal, The Veterinary Record.*

Basic Abstracts and Indexes

Biological Abstracts; CAB Abstracts; Index Veterinarius; PUBMED; Scopus; Web of Science.

4959. *American Animal Hospital Association. Journal.* Former titles (until 1968): *Animal Hospital; American Animal Hospital Association Bulletin.* [ISSN: 0587-2871] 1965. bi-m. Members, USD 39; Non-members, USD 107. Ed(s): Alan H Rebar. American Animal Hospital Association, 12575 W Bayaud Ave, Lakewood, CO 80228; info@aaha.org; https://www.aaha.org/. Illus., index, adv. Refereed. Vol. ends: Nov/Dec. Microform: PQC. *Indexed:* A22, C45. *Aud.:* Ac, Sa.

Journal of the American Animal Hospital Association, or *JAAHA*, is the official publication of the American Animal Hospital Association, and is available bimonthly in print and online. Articles appearing in the journal are peer-reviewed and address the interests of practitioners in small-animal medicine and surgery. The article topics and content adhere to the journal's target audience of clinical practice veterinarians and team members. Article submissions are categorized as original studies, retrospective studies, case series, case reports, or review articles, and report predominately on issues related to small animals. The journal also publishes veterinary practice guidelines developed by the association on such topics as canine life stage, dental problems, weight management, and behavior. The online version of the journal includes issues from volume 31 (1995) to the current issue. This journal is recommended for libraries that support all levels of veterinary medicine programs. URL: www.jaaha.org

4960. *American Journal of Veterinary Research.* [ISSN: 0002-9645] 1940. m. USD 260 combined subscription domestic (print & online eds.); USD 270 combined subscription foreign (print & online eds.); USD 40 per issue domestic). Ed(s): Dr. Kurt J Matushek, Nicholas T. De Luca. American Veterinary Medical Association, 1931 N Meacham Rd, Ste 100, Schaumburg, IL 60173-4360; llarson@avma.org; http://www.avma.org. Illus., index, adv. Refereed. Vol. ends: Dec. Microform: PMC; PQC. *Indexed:* A01, A22, Agr, C45. *Aud.:* Ac, Sa.

The *American Journal of Veterinary Research* is one of the two major journals owned and published by the American Veterinary Medical Association. The journal is available in both online and print formats, and it publishes peer-reviewed reports of applied research in veterinary medicine and associated biological sciences. Articles aim to "translate laboratory research and preclinical studies to the development of clinical trials and clinical practice." It is also noted that "reports of laboratory animal studies and studies involving the use of animals as experimental models of human diseases are considered only when the study results are of demonstrable benefit to the species used in the research or to another species of veterinary interest." Articles are grouped by topic or body system, with news content at the front of each issue. The association states that this journal is one of the most widely circulated veterinary research journals in the world. This title is highly recommended for both medical and academic libraries that support veterinary medicine programs, medicine, or graduate programs such as in animal science where research of this type would be relevant. URL: http://avmajournals.avma.org

4961. *American Veterinary Medical Association. Journal.* Incorporates (1899-1913): *American Veterinary Medical Association. Proceedings;* (1950-1964): *American Veterinary Medical Association. Annual Meeting. Scientific Proceedings;* Which was formerly (until 1956): *American Veterinary Medical Association. Annual Meeting. Proceedings.* [ISSN: 0003-1488] 1877. s-m. USD 260 combined subscription domestic (print & online eds.); USD 270 combined subscription foreign (print & online eds.); USD 40 per issue domestic). Ed(s): Dr. Kurt J Matushek, Nicholas

T. De Luca. American Veterinary Medical Association, 1931 N Meacham Rd, Ste 100, Schaumburg, IL 60173-4360; llarson@avma.org; http://www.avma.org. Illus., index, adv. Refereed. Circ: 77100 Paid. Microform: BHP; PQC. *Indexed:* A01, A22, Agr, C45. *Bk. rev.:* 2-3, 200-400 words. *Aud.:* Ac, Sa.

This is the official publication of the American Veterinary Medical Association (AVMA) and is published twice per month. The stated aim is to "promote the science and art of veterinary medicine and to provide a forum for discussion and dissemination of ideas important to the profession," and it essentially serves as the voice of the veterinary profession. Articles are peer-reviewed and include reports of clinical research, feature articles, and regular columns of interest to veterinarians in a variety of practice situations. The news and classified-ad sections are posted online ten days to two weeks before they are delivered in print. All issues published since volume 216 (2000) are available online and are searchable. The "Veterinary Medicine Today" section promotes continuing education through didactic exercises, case discussions, and updates on clinical topics. Not every feature is published in every issue. The "Scientific Reports" section contains original studies, clinical reports, and review articles, with content in this section further subdivided, such as "Small Animal/Exotic" or "Equine." The journal draws article content from the AVMA's research publication, *American Journal of Veterinary Research.* Information on upcoming meetings and continuing education opportunities are included in a calendar section. Book reviews are occasionally included in the journal, and may help identify new veterinary-related books for a library collection or to the interested reader. While membership in the AVMA includes a choice of a subscription to this journal or the association's other publication, this journal is a must-have for a veterinary medicine collection. URL: http://avmajournals.avma.org

4962. *Australian Veterinary Journal.* Formerly (until 1927): *Australian Veterinary Association. Journal.* [ISSN: 0005-0423] 1925. m. GBP 535. Ed(s): Anne Jackson. Wiley-Blackwell Publishing Ltd., The Atrium, Southern Gate, Chichester, PO19 8QG, United Kingdom; cs-journals@wiley.com; http://onlinelibrary.wiley.com/. Illus., index, adv. Sample. Refereed. Vol. ends: Dec. Reprint: PSC. *Indexed:* A22, Agr, BRI, C45, E01. *Bk. rev.:* 1-3, 300-600 words. *Aud.:* Ac, Sa.

The *Australian Veterinary Journal* is the official journal of the Australian Veterinary Association. Scientific and clinical articles are peer-reviewed, and a typical issue includes original research and reviews, case reports and series, clinical updates, and letters on all aspects of veterinary science, particularly their significance to Australasian veterinary medicine. The content is easily readable and includes many color photos, but will appeal mostly to the target audience of veterinary professionals, as they would gain the most from the clinical and scientific articles. As the premier veterinary science journal for Australian Veterinary Association members and subscribers, this journal provides a uniquely Australian perspective, including indigenous species and issues specific to geographic locations in Australia. The journal provides equal parts association news and scientific articles, with the research articles subdivided into sections on production animals, equine, small animals, wildlife and zoos, and avian. This journal also includes book reviews that would be helpful to identifying veterinary-related books for a library collection. Diagnostic challenge articles are intended to "highlight the usefulness of investigative techniques in formulating a diagnosis." The online format provides access to issues dating back to volume 1 (1925). The publisher, John Wiley & Sons, Inc., includes an option for authors to pay charges that would make their article freely available so an issue may have one or two articles designated with the Open Access symbol. This journal is most appropriate for academic institutions with a veterinary or animal science program. URL: http://onlinelibrary.wiley.com/journal/10.1111/%28ISSN%291751-0813

4963. *Avian Diseases.* [ISSN: 0005-2086] 1957. q. Individuals, USD 343; Free to members. American Association of Avian Pathologists, Inc., 12627 San Jose Blvd, Ste 202, Jacksonville, FL 32223; aaap@aaap.info; http://www.aaap.info/index.html. Illus., index. Refereed. Vol. ends: Oct/Dec. Microform: WSH; PMC; PQC. *Indexed:* A22, Agr, C45, E01. *Aud.:* Ac, Sa.

An international journal published by the American Association of Avian Pathologists, whose mission is to enhance scientific knowledge and promote avian health. Journal issues consist of original basic or clinical research from various disciplines, including microbiology, immunology, pathology, and epidemiology. Papers on avian diseases of poultry, pet, and wild birds that are relevant to etiology, pathogenesis, diagnosis, treatment, and control are accepted. This quarterly journal includes a hefty 20 to 30 articles, averaging six to eight pages in length, with the abstracts provided in both English and Spanish. Included at the back of the journal is the table of contents from another related journal, *Avian Pathology.* The online version of the journal, for both members and subscribers, features a mobile-friendly website. This journal is recommended for libraries that support veterinary or animal science programs, libraries that serve clientele in the poultry industry, and special collections at research facilities that support avian diagnostics. URL: www.aaapjournals.info/avdi

4964. *Canadian Journal of Veterinary Research (Online).* [ISSN: 1928-9022] 2010. q. Free. Canadian Veterinary Medical Association, 339 Booth St, Ottawa, ON K1R 7K1, Canada; admin@cvma-acmv.org ; http://canadianveterinarians.net. Adv. Refereed. *Aud.:* Ac, Sa.

This is a quarterly, peer-reviewed research publication of the Canadian Veterinary Medical Association, which is only available in an online format. Though it ceased as a print publication in 2010, this research journal maintains an international readership through the publishing of high-quality scientific papers in the field of veterinary medicine. The journal publishes about 10 to 12 articles per issue of original research in veterinary and comparative medicine. The content is predominately review articles, short communications, or full articles, and does not include other news, editorials, or letters. In the print format, the abstracts were written in both English and French, but this is not apparent in the current online version. Journal issues are freely available in PubMed for earlier titles of the journal back to volume 1 (1937) and up through the current title for all but the latest six months. The subscription access on the Ingentaconnect platform includes volume 74 (2010) through the current issue. This journal is recommended for libraries that serve veterinary, animal science, or medical programs, and particularly for libraries located in North America. URLs: www.ncbi.nlm.nih.gov/pmc/journals/133/; www.ingentaconnect.com/content/cvma/cjvr

4965. *The Canadian Veterinary Journal.* [ISSN: 0008-5286] 1960. m. Free to members; Non-members, CAD 170. Ed(s): Carlton Gyles, Heather Broughton. Canadian Veterinary Medical Association, 339 Booth St, Ottawa, ON K1R 7K1, Canada; admin@cvma-acmv.org ; http://canadianveterinarians.net. Illus., index, adv. Refereed. Vol. ends: Dec. Microform: PMC; PQC. *Indexed:* A22, Agr, C45. *Bk. rev.:* 1-6, 300-700 words. *Aud.:* Ac, Sa.

The Canadian Veterinary Journal is a monthly journal of the Canadian Veterinary Medical Association, which aims to "educate by informing readers of progress in clinical veterinary medicine, clinical veterinary research, and related fields of endeavor." The journal claims to be the "voice of veterinary medicine in Canada" with the key objective to promote the art and science of veterinary medicine and the betterment of animal health. Regular content includes research and review articles, case reports, a student paper publication, news, content of interest to veterinary practice management, book reviews, letters, and a section of classified advertisements. There is also a "Quiz Corner" section with four or five questions, often taken from a veterinary board prep text. Articles are written in English, but abstracts, section headings, news, and other brief communications are in both English and French. The journal notes that it is print-based and directs users to PubMed Central for older issues, but association membership includes access to interactive pdfs. The free online access through PubMed Central from volume 1 (1960) to the present does, however, exclude the most recent six months. The journal states that it is intended for the veterinary practitioner, but those studying veterinary medicine or animal science would also find the content relevant. URLs: www.ncbi.nlm.nih.gov/pmc/; www.canadianveterinarians.net/science-knowledge/cvj

4966. *D V M 360.* Formerly (until 2013): *D V M.* [ISSN: 2326-0688] 1969. m. Ed(s): Kristi Reimer. U B M Advanstar Communications, Inc., 8033 Flint, Lenexa, KS 66214; info@advanstar.com; http://ubmadvanstar.com//. Illus., adv. Vol. ends: Dec. Microform: PQC. *Indexed:* A01, A22, BRI. *Aud.:* Ga, Ac, Sa.

This title was formerly known as *DVM Newsmagazine* until 2013, when the title changed to *dvm360* to more closely resemble the layout of the online dvm360.com site. In print, this is a larger-format publication (10.5" x 14") that "provides unbiased multimedia reporting on all issues affecting the veterinary profession." It is a heavily illustrated newsmagazine that contains both short news entries and longer feature stories, with some of the shorter stories continuing online. In general, the graphical presentation of information makes it easy to scan, but there is also more advertising content sandwiched in between the articles. The eight to ten pages of product information would likely be of interest to many readers, as would the employment opportunities and the calendar of meetings. The clinical content is authoritative and presents topics of a practical nature, such as "A safer way to place chest tubes," "Top 5 toxins in companion birds," and "Managing glaucoma in your equine patients." Articles often come with cited references and pictures illustrating procedures. Online is an eye-catching site that pulls information from several different publications (*Veterinary Medicine, Veterinary Economics,* and *Firstline*) with multiple methods of navigating the site by section or subject; but this also poses some difficulty in locating the specific page within the individual issues of *dvm360,* but they are there. The *dvm360* website has the advantage of including the print content along with more current breaking news. Many of the articles could be understood and are of interest to the general adult reader, but the target audience is the practitioner and team. This magazine is highly recommended for libraries that support veterinary medicine programs. URL: http://veterinarynews.dvm360.com/sourceissues

4967. *Equine Veterinary Journal.* [ISSN: 0425-1644] 1968. bi-m. GBP 622. Ed(s): Celia M Marr. John Wiley & Sons, Inc., 111 River St, Hoboken, NJ 07030; cs-journals@wiley.com; http://onlinelibrary.wiley.com. Illus., index, adv. Refereed. Vol. ends: Nov. Reprint: PSC. *Indexed:* A22, Agr, C45, E01. *Aud.:* Ac, Sa.

In 1968, the British Equine Veterinary Association undertook the task to issue its own publication, calling it the *Equine Veterinary Journal.* Its stature has grown so that it is now the most respected international scientific equine journal in the world. *Equine Veterinary Journal* publishes evidence to improve clinical practice or expand scientific knowledge underpinning equine veterinary medicine. The average issue contains 12 to 14 full-length articles on original research, plus one to three short communications, and case reports on such diverse topics as dermatology, exercise, anatomy, ergonomics, pain therapy, surgery, behavior, reproduction, and racing. Many of the figures and illustrations are in color. A selection of articles are posted online, ahead of print, in the "Early View" section of the online journal. A must for veterinary libraries, equine practitioners, and libraries that serve colleges with equestrian programs or those conducting equine research. Full text is available from volume 1. URL: http://onlinelibrary.wiley.com/journal/10.1001/(ISSN)2042-3306

4968. *Journal of Avian Medicine and Surgery.* Former titles (until 1995): *Association of Avian Veterinarians. Journal;* (until 1989): *A A V Today;* (until 1987): *A.V.A. Newsletter.* [ISSN: 1082-6742] 1980. q. Free to members; USD 240 combined subscription in US & Canada (print & online eds.)). Ed(s): James W Carpenter, Chris Brower. Association of Avian Veterinarians, PO Box 9, Teaneck, NJ 07666; office@aav.org; http://www.aav.org. Illus., index, adv. Refereed. Vol. ends: Dec. *Indexed:* A01, A22, BRI, C45, E01. *Bk. rev.:* 1-2, 400-500 words. *Aud.:* Ac, Sa.

The *Journal of Avian Medicine and Surgery* is published quarterly by the Association of Avian Veterinarians (AAV). It is an international journal on the medicine and surgery of captive and wild birds. It publishes original research, clinical reports, review articles, retrospective studies, case reports, editorials, and research briefs. In addition, it has featured sections including "What's Your Diagnosis?," "Selected Abstracts from the Literature," and "Round Table Discussions." There are also book and DVD reviews, and a calendar of upcoming meetings. The illustrations are chiefly in black and white, with an occasional use of color. The journal is essential for the avian practitioner and is highly recommended for zoo and veterinary libraries. Full text for earlier titles of the journal back to volumes 1 through to volume 27 (2013) are available from JSTOR. Online full text is available from volume 14 (2000) to the most current issue through BioOne. URL: www.bioone.org/loi/avms

4969. *Journal of Exotic Pet Medicine.* Formerly (until 2006): *Seminars in Avian and Exotic Pet Medicine.* [ISSN: 1557-5063] 1992. q. USD 893. Elsevier Inc., 1600 John F Kennedy Blvd, Philadelphia, PA 19103; usinfo-f@elsevier.com; https://www.elsevier.com. Illus., index, adv. Refereed. Vol. ends: Dec. *Indexed:* C45. *Aud.:* Ac, Sa.

Journal of Exotic Pet Medicine is the official journal of the Association of Exotic Mammal Veterinarians and strives to be "the most complete resource for practitioners who treat avian and exotic pets." Each issue is guest edited by an authority on a particular topic that is then the focus of five or six articles by invited experts in the "Topics in Medicine and Surgery" section. The featured articles typically discuss the topic as it applies to various groups of exotic animals. Some examples of topics have included clinical therapeutics, welfare issues, unusual exotic pets, field techniques, and neurology. The journal is peer-reviewed, with most issues containing research and review articles, case reports, industry news, diagnostic challenges, and practice management. In the online format, the publisher site provides easy navigation to other articles in the issue, recommended articles, citing articles, and related book content (from the publisher's vast resources). This journal is recommended for veterinary and zoo libraries, as the content is written for an audience of avian and exotic animal practitioners. The variety of exotic animals covered in the articles, and the detailed captions for the accompanying pictures, could also be of interest to other adult readers. Online full-text articles are available from volume 15 (2006) to the current issue on the ScienceDirect platform, with issues from volumes 4-14 (1995-2005) on a separate page for the former title, *Seminars in Avian and Exotic Pet Medicine.* URL: www.sciencedirect.com/science/journal/15575063

4970. *Journal of Feline Medicine and Surgery.* [ISSN: 1098-612X] 1999. m. USD 959 (print & online eds.)). Ed(s): Margie Scherk. Sage Publications Ltd., 1 Oliver's Yard, 55 City Rd, London, EC1Y 1SP, United Kingdom; info@sagepub.com; https://www.sagepub.com/. Illus., adv. Sample. Refereed. Reprint: PSC. *Indexed:* A22, Agr, C45, E01. *Bk. rev.:* 1, 200-300 words. *Aud.:* Ac, Sa.

The *Journal of Feline Medicine and Surgery* is an international journal, and the official journal of both the International Society of Feline Medicine (ISFM) and the American Association of Feline Practitioners (AAFP). It is aimed at both practitioners and researchers with an interest in clinical veterinary health care of domestic cats. It may be the only scientific, peer-reviewed journal in the world devoted exclusively to feline medicine and surgery. Due to the unique publishing format, the following is quoted directly from the journal: "The journal is published monthly in two formats - Classic' editions (published in February, April, June, August, October, and December) containing high quality original papers on all aspects of feline medicine and surgery, including basic research relevant to clinical practice; and dedicated 'Clinical Practice' editions (published in January, March, May, July, September, and November) primarily containing commissioned opinionated review articles [that] provid[e] state of the art information for feline clinicians, along with other relevant articles such as case reports." The journal uses a substantial amount of color illustrations. An international news section provides information about feline veterinary meetings, society news, new developments, book reviews, and relevant issues from other publications and meetings. In May 2015, a sister journal was launched, *Journal of Feline Medicine and Surgery Open Reports* for open-access content. This journal is a must for the feline practitioner, and should be considered a basic title for veterinary libraries. Online full text is available from volume 1 (1999). URL: http://jfm.sagepub.com/

4971. *Journal of Small Animal Practice.* [ISSN: 0022-4510] 1960. m. GBP 584. Ed(s): Carmel T Mooney. Wiley-Blackwell Publishing Ltd., The Atrium, Southern Gate, Chichester, PO19 8QG, United Kingdom; cs-journals@wiley.com; http://onlinelibrary.wiley.com. Illus., index, adv. Sample. Refereed. Vol. ends: Dec. Reprint: PSC. *Indexed:* A22, Agr, BRI, C45, E01. *Bk. rev.:* 1, 300-375 words. *Aud.:* Ac, Sa.

The *Journal of Small Animal Practice* is the monthly, peer-reviewed journal of the British Small Animal Veterinary Association (BSAVA) and the World Small Animal Veterinary Association (WSAVA). The aims and scope of the journal are to integrate clinical research papers and case reports that cover all aspects of medicine and surgery relating to dogs, cats, and other small animals, and by distributing that information, to promote best practice. Issues consist of original articles, review articles, invited editorials, guidelines issued by the associations, book reviews, and other scientific and educational information from around the world. Topics of recently published articles have included: "Health screening to identify opportunities to improve preventive medicine in cats and dogs," "Bodyweight and body condition score in rabbits on four different feeding regimes," "Prevalence of physiological heart murmurs in a population of 95 healthy young adult dogs," and "Backyard poultry: legislation, zoonoses and disease prevention." The primary audience is veterinarians engaged in small-animal medicine, and this journal is highly recommended for veterinary libraries. All issues dating back to volume 1 (1960) have been digitized and are available on the Wiley Online Library platform. URL: http://onlinelibrary.wiley.com/journal/10.1111/(ISSN)1748-5827

4972. *Journal of Swine Health and Production.* Former titles (until 2001): *Swine Health and Production;* (until 1993): *American Association of Swine Practitioners. Newsletter.* [ISSN: 1537-209X] 1993. bi-m. Free to members; Non-members, USD 140. American Association of Swine Veterinarians, 830 26th St, Perry, IA 50220; aasv@aasv.org; http://www.aasv.org. Refereed. Vol. ends: Nov/Dec. *Indexed:* Agr, C45. *Aud.:* Ac, Sa.

The *Journal of Swine Health & Production* (*JSHAP*) is a peer-reviewed title published six times per year by the American Association of Swine Veterinarians (AASV). The journal publishes practical and scientific information that is relevant to both the veterinary practitioner and the international research and academic community. Topics covered focus on applied swine health and production, including the diagnosis, treatment, prevention, and eradication of swine diseases; also covered are welfare; public health; biosecurity; antimicrobial use and resistance; economics; and facility design. Issues are typically about 50 pages in length and contain original research, brief communications, case reports, literature reviews, commentaries, diagnostic notes, production tools, practice tips, as well as association news. Full text of the journal is available in an open-access edition, with issues dating back to volume 1 (1993), while subscriptions for print copies are also available and are a benefit of AASV membership. URL: https://www.aasv.org/shap/issues/index.html

4973. *Journal of Veterinary Internal Medicine.* [ISSN: 0891-6640] 1987. bi-m. GBP 479 (print & online eds.)). Ed(s): Kenneth W Hinchcliff, Stephen P DiBartola. Wiley-Blackwell Publishing, Inc., 111 River St, Hoboken, NJ 07030; http://onlinelibrary.wiley.com. Illus., index, adv. Sample. Refereed. Reprint: PSC. *Indexed:* A01, A22, Agr, C45, E01. *Aud.:* Ac, Sa.

This is the official journal of the American College of Veterinary Internal Medicine (ACVIM), which is the international certifying organization for veterinary specialists in cardiology, large-animal internal medicine, neurology, oncology, and small-animal internal medicine. It is also the official journal for the European College of Veterinary Internal Medicine, the European College of Veterinary Neurology, and the European College of Equine Internal Medicine. The journal aims to "advance veterinary medical knowledge and improve the lives of animals by publication of authoritative scientific articles of animal diseases." This title is published six times per year, and issues are quite substantial, with 25 to 35 articles that are, on average, six to ten pages in length, on topics such as cardiology, neurology, oncology, immunology, infectious disease, nutrition/metabolism, pharmacology, theriogenology, epidemiology, and muscle disease. Captions for some of the article figures indicate that color versions of the images are available in the online issue. In January 2015, the *Journal of Veterinary Internal Medicine* moved to an online, open-access format, but it has also provided free access to journal articles back to volume 1(1987). This journal is a must-have for libraries that support a veterinary program. URL: www.wileyonlinelibrary.com/journal/jvim

4974. *Journal of Veterinary Medical Education.* [ISSN: 0748-321X] 1974. q. CAD 390. Ed(s): Daryl J Buss. University of Toronto Press, Journals Division, 5201 Dufferin St, Toronto, ON M3H 5T8, Canada; journals@utpress.utoronto.ca; http://www.utpjournals.com. Illus., adv. Refereed. Circ: 3392. Vol. ends: Dec. Microform: PQC. *Indexed:* A22, C45. *Aud.:* Ac, Sa.

The official publication of the Association of American Veterinary Medical Colleges, this is the journal to read if you are interested in veterinary medical education, as it is the only one in any language devoted to the subject. It is an internationally distributed title whose purpose is to provide a forum for the exchange of ideas, research, and discoveries about veterinary medical education. "The journal's areas of focus include: best practices and educational methods in veterinary education; recruitment, training, and mentoring of students at all levels of education, including undergraduate, graduate, veterinary technology, and continuing education; clinical instruction and assessment; institutional policy; and other challenges and issues faced by veterinary educators domestically and internationally." It is a useful journal to monitor for information regarding changes in the profession and how veterinary colleges are reacting to the changes. Most of the issues are theme specific. Examples of this include "Innovations in Veterinary Medical Education," "40 Years of Service to Veterinary Medical Education," "Veterinary Medical Simulations," and "Primary Health Care Education." Readership will mostly be limited to teaching faculty, veterinary college administrators, members of curriculum committees, and continuing-education personnel. This is a necessary title in veterinary school libraries and should be considered for libraries that support animal technician programs. Full text online is available from volume 33 (2006). URL: http://jvme.utpjournals.press/loi/jvme#

4975. *Journal of Wildlife Diseases.* Former titles (until 1970): *Wildlife Disease Association. Bulletin;* (until 1965): *Wildlife Disease Association. Newsletter.* [ISSN: 0090-3558] 1965. q. Free to members. Ed(s): Kristen Anderson, James Mills. Wildlife Disease Association, Inc., PO Box 7065, Lawrence, KS 66044-7065; wda@allenpress.com; http://www.wildlifedisease.org. Illus., index, adv. Sample. Refereed. Vol. ends: Oct. *Indexed:* A22, Agr, C45. *Bk. rev.:* 1-5, 500-600 words. *Aud.:* Ac, Sa.

The *Journal of Wildlife Diseases* (*JWD*) is a quarterly journal of the Wildlife Disease Association (WDA). This title publishes the results of original research and observations of factors that impact "the health and survival of free-living or occasionally captive populations of wild animals, including fish, amphibians, reptiles, birds, and mammals." Issues include approximately 20 to 30 articles that encompass research, wildlife disease investigations, case reports, and review articles that are 8 to 12 pages in length, with 2 to 14 short communications per issue, letters, and an occasional book review. Online access to this journal includes coverage back to volume 1 (1965), with all but the most recent six issues available as open access. This journal is recommended for libraries that support veterinary programs or other science programs that involve wildlife. URL: www.jwildlifedis.org/

4976. *Journal of Zoo and Wildlife Medicine.* Formerly (until 1989): *Journal of Zoo Animal Medicine.* [ISSN: 1042-7260] 1971. q. USD 336 (print & online eds.) Individuals, USD 163 (print & online eds.)). American Association of Zoo Veterinarians, 581705 White Oak Rd, Yulee, FL 32097; admin@aazv.org; http://www.aazv.org. Illus., index, adv. Refereed. Vol. ends: Dec. *Indexed:* A22, C45, E01. *Bk. rev.:* 2-3, 300-500 words. *Aud.:* Ac, Sa.

The American Association of Zoo Veterinarians has as its official publication the *Journal of Zoo and Wildlife Medicine*. It is considered one of the major sources of information in zoological medicine. The journal emphasizes original research findings, clinical observations, and case reports in the field of veterinary medicine that deal with captive and free-ranging wild animals, and it has the stated goal "to improve the husbandry, preventive medicine and research required to preserve these animals." It also publishes editorials, review articles, and special reports. A typical issue has 15 to 20 full-length articles, plus three or four case reports and 12 to 16 brief communications. The book reviews are exceptionally well written and useful to librarians doing collection development. Abstracts of selected articles that appear elsewhere in the literature are included in each issue. An interesting regular feature, "Clinical Challenge," gives insight into how difficult cases were solved and/or resolved. All of the illustrative material is mostly in black-and-white. This high-quality research publication is a must for zoo and veterinary libraries, and perhaps for libraries that support marine biology programs. Full text back to 2009 can be found on the association web site. http://zoowildlifejournal.com/loi/zamd. However, full text is also available back to volume 31 (2000) through BioOne. URL: www.bioone.org/loi/zamd

4977. *Research in Veterinary Science.* [ISSN: 0034-5288] 1960. bi-m. EUR 1654. Ed(s): P Pasquali. Elsevier Ltd, 125 London Wall, London, EC2Y 5AS, United Kingdom; corporate.sales@elsevier.com; http://www.elsevier.com. Illus., index, adv. Sample. Refereed. Vol. ends: Nov. Microform: PMC; PQC. *Indexed:* A01, A22, Agr, C45, E01. *Aud.:* Ac, Sa.

This is the official journal of the Association for Veterinary Teaching and Research Work, a U.K.-based organization "for people engaged primarily in veterinary teaching and research." Issues of this international journal include original research articles, reviews, and short communications, and they generally do not include editorials, letters, or other news. Articles cover all species of animals, as well as a variety of subjects such as anatomy, epidemiology, immunology, nutrition, parasitology, surgery, virology, and welfare. Issues typically contain 30 to 35 articles of five to eight pages in length. This journal is recommended for veterinary libraries, though some medical libraries might find the comparative medicine content useful as well. URL: www.sciencedirect.com/science/journal/00345288/95

4978. *Topics in Companion Animal Medicine.* Former titles (until 2008): *Clinical Techniques in Small Animal Practice;* (until 1997): *Seminars in Veterinary Medicine and Surgery: Small Animal.* [ISSN: 1938-9736] 1986. q. USD 820. Ed(s): Deborah S Greco. Elsevier BV, Radarweg 29, Amsterdam, 1043 NX, Netherlands; info@elsevier.com; https://www.elsevier.com. Illus., index, adv. Refereed. Vol. ends: Nov. *Indexed:* A22, Agr, C45. *Aud.:* Ac, Sa.

Topics in Companion Animal Medicine is a peer-reviewed journal focused on the most recent advances in companion animal medicine. The journal is published quarterly and usually contains 10 to 12 articles of approximately three to five pages in length, with each issue having a major theme. Articles on the latest developments and techniques regarding an important topic in veterinary medicine are guest edited by a leading expert in the field. Color photographs accompany most articles, truly illustrating the technique or procedure discussed in the article. The journal accepts original research articles, case reports, and review articles, and publishes timely editorials that address issues that affect the companion animal practitioner. Recent themes of journal issues have been advances in rehabilitation, approaches to pain management, pituitary disorders, and pancreatitis. This journal is recommended for veterinary libraries. URL: www.companimalmed.com/

4979. *Veterinary Clinics of North America: Equine Practice.* Supersedes in part (in 1985): *The Veterinary Clinics of North America. Large Animal Practice;* Which superseded in part (in 1979): *Veterinary Clinics of North America.* [ISSN: 0749-0739] 1971. 3x/yr. USD 737. Elsevier BV, Radarweg 29, Amsterdam, 1043 NX, Netherlands; info@elsevier.com; https://www.elsevier.com. Illus., index. Refereed. Vol. ends: Dec. *Indexed:* A22, Agr, C45. *Aud.:* Ac, Sa.

Veterinary Clinics of North America: Equine Practice is one of four journals in the *Veterinary Clinics of North America* series. A guest editor leads each themed issue and compiles contributions of 12 or 13 review articles from experts on the featured topic. Print issues are published in hardcover three times per year. The journal aims to report current and latest advances that are directly applicable to the treatment of horses. Recent issues have covered respiratory medicine and surgery, equine pathology and laboratory diagnostics, standing surgery, equine dermatology, and advances in equine dentistry. Online issues are available from volume 18 (2002) to the current issue. This journal is essential for equine practitioners, as well as for veterinary and animal science collections. URL: www.elsevier.com/journals/veterinary-clinics-of-north-america-equine-practice/0749-0739

4980. *Veterinary Clinics of North America: Exotic Animal Practice.* [ISSN: 1094-9194] 1998. 3x/yr. USD 657. Elsevier BV, Radarweg 29, Amsterdam, 1043 NX, Netherlands; https://www.elsevier.com. Illus., index. Refereed. Vol. ends: Sep. *Indexed:* C45. *Aud.:* Ac, Sa.

Veterinary Clinics of North America: Exotic Animal Practice is one of four journals in the Veterinary Clinics of North America series. A guest editor leads each themed issue and compiles contributions of nine or ten review articles from experts on the featured topic. Print issues are published in hardcover three times per year. The journal aims to report current and latest advances in the treatment of exotic animals. Recent issues have covered clinical and diagnostic pathology, new and emerging diseases, nutrition, hematology, and wellness and environmental enrichment. Online issues are available from volume 5 (2002) to the current issue. This journal is highly recommended for veterinary libraries and for wildlife or zoo library collections. URL: www.elsevier.com/journals/veterinary-clinics-of-north-america-exotic-animal-practice/1094-9194

4981. *Veterinary Clinics of North America: Food Animal Practice.* Supersedes in part (in 1985): *The Veterinary Clinics of North America. Large Animal Practice;* Which superseded in part (in 1979): *Veterinary Clinics of North America.* [ISSN: 0749-0720] 1971. 3x/yr. USD 601. Elsevier BV, Radarweg 29, Amsterdam, 1043 NX, Netherlands; info@elsevier.com; https://www.elsevier.com/. Illus., index. Refereed. Vol. ends: Nov. *Indexed:* A22, Agr, C45. *Aud.:* Ac, Sa.

Veterinary Clinics of North America: Food Animal Practice is one of four journals in the Veterinary Clinics of North America series. A guest editor leads each themed issue and compiles contributions of 10 to 12 review articles from experts on the featured topic. Print issues are published in hardcover three times per year. The journal aims to report current and latest advances in the treatment of food animals (cattle, sheep, goats, llama, camelids, and the like). Recent issues have covered feedlot processing and arrival cattle management, ruminant toxicology, therapeutics and control of sheep and goat diseases, alpaca and llama health management, and production animal ophthalmology. Online issues are available from volume 18 (2002) to the current issue. This journal is recommended for libraries that support animal science and veterinary programs. URL: www.elsevier.com/journals/veterinary-clinics-of-north-america-food-animal-practice/0749-0720

4982. *Veterinary Clinics of North America: Small Animal Practice.* Supersedes in part (in 1979): *Veterinary Clinics of North America.* [ISSN: 0195-5616] 1971. bi-m. USD 876. Elsevier BV, Radarweg 29, Amsterdam, 1043 NX, Netherlands; https://www.elsevier.com. Illus., index. Refereed. Vol. ends: Nov. Microform: MIM; PQC. *Indexed:* A22, Agr, C45. *Aud.:* Ac, Sa.

Veterinary Clinics of North America: Small Animal Practice is one of the older of the titles in the Veterinary Clinics of North America series. A guest editor leads each themed issue and compiles contributions of 12 or 13 review articles from experts on the featured topic. Print issues are published in hardcover six times per year. The journal aims to report current and latest advances in the treatment of small animals such as cats and dogs. Recent issues have covered urology, soft-tissue surgery, infection control, rehabilitation and physical therapy, clinical nutrition, behavior, and pediatrics. Online issues are available from volume 25 (1996) to the current issue. This journal is essential for a veterinary medicine collection. URL: www.elsevier.com/journals/veterinary-clinics-of-north-america-small-animal-practice/0195-5616

4983. *Veterinary Economics: business solutions for practicing veterinarians.* [ISSN: 0042-4862] 1960. m. Ed(s): Amanda Bertholf, Kristi Reimer. U B M Advanstar Communications, Inc., 6200 Canoga Ave, 2nd Fl, Woodland Hills, CA 91367; info@advanstar.com; http://ubmadvanstar.com//. Illus., index, adv. Refereed. Vol. ends: Dec. Microform: PQC. *Indexed:* ATI, B01. *Aud.:* Ac, Sa.

Veterinary Economics is a monthly professional trade magazine for practicing veterinarians, available in both print and digital format. It broadly covers the business side of veterinary medicine, such as practice management, personnel issues, communication, practice finances, personal finances, client relations, work-life balance, and industry trends. The publication offers practical advice in the form of tips on client education, marketing, investing, staff rewards, hospital design, and hospital maintenance. In addition to the cover story, regular sections of the magazine include "Practice tips," "Practice with heart," "Data center," "Hospital design," "Benchmarks," "Industry issues," "Personal finance," and "Hot button"; infographics or other tools accompany many of the articles to emphasize the important points. The magazine accepts and compensates for a limited number of unsolicited freelance submissions, which may include interviews, case-study examples of practitioners' experiences, feedback on a new veterinary product, and tips. (A supplement included with this magazine is *Firstline,* a professional trade magazine aimed at other members of the veterinary team, such as receptionists, veterinary assistants, technicians, and practice managers.) Published by Advanstar Communications, this title can be found on the *dvm360* platform, and it benefits from the same graphics-packed content. The "Data Center" column is a good source of market data for practitioners on issues such as client perceptions of particular services, revenue analysis, regional analysis of staff pay, and job satisfaction. Issues are available online from December 2003 to the current. *Veterinary Economics* is recommended for veterinary libraries and other collections that serve veterinary staff and practitioners, though most adult readers could readily understand the article content. URL: http://veterinarybusiness.dvm360.com/sourceissues

4984. ***The Veterinary Journal.*** Former titles (until 1997): *British Veterinary Journal;* (until 1949): *The Veterinary Journal;* (until 1900): *The Veterinary Journal and Annals of Comparative Pathology.* [ISSN: 1090-0233] 1875. m. EUR 2243. Ed(s): Adrian Philbey, Annette Litster. Elsevier Ltd, 125 London Wall, London, EC2Y 5AS, United Kingdom; corporate.sales@elsevier.com; http://www.elsevier.com. Illus., index, adv. Sample. Refereed. Vol. ends: Dec. Microform: PMC; PQC. Reprint: PSC. *Indexed:* A01, A22, Agr, C45, E01. *Bk. rev.:* 4-6, 300-500 words; signed. *Aud.:* Ac.

Tracing its history back to 1875, *The Veterinary Journal* has the distinction of being the longest-running English-language veterinary journal. It is international in scope and publishes original papers and reviews on all aspects of veterinary science, with particular emphasis on animal health and preventive medicine. It commissions topical reviews and commentaries on features of major importance. Research areas include infectious diseases, applied biochemistry, parasitology, endocrinology, microbiology, immunology, pathology, pharmacology, physiology, molecular biology, immunogenetics, surgery, ophthalmology, dermatology, and oncology. Papers are published under three categories: "Guest Editorials," "Commissioned Topical Reviews," and "Original Articles." The journal also publishes book reviews and has a short communications section. The guest editorials are informative and often thought-provoking. The use of photographic materials is minimal, with a greater reliance on charts, tables, and graphs. Collection development librarians will enjoy the signed book reviews. This should be considered a basic title for veterinary science collections. Online full-text coverage, available since 1997, is through ScienceDirect. URL: www.sciencedirect.com/science/journal/10900233

4985. ***Veterinary Medicine.*** Formerly (until 1985): *Veterinary Medicine - Small Animal Clinician.* [ISSN: 8750-7943] 1905. m. Ed(s): Mindy Valcarcel, Margaret Rampey. Advanstar Veterinary Healthcare Communications, 8033 Flint, Lenexa, KS 66214; info@advanstar.com; http://ubmadvanstar.com/. Illus., index, adv. Refereed. Vol. ends: Dec. Microform: PQC. *Indexed:* A01, A22, Agr, BRI, C45. *Aud.:* Ac, Sa.

This is a well-respected journal in American veterinary medicine, having begun publication in 1905. It has undergone serious competition in recent years due to specialization within the profession, but it still provides "concise, credible, and essential information on the most common and emerging diagnostic and therapeutic problems seen in companion-animal practice." Therefore, the emphasis is on articles that present a how-to approach to guide practicing veterinarians in selecting better diagnostic and therapeutic strategies; hence, the articles are more clinical than research-oriented. Due to its practical nature, and because the articles are concise, to the point, and well illustrated in color, this journal is popular with practicing veterinarians. Since January 2000, the journal has focused exclusively on companion animals and exotics. Other regularly featured columns are the "Journal Scan," which reviews the literature, and the "Idea Exchange," where practitioners can submit practical practice tips. Frequently, one to three video clips are linked that can be viewed online. A new feature is a removable section that includes a toolkit on a specific topic, i.e., senior care, vaccines, tick control, flea control, and dental care. The same insert also appears in another journal, *Veterinary Economics,* which is issued by the same publisher. Online is an eye-catching site that pulls information from several different publications (*dvm360, Veterinary Economics,* and *Firstline*), with multiple methods of navigating the site by section or subject, though this site also poses some difficulty in locating the specific page with the individual issues of *Veterinary Medicine*; meanwhile, there are issues back to 2004 available. This is a recommended title for the small-animal practitioner, veterinary science collections, and libraries that serve veterinary technician programs. URL: http://veterinarymedicine.dvm360.com/sourceissues

4986. ***Veterinary Pathology.*** Formerly (until 1971): *Pathologia Veterinaria.* [ISSN: 0300-9858] 1964. bi-m. USD 511 (print & online eds.)). Ed(s): Jeff L Caswell. Sage Publications, Inc., 2455 Teller Rd, Thousand Oaks, CA 91320; info@sagepub.com; http://www.sagepub.com/. Illus., index, adv. Sample. Refereed. Vol. ends: Nov. Reprint: PSC. *Indexed:* A22, Agr, C45, E01. *Bk. rev.:* 1-2, 250-350 words. *Aud.:* Ac, Sa.

Veterinary Pathology is a journal of basic and applied research and the official journal of three different pathology associations: the American College of Veterinary Pathologists, the European College of Veterinary Pathologists, and the Japanese College of Veterinary Pathologists. Published six times per year, it reports international research involving domestic and laboratory animals, wildlife, marine and zoo animals, and poultry. Each issue features original articles, in-depth reviews, brief communications, and unique case reports that are grouped into sections such as "Oncology," "Infectious Disease," "Domestic Animals," "Nondomestic, Exotic, Wildlife and Zoo Animals," and "Laboratory Animals." Book reviews are occasionally included in the journal, and may help identify new veterinary-related books for a library collection or for the interested reader. The journal states it is "written for veterinary pathologists, veterinary diagnostic laboratory staff, toxicologic pathologists, comparative pathologists, medical pathology researchers, environmental scientists, and others involved in veterinary diagnosis and animal research across all animal species." Recent topics covered have included cancer diagnosis and prognosis, diseases linked with the environment, genetically modified animals, xenobiotic injury, and zoonotics. Issues are available online from volume 1 (1964) to the current. This journal is recommended for libraries that support veterinary programs or diagnostic laboratories. URL: http://vet.sagepub.com/

4987. ***The Veterinary Record.*** [ISSN: 0042-4900] 1888. w. Individuals, GBP 482 (print & online eds.)). Ed(s): Alexander John Trees, Dr. Alastair MacMillan. B M J Group, BMA House, Tavistock Sq, London, WC1H 9JR, United Kingdom; info.adc@bmj.com; http://www.bmj.com/. Illus., adv. Sample. Refereed. Vol. ends: Dec. *Indexed:* A01, A22, Agr, C45. *Bk. rev.:* 1-3, 400-750 words. *Aud.:* Ac, Sa.

The Veterinary Record is the official journal of the British Veterinary Association (BVA) and has been published weekly since 1888. Regular features of the publication are "News and Reports," "News in Brief," "Surveillance," "Research," "Research Digest," "Viewpoint," "Books," "Gazette," "Letters, and "Vet Record Career." The news sections report association business or issues deemed important to the members, particularly veterinary-related concerns in the United Kingdom. Three or four original research papers on a wide range of veterinary topics are typically included in each issue, as are selected highlights from other journals in the digest section. The online journal content includes full text of articles back to volume 138 (1996), and only abstracts or tables of contents for issues back to 1950. This journal is highly recommended for veterinary libraries. URL: http://veterinaryrecord.bmj.com/

4988. ***Veterinary Surgery.*** Incorporates (1974-198?): *Veterinary Anesthesia;* Formerly (until 1978): *Journal of Veterinary Surgery.* [ISSN: 0161-3499] 1978. 8x/yr. GBP 655. Ed(s): Giselle E Hosgood, Linda Dahlgren. Wiley-Blackwell Publishing, Inc., 111 River St, Hoboken, NJ 07030; http://onlinelibrary.wiley.com. Illus., index, adv. Sample. Refereed. Vol. ends: Nov/Dec. Reprint: PSC. *Indexed:* A22, Agr, C45, E01. *Aud.:* Ac, Sa.

Veterinary Surgery is the official publication of both the American College of Veterinary Surgeons and European College of Veterinary Surgeons. The journal is published eight times per year in both print and online. Articles appearing in the journal are original and peer-reviewed, and cover the latest developments in veterinary surgery and the anesthetic management of animals. Published content is intended to present "timely articles on surgical techniques, diagnostic aims, care of infections, and advances in knowledge of metabolism as it affects the surgical patient." Most articles are categorized as either research or clinical in nature, with meeting abstracts included at the back of the journal. The online version of the journal includes issues from volume 1 (1971) to the current. This journal is recommended for veterinary library collections. URL: http://onlinelibrary.wiley.com/journal/10.1111/(ISSN)1532-950X

■ WEDDINGS

Lindsay Brownfield, Reference and Instruction Librarian, University of Nebraska-Kearney, Kearney, NE; brownfieldlj@unk.edu

Introduction

Bridal surveys from 2017 place the average wedding costs in the United States between $27,000 and $36,000. Showcasing a vast array of products, wedding magazines and their accompanying web sites are the go-to source for inquisitive brides investigating the options available for planning their big day.

The magazines reviewed range from basic coverage of affordable goods to a compendium of high-end resources for the bride with the near-limitless budget. All cover the standard fare of fashion, furnishings, jewelry, beauty products, wedding destinations, honeymoon options, registry suggestions, and china. Most are advertisement-heavy, with varying amounts of editorial content; all display gorgeous photography.

Basic Periodicals

Sa: *Bride's, The Knot Weddings.*

Basic Abstracts and Indexes

MAS Ultra: School Edition; Reader's Guide to Periodical Literature.

4989. ***Bridal Guide.*** [ISSN: 0882-7451] 1985. bi-m. USD 9.95. Ed(s): Diane Forden. RFP LLC, 228 E 45th St, 11th Fl, New York, NY 10017; http://www.BridalGuidemag.com. Illus., adv. Circ: 109927. Vol. ends: Dec (No. 6). *Aud.:* Sa.

Bridal Guide takes a traditional approach to wedding resources: displays of dresses, china, and furnishings are interwoven with short features on fashion, registry suggestions, honeymoon destinations, and advice on how to handle sticky relations within the wedding party and with the in-laws. Real-life weddings are portrayed, as well. The products advertised include some high-end gowns and expensive jewelry, but most of the resources are accessible for the budget-conscious bride. Its web site, similarly, is filled with many advice features, as well as multiple links for registry suggestions and fashion tips. *Bridal Guide* is more practical than out-of-this-world dreamy, and thus is more useful for the majority of brides than some wedding magazines. URL: www.bridalguide.com

4990. ***Bride's.*** Former titles (until 1995): *Bride's and Your New Home;* (until 1992): *Bride's.* [ISSN: 1084-1628] 19??. bi-m. USD 10. Conde Nast Publications, Inc., 1 World Trade Center, New York, NY 10007; communications@condenast.com; http://www.condenast.com. Illus., adv. Microform: PQC. *Indexed:* A22. *Aud.:* Sa.

This magazine is best for the bride who wants to read about weddings and honeymoons, rather than just be assaulted by a storm of graphic images and advertisements. It contains more editorial text than most of the other wedding magazines reviewed. Including lots of ideas and advice on the standard topics (fashion, jewelry, beauty, etiquette, honeymoon destinations, and relationships), the magazine offers feature essays that are fairly long and comprehensive. A wedding countdown that spells out standard tasks that are involved in most weddings is included. Visually, this magazine includes people of different ethnicities and races, as well as "normal-sized" brides, not just exquisitely thin and ethereal models. The variety and arrangement of text and photographs make *Bride's* easy to browse as well as to read from cover to cover. The web site similarly provides multiple ideas for engagement rings, honeymoon destinations, and dresses galore for all members of the wedding party. Overall, *Bride's* is a basic resource for someone planning a wedding with a good mix of advice and inspiration. URL: www.brides.com

4991. ***Grace Ormonde Wedding Style.*** [ISSN: 1554-1185] 1998. s-a. USD 25; USD 16 per issue. Ed(s): Grace Ormonde. Elegant Publishing, Inc., PO Box 89, Barrington, RI 02806; admin@weddingstylemagazine.com. Adv. *Aud.:* Sa.

Grace Ormonde Wedding Style stands out from the other publications reviewed as a magazine directed to a very upscale audience. For the bride with an unlimited budget, this magazine offers many resources; for others, it provides visually captivating visions for any bride to dream about. A beautifully designed spread of luscious photographs illustrates the standard wedding magazine content: fashion, cakes, honeymoon locales, jewelry, floral design, and registry suggestions. Exquisite runway-style bridal dresses and exotic locations for destination weddings are featured. The real-life weddings features are short cameos without the comprehensive coverage given in some of the other wedding magazines. The magazine includes a "Platinum List" of vendors and wedding resources, organized by state. These resources are also available in searchable format on the web site. The web site continues the same sumptuous style and open feel of the magazine - in fact, some of the features include page-turning as if one is reading the print version. It includes resources and vendors recommended by Grace Ormonde and gives the bride the opportunity to hire the Grace Ormonde wedding planning team! A sister magazine, *Grace Ormonde Wedding Style New England,* focuses specifically on vendors and products available to the New England bride. Beautiful to look at, this magazine - which styles itself as "The Luxury Wedding Source" - offers less of practical value for most budget-conscious brides, but provides a delicious array of luxury products and decorating ideas as inspiration for all who read it. URL: www.weddingstylemagazine.com

4992. ***Inside Weddings: the insider's guide to wedding inspiration.*** [ISSN: 1552-4647] 2003. q. USD 16 combined subscription domestic (print & online eds.); USD 40 Canada; USD 125 foreign). Ed(s): Walt Shepard. Inside Weddings, t 6255 W. Sunset Blvd., Suite 860, Los Angeles, CA 90028; http://insideweddings.com/. Illus., adv. *Aud.:* Sa.

Although this magazine includes the standard fare of fashion, beauty, china, jewelry, honeymoon ideas, and registry gifts portrayed primarily through advertisements, *Inside Weddings* distinguishes itself in its organization and focus. Its real-life wedding features include eight to ten couples, and it devotes substantial space (six to ten pages) to each wedding experience. Although rich with photographs, it has considerable text that gives a good sense of the real people profiled; extensive detail on the featured weddings is included. There is also a "Runway Report" that exhibits more than 400 gowns from more than 40 designers, grouped by designer; this format focuses the review of dresses and makes it easier for the reader to compare gowns than if they were spread throughout the issue. One drawback is that this format does not include store and availability information with the dresses, although some of it can be found elsewhere in the magazine. At the end of the issue, there are a few pages of expert advice on various topics, such as etiquette and photography. The tone of the magazine is more editorial than graphic, although there are abundant photographs providing inspiration to the bride. The accompanying web site includes many links to wedding products, including gift ideas, beauty and fashion productions, and other wedding resources. Organized topically (for example, dresses, hairstyles, shoes, flowers, cakes, bridesmaids' dresses), the web site includes only its recommended vendors, reflecting the magazine's "commitment to limiting advertisers to professionals with whom we've worked, business we've reference checked, or companies we know extremely well by reputation" ("Editor's Letter"). Archived features on real-life weddings and expert advice from prior issues are included in the web site. Together, the magazine and the web site give a very balanced approach to editorial content and beautiful photography, making the presentation of the material manageable for the reader. URL: www.insideweddings.com

4993. ***The Knot Weddings Magazine.*** Formerly (until 19??): *The Knot Wedding Gowns.* 1999. s-a. XO Group Inc., 462 Broadway, 6th Fl, New York, NY 10013; salesinfo@theknot.com. *Aud.:* Sa.

Formerly known as *The Knot Wedding Gowns, The Knot Weddings Magazine* focuses primarily on wedding dresses, although there are many advertisements for other wedding products. The web site acts as a portal through which these and other wedding-related products can be purchased by clicking on vendor links; it serves as a leading retail vendor of wedding products and accessories. *The Knot Weddings Magazine* offers a photographic gallery of inspiration for any bride. The costs of the dresses cover a wide spectrum that gives the most budget-conscious some affordable options. Although practical wedding and couples advice is sprinkled throughout, the sheer mass of material (more than 500 pages per issue) makes this magazine a bit hard to read. The content includes the usual wedding magazine fare - fashion, jewelry, china, and furnishings - but it has the feel of a Sears Roebuck catalog, with a little of everything. The honeymoon destinations section gives brief descriptions of the different locales as well as tips on weather and travel logistics, in addition to photographs and brief descriptions of resorts in that area. Further, although bridal gown advertisements are throughout the magazine, there is a specific section, "The Look Book," which includes photographs of wedding gowns arranged alphabetically by designer. Each dress is linked to store information through links to the designer through the magazine's web site (http://theknot.com) and the designer's own web site (referenced on each page), as well as to the store directory in the back of the print magazine, which includes full contact information for each store that carries the dress. Lastly, special issues, including an annual "Best of Weddings" issue, published annually, feature similar vendor information, organized by region of the country, with ratings by real brides in each region who vote for their favorite resources. There are also quarterly regional magazines that provide localized content in terms of shopping resources. Real-life weddings featured in the regional magazines focus on couples specific to each region. Together, *The Knot Weddings* publications and web site provide an extensive and comprehensive one-stop location for a bride's shopping.

■ WORLD WIDE WEB

See also Business; Communications; Computers and Information Technology; Electronics; Engineering and Technology; and Library and Information Science sections.

Sasha Bishop, Technology Services/Instruction Librarian, Technical College of the Lowcountry, 921 Ribaut Road, Beaufort, SC 29902; sbishop@tcl.edu

Introduction

The World Wide Web—its uses, its venues for access, and its attendant issues of privacy and security—continues to be a subject ripe for research, exploration, and debate. The publications considered here take on the complicated subject that is the Web in a variety of ways. Broadly, the titles in this section may be divided into those that consider Web issues from the general user's perspective; those aimed at scholars or professionals working in tech-related fields; and those publications that collect and review the ever-growing trove of resources on the Web in an attempt to spotlight the standouts in specific subject areas. There are publications here that will primarily appeal to researchers and scholars, several that are tailor-made for librarians and educators, and a handful that will likely appeal to Web users at all levels and all ranges of interest and expertise. Despite varying audiences, common themes abound. User behavior and decision-making online are frequent topics, as is social media and its impact upon both the user and society at large. The Internet of Things and the Web of Things also make appearances throughout these publications and represent a growing field of discussion and research. The expansion of the Web from our computers to our phones, fitness trackers, health monitors, home entertainment systems, vehicles, and buildings brings with it privacy and security concerns, another major theme of Web-focused publications. Each of the titles reviewed here speaks to these issues, addressing everything from legal ramifications to specific network architecture concerns, with the common goal of making sense of the rapidly changing Web and how it impacts its users.

Please note: The EFFector Online Newsletter has been deleted from this section for three reasons:(1) The latest issue we could find was for January 2017 (this is being written in July 2017, and most volumes of the newsletter have had 5 to 10 issues out by this point); (2) Repeated attempts to reach the Electronic Frontier Foundation resulted in no response; (3) much of the content from the newsletter has moved to the DeepLinks Blog (https://www.eff.org/deeplinks?type=blog).

Basic Periodicals

First Monday, I E E E Internet Computing, Internet Research, The Scout Report, Wired.

Basic Abstracts and Indexes

Academic Search Premier, INSPEC, Reader's Guide to Periodical Literature, ScienceDirect.

4994. *A C M Transactions on Internet Technology.* [ISSN: 1533-5399] 2001. q. USD 900 (print & online eds.)). Ed(s): Munindar P Singh. Association for Computing Machinery, PO Box 30777, New York, NY 10087; acmhelp@acm.org; https://www.acm.org. Refereed. *Aud.:* Ac, Sa.

According to the publication website, Transactions on Internet Technology (TOIT) "brings together many computing disciplines including computer software engineering, computer programming languages, middleware, database management, security, knowledge discovery and data mining, networking and distributed systems, communications, performance and scalability." A peer-reviewed publication of the Association for Computing Machinery, TOIT's editorial staff represent computer science departments and companies in an array of nations. Contact information for authors is provided, as well as information on the grants, awards, and projects that supported each work. The articles are highly technical and thoroughly referenced. Recent special issues have focused on the Internet of Things and advances in social computing. Additional articles in recent issues have addressed pattern mining, irony detection in Twitter, and cloud infrastructures. Recommended for academic libraries that serve computer science and engineering programs, and any collections utilized by researchers in the field of Internet technology.

4995. *A C M Transactions on the Web.* [ISSN: 1559-1131] 2007. q. USD 759 (print & online eds.)). Ed(s): Marianne Winslett, Brian D. Davison. Association for Computing Machinery, PO Box 30777, New York, NY 10087; acmhelp@acm.org; https://www.acm.org. Refereed. *Aud.:* Ac, Sa.

A publication of the Association for Computing Machinery (ACM), *Transactions on the Web* (*TWEB*) features research on web content and the technology that makes that content run. Among its chief focuses are browsers and web interfaces, e-commerce, electronic publishing, the semantic web, web engineering, and web services. Its international body of editors hail largely from educational institutions. Articles from recent issues include "Information Sharing by Viewers Via Second Screens for In-Real-Life Events," "A Large-Scale Evaluation of U.S. Financial Institutions' Standardized Privacy Notices," and "Prediction and Predictability for Search Query Acceleration." This publication is recommended for academic libraries that serve computer science and web design programs and for special libraries that serve research endeavors related to the web.

4996. *e-Service Journal: a journal of electronic services in the public and private sectors.* [ISSN: 1528-8226] 2001. 3x/yr. USD 180 (print & online eds.)). Ed(s): Amit Deokar, Marissa McGee. Indiana University Press, Office of Scholarly Publishing, Herman B Wells Library 350, Bloomington, IN 47405; iuporder@indiana.edu; http://iupress.indiana.edu/ . Illus., adv. Refereed. Reprint: PSC. *Indexed:* A22, B01, E01. *Aud.:* Ga, Ac, Sa.

Indiana University Press's *e-Service Journal* publishes "innovative research on the design, delivery, and impact of electronic services via a variety of computing applications and communications technologies." The publication's editors, advisory board, and contributors represent business, law, information science, and computer science programs. Both the public and private sector issues are given consideration in the journal. Many *e-Service* articles discuss the progress made and barriers encountered in the adoption of e-services in contexts such as government information systems and large-scale public sector projects. Articles often address how to reconcile the technical realities faced by IT architects and the needs of e-service users. Topics include everything from e-voting to Internet banking, to consumer health-care services. This refereed journal is a useful publication for those researching the web's role in the areas of business, health care, and government. Primarily recommended for academic and special libraries that serve researchers in these areas.

Educause Review. See Computers and Information Technology/ Professional Journals section.

4997. *EFFector Online Newsletter.* Former titles (until 2002): *EFFector;* (until 1997): *EFFector Online;* (until 1991): *E F F News.* 1991. irreg. 1-4/mo. Free. Ed(s): Stanton McCandlish. Electronic Frontier Foundation, 454 Shotwell St., San Francisco, CA 94110; information@eff.org; http://www.eff.org/. *Aud.:* Ac, Sa, Ga.

The online newsletter *EFFector* is published by the Electronic Frontier Foundation, an organization that pursues legal cases in the arena of digital rights. EFF's advisory board is composed of lawyers, digital rights experts, website creators, and computer industry luminaries. The main EFF website is updated regularly and covers issues related to surveillance, online privacy and security, and digital free speech. Recent subjects include net neutrality, censorship of controversial online content, and the potential benefits to removing DRM locks. A selection of back issues of the newsletter is available online, but readers wanting regular content updates should sign up on the EFF site to receive emailed issues of the newsletter, which in addition to featured stories also includes updates on current legislative issues and events related to digital rights. This free resource is a valuable source of passionately opinionated news focused on digital rights-related topics, not to mention an extremely entertaining read, and it should be of interest to anyone following the interplay of law, government, industry, and the digital frontier.

eWEEK. See Computers and Information Technology/Popular Titles section.

4998. *First Monday (Chicago).* [ISSN: 1396-0466] 1996. m. Ed(s): Edward J Valauskas. First Monday Editorial Group, c/o Edward Valauskas, Chief Editor, 9480 Lakeview, PO Box 638, Bridgman, MI 49106. Illus. Refereed. *Indexed:* BRI, CBRI, MLA-IB. *Bk. rev.:* 5-10, 500-1,500 words. *Aud.:* Ga, Ac.

Published by the University of Illinois at Chicago, First Monday has been going strong for more than 21 years and has published more than 1,600 articles in more than 250 issues. "One of the first openly accessible, peer-reviewed journals solely devoted to research about the Internet," *First Monday*'s globe-spanning editorial board and contributors have covered a massive number of issues related to the Web over the years, including the open-source movement, social networking, open online courses, Wikipedia, search engines, trolling, big data, and the Internet of things. While some articles explore technical issues, many focus on the cultural importance of various Internet technologies and trends. Articles often investigate the behavior of Internet users and the intersection of the Internet with education, media, and politics. A few recent article titles include "How Do Saudi Youth Engage with Social Media?", "The Rise of Reading Analytics and the Emerging Calculus of Reader Privacy in the Digital World," and "The Social Media Logic of Political Interaction: Exploring Citizens' and Politicians' Relationship on Facebook and Twitter." Online archives of *First Monday* date back to 1996, making this not only a useful resource for tracking current web developments but also as a lens into how the Internet and our views of it have evolved over the years. Recommended for public and academic libraries, and anyone interested in the past, present, and future of the web.

4999. *I E E E Internet Computing.* [ISSN: 1089-7801] 1997. bi-m. USD 1385. Ed(s): George Pallis. Institute of Electrical and Electronics Engineers, 445 Hoes Ln, Piscataway, NJ 08854; contactcenter@ieee.org; http://www.ieee.org. Illus., index, adv. Refereed. Vol. ends: Dec. *Indexed:* A22, CompLI. *Aud.:* Ac, Sa.

A publication of the Institute of Electrical and Electronics Engineers (IEEE), *IEEE Internet Computing* is billed as "a crossroads between academic researchers and software professionals." Topics covered in its peer-reviewed articles (as well as industry reports, columns, and tutorials) range from applications and architectures to information management, security, and standards. Recent issues have focused on the fog computing, information and communication technology (ICT) for smart industries, and network function virtualization. The editorial board includes representation from academia and industry. IC's editorial musings on the future of the Internet coupled with lengthier articles on current trends in computing technology make for an entertaining and informative read on developments in the field. Useful for both researchers and practitioners in the industry, this publication is recommended for academic libraries that serve web design and computer science programs, libraries that serve industry professionals, and any library with a readership interested in following the continuing evolution and expansion of the Internet.

5000. *The Information Advisor's Guide to Internet Research.* Formed by the merger of (1988-2013): *The Information Advisor;* (1996-2013): *The Cyberskeptic's Guide to Internet Research.* [ISSN: 2333-2336] 2013. 10x/yr. USD 225.50. Ed(s): Robert Berkman. Information Today, Inc., 143 Old Marlton Pike, Medford, NJ 08055; custserv@infotoday.com; http://www.infotoday.com. Sample. *Indexed:* BRI. *Aud.:* Ga, Sa.

A publication of Information Today, this newsletter is the result of a merger of *The Cyberskeptic's Guide to Internet Research* and *The Information Advisor.* Edited by Information Advisor editor Robert Berkman and Online Searcher senior editor Barbara Quint, *The Information Advisor's Guide to Internet Research* provides "critical analysis of free and fee-based information resources, web-based services, and search strategies to help you maximize your research time and keep you up-to-date on the internet's role in research." The authors of the reviews (mainly librarians and specialists in Internet research) consider various aspects of the selected sites and tools, including user-friendliness, cost, and overall usefulness. In the lengthiest reviews, major web sites and tools are explored in depth. Recent products and sites considered include Ballotopedia: The Encyclopedia of American Politics, Dow Jones's Factivia, and Our World in Data, a site that focuses on changing living conditions worldwide. *The Information Advisor's Guide* examines established sites and tools, start-ups, and lesser-known entities on the web, and the reviews are thorough, honest, and readable. This publication will be useful to large public libraries, academic libraries, and any institution that serves information professionals and educators looking to stay on top of web resources.

5001. *International Journal of Hyperconnectivity and the Internet of Things.* [ISSN: 2473-4365] 2017. s-a. USD 870. Ed(s): Maurice Dawson. I G I Global, 701 E Chocolate Ave, Ste 200, Hershey, PA 17033; eresources@igi-global.com; http://www.igi-global.com. Refereed. *Aud.:* Ac.

Research on the Internet of Things and the Web of Things abounds in web-related publications of late, as the Internet continues to make its way off our computer screens and into the various technologies that surround us in our homes, cities, vehicles, and so on. According to the homepage of the International Journal of Hyperconnectivity and the Internet of Things, the journal's mission is "to explore a range of related topics and generate research debates in relation to cyber security, hyperconnectivity, Internet of Things (IoT), Web of Things (WoT), and Internet of Everything (IoE). Targeting researchers, practitioners, academicians, government officials, military professionals, and other industry professionals, *IJHIoT* provides a forum to discuss technical, human, societal, and policy issues in relation to hyperconnectivity, and IoT." Its editor in chief and editorial board represent a range of universities, largely in the United States. At the time of this review, only one issue has been published, with another forthcoming, but based upon review of the current issue, readers can expect articles of a technical nature. Extensive author information is provided, and articles are thoroughly referenced. Titles from the inaugural issue include "Internet of Things: Privacy and Security Implications" and "Tails Linux Operating System: Remaining Anonymous with the Assistance of an Incognito System in Times of High Surveillance." This publication will likely be of use to academic and special libraries that serve computer science and engineering students and researchers, particularly those with a focus on the Internet of Things.

5002. *International Journal of Web Information Systems.* [ISSN: 1744-0084] 2005. 5x/yr. EUR 676 (print & online eds.) (excluding UK)). Ed(s): David Taniar, Dr. Eric Pardede. Emerald Publishing Limited, Howard House, Wagon Ln, Bingley, BD16 1WA, United Kingdom; emerald@emeraldinsight.com; http://www.emeraldinsight.com. Sample. Refereed. Reprint: PSC. *Aud.:* Ac, Sa.

According to the publication website, the primary audience for the *International Journal of Web Information Systems includes "academics, students, developers, engineers, innovators, research strategists and IT-managers who are looking visionary concepts and stimulating ideas in Web information systems at both the theory and application levels." The topics covered in IJWIS* include web searching, web semantics, mobile solutions, databases, and systems used in e-commerce and online education. *IJWIS* boasts an international group of editors, associate editors, and editorial advisory board, mainly representing university computer science departments. Articles tend to be highly technical; recent titles include "Formal Analysis and Verification Support for Reactive Rule-Based Web Agents," "Pushing Similarity Joins Down to the Storage Layer in XML Databases," and "A Qos-Aware Approach for Runtime Discovery, Selection and Composition of Semantic Web Services." Detailed abstracts describe the purpose, design, findings, and value of the work. This publication is recommended for academic and research libraries with computer science and engineering or information science collections.

5003. ***International Journal of Web Services Research: an international source for researchers and engineers in the field of web services.*** [ISSN: 1545-7362] 2004. q. USD 840. Ed(s): Liang-Jie Zhang. I G I Global, 701 E Chocolate Ave, Ste 200, Hershey, PA 17033; eresources@igi-global.com; http://www.igi-global.com. Refereed. *Indexed:* A22, E01. *Aud.:* Ac, Sa.

A publication of the Information Resources Management Association, the *International Journal of Web Services Research* (*IJWSR*) "is designed to be a valuable resource providing leading technologies, development, ideas, and trends to an international readership of researchers and engineers in the field of Web Services." Its editor-in-chief is the senior vice president, chief scientist, and director of research at the Kingdee International Software Group, and *IJWSR*'s editorial review board represents many nations, with the bulk of its associate editors hailing from U.S. universities. Author information included with each paper details author interests and current research. *IJWSR* covers a variety of topics related to the web, such as web service architecture, security, the mathematical foundations of computing, and quality of web services. An editorial preface describes the theme of the issue and gives a synopsis of each article. The issue that focuses on big data, for example, includes papers entitled "Association Rule Mining of Personal Hobbies in Social Networks" and "A Fastest Patchwise Histogram Construction Algorithm based on Cloud-Computing Architecture." This publication is likely to be a good fit for academic and research libraries with computer science or web engineering collections.

5004. ***Internet Research.*** Formerly (until 1993): *Electronic Networking.* [ISSN: 1066-2243] 1991. 6x/yr. EUR 3728 print & online eds. (excluding UK)). Ed(s): M.K Cheung. Emerald Publishing Limited, Howard House, Wagon Ln, Bingley, BD16 1WA, United Kingdom; emerald@emeraldinsight.com; http://www.emeraldinsight.com. Illus. Sample. Refereed. Vol. ends: Dec. Reprint: PSC. *Indexed:* A01, A22, CompLI, E01, ISTA. *Aud.:* Ac, Sa.

Internet Research publishes articles focused on the social, political, economic, and ethical implications of widespread use of the Internet. User behavior is a frequent topic and is examined in relation to online gaming, e-commerce and advertising outreach, and social networking and knowledge sharing. *IR*'s associate editors and advisory editorial board members represent a range of nationalities and universities. Articles in this refereed publication are thoroughly referenced, and often focus on a particular type of web page or service, such as blogs, virtual knowledge-sharing communities, and social networking sites. Recent articles include "Anxiety about Electronic Data Hacking: Predictors and Relations with Digital Privacy Protection Behavior," and "Effectiveness of Online Consumer Reviews: The Influence of Valence, Reviewer Ethnicity, Social Distance and Source Trustworthiness." Each article is thoroughly referenced and includes author information, and information about the grants and financial support for each study is also provided. The papers published in *Internet Research* should be valuable to large academic libraries and research libraries with a strong focus on web design and Internet research.

5005. ***Network World (Online).*** Formerly: *Network World Fusion.* [ISSN: 1944-7655] 2013. w. Ed(s): John Dix. Network World Inc., 492 Old Connecticut Path, Framingham, MA 01701; editorialinquiry@nww.com; http://www.nwfusion.com. Illus., adv. *Bk. rev.:* 3-4, 200 words. *Aud.:* Ga, Sa.

Owned by International Data Group (IDG), the *Network World* site and accompanying daily newsletters provide news and articles related to the tech industry, "with an editorial focus on delivering news, opinion, and analytical tools for key decision makers who architect, deploy, and manage business solutions." Among its many topics are security, cloud computing, the Internet of things, infrastructure management, mobile and wireless tech, and software. Product reviews and advertisements take up a large part of the site, making it a good resource for industry professionals in charge of product decisions. *NW* also features blogs, whitepapers, and scans of technology useful for specific consumers or purposes. While much of the content is available without registration, users may also sign up with an email address for access to free "Insider" content. Readers may also opt to receive a free daily newsletter in their areas of interest. Topics include daily news, voices of networking, IT best practices, and network/systems management. Although it is primarily aimed at network IT professionals (particularly executives), *NW* will also be helpful to computer-savvy readers who want to stay abreast of current trends in computing. Recommended for any collection that serves network and IT professionals.

5006. ***The Scout Report.*** [ISSN: 1092-3861] 1994. w. Free. University of Wisconsin at Madison, Computer Sciences Department, 1210 West Dayton St, Madison, WI 53706; lab@cs.wisc.edu ; http://www.cs.wisc.edu/. *Aud.:* Ems, Hs, Ac.

The Scout Report, a free online publication, "provides a fast, convenient way to stay informed of valuable STEM and humanities resources on the Internet." The signature publication of the Internet Scout Research Group (part of the University of Wisconsin Madison's College of Letters and Sciences), the *Scout Report* has been highlighting various online resources and tools since its first publication in 1994. According to their "About Us" page, a team of librarians and subject specialists investigate and annotate each resource. Published most Fridays of the year, issues include sections on research and education, general interest, network tools, and items in the news. Recent reviews have covered everything from the sites Austen Said: Patterns of Diction in Jane Austen's Major Novels (in "Research and Education") and Adrift: The Secret World of Space Junk ("General Interest") to the text messaging app Signal Private Messenger ("Network Tools"). Full *Scout Report* back issues are accessible through the site, and users can have issues emailed to them as well. Readers in search of resources for specific subjects will want to take advantage of the searchable archives, where users can perform keyword searches to locate previously reviewed sites. Users can also rate or comment on the resources reviewed. This is an excellent resource for librarians (particularly those working in school and academic libraries), teachers, and anyone who has trouble staying on top of the many web resources popping up daily.

5007. ***Wired.*** [ISSN: 1059-1028] 1993. m. USD 19.99 combined subscription domestic (print & online eds.); USD 40 combined subscription Canada (print & online eds.); USD 70 combined subscription elsewhere (print & online eds.)). Ed(s): Scott Dadich. Conde Nast Publications Inc., Wired Ventures Ltd., PO Box 37706, Boone, IA 50037; http://www.condenast.com. Illus., adv. Vol. ends: Dec. *Indexed:* A22, BRI, MLA-IB. *Bk. rev.:* 5-8, 100 words. *Aud.:* Hs, Ga.

The Conde Nast publication *Wired* covers not just the web but all things digital, as it delves into pop culture, media, politics, science, business, and technology at large. The reader never knows what strange, scattered topics will lie between the covers of *Wired*'s very busy but always entertaining website. Articles cover everything from work-related tech tools to science fiction books and TV shows, to meditations on how we interact with the Internet and our many digital devices. *Wired* divides its content broadly into categories: Business, Culture, Design, Gear, Science, Security, and Transportation. Much of the content of the magazine is available on the *Wired* website, and digital editions are available for download to various tablets. The publication also has a YouTube channel and will deliver e-newsletters to those who provide an email address. This is a glossy, colorful, ad-heavy publication that makes for entertaining reading on a variety of subjects. Recommended for public library collections, as well as high school media centers and college libraries.

■ ZOOLOGY

General/Entomology/Herpetology/Invertebrates/Mammalogy

See also Biology; Birds; Ecology; Fish, Fisheries, and Aquaculture; and Marine Science and Technology sections.

Michelle Wilde; Michelle.Wilde@ColoState.Edu

Introduction

Zoology is the study of animal life, ranging from one-celled organisms, such as amoebas, to more complex multicellular organisms such as animals. Although humans are considered animals, most definitions of zoology cover animals up to the non-human primates.

As a branch of biology, modern zoology encompasses the study of all aspects of animal life, including anatomy, physiology, taxonomy, evolution, ethology (animal behavior), behavioral ecology, group dynamics, and zoogeography. While zoology initially focused on describing the animal world, as science has progressed the discipline has expanded to include aspects of other scientific disciplines. Today the field of zoology includes a laboratory component in which scientists study animal life at a microscopic level, and the zoological literature includes topics such as genetics, cell biology, biochemical processes, and more.

The complexity of the discipline of zoology is reflected in the journal literature, which includes titles relevant to general zoology topics, as well as some titles that focus on specific species. Other sections include biology, birds (ornithology), and fish (ichthyology, fisheries, and aquaculture), so these topics have not been included in the zoology section.

The target audience of most of these journals is professionals working in the zoological disciplines, so these titles will be most appropriate for academic libraries. However, upper-level undergraduates and zoology enthusiasts will likely find some of the articles to be accessible, and some larger public libraries will find some of these titles to be appropriate for their collections.

Online access is now the standard for zoology journals, and some of the titles are adding supplemental content such as audio, video, discussion boards, and altmetrics to their websites. Although only a few titles on this list are fully open access, zoology journals are starting to embrace open science. Many journals require authors to publish open data sets with articles, and most publishers offer authors the opportunity to make articles open access for a fee.

Basic Periodicals

Animal Behaviour, Annual Review of Entomology, Behavioral Ecology, Herpetologica, Integrative & Comparative Biology, The Journal of Experimental Biology, Journal of Experimental Zoology. Part B, Systematic Entomology, Mammal Review.

Basic Abstracts and Indexes

Biological Abstracts, Biological Abstracts/RRM, Biological and Agricultural Index, Biology Digest, CAB Abstracts; Current Contents/Life Sciences, Zoological Record.

General

The American Naturalist. See Ecology section.

5008. ***Animal Behaviour.*** Former titles (until 1958): *British Journal of Animal Behaviour;* (until 1953): *Bulletin of Animal Behaviour.* [ISSN: 0003-3472] 1938. m. EUR 2244. Elsevier Ltd, 125 London Wall, London, EC2Y 5AS, United Kingdom; corporate.sales@elsevier.com; http://www.elsevier.com. Illus., index, adv. Sample. Refereed. Microform: PMC; PQC. Reprint: PSC. *Indexed:* A01, A22, Agr, BRI, C45, E01, MLA-IB. *Bk. rev.:* Occasional, 500-1,400 words. *Aud.:* Ac, Sa.

Animal Behaviour is published for the Association for the Study of Animal Behaviour in collaboration with the Animal Behavior Society. It publishes "critical reviews, original papers, and research articles on all aspects of animal behavior," including humans, and coverage includes behavioral ecology, evolution of behavior, population biology, sensory behavior, navigation and migration, and more. The online edition publishes "Virtual Special Issues" that compile selections of "interesting papers" published in "the last few years." This title should be considered nearly essential for academic libraries. This journal offers an open-access option for authors, so some articles may be freely available.

5009. ***Behavioral Ecology.*** [ISSN: 1045-2249] 1990. bi-m. EUR 1203. Ed(s): Leigh Simmons. Oxford University Press, 2001 Evans Rd, Cary, NC 27513; https://academic.oup.com/journals. Adv. Sample. Refereed. Reprint: PSC. *Indexed:* A01, A22, C45, E01. *Aud.:* Ac, Sa.

Behavioral Ecology, the official journal of the International Society for Behavioral Ecology, covers all aspects of behavioral ecology, including empirical and theoretical work. Covering the entire spectrum of behaving organisms, the journal includes articles on plants, invertebrates, vertebrates, and humans. The journal addresses the field broadly, dealing with "the use of ecological and evolutionary processes to explain the occurrence and adaptive significance of behavior patterns; the use of behavioral processes to predict ecological patterns, and empirical, comparative analyses relating behavior to the environment in which it occurs." Original articles, review articles, and a forum section with commentaries on recent issues are all included. This journal is generally appropriate for academic audiences, and articles are suitable for undergraduates through specialists. For non-academics, the journal provides a "lay summary" on the online journal table of contents for each article that is designed to "interpret the context and significance of our published papers in a manner intelligible to interested nonspecialists." Data archiving is mandated for all published articles, and there is an open-access option for authors, so some articles may be freely available.

5010. ***Behavioral Ecology and Sociobiology.*** [ISSN: 0340-5443] 1976. m. EUR 7224 (print & online eds.)). Ed(s): J F A Traniello, T C M Bakker. Springer, Tiergartenstr 17, Heidelberg, 69121, Germany. Adv. Refereed. Reprint: PSC. *Indexed:* A22, Agr, C45, CJPI, E01. *Aud.:* Ac, Sa.

Behavioral Ecology and Sociobiology publishes original research papers and occasional review articles "dealing with quantitative empirical and theoretical studies in the analysis of animal behavior at the level of the individual, group, population, community, and species." In 2017 the journal implemented "Continuous Article Publishing," a model that published articles as they are accepted, with an "Article CitationID" replacing the page numbers. A "Featured Student Research Paper" section highlights "original publications that result from graduate or undergraduate student research and carry the name of the student as the lead author" in each issue. Appropriate for advanced undergraduates through specialists.

5011. ***Frontiers in Zoology.*** [ISSN: 1742-9994] 2004. irreg. Free. Ed(s): Diethard Tautz, Jurgen Heinze. BioMed Central Ltd., Fl 6, 236 Gray's Inn Rd, London, WC1X 8HB, United Kingdom; info@biomedcentral.com; https://www.biomedcentral.com. Adv. Refereed. *Indexed:* A01. *Bk. rev.:* Number and length vary. *Aud.:* Ac, Sa.

A peer-reviewed open-access title supported by the Deutsche Zoologische Gesellschaft, one of the world's largest and oldest zoological societies, *Frontiers in Zoology* publishes a wide range of article types, including research articles, book reviews, commentaries, debate articles, hypotheses, methodology articles, review articles, and short reports. The journal focuses on zoology as a whole, seeking "to represent and re-unite the various disciplines that look at animal life from different perspectives" and to provide a "basis for a comprehensive understanding of zoological phenomena." Links are provided for author and related-article searching and article metrics, and users may post and read comments on the published articles. Content is specialized, but most papers should be accessible to advanced undergraduates. URL: www.frontiersinzoology.com

5012. ***Integrative & Comparative Biology.*** Formerly (until 2002): *American Zoologist.* [ISSN: 1540-7063] 1961. bi-m. EUR 907. Ed(s): Lynn Martin. Oxford University Press, Great Clarendon St, Oxford, OX2 6DP, United Kingdom; onlinequeries.uk@oup.com; http://global.oup.com. Illus., adv. Sample. Refereed. Microform: PQC. Reprint: PSC. *Indexed:* A01, A22, Agr, BRI, C45, E01. *Bk. rev.:* Number and length vary. *Aud.:* Ac, Sa.

Published by the Society for Integrative and Comparative Biology, this journal was formerly titled *American Zoologist*, and it is an important journal in the study of zoology. Individual issues are generally organized around one or two common themes and are typically based on symposia from the annual meeting. In recent years, the journal has branched out and is now also offering a variety of other article types, including "invited reviews, perspectives, and proceedings from meeting workshops and other events." While original papers are sometimes published, the primary content is review articles and synthetic papers of general interest to comparative biologists. The journal covers all areas of biology, and its mission is to "integrate the varying disciplines in this broad field, while maintaining the highest scientific quality." The method of publishing subject-based issues makes this title especially useful for undergraduates, even though the primary audience is specialists. An essential purchase for academic libraries.

Journal of Animal Ecology. See Ecology section.

Journal of Animal Science. See Agriculture section.

5013. *The Journal of Experimental Biology.* Formerly (until 1930): *British Journal of Experimental Biology.* [ISSN: 0022-0949] 1923. s-m. USD 3102 (print & online eds.)). Ed(s): Dr. Hans Hoppeler. The Company of Biologists Ltd., 140 Cowley Rd, Cambridge, CB4 0DL, United Kingdom; sales@biologists.com; http://www.biologists.org. Illus., index. Sample. Refereed. *Indexed:* A01, A22, C45. *Bk. rev.:* 0-1, 750-1,000 words. *Aud.:* Ac, Sa.

The Journal of Experimental Biology publishes "papers on the form and function of living organisms at all levels of biological organisation, from the molecular and subcellular to the integrated whole animal." The journal publishes primary research articles, themed special issues, book reviews, editorials, and historical articles. Additionally, *JEB* commissions "review-based articles aimed at synthesising the latest advances in the field, putting forward new hypotheses to provoke debate and inspire new research directions." The online version provides supplementary data, and a forum is sometimes linked to the commentaries. Although published by a nonprofit company, this title is expensive. However, after a six-month embargo, all articles become freely available, and an open-access option is offered to authors who want their articles to be immediately available. This is an essential title for most academic libraries, as the articles have broad disciplinary appeal and are accessible to a wide range of readers.

5014. *Journal of Experimental Zoology. Part B: Molecular and Developmental Evolution.* Supersedes in part (in 2003): *The Journal of Experimental Zoology.* [ISSN: 1552-5007] 1904. 8x/yr. Ed(s): Ehab Abouheif. John Wiley & Sons, Inc., 111 River St, Hoboken, NJ 07030; cs-journals@wiley.com; http://onlinelibrary.wiley.com. Adv. Refereed. *Indexed:* A22, C45. *Aud.:* Ac, Sa.

An influential title in developmental evolution, "a branch of evolutionary biology that integrates evidence and concepts from developmental biology, phylogenetics, comparative morphology, evolutionary genetics and increasingly also genomics, systems biology as well as synthetic biology to gain a causal understanding of the structure and evolution of organisms." Contents are primarily papers reporting on original research and tend to be more than ten pages long. Review articles, editorials, and commentaries also appear occasionally. Many articles appear online before the print. This journal is participating in a transparent peer review pilot, and peer review information for each article is available on Publons. Only the most advanced undergraduates will find this title accessible, and since the journal is very expensive, it should be purchased primarily with graduate students and faculty in mind in cases where schools support such research.

5015. *Journal of Zoology.* Formed by the 1987 merger of: *Journal of Zoology. Series A; Journal of Zoology. Series B;* Which incorporated (1833-1984): *Zoological Society of London. Transactions;* Both A & B superseded in part (in 1984): *Journal of Zoology;* Which was formerly (until 1965): *Zoological Society of London. Proceedings;* Which was formed by the 1944 merger of: *Zoological Society of London. Proceedings. Series A; Zoological Society of London. Proceedings. Series B.* [ISSN: 0952-8369] 1987. m. GBP 2137. Ed(s): Nigel Bennett. Wiley-Blackwell Publishing Ltd., The Atrium, Southern Gate, Chichester, PO19 8QG, United Kingdom; cs-journals@wiley.com; http://onlinelibrary.wiley.com. Adv. Sample. Refereed. Reprint: PSC. *Indexed:* A01, A22, Agr, C45, E01. *Aud.:* Ac, Sa.

Published by the Zoological Society of London, this interdisciplinary journal publishes "hypothesis-driven" articles on topics that are of broad interest, including "animal behaviour, ecology, physiology, anatomy, developmental biology, evolution, systematics, genetics and genomics," encouraging "research that explores the interface between these disciplines." Articles are mostly original research and tend to be six to nine pages long. Longer review articles and articles on current issues are published periodically. Although this journal is appropriate for scientists, the articles will also be accessible to a general audience.

5016. *Linnean Society. Zoological Journal (Online): an international journal.* [ISSN: 1096-3642] 1855. m. GBP 2336. Ed(s): Dr. Louise Allcock. Wiley-Blackwell Publishing Ltd., The Atrium, Southern Gate, Chichester, PO19 8QG, United Kingdom; cs-journals@wiley.com; http://onlinelibrary.wiley.com. Illus., adv. Refereed. *Bk. rev.:* 1. *Aud.:* Ac, Sa.

One of three titles published by the venerable Linnean Society, this journal "publishes papers on systematic and evolutionary zoology and comparative, functional and other studies where relevant to these areas." Both living and extinct animals are covered, and the contents are primarily original research articles. Review articles are also occasionally published, and some issues also contain book reviews. The primary audience is zoologists, and editors seek papers with broad appeal to the zoological community. The content is appropriate for research institutions, as the articles are technical in nature and aimed at specialists in the field. Since 2016, this journal is published online-only.

Systematic Biology. See Biology/General section.

5017. *Zoologica Scripta: an international journal of systematic zoology.* Supersedes (in 1971): *Arkiv for Zoologi;* Incorporates (in 1976): *Norwegian Journal of Zoology;* Which was formerly (until 1971): *Nytt Magasin for Zoologi;* Which superseded in part (in 1952): *Nytt Magasin for Naturvidenskapene;* Which was formerly (until 1935): *Magazin for Naturvidenskaberne.* [ISSN: 0300-3256] 1903. bi-m. GBP 2270. Ed(s): Per Sundberg. Wiley-Blackwell Publishing Ltd., The Atrium, Southern Gate, Chichester, PO19 8QG, United Kingdom; cs-journals@wiley.com; http://onlinelibrary.wiley.com. Illus., adv. Sample. Refereed. Microform: PQC. Reprint: PSC. *Indexed:* A01, A22, C45, E01. *Bk. rev.:* Occasional. *Aud.:* Ac, Sa.

A joint publication of the Norwegian Academy of Science and Letters and the Royal Swedish Academy of Sciences, *Zoologica Scripta* is one of the more important titles in systematic zoology, focusing on "understanding evolutionary relationships among taxa and as well as zoological classification." Original theoretical, empirical, and methodological articles make up most of the contents, with a scattering of review articles and book reviews and letters. Papers vary greatly in length and tend to be quite sophisticated. The primary audience will be graduate students and researchers, although advanced undergraduates may also utilize the content.

Entomology

5018. *Annual Review of Entomology.* [ISSN: 0066-4170] 1956. a. USD 431 (print & online eds.)). Ed(s): Angela E Douglas. Annual Reviews, PO Box 10139, Palo Alto, CA 94303; service@annualreviews.org; http://www.annualreviews.org. Refereed. Reprint: PSC. *Indexed:* A01, A22, Agr, C45, MLA-IB. *Aud.:* Ac, Sa.

Published by Annual Reviews, papers are generally review articles of 15 pages or longer, covering "significant developments in the field of entomology, including biochemistry and physiology, morphology and development, behavior and neuroscience, ecology, agricultural entomology and pest management," and more. Papers appear online about a month before the print volume is published, so libraries should consider electronic access. This serial is a must for all medium- to large-sized academic libraries, and would be considered a good choice by smaller libraries that seek to add some coverage of entomology to their collection.

5019. *Journal of Insect Physiology.* [ISSN: 0022-1910] 1957. m. EUR 4709. Ed(s): F Pennacchio. Pergamon Press, The Blvd, Langford Ln, E Park, Kidlington, OX5 1GB, United Kingdom; JournalsCustomerServiceEMEA@elsevier.com; http://www.elsevier.com. Illus., adv. Sample. Refereed. Microform: MIM; PQC. *Indexed:* A01, A22, Agr, C45. *Aud.:* Ac, Sa.

A publication of the Entomological Society of America, this is the leading title in the physiology of insects, and papers on the physiology of other arthropods may be included if they are of general interest. Covered topics include "endocrinology (in relation to moulting, reproduction and metabolism), pheromones, neurobiology (cellular, integrative, and developmental), physiological pharmacology, nutrition (food selection, digestion, and absorption), homeostasis, excretion, reproduction and behaviour." While articles are primarily original research, the journal has been publishing an increasing number of review articles. Highly technical writing and very specialized subject matter make this title appropriate for graduate students and faculty.

5020. ***Systematic Entomology.*** Former titles (until 1976): *Journal of Entomology. Series B. Taxonomy & Systematics;* (until 1975): *Journal of Entomology. Series B. Taxonomy;* (until 1971): *Royal Entomological Society of London. Series B: Taxonomy. Proceedings; Stylops;* Which superseded in part (in 1936): *Royal Entomological Society of London. Proceedings;* Which was formerly (until 1933): *Entomological Society of London. Proceedings.* [ISSN: 0307-6970] 1932. q. GBP 1528. Ed(s): Thomas J Simonsen, Peter S Cranston. Wiley-Blackwell Publishing Ltd., The Atrium, Southern Gate, Chichester, PO19 8QG, United Kingdom; cs-journals@wiley.com; http://onlinelibrary.wiley.com. Illus., index, adv. Sample. Refereed. Vol. ends: Oct/Dec. Microform: PQC. Reprint: PSC. *Indexed:* A01, A22, Agr, BRI, C45, E01. *Bk. rev.:* 0-3, 500-800 words. *Aud.:* Ac, Sa.

This journal publishes "original papers on insect systematics, phylogenetics and integrative taxonomy, with a preference for general-interest papers of broad biological, evolutionary or zoogeographical relevance." Research articles, review articles, editorials, technical comments, and book and software reviews are all included. The journal has an "Opinion Piece" section that encourages "non-polemical debate on pressing issues in our field." Articles are very specialized, and the primary audience is entomologists, although evolutionary biologists and zoologists may also find the journal useful.

Herpetology

5021. ***Herpetologica.*** [ISSN: 0018-0831] 1936. q. USD 475 (print & online eds.)). Ed(s): Jane Cigard, Stephen Mullin. Allen Press, Inc., 810 E 10th St, Lawrence, KS 66044; https://www2.allenpress.com/. Illus. Refereed. Microform: PQC. *Indexed:* A01, A22, C45, E01. *Aud.:* Ac, Sa.

Herpetologica publishes original papers dealing with the biology of amphibians and reptiles. It is one of the two major publications of the Herpetologists League, along with *Herpetological Monographs.* Original research is published, with emphasis given to theoretical or quantitative papers, and article formats include research reports, reviews, editorials, and case letters. Articles vary in length, with most being six to ten pages long. Although aimed toward specialists, articles are generally well written, and some will be accessible to undergraduates. As of 2019 four issues a year will be published online, and the print version will be published annually in one full volume.

5022. ***Herpetological Journal.*** Formerly (until 1985): *British Journal of Herpetology.* [ISSN: 0268-0130] 1948. q. Free to members. Ed(s): Eluned Price, Mr. Chris Barratt. British Herpetological Society, 11, Strathmore Pl, Montrose, Angus, DD10 8LQ, United Kingdom; info@thebhs.org; http://www.thebhs.org/. Adv. Refereed. *Indexed:* A01, A22, C45. *Bk. rev.:* Number and length vary. *Aud.:* Ac, Sa.

Published quarterly by the British Herpetological Society, *The Herpetological Journal* disseminates papers and features on a wide range of reptile and amphibian biology. Experimental, observational, and theoretical studies are published along with occasional reviews and book reviews. Content is appropriate for upper-level undergraduates and above, as well as the interested lay reader. Online content is available from 1985 forward, and as of January 2017, the journal is only available online via the British Herpetological Society website. Authors may make individual articles open access, an option that is free for society members, and over 25 years of backfile content is available for free online.

5023. ***Journal of Herpetology.*** Supersedes in part (in 1968): *Ohio Herpetological Society. Journal;* Which was formerly (until 1959): *Ohio Herpetological Society. Tri-Monthly Report.* [ISSN: 0022-1511] 1958. q. Free to members. Ed(s): Paul E Bartelt, Tiffany M Doan-Costa. Society for the Study of Amphibians and Reptiles, Publications Secretary, PO Box 58517, Salt Lake City, UT 84158; ssar@herplit.com; http://ssarherps.org/. Illus. Refereed. *Indexed:* A01, A22, C45, E01. *Aud.:* Ac, Sa.

Published by the Society for the Study of Amphibians and Reptiles, this quarterly journal "publishes original taxonomy and hypothesis-driven research on the biology of amphibians and/or reptiles." Subjects may include "research on the evolution, genetics, ecology, behavior, physiology, morphology, development, conservation, education, and management of herpetofaunal species." Articles are usually under ten pages long and are accessible to upper-level undergraduates and above. Many issues contain articles grouped around a particular subtopic.

Invertebrates

5024. ***Invertebrate Biology.*** Former titles (until 1995): *American Microscopical Society. Transactions;* (until 1895): *American Microscopical Society. Proceedings;* (until 1892): *American Society of Microscopists. Proceedings.* [ISSN: 1077-8306] 1879. q. Ed(s): Michael W Hart. Wiley-Blackwell Publishing, Inc., 350 Main St, Malden, MA 02148; http://onlinelibrary.wiley.com. Illus., adv. Sample. Refereed. Reprint: PSC. *Indexed:* A01, A22, Agr, C45, E01. *Aud.:* Ac, Sa.

One of the oldest journals in the United States, *Invertebrate Biology* has been published continuously, under various titles, since 1879. The title "presents fundamental advances in our understanding of the structure, function, ecology, and evolution of the invertebrates" and covers all aspects of invertebrate animals, including morphology and ultrastructure, genetics, phylogenetics and evolution, physiology and ecology, neurobiology, behavior and biomechanics, reproduction and development, and cell and molecular biology. Content is almost entirely original research papers of ten or more pages, and the journal is published by the American Microscopical Society.

5025. ***Malacologia.*** [ISSN: 0076-2997] 1962. irreg. USD 53 (Individuals, USD 38; Free to members). Ed(s): George M Davis. Institute of Malacology, PO Box 385, Haddonfield, NJ 08033. Refereed. *Indexed:* A22, C45. *Aud.:* Ac, Sa.

Published by the Institute of Malacology, this journal specializes in original research on the Mollusca and includes long papers and monographic treatments covering "diverse topics such as systematics, ecology, biogeography, parasitology, genetics, evolution, biodiversity modeling, physiology, invasion biology, aquaculture, and fisheries." Occasional symposia are published, but manuscripts on single topics are encouraged. Short papers may be published as research notes, and historical notes and letters are also included. Articles are technical and typically eight pages or longer. The primary audience is researchers on Mollusca, and the content will be appropriate for institutions with programs in this area. Pre-2006 content is open access and freely available at the Biodiversity Heritage Library site.

Mammalogy

5026. ***American Journal of Primatology (Online).*** [ISSN: 1098-2345] 1981. m. GBP 2907. Ed(s): Paul A Garber. John Wiley & Sons, Inc., 111 River St, Hoboken, NJ 07030; cs-journals@wiley.com; http://onlinelibrary.wiley.com. Adv. Refereed. *Bk. rev.:* Number and length vary. *Aud.:* Ac, Sa.

The official journal of the American Society of Primatologists covers all aspects of primatology with the goal "to provide a forum for the exchange of ideas and findings among primatologists and to convey our increasing understanding of this order of animals to specialists and interested readers alike." Contents are primarily original research articles, but also include review articles, commentaries, brief reports, research articles, and book and media reviews. Special topic-based issues are published several times each year. Articles are appropriate for upper-level undergraduates and above, and should be accessible to the educated lay reader. The journal is published online, with print copies available through a third-party service.

5027. ***International Journal of Primatology.*** [ISSN: 0164-0291] 1980. bi-m. EUR 1678 (print & online eds.)). Ed(s): Joanna M Setchell. Springer New York LLC, 233 Spring St, New York, NY 10013; customerservice@springer.com; http://www.springer.com. Adv. Refereed. Microform: PQC. Reprint: PSC. *Indexed:* A01, A22, Agr, BRI, C45, E01, IBSS. *Bk. rev.:* Number and length vary. *Aud.:* Ac, Sa.

The official publication of the International Primatological Society, the *International Journal of Primatology* is a "multidisciplinary forum devoted to current research in fundamental primatology." As one would expect given the subject matter, "the journal gathers laboratory and field studies from such diverse disciplines as anthropology, anatomy, ethology, paleontology, psychology, sociology, and zoology." Articles tend to be long and technical and include "original research articles, reviews, commentaries, and book reviews." While accessible to advanced undergraduates, articles are most appropriate for graduate students and researchers. The journal gives special emphasis to articles that report on threatened or endangered species.

5028. *Journal of Mammalian Evolution.* [ISSN: 1064-7554] 1993. q. EUR 638 (print & online eds.)). Ed(s): John R Wible. Springer New York LLC, 233 Spring St, New York, NY 10013; customerservice@springer.com; http://www.springer.com. Adv. Sample. Refereed. Microform: PQC. Reprint: PSC. *Indexed:* A01, A22, Agr, BRI, E01. *Bk. rev.:* Number and length vary. *Aud.:* Ac, Sa.

The official journal of the Society for the Study of Mammalian Evolution, the *Journal of Mammalian Evolution* describes itself as "a multidisciplinary forum devoted to studies on the comparative morphology, molecular biology, paleobiology, genetics, developmental and reproductive biology, biogeography, systematics, ethology and ecology, and population dynamics of mammals and the ways these diverse data can be analyzed for the reconstruction of mammalian evolution." Research published in this journal may focus on laboratory work or field studies and includes original research and reviews.

5029. *Journal of Mammalogy.* [ISSN: 0022-2372] 1919. m. EUR 356. Ed(s): Joseph F Merritt. Oxford University Press, 2001 Evans Rd, Cary, NC 27513; custserv.us@oup.com; https://academic.oup.com/journals. Illus., index. Refereed. Vol. ends: Nov. Microform: PMC; PQC. Reprint: PSC. *Indexed:* A01, A22, Agr, BRI, C45, E01. *Bk. rev.:* 1-3, 800-2,100 words. *Aud.:* Ac, Sa.

Published by the American Society of Mammalogists, this journal presents original research on "all aspects of the biology of mammals," including "mammalian behavior, conservation, ecology, genetics, morphology, physiology, and taxonomy." Terrestrial as well as marine mammals are covered, and articles include reports on newly found species. In addition to research articles, the journal publishes society news, book reviews, and obituaries, and it occasionally groups articles together in a special feature section. Articles published after 1996 are available freely online, with a one-year embargo on new content. A longstanding title, the *Journal of Mammalogy* is attractively priced and useful for undergraduates and general readers, as well as specialists.

5030. *Mammal Review.* Formerly (until 1970): *Mammal Society. Bulletin.* [ISSN: 0305-1838] 1970. q. GBP 705. Ed(s): Nancy Jennings. Wiley-Blackwell Publishing Ltd., The Atrium, Southern Gate, Chichester, PO19 8QG, United Kingdom; cs-journals@wiley.com; http://onlinelibrary.wiley.com. Adv. Sample. Refereed. Microform: PQC. Reprint: PSC. *Indexed:* A01, A22, Agr, C45, E01. *Aud.:* Ac, Sa.

Published by The Mammal Society, this British title covers all areas of mammalian biology and ecology. The contents are primarily review articles, with an emphasis on "hypothesis-driven analytical and systematic reviews of current theoretical and applied research on mammals, meta-analyses, practical assessments of techniques for studying mammals and large-scale considerations of the status, conservation and management of mammals." Short communications and original research are occasionally published, as well as "perspectives" that give authors a venue for presenting original points of view. Articles are long, technical, and most suited to specialists.

Marine Mammal Science. See Marine Science and Technology/Marine Biology section.

TITLE INDEX

The numbers in this index refer to entry numbers in the text, not page numbers. Titles in boldface have been designated basic periodicals in a given subject area.

D

F

G

H

J

K

L

N

O

P

Q

R

S

U

V

W

X

Y

Z

SUBJECT INDEX

B

C

F

G

H

I

J

K

M

N

O

P

Q

R

S

U

V

Z